SELF-PRONOUNCING EDITION

THE
Holy Bible

REVISED STANDARD VERSION

CONTAINING THE

Old and New Testaments

TRANSLATED FROM THE ORIGINAL TONGUES
BEING THE VERSION SET FORTH A.D. 1611
REVISED A.D. 1881-1885 AND A.D. 1901
COMPARED WITH THE MOST ANCIENT
AUTHORITIES AND REVISED
A.D. 1946-1

A MERIDIAN BOOK

MERIDIAN
Published by the Penguin Group
Penguin Books USA Inc., 375 Hudson Street, New York, New York 10014, U.S.A.
Penguin Books Ltd, 27 Wrights Lane, London W8 5TZ, England
Penguin Books Australia Ltd, Ringwood, Victoria, Australia
Penguin Books Canada Ltd, 10 Alcorn Avenue, Toronto, Ontario, Canada, M4V 3B2
Penguin Books (N.Z.) Ltd, 182-190 Wairau Road, Auckland 10, New Zealand

Penguin Books Ltd, Registered Offices: Harmondsworth, Middlesex, England

Published by Meridian, an imprint of New American Library, a division of Penguin Books USA Inc.

First Meridian Printing, November, 1974
22 21 20 19 18 17 16 15

REGISTERED TRADEMARK—MARCA REGISTRADA

Printed in the United States of America

PREFACE

THE Revised Standard Version of the Bible is an authorized revision of the American Standard Version, published in 1901, which was a revision of the King James Version, published in 1611.

The first English version of the Scriptures made by direct translation from the original Hebrew and Greek, and the first to be printed, was the work of William Tyndale. He met bitter opposition. He was accused of willfully perverting the meaning of the Scriptures, and his New Testaments were ordered to be burned as "untrue translations." He was finally betrayed into the hands of his enemies, and in October 1536, was publicly executed and burned at the stake.

Yet Tyndale's work became the foundation of subsequent English versions, notably those of Coverdale, 1535; Thomas Matthew (probably a pseudonym for John Rogers), 1537; the Great Bible, 1539; the Geneva Bible, 1560; and the Bishops' Bible, 1568. In 1582 a translation of the New Testament, made from the Latin Vulgate by Roman Catholic scholars, was published at Rheims.

The translators who made the King James Version took into account all of these preceding versions; and comparison shows that it owes something to each of them. It kept felicitous phrases and apt expressions, from whatever source, which had stood the test of public usage. It owed most, especially in the New Testament, to Tyndale.

The King James Version had to compete with the Geneva Bible in popular use; but in the end it prevailed, and for more than two and a half centuries no other authorized translation of the Bible into English was made. The King James Version became the "Authorized Version" of the English-speaking peoples.

The King James Version has with good reason been termed "the noblest monument of English prose." Its revisers in 1881 expressed admiration for "its simplicity, its dignity, its power, its happy turns of expression . . . the music of its cadences, and the felicities of its rhythm." It entered, as no other book has, into the making of the personal character and the public institutions of the English-speaking peoples. We owe to it an incalculable debt.

Yet the King James Version has grave defects. By the middle of the nineteenth century, the development of Biblical studies and the discovery of many manuscripts more ancient than those upon which the King James Version was based, made it manifest that these defects are so many and so serious as to call for revision of the English translation. The task was undertaken, by authority of the Church of England, in 1870. The English Revised Version of the Bible was published in 1881–1885; and the American Standard Version, its variant embodying the preferences of the American scholars associated in the work, was published in 1901.

Because of unhappy experience with unauthorized publications in the two decades between 1881 and 1901, which tampered with the text of the English Revised Version in the supposed interest of the American public, the American Standard Version was copyrighted, to protect the text from unauthorized changes. In 1928 this copyright was acquired by the International Council of Religious Education, and thus passed into the ownership of the churches of the United States and Canada which were associated in this Council through their boards of education and publication.

The Council appointed a committee of scholars to have charge of the text of the American Standard Version and to undertake inquiry as to whether further revision was necessary. For more than two years the Committee worked upon the problem of whether or not revision should be undertaken; and if so, what should be its nature and extent. In the end the decision was reached that there is need for a thorough revision of the version of 1901, which will stay as close to the Tyndale-King James tradition as it can in the light of our present knowledge of the Hebrew and Greek texts and their meaning on the one hand, and our present understanding of English on the other.

In 1937 the revision was authorized by vote of the Council, which directed that the resulting version should "embody the best results of modern scholarship as to the meaning of the Scriptures, and express this meaning in English diction which is designed for use in public and private worship and preserves those qualities which have given to the King James Version a supreme place in English literature."

Thirty-two scholars have served as members of the Committee charged with making the revision, and they have secured the review and counsel of an Advisory Board of fifty representatives of the cooperating denominations. The Committee has worked in two sections, one dealing with the Old Testament and one with the New Testament. Each section has submitted its work to the scrutiny of the members of the other section; and the charter of the Committee requires that all changes be agreed upon by a two-thirds vote of the total membership of the Committee. The Revised Standard Version of the New Testament was published in 1946. The publication of the Revised Standard Version of the Bible, containing the Old and New Testaments, was authorized by vote of the National Council of the Churches of Christ in the U.S.A. in 1951.

The problem of establishing the correct Hebrew and Aramaic text of the Old Testament is very different from the corresponding problem in the New Testament. For the New Testament we have a large number of Greek manuscripts, preserving many variant forms of the text. Some of them were made only two or three centuries later than the original composition of the books. For the Old Testament only late manuscripts survive, all (with the exception of the Dead Sea texts of Isaiah and Habakkuk and some fragments of other books) based on a standardized form of the text established many centuries after the books were written.

The present revision is based on the consonantal Hebrew and Aramaic text as fixed early in the Christian era and revised by Jewish scholars (the "Masoretes") of the sixth to ninth centuries. The vowel signs, which were added by the Masoretes, are accepted also in the main, but where a more probable and convincing reading can be obtained by assuming different vowels, this has been done. No notes are given in such cases, because the vowel points are less ancient and reliable than the consonants.

Departures from the consonantal text of the best manuscripts have been made only where it seems clear that errors in copying had been made before the text was standardized. Most of the corrections adopted are based on the ancient versions (translations into Greek, Aramaic, Syriac, and Latin), which were made before the time of the Masoretic revision and therefore reflect earlier forms of the text. In every such instance a footnote specifies the version or versions from which the correction has been derived, and also gives a translation of the Masoretic Text.

Sometimes it is evident that the text has suffered in transmission, but none of the versions provides a satisfactory restoration. Here we can only follow the best judgment of competent scholars as to the most probable reconstruction of the original text. Such corrections are indicated in the footnotes by the abbreviation *Cn*, and a translation of the Masoretic Text is added.

The discovery of the meaning of the text, once the best readings have been established, is aided by many new resources for understanding the original languages. Much progress has been made in the historical and comparative study of these languages. A vast quantity of writings in related

Semitic languages, some of them only recently discovered, has greatly enlarged our knowledge of the vocabulary and grammar of Biblical Hebrew and Aramaic. Sometimes the present translation will be found to render a Hebrew word in a sense quite different from that of the traditional interpretation. It has not been felt necessary in such cases to attach a footnote, because no change in the text is involved and it may be assumed that the new rendering was not adopted without convincing evidence. The analysis of religious texts from the ancient Near East has made clearer the significance of ideas and practices recorded in the Old Testament. Many difficulties and obscurities, of course, remain. Where the choice between two meanings is particularly difficult or doubtful, we have given an alternative rendering in a footnote. If in the judgment of the Committee the meaning of a passage is quite uncertain or obscure, either because of corruption in the text or because of the inadequacy of our present knowledge of the language, that fact is indicated by a note. It should not be assumed, however, that the Committee was entirely sure or unanimous concerning every rendering not so indicated. To record all minority views was obviously out of the question.

A major departure from the practice of the American Standard Version is the rendering of the Divine Name, the "Tetragrammaton." The American Standard Version used the term "Jehovah"; the King James Version had employed this in four places, but everywhere else, except in three cases where it was employed as part of a proper name, used the English word LORD (or in certain cases GOD) printed in capitals. The present revision returns to the procedure of the King James Version, which follows the precedent of the ancient Greek and Latin translators and the long established practice in the reading of the Hebrew scriptures in the synagogue. While it is almost if not quite certain that the Name was originally pronounced "Yahweh," this pronunciation was not indicated when the Masoretes added vowel signs to the consonantal Hebrew text. To the four consonants YHWH of the Name, which had come to be regarded as too sacred to be pronounced, they attached vowel signs indicating that in its place should be read the Hebrew word *Adonai* meaning "Lord" (or *Elohim* meaning "God"). The ancient Greek translators substituted the word *Kyrios* (Lord) for the Name. The Vulgate likewise used the Latin word *Dominus*. The form "Jehovah" is of late medieval origin; it is a combination of the consonants of the Divine Name and the vowels attached to it by the Masoretes but belonging to an entirely different word. The sound of Y is represented by J and the sound of W by V, as in Latin. For two reasons the Committee has returned to the more familiar usage of the King James Version: (1) the word "Jehovah" does not accurately represent any form of the Name ever used in Hebrew; and (2) the use of any proper name for the one and only God, as though there were other gods from whom He had to be distinguished, was discontinued in Judaism before the Christian era and is entirely inappropriate for the universal faith of the Christian Church.

The King James Version of the New Testament was based upon a Greek text that was marred by mistakes, containing the accumulated errors of fourteen centuries of manuscript copying. It was essentially the Greek text of the New Testament as edited by Beza, 1589, who closely followed that published by Erasmus, 1516–1535, which was based upon a few medieval manuscripts. The earliest and best of the eight manuscripts which Erasmus consulted was from the tenth century, and he made the least use of it because it differed most from the commonly received text; Beza had access to two manuscripts of great value, dating from the fifth and sixth centuries, but he made very little use of them because they differed from the text published by Erasmus.

We now possess many more ancient manuscripts of the New Testament, and are far better equipped to seek to recover the original wording of the Greek text. The evidence for the text of the books of the New Testament is better than for any other ancient book, both in the number of extant manuscripts and in the nearness of the date of some of these manuscripts to the date when the book was originally written.

The revisers in the 1870's had most of the evidence that we now have for the Greek text, though the most ancient of all extant manuscripts of the Greek New Testament were not discovered until 1931. But they lacked the resources which discoveries within the past eighty years have afforded for understanding the vocabulary, grammar and idioms of the Greek New Testament. An amazing body of Greek papyri has been unearthed in Egypt since the 1870's—private letters, official reports, wills, business accounts, petitions, and other such trivial, everyday recordings of the activities of human beings. In 1895 appeared the first of Adolf Deissmann's studies of these ordinary materials. He proved that many words which had hitherto been assumed to belong to what was called "Biblical Greek" were current in the spoken vernacular of the first century A.D. The New Testament was written in the Koine, the common Greek which was spoken and understood practically everywhere throughout the Roman Empire in the early centuries of the Christian era. This development in the study of New Testament Greek has come since the work on the English Revised Version and the American Standard Version was done, and at many points sheds new light upon the meaning of the Greek text.

A major reason for revision of the King James Version, which is valid for both the Old Testament and the New Testament, is the change since 1611 in English usage. Many forms of expression have become archaic, while still generally intelligible—the use of thou, thee, thy, thine and the verb endings -est and -edst, the verb endings -eth and -th, it came to pass that, whosoever, whatsoever, insomuch that, because that, for that, unto, howbeit, peradventure, holden, aforetime, must needs, would fain, behooved, to you-ward, etc. Other words are obsolete and no longer understood by the common reader. The greatest problem, however, is presented by the English words which are still in constant use but now convey a different meaning from that which they had in 1611 and in the King James Version. These words were once accurate translations of the Hebrew and Greek Scriptures; but now, having changed in meaning, they have become misleading. They no longer say what the King James translators meant them to say.

The King James Version uses the word "let" in the sense of "hinder," "prevent" to mean "precede," "allow" in the sense of "approve," "communicate" for "share," "conversation" for "conduct," "comprehend" for "overcome," "ghost" for "spirit," "wealth" for "well-being," "allege" for "prove," "demand" for "ask," "take no thought" for "be not anxious," "purchase a good degree" for "gain a good standing," etc. The Greek word for "immediately" is translated in the King James Version not only by "immediately" and "straightway" but also by the terms "anon," "by and by," and "presently." There are more than three hundred such English words which are used in the King James Version in a sense substantially different from that which they now convey. It not only does the King James translators no honor, but it is quite unfair to them and to the truth which they understood and expressed, to retain these words which now convey meanings they did not intend.

The Revised Standard Version of the Bible, containing the Old and New Testaments, was published on September 30, 1952, and has met with wide acceptance. This preface does not undertake to set forth in detail the lines along which the revision proceeded. That is done in pamphlets entitled *An Introduction to the Revised Standard Version of the Old Testament* and *An Introduction to the Revised Standard Version of the New Testament*, written by members of the Committee and designed to help the general public to understand the main principles which have guided this comprehensive revision of the King James and American Standard versions.

These principles were reaffirmed by the Committee in 1959, in connection with a study of criticisms and suggestions from various readers. As a result, a few changes have been authorized for the present and subsequent editions. Most of these are corrections of punctuation, capitalization, or footnotes. Some changes of words or phrases are made in the interest of consistency, clarity or accuracy of translation. Examples of such changes are "from," Job 19.26; "bread," Matthew 7.9; 1 Corinthians 10.17; "is he," Matthew 21.9 and parallels; "the Son," Matthew 27.54; Mark 15.39; "ask nothing of me," John 16.23; "for this life only," 1 Corinthians 15.19; "the husband of one wife," 1 Timothy 3.2, 12; Titus 1.6.

All the reasons which led to the demand for revision of the King James Version in the nineteenth century are still valid, and are even more cogent now than then. We have had a freer charter than our predecessors in the 1870's in that we have not been required, as they were, to limit the language of the English Bible to the vocabulary of the Elizabethan age. But we hope that we have not taken undue advantage of that freedom. The Revised Standard Version is not a new translation in the language of today. It is not a paraphrase which aims at striking idioms. It is a revision which seeks to preserve all that is best in the English Bible as it has been known and used through the years. It is intended for use in public and private worship, not merely for reading and instruction. We have resisted the temptation to use phrases that are merely current usage, and have sought to put the message of the Bible in simple, enduring words that are worthy to stand in the great Tyndale-King James tradition. We are glad to say, with the King James translators: "Truly (good Christian Reader) we never thought from the beginning, that we should need to make a new Translation, nor yet to make of a bad one a good one . . . but to make a good one better."

The Bible is more than a historical document to be preserved. And it is more than a classic of English literature to be cherished and admired. It is a record of God's dealing with men, of God's revelation of Himself and His will. It records the life and work of Him in whom the Word of God became flesh and dwelt among men. The Bible carries its full message, not to those who regard it simply as a heritage of the past or praise its literary style, but to those who read it that they may discern and understand God's Word to men. That Word must not be disguised in phrases that are no longer clear, or hidden under words that have changed or lost their meaning. It must stand forth in language that is direct and plain and meaningful to people today. It is our hope and our earnest prayer that this Revised Standard Version of the Bible may be used by God to speak to men in these momentous times, and to help them to understand and believe and obey His Word.

THE NAMES AND ORDER OF THE BOOKS OF THE

OLD AND NEW TESTAMENTS

THE OLD TESTAMENT

	Page	*Chaps*
Genesis	1	50
Exodus	47	40
Leviticus	86	27
Numbers	114	36
Deuteronomy	155	34
Joshua	190	24
Judges	213	21
Ruth	236	4
1 Samuel	239	31
2 Samuel	269	24
1 Kings	295	22
2 Kings	325	25
1 Chronicles	354	29
2 Chronicles	380	36
Ezra	412	10
Nehemiah	422	13
Esther	435	10
Job	442	42
Psalms	475	150
Proverbs	560	31
Ecclesiastes	587	12
Song of Solomon	594	8
Isaiah	599	66
Jeremiah	662	52
Lamentations	722	5
Ezekiel	729	48
Daniel	778	12
Hosea	792	14
Joel	802	3
Amos	806	9
Obadiah	813	1
Jonah	815	4
Micah	817	7
Nahum	823	3
Habakkuk	825	3
Zephaniah	828	3
Haggai	831	2
Zechariah	833	14
Malachi	841	4

THE NEW TESTAMENT

	Page	*Chaps*
Matthew	1	28
Mark	32	16
Luke	52	24
John	86	21
Acts	111	28
Romans	141	16
1 Corinthians	155	16
2 Corinthians	168	13
Galatians	176	6
Ephesians	180	6
Philippians	184	4
Colossians	187	4
1 Thessalonians	190	5
2 Thessalonians	193	3
1 Timothy	195	6
2 Timothy	198	4
Titus	200	3
Philemon	202	1
Hebrews	203	13
James	213	5
1 Peter	216	5
2 Peter	219	3
1 John	222	5
2 John	225	1
3 John	226	1
Jude	226	1
Revelation	227	22

ABBREVIATIONS AND CROSS REFERENCES

ABBREVIATIONS

References to quoted and parallel passages are given following the notes on pages where these are relevant. The following abbreviations are used for the books of the Bible:

OLD TESTAMENT

Gen	Genesis	Eccles	Ecclesiastes
Ex	Exodus	Song	Song of Solomon
Lev	Leviticus	Is	Isaiah
Num	Numbers	Jer	Jeremiah
Deut	Deuteronomy	Lam	Lamentations
Josh	Joshua	Ezek	Ezekiel
Judg	Judges	Dan	Daniel
Ruth	Ruth	Hos	Hosea
1 Sam	1 Samuel	Joel	Joel
2 Sam	2 Samuel	Amos	Amos
1 Kings	1 Kings	Obad	Obadiah
2 Kings	2 Kings	Jon	Jonah
1 Chron	1 Chronicles	Mic	Micah
2 Chron	2 Chronicles	Nahum	Nahum
Ezra	Ezra	Hab	Habakkuk
Neh	Nehemiah	Zeph	Zephaniah
Esther	Esther	Hag	Haggai
Job	Job	Zech	Zechariah
Ps	Psalms	Mal	Malachi
Prov	Proverbs		

NEW TESTAMENT

Mt	Matthew	1 Tim	1 Timothy
Mk	Mark	2 Tim	2 Timothy
Lk	Luke	Tit	Titus
Jn	John	Philem	Philemon
Acts	Acts of the Apostles	Heb	Hebrews
Rom	Romans	Jas	James
1 Cor	1 Corinthians	1 Pet	1 Peter
2 Cor	2 Corinthians	2 Pet	2 Peter
Gal	Galatians	1 Jn	1 John
Eph	Ephesians	2 Jn	2 John
Phil	Philippians	3 Jn	3 John
Col	Colossians	Jude	Jude
1 Thess	1 Thessalonians	Rev	Revelation
2 Thess	2 Thessalonians		

In the notes to the books of the Old Testament, the following abbreviations are used: Ms for manuscript; Mss for manuscripts. Heb denotes the Hebrew of the consonantal Masoretic Text of the Old Testament; and MT denotes the Hebrew of the pointed Masoretic Text of the Old Testament.

ABBREVIATIONS AND CROSS REFERENCES

The ancient versions of the Old Testament are indicated by:

Gk	Septuagint, Greek Version of Old Testament
Sam	Samaritan Hebrew Text of Old Testament
Syr	Syriac Version of Old Testament
Tg	Targum
Vg	Vulgate, Latin Version of Old Testament

Cn indicates a correction made where the text has suffered in transmission and the versions provide no satisfactory restoration but the Committee agrees with the judgment of competent scholars as to the most probable reconstruction of the original text.

CROSS REFERENCES

Cross references for the thought or theme of an entire verse are given first; further references are put in the order of the words in the verse to which they pertain. These references are kept in the same order as the books of the Bible for each sentence, word, or phrase under consideration. For example: The first reference to Matthew 9.36 (Mk 6.34) refers to the whole verse; the next two references (Mt 14.14; 15.32) apply to the phrase "When he saw the crowds, he had compassion for them"; and the last two references (Num 27.17; Zech 10.2) apply to "helpless, like sheep without a shepherd." The reader is referred to the Preface for a further statement of policy concerning text and notes.

KEY TO PRONUNCIATION

In this edition of the Revised Standard Version of the Holy Bible a pronunciation system has been added so that the reader may easily read and pronounce the proper names. The pronunciation marks are shown in the list below. The names are separated into syllables, and an accent mark (ʹ) is placed after the syllable that is to receive the main stress. Pronunciation is shown only for those proper names that are not well known in English. It is not shown for common given names (such as *Benjamin*), common geographical place names (such as *Ethiopia*), or subjects of common reference (such as *Pharaoh*). Each name is pronounced only the first time it appears in any given verse.

a as in cat	ȯ as in cȯmply
ā " " cāke	u " " up
ä " " cär	ū " " ūse
ȧ " " ȧbout	ü " " rüle
â " " câre	u̇ " " focu̇s
e " " ten	ũr " " fũrther
ē " " ēven	y " " happy
ė " " agėnt or fathėr	ȳ " " lȳre
ẽr " " hẽrd	
i " " it or sanity	äi = i as in äisle
ī " " bīte	ch = k " " ache
ĩ " " bĩrd	ċ = s " " ċite
o " " lot	ġ = j " " ġem
ō " " gō	ṡ = z " " thoṡe
ô " " hôrn	ẋ = z " " ẋylophone

All other consonants are pronounced with their usual sounds in English, as ph = f, c = k, etc.

THE
Old Testament

THE FIRST BOOK OF MOSES

COMMONLY CALLED

GENESIS

1 In the beginning God created[a]
the heavens and the earth. 2 The
earth was without form and void, and
darkness was upon the face of the
deep; and the Spirit[b] of God was moving over the face of the waters.
3 And God said, "Let there be
light"; and there was light. 4 And God
saw that the light was good; and God
separated the light from the darkness.
5 God called the light Day, and the
darkness he called Night. And there
was evening and there was morning,
one day.
6 And God said, "Let there be a
firmament in the midst of the waters,
and let it separate the waters from the
waters." 7 And God made the firmament and separated the waters which
were under the firmament from the
waters which were above the firmament. And it was so. 8 And God called
the firmament Heaven. And there was
evening and there was morning, a
second day.
9 And God said, "Let the waters
under the heavens be gathered together into one place, and let the dry
land appear." And it was so. 10 God
called the dry land Earth, and the
waters that were gathered together he
called Seas. And God saw that it was
good. 11 And God said, "Let the earth
put forth vegetation, plants yielding
seed, and fruit trees bearing fruit in
which is their seed, each according to
its kind, upon the earth." And it was
so. 12 The earth brought forth vegetation, plants yielding seed according to
their own kinds, and trees bearing fruit
in which is their seed, each according
to its kind. And God saw that it was
good. 13 And there was evening and
there was morning, a third day.
14 And God said, "Let there be
lights in the firmament of the heavens
to separate the day from the night;
and let them be for signs and for
seasons and for days and years, 15 and
let them be lights in the firmament of
the heavens to give light upon the
earth." And it was so. 16 And God
made the two great lights, the greater
light to rule the day, and the lesser
light to rule the night; he made the
stars also. 17 And God set them in the
firmament of the heavens to give light
upon the earth, 18 to rule over the day
and over the night, and to separate
the light from the darkness. And God
saw that it was good. 19 And there was
evening and there was morning, a
fourth day.
20 And God said, "Let the waters
bring forth swarms of living creatures,
and let birds fly above the earth across
the firmament of the heavens." 21 So
God created the great sea monsters
and every living creature that moves,
with which the waters swarm, according to their kinds, and every winged
bird according to its kind. And God
saw that it was good. 22 And God
blessed them, saying, "Be fruitful and
multiply and fill the waters in the seas,
and let birds multiply on the earth."
23 And there was evening and there
was morning, a fifth day.
24 And God said, "Let the earth
bring forth living creatures according
to their kinds: cattle and creeping
things and beasts of the earth according to their kinds." And it was so.
25 And God made the beasts of the
earth according to their kinds and the
cattle according to their kinds, and
everything that creeps upon the
ground according to its kind. And God
saw that it was good.
26 Then God said, "Let us make
man in our image, after our likeness;
and let them have dominion over the
fish of the sea, and over the birds of
the air, and over the cattle, and over
all the earth, and over every creeping
thing that creeps upon the earth."
27 So God created man in his own
image, in the image of God he created

[a] Or *When God began to create* [b] Or *wind*
1.1: Jn 1.1. **1.26-27:** Gen 5.1; Mt 19.4; Mk 10.6; Col 3.10; Jas 3.9.

him; male and female he created them.
28 And God blessed them, and God
said to them, "Be fruitful and multiply,
and fill the earth and subdue it; and
have dominion over the fish of the sea
and over the birds of the air and over
every living thing that moves upon
the earth." 29 And God said, "Behold,
I have given you every plant yielding
seed which is upon the face of all the
earth, and every tree with seed in its
fruit; you shall have them for food.
30 And to every beast of the earth, and
to every bird of the air, and to everything that creeps on the earth, everything that has the breath of life, I have
given every green plant for food." And
it was so. 31 And God saw everything
that he had made, and behold, it was
very good. And there was evening and
there was morning, a sixth day.

2 Thus the heavens and the earth
were finished, and all the host of
them. 2 And on the seventh day God
finished his work which he had done,
and he rested on the seventh day from
all his work which he had done. 3 So
God blessed the seventh day and
hallowed it, because on it God rested
from all his work which he had done
in creation.

4 These are the generations of the
heavens and the earth when they were
created.

In the day that the LORD God made
the earth and the heavens, 5 when no
plant of the field was yet in the earth
and no herb of the field had yet sprung
up—for the LORD God had not caused
it to rain upon the earth, and there
was no man to till the ground; 6 but a
mist[c] went up from the earth and
watered the whole face of the ground—
7 then the LORD God formed man of
dust from the ground, and breathed
into his nostrils the breath of life; and
man became a living being. 8 And the
LORD God planted a garden in Eden,
in the east; and there he put the man
whom he had formed. 9 And out of the
ground the LORD God made to grow
every tree that is pleasant to the sight
and good for food, the tree of life also
in the midst of the garden, and the
tree of the knowledge of good and evil.

10 A river flowed out of Eden to
water the garden, and there it divided
and became four rivers. 11 The name
of the first is Pī'shon; it is the one
which flows around the whole land of
Hav'i·lȧh, where there is gold; 12 and
the gold of that land is good; bdellium
and onyx stone are there. 13 The name
of the second river is Gī'hon; it is the
one which flows around the whole land
of Cush. 14 And the name of the third
river is Tī'gris, which flows east of
Assyria. And the fourth river is the
Eū·phrā'tēṡ.

15 The LORD God took the man
and put him in the garden of Eden to
till it and keep it. 16 And the LORD God
commanded the man, saying, "You
may freely eat of every tree of the
garden; 17 but of the tree of the knowledge of good and evil you shall not
eat, for in the day that you eat of it
you shall die."

18 Then the LORD God said, "It is
not good that the man should be
alone; I will make him a helper fit for
him." 19 So out of the ground the
LORD God formed every beast of the
field and every bird of the air, and
brought them to the man to see what
he would call them; and whatever the
man called every living creature, that
was its name. 20 The man gave names
to all cattle, and to the birds of the air,
and to every beast of the field; but for
the man there was not found a helper
fit for him. 21 So the LORD God caused
a deep sleep to fall upon the man, and
while he slept took one of his ribs and
closed up its place with flesh; 22 and
the rib which the LORD God had taken
from the man he made into a woman
and brought her to the man. 23 Then
the man said,

"This at last is bone of my bones
and flesh of my flesh;
she shall be called Woman,[d]
because she was taken out of
Man."[e]

24 Therefore a man leaves his father
and his mother and cleaves to his wife,
and they become one flesh. 25 And the
man and his wife were both naked,
and were not ashamed.

3 Now the serpent was more subtle
than any other wild creature that
the LORD God had made. He said to
the woman, "Did God say, 'You shall
not eat of any tree of the garden'?"
2 And the woman said to the serpent,
"We may eat of the fruit of the trees

[c] Or *flood* [d] Heb *ishshah* [e] Heb *ish*

2.1-3: Ex 20.11. **2.2:** Heb 4.4, 10. **2.7:** 1 Cor 15.45, 47. **2.9:** Rev 2.7; 22.2, 14, 19.
2.24: Mt 19.5; Mk 10.7; 1 Cor 6.16; Eph 5.31. **3.1:** Rev 12.9; 20.2.

of the garden; 3 but God said, 'You
shall not eat of the fruit of the tree
which is in the midst of the garden,
neither shall you touch it, lest you
die.' " 4 But the serpent said to the
woman, "You will not die. 5 For God
knows that when you eat of it your
eyes will be opened, and you will be
like God, knowing good and evil." 6 So
when the woman saw that the tree was
good for food, and that it was a delight
to the eyes, and that the tree was to be
desired to make one wise, she took of
its fruit and ate; and she also gave some
to her husband, and he ate. 7 Then the
eyes of both were opened, and they
knew that they were naked; and they
sewed fig leaves together and made
themselves aprons.

8 And they heard the sound of the
LORD God walking in the garden in
the cool of the day, and the man and
his wife hid themselves from the presence of the LORD God among the trees
of the garden. 9 But the LORD God
called to the man, and said to him,
"Where are you?" 10 And he said, "I
heard the sound of thee in the garden,
and I was afraid, because I was naked;
and I hid myself." 11 He said, "Who
told you that you were naked? Have
you eaten of the tree of which I commanded you not to eat?" 12 The man
said, "The woman whom thou gavest
to be with me, she gave me fruit of the
tree, and I ate." 13 Then the LORD
God said to the woman, "What is this
that you have done?" The woman
said, "The serpent beguiled me, and
I ate."

14 The LORD God said to the serpent,
"Because you have done this,
cursed are you above all cattle,
and above all wild animals;
upon your belly you shall go,
and dust you shall eat
all the days of your life.
15 I will put enmity between you and
the woman,
and between your seed and her
seed;
he shall bruise your head,
and you shall bruise his heel."
16 To the woman he said,
"I will greatly multiply your pain in
childbearing;
in pain you shall bring forth
children,
yet your desire shall be for your
husband,
and he shall rule over you."
17 And to Adam he said,
"Because you have listened to the
voice of your wife,
and have eaten of the tree
of which I commanded you,
'You shall not eat of it,'
cursed is the ground because of you;
in toil you shall eat of it all the
days of your life;
18 thorns and thistles it shall bring
forth to you;
and you shall eat the plants of the
field.
19 In the sweat of your face
you shall eat bread
till you return to the ground,
for out of it you were taken;
you are dust,
and to dust you shall return."

20 The man called his wife's name
Eve,[f] because she was the mother of
all living. 21 And the LORD God made
for Adam and for his wife garments of
skins, and clothed them.

22 Then the LORD God said, "Behold, the man has become like one of
us, knowing good and evil; and now,
lest he put forth his hand and take also
of the tree of life, and eat, and live for
ever"—23 therefore the LORD God sent
him forth from the garden of Eden, to
till the ground from which he was
taken. 24 He drove out the man; and at
the east of the garden of Eden he
placed the cherubim, and a flaming
sword which turned every way, to
guard the way to the tree of life.

4 Now Adam knew Eve his wife,
and she conceived and bore Cain,
saying, "I have gotten[g] a man with the
help of the LORD." 2 And again, she
bore his brother Abel. Now Abel was
a keeper of sheep, and Cain a tiller of
the ground. 3 In the course of time
Cain brought to the LORD an offering
of the fruit of the ground, 4 and Abel
brought of the firstlings of his flock
and of their fat portions. And the
LORD had regard for Abel and his
offering, 5 but for Cain and his offering
he had no regard. So Cain was very
angry, and his countenance fell. 6 The
LORD said to Cain, "Why are you
angry, and why has your countenance
fallen? 7 If you do well, will you not be

[f] The name in Hebrew resembles the word for *living* [g] Heb *qanah*, get

3.4: 2 Cor 11.3. **3.13:** 2 Cor 11.3. **3.14-15:** Rev 12.9; 20.2. **3.17-18:** Heb 6.8.
3.22, 24: Rev 2.7; 22.2, 14, 19. **4.4:** Heb 11.4.

accepted? And if you do not do well,
sin is couching at the door; its desire is for you, but you must master
it."

8 Cain said to Abel his brother,
"Let us go out to the field."[h] And
when they were in the field, Cain rose
up against his brother Abel, and killed
him. 9 Then the LORD said to Cain,
"Where is Abel your brother?" He
said, "I do not know; am I my
brother's keeper?" 10And the LORD
said, "What have you done? The voice
of your brother's blood is crying to me
from the ground. 11And now you are
cursed from the ground, which has
opened its mouth to receive your
brother's blood from your hand.
12 When you till the ground, it shall no
longer yield to you its strength; you
shall be a fugitive and a wanderer on
the earth." 13 Cain said to the LORD,
"My punishment is greater than I can
bear. 14 Behold, thou hast driven me
this day away from the ground; and
from thy face I shall be hidden; and I
shall be a fugitive and a wanderer on
the earth, and whoever finds me will
slay me." 15 Then the LORD said to
him, "Not so![i] If any one slays Cain,
vengeance shall be taken on him sevenfold." And the LORD put a mark on
Cain, lest any who came upon him
should kill him. 16 Then Cain went
away from the presence of the LORD,
and dwelt in the land of Nod,[j] east of
Eden.

17 Cain knew his wife, and she conceived and bore Ē'nŏch; and he built
a city, and called the name of the city
after the name of his son, Enoch. 18 To
Ē'nŏch was born Ī'rad; and Irad was
the father of Me·hū'jā-el, and Mehuja-
el the father of Me·thū'shā-el, and
Methusha-el the father of Lā'mech.
19And Lā'mech took two wives; the
name of the one was Ā'dăh, and the
name of the other Zĭl'lăh. 20Ā'dăh bore
Jā'băl; he was the father of those who
dwell in tents and have cattle. 21 His
brother's name was Jū'băl; he was the
father of all those who play the lyre
and pipe. 22 Zĭl'lăh bore Tū'băl-cāin;
he was the forger of all instruments of
bronze and iron. The sister of Tubal-
cain was Nā'ă·măh.

23 Lā'mech said to his wives:
"Ā'dăh and Zĭl'lăh, hear my voice;
you wives of Lamech, hearken to
what I say:
I have slain a man for wounding me,
a young man for striking me.
24 If Cain is avenged sevenfold,
truly Lā'mech seventy-seven-
fold."

25 And Adam knew his wife again,
and she bore a son and called his name
Seth, for she said, "God has appointed
for me another child instead of Abel,
for Cain slew him." 26 To Seth also a
son was born, and he called his name
Ē'nŏsh. At that time men began to call
upon the name of the LORD.

5 This is the book of the generations of Adam. When God created
man, he made him in the likeness of
God. 2 Male and female he created
them, and he blessed them and named
them Man when they were created.
3 When Adam had lived a hundred and
thirty years, he became the father of a
son in his own likeness, after his image,
and named him Seth. 4 The days of
Adam after he became the father of
Seth were eight hundred years; and he
had other sons and daughters. 5 Thus
all the days that Adam lived were nine
hundred and thirty years; and he
died.

6 When Seth had lived a hundred
and five years, he became the father of
Ē'nŏsh. 7 Seth lived after the birth
of Ē'nŏsh eight hundred and seven
years, and had other sons and daughters. 8 Thus all the days of Seth were
nine hundred and twelve years; and
he died.

9 When Ē'nŏsh had lived ninety
years, he became the father of Kē'năn.
10 Ē'nŏsh lived after the birth of Kē'-
năn eight hundred and fifteen years,
and had other sons and daughters.
11 Thus all the days of Ē'nŏsh were
nine hundred and five years; and he
died.

12 When Kē'năn had lived seventy
years, he became the father of Ma-
hal'ă·lel. 13 Kē'năn lived after the
birth of Ma-hal'ă·lel eight hundred
and forty years, and had other sons
and daughters. 14 Thus all the days of
Kē'năn were nine hundred and ten
years; and he died.

15 When Ma-hal'ă·lel had lived
sixty-five years, he became the father
of Jâr'ĕd. 16 Ma-hal'ă·lel lived after

[h] Sam Gk Syr Compare Vg: Heb lacks *Let us go out to the field* [i] Gk Syr Vg: Heb *Therefore*
[j] That is *Wandering*
4.8: 1 Jn 3.12. **5.1**: Gen 1.27.

the birth of Jâr'ĕd eight hundred and
thirty years, and had other sons and
daughters. 17 Thus all the days of Ma-
hal'ă·lel were eight hundred and ninety-
five years; and he died.

18 When Jâr'ĕd had lived a hundred
and sixty-two years he became the
father of E'nŏch. 19 Jâr'ĕd lived after
the birth of E'nŏch eight hundred
years, and had other sons and daughters. 20 Thus all the days of Jâr'ĕd were
nine hundred and sixty-two years; and
he died.

21 When E'nŏch had lived sixty-
five years, he became the father of
Mĕ·thü'sĕ·lăh. 22 E'nŏch walked with
God after the birth of Mĕ·thü'sĕ·lăh
three hundred years, and had other
sons and daughters. 23 Thus all the
days of E'nŏch were three hundred
and sixty-five years. 24 E'nŏch walked
with God; and he was not, for God
took him.

25 When Mĕ·thü'sĕ·lăh had lived a
hundred and eighty-seven years, he
became the father of Lā'mech. 26 Mĕ-
thü'sĕ·lăh lived after the birth of
Lā'mech seven hundred and eighty-
two years, and had other sons and
daughters. 27 Thus all the days of
Mĕ·thü'sĕ·lăh were nine hundred and
sixty-nine years; and he died.

28 When Lā'mech had lived a hundred and eighty-two years, he became
the father of a son, 29 and called his
name Noah, saying, "Out of the
ground which the LORD has cursed
this one shall bring us relief from our
work and from the toil of our hands."
30 Lā'mech lived after the birth of
Noah five hundred and ninety-five
years, and had other sons and daughters. 31 Thus all the days of Lā'mech
were seven hundred and seventy-seven
years; and he died.

32 After Noah was five hundred
years old, Noah became the father of
Shem, Ham, and Jā'pheth.

6 When men began to multiply on
the face of the ground, and daughters were born to them, 2 the sons of
God saw that the daughters of men
were fair; and they took to wife such
of them as they chose. 3 Then the
LORD said, "My spirit shall not abide
in man for ever, for he is flesh, but his
days shall be a hundred and twenty
years." 4 The Neph'i·lim were on the
earth in those days, and also afterward,
when the sons of God came in to the
daughters of men, and they bore
children to them. These were the
mighty men that were of old, the men
of renown.

5 The LORD saw that the wickedness of man was great in the earth,
and that every imagination of the
thoughts of his heart was only evil
continually. 6 And the LORD was sorry
that he had made man on the earth,
and it grieved him to his heart. 7 So
the LORD said, "I will blot out man
whom I have created from the face of
the ground, man and beast and creeping things and birds of the air, for I
am sorry that I have made them."
8 But Noah found favor in the eyes of
the LORD.

9 These are the generations of
Noah. Noah was a righteous man,
blameless in his generation; Noah
walked with God. 10 And Noah had
three sons, Shem, Ham, and Jā'-
pheth.

11 Now the earth was corrupt in
God's sight, and the earth was filled
with violence. 12 And God saw the
earth, and behold, it was corrupt; for
all flesh had corrupted their way upon
the earth. 13 And God said to Noah,
"I have determined to make an end
of all flesh; for the earth is filled with
violence through them; behold, I will
destroy them with the earth. 14 Make
yourself an ark of gopher wood; make
rooms in the ark, and cover it inside
and out with pitch. 15 This is how you
are to make it: the length of the ark
three hundred cubits, its breadth fifty
cubits, and its height thirty cubits.
16 Make a roof[k] for the ark, and finish
it to a cubit above; and set the door of
the ark in its side; make it with lower,
second, and third decks. 17 For behold, I will bring a flood of waters
upon the earth, to destroy all flesh in
which is the breath of life from under
heaven; everything that is on the earth
shall die. 18 But I will establish my
covenant with you; and you shall come
into the ark, you, your sons, your wife,
and your sons' wives with you. 19 And
of every living thing of all flesh, you
shall bring two of every sort into the
ark, to keep them alive with you; they
shall be male and female. 20 Of the
birds according to their kinds, and of
the animals according to their kinds,

[k] Or *Window*
5.24: Heb 11.5. **6.4:** Num 13.33.

of every creeping thing of the ground
according to its kind, two of every sort
shall come in to you, to keep them
alive. 21 Also take with you every sort
of food that is eaten, and store it up;
and it shall serve as food for you and
for them." 22 Noah did this; he did all
that God commanded him.

7 Then the LORD said to Noah,
"Go into the ark, you and all your
household, for I have seen that you are
righteous before me in this generation.
2 Take with you seven pairs of all clean
animals, the male and his mate; and a
pair of the animals that are not clean,
the male and his mate; 3 and seven
pairs of the birds of the air also, male
and female, to keep their kind alive
upon the face of all the earth. 4 For in
seven days I will send rain upon the
earth forty days and forty nights; and
every living thing that I have made I
will blot out from the face of the
ground." 5 And Noah did all that the
LORD had commanded him.

6 Noah was six hundred years old
when the flood of waters came upon
the earth. 7 And Noah and his sons and
his wife and his sons' wives with him
went into the ark, to escape the waters
of the flood. 8 Of clean animals, and
of animals that are not clean, and of
birds, and of everything that creeps on
the ground, 9 two and two, male and
female, went into the ark with Noah,
as God had commanded Noah. 10 And
after seven days the waters of the flood
came upon the earth.

11 In the six hundredth year of
Noah's life, in the second month, on
the seventeenth day of the month, on
that day all the fountains of the great
deep burst forth, and the windows of
the heavens were opened. 12 And rain
fell upon the earth forty days and forty
nights. 13 On the very same day Noah
and his sons, Shem and Ham and
Jā'pheth, and Noah's wife and the
three wives of his sons with them
entered the ark, 14 they and every
beast according to its kind, and all the
cattle according to their kinds, and
every creeping thing that creeps on
the earth according to its kind, and
every bird according to its kind, every
bird of every sort. 15 They went into
the ark with Noah, two and two of all
flesh in which there was the breath of
life. 16 And they that entered, male and
female of all flesh, went in as God had
commanded him; and the LORD shut
him in.

17 The flood continued forty days
upon the earth; and the waters increased, and bore up the ark, and it
rose high above the earth. 18 The
waters prevailed and increased greatly
upon the earth; and the ark floated on
the face of the waters. 19 And the waters
prevailed so mightily upon the earth
that all the high mountains under the
whole heaven were covered; 20 the
waters prevailed above the mountains,
covering them fifteen cubits deep.
21 And all flesh died that moved upon
the earth, birds, cattle, beasts, all
swarming creatures that swarm upon
the earth, and every man; 22 everything on the dry land in whose nostrils
was the breath of life died. 23 He
blotted out every living thing that was
upon the face of the ground, man and
animals and creeping things and birds
of the air; they were blotted out from
the earth. Only Noah was left, and
those that were with him in the ark.
24 And the waters prevailed upon the
earth a hundred and fifty days.

8 But God remembered Noah and
all the beasts and all the cattle that
were with him in the ark. And God
made a wind blow over the earth, and
the waters subsided; 2 the fountains
of the deep and the windows of the
heavens were closed, the rain from the
heavens was restrained, 3 and the
waters receded from the earth continually. At the end of a hundred and
fifty days the waters had abated; 4 and
in the seventh month, on the seventeenth day of the month, the ark came
to rest upon the mountains of Ar'ȧ·rat.
5 And the waters continued to abate
until the tenth month; in the tenth
month, on the first day of the month,
the tops of the mountains were seen.

6 At the end of forty days Noah
opened the window of the ark which
he had made, 7 and sent forth a raven;
and it went to and fro until the waters
were dried up from the earth. 8 Then
he sent forth a dove from him, to see
if the waters had subsided from the
face of the ground; 9 but the dove
found no place to set her foot, and she
returned to him to the ark, for the
waters were still on the face of the
whole earth. So he put forth his hand
and took her and brought her into the
ark with him. 10 He waited another

7.7: Mt 24.38; Lk 17.27.

seven days, and again he sent forth the
dove out of the ark; 11 and the dove
came back to him in the evening, and
lo, in her mouth a freshly plucked
olive leaf; so Noah knew that the waters
had subsided from the earth. 12 Then
he waited another seven days, and
sent forth the dove; and she did not
return to him any more.

13 In the six hundred and first
year, in the first month, the first day
of the month, the waters were dried
from off the earth; and Noah removed
the covering of the ark, and looked,
and behold, the face of the ground was
dry. 14 In the second month, on the
twenty-seventh day of the month, the
earth was dry. 15 Then God said to
Noah, 16 "Go forth from the ark, you
and your wife, and your sons and your
sons' wives with you. 17 Bring forth
with you every living thing that is with
you of all flesh—birds and animals and
every creeping thing that creeps on the
earth—that they may breed abundantly on the earth, and be fruitful and
multiply upon the earth." 18 So Noah
went forth, and his sons and his wife
and his sons' wives with him. 19 And
every beast, every creeping thing, and
every bird, everything that moves
upon the earth, went forth by families
out of the ark.

20 Then Noah built an altar to the
LORD, and took of every clean animal
and of every clean bird, and offered
burnt offerings on the altar. 21 And
when the LORD smelled the pleasing
odor, the LORD said in his heart, "I
will never again curse the ground because of man, for the imagination of
man's heart is evil from his youth;
neither will I ever again destroy every
living creature as I have done. 22 While
the earth remains, seedtime and harvest, cold and heat, summer and
winter, day and night, shall not cease."

9 And God blessed Noah and his
sons, and said to them, "Be fruitful and multiply, and fill the earth.
2 The fear of you and the dread of you
shall be upon every beast of the earth,
and upon every bird of the air, upon
everything that creeps on the ground
and all the fish of the sea; into your
hand they are delivered. 3 Every moving thing that lives shall be food for
you; and as I gave you the green plants,
I give you everything. 4 Only you shall
not eat flesh with its life, that is, its
blood. 5 For your lifeblood I will surely
require a reckoning; of every beast I
will require it and of man; of every
man's brother I will require the life of
man. 6 Whoever sheds the blood of
man, by man shall his blood be shed;
for God made man in his own image.
7 And you, be fruitful and multiply,
bring forth abundantly on the earth
and multiply in it."

8 Then God said to Noah and to
his sons with him, 9 "Behold, I establish my covenant with you and your
descendants after you, 10 and with
every living creature that is with you,
the birds, the cattle, and every beast
of the earth with you, as many as
came out of the ark.[l] 11 I establish my
covenant with you, that never again
shall all flesh be cut off by the waters
of a flood, and never again shall there
be a flood to destroy the earth." 12 And
God said, "This is the sign of the
covenant which I make between me
and you and every living creature that
is with you, for all future generations:
13 I set my bow in the cloud, and it
shall be a sign of the covenant between
me and the earth. 14 When I bring
clouds over the earth and the bow is
seen in the clouds, 15 I will remember
my covenant which is between me and
you and every living creature of all
flesh; and the waters shall never again
become a flood to destroy all flesh.
16 When the bow is in the clouds, I
will look upon it and remember the
everlasting covenant between God and
every living creature of all flesh that
is upon the earth." 17 God said to
Noah, "This is the sign of the covenant which I have established between
me and all flesh that is upon the
earth."

18 The sons of Noah who went
forth from the ark were Shem, Ham,
and Jā'pheth. Ham was the father of
Canaan. 19 These three were the sons
of Noah; and from these the whole
earth was peopled.

20 Noah was the first tiller of the
soil. He planted a vineyard; 21 and he
drank of the wine, and became drunk,
and lay uncovered in his tent. 22 And
Ham, the father of Canaan, saw the
nakedness of his father, and told his
two brothers outside. 23 Then Shem
and Jā'pheth took a garment, laid it

[l] Gk: Heb repeats *every beast of the earth*
9.4: Lev 7.26-27; 17.10-14; Deut 12.16, 23.

upon both their shoulders, and walked
backward and covered the nakedness
of their father; their faces were turned
away, and they did not see their
father's nakedness. 24 When Noah
awoke from his wine and knew what
his youngest son had done to him,
25 he said,
"Cursed be Canaan;
a slave of slaves shall he be to his
brothers."
26 He also said,
"Blessed by the LORD my God be
Shem;[m]
and let Canaan be his slave.
27 God enlarge Jā'pheth,
and let him dwell in the tents of
Shem;
and let Canaan be his slave."
28 After the flood Noah lived three
hundred and fifty years. 29 All the days
of Noah were nine hundred and fifty
years; and he died.

10 These are the generations of the
sons of Noah, Shem, Ham, and
Jā'pheth; sons were born to them after
the flood.
2 The sons of Jā'pheth: Gō'mėr,
Mā'gog, Mad'āi, Jā'vȧn, Tü'bȧl, Mē'-
shech, and Tī'rȧs. 3 The sons of Gō'-
mėr: Ash'kė·naz, Rī'phȧth, and Tō-
gär'mȧh. 4 The sons of Jā'vȧn: E·lī'-
shȧh, Tär'shish, Kit'tim, and Do'dȧ-
nim. 5 From these the coastland
peoples spread. These are the sons of
Jā'pheth[n] in their lands, each with his
own language, by their families, in
their nations.
6 The sons of Ham: Cush, Egypt,
Püt, and Canaan. 7 The sons of Cush:
Sē'bȧ, Hav'i·lȧh, Sab'tȧh, Rā'ȧ·mȧh,
and Sab'tė·cȧ. The sons of Raamah:
Sheba and Dē'dan. 8 Cush became the
father of Nimrod; he was the first on
earth to be a mighty man. 9 He was a
mighty hunter before the LORD; therefore it is said, "Like Nimrod a mighty
hunter before the LORD." 10 The beginning of his kingdom was Bā'bėl,
Ē'rech, and Ac'cad, all of them in the
land of Shī'när. 11 From that land he
went into Assyria, and built Nin'ė·vėh,
Re·hō'both-Ir, Cā'lȧh, and 12 Rē'sėn
between Nin'ė·vėh and Cā'lȧh; that is
the great city. 13 Egypt became the
father of Lü'dim, An'ȧ·mim, Lē·hä'-
bim, Naph'tū·him, 14 Path·rü'sim,
Cas·lü'him (whence came the Philistines), and Caph'tȯ·rim.
15 Canaan became the father of
Sī'don his first-born, and Heth, 16 and
the Jeb'ū·sītes, the Am'ȯ·rītes, the
Gīr'gȧ·shītes, 17 the Hī'vītes, the Ärk'-
ītes, the Sī'nītes, 18 the Är'vȧ·dītes, the
Zem'ȧ·rītes, and the Hā'mȧ·thītes.
Afterward the families of the Canaanites spread abroad. 19 And the territory
of the Canaanites extended from
Sī'don, in the direction of Gē'rär, as
far as Gā'zȧ, and in the direction of
Sod'ȯm, Gȯ·môr'rȧh, Ad'mȧh, and
Ze·boi'im, as far as Lā'shȧ. 20 These
are the sons of Ham, by their families,
their languages, their lands, and their
nations.
21 To Shem also, the father of all
the children of Ē'bėr, the elder brother
of Jā'pheth, children were born. 22 The
sons of Shem: Ē'lȧm, As'shür, Är-
pach'shad, Lüd, and Âr'ȧm. 23 The
sons of Âr'ȧm: Ūz, Hül, Gē'thėr, and
Mash. 24 Är·pach'shad became the
father of Shē'lȧh; and Shelah became
the father of Ē'bėr. 25 To Ē'bėr were
born two sons: the name of the one was
Pē'leg,[o] for in his days the earth was
divided, and his brother's name was
Jok'tan. 26 Jok'tan became the father
of Al·mō'dad, Shē'leph, Hā·zär·mā'-
veth, Jē'rȧh, 27 Hȧ·dôr'ȧm, Ū'zȧl,
Dik'lȧh, 28 Ō'bȧl, Ȧ·bim'ȧ-el, Sheba,
29 Ō'phīr, Hav'i·lȧh, and Jō'bab; all
these were the sons of Jok'tan. 30 The
territory in which they lived extended
from Mē'shȧ in the direction of Sē'phȧr
to the hill country of the east. 31 These
are the sons of Shem, by their families,
their languages, their lands, and their
nations.
32 These are the families of the sons
of Noah, according to their genealogies, in their nations; and from these
the nations spread abroad on the earth
after the flood.

11 Now the whole earth had one
language and few words. 2 And as
men migrated from the east, they found
a plain in the land of Shī'när and
settled there. 3 And they said to one
another, "Come, let us make bricks, and
burn them thoroughly." And they had
brick for stone, and bitumen for mortar.
4 Then they said, "Come, let us build
ourselves a city, and a tower with its
top in the heavens, and let us make a
name for ourselves, lest we be scattered
abroad upon the face of the whole
earth." 5 And the LORD came down to

[m] Or *Blessed be the* LORD, *the God of Shem*
[n] Supplied from verses 20, 31. Heb lacks *These are the sons of Japheth* [o] That is *Division*

see the city and the tower, which the
sons of men had built. 6And the LORD
said, "Behold, they are one people,
and they have all one language; and
this is only the beginning of what they
will do; and nothing that they propose
to do will now be impossible for them.
7 Come, let us go down, and there
confuse their language, that they may
not understand one another's speech."
8 So the LORD scattered them abroad
from there over the face of all the
earth, and they left off building the
city. 9 Therefore its name was called
Bā′bėl, because there the LORD confused[p] the language of all the earth;
and from there the LORD scattered
them abroad over the face of all the
earth.

10 These are the descendants of
Shem. When Shem was a hundred
years old, he became the father of
Ăr·pach′shad two years after the flood;
11 and Shem lived after the birth of
Ăr·pach′shad five hundred years, and
had other sons and daughters.

12 When Ăr·pach′shad had lived
thirty-five years, he became the father
of Shē′lȧh; 13 and Ăr·pach′shad lived
after the birth of Shē′lȧh four hundred
and three years, and had other sons
and daughters.

14 When Shē′lȧh had lived thirty
years, he became the father of Ē′bėr;
15 and Shē′lȧh lived after the birth
of Ē′bėr four hundred and three
years, and had other sons and daughters.

16 When Ē′bėr had lived thirty-
four years, he became the father of
Pē′leg; 17 and Ē′bėr lived after the
birth of Pē′leg four hundred and thirty
years, and had other sons and
daughters.

18 When Pē′leg had lived thirty
years, he became the father of Rē′ü;
19 and Pē′leg lived after the birth of
Rē′ü two hundred and nine years, and
had other sons and daughters.

20 When Rē′ü had lived thirty-two
years, he became the father of Sē′-
ru̇g; 21 and Rē′ü lived after the birth
of Sē′ru̇g two hundred and seven
years, and had other sons and daughters.

22 When Sē′ru̇g had lived thirty
years, he became the father of Nā′hôr;
23 and Sē′ru̇g lived after the birth of
Nā′hôr two hundred years, and had
other sons and daughters.

24 When Nā′hôr had lived twenty-
nine years, he became the father of
Tē′rȧh; 25 and Nā′hôr lived after the
birth of Tē′rȧh a hundred and nineteen years, and had other sons and
daughters.

26 When Tē′rȧh had lived seventy
years, he became the father of Abram,
Nā′hôr, and Hâr′ȧn.

27 Now these are the descendants
of Tē′rȧh. Terah was the father of
Abram, Nā′hôr, and Hâr′ȧn; and Haran
was the father of Lot. 28 Hâr′ȧn died
before his father Tē′rȧh in the land of
his birth, in Ŭr of the Chal·dē′ȧnṡ.
29And Abram and Nā′hôr took wives;
the name of Abram's wife was Sâr′äi,
and the name of Nahor's wife, Mil′cȧh,
the daughter of Hâr′ȧn the father of
Milcah and Iṡ′cȧh. 30 Now Sâr′äi was
barren; she had no child.

31 Tē′rȧh took Abram his son and
Lot the son of Hâr′ȧn, his grandson,
and Sâr′äi his daughter-in-law, his son
Abram's wife, and they went forth
together from Ŭr of the Chal·dē′ȧnṡ to
go into the land of Canaan; but when
they came to Haran, they settled there.
32 The days of Tē′rȧh were two hundred and five years; and Terah died
in Hâr′ȧn.

12 Now the LORD said to Abram,
"Go from your country and your
kindred and your father's house to the
land that I will show you. 2And I will
make of you a great nation, and I will
bless you, and make your name great,
so that you will be a blessing. 3 I will
bless those who bless you, and him
who curses you I will curse; and by
you all the families of the earth shall
bless themselves."[q]

4 So Abram went, as the LORD had
told him; and Lot went with him.
Abram was seventy-five years old when
he departed from Hâr′ȧn. 5And
Abram took Sâr′äi his wife, and Lot
his brother's son, and all their possessions which they had gathered, and
the persons that they had gotten in
Hâr′ȧn; and they set forth to go to the
land of Canaan. When they had come
to the land of Canaan, 6Abram passed
through the land to the place at Shē′-
chem, to the oak[r] of Mō′reh. At that
time the Canaanites were in the land.

[p] Compare Heb *balal*, confuse [q] Or *in you all the families of the earth will be blessed* [r] Or *terebinth*
12.1: Acts 7.3; Heb 11.8. **12.2**: Gen 15.5; 17.4-5; 18.18; 22.17; 28.14; 32.12; 35.11; 46.3.
12.3: Gen 18.18; 22.17-18; 26.4; 28.14; Gal 3.8.

7 Then the LORD appeared to Abram,
and said, "To your descendants I will
give this land." So he built there an
altar to the LORD, who had appeared
to him. 8 Thence he removed to the
mountain on the east of Beth'ĕl, and
pitched his tent, with Bethel on the
west and Ä̆i on the east; and there he
built an altar to the LORD and called
on the name of the LORD. 9And Abram
journeyed on, still going toward the
Negeb.

10 Now there was a famine in the
land. So Abram went down to Egypt
to sojourn there, for the famine was
severe in the land. 11 When he was
about to enter Egypt, he said to Sâr'äi
his wife, "I know that you are a woman
beautiful to behold; 12 and when the
Egyptians see you, they will say, 'This
is his wife'; then they will kill me, but
they will let you live. 13 Say you are
my sister, that it may go well with me
because of you, and that my life may
be spared on your account." 14 When
Abram entered Egypt the Egyptians
saw that the woman was very beautiful.
15And when the princes of Pharaoh
saw her, they praised her to Pharaoh.
And the woman was taken into Pharaoh's house. 16And for her sake he
dealt well with Abram; and he had
sheep, oxen, he-asses, menservants,
maidservants, she-asses, and camels.

17 But the LORD afflicted Pharaoh
and his house with great plagues because of Sâr'äi, Abram's wife. 18 So
Pharaoh called Abram, and said,
"What is this you have done to me?
Why did you not tell me that she was
your wife? 19 Why did you say, 'She
is my sister,' so that I took her for my
wife? Now then, here is your wife, take
her, and be gone." 20And Pharaoh
gave men orders concerning him; and
they set him on the way, with his wife
and all that he had.

13 So Abram went up from Egypt,
he and his wife, and all that he
had, and Lot with him, into the Negeb.

2 Now Abram was very rich in
cattle, in silver, and in gold. 3And he
journeyed on from the Negeb as far as
Beth'ĕl, to the place where his tent
had been at the beginning, between
Bethel and Ä̆i, 4 to the place where he
had made an altar at the first; and
there Abram called on the name of the
LORD. 5And Lot, who went with
Abram, also had flocks and herds and
tents, 6 so that the land could not
support both of them dwelling together; for their possessions were so
great that they could not dwell together, 7 and there was strife between
the herdsmen of Abram's cattle and
the herdsmen of Lot's cattle. At that
time the Canaanites and the Per'iz·zītes
dwelt in the land.

8 Then Abram said to Lot, "Let
there be no strife between you and me,
and between your herdsmen and my
herdsmen; for we are kinsmen. 9 Is
not the whole land before you? Separate yourself from me. If you take the
left hand, then I will go to the right;
or if you take the right hand, then I
will go to the left." 10And Lot lifted
up his eyes, and saw that the Jordan
valley was well watered everywhere
like the garden of the LORD, like the
land of Egypt, in the direction of
Zō'är; this was before the LORD destroyed Sod'ŏm and Gŏ·môr'rȧh. 11 So
Lot chose for himself all the Jordan
valley, and Lot journeyed east; thus
they separated from each other.
12Abram dwelt in the land of Canaan,
while Lot dwelt among the cities of
the valley and moved his tent as far as
Sod'ŏm. 13 Now the men of Sod'ŏm
were wicked, great sinners against the
LORD.

14 The LORD said to Abram, after
Lot had separated from him, "Lift up
your eyes, and look from the place
where you are, northward and southward and eastward and westward;
15 for all the land which you see I will
give to you and to your descendants for
ever. 16 I will make your descendants
as the dust of the earth; so that if one
can count the dust of the earth, your
descendants also can be counted.
17Arise, walk through the length and
the breadth of the land, for I will give
it to you." 18 So Abram moved his
tent, and came and dwelt by the oaks[s]
of Mam're, which are at Hē'brŏn; and
there he built an altar to the LORD.

14 In the days of Am'rȧ·phel king
of Shī'när, Âr'i·och king of El·lä'-
sȧr, Ched-or-lȧ ō'mẽr king of Ē'lȧm,
and Tī'dȧl king of Goi'im, 2 these
kings made war with Bē'rȧ king of
Sod'ŏm, Bir'shȧ king of Gŏ·môr'rȧh,

[s] Or *terebinths*

12.7: Gen 13.15; 15.18; 17.8; 24.7; 26.3; 28.4, 13; 35.12; 48.4; Acts 7.5; Gal 3.16.
12.10-20: Gen 20.1-18; 26.7-11. **13.15:** Acts 7.5; Gal 3.16

Shī'nȧb king of Ad'mȧh, Shem·ē'bėr
king of Ze·boi'im, and the king of
Bē'lȧ (that is, Zō'är). 3 And all these
joined forces in the Valley of Sid'dim
(that is, the Salt Sea). 4 Twelve years
they had served Ched-or-lȧ·ō'mėr, but
in the thirteenth year they rebelled.
5 In the fourteenth year Ched-or-lȧ·ō'-
mėr and the kings who were with him
came and subdued the Reph'ȧ·im in
Ash'te·roth-kär·nā'im, the Zū'zim in
Ham, the Ē'mim in Shā'veh-kīr·i·ȧ-
thā'im, 6 and the Hôr'ītes in their
Mount Sē'ir as far as El-pâr'ȧn on the
border of the wilderness; 7 then they
turned back and came to En·mish'pat
(that is, Kā'desh), and subdued all the
country of the Ȧ·mal'ė·kītes, and also
the Am'ȯ·rītes who dwelt in Haz'ȧ·zon-
tā'mȧr. 8 Then the king of Sod'ȯm,
the king of Gȯ·môr'rȧh, the king of
Ad'mȧh, the king of Ze·boi'im, and
the king of Bē'lȧ (that is, Zō'är) went
out, and they joined battle in the
Valley of Sid'dim 9 with Ched-or-
lȧ·ō'mėr king of Ē'lȧm, Tī'dȧl king of
Goi'im, Am'rȧ·phel king of Shī'när,
and Âr'i·och king of El·lä'sȧr, four
kings against five. 10 Now the Valley of
Sid'dim was full of bitumin pits; and
as the kings of Sod'ȯm and Gȯ·môr'rȧh
fled, some fell into them, and the rest
fled to the mountain. 11 So the enemy
took all the goods of Sod'ȯm and
Gȯ·môr'rȧh, and all their provisions,
and went their way; 12 they also took
Lot, the son of Abram's brother, who
dwelt in Sod'ȯm, and his goods, and
departed.

13 Then one who had escaped
came, and told Abram the Hebrew,
who was living by the oaks[s] of Mam're
the Am'ȯ·rīte, brother of Esh'cȯl and
of Ā'nėr; these were allies of Abram.
14 When Abram heard that his kinsman had been taken captive, he led
forth his trained men, born in his
house, three hundred and eighteen of
them, and went in pursuit as far as
Dan. 15 And he divided his forces
against them by night, he and his
servants, and routed them and pursued
them to Hō'bȧh, north of Damascus.
16 Then he brought back all the goods,
and also brought back his kinsman Lot
with his goods, and the women and
the people.

17 After his return from the defeat
of Ched-or-lȧ·ō'mėr and the kings who
were with him, the king of Sod'ȯm
went out to meet him at the Valley of
Shā'veh (that is, the King's Valley).
18 And Mel-chiz'ė·dek king of Salem
brought out bread and wine; he was
priest of God Most High. 19 And he
blessed him and said,

"Blessed be Abram by God Most
High,
maker of heaven and earth;
20 and blessed be God Most High,
who has delivered your enemies
into your hand!"

And Abram gave him a tenth of everything. 21 And the king of Sod'ȯm said
to Abram, "Give me the persons, but
take the goods for yourself." 22 But
Abram said to the king of Sod'ȯm, "I
have sworn to the LORD God Most
High, maker of heaven and earth,
23 that I would not take a thread or a
sandal-thong or anything that is yours,
lest you should say, 'I have made
Abram rich.' 24 I will take nothing but
what the young men have eaten, and
the share of the men who went with
me; let Ā'nėr, Esh'cȯl, and Mam're
take their share."

15 After these things the word of
the LORD came to Abram in a
vision, "Fear not, Abram, I am your
shield; your reward shall be very
great." 2 But Abram said, "O Lord
GOD, what wilt thou give me, for I
continue childless, and the heir of my
house is Ē·lī·ē'zėr of Damascus?"
3 And Abram said, "Behold, thou hast
given me no offspring; and a slave
born in my house will be my heir."
4 And behold, the word of the LORD
came to him, "This man shall not be
your heir; your own son shall be your
heir." 5 And he brought him outside
and said, "Look toward heaven, and
number the stars, if you are able to
number them." Then he said to him,
"So shall your descendants be." 6 And
he believed the LORD; and he reckoned
it to him as righteousness.

7 And he said to him, "I am the
LORD who brought you from Ūr of the
Chal·dē'ȧns, to give you this land to
possess." 8 But he said, "O Lord GOD,
how am I to know that I shall possess
it?" 9 He said to him, "Bring me a

[s] Or *terebinths*

14.17-20: Heb 7.1-10. **15.4:** Gen 17.16, 21; 18.10; 21.2. **15.5:** Rom 4.18; Heb 11.12.
15.6: Rom 4.3, 9, 22-23; Gal 3.6.

heifer three years old, a she-goat three
years old, a ram three years old, a
turtledove, and a young pigeon."
10 And he brought him all these, cut
them in two, and laid each half over
against the other; but he did not cut
the birds in two. 11 And when birds of
prey came down upon the carcasses,
Abram drove them away.
12 As the sun was going down, a
deep sleep fell on Abram; and lo, a
dread and great darkness fell upon
him. 13 Then the LORD said to Abram,
"Know of a surety that your descendants will be sojourners in a land that is
not theirs, and will be slaves there, and
they will be oppressed for four hundred years; 14 but I will bring judgment on the nation which they serve,
and afterward they shall come out with
great possessions. 15 As for yourself,
you shall go to your fathers in peace;
you shall be buried in a good old age.
16 And they shall come back here in
the fourth generations; for the iniquity
of the Am'ŏ·rītes is not yet complete."
17 When the sun had gone down
and it was dark, behold, a smoking fire
pot and a flaming torch passed between
these pieces. 18 On that day the LORD
made a covenant with Abram, saying,
"To your descendants I give this land,
from the river of Egypt to the great
river, the river Eū·phrā'tēṡ, 19 the land
of the Ken'ītes, the Ken'iz·zītes, the
Kad'mȯ·nītes, 20 the Hit'tītes, the Per'-
iz·zītes, the Reph'ȧ·im, 21 the Am'ȯ-
rītes, the Canaanites, the Gīr'gȧ·shītes
and the Jeb'ū·sītes."

16 Now Sâr'äi, Abram's wife, bore
him no children. She had an
Egyptian maid whose name was
Hā'gȧr; 2 and Sâr'äi said to Abram,
"Behold now, the LORD has prevented
me from bearing children; go in to my
maid; it may be that I shall obtain
children by her." And Abram hearkened to the voice of Sarai. 3 So, after
Abram had dwelt ten years in the land
of Canaan, Sâr'äi, Abram's wife, took
Hā'gȧr the Egyptian, her maid, and
gave her to Abram her husband as a
wife. 4 And he went in to Hā'gȧr, and
she conceived; and when she saw that
she had conceived, she looked with
contempt on her mistress. 5 And Sâr'äi
said to Abram, "May the wrong done
to me be on you! I gave my maid to
your embrace, and when she saw that
she had conceived, she looked on me
with contempt. May the LORD judge
between you and me!" 6 But Abram
said to Sâr'äi, "Behold, your maid is in
your power; do to her as you please."
Then Sarai dealt harshly with her, and
she fled from her.
7 The angel of the LORD found her
by a spring of water in the wilderness,
the spring on the way to Shūr. 8 And he
said, "Hā'gȧr, maid of Sâr'äi, where
have you come from and where are
you going?" She said, "I am fleeing
from my mistress Sarai." 9 The angel
of the LORD said to her, "Return to
your mistress, and submit to her."
10 The angel of the LORD also said to
her, "I will so greatly multiply your
descendants that they cannot be
numbered for multitude." 11 And the
angel of the LORD said to her, "Behold, you are with child, and shall
bear a son; you shall call his name
Ish'mȧ·el;[t] because the LORD has given
heed to your affliction. 12 He shall be
a wild ass of a man, his hand against
every man and every man's hand
against him; and he shall dwell over
against all his kinsmen." 13 So she
called the name of the LORD who
spoke to her, "Thou art a God of
seeing"; for she said, "Have I really
seen God and remained alive after seeing him?"[u] 14 Therefore the well was
called Bē'ėr-lä'häi-roi;[v] it lies between
Kā'desh and Bē'red.
15 And Hā'gȧr bore Abram a son;
and Abram called the name of his son,
whom Hagar bore, Ish'mȧ·el. 16 Abram
was eighty-six years old when Hā'gȧr
bore Ish'mȧ·el to Abram.

17 When Abram was ninety-nine
years old the LORD appeared to
Abram, and said to him, "I am God
Almighty;[w] walk before me, and be
blameless. 2 And I will make my covenant between me and you, and will
multiply you exceedingly." 3 Then
Abram fell on his face; and God said
to him, 4 "Behold, my covenant is
with you, and you shall be the father
of a multitude of nations. 5 No longer
shall your name be Abram,[x] but your
name shall be Abraham;[y] for I have
made you the father of a multitude of

[t] That is *God hears* [u] Cn: Heb *have I even here seen after him who sees me?*
[v] That is *the well of one who sees and lives* [w] Heb *El Shaddai* [x] That is *exalted father*
[y] Here taken to mean *father of a multitude*
15.13-14: Acts 7.6-7. **15.18:** Gen 17.2, 7, 9-14, 21. **17.5:** Rom 4.17.

nations. 6 I will make you exceedingly
fruitful; and I will make nations of
you, and kings shall come forth from
you. 7And I will establish my covenant
between me and you and your descendants after you throughout their generations for an everlasting covenant, to be
God to you and to your descendants
after you. 8And I will give to you, and
to your descendants after you, the land
of your sojournings, all the land of
Canaan, for an everlasting possession;
and I will be their God."
9 And God said to Abraham, "As
for you, you shall keep my covenant,
you and your descendants after you
throughout their generations. 10 This
is my covenant, which you shall keep,
between me and you and your descendants after you: Every male among
you shall be circumcised. 11 You shall
be circumcised in the flesh of your
foreskins, and it shall be a sign of the
covenant between me and you. 12 He
that is eight days old among you shall
be circumcised; every male throughout your generations, whether born in
your house, or bought with your
money from any foreigner who is not
of your offspring, 13 both he that is
born in your house and he that is
bought with your money, shall be
circumcised. So shall my covenant be
in your flesh an everlasting covenant.
14Any uncircumcised male who is not
circumcised in the flesh of his foreskin
shall be cut off from his people; he has
broken my covenant."
15 And God said to Abraham, "As
for Sâr'äi your wife, you shall not call
her name Sarai, but Sarah shall be her
name. 16 I will bless her, and moreover I will give you a son by her; I
will bless her, and she shall be a mother
of nations; kings of peoples shall come
from her." 17 Then Abraham fell on
his face and laughed, and said to himself, "Shall a child be born to a man
who is a hundred years old? Shall
Sarah, who is ninety years old, bear a
child?" 18And Abraham said to God,
"O that Ish'mȧ-el might live in thy
sight!" 19 God said, "No, but Sarah
your wife shall bear you a son, and you
shall call his name Isaac.[z] I will
establish my covenant with him as an
everlasting covenant for his descendants after him. 20As for Ish'mȧ-el, I
have heard you; behold, I will bless
him and make him fruitful and multiply him exceedingly; he shall be the
father of twelve princes, and I will
make him a great nation. 21 But I will
establish my covenant with Isaac,
whom Sarah shall bear to you at this
season next year."
22 When he had finished talking
with him, God went up from Abraham.
23 Then Abraham took Ish'mȧ-el his
son and all the slaves born in his house
or bought with his money, every male
among the men of Abraham's house,
and he circumcised the flesh of their
foreskins that very day, as God had
said to him. 24Abraham was ninety-
nine years old when he was circumcised in the flesh of his foreskin. 25And
Ish'mȧ-el his son was thirteen years
old when he was circumcised in the
flesh of his foreskin. 26 That very day
Abraham and his son Ish'mȧ-el were
circumcised; 27 and all the men of his
house, those born in the house and
those bought with money from a
foreigner, were circumcised with him.

18 And the LORD appeared to him
by the oaks[a] of Mam're, as he sat
at the door of his tent in the heat of
the day. 2 He lifted up his eyes and
looked, and behold, three men stood
in front of him. When he saw them,
he ran from the tent door to meet
them, and bowed himself to the earth,
3 and said, "My lord, if I have found
favor in your sight, do not pass by
your servant. 4 Let a little water be
brought, and wash your feet, and rest
yourselves under the tree, 5 while I
fetch a morsel of bread, that you may
refresh yourselves, and after that you
may pass on—since you have come to
your servant." So they said, "Do as
you have said." 6And Abraham hastened into the tent to Sarah, and said,
"Make ready quickly three measures[b]
of fine meal, knead it, and make
cakes." 7And Abraham ran to the herd,
and took a calf, tender and good, and
gave it to the servant, who hastened to
prepare it. 8 Then he took curds, and
milk, and the calf which he had prepared, and set it before them; and he
stood by them under the tree while
they ate.
9 They said to him, "Where is
Sarah your wife?" And he said, "She
is in the tent." 10 The LORD said, "I
will surely return to you in the spring,

[z] That is *he laughs* [a] Or *terebinths* [b] Heb *seahs*

17.7: Lk 1.55; Gal 3.16. 17.8: Acts 7.5. 17.10: Acts 7.8. 17.11-14: Gen 17.24; 21.4. 18.10: Rom 9.9.

and Sarah your wife shall have a son."
And Sarah was listening at the tent
door behind him. 11 Now Abraham
and Sarah were old, advanced in age;
it had ceased to be with Sarah after the
manner of women. 12 So Sarah laughed
to herself, saying, "After I have grown
old, and my husband is old, shall I
have pleasure?" 13 The LORD said to
Abraham, "Why did Sarah laugh, and
say, 'Shall I indeed bear a child, now
that I am old?' 14 Is anything too hard[c]
for the LORD? At the appointed time I
will return to you, in the spring, and
Sarah shall have a son." 15 But Sarah
denied, saying, "I did not laugh"; for
she was afraid. He said, "No, but you
did laugh."

16 Then the men set out from
there, and they looked toward Sod'ŏm;
and Abraham went with them to set
them on their way. 17 The LORD said,
"Shall I hide from Abraham what I
am about to do, 18 seeing that Abraham
shall become a great and mighty nation, and all the nations of the earth
shall bless themselves by him?[d] 19 No,
for I have chosen[e] him, that he may
charge his children and his household
after him to keep the way of the LORD
by doing righteousness and justice; so
that the LORD may bring to Abraham
what he has promised him." 20 Then
the LORD said, "Because the outcry
against Sod'ŏm and Gŏ·môr'rah is
great and their sin is very grave, 21 I
will go down to see whether they have
done altogether according to the outcry which has come to me; and if not,
I will know."

22 So the men turned from there,
and went toward Sod'ŏm; but Abraham still stood before the LORD.
23 Then Abraham drew near, and said,
"Wilt thou indeed destroy the righteous with the wicked? 24 Suppose there
are fifty righteous within the city; wilt
thou then destroy the place and not
spare it for the fifty righteous who are
in it? 25 Far be it from thee to do such
a thing, to slay the righteous with the
wicked, so that the righteous fare as
the wicked! Far be that from thee!
Shall not the Judge of all the earth do
right?" 26And the LORD said, "If I
find at Sod'ŏm fifty righteous in the
city, I will spare the whole place for
their sake." 27Abraham answered, "Behold, I have taken upon myself to
speak to the LORD, I who am but dust
and ashes. 28 Suppose five of the fifty
righteous are lacking? Wilt thou destroy the whole city for lack of five?"
And he said, "I will not destroy it if I
find forty-five there." 29Again he
spoke to him, and said, "Suppose forty
are found there." He answered, "For
the sake of forty I will not do it."
30 Then he said, "Oh let not the Lord
be angry, and I will speak. Suppose
thirty are found there." He answered,
"I will not do it, if I find thirty there."
31 He said, "Behold, I have taken upon
myself to speak to the Lord. Suppose
twenty are found there." He answered, "For the sake of twenty I will
not destroy it." 32 Then he said, "Oh
let not the Lord be angry, and I will
speak again but this once. Suppose ten
are found there." He answered, "For
the sake of ten I will not destroy it."
33And the LORD went his way, when
he had finished speaking to Abraham;
and Abraham returned to his place.

19 The two angels came to Sod'ŏm
in the evening; and Lot was
sitting in the gate of Sodom. When Lot
saw them, he rose to meet them, and
bowed himself with his face to the
earth, 2 and said, "My lords, turn
aside, I pray you, to your servant's
house and spend the night, and wash
your feet; then you may rise up early
and go on your way." They said, "No;
we will spend the night in the street."
3 But he urged them strongly; so they
turned aside to him and entered his
house; and he made them a feast, and
baked unleavened bread, and they ate.
4 But before they lay down, the men
of the city, the men of Sod'ŏm, both
young and old, all the people to the
last man, surrounded the house; 5 and
they called to Lot, "Where are the men
who came to you tonight? Bring them
out to us, that we may know them."
6 Lot went out of the door to the men,
shut the door after him, 7 and said,
"I beg you, my brothers, do not act so
wickedly. 8 Behold, I have two daughters who have not known man; let me
bring them out to you, and do to them
as you please; only do nothing to these
men, for they have come under the
shelter of my roof." 9 But they said,
"Stand back!" And they said, "This
fellow came to sojourn, and he would
play the judge! Now we will deal worse

[c] Or *wonderful* [d] Or *in him all the families of the earth shall be blessed* [e] Heb *known*
18.12: 1 Pet 3.6. **18.14:** Mt 19.26; Mk 10.27; Lk 1.37; Rom 9.9. **18.18:** Gal 3.8.

with you than with them." Then they
pressed hard against the man Lot, and
drew near to break the door. 10 But
the men put forth their hands and
brought Lot into the house to them,
and shut the door. 11 And they struck
with blindness the men who were at
the door of the house, both small and
great, so that they wearied themselves
groping for the door.

12 Then the men said to Lot, "Have
you any one else here? Sons-in-law,
sons, daughters, or any one you have
in the city, bring them out of the
place; 13 for we are about to destroy
this place, because the outcry against
its people has become great before the
LORD, and the LORD has sent us to
destroy it." 14 So Lot went out and
said to his sons-in-law, who were to
marry his daughters, "Up, get out of
this place; for the LORD is about to
destroy the city." But he seemed to
his sons-in-law to be jesting.

15 When morning dawned, the
angels urged Lot, saying, "Arise, take
your wife and your two daughters who
are here, lest you be consumed in the
punishment of the city." 16 But he
lingered; so the men seized him and
his wife and his two daughters by the
hand, the LORD being merciful to him,
and they brought him forth and set
him outside the city. 17 And when they
had brought them forth, they[f] said,
"Flee for your life; do not look back
or stop anywhere in the valley; flee to
the hills, lest you be consumed." 18 And
Lot said to them, "Oh, no, my lords;
19 behold, your servant has found favor
in your sight, and you have shown me
great kindness in saving my life; but I
cannot flee to the hills, lest the disaster
overtake me, and I die. 20 Behold,
yonder city is near enough to flee to,
and it is a little one. Let me escape
there—is it not a little one?—and my
life will be saved!" 21 He said to him,
"Behold, I grant you this favor also,
that I will not overthrow the city of
which you have spoken. 22 Make haste,
escape there; for I can do nothing till
you arrive there." Therefore the name
of the city was called Zō'är.[g] 23 The
sun had risen on the earth when Lot
came to Zō'är.

24 Then the LORD rained on Sod'-
ŏm and Gȯ·môr'rȧh brimstone and fire
from the LORD out of heaven; 25 and
he overthrew those cities, and all the
valley, and all the inhabitants of the
cities, and what grew on the ground.
26 But Lot's wife behind him looked
back, and she became a pillar of salt.
27 And Abraham went early in the
morning to the place where he had
stood before the LORD; 28 and he
looked down toward Sod'ŏm and
Gȯ·môr'rȧh and toward all the land of
the valley, and beheld, and lo, the
smoke of the land went up like the
smoke of a furnace.

29 So it was that, when God destroyed the cities of the valley, God
remembered Abraham, and sent Lot
out of the midst of the overthrow,
when he overthrew the cities in which
Lot dwelt.

30 Now Lot went up out of Zō'är,
and dwelt in the hills with his two
daughters, for he was afraid to dwell
in Zoar; so he dwelt in a cave with his
two daughters. 31 And the first-born
said to the younger, "Our father is old,
and there is not a man on earth to
come in to us after the manner of all
the earth. 32 Come, let us make our
father drink wine, and we will lie with
him, that we may preserve offspring
through our father." 33 So they made
their father drink wine that night; and
the first-born went in, and lay with her
father; he did not know when she lay
down or when she arose. 34 And on the
next day, the first-born said to the
younger, "Behold, I lay last night with
my father; let us make him drink wine
tonight also; then you go in and lie
with him, that we may preserve offspring through our father." 35 So they
made their father drink wine that night
also; and the younger arose, and lay
with him; and he did not know when
she lay down nor when she arose.
36 Thus both the daughters of Lot
were with child by their father. 37 The
first-born bore a son, and called his
name Mō'ab; he is the father of the
Mō'ȧb·ītes to this day. 38 The younger
also bore a son, and called his name
Ben-am'mī; he is the father of the
Am'mȯ·nītes to this day.

20 From there Abraham journeyed toward the territory of
the Negeb, and dwelt between Kā'-
desh and Shūr; and he sojourned in
Gē'rär. 2 And Abraham said of Sarah
his wife, "She is my sister." And

[f] Gk Syr Vg: Heb *he* [g] That is *Little*

19.24-25: Lk 17.29. **19.26:** Lk 17.32. **19.28:** Rev 9.2.

A·bim'ĕ·lech king of Gē'rär sent and
took Sarah. 3 But God came to A·bim'-
ĕ·lech in a dream by night, and said to
him, "Behold, you are a dead man,
because of the woman whom you have
taken; for she is a man's wife." 4 Now
A·bim'ĕ·lech had not approached her;
so he said, "Lord, wilt thou slay an
innocent people? 5 Did he not himself
say to me, 'She is my sister'? And she
herself said, 'He is my brother.' In the
integrity of my heart and the innocence of my hands I have done this."
6 Then God said to him in the dream,
"Yes, I know that you have done this
in the integrity of your heart, and it
was I who kept you from sinning
against me; therefore I did not let you
touch her. 7 Now then restore the
man's wife; for he is a prophet, and he
will pray for you, and you shall live.
But if you do not restore her, know
that you shall surely die, you, and all
that are yours."

8 So A·bim'ĕ·lech rose early in the
morning, and called all his servants,
and told them all these things; and the
men were very much afraid. 9 Then
A·bim'ĕ·lech called Abraham, and said
to him, "What have you done to us?
And how have I sinned against you,
that you have brought on me and my
kingdom a great sin? You have done
to me things that ought not to be
done." 10 And A·bim'ĕ·lech said to
Abraham, "What were you thinking
of, that you did this thing?" 11 Abraham said, "I did it because I thought,
There is no fear of God at all in this
place, and they will kill me because of
my wife. 12 Besides she is indeed my
sister, the daughter of my father but
not the daughter of my mother; and
she became my wife. 13 And when God
caused me to wander from my father's
house, I said to her, 'This is the kindness you must do me: at every place
to which we come, say of me, He is my
brother.' " 14 Then A·bim'ĕ·lech took
sheep and oxen, and male and female
slaves, and gave them to Abraham,
and restored Sarah his wife to him.
15 And A·bim'ĕ·lech said, "Behold, my
land is before you; dwell where it
pleases you." 16 To Sarah he said,
"Behold, I have given your brother a
thousand pieces of silver; it is your
vindication in the eyes of all who are
with you; and before every one you
are righted." 17 Then Abraham prayed
to God; and God healed A·bim'ĕ-
lech, and also healed his wife and
female slaves so that they bore children. 18 For the LORD had closed
all the wombs of the house of A·bim'-
ĕ·lech because of Sarah, Abraham's
wife.

21 The LORD visited Sarah as he
had said, and the LORD did to
Sarah as he had promised. 2 And Sarah
conceived, and bore Abraham a son in
his old age at the time of which God
had spoken to him. 3 Abraham called
the name of his son who was born to
him, whom Sarah bore him, Isaac.
4 And Abraham circumcised his son
Isaac when he was eight days old, as
God had commanded him. 5 Abraham
was a hundred years old when his son
Isaac was born to him. 6 And Sarah
said, "God has made laughter for me;
every one who hears will laugh over
me." 7 And she said, "Who would have
said to Abraham that Sarah would
suckle children? Yet I have borne him
a son in his old age."

8 And the child grew, and was
weaned; and Abraham made a great
feast on the day that Isaac was weaned.
9 But Sarah saw the son of Hā'gàr the
Egyptian, whom she had borne to
Abraham, playing with her son Isaac.[h]
10 So she said to Abraham, "Cast out
this slave woman with her son; for the
son of this slave woman shall not be
heir with my son Isaac." 11 And the
thing was very displeasing to Abraham
on account of his son. 12 But God said
to Abraham, "Be not displeased because of the lad and because of your
slave woman; whatever Sarah says to
you, do as she tells you, for through
Isaac shall your descendants be
named. 13 And I will make a nation of
the son of the slave woman also, because he is your offspring." 14 So
Abraham rose early in the morning,
and took bread and a skin of water,
and gave it to Hā'gàr, putting it on her
shoulder, along with the child, and
sent her away. And she departed, and
wandered in the wilderness of Beer-
sheba.

15 When the water in the skin was
gone, she cast the child under one of
the bushes. 16 Then she went, and sat
down over against him a good way off,
about the distance of a bowshot; for

h Gk Vg: Heb lacks *with her son Isaac*

21.4: Acts 7.8. **21.10:** Gal 4.30. **21.12:** Rom 9.7; Heb 11.18.

she said, "Let me not look upon the
death of the child." And as she sat over
against him, the child lifted up his
voice[i] and wept. 17And God heard the
voice of the lad; and the angel of God
called to Hā'gȧr from heaven, and said
to her, "What troubles you, Hagar?
Fear not; for God has heard the voice
of the lad where he is. 18Arise, lift up
the lad, and hold him fast with your
hand; for I will make him a great
nation." 19 Then God opened her
eyes, and she saw a well of water; and
she went, and filled the skin with
water, and gave the lad a drink. 20And
God was with the lad, and he grew up;
he lived in the wilderness, and became
an expert with the bow. 21 He lived in
the wilderness of Pâr'an; and his
mother took a wife for him from the
land of Egypt.

22 At that time Ȧ·bim'ė·lech and
Phī'col the commander of his army
said to Abraham, "God is with you in
all that you do; 23 now therefore swear
to me here by God that you will not
deal falsely with me or with my offspring or with my posterity, but as I
have dealt loyally with you, you will
deal with me and with the land where
you have sojourned." 24And Abraham
said, "I will swear."

25 When Abraham complained to
Ȧ·bim'ė·lech about a well of water
which Abimelech's servants had
seized, 26Ȧ·bim'ė·lech said, "I do not
know who has done this thing; you
did not tell me, and I have not heard
of it until today." 27 So Abraham took
sheep and oxen and gave them to
Ȧ·bim'ė·lech, and the two men made
a covenant. 28Abraham set seven ewe
lambs of the flock apart. 29And Ȧ·bim'-
ė·lech said to Abraham, "What is the
meaning of these seven ewe lambs
which you have set apart?" 30 He said,
"These seven ewe lambs you will take
from my hand, that you may be a
witness for me that I dug this well."
31 Therefore that place was called
Beer-sheba;[j] because there both of
them swore an oath. 32 So they made
a covenant at Beer-sheba. Then
Ȧ·bim'ė·lech and Phī'col the commander of his army rose up and
returned to the land of the Philistines.
33Abraham planted a tamarisk tree in
Beer-sheba, and called there on the
name of the LORD, the Everlasting
God. 34And Abraham sojourned many
days in the land of the Philistines.

22 After these things God tested
Abraham, and said to him,
"Abraham!" And he said, "Here am
I." 2 He said, "Take your son, your
only son Isaac, whom you love, and go
to the land of Mō·rī'ȧh, and offer him
there as a burnt offering upon one of
the mountains of which I shall tell
you." 3 So Abraham rose early in the
morning, saddled his ass, and took two
of his young men with him, and his
son Isaac; and he cut the wood for the
burnt offering, and arose and went to
the place of which God had told him.
4 On the third day Abraham lifted up
his eyes and saw the place afar off.
5 Then Abraham said to his young
men, "Stay here with the ass; I and
the lad will go yonder and worship,
and come again to you." 6And Abraham took the wood of the burnt offering, and laid it on Isaac his son; and
he took in his hand the fire and the
knife. So they went both of them together. 7And Isaac said to his father
Abraham, "My father!" And he said,
"Here am I, my son." He said, "Behold, the fire and the wood; but where
is the lamb for a burnt offering?"
8Abraham said, "God will provide
himself the lamb for a burnt offering,
my son." So they went both of them
together.

9 When they came to the place of
which God had told him, Abraham
built an altar there, and laid the wood
in order, and bound Isaac his son, and
laid him on the altar, upon the wood.
10 Then Abraham put forth his hand,
and took the knife to slay his son.
11 But the angel of the LORD called to
him from heaven, and said, "Abraham,
Abraham!" And he said, "Here am
I." 12 He said, "Do not lay your hand
on the lad or do anything to him; for
now I know that you fear God, seeing
you have not withheld your son, your
only son, from me." 13And Abraham
lifted up his eyes and looked, and behold, behind him was a ram, caught
in a thicket by his horns; and Abraham
went and took the ram, and offered it
up as a burnt offering instead of his
son. 14 So Abraham called the name of
that place The LORD will provide;[k] as
it is said to this day, "On the mount of
the LORD it shall be provided."[l]

[i] Gk: Heb *she lifted up her voice* [j] That is *Well of seven* or *Well of the oath* [k] Or *see* [l] Or *he will be seen*
21.31: Gen 26.33. **22.1-18:** Heb 11.17-19. **22.9-10, 12:** Jas 2.21.

15 And the angel of the LORD called to Abraham a second time from heaven, 16 and said, "By myself I have sworn, says the LORD, because you have done this, and have not withheld your son, your only son, 17 I will indeed bless you, and I will multiply your descendants as the stars of heaven and as the sand which is on the seashore. And your descendants shall possess the gate of their enemies, 18 and by your descendants shall all the nations of the earth bless themselves, because you have obeyed my voice." 19 So Abraham returned to his young men, and they arose and went together to Beer-sheba; and Abraham dwelt at Beer-sheba.

20 Now after these things it was told Abraham, "Behold, Mil'cȧh also has borne children to your brother Nā'hôr: 21 Uz the first-born, Buz his brother, Ke·mū'el the father of Âr'ȧm, 22 Chē'sed, Hā'zō, Pil'dash, Jid'laph, and Be·thū'el." 23 Be·thū'el became the father of Rebekah. These eight Mil'cȧh bore to Nā'hôr, Abraham's brother. 24 Moreover, his concubine, whose name was Reü'mȧh, bore Tē'bȧh, Gā'hȧm, Tā'hash, and Mā'ȧ·cȧh.

23 Sarah lived a hundred and twenty-seven years; these were the years of the life of Sarah. 2 And Sarah died at Kīr'i·ȧth-är'bȧ (that is, Hē'brȯn) in the land of Canaan; and Abraham went in to mourn for Sarah and to weep for her. 3 And Abraham rose up from before his dead, and said to the Hit'tītes, 4 "I am a stranger and a sojourner among you; give me property among you for a burying place, that I may bury my dead out of my sight." 5 The Hit'tītes answered Abraham, 6 "Hear us, my lord; you are a mighty prince among us. Bury your dead in the choicest of our sepulchres; none of us will withhold from you his sepulchre, or hinder you from burying your dead." 7 Abraham rose and bowed to the Hit'tītes, the people of the land. 8 And he said to them, "If you are willing that I should bury my dead out of my sight, hear me, and entreat for me Ē'phrȯn the son of Zō'här, 9 that he may give me the cave of Mach-pē'lȧh, which he owns; it is at the end of his field. For the full price let him give it to me in your presence as a possession for a burying place." 10 Now Ē'phrȯn was sitting among the Hit'tītes; and Ephron the Hittite answered Abraham in the hearing of the Hittites, of all who went in at the gate of his city, 11 "No, my lord, hear me; I give you the field, and I give you the cave that is in it; in the presence of the sons of my people I give it to you; bury your dead." 12 Then Abraham bowed down before the people of the land. 13 And he said to Ē'phrȯn in the hearing of the people of the land, "But if you will, hear me; I will give the price of the field; accept it from me, that I may bury my dead there." 14 Ē'phrȯn answered Abraham, 15 "My lord, listen to me; a piece of land worth four hundred shekels of silver, what is that between you and me? Bury your dead." 16 Abraham agreed with Ē'phrȯn; and Abraham weighed out for Ephron the silver which he had named in the hearing of the Hit'tītes, four hundred shekels of silver, according to the weights current among the merchants.

17 So the field of Ē'phrȯn in Mach-pē'lȧh, which was to the east of Mam're, the field with the cave which was in it and all the trees that were in the field, throughout its whole area, was made over 18 to Abraham as a possession in the presence of the Hit'tītes, before all who went in at the gate of his city. 19 After this, Abraham buried Sarah his wife in the cave of the field of Mach-pē'lȧh east of Mam're (that is, Hē'brȯn) in the land of Canaan. 20 The field and the cave that is in it were made over to Abraham as a possession for a burying place by the Hit'tītes.

24 Now Abraham was old, well advanced in years; and the LORD had blessed Abraham in all things. 2 And Abraham said to his servant, the oldest of his house, who had charge of all that he had, "Put your hand under my thigh, 3 and I will make you swear by the LORD, the God of heaven and of the earth, that you will not take a wife for my son from the daughters of the Canaanites, among whom I dwell, 4 but will go to my country and to my kindred, and take a wife for my son Isaac." 5 The servant said to him, "Perhaps the woman may not be willing to follow me to this land; must I then take your

22.16-17: Lk 1.73; Heb 6.13-14; 11.12. **22.18:** Acts 3.25; Gal 3.16. **23.4:** Heb 11.9, 13. **23.16-17:** Acts 7.16.

son back to the land from which you
came?" 6 Abraham said to him, "See
to it that you do not take my son back
there. 7 The LORD, the God of heaven,
who took me from my father's house
and from the land of my birth, and
who spoke to me and swore to me, 'To
your descendants I will give this land,'
he will send his angel before you, and
you shall take a wife for my son from
there. 8 But if the woman is not willing
to follow you, then you will be free
from this oath of mine; only you must
not take my son back there." 9 So the
servant put his hand under the thigh
of Abraham his master, and swore to
him concerning this matter.

10 Then the servant took ten of his
master's camels and departed, taking
all sorts of choice gifts from his master;
and he arose, and went to Mes·ȯ·pȯ-
tā'mi·ȧ, to the city of Nā'hôr. 11 And
he made the camels kneel down outside the city by the well of water at
the time of evening, the time when
women go out to draw water. 12 And
he said, "O LORD, God of my master
Abraham, grant me success today, I
pray thee, and show steadfast love to
my master Abraham. 13 Behold, I am
standing by the spring of water, and
the daughters of the men of the city
are coming out to draw water. 14 Let
the maiden to whom I shall say, 'Pray
let down your jar that I may drink,'
and who shall say, 'Drink, and I will
water your camels'—let her be the one
whom thou hast appointed for thy
servant Isaac. By this I shall know
that thou hast shown steadfast love to
my master."

15 Before he had done speaking,
behold, Rebekah, who was born to
Be·thū'el the son of Mil'cȧh, the wife
of Nā'hôr, Abraham's brother, came
out with her water jar upon her
shoulder. 16 The maiden was very fair
to look upon, a virgin, whom no man
had known. She went down to the
spring, and filled her jar, and came up.
17 Then the servant ran to meet her,
and said, "Pray give me a little water
to drink from your jar." 18 She said,
"Drink, my lord"; and she quickly let
down her jar upon her hand, and gave
him a drink. 19 When she had finished
giving him a drink, she said, "I will
draw for your camels also, until they
have done drinking." 20 So she quickly
emptied her jar into the trough and
ran again to the well to draw, and she
drew for all his camels. 21 The man
gazed at her in silence to learn whether
the LORD had prospered his journey
or not.

22 When the camels had done drinking, the man took a gold ring weighing
a half shekel, and two bracelets for her
arms weighing ten gold shekels, 23 and
said, "Tell me whose daughter you
are. Is there room in your father's
house for us to lodge in?" 24 She said
to him, "I am the daughter of Be·thū'el
the son of Mil'cȧh, whom she bore to
Nā'hôr." 25 She added, "We have
both straw and provender enough, and
room to lodge in." 26 The man bowed
his head and worshiped the LORD,
27 and said, "Blessed be the LORD, the
God of my master Abraham, who has
not forsaken his steadfast love and his
faithfulness toward my master. As for
me, the LORD has led me in the way
to the house of my master's kinsmen."

28 Then the maiden ran and told
her mother's household about these
things. 29 Rebekah had a brother
whose name was Lā'bȧn; and Laban
ran out to the man, to the spring.
30 When he saw the ring, and the
bracelets on his sister's arms, and
when he heard the words of Rebekah
his sister, "Thus the man spoke to
me," he went to the man; and behold,
he was standing by the camels at the
spring. 31 He said, "Come in, O
blessed of the LORD; why do you stand
outside? For I have prepared the
house and a place for the camels."
32 So the man came into the house;
and Lā'bȧn ungirded the camels, and
gave him straw and provender for the
camels, and water to wash his feet and
the feet of the men who were with him.
33 Then food was set before him to
eat; but he said, "I will not eat until I
have told my errand." He said, "Speak
on."

34 So he said, "I am Abraham's
servant. 35 The LORD has greatly
blessed my master, and he has become
great; he has given him flocks and
herds, silver and gold, menservants
and maidservants, camels and asses.
36 And Sarah my master's wife bore a
son to my master when she was old;
and to him he has given all that he has.
37 My master made me swear, saying,
'You shall not take a wife for my son
from the daughters of the Canaanites,
in whose land I dwell; 38 but you shall
go to my father's house and to my

kindred, and take a wife for my son.'
39 I said to my master, 'Perhaps the
woman will not follow me.' 40 But he
said to me, 'The LORD, before whom
I walk, will send his angel with you
and prosper your way; and you shall
take a wife for my son from my kindred
and from my father's house; 41 then
you will be free from my oath, when
you come to my kindred; and if they
will not give her to you, you will be
free from my oath.'

42 "I came today to the spring, and
said, 'O LORD, the God of my master
Abraham, if now thou wilt prosper the
way which I go, 43 behold, I am standing by the spring of water; let the
young woman who comes out to draw,
to whom I shall say, "Pray give me a
little water from your jar to drink,"
44 and who will say to me, "Drink,
and I will draw for your camels also," let her be the woman whom the
LORD has appointed for my master's
son.'

45 "Before I had done speaking in
my heart, behold, Rebekah came out
with her water jar on her shoulder;
and she went down to the spring, and
drew. I said to her, 'Pray let me drink.'
46 She quickly let down her jar from
her shoulder, and said, 'Drink, and I
will give your camels drink also.' So I
drank, and she gave the camels drink
also. 47 Then I asked her, 'Whose
daughter are you?' She said, 'The
daughter of Be·thū'el, Nā'hôr's son,
whom Mil'cȧh bore to him.' So I put
the ring on her nose, and the bracelets
on her arms. 48 Then I bowed my
head and worshiped the LORD, and
blessed the LORD, the God of my
master Abraham, who had led me by
the right way to take the daughter of
my master's kinsman for his son.
49 Now then, if you will deal loyally
and truly with my master, tell me; and
if not, tell me; that I may turn to the
right hand or to the left."

50 Then Lā'bȧn and Be·thū'el answered, "The thing comes from the
LORD; we cannot speak to you bad or
good. 51 Behold, Rebekah is before
you, take her and go, and let her be
the wife of your master's son, as the
LORD has spoken."

52 When Abraham's servant heard
their words, he bowed himself to the
earth before the LORD. 53 And the
servant brought forth jewelry of silver
and of gold, and raiment, and gave
them to Rebekah; he also gave to her
brother and to her mother costly ornaments. 54 And he and the men who
were with him ate and drank, and they
spent the night there. When they
arose in the morning, he said, "Send
me back to my master." 55 Her brother
and her mother said, "Let the maiden
remain with us a while, at least ten
days; after that she may go." 56 But
he said to them, "Do not delay me,
since the LORD has prospered my way;
let me go that I may go to my master."
57 They said, "We will call the maiden,
and ask her." 58 And they called Rebekah, and said to her, "Will you go
with this man?" She said, "I will go."
59 So they sent away Rebekah their
sister and her nurse, and Abraham's
servant and his men. 60 And they
blessed Rebekah, and said to her,
"Our sister, be the mother of thousands of ten thousands; and may your
descendants possess the gate of those
who hate them!" 61 Then Rebekah
and her maids arose, and rode upon
the camels and followed the man; thus
the servant took Rebekah, and went
his way.

62 Now Isaac had come from[n] Bē'ėr-
lä'häi-roi, and was dwelling in the
Negeb. 63 And Isaac went out to
meditate in the field in the evening;
and he lifted up his eyes and looked,
and behold, there were camels coming.
64 And Rebekah lifted up her eyes, and
when she saw Isaac, she alighted from
the camel, 65 and said to the servant,
"Who is the man yonder, walking in
the field to meet us?" The servant said,
"It is my master." So she took her veil
and covered herself. 66 And the servant
told Isaac all the things that he had
done. 67 Then Isaac brought her into
the tent,[o] and took Rebekah, and she
became his wife; and he loved her. So
Isaac was comforted after his mother's
death.

25 Abraham took another wife,
whose name was Ke·tü'rȧh.
2 She bore him Zim'ran, Jok'shȧn,
Mē'dan, Mid'i·ȧn, Ish'bak, and Shü'-
ȧh. 3 Jok'shȧn was the father of Sheba
and Dē'dan. The sons of Dedan were
Ȧs·shü'rim, Le·tū'shim, and Le-um'-
mim. 4 The sons of Mid'i·ȧn were
Ē'phȧh, Ē'phėr, Hā'nȯch, Ȧ·bī'dȧ, and
El·dā'ȧh. All these were the children
of Ke·tü'rȧh. 5 Abraham gave all he

[n] Syr Tg: Heb *from coming to* [o] Heb adds *Sarah his mother*

had to Isaac. 6 But to the sons of his
concubines Abraham gave gifts, and
while he was still living he sent them
away from his son Isaac, eastward to
the east country.

7 These are the days of the years of
Abraham's life, a hundred and seventy-
five years. 8 Abraham breathed his last
and died in a good old age, an old man
and full of years, and was gathered to
his people. 9 Isaac and Ish'mȧ·el his
sons buried him in the cave of Mach-
pē'lȧh, in the field of Ē'phrȯn the son
of Zō'här the Hit'tīte, east of Mam're,
10 the field which Abraham purchased
from the Hit'tītes. There Abraham was
buried, with Sarah his wife. 11 After
the death of Abraham God blessed
Isaac his son. And Isaac dwelt at
Bē'ėr-lä'häi-roi.

12 These are the descendants of
Ish'mȧ·el, Abraham's son, whom
Hā'gȧr the Egyptian, Sarah's maid,
bore to Abraham. 13 These are the
names of the sons of Ish'mȧ·el, named
in the order of their birth: Ne·bā'ioth,
the first-born of Ishmael; and Kē'där,
Ad'bē·el, Mib'sȧm, 14 Mish'mȧ, Dü'-
mȧh, Mas'sȧ, 15 Hā'dad, Tē'mȧ, Jē'-
tūr, Nā'phish, and Ked'e·mȧh. 16 These
are the sons of Ish'mȧ·el and these are
their names, by their villages and by
their encampments, twelve princes
according to their tribes. 17 (These are
the years of the life of Ish'mȧ·el, a hundred and thirty-seven years; he
breathed his last and died, and was
gathered to his kindred.) 18 They
dwelt from Hav'i·lȧh to Shûr, which
is opposite Egypt in the direction of
Assyria; he settled[p] over against all his
people.

19 These are the descendants of
Isaac, Abraham's son: Abraham was
the father of Isaac, 20 and Isaac was
forty years old when he took to wife
Rebekah, the daughter of Be·thū'el
the Ar·ȧ·mē'ȧn of Pad'dȧn-âr'ȧm, the
sister of Lā'bȧn the Aramean. 21 And
Isaac prayed to the LORD for his wife,
because she was barren; and the LORD
granted his prayer, and Rebekah his
wife conceived. 22 The children strug-
gled together within her; and she said,
"If it is thus, why do I live?"[q] So she
went to inquire of the LORD. 23 And the
LORD said to her,

"Two nations are in your womb,
and two peoples, born of you,
shall be divided;
the one shall be stronger than the
other,
the elder shall serve the younger."
24 When her days to be delivered were
fulfilled, behold, there were twins in
her womb. 25 The first came forth red,
all his body like a hairy mantle; so they
called his name Esau. 26 Afterward his
brother came forth, and his hand had
taken hold of Esau's heel; so his name
was called Jacob.[r] Isaac was sixty
years old when she bore them.

27 When the boys grew up, Esau
was a skilful hunter, a man of the field,
while Jacob was a quiet man, dwelling
in tents. 28 Isaac loved Esau, because
he ate of his game; but Rebekah loved
Jacob.

29 Once when Jacob was boiling
pottage, Esau came in from the field,
and he was famished. 30 And Esau said
to Jacob, "Let me eat some of that red
pottage, for I am famished!" (Therefore his name was called Ē'dȯm.[s])
31 Jacob said, "First sell me your birthright." 32 Esau said, "I am about to
die; of what use is a birthright to me?"
33 Jacob said, "Swear to me first."[t] So
he swore to him, and sold his birthright to Jacob. 34 Then Jacob gave
Esau bread and pottage of lentils, and
he ate and drank, and rose and went
his way. Thus Esau despised his
birthright.

26 Now there was a famine in the
land, besides the former famine
that was in the days of Abraham. And
Isaac went to Gē'rär, to Ȧ·bim'ė·lech
king of the Philistines. 2 And the LORD
appeared to him, and said, "Do not go
down to Egypt; dwell in the land of
which I shall tell you. 3 Sojourn in
this land, and I will be with you, and
will bless you; for to you and to your
descendants I will give all these lands,
and I will fulfil the oath which I
swore to Abraham your father. 4 I will
multiply your descendants as the stars
of heaven, and will give to your descendants all these lands; and by your
descendants all the nations of the
earth shall bless themselves: 5 because
Abraham obeyed my voice and kept
my charge, my commandments, my
statutes, and my laws."

6 So Isaac dwelt in Gē'rär. 7 When

[p] Heb *fell* [q] Syr: Heb obscure [r] That is *He takes by the heel* or *He supplants* [s] That is *Red*
[t] Heb *today*
25.13-16: 1 Chron 1.29-31.

the men of the place asked him about
his wife, he said, "She is my sister";
for he feared to say, "My wife,"
thinking, "lest the men of the place
should kill me for the sake of Rebekah"; because she was fair to look
upon. 8 When he had been there a
long time, A·bim'ė·lech king of the
Philistines looked out of a window and
saw Isaac fondling Rebekah his wife.
9 So A·bim'ė·lech called Isaac, and
said, "Behold, she is your wife; how
then could you say, 'She is my sister'?"
Isaac said to him, "Because I thought,
'Lest I die because of her.' " 10 A·bim'-
ė·lech said, "What is this you have
done to us? One of the people might
easily have lain with your wife, and
you would have brought guilt upon
us." 11 So A·bim'ė·lech warned all the
people, saying, "Whoever touches
this man or his wife shall be put to
death."

12 And Isaac sowed in that land,
and reaped in the same year a hundredfold. The LORD blessed him, 13 and
the man became rich, and gained more
and more until he became very
wealthy. 14 He had possessions of
flocks and herds, and a great household,
so that the Philistines envied him.
15 (Now the Philistines had stopped
and filled with earth all the wells which
his father's servants had dug in the
days of Abraham his father.) 16 And
A·bim'ė·lech said to Isaac, "Go away
from us; for you are much mightier
than we."

17 So Isaac departed from there,
and encamped in the valley of Gē'rär
and dwelt there. 18 And Isaac dug again
the wells of water which had been dug
in the days of Abraham his father; for
the Philistines had stopped them after
the death of Abraham; and he gave
them the names which his father had
given them. 19 But when Isaac's servants dug in the valley and found there
a well of springing water, 20 the herdsmen of Gē'rär quarreled with Isaac's
herdsmen, saying, "The water is
ours." So he called the name of the
well E'sek,[u] because they contended
with him. 21 Then they dug another
well, and they quarreled over that
also; so he called its name Sit'nȧh.[v]
22 And he moved from there and dug
another well, and over that they did
not quarrel; so he called its name
Re·hō'both,[w] saying, "For now the
LORD has made room for us, and we
shall be fruitful in the land."

23 From there he went up to Beer-
sheba. 24 And the LORD appeared to
him the same night and said, "I am
the God of Abraham your father; fear
not, for I am with you and will bless
you and multiply your descendants for
my servant Abraham's sake." 25 So he
built an altar there and called upon the
name of the LORD, and pitched his
tent there. And there Isaac's servants
dug a well.

26 Then A·bim'ė·lech went to him
from Gē'rär with A·huz'zȧth his ad-
viser and Phī'col the commander of his
army. 27 Isaac said to them, "Why
have you come to me, seeing that you
hate me and have sent me away from
you?" 28 They said, "We see plainly
that the LORD is with you; so we say,
let there be an oath between you and
us, and let us make a covenant with
you, 29 that you will do us no harm,
just as we have not touched you and
have done to you nothing but good
and have sent you away in peace. You
are now the blessed of the LORD." 30 So
he made them a feast, and they ate and
drank. 31 In the morning they rose
early and took oath with one another;
and Isaac set them on their way, and
they departed from him in peace.
32 That same day Isaac's servants
came and told him about the well
which they had dug, and said to him,
"We have found water." 33 He called
it Shī'bȧh; therefore the name of the
city is Beer-sheba to this day.

34 When Esau was forty years old,
he took to wife Judith the daughter of
Be-ē'rī the Hit'tīte, and Bas'ė·math
the daughter of E'lon the Hittite;
35 and they made life bitter for Isaac
and Rebekah.

27 When Isaac was old and his
eyes were dim so that he could
not see, he called Esau his older son,
and said to him, "My son"; and he
answered, "Here I am." 2 He said,
"Behold, I am old; I do not know the
day of my death. 3 Now then, take
your weapons, your quiver and your
bow, and go out to the field, and hunt
game for me, 4 and prepare for me
savory food, such as I love, and bring
it to me that I may eat; that I may
bless you before I die."

[u] That is *Contention* [v] That is *Enmity* [w] That is *Broad places* or *Room*
26.33: Gen 21.31.

5 Now Rebekah was listening when
Isaac spoke to his son Esau. So when
Esau went to the field to hunt for
game and bring it, 6 Rebekah said to
her son Jacob, "I heard your father
speak to your brother Esau, 7 'Bring
me game, and prepare for me savory
food, that I may eat it, and bless you
before the LORD before I die.' 8 Now
therefore, my son, obey my word as I
command you. 9 Go to the flock, and
fetch me two good kids, that I may
prepare from them savory food for
your father, such as he loves; 10 and
you shall bring it to your father to eat,
so that he may bless you before he
dies." 11 But Jacob said to Rebekah
his mother, "Behold, my brother is a
hairy man, and I am a smooth man.
12 Perhaps my father will feel me, and
I shall seem to be mocking him, and
bring a curse upon myself and not a
blessing." 13 His mother said to him,
"Upon me be your curse, my son;
only obey my word, and go, fetch them
to me." 14 So he went and took them
and brought them to his mother; and
his mother prepared savory food, such
as his father loved. 15 Then Rebekah
took the best garments of Esau her
older son, which were with her in the
house, and put them on Jacob her
younger son; 16 and the skins of the
kids she put upon his hands and upon
the smooth part of his neck 17 and she
gave the savory food and the bread,
which she had prepared, into the hand
of her son Jacob.

18 So he went in to his father, and
said, "My father"; and he said, "Here
I am; who are you, my son?" 19 Jacob
said to his father, "I am Esau your
first-born. I have done as you told me;
now sit up and eat of my game, that
you may bless me." 20 But Isaac said
to his son, "How is it that you have
found it so quickly, my son?" He
answered, "Because the LORD your
God granted me success." 21 Then
Isaac said to Jacob, "Come near, that
I may feel you, my son, to know
whether you are really my son Esau or
not." 22 So Jacob went near to Isaac
his father, who felt him and said, "The
voice is Jacob's voice, but the hands
are the hands of Esau." 23 And he did
not recognize him, because his hands
were hairy like his brother Esau's
hands; so he blessed him. 24 He said,
"Are you really my son Esau?" He
answered, "I am." 25 Then he said,
"Bring it to me, that I may eat of my
son's game and bless you." So he
brought it to him, and he ate; and he
brought him wine, and he drank.
26 Then his father Isaac said to him,
"Come near and kiss me, my son."
27 So he came near and kissed him;
and he smelled the smell of his garments, and blessed him, and said,

"See, the smell of my son
is as the smell of a field which the
LORD has blessed!
28 May God give you of the dew of
heaven,
and of the fatness of the earth,
and plenty of grain and wine.
29 Let peoples serve you,
and nations bow down to you.
Be lord over your brothers,
and may your mother's sons bow
down to you.
Cursed be every one who curses you,
and blessed be every one who blesses
you!"

30 As soon as Isaac had finished
blessing Jacob, when Jacob had
scarcely gone out from the presence of
Isaac his father, Esau his brother came
in from his hunting. 31 He also prepared savory food, and brought it to
his father. And he said to his father,
"Let my father arise, and eat of his
son's game, that you may bless me."
32 His father Isaac said to him, "Who
are you?" He answered, "I am your
son, your first-born, Esau." 33 Then
Isaac trembled violently, and said,
"Who was it then that hunted game
and brought it to me, and I ate it all[x]
before you came, and I have blessed
him?—yes, and he shall be blessed."
34 When Esau heard the words of his
father, he cried out with an exceedingly great and bitter cry, and said to
his father, "Bless me, even me also, O
my father!" 35 But he said, "Your
brother came with guile, and he has
taken away your blessing." 36 Esau
said, "Is he not rightly named Jacob?
For he has supplanted me these two
times. He took away my birthright;
and behold, now he has taken away
my blessing." Then he said, "Have
you not reserved a blessing for me?"
37 Isaac answered Esau, "Behold, I
have made him your lord, and all his
brothers I have given to him for ser-

[x] Cn: Heb *of all*
27.5: Gen 12.3; Num 24.9.

vants, and with grain and wine I have
sustained him. What then can I do
for you, my son?" 38 Esau said to his
father, "Have you but one blessing,
my father? Bless me, even me also, O
my father." And Esau lifted up his
voice and wept.

39 Then Isaac his father answered
him:

"Behold, away from[y] the fatness of
the earth shall your dwelling be,
and away from[y] the dew of heaven
on high.
40 By your sword you shall live,
and you shall serve your brother;
but when you break loose
you shall break his yoke from
your neck."

41 Now Esau hated Jacob because
of the blessing with which his father
had blessed him, and Esau said to himself, "The days of mourning for my
father are approaching; then I will kill
my brother Jacob." 42 But the words
of Esau her older son were told to
Rebekah; so she sent and called Jacob
her younger son, and said to him, "Behold, your brother Esau comforts himself by planning to kill you. 43 Now
therefore, my son, obey my voice;
arise, flee to Lā'bȧn my brother in
Hâr'ȧn, 44 and stay with him a while,
until your brother's fury turns away;
45 until your brother's anger turns
away, and he forgets what you have
done to him; then I will send, and
fetch you from there. Why should I
be bereft of you both in one day?"

46 Then Rebekah said to Isaac, "I
am weary of my life because of the
Hit'tīte women. If Jacob marries one
of the Hittite women such as these,
one of the women of the land, what
good will my life be to me?"

28 1 Then Isaac called Jacob and
blessed him, and charged him, "You
shall not marry one of the Canaanite
women. 2 Arise, go to Pad'dȧn-âr'ȧm to
the house of Be·thū'el your mother's
father; and take as wife from there one
of the daughters of Lā'bȧn your
mother's brother. 3 God Almighty[z]
bless you and make you fruitful and
multiply you, that you may become a
company of peoples. 4 May he give the
blessing of Abraham to you and to
your descendants with you, that you
may take possession of the land of your
sojournings which God gave to Abraham!" 5 Thus Isaac sent Jacob away;
and he went to Pad'dȧn-âr'ȧm to
Lā'bȧn, the son of Be·thū'el the Ar·ȧ·
mē'ȧn, the brother of Rebekah, Jacob's
and Esau's mother.

6 Now Esau saw that Isaac had
blessed Jacob and sent him away to
Pad'dȧn-âr'ȧm to take a wife from
there, and that as he blessed him he
charged him, "You shall not marry one
of the Canaanite women," 7 and that
Jacob had obeyed his father and his
mother and gone to Pad'dȧn-âr'ȧm.
8 So when Esau saw that the Canaanite
women did not please Isaac his father,
9 Esau went to Ish'mȧ·el and took to
wife, besides the wives he had, Mā'hȧ-
lath the daughter of Ishmael Abraham's son, the sister of Ne·bā'ioth.

10 Jacob left Beer-sheba, and went
toward Hâr'ȧn. 11 And he came to a
certain place, and stayed there that
night, because the sun had set. Taking
one of the stones of the place, he put
it under his head and lay down in that
place to sleep. 12 And he dreamed that
there was a ladder set up on the earth,
and the top of it reached to heaven;
and behold, the angels of God were
ascending and descending on it! 13 And
behold, the LORD stood above it[a] and
said, "I am the LORD, the God of
Abraham your father and the God of
Isaac; the land on which you lie I will
give to you and to your descendants;
14 and your descendants shall be like
the dust of the earth, and you shall
spread abroad to the west and to the
east and to the north and to the south;
and by you and your descendants shall
all the families of the earth bless themselves.[b] 15 Behold, I am with you and
will keep you wherever you go, and
will bring you back to this land; for I
will not leave you until I have done
that of which I have spoken to you."
16 Then Jacob awoke from his sleep
and said, "Surely the LORD is in this
place; and I did not know it." 17 And
he was afraid, and said, "How awesome is this place! This is none other
than the house of God, and this is the
gate of heaven."

18 So Jacob rose early in the morning and he took the stone which he had
put under his head and set it up for a
pillar and poured oil on the top of it.
19 He called the name of that place
Beth'ĕl;[c] but the name of the city was
Luz at the first. 20 Then Jacob made
a vow, saying, "If God will be with

[y] Or *of* [z] Heb *El Shaddai* [a] Or *beside him* [b] Or *be blessed* [c] That is *The house of God*

me, and will keep me in this way that
I go, and will give me bread to eat and
clothing to wear, 21 so that I come
again to my father's house in peace,
then the LORD shall be my God, 22 and
this stone, which I have set up for a
pillar, shall be God's house; and of all
that thou givest me I will give the
tenth to thee."

29 Then Jacob went on his journey, and came to the land of the
people of the east. 2As he looked, he
saw a well in the field, and lo, three
flocks of sheep lying beside it; for out
of that well the flocks were watered.
The stone on the well's mouth was
large, 3 and when all the flocks were
gathered there, the shepherds would
roll the stone from the mouth of the
well, and water the sheep, and put the
stone back in its place upon the mouth
of the well.

4 Jacob said to them, "My brothers,
where do you come from?" They said,
"We are from Hâr'ån." 5 He said to
them, "Do you know Lā'bån the son of
Nā'hôr?" They said, "We know him."
6 He said to them, "Is it well with
him?" They said, "It is well; and see,
Rachel his daughter is coming with the
sheep!" 7 He said, "Behold, it is still
high day, it is not time for the animals
to be gathered together; water the
sheep, and go, pasture them." 8 But
they said, "We cannot until all the
flocks are gathered together, and the
stone is rolled from the mouth of the
well; then we water the sheep."

9 While he was still speaking with
them, Rachel came with her father's
sheep; for she kept them. 10 Now when
Jacob saw Rachel the daughter of
Lā'bån his mother's brother, and the
sheep of Laban his mother's brother,
Jacob went up and rolled the stone
from the well's mouth, and watered the
flock of Laban his mother's brother.
11 Then Jacob kissed Rachel, and wept
aloud. 12And Jacob told Rachel that he
was her father's kinsman, and that he
was Rebekah's son; and she ran and
told her father.

13 When Lā'bån heard the tidings
of Jacob his sister's son, he ran to meet
him, and embraced him and kissed
him, and brought him to his house.
Jacob told Laban all these things,
14 and Lā'bån said to him, "Surely you
are my bone and my flesh!" And he
stayed with him a month.

15 Then Lā'bån said to Jacob, "Because you are my kinsman, should you
therefore serve me for nothing? Tell
me, what shall your wages be?" 16 Now
Lā'bån had two daughters; the name
of the older was Leah, and the name
of the younger was Rachel. 17 Leah's
eyes were weak, but Rachel was
beautiful and lovely. 18 Jacob loved
Rachel; and he said, "I will serve you
seven years for your younger daughter
Rachel." 19 Lā'bån said, "It is better
that I give her to you than that I
should give her to any other man; stay
with me." 20 So Jacob served seven
years for Rachel, and they seemed to
him but a few days because of the love
he had for her.

21 Then Jacob said to Lā'bån,
"Give me my wife that I may go in to
her, for my time is completed." 22 So
Lā'bån gathered together all the men
of the place, and made a feast. 23 But
in the evening he took his daughter
Leah and brought her to Jacob; and he
went in to her. 24 (Lā'bån gave his
maid Zil'påh to his daughter Leah to
be her maid.) 25And in the morning,
behold, it was Leah; and Jacob said to
Lā'bån, "What is this you have done
to me? Did I not serve with you for
Rachel? Why then have you deceived
me?" 26 Lā'bån said, "It is not so done
in our country, to give the younger before the first-born. 27 Complete the
week of this one, and we will give you
the other also in return for serving me
another seven years." 28 Jacob did so,
and completed her week; then Lā'bån
gave him his daughter Rachel to wife.
29 (Lā'bån gave his maid Bil'håh to
his daughter Rachel to be her maid.)
30 So Jacob went in to Rachel also,
and he loved Rachel more than Leah,
and served Lā'bån for another seven
years.

31 When the LORD saw that Leah
was hated, he opened her womb; but
Rachel was barren. 32And Leah conceived and bore a son, and she called
his name Reuben;[d] for she said, "Because the LORD has looked upon my
affliction; surely now my husband will
love me." 33 She conceived again and
bore a son, and said, "Because the
LORD has heard[e] that I am hated, he
has given me this son also"; and she
called his name Simeon. 34Again she
conceived and bore a son, and said,
"Now this time my husband will be

[d] That is *See, a son* [e] Heb *shama*

joined[f] to me, because I have borne
him three sons"; therefore his name
was called Levi. 35 And she conceived
again and bore a son, and said, "This
time I will praise[g] the LORD"; therefore she called his name Judah; then
she ceased bearing.

30 When Rachel saw that she bore
Jacob no children, she envied
her sister; and she said to Jacob, "Give
me children, or I shall die!" 2 Jacob's
anger was kindled against Rachel, and
he said, "Am I in the place of God,
who has withheld from you the fruit
of the womb?" 3 Then she said, "Here
is my maid Bil'hȧh; go in to her, that
she may bear upon my knees, and
even I may have children through her."
4 So she gave him her maid Bil'hȧh as
a wife; and Jacob went in to her. 5 And
Bil'hȧh conceived and bore Jacob a
son. 6 Then Rachel said, "God has
judged me, and has also heard my
voice and given me a son"; therefore
she called his name Dan.[h] 7 Rachel's
maid Bil'hȧh conceived again and
bore Jacob a second son. 8 Then
Rachel said, "With mighty wrestlings
I have wrestled[i] with my sister, and
have prevailed"; so she called his
name Naph'tȧ·lī.

9 When Leah saw that she had
ceased bearing children, she took her
maid Zil'pȧh and gave her to Jacob as
a wife. 10 Then Leah's maid Zil'pȧh
bore Jacob a son. 11 And Leah said,
"Good fortune!" so she called his name
Gad.[j] 12 Leah's maid Zil'pȧh bore
Jacob a second son. 13 And Leah said,
"Happy am I! For the women will call
me happy"; so she called his name
Ash'ėr.[k]

14 In the days of wheat harvest
Reuben went and found mandrakes in
the field, and brought them to his
mother Leah. Then Rachel said to
Leah, "Give me, I pray, some of your
son's mandrakes." 15 But she said to
her, "Is it a small matter that you have
taken away my husband? Would you
take away my son's mandrakes also?"
Rachel said, "Then he may lie with
you tonight for your son's mandrakes."
16 When Jacob came from the field in
the evening, Leah went out to meet
him, and said, "You must come in to
me; for I have hired you with my son's
mandrakes." So he lay with her that
night. 17 And God hearkened to Leah,
and she conceived and bore Jacob a
fifth son. 18 Leah said, "God has given
me my hire[l] because I gave my maid
to my husband"; so she called his
name Is'sȧ·chär. 19 And Leah conceived
again, and she bore Jacob a sixth son.
20 Then Leah said, "God has endowed
me with a good dowry; now my husband will honor[m] me, because I have
borne him six sons"; so she called his
name Zeb'ū·lu̇n. 21 Afterwards she bore
a daughter, and called her name Dinah.
22 Then God remembered Rachel, and
God hearkened to her and opened her
womb. 23 She conceived and bore a
son, and said, "God has taken away
my reproach"; 24 and she called his
name Joseph,[n] saying, "May the LORD
add to me another son!"

25 When Rachel had borne Joseph,
Jacob said to Lā'bȧn, "Send me away,
that I may go to my own home and
country. 26 Give me my wives and my
children for whom I have served you,
and let me go; for you know the service
which I have given you." 27 But Lā'bȧn
said to him, "If you will allow me to
say so, I have learned by divination
that the LORD has blessed me because
of you; 28 name your wages, and I will
give it." 29 Jacob said to him, "You
yourself know how I have served you,
and how your cattle have fared with
me. 30 For you had little before I came,
and it has increased abundantly; and
the LORD has blessed you wherever I
turned. But now when shall I provide
for my own household also?" 31 He
said, "What shall I give you?" Jacob
said, "You shall not give me anything;
if you will do this for me, I will again
feed your flock and keep it: 32 let me
pass through all your flock today, removing from it every speckled and
spotted sheep and every black lamb,
and the spotted and speckled among
the goats; and such shall be my wages.
33 So my honesty will answer for me
later, when you come to look into my
wages with you. Every one that is not
speckled and spotted among the goats
and black among the lambs, if found
with me, shall be counted stolen."
34 Lā'bȧn said, "Good! Let it be as you
have said." 35 But that day Lā'bȧn
removed the he-goats that were striped
and spotted, and all the she-goats that
were speckled and spotted, every one
that had white on it, and every lamb

[f] Heb *lawah* [g] Heb *hodah* [h] That is *He judged* [i] Heb *niphtal* [j] That is *Fortune* [k] That is *Happy*
[l] Heb *sakar* [m] Heb *zabal* [n] That is *He adds*

that was black, and put them in charge
of his sons; 36 and he set a distance of
three days' journey between himself
and Jacob; and Jacob fed the rest of
Lā'bȧn's flock.

37 Then Jacob took fresh rods of
poplar and almond and plane, and
peeled white streaks in them, exposing
the white of the rods. 38 He set the rods
which he had peeled in front of the
flocks in the runnels, that is, the watering troughs, where the flocks came to
drink. And since they bred when they
came to drink, 39 the flocks bred in
front of the rods and so the flocks
brought forth striped, speckled, and
spotted. 40And Jacob separated the
lambs, and set the faces of the flocks
toward the striped and all the black in
the flock of Lā'bȧn; and he put his own
droves apart, and did not put them
with Laban's flock. 41 Whenever the
stronger of the flock were breeding
Jacob laid the rods in the runnels before the eyes of the flock, that they
might breed among the rods, 42 but
for the feebler of the flock he did not
lay them there; so the feebler were
Lā'bȧn's, and the stronger Jacob's.
43 Thus the man grew exceedingly
rich, and had large flocks, maidservants and menservants, and camels
and asses.

31 Now Jacob heard that the sons
of Lā'bȧn were saying, "Jacob
has taken all that was our father's;
and from what was our father's he has
gained all this wealth." 2And Jacob
saw that Lā'bȧn did not regard him
with favor as before. 3 Then the LORD
said to Jacob, "Return to the land of
your fathers and to your kindred, and
I will be with you." 4 So Jacob sent
and called Rachel and Leah into the
field where his flock was, 5 and said to
them, "I see that your father does not
regard me with favor as he did before.
But the God of my father has been
with me. 6 You know that I have
served your father with all my strength;
7 yet your father has cheated me and
changed my wages ten times, but God
did not permit him to harm me. 8 If
he said, 'The spotted shall be your
wages,' then all the flock bore spotted;
and if he said, 'The striped shall be
your wages,' then all the flock bore
striped. 9 Thus God has taken away
the cattle of your father, and given
them to me. 10 In the mating season
of the flock I lifted up my eyes, and
saw in a dream that the he-goats which
leaped upon the flock were striped,
spotted, and mottled. 11 Then the
angel of God said to me in the dream,
'Jacob,' and I said, 'Here I am!' 12And
he said, 'Lift up your eyes and see, all
the goats that leap upon the flock are
striped, spotted, and mottled; for I
have seen all that Lā'bȧn is doing to
you. 13 I am the God of Beth'ėl, where
you anointed a pillar and made a vow
to me. Now arise, go forth from this
land, and return to the land of your
birth.' " 14 Then Rachel and Leah
answered him, "Is there any portion
or inheritance left to us in our father's
house? 15Are we not regarded by him
as foreigners? For he has sold us, and
he has been using up the money given
for us. 16All the property which God
has taken away from our father belongs
to us and to our children; now then,
whatever God has said to you, do."

17 So Jacob arose, and set his sons
and his wives on camels, 18 and he
drove away all his cattle, all his livestock which he had gained, the cattle
in his possession which he had acquired
in Pad'dȧn-âr'ȧm, to go to the land of
Canaan to his father Isaac. 19 Lā'bȧn
had gone to shear his sheep, and
Rachel stole her father's household
gods. 20And Jacob outwitted Lā'bȧn
the Ar·ȧ·mē'ȧn, in that he did not tell
him that he intended to flee. 21 He fled
with all that he had, and arose and
crossed the Eū·phrā'tēṡ, and set his
face toward the hill country of Gilead.

22 When it was told Lā'bȧn on the
third day that Jacob had fled, 23 he
took his kinsmen with him and pursued
him for seven days and followed close
after him into the hill country of
Gilead. 24 But God came to Lā'bȧn the
Ar·ȧ·mē'ȧn in a dream by night, and
said to him, "Take heed that you say
not a word to Jacob, either good or
bad."

25 And Lā'bȧn overtook Jacob.
Now Jacob had pitched his tent in the
hill country, and Laban with his kinsmen encamped in the hill country of
Gilead. 26And Lā'bȧn said to Jacob,
"What have you done, that you have
cheated me, and carried away my
daughters like captives of the sword?
27 Why did you flee secretly, and cheat
me, and did not tell me, so that I
might have sent you away with mirth
and songs, with tambourine and lyre?
28And why did you not permit me to

kiss my sons and my daughters farewell? Now you have done foolishly.
29 It is in my power to do you harm;
but the God of your father spoke to
me last night, saying, 'Take heed that
you speak to Jacob neither good nor
bad.' 30 And now you have gone away
because you longed greatly for your
father's house, but why did you steal
my gods?" 31 Jacob answered Lā'bȧn,
"Because I was afraid, for I thought
that you would take your daughters
from me by force. 32 Any one with
whom you find your gods shall not
live. In the presence of our kinsmen
point out what I have that is yours,
and take it." Now Jacob did not know
that Rachel had stolen them.

33 So Lā'bȧn went into Jacob's
tent, and into Leah's tent, and into
the tent of the two maidservants, but
he did not find them. And he went
out of Leah's tent, and entered
Rachel's. 34 Now Rachel had taken the
household gods and put them in the
camel's saddle, and sat upon them.
Lā'bȧn felt all about the tent, but did
not find them. 35 And she said to her
father, "Let not my lord be angry
that I cannot rise before you, for the
way of women is upon me." So he
searched, but did not find the household gods.

36 Then Jacob became angry, and
upbraided Lā'bȧn; Jacob said to Laban, "What is my offense? What is my
sin, that you have hotly pursued me?
37 Although you have felt through all
my goods, what have you found of all
your household goods? Set it here before my kinsmen and your kinsmen,
that they may decide between us two.
38 These twenty years I have been
with you; your ewes and your she-
goats have not miscarried, and I have
not eaten the rams of your flocks.
39 That which was torn by wild beasts
I did not bring to you; I bore the loss
of it myself; of my hand you required
it, whether stolen by day or stolen by
night. 40 Thus I was, by day the heat
consumed me, and the cold by night,
and my sleep fled from my eyes.
41 These twenty years I have been in
your house; I served you fourteen
years for your two daughters, and six
years for your flock, and you have
changed my wages ten times. 42 If the
God of my father, the God of Abraham and the Fear of Isaac, had not
been on my side, surely now you
would have sent me away empty-
handed. God saw my affliction and the
labor of my hands, and rebuked you
last night."

43 Then Lā'bȧn answered and said
to Jacob, "The daughters are my
daughters, the children are my children, the flocks are my flocks, and all
that you see is mine. But what can I
do this day to these my daughters, or
to their children whom they have
borne? 44 Come now, let us make a
covenant, you and I; and let it be a
witness between you and me." 45 So
Jacob took a stone, and set it up as a
pillar. 46 And Jacob said to his kinsmen, "Gather stones," and they took
stones, and made a heap; and they ate
there by the heap. 47 Lā'bȧn called it
Jē'gȧr-sā·hȧ·dū'thȧ:[o] but Jacob called
it Gal'ē·ed.[p] 48 Lā'bȧn said, "This heap
is a witness between you and me today." Therefore he named it Gal'ē·ed,
49 and the pillar[q] Miz'pȧh,[r] for he said,
"The LORD watch between you and
me, when we are absent one from the
other. 50 If you ill-treat my daughters,
or if you take wives besides my daughters, although no man is with us,
remember, God is witness between
you and me."

51 Then Lā'bȧn said to Jacob, "See
this heap and the pillar, which I have
set between you and me. 52 This heap
is a witness, and the pillar is a witness,
that I will not pass over this heap to
you, and you will not pass over this
heap and this pillar to me, for harm.
53 The God of Abraham and the God
of Nā'hôr, the God of their father,
judge between us." So Jacob swore by
the Fear of his father Isaac, 54 and
Jacob offered a sacrifice on the mountain and called his kinsmen to eat
bread; and they ate bread and tarried
all night on the mountain.

55[s] Early in the morning Lā'bȧn
arose, and kissed his grandchildren
and his daughters and blessed them;
then he departed and returned home.

32 Jacob went on his way and the
angels of God met him; 2 and
when Jacob saw them he said, "This
is God's army!" So he called the name
of that place Mā·hȧ·nā'im.[t]

[o] In Aramaic *The heap of witness* [p] In Hebrew *The heap of witness*
[q] Compare Sam: Heb lacks *the pillar* [r] That is *Watchpost* [s] Ch 32.1 in Heb
[t] Here taken to mean *Two armies*

3 And Jacob sent messengers before
him to Esau his brother in the land of
Sē'ir, the country of Ē'dŏm, 4 instructing them, "Thus you shall say to my
lord Esau: Thus says your servant
Jacob, 'I have sojourned with Lā'băn,
and stayed until now; 5 and I have
oxen, asses, flocks, menservants, and
maidservants; and I have sent to tell
my lord, in order that I may find favor
in your sight.' "
6 And the messengers returned to
Jacob, saying, "We came to your
brother Esau, and he is coming to
meet you, and four hundred men with
him." 7 Then Jacob was greatly afraid
and distressed; and he divided the
people that were with him, and the
flocks and herds and camels, into two
companies, 8 thinking, "If Esau comes
to the one company and destroys it,
then the company which is left will
escape."
9 And Jacob said, "O God of my
father Abraham and God of my father
Isaac, O LORD who didst say to me,
'Return to your country and to your
kindred, and I will do you good,' 10 I
am not worthy of the least of all the
steadfast love and all the faithfulness
which thou hast shown to thy servant,
for with only my staff I crossed this
Jordan; and now I have become two
companies. 11 Deliver me, I pray thee,
from the hand of my brother, from the
hand of Esau, for I fear him, lest he
come and slay us all, the mothers with
the children. 12 But thou didst say, 'I
will do you good, and make your
descendants as the sand of the sea,
which cannot be numbered for
multitude.' "
13 So he lodged there that night,
and took from what he had with him
a present for his brother Esau, 14 two
hundred she-goats and twenty he-
goats, two hundred ewes and twenty
rams, 15 thirty milch camels and their
colts, forty cows and ten bulls, twenty
she-asses and ten he-asses. 16 These
he delivered into the hand of his
servants, every drove by itself, and
said to his servants, "Pass on before
me, and put a space between drove
and drove." 17 He instructed the foremost, "When Esau my brother meets
you, and asks you, 'To whom do you
belong? Where are you going? And
whose are these before you?' 18 then
you shall say, 'They belong to your
servant Jacob; they are a present sent
to my lord Esau; and moreover he is
behind us.' " 19 He likewise instructed
the second and the third and all who
followed the droves, "You shall say
the same thing to Esau when you meet
him, 20 and you shall say, 'Moreover
your servant Jacob is behind us.' " For
he thought, "I may appease him with
the present that goes before me, and
afterwards I shall see his face; perhaps
he will accept me." 21 So the present
passed on before him; and he himself
lodged that night in the camp.
22 The same night he arose and
took his two wives, his two maids, and
his eleven children, and crossed the
ford of the Jab'bŏk. 23 He took them
and sent them across the stream, and
likewise everything that he had. 24 And
Jacob was left alone; and a man
wrestled with him until the breaking
of the day. 25 When the man saw that
he did not prevail against Jacob, he
touched the hollow of his thigh; and
Jacob's thigh was put out of joint as
he wrestled with him. 26 Then he said,
"Let me go, for the day is breaking."
But Jacob said, "I will not let you go,
unless you bless me." 27 And he said
to him, "What is your name?" And
he said, "Jacob." 28 Then he said,
"Your name shall no more be called
Jacob, but Israel,[u] for you have striven
with God and with men, and have
prevailed." 29 Then Jacob asked him,
"Tell me, I pray, your name." But he
said, "Why is it that you ask my
name?" And there he blessed him.
30 So Jacob called the name of the
place Pė·nī'el,[v] saying, "For I have
seen God face to face, and yet my life
is preserved." 31 The sun rose upon
him as he passed Pė·nū'el, limping
because of his thigh. 32 Therefore to
this day the Israelites do not eat the
sinew of the hip which is upon the hollow of the thigh, because he touched
the hollow of Jacob's thigh on the
sinew of the hip.
33 And Jacob lifted up his eyes
and looked, and behold, Esau
was coming, and four hundred men
with him. So he divided the children
among Leah and Rachel and the two
maids. 2 And he put the maids with
their children in front, then Leah with
her children, and Rachel and Joseph
last of all. 3 He himself went on before
them, bowing himself to the ground

[u] That is *He who strives with God* or *God strives* [v] That is *The face of God*

seven times, until he came near to his
brother.
4 But Esau ran to meet him, and
embraced him, and fell on his neck
and kissed him, and they wept. 5 And
when Esau raised his eyes and saw the
women and children, he said, "Who
are these with you?" Jacob said, "The
children whom God has graciously
given your servant." 6 Then the maids
drew near, they and their children,
and bowed down; 7 Leah likewise and
her children drew near and bowed
down; and last Joseph and Rachel
drew near, and they bowed down.
8 Esau said, "What do you mean by
all this company which I met?" Jacob
answered, "To find favor in the sight
of my lord." 9 But Esau said, "I have
enough, my brother; keep what you
have for yourself." 10 Jacob said, "No,
I pray you, if I have found favor in
your sight, then accept my present
from my hand; for truly to see your
face is like seeing the face of God, with
such favor have you received me.
11 Accept, I pray you, my gift that is
brought to you, because God has
dealt graciously with me, and because
I have enough." Thus he urged him,
and he took it.
12 Then Esau said, "Let us journey
on our way, and I will go before you."
13 But Jacob said to him, "My lord
knows that the children are frail, and
that the flocks and herds giving suck
are a care to me; and if they are over-
driven for one day, all the flocks will
die. 14 Let my lord pass on before his
servant, and I will lead on slowly,
according to the pace of the cattle
which are before me and according to
the pace of the children, until I come
to my lord in Sē′ir."
15 So Esau said, "Let me leave with
you some of the men who are with
me." But he said, "What need is there?
Let me find favor in the sight of my
lord." 16 So Esau returned that day
on his way to Sē′ir. 17 But Jacob
journeyed to Suc′coth,[w] and built himself a house, and made booths for his
cattle; therefore the name of the place
is called Succoth.
18 And Jacob came safely to the
city of Shē′chem, which is in the land
of Canaan, on his way from Pad′dăn-
ăr′ăm; and he camped before the city.
19 And from the sons of Hā′mor, Shē′-
chem's father, he bought for a hundred
pieces of money[x] the piece of land on
which he had pitched his tent. 20 There
he erected an altar and called it El-
El′ō·hē-Iṡ′rȧ·el.[y]

34 Now Dinah the daughter of
Leah, whom she had borne to
Jacob, went out to visit the women of
the land; 2 and when Shē′chem the son
of Hā′mor the Hī′vīte, the prince of
the land, saw her, he seized her and
lay with her and humbled her. 3 And
his soul was drawn to Dinah the
daughter of Jacob; he loved the maiden
and spoke tenderly to her. 4 So Shē′-
chem spoke to his father Hā′mor, saying, "Get me this maiden for my
wife." 5 Now Jacob heard that he had
defiled his daughter Dinah; but his
sons were with his cattle in the field,
so Jacob held his peace until they came.
6 And Hā′mor the father of Shē′chem
went out to Jacob to speak with him.
7 The sons of Jacob came in from the
field when they heard of it; and the
men were indignant and very angry,
because he had wrought folly in Israel
by lying with Jacob's daughter, for
such a thing ought not to be done.
8 But Hā′mor spoke with them,
saying, "The soul of my son Shē′chem
longs for your daughter; I pray you,
give her to him in marriage. 9 Make
marriages with us; give your daughters
to us, and take our daughters for yourselves. 10 You shall dwell with us; and
the land shall be open to you; dwell
and trade in it, and get property in it."
11 Shē′chem also said to her father and
to her brothers, "Let me find favor in
your eyes, and whatever you say to me
I will give. 12 Ask of me ever so much
as marriage present and gift, and I will
give according as you say to me;
only give me the maiden to be my
wife."
13 The sons of Jacob answered
Shē′chem and his father Hā′mor deceitfully, because he had defiled their
sister Dinah. 14 They said to them,
"We cannot do this thing, to give our
sister to one who is uncircumcised, for
that would be a disgrace to us. 15 Only
on this condition will we consent to
you: that you will become as we are
and every male of you be circumcised.
16 Then we will give our daughters to
you, and we will take your daughters
to ourselves, and we will dwell with
you and become one people. 17 But if
you will not listen to us and be cir-

[w] That is *Booths* [x] Heb *a hundred qesitas* [y] That is *God, the God of Israel*

cumcised, then we will take our daughter, and we will be gone."
18 Their words pleased Hā'mor
and Hamor's son Shē'chem. 19And
the young man did not delay to do
the thing, because he had delight in
Jacob's daughter. Now he was the
most honored of all his family. 20 So
Hā'mor and his son Shē'chem came to
the gate of their city and spoke to the
men of their city, saying, 21 "These
men are friendly with us; let them
dwell in the land and trade in it, for
behold, the land is large enough for
them; let us take their daughters in
marriage, and let us give them our
daughters. 22 Only on this condition
will the men agree to dwell with us,
to become one people: that every male
among us be circumcised as they are
circumcised. 23 Will not their cattle,
their property and all their beasts be
ours? Only let us agree with them, and
they will dwell with us." 24And all
who went out of the gate of his city
hearkened to Hā'mor and his son
Shē'chem; and every male was circumcised, all who went out of the gate
of his city.
25 On the third day, when they
were sore, two of the sons of Jacob,
Simeon and Levi, Dinah's brothers,
took their swords and came upon the
city unawares, and killed all the males.
26 They slew Hā'mor and his son Shē'-
chem with the sword, and took Dinah
out of Shechem's house, and went
away. 27And the sons of Jacob came
upon the slain, and plundered the city,
because their sister had been defiled;
28 they took their flocks and their
herds, their asses, and whatever was
in the city and in the field; 29 all their
wealth, all their little ones and their
wives, all that was in the houses, they
captured and made their prey. 30 Then
Jacob said to Simeon and Levi, "You
have brought trouble on me by making
me odious to the inhabitants of the
land, the Canaanites and the Per'iz-
zītes; my numbers are few, and if they
gather themselves against me and
attack me, I shall be destroyed, both
I and my household." 31 But they
said, "Should he treat our sister as a
harlot?"

35 God said to Jacob, "Arise, go
up to Beth'ĕl, and dwell there;
and make there an altar to the God
who appeared to you when you fled
from your brother Esau." 2 So Jacob
said to his household and to all who
were with him, "Put away the foreign
gods that are among you, and purify
yourselves, and change your garments; 3 then let us arise and go up to
Beth'ĕl, that I may make there an
altar to the God who answered me in
the day of my distress and has been
with me wherever I have gone." 4 So
they gave to Jacob all the foreign gods
that they had, and the rings that were
in their ears; and Jacob hid them under
the oak which was near Shē'chem.
5 And as they journeyed, a terror
from God fell upon the cities that
were round about them, so that they
did not pursue the sons of Jacob. 6And
Jacob came to Luz (that is, Beth'ĕl),
which is in the land of Canaan, he and
all the people who were with him,
7 and there he built an altar, and called
the place El-beth'ĕl,[z] because there
God had revealed himself to him when
he fled from his brother. 8And Deb'ō-
râh, Rebekah's nurse, died, and she
was buried under an oak below Beth'ĕl;
so the name of it was called Al'lŏn-
bac'ŭth.[a]
9 God appeared to Jacob again,
when he came from Pad'dăn-ăr'ăm,
and blessed him. 10And God said to
him, "Your name is Jacob; no longer
shall your name be called Jacob, but
Israel shall be your name." So his
name was called Israel. 11And God
said to him, "I am God Almighty:[b] be
fruitful and multiply; a nation and a
company of nations shall come from
you, and kings shall spring from you.
12 The land which I gave to Abraham
and Isaac I will give to you, and I will
give the land to your descendants after
you." 13 Then God went up from him
in the place where he had spoken with
him. 14And Jacob set up a pillar in the
place where he had spoken with him,
a pillar of stone; and he poured out a
drink offering on it, and poured oil on
it. 15 So Jacob called the name of the
place where God had spoken with him,
Beth'ĕl.
16 Then they journeyed from
Beth'ĕl; and when they were still some
distance from Eph'rath, Rachel travailed, and she had hard labor. 17And
when she was in her hard labor, the
midwife said to her, "Fear not; for
now you will have another son." 18And
as her soul was departing (for she

[z] That is *God of Bethel* [a] That is *Oak of weeping* [b] Heb *El Shaddai*

died), she called his name Ben-ō'nī;[c]
but his father called his name Benjamin.[d] 19 So Rachel died, and she was
buried on the way to Eph'rath (that is,
Bethlehem), 20 and Jacob set up a
pillar upon her grave; it is the pillar of
Rachel's tomb, which is there to this
day. 21 Israel journeyed on, and pitched
his tent beyond the tower of Ē'dėr.

22 While Israel dwelt in that land
Reuben went and lay with Bil'hȧh his
father's concubine; and Israel heard
of it.

Now the sons of Jacob were twelve.
23 The sons of Leah: Reuben (Jacob's
first-born), Simeon, Levi, Judah, Is'-
sȧ·chär, and Zeb'ū·lŭn. 24 The sons of
Rachel: Joseph and Benjamin. 25 The
sons of Bil'hȧh, Rachel's maid: Dan
and Naph'tȧ·lī. 26 The sons of Zil'pȧh,
Leah's maid: Gad and Ash'ėr. These
were the sons of Jacob who were born
to him in Pad'dȧn-âr'ȧm.

27 And Jacob came to his father
Isaac at Mam're, or Kĭr'i·ath-är'bȧ
(that is, Hē'brȯn), where Abraham and
Isaac had sojourned. 28 Now the days
of Isaac were a hundred and eighty
years. 29 And Isaac breathed his last;
and he died and was gathered to his
people, old and full of days; and his
sons Esau and Jacob buried him.

36 These are the descendants of
Esau (that is, Ē'dȯm). 2 Esau
took his wives from the Canaanites:
Ā'dȧh the daughter of Ē'lon the Hit'-
tīte, Ō·hol·i·bā'mȧh the daughter of
An'ȧh the son[e] of Zib'ē·ȯn the Hī'vīte,
3 and Bas'ė·math, Ish'mȧ·el's daughter, the sister of Ne·bā'ioth. 4 And
Ā'dȧh bore to Esau, E·lī'phaz; Bas'ė-
math bore Reü'el; 5 and Ō·hol·i·bā'-
mȧh bore Jē'ush, Jā'lȧm, and Kō'rȧh.
These are the sons of Esau who were
born to him in the land of Canaan.

6 Then Esau took his wives, his
sons, his daughters, and all the members of his household, his cattle, all his
beasts, and all his property which he
had acquired in the land of Canaan;
and he went into a land away from his
brother Jacob. 7 For their possessions
were too great for them to dwell together; the land of their sojournings
could not support them because of
their cattle. 8 So Esau dwelt in the hill
country of Sē'ir; Esau is Ē'dȯm.

9 These are the descendants of Esau
the father of the Ē'dȯ·mītes in the hill
country of Sē'ir. 10 These are the
names of Esau's sons: E·lī'phaz the son
of Ā'dȧh the wife of Esau, Reü'el the
son of Bas'ė·math the wife of Esau.
11 The sons of E·lī'phaz were Tē'mȧn,
Ō'mär, Zē'phō, Gā'tam, and Kē'naz.
12 (Tim'nȧ was a concubine of E·lī'-
phaz, Esau's son; she bore Am'ȧ·lek to
Eliphaz.) These are the sons of Ā'dȧh,
Esau's wife. 13 These are the sons of
Reü'el: Nā'hath, Zē'rȧh, Sham'mȧh,
and Miz'zȧh. These are the sons of
Bas'ė·math, Esau's wife. 14 These are
the sons of Ō·hol·i·bā'mȧh the daughter of An'ȧh the son[f] of Zib'ē·ȯn,
Esau's wife: she bore to Esau Jē'ush,
Jā'lȧm, and Kō'rȧh.

15 These are the chiefs of the sons
of Esau. The sons of E·lī'phaz the first-
born of Esau: the chiefs Tē'mȧn,
Ō'mär, Zē'phō, Kē'naz, 16 Kō'rȧh,
Gā'tam, and Am'ȧ·lek; these are the
chiefs of E·lī'phaz in the land of Ē'dȯm;
they are the sons of Ā'dȧh. 17 These
are the sons of Reü'el, Esau's son: the
chiefs Nā'hath, Zē'rȧh, Sham'mȧh,
and Miz'zȧh; these are the chiefs of
Reuel in the land of Ē'dȯm; they are
the sons of Bas'ė·math, Esau's wife.
18 These are the sons of Ō·hol·i·bā'-
mȧh, Esau's wife: the chiefs Jē'ush,
Jā'lȧm, and Kō'rȧh; these are the chiefs
born of Oholibamah the daughter of
An'ȧh, Esau's wife. 19 These are the
sons of Esau (that is, Ē'dȯm), and
these are their chiefs.

20 These are the sons of Sē'ir the
Hôr'īte, the inhabitants of the land:
Lō'tan, Shō'bȧl, Zib'ē·ȯn, An'ȧh,
21 Dī'shon, Ē'zėr, and Dī'shan; these
are the chiefs of the Hôr'ītes, the sons
of Sē'ir in the land of Ē'dȯm. 22 The
sons of Lō'tan were Hō'rī and Hē'-
mȧn; and Lotan's sister was Tim'nȧ.
23 These are the sons of Shō'bȧl: Al'-
vȧn, Man'ȧ·hath, Ē'bȧl, Shē'phō, and
Ō'nȧm. 24 These are the sons of Zib'ē-
ȯn: Ā'iȧh and An'ȧh; he is the Anah
who found the hot springs in the wilderness, as he pastured the asses of
Zibeon his father. 25 These are the
children of An'ȧh: Dī'shon and Ō·hol·i-
bā'mȧh the daughter of Anah. 26 These
are the sons of Dī'shon: Hem'dȧn,
Esh'bȧn, Ith'ran, and Chē'rȧn. 27 These
are the sons of Ē'zėr: Bil'han, Zā'ȧ·van,
and Ā'kȧn. 28 These are the sons of

[c] That is *Son of my sorrow* [d] That is *Son of the right hand* or *Son of the South*
[e] Sam Gk Syr: Heb *daughter* [f] Gk Syr: Heb *daughter*
36.2: Gen 26.34; 28.9. 36.20-28: 1 Chron 1.38-42.

Dī′shan: Uz and Âr′ȧn. 29 These are
the chiefs of the Hôr′ītes: the chiefs
Lō′tan, Shō′bȧl, Zib′ē·ȯn, An′ȧh,
30 Dī′shon, Ē′zẽr, and Dī′shan; these
are the chiefs of the Hôr′ītes, according to their clans in the land of Sē′ir.

31 These are the kings who reigned
in the land of Ē′dȯm, before any king
reigned over the Israelites. 32 Bē′lȧ the
son of Bē′ôr reigned in Ē′dȯm, the
name of his city being Din′hȧ·bȧh.
33 Bē′lȧ died, and Jō′bab the son of
Zē′rȧh of Boz′rȧh reigned in his stead.
34 Jō′bab died, and Hū′shȧm of the
land of the Tē′mȧ·nītes reigned in his
stead. 35 Hū′shȧm died, and Hā′dad
the son of Bē′dad, who defeated Mid′-
i·ȧn in the country of Mō′ab, reigned
in his stead, the name of his city being
Ā′vith. 36 Hā′dad died, and Sam′lȧh
of Mas·rē′kȧh reigned in his stead.
37 Sam′lȧh died, and Shā′ụl of Re·hō′-
both on the Eū·phrā′tēṣ reigned in his
stead. 38 Shā′ụl died, and Bā′ȧl-hā′-
nȧn the son of Ach′bôr reigned in his
stead. 39 Bā′ȧl-hā′nȧn the son of Ach′-
bôr died, and Hā′dȧr reigned in his
stead, the name of his city being Pā′ụ;
his wife's name was Me·het′ȧ·bẹl, the
daughter of Mā′tred, daughter of
Mē′zȧ·hab.

40 These are the names of the chiefs
of Esau, according to their families and
their dwelling places, by their names:
the chiefs Tim′nȧ, Al′vȧh, Jē′theth,
41 Ō·hol·i·bā′mȧh, Ē′lȧh, Pī′non, 42 Kē′-
naz, Tē′mȧn, Mib′zär, 43 Mag′di·el,
and Ī′rȧm; these are the chiefs of
Ē′dȯm (that is, Esau, the father of
Edom), according to their dwelling
places in the land of their possession.

37 Jacob dwelt in the land of his
father's sojournings, in the land
of Canaan. 2 This is the history of the
family of Jacob.

Joseph, being seventeen years old,
was shepherding the flock with his
brothers; he was a lad with the sons of
Bil′hȧh and Zil′pȧh, his father's wives;
and Joseph brought an ill report of
them to their father. 3 Now Israel
loved Joseph more than any other of
his children, because he was the son
of his old age; and he made him a long
robe with sleeves. 4 But when his
brothers saw that their father loved
him more than all his brothers, they
hated him, and could not speak peaceably to him.

5 Now Joseph had a dream, and
when he told it to his brothers they
only hated him the more. 6 He said to
them, "Hear this dream which I have
dreamed: 7 behold, we were binding
sheaves in the field, and lo, my sheaf
arose and stood upright; and behold,
your sheaves gathered round it, and
bowed down to my sheaf." 8 His
brothers said to him, "Are you indeed
to reign over us? Or are you indeed to
have dominion over us?" So they
hated him yet more for his dreams and
for his words. 9 Then he dreamed
another dream, and told it to his
brothers, and said, "Behold, I have
dreamed another dream; and behold,
the sun, the moon, and eleven stars
were bowing down to me." 10 But
when he told it to his father and to his
brothers, his father rebuked him, and
said to him, "What is this dream that
you have dreamed? Shall I and your
mother and your brothers indeed come
to bow ourselves to the ground before
you?" 11 And his brothers were jealous
of him, but his father kept the saying
in mind.

12 Now his brothers went to pasture their father's flock near Shē′chem.
13 And Israel said to Joseph, "Are not
your brothers pasturing the flock at
Shē′chem? Come, I will send you to
them." And he said to him, "Here I
am." 14 So he said to him, "Go now,
see if it is well with your brothers, and
with the flock; and bring me word
again." So he sent him from the valley
of Hē′brȯn, and he came to Shē′chem.
15 And a man found him wandering in
the fields; and the man asked him,
"What are you seeking?" 16 "I am
seeking my brothers," he said, "tell
me, I pray you, where they are pasturing the flock." 17 And the man said,
"They have gone away, for I heard
them say, 'Let us go to Dō′thȧn.' " So
Joseph went after his brothers, and
found them at Dothan. 18 They saw
him afar off, and before he came near
to them they conspired against him to
kill him. 19 They said to one another,
"Here comes this dreamer. 20 Come
now, let us kill him and throw him
into one of the pits; then we shall say
that a wild beast has devoured him,
and we shall see what will become of
his dreams." 21 But when Reuben
heard it, he delivered him out of their
hands, saying, "Let us not take his
life." 22 And Reuben said to them,

36.31-43: 1 Chron 1.43-53. **37.11, 28:** Acts 7.9.

"Shed no blood; cast him into this pit
here in the wilderness, but lay no hand
upon him"—that he might rescue him
out of their hand, to restore him to his
father. 23 So when Joseph came to his
brothers, they stripped him of his
robe, the long robe with sleeves that
he wore; 24 and they took him and cast
him into a pit. The pit was empty,
there was no water in it.

25 Then they sat down to eat; and
looking up they saw a caravan of
Ish'mȧ·el·ītes coming from Gilead,
with their camels bearing gum, balm,
and myrrh, on their way to carry it
down to Egypt. 26 Then Judah said to
his brothers, "What profit is it if we
slay our brother and conceal his blood?
27 Come, let us sell him to the Ish'mȧ-
el·ītes, and let not our hand be upon
him, for he is our brother, our own
flesh." And his brothers heeded him.
28 Then Mid'i·ȧ·nīte traders passed by;
and they drew Joseph up and lifted
him out of the pit, and sold him to
the Ish'mȧ·el·ītes for twenty shekels
of silver; and they took Joseph to
Egypt.

29 When Reuben returned to the
pit and saw that Joseph was not in the
pit, he rent his clothes 30 and returned
to his brothers, and said, "The lad is
gone; and I, where shall I go?" 31 Then
they took Joseph's robe, and killed a
goat, and dipped the robe in the blood;
32 and they sent the long robe with
sleeves and brought it to their father,
and said, "This we have found; see
now whether it is your son's robe or
not." 33 And he recognized it, and said,
"It is my son's robe; a wild beast has
devoured him; Joseph is without doubt
torn to pieces." 34 Then Jacob rent his
garments, and put sackcloth upon his
loins, and mourned for his son many
days. 35 All his sons and all his daughters rose up to comfort him; but he
refused to be comforted and said, "No,
I shall go down to Shē'ōl to my son,
mourning." Thus his father wept for
him. 36 Meanwhile the Mid'i·ȧ·nītes
had sold him in Egypt to Pot'i-phȧr,
an officer of Pharaoh, the captain of
the guard.

38 It happened at that time that
Judah went down from his
brothers, and turned in to a certain
Ȧ·dul'lȧ·mīte, whose name was Hī'rȧh.
2 There Judah saw the daughter of a
certain Canaanite whose name was
Shü'ȧ; he married her and went in to
her, 3 and she conceived and bore a
son, and he called his name Ĕr. 4 Again
she conceived and bore a son, and she
called his name Ō'nȧn. 5 Yet again
she bore a son, and she called his name
Shē'lȧh. She[g] was in Chē'zib when she
bore him. 6 And Judah took a wife for
Ĕr his first-born, and her name was
Tā'mär. 7 But Ĕr, Judah's first-born,
was wicked in the sight of the LORD;
and the LORD slew him. 8 Then Judah
said to Ō'nȧn, "Go in to your brother's
wife, and perform the duty of a brother-
in-law to her, and raise up offspring
for your brother." 9 But Ō'nȧn knew
that the offspring would not be his; so
when he went in to his brother's wife
he spilled the semen on the ground,
lest he should give offspring to his
brother. 10 And what he did was displeasing in the sight of the LORD, and
he slew him also. 11 Then Judah said
to Tā'mär his daughter-in-law, "Remain a widow in your father's house,
till Shē'lȧh my son grows up"—for he
feared that he would die, like his
brothers. So Tamar went and dwelt in
her father's house.

12 In course of time the wife of
Judah, Shü'ȧ's daughter, died; and
when Judah was comforted, he went
up to Tim'nȧh to his sheepshearers,
he and his friend Hī'rȧh the Ȧ·dul'lȧ-
mīte. 13 And when Tā'mär was told,
"Your father-in-law is going up to
Tim'nȧh to shear his sheep," 14 she
put off her widow's garments, and put
on a veil, wrapping herself up, and sat
at the entrance to E·nā'im, which is on
the road to Tim'nȧh; for she saw that
Shē'lȧh was grown up, and she had
not been given to him in marriage.
15 When Judah saw her, he thought
her to be a harlot, for she had covered
her face. 16 He went over to her at the
road side, and said, "Come, let me
come in to you," for he did not know
that she was his daughter-in-law. She
said, "What will you give me, that you
may come in to me?" 17 He answered,
"I will send you a kid from the flock."
And she said, "Will you give me a
pledge, till you send it?" 18 He said,
"What pledge shall I give you?" She
replied, "Your signet and your cord,
and your staff that is in your hand."
So he gave them to her, and went in to
her, and she conceived by him. 19 Then
she arose and went away, and taking

g Gk: Heb *He*

off her veil she put on the garments of
her widowhood.
20 When Judah sent the kid by his
friend the A·dul'lȧ·mīte, to receive the
pledge from the woman's hand, he
could not find her. 21 And he asked the
men of the place, "Where is the harlot[h]
who was at E·nā'im by the wayside?"
And they said, "No harlot[h] has been
here." 22 So he returned to Judah, and
said, "I have not found her; and also
the men of the place said, 'No harlot[h]
has been here.' " 23 And Judah replied,
"Let her keep the things as her own,
lest we be laughed at; you see, I sent
this kid, and you could not find her."
24 About three months later Judah
was told, "Tā'mär your daughter-in-
law has played the harlot; and moreover she is with child by harlotry."
And Judah said, "Bring her out, and
let her be burned." 25 As she was being
brought out, she sent word to her
father-in-law, "By the man to whom
these belong, I am with child." And
she said, "Mark, I pray you, whose
these are, the signet and the cord and
the staff." 26 Then Judah acknowledged them and said, "She is more
righteous than I, inasmuch as I did
not give her to my son Shē'lȧh." And
he did not lie with her again.
27 When the time of her delivery
came, there were twins in her womb.
28 And when she was in labor, one put
out a hand; and the midwife took and
bound on his hand a scarlet thread,
saying, "This came out first." 29 But
as he drew back his hand, behold, his
brother came out; and she said, "What
a breach you have made for yourself!"
Therefore his name was called Per'ez.[i]
30 Afterward his brother came out with
the scarlet thread upon his hand; and
his name was called Zē'rȧh.

39 Now Joseph was taken down
to Egypt, and Pot'i-phȧr, an
officer of Pharaoh, the captain of the
guard, an Egyptian, bought him from
the Ish'mȧ·el·ītes who had brought
him down there. 2 The LORD was with
Joseph, and he became a successful
man; and he was in the house of his
master the Egyptian, 3 and his master
saw that the LORD was with him, and
that the LORD caused all that he did to
prosper in his hands. 4 So Joseph
found favor in his sight and attended
him, and he made him overseer of his
house and put him in charge of all
that he had. 5 From the time that he
made him overseer in his house and
over all that he had the LORD blessed
the Egyptian's house for Joseph's
sake; the blessing of the LORD was
upon all that he had, in house and
field. 6 So he left all that he had in
Joseph's charge; and having him he
had no concern for anything but the
food which he ate.
Now Joseph was handsome and
good-looking. 7 And after a time his
master's wife cast her eyes upon Joseph, and said, "Lie with me." 8 But
he refused and said to his master's
wife, "Lo, having me my master has
no concern about anything in the
house, and he has put everything that
he has in my hand; 9 he is not greater
in this house than I am; nor has he
kept back anything from me except
yourself, because you are his wife; how
then can I do this great wickedness,
and sin against God?" 10 And although
she spoke to Joseph day after day, he
would not listen to her, to lie with her
or to be with her. 11 But one day,
when he went into the house to do his
work and none of the men of the house
was there in the house, 12 she caught
him by his garment, saying, "Lie with
me." But he left his garment in her
hand, and fled and got out of the
house. 13 And when she saw that he
had left his garment in her hand, and
had fled out of the house, 14 she called
to the men of her household and said
to them, "See, he has brought among
us a Hebrew to insult us; he came in
to me to lie with me and I cried out
with a loud voice; 15 and when he
heard that I lifted up my voice and
cried, he left his garment with me, and
fled and got out of the house." 16 Then
she laid up his garment by her until
his master came home, 17 and she told
him the same story, saying, "The
Hebrew servant, whom you have
brought among us, came in to me to
insult me; 18 but as soon as I lifted up
my voice and cried, he left his garment with me, and fled out of the
house."
19 When his master heard the words
which his wife spoke to him, "This is
the way your servant treated me," his
anger was kindled. 20 And Joseph's
master took him and put him into the

[h] Or *cult prostitute* [i] That is *A breach*
39.1-2, 21: Acts 7.9.

prison, the place where the king's
prisoners were confined, and he was
there in prison. 21 But the LORD was
with Joseph and showed him steadfast
love, and gave him favor in the sight
of the keeper of the prison. 22And the
keeper of the prison committed to
Joseph's care all the prisoners who
were in the prison; and whatever was
done there, he was the doer of it; 23 the
keeper of the prison paid no heed to
anything that was in Joseph's care,
because the LORD was with him; and
whatever he did, the LORD made it
prosper.

40 Some time after this, the butler
of the king of Egypt and his
baker offended their lord the king of
Egypt. 2And Pharaoh was angry with
his two officers, the chief butler and
the chief baker, 3 and he put them in
custody in the house of the captain of
the guard, in the prison where Joseph
was confined. 4 The captain of the
guard charged Joseph with them, and
he waited on them; and they continued
for some time in custody. 5And one
night they both dreamed—the butler
and the baker of the king of Egypt,
who were confined in the prison—each
his own dream, and each dream with
its own meaning. 6 When Joseph came
to them in the morning and saw them,
they were troubled. 7 So he asked
Pharaoh's officers who were with him
in custody in his master's house, "Why
are your faces downcast today?" 8 They
said to him, "We have had dreams,
and there is no one to interpret them."
And Joseph said to them, "Do not
interpretations belong to God? Tell
them to me, I pray you."

9 So the chief butler told his dream
to Joseph, and said to him, "In my
dream there was a vine before me,
10 and on the vine there were three
branches; as soon as it budded, its
blossoms shot forth, and the clusters
ripened into grapes. 11 Pharaoh's cup
was in my hand; and I took the grapes
and pressed them into Pharaoh's cup,
and placed the cup in Pharaoh's hand."
12 Then Joseph said to him, "This is
its interpretation: the three branches
are three days; 13 within three days
Pharaoh will lift up your head and
restore you to your office; and you
shall place Pharaoh's cup in his hand
as formerly, when you were his butler.
14 But remember me, when it is well
with you, and do me the kindness, I
pray you, to make mention of me to
Pharaoh, and so get me out of this
house. 15 For I was indeed stolen out
of the land of the Hebrews; and here
also I have done nothing that they
should put me into the dungeon."

16 When the chief baker saw that
the interpretation was favorable, he
said to Joseph, "I also had a dream:
there were three cake baskets on my
head, 17 and in the uppermost basket
there were all sorts of baked food for
Pharaoh, but the birds were eating it
out of the basket on my head." 18And
Joseph answered, "This is its interpretation: the three baskets are three days;
19 within three days Pharaoh will lift
up your head—from you!—and hang
you on a tree; and the birds will eat
the flesh from you."

20 On the third day, which was
Pharaoh's birthday, he made a feast
for all his servants, and lifted up the
head of the chief butler and the head
of the chief baker among his servants.
21 He restored the chief butler to his
butlership, and he placed the cup in
Pharaoh's hand; 22 but he hanged the
chief baker, as Joseph had interpreted
to them. 23 Yet the chief butler did not
remember Joseph, but forgot him.

41 After two whole years, Pharaoh
dreamed that he was standing by
the Nile, 2 and behold, there came up
out of the Nile seven cows sleek and
fat, and they fed in the reed grass.
3And behold, seven other cows, gaunt
and thin, came up out of the Nile after
them, and stood by the other cows on
the bank of the Nile. 4And the gaunt
and thin cows ate up the seven sleek
and fat cows. And Pharaoh awoke.
5And he fell asleep and dreamed a
second time; and behold, seven ears of
grain, plump and good, were growing
on one stalk. 6And behold, after them
sprouted seven ears, thin and blighted
by the east wind. 7And the thin ears
swallowed up the seven plump and
full ears. And Pharaoh awoke, and behold, it was a dream. 8 So in the
morning his spirit was troubled; and
he sent and called for all the magicians
of Egypt and all its wise men; and
Pharaoh told them his dream, but
there was none who could interpret it[l]
to Pharaoh.

9 Then the chief butler said to
Pharaoh, "I remember my faults to-

[l] Gk: Heb *them*

day. 10 When Pharaoh was angry with
his servants, and put me and the chief
baker in custody in the house of the
captain of the guard, 11 we dreamed
on the same night, he and I, each
having a dream with its own meaning.
12 A young Hebrew was there with us,
a servant of the captain of the guard;
and when we told him, he interpreted
our dreams to us, giving an interpretation to each man according to his
dream. 13 And as he interpreted to us,
so it came to pass; I was restored to
my office, and the baker was hanged."

14 Then Pharaoh sent and called
Joseph, and they brought him hastily
out of the dungeon; and when he had
shaved himself and changed his clothes,
he came in before Pharaoh. 15 And
Pharaoh said to Joseph, "I have had
a dream, and there is no one who can
interpret it; and I have heard it said of
you that when you hear a dream you
can interpret it." 16 Joseph answered
Pharaoh, "It is not in me; God will
give Pharaoh a favorable answer."
17 Then Pharaoh said to Joseph, "Behold, in my dream I was standing on
the banks of the Nile; 18 and seven
cows, fat and sleek, came up out of the
Nile and fed in the reed grass; 19 and
seven other cows came up after them,
poor and very gaunt and thin, such as
I had never seen in all the land of
Egypt. 20 And the thin and gaunt cows
ate up the first seven fat cows, 21 but
when they had eaten them no one
would have known that they had
eaten them, for they were still as gaunt
as at the beginning. Then I awoke.
22 I also saw in my dream seven ears
growing on one stalk, full and good;
23 and seven ears, withered, thin, and
blighted by the east wind, sprouted
after them, 24 and the thin ears swallowed up the seven good ears. And I
told it to the magicians, but there was
no one who could explain it to me."

25 Then Joseph said to Pharaoh,
"The dream of Pharaoh is one; God
has revealed to Pharaoh what he is
about to do. 26 The seven good cows
are seven years, and the seven good
ears are seven years; the dream is one.
27 The seven lean and gaunt cows that
came up after them are seven years,
and the seven empty ears blighted by
the east wind are also seven years of
famine. 28 It is as I told Pharaoh, God
has shown to Pharaoh what he is about
to do. 29 There will come seven years
of great plenty throughout all the land
of Egypt, 30 but after them there will
arise seven years of famine, and all the
plenty will be forgotten in the land of
Egypt; the famine will consume the
land, 31 and the plenty will be unknown in the land by reason of that
famine which will follow, for it will be
very grievous. 32 And the doubling of
Pharaoh's dream means that the thing
is fixed by God, and God will shortly
bring it to pass. 33 Now therefore let
Pharaoh select a man discreet and wise,
and set him over the land of Egypt.
34 Let Pharaoh proceed to appoint
overseers over the land, and take the
fifth part of the produce of the land of
Egypt during the seven plenteous
years. 35 And let them gather all the
food of these good years that are
coming, and lay up grain under the
authority of Pharaoh for food in the
cities, and let them keep it. 36 That
food shall be a reserve for the land
against the seven years of famine which
are to befall the land of Egypt, so that
the land may not perish through the
famine."

37 This proposal seemed good to
Pharaoh and to all his servants. 38 And
Pharaoh said to his servants, "Can we
find such a man as this, in whom is the
Spirit of God?" 39 So Pharaoh said to
Joseph, "Since God has shown you all
this, there is none so discreet and wise
as you are; 40 you shall be over my
house, and all my people shall order
themselves as you command; only as
regards the throne will I be greater
than you." 41 And Pharaoh said to
Joseph, "Behold, I have set you over
all the land of Egypt." 42 Then Pharaoh took his signet ring from his hand,
and put it on Joseph's hand, and
arrayed him in garments of fine linen,
and put a gold chain about his neck;
43 and he made him to ride in his
second chariot; and they cried before
him, "Bow the knee!"[k] Thus he set
him over all the land of Egypt. 44 Moreover Pharaoh said to Joseph, "I am
Pharaoh, and without your consent no
man shall lift up hand or foot in all the
land of Egypt." 45 And Pharaoh called
Joseph's name Zaph'ĕ·nath-pȧ·nē'ăh;
and he gave him in marriage As'ĕ-
nath, the daughter of Pō·tĭ'phĕ·rȧ

k Abrek, probably an Egyptian word similar in sound to the Hebrew word meaning *to kneel*
41.38-45: Acts 7.10.

priest of On. So Joseph went out over
the land of Egypt.
46 Joseph was thirty years old when
he entered the service of Pharaoh king
of Egypt. And Joseph went out from
the presence of Pharaoh, and went
through all the land of Egypt. 47 During the seven plenteous years the earth
brought forth abundantly, 48 and he
gathered up all the food of the seven
years when there was plenty[l] in the
land of Egypt, and stored up food in
the cities; he stored up in every city
the food from the fields around it.
49 And Joseph stored up grain in great
abundance like the sand of the sea,
until he ceased to measure it, for it
could not be measured.
50 Before the year of famine came,
Joseph had two sons, whom As'ė·nath,
the daughter of Pō·ti'phė·rȧ priest of
On, bore to him. 51 Joseph called the
name of the first-born Mȧ·nas'sėh,[m]
"For," he said, "God has made me
forget all my hardship and all my
father's house." 52 The name of the
second he called E'phrȧ·im,[n] "For
God has made me fruitful in the land
of my affliction."
53 The seven years of plenty that
prevailed in the land of Egypt came
to an end; 54 and the seven years of
famine began to come, as Joseph had
said. There was famine in all lands;
but in all the land of Egypt there was
bread. 55 When all the land of Egypt
was famished, the people cried to
Pharaoh for bread; and Pharaoh said
to all the Egyptians, "Go to Joseph;
what he says to you, do." 56 So when
the famine had spread over all the
land, Joseph opened all the storehouses,[o] and sold to the Egyptians, for
the famine was severe in the land of
Egypt. 57 Moreover, all the earth came
to Egypt to Joseph to buy grain, because the famine was severe over all
the earth.

42 When Jacob learned that there
was grain in Egypt, he said to
his sons, "Why do you look at one
another?" 2 And he said, "Behold, I
have heard that there is grain in Egypt;
go down and buy grain for us there,
that we may live, and not die." 3 So
ten of Joseph's brothers went down to
buy grain in Egypt. 4 But Jacob did
not send Benjamin, Joseph's brother,
with his brothers, for he feared that
harm might befall him. 5 Thus the
sons of Israel came to buy among the
others who came, for the famine was
in the land of Canaan.
6 Now Joseph was governor over
the land; he it was who sold to all the
people of the land. And Joseph's
brothers came, and bowed themselves
before him with their faces to the
ground. 7 Joseph saw his brothers,
and knew them, but he treated them
like strangers and spoke roughly to
them. "Where do you come from?"
he said. They said, "From the land of
Canaan, to buy food." 8 Thus Joseph
knew his brothers, but they did not
know him. 9 And Joseph remembered
the dreams which he had dreamed of
them; and he said to them, "You are
spies, you have come to see the weakness of the land." 10 They said to him,
"No, my lord, but to buy food have
your servants come. 11 We are all sons
of one man, we are honest men, your
servants are not spies." 12 He said to
them, "No, it is the weakness of the
land that you have come to see." 13 And
they said, "We, your servants, are
twelve brothers, the sons of one man
in the land of Canaan; and behold, the
youngest is this day with our father,
and one is no more." 14 But Joseph
said to them, "It is as I said to you,
you are spies. 15 By this you shall be
tested: by the life of Pharaoh, you shall
not go from this place unless your
youngest brother comes here. 16 Send
one of you, and let him bring your
brother, while you remain in prison,
that your words may be tested, whether
there is truth in you; or else, by the
life of Pharaoh, surely you are spies."
17 And he put them altogether in
prison for three days.
18 On the third day Joseph said to
them, "Do this and you will live, for
I fear God: 19 if you are honest men,
let one of your brothers remain confined in your prison, and let the rest
go and carry grain for the famine of
your households, 20 and bring your
youngest brother to me; so your words
will be verified, and you shall not die."
And they did so. 21 Then they said to
one another, "In truth we are guilty
concerning our brother, in that we saw
the distress of his soul, when he be-

[l] Sam Gk: Heb *which were* [m] That is *Making to forget* [n] From a Hebrew word meaning *to be fruitful*
[o] Gk Vg Compare Syr: Heb *all that was in them*
41.54: Acts 7.11. **42.2:** Acts 7.12. **42.5:** Acts 7.11.

sought us and we would not listen;
therefore is this distress come upon
us." 22And Reuben answered them,
"Did I not tell you not to sin against
the lad? But you would not listen. So
now there comes a reckoning for his
blood." 23 They did not know that
Joseph understood them, for there was
an interpreter between them. 24 Then
he turned away from them and wept;
and he returned to them and spoke to
them. And he took Simeon from them
and bound him before their eyes.
25And Joseph gave orders to fill their
bags with grain, and to replace every
man's money in his sack, and to give
them provisions for the journey. This
was done for them.

26 Then they loaded their asses
with their grain, and departed. 27And
as one of them opened his sack to give
his ass provender at the lodging place,
he saw his money in the mouth of his
sack; 28 and he said to his brothers,
"My money has been put back; here
it is in the mouth of my sack!" At this
their hearts failed them, and they
turned trembling to one another, saying, "What is this that God has done
to us?"

29 When they came to Jacob their
father in the land of Canaan, they told
him all that had befallen them, saying,
30 "The man, the lord of the land,
spoke roughly to us, and took us to
be spies of the land. 31 But we said to
him, 'We are honest men, we are not
spies, 32 we are twelve brothers, sons
of our father; one is no more, and the
youngest is this day with our father in
the land of Canaan.' 33 Then the man,
the lord of the land, said to us, 'By
this I shall know that you are honest
men: leave one of your brothers with
me, and take grain for the famine of
your households, and go your way.
34 Bring your youngest brother to me;
then I shall know that you are not
spies but honest men, and I will deliver
to you your brother, and you shall
trade in the land.' "

35 As they emptied their sacks, behold, every man's bundle of money
was in his sack; and when they and
their father saw their bundles of
money, they were dismayed. 36And
Jacob their father said to them, "You
have bereaved me of my children:
Joseph is no more, and Simeon is no
more, and now you would take Benjamin; all this has come upon me."
37 Then Reuben said to his father,
"Slay my two sons if I do not bring
him back to you; put him in my hands,
and I will bring him back to you."
38 But he said, "My son shall not go
down with you, for his brother is dead,
and he only is left. If harm should
befall him on the journey that you are
to make, you would bring down my
gray hairs with sorrow to Shē'ōl."

43 Now the famine was severe in
the land. 2And when they had
eaten the grain which they had brought
from Egypt, their father said to them,
"Go again, buy us a little food." 3 But
Judah said to him, "The man solemnly warned us, saying, 'You shall
not see my face, unless your brother
is with you.' 4 If you will send our
brother with us, we will go down and
buy you food; 5 but if you will not
send him, we will not go down, for the
man said to us, 'You shall not see my
face, unless your brother is with you.' "
6 Israel said, "Why did you treat me
so ill as to tell the man that you had
another brother?" 7 They replied,
"The man questioned us carefully
about ourselves and our kindred, saying, 'Is your father still alive? Have
you another brother?' What we told
him was in answer to these questions;
could we in any way know that he
would say, 'Bring your brother down'?"
8And Judah said to Israel his father,
"Send the lad with me, and we will
arise and go, that we may live and not
die, both we and you and also our
little ones. 9 I will be surety for him;
of my hand you shall require him. If
I do not bring him back to you and
set him before you, then let me bear
the blame for ever; 10 for if we had not
delayed, we would now have returned
twice."

11 Then their father Israel said to
them, "If it must be so, then do this:
take some of the choice fruits of the
land in your bags, and carry down to
the man a present, a little balm and a
little honey, gum, myrrh, pistachio
nuts, and almonds. 12 Take double the
money with you; carry back with you
the money that was returned in the
mouth of your sacks; perhaps it was
an oversight. 13 Take also your
brother, and arise, go again to the
man; 14 may God Almighty[p] grant you
mercy before the man, that he may

[p] Heb *El Shaddai*

send back your other brother and
Benjamin. If I am bereaved of my
children, I am bereaved." 15 So the
men took the present, and they took
double the money with them, and
Benjamin; and they arose and went
down to Egypt, and stood before
Joseph.

16 When Joseph saw Benjamin
with them, he said to the steward of
his house, "Bring the men into the
house, and slaughter an animal and
make ready, for the men are to dine
with me at noon." 17 The man did as
Joseph bade him, and brought the
men to Joseph's house. 18 And the men
were afraid because they were brought
to Joseph's house, and they said, "It
is because of the money, which was
replaced in our sacks the first time,
that we are brought in, so that he may
seek occasion against us and fall upon
us, to make slaves of us and seize our
asses." 19 So they went up to the
steward of Joseph's house, and spoke
with him at the door of the house,
20 and said, "Oh, my lord, we came
down the first time to buy food; 21 and
when we came to the lodging place we
opened our sacks, and there was every
man's money in the mouth of his sack,
our money in full weight; so we have
brought it again with us, 22 and we
have brought other money down in
our hand to buy food. We do not know
who put our money in our sacks."
23 He replied, "Rest assured, do not
be afraid; your God and the God of
your father must have put treasure in
your sacks for you; I received your
money." Then he brought Simeon out
to them. 24 And when the man had
brought the men into Joseph's house,
and given them water, and they had
washed their feet, and when he had
given their asses provender, 25 they
made ready the present for Joseph's
coming at noon, for they heard that
they should eat bread there.

26 When Joseph came home, they
brought into the house to him the
present which they had with them,
and bowed down to him to the ground.
27 And he inquired about their welfare,
and said, "Is your father well, the old
man of whom you spoke? Is he still
alive?" 28 They said, "Your servant
our father is well, he is still alive."
And they bowed their heads and made
obeisance. 29 And he lifted up his eyes,
and saw his brother Benjamin, his
mother's son, and said, "Is this your
youngest brother, of whom you spoke
to me? God be gracious to you, my
son!" 30 Then Joseph made haste, for
his heart yearned for his brother, and
he sought a place to weep. And he
entered his chamber and wept there.
31 Then he washed his face and came
out; and controlling himself he said,
"Let food be served." 32 They served
him by himself, and them by themselves, and the Egyptians who ate with
him by themselves, because the Egyptians might not eat bread with the
Hebrews, for that is an abomination
to the Egyptians. 33 And they sat before
him, the first-born according to his
birthright and the youngest according
to his youth; and the men looked at
one another in amazement. 34 Portions
were taken to them from Joseph's
table, but Benjamin's portion was five
times as much as any of theirs. So they
drank and were merry with him.

44 Then he commanded the
steward of his house, "Fill the
men's sacks with food, as much as
they can carry, and put each man's
money in the mouth of his sack, 2 and
put my cup, the silver cup, in the
mouth of the sack of the youngest,
with his money for the grain." And he
did as Joseph told him. 3 As soon as
the morning was light, the men were
sent away with their asses. 4 When
they had gone but a short distance from
the city, Joseph said to his steward,
"Up, follow after the men; and when
you overtake them, say to them, 'Why
have you returned evil for good? Why
have you stolen my silver cup?[q] 5 Is it
not from this that my lord drinks, and
by this that he divines? You have
done wrong in so doing.' "

6 When he overtook them, he spoke
to them these words. 7 They said to
him, "Why does my lord speak such
words as these? Far be it from your
servants that they should do such a
thing! 8 Behold, the money which we
found in the mouth of our sacks, we
brought back to you from the land of
Canaan; how then should we steal
silver or gold from your lord's house?
9 With whomever of your servants it
be found, let him die, and we also will
be my lord's slaves." 10 He said, "Let
it be as you say: he with whom it is
found shall be my slave, and the rest

[q] Gk Compare Vg: Heb lacks *Why have you stolen my silver cup?*

of you shall be blameless." 11 Then
every man quickly lowered his sack to
the ground, and every man opened his
sack. 12 And he searched, beginning
with the eldest and ending with the
youngest; and the cup was found in
Benjamin's sack. 13 Then they rent
their clothes, and every man loaded
his ass, and they returned to the city.
14 When Judah and his brothers
came to Joseph's house, he was still
there; and they fell before him to the
ground. 15 Joseph said to them, "What
deed is this that you have done? Do
you not know that such a man as I
can indeed divine?" 16 And Judah said,
"What shall we say to my lord? What
shall we speak? Or how can we clear
ourselves? God has found out the
guilt of your servants; behold, we are
my lord's slaves, both we and he also
in whose hand the cup has been
found." 17 But he said, "Far be it from
me that I should do so! Only the man
in whose hand the cup was found shall
be my slave; but as for you, go up in
peace to your father."
18 Then Judah went up to him and
said, "O my lord, let your servant, I
pray you, speak a word in my lord's
ears, and let not your anger burn
against your servant; for you are like
Pharaoh himself. 19 My lord asked his
servants, saying, 'Have you a father,
or a brother?' 20 And we said to my
lord, 'We have a father, an old man,
and a young brother, the child of his
old age; and his brother is dead, and
he alone is left of his mother's children; and his father loves him.' 21 Then
you said to your servants, 'Bring him
down to me, that I may set my eyes
upon him.' 22 We said to my lord, 'The
lad cannot leave his father, for if he
should leave his father, his father
would die.' 23 Then you said to your
servants, 'Unless your youngest brother comes down with you, you shall
see my face no more.' 24 When we went
back to your servant my father we
told him the words of my lord. 25 And
when our father said, 'Go again, buy
us a little food,' 26 we said, 'We cannot
go down. If our youngest brother goes
with us, then we will go down; for we
cannot see the man's face unless our
youngest brother is with us.' 27 Then
your servant my father said to us,
'You know that my wife bore me two
sons; 28 one left me, and I said, Surely
he has been torn to pieces; and I have
never seen him since. 29 If you take this
one also from me, and harm befalls
him, you will bring down my gray hairs
in sorrow to Shē'ōl.' 30 Now therefore,
when I come to your servant my
father, and the lad is not with us, then,
as his life is bound up in the lad's life,
31 when he sees that the lad is not with
us, he will die; and your servants will
bring down the gray hairs of your
servant our father with sorrow to
Shē'ōl. 32 For your servant became
surety for the lad to my father, saying,
'If I do not bring him back to you,
then I shall bear the blame in the sight
of my father all my life.' 33 Now therefore, let your servant, I pray you,
remain instead of the lad as a slave to
my lord; and let the lad go back with
his brothers. 34 For how can I go back
to my father if the lad is not with me?
I fear to see the evil that would come
upon my father."

45 Then Joseph could not control
himself before all those who
stood by him; and he cried, "Make
every one go out from me." So no one
stayed with him when Joseph made
himself known to his brothers. 2 And
he wept aloud, so that the Egyptians
heard it, and the household of Pharaoh
heard it. 3 And Joseph said to his
brothers, "I am Joseph; is my father
still alive?" But his brothers could not
answer him, for they were dismayed
at his presence.
4 So Joseph said to his brothers,
"Come near to me, I pray you." And
they came near. And he said, "I am
your brother, Joseph, whom you sold
into Egypt. 5 And now do not be distressed, or angry with yourselves, because you sold me here; for God sent
me before you to preserve life. 6 For
the famine has been in the land these
two years; and there are yet five years
in which there will be neither plowing
nor harvest. 7 And God sent me before
you to preserve for you a remnant on
earth, and to keep alive for you many
survivors. 8 So it was not you who
sent me here, but God; and he has
made me a father to Pharaoh, and lord
of all his house and ruler over all the
land of Egypt. 9 Make haste and go
up to my father and say to him, 'Thus
says your son Joseph, God has made
me lord of all Egypt; come down to me,
do not tarry; 10 you shall dwell in the

45.1: Acts 7.13.

land of Gō'shėn, and you shall be near
me, you and your children and your
children's children, and your flocks,
your herds, and all that you have;
11 and there I will provide for you, for
there are yet five years of famine to
come; lest you and your household,
and all that you have, come to poverty.'
12 And now your eyes see, and the eyes
of my brother Benjamin see, that it is
my mouth that speaks to you. 13 You
must tell my father of all my splendor
in Egypt, and of all that you have seen.
Make haste and bring my father down
here." 14 Then he fell upon his brother
Benjamin's neck and wept; and Benjamin wept upon his neck. 15 And he
kissed all his brothers and wept upon
them; and after that his brothers talked
with him.

16 When the report was heard in
Pharaoh's house, "Joseph's brothers
have come," it pleased Pharaoh and
his servants well. 17 And Pharaoh said
to Joseph, "Say to your brothers, 'Do
this: load your beasts and go back to
the land of Canaan; 18 and take your
father and your households, and come
to me, and I will give you the best of
the land of Egypt, and you shall eat
the fat of the land.' 19 Command them[r]
also, 'Do this: take wagons from the
land of Egypt for your little ones and
for your wives, and bring your father,
and come. 20 Give no thought to your
goods, for the best of all the land of
Egypt is yours.'"

21 The sons of Israel did so; and
Joseph gave them wagons, according
to the command of Pharaoh, and gave
them provisions for the journey. 22 To
each and all of them he gave festal
garments; but to Benjamin he gave
three hundred shekels of silver and
five festal garments. 23 To his father
he sent as follows: ten asses loaded
with the good things of Egypt, and
ten she-asses loaded with grain, bread,
and provision for his father on the
journey. 24 Then he sent his brothers
away, and as they departed, he said to
them, "Do not quarrel on the way."
25 So they went up out of Egypt, and
came to the land of Canaan to their
father Jacob. 26 And they told him,
"Joseph is still alive, and he is ruler
over all the land of Egypt." And his
heart fainted, for he did not believe
them. 27 But when they told him all
the words of Joseph, which he had
said to them, and when he saw the
wagons which Joseph had sent to
carry him, the spirit of their father
Jacob revived; 28 and Israel said, "It
is enough; Joseph my son is still alive;
I will go and see him before I die."

46 So Israel took his journey with
all that he had, and came to
Beer-sheba, and offered sacrifices to
the God of his father Isaac. 2 And God
spoke to Israel in visions of the night,
and said, "Jacob, Jacob." And he said,
"Here am I." 3 Then he said, "I am
God, the God of your father; do not
be afraid to go down to Egypt; for I
will there make of you a great nation.
4 I will go down with you to Egypt,
and I will also bring you up again; and
Joseph's hand shall close your eyes."
5 Then Jacob set out from Beer-sheba;
and the sons of Israel carried Jacob
their father, their little ones, and their
wives, in the wagons which Pharaoh
had sent to carry him. 6 They also
took their cattle and their goods, which
they had gained in the land of Canaan,
and came into Egypt, Jacob and all
his offspring with him, 7 his sons, and
his sons' sons with him, his daughters, and his sons' daughters; all his
offspring he brought with him into
Egypt.

8 Now these are the names of the
descendants of Israel, who came into
Egypt, Jacob and his sons. Reuben,
Jacob's first-born, 9 and the sons of
Reuben: Hā'nŏch, Pal'lü, Hez'rŏn, and
Cär'mī. 10 The sons of Simeon: Jė-
mū'ėl, Jā'min, Ō'had, Jā'chin, Zō'här,
and Shā'ŭl, the son of a Canaanitish
woman. 11 The sons of Levi: Gēr'shŏn,
Kō'hath, and Mė·rār'ī. 12 The sons of
Judah: Ēr, Ō'năn, Shē'lȧh, Per'ez, and
Zē'rȧh (but Er and Onan died in the
land of Canaan); and the sons of Perez
were Hez'rŏn and Hā'mŭl. 13 The
sons of Is'sȧ·chär: Tō'lȧ, Pū'vȧh, Iōb,
and Shim'rŏn. 14 The sons of Zeb'ū-
lŭn: Sē'rėd, Ē'lon, and Jäh'lē·ėl
15 (these are the sons of Leah, whom
she bore to Jacob in Pad'dȧn-âr'ȧm,
together with his daughter Dinah;
altogether his sons and his daughters
numbered thirty-three). 16 The sons
of Gad: Ziph'ī·ŏn, Hag'gī, Shü'nī,
Ez'bŏn, Ē'rī, Ȧ·rō'dī, and Ȧ·rē'lī.
17 The sons of Ash'ėr: Im'nȧh, Ish'-
vȧh, Ish'vī, Bė·rī'ȧh, with Sē'rȧh their

[r] Compare Gk Vg: Heb *you are commanded*
46.6: Acts 7.14-15. 46.8-27: Ex 1.1-4; Num 26.4-50.

sister. And the sons of Beriah: Hē'ber
and Mal'chi·el 18 (these are the sons of
Zil'pȧh, whom Lā'bȧn gave to Leah
his daughter; and these she bore to
Jacob—sixteen persons). 19 The sons
of Rachel, Jacob's wife: Joseph and
Benjamin. 20And to Joseph in the land
of Egypt were born Mȧ·nas'sėh and
E'phrȧ·im, whom As'ė·nath, the daughter of Pō·ti'phė·rȧ the priest of On,
bore to him. 21And the sons of Benjamin: Bē'lȧ, Bē'chėr, Ash'bel, Gē'rȧ,
Nā'ȧ·man, E'hī, Rosh, Mup'pim,
Hup'pim, and Ȧrd 22 (these are the
sons of Rachel, who were born to
Jacob—fourteen persons in all). 23 The
sons of Dan: Hū'shim. 24 The sons of
Naph'tȧ·lī: Jäh'zē·ėl, Gū'nī, Jē'zėr,
and Shil'lem 25 (these are the sons of
Bil'hȧh, whom Lā'bȧn gave to Rachel
his daughter, and these she bore to
Jacob—seven persons in all). 26All the
persons belonging to Jacob who came
into Egypt, who were his own offspring, not including Jacob's sons'
wives, were sixty-six persons in all;
27 and the sons of Joseph, who were
born to him in Egypt, were two; all
the persons of the house of Jacob, that
came into Egypt, were seventy.

28 He sent Judah before him to
Joseph, to appear[s] before him in Gō'-
shėn; and they came into the land of
Goshen. 29 Then Joseph made ready
his chariot and went up to meet Israel
his father in Gō'shėn; and he presented
himself to him, and fell on his neck,
and wept on his neck a good while.
30 Israel said to Joseph, "Now let me
die, since I have seen your face and
know that you are still alive." 31 Joseph
said to his brothers and to his father's
household, "I will go up and tell
Pharaoh, and will say to him, 'My
brothers and my father's household,
who were in the land of Canaan, have
come to me; 32 and the men are
shepherds, for they have been keepers
of cattle; and they have brought their
flocks, and their herds, and all that
they have.' 33 When Pharaoh calls you,
and says, 'What is your occupation?'
34 you shall say, 'Your servants have
been keepers of cattle from our youth
even until now, both we and our
fathers,' in order that you may dwell
in the land of Gō'shėn; for every
shepherd is an abomination to the
Egyptians."

[s] Sam Syr Compare Gk Vg: Heb *to show the way*
46.27: Acts 7.14.

47 So Joseph went in and told
Pharaoh, "My father and my
brothers, with their flocks and herds
and all that they possess, have come
from the land of Canaan; they are now
in the land of Gō'shėn." 2And from
among his brothers he took five men
and presented them to Pharaoh. 3 Pharaoh said to his brothers, "What is your
occupation?" And they said to Pharaoh, "Your servants are shepherds, as
our fathers were." 4 They said to
Pharaoh, "We have come to sojourn
in the land; for there is no pasture for
your servants' flocks, for the famine is
severe in the land of Canaan; and now,
we pray you, let your servants dwell
in the land of Gō'shėn." 5 Then Pharaoh said to Joseph, "Your father and
your brothers have come to you. 6 The
land of Egypt is before you; settle your
father and your brothers in the best of
the land; let them dwell in the land of
Gō'shėn; and if you know any able
men among them, put them in charge
of my cattle."

7 Then Joseph brought in Jacob his
father, and set him before Pharaoh,
and Jacob blessed Pharaoh. 8And
Pharaoh said to Jacob, "How many
are the days of the years of your life?"
9And Jacob said to Pharaoh, "The
days of the years of my sojourning are
a hundred and thirty years; few and
evil have been the days of the years of
my life, and they have not attained to
the days of the years of the life of my
fathers in the days of their sojourning."
10And Jacob blessed Pharaoh, and
went out from the presence of Pharaoh.
11 Then Joseph settled his father and
his brothers, and gave them a possession in the land of Egypt, in the best
of the land, in the land of Ram'ė·sēs,
as Pharaoh had commanded. 12And
Joseph provided his father, his
brothers, and all his father's household
with food, according to the number
of their dependents.

13 Now there was no food in all the
land; for the famine was very severe,
so that the land of Egypt and the land
of Canaan languished by reason of the
famine. 14And Joseph gathered up all
the money that was found in the land
of Egypt and in the land of Canaan,
for the grain which they bought; and
Joseph brought the money into Pharaoh's house. 15And when the money

was all spent in the land of Egypt and
in the land of Canaan, all the Egyptians came to Joseph, and said, "Give
us food; why should we die before
your eyes? For our money is gone."
16And Joseph answered, "Give your
cattle, and I will give you food in
exchange for your cattle, if your money
is gone." 17So they brought their
cattle to Joseph; and Joseph gave them
food in exchange for the horses, the
flocks, the herds, and the asses: and he
supplied them with food in exchange
for all their cattle that year. 18And
when that year was ended, they came
to him the following year, and said to
him, "We will not hide from my lord
that our money is all spent; and the
herds of cattle are my lord's; there is
nothing left in the sight of my lord
but our bodies and our lands. 19Why
should we die before your eyes, both
we and our land? Buy us and our land
for food, and we with our land will be
slaves to Pharaoh; and give us seed,
that we may live, and not die, and
that the land may not be desolate."
20 So Joseph bought all the land of
Egypt for Pharaoh; for all the Egyptians sold their fields, because the
famine was severe upon them. The
land became Pharaoh's; 21and as for
the people, he made slaves of them[t]
from one end of Egypt to the other.
22Only the land of the priests he did
not buy; for the priests had a fixed
allowance from Pharaoh, and lived on
the allowance which Pharaoh gave
them; therefore they did not sell their
land. 23Then Joseph said to the people, "Behold, I have this day bought
you and your land for Pharaoh. Now
here is seed for you, and you shall sow
the land. 24And at the harvests you
shall give a fifth to Pharaoh, and four
fifths shall be your own, as seed for
the field and as food for yourselves and
your households, and as food for your
little ones." 25And they said, "You
have saved our lives; may it please my
lord, we will be slaves to Pharaoh."
26So Joseph made it a statute concerning the land of Egypt, and it stands
to this day, that Pharaoh should have
the fifth; the land of the priests alone
did not become Pharaoh's.
27 Thus Israel dwelt in the land of
Egypt, in the land of Gō'shėn; and
they gained possessions in it, and were
fruitful and multiplied exceedingly.
28And Jacob lived in the land of Egypt
seventeen years; so the days of Jacob,
the years of his life, were a hundred
and forty-seven years.
29 And when the time drew near
that Israel must die, he called his son
Joseph and said to him, "If now I
have found favor in your sight, put
your hand under my thigh, and promise to deal loyally and truly with me.
Do not bury me in Egypt, 30but let
me lie with my fathers; carry me out
of Egypt and bury me in their burying
place." He answered, "I will do as you
have said." 31And he said, "Swear to
me"; and he swore to him. Then Israel
bowed himself upon the head of his bed.
48 After this Joseph was told,
"Behold, your father is ill"; so
he took with him his two sons, Mȧ-
nas'sėh and E'phrȧ·im. 2And it was
told to Jacob, "Your son Joseph has
come to you"; then Israel summoned
his strength, and sat up in bed. 3And
Jacob said to Joseph, "God Almighty[u]
appeared to me at Luz in the land of
Canaan and blessed me, 4and said to
me, 'Behold, I will make you fruitful,
and multiply you, and I will make of
you a company of peoples, and will
give this land to your descendants
after you for an everlasting possession.' 5And now your two sons, who
were born to you in the land of Egypt
before I came to you in Egypt, are
mine; E'phrȧ·im and Mȧ·nas'sėh shall
be mine, as Reuben and Simeon are.
6And the offspring born to you after
them shall be yours; they shall be
called by the name of their brothers in
their inheritance. 7For when I came
from Pad'dȧn, Rachel to my sorrow
died in the land of Canaan on the way,
when there was still some distance to
go to Eph'rath; and I buried her there
on the way to Ephrath (that is,
Bethlehem)."
8 When Israel saw Joseph's sons,
he said, "Who are these?" 9Joseph
said to his father, "They are my sons,
whom God has given me here." And
he said, "Bring them to me, I pray
you, that I may bless them." 10Now
the eyes of Israel were dim with age,
so that he could not see. So Joseph
brought them near him; and he kissed
them and embraced them. 11And
Israel said to Joseph, "I had not
thought to see your face; and lo, God
has let me see your children also."

[t] Sam Gk Compare Vg: Heb *he removed them to the cities* [u] Heb *El Shaddai*

12 Then Joseph removed them from
his knees, and he bowed himself with
his face to the earth. 13And Joseph
took them both, E'phrȧ·im in his right
hand toward Israel's left hand, and
Mȧ·nas'sėh in his left hand toward
Israel's right hand, and brought them
near him. 14And Israel stretched out
his right hand and laid it upon the head
of E'phrȧ·im, who was the younger,
and his left hand upon the head of
Mȧ·nas'sėh, crossing his hands, for
Manasseh was the first-born. 15And
he blessed Joseph, and said,

"The God before whom my fathers
Abraham and Isaac walked,
the God who has led me all my life
long to this day,
16 the angel who has redeemed me
from all evil, bless the lads;
and in them let my name be perpetuated,
and the name of my
fathers Abraham and Isaac;
and let them grow into a multitude
in the midst of the earth."

17 When Joseph saw that his father
laid his right hand upon the head of
E'phrȧ·im, it displeased him; and he
took his father's hand, to remove it
from Ephraim's head to Mȧ·nas'sėh's
head. 18And Joseph said to his father,
"Not so, my father; for this one is the
first-born; put your right hand upon
his head." 19 But his father refused,
and said, "I know, my son, I know;
he also shall become a people, and he
also shall be great; nevertheless his
younger brother shall be greater than
he, and his descendants shall become
a multitude of nations." 20 So he
blessed them that day, saying,

"By you Israel will pronounce
blessings, saying,
'God make you as E'phrȧ·im and as
Mȧ·nas'sėh' ";

and thus he put Ephraim before Manasseh.
21 Then Israel said to Joseph,
"Behold, I am about to die, but God
will be with you, and will bring you
again to the land of your fathers.
22 Moreover I have given to you rather
than to your brothers one mountain
slope[v] which I took from the hand of
the Am'ȯ·rītes with my sword and
with my bow."

49 Then Jacob called his sons, and
said, "Gather yourselves together,
that I may tell you what shall
befall you in days to come.

2 Assemble and hear, O sons of Jacob,
and hearken to Israel your father.

3 Reuben, you are my first-born,
my might, and the first fruits of
my strength,
pre-eminent in pride and pre-eminent
in power.
4 Unstable as water, you shall not
have pre-eminence
because you went up to your
father's bed;
then you defiled it—you[w] went
up to my couch!

5 Simeon and Levi are brothers;
weapons of violence are their
swords.
6 O my soul, come not into their
council;
O my spirit,[x] be not joined to
their company;
for in their anger they slay men,
and in their wantonness they
hamstring oxen.
7 Cursed be their anger, for it is
fierce;
and their wrath, for it is cruel!
I will divide them in Jacob
and scatter them in Israel.

8 Judah, your brothers shall praise
you;
your hand shall be on the neck of
your enemies;
your father's sons shall bow down
before you.
9 Judah is a lion's whelp;
from the prey, my son, you have
gone up.
He stooped down, he couched as a
lion,
and as a lioness; who dares rouse
him up?
10 The scepter shall not depart from
Judah,
nor the ruler's staff from between
his feet,
until he comes to whom it belongs;[y]
and to him shall be the obedience
of the peoples.
11 Binding his foal to the vine
and his ass's colt to the choice
vine,
he washes his garments in wine

[v] Heb *shekem*, shoulder [w] Gk Syr Tg: Heb *he* [x] Or *glory*
[y] Syr Compare Tg: Heb *until Shiloh comes* or *until he comes to Shiloh*
49.9-10: Num 24.9; Rev 5.5.

and his vesture in the blood of grapes;
12 his eyes shall be red with wine,
and his teeth white with milk.

13 Zeb′ū·lŭn shall dwell at the shore of the sea;
he shall become a haven for ships,
and his border shall be at Sī′don.

14 Is′sȧ·chär is a strong ass,
crouching between the sheep-folds;
15 he saw that a resting place was good,
and that the land was pleasant;
so he bowed his shoulder to bear,
and became a slave at forced labor.

16 Dan shall judge his people
as one of the tribes of Israel.
17 Dan shall be a serpent in the way,
a viper by the path,
that bites the horse's heels
so that his rider falls backward.
18 I wait for thy salvation, O LORD.

19 Raiders[z] shall raid Gad,
but he shall raid at their heels.

20 Ash′ẽr′s food shall be rich,
and he shall yield royal dainties.

21 Naph′tȧ·lī is a hind let loose,
that bears comely fawns.[a]

22 Joseph is a fruitful bough,
a fruitful bough by a spring;
his branches run over the wall.
23 The archers fiercely attacked him,
shot at him, and harassed him sorely;
24 yet his bow remained unmoved,
his arms[b] were made agile
by the hands of the Mighty One of Jacob
(by the name of the Shepherd, the Rock of Israel),
25 by the God of your father who will help you
by God Almighty[u] who will bless you
with blessings of heaven above,
blessings of the deep that couches beneath,
blessings of the breasts and of the womb.
26 The blessings of your father
are mighty beyond the blessings
of the eternal mountains,[c]
the bounties of the everlasting hills;
may they be on the head of Joseph,
and on the brow of him who was separate from his brothers.

27 Benjamin is a ravenous wolf,
in the morning devouring the prey,
and at even dividing the spoil."

28 All these are the twelve tribes of
Israel; and this is what their father
said to them as he blessed them, blessing each with the blessing suitable to
him. 29 Then he charged them, and
said to them, "I am to be gathered to
my people; bury me with my fathers
in the cave that is in the field of
E′phrȯn the Hit′tīte, 30 in the cave
that is in the field at Mach-pē′lȧh, to
the east of Mam′re, in the land of
Canaan, which Abraham bought with
the field from E′phrȯn the Hit′tīte to
possess as a burying place. 31 There
they buried Abraham and Sarah his
wife; there they buried Isaac and
Rebekah his wife; and there I buried
Leah—32 the field and the cave that
is in it were purchased from the Hit′-
tītes." 33 When Jacob finished charging his sons, he drew up his feet into
the bed, and breathed his last, and
was gathered to his people.

50 Then Joseph fell on his father's
face, and wept over him, and
kissed him. 2 And Joseph commanded
his servants the physicians to embalm
his father. So the physicians embalmed
Israel; 3 forty days were required for
it, for so many are required for em-
balming. And the Egyptians wept for
him seventy days.

4 And when the days of weeping
for him were past, Joseph spoke to the
household of Pharaoh, saying, "If now
I have found favor in your eyes, speak,
I pray you, in the ears of Pharaoh,
saying, 5 My father made me swear,
saying, 'I am about to die: in my tomb
which I hewed out for myself in the
land of Canaan, there shall you bury
me.' Now therefore let me go up, I
pray you, and bury my father; then I
will return." 6 And Pharaoh answered,
"Go up, and bury your father, as he
made you swear." 7 So Joseph went up
to bury his father; and with him went
up all the servants of Pharaoh, the

[z] Heb *gedud*, a raiding troop [a] Or *who gives beautiful words*
[b] Heb *the arms of his hands* [u] Heb *El Shaddai* [c] Compare Gk: Heb *of my progenitors to*

elders of his household, and all the
elders of the land of Egypt, 8 as well
as all the household of Joseph, his
brothers, and his father's household;
only their children, their flocks, and
their herds were left in the land of
Gō′shėn. 9 And there went up with him
both chariots and horsemen; it was a
very great company. 10 When they
came to the threshing floor of Ā′tad,
which is beyond the Jordan, they
lamented there with a very great and
sorrowful lamentation; and he made
a mourning for his father seven days.
11 When the inhabitants of the land,
the Canaanites, saw the mourning on
the threshing floor of Ā′tad, they said,
"This is a grievous mourning to the
Egyptians." Therefore the place was
named Ā′bėl-miz′rȧ·im;[d] it is beyond
the Jordan. 12 Thus his sons did for
him as he had commanded them;
13 for his sons carried him to the land
of Canaan, and buried him in the cave
of the field at Mach-pē′lȧh, to the east
of Mam′re, which Abraham bought
with the field from Ē′phrȯn the Hit′-
tīte, to possess as a burying place.
14 After he had buried his father,
Joseph returned to Egypt with his
brothers and all who had gone up with
him to bury his father.

15 When Joseph's brothers saw that
their father was dead, they said, "It
may be that Joseph will hate us and
pay us back for all the evil which we
did to him." 16 So they sent a message
to Joseph, saying, "Your father gave
this command before he died, 17 'Say
to Joseph, Forgive, I pray you, the
transgression of your brothers and
their sin, because they did evil to you.'
And now, we pray you, forgive the
transgression of the servants of the
God of your father." Joseph wept
when they spoke to him. 18 His
brothers also came and fell down before him, and said, "Behold, we are
your servants." 19 But Joseph said to
them, "Fear not, for am I in the place
of God? 20 As for you, you meant evil
against me; but God meant it for good,
to bring it about that many people
should be kept alive, as they are today.
21 So do not fear; I will provide for
you and your little ones." Thus he
reassured them and comforted them.

22 So Joseph dwelt in Egypt, he
and his father's house; and Joseph
lived a hundred and ten years. 23 And
Joseph saw Ē′phrȧ·im's children of
the third generation; the children also
of Mā′chir the son of Mȧ·nas′sėh were
born upon Joseph's knees. 24 And
Joseph said to his brothers, "I am
about to die; but God will visit you,
and bring you up out of this land to
the land which he swore to Abraham,
to Isaac, and to Jacob." 25 Then
Joseph took an oath of the sons of
Israel, saying, "God will visit you, and
you shall carry up my bones from
here." 26 So Joseph died, being a
hundred and ten years old; and they
embalmed him, and he was put in a
coffin in Egypt.

THE SECOND BOOK OF MOSES

COMMONLY CALLED

EXODUS

1 These are the names of the sons of
Israel who came to Egypt with
Jacob, each with his household:
2 Reuben, Simeon, Levi, and Judah,
3 Is′sȧ·chär, Zeb′ū·lụn, and Benjamin,
4 Dan and Naph′tȧ·lī, Gad and
Ash′ėr. 5 All the offspring of Jacob were
seventy persons; Joseph was already
in Egypt. 6 Then Joseph died, and all
his brothers, and all that generation.
7 But the descendants of Israel were
fruitful and increased greatly; they
multiplied and grew exceedingly
strong; so that the land was filled
with them.

8 Now there arose a new king over

[d] That is *meadow* (or *mourning*) *of Egypt*

50.13: Acts 7.16. **1.1-4:** Gen 46.8-27; Num 26.4-50. **1.5-8:** Acts 7.14-18.

Egypt, who did not know Joseph.
9 And he said to his people, "Behold,
the people of Israel are too many and
too mighty for us. 10 Come, let us deal
shrewdly with them, lest they multiply, and, if war befall us, they join our
enemies and fight against us and escape
from the land." 11 Therefore they set
taskmasters over them to afflict them
with heavy burdens; and they built
for Pharaoh store-cities, Pī′thom and
Rȧ-am′sēṡ. 12 But the more they were
oppressed, the more they multiplied
and the more they spread abroad. And
the Egyptians were in dread of the
people of Israel. 13 So they made the
people of Israel serve with rigor,
14 and made their lives bitter with
hard service, in mortar and brick, and
in all kinds of work in the field; in all
their work they made them serve with
rigor.

15 Then the king of Egypt said to
the Hebrew midwives, one of whom
was named Shiph′rȧh and the other
Pū′ȧh, 16 "When you serve as midwife
to the Hebrew women, and see them
upon the birthstool, if it is a son, you
shall kill him; but if it is a daughter,
she shall live." 17 But the midwives
feared God, and did not do as the king
of Egypt commanded them, but let
the male children live. 18 So the king
of Egypt called the midwives, and said
to them, "Why have you done this,
and let the male children live?" 19 The
midwives said to Pharaoh, "Because
the Hebrew women are not like the
Egyptian women; for they are vigorous
and are delivered before the midwife
comes to them." 20 So God dealt well
with the midwives; and the people
multiplied and grew very strong. 21 And
because the midwives feared God he
gave them families. 22 Then Pharaoh
commanded all his people, "Every son
that is born to the Hebrews[a] you shall
cast into the Nile, but you shall let
every daughter live."

2 Now a man from the house of
Levi went and took to wife a
daughter of Levi. 2 The woman conceived and bore a son; and when she
saw that he was a goodly child, she hid
him three months. 3 And when she
could hide him no longer she took for
him a basket made of bulrushes, and
daubed it with bitumen and pitch; and
she put the child in it and placed it
among the reeds at the river's brink.
4 And his sister stood at a distance, to
know what would be done to him.
5 Now the daughter of Pharaoh came
down to bathe at the river, and her
maidens walked beside the river; she
saw the basket among the reeds and
sent her maid to fetch it. 6 When she
opened it she saw the child; and lo,
the babe was crying. She took pity on
him and said, "This is one of the Hebrews' children." 7 Then his sister
said to Pharaoh's daughter, "Shall I
go and call you a nurse from the
Hebrew women to nurse the child for
you?" 8 And Pharaoh's daughter said
to her, "Go." So the girl went and
called the child's mother. 9 And Pharaoh's daughter said to her, "Take this
child away, and nurse him for me, and
I will give you your wages." So the
woman took the child and nursed him.
10 And the child grew, and she brought
him to Pharaoh's daughter, and he became her son; and she named him
Moses,[b] for she said, "Because I drew
him out[c] of the water."

11 One day, when Moses had grown
up, he went out to his people and
looked on their burdens; and he saw
an Egyptian beating a Hebrew, one of
his people. 12 He looked this way and
that, and seeing no one he killed the
Egyptian and hid him in the sand.
13 When he went out the next day,
behold, two Hebrews were struggling
together; and he said to the man that
did the wrong, "Why do you strike
your fellow?" 14 He answered, "Who
made you a prince and a judge over
us? Do you mean to kill me as you
killed the Egyptian?" Then Moses
was afraid, and thought, "Surely the
thing is known." 15 When Pharaoh
heard of it, he sought to kill Moses.

But Moses fled from Pharaoh, and
stayed in the land of Mid′i-ȧn; and he
sat down by a well. 16 Now the priest
of Mid′i-ȧn had seven daughters; and
they came and drew water, and filled
the troughs to water their father's
flock. 17 The shepherds came and
drove them away; but Moses stood up
and helped them, and watered their
flock. 18 When they came to their
father Reü′el, he said, "How is it that
you have come so soon today?" 19 They

[a] Sam Gk Tg: Heb lacks *to the Hebrews* [b] Heb *Mosheh* [c] Heb *mashah*

1.10-11, 22: Acts 7.19. **2.2:** Acts 7.20; Heb 11.23. **2.5, 10:** Acts 7.21. **2.11:** Acts 7.23; Heb 11.24. **2.12:** Acts 7.24. **2.14:** Acts 7.27-28. **2.15, 22:** Acts 7.29.

said, "An Egyptian delivered us out
of the hand of the shepherds, and even
drew water for us and watered the
flock." 20 He said to his daughters,
"And where is he? Why have you left
the man? Call him, that he may eat
bread." 21And Moses was content to
dwell with the man, and he gave Moses
his daughter Zip·pō′rȧh. 22 She bore a
son, and he called his name Gẽr′shȯm;
for he said, "I have been a sojourner[d]
in a foreign land."

23 In the course of those many days
the king of Egypt died. And the people
of Israel groaned under their bondage,
and cried out for help, and their cry
under bondage came up to God. 24And
God heard their groaning, and God
remembered his covenant with Abraham, with Isaac, and with Jacob.
25And God saw the people of Israel,
and God knew their condition.

3 Now Moses was keeping the flock
of his father-in-law, Jethro, the
priest of Mid′i·ȧn; and he led his flock to
the west side of the wilderness, and
came to Hō′reb, the mountain of God.
2And the angel of the LORD appeared to
him in a flame of fire out of the midst of
a bush; and he looked, and lo, the bush
was burning, yet it was not consumed.
3And Moses said, "I will turn aside
and see this great sight, why the bush
is not burnt." 4 When the LORD saw
that he turned aside to see, God
called to him out of the bush, "Moses,
Moses!" And he said, "Here am I."
5 Then he said, "Do not come near;
put off your shoes from your feet, for
the place on which you are standing
is holy ground." 6And he said, "I am
the God of your father, the God of
Abraham, the God of Isaac, and the
God of Jacob." And Moses hid his
face, for he was afraid to look at God.

7 Then the LORD said, "I have seen
the affliction of my people who are in
Egypt, and have heard their cry because of their taskmasters; I know
their sufferings, 8 and I have come
down to deliver them out of the hand
of the Egyptians, and to bring them
up out of that land to a good and broad
land, a land flowing with milk and
honey, to the place of the Canaanites,
the Hit′tītes, the Am′ȯ·rītes, the Per′-
iz·zītes, the Hī′vītes, and the Jeb′ū-
sītes. 9And now, behold, the cry of the
people of Israel has come to me, and
I have seen the oppression with which
the Egyptians oppress them. 10 Come,
I will send you to Pharaoh that you
may bring forth my people, the sons
of Israel, out of Egypt." 11 But Moses
said to God, "Who am I that I should
go to Pharaoh, and bring the sons of
Israel out of Egypt?" 12 He said, "But
I will be with you; and this shall be
the sign for you, that I have sent you:
when you have brought forth the people out of Egypt, you shall serve God
upon this mountain."

13 Then Moses said to God, "If I
come to the people of Israel and say
to them, 'The God of your fathers has
sent me to you,' and they ask me,
'What is his name?' what shall I say
to them?" 14 God said to Moses, "I
AM WHO I AM."[e] And he said, "Say
this to the people of Israel, 'I AM has
sent me to you.' " 15 God also said to
Moses, "Say this to the people of
Israel, 'The LORD,[f] the God of your
fathers, the God of Abraham, the God
of Isaac, and the God of Jacob, has
sent me to you': this is my name for
ever, and thus I am to be remembered
throughout all generations. 16 Go and
gather the elders of Israel together,
and say to them, 'The LORD, the God
of your fathers, the God of Abraham,
of Isaac, and of Jacob, has appeared to
me, saying, "I have observed you and
what has been done to you in Egypt;
17 and I promise that I will bring you
up out of the affliction of Egypt, to the
land of the Canaanites, the Hit′tītes,
the Am′ȯ·rītes, the Per′iz·zītes, the
Hī′vītes, and the Jeb′ū·sītes, a land
flowing with milk and honey." ' 18And
they will hearken to your voice; and
you and the elders of Israel shall go to
the king of Egypt and say to him, 'The
LORD, the God of the Hebrews, has
met with us; and now, we pray you,
let us go a three days' journey into the
wilderness, that we may sacrifice to
the LORD our God.' 19 I know that the
king of Egypt will not let you go unless
compelled by a mighty hand.[g] 20 So I
will stretch out my hand and smite
Egypt with all the wonders which I

[d] Heb *ger* [e] Or I AM WHAT I AM or I WILL BE WHAT I WILL BE
[f] The word LORD when spelled with capital letters, stands for the divine name, *YHWH*, which is here connected with the verb *hayah*, to be [g] Gk Vg: Heb *no, not by a mighty hand*

2.24: Acts 7.34. **3.2:** Acts 7.30. **3.1-4, 17:** Ex 6.2-13. **3.5:** Acts 7.33.
3.6: Mt 22.32; Mk 12.26; Lk 20.37; Acts 3.13; 7.32.

will do in it; after that he will let you
go. 21 And I will give this people favor
in the sight of the Egyptians; and when
you go, you shall not go empty, 22 but
each woman shall ask of her neighbor, and of her who sojourns in her
house, jewelry of silver and of gold,
and clothing, and you shall put them
on your sons and on your daughters;
thus you shall despoil the Egyptians."

4 Then Moses answered, "But behold, they will not believe me or
listen to my voice, for they will say,
'The LORD did not appear to you.' "
2 The LORD said to him, "What is that
in your hand?" He said, "A rod."
3 And he said, "Cast it on the ground."
So he cast it on the ground, and it
became a serpent; and Moses fled from
it. 4 But the LORD said to Moses, "Put
out your hand, and take it by the
tail"—so he put out his hand and
caught it, and it became a rod in his
hand—5 "that they may believe that
the LORD, the God of their fathers, the
God of Abraham, the God of Isaac,
and the God of Jacob, has appeared
to you." 6 Again, the LORD said to him,
"Put your hand into your bosom."
And he put his hand into his bosom;
and when he took it out, behold, his
hand was leprous, as white as snow.
7 Then God said, "Put your hand
back into your bosom." So he put his
hand back into his bosom; and when
he took it out, behold, it was restored
like the rest of his flesh. 8 "If they will
not believe you," God said, "or heed
the first sign, they may believe the
latter sign. 9 If they will not believe
even these two signs or heed your
voice, you shall take some water from
the Nile and pour it upon the dry
ground; and the water which you shall
take from the Nile will become blood
upon the dry ground."

10 But Moses said to the LORD,
"Oh, my LORD, I am not eloquent,
either heretofore or since thou hast
spoken to thy servant; but I am slow
of speech and of tongue." 11 Then the
LORD said to him, "Who has made
man's mouth? Who makes him dumb,
or deaf, or seeing, or blind? Is it not
I, the LORD? 12 Now therefore go, and
I will be with your mouth and teach
you what you shall speak." 13 But he
said, "Oh, my Lord, send, I pray,
some other person." 14 Then the anger
of the LORD was kindled against Moses
and he said, "Is there not Aaron, your
brother, the Levite? I know that he
can speak well; and behold, he is
coming out to meet you, and when he
sees you he will be glad in his heart.
15 And you shall speak to him and put
the words in his mouth; and I will be
with your mouth and with his mouth,
and will teach you what you shall do.
16 He shall speak for you to the people;
and he shall be a mouth for you, and
you shall be to him as God. 17 And you
shall take in your hand this rod, with
which you shall do the signs."

18 Moses went back to Jethro his
father-in-law and said to him, "Let
me go back, I pray, to my kinsmen in
Egypt and see whether they are still
alive." And Jethro said to Moses, "Go
in peace." 19 And the LORD said to
Moses in Mid'i·ȧn, "Go back to
Egypt; for all the men who were seeking your life are dead." 20 So Moses
took his wife and his sons and set
them on an ass, and went back to the
land of Egypt; and in his hand Moses
took the rod of God.

21 And the LORD said to Moses,
"When you go back to Egypt, see that
you do before Pharaoh all the miracles
which I have put in your power; but I
will harden his heart, so that he will
not let the people go. 22 And you shall
say to Pharaoh, 'Thus says the LORD,
Israel is my first-born son, 23 and I say
to you, "Let my son go that he may
serve me"; if you refuse to let him go,
behold, I will slay your first-born
son.' "

24 At a lodging place on the way
the LORD met him and sought to kill
him. 25 Then Zip·pō'rȧh took a flint
and cut off her son's foreskin, and
touched Moses' feet with it, and said,
"Surely you are a bridegroom of blood
to me!" 26 So he let him alone. Then
it was that she said, "You are a bridegroom of blood," because of the
circumcision.

27 The LORD said to Aaron, "Go
into the wilderness to meet Moses."
So he went, and met him at the
mountain of God and kissed him.
28 And Moses told Aaron all the words
of the LORD with which he had sent
him, and all the signs which he had
charged him to do. 29 Then Moses and
Aaron went and gathered together all
the elders of the people of Israel.

4.19: Acts 7.34.

30And Aaron spoke all the words which
the LORD had spoken to Moses, and
did the signs in the sight of the people.
31And the people believed; and when
they heard that the LORD had visited
the people of Israel and that he had
seen their affliction, they bowed their
heads and worshiped.

5 Afterward Moses and Aaron went
to Pharaoh and said, "Thus says
the LORD, the God of Israel, 'Let my
people go, that they may hold a feast
to me in the wilderness.' " 2 But Pharaoh said, "Who is the LORD, that I
should heed his voice and let Israel
go? I do not know the LORD, and moreover I will not let Israel go." 3 Then
they said, "The God of the Hebrews
has met with us; let us go, we pray, a
three days' journey into the wilderness, and sacrifice to the LORD our
God, lest he fall upon us with pestilence or with the sword." 4 But the
king of Egypt said to them, "Moses
and Aaron, why do you take the people
away from their work? Get to your
burdens." 5And Pharaoh said, "Behold, the people of the land are now
many and you make them rest from
their burdens!" 6 The same day Pharaoh commanded the taskmasters of the
people and their foremen, 7 "You shall
no longer give the people straw to
make bricks, as heretofore; let them
go and gather straw for themselves.
8 But the number of bricks which they
made heretofore you shall lay upon
them, you shall by no means lessen it;
for they are idle; therefore they cry,
'Let us go and offer sacrifice to our
God.' 9 Let heavier work be laid upon
the men that they may labor at it and
pay no regard to lying words."

10 So the taskmasters and the foremen of the people went out and said
to the people, "Thus says Pharaoh, 'I
will not give you straw. 11 Go yourselves, get your straw wherever you
can find it; but your work will not be
lessened in the least.' " 12 So the people were scattered abroad throughout
all the land of Egypt, to gather stubble
for straw. 13 The taskmasters were
urgent, saying, "Complete your work,
your daily task, as when there was
straw." 14And the foremen of the
people of Israel, whom Pharaoh's taskmasters had set over them, were
beaten, and were asked, "Why have
you not done all your task of making
bricks today, as hitherto?"

15 Then the foremen of the people
of Israel came and cried to Pharaoh,
"Why do you deal thus with your
servants? 16 No straw is given to your
servants, yet they say to us, 'Make
bricks!' And behold, your servants are
beaten; but the fault is in your own
people." 17 But he said, "You are idle,
you are idle; therefore you say, 'Let us
go and sacrifice to the LORD.' 18 Go
now, and work; for no straw shall be
given you, yet you shall deliver the
same number of bricks." 19 The foremen of the people of Israel saw that
they were in evil plight, when they
said, "You shall by no means lessen
your daily number of bricks." 20 They
met Moses and Aaron, who were waiting for them, as they came forth from
Pharaoh; 21 and they said to them,
"The LORD look upon you and judge,
because you have made us offensive in
the sight of Pharaoh and his servants,
and have put a sword in their hand to
kill us."

22 Then Moses turned again to the
LORD and said, "O LORD, why hast
thou done evil to this people? Why
didst thou ever send me? 23 For since
I came to Pharaoh to speak in thy
name, he has done evil to this people,
and thou hast not delivered thy people
6 at all." 1 But the LORD said to
Moses, "Now you shall see what
I will do to Pharaoh; for with a strong
hand he will send them out, yea, with
a strong hand he will drive them out
of his land."

2 And God said to Moses, "I am
the LORD. 3 I appeared to Abraham, to
Isaac, and to Jacob, as God Almighty,[h]
but by my name the LORD I did not
make myself known to them. 4 I also
established my covenant with them,
to give them the land of Canaan, the
land in which they dwelt as sojourners.
5 Moreover I have heard the groaning
of the people of Israel whom the
Egyptians hold in bondage and I have
remembered my covenant. 6 Say therefore to the people of Israel, 'I am the
LORD, and I will bring you out from
under the burdens of the Egyptians,
and I will deliver you from their
bondage, and I will redeem you with
an outstretched arm and with great
acts of judgment, 7 and I will take you

[h] Heb *El Shaddai*
6.1, 6: Acts 13.17.

for my people, and I will be your God;
and you shall know that I am the LORD
your God, who has brought you out
from under the burdens of the Egyptians. 8 And I will bring you into the
land which I swore to give to Abraham,
to Isaac, and to Jacob; I will give it to
you for a possession. I am the LORD.' "
9 Moses spoke thus to the people of
Israel; but they did not listen to Moses,
because of their broken spirit and their
cruel bondage.
10 And the LORD said to Moses,
11 "Go in, tell Pharaoh king of Egypt
to let the people of Israel go out of his
land." 12 But Moses said to the LORD,
"Behold, the people of Israel have not
listened to me; how then shall Pharaoh
listen to me, who am a man of uncircumcised lips?" 13 But the LORD
spoke to Moses and Aaron, and gave
them a charge to the people of Israel
and to Pharaoh king of Egypt to bring
the people of Israel out of the land of
Egypt.
14 These are the heads of their
fathers' houses: the sons of Reuben,
the first-born of Israel: Hā'nŏch, Pal'-
lü, Hez'rŏn, and Cär'mī; these are the
families of Reuben. 15 The sons of
Simeon: Jė·mū'ėl, Jā'min, Ō'had,
Jā'chin, Zō'här, and Shā'ŭl, the
son of a Canaanite woman; these
are the families of Simeon. 16 These
are the names of the sons of Levi
according to their generations: Gẽr'-
shŏn, Kō'hath, and Mė·rär'ī, the years
of the life of Levi being a hundred and
thirty-seven years. 17 The sons of
Gẽr'shŏn: Lib'nī and Shim'ē-ī, by
their families. 18 The sons of Kō'hath:
Am'ram, Iz'här, Hē'brŏn, and Uz'zi·el,
the years of the life of Kohath being a
hundred and thirty-three years. 19 The
sons of Mė·rär'ī: Mäh'lī and Mū'shī.
These are the families of the Levites
according to their generations. 20 Am'-
ram took to wife Joch'ė·bed his father's
sister and she bore him Aaron and
Moses, the years of the life of Amram
being one hundred and thirty-seven
years. 21 The sons of Iz'här: Kō'rȧh,
Nē'pheg, and Zich'rī. 22 And the sons
of Uz'zi·el: Mish'ȧ-el, El'zȧ·phan, and
Sith'rī. 23 Aaron took to wife E·li'shė-
bȧ, the daughter of Am·min'ȧ·dab and
the sister of Näh'shŏn; and she bore
him Nā'dab, Ȧ·bī'hū, El·ē·ā'zär, and
Ith'ȧ·mär. 24 The sons of Kō'rȧh:
As'sir, El·kā'nȧh, and Ȧ·bī'ȧ·saph;
these are the families of the Kō'rȧ-
hītes. 25 El·ē·ā'zär, Aaron's son, took
to wife one of the daughters of Pū'ti-
el; and she bore him Phin'ė·hȧs. These
are the heads of the fathers' houses of
the Levites by their families.
26 These are the Aaron and Moses
to whom the LORD said: "Bring out
the people of Israel from the land of
Egypt by their hosts." 27 It was they
who spoke to Pharaoh king of Egypt
about bringing out the people of Israel from Egypt, this Moses and this
Aaron.
28 On the day when the LORD
spoke to Moses in the land of Egypt,
29 the LORD said to Moses, "I am the
LORD; tell Pharaoh king of Egypt all
that I say to you." 30 But Moses said
to the LORD, "Behold, I am of uncircumcised lips; how then shall Pharaoh
7 listen to me?" 1 And the LORD said
to Moses, "See, I make you as God
to Pharaoh; and Aaron your brother
shall be your prophet. 2 You shall
speak all that I command you; and
Aaron your brother shall tell Pharaoh
to let the people of Israel go out of his
land. 3 But I will harden Pharaoh's
heart, and though I multiply my signs
and wonders in the land of Egypt,
4 Pharaoh will not listen to you; then
I will lay my hand upon Egypt and
bring forth my hosts, my people the
sons of Israel, out of the land of Egypt
by great acts of judgment. 5 And the
Egyptians shall know that I am the
LORD, when I stretch forth my hand
upon Egypt and bring out the people
of Israel from among them." 6 And
Moses and Aaron did so; they did as
the LORD commanded them. 7 Now
Moses was eighty years old, and Aaron
eighty-three years old, when they
spoke to Pharaoh.
8 And the LORD said to Moses and
Aaron, 9 "When Pharaoh says to you,
'Prove yourselves by working a miracle,' then you shall say to Aaron, 'Take
your rod and cast it down before
Pharaoh, that it may become a serpent.' " 10 So Moses and Aaron went
to Pharaoh and did as the LORD commanded; Aaron cast down his rod before Pharaoh and his servants, and it
became a serpent. 11 Then Pharaoh
summoned the wise men and the
sorcerers; and they also, the magicians

6.14-16: Gen 46.8-11; Num 26.5-14. **6.16-19:** Num 3.15-20; 26.57-58; 1 Chron 6.1, 16-19.
6.20-23: Num 26.58-60. **7.3:** Acts 7.36.

of Egypt, did the same by their secret
arts. 12 For every man cast down his
rod, and they became serpents. But
Aaron's rod swallowed up their rods.
13 Still Pharaoh's heart was hardened,
and he would not listen to them; as
the LORD had said.

14 Then the LORD said to Moses,
"Pharaoh's heart is hardened, he refuses to let the people go. 15 Go to
Pharaoh in the morning, as he is going
out to the water; wait for him by the
river's brink, and take in your hand
the rod which was turned into a serpent. 16 And you shall say to him, 'The
LORD, the God of the Hebrews, sent
me to you, saying, "Let my people go,
that they may serve me in the wilderness; and behold, you have not yet
obeyed." 17 Thus says the LORD, "By
this you shall know that I am the
LORD: behold, I will strike the water
that is in the Nile with the rod that is
in my hand, and it shall be turned to
blood, 18 and the fish in the Nile shall
die, and the Nile shall become foul,
and the Egyptians will loathe to drink
water from the Nile."'" 19 And the
LORD said to Moses, "Say to Aaron,
'Take your rod and stretch out your
hand over the waters of Egypt, over
their rivers, their canals, and their
ponds, and all their pools of water,
that they may become blood; and
there shall be blood throughout all the
land of Egypt, both in vessels of wood
and in vessels of stone.'"

20 Moses and Aaron did as the
LORD commanded; in the sight of
Pharaoh and in the sight of his servants, he lifted up the rod and struck
the water that was in the Nile, and all
the water that was in the Nile turned
to blood. 21 And the fish in the Nile
died; and the Nile became foul, so that
the Egyptians could not drink water
from the Nile; and there was blood
throughout all the land of Egypt.
22 But the magicians of Egypt did the
same by their secret arts; so Pharaoh's
heart remained hardened, and he
would not listen to them; as the LORD
had said. 23 Pharaoh turned and went
into his house, and he did not lay even
this to heart. 24 And all the Egyptians
dug round about the Nile for water to
drink, for they could not drink the
water of the Nile.

25 Seven days passed after the
8 [i]LORD had struck the Nile. 1 Then
the LORD said to Moses, "Go in
to Pharaoh and say to him, 'Thus says
the LORD, "Let my people go, that
they may serve me. 2 But if you refuse
to let them go, behold, I will plague
all your country with frogs; 3 the Nile
shall swarm with frogs which shall
come up into your house, and into
your bedchamber and on your bed,
and into the houses of your servants
and of your people,[j] and into your
ovens and your kneading bowls; 4 the
frogs shall come up on you and on your
people and on all your servants."'"
5 [k]And the LORD said to Moses, "Say
to Aaron, 'Stretch out your hand with
your rod over the rivers, over the
canals, and over the pools, and cause
frogs to come upon the land of
Egypt!'" 6 So Aaron stretched out his
hand over the waters of Egypt; and
the frogs came up and covered the
land of Egypt. 7 But the magicians
did the same by their secret arts, and
brought frogs upon the land of Egypt.

8 Then Pharaoh called Moses and
Aaron, and said, "Entreat the LORD to
take away the frogs from me and from
my people; and I will let the people go
to sacrifice to the LORD." 9 Moses said
to Pharaoh, "Be pleased to command
me when I am to entreat, for you and
for your servants and for your people,
that the frogs be destroyed from you
and your houses and be left only in
the Nile." 10 And he said, "Tomorrow."
Moses said, "Be it as you say, that you
may know that there is no one like the
LORD our God. 11 The frogs shall depart from you and your houses and
your servants and your people; they
shall be left only in the Nile." 12 So
Moses and Aaron went out from Pharaoh; and Moses cried to the LORD concerning the frogs, as he had agreed
with Pharaoh.[l] 13 And the LORD did
according to the word of Moses; the
frogs died out of the houses and court-
yards and out of the fields. 14 And they
gathered them together in heaps, and
the land stank. 15 But when Pharaoh
saw that there was a respite, he
hardened his heart, and would not
listen to them; as the LORD had said.

16 Then the LORD said to Moses,
"Say to Aaron, 'Stretch out your rod
and strike the dust of the earth, that
it may become gnats throughout all

[i] Ch 7.26 in Heb [j] Gk: Heb *upon your people* [k] Ch 8.1 in Heb
[l] Or *which he had brought upon Pharaoh*

the land of Egypt.' " 17 And they did
so; Aaron stretched out his hand with
his rod, and struck the dust of the
earth, and there came gnats on man
and beast; all the dust of the earth became gnats throughout all the land of
Egypt. 18 The magicians tried by their
secret arts to bring forth gnats, but
they could not. So there were gnats on
man and beast. 19 And the magicians
said to Pharaoh, "This is the finger of
God." But Pharaoh's heart was hardened, and he would not listen to them;
as the LORD had said.

20 Then the LORD said to Moses,
"Rise up early in the morning and
wait for Pharaoh, as he goes out to the
water, and say to him, 'Thus says the
LORD, "Let my people go, that they
may serve me. 21 Else, if you will not
let my people go, behold, I will send
swarms of flies on you and your servants and your people, and into your
houses; and the houses of the Egyptians shall be filled with swarms of
flies, and also the ground on which
they stand. 22 But on that day I will
set apart the land of Gō'shĕn, where
my people dwell, so that no swarms of
flies shall be there; that you may know
that I am the LORD in the midst of the
earth. 23 Thus I will put a division[m]
between my people and your people.
By tomorrow shall this sign be." ' "
24 And the LORD did so; there came
great swarms of flies into the house of
Pharaoh and into his servants' houses,
and in all the land of Egypt the land
was ruined by reason of the flies.

25 Then Pharaoh called Moses and
Aaron, and said, "Go, sacrifice to your
God within the land." 26 But Moses
said, "It would not be right to do so;
for we shall sacrifice to the LORD our
God offerings abominable to the Egyptians. If we sacrifice offerings abominable to the Egyptians before their
eyes, will they not stone us? 27 We must
go three days' journey into the wilderness and sacrifice to the LORD our God
as he will command us." 28 So Pharaoh
said, "I will let you go, to sacrifice to
the LORD your God in the wilderness;
only you shall not go very far away.
Make entreaty for me." 29 Then Moses
said, "Behold, I am going out from
you and I will pray to the LORD that
the swarms of flies may depart from
Pharaoh, from his servants, and from
his people, tomorrow; only let not
Pharaoh deal falsely again by not
letting the people go to sacrifice to the
LORD." 30 So Moses went out from
Pharaoh and prayed to the LORD.
31 And the LORD did as Moses asked,
and removed the swarms of flies from
Pharaoh, from his servants, and from
his people; not one remained. 32 But
Pharaoh hardened his heart this time
also, and did not let the people go.

9 Then the LORD said to Moses,
"Go in to Pharaoh, and say to him,
'Thus says the LORD, the God of the
Hebrews, "Let my people go, that
they may serve me. 2 For if you refuse
to let them go and still hold them,
3 behold, the hand of the LORD will
fall with a very severe plague upon
your cattle which are in the field, the
horses, the asses, the camels, the herds,
and the flocks. 4 But the LORD will
make a distinction between the cattle
of Israel and the cattle of Egypt, so
that nothing shall die of all that belongs
to the people of Israel." ' " 5 And the
LORD set a time, saying, "Tomorrow
the LORD will do this thing in the
land." 6 And on the morrow the LORD
did this thing; all the cattle of the
Egyptians died, but of the cattle of
the people of Israel not one died. 7 And
Pharaoh sent, and behold, not one of
the cattle of the Israelites was dead.
But the heart of Pharaoh was hardened, and he did not let the people go.

8 And the LORD said to Moses and
Aaron, "Take handfuls of ashes from
the kiln, and let Moses throw them
toward heaven in the sight of Pharaoh.
9 And it shall become fine dust over all
the land of Egypt, and become boils
breaking out in sores on man and
beast throughout all the land of
Egypt." 10 So they took ashes from
the kiln, and stood before Pharaoh,
and Moses threw them toward heaven,
and it became boils breaking out in
sores on man and beast. 11 And the
magicians could not stand before
Moses because of the boils, for the
boils were upon the magicians and
upon all the Egyptians. 12 But the
LORD hardened the heart of Pharaoh,
and he did not listen to them; as the
LORD had spoken to Moses.

13 Then the LORD said to Moses,
"Rise up early in the morning and
stand before Pharaoh, and say to him,
'Thus says the LORD, the God of the
Hebrews, "Let my people go, that

[m] Gk Vg: Heb *set redemption*

they may serve me. [14] For this time I
will send all my plagues upon your
heart, and upon your servants and
your people, that you may know that
there is none like me in all the earth.
[15] For by now I could have put forth
my hand and struck you and your
people with pestilence, and you would
have been cut off from the earth; [16] but
for this purpose have I let you live, to
show you my power, so that my name
may be declared throughout all the
earth. [17] You are still exalting yourself
against my people, and will not let
them go. [18] Behold, tomorrow about
this time I will cause very heavy hail
to fall, such as never has been in Egypt
from the day it was founded until
now. [19] Now therefore send, get your
cattle and all that you have in the
field into safe shelter; for the hail shall
come down upon every man and beast
that is in the field and is not brought
home, and they shall die." ' " [20] Then
he who feared the word of the LORD
among the servants of Pharaoh made
his slaves and his cattle flee into the
houses; [21] but he who did not regard
the word of the LORD left his slaves
and his cattle in the field.

22 And the LORD said to Moses,
"Stretch forth your hand toward
heaven, that there may be hail in all
the land of Egypt, upon man and beast
and every plant of the field, throughout
the land of Egypt." [23] Then Moses
stretched forth his rod toward heaven;
and the LORD sent thunder and hail,
and fire ran down to the earth. And
the LORD rained hail upon the land
of Egypt; [24] there was hail, and fire
flashing continually in the midst of
the hail, very heavy hail, such as had
never been in all the land of Egypt
since it became a nation. [25] The hail
struck down everything that was in
the field throughout all the land of
Egypt, both man and beast; and the
hail struck down every plant of the
field, and shattered every tree of the
field. [26] Only in the land of Gō'shĕn,
where the people of Israel were, there
was no hail.

27 Then Pharaoh sent, and called
Moses and Aaron, and said to them,
"I have sinned this time; the LORD is
in the right, and I and my people are
in the wrong. [28] Entreat the LORD; for
there has been enough of this thunder
and hail; I will let you go, and you
shall stay no longer." [29] Moses said to
him, "As soon as I have gone out of
the city, I will stretch out my hands to
the LORD; the thunder will cease, and
there will be no more hail, that you
may know that the earth is the LORD's.
[30] But as for you and your servants,
I know that you do not yet fear the
LORD God." [31] (The flax and the
barley were ruined, for the barley was
in the ear and the flax was in bud.
[32] But the wheat and the spelt were
not ruined, for they are late in coming
up.) [33] So Moses went out of the city
from Pharaoh, and stretched out his
hands to the LORD; and the thunder
and the hail ceased, and the rain no
longer poured upon the earth. [34] But
when Pharaoh saw that the rain and
the hail and the thunder had ceased,
he sinned yet again, and hardened his
heart, he and his servants. [35] So the
heart of Pharaoh was hardened, and
he did not let the people of Israel go;
as the LORD had spoken through
Moses.

10 Then the LORD said to Moses,
"Go in to Pharaoh; for I have
hardened his heart and the heart of his
servants, that I may show these signs
of mine among them, [2] and that you
may tell in the hearing of your son and
of your sons' son how I have made
sport of the Egyptians and what signs
I have done among them; that you
may know that I am the LORD."

3 So Moses and Aaron went in to
Pharaoh, and said to him, "Thus says
the LORD, the God of the Hebrews,
'How long will you refuse to humble
yourself before me? Let my people go,
that they may serve me. [4] For if you
refuse to let my people go, behold,
tomorrow I will bring locusts into your
country, [5] and they shall cover the face
of the land, so that no one can see the
land; and they shall eat what is left to
you after the hail, and they shall eat
every tree of yours which grows in the
field, [6] and they shall fill your houses,
and the houses of all your servants and
of all the Egyptians; as neither your
fathers nor your grandfathers have
seen, from the day they came on earth
to this day.' " Then he turned and
went out from Pharaoh.

7 And Pharaoh's servants said to
him, "How long shall this man be a
snare to us? Let the men go, that they
may serve the LORD their God; do you

9.16: Rom 9.17.

not yet understand that Egypt is
ruined?" 8 So Moses and Aaron were
brought back to Pharaoh; and he said
to them, "Go, serve the LORD your
God; but who are to go?" 9 And Moses
said, "We will go with our young and
our old; we will go with our sons and
daughters and with our flocks and
herds, for we must hold a feast to the
LORD." 10 And he said to them, "The
LORD be with you, if ever I let you and
your little ones go! Look, you have
some evil purpose in mind.[n] 11 No!
Go, the men among you, and serve the
LORD, for that is what you desire."
And they were driven out from Pharaoh's presence.

12 Then the LORD said to Moses,
"Stretch out your hand over the land
of Egypt for the locusts, that they
may come upon the land of Egypt, and
eat every plant in the land, all that the
hail has left." 13 So Moses stretched
forth his rod over the land of Egypt,
and the LORD brought an east wind
upon the land all that day and all that
night; and when it was morning the
east wind had brought the locusts.
14 And the locusts came up over all the
land of Egypt, and settled on the whole
country of Egypt, such a dense swarm
of locusts as had never been before,
nor ever shall be again. 15 For they
covered the face of the whole land, so
that the land was darkened, and they
ate all the plants in the land and all the
fruit of the trees which the hail had
left; not a green thing remained, neither
tree nor plant of the field, through all
the land of Egypt. 16 Then Pharaoh
called Moses and Aaron in haste, and
said, "I have sinned against the LORD
your God, and against you. 17 Now
therefore, forgive my sin, I pray you,
only this once, and entreat the LORD
your God only to remove this death
from me." 18 So he went out from
Pharaoh, and entreated the LORD.
19 And the LORD turned a very strong
west wind, which lifted the locusts and
drove them into the Red Sea; not a
single locust was left in all the country
of Egypt. 20 But the LORD hardened
Pharaoh's heart, and he did not let the
children of Israel go.

21 Then the LORD said to Moses,
"Stretch out your hand toward heaven
that there may be darkness over the
land of Egypt, a darkness to be felt."
22 So Moses stretched out his hand
toward heaven, and there was thick
darkness in all the land of Egypt three
days; 23 they did not see one another,
nor did any rise from his place for
three days; but all the people of Israel
had light where they dwelt. 24 Then
Pharaoh called Moses, and said, "Go,
serve the LORD; your children also may
go with you; only let your flocks and
your herds remain behind." 25 But
Moses said, "You must also let us
have sacrifices and burnt offerings,
that we may sacrifice to the LORD our
God. 26 Our cattle also must go with
us; not a hoof shall be left behind, for
we must take of them to serve the
LORD our God, and we do not know
with what we must serve the LORD
until we arrive there." 27 But the LORD
hardened Pharaoh's heart, and he
would not let them go. 28 Then Pharaoh said to him, "Get away from me;
take heed to yourself; never see my
face again; for in the day you see
my face you shall die." 29 Moses said,
"As you say! I will not see your face
again."

11 The LORD said to Moses, "Yet
one plague more I will bring upon
Pharaoh and upon Egypt; afterwards
he will let you go hence; when he lets
you go, he will drive you away completely. 2 Speak now in the hearing of
the people, that they ask, every man
of his neighbor and every woman of
her neighbor, jewelry of silver and of
gold." 3 And the LORD gave the people
favor in the sight of the Egyptians.
Moreover, the man Moses was very
great in the land of Egypt, in the sight
of Pharaoh's servants and in the sight
of the people.

4 And Moses said, "Thus says the
LORD: About midnight I will go forth
in the midst of Egypt; 5 and all the
first-born in the land of Egypt shall
die, from the first-born of Pharaoh
who sits upon his throne, even to the
first-born of the maidservant who is
behind the mill; and all the first-born
of the cattle. 6 And there shall be a
great cry throughout all the land of
Egypt, such as there has never been,
nor ever shall be again. 7 But against
any of the people of Israel, either man
or beast, not a dog shall growl; that
you may know that the LORD makes a
distinction between the Egyptians and
Israel. 8 And all these your servants
shall come down to me, and bow down

[n] Heb *before your face*

to me, saying, 'Get you out, and all
the people who follow you.' And after
that I will go out." And he went out
from Pharaoh in hot anger. 9 Then the
LORD said to Moses, "Pharaoh will not
listen to you; that my wonders may be
multiplied in the land of Egypt."

10 Moses and Aaron did all these
wonders before Pharaoh; and the LORD
hardened Pharaoh's heart, and he did
not let the people of Israel go out of
his land.

12 The LORD said to Moses and
Aaron in the land of Egypt,
2 "This month shall be for you the
beginning of months; it shall be the
first month of the year for you. 3 Tell
all the congregation of Israel that on
the tenth day of this month they shall
take every man a lamb according to
their fathers' houses, a lamb for a
household; 4 and if the household is
too small for a lamb, then a man and
his neighbor next to his house shall
take according to the number of
persons; according to what each can
eat you shall make your count for the
lamb. 5 Your lamb shall be without
blemish, a male a year old; you shall
take it from the sheep or from the
goats; 6 and you shall keep it until the
fourteenth day of this month, when
the whole assembly of the congregation of Israel shall kill their lambs in
the evening.[o] 7 Then they shall take
some of the blood, and put it on the
two doorposts and the lintel of the
houses in which they eat them. 8 They
shall eat the flesh that night, roasted;
with unleavened bread and bitter
herbs they shall eat it. 9 Do not eat
any of it raw or boiled with water, but
roasted, its head with its legs and its
inner parts. 10 And you shall let none
of it remain until the morning, anything that remains until the morning
you shall burn. 11 In this manner you
shall eat it: your loins girded, your
sandals on your feet, and your staff in
your hand; and you shall eat it in
haste. It is the LORD's passover. 12 For
I will pass through the land of Egypt
that night, and I will smite all the
first-born in the land of Egypt, both
man and beast; and on all the gods of
Egypt I will execute judgments: I am
the LORD. 13 The blood shall be a sign
for you, upon the houses where you
are; and when I see the blood, I will
pass over you, and no plague shall fall
upon you to destroy you, when I smite
the land of Egypt.

14 "This day shall be for you a
memorial day, and you shall keep it
as a feast to the LORD; throughout
your generations you shall observe it
as an ordinance for ever. 15 Seven days
you shall eat unleavened bread; on the
first day you shall put away leaven out
of your houses, for if any one eats
what is leavened, from the first day
until the seventh day, that person shall
be cut off from Israel. 16 On the first
day you shall hold a holy assembly,
and on the seventh day a holy assembly; no work shall be done on those
days; but what every one must eat,
that only may be prepared by you.
17 And you shall observe the feast of
unleavened bread, for on this very day
I brought your hosts out of the land
of Egypt: therefore you shall observe
this day, throughout your generations,
as an ordinance for ever. 18 In the first
month, on the fourteenth day of the
month at evening, you shall eat unleavened bread, and so until the
twenty-first day of the month at
evening. 19 For seven days no leaven
shall be found in your houses; for if
any one eats what is leavened, that
person shall be cut off from the congregation of Israel, whether he is a
sojourner or a native of the land.
20 You shall eat nothing leavened; in
all your dwellings you shall eat unleavened bread."

21 Then Moses called all the elders
of Israel, and said to them, "Select
lambs for yourselves according to your
families, and kill the passover lamb.
22 Take a bunch of hyssop and dip it
in the blood which is in the basin, and
touch the lintel and the two doorposts
with the blood which is in the basin;
and none of you shall go out of the
door of his house until the morning.
23 For the LORD will pass through to
slay the Egyptians; and when he sees
the blood on the lintel and on the two
doorposts, the LORD will pass over the
door, and will not allow the destroyer
to enter your houses to slay you. 24 You
shall observe this rite as an ordinance
for you and for your sons for ever.
25 And when you come to the land
which the LORD will give you, as he
has promised, you shall keep this

[o] Heb *between the two evenings*
12.13: Heb 11.28.

service. 26And when your children say
to you, 'What do you mean by this
service?' 27 you shall say, 'It is the
sacrifice of the LORD's passover, for
he passed over the houses of the people
of Israel in Egypt, when he slew the
Egyptians but spared our houses.' "
And the people bowed their heads and
worshiped.

28 Then the people of Israel went
and did so; as the LORD had commanded Moses and Aaron, so they did.

29 At midnight the LORD smote all
the first-born in the land of Egypt,
from the first-born of Pharaoh who
sat on his throne to the first-born of
the captive who was in the dungeon,
and all the first-born of the cattle.
30And Pharaoh rose up in the night,
he, and all his servants, and all the
Egyptians; and there was a great cry
in Egypt, for there was not a house
where one was not dead. 31And he
summoned Moses and Aaron by night,
and said, "Rise up, go forth from
among my people, both you and the
people of Israel; and go, serve the
LORD, as you have said. 32 Take your
flocks and your herds, as you have
said, and be gone; and bless me also!"

33 And the Egyptians were urgent
with the people, to send them out of
the land in haste; for they said, "We
are all dead men." 34 So the people
took their dough before it was leavened, their kneading bowls being
bound up in their mantles on their
shoulders. 35 The people of Israel had
also done as Moses told them, for they
had asked of the Egyptians jewelry of
silver and of gold, and clothing; 36 and
the LORD had given the people favor
in the sight of the Egyptians, so that
they let them have what they asked.
Thus they despoiled the Egyptians.

37 And the people of Israel journeyed from Ram'ĕ·sēs to Suc'coth,
about six hundred thousand men on
foot, besides women and children. 38A
mixed multitude also went up with
them, and very many cattle, both
flocks and herds. 39And they baked
unleavened cakes of the dough which
they had brought out of Egypt, for it
was not leavened, because they were
thrust out of Egypt and could not
tarry, neither had they prepared for
themselves any provisions.

40 The time that the people of
Israel dwelt in Egypt was four hundred
and thirty years. 41And at the end of
four hundred and thirty years, on that
very day, all the hosts of the LORD
went out from the land of Egypt. 42 It
was a night of watching by the LORD,
to bring them out of the land of Egypt;
so this same night is a night of watching kept to the LORD by all the people
of Israel throughout their generations.

43 And the LORD said to Moses and
Aaron, "This is the ordinance of the
passover: no foreigner shall eat of it;
44 but every slave that is bought for
money may eat of it after you have
circumcised him. 45 No sojourner or
hired servant may eat of it. 46 In one
house shall it be eaten; you shall not
carry forth any of the flesh outside the
house; and you shall not break a bone
of it. 47All the congregation of Israel
shall keep it. 48And when a stranger
shall sojourn with you and would keep
the passover to the LORD, let all his
males be circumcised, then he may
come near and keep it; he shall be as
a native of the land. But no uncircumcised person shall eat of it. 49 There
shall be one law for the native and for
the stranger who sojourns among you."

50 Thus did all the people of Israel;
as the LORD commanded Moses and
Aaron, so they did. 51And on that very
day the LORD brought the people of
Israel out of the land of Egypt by
their hosts.

13 The LORD said to Moses,
2 "Consecrate to me all the first-
born; whatever is the first to open the
womb among the people of Israel,
both of man and of beast, is mine."

3 And Moses said to the people,
"Remember this day, in which you
came out from Egypt, out of the house
of bondage, for by strength of hand
the LORD brought you out from this
place; no leavened bread shall be eaten.
4 This day you are to go forth, in the
month of A'bib. 5And when the LORD
brings you into the land of the Canaanites, the Hit'tītes, the Am'ŏ·rītes, the
Hī'vītes, and the Jeb'ū·sītes, which he
swore to your fathers to give you, a
land flowing with milk and honey, you
shall keep this service in this month.
6 Seven days you shall eat unleavened
bread, and on the seventh day there
shall be a feast to the LORD. 7 Un-

12.40: Acts 7.6. **12.46:** Num 9.12; Jn 19.36. **12.49:** Lev 24.22; Num 9.14; 15.15-16, 29.
13.2: Lk 2.23.

leavened bread shall be eaten for seven
days; no leavened bread shall be seen
with you, and no leaven shall be seen
with you in all your territory. 8 And
you shall tell your son on that day, 'It
is because of what the LORD did for
me when I came out of Egypt.' 9 And
it shall be to you as a sign on your
hand and as a memorial between your
eyes, that the law of the LORD may be
in your mouth; for with a strong hand
the LORD has brought you out of
Egypt. 10 You shall therefore keep this
ordinance at its appointed time from
year to year.

11 "And when the LORD brings you
into the land of the Canaanites, as he
swore to you and your fathers, and
shall give it to you, 12 you shall set
apart to the LORD all that first opens
the womb. All the firstlings of your
cattle that are males shall be the
LORD's. 13 Every firstling of an ass you
shall redeem with a lamb, or if you
will not redeem it you shall break its
neck. Every first-born of man among
your sons you shall redeem. 14 And
when in time to come your son asks
you, 'What does this mean?' you shall
say to him, 'By strength of hand the
LORD brought us out of Egypt, from
the house of bondage. 15 For when
Pharaoh stubbornly refused to let us
go, the LORD slew all the first-born in
the land of Egypt, both the first-born
of man and the first-born of cattle.
Therefore I sacrifice to the LORD all
the males that first open the womb;
but all the first-born of my sons I
redeem.' 16 It shall be as a mark on
your hand or frontlets between your
eyes; for by a strong hand the LORD
brought us out of Egypt."

17 When Pharaoh let the people go,
God did not lead them by way of the
land of the Philistines, although that
was near; for God said, "Lest the
people repent when they see war, and
return to Egypt." 18 But God led the
people round by the way of the wilderness toward the Red Sea. And the
people of Israel went up out of the
land of Egypt equipped for battle.
19 And Moses took the bones of
Joseph with him; for Joseph had
solemnly sworn the people of Israel,
saying, "God will visit you; then you
must carry my bones with you from
here." 20 And they moved on from
Suc'coth, and encamped at E'thȧm, on
the edge of the wilderness. 21 And the
LORD went before them by day in a
pillar of cloud to lead them along the
way, and by night in a pillar of fire to
give them light, that they might travel
by day and by night; 22 the pillar of
cloud by day and the pillar of fire by
night did not depart from before the
people.

14 Then the LORD said to Moses,
2 "Tell the people of Israel to
turn back and encamp in front of Pī-
hȧ-hī'roth, between Mig'dōl and the
sea, in front of Bā'ȧl-zē'phon; you
shall encamp over against it, by the
sea. 3 For Pharaoh will say of the
people of Israel, 'They are entangled
in the land; the wilderness has shut
them in.' 4 And I will harden Pharaoh's
heart, and he will pursue them and I
will get glory over Pharaoh and all his
host; and the Egyptians shall know
that I am the LORD." And they did so.

5 When the king of Egypt was told
that the people had fled, the mind of
Pharaoh and his servants was changed
toward the people, and they said,
"What is this we have done, that we
have let Israel go from serving us?"
6 So he made ready his chariot and
took his army with him, 7 and took six
hundred picked chariots and all the
other chariots of Egypt with officers
over all of them. 8 And the LORD hardened the heart of Pharaoh king of
Egypt and he pursued the people of
Israel as they went forth defiantly.
9 The Egyptians pursued them, all
Pharaoh's horses and chariots and his
horsemen and his army, and overtook
them encamped at the sea, by Pī-hȧ-
hī'roth, in front of Bā'ȧl-zē'phon.

10 When Pharaoh drew near, the
people of Israel lifted up their eyes,
and behold, the Egyptians were marching after them; and they were in great
fear. And the people of Israel cried
out to the LORD; 11 and they said to
Moses, "Is it because there are no
graves in Egypt that you have taken us
away to die in the wilderness? What
have you done to us, in bringing us
out of Egypt? 12 Is not this what we
said to you in Egypt, 'Let us alone and
let us serve the Egyptians'? For it
would have been better for us to serve
the Egyptians than to die in the wilderness." 13 And Moses said to the people,
"Fear not, stand firm, and see the
salvation of the LORD, which he will

13.12,15: Lk 2.23. **13.19:** Gen 50.25. **14.8:** Acts 13.17. **14.12:** Ex 16.3; 17.3.

work for you today; for the Egyptians
whom you see today, you shall never
see again. 14 The LORD will fight for
you, and you have only to be still."
15 The LORD said to Moses, "Why do
you cry to me? Tell the people of
Israel to go forward. 16 Lift up your
rod, and stretch out your hand over
the sea and divide it, that the people
of Israel may go on dry ground through
the sea. 17 And I will harden the hearts
of the Egyptians so that they shall go
in after them, and I will get glory over
Pharaoh and all his host, his chariots,
and his horsemen. 18 And the Egyptians shall know that I am the LORD,
when I have gotten glory over Pharaoh, his chariots, and his horsemen."
19 Then the angel of God who
went before the host of Israel moved
and went behind them; and the pillar
of cloud moved from before them and
stood behind them, 20 coming between
the host of Egypt and the host of Israel.
And there was the cloud and the darkness; and the night passed[p] without
one coming near the other all night.
21 Then Moses stretched out his
hand over the sea; and the LORD drove
the sea back by a strong east wind all
night, and made the sea dry land, and
the waters were divided. 22 And the
people of Israel went into the midst of
the sea on dry ground, the waters
being a wall to them on their right
hand and on their left. 23 The Egyptians pursued, and went in after them
into the midst of the sea, all Pharaoh's
horses, his chariots, and his horsemen.
24 And in the morning watch the LORD
in the pillar of fire and of cloud looked
down upon the host of the Egyptians,
and discomfited the host of the Egyptians, 25 clogging[q] their chariot wheels
so that they drove heavily; and the
Egyptians said, "Let us flee from before Israel; for the LORD fights for
them against the Egyptians."
26 Then the LORD said to Moses,
"Stretch out your hand over the sea,
that the water may come back upon
the Egyptians, upon their chariots,
and upon their horsemen." 27 So
Moses stretched forth his hand over
the sea, and the sea returned to its
wonted flow when the morning appeared; and the Egyptians fled into it,
and the LORD routed[r] the Egyptians
in the midst of the sea. 28 The waters
returned and covered the chariots and
the horsemen and all the host[s] of
Pharaoh that had followed them into
the sea; not so much as one of them
remained. 29 But the people of Israel
walked on dry ground through the sea,
the waters being a wall to them on
their right hand and on their left.
30 Thus the LORD saved Israel that
day from the hand of the Egyptians;
and Israel saw the Egyptians dead
upon the seashore. 31 And Israel saw
the great work which the LORD did
against the Egyptians, and the people
feared the LORD; and they believed in
the LORD and in his servant Moses.

15 Then Moses and the people of
Israel sang this song to the LORD,
saying,

"I will sing to the LORD, for he has
triumphed gloriously;
the horse and his rider[t] he has
thrown into the sea.
2 The LORD is my strength and my
song,
and he has become my salvation;
this is my God, and I will praise
him,
my father's God, and I will exalt
him.
3 The LORD is a man of war;
the LORD is his name.

4 "Pharaoh's chariots and his host he
cast into the sea;
and his picked officers are sunk in
the Red Sea.
5 The floods cover them;
they went down into the depths
like a stone.
6 Thy right hand, O LORD, glorious in
power,
thy right hand, O LORD, shatters
the enemy.
7 In the greatness of thy majesty thou
overthrowest thy adversaries;
thou sendest forth thy fury, it
consumes them like stubble.
8 At the blast of thy nostrils the
waters piled up,
the floods stood up in a heap;
the deeps congealed in the heart
of the sea.
9 The enemy said, 'I will pursue, I
will overtake,
I will divide the spoil, my desire
shall have its fill of them.
I will draw my sword, my hand
shall destroy them.'

[p] Gk: Heb *and it lit up the night* [q] Or *binding*. Sam Gk Syr: Heb *removing* [r] Heb *shook off*
[s] Gk Syr: Heb *to all the host* [t] Or *its chariot*

10 Thou didst blow with thy wind, the
sea covered them;
they sank as lead in the mighty
waters.

11 "Who is like thee, O LORD, among
the gods?
Who is like thee, majestic in
holiness,
terrible in glorious deeds, doing
wonders?
12 Thou didst stretch out thy right
hand,
the earth swallowed them.

13 "Thou hast led in thy steadfast love
the people whom thou hast
redeemed,
thou hast guided them by thy
strength to thy holy abode.
14 The peoples have heard, they
tremble;
pangs have seized on the inhabitants of Phi·lis'ti·ȧ.
15 Now are the chiefs of Ē'dȯm dismayed;
the leaders of Mō'ab, trembling
seizes them;
all the inhabitants of Canaan have
melted away.
16 Terror and dread fall upon them;
because of the greatness of thy
arm, they are as still as a stone,
till thy people, O LORD, pass by,
till the people pass by whom thou
hast purchased.
17 Thou wilt bring them in, and plant
them on thy own mountain,
the place, O LORD, which thou
hast made for thy abode,
the sanctuary, O LORD, which thy
hands have established.
18 The LORD will reign for ever and
ever."

19 For when the horses of Pharaoh
with his chariots and his horsemen
went into the sea, the LORD brought
back the waters of the sea upon them;
but the people of Israel walked on dry
ground in the midst of the sea. 20 Then
Miriam, the prophetess, the sister of
Aaron, took a timbrel in her hand; and
all the women went out after her with
timbrels and dancing. 21 And Miriam
sang to them:

"Sing to the LORD, for he has triumphed gloriously;
the horse and his rider he has thrown
into the sea."

22 Then Moses led Israel onward
from the Red Sea, and they went into
the wilderness of Shür; they went
three days in the wilderness and found
no water. 23 When they came to
Mâr'ȧh, they could not drink the
water of Marah because it was bitter;
therefore it was named Marah.[u] 24 And
the people murmured against Moses,
saying, "What shall we drink?" 25 And
he cried to the LORD; and the LORD
showed him a tree, and he threw it into
the water, and the water became sweet.

There the LORD[v] made for them a
statute and an ordinance and there he
proved them, 26 saying, "If you will
diligently hearken to the voice of the
LORD your God, and do that which is
right in his eyes, and give heed to his
commandments and keep all his
statutes, I will put none of the diseases
upon you which I put upon the Egyptians; for I am the LORD, your healer."

27 Then they came to Ē'lim, where
there were twelve springs of water
and seventy palm trees; and they encamped there by the water.

16 They set out from Ē'lim, and
all the congregation of the people
of Israel came to the wilderness of Sin,
which is between Elim and Sinai, on
the fifteenth day of the second month
after they had departed from the land
of Egypt. 2 And the whole congregation of the people of Israel murmured
against Moses and Aaron in the wilderness, 3 and said to them, "Would that
we had died by the hand of the LORD
in the land of Egypt, when we sat by
the fleshpots and ate bread to the full;
for you have brought us out into this
wilderness to kill this whole assembly
with hunger."

4 Then the LORD said to Moses,
"Behold, I will rain bread from heaven
for you; and the people shall go out
and gather a day's portion every day,
that I may prove them, whether they
will walk in my law or not. 5 On the
sixth day, when they prepare what
they bring in, it will be twice as much
as they gather daily." 6 So Moses and
Aaron said to all the people of Israel,
"At evening you shall know that it was
the LORD who brought you out of the
land of Egypt, 7 and in the morning
you shall see the glory of the LORD,
because he has heard your murmurings against the LORD. For what are

[u] That is *Bitterness* [v] Heb *he*
16.3: Ex 14.12; 17.3. **16.4:** Jn 6.31.

we, that you murmur against us?"
8 And Moses said, "When the LORD
gives you in the evening flesh to eat
and in the morning bread to the full,
because the LORD has heard your
murmurings which you murmur
against him—what are we? Your
murmurings are not against us but
against the LORD."

9 And Moses said to Aaron, "Say
to the whole congregation of the people of Israel, 'Come near before the
LORD, for he has heard your murmurings.'" 10 And as Aaron spoke to the
whole congregation of the people of
Israel, they looked toward the wilderness, and behold, the glory of the
LORD appeared in the cloud. 11 And
the LORD said to Moses, 12 "I have
heard the murmurings of the people
of Israel; say to them, 'At twilight you
shall eat flesh, and in the morning you
shall be filled with bread; then you
shall know that I am the LORD your
God.'"

13 In the evening quails came up
and covered the camp; and in the
morning dew lay round about the
camp. 14 And when the dew had gone
up, there was on the face of the wilderness a fine, flake-like thing, fine as
hoarfrost on the ground. 15 When the
people of Israel saw it, they said to
one another, "What is it?"[w] For they
did not know what it was. And Moses
said to them, "It is the bread which
the LORD has given you to eat. 16 This
is what the LORD has commanded:
'Gather of it, every man of you, as
much as he can eat; you shall take an
omer apiece, according to the number
of the persons whom each of you has
in his tent.'" 17 And the people of
Israel did so; they gathered, some
more, some less. 18 But when they
measured it with an omer, he that
gathered much had nothing over, and
he that gathered little had no lack;
each gathered according to what he
could eat. 19 And Moses said to them,
"Let no man leave any of it till the
morning." 20 But they did not listen
to Moses; some left part of it till the
morning, and it bred worms and became foul; and Moses was angry with
them. 21 Morning by morning they
gathered it, each as much as he could
eat; but when the sun grew hot, it
melted.

22 On the sixth day they gathered
twice as much bread, two omers apiece;
and when all the leaders of the congregation came and told Moses, 23 he
said to them, "This is what the LORD
has commanded: 'Tomorrow is a day
of solemn rest, a holy sabbath to the
LORD; bake what you will bake and
boil what you will boil, and all that is
left over lay by to be kept till the
morning.'" 24 So they laid it by till
the morning, as Moses bade them; and
it did not become foul, and there were
no worms in it. 25 Moses said, "Eat it
today, for today is a sabbath to the
LORD; today you will not find it in the
field. 26 Six days you shall gather it;
but on the seventh day, which is a
sabbath, there will be none." 27 On
the seventh day some of the people
went out to gather, and they found
none. 28 And the LORD said to Moses,
"How long do you refuse to keep my
commandments and my laws? 29 See!
The LORD has given you the sabbath,
therefore on the sixth day he gives you
bread for two days; remain every man
of you in his place, let no man go out
of his place on the seventh day." 30 So
the people rested on the seventh day.

31 Now the house of Israel called
its name manna; it was like coriander
seed, white, and the taste of it was like
wafers made with honey. 32 And Moses
said, "This is what the LORD has
commanded: 'Let an omer of it be
kept throughout your generations, that
they may see the bread with which I
fed you in the wilderness, when I
brought you out of the land of
Egypt.'" 33 And Moses said to Aaron,
"Take a jar, and put an omer of manna
in it, and place it before the LORD, to
be kept throughout your generations."
34 As the LORD commanded Moses, so
Aaron placed it before the testimony,
to be kept. 35 And the people of Israel
ate the manna forty years, till they
came to a habitable land; they ate the
manna, till they came to the border of
the land of Canaan. 36 (An omer is the
tenth part of an ephah.)

17 All the congregation of the people of Israel moved on from the
wilderness of Sin by stages, according
to the commandment of the LORD,
and camped at Reph'i·dim; but there
was no water for the people to drink.
2 Therefore the people found fault

[w] Or "*It is manna.*" Heb *man hu*
16.13: Jn 6.31. **16.18:** 2 Cor 8.15.

with Moses, and said, "Give us water
to drink." And Moses said to them,
"Why do you find fault with me? Why
do you put the LORD to the proof?"
3 But the people thirsted there for
water, and the people murmured
against Moses, and said, "Why did
you bring us up out of Egypt, to kill
us and our children and our cattle with
thirst?" 4 So Moses cried to the LORD,
"What shall I do with this people?
They are almost ready to stone me."
5 And the LORD said to Moses, "Pass
on before the people, taking with you
some of the elders of Israel; and take
in your hand the rod with which you
struck the Nile, and go. 6 Behold, I
will stand before you there on the rock
at Hō'reb; and you shall strike the
rock, and water shall come out of it,
that the people may drink." And
Moses did so, in the sight of the elders
of Israel. 7 And he called the name of
the place Mas'sȧh[x] and Mer'i·bȧh,[y] because of the faultfinding of the children
of Israel, and because they put the
LORD to the proof by saying, "Is the
LORD among us or not?"

8 Then came Am'ȧ·lek and fought
with Israel at Reph'i·dim. 9 And Moses
said to Joshua, "Choose for us men,
and go out, fight with Am'ȧ·lek;
tomorrow I will stand on the top of
the hill with the rod of God in my
hand." 10 So Joshua did as Moses told
him, and fought with Am'ȧ·lek; and
Moses, Aaron, and Hũr went up to
the top of the hill. 11 Whenever Moses
held up his hand, Israel prevailed; and
whenever he lowered his hand, Am'ȧ-
lek prevailed. 12 But Moses' hands
grew weary; so they took a stone and
put it under him, and he sat upon it,
and Aaron and Hũr held up his hands,
one on one side, and the other on the
other side; so his hands were steady
until the going down of the sun. 13 And
Joshua mowed down Am'ȧ·lek and his
people with the edge of the sword.

14 And the LORD said to Moses,
"Write this as a memorial in a book
and recite it in the ears of Joshua, that
I will utterly blot out the remembrance
of Am'ȧ·lek from under heaven."
15 And Moses built an altar and called
the name of it, The LORD is my banner,
16 saying, "A hand upon the banner
of the LORD![z] The LORD will have war
with Am'ȧ·lek from generation to
generation."

18 Jethro, the priest of Mid'i·ȧn,
Moses' father-in-law, heard of
all that God had done for Moses and
for Israel his people, how the LORD
had brought Israel out of Egypt. 2 Now
Jethro, Moses' father-in-law, had
taken Zip·pō'rȧh, Moses' wife, after he
had sent her away, 3 and her two sons,
of whom the name of the one was
Gẽr'shȯm (for he said, "I have been a
sojourner[a] in a foreign land"), 4 and
the name of the other, E·lī·ē'zẽr[b] (for
he said, "The God of my father was
my help, and delivered me from the
sword of Pharaoh"). 5 And Jethro,
Moses' father-in-law, came with his
sons and his wife to Moses in the
wilderness where he was encamped at
the mountain of God. 6 And when one
told Moses, "Lo,[c] your father-in-law
Jethro is coming to you with your wife
and her two sons with her," 7 Moses
went out to meet his father-in-law, and
did obeisance and kissed him; and they
asked each other of their welfare, and
went into the tent. 8 Then Moses told
his father-in-law all that the LORD had
done to Pharaoh and to the Egyptians
for Israel's sake, all the hardship that
had come upon them in the way, and
how the LORD had delivered them.
9 And Jethro rejoiced for all the good
which the LORD had done to Israel, in
that he had delivered them out of the
hand of the Egyptians.

10 And Jethro said, "Blessed be the
LORD, who has delivered you out of
the hands of the Egyptians and out of
the hand of Pharaoh. 11 Now I know
that the LORD is greater than all gods,
because he delivered the people from
under the hand of the Egyptians,[d]
when they dealt arrogantly with
them." 12 And Jethro, Moses' father-
in-law, offered[e] a burnt offering and
sacrifices to God; and Aaron came
with all the elders of Israel to eat bread
with Moses' father-in-law before God.

13 On the morrow Moses sat to
judge the people, and the people stood
about Moses from morning till evening. 14 When Moses' father-in-law
saw all that he was doing for the people, he said, "What is this that you are
doing for the people? Why do you sit
alone, and all the people stand about

[x] That is *Proof* [y] That is *Contention* [z] Cn: Heb obscure [a] Heb *ger* [b] Heb *Eli*, my God *ezer*, help
[c] Sam Gk Syr: Heb *I* [d] Transposing the last clause of v. 10 to v. 11 [e] Syr Tg Vg: Heb *took*
17.3: 14.12; 16.3. 17.14: Deut 25.17-19; 1 Sam 15.2-9. 18.3-4: Acts 7.29.

you from morning till evening?" 15And
Moses said to his father-in-law, "Because the people come to me to inquire
of God; 16 when they have a dispute,
they come to me and I decide between
a man and his neighbor, and I make
them know the statutes of God and
his decisions." 17 Moses' father-in-
law said to him, "What you are doing
is not good. 18 You and the people
with you will wear yourselves out, for
the thing is too heavy for you; you are
not able to perform it alone. 19 Listen
now to my voice; I will give you
counsel, and God be with you! You
shall represent the people before God,
and bring their cases to God; 20 and
you shall teach them the statutes and
the decisions, and make them know
the way in which they must walk and
what they must do. 21 Moreover choose
able men from all the people, such as
fear God, men who are trustworthy
and who hate a bribe; and place such
men over the people as rulers of thousands, of hundreds, of fifties, and of
tens. 22And let them judge the people
at all times; every great matter they
shall bring to you, but any small
matter they shall decide themselves;
so it will be easier for you, and they
will bear the burden with you. 23 If
you do this, and God so commands
you, then you will be able to endure,
and all this people also will go to their
place in peace."

24 So Moses gave heed to the voice
of his father-in-law and did all that he
had said. 25 Moses chose able men out
of all Israel, and made them heads
over the people, rulers of thousands,
of hundreds, of fifties, and of tens.
26And they judged the people at all
times; hard cases they brought to
Moses, but any small matter they
decided themselves. 27 Then Moses
let his father-in-law depart, and he
went his way to his own country.

19 On the third new moon after the
people of Israel had gone forth
out of the land of Egypt, on that day
they came into the wilderness of Sinai.
2And when they set out from Reph'i-
dim and came into the wilderness of
Sinai, they encamped in the wilderness; and there Israel encamped before
the mountain. 3And Moses went up to
God, and the LORD called to him out
of the mountain, saying, "Thus you
shall say to the house of Jacob, and tell
the people of Israel: 4 You have seen
what I did to the Egyptians, and how
I bore you on eagles' wings and
brought you to myself. 5 Now therefore, if you will obey my voice and
keep my covenant, you shall be my
own possession among all peoples; for
all the earth is mine, 6 and you shall
be to me a kingdom of priests and a
holy nation. These are the words which
you shall speak to the children of
Israel."

7 So Moses came and called the
elders of the people, and set before
them all these words which the LORD
had commanded him. 8And all the
people answered together and said,
"All that the LORD has spoken we will
do." And Moses reported the words of
the people to the LORD. 9And the
LORD said to Moses, "Lo, I am coming
to you in a thick cloud, that the people
may hear when I speak with you, and
may also believe you for ever."

Then Moses told the words of the
people to the LORD. 10And the LORD
said to Moses, "Go to the people and
consecrate them today and tomorrow,
and let them wash their garments,
11 and be ready by the third day; for
on the third day the LORD will come
down upon Mount Sinai in the sight
of all the people. 12And you shall set
bounds for the people round about,
saying, 'Take heed that you do not go
up into the mountain or touch the
border of it; whoever touches the
mountain shall be put to death; 13 no
hand shall touch him, but he shall be
stoned or shot; whether beast or man,
he shall not live.' When the trumpet
sounds a long blast, they shall come
up to the mountain." 14 So Moses
went down from the mountain to the
people, and consecrated the people;
and they washed their garments. 15And
he said to the people, "Be ready by
the third day; do not go near a
woman."

16 On the morning of the third day
there were thunders and lightnings,
and a thick cloud upon the mountain,
and a very loud trumpet blast, so that
all the people who were in the camp
trembled. 17 Then Moses brought the
people out of the camp to meet God;
and they took their stand at the foot
of the mountain. 18And Mount Sinai
was wrapped in smoke, because the
LORD descended upon it in fire; and

19.5-6: Deut 7.6; 14.2, 21; 26.19; Tit 2.14; 1 Pet 2.9; Rev 1.6; 5.10. **19.12-19:** Heb 12.18-20.

the smoke of it went up like the smoke
of a kiln, and the whole mountain
quaked greatly. 19 And as the sound of
the trumpet grew louder and louder,
Moses spoke, and God answered him
in thunder. 20 And the LORD came
down upon Mount Sinai, to the top
of the mountain; and the LORD called
Moses to the top of the mountain, and
Moses went up. 21 And the LORD said
to Moses, "Go down and warn the
people, lest they break through to the
LORD to gaze and many of them perish. 22 And also let the priests who come
near to the LORD consecrate themselves, lest the LORD break out upon
them." 23 And Moses said to the
LORD, "The people cannot come up
to Mount Sinai; for thou thyself didst
charge us, saying, 'Set bounds about
the mountain, and consecrate it.' "
24 And the LORD said to him, "Go
down, and come up bringing Aaron
with you; but do not let the priests
and the people break through to come
up to the LORD, lest he break out
against them." 25 So Moses went down
to the people and told them.

20 And God spoke all these words,
saying,
2 "I am the LORD your God, who
brought you out of the land of Egypt,
out of the house of bondage.

3 "You shall have no other gods
before[f] me.

4 "You shall not make for yourself
a graven image, or any likeness of anything that is in heaven above, or that
is in the earth beneath, or that is in the
water under the earth; 5 you shall not
bow down to them or serve them; for
I the LORD your God am a jealous
God, visiting the iniquity of the fathers
upon the children to the third and the
fourth generation of those who hate
me, 6 but showing steadfast love to
thousands of those who love me and
keep my commandments.

7 "You shall not take the name of
the LORD your God in vain; for the
LORD will not hold him guiltless who
takes his name in vain.

8 "Remember the sabbath day, to
keep it holy. 9 Six days you shall labor,
and do all your work; 10 but the
seventh day is a sabbath to the LORD
your God; in it you shall not do any
work, you, or your son, or your daughter, your manservant, or your maidservant, or your cattle, or the sojourner who is within your gates; 11 for
in six days the LORD made heaven and
earth, the sea, and all that is in them,
and rested the seventh day; therefore
the LORD blessed the sabbath day and
hallowed it.

12 "Honor your father and your
mother, that your days may be long
in the land which the LORD your God
gives you.

13 "You shall not kill.

14 "You shall not commit adultery.

15 "You shall not steal.

16 "You shall not bear false witness
against your neighbor.

17 "You shall not covet your neighbor's house; you shall not covet your
neighbor's wife, or his manservant, or
his maidservant, or his ox, or his ass,
or anything that is your neighbor's."

18 Now when all the people perceived the thunderings and the lightnings and the sound of the trumpet
and the mountain smoking, the people
were afraid and trembled; and they
stood afar off, 19 and said to Moses,
"You speak to us, and we will hear;
but let not God speak to us, lest we
die." 20 And Moses said to the people,
"Do not fear; for God has come to
prove you, and that the fear of him
may be before your eyes, that you
may not sin."

21 And the people stood afar off,
while Moses drew near to the thick
darkness where God was. 22 And the
LORD said to Moses, "Thus you shall
say to the people of Israel: 'You have
seen for yourselves that I have talked
with you from heaven. 23 You shall not
make gods of silver to be with me, nor
shall you make for yourselves gods of
gold. 24 An altar of earth you shall
make for me and sacrifice on it your

[f] Or *besides*

20.2-17: Deut 5.6-21. **20.3:** Ex 20.23; Deut 5.7.
20.4: Ex 20.23; 34.17; Lev 19.4; 26.1; Deut 4.15-19; 5.8; 27.15.
20.5-6: Ex 23.24; 34.6-7, 14; Deut 4.24; 5.9-10; 7.9. **20.7:** Lev 19.12; Deut 5.11.
20.8: Ex 23.12; 31.12-17; 34.21; 35.2-3; Lev 19.3; Deut 5.12-15.
20.12-16: Mt 19.18-19; Mk 10.19; Lk 18.20. **20.12:** Lev 19.3; Deut 5.16; Mt 15.4; Mk 7.10; Eph 6.2.
20.13: Gen 9.6; Ex 21.12; Lev 24.17; Deut 5.17; Mt 5.21; Jas 2.11. **20.13-17:** Rom 13.9.
20.14: Lev 20.10; Deut 5.18; Mt 5.27; Rom 7.7. **20.15:** Lev 19.11; Deut 5.19.
20.16: Ex 23.1; Deut 5.20. **20.17:** Deut 5.21; Rom 7.7. **20.23:** Ex 20.3-4; 34.17; Deut 27.15.
20.24: Ex 27.1-8; Deut 12.5; 26.2.

burnt offerings and your peace offerings, your sheep and your oxen; in
every place where I cause my name to
be remembered I will come to you
and bless you. 25 And if you make me
an altar of stone, you shall not build
it of hewn stones; for if you wield your
tool upon it you profane it. 26 And you
shall not go up by steps to my altar,
that your nakedness be not exposed
on it.'

21 "Now these are the ordinances
which you shall set before them.
2 When you buy a Hebrew slave, he
shall serve six years, and in the seventh
he shall go out free, for nothing. 3 If
he comes in single, he shall go out
single; if he comes in married, then
his wife shall go out with him. 4 If his
master gives him a wife and she bears
him sons or daughters, the wife and
her children shall be her master's and
he shall go out alone. 5 But if the slave
plainly says, 'I love my master, my
wife, and my children; I will not go
out free,' 6 then his master shall bring
him to God, and he shall bring him
to the door or the doorpost; and his
master shall bore his ear through with
an awl; and he shall serve him for life.

7 "When a man sells his daughter
as a slave, she shall not go out as the
male slaves do. 8 If she does not please
her master, who has designated her[g]
for himself, then he shall let her be
redeemed; he shall have no right to sell
her to a foreign people, since he has
dealt faithlessly with her. 9 If he desig-
nates her for his son, he shall deal with
her as with a daughter. 10 If he takes
another wife to himself, he shall not
diminish her food, her clothing, or
her marital rights. 11 And if he does
not do these three things for her, she
shall go out for nothing, without payment of money.

12 "Whoever strikes a man so that
he dies shall be put to death. 13 But if
he did not lie in wait for him, but God
let him fall into his hand, then I will
appoint for you a place to which he
may flee. 14 But if a man willfully
attacks another to kill him treacherously, you shall take him from my
altar, that he may die.

15 "Whoever strikes his father or
his mother shall be put to death.

16 "Whoever steals a man, whether
he sells him or is found in possession
of him, shall be put to death.

17 "Whoever curses his father or
his mother shall be put to death.

18 "When men quarrel and one
strikes the other with a stone or with
his fist and the man does not die but
keeps his bed, 19 then if the man rises
again and walks abroad with his staff,
he that struck him shall be clear; only
he shall pay for the loss of his time,
and shall have him thoroughly healed.

20 "When a man strikes his slave,
male or female, with a rod and the
slave dies under his hand, he shall be
punished. 21 But if the slave survives
a day or two, he is not to be punished;
for the slave is his money.

22 "When men strive together, and
hurt a woman with child, so that there
is a miscarriage, and yet no harm
follows, the one who hurt her shall[h]
be fined, according as the woman's
husband shall lay upon him; and he
shall pay as the judges determine. 23 If
any harm follows, then you shall give
life for life, 24 eye for eye, tooth for
tooth, hand for hand, foot for foot,
25 burn for burn, wound for wound,
stripe for stripe.

26 "When a man strikes the eye of
his slave, male or female, and destroys
it, he shall let the slave go free for the
eye's sake. 27 If he knocks out the
tooth of his slave, male or female, he
shall let the slave go free for the
tooth's sake.

28 "When an ox gores a man or a
woman to death, the ox shall be
stoned, and its flesh shall not be eaten;
but the owner of the ox shall be clear.
29 But if the ox has been accustomed
to gore in the past, and its owner has
been warned but has not kept it in,
and it kills a man or a woman, the ox
shall be stoned, and its owner also
shall be put to death. 30 If a ransom is
laid on him, then he shall give for the
redemption of his life whatever is laid
upon him. 31 If it gores a man's son
or daughter, he shall be dealt with
according to this same rule. 32 If the
ox gores a slave, male or female, the
owner shall give to their master thirty
shekels of silver, and the ox shall be
stoned.

[g] Another reading is *so that he has not designated her* [h] Heb *he shall*

20.25: Deut 27.5-6. **21.2-11:** Lev 25.39-46; Deut 15.12-18.
21.12: Ex 20.13; Lev 24.17; Deut 5.17; Mt 5.21. **21.13:** Num 35.10-34; Deut 19.1-13; Josh 20.1-9.
21.16: Deut 24.7. **21.17:** Lev 20.9; Mt 15.4; Mk 7.10. **21.23-25:** Lev 24.19-20; Deut 19.21; Mt 5.38.

33 "When a man leaves a pit open,
or when a man digs a pit and does not
cover it, and an ox or an ass falls into
it, 34 the owner of the pit shall make
it good; he shall give money to its
owner, and the dead beast shall be
his.

35 "When one man's ox hurts another's, so that it dies, then they shall
sell the live ox and divide the price of
it; and the dead beast also they shall
divide. 36 Or if it is known that the ox
has been accustomed to gore in the
past, and its owner has not kept it in,
he shall pay ox for ox, and the dead
beast shall be his.

22[i] "If a man steals an ox or a
sheep, and kills it or sells it, he
shall pay five oxen for an ox, and four
sheep for a sheep.[j] He shall make
restitution; if he has nothing, then he
shall be sold for his theft. 4 If the
stolen beast is found alive in his possession, whether it is an ox or an ass
or a sheep, he shall pay double.

2[k] "If a thief is found breaking in,
and is struck so that he dies, there
shall be no bloodguilt for him; 3 but
if the sun has risen upon him, there
shall be bloodguilt for him.

5 "When a man causes a field or
vineyard to be grazed over, or lets his
beast loose and it feeds in another
man's field, he shall make restitution
from the best in his own field and in
his own vineyard.

6 "When fire breaks out and catches
in thorns so that the stacked grain or
the standing grain or the field is consumed, he that kindled the fire shall
make full restitution.

7 "If a man delivers to his neighbor
money or goods to keep, and it is
stolen out of the man's house, then, if
the thief is found, he shall pay double.
8 If the thief is not found, the owner
of the house shall come near to God,
to show whether or not he has put his
hand to his neighbor's goods.

9 "For every breach of trust,
whether it is for ox, for ass, for sheep,
for clothing, or for any kind of lost
thing, of which one says, 'This is it,'
the case of both parties shall come before God; he whom God shall condemn shall pay double to his neighbor.

10 "If a man delivers to his neighbor an ass or an ox or a sheep or any
beast to keep, and it dies or is hurt or
is driven away, without any one seeing
it, 11 an oath by the LORD shall be
between them both to see whether he
has not put his hand to his neighbor's
property; and the owner shall accept
the oath, and he shall not make restitution. 12 But if it is stolen from him, he
shall make restitution to its owner. 13 If
it is torn by beasts, let him bring it as
evidence; he shall not make restitution
for what has been torn.

14 "If a man borrows anything of
his neighbor, and it is hurt or dies, the
owner not being with it, he shall make
full restitution. 15 If the owner was
with it, he shall not make restitution;
if it was hired, it came for its hire.[l]

16 "If a man seduces a virgin who
is not betrothed, and lies with her, he
shall give the marriage present for her,
and make her his wife. 17 If her father
utterly refuses to give her to him, he
shall pay money equivalent to the
marriage present for virgins.

18 "You shall not permit a sorceress to live.

19 "Whoever lies with a beast shall
be put to death.

20 "Whoever sacrifices to any god,
save to the LORD only, shall be utterly
destroyed.

21 "You shall not wrong a stranger
or oppress him, for you were strangers
in the land of Egypt. 22 You shall not
afflict any widow or orphan. 23 If you
do afflict them, and they cry out to
me, I will surely hear their cry; 24 and
my wrath will burn, and I will kill you
with the sword, and your wives shall
become widows and your children
fatherless.

25 "If you lend money to any of my
people with you who is poor, you shall
not be to him as a creditor, and you
shall not exact interest from him. 26 If
ever you take your neighbor's garment
in pledge, you shall restore it to him
before the sun goes down; 27 for that
is his only covering, it is his mantle for
his body; in what else shall he sleep?

[i] Ch 21.37 in Heb
[j] Restoring the second half of verse 3 with 4 to their place immediately following verse 1
[k] Ch 22.1 in Heb [l] Or *it is reckoned in* (Heb *comes into*) *its hire*
22.7-15: Lev 5.14-6.7; Num 5.5-8. **22.16-17:** Deut 22.28-29. **22.18:** Lev 20.27; Deut 18.10.
22.19: Lev 18.23; 20.15-16; Deut 27.21. **22.21:** Ex 23.9; Lev 19.33-34; Deut 27.19.
22.22: Deut 24.17. **22.25-27:** Lev 25.36-37; Deut 23.19-20.

And if he cries to me, I will hear, for
I am compassionate.
28 "You shall not revile God, nor
curse a ruler of your people.
29 "You shall not delay to offer
from the fulness of your harvest and
from the outflow of your presses.
"The first-born of your sons you
shall give to me. 30 You shall do likewise with your oxen and with your
sheep: seven days it shall be with its
dam; on the eighth day you shall give
it to me.
31 "You shall be men consecrated
to me; therefore you shall not eat any
flesh that is torn by beasts in the field;
you shall cast it to the dogs.
23 "You shall not utter a false
report. You shall not join hands
with a wicked man, to be a malicious
witness. 2 You shall not follow a
multitude to do evil; nor shall you
bear witness in a suit, turning aside
after a multitude, so as to pervert
justice; 3 nor shall you be partial to a
poor man in his suit.
4 "If you meet your enemy's ox or
his ass going astray, you shall bring it
back to him. 5 If you see the ass of one
who hates you lying under its burden,
you shall refrain from leaving him with
it, you shall help him to lift it up.[m]
6 "You shall not pervert the justice
due to your poor in his suit. 7 Keep
far from a false charge, and do not
slay the innocent and righteous, for I
will not acquit the wicked. 8 And you
shall take no bribe, for a bribe blinds
the officials, and subverts the cause of
those who are in the right.
9 "You shall not oppress a stranger;
you know the heart of a stranger, for
you were strangers in the land of
Egypt.
10 "For six years you shall sow
your land and gather in its yield; 11 but
the seventh year you shall let it rest
and lie fallow, that the poor of your
people may eat; and what they leave
the wild beasts may eat. You shall do
likewise with your vineyard, and with
your olive orchard.
12 "Six days you shall do your
work, but on the seventh day you shall
rest; that your ox and your ass may
have rest, and the son of your bond-
maid, and the alien, may be refreshed.
13 Take heed to all that I have said to
you; and make no mention of the
names of other gods, nor let such be
heard out of your mouth.
14 "Three times in the year you
shall keep a feast to me. 15 You shall
keep the feast of unleavened bread; as
I commanded you, you shall eat unleavened bread for seven days at the
appointed time in the month of Ā'bib,
for in it you came out of Egypt. None
shall appear before me empty-handed.
16 You shall keep the feast of harvest,
of the first fruits of your labor, of
what you sow in the field. You shall
keep the feast of ingathering at the
end of the year, when you gather in
from the field the fruit of your labor.
17 Three times in the year shall all
your males appear before the Lord
GOD.
18 "You shall not offer the blood
of my sacrifice with leavened bread,
or let the fat of my feast remain until
the morning.
19 "The first of the first fruits of
your ground you shall bring into the
house of the LORD your God.
"You shall not boil a kid in its
mother's milk.
20 "Behold, I send an angel before
you, to guard you on the way and to
bring you to the place which I have
prepared. 21 Give heed to him and
hearken to his voice, do not rebel
against him, for he will not pardon
your transgression; for my name is in
him.
22 "But if you hearken attentively
to his voice and do all that I say, then
I will be an enemy to your enemies
and an adversary to your adversaries.
23 "When my angel goes before
you, and brings you in to the Am'ŏ-
rītes, and the Hit'tītes, and the Per'iz-
zītes, and the Canaanites, the Hī'vītes,
and the Jeb'ū-sītes, and I blot them
out, 24 you shall not bow down to
their gods, nor serve them, nor do
according to their works, but you shall
utterly overthrow them and break their

[m] Gk: Heb obscure

22.28: Acts 23.5. **22.29:** Ex 23.16, 19; Deut 26.2-11; Ex 13.2, 11-16.
22.31: Ex 19.6; Lev 11.44; 19.1; 7.24; 17.15. **23.1:** Ex 20.16; 23.7; Deut 5.20; 19.15-21.
23.3, 6: Lev 19.15. **23.7:** Ex 20.16; 23.1. **23.8:** Deut 16.19.
23.9: Ex 22.21; Lev 19.33-34; Deut 27.19. **23.10-11:** Lev 25.1-7.
23.12: Ex 20.8-11; 31.15-17; 34.21; 35.2; Deut 5.12-15.
23.14-17: Ex 34.22-24; Lev 23.1-44; Deut 16.1-17. **23.18:** Ex 12.10; Ex 34.25; Lev 2.11; Lev 7.15.
23.19: Ex 22.29; 34.26; Deut 26.2-11; 14.21.

pillars in pieces. 25 You shall serve the
LORD your God, and I[n] will bless your
bread and your water; and I will take
sickness away from the midst of you.
26 None shall cast her young or be
barren in your land; I will fulfil the
number of your days. 27 I will send
my terror before you, and will throw
into confusion all the people against
whom you shall come, and I will make
all your enemies turn their backs to
you. 28 And I will send hornets before
you, which shall drive out Hī'vīte,
Canaanite, and Hit'tīte from before
you. 29 I will not drive them out from
before you in one year, lest the land
become desolate and the wild beasts
multiply against you. 30 Little by little
I will drive them out from before you,
until you are increased and possess the
land. 31 And I will set your bounds
from the Red Sea to the sea of the
Philistines, and from the wilderness
to the Eū·phrā'tēs; for I will deliver
the inhabitants of the land into your
hand, and you shall drive them out
before you. 32 You shall make no
covenant with them or with their gods.
33 They shall not dwell in your land,
lest they make you sin against me; for
if you serve their gods, it will surely
be a snare to you."

24 And he said to Moses, "Come
up to the LORD, you and Aaron,
Nā'dab, and A·bī'hū, and seventy of
the elders of Israel, and worship afar
off. 2 Moses alone shall come near to
the LORD; but the others shall not
come near, and the people shall not
come up with him."

3 Moses came and told the people
all the words of the LORD and all the
ordinances; and all the people answered
with one voice, and said, "All the
words which the LORD has spoken we
will do." 4 And Moses wrote all the
words of the LORD. And he rose early
in the morning, and built an altar at
the foot of the mountain, and twelve
pillars, according to the twelve tribes
of Israel. 5 And he sent young men of
the people of Israel, who offered burnt
offerings and sacrificed peace offerings
of oxen to the LORD. 6 And Moses took
half of the blood and put it in basins,
and half of the blood he threw against
the altar. 7 Then he took the book of
the covenant, and read it in the hearing
of the people; and they said, "All that
the LORD has spoken we will do, and
we will be obedient." 8 And Moses
took the blood and threw it upon the
people, and said, "Behold the blood of
the covenant which the LORD has
made with you in accordance with all
these words."

9 Then Moses and Aaron, Nā'dab,
and A·bī'hū, and seventy of the elders
of Israel went up, 10 and they saw the
God of Israel; and there was under
his feet as it were a pavement of
sapphire stone, like the very heaven
for clearness. 11 And he did not lay his
hand on the chief men of the people
of Israel; they beheld God, and ate
and drank.

12 The LORD said to Moses, "Come
up to me on the mountain, and wait
there; and I will give you the tables of
stone, with the law and the commandment, which I have written for their
instruction." 13 So Moses rose with
his servant Joshua, and Moses went
up into the mountain of God. 14 And
he said to the elders, "Tarry here for
us, until we come to you again; and,
behold, Aaron and Hûr are with you;
whoever has a cause, let him go to
them."

15 Then Moses went up on the
mountain, and the cloud covered the
mountain. 16 The glory of the LORD
settled on Mount Sinai, and the cloud
covered it six days; and on the seventh
day he called to Moses out of the midst
of the cloud. 17 Now the appearance
of the glory of the LORD was like a
devouring fire on the top of the mountain in the sight of the people of Israel.
18 And Moses entered the cloud, and
went up on the mountain. And Moses
was on the mountain forty days and
forty nights.

25 The LORD said to Moses,
2 "Speak to the people of Israel,
that they take for me an offering; from
every man whose heart makes him
willing you shall receive the offering
for me. 3 And this is the offering which
you shall receive from them: gold,
silver, and bronze, 4 blue and purple
and scarlet stuff and fine twined linen,
goats' hair, 5 tanned rams' skins, goatskins, acacia wood, 6 oil for the lamps,
spices for the anointing oil and for the
fragrant incense, 7 onyx stones, and

n Gk Vg: Heb *he*

24.8: Mt 26.28; Mk 14.24; Lk 22.20; 1 Cor 11.25; Heb 9.20; 10.29. **24.12:** 2 Cor 3.3.
25-31: Ex 35-40. **25.2-8:** Ex 35.4-9.

stones for setting, for the ephod and
for the breastpiece. 8And let them
make me a sanctuary, that I may dwell
in their midst. 9According to all that
I show you concerning the pattern of
the tabernacle, and of all its furniture,
so you shall make it.

10 "They shall make an ark of
acacia wood; two cubits and a half
shall be its length, a cubit and a half
its breadth, and a cubit and a half its
height. 11And you shall overlay it with
pure gold, within and without shall
you overlay it, and you shall make
upon it a molding of gold round about.
12And you shall cast four rings of gold
for it and put them on its four feet,
two rings on the one side of it, and two
rings on the other side of it. 13 You
shall make poles of acacia wood, and
overlay them with gold. 14And you
shall put the poles into the rings on
the sides of the ark, to carry the ark
by them. 15 The poles shall remain in
the rings of the ark; they shall not be
taken from it. 16And you shall put
into the ark the testimony which I
shall give you. 17 Then you shall make
a mercy seat[o] of pure gold; two cubits
and a half shall be its length, and a
cubit and a half its breadth. 18And
you shall make two cherubim of gold;
of hammered work shall you make
them, on the two ends of the mercy
seat. 19 Make one cherub on the one
end, and one cherub on the other end;
of one piece with the mercy seat shall
you make the cherubim on its two
ends. 20 The cherubim shall spread
out their wings above, overshadowing
the mercy seat with their wings, their
faces one to another; toward the mercy
seat shall the faces of the cherubim
be. 21And you shall put the mercy
seat on the top of the ark; and in the
ark you shall put the testimony that I
shall give you. 22 There I will meet with
you, and from above the mercy seat,
from between the two cherubim that
are upon the ark of the testimony, I
will speak with you of all that I will
give you in commandment for the
people of Israel.

23 "And you shall make a table of
acacia wood; two cubits shall be its
length, a cubit its breadth, and a cubit
and a half its height. 24 You shall overlay it with pure gold, and make a
molding of gold around it. 25And you
shall make around it a frame a handbreadth wide, and a molding of gold
around the frame. 26And you shall
make for it four rings of gold, and
fasten the rings to the four corners at
its four legs. 27 Close to the frame the
rings shall lie, as holders for the poles
to carry the table. 28 You shall make
the poles of acacia wood, and overlay
them with gold, and the table shall be
carried with these. 29And you shall
make its plates and dishes for incense,
and its flagons and bowls with which
to pour libations; of pure gold you
shall make them. 30And you shall set
the bread of the Presence on the table
before me always.

31 "And you shall make a lampstand of pure gold. The base and the
shaft of the lampstand shall be made
of hammered work; its cups, its capitals, and its flowers shall be of one
piece with it; 32 and there shall be six
branches going out of its sides, three
branches of the lampstand out of one
side of it and three branches of the
lampstand out of the other side of it;
33 three cups made like almonds, each
with capital and flower, on one branch,
and three cups made like almonds,
each with capital and flower, on the
other branch—so for the six branches
going out of the lampstand; 34 and on
the lampstand itself four cups made
like almonds, with their capitals and
flowers, 35 and a capital of one piece
with it under each pair of the six
branches going out from the lampstand. 36 Their capitals and their
branches shall be of one piece with it,
the whole of it one piece of hammered
work of pure gold. 37And you shall
make the seven lamps for it; and the
lamps shall be set up so as to give
light upon the space in front of it.
38 Its snuffers and their trays shall be
of pure gold. 39 Of a talent of pure
gold shall it be made, with all these
utensils. 40And see that you make them
after the pattern for them, which is
being shown you on the mountain.

26 "Moreover you shall make the
tabernacle with ten curtains of
fine twined linen and blue and purple
and scarlet stuff; with cherubim skilfully worked shall you make them.
2 The length of each curtain shall be

[o] Or *cover*

25.10-22: Ex 37.1-9. **25.23-30:** Ex 37.10-15. **25.30:** Ex 39.36; 40.23; Lev 24.5-9.
25.31-40: Ex 37.17-24. **25.40:** Acts 7.44; Heb 8.5. **26.1-14:** Ex 36.8-19.

twenty-eight cubits, and the breadth
of each curtain four cubits; all the
curtains shall have one measure. 3 Five
curtains shall be coupled to one
another; and the other five curtains
shall be coupled to one another. 4 And
you shall make loops of blue on the
edge of the outmost curtain in the first
set; and likewise you shall make loops
on the edge of the outmost curtain in
the second set. 5 Fifty loops you shall
make on the one curtain, and fifty
loops you shall make on the edge of
the curtain that is in the second set;
the loops shall be opposite one another.
6 And you shall make fifty clasps of
gold, and couple the curtains one to
the other with the clasps, that the
tabernacle may be one whole.

7 "You shall also make curtains of
goats' hair for a tent over the tabernacle; eleven curtains shall you make.
8 The length of each curtain shall be
thirty cubits, and the breadth of each
curtain four cubits; the eleven curtains
shall have the same measure. 9 And you
shall couple five curtains by themselves, and six curtains by themselves,
and the sixth curtain you shall double
over at the front of the tent. 10 And
you shall make fifty loops on the edge
of the curtain that is outmost in one
set, and fifty loops on the edge of the
curtain which is outmost in the second
set.

11 "And you shall make fifty clasps
of bronze, and put the clasps into the
loops, and couple the tent together
that it may be one whole. 12 And the
part that remains of the curtains of the
tent, the half curtain that remains,
shall hang over the back of the tabernacle. 13 And the cubit on the one side,
and the cubit on the other side, of
what remains in the length of the
curtains of the tent shall hang over the
sides of the tabernacle, on this side
and that side, to cover it. 14 And you
shall make for the tent a covering of
tanned rams' skins and goatskins.

15 "And you shall make upright
frames for the tabernacle of acacia
wood. 16 Ten cubits shall be the length
of a frame, and a cubit and a half the
breadth of each frame. 17 There shall
be two tenons in each frame, for fitting
together; so shall you do for all the
frames of the tabernacle. 18 You shall
make the frames for the tabernacle:
twenty frames for the south side; 19 and
forty bases of silver you shall make
under the twenty frames, two bases
under one frame for its two tenons,
and two bases under another frame for
its two tenons; 20 and for the second
side of the tabernacle, on the north
side twenty frames, 21 and their forty
bases of silver, two bases under one
frame, and two bases under another
frame; 22 and for the rear of the
tabernacle westward you shall make
six frames. 23 And you shall make two
frames for corners of the tabernacle in
the rear; 24 they shall be separate
beneath, but joined at the top, at the
first ring; thus shall it be with both of
them; they shall form the two corners.
25 And there shall be eight frames, with
their bases of silver, sixteen bases; two
bases under one frame, and two bases
under another frame.

26 "And you shall make bars of
acacia wood, five for the frames of the
one side of the tabernacle, 27 and five
bars for the frames of the other side of
the tabernacle, and five bars for the
frames of the side of the tabernacle at
the rear westward. 28 The middle bar,
halfway up the frames, shall pass
through from end to end. 29 You shall
overlay the frames with gold, and
shall make their rings of gold for
holders for the bars; and you shall
overlay the bars with gold. 30 And you
shall erect the tabernacle according to
the plan for it which has been shown
you on the mountain.

31 "And you shall make a veil of
blue and purple and scarlet stuff and
fine twined linen; in skilled work shall
it be made, with cherubim; 32 and you
shall hang it upon four pillars of acacia
overlaid with gold, with hooks of
gold, upon four bases of silver. 33 And
you shall hang the veil from the clasps,
and bring the ark of the testimony in
thither within the veil; and the veil
shall separate for you the holy place
from the most holy. 34 You shall put
the mercy seat upon the ark of the
testimony in the most holy place. 35 And
you shall set the table outside the veil,
and the lampstand on the south side
of the tabernacle opposite the table;
and you shall put the table on the
north side.

36 "And you shall make a screen
for the door of the tent, of blue and
purple and scarlet stuff and fine twined
linen, embroidered with needlework.

26.15-29: Ex 36.20-34. **26.31-37:** Ex 36.35-38.

37 And you shall make for the screen
five pillars of acacia, and overlay them
with gold; their hooks shall be of gold,
and you shall cast five bases of bronze
for them.

27 "You shall make the altar of
acacia wood, five cubits long
and five cubits broad; the altar shall
be square, and its height shall be three
cubits. 2 And you shall make horns for
it on its four corners; its horns shall be
of one piece with it, and you shall
overlay it with bronze. 3 You shall
make pots for it to receive its ashes,
and shovels and basins and forks and
firepans; all its utensils you shall make
of bronze. 4 You shall also make for
it a grating, a network of bronze; and
upon the net you shall make four
bronze rings at its four corners. 5 And
you shall set it under the ledge of the
altar so that the net shall extend halfway down the altar. 6 And you shall
make poles for the altar, poles of acacia
wood, and overlay them with bronze,
7 and the poles shall be put through
the rings, so that the poles shall be
upon the two sides of the altar, when
it is carried. 8 You shall make it hollow,
with boards; as it has been shown you
on the mountain, so shall it be made.

9 "You shall make the court of the
tabernacle. On the south side the court
shall have hangings of fine twined linen
a hundred cubits long for one side;
10 their pillars shall be twenty and
their bases twenty, of bronze, but the
hooks of the pillars and their fillets
shall be of silver. 11 And likewise for
its length on the north side there shall
be hangings a hundred cubits long,
their pillars twenty and their bases
twenty, of bronze, but the hooks of
the pillars and their fillets shall be of
silver. 12 And for the breadth of the
court on the west side there shall be
hangings for fifty cubits, with ten
pillars and ten bases. 13 The breadth
of the court on the front to the east
shall be fifty cubits. 14 The hangings
for the one side of the gate shall be
fifteen cubits, with three pillars and
three bases. 15 On the other side the
hangings shall be fifteen cubits, with
three pillars and three bases. 16 For
the gate of the court there shall be a
screen twenty cubits long, of blue and
purple and scarlet stuff and fine
twined linen, embroidered with
needlework; it shall have four pillars
and with them four bases. 17 All the
pillars around the court shall be filleted
with silver; their hooks shall be of
silver, and their bases of bronze. 18 The
length of the court shall be a hundred
cubits, the breadth fifty, and the
height five cubits, with hangings of
fine twined linen and bases of bronze.
19 All the utensils of the tabernacle for
every use, and all its pegs and all the
pegs of the court, shall be of bronze.

20 "And you shall command the
people of Israel that they bring to you
pure beaten olive oil for the light, that
a lamp may be set up to burn continually. 21 In the tent of meeting, outside the veil which is before the testimony, Aaron and his sons shall tend
it from evening to morning before the
LORD. It shall be a statute for ever to
be observed throughout their generations by the people of Israel.

28 "Then bring near to you
Aaron your brother, and his
sons with him, from among the people
of Israel, to serve me as priests—Aaron
and Aaron's sons, Nā'dab and Ȧ·bī'hū,
El·ē·ā'zȧr and Ith'ȧ·mär. 2 And you
shall make holy garments for Aaron
your brother, for glory and for beauty.
3 And you shall speak to all who have
ability, whom I have endowed with an
able mind, that they make Aaron's
garments to consecrate him for my
priesthood. 4 These are the garments
which they shall make: a breastpiece,
an ephod, a robe, a coat of checker
work, a turban, and a girdle; they shall
make holy garments for Aaron your
brother and his sons to serve me as
priests.

5 "They shall receive gold, blue
and purple and scarlet stuff, and fine
twined linen. 6 And they shall make the
ephod of gold, of blue and purple and
scarlet stuff, and of fine twined linen,
skilfully worked. 7 It shall have two
shoulder-pieces attached to its two
edges, that it may be joined together.
8 And the skilfully woven band upon
it, to gird it on, shall be of the same
workmanship and materials, of gold,
blue and purple and scarlet stuff, and
fine twined linen. 9 And you shall take
two onyx stones, and engrave on them
the names of the sons of Israel, 10 six
of their names on the one stone, and
the names of the remaining six on the
other stone, in the order of their birth.
11 As a jeweler engraves signets, so

27.1-8: Ex 38.1-7. **27.9-19:** Ex 38.9-20. **27.20-21:** Lev 24.1-4. **28.6-12:** Ex 39.2-7.

shall you engrave the two stones with
the names of the sons of Israel; you
shall enclose them in settings of gold
filigree. 12And you shall set the two
stones upon the shoulder-pieces of the
ephod, as stones of remembrance for
the sons of Israel; and Aaron shall
bear their names before the LORD upon
his two shoulders for remembrance.
13And you shall make settings of gold
filigree, 14 and two chains of pure gold,
twisted like cords; and you shall attach
the corded chains to the settings.

15 "And you shall make a breastpiece of judgment, in skilled work;
like the work of the ephod you shall
make it; of gold, blue and purple and
scarlet stuff, and fine twined linen
shall you make it. 16 It shall be square
and double, a span its length and a
span its breadth. 17And you shall set
in it four rows of stones. A row of
sardius, topaz, and carbuncle shall be
the first row; 18 and the second row
an emerald, a sapphire, and a diamond;
19 and the third row a jacinth, an
agate, and an amethyst; 20 and the
fourth row a beryl, an onyx, and a
jasper; they shall be set in gold filigree.
21 There shall be twelve stones with
their names according to the names of
the sons of Israel; they shall be like
signets, each engraved with its name,
for the twelve tribes. 22And you shall
make for the breastpiece twisted chains
like cords, of pure gold; 23 and you
shall make for the breastpiece two
rings of gold, and put the two rings on
the two edges of the breastpiece. 24And
you shall put the two cords of gold in
the two rings at the edges of the
breastpiece; 25 the two ends of the two
cords you shall attach to the two
settings of filigree, and so attach it in
front to the shoulder-pieces of the
ephod. 26And you shall make two
rings of gold, and put them at the two
ends of the breastpiece, on its inside
edge next to the ephod. 27And you
shall make two rings of gold, and
attach them in front to the lower part
of the two shoulder-pieces of the
ephod, at its joining above the skilfully woven band of the ephod. 28And
they shall bind the breastpiece by its
rings to the rings of the ephod with a
lace of blue, that it may lie upon the
skilfully woven band of the ephod,
and that the breastpiece shall not come
loose from the ephod. 29 So Aaron
shall bear the names of the sons of
Israel in the breastpiece of judgment
upon his heart, when he goes into the
holy place, to bring them to continual
remembrance before the LORD. 30And
in the breastpiece of judgment you
shall put the Ū'rim and the Thum'-
mim, and they shall be upon Aaron's
heart, when he goes in before the
LORD; thus Aaron shall bear the
judgment of the people of Israel upon
his heart before the LORD continually.

31 "And you shall make the robe
of the ephod all of blue. 32 It shall have
in it an opening for the head, with a
woven binding around the opening,
like the opening in a garment,[p] that it
may not be torn. 33 On its skirts you
shall make pomegranates of blue and
purple and scarlet stuff, around its
skirts, with bells of gold between them,
34 a golden bell and a pomegranate, a
golden bell and a pomegranate, round
about on the skirts of the robe. 35And
it shall be upon Aaron when he
ministers, and its sound shall be heard
when he goes into the holy place before
the LORD, and when he comes out, lest
he die.

36 "And you shall make a plate of
pure gold, and engrave on it, like the
engraving of a signet, 'Holy to the
LORD.' 37And you shall fasten it on
the turban by a lace of blue; it shall be
on the front of the turban. 38 It shall
be upon Aaron's forehead, and Aaron
shall take upon himself any guilt
incurred in the holy offering which the
people of Israel hallow as their holy
gifts; it shall always be upon his forehead, that they may be accepted before
the LORD.

39 "And you shall weave the coat
in checker work of fine linen, and you
shall make a turban of fine linen, and
you shall make a girdle embroidered
with needlework.

40 "And for Aaron's sons you shall
make coats and girdles and caps; you
shall make them for glory and beauty.
41And you shall put them upon Aaron
your brother, and upon his sons with
him, and shall anoint them and ordain
them and consecrate them, that they
may serve me as priests. 42And you
shall make for them linen breeches to
cover their naked flesh; from the loins
to the thighs they shall reach; 43 and

[p] The Hebrew word is of uncertain meaning

28.15-28: Ex 39.8-21 **28.31-34:** Ex 39.22-26. **28.36-37:** Ex 39.30-31 **28.39-40, 42:** Ex 39.27-29.

they shall be upon Aaron, and upon
his sons, when they go into the tent
of meeting, or when they come near
the altar to minister in the holy place;
lest they bring guilt upon themselves
and die. This shall be a perpetual
statute for him and for his descendants
after him.

29 "Now this is what you shall do
to them to consecrate them, that
they may serve me as priests. Take
one young bull and two rams without
blemish, 2 and unleavened bread, unleavened cakes mixed with oil, and
unleavened wafers spread with oil. You
shall make them of fine wheat flour.
3 And you shall put them in one basket
and bring them in the basket, and
bring the bull and the two rams. 4 You
shall bring Aaron and his sons to the
door of the tent of meeting, and wash
them with water. 5 And you shall take
the garments, and put on Aaron the
coat and the robe of the ephod, and
the ephod, and the breastpiece, and
gird him with the skilfully woven band
of the ephod; 6 and you shall set the
turban on his head, and put the holy
crown upon the turban. 7 And you
shall take the anointing oil, and pour
it on his head and anoint him. 8 Then
you shall bring his sons, and put coats
on them, 9 and you shall gird them
with girdles[q] and bind caps on them;
and the priesthood shall be theirs by
a perpetual statute. Thus you shall
ordain Aaron and his sons.

10 "Then you shall bring the bull
before the tent of meeting. Aaron and
his sons shall lay their hands upon the
head of the bull, 11 and you shall kill
the bull before the LORD, at the door
of the tent of meeting, 12 and shall take
part of the blood of the bull and put
it upon the horns of the altar with your
finger, and the rest of[r] the blood you
shall pour out at the base of the altar.
13 And you shall take all the fat that
covers the entrails, and the appendage
of the liver, and the two kidneys with
the fat that is on them, and burn them
upon the altar. 14 But the flesh of the
bull, and its skin, and its dung, you
shall burn with fire outside the camp;
it is a sin offering.

15 "Then you shall take one of the
rams, and Aaron and his sons shall lay
their hands upon the head of the ram,
16 and you shall slaughter the ram, and
shall take its blood and throw it against
the altar round about. 17 Then you
shall cut the ram into pieces, and wash
its entrails and its legs, and put them
with its pieces and its head, 18 and
burn the whole ram upon the altar; it
is a burnt offering to the LORD; it is a
pleasing odor, an offering by fire to
the LORD.

19 "You shall take the other ram;
and Aaron and his sons shall lay their
hands upon the head of the ram,
20 and you shall kill the ram, and take
part of its blood and put it upon the
tip of the right ear of Aaron and upon
the tips of the right ears of his sons,
and upon the thumbs of their right
hands, and upon the great toes of their
right feet, and throw the rest of the
blood against the altar round about.
21 Then you shall take part of the
blood that is on the altar, and of the
anointing oil, and sprinkle it upon
Aaron and his garments, and upon his
sons and his sons' garments with him;
and he and his garments shall be holy,
and his sons and his sons' garments
with him.

22 "You shall also take the fat of
the ram, and the fat tail, and the fat
that covers the entrails, and the appendage of the liver, and the two
kidneys with the fat that is on them,
and the right thigh (for it is a ram of
ordination), 23 and one loaf of bread,
and one cake of bread with oil, and
one wafer, out of the basket of unleavened bread that is before the
LORD; 24 and you shall put all these in
the hands of Aaron and in the hands
of his sons, and wave them for a wave
offering before the LORD. 25 Then you
shall take them from their hands, and
burn them on the altar in addition to
the burnt offering, as a pleasing odor
before the LORD; it is an offering by
fire to the LORD.

26 "And you shall take the breast
of the ram of Aaron's ordination and
wave it for a wave offering before the
LORD; and it shall be your portion.
27 And you shall consecrate the breast
of the wave offering, and the thigh of
the priests' portion, which is waved,
and which is offered from the ram of
ordination, since it is for Aaron and
for his sons. 28 It shall be for Aaron
and his sons as a perpetual due from
the people of Israel, for it is the priests'

[q] Gk; Heb *girdles, Aaron and his sons* [r] Heb *all*
29.1-37: Lev 8.1-34. **29.18:** Eph 5.2; Phil 4.18.

portion to be offered by the people of
Israel from their peace offerings; it is
their offering to the LORD.
29 "The holy garments of Aaron
shall be for his sons after him, to be
anointed in them and ordained in them.
30 The son who is priest in his place
shall wear them seven days, when he
comes into the tent of meeting to
minister in the holy place.
31 "You shall take the ram of ordination, and boil its flesh in a holy place;
32 and Aaron and his sons shall eat the
flesh of the ram and the bread that is
in the basket, at the door of the tent
of meeting. 33 They shall eat those
things with which atonement was
made, to ordain and consecrate them,
but an outsider shall not eat of them,
because they are holy. 34 And if any of
the flesh for the ordination, or of the
bread, remain until the morning, then
you shall burn the remainder with fire;
it shall not be eaten, because it is holy.
35 "Thus you shall do to Aaron and
to his sons, according to all that I have
commanded you; through seven days
shall you ordain them, 36 and every
day you shall offer a bull as a sin offering for atonement. Also you shall offer
a sin offering for the altar, when you
make atonement for it, and shall
anoint it, to consecrate it. 37 Seven
days you shall make atonement for
the altar, and consecrate it, and the
altar shall be most holy; whatever
touches the altar shall become holy.
38 "Now this is what you shall
offer upon the altar: two lambs a year
old day by day continually. 39 One
lamb you shall offer in the morning,
and the other lamb you shall offer in
the evening; 40 and with the first lamb
a tenth measure of fine flour mingled
with a fourth of a hin of beaten oil, and
a fourth of a hin of wine for a libation.
41 And the other lamb you shall offer
in the evening, and shall offer with it
a cereal offering and its libation, as in
the morning, for a pleasing odor, an
offering by fire to the LORD. 42 It shall
be a continual burnt offering throughout your generations at the door of the
tent of meeting before the LORD, where
I will meet with you, to speak there
to you. 43 There I will meet with the
people of Israel, and it shall be sanctified by my glory; 44 I will consecrate
the tent of meeting and the altar;
Aaron also and his sons I will consecrate, to serve me as priests. 45 And I
will dwell among the people of Israel,
and will be their God. 46 And they shall
know that I am the LORD their God,
who brought them forth out of the
land of Egypt that I might dwell
among them; I am the LORD their God.

30 "You shall make an altar to
burn incense upon; of acacia
wood shall you make it. 2 A cubit shall
be its length, and a cubit its breadth;
it shall be square, and two cubits shall
be its height; its horns shall be of one
piece with it. 3 And you shall overlay it
with pure gold, its top and its sides
round about and its horns; and you
shall make for it a molding of gold
round about. 4 And two golden rings
shall you make for it; under its molding
on two opposite sides of it shall you
make them, and they shall be holders
for poles with which to carry it. 5 You
shall make the poles of acacia wood,
and overlay them with gold. 6 And you
shall put it before the veil that is by
the ark of the testimony, before the
mercy seat that is over the testimony,
where I will meet with you. 7 And
Aaron shall burn fragrant incense on
it; every morning when he dresses the
lamps he shall burn it, 8 and when
Aaron sets up the lamps in the evening,
he shall burn it, a perpetual incense
before the LORD throughout your generations. 9 You shall offer no unholy
incense thereon, nor burnt offering,
nor cereal offering; and you shall pour
no libation thereon. 10 Aaron shall make
atonement upon its horns once a year;
with the blood of the sin offering of
atonement he shall make atonement
for it once in the year throughout your
generations; it is most holy to the
LORD.
11 The LORD said to Moses,
12 "When you take the census of the
people of Israel, then each shall give a
ransom for himself to the LORD when
you number them, that there be no
plague among them when you number
them. 13 Each who is numbered in the
census shall give this: half a shekel
according to the shekel of the sanctuary (the shekel is twenty gerahs), half
a shekel as an offering to the LORD.
14 Every one who is numbered in the
census, from twenty years old and upward, shall give the LORD's offering.
15 The rich shall not give more, and
the poor shall not give less, than the

29.38-42: Num 28.3-10. **30.1-5:** Ex 37.25-29. **30.11-16:** Ex 38.25-26.

half shekel, when you give the LORD's
offering to make atonement for yourselves. 16 And you shall take the atonement money from the people of Israel,
and shall appoint it for the service of
the tent of meeting; that it may bring
the people of Israel to remembrance
before the LORD, so as to make atonement for yourselves."
17 The LORD said to Moses,
18 "You shall also make a laver of
bronze, with its base of bronze, for
washing. And you shall put it between
the tent of meeting and the altar, and
you shall put water in it, 19 with which
Aaron and his sons shall wash their
hands and their feet. 20 When they go
into the tent of meeting, or when they
come near the altar to minister, to
burn an offering by fire to the LORD,
they shall wash with water, lest they
die. 21 They shall wash their hands
and their feet, lest they die: it shall be
a statute for ever to them, even to him
and to his descendants throughout
their generations."
22 Moreover, the LORD said to
Moses, 23 "Take the finest spices: of
liquid myrrh five hundred shekels, and
of sweet-smelling cinnamon half as
much, that is, two hundred and fifty,
and of aromatic cane two hundred and
fifty, 24 and of cassia five hundred,
according to the shekel of the sanctuary, and of olive oil a hin; 25 and you
shall make of these a sacred anointing
oil blended as by the perfumer; a holy
anointing oil it shall be. 26 And you
shall anoint with it the tent of meeting
and the ark of the testimony, 27 and
the table and all its utensils, and the
lampstand and its utensils, and the
altar of incense, 28 and the altar of
burnt offering with all its utensils and
the laver and its base; 29 you shall
consecrate them, that they may be
most holy; whatever touches them will
become holy. 30 And you shall anoint
Aaron and his sons, and consecrate
them, that they may serve me as priests.
31 And you shall say to the people of
Israel, 'This shall be my holy anointing
oil throughout your generations. 32 It
shall not be poured upon the bodies
of ordinary men, and you shall make
no other like it in composition; it is
holy, and it shall be holy to you.
33 Whoever compounds any like it or
whoever puts any of it on an outsider
shall be cut off from his people.' "
34 And the LORD said to Moses,
"Take sweet spices, stacte, and ony-
cha, and galbanum, sweet spices with
pure frankincense (of each shall there
be an equal part), 35 and make an
incense blended as by the perfumer,
seasoned with salt, pure and holy;
36 and you shall beat some of it very
small, and put part of it before the
testimony in the tent of meeting where
I shall meet with you; it shall be for
you most holy. 37 And the incense which
you shall make according to its composition, you shall not make for yourselves; it shall be for you holy to the
LORD. 38 Whoever makes any like it to
use as perfume shall be cut off from
his people."
31 The LORD said to Moses, 2 "See,
I have called by name Bez'à·lel
the son of Ū'rī, son of Hûr, of the
tribe of Judah: 3 and I have filled him
with the Spirit of God, with ability
and intelligence, with knowledge and
all craftsmanship, 4 to devise artistic
designs, to work in gold, silver, and
bronze, 5 in cutting stones for setting,
and in carving wood, for work in every
craft. 6 And behold, I have appointed
with him Ō·hō'lĭ·ab, the son of À·his'-
à·mach, of the tribe of Dan; and I have
given to all able men ability, that they
may make all that I have commanded
you: 7 the tent of meeting, and th ark
of the testimony, and the mercy seat
that is thereon, and all the furnishings
of the tent, 8 the table and its utensils,
and the pure lampstand with all its
utensils, and the altar of incense, 9 and
the altar of burnt offering with all its
utensils, and the laver and its base,
10 and the finely worked garments, the
holy garments for Aaron the priest and
the garments of his sons, for their
service as priests, 11 and the anointing
oil and the fragrant incense for the
holy place. According to all that I have
commanded you they shall do."
12 And the LORD said to Moses,
13 "Say to the people of Israel, 'You
shall keep my sabbaths, for this is a
sign between me and you throughout
your generations, that you may know
that I, the LORD, sanctify you. 14 You
shall keep the sabbath, because it is
holy for you; every one who profanes
it shall be put to death; whoever does
any work on it, that soul shall be cut
off from among his people. 15 Six days
shall work be done, but the seventh

30.18: Ex 38.8. **30.22-33:** Ex 37.29. **31.1-6:** Ex 35.30-36.1. **31.12-17:** Ex 20.8; 23.12; 35.2; Deut 5.12-15.

day is a sabbath of solemn rest, holy to
the LORD; whoever does any work on
the sabbath day shall be put to death.
16 Therefore the people of Israel shall
keep the sabbath, observing the sabbath throughout their generations, as
a perpetual covenant. 17 It is a sign for
ever between me and the people of
Israel that in six days the LORD made
heaven and earth, and on the seventh
day he rested, and was refreshed.' "
18 And he gave to Moses, when he
had made an end of speaking with him
upon Mount Sinai, the two tables of
the testimony, tables of stone, written
with the finger of God.

32 When the people saw that
Moses delayed to come down
from the mountain, the people gathered
themselves together to Aaron, and said
to him, "Up, make us gods, who shall
go before us; as for this Moses, the
man who brought us up out of the
land of Egypt, we do not know what
has become of him." 2 And Aaron said
to them, "Take off the rings of gold
which are in the ears of your wives,
your sons, and your daughters, and
bring them to me." 3 So all the people
took off the rings of gold which were
in their ears, and brought them to
Aaron. 4 And he received the gold at
their hand, and fashioned it with a
graving tool, and made a molten calf;
and they said, "These are your gods,
O Israel, who brought you up out of
the land of Egypt!" 5 When Aaron
saw this, he built an altar before it;
and Aaron made proclamation and
said, "Tomorrow shall be a feast to the
LORD." 6 And they rose up early on
the morrow, and offered burnt offerings and brought peace offerings; and
the people sat down to eat and drink,
and rose up to play.
7 And the LORD said to Moses,
"Go down; for your people, whom you
brought up out of the land of Egypt,
have corrupted themselves; 8 they have
turned aside quickly out of the way
which I commanded them; they have
made for themselves a molten calf, and
have worshiped it and sacrificed to it,
and said, 'These are your gods, O
Israel, who brought you up out of the
land of Egypt!' " 9 And the LORD said
to Moses, "I have seen this people,
and behold, it is a stiff-necked people;
10 now therefore let me alone, that my
wrath may burn hot against them and
I may consume them; but of you I will
make a great nation."
11 But Moses besought the LORD
his God, and said, "O LORD, why does
thy wrath burn hot against thy people,
whom thou hast brought forth out of
the land of Egypt with great power
and with a mighty hand? 12 Why
should the Egyptians say, 'With evil
intent did he bring them forth, to slay
them in the mountains, and to consume
them from the face of the earth'? Turn
from thy fierce wrath, and repent of
this evil against thy people. 13 Remember Abraham, Isaac, and Israel,
thy servants, to whom thou didst
swear by thine own self, and didst say
to them, 'I will multiply your descendants as the stars of heaven, and all this
land that I have promised I will give
to your descendants, and they shall
inherit it for ever.' " 14 And the LORD
repented of the evil which he thought
to do to his people.
15 And Moses turned, and went
down from the mountain with the two
tables of the testimony in his hands,
tables that were written on both sides;
on the one side and on the other were
they written. 16 And the tables were
the work of God, and the writing was
the writing of God, graven upon the
tables. 17 When Joshua heard the noise
of the people as they shouted, he said
to Moses, "There is a noise of war in
the camp." 18 But he said, "It is not
the sound of shouting for victory, or
the sound of the cry of defeat, but the
sound of singing that I hear." 19 And
as soon as he came near the camp and
saw the calf and the dancing, Moses'
anger burned hot, and he threw the
tables out of his hands and broke them
at the foot of the mountain. 20 And he
took the calf which they had made, and
burnt it with fire, and ground it to
powder, and scattered it upon the
water, and made the people of Israel
drink it.
21 And Moses said to Aaron, "What
did this people do to you that you have
brought a great sin upon them?" 22 And
Aaron said, "Let not the anger of my
lord burn hot; you know the people,
that they are set on evil. 23 For they
said to me, 'Make us gods, who shall
go before us; as for this Moses, the
man who brought us up out of the land
of Egypt, we do not know what has
become of him.' 24 And I said to them,

32.1-6: Acts 7.40-41. **32.6:** 1 Cor 10.7. **32.9-14:** Ex 32.31-35; Num 14.11-25. **32.23:** Acts 7.40.

'Let any who have gold take it off'; so
they gave it to me, and I threw it into
the fire, and there came out this calf."

25 And when Moses saw that the
people had broken loose (for Aaron
had let them break loose, to their shame
among their enemies), 26 then Moses
stood in the gate of the camp, and
said, "Who is on the LORD's side?
Come to me." And all the sons of Levi
gathered themselves together to him.
27 And he said to them, "Thus says the
LORD God of Israel, 'Put every man
his sword on his side, and go to and
fro from gate to gate throughout the
camp, and slay every man his brother,
and every man his companion, and
every man his neighbor.' " 28 And the
sons of Levi did according to the word
of Moses; and there fell of the people
that day about three thousand men.
29 And Moses said, "Today you have
ordained yourselves[s] for the service of
the LORD, each one at the cost of his
son and of his brother, that he may
bestow a blessing upon you this day."

30 On the morrow Moses said to
the people, "You have sinned a great
sin. And now I will go up to the LORD;
perhaps I can make atonement for
your sin." 31 So Moses returned to the
LORD and said, "Alas, this people have
sinned a great sin; they have made for
themselves gods of gold. 32 But now,
if thou wilt forgive their sin—and if
not, blot me, I pray thee, out of thy
book which thou hast written." 33 But
the LORD said to Moses, "Whoever has
sinned against me, him will I blot out
of my book. 34 But now go, lead the
people to the place of which I have
spoken to you; behold, my angel shall
go before you. Nevertheless, in the
day when I visit, I will visit their sin
upon them."

35 And the LORD sent a plague
upon the people, because they made
the calf which Aaron made.

33 The LORD said to Moses,
"Depart, go up hence, you and
the people whom you have brought up
out of the land of Egypt, to the land
of which I swore to Abraham, Isaac,
and Jacob, saying, 'To your descendants I will give it.' 2 And I will send an
angel before you, and I will drive out
the Canaanites, the Am'ŏ-rites, the
Hit'tītes, the Per'iz-zītes, the Hī'vītes,
and the Jeb'ū-sītes. 3 Go up to a land
flowing with milk and honey; but I
will not go up among you, lest I consume you in the way, for you are a
stiff-necked people."

4 When the people heard these evil
tidings, they mourned; and no man
put on his ornaments. 5 For the LORD
had said to Moses, "Say to the people
of Israel, 'You are a stiff-necked people; if for a single moment I should go
up among you, I would consume you.
So now put off your ornaments from
you, that I may know what to do with
you.' " 6 Therefore the people of Israel
stripped themselves of their ornaments, from Mount Hō'reb onward.

7 Now Moses used to take the tent
and pitch it outside the camp, far off
from the camp; and he called it the
tent of meeting. And every one who
sought the LORD would go out to the
tent of meeting, which was outside the
camp. 8 Whenever Moses went out to
the tent, all the people rose up, and
every man stood at his tent door, and
looked after Moses, until he had gone
into the tent. 9 When Moses entered
the tent, the pillar of cloud would
descend and stand at the door of the
tent, and the LORD would speak with
Moses. 10 And when all the people saw
the pillar of cloud standing at the door
of the tent, all the people would rise
up and worship, every man at his tent
door. 11 Thus the LORD used to speak
to Moses face to face, as a man speaks
to his friend. When Moses turned
again into the camp, his servant Joshua
the son of Nun, a young man, did not
depart from the tent.

12 Moses said to the LORD, "See,
thou sayest to me, 'Bring up this
people'; but thou hast not let me know
whom thou wilt send with me. Yet
thou hast said, 'I know you by name,
and you have also found favor in my
sight.' 13 Now therefore, I pray thee,
if I have found favor in thy sight, show
me now thy ways, that I may know
thee and find favor in thy sight. Consider too that this nation is thy people." 14 And he said, "My presence
will go with you, and I will give you
rest." 15 And he said to him, "If thy
presence will not go with me, do not
carry us up from here. 16 For how
shall it be known that I have found
favor in thy sight, I and thy people?
Is it not in thy going with us, so that

[s] Gk Vg See Tg: Heb *ordain yourselves*
32.32-33: Rev 3.5. **33.3:** Acts 7.51. **33.11:** Num 12.8; Deut 34.10.

we are distinct, I and thy people, from
all other people that are upon the face
of the earth?"
17 And the LORD said to Moses,
"This very thing that you have spoken
I will do; for you have found favor in
my sight, and I know you by name."
18 Moses said, "I pray thee, show me
thy glory." 19 And he said, "I will make
all my goodness pass before you, and
will proclaim before you my name
'The LORD'; and I will be gracious to
whom I will be gracious, and will show
mercy on whom I will show mercy.
20 But," he said, "you cannot see my
face; for man shall not see me and
live." 21 And the LORD said, "Behold,
there is a place by me where you shall
stand upon the rock; 22 and while my
glory passes by I will put you in a
cleft of the rock, and I will cover you
with my hand until I have passed by;
23 then I will take away my hand, and
you shall see my back; but my face
shall not be seen."

34 The LORD said to Moses,
"Cut two tables of stone like the
first; and I will write upon the tables
the words that were on the first tables,
which you broke. 2 Be ready in the
morning, and come up in the morning
to Mount Sinai, and present yourself
there to me on the top of the mountain. 3 No man shall come up with you,
and let no man be seen throughout all
the mountain; let no flocks or herds
feed before that mountain." 4 So Moses
cut two tables of stone like the first;
and he rose early in the morning and
went up on Mount Sinai, as the LORD
had commanded him, and took in his
hand two tables of stone. 5 And the
LORD descended in the cloud and stood
with him there, and proclaimed the
name of the LORD. 6 The LORD passed
before him, and proclaimed, "The LORD,
the LORD, a God merciful and gracious,
slow to anger, and abounding in steadfast love and faithfulness, 7 keeping
steadfast love for thousands, forgiving
iniquity and transgression and sin, but
who will by no means clear the guilty,
visiting the iniquity of the fathers upon
the children and the children's children, to the third and the fourth generation." 8 And Moses made haste to
bow his head toward the earth, and
worshiped. 9 And he said, "If now I
have found favor in thy sight, O Lord,
let the Lord, I pray thee, go in the
midst of us, although it is a stiff-
necked people; and pardon our iniquity and our sin, and take us for thy
inheritance."
10 And he said, "Behold, I make a
covenant. Before all your people I will
do marvels, such as have not been
wrought in all the earth or in any
nation; and all the people among
whom you are shall see the work of
the LORD; for it is a terrible thing that
I will do with you.
11 "Observe what I command you
this day. Behold, I will drive out before you the Am'ŏ-rītes, the Canaanites, the Hit'tītes, the Per'iz-zītes, the
Hī'vītes, and the Jeb'ū-sītes. 12 Take
heed to yourself, lest you make a
covenant with the inhabitants of the
land whither you go, lest it become a
snare in the midst of you. 13 You shall
tear down their altars, and break their
pillars, and cut down their Ȧ-shē'rim
14 (for you shall worship no other god,
for the LORD, whose name is Jealous,
is a jealous God), 15 lest you make a
covenant with the inhabitants of the
land, and when they play the harlot
after their gods and sacrifice to their
gods and one invites you, you eat of
his sacrifice, 16 and you take of their
daughters for your sons, and their
daughters play the harlot after their
gods and make your sons play the
harlot after their gods.
17 "You shall make for yourself no
molten gods.
18 "The feast of unleavened bread
you shall keep. Seven days you shall
eat unleavened bread, as I commanded
you, at the time appointed in the
month Ā'bib; for in the month Abib
you came out from Egypt. 19 All that
opens the womb is mine, all your
male[x] cattle, the firstlings of cow and
sheep. 20 The firstling of an ass you
shall redeem with a lamb, or if you
will not redeem it you shall break its
neck. All the first-born of your sons
you shall redeem. And none shall
appear before me empty.
21 "Six days you shall work, but
on the seventh day you shall rest; in
plowing time and in harvest you shall

[x] Gk Theodotion Vg Tg: Heb uncertain

33.19: Rom 9.15. **34.6:** Num 14.18; Neh 9.17; Ps 86.15; 103.8; 145.8; Jon 4.2.
34.14: Ex 20.5; 34.7; Deut 4.24; 5.9. **34.17:** Ex 20.4. **34.18:** Ex 12.15-20. **34.19-20:** Ex 13.2, 11-16.
34.21: Ex 20.8-10; 23.12; 31.12-17; 35.2; Deut 5.12-15.

rest. 22And you shall observe the feast
of weeks, the first fruits of wheat
harvest, and the feast of ingathering
at the year's end. 23 Three times in the
year shall all your males appear before
the LORD God, the God of Israel.
24 For I will cast out nations before
you, and enlarge your borders; neither
shall any man desire your land, when
you go up to appear before the LORD
your God three times in the year.

25 "You shall not offer the blood
of my sacrifice with leaven; neither
shall the sacrifice of the feast of the
passover be left until the morning.
26 The first of the first fruits of your
ground you shall bring to the house of
the LORD your God. You shall not boil
a kid in its mother's milk."

27 And the LORD said to Moses,
"Write these words; in accordance
with these words I have made a covenant with you and with Israel." 28And
he was there with the LORD forty days
and forty nights; he neither ate bread
nor drank water. And he wrote upon
the tables the words of the covenant,
the ten commandments.[t]

29 When Moses came down from
Mount Sinai, with the two tables of
the testimony in his hand as he came
down from the mountain, Moses did
not know that the skin of his face shone
because he had been talking with God.
30And when Aaron and all the people
of Israel saw Moses, behold, the skin
of his face shone, and they were afraid
to come near him. 31 But Moses called
to them; and Aaron and all the leaders
of the congregation returned to him,
and Moses talked with them. 32And
afterward all the people of Israel came
near, and he gave them in commandment all that the LORD had spoken
with him in Mount Sinai. 33And when
Moses had finished speaking with
them, he put a veil on his face; 34 but
whenever Moses went in before the
LORD to speak with him, he took the
veil off, until he came out; and when
he came out, and told the people of
Israel what he was commanded, 35 the
people of Israel saw the face of Moses,
that the skin of Moses' face shone; and
Moses would put the veil upon his
face again, until he went in to speak
with him.

35 Moses assembled all the congregation of the people of Israel,
and said to them, "These are the things
which the LORD has commanded you
to do. 2 Six days shall work be done,
but on the seventh day you shall have
a holy sabbath of solemn rest to the
LORD; whoever does any work on it
shall be put to death;3 you shall kindle
no fire in all your habitations on the
sabbath day."

4 Moses said to all the congregation
of the people of Israel, "This is the
thing which the LORD has commanded. 5 Take from among you an
offering to the LORD; whoever is of
a generous heart, let him bring the
LORD's offering: gold, silver, and
bronze; 6 blue and purple and scarlet
stuff and fine twined linen; goats' hair,
7 tanned rams' skins, and goatskins;
acacia wood, 8 oil for the light, spices
for the anointing oil and for the
fragrant incense, 9 and onyx stones and
stones for setting, for the ephod and
for the breastpiece.

10 "And let every able man among
you come and make all that the LORD
has commanded: the tabernacle, 11 its
tent and its covering, its hooks and
its frames, its bars, its pillars, and its
bases; 12 the ark with its poles, the
mercy seat, and the veil of the screen;
13 the table with its poles and all its
utensils, and the bread of the Presence;
14 the lampstand also for the light, with
its utensils and its lamps, and the oil
for the light; 15 and the altar of incense, with its poles, and the anointing
oil and the fragrant incense, and the
screen for the door, at the door of the
tabernacle; 16 the altar of burnt offering, with its grating of bronze, its poles,
and all its utensils, the laver and its
base; 17 the hangings of the court, its
pillars and its bases, and the screen
for the gate of the court; 18 the pegs
of the tabernacle and the pegs of the
court, and their cords; 19 the finely
wrought garments for ministering in
the holy place, the holy garments for
Aaron the priest, and the garments of
his sons, for their service as priests."

20 Then all the congregation of the
people of Israel departed from the
presence of Moses. 21And they came,
every one whose heart stirred him,

[t] Heb *words*

34.22-24: Ex 23.14-17; Lev 23.1-44; Deut 16.1-17. **34.25:** Ex 23.18; Lev 2.11; Ex 12.10.
34.26: Ex 23.19; Deut 14.21; 26.2-11. **34.29-35:** 2 Cor 3.7-16.
35.2-3: Ex 23.12; 31.12-17; 34.21; Deut 5.12-15. **35.4-9:** Ex 25.1-9.

and every one whose spirit moved him,
and brought the LORD's offering to be
used for the tent of meeting, and for
all its service, and for the holy garments. 22 So they came, both men and
women; all who were of a willing heart
brought brooches and earrings and
signet rings and armlets, all sorts of
gold objects, every man dedicating an
offering of gold to the LORD. 23 And
every man with whom was found blue
or purple or scarlet stuff or fine linen
or goats' hair or tanned rams' skins or
goatskins, brought them. 24 Every one
who could make an offering of silver
or bronze brought it as the LORD's
offering; and every man with whom
was found acacia wood of any use in
the work, brought it. 25 And all women
who had ability spun with their hands,
and brought what they had spun in
blue and purple and scarlet stuff and
fine twined linen; 26 all the women
whose hearts were moved with ability
spun the goats' hair. 27 And the leaders
brought onyx stones and stones to be
set, for the ephod and for the breastpiece, 28 and spices and oil for the
light, and for the anointing oil, and for
the fragrant incense. 29 All the men
and women, the people of Israel,
whose heart moved them to bring anything for the work which the LORD
had commanded by Moses to be done,
brought it as their freewill offering to
the LORD.

30 And Moses said to the people of
Israel, "See, the LORD has called by
name Bez'ȧ·lel the son of Ū'rī, son of
Hūr, of the tribe of Judah; 31 and he
has filled him with the Spirit of God,
with ability, with intelligence, with
knowledge, and with all craftsmanship, 32 to devise artistic designs, to
work in gold and silver and bronze,
33 in cutting stones for setting, and in
carving wood, for work in every skilled
craft. 34 And he has inspired him to
teach, both him and Ō·hō'li·ab the son
of Ȧ·his'ȧ·mach of the tribe of Dan.
35 He has filled them with ability to do
every sort of work done by a craftsman
or by a designer or by an embroiderer
in blue and purple and scarlet stuff
and fine twined linen, or by a weaver—
by any sort of workman or skilled
36 designer. 1 Bez'ȧ·lel and Ō·hō'-
li·ab and every able man in
whom the LORD has put ability and
intelligence to know how to do any
work in the construction of the sanctuary shall work in accordance with all
that the LORD has commanded."

2 And Moses called Bez'ȧ·lel and
Ō·hō'li·ab and every able man in whose
mind the LORD had put ability, every
one whose heart stirred him up to
come to do the work; 3 and they
received from Moses all the freewill
offering which the people of Israel had
brought for doing the work on the
sanctuary. They still kept bringing him
freewill offerings every morning, 4 so
that all the able men who were doing
every sort of task on the sanctuary
came, each from the task that he was
doing, 5 and said to Moses, "The people bring much more than enough for
doing the work which the LORD has
commanded us to do." 6 So Moses
gave command, and word was proclaimed throughout the camp, "Let
neither man nor woman do anything
more for the offering for the sanctuary." So the people were restrained
from bringing; 7 for the stuff they had
was sufficient to do all the work, and
more.

8 And all the able men among the
workmen made the tabernacle with
ten curtains; they were made of fine
twined linen and blue and purple and
scarlet stuff, with cherubim skilfully
worked. 9 The length of each curtain
was twenty-eight cubits, and the
breadth of each curtain four cubits; all
the curtains had the same measure.

10 And he coupled five curtains to
one another, and the other five curtains
he coupled to one another. 11 And he
made loops of blue on the edge of the
outmost curtain of the first set; likewise he made them on the edge of the
outmost curtain of the second set;
12 he made fifty loops on the one
curtain, and he made fifty loops on the
edge of the curtain that was in the
second set; the loops were opposite one
another. 13 And he made fifty clasps of
gold, and coupled the curtains one to
the other with clasps; so the tabernacle
was one whole.

14 He also made curtains of goats'
hair for a tent over the tabernacle; he
made eleven curtains. 15 The length
of each curtain was thirty cubits, and
the breadth of each curtain four cubits;
the eleven curtains had the same measure. 16 He coupled five curtains by
themselves, and six curtains by them-

35.30-36.1: Ex 31.1-6. **36.8-19:** Ex 26.1-14.

selves. 17 And he made fifty loops on
the edge of the outmost curtain of the
one set, and fifty loops on the edge of
the other connecting curtain. 18 And
he made fifty clasps of bronze to couple
the tent together that it might be one
whole. 19 And he made for the tent a
covering of tanned rams' skins and
goatskins.

20 Then he made the upright
frames for the tabernacle of acacia
wood. 21 Ten cubits was the length of
a frame, and a cubit and a half the
breadth of each frame. 22 Each frame
had two tenons, for fitting together;
he did this for all the frames of the
tabernacle. 23 The frames for the
tabernacle he made thus: twenty
frames for the south side; 24 and he
made forty bases of silver under the
twenty frames, two bases under one
frame for its two tenons, and two bases
under another frame for its two tenons. 25 And for the second side of the
tabernacle, on the north side, he made
twenty frames 26 and their forty bases
of silver, two bases under one frame
and two bases under another frame.
27 And for the rear of the tabernacle
westward he made six frames. 28 And
he made two frames for corners of the
tabernacle in the rear. 29 And they were
separate beneath, but joined at the
top, at the first ring; he made two of
them thus, for the two corners. 30 There
were eight frames with their bases of
silver: sixteen bases, under every frame
two bases.

31 And he made bars of acacia
wood, five for the frames of the one
side of the tabernacle, 32 and five bars
for the frames of the other side of the
tabernacle, and five bars for the frames
of the tabernacle at the rear westward.
33 And he made the middle bar to pass
through from end to end halfway up
the frames. 34 And he overlaid the
frames with gold, and made their rings
of gold for holders for the bars, and
overlaid the bars with gold.

35 And he made the veil of blue
and purple and scarlet stuff and fine
twined linen; with cherubim skilfully
worked he made it. 36 And for it he
made four pillars of acacia, and overlaid them with gold; their hooks were
of gold, and he cast for them four bases
of silver. 37 He also made a screen for
the door of the tent, of blue and purple
and scarlet stuff and fine twined linen,
embroidered with needlework; 38 and
its five pillars with their hooks. He
overlaid their capitals, and their fillets
were of gold, but their five bases were
of bronze.

37 Bez'a·lel made the ark of acacia
wood; two cubits and a half was
its length, a cubit and a half its breadth,
and a cubit and a half its height. 2 And
he overlaid it with pure gold within
and without, and made a molding of
gold around it. 3 And he cast for it four
rings of gold for its four corners, two
rings on its one side and two rings on
its other side. 4 And he made poles of
acacia wood, and overlaid them with
gold, 5 and put the poles into the rings
on the sides of the ark, to carry the
ark. 6 And he made a mercy seat of pure
gold; two cubits and a half was its
length, and a cubit and a half its
breadth. 7 And he made two cherubim
of hammered gold; on the two ends of
the mercy seat he made them, 8 one
cherub on the one end, and one cherub
on the other end; of one piece with the
mercy seat he made the cherubim on
its two ends. 9 The cherubim spread
out their wings above, overshadowing
the mercy seat with their wings, with
their faces one to another; toward the
mercy seat were the faces of the
cherubim.

10 He also made the table of acacia
wood; two cubits was its length, a cubit
its breadth, and a cubit and a half its
height; 11 and he overlaid it with pure
gold, and made a molding of gold
around it. 12 And he made around it a
frame a handbreadth wide, and made
a molding of gold around the frame.
13 He cast for it four rings of gold, and
fastened the rings to the four corners
at its four legs. 14 Close to the frame
were the rings, as holders for the poles
to carry the table. 15 He made the poles
of acacia wood to carry the table, and
overlaid them with gold. 16 And he
made the vessels of pure gold which
were to be upon the table, its plates
and dishes for incense, and its bowls
and flagons with which to pour
libations.

17 He also made the lampstand of
pure gold. The base and the shaft of
the lampstand were made of hammered work; its cups, its capitals, and
its flowers were of one piece with it.

36.20-34: Ex 26.15-29. **36.35-38:** Ex 26.31-37. **37.1-9:** Ex 25.10-22. **37.10-16:** Ex 25.23-29. **37.17-24:** Ex 25.31-39.

18And there were six branches going
out of its sides, three branches of the
lampstand out of one side of it and
three branches of the lampstand out
of the other side of it; 19 three cups
made like almonds, each with capital
and flower, on one branch, and three
cups made like almonds, each with
capital and flower, on the other
branch—so for the six branches going
out of the lampstand. 20And on the
lampstand itself were four cups made
like almonds, with their capitals and
flowers, 21 and a capital of one piece
with it under each pair of the six
branches going out of it. 22 Their capitals and their branches were of one
piece with it; the whole of it was one
piece of hammered work of pure gold.
23And he made its seven lamps and its
snuffers and its trays of pure gold.
24 He made it and all its utensils of a
talent of pure gold.

25 He made the altar of incense of
acacia wood; its length was a cubit, and
its breadth was a cubit; it was square,
and two cubits was its height; its horns
were of one piece with it. 26 He overlaid it with pure gold, its top, and its
sides round about, and its horns; and
he made a molding of gold round about
it, 27 and made two rings of gold on it
under its molding, on two opposite
sides of it, as holders for the poles with
which to carry it. 28And he made the
poles of acacia wood, and overlaid
them with gold.

29 He made the holy anointing oil
also, and the pure fragrant incense,
blended as by the perfumer.

38 He made the altar of burnt
offering also of acacia wood; five
cubits was its length, and five cubits
its breadth; it was square, and three
cubits was its height. 2 He made horns
for it on its four corners; its horns
were of one piece with it, and he overlaid it with bronze. 3And he made all
the utensils of the altar, the pots, the
shovels, the basins, the forks, and the
firepans: all its utensils he made of
bronze. 4And he made for the altar a
grating, a network of bronze, under
its ledge, extending halfway down.
5 He cast four rings on the four corners
of the bronze grating as holders for
the poles; 6 he made the poles of acacia
wood, and overlaid them with bronze.
7And he put the poles through the
rings on the sides of the altar, to carry
it with them; he made it hollow, with
boards.

8 And he made the laver of bronze
and its base of bronze, from the mirrors
of the ministering women who ministered at the door of the tent of
meeting.

9 And he made the court; for the
south side the hangings of the court
were of fine twined linen, a hundred
cubits; 10 their pillars were twenty and
their bases twenty, of bronze, but the
hooks of the pillars and their fillets
were of silver. 11And for the north side
a hundred cubits, their pillars twenty,
their bases twenty, of bronze, but the
hooks of the pillars and their fillets
were of silver. 12And for the west side
were hangings of fifty cubits, their
pillars ten, and their sockets ten; the
hooks of the pillars and their fillets
were of silver. 13And for the front to
the east, fifty cubits. 14 The hangings
for one side of the gate were fifteen
cubits, with three pillars and three
bases. 15And so for the other side; on
this hand and that hand by the gate of
the court were hangings of fifteen
cubits, with three pillars and three
bases. 16All the hangings round about
the court were of fine twined linen.
17And the bases for the pillars were of
bronze, but the hooks of the pillars
and their fillets were of silver; the overlaying of their capitals was also of
silver, and all the pillars of the court
were filleted with silver. 18And the
screen for the gate of the court was
embroidered with needlework in blue
and purple and scarlet stuff and fine
twined linen; it was twenty cubits long
and five cubits high in its breadth,
corresponding to the hangings of the
court. 19And their pillars were four;
their four bases were of bronze, their
hooks of silver, and the overlaying of
their capitals and their fillets of silver.
20And all the pegs for the tabernacle
and for the court round about were of
bronze.

21 This is the sum of the things for
the tabernacle, the tabernacle of the
testimony, as they were counted at the
commandment of Moses, for the work
of the Levites under the direction of
Ith'ȧ·mär the son of Aaron the priest.
22 Bez'ȧ·lel the son of Ū'rī, son of
Hŭr, of the tribe of Judah, made all
that the LORD commanded Moses;
23 and with him was Ō·hō'li·ab the son

37.25-29: Ex 30.1-5. **38.1-7:** Ex 27.1-8. **38.8:** Ex 30.18. **38.9-20:** Ex 27.9-19.

of A·his'ȧ·mach, of the tribe of Dan,
a craftsman and designer and embroiderer in blue and purple and
scarlet stuff and fine twined linen.

24 All the gold that was used for
the work, in all the construction of the
sanctuary, the gold from the offering,
was twenty-nine talents and seven
hundred and thirty shekels, by the
shekel of the sanctuary. 25 And the
silver from those of the congregation
who were numbered was a hundred
talents and a thousand seven hundred
and seventy-five shekels, by the shekel
of the sanctuary: 26 a beka a head
(that is, half a shekel, by the shekel of
the sanctuary), for every one who was
numbered in the census, from twenty
years old and upward, for six hundred
and three thousand, five hundred and
fifty men. 27 The hundred talents of
silver were for casting the bases of the
sanctuary, and the bases of the veil; a
hundred bases for the hundred talents,
a talent for a base. 28 And of the thousand seven hundred and seventy-five
shekels he made hooks for the pillars,
and overlaid their capitals and made
fillets for them. 29 And the bronze that
was contributed was seventy talents,
and two thousand and four hundred
shekels; 30 with it he made the bases
for the door of the tent of meeting,
the bronze altar and the bronze grating
for it and all the utensils of the altar,
31 the bases round about the court,
and the bases of the gate of the court,
all the pegs of the tabernacle, and all
the pegs round about the court.

39 And of the blue and purple
and scarlet stuff they made
finely wrought garments, for ministering in the holy place; they made the
holy garments for Aaron; as the LORD
had commanded Moses.

2 And he made the ephod of gold,
blue and purple and scarlet stuff, and
fine twined linen. 3 And gold leaf was
hammered out and cut into threads
to work into the blue and purple and
the scarlet stuff, and into the fine
twined linen, in skilled design. 4 They
made for the ephod shoulder-pieces,
joined to it at its two edges. 5 And the
skilfully woven band upon it, to gird
it on, was of the same materials and
workmanship, of gold, blue and purple
and scarlet stuff, and fine twined linen;
as the LORD had commanded Moses.

6 The onyx stones were prepared,
enclosed in settings of gold filigree and
engraved like the engravings of a signet, according to the names of the sons
of Israel. 7 And he set them on the shoulder-pieces of the ephod, to be stones
of remembrance for the sons of Israel;
as the LORD had commanded Moses.

8 He made the breastpiece, in
skilled work, like the work of the
ephod, of gold, blue and purple and
scarlet stuff, and fine twined linen. 9 It
was square; the breastpiece was made
double, a span its length and a span
its breadth when doubled. 10 And they
set in it four rows of stones. A row of
sardius, topaz, and carbuncle was the
first row; 11 and the second row, an
emerald, a sapphire, and a diamond;
12 and the third row, a jacinth, an
agate, and an amethyst; 13 and the
fourth row, a beryl, an onyx, and a
jasper; they were enclosed in settings
of gold filigree. 14 There were twelve
stones with their names according to
the names of the sons of Israel; they
were like signets, each engraved with
its name, for the twelve tribes. 15 And
they made on the breastpiece twisted
chains like cords, of pure gold; 16 and
they made two settings of gold filigree
and two gold rings, and put the two
rings on the two edges of the breastpiece; 17 and they put the two cords
of gold in the two rings at the edges
of the breastpiece. 18 Two ends of the
two cords they had attached to the
two settings of filigree; thus they
attached it in front to the shoulder-
pieces of the ephod. 19 Then they
made two rings of gold, and put them
at the two ends of the breastpiece, on
its inside edge next to the ephod.
20 And they made two rings of gold,
and attached them in front to the
lower part of the two shoulder-pieces
of the ephod, at its joining above the
skilfully woven band of the ephod.
21 And they bound the breastpiece by
its rings to the rings of the ephod with
a lace of blue, so that it should lie upon
the skilfully woven band of the ephod,
and that the breastpiece should not
come loose from the ephod; as the
LORD had commanded Moses.

22 He also made the robe of the
ephod woven all of blue; 23 and the
opening of the robe in it was like the
opening in a garment, with a binding
around the opening, that it might not
be torn. 24 On the skirts of the robe

38.25-26: Ex 30.11-16. **39.2-7:** Ex 28.6-12. **39.8-21:** Ex 28.15-28. **39.22-26:** Ex 28.31-34.

they made pomegranates of blue and
purple and scarlet stuff and fine
twined linen. 25 They also made bells
of pure gold, and put the bells between
the pomegranates upon the skirts of
the robe round about, between the
pomegranates; 26 a bell and a pomegranate, a bell and a pomegranate
round about upon the skirts of the
robe for ministering; as the LORD had
commanded Moses.

27 They also made the coats, woven
of fine linen, for Aaron and his sons,
28 and the turban of fine linen, and
the caps of fine linen, and the linen
breeches of fine twined linen, 29 and
the girdle of fine twined linen and of
blue and purple and scarlet stuff, embroidered with needlework; as the
LORD had commanded Moses.

30 And they made the plate of the
holy crown of pure gold, and wrote
upon it an inscription, like the engraving of a signet, "Holy to the LORD."
31 And they tied to it a lace of blue, to
fasten it on the turban above; as the
LORD had commanded Moses.

32 Thus all the work of the tabernacle of the tent of meeting was finished; and the people of Israel had
done according to all that the LORD
had commanded Moses; so had they
done. 33 And they brought the tabernacle to Moses, the tent and all its
utensils, its hooks, its frames, its bars,
its pillars, and its bases; 34 the covering
of tanned rams' skins and goatskins,
and the veil of the screen; 35 the ark of
the testimony with its poles and the
mercy seat; 36 the table with all its
utensils, and the bread of the Presence;
37 the lampstand of pure gold and its
lamps with the lamps set and all its
utensils, and the oil for the light; 38 the
golden altar, the anointing oil and the
fragrant incense, and the screen for
the door of the tent; 39 the bronze
altar, and its grating of bronze, its
poles, and all its utensils; the laver and
its base; 40 the hangings of the court,
its pillars, and its bases, and the screen
for the gate of the court, its cords, and
its pegs; and all the utensils for the
service of the tabernacle, for the tent
of meeting; 41 the finely worked garments for ministering in the holy place,
the holy garments for Aaron the
priest, and the garments of his sons to
serve as priests. 42 According to all that
the LORD had commanded Moses, so
the people of Israel had done all the
work. 43 And Moses saw all the work,
and behold, they had done it; as the
LORD had commanded, so had they
done it. And Moses blessed them.

40 The LORD said to Moses,
2 "On the first day of the first
month you shall erect the tabernacle of
the tent of meeting. 3 And you shall
put in it the ark of the testimony, and
you shall screen the ark with the veil.
4 And you shall bring in the table, and
set its arrangements in order; and you
shall bring in the lampstand, and set
up its lamps. 5 And you shall put the
golden altar for incense before the ark
of the testimony, and set up the screen
for the door of the tabernacle. 6 You
shall set the altar of burnt offering before the door of the tabernacle of the
tent of meeting, 7 and place the laver
between the tent of meeting and the
altar, and put water in it. 8 And you
shall set up the court round about, and
hang up the screen for the gate of the
court. 9 Then you shall take the anointing oil, and anoint the tabernacle and
all that is in it, and consecrate it and
all its furniture; and it shall become
holy. 10 You shall also anoint the altar
of burnt offering and all its utensils,
and consecrate the altar; and the altar
shall be most holy. 11 You shall also
anoint the laver and its base, and consecrate it. 12 Then you shall bring
Aaron and his sons to the door of the
tent of meeting, and shall wash them
with water, 13 and put upon Aaron the
holy garments, and you shall anoint
him and consecrate him, that he may
serve me as priest. 14 You shall bring
his sons also and put coats on them,
15 and anoint them, as you anointed
their father, that they may serve me as
priests: and their anointing shall admit
them to a perpetual priesthood
throughout their generations."

16 Thus did Moses; according to
all that the LORD commanded him, so
he did. 17 And in the first month in the
second year, on the first day of the
month, the tabernacle was erected.
18 Moses erected the tabernacle; he
laid its bases, and set up its frames,
and put in its poles, and raised up its
pillars; 19 and he spread the tent over
the tabernacle, and put the covering of
the tent over it, as the LORD had commanded Moses. 20 And he took the
testimony and put it into the ark, and

39.27-29: Ex 28.39-40, 42. **39.30-31:** Ex 28.36-37. **39.36:** Ex 25.30; 40.23; Lev 24.5-9.

put the poles on the ark, and set the
mercy seat above on the ark; 21 and he
brought the ark into the tabernacle,
and set up the veil of the screen, and
screened the ark of the testimony; as
the LORD had commanded Moses.
22And he put the table in the tent of
meeting, on the north side of the
tabernacle, outside the veil, 23 and set
the bread in order on it before the
LORD; as the LORD had commanded
Moses. 24And he put the lampstand in
the tent of meeting, opposite the table
on the south side of the tabernacle,
25 and set up the lamps before the
LORD; as the LORD had commanded
Moses. 26And he put the golden altar
in the tent of meeting before the veil,
27 and burnt fragrant incense upon it;
as the LORD had commanded Moses.
28And he put in place the screen for
the door of the tabernacle. 29And he
set the altar of burnt offering at the
door of the tabernacle of the tent of
meeting, and offered upon it the burnt
offering and the cereal offering; as the
LORD had commanded Moses. 30And
he set the laver between the tent of
meeting and the altar, and put water
in it for washing, 31 with which Moses
and Aaron and his sons washed their
hands and their feet; 32 when they
went into the tent of meeting, and
when they approached the altar, they
washed; as the LORD commanded
Moses. 33And he erected the court
round the tabernacle and the altar, and
set up the screen of the gate of the
court. So Moses finished the work.

34 Then the cloud covered the tent
of meeting, and the glory of the LORD
filled the tabernacle. 35And Moses was
not able to enter the tent of meeting,
because the cloud abode upon it, and
the glory of the LORD filled the tabernacle. 36 Throughout all their journeys,
whenever the cloud was taken up from
over the tabernacle, the people of
Israel would go onward; 37 but if the
cloud was not taken up, then they did
not go onward till the day that it was
taken up. 38 For throughout all their
journeys the cloud of the LORD was
upon the tabernacle by day, and fire
was in it by night, in the sight of all
the house of Israel.

THE THIRD BOOK OF MOSES

COMMONLY CALLED

LEVITICUS

1 The LORD called Moses, and spoke
to him from the tent of meeting,
saying, 2 "Speak to the people of Israel,
and say to them, When any man of you
brings an offering to the LORD, you
shall bring your offering of cattle from
the herd or from the flock.

3 "If his offering is a burnt offering
from the herd, he shall offer a male
without blemish; he shall offer it at
the door of the tent of meeting, that
he may be accepted before the LORD;
4 he shall lay his hand upon the head
of the burnt offering, and it shall be
accepted for him to make atonement
for him. 5 Then he shall kill the bull
before the LORD; and Aaron's sons the
priests shall present the blood, and
throw the blood round about against
the altar that is at the door of the tent
of meeting. 6And he shall flay the
burnt offering and cut it into pieces;
7 and the sons of Aaron the priest shall
put fire on the altar, and lay wood in
order upon the fire; 8 and Aaron's sons
the priests shall lay the pieces, the
head, and the fat, in order upon the
wood that is on the fire upon the altar;
9 but its entrails and its legs he shall
wash with water. And the priest shall
burn the whole on the altar, as a burnt
offering, an offering by fire, a pleasing
odor to the LORD.

10 "If his gift for a burnt offering
is from the flock, from the sheep or
goats, he shall offer a male without
blemish; 11 and he shall kill it on the
north side of the altar before the LORD,

40.23: Ex 25.30; 39.36; Lev 24.5-9. **40.30-32:** Ex 30.18-21. **40.34:** Rev 15.8.

and Aaron's sons the priests shall
throw its blood against the altar round
about. 12 And he shall cut it into pieces,
with its head and its fat, and the priest
shall lay them in order upon the wood
that is on the fire upon the altar; 13 but
the entrails and the legs he shall wash
with water. And the priest shall offer
the whole, and burn it on the altar; it
is a burnt offering, an offering by fire,
a pleasing odor to the LORD.

14 "If his offering to the LORD is a
burnt offering of birds, then he shall
bring his offering of turtledoves or of
young pigeons. 15 And the priest shall
bring it to the altar and wring off its
head, and burn it on the altar; and its
blood shall be drained out on the side
of the altar; 16 and he shall take away
its crop with the feathers, and cast it
beside the altar on the east side, in the
place for ashes; 17 he shall tear it by
its wings, but shall not divide it
asunder. And the priest shall burn it
on the altar, upon the wood that is on
the fire; it is a burnt offering, an offering by fire, a pleasing odor to the
LORD.

2 "When any one brings a cereal
offering as an offering to the LORD,
his offering shall be of fine flour; he
shall pour oil upon it, and put frankincense on it, 2 and bring it to Aaron's
sons the priests. And he shall take
from it a handful of the fine flour and
oil, with all of its frankincense; and the
priest shall burn this as its memorial
portion upon the altar, an offering by
fire, a pleasing odor to the LORD. 3 And
what is left of the cereal offering shall
be for Aaron and his sons; it is a most
holy part of the offerings by fire to
the LORD.

4 "When you bring a cereal offering
baked in the oven as an offering, it
shall be unleavened cakes of fine flour
mixed with oil, or unleavened wafers
spread with oil. 5 And if your offering
is a cereal offering baked on a griddle,
it shall be of fine flour unleavened,
mixed with oil; 6 you shall break it in
pieces, and pour oil on it; it is a cereal
offering. 7 And if your offering is a
cereal offering cooked in a pan, it shall
be made of fine flour with oil. 8 And
you shall bring the cereal offering that
is made of these things to the LORD;
and when it is presented to the priest,
he shall bring it to the altar. 9 And the
priest shall take from the cereal offering its memorial portion and burn this
on the altar, an offering by fire, a
pleasing odor to the LORD. 10 And what
is left of the cereal offering shall be for
Aaron and his sons; it is a most holy
part of the offerings by fire to the
LORD.

11 "No cereal offering which you
bring to the LORD shall be made with
leaven; for you shall burn no leaven
nor any honey as an offering by fire
to the LORD. 12 As an offering of first
fruits you may bring them to the
LORD, but they shall not be offered on
the altar for a pleasing odor. 13 You
shall season all your cereal offerings
with salt; you shall not let the salt of
the covenant with your God be lacking
from your cereal offering; with all your
offerings you shall offer salt.

14 "If you offer a cereal offering of
first fruits to the LORD, you shall offer
for the cereal offering of your first
fruits crushed new grain from fresh
ears, parched with fire. 15 And you
shall put oil upon it, and lay frankincense on it; it is a cereal offering.
16 And the priest shall burn as its
memorial portion part of the crushed
grain and of the oil with all of its
frankincense; it is an offering by fire
to the LORD.

3 "If a man's offering is a sacrifice
of peace offering, if he offers an
animal from the herd, male or female,
he shall offer it without blemish before
the LORD. 2 And he shall lay his hand
upon the head of his offering and kill
it at the door of the tent of meeting;
and Aaron's sons the priests shall
throw the blood against the altar round
about. 3 And from the sacrifice of the
peace offering, as an offering by fire to
the LORD, he shall offer the fat covering the entrails and all the fat that is
on the entrails, 4 and the two kidneys
with the fat that is on them at the loins,
and the appendage of the liver which
he shall take away with the kidneys.
5 Then Aaron's sons shall burn it on
the altar upon the burnt offering,
which is upon the wood on the fire; it
is an offering by fire, a pleasing odor
to the LORD.

6 "If his offering for a sacrifice of
peace offering to the LORD is an
animal from the flock, male or female,
he shall offer it without blemish. 7 If
he offers a lamb for his offering, then
he shall offer it before the LORD, 8 lay-

3.1-17: Lev 7.11-18.

ing his hand upon the head of his
offering and killing it before the tent
of meeting; and Aaron's sons shall
throw its blood against the altar round
about. 9 Then from the sacrifice of the
peace offering as an offering by fire to
the LORD he shall offer its fat, the fat
tail entire, taking it away close by the
backbone, and the fat that covers the
entrails, and all the fat that is on the
entrails, 10 and the two kidneys with
the fat that is on them at the loins, and
the appendage of the liver which he
shall take away with the kidneys. 11 And
the priest shall burn it on the altar as
food offered by fire to the LORD.

12 "If his offering is a goat, then he
shall offer it before the LORD, 13 and
lay his hand upon its head, and kill it
before the tent of meeting; and the sons
of Aaron shall throw its blood against
the altar round about. 14 Then he shall
offer from it, as his offering for an
offering by fire to the LORD, the fat
covering the entrails, and all the fat
that is on the entrails, 15 and the two
kidneys with the fat that is on them
at the loins, and the appendage of the
liver which he shall take away with the
kidneys. 16 And the priest shall burn
them on the altar as food offered by
fire for a pleasing odor. All fat is the
LORD's. 17 It shall be a perpetual
statute throughout your generations,
in all your dwelling places, that you
eat neither fat nor blood."

4 And the LORD said to Moses,
2 "Say to the people of Israel, If
any one sins unwittingly in any of the
things which the LORD has commanded
not to be done, and does any one of
them, 3 if it is the anointed priest who
sins, thus bringing guilt on the people,
then let him offer for the sin which he
has committed a young bull without
blemish to the LORD for a sin offering.
4 He shall bring the bull to the door
of the tent of meeting before the LORD,
and lay his hand on the head of the
bull, and kill the bull before the LORD.
5 And the anointed priest shall take
some of the blood of the bull and bring
it to the tent of meeting; 6 and the
priest shall dip his finger in the blood
and sprinkle part of the blood seven
times before the LORD in front of the
veil of the sanctuary. 7 And the priest
shall put some of the blood on the
horns of the altar of fragrant incense
before the LORD which is in the tent
of meeting, and the rest of the blood
of the bull he shall pour out at the base
of the altar of burnt offering which is
at the door of the tent of meeting. 8 And
all the fat of the bull of the sin offering
he shall take from it, the fat that covers
the entrails and all the fat that is on the
entrails, 9 and the two kidneys with
the fat that is on them at the loins, and
the appendage of the liver which he
shall take away with the kidneys 10 (just
as these are taken from the ox of the
sacrifice of the peace offerings), and
the priest shall burn them upon the
altar of burnt offering. 11 But the skin
of the bull and all its flesh, with its
head, its legs, its entrails, and its dung,
12 the whole bull he shall carry forth
outside the camp to a clean place,
where the ashes are poured out, and
shall burn it on a fire of wood; where
the ashes are poured out it shall be
burned.

13 "If the whole congregation of
Israel commits a sin unwittingly and
the thing is hidden from the eyes of
the assembly, and they do any one of
the things which the LORD has commanded not to be done and are guilty;
14 when the sin which they have committed becomes known, the assembly
shall offer a young bull for a sin offering and bring it before the tent of
meeting; 15 and the elders of the congregation shall lay their hands upon
the head of the bull before the LORD,
and the bull shall be killed before the
LORD. 16 Then the anointed priest
shall bring some of the blood of the
bull to the tent of meeting, 17 and the
priest shall dip his finger in the blood
and sprinkle it seven times before the
LORD in front of the veil. 18 And he
shall put some of the blood on the
horns of the altar which is in the tent
of meeting before the LORD; and the
rest of the blood he shall pour out at
the base of the altar of burnt offering
which is at the door of the tent of
meeting. 19 And all its fat he shall take
from it and burn upon the altar.
20 Thus shall he do with the bull; as
he did with the bull of the sin offering,
so shall he do with this; and the priest
shall make atonement for them, and
they shall be forgiven. 21 And he shall
carry forth the bull outside the camp,
and burn it as he burned the first bull;
it is the sin offering for the assembly.

22 "When a ruler sins, doing un-

4.2-12: Num 15.27-29. **4.13-21:** Num 15.22-26.

wittingly any one of all the things
which the LORD his God has commanded not to be done, and is guilty,
23 if the sin which he has committed
is made known to him, he shall bring
as his offering a goat, a male without
blemish, 24 and shall lay his hand upon
the head of the goat, and kill it in the
place where they kill the burnt offering before the LORD; it is a sin offering.
25 Then the priest shall take some of
the blood of the sin offering with his
finger and put it on the horns of the
altar of burnt offering, and pour out
the rest of its blood at the base of the
altar of burnt offering. 26 And all its
fat he shall burn on the altar, like the
fat of the sacrifice of peace offerings;
so the priest shall make atonement for
him for his sin, and he shall be forgiven.

27 "If any one of the common people sins unwittingly in doing any one
of the things which the LORD has commanded not to be done, and is guilty,
28 when the sin which he has committed is made known to him he shall
bring for his offering a goat, a female
without blemish, for his sin which he
has committed. 29 And he shall lay his
hand on the head of the sin offering,
and kill the sin offering in the place of
burnt offering. 30 And the priest shall
take some of its blood with his finger
and put it on the horns of the altar of
burnt offering, and pour out the rest
of its blood at the base of the altar.
31 And all its fat he shall remove, as
the fat is removed from the peace
offerings, and the priest shall burn it
upon the altar for a pleasing odor to
the LORD; and the priest shall make
atonement for him, and he shall be
forgiven.

32 "If he brings a lamb as his offering for a sin offering, he shall bring a
female without blemish, 33 and lay his
hand upon the head of the sin offering,
and kill it for a sin offering in the place
where they kill the burnt offering.
34 Then the priest shall take some of
the blood of the sin offering with his
finger and put it on the horns of the
altar of burnt offering, and pour out
the rest of its blood at the base of
the altar. 35 And all its fat he shall
remove as the fat of the lamb is removed from the sacrifice of peace
offerings, and the priest shall burn it
on the altar, upon the offerings by fire
to the LORD; and the priest shall make
atonement for him for the sin which
he has committed, and he shall be
forgiven.

5 "If any one sins in that he hears
a public adjuration to testify and
though he is a witness, whether he has
seen or come to know the matter, yet
does not speak, he shall bear his
iniquity. 2 Or if any one touches an
unclean thing, whether the carcass of
an unclean beast or a carcass of unclean cattle or a carcass of unclean
swarming things, and it is hidden from
him, and he has become unclean, he
shall be guilty. 3 Or if he touches
human uncleanness, of whatever sort
the uncleanness may be with which
one becomes unclean, and it is hidden
from him, when he comes to know it
he shall be guilty. 4 Or if any one
utters with his lips a rash oath to do
evil or to do good, any sort of rash oath
that men swear, and it is hidden from
him, when he comes to know it he
shall in any of these be guilty. 5 When
a man is guilty in any of these, he shall
confess the sin he has committed,
6 and he shall bring his guilt offering
to the LORD for the sin which he has
committed, a female from the flock, a
lamb or a goat, for a sin offering; and
the priest shall make atonement for
him for his sin.

7 "But if he cannot afford a lamb,
then he shall bring, as his guilt offering
to the LORD for the sin which he has
committed, two turtledoves or two
young pigeons, one for a sin offering
and the other for a burnt offering.
8 He shall bring them to the priest,
who shall offer first the one for the sin
offering; he shall wring its head from
its neck, but shall not sever it, 9 and
he shall sprinkle some of the blood of
the sin offering on the side of the altar,
while the rest of the blood shall be
drained out at the base of the altar; it
is a sin offering. 10 Then he shall offer
the second for a burnt offering according to the ordinance; and the priest
shall make atonement for him for the
sin which he has committed, and he
shall be forgiven.

11 "But if he cannot afford two
turtledoves or two young pigeons,
then he shall bring, as his offering for
the sin which he has committed, a
tenth of an ephah of fine flour for a sin
offering; he shall put no oil upon it,
and shall put no frankincense on it, for
it is a sin offering. 12 And he shall bring
it to the priest, and the priest shall

take a handful of it as its memorial
portion and burn this on the altar,
upon the offerings by fire to the LORD;
it is a sin offering. 13 Thus the priest
shall make atonement for him for the
sin which he has committed in any one
of these things, and he shall be forgiven. And the remainder shall be for
the priest, as in the cereal offering."
14 The LORD said to Moses, 15 "If
any one commits a breach of faith and
sins unwittingly in any of the holy
things of the LORD, he shall bring, as
his guilt offering to the LORD, a ram
without blemish out of the flock,
valued by you in shekels of silver,
according to the shekel of the sanctuary; it is a guilt offering. 16 He shall
also make restitution for what he has
done amiss in the holy thing, and shall
add a fifth to it and give it to the priest;
and the priest shall make atonement
for him with the ram of the guilt offering, and he shall be forgiven.
17 "If any one sins, doing any of
the things which the LORD has commanded not to be done, though he
does not know it, yet he is guilty and
shall bear his iniquity. 18 He shall
bring to the priest a ram without
blemish out of the flock, valued by you
at the price for a guilt offering, and
the priest shall make atonement for
him for the error which he committed
unwittingly, and he shall be forgiven.
19 It is a guilt offering; he is guilty
before the LORD."
6[a] The LORD said to Moses, 2 "If
any one sins and commits a breach
of faith against the LORD by deceiving
his neighbor in a matter of deposit or
security, or through robbery, or if he
has oppressed his neighbor 3 or has
found what was lost and lied about
it, swearing falsely—in any of all the
things which men do and sin therein,
4 when one has sinned and become
guilty, he shall restore what he took by
robbery, or what he got by oppression,
or the deposit which was committed
to him, or the lost thing which he
found, 5 or anything about which he
has sworn falsely; he shall restore it in
full, and shall add a fifth to it, and
give it to him to whom it belongs, on
the day of his guilt offering. 6 And he
shall bring to the priest his guilt offering to the LORD, a ram without blemish
out of the flock, valued by you at the
price for a guilt offering; 7 and the
priest shall make atonement for him
before the LORD, and he shall be forgiven for any of the things which one
may do and thereby become guilty."
8[b] The LORD said to Moses, 9 "Command Aaron and his sons, saying,
This is the law of the burnt offering.
The burnt offering shall be on the
hearth upon the altar all night until the
morning, and the fire of the altar shall
be kept burning on it. 10 And the priest
shall put on his linen garment, and put
his linen breeches upon his body, and
he shall take up the ashes to which
the fire has consumed the burnt offering on the altar, and put them beside
the altar. 11 Then he shall put off his
garments, and put on other garments,
and carry forth the ashes outside the
camp to a clean place. 12 The fire on
the altar shall be kept burning on it,
it shall not go out; the priest shall burn
wood on it every morning, and he shall
lay the burnt offering in order upon it,
and shall burn on it the fat of the peace
offerings. 13 Fire shall be kept burning
upon the altar continually; it shall not
go out.
14 "And this is the law of the cereal
offering. The sons of Aaron shall offer
it before the LORD, in front of the
altar. 15 And one shall take from it a
handful of the fine flour of the cereal
offering with its oil and all the frankincense which is on the cereal offering,
and burn this as its memorial portion
on the altar, a pleasing odor to the
LORD. 16 And the rest of it Aaron and
his sons shall eat; it shall be eaten unleavened in a holy place; in the court
of the tent of meeting they shall eat it.
17 It shall not be baked with leaven. I
have given it as their portion of my
offerings by fire; it is a thing most
holy, like the sin offering and the guilt
offering. 18 Every male among the
children of Aaron may eat of it, as
decreed for ever throughout your generations, from the LORD's offerings by
fire; whoever touches them shall become holy."
19 The LORD said to Moses, 20 "This
is the offering which Aaron and his
sons shall offer to the LORD on the day
when he is anointed: a tenth of an
ephah of fine flour as a regular cereal
offering, half of it in the morning and
half in the evening. 21 It shall be made

[a] Ch 5.20 in Heb [b] Ch 6.1 in Heb
6.1-7: Ex 22.7-15; Num 5.5-8.

with oil on a griddle; you shall bring
it well mixed, in baked[c] pieces like a
cereal offering, and offer it for a pleasing odor to the LORD. 22 The priest
from among Aaron's sons, who is
anointed to succeed him, shall offer
it to the LORD as decreed for ever; the
whole of it shall be burned. 23 Every
cereal offering of a priest shall be
wholly burned; it shall not be eaten."

24 The LORD said to Moses, 25 "Say
to Aaron and his sons, This is the law
of the sin offering. In the place where
the burnt offering is killed shall the
sin offering be killed before the LORD;
it is most holy. 26 The priest who
offers it for sin shall eat it; in a holy
place it shall be eaten, in the court
of the tent of meeting. 27 Whatever[d]
touches its flesh shall be holy; and
when any of its blood is sprinkled on
a garment, you shall wash that on
which it was sprinkled in a holy place.
28 And the earthen vessel in which it
is boiled shall be broken; but if it is
boiled in a bronze vessel, that shall be
scoured, and rinsed in water. 29 Every
male among the priests may eat of it;
it is most holy. 30 But no sin offering
shall be eaten from which any blood
is brought into the tent of meeting to
make atonement in the holy place; it
shall be burned with fire.

7 "This is the law of the guilt offering. It is most holy; 2 in the place
where they kill the burnt offering they
shall kill the guilt offering, and its
blood shall be thrown on the altar
round about. 3 And all its fat shall be
offered, the fat tail, the fat that covers
the entrails, 4 the two kidneys with the
fat that is on them at the loins, and
the appendage of the liver which he
shall take away with the kidneys; 5 the
priests shall burn them on the altar as
an offering by fire to the LORD; it is a
guilt offering. 6 Every male among the
priests may eat of it; it shall be eaten
in a holy place; it is most holy. 7 The
guilt offering is like the sin offering,
there is one law for them; the priest
who makes atonement with it shall
have it. 8 And the priest who offers any
man's burnt offering shall have for
himself the skin of the burnt offering
which he has offered. 9 And every cereal
offering baked in the oven and all that
is prepared on a pan or a griddle shall
belong to the priest who offers it.
10 And every cereal offering, mixed
with oil or dry, shall be for all the sons
of Aaron, one as well as another.

11 "And this is the law of the
sacrifice of peace offerings which one
may offer to the LORD. 12 If he offers it
for a thanksgiving, then he shall offer
with the thank offering unleavened
cakes mixed with oil, unleavened
wafers spread with oil, and cakes of fine
flour well mixed with oil. 13 With the
sacrifice of his peace offerings for
thanksgiving he shall bring his offering
with cakes of leavened bread. 14 And of
such he shall offer one cake from each
offering, as an offering to the LORD; it
shall belong to the priest who throws
the blood of the peace offerings. 15 And
the flesh of the sacrifice of his peace
offerings for thanksgiving shall be
eaten on the day of his offering; he
shall not leave any of it until the morning. 16 But if the sacrifice of his offering is a votive offering or a freewill
offering, it shall be eaten on the day
that he offers his sacrifice, and on the
morrow what remains of it shall be
eaten, 17 but what remains of the flesh
of the sacrifice on the third day shall
be burned with fire. 18 If any of the
flesh of the sacrifice of his peace offering is eaten on the third day, he who
offers it shall not be accepted, neither
shall it be credited to him; it shall be
an abomination, and he who eats of it
shall bear his iniquity.

19 "Flesh that touches any unclean
thing shall not be eaten; it shall be
burned with fire. All who are clean
may eat flesh, 20 but the person who
eats of the flesh of the sacrifice of the
LORD's peace offerings while an uncleanness is on him, that person shall
be cut off from his people. 21 And if
any one touches an unclean thing,
whether the uncleanness of man or an
unclean beast or any unclean abomination, and then eats of the flesh of the
sacrifice of the LORD's peace offerings,
that person shall be cut off from his
people."

22 The LORD said to Moses, 23 "Say
to the people of Israel, You shall eat
no fat, of ox, or sheep, or goat. 24 The
fat of an animal that dies of itself, and
the fat of one that is torn by beasts,
may be put to any other use, but on
no account shall you eat it. 25 For
every person who eats of the fat of
an animal of which an offering by
fire is made to the LORD shall be cut

Meaning of Heb is uncertain [d] Or *Whoever*

off from his people. 26 Moreover you
shall eat no blood whatever, whether
of fowl or of animal, in any of your
dwellings. 27 Whoever eats any blood,
that person shall be cut off from his
people."

28 The LORD said to Moses, 29 "Say
to the people of Israel, He that offers
the sacrifice of his peace offerings to
the LORD shall bring his offering to
the LORD; from the sacrifice of his
peace offerings 30 he shall bring with
his own hands the offerings by fire to
the LORD; he shall bring the fat with
the breast, that the breast may be
waved as a wave offering before the
LORD. 31 The priest shall burn the fat
on the altar, but the breast shall be for
Aaron and his sons. 32 And the right
thigh you shall give to the priest as an
offering from the sacrifice of your
peace offerings; 33 he among the sons
of Aaron who offers the blood of the
peace offerings and the fat shall have
the right thigh for a portion. 34 For
the breast that is waved and the thigh
that is offered I have taken from the
people of Israel, out of the sacrifices
of their peace offerings, and have given
them to Aaron the priest and to his
sons, as a perpetual due from the
people of Israel. 35 This is the portion
of Aaron and of his sons from the
offerings made by fire to the LORD,
consecrated to them on the day they
were presented to serve as priests of
the LORD; 36 the LORD commanded
this to be given them by the people of
Israel, on the day that they were
anointed; it is a perpetual due throughout their generations."

37 This is the law of the burnt
offering, of the cereal offering, of
the sin offering, of the guilt offering,
of the consecration, and of the
peace offerings, 38 which the LORD
commanded Moses on Mount Sinai,
on the day that he commanded the
people of Israel to bring their offerings
to the LORD, in the wilderness of
Sinai.

8 The LORD said to Moses, 2 "Take
Aaron and his sons with him, and
the garments, and the anointing oil,
and the bull of the sin offering, and
the two rams, and the basket of unleavened bread; 3 and assemble all the
congregation at the door of the tent of
meeting." 4 And Moses did as the LORD
commanded him; and the congregation
was assembled at the door of the tent
of meeting.

5 And Moses said to the congregation, "This is the thing which the
LORD has commanded to be done."
6 And Moses brought Aaron and his
sons, and washed them with water.
7 And he put on him the coat, and
girded him with the girdle, and clothed
him with the robe, and put the ephod
upon him, and girded him with the
skilfully woven band of the ephod,
binding it to him therewith. 8 And he
placed the breastpiece on him, and in
the breastpiece he put the U'rim and
the Thum'mim. 9 And he set the turban
upon his head, and on the turban, in
front, he set the golden plate, the holy
crown, as the LORD commanded
Moses.

10 Then Moses took the anointing
oil, and anointed the tabernacle and
all that was in it, and consecrated
them. 11 And he sprinkled some of it
on the altar seven times, and anointed
the altar and all its utensils, and the
laver and its base, to consecrate them.
12 And he poured some of the anointing
oil on Aaron's head, and anointed him,
to consecrate him. 13 And Moses
brought Aaron's sons, and clothed
them with coats, and girded them with
girdles, and bound caps on them, as
the LORD commanded Moses.

14 Then he brought the bull of the
sin offering; and Aaron and his sons
laid their hands upon the head of the
bull of the sin offering. 15 And Moses
killed it, and took the blood, and with
his finger put it on the horns of the
altar round about, and purified the
altar, and poured out the blood at the
base of the altar, and consecrated it,
to make atonement for it. 16 And he
took all the fat that was on the entrails,
and the appendage of the liver, and
the two kidneys with their fat, and
Moses burned them on the altar. 17 But
the bull, and its skin, and its flesh, and
its dung, he burned with fire outside
the camp, as the LORD commanded
Moses.

18 Then he presented the ram of
the burnt offering; and Aaron and his
sons laid their hands on the head of
the ram. 19 And Moses killed it, and
threw the blood upon the altar round
about. 20 And when the ram was cut
into pieces, Moses burned the head
and the pieces and the fat. 21 And when

8.1-36: Ex 29.1-37.

the entrails and the legs were washed
with water, Moses burned the whole
ram on the altar, as a burnt offering, a
pleasing odor, an offering by fire to
the LORD, as the LORD commanded
Moses.
22 Then he presented the other
ram, the ram of ordination; and Aaron
and his sons laid their hands on the
head of the ram. 23And Moses killed
it, and took some of its blood and put
it on the tip of Aaron's right ear and on
the thumb of his right hand and on
the great toe of his right foot. 24And
Aaron's sons were brought, and Moses
put some of the blood on the tips of
their right ears and on the thumbs of
their right hands and on the great toes
of their right feet; and Moses threw
the blood upon the altar round about.
25 Then he took the fat, and the fat
tail, and all the fat that was on the
entrails, and the appendage of the
liver, and the two kidneys with their
fat, and the right thigh; 26 and out of
the basket of unleavened bread which
was before the LORD he took one unleavened cake, and one cake of bread
with oil, and one wafer, and placed
them on the fat and on the right thigh;
27 and he put all these in the hands of
Aaron and in the hands of his sons,
and waved them as a wave offering
before the LORD. 28 Then Moses took
them from their hands, and burned
them on the altar with the burnt
offering, as an ordination offering, a
pleasing odor, an offering by fire to the
LORD. 29And Moses took the breast,
and waved it for a wave offering before the LORD; it was Moses' portion of
the ram of ordination, as the LORD
commanded Moses.
30 Then Moses took some of the
anointing oil and of the blood which
was on the altar, and sprinkled it upon
Aaron and his garments, and also upon
his sons and his sons' garments; so he
consecrated Aaron and his garments,
and his sons and his sons' garments
with him.
31 And Moses said to Aaron and
his sons, "Boil the flesh at the door of
the tent of meeting, and there eat it
and the bread that is in the basket of
ordination offerings, as I commanded,
saying, 'Aaron and his sons shall eat
it'; 32 and what remains of the flesh
and the bread you shall burn with
fire. 33And you shall not go out from
the door of the tent of meeting for
seven days, until the days of your
ordination are completed, for it will
take seven days to ordain you. 34As has
been done today, the LORD has commanded to be done to make atonement
for you. 35At the door of the tent of
meeting you shall remain day and
night for seven days, performing what
the LORD has charged, lest you die;
for so I am commanded." 36And
Aaron and his sons did all the things
which the LORD commanded by
Moses.

9 On the eighth day Moses called
Aaron and his sons and the elders
of Israel; 2 and he said to Aaron, "Take
a bull calf for a sin offering, and a ram
for a burnt offering, both without
blemish, and offer them before the
LORD. 3And say to the people of Israel,
'Take a male goat for a sin offering,
and a calf and a lamb, both a year old
without blemish, for a burnt offering,
4 and an ox and a ram for peace offerings, to sacrifice before the LORD, and
a cereal offering mixed with oil; for today the LORD will appear to you.'"
5And they brought what Moses commanded before the tent of meeting;
and all the congregation drew near and
stood before the LORD. 6And Moses
said, "This is the thing which the LORD
commanded you to do; and the glory
of the LORD will appear to you."
7 Then Moses said to Aaron, "Draw
near to the altar, and offer your sin
offering and your burnt offering, and
make atonement for yourself and for
the people; and bring the offering of
the people, and make atonement for
them; as the LORD has commanded."
8 So Aaron drew near to the altar,
and killed the calf of the sin offering,
which was for himself. 9And the sons
of Aaron presented the blood to him,
and he dipped his finger in the blood
and put it on the horns of the altar,
and poured out the blood at the base
of the altar; 10 but the fat and the
kidneys and the appendage of the liver
from the sin offering he burned upon
the altar, as the LORD commanded
Moses. 11 The flesh and the skin he
burned with fire outside the camp.
12 And he killed the burnt offering;
and Aaron's sons delivered to him the
blood, and he threw it on the altar
round about. 13And they delivered the
burnt offering to him, piece by piece,
and the head; and he burned them
upon the altar. 14And he washed the

entrails and the legs, and burned them
with the burnt offering on the altar.
15 Then he presented the people's
offering, and took the goat of the sin
offering which was for the people, and
killed it, and offered it for sin, like the
first sin offering. 16 And he presented
the burnt offering, and offered it according to the ordinance. 17 And he
presented the cereal offering, and
filled his hand from it, and burned it
upon the altar, besides the burnt offering of the morning.
18 He killed the ox also and the
ram, the sacrifice of peace offerings for
the people; and Aaron's sons delivered
to him the blood, which he threw upon
the altar round about, 19 and the fat of
the ox and of the ram, the fat tail, and
that which covers the entrails, and the
kidneys, and the appendage of the
liver; 20 and they put the fat upon the
breasts, and he burned the fat upon
the altar, 21 but the breasts and the
right thigh Aaron waved for a wave
offering before the LORD; as Moses
commanded.
22 Then Aaron lifted up his hands
toward the people and blessed them;
and he came down from offering the
sin offering and the burnt offering and
the peace offerings. 23 And Moses and
Aaron went into the tent of meeting;
and when they came out they blessed
the people, and the glory of the LORD
appeared to all the people. 24 And fire
came forth from before the LORD and
consumed the burnt offering and the
fat upon the altar; and when all the
people saw it, they shouted, and fell
on their faces.

10 Now Nā′dab and A·bī′hū, the
sons of Aaron, each took his
censer, and put fire in it, and laid
incense on it, and offered unholy fire
before the LORD, such as he had not
commanded them. 2 And fire came
forth from the presence of the LORD
and devoured them, and they died before the LORD. 3 Then Moses said to
Aaron, "This is what the LORD has said,
'I will show myself holy among those
who are near me, and before all the
people I will be glorified.' " And Aaron
held his peace.
4 And Moses called Mish′a-el and
El′za·phan, the sons of Uz′zi·el the
uncle of Aaron, and said to them,
"Draw near, carry your brethren from
before the sanctuary out of the camp."
5 So they drew near, and carried them
in their coats out of the camp, as
Moses had said. 6 And Moses said to
Aaron and to El·ē·ā′zȧr and Ith′ȧ·mär,
his sons, "Do not let the hair of your
heads hang loose, and do not rend your
clothes, lest you die, and lest wrath
come upon all the congregation; but
your brethren, the whole house of
Israel, may bewail the burning which
the LORD has kindled. 7 And do not go
out from the door of the tent of meeting, lest you die; for the anointing oil
of the LORD is upon you." And
they did according to the word of
Moses.
8 And the LORD spoke to Aaron,
saying, 9 "Drink no wine nor strong
drink, you nor your sons with you,
when you go into the tent of meeting,
lest you die; it shall be a statute for
ever throughout your generations.
10 You are to distinguish between the
holy and the common, and between
the unclean and the clean; 11 and you
are to teach the people of Israel all the
statutes which the LORD has spoken
to them by Moses."
12 And Moses said to Aaron and
to El·ē·ā′zȧr and Ith′ȧ·mär, his sons
who were left, "Take the cereal offering that remains of the offerings by
fire to the LORD, and eat it unleavened
beside the altar, for it is most holy;
13 you shall eat it in a holy place,
because it is your due and your sons'
due, from the offerings by fire to the
LORD; for so I am commanded. 14 But
the breast that is waved and the thigh
that is offered you shall eat in any
clean place, you and your sons and
your daughters with you; for they are
given as your due and your sons' due,
from the sacrifices of the peace offering
of the people of Israel. 15 The thigh
that is offered and the breast that is
waved they shall bring with the offerings by fire of the fat, to wave for a
wave offering before the LORD, and it
shall be yours, and your sons' with
you, as a due for ever; as the LORD has
commanded."
16 Now Moses diligently inquired
about the goat of the sin offering, and
behold, it was burned! And he was
angry with El·ē·ā′zȧr and Ith′ȧ·mär,
the sons of Aaron who were left, saying, 17 "Why have you not eaten the
sin offering in the place of the sanctuary, since it is a thing most holy and

9.18-21: Lev 3.1-11. **10.8:** Ezek 44.21. **10.12-13:** Lev 6.14-18. **10.14-15:** Lev 7.30-34.

has been given to you that you may bear the iniquity of the congregation, to make atonement for them before the LORD? 18 Behold, its blood was not brought into the inner part of the sanctuary. You certainly ought to have eaten it in the sanctuary, as I commanded." 19And Aaron said to Moses, "Behold, today they have offered their sin offering and their burnt offering before the LORD; and yet such things as these have befallen me! If I had eaten the sin offering today, would it have been acceptable in the sight of the LORD?" 20And when Moses heard that, he was content.

11 And the LORD said to Moses and Aaron, 2 "Say to the people of Israel, These are the living things which you may eat among all the beasts that are on the earth. 3 Whatever parts the hoof and is cloven-footed and chews the cud, among the animals, you may eat. 4 Nevertheless among those that chew the cud or part the hoof, you shall not eat these: The camel, because it chews the cud but does not part the hoof, is unclean to you. 5And the rock badger, because it chews the cud but does not part the hoof, is unclean to you. 6And the hare, because it chews the cud but does not part the hoof, is unclean to you. 7And the swine, because it parts the hoof and is cloven-footed but does not chew the cud, is unclean to you. 8 Of their flesh you shall not eat, and their carcasses you shall not touch; they are unclean to you.

9 "These you may eat, of all that are in the waters. Everything in the waters that has fins and scales, whether in the seas or in the rivers, you may eat. 10 But anything in the seas or the rivers that has not fins and scales, of the swarming creatures in the waters and of the living creatures that are in the waters, is an abomination to you. 11 They shall remain an abomination to you; of their flesh you shall not eat, and their carcasses you shall have in abomination. 12 Everything in the waters that has not fins and scales is an abomination to you.

13 "And these you shall have in abomination among the birds, they shall not be eaten, they are an abomination: the eagle, the carrion vulture, the osprey, 14 the kite, the falcon according to its kind, 15 every raven according to its kind, 16 the ostrich, the nighthawk, the sea gull, the hawk according to its kind, 17 the owl, the cormorant, the ibis, 18 the water hen, the pelican, the carrion vulture, 19 the stork, the heron according to its kind, the hoopoe, and the bat.

20 "All winged insects that go upon all fours are an abomination to you. 21 Yet among the winged insects that go on all fours you may eat those which have legs above their feet, with which to leap on the earth. 22 Of them you may eat: the locust according to its kind, the bald locust according to its kind, the cricket according to its kind, and the grasshopper according to its kind. 23 But all other winged insects which have four feet are an abomination to you.

24 "And by these you shall become unclean; whoever touches their carcass shall be unclean until the evening, 25 and whoever carries any part of their carcass shall wash his clothes and be unclean until the evening. 26 Every animal which parts the hoof but is not cloven-footed or does not chew the cud is unclean to you; every one who touches them shall be unclean. 27And all that go on their paws, among the animals that go on all fours, are unclean to you; whoever touches their carcass shall be unclean until the evening, 28 and he who carries their carcass shall wash his clothes and be unclean until the evening; they are unclean to you.

29 "And these are unclean to you among the swarming things that swarm upon the earth: the weasel, the mouse, the great lizard according to its kind, 30 the gecko, the land crocodile, the lizard, the sand lizard, and the chameleon. 31 These are unclean to you among all that swarm; whoever touches them when they are dead shall be unclean until the evening. 32And anything upon which any of them falls when they are dead shall be unclean, whether it is an article of wood or a garment or a skin or a sack, any vessel that is used for any purpose; it must be put into water, and it shall be unclean until the evening; then it shall be clean. 33And if any of them falls into any earthen vessel, all that is in it shall be unclean, and you shall break it. 34Any food in it which may be eaten, upon which water may come, shall be

11.2-47: Deut 14.3-21.

unclean; and all drink wh ch may be
drunk from every such vessel shall be
unclean. 35 And everything upon which
any part of their carcass falls shall be
unclean; whether oven or stove, it
shall be broken in pieces; they are unclean, and shall be unclean to you.
36 Nevertheless a spring or a cistern
holding water shall be clean; but whatever touches their carcass shall be unclean. 37 And if any part of their carcass
falls upon any seed for sowing that is
to be sown, it is clean; 38 but if water
is put on the seed and any part of their
carcass falls on it, it is unclean to you.
39 "And if any animal of which you
may eat dies, he who touches its carcass shall be unclean until the evening,
40 and he who eats of its carcass shall
wash his clothes and be unclean until
the evening; he also who carries the
carcass shall wash his clothes and be
unclean until the evening.
41 "Every swarming thing that
swarms upon the earth is an abomination; it shall not be eaten. 42 Whatever
goes on its belly, and whatever goes on
all fours, or whatever has many feet,
all the swarming things that swarm
upon the earth, you shall not eat; for
they are an abomination. 43 You shall
not make yourselves abominable with
any swarming thing that swarms; and
you shall not defile yourselves with
them, lest you become unclean. 44 For
I am the LORD your God; consecrate
yourselves therefore, and be holy, for
I am holy. You shall not defile yourselves with any swarming thing that
crawls upon the earth. 45 For I am the
LORD who brought you up out of the
land of Egypt, to be your God; you
shall therefore be holy, for I am holy."
46 This is the law pertaining to
beast and bird and every living creature that moves through the waters
and every creature that swarms upon
the earth, 47 to make a distinction between the unclean and the clean and
between the living creature that may
be eaten and the living creature that
may not be eaten.

12 The LORD said to Moses, 2 "Say
to the people of Israel, If a
woman conceives, and bears a male
child, then she shall be unclean seven
days; as at the time of her menstrua-
tion, she shall be unclean. 3 And on the
eighth day the flesh of his foreskin
shall be circumcised. 4 Then she shall
continue for thirty-three days in the
blood of her purifying; she shall not
touch any hallowed thing, nor come
into the sanctuary, until the days of
her purifying are completed. 5 But if
she bears a female child, then she shall
be unclean two weeks, as in her men-
struation; and she shall continue in the
blood of her purifying for sixty-six
days.
6 "And when the days of her purifying are completed, whether for a son
or for a daughter, she shall bring to
the priest at the door of the tent of
meeting a lamb a year old for a burnt
offering, and a young pigeon or a
turtledove for a sin offering, 7 and he
shall offer it before the LORD, and
make atonement for her; then she
shall be clean from the flow of her
blood. This is the law for her who
bears a child, either male or female.
8 And if she cannot afford a lamb, then
she shall take two turtledoves or two
young pigeons, one for a burnt offering
and the other for a sin offering, and
the priest shall make atonement for
her, and she shall be clean."

13 The LORD said to Moses and
Aaron, 2 "When a man has on
the skin of his body a swelling or an
eruption or a spot, and it turns into a
leprous disease on the skin of his body,
then he shall be brought to Aaron the
priest or to one of his sons the priests,
3 and the priest shall examine the
diseased spot on the skin of his body;
and if the hair in the diseased spot has
turned white and the disease appears
to be deeper than the skin of his body,
it is a leprous disease; when the priest
has examined him he shall pronounce
him unclean. 4 But if the spot is white
in the skin of his body, and appears no
deeper than the skin, and the hair in
it has not turned white, the priest shall
shut up the diseased person for seven
days; 5 and the priest shall examine
him on the seventh day, and if in his
eyes the disease is checked and the
disease has not spread in the skin, then
the priest shall shut him up seven days
more; 6 and the priest shall examine
him again on the seventh day, and if
the diseased spot is dim and the
disease has not spread in the skin, then
the priest shall pronounce him clean;
it is only an eruption; and he shall
wash his clothes, and be clean. 7 But
if the eruption spreads in the skin, after

11.44-45: Lev 19.2; 20.7, 26; 1 Pet 1.16. **11.46:** Num 5.2-3. **12.1-8:** Lk 2.22-24.

he has shown himself to the priest for
his cleansing, he shall appear again before the priest; 8 and the priest shall
make an examination, and if the eruption has spread in the skin, then the
priest shall pronounce him unclean; it
is leprosy.

9 "When a man is afflicted with
leprosy, he shall be brought to the
priest; 10 and the priest shall make an
examination, and if there is a white
swelling in the skin, which has turned
the hair white, and there is quick raw
flesh in the swelling, 11 it is a chronic
leprosy in the skin of his body, and the
priest shall pronounce him unclean; he
shall not shut him up, for he is unclean. 12 And if the leprosy breaks out
in the skin, so that the leprosy covers
all the skin of the diseased person from
head to foot, so far as the priest can
see, 13 then the priest shall make an
examination, and if the leprosy has
covered all his body, he shall pronounce him clean of the disease; it has
all turned white, and he is clean. 14 But
when raw flesh appears on him, he
shall be unclean. 15 And the priest shall
examine the raw flesh, and pronounce
him unclean; raw flesh is unclean, for
it is leprosy. 16 But if the raw flesh
turns again and is changed to white,
then he shall come to the priest, 17 and
the priest shall examine him, and if
the disease has turned white, then the
priest shall pronounce the diseased
person clean; he is clean.

18 "And when there is in the skin
of one's body a boil that has healed,
19 and in the place of the boil there
comes a white swelling or a reddish-
white spot, then it shall be shown to
the priest; 20 and the priest shall make
an examination, and if it appears
deeper than the skin and its hair has
turned white, then the priest shall pronounce him unclean; it is the disease
of leprosy, it has broken out in the boil.
21 But if the priest examines it, and the
hair on it is not white and it is not
deeper than the skin, but is dim, then
the priest shall shut him up seven days;
22 and if it spreads in the skin, then
the priest shall pronounce him unclean; it is diseased. 23 But if the spot
remains in one place and does not
spread, it is the scar of the boil; and
the priest shall pronounce him clean.

24 "Or, when the body has a burn
on its skin and the raw flesh of the
burn becomes a spot, reddish-white or
white, 25 the priest shall examine it,
and if the hair in the spot has turned
white and it appears deeper than the
skin, then it is leprosy; it has broken
out in the burn, and the priest shall
pronounce him unclean; it is a leprous
disease. 26 But if the priest examines
it, and the hair in the spot is not white
and it is no deeper than the skin, but
is dim, the priest shall shut him up
seven days, 27 and the priest shall
examine him the seventh day; if it is
spreading in the skin, then the priest
shall pronounce him unclean; it is a
leprous disease. 28 But if the spot remains in one place and does not spread
in the skin, but is dim, it is a swelling
from the burn, and the priest shall pronounce him clean; for it is the scar of
the burn.

29 "When a man or woman has a
disease on the head or the beard, 30 the
priest shall examine the disease; and if
it appears deeper than the skin, and
the hair in it is yellow and thin, then
the priest shall pronounce him unclean; it is an itch, a leprosy of the
head or the beard. 31 And if the priest
examines the itching disease, and it
appears no deeper than the skin and
there is no black hair in it, then the
priest shall shut up the person with the
itching disease for seven days, 32 and
on the seventh day the priest shall examine the disease; and if the itch has
not spread, and there is in it no yellow
hair, and the itch appears to be no
deeper than the skin, 33 then he shall
shave himself, but the itch he shall not
shave; and the priest shall shut up the
person with the itching disease for
seven days more; 34 and on the seventh
day the priest shall examine the itch,
and if the itch has not spread in the
skin and it appears to be no deeper
than the skin, then the priest shall pronounce him clean; and he shall wash
his clothes, and be clean. 35 But if the
itch spreads in the skin after his
cleansing, 36 then the priest shall examine him, and if the itch has spread
in the skin, the priest need not seek for
the yellow hair; he is unclean. 37 But
if in his eyes the itch is checked, and
black hair has grown in it, the itch is
healed, he is clean; and the priest shall
pronounce him clean.

38 "When a man or a woman has
spots on the skin of the body, white
spots, 39 the priest shall make an examination, and if the spots on the skin

of the body are of a dull white, it is
tetter that has broken out in the skin;
he is clean.
40 "If a man's hair has fallen from
his head, he is bald but he is clean.
41 And if a man's hair has fallen from
his forehead and temples, he has baldness of the forehead but he is clean.
42 But if there is on the bald head or
the bald forehead a reddish-white diseased spot, it is leprosy breaking out
on his bald head or his bald forehead.
43 Then the priest shall examine him,
and if the diseased swelling is reddish-
white on his bald head or on his bald
forehead, like the appearance of leprosy
in the skin of the body, 44 he is a
leprous man, he is unclean; the priest
must pronounce him unclean; his disease is on his head.
45 "The leper who has the disease
shall wear torn clothes and let the hair
of his head hang loose, and he shall
cover his upper lip and cry, 'Unclean,
unclean.' 46 He shall remain unclean
as long as he has the disease; he is unclean; he shall dwell alone in a habitation outside the camp.
47 "When there is a leprous disease
in a garment, whether a woolen or a
linen garment, 48 in warp or woof of
linen or wool, or in a skin or in anything made of skin, 49 if the disease
shows greenish or reddish in the garment, whether in warp or woof or in
skin or in anything made of skin, it is
a leprous disease and shall be shown
to the priest. 50 And the priest shall
examine the disease, and shut up that
which has the disease for seven days;
51 then he shall examine the disease on
the seventh day. If the disease has
spread in the garment, in warp or
woof, or in the skin, whatever be the
use of the skin, the disease is a malignant leprosy; it is unclean. 52 And he
shall burn the garment, whether diseased in warp or woof, woolen or linen,
or anything of skin, for it is a malignant
leprosy; it shall be burned in the fire.
53 "And if the priest examines, and
the disease has not spread in the garment in warp or woof or in anything
of skin, 54 then the priest shall command that they wash the thing in
which is the disease, and he shall shut
it up seven days more; 55 and the priest
shall examine the diseased thing after
it has been washed. And if the diseased
spot has not changed color, though the
disease has not spread, it is unclean;
you shall burn it in the fire, whether
the leprous spot is on the back or on
the front.
56 "But if the priest examines, and
the disease is dim after it is washed,
he shall tear the spot out of the garment or the skin or the warp or woof;
57 then if it appears again in the garment, in warp or woof, or in anything
of skin, it is spreading; you shall burn
with fire that in which is the disease.
58 But the garment, warp or woof, or
anything of skin from which the disease departs when you have washed it,
shall then be washed a second time,
and be clean."
59 This is the law for a leprous
disease in a garment of wool or linen,
either in warp or woof, or in anything
of skin, to decide whether it is clean
or unclean.

14 The LORD said to Moses, 2 "This
shall be the law of the leper for
the day of his cleansing. He shall be
brought to the priest; 3 and the priest
shall go out of the camp, and the
priest shall make an examination.
Then, if the leprous disease is healed
in the leper, 4 the priest shall command
them to take for him who is to be
cleansed two living clean birds and
cedarwood and scarlet stuff and hyssop; 5 and the priest shall command
them to kill one of the birds in an
earthen vessel over running water. 6 He
shall take the living bird with the
cedarwood and the scarlet stuff and the
hyssop, and dip them and the living
bird in the blood of the bird that was
killed over the running water; 7 and he
shall sprinkle it seven times upon him
who is to be cleansed of leprosy; then
he shall pronounce him clean, and shall
let the living bird go into the open
field. 8 And he who is to be cleansed
shall wash his clothes, and shave off
all his hair, and bathe himself in water,
and he shall be clean; and after that he
shall come into the camp, but shall
dwell outside his tent seven days.
9 And on the seventh day he shall shave
all his hair off his head; he shall shave
off his beard and his eyebrows, all his
hair. Then he shall wash his clothes,
and bathe his body in water, and he
shall be clean.
10 "And on the eighth day he shall
take two male lambs without blemish,
and one ewe lamb a year old without

14.2-32: Mt 8.4; Mk 1.44; Lk 5.14; 17.14.

blemish, and a cereal offering of three
tenths of an ephah of fine flour mixed
with oil, and one log of oil. 11 And the
priest who cleanses him shall set the
man who is to be cleansed and these
things before the LORD, at the door of
the tent of meeting. 12 And the priest
shall take one of the male lambs, and
offer it for a guilt offering, along with
the log of oil, and wave them for a
wave offering before the LORD; 13 and
he shall kill the lamb in the place
where they kill the sin offering and the
burnt offering, in the holy place; for
the guilt offering, like the sin offering,
belongs to the priest; it is most holy.
14 The priest shall take some of the
blood of the guilt offering, and the
priest shall put it on the tip of the
right ear of him who is to be cleansed,
and on the thumb of his right hand,
and on the great toe of his right foot.
15 Then the priest shall take some of
the log of oil, and pour it into the palm
of his own left hand, 16 and dip his
right finger in the oil that is in his left
hand, and sprinkle some oil with his
finger seven times before the LORD.
17 And some of the oil that remains in
his hand the priest shall put on the tip
of the right ear of him who is to be
cleansed, and on the thumb of his
right hand, and on the great toe of his
right foot, upon the blood of the guilt
offering; 18 and the rest of the oil that
is in the priest's hand he shall put on
the head of him who is to be cleansed.
Then the priest shall make atonement
for him before the LORD. 19 The priest
shall offer the sin offering, to make
atonement for him who is to be
cleansed from his uncleanness. And
afterward he shall kill the burnt offering; 20 and the priest shall offer the
burnt offering and the cereal offering
on the altar. Thus the priest shall make
atonement for him, and he shall be
clean.

21 "But if he is poor and cannot
afford so much, then he shall take one
male lamb for a guilt offering to be
waved, to make atonement for him,
and a tenth of an ephah of fine flour
mixed with oil for a cereal offering,
and a log of oil; 22 also two turtledoves
or two young pigeons, such as he can
afford; the one shall be a sin offering
and the other a burnt offering. 23 And
on the eighth day he shall bring them
for his cleansing to the priest, to the
door of the tent of meeting, before the
LORD; 24 and the priest shall take the
lamb of the guilt offering, and the log
of oil, and the priest shall wave them
for a wave offering before the LORD.
25 And he shall kill the lamb of the
guilt offering; and the priest shall take
some of the blood of the guilt offering,
and put it on the tip of the right ear
of him who is to be cleansed, and on
the thumb of his right hand, and on
the great toe of his right foot. 26 And
the priest shall pour some of the oil
into the palm of his own left hand;
27 and shall sprinkle with his right
finger some of the oil that is in his left
hand seven times before the LORD;
28 and the priest shall put some of the
oil that is in his hand on the tip of the
right ear of him who is to be cleansed,
and on the thumb of his right hand,
and the great toe of his right foot, in
the place where the blood of the guilt
offering was put; 29 and the rest of the
oil that is in the priest's hand he shall
put on the head of him who is to be
cleansed, to make atonement for him
before the LORD. 30 And he shall offer,
of the turtledoves or young pigeons
such as he can afford, 31 one[x] for a sin
offering and the other for a burnt
offering, along with a cereal offering;
and the priest shall make atonement
before the LORD for him who is being
cleansed. 32 This is the law for him in
whom is a leprous disease, who cannot
afford the offerings for his cleansing."

33 The LORD said to Moses and
Aaron, 34 "When you come into the
land of Canaan, which I give you for
a possession, and I put a leprous disease in a house in the land of your
possession, 35 then he who owns the
house shall come and tell the priest,
'There seems to me to be some sort of
disease in my house.' 36 Then the
priest shall command that they empty
the house before the priest goes to
examine the disease, lest all that is in
the house be declared unclean; and
afterward the priest shall go in to see
the house. 37 And he shall examine the
disease; and if the disease is in the walls
of the house with greenish or reddish
spots, and if it appears to be deeper
than the surface, 38 then the priest
shall go out of the house to the door of
the house, and shut up the house seven
days. 39 And the priest shall come again
on the seventh day, and look; and if

[x] Gk Syr: Heb *afford, 31 such as he can afford, one*

the disease has spread in the walls of
the house, 40 then the priest shall command that they take out the stones in
which is the disease and throw them
into an unclean place outside the city;
41 and he shall cause the inside of the
house to be scraped round about, and
the plaster that they scrape off they
shall pour into an unclean place outside the city; 42 then they shall take
other stones and put them in the place
of those stones, and he shall take other
plaster and plaster the house.

43 "If the disease breaks out again
in the house, after he has taken out the
stones and scraped the house and
plastered it, 44 then the priest shall go
and look; and if the disease has spread
in the house, it is a malignant leprosy
in the house; it is unclean. 45 And he
shall break down the house, its stones
and timber and all the plaster of the
house; and he shall carry them forth
out of the city to an unclean place.
46 Moreover he who enters the house
while it is shut up shall be unclean
until the evening; 47 and he who lies
down in the house shall wash his
clothes; and he who eats in the house
shall wash his clothes.

48 "But if the priest comes and
makes an examination, and the disease
has not spread in the house after the
house was plastered, then the priest
shall pronounce the house clean, for
the disease is healed. 49 And for the
cleansing of the house he shall take
two small birds, with cedarwood and
scarlet stuff and hyssop, 50 and shall
kill one of the birds in an earthen
vessel over running water, 51 and shall
take the cedarwood and the hyssop and
the scarlet stuff, along with the living
bird, and dip them in the blood of the
bird that was killed and in the running
water, and sprinkle the house seven
times. 52 Thus he shall cleanse the
house with the blood of the bird, and
with the running water, and with the
living bird, and with the cedarwood
and hyssop and scarlet stuff; 53 and he
shall let the living bird go out of the
city into the open field; so he shall
make atonement for the house, and it
shall be clean."

54 This is the law for any leprous
disease: for an itch, 55 for leprosy in a
garment or in a house, 56 and for a
swelling or an eruption or a spot, 57 to
show when it is unclean and when it
is clean. This is the law for leprosy.

15 The LORD said to Moses and
Aaron, 2 "Say to the people of
Israel, When any man has a discharge
from his body, his discharge is unclean. 3 And this is the law of his uncleanness for a discharge: whether his
body runs with his discharge, or his
body is stopped from discharge, it is
uncleanness in him. 4 Every bed on
which he who has the discharge lies
shall be unclean; and everything on
which he sits shall be unclean. 5 And
any one who touches his bed shall
wash his clothes, and bathe himself in
water, and be unclean until the evening. 6 And whoever sits on anything
on which he who has the discharge has
sat shall wash his clothes, and bathe
himself in water, and be unclean until
the evening. 7 And whoever touches the
body of him who has the discharge
shall wash his clothes, and bathe himself in water, and be unclean until the
evening. 8 And if he who has the
discharge spits on one who is clean,
then he shall wash his clothes, and
bathe himself in water, and be unclean
until the evening. 9 And any saddle on
which he who has the discharge rides
shall be unclean. 10 And whoever
touches anything that was under him
shall be unclean until the evening; and
he who carries such a thing shall wash
his clothes, and bathe himself in water,
and be unclean until the evening.
11 Any one whom he that has the discharge touches without having rinsed
his hands in water shall wash his
clothes, and bathe himself in water,
and be unclean until the evening.
12 And the earthen vessel which he who
has the discharge touches shall be
broken; and every vessel of wood shall
be rinsed in water.

13 "And when he who has a discharge is cleansed of his discharge,
then he shall count for himself seven
days for his cleansing, and wash his
clothes; and he shall bathe his body
in running water, and shall be clean.
14 And on the eighth day he shall take
two turtledoves or two young pigeons,
and come before the LORD to the door
of the tent of meeting, and give them
to the priest; 15 and the priest shall
offer them, one for a sin offering and
the other for a burnt offering; and the
priest shall make atonement for him
before the LORD for his discharge.

16 "And if a man has an emission
of semen, he shall bathe his whole

body in water, and be unclean until the
evening. 17 And every garment and
every skin on which the semen comes
shall be washed with water, and be
unclean until the evening. 18 If a man
lies with a woman and has an emission
of semen, both of them shall bathe
themselves in water, and be unclean
until the evening.

19 "When a woman has a discharge
of blood which is her regular discharge
from her body, she shall be in her
impurity for seven days, and whoever
touches her shall be unclean until the
evening. 20 And everything upon which
she lies during her impurity shall be
unclean; everything also upon which
she sits shall be unclean. 21 And whoever touches her bed shall wash his
clothes, and bathe himself in water,
and be unclean until the evening.
22 And whoever touches anything upon
which she sits shall wash his clothes,
and bathe himself in water, and be
unclean until the evening; 23 whether
it is the bed or anything upon which
she sits, when he touches it he shall be
unclean until the evening. 24 And if any
man lies with her, and her impurity is
on him, he shall be unclean seven days;
and every bed on which he lies shall
be unclean.

25 "If a woman has a discharge of
blood for many days, not at the time
of her impurity, or if she has a discharge beyond the time of her impurity, all the days of the discharge
she shall continue in uncleanness; as
in the days of her impurity, she shall
be unclean. 26 Every bed on which she
lies, all the days of her discharge, shall
be to her as the bed of her impurity;
and everything on which she sits shall
be unclean, as in the uncleanness of
her impurity. 27 And whoever touches
these things shall be unclean, and shall
wash his clothes, and bathe himself in
water, and be unclean until the evening. 28 But if she is cleansed of her
discharge, she shall count for herself
seven days, and after that she shall be
clean. 29 And on the eighth day she
shall take two turtledoves or two young
pigeons, and bring them to the priest,
to the door of the tent of meeting.
30 And the priest shall offer one for a
sin offering and the other for a burnt
offering; and the priest shall make
atonement for her before the LORD for
her unclean discharge.

31 "Thus you shall keep the people
of Israel separate from their uncleanness, lest they die in their uncleanness
by defiling my tabernacle that is in
their midst."

32 This is the law for him who has
a discharge and for him who has an
emission of semen, becoming unclean
thereby; 33 also for her who is sick with
her impurity; that is, for any one, male
or female, who has a discharge, and
for the man who lies with a woman
who is unclean.

16 The LORD spoke to Moses, after
the death of the two sons of
Aaron, when they drew near before the
LORD and died; 2 and the LORD said to
Moses, "Tell Aaron your brother not
to come at all times into the holy place
within the veil, before the mercy seat
which is upon the ark, lest he die; for
I will appear in the cloud upon the
mercy seat. 3 But thus shall Aaron
come into the holy place: with a young
bull for a sin offering and a ram for a
burnt offering. 4 He shall put on the
holy linen coat, and shall have the
linen breeches on his body, be girded
with the linen girdle, and wear the
linen turban; these are the holy garments. He shall bathe his body in
water, and then put them on. 5 And he
shall take from the congregation of
the people of Israel two male goats for
a sin offering, and one ram for a burnt
offering.

6 "And Aaron shall offer the bull
as a sin offering for himself, and shall
make atonement for himself and for
his house. 7 Then he shall take the two
goats, and set them before the LORD at
the door of the tent of meeting; 8 and
Aaron shall cast lots upon the two
goats, one lot for the LORD and the
other lot for Ȧ·zā'zĕl. 9 And Aaron shall
present the goat on which the lot fell
for the LORD, and offer it as a sin
offering; 10 but the goat on which the
lot fell for Ȧ·zā'zĕl shall be presented
alive before the LORD to make atonement over it, that it may be sent away
into the wilderness to Azazel.

11 "Aaron shall present the bull as
a sin offering for himself, and shall
make atonement for himself and for
his house; he shall kill the bull as a sin
offering for himself. 12 And he shall
take a censer full of coals of fire from
the altar before the LORD, and two
handfuls of sweet incense beaten

15.24: Lev 18.19; 20.18. **16.2, 12:** Heb 6.19; 9.7, 25.

small; and he shall bring it within the
veil 13 and put the incense on the fire
before the LORD, that the cloud of the
incense may cover the mercy seat
which is upon the testimony, lest he
die; 14 and he shall take some of the
blood of the bull, and sprinkle it with
his finger on the front of the mercy
seat, and before the mercy seat he shall
sprinkle the blood with his finger seven
times.

15 "Then he shall kill the goat of
the sin offering which is for the people,
and bring its blood within the veil, and
do with its blood as he did with the
blood of the bull, sprinkling it upon
the mercy seat and before the mercy
seat; 16 thus he shall make atonement
for the holy place, because of the
uncleannesses of the people of Israel,
and because of their transgressions, all
their sins; and so he shall do for the
tent of meeting, which abides with
them in the midst of their uncleannesses. 17 There shall be no man in the
tent of meeting when he enters to
make atonement in the holy place until
he comes out and has made atonement
for himself and for his house and for
all the assembly of Israel. 18 Then he
shall go out to the altar which is before
the LORD and make atonement for it,
and shall take some of the blood of the
bull and of the blood of the goat, and
put it on the horns of the altar round
about. 19 And he shall sprinkle some of
the blood upon it with his finger seven
times, and cleanse it and hallow it from
the uncleannesses of the people of
Israel.

20 "And when he has made an end
of atoning for the holy place and the
tent of meeting and the altar, he shall
present the live goat; 21 and Aaron
shall lay both his hands upon the head
of the live goat, and confess over him
all the iniquities of the people of
Israel, and all their transgressions, all
their sins; and he shall put them upon
the head of the goat, and send him
away into the wilderness by the hand
of a man who is in readiness. 22 The
goat shall bear all their iniquities upon
him to a solitary land; and he shall let
the goat go in the wilderness.

23 "Then Aaron shall come into
the tent of meeting, and shall put off
the linen garments which he put on
when he went into the holy place, and
shall leave them there; 24 and he shall
bathe his body in water in a holy place,
and put on his garments, and come
forth, and offer his burnt offering and
the burnt offering of the people, and
make atonement for himself and for
the people. 25 And the fat of the sin
offering he shall burn upon the altar.
26 And he who lets the goat go to
A·zā'zėl shall wash his clothes and
bathe his body in water, and afterward
he may come into the camp. 27 And
the bull for the sin offering and the
goat for the sin offering, whose blood
was brought in to make atonement in
the holy place, shall be carried forth
outside the camp; their skin and their
flesh and their dung shall be burned
with fire. 28 And he who burns them
shall wash his clothes and bathe his
body in water, and afterward he may
come into the camp.

29 "And it shall be a statute to you
for ever that in the seventh month, on
the tenth day of the month, you shall
afflict yourselves, and shall do no
work, either the native or the stranger
who sojourns among you; 30 for on
this day shall atonement be made for
you, to cleanse you; from all your sins
you shall be clean before the LORD.
31 It is a sabbath of solemn rest to you,
and you shall afflict yourselves; it is a
statute for ever. 32 And the priest who
is anointed and consecrated as priest
in his father's place shall make atonement, wearing the holy linen garments;
33 he shall make atonement for the
sanctuary, and he shall make atonement for the tent of meeting and for
the altar, and he shall make atonement
for the priests and for all the people of
the assembly. 34 And this shall be an
everlasting statute for you, that atonement may be made for the people of
Israel once in the year because of all
their sins." And Moses did as the LORD
commanded him.

17 And the LORD said to Moses,
2 "Say to Aaron and his sons, and
to all the people of Israel, This is the
thing which the LORD has commanded.
3 If any man of the house of Israel kills
an ox or a lamb or a goat in the camp,
or kills it outside the camp, 4 and does
not bring it to the door of the tent of
meeting, to offer it as a gift to the
LORD before the tabernacle of the
LORD, bloodguilt shall be imputed to
that man; he has shed blood; and that
man shall be cut off from among his

16.27: Heb 13.11.

people. 5 This is to the end that the
people of Israel may bring their sacrifices which they slay in the open field,
that they may bring them to the LORD,
to the priest at the door of the tent of
meeting, and slay them as sacrifices of
peace offerings to the LORD; 6 and the
priest shall sprinkle the blood on the
altar of the LORD at the door of the
tent of meeting, and burn the fat for
a pleasing odor to the LORD. 7 So they
shall no more slay their sacrifices for
satyrs, after whom they play the
harlot. This shall be a statute for ever
to them throughout their generations.

8 "And you shall say to them, Any
man of the house of Israel, or of the
strangers that sojourn among them,
who offers a burnt offering or sacrifice,
9 and does not bring it to the door of
the tent of meeting, to sacrifice it to
the LORD; that man shall be cut off
from his people.

10 "If any man of the house of
Israel or of the strangers that sojourn
among them eats any blood, I will set
my face against that person who eats
blood, and will cut him off from among
his people. 11 For the life of the flesh
is in the blood; and I have given it for
you upon the altar to make atonement
for your souls; for it is the blood that
makes atonement, by reason of the life.
12 Therefore I have said to the people
of Israel, No person among you shall
eat blood, neither shall any stranger
who sojourns among you eat blood.
13 Any man also of the people of Israel,
or of the strangers that sojourn among
them, who takes in hunting any beast
or bird that may be eaten shall
pour out its blood and cover it with
dust.

14 "For the life of every creature
is the blood of it;[e] therefore I have said
to the people of Israel, You shall not
eat the blood of any creature, for the
life of every creature is its blood; whoever eats it shall be cut off. 15 And
every person that eats what dies of
itself or what is torn by beasts, whether
he is a native or a sojourner, shall wash
his clothes, and bathe himself in water,
and be unclean until the evening; then
he shall be clean. 16 But if he does not
wash them or bathe his flesh, he shall
bear his iniquity."

18 And the LORD said to Moses,
2 "Say to the people of Israel, I
am the LORD your God. 3 You shall
not do as they do in the land of Egypt,
where you dwelt, and you shall not do
as they do in the land of Canaan, to
which I am bringing you. You shall
not walk in their statutes. 4 You shall
do my ordinances and keep my statutes
and walk in them. I am the LORD your
God. 5 You shall therefore keep my
statutes and my ordinances, by doing
which a man shall live: I am the LORD.

6 "None of you shall approach any
one near of kin to him to uncover
nakedness. I am the LORD. 7 You shall
not uncover the nakedness of your
father, which is the nakedness of your
mother; she is your mother, you shall
not uncover her nakedness. 8 You shall
not uncover the nakedness of your
father's wife; it is your father's nakedness. 9 You shall not uncover the
nakedness of your sister, the daughter
of your father or the daughter of your
mother, whether born at home or born
abroad. 10 You shall not uncover the
nakedness of your son's daughter or of
your daughter's daughter, for their
nakedness is your own nakedness.
11 You shall not uncover the nakedness
of your father's wife's daughter, begotten by your father, since she is your
sister. 12 You shall not uncover the
nakedness of your father's sister; she
is your father's near kinswoman. 13 You
shall not uncover the nakedness of
your mother's sister, for she is your
mother's near kinswoman. 14 You shall
not uncover the nakedness of your
father's brother, that is, you shall not
approach his wife; she is your aunt.
15 You shall not uncover the nakedness
of your daughter-in-law; she is your
son's wife, you shall not uncover her
nakedness. 16 You shall not uncover
the nakedness of your brother's wife;
she is your brother's nakedness. 17 You
shall not uncover the nakedness of a
woman and of her daughter, and you
shall not take her son's daughter or
her daughter's daughter to uncover her
nakedness; they are your[f] near kins-
women; it is wickedness. 18 And you
shall not take a woman as a rival wife
to her sister, uncovering her nakedness
while her sister is yet alive.

[e] Gk Syr Compare Vg: Heb *for the life of all flesh, its blood is in its life* [f] Gk: Heb lacks *your*

17.10-16: Lev 3.17; 7.26-27; 19.26; Deut 12.16, 23-25. **18.5:** Lk 10.28; Rom 10.5; Gal 3.12.
18.7: Lev 20.11. **18.9, 11:** Lev 20.17; Deut 27.22. **18.12:** Lev 20.19. **18.14:** Lev 20.20.
18.15: Lev 20.12. **18.16:** Lev 20.21. **18.17:** Lev 20.14.

19 "You shall not approach a woman
to uncover her nakedness while she is
in her menstrual uncleanness. 20 And
you shall not lie carnally with your
neighbor's wife, and defile yourself
with her. 21 You shall not give any of
your children to devote them by fire
to Mō'lech, and so profane the name
of your God: I am the LORD. 22 You
shall not lie with a male as with a
woman; it is an abomination. 23 And
you shall not lie with any beast and
defile yourself with it, neither shall any
woman give herself to a beast to lie
with it: it is perversion.

24 "Do not defile yourselves by any
of these things, for by all these the
nations I am casting out before you
defiled themselves; 25 and the land
became defiled, so that I punished its
iniquity, and the land vomited out its
inhabitants. 26 But you shall keep my
statutes and my ordinances and do
none of these abominations, either the
native or the stranger who sojourns
among you 27 (for all of these abominations the men of the land did, who
were before you, so that the land
became defiled); 28 lest the land vomit
you out, when you defile it, as it
vomited out the nation that was before
you. 29 For whoever shall do any of
these abominations, the persons that
do them shall be cut off from among
their people. 30 So keep my charge
never to practice any of these abominable customs which were practiced
before you, and never to defile yourselves by them: I am the LORD your
God."

19 And the LORD said to Moses,
2 "Say to all the congregation of
the people of Israel, You shall be holy;
for I the LORD your God am holy.
3 Every one of you shall revere his
mother and his father, and you shall
keep my sabbaths: I am the LORD your
God. 4 Do not turn to idols or make
for yourselves molten gods: I am the
LORD your God.

5 "When you offer a sacrifice of
peace offerings to the LORD, you shall
offer it so that you may be accepted.
6 It shall be eaten the same day you
offer it, or on the morrow; and anything left over until the third day shall
be burned with fire. 7 If it is eaten at
all on the third day, it is an abomination; it will not be accepted, 8 and
every one who eats it shall bear his
iniquity, because he has profaned a
holy thing of the LORD; and that person
shall be cut off from his people.

9 "When you reap the harvest of
your land, you shall not reap your
field to its very border, neither shall
you gather the gleanings after your
harvest. 10 And you shall not strip your
vineyard bare, neither shall you gather
the fallen grapes of your vineyard; you
shall leave them for the poor and for
the sojourner: I am the LORD your
God.

11 "You shall not steal, nor deal
falsely, nor lie to one another. 12 And
you shall not swear by my name falsely,
and so profane the name of your God:
I am the LORD.

13 "You shall not oppress your
neighbor or rob him. The wages of a
hired servant shall not remain with you
all night until the morning. 14 You
shall not curse the deaf or put a
stumbling block before the blind, but
you shall fear your God: I am the
LORD.

15 "You shall do no injustice in
judgment; you shall not be partial to
the poor or defer to the great, but in
righteousness shall you judge your
neighbor. 16 You shall not go up and
down as a slanderer among your people, and you shall not stand forth
against the life[g] of your neighbor: I
am the LORD.

17 "You shall not hate your brother
in your heart, but you shall reason with
your neighbor, lest you bear sin because of him. 18 You shall not take
vengeance or bear any grudge against
the sons of your own people, but you
shall love your neighbor as yourself: I
am the LORD.

19 "You shall keep my statutes. You
shall not let your cattle breed with a
different kind; you shall not sow your
field with two kinds of seed; nor shall
there come upon you a garment of
cloth made of two kinds of stuff.

20 "If a man lies carnally with a

[g] Heb *blood*

18.19: Lev 15.24; 20.18. **18.21:** Lev 20.2-5. **18.22:** Lev 20.13; Deut 23.18.
18.23: Ex 22.19; Lev 20.15-16; Deut 27.21. **19.2:** Lev 11.44-45; 20.7, 26; 1 Pet 1.16.
19.3, 30: Ex 20.12; Deut 5.16; Ex 20.8; 23.12; 34.21; 35.23; Deut 5.12-15. **19.4:** Ex 20.4; Lev 26.1; Deut 4.15-19; 27.15. **19.9-10:** Lev 23.22; Deut 24.20-21. **19.11:** Ex 20.15-16; Deut 5.19. **19.12:** Ex 20.7; Deut 5.11; Mt 5.33. **19.13:** Deut 24.15; Jas 5.4. **19.14:** Deut 27.18. **19.15:** Ex 23.6; Deut 1.17.
19.18: Mt 5.43; 19.19; 22.39; Mk 12.31; Lk 10.27; Rom 13.9; Gal 5.14; Jas 2.8. **19.19:** Deut 22.9, 11.

woman who is a slave, betrothed to
another man and not yet ransomed or
given her freedom, an inquiry shall be
held. They shall not be put to death,
because she was not free; 21 but he
shall bring a guilt offering for himself
to the LORD, to the door of the tent of
meeting, a ram for a guilt offering.
22 And the priest shall make atonement
for him with the ram of the guilt offering before the LORD for his sin which
he has committed; and the sin which
he has committed shall be forgiven him.

23 "When you come into the land
and plant all kinds of trees for food,
then you shall count their fruit as
forbidden;[h] three years it shall be forbidden to you, it must not be eaten.
24 And in the fourth year all their fruit
shall be holy, an offering of praise to
the LORD. 25 But in the fifth year you
may eat of their fruit, that they may
yield more richly for you: I am the
LORD your God.

26 "You shall not eat any flesh with
the blood in it. You shall not practice
augury or witchcraft. 27 You shall not
round off the hair on your temples or
mar the edges of your beard. 28 You
shall not make any cuttings in your
flesh on account of the dead or tattoo
any marks upon you: I am the LORD.

29 "Do not profane your daughter
by making her a harlot, lest the land
fall into harlotry and the land become
full of wickedness. 30 You shall keep
my sabbaths and reverence my sanctuary: I am the LORD.

31 "Do not turn to mediums or
wizards; do not seek them out, to be
defiled by them: I am the LORD your
God.

32 "You shall rise up before the
hoary head, and honor the face of an
old man, and you shall fear your God:
I am the LORD.

33 "When a stranger sojourns with
you in your land, you shall not do him
wrong. 34 The stranger who sojourns
with you shall be to you as the native
among you, and you shall love him as
yourself; for you were strangers in the
land of Egypt: I am the LORD your
God.

35 "You shall do no wrong in judgment, in measures of length or weight
or quantity. 36 You shall have just
balances, just weights, a just ephah,
and a just hin: I am the LORD your
God, who brought you out of the land
of Egypt. 37 And you shall observe all
my statutes and all my ordinances,
and do them: I am the LORD."

20 The LORD said to Moses, 2 "Say
to the people of Israel, Any
man of the people of Israel, or of the
strangers that sojourn in Israel, who
gives any of his children to Mō'lech
shall be put to death; the people
of the land shall stone him with stones.
3 I myself will set my face against that
man, and will cut him off from among
his people, because he has given one
of his children to Mō'lech, defiling my
sanctuary and profaning my holy
name. 4 And if the people of the land
do at all hide their eyes from that man,
when he gives one of his children to
Mō'lech, and do not put him to death,
5 then I will set my face against that
man and against his family, and will
cut them off from among their people,
him and all who follow him in playing
the harlot after Mō'lech.

6 "If a person turns to mediums
and wizards, playing the harlot after
them, I will set my face against that
person, and will cut him off from
among his people. 7 Consecrate yourselves therefore, and be holy; for I am
the LORD your God. 8 Keep my
statutes, and do them; I am the LORD
who sanctify you. 9 For every one who
curses his father or his mother shall
be put to death; he has cursed his
father or his mother, his blood is upon
him.

10 "If a man commits adultery
with the wife of[l] his neighbor, both
the adulterer and the adulteress shall
be put to death. 11 The man who lies
with his father's wife has uncovered
his father's nakedness; both of them
shall be put to death, their blood is
upon them. 12 If a man lies with his
daughter-in-law, both of them shall
be put to death; they have committed
incest, their blood is upon them. 13 If
a man lies with a male as with a
woman, both of them have committed

[h] Heb *their uncircumcision* [l] Heb repeats *if a man commits adultery with the wife of*

19.26: Lev 3.17; 7.26-27; 17.10-16; Deut 12.16, 23-25; 18.10. **19.27:** Lev 21.5; Deut 14.1.
19.29: Deut 23.17-18. **19.30:** Ex 20.8-11; 23.12; 34.21; 35.2-3; Lev 19.3; 26.2; Deut 5.12-15.
19.31: Lev 20.6, 27. **19.33:** Ex 22.21. **20.2-5:** Lev 18.21. **20.6:** Lev 19.31.
20.7: Lev 11.44-45; 19.2; 20.26; 1 Pet 1.16. **20.9:** Ex 21.17; Deut 27.16.
20.10: Ex 20.14; Lev 18.20; Deut 5.18. **20.11:** Lev 18.7-8. **20.12:** Lev 18.15. **20.13:** Lev 18.22.

an abomination; they shall be put to
death, their blood is upon them. 14 If
a man takes a wife and her mother
also, it is wickedness; they shall be
burned with fire, both he and they,
that there may be no wickedness
among you. 15 If a man lies with a
beast, he shall be put to death; and
you shall kill the beast. 16 If a woman
approaches any beast and lies with it,
you shall kill the woman and the
beast; they shall be put to death, their
blood is upon them.

17 "If a man takes his sister, a
daughter of his father or a daughter of
his mother, and sees her nakedness,
and she sees his nakedness, it is a
shameful thing, and they shall be cut
off in the sight of the children of their
people; he has uncovered his sister's
nakedness, he shall bear his iniquity.
18 If a man lies with a woman having
her sickness, and uncovers her nakedness, he has made naked her fountain,
and she has uncovered the fountain of
her blood; both of them shall be cut off
from among their people. 19 You shall
not uncover the nakedness of your
mother's sister or of your father's
sister, for that is to make naked one's
near kin; they shall bear their iniquity.
20 If a man lies with his uncle's wife,
he has uncovered his uncle's nakedness; they shall bear their sin, they
shall die childless. 21 If a man takes
his brother's wife, it is impurity; he
has uncovered his brother's nakedness,
they shall be childless.

22 "You shall therefore keep all my
statutes and all my ordinances, and do
them; that the land where I am bringing you to dwell may not vomit you
out. 23 And you shall not walk in the
customs of the nation which I am
casting out before you; for they did all
these things, and therefore I abhorred
them. 24 But I have said to you, 'You
shall inherit their land, and I will give
it to you to possess, a land flowing
with milk and honey.' I am the LORD
your God, who have separated you
from the peoples. 25 You shall therefore make a distinction between the
clean beast and the unclean, and between the unclean bird and the clean;
you shall not make yourselves abominable by beast or by bird or by anything with which the ground teems,
which I have set apart for you to hold
unclean. 26 You shall be holy to me;
for I the LORD am holy, and have
separated you from the peoples, that
you should be mine.

27 "A man or a woman who is a
medium or a wizard shall be put to
death; they shall be stoned with stones,
their blood shall be upon them."

21 And the LORD said to Moses,
"Speak to the priests, the sons of
Aaron, and say to them that none of
them shall defile himself for the dead
among his people, 2 except for his
nearest of kin, his mother, his father,
his son, his daughter, his brother, 3 or
his virgin sister (who is near to him
because she has had no husband; for
her he may defile himself). 4 He shall
not defile himself as a husband among
his people and so profane himself.
5 They shall not make tonsures upon
their heads, nor shave off the edges of
their beards, nor make any cuttings in
their flesh. 6 They shall be holy to
their God, and not profane the name
of their God; for they offer the offerings by fire to the LORD, the bread of
their God; therefore they shall be
holy. 7 They shall not marry a harlot
or a woman who has been defiled;
neither shall they marry a woman
divorced from her husband; for the
priest is holy to his God. 8 You shall
consecrate him, for he offers the bread
of your God; he shall be holy to you;
for I the LORD, who sanctify you, am
holy. 9 And the daughter of any priest,
if she profanes herself by playing the
harlot, profanes her father; she shall
be burned with fire.

10 "The priest who is chief among
his brethren, upon whose head the
anointing oil is poured, and who has
been consecrated to wear the garments,
shall not let the hair of his head hang
loose, nor rend his clothes; 11 he shall
not go in to any dead body, nor defile
himself, even for his father or for his
mother; 12 neither shall he go out of
the sanctuary, nor profane the sanctuary of his God; for the consecration of
the anointing oil of his God is upon
him: I am the LORD. 13 And he shall
take a wife in her virginity. 14 A widow,
or one divorced, or a woman who has
been defiled, or a harlot, these he shall
not marry; but he shall take to wife a

20.14: Lev 18.17; Deut 27.23. **20.15-16:** Lev 18.23. **20.17:** Lev 18.9.
20.18: Lev 15.24; 18.19. **20.19:** Lev 18.12-13. **20.20:** Lev 18.14. **20.21:** Lev 18.16. **20.26:** Lev 20.7.
20.27: Lev 19.31; 20.6. **21.1-3:** Ezek 44.25. **21.5:** Lev 19.27; Deut 14.1.

virgin of his own people, 15 that he
may not profane his children among
his people; for I am the LORD who
sanctify him."
16 And the LORD said to Moses,
17 "Say to Aaron, None of your descendants throughout their generations
who has a blemish may approach to
offer the bread of his God. 18 For no
one who has a blemish shall draw near,
a man blind or lame, or one who has a
mutilated face or a limb too long, 19 or
a man who has an injured foot or an
injured hand, 20 or a hunchback, or
a dwarf, or a man with a defect in his
sight or an itching disease or scabs or
crushed testicles; 21 no man of the
descendants of Aaron the priest who
has a blemish shall come near to offer
the LORD's offerings by fire; since he
has a blemish, he shall not come near
to offer the bread of his God. 22 He
may eat the bread of his God, both of
the most holy and of the holy things,
23 but he shall not come near the veil
or approach the altar, because he has
a blemish, that he may not profane
my sanctuaries; for I am the LORD
who sanctify them." 24 So Moses spoke
to Aaron and to his sons and to all the
people of Israel.
22 And the LORD said to Moses,
2 "Tell Aaron and his sons to
keep away from the holy things of the
people of Israel, which they dedicate
to me, so that they may not profane
my holy name: I am the LORD. 3 Say
to them, 'If any one of all your descendants throughout your generations
approaches the holy things, which the
people of Israel dedicate to the LORD,
while he has an uncleanness, that
person shall be cut off from my
presence: I am the LORD. 4 None of
the line of Aaron who is a leper or
suffers a discharge may eat of the holy
things until he is clean. Whoever
touches anything that is unclean
through contact with the dead or a
man who has had an emission of
semen, 5 and whoever touches a creeping thing by which he may be made
unclean or a man from whom he may
take uncleanness, whatever his uncleanness may be—6 the person who
touches any such shall be unclean
until the evening and shall not eat of
the holy things unless he has bathed
his body in water. 7 When the sun is
down he shall be clean; and afterward
he may eat of the holy things, because
such are his food. 8 That which dies
of itself or is torn by beasts he shall
not eat, defiling himself by it: I am the
LORD.' 9 They shall therefore keep my
charge, lest they bear sin for it and die
thereby when they profane it: I am
the LORD who sanctify them.
10 "An outsider shall not eat of a
holy thing. A sojourner of the priest's
or a hired servant shall not eat of a holy
thing; 11 but if a priest buys a slave as
his property for money, the slave may
eat of it; and those that are born in his
house may eat of his food. 12 If a
priest's daughter is married to an outsider she shall not eat of the offering
of the holy things. 13 But if a priest's
daughter is a widow or divorced, and
has no child, and returns to her father's
house, as in her youth, she may eat of
her father's food; yet no outsider shall
eat of it. 14 And if a man eats of a holy
thing unwittingly, he shall add the
fifth of its value to it, and give the holy
thing to the priest. 15 The priests shall
not profane the holy things of the people of Israel, which they offer to the
LORD, 16 and so cause them to bear
iniquity and guilt, by eating their holy
things: for I am the LORD who sanctify
them."
17 And the LORD said to Moses,
18 "Say to Aaron and his sons and all
the people of Israel, When any one of
the house of Israel or of the sojourners
in Israel presents his offering, whether
in payment of a vow or as a freewill
offering which is offered to the LORD
as a burnt offering, 19 to be accepted
you shall offer a male without blemish,
of the bulls or the sheep or the goats.
20 You shall not offer anything that
has a blemish, for it will not be acceptable for you. 21 And when any one
offers a sacrifice of peace offerings to
the LORD, to fulfil a vow or as a freewill offering, from the herd or from
the flock, to be accepted it must be
perfect; there shall be no blemish in it.
22 Animals blind or disabled or mutilated or having a discharge or an itch
or scabs, you shall not offer to the
LORD or make of them an offering by
fire upon the altar to the LORD. 23 A
bull or a lamb which has a part too
long or too short you may present for
a freewill offering; but for a votive
offering it cannot be accepted. 24 Any
animal which has its testicles bruised

22.12: Lev 7.31-36.

or crushed or torn or cut, you shall
not offer to the LORD or sacrifice within your land; 25 neither shall you offer
as the bread of your God any such
animals gotten from a foreigner. Since
there is a blemish in them, because of
their mutilation, they will not be
accepted for you."
26 And the LORD said to Moses,
27 "When a bull or sheep or goat is
born, it shall remain seven days with
its mother; and from the eighth day
on it shall be acceptable as an offering
by fire to the LORD. 28 And whether
the mother is a cow or a ewe, you shall
not kill both her and her young in one
day. 29 And when you sacrifice a sacrifice of thanksgiving to the LORD, you
shall sacrifice it so that you may be accepted. 30 It shall be eaten on the
same day, you shall leave none of it
until morning: I am the LORD.
31 "So you shall keep my commandments and do them: I am the
LORD. 32 And you shall not profane my
holy name, but I will be hallowed
among the people of Israel; I am the
LORD who sanctify you, 33 who brought
you out of the land of Egypt to be
your God: I am the LORD."

23 The LORD said to Moses,
2 "Say to the people of Israel,
The appointed feasts of the LORD
which you shall proclaim as holy
convocations, my appointed feasts, are
these. 3 Six days shall work be done;
but on the seventh day is a sabbath of
solemn rest, a holy convocation; you
shall do no work; it is a sabbath to the
LORD in all your dwellings.
4 "These are the appointed feasts
of the LORD, the holy convocations,
which you shall proclaim at the time
appointed for them. 5 In the first
month, on the fourteenth day of the
month in the evening,[j] is the LORD's
passover. 6 And on the fifteenth day of
the same month is the feast of unleavened bread to the LORD; seven
days you shall eat unleavened bread.
7 On the first day you shall have a holy
convocation; you shall do no laborious
work. 8 But you shall present an offering by fire to the LORD seven days; on
the seventh day is a holy convocation;
you shall do no laborious work."
9 And the LORD said to Moses,
10 "Say to the people of Israel, When
you come into the land which I give
you and reap its harvest, you shall
bring the sheaf of the first fruits of
your harvest to the priest; 11 and he
shall wave the sheaf before the LORD,
that you may find acceptance; on the
morrow after the sabbath the priest
shall wave it. 12 And on the day when
you wave the sheaf, you shall offer a
male lamb a year old without blemish
as a burnt offering to the LORD. 13 And
the cereal offering with it shall be two
tenths of an ephah of fine flour mixed
with oil, to be offered by fire to the
LORD, a pleasing odor; and the drink
offering with it shall be of wine, a
fourth of a hin. 14 And you shall eat
neither bread nor grain parched or
fresh until this same day, until you
have brought the offering of your God:
it is a statute for ever throughout your
generations in all your dwellings.
15 "And you shall count from the
morrow after the sabbath, from the day
that you brought the sheaf of the wave
offering; seven full weeks shall they be,
16 counting fifty days to the morrow
after the seventh sabbath; then you
shall present a cereal offering of new
grain to the LORD. 17 You shall bring
from your dwellings two loaves of
bread to be waved, made of two tenths
of an ephah; they shall be of fine flour,
they shall be baked with leaven, as
first fruits to the LORD. 18 And you
shall present with the bread seven
lambs a year old without blemish, and
one young bull, and two rams; they
shall be a burnt offering to the LORD,
with their cereal offering and their
drink offerings, an offering by fire, a
pleasing odor to the LORD. 19 And you
shall offer one male goat for a sin
offering, and two male lambs a year
old as a sacrifice of peace offerings.
20 And the priest shall wave them with
the bread of the first fruits as a wave
offering before the LORD, with the two
lambs; they shall be holy to the LORD
for the priest. 21 And you shall make
proclamation on the same day; you
shall hold a holy convocation; you shall
do no laborious work: it is a statute for
ever in all your dwellings throughout
your generations.
22 "And when you reap the harvest
of your land, you shall not reap your
field to its very border, nor shall you
gather the gleanings after your harvest;
you shall leave them for the poor and

[j] Heb *between the two evenings*

23.1-44: Ex 23.14-17; 34.22-24; Deut 16.1-17. **23.22:** Lev 19.9-10; Deut 24.20-21.

for the stranger: I am the LORD your
God."
23 And the LORD said to Moses,
24 "Say to the people of Israel, In the
seventh month, on the first day of
the month, you shall observe a day of
solemn rest, a memorial proclaimed
with blast of trumpets, a holy convocation. 25 You shall do no laborious
work; and you shall present an offering
by fire to the LORD."
26 And the LORD said to Moses,
27 "On the tenth day of this seventh
month is the day of atonement; it shall
be for you a time of holy convocation,
and you shall afflict yourselves and
present an offering by fire to the LORD.
28 And you shall do no work on this
same day; for it is a day of atonement,
to make atonement for you before the
LORD your God. 29 For whoever is not
afflicted on this same day shall be cut
off from his people. 30 And whoever
does any work on this same day, that
person I will destroy from among his
people. 31 You shall do no work: it is
a statute for ever throughout your
generations in all your dwellings. 32 It
shall be to you a sabbath of solemn
rest, and you shall afflict yourselves;
on the ninth day of the month beginning at evening, from evening to
evening shall you keep your sabbath."
33 And the LORD said to Moses,
34 "Say to the people of Israel, On the
fifteenth day of this seventh month
and for seven days is the feast of
booths[k] to the LORD. 35 On the first
day shall be a holy convocation; you
shall do no laborious work. 36 Seven
days you shall present offerings by fire
to the LORD; on the eighth day you
shall hold a holy convocation and present an offering by fire to the LORD; it
is a solemn assembly; you shall do no
laborious work.
37 "These are the appointed feasts
of the LORD, which you shall proclaim
as times of holy convocation, for presenting to the LORD offerings by fire,
burnt offerings and cereal offerings,
sacrifices and drink offerings, each on
its proper day; 38 besides the sabbaths
of the LORD, and besides your gifts,
and besides all your votive offerings,
and besides all your freewill offerings,
which you give to the LORD.
39 "On the fifteenth day of the
seventh month, when you have gathered in the produce of the land, you
shall keep the feast of the LORD seven
days; on the first day shall be a solemn
rest, and on the eighth day shall be a
solemn rest. 40 And you shall take on
the first day the fruit of goodly trees,
branches of palm trees, and boughs of
leafy trees, and willows of the brook;
and you shall rejoice before the LORD
your God seven days. 41 You shall
keep it as a feast to the LORD seven
days in the year; it is a statute for ever
throughout your generations; you shall
keep it in the seventh month. 42 You
shall dwell in booths for seven days;
all that are native in Israel shall dwell
in booths, 43 that your generations may
know that I made the people of Israel
dwell in booths when I brought them
out of the land of Egypt: I am the
LORD your God."
44 Thus Moses declared to the people of Israel the appointed feasts of
the LORD.

24 The LORD said to Moses,
2 "Command the people of Israel to bring you pure oil from beaten
olives for the lamp, that a light may be
kept burning continually. 3 Outside
the veil of the testimony, in the tent of
meeting, Aaron shall keep it in order
from evening to morning before the
LORD continually; it shall be a statute
for ever throughout your generations.
4 He shall keep the lamps in order
upon the lampstand of pure gold before the LORD continually.
5 "And you shall take fine flour,
and bake twelve cakes of it; two tenths
of an ephah shall be in each cake. 6 And
you shall set them in two rows, six in
a row, upon the table of pure gold.
7 And you shall put pure frankincense
with each row, that it may go with the
bread as a memorial portion to be
offered by fire to the LORD. 8 Every
sabbath day Aaron shall set it in order
before the LORD continually on behalf
of the people of Israel as a covenant
for ever. 9 And it shall be for Aaron and
his sons, and they shall eat it in a holy
place, since it is for him a most holy
portion out of the offerings by fire to
the LORD, a perpetual due."
10 Now an Israelite woman's son,
whose father was an Egyptian, went
out among the people of Israel; and
the Israelite woman's son and a man

[k] Or *tabernacles*

24.1-4: Ex 27.20-21. **24.5-9:** Ex 25.30; 39.36; 40.23; Mt 12.4; Mk 2.26; Lk 6.4.

of Israel quarreled in the camp, 11 and
the Israelite woman's son blasphemed
the Name, and cursed. And they
brought him to Moses. His mother's
name was She·lō'mith, the daughter
of Dib'rī, of the tribe of Dan. 12 And
they put him in custody, till the will
of the LORD should be declared to
them.

13 And the LORD said to Moses,
14 "Bring out of the camp him who
cursed; and let all who heard him lay
their hands upon his head, and let all
the congregation stone him. 15 And say
to the people of Israel, Whoever curses
his God shall bear his sin. 16 He who
blasphemes the name of the LORD
shall be put to death; all the congregation shall stone him; the sojourner as
well as the native, when he blasphemes
the Name, shall be put to death. 17 He
who kills a man shall be put to death.
18 He who kills a beast shall make it
good, life for life. 19 When a man
causes a disfigurement in his neighbor,
as he has done it shall be done to him,
20 fracture for fracture, eye for eye,
tooth for tooth; as he has disfigured a
man, he shall be disfigured. 21 He who
kills a beast shall make it good; and he
who kills a man shall be put to death.
22 You shall have one law for the sojourner and for the native; for I am
the LORD your God." 23 So Moses
spoke to the people of Israel; and they
brought him who had cursed out of
the camp, and stoned him with stones.
Thus the people of Israel did as the
LORD commanded Moses.

25 The LORD said to Moses on
Mount Sinai, 2 "Say to the people of Israel, When you come into the
land which I give you, the land shall
keep a sabbath to the LORD. 3 Six years
you shall sow your field, and six years
you shall prune your vineyard, and
gather in its fruits; 4 but in the seventh
year there shall be a sabbath of solemn
rest for the land, a sabbath to the
LORD; you shall not sow your field or
prune your vineyard. 5 What grows of
itself in your harvest you shall not
reap, and the grapes of your undressed
vine you shall not gather; it shall be a
year of solemn rest for the land. 6 The
sabbath of the land shall provide food
for you, for yourself and for your male
and female slaves and for your hired
servant and the sojourner who lives
with you; 7 for your cattle also and for
the beasts that are in your land all its
yield shall be for food.

8 "And you shall count seven weeks[l]
of years, seven times seven years, so
that the time of the seven weeks of
years shall be to you forty-nine years.
9 Then you shall send abroad the loud
trumpet on the tenth day of the seventh
month; on the day of atonement you
shall send abroad the trumpet throughout all your land. 10 And you shall
hallow the fiftieth year, and proclaim
liberty throughout the land to all its
inhabitants; it shall be a jubilee for you,
when each of you shall return to his
property and each of you shall return
to his family. 11 A jubilee shall that
fiftieth year be to you; in it you shall
neither sow, nor reap what grows of
itself, nor gather the grapes from the
undressed vines. 12 For it is a jubilee;
it shall be holy to you; you shall eat
what it yields out of the field.

13 "In this year of jubilee each of
you shall return to his property. 14 And
if you sell to your neighbor or buy
from your neighbor, you shall not
wrong one another. 15 According to the
number of years after the jubilee, you
shall buy from your neighbor, and
according to the number of years for
crops he shall sell to you. 16 If the
years are many you shall increase the
price, and if the years are few you shall
diminish the price, for it is the number
of crops that he is selling to you. 17 You
shall not wrong one another, but you
shall fear your God; for I am the LORD
your God.

18 "Therefore you shall do my
statutes, and keep my ordinances and
perform them; so you will dwell in the
land securely. 19 The land will yield
its fruit, and you will eat your fill, and
dwell in it securely. 20 And if you say,
'What shall we eat in the seventh year,
if we may not sow or gather in our
crop?' 21 I will command my blessing
upon you in the sixth year, so that it
will bring forth fruit for three years.
22 When you sow in the eighth year,
you will be eating old produce; until
the ninth year, when its produce comes
in, you shall eat the old. 23 The land
shall not be sold in perpetuity, for the
land is mine; for you are strangers and

[l] Or *sabbaths*

24.19-20: Ex 21.23-25; Deut 19.21; Mt 5.38. **24.22:** Ex 12.49; Num 9.14; 15.15-16, 29.
25.2-7: Ex 23.10-11.

sojourners with me. 24 And in all the
country you possess, you shall grant a
redemption of the land.
25 "If your brother becomes poor,
and sells part of his property, then his
next of kin shall come and redeem
what his brother has sold. 26 If a man
has no one to redeem it, and then himself becomes prosperous and finds
sufficient means to redeem it, 27 let
him reckon the years since he sold it
and pay back the overpayment to the
man to whom he sold it; and he shall
return to his property. 28 But if he has
not sufficient means to get it back for
himself, then what he sold shall remain
in the hand of him who bought it until
the year of jubilee; in the jubilee it
shall be released, and he shall return
to his property.
29 "If a man sells a dwelling house
in a walled city, he may redeem it
within a whole year after its sale; for
a full year he shall have the right of
redemption. 30 If it is not redeemed
within a full year, then the house that
is in the walled city shall be made sure
in perpetuity to him who bought it,
throughout his generations; it shall
not be released in the jubilee. 31 But
the houses of the villages which have
no wall around them shall be reckoned
with the fields of the country; they
may be redeemed, and they shall be
released in the jubilee. 32 Nevertheless
the cities of the Levites, the houses in
the cities of their possession, the Levites may redeem at any time. 33 And
if one of the Levites does not exercise[m]
his right of redemption, then the house
that was sold in a city of their possession shall be released in the jubilee; for
the houses in the cities of the Levites
are their possession among the people
of Israel. 34 But the fields of common
land belonging to their cities may not
be sold; for that is their perpetual
possession.
35 "And if your brother becomes
poor, and cannot maintain himself
with you, you shall maintain him; as
a stranger and a sojourner he shall live
with you. 36 Take no interest from him
or increase, but fear your God; that
your brother may live beside you.
37 You shall not lend him your money
at interest, nor give him your food for
profit. 38 I am the LORD your God,
who brought you forth out of the land
of Egypt to give you the land of
Canaan, and to be your God.
39 "And if your brother becomes
poor beside you, and sells himself to
you, you shall not make him serve as
a slave: 40 he shall be with you as a
hired servant and as a sojourner. He
shall serve with you until the year of
the jubilee; 41 then he shall go out from
you, he and his children with him, and
go back to his own family, and return
to the possession of his fathers. 42 For
they are my servants, whom I brought
forth out of the land of Egypt; they
shall not be sold as slaves. 43 You shall
not rule over him with harshness, but
shall fear your God. 44 As for your
male and female slaves whom you may
have: you may buy male and female
slaves from among the nations that are
round about you. 45 You may also buy
from among the strangers who sojourn
with you and their families that are
with you, who have been born in your
land; and they may be your property.
46 You may bequeath them to your
sons after you, to inherit as a possession
for ever; you may make slaves of them,
but over your brethren the people of
Israel you shall not rule, one over
another, with harshness.
47 "If a stranger or sojourner with
you becomes rich, and your brother
beside him becomes poor and sells
himself to the stranger or sojourner
with you, or to a member of the stranger's family, 48 then after he is sold he
may be redeemed; one of his brothers
may redeem him, 49 or his uncle, or
his cousin may redeem him, or a near
kinsman belonging to his family may
redeem him; or if he grows rich he
may redeem himself. 50 He shall
reckon with him who bought him from
the year when he sold himself to him
until the year of jubilee, and the price
of his release shall be according to the
number of years; the time he was with
his owner shall be rated as the time of
a hired servant. 51 If there are still
many years, according to them he shall
refund out of the price paid for him
the price for his redemption. 52 If
there remain but a few years until the
year of jubilee, he shall make a reckoning with him; according to the years of
service due from him he shall refund
the money for his redemption. 53 As a
servant hired year by year shall he be

[m] Compare Vg: Heb *exercises*
25.35: Deut 15.7-11. **25.36:** Ex 22.25; Deut 23.19-20. **25.39-43:** Ex 21.2-6; Deut 15.12-18.

with him; he shall not rule with harshness over him in your sight. 54 And if
he is not redeemed by these means,
then he shall be released in the year of
jubilee, he and his children with him.
55 For to me the people of Israel are
servants, they are my servants whom
I brought forth out of the land of
Egypt: I am the LORD your God.

26 "You shall make for yourselves
no idols and erect no graven
image or pillar, and you shall not set
up a figured stone in your land, to bow
down to them; for I am the LORD your
God. 2 You shall keep my sabbaths
and reverence my sanctuary: I am the
LORD.

3 "If you walk in my statutes and
observe my commandments and do
them, 4 then I will give you your rains
in their season, and the land shall
yield its increase, and the trees of the
field shall yield their fruit. 5 And your
threshing shall last to the time of
vintage, and the vintage shall last to
the time for sowing; and you shall eat
your bread to the full, and dwell in
your land securely. 6 And I will give
peace in the land, and you shall lie
down, and none shall make you afraid;
and I will remove evil beasts from the
land, and the sword shall not go
through your land. 7 And you shall
chase your enemies, and they shall fall
before you by the sword. 8 Five of you
shall chase a hundred, and a hundred
of you shall chase ten thousand; and
your enemies shall fall before you by
the sword. 9 And I will have regard for
you and make you fruitful and multiply
you, and will confirm my covenant
with you. 10 And you shall eat old store
long kept, and you shall clear out the
old to make way for the new. 11 And I
will make my abode among you, and
my soul shall not abhor you. 12 And I
will walk among you, and will be your
God, and you shall be my people. 13 I
am the LORD your God, who brought
you forth out of the land of Egypt,
that you should not be their slaves;
and I have broken the bars of your
yoke and made you walk erect.

14 "But if you will not hearken to
me, and will not do all these commandments, 15 if you spurn my statutes, and if your soul abhors my
ordinances, so that you will not do all
my commandments, but break my
covenant, 16 I will do this to you: I
will appoint over you sudden terror,
consumption, and fever that waste the
eyes and cause life to pine away. And
you shall sow your seed in vain, for
your enemies shall eat it; 17 I will set
my face against you, and you shall be
smitten before your enemies; those
who hate you shall rule over you, and
you shall flee when none pursues you.
18 And if in spite of this you will not
hearken to me, then I will chastise you
again sevenfold for your sins, 19 and
I will break the pride of your power,
and I will make your heavens like iron
and your earth like brass; 20 and your
strength shall be spent in vain, for
your land shall not yield its increase,
and the trees of the land shall not
yield their fruit.

21 "Then if you walk contrary to
me, and will not hearken to me, I will
bring more plagues upon you, sevenfold as many as your sins. 22 And I will
let loose the wild beasts among you,
which shall rob you of your children,
and destroy your cattle, and make you
few in number, so that your ways shall
become desolate.

23 "And if by this discipline you
are not turned to me, but walk contrary to me, 24 then I also will walk
contrary to you, and I myself will smite
you sevenfold for your sins. 25 And I
will bring a sword upon you, that shall
execute vengeance for the covenant;
and if you gather within your cities I
will send pestilence among you, and
you shall be delivered into the hand
of the enemy. 26 When I break your
staff of bread, ten women shall bake
your bread in one oven, and shall
deliver your bread again by weight;
and you shall eat, and not be satisfied.

27 "And if in spite of this you will
not hearken to me, but walk contrary
to me, 28 then I will walk contrary to
you in fury, and chastise you myself
sevenfold for your sins. 29 You shall
eat the flesh of your sons, and you shall
eat the flesh of your daughters. 30 And
I will destroy your high places, and
cut down your incense altars, and cast
your dead bodies upon the dead bodies
of your idols; and my soul will abhor
you. 31 And I will lay your cities waste,
and will make your sanctuaries deso-

26.1: Lev 19.4; Ex 20.4, 23; Deut 4.15-18; 27.15.
26.2: Ex 20.8; 23.12; 34.21; 35.2-3; Lev 19.3, 30; Deut 5.12-15. **26.3-13:** Deut 7.12-26; 28.1-14.
26.11-12: 2 Cor 6.16. **26.14-45:** Deut 28.16-68.

late, and I will not smell your pleasing
odors. 32And I will devastate the land,
so that your enemies who settle in it
shall be astonished at it. 33And I will
scatter you among the nations, and I
will unsheathe the sword after you;
and your land shall be desolation, and
your cities shall be a waste.

34 "Then the land shall enjoy[n] its
sabbaths as long as it lies desolate,
while you are in your enemies' land;
then the land shall rest, and enjoy[n] its
sabbaths. 35As long as it lies desolate
it shall have rest, the rest which it had
not in your sabbaths when you dwelt
upon it. 36And as for those of you that
are left, I will send faintness into their
hearts in the lands of their enemies;
the sound of a driven leaf shall put
them to flight, and they shall flee as
one flees from the sword, and they
shall fall when none pursues. 37 They
shall stumble over one another, as if
to escape a sword, though none pursues; and you shall have no power to
stand before your enemies. 38And you
shall perish among the nations, and the
land of your enemies shall eat you up.
39And those of you that are left shall
pine away in your enemies' lands because of their iniquity; and also because
of the iniquities of their fathers they
shall pine away like them.

40 "But if they confess their iniquity and the iniquity of their fathers
in their treachery which they committed against me, and also in walking
contrary to me, 41 so that I walked
contrary to them and brought them
into the land of their enemies; if then
their uncircumcised heart is humbled
and they make amends for their iniquity; 42 then I will remember my
covenant with Jacob, and I will remember my covenant with Isaac and
my covenant with Abraham, and I will
remember the land. 43 But the land
shall be left by them, and enjoy[n] its
sabbaths while it lies desolate without
them; and they shall make amends for
their iniquity, because they spurned
my ordinances, and their soul abhorred
my statutes. 44 Yet for all that, when
they are in the land of their enemies,
I will not spurn them, neither will I
abhor them so as to destroy them
utterly and break my covenant with
them; for I am the LORD their God;
45 but I will for their sake remember
the covenant with their forefathers,
whom I brought forth out of the land
of Egypt in the sight of the nations,
that I might be their God: I am the
LORD."

46 These are the statutes and ordinances and laws which the LORD made
between him and the people of Israel
on Mount Sinai by Moses.

27 The LORD said to Moses,
2 "Say to the people of Israel,
When a man makes a special vow of
persons to the LORD at your valuation,
3 then your valuation of a male from
twenty years old up to sixty years old
shall be fifty shekels of silver, according to the shekel of the sanctuary. 4 If
the person is a female, your valuation
shall be thirty shekels. 5 If the person
is from five years old up to twenty
years old, your valuation shall be for
a male twenty shekels, and for a female
ten shekels. 6 If the person is from a
month old up to five years old, your
valuation shall be for a male five
shekels of silver, and for a female your
valuation shall be three shekels of
silver. 7And if the person is sixty years
old and upward, then your valuation
for a male shall be fifteen shekels, and
for a female ten shekels. 8And if a man
is too poor to pay your valuation, then
he shall bring the person before the
priest, and the priest shall value him;
according to the ability of him who
vowed the priest shall value him.

9 "If it is an animal such as men
offer as an offering to the LORD, all of
such that any man gives to the LORD
is holy. 10 He shall not substitute anything for it or exchange it, a good for
a bad, or a bad for a good; and if he
makes any exchange of beast for beast,
then both it and that for which it is
exchanged shall be holy. 11And if it is
an unclean animal such as is not offered
as an offering to the LORD, then the
man shall bring the animal before the
priest, 12 and the priest shall value it
as either good or bad; as you, the priest,
value it, so it shall be. 13 But if he
wishes to redeem it, he shall add a
fifth to the valuation.

14 "When a man dedicates his
house to be holy to the LORD, the
priest shall value it as either good or
bad; as the priest values it, so it shall
stand. 15And if he who dedicates it
wishes to redeem his house, he shall

[n] Or *pay for*
26.40-41: Acts 7.51.

add a fifth of the valuation in money
to it, and it shall be his.
16 "If a man dedicates to the LORD
part of the land which is his by
inheritance, then your valuation shall
be according to the seed for it; a
sowing of a homer of barley shall be
valued at fifty shekels of silver. 17 If
he dedicates his field from the year of
jubilee, it shall stand at your full
valuation; 18 but if he dedicates his
field after the jubilee, then the priest
shall compute the money-value for it
according to the years that remain until
the year of jubilee, and a deduction
shall be made from your valuation.
19 And if he who dedicates the field
wishes to redeem it, then he shall add
a fifth of the valuation in money to it,
and it shall remain his. 20 But if he
does not wish to redeem the field, or
if he has sold the field to another man,
it shall not be redeemed any more;
21 but the field, when it is released in
the jubilee, shall be holy to the LORD,
as a field that has been devoted; the
priest shall be in posesssion of it. 22 If
he dedicates to the LORD a field which
he has bought, which is not a part of
his possession by inheritance, 23 then
the priest shall compute the valuation
for it up to the year of jubilee, and the
man shall give the amount of the
valuation on that day as a holy thing
to the LORD. 24 In the year of jubilee
the field shall return to him from whom
it was bought, to whom the land
belongs as a possession by inheritance.
25 Every valuation shall be according
to the shekel of the sanctuary: twenty
gerahs shall make a shekel.
26 "But a firstling of animals, which
as a firstling belongs to the LORD, no
man may dedicate; whether ox or
sheep, it is the LORD'S. 27 And if it is an
unclean animal, then he shall buy it
back at your valuation, and add a fifth
to it; or, if it is not redeemed, it shall
be sold at your valuation.
28 "But no devoted thing that a
man devotes to the LORD, of anything
that he has, whether of man or beast,
or of his inherited field, shall be sold
or redeemed; every devoted thing is
most holy to the LORD. 29 No one
devoted, who is to be utterly destroyed
from among men, shall be ransomed;
he shall be put to death.
30 "All the tithe of the land,
whether of the seed of the land or of
the fruit of the trees, is the LORD'S; it
is holy to the LORD. 31 If a man wishes
to redeem any of his tithe, he shall add
a fifth to it. 32 And all the tithe of herds
and flocks, every tenth animal of all
that pass under the herdsman's staff,
shall be holy to the LORD. 33 A man
shall not inquire whether it is good or
bad, neither shall he exchange it; and
if he exchanges it, then both it and
that for which it is exchanged shall be
holy; it shall not be redeemed."
34 These are the commandments
which the LORD commanded Moses
for the people of Israel on Mount
Sinai.

THE FOURTH BOOK OF MOSES

COMMONLY CALLED

NUMBERS

1 The LORD spoke to Moses in the
wilderness of Sinai, in the tent of
meeting, on the first day of the second
month, in the second year after they
had come out of the land of Egypt,
saying, 2 "Take a census of all the
congregation of the people of Israel,
by families, by fathers' houses, according to the number of names, every
male, head by head; 3 from twenty
years old and upward, all in Israel who
are able to go forth to war, you and
Aaron shall number them, company
by company. 4 And there shall be with
you a man from each tribe, each man
being the head of the house of his
fathers. 5 And these are the names of
the men who shall attend you. From

27.28: Num 18.14. **1.1-46:** Num 26.1-51.

Reuben, E·lī'zūr the son of Shed'ē·ŭr;
6 from Simeon, She·lü'mi-el the son of
Zü·ri·shad'däi; 7 from Judah, Näh'-
shŏn the son of Am·min'ȧ·dab; 8 from
Is'sȧ·chär, Nė·than'el the son of Zü'ȧr;
9 from Zeb'ū·lŭn, E·lī'ab the son of
Hē'lon; 10 from the sons of Joseph,
from Ē'phrȧ·im, E·lish'ȧ·mȧ the son
of Am·mī'hŭd, and from Mȧ·nas'sėh,
Gȧ·mā'li·ėl the son of Pė·däh'zŭr;
11 from Benjamin, Ȧ·bī'dȧn the son of
Gid·ē·ō'ni; 12 from Dan, Ā·hī·ē'zėr the
son of Am·mi·shad'däi; 13 from Ash'ėr,
Pā'gi·el the son of Ōch'rȧn; 14 from
Gad, E·lī'ȧ·saph the son of Deü'el;
15 from Naph'tȧ·lī, Ȧ·hī'rȧ the son of
Ē'nan." 16 These were the ones chosen
from the congregation, the leaders of
their ancestral tribes, the heads of the
clans of Israel.

17 Moses and Aaron took these men
who have been named, 18 and on the
first day of the second month, they
assembled the whole congregation together, who registered themselves by
families, by fathers' houses, according
to the number of names from twenty
years old and upward, head by head,
19 as the LORD commanded Moses. So
he numbered them in the wilderness
of Sinai.

20 The people of Reuben, Israel's
first-born, their generations, by their
families, by their fathers' houses, according to the number of names, head
by head, every male from twenty years
old and upward, all who were able to
go forth to war; 21 the number of the
tribe of Reuben was forty-six thousand five hundred.

22 Of the people of Simeon, their
generations, by their families, by their
fathers' houses, those of them that
were numbered, according to the
number of names, head by head, every
male from twenty years old and upward, all who were able to go forth to
war: 23 the number of the tribe of
Simeon was fifty-nine thousand three
hundred.

24 Of the people of Gad, their generations, by their families, by their
fathers' houses, according to the
number of the names, from twenty
years old and upward, all who were
able to go forth to war: 25 the number of the tribe of Gad was forty-
five thousand six hundred and
fifty.

26 Of the people of Judah, their
generations, by their families, by their
fathers' houses, according to the
number of names, from twenty years
old and upward, every man able to go
forth to war: 27 the number of the
tribe of Judah was seventy-four thousand six hundred.

28 Of the people of Is'sȧ·chär, their
generations, by their families, by their
fathers' houses, according to the number of names, from twenty years old
and upward, every man able to go
forth to war: 29 the number of the
tribe of Is'sȧ·chär was fifty-four thousand four hundred.

30 Of the people of Zeb'ū·lŭn, their
generations, by their families, by their
fathers' houses, according to the number of names, from twenty years old
and upward, every man able to go
forth to war: 31 the number of the tribe
of Zeb'ū·lŭn was fifty-seven thousand
four hundred.

32 Of the people of Joseph, namely,
of the people of Ē'phrȧ·im, their generations, by their families, by their
fathers' houses, according to the number of names, from twenty years old
and upward, every man able to go
forth to war: 33 the number of the
tribe of Ē'phrȧ·im was forty thousand
five hundred.

34 Of the people of Mȧ·nas'sėh,
their generations, by their families, by
their fathers' houses, according to the
number of names, from twenty years
old and upward, every man able to go
forth to war: 35 the number of the
tribe of Mȧ·nas'sėh was thirty-two
thousand two hundred.

36 Of the people of Benjamin, their
generations, by their families, by their
fathers' houses, according to the number of names, from twenty years old
and upward, every man able to go
forth to war: 37 the number of the
tribe of Benjamin was thirty-five thousand four hundred.

38 Of the people of Dan, their
generations, by their families, by their
fathers' houses, according to the number of names, from twenty years old
and upward, every man able to go
forth to war: 39 the number of the tribe
of Dan was sixty-two thousand seven
hundred.

40 Of the people of Ash'ėr, their
generations, by their families, by their
fathers' houses, according to the number of names, from twenty years old
and upward, every man able to go
forth to war: 41 the number of the tribe

of Ash'ėr was forty-one thousand five
hundred.
42 Of the people of Naph'tȧ·lī, their
generations, by their families, by their
fathers' houses, according to the number of names, from twenty years old
and upward, every man able to go
forth to war: 43 the number of the tribe
of Naph'tȧ·lī was fifty-three thousand
four hundred.
44 These are those who were numbered, whom Moses and Aaron numbered with the help of the leaders of
Israel, twelve men, each representing
his fathers' house. 45 So the whole
number of the people of Israel, by
their fathers' houses, from twenty
years old and upward, every man able
to go forth to war in Israel—46 their
whole number was six hundred and
three thousand five hundred and fifty.
47 But the Levites were not numbered by their ancestral tribe along
with them. 48 For the LORD said to
Moses, 49 "Only the tribe of Levi you
shall not number, and you shall not
take a census of them among the people
of Israel; 50 but appoint the Levites
over the tabernacle of the testimony,
and over all its furnishings, and over
all that belongs to it; they are to carry
the tabernacle and all its furnishings,
and they shall tend it, and shall encamp around the tabernacle. 51 When
the tabernacle is to set out, the Levites
shall take it down; and when the tabernacle is to be pitched, the Levites shall
set it up. And if any one else comes
near, he shall be put to death. 52 The
people of Israel shall pitch their tents
by their companies, every man by his
own camp and every man by his own
standard; 53 but the Levites shall encamp around the tabernacle of the
testimony, that there may be no wrath
upon the congregation of the people of
Israel; and the Levites shall keep
charge of the tabernacle of the testimony." 54 Thus did the people of
Israel; they did according to all that
the LORD commanded Moses.
2 The LORD said to Moses and
Aaron, 2 "The people of Israel
shall encamp each by his own standard, with the ensigns of their fathers'
houses; they shall encamp facing the
tent of meeting on every side. 3 Those
to encamp on the east side toward the
sunrise shall be of the standard of
the camp of Judah by their companies,
the leader of the people of Judah being
Näh'shȯn the son of Am·min'ȧ·dab,
4 his host as numbered being seventy-
four thousand six hundred. 5 Those to
encamp next to him shall be the tribe
of Is'sȧ·chär, the leader of the people
of Issachar being Nė·than'el the son
of Zü'ȧr, 6 his host as numbered being
fifty-four thousand four hundred.
7 Then the tribe of Zeb'ū·lůn, the
leader of the people of Zebulun being
E·lī'ab the son of Hē'lon, 8 his host as
numbered being fifty-seven thousand
four hundred. 9 The whole number of
the camp of Judah, by their companies,
is a hundred and eighty-six thousand
four hundred. They shall set out first
on the march.
10 "On the south side shall be the
standard of the camp of Reuben by
their companies, the leader of the people of Reuben being E·lī'zůr the son
of Shed'ē·ůr, 11 his host as numbered
being forty-six thousand five hundred.
12 And those to encamp next to him
shall be the tribe of Simeon, the leader
of the people of Simeon being She·lü'-
mi-el the son of Zü·ri·shad'däi, 13 his
host as numbered being fifty-nine
thousand three hundred. 14 Then the
tribe of Gad, the leader of the people
of Gad being E·lī'ȧ·saph the son of
Reü'el, 15 his host as numbered being
forty-five thousand six hundred and
fifty. 16 The whole number of the
camp of Reuben, by their companies,
is a hundred and fifty-one thousand
four hundred and fifty. They shall set
out second.
17 "Then the tent of meeting shall
set out, with the camp of the Levites
in the midst of the camps; as they
encamp, so shall they set out, each in
position, standard by standard.
18 "On the west side shall be the
standard of the camp of E'phrȧ·im by
their companies, the leader of the
people of Ephraim being E·lish'ȧ·mȧ
the son of Am·mī'hůd, 19 his host as
numbered being forty thousand five
hundred. 20 And next to him shall be
the tribe of Mȧ·nas'sėh, the leader of
the people of Manasseh being Gȧ·mā'-
li·ėl the son of Pė·däh'zůr, 21 his host
as numbered being thirty-two thousand two hundred. 22 Then the tribe of
Benjamin, the leader of the people
of Benjamin being Ȧ·bī'dȧn the son of
Gid·ē·ō'ni, 23 his host as numbered being thirty-five thousand four hundred.

1.47: Num 2.33. **1.50-53:** Num 3.5-8, 21-37; 4.1-33; 8.19; 18.3-4, 23.

24 The whole number of the camp of
Ē'phrȧ·im, by their companies, is a
hundred and eight thousand one hundred. They shall set out third on the
march.

25 "On the north side shall be the
standard of the camp of Dan by their
companies, the leader of the people of
Dan being Ā·hī·ē'zėr the son of Am-
mi·shad'dāi, 26 his host as numbered
being sixty-two thousand seven hundred. 27 And those to encamp next to
him shall be the tribe of Ash'ėr, the
leader of the people of Asher being
Pā'gi·el the son of Ōch'rȧn, 28 his host
as numbered being forty-one thousand
five hundred. 29 Then the tribe of
Naph'tȧ·lī, the leader of the people of
Naphtali being Ȧ·hī'rȧ the son of
Ē'nan, 30 his host as numbered being
fifty-three thousand four hundred.
31 The whole number of the camp of
Dan is a hundred and fifty-seven
thousand six hundred. They shall set
out last, standard by standard."

32 These are the people of Israel as
numbered by their fathers' houses; all
in the camps who were numbered by
their companies were six hundred and
three thousand five hundred and fifty.
33 But the Levites were not numbered
among the people of Israel, as the
LORD commanded Moses.

34 Thus did the people of Israel.
According to all that the LORD commanded Moses, so they encamped by
their standards, and so they set out,
every one in his family, according to
his fathers' house.

3 These are the generations of
Aaron and Moses at the time when
the LORD spoke with Moses on Mount
Sinai. 2 These are the names of the
sons of Aaron: Nā'dab the first-born,
and Ȧ·bī'hū, El·ē·ā'zȧr, and Ith'ȧ·mär;
3 these are the names of the sons of
Aaron, the anointed priests, whom he
ordained to minister in the priest's
office. 4 But Nā'dab and Ȧ·bī'hū died
before the LORD when they offered
unholy fire before the LORD in the
wilderness of Sinai; and they had no
children. So El·ē·ā'zȧr and Ith'ȧ·mär
served as priests in the lifetime of
Aaron their father.

5 And the LORD said to Moses,
6 "Bring the tribe of Levi near, and
set them before Aaron the priest, that
they may minister to him. 7 They shall
perform duties for him and for the
whole congregation before the tent of
meeting, as they minister at the tabernacle; 8 they shall have charge of all
the furnishings of the tent of meeting,
and attend to the duties for the people
of Israel as they minister at the tabernacle. 9 And you shall give the Levites
to Aaron and his sons; they are wholly
given to him from among the people
of Israel. 10 And you shall appoint
Aaron and his sons, and they shall
attend to their priesthood; but if any
one else comes near, he shall be put
to death."

11 And the LORD said to Moses,
12 "Behold, I have taken the Levites
from among the people of Israel instead of every first-born that opens the
womb among the people of Israel. The
Levites shall be mine, 13 for all the
first-born are mine; on the day that I
slew all the first-born in the land of
Egypt, I consecrated for my own all
the first-born in Israel, both of man
and of beast; they shall be mine: I am
the LORD."

14 And the LORD said to Moses in
the wilderness of Sinai, 15 "Number
the sons of Levi, by fathers' houses
and by families; every male from a
month old and upward you shall number." 16 So Moses numbered them
according to the word of the LORD, as
he was commanded. 17 And these were
the sons of Levi by their names: Gēr'-
shȯn and Kō'hath and Mė·rär'ī. 18 And
these are the names of the sons of
Gēr'shȯn by their families: Lib'nī and
Shim'ē-ī. 19 And the sons of Kō'hath
by their families: Am'ram, Iz'här,
Hē'brȯn, and Uz'zi·el. 20 And the sons
of Mė·rär'ī by their families: Mäh'lī
and Mū'shī. These are the families of
the Levites, by their fathers' houses.

21 Of Gēr'shȯn were the family of
the Lib'nītes and the family of the
Shim'ē-ītes; these were the families of
the Gēr'shȯ·nītes. 22 Their number
according to the number of all the
males from a month old and upward
was[a] seven thousand five hundred.
23 The families of the Gēr'shȯ·nītes
were to encamp behind the tabernacle
on the west, 24 with Ē·lī'ȧ·saph, the son
of Lā'ėl as head of the fathers' house
of the Gēr'shȯ·nītes. 25 And the charge

[a] Heb *their number was*

3.2: Num 26.60. 3.5-13: Num 8.6-26. 3.5-8: Num 1.50-53; 3.21-37; 4.1-33; 8.19.
3.11-13: Num 3.45; 8.18. 3.15-34: Num 4.34-49. 3.17-20: Ex 6.16, 22.

of the sons of Gēr'shŏn in the tent of
meeting was to be the tabernacle, the
tent with its covering, the screen for
the door of the tent of meeting, 26 the
hangings of the court, the screen for
the door of the court which is around
the tabernacle and the altar, and its
cords; all the service pertaining to
these.

27 Of Kō'hath were the family of
the Am'rȧ·mītes, and the family of the
Iz·här'ītes, and the family of the Hē'-
brŏ·nītes, and the family of the Uz·zī'-
ė·lītes; these are the families of the
Kō'hȧ·thītes. 28 According to the number of all the males, from a month old
and upward, there were eight thousand
six hundred, attending to the duties of
the sanctuary. 29 The families of the
sons of Kō'hath were to encamp on
the south side of the tabernacle, 30 with
El·i·zā'phȧn the son of Uz'zi·el as head
of the fathers' house of the families of
the Kō'hȧ·thītes. 31 And their charge
was to be the ark, the table, the lampstand, the altars, the vessels of the
sanctuary with which the priests minister, and the screen; all the service
pertaining to these. 32 And El·ē·ā'zȧr
the son of Aaron the priest was to be
chief over the leaders of the Levites,
and to have oversight of those who
had charge of the sanctuary.

33 Of Mė·rär'ī were the family of
the Mäh'lītes and the family of the
Mū'shītes: these are the families of
Merari. 34 Their number according to
the number of all the males from a
month old and upward was six thousand two hundred. 35 And the head of
the fathers' house of the families of
Mė·rär'ī was Zū'ri·el the son of Ab·i-
hā'il; they were to encamp on the
north side of the tabernacle. 36 And the
appointed charge of the sons of Mė-
rär'ī was to be the frames of the tabernacle, the bars, the pillars, the bases,
and all their accessories; all the service
pertaining to these; 37 also the pillars
of the court round about, with their
bases and pegs and cords.

38 And those to encamp before the
tabernacle on the east, before the tent
of meeting toward the sunrise, were
Moses and Aaron and his sons, having
charge of the rites within the sanctuary,
whatever had to be done for the people
of Israel; and any one else who came
near was to be put to death. 39 All who
were numbered of the Levites, whom
Moses and Aaron numbered at the
commandment of the LORD, by families, all the males from a month old
and upward, were twenty-two thousand.

40 And the LORD said to Moses,
"Number all the first-born males of
the people of Israel, from a month old
and upward, taking their number by
names. 41 And you shall take the
Levites for me—I am the LORD—
instead of all the first-born among the
people of Israel, and the cattle of the
Levites instead of all the firstlings
among the cattle of the people of
Israel." 42 So Moses numbered all the
first-born among the people of Israel,
as the LORD commanded him. 43 And
all the first-born males, according to
the number of names, from a month
old and upward as numbered were
twenty-two thousand two hundred
and seventy-three.

44 And the LORD said to Moses,
45 "Take the Levites instead of all the
first-born among the people of Israel,
and the cattle of the Levites instead of
their cattle; and the Levites shall be
mine: I am the LORD. 46 And for the
redemption of the two hundred and
seventy-three of the first-born of the
people of Israel, over and above the
number of the male Levites, 47 you
shall take five shekels apiece; reckoning by the shekel of the sanctuary, the
shekel of twenty gerahs, you shall take
them, 48 and give the money by which
the excess number of them is redeemed
to Aaron and his sons." 49 So Moses
took the redemption money from those
who were over and above those redeemed by the Levites; 50 from the
first-born of the people of Israel he
took the money, one thousand three
hundred and sixty-five shekels, reckoned by the shekel of the sanctuary;
51 and Moses gave the redemption
money to Aaron and his sons, according to the word of the LORD, as the
LORD commanded Moses.

4 The LORD said to Moses and
Aaron, 2 "Take a census of the
sons of Kō'hath from among the sons
of Levi, by their families and their
fathers' houses, 3 from thirty years old
up to fifty years old, all who can enter
the service, to do the work in the tent
of meeting. 4 This is the service of the
sons of Kō'hath in the tent of meeting:
the most holy things. 5 When the

3.45: Num 3.11-13; 8.18. **4.1-33:** Num 1.50-53; 3.5-8, 21-37; 8.19; 18.3-4, 23.

camp is to set out, Aaron and his sons
shall go in and take down the veil of
the screen, and cover the ark of the
testimony with it; 6 then they shall put
on it a covering of goatskin, and spread
over that a cloth all of blue, and shall
put in its poles. 7And over the table of
the bread of the Presence they shall
spread a cloth of blue, and put upon
it the plates, the dishes for incense,
the bowls, and the flagons for the
drink offering; the continual bread also
shall be on it; 8 then they shall spread
over them a cloth of scarlet, and cover
the same with a covering of goatskin,
and shall put in its poles. 9And they
shall take a cloth of blue, and cover the
lampstand for the light, with its lamps,
its snuffers, its trays, and all the vessels
for oil with which it is supplied: 10 and
they shall put it with all its utensils in
a covering of goatskin and put it upon
the carrying frame. 11And over the
golden altar they shall spread a cloth
of blue, and cover it with a covering
of goatskin, and shall put in its poles;
12 and they shall take all the vessels of
the service which are used in the
sanctuary, and put them in a cloth of
blue, and cover them with a covering
of goatskin, and put them on the
carrying frame. 13And they shall take
away the ashes from the altar, and
spread a purple cloth over it; 14 and
they shall put on it all the utensils of
the altar, which are used for the
service there, the firepans, the forks,
the shovels, and the basins, all the
utensils of the altar; and they shall
spread upon it a covering of goatskin,
and shall put in its poles. 15And when
Aaron and his sons have finished
covering the sanctuary and all the
furnishings of the sanctuary, as the
camp sets out, after that the sons of
Kō'hath shall come to carry these, but
they must not touch the holy things,
lest they die. These are the things of
the tent of meeting which the sons of
Kohath are to carry.

16 "And El·ē·ā'zär the son of Aaron
the priest shall have charge of the oil
for the light, the fragrant incense, the
continual cereal offering, and the
anointing oil, with the oversight of all
the tabernacle and all that is in it, of
the sanctuary and its vessels."

17 The LORD said to Moses and
Aaron, 18 "Let not the tribe of the
families of the Kō'hȧ·thītes be destroyed from among the Levites; 19 but
deal thus with them, that they may
live and not die when they come near
to the most holy things: Aaron and his
sons shall go in and appoint them each
to his task and to his burden, 20 but
they shall not go in to look upon the
holy things even for a moment, lest
they die."

21 The LORD said to Moses,
22 "Take a census of the sons of Gẽr'-
shȯn also, by their families and their
fathers' houses; 23 from thirty years
old up to fifty years old, you shall
number them, all who can enter for
service, to do the work in the tent of
meeting. 24 This is the service of the
families of the Gẽr'shȯ·nītes, in serving
and bearing burdens: 25 they shall
carry the curtains of the tabernacle,
and the tent of meeting with its covering, and the covering of goatskin that
is on top of it, and the screen for the
door of the tent of meeting, 26 and the
hangings of the court, and the screen
for the entrance of the gate of the
court which is around the tabernacle
and the altar, and their cords, and all
the equipment for their service; and
they shall do all that needs to be done
with regard to them. 27All the service
of the sons of the Gẽr'shȯ·nītes shall
be at the command of Aaron and his
sons, in all that they are to carry, and
in all that they have to do; and you
shall assign to their charge all that
they are to carry. 28 This is the service
of the families of the sons of the Gẽr'-
shȯ·nītes in the tent of meeting, and
their work is to be under the oversight
of Ith'ȧ·mär the son of Aaron the priest.

29 "As for the sons of Mė·rär'ī, you
shall number them by their families and their fathers' houses; 30 from
thirty years old up to fifty years old,
you shall number them, every one
that can enter the service, to do the
work of the tent of meeting. 31And
this is what they are charged to carry,
as the whole of their service in the tent
of meeting: the frames of the tabernacle, with its bars, pillars, and bases,
32 and the pillars of the court round
about with their bases, pegs, and cords,
with all their equipment and all their
accessories; and you shall assign by
name the objects which they are required to carry. 33 This is the service
of the families of the sons of Mė·rär'ī,
the whole of their service in the tent
of meeting, under the hand of Ith'ȧ-
mär the son of Aaron the priest."

34 And Moses and Aaron and the
leaders of the congregation numbered
the sons of the Kō'hȧ·thītes, by their
families and their fathers' houses,
35 from thirty years old up to fifty
years old, every one that could enter
the service, for work in the tent of
meeting; 36 and their number by
families was two thousand seven hundred and fifty. 37 This was the number
of the families of the Kō'hȧ·thītes, all
who served in the tent of meeting,
whom Moses and Aaron numbered
according to the commandment of the
LORD by Moses.

38 The number of the sons of
Gẽr'shȯn, by their families and their
fathers' houses, 39 from thirty years
old up to fifty years old, every one that
could enter the service for work in the
tent of meeting—40 their number by
their families and their fathers' houses
was two thousand six hundred and
thirty. 41 This was the number of the
families of the sons of Gẽr'shȯn, all
who served in the tent of meeting,
whom Moses and Aaron numbered
according to the commandment of the
LORD.

42 The number of the families of
the sons of Mė·rär'ī, by their families
and their fathers' houses, 43 from thirty
years old up to fifty years old, every
one that could enter the service, for
work in the tent of meeting—44 their
number by families was three thousand
two hundred. 45 These are those who
were numbered of the families of the
sons of Mė·rär'ī, whom Moses and
Aaron numbered according to the
commandment of the LORD by Moses.

46 All those who were numbered of
the Levites, whom Moses and Aaron
and the leaders of Israel numbered, by
their families and their fathers' houses,
47 from thirty years old up to fifty
years old, every one that could enter
to do the work of service and the work
of bearing burdens in the tent of meeting, 48 those who were numbered of
them were eight thousand five hundred
and eighty. 49 According to the commandment of the LORD through Moses
they were appointed, each to his task
of serving or carrying; thus they were
numbered by him, as the LORD commanded Moses.

5 The LORD said to Moses, 2 "Command the people of Israel that they
put out of the camp every leper, and
every one having a discharge, and
every one that is unclean through contact with the dead; 3 you shall put out
both male and female, putting them
outside the camp, that they may not
defile their camp, in the midst of which
I dwell." 4 And the people of Israel did
so, and drove them outside the camp;
as the LORD said to Moses, so the people of Israel did.

5 And the LORD said to Moses,
6 "Say to the people of Israel, When
a man or woman commits any of the
sins that men commit by breaking
faith with the LORD, and that person
is guilty, 7 he shall confess his sin
which he has committed; and he shall
make full restitution for his wrong,
adding a fifth to it, and giving it to him
to whom he did the wrong. 8 But if
the man has no kinsman to whom
restitution may be made for the wrong,
the restitution for wrong shall go to
the LORD for the priest, in addition to
the ram of atonement with which
atonement is made for him. 9 And every
offering, all the holy things of the
people of Israel, which they bring to
the priest, shall be his; 10 and every
man's holy things shall be his; whatever any man gives to the priest shall
be his."

11 And the LORD said to Moses,
12 "Say to the people of Israel, If any
man's wife goes astray and acts unfaithfully against him, 13 if a man lies
with her carnally, and it is hidden
from the eyes of her husband, and she
is undetected though she has defiled
herself, and there is no witness against
her, since she was not taken in the act;
14 and if the spirit of jealousy comes
upon him, and he is jealous of his wife
who has defiled herself; or if the spirit
of jealousy comes upon him, and he is
jealous of his wife, though she has not
defiled herself; 15 then the man shall
bring his wife to the priest, and bring
the offering required of her, a tenth of
an ephah of barley meal; he shall pour
no oil upon it and put no frankincense
on it, for it is a cereal offering of
jealousy, a cereal offering of remembrance, bringing iniquity to remembrance.

16 "And the priest shall bring her
near, and set her before the LORD;
17 and the priest shall take holy water
in an earthen vessel, and take some of
the dust that is on the floor of the

4.34-49: Num 3.15-34. **5.2-3:** Num 12.14-15. **5.5-8:** Ex 22.7-15; Lev 6.1-7.

tabernacle and put it into the water.
18 And the priest shall set the woman
before the LORD, and unbind the hair
of the woman's head, and place in her
hands the cereal offering of remembrance, which is the cereal offering of
jealousy. And in his hand the priest
shall have the water of bitterness that
brings the curse. 19 Then the priest
shall make her take an oath, saying,
'If no man has lain with you, and if
you have not turned aside to uncleanness, while you were under your husband's authority, be free from this
water of bitterness that brings the
curse. 20 But if you have gone astray,
though you are under your husband's
authority, and if you have defiled yourself, and some man other than your
husband has lain with you, 21 then'
(let the priest make the woman take
the oath of the curse, and say to the
woman) 'the LORD make you an execration and an oath among your people, when the LORD makes your thigh
fall away and your body swell; 22 may
this water that brings the curse pass
into your bowels and make your body
swell and your thigh fall away.' And
the woman shall say, 'Amen, Amen.'

23 "Then the priest shall write
these curses in a book, and wash them
off into the water of bitterness; 24 and
he shall make the woman drink the
water of bitterness that brings the
curse, and the water that brings the
curse shall enter into her and cause
bitter pain. 25 And the priest shall take
the cereal offering of jealousy out of
the woman's hand, and shall wave the
cereal offering before the LORD and
bring it to the altar; 26 and the priest
shall take a handful of the cereal offering, as its memorial portion, and burn
it upon the altar, and afterward shall
make the woman drink the water.
27 And when he has made her drink
the water, then, if she has defiled herself and has acted unfaithfully against
her husband, the water that brings the
curse shall enter into her and cause
bitter pain, and her body shall swell,
and her thigh shall fall away, and the
woman shall become an execration
among her people. 28 But if the woman
has not defiled herself and is clean,
then she shall be free and shall conceive children.

29 "This is the law in cases of
jealousy, when a wife, though under
her husband's authority, goes astray
and defiles herself, 30 or when the
spirit of jealousy comes upon a man
and he is jealous of his wife; then he
shall set the woman before the LORD,
and the priest shall execute upon her
all this law. 31 The man shall be free
from iniquity, but the woman shall
bear her iniquity."

6 And the LORD said to Moses,
2 "Say to the people of Israel,
When either a man or a woman makes
a special vow, the vow of a Naz'i·rite,[b]
to separate himself to the LORD, 3 he
shall separate himself from wine and
strong drink; he shall drink no vinegar
made from wine or strong drink, and
shall not drink any juice of grapes or
eat grapes, fresh or dried. 4 All the days
of his separation[c] he shall eat nothing
that is produced by the grapevine, not
even the seeds or the skins.

5 "All the days of his vow of separation no razor shall come upon his
head; until the time is completed for
which he separates himself to the
LORD, he shall be holy; he shall let the
locks of hair of his head grow long.

6 "All the days that he separates
himself to the LORD he shall not go
near a dead body. 7 Neither for his
father nor for his mother, nor for
brother or sister, if they die, shall he
make himself unclean; because his
separation to God is upon his head.
8 All the days of his separation he is
holy to the LORD.

9 "And if any man dies very suddenly beside him, and he defiles his
consecrated head, then he shall shave
his head on the day of his cleansing;
on the seventh day he shall shave it.
10 On the eighth day he shall bring
two turtledoves or two young pigeons
to the priest to the door of the tent of
meeting, 11 and the priest shall offer
one for a sin offering and the other for
a burnt offering, and make atonement
for him, because he sinned by reason
of the dead body. And he shall consecrate his head that same day, 12 and
separate himself to the LORD for the
days of his separation, and bring a
male lamb a year old for a guilt offering; but the former time shall be void,
because his separation was defiled.

13 "And this is the law for the
Naz'i·rite, when the time of his separa-

[b] That is *one separated* or *one consecrated* [c] Or *Naziriteship*
6.3: Lk 1.15. 6.13-21: Acts 21.24, 26.

tion has been completed: he shall be
brought to the door of the tent of
meeting, 14 and he shall offer his gift
to the LORD, one male lamb a year old
without blemish for a burnt offering,
and one ewe lamb a year old without
blemish as a sin offering, and one ram
without blemish as a peace offering,
15 and a basket of unleavened bread,
cakes of fine flour mixed with oil, and
unleavened wafers spread with oil, and
their cereal offering and their drink
offerings. 16 And the priest shall present them before the LORD and offer
his sin offering and his burnt offering,
17 and he shall offer the ram as a
sacrifice of peace offering to the LORD,
with the basket of unleavened bread;
the priest shall offer also its cereal
offering and its drink offering. 18 And
the Naz′i·rīte shall shave his consecrated head at the door of the tent of
meeting, and shall take the hair from
his consecrated head and put it on the
fire which is under the sacrifice of the
peace offering. 19 And the priest shall
take the shoulder of the ram, when it
is boiled, and one unleavened cake out
of the basket, and one unleavened
wafer, and shall put them upon the
hands of the Naz′i·rīte, after he has
shaven the hair of his consecration,
20 and the priest shall wave them for
a wave offering before the LORD; they
are a holy portion for the priest, together with the breast that is waved
and the thigh that is offered; and after
that the Naz′i·rīte may drink wine.

21 "This is the law for the Naz′i-
rīte who takes a vow. His offering to
the LORD shall be according to his vow
as a Nazirite, apart from what else he
can afford; in accordance with the
vow which he takes, so shall he do
according to the law for his separation
as a Nazirite."

22 The LORD said to Moses, 23 "Say
to Aaron and his sons, Thus you shall
bless the people of Israel: you shall
say to them,

24 The LORD bless you and keep you:
25 The LORD make his face to shine
upon you, and be gracious to you:
26 The LORD lift up his countenance
upon you, and give you peace.

27 "So shall they put my name
upon the people of Israel, and I will
bless them."

7 On the day when Moses had
finished setting up the tabernacle,
and had anointed and consecrated it
with all its furnishings, and had
anointed and consecrated the altar with
all its utensils, 2 the leaders of Israel,
heads of their fathers' houses, the
leaders of the tribes, who were over
those who were numbered, 3 offered
and brought their offerings before the
LORD, six covered wagons and twelve
oxen, a wagon for every two of the
leaders, and for each one an ox; they
offered them before the tabernacle.
4 Then the LORD said to Moses,
5 "Accept these from them, that they
may be used in doing the service of
the tent of meeting, and give them to
the Levites, to each man according to
his service." 6 So Moses took the
wagons and the oxen, and gave them
to the Levites. 7 Two wagons and
four oxen he gave to the sons of Gĕr′-
shŏn, according to their service; 8 and
four wagons and eight oxen he gave to
the sons of Mė·rãr′ī, according to their
service, under the direction of Ĭth′ȧ-
mär the son of Aaron the priest. 9 But
to the sons of Kō′hath he gave none,
because they were charged with the
care of the holy things which had to
be carried on the shoulder. 10 And the
leaders offered offerings for the dedication of the altar on the day it was
anointed; and the leaders offered their
offering before the altar. 11 And the
LORD said to Moses, "They shall offer
their offerings, one leader each day,
for the dedication of the altar."

12 He who offered his offering the
first day was Näh′shŏn the son of
Am·min′ȧ·dab, of the tribe of Judah;
13 and his offering was one silver plate
whose weight was a hundred and thirty
shekels, one silver basin of seventy
shekels, according to the shekel of the
sanctuary, both of them full of fine
flour mixed with oil for a cereal offering; 14 one golden dish of ten shekels,
full of incense; 15 one young bull, one
ram, one male lamb a year old, for a
burnt offering; 16 one male goat for a
sin offering; 17 and for the sacrifice of
peace offerings, two oxen, five rams,
five male goats, and five male lambs a
year old. This was the offering of
Näh′shŏn the son of Am·min′ȧ·dab.

18 On the second day Nė·than′el
the son of Zü′ȧr, the leader of Is′sȧ-
chär, made an offering; 19 he offered
for his offering one silver plate, whose
weight was a hundred and thirty
shekels, one silver basin of seventy
shekels, according to the shekel of the

sanctuary, both of them full of fine
flour mixed with oil for a cereal offering; 20 one golden dish of ten shekels,
full of incense; 21 one young bull, one
ram, one male lamb a year old, for a
burnt offering; 22 one male goat for a
sin offering; 23 and for the sacrifice of
peace offerings, two oxen, five rams,
five male goats, and five male lambs a
year old. This was the offering of
Nė·than'el the son of Zū'ȧr.

24 On the third day E·lī'ab the son
of Hē'lon, the leader of the men of
Zeb'ū·lu̇n: 25 his offering was one
silver plate, whose weight was a hundred and thirty shekels, one silver
basin of seventy shekels, according to
the shekel of the sanctuary, both of
them full of fine flour mixed with oil
for a cereal offering; 26 one golden dish
of ten shekels, full of incense; 27 one
young bull, one ram, one male lamb a
year old, for a burnt offering; 28 one
male goat for a sin offering; 29 and for
the sacrifice of peace offerings, two
oxen, five rams, five male goats, and
five male lambs a year old. This was
the offering of E·lī'ab the son of Hē'lon.

30 On the fourth day E·lī'zu̇r the
son of Shed'ē·u̇r, the leader of the men
of Reuben: 31 his offering was one
silver plate whose weight was a hundred and thirty shekels, one silver
basin of seventy shekels, according to
the shekel of the sanctuary, both of
them full of fine flour mixed with oil
for a cereal offering; 32 one golden dish
of ten shekels, full of incense; 33 one
young bull, one ram, one male lamb a
year old, for a burnt offering; 34 one
male goat for a sin offering; 35 and for
the sacrifice of peace offerings, two
oxen, five rams, five male goats, and
five male lambs a year old. This was
the offering of E·lī'zu̇r the son of
Shed'ē·u̇r.

36 On the fifth day She·lü'mi-el the
son of Zü·ri·shad'däi, the leader of the
men of Simeon: 37 his offering was one
silver plate, whose weight was a hundred and thirty shekels, one silver
basin of seventy shekels, according to
the shekel of the sanctuary, both of
them full of fine flour mixed with oil
for a cereal offering; 38 one golden dish
of ten shekels, full of incense; 39 one
young bull, one ram, one male lamb
a year old, for a burnt offering; 40 one
male goat for a sin offering; 41 and for
the sacrifice of peace offerings, two
oxen, five rams, five male goats, and
five male lambs a year old. This was
the offering of She·lü'mi-el the son of
Zü·ri·shad'däi.

42 On the sixth day E·lī'ȧ·saph the
son of Deü'el, the leader of the men of
Gad: 43 his offering was one silver
plate, whose weight was a hundred
and thirty shekels, one silver basin of
seventy shekels, according to the shekel
of the sanctuary, both of them full
of fine flour mixed with oil for a
cereal offering; 44 one golden dish
of ten shekels, full of incense; 45 one
young bull, one ram, one male lamb
a year old, for a burnt offering;
46 one male goat for a sin offering;
47 and for the sacrifice of peace offerings, two oxen, five rams, five male
goats, and five male lambs a year old.
This was the offering of E·lī'ȧ·saph the
son of Deü'el.

48 On the seventh day E·lish'ȧ·mȧ
the son of Am·mī'hu̇d, the leader of
the men of E'phrȧ·im: 49 his offering
was one silver plate, whose weight was
a hundred and thirty shekels, one
silver basin of seventy shekels, according to the shekel of the sanctuary, both
of them full of fine flour mixed with
oil for a cereal offering; 50 one golden
dish of ten shekels, full of incense;
51 one young bull, one ram, one male
lamb a year old, for a burnt offering;
52 one male goat for a sin offering;
53 and for the sacrifice of peace offerings, two oxen, five rams, five male
goats, and five male lambs a year old.
This was the offering of E·lish'ȧ·mȧ
the son of Am·mī'hu̇d.

54 On the eighth day Gȧ·mā'li·ėl
the son of Pė·däh'zu̇r, the leader of the
men of Mȧ·nas'sėh: 55 his offering was
one silver plate, whose weight was a
hundred and thirty shekels, one silver
basin of seventy shekels, according to
the shekel of the sanctuary, both of
them full of fine flour mixed with oil
for a cereal offering; 56 one golden dish
of ten shekels, full of incense; 57 one
young bull, one ram, one male lamb a
year old, for a burnt offering; 58 one
male goat for a sin offering; 59 and for
the sacrifice of peace offerings, two
oxen, five rams, five male goats, and
five male lambs a year old. This was
the offering of Gȧ·mā'li·ėl the son of
Pė·däh'zu̇r.

60 On the ninth day A·bī'dȧn the
son of Gid·ē·ō'ni, the leader of the men
of Benjamin: 61 his offering was one
silver plate, whose weight was a hun-

dred and thirty shekels, one silver
basin of seventy shekels, according to
the shekel of the sanctuary, both of
them full of fine flour mixed with oil
for a cereal offering; 62 one golden dish
of ten shekels, full of incense; 63 one
young bull, one ram, one male lamb a
year old, for a burnt offering; 64 one
male goat for a sin offering; 65 and for
the sacrifice of peace offerings, two
oxen, five rams, five male goats, and
five male lambs a year old. This was
the offering of A·bī'dȧn the son of
Gid·ē·ō'ni.

66 On the tenth day Ā·hi·ē'zėr the
son of Am·mi·shad'dāi, the leader of
the men of Dan: 67 his offering was one
silver plate, whose weight was a hundred and thirty shekels, one silver basin
of seventy shekels, according to the
shekel of the sanctuary, both of them
full of fine flour mixed with oil for a
cereal offering; 68 one golden dish of
ten shekels, full of incense; 69 one
young bull, one ram, one male lamb a
year old, for a burnt offering; 70 one
male goat for a sin offering; 71 and for
the sacrifice of peace offerings, two
oxen, five rams, five male goats, and
five male lambs a year old. This was
the offering of Ā·hi·ē'zėr the son of
Am·mi·shad'dāi.

72 On the eleventh day Pā'gi·el the
son of Ōch'rȧn, the leader of the men
of Ash'ėr: 73 his offering was one silver
plate, whose weight was a hundred
and thirty shekels, one silver basin of
seventy shekels, according to the
shekel of the sanctuary, both of them
full of fine flour mixed with oil for a
cereal offering; 74 one golden dish of
ten shekels, full of incense; 75 one
young bull, one ram, one male lamb a
year old, for a burnt offering; 76 one
male goat for a sin offering; 77 and for
the sacrifice of peace offerings, two
oxen, five rams, five male goats, and
five male lambs a year old. This was
the offering of Pā'gi·el the son of
Ōch'rȧn.

78 On the twelfth day A·hī'rȧ the
son of Ē'nan, the leader of the men of
Naph'tȧ·lī: 79 his offering was one
silver plate, whose weight was a hundred and thirty shekels, one silver
basin of seventy shekels, according to
the shekel of the sanctuary, both of
them full of fine flour mixed with oil
for a cereal offering; 80 one golden dish
of ten shekels, full of incense; 81 one
young bull, one ram, one male lamb a
year old, for a burnt offering; 82 one
male goat for a sin offering; 83 and for
the sacrifice of peace offerings, two
oxen, five rams, five male goats, and
five male lambs a year old. This
was the offering of A·hī'rȧ the son of
Ē'nan.

84 This was the dedication offering
for the altar, on the day when it was
anointed, from the leaders of Israel:
twelve silver plates, twelve silver
basins, twelve golden dishes, 85 each
silver plate weighing a hundred and
thirty shekels and each basin seventy,
all the silver of the vessels two thousand four hundred shekels according
to the shekel of the sanctuary, 86 the
twelve golden dishes, full of incense,
weighing ten shekels apiece according
to the shekel of the sanctuary, all the
gold of the dishes being a hundred and
twenty shekels; 87 all the cattle for the
burnt offering twelve bulls, twelve
rams, twelve male lambs a year old,
with their cereal offering; and twelve
male goats for a sin offering; 88 and all
the cattle for the sacrifice of peace
offerings twenty-four bulls, the rams
sixty, the male goats sixty, the male
lambs a year old sixty. This was the
dedication offering for the altar, after
it was anointed.

89 And when Moses went into the
tent of meeting to speak with the LORD,
he heard the voice speaking to him
from above the mercy seat that was
upon the ark of the testimony, from
between the two cherubim; and it
spoke to him.

8 Now the LORD said to Moses,
2 "Say to Aaron, When you set up
the lamps, the seven lamps shall give
light in front of the lampstand." 3 And
Aaron did so; he set up its lamps to
give light in front of the lampstand, as
the LORD commanded Moses. 4 And
this was the workmanship of the lampstand, hammered work of gold; from
its base to its flowers, it was hammered
work; according to the pattern which
the LORD had shown Moses, so he
made the lampstand.

5 And the LORD said to Moses,
6 "Take the Levites from among the
people of Israel, and cleanse them. 7 And
thus you shall do to them, to cleanse
them: sprinkle the water of expiation
upon them, and let them go with a
razor over all their body, and wash

8.6-26: Num 3.5-13.

their clothes and cleanse themselves.
8 Then let them take a young bull and
its cereal offering of fine flour mixed
with oil, and you shall take another
young bull for a sin offering. 9 And you
shall present the Levites before the
tent of meeting, and assemble the
whole congregation of the people of
Israel. 10 When you present the Levites before the LORD, the people of
Israel shall lay their hands upon the
Levites, 11 and Aaron shall offer the
Levites before the LORD as a wave
offering from the people of Israel, that
it may be theirs to do the service of the
LORD. 12 Then the Levites shall lay
their hands upon the heads of the
bulls; and you shall offer the one for a
sin offering and the other for a burnt
offering to the LORD, to make atonement for the Levites. 13 And you shall
cause the Levites to attend Aaron and
his sons, and shall offer them as a wave
offering to the LORD.

14 "Thus you shall separate the
Levites from among the people of
Israel, and the Levites shall be mine.
15 And after that the Levites shall go
in to do service at the tent of meeting,
when you have cleansed them and
offered them as a wave offering. 16 For
they are wholly given to me from
among the people of Israel; instead of
all that open the womb, the first-born
of all the people of Israel, I have taken
them for myself. 17 For all the first-
born among the people of Israel are
mine, both of man and of beast; on the
day that I slew all the first-born in the
land of Egypt I consecrated them for
myself, 18 and I have taken the Levites
instead of all the first-born among the
people of Israel. 19 And I have given
the Levites as a gift to Aaron and his
sons from among the people of Israel,
to do the service for the people of
Israel at the tent of meeting, and to
make atonement for the people of
Israel, that there may be no plague
among the people of Israel in case the
people of Israel should come near the
sanctuary."

20 Thus did Moses and Aaron and
all the congregation of the people of
Israel to the Levites; according to all
that the LORD commanded Moses concerning the Levites, the people of
Israel did to them. 21 And the Levites
purified themselves from sin, and
washed their clothes; and Aaron offered
them as a wave offering before the
LORD, and Aaron made atonement for
them to cleanse them. 22 And after that
the Levites went in to do their service
in the tent of meeting in attendance
upon Aaron and his sons; as the LORD
had commanded Moses concerning the
Levites, so they did to them.

23 And the LORD said to Moses,
24 "This is what pertains to the Levites: from twenty-five years old and
upward they shall go in to perform the
work in the service of the tent of meeting; 25 and from the age of fifty years
they shall withdraw from the work of
the service and serve no more, 26 but
minister to their brethren in the tent
of meeting, to keep the charge, and
they shall do no service. Thus shall
you do to the Levites in assigning their
duties."

9 And the LORD spoke to Moses in
the wilderness of Sinai, in the first
month of the second year after they
had come out of the land of Egypt,
saying, 2 "Let the people of Israel keep
the passover at its appointed time. 3 On
the fourteenth day of this month, in
the evening, you shall keep it at its
appointed time; according to all its
statutes and all its ordinances you shall
keep it." 4 So Moses told the people
of Israel that they should keep the
passover. 5 And they kept the passover
in the first month, on the fourteenth
day of the month, in the evening, in
the wilderness of Sinai; according to
all that the LORD commanded Moses,
so the people of Israel did. 6 And there
were certain men who were unclean
through touching the dead body of a
man, so that they could not keep the
passover on that day; and they came
before Moses and Aaron on that day;
7 and those men said to him, "We are
unclean through touching the dead
body of a man; why are we kept from
offering the LORD's offering at its
appointed time among the people of
Israel?" 8 And Moses said to them,
"Wait, that I may hear what the LORD
will command concerning you."

9 The LORD said to Moses, 10 "Say
to the people of Israel, If any man of
you or of your descendants is unclean
through touching a dead body, or is
afar off on a journey, he shall still keep
the passover to the LORD. 11 In the
second month on the fourteenth day
in the evening they shall keep it; they

8.18: Num 3.11-13, 45. **9.1-5:** Ex 12.1-14, 21-28.

shall eat it with unleavened bread and
bitter herbs. 12 They shall leave none
of it until the morning, nor break a
bone of it; according to all the statute
for the passover they shall keep it.
13 But the man who is clean and is not
on a journey, yet refrains from keeping
the passover, that person shall be cut
off from his people, because he did not
offer the LORD's offering at its appointed time; that man shall bear his
sin. 14 And if a stranger sojourns among
you, and will keep the passover to the
LORD, according to the statute of the
passover and according to its ordinance, so shall he do; you shall have
one statute, both for the sojourner and
for the native."

15 On the day that the tabernacle
was set up, the cloud covered the tabernacle, the tent of the testimony; and
at evening it was over the tabernacle
like the appearance of fire until morning. 16 So it was continually; the cloud
covered it by day,[d] and the appearance
of fire by night. 17 And whenever the
cloud was taken up from over the tent,
after that the people of Israel set out;
and in the place where the cloud
settled down, there the people of Israel
encamped. 18 At the command of the
LORD the people of Israel set out, and
at the command of the LORD they encamped; as long as the cloud rested
over the tabernacle, they remained in
camp. 19 Even when the cloud continued over the tabernacle many days,
the people of Israel kept the charge of
the LORD, and did not set out. 20 Sometimes the cloud was a few days over
the tabernacle, and according to the
command of the LORD they remained
in camp; then according to the command of the LORD they set out. 21 And
sometimes the cloud remained from
evening until morning; and when the
cloud was taken up in the morning,
they set out, or if it continued for a
day and a night, when the cloud was
taken up they set out. 22 Whether it
was two days, or a month, or a longer
time, that the cloud continued over
the tabernacle, abiding there, the people of Israel remained in camp and
did not set out; but when it was taken
up they set out. 23 At the command of
the LORD they encamped, and at the
command of the LORD they set out;
they kept the charge of the LORD,
at the command of the LORD by
Moses.

10 The LORD said to Moses,
2 "Make two silver trumpets; of
hammered work you shall make them;
and you shall use them for summoning
the congregation, and for breaking
camp. 3 And when both are blown, all
the congregation shall gather themselves to you at the entrance of the tent
of meeting. 4 But if they blow only
one, then the leaders, the heads of the
tribes of Israel, shall gather themselves
to you. 5 When you blow an alarm,
the camps that are on the east side
shall set out. 6 And when you blow an
alarm the second time, the camps that
are on the south side shall set out. An
alarm is to be blown whenever they
are to set out. 7 But when the assembly
is to be gathered together, you shall
blow, but you shall not sound an
alarm. 8 And the sons of Aaron, the
priests, shall blow the trumpets. The
trumpets shall be to you for a perpetual
statute throughout your generations.
9 And when you go to war in your land
against the adversary who oppresses
you, then you shall sound an alarm
with the trumpets, that you may be
remembered before the LORD your
God, and you shall be saved from your
enemies. 10 On the day of your gladness also, and at your appointed feasts,
and at the beginnings of your months,
you shall blow the trumpets over your
burnt offerings and over the sacrifices
of your peace offerings; they shall serve
you for remembrance before your God;
I am the LORD your God."

11 In the second year, in the second
month, on the twentieth day of the
month, the cloud was taken up from
over the tabernacle of the testimony,
12 and the people of Israel set out by
stages from the wilderness of Sinai;
and the cloud settled down in the
wilderness of Pâr′an. 13 They set out
for the first time at the command of
the LORD by Moses. 14 The standard
of the camp of the men of Judah set
out first by their companies; and over
their host was Näh′shŏn the son of
Am·min′ȧ·dab. 15 And over the host of
the tribe of the men of Is′sȧ·chär was
Nė·than′el the son of Zü′ȧr. 16 And
over the host of the tribe of the men
of Zeb′ū·lŭn was E·lī′ab the son of
Hē′lon.

[d] Gk Syr Vg: Heb lacks *by day*
9.12: Ex 12.46; Jn 19.36. **9.15-23:** Ex 40.36-38.

17 And when the tabernacle was
taken down, the sons of Gēr′shŏn and
the sons of Mė·rär′ī, who carried the
tabernacle, set out. 18 And the standard
of the camp of Reuben set out by their
companies; and over their host was
E·lī′zŭr the son of Shed′ē·ŭr. 19 And
over the host of the tribe of the men
of Simeon was She·lü′mi-el the son of
Zü·ri·shad′däi. 20 And over the host of
the tribe of the men of Gad was E·lī′ȧ-
saph the son of Deü′el.

21 Then the Kō′hȧ·thītes set out,
carrying the holy things, and the
tabernacle was set up before their
arrival. 22 And the standard of the
camp of the men of E′phrȧ·im set out
by their companies; and over their host
was E·lish′ȧ·mȧ the son of Am·mī′hŭd.
23 And over the host of the tribe of the
men of Mȧ·nas′sėh was Gȧ·mā′li·ėl the
son of Pė·däh′zŭr. 24 And over the host
of the tribe of the men of Benjamin
was Ȧ·bī′dȧn the son of Gid·ē·ō′ni.

25 Then the standard of the camp
of the men of Dan, acting as the rear
guard of all the camps, set out by their
companies; and over their host was
Ā·hi·ē′zėr the son of Am·mi·shad′däi.
26 And over the host of the tribe of the
men of Ash′ėr was Pā′gi·el the son of
Ōch′rȧn. 27 And over the host of the
tribe of the men of Naph′tȧ·lī was
Ȧ·hī′rȧ the son of Ē′nan. 28 This was
the order of march of the people of
Israel according to their hosts, when
they set out.

29 And Moses said to Hō′bab the
son of Reü′el the Mid′i·ȧn·ite, Moses'
father-in-law, "We are setting out for
the place of which the LORD said, 'I
will give it to you'; come with us, and
we will do you good; for the LORD has
promised good to Israel." 30 But he
said to him, "I will not go; I will
depart to my own land and to my
kindred." 31 And he said, "Do not
leave us, I pray you, for you know
how we are to encamp in the wilderness, and you will serve as eyes for us.
32 And if you go with us, whatever good
the LORD will do to us, the same will
we do to you."

33 So they set out from the mount
of the LORD three days' journey; and
the ark of the covenant of the LORD
went before them three days' journey,
to seek out a resting place for them.
34 And the cloud of the LORD was over
them by day, whenever they set out
from the camp.

35 And whenever the ark set out,
Moses said, "Arise, O LORD, and let
thy enemies be scattered; and let them
that hate thee flee before thee." 36 And
when it rested, he said, "Return, O
LORD, to the ten thousand thousands
of Israel."

11 And the people complained in
the hearing of the LORD about
their misfortunes; and when the LORD
heard it, his anger was kindled, and
the fire of the LORD burned among
them, and consumed some outlying
parts of the camp. 2 Then the people
cried to Moses; and Moses prayed to
the LORD, and the fire abated. 3 So
the name of that place was called
Tab′ė·rȧh,[e] because the fire of the
LORD burned among them.

4 Now the rabble that was among
them had a strong craving; and the
people of Israel also wept again, and
said, "O that we had meat to eat!
5 We remember the fish we ate in
Egypt for nothing, the cucumbers, the
melons, the leeks, the onions, and the
garlic; 6 but now our strength is dried
up, and there is nothing at all but this
manna to look at."

7 Now the manna was like coriander
seed, and its appearance like that of
bdellium. 8 The people went about
and gathered it, and ground it in mills
or beat it in mortars, and boiled it in
pots, and made cakes of it; and the
taste of it was like the taste of cakes
baked with oil. 9 When the dew fell
upon the camp in the night, the manna
fell with it.

10 Moses heard the people weeping
throughout their families, every man
at the door of his tent; and the anger
of the LORD blazed hotly, and Moses
was displeased. 11 Moses said to the
LORD, "Why hast thou dealt ill with
thy servant? And why have I not
found favor in thy sight, that thou
dost lay the burden of all this people
upon me? 12 Did I conceive all this
people? Did I bring them forth, that
thou shouldst say to me, 'Carry them
in your bosom, as a nurse carries the
sucking child, to the land which thou
didst swear to give their fathers?'
13 Where am I to get meat to give to
all this people? For they weep before
me and say, 'Give us meat, that we

[e] That is *Burning*

10.35: Ps 68.1-2. **11.4:** 1 Cor 10.6.

may eat.' 14 I am not able to carry all
this people alone, the burden is too
heavy for me. 15 If thou wilt deal thus
with me, kill me at once, if I find favor
in thy sight, that I may not see my
wretchedness."

16 And the LORD said to Moses,
"Gather for me seventy men of the
elders of Israel, whom you know to be
the elders of the people and officers
over them; and bring them to the tent
of meeting, and let them take their
stand there with you. 17 And I will
come down and talk with you there;
and I will take some of the spirit which
is upon you and put it upon them; and
they shall bear the burden of the
people with you, that you may not
bear it yourself alone. 18 And say to the
people, 'Consecrate yourselves for tomorrow, and you shall eat meat; for
you have wept in the hearing of the
LORD, saying, "Who will give us meat
to eat? For it was well with us in
Egypt." Therefore the LORD will give
you meat, and you shall eat. 19 You
shall not eat one day, or two days, or
five days, or ten days, or twenty days,
20 but a whole month, until it comes
out at your nostrils and becomes loathsome to you, because you have rejected
the LORD who is among you, and have
wept before him, saying, "Why did we
come forth out of Egypt?" ' " 21 But
Moses said, "The people among whom
I am number six hundred thousand on
foot; and thou hast said, 'I will give
them meat, that they may eat a whole
month!' 22 Shall flocks and herds be
slaughtered for them, to suffice them?
Or shall all the fish of the sea be gathered together for them, to suffice
them?" 23 And the LORD said to Moses,
"Is the LORD's hand shortened? Now
you shall see whether my word will
come true for you or not."

24 So Moses went out and told the
people the words of the LORD; and he
gathered seventy men of the elders of
the people, and placed them round
about the tent. 25 Then the LORD came
down in the cloud and spoke to him,
and took some of the spirit that was
upon him and put it upon the seventy
elders; and when the spirit rested upon
them, they prophesied. But they did
so no more.

26 Now two men remained in the
camp, one named El'dad, and the
other named Mē'dad, and the spirit
rested upon them; they were among
those registered, but they had not gone
out to the tent, and so they prophesied
in the camp. 27 And a young man ran
and told Moses, "El'dad and Mē'dad
are prophesying in the camp." 28 And
Joshua the son of Nun, the minister of
Moses, one of his chosen men, said,
"My lord Moses, forbid them." 29 But
Moses said to him, "Are you jealous
for my sake? Would that all the
LORD's people were prophets, that the
LORD would put his spirit upon them!"
30 And Moses and the elders of Israel
returned to the camp.

31 And there went forth a wind
from the LORD, and it brought quails
from the sea, and let them fall beside
the camp, about a day's journey on
this side and a day's journey on the
other side, round about the camp, and
about two cubits above the face of the
earth. 32 And the people rose all that
day, and all night, and all the next
day, and gathered the quails; he who
gathered least gathered ten homers;
and they spread them out for themselves all around the camp. 33 While
the meat was yet between their teeth,
before it was consumed, the anger of
the LORD was kindled against the people, and the LORD smote the people
with a very great plague. 34 Therefore
the name of that place was called Kib'-
roth-hat·tā'ȧ·vȧh,[f] because there they
buried the people who had the craving.
35 From Kib'roth-hat·tā'ȧ·vȧh the
people journeyed to Hȧ·zē'roth; and
they remained at Hazeroth.

12 Miriam and Aaron spoke against
Moses because of the Cushite
woman whom he had married, for he
had married a Cushite woman; 2 and
they said, "Has the LORD indeed
spoken only through Moses? Has he
not spoken through us also?" And the
LORD heard it. 3 Now the man Moses
was very meek, more than all men that
were on the face of the earth. 4 And
suddenly the LORD said to Moses and
to Aaron and Miriam, "Come out, you
three, to the tent of meeting." And
the three of them came out. 5 And the
LORD came down in a pillar of cloud,
and stood at the door of the tent, and
called Aaron and Miriam; and they
both came forward. 6 And he said,
"Hear my words: If there is a prophet

[f] That is *Graves of craving*
11.34: 1 Cor 10.6.

among you, I the LORD make myself
known to him in a vision, I speak with
him in a dream. 7 Not so with my
servant Moses; he is entrusted with all
my house. 8 With him I speak mouth
to mouth, clearly, and not in dark
speech; and he beholds the form of the
LORD. Why then were you not afraid
to speak against my servant Moses?"
9 And the anger of the LORD was
kindled against them, and he departed;
10 and when the cloud removed from
over the tent, behold, Miriam was
leprous, as white as snow. And Aaron
turned towards Miriam, and behold,
she was leprous. 11 And Aaron said to
Moses, "Oh, my lord, do not[g] punish
us because we have done foolishly and
have sinned. 12 Let her not be as one
dead, of whom the flesh is half consumed when he comes out of his
mother's womb." 13 And Moses cried
to the LORD, "Heal her, O God, I
beseech thee." 14 But the LORD said to
Moses, "If her father had but spit in
her face, should she not be shamed
seven days? Let her be shut up outside
the camp seven days, and after that
she may be brought in again." 15 So
Miriam was shut up outside the camp
seven days; and the people did not set
out on the march till Miriam was
brought in again. 16 After that the people set out from Hȧ·zē'roth, and encamped in the wilderness of Pâr'an.

13 The LORD said to Moses,
2 "Send men to spy out the land
of Canaan, which I give to the people
of Israel; from each tribe of their
fathers shall you send a man, every one
a leader among them." 3 So Moses sent
them from the wilderness of Pâr'an,
according to the command of the
LORD, all of them men who were heads
of the people of Israel. 4 And these were
their names: From the tribe of Reuben,
Sham'mū-ȧ the son of Zac'cūr; 5 from
the tribe of Simeon, Shā'phȧt the son
of Hō'rī; 6 from the tribe of Judah,
Caleb the son of Jė·phün'nėh; 7 from
the tribe of Is'sȧ·chär, I'gal the son of
Joseph; 8 from the tribe of Ē'phrȧ·im,
Hō·shē'ȧ the son of Nun; 9 from the
tribe of Benjamin, Pal'tī the son of
Rā'phū; 10 from the tribe of Zeb'ū·lŭn,
Gad'di·el the son of Sō'dī; 11 from the
tribe of Joseph (that is from the
tribe of Mȧ·nas'sėh), Gad'dī the son of
Sü'sī; 12 from the tribe of Dan, Am'-
mi·el the son of Gė·mal'lī; 13 from the
tribe of Ash'ėr, Sē'thŭr the son of
Michael; 14 from the tribe of Naph'tȧ-
lī, Näh'bī the son of Voph'sī; 15 from
the tribe of Gad, Gė·ū'el the son of
Mā'chī. 16 These were the names of
the men whom Moses sent to spy out
the land. And Moses called Hō·shē'ȧ
the son of Nun Joshua.
17 Moses sent them to spy out the
land of Canaan, and said to them,
"Go up into the Negeb yonder, and
go up into the hill country, 18 and see
what the land is, and whether the people who dwell in it are strong or weak,
whether they are few or many, 19 and
whether the land that they dwell in is
good or bad, and whether the cities
that they dwell in are camps or strongholds, 20 and whether the land is rich
or poor, and whether there is wood in
it or not. Be of good courage, and
bring some of the fruit of the land."
Now the time was the season of the
first ripe grapes.
21 So they went up and spied out
the land from the wilderness of Zin to
Rē'hob, near the entrance of Hā'math.
22 They went up into the Negeb, and
came to Hē'brŏn; and Ȧ·hī'mȧn, Shē'-
shäi, and Tal'mäi, the descendants of
Ā'nak, were there. (Hebron was built
seven years before Zō'ȧn in Egypt.)
23 And they came to the Valley of Esh'-
cŏl, and cut down from there a branch
with a single cluster of grapes, and
they carried it on a pole between two
of them; they brought also some pomegranates and figs. 24 That place was
called the Valley of Esh'cŏl,[h] because
of the cluster which the men of Israel
cut down from there.
25 At the end of forty days they
returned from spying out the land.
26 And they came to Moses and Aaron
and to all the congregation of the people of Israel in the wilderness of Pâr'-
an, at Kā'desh; they brought back
word to them and to all the congregation, and showed them the fruit of the
land. 27 And they told him, "We came
to the land to which you sent us; it
flows with milk and honey, and this is
its fruit. 28 Yet the people who dwell
in the land are strong, and the cities
are fortified and very large; and besides, we saw the descendants of Ā'nak
there. 29 The Ȧ·mal'ė·kites dwell in
the land of the Negeb; the Hit'tites,

[g] Heb *lay not sin upon us* [h] That is *Cluster*
12.7: Heb 3.2, 5-6. 12.8: Ex 33.11; Deut 34.10.

the Jeb'ū·sites, and the Am'ô·rītes
dwell in the hill country; and the
Canaanites dwell by the sea, and along
the Jordan."
30 But Caleb quieted the people before Moses, and said, "Let us go up
at once, and occupy it; for we are well
able to overcome it." 31 Then the men
who had gone up with him said, "We
are not able to go up against the people; for they are stronger than we."
32 So they brought to the people of
Israel an evil report of the land which
they had spied out, saying, "The land,
through which we have gone, to spy it
out, is a land that devours its inhabitants; and all the people that we saw in
it are men of great stature. 33 And there
we saw the Neph'i·lim (the sons of
Ā'nak, who come from the Nephilim);
and we seemed to ourselves like grasshoppers, and so we seemed to them."

14 Then all the congregation raised
a loud cry; and the people wept
that night. 2 And all the people of Israel
murmured against Moses and Aaron;
the whole congregation said to them,
"Would that we had died in the land
of Egypt! Or would that we had died
in this wilderness! 3 Why does the
LORD bring us into this land, to fall by
the sword? Our wives and our little
ones will become a prey; would it
not be better for us to go back to
Egypt?"
4 And they said to one another,
"Let us choose a captain, and go back
to Egypt." 5 Then Moses and Aaron
fell on their faces before all the assembly of the congregation of the people
of Israel. 6 And Joshua the son of Nun
and Caleb the son of Jė·phŭn'nėh, who
were among those who had spied out
the land, rent their clothes, 7 and said
to all the congregation of the people of
Israel, "The land, which we passed
through to spy it out, is an exceedingly
good land. 8 If the LORD delights in
us, he will bring us into this land and
give it to us, a land which flows with
milk and honey. 9 Only, do not rebel
against the LORD; and do not fear the
people of the land, for they are bread
for us; their protection is removed
from them, and the LORD is with us;
do not fear them." 10 But all the congregation said to stone them with
stones.
Then the glory of the LORD appeared at the tent of meeting to all the
people of Israel. 11 And the LORD said
to Moses, "How long will this people
despise me? And how long will they
not believe in me, in spite of all the
signs which I have wrought among
them? 12 I will strike them with the
pestilence and disinherit them, and I
will make of you a nation greater and
mightier than they."
13 But Moses said to the LORD,
"Then the Egyptians will hear of it,
for thou didst bring up this people in
thy might from among them, 14 and
they will tell the inhabitants of this
land. They have heard that thou, O
LORD, art in the midst of this people;
for thou, O LORD, art seen face to face,
and thy cloud stands over them and
thou goest before them, in a pillar of
cloud by day and in a pillar of fire by
night. 15 Now if thou dost kill this
people as one man, then the nations
who have heard thy fame will say,
16 'Because the LORD was not able to
bring this people into the land which
he swore to give to them, therefore he
has slain them in the wilderness.'
17 And now, I pray thee, let the power
of the LORD be great as thou hast
promised, saying, 18 'The LORD is
slow to anger, and abounding in steadfast love, forgiving iniquity and transgression, but he will by no means clear
the guilty, visiting the iniquity of
fathers upon children, upon the third
and upon the fourth generation.'
19 Pardon the iniquity of this people,
I pray thee, according to the greatness
of thy steadfast love, and according as
thou hast forgiven this people, from
Egypt even until now."
20 Then the LORD said, "I have
pardoned, according to your word;
21 but truly, as I live, and as all the
earth shall be filled with the glory of
the LORD, 22 none of the men who
have seen my glory and my signs
which I wrought in Egypt and in the
wilderness, and yet have put me to
the proof these ten times and have not
hearkened to my voice, 23 shall see the
land which I swore to give to their
fathers; and none of those who despised
me shall see it. 24 But my servant
Caleb, because he has a different spirit
and has followed me fully, I will bring
into the land into which he went, and
his descendants shall possess it.
25 Now, since the A·mal'ė·kites and the
Canaanites dwell in the valleys, turn

13.33: Gen 6.4. **14.3:** Acts 7.39. **14.11-25:** Ex 32.9-14, 31-35. **14.22-23:** Heb 3.18.

tomorrow and set out for the wilderness by the way to the Red Sea."
26 And the LORD said to Moses and
to Aaron, 27 "How long shall this
wicked congregation murmur against
me? I have heard the murmurings of
the people of Israel, which they murmur against me. 28 Say to them, 'As
I live,' says the LORD, 'what you have
said in my hearing I will do to you:
29 your dead bodies shall fall in this
wilderness; and of all your number,
numbered from twenty years old and
upward, who have murmured against
me, 30 not one shall come into the land
where I swore that I would make you
dwell, except Caleb the son of Jė-
phün'nėh and Joshua the son of Nun.
31 But your little ones, who you said
would become a prey, I will bring in,
and they shall know the land which
you have despised. 32 But as for you,
your dead bodies shall fall in this
wilderness. 33 And your children shall
be shepherds in the wilderness forty
years, and shall suffer for your faithlessness, until the last of your dead
bodies lies in the wilderness. 34 According to the number of the days in which
you spied out the land, forty days, for
every day a year, you shall bear your
iniquity, forty years, and you shall
know my displeasure.' 35 I, the LORD,
have spoken; surely this will I do to
all this wicked congregation that are
gathered together against me: in this
wilderness they shall come to a full
end, and there they shall die."
36 And the men whom Moses sent
to spy out the land, and who returned
and made all the congregation to murmur against him by bringing up an
evil report against the land, 37 the men
who brought up an evil report of the
land, died by plague before the LORD.
38 But Joshua the son of Nun and
Caleb the son of Jė·phün'nėh remained
alive, of those men who went to spy
out the land.
39 And Moses told these words to
all the people of Israel, and the people
mourned greatly. 40 And they rose early
in the morning, and went up to the
heights of the hill country, saying,
"See, we are here, we will go up to the
place which the LORD has promised;
for we have sinned." 41 But Moses
said, "Why now are you transgressing
the command of the LORD, for that
will not succeed? 42 Do not go up lest
you be struck down before your
enemies, for the LORD is not among
you. 43 For there the A·mal'ė·kites and
the Canaanites are before you, and you
shall fall by the sword; because you
have turned back from following the
LORD, the LORD will not be with you."
44 But they presumed to go up to the
heights of the hill country, although
neither the ark of the covenant of the
LORD, nor Moses, departed out of the
camp. 45 Then the A·mal'ė·kites and
the Canaanites who dwell in that hill
country came down, and defeated
them and pursued them, even to
Hôr'māh.

15 The LORD said to Moses, 2 "Say
to the people of Israel, When you
come into the land you are to inhabit,
which I give you, 3 and you offer to
the LORD from the herd or from the
flock an offering by fire or a burnt
offering or a sacrifice, to fulfil a vow
or as a freewill offering or at your
appointed feasts, to make a pleasing
odor to the LORD, 4 then he who brings
his offering shall offer to the LORD a
cereal offering of a tenth of an ephah
of fine flour, mixed with a fourth of a
hin of oil; 5 and wine for the drink
offering, a fourth of a hin, you shall
prepare with the burnt offering, or for
the sacrifice, for each lamb. 6 Or for a
ram, you shall prepare for a cereal
offering two tenths of an ephah of fine
flour mixed with a third of a hin of
oil; 7 and for the drink offering you
shall offer a third of a hin of wine, a
pleasing odor to the LORD. 8 And when
you prepare a bull for a burnt offering,
or for a sacrifice, to fulfil a vow, or for
peace offerings to the LORD, 9 then one
shall offer with the bull a cereal offering of three tenths of an ephah of fine
flour, mixed with half a hin of oil,
10 and you shall offer for the drink
offering half a hin of wine, as an offering by fire, a pleasing odor to the
LORD.
11 "Thus it shall be done for each
bull or ram, or for each of the male
lambs or the kids. 12 According to the
number that you prepare, so shall you
do with every one according to their
number. 13 All who are native shall do
these things in this way, in offering an
offering by fire, a pleasing odor to the
LORD. 14 And if a stranger is sojourning
with you, or any one is among you
throughout your generations, and he

14.29: Heb 3.17. **14.33:** Acts 7.36. **15.14:** Ex 12.49; Lev 24.22; Num 15.15-16, 29.

wishes to offer an offering by fire, a
pleasing odor to the LORD, he shall do
as you do. 15 For the assembly, there
shall be one statute for you and for
the stranger who sojourns with you, a
perpetual stature throughout your
generations; as you are, so shall the sojourner be before the LORD. 16 One
law and one ordinance shall be for you
and for the stranger who sojourns
with you."

17 The LORD said to Moses, 18 "Say
to the people of Israel, When you come
into the land to which I bring you
19 and when you eat of the food of the
land, you shall present an offering to
the LORD. 20 Of the first of your coarse
meal you shall present a cake as an
offering; as an offering from the
threshing floor, so shall you present it.
21 Of the first of your coarse meal you
shall give to the LORD an offering
throughout your generations.

22 "But if you err, and do not
observe all these commandments
which the LORD has spoken to Moses,
23 all that the LORD has commanded
you by Moses, from the day that the
LORD gave commandment, and onward throughout your generations,
24 then if it was done unwittingly without the knowledge of the congregation,
all the congregation shall offer one
young bull for a burnt offering, a
pleasing odor to the LORD, with its
cereal offering and its drink offering,
according to the ordinance, and one
male goat for a sin offering. 25 And the
priest shall make atonement for all the
congregation of the people of Israel,
and they shall be forgiven; because it
was an error, and they have brought
their offering, an offering by fire to
the LORD, and their sin offering before
the LORD, for their error. 26 And all the
congregation of the people of Israel
shall be forgiven, and the stranger who
sojourns among them, because the
whole population was involved in the
error.

27 "If one person sins unwittingly,
he shall offer a female goat a year old
for a sin offering. 28 And the priest
shall make atonement before the LORD
for the person who commits an error,
when he sins unwittingly, to make
atonement for him; and he shall be
forgiven. 29 You shall have one law for
him who does anything unwittingly,
for him who is native among the people
of Israel, and for the stranger who sojourns among them. 30 But the person
who does anything with a high hand,
whether he is native or a sojourner,
reviles the LORD, and that person shall
be cut off from among his people.
31 Because he has despised the word
of the LORD, and has broken his commandment, that person shall be utterly
cut off; his iniquity shall be upon him."

32 While the people of Israel were
in the wilderness, they found a man
gathering sticks on the sabbath day.
33 And those who found him gathering
sticks brought him to Moses and
Aaron, and to all the congregation.
34 They put him in custody, because
it had not been made plain what should
be done to him. 35 And the LORD said
to Moses, "The man shall be put to
death; all the congregation shall stone
him with stones outside the camp."
36 And all the congregation brought
him outside the camp, and stoned him
to death with stones, as the LORD commanded Moses.

37 The LORD said to Moses,
38 "Speak to the people of Israel, and
bid them to make tassels on the corners
of their garments throughout their
generations, and to put upon the tassel
of each corner a cord of blue; 39 and it
shall be to you a tassel to look upon
and remember all the commandments
of the LORD, to do them, not to follow
after your own heart and your own
eyes, which you are inclined to go
after wantonly. 40 So you shall remember and do all my commandments, and be holy to your God. 41 I
am the LORD your God, who brought
you out of the land of Egypt, to be
your God: I am the LORD your God."

16 Now Kō'rȧh the son of Iz'här,
son of Kō'hath, son of Levi, and
Dā'thȧn and A·bī'rȧm the sons of
E·lī'ab, and On the son of Pē'leth,
sons of Reuben, 2 took men; and they
rose up before Moses, with a number
of the people of Israel, two hundred
and fifty leaders of the congregation,
chosen from the assembly, well-known
men; 3 and they assembled themselves
together against Moses and against
Aaron, and said to them, "You have
gone too far! For all the congregation
are holy, every one of them, and the
LORD is among them; why then do you
exalt yourselves above the assembly of
the LORD?" 4 When Moses heard it,

15.17-21: Ex 34.26; Lev 23.14. 15.22-26: Lev 4.13-21. 15.27-29: Lev 4.2-12. 15.38-40: Deut 22.12.

he fell on his face; 5 and he said to
Kō'rȧh and all his company, "In the
morning the LORD will show who is
his, and who is holy, and will cause
him to come near to him; him whom
he will choose he will cause to come
near to him. 6 Do this: take censers,
Kō'rȧh and all his company; 7 put fire
in them and put incense upon them
before the LORD tomorrow, and the
man whom the LORD chooses shall be
the holy one. You have gone too far,
sons of Levi!" 8And Moses said to
Kō'rȧh, "Hear now, you sons of Levi:
9 is it too small a thing for you that
the God of Israel has separated you
from the congregation of Israel, to
bring you near to himself, to do service
in the tabernacle of the LORD, and to
stand before the congregation to minister to them; 10 and that he has brought
you near him, and all your brethren
the sons of Levi with you? And would
you seek the priesthood also? 11 Therefore it is against the LORD that you and
all your company have gathered together; what is Aaron that you murmur
against him?"
12 And Moses sent to call Dā'thȧn
and Ȧ·bī'rȧm the sons of E·lī'ab; and
they said, "We will not come up. 13 Is
it a small thing that you have brought
us up out of a land flowing with milk
and honey, to kill us in the wilderness,
that you must also make yourself a
prince over us? 14 Moreover you have
not brought us into a land flowing with
milk and honey, nor given us inheritance of fields and vineyards. Will you
put out the eyes of these men? We
will not come up."
15 And Moses was very angry, and
said to the LORD, "Do not respect their
offering. I have not taken one ass from
them, and I have not harmed one of
them." 16And Moses said to Kō'rȧh,
"Be present, you and all your company, before the LORD, you and they,
and Aaron, tomorrow; 17 and let every
one of you take his censer, and put
incense upon it, and every one of you
bring before the LORD his censer,
two hundred and fifty censers; you
also, and Aaron, each his censer." 18 So
every man took his censer, and they
put fire in them and laid incense upon
them, and they stood at the entrance
of the tent of meeting with Moses and
Aaron. 19 Then Kō'rȧh assembled all
the congregation against them at the
entrance of the tent of meeting. And
the glory of the LORD appeared to all
the congregation.
20 And the LORD said to Moses and
to Aaron, 21 "Separate yourselves from
among this congregation, that I may
consume them in a moment." 22And
they fell on their faces, and said, "O
God, the God of the spirits of all
flesh, shall one man sin, and wilt thou
be angry with all the congregation?"
23And the LORD said to Moses,
24 "Say to the congregation, Get away
from about the dwelling of Kō'rȧh,
Dā'thȧn, and Ȧ·bī'rȧm."
25 Then Moses rose and went to
Dā'thȧn and Ȧ·bī'rȧm; and the elders
of Israel followed him. 26And he said
to the congregation, "Depart, I pray
you, from the tents of these wicked
men, and touch nothing of theirs, lest
you be swept away with all their sins."
27 So they got away from about the
dwelling of Kō'rȧh, Dā'thȧn, and
Ȧ·bī'rȧm; and Dathan and Abiram
came out and stood at the door of their
tents, together with their wives, their
sons, and their little ones. 28And Moses
said, "Hereby you shall know that the
LORD has sent me to do all these works,
and that it has not been of my own
accord. 29 If these men die the common death of all men, or if they are
visited by the fate of all men, then the
LORD has not sent me. 30 But if the
LORD creates something new, and the
ground opens its mouth, and swallows
them up, with all that belongs to them,
and they go down alive into Shē'ōl,
then you shall know that these men
have despised the LORD."
31 And as he finished speaking all
these words, the ground under them
split asunder; 32 and the earth opened
its mouth and swallowed them up,
with their households and all the men
that belonged to Kō'rȧh and all their
goods. 33 So they and all that belonged
to them went down alive into Shē'ōl;
and the earth closed over them, and
they perished from the midst of the
assembly. 34And all Israel that were
round about them fled at their cry; for
they said, "Lest the earth swallow
us up!" 35And fire came forth from the
LORD, and consumed the two hundred
and fifty men offering the incense.
36[l] Then the LORD said to Moses,

[l] Ch 17.1 in Heb
16.5: 2 Tim 2.19.

37 "Tell El·ē·ā'zār the son of Aaron
the priest to take up the censers out of
the blaze; then scatter the fire far and
wide. For they are holy, 38 the censers
of these men who have sinned at the
cost of their lives; so let them be made
into hammered plates as a covering for
the altar, for they offered them before
the LORD; therefore they are holy.
Thus they shall be a sign to the people
of Israel." 39 So El·ē·ā'zār the priest
took the bronze censers, which those
who were burned had offered; and
they were hammered out as a covering
for the altar, 40 to be a reminder to the
people of Israel, so that no one who is
not a priest, who is not of the descendants of Aaron, should draw near to
burn incense before the LORD, lest he
become as Kō'rah and as his company
—as the LORD said to El·ē·ā'zār
through Moses.

41 But on the morrow all the
congregation of the people of Israel
murmured against Moses and against
Aaron, saying, "You have killed the
people of the LORD." 42 And when the
congregation had assembled against
Moses and against Aaron, they turned
toward the tent of meeting; and behold, the cloud covered it, and the
glory of the LORD appeared. 43 And
Moses and Aaron came to the front of
the tent of meeting, 44 and the LORD
said to Moses, 45 "Get away from the
midst of this congregation, that I may
consume them in a moment." And
they fell on their faces. 46 And Moses
said to Aaron, "Take your censer, and
put fire therein from off the altar, and
lay incense on it, and carry it quickly
to the congregation, and make atonement for them; for wrath has gone
forth from the LORD, the plague has
begun." 47 So Aaron took it as Moses
said, and ran into the midst of the
assembly; and behold, the plague had
already begun among the people; and
he put on the incense, and made
atonement for the people. 48 And he
stood between the dead and the living;
and the plague was stopped. 49 Now
those who died by the plague were
fourteen thousand seven hundred, besides those who died in the affair of
Kō'rah. 50 And Aaron returned to
Moses at the entrance of the tent
of meeting, when the plague was
stopped.

17 The LORD said to Moses,
2 "Speak to the people of Israel,
and get from them rods, one for each
fathers' house, from all their leaders
according to their fathers' houses,
twelve rods. Write each man's name
upon his rod, 3 and write Aaron's
name upon the rod of Levi. For there
shall be one rod for the head of each
fathers' house. 4 Then you shall
deposit them in the tent of meeting
before the testimony, where I meet
with you. 5 And the rod of the man
whom I choose shall sprout; thus I
will make to cease from me the murmurings of the people of Israel, which
they murmur against you." 6 Moses
spoke to the people of Israel; and all
their leaders gave him rods, one for
each leader, according to their fathers'
houses, twelve rods; and the rod of
Aaron was among their rods. 7 And
Moses deposited the rods before the
LORD in the tent of the testimony.

8 And on the morrow Moses went
into the tent of the testimony; and behold, the rod of Aaron for the house
of Levi had sprouted and put forth
buds, and produced blossoms, and it
bore ripe almonds. 9 Then Moses
brought out all the rods from before
the LORD to all the people of Israel;
and they looked, and each man took
his rod. 10 And the LORD said to Moses,
"Put back the rod of Aaron befoɪe the
testimony, to be kept as a sign for the
rebels, that you may make an end of
their murmurings against me, lest they
die." 11 Thus did Moses; as the LORD
commanded him, so he did.

12 And the people of Israel said to
Moses, "Behold, we perish, we are undone, we are all undone. 13 Every one
who comes near, who comes near to
the tabernacle of the LORD, shall die.
Are we all to perish?"

18 So the LORD said to Aaron,
"You and your sons and your
fathers' house with you shall bear
iniquity in connection with the sanctuary; and you and your sons with you
shall bear iniquity in connection with
your priesthood. 2 And with you bring
your brethren also, the tribe of Levi,
the tribe of your father, that they may
join you, and minister to you while
you and your sons with you are before
the tent of the testimony. 3 They shall
attend you and attend to all duties of

[l] Ch 17.16 in Heb
18.3-4, 23: Num 1.50-53; 3.5-8, 21-37; 4.1-33; 8.19.

the tent; but shall not come near to
the vessels of the sanctuary or to the
altar, lest they, and you, die. 4 They
shall join you, and attend to the tent
of meeting, for all the service of the
tent; and no one else shall come near
you. 5 And you shall attend to the
duties of the sanctuary and the duties
of the altar, that there be wrath no
more upon the people of Israel. 6 And
behold, I have taken your brethren
the Levites from among the people of
Israel; they are a gift to you, given to
the LORD, to do the service of the tent
of meeting. 7 And you and your sons
with you shall attend to your priesthood for all that concerns the altar and
that is within the veil; and you shall
serve. I give your priesthood as a
gift,[k] and any one else who comes near
shall be put to death."

8 Then the LORD said to Aaron,
"And behold, I have given you whatever is kept of the offerings made to
me, all the consecrated things of the
people of Israel; I have given them to
you as a portion, and to your sons as
a perpetual due. 9 This shall be yours
of the most holy things, reserved from
the fire; every offering of theirs, every
cereal offering of theirs and every sin
offering of theirs and every guilt offering of theirs, which they render to me,
shall be most holy to you and to your
sons. 10 In a most holy place shall you
eat of it; every male may eat of it; it is
holy to you. 11 This also is yours, the
offering of their gift, all the wave offerings of the people of Israel; I have
given them to you, and to your sons
and daughters with you, as a perpetual
due; every one who is clean in your
house may eat of it. 12 All the best of
the oil, and all the best of the wine and
of the grain, the first fruits of what they
give to the LORD, I give to you. 13 The
first ripe fruits of all that is in their
land, which they bring to the LORD,
shall be yours; every one who is clean
in your house may eat of it. 14 Every
devoted thing in Israel shall be yours.
15 Everything that opens the womb of
all flesh, whether man or beast, which
they offer to the LORD, shall be yours;
nevertheless the first-born of man you
shall redeem, and the firstling of unclean beasts you shall redeem. 16 And
their redemption price (at a month old
you shall redeem them) you shall fix
at five shekels in silver, according to
the shekel of the sanctuary, which is
twenty gerahs. 17 But the firstling of
a cow, or the firstling of a sheep, or
the firstling of a goat, you shall not
redeem; they are holy. You shall
sprinkle their blood upon the altar,
and shall burn their fat as an offering
by fire, a pleasing odor to the LORD;
18 but their flesh shall be yours, as the
breast that is waved and as the right
thigh is yours. 19 All the holy offerings
which the people of Israel present to
the LORD I give to you, and to your
sons and daughters with you, as a perpetual due; it is a covenant of salt for
ever before the LORD for you and for
your offspring with you." 20 And the
LORD said to Aaron, "You shall have
no inheritance in their land, neither
shall you have any portion among
them; I am your portion and your
inheritance among the people of Israel.

21 "To the Levites I have given
every tithe in Israel for an inheritance,
in return for their service which they
serve, their service in the tent of meeting. 22 And henceforth the people of
Israel shall not come near the tent of
meeting, lest they bear sin and die.
23 But the Levites shall do the service
of the tent of meeting, and they shall
bear their iniquity; it shall be a perpetual statute throughout your generations; and among the people of Israel
they shall have no inheritance. 24 For
the tithe of the people of Israel, which
they present as an offering to the LORD,
I have given to the Levites for an
inheritance; therefore I have said of
them that they shall have no inheritance among the people of Israel."

25 And the LORD said to Moses,
26 "Moreover you shall say to the
Levites, 'When you take from the
people of Israel the tithe which I have
given you from them for your inheritance, then you shall present an offering
from it to the LORD, a tithe of the tithe.
27 And your offering shall be reckoned
to you as though it were the grain of
the threshing floor, and as the fulness
of the wine press. 28 So shall you also
present an offering to the LORD from
all your tithes, which you receive from
the people of Israel; and from it you
shall give the LORD's offering to Aaron
the priest. 29 Out of all the gifts to you,
you shall present every offering due

[k] Heb *service of gift*
18.14: Lev 27.28. **18.19:** 2 Chron 13.5.

to the LORD, from all the best of them,
giving the hallowed part from them.'
30 Therefore you shall say to them,
'When you have offered from it the
best of it, then the rest shall be reckoned to the Levites as produce of the
threshing floor, and as produce of the
wine press; 31 and you may eat it in
any place, you and your households;
for it is your reward in return for your
service in the tent of meeting. 32And
you shall bear no sin by reason of it,
when you have offered the best of it.
And you shall not profane the holy
things of the people of Israel, lest you
die.' "

19 Now the LORD said to Moses
and to Aaron, 2 "This is the
statute of the law which the LORD has
commanded: Tell the people of Israel
to bring you a red heifer without
defect, in which there is no blemish,
and upon which a yoke has never
come. 3And you shall give her to
El·ē·ā'zär the priest, and she shall be
taken outside the camp and slaughtered
before him; 4 and El·ē·ā'zär the priest
shall take some of her blood with his
finger, and sprinkle some of her blood
toward the front of the tent of meeting
seven times. 5And the heifer shall be
burned in his sight; her skin, her flesh,
and her blood, with her dung, shall be
burned; 6 and the priest shall take
cedarwood and hyssop and scarlet stuff,
and cast them into the midst of the
burning of the heifer. 7 Then the priest
shall wash his clothes and bathe his
body in water, and afterwards he shall
come into the camp; and the priest
shall be unclean until evening. 8 He
who burns the heifer shall wash his
clothes in water and bathe his body in
water, and shall be unclean until evening. 9And a man who is clean shall
gather up the ashes of the heifer, and
deposit them outside the camp in a
clean place; and they shall be kept for
the congregation of the people of
Israel for the water for impurity, for
the removal of sin. 10And he who
gathers the ashes of the heifer shall
wash his clothes, and be unclean until
evening. And this shall be to the people
of Israel, and to the stranger who sojourns among them, a perpetual
statute.

11 "He who touches the dead body
of any person shall be unclean seven
days; 12 he shall cleanse himself with
the water on the third day and on the
seventh day, and so be clean; but if he
does not cleanse himself on the third
day and on the seventh day, he will
not become clean. 13 Whoever touches
a dead person, the body of any man
who has died, and does not cleanse
himself, defiles the tabernacle of the
LORD, and that person shall be cut off
from Israel; because the water for
impurity was not thrown upon him,
he shall be unclean; his uncleanness is
still on him.

14 "This is the law when a man dies
in a tent: every one who comes into
the tent, and every one who is in the
tent, shall be unclean seven days.
15And every open vessel, which has no
cover fastened upon it, is unclean.
16 Whoever in the open field touches
one who is slain with a sword, or a
dead body, or a bone of a man, or a
grave, shall be unclean seven days.
17 For the unclean they shall take some
ashes of the burnt sin offering, and
running water shall be added in a
vessel; 18 then a clean person shall
take hyssop, and dip it in the water,
and sprinkle it upon the tent, and
upon all the furnishings, and upon the
persons who were there, and upon him
who touched the bone, or the slain, or
the dead, or the grave; 19 and the clean
person shall sprinkle upon the unclean
on the third day and on the seventh
day; thus on the seventh day he
shall cleanse him, and he shall wash
his clothes and bathe himself in
water, and at evening he shall be
clean.

20 "But the man who is unclean
and does not cleanse himself, that
person shall be cut off from the midst
of the assembly, since he has defiled
the sanctuary of the LORD; because the
water for impurity has not been thrown
upon him, he is unclean. 21And it
shall be a perpetual statute for them.
He who sprinkles the water for impurity shall wash his clothes; and he
who touches the water for impurity
shall be unclean until evening. 22And
whatever the unclean person touches
shall be unclean; and any one who
touches it shall be unclean until
evening."

20 And the people of Israel, the
whole congregation, came into
the wilderness of Zin in the first month,
and the people stayed in Kā'desh; and
Miriam died there, and was buried
there.

2 Now there was no water for the
congregation; and they assembled
themselves together against Moses and
against Aaron. 3 And the people contended with Moses, and said, "Would
that we had died when our brethren
died before the LORD! 4 Why have you
brought the assembly of the LORD into
this wilderness, that we should die
here, both we and our cattle? 5 And
why have you made us come up out of
Egypt, to bring us to this evil place?
It is no place for grain, or figs, or vines,
or pomegranates; and there is no
water to drink." 6 Then Moses and
Aaron went from the presence of the
assembly to the door of the tent of
meeting, and fell on their faces. And
the glory of the LORD appeared to
them, 7 and the LORD said to Moses,
8 "Take the rod, and assemble the
congregation, you and Aaron your
brother, and tell the rock before their
eyes to yield its water; so you shall
bring water out of the rock for them;
so you shall give drink to the congregation and their cattle." 9 And Moses
took the rod from before the LORD, as
he commanded him.

10 And Moses and Aaron gathered
the assembly together before the rock,
and he said to them, "Hear now, you
rebels; shall we bring forth water for
you out of this rock?" 11 And Moses
lifted up his hand and struck the rock
with his rod twice; and water came
forth abundantly, and the congregation drank, and their cattle. 12 And the
LORD said to Moses and Aaron, "Because you did not believe in me, to
sanctify me in the eyes of the people
of Israel, therefore you shall not bring
this assembly into the land which I
have given them." 13 These are the
waters of Mer'i·bàh,[l] where the people
of Israel contended with the LORD,
and he showed himself holy among
them.

14 Moses sent messengers from
Kā'desh to the king of Ē'dŏm, "Thus
says your brother Israel: You know all
the adversity that has befallen us:
15 how our fathers went down to Egypt,
and we dwelt in Egypt a long time; and
the Egyptians dealt harshly with us
and our fathers; 16 and when we cried
to the LORD, he heard our voice, and
sent an angel and brought us forth out
of Egypt; and here we are in Kā'desh,
a city on the edge of your territory.
17 Now let us pass through your land.
We will not pass through field or vineyard, neither will we drink water from
a well; we will go along the King's
Highway, we will not turn aside to the
right hand or to the left, until we have
passed through your territory." 18 But
Ē'dŏm said to him, "You shall not pass
through, lest I come out with the
sword against you." 19 And the people
of Israel said to him, "We will go up
by the highway; and if we drink of your
water, I and my cattle, then I will pay
for it; let me only pass through on
foot, nothing more." 20 But he said,
"You shall not pass through." And
Ē'dŏm came out against them with
many men, and with a strong force.
21 Thus Ē'dŏm refused to give Israel
passage through his territory; so Israel
turned away from him.

22 And they journeyed from Kā'-
desh, and the people of Israel, the
whole congregation, came to Mount
Hôr. 23 And the LORD said to Moses
and Aaron at Mount Hôr, on the
border of the land of Ē'dŏm, 24 "Aaron
shall be gathered to his people; for he
shall not enter the land which I have
given to the people of Israel, because
you rebelled against my command at
the waters of Mer'i·bàh. 25 Take Aaron
and El·ē·ā'zàr his son, and bring them
up to Mount Hôr; 26 and strip Aaron
of his garments, and put them upon
El·ē·ā'zàr his son; and Aaron shall be
gathered to his people, and shall die
there." 27 Moses did as the LORD commanded; and they went up Mount Hôr
in the sight of all the congregation.
28 And Moses stripped Aaron of his
garments, and put them upon El·ē·ā'-
zàr his son; and Aaron died there on
the top of the mountain. Then Moses
and Eleazar came down from the
mountain. 29 And when all the congregation saw that Aaron was dead, all the
house of Israel wept for Aaron thirty
days.

21 When the Canaanite, the king of
Âr'àd, who dwelt in the Negeb,
heard that Israel was coming by the
way of Ath'à·rim, he fought against
Israel, and took some of them captive.
2 And Israel vowed a vow to the LORD,
and said, "If thou wilt indeed give this
people into my hand, then I will
utterly destroy their cities." 3 And the

[l] That is *Contention*
20.2-13: Ex 17.2-7. **20.25-29:** Num 33.38-39. **21.1:** Num 33.40.

Lord hearkened to the voice of Israel,
and gave over the Canaanites; and they
utterly destroyed them and their cities;
so the name of the place was called
Hôr'mȧh.[m]
4 From Mount Hôr they set out by
the way to the Red Sea, to go around
the land of Ē'dȯm; and the people became impatient on the way. 5And the
people spoke against God and against
Moses, "Why have you brought us up
out of Egypt to die in the wilderness?
For there is no food and no water, and
we loathe this worthless food." 6 Then
the Lord sent fiery serpents among the
people, and they bit the people, so that
many people of Israel died. 7And the
people came to Moses, and said, "We
have sinned, for we have spoken
against the Lord and against you;
pray to the Lord, that he take away
the serpents from us." So Moses
prayed for the people. 8And the Lord
said to Moses, "Make a fiery serpent,
and set it on a pole; and every one who
is bitten, when he sees it, shall live."
9 So Moses made a bronze serpent,
and set it on a pole; and if a serpent
bit any man, he would look at the
bronze serpent and live.
10 And the people of Israel set out,
and encamped in Ō'both. 11And they
set out from Ō'both, and encamped at
I'ye-ab'ȧ·rim, in the wilderness which
is opposite Mō'ab, toward the sunrise.
12 From there they set out, and encamped in the Valley of Zē'red.
13 From there they set out, and encamped on the other side of the Är'-
non, which is in the wilderness, that
extends from the boundary of the
Am'ȯ·rītes; for the Arnon is the boundary of Mō'ab, between Moab and the
Amorites. 14 Wherefore it is said in the
Book of the Wars of the Lord,

"Wä'heb in Sü'phȧh,
and the valleys of the Är'non,
15 and the slope of the valleys
that extends to the seat of Är,
and leans to the border of Mō'ab."

16 And from there they continued
to Beer;[n] that is the well of which the
Lord said to Moses, "Gather the people together, and I will give them
water." 17 Then Israel sang this song:

"Spring up, O well!—Sing to it!—
18 the well which the princes dug,
which the nobles of the people
delved,
with the scepter and with their
staves."

And from the wilderness they went on
to Mat'tȧ·nȧh, 19 and from Mat'tȧ·nȧh
to Nȧ·hal'i·el, and from Nahaliel to
Bā'moth, 20 and from Bā'moth to the
valley lying in the region of Mō'ab by
the top of Pis'gȧh which looks down
upon the desert.[o]
21 Then Israel sent messengers to
Sī'hon king of the Am'ȯ·rītes, saying,
22 "Let me pass through your land; we
will not turn aside into field or vineyard; we will not drink the water of a
well; we will go by the King's Highway, until we have passed through your
territory." 23 But Sī'hon would not
allow Israel to pass through his territory. He gathered all his men together,
and went out against Israel to the wilderness, and came to Jā'haz, and
fought against Israel. 24And Israel
slew him with the edge of the sword,
and took possession of his land from
the Är'non to the Jab'bȯk, as far as to
the Am'mȯ·nītes; for Jā'zėr was the
boundary of the Ammonites.[p] 25And
Israel took all these cities, and Israel
settled in all the cities of the Am'ȯ-
rītes, in Hesh'bȯn, and in all its villages. 26 For Hesh'bȯn was the city of
Sī'hon the king of the Am'ȯ·rītes, who
had fought against the former king of
Mō'ab and taken all his land out of his
hand, as far as the Är'non. 27 Therefore the ballad singers say,

"Come to Hesh'bȯn, let it be
built,
let the city of Sī'hon be established.
28 For fire went forth from Hesh'bȯn,
flame from the city of Sī'hon.
It devoured Är of Mō'ab,
the lords of the heights of the
Är'non.
29 Woe to you, O Mō'ab!
You are undone, O people of
Chē'mosh!
He has made his sons fugitives,
and his daughters captives,
to an Am'ȯ·rīte king, Sī'hon.
30 So their posterity perished from
Hesh'bȯn,[q] as far as Dī'bon,
and we laid waste until fire spread
to Med'ė·bȧ."[r]

[m] Heb *Destruction* [n] That is *Well* [o] Or *Jeshimon* [p] Gk: Heb *the boundary of the Ammonites was strong*
[q] Gk: Heb *we have shot at them. Heshbon has perished*
[r] Compare Sam and Gk: Heb *we have laid waste to Nophah which to Medebah*
21.21-30: Deut 2.26-37.

31 Thus Israel dwelt in the land of
the Am'ŏ·rītes. 32And Moses sent to
spy out Jā'zėr; and they took its villages, and dispossessed the Am'ŏ·rītes
that were there. 33 Then they turned
and went up by the way to Bā'shăn;
and Og the king of Bashan came out
against them, he and all his people, to
battle at Ed'rē-ī. 34 But the LORD said
to Moses, "Do not fear him; for I have
given him into your hand, and all his
people, and his land; and you shall do
to him as you did to Sī'hon king of the
Am'ŏ·rītes, who dwelt at Hesh'bŏn."
35 So they slew him, and his sons, and
all his people, until there was not one
survivor left to him; and they possessed
his land.

22 Then the people of Israel set
out, and encamped in the plains
of Mō'ab beyond the Jordan at
Jericho. 2And Bā'lak the son of Zip'pôr
saw all that Israel had done to the
Am'ŏ·rītes. 3And Mō'ab was in great
dread of the people, because they were
many; Moab was overcome with fear
of the people of Israel. 4And Mō'ab
said to the elders of Mid'ĭ·ăn, "This
horde will now lick up all that is
round about us, as the ox licks up the
grass of the field." So Bā'lak the son
of Zip'pôr, who was king of Mō'ab at
that time, 5 sent messengers to Balaam the son of Bē'ôr at Pē'thôr, which
is near the River, in the land of Am'aw
to call him, saying, "Behold, a people
has come out of Egypt; they cover the
face of the earth, and they are dwelling
opposite me. 6 Come now, curse this
people for me, since they are too
mighty for me; perhaps I shall be able
to defeat them and drive them from
the land; for I know that he whom you
bless is blessed, and he whom you
curse is cursed."

7 So the elders of Mō'ab and the
elders of Mid'ĭ·ăn departed with the
fees for divination in their hand; and
they came to Balaam, and gave him
Bā'lak's message. 8And he said to
them, "Lodge here this night, and I
will bring back word to you, as the
LORD speaks to me"; so the princes of
Mō'ab stayed with Balaam. 9And God
came to Balaam and said, "Who are
these men with you?" 10And Balaam
said to God, "Bā'lak the son of Zip'-
pôr, king of Mō'ab, has sent to me,
saying, 11 'Behold, a people has come
out of Egypt, and it covers the face of
the earth; now come, curse them for
me; perhaps I shall be able to fight
against them and drive them out.' "
12 God said to Balaam, "You shall not
go with them; you shall not curse the
people, for they are blessed." 13 So
Balaam rose in the morning, and said
to the princes of Bā'lak, "Go to your
own land; for the LORD has refused to
let me go with you." 14 So the princes
of Mō'ab rose and went to Bā'lak, and
said, "Balaam refuses to come with
us."

15 Once again Bā'lak sent princes,
more in number and more honorable
than they. 16And they came to Balaam
and said to him, "Thus says Bā'lak
the son of Zip'pôr: 'Let nothing hinder
you from coming to me; 17 for I will
surely do you great honor, and whatever you say to me I will do; come,
curse this people for me.' " 18 But
Balaam answered and said to the
servants of Bā'lak, "Though Balak
were to give me his house full of silver
and gold, I could not go beyond the
command of the LORD my God, to do
less or more. 19 Pray, now, tarry here
this night also, that I may know what
more the LORD will say to me." 20And
God came to Balaam at night and said
to him, "If the men have come to call
you, rise, go with them; but only what
I bid you, that shall you do."

21 So Balaam rose in the morning,
and saddled his ass, and went with the
princes of Mō'ab. 22 But God's anger
was kindled because he went; and the
angel of the LORD took his stand in
the way as his adversary. Now he was
riding on the ass, and his two servants
were with him. 23And the ass saw the
angel of the LORD standing in the
road, with a drawn sword in his hand;
and the ass turned aside out of the
road, and went into the field; and Balaam struck the ass, to turn her into
the road. 24 Then the angel of the
LORD stood in a narrow path between
the vineyards, with a wall on either
side. 25And when the ass saw the angel
of the LORD, she pushed against the
wall, and pressed Balaam's foot against
the wall; so he struck her again.
26 Then the angel of the LORD went
ahead, and stood in a narrow place,
where there was no way to turn either
to the right or to the left. 27 When the
ass saw the angel of the LORD, she lay
down under Balaam; and Balaam's

21.33-35: Deut 3.1-7. 22.1: Num 33.48.

anger was kindled, and he struck the
ass with his staff. 28 Then the LORD
opened the mouth of the ass, and she
said to Balaam, "What have I done to
you, that you have struck me these
three times?" 29 And Balaam said to
the ass, "Because you have made
sport of me I wish I had a sword in
my hand, for then I would kill you."
30 And the ass said to Balaam, "Am I
not your ass, upon which you have
ridden all your life long to this day?
Was I ever accustomed to do so to
you?" And he said, "No."

31 Then the LORD opened the eyes
of Balaam, and he saw the angel of the
LORD standing in the way, with his
drawn sword in his hand; and he
bowed his head, and fell on his face.
32 And the angel of the LORD said to
him, "Why have you struck your ass
these three times? Behold, I have come
forth to withstand you, because your
way is perverse before me; and the
ass saw me, and turned aside before
me these three times. If she had not
turned aside from me, surely just now
I would have slain you and let her
live." 34 Then Balaam said to the angel
of the LORD, "I have sinned, for I did
not know that thou didst stand in the
road against me. Now therefore, if it
is evil in thy sight, I will go back
again." 35 And the angel of the LORD
said to Balaam, "Go with the men; but
only the word which I bid you, that
shall you speak." So Balaam went on
with the princes of Bā'lak.

36 When Bā'lak heard that Balaam
had come, he went out to meet him at
the city of Mō'ab, on the boundary
formed by the Ăr'non, at the extremity
of the boundary. 37 And Bā'lak said to
Balaam, "Did I not send to you to call
you? Why did you not come to me?
Am I not able to honor you?" 38 Balaam said to Bā'lak, "Lo, I have come
to you! Have I now any power at all to
speak anything? The word that God
puts in my mouth, that must I
speak." 39 Then Balaam went with
Bā'lak, and they came to Kĭr'i·ath-
hū'zŏth. 40 And Bā'lak sacrificed oxen
and sheep, and sent to Balaam and to
the princes who were with him.

41 And on the morrow Bā'lak took
Balaam and brought him up to Bā'-
mŏth-bā'ăl; and from there he saw the
23 nearest of the people. 1 And Balaam said to Bā'lak, "Build for
me here seven altars, and provide for
me here seven bulls and seven rams."
2 Bā'lak did as Balaam had said; and
Balak and Balaam offered on each altar
a bull and a ram. 3 And Balaam said to
Bā'lak, "Stand beside your burnt offering, and I will go; perhaps the LORD
will come to meet me; and whatever
he shows me I will tell you." And he
went to a bare height. 4 And God met
Balaam; and Balaam said to him, "I
have prepared the seven altars, and I
have offered upon each altar a bull and
a ram." 5 And the LORD put a word in
Balaam's mouth, and said, "Return
to Bā'lak, and thus you shall speak."
6 And he returned to him, and lo, he
and all the princes of Mō'ab were
standing beside his burnt offering.
7 And Balaam took up his discourse,
and said,

"From Ā'răm Bā'lak has brought
me,
the king of Mō'ab from the eastern
mountains:
'Come, curse Jacob for me,
and come, denounce Israel!'
8 How can I curse whom God has not
cursed?
How can I denounce whom the
LORD has not denounced?
9 For from the top of the mountains
I see him,
from the hills I behold him;
lo, a people dwelling alone,
and not reckoning itself among
the nations!
10 Who can count the dust of Jacob,
or number the fourth part[s] of
Israel?
Let me die the death of the righteous,
and let my end be like his!"

11 And Bā'lak said to Balaam,
"What have you done to me? I took
you to curse my enemies, and behold,
you have done nothing but bless
them." 12 And he answered, "Must I
not take heed to speak what the LORD
puts in my mouth?"

13 And Bā'lak said to him, "Come
with me to another place, from which
you may see them; you shall see only
the nearest of them, and shall not see
them all; then curse them for me from
there." 14 And he took him to the field
of Zō'phim, to the top of Pĭs'găh, and
built seven altars, and offered a bull
and a ram on each altar. 15 Balaam said
to Bā'lak, "Stand here beside your
burnt offering, while I meet the LORD

[s] Or *dust clouds*

yonder." 16And the LORD met Balaam
and put a word in his mouth, and said,
"Return to Bā'lak, and thus shall you
speak." 17And he came to him, and,
lo, he was standing beside his burnt
offering, and the princes of Mō'ab
with him. And Bā'lak said to him,
"What has the LORD spoken?" 18And
Balaam took up his discourse, and
said,

"Rise, Bā'lak, and hear;
hearken to me, O son of Zip'-pôr:
19 God is not man, that he should lie,
or a son of man, that he should repent.
Has he said, and will he not do it?
Or has he spoken, and will he not fulfil it?
20 Behold, I received a command to bless:
he has blessed, and I cannot revoke it.
21 He has not beheld misfortune in Jacob;
nor has he seen trouble in Israel.
The LORD their God is with them,
and the shout of a king is among them.
22 God brings them out of Egypt;
they have as it were the horns of the wild ox.
23 For there is no enchantment against Jacob,
no divination against Israel;
now it shall be said of Jacob and Israel,
'What has God wrought!'
24 Behold, a people! As a lioness it rises up
and as a lion it lifts itself;
it does not lie down till it devours the prey,
and drinks the blood of the slain."

25 And Bā'lak said to Balaam,
"Neither curse them at all, nor bless
them at all." 26 But Balaam answered
Bā'lak, "Did I not tell you, 'All that
the LORD says, that I must do'?"
27And Bā'lak said to Balaam, "Come
now, I will take you to another place;
perhaps it will please God that you
may curse them for me from there."
28 So Bā'lak took Balaam to the top of
Pē'ôr, that overlooks the desert.[t] 29And
Balaam said to Bā'lak, "Build for me
here seven altars, and provide for me
here seven bulls and seven rams."
30And Bā'lak did as Balaam had said,
and offered a bull and a ram on each
altar.

24 When Balaam saw that it
pleased the LORD to bless Israel,
he did not go, as at other times, to look
for omens, but set his face toward the
wilderness. 2And Balaam lifted up his
eyes, and saw Israel encamping tribe
by tribe. And the Spirit of God came
upon him, 3 and he took up his discourse, and said,

"The oracle of Balaam the son of Bē'ôr,
the oracle of the man whose eye is opened,[u]
4 the oracle of him who hears the words of God,
who sees the vision of the Almighty,
falling down, but having his eyes uncovered:
5 how fair are your tents, O Jacob,
your encampments, O Israel!
6 Like valleys that stretch afar,
like gardens beside a river,
like aloes that the LORD has planted,
like cedar trees beside the waters.
7 Water shall flow from his buckets,
and his seed shall be in many waters,
his king shall be higher that Ā'gag,
and his kingdom shall be exalted.
8 God brings him out of Egypt;
he has as it were the horns of the wild ox,
he shall eat up the nations his adversaries,
and shall break their bones in pieces,
and pierce them through with his arrows.
9 He couched, he lay down like a lion,
and like a lioness; who will rouse him up?
Blessed be every one who blesses you,
and cursed be every one who curses you."

10 And Bā'lak's anger was kindled
against Balaam, and he struck his
hands together; and Balak said to Balaam,
"I called you to curse my
enemies, and behold, you have blessed
them these three times. 11 Therefore
now flee to your place; I said, 'I will
certainly honor you,' but the LORD has
held you back from honor." 12And
Balaam said to Bā'lak, "Did I not tell
your messengers whom you sent to me,

[t] Or *Jeshimon* [u] Or *closed* or *perfect*
24.9: Gen 49.9.

13 'If Bā'lak should give me his house
full of silver and gold, I would not be
able to go beyond the word of the
LORD, to do either good or bad of my
own will; what the LORD speaks, that
will I speak'? 14 And now, behold, I
am going to my people; come, I will
let you know what this people will do
to your people in the latter days."
15 And he took up his discourse, and
said,

"The oracle of Balaam the son of
Bē'ôr,
the oracle of the man whose eye
is opened,[v]
16 the oracle of him who hears the
words of God,
and knows the knowledge of the
Most High,
who sees the vision of the Almighty,
falling down, but having his eyes
uncovered:
17 I see him, but not now;
I behold him, but not nigh:
a star shall come forth out of Jacob,
and a scepter shall rise out of
Israel;
it shall crush the forehead[w] of Mō'ab,
and break down all the sons of
Sheth.
18 Ē'dȯm shall be dispossessed,
Sē'ir also, his enemies, shall be
dispossessed,
while Israel does valiantly.
19 By Jacob shall dominion be exercised,
and the survivors of cities be
destroyed!"

20 Then he looked on Am'ȧ·lek, and
took up his discourse, and said,
"Amalek was the first of the nations,
but in the end he shall come to
destruction."

21 And he looked on the Ken'īte,
and took up his discourse, and said,
"Enduring is your dwelling place,
and your nest is set in the rock;
22 nevertheless Kāin shall be wasted.
How long shall As'shür take you
away captive?"

23 And he took up his discourse,
and said,
"Alas, who shall live when God does
this?
24 But ships shall come from Kit'-
tim and shall afflict As'shür
and Ē'bėr;
and he also shall come to destruction."

25 Then Balaam rose, and went
back to his place; and Bā'lak also went
his way.

25 While Israel dwelt in Shit'tim
the people began to play the
harlot with the daughters of Mō'ab.
2 These invited the people to the sacrifices of their gods, and the people ate,
and bowed down to their gods. 3 So
Israel yoked himself to Bā'ȧl of Pē'ôr.
And the anger of the LORD was kindled
against Israel; 4 and the LORD said to
Moses, "Take all the chiefs of the people, and hang them in the sun before
the LORD, that the fierce anger of the
LORD may turn away from Israel."
5 And Moses said to the judges of
Israel, "Every one of you slay his men
who have yoked themselves to Bā'ȧl
of Pē'ôr."

6 And behold, one of the people of
Israel came and brought a Mid'i·ȧ·nīte
woman to his family, in the sight of
Moses and in the sight of the whole
congregation of the people of Israel,
while they were weeping at the door of
the tent of meeting. 7 When Phin'ė·hȧs
the son of El·ē·ā'zȧr, son of Aaron the
priest, saw it, he rose and left the
congregation, and took a spear in his
hand 8 and went after the man of
Israel into the inner room, and pierced
both of them, the man of Israel and
the woman, through her body. Thus
the plague was stayed from the people
of Israel. 9 Nevertheless those that
died by the plague were twenty-four
thousand.

10 And the LORD said to Moses,
11 "Phin'ė·hȧs the son of El·ē·ā'zȧr,
son of Aaron the priest, has turned
back my wrath from the people of
Israel, in that he was jealous with my
jealousy among them, so that I did not
consume the people of Israel in my
jealousy. 12 Therefore say, 'Behold, I
give to him my covenant of peace;
13 and it shall be to him, and to his
descendants after him, the covenant of
a perpetual priesthood, because he was
jealous for his God, and made atonement for the people of Israel.' "

14 The name of the slain man of
Israel, who was slain with the Mid'i·ȧ-
nīte woman, was Zim'rī the son of
Sā'lü, head of a fathers' house belonging to the Simeonites. 15 And the name
of the Mid'i·ȧ·nīte woman who was
slain was Coz'bī the daughter of Zûr,
who was the head of the people of a
fathers' house in Mid'i·ȧn.

[v] Or *closed* or *perfect* [w] Heb *corners* (of the head)

16 And the LORD said to Moses,
17 "Harass the Mid'i·ȧ·nītes, and smite
them; 18 for they have harassed you
with their wiles, with which they beguiled you in the matter of Pē'ôr, and
in the matter of Coz'bī, the daughter
of the prince of Mid'i·ȧn, their sister,
who was slain on the day of the plague
on account of Pē'ôr."

26 After the plague the LORD said
to Moses and to El·ē·ā'zȧr the
son of Aaron, the priest, 2 "Take a
census of all the congregation of the
people of Israel, from twenty years old
and upward, by their fathers' houses,
all in Israel who are able to go forth
to war." 3 And Moses and El·ē·ā'zȧr
the priest spoke with them in the plains
of Mō'ab by the Jordan at Jericho,
saying, 4 "Take a census of the people,[x] from twenty years old and upward," as the LORD commanded
Moses. The people of Israel, who came
forth out of the land of Egypt, were:

5 Reuben, the first-born of Israel;
the sons of Reuben: of Hā'noch, the
family of the Hā'nȯ·chītes; of Pal'lü,
the family of the Pal'lü·ītes; 6 of Hez'-
rȯn, the family of the Hez'rȯ·nītes; of
Cär'mī, the family of the Cär'mītes.
7 These are the families of the Reubenites; and their number was forty-three
thousand seven hundred and thirty.
8 And the sons of Pal'lü: E·lī'ab. 9 The
sons of E·lī'ab: Nem'ū-el, Dā'thȧn, and
A·bī'rȧm. These are the Dathan and
Abiram, chosen from the congregation, who contended against Moses
and Aaron in the company of Kō'rȧh,
when they contended against the
LORD, 10 and the earth opened its
mouth and swallowed them up together with Kō'rȧh, when that company died, when the fire devoured two
hundred and fifty men; and they became a warning. 11 Notwithstanding,
the sons of Kō'rȧh did not die.

12 The sons of Simeon according to
their families: of Nem'ū-el, the family
of the Nem'ū-ė·lītes; of Jā'min, the
family of the Jā'mi·nītes; of Jā'chin,
the family of the Jā'chi·nītes; 13 of
Zē'rȧh, the family of the Zē'rȧ·hītes; of
Shā'ūl, the family of the Shā'ū·lītes.
14 These are the families of the
Simeonites, twenty-two thousand two
hundred.

15 The sons of Gad according to
their families: of Zē'phon, the family
of the Zē'phȯ·nītes; of Hag'gī, the
family of the Hag'gītes; of Shü'nī, the
family of the Shü'nītes; 16 of Oz'nī,
the family of the Oz'nītes; of Ē'rī, the
family of the Ē'rītes; 17 of Âr'ȯd, the
family of the Âr'ȯ·dītes; of A·rē'lī, the
family of the A·rē'lītes. 18 These are
the families of the sons of Gad according to their number, forty thousand
five hundred.

19 The sons of Judah were Ēr and
Ō'nȧn; and Er and Onan died in the
land of Canaan. 20 And the sons of
Judah according to their families were:
of Shē'lȧh, the family of the Shė·lā'-
nītes; of Per'ez, the family of the
Per'ė·zītes; of Zē'rȧh, the family of the
Zē'rȧ·hītes. 21 And the sons of Per'ez
were: of Hez'rȯn, the family of the
Hez'rȯ·nītes; of Hā'mul, the family of
the Hā'mu·lītes. 22 These are the
families of Judah according to their
number, seventy-six thousand five
hundred.

23 The sons of Is'sȧ·chär according
to their families: of Tō'lȧ, the family
of the Tō'lȧ·ītes; of Pū'vȧh, the family
of the Pū'nītes; 24 of Jash'ub, the
family of the Jash'u·bītes; of Shim'rȯn,
the family of the Shim'rȯ·nītes.
25 These are the families of Is'sȧ·chär
according to their number, sixty-four
thousand three hundred.

26 The sons of Zeb'ū·lun, according
to their families: of Ser'ėd, the family
of the Ser'ė·dītes; of Ē'lon, the family
of the Ē'lȯ·nītes; of Jäh'lē·ėl, the family
of the Jäh'lē·ė·lītes. 27 These are the
families of the Ze·bū'lu·nītes according to their number, sixty thousand
five hundred.

28 The sons of Joseph according to
their families: Mȧ·nas'sėh and Ē'phrȧ-
im. 29 The sons of Mȧ·nas'sėh: of
Mā'chir, the family of the Mā'chi·rītes;
and Machir was the father of Gilead;
of Gilead, the family of the Gil'ē·ȧ-
dītes. 30 These are the sons of Gilead:
of I·ē'zėr, the family of the I·ē'zė·rītes;
of Hē'lek, the family of the Hē'lė·kītes;
31 and of As'ri·el, the family of the
As'ri·ė·lītes; and of Shē'chem, the
family of the Shē'chė·mītes; 32 and of
She·mī'dȧ, the family of the She·mī'dȧ-
ītes; and of Hē'phėr, the family of the
Hē'phė·rītes. 33 Now Ze·loph'ė·had
the son of Hē'phėr had no sons, but
daughters: and the names of the daughters of Zelophehad were Mäh'lȧh,

[x] Supplying *take a census of the people* Compare verse 2
26.5-51: Num 1.22-46.

Noah, Hog'lȧh, Mil'cȧh, and Tīr'zȧh.
34 These are the families of Mȧ·nas'-
sėh; and their number was fifty-two
thousand seven hundred.
35 These are the sons of Ē'phrȧ·im
according to their families: of Shü'thė-
lȧh, the family of the Shü'thė·lā'hītes;
of Bē'chėr, the family of the Bē'chė-
rītes; of Tā'han, the family of the
Tā'hȧ·nītes. 36 And these are the sons
of Shü'thė·lȧh: of Ē'rȧn, the family of
the Ē'rȧ·nītes. 37 These are the families
of the sons of Ē'phrȧ·im according to
their number, thirty-two thousand
five hundred. These are the sons of
Joseph according to their families.
38 The sons of Benjamin according
to their families: of Bē'lȧ, the family
of the Bē'lȧ-ītes; of Ash'bėl, the family
of the Ash'bė·lītes; of Ȧ·hī'rȧm, the
family of the Ȧ·hī'rȧ·mītes; 39 of She-
phü'phȧm, the family of the Shü'phȧ-
mītes; of Hū'pham, the family of the
Hū'phȧ·mītes. 40 And the sons of Bē'lȧ
were Ärd and Nā'ȧ·mȧn: of Ard, the
family of the Är'dītes; of Naaman, the
family of the Nā'ȧ·mītes. 41 These are
the sons of Benjamin according to
their families; and their number was
forty-five thousand six hundred.
42 These are the sons of Dan according to their families: of Shü'hȧm,
the family of the Shü'hȧ·mītes. These
are the families of Dan according to
their families. 43 All the families of the
Shü'hȧ·mītes, according to their number, were sixty-four thousand four
hundred.
44 The sons of Ash'ėr according to
their families: of Im'nȧh, the family of
the Im'nītes; of Ish'vī, the family of
the Ish'vītes; of Bē·rī'ȧh, the family of
the Bē·rī'ītes. 45 Of the sons of Bē·rī'ȧh:
of Hē'bėr, the family of the Hē'bė·rītes;
of Mal'chi-el, the family of the Mal'-
chi-ė·lītes. 46 And the name of the
daughter of Ash'ėr was Ser'ȧh. 47 These
are the families of the sons of Ash'ėr
according to their number, fifty-three
thousand four hundred.
48 The sons of Naph'tȧ·lī according
to their families: of Jäh'rē·ėl, the family
of the Jäh'rē·ė·lītes; of Gū'nī, the
fami y of the Gū'nītes; 49 of Jē'zėr, the
family of the Jē'zė·rītes; of Shil'lėm,
the family of the Shil'lė·mītes. 50 These
are the families of Naph'tȧ·lī according
to their families; and their number was
forty-five thousand four hundred.
51 This was the number of the people of Israel, six hundred and one
thousand seven hundred and thirty.
52 The LORD said to Moses: 53 "To
these the land shall be divided for
inheritance according to the number
of names. 54 To a large tribe you shall
give a large inheritance, and to a small
tribe you shall give a small inheritance;
every tribe shall be given its inheritance according to its numbers. 55 But
the land shall be divided by lot;
according to the names of the tribes
of their fathers they shall inherit.
56 Their inheritance shall be divided
according to lot between the larger and
the smaller."
57 These are the Levites as numbered according to their families: of
Gĕr'shȯn, the family of the Gĕr'shȯ-
nītes; of Kō'hath, the family of the
Kō'hȧ·thītes; of Mė·rär'ī, the family of
the Mė·rär'ītes. 58 These are the families of Levi: the family of the Lib'-
nītes, the family of the Hē'brȯ·nītes,
the family of the Mäh'lītes, the family
of the Mū'shītes, the family of the
Kō'rȧ·hītes. And Kō'hath was the
father of Am'ram. 59 The name of
Am'ram's wife was Joch'ė·bed the
daughter of Levi, who was born to
Levi in Egypt; and she bore to Amram
Aaron and Moses and Miriam their
sister. 60 And to Aaron were born Nā'-
dab, Ȧ·bī'hū, El·ē·ā'zȧr and Ith'ȧ·mär.
61 But Nā'dab and Ȧ·bī'hū died when
they offered unholy fire before the
LORD. 62 And those numbered of them
were twenty-three thousand, every
male from a month old and upward;
for they were not numbered among
the people of Israel, because there was
no inheritance given to them among
the people of Israel.
63 These were those numbered by
Moses and El·ē·ā'zȧr the priest, who
numbered the people of Israel in the
plains of Mō'ȧb by the Jordan at
Jericho. 64 But among these there was
not a man of those numbered by Moses
and Aaron the priest, who had numbered the people of Israel in the wilderness of Sinai. 65 For the LORD had
said of them, "They shall die in the
wilderness." There was not left a man
of them, except Caleb the son of
Jė·phün'nėh and Joshua the son of Nun.
27 Then drew near the daughters
of Ze·loph'ė·had the son of Hē'-
phėr, son of Gilead, son of Mā'chir,
son of Mȧ·nas'sėh, from the families of

26.57-62: Num 1.47-49. **26.64-65:** Num 14.26-35. **27.1-11:** Num 36.1-12.

Manasseh the son of Joseph. The
names of his daughters were: Mäh′läh,
Noah, Hog′läh, Mil′cäh, and Tĭr′zäh.
2And they stood before Moses, and
before El·ē·ā′zär the priest, and before
the leaders and all the congregation,
at the door of the tent of meeting, saying, 3 "Our father died in the wilderness; he was not among the company
of those who gathered themselves together against the LORD in the company of Kō′räh, but died for his own
sin; and he had no sons. 4 Why should
the name of our father be taken away
from his family, because he had no
son? Give to us a possession among
our father's brethren."

5 Moses brought their case before
the LORD. 6And the LORD said to
Moses, 7 "The daughters of Ze·loph′-
ė·had are right; you shall give them
possession of an inheritance among
their father's brethren and cause the
inheritance of their father to pass to
them. 8And you shall say to the people
of Israel, 'If a man dies, and has no
son, then you shall cause his inheritance to pass to his daughter. 9And if
he has no daughter, then you shall
give his inheritance to his brothers.
10And if he has no brothers, then you
shall give his inheritance to his father's
brothers. 11And if his father has no
brothers, then you shall give his inheritance to his kinsman that is next
to him of his family, and he shall
possess it. And it shall be to the people
of Israel a statute and ordinance, as
the LORD commanded Moses.' "

12 The LORD said to Moses, "Go
up into this mountain of Ab′ȧ·rim, and
see the land which I have given to the
people of Israel. 13And when you have
seen it, you also shall be gathered to
your people, as your brother Aaron
was gathered, 14 because you rebelled
against my word in the wilderness of
Zin during the strife of the congregation, to sanctify me at the waters before
their eyes." (These are the waters of
Mer′i·bäh of Kā′desh in the wilderness
of Zin.) 15 Moses said to the LORD,
16 "Let the LORD, the God of the
spirits of all flesh, appoint a man over
the congregation, 17 who shall go out
before them and come in before them,
who shall lead them out and bring
them in; that the congregation of the
LORD may not be as sheep which have
no shepherd." 18And the LORD said to
Moses, "Take Joshua the son of Nun,
a man in whom is the spirit, and lay
your hand upon him; 19 cause him to
stand before El·ē·ā′zär the priest and
all the congregation, and you shall
commission him in their sight. 20 You
shall invest him with some of your
authority, that all the congregation of
the people of Israel may obey. 21And
he shall stand before El·ē·ā′zär the
priest, who shall inquire for him by
the judgment of the Ū′rim before the
LORD; at his word they shall go out,
and at his word they shall come in,
both he and all the people of Israel
with him, the whole congregation."
22And Moses did as the LORD commanded him; he took Joshua and
caused him to stand before El·ē·ā′zär
the priest and the whole congregation,
23 and he laid his hands upon him,
and commissioned him as the LORD
directed through Moses.

28 The LORD said to Moses,
2 "Command the people of
Israel, and say to them, 'My offering,
my food for my offerings by fire, my
pleasing odor, you shall take heed to
offer to me in its due season.' 3And
you shall say to them, This is the
offering by fire which you shall offer
to the LORD: two male lambs a year
old without blemish, day by day, as a
continual offering. 4 The one lamb you
shall offer in the morning, and the
other lamb you shall offer in the evening; 5 also a tenth of an ephah of fine
flour for a cereal offering, mixed with
a fourth of a hin of beaten oil. 6 It is a
continual burnt offering, which was
ordained at Mount Sinai for a pleasing
odor, an offering by fire to the LORD.
7 Its drink offering shall be a fourth of
a hin for each lamb; in the holy place
you shall pour out a drink offering of
strong drink to the LORD. 8 The other
lamb you shall offer in the evening;
like the cereal offering of the morning,
and like its drink offering, you shall
offer it as an offering by fire, a pleasing
odor to the LORD.

9 "On the sabbath day two male
lambs a year old without blemish, and
two tenths of an ephah of fine flour for
a cereal offering, mixed with oil, and
its drink offering: 10 this is the burnt
offering of every sabbath, besides the
continual burnt offering and its drink
offering.

11 "At the beginnings of your

27.12-14: Deut 3.23-27; 32.48-52. **27.18-23:** Deut 3.28. **28.3-8:** Ex 29.38-42.

months you shall offer a burnt offering
to the LORD: two young bulls, one
ram, seven male lambs a year old without blemish; 12 also three tenths of an
ephah of fine flour for a cereal offering,
mixed with oil, for each bull; and two
tenths of fine flour for a cereal offering,
mixed with oil, for the one ram; 13 and
a tenth of fine flour mixed with oil as
a cereal offering for every lamb; for a
burnt offering of pleasing odor, an
offering by fire to the LORD. 14 Their
drink offering shall be half a hin of
wine for a bull, a third of a hin for a
ram, and a fourth of a hin for a lamb;
this is the burnt offering of each
month throughout the months of the
year. 15 Also one male goat for a sin
offering to the LORD; it shall be offered
besides the continual burnt offering
and its drink offering.

16 "On the fourteenth day of the
first month is the LORD's passover.
17 And on the fifteenth day of this
month is a feast; seven days shall unleavened bread be eaten. 18 On the
first day there shall be a holy convocation: you shall do no laborious work,
19 but offer an offering by fire, a burnt
offering to the LORD: two young bulls,
one ram, and seven male lambs a year
old; see that they are without blemish;
20 also their cereal offering of fine
flour mixed with oil; three tenths of an
ephah shall you offer for a bull, and
two tenths for a ram; 21 a tenth shall
you offer for each of the seven lambs;
22 also one male goat for a sin offering,
to make atonement for you. 23 You
shall offer these besides the burnt
offering of the morning, which is for
a continual burnt offering. 24 In the
same way you shall offer daily, for
seven days, the food of an offering by
fire, a pleasing odor to the LORD; it
shall be offered besides the continual
burnt offering and its drink offering.
25 And on the seventh day you shall
have a holy convocation; you shall do
no laborious work.

26 "On the day of the first fruits,
when you offer a cereal offering of new
grain to the LORD at your feast of
weeks, you shall have a holy convocation; you shall do no laborious work,
27 but offer a burnt offering, a pleasing
odor to the LORD: two young bulls,
one ram, seven male lambs a year old;
28 also their cereal offering of fine
flour mixed with oil, three tenths of an
ephah for each bull, two tenths for one
ram, 29 a tenth for each of the seven
lambs; 30 with one male goat, to make
atonement for you. 31 Besides the continual burnt offering and its cereal
offering, you shall offer them and their
drink offering. See that they are without blemish.

29 "On the first day of the seventh
month you shall have a holy
convocation; you shall do no laborious
work. It is a day for you to blow the
trumpets, 2 and you shall offer a burnt
offering, a pleasing odor to the LORD:
one young bull, one ram, seven male
lambs a year old without blemish;
3 also their cereal offering of fine flour
mixed with oil, three tenths of an
ephah for the bull, two tenths for the
ram, 4 and one tenth for each of the
seven lambs; 5 with one male goat for
a sin offering, to make atonement for
you; 6 besides the burnt offering of the
new moon, and its cereal offering, and
the continual burnt offering and its
cereal offering, and their drink offering, according to the ordinance for
them, a pleasing odor, an offering by
fire to the LORD.

7 "On the tenth day of this seventh
month you shall have a holy convocation, and afflict yourselves; you shall
do no work, 8 but you shall offer a
burnt offering to the LORD, a pleasing
odor: one young bull, one ram, seven
male lambs a year old; they shall be to
you without blemish; 9 and their cereal
offering of fine flour mixed with oil,
three tenths of an ephah for the bull,
two tenths for the one ram, 10 a tenth
for each of the seven lambs: 11 also one
male goat for a sin offering, besides
the sin offering of atonement, and the
continual burnt offering and its cereal
offering, and their drink offerings.

12 "On the fifteenth day of the
seventh month you shall have a holy
convocation; you shall do no laborious
work, and you shall keep a feast to the
LORD seven days; 13 and you shall offer
a burnt offering, an offering by fire, a
pleasing odor to the LORD, thirteen
young bulls, two rams, fourteen male
lambs a year old; they shall be without
blemish; 14 and their cereal offering of
fine flour mixed with oil, three tenths

28.16: Ex 12.1-14, 21-27; Lev 23.5; Deut 16.1-2, 5-7. **28.17-25**: Ex 12.15-20; Lev 23.6-8; Deut 16.3-4, 8.
28.26-31: Ex 23.16; 34.22; Lev 23.15-21; Deut 16.9-12. **29.1-6**: Ex 23.16; 34.22; Lev 23.23-25.
29.7-11: Lev 16.29-34; 23.26-32. **29.12-34**: Lev 33.33-35.

of an ephah for each of the thirteen
bulls, two tenths for each of the two
rams, 15 and a tenth for each of the
fourteen lambs; 16 also one male goat
for a sin offering, besides the continual
burnt offering, its cereal offering and
its drink offering.
17 "On the second day twelve
young bulls, two rams, fourteen male
lambs a year old without blemish,
18 with the cereal offering and the
drink offerings for the bulls, for the
rams, and for the lambs, by number,
according to the ordinance; 19 also one
male goat for a sin offering, besides
the continual burnt offering and its
cereal offering, and their drink offerings.
20 "On the third day eleven bulls,
two rams, fourteen male lambs a year
old without blemish, 21 with the cereal
offering and the drink offerings for the
bulls, for the rams, and for the lambs,
by number, according to the ordinance;
22 also one male goat for a sin offering,
besides the continual burnt offering
and its cereal offering and its drink
offering.
23 "On the fourth day ten bulls,
two rams, fourteen male lambs a year
old without blemish, 24 with the cereal
offering and the drink offerings for the
bulls, for the rams, and for the lambs,
by number, according to the ordinance; 25 also one male goat for a sin
offering, besides the continual burnt
offering, its cereal offering and its
drink offering.
26 "On the fifth day nine bulls, two
rams, fourteen male lambs a year old
without blemish, 27 with the cereal
offering and the drink offerings for the
bulls, for the rams, and for the lambs,
by number, according to the ordinance; 28 also one male goat for a sin
offering; besides the continual burnt
offerings and its cereal offering and its
drink offering.
29 "On the sixth day eight bulls,
two rams, fourteen male lambs a year
old without blemish, 30 with the cereal
offering and the drink offerings for the
bulls, for the rams, and for the lambs,
by number, according to the ordinance; 31 also one male goat for a sin
offering; besides the continual burnt
offering, its cereal offering, and its
drink offerings.
32 "On the seventh day seven bulls,
two rams, fourteen male lambs a year
old without blemish, 33 with the cereal
offering and the drink offerings for
the bulls, for the rams, and for the
lambs, by number, according to the
ordinance; 34 also one male goat for a
sin offering; besides the continual
burnt offering, its cereal offering, and
its drink offering.
35 "On the eighth day you shall
have a solemn assembly: you shall do
no laborious work, 36 but you shall
offer a burnt offering, an offering by
fire, a pleasing odor to the LORD: one
bull, one ram, seven male lambs a year
old without blemish, 37 and the cereal
offering and the drink offerings for the
bull, for the ram, and for the lambs,
by number, according to the ordinance; 38 also one male goat for a sin
offering; besides the continual burnt
offering and its cereal offering and its
drink offering.
39 "These you shall offer to the
LORD at your appointed feasts, in
addition to your votive offerings and
your freewill offerings, for your burnt
offerings, and for your cereal offerings,
and for your drink offerings, and for
your peace offerings."
40[y] And Moses told the people of
Israel everything just as the LORD had
commanded Moses.

30 Moses said to the heads of the
tribes of the people of Israel,
"This is what the LORD has commanded. 2 When a man vows a vow
to the LORD, or swears an oath to bind
himself by a pledge, he shall not break
his word; he shall do according to all
that proceeds out of his mouth. 3 Or
when a woman vows a vow to the
LORD, and binds herself by a pledge,
while within her father's house, in her
youth, 4 and her father hears of her
vow and of her pledge by which she has
bound herself, and says nothing to her;
then all her vows shall stand, and every
pledge by which she has bound herself
shall stand. 5 But if her father expresses
disapproval to her on the day that he
hears of it, no vow of hers, no pledge
by which she has bound herself, shall
stand; and the LORD will forgive her,
because her father opposed her. 6 And
if she is married to a husband, while
under her vows or any thoughtless
utterance of her lips by which she has
bound herself, 7 and her husband hears

[y] Ch 30.1 in Heb
29.35-38: Lev 23.36. **30.2-16:** Deut 23.21-23. **30.2:** Mt 5.33.

of it, and says nothing to her on the
day that he hears; then her vows shall
stand, and her pledges by which she
has bound herself shall stand. 8 But if,
on the day that her husband comes to
hear of it, he expresses disapproval,
then he shall make void her vow which
was on her, and the thoughtless utterance of her lips, by which she bound
herself; and the LORD will forgive her.
9 But any vow of a widow or of a
divorced woman, anything by which
she has bound herself, shall stand
against her. 10 And if she vowed in her
husband's house, or bound herself by
a pledge with an oath, 11 and her
husband heard of it, and said nothing
to her, and did not oppose her; then
all her vows shall stand, and every
pledge by which she bound herself
shall stand. 12 But if her husband
makes them null and void on the day
that he hears them, then whatever proceeds out of her lips concerning her
vows, or concerning her pledge of herself, shall not stand: her husband has
made them void, and the LORD will
forgive her. 13 Any vow and any binding
oath to afflict herself, her husband may
establish, or her husband may make
void. 14 But if her husband says
nothing to her from day to day, then
he establishes all her vows, or all her
pledges, that are upon her; he has
established them, because he said
nothing to her on the day that he heard
of them. 15 But if he makes them null
and void after he has heard of them,
then he shall bear her iniquity."

16 These are the statutes which the
LORD commanded Moses, as between
a man and his wife, and between a
father and his daughter, while in her
youth, within her father's house.

31 The LORD said to Moses,
2 "Avenge the people of Israel on
the Mid'i·ȧ·nītes; afterward you shall
be gathered to your people." 3 And
Moses said to the people, "Arm men
from among you for the war, that they
may go against Mid'i·ȧn, to execute
the LORD's vengeance on Midian.
4 You shall send a thousand from each
of the tribes of Israel to the war." 5 So
there were provided, out of the thousands of Israel, a thousand from each
tribe, twelve thousand armed for war.
6 And Moses sent them to the war, a
thousand from each tribe, together
with Phin'ē·hȧs the son of El·ē·ā'zȧr
the priest, with the vessels of the
sanctuary and the trumpets for the
alarm in his hand. 7 They warred
against Mid'i·ȧn, as the LORD commanded Moses, and slew every male.
8 They slew the kings of Mid'i·ȧn with
the rest of their slain, Ē'vī, Rē'kem,
Zūr, Hūr, and Rē'bȧ, the five kings of
Mid'i·ȧn; and they also slew Balaam
the son of Bē'ôr with the sword. 9 And
the people of Israel took captive the
women of Mid'i·ȧn and their little
ones; and they took as booty all their
cattle, their flocks, and all their goods.
10 All their cities in the places where
they dwelt, and all their encampments,
they burned with fire, 11 and took all
the spoil and all the booty, both of man
and of beast. 12 Then they brought the
captives and the booty and the spoil
to Moses, and to El·ē·ā'zȧr the priest,
and to the congregation of the people
of Israel, at the camp on the plains
of Mō'ab by the Jordan at Jericho.

13 Moses, and El·ē·ā'zȧr the priest,
and all the leaders of the congregation,
went forth to meet them outside the
camp. 14 And Moses was angry with
the officers of the army, the commanders of thousands and the commanders of hundreds, who had come
from service in the war. 15 Moses said
to them, "Have you let all the women
live? 16 Behold, these caused the people of Israel, by the counsel of Balaam,
to act treacherously against the LORD
in the matter of Pē'ôr, and so the
plague came among the congregation
of the LORD. 17 Now therefore, kill
every male among the little ones, and
kill every woman who has known man
by lying with him. 18 But all the young
girls who have not known man by
lying with him, keep alive for yourselves. 19 Encamp outside the camp
seven days; whoever of you has killed
any person, and whoever has touched
any slain, purify yourselves and your
captives on the third day and on the
seventh day. 20 You shall purify every
garment, every article of skin, all work
of goats' hair, and every article of
wood."

21 And El·ē·ā'zȧr the priest said to
the men of war who had gone to battle:
"This is the statute of the law which
the LORD has commanded Moses:
22 only the gold, the silver, the bronze,
the iron, the tin, and the lead, 23 everything that can stand the fire, you shall

31.16: Rev 2.14.

pass through the fire, and it shall be
clean. Nevertheless it shall also be
purified with the water of impurity;
and whatever cannot stand the fire,
you shall pass through the water.
24 You must wash your clothes on the
seventh day, and you shall be clean;
and afterward you shall come into the
camp."

25 The LORD said to Moses,
26 "Take the count of the booty that
was taken, both of man and of beast,
you and El·ē·ā'zȧr the priest and the
heads of the fathers' houses of the congregation; 27 and divide the booty into
two parts, between the warriors who
went out to battle and all the congregation. 28 And levy for the LORD a
tribute from the men of war who went
out to battle, one out of five hundred,
of the persons and of the oxen and of
the asses and of the flocks; 29 take it
from their half, and give it to El·ē·ā'zȧr
the priest as an offering to the LORD.
30 And from the people of Israel's half
you shall take one drawn out of every
fifty, of the persons, of the oxen, of
the asses, and of the flocks, of all the
cattle, and give them to the Levites
who have charge of the tabernacle of
the LORD." 31 And Moses and El·ē·ā'-
zȧr the priest did as the LORD commanded Moses.

32 Now the booty remaining of the
spoil that the men of war took was:
six hundred and seventy-five thousand
sheep, 33 seventy-two thousand cattle,
34 sixty-one thousand asses, 35 and
thirty-two thousand persons in all,
women who had not known man by
lying with him. 36 And the half, the
portion of those who had gone out to
war, was in number three hundred and
thirty-seven thousand five hundred
sheep, 37 and the LORD's tribute of
sheep was six hundred and seventy-
five. 38 The cattle were thirty-six thousand, of which the LORD's tribute was
seventy-two. 39 The asses were thirty
thousand five hundred, of which the
LORD's tribute was sixty-one. 40 The
persons were sixteen thousand, of
which the LORD's tribute was thirty-
two persons. 41 And Moses gave the
tribute, which was the offering for the
LORD, to El·ē·ā'zȧr the priest, as the
LORD commanded Moses.

42 From the people of Israel's half,
which Moses separated from that of
the men who had gone to war—43 now
the congregation's half was three hundred and thirty-seven thousand five
hundred sheep, 44 thirty-six thousand
cattle, 45 and thirty thousand five hundred asses, 46 and sixteen thousand
persons—47 from the people of Israel's
half Moses took one of every fifty,
both of persons and of beasts, and
gave them to the Levites who had
charge of the tabernacle of the LORD;
as the LORD commanded Moses.

48 Then the officers who were over
the thousands of the army, the captains
of thousands and the captains of hundreds, came near to Moses, 49 and said
to Moses, "Your servants have counted
the men of war who are under our
command, and there is not a man
missing from us. 50 And we have
brought the LORD's offering, what each
man found, articles of gold, armlets
and bracelets, signet rings, earrings,
and beads, to make atonement for ourselves before the LORD." 51 And Moses
and El·ē·ā'zȧr the priest received from
them the gold, all wrought articles.
52 And all the gold of the offering that
they offered to the LORD, from the
commanders of thousands and the
commanders of hundreds, was sixteen
thousand seven hundred and fifty
shekels. 53 (The men of war had taken
booty, every man for himself.) 54 And
Moses and El·ē·ā'zȧr the priest received the gold from the commanders
of thousands and of hundreds, and
brought it into the tent of meeting, as
a memorial for the people of Israel
before the LORD.

32 Now the sons of Reuben and
the sons of Gad had a very great
multitude of cattle; and they saw the
land of Jā'zėr and the land of Gilead,
and behold, the place was a place for
cattle. 2 So the sons of Gad and the
sons of Reuben came and said to Moses
and to El·ē·ā'zȧr the priest and to the
leaders of the congregation, 3 "At'ȧ-
roth, Dī'bon, Jā'zėr, Nim'rȧh, Hesh'-
bȯn, E·lė·ā'lėh, Sē'bam, Nē'bō, and
Bē'on, 4 the land which the LORD
smote before the congregation of
Israel, is a land for cattle; and your
servants have cattle." 5 And they said,
"If we have found favor in your sight,
let this land be given to your servants
for a possession; do not take us across
the Jordan."

6 But Moses said to the sons of Gad
and to the sons of Reuben, "Shall
your brethren go to the war while you
sit here? 7 Why will you discourage the

heart of the people of Israel from going
over into the land which the LORD has
given them? 8 Thus did your fathers,
when I sent them from Kā'desh-bär'-
nē·ȧ to see the land. 9 For when they
went up to the Valley of Esh'cȯl, and
saw the land, they discouraged the
heart of the people of Israel from going into the land which the LORD had
given them. 10And the LORD's anger
was kindled on that day, and he swore,
saying, 11 'Surely none of the men who
came up out of Egypt, from twenty
years old and upward, shall see the
land which I swore to give to Abraham, to Isaac, and to Jacob, because
they have not wholly followed me;
12 none except Caleb the son of Jė-
phün'nėh the Ken'iz·zīte and Joshua
the son of Nun, for they have wholly
followed the LORD.' 13And the LORD's
anger was kindled against Israel, and
he made them wander in the wilderness forty years, until all the generation that had done evil in the sight of
the LORD was consumed. 14And behold, you have risen in your fathers'
stead, a brood of sinful men, to increase
still more the fierce anger of the LORD
against Israel! 15 For if you turn away
from following him, he will again abandon them in the wilderness; and you
will destroy all this people."

16 Then they came near to him,
and said, "We will build sheepfolds
here for our flocks, and cities for our
little ones, 17 but we will take up arms,
ready to go before the people of Israel,
until we have brought them to their
place; and our little ones shall live in
the fortified cities because of the inhabitants of the land. 18 We will not
return to our homes until the people
of Israel have inherited each his
inheritance. 19 For we will not inherit
with them on the other side of the
Jordan and beyond; because our inheritance has come to us on this side
of the Jordan to the east." 20 So Moses
said to them, "If you will do this, if
you will take up arms to go before the
LORD for the war, 21 and every armed
man of you will pass over the Jordan
before the LORD, until he has driven
out his enemies from before him 22 and
the land is subdued before the LORD;
then after that you shall return and be
free of obligation to the LORD and to
Israel; and this land shall be your possession before the LORD. 23 But if you
will not do so, behold, you have sinned
against the LORD; and be sure your sin
will find you out. 24 Build cities for
your little ones, and folds for your
sheep; and do what you have promised." 25And the sons of Gad and the
sons of Reuben said to Moses, "Your
servants will do as my lord commands.
26 Our little ones, our wives, our flocks,
and all our cattle, shall remain there
in the cities of Gilead; 27 but your servants will pass over, every man who
is armed for war, before the LORD to
battle, as my lord orders."

28 So Moses gave command concerning them to El·ē·ā'zȧr the priest,
and to Joshua the son of Nun, and to
the heads of the fathers' houses of the
tribes of the people of Israel. 29And
Moses said to them, "If the sons of
Gad and the sons of Reuben, every
man who is armed to battle before the
LORD, will pass with you over the
Jordan and the land shall be subdued
before you, then you shall give them
the land of Gilead for a possession;
30 but if they will not pass over with
you armed, they shall have possessions
among you in the land of Canaan."
31And the sons of Gad and the sons of
Reuben answered, "As the LORD has
said to your servants, so we will do.
32 We will pass over armed before
the LORD into the land of Canaan, and
the possession of our inheritance shall
remain with us beyond the Jordan."

33 And Moses gave to them, to the
sons of Gad and to the sons of Reuben
and to the half-tribe of Mȧ·nas'sėh the
son of Joseph, the kingdom of Sī'hon
king of the Am'ȯ·rītes and the kingdom of Og king of Bā'shȧn, the land and
its cities with their territories, the cities
of the land throughout the country.
34And the sons of Gad built Dī'bon,
At'ȧ·roth, Ȧ·rō'ėr, 35At'roth-shō'phȧn,
Jā'zėr, Jog'be·häh, 36 Beth-nim'rȧh
and Beth-hâr'ȧn, fortified cities, and
folds for sheep. 37And the sons of Reuben built Hesh'bȯn, Ē·lė·ā'lėh, Kīr·i·ȧ-
thā'im, 38 Nē'bō, and Bā'ȧl-mē'ȯn
(their names to be changed), and Sib'-
mȧh; and they gave other names to the
cities which they built. 39And the sons
of Mā'chir the son of Mȧ·nas'sėh went
to Gilead and took it, and dispossessed
the Am'ȯ·rītes who were in it. 40And
Moses gave Gilead to Mā'chir the son
of Mȧ·nas'sėh, and he settled in it.
41And Jā'ir the son of Mȧ·nas'sėh went
and took their villages, and called them

Hav'vȯth-jā'ir.[z] 42And Nō'bȧh went
and took Kē'nath and its villages, and
called it Nobah, after his own name.

33 These are the stages of the
people of Israel, when they
went forth out of the land of Egypt
by their hosts under the leadership of
Moses and Aaron. 2 Moses wrote down
their starting places, stage by stage,
by command of the LORD; and these
are their stages according to their
starting places. 3 They set out from
Ram'ė·sēṡ in the first month, on the
fifteenth day of the first month; on the
day after the passover the people of
Israel went out triumphantly in the
sight of all the Egyptians, 4 while the
Egyptians were burying all their first-
born, whom the LORD had struck down
among them; upon their gods also the
LORD executed judgments.

5 So the people of Israel set out
from Ram'ė·sēṡ, and encamped at
Suc'coth. 6And they set out from Suc'-
coth, and encamped at Ē'thȧm, which
is on the edge of the wilderness. 7And
they set out from Ē'thȧm, and turned
back to Pī-hȧ·hī'roth, which is east of
Bā'ȧl-zē'phȯn; and they encamped before Mig'dōl. 8And they set out from
before Hȧ·hī'roth, and passed through
the midst of the sea into the wilderness, and they went a three days' journey in the wilderness of Ē'thȧm, and
encamped at Mâr'ȧh. 9And they set
out from Mâr'ȧh, and came to Ē'lim;
at Elim there were twelve springs of
water and seventy palm trees, and they
encamped there. 10And they set out
from Ē'lim, and encamped by the Red
Sea. 11And they set out from the Red
Sea, and encamped in the wilderness
of Sin. 12And they set out from the
wilderness of Sin, and encamped at
Doph'kȧh. 13And they set out from
Doph'kȧh, and encamped at Ā'lụsh.
14And they set out from Ā'lụsh, and
encamped at Reph'i·dim, where there
was no water for the people to drink.
15And they set out from Reph'i·dim,
and encamped in the wilderness of
Sinai. 16And they set out from the
wilderness of Sinai, and encamped at
Kib'roth-ha·tā'ȧ·vȧh. 17And they set
out from Kib'roth-ha·tā'ȧ·vȧh, and encamped at Hȧ·zē'roth. 18And they set
out from Hȧ·zē'roth, and encamped at
Rith'mȧh. 19And they set out from
Rith'mȧh, and encamped at Rim'mon-
per'ez. 20And they set out from Rim'-
mon-per'ez, and encamped at Lib'nȧh.
21And they set out from Lib'nȧh, and
encamped at Ris'sȧh. 22And they set
out from Ris'sȧh, and encamped at
Kē·hė·lā'thȧh. 23And they set out from
Kē·hė·lā'thȧh, and encamped at Mount
Shē'phẽr. 24And they set out from
Mount Shē'phẽr, and encamped at
Hȧ·rā'dȧh. 25And they set out from
Hȧ·rā'dȧh, and encamped at Mak·hē'-
lȯth. 26And they set out from Mak-
hē'lȯth, and encamped at Tā'hath.
27And they set out from Tā'hath, and
encamped at Ter'ȧh. 28And they set
out from Ter'ȧh, and encamped at
Mith'kȧh. 29And they set out from
Mith'kȧh, and encamped at Hash·mō'-
nȧh. 30And they set out from Hash-
mō'nȧh, and encamped at Mō·sē'rȯth.
31And they set out from Mō·sē'rȯth,
and encamped at Bē'ne-jā'ȧ·kȧn. 32And
they set out from Bē'ne-jā'ȧ·kȧn, and
encamped at Hôr-hȧg·gid'gad. 33And
they set out from Hôr-hȧg·gid'gad, and
encamped at Jot'bȧ·thȧh. 34And they
set out from Jot'bȧ·thȧh, and encamped at Ȧ·brō'nȧh. 35And they set
out from Ȧ·brō'nȧh, and encamped at
Ē'zi·on-gē'bẽr. 36And they set out
from Ē'zi·on-gē'bẽr, and encamped in
the wilderness of Zin (that is, Kā'-
desh). 37And they set out from Kā'-
desh, and encamped at Mount Hôr,
on the edge of the land of Ē'dȯm.

38 And Aaron the priest went up
Mount Hôr at the command of the
LORD, and died there, in the fortieth
year after the people of Israel had
come out of the land of Egypt, on the
first day of the fifth month. 39And
Aaron was a hundred and twenty-
three years old when he died on
Mount Hôr.

40 And the Canaanite, the king of
Âr'ȧd, who dwelt in the Negeb in the
land of Canaan, heard of the coming
of the people of Israel.

41 And they set out from Mount
Hôr, and encamped at Zal·mō'nȧh.
42And they set out from Zal·mō'nȧh,
and encamped at Pū'non. 43And they
set out from Pū'non, and encamped at
Ō'both. 44And they set out from
Ō'both, and encamped at Ī'ye-ab'ȧ-
rim, in the territory of Mō'ab. 45And
they set out from Ī'yim, and encamped
at Dī'bon-gad. 46And they set out from
Dī'bon-gad, and encamped at Al'mȯn-

[z] That is *the villages of Jair*
33.38-39: Num 20.23-29; Deut 10.6.

dib·lȧ·thā'im. 47 And they set out from
Al'mȯn-dib·lȧ·thā'im, and encamped
in the mountains of Ab'ȧ·rim, before
Nē'bō. 48 And they set out from the
mountains of Ab'ȧ·rim, and encamped
in the plains of Mō'ab by the Jordan
at Jericho; 49 they encamped by the
Jordan from Beth-jesh'i·moth as far as
Ā'bėl-shit'tim in the plains of Mō'ab.
50 And the LORD said to Moses in
the plains of Mō'ab by the Jordan at
Jericho, 51 "Say to the people of Israel,
When you pass over the Jordan into
the land of Canaan, 52 then you shall
drive out all the inhabitants of the land
from before you, and destroy all their
figured stones, and destroy all their
molten images, and demolish all their
high places; 53 and you shall take
possession of the land and settle in it,
for I have given the land to you to
possess it. 54 You shall inherit the land
by lot according to your families; to a
large tribe you shall give a large inheritance, and to a small tribe you shall
give a small inheritance; wherever the
lot falls to any man, that shall be his;
according to the tribes of your fathers
you shall inherit. 55 But if you do not
drive out the inhabitants of the land
from before you, then those of them
whom you let remain shall be as pricks
in your eyes and thorns in your sides,
and they shall trouble you in the land
where you dwell. 56 And I will do to
you as I thought to do to them."
34 The LORD said to Moses,
2 "Command the people of Israel, and say to them, When you enter
the land of Canaan (this is the land
that shall fall to you for an inheritance,
the land of Canaan in its full extent),
3 your south side shall be from the
wilderness of Zin along the side of
Ē'dȯm, and your southern boundary
shall be from the end of the Salt Sea
on the east; 4 and your boundary shall
turn south of the ascent of Ak·rab'bim,
and cross to Zin, and its end shall be
south of Kā'desh-bär'nē·ȧ; then it shall
go on to Hā'zär-ad'dȧr, and pass along
to Az'mȯn; 5 and the boundary shall
turn from Az'mȯn to the Brook of
Egypt, and its termination shall be at
the sea.
6 "For the western boundary, you
shall have the Great Sea and its[a] coast;
this shall be your western boundary.
7 "This shall be your northern
boundary: from the Great Sea you
shall mark out your line to Mount
Hôr; 8 from Mount Hôr you shall mark
it out to the entrance of Hā'math, and
the end of the boundary shall be at
Zē'dad; 9 then the boundary shall extend to Ziph'rȯn, and its end shall be
at Hā'zär-ē'nȧn; this shall be your
northern boundary.
10 "You shall mark out your eastern boundary from Hā'zär-ē'nȧn to
Shē'pham; 11 and the boundary shall
go down from Shē'pham to Rib'lȧh on
the east side of Ā'in; and the boundary
shall go down, and reach to the
shoulder of the sea of Chim'nė-reth on
the east; 12 and the boundary shall go
down to the Jordan, and its end shall
be at the Salt Sea. This shall be your
land with its boundaries all round."
13 Moses commanded the people of
Israel, saying, "This is the land which
you shall inherit by lot, which the
LORD has commanded to give to the
nine tribes and to the half-tribe; 14 for
the tribe of the sons of Reuben by
fathers' houses and the tribe of the
sons of Gad by their fathers' houses
have received their inheritance, and
also the half-tribe of Mȧ·nas'sėh;
15 the two tribes and the half-tribe
have received their inheritance beyond
the Jordan at Jericho eastward, toward
the sunrise."
16 The LORD said to Moses,
17 "These are the names of the men
who shall divide the land to you for
inheritance: El·ē·ā'zȧr the priest and
Joshua the son of Nun. 18 You shall
take one leader of every tribe, to divide
the land for inheritance. 19 These are
the names of the men: Of the tribe of
Judah, Caleb the son of Jė·phün'nėh.
20 Of the tribe of the sons of Simeon,
She·mū'el the son of Am·mī'hȯd.
21 Of the tribe of Benjamin, E·lī'dad
the son of Chis'lȯn. 22 Of the tribe of
the sons of Dan a leader, Buk'kī the
son of Jog'lī. 23 Of the sons of Joseph:
of the tribe of the sons of Mȧ·nas'sėh
a leader, Han'ni·el the son of Ē'phod.
24 And of the tribe of the sons of
Ē'phrȧ·im a leader, Ke·mū'el the son
of Shiph'tȧn. 25 Of the tribe of the sons
of Zeb'ū·lȯn a leader, El·i·zā'phȧn the
son of Pär'nach. 26 Of the tribe of the
sons of Is'sȧ·chär a leader, Pal'ti·el
the son of Az'zȧn. 27 And of the tribe
of the sons of Ash'ėr a leader, Ȧ·hī'hȯd

[a] Syr: Heb lacks *its*

33.52: Ex 23.24; Deut 7.5; 12.3. **34.3-5**: Josh 15.1-4. **34.13-15**: Josh 14.1-5.

the son of Shė·lō'mī. 28 Of the tribe
of the sons of Naph'tȧ·lī a leader, Pe-
däh'el the son of Am·mī'hůd. 29 These
are the men whom the LORD commanded to divide the inheritance for
the people of Israel in the land of
Canaan."

35 The LORD said to Moses in the
plains of Mō'ab by the Jordan
at Jericho, 2 "Command the people of
Israel, that they give to the Levites,
from the inheritance of their possession, cities to dwell in; and you shall
give to the Levites pasture lands round
about the cities. 3 The cities shall be
theirs to dwell in, and their pasture
lands shall be for their cattle and for
their livestock and for all their beasts.
4 The pasture lands of the cities, which
you shall give to the Levites, shall
reach from the wall of the city outward a thousand cubits all round.
5 And you shall measure, outside the
city, for the east side two thousand
cubits, and for the south side two
thousand cubits, and for the west side
two thousand cubits, and for the north
side two thousand cubits, the city being in the middle; this shall belong to
them as pasture land for their cities.
6 The cities which you give to the
Levites shall be the six cities of refuge,
where you shall permit the manslayer
to flee, and in addition to them you
shall give forty-two cities. 7 All the
cities which you give to the Levites
shall be forty-eight, with their pasture
lands. 8 And as for the cities which you
shall give from the possession of the
people of Israel, from the larger tribes
you shall take many, and from the
smaller tribes you shall take few; each,
in proportion to the inheritance which
it inherits, shall give of its cities to the
Levites."

9 And the LORD said to Moses,
10 "Say to the people of Israel, When
you cross the Jordan into the land of
Canaan, 11 then you shall select cities
to be cities of refuge for you, that the
manslayer who kills any person without intent may flee there. 12 The cities
shall be for you a refuge from the
avenger, that the manslayer may not
die until he stands before the congregation for judgment. 13 And the cities
which you give shall be your six cities
of refuge. 14 You shall give three cities
beyond the Jordan, and three cities in
the land of Canaan, to be cities of
refuge. 15 These six cities shall be for
refuge for the people of Israel, and for
the stranger and for the sojourner
among them, that any one who kills
any person without intent may flee
there.

16 "But if he struck him down with
an instrument of iron, so that he died,
he is a murderer; the murderer shall
be put to death. 17 And if he struck him
down with a stone in the hand, by
which a man may die, and he died, he
is a murderer; the murderer shall be
put to death. 18 Or if he struck him
down with a weapon of wood in the
hand, by which a man may die, and
he died, he is a murderer; the murderer
shall be put to death. 19 The avenger
of blood shall himself put the murderer
to death; when he meets him, he shall
put him to death. 20 And if he stabbed
him from hatred, or hurled at him,
lying in wait, so that he died, 21 or in
enmity struck him down with his hand,
so that he died, then he who struck the
blow shall be put to death; he is a
murderer; the avenger of blood shall
put the murderer to death, when he
meets him.

22 "But if he stabbed him suddenly
without enmity, or hurled anything on
him without lying in wait, 23 or used
a stone, by which a man may die, and
without seeing him cast it upon him,
so that he died, though he was not his
enemy, and did not seek his harm;
24 then the congregation shall judge between the manslayer and the avenger
of blood, in accordance with these
ordinances; 25 and the congregation
shall rescue the manslayer from the
hand of the avenger of blood, and the
congregation shall restore him to his
city of refuge, to which he had fled,
and he shall live in it until the death
of the high priest who was anointed
with the holy oil. 26 But if the manslayer shall at any time go beyond the
bounds of his city of refuge to which
he fled, 27 and the avenger of blood
finds him outside the bounds of his
city of refuge, and the avenger of
blood slays the manslayer, he shall not
be guilty of blood. 28 For the man
must remain in his city of refuge until
the death of the high priest; but after
the death of the high priest the manslayer may return to the land of his
possession.

29 "And these things shall be for a

35.1-8: Lev 25.32-34; Josh 21.1-42. **35.6, 9-34:** Deut 19.1-13.

statute and ordinance to you throughout your generations in all your dwellings. 30 If any one kills a person, the
murderer shall be put to death on the
evidence of witnesses; but no person
shall be put to death on the testimony
of one witness. 31 Moreover you shall
accept no ransom for the life of a
murderer, who is guilty of death; but
he shall be put to death. 32 And you
shall accept no ransom for him who
has fled to his city of refuge, that he
may return to dwell in the land before
the death of the high priest. 33 You
shall not thus pollute the land in which
you live; for blood pollutes the land,
and no expiation can be made for the
land, for the blood that is shed in it,
except by the blood of him who shed
it. 34 You shall not defile the land in
which you live, in the midst of which
I dwell; for I the LORD dwell in the
midst of the people of Israel."

36 The heads of the fathers'
houses of the families of the
sons of Gilead the son of Mā'chir, son
of Ma·nas'sėh, of the fathers' houses
of the sons of Joseph, came near and
spoke before Moses and before the
leaders, the heads of the fathers'
houses of the people of Israel; 2 they
said, "The LORD commanded my lord
to give the land for inheritance by lot
to the people of Israel; and my lord
was commanded by the LORD to give
the inheritance of Ze·loph'ė·had our
brother to his daughters. 3 But if they
are married to any of the sons of the
other tribes of the people of Israel
then their inheritance will be taken
from the inheritance of our fathers, and
added to the inheritance of the tribe
to which they belong; so it will be
taken away from the lot of our inheritance. 4 And when the jubilee of the
people of Israel comes, then their inheritance will be added to the inheritance of the tribe to which they belong;
and their inheritance will be taken
from the inheritance of the tribe of
our fathers."

5 And Moses commanded the people of Israel according to the word of
the LORD, saying, "The tribe of the
sons of Joseph is right. 6 This is what
the LORD commands concerning the
daughters of Ze·loph'ė·had, 'Let them
marry whom they think best; only,
they shall marry within the family of
the tribe of their father. 7 The inheritance of the people of Israel shall not
be transferred from one tribe to
another; for every one of the people of
Israel shall cleave to the inheritance
of the tribe of his fathers. 8 And every
daughter who possesses an inheritance
in any tribe of the people of Israel
shall be wife to one of the family of the
tribe of her father, so that every one
of the people of Israel may possess
the inheritance of his fathers. 9 So no
inheritance shall be transferred from
one tribe to another; for each of the
tribes of the people of Israel shall
cleave to its own inheritance.' "

10 The daughters of Ze·loph'ė·had
did as the LORD commanded Moses;
11 for Mäh'lȧh, Tīr'zȧh, Hog'lȧh, Mil'-
cȧh, and Noah, the daughters of
Ze·loph'ė·had, were married to sons of
their father's brothers. 12 They were
married into the families of the sons of
Mȧ·nas'sėh the son of Joseph, and
their inheritance remained in the tribe
of the family of their father.

13 These are the commandments
and the ordinances which the LORD
commanded by Moses to the people of
Israel in the plains of Mō'ab by the
Jordan at Jericho.

THE FIFTH BOOK OF MOSES

COMMONLY CALLED

DEUTERONOMY

1 These are the words that Moses spoke to all Israel beyond the Jordan in the wilderness, in the Ar'ȧ·bȧh over against Süph, between Pâr'an and Tō'phel, Lā'bȧn, Hȧ·zē'roth, and Dī'zȧ·hab. 2 It is eleven days' journey from Hō'reb by the way of Mount Sē'ir to Kā'desh-bär'nē·ȧ. 3 And in the fortieth year, on the first day of the eleventh month, Moses spoke to the people of Israel according to all that the LORD had given him in commandment to them, 4 after he had defeated Sī'hon the king of the Am'ȯ·rītes, who lived in Hesh'bȯn, and Og the king of Bā'shȧn, who lived in Ash'tȧ·roth and in Ed'rē-ī. 5 Beyond the Jordan, in the land of Mō'ab, Moses undertook to explain this law, saying, 6 "The LORD our God said to us in Hō'reb, 'You have stayed long enough at this mountain; 7 turn and take your journey, and go to the hill country of the Am'ȯ·rītes, and to all their neighbors in the Ar'ȧ·bȧh, in the hill country and in the lowland, and in the Negeb, and by the seacoast, the land of the Canaanites, and Lebanon, as far as the great river, the river Eū·phrā'tēs. 8 Behold, I have set the land before you; go in and take possession of the land which the LORD swore to your fathers, to Abraham, to Isaac, and to Jacob, to give to them and to their descendants after them.'

9 "At that time I said to you, 'I am not able alone to bear you; 10 the LORD your God has multiplied you, and behold, you are this day as the stars of heaven for multitude. 11 May the LORD, the God of your fathers, make you a thousand times as many as you are, and bless you, as he has promised you! 12 How can I bear alone the weight and burden of you and your strife? 13 Choose wise, understanding, and experienced men, according to your tribes, and I will appoint them as your heads.' 14 And you answered me, 'The thing that you have spoken is good for us to do.' 15 So I took the heads of your tribes, wise and experienced men, and set them as heads over you, commanders of thousands, commanders of hundreds, commanders of fifties, commanders of tens, and officers, throughout your tribes. 16 And I charged your judges at that time, 'Hear the cases between your brethren, and judge righteously between a man and his brother or the alien that is with him. 17 You shall not be partial in judgment; you shall hear the small and the great alike; you shall not be afraid of the face of man, for the judgment is God's; and the case that is too hard for you, you shall bring to me, and I will hear it.' 18 And I commanded you at that time all the things that you should do.

19 "And we set out from Hō'reb, and went through all that great and terrible wilderness which you saw, on the way to the hill country of the Am'ȯ·rītes, as the LORD our God commanded us; and we came to Kā'desh-bär'nē·ȧ. 20 And I said to you, 'You have come to the hill country of the Am'ȯ·rītes, which the LORD our God gives us. 21 Behold, the LORD your God has set the land before you; go up, take possession, as the LORD, the God of your fathers, has told you; do not fear or be dismayed.' 22 Then all of you came near me, and said, 'Let us send men before us, that they may explore the land for us, and bring us word again of the way by which we must go up and the cities into which we shall come.' 23 The thing seemed good to me, and I took twelve men of you, one man for each tribe; 24 and they turned and went up into the hill country, and came to the Valley of Esh'cȯl and spied it out. 25 And they took in their hands some of the fruit of the land and brought it down to us, and brought us word again, and said, 'It is a good land which the LORD our God gives us.'

26 "Yet you would not go up, but

1.9-15: Num 11.10-25. 1.16-18: Ex 18.25-26. 1.22-46: Num 13.1-14. 45; 32.8-13.

rebelled against the command of the
LORD your God; 27 and you murmured
in your tents, and said, 'Because the
LORD hated us he has brought us forth
out of the land of Egypt, to give us
into the hand of the Am'ŏ·rītes, to
destroy us. 28 Whither are we going
up? Our brethren have made our
hearts melt, saying, "The people are
greater and taller then we; the cities
are great and fortified up to heaven;
and moreover we have seen the sons
of the An'ȧ·kim there." ' 29 Then I
said to you, 'Do not be in dread or
afraid of them. 30 The LORD your God
who goes before you will himself fight
for you, just as he did for you in
Egypt before your eyes, 31 and in the
wilderness, where you have seen how
the LORD your God bore you, as a man
bears his son, in all the way that you
went until you came to this place.'
32 Yet in spite of this word you did not
believe the LORD your God, 33 who
went before you in the way to seek you
out a place to pitch your tents, in fire
by night, to show you by what way
you should go, and in the cloud by day.

34 "And the LORD heard your
words, and was angered, and he swore,
35 'Not one of these men of this evil
generation shall see the good land
which I swore to give to your fathers,
36 except Caleb the son of Jė·phŭn'-
nėh; he shall see it, and to him and to
his children I will give the land upon
which he has trodden, because he has
wholly followed the LORD!' 37 The
LORD was angry with me also on your
account, and said, 'You also shall not
go in there; 38 Joshua the son of Nun,
who stands before you, he shall enter;
encourage him, for he shall cause Israel
to inherit it. 39 Moreover your little
ones, who you said would become a
prey, and your children, who this day
have no knowledge of good or evil,
shall go in there, and to them I will
give it, and they shall possess it. 40 But
as for you, turn, and journey into the
wilderness in the direction of the Red
Sea.'

41 "Then you answered me, 'We
have sinned against the LORD; we will
go up and fight, just as the LORD our
God commanded us.' And every man
of you girded on his weapons of war,
and thought it easy to go up into the
hill country. 42 And the LORD said to
me, 'Say to them, Do not go up or
fight, for I am not in the midst of you;
lest you be defeated before your
enemies.' 43 So I spoke to you, and
you would not hearken; but you
rebelled against the command of the
LORD, and were presumptuous and
went up into the hill country. 44 Then
the Am'ŏ·rītes who lived in that hill
country came out against you and
chased you as bees do and beat you
down in Sē'ir as far as Hôr'mȧh.
45 And you returned and wept before
the LORD; but the LORD did not
hearken to your voice or give ear to
you. 46 So you remained at Kā'desh
many days, the days that you remained
there.

2 "Then we turned, and journeyed
into the wilderness in the direction
of the Red Sea, as the LORD told me;
and for many days we went about
Mount Sē'ir. 2 Then the LORD said
to me, 3 'You have been going about
this mountain country long enough;
turn northward. 4 And command the
people, You are about to pass through
the territory of your brethren the sons
of Esau, who live in Sē'ir; and they
will be afraid of you. So take good
heed; 5 do not contend with them; for
I will not give you any of their land,
no, not so much as for the sole of the
foot to tread on, because I have given
Mount Sē'ir to Esau as a possession.
6 You shall purchase food from them
for money, that you may eat; and you
shall also buy water of them for money,
that you may drink. 7 For the LORD
your God has blessed you in all the
work of your hands; he knows your
going through this great wilderness;
these forty years the LORD your God
has been with you; you have lacked
nothing.' 8 So we went on, away from
our brethren the sons of Esau who
live in Sē'ir, away from the Ar'ȧ·bȧh
road from Ē'lath and Ē'zi·on-gē'bėr.

"And we turned and went in the
direction of the wilderness of Mō'ab.
9 And the LORD said to me, 'Do not
harass Mō'ab or contend with them in
battle, for I will not give you any of
their land for a possession, because I
have given Ăr to the sons of Lot for a
possession.' 10 (The Ē'mim formerly
lived there, a people great and many,
and tall as the Ăn'ȧ·kim; 11 like the
An'ȧ·kim they are also known as
Reph'ȧ·im, but the Mō'ȧb·ītes call
them Ē'mim. 12 The Hôr'ītes also lived

1.31: Acts 13.18. **2.1-8:** Num 21.4-20.

in Sē'ir formerly, but the sons of Esau
dispossessed them, and destroyed
them from before them, and settled in
their stead; as Israel did to the land of
their possession, which the LORD gave
to them.) 13 'Now rise up, and go over
the brook Zē'red.' So we went over the
brook Zered. 14 And the time from our
leaving Kā'desh-bär'nē·ȧ until we
crossed the brook Zē'red was thirty-
eight years, until the entire generation,
that is, the men of war, had perished
from the camp, as the LORD had sworn
to them. 15 For indeed the hand of the
LORD was against them, to destroy
them from the camp, until they had
perished.

16 "So when all the men of war had
perished and were dead from among
the people, 17 the LORD said to me,
18 'This day you are to pass over the
boundary of Mō'ab at Ăr; 19 and when
you approach the frontier of the sons
of Am'mȯn, do not harass them or
contend with them, for I will not give
you any of the land of the sons of
Ammon as a possession, because I have
given it to the sons of Lot for a possession.' 20 (That also is known as a land
of Reph'ȧ·im; Rephaim formerly lived
there, but the Am'mȯ·nītes call them
Zam·zum'mim, 21 a people great and
many, and tall as the Ăn'ȧ·kim; but
the LORD destroyed them before them;
and they dispossessed them, and
settled in their stead; 22 as he did for
the sons of Esau, who live in Sē'ir,
when he destroyed the Hôr'ītes before
them, and they dispossessed them,
and settled in their stead even to this
day. 23 As for the Av'vim, who lived in
villages as far as Gā'zȧ, the Caph'tȯ-
rim, who came from Caph'tor, destroyed them and settled in their stead.)
24 'Rise up, take your journey, and go
over the valley of the Ăr'non; behold,
I have given into your hand Sī'hon
the Am'ȯ·rīte, king of Hesh'bȯn, and
his land; begin to take possession, and
contend with him in battle. 25 This
day I will begin to put the dread and
fear of you upon the peoples that are
under the whole heaven, who shall
hear the report of you and shall tremble
and be in anguish because of you.'

26 " So I sent messengers from the
wilderness of Ked'ė·moth to Sī'hon
the king of Hesh'bȯn, with words of
peace, saying, 27 'Let me pass through
your land; I will go only by the road,
I will turn aside neither to the right
nor to the left. 28 You shall sell me
food for money, that I may eat, and
give me water for money, that I may
drink; only let me pass through on
foot, 29 as the sons of Esau who live in
Sē'ir and the Mō'ȧb·ītes who live in
Ăr did for me, until I go over the
Jordan into the land which the LORD
our God gives to us.' 30 But Sī'hon
the king of Hesh'bȯn would not let us
pass by him; for the LORD your God
hardened his spirit and made his heart
obstinate, that he might give him into
your hand, as at this day. 31 And the
LORD said to me, 'Behold, I have begun to give Sī'hon and his land over
to you; begin to take possession, that
you may occupy his land.' 32 Then
Sī'hon came out against us, he and all
his people, to battle at Jā'haz. 33 And
the LORD our God gave him over to us;
and we defeated him and his sons and
all his people. 34 And we captured all
his cities at that time and utterly destroyed every city, men, women, and
children; we left none remaining; 35 only
the cattle we took as spoil for ourselves,
with the booty of the cities which we
captured. 36 From Ȧ·rō'ėr, which is on
the edge of the valley of the Ăr'non,
and from the city that is in the valley,
as far as Gilead, there was not a city
too high for us; the LORD our God gave
all into our hands. 37 Only to the land
of the sons of Am'mȯn you did not
draw near, that is, to all the banks of
the river Jab'bȯk and the cities of the
hill country, and wherever the LORD
our God forbade us.

3 "Then we turned and went up
the way to Bā'shȧn; and Og the
king of Bashan came out against us,
he and all his people, to battle at
Ed'rē-ī. 2 But the LORD said to me,
'Do not fear him; for I have given him
and all his people and his land into
your hand; and you shall do to him as
you did to Sī'hon the king of the
Am'ȯ·rītes, who dwelt at Hesh'bȯn.'
3 So the LORD our God gave into our
hand Og also, the king of Bā'shȧn, and
all his people; and we smote him until
no survivor was left to him. 4 And we
took all his cities at that time—there
was not a city which we did not take
from them—sixty cities, the whole
region of Ăr'gȯb, the kingdom of Og
in Bā'shȧn. 5 All these were cities fortified with high walls, gates, and bars,

2.26-37: Num 21.21-32. 3.1-11: Num 21.33-35.

besides very many unwalled villages.
6 And we utterly destroyed them, as
we did to Sī'hon the king of Hesh'-
bȯn, destroying every city, men,
women, and children. 7 But all the
cattle and the spoil of the cities we
took as our booty. 8 So we took the
land at that time out of the hand of the
two kings of the Am'ȯ·rītes who were
beyond the Jordan, from the valley of
the Är'non to Mount Hĕr'mȯn 9 (the
Sī·dō'ni·ȧnṡ call Hĕr'mȯn Sir'i·ȯn,
while the Am'ȯ·rītes call it Sē'nir),
10 all the cities of the tableland and all
Gilead and all Bā'shȧn, as far as Sal'ė-
cȧh and Ed'rē-ī, cities of the kingdom
of Og in Bashan. 11 (For only Og the
king of Bā'shȧn was left of the remnant
of the Reph'ȧ·im; behold, his bedstead
was a bedstead of iron; is it not in
Rab'bȧh of the Am'mȯ·nītes? Nine
cubits was its length, and four cubits
its breadth, according to the common
cubit.[a])

12 "When we took possession of this
land at that time, I gave to the
Reubenites and the Gadites the territory beginning at Ȧ·rō'ėr, which is
on the edge of the valley of the Är'non,
and half the hill country of Gilead
with its cities; 13 the rest of Gilead,
and all Bā'shȧn, the kingdom of Og,
that is, all the region of Är'gȯb, I gave
to the half-tribe of Mȧ·nas'sėh. (The
whole of that Bashan is called the land
of Reph'ȧ·im. 14 Jā'ir the Mȧ·nas'sīte
took all the region of Är'gȯb, that is,
Bā'shȧn, as far as the border of the
Gesh'ū·rītes and the Mā-ac'ȧ·thītes,
and called the villages after his own
name, Hav'vȯth-jā'ir, as it is to this
day.) 15 To Mā'chir I gave Gilead,
16 and to the Reubenites and the
Gadites I gave the territory from
Gilead as far as the valley of the
Är'non, with the middle of the valley
as a boundary, as far over as the river
Jab'bȯk, the boundary of the Am'mȯ-
nītes; 17 the Ar'ȧ·bȧh also, with the
Jordan as the boundary, from Chin'-
nė·reth as far as the sea of the Arabah,
the Salt Sea, under the slopes of
Piṡ'gȧh on the east.

18 "And I commanded you at that
time, saying, 'The LORD your God has
given you this land to possess; all your
men of valor shall pass over armed before your brethren the people of Israel.
19 But your wives, your little ones, and
your cattle (I know that you have
many cattle) shall remain in the cities
which I have given you, 20 until the
LORD gives rest to your brethren, as
to you, and they also occupy the land
which the LORD your God gives them
beyond the Jordan; then you shall
return every man to his possession
which I have given you.' 21 And I commanded Joshua at that time, 'Your eyes
have seen all that the LORD your God
has done to these two kings; so will
the LORD do to all the kingdoms into
which you are going over. 22 You shall
not fear them; for it is the LORD your
God who fights for you.'

23 "And I besought the LORD at
that time, saying, 24 'O Lord GOD,
thou hast only begun to show thy
servant thy greatness and thy mighty
hand; for what god is there in heaven
or on earth who can do such works and
mighty acts as thine? 25 Let me go over,
I pray, and see the good land beyond
the Jordan, that goodly hill country,
and Lebanon.' 26 But the LORD was
angry with me on your account, and
would not hearken to me; and the
LORD said to me, 'Let it suffice you;
speak no more to me of this matter.
27 Go up to the top of Piṡ'gȧh, and lift
up your eyes westward and northward
and southward and eastward, and behold it with your eyes; for you shall
not go over this Jordan. 28 But charge
Joshua, and encourage and strengthen
him; for he shall go over at the head of
this people, and he shall put them in
possession of the land which you shall
see.' 29 So we remained in the valley
opposite Beth-pē'ôr.

4 "And now, O Israel, give heed to
the statutes and the ordinances
which I teach you, and do them; that
you may live, and go in and take possession of the land which the LORD,
the God of your fathers, gives you.
2 You shall not add to the word which
I command you, nor take from it; that
you may keep the commandments of
the LORD your God which I command
you. 3 Your eyes have seen what the
LORD did at Bā'ȧl-pē'ôr; for the LORD
your God destroyed from among you
all the men who followed the Bā'ȧl of
Pē'ôr; 4 but you who held fast to the
LORD your God are all alive this day.
5 Behold, I have taught you statutes
and ordinances, as the LORD my God

[a] Heb *cubit of a man*

3.12-20: Num 32. **3.23-27:** Num 27.12-14; Deut 32.48-52. **4.2:** Rev 22.18-19.

commanded me, that you should do
them in the land which you are entering to take possession of it. 6 Keep
them and do them; for that will be
your wisdom and your understanding
in the sight of the peoples, who, when
they hear all these statutes, will say,
'Surely this great nation is a wise and
understanding people.' 7 For what
great nation is there that has a god so
near to it as the LORD our God is to us,
whenever we call upon him? 8 And
what great nation is there, that has
statutes and ordinances so righteous
as all this law which I set before you
this day?

9 "Only take heed, and keep your
soul diligently, lest you forget the
things which your eyes have seen, and
lest they depart from your heart all
the days of your life; make them known
to your children and your children's
children—10 how on the day that you
stood before the LORD your God at
Hō'reb, the LORD said to me, 'Gather
the people to me, that I may let them
hear my words, so that they may learn
to fear me all the days that they live
upon the earth, and that they may
teach their children so.' 11 And you
came near and stood at the foot of the
mountain, while the mountain burned
with fire to the heart of heaven,
wrapped in darkness, cloud, and gloom.
12 Then the LORD spoke to you out of
the midst of the fire; you heard the
sound of words, but saw no form; there
was only a voice. 13 And he declared to
you his covenant, which he commanded you to perform, that is, the
ten commandments;[b] and he wrote
them upon two tables of stone. 14 And
the LORD commanded me at that time
to teach you statutes and ordinances,
that you might do them in the land
which you are going over to possess.

15 "Therefore take good heed to
yourselves. Since you saw no form on
the day that the LORD spoke to you at
Hō'reb out of the midst of the fire,
16 beware lest you act corruptly by
making a graven image for yourselves,
in the form of any figure, the likeness
of male or female, 17 the likeness of
any beast that is on the earth, the likeness of any winged bird that flies in
the air, 18 the likeness of anything that
creeps on the ground, the likeness of
any fish that is in the water under the
earth. 19 And beware lest you lift up
your eyes to heaven, and when you see
the sun and the moon and the stars,
all the host of heaven, you be drawn
away and worship them and serve
them, things which the LORD your
God has allotted to all the peoples
under the whole heaven. 20 But the
LORD has taken you, and brought you
forth out of the iron furnace, out of
Egypt, to be a people of his own possession, as at this day. 21 Furthermore
the LORD was angry with me on your
account, and he swore that I should
not cross the Jordan, and that I should
not enter the good land which the
LORD your God gives you for an inheritance. 22 For I must die in this
land, I must not go over the Jordan;
but you shall go over and take possession of that good land. 23 Take heed
to yourselves, lest you forget the covenant of the LORD your God, which he
made with you, and make a graven
image in the form of anything which
the LORD your God has forbidden you.
24 For the LORD your God is a devouring fire, a jealous God.

25 "When you beget children and
children's children, and have grown
old in the land, if you act corruptly by
making a graven image in the form of
anything, and by doing what is evil in
the sight of the LORD your God, so as
to provoke him to anger, 26 I call
heaven and earth to witness against
you this day, that you will soon utterly
perish from the land which you are
going over the Jordan to possess; you
will not live long upon it, but will be
utterly destroyed. 27 And the LORD will
scatter you among the peoples, and you
will be left few in number among the
nations where the LORD will drive you.
28 And there you will serve gods of
wood and stone, the work of men's
hands, that neither see, nor hear, nor
eat, nor smell. 29 But from there you
will seek the LORD your God, and you
will find him, if you search after him
with all your heart and with all your
soul. 30 When you are in tribulation,
and all these things come upon you in
the latter days, you will return to the
LORD your God and obey his voice,
31 for the LORD your God is a merciful
God; he will not fail you or destroy
you or forget the covenant with your
fathers which he swore to them.

[b] Heb *words*

4.9-14: Ex 19.1-21. **4.24:** Heb 12.29.

32 "For ask now of the days that
are past, which were before you, since
the day that God created man upon
the earth, and ask from one end of
heaven to the other, whether such a
great thing as this has ever happened
or was ever heard of. 33 Did any people
ever hear the voice of a god speaking
out of the midst of the fire, as you have
heard, and still live? 34 Or has any god
ever attempted to go and take a nation
for himself from the midst of another
nation, by trials, by signs, by wonders,
and by war, by a mighty hand and an
outstretched arm, and by great terrors,
according to all that the LORD your
God did for you in Egypt before your
eyes? 35 To you it was shown, that you
might know that the LORD is God;
there is no other besides him. 36 Out
of heaven he let you hear his voice,
that he might discipline you; and on
earth he let you see his great fire, and
you heard his words out of the midst
of the fire. 37 And because he loved
your fathers and chose their descendants after them, and brought you out
of Egypt with his own presence, by
his great power, 38 driving out before
you nations greater and mightier than
yourselves, to bring you in, to give you
their land for an inheritance, as at this
day; 39 know therefore this day, and
lay it to your heart, that the LORD is
God in heaven above and on the earth
beneath; there is no other. 40 Therefore you shall keep his statutes and his
commandments, which I command
you this day, that it may go well with
you, and with your children after you,
and that you may prolong your days
in the land which the LORD your God
gives you for ever."

41 Then Moses set apart three cities
in the east beyond the Jordan, 42 that
the manslayer might flee there, who
kills his neighbor unintentionally,
without being at enmity with him in
time past, and that by fleeing to one
of these cities he might save his life:
43 Bē'zėr in the wilderness on the
tableland for the Reubenites, and Rā'-
moth in Gilead for the Gadites, and
Gō'lȧn in Bā'shȧn for the Mȧ·nas'sītes.

44 This is the law which Moses set
before the children of Israel; 45 these
are the testimonies, the statutes, and
the ordinances, which Moses spoke to
the children of Israel when they came
out of Egypt, 46 beyond the Jordan in
the valley opposite Beth-pē'ôr, in the
land of Sī'hon the king of the Am'ō-
rītes, who lived at Hesh'bȯn, whom
Moses and the children of Israel defeated when they came out of Egypt.
47 And they took possession of his land
and the land of Og the king of Bā'shȧn,
the two kings of the Am'ō·rītes, who
lived to the east beyond the Jordan;
48 from Ȧ·rō'ėr, which is on the edge
of the valley of the Är'non, as far as
Mount Sir'ī·ȯn[c] (that is, Hẽr'mȯn),
49 together with all the Ar'ȧ·bȧh on
the east side of the Jordan as far as
the Sea of the Arabah, under the slopes
of Piṡ'gȧh.

5 And Moses summoned all Israel,
and said to them, "Hear, O Israel,
the statutes and the ordinances which
I speak in your hearing this day, and
you shall learn them and be careful to
do them. 2 The LORD our God made
a covenant with us in Hō'reb. 3 Not
with our fathers did the LORD make
this covenant, but with us, who are all
of us here alive this day. 4 The LORD
spoke with you face to face at the
mountain, out of the midst of the fire,
5 while I stood between the LORD and
you at that time, to declare to you the
word of the LORD; for you were afraid
because of the fire, and you did not
go up into the mountain. He said:

6 " 'I am the LORD your God, who
brought you out of the land of Egypt,
out of the house of bondage.

7 " 'You shall have no other gods
before[d] me.

8 " 'You shall not make for yourself
a graven image, or any likeness of any
thing that is in heaven above, or that
is on the earth beneath, or that is in
the water under the earth; 9 you shall
not bow down to them or serve them;
for I the LORD your God am a jealous
God, visiting the iniquity of the fathers
upon the children to the third and
fourth generation of those who hate
me, 10 but showing steadfast love to
thousands of those who love me and
keep my commandments.

11 " 'You shall not take the name of
the LORD your God in vain: for the
LORD will not hold him guiltless who
takes his name in vain.

12 " 'Observe the sabbath day, to
keep it holy, as the LORD your God
commanded you. 13 Six days you shall

[c] Syr: Heb *Sion* [d] Or *besides*

4.35: Mk 12.32. 4.41-43: Num 35.6, 9-34; Deut 19.2-13; Josh 20.7-9. 5.6-21: Ex 20.2-17.

labor, and do all your work; 14 but the
seventh day is a sabbath to the LORD
your God; in it you shall not do any
work, you, or your son, or your daughter, or your manservant, or your maidservant, or your ox, or your ass, or any
of your cattle, or the sojourner who is
within your gates, that your manservant and your maidservant may rest as
well as you. 15 You shall remember
that you were a servant in the land of
Egypt, and the LORD your God
brought you out thence with a mighty
hand and an outstretched arm; therefore the LORD your God commanded
you to keep the sabbath day.
16 " 'Honor your father and your
mother, as the LORD your God commanded you, that your days may be
prolonged, and that it may go well with
you, in the land which the LORD your
God gives you.
17 " 'You shall not kill.
18 " 'Neither shall you commit
adultery.
19 " 'Neither shall you steal.
20 " 'Neither shall you bear false
witness against your neighbor.
21 " 'Neither shall you covet your
neighbor's wife; and you shall not desire your neighbor's house, his field,
or his manservant, or his maidservant,
his ox, or his ass, or anything that is
your neighbor's.'
22 "These words the LORD spoke
to all your assembly at the mountain
out of the midst of the fire, the cloud,
and the thick darkness, with a loud
voice; and he added no more. And he
wrote them upon two tables of stone,
and gave them to me. 23 And when you
heard the voice out of the midst of the
darkness, while the mountain was
burning with fire, you came near to
me, all the heads of your tribes, and
your elders; 24 and you said, 'Behold,
the LORD our God has shown us his
glory and greatness, and we have heard
his voice out of the midst of the fire;
we have this day seen God speak with
man and man still live. 25 Now therefore why should we die? For this great
fire will consume us; if we hear the
voice of the LORD our God any more,
we shall die. 26 For who is there of all
flesh, that has heard the voice of the
living God speaking out of the midst
of fire, as we have, and has still lived?
27 Go near, and hear all that the LORD
our God will say; and speak to us all
that the LORD our God will speak to
you; and we will hear and do it.'
28 "And the LORD heard your
words, when you spoke to me; and the
LORD said to me, 'I have heard the
words of this people, which they have
spoken to you; they have rightly said
all that they have spoken. 29 Oh that
they had such a mind as this always, to
fear me and to keep all my commandments, that it might go well with them
and with their children for ever! 30 Go
and say to them, "Return to your
tents." 31 But you, stand here by me,
and I will tell you all the commandment and the statutes and the ordinances which you shall teach them,
that they may do them in the land
which I give them to possess.' 32 You
shall be careful to do therefore as the
LORD your God has commanded you;
you shall not turn aside to the right
hand or to the left. 33 You shall walk
in all the way which the LORD your
God has commanded you, that you
may live, and that it may go well with
you, and that you may live long in the
land which you shall possess.

6 "Now this is the commandment, the statutes, and the ordinances which the LORD your God
commanded me to teach you, that you
may do them in the land to which
you are going over, to possess it; 2 that
you may fear the LORD your God, you
and your son and your son's son, by
keeping all his statutes and his commandments, which I command you,
all the days of your life; and that your
days may be prolonged. 3 Hear therefore, O Israel, and be careful to do
them; that it may go well with you, and
that you may multiply greatly, as the
LORD, the God of your fathers, has
promised you, in a land flowing with
milk and honey.
4 "Hear, O Israel: The LORD our
God is one LORD;[e] 5 and you shall love
the LORD your God with all your
heart, and with all your soul, and with
all your might. 6 And these words
which I command you this day shall

[e] Or *the* LORD *our God, the* LORD *is one* Or *the* LORD *is our God, the* LORD *is one* Or *the* LORD *is our God, the* LORD *alone*

5.14: Ex 20.8-11; 23.12. **5.16-20:** Mt 19.18-19; Mk 10.19; Lk 18.20. **5.16:** Mt 15.4; Mk 7.10; Eph 6.3. **5.17-18:** Jas 2.11. **5.17-21:** Rom 13.9. **5.18:** Mt 5.27; Rom 7.7. **5.21:** Rom 7.7. **5.22-27:** Ex 20.18-21. **6.4-5:** Mt 22.37; Mk 12.29-30; Lk 10.27. **6.6-9:** Deut 6.20-25; 11.18-20.

be upon your heart; 7 and you shall
teach them diligently to your children,
and shall talk of them when you sit in
your house, and when you walk by the
way, and when you lie down, and when
you rise. 8And you shall bind them as
a sign upon your hand, and they shall
be as frontlets between your eyes.
9And you shall write them on the doorposts of your house and on your gates.

10 "And when the LORD your God
brings you into the land which he
swore to your fathers, to Abraham, to
Isaac, and to Jacob, to give you, with
great and goodly cities, which you did
not build, 11 and houses full of all
good things, which you did not fill, and
cisterns hewn out, which you did not
hew, and vineyards and olive trees,
which you did not plant, and when you
eat and are full, 12 then take heed lest
you forget the LORD, who brought you
out of the land of Egypt, out of the
house of bondage. 13 You shall fear the
LORD your God; you shall serve him,
and swear by his name. 14 You shall
not go after other gods, of the gods of
the peoples who are round about you;
15 for the LORD your God in the midst
of you is a jealous God; lest the anger
of the LORD your God be kindled
against you, and he destroy you from
off the face of the earth.

16 "You shall not put the LORD
your God to the test, as you tested him
at Mas'sah. 17 You shall diligently
keep the commandments of the LORD
your God, and his testimonies, and his
statutes, which he has commanded
you. 18And you shall do what is right
and good in the sight of the LORD,
that it may go well with you, and that
you may go in and take possession of
the good land which the LORD swore
to give to your fathers 19 by thrusting
out all your enemies from before you,
as the LORD has promised.

20 "When your son asks you in
time to come, 'What is the meaning of
the testimonies and the statutes and
the ordinances which the LORD our
God has commanded you?' 21 then you
shall say to your son, 'We were Pharaoh's slaves in Egypt; and the LORD
brought us out of Egypt with a mighty
hand; 22 and the LORD showed signs
and wonders, great and grievous,
against Egypt and against Pharaoh
and all his household, before our eyes;
23 and he brought us out from there,
that he might bring us in and give us
the land which he swore to give to our
fathers. 24And the LORD commanded
us to do all these statutes, to fear the
LORD our God, for our good always,
that he might preserve us alive, as at
this day. 25And it will be righteousness
for us, if we are careful to do all this
commandment before the LORD our
God, as he has commanded us.'

7 "When the LORD your God
brings you into the land which you
are entering to take possession of it,
and clears away many nations before
you, the Hit'tītes, the Gĩr'gȧ·shītes,
the Am'ŏ·rītes, the Canaanites, the
Per'iz·zītes, the Hī'vītes, and the Jeb'-
ū·sītes, seven nations greater and
mightier than yourselves, 2 and when
the LORD your God gives them over to
you, and you defeat them; then you
must utterly destroy them; you shall
make no covenant with them, and
show no mercy to them. 3 You shall
not make marriages with them, giving
your daughters to their sons or taking
their daughters for your sons. 4 For
they would turn away your sons from
following me, to serve other gods; then
the anger of the LORD would be kindled
against you, and he would destroy you
quickly. 5 But thus shall you deal with
them: you shall break down their
altars, and dash in pieces their pillars,
and hew down their A·shē'rim, and
burn their graven images with fire.

6 "For you are a people holy to the
LORD your God; the LORD your God
has chosen you to be a people for his
own possession, out of all the peoples
that are on the face of the earth. 7 It
was not because you were more in
number than any other people that the
LORD set his love upon you and chose
you, for you were the fewest of all
peoples; 8 but it is because the LORD
loves you, and is keeping the oath
which he swore to your fathers, that
the LORD has brought you out with a
mighty hand, and redeemed you from
the house of bondage, from the hand
of Pharaoh king of Egypt. 9 Know
therefore that the LORD your God is
God, the faithful God who keeps covenant and steadfast love with those who
love him and keep his commandments,

6.8: Ex 13.9, 16; Deut 11.18. **6.13:** Mt 4.10; Lk 4.8. **6.16:** Mt 4.7; Lk 4.12. **7.1:** Acts 13.19.
7.2-4: Ex 23.32-33; 34.12, 15-16. **7.3:** Ex 34.15-16. **7.5:** Ex 23.24; 34.13; Num 33.52; Deut 12.3.
7.6: Ex. 19.5; 22.3; Lev 11.44-45; 19.2; 20.7, 26; Num 15.40; Deut 14.2, 21; 26.19; 28.9.

to a thousand generations, 10 and requites to their face those who hate him, by destroying them; he will not be slack with him who hates him, he will requite him to his face. 11 You shall therefore be careful to do the commandment, and the statutes, and the ordinances, which I command you this day.

12 "And because you hearken to these ordinances, and keep and do them, the LORD your God will keep with you the covenant and the steadfast love which he swore to your fathers to keep; 13 he will love you, bless you, and multiply you; he will also bless the fruit of your body and the fruit of your ground, your grain and your wine and your oil, the increase of your cattle and the young of your flock, in the land which he swore to your fathers to give you. 14 You shall be blessed above all peoples; there shall not be male or female barren among you, or among your cattle. 15 And the LORD will take away from you all sickness; and none of the evil diseases of Egypt, which you knew, will he inflict upon you, but he will lay them upon all who hate you. 16 And you shall destroy all the peoples that the LORD your God will give over to you, your eye shall not pity them; neither shall you serve their gods, for that would be a snare to you.

17 "If you say in your heart, 'These nations are greater than I; how can I dispossess them?' 18 you shall not be afraid of them, but you shall remember what the LORD your God did to Pharaoh and to all Egypt, 19 the great trials which your eyes saw, the signs, the wonders, the mighty hand, and the outstretched arm, by which the LORD your God brought you out; so will the LORD your God do to all the peoples of whom you are afraid. 20 Moreover the LORD your God will send hornets among them, until those who are left and hide themselves from you are destroyed. 21 You shall not be in dread of them; for the LORD your God is in the midst of you, a great and terrible God. 22 The LORD your God will clear away these nations before you little by little; you may not make an end of them at once,[f] lest the wild beasts grow too numerous for you. 23 But the LORD your God will give them over to you, and throw them into great confusion, until they are destroyed. 24 And he will give their kings into your hand, and you shall make their name perish from under heaven; not a man shall be able to stand against you, until you have destroyed them. 25 The graven images of their gods you shall burn with fire; you shall not covet the silver or the gold that is on them, or take it for yourselves, lest you be ensnared by it; for it is an abomination to the LORD your God. 26 And you shall not bring an abominable thing into your house, and become accursed like it; you shall utterly detest and abhor it; for it is an accursed thing.

8 "All the commandment which I command you this day you shall be careful to do, that you may live and multiply, and go in and possess the land which the LORD swore to give to your fathers. 2 And you shall remember all the way which the LORD your God has led you these forty years in the wilderness, that he might humble you, testing you to know what was in your heart, whether you would keep his commandments, or not. 3 And he humbled you and let you hunger and fed you with manna, which you did not know, nor did your fathers know; that he might make you know that man does not live by bread alone, but that man lives by everything that proceeds out of the mouth of the LORD. 4 Your clothing did not wear out upon you, and your foot did not swell, these forty years. 5 Know then in your heart that, as a man disciplines his son, the LORD your God disciplines you. 6 So you shall keep the commandments of the LORD your God, by walking in his ways and by fearing him. 7 For the LORD your God is bringing you into a good land, a land of brooks of water, of fountains and springs, flowing forth in valleys and hills, 8 a land of wheat and barley, of vines and fig trees and pomegranates, a land of olive trees and honey, 9 a land in which you will eat bread without scarcity, in which you will lack nothing, a land whose stones are iron, and out of whose hills you can dig copper. 10 And you shall eat and be full, and you shall bless the LORD your God for the good land he has given you.

11 "Take heed lest you forget the LORD your God, by not keeping his

[f] Or *quickly*

8.3: Mt 4.4; Lk 4.4.

commandments and his ordinances
and his statutes, which I command you
this day: 12 lest, when you have eaten
and are full, and have built goodly
houses and live in them, 13 and when
your herds and flocks multiply, and
your silver and gold is multiplied, and
all that you have is multiplied, 14 then
your heart be lifted up, and you forget
the LORD your God, who brought you
out of the land of Egypt, out of the
house of bondage, 15 who led you
through the great and terrible wilderness, with its fiery serpents and scorpions and thirsty ground where there
was no water, who brought you water
out of the flinty rock, 16 who fed you
in the wilderness with manna which
your fathers did not know, that he
might humble you and test you, to do
you good in the end. 17 Beware lest
you say in your heart, 'My power and
the might of my hand have gotten me
this wealth.' 18 You shall remember
the LORD your God, for it is he who
gives you power to get wealth; that he
may confirm his covenant which he
swore to your fathers, as at this day.
19And if you forget the LORD your God
and go after other gods and serve them
and worship them, I solemnly warn
you this day that you shall surely
perish. 20 Like the nations that the
LORD makes to perish before you, so
shall you perish, because you would
not obey the voice of the LORD your
God.

9 "Hear, O Israel; you are to pass
over the Jordan this day, to go in
to dispossess nations greater and
mightier than yourselves, cities great
and fortified up to heaven, 2 a people
great and tall, the sons of the An'ă·kim,
whom you know, and of whom you
have heard it said, 'Who can stand before the sons of Ā'nak? 3 Know therefore this day that he who goes over
before you as a devouring fire is the
LORD your God; he will destroy them
and subdue them before you; so you
shall drive them out, and make them
perish quickly, as the LORD has promised you.

4 "Do not say in your heart, after
the LORD your God has thrust them
out before you, 'It is because of my
righteousness that the LORD has
brought me in to possess this land';
whereas it is because of the wickedness
of these nations that the LORD is
driving them out before you. 5 Not because of your righteousness or the
uprightness of your heart are you going
in to possess their land; but because
of the wickedness of these nations the
LORD your God is driving them out
from before you, and that he may confirm the word which the Lord swore
to your fathers, to Abraham, to Isaac,
and to Jacob.

6 "Know therefore, that the LORD
your God is not giving you this good
land to possess because of your righteousness; for you are a stubborn people. 7 Remember and do not forget
how you provoked the LORD your God
to wrath in the wilderness; from the
day you came out of the land of Egypt,
until you came to this place, you have
been rebellious against the LORD.
8 Even at Hō'reb you provoked the
LORD to wrath, and the LORD was so
angry with you that he was ready to
destroy you. 9 When I went up the
mountain to receive the tables of stone,
the tables of the covenant which the
LORD made with you, I remained on
the mountain forty days and forty
nights; I neither ate bread nor drank
water. 10And the LORD gave me the
two tables of stone written with the
finger of God; and on them were all
the words which the LORD had spoken
with you on the mountain out of the
midst of the fire on the day of the
assembly. 11And at the end of forty
days and forty nights the LORD gave
me the two tables of stone, the tables
of the covenant. 12 Then the LORD
said to me, 'Arise, go down quickly
from here; for your people whom you
have brought from Egypt have acted
corruptly; they have turned aside
quickly out of the way which I commanded them; they have made themselves a molten image.'

13 "Furthermore the LORD said to
me, 'I have seen this people, and behold, it is a stubborn people; 14 let me
alone, that I may destroy them and blot
out their name from under heaven;
and I will make of you a nation mightier
and greater than they.' 15 So I turned
and came down from the mountain,
and the mountain was burning with
fire; and the two tables of the covenant
were in my two hands. 16And I looked,
and behold, you had sinned against the
LORD your God; you had made yourselves a molten calf; you had turned

9.3: Heb 12.29. 9.8-21: Ex 32.7-20.

aside quickly from the way which the
LORD had commanded you. 17 So I
took hold of the two tables, and cast
them out of my two hands, and broke
them before your eyes. 18 Then I lay
prostrate before the LORD as before,
forty days and forty nights; I neither
ate bread nor drank water, because of
all the sin which you had committed,
in doing what was evil in the sight of
the LORD, to provoke him to anger.
19 For I was afraid of the anger and
hot displeasure which the LORD bore
against you, so that he was ready to
destroy you. But the LORD hearkened
to me that time also. 20 And the LORD
was so angry with Aaron that he was
ready to destroy him; and I prayed for
Aaron also at the same time. 21 Then
I took the sinful thing, the calf which
you had made, and burned it with fire
and crushed it, grinding it very small,
until it was as fine as dust; and I threw
the dust of it into the brook that
descended out of the mountain.

22 "At Tab′ė·rȧh also, and at Mas′-
sȧh, and at Kib′roth-hȧt·tā′ȧ·vȧh, you
provoked the LORD to wrath. 23 And
when the LORD sent you from Kā′desh-
bär′nē·ȧ, saying, 'Go up and take possession of the land which I have given
you,' then you rebelled against the
commandment of the LORD your God,
and did not believe him or obey his
voice. 24 You have been rebellious
against the LORD from the day that I
knew you.

25 "So I lay prostrate before the
LORD for these forty days and forty
nights, because the LORD had said he
would destroy you. 26 And I prayed to
the LORD, 'O LORD God, destroy not
thy people and thy heritage, whom
thou hast redeemed through thy greatness, whom thou hast brought out of
Egypt with a mighty hand. 27 Remember thy servants, Abraham, Isaac, and
Jacob; do not regard the stubbornness
of this people, or their wickedness, or
their sin, 28 lest the land from which
thou didst bring us say, "Because the
LORD was not able to bring them into
the land which he promised them, and
because he hated them, he has brought
them out to slay them in the wilderness." 29 For they are thy people and
thy heritage, whom thou didst bring
out by thy great power and by thy out
stretched arm.'

10 "At that time the LORD said to
me, 'Hew two tables of stone like
the first, and come up to me on the
mountain, and make an ark of wood.
2 And I will write on the tables the
words that were on the first tables
which you broke, and you shall put
them in the ark.' 3 So I made an ark
of acacia wood, and hewed two tables
of stone like the first, and went up the
mountain with the two tables in my
hand. 4 And he wrote on the tables, as
at the first writing, the ten commandments[g] which the LORD had spoken to
you on the mountain out of the midst
of the fire on the day of the assembly;
and the LORD gave them to me. 5 Then
I turned and came down from the
mountain, and put the tables in the
ark which I had made; and there they
are, as the LORD commanded me.

6 (The people of Israel journeyed
from Bė-ēr′ōth Bē′ne-jā′ȧ·kȧn[h] to Mō-
sē′rȧh. There Aaron died, and there
he was buried; and his son El·ē·ā′zȧr
ministered as priest in his stead. 7 From
there they journeyed to Gud′gō·dȧh,
and from Gudgodah to Jot′bȧ·thȧh, a
land with brooks of water. 8 At that
time the LORD set apart the tribe of Levi
to carry the ark of the covenant of the
LORD, to stand before the LORD to
minister to him and to bless in his
name, to this day. 9 Therefore Levi
has no portion or inheritance with his
brothers; the LORD is his inheritance,
as the LORD your God said to him.)

10 "I stayed on the mountain, as at
the first time, forty days and forty
nights, and the LORD hearkened to me
that time also; the LORD was unwilling
to destroy you. 11 And the LORD said
to me, 'Arise, go on your journey at the
head of the people, that they may go
in and possess the land, which I swore
to their fathers to give them.'

12 "And now, Israel, what does the
LORD our God require of you, but to
fear the LORD your God, to walk in all
his ways, to love him, to serve the
LORD your God with all your heart
and with all your soul, 13 and to keep
the commandments and statutes of the
LORD, which I command you this day
for your good? 14 Behold, to the LORD
your God belong heaven and the
heaven of heavens, the earth with all
that is in it; 15 yet the LORD set his
heart in love upon your fathers and

[g] Heb *words* [h] Or *the wells of the Bene-jaakan*
9.25-29: Ex 32.11-14.

chose their descendants after them,
you above all peoples, as at this day.
16 Circumcise therefore the foreskin of
your heart, and be no longer stubborn.
17 For the LORD your God is God of
gods and Lord of lords, the great, the
mighty, and the terrible God, who is
not partial and takes no bribe. 18 He
executes justice for the fatherless and
the widow, and loves the sojourner,
giving him food and clothing. 19 Love
the sojourner therefore; for you were
sojourners in the land of Egypt. 20 You
shall fear the LORD your God; you
shall serve him and cleave to him, and
by his name you shall swear. 21 He is
your praise; he is your God, who has
done for you these great and terrible
things which your eyes have seen.
22 Your fathers went down to Egypt
seventy persons; and now the LORD
your God has made you as the stars of
heaven for multitude.

11 "You shall therefore love the
LORD your God, and keep his
charge, his statutes, his ordinances,
and his commandments always. 2 And
consider this day (since I am not
speaking to your children who have
not known or seen it), consider the
discipline[i] of the LORD your God, his
greatness, his mighty hand and his outstretched arm, 3 his signs and his
deeds which he did in Egypt to Pharaoh the king of Egypt and to all his
land; 4 and what he did to the army
of Egypt, to their horses and to their
chariots; how he made the water of
the Red Sea overflow them as they
pursued after you, and how the LORD
has destroyed them to this day; 5 and
what he did to you in the wilderness,
until you came to this place; 6 and
what he did to Dā'thăn and A·bī'răm
the sons of E·lī'ăb, son of Reuben;
how the earth opened its mouth and
swallowed them up, with their households, their tents, and every living
thing that followed them, in the midst
of all Israel; 7 for your eyes have seen
all the great work of the LORD which
he did.

8 "You shall therefore keep all the
commandment which I command you
this day, that you may be strong, and
go in and take possession of the land
which you are going over to possess,
9 and that you may live long in the land
which the LORD swore to your fathers
to give to them and to their descendants, a land flowing with milk and
honey. 10 For the land which you are
entering to take possession of it is not
like the land of Egypt, from which you
have come, where you sowed your seed
and watered it with your feet, like a
garden of vegetables; 11 but the land
which you are going over to possess
is a land of hills and valleys, which
drinks water by the rain from heaven,
12 a land which the LORD your God
cares for; the eyes of the LORD your
God are always upon it, from the
beginning of the year to the end of the
year.

13 "And if you will obey my commandments which I command you
this day, to love the LORD your God,
and to serve him with all your heart
and with all your soul, 14 he[j] will give
the rain for your land in its season,
the early rain and the later rain, that
you may gather in your grain and your
wine and your oil. 15 And he[j] will give
grass in your fields for your cattle, and
you shall eat and be full. 16 Take heed
lest your heart be deceived, and you
turn aside and serve other gods and
worship them, 17 and the anger of the
LORD be kindled against you, and he
shut up the heavens, so that there be
no rain, and the land yield no fruit,
and you perish quickly off the good
land which the LORD gives you.

18 "You shall therefore lay up these
words of mine in your heart and in
your soul; and you shall bind them as
a sign upon your hand, and they shall
be as frontlets between your eyes.
19 And you shall teach them to your
children, talking of them when you are
sitting in your house, and when you
are walking by the way, and when you
lie down, and when you rise. 20 And
you shall write them upon the doorposts of your house and upon your
gates, 21 that your days and the days
of your children may be multiplied in
the land which the LORD swore to
your fathers to give them, as long as
the heavens are above the earth. 22 For
if you will be careful to do all this
commandment which I command you
to do, loving the LORD your God,
walking in all his ways, and cleaving
to him, 23 then the LORD will drive out
all these nations before you, and you
will dispossess nations greater and

[i] Or *instruction* [j] Sam Gk Vg: Heb *I*

10.17: Acts 10.34; Gal 2.6; Rev 17.14; 19.16. **10.19:** Ex 22.21; 23.9; Lev 19.34. **10.22:** Acts 7.14.

mightier than yourselves. 24 Every
place on which the sole of your foot
treads shall be yours; your territory
shall be from the wilderness and
Lebanon and from the River, the river
Eū·phrā'tēṡ, to the western sea. 25 No
man shall be able to stand against you;
the LORD your God will lay the fear of
you and the dread of you upon all the
land that you shall tread, as he promised you.

26 "Behold, I set before you this
day a blessing and a curse: 27 the
blessing, if you obey the commandments of the Lord your God, which
I command you this day, 28 and the
curse, if you do not obey the commandments of the LORD your God,
but turn aside from the way which I
command you this day, to go after
other gods which you have not known.
29 And when the LORD your God brings
you into the land which you are entering to take possession of it, you shall
set the blessing on Mount Gĕr'i·zim
and the curse on Mount Ē'bȧl. 30 Are
they not beyond the Jordan, west of
the road, toward the going down of
the sun, in the land of the Canaanites
who live in the Ar'ȧ·bȧh, over against
Gil'gȧl, beside the oak[k] of Mō'reh?
31 For you are to pass over the Jordan
to go in to take possession of the land
which the LORD your God gives you;
and when you possess it and live in it,
32 you shall be careful to do all the
statutes and the ordinances which I
set before you this day.

12 "These are the statutes and
ordinances which you shall be
careful to do in the land which the
LORD, the God of your fathers, has
given you to possess, all the days that
you live upon the earth. 2 You shall
surely destroy all the places where the
nations whom you shall dispossess
served their gods, upon the high mountains and upon the hills and under
every green tree; 3 you shall tear down
their altars, and dash in pieces their
pillars, and burn their A·shē'rim with
fire; you shall hew down the graven
images of their gods, and destroy their
name out of that place. 4 You shall not
do so to the LORD your God. 5 But you
shall seek the place which the LORD
your God will choose out of all your
tribes to put his name and make his
habitation there; thither you shall go,
6 and thither you shall bring your
burnt offerings and your sacrifices,
your tithes and the offering that you
present, your votive offerings, your
freewill offerings, and the firstlings of
your herd and of your flock; 7 and
there you shall eat before the LORD
your God, and you shall rejoice, you
and your households, in all that you
undertake, in which the LORD your
God has blessed you. 8 You shall not
do according to all that we are doing
here this day, every man doing whatever is right in his own eyes; 9 for you
have not as yet come to the rest and
to the inheritance which the LORD
your God gives you. 10 But when you
go over the Jordan, and live in the
land which the LORD your God gives
you to inherit, and when he gives you
rest from all your enemies round
about, so that you live in safety, 11 then
to the place which the LORD your God
will choose, to make his name dwell
there, thither you shall bring all that
I command you: your burnt offerings
and your sacrifices, your tithes and the
offering that you present, and all your
votive offerings which you vow to the
LORD. 12 And you shall rejoice before
the LORD your God, you and your sons
and your daughters, your menservants
and your maidservants, and the Levite
that is within your towns, since he has
no portion or inheritance with you.
13 Take heed that you do not offer your
burnt offerings at every place that you
see; 14 but at the place which the LORD
will choose in one of your tribes, there
you shall offer your burnt offerings,
and there you shall do all that I am
commanding you.

15 "However, you may slaughter
and eat flesh within any of your towns,
as much as you desire, according to
the blessing of the LORD your God
which he has given you; the unclean
and the clean may eat of it, as of the
gazelle and as of the hart. 16 Only you
shall not eat the blood; you shall pour
it out upon the earth like water. 17 You
may not eat within your towns the
tithe of your grain or of your wine or
of your oil, or the firstlings of your
herd or of your flock, or any of your
votive offerings which you vow, or
your freewill offerings, or the offering
that you present; 18 but you shall eat
them before the LORD your God in

[k] Gk Syr: See Gen 12.6. Heb *oaks* or *terebinths*
12.1-28: Ex 20.24. **12.16, 23:** Lev 17.10-14; 19.26.

the place which the LORD your God
will choose, you and your son and
your daughter, your manservant and
your maidservant, and the Levite who
is within your towns; and you shall
rejoice before the LORD your God in
all that you undertake. 19 Take heed
that you do not forsake the Levite as
long as you live in your land.
20 "When the LORD your God enlarges your territory, as he has promised you, and you say, 'I will eat
flesh,' because you crave flesh, you
may eat as much flesh as you desire.
21 If the place which the LORD your
God will choose to put his name there
is too far from you, then you may kill
any of your herd or your flock, which
the LORD has given you, as I have
commanded you; and you may eat
within your towns as much as you
desire. 22 Just as the gazelle or the
hart is eaten, so you may eat of it; the
unclean and the clean alike may eat
of it. 23 Only be sure that you do not
eat the blood; for the blood is the life,
and you shall not eat the life with the
flesh. 24 You shall not eat it; you shall
pour it out upon the earth like water.
25 You shall not eat it; that all may go
well with you and with your children
after you, when you do what is right
in the sight of the LORD. 26 But the
holy things which are due from you,
and your votive offerings, you shall
take, and you shall go to the place
which the LORD will choose, 27 and
offer your burnt offerings, the flesh
and the blood, on the altar of the LORD
your God; the blood of your sacrifices
shall be poured out on the altar of the
LORD your God, but the flesh you may
eat. 28 Be careful to heed all these
words which I command you, that it
may go well with you and with your
children after you for ever, when you
do what is good and right in the sight
of the LORD your God.
29 "When the LORD your God cuts
off before you the nations whom you
go in to dispossess, and you dispossess
them and dwell in their land, 30 take
heed that you be not ensnared to follow
them, after they have been destroyed
before you, and that you do not inquire
about their gods, saying, 'How did
these nations serve their gods?—that
I also may do likewise.' 31 You shall
not do so to the LORD your God; for
every abominable thing which the
LORD hates they have done for their
gods; for they even burn their sons
and their daughters in the fire to their
gods.
32[l] "Everything that I command
you you shall be careful to do; you
shall not add to it or take from it.

13 "If a prophet arises among you,
or a dreamer of dreams, and gives
you a sign or a wonder, 2 and the sign
or wonder which he tells you comes to
pass, and if he says, 'Let us go after
other gods,' which you have not known,
'and let us serve them,' 3 you shall not
listen to the words of that prophet or
to that dreamer of dreams; for the
LORD your God is testing you, to
know whether you love the LORD your
God with all your heart and with all
your soul. 4 You shall walk after the
LORD your God and fear him, and
keep his commandments and obey his
voice, and you shall serve him and
cleave to him. 5 But that prophet or
that dreamer of dreams shall be put
to death, because he has taught rebellion against the LORD your God, who
brought you out of the land of Egypt
and redeemed you out of the house of
bondage, to make you leave the way
in which the LORD your God commanded you to walk. So you shall
purge the evil from the midst of you.
6 "If your brother, the son of your
mother, or your son, or your daughter,
or the wife of your bosom, or your
friend who is as your own soul, entices
you secretly, saying, 'Let us go and
serve other gods,' which neither you
nor your fathers have known, 7 some
of the gods of the peoples that are
round about you, whether near you or
far off from you, from the one end of
the earth to the other, 8 you shall not
yield to him or listen to him, nor shall
your eye pity him, nor shall you spare
him, nor shall you conceal him; 9 but
you shall kill him; your hand shall
be first against him to put him to death,
and afterwards the hand of all the
people. 10 You shall stone him to
death with stones, because he sought
to draw you away from the LORD your
God, who brought you out of the land
of Egypt, out of the house of bondage.
11 And all Israel shall hear, and fear,
and never again do any such wickedness as this among you.

[l] Ch 13.1 in Heb
12.29-32: Ex 23.24; 34.12-14; Num 33.52.

12 "If you hear in one of your cities,
which the LORD your God gives you
to dwell there, 13 that certain base
fellows have gone out among you and
have drawn away the inhabitants of
the city, saying, 'Let us go and serve
other gods,' which you have not
known, 14 then you shall inquire and
make search and ask diligently; and behold, if it be true and certain that such
an abominable thing has been done
among you, 15 you shall surely put the
inhabitants of that city to the sword,
destroying it utterly, all who are in it
and its cattle, with the edge of the
sword. 16 You shall gather all its spoil
into the midst of its open square, and
burn the city and all its spoil with fire,
as a whole burnt offering to the LORD
your God; it shall be a heap for ever,
it shall not be built again. 17 None of
the devoted things shall cleave to your
hand; that the LORD may turn from
the fierceness of his anger, and show
you mercy, and have compassion on
you, and multiply you, as he swore to
your fathers, 18 if you obey the voice
of the LORD your God, keeping all his
commandments which I command you
this day, and doing what is right in
the sight of the LORD your God.

14 "You are the sons of the LORD
your God; you shall not cut yourselves or make any baldness on your
foreheads for the dead. 2 For you are
a people holy to the LORD your God,
and the LORD has chosen you to be a
people for his own possession, out of
all the peoples that are on the face of
the earth.

3 "You shall not eat any abominable
thing. 4 These are the animals you may
eat: the ox, the sheep, the goat, 5 the
hart, the gazelle, the roebuck, the wild
goat, the ibex, the antelope, and the
mountain-sheep. 6 Every animal that
parts the hoof and has the hoof cloven
in two, and chews the cud, among the
animals, you may eat. 7 Yet of those
that chew the cud or have the hoof
cloven you shall not eat these: the
camel, the hare, and the rock badger,
because they chew the cud but do not
part the hoof, are unclean for you.
8 And the swine, because it parts the
hoof but does not chew the cud, is unclean for you. Their flesh you shall not
eat, and their carcasses you shall not
touch.

9 "Of all that are in the waters you
may eat these: whatever has fins and
scales you may eat. 10 And whatever
does not have fins and scales you shall
not eat; it is unclean for you.

11 "You may eat all clean birds.
12 But these are the ones which you
shall not eat: the eagle, the vulture,
the osprey, 13 the buzzard, the kite,
after their kinds; 14 every raven after
its kind; 15 the ostrich, the nighthawk,
the sea gull, the hawk, after their
kinds; 16 the little owl and the great
owl, the water hen 17 and the pelican,
the carrion vulture and the cormorant,
18 the stork, the heron, after their
kinds; the hoopoe and the bat. 19 And
all winged insects are unclean for you;
they shall not be eaten. 20 All clean
winged things you may eat.

21 "You shall not eat anything that
dies of itself; you may give it to the
alien who is within your towns, that
he may eat it, or you may sell it to a
foreigner; for you are a people holy to
the LORD your God.

"You shall not boil a kid in its
mother's milk.

22 "You shall tithe all the yield of
your seed, which comes forth from the
field year by year. 23 And before the
LORD your God, in the place which
he will choose, to make his name dwell
there, you shall eat the tithe of your
grain, of your wine, and of your oil,
and the firstlings of your herd and
flock; that you may learn to fear the
LORD your God always. 24 And if the
way is too long for you, so that you
are not able to bring the tithe, when
the LORD your God blesses you, because the place is too far from you,
which the LORD your God chooses, to
set his name there, 25 then you shall
turn it into money, and bind up the
money in your hand, and go to the
place which the LORD your God
chooses, 26 and spend the money for
whatever you desire, oxen, or sheep,
or wine or strong drink, whatever your
appetite craves; and you shall eat there
before the LORD your God and rejoice,
you and your household. 27 And you
shall not forsake the Levite who is
within your towns, for he has no portion or inheritance with you.

28 "At the end of every three years
you shall bring forth all the tithe of
your produce in the same year, and lay

14.1: Lev 19.28. **14.2:** Ex 19.5-6; Deut 26.19; Tit 2.14; 1 Pet 2.9; Rev 1.6; 5.10. **14.3-20:** Lev 11.2-23. **14.21:** Lev 11.39-40; 17.15; Ex 23.19; 34.26. **14.22-29:** Lev 27.30-33; Num 18.21-32.

it up within your towns; 29 and the Levite, because he has no portion or inheritance with you, and the sojourner, the fatherless, and the widow, who are within your towns, shall come and eat and be filled; that the LORD your God may bless you in all the work of your hands that you do.

15 "At the end of every seven years you shall grant a release. 2 And this is the manner of the release: every creditor shall release what he has lent to his neighbor; he shall not exact it of his neighbor, his brother, because the LORD's release has been proclaimed. 3 Of a foreigner you may exact it; but whatever of yours is with your brother your hand shall release. 4 But there will be no poor among you (for the LORD will bless you in the land which the LORD your God gives you for an inheritance to possess), 5 if only you will obey the voice of the LORD your God, being careful to do all this commandment which I command you this day. 6 For the LORD your God will bless you, as he promised you, and you shall lend to many nations, but you shall not borrow; and you shall rule over many nations, but they shall not rule over you.

7 "If there is among you a poor man, one of your brethren, in any of your towns within your land which the LORD your God gives you, you shall not harden your heart or shut your hand against your poor brother, 8 but you shall open your hand to him, and lend him sufficient for his need, whatever it may be. 9 Take heed lest there be a base thought in your heart, and you say, 'The seventh year, the year of release is near,' and your eye be hostile to your poor brother, and you give him nothing, and he cry to the LORD against you, and it be sin in you. 10 You shall give to him freely, and your heart shall not be grudging when you give to him; because for this the LORD your God will bless you in all your work and in all that you undertake. 11 For the poor will never cease out of the land; therefore I command you, You shall open wide your hand to your brother, to the needy and to the poor, in the land.

12 "If your brother, a Hebrew man, or a Hebrew woman, is sold to you, he shall serve you six years, and in the seventh year you shall let him go free from you. 13 And when you let him go free from you, you shall not let him go empty-handed; 14 you shall furnish him liberally out of your flock, out of your threshing floor, and out of your wine press; as the LORD your God has blessed you, you shall give to him. 15 You shall remember that you were a slave in the land of Egypt, and the LORD your God redeemed you; therefore I command you this today. 16 But if he says to you, 'I will not go out from you,' because he loves you and your household, since he fares well with you, 17 then you shall take an awl, and thrust it through his ear into the door, and he shall be your bondman for ever. And to your bondwoman you shall do likewise. 18 It shall not seem hard to you, when you let him go free from you; for at half the cost of a hired servant he has served you six years. So the LORD your God will bless you in all that you do.

19 "All the firstling males that are born of your herd and flock you shall consecrate to the LORD your God; you shall do no work with the firstling of your herd, nor shear the firstling of your flock. 20 You shall eat it, you and your household, before the LORD your God year by year at the place which the LORD will choose. 21 But if it has any blemish, if it is lame or blind, or has any serious blemish whatever, you shall not sacrifice it to the LORD your God. 22 You shall eat it within your towns; the unclean and the clean alike may eat it, as though it were a gazelle or a hart. 23 Only you shall not eat its blood; you shall pour it out on the ground like water.

16 "Observe the month of Ā'bib, and keep the passover to the LORD your God; for in the month of Abib the LORD your God brought you out of Egypt by night. 2 And you shall offer the passover sacrifice to the LORD your God, from the flock or the herd, at the place which the LORD will choose, to make his name dwell there. 3 You shall eat no leavened bread with it; seven days you shall eat it with unleavened bread, the bread of affliction—for you came out of the land of Egypt in hurried flight—that all the days of your life you may remember the day when you came out of the land

15.12-18: Ex 21.2-11; Lev 25.39-46. 15.19-23: Ex 13.11-12; 22.30; 34.19; Num 18.17-18.
16.1-17: Ex 23.14-17; Lev 23; Num 28-29.

of Egypt. 4 No leaven shall be seen
with you in all your territory for seven
days; nor shall any of the flesh which
you sacrifice on the evening of the first
day remain all night until morning.
5 You may not offer the passover
sacrifice within any of your towns
which the LORD your God gives you;
6 but at the place which the LORD your
God will choose, to make his name
dwell in it, there you shall offer the
passover sacrifice, in the evening at
the going down of the sun, at the time
you came out of Egypt. 7 And you
shall boil it and eat it at the place which
the LORD your God will choose; and in
the morning you shall turn and go to
your tents. 8 For six days you shall eat
unleavened bread; and on the seventh
day there shall be a solemn assembly
to the LORD your God; you shall do
no work on it.

9 "You shall count seven weeks;
begin to count the seven weeks from
the time you first put the sickle to the
standing grain. 10 Then you shall keep
the feast of weeks to the LORD your
God with the tribute of a freewill
offering from your hand, which you
shall give as the LORD your God blesses
you; 11 and you shall rejoice before the
LORD your God, you and your son and
your daughter, your manservant and
your maidservant, the Levite who is
within your towns, the sojourner, the
fatherless, and the widow who are
among you, at the place which the
LORD your God will choose, to make
his name dwell there. 12 You shall
remember that you were a slave in
Egypt; and you shall be careful to
observe these statutes.

13 "You shall keep the feast of
booths seven days, when you make
your ingathering from your threshing
floor and your wine press; 14 you shall
rejoice in your feast, you and your son
and your daughter, your manservant
and your maidservant, the Levite, the
sojourner, the fatherless, and the
widow who are within your towns.
15 For seven days you shall keep the
feast to the LORD your God at the
place which the LORD will choose; because the LORD your God will bless
you in all your produce and in all the
work of your hands, so that you will
be altogether joyful.

16 "Three times a year all your
males shall appear before the LORD
your God at the place which he will
choose: at the feast of unleavened
bread, at the feast of weeks, and at the
feast of booths. They shall not appear
before the LORD empty-handed;
17 every man shall give as he is able,
according to the blessing of the LORD
your God which he has given you.

18 "You shall appoint judges and
officers in all your towns which the
LORD your God gives you, according
to your tribes; and they shall judge
the people with righteous judgment.
19 You shall not pervert justice; you
shall not show partiality; and you shall
not take a bribe, for a bribe blinds the
eyes of the wise and subverts the cause
of the righteous. 20 Justice, and only
justice, you shall follow, that you may
live and inherit the land which the
LORD your God gives you.

21 "You shall not plant any tree as
an A·shē'rȧh beside the altar of the
LORD your God which you shall make.
22 And you shall not set up a pillar,
which the LORD your God hates.

17 "You shall not sacrifice to the
LORD your God an ox or a sheep
in which is a blemish, any defect whatever; for that is an abomination to the
LORD your God.

2 "If there is found among you,
within any of your towns which the
LORD your God gives you, a man or
woman who does what is evil in the
sight of the LORD your God, in transgressing his covenant, 3 and has gone
and served other gods and worshiped
them, or the sun or the moon or any
of the host of heaven, which I have
forbidden, 4 and it is told you and you
hear of it; then you shall inquire
diligently, and if it is true and certain
that such an abominable thing has
been done in Israel, 5 then you shall
bring forth to your gates that man or
woman who has done this evil thing,
and you shall stone that man or woman
to death with stones. 6 On the evidence
of two witnesses or of three witnesses
he that is to die shall be put to death;
a person shall not be put to death on
the evidence of one witness. 7 The
hand of the witnesses shall be first
against him to put him to death, and
afterward the hand of all the people.

16.19: Ex 23.6-9; Lev 19.15. **16.21-22:** Lev 26.1. **17.1:** Lev 22.17-24. **17.2-7:** Ex 22.20.
17.6: Num 35.30; Deut 19.15; Mt 18.16; 2 Cor 13.1; 1 Tim 5.19; Heb 10.28.
17.7: Deut 19.19; 1 Cor 5.13.

So you shall purge the evil from the
midst of you.
8 "If any case arises requiring decision between one kind of homicide
and another, one kind of legal right
and another, or one kind of assault and
another, any case within your towns
which is too difficult for you, then you
shall arise and go up to the place which
the LORD your God will choose, [9] and
coming to the Levitical priests, and to
the judge who is in office in those days,
you shall consult them, and they shall
declare to you the decision. [10] Then
you shall do according to what they
declare to you from that place which
the LORD will choose; and you shall be
careful to do according to all that they
direct you; [11] according to the instructions which they give you, and according to the decision which they pronounce to you, you shall do; you shall
not turn aside from the verdict which
they declare to you, either to the right
hand or to the left. [12] The man who
acts presumptuously, by not obeying
the priest who stands to minister there
before the LORD your God, or the
judge, that man shall die; so you shall
purge the evil from Israel. [13]And all
the people shall hear, and fear, and not
act presumptuously again.
14 "When you come to the land
which the LORD your God gives you,
and you possess it and dwell in it, and
then say, 'I will set a king over me, like
all the nations that are round about
me'; [15] you may indeed set as king over
you him whom the LORD your God
will choose. One from among your
brethren you shall set as king over
you; you may not put a foreigner over
you, who is not your brother. [16] Only
he must not multiply horses for himself, or cause the people to return to
Egypt in order to multiply horses,
since the LORD has said to you, 'You
shall never return that way again.'
[17]And he shall not multiply wives for
himself, lest his heart turn away;
nor shall he greatly multiply for himself silver and gold.
18 "And when he sits on the throne
of his kingdom, he shall write for himself in a book a copy of this law, from
that which is in charge of the Levitical
priests; [19] and it shall be with him, and
he shall read in it all the days of his
life, that he may learn to fear the LORD
his God, by keeping all the words of
this law and these statutes, and doing
them; [20] that his heart may not be
lifted up above his brethren, and that
he may not turn aside from the commandment, either to the right hand or
to the left; so that he may continue
long in his kingdom, he and his children, in Israel.

18 "The Levitical priests, that is,
all the tribe of Levi, shall have
no portion or inheritance with Israel;
they shall eat the offerings by fire to
the LORD, and his rightful dues. [2] They
shall have no inheritance among their
brethren; the LORD is their inheritance,
as he promised them. [3]And this shall
be the priests' due from the people,
from those offering a sacrifice, whether
it be ox or sheep: they shall give to the
priest the shoulder and the two cheeks
and the stomach. [4] The first fruits of
your grain, of your wine and of your
oil, and the first of the fleece of your
sheep, you shall give him. [5] For the
LORD your God has chosen him out of
all your tribes, to stand and minister
in the name of the LORD, him and his
sons for ever.
6 "And if a Levite comes from any
of your towns out of all Israel, where
he lives—and he may come when he
desires—to the place which the LORD
will choose, [7] then he may minister in
the name of the LORD his God, like all
his fellow-Levites who stand to minister there before the LORD. [8] They
shall have equal portions to eat, besides what he receives from the sale
of his patrimony.[m]
9 "When you come into the land
which the LORD your God gives you,
you shall not learn to follow the
abominable practices of those nations.
[10] There shall not be found among you
any one who burns his son or his
daughter as an offering,[n] any one who
practices divination, a soothsayer, or
an augur, or a sorcerer, [11] or a charmer,
or a medium, or a wizard, or a necro-
mancer. [12] For whoever does these
things is an abomination to the LORD;
and because of these abominable practices the LORD your God is driving
them out before you. [13] You shall be
blameless before the LORD your God.
[14] For these nations, which you are
about to dispossess, give heed to soothsayers and to diviners; but as for you,

[m] Heb obscure [n] Heb *makes his son or his daughter pass through the fire*

18.1-8: Num 18.20-24. **18.10-11:** Ex 22.18; Lev 19.26, 31; 20.6, 27. **18.13:** Mt 5.48.

the LORD your God has not allowed
you so to do.
15 "The LORD your God will raise
up for you a prophet like me from
among you, from your brethren—him
you shall heed—16 just as you desired
of the LORD your God at Hō'reb on the
day of the assembly, when you said,
'Let me not hear again the voice of the
LORD my God, or see this great fire
any more, lest I die.' 17And the LORD
said to me, 'They have rightly said all
that they have spoken. 18 I will raise
up for them a prophet like you from
among their brethren; and I will put
my words in his mouth, and he shall
speak to them all that I command him.
19And whoever will not give heed to
my words which he shall speak in my
name, I myself will require it of him.
20 But the prophet who presumes to
speak a word in my name which I have
not commanded him to speak, or who
speaks in the name of other gods, that
same prophet shall die.' 21And if you
say in your heart, 'How may we know
the word which the LORD has not
spoken?'—22when a prophet speaks
in the name of the LORD, if the word
does not come to pass or come true,
that is a word which the LORD has not
spoken; the prophet has spoken it
presumptuously, you need not be
afraid of him.

19 "When the LORD your God
cuts off the nations whose land
the LORD your God gives you, and you
dispossess them and dwell in their
cities and in their houses, 2 you shall
set apart three cities for you in the
land which the LORD your God gives
you to possess. 3 You shall prepare the
roads, and divide into three parts the
area of the land which the LORD your
God gives you as a possession, so that
any manslayer can flee to them.
4 "This is the provision for the
manslayer, who by fleeing there may
save his life. If any one kills his
neighbor unintentionally without having been at enmity with him in time
past—5 as when a man goes into the
forest with his neighbor to cut wood,
and his hand swings the axe to cut
down a tree, and the head slips from
the handle and strikes his neighbor so
that he dies—he may flee to one of
these cities and save his life; 6 lest the
avenger of blood in hot anger pursue
the manslayer and overtake him, because the way is long, and wound him
mortally, though the man did not
deserve to die, since he was not at
enmity with his neighbor in time past.
7 Therefore I command you, You shall
set apart three cities. 8And if the LORD
your God enlarges your border, as he
has sworn to your fathers, and gives
you all the land which he promised to
give to your fathers—9 provided you
are careful to keep all this commandment, which I command you this day,
by loving the LORD your God and by
walking ever in his ways—then you
shall add three other cities to these
three, 10 lest innocent blood be shed in
your land which the LORD your God
gives you for an inheritance, and so
the guilt of bloodshed be upon you.
11 "But if any man hates his neighbor, and lies in wait for him, and
attacks him, and wounds him mortally
so that he dies, and the man flees into
one of these cities, 12 then the elders
of his city shall send and fetch him
from there, and hand him over to the
avenger of blood, so that he may die.
13 Your eye shall not pity him, but you
shall purge the guilt of innocent blood[o]
from Israel, so that it may be well
with you.
14 "In the inheritance which you
will hold in the land that the LORD
your God gives you to possess, you
shall not remove your neighbor's landmark, which the men of old have set.
15 "A single witness shall not prevail against a man for any crime or for
any wrong in connection with any
offense that he has committed; only
on the evidence of two witnesses, or of
three witnesses, shall a charge be sustained. 16 If a malicious witness rises
against any man to accuse him of
wrongdoing, 17 then both parties to
the dispute shall appear before the
LORD, before the priests and the judges
who are in office in those days; 18 the
judges shall inquire diligently, and if
the witness is a false witness and has
accused his brother falsely, 19 then you
shall do to him as he had meant to do
to his brother; so you shall purge the
evil from the midst of you. 20And the

o Or *the blood of the innocent*

18.15-19: Acts 3.22-23; 7.37. **19.1-13:** Ex 21.12-14; Num 35.
19.15: Num 35.30; Deut 17.6; Mt 18.16; 2 Cor 13.1; 1 Tim 5.19; Heb 10.28.
19.16-20: Ex 20.16; 23.1; Lev 19.16; Deut 5.20. **19.19:** 1 Cor 5.13.

rest shall hear, and fear, and shall
never again commit any such evil
among you. 21 Your eye shall not pity;
it shall be life for life, eye for eye,
tooth for tooth, hand for hand, foot
for foot.

20 "When you go forth to war
against your enemies, and see
horses and chariots and an army larger
than your own, you shall not be afraid
of them; for the LORD your God is
with you, who brought you up out of
the land of Egypt. 2 And when you draw
near to the battle, the priest shall come
forward and speak to the people, 3 and
shall say to them, 'Hear, O Israel, you
draw near this day to battle against
your enemies: let not your heart faint;
do not fear, or tremble, or be in dread
of them; 4 for the LORD your God is
he that goes with you, to fight for you
against your enemies, to give you the
victory.' 5 Then the officers shall speak
to the people, saying, 'What man is
there that has built a new house and
has not dedicated it? Let him go back
to his house, lest he die in the battle
and another man dedicate it. 6 And
what man is there that has planted a
vineyard and has not enjoyed its fruit?
Let him go back to his house, lest he
die in the battle and another man enjoy
its fruit. 7 And what man is there that
has betrothed a wife and has not taken
her? Let him go back to his house, lest
he die in the battle and another man
take her.' 8 And the officers shall speak
further to the people, and say, 'What
man is there that is fearful and fainthearted? Let him go back to his house,
lest the heart of his fellows melt as his
heart.' 9 And when the officers have
made an end of speaking to the people,
then commanders shall be appointed
at the head of the people.

10 "When you draw near to a city
to fight against it, offer terms of peace
to it. 11 And if its answer to you is peace
and it opens to you, then all the people
who are found in it shall do forced
labor for you and shall serve you.
12 But if it makes no peace with you,
but makes war against you, then you
shall besiege it; 13 and when the LORD
your God gives it into your hand you
shall put all its males to the sword,
14 but the women and the little ones,
the cattle, and everything else in the
city, all its spoil, you shall take as booty
for yourselves; and you shall enjoy the
spoil of your enemies, which the LORD
your God has given you. 15 Thus you
shall do to all the cities which are very
far from you, which are not cities of
the nations here. 16 But in the cities of
these peoples that the LORD your God
gives you for an inheritance, you
shall save alive nothing that breathes,
17 but you shall utterly destroy them,
the Hit'tites and the Am'ŏ·rītes, the
Canaanites and the Per'iz·zītes, the Hī'-
vītes and the Jeb'ū·sītes, as the LORD
your God has commanded; 18 that they
may not teach you to do according to
all their abominable practices which
they have done in the service of their
gods, and so to sin against the LORD
your God.

19 "When you besiege a city for a
long time, making war against it in
order to take it, you shall not destroy
its trees by wielding an axe against
them; for you may eat of them, but you
shall not cut them down. Are the trees
in the field men that they should be
besieged by you? 20 Only the trees
which you know are not trees for food
you may destroy and cut down that
you may build siegeworks against the
city that makes war with you, until it
falls.

21 "If in the land which the LORD
your God gives you to possess,
any one is found slain, lying in the
open country, and it is not known who
killed him, 2 then your elders and your
judges shall come forth, and they shall
measure the distance to the cities
which are around him that is slain;
3 and the elders of the city which is
nearest to the slain man shall take a
heifer which has never been worked
and which has not pulled in the yoke.
4 And the elders of that city shall bring
the heifer down to a valley with running water, which is neither plowed
nor sown, and shall break the heifer's
neck there in the valley. 5 And the
priests the sons of Levi shall come
forward, for the LORD your God has
chosen them to minister to him and to
bless in the name of the LORD, and by
their word every dispute and every
assault shall be settled. 6 And all the
elders of that city nearest to the slain
man shall wash their hands over the
heifer whose neck was broken in the
valley; 7 and they shall testify, 'Our
hands did not shed this blood, neither
did our eyes see it shed. 8 Forgive, O

19.21: Ex 21.23-26; Lev 24.20; Mt 5.38.

LORD, thy people Israel, whom thou
hast redeemed, and set not the guilt of
innocent blood in the midst of thy
people Israel; but let the guilt of blood
be forgiven them.' 9 So you shall purge
the guilt of innocent blood from your
midst, when you do what is right in the
sight of the LORD.

10 "When you go forth to war
against your enemies, and the LORD
your God gives them into your hands,
and you take them captive, 11 and see
among the captives a beautiful woman,
and you have desire for her and would
take her for yourself as wife, 12 then
you shall bring her home to your house,
and she shall shave her head and pare
her nails. 13 And she shall put off her
captive's garb, and shall remain in
your house and bewail her father and
her mother a full month; after that you
may go in to her, and be her husband,
and she shall be your wife. 14 Then, if
you have no delight in her, you shall
let her go where she will; but you shall
not sell her for money, you shall not
treat her as a slave, since you have
humiliated her.

15 "If a man has two wives, the one
loved and the other disliked, and they
have borne him children, both the
loved and the disliked, and if the first-
born son is hers that is disliked, 16 then
on the day when he assigns his possessions as an inheritance to his sons, he
may not treat the son of the loved as
the first-born in preference to the son
of the disliked, who is the first-born,
17 but he shall acknowledge the first-
born, the son of the disliked, by giving
him a double portion of all that he has,
for he is the first issue of his strength;
the right of the first-born is his.

18 "If a man has a stubborn and
rebellious son, who will not obey the
voice of his father or the voice of his
mother, and though they chastise him,
will not give heed to them, 19 then his
father and his mother shall take hold
of him and bring him out to the elders
of his city at the gate of the place where
he lives, 20 and they shall say to the
elders of his city, 'This our son is
stubborn and rebellious, he will not
obey our voice; he is a glutton and a
drunkard.' 21 Then all the men of the
city shall stone him to death with
stones; so you shall purge the evil from
your midst; and all Israel shall hear,
and fear.

22 "And if a man has committed a
crime punishable by death and he is
put to death, and you hang him on a
tree, 23 his body shall not remain all
night upon the tree, but you shall bury
him the same day, for a hanged man is
accursed by God; you shall not defile
your land which the LORD your God
gives you for an inheritance.

22 "You shall not see your brother's ox or his sheep go astray,
and withhold your help[p] from them;
you shall take them back to your
brother. 2 And if he is not near you,
or if you do not know him, you shall
bring it home to your house, and it
shall be with you until your brother
seeks it; then you shall restore it to
him. 3 And so you shall do with his ass;
so you shall do with his garment; so
you shall do with any lost thing of
your brother's, which he loses and you
find; you may not withhold your help.
4 You shall not see your brother's
ass or his ox fallen down by the way,
and withhold your help[p] from them;
you shall help him to lift them up
again.

5 "A woman shall not wear anything that pertains to a man, nor shall
a man put on a woman's garment; for
whoever does these things is an abomination to the LORD your God.

6 "If you chance to come upon a
bird's nest, in any tree or on the
ground, with young ones or eggs and
the mother sitting upon the young or
upon the eggs, you shall not take the
mother with the young; 7 you shall let
the mother go, but the young you may
take to yourself; that it may go well
with you, and that you may live long.

8 "When you build a new house,
you shall make a parapet for your roof,
that you may not bring the guilt of
blood upon your house, if any one fall
from it.

9 "You shall not sow your vineyard
with two kinds of seed, lest the whole
yield be forfeited to the sanctuary,[q] the
crop which you have sown and the
yield of the vineyard. 10 You shall not
plow with an ox and an ass together.
11 You shall not wear a mingled stuff,
wool and linen together.

12 "You shall make yourself tassels

[p] Heb *hide yourself* [q] Heb *become holy*

21.18-21: Ex 20.12; 21.15, 17; Lev 20.9; Deut 5.16; 27.16. 21.22: Acts 5.30; 10.39. 21.23: Gal 3.13. 22.1-4: Ex 23.4-5. 22.9-11: Lev 19.19. 22.12: Num 15.37-41.

on the four corners of your cloak with
which you cover yourself.
13 "If any man takes a wife, and
goes in to her, and then spurns her,
14 and charges her with shameful conduct, and brings an evil name upon
her, saying, 'I took this woman, and
when I came near her, I did not find
in her the tokens of virginity,' 15 then
the father of the young woman and
her mother shall take and bring out the
tokens of her virginity to the elders of
the city in the gate; 16 and the father
of the young woman shall say to the
elders, 'I gave my daughter to this man
to wife, and he spurns her; 17 and lo,
he has made shameful charges against
her, saying, "I did not find in your
daughter the tokens of virginity." And
yet these are the tokens of my daughter's virginity.' And they shall spread
the garment before the elders of the
city. 18 Then the elders of that city
shall take the man and whip him;
19 and they shall fine him a hundred
shekels of silver, and give them to the
father of the young woman, because
he has brought an evil name upon a
virgin of Israel; and she shall be his
wife; he may not put her away all his
days. 20 But if the thing is true, that
the tokens of virginity were not found
in the young woman, 21 then they shall
bring out the young woman to the door
of her father's house, and the men of
her city shall stone her to death with
stones, because she has wrought folly
in Israel by playing the harlot in her
father's house; so you shall purge the
evil from the midst of you.
22 "If a man is found lying with the
wife of another man, both of them
shall die, the man who lay with the
woman, and the woman; so you shall
purge the evil from Israel.
23 "If there is a betrothed virgin,
and a man meets her in the city and
lies with her, 24 then you shall bring
them both out to the gate of that city,
and you shall stone them to death with
stones, the young woman because she
did not cry for help though she was in
the city, and the man because he
violated his neighbor's wife; so you
shall purge the evil from the midst of
you.
25 "But if in the open country a
man meets a young woman who is
betrothed, and the man seizes her and
lies with her, then only the man who
lay with her shall die. 26 But to the
young woman you shall do nothing; in
the young woman there is no offense
punishable by death, for this case is
like that of a man attacking and mur-
dering his neighbor; 27 because he
came upon her in the open country,
and though the betrothed young
woman cried for help there was no one
to rescue her.
28 "If a man meets a virgin who is
not betrothed, and seizes her and lies
with her, and they are found, 29 then
the man who lay with her shall give
to the father of the young woman fifty
shekels of silver, and she shall be
his wife, because he has violated
her; he may not put her away all his
days.
30[r] "A man shall not take his
father's wife, nor shall he uncover her
who is his father's.[s]

23 "He whose testicles are crushed
or whose male member is cut
off shall not enter the assembly of the
LORD.
2 "No bastard shall enter the assembly of the LORD; even to the tenth
generation none of his descendants
shall enter the assembly of the LORD.
3 "No Am'mo·nite or Mō'ab·ite
shall enter the assembly of the LORD;
even to the tenth generation none belonging to them shall enter the assembly of the LORD for ever; 4 because
they did not meet you with bread and
with water on the way, when you came
forth out of Egypt, and because they
hired against you Balaam the son of
Bē'ôr from Pē'thôr of Mes·o·po·tā'-
mi·a, to curse you. 5 Nevertheless the
LORD your God would not hearken to
Balaam; but the LORD your God turned
the curse into a blessing for you, because the LORD your God loved you.
6 You shall not seek their peace or
their prosperity all your days for ever.
7 "You shall not abhor an E'dom-
ite, for he is your brother; you shall
not abhor an Egyptian, because you
were a sojourner in his land. 8 The
children of the third generation that
are born to them may enter the assembly of the LORD.
9 "When you go forth against your
enemies and are in camp, then you

[r] Ch 23.1. in Heb [s] Heb *uncover his father's skirt*
22.21: 1 Cor 5.13. 22.22-27: Ex 20.14; Lev 18.20; 20.10; Deut 5.18. 22.24: 1 Cor 5.13.
22.28-29: Ex 22.16-17.

shall keep yourself from every evil
thing.
10 “If there is among you any man
who is not clean by reason of what
chances to him by night, then he shall
go outside the camp, he shall not come
within the camp; 11 but when evening
comes on, he shall bathe himself in
water, and when the sun is down, he
may come within the camp.
12 “You shall have a place outside
the camp and you shall go out to it;
13 and you shall have a stick with your
weapons; and when you sit down outside, you shall dig a hole with it, and
turn back and cover up your excre-
ment. 14 Because the LORD your God
walks in the midst of your camp, to
save you and to give up your enemies
before you, therefore your camp must
be holy, that he may not see anything
indecent among you, and turn away
from you.
15 “You shall not give up to his
master a slave who has escaped from
his master to you; 16 he shall dwell with
you, in your midst, in the place which
he shall choose within one of your
towns, where it pleases him best; you
shall not oppress him.
17 “There shall be no cult prostitute of the daughters of Israel, neither
shall there be a cult prostitute of the
sons of Israel. 18 You shall not bring
the hire of a harlot, or the wages of a
dog,[t] into the house of the LORD your
God in payment for any vow; for both
of these are an abomination to the
LORD your God.
19 “You shall not lend upon interest to your brother, interest on
money, interest on victuals, interest
on anything that is lent for interest.
20 To a foreigner you may lend upon
interest, but to your brother you shall
not lend upon interest; that the LORD
your God may bless you in all that you
undertake in the land which you are
entering to take possession of it.
21 “When you make a vow to the
LORD your God, you shall not be slack
to pay it; for the LORD your God will
surely require it of you, and it would
be sin in you. 22 But if you refrain
from vowing, it shall be no sin in you.
23 You shall be careful to perform
what has passed your lips, for you have
voluntarily vowed to the LORD your
God what you have promised with
your mouth.
24 “When you go into your neighbor's vineyard, you may eat your fill
of grapes, as many as you wish, but
you shall not put any in your vessel.
25 When you go into your neighbor's
standing grain, you may pluck the ears
with your hand, but you shall not put
a sickle to your neighbor's standing
grain.

24 “When a man takes a wife and
marries her, if then she finds no
favor in his eyes because he has found
some indecency in her, and he writes
her a bill of divorce and puts it in her
hand and sends her out of his house,
and she departs out of his house, 2 and
if she goes and becomes another man's
wife, 3 and the latter husband dislikes
her and writes her a bill of divorce and
puts it in her hand and sends her out
of his house, or if the latter husband
dies, who took her to be his wife, 4 then
her former husband, who sent her
away, may not take her again to be his
wife, after she has been defiled; for
that is an abomination before the
LORD, and you shall not bring guilt
upon the land which the LORD your
God gives you for an inheritance.
5 “When a man is newly married,
he shall not go out with the army or be
charged with any business; he shall be
free at home one year, to be happy with
his wife whom he has taken.
6 “No man shall take a mill or an
upper millstone in pledge; for he
would be taking a life in pledge.
7 “If a man is found stealing one of
his brethren, the people of Israel,
and if he treats him as a slave or sells
him, then that thief shall die; so you
shall purge the evil from the midst of
you.
8 “Take heed, in an attack of leprosy, to be very careful to do according to all that the Levitical priests shall
direct you; as I commanded them, so
you shall be careful to do. 9 Remember
what the LORD your God did to
Miriam on the way as you came forth
out of Egypt.
10 “When you make your neighbor
a loan of any sort, you shall not go
into his house to fetch his pledge.
11 You shall stand outside, and the
man to whom you make the loan shall

[t] Or *sodomite*

23.19: Ex 22.26; Lev 25.35-37. **23.21-23:** Num 30.2-16. **24.1:** Mt 5.31; 19.7; Mk 10.4.
24.6, 10-13: Ex 22.26-27. **24.7:** Ex 21.16; 1 Cor 5.13. **24.8-9:** Lev 13-14.

bring the pledge out to you. 12And if
he is a poor man, you shall not sleep
in his pledge; 13 when the sun goes
down, you shall restore to him the
pledge that he may sleep in his cloak
and bless you; and it shall be righteousness to you before the LORD your
God.
14 "You shall not oppress a hired
servant who is poor and needy,
whether he is one of your brethren or
one of the sojourners who are in your
land within your towns; 15 you shall
give him his hire on the day he earns
it, before the sun goes down (for he is
poor, and sets his heart upon it); lest
he cry against you to the LORD, and it
be sin in you.
16 "The fathers shall not be put to
death for the children, nor shall the
children be put to death for the fathers;
every man shall be put to death for his
own sin.
17 "You shall not pervert the justice
due to the sojourner or to the fatherless, or take a widow's garment in
pledge; 18 but you shall remember that
you were a slave in Egypt and the
LORD your God redeemed you from
there; therefore I command you to do
this.
19 "When you reap your harvest in
your field, and have forgotten a sheaf
in the field, you shall not go back to
get it; it shall be for the sojourner, the
fatherless, and the widow; that the
LORD your God may bless you in all
the work of your hands. 20 When you
beat your olive trees, you shall not go
over the boughs again; it shall be for
the sojourner, the fatherless, and the
widow. 21 When you gather the grapes
of your vineyard, you shall not glean
it afterward; it shall be for the sojourner, the fatherless, and the widow.
22 You shall remember that you were
a slave in the land of Egypt; therefore I command you to do this.

25 "If there is a dispute between
men, and they come into court,
and the judges decide between them,
acquitting the innocent and condemning the guilty, 2 then if the guilty man
deserves to be beaten, the judge shall
cause him to lie down and be beaten
in his presence with a number of
stripes in proportion to his offense.
3 Forty stripes may be given him, but
not more; lest, if one should go on to
beat him with more stripes than these,
your brother be degraded in your sight.
4 "You shall not muzzle an ox when
it treads out the grain.
5 "If brothers dwell together, and
one of them dies and has no son, the
wife of the dead shall not be married
outside the family to a stranger; her
husband's brother shall go in to her,
and take her as his wife, and perform
the duty of a husband's brother to her.
6And the first son whom she bears
shall succeed to the name of his
brother who is dead, that his name
may not be blotted out of Israel. 7And
if the man does not wish to take his
brother's wife, then his brother's wife
shall go up to the gate to the elders,
and say, 'My husband's brother refuses
to perpetuate his brother's name in
Israel; he will not perform the duty of
a husband's brother to me.' 8 Then
the elders of his city shall call him, and
speak to him: and if he persists, saying,
'I do not wish to take her,' 9 then his
brother's wife shall go up to him in
the presence of the elders, and pull his
sandal off his foot, and spit in his face;
and she shall answer and say, 'So shall
it be done to the man who does not
build up his brother's house.' 10And
the name of his house[u] shall be called
in Israel, The house of him that had
his sandal pulled off.
11 "When men fight with one another, and the wife of the one draws
near to rescue her husband from the
hand of him who is beating him, and
puts out her hand and seizes him by
the private parts, 12 then you shall cut
off her hand; your eye shall have no
pity.
13 "You shall not have in your bag
two kinds of weights, a large and a
small. 14 You shall not have in your
house two kinds of measures, a large
and a small. 15A full and just weight
you shall have, a full and just measure
you shall have; that your days may be
prolonged in the land which the LORD
your God gives you. 16 For all who do
such things, all who act dishonestly,
are an abomination to the LORD your
God.
17 "Remember what Am'a·lek did

[u] Heb *its name*
24.14-15: Lev 19.13; Jas 5.4. **24.17-18:** Ex 22.21-24; 23.9; Lev 19.33-34. **24.19-22:** Lev 19.9-10; 23.22.
25.4: 1 Cor 9.9; 1 Tim 5.18. **25.5-6:** Mt 22.24; Mk 12.19; Lk 20.28. **25.13-16:** Lev 19.35-36.
25.17-19: Ex 17.14; 1 Sam 15.

to you on the way as you came out of
Egypt, 18 how he attacked you on the
way, when you were faint and weary,
and cut off at your rear all who lagged
behind you; and he did not fear God.
19 Therefore when the LORD your God
has given you rest from all your enemies round about, in the land which
the LORD your God gives you for an
inheritance to possess, you shall blot
out the remembrance of Am'ȧ·lek from
under heaven; you shall not forget.

26 "When you come into the land
which the LORD your God gives
you for an inheritance, and have taken
possession of it, and live in it, 2 you
shall take some of the first of all the
fruit of the ground, which you harvest
from your land that the LORD your
God gives you, and you shall put it in
a basket, and you shall go to the place
which the LORD your God will choose,
to make his name to dwell there. 3 And
you shall go to the priest who is in
office at that time, and say to him, 'I
declare this day to the LORD your God
that I have come into the land which
the LORD swore to our fathers to give
us.' 4 Then the priest shall take the
basket from your hand, and set it down
before the altar of the LORD your God.

5 "And you shall make response before the LORD your God, 'A wandering
Ar·ȧ·mē'ȧn was my father; and he went
down into Egypt and sojourned there,
few in number; and there he became
a nation, great, mighty, and populous.
6 And the Egyptians treated us harshly,
and afflicted us, and laid upon us hard
bondage. 7 Then we cried to the LORD
the God of our fathers, and the LORD
heard our voice, and saw our affliction,
our toil, and our oppression; 8 and the
LORD brought us out of Egypt with a
mighty hand and an outstretched arm,
with great terror, with signs and wonders; 9 and he brought us into this
place and gave us this land, a land
flowing with milk and honey. 10 And
behold, now I bring the first of the
fruit of the ground, which thou, O
LORD, hast given me.' And you shall set
it down before the LORD your God,
and worship before the LORD your
God; 11 and you shall rejoice in all the
good which the LORD your God has
given to you and to your house, you,
and the Levite, and the sojourner who
is among you.

12 "When you have finished paying
all the tithe of your produce in the
third year, which is the year of tithing,
giving it to the Levite, the sojourner,
the fatherless, and the widow, that
they may eat within your towns and
be filled, 13 then you shall say before
the LORD your God, 'I have removed
the sacred portion out of my house,
and moreover I have given it to the
Levite, the sojourner, the fatherless,
and the widow, according to all thy
commandment which thou hast commanded me; I have not transgressed
any of thy commandments, neither
have I forgotten them; 14 I have not
eaten of the tithe while I was mourning,
or removed any of it while I was unclean, or offered any of it to the dead;
I have obeyed the voice of the LORD
my God, I have done according to all
that thou hast commanded me. 15 Look
down from thy holy habitation, from
heaven, and bless thy people Israel
and the ground which thou hast given
us, as thou didst swear to our fathers,
a land flowing with milk and honey.'

16 "This day the LORD your God
commands you to do these statutes
and ordinances; you shall therefore be
careful to do them with all your heart
and with all your soul. 17 You have
declared this day concerning the LORD
that he is your God, and that you will
walk in his ways, and keep his statutes
and his commandments and his ordinances, and will obey his voice; 18 and
the LORD has declared this day concerning you that you are a people for
his own possession, as he has promised
you, and that you are to keep all his
commandments, 19 that he will set you
high above all nations that he has
made, in praise and in fame and in
honor, and that you shall be a people
holy to the LORD your God, as he has
spoken."

27 Now Moses and the elders of
Israel commanded the people,
saying, "Keep all the commandment
which I command you this day. 2 And
on the day you pass over the Jordan to
the land which the LORD your God
gives you, you shall set up large stones,
and plaster them with plaster; 3 and
you shall write upon them all the
words of this law, when you pass over
to enter the land which the LORD your
God gives you, a land flowing with
milk and honey, as the LORD, the God
of your fathers, has promised you.

26.1-11: Ex 22.29; 23.19; 34.26; Num 18.12-13.

4 And when you have passed over the
Jordan, you shall set up these stones,
concerning which I command you this
day, on Mount Ē'bȧl, and you shall
plaster them with plaster. 5 And there
you shall build an altar to the LORD
your God, an altar of stones; you shall
lift up no iron tool upon them. 6 You
shall build an altar to the LORD your
God of unhewn[v] stones; and you shall
offer burnt offerings on it to the LORD
your God; 7 and you shall sacrifice
peace offerings, and shall eat there; and
you shall rejoice before the LORD your
God. 8 And you shall write upon the
stones all the words of this law very
plainly."

9 And Moses and the Levitical
priests said to all Israel, "Keep silence
and hear, O Israel: this day you have
become the people of the LORD your
God. 10 You shall therefore obey the
voice of the LORD your God, keeping
his commandments and his statutes,
which I command you this day."

11 And Moses charged the people
the same day, saying, 12 "When you
have passed over the Jordan, these
shall stand upon Mount Gĕr'i·zim to
bless the people: Simeon, Levi, Judah,
Is'sȧ·chär, Joseph, and Benjamin.
13 And these shall stand upon Mount
Ē'bȧl for the curse: Reuben, Gad,
Ash'ẽr, Zeb'ū·lŭn, Dan, and Naph'tȧ-
lī. 14 And the Levites shall declare to
all the men of Israel with a loud voice:

15 " 'Cursed be the man who makes
a graven or molten image, an abomination to the LORD, a thing made by the
hands of a craftsman, and sets it up in
secret.' And all the people shall answer
and say, 'Amen.'

16 " 'Cursed be he who dishonors
his father or his mother.' And all the
people shall say, 'Amen.'

17 " 'Cursed be he who removes his
neighbor's landmark.' And all the people shall say, 'Amen.'

18 " 'Cursed be he who misleads a
blind man on the road.' And all the
people shall say, 'Amen.'

19 " 'Cursed be he who perverts the
justice due to the sojourner, the fatherless, and the widow.' And all the
people shall say, 'Amen.'

20 " 'Cursed be he who lies with
his father's wife, because he has uncovered her who is his father's.'[w] And
all the people shall say, 'Amen.'

21 " 'Cursed be he who lies with
any kind of beast.' And all the people
shall say, 'Amen.'

22 " 'Cursed be he who lies with
his sister, whether the daughter of his
father or the daughter of his mother.'
And all the people shall say, 'Amen.'

23 " 'Cursed be he who lies with
his mother-in-law.' And all the people
shall say, 'Amen.'

24 " 'Cursed be he who slays his
neighbor in secret.' And all the people
shall say, 'Amen.'

25 " 'Cursed be he who takes a
bribe to slay an innocent person.' And
all the people shall say, 'Amen.'

26 " 'Cursed be he who does not
confirm the words of this law by doing
them.' And all the people shall say,
'Amen.'

28 "And if you obey the voice of
the LORD your God, being careful to do all his commandments which
I command you this day, the LORD
your God will set you high above all
the nations of the earth. 2 And all these
blessings shall come upon you and
overtake you, if you obey the voice of
the LORD your God. 3 Blessed shall you
be in the city, and blessed shall you be
in the field. 4 Blessed shall be the fruit
of your body, and the fruit of your
ground, and the fruit of your beasts,
the increase of your cattle, and the
young of your flock. 5 Blessed shall be
your basket and your kneading-trough.
6 Blessed shall you be when you come
in, and blessed shall you be when you
go out.

7 "The LORD will cause your enemies who rise against you to be defeated before you; they shall come out
against you one way, and flee before
you seven ways. 8 The LORD will command the blessing upon you in your
barns, and in all that you undertake;
and he will bless you in the land which
the LORD your God gives you. 9 The
LORD will establish you as a people
holy to himself, as he has sworn to you,
if you keep the commandments of the

[v] Heb *whole* [w] Heb *uncovered his father's skirt*

27.15: Ex 20.4, 23; 34.17; Lev 19.4; 26.1; Deut 4.16, 23, 25; 5.8; 7.25.
27.16: Ex 20.12; 21.15, 17; Lev 20.9; Deut 5.16; 21.18-21. **27.18:** Lev 19.14.
27.19: Ex 22.21-24; 23.9; Lev 19. 33-34; Deut 24.17-18. **27.20:** Lev 18.8; 20.11; Deut 22.30.
27.21: Ex 22.19; Lev 18.23; 20.15. **27.22:** Lev 18.9; 20.17. **27.23:** Lev 18.17; 20.14. **27.26:** Gal 3.10.
28: Lev 26.3-45.

LORD your God, and walk in his ways.
10 And all the peoples of the earth shall
see that you are called by the name of
the LORD; and they shall be afraid of
you. 11 And the LORD will make you
abound in prosperity, in the fruit of
your body, and in the fruit of your
cattle, and in the fruit of your ground,
within the land which the LORD swore
to your fathers to give you. 12 The
LORD will open to you his good treasury the heavens, to give the rain of
your land in its season and to bless all
the work of your hands; and you shall
lend to many nations, but you shall not
borrow. 13 And the LORD will make
you the head, and not the tail; and you
shall tend upward only, and not downward; if you obey the commandments
of the LORD your God, which I command you this day, being careful to do
them, 14 and if you do not turn aside
from any of the words which I command you this day, to the right hand
or to the left, to go after other gods to
serve them.

15 "But if you will not obey the
voice of the LORD your God or be
careful to do all his commandments
and his statutes which I command you
this day, then all these curses shall
come upon you and overtake you.
16 Cursed shall you be in the city, and
cursed shall you be in the field.
17 Cursed shall be your basket and
your kneading-trough. 18 Cursed shall
be the fruit of your body, and the fruit
of your ground, the increase of your
cattle, and the young of your flock.
19 Cursed shall you be when you come
in, and cursed shall you be when you
go out.

20 "The LORD will send upon you
curses, confusion, and frustration, in
all that you undertake to do, until you
are destroyed and perish quickly, on
account of the evil of your doings, because you have forsaken me. 21 The
LORD will make the pestilence cleave
to you until he has consumed you off
the land which you are entering to take
possession of it. 22 The LORD will smite
you with consumption, and with fever,
inflammation, and fiery heat, and with
drought,[x] and with blasting, and with
mildew; they shall pursue you until
you perish. 23 And the heavens over
your head shall be brass, and the earth
under you shall be iron. 24 The LORD
will make the rain of your land powder
and dust; from heaven it shall come
down upon you until you are destroyed.

25 "The LORD will cause you to be
defeated before your enemies; you
shall go out one way against them, and
flee seven ways before them; and you
shall be a horror to all the kingdoms
of the earth. 26 And your dead body
shall be food for all birds of the air,
and for the beasts of the earth; and
there shall be no one to frighten them
away. 27 The LORD will smite you
with the boils of Egypt, and with the
ulcers and the scurvy and the itch, of
which you cannot be healed. 28 The
LORD will smite you with madness and
blindness and confusion of mind;
29 and you shall grope at noonday, as
the blind grope in darkness, and you
shall not prosper in your ways; and
you shall be only oppressed and robbed
continually, and there shall be no one
to help you. 30 You shall betroth a
wife, and another man shall lie with
her; you shall build a house, and you
shall not dwell in it; you shall plant a
vineyard, and you shall not use the
fruit of it. 31 Your ox shall be slain
before your eyes, and you shall not eat
of it; your ass shall be violently taken
away before your face, and shall not
be restored to you; your sheep shall be
given to your enemies, and there shall
be no one to help you. 32 Your sons
and your daughters shall be given to
another people, while your eyes look
on and fail with longing for them all
the day; and it shall not be in the
power of your hand to prevent it. 33 A
nation which you have not known shall
eat up the fruit of your ground and of
all your labors; and you shall be only
oppressed and crushed continually;
34 so that you shall be driven mad by
the sight which your eyes shall see.
35 The LORD will smite you on the
knees and on the legs with grievous
boils of which you cannot be healed,
from the sole of your foot to the crown
of your head.

36 "The LORD will bring you, and
your king whom you set over you, to a
nation that neither you nor your
fathers have known; and there you shall
serve other gods, of wood and stone.
37 And you shall become a horror, a
proverb, and a byword, among all the
peoples where the LORD will lead you
away. 38 You shall carry much seed into

[x] Another reading is *sword*

the field, and shall gather little in; for
the locust shall consume it. 39 You shall
plant vineyards and dress them, but
you shall neither drink of the wine nor
gather the grapes; for the worm shall
eat them. 40 You shall have olive trees
throughout all your territory, but you
shall not anoint yourself with the oil;
for your olives shall drop off. 41 You
shall beget sons and daughters, but
they shall not be yours; for they shall
go into captivity. 42 All your trees and
the fruit of your ground the locust
shall possess. 43 The sojourner who is
among you shall mount above you
higher and higher; and you shall come
down lower and lower. 44 He shall lend
to you, and you shall not lend to him;
he shall be the head, and you shall be
the tail. 45 All these curses shall come
upon you and pursue you and overtake
you, till you are destroyed, because
you did not obey the voice of the LORD
your God, to keep his commandments
and his statutes which he commanded
you. 46 They shall be upon you as a
sign and a wonder, and upon your
descendants for ever.

47 "Because you did not serve the
LORD your God with joyfulness and
gladness of heart, by reason of the
abundance of all things, 48 therefore
you shall serve your enemies whom
the LORD will send against you, in
hunger and thirst, in nakedness, and
in want of all things; and he will put
a yoke of iron upon your neck, until
he has destroyed you. 49 The LORD
will bring a nation against you from
afar, from the end of the earth, as
swift as the eagle flies, a nation whose
language you do not understand, 50 a
nation of stern countenance, who shall
not regard the person of the old or
show favor to the young, 51 and shall
eat the offspring of your cattle and the
fruit of your ground, until you are
destroyed; who also shall not leave
you grain, wine, or oil, the increase of
your cattle or the young of your flock,
until they have caused you to perish.
52 They shall besiege you in all your
towns, until your high and fortified
walls, in which you trusted, come
down throughout all your land; and
they shall besiege you in all your towns
throughout all your land, which the
LORD your God has given you. 53 And
you shall eat the offspring of your own
body, the flesh of your sons and
daughters, whom the LORD your God
has given you, in the siege and in the
distress with which your enemies shall
distress you. 54 The man who is the
most tender and delicately bred among
you will grudge food to his brother, to
the wife of his bosom, and to the last
of the children who remain to him;
55 so that he will not give to any of
them any of the flesh of his children
whom he is eating, because he has
nothing left him, in the siege and in
the distress with which your enemy
shall distress you in all your towns.
56 The most tender and delicately bred
woman among you, who would not
venture to set the sole of her foot upon
the ground because she is so delicate
and tender, will grudge to the husband
of her bosom, to her son and to her
daughter, 57 her afterbirth that come
out from between her feet and her
children whom she bears, because she
will eat them secretly, for want of all
things, in the siege and in the distress
with which your enemy shall distress
you in your towns.

58 "If you are not careful to do all
the words of this law which are written
in this book, that you may fear this
glorious and awful name, the LORD
your God, 59 then the LORD will bring
on you and your offspring extraordinary afflictions, afflictions severe
and lasting, and sicknesses grievous
and lasting. 60 And he will bring upon
you again all the diseases of Egypt,
which you were afraid of; and they
shall cleave to you. 61 Every sickness
also, and every affliction which is not
recorded in the book of this law, the
LORD will bring upon you, until you
are destroyed. 62 Whereas you were as
the stars of heaven for multitude, you
shall be left few in number; because
you did not obey the voice of the LORD
your God. 63 And as the LORD took
delight in doing you good and multiplying you, so the LORD will take delight in bringing ruin upon you and
destroying you; and you shall be
plucked off the land which you are
entering to take possession of it. 64 And
the LORD will scatter you among all
peoples, from one end of the earth to
the other; and there you shall serve
other gods, of wood and stone, which
neither you nor your fathers have
known. 65 And among these nations
you shall find no ease, and there shall

28.49: 1 Cor 14.21.

be no rest for the sole of your foot; but
the LORD will give you there a trembling heart, and failing eyes, and a
languishing soul; 66 your life shall hang
in doubt before you; night and day
you shall be in dread, and have no
assurance of your life. 67 In the morning you shall say, 'Would it were
evening!' and at evening you shall say,
'Would it were morning!' because of
the dread which your heart shall fear,
and the sights which your eyes shall
see. 68 And the LORD will bring you
back in ships to Egypt, a journey
which I promised that you should never
make again; and there you shall offer
yourselves for sale to your enemies as
male and female slaves, but no man
will buy you."

29[y] These are the words of the
covenant which the LORD commanded Moses to make with the people of Israel in the land of Mō'ab,
besides the covenant which he had
made with them at Hō'reb.

2[z] And Moses summoned all Israel
and said to them: "You have seen all
that the LORD did before your eyes in
the land of Egypt, to Pharaoh and to
all his servants and to all his land,
3 the great trials which your eyes saw,
the signs, and those great wonders;
4 but to this day the LORD has not
given you a mind to understand, or
eyes to see, or ears to hear. 5 I have led
you forty years in the wilderness; your
clothes have not worn out upon you,
and your sandals have not worn off
your feet; 6 you have not eaten bread,
and you have not drunk wine or strong
drink; that you may know that I am
the LORD your God. 7 And when you
came to this place, Sī'hon the king of
Hesh'bȯn and Og the king of Bā'shȧn
came out against us to battle, but we
defeated them; 8 we took their land,
and gave it for an inheritance to the
Reubenites, the Gadites, and the half-
tribe of the Mȧ·nas'sītes. 9 Therefore
be careful to do the words of this covenant, that you may prosper[a] in all that
you do.

10 "You stand this day all of you
before the LORD your God; the heads
of your tribes,[b] your elders, and your
officers, all the men of Israel, 11 your
little ones, your wives, and the sojourner who is in your camp, both he
who hews your wood and he who
draws your water, 12 that you may
enter into the sworn covenant of the
LORD your God, which the LORD your
God makes with you this day; 13 that
he may establish you this day as his
people, and that he may be your God,
as he promised you, and as he swore
to your fathers, to Abraham, to Isaac,
and to Jacob. 14 Nor is it with you
only that I make this sworn covenant,
15 but with him who is not here with
us this day as well as with him who
stands here with us this day before the
LORD our God.

16 "You know how we dwelt in the
land of Egypt, and how we came
through the midst of the nations
through which you passed; 17 and you
have seen their detestable things, their
idols of wood and stone, of silver and
gold, which were among them. 18 Beware lest there be among you a man or
woman or family or tribe, whose heart
turns away this day from the LORD
our God to go and serve the gods of
those nations; lest there be among you
a root bearing poisonous and bitter
fruit, 19 one who, when he hears the
words of this sworn covenant, blesses
himself in his heart, saying, 'I shall be
safe, though I walk in the stubbornness of my heart.' This would lead to
the sweeping away of moist and dry
alike. 20 The LORD would not pardon
him, but rather the anger of the LORD
and his jealousy would smoke against
that man, and the curses written in
this book would settle upon him, and
the LORD would blot out his name
from under heaven. 21 And the LORD
would single him out from all the tribes
of Israel for calamity, in accordance
with all the curses of the covenant
written in this book of the law. 22 And
the generation to come, your children
who rise up after you, and the foreigner
who comes from a far land, would say,
when they see the afflictions of that
land and the sicknesses with which the
LORD has made it sick—23 the whole
land brimstone and salt, and a burnt-
out waste, unsown, and growing nothing, where no grass can sprout, an
overthrow like that of Sod'ȯm and
Gȯ·môr'rȧh, Ad'mȧh and Ze·boi'im,
which the LORD overthrew in his anger
and wrath—24 yea, all the nations
would say, 'Why has the LORD done
thus to this land? What means the heat

[y] Ch 28.69 in Heb [z] Ch 29.1 in Heb [a] Or *deal wisely* [b] Gk Syr: Heb *your heads, your tribes*
29.4: Rom 11.8 **29.18:** Acts 8.23; Heb 12.15.

of this great anger?' 25 Then men
would say, 'It is because they forsook
the covenant of the LORD, the God of
their fathers, which he made with
them when he brought them out of
the land of Egypt, 26 and went and
served other gods and worshiped them,
gods whom they had not known and
whom he had not allotted to them;
27 therefore the anger of the LORD was
kindled against this land, bringing
upon it all the curses written in this
book; 28 and the LORD uprooted them
from their land in anger and fury and
great wrath, and cast them into
another land, as at this day.'

29 "The secret things belong to the
LORD our God; but the things that are
revealed belong to us and to our
children for ever, that we may do all
the words of this law.

30 "And when all these things
come upon you, the blessing and
the curse, which I have set before you,
and you call them to mind among all
the nations where the LORD your God
has driven you, 2 and return to the
LORD your God, you and your children, and obey his voice in all that I
command you this day, with all your
heart and with all your soul; 3 then
the LORD your God will restore your
fortunes, and have compassion upon
you, and he will gather you again from
all the peoples where the LORD your
God has scattered you. 4 If your outcasts are in the uttermost parts of
heaven, from there the LORD your God
will gather you, and from there he will
fetch you; 5 and the LORD your God
will bring you into the land which
your fathers possessed, that you may
possess it; and he will make you more
prosperous and numerous that your
fathers. 6And the LORD your God will
circumcise your heart and the heart of
your offspring, so that you will love
the LORD your God with all your heart
and with all your soul, that you may
live. 7And the LORD your God will put
all these curses upon your foes and
enemies who persecuted you. 8And
you shall again obey the voice of the
LORD, and keep all his commandments
which I command you this day. 9 The
LORD your God will make you abundantly prosperous in all the work of
your hand, in the fruit of your body,
and in the fruit of your cattle, and in
the fruit of your ground; for the LORD
will again take delight in prospering
you, as he took delight in your fathers,
10 if you obey the voice of the LORD
your God, to keep his commandments
and his statutes which are written in
this book of the law, if you turn to the
LORD your God with all your heart
and with all your soul.

11 "For this commandment which
I command you this day is not too
hard for you, neither is it far off. 12 It
is not in heaven, that you should say,
'Who will go up for us to heaven, and
bring it to us, that we may hear it and
do it?' 13 Neither is it beyond the sea,
that you should say, 'Who will go over
the sea for us, and bring it to us, that
we may hear it and do it?' 14 But the
word is very near you; it is in your
mouth and in your heart, so that you
can do it.

15 "See, I have set before you this
day life and good, death and evil. 16 If
you obey the commandments of the
LORD your God[c] which I command
you this day, by loving the LORD your
God, by walking in his ways, and by
keeping his commandments and his
statutes and his ordinances, then you
shall live and multiply, and the LORD
your God will bless you in the land
which you are entering to take possession of it. 17 But if your heart turns
away, and you will not hear, but are
drawn away to worship other gods and
serve them, 18 I declare to you this day,
that you shall perish; you shall not live
long in the land which you are going
over the Jordan to enter and possess.
19 I call heaven and earth to witness
against you this day, that I have set
before you life and death, blessing and
curse; therefore choose life, that you
and your descendants may live, 20 loving the LORD your God, obeying his
voice, and cleaving to him; for that
means life to you and length of days,
that you may dwell in the land which
the LORD swore to your fathers, to
Abraham, to Isaac, and to Jacob, to
give them."

31 So Moses continued to speak
these words to all Israel. 2And he
said to them, "I am a hundred and
twenty years old this day; I am no
longer able to go out and come in. The
LORD has said to me, 'You shall not
go over this Jordan.' 3 The LORD your

[c] Gk: Heb lacks *If you obey the commandments of the* LORD *your God*
30.4: Mt 24.31; Mk 13.27. **30.12-13:** Rom 10.6-7. **30.14:** Rom 10.8.

God himself will go over before you;
he will destroy these nations before
you, so that you shall dispossess them;
and Joshua will go over at your head,
as the LORD has spoken. 4 And the
LORD will do to them as he did to
Si'hon and Og, the kings of the Am'ō-
rites, and to their land, when he destroyed them. 5 And the LORD will give
them over to you, and you shall do to
them according to all the commandment which I have commanded you.
6 Be strong and of good courage, do
not fear or be in dread of them: for it
is the LORD your God who goes with
you; he will not fail you or forsake
you."

7 Then Moses summoned Joshua,
and said to him in the sight of all
Israel, "Be strong and of good courage;
for you shall go with this people into
the land which the LORD has sworn to
their fathers to give them; and you
shall put them in possession of it. 8 It
is the LORD who goes before you; he
will be with you, he will not fail you
or forsake you; do not fear or be dismayed."

9 And Moses wrote this law, and
gave it to the priests the sons of Levi,
who carried the ark of the covenant of
the LORD, and to all the elders of
Israel. 10 And Moses commanded them,
"At the end of every seven years, at
the set time of the year of release, at
the feast of booths, 11 when all Israel
comes to appear before the LORD your
God at the place which he will choose,
you shall read this law before all Israel
in their hearing. 12 Assemble the people, men, women, and little ones, and
the sojourner within your towns, that
they may hear and learn to fear the
LORD your God, and be careful to do
all the words of this law, 13 and that
their children, who have not known it,
may hear and learn to fear the LORD
your God, as long as you live in the
land which you are going over the
Jordan to possess."

14 And the LORD said to Moses,
"Behold, the days approach when you
must die; call Joshua, and present
yourselves in the tent of meeting, that
I may commission him." And Moses
and Joshua went and presented themselves in the tent of meeting. 15 And
the LORD appeared in the tent in a
pillar of cloud; and the pillar of cloud
stood by the door of the tent.

16 And the LORD said to Moses,
"Behold, you are about to sleep with
your fathers; then this people will rise
and play the harlot after the strange
gods of the land, where they go to be
among them, and they will forsake me
and break my covenant which I have
made with them. 17 Then my anger
will be kindled against them in that
day, and I will forsake them and hide
my face from them, and they will be
devoured; and many evils and troubles
will come upon them, so that they will
say in that day, 'Have not these evils
come upon us because our God is not
among us?' 18 And I will surely hide
my face in that day on account of all
the evil which they have done, because
they have turned to other gods. 19 Now
therefore write this song, and teach it
to the people of Israel; put it in their
mouths, that this song may be a
witness for me against the people of
Israel. 20 For when I have brought
them into the land flowing with milk
and honey, which I swore to give to
their fathers, and they have eaten and
are full and grown fat, they will turn
to other gods and serve them, and
despise me and break my covenant.
21 And when many evils and troubles
have come upon them, this song shall
confront them as a witness (for it will
live unforgotten in the mouths of their
descendants); for I know the purposes
which they are already forming, before
I have brought them into the land that
I swore to give." 22 So Moses wrote
this song the same day, and taught it
to the people of Israel.

23 And the LORD commissioned
Joshua the son of Nun and said, "Be
strong and of good courage; for you
shall bring the children of Israel into
the land which I swore to give them:
I will be with you."

24 When Moses had finished writing the words of this law in a book, to
the very end, 25 Moses commanded the
Levites who carried the ark of the
covenant of the LORD, 26 "Take this
book of the law, and put it by the side
of the ark of the covenant of the LORD
your God, that it may be there for a
witness against you. 27 For I know how
rebellious and stubborn you are; behold, while I am yet alive with you,
today you have been rebellious against
the LORD; how much more after my
death! 28 Assemble to me all the elders

31.6, 8: Heb 13.5.

of your tribes, and your officers, that
I may speak these words in their ears
and call heaven and earth to witness
against them. 29 For I know that after
my death you will surely act corruptly,
and turn aside from the way which I
have commanded you; and in the days
to come evil will befall you, because
you will do what is evil in the sight of
the Lord, provoking him to anger
through the work of your hands."
30 Then Moses spoke the words of
this song until they were finished, in
the ears of all the assembly of Israel:

32 "Give ear, O heavens, and I will speak;
and let the earth hear the words of my mouth.
2 May my teaching drop as the rain,
my speech distil as the dew,
as the gentle rain upon the tender grass,
and as the showers upon the herb.
3 For I will proclaim the name of the LORD.
Ascribe greatness to our God!

4 "The Rock, his work is perfect;
for all his ways are justice.
A God of faithfulness and without iniquity,
just and right is he.
5 They have dealt corruptly with him,
they are no longer his children because of their blemish;
they are a perverse and crooked generation.
6 Do you thus requite the LORD,
you foolish and senseless people?
Is not he your father, who created you,
who made you and established you?
7 Remember the days of old,
consider the years of many generations;
ask your father, and he will show you;
your elders, and they will tell you.
8 When the Most High gave to the nations their inheritance,
when he separated the sons of men,
he fixed the bounds of the peoples
according to the number of the sons of God.[d]
9 For the LORD's portion is his people,
Jacob his allotted heritage.

10 "He found him in a desert land,
and in the howling waste of the wilderness;
he encircled him, he cared for him,
he kept him as the apple of his eye.
11 Like an eagle that stirs up its nest,
that flutters over its young,
spreading out its wings, catching them,
bearing them on its pinions,
12 the LORD alone did lead him,
and there was no foreign god with him.
13 He made him ride on the high places of the earth,
and he ate the produce of the field;
and he made him suck honey out of the rock,
and oil out of the flinty rock.
14 Curds from the herd, and milk from the flock,
with fat of lambs and rams,
herds of Bā'shǎn and goats,
with the finest of the wheat—
and of the blood of the grape you drank wine.

15 "But Jesh'ū·rǔn waxed fat, and kicked;
you waxed fat, you grew thick, you became sleek;
then he forsook God who made him,
and scoffed at the Rock of his salvation.
16 They stirred him to jealousy with strange gods;
with abominable practices they provoked him to anger.
17 They sacrificed to demons which were no gods,
to gods they had never known,
to new gods that had come in of late,
whom your fathers had never dreaded.
18 You were unmindful of the Rock that begot[e] you,
and you forgot the God who gave you birth.

19 "The LORD saw it, and spurned them,
because of the provocation of his sons and his daughters.
20 And he said, 'I will hide my face from them,
I will see what their end will be,
for they are a perverse generation,

[d] Compare Gk: Heb *Israel* [e] Or *bore*
32.5: Phil 2.15. 32.17: 1 Cor 10.20.

children in whom is no faithfulness.
21 They have stirred me to jealousy
with what is no god;
they have provoked me with their
idols.
So I will stir them to jealousy with
those who are no people;
I will provoke them with a foolish
nation.
22 For a fire is kindled by my anger,
and it burns to the depths of
Shē'ōl,
devours the earth and its increase,
and sets on fire the foundations
of the mountains.

23 " 'And I will heap evils upon them;
I will spend my arrows upon them;
24 they shall be wasted with hunger,
and devoured with burning heat
and poisonous pestilence;
and I will send the teeth of beasts
against them,
with venom of crawling things
of the dust.
25 In the open the sword shall bereave,
and in the chambers shall be
terror,
destroying both young man and
virgin,
the sucking child with the man
of gray hairs.
26 I would have said, "I will scatter
them afar,
I will make the remembrance of
them cease from among men,"
27 had I not feared provocation by the
enemy,
lest their adversaries should judge
amiss,
lest they should say, "Our hand is
triumphant,
the LORD has not wrought all
this." '

28 "For they are a nation void of
counsel,
and there is no understanding in
them.
29 If they were wise, they would understand this,
they would discern their latter
end!
30 How should one chase a thousand,
and two put ten thousand to
flight,
unless their Rock had sold them,
and the LORD had given them up?
31 For their rock is not as our Rock,
even our enemies themselves being judges.
32 For their vine comes from the vine
of Sod'ŏm,
and from the fields of Gŏ·môr'răh;
their grapes are grapes of poison,
their clusters are bitter;
33 their wine is the poison of serpents,
and the cruel venom of asps.

34 "Is not this laid up in store with
me,
sealed up in my treasuries?
35 Vengeance is mine, and recompense,
for the time when their foot shall
slip;
for the day of their calamity is at
hand,
and their doom comes swiftly.
36 For the LORD will vindicate his
people
and have compassion on his
servants,
when he sees that their power is
gone,
and there is none remaining, bond
or free.
37 Then he will say, 'Where are their
gods,
the rock in which they took refuge,
38 who ate the fat of their sacrifices,
and drank the wine of their drink
offering?
Let them rise up and help you,
let them be your protection!

39 " 'See now that I, even I, am he,
and there is no god beside me;
I kill and I make alive;
I wound and I heal;
and there is none that can deliver
out of my hand.
40 For I lift up my hand to heaven,
and swear, As I live for ever,
41 if I whet my glittering sword,[f]
and my hand takes hold on
judgment,
I will take vengeance on my adversaries,
and will requite those who hate
me.
42 I will make my arrows drunk with
blood,
and my sword shall devour flesh—
with the blood of the slain and the
captives,
from the long-haired heads of the
enemy.'

[f] Heb *the lightning of my sword*

32.21: Rom 10.19; 11.11; 1 Cor 10.22. 32.35: Rom 12.19; Heb 10.30.

43 "Praise his people, O you nations;
for he avenges the blood of his servants,
and takes vengeance on his adversaries,
and makes expiation for the land of his people."[g]

44 Moses came and recited all the
words of this song in the hearing of
the people, he and Joshua[h] the son of
Nun. 45 And when Moses had finished
speaking all these words to all Israel,
46 he said to them, "Lay to heart all
the words which I enjoin upon you
this day, that you may command them
to your children, that they may be
careful to do all the words of this law.
47 For it is no trifle for you, but it is
your life, and thereby you shall live
long in the land which you are going
over the Jordan to possess."

48 And the LORD said to Moses
that very day, 49 "Ascend this mountain of the Ab'ȧ-rim, Mount Nē'bō,
which is in the land of Mō'ab, opposite
Jericho; and view the land of Canaan,
which I give to the people of Israel for
a possession; 50 and die on the mountain which you ascend, and be gathered
to your people, as Aaron your brother
died in Mount Hôr and was gathered
to his people; 51 because you broke
faith with me in the midst of the people
of Israel at the waters of Mer'i-bäth-
kā'desh, in the wilderness of Zin; because you did not revere me as holy
in the midst of the people of Israel.
52 For you shall see the land before
you; but you shall not go there, into
the land which I give to the people of
Israel."

33 This is the blessing with which
Moses the man of God blessed
the children of Israel before his death.
2 He said,
"The LORD came from Sinai,
and dawned from Sē'ir upon us;[i]
he shone forth from Mount Pâr'an,
he came from the ten thousands of holy ones,
with flaming fire[j] at his right hand.
3 Yea, he loved his people;[k]
all those consecrated to him were in his[x] hand;
so they followed[l] in thy steps,
receiving direction from thee,
4 when Moses commanded us a law,
as a possession for the assembly of Jacob.
5 Thus the LORD became king in Jesh'ū·rŭn,
when the heads of the people were gathered,
all the tribes of Israel together.

6 "Let Reuben live, and not die,
nor let his men be few."

7 And this he said of Judah:
"Hear, O LORD, the voice of Judah,
and bring him in to his people.
With thy hands contend[l] for him,
and be a help against his adversaries."

8 And of Levi he said,
"Give to Levi[m] thy Thum'mim,
and thy Ū'rim to thy godly one,
whom thou didst test at Mas'sȧh,
with whom thou didst strive at the waters of Mer'i·bȧh;
9 who said of his father and mother,
'I regard them not';
he disowned his brothers,
and ignored his children.
For they observed thy word,
and kept thy covenant.
10 They shall teach Jacob thy ordinances,
and Israel thy law;
they shall put incense before thee,
and whole burnt offering upon thy altar.
11 Bless, O LORD, his substance,
and accept the work of his hands;
crush the loins of his adversaries,
of those that hate him, that they rise not again."

12 Of Benjamin he said,
"The beloved of the LORD,
he dwells in safety by him;
he encompasses him all the day long,
and makes his dwelling between his shoulders."

13 And of Joseph he said,
"Blessed by the LORD be his land,
with the choicest gifts of heaven above,[n]

[g] Gk Vg: Heb *his land his people* [h] Gk Syr Vg: Heb *Hoshea* Gk Syr Vg: Heb *them*
[i] The meaning of the Hebrew word is uncertain [k] Gk: Heb *peoples* [x] Heb *thy*
[l] Cn: Heb *with his hands he contended* [m] Gk: Heb lacks *Give to Levi*
[n] Two Heb Mss and Tg: Heb *with the dew*
32.43: Rom 15.10; Heb 1.6 (Septuagint); Rev 6.10; 19.2.

and of the deep that couches
beneath,
14 with the choicest fruits of the sun,
and the rich yield of the months,
15 with the finest produce of the
ancient mountains,
and the abundance of the everlasting hills,
16 with the best gifts of the earth and
its fulness,
and the favor of him that dwelt
in the bush.
Let these come upon the head of
Joseph,
and upon the crown of the head
of him that is prince among
his brothers.
17 His firstling bull has majesty,
and his horns are the horns of a
wild ox;
with them he shall push the peoples,
all of them, to the ends of the
earth;
such are the ten thousands of
Ē'phrȧ·im,
and such are the thousands of
Mȧ·nas'sėh."

18 And of Zeb'ū·lŭn he said,
"Rejoice, Zebulun, in your going
out;
and Is'sȧ·chär, in your tents.
19 They shall call peoples to their
mountain;
there they offer right sacrifices;
for they suck the affluence of the
seas
and the hidden treasures of the
sand."

20 And of Gad he said,
"Blessed be he who enlarges Gad!
Gad couches like a lion,
he tears the arm, and the crown
of the head.
21 He chose the best of the land for
himself,
for there a commander's portion
was reserved;
and he came to the heads of the
people,
with Israel he executed the commands
and just decrees of the LORD."

22 And of Dan he said,
"Dan is a lion's whelp,
that leaps forth from Bā'shȧn."

23 And of Naph'tȧ·lī he said,
"O Naphtali, satisfied with favor,
and full of the blessing of the
LORD,
possess the lake and the south."

24 And of Ash'ėr he said,
"Blessed above sons be Asher;
let him be the favorite of his
brothers,
and let him dip his foot in oil.
25 Your bars shall be iron and bronze;
and as your days, so shall your
strength be.

26 "There is none like God, O Jesh'ū-
rŭn,
who rides through the heavens
to your help,
and in his majesty through the
skies.
27 The eternal God is your dwelling
place,
and underneath are the everlasting arms.
And he thrust out the enemy before
you,
and said, Destroy.
28 So Israel dwelt in safety,
the fountain of Jacob alone,
in a land of grain and wine;
yea, his heavens drop down
dew.
29 Happy are you, O Israel! Who is like
you,
a people saved by the LORD,
the shield of your help,
and the sword of your triumph!
Your enemies shall come fawning to
you;
and you shall tread upon their
high places."

34 And Moses went up from the
plains of Mō'ab to Mount
Nē'bō, to the top of Pis'gȧh, which is
opposite Jericho. And the LORD
showed him all the land, Gilead as far
as Dan, 2 all Naph'tȧ·lī, the land of
Ē'phrȧ·im and Mȧ·nas'sėh, all the land
of Judah as far as the Western Sea,
3 the Negeb, and the Plain, that is, the
valley of Jericho the city of palm trees,
as far as Zō'är. 4 And the LORD said to
him, "This is the land of which I
swore to Abraham, to Isaac, and to
Jacob, 'I will give it to your descendants.' I have let you see it with your
eyes, but you shall not go over there."
5 So Moses the servant of the LORD
died there in the land of Mō'ab,
according to the word of the LORD,
6 and he buried him in the valley in
the land of Mō'ab opposite Beth-

pē'ôr; but no man knows the place of
his burial to this day. 7 Moses was a
hundred and twenty years old when
he died; his eye was not dim, nor his
natural force abated. 8And the people
of Israel wept for Moses in the plains
of Mō'ab thirty days; then the days of
weeping and mourning for Moses
were ended.

9 And Joshua the son of Nun was
full of the spirit of wisdom, for Moses
had laid his hands upon him; so the
people of Israel obeyed him, and did
as the LORD had commanded Moses.
10And there has not arisen a prophet
since in Israel like Moses, whom the
LORD knew face to face, 11 none like
him for all the signs and the wonders
which the LORD sent him to do in the
land of Egypt, to Pharaoh and to all
his servants and to all his land, 12 and
for all the mighty power and all the
great and terrible deeds which Moses
wrought in the sight of all Israel.

THE BOOK OF

JOSHUA

1 After the death of Moses the servant of the LORD, the LORD said to
Joshua the son of Nun, Moses' minister, 2 "Moses my servant is dead; now
therefore arise, go over this Jordan,
you and all this people, into the land
which I am giving to them, to the
people of Israel. 3 Every place that the
sole of your foot will tread upon I have
given to you, as I promised to Moses.
4 From the wilderness and this Lebanon as far as the great river, the river
Eū·phrā'tēs, all the land of the Hit'-
tītes to the Great Sea toward the going
down of the sun shall be your territory.
5 No man shall be able to stand before
you all the days of your life; as I was
with Moses, so I will be with you; I
will not fail you or forsake you. 6 Be
strong and of good courage; for you
shall cause this people to inherit the
land which I swore to their fathers to
give them. 7 Only be strong and very
courageous, being careful to do according to all the law which Moses my
servant commanded you; turn not
from it to the right hand or to the left,
that you may have good success
wherever you go. 8 This book of the
law shall not depart out of your mouth,
but you shall meditate on it day and
night, that you may be careful to do
according to all that is written in it;
for then you shall make your way
prosperous, and then you shall have
good success. 9 Have I not commanded you? Be strong and of good
courage; be not frightened, neither be
dismayed; for the LORD your God is
with you wherever you go."

10 Then Joshua commanded the
officers of the people, 11 "Pass through
the camp, and command the people,
'Prepare your provisions; for within
three days you are to pass over this
Jordan, to go in to take possession of
the land which the LORD your God
gives you to possess.' "

12 And to the Reubenites, the
Gadites, and the half-tribe of Ma·nas'-
sėh Joshua said, 13 "Remember the
word which Moses the servant of the
LORD commanded you, saying, 'The
LORD your God is providing you a
place to rest, and will give you this
land.' 14 Your wives, your little ones,
and your cattle shall remain in the land
which Moses gave you beyond the
Jordan; but all the men of valor among
you shall pass over armed before your
brethren and shall help them, 15 until
the LORD gives rest to your brethren
as well as to you, and they also take
possession of the land which the LORD
your God is giving them; then you
shall return to the land of your possession, and shall possess it, the land
which Moses the servant of the LORD
gave you beyond the Jordan toward the
sunrise." 16And they answered Joshua,
"All that you have commanded us we
will do, and wherever you send us we
will go. 17 Just as we obeyed Moses in
all things, so we will obey you; only

34.10: Num 12.6-8. **1.5:** Heb 13.5. **1.12-18:** Josh 22.1-34; Num 32.20-22.

may the LORD your God be with you,
as he was with Moses! 18 Whoever
rebels against your commandment and
disobeys your words, whatever you
command him, shall be put to death.
Only be strong and of good courage."

2 And Joshua the son of Nun sent
two men secretly from Shit'tim as
spies, saying, "Go, view the land,
especially Jericho." And they went,
and came into the house of a harlot
whose name was Rā'hab, and lodged
there. 2 And it was told the king of
Jericho, "Behold, certain men of Israel
have come here tonight to search out
the land." 3 Then the king of Jericho
sent to Rā'hab, saying, "Bring forth
the men that have come to you, who
entered your house; for they have
come to search out all the land." 4 But
the woman had taken the two men and
hidden them; and she said, "True, men
came to me, but I did not know where
they came from; 5 and when the gate
was to be closed, at dark, the men
went out; where the men went I do
not know; pursue them quickly, for
you will overtake them." 6 But she had
brought them up to the roof, and hid
them with the stalks of flax which she
had laid in order on the roof. 7 So the
men pursued after them on the way to
the Jordan as far as the fords; and as
soon as the pursuers had gone out, the
gate was shut.

8 Before they lay down, she came
up to them on the roof, 9 and said to
the men, "I know that the LORD has
given you the land, and that the fear
of you has fallen upon us, and that all
the inhabitants of the land melt away
before you. 10 For we have heard how
the LORD dried up the water of the
Red Sea before you when you came
out of Egypt, and what you did to the
two kings of the Am'o·rites that were
beyond the Jordan, to Sī'hon and Og,
whom you utterly destroyed. 11 And as
soon as we heard it, our hearts melted,
and there was no courage left in any
man, because of you; for the LORD
your God is he who is God in heaven
above and on earth beneath. 12 Now
then, swear to me by the LORD that as
I have dealt kindly with you, you also
will deal kindly with my father's house,
and give me a sure sign, 13 and save
alive my father and mother, my
brothers and sisters, and all who belong to them, and deliver our lives
from death." 14 And the men said to
her, "Our life for yours! If you do not
tell this business of ours, then we will
deal kindly and faithfully with you
when the LORD gives us the land."

15 Then she let them down by a
rope through the window, for her
house was built into the city wall, so
that she dwelt in the wall. 16 And she
said to them, "Go into the hills, lest
the pursuers meet you; and hide yourselves there three days, until the
pursuers have returned; then afterward you may go your way." 17 The
men said to her, "We will be guiltless
with respect to this oath of yours
which you have made us swear. 18 Behold, when we come into the land, you
shall bind this scarlet cord in the
window through which you let us
down; and you shall gather into your
house your father and mother, your
brothers, and all your father's household. 19 If any one goes out of the
doors of your house into the street, his
blood shall be upon his head, and we
shall be guiltless; but if a hand is laid
upon any one who is with you in the
house, his blood shall be on our head.
20 But if you tell this business of ours,
then we shall be guiltless with respect
to your oath which you have made us
swear." 21 And she said, "According
to your words, so be it." Then she
sent them away, and they departed;
and she bound the scarlet cord in the
window.

22 They departed, and went into
the hills, and remained there three
days, until the pursuers returned; for
the pursuers had made search all
along the way and found nothing.
23 Then the two men came down again
from the hills, and passed over and
came to Joshua the son of Nun; and
they told him all that had befallen
them. 24 And they said to Joshua,
"Truly the LORD has given all the
land into our hands; and moreover all
the inhabitants of the land are fainthearted because of us."

3 Early in the morning Joshua rose
and set out from Shit'tim, with all
the people of Israel; and they came to
the Jordan, and lodged there before
they passed over. 2 At the end of three
days the officers went through the
camp 3 and commanded the people,
"When you see the ark of the covenant
of the LORD your God being carried
by the Levitical priests, then you shall
set out from your place and follow it,

4 that you may know the way you shall
go, for you have not passed this way
before. Yet there shall be a space between you and it, a distance of about
two thousand cubits; do not come near
it." 5 And Joshua said to the people,
"Sanctify yourselves; for tomorrow the
LORD will do wonders among you."
6 And Joshua said to the priests, "Take
up the ark of the covenant, and pass on
before the people." And they took up
the ark of the covenant, and went before the people.

7 And the LORD said to Joshua,
"This day I will begin to exalt you in
the sight of all Israel, that they may
know that, as I was with Moses, so I
will be with you. 8 And you shall command the priests who bear the ark of
the covenant, 'When you come to the
brink of the waters of the Jordan, you
shall stand still in the Jordan.' " 9 And
Joshua said to the people of Israel,
"Come hither, and hear the words of
the LORD your God." 10 And Joshua
said, "Hereby you shall know that the
living God is among you, and that he
will without fail drive out from before
you the Canaanites, the Hit'tītes, the
Hī'vītes, the Per'iz·zītes, the Gīr'gȧ-
shites, the Am'ō·rītes, and the Jeb'ū-
sītes. 11 Behold, the ark of the covenant
of the Lord of all the earth is to pass
over before you into the Jordan. 12 Now
therefore take twelve men from the
tribes of Israel, from each tribe a man.
13 And when the soles of the feet of the
priests who bear the ark of the LORD,
the Lord of all the earth, shall rest in
the waters of the Jordan, the waters
of the Jordan shall be stopped from
flowing, and the waters coming
down from above shall stand in one
heap."

14 So, when the people set out from
their tents, to pass over the Jordan
with the priests bearing the ark of the
covenant before the people, 15 and
when those who bore the ark had come
to the Jordan, and the feet of the priests
bearing the ark were dipped in the
brink of the water (the Jordan overflows all its banks throughout the time
of harvest), 16 the waters coming down
from above stood and rose up in a
heap far off, at Adam, the city that is
beside Zar'ē·than, and those flowing
down toward the sea of the Ar'ȧ·bȧh,
the Salt Sea, were wholly cut off; and
the people passed over opposite Jericho. 17 And while all Israel were passing over on dry ground, the priests
who bore the ark of the covenant of
the LORD stood on dry ground in the
midst of the Jordan, until all the nation
finished passing over the Jordan.

4 When all the nation had finished
passing over the Jordan, the LORD
said to Joshua, 2 "Take twelve men
from the people, from each tribe a
man, 3 and command them, 'Take
twelve stones from here out of the
midst of the Jordan, from the very
place where the priests' feet stood, and
carry them over with you, and lay
them down in the place where you
lodge tonight.' " 4 Then Joshua called
the twelve men from the people of
Israel, whom he had appointed, a man
from each tribe; 5 and Joshua said to
them, "Pass on before the ark of the
LORD your God in the midst of the
Jordan, and take up each of you a
stone upon his shoulder, according to
the number of the tribes of the people
of Israel, 6 that this may be a sign
among you, when your children ask
in time to come, 'What do those stones
mean to you?' 7 Then you shall tell
them that the waters of the Jordan
were cut off before the ark of the covenant of the LORD; when it passed over
the Jordan, the waters of the Jordan
were cut off. So these stones shall be
to the people of Israel a memorial for
ever."

8 And the men of Israel did as
Joshua commanded, and took up
twelve stones out of the midst of the
Jordan, according to the number of
the tribes of the people of Israel, as
the LORD told Joshua; and they carried
them over with them to the place
where they lodged, and laid them down
there. 9 And Joshua set up twelve
stones in the midst of the Jordan, in
the place where the feet of the priests
bearing the ark of the covenant had
stood; and they are there to this day.
10 For the priests who bore the ark
stood in the midst of the Jordan, until
everything was finished that the LORD
commanded Joshua to tell the people,
according to all that Moses had commanded Joshua.

The people passed over in haste;
11 and when all the people had finished
passing over, the ark of the LORD and
the priests passed over before the people. 12 The sons of Reuben and the
sons of Gad and the half-tribe of
Mȧ·nas'sėh passed over armed before

the people of Israel, as Moses had
bidden them; 13 about forty thousand
ready armed for war passed over before the LORD for battle, to the plains
of Jericho. 14 On that day the LORD
exalted Joshua in the sight of all Israel;
and they stood in awe of him, as they
had stood in awe of Moses, all the days
of his life.

15 And the LORD said to Joshua,
16 "Command the priests who bear the
ark of the testimony to come up out
of the Jordan." 17 Joshua therefore
commanded the priests, "Come up
out of the Jordan." 18 And when the
priests bearing the ark of the covenant
of the LORD came up from the midst
of the Jordan, and the soles of the
priests' feet were lifted up on dry
ground, the waters of the Jordan returned to their place and overflowed
all its banks, as before.

19 The people came up out of the
Jordan on the tenth day of the first
month, and they encamped in Gil'găl
on the east border of Jericho. 20 And
those twelve stones, which they took
out of the Jordan, Joshua set up in
Gil'găl. 21 And he said to the people of
Israel, "When your children ask their
fathers in time to come, 'What do
these stones mean?' 22 then you shall
let your children know, 'Israel passed
over this Jordan on dry ground.' 23 For
the LORD your God dried up the waters
of the Jordan for you until you passed
over, as the LORD your God did to the
Red Sea, which he dried up for us
until we passed over, 24 so that all the
peoples of the earth may know that the
hand of the LORD is mighty; that
you may fear the LORD your God
forever."

5 When all the kings of the Am'ō-
rites that were beyond the Jordan
to the west, and all the kings of the
Canaanites that were by the sea, heard
that the LORD had dried up the waters
of the Jordan for the people of Israel
until they had crossed over, their heart
melted, and there was no longer any
spirit in them, because of the people
of Israel.

2 At that time the LORD said to
Joshua, "Make flint knives and circumcise the people of Israel again the
second time." 3 So Joshua made flint
knives, and circumcised the people of
Israel at Gib'ē·ăth-hȧ·är'ȧ·loth.[a] 4 And
this is the reason why Joshua circumcised them: all the males of the people
who came out of Egypt, all the men of
war, had died on the way in the wilderness after they had come out of Egypt.
5 Though all the people who came out
had been circumcised, yet all the people that were born on the way in the
wilderness after they had come out of
Egypt had not been circumcised. 6 For
the people of Israel walked forty years
in the wilderness, till all the nation,
the men of war that came forth out of
Egypt, perished, because they did not
hearken to the voice of the LORD; to
them the LORD swore that he would
not let them see the land which the
LORD had sworn to their fathers to
give us, a land flowing with milk and
honey. 7 So it was their children, whom
he raised up in their stead, that Joshua
circumcised; for they were uncircumcised, because they had not been circumcised on the way.

8 When the circumcising of all the
nation was done, they remained in
their places in the camp till they were
healed. 9 And the LORD said to Joshua,
"This day I have rolled away the
reproach of Egypt from you." And so
the name of that place is called Gil'-
găl[b] to this day.

10 While the people of Israel were
encamped in Gil'găl they kept the
passover on the fourteenth day of the
month at evening in the plains of
Jericho. 11 And on the morrow after the
passover, on that very day, they ate of
the produce of the land, unleavened
cakes and parched grain. 12 And the
manna ceased on the morrow, when
they ate of the produce of the land;
and the people of Israel had manna no
more, but ate of the fruit of the land
of Canaan that year.

13 When Joshua was by Jericho, he
lifted up his eyes and looked, and behold, a man stood before him with his
drawn sword in his hand; and Joshua
went to him and said to him, "Are you
for us, or for our adversaries?" 14 And
he said, "No; but as commander of
the army of the LORD I have now
come." And Joshua fell on his face to
the earth, and worshiped, and said to
him, "What does my lord bid his servant?" 15 And the commander of the
LORD's army said to Joshua, "Put off
your shoes from your feet; for the
place where you stand is holy." And
Joshua did so.

[a] That is *the hill of the foreskins* [b] From Heb *galal* to roll

6 Now Jericho was shut up from within and from without because of the people of Israel; none went out, and none came in. 2 And the LORD said to Joshua, "See, I have given into your hand Jericho, with its king and mighty men of valor. 3 You shall march around the city, all the men of war going around the city once. Thus shall you do for six days. 4 And seven priests shall bear seven trumpets of rams' horns before the ark; and on the seventh day you shall march around the city seven times, the priests blowing the trumpets. 5 And when they make a long blast with the ram's horn, as soon as you hear the sound of the trumpet, then all the people shall shout with a great shout; and the wall of the city will fall down flat, and the people shall go up every man straight before him." 6 So Joshua the son of Nun called the priests and said to them, "Take up the ark of the covenant, and let seven priests bear seven trumpets of rams' horns before the ark of the LORD." 7 And he said to the people, "Go forward; march around the city, and let the armed men pass on before the ark of the LORD."

8 And as Joshua had commanded the people, the seven priests bearing the seven trumpets of rams' horns before the LORD went forward, blowing the trumpets, with the ark of the covenant of the LORD following them. 9 And the armed men went before the priests who blew the trumpets, and the rear guard came after the ark, while the trumpets blew continually. 10 But Joshua commanded the people, "You shall not shout or let your voice be heard, neither shall any word go out of your mouth, until the day I bid you shout; then you shall shout." 11 So he caused the ark of the LORD to compass the city, going about it once; and they came into the camp, and spent the night in the camp.

12 Then Joshua rose early in the morning, and the priests took up the ark of the LORD. 13 And the seven priests bearing the seven trumpets of rams' horns before the ark of the LORD passed on, blowing the trumpets continually; and the armed men went before them, and the rear guard came after the ark of the LORD, while the trumpets blew continually. 14 And the second day they marched around the city once, and returned into the camp. So they did for six days.

15 On the seventh day they rose early at the dawn of day, and marched around the city in the same manner seven times: it was only on that day they marched around the city seven times. 16 And at the seventh time, when the priests had blown the trumpets, Joshua said to the people, "Shout; for the LORD has given you the city. 17 And the city and all that is within it shall be devoted to the LORD for destruction; only Rā'hab the harlot and all who are with her in her house shall live, because she hid the messengers that we sent. 18 But you, keep yourselves from the things devoted to destruction, lest when you have devoted them you take any of the devoted things and make the camp of Israel a thing for destruction, and bring trouble upon it. 19 But all silver and gold, and vessels of bronze and iron, are sacred to the LORD; they shall go into the treasury of the LORD." 20 So the people shouted, and the trumpets were blown. As soon as the people heard the sound of the trumpet, the people raised a great shout, and the wall fell down flat, so that the people went up into the city, every man straight before him, and they took the city. 21 Then they utterly destroyed all in the city, both men and women, young and old, oxen, sheep, and asses, with the edge of the sword.

22 And Joshua said to the two men who had spied out the land, "Go into the harlot's house, and bring out from it the woman, and all who belong to her, as you swore to her." 23 So the young men who had been spies went in, and brought out Rā'hab, and her father and mother and brothers and all who belonged to her; and they brought all her kindred, and set them outside the camp of Israel. 24 And they burned the city with fire, and all within it; only the silver and gold, and the vessels of bronze and of iron, they put into the treasury of the house of the LORD. 25 But Rā'hab the harlot, and her father's household, and all who belonged to her, Joshua saved alive; and she dwelt in Israel to this day, because she hid the messengers whom Joshua sent to spy out Jericho.

26 Joshua laid an oath upon them at that time, saying, "Cursed before

6.26: 1 Kings 16.34.

the LORD be the man that rises up and
rebuilds this city, Jericho.

At the cost of his first-born shall
he lay its foundation,
and at the cost of his youngest son
shall he set up its gates."

27 So the LORD was with Joshua;
and his fame was in all the land.

7 But the people of Israel broke
faith in regard to the devoted
things; for Ā′chȧn the son of Cär′mī,
son of Zab′dī, son of Zē′rȧh, of the
tribe of Judah, took some of the devoted things; and the anger of the
LORD burned against the people of
Israel.

2 Joshua sent men from Jericho to
Äi, which is near Beth-ā′vėn, east of
Beth′ėl, and said to them, "Go up and
spy out the land." And the men went
up and spied out Ai. 3And they returned to Joshua, and said to him,
"Let not all the people go up, but let
about two or three thousand men go
up and attack Äi; do not make the
whole people toil up there, for they
are but few." 4 So about three thousand went up there from the people;
and they fled before the men of Äi,
5 and the men of Äi killed about thirty-
six men of them, and chased them before the gate as far as Sheb′ȧ·rim, and
slew them at the descent. And the
hearts of the people melted, and became as water.

6 Then Joshua rent his clothes, and
fell to the earth upon his face before
the ark of the LORD until the evening,
he and the elders of Israel; and they
put dust upon their heads. 7And
Joshua said, "Alas, O Lord GOD, why
hast thou brought this people over the
Jordan at all, to give us into the hands
of the Am′ȯ·rītes, to destroy us?
Would that we had been content to
dwell beyond the Jordan! 8 O Lord,
what can I say, when Israel has turned
their backs before their enemies! 9 For
the Canaanites and all the inhabitants
of the land will hear of it, and will
surround us, and cut off our name
from the earth; and what wilt thou do
for thy great name?"

10 The LORD said to Joshua, "Arise,
why have you thus fallen upon your
face? 11 Israel has sinned; they have
transgressed my covenant which I
commanded them; they have taken
some of the devoted things; they have
stolen, and lied, and put them among
their own stuff. 12 Therefore the people of Israel cannot stand before their
enemies; they turn their backs before
their enemies, because they have become a thing for destruction. I will be
with you no more, unless you destroy
the devoted things from among you.
13 Up, sanctify the people, and say,
'Sanctify yourselves for tomorrow; for
thus says the LORD, God of Israel,
"There are devoted things in the midst
of you, O Israel; you cannot stand
before your enemies, until you take
away the devoted things from among
you." 14 In the morning therefore you
shall be brought near by your tribes;
and the tribe which the LORD takes
shall come near by families; and the
family which the LORD takes shall
come near by households; and the
household which the LORD takes shall
come near man by man. 15And he who
is taken with the devoted things shall
be burned with fire, he and all that he
has, because he has transgressed the
covenant of the LORD, and because he
has done a shameful thing in Israel.' "

16 So Joshua rose early in the morning, and brought Israel near tribe by
tribe, and the tribe of Judah was taken;
17 and he brought near the families of
Judah, and the family of the Zē′rȧ·hītes
was taken; and he brought near the
family of the Zerahites man by man,
and Zab′dī was taken; 18 and he
brought near his household man by
man, and Ā′chȧn the son of Cär′mī,
son of Zab′dī, son of Zē′rȧh of the
tribe of Judah, was taken. 19 Then
Joshua said to Ā′chȧn, "My son, give
glory to the LORD God of Israel, and
render praise to him; and tell me now
what you have done; do not hide it
from me." 20And Ā′chȧn answered
Joshua, "Of a truth I have sinned
against the LORD God of Israel, and
this is what I did: 21 when I saw among
the spoil a beautiful mantle from
Shī′när, and two hundred shekels of
silver, and a bar of gold weighing fifty
shekels, then I coveted them, and took
them; and behold, they are hidden in
the earth inside my tent, with the silver
underneath."

22 So Joshua sent messengers, and
they ran to the tent; and behold, it was
hidden in his tent with the silver underneath. 23And they took them out of
the tent and brought them to Joshua
and all the people of Israel; and they
laid them down before the LORD.
24And Joshua and all Israel with him

took Ā'chăn the son of Zē'răh, and the
silver and the mantle and the bar of
gold, and his sons and daughters, and
his oxen and asses and sheep, and his
tent, and all that he had; and they
brought them up to the Valley of
Ā'chôr. 25 And Joshua said, "Why did
you bring trouble on us? The LORD
brings trouble on you today." And all
Israel stoned him with stones; they
burned them with fire, and stoned
them with stones. 26 And they raised
over him a great heap of stones that
remains to this day; then the LORD
turned from his burning anger. Therefore to this day the name of that place
is called the Valley of Ā'chôr.[c]

8 And the LORD said to Joshua,
"Do not fear or be dismayed; take
all the fighting men with you, and
arise, go up to Ăi; see, I have given
into your hand the king of Ai, and his
people, his city, and his land; 2 and
you shall do to Ăi and its king as you
did to Jericho and its king; only its
spoil and its cattle you shall take as
booty for yourselves; lay an ambush
against the city, behind it."

3 So Joshua arose, and all the fighting men, to go up to Ăi; and Joshua
chose thirty thousand mighty men of
valor, and sent them forth by night.
4 And he commanded them, "Behold,
you shall lie in ambush against the city,
behind it; do not go very far from the
city, but hold yourselves all in readiness; 5 and I, and all the people who
are with me, will approach the city.
And when they come out against us, as
before, we shall flee before them; 6 and
they will come out after us, till we have
drawn them away from the city; for
they will say, 'They are fleeing from
us, as before.' So we will flee from
them; 7 then you shall rise up from the
ambush, and seize the city; for the
LORD your God will give it into your
hand. 8 And when you have taken the
city, you shall set the city on fire,
doing as the LORD has bidden; see, I
have commanded you." 9 So Joshua
sent them forth; and they went to the
place of ambush, and lay between
Beth'ĕl and Ăi, to the west of Ai; but
Joshua spent that night among the
people.

10 And Joshua arose early in the
morning and mustered the people, and
went up, with the elders of Israel, before the people to Ăi. 11 And all the
fighting men who were with him went
up, and drew near before the city, and
encamped on the north side of Ăi, with
a ravine between them and Ai. 12 And
he took about five thousand men, and
set them in ambush between Beth'ĕl
and Ăi, to the west of the city. 13 So
they stationed the forces, the main
encampment which was north of the
city and its rear guard west of the city.
But Joshua spent that night in the
valley. 14 And when the king of Ăi saw
this he and all his people, the men of
the city, made haste and went out
early to the descent[d] toward the Ar'ă-
băh to meet Israel in battle; but he did
not know that there was an ambush
against him behind the city. 15 And
Joshua and all Israel made a pretense
of being beaten before them, and fled
in the direction of the wilderness.
16 So all the people who were in the
city were called together to pursue
them, and as they pursued Joshua they
were drawn away from the city.
17 There was not a man left in Ăi or
Beth'ĕl, who did not go out after
Israel; they left the city open, and
pursued Israel.

18 Then the LORD said to Joshua,
"Stretch out the javelin that is in your
hand toward Ăi; for I will give it into
your hand." And Joshua stretched out
the javelin that was in his hand toward
the city. 19 And the ambush rose
quickly out of their place, and as soon
as he had stretched out his hand, they
ran and entered the city and took it;
and they made haste to set the city on
fire. 20 So when the men of Ăi looked
back, behold, the smoke of the city
went up to heaven; and they had no
power to flee this way or that, for the
people that fled to the wilderness
turned back upon the pursuers. 21 And
when Joshua and all Israel saw that
the ambush had taken the city, and
that the smoke of the city went up,
then they turned back and smote the
men of Ăi. 22 And the others came forth
from the city against them; so they
were in the midst of Israel, some on
this side, and some on that side; and
Israel smote them, until there was left
none that survived or escaped. 23 But
the king of Ăi they took alive, and
brought him to Joshua.

24 When Israel had finished slaughtering all the inhabitants of Ăi in the
open wilderness where they pursued

[c] That is *Trouble* [d] Cn: Heb *appointed time*

them and all of them to the very last
had fallen by the edge of the sword, all
Israel returned to Ai, and smote it
with the edge of the sword. 25 And all
who fell that day, both men and
women, were twelve thousand, all the
people of Äi. 26 For Joshua did not
draw back his hand, with which he
stretched out the javelin, until he had
utterly destroyed all the inhabitants
of Äi. 27 Only the cattle and the spoil
of that city Israel took as their booty,
according to the word of the LORD
which he commanded Joshua. 28 So
Joshua burned Äi, and made it for ever
a heap of ruins, as it is to this day.
29 And he hanged the king of Äi on a
tree until evening; and at the going
down of the sun Joshua commanded,
and they took his body down from the
tree, and cast it at the entrance of the
gate of the city, and raised over it a
great heap of stones, which stands
there to this day.

30 Then Joshua built an altar in
Mount Ē'băl to the LORD, the God of
Israel, 31 as Moses the servant of the
LORD had commanded the people of
Israel, as it is written in the book of
the law of Moses, "an altar of unhewn
stones, upon which no man has lifted
an iron tool"; and they offered on it
burnt offerings to the LORD, and
sacrificed peace offerings. 32 And there,
in the presence of the people of Israel,
he wrote upon the stones a copy of
the law of Moses, which he had written.
33 And all Israel, sojourner as well as
homeborn, with their elders and
officers and their judges, stood on
opposite sides of the ark before the
Levitical priests who carried the ark of
the covenant of the LORD, half of them
in front of Mount Gĕr'i·zim and half
of them in front of Mount Ē'băl, as
Moses the servant of the LORD had
commanded at the first, that they
should bless the people of Israel. 34 And
afterward he read all the words of the
law, the blessing and the curse, according to all that is written in the book of
the law. 35 There was not a word of
all that Moses commanded which
Joshua did not read before all the
assembly of Israel, and the women,
and the little ones, and the sojourners
who lived among them.

9 When all the kings who were beyond the Jordan in the hill country
and in the lowland all along the coast
of the Great Sea toward Lebanon, the
Hit'tītes, the Am'ŏ·rītes, the Canaanites, the Per'iz·zītes, the Hī'vītes, and
the Jeb'ū·sītes, heard of this, 2 they
gathered together with one accord to
fight Joshua and Israel.

3 But when the inhabitants of Gib'-
ē·ŏn heard what Joshua had done to
Jericho and to Äi, 4 they on their part
acted with cunning, and went and
made ready provisions, and took worn-
out sacks upon their asses, and wineskins, worn-out and torn and mended,
5 with worn-out, patched sandals on
their feet, and worn-out clothes; and
all their provisions were dry and
moldy. 6 And they went to Joshua in
the camp at Gil'găl, and said to him
and to the men of Israel, "We have
come from a far country; so now make
a covenant with us." 7 But the men of
Israel said to the Hī'vītes, "Perhaps
you live among us; then how can we
make a covenant with you?" 8 They
said to Joshua, "We are your servants."
And Joshua said to them, "Who are
you? And where do you come from?"
9 They said to him, "From a very far
country your servants have come, because of the name of the LORD your
God; for we have heard a report of
him, and all that he did in Egypt,
10 and all that he did to the two kings
of the Am'ŏ·rītes who were beyond the
Jordan, Sī'hon the king of Hesh'bŏn,
and Og king of Bā'shăn, who dwelt in
Ash'tă·roth. 11 And our elders and all
the inhabitants of our country said to
us, 'Take provisions in your hand for
the journey, and go to meet them, and
say to them, "We are your servants;
come now, make a covenant with us."'
12 Here is our bread; it was still warm
when we took it from our houses as
our food for the journey, on the day
we set forth to come to you, but now,
behold, it is dry and moldy; 13 these
wineskins were new when we filled
them, and behold, they are burst; and
these garments and shoes of ours are
worn out from the very long journey."
14 So the men partook of their provisions, and did not ask direction from
the LORD. 15 And Joshua made peace
with them, and made a covenant with
them, to let them live; and the leaders
of the congregation swore to them.

16 At the end of three days after
they had made a covenant with them,
they heard that they were their neigh-

8.30-35: Deut 27.2-8.

bors, and that they dwelt among them.
17 And the people of Israel set out and
reached their cities on the third day.
Now their cities were Gib'ē·ȯn,
Chē·phī'rȧh, Bė-ēr'ȯth, and Kĭr'i·ath-
jē'ȧ·rim. 18 But the people of Israel
did not kill them, because the leaders
of the congregation had sworn to them
by the LORD, the God of Israel. Then
all the congregation murmured against
the leaders. 19 But all the leaders said
to all the congregation, "We have
sworn to them by the LORD, the God
of Israel, and now we may not touch
them. 20 This we will do to them, and
let them live, lest wrath be upon us,
because of the oath which we swore
to them." 21 And the leaders said to
them, "Let them live." So they became hewers of wood and drawers of
water for all the congregation, as the
leaders had said of them.

22 Joshua summoned them, and he
said to them, "Why did you deceive
us, saying, 'We are very far from you,'
when you dwell among us? 23 Now
therefore you are cursed, and some of
you shall always be slaves, hewers of
wood and drawers of water for the
house of my God." 24 They answered
Joshua, "Because it was told to your
servants for a certainty that the LORD
your God had commanded his servant
Moses to give you all the land, and to
destroy all the inhabitants of the land
from before you; so we feared greatly
for our lives because of you, and did
this thing. 25 And now, behold, we are
in your hand: do as it seems good and
right in your sight to do to us." 26 So
he did to them, and delivered them
out of the hand of the people of Israel;
and they did not kill them. 27 But
Joshua made them that day hewers of
wood and drawers of water for the
congregation and for the altar of the
LORD, to continue to this day, in the
place which he should choose.

10 When Ȧ·dō'ni-zē'dek king of
Jerusalem heard how Joshua had
taken Āi, and had utterly destroyed it,
doing to Ai and its king as he had done
to Jericho and its king, and how the
inhabitants of Gib'ē·ȯn had made
peace with Israel and were among
them, 2 he[x] feared greatly, because
Gib'ē·ȯn was a great city, like one of
the royal cities, and because it was
greater then Āi, and all its men were
mighty. 3 So Ȧ·dō'ni-zē'dek king of
Jerusalem sent to Hō'ham king of
Hē'brȯn, to Pī'rȧm king of Jär'muth,
to Jȧ·phī'ȧ king of Lā'chish, and to
Dē'bir king of Eg'lon, saying, 4 "Come
up to me, and help me, and let us smite
Gib'ē·ȯn; for it has made peace with
Joshua and with the people of Israel."
5 Then the five kings of the Am'ȯ·rītes,
the king of Jerusalem, the king of
Hē'brȯn, the king of Jär'muth, the
king of Lā'chish, and the king of
Eg'lon, gathered their forces, and
went up with all their armies and
encamped against Gib'ē·ȯn, and made
war against it.

6 And the men of Gib'ē·ȯn sent to
Joshua at the camp in Gil'gȧl, saying,
"Do not relax your hand from your
servants; come up to us quickly, and
save us, and help us; for all the kings
of the Am'ȯ·rītes that dwell in the hill
country are gathered against us." 7 So
Joshua went up from Gil'gȧl, he and
all the people of war with him, and all
the mighty men of valor. 8 And the
LORD said to Joshua, "Do not fear
them, for I have given them into your
hands; there shall not a man of them
stand before you." 9 So Joshua came
upon them suddenly, having marched
up all night from Gil'gȧl. 10 And the
LORD threw them into a panic before
Israel, who slew them with a great
slaughter at Gib'ē·ȯn, and chased them
by the way of the ascent of Beth-hō'-
ron, and smote them as far as Ȧ·zē'kȧh
and Mak·kē'dȧh. 11 And as they fled
before Israel, while they were going
down the ascent of Beth-hō'ron, the
LORD threw down great stones from
heaven upon them as far as Ȧ·zē'kȧh,
and they died; there were more who
died because of the hailstones than
the men of Israel killed with the sword.

12 Then spoke Joshua to the LORD
in the day when the LORD gave the
Am'ȯ·rītes over to the men of Israel;
and he said in the sight of Israel,

"Sun, stand thou still at Gib'ē·ȯn,
and thou Moon in the valley of
Āi'jȧ·lon."
13 And the sun stood still, and the
moon stayed,
until the nation took vengeance on
their enemies.

Is this not written in the Book of
Jash'ȧr? The sun stayed in the midst
of heaven, and did not hasten to go
down for about a whole day. 14 There
has been no day like it before or since,

x Heb *they*

when the LORD hearkened to the voice
of a man; for the LORD fought for
Israel.
15 Then Joshua returned, and all
Israel with him, to the camp at Gil'găl.
16 These five kings fled, and hid
themselves in the cave at Mak·kē'dȧh.
17And it was told Joshua, "The five
kings have been found, hidden in the
cave at Mak·kē'dȧh." 18And Joshua
said, "Roll great stones against the
mouth of the cave, and set men by it
to guard them; 19 but do not stay there
yourselves, pursue your enemies, fall
upon their rear, do not let them enter
their cities; for the LORD your God has
given them into your hand." 20 When
Joshua and the men of Israel had
finished slaying them with a very great
slaughter, until they were wiped out,
and when the remnant which remained of them had entered into the
fortified cities, 21 all the people returned safe to Joshua in the camp at
Mak·kē'dȧh; not a man moved his
tongue against any of the people of
Israel.
22 Then Joshua said, "Open the
mouth of the cave, and bring those
five kings out to me from the cave."
23And they did so, and brought those
five kings out to him from the cave,
the king of Jerusalem, the king of
Hē'brȯn, the king of Jär'muth, the
king of Lā'chish, and the king of
Eg'lon. 24And when they brought those
kings out to Joshua, Joshua summoned
all the men of Israel, and said to the
chiefs of the men of war who had gone
with him, "Come near, put your feet
upon the necks of these kings." Then
they came near, and put their feet on
their necks. 25And Joshua said to
them, "Do not be afraid or dismayed;
be strong and of good courage; for thus
the LORD will do to all your enemies
against whom you fight." 26And afterward Joshua smote them and put
them to death, and he hung them on
five trees. And they hung upon the
trees until evening; 27 but at the time
of the going down of the sun, Joshua
commanded, and they took them down
from the trees, and threw them into
the cave where they had hidden themselves, and they set great stones against
the mouth of the cave, which remain
to this very day.
28 And Joshua took Mak·kē'dȧh on
that day, and smote it and its king with
the edge of the sword; he utterly
destroyed every person in it, he left
none remaining; and he did to the
king of Makkedah as he had done to
the king of Jericho.
29 Then Joshua passed on from
Mak·kē'dȧh, and all Israel with him,
to Lib'nȧh, and fought against Lib-
nah; 30 and the LORD gave it also and
its king into the hand of Israel; and he
smote it with the edge of the sword,
and every person in it; he left none
remaining in it; and he did to its king
as he had done to the king of Jericho.
31 And Joshua passed on from
Lib'nȧh, and all Israel with him, to
Lā'chish, and laid siege to it, and
assaulted it: 32 and the LORD gave
Lā'chish into the hand of Israel, and
he took it on the second day, and
smote it with the edge of the sword,
and every person in it, as he had
done to Lib'nȧh.
33 Then Hō'ram king of Gē'zėr
came up to help Lā'chish; and Joshua
smote him and his people, until he left
none remaining.
34 And Joshua passed on with all
Israel from Lā'chish to Eg'lon; and
they laid siege to it, and assaulted it;
35 and they took it on that day, and
smote it with the edge of the sword;
and every person in it he utterly destroyed that day, as he had done to
Lā'chish.
36 Then Joshua went up with all
Israel from Eg'lon to Hē'brȯn; and
they assaulted it, 37 and took it, and
smote it with the edge of the sword,
and its king and its towns, and every
person in it; he left none remaining,
as he had done to Eg'lon, and utterly
destroyed it with every person in it.
38 Then Joshua, with all Israel,
turned back to Dē'bir and assaulted it,
39 and he took it with its king and all
its towns; and they smote them with
the edge of the sword, and utterly
destroyed every person in it; he left
none remaining; as he had done to
Hē'brȯn and to Lib'nȧh and its king,
so he did to Dē'bir and to its king.
40 So Joshua defeated the whole
land, the hill country and the Negeb
and the lowland and the slopes, and
all their kings; he left none remaining,
but utterly destroyed all that breathed,
as the LORD God of Israel commanded.
41And Joshua defeated them from
Kā'desh-bär'nē·ȧ to Gā'zȧ, and all the
country of Gō'shėn, as far as Gib'ē·ȯn.
42And Joshua took all these kings and

their land at one time, because the
LORD God of Israel fought for Israel.
43 Then Joshua returned, and all Israel
with him, to the camp at Gil'găl.

11 When Jā'bin king of Hā'zôr
heard of this, he sent to Jō'bab
king of Mā'don, and to the king of
Shim'rŏn, and to the king of Ach'-
shaph, 2 and to the kings who were in
the northern hill country, and in the
Ar'ă·băh south of Chin'nĕ·roth, and
in the lowland, and in Nā'photh-dôr
on the west, 3 to the Canaanites in the
east and the west, the Am'ŏ·rītes, the
Hit'tītes, the Per'iz·zītes, and the Jeb'-
ū·sītes in the hill country, and the
Hī'vītes under Hēr'mŏn in the land of
Miz'păh. 4 And they came out, with all
their troops, a great host, in number
like the sand that is upon the seashore,
with very many horses and chariots.
5 And all these kings joined their forces
and came and encamped together at
the waters of Mē'rom, to fight with
Israel.

6 And the LORD said to Joshua,
"Do not be afraid of them, for tomorrow at this time I will give over all
of them, slain, to Israel; you shall hamstring their horses, and burn their
chariots with fire." 7 So Joshua came
suddenly upon them with all his people of war, by the waters of Mē'rom,
and fell upon them. 8 And the LORD
gave them into the hand of Israel, who
smote them and chased them as far as
Great Sī'don and Mis'rē·photh-mā'im,
and eastward as far as the valley of
Miz'peh; and they smote them, until
they left none remaining. 9 And Joshua
did to them as the LORD bade him; he
hamstrung their horses, and burned
their chariots with fire.

10 And Joshua turned back at that
time, and took Hā'zôr, and smote its
king with the sword; for Hazor formerly was the head of all those kingdoms. 11 And they put to the sword all
who were in it, utterly destroying them;
there was none left that breathed, and
he burned Hā'zôr with fire. 12 And all
the cities of those kings, and all their
kings, Joshua took, and smote them
with the edge of the sword, utterly
destroying them, as Moses the servant
of the LORD had commanded. 13 But
none of the cities that stood on mounds
did Israel burn, except Hā'zôr only;
that Joshua burned. 14 And all the spoil
of these cities and the cattle, the people
of Israel took for their booty; but every
man they smote with the edge of the
sword, until they had destroyed them,
and they did not leave any that
breathed. 15 As the LORD had commanded Moses his servant, so Moses
commanded Joshua, and so Joshua
did; he left nothing undone of all that
the LORD had commanded Moses.

16 So Joshua took all that land, the
hill country and all the Negeb and all
the land of Gō'shĕn and the lowland
and the Ar'ă·băh and the hill country
of Israel and its lowland 17 from Mount
Hā'lak, that rises toward Sē'ir, as far
as Bā'ăl-gad in the valley of Lebanon
below Mount Hēr'mŏn. And he took
all their kings, and smote them, and
put them to death. 18 Joshua made
war a long time with all those kings.
19 There was not a city that made
peace with the people of Israel, except
the Hī'vītes, the inhabitants of Gib'ē-
ŏn; they took all in battle. 20 For it was
the LORD's doing to harden their
hearts that they should come against
Israel in battle, in order that they
should be utterly destroyed, and should
receive no mercy but be exterminated,
as the LORD commanded Moses.

21 And Joshua came at that time,
and wiped out the An'ă·kim from the
hill country, from Hē'brŏn, from Dē'-
bir, from Ā'nab, and from all the hill
country of Judah, and from all the hill
country of Israel; Joshua utterly destroyed them with their cities. 22 There
was none of the An'ă·kim left in the
land of the people of Israel; only in
Gā'ză, in Gath, and in Ash'dod, did
some remain. 23 So Joshua took the
whole land, according to all that the
LORD had spoken to Moses; and
Joshua gave it for an inheritance to
Israel according to their tribal allotments. And the land had rest from war.

12 Now these are the kings of the
land, whom the people of Israel
defeated, and took possession of their
land beyond the Jordan toward the
sunrising, from the valley of the
Ār'non to Mount Hēr'mŏn, with all
the Ar'ă·băh eastward: 2 Sī'hon king of
the Am'ŏ·rītes who dwelt at Hesh'bŏn,
and ruled from Ā·rō'ĕr, which is on
the edge of the valley of the Ār'non,
and from the middle of the valley as
far as the river Jab'bŏk, the boundary
of the Am'mŏ·nītes, that is, half of
Gilead, 3 and the Ar'ă·băh to the Sea
of Chin'nĕ·roth eastward, and in the
direction of Beth-jesh'i·moth, to the

sea of the Arabah, the Salt Sea, southward to the foot of the slopes of Pis'-
gȧh; 4 and Og[e] king of Bā'shȧn, one of
the remnant of the Reph'ȧ·im, who
dwelt at Ash'tȧ·roth and at Ed'rē-ī
5 and ruled over Mount Hẽr'mȯn and
Sal'ė·cȧh and all Bā'shȧn to the boundary of the Gesh'ū·rītes and the Mā-
ac'ȧ·thītes, and over half of Gilead to
the boundary of Sī'hon king of Hesh'-
bȯn. 6 Moses, the servant of the LORD,
and the people of Israel defeated them;
and Moses the servant of the LORD
gave their land for a possession to the
Reubenites and the Gadites and the
half-tribe of Mȧ·nas'sėh.

7 And these are the kings of the
land whom Joshua and the people of
Israel defeated on the west side of the
Jordan, from Bā'ȧl-gad in the valley of
Lebanon to Mount Hā'lak, that rises
toward Sē'ir (and Joshua gave their
land to the tribes of Israel as a possession according to their allotments, 8 in
the hill country, in the lowland, in the
Ar'ȧ·bȧh, in the slopes, in the wilderness, and in the Negeb, the land of the
Hit'tītes, the Am'ȯ·rītes, the Canaanites, the Per'iz·zītes, the Hī'vītes, and
the Jeb'ū·sītes): 9 the king of Jericho,
one; the king of Ä'i, which is beside
Beth'ėl, one; 10 the king of Jerusalem,
one; the king of Hē'brȯn, one; 11 the
king of Jär'muth, one; the king of
Lā'chish, one; 12 the king of Eg'lon,
one; the king of Gē'zėr, one; 13 the
king of Dē'bir, one; the king of Gē'dėr,
one; 14 the king of Hôr'mȧh, one; the
king of Âr'ȧd, one; 15 the king of
Lib'nȧh, one; the king of Ȧ·dul'lȧm,
one; 16 the king of Mak·kē'dȧh, one;
the king of Beth'ėl, one; 17 the king of
Tap'pū-ȧh, one; the king of Hē'phėr,
one; 18 the king of Ā'phek, one; the
king of La·shâr'on, one; 19 the king of
Mā'don, one; the king of Hā'zôr, one;
20 the king of Shim'ron-mē'ron, one;
the king of Ach'shaph, one; 21 the king
of Tā'ȧ·nach, one; the king of Mė-
gid'dō, one; 22 the king of Kē'desh,
one; the king of Jok'nē-am in Cär'mėl,
one; 23 the king of Dôr in Nā'phath-
dôr, one; the king of Goi'im in
Galilee,[f] one; 24 the king of Tīr'zȧh;
one: in all, thirty-one kings.

13 Now Joshua was old and advanced in years; and the LORD
said to him, "You are old and advanced
in years, and there remains yet very
much land to be possessed. 2 This is
the land that yet remains: all the
regions of the Philistines, and all those
of the Gesh'ū·rītes 3 (from the Shī'hôr,
which is east of Egypt, northward to
the boundary of Ek'rȯn, it is reckoned
as Canaanite; there are five rulers of
the Philistines, those of Gā'zȧ, Ash'-
dod, Ash'kė·lon, Gath, and Ek'rȯn),
and those of the Av'vim, 4 in the south,
all the land of the Canaanites, and
Me-âr'ȧh which belongs to the Sī·dō'-
ni·ȧnṡ, to Ā'phek, to the boundary of
the Am'ȯ·rītes, 5 and the land of the
Geb'ȧ·lītes, and all Lebanon, toward
the sunrising, from Bā'ȧl-gad below
Mount Hẽr'mȯn to the entrance of
Hā'math, 6 all the inhabitants of the
hill country from Lebanon to Mis'rē-
photh-mā'im, even all the Sī·dō'ni·ȧnṡ.
I will myself drive them out from before the people of Israel; only allot the
land to Israel for an inheritance, as I
have commanded you. 7 Now therefore divide this land for an inheritance
to the nine tribes and half the tribe of
Mȧ·nas'sėh."

8 With the other half of the tribe
of Mȧ·nas'sėh[g] the Reubenites and the
Gadites received their inheritance,
which Moses gave them, beyond the
Jordan eastward, as Moses the servant
of the LORD gave them: 9 from Ȧ·rō'ėr,
which is on the edge of the valley of
the Är'non, and the city that is in the
middle of the valley, and all the tableland of Med'ė·bȧ as far as Dī'bon;
10 and all the cities of Sī'hon king of
the Am'ȯ·rītes, who reigned in Hesh'-
bȯn, as far as the boundary of the
Am'mȯ·nītes; 11 and Gilead, and the
region of the Gesh'ū·rītes and Mā-
ac'ȧ·thītes, and all Mount Hẽr'mȯn,
and all Bā'shȧn to Sal'ė·cȧh; 12 all the
kingdom of Og in Bā'shȧn, who
reigned in Ash'tȧ·roth and in Ed'rē-ī
(he alone was left of the remnant of the
Reph'ȧ·im); these Moses had defeated
and driven out. 13 Yet the people of
Israel did not drive out the Gesh'ū-
rītes or the Mā-ac'ȧ·thītes; but Gē'shūr
and Mā'ȧ·cath dwell in the midst of
Israel to this day.

14 To the tribe of Levi alone Moses gave no inheritance; the offerings by fire to the LORD God of Israel
are their inheritance, as he said to
him.

15 And Moses gave an inheritance
to the tribe of the Reubenites according to their families. 16 So their terri-

[e] Gk: Heb *the boundary of Og* [f] Gk: Heb *Gilgal* [g] Cn: Heb *With it*

tory was from Ȧ·rō'ėr, which is on the
edge of the valley of the Ăr'non, and
the city that is in the middle of the
valley, and all the tableland by Med'ė-
bȧ; 17 with Hesh'bȯn, and all its cities
that are in the tableland; Dī'bon, and
Bā'moth-bā'ȧl, and Beth-bā'ȧl-mē'on,
18 and Jā'haz, and Ked'ē·moth, and
Meph'ȧ-ath, 19 and Kĭr·ĭ·ȧ·thā'im, and
Sib'mȧh, and Zē'reth-shā'hȧr on the
hill of the valley, 20 and Beth-pē'ôr,
and the slopes of Pis'gȧh, and Beth-
jesh'i·moth, 21 that is, all the cities of
the tableland, and all the kingdom of
Sī'hon king of the Am'ȯ·rites, who
reigned in Hesh'bȯn, whom Moses defeated with the leaders of Mid'i·ȧn,
Ē'vī and Rē'kem and Zūr and Hūr and
Rē'bȧ, the princes of Sihon, who
dwelt in the land. 22 Balaam also, the
son of Bē'ôr, the soothsayer, the people
of Israel killed with the sword among
the rest of their slain. 23 And the border
of the people of Reuben was the
Jordan as a boundary. This was the
inheritance of the Reubenites, according to their families with their cities
and villages.

24 And Moses gave an inheritance
also to the tribe of the Gadites, according to their families. 25 Their territory
was Jā'zėr, and all the cities of Gilead,
and half the land of the Am'mȯ·nītes,
to Ȧ·rō'ėr, which is east of Rab'bȧh,
26 and from Hesh'bȯn to Rā'mȧth-
miz'peh and Bet'ō·nim, and from Mā-
hȧ·nā'im to the territory of Dē'bir,[h]
27 and in the valley Beth-hā'ram,
Beth-nim'rȧh, Suc'coth, and Zā'phon,
the rest of the kingdom of Sī'hon king
of Hesh'bȯn, having the Jordan as a
boundary, to the lower end of the Sea
of Chin'nė·reth, eastward beyond the
Jordan. 28 This is the inheritance of
the Gadites according to their families,
with their cities and villages.

29 And Moses gave an inheritance
to the half-tribe of Mȧ·nas'sėh; it was
allotted to the half-tribe of the Mȧ-
nas'sītes according to their families.
30 Their region extended from Mā·hȧ-
nā'im, through all Bā'shȧn, the whole
kingdom of Og king of Bashan, and
all the towns of Jā'ir, which are in
Bashan, sixty cities, 31 and half Gilead,
and Ash'tȧ·roth, and Ed'rē-ī, the cities
of the kingdom of Og in Bā'shȧn; these
were allotted to the people of Mā'chir
the son of Mȧ·nas'sėh for the half of
the Mā'chi·rītes according to their
families.

32 These are the inheritances which
Moses distributed in the plains of
Mō'ab, beyond the Jordan east of
Jericho. 33 But to the tribe of Levi
Moses gave no inheritance; the LORD
God of Israel is their inheritance, as
he said to them.

14 And these are the inheritances
which the people of Israel received in the land of Canaan, which
El·ė·ā'zȧr the priest, and Joshua the
son of Nun, and the heads of the
fathers' houses of the tribes of the people of Israel distributed to them.
2 Their inheritance was by lot, as the
LORD had commanded Moses for the
nine and one-half tribes. 3 For Moses
had given an inheritance to the two
and one-half tribes beyond the Jordan;
but to the Levites he gave no inheritance among them. 4 For the people of
Joseph were two tribes, Mȧ·nas'sėh
and Ē'phrȧ·im; and no portion was
given to the Levites in the land, but
only cities to dwell in, with their
pasture lands for their cattle and their
substance. 5 The people of Israel did
as the LORD commanded Moses; they
allotted the land.

6 Then the people of Judah came
to Joshua at Gil'gȧl; and Caleb the son
of Jė·phün'nėh the Ken'iz·zīte said to
him, "You know what the LORD said
to Moses the man of God in Kā'desh-
bär'nē·ȧ concerning you and me. 7 I
was forty years old when Moses the
servant of the LORD sent me from
Kā'desh-bär'nē·ȧ to spy out the land;
and I brought him word again as it
was in my heart. 8 But my brethren
who went up with me made the heart
of the people melt; yet I wholly followed the LORD my God. 9 And Moses
swore on that day, saying, 'Surely the
land on which your foot has trodden
shall be an inheritance for you and
your children for ever, because you
have wholly followed the LORD my
God.' 10 And now, behold, the LORD
has kept me alive, as he said, these
forty-five years since the time that the
LORD spoke this word to Moses, while
Israel walked in the wilderness; and
now, lo, I am this day eighty-five years
old. 11 I am still as strong to this day as
I was in the day that Moses sent me; my
strength now is as my strength was

[h] Gk Syr Vg: Heb *Lidebir*
14.6-15: Num 13.6, 30; 14.6, 24, 30.

then, for war, and for going and
coming. 12 So now give me this hill
country of which the LORD spoke on
that day; for you heard on that day
how the An'a·kim were there, with
great fortified cities; it may be that the
LORD will be with me, and I shall drive
them out as the LORD said."

13 Then Joshua blessed him; and
he gave Hē'bron to Caleb the son of
Je·phün'neh for an inheritance. 14 So
Hē'bron became the inheritance of
Caleb the son of Je·phün'neh the
Ken'iz·zīte to this day, because he
wholly followed the LORD, the God of
Israel. 15 Now the name of Hē'bron
formerly was Kïr'i·ath-är'ba;[l] this
Är'ba was the greatest man among the
An'a·kim. And the land had rest from
war.

15 The lot for the tribe of the people of Judah according to their
families reached southward to the
boundary of E'dom, to the wilderness
of Zin at the farthest south. 2 And their
south boundary ran from the end of
the Salt Sea, from the bay that faces
southward; 3 it goes out southward of
the ascent of Ak·rab'bim, passes along
to Zin, and goes up south of Kā'desh-
bär'nē·a, along by Hez'ron, up to
Ad'där, turns about to Kär'ka, 4 passes
along to Az'mon, goes out by the Brook
of Egypt, and comes to its end at the
sea. This shall be your south boundary. 5 And the east boundary is the
Salt Sea, to the mouth of the Jordan.
And the boundary on the north side
runs from the bay of the sea at the
mouth of the Jordan; 6 and the boundary goes up to Beth-hog'lah, and passes
along north of Beth-ar'a·bah; and the
boundary goes up to the stone of Bō'han
the son of Reuben; 7 and the boundary
goes up to Dē'bir from the Valley of
Ā'chôr, and so northward, turning toward Gil'gal, which is opposite the
ascent of A·dum'mim, which is on the
south side of the valley; and the boundary passes along to the waters of
En-shē'mesh, and ends at En-rō'gel;
8 then the boundary goes up by the
valley of the son of Hin'nom at the
southern shoulder of the Jeb'ū·site
(that is, Jerusalem); and the boundary
goes up to the top of the mountain
that lies over against the valley of
Hinnom, on the west, at the northern
end of the valley of Reph'a·im; 9 then
the boundary extends from the top of
the mountain to the spring of the
Waters of Neph·tō'ah, and from there
to the cities of Mount E'phron; then
the boundary bends round to Bā'a·lah
(that is, Kïr'i·ath-jē'a·rim); 10 and the
boundary circles west of Bā'a·lah to
Mount Sē'ir, passes along to the
northern shoulder of Mount Jē'a·rim
(that is, Ches'a·lon), and goes down to
Beth-shē'mesh, and passes along by
Tim'nah; 11 the boundary goes out to
the shoulder of the hill north of Ek'-
ron, then the boundary bends round
to Shik'ke·ron, and passes along to
Mount Bā'a·lah, and goes out to Jab'-
nē·el; then the boundary comes to an
end at the sea. 12 And the west boundary was the Great Sea with its coast-
line. This is the boundary round about
the people of Judah according to their
families.

13 According to the commandment
of the LORD to Joshua, he gave to
Caleb the son of Je·phün'neh a portion
among the people of Judah, Kïr'i·ath-
är'ba, that is, Hē'bron (Är'ba was the
father of Ā'nak). 14 And Caleb drove
out from there the three sons of Ā'nak,
Shē'shäi and A·hī'man and Tal'mī, the
descendants of Anak. 15 And he went
up from there against the inhabitants
of Dē'bir; now the name of Debir
formerly was Kïr'i·ath-sē'pher. 16 And
Caleb said, "Whoever smites Kïr'i·ath-
sē'pher, and takes it, to him will I give
Ach'sah my daughter as wife." 17 And
Oth'ni-el the son of Kē'naz, the
brother of Caleb, took it; and he gave
him Ach'sah his daughter as wife.
18 When she came to him, she urged
him to ask her father for a field; and
she alighted from her ass, and Caleb
said to her, "What do you wish?"
19 She said to him, "Give me a present;
since you have set me in the land of the
Negeb, give me also springs of water."
And Caleb gave her the upper springs
and the lower springs.

20 This is the inheritance of the
tribe of the people of Judah according
to their families. 21 The cities belonging to the tribe of the people of Judah
in the extreme South, toward the
boundary of E'dom, were Kab'zē·el,
E'der, Jā'gūr, 22 Kī'nah, Di·mō'nah,
A·dā'dah, 23 Kē'desh, Hā'zôr, Ith'nan,
24 Ziph, Tē'lem, Be-ā'loth, 25 Hā'zôr-
ha·dat'tah, Kēr'i-oth-hez'ron (that is,

[l] That is *The city of Arba*
15.14-19: Judg 1.10-15, 20.

Hā'zôr), 26 Ā'mam, Shē'mȧ, Mō'lȧ·dȧh,
27 Hā'zär-gad'dȧh, Hesh'mȯn, Beth-
pel'et, 28 Hā'zär-shü'ăl, Beer-sheba,
Biz·i·ȯ·thī'ȧh, 29 Bā'ȧ·lȧh, I'im, E'zem,
30 El·tō'lad, Chē'sil, Hôr'mȧh, 31 Zik'-
lag, Mad·man'nȧh, San·san'nȧh, 32 Lė-
bā'oth, Shil'him, Ā'in, and Rim'mon:
in all, twenty-nine cities, with their
villages.
33 And in the lowland, Esh'tā-ol,
Zō'rȧh, Ash'nȧh, 34 Zȧ·nō'ȧh, En-gan'-
nim, Tap'pū-ȧh, E'nam, 35 Jär'muth,
Ȧ·dul'lȧm, Sō'cōh, Ȧ·zē'kȧh, 36 Shā·ȧ-
rā'im, Ad·i·thā'im, Ge·dē'rȧh, Ge·dē-
roth·ā'im: fourteen cities with their
villages.
37 Zē'nȧn, Hȧ·dash'ȧh, Mig'dȧl-
gad, 38 Dī'lē·ȧn, Miz'peh, Jok'thē-el,
39 Lā'chish, Boz'kath, Eg'lon, 40 Cab'-
bon, Läh'mȧm, Chit'lish, 41 Ge·dē'-
roth, Beth-dā'gon, Nā'ȧ·mȧh, and
Mak·kē'dȧh: sixteen cities with their
villages.
42 Lib'nȧh, E'thėr, Ā'shȧn, 43 Iph'-
tȧh, Ash'nȧh, Nē'zib, 44 Kē·ī'lȧh, Ach'-
zib, and Mȧ·rē'shȧh: nine cities with
their villages.
45 Ek'rȯn, with its towns and its
villages; 46 from Ek'rȯn to the sea, all
that were by the side of Ash'dod, with
their villages.
47 Ash'dod, its towns and its villages; Gā'zȧ, its towns and its villages;
to the Brook of Egypt, and the Great
Sea with its coast-line.
48 And in the hill country, Shā'mir,
Jat'tir, Sō'cōh, 49 Dan'nȧh, Kīr'i·ath-
san'nȧh (that is, Dē'bir), 50 Ā'nab,
Esh'tē·mōh, Ā'nim, 51 Gō'shėn, Hō'-
lon, and Gī'lōh: eleven cities with their
villages.
52 Arab, Dü'mȧh, E'shan, 53 Jā'nim,
Beth-tap'pū-ȧh, Ȧ·phē'kȧh, 54 Hum'-
tȧh, Kīr'i·ath-är'bȧ (that is, Hē'brȯn),
and Zī'ôr: nine cities with their villages.
55 Mā'on, Cär'mėl, Ziph, Jut'tȧh,
56 Jez'rē·ėl, Jok'dē-am, Zȧ·nō'ȧh,
57 Kain, Gib'ē-ȧh, and Tim'nȧh: ten
cities with their villages.
58 Hal'hul, Beth'-zūr, Gē'dôr,
59 Mā'ȧ·rath, Beth-ā'noth, and El'tē-
kon: six cities with their villages.
60 Kīr'i·ath-bā'ăl (that is, Kīr'i·ath-
jē'ȧ·rim), and Rab'bȧh: two cities with
their villages.
61 In the wilderness, Beth-ar'ȧ·bȧh,
Mid'din, Sė·cā'cȧh, 62 Nib'shan, the
City of Salt, and En-gē'dī: six cities
with their villages.
63 But the Jeb'ū·sītes, the inhabitants of Jerusalem, the people of Judah
could not drive out; so the Jebusites
dwell with the people of Judah at
Jerusalem to this day.

16 The allotment of the descendants of Joseph went from the
Jordan by Jericho, east of the waters
of Jericho, into the wilderness, going
up from Jericho into the hill country
to Beth'ėl; 2 then going from Beth'ėl
to Luz, it passes along to At'ȧ·roth, the
territory of the Är'chītes; 3 then it goes
down westward to the territory of the
Japh'lė·tītes, as far as the territory of
Lower Beth-hō'ron, then to Gē'zėr,
and it ends at the sea.
4 The people of Joseph, Mȧ·nas'-
sėh and E'phrȧ·im, received their inheritance.
5 The territory of the E'phrȧ·im-
ītes by their families was as follows:
the boundary of their inheritance on
the east was At'ȧ·roth-ad'där as far as
Upper Beth-hō'ron, 6 and the boundary goes thence to the sea; on the
north is Mich·mē'thath; then on the
east the boundary turns round toward
Tā'ȧ·nath-shī'lōh, and passes along beyond it on the east to Jȧ·nō'ȧh, 7 then
it goes down from Jȧ·nō'ȧh to At'ȧ·roth
and to Nā'ȧ·rȧh, and touches Jericho,
ending at the Jordan. 8 From Tap'pū-
ȧh the boundary goes westward to the
brook Kā'nȧh, and ends at the sea.
Such is the inheritance of the tribe of
the E'phrȧ·im·ītes by their families,
9 together with the towns which were
set apart for the E'phrȧ·im·ītes within
the inheritance of the Mȧ·nas'sītes, all
those towns with their villages. 10 However they did not drive out the Canaanites that dwelt in Gē'zėr: so the
Canaanites have dwelt in the midst of
E'phrȧ·im to this day but have become
slaves to do forced labor.

17 Then allotment was made to the
tribe of Mȧ·nas'sėh, for he was
the first-born of Joseph. To Mā'chir
the first-born of Manasseh, the father
of Gilead, were allotted Gilead and
Bā'shȧn, because he was a man of war.
2 And allotments were made to the rest
of the tribe of Mȧ·nas'sėh, by their
families, Ā·bi·ē'zėr, Hē'lek, As'ri-el,
Shē'chem, Hē'phėr, and She·mī'dȧ;
these were the male descendants of
Manasseh the son of Joseph, by their
families.
3 Now Ze·loph'ė·had the son of

15.63: Judg 1.21; 2 Sam 5.6. 16.10: Judg 1.29. 17.3-4: Num 26.33; 27.1-7.

Hē'phėr, son of Gilead, son of Mā'chir,
son of Mȧ·nas'sėh, had no sons, but
only daughters; and these are the
names of his daughters: Mäh'lȧh,
Noah, Hog'lȧh, Mil'cȧh, and Tĭr'zȧh.
4 They came before El·ē·ā'zȧr the
priest and Joshua the son of Nun and
the leaders, and said, "The LORD
commanded Moses to give us an inheritance along with our brethren."
So according to the commandment of
the LORD he gave them an inheritance
among the brethren of their father.
5 Thus there fell to Mȧ·nas'sėh ten
portions, besides the land of Gilead
and Bā'shȧn, which is on the other side
of the Jordan; 6 because the daughters
of Mȧ·nas'sėh received an inheritance
along with his sons. The land of
Gilead was allotted to the rest of the
Mȧ·nas'sītes.

7 The territory of Mȧ·nas'sėh
reached from Ash'ėr to Mich·mē'thath,
which is east of Shē'chem; then the
boundary goes along southward to the
inhabitants of En-tap'pū-ȧh. 8 The
land of Tap'pū-ȧh belonged to Mȧ-
nas'sėh, but the town of Tappu-ah on
the boundary of Manasseh belonged
to the sons of Ē'phrȧ·im. 9 Then the
boundary went down to the brook
Kā'nȧh. The cities here, to the south
of the brook, among the cities of
Mȧ·nas'sėh, belong to Ē'phrȧ·im.
Then the boundary of Manasseh goes
on the north side of the brook and
ends at the sea; 10 the land to the south
being Ē'phrȧ·im's and that to the
north being Mȧ·nas'sėh's, with the sea
forming its boundary; on the north
Ash'ėr is reached, and on the east
Is'sȧ·chär. 11 Also in Is'sȧ·chär and in
Ash'ėr Mȧ·nas'sėh had Beth-shē'ȧn
and its villages, and Ib'lē-am and its
villages, and the inhabitants of Dôr
and its villages, and the inhabitants of
En'-dôr and its villages, and the inhabitants of Tā'ȧ·nach and its villages,
and the inhabitants of Mė·gid'dō and
its villages; the third is Nā'phath.[j]
12 Yet the sons of Mȧ·nas'sėh could
not take possession of those cities; but
the Canaanites persisted in dwelling in
that land. 13 But when the people of
Israel grew strong, they put the
Canaanites to forced labor, and did not
utterly drive them out.

14 And the tribe of Joseph spoke to
Joshua, saying, "Why have you given
me but one lot and one portion as an
inheritance, although I am a numerous
people, since hitherto the LORD has
blessed me?" 15 And Joshua said to
them, "If you are a numerous people,
go up to the forest, and there clear
ground for yourselves in the land of
the Per'iz·zītes and the Reph'ȧ·im,
since the hill country of Ē'phrȧ·im is
too narrow for you." 16 The tribe of
Joseph said, "The hill country is not
enough for us; yet all the Canaanites
who dwell in the plain have chariots of
iron, both those in Beth-shē'ȧn and
its villages and those in the Valley of
Jez'rē·ėl." 17 Then Joshua said to the
house of Joseph, to Ē'phrȧ·im and
Mȧ·nas'sėh, "You are a numerous
people, and have great power; you
shall not have one lot only, 18 but the
hill country shall be yours, for though
it is a forest, you shall clear it and
possess it to its farthest borders; for
you shall drive out the Canaanites,
though they have chariots of iron, and
though they are strong."

18 Then the whole congregation of
the people of Israel assembled at
Shī'lōh, and set up the tent of meeting
there; the land lay subdued before
them.

2 There remained among the people
of Israel seven tribes whose inheritance
had not yet been apportioned. 3 So
Joshua said to the people of Israel,
"How long will you be slack to go in
and take possession of the land, which
the LORD, the God of your fathers, has
given you? 4 Provide three men from
each tribe, and I will send them out
that they may set out and go up and
down the land, writing a description
of it with a view to their inheritances,
and then come to me. 5 They shall
divide it into seven portions, Judah
continuing in his territory on the south,
and the house of Joseph in their territory on the north. 6 And you shall
describe the land in seven divisions
and bring the description here to me;
and I will cast lots for you here before
the LORD our God. 7 The Levites have
no portion among you, for the priesthood of the LORD is their heritage; and
Gad and Reuben and half the tribe of
Mȧ·nas'sėh have received their inheritance beyond the Jordan eastward,
which Moses the servant of the LORD
gave them."

[j] Heb obscure
17.11-13: Judg 1.27-28.

8 So the men started on their way; and Joshua charged those who went to write the description of the land, saying, "Go up and down and write a description of the land, and come again to me; and I will cast lots for you here before the LORD in Shī'lōh." 9 So the men went and passed up and down in the land and set down in a book a description of it by towns in seven divisions; then they came to Joshua in the camp at Shī'lōh, 10 and Joshua cast lots for them in Shī'lōh before the LORD; and there Joshua apportioned the land to the people of Israel, to each his portion.

11 The lot of the tribe of Benjamin according to its families came up, and the territory allotted to it fell between the tribe of Judah and the tribe of Joseph. 12 On the north side their boundary began at the Jordan; then the boundary goes up to the shoulder north of Jericho, then up through the hill country westward; and it ends at the wilderness of Beth-ā'vėn. 13 From there the boundary passes along southward in the direction of Luz, to the shoulder of Luz (the same is Beth'ėl), then the boundary goes down to At'ȧ·roth-ad'där, upon the mountain that lies south of Lower Beth-hō'ron. 14 Then the boundary goes in another direction, turning on the western side southward from the mountain that lies to the south, opposite Beth-hō'ron, and it ends at Kïr'i·ath-bā'ȧl (that is, Kïr'i·ath-jē'ȧ·rim), a city belonging to the tribe of Judah. This forms the western side. 15 And the southern side begins at the outskirts of Kïr'i·ath-jē'ȧ·rim; and the boundary goes from there to E'phrȯn,[k] to the spring of the Waters of Neph·tō'ȧh; 16 then the boundary goes down to the border of the mountain that overlooks the valley of the son of Hin'nȯm, which is at the north end of the valley of Reph'ȧ·im; and it then goes down the valley of Hinnom, south of the shoulder of the Jeb'ū·sītes, and downward to En-rō'gel; 17 then it bends in a northerly direction going on to En-shē'mesh, and thence goes to Ge·lĭ'loth, which is opposite the ascent of A·dum'mim; then it goes down to the Stone of Bō'han the son of Reuben; 18 and passing on to the north of the shoulder of Beth-ar'ȧ·bȧh[l] it goes down to the Ar'ȧ·bȧh; 19 then the boundary passes on to the north of the shoulder of Beth-hog'lȧh; and the boundary ends at the northern bay of the Salt Sea, at the south end of the Jordan; this is the southern border. 20 The Jordan forms its boundary on the eastern side. This is the inheritance of the tribe of Benjamin, according to its families, boundary by boundary round about.

21 Now the cities of the tribe of Benjamin according to their families were Jericho, Beth-hog'lȧh, E'mek-kē'ziz, 22 Beth-ar'ȧ·bȧh, Zem·ȧ·rā'im, Beth'ėl, 23 Av'vim, Pâr'ȧh, Oph'rȧh, 24 Chē'phär-am'mȯ·nī, Oph'nī, Gē'bȧ—twelve cities with their villages: 25 Gib'ē·ȯn, Rā'mȧh, Bė-ēr'ȯth, 26 Miz'peh, Che·phī'rȧh, Mō'zȧh, 27 Rē'kem, Ïr'pē·ėl, Tar'ȧ·lȧh, 28 Zē'lȧ, Ha-ē'leph, Jē'bus[m] (that is, Jerusalem), Gib'ē-ȧh[n] and Kïr'i·ath-jē'ȧ·rim[o]—fourteen cities with their villages. This is the inheritance of the tribe of Benjamin according to its families.

19 The second lot came out for Simeon, for the tribe of Simeon, according to its families; and its inheritance was in the midst of the inheritance of the tribe of Judah. 2 And it had for its inheritance Beer-sheba, Sheba, Mō'lȧ·dȧh, 3 Hā·zär·shü'ȧl, Bā'lȧh, E'zem, 4 El·tō'lad, Bē'thul, Hôr'mȧh, 5 Zik'lag, Beth-mär'cȧ·both, Hā'zär-sü'sȧh, 6 Beth-lė·bā'oth, and Shȧ·rü'hen—thirteen cities with their villages; 7 En-rim'mon, E'thėr, and A'shȧn—four cities with their villages; 8 together with all the villages round about these cities as far as Bā'ȧ·lath-bē'ėr, Rā'mȧh of the Negeb. This was the inheritance of the tribe of Simeon according to its families. 9 The inheritance of the tribe of Simeon formed part of the territory of Judah; because the portion of the tribe of Judah was too large for them, the tribe of Simeon obtained an inheritance in the midst of their inheritance.

10 The third lot came up for the tribe of Zeb'ū·lün, according to its families. And the territory of its inheritance reached as far as Sā'rid; 11 then its boundary goes up westward, and on to Mar'ē·ȧl, and touches Dab'bė·sheth, then the brook which is east of Jok'nē-am; 12 from Sā'rid it goes in the other direction eastward toward the sunrise to the boundary of

[k] Cn See 15.9 Heb *westward* [l] Gk: Heb *to the shoulder over against the Arabah*
[m] Gk Syr Vg: Heb *the Jebusite* [n] Heb *Gibeath* [o] Gk: Heb *Kiriath*

Chis'loth-tā'bôr; thence it goes to
Dab'ė·rath, then up to Jȧ·phī'ȧ; 13 from
there it passes along on the east toward
the sunrise to Gath-hē'phėr, to Eth-
kā'zin, and going on to Rim'mon it
bends toward Nē'ȧh; 14 then on the
north the boundary turns about to
Han'nȧ·thon, and it ends at the valley
of Iph'tȧh·el; 15 and Kat'tȧth, Nȧ·hal'-
ȧl, Shim'rȯn, I'dȧ·lȧh, and Bethlehem
—twelve cities with their villages.
16 This is the inheritance of the tribe
of Zeb'ū·lun, according to its families
—these cities with their villages.

17 The fourth lot came out for
Is'sȧ·chär, for the tribe of Issachar,
according to its families. 18 Its territory included Jez'rē·ėl, Che·sul'loth,
Shü'nem, 19 Haph'ȧ·rā-im, Shī'on,
A·nā'hȧ·rath, 20 Rab'bith, Kish'i·on,
Ē'bez, 21 Rē'meth, En-gan'nim, En-
had'dȧh, Beth-paz'zez; 22 the boundary also touches Tā'bôr, Shȧ·ha-
zü'mȧh, and Beth-shē'mesh, and its
boundary ends at the Jordan—sixteen
cities with their villages. 23 This is the
inheritance of the tribe of Is'sȧ·chär,
according to its families—the cities
with their villages.

24 The fifth lot came out for the
tribe of Ash'ėr according to its families.
25 Its territory included Hel'kath,
Hā'lī, Bē'ten, Ach'shaph, 26 Al·lam'mė-
lech, Ā'mad, and Mī'shȧl; on the west
it touches Cär'mėl and Shī·hôr·lib'-
nath, 27 then it turns eastward, it goes
to Beth-dā'gon, and touches Zeb'ū·lun
and the valley of Iph'tȧh·el northward
to Beth-ē'mek and Nē·ī'el; then it continues in the north to Cā'bul, 28 Ē'bron,
Rē'hob, Ham'mȯn, Kā'nȧh, as far as
Sī'don the Great; 29 then the boundary
turns to Rā'mȧh, reaching to the fortified city of Tyre; then the boundary
turns to Hō'sȧh, and it ends at the
sea; Mȧ·hā'lȧb,[p] Ach'zib, 30 Um'-
mȧh, Ā'phek and Rē'hob—twenty-
two cities with their villages. 31 This
is the inheritance of the tribe of
Ash'ėr according to its families—
these cities with their villages.

32 The sixth lot came out for the
tribe of Naph'tȧ·lī, for the tribe of
Naphtali, according to its families.
33 And its boundary ran from Hē'leph,
from the oak in Zā-ȧ·nan'nim, and
Ad'ȧ·mī-nek'eb, and Jab'nē·ėl, as far
as Lak'kum; and it ended at the Jordan;
34 then the boundary turns westward
to Az'noth-tā'bôr, and goes from there
to Huz'kok, touching Zeb'ū·lun at the
south, and Ash'ėr on the west, and
Judah on the east at the Jordan. 35 The
fortified cities are Zid'dim, Zēr, Ham'-
math, Rak'kath, Chin'nė·reth, 36 Ad'ȧ-
mȧh, Rā'mȧh, Hā'zôr, 37 Kē'desh,
Ed'rē-ī, En-hā'zôr, 38 Yī'ron, Mig'dȧl-
el, Hō'rem, Beth-ā'nath, and Beth-
shē'mesh—nineteen cities with their
villages. 39 This in the inheritance of
the tribe of Naph'tȧ·lī according to
its families—the cities with their
villages.

40 The seventh lot came out for the
tribe of Dan, according to its families.
41 And the territory of its inheritance included Zō'rȧh, Esh'tā-ol, Īr·shē'mesh,
42 Shā-ȧ·lab'bin, Äi'jȧ·lon, Ith'lȧh,
43 Ē'lon, Tim'nȧh, Ek'rȯn, 44 El'tē·kėh,
Gib'bė·thon, Bā'ȧ·lath, 45 Jē'hud,
Ben'ē-bē'rak, Gath-rim'mon, 46 and
Mē-jär'kon and Rak'kon with the territory over against Jop'pȧ. 47 When the
territory of the Danites was lost to
them, the Danites went up and fought
against Lē'shem, and after capturing
it and putting it to the sword they
took possession of it and settled in it,
calling Leshem, Dan, after the name
of Dan their ancestor. 48 This is the
inheritance of the tribe of Dan, according to their families—these cities with
their villages.

49 When they had finished distrib-
uting the several territories of the land
as inheritances, the people of Israel
gave an inheritance among them to
Joshua the son of Nun. 50 By command
of the LORD they gave him the city
which he asked, Tim'nath-sē'rȧh in
the hill country of Ē'phrȧ·im; and he
rebuilt the city, and settled in it.

51 These are the inheritances which
El·ē·ā'zȧr the priest and Joshua the son
of Nun and the heads of the fathers'
houses of the tribes of the people of
Israel distributed by lot at Shī'lōh before the LORD, at the door of the tent
of meeting. So they finished dividing
the land.

20 Then the LORD said to Joshua,
2 "Say to the people of Israel,
'Appoint the cities of refuge, of which
I spoke to you through Moses, 3 that
the manslayer who kills any person
without intent or unwittingly may flee
there; they shall be for you a refuge
from the avenger of blood. 4 He shall

[p] Cn Compare Gk: Heb *Mehebel*

19.47: Judg 18.27-31. **20.2-9:** Num 35.6-34; Deut 4.41-43; 19.1-13.

flee to one of these cities and shall
stand at the entrance of the gate of the
city, and explain his case to the elders
of that city; then they shall take him
into the city, and give him a place, and
he shall remain with them. 5 And if
the avenger of blood pursues him, they
shall not give up the slayer into his
hand; because he killed his neighbor
unwittingly, having had no enmity
against him in times past. 6 And he shall
remain in that city until he has stood
before the congregation for judgment,
until the death of him who is high
priest at the time: then the slayer may
go again to his own town and his own
home, to the town from which he
fled.' "

7 So they set apart Kē'desh in
Galilee in the hill country of Naph'tȧ-
lī, and Shē'chem in the hill country of
Ē'phrȧ·im, and Kĭr'i·ath-är'bȧ (that is,
Hē'brȯn) in the hill country of Judah.
8 And beyond the Jordan east of Jericho,
they appointed Bē'zėr in the wilderness
on the tableland, from the tribe of
Reuben, and Rā'moth in Gilead, from
the tribe of Gad, and Gō'lan in Bā'-
shȧn, from the tribe of Mȧ·nas'sėh.
9 These were the cities designated for
all the people of Israel, and for the
stranger sojourning among them, that
any one who killed a person without
intent could flee there, so that he might
not die by the hand of the avenger of
blood, till he stood before the congregation.

21 Then the heads of the fathers'
houses of the Levites came to
El·ē·ā'zȧr the priest and to Joshua the
son of Nun and to the heads of the
fathers' houses of the tribes of the people of Israel; 2 and they said to them
at Shī'lōh in the land of Canaan, "The
LORD commanded through Moses that
we be given cities to dwell in, along
with their pasture lands for our cattle."
3 So by command of the LORD the
people of Israel gave to the Levites
the following cities and pasture lands
out of their inheritance.

4 The lot came out for the families
of the Kō'hȧ·thītes. So those Levites
who were descendants of Aaron the
priest received by lot from the tribes
of Judah, Simeon, and Benjamin,
thirteen cities.

5 And the rest of the Kō'hȧ·thītes
received by lot from the families of the
tribe of Ē'phrȧ·im, from the tribe of
Dan and the half-tribe of Mȧ·nas'sėh,
ten cities.

6 The Gēr'shȯ·nītes received by lot
from the families of the tribe of Is'sȧ-
chär, from the tribe of Ash'ėr, from
the tribe of Naph'tȧ·lī, and from the
half-tribe of Mȧ·nas'sėh in Bā'shȧn,
thirteen cities.

7 The Mė·râr'ītes according to their
families received from the tribe of
Reuben, the tribe of Gad, and the
tribe of Zeb'ū·lŭn, twelve cities.

8 These cities and their pasture
lands the people of Israel gave by lot
to the Levites, as the LORD had commanded through Moses.

9 Out of the tribe of Judah and the
tribe of Simeon they gave the following
cities mentioned by name, 10 which
went to the descendants of Aaron, one
of the families of the Kō'hȧ·thītes who
belonged to the Levites; since the lot
fell to them first. 11 They gave them
Kĭr'i·ath-är'bȧ (Är'bȧ being the father
of Ā'nak), that is Hē'brȯn, in the hill
country of Judah, along with the pasture lands round about it. 12 But the
fields of the city and its villages had
been given to Caleb the son of Jė-
phŭn'nėh as his possession.

13 And to the descendants of Aaron
the priest they gave Hē'brȯn, the city
of refuge for the slayer, with its pasture
lands, Lib'nȧh with its pasture lands,
14 Jat'tir with its pasture lands, Esh-
tė·mō'ȧ with its pasture lands, 15 Hō'-
lon with its pasture lands, Dē'bir with
its pasture lands, 16 Ā'in with its pasture lands, Jut'tȧh with its pasture
lands, Beth-shē'mesh with its pasture
lands—nine cities out of these two
tribes; 17 then out of the tribe of Benjamin, Gibeon with its pasture lands,
Gē'bȧ with its pasture lands, 18 An'ȧ-
thoth with its pasture lands, and
Al'mon with its pasture lands—four
cities. 19 The cities of the descendants
of Aaron, the priests, were in all thirteen cities with their pasture lands.

20 As to the rest of the Kō'hȧ·thītes
belonging to the Kohathite families of
the Levites, the cities allotted to them
were out of the tribe of Ē'phrȧ·im.
21 To them were given Shē'chem, the
city of refuge for the slayer, with its
pasture lands in the hill country of
Ē'phrȧ·im, Gē'zėr with its pasture
lands, 22 Kib'zȧ-im with its pasture
lands, Beth-hō'ron with its pasture
lands—four cities; 23 and out of the

21.1-42: Num 35.1-8; 1 Chron 6.54-81.

tribe of Dan, El'tē·kė with its pasture
lands, Gib'bė·thon with its pasture
lands, 24 Ai'jȧ·lon with its pasture lands,
Gath-rim'mon with its pasture lands—
four cities; 25 and out of the half-tribe
of Mȧ·nas'sėh, Tā'ȧ·nach with its pasture lands, and Gath-rim'mon with
its pasture lands—two cities. 26 The
cities of the families of the rest of the
Kō'hȧ·thītes were ten in all with their
pasture lands.

27 And to the Gēr'shȯ·nītes, one of
the families of the Levites, were given
out of the half-tribe of Mȧ·nas'sėh,
Gō'lan in Bā'shȧn with its pasture
lands, the city of refuge for the slayer,
and Be-esh'tē·rȧh with its pasture
lands—two cities; 28 and out of the
tribe of Is'sȧ·chär, Kish'i·on with its
pasture lands, Dab'ė·rath with its pasture lands, 29 Jär'muth with its pasture
lands, En-gan'nim with its pasture
lands—four cities; 30 and out of the
tribe of Ash'ėr, Mī'shȧl with its pasture lands, Ab'don with its pasture
lands, 31 Hel'kath with its pasture
lands, and Rē'hob with its pasture
lands—four cities; 32 and out of the
tribe of Naph'tȧ·lī, Kē'desh in Galilee
with its pasture lands, the city of refuge
for the slayer, Ham'moth-dôr with its
pasture lands, and Kär'tȧn with its pasture lands—three cities. 33 The cities
of the several families of the Gēr'shȯ-
nītes were in all thirteen cities with
their pasture lands.

34 And to the rest of the Levites,
the Mė·râr'īte families, were given out
of the tribe of Zeb'ū·lŭn, Jok'nē-am
with its pasture lands, Kär'tȧh with its
pasture lands, 35 Dim'nȧh with its
pasture lands, Nȧ·hal'ȧl with its pasture lands—four cities; 36 and out of
the tribe of Reuben, Bē'zėr with its
pasture lands, Jā'haz with its pasture
lands, 37 Ked'ē·moth with its pasture
lands, and Meph'ȧ-ath with its pasture
lands—four cities; 38 and out of the
tribe of Gad, Rā'moth in Gilead with
its pasture lands, the city of refuge for
the slayer, Mā·hȧ·nā'im with its pasture lands, 39 Hesh'bȯn with its pasture lands, Jā'zėr with its pasture lands
—four cities in all. 40 As for the cities
of the several Mė·râr'īte families, that
is, the remainder of the families of the
Levites, those allotted to them were
in all twelve cities.

41 The cities of the Levites in the
midst of the possession of the people
of Israel were in all forty-eight cities
with their pasture lands. 42 These
cities had each its pasture lands round
about it; so it was with all these
cities.

43 Thus the LORD gave to Israel
all the land which he swore to give to
their fathers; and having taken possession of it, they settled there. 44 And the
LORD gave them rest on every side just
as he had sworn to their fathers; not
one of all their enemies had withstood
them, for the LORD had given all their
enemies into their hands. 45 Not one
of all the good promises which the
LORD had made to the house of Israel
had failed; all came to pass.

22 Then Joshua summoned the
Reubenites, and the Gadites,
and the half-tribe of Mȧ·nas'sėh, 2 and
said to them, "You have kept all that
Moses the servant of the LORD commanded you, and have obeyed my
voice in all that I have commanded
you; 3 you have not forsaken your
brethren these many days, down to
this day, but have been careful to keep
the charge of the LORD your God.
4 And now the LORD your God has
given rest to your brethren, as he
promised them; therefore turn and go
to your home in the land where your
possession lies, which Moses the servant of the LORD gave you on the other
side of the Jordan. 5 Take good care
to observe the commandment and the
law which Moses the servant of the
LORD commanded you, to love the
LORD your God, and to walk in all his
ways, and to keep his commandments,
and to cleave to him, and to serve him
with all your heart and with all your
soul." 6 So Joshua blessed them, and
sent them away; and they went to their
homes.

7 Now to the one half of the tribe
of Mȧ·nas'sėh Moses had given a
possession in Bā'shȧn; but to the other
half Joshua had given a possession beside their brethren in the land west of
the Jordan. And when Joshua sent
them away to their homes and blessed
them, 8 he said to them, "Go back to
your homes with much wealth, and
with very many cattle, with silver,
gold, bronze, and iron, and with much
clothing; divide the spoil of your
enemies with your brethren." 9 So the
Reubenites and the Gadites and the
half-tribe of Mȧ·nas'sėh returned

22.1-34: Josh 1.12-18; Num 32.20-22.

home, parting from the people of
Israel at Shī′lōh, which is in the land
of Canaan, to go to the land of Gilead,
their own land of which they had
possessed themselves by command of
the Lord through Moses.

10 And when they came to the region about the Jordan, that lies in the
land of Canaan, the Reubenites and
the Gadites and the half-tribe of Mȧ-
nas′sėh built there an altar by the
Jordan, an altar of great size. 11 And
the people of Israel heard say, "Behold, the Reubenites and the Gadites
and the half-tribe of Mȧ·nas′sėh have
built an altar at the frontier of the land
of Canaan, in the region about the
Jordan, on the side that belongs to the
people of Israel." 12 And when the people of Israel heard of it, the whole
assembly of the people of Israel gathered at Shī′lōh, to make war against
them.

13 Then the people of Israel sent to
the Reubenites and the Gadites and
the half-tribe of Mȧ·nas′sėh, in the
land of Gilead, Phin′ė·hȧs the son of
El·ē·ā′zȧr the priest, 14 and with him
ten chiefs, one from each of the tribal
families of Israel, every one of them
the head of a family among the clans
of Israel. 15 And they came to the
Reubenites, the Gadites, and the half-
tribe of Mȧ·nas′sėh, in the land of
Gilead, and they said to them, 16 "Thus
says the whole congregation of the
Lord, 'What is this treachery which
you have committed against the God
of Israel in turning away this day from
following the Lord, by building yourselves an altar this day in rebellion
against the Lord? 17 Have we not had
enough of the sin at Pē′ôr from which
even yet we have not cleansed ourselves, and for which there came a
plague upon the congregation of the
Lord, 18 that you must turn away this
day from following the Lord? And if
you rebel against the Lord today he
will be angry with the whole congregation of Israel tomorrow. 19 But now,
if your land is unclean, pass over into
the Lord's land where the Lord's
tabernacle stands, and take for yourselves a possession among us; only do
not rebel against the Lord, or make us
as rebels by building yourselves an
altar other than the altar of the Lord
our God. 20 Did not Ā′chȧn the son of
Zē′rȧh break faith in the matter of the
devoted things, and wrath fell upon all
the congregation of Israel? And he did
not perish alone for his iniquity.' "

21 Then the Reubenites, the Gadites, and the half-tribe of Mȧ·nas′sėh
said in answer to the heads of the
families of Israel, 22 "The Mighty
One, God, the Lord! The Mighty
One, God, the Lord! He knows; and
let Israel itself know! If it was in rebellion or in breach of faith toward the
Lord, spare us not today 23 for building an altar to turn away from following the Lord; or if we did so to offer
burnt offerings or cereal offerings or
peace offerings on it, may the Lord
himself take vengeance. 24 Nay, but we
did it from fear that in time to come
your children might say to our children, 'What have you to do with the
Lord, the God of Israel? 25 For the
Lord has made the Jordan a boundary
between us and you, you Reubenites
and Gadites; you have no portion in
the Lord.' So your children might
make our children cease to worship the
Lord. 26 Therefore we said, 'Let us
now build an altar, not for burnt offering, nor for sacrifice, 27 but to be a
witness between us and you, and between the generations after us, that we
do perform the service of the Lord in
his presence with our burnt offerings
and sacrifices and peace offerings; lest
your children say to our children in
time to come, "You have no portion in
the Lord." ' 28 And we thought, If
this should be said to us or to our
descendants in time to come, we
should say, 'Behold the copy of the
altar of the Lord, which our fathers
made, not for burnt offerings, nor for
sacrifice, but to be a witness between
us and you.' 29 Far be it from us that
we should rebel against the Lord, and
turn away this day from following the
Lord by building an altar for burnt
offering, cereal offering, or sacrifice,
other than the altar of the Lord our
God that stands before his tabernacle!"

30 When Phin′ė·hȧs the priest and
the chiefs of the congregation, the
heads of the families of Israel who
were with him, heard the words that
the Reubenites and the Gadites and
the Mȧ·nas′sītes spoke, it pleased them
well. 31 And Phin′ė·hȧs the son of El·ē-
ā′zȧr the priest said to the Reubenites
and the Gadites and the Mȧ·nas′sītes,
"Today we know that the Lord is in
the midst of us, because you have not
committed this treachery against the

LORD; now you have saved the people
of Israel from the hand of the LORD."
32 Then Phin'ė·hȧs the son of El·ē-
ā'zȧr the priest, and the chiefs, returned
from the Reubenites and the Gadites
in the land of Gilead to the land of
Canaan, to the people of Israel, and
brought back word to them. 33 And the
report pleased the people of Israel;
and the people of Israel blessed God
and spoke no more of making war
against them, to destroy the land
where the Reubenites and the Gadites
were settled. 34 The Reubenites and
the Gadites called the altar Witness;
"For," said they, "it is a witness between us that the LORD is God."

23 A long time afterward, when
the LORD had given rest to Israel
from all their enemies round about,
and Joshua was old and well advanced
in years, 2 Joshua summoned all Israel,
their elders and heads, their judges and
officers, and said to them, "I am now
old and well advanced in years; 3 and
you have seen all that the LORD your
God has done to all these nations for
your sake, for it is the LORD your God
who has fought for you. 4 Behold, I
have allotted to you as an inheritance
for your tribes those nations that remain, along with all the nations that I
have already cut off, from the Jordan
to the Great Sea in the west. 5 The
LORD your God will push them back
before you, and drive them out of your
sight; and you shall possess their land,
as the LORD your God promised you.
6 Therefore be very steadfast to keep
and do all that is written in the book
of the law of Moses, turning aside from
it neither to the right hand nor to the
left, 7 that you may not be mixed with
these nations left here among you, or
make mention of the names of their
gods, or swear by them, or serve them,
or bow down yourselves to them, 8 but
cleave to the LORD your God as you
have done to this day. 9 For the LORD
has driven out before you great and
strong nations; and as for you, no man
has been able to withstand you to this
day. 10 One man of you puts to flight
a thousand, since it is the LORD your
God who fights for you, as he promised you. 11 Take good heed to yourselves, therefore, to love the LORD your
God. 12 For if you turn back, and join
the remnant of these nations left here
among you, and make marriages with
them, so that you marry their women
and they yours, 13 know assuredly that
the LORD your God will not continue
to drive out these nations before you;
but they shall be a snare and a trap for
you, a scourge on your sides, and
thorns in your eyes, till you perish
from off this good land which the
LORD your God has given you.
14 "And now I am about to go the
way of all the earth, and you know in
your hearts and souls, all of you, that
not one thing has failed of all the good
things which the LORD your God promised concerning you; all have come to
pass for you, not one of them has
failed. 15 But just as all the good things
which the LORD your God promised
concerning you have been fulfilled for
you, so the LORD will bring upon you
all the evil things, until he have destroyed you from off this good land
which the LORD your God has given
you, 16 if you transgress the covenant
of the LORD your God, which he commanded you, and go and serve other
gods and bow down to them. Then the
anger of the LORD will be kindled
against you, and you shall perish
quickly from off the good land which
he has given to you."

24 Then Joshua gathered all the
tribes of Israel to Shē'chem, and
summoned the elders, the heads, the
judges, and the officers of Israel; and
they presented themselves before God.
2 And Joshua said to all the people,
"Thus says the LORD, the God of Israel,
'Your fathers lived of old beyond the
Eū·phrā'tēṡ, Tē'rȧh, the father of
Abraham and of Nā'hôr; and they
served other gods. 3 Then I took your
father Abraham from beyond the River
and led him through all the land of
Canaan, and made his offspring many.
I gave him Isaac; 4 and to Isaac I gave
Jacob and Esau. And I gave Esau the
hill country of Sē'ir to possess, but
Jacob and his children went down to
Egypt. 5 And I sent Moses and Aaron,
and I plagued Egypt with what I did
in the midst of it; and afterwards I
brought you out. 6 Then I brought your
fathers out of Egypt, and you came to
the sea; and the Egyptians pursued
your fathers with chariots and horsemen to the Red Sea. 7 And when they
cried to the LORD, he put darkness
between you and the Egyptians, and
made the sea come upon them and cover
them; and your eyes saw what I did to
Egypt; and you lived in the wilderness

a long time. 8 Then I brought you to
the land of the Am'ȯ·rītes, who lived
on the other side of the Jordan; they
fought with you, and I gave them into
your hand, and you took possession of
their land, and I destroyed them before you. 9 Then Bā'lak the son of
Zip'pôr, king of Mō'ab, arose and
fought against Israel; and he sent and
invited Balaam the son of Bē'ôr to
curse you, 10 but I would not listen to
Balaam; therefore he blessed you; so
I delivered you out of his hand. 11 And
you went over the Jordan and came to
Jericho, and the men of Jericho fought
against you, and also the Am'ȯ·rītes,
the Per'iz·zītes, the Canaanites, the
Hit'tītes, the Gĩr'gȧ·shītes, the Hī'-
vītes, and the Jeb'ū·sītes; and I gave
them into your hand. 12 And I sent the
hornet before you, which drove them
out before you, the two kings of the
Am'ȯ·rītes; it was not by your sword
or by your bow. 13 I gave you a land
on which you had not labored, and
cities which you had not built, and
you dwell therein; you eat the fruit of
vineyards and oliveyards which you
did not plant.'

14 "Now therefore fear the LORD,
and serve him in sincerity and in faithfulness; put away the gods which your
fathers served beyond the River, and
in Egypt, and serve the LORD. 15 And
if you be unwilling to serve the LORD,
choose this day whom you will serve,
whether the gods your fathers served
in the region beyond the River, or the
gods of the Am'ȯ·rītes in whose land
you dwell; but as for me and my house,
we will serve the LORD."

16 Then the people answered, "Far
be it from us that we should forsake the
LORD, to serve other gods; 17 for it is
the LORD our God who brought us
and our fathers up from the land of
Egypt, out of the house of bondage,
and who did those great signs in our
sight, and preserved us in all the way
that we went, and among all the peoples through whom we passed; 18 and
the LORD drove out before us all the
peoples, the Am'ȯ·rītes who lived in
the land; therefore we also will serve
the LORD, for he is our God."

19 But Joshua said to the people,
"You cannot serve the LORD; for he is
a holy God; he is a jealous God; he will
not forgive your transgressions or your
sins. 20 If you forsake the LORD and
serve foreign gods, then he will turn
and do you harm, and consume you,
after having done you good." 21 And
the people said to Joshua, "Nay; but
we will serve the LORD." 22 Then
Joshua said to the people, "You are
witnesses against yourselves that you
have chosen the LORD, to serve him."
And they said, "We are witnesses."
23 He said, "Then put away the foreign
gods which are among you, and incline
your heart to the LORD, the God of
Israel." 24 And the people said to
Joshua, "The LORD our God we will
serve, and his voice we will obey."
25 So Joshua made a covenant with the
people that day, and made statutes and
ordinances for them at Shē'chem.
26 And Joshua wrote these words in the
book of the law of God; and he took a
great stone, and set it up there under
the oak in the sanctuary of the LORD.
27 And Joshua said to all the people,
"Behold, this stone shall be a witness
against us; for it has heard all the words
of the LORD which he spoke to us;
therefore it shall be a witness against
you, lest you deal falsely with your
God." 28 So Joshua sent the people away, every man to his inheritance.

29 After these things Joshua the son
of Nun, the servant of the LORD, died,
being a hundred and ten years old.
30 And they buried him in his own inheritance at Tim'nath-sē'rȧh, which is
in the hill country of Ē'phrȧ·im, north
of the mountain of Gā'ash.

31 And Israel served the LORD all
the days of Joshua, and all the days of
the elders who outlived Joshua and
had known all the work which the
LORD did for Israel.

32 The bones of Joseph which the
people of Israel brought up from
Egypt were buried at Shē'chem, in the
portion of ground which Jacob bought
from the sons of Hā'mor the father of
Shechem for a hundred pieces of
money;[q] it became an inheritance of
the descendants of Joseph.

33 And El·ē·ā'zȧr the son of Aaron
died; and they buried him at Gib'ē-ȧh,
the town of Phin'ė·hȧs his son, which
had been given him in the hill country
of Ē'phrȧ·im.

[q] Heb *qesitah*
24.32: Gen 50.24-25; Ex 13.19; Acts 7.16.

THE BOOK OF
JUDGES

1 After the death of Joshua the people of Israel inquired of the LORD,
"Who shall go up first for us against
the Canaanites, to fight against them?"
2 The LORD said, "Judah shall go up;
behold, I have given the land into his
hand." 3 And Judah said to Simeon his
brother, "Come up with me into the
territory allotted to me, that we may
fight against the Canaanites; and I likewise will go with you into the territory
allotted to you." So Simeon went with
him. 4 Then Judah went up and the
LORD gave the Canaanites and the
Per′iz·zītes into their hand; and they
defeated ten thousand of them at Bē′-
zek. 5 They came upon Ȧ·dō′nī-bē′zek
at Bē′zek, and fought against him, and
defeated the Canaanites and the Per′-
iz·zītes. 6 Ȧ·dō′nī-bē′zek fled; but they
pursued him, and caught him, and cut
off his thumbs and his great toes. 7 And
Ȧ·dō′nī-bē′zek said, "Seventy kings
with their thumbs and their great toes
cut off used to pick up scraps under
my table; as I have done, so God has
requited me." And they brought him
to Jerusalem, and he died there.
8 And the men of Judah fought
against Jerusalem, and took it, and
smote it with the edge of the sword,
and set the city on fire. 9 And afterward
the men of Judah went down to fight
against the Canaanites who dwelt in
the hill country, in the Negeb, and in
the lowland. 10 And Judah went against
the Canaanites who dwelt in Hē′brȯn
(now the name of Hebron was formerly Kĭr′i·ath-är′bȧ); and they defeated Shē′shäi and Ȧ·hī′mȧn and
Tal′mäi.
11 From there they went against
the inhabitants of Dē′bir. The name
of Debir was formerly Kĭr′i·ath-sē′-
phėr. 12 And Caleb said, "He who
attacks Kĭr′i·ath-sē′phėr and takes it,
I will give him Ach′sȧh my daughter
as wife." 13 And Oth′ni-el the son of
Kē′naz, Caleb's younger brother, took
it; and he gave him Ach′sȧh his
daughter as wife. 14 When she came
to him, she urged him to ask her father
for a field; and she alighted from her
ass, and Caleb said to her, "What do
you wish?" 15 She said to him, "Give
me a present; since you have set me in
the land of the Negeb, give me also
springs of water." And Caleb gave her
the upper springs and the lower
springs.
16 And the descendants of the
Ken′īte, Moses' father-in-law, went up
with the people of Judah from the city
of palms into the wilderness of Judah,
which lies in the Negeb near Âr′ȧd;
and they went and settled with the
people. 17 And Judah went with
Simeon his brother, and they defeated
the Canaanites who inhabited Zē′-
phath, and utterly destroyed it. So the
name of the city was called Hôr′mȧh.
18 Judah also took Gā′zȧ with its
territory, and Ash′kė·lon with its territory, and Ek′rȯn with its territory.
19 And the LORD was with Judah, and
he took possession of the hill country,
but he could not drive out the inhabitants of the plain, because they had
chariots of iron. 20 And Hē′brȯn was
given to Caleb, as Moses had said; and
he drove out from it the three sons of
Ā′nak. 21 But the people of Benjamin
did not drive out the Jeb′ū·sītes who
dwelt in Jerusalem; so the Jebusites
have dwelt with the people of Benjamin in Jerusalem to this day.
22 The house of Joseph also went
up against Beth′ėl; and the LORD was
with them. 23 And the house of Joseph
sent to spy out Beth′ėl. (Now the name
of the city was formerly Luz). 24 And
the spies saw a man coming out of the
city, and they said to him, "Pray, show
us the way into the city, and we will
deal kindly with you." 25 And he
showed them the way into the city;
and they smote the city with the edge
of the sword, but they let the man and
all his family go. 26 And the man went
to the land of the Hit′tītes and built a
city, and called its name Luz; that is
its name to this day.

1.10: Josh 15.13-19. 1.10-15: Josh 15.14-19. 1.20: Josh 15.14.
1.21: Josh 15.63.

27 Mȧ·nas'sėh did not drive out the
inhabitants of Beth-shē'ȧn and its villages, or Tā'ȧ·nach and its villages, or
the inhabitants of Dôr and its villages,
or the inhabitants of Ib'lē·ȧm and its
villages, or the inhabitants of Mė·gid'-
dō and its villages; but the Canaanites
persisted in dwelling in that land.
28 When Israel grew strong, they put
the Canaanites to forced labor, but
did not utterly drive them out.
29 And E'phrȧ·im did not drive out
the Canaanites who dwelt in Gē'zėr;
but the Canaanites dwelt in Gezer
among them.
30 Zeb'ū·lŭn did not drive out the
inhabitants of Kit'ron, or the inhabitants of Nȧ·hal'ol; but the Canaanites
dwelt among them, and became subject to forced labor.
31 Ash'ėr did not drive out the inhabitants of Ac'cō, or the inhabitants
of Sī'don, or of Ăh'lab, or of Ach'zib,
or of Hel'bȧh, or of Ā'phik, or of
Rē'hob; 32 but the Ash'ė·rītes dwelt
among the Canaanites, the inhabitants
of the land; for they did not drive
them out.
33 Naph'tȧ·lī did not drive out the
inhabitants of Beth-shē'mesh, or the
inhabitants of Beth-ā'nath, but dwelt
among the Canaanites, the inhabitants
of the land; nevertheless the inhabitants of Beth-shemesh and of Beth-
anath became subject to forced labor
for them.
34 The Am'ō·rītes pressed the
Danites back into the hill country, for
they did not allow them to come down
to the plain; 35 the Am'ō·rītes persisted
in dwelling in Här-hē'rēs, in Ai'jȧ·lon,
and in Shā-al'bim, but the hand of the
house of Joseph rested heavily upon
them, and they became subject to
forced labor. 36 And the border of the
Am'ō·rītes ran from the ascent of
Ȧ·krab'bim, from Sē'lȧ and upward.

2 Now the angel of the LORD went
up from Gil'gȧl to Bō'chim. And
he said, "I brought you up from Egypt,
and brought you into the land which I
swore to give to your fathers. I said 'I
will never break my covenant with
you, 2 and you shall make no covenant
with the inhabitants of this land; you
shall break down their altars.' But you
have not obeyed my command. What
is this you have done? 3 So now I say,
I will not drive them out before you;
but they shall become adversaries[a] to
you, and their gods shall be a snare
to you." 4 When the angel of the LORD
spoke these words to all the people of
Israel, the people lifted up their voices
and wept. 5 And they called the name
of that place Bō'chim;[b] and they sacrificed there to the LORD.
6 When Joshua dismissed the people, the people of Israel went each to
his inheritance to take possession of
the land. 7 And the people served the
LORD all the days of Joshua, and all
the days of the elders who outlived
Joshua, who had seen all the great
work which the LORD had done for
Israel. 8 And Joshua the son of Nun,
the servant of the LORD, died at the
age of one hundred and ten years.
9 And they buried him within the
bounds of his inheritance in Tim'nath-
hē'rēs, in the hill country of E'phrȧ·im,
north of the mountain of Gā'ash.
10 And all that generation also were
gathered to their fathers; and there
arose another generation after them,
who did not know the LORD or
the work which he had done for
Israel.
11 And the people of Israel did
what was evil in the sight of the LORD
and served the Bā'ȧls; 12 and they forsook the LORD, the God of their fathers,
who had brought them out of the land
of Egypt; they went after other gods,
from among the gods of the peoples
who were round about them, and
bowed down to them; and they provoked the LORD to anger. 13 They forsook the LORD, and served the Bā'ȧls
and the Ash'tȧ·roth. 14 So the anger of
the LORD was kindled against Israel,
and he gave them over to plunderers,
who plundered them; and he sold them
into the power of their enemies round
about, so that they could no longer
withstand their enemies. 15 Whenever
they marched out, the hand of the
LORD was against them for evil, as the
LORD had warned, and as the LORD
had sworn to them; and they were in
sore straits.
16 Then the LORD raised up judges,
who saved them out of the power of
those who plundered them. 17 And yet
they did not listen to their judges; for
they played the harlot after other gods
and bowed down to them; they soon
turned aside from the way in which

[a] Vg Old Latin Compare Gk: Heb *sides* [b] That is *Weepers*
1.27-28: Josh 17.11-13. 1.29: Josh 16.10. 2.6-9: Josh 24.28-31.

their fathers had walked, who had
obeyed the commandments of the
LORD, and they did not do so. 18 Whenever the LORD raised up judges for
them, the LORD was with the judge,
and he saved them from the hand of
their enemies all the days of the judge;
for the LORD was moved to pity by
their groaning because of those who
afflicted and oppressed them. 19 But
whenever the judge died, they turned
back and behaved worse than their
fathers, going after other gods, serving
them and bowing down to them; they
did not drop any of their practices or
their stubborn ways. 20 So the anger
of the LORD was kindled against Israel;
and he said, "Because this people have
transgressed my covenant which I
commanded their fathers, and have
not obeyed my voice, 21 I will not
henceforth drive out before them any
of the nations that Joshua left when he
died, 22 that by them I may test Israel,
whether they will take care to walk in
the way of the LORD as their fathers
did, or not." 23 So the LORD left those
nations, not driving them out at once,
and he did not give them into the
power of Joshua.

3 Now these are the nations which
the LORD left, to test Israel by
them, that is, all in Israel who had no
experience of any war in Canaan; 2 it
was only that the generations of the
people of Israel might know war, that
he might teach war to such at least as
had not known it before. 3 These are
the nations: the five lords of the
Philistines, and all the Canaanites, and
the Sī·dō'ni·ȧnṡ, and the Hī'vītes who
dwelt on Mount Lebanon, from Mount
Bā'ȧl-hēr'mȯn as far as the entrance of
Hā'math. 4 They were for the testing
of Israel, to know whether Israel
would obey the commandments of the
LORD, which he commanded their
fathers by Moses. 5 So the people of
Israel dwelt among the Canaanites, the
Hit'tītes, the Am'ȯ·rītes, the Per'iz-
zītes, the Hī'vītes, and the Jeb'ū·sītes;
6 and they took their daughters to
themselves for wives, and their own
daughters they gave to their sons; and
they served their gods.

7 And the people of Israel did what
was evil in the sight of the LORD, forgetting the LORD their God, and serving the Bā'ȧlṡ and the Ȧ·shē'roth.
8 Therefore the anger of the LORD was
kindled against Israel, and he sold
them into the hand of Cū'shan-rish·ȧ-
thā'im king of Mes·ȯ·pȯ·tā'mi·ȧ; and
the people of Israel served Cushan-
rishathaim eight years. 9 But when the
people of Israel cried to the LORD,
the LORD raised up a deliverer for the
people of Israel, who delivered them,
Oth'ni-el the son of Kē'naz, Caleb's
younger brother. 10 The Spirit of the
LORD came upon him, and he judged
Israel; he went out to war, and the
LORD gave Cū'shan-rish·ȧ·thā'im king
of Mes·ȯ·pȯ·tā'mi·ȧ into his hand; and
his hand prevailed over Cushan-
rishathaim. 11 So the land had rest
forty years. Then Oth'ni-el the son of
Kē'naz died.

12 And the people of Israel again
did what was evil in the sight of the
LORD; and the LORD strengthened
Eg'lon the king of Mō'ab against Israel, because they had done what was
evil in the sight of the LORD. 13 He
gathered to himself the Am'mȯ·nītes
and the Ȧ·mal'ė·kītes, and went and
defeated Israel; and they took possession of the city of palms. 14 And the
people of Israel served Eg'lon the king
of Mō'ab eighteen years.

15 But when the people of Israel
cried to the LORD, the LORD raised up
for them a deliverer, E'hud, the son of
Gē'rȧ, the Benjaminite, a left-handed
man. The people of Israel sent tribute
by him to Eg'lon the king of Mō'ab.
16 And E'hud made for himself a sword
with two edges, a cubit in length; and
he girded it on his right thigh under
his clothes. 17 And he presented the
tribute to Eg'lon king of Mō'ab. Now
Eglon was a very fat man. 18 And when
E'hud had finished presenting the
tribute, he sent away the people that
carried the tribute. 19 But he himself
turned back at the sculptured stones
near Gil'gȧl, and said, "I have a secret
message for you, O king." And he
commanded, "Silence." And all his
attendants went out from his presence.
20 And E'hud came to him, as he was
sitting alone in his cool roof chamber.
And Ehud said, "I have a message
from God for you." And he arose from
his seat. 21 And E'hud reached with his
left hand, took the sword from his right
thigh, and thrust it into his belly;
22 and the hilt also went in after the
blade, and the fat closed over the
blade, for he did not draw the sword
out of his belly; and the dirt came out.
23 Then E'hud went out into the

vestibule,[c] and closed the doors of the
roof chamber upon him, and locked
them.
24 When he had gone, the servants
came; and when they saw that the
doors of the roof chamber were locked,
they thought, "He is only relieving
himself in the closet of the cool
chamber." 25And they waited till they
were utterly at a loss; but when he still
did not open the doors of the roof
chamber, they took the key and opened
them; and there lay their lord dead on
the floor.
26 Ē'hud escaped while they delayed, and passed beyond the sculptured stones, and escaped to Sē-ī'rȧh.
27 When he arrived, he sounded the
trumpet in the hill country of Ē'phrȧ-
im; and the people of Israel went down
with him from the hill country, having
him at their head. 28And he said to
them, "Follow after me; for the LORD
has given your enemies the Mō'ȧb·ītes
into your hand." So they went down
after him, and seized the fords of the
Jordan against the Moabites, and
allowed not a man to pass over. 29And
they killed at that time about ten thousand of the Mō'ȧb·ītes, all strong, able-
bodied men; not a man escaped. 30 So
Mō'ab was subdued that day under the
hand of Israel. And the land had rest
for eighty years.
31 After him was Sham'gär the son
of Ā'nath, who killed six hundred of
the Philistines with an oxgoad; and he
too delivered Israel.
4 And the people of Israel again did
what was evil in the sight of the
LORD, after Ē'hud died. 2And the LORD
sold them into the hand of Jā'bin king
of Canaan, who reigned in Hā'zôr; the
commander of his army was Sis'ėr·ȧ,
who dwelt in Hȧ·rō'sheth-hȧ-goi'im.
3 Then the people of Israel cried to
the LORD for help; for he had nine
hundred chariots of iron, and oppressed the people of Israel cruelly for
twenty years.
4 Now Deb'ȯ·rȧh, a prophetess, the
wife of Lap'pi·doth, was judging Israel
at that time. 5 She used to sit under
the palm of Deb'ȯ·rȧh between Rā'-
mȧh and Beth'ėl in the hill country of
Ē'phrȧ·im; and the people of Israel
came up to her for judgment. 6 She
sent and summoned Bâr'ȧk the son of
Ȧ·bin'ō-am from Kē'desh in Naph'tȧ-
lī, and said to him, "The LORD, the
God of Israel, commands you, 'Go,
gather your men at Mount Tā'bôr,
taking ten thousand from the tribe of
Naphtali and the tribe of Zeb'ū·lůn.
7And I will draw out Sis'ėr·ȧ, the
general of Jā'bin's army, to meet you
by the river Kī'shon with his chariots
and his troops; and I will give him into
your hand.'" 8 Bâr'ȧk said to her, "If
you will go with me, I will go; but if
you will not go with me, I will not
go." 9And she said, "I will surely go
with you; nevertheless, the road on
which you are going will not lead to
your glory, for the LORD will sell
Sis'ėr·ȧ into the hand of a woman."
Then Deb'ȯ·rȧh arose, and went with
Bâr'ȧk to Kē'desh. 10And Bâr'ȧk summoned Zeb'ū·lůn and Naph'tȧ·lī to
Kē'desh; and ten thousand men went
up at his heels; and Deb'ȯ·rȧh went up
with him.
11 Now Hē'bėr the Ken'īte had
separated from the Kenites, the descendants of Hō'bab the father-in-law
of Moses, and had pitched his tent as
far away as the oak in Zā-ȧ·nan'nim,
which is near Kē'desh.
12 When Sis'ėr·ȧ was told that
Bâr'ȧk the son of Ȧ·bin'ō-am had gone
up to Mount Tā'bôr, 13 Sis'ėr·ȧ called
out all his chariots, nine hundred
chariots of iron, and all the men who
were with him, from Hȧ·rō'sheth-hȧ-
goi'im to the river Kī'shon. 14And
Deb'ȯ·rȧh said to Bâr'ȧk, "Up! For
this is the day in which the LORD has
given Sis'ėr·ȧ into your hand. Does
not the LORD go out before you?" So
Barak went down from Mount Tā'bôr
with ten thousand men following him.
15And the LORD routed Sis'ėr·ȧ and all
his chariots and all his army before
Bâr'ȧk at the edge of the sword; and
Sisera alighted from his chariot and
fled away on foot. 16And Bâr'ȧk pursued the chariots and the army to
Hȧ·rō'sheth-hȧ-goi'im, and all the
army of Sis'ėr·ȧ fell by the edge of the
sword; not a man was left.
17 But Sis'ėr·ȧ fled away on foot to
the tent of Jā'ėl, the wife of Hē'bėr the
Ken'īte; for there was peace between
Jā'bin the king of Hā'zôr and the house
of Heber the Kenite. 18And Jā'ėl came
out to meet Sis'ėr·ȧ, and said to him,
"Turn aside, my lord, turn aside to
me; have no fear." So he turned aside
to her into the tent, and she covered
him with a rug. 19And he said to her,

[c] The meaning of the Hebrew word is unknown

"Pray, give me a little water to drink;
for I am thirsty." So she opened a skin
of milk and gave him a drink and
covered him. 20And he said to her,
"Stand at the door of the tent, and if
any man comes and asks you, 'Is any
one here?' say, No." 21 But Jā'ĕl the
wife of Hē'bẽr took a tent peg, and
took a hammer in her hand, and went
softly to him and drove the peg into
his temple, till it went down into the
ground, as he was lying fast asleep from
weariness. So he died. 22And behold,
as Bâr'ăk pursued Sis'ẽr·ȧ, Jā'ĕl went
out to meet him, and said to him,
"Come, and I will show you the man
whom you are seeking." So he went
in to her tent; and there lay Sisera
dead, with the tent peg in his temple.
23 So on that day God subdued
Jā'bin the king of Canaan before the
people of Israel. 24And the hand of the
people of Israel bore harder and harder
on Jā'bin the king of Canaan, until
they destroyed Jabin king of Canaan.

5 Then sang Deb'ō·rȧh and Bâr'ăk the son of A·bin'ō-am on that day:

2 "That the leaders took the lead in Israel,
that the people offered themselves willingly,
bless[d] the LORD!

3 "Hear, O kings; give ear, O princes;
to the LORD I will sing,
I will make melody to the LORD, the God of Israel.

4 "LORD, when thou didst go forth from Sē'ir,
when thou didst march from the region of E'dom,
the earth trembled,
and the heavens dropped,
yea, the clouds dropped water.
5 The mountains quaked before the LORD,
yon Sinai before the LORD, the God of Israel.

6 "In the days of Sham'gär, son of A'nath,
in the days of Jā'ĕl, caravans ceased
and travelers kept to the byways.
7 The peasantry ceased in Israel, they ceased
until you arose, Deb'ō·rȧh,
arose as a mother in Israel.
8 When new gods were chosen,
then war was in the gates.
Was shield or spear to be seen
among forty thousand in Israel?
9 My heart goes out to the commanders of Israel
who offered themselves willingly among the people.
Bless the LORD.

10 "Tell of it, you who ride on tawny asses,
you who sit on rich carpets[e]
and you who walk by the way.
11 To the sound of musicians[e] at the watering places,
there they repeat the triumphs of the LORD,
the triumphs of his peasantry in Israel.

"Then down to the gates marched the people of the LORD.

12 "Awake, awake, Deb'ō·rȧh!
Awake, awake, utter a song!
Arise, Bâr'ăk, lead away your captives,
O son of A·bin'ō-am.
13 Then down marched the remnant of the noble;
the people of the LORD marched down for him[f] against the mighty.
14 From E'phrȧ·im they set out thither[x] into the valley,[g]
following you, Benjamin, with your kinsmen;
from Mā'chir marched down the commanders,
and from Zeb'ū·lŭn those who bear the marshal's staff;
15 the princes of Is'sȧ·chär came with Deb'ō·rȧh,
and Issachar faithful to Bâr'ăk;
into the valley they rushed forth at his heels.
Among the clans of Reuben
there were great searchings of heart.
16 Why did you tarry among the sheepfolds,
to hear the piping for the flocks?
Among the clans of Reuben
there were great searchings of heart.
17 Gilead stayed beyond the Jordan;

[d] Or *You who offered yourselves willingly among the people, bless*
[e] The meaning of the Hebrew word is uncertain [f] Gk: Heb *me*
[x] Cn: Heb *From Ephraim their root* [g] Gk: Heb *in Amalek*

and Dan, why did he abide with
the ships?
Ash'ėr sat still at the coast of the
sea,
settling down by his landings.
18 Zeb'ū·lŭn is a people that jeoparded
their lives to the death;
Naph'tȧ·lī too, on the heights of
the field.

19 "The kings came, they fought;
then fought the kings of Canaan,
at Tā'ȧ·nach, by the waters of
Mė·gid'dō;
they got no spoils of silver.
20 From heaven fought the stars,
from their courses they fought
against Sis'ėr·ȧ.
21 The torrent Kī'shon swept them
away,
the onrushing torrent, the torrent
Kishon.
March on, my soul, with might!

22 "Then loud beat the horses' hoofs
with the galloping, galloping of
his steeds.

23 "Curse Mē'roz, says the angel of
the LORD,
curse bitterly its inhabitants,
because they came not to the help
of the LORD,
to the help of the LORD against
the mighty.

24 "Most blessed of women be Jā'ėl,
the wife of Hē'bėr the Ken'īte,
of tent-dwelling women most
blessed.
25 He asked water and she gave him
milk,
she brought him curds in a lordly
bowl.
26 She put her hand to the tent peg
and her right hand to the workmen's mallet;
she struck Sis'ėr·ȧ a blow,
she crushed his head,
she shattered and pierced his
temple.
27 He sank, he fell,
he lay still at her feet;
at her feet he sank, he fell;
where he sank, there he fell dead.

28 "Out of the window she peered,
the mother of Sis'ėr·ȧ gazed[h]
through the lattice:
'Why is his chariot so long in
coming?
Why tarry the hoofbeats of his
chariots?'
29 Her wisest ladies make answer,
nay, she gives answer to herself,
30 'Are they not finding and dividing
the spoil?—
A maiden or two for every man;
spoil of dyed stuffs for Sis'ėr·ȧ,
spoil of dyed stuffs embroidered,
two pieces of dyed work embroidered for my neck as spoil?'

31 "So perish all thine enemies,
O LORD!
But thy friends be like the sun as
he rises in his might."

And the land had rest for forty years.
6 The people of Israel did what was
evil in the sight of the LORD; and
the LORD gave them into the hand of
Mid'i·ȧn seven years. 2 And the hand
of Mid'i·ȧn prevailed over Israel; and
because of Midian the people of Israel
made for themselves the dens which
are in the mountains, and the caves
and the strongholds. 3 For whenever
the Israelites put in seed the Mid'i·ȧ-
nītes and the A·mal'ė·kītes and the
people of the East would come up and
attack them; 4 they would encamp
against them and destroy the produce
of the land, as far as the neighborhood
of Gā'zȧ, and leave no sustenance in
Israel, and no sheep or ox or ass. 5 For
they would come up with their cattle
and their tents, coming like locusts for
numbers; both they and their camels
could not be counted; so that they
wasted the land as they came in. 6 And
Israel was brought very low because
of Mid'i·ȧn; and the people of Israel
cried for help to the LORD.
7 When the people of Israel cried
to the LORD on account of the Mid'i-
ȧ·nītes, 8 the LORD sent a prophet to
the people of Israel; and he said to
them, "Thus says the LORD, the God
of Israel: I led you up from Egypt, and
brought you out of the house of bondage; 9 and I delivered you from the
hand of the Egyptians, and from the
hand of all who oppressed you, and
drove them out before you, and gave
you their land; 10 and I said to you, 'I
am the LORD your God; you shall not
pay reverence to the gods of the Am'ȯ-

[h] Gk Compare Tg: Heb *exclaimed*
5.31: Rev 1.16.

rītes, in whose land you dwell.' But
you have not given heed to my voice."
11 Now the angel of the LORD came
and sat under the oak at Oph'rȧh,
which belonged to Jō'ash the Ā·bi·ez'-
rīte, as his son Gideon was beating out
wheat in the wine press, to hide it
from the Mid'i·ȧ·nītes. 12 And the angel
of the LORD appeared to him and said
to him, "The LORD is with you, you
mighty man of valor." 13 And Gideon
said to him, "Pray, sir, if the LORD is
with us, why then has all this befallen
us? And where are all his wonderful
deeds which our fathers recounted to
us, saying, 'Did not the LORD bring us
up from Egypt?' But now the LORD
has cast us off, and given us into the
hand of Mid'i·ȧn." 14 And the LORD
turned to him and said, "Go in this
might of yours and deliver Israel from
the hand of Mid'i·ȧn; do not I send
you?" 15 And he said to him, "Pray,
Lord, how can I deliver Israel? Behold,
my clan is the weakest in Mȧ·nas'sėh,
and I am the least in my family."
16 And the LORD said to him, "But I
will be with you, and you shall smite
the Mid'i·ȧ·nītes as one man." 17 And
he said to him, "If now I have found
favor with thee, then show me a sign
that it is thou who speakest with me.
18 Do not depart from here, I pray
thee, until I come to thee, and bring
out my present, and set it before thee."
And he said, "I will stay till you
return."

19 So Gideon went into his house
and prepared a kid, and unleavened
cakes from an ephah of flour; the meat
he put in a basket, and the broth he
put in a pot, and brought them to him
under the oak and presented them.
20 And the angel of God said to him,
"Take the meat and the unleavened
cakes, and put them on this rock, and
pour the broth over them." And he
did so. 21 Then the angel of the LORD
reached out the tip of the staff that was
in his hand, and touched the meat and
the unleavened cakes; and there sprang
up fire from the rock and consumed
the flesh and the unleavened cakes;
and the angel of the LORD vanished
from his sight. 22 Then Gideon perceived that he was the angel of the
LORD; and Gideon said, "Alas, O Lord
GOD! For now I have seen the angel
of the LORD face to face." 23 But the
LORD said to him, "Peace be to you;
do not fear, you shall not die." 24 Then
Gideon built an altar there to the
LORD, and called it, The LORD is peace.
To this day it still stands at Oph'rȧh,
which belongs to the Ā·bi·ez'rītes.

25 That night the LORD said to him,
"Take your father's bull, the second
bull seven years old, and pull down the
altar of Bā'ȧl which your father has,
and cut down the Ȧ·shē'rȧh that is beside it; 26 and build an altar to the
LORD your God on the top of the
stronghold here, with stones laid in
due order; then take the second bull,
and offer it as a burnt offering with the
wood of the Ȧ·shē'rȧh which you shall
cut down." 27 So Gideon took ten men
of his servants, and did as the LORD
had told him; but because he was too
afraid of his family and the men of the
town to do it by day, he did it by night.

28 When the men of the town rose
early in the morning, behold, the altar
of Bā'ȧl was broken down, and the
Ȧ·shē'rȧh beside it was cut down, and
the second bull was offered upon the
altar which had been built. 29 And they
said to one another, "Who has done
this thing?" And after they had made
search and inquired, they said, "Gideon the son of Jō'ash has done this
thing." 30 Then the men of the town
said to Jō'ash, "Bring out your son,
that he may die, for he has pulled
down the altar of Bā'ȧl and cut down
the Ȧ·shē'rȧh beside it." 31 But Jō'ash
said to all who were arrayed against
him, "Will you contend for Bā'ȧl? Or
will you defend his cause? Whoever
contends for him shall be put to death
by morning. If he is a god, let him
contend for himself, because his altar
has been pulled down." 32 Therefore
on that day he was called Jer·ub·bā'ȧl,
that is to say, "Let Bā'ȧl contend
against him," because he pulled down
his altar.

33 Then all the Mid'i·ȧ·nītes and
the Ȧ·mal'ė·kītes and the people of the
East came together, and crossing the
Jordan they encamped in the Valley of
Jez'rē·ėl. 34 But the Spirit of the LORD
took possession of Gideon; and he
sounded the trumpet, and the Ā·bi·ez'-
rītes were called out to follow him.
35 And he sent messengers throughout
all Mȧ·nas'sėh; and they too were
called out to follow him. And he sent
messengers to Ash'ėr, Zeb'ū·lŭn, and
Naph'tȧ·lī; and they went up to meet
them.

36 Then Gideon said to God, "If

thou wilt deliver Israel by my hand,
as thou hast said, 37 behold, I am laying a fleece of wool on the threshing
floor; if there is dew on the fleece alone,
and it is dry on all the ground, then I
shall know that thou wilt deliver Israel
by my hand, as thou hast said." 38And
it was so. When he rose early next
morning and squeezed the fleece, he
wrung enough dew from the fleece to
fill a bowl with water. 39 Then Gideon
said to God, "Let not thy anger burn
against me, let me speak but this once;
pray, let me make trial only this once
with the fleece; pray, let it be dry only
on the fleece, and on all the ground let
there be dew." 40And God did so that
night; for it was dry on the fleece only,
and on all the ground there was dew.

7 Then Jer·ub·bā'ȧl (that is, Gideon) and all the people who were
with him rose early and encamped
beside the spring of Hâr'od; and the
camp of Mid'i·ȧn was north of them,
by the hill of Mō'reh, in the valley.

2 The LORD said to Gideon, "The
people with you are too many for me
to give the Mid'i·ȧ·nītes into their
hand, lest Israel vaunt themselves
against me, saying, 'My own hand has
delivered me.' 3 Now therefore proclaim in the ears of the people, saying,
'Whoever is fearful and trembling, let
him return home.'" And Gideon
tested them;[i] twenty-two thousand
returned, and ten thousand remained.

4 And the LORD said to Gideon,
"The people are still too many; take
them down to the water and I will test
them for you there; and he of whom I
say to you, 'This man shall go with
you,' shall go with you; and any of
whom I say to you, 'This man shall not
go with you,' shall not go." 5 So he
brought the people down to the water;
and the LORD said to Gideon, "Every
one that laps the water with his tongue,
as a dog laps, you shall set by himself;
likewise every one that kneels down to
drink." 6And the number of those that
lapped, putting their hands to their
mouths, was three hundred men; but
all the rest of the people knelt down to
drink water. 7And the LORD said to
Gideon, "With the three hundred men
that lapped I will deliver you, and give
the Mid'i·ȧ·nītes into your hand; and
let all the others go every man to his
home." 8 So he took the jars of the
people from their hands,[j] and their
trumpets; and he sent all the rest of
Israel every man to his tent, but
retained the three hundred men; and
the camp of Mid'i·ȧn was below him
in the valley.

9 That same night the LORD said to
him, "Arise, go down against the
camp; for I have given it into your
hand. 10 But if you fear to go down,
go down to the camp with Pū'rȧh your
servant; 11 and you shall hear what
they say, and afterward your hands
shall be strengthened to go down
against the camp." Then he went
down with Pū'rȧh his servant to the
outposts of the armed men that were
in the camp. 12And the Mid'i·ȧ·nītes
and the Ȧ·mal'ė·kītes and all the people
of the East lay along the valley like
locusts for multitude; and their camels
were without number, as the sand
which is upon the seashore for multitude. 13 When Gideon came, behold,
a man was telling a dream to his
comrade; and he said, "Behold, I
dreamed a dream; and lo, a cake of
barley bread tumbled into the camp of
Mid'i·ȧn, and came to the tent, and
struck it so that it fell, and turned it
upside down, so that the tent lay flat."
14And his comrade answered, "This
is no other than the sword of Gideon
the son of Jō'ash, a man of Israel; into
his hand God has given Mid'i·ȧn and
all the host."

15 When Gideon heard the telling
of the dream and its interpretation, he
worshiped; and he returned to the
camp of Israel, and said, "Arise; for
the LORD has given the host of Mid'i-
ȧn into your hand." 16And he divided
the three hundred men into three
companies, and put trumpets into the
hands of all of them and empty jars,
with torches inside the jars. 17And he
said to them, "Look at me, and do
likewise; when I come to the outskirts
of the camp, do as I do. 18 When I
blow the trumpet, I and all who are
with me, then blow the trumpets also
on every side of all the camp, and
shout, 'For the LORD and for Gideon.'"

19 So Gideon and the hundred men
who were with him came to the outskirts of the camp at the beginning of
the middle watch, when they had just
set the watch; and they blew the
trumpets and smashed the jars that
were in their hands. 20And the three
companies blew the trumpets and

[i] Cn: Heb *and depart from Mount Gilead* [j] Cn: Heb *the people took provisions in their hands*

broke the jars, holding in their left
hands the torches, and in their right
hands the trumpets to blow; and they
cried, "A sword for the LORD and for
Gideon!" 21 They stood every man in
his place round about the camp, and
all the army ran; they cried out and
fled. 22 When they blew the three hundred trumpets, the LORD set every
man's sword against his fellow and
against all the army; and the army fled
as far as Beth-shit'tȧh toward Zer'ė-
rȧh,[k] as far as the border of Ā'bėl-
mė·hō'lȧh, by Tab'bath. 23And the
men of Israel were called out from
Naph'tȧ·lī and from Ash'ėr and from
all Mȧ·nas'sėh, and they pursued after
Mid'i·ȧn.

24 And Gideon sent messengers
throughout all the hill country of
E'phrȧ·im, saying, "Come down
against the Mid'i·ȧ·nītes and seize the
waters against them, as far as Beth-
bâr'ȧh, and also the Jordan." So all the
men of Ephraim were called out, and
they seized the waters as far as Beth-
barah, and also the Jordan. 25And they
took the two princes of Mid'i·ȧn, Ôr'eb
and Zē'eb; they killed Oreb at the rock
of Oreb, and Zeeb they killed at the
wine press of Zeeb, as they pursued
Mid'i·ȧn; and they brought the heads
of Oreb and Zeeb to Gideon beyond
the Jordan.

8 And the men of E'phrȧ·im said to
him, "What is this that you have
done to us, not to call us when you
went to fight with Mid'i·ȧn?" And they
upbraided him violently. 2And he said
to them, "What have I done now in
comparison with you? Is not the gleaning of the grapes of E'phrȧ·im better
than the vintage of Ā·bi·ē'zėr? 3 God
has given into your hands the princes
of Mid'i·ȧn, Ôr'eb and Zē'eb; what
have I been able to do in comparison
with you?" Then their anger against
him was abated, when he had said
this.

4 And Gideon came to the Jordan
and passed over, he and the three hundred men who were with him, faint
yet pursuing. 5 So he said to the men
of Suc'coth, "Pray, give loaves of
bread to the people who follow me;
for they are faint, and I am pursuing
after Zē'bȧh and Zal·mun'nȧ, the kings
of Mid'i·ȧn." 6And the officials of
Suc'coth said, "Are Zē'bȧh and Zal-
mun'nȧ already in your hand, that we
should give bread to your army?"
7And Gideon said, "Well then, when
the LORD has given Zē'bȧh and Zal-
mun'nȧ into my hand, I will flail your
flesh with the thorns of the wilderness
and with briers." 8And from there he
went up to Pė·nū'el, and spoke to them
in the same way; and the men of
Penuel answered him as the men of
Suc'coth had answered. 9And he said
to the men of Pė·nū'el, "When I come
again in peace, I will break down this
tower."

10 Now Zē'bȧh and Zal·mun'nȧ
were in Kär'kôr with their army, about
fifteen thousand men, all who were left
of all the army of the people of the
East; for there had fallen a hundred
and twenty thousand men who drew
the sword. 11And Gideon went up by
the caravan route east of Nō'bȧh and
Jog'be·hȧh, and attacked the army; for
the army was off its guard. 12And
Zē'bȧh and Zal·mun'nȧ fled; and he
pursued them and took the two kings
of Mid'i·ȧn, Zebah and Zalmunna, and
he threw all the army into a panic.

13 Then Gideon the son of Jō'ash
returned from the battle by the ascent
of Hē'rēs. 14And he caught a young
man of Suc'coth, and questioned him;
and he wrote down for him the officials
and elders of Succoth, seventy-seven
men. 15And he came to the men of
Suc'coth, and said, "Behold Zē'bȧh
and Zal·mun'nȧ, about whom you
taunted me, saying, 'Are Zebah and
Zalmunna already in your hand, that
we should give bread to your men who
are faint?' " 16And he took the elders
of the city and he took thorns of the
wilderness and briers and with them
taught the men of Suc'coth. 17And he
broke down the tower of Pė·nū'el, and
slew the men of the city.

18 Then he said to Zē'bȧh and
Zal·mun'nȧ, "Where are the men
whom you slew at Tā'bôr?" They
answered, "As you are, so were they,
every one of them; they resembled the
sons of a king." 19And he said, "They
were my brothers, the sons of my
mother; as the LORD lives, if you had
saved them alive, I would not slay
you." 20And he said to Jē'thėr his first-
born, "Rise, and slay them." But the
youth did not draw his sword; for he
was afraid, because he was still a youth.
21 Then Zē'bȧh and Zal·mun'nȧ said,
"Rise yourself, and fall upon us; for as

[k] Another reading is *Zeredah*

the man is, so is his strength." And
Gideon arose and slew Zebah and
Zalmunna; and he took the crescents
that were on the necks of their camels.
22 Then the men of Israel said to
Gideon, "Rule over us, you and your
son and your grandson also; for you
have delivered us out of the hand of
Mid'i·ȧn." 23 Gideon said to them, "I
will not rule over you, and my son will
not rule over you; the LORD will rule
over you." 24 And Gideon said to them,
"Let me make a request of you; give
me every man of you the earrings of
his spoil." (For they had golden earrings, because they were Ish'mȧ·el-
ites.) 25 And they answered, "We will
willingly give them." And they spread
a garment, and every man cast in it
the earrings of his spoil. 26 And the
weight of the golden earrings that he
requested was one thousand seven
hundred shekels of gold; besides the
crescents and the pendants and the
purple garments worn by the kings of
Mid'i·ȧn, and besides the collars that
were about the necks of their camels.
27 And Gideon made an ephod of it
and put it in his city, in Oph'rȧh; and
all Israel played the harlot after it
there, and it became a snare to Gideon
and to his family. 28 So Mid'i·ȧn was
subdued before the people of Israel,
and they lifted up their heads no more.
And the land had rest forty years in
the days of Gideon.
29 Jer·ub·bā'ăl the son of Jō'ash
went and dwelt in his own house.
30 Now Gideon had seventy sons, his
own offspring, for he had many wives.
31 And his concubine who was in Shē'-
chem also bore him a son, and he
called his name Ȧ·bim'ė·lech. 32 And
Gideon the son of Jō'ash died in a good
old age, and was buried in the tomb of
Jō'ash his father, at Oph'rȧh of the
Ā·bi·ez'rītes.
33 As soon as Gideon died, the people of Israel turned again and played
the harlot after the Bā'ăls, and made
Bā'ăl-bē'rith their god. 34 And the people of Israel did not remember the
LORD their God, who had rescued
them from the hand of all their enemies
on every side; 35 and they did not show
kindness to the family of Jer·ub·bā'ăl
(that is, Gideon) in return for all the
good that he had done to Israel.
9 Now Ȧ·bim'ė·lech the son of Jer-
ub·bā'ăl went to Shē'chem to his
mother's kinsmen and said to them and
to the whole clan of his mother's
family, 2 "Say in the ears of all the
citizens of Shē'chem, 'Which is better
for you, that all seventy of the sons of
Jer·ub·bā'ăl rule over you, or that one
rule over you?' Remember also that I
am your bone and your flesh." 3 And
his mother's kinsmen spoke all these
words on his behalf in the ears of all
the men of Shē'chem; and their hearts
inclined to follow Ȧ·bim'ė·lech, for
they said, "He is our brother." 4 And
they gave him seventy pieces of silver
out of the house of Bā'ăl-bē'rith with
which Ȧ·bim'ė·lech hired worthless
and reckless fellows, who followed him.
5 And he went to his father's house at
Oph'rȧh, and slew his brothers the
sons of Jer·ub·bā'ăl, seventy men, upon
one stone; but Jō'thȧm the youngest
son of Jerubbaal was left, for he hid
himself. 6 And all the citizens of Shē'-
chem came together, and all Beth-
mil'lō, and they went and made
Ȧ·bim'ė·lech king, by the oak of the
pillar at Shechem.
7 When it was told to Jō'thȧm, he
went and stood on the top of Mount
Gĕr'i·zim, and cried aloud and said to
them, "Listen to me, you men of Shē'-
chem, that God may listen to you.
8 The trees once went forth to anoint
a king over them; and they said to the
olive tree, 'Reign over us.' 9 But the
olive tree said to them, 'Shall I leave
my fatness, by which gods and men
are honored, and go to sway over the
trees?' 10 And the trees said to the fig
tree, 'Come you, and reign over us.'
11 But the fig tree said to them, 'Shall
I leave my sweetness and my good
fruit, and go to sway over the trees?'
12 And the trees said to the vine, 'Come
you, and reign over us.' 13 But the
vine said to them, 'Shall I leave my
wine which cheers gods and men, and
go to sway over the trees?' 14 Then all
the trees said to the bramble, 'Come
you, and reign over us.' 15 And the
bramble said to the trees, 'If in good
faith you are anointing me king over
you, then come and take refuge in my
shade; but if not, let fire come out of
the bramble and devour the cedars of
Lebanon.'
16 "Now therefore, if you acted in
good faith and honor when you made
Ȧ·bim'ė·lech king, and if you have
dealt well with Jer·ub·bā'ăl and his
house, and have done to him as his
deeds deserved— 17 for my father

fought for you, and risked his life, and
rescued you from the hand of Mid'i-
ȧn; 18 and you have risen up against
my father's house this day, and have
slain his sons, seventy men on one
stone, and have made A·bim'ė·lech,
the son of his maidservant, king over
the citizens of Shē'chem, because he
is your kinsman— 19 if you then have
acted in good faith and honor with
Jer·ub·bā'ȧl and with his house this
day, then rejoice in A·bim'ė·lech, and
let him also rejoice in you; 20 but if
not, let fire come out from A·bim'ė-
lech, and devour the citizens of Shē'-
chem, and Beth-mil'lō; and let fire
come out from the citizens of Shechem,
and from Beth-millo, and devour
Abimelech." 21 And Jō'thȧm ran away
and fled, and went to Beer and dwelt
there, for fear of A·bim'ė·lech his
brother.

22 A·bim'ė·lech ruled over Israel
three years. 23 And God sent an evil
spirit between A·bim'ė·lech and the
men of Shē'chem; and the men of
Shechem dealt treacherously with
Abimelech; 24 that the violence done
to the seventy sons of Jer·ub·bā'ȧl
might come and their blood be laid
upon A·bim'ė·lech their brother, who
slew them, and upon the men of Shē'-
chem, who strengthened his hands to
slay his brothers. 25 And the men of
Shē'chem put men in ambush against
him on the mountain tops, and they
robbed all who passed by them along
the way; and it was told A·bim'ė·lech.

26 And Gā'ȧl the son of Ē'bed
moved into Shē'chem with his kinsmen; and the men of Shechem put
confidence in him. 27 And they went
out into the field, and gathered the
grapes from their vineyards and trod
them, and held festival, and went into
the house of their god, and ate and
drank and reviled A·bim'ė·lech. 28 And
Gā'ȧl the son of Ē'bed said, "Who is
A·bim'ė·lech, and who are we of Shē'-
chem, that we should serve him? Did
not the son of Jer·ub·bā'ȧl and Zē'bul
his officer serve the men of Hā'mor
the father of Shechem? Why then
should we serve him? 29 Would that
this people were under my hand! then
I would remove A·bim'ė·lech. I would
say[l] to Abimelech, 'Increase your
army, and come out.' "

30 When Zē'bul the ruler of the
city heard the words of Gā'ȧl the son
of Ē'bed, his anger was kindled. 31 And
he sent messengers to A·bim'ė·lech at
A·rü'mȧh,[m] saying, "Behold, Gā'ȧl the
son of Ē'bed and his kinsmen have
come to Shē'chem, and they are
stirring up[n] the city against you. 32 Now
therefore, go by night, you and the
men that are with you, and lie in wait
in the fields. 33 Then in the morning,
as soon as the sun is up, rise early and
rush upon the city; and when he and
the men that are with him come out
against you, you may do to them as
occasion offers."

34 And A·bim'ė·lech and all the
men that were with him rose up by
night, and laid wait against Shē'chem
in four companies. 35 And Gā'ȧl the
son of Ē'bed went out and stood in the
entrance of the gate of the city; and
A·bim'ė·lech and the men that were
with him rose from the ambush. 36 And
when Gā'ȧl saw the men, he said to
Zē'bul, "Look, men are coming down
from the mountain tops!" And Zebul
said to him, "You see the shadow of
the mountains as if they were men."
37 Gā'ȧl spoke again and said, "Look,
men are coming down from the center
of the land, and one company is coming
from the direction of the Diviners'
Oak." 38 Then Zē'bul said to him,
"Where is your mouth now, you who
said, 'Who is A·bim'ė·lech, that we
should serve him?' Are not these the
men whom you despised? Go out now
and fight with them." 39 And Gā'ȧl
went out at the head of the men of
Shē'chem, and fought with A·bim'ė-
lech. 40 And A·bim'ė·lech chased him,
and he fled before him; and many fell
wounded, up to the entrance of the
gate. 41 And A·bim'ė·lech dwelt at
A·rü'mȧh; and Zē'bul drove out Gā'ȧl
and his kinsmen, so that they could
not live on at Shē'chem.

42 On the following day the men
went out into the fields. And A·bim'ė-
lech was told. 43 He took his men and
divided them into three companies,
and laid wait in the fields; and he
looked and saw the men coming out
of the city, and he rose against them
and slew them. 44 A·bim'ė·lech and the
company[o] that was with him rushed
forward and stood at the entrance of
the gate of the city, while the two
companies rushed upon all who were

[l] Gk: Heb *and he said* [m] Cn See 9.41. Heb *Tormah* [n] Cn: Heb *besieging*
[o] Vg and some Mss of Gk: Heb *companies*

in the fields and slew them. 45And
A·bim'ė·lech fought against the city
all that day; he took the city, and killed
the people that were in it; and he razed
the city and sowed it with salt.

46 When all the people of the
Tower of Shē'chem heard of it, they
entered the stronghold of the house of
El-bē'rith. 47A·bim'ė·lech was told that
all the people of the Tower of Shē'-
chem were gathered together. 48And
A·bim'ė·lech went up to Mount Zal'-
mon, he and all the men that were
with him; and Abimelech took an axe
in his hand, and cut down a bundle of
brushwood, and took it up and laid it
on his shoulder. And he said to the
men that were with him, "What you
have seen me do, make haste to do, as
I have done." 49 So every one of the
people cut down his bundle and following A·bim'ė·lech put it against the
stronghold, and they set the stronghold on fire over them, so that all the
people of the Tower of Shē'chem also
died, about a thousand men and
women.

50 Then A·bim'ė·lech went to Thē'-
bez, and encamped against Thebez,
and took it. 51 But there was a strong
tower within the city, and all the people of the city fled to it, all the men
and women, and shut themselves in;
and they went to the roof of the tower.
52And A·bim'ė·lech came to the tower,
and fought against it, and drew near
to the door of the tower to burn it with
fire. 53And a certain woman threw an
upper millstone upon A·bim'ė·lech's
head, and crushed his skull. 54 Then
he called hastily to the young man his
armor-bearer, and said to him, "Draw
your sword and kill me, lest men say
of me, 'A woman killed him.' " And
his young man thrust him through,
and he died. 55And when the men of
Israel saw that A·bim'ė·lech was dead,
they departed every man to his home.
56 Thus God requited the crime of
A·bim'ė·lech, which he committed
against his father in killing his seventy
brothers; 57 and God also made all
the wickedness of the men of Shē'-
chem fall back upon their heads, and
upon them came the curse of Jō'thȧm
the son of Jer·ub·bā'ȧl.

10 After A·bim'ė·lech there arose
to deliver Israel Tō'lȧ the son of
Pū'ȧh, son of Dō'dō, a man of Is'sȧ-
chär; and he lived at Shā'mir in the
hill country of Ē'phrȧ·im. 2And he
judged Israel twenty-three years. Then
he died, and was buried at Shā'mir.

3 After him arose Jā'ir the Gileadite,
who judged Israel twenty-two years.
4And he had thirty sons who rode on
thirty asses; and they had thirty cities,
called Hāv'voth-jā'ir to this day, which
are in the land of Gilead. 5And Jā'ir
died, and was buried in Kā'mon.

6 And the people of Israel again did
what was evil in the sight of the LORD,
and served the Bā'ȧls and the Ash'tȧ-
roth, the gods of Syria, the gods of
Sī'don, the gods of Mō'ab, the gods
of the Am'mȯ·nītes, and the gods of
the Philistines; and they forsook the
LORD, and did not serve him. 7And
the anger of the LORD was kindled
against Israel, and he sold them into
the hand of the Philistines and into
the hand of the Am'mȯ·nītes, 8 and
they crushed and oppressed the children of Israel that year. For eighteen
years they oppressed all the people of
Israel that were beyond the Jordan in
the land of the Am'ȯ·rītes, which is in
Gilead. 9And the Am'mȯ·nītes crossed
the Jordan to fight also against Judah
and against Benjamin and against the
house of Ē'phrȧ·im; so that Israel was
sorely distressed.

10 And the people of Israel cried to
the LORD, saying, "We have sinned
against thee, because we have forsaken
our God and have served the Bā'ȧls."
11And the LORD said to the people of
Israel, "Did I not deliver you from
the Egyptians and from the Am'ȯ·rītes,
from the Am'mȯ·nītes and from the
Philistines? 12 The Sī·dō'ni·ȧns also,
and the A·mal'ė·kītes, and the Mā'ȯ-
nītes, oppressed you; and you cried to
me, and I delivered you out of their
hand. 13 Yet you have forsaken me
and served other gods; therefore I will
deliver you no more. 14 Go and cry to
the gods whom you have chosen; let
them deliver you in the time of your
distress." 15And the people of Israel
said to the LORD, "We have sinned; do
to us whatever seems good to thee;
only deliver us, we pray thee, this
day." 16 So they put away the foreign
gods from among them and served the
LORD; and he became indignant over
the misery of Israel.

17 Then the Am'mȯ·nītes were
called to arms, and they encamped in
Gilead; and the people of Israel came
together, and they encamped at Miz'-
pȧh. 18And the people, the leaders of

Gilead, said one to another, "Who is
the man that will begin to fight against
the Am'mȯ·nītes? He shall be head
over all the inhabitants of Gilead."

11 Now Jeph'thȧh the Gileadite
was a mighty warrior, but he was
the son of a harlot. Gilead was the
father of Jephthah. 2 And Gilead's wife
also bore him sons; and when his wife's
sons grew up, they thrust Jeph'thȧh
out, and said to him, "You shall not
inherit in our father's house; for you
are the son of another woman." 3 Then
Jeph'thȧh fled from his brothers, and
dwelt in the land of Tob; and worthless fellows collected round Jephthah,
and went raiding with him.

4 After a time the Am'mȯ·nītes
made war against Israel. 5 And when
the Am'mȯ·nītes made war against
Israel, the elders of Gilead went to
bring Jeph'thȧh from the land of Tob;
6 and they said to Jeph'thȧh, "Come
and be our leader, that we may fight
with the Am'mȯ·nītes." 7 But Jeph'-
thȧh said to the elders of Gilead, "Did
you not hate me, and drive me out of
my father's house? Why have you
come to me now when you are in
trouble?" 8 And the elders of Gilead
said to Jeph'thȧh, "That is why we
have turned to you now, that you may
go with us and fight with the Am'mȯ-
nītes, and be our head over all the inhabitants of Gilead." 9 Jeph'thȧh said
to the elders of Gilead, "If you bring
me home again to fight with the Am'-
mȯ·nītes, and the LORD gives them
over to me, I will be your head." 10 And
the elders of Gilead said to Jeph'thȧh,
"The LORD will be witness between
us; we will surely do as you say." 11 So
Jeph'thȧh went with the elders of
Gilead, and the people made him head
and leader over them; and Jephthah
spoke all his words before the LORD
at Miz'pȧh.

12 Then Jeph'thȧh sent messengers
to the king of the Am'mȯ·nītes and
said, "What have you against me, that
you have come to me to fight against
my land?" 13 And the king of the
Am'mȯ·nītes answered the messengers
of Jeph'thȧh, "Because Israel on
coming from Egypt took away my
land, from the Är'non to the Jab'bȯk
and to the Jordan; now therefore
restore it peaceably." 14 And Jeph'-
thȧh sent messengers again to the king
of the Am'mȯ·nītes 15 and said to him,
"Thus says Jeph'thȧh: Israel did not
take away the land of Mō'ab or the
land of the Am'mȯ·nītes, 16 but when
they came up from Egypt, Israel went
through the wilderness to the Red Sea
and came to Kā'desh. 17 Israel then
sent messengers to the king of Ē'dȯm,
saying, 'Let us pass, we pray, through
your land'; but the king of Edom
would not listen. And they sent also
to the king of Mō'ab, but he would
not consent. So Israel remained at
Kā'desh. 18 Then they journeyed
through the wilderness, and went
around the land of Ē'dȯm and the land
of Mō'ab, and arrived on the east side
of the land of Moab, and camped on
the other side of the Är'non; but they
did not enter the territory of Moab,
for the Arnon was the boundary of
Moab. 19 Israel then sent messengers
to Sī'hon king of the Am'ȯ·rītes, king
of Hesh'bȯn; and Israel said to him,
'Let us pass, we pray, through your
land to our country.' 20 But Sī'hon
did not trust Israel to pass through his
territory; so Sihon gathered all his
people together, and encamped at
Jā'haz, and fought with Israel. 21 And
the LORD, the God of Israel, gave
Sī'hon and all his people into the hand
of Israel, and they defeated them; so
Israel took possession of all the land
of the Am'ȯ·rītes, who inhabited that
country. 22 And they took possession
of all the territory of the Am'ȯ·rītes
from the Är'non to the Jab'bȯk and
from the wilderness to the Jordan.
23 So then the LORD, the God of Israel,
dispossessed the Am'ȯ·rītes from before his people Israel; and are you to
take possession of them? 24 Will you
not possess what Chē'mosh your god
gives you to possess? And all that the
LORD our God has dispossessed before
us, we will possess. 25 Now are you
any better than Bā'lak the son of
Zip'pôr, king of Mō'ab? Did he ever
strive against Israel, or did he ever go
to war with them? 26 While Israel
dwelt in Hesh'bȯn and its villages, and
in Ȧ·rō'ėr and its villages, and in all
the cities that are on the banks of the
Är'non, three hundred years, why did
you not recover them within that
time? 27 I therefore have not sinned
against you, and you do me wrong by
making war on me; the LORD, the
Judge, decide this day between the
people of Israel and the people of
Am'mȯn." 28 But the king of the
Am'mȯ·nītes did not heed the mes-

sage of Jeph'thȧh which he sent to
him.
29 Then the Spirit of the LORD
came upon Jeph'thȧh, and he passed
through Gilead and Mȧ·nas'sėh, and
passed on to Miz'pȧh of Gilead, and
from Mizpah of Gilead he passed on
to the Am'mȯ·nītes. 30 And Jeph'thȧh
made a vow to the LORD, and said,
"If thou wilt give the Am'mȯ·nītes into my hand, 31 then whoever comes
forth from the doors of my house to
meet me, when I return victorious
from the Am'mȯ·nītes, shall be the
LORD's, and I will offer him up for a
burnt offering." 32 So Jeph'thȧh
crossed over to the Am'mȯ·nītes to
fight against them; and the LORD gave
them into his hand. 33 And he smote
them from Ȧ·rō'ėr to the neighborhood
of Min'nith, twenty cities, and as far
as Ā·bėl-ker'ȧ·mim, with a very great
slaughter. So the Am'mȯ·nītes were
subdued before the people of Israel.
34 Then Jeph'thȧh came to his
home at Miz'pȧh; and behold, his
daughter came out to meet him with
timbrels and with dances; she was his
only child; beside her he had neither
son nor daughter. 35 And when he saw
her, he rent his clothes, and said,
"Alas, my daughter! you have brought
me very low, and you have become the
cause of great trouble to me; for I have
opened my mouth to the LORD, and I
cannot take back my vow." 36 And she
said to him, "My father, if you have
opened your mouth to the LORD, do
to me according to what has gone forth
from your mouth, now that the LORD
has avenged you on your enemies, on
the Am'mȯ·nītes." 37 And she said to
her father, "Let this thing be done for
me; let me alone two months, that I
may go and wander[p] on the mountains,
and bewail my virginity, I and my
companions." 38 And he said, "Go."
And he sent her away for two months;
and she departed, she and her companions, and bewailed her virginity
upon the mountains. 39 And at the end
of two months, she returned to her
father, who did with her according to
his vow which he had made. She had
never known a man. And it became a
custom in Israel 40 that the daughters
of Israel went year by year to lament
the daughter of Jeph'thȧh the Gileadite four days in the year.

12 The men of E'phrȧ·im were
called to arms, and they crossed
to Zā'phȯn and said to Jeph'thȧh,
"Why did you cross over to fight
against the Am'mȯ·nītes, and did not
call us to go with you? We will burn
your house over you with fire." 2 And
Jeph'thȧh said to them, "I and my
people had a great feud with the
Am'mȯ·nītes; and when I called you,
you did not deliver me from their
hand. 3 And when I saw that you
would not deliver me, I took my life
in my hand, and crossed over against
the Am'mȯ·nītes, and the LORD gave
them into my hand; why then have you
come up to me this day, to fight against
me?" 4 Then Jeph'thȧh gathered all
the men of Gilead and fought with
E'phrȧ·im; and the men of Gilead
smote Ephraim, because they said,
"You are fugitives of Ephraim, you
Gileadites, in the midst of Ephraim
and Mȧ·nas'sėh." 5 And the Gileadites
took the fords of the Jordan against the
E'phrȧ·im·ītes. And when any of the
fugitives of E'phrȧ·im said, "Let me
go over," the men of Gilead said to
him, "Are you an Ephraimite?" When
he said, "No," 6 they said to him,
"Then say Shib'bȯ·lėth," and he said,
"Sib'bȯ·lėth," for he could not pronounce it right; then they seized him
and slew him at the fords of the Jordan.
And there fell at that time forty-two
thousand of the E'phrȧ·im·ītes.
7 Jeph'thȧh judged Israel six years.
Then Jephthah the Gileadite died, and
was buried in his city in Gilead[q].
8 After him Ib'zȧn of Bethlehem
judged Israel. 9 He had thirty sons;
and thirty daughters he gave in marriage outside his clan, and thirty
daughters he brought in from outside
for his sons. And he judged Israel
seven years. 10 Then Ib'zȧn died, and
was buried at Bethlehem.
11 After him E'lon the Zeb'ū·lŭ-
nīte judged Israel; and he judged Israel
ten years. 12 Then E'lon the Zeb'ū·lŭ-
nīte died, and was buried at Ai'jȧ·lon
in the land of Zeb'ū·lŭn.
13 After him Ab'don the son of
Hil'lel the Pir'ȧ·thȯ·nīte judged Israel.
14 He had forty sons and thirty grandsons, who rode on seventy asses; and
he judged Israel eight years. 15 Then
Ab'don the son of Hil'lel the Pir'ȧ·thȯ-
nīte died, and was buried at Pir'ȧ·thon

[p] Cn: Heb *go down*
[q] Gk: Heb *in the cities of Gilead*

in the land of E'phrȧ·im, in the hill
country of the Ȧ·mal'ĕ·kītes.

13 And the people of Israel again
did what was evil in the sight of
the LORD; and the LORD gave them
into the hand of the Philistines for
forty years.

2 And there was a certain man of
Zō'rȧh, of the tribe of the Danites,
whose name was Mȧ·nō'ăh; and his
wife was barren and had no children.
3 And the angel of the LORD appeared
to the woman and said to her, "Behold, you are barren and have no children; but you shall conceive and bear
a son. 4 Therefore beware, and drink
no wine or strong drink, and eat
nothing unclean, 5 for lo, you shall
conceive and bear a son. No razor
shall come upon his head, for the boy
shall be a Naz'i·rite to God from birth;
and he shall begin to deliver Israel
from the hand of the Philistines."
6 Then the woman came and told her
husband, "A man of God came to me,
and his countenance was like the
countenance of the angel of God, very
terrible; I did not ask him whence he
was, and he did not tell me his name;
7 but he said to me, 'Behold, you shall
conceive and bear a son; so then drink
no wine or strong drink, and eat
nothing unclean, for the boy shall be
a Naz'i·rite to God from birth to the
day of his death.' "

8 Then Mȧ·nō'ăh entreated the
LORD, and said, "O, LORD, I pray thee,
let the man of God whom thou didst
send come again to us, and teach us
what we are to do with the boy that
will be born." 9 And God listened to
the voice of Mȧ·nō'ăh, and the angel
of God came again to the woman as
she sat in the field; but Manoah her
husband was not with her. 10 And the
woman ran in haste and told her
husband, "Behold, the man who came
to me the other day has appeared to
me." 11 And Mȧ·nō'ăh arose and went
after his wife, and came to the man
and said to him, "Are you the man
who spoke to this woman?" And he
said, "I am." 12 And Mȧ·nō'ăh said,
"Now when your words come true,
what is to be the boy's manner of life,
and what is he to do?" 13 And the angel
of the LORD said to Mȧ·nō'ăh, "Of all
that I said to the woman let her beware. 14 She may not eat of anything
that comes from the vine, neither let
her drink wine or strong drink, or eat
any unclean thing; all that I commanded her let her observe."

15 Mȧ·nō'ăh said to the angel of the
LORD, "Pray, let us detain you, and
prepare a kid for you." 16 And the angel
of the LORD said to Mȧ·nō'ăh, "If you
detain me, I will not eat of your food;
but if you make ready a burnt offering,
then offer it to the LORD." (For
Manoah did not know that he was the
angel of the LORD.) 17 And Mȧ·nō'ăh
said to the angel of the LORD, "What
is your name, so that, when your words
come true, we may honor you?" 18 And
the angel of the LORD said to him,
"Why do you ask my name, seeing it is
wonderful?" 19 So Mȧ·nō'ăh took the
kid with the cereal offering, and offered
it upon the rock to the LORD, to him
who works[r] wonders[s]. 20 And when the
flame went up toward heaven from the
altar, the angel of the LORD ascended
in the flame of the altar while Mȧ·nō'ăh
and his wife looked on; and they fell
on their faces to the ground.

21 The angel of the LORD appeared
no more to Mȧ·nō'ăh and to his wife.
Then Manoah knew that he was the
angel of the LORD. 22 And Mȧ·nō'ăh
said to his wife, "We shall surely die,
for we have seen God." 23 But his wife
said to him, "If the LORD had meant
to kill us, he would not have accepted
a burnt offering and a cereal offering
at our hands, or shown us all these
things, or now announced to us such
things as these." 24 And the woman
bore a son, and called his name Samson; and the boy grew, and the LORD
blessed him. 25 And the Spirit of the
LORD began to stir him in Mā'hȧ-
nĕh-dan, between Zō'rȧh and Esh'-
tā-ol.

14 Samson went down to Tim'nȧh,
and at Timnah he saw one of the
daughters of the Philistines. 2 Then he
came up, and told his father and
mother, "I saw one of the daughters
of the Philistines at Tim'nȧh; now get
her for me as my wife." 3 But his father
and mother said to him, "Is there not
a woman among the daughters of your
kinsmen, or among all our people, that
you must go to take a wife from the
uncircumcised Philistines?" But Samson said to his father, "Get her for me;
for she pleases me well."

[r] Gk Vg: Heb *and working* [s] Heb *wonders, while Manoah and his wife looked on*
13.4-5: Lk 1.15. 13.24: Lk 2.40.

4 His father and mother did not
know that it was from the LORD; for
he was seeking an occasion against the
Philistines. At that time the Philistines
had dominion over Israel.

5 Then Samson went down with
his father and mother to Tim'nah, and
he came to the vineyards of Timnah.
And behold, a young lion roared
against him; 6 and the Spirit of the
LORD came mightily upon him, and
he tore the lion asunder as one tears a
kid; and he had nothing in his hand.
But he did not tell his father or his
mother what he had done. 7 Then he
went down and talked with the woman;
and she pleased Samson well. 8 And
after a while he returned to take her;
and he turned aside to see the carcass
of the lion, and behold, there was a
swarm of bees in the body of the lion,
and honey. 9 He scraped it out into his
hands, and went on, eating as he went;
and he came to his father and mother,
and gave some to them, and they ate.
But he did not tell them that he had
taken the honey from the carcass of
the lion.

10 And his father went down to the
woman, and Samson made a feast
there; for so the young men used to do.
11 And when the people saw him, they
brought thirty companions to be with
him. 12 And Samson said to them,
"Let me now put a riddle to you; if
you can tell me what it is, within the
seven days of the feast, and find it out,
then I will give you thirty linen garments and thirty festal garments;
13 but if you cannot tell me what it is,
then you shall give me thirty linen
garments and thirty festal garments."
And they said to him, "Put your riddle,
that we may hear it." 14 And he said to
them,

"Out of the eater came something
to eat.
Out of the strong came something
sweet."

And they could not in three days tell
what the riddle was.

15 On the fourth[t] day they said to
Samson's wife, "Entice your husband
to tell us what the riddle is, lest we
burn you and your father's house with
fire. Have you invited us here to
impoverish us?" 16 And Samson's wife
wept before him, and said, "You only
hate me, you do not love me; you have
put a riddle to my countrymen, and
you have not told me what is is." And
he said to her, "Behold, I have not
told my father nor my mother, and
shall I tell you?" 17 She wept before
him the seven days that their feast
lasted; and on the seventh day he told
her, because she pressed him hard.
Then she told the riddle to her countrymen. 18 And the men of the city said to
him on the seventh day before the sun
went down,

"What is sweeter than honey?
What is stronger than a lion?"

And he said to them,

"If you had not plowed with my
heifer,
you would not have found out my
riddle."

19 And the Spirit of the LORD came
mightily upon him, and he went down
to Ash'ke-lon and killed thirty men of
the town, and took their spoil and gave
the festal garments to those who had
told the riddle. In hot anger he went
back to his father's house. 20 And Samson's wife was given to his companion,
who had been his best man.

15 After a while, at the time of
wheat harvest, Samson went to
visit his wife with a kid; and he said,
"I will go in to my wife in the chamber." But her father would not allow
him to go in. 2 And her father said, "I
really thought that you utterly hated
her; so I gave her to your companion.
Is not her younger sister fairer than
she? Pray take her instead." 3 And Samson said to them, "This time I shall be
blameless in regard to the Philistines,
when I do them mischief." 4 So Samson went and caught three hundred
foxes, and took torches; and he turned
them tail to tail, and put a torch between each pair of tails. 5 And when
he had set fire to the torches, he let the
foxes go into the standing grain of
the Philistines, and burned up the
shocks and the standing grain, as well
as the olive orchards. 6 Then the
Philistines said, "Who has done this?"
And they said, "Samson, the son-in-
law of the Tim'nite, because he has
taken his wife and given her to his
companion." And the Philistines came
up, and burned her and her father with
fire. 7 And Samson said to them, "If
this is what you do, I swear I will be
avenged upon you, and after that I
will quit." 8 And he smote them hip
and thigh with great slaughter; and he

[t] Gk Syr: Heb *seventh*

went down and stayed in the cleft of
the rock of Ē'tam.
9 Then the Philistines came up and
encamped in Judah, and made a raid
on Lē'hī. 10 And the men of Judah
said, "Why have you come up against
us?" They said, "We have come up to
bind Samson, to do to him as he did
to us." 11 Then three thousand men
of Judah went down to the cleft of the
rock of Ē'tam, and said to Samson,
"Do you not know that the Philistines
are rulers over us? What then is this
that you have done to us?" And he
said to them, "As they did to me, so
have I done to them." 12 And they said
to him, "We have come down to bind
you, that we may give you into the
hands of the Philistines." And Samson
said to them, "Swear to me that you
will not fall upon me yourselves."
13 They said to him, "No; we will only
bind you and give you into their hands;
we will not kill you." So they bound
him with two new ropes, and brought
him up from the rock.
14 When he came to Lē'hī, the
Philistines came shouting to meet him;
and the Spirit of the LORD came
mightily upon him, and the ropes
which were on his arms became as
flax that has caught fire, and his bonds
melted off his hands. 15 And he found
a fresh jawbone of an ass, and put out
his hand and seized it, and with it he
slew a thousand men. 16 And Samson
said,

"With the jawbone of an ass,
heaps upon heaps,
with the jawbone of an ass
have I slain a thousand men."

17 When he had finished speaking, he
threw away the jawbone out of his
hand; and that place was called
Rā'mȧth-lē'hī.[u]
18 And he was very thirsty, and he
called on the LORD and said, "Thou
hast granted this great deliverance by
the hand of thy servant; and shall I
now die of thirst, and fall into the
hands of the uncircumcised?" 19 And
God split open the hollow place that
is at Lē'hī, and there came water from
it; and when he drank, his spirit returned, and he revived. Therefore the
name of it was called En-hak·kōr'ē;[v] it
is at Lehi to this day. 20 And he judged
Israel in the days of the Philistines
twenty years.

16 Samson went to Gā'zȧ, and
there he saw a harlot, and he went
in to her. 2 The Gā'zītes were told,
"Samson has come here," and they
surrounded the place and lay in wait
for him all night at the gate of the city.
They kept quiet all night, saying,
"Let us wait till the light of the morning; then we will kill him." 3 But Samson lay till midnight, and at midnight
he arose and took hold of the doors of
the gate of the city and the two posts,
and pulled them up, bar and all, and
put them on his shoulders and carried
them to the top of the hill that is before Hē'brȯn.
4 After this he loved a woman in
the valley of Sō'rek, whose name was
Dē·lī'lȧh. 5 And the lords of the Philistines came to her and said to her,
"Entice him, and see wherein his great
strength lies, and by what means we
may overpower him, that we may
bind him to subdue him; and we will
each give you eleven hundred pieces
of silver." 6 And Dē·lī'lȧh said to Samson, "Please tell me wherein your great
strength lies, and how you might be
bound, that one could subdue you."
7 And Samson said to her, "If they
bind me with seven fresh bowstrings
which have not been dried, then I shall
become weak, and be like any other
man." 8 Then the lords of the Philistines brought her seven fresh bowstrings which had not been dried, and
she bound him with them. 9 Now she
had men lying in wait in an inner
chamber. And she said to him, "The
Philistines are upon you, Samson!"
But he snapped the bowstrings, as a
string of tow snaps when it touches the
fire. So the secret of his strength was
not known.
10 And Dē·lī'lȧh said to Samson,
"Behold, you have mocked me, and
told me lies; please tell me how you
might be bound." 11 And he said to
her, "If they bind me with new ropes
that have not been used, then I shall
become weak, and be like any other
man." 12 So Dē·lī'lȧh took new ropes
and bound him with them, and said to
him, "The Philistines are upon you,
Samson!" And the men lying in wait
were in an inner chamber. But he
snapped the ropes off his arms like a
thread.
13 And Dē·lī'lȧh said to Samson,
"Until now you have mocked me, and

[u] That is *The hill of the jawbone* [v] That is *The spring of him who called*

told me lies; tell me how you might be
bound." And he said to her, "If you
weave the seven locks of my head with
the web and make it tight with the
pin, then I shall become weak, and be
like any other man." 14 So while he
slept, Dē·lī'lȧh took the seven locks of
his head and wove them into the web.[w]
And she made them tight with the pin,
and said to him, "The Philistines are
upon you, Samson!" But he awoke
from his sleep, and pulled away the
pin, the loom, and the web.

15 And she said to him, "How can
you say, 'I love you,' when your heart
is not with me? You have mocked me
these three times, and you have not
told me wherein your great strength
lies." 16 And when she pressed him
hard with her words day after day, and
urged him, his soul was vexed to death.
17 And he told her all his mind, and
said to her, "A razor has never come
upon my head; for I have been a
Naz'i·rīte to God from my mother's
womb. If I be shaved, then my strength
will leave me, and I shall become
weak, and be like any other man."

18 When Dē·lī'lȧh saw that he had
told her all his mind, she sent and
called the lords of the Philistines, saying, "Come up this once, for he has
told me all his mind." Then the lords
of the Philistines came up to her, and
brought the money in their hands.
19 She made him sleep upon her knees;
and she called a man, and had him
shave off the seven locks of his head.
Then she began to torment him, and
his strength left him. 20 And she said,
"The Philistines are upon you, Samson!" And he awoke from his sleep,
and said, "I will go out as at other
times, and shake myself free." And he
did not know that the LORD had left
him. 21 And the Philistines seized him
and gouged out his eyes, and brought
him down to Gā'zȧ, and bound him
with bronze fetters; and he ground at
the mill in the prison. 22 But the hair
of his head began to grow again after
it had been shaved.

23 Now the lords of the Philistines
gathered to offer a great sacrifice to
Dā'gon their god, and to rejoice; for
they said, "Our god has given Samson
our enemy into our hand." 24 And
when the people saw him, they praised
their god; for they said, "Our god has
given our enemy into our hand, the
ravager of our country, who has slain
many of us." 25 And when their hearts
were merry, they said, "Call Samson,
that he may make sport for us." So
they called Samson out of the prison,
and he made sport before them. They
made him stand between the pillars;
26 and Samson said to the lad who
held him by the hand, "Let me feel
the pillars on which the house rests,
that I may lean against them." 27 Now
the house was full of men and women;
all the lords of the Philistines were
there, and on the roof there were about
three thousand men and women, who
looked on while Samson made sport.

28 Then Samson called to the LORD
and said, "O Lord GOD, remember
me, I pray thee, and strengthen me,
I pray thee, only this once, O God,
that I may be avenged upon the Philistines for one of my two eyes." 29 And
Samson grasped the two middle pillars
upon which the house rested, and he
leaned his weight upon them, his right
hand on the one and his left hand on
the other. 30 And Samson said, "Let
me die with the Philistines." Then he
bowed with all his might; and the
house fell upon the lords and upon all
the people that were in it. So the dead
whom he slew at his death were more
than those whom he had slain during
his life. 31 Then his brothers and all
his family came down and took him
and brought him up and buried him
between Zō'rȧh and Esh'tā-ol in the
tomb of Mȧ·nō'ȧh his father. He had
judged Israel twenty years.

17 There was a man of the hill
country of E'phrȧ·im, whose
name was Mī'cȧh. 2 And he said to his
mother, "The eleven hundred pieces
of silver which were taken from you,
about which you uttered a curse, and
also spoke it in my ears, behold, the
silver is with me; I took it." And his
mother said, "Blessed be my son by
the LORD." 3 And he restored the eleven
hundred pieces of silver to his mother;
and his mother said, "I consecrate the
silver to the LORD from my hand for
my son, to make a graven image and a
molten image; now therefore I will
restore it to you." 4 So when he restored the money to his mother, his
mother took two hundred pieces of
silver, and gave it to the silversmith,
who made it into a graven image and a
molten image; and it was in the house

[w] Compare Gk: Heb lacks *and make it tight . . . into the web*

of Mī′cȧh. 5And the man Mī′cȧh had
a shrine, and he made an ephod and
teraphim, and installed one of his sons,
who became his priest. 6 In those days
there was no king in Israel; every man
did what was right in his own eyes.
7 Now there was a young man of
Bethlehem in Judah, of the family of
Judah, who was a Levite; and he sojourned there. 8And the man departed
from the town of Bethlehem in Judah,
to live where he could find a place; and
as he journeyed, he came to the hill
country of Ē′phrȧ·im to the house of
Mī′cȧh. 9And Mī′cȧh said to him,
"From where do you come?" And he
said to him, "I am a Levite of Bethlehem in Judah, and I am going to sojourn where I may find a place."
10And Mī′cȧh said to him, "Stay with
me, and be to me a father and a priest,
and I will give you ten pieces of silver
a year, and a suit of apparel, and your
living."[w] 11And the Levite was content
to dwell with the man; and the young
man became to him like one of his
sons. 12And Mī′cȧh installed the Levite, and the young man became his
priest, and was in the house of Mī′cȧh.
13 Then Mī′cȧh said, "Now I know that
the LORD will prosper me, because I
have a Levite as priest."

18 In those days there was no king
in Israel. And in those days the
tribe of the Danites was seeking for itself an inheritance to dwell in; for until
then no inheritance among the tribes
of Israel had fallen to them. 2 So the
Danites sent five able men from the
whole number of their tribe, from
Zō′rȧh and from Esh′tā-ol, to spy out
the land and to explore it; and they
said to them, "Go and explore the
land." And they came to the hill
country of Ē′phrȧ·im, to the house of
Mī′cȧh, and lodged there. 3 When they
were by the house of Mī′cȧh, they
recognized the voice of the young
Levite; and they turned aside and said
to him, "Who brought you here? What
are you doing in this place? What is
your business here?" 4And he said to
them, "Thus and thus has Mī′cȧh
dealt with me: he has hired me, and I
have become his priest." 5And they
said to him, "Inquire of God, we pray
thee, that we may know whether the
journey on which we are setting out
will succeed." 6And the priest said to
them, "Go in peace. The journey on
which you go is under the eye of the
LORD."
7 Then the five men departed, and
came to Lā′ish, and saw the people
who were there, how they dwelt in
security, after the manner of the Sī-
dō′ni·ȧnṡ, quiet and unsuspecting,
lacking[x] nothing that is in the earth,
and possessing wealth, and how they
were far from the Sidonians and had
no dealings with any one. 8And when
they came to their brethren at Zō′rȧh
and Esh′tā-ol, their brethren said to
them, "What do you report?" 9 They
said, "Arise, and let us go up against
them; for we have seen the land, and
behold, it is very fertile. And will you
do nothing? Do not be slow to go, and
enter in and possess the land. 10 When
you go, you will come to an unsuspecting people. The land is broad; yea,
God has given it into your hands, a
place where there is no lack of anything that is in the earth."
11 And six hundred men of the
tribe of Dan, armed with weapons of
war, set forth from Zō′rȧh and Esh′-
tā-ol, 12 and went up and encamped at
Kĭr′i·ath-jē′ȧ·rim in Judah. On this
account that place is called Mā′hȧ·nėh-
dan[y] to this day; behold, it is west of
Kiriath-jearim. 13And they passed on
from there to the hill country of
Ē′phrȧ·im, and came to the house of
Mī′cȧh.
14 Then the five men who had gone
to spy out the country of Lā′ish said to
their brethren, "Do you know that in
these houses there are an ephod, teraphim, a graven image, and a molten
image? Now therefore consider what
you will do." 15And they turned aside
thither, and came to the house of the
young Levite, at the home of Mī′cȧh,
and asked him of his welfare. 16 Now
the six hundred men of the Danites,
armed with their weapons of war,
stood by the entrance of the gate;
17 and the five men who had gone to
spy out the land went up, and entered
and took the graven image, the ephod,
the teraphim, and the molten image,
while the priest stood by the entrance
of the gate with the six hundred men
armed with weapons of war. 18And
when these went into Mī′cȧh's house

[w] Heb *living, and the Levite went* [x] Cn Compare 18.10. The Hebrew text is uncertain
[y] That is *Camp of Dan*
18.7: Judg 18.27-28.

and took the graven image, the ephod,
the teraphim, and the molten image,
the priest said to them, "What are you
doing?" 19 And they said to him,
"Keep quiet, put your hand upon
your mouth, and come with us, and be
to us a father and a priest. Is it better
for you to be priest to the house of one
man, or to be priest to a tribe and
family in Israel?" 20 And the priest's
heart was glad; he took the ephod, and
the teraphim, and the graven image,
and went in the midst of the people.

21 So they turned and departed,
putting the little ones and the cattle
and the goods in front of them. 22 When
they were a good way from the home
of Mī′cah, the men who were in the
houses near Micah's house were called
out, and they overtook the Danites.
23 And they shouted to the Danites,
who turned round and said to Mī′cah,
"What ails you that you come with
such a company?" 24 And he said,
"You take my gods which I made, and
the priest, and go away, and what have
I left? How then do you ask me, 'What
ails you?' " 25 And the Danites said to
him, "Do not let your voice be heard
among us, lest angry fellows fall upon
you, and you lose your life with the
lives of your household." 26 Then the
Danites went their way; and when
Mī′cah saw that they were too strong
for him, he turned and went back to
his home.

27 And taking what Mī′cah had
made, and the priest who belonged to
him, the Danites came to Lā′ish, to a
people quiet and unsuspecting, and
smote them with the edge of the
sword, and burned the city with fire.
28 And there was no deliverer because
it was far from Sī′don, and they had
no dealings with any one. It was in the
valley which belongs to Beth-rē′hob.
And they rebuilt the city, and dwelt in
it. 29 And they named the city Dan,
after the name of Dan their ancestor,
who was born to Israel; but the name
of the city was Lā′ish at the first.
30 And the Danites set up the graven
image for themselves; and Jonathan
the son of Gēr′shom, son of Moses,[z]
and his sons were priests to the tribe
of the Danites until the day of the
captivity of the land. 31 So they set up
Mī′cah's graven image which he made,
as long as the house of God was at
Shī′lōh.

19 In those days, when there was
no king in Israel, a certain Levite
was sojourning in the remote parts of
the hill country of E′phra·im, who
took to himself a concubine from
Bethlehem in Judah. 2 And his concubine became angry with[a] him, and
she went away from him to her father's
house at Bethlehem in Judah, and was
there some four months. 3 Then her
husband arose and went after her, to
speak kindly to her and bring her
back. He had with him his servant and
a couple of asses. And he came[b] to her
father's house; and when the girl's
father saw him, he came with joy to
meet him. 4 And his father-in-law, the
girl's father, made him stay, and he
remained with him three days; so they
ate and drank, and lodged there. 5 And
on the fourth day they arose early in
the morning, and he prepared to go;
but the girl's father said to his son-in-
law, "Strengthen your heart with a
morsel of bread, and after that you
may go." 6 So the two men sat and ate
and drank together; and the girl's
father said to the man, "Be pleased to
spend the night, and let your heart be
merry." 7 And when the man rose up
to go, his father-in-law urged him, till
he lodged there again. 8 And on the
fifth day he arose early in the morning
to depart; and the girl's father said,
"Strengthen your heart, and tarry until
the day declines." So they ate, both
of them. 9 And when the man and his
concubine and his servant rose up to
depart, his father-in-law, the girl's
father, said to him, "Behold, now the
day has waned toward evening; pray
tarry all night. Behold, the day draws
to its close; lodge here and let your
heart be merry; and tomorrow you
shall arise early in the morning for
your journey, and go home."

10 But the man would not spend
the night; he rose up and departed,
and arrived opposite Jē′bus (that is,
Jerusalem). He had with him a couple
of saddled asses, and his concubine
was with him. 11 When they were near
Jē′bus, the day was far spent, and the
servant said to his master, "Come now,
let us turn aside to this city of the
Jeb′ū·sites, and spend the night in it."
12 And his master said to him, "We

[z] Another reading is *Manasseh* [a] Gk Old Latin: Heb *played the harlot against*
[b] Gk: Heb *she brought him*

will not turn aside into the city of
foreigners, who do not belong to the
people of Israel; but we will pass on to
Gib′ē-ȧh." 13 And he said to his servant, "Come and let us draw near to
one of these places, and spend the
night at Gib′ē-ȧh or at Rā′mȧh." 14 So
they passed on and went their way;
and the sun went down on them near
Gib′ē-ȧh, which belongs to Benjamin,
15 and they turned aside there, to go
in and spend the night at Gib′ē-ȧh.
And he went in and sat down in the
open square of the city; for no man
took them into his house to spend the
night.

16 And behold, an old man was
coming from his work in the field at
evening; the man was from the hill
country of Ē′phrȧ·im, and he was sojourning in Gib′ē-ȧh; the men of the
place were Benjaminites. 17 And he
lifted up his eyes, and saw the wayfarer
in the open square of the city; and the
old man said, "Where are you going?
and whence do you come?" 18 And he
said to him, "We are passing from
Bethlehem in Judah to the remote
parts of the hill country of Ē′phrȧ·im,
from which I come. I went to Bethlehem in Judah; and I am going to my
home;[c] and nobody takes me into his
house. 19 We have straw and provender
for our asses, with bread and wine for
me and your maidservant and the
young man with your servants; there
is no lack of anything." 20 And the old
man said, "Peace be to you; I will care
for all your wants; only, do not spend
the night in the square." 21 So he
brought him into his house, and gave
the asses provender; and they washed
their feet, and ate and drank.

22 As they were making their hearts
merry, behold, the men of the city,
base fellows, beset the house round
about, beating on the door; and they
said to the old man, the master of the
house, "Bring out the man who came
into your house, that we may know
him." 23 And the man, the master of
the house, went out to them and said
to them, "No, my brethren, do not act
so wickedly; seeing that this man has
come into my house, do not do this
vile thing. 24 Behold, here are my
virgin daughter and his concubine; let
me bring them out now. Ravish them
and do with them what seems good to
you; but against this man do not do so
vile a thing." 25 But the men would
not listen to him. So the man seized
his concubine, and put her out to
them; and they knew her, and abused
her all night until the morning. And
as the dawn began to break, they let
her go. 26 And as morning appeared,
the woman came and fell down at the
door of the man's house where her
master was, till it was light.

27 And her master rose up in the
morning, and when he opened the
doors of the house and went out to go
on his way, behold, there was his
concubine lying at the door of the
house, with her hands on the threshold. 28 He said to her, "Get up, let us
be going." But there was no answer.
Then he put her upon the ass; and the
man rose up and went away to his
home. 29 And when he entered his
house, he took a knife, and laying hold
of his concubine he divided her, limb
by limb, into twelve pieces, and sent
her throughout all the territory of
Israel. 30 And all who saw it said,
"Such a thing has never happened or
been seen from the day that the people
of Israel came up out of the land of
Egypt until this day; consider it, take
counsel, and speak."

20 Then all the people of Israel
came out, from Dan to Beer-
sheba, including the land of Gilead,
and the congregation assembled as one
man to the LORD at Miz′pȧh. 2 And the
chiefs of all the people, of all the tribes
of Israel, presented themselves in the
assembly of the people of God, four
hundred thousand men on foot that
drew the sword. 3 (Now the Benjaminites heard that the people of Israel
had gone up to Miz′pȧh.) And the
people of Israel said, "Tell us, how
was this wickedness brought to pass?"
4 And the Levite, the husband of the
woman who was murdered, answered
and said, "I came to Gib′ē-ȧh that belongs to Benjamin, I and my concubine, to spend the night. 5 And the men
of Gib′ē-ȧh rose against me, and beset
the house round about me by night;
they meant to kill me, and they
ravished my concubine, and she is dead.
6 And I took my concubine and cut her
in pieces, and sent her throughout all
the country of the inheritance of Israel; for they have committed abomination and wantonness in Israel.
7 Behold, you people of Israel, all of

[c] Gk Compare 19.29. Heb *to the house of the* LORD

you, give your advice and counsel here."

8 And all the people arose as one man, saying, "We will not any of us go to his tent, and none of us will return to his house. 9 But now this is what we will do to Gib'ē-ȧh: we will go up against it by lot, 10 and we will take ten men of a hundred throughout all the tribes of Israel, and a hundred of a thousand, and a thousand of ten thousand, to bring provisions for the people, that when they come they may requite Gib'ē-ȧh of Benjamin, for all the wanton crime which they have committed in Israel." 11 So all the men of Israel gathered against the city, united as one man.

12 And the tribes of Israel sent men through all the tribe of Benjamin, saying, "What wickedness is this that has taken place among you? 13 Now therefore give up the men, the base fellows in Gib'ē-ȧh, that we may put them to death, and put away evil from Israel." But the Benjaminites would not listen to the voice of their brethren, the people of Israel. 14And the Benjaminites came together out of the cities to Gib'ē-ȧh, to go out to battle against the people of Israel. 15And the Benjaminites mustered out of their cities on that day twenty-six thousand men that drew the sword, besides the inhabitants of Gib'ē-ȧh, who mustered seven hundred picked men. 16Among all these were seven hundred picked men who were left-handed; every one could sling a stone at a hair, and not miss. 17And the men of Israel, apart from Benjamin, mustered four hundred thousand men that drew sword; all these were men of war.

18 The people of Israel arose and went up to Beth'ĕl, and inquired of God, "Which of us shall go up first to battle against the Benjaminites?" And the LORD said, "Judah shall go up first."

19 Then the people of Israel rose in the morning, and encamped against Gib'ē-ȧh. 20And the men of Israel went out to battle against Benjamin; and the men of Israel drew up the battle line against them at Gib'ē-ȧh. 21 The Benjaminites came out of Gib'ē-ȧh, and felled to the ground on that day twenty-two thousand men of the Israelites. 22 But the people, the men of Israel, took courage, and again formed the battle line in the same place where they had formed it on the first day. 23And the people of Israel went up and wept before the LORD until the evening; and they inquired of the LORD, "Shall we again draw near to battle against our brethren the Benjaminites?" And the LORD said, "Go up against them."

24 So the people of Israel came near against the Benjaminites the second day. 25And Benjamin went against them out of Gib'ē-ȧh the second day, and felled to the ground eighteen thousand men of the people of Israel; all these were men who drew the sword. 26 Then all the people of Israel, the whole army, went up and came to Beth'ĕl and wept; they sat there before the LORD, and fasted that day until evening, and offered burnt offerings and peace offerings before the LORD. 27And the people of Israel inquired of the LORD (for the ark of the covenant of God was there in those days, 28 and Phin'ē·hȧs the son of El·ē·ā'zȧr, son of Aaron, ministered before it in those days), saying, "Shall we yet again go out to battle against our brethren the Benjaminites, or shall we cease?" And the LORD said, "Go up; for tomorrow I will give them into your hand."

29 So Israel set men in ambush round about Gib'ē-ȧh. 30And the people of Israel went up against the Benjaminites on the third day, and set themselves in array against Gib'ē-ȧh, as at other times. 31And the Benjaminites went out against the people, and were drawn away from the city; and as at other times they began to smite and kill some of the people, in the highways, one of which goes up to Beth'ĕl and the other to Gib'ē-ȧh, and in the open country, about thirty men of Israel. 32And the Benjaminites said, "They are routed before us, as at the first." But the men of Israel said, "Let us flee, and draw them away from the city to the highways." 33And all the men of Israel rose up out of their place, and set themselves in array at Bā'ȧl-tā'mär; and the men of Israel who were in ambush rushed out of their place west[d] of Gē'bȧ. 34And there came against Gib'ē-ȧh ten thousand picked men out of all Israel, and the battle was hard; but the Benjaminites did not know that disaster was close upon them. 35And the LORD defeated

[d] Gk Vg: Heb *in the plain*

Benjamin before Israel; and the men
of Israel destroyed twenty-five thousand one hundred men of Benjamin
that day; all these were men who drew
the sword. 36 So the Benjaminites saw
that they were defeated.

The men of Israel gave ground to
Benjamin, because they trusted to the
men in ambush whom they had set
against Gib′ē-ȧh. 37 And the men in
ambush made haste and rushed upon
Gib′ē-ȧh; the men in ambush moved
out and smote all the city with the edge
of the sword. 38 Now the appointed
signal between the men of Israel and
the men in ambush was that when they
made a great cloud of smoke rise up
out of the city 39 the men of Israel
should turn in battle. Now Benjamin
had begun to smite and kill about
thirty men of Israel; they said,
"Surely they are smitten down before
us, as in the first battle." 40 But when
the signal began to rise out of the city
in a column of smoke, the Benjaminites
looked behind them; and behold, the
whole of the city went up in smoke to
heaven. 41 Then the men of Israel
turned, and the men of Benjamin were
dismayed, for they saw that disaster
was close upon them. 42 Therefore they
turned their backs before the men of
Israel in the direction of the wilderness; but the battle overtook them,
and those who came out of the cities
destroyed them in the midst of them.
43 Cutting down[e] the Benjaminites,
they pursued them and trod them
down from Nō′hȧh[f] as far as opposite
Gib′ē-ȧh on the east. 44 Eighteen thousand men of Benjamin fell, all of them
men of valor. 45 And they turned and
fled toward the wilderness to the rock
of Rim′mon; five thousand men of
them were cut down in the highways,
and they were pursued hard to Gī′-
dom, and two thousand men of them
were slain. 46 So all who fell that day
of Benjamin were twenty-five thousand men that drew the sword, all of
them men of valor. 47 But six hundred
men turned and fled toward the wilderness to the rock of Rim′mon, and
abode at the rock of Rimmon four
months. 48 And the men of Israel
turned back against the Benjaminites,
and smote them with the edge of the
sword, men and beasts and all that they
found. And all the towns which they
found they set on fire.

21 Now the men of Israel had
sworn at Miz′pȧh, "No one of us
shall give his daughter in marriage to
Benjamin." 2 And the people came to
Beth′ėl, and sat there till evening before God, and they lifted up their
voices and wept bitterly. 3 And they
said, "O LORD, the God of Israel, why
has this come to pass in Israel, that
there should be today one tribe lacking
in Israel?" 4 And on the morrow the
people rose early, and built there an
altar, and offered burnt offerings and
peace offerings. 5 And the people of
Israel said, "Which of all the tribes of
Israel did not come up in the assembly
to the LORD?" For they had taken a
great oath concerning him who did
not come up to the LORD to Miz′pȧh,
saying, "He shall be put to death."
6 And the people of Israel had compassion for Benjamin their brother,
and said, "One tribe is cut off from
Israel this day. 7 What shall we do for
wives for those who are left, since we
have sworn by the LORD that we will
not give them any of our daughters
for wives?"

8 And they said, "What one is there
of the tribes of Israel that did not come
up to the LORD to Miz′pȧh?" And
behold, no one had come to the camp
from Jā′besh-gil′ē·ȧd, to the assembly.
9 For when the people were mustered,
behold, not one of the inhabitants of
Jā′besh-gil′ē·ȧd was there. 10 So the
congregation sent thither twelve thousand of their bravest men, and commanded them, "Go and smite the
inhabitants of Jā′besh-gil′ē·ȧd with
the edge of the sword; also the women
and the little ones. 11 This is what you
shall do; every male and every woman
that has lain with a male you shall
utterly destroy." 12 And they found
among the inhabitants of Jā′besh-
gil′ē·ȧd four hundred young virgins
who had not known man by lying with
him; and they brought them to the
camp at Shī′lōh, which is in the land
of Canaan.

13 Then the whole congregation
sent word to the Benjaminites who
were at the rock of Rim′mon, and proclaimed peace to them. 14 And Benjamin returned at that time; and they
gave them the women whom they had
saved alive of the women of Jā′besh-
gil′ē·ȧd; but they did not suffice for
them. 15 And the people had compas-

[e] Gk: Heb *surrounding* [f] Gk: Heb (*at their*) *resting place*

sion on Benjamin because the LORD
had made a breach in the tribes of
Israel.
16 Then the elders of the congregation said, "What shall we do for wives
for those who are left, since the women
are destroyed out of Benjamin?" 17 And
they said, "There must be an inheritance for the survivors of Benjamin,
that a tribe be not blotted out from
Israel. 18 Yet we cannot give them
wives of our daughters." For the people of Israel had sworn, "Cursed be
he who gives a wife to Benjamin."
19 So they said, "Behold, there is the
yearly feast of the LORD at Shī'lōh,
which is north of Beth'ĕl, on the east
of the highway that goes up from
Bethel to Shē'chem, and south of
Lė·bō'nȧh." 20 And they commanded
the Benjaminites, saying, "Go and lie
in wait in the vineyards, 21 and watch;
if the daughters of Shī'lōh come out
to dance in the dances, then come out
of the vineyards and seize each man
his wife from the daughters of Shiloh,
and go to the land of Benjamin. 22 And
when their fathers or their brothers
come to complain to us, we will say to
them, 'Grant them graciously to us;
because we did not take for each man
of them his wife in battle, neither did
you give them to them, else you would
now be guilty.' " 23 And the Benjaminites did so, and took their wives,
according to their number, from the
dancers whom they carried off; then
they went and returned to their inheritance, and rebuilt the towns,
and dwelt in them. 24 And the people of Israel departed from there at
that time, every man to his tribe
and family, and they went out
from there every man to his inheritance.
25 In those days there was no king
in Israel; every man did what was
right in his own eyes.

THE BOOK OF

RUTH

1 In the days when the judges ruled
there was a famine in the land, and
a certain man of Bethlehem in Judah
went to sojourn in the country of
Mō'ab, he and his wife and his two
sons. 2 The name of the man was
E·lim'ė·lech and the name of his wife
Nā'ō·mī, and the names of his two sons
were Mäh'lon and Chil'i·ŏn; they were
Eph'rȧ·thītes from Bethlehem in
Judah. They went into the country of
Mō'ab and remained there. 3 But
E·lim'ė·lech, the husband of Nā'ō·mī,
died, and she was left with her two
sons. 4 These took Mō'ăb·īte wives;
the name of the one was Ôr'pȧh and
the name of the other Ruth. They lived
there about ten years; 5 and both
Mäh'lon and Chil'i·ŏn died, so that
the woman was bereft of her two sons
and her husband.
6 Then she started with her daugh-
ters-in-law to return from the country
of Mō'ab, for she had heard in the
country of Moab that the LORD had
visited his people and given them food.
7 So she set out from the place where
she was, with her two daughters-in-
law, and they went on the way to
return to the land of Judah. 8 But
Nā'ō·mī said to her two daughters-in-
law, "Go, return each of you to her
mother's house. May the LORD deal
kindly with you, as you have dealt
with the dead and with me. 9 The LORD
grant that you may find a home, each
of you in the house of her husband!"
Then she kissed them, and they lifted
up their voices and wept. 10 And they
said to her, "No, we will return with
you to your people." 11 But Nā'ō·mī
said, "Turn back, my daughters, why
will you go with me? Have I yet sons
in my womb that they may become
your husbands? 12 Turn back, my
daughters, go your way, for I am too
old to have a husband. If I should say
I have hope, even if I should have a
husband this night and should bear
sons, 13 would you therefore wait till
they were grown? Would you therefore refrain from marrying? No, my

daughters, for it is exceedingly bitter
to me for your sake that the hand of
the LORD has gone forth against me."
14 Then they lifted up their voices and
wept again; and Ôr′păh kissed her
mother-in-law, but Ruth clung to
her.

15 And she said, "See, your sister-
in-law has gone back to her people and
to her gods; return after your sister-in-
law." 16 But Ruth said, "Entreat me
not to leave you or to return from
following you; for where you go I will
go, and where you lodge I will lodge;
your people shall be my people, and
your God my God; 17 where you die
I will die, and there will I be buried.
May the LORD do so to me and more
also if even death parts me from you."
18 And when Nā′ŏ·mī saw that she was
determined to go with her, she said no
more.

19 So the two of them went on until
they came to Bethlehem. And when
they came to Bethlehem, the whole
town was stirred because of them; and
the women said, "Is this Nā′ŏ·mī?"
20 She said to them, "Do not call me
Nā′ŏ·mī,[a] call me Mâr′ă,[b] for the
Almighty has dealt very bitterly with
me. 21 I went away full, and the LORD
has brought me back empty. Why call
me Nā′ŏ·mī, when the LORD has
afflicted[c] me and the Almighty has
brought calamity upon me?"

22 So Nā′ŏ·mī returned, and Ruth
the Mō′ăb·īt·ĕss her daughter-in-law
with her, who returned from the
country of Mō′ăb. And they came to
Bethlehem at the beginning of barley
harvest.

2 Now Nā′ŏ·mī had a kinsman of
her husband's, a man of wealth, of
the family of Ĕ·lĭm′ĕ·lĕch, whose name
was Bō′ăz. 2 And Ruth the Mō′ăb·īt·ĕss
said to Nā′ŏ·mī, "Let me go to the
field, and glean among the ears of grain
after him in whose sight I shall find
favor." And she said to her, "Go, my
daughter." 3 So she set forth and went
and gleaned in the field after the
reapers; and she happened to come to
the part of the field belonging to Bō′ăz,
who was of the family of Ĕ·lĭm′ĕ·lĕch.
4 And behold, Bō′ăz came from Bethlehem; and he said to the reapers,
"The LORD be with you!" And they
answered, "The LORD bless you."
5 Then Bō′ăz said to his servant who
was in charge of the reapers, "Whose
maiden is this?" 6 And the servant who
was in charge of the reapers answered,
"It is the Mō′ăb·īte maiden, who came
back with Nā′ŏ·mī from the country of
Mō′ăb. 7 She said, 'Pray, let me glean
and gather among the sheaves after the
reapers.' So she came, and she has
continued from early morning until
now, without resting even for a
moment."[d]

8 Then Bō′ăz said to Ruth, "Now,
listen, my daughter, do not go to glean
in another field or leave this one, but
keep close to my maidens. 9 Let your
eyes be upon the field which they are
reaping, and go after them. Have I not
charged the young men not to molest
you? And when you are thirsty, go to
the vessels and drink what the young
men have drawn." 10 Then she fell on
her face, bowing to the ground, and
said to him, "Why have I found favor
in your eyes, that you should take
notice of me, when I am a foreigner?"
11 But Bō′ăz answered her, "All that
you have done for your mother-in-law
since the death of your husband has
been fully told me, and how you left
your father and mother and your
native land and came to a people that
you did not know before. 12 The LORD
recompense you for what you have
done, and a full reward be given you
by the LORD, the God of Israel, under
whose wings you have come to take
refuge!" 13 Then she said, "You are
most gracious to me, my lord, for you
have comforted me and spoken kindly
to your maidservant, though I am not
one of your maidservants."

14 And at mealtime Bō′ăz said to
her, "Come here, and eat some bread,
and dip your morsel in the wine." So
she sat beside the reapers, and he
passed to her parched grain; and she
ate until she was satisfied, and she had
some left over. 15 When she rose to
glean, Bō′ăz instructed his young men,
saying, "Let her glean even among the
sheaves, and do not reproach her.
16 And also pull out some from the
bundles for her, and leave it for her to
glean, and do not rebuke her."

17 So she gleaned in the field until
evening; then she beat out what she
had gleaned, and it was about an ephah
of barley. 18 And she took it up and
went into the city; she showed her

[a] That is *Pleasant* [b] That is *Bitter* [c] Gk Syr Vg: Heb *testified against*
[d] Compare Gk Vg: the meaning of the Hebrew text is uncertain

mother-in-law what she had gleaned,
and she also brought out and gave her
what food she had left over after being
satisfied. 19And her mother-in-law said
to her, "Where did you glean today?
And where have you worked? Blessed
be the man who took notice of you."
So she told her mother-in-law with
whom she had worked, and said, "The
man's name with whom I worked today is Bō'az." 20And Nā'ō·mī said to
her daughter-in-law, "Blessed be he
by the LORD, whose kindness has not
forsaken the living or the dead!"
Naomi also said to her, "The man is a
relative of ours, one of our nearest
kin." 21And Ruth the Mō'ăb·ĭt·ĕss
said, "Besides, he said to me, 'You
shall keep close by my servants, till
they have finished all my harvest.' "
22And Nā'ō·mī said to Ruth, her
daughter-in-law, "It is well, my
daughter, that you go out with his
maidens, lest in another field you be
molested." 23 So she kept close to the
maidens of Bō'az, gleaning until the
end of the barley and wheat harvests;
and she lived with her mother-in-
law.

3 Then Nā'ō·mī her mother-in-law
said to her, "My daughter, should
I not seek a home for you, that it may
be well with you? 2 Now is not Bō'az
our kinsman, with whose maidens you
were? See, he is winnowing barley tonight at the threshing floor. 3 Wash
therefore and anoint yourself, and put
on your best clothes and go down to
the threshing floor; but do not make
yourself known to the man until he
has finished eating and drinking. 4 But
when he lies down, observe the place
where he lies; then, go and uncover
his feet and lie down; and he will tell
you what to do." 5And she replied,
"All that you say I will do."

6 So she went down to the threshing
floor and did just as her mother-in-law
had told her. 7And when Bō'az had
eaten and drunk, and his heart was
merry, he went to lie down at the end
of the heap of grain. Then she came
softly, and uncovered his feet, and lay
down. 8At midnight the man was
startled, and turned over, and behold,
a woman lay at his feet! 9 He said,
"Who are you?" And she answered,
"I am Ruth, your maidservant; spread
your skirt over your maidservant, for
you are next of kin." 10And he said,
"May you be blessed by the LORD, my
daughter; you have made this last
kindness greater than the first, in that
you have not gone after young men,
whether poor or rich. 11And now, my
daughter, do not fear, I will do for
you all that you ask, for all my fellow
townsmen know that you are a woman
of worth. 12And now it is true that I
am a near kinsman, yet there is a
kinsman nearer than I. 13 Remain this
night, and in the morning, if he will
do the part of the next of kin for you,
well; let him do it; but if he is not willing to do the part of the next of kin for
you, then, as the LORD lives, I will do
the part of the next of kin for you. Lie
down until the morning."

14 So she lay at his feet until the
morning, but arose before one could
recognize another; and he said, "Let
it not be known that the woman came
to the threshing floor." 15And he said,
"Bring the mantle you are wearing and
hold it out." So she held it, and he
measured out six measures of barley,
and laid it upon her; then she went
into the city. 16And when she came to
her mother-in-law, she said, "How did
you fare, my daughter?" Then she
told her all that the man had done for
her, 17 saying, "These six measures of
barley he gave to me, for he said, 'You
must not go back empty-handed to
your mother-in-law.' " 18 She replied,
"Wait, my daughter, until you learn
how the matter turns out, for the man
will not rest, but will settle the matter
today."

4 And Bō'az went up to the gate
and sat down there; and behold,
the next of kin, of whom Boaz had
spoken, came by. So Boaz said, "Turn
aside, friend; sit down here"; and he
turned aside and sat down. 2And he
took ten men of the elders of the city,
and said, "Sit down here"; so they sat
down. 3 Then he said to the next of kin,
"Nā'ō·mī, who has come back from
the country of Mō'ab, is selling the
parcel of land which belonged to our
kinsman E·lim'ĕ·lech. 4 So I thought
I would tell you of it, and say, Buy it
in the presence of those sitting here,
and in the presence of the elders of my
people. If you will redeem it, redeem
it; but if you will not, tell me, that I
may know, for there is no one besides
you to redeem it, and I come after
you." And he said, "I will redeem it."
5 Then Bō'az said, "The day you buy
the field from the hand of Nā'ō·mī, you

are also buying Ruth[e] the Mō′ab·īt·ĕss,
the widow of the dead, in order to
restore the name of the dead to his
inheritance." 6 Then the next of kin
said, "I cannot redeem it for myself,
lest I impair my own inheritance. Take
my right of redemption yourself, for I
cannot redeem it."
7 Now this was the custom in former times in Israel concerning redeem-
ing and exchanging: to confirm a
transaction, the one drew off his sandal
and gave it to the other, and this was
the manner of attesting in Israel. 8 So
when the next of kin said to Bō′az,
"Buy it for yourself," he drew off his
sandal. 9 Then Bō′az said to the elders
and all the people, "You are witnesses
this day that I have bought from the
hand of Nā′ŏ·mī all that belonged to
Ē·lim′ĕ·lech and all that belonged to
Chil′i·ŏn and to Mäh′lon. 10 Also Ruth
the Mō′ȧb·īt·ĕss, the widow of Mäh′-
lon, I have bought to be my wife, to
perpetuate the name of the dead in his
inheritance, that the name of the dead
may not be cut off from among his
brethren and from the gate of his
native place; you are witnesses this
day." 11 Then all the people who were
at the gate, and the elders, said, "We
are witnesses. May the LORD make the
woman, who is coming into your house,
like Rachel and Leah, who together
built up the house of Israel. May you
prosper in Eph′rȧ·thȧh and be renowned in Bethlehem; 12 and may your
house be like the house of Per′-
ez, whom Tā′mär bore to Judah, because of the children that the LORD
will give you by this young woman."
13 So Bō′az took Ruth and she became his wife; and he went into her,
and the LORD gave her conception, and
she bore a son. 14 Then the women
said to Nā′ŏ·mī, "Blessed be the LORD,
who has not left you this day without
next of kin; and may his name be
renowned in Israel! 15 He shall be to
you a restorer of life and a nourisher
of your old age; for your daughter-in-
law who loves you, who is more to you
than seven sons, has borne him."
16 Then Nā′ŏ·mī took the child and
laid him in her bosom, and became his
nurse. 17 And the women of the neighborhood gave him a name, saying, "A
son has been born to Nā′ŏ·mī." They
named him Ō′bed; he was the father
of Jesse, the father of David.
18 Now these are the descendants
of Per′ez: Perez was the father of
Hez′rŏn, 19 Hez′rŏn of Räm, Ram of
Am·min′ȧ·dab, 20 Am·min′ȧ·dab of
Näh′shŏn, Nahshon of Sal′mŏn, 21 Sal′-
mŏn of Bō′az, Boaz of Ō′bed, 22 Ō′bed
of Jesse, and Jesse of David.

THE FIRST BOOK OF

SAMUEL

1 There was a certain man of Rā·mȧ-
thā′im-zō′phim of the hill country
of Ē′phrȧ·im, whose name was El·kā′-
nȧh the son of Je·rō′ham, son of E·lī′-
hū, son of Tō′hū, son of Zuph, an
Ē′phrȧ·im·īte. 2 He had two wives; the
name of the one was Hannah, and the
name of the other Pė·nin′nȧh. And
Peninnah had children, but Hannah
had no children.
3 Now this man used to go up year
by year from his city to worship and
to sacrifice to the LORD of hosts at
Shī′lōh, where the two sons of Eli,
Hoph′nī and Phin′ė·hȧs, were priests
of the LORD. 4 On the day when El-
kā′nȧh sacrificed, he would give portions to Pė·nin′nȧh his wife and to all
her sons and daughters; 5 and, although[a] he loved Hannah, he would
give Hannah only one portion, because
the LORD had closed her womb. 6 And
her rival used to provoke her sorely, to
irritate her, because the LORD had
closed her womb. 7 So it went on year
by year; as often as she went up to the
house of the LORD, she used to provoke
her. Therefore Hannah wept and
would not eat. 8 And El·kā′nȧh, her
husband, said to her, "Hannah, why

[e] Old Latin Vg: Heb *of Naomi and from Ruth* [a] Gk: Heb obscure
4.7: Deut 25.8-10.

do you weep? And why do you not
eat? And why is your heart sad? Am I
not more to you than ten sons?"
9 After they had eaten and drunk in
Shī'lōh, Hannah rose. Now Eli the
priest was sitting on the seat beside
the doorpost of the temple of the
LORD. 10 She was deeply distressed
and prayed to the LORD, and wept
bitterly. 11 And she vowed a vow and
said, "O LORD of hosts, if thou wilt
indeed look on the affliction of thy
maidservant, and remember me, and
not forget thy maidservant, but wilt
give to thy maidservant a son, then I
will give him to the LORD all the days
of his life, and no razor shall touch his
head."
12 As she continued praying before
the LORD, Eli observed her mouth.
13 Hannah was speaking in her heart;
only her lips moved, and her voice was
not heard; therefore Eli took her to be
a drunken woman. 14 And Eli said to
her, "How long will you be drunken?
Put away your wine from you." 15 But
Hannah answered, "No, my lord, I am
a woman sorely troubled; I have drunk
neither wine nor strong drink, but I
have been pouring out my soul before
the LORD. 16 Do not regard your maidservant as a base woman, for all along
I have been speaking out of my great
anxiety and vexation." 17 Then Eli
answered, "Go in peace, and the God
of Israel grant your petition which you
have made to him." 18 And she said,
"Let your maidservant find favor in
your eyes." Then the woman went her
way and ate, and her countenance was
no longer sad.
19 They rose early in the morning
and worshiped before the LORD; then
they went back to their house at Rā'-
māh. And El·kā'nȧh knew Hannah his
wife, and the LORD remembered her;
20 and in due time Hannah conceived
and bore a son, and she called his name
Samuel, for she said, "I have asked
him of the LORD."
21 And the man El·kā'nȧh and all
his house went up to offer to the LORD
the yearly sacrifice, and to pay his
vow. 22 But Hannah did not go up, for
she said to her husband, "As soon as
the child is weaned, I will bring him,
that he may appear in the presence of
the LORD, and abide there for ever."
23 El·kā'nȧh her husband said to her,
"Do what seems best to you, wait
until you have weaned him; only, may
the LORD establish his word." So the
woman remained and nursed her son,
until she weaned him. 24 And when
she had weaned him, she took him up
with her, along with a three-year-old
bull,[b] an ephah of flour, and a skin of
wine; and she brought him to the house
of the LORD at Shī'lōh; and the child
was young. 25 Then they slew the bull,
and they brought the child to Eli.
26 And she said, "Oh, my lord! As you
live, my lord, I am the woman who
was standing here in your presence,
praying to the LORD. 27 For this child
I prayed; and the LORD has granted
me my petition which I made to him.
28 Therefore I have lent him to the
LORD; as long as he lives, he is lent to
the LORD."
And they[x] worshiped the LORD there.

2 Hannah also prayed and said,
"My heart exults in the LORD;
my strength is exalted in the LORD.
My mouth derides my enemies,
because I rejoice in thy salvation.

2 "There is none holy like the LORD,
there is none besides thee;
there is no rock like our God.
3 Talk no more so very proudly,
let not arrogance come from your mouth;
for the LORD is a God of knowledge,
and by him actions are weighed.
4 The bows of the mighty are broken,
but the feeble gird on strength.
5 Those who were full have hired themselves out for bread,
but those who were hungry have ceased to hunger.
The barren has borne seven,
but she who has many children is forlorn.
6 The LORD kills and brings to life;
he brings down to Shē'ōl and raises up.
7 The LORD makes poor and makes rich;
he brings low, he also exalts.
8 He raises up the poor from the dust;
he lifts the needy from the ash heap,
to make them sit with princes
and inherit a seat of honor.
For the pillars of the earth are the LORD's,
and on them he has set the world.

[b] Gk Syr: Heb *three bulls* [x] Heb *he*
2.1-10: Lk 1.46-55.

9 "He will guard the feet of his faithful ones;
but the wicked shall be cut off in darkness;
for not by might shall a man prevail.
10 The adversaries of the LORD shall be broken to pieces;
against them he will thunder in heaven.
The LORD will judge the ends of the earth;
he will give strength to his king,
and exalt the power of his anointed."

11 Then El·kā′nah went home to
Rā′mah. And the boy ministered to
the LORD, in the presence of Eli the
priest.

12 Now the sons of Eli were worthless men; they had no regard for the
LORD. 13 The custom of the priests
with the people was that when any
man offered sacrifice, the priest's servant would come, while the meat was
boiling, with a three-pronged fork in
his hand, 14 and he would thrust it
into the pan, or kettle, or caldron, or
pot; all that the fork brought up the
priest would take for himself.[c] So they
did at Shī′lōh to all the Israelites who
came there. 15 Moreover, before the fat
was burned, the priest's servant would
come and say to the man who was
sacrificing, "Give meat for the priest
to roast; for he will not accept boiled
meat from you, but raw." 16 And if the
man said to him, "Let them burn the
fat first, and then take as much as you
wish," he would say, "No, you must
give it now; and if not, I will take it by
force." 17 Thus the sin of the young
men was very great in the sight of the
LORD; for the men treated the offering
of the LORD with contempt.

18 Samuel was ministering before
the LORD, a boy girded with a linen
ephod. 19 And his mother used to make
for him a little robe and take it to him
each year, when she went up with her
husband to offer the yearly sacrifice.
20 Then Eli would bless El·kā′nah and
his wife, and say, "The LORD give you
children by this woman for the loan
which she lent to[d] the LORD"; so then
they would return to their home.

21 And the LORD visited Hannah,
and she conceived and bore three sons
and two daughters. And the boy Samuel grew in the presence of the LORD.

22 Now Eli was very old, and he
heard all that his sons were doing to
all Israel, and how they lay with the
women who served at the entrance to
the tent of meeting. 23 And he said to
them, "Why do you do such things?
For I hear of your evil dealings from
all the people. 24 No, my sons; it is no
good report that I hear the people of
the LORD spreading abroad. 25 If a
man sins against a man, God will
mediate for him; but if a man sins
against the LORD, who can intercede
for him?" But they would not listen to
the voice of their father; for it was the
will of the LORD to slay them.

26 Now the boy Samuel continued
to grow both in stature and in favor
with the LORD and with men.

27 And there came a man of God to
Eli, and said to him, "Thus the LORD
has said, 'I revealed[e] myself to the
house of your father when they were
in Egypt subject to the house of
Pharaoh. 28 And I chose him out of all
the tribes of Israel to be my priest, to
go up to my altar, to burn incense, to
wear an ephod before me; and I gave
to the house of your father all my
offerings by fire from the people of
Israel. 29 Why then look with greedy
eye at[f] my sacrifices and my offerings
which I commanded, and honor your
sons above me by fattening yourselves
upon the choicest parts of every offering of my people Israel?' 30 Therefore
the LORD the God of Israel declares:
'I promise that your house and the
house of your father should go in and
out before me for ever'; but now the
LORD declares: 'Far be it from me; for
those who honor me I will honor, and
those who despise me shall be lightly
esteemed. 31 Behold, the days are
coming, when I will cut off your
strength and the strength of your
father's house, so that there will not
be an old man in your house. 32 Then
in distress you will look with envious
eye on all the prosperity which shall be
bestowed upon Israel; and there shall
not be an old man in your house for
ever. 33 The man of you whom I shall
not cut off from my altar shall be
spared to weep out his[g] eyes and grieve
his[g] heart; and all the increase of your

[c] Gk Syr Vg: Heb *with it* [d] Or *for the petition which she asked of* [e] Gk Tg: Heb *Did I reveal*
[f] Or *treat with scorn* Gk: Heb *kick at* [g] Gk: Heb *your*
2.26: Lk 2.52.

house shall die by the sword of men.[h]
34 And this which shall befall your
two sons, Hoph'nī and Phin'ĕ·hȧs,
shall be the sign to you: both of them
shall die on the same day. 35 And I will
raise up for myself a faithful priest,
who shall do according to what is in
my heart and in my mind; and I will
build him a sure house, and he shall
go in and out before my anointed for
ever. 36 And every one who is left in
your house shall come to implore him
for a piece of silver or a loaf of bread,
and shall say, "Put me, I pray you, in
one of the priest's places, that I may
eat a morsel of bread." ' "

3 Now the boy Samuel was ministering to the LORD under Eli.
And the word of the LORD was rare in
those days; there was no frequent
vision.

2 At that time Eli, whose eyesight
had begun to grow dim, so that he
could not see, was lying down in his
own place; 3 the lamp of God had not
yet gone out, and Samuel was lying
down within the temple of the LORD,
where the ark of God was. 4 Then the
LORD called, "Samuel! Samuel!"[i] and
he said, "Here I am!" 5 and ran to Eli,
and said, "Here I am, for you called
me." But he said, "I did not call; lie
down again." So he went and lay
down. 6 And the LORD called again,
"Samuel!" And Samuel arose and
went to Eli, and said, "Here I am, for
you called me." But he said, "I did
not call, my son; lie down again."
7 Now Samuel did not yet know the
LORD, and the word of the LORD had
not yet been revealed to him. 8 And the
LORD called Samuel again the third
time. And he arose and went to Eli,
and said, "Here I am, for you called
me." Then Eli perceived that the LORD
was calling the boy. 9 Therefore Eli
said to Samuel, "Go, lie down; and if
he calls you, you shall say, 'Speak,
LORD, for thy servant hears.' " So
Samuel went and lay down in his place.

10 And the LORD came and stood
forth, calling as at other times, "Samuel! Samuel!" And Samuel said,
"Speak, for thy servant hears."
11 Then the LORD said to Samuel,
"Behold, I am about to do a thing in
Israel, at which the two ears of every
one that hears it will tingle. 12 On that
day I will fulfil against Eli all that I
have spoken concerning his house,
from beginning to end. 13 And I tell
him that I am about to punish his
house for ever, for the iniquity which
he knew, because his sons were blaspheming God,[j] and he did not restrain
them. 14 Therefore I swear to the
house of Eli that the iniquity of Eli's
house shall not be expiated by sacrifice
or offering for ever."

15 Samuel lay until morning; then
he opened the doors of the house of
the LORD. And Samuel was afraid to
tell the vision to Eli. 16 But Eli called
Samuel and said, "Samuel, my son."
And he said, "Here I am." 17 And Eli
said, "What was it that he told you?
Do not hide it from me. May God do
so to you and more also, if you hide
anything from me of all that he told
you." 18 So Samuel told him everything and hid nothing from him. And
he said, "It is the LORD; let him do
what seems good to him."

19 And Samuel grew, and the LORD
was with him and let none of his words
fall to the ground. 20 And all Israel
from Dan to Beer-sheba knew that
Samuel was established as a prophet of
the LORD. 21 And the LORD appeared
again at Shī'lōh, for the LORD revealed
himself to Samuel at Shiloh by the
word of the LORD.

4 1 And the word of Samuel came
to all Israel.

Now Israel went out to battle against
the Philistines; they encamped at Eb-
ĕn·ē'zėr, and the Philistines encamped
at Ā'phek. 2 The Philistines drew up
in line against Israel, and when the
battle spread, Israel was defeated by
the Philistines, who slew about four
thousand men on the field of battle.
3 And when the troops came to the
camp, the elders of Israel said, "Why
has the LORD put us to rout today before the Philistines? Let us bring the
ark of the covenant of the LORD here
from Shī'lōh, that he may come among
us and save us from the power of our
enemies." 4 So the people sent to
Shī'lōh, and brought from there the
ark of the covenant of the LORD of
hosts, who is enthroned on the cherubim; and the two sons of Eli, Hoph'nī
and Phin'ĕ·hȧs, were there with the
ark of the covenant of God.

5 When the ark of the covenant of
the LORD came into the camp, all
Israel gave a mighty shout, so that the
earth resounded. 6 And when the Phil-

[h] Gk: Heb *die as men* [i] Gk See 3.10: Heb *the* LORD *called Samuel* [j] Another reading is *for themselves*

istines heard the noise of the shouting,
they said, "What does this great shouting in the camp of the Hebrews mean?"
And when they learned that the ark of
the LORD had come to the camp, 7 the
Philistines were afraid; for they said,
"A god has come into the camp." And
they said, "Woe to us! For nothing like
this has happened before. 8 Woe to us!
Who can deliver us from the power of
these mighty gods? These are the gods
who smote the Egyptians with every
sort of plague in the wilderness. 9 Take
courage, and acquit yourselves like
men, O Philistines, lest you become
slaves to the Hebrews as they have
been to you; acquit yourselves like
men and fight."

10 So the Philistines fought, and
Israel was defeated, and they fled,
every man to his home; and there was
a very great slaughter, for there fell of
Israel thirty thousand foot soldiers.
11 And the ark of God was captured;
and the two sons of Eli, Hoph'nī and
Phin'ė·hȧs, were slain.

12 A man of Benjamin ran from the
battle line, and came to Shī'lōh the
same day, with his clothes rent and
with earth upon his head. 13 When he
arrived, Eli was sitting upon his seat
by the road watching, for his heart
trembled for the ark of God. And when
the man came into the city and told the
news, all the city cried out. 14 When
Eli heard the sound of the outcry, he
said, "What is this uproar?" Then the
man hastened and came and told Eli.
15 Now Eli was ninety-eight years old
and his eyes were set, so that he could
not see. 16 And the man said to Eli, "I
am he who has come from the battle;
I fled from the battle today." And he
said, "How did it go, my son?" 17 He
who brought the tidings answered and
said, "Israel has fled before the Philistines, and there has also been a great
slaughter among the people; your two
sons also, Hoph'nī and Phin'ė·hȧs, are
dead, and the ark of God has been
captured." 18 When he mentioned the
ark of God, Eli fell over backward from
his seat by the side of the gate; and his
neck was broken and he died, for he
was an old man, and heavy. He had
judged Israel forty years.

19 Now his daughter-in-law, the
wife of Phin'ė·hȧs, was with child,
about to give birth. And when she
heard the tidings that the ark of God
was captured, and that her father-in-
law and her husband were dead, she
bowed and gave birth; for her pains
came upon her. 20 And about the time
of her death the women attending her
said to her, "Fear not, for you have
borne a son." But she did not answer
or give heed. 21 And she named the
child Ich'ȧ·bod, saying, "The glory
has departed from Israel!" because the
ark of God had been captured and because of her father-in-law and her husband. 22 And she said, "The glory has
departed from Israel, for the ark of
God has been captured."

5 When the Philistines captured
the ark of God, they carried it from
Eb·ėn·ē'zėr to Ash'dod; 2 then the
Philistines took the ark of God and
brought it into the house of Dā'gon
and set it up beside Dagon. 3 And when
the people of Ash'dod rose early the
next day, behold, Dā'gon had fallen
face downward on the ground before
the ark of the LORD. So they took
Dagon and put him back in his place.
4 But when they rose early on the next
morning, behold, Dā'gon had fallen
face downward on the ground before
the ark of the LORD, and the head of
Dagon and both his hands were lying
cut off upon the threshold; only the
trunk of Dagon was left to him. 5 This
is why the priests of Dā'gon and all
who enter the house of Dagon do not
tread on the threshold of Dagon in
Ash'dod to this day.

6 The hand of the LORD was heavy
upon the people of Ash'dod, and he
terrified and afflicted them with
tumors, both Ashdod and its territory.
7 And when the men of Ash'dod saw
how things were, they said, "The ark
of the God of Israel must not remain
with us; for his hand is heavy upon us
and upon Dā'gon our god." 8 So they
sent and gathered together all the lords
of the Philistines, and said, "What
shall we do with the ark of the God of
Israel?" They answered, "Let the ark
of the God of Israel be brought
around to Gath." So they brought the
ark of the God of Israel there. 9 But
after they had brought it around, the
hand of the LORD was against the city,
causing a very great panic, and he
afflicted the men of the city, both
young and old, so that tumors broke
out upon them. 10 So they sent the ark
of God to Ek'rŏn. But when the ark of
God came to Ekron, the people of
Ekron cried out, "They have brought

around to us the ark of the God of
Israel to slay us and our people."
11 They sent therefore and gathered
together all the lords of the Philistines,
and said, "Send away the ark of the
God of Israel, and let it return to its
own place, that it may not slay us and
our people." For there was a deathly
panic throughout the whole city. The
hand of God was very heavy there;
12 the men who did not die were
stricken with tumors, and the cry of
the city went up to heaven.

6 The ark of the LORD was in the
country of the Philistines seven
months. 2And the Philistines called for
the priests and the diviners and said,
"What shall we do with the ark of the
LORD? Tell us with what we shall send
it to its place." 3 They said, "If you send
away the ark of the God of Israel, do
not send it empty, but by all means
return him a guilt offering. Then you
will be healed, and it will be known to
you why his hand does not turn away
from you." 4And they said, "What is
the guilt offering that we shall return
to him?" They answered, "Five golden
tumors and five golden mice, according
to the number of the lords of the Philistines; for the same plague was upon
all of you and upon your lords. 5 So
you must make images of your tumors
and images of your mice that ravage
the land, and give glory to the God of
Israel; perhaps he will lighten his hand
from off you and your gods and your
land. 6 Why should you harden your
hearts as the Egyptians and Pharaoh
hardened their hearts? After he had
made sport of them, did not they let
the people go, and they departed?
7 Now then, take and prepare a new
cart and two milch cows upon which
there has never come a yoke, and yoke
the cows to the cart, but take their
calves home, away from them. 8And
take the ark of the LORD and place it
on the cart, and put in a box at its side
the figures of gold, which you are
returning to him as a guilt offering.
Then send it off, and let it go its way.
9And watch; if it goes up on the way
to its own land, to Beth-shē'mesh,
then it is he who has done us this great
harm; but if not, then we shall know
that it is not his hand that struck us,
it happened to us by chance."

10 The men did so, and took two
milch cows and yoked them to the cart,
and shut up their calves at home.
11And they put the ark of the LORD on
the cart, and the box with the golden
mice and the images of their tumors.
12And the cows went straight in the
direction of Beth-shē'mesh along one
highway, lowing as they went; they
turned neither to the right nor to the
left, and the lords of the Philistines
went after them as far as the border of
Beth-shemesh. 13 Now the people of
Beth-shē'mesh were reaping their
wheat harvest in the valley; and when
they lifted up their eyes and saw the
ark, they rejoiced to see it. 14 The cart
came into the field of Joshua of Beth-
shē'mesh, and stopped there. A great
stone was there; and they split up the
wood of the cart and offered the cows
as a burnt offering to the LORD. 15And
the Levites took down the ark of the
LORD and the box that was beside it,
in which were the golden figures, and
set them upon the great stone; and the
men of Beth-shē'mesh offered burnt
offerings and sacrificed sacrifices on
that day to the LORD. 16And when the
five lords of the Philistines saw it, they
returned that day to Ek'rȯn.

17 These are the golden tumors,
which the Philistines returned as a
guilt offering to the LORD: one for
Ash'dod, one for Gā'zȧ, one for Ash'-
kė·lon, one for Gath, one for Ek'rȯn;
18 also the golden mice, according to
the number of all the cities of the
Philistines belonging to the five lords,
both fortified cities and unwalled villages. The great stone, beside which
they set down the ark of the LORD, is a
witness to this day in the field of
Joshua of Beth-shē'mesh.

19 And he slew some of the men of
Beth-shē'mesh, because they looked
into the ark of the LORD; he slew
seventy men of them,[k] and the people
mourned because the LORD had made
a great slaughter among the people.
20 Then the men of Beth-shē'mesh
said, "Who is able to stand before the
LORD, this holy God? And to whom
shall he go up away from us?" 21 So
they sent messengers to the inhabitants
of Kīr'i·ath-jē'ȧ·rim, saying, "The
Philistines have returned the ark of the
LORD. Come down and take it up to
7 you." 1And the men of Kīr'i·ath-
jē'ȧ·rim came and took up the ark
of the LORD, and brought it to the
house of A·bin'ȧ·dab on the hill; and

[k] Cn: Heb *of the people seventy men, fifty thousand men*

they consecrated his son, El·ē·ā'zȧr, to
have charge of the ark of the LORD.
2 From the day that the ark was lodged
at Kĭr'i·ath-jē'ȧ·rim, a long time
passed, some twenty years, and all the
house of Israel lamented after the
LORD.
3 Then Samuel said to all the house
of Israel, "If you are returning to the
LORD with all your heart, then put
away the foreign gods and the Ash'tȧ-
roth from among you, and direct your
heart to the LORD, and serve him only,
and he will deliver you out of the hand
of the Philistines." 4 So Israel put
away the Bā'ȧls and the Ash'tȧ·roth,
and they served the LORD only.
5 Then Samuel said, "Gather all
Israel at Miz'pȧh, and I will pray to
the LORD for you." 6 So they gathered
at Miz'pȧh, and drew water and poured
it out before the LORD, and fasted on
that day, and said there, "We have
sinned against the LORD." And Samuel
judged the people of Israel at Mizpah.
7 Now when the Philistines heard that
the people of Israel had gathered at
Miz'pȧh, the lords of the Philistines
went up against Israel. And when the
people of Israel heard of it they were
afraid of the Philistines. 8And the people of Israel said to Samuel, "Do not
cease to cry to the LORD our God for
us, that he may save us from the hand
of the Philistines." 9 So Samuel took
a sucking lamb and offered it as a
whole burnt offering to the LORD; and
Samuel cried to the LORD for Israel,
and the LORD answered him. 10As
Samuel was offering up the burnt
offering, the Philistines drew near to
attack Israel; but the LORD thundered
with a mighty voice that day against
the Philistines and threw them into
confusion; and they were routed before
Israel. 11And the men of Israel went
out of Miz'pȧh and pursued the Philistines, and smote them, as far as below
Beth'-cär.
12 Then Samuel took a stone and
set it up between Miz'pȧh and Je·shā'-
nȧh,[l] and called its name Eb·ĕn·ē'zẽr;[m]
for he said, "Hitherto the LORD has
helped us." 13 So the Philistines were
subdued and did not again enter the
territory of Israel. And the hand of the
LORD was against the Philistines all the
days of Samuel. 14 The cities which the
Philistines had taken from Israel were
restored to Israel, from Ek'rŏn to Gath;
and Israel rescued their territory from
the hand of the Philistines. There was
peace also between Israel and the
Am'ô·rītes.
15 Samuel judged Israel all the days
of his life. 16And he went on a circuit
year by year to Beth'ĕl, Gil'gȧl, and
Miz'pȧh; and he judged Israel in all
these places. 17 Then he would come
back to Rā'mȧh, for his home was
there, and there also he administered
justice to Israel. And he built there an
altar to the LORD.

8 When Samuel became old, he
made his sons judges over Israel.
2 The name of his first-born son was
Jō'ĕl, and the name of his second,
A·bī'jȧh; they were judges in Beer-
sheba. 3 Yet his sons did not walk in
his ways, but turned aside after gain;
they took bribes and perverted justice.
4 Then all the elders of Israel gathered together and came to Samuel at
Rā'mȧh, 5 and said to him, "Behold,
you are old and your sons do not walk
in your ways; now appoint for us a king
to govern us like all the nations." 6 But
the thing displeased Samuel when they
said, "Give us a king to govern us."
And Samuel prayed to the LORD. 7And
the LORD said to Samuel, "Hearken to
the voice of the people in all that they
say to you; for they have not rejected
you, but they have rejected me from
being king over them. 8According to
all the deeds which they have done to
me,[n] from the day I brought them up
out of Egypt even to this day, forsaking
me and serving other gods, so they are
also doing to you. 9 Now then, hearken
to their voice; only, you shall solemnly
warn them, and show them the ways
of the king who shall reign over them."
10 So Samuel told all the words of
the LORD to the people who were asking a king from him. 11 He said,
"These will be the ways of the king
who will reign over you: he will take
your sons and appoint them to his
chariots and to be his horsemen, and
to run before his chariots; 12 and he
will appoint for himself commanders
of thousands and commanders of
fifties, and some to plow his ground
and to reap his harvest, and to make
his implements of war and the equipment of his chariots. 13 He will take
your daughters to be perfumers and
cooks and bakers. 14 He will take the
best of your fields and vineyards and

[l] Gk Syr: Heb *Shen* [m] That is *Stone of help* [n] Gk: Heb lacks *to me*

olive orchards and give them to his
servants. 15 He will take the tenth of
your grain and of your vineyards and
give it to his officers and to his servants. 16 He will take your menservants
and maidservants, and the best of your
cattle[o] and your asses, and put them
to his work. 17 He will take the tenth
of your flocks, and you shall be his
slaves. 18 And in that day you will cry
out because of your king, whom you
have chosen for yourselves; but the
LORD will not answer you in that
day."

19 But the people refused to listen
to the voice of Samuel; and they said,
"No! but we will have a king over us,
20 that we also may be like all the
nations, and that our king may govern
us and go out before us and fight our
battles." 21 And when Samuel had
heard all the words of the people, he
repeated them in the ears of the LORD.
22 And the LORD said to Samuel,
"Hearken to their voice, and make
them a king." Samuel then said to the
men of Israel, "Go every man to his
city."

9 There was a man of Benjamin
whose name was Kish, the son of
A·bī'ĕl, son of Zē'rôr, son of Bė·cō'-
rath, son of A·phī'ăh, a Benjaminite,
a man of wealth; 2 and he had a son
whose name was Saul, a handsome
young man. There was not a man
among the people of Israel more handsome than he; from his shoulders upward he was taller than any of the
people.

3 Now the asses of Kish, Saul's
father, were lost. So Kish said to Saul
his son, "Take one of the servants with
you, and arise, go and look for the
asses." 4 And they[p] passed through the
hill country of Ē'phră·im and passed
through the land of Shal'i·shăh, but
they did not find them. And they
passed through the land of Shā'ă·lim,
but they were not there. Then they
passed through the land of Benjamin,
but did not find them.

5 When they came to the land of
Zuph, Saul said to his servant who
was with him, "Come, let us go back,
lest my father cease to care about the
asses and become anxious about us."
6 But he said to him, "Behold, there is
a man of God in this city, and he is a
man that is held in honor; all that he
says comes true. Let us go there; perhaps he can tell us about the journey
on which we have set out." 7 Then
Saul said to his servant, "But if we go,
what can we bring the man? For the
bread in our sacks is gone, and there
is no present to bring to the man of
God. What have we?" 8 The servant
answered Saul again, "Here, I have
with me the fourth part of a shekel of
silver, and I will give it to the man of
God, to tell us our way." 9 (Formerly
in Israel, when a man went to inquire
of God, he said, "Come, let us go to
the seer"; for he who is now called a
prophet was formerly called a seer.)
10 And Saul said to his servant, "Well
said; come, let us go." So they went
to the city where the man of God was.

11 As they went up the hill to the
city, they met young maidens coming
out to draw water, and said to them,
"Is the seer here?" 12 They answered,
"He is; behold, he is just ahead of you.
Make haste; he has come just now to
the city, because the people have a
sacrifice today on the high place. 13 As
soon as you enter the city, you will
find him, before he goes up to the
high place to eat; for the people will
not eat till he comes, since he must
bless the sacrifice; afterward those eat
who are invited. Now go up, for you
will meet him immediately." 14 So
they went up to the city. As they were
entering the city, they saw Samuel
coming out toward them on his way
up to the high place.

15 Now the day before Saul came,
the LORD had revealed to Samuel:
16 "Tomorrow about this time I will
send to you a man from the land of
Benjamin, and you shall anoint him to
be prince over my people Israel. He
shall save my people from the hand of
the Philistines; for I have seen the
affliction of[q] my people, because their
cry has come to me." 17 When Samuel
saw Saul, the LORD told him, "Here is
the man of whom I spoke to you! He
it is who shall rule over my people."
18 Then Saul approached Samuel in
the gate, and said, "Tell me where is
the house of the seer?" 19 Samuel answered Saul, "I am the seer; go up
before me to the high place, for today
you shall eat with me, and in the
morning I will let you go and will tell
you all that is on your mind. 20 As for
your asses that were lost three days
ago, do not set your mind on them, for

[o] Gk: Heb *young men* [p] Gk Vg: Heb *he* [q] Gk: Heb lacks *the affliction of*

they have been found. And for whom
is all that is desirable in Israel? Is it
not for you and for all your father's
house?" 21 Saul answered, "Am I not
a Benjaminite, from the least of the
tribes of Israel? And is not my family
the humblest of all the families of the
tribe of Benjamin? Why then have you
spoken to me in this way?"

22 Then Samuel took Saul and his
servant and brought them into the hall
and gave them a place at the head of
those who had been invited, who were
about thirty persons. 23And Samuel
said to the cook, "Bring the portion I
gave you, of which I said to you, 'Put
it aside.' " 24 So the cook took up the
leg and the upper portion[r] and set them
before Saul; and Samuel said, "See,
what was kept is set before you. Eat;
because it was kept for you until the
hour appointed, that you might eat
with the guests."[s]

So Saul ate with Samuel that day.
25And when they came down from the
high place into the city, a bed was
spread for Saul[t] upon the roof, and he
lay down to sleep. 26 Then at the
break of dawn[u] Samuel called to Saul
upon the roof, "Up, that I may send
you on your way." So Saul arose, and
both he and Samuel went out into the
street.

27 As they were going down to the
outskirts of the city, Samuel said to
Saul, "Tell the servant to pass on before us, and when he has passed on
stop here yourself for a while, that I
may make known to you the word of
God."

10 Then Samuel took a vial of oil
and poured it on his head, and
kissed him and said, "Has not the
LORD anointed you to be prince over
his people Israel? And you shall reign
over the people of the LORD and you
will save them from the hand of their
enemies round about. And this shall
be the sign to you that the LORD has
anointed you to be prince[w] over his
heritage. 2 When you depart from me
today you will meet two men by
Rachel's tomb in the territory of Benjamin at Zel'zăh, and they will say to
you, 'The asses which you went to
seek are found, and now your father
has ceased to care about the asses and
is anxious about you, saying, "What
shall I do about my son?" ' 3 Then you
shall go on from there further and
come to the oak of Tā'bôr; three men
going up to God at Beth'ĕl will meet
you there, one carrying three kids,
another carrying three loaves of bread,
and another carrying a skin of wine.
4And they will greet you and give you
two loaves of bread, which you shall
accept from their hand. 5After that you
shall come to Gib'ē·ath·e·lō'him,[x]
where there is a garrison of the Philistines; and there, as you come to the
city, you will meet a band of prophets
coming down from the high place with
harp, tambourine, flute, and lyre before them, prophesying. 6 Then the
spirit of the LORD will come mightily
upon you, and you shall prophesy with
them and be turned into another man.
7 Now when these signs meet you, do
whatever your hand finds to do, for
God is with you. 8And you shall go
down before me to Gil'găl; and behold, I am coming to you to offer
burnt offerings and to sacrifice peace
offerings. Seven days you shall wait,
until I come to you and show you what
you shall do."

9 When he turned his back to leave
Samuel, God gave him another heart;
and all these signs came to pass that
day. 10 When they came to Gib'ē-ăh,[z]
behold, a band of prophets met him;
and the spirit of God came mightily
upon him, and he prophesied among
them. 11And when all who knew him
before saw how he prophesied with
the prophets, the people said to one
another, "What has come over the son
of Kish? Is Saul also among the prophets?" 12And a man of the place answered, "And who is their father?"
Therefore it became a proverb, "Is
Saul also among the prophets?"
13 When he had finished prophesying,
he came to the high place.

14 Saul's uncle said to him and to
his servant, "Where did you go?" And
he said, "To seek the asses; and when
we saw they were not to be found, we
went to Samuel." 15And Saul's uncle
said, "Pray, tell me what Samuel said
to you." 16And Saul said to his uncle,

[r] Heb obscure [s] Cn: Heb *saying, I have invited the people* [t] Gk: Heb *and he spoke with Saul*
[u] Gk: Heb *and they arose early and at break of dawn*
[w] Gk: Heb lacks *over his people Israel? And you shall . . . to be prince* [x] Or *the hill of God*
[z] Or *the hill*
10.11-12: 1 Sam 19.23-24.

"He told us plainly that the asses had
been found." But about the matter of
the kingdom, of which Samuel had
spoken, he did not tell him anything.
17 Now Samuel called the people
together to the LORD at Miz'pȧh;
18 and he said to the people of Israel,
"Thus says the LORD, the God of
Israel, 'I brought up Israel out of
Egypt, and I delivered you from the
hand of the Egyptians and from the
hand of all the kingdoms that were
oppressing you.' 19 But you have this
day rejected your God, who saves you
from all your calamities and your distresses; and you have said, 'No! but set
a king over us.' Now therefore present
yourselves before the LORD by your
tribes and by your thousands."
20 Then Samuel brought all the
tribes of Israel near, and the tribe of
Benjamin was taken by lot. 21 He
brought the tribe of Benjamin near by
its families, and the family of the
Mā'trītes was taken by lot; finally he
brought the family of the Matrites
near man by man,[a] and Saul the son
of Kish was taken by lot. But when
they sought him, he could not be
found. 22 So they inquired again of the
LORD, "Did the man come hither?"[b]
and the LORD said, "Behold, he has
hidden himself among the baggage."
23 Then they ran and fetched him from
there; and when he stood among the
people, he was taller than any of the
people from his shoulders upward.
24 And Samuel said to all the people,
"Do you see him whom the LORD has
chosen? There is none like him among
all the people." And all the people
shouted, "Long live the king!"
25 Then Samuel told the people the
rights and duties of the kingship; and
he wrote them in a book and laid it up
before the LORD. Then Samuel sent
all the people away, each one to his
home. 26 Saul also went to his home
at Gib'ē-ȧh, and with him went men
of valor whose hearts God had
touched. 27 But some worthless fellows
said, "How can this man save us?"
And they despised him, and brought
him no present. But he held his peace.
11 Then Nā'hash the Am'mȯ·nīte
went up and besieged Jā'besh-
gil'ē·ȧd; and all the men of Jā'besh said
to Nahash, "Make a treaty with us, and
we will serve you." 2 But Nā'hash the
Am'mȯ·nīte said to them, "On this
condition I will make a treaty with
you, that I gouge out all your right
eyes, and thus put disgrace upon all
Israel." 3 The elders of Jā'besh said to
him, "Give us seven days respite that
we may send messengers through all
the territory of Israel. Then, if there is
no one to save us, we will give ourselves up to you." 4 When the messengers came to Gib'ē-ȧh of Saul, they
reported the matter in the ears of the
people; and all the people wept aloud.
5 Now Saul was coming from the
field behind the oxen; and Saul said,
"What ails the people, that they are
weeping?" So they told him the tidings
of the men of Jā'besh. 6 And the spirit
of God came mightily upon Saul when
he heard these words, and his anger
was greatly kindled. 7 He took a yoke
of oxen, and cut them in pieces and
sent them throughout all the territory
of Israel by the hand of messengers,
saying, "Whoever does not come out
after Saul and Samuel so shall it be
done to his oxen!" Then the dread of
the LORD fell upon the people, and
they came out as one man. 8 When he
mustered them at Bē'zek, the men of
Israel were three hundred thousand,
and the men of Judah thirty thousand.
9 And they said to the messengers who
had come, "Thus shall you say to the
men of Jā'besh-gil'ē·ȧd: 'Tomorrow,
by the time the sun is hot, you shall
have deliverance.'" When the messengers came and told the men of
Jā'besh, they were glad. 10 Therefore
the men of Jā'besh said, "Tomorrow
we will give ourselves up to you, and
you may do to us whatever seems good
to you." 11 And on the morrow Saul
put the people in three companies; and
they came into the midst of the camp
in the morning watch, and cut down
the Am'mȯ·nītes until the heat of the
day; and those who survived were
scattered, so that no two of them were
left together.
12 Then the people said to Samuel,
"Who is it that said, 'Shall Saul reign
over us?' Bring the men, that we may
put them to death." 13 But Saul said,
"Not a man shall be put to death this
day, for today the LORD has wrought
deliverance in Israel." 14 Then Samuel said to the people, "Come, let us
go to Gil'gȧl and there renew the kingdom." 15 So all the people went to
Gil'gȧl, and there they made Saul king

Gk: Heb lacks *finally . . . man by man* [b] Gk: Heb *Is there yet a man to come hither?*

before the LORD in Gilgal. There they
sacrificed peace offerings before the
LORD, and there Saul and all the men
of Israel rejoiced greatly.

12 And Samuel said to all Israel,
"Behold, I have hearkened to
your voice in all that you have said to
me, and have made a king over you.
2 And now, behold, the king walks before you; and I am old and gray, and
behold, my sons are with you; and I
have walked before you from my
youth until this day. 3 Here I am;
testify against me before the LORD and
before his anointed. Whose ox have I
taken? Or whose ass have I taken? Or
whom have I defrauded? Whom have
I oppressed? Or from whose hand have
I taken a bribe to blind my eyes with
it? Testify against me[c] and I will restore it to you." 4 They said, "You
have not defrauded us or oppressed us
or taken anything from any man's
hand." 5 And he said to them, "The
LORD is witness against you, and his
anointed is witness this day, that
you have not found anything in my
hand." And they said, "He is witness."

6 And Samuel said to the people,
"The LORD is witness,[d] who appointed
Moses and Aaron and brought your
fathers up out of the land of Egypt.
7 Now therefore stand still, that I may
plead with you before the LORD concerning all the saving deeds of the LORD
which he performed for you and for
your fathers. 8 When Jacob went into
Egypt and the Egyptians oppressed
them,[e] then your fathers cried to the
LORD and the LORD sent Moses and
Aaron, who brought forth your fathers
out of Egypt, and made them dwell in
this place. 9 But they forgot the LORD
their God; and he sold them into the
hand of Sis'ĕr·ȧ, commander of the
army of Jā'bin king of[f] Hā'zôr, and
into the hand of the Philistines, and
into the hand of the king of Mō'ab;
and they fought against them. 10 And
they cried to the LORD, and said, 'We
have sinned, because we have forsaken
the LORD, and have served the Bā'ăls
and the Ash'tė·roth; but now deliver
us out of the hand of our enemies, and
we will serve thee.' 11 And the LORD
sent Jer·ub·bā'ăl and Bâr'ăk,[g] and
Jeph'thăh, and Samuel, and delivered
you out of the hand of your enemies
on every side; and you dwelt in safety.
12 And when you saw that Nā'hash the
king of the Am'mȯ·nītes came against
you, you said to me, 'No, but a king
shall reign over us,' when the LORD
your God was your king. 13 And now
behold the king whom you have
chosen, for whom you have asked; behold, the LORD has set a king over you.
14 If you will fear the LORD and serve
him and hearken to his voice and not
rebel against the commandment of the
LORD, and if both you and the king
who reigns over you will follow the
LORD your God, it will be well; 15 but
if you will not hearken to the voice of
the LORD, but rebel against the commandment of the LORD, then the hand
of the LORD will be against you and
your king.[h] 16 Now therefore stand
still and see this great thing, which the
LORD will do before your eyes. 17 Is it
not wheat harvest today? I will call
upon the LORD, that he may send
thunder and rain; and you shall know
and see that your wickedness is great,
which you have done in the sight of
the LORD, in asking for yourselves a
king." 18 So Samuel called upon the
LORD, and the LORD sent thunder and
rain that day; and all the people greatly
feared the LORD and Samuel.

19 And all the people said to Samuel, "Pray for your servants to the
LORD your God, that we may not die;
for we have added to all our sins this
evil, to ask for ourselves a king." 20 And
Samuel said to the people, "Fear not;
you have done all this evil, yet do not
turn aside from following the LORD,
but serve the LORD with all your heart;
21 and do not turn aside after[i] vain
things which cannot profit or save, for
they are vain. 22 For the LORD will not
cast away his people, for his great
name's sake, because it has pleased the
LORD to make you a people for himself. 23 Moreover as for me, far be it
from me that I should sin against the
LORD by ceasing to pray for you; and
I will instruct you in the good and the
right way. 24 Only fear the LORD, and
serve him faithfully with all your heart;
for consider what great things he has
done for you. 25 But if you still do
wickedly, you shall be swept away,
both you and your king."

[c] Gk: Heb lacks *Testify against me* [d] Gk: Heb lacks *is witness*
[e] Gk: Heb lacks *and the Egyptians oppressed them* [f] Gk: Heb lacks *Jabin king of* [g] Gk Syr: Heb *Bedan*
[h] Gk: Heb *fathers* [i] Gk Syr Tg Vg: Heb *because after*

13 Saul was . . .[j] years old when he
began to reign; and he reigned
. . . and two[k] years over Israel.
2 Saul chose three thousand men of
Israel; two thousand were with Saul
in Mich'mash and the hill country of
Beth'ĕl, and a thousand were with
Jonathan in Gib'ē-ȧh of Benjamin; the
rest of the people he sent home, every
man to his tent. 3 Jonathan defeated
the garrison of the Philistines which
was at Gē'bȧ; and the Philistines heard
of it. And Saul blew the trumpet
throughout all the land, saying, "Let
the Hebrews hear." 4And all Israel
heard it said that Saul had defeated
the garrison of the Philistines, and also
that Israel had become odious to the
Philistines. And the people were called
out to join Saul at Gil'gȧl.
5 And the Philistines mustered to
fight with Israel, thirty thousand
chariots, and six thousand horsemen,
and troops like the sand on the seashore in multitude; they came up and
encamped in Mich'mash, to the east
of Beth-ā'vėn. 6 When the men of
Israel saw that they were in straits (for
the people were hard pressed), the
people hid themselves in caves and in
holes and in rocks and in tombs and
in cisterns, 7 or crossed the fords of
the Jordan[l] to the land of Gad and
Gilead. Saul was still at Gil'gȧl, and
all the people followed him trembling.
8 He waited seven days, the time
appointed by Samuel; but Samuel did
not come to Gil'gȧl, and the people
were scattering from him. 9 So Saul
said, "Bring the burnt offering here to
me, and the peace offerings." And he
offered the burnt offering. 10As soon
as he had finished offering the burnt
offering, behold, Samuel came; and
Saul went out to meet him and salute
him. 11 Samuel said, "What have you
done?" And Saul said, "When I saw
that the people were scattering from
me, and that you did not come within
the days appointed, and that the Philistines had mustered at Mich'mash, 12 I
said, 'Now the Philistines will come
down upon me at Gil'gȧl, and I have
not entreated the favor of the LORD';
so I forced myself, and offered the
burnt offering." 13And Samuel said to
Saul, "You have done foolishly; you
have not kept the commandment of
the LORD your God, which he commanded you; for now the LORD would
have established your kingdom over
Israel for ever. 14 But now your kingdom shall not continue; the LORD has
sought out a man after his own heart;
and the LORD has appointed him to
be prince over his people, because you
have not kept what the LORD commanded you." 15And Samuel arose,
and went up from Gil'gȧl to Gib'ē-ȧh
of Benjamin.
And Saul numbered the people who
were present with him, about six hundred men. 16And Saul, and Jonathan
his son, and the people who were present with them, stayed in Gē'bȧ of Benjamin; but the Philistines encamped
in Mich'mash. 17And raiders came out
of the camp of the Philistines in three
companies; one company turned toward Oph'rȧh, to the land of Shü'ȧl,
18 another company turned toward
Beth-hō'ron, and another company
turned toward the border that looks
down upon the valley of Ze·bō'im toward the wilderness.
19 Now there was no smith to be
found throughout all the land of
Israel; for the Philistines said, "Lest
the Hebrews make themselves swords
or spears"; 20 but every one of the
Israelites went down to the Philistines
to sharpen his plowshare, his mattock,
his axe, or his sickle;[m] 21 and the charge
was a pim for the plowshares and for
the mattocks, and a third of a shekel
for sharpening the axes and for setting
the goads.[n] 22 So on the day of the
battle there was neither sword nor
spear found in the hand of any of the
people with Saul and Jonathan; but
Saul and Jonathan his son had them.
23And the garrison of the Philistines
went out to the pass of Mich'mash.
14 One day Jonathan the son of
Saul said to the young man who
bore his armor, "Come, let us go over
to the Philistine garrison on yonder
side." But he did not tell his father.
2 Saul was staying in the outskirts of
Gib'ē-ȧh under the pomegranate tree
which is at Mig'rȯn; the people who
were with him were about six hundred
men, 3 and Ȧ·hī'jȧh the son of Ȧ·hī'tŭb,
Ich'ȧ·bod's brother, son of Phin'ė·hȧs,
son of Eli, the priest of the LORD in
Shī'lōh, wearing an ephod. And the

[j] The number is lacking in Heb [k] *Two* is not the entire number. Something has dropped out.
[l] Cn: Heb *Hebrews crossed the Jordan* [m] Gk: Heb *plowshare* [n] The Heb of this verse is obscure
13.14: Acts 13.22.

people did not know that Jonathan had
gone. 4 In the pass,[o] by which Jonathan
sought to go over to the Philistine garrison, there was a rocky crag on the
one side and a rocky crag on the other
side; the name of the one was Bō′zez,
and the name of the other Sē′neh.
5 The one crag rose on the north in
front of Mich′mash, and the other on
the south in front of Gē′bȧ.

6 And Jonathan said to the young
man who bore his armor, "Come, let
us go over to the garrison of these uncircumcised; it may be that the LORD
will work for us; for nothing can hinder
the LORD from saving by many or by
few." 7 And his armor-bearer said to
him, "Do all that your mind inclines
to;[p] behold, I am with you, as is your
mind so is mine."[q] 8 Then said
Jonathan, "Behold, we will cross over
to the men, and we will show ourselves
to them. 9 If they say to us, 'Wait until
we come to you,' then we will stand
still in our place, and we will not go
up to them. 10 But if they say, 'Come
up to us,' then we will go up; for the
LORD has given them into our hand.
And this shall be the sign to us." 11 So
both of them showed themselves to
the garrison of the Philistines; and the
Philistines said, "Look, Hebrews are
coming out of the holes where they
have hid themselves." 12 And the men
of the garrison hailed Jonathan and his
armor-bearer, and said, "Come up to
us, and we will show you a thing."
And Jonathan said to his armor-bearer,
"Come up after me; for the LORD has
given them into the hand of Israel."
13 Then Jonathan climbed up on his
hands and feet, and his armor-bearer
after him. And they fell before Jonathan, and his armor-bearer killed them
after him; 14 and that first slaughter,
which Jonathan and his armor-bearer
made, was of about twenty men within
as it were half a furrow's length in an
acre[r] of land. 15 And there was a panic
in the camp, in the field, and among
all the people; the garrison and even
the raiders trembled; the earth quaked;
and it became a very great panic.

16 And the watchmen of Saul in
Gib′ē-ȧh of Benjamin looked; and behold, the multitude was surging hither
and thither.[s] 17 Then Saul said to the
people who were with him, "Number
and see who has gone from us." And
when they had numbered, behold,
Jonathan and his armor-bearer were
not there. 18 And Saul said to A·hī′jȧh,
"Bring hither the ark of God." For the
ark of God went at that time with the
people of Israel. 19 And while Saul was
talking to the priest, the tumult in the
camp of the Philistines increased more
and more; and Saul said to the priest,
"Withdraw your hand." 20 Then Saul
and all the people who were with him
rallied and went into the battle; and
behold, every man's sword was against
his fellow, and there was very great
confusion. 21 Now the Hebrews who
had been with the Philistines before
that time and who had gone up with
them into the camp, even they also
turned to be with[t] the Israelites who
were with Saul and Jonathan. 22 Likewise, when all the men of Israel who
had hid themselves in the hill country
of Ē′phrȧ·im heard that the Philistines
were fleeing, they too followed hard
after them in the battle. 23 So the
LORD delivered Israel that day; and
the battle passed beyond Beth-ā′-
vėn.

24 And the men of Israel were distressed that day; for Saul laid an oath
on the people, saying, "Cursed be the
man who eats food until it is evening
and I am avenged on my enemies." So
none of the people tasted food. 25 And
all the people[u] came into the forest; and
there was honey on the ground. 26 And
when the people entered the forest,
behold, the honey was dropping, but
no man put his hand to his mouth; for
the people feared the oath. 27 But
Jonathan had not heard his father
charge the people with the oath; so he
put forth the tip of the staff that was
in his hand, and dipped it in the honeycomb, and put his hand to his mouth;
and his eyes became bright. 28 Then
one of the people said, "Your father
strictly charged the people with an
oath, saying, 'Cursed be the man who
eats food this day.'" And the people
were faint. 29 Then Jonathan said,
"My father has troubled the land; see
how my eyes have become bright, because I tasted a little of this honey.
30 How much better if the people had
eaten freely today of the spoil of their
enemies which they found; for now the

[o] Heb *between the passes* [p] Gk: Heb *Do all that is in your mind. Turn* [q] Gk: Heb lacks *so is mine*
[r] Heb *yoke* [s] Gk: Heb *they went and thither* [t] Gk Syr Vg Tg: Heb *round about, they also, to be with*
[u] Heb *land*

slaughter among the Philistines has not
been great."
31 They struck down the Philistines
that day from Mich′mash to Ai′jȧ·lon.
And the people were very faint; 32 the
people flew upon the spoil, and took
sheep and oxen and calves, and slew
them on the ground; and the people
ate them with the blood. 33 Then they
told Saul, "Behold, the people are sinning against the LORD, by eating with
the blood." And he said, "You have
dealt treacherously; roll a great stone
to me here."[v] 34 And Saul said, "Disperse yourselves among the people,
and say to them, 'Let every man bring
his ox or his sheep, and slay them here,
and eat; and do not sin against the
LORD by eating with the blood.' " So
every one of the people brought his ox
with him that night, and slew them
there. 35 And Saul built an altar to the
LORD; it was the first altar that he
built to the LORD.
36 Then Saul said, "Let us go down
after the Philistines by night and
despoil them until the morning light;
let us not leave a man of them." And
they said, "Do whatever seems good
to you." But the priest said, "Let us
draw near hither to God." 37 And Saul
inquired of God, "Shall I go down
after the Philistines? Wilt thou give
them into the hand of Israel?" But he
did not answer him that day. 38 And
Saul said, "Come hither, all you leaders
of the people; and know and see how
this sin has arisen today. 39 For as the
LORD lives who saves Israel, though it
be in Jonathan my son, he shall surely
die." But there was not a man among
all the people that answered him.
40 Then he said to all Israel, "You shall
be on one side, and I and Jonathan my
son will be on the other side." And the
people said to Saul, "Do what seems
good to you." 41 Therefore Saul said,
"O LORD God of Israel, why hast thou
not answered thy servant this day? If
this guilt is in me or in Jonathan my
son, O LORD, God of Israel, give
Ū′rim; but if this guilt is in thy people
Israel,[w] give Thum′mim." And Jonathan and Saul were taken, but the
people escaped. 42 Then Saul said,
"Cast the lot between me and my son
Jonathan." And Jonathan was taken.
43 Then Saul said to Jonathan,
"Tell me what you have done." And
Jonathan told him, "I tasted a little
honey with the tip of the staff that was
in my hand; here I am, I will die."
44 And Saul said, "God do so to me
and more also; you shall surely die,
Jonathan." 45 Then the people said to
Saul, "Shall Jonathan die, who has
wrought this great victory in Israel?
Far from it! As the LORD lives, there
shall not one hair of his head fall to the
ground; for he has wrought with God
this day." So the people ransomed
Jonathan, that he did not die. 46 Then
Saul went up from pursuing the Philistines; and the Philistines went to their
own place.
47 When Saul had taken the kingship over Israel, he fought against all
his enemies on every side, against
Mō′ab, against the Am′mȯ·nītes,
against E′dȯm, against the kings of
Zō′bȧh, and against the Philistines;
wherever he turned he put them to the
worse. 48 And he did valiantly, and
smote the Ȧ·mal′ė·kītes, and delivered
Israel out of the hands of those who
plundered them.
49 Now the sons of Saul were Jonathan, Ish′vī, and Mal′chī·shü′ȧ; and
the names of his two daughters were
these: the name of the first-born was
Mē′reb, and the name of the younger
Mī′chȧl; 50 and the name of Saul's
wife was Ȧ·hin′ō-am the daughter of
Ȧ·him′ȧ-az. And the name of the commander of his army was Abner the son
of Nēr, Saul's uncle; 51 Kish was the
father of Saul, and Nēr the father of
Abner was the son of Ȧ·bī′ėl.
52 There was hard fighting against
the Philistines all the days of Saul; and
when Saul saw any strong man, or any
valiant man, he attached him to himself.

15 And Samuel said to Saul, "The
LORD sent me to anoint you king
over his people Israel; now therefore
hearken to the words of the LORD.
2 Thus says the LORD of hosts, 'I will
punish what Am′ȧ·lek did to Israel in
opposing them on the way, when they
came up out of Egypt. 3 Now go and
smite Am′ȧ·lek, and utterly destroy all
that they have; do not spare them, but
kill both man and woman, infant and
suckling, ox and sheep, camel and
ass.' "
4 So Saul summoned the people,
and numbered them in Tė·lā′im, two

[v] Gk: Heb *this day* [w] Vg Compare Gk: Heb *Saul said to the* LORD, *the God of Israel*
14.49: 1 Sam 31.2; 1 Chron 10.2.

hundred thousand men on foot, and
ten thousand men of Judah. 5 And Saul
came to the city of Am'ȧ·lek, and lay
in wait in the valley. 6 And Saul said
to the Ken'ītes, "Go, depart, go down
from among the Ȧ·mal'ė·kītes, lest I
destroy you with them; for you showed
kindness to all the people of Israel
when they came up out of Egypt." So
the Kenites departed from among the
Amalekites. 7 And Saul defeated the
Ȧ·mal'ė·kītes, from Hav'i·lȧh as far as
Shür, which is east of Egypt. 8 And he
took Ā'gag the king of the Ȧ·mal'ė·kītes
alive, and utterly destroyed all the people with the edge of the sword. 9 But
Saul and the people spared Ā'gag, and
the best of the sheep and of the oxen
and of the fatlings, and the lambs, and
all that was good, and would not utterly
destroy them; all that was despised and
worthless they utterly destroyed.

10 The word of the LORD came to
Samuel: 11 "I repent that I have made
Saul king; for he has turned back from
following me, and has not performed
my commandments." And Samuel was
angry; and he cried to the LORD all
night. 12 And Samuel rose early to meet
Saul in the morning; and it was told
Samuel, "Saul came to Cär'mėl, and
behold, he set up a monument for himself and turned, and passed on, and
went down to Gil'gȧl." 13 And Samuel
came to Saul, and Saul said to him,
"Blessed be you to the LORD; I have
performed the commandment of the
LORD." 14 And Samuel said, "What
then is this bleating of the sheep in
my ears, and the lowing of the oxen
which I hear?" 15 Saul said, "They
have brought them from the Ȧ·mal'ė-
kītes; for the people spared the best of
the sheep and of the oxen, to sacrifice
to the LORD your God; and the rest we
have utterly destroyed." 16 Then Samuel said to Saul, "Stop! I will tell you
what the LORD said to me this night."
And he said to him, "Say on."

17 And Samuel said, "Though you
are little in your own eyes, are you not
the head of the tribes of Israel? The
LORD anointed you king over Israel.
18 And the LORD sent you on a mission,
and said, 'Go, utterly destroy the
sinners, the Ȧ·mal'ė·kītes, and fight
against them until they are consumed.'
19 Why then did you not obey the
voice of the LORD? Why did you swoop
on the spoil, and do what was evil in
the sight of the LORD?" 20 And Saul
said to Samuel, "I have obeyed the
voice of the LORD, I have gone on the
mission on which the LORD sent me, I
have brought Ā'gag the king of Am'ȧ-
lek, and I have utterly destroyed the
Ȧ·mal'ė·kītes. 21 But the people took
of the spoil, sheep and oxen, the best
of the things devoted to destruction,
to sacrifice to the LORD your God in
Gil'gȧl." 22 And Samuel said,

"Has the LORD as great delight in
burnt offerings and sacrifices,
as in obeying the voice of the
LORD?
Behold, to obey is better than
sacrifice,
and to hearken than the fat of
rams.
23 For rebellion is as the sin of
divination,
and stubbornness is as iniquity
and idolatry.
Because you have rejected the word
of the LORD,
he has also rejected you from
being king."

24 And Saul said to Samuel, "I
have sinned; for I have transgressed
the commandment of the LORD and
your words, because I feared the people and obeyed their voice. 25 Now
therefore, I pray, pardon my sin, and
return with me, that I may worship
the LORD." 26 And Samuel said to
Saul, "I will not return with you; for
you have rejected the word of the
LORD, and the LORD has rejected you
from being king over Israel." 27 As
Samuel turned to go away, Saul laid
hold upon the skirt of his robe, and it
tore. 28 And Samuel said to him, "The
LORD has torn the kingdom of Israel
from you this day, and has given it to
a neighbor of yours, who is better than
you. 29 And also the Glory of Israel will
not lie or repent; for he is not a man,
that he should repent." 30 Then he
said, "I have sinned; yet honor me
now before the elders of my people
and before Israel, and return with me,
that I may worship the LORD your
God." 31 So Samuel turned back after
Saul; and Saul worshiped the LORD.

32 Then Samuel said, "Bring here
to me Ā'gag the king of the Ȧ·mal'ė-
kītes." And Agag came to him cheerfully. Agag said, "Surely the bitterness
of death is past." 33 And Samuel said,
"As your sword has made women

15.22: Mk 12.33.

childless, so shall your mother be
childless among women." And Samuel
hewed Ā'gag in pieces before the
LORD in Gil'gȧl.
34 Then Samuel went to Rā'mȧh;
and Saul went up to his house in
Gib'ē-ȧh of Saul. 35 And Samuel did
not see Saul again until the day of his
death, but Samuel grieved over Saul.
And the LORD repented that he had
made Saul king over Israel.
16 The LORD said to Samuel,
"How long will you grieve over
Saul, seeing I have rejected him from
being king over Israel? Fill your horn
with oil, and go; I will send you to
Jesse the Bethlehemite, for I have provided for myself a king among his
sons." 2 And Samuel said, "How can
I go? If Saul hears it, he will kill me."
And the LORD said, "Take a heifer
with you, and say, 'I have come to sacrifice to the LORD.' 3 And invite Jesse
to the sacrifice, and I will show you
what you shall do; and you shall anoint
for me him whom I name to you."
4 Samuel did what the LORD commanded, and came to Bethlehem. The
elders of the city came to meet him
trembling, and said, "Do you come
peaceably?" 5 And he said, "Peaceably;
I have come to sacrifice to the LORD;
consecrate yourselves, and come with
me to the sacrifice." And he consecrated Jesse and his sons, and invited
them to the sacrifice.
6 When they came, he looked on
Ē·li'ab and thought, "Surely the
LORD's anointed is before him." 7 But
the LORD said to Samuel, "Do not
look on his appearance or on the height
of his stature, because I have rejected
him; for the LORD sees not as man
sees; man looks on the outward appearance, but the LORD looks on the heart."
8 Then Jesse called Ȧ·bin'ȧ·dab, and
made him pass before Samuel. And he
said, "Neither has the LORD chosen
this one." 9 Then Jesse made Sham'-
mȧh pass by. And he said, "Neither
has the LORD chosen this one." 10 And
Jesse made seven of his sons pass before Samuel. And Samuel said to Jesse,
"The LORD has not chosen these."
11 And Samuel said to Jesse, "Are all
your sons here?" And he said, "There
remains yet the youngest, but behold,
he is keeping the sheep." And Samuel
said to Jesse, "Send and fetch him;
for we will not sit down till he comes
here." 12 And he sent, and brought
him in. Now he was ruddy, and had
beautiful eyes, and was handsome.
And the LORD said, "Arise, anoint
him; for this is he." 13 Then Samuel
took the horn of oil, and anointed him
in the midst of his brothers; and the
Spirit of the LORD came mightily upon
David from that day forward. And
Samuel rose up, and went to Rā'mȧh.
14 Now the Spirit of the LORD
departed from Saul, and an evil spirit
from the LORD tormented him. 15 And
Saul's servants said to him, "Behold
now, an evil spirit from God is tor-
menting you. 16 Let our lord now
command your servants, who are before you, to seek out a man who is
skilful in playing the lyre; and when
the evil spirit from God is upon you,
he will play it, and you will be well."
17 So Saul said to his servants, "Provide for me a man who can play well,
and bring him to me." 18 One of the
young men answered, "Behold, I have
seen a son of Jesse the Bethlehemite,
who is skilful in playing, a man of
valor, a man of war, prudent in speech,
and a man of good presence; and the
LORD is with him." 19 Therefore Saul
sent messengers to Jesse, and said,
"Send me David your son, who is with
the sheep." 20 And Jesse took an ass
laden with bread, and a skin of wine
and a kid, and sent them by David his
son to Saul. 21 And David came to Saul,
and entered his service. And Saul loved
him greatly, and he became his armor-
bearer. 22 And Saul sent to Jesse, saying, "Let David remain in my service,
for he has found favor in my sight."
23 And whenever the evil spirit from
God was upon Saul, David took the
lyre and played it with his hand; so
Saul was refreshed, and was well, and
the evil spirit departed from him.
17 Now the Philistines gathered
their armies for battle; and they
were gathered at Sō'cōh, which belongs to Judah, and encamped between Socoh and Ȧ·zē'kȧh, in Ē'phĕs-
dam'mim. 2 And Saul and the men of
Israel were gathered, and encamped
in the valley of Ē'lȧh, and drew up in
line of battle against the Philistines.
3 And the Philistines stood on the
mountain on the one side, and Israel
stood on the mountain on the other
side, with a valley between them. 4 And
there came out from the camp of the
Philistines a champion named Goliath,
of Gath, whose height was six cubits

and a span. 5 He had a helmet of
bronze on his head, and he was armed
with a coat of mail, and the weight of
the coat was five thousand shekels of
bronze. 6And he had greaves of bronze
upon his legs, and a javelin of bronze
slung between his shoulders. 7And the
shaft of his spear was like a weaver's
beam, and his spear's head weighed
six hundred shekels of iron; and his
shield-bearer went before him. 8 He
stood and shouted to the ranks of
Israel, "Why have you come out to
draw up for battle? Am I not a Philistine, and are you not servants of Saul?
Choose a man for yourselves, and let
him come down to me. 9 If he is able
to fight with me and kill me, then we
will be your servants; but if I prevail
against him and kill him, then you
shall be our servants and serve us."
10And the Philistine said, "I defy the
ranks of Israel this day; give me a man,
that we may fight together." 11 When
Saul and all Israel heard these words
of the Philistine, they were dismayed
and greatly afraid.

12 Now David was the son of an
Eph'rȧ·thīte of Bethlehem in Judah,
named Jesse, who had eight sons. In
the days of Saul the man was already
old and advanced in years.[x] 13 The
three eldest sons of Jesse had followed
Saul to the battle; and the names of
his three sons who went to the battle
were E·lī'ab the first-born, and next to
him Ȧ·bin'ȧ·dab, and the third Sham'-
mȧh. 14 David was the youngest; the
three eldest followed Saul, 15 but
David went back and forth from Saul
to feed his father's sheep at Bethlehem.
16 For forty days the Philistine came
forward and took his stand, morning
and evening.

17 And Jesse said to David his son,
"Take for your brothers an ephah of
this parched grain, and these ten
loaves, and carry them quickly to the
camp to your brothers; 18 also take
these ten cheeses to the commander of
their thousand. See how your brothers
fare, and bring some token from them."

19 Now Saul, and they, and all the
men of Israel, were in the valley of
E'lȧh, fighting with the Philistines.
20And David rose early in the morning,
and left the sheep with a keeper, and
took the provisions, and went, as Jesse
had commanded him; and he came to
the encampment as the host was going
forth to the battle line, shouting the
war cry. 21And Israel and the Philistines drew up for battle, army against
army. 22And David left the things in
charge of the keeper of the baggage,
and ran to the ranks, and went and
greeted his brothers. 23As he talked
with them, behold, the champion, the
Philistine of Gath, Goliath by name,
came up out of the ranks of the Philistines, and spoke the same words as
before. And David heard him.

24 All the men of Israel, when they
saw the man, fled from him, and were
much afraid. 25And the men of Israel
said, "Have you seen this man who
has come up? Surely he has come up
to defy Israel; and the man who kills
him, the king will enrich with great
riches, and will give him his daughter,
and make his father's house free in
Israel." 26And David said to the men
who stood by him, "What shall be
done for the man who kills this Philistine, and takes away the reproach from
Israel? For who is this uncircumcised
Philistine, that he should defy the
armies of the living God?" 27And the
people answered him in the same way,
"So shall it be done to the man who
kills him."

28 Now E·lī'ab his eldest brother
heard when he spoke to the men; and
Eliab's anger was kindled against
David, and he said, "Why have you
come down? And with whom have you
left those few sheep in the wilderness?
I know your presumption, and the
evil of your heart; for you have come
down to see the battle." 29And David
said, "What have I done now? Was it
not but a word?" 30And he turned
away from him toward another, and
spoke in the same way; and the people
answered him again as before.

31 When the words which David
spoke were heard, they repeated them
before Saul; and he sent for him. 32And
David said to Saul, "Let no man's
heart fail because of him; your servant
will go and fight with this Philistine."
33And Saul said to David, "You are
not able to go against this Philistine to
fight with him; for you are but a youth,
and he has been a man of war from
his youth." 34 But David said to Saul,
"Your servant used to keep sheep for
his father; and when there came a
lion, or a bear, and took a lamb from
the flock, 35 I went after him and

[x] Gk Syr: Heb *among men*

smote him and delivered it out of his
mouth; and if he arose against me, I
caught him by his beard, and smote
him and killed him. 36 Your servant
has killed both lions and bears; and
this uncircumcised Philistine shall be
like one of them, seeing he has defied
the armies of the living God." 37And
David said, "The LORD who delivered
me from the paw of the lion and from
the paw of the bear, will deliver me
from the hand of this Philistine." And
Saul said to David, "Go, and the LORD
be with you!" 38 Then Saul clothed
David with his armor; he put a helmet
of bronze on his head, and clothed him
with a coat of mail. 39And David girded
his sword over his armor, and he tried
in vain to go, for he was not used to
them. Then David said to Saul, "I
cannot go with these; for I am not
used to them." And David put them
off. 40 Then he took his staff in his
hand, and chose five smooth stones
from the brook, and put them in his
shepherd's bag or wallet; his sling was
in his hand, and he drew near to the
Philistine.

41 And the Philistine came on and
drew near to David, with his shield-
bearer in front of him. 42And when
the Philistine looked, and saw David,
he disdained him; for he was but a
youth, ruddy and comely in appearance. 43And the Philistine said to
David, "Am I a dog, that you come to
me with sticks?" And the Philistine
cursed David by his gods. 44 The
Philistine said to David, "Come to me,
and I will give your flesh to the birds
of the air and to the beasts of the field."
45 Then David said to the Philistine,
"You come to me with a sword and
with a spear and with a javelin; but I
come to you in the name of the LORD
of hosts, the God of the armies of
Israel, whom you have defied. 46 This
day the LORD will deliver you into my
hand, and I will strike you down, and
cut off your head; and I will give the
dead bodies of the host of the Philistines this day to the birds of the air
and to the wild beasts of the earth; that
all the earth may know that there is
a God in Israel, 47 and that all this
assembly may know that the LORD
saves not with sword and spear; for
the battle is the LORD's and he will
give you into our hand."

48 When the Philistine arose and
came and drew near to meet David,
David ran quickly toward the battle
line to meet the Philistine. 49And
David put his hand in his bag and took
out a stone, and slung it, and struck
the Philistine on his forehead; the stone
sank into his forehead, and he fell on
his face to the ground.

50 So David prevailed over the
Philistine with a sling and with a stone,
and struck the Philistine, and killed
him; there was no sword in the hand
of David. 51 Then David ran and
stood over the Philistine, and took his
sword and drew it out of its sheath,
and killed him, and cut off his head
with it. When the Philistines saw that
their champion was dead, they fled.
52And the men of Israel and Judah
rose with a shout and pursued the
Philistines as far as Gath[y] and the gates
of Ek′rŏn, so that the wounded Philistines fell on the way from Shā-ȧ·rā′im
as far as Gath and Ekron. 53And the
Israelites came back from chasing the
Philistines, and they plundered their
camp. 54And David took the head of
the Philistine and brought it to Jerusalem; but he put his armor in his tent.

55 When Saul saw David go forth
against the Philistine, he said to Abner,
the commander of the army, "Abner,
whose son is this youth?" And Abner
said, "As your soul lives, O king, I
cannot tell." 56And the king said,
"Inquire whose son the stripling is."
57And as David returned from the
slaughter of the Philistine, Abner took
him, and brought him before Saul
with the head of the Philistine in his
hand. 58And Saul said to him, "Whose
son are you, young man?" And David
answered, "I am the son of your servant Jesse the Bethlehemite."

18 When he had finished speaking
to Saul, the soul of Jonathan was
knit to the soul of David, and Jonathan
loved him as his own soul. 2And Saul
took him that day, and would not let
him return to his father's house. 3 Then
Jonathan made a covenant with
David, because he loved him as his
own soul. 4And Jonathan stripped himself of the robe that was upon him, and
gave it to David, and his armor, and
even his sword and his bow and his
girdle. 5And David went out and was
successful wherever Saul sent him; so
that Saul set him over the men of war.
And this was good in the sight of all the

[y] Gk: Heb *Gai*

people and also in the sight of Saul's
servants.
6 As they were coming home, when
David returned from slaying the Philistine, the women came out of all the
cities of Israel, singing and dancing,
to meet King Saul, with timbrels, with
songs of joy, and with instruments[z] of
music. 7 And the women sang to one
another as they made merry,

"Saul has slain his thousands,
and David his ten thousands."

8 And Saul was very angry, and this
saying displeased him; he said, "They
have ascribed to David ten thousands,
and to me they have ascribed thousands; and what more can he have but
the kingdom?" 9 And Saul eyed David
from that day on.
10 And on the morrow an evil spirit
from God rushed upon Saul, and he
raved within his house, while David
was playing the lyre, as he did day by
day. Saul had his spear in his hand;
11 and Saul cast the spear, for he
thought, "I will pin David to the
wall." But David evaded him twice.
12 Saul was afraid of David, because the LORD was with him but had
departed from Saul. 13 So Saul removed him from his presence, and
made him a commander of a thousand;
and he went out and came in before
the people. 14 And David had success
in all his undertakings; for the LORD
was with him. 15 And when Saul saw
that he had great success, he stood in
awe of him. 16 But all Israel and Judah
loved David; for he went out and came
in before them.
17 Then Saul said to David, "Here
is my elder daughter Mē'rab; I will
give her to you for a wife; only be
valiant for me and fight the LORD's
battles." For Saul thought, "Let not
my hand be upon him, but let the hand
of the Philistines be upon him." 18 And
David said to Saul, "Who am I, and
who are my kinsfolk, my father's
family in Israel, that I should be son-
in-law to the king?" 19 But at the time
when Mē'rab, Saul's daughter, should
have been given to David, she was
given to Ā'dri·el the Mė·hō'lȧ·thīte for
a wife.
20 Now Saul's daughter Mī'chȧl
loved David; and they told Saul, and
the thing pleased him. 21 Saul thought,
"Let me give her to him, that she may
be a snare for him, and that the hand
of the Philistines may be against him."
Therefore Saul said to David a second
time,[a] "You shall now be my son-in-
law." 22 And Saul commanded his servants, "Speak to David in private and
say, 'Behold, the king has delight in
you, and all his servants love you; now
then become the king's son-in-law.' "
23 And Saul's servants spoke those
words in the ears of David. And David
said, "Does it seem to you a little thing
to become the king's son-in-law, seeing
that I am a poor man and of no repute?" 24 And the servants of Saul told
him, "Thus and so did David speak."
25 Then Saul said, "Thus shall you
say to David, 'The king desires no
marriage present except a hundred
foreskins of the Philistines, that he may
be avenged of the king's enemies.' "
Now Saul thought to make David fall
by the hand of the Philistines. 26 And
when his servants told David these
words, it pleased David well to be the
king's son-in-law. Before the time had
expired, 27 David arose and went, along
with his men, and killed two hundred
of the Philistines; and David brought
their foreskins, which were given in
full number to the king, that he might
become the king's son-in-law. And
Saul gave him his daughter Mī'chȧl
for a wife. 28 But when Saul saw and
knew that the LORD was with David,
and that all Israel[b] loved him, 29 Saul
was still more afraid of David. So
Saul was David's enemy continually.
30 Then the princes of the Philistines came out to battle, and as often
as they came out David had more
success than all the servants of Saul;
so that his name was highly esteemed.

19 And Saul spoke to Jonathan his
son and to all his servants, that
they should kill David. But Jonathan,
Saul's son, delighted much in David.
2 And Jonathan told David, "Saul my
father seeks to kill you; therefore take
heed to yourself in the morning, stay
in a secret place and hide yourself;
3 and I will go out and stand beside
my father in the field where you are,
and I will speak to my father about
you; and if I learn anything I will tell
you." 4 And Jonathan spoke well of
David to Saul his father, and said to
him, "Let not the king sin against his
servant David; because he has not

[z] Or *triangles*, or *three-stringed instruments* [a] Heb *by two* [b] Gk: Heb *Michal, Saul's daughter*
18.7: 1 Sam 21.11; 29.5.

sinned against you, and because his
deeds have been of good service to you;
5 for he took his life in his hand and
he slew the Philistine, and the LORD
wrought a great victory for all Israel.
You saw it, and rejoiced; why then will
you sin against innocent blood by
killing David without cause?" 6 And
Saul hearkened to the voice of Jonathan; Saul swore, "As the LORD lives,
he shall not be put to death." 7 And
Jonathan called David, and Jonathan
showed him all these things. And
Jonathan brought David to Saul, and
he was in his presence as before.

8 And there was war again; and
David went out and fought with the
Philistines, and made a great slaughter
among them, so that they fled before
him. 9 Then an evil spirit from the
LORD came upon Saul, as he sat in his
house with his spear in his hand; and
David was playing the lyre. 10 And Saul
sought to pin David to the wall with
the spear; but he eluded Saul, so that
he struck the spear into the wall. And
David fled, and escaped.

11 That night Saul[x] sent messengers to David's house to watch him,
that he might kill him in the morning.
But Mī'chal, David's wife, told him,
"If you do not save your life tonight,
tomorrow you will be killed." 12 So
Mī'chal let David down through the
window; and he fled away and escaped.
13 Mī'chal took an image[c] and laid it
on the bed and put a pillow[d] of goats'
hair at its head, and covered it with
the clothes. 14 And when Saul sent
messengers to take David, she said,
"He is sick." 15 Then Saul sent the messengers to see David, saying, "Bring
him up to me in the bed, that I may
kill him." 16 And when the messengers
came in, behold, the image[c] was in the
bed, with the pillow[d] of goats' hair at
its head. 17 Saul said to Mī'chal, "Why
have you deceived me thus, and let my
enemy go, so that he has escaped?"
And Michal answered Saul, "He said
to me, 'Let me go; why should I kill
you?' "

18 Now David fled and escaped,
and he came to Samuel at Rā'mah, and
told him all that Saul had done to him.
And he and Samuel went and dwelt at
Nā'ōth. 19 And it was told Saul, "Behold, David is at Nā'ōth in Rā'mah."
20 Then Saul sent messengers to take
David; and when they saw the company of the prophets prophesying, and
Samuel standing as head over them,
the Spirit of God came upon the messengers of Saul, and they also prophesied. 21 When it was told Saul, he
sent other messengers, and they also
prophesied. And Saul sent messengers
again the third time, and they also
prophesied. 22 Then he himself went
to Rā'mah, and came to the great well
that is in Sē'cū; and he asked, "Where
are Samuel and David?" And one said,
"Behold, they are at Nā'ōth in Ramah." 23 And he went from[f] there to
Nā'ōth in Rā'mah; and the Spirit of
God came upon him also, and as he
went he prophesied, until he came to
Naioth in Ramah. 24 And he too
stripped off his clothes, and he too
prophesied before Samuel, and lay
naked all that day and all that night.
Hence it is said, "Is Saul also among
the prophets?"

20 Then David fled from Nā'ōth
in Rā'mah, and came and said
before Jonathan, "What have I done?
What is my guilt? And what is my sin
before your father, that he seeks my
life?" 2 And he said to him, "Far from
it! You shall not die. Behold, my father
does nothing either great or small without disclosing it to me; and why should
my father hide this from me? It is not
so." 3 But David replied,[g] "Your
father knows well that I have found
favor in your eyes; and he thinks, 'Let
not Jonathan know this, lest he be
grieved.' But truly, as the LORD lives
and as your soul lives, there is but a
step between me and death." 4 Then
said Jonathan to David, "Whatever
you say, I will do for you." 5 David
said to Jonathan, "Behold, tomorrow
is the new moon, and I should not fail
to sit at table with the king; but let
me go, that I may hide myself in the
field till the third day at evening. 6 If
your father misses me at all, then say,
'David earnestly asked leave of me to
run to Bethlehem his city; for there is
a yearly sacrifice there for all the
family.' 7 If he says, 'Good!' it will be
well with your servant; but if he is
angry, then know that evil is determined by him. 8 Therefore deal kindly
with your servant, for you have brought

[x] Gk Old Latin: Heb *escaped that night.* 11 *And Saul* [c] Heb *teraphim*
[d] The meaning of the Hebrew word is uncertain [f] Gk: Heb lacks *from* [g] Gk: Heb *swore again*
19.23-24: 1 Sam 10.10-12.

your servant into a sacred covenant[h]
with you. But if there is guilt in me,
slay me yourself; for why should you
bring me to your father?" 9 And Jonathan said, "Far be it from you! If I
knew that it was determined by my
father that evil should come upon you,
would I not tell you?" 10 Then said
David to Jonathan, "Who will tell me
if your father answers you roughly?"
11 And Jonathan said to David, "Come,
let us go out into the field." So they
both went out into the field.

12 And Jonathan said to David,
"The LORD, the God of Israel, be
witness![i] When I have sounded my
father, about this time tomorrow, or
the third day, behold, if he is well
disposed toward David, shall I not
then send and disclose it to you? 13 But
should it please my father to do you
harm, the LORD do so to Jonathan, and
more also, if I do not disclose it to you,
and send you away, that you may go
in safety. May the LORD be with you,
as he has been with my father. 14 If I
am still alive, show me the loyal love of
the LORD, that I may not die;[j] 15 and
do not cut off your loyalty from my
house for ever. When the LORD cuts
off every one of the enemies of David
from the face of the earth, 16 let not
the name of Jonathan be cut off from
the house of David.[k] And may the
LORD take vengeance on David's
enemies." 17 And Jonathan made David
swear again by his love for him; for he
loved him as he loved his own soul.

18 Then Jonathan said to him, "Tomorrow is the new moon; and you will
be missed, because your seat will be
empty. 19 And on the third day you
will be greatly missed;[l] then go to the
place where you hid yourself when the
matter was in hand, and remain beside
yonder stone heap.[m] 20 And I will shoot
three arrows to the side of it, as though
I shot at a mark. 21 And behold, I will
send the lad, saying, 'Go, find the
arrows.' If I say to the lad, 'Look, the
arrows are on this side of you, take
them,' then you are to come, for, as
the LORD lives, it is safe for you and
there is no danger. 22 But if I say to
the youth, 'Look, the arrows are beyond you,' then go; for the LORD has
sent you away. 23 And as for the matter
of which you and I have spoken, behold, the LORD is between you and me
for ever."

24 So David hid himself in the
field; and when the new moon came,
the king sat down to eat food. 25 The
king sat upon his seat, as at other times,
upon the seat by the wall; Jonathan
sat opposite,[n] and Abner sat by Saul's
side, but David's place was empty.

26 Yet Saul did not say anything
that day; for he thought, "Something
has befallen him; he is not clean,
surely he is not clean." 27 But on the
second day, the morrow after the new
moon, David's place was empty. And
Saul said to Jonathan his son, "Why
has not the son of Jesse come to the
meal, either yesterday or today?"
28 Jonathan answered Saul, "David
earnestly asked leave of me to go to
Bethlehem; 29 he said, 'Let me go; for
our family holds a sacrifice in the city,
and my brother has commanded me
to be there. So now, if I have found
favor in your eyes, let me get away,
and see my brothers.' For this reason
he has not come to the king's table."

30 Then Saul's anger was kindled
against Jonathan, and he said to him,
"You son of a perverse, rebellious
woman, do I not know that you have
chosen the son of Jesse to your own
shame, and to the shame of your
mother's nakedness? 31 For as long as
the son of Jesse lives upon the earth,
neither you nor your kingdom shall be
established. Therefore send and fetch
him to me, for he shall surely die."
32 Then Jonathan answered Saul his
father, "Why should he be put to
death? What has he done?" 33 But Saul
cast his spear at him to smite him; so
Jonathan knew that his father was
determined to put David to death.
34 And Jonathan rose from the table in
fierce anger and ate no food the second
day of the month, for he was grieved
for David, because his father had disgraced him.

35 In the morning Jonathan went
out into the field to the appointment
with David, and with him a little lad.
36 And he said to his lad, "Run and
find the arrows which I shoot." As the
lad ran, he shot an arrow beyond him.
37 And when the lad came to the place
of the arrow which Jonathan had shot,
Jonathan called after the lad and said,

[h] Heb *a covenant of the* LORD [i] Heb lacks *be witness* [j] Heb uncertain
[k] Gk: Heb *earth, and Jonathan made a covenant with the house of David* [l] Gk: Heb *go down quickly*
[m] Gk: Heb *the stone Ezel* [n] Cn See Gk: Heb *stood up*

"Is not the arrow beyond you?" 38And
Jonathan called after the lad, "Hurry,
make haste, stay not." So Jonathan's
lad gathered up the arrows, and came
to his master. 39 But the lad knew
nothing; only Jonathan and David
knew the matter. 40And Jonathan gave
his weapons to his lad, and said to
him, "Go and carry them to the city."
41And as soon as the lad had gone,
David rose from beside the stone heap[o]
and fell on his face to the ground, and
bowed three times; and they kissed
one another, and wept with one
another, until David recovered himself.[p]
42 Then Jonathan said to David,
"Go in peace, forasmuch as we have
sworn both of us in the name of the
LORD, saying, 'The LORD shall be
between me and you, and between my
descendants and your descendants, for
ever.'" And he rose and departed;
and Jonathan went into the city.[q]

21 [r] Then came David to Nob
to A·him'ĕ·lech the priest; and
Ahimelech came to meet David trembling,
and said to him, "Why are you
alone, and no one with you?" 2And
David said to A·him'ĕ·lech the priest,
"The king has charged me with a
matter, and said to me, 'Let no one
know anything of the matter about
which I send you, and with which I
have charged you.' I have made an
appointment with the young men for
such and such a place. 3 Now then,
what have you at hand? Give me five
loaves of bread, or whatever is here."
4And the priest answered David, "I
have no common bread at hand, but
there is holy bread; if only the young
men have kept themselves from
women." 5And David answered the
priest, "Of a truth women have been
kept from us as always when I go on
an expedition; the vessels of the young
men are holy, even when it is a common
journey; how much more today
will their vessels be holy?" 6 So the
priest gave him the holy bread; for
there was no bread there but the bread
of the Presence, which is removed from
before the LORD, to be replaced by
hot bread on the day it is taken
away.
7 Now a certain man of the servants
of Saul was there that day, detained
before the LORD; his name was Dō'eg
the E'dŏm·īte, the chief of Saul's
herdsmen.
8 And David said to A·him'ĕ·lech,
"And have you not here a spear or a
sword at hand? For I have brought
neither my sword nor my weapons
with me, because the king's business
required haste." 9And the priest said,
"The sword of Goliath the Philistine,
whom you killed in the valley of
E'lăh, behold, it is here wrapped in a
cloth behind the ephod; if you will
take that, take it, for there is none but
that here." And David said, "There
is none like that; give it to me."
10 And David rose and fled that day
from Saul, and went to Ā'chish the
king of Gath. 11And the servants of
Ā'chish said to him, "Is not this David
the king of the land? Did they not sing
to one another of him in dances,

'Saul has slain his thousands,
and David his ten thousands'?"

12And David took these words to
heart, and was much afraid of Ā'chish
the king of Gath. 13 So he changed
his behavior before them, and feigned
himself mad in their hands, and made
marks on the doors of the gate, and let
his spittle run down his beard. 14 Then
said Ā'chish to his servants, "Lo, you
see the man is mad; why then have
you brought him to me? 15 Do I lack
madmen, that you have brought this
fellow to play the madman in my
presence? Shall this fellow come into
my house?"

22 David departed from there and
escaped to the cave of A·dul'lăm;
and when his brothers and all his
father's house heard it, they went down
there to him. 2And every one who was
in distress, and every one who was in
debt, and every one who was discontented,
gathered to him; and he became
captain over them. And there
were with him about four hundred men.
3 And David went from there to
Miz'peh of Mō'ab; and he said to the
king of Moab, "Pray let my father and
my mother stay[s] with you, till I know
what God will do for me." 4And he
left them with the king of Mō'ab, and
they stayed with him all the time that
David was in the stronghold. 5 Then
the prophet Gad said to David, "Do
not remain in the stronghold; depart,
and go into the land of Judah." So

[o] Gk: Heb *from beside the south* [p] Or *exceeded* [q] This sentence is 21.1 in Heb [r] Ch 21.2 in Heb
[s] Syr Vg: Heb *come out*
21.11: 1 Sam 18.7; 29.5.

David departed, and went into the
forest of Hē'reth.
6 Now Saul heard that David was
discovered, and the men who were
with him. Saul was sitting at Gib'ē-ȧh,
under the tamarisk tree on the height,
with his spear in his hand, and all his
servants were standing about him.
7 And Saul said to his servants who
stood about him, "Hear now, you
Benjaminites; will the son of Jesse give
every one of you fields and vineyards,
will he make you all commanders of
thousands and commanders of hundreds, 8 that all of you have conspired
against me? No one discloses to me
when my son makes a league with the
son of Jesse, none of you is sorry for
me or discloses to me that my son has
stirred up my servant against me, to
lie in wait, as at this day." 9 Then
answered Dō'eg the E'dȯm·īte, who
stood by the servants of Saul, "I saw
the son of Jesse coming to Nob, to
Ȧ·him'ė·lech the son of Ȧ·hī'tu̇b, 10 and
he inquired of the LORD for him, and
gave him provisions, and gave him
the sword of Goliath the Philistine."
11 Then the king sent to summon
Ȧ·him'ė·lech the priest, the son of
Ȧ·hī'tu̇b, and all his father's house,
the priests who were at Nob; and all
of them came to the king. 12 And Saul
said, "Hear now, son of Ȧ·hī'tu̇b." And
he answered, "Here I am, my lord."
13 And Saul said to him, "Why have
you conspired against me, you and the
son of Jesse, in that you have given
him bread and a sword, and have inquired of God for him, so that he has
risen against me, to lie in wait, as at
this day?" 14 Then Ȧ·him'ė·lech answered the king, "And who among all
your servants is so faithful as David,
who is the king's son-in-law, and
captain over[t] your bodyguard, and
honored in your house? 15 Is today the
first time that I have inquired of God
for him? No! Let not the king impute
anything to his servant or to all the
house of my father; for your servant
has known nothing of all this, much
or little." 16 And the king said, "You
shall surely die, Ȧ·him'ė·lech, you and
all your father's house." 17 And the
king said to the guard who stood about
him, "Turn and kill the priests of the
LORD; because their hand also is with
David, and they knew that he fled,
and did not disclose it to me." But
the servants of the king would not put
forth their hand to fall upon the priests
of the LORD. 18 Then the king said to
Dō'eg, "You turn and fall upon the
priests." And Doeg the E'dȯm·īte
turned and fell upon the priests, and
he killed on that day eighty-five persons who wore the linen ephod. 19 And
Nob, the city of the priests, he put to
the sword; both men and women,
children and sucklings, oxen, asses
and sheep, he put to the sword.
20 But one of the sons of Ȧ·him'ė-
lech the son of Ȧ·hī'tu̇b, named Ȧ·bī'ȧ-
thär, escaped and fled after David.
21 And Ȧ·bī'ȧ·thär told David that Saul
had killed the priests of the LORD.
22 And David said to Ȧ·bī'ȧ·thär, "I
knew on that day, when Dō'eg the
E'dȯm·īte was there, that he would
surely tell Saul. I have occasioned the
death of all the persons of your father's
house. 23 Stay with me, fear not; for
he that seeks my life seeks your life;
with me you shall be in safekeeping."

23 Now they told David, "Behold, the Philistines are fighting
against Kē·ī'lȧh, and are robbing the
threshing floors." 2 Therefore David
inquired of the LORD, "Shall I go and
attack these Philistines?" And the
LORD said to David, "Go and attack
the Philistines and save Kē·ī'lȧh."
3 But David's men said to him, "Behold, we are afraid here in Judah; how
much more then if we go to Kē·ī'lȧh
against the armies of the Philistines?"
4 Then David inquired of the LORD
again. And the LORD answered him,
"Arise, go down to Kē·ī'lȧh; for I will
give the Philistines into your hand."
5 And David and his men went to
Kē·ī'lȧh, and fought with the Philistines, and brought away their cattle,
and made a great slaughter among
them. So David delivered the inhabitants of Keilah.
6 When Ȧ·bī'ȧ·thär the son of
Ȧ·him'ė·lech fled to David to Kē·ī'lȧh,
he came down with an ephod in his
hand. 7 Now it was told Saul that
David had come to Kē·ī'lȧh. And Saul
said, "God has given him into my
hand; for he has shut himself in by
entering a town that has gates and
bars." 8 And Saul summoned all the
people to war, to go down to Kē·ī'lȧh,
to besiege David and his men. 9 David
knew that Saul was plotting evil
against him; and he said to Ȧ·bī'ȧ·thär

[t] Gk Tg: Heb *and has turned aside to*

the priest, "Bring the ephod here."
10 Then said David, "O LORD, the God
of Israel, thy servant has surely heard
that Saul seeks to come to Kē·ī'lȧh, to
destroy the city on my account. 11 Will
the men of Kē·ī'lȧh surrender me into
his hand? Will Saul come down, as
thy servant has heard? O LORD, the
God of Israel, I beseech thee, tell thy
servant." And the LORD said, "He
will come down." 12 Then said David,
"Will the men of Kē·ī'lȧh surrender
me and my men into the hand of
Saul?" And the LORD said, "They will
surrender you." 13 Then David and
his men, who were about six hundred,
arose and departed from Kē·ī'lȧh, and
they went wherever they could go.
When Saul was told that David had
escaped from Keilah, he gave up the
expedition. 14 And David remained in
the strongholds in the wilderness, in
the hill country of the Wilderness of
Ziph. And Saul sought him every day,
but God did not give him into his hand.

15 And David was afraid because[u]
Saul had come out to seek his life.
David was in the Wilderness of Ziph
at Hō'resh. 16 And Jonathan, Saul's
son, rose, and went to David at Hō'-
resh, and strengthened his hand in God.
17 And he said to him, "Fear not; for
the hand of Saul my father shall not
find you; you shall be king over Israel,
and I shall be next to you; Saul my
father also knows this." 18 And the two
of them made a covenant before the
LORD; David remained at Hō'resh,
and Jonathan went home.

19 Then the Ziphites went up to
Saul at Gib'ē-ȧh, saying, "Does not
David hide among us in the strongholds at Hō'resh, on the hill of Hȧ·chī'-
lȧh, which is south of Jē·shī'mon?
20 Now come down, O king, according
to all your heart's desire to come down;
and our part shall be to surrender him
into the king's hand." 21 And Saul said,
"May you be blessed by the LORD; for
you have had compassion on me.
22 Go, make yet more sure; know and
see the place where his haunt is, and
who has seen him there; for it is told
me that he is very cunning. 23 See
therefore, and take note of all the lurking places where he hides, and come
back to me with sure information.
Then I will go with you; and if he is
in the land, I will search him out
among all the thousands of Judah."
24 And they arose, and went to Ziph
ahead of Saul.

Now David and his men were in the
wilderness of Mā'on, in the Ar'ȧ·bȧh
to the south of Jē·shī'mon. 25 And Saul
and his men went to seek him. And
David was told; therefore he went
down to the rock which is[v] in the
wilderness of Mā'on. And when Saul
heard that, he pursued after David in
the wilderness of Maon. 26 Saul went
on one side of the mountain, and David
and his men on the other side of the
mountain; and David was making
haste to get away from Saul, as Saul
and his men were closing in upon
David and his men to capture them,
27 when a messenger came to Saul,
saying, "Make haste and come; for the
Philistines have made a raid upon the
land." 28 So Saul returned from pursuing after David, and went against
the Philistines; therefore that place
was called the Rock of Escape. 29 [w]And
David went up from there, and dwelt
in the strongholds of En-gē'dī.

24 When Saul returned from following the Philistines, he was
told, "Behold, David is in the wilderness of En-gē'dī." 2 Then Saul took
three thousand chosen men out of all
Israel, and went to seek David and his
men in front of the Wildgoats' Rocks.
3 And he came to the sheepfolds by
the way, where there was a cave; and
Saul went in to relieve himself. Now
David and his men were sitting in the
innermost parts of the cave. 4 And the
men of David said to him, "Here is
the day of which the LORD said to you,
'Behold, I will give your enemy into
your hand, and you shall do to him
as it shall seem good to you.' " Then
David arose and stealthily cut off the
skirt of Saul's robe. 5 And afterward
David's heart smote him, because he
had cut off Saul's skirt. 6 He said to
his men, "The LORD forbid that I
should do this thing to my lord, the
LORD's anointed, to put forth my hand
against him, seeing he is the LORD's
anointed." 7 So David persuaded his
men with these words, and did not
permit them to attack Saul. And Saul
rose up and left the cave, and went
upon his way.

8 Afterward David also arose, and
went out of the cave, and called after

[u] Or *saw that* [v] Gk: Heb *and dwelt* [w] Ch 24.1 in Heb
24.1-22: 1 Sam 26.1-25.

Saul, "My lord the king!" And when
Saul looked behind him, David bowed
with his face to the earth, and did
obeisance. 9 And David said to Saul,
"Why do you listen to the words of
men who say, 'Behold, David seeks
your hurt'? 10 Lo, this day your eyes
have seen how the LORD gave you today into my hand in the cave; and
some bade me kill you, but I[x] spared
you. I said, 'I will not put forth my
hand against my lord; for he is the
LORD's anointed.' 11 See, my father,
see the skirt of your robe in my hand;
for by the fact that I cut off the skirt
of your robe, and did not kill you, you
may know and see that there is no
wrong or treason in my hands. I have
not sinned against you, though you
hunt my life to take it. 12 May the
LORD judge between me and you, may
the LORD avenge me upon you; but
my hand shall not be against you.
13 As the proverb of the ancients says,
'Out of the wicked comes forth
wickedness'; but my hand shall not be
against you. 14 After whom has the
king of Israel come out? After whom
do you pursue? After a dead dog! After
a flea! 15 May the LORD therefore be
judge, and give sentence between me
and you, and see to it, and plead
my cause, and deliver me from your
hand."

16 When David had finished speaking these words to Saul, Saul said, "Is
this your voice, my son David?" And
Saul lifted up his voice and wept.
17 He said to David, "You are more
righteous than I; for you have repaid
me good, whereas I have repaid you
evil. 18 And you have declared this day
how you have dealt well with me, in
that you did not kill me when the
LORD put me into your hands. 19 For
if a man finds his enemy, will he let
him go away safe? So may the LORD
reward you with good for what you
have done to me this day. 20 And now,
behold, I know that you shall surely
be king, and that the kingdom of Israel
shall be established in your hand.
21 Swear to me therefore by the LORD
that you will not cut off my descendants after me, and that you will not
destroy my name out of my father's
house." 22 And David swore this to
Saul. Then Saul went home; but
David and his men went up to the
stronghold.

x Gk Syr Tg: Heb *you*

25 Now Samuel died; and all Israel assembled and mourned for
him, and they buried him in his house
at Rā'mȧh.

Then David rose and went down to
the wilderness of Pâr'an. 2 And there
was a man in Mā'on, whose business
was in Cär'mėl. The man was very
rich; he had three thousand sheep and
a thousand goats. He was shearing his
sheep in Carmel. 3 Now the name of
the man was Nā'bal, and the name of
his wife Ab'i·gāil. The woman was of
good understanding and beautiful, but
the man was churlish and ill-behaved;
he was a Calebite. 4 David heard in
the wilderness that Nā'bal was shearing his sheep. 5 So David sent ten
young men; and David said to the
young men, "Go up to Cär'mėl, and
go to Nā'bal, and greet him in my
name. 6 And thus you shall salute him:
'Peace be to you, and peace be to your
house, and peace be to all that you
have. 7 I hear that you have shearers;
now your shepherds have been with
us, and we did them no harm, and they
missed nothing, all the time they were
in Cär'mėl. 8 Ask your young men, and
they will tell you. Therefore let my
young men find favor in your eyes; for
we come on a feast day. Pray, give
whatever you have at hand to your
servants and to your son David.' "

9 When David's young men came,
they said all this to Nā'bal in the name
of David; and then they waited. 10 And
Nā'bal answered David's servants,
"Who is David? Who is the son of
Jesse? There are many servants nowa-
days who are breaking away from their
masters. 11 Shall I take my bread and
my water and my meat that I have
killed for my shearers, and give it to
men who come from I do not know
where?" 12 So David's young men
turned away, and came back and told
him all this. 13 And David said to his
men, "Every man gird on his sword!"
And every man of them girded on his
sword; David also girded on his sword;
and about four hundred men went up
after David, while two hundred remained with the baggage.

14 But one of the young men told
Ab'i·gāil, Nā'bal's wife, "Behold,
David sent messengers out of the
wilderness to salute our master; and
he railed at them. 15 Yet the men were
very good to us, and we suffered no

harm, and we did not miss anything
when we were in the fields, as long as
we went with them; 16 they were a wall
to us both by night and by day, all the
while we were with them keeping the
sheep. 17 Now therefore know this and
consider what you should do; for evil
is determined against our master and
against all his house, and he is so ill-
natured that one cannot speak to him."

18 Then Ab'i·gāil made haste, and
took two hundred loaves, and two
skins of wine, and five sheep ready
dressed, and five measures of parched
grain, and a hundred clusters of
raisins, and two hundred cakes of figs,
and laid them on asses. 19 And she said
to her young men, "Go on before me;
behold, I come after you." But she did
not tell her husband Nā'bal. 20 And as
she rode on the ass, and came down
under cover of the mountain, behold,
David and his men came down toward
her; and she met them. 21 Now David
had said, "Surely in vain have I
guarded all that this fellow has in the
wilderness, so that nothing was missed
of all that belonged to him; and he has
returned me evil for good. 22 God do
so to David[y] and more also, if by
morning I leave so much as one male
of all who belong to him."

23 When Ab'i·gāil saw David, she
made haste, and alighted from the ass,
and fell before David on her face, and
bowed to the ground. 24 She fell at his
feet and said, "Upon me alone, my
lord, be the guilt; pray let your handmaid speak in your ears, and hear the
words of your handmaid. 25 Let not
my lord regard this ill-natured fellow,
Nā'bal; for as his name is, so is he;
Nabal[z] is his name, and folly is with
him; but I your handmaid did not see
the young men of my lord, whom you
sent. 26 Now then, my lord, as the
LORD lives, and as your soul lives, seeing the LORD has restrained you from
bloodguilt, and from taking vengeance
with your own hand, now then let
your enemies and those who seek to
do evil to my lord be as Nā'bal. 27 And
now let this present which your servant
has brought to my lord be given to the
young men who follow my lord.
28 Pray forgive the trespass of your
handmaid; for the LORD will certainly
make my lord a sure house, because
my lord is fighting the battles of the
LORD; and evil shall not be found in
you so long as you live. 29 If men rise
up to pursue you and to seek your life,
the life of my lord shall be bound in
the bundle of the living in the care of
the LORD your God; and the lives of
your enemies he shall sling out as from
the hollow of a sling. 30 And when the
LORD has done to my lord according
to all the good that he has spoken concerning you, and has appointed you
prince over Israel, 31 my lord shall
have no cause of grief, or pangs of
conscience, for having shed blood
without cause or for my lord taking
vengeance himself. And when the LORD
has dealt well with my lord, then
remember your handmaid."

32 And David said to Ab'i·gāil,
"Blessed be the LORD, the God of
Israel, who sent you this day to meet
me! 33 Blessed be your discretion, and
blessed be you, who have kept me this
day from bloodguilt and from avenging
myself with my own hand! 34 For as
surely as the LORD the God of Israel
lives, who has restrained me from
hurting you, unless you had made haste
and come to meet me, truly by morning there had not been left to Nā'bal
so much as one male." 35 Then David
received from her hand what she had
brought him; and he said to her, "Go
up in peace to your house; see, I have
hearkened to your voice, and I have
granted your petition."

36 And Ab'i·gāil came to Nā'bal;
and, lo, he was holding a feast in his
house, like the feast of a king. And
Nabal's heart was merry within him,
for he was very drunk; so she told him
nothing at all until the morning light.
37 And in the morning, when the wine
had gone out of Nā'bal, his wife told
him these things, and his heart died
within him, and he became as a stone.
38 And about ten days later the LORD
smote Nā'bal; and he died.

39 When David heard that Nā'bal
was dead, he said, "Blessed be the
LORD who has avenged the insult I
received at the hand of Nabal, and has
kept back his servant from evil; the
LORD has returned the evil-doing of
Nabal upon his own head." Then David
sent and wooed Ab'i·gāil, to make her
his wife. 40 And when the servants of
David came to Ab'i·gāil at Cär'mĕl,
they said to her, "David has sent us to
you to take you to him as his wife."
41 And she rose and bowed with her

[y] Gk Compare Syr: Heb *the enemies of David* [z] That is *fool*

face to the ground, and said, "Behold,
your handmaid is a servant to wash
the feet of the servants of my lord."
42 And Ab'i·gāil made haste and rose
and mounted on an ass, and her five
maidens attended her; she went after
the messengers of David, and became
his wife.
43 David also took Ȧ·hin'ō-am of
Jez'rē·ėl; and both of them became his
wives. 44 Saul had given Mī'chȧl his
daughter, David's wife, to Pal'tī the
son of Lā'ish, who was of Gal'lim.

26 Then the Ziphites came to
Saul at Gib'ē-ȧh, saying, "Is
not David hiding himself on the hill
of Hȧ·chī'lȧh, which is on the east of
Jē·shī'mon?" 2 So Saul arose and went
down to the wilderness of Ziph, with
three thousand chosen men of Israel,
to seek David in the wilderness of
Ziph. 3 And Saul encamped on the hill
of Hȧ·chī'lȧh, which is beside the road
on the east of Jē·shī'mon. But David
remained in the wilderness; and when
he saw that Saul came after him into
the wilderness, 4 David sent out spies,
and learned of a certainty that Saul
had come. 5 Then David rose and came
to the place where Saul had encamped;
and David saw the place where Saul
lay, with Abner the son of Nēr, the
commander of his army; Saul was
lying within the encampment, while
the army was encamped around him.
6 Then David said to Ȧ·him'ė·lech
the Hit'tīte, and to Jō'ab's brother
Ȧ·bi'shäi the son of Zė·rü'i·ȧh, "Who
will go down with me into the camp
to Saul?" And Abishai said, "I will go
down with you." 7 So David and Ȧ·bi'-
shäi went to the army by night; and
there lay Saul sleeping within the encampment, with his spear stuck in the
ground at his head; and Abner and the
army lay around him. 8 Then said
Ȧ·bi'shäi to David, "God has given
your enemy into your hand this day;
now therefore let me pin him to the
earth with one stroke of the spear, and
I will not strike him twice." 9 But
David said to Ȧ·bi'shäi, "Do not
destroy him; for who can put forth his
hand against the LORD's anointed, and
be guiltless?" 10 And David said, "As
the LORD lives, the LORD will smite
him; or his day shall come to die; or
he shall go down into battle and perish.
11 The LORD forbid that I should put
forth my hand against the LORD's
anointed; but take now the spear that
is at his head, and the jar of water, and
let us go." 12 So David took the spear
and the jar of water from Saul's head;
and they went away. No man saw it,
or knew it, nor did any awake; for they
were all asleep, because a deep sleep
from the LORD had fallen upon them.
13 Then David went over to the
other side, and stood afar off on the
top of the mountain, with a great space
between them; 14 and David called to
the army, and to Abner the son of Nēr,
saying, "Will you not answer, Abner?"
Then Abner answered, "Who are you
that calls to the king?" 15 And David
said to Abner, "Are you not a man?
Who is like you in Israel? Why then
have you not kept watch over your
lord the king? For one of the people
came in to destroy the king your lord.
16 This thing that you have done is not
good. As the LORD lives, you deserve
to die, because you have not kept watch
over your lord, the LORD's anointed.
And now see where the king's spear is,
and the jar of water that was at his
head."
17 Saul recognized David's voice,
and said, "Is this your voice, my son
David?" And David said, "It is my
voice, my lord, O king." 18 And he
said, "Why does my lord pursue after
his servant? For what have I done?
What guilt is on my hands? 19 Now
therefore let my lord the king hear
the words of his servant. If it is the
LORD who has stirred you up against
me, may he accept an offering; but if
it is men, may they be cursed before
the LORD, for they have driven me out
this day that I should have no share in
the heritage of the LORD, saying, 'Go,
serve other gods.' 20 Now therefore,
let not my blood fall to the earth away
from the presence of the LORD; for the
king of Israel has come out to seek my
life,[a] like one who hunts a partridge in
the mountains."
21 Then Saul said, "I have done
wrong; return, my son David, for I will
no more do you harm, because my life
was precious in your eyes this day;
behold, I have played the fool, and
have erred exceedingly." 22 And David
made answer, "Here is the spear, O
king! Let one of the young men come
over and fetch it. 23 The LORD rewards

[a] Gk: Heb *a flea* (as in 24.14)
26.1-25: 1 Sam 24.1-22.

every man for his righteousness and
his faithfulness; for the LORD gave you
into my hand today, and I would not
put forth my hand against the LORD's
anointed. 24 Behold, as your life was
precious this day in my sight, so may
my life be precious in the sight of the
LORD, and may he deliver me out of
all tribulation." 25 Then Saul said to
David, "Blessed be you, my son David!
You will do many things and will succeed in them." So David went his way,
and Saul returned to his place.

27 And David said in his heart,
"I shall now perish one day by
the hand of Saul; there is nothing
better for me than that I should escape
to the land of the Philistines; then Saul
will despair of seeking me any longer
within the borders of Israel, and I shall
escape out of his hand." 2 So David
arose and went over, he and the six
hundred men who were with him, to
Ā'chish the son of Mā'och, king of
Gath. 3 And David dwelt with Ā'chish
at Gath, he and his men, every man
with his household, and David with
his two wives, A·hin'ō-am of Jez'rē·ĕl,
and Ab'i·gāil of Cär'mĕl, Nā'bal's
widow. 4 And when it was told Saul
that David had fled to Gath, he sought
for him no more.

5 Then David said to Ā'chish, "If
I have found favor in your eyes, let a
place be given me in one of the
country towns, that I may dwell there;
for why should your servant dwell in
the royal city with you?" 6 So that day
Ā'chish gave him Zik'lag; therefore
Ziklag has belonged to the kings of
Judah to this day. 7 And the number
of the days that David dwelt in the
country of the Philistines was a year
and four months.

8 Now David and his men went up,
and made raids upon the Gesh'ū·rītes,
the Gĭr'zītes, and the A·mal'ĕ·kītes;
for these were the inhabitants of the
land from of old, as far as Shûr, to
the land of Egypt. 9 And David smote
the land, and left neither man nor
woman alive, but took away the sheep,
the oxen, the asses, the camels, and
the garments, and came back to
Ā'chish. 10 When Ā'chish asked,
"Against whom[b] have you made a raid
today?" David would say, "Against
the Negeb of Judah," or "Against the
Negeb of the Je·räh'mē·ĕ·lītes," or,
"Against the Negeb of the Ken'ītes."
11 And David saved neither man nor
woman alive, to bring tidings to Gath,
thinking, "Lest they should tell about
us, and say, 'So David has done.' "
Such was his custom all the while he
dwelt in the country of the Philistines.
12 And Ā'chish trusted David, thinking,
"He has made himself utterly abhorred
by his people Israel; therefore he shall
be my servant always."

28 In those days the Philistines
gathered their forces for war, to
fight against Israel. And Ā'chish said
to David, "Understand that you and
your men are to go out with me in the
army." 2 David said to Ā'chish, "Very
well, you shall know what your servant
can do." And Achish said to David,
"Very well, I will make you my bodyguard for life."

3 Now Samuel had died, and all
Israel had mourned for him and buried
him in Rā'măh, his own city. And Saul
had put the mediums and the wizards
out of the land. 4 The Philistines
assembled, and came and encamped at
Shü'nem; and Saul gathered all Israel,
and they encamped at Gil·bō'ă. 5 When
Saul saw the army of the Philistines,
he was afraid, and his heart trembled
greatly. 6 And when Saul inquired of
the LORD, the LORD did not answer
him, either by dreams, or by Ū'rim,
or by prophets. 7 Then Saul said to
his servants, "Seek out for me a
woman who is a medium, that I may
go to her and inquire of her." And his
servants said to him, "Behold, there
is a medium at En'-dôr."

8 So Saul disguised himself and put
on other garments, and went, he and
two men with him; and they came to
the woman by night. And he said,
"Divine for me by a spirit, and bring
up for me whomever I shall name to
you." 9 The woman said to him,
"Surely you know what Saul has done,
how he has cut off the mediums and
the wizards from the land. Why then
are you laying a snare for my life to
bring about my death?" 10 But Saul
swore to her by the LORD, "As the
LORD lives, no punishment shall come
upon you for this thing." 11 Then the
woman said, "Whom shall I bring up
for you?" He said, "Bring up Samuel
for me." 12 When the woman saw
Samuel, she cried out with a loud voice;
and the woman said to Saul, "Why
have you deceived me? You are Saul."

[b] Gk Vg: Heb lacks *whom*

13 The king said to her, "Have no fear;
what do you see?" And the woman
said to Saul, "I see a god coming up
out of the earth." 14 He said to her,
"What is his appearance?" And she
said, "An old man is coming up; and
he is wrapped in a robe." And Saul
knew that it was Samuel, and he bowed
with his face to the ground, and did
obeisance.

15 Then Samuel said to Saul, "Why
have you disturbed me by bringing
me up?" Saul answered, "I am in great
distress; for the Philistines are warring
against me, and God has turned away
from me and answers me no more,
either by prophets or by dreams; therefore I have summoned you to tell me
what I shall do." 16 And Samuel said,
"Why then do you ask me, since the
LORD has turned from you and become
your enemy? 17 The LORD has done to
you as he spoke by me; for the LORD
has torn the kingdom out of your hand,
and given it to your neighbor, David.
18 Because you did not obey the voice
of the LORD and did not carry out his
fierce wrath against Am'ȧ·lek, therefore the LORD has done this thing to
you this day. 19 Moreover the LORD
will give Israel also with you into the
hand of the Philistines; and tomorrow
you and your sons shall be with me;
the LORD will give the army of Israel
also into the hand of the Philistines."

20 Then Saul fell at once full length
upon the ground, filled with fear because of the words of Samuel; and
there was no strength in him, for he
had eaten nothing all day and all
night. 21 And the woman came to Saul,
and when she saw that he was terrified,
she said to him, "Behold, your handmaid has hearkened to you; I have
taken my life in my hand, and have
hearkened to what you have said to me.
22 Now therefore, you also hearken to
your handmaid; let me set a morsel of
bread before you; and eat, that you
may have strength when you go on
your way." 23 He refused, and said, "I
will not eat." But his servants, together
with the woman, urged him; and he
hearkened to their words. So he arose
from the earth, and sat upon the bed.
24 Now the woman had a fatted calf in
the house, and she quickly killed it,
and she took flour, and kneaded it and
baked unleavened bread of it, 25 and
she put it before Saul and his servants;
and they ate. Then they rose and went
away that night.

29 Now the Philistines gathered
all their forces at Ā'phek; and
the Israelites were encamped by the
fountain which is in Jez'rē·ėl. 2 As the
lords of the Philistines were passing on
by hundreds and by thousands, and
David and his men were passing on in
the rear with Ā'chish, 3 the commanders of the Philistines said, "What
are these Hebrews doing here?" And
Ā'chish said to the commanders of the
Philistines, "Is not this David, the
servant of Saul, king of Israel, who has
been with me now for days and years,
and since he deserted to me I have
found no fault in him to this day." 4 But
the commanders of the Philistines were
angry with him; and the commanders
of the Philistines said to him, "Send
the man back, that he may return to
the place to which you have assigned
him; he shall not go down with us to
battle, lest in the battle he become an
adversary to us. For how could this
fellow reconcile himself to his lord?
Would it not be with the heads of the
men here? 5 Is not this David, of whom
they sing to one another in dances,

'Saul has slain his thousands,
and David his ten thousands'?"

6 Then Ā'chish called David and
said to him, "As the LORD lives, you
have been honest, and to me it seems
right that you should march out and in
with me in the campaign; for I have
found nothing wrong in you from the
day of your coming to me to this day.
Nevertheless the lords do not approve
of you. 7 So go back now; and go
peaceably, that you may not displease
the lords of the Philistines." 8 And
David said to Ā'chish, "But what have
I done? What have you found in your
servant from the day I entered your
service until now, that I may not go
and fight against the enemies of my
lord the king?" 9 And Ā'chish made
answer to David, "I know that you are
as blameless in my sight as an angel of
God; nevertheless the commanders of
the Philistines have said, 'He shall not
go up with us to the battle.' 10 Now
then rise early in the morning with the
servants of your lord who came with
you; and start early in the morning,
and depart as soon as you have light."
11 So David set out with his men early
in the morning, to return to the land

29.5: 1 Sam 18.7; 21.11.

of the Philistines. But the Philistines
went up to Jez′rē·ĕl.

30 Now when David and his men
came to Zik′lag on the third day,
the Ȧ·mal′ė·kītes had made a raid upon
the Negeb and upon Ziklag. They had
overcome Ziklag, and burned it with
fire, 2 and taken captive the women
and all[c] who were in it, both small and
great; they killed no one, but carried
them off, and went their way. 3And
when David and his men came to the
city, they found it burned with fire,
and their wives and sons and daughters
taken captive. 4 Then David and the
people who were with him raised their
voices and wept, until they had no
more strength to weep. 5 David's two
wives also had been taken captive,
Ȧ·hin′ō-am of Jez′rē·ĕl, and Ab′i·gāil
the widow of Nā′bal of Cär′mĕl. 6And
David was greatly distressed; for the
people spoke of stoning him, because
all the people were bitter in soul, each
for his sons and daughters. But David
strengthened himself in the LORD his
God.

7 And David said to Ȧ·bī′ȧ·thär the
priest, the son of Ȧ·him′ė·lech, "Bring
me the ephod." So Abiathar brought
the ephod to David. 8And David inquired of the LORD, "Shall I pursue
after this band? Shall I overtake
them?" He answered him, "Pursue; for
you shall surely overtake and shall
surely rescue." 9 So David set out, and
the six hundred men who were with
him, and they came to the brook Bē′-
sôr, where those stayed who were left
behind. 10 But David went on with the
pursuit, he and four hundred men;
two hundred stayed behind, who were
too exhausted to cross the brook Bē′sôr.

11 They found an Egyptian in the
open country, and brought him to
David; and they gave him bread and
he ate, they gave him water to drink,
12 and they gave him a piece of a cake
of figs and two clusters of raisins. And
when he had eaten, his spirit revived;
for he had not eaten bread or drunk
water for three days and three nights.
13And David said to him, "To whom
do you belong? And where are you
from?" He said, "I am a young man of
Egypt, servant to an Ȧ·mal′ė·kīte; and
my master left me behind because I
fell sick three days ago. 14 We had
made a raid upon the Negeb of the
Cher′ė·thītes and upon that which belongs to Judah and upon the Negeb of
Caleb; and we burned Zik′lag with
fire." 15And David said to him, "Will
you take me down to this band?" And
he said, "Swear to me by God, that
you will not kill me, or deliver me into
the hands of my master, and I will
take you down to this band."

16 And when he had taken him
down, behold, they were spread abroad
over all the land, eating and drinking
and dancing, because of all the great
spoil they had taken from the land of
the Philistines and from the land of
Judah. 17And David smote them from
twilight until the evening of the next
day; and not a man of them escaped,
except four hundred young men, who
mounted camels and fled. 18 David recovered all that the Ȧ·mal′ė·kītes had
taken; and David rescued his two
wives. 19 Nothing was missing, whether
small or great, sons or daughters, spoil
or anything that had been taken; David
brought back all. 20 David also captured all the flocks and herds; and the
people drove those cattle before him,[d]
and said, "This is David's spoil."

21 Then David came to the two
hundred men, who had been too exhausted to follow David, and who had
been left at the brook Bē′sôr; and they
went out to meet David and to meet
the people who were with him; and
when David drew near to the people
he saluted them. 22 Then all the wicked
and base fellows among the men who
had gone with David said, "Because
they did not go with us, we will not
give them any of the spoil which we
have recovered, except that each man
may lead away his wife and children,
and depart." 23 But David said, "You
shall not do so, my brothers, with what
the LORD has given us; he has preserved us and given into our hand the
band that came against us. 24 Who
would listen to you in this matter? For
as his share is who goes down into the
battle, so shall his share be who stays
by the baggage; they shall share alike."
25And from that day forward he made
it a statute and an ordinance for
Israel to this day.

26 When David came to Zik′lag, he
sent part of the spoil to his friends, the
elders of Judah, saying, "Here is a
present for you from the spoil of the
enemies of the LORD"; 27 it was for
those in Beth′ĕl, in Rā′moth of the

[c] Gk: Heb lacks *and all* [d] Cn: Heb *they drove before those cattle*

Negeb, in Jat'tîr, 28 in A·rō'ėr, in
Siph'moth, in Esh·tė·mō'ȧ, 29 in Rā'-
cȧl, in the cities of the Jė·räh'mē·ė·lītes,
in the cities of the Ken'ītes, 30 in
Hôr'mȧh, in Bôr·ash'ȧn, in Ā'thach,
31 in Hē'brȯn, for all the places where
David and his men had roamed.

31 Now the Philistines fought
against Israel; and the men of
Israel fled before the Philistines, and
fell slain on Mount Gil·bō'ȧ. 2And the
Philistines overtook Saul and his sons;
and the Philistines slew Jonathan and
A·bin'ȧ·dab and Mal'chī·shü'ȧ, the
sons of Saul. 3 The battle pressed hard
upon Saul, and the archers found him;
and he was badly wounded by the
archers. 4 Then Saul said to his armor-
bearer, "Draw your sword, and thrust
me through with it, lest these uncircumcised come and thrust me through,
and make sport of me." But his armor-
bearer would not; for he feared greatly.
Therefore Saul took his own sword,
and fell upon it. 5And when his armor-
bearer saw that Saul was dead, he also
fell upon his sword, and died with him.
6 Thus Saul died, and his three sons,
and his armor-bearer, and all his men,
on the same day together. 7And when
the men of Israel who were on the
other side of the valley and those beyond the Jordan saw that the men of
Israel had fled and that Saul and his
sons were dead, they forsook their
cities and fled; and the Philistines
came and dwelt in them.

8 On the morrow, when the Philistines came to strip the slain, they
found Saul and his three sons fallen on
Mount Gil·bō'ȧ. 9And they cut off his
head, and stripped off his armor, and
sent messengers throughout the land
of the Philistines, to carry the good
news to their idols[e] and to the people.
10 They put his armor in the temple of
Ash'tȧ·roth; and they fastened his body
to the wall of Beth'-shan. 11 But when
the inhabitants of Jā'besh-gil'ē·ȧd
heard what the Philistines had done to
Saul, 12 all the valiant men arose, and
went all night, and took the body of
Saul and the bodies of his sons from
the wall of Beth'-shan; and they came
to Jā'besh and burnt them there. 13And
they took their bones and buried them
under the tamarisk tree in Jā'besh,
and fasted seven days.

THE SECOND BOOK OF

SAMUEL

1 After the death of Saul, when
David had returned from the
slaughter of the A·mal'ė·kītes, David
remained two days in Zik'lag; 2 and
on the third day, behold, a man came
from Saul's camp, with his clothes rent
and earth upon his head. And when
he came to David, he fell to the
ground and did obeisance. 3 David
said to him, "Where do you come
from?" And he said to him, "I have
escaped from the camp of Israel."
4And David said to him, "How did it
go? Tell me." And he answered, "The
people have fled from the battle, and
many of the people also have fallen
and are dead; and Saul and his son
Jonathan are also dead." 5 Then David
said to the young man who told him,
"How do you know that Saul and his
son Jonathan are dead?" 6And the
young man who told him said, "By
chance I happened to be on Mount
Gil·bō'ȧ; and there was Saul leaning
upon his spear; and lo, the chariots
and the horsemen were close upon
him. 7And when he looked behind
him, he saw me, and called to me. And
I answered, 'Here I am.' 8And he said
to me, 'Who are you?' I answered him,
'I am an A·mal'ė·kīte.' 9And he said to
me, 'Stand beside me and slay me; for
anguish has seized me, and yet my life
still lingers.' 10 So I stood beside him,
and slew him, because I was sure that
he could not live after he had fallen;
and I took the crown which was on
his head and the armlet which was on

[e] Gk Compare 1 Chron 10.9: Heb *to the house of their idols*

31.1-13: 2 Sam 1.6-10; 1 Chron 10.1-12. 1.6-10: 1 Sam 31.1-13; 1 Chron 10.1-12.

his arm, and I have brought them here
to my lord."
11 Then David took hold of his
clothes, and rent them; and so did all
the men who were with him; 12 and
they mourned and wept and fasted
until evening for Saul and for Jonathan
his son and for the people of the LORD
and for the house of Israel, because
they had fallen by the sword. 13 And
David said to the young man who told
him, "Where do you come from?"
And he answered, "I am the son of a
sojourner, an A·mal'ė·kite." 14 David
said to him, "How is it you were not
afraid to put forth your hand to destroy
the LORD's anointed?" 15 Then David
called one of the young men and said,
"Go, fall upon him." And he smote
him so that he died. 16 And David said
to him, "Your blood be upon your
head; for your own mouth has testified
against you, saying, 'I have slain the
LORD's anointed.' "
17 And David lamented with this
lamentation over Saul and Jonathan
his son, 18 and he said it[a] should be
taught to the people of Judah; behold,
it is written in the Book of Jash'ăr.[b]
He said:

19 "Thy glory, O Israel, is slain upon
thy high places!
How are the mighty fallen!
20 Tell it not in Gath,
publish it not in the streets of
Ash'kė·lon;
lest the daughters of the Philistines
rejoice,
lest the daughters of the uncircumcised exult.

21 "Ye mountains of Gil·bō'ă,
let there be no dew or rain upon
you,
nor upsurging of the deep![c]
For there the shield of the mighty
was defiled,
the shield of Saul, not anointed
with oil.

22 "From the blood of the slain,
from the fat of the mighty,
the bow of Jonathan turned not
back,
and the sword of Saul returned
not empty.

23 "Saul and Jonathan, beloved and
lovely!
In life and in death they were not
divided;
they were swifter than eagles,
they were stronger than lions.

24 "Ye daughters of Israel, weep over
Saul,
who clothed you daintily in
scarlet,
who put ornaments of gold upon
your apparel.

25 "How are the mighty fallen
in the midst of the battle!

"Jonathan lies slain upon thy high
places.
26 I am distressed for you, my
brother Jonathan;
very pleasant have you been to
me;
your love to me was wonderful,
passing the love of women.

27 "How are the mighty fallen,
and the weapons of war perished!"

2 After this David inquired of the
LORD, "Shall I go up into any of
the cities of Judah?" And the LORD
said to him, "Go up." David said, "To
which shall I go up?" And he said,
"To Hē'brŏn." 2 So David went up
there, and his two wives also, A·hin'ō-
am of Jez'rē·ĕl, and Ab'ĭ·găil the widow
of Nā'bal of Cär'mĕl. 3 And David
brought up his men who were with
him, every one with his household; and
they dwelt in the towns of Hē'brŏn.
4 And the men of Judah came, and
there they anointed David king over
the house of Judah.
When they told David, "It was the
men of Jā'besh-gil'ē·ăd who buried
Saul," 5 David sent messengers to the
men of Jā'besh-gil'ē·ăd, and said to
them, "May you be blessed by the
LORD, because you showed this
loyalty to Saul your lord, and buried
him! 6 Now may the LORD show steadfast love and faithfulness to you! And
I will do good to you because you have
done this thing. 7 Now therefore let
your hands be strong, and be valiant;
for Saul your lord is dead, and the
house of Judah has anointed me king
over them."
8 Now Abner the son of Nēr, commander of Saul's army, had taken
Ish-bō'sheth the son of Saul, and

[a] Gk: Heb *the Bow* [b] Or *The upright*
[c] Cn: Heb *fields of offerings*

brought him over to Mā·hȧ·nā′im;
9 and he made him king over Gilead
and the Ash′ū·rītes and Jez′rē·ĕl and
Ē′phrȧ·im and Benjamin and all Israel.
10 Ish-bō′sheth, Saul's son, was forty
years old when he began to reign over
Israel, and he reigned two years. But
the house of Judah followed David.
11 And the time that David was king in
Hē′brȯn over the house of Judah was
seven years and six months.

12 Abner the son of Nēr, and the
servants of Ish-bō′sheth the son of
Saul, went out from Mā·hȧ·nā′im to
Gib′ē·ŏn. 13 And Jō′ab the son of
Zė·rü′i·ȧh, and the servants of David,
went out and met them at the pool of
Gib′ē·ŏn; and they sat down, the one
on the one side of the pool, and the
other on the other side of the pool.
14 And Abner said to Jō′ab, "Let the
young men arise and play before us."
And Joab said, "Let them arise."
15 Then they arose and passed over by
number, twelve for Benjamin and Ish-
bō′sheth the son of Saul, and twelve of
the servants of David. 16 And each
caught his opponent by the head, and
thrust his sword in his opponent's
side; so they fell down together. Therefore that place was called Hel′kath-
haz·zū′rim,[d] which is at Gib′ē·ŏn.
17 And the battle was very fierce that
day; and Abner and the men of Israel
were beaten before the servants of
David.

18 And the three sons of Zė·rü′i·ȧh
were there, Jō′ab, Ȧ·bi′shăi, and As′ȧ-
hel. Now Asahel was as swift of foot
as a wild gazelle; 19 and As′ȧ·hel pursued Abner, and as he went he turned
neither to the right hand nor to the
left from following Abner. 20 Then
Abner looked behind him and said,
"Is it you, As′ȧ·hel?" And he answered, "It is I." 21 Abner said to him,
"Turn aside to your right hand or to
your left, and seize one of the young
men, and take his spoil." But As′ȧ·hel
would not turn aside from following
him. 22 And Abner said again to As′ȧ-
hel, "Turn aside from following me;
why should I smite you to the ground?
How then could I lift up my face to
your brother Jō′ab?" 23 But he refused
to turn aside; therefore Abner smote
him in the belly with the butt of his
spear, so that the spear came out at his
back; and he fell there, and died where
he was. And all who came to the place
where As′ȧ·hel had fallen and died,
stood still.

24 But Jō′ab and Ȧ·bi′shăi pursued
Abner; and as the sun was going down
they came to the hill of Am′mȧh,
which lies before Gī′ȧh on the way to
the wilderness of Gib′ē·ŏn. 25 And the
Benjaminites gathered themselves together behind Abner, and became one
band, and took their stand on the top
of a hill. 26 Then Abner called to Jō′ab,
"Shall the sword devour for ever? Do
you not know that the end will be
bitter? How long will it be before you
bid your people turn from the pursuit
of their brethren?" 27 And Jō′ab said,
"As God lives, if you had not spoken,
surely the men would have given up
the pursuit of their brethren in the
morning." 28 So Jō′ab blew the trumpet; and all the men stopped, and
pursued Israel no more, nor did they
fight any more.

29 And Abner and his men went all
that night through the Ar′ȧ·bȧh; they
crossed the Jordan, and marching the
whole forenoon they came to Mā·hȧ-
nā′im. 30 Jō′ab returned from the pursuit of Abner; and when he had
gathered all the people together, there
were missing of David's servants nineteen men besides As′ȧ·hel. 31 But the
servants of David had slain of Benjamin three hundred and sixty of Abner's
men. 32 And they took up As′ȧ·hel, and
buried him in the tomb of his father,
which was at Bethlehem. And Jō′-
ab and his men marched all night,
and the day broke upon them at
Hē′brȯn.

3 There was a long war between the
house of Saul and the house of
David; and David grew stronger and
stronger, while the house of Saul became weaker and weaker.

2 And sons were born to David at
Hē′brȯn: his first-born was Am′non,
of Ȧ·hin′ō-am of Jez′rē·ĕl; 3 and his
second, Chil′ē-ab, of Ab′i·găil the
widow of Nā′bal of Cär′mĕl; and the
third, Ab′sȧ·lȯm the son of Mā·ȧ·cȧh
the daughter of Tal′măi king of Gē′-
shūr; 4 and the fourth, Ad·ȯ·nī′jȧh the
son of Hag′gith; and the fifth, Sheph-
ȧ·tī′ȧh the son of Ȧ·bī′tȧl; 5 and the
sixth, Ith′rē-am of Eg′lȧh, David's
wife. These were born to David in
Hē′brȯn.

[d] That is *the field of sword-edges*
3.2-5: 1 Chron 3.1-4.

6 While there was war between the
house of Saul and the house of David,
Abner was making himself strong in
the house of Saul. 7 Now Saul had a
concubine, whose name was Riz'pȧh,
the daughter of Ăi'ȧh; and Ish-bō'-
sheth said to Abner, "Why have you
gone in to my father's concubine?"
8 Then Abner was very angry over the
words of Ish-bō'sheth, and said, "Am
I a dog's head of Judah? This day I
keep showing loyalty to the house of
Saul your father, to his brothers, and
to his friends, and have not given you
into the hand of David; and yet you
charge me today with a fault concerning a woman. 9 God do so to Abner,
and more also, if I do not accomplish
for David what the LORD has sworn to
him, 10 to transfer the kingdom from
the house of Saul, and set up the
throne of David over Israel and over
Judah, from Dan to Beer-sheba."
11 And Ish-bō'sheth could not answer
Abner another word, because he feared
him.

12 And Abner sent messengers to
David at Hē'brŏn,[e] saying, "To whom
does the land belong? Make your
covenant with me, and behold, my
hand shall be with you to bring over
all Israel to you." 13 And he said,
"Good; I will make a covenant with
you; but one thing I require of you;
that is, you shall not see my face, unless
you first bring Mī'chȧl, Saul's daughter, when you come to see my face."
14 Then David sent messengers to Ish-
bō'sheth Saul's son, saying, "Give me
my wife Mī'chȧl, whom I betrothed at
the price of a hundred foreskins of the
Philistines." 15 And Ish-bō'sheth sent,
and took her from her husband Pal'-
ti-el the son of Lā'ish. 16 But her husband went with her, weeping after her
all the way to Bȧ-hū'rim. Then Abner
said to him, "Go, return"; and he
returned.

17 And Abner conferred with the
elders of Israel, saying, "For some
time past you have been seeking David
as king over you. 18 Now then bring
it about; for the LORD has promised
David, saying, 'By the hand of my
servant David I will save my people
Israel from the hand of the Philistines, and from the hand of all their
enemies.' " 19 Abner also spoke to Benjamin; and then Abner went to tell
David at Hē'brŏn all that Israel and
the whole house of Benjamin thought
good to do.

20 When Abner came with twenty
men to David at Hē'brŏn, David made
a feast for Abner and the men who
were with him. 21 And Abner said to
David, "I will arise and go, and will
gather all Israel to my lord the king,
that they may make a covenant with
you, and that you may reign over all
that your heart desires." So David
sent Abner away; and he went in peace.

22 Just then the servants of David
arrived with Jō'ab from a raid, bringing much spoil with them. But Abner
was not with David at Hē'brŏn, for he
had sent him away, and he had gone
in peace. 23 When Jō'ab and all the
army that was with him came, it was
told Joab, "Abner the son of Nēr came
to the king, and he has let him go, and
he has gone in peace." 24 Then Jō'ab
went to the king and said, "What have
you done? Behold, Abner came to you;
why is it that you have sent him away,
so that he is gone? 25 You know that
Abner the son of Nēr came to deceive
you, and to know your going out and
your coming in, and to know all that
you are doing."

26 When Jō'ab came out from
David's presence, he sent messengers
after Abner, and they brought him
back from the cistern of Sī'rȧh; but
David did not know about it. 27 And
when Abner returned to Hē'brŏn,
Jō'ab took him aside into the midst of
the gate to speak with him privately,
and there he smote him in the belly,
so that he died, for the blood of
As'ȧ-hel his brother. 28 Afterward, when
David heard of it, he said, "I and my
kingdom are for ever guiltless before
the LORD for the blood of Abner the
son of Nēr. 29 May it fall upon the
head of Jō'ab, and upon all his father's
house; and may the house of Joab never
be without one who has a discharge,
or who is leprous, or who holds a
spindle, or who is slain by the sword,
or who lacks bread!" 30 So Jō'ab and
Ȧ-bi'shāi his brother slew Abner, because he had killed their brother As'ȧ-
hel in the battle at Gib'ē-ŏn.

31 Then David said to Jō'ab and to
all the people who were with him,
"Rend your clothes, and gird on sackcloth, and mourn before Abner." And
King David followed the bier. 32 They
buried Abner at Hē'brŏn; and the king

[e] Gk: Heb *where he was*

lifted up his voice and wept at the
grave of Abner; and all the people
wept. [33]And the king lamented for
Abner, saying,

"Should Abner die as a fool dies?
[34] Your hands were not bound,
your feet were not fettered;
as one falls before the wicked
you have fallen."

And all the people wept again over
him. [35] Then all the people came to
persuade David to eat bread while it
was yet day; but David swore, saying,
"God do so to me and more also, if I
taste bread or any thing else till the sun
goes down!" [36]And all the people took
notice of it, and it pleased them; as
everything that the king did pleased
all the people. [37] So all the people and
all Israel understood that day that it
had not been the king's will to slay
Abner the son of Nēr. [38]And the king
said to his servants, "Do you not know
that a prince and a great man has fallen
this day in Israel? [39]And I am this day
weak, though anointed king; these men
the sons of Zė·rü'i·ȧh are too hard for
me. The LORD requite the evildoer
according to his wickedness!"

4 When Ish-bō'sheth, Saul's son,
heard that Abner had died at
Hē'brȯn, his courage failed, and all
Israel was dismayed. [2] Now Saul's son
had two men who were captains of
raiding bands; the name of the one was
Bā'ȧ·nȧh, and the name of the other
Rē'chab, sons of Rim'mon a man of
Benjamin from Bė-ēr'ŏth (for Be-eroth
also is reckoned to Benjamin; [3] the
Bė-ēr'ȯ·thītes fled to Git·tā'im, and
have been sojourners there to this day).

4 Jonathan, the son of Saul, had a
son who was crippled in his feet. He
was five years old when the news about
Saul and Jonathan came from Jez'rē·ėl;
and his nurse took him up, and fled;
and, as she fled in her haste, he fell,
and became lame. And his name was
Me·phib'ȯ·sheth.

5 Now the sons of Rim'mon the
Bė-ēr'ȯ·thīte, Rē'chab and Bā'ȧ·nȧh,
set out, and about the heat of the day
they came to the house of Ish-bō'sheth,
as he was taking his noonday rest.
[6]And behold, the doorkeeper of the
house had been cleaning wheat, but
she grew drowsy and slept; so Rē'chab
and Bā'ȧ·nȧh his brother slipped in.[f]
[7] When they came into the house, as
he lay on his bed in his bedchamber,
they smote him, and slew him, and
beheaded him. They took his head,
and went by the way of the Ar'ȧ·bȧh
all night, [8] and brought the head of
Ish-bō'sheth to David at Hē'brȯn. And
they said to the king, "Here is the head
of Ish-bosheth, the son of Saul, your
enemy, who sought your life; the LORD
has avenged my lord the king this day
on Saul and on his offspring." [9] But
David answered Rē'chab and Bā'ȧ·nȧh
his brother, the sons of Rim'mon the
Bė-ēr'ȯ·thīte, "As the LORD lives, who
has redeemed my life out of every adversity, [10] when one told me, 'Behold,
Saul is dead,' and thought he was
bringing good news, I seized him and
slew him at Zik'lag, which was the
reward I gave him for his news. [11] How
much more, when wicked men have
slain a righteous man in his own house
upon his bed, shall I not now require
his blood at your hand, and destroy
you from the earth?" [12]And David
commanded his young men, and they
killed them, and cut off their hands and
feet, and hanged them beside the pool
at Hē'brȯn. But they took the head of
Ish-bō'sheth, and buried it in the tomb
of Abner at Hebron.

5 Then all the tribes of Israel came
to David at Hē'brȯn, and said,
"Behold, we are your bone and flesh.
[2] In times past, when Saul was king
over us, it was you that led out and
brought in Israel; and the LORD said
to you, 'You shall be shepherd of my
people Israel, and you shall be prince
over Israel.' " [3] So all the elders of
Israel came to the king at Hē'brȯn; and
King David made a covenant with
them at Hebron before the LORD, and
they anointed David king over Israel.
[4] David was thirty years old when he
began to reign, and he reigned forty
years. [5]At Hē'brȯn he reigned over
Judah seven years and six months; and
at Jerusalem he reigned over all Israel
and Judah thirty-three years.

6 And the king and his men went
to Jerusalem against the Jeb'ū·sītes,
the inhabitants of the land, who said
to David, "You will not come in here,
but the blind and the lame will ward
you off"—thinking, "David cannot
come in here." [7] Nevertheless David

[f] Gk: Heb [6]*And hither they came into the midst of the house fetching wheat; and they smote him in the belly; and Rechab and Baanah his brother escaped*

5.1-3: 1 Chron 11.1-3. 5.4-5: 1 Chron 3.4. 5.6-10: 1 Chron 11.4-9.

took the stronghold of Zion, that is,
the city of David. 8And David said on
that day, "Whoever would smite the
Jeb'ū·sītes, let him get up the water
shaft to attack the lame and the blind,
who are hated by David's soul." Therefore it is said, "The blind and the lame
shall not come into the house." 9And
David dwelt in the stronghold, and
called it the city of David. And David
built the city round about from the
Mil'lō inward. 10And David became
greater and greater, for the LORD, the
God of hosts, was with him.

11 And Hiram king of Tȳre sent
messengers to David, and cedar trees,
also carpenters and masons who built
David a house. 12And David perceived
that the LORD had established him
king over Israel, and that he had
exalted his kingdom for the sake of
his people Israel.

13 And David took more concubines and wives from Jerusalem, after
he came from Hē'brȯn; and more sons
and daughters were born to David.
14And these are the names of those
who were born to him in Jerusalem:
Sham'mū-ȧ, Shō'bab, Nathan, Solomon, 15 Ib'hār, E·lī'shü-ȧ, Nē'pheg,
Jȧ·phī'ȧ, 16 E·lish'ȧ·mȧ, E·lī'ȧ·dȧ, and
E·liph'ė·let.

17 When the Philistines heard that
David had been anointed king over
Israel, all the Philistines went up in
search of David; but David heard of
it and went down to the stronghold.
18 Now the Philistines had come and
spread out in the valley of Reph'ȧ·im.
19And David inquired of the LORD,
"Shall I go up against the Philistines?
Wilt thou give them into my hand?"
And the LORD said to David, "Go up;
for I will certainly give the Philistines
into your hand." 20And David came
to Bā'ȧl-pe·rā'zim, and David defeated
them there; and he said, "The LORD
has broken through[g] my enemies before me, like a bursting flood." Therefore the name of that place is called
Baal-perazim.[h] 21And the Philistines
left their idols there, and David and
his men carried them away.

22 And the Philistines came up yet
again, and spread out in the valley of
Reph'ȧ·im. 23And when David inquired of the LORD, he said, "You
shall not go up; go around to their
rear, and come upon them opposite
the balsam trees. 24And when you hear
the sound of marching in the tops of
the balsam trees, then bestir yourself;
for then the LORD has gone out before
you to smite the army of the Philistines." 25And David did as the LORD
commanded him, and smote the Philistines from Gē'bȧ to Gē'zėr.

6 David again gathered all the
chosen men of Israel, thirty thousand. 2And David arose and went with
all the people who were with him from
Bā'ȧ·lē-jü'dȧh, to bring up from there
the ark of God, which is called by the
name of the LORD of hosts who sits
enthroned on the cherubim. 3And
they carried the ark of God upon a
new cart, and brought it out of the
house of A·bin'ȧ·dab which was on
the hill; and Uz'zȧh and A·hī'ō,[i] the
sons of Abinadab, were driving the
new cart[j] 4 with the ark of God; and
A·hī'ō[i] went before the ark. 5And
David and all the house of Israel were
making merry before the LORD with
all their might, with songs[k] and lyres
and harps and tambourines and casta-
nets and cymbals.

6 And when they came to the
threshing floor of Nā'con, Uz'zȧh put
out his hand to the ark of God and
took hold of it, for the oxen stumbled.
7And the anger of the LORD was
kindled against Uz'zȧh; and God smote
him there because he put forth his
hand to the ark;[l] and he died there
beside the ark of God. 8And David
was angry because the LORD had
broken forth upon Uz'zȧh; and that
place is called Per'ez-uz'zȧh,[m] to this
day. 9And David was afraid of the LORD
that day; and he said, "How can the
ark of the LORD come to me?" 10 So
David was not willing to take the ark
of the LORD into the city of David; but
David took it aside to the house of
Ō'bed-ē'dȯm the Git'tīte. 11And the
ark of the LORD remained in the house
of Ō'bed-ē'dȯm the Git'tīte three
months; and the LORD blessed Obed-
edom and all his household.

[g] Heb *paraz* [h] That is *Lord of breaking through* [i] Or *and his brother*
[j] Compare Gk: Heb *the new cart, and brought it out of the house of Abinadab which was on the hill*
[k] Gk 1 Chron 13.8: Heb *fir-trees* [l] 1 Chron 13.10: Heb uncertain
[m] That is *The breaking forth upon Uzzah*

5.11-12: 1 Chron 14.1-2. **5.14-16:** 1 Chron 3.5-8; 14.3-7. **5.17-21:** 1 Chron 14.8-12.
5.22-25: 1 Chron 14.13-16. **6.1-11:** 1 Chron 13.1-14.

12 And it was told King David,
"The LORD has blessed the household
of Ō'bed-ē'dŏm and all that belongs to
him, because of the ark of God." So
David went and brought up the ark of
God from the house of Obed-edom to
the city of David with rejoicing; 13 and
when those who bore the ark of the
LORD had gone six paces, he sacrificed
an ox and a fatling. 14 And David
danced before the LORD with all his
might; and David was girded with a
linen ephod. 15 So David and all the
house of Israel brought up the ark of
the LORD with shouting, and with the
sound of the horn.

16 As the ark of the LORD came
into the city of David, Mī'chăl the
daughter of Saul looked out of the
window, and saw King David leaping
and dancing before the LORD; and she
despised him in her heart. 17 And they
brought in the ark of the LORD, and
set it in its place, inside the tent which
David had pitched for it; and David
offered burnt offerings and peace offerings before the LORD. 18 And when
David had finished offering the burnt
offerings and the peace offerings, he
blessed the people in the name of the
LORD of hosts, 19 and distributed among
all the people, the whole multitude of
Israel, both men and women, to
each a cake of bread, a portion of
meat,[n] and a cake of raisins. Then
all the people departed, each to his
house.

20 And David returned to bless his
household. But Mī'chăl the daughter
of Saul came out to meet David, and
said, "How the king of Israel honored
himself today, uncovering himself today before the eyes of his servants'
maids, as one of the vulgar fellows
shamelessly uncovers himself!" 21 And
David said to Mī'chăl, "It was before
the LORD, who chose me above your
father, and above all his house, to
appoint me as prince over Israel, the
people of the LORD—and I will make
merry before the LORD. 22 I will make
myself yet more contemptible than
this, and I will be abased in your[o] eyes;
but by the maids of whom you have
spoken, by them I shall be held in
honor." 23 And Mī'chăl the daughter
of Saul had no child to the day of her
death.

7 Now when the king dwelt in his
house, and the LORD had given
him rest from all his enemies round
about, 2 the king said to Nathan the
prophet, "See now, I dwell in a house
of cedar, but the ark of God dwells in
a tent." 3 And Nathan said to the king,
"Go, do all that is in your heart; for
the LORD is with you."

4 But that same night the word of
the LORD came to Nathan, 5 "Go and
tell my servant David, 'Thus says the
LORD: Would you build me a house to
dwell in? 6 I have not dwelt in a house
since the day I brought up the people
of Israel from Egypt to this day, but
I have been moving about in a tent for
my dwelling. 7 In all places where I
have moved with all the people of
Israel, did I speak a word with any of
the judges[p] of Israel, whom I commanded to shepherd my people Israel,
saying, "Why have you not built me a
house of cedar?"' 8 Now therefore
thus you shall say to my servant David,
'Thus says the LORD of hosts, I took
you from the pasture, from following
the sheep, that you should be prince
over my people Israel; 9 and I have
been with you wherever you went, and
have cut off all your enemies from before you; and I will make for you a
great name, like the name of the great
ones of the earth. 10 And I will appoint
a place for my people Israel, and will
plant them, that they may dwell in
their own place, and be disturbed no
more; and violent men shall afflict
them no more, as formerly, 11 from
the time that I appointed judges over
my people Israel; and I will give you
rest from all your enemies. Moreover
the LORD declares to you that the
LORD will make you a house. 12 When
your days are fulfilled and you lie
down with your fathers, I will raise up
your offspring after you, who shall
come forth from your body, and I will
establish his kingdom. 13 He shall
build a house for my name, and I will
establish the throne of his kingdom for
ever. 14 I will be his father, and he shall
be my son. When he commits iniquity,
I will chasten him with the rod of men,
with the stripes of the sons of men;
15 but I will not take[q] my steadfast
love from him, as I took it from Saul,
whom I put away from before you.

[n] Vg: Heb uncertain [o] Gk: Heb *my* [p] 1 Chron 17.6: Heb *tribes*
[q] Gk Syr Vg 1 Chron 17.13: Heb *shall not depart*
6.12-19: 1 Chron 15.1-16.3. 7.1-29: 1 Chron 17.1-27. 7.14: Heb 1.5.

16 And your house and your kingdom
shall be made sure for ever before me;
your throne shall be established for
ever.' " 17 In accordance with all these
words, and in accordance with all this
vision, Nathan spoke to David.

18 Then King David went in and
sat before the LORD, and said, "Who
am I, O Lord GOD, and what is my
house, that thou hast brought me thus
far? 19 And yet this was a small thing
in thy eyes, O Lord GOD; thou hast
spoken also of thy servant's house for
a great while to come, and hast shown
me future generations,[r] O Lord GOD!
20 And what more can David say to
thee? For thou knowest thy servant, O
Lord GOD! 21 Because of thy promise,
and according to thy own heart, thou
hast wrought all this greatness, to make
thy servant know it. 22 Therefore thou
art great, O LORD God; for there is
none like thee, and there is no God besides thee, according to all that we have
heard with our ears. 23 What other[s]
nation on earth is like thy people
Israel, whom God went to redeem to
be his people, making himself a name,
and doing for them[t] great and terrible
things, by driving out[u] before his
people a nation and its gods?[v] 24 And
thou didst establish for thyself thy
people Israel to be thy people for ever;
and thou, O LORD, didst become their
God. 25 And now, O LORD God, confirm
for ever the word which thou hast
spoken concerning thy servant and
concerning his house, and do as thou
hast spoken; 26 and thy name will be
magnified for ever, saying, 'The LORD
of hosts is God over Israel,' and the
house of thy servant David will be
established before thee. 27 For thou, O
LORD of hosts, the God of Israel, hast
made this revelation to thy servant,
saying, 'I will build you a house'; therefore thy servant has found courage to
pray this prayer to thee. 28 And now,
O Lord GOD, thou art God, and thy
words are true, and thou hast promised
this good thing to thy servant; 29 now
therefore may it please thee to bless
the house of thy servant, that it may
continue for ever before thee; for thou,
O Lord GOD, hast spoken, and with
thy blessing shall the house of thy
servant be blessed for ever."

8 After this David defeated the
Philistines and subdued them, and
David took Meth'eg-am'mȧh out of
the hand of the Philistines.

2 And he defeated Mō'ab, and
measured them with a line, making
them lie down on the ground; two lines
he measured to be put to death, and
one full line to be spared. And the
Mō'ȧb·ītes became servants to David
and brought tribute.

3 David also defeated Had·ȧ·dē'zėr
the son of Rē'hob, king of Zō'bȧh, as
he went to restore his power at the
river Eū·phrā'tēṡ. 4 And David took
from him a thousand and seven hundred horsemen, and twenty thousand
foot soldiers; and David hamstrung all
the chariot horses, but left enough for
a hundred chariots. 5 And when the
Syrians of Damascus came to help
Had·ȧ·dē'zėr king of Zō'bȧh, David
slew twenty-two thousand men of the
Syrians. 6 Then David put garrisons
in Âr'ȧm of Damascus; and the Syrians
became servants to David and brought
tribute. And the LORD gave victory to
David wherever he went. 7 And David
took the shields of gold which were
carried by the servants of Had·ȧ·dē'-
zėr, and brought them to Jerusalem.
8 And from Bē'tȧh and from Be·rō'-
thäi, cities of Had·ȧ·dē'zėr, King
David took very much bronze.

9 When Tō'ī king of Hā'math heard
that David had defeated the whole
army of Had·ȧ·dē'zėr, 10 Tō'ī sent his
son Jō'rȧm to King David, to greet
him, and to congratulate him because
he had fought against Had·ȧ·dē'zėr and
defeated him; for Hadadezer had often
been at war with Toi. And Joram
brought with him articles of silver, of
gold, and of bronze; 11 these also King
David dedicated to the LORD, together
with the silver and gold which he dedicated from all the nations he subdued,
12 from Ē'dȯm, Mō'ab, the Am'mȯ-
nītes, the Philistines, Am'ȧ·lek, and
from the spoil of Had·ȧ·dē'zėr the son
of Rē'hob, king of Zō'bȧh.

13 And David won a name for himself. When he returned, he slew
eighteen thousand Ē'dȯm·ītes[w] in the
Valley of Salt. 14 And he put garrisons
in Ē'dȯm; throughout all Edom he put
garrisons, and all the Ē'dȯm·ītes be-

[r] Cn: Heb *this is the law for man* [s] Gk: Heb *one* [t] Heb *you* [u] Gk 1 Chron 17.21: Heb *for your land*
[v] Heb *before thy people, whom thou didst redeem for thyself from Egypt, nations and its gods*
[w] Gk: Heb *returned from smiting eighteen thousand Syrians*
8.1-14: 1 Chron 18.1-13.

came David's servants. And the LORD
gave victory to David wherever he
went.

15 So David reigned over all Israel;
and David administered justice and
equity to all his people. 16 And Jō'ab
the son of Zė·rü'i·ȧh was over the
army; and Je·hosh'ȧ·phat the son of
Ȧ·hī'lụd was recorder; 17 and Zā'dok
the son of Ȧ·hī'tụb and Ȧ·him'ė·lech
the son of Ȧ·bī'ȧ·thär were priests; and
Se·räi'ȧh was secretary; 18 and Be·nā'-
iȧh the son of Je·hoi'ȧ·dȧ was over[x] the
Cher'ė·thītes and the Pel'ė·thītes; and
David's sons were priests.

9 And David said, "Is there still
any one left of the house of Saul,
that I may show him kindness for
Jonathan's sake?" 2 Now there was a
servant of the house of Saul whose
name was Zī'bȧ, and they called him
to David; and the king said to him,
"Are you Ziba?" And he said, "Your
servant is he." 3 And the king said, "Is
there not still some one of the house
of Saul, that I may show the kindness
of God to him?" Zī'bȧ said to the king,
"There is still a son of Jonathan; he is
crippled in his feet." 4 The king said
to him, "Where is he?" And Zī'bȧ said
to the king, "He is in the house of
Mā'chir the son of Am'mi·el, at Lō-
dē'bär." 5 Then King David sent and
brought him from the house of Mā'-
chir the son of Am'mi·el, at Lō-dē'bär.
6 And Me·phib'ȯ·sheth the son of Jonathan, son of Saul, came to David, and
fell on his face and did obeisance. And
David said, "Mephibosheth!" And he
answered, "Behold, your servant."
7 And David said to him, "Do not fear;
for I will show you kindness for the
sake of your father Jonathan, and I
will restore to you all the land of Saul
your father; and you shall eat at my
table always." 8 And he did obeisance,
and said, "What is your servant, that
you should look upon a dead dog such
as I?"

9 Then the king called Zī'bȧ, Saul's
servant, and said to him, "All that belonged to Saul and to all his house I
have given to your master's son. 10 And
you and your sons and your servants shall till the land for him, and
shall bring in the produce, that your
master's son may have bread to eat; but
Me·phib'ȯ·sheth your master's son shall
always eat at my table." Now Zī'bȧ
had fifteen sons and twenty servants.
11 Then Zī'bȧ said to the king, "According to all that my lord the king
commands his servant, so will your
servant do." So Me·phib'ȯ·sheth ate at
David's[y] table, like one of the king's
sons. 12 And Me·phib'ȯ·sheth had a
young son, whose name was Mī'cȧ.
And all who dwelt in Zī'bȧ's house
became Mephibosheth's servants. 13 So
Me·phib'ȯ·sheth dwelt in Jerusalem;
for he ate always at the king's table.
Now he was lame in both his feet.

10 After this the king of the Am'-
mȯ·nītes died, and Hā'nụn his
son reigned in his stead. 2 And David
said, "I will deal loyally with Hā'nụn
the son of Nā'hash, as his father dealt
loyally with me." So David sent by
his servants to console him concerning
his father. And David's servants came
into the land of the Am'mȯ·nītes. 3 But
the princes of the Am'mȯ·nītes said to
Hā'nụn their lord, "Do you think,
because David has sent comforters to
you, that he is honoring your father?
Has not David sent his servants to you
to search the city, and to spy it out,
and to overthrow it?" 4 So Hā'nụn
took David's servants, and shaved off
half the beard of each, and cut off their
garments in the middle, at their hips,
and sent them away. 5 When it was
told David, he sent to meet them, for
the men were greatly ashamed. And
the king said, "Remain at Jericho until
your beards have grown, and then return."

6 When the Am'mȯ·nītes saw that
they had become odious to David, the
Ammonites sent and hired the Syrians
of Beth-rē'hob, and the Syrians of
Zō'bȧh, twenty thousand foot soldiers,
and the king of Mā'ȧ·cȧh with a thousand men, and the men of Tōb, twelve
thousand men. 7 And when David
heard of it, he sent Jō'ab and all the
host of the mighty men. 8 And the
Am'mȯ·nītes came out and drew up
in battle array at the entrance of the
gate; and the Syrians of Zō'bȧh and
of Rē'hob, and the men of Tōb and
Mā'ȧ·cȧh, were by themselves in the
open country.

9 When Jō'ab saw that the battle
was set against him both in front and
in the rear, he chose some of the
picked men of Israel, and arrayed them
against the Syrians; 10 the rest of his

[x] Syr Tg Vg 20.23; 1 Chron 18.17: Heb lacks *was over* [y] Gk: Heb *my*
8.15-18: 2 Sam 20.23-26; 1 Chron 18.14-17. 10.1-19: 1 Chron 19.1-19.

men he put in the charge of A·bi'shäi
his brother, and he arrayed them
against the Am'mȯ·nītes. 11And he
said, "If the Syrians are too strong for
me, then you shall help me; but if the
Am'mȯ·nītes are too strong for you,
then I will come and help you. 12 Be
of good courage, and let us play the
man for our people, and for the cities
of our God; and may the LORD do
what seems good to him." 13 So Jō'ab
and the people who were with him
drew near to battle against the Syrians;
and they fled before him. 14And when
the Am'mȯ·nītes saw that the Syrians
fled, they likewise fled before A·bi'-
shäi, and entered the city. Then Jō'ab
returned from fighting against the
Ammonites, and came to Jerusalem.
15 But when the Syrians saw that
they had been defeated by Israel, they
gathered themselves together. 16And
Had·ȧ·dē'zėr sent, and brought out the
Syrians who were beyond the Eū-
phrā'tēṡ;[z] and they came to Hē'lȧm,
with Shō'bach the commander of the
army of Hadadezer at their head. 17And
when it was told David, he gathered
all Israel together, and crossed the
Jordan, and came to Hē'lȧm. And the
Syrians arrayed themselves against
David, and fought with him. 18And
the Syrians fled before Israel; and
David slew of the Syrians the men of
seven hundred chariots, and forty
thousand horsemen, and wounded
Shō'bach the commander of their army,
so that he died there. 19And when all
the kings who were servants of Had·ȧ-
dē'zėr saw that they had been defeated
by Israel, they made peace with Israel,
and became subject to them. So the
Syrians feared to help the Am'mȯ·nītes
any more.

11 In the spring of the year, the
time when kings go forth to
battle, David sent Jō'ab, and his servants with him, and all Israel; and
they ravaged the Am'mȯ·nītes, and besieged Rab'bȧh. But David remained
at Jerusalem.
2 It happened, late one afternoon,
when David arose from his couch and
was walking upon the roof of the
king's house, that he saw from the roof
a woman bathing; and the woman was
very beautiful. 3And David sent and
inquired about the woman. And one
said, "Is not this Bath·shē'bȧ, the
daughter of E·lī'ȧm, the wife of Ū·rī'ȧh
the Hit'tīte?" 4 So David sent messengers, and took her; and she came
to him, and he lay with her. (Now she
was purifying herself from her uncleanness.) Then she returned to her
house. 5And the woman conceived;
and she sent and told David, "I am
with child."
6 So David sent word to Jō'ab,
"Send me Ū·rī'ȧh the Hit'tīte." And
Joab sent Uriah to David. 7 When
Ū·rī'ȧh came to him, David asked how
Jō'ab was doing, and how the people
fared, and how the war prospered.
8 Then David said to Ū·rī'ȧh, "Go
down to your house, and wash your
feet." And Uriah went out of the
king's house, and there followed him
a present from the king. 9 But Ū·rī'ȧh
slept at the door of the king's house
with all the servants of his lord, and
did not go down to his house. 10 When
they told David, "Ū·rī'ȧh did not go
down to his house," David said to
Uriah, "Have you not come from a
journey? Why did you not go down to
your house?" 11 Ū·rī'ȧh said to David,
"The ark and Israel and Judah dwell
in booths; and my lord Jō'ab and the
servants of my lord are camping in the
open field; shall I then go to my house,
to eat and to drink, and to lie with my
wife? As you live, and as your soul
lives, I will not do this thing." 12 Then
David said to Ū·rī'ȧh, "Remain here
today also, and tomorrow I will let you
depart." So Uriah remained in Jerusalem that day, and the next. 13And
David invited him, and he ate in his
presence and drank, so that he made
him drunk; and in the evening he went
out to lie on his couch with the servants
of his lord, but he did not go down to
his house.
14 In the morning David wrote a
letter to Jō'ab, and sent it by the hand
of Ū·rī'ȧh. 15 In the letter he wrote,
"Set Ū·rī'ȧh in the forefront of the
hardest fighting, and then draw back
from him, that he may be struck down,
and die." 16And as Jō'ab was besieging
the city, he assigned Ū·rī'ȧh to the
place where he knew there were valiant
men. 17And the men of the city came
out and fought with Jō'ab; and some
of the servants of David among the
people fell. Ū·rī'ȧh the Hit'tīte was
slain also. 18 Then Jō'ab sent and told

z Heb *river*
11.1: 1 Chron 20.1.

David all the news about the fighting;
19 and he instructed the messenger,
"When you have finished telling all
the news about the fighting to the king,
20 then, if the king's anger rises, and
if he says to you, 'Why did you go so
near the city to fight? Did you not
know that they would shoot from the
wall? 21 Who killed A·bim'ė·lech the
son of Je·rub'bė·sheth? Did not a
woman cast an upper millstone upon
him from the wall, so that he died at
Thē'bez? Why did you go so near the
wall?' then you shall say, 'Your servant Ū·rī'ȧh the Hit'tīte is dead
also.' "

22 So the messenger went, and
came and told David all that Jō'ab had
sent him to tell. 23 The messenger said
to David, "The men gained an advantage over us, and came out against us
in the field; but we drove them back
to the entrance of the gate. 24 Then the
archers shot at your servants from the
wall; some of the king's servants are
dead; and your servant Ū·rī'ȧh the
Hit'tīte is dead also." 25 David said to
the messenger, "Thus shall you say to
Jō'ab, 'Do not let this matter trouble
you, for the sword devours now one
and now another; strengthen your
attack upon the city, and overthrow
it.' And encourage him."

26 When the wife of Ū·rī'ȧh heard
that Uriah her husband was dead, she
made lamentation for her husband.
27 And when the mourning was over,
David sent and brought her to his
house, and she became his wife, and
bore him a son. But the thing that
David had done displeased the LORD.

12 And the LORD sent Nathan to
David. He came to him, and said
to him, "There were two men in a
certain city, the one rich and the other
poor. 2 The rich man had very many
flocks and herds; 3 but the poor man
had nothing but one little ewe lamb,
which he had bought. And he brought
it up, and it grew up with him and
with his children; it used to eat of his
morsel, and drink from his cup, and
lie in his bosom, and it was like a
daughter to him. 4 Now there came a
traveler to the rich man, and he was
unwilling to take one of his own flock
or herd to prepare for the wayfarer
who had come to him, but he took the
poor man's lamb, and prepared it for
the man who had come to him."
5 Then David's anger was greatly
kindled against the man; and he said
to Nathan, "As the LORD lives, the
man who has done this deserves to
die; 6 and he shall restore the lamb
fourfold, because he did this thing,
and because he had no pity."

7 Nathan said to David, "You are
the man. Thus says the LORD, the God
of Israel, 'I anointed you king over
Israel, and I delivered you out of the
hand of Saul; 8 and I gave you your
master's house, and your master's
wives into your bosom, and gave you
the house of Israel and of Judah; and
if this were too little, I would add to
you as much more. 9 Why have you
despised the word of the LORD, to do
what is evil in his sight? You have
smitten Ū·rī'ȧh the Hit'tīte with the
sword, and have taken his wife to be
your wife, and have slain him with the
sword of the Am'mō·nītes. 10 Now therefore the sword shall never depart from
your house, because you have despised
me, and have taken the wife of Ū·rī'ȧh
the Hit'tīte to be your wife.' 11 Thus
says the LORD, 'Behold, I will raise up
evil against you out of your own house;
and I will take your wives before your
eyes, and give them to your neighbor,
and he shall lie with your wives in the
sight of this sun. 12 For you did it
secretly; but I will do this thing before
all Israel, and before the sun.' "
13 David said to Nathan, "I have
sinned against the LORD." And Nathan
said to David, "The LORD also has
put away your sin; you shall not die.
14 Nevertheless, because by this deed
you have utterly scorned the LORD,[a]
the child that is born to you shall
die." 15 Then Nathan went to his
house.

And the LORD struck the child that
Ū·rī'ȧh's wife bore to David, and it
became sick. 16 David therefore besought God for the child; and David
fasted, and went in and lay all night
upon the ground. 17 And the elders of
his house stood beside him, to raise
him from the ground; but he would
not, nor did he eat food with them.
18 On the seventh day the child died.
And the servants of David feared to
tell him that the child was dead; for
they said, "Behold, while the child
was yet alive, we spoke to him, and he
did not listen to us; how then can we
say to him the child is dead? He may

[a] Heb *the enemies of the* LORD

do himself some harm." 19 But when
David saw that his servants were
whispering together, David perceived
that the child was dead; and David
said to his servants, "Is the child
dead?" They said, "He is dead."
20 Then David arose from the earth,
and washed, and anointed himself, and
changed his clothes; and he went into
the house of the LORD, and worshiped;
he then went to his own house; and
when he asked, they set food before
him, and he ate. 21 Then his servants
said to him, "What is this thing that
you have done? You fasted and wept
for the child while it was alive; but
when the child died, you arose and ate
food." 22 He said, "While the child
was still alive, I fasted and wept; for I
said, 'Who knows whether the LORD
will be gracious to me, that the child
may live?' 23 But now he is dead; why
should I fast? Can I bring him back
again? I shall go to him, but he will
not return to me."

24 Then David comforted his wife,
Bath-shē'bȧ, and went in to her, and
lay with her; and she bore a son, and
he called his name Solomon. And the
LORD loved him, 25 and sent a message
by Nathan the prophet; so he called
his name Jed-i-dī'ȧh,[b] because of the
LORD.

26 Now Jō'ab fought against Rab'-
bȧh of the Am'mȯ-nītes, and took the
royal city. 27 And Jō'ab sent messengers
to David, and said, "I have fought
against Rab'bȧh; moreover, I have
taken the city of waters. 28 Now, then,
gather the rest of the people together,
and encamp against the city, and take
it; lest I take the city, and it be called
by my name." 29 So David gathered
all the people together and went to
Rab'bȧh, and fought against it and
took it. 30 And he took the crown of
their king[c] from his head; the weight
of it was a talent of gold, and in it was
a precious stone; and it was placed on
David's head. And he brought forth
the spoil of the city, a very great
amount. 31 And he brought forth the
people who were in it, and set them
to labor with saws and iron picks and
iron axes, and made them toil at[d] the
brickkilns; and thus he did to all the
cities of the Am'mȯ-nītes. Then David
and all the people returned to Jerusalem.

13 Now Ab'sȧ-lȯm, David's son,
had a beautiful sister, whose
name was Tā'mär; and after a time
Am'non, David's son, loved her. 2 And
Am'non was so tormented that he
made himself ill because of his sister
Tā'mär; for she was a virgin, and it
seemed impossible to Amnon to do
anything to her. 3 But Am'non had a
friend, whose name was Jon'ȧ-dab, the
son of Shim'ē-ȧh, David's brother;
and Jonadab was a very crafty man.
4 And he said to him, "O son of the
king, why are you so haggard morning
after morning? Will you not tell me?"
Am'non said to him, "I love Tā'mär,
my brother Ab'sȧ-lȯm's sister." 5 Jon'-
ȧ-dab said to him, "Lie down on your
bed, and pretend to be ill; and when
your father comes to see you, say to
him, 'Let my sister Tā'mär come and
give me bread to eat, and prepare the
food in my sight, that I may see it,
and eat it from her hand.'" 6 So
Am'non lay down, and pretended to
be ill; and when the king came to see
him, Amnon said to the king, "Pray
let my sister Tā'mär come and make
a couple of cakes in my sight, that I
may eat from her hand."

7 Then David sent home to Tā'mär,
saying, "Go to your brother Am'non's
house, and prepare food for him."
8 So Tā'mär went to her brother
Am'non's house, where he was lying
down. And she took dough, and
kneaded it, and made cakes in his
sight, and baked the cakes. 9 And she
took the pan and emptied it out before
him, but he refused to eat. And Am'-
non said, "Send out every one from
me." So every one went out from him.
10 Then Am'non said to Tā'mär,
"Bring the food into the chamber, that
I may eat from your hand." And
Tamar took the cakes she had made,
and brought them into the chamber to
Amnon her brother. 11 But when she
brought them near him to eat, he took
hold of her, and said to her, "Come,
lie with me, my sister." 12 She answered him, "No, my brother, do not
force me; for such a thing is not done
in Israel; do not do this wanton folly.
13 As for me, where could I carry my
shame? And as for you, you would be
as one of the wanton fools in Israel.
Now therefore, I pray you, speak to
the king; for he will not withhold me

[b] That is *beloved of the* LORD [c] Or *Milcom* See Zeph 1.5 [d] Cn: Heb *pass through*
12.26-31: 1 Chron 20.1-3.

from you." 14 But he would not listen
to her; and being stronger than she, he
forced her, and lay with her.
15 Then Am′non hated her with
very great hatred; so that the hatred
with which he hated her was greater
than the love with which he had loved
her. And Amnon said to her, "Arise,
be gone." 16 But she said to him, "No,
my brother; for this wrong in sending
me away is greater than the other
which you did to me."[e] But he would
not listen to her. 17 He called the
young man who served him and said,
"Put this woman out of my presence,
and bolt the door after her." 18 Now
she was wearing a long robe with
sleeves; for thus were the virgin
daughters of the king clad of old.[f] So
his servant put her out, and bolted the
door after her. 19 And Tā′mär put ashes
on her head, and rent the long robe
which she wore; and she laid her hand
on her head, and went away, crying
aloud as she went.
20 And her brother Ab′sȧ·lôm said
to her, "Has Am′non your brother
been with you? Now hold your peace,
my sister; he is your brother; do not
take this to heart." So Tā′mär dwelt,
a desolate woman, in her brother
Absalom's house. 21 When King David
heard of all these things, he was very
angry. 22 But Ab′sȧ·lôm spoke to
Am′non neither good nor bad; for
Absalom hated Amnon, because he
had forced his sister Tā′mär.
23 After two full years Ab′sȧ·lôm
had sheepshearers at Bā·ȧl-hā′zôr,
which is near Ē′phrȧ·im, and Absalom
invited all the king's sons. 24 And
Ab′sȧ·lôm came to the king, and said,
"Behold, your servant has sheepshearers; pray let the king and his
servants go with your servant." 25 But
the king said to Ab′sȧ·lôm, "No, my
son, let us not all go, lest we be burdensome to you." He pressed him, but he
would not go but gave him his blessing.
26 Then Ab′sȧ·lôm said, "If not, pray
let my brother Am′non go with us."
And the king said to him, "Why should
he go with you?" 27 But Ab′sȧ·lôm
pressed him until he let Am′non and
all the king's sons go with him. 28 Then
Ab′sȧ·lôm commanded his servants,
"Mark when Am′non's heart is merry
with wine, and when I say to you,
'Strike Amnon,' then kill him. Fear
not; have I not commanded you? Be
courageous and be valiant." 29 So the
servants of Ab′sȧ·lôm did to Am′non
as Absalom had commanded. Then all
the king's sons arose, and each mounted
his mule and fled.
30 While they were on the way,
tidings came to David, "Ab′sȧ·lôm has
slain all the king's sons, and not one
of them is left." 31 Then the king
arose, and rent his garments, and lay
on the earth; and all his servants who
were standing by rent their garments.
32 But Jon′ȧ·dab the son of Shim′ē-āh,
David's brother, said, "Let not my
lord suppose that they have killed all
the young men the king's sons, for
Am′non alone is dead, for by the command of Ab′sȧ·lôm this has been determined from the day he forced his
sister Tā′mär. 33 Now therefore let not
my lord the king so take it to heart as
to suppose that all the king's sons are
dead; for Am′non alone is dead."
34 But Ab′sȧ·lôm fled. And the
young man who kept the watch lifted
up his eyes, and looked, and behold,
many people were coming from the
Hor·ō·nā′im road[g] by the side of the
mountain. 35 And Jon′ȧ·dab said to
the king, "Behold, the king's sons
have come; as your servant said, so it
has come about." 36 And as soon as he
had finished speaking, behold, the
king's sons came, and lifted up their
voice and wept; and the king also
and all his servants wept very bitterly.
37 But Ab′sȧ·lôm fled, and went to
Tal′mäi the son of Am·mī′hŭd, king
of Gē′shŭr. And David mourned for
his son day after day. 38 So Ab′sȧ·lôm
fled, and went to Gē′shŭr, and was
there three years. 39 And the spirit[h] of
the king longed to go forth to Ab′sȧ-
lôm; for he was comforted about
Am′non, seeing he was dead.

14 Now Jō′ab the son of Zė·rü′i·āh
perceived that the king's heart
went out to Ab′sȧ·lôm. 2 And Jō′ab
sent to Te·kō′ȧ, and fetched from
there a wise woman, and said to her,
"Pretend to be a mourner, and put on
mourning garments; do not anoint
yourself with oil, but behave like a
woman who has been mourning many
days for the dead; 3 and go to the king,

[e] Cn Compare Gk Vg: Heb *No, for this great wrong in sending me away is* (*worse*) *than the other which you did to me* [f] Cn: Heb *clad in robes* [g] Cn Compare Gk: Heb *the road behind him*
[h] Gk: Heb *David*

and speak thus to him." So Jō'ab put
the words in her mouth.
4 When the woman of Te·kō'ȧ came
to the king, she fell on her face to the
ground, and did obeisance, and said,
"Help, O king." 5 And the king said
to her, "What is your trouble?" She
answered, "Alas, I am a widow; my
husband is dead. 6 And your handmaid
had two sons, and they quarreled with
one another in the field; there was no
one to part them, and one struck the
other and killed him. 7 And now the
whole family has risen against your
handmaid, and they say, 'Give up the
man who struck his brother, that we
may kill him for the life of his brother
whom he slew'; and so they would
destroy the heir also. Thus they would
quench my coal which is left, and leave
to my husband neither name nor
remnant upon the face of the earth."
8 Then the king said to the woman,
"Go to your house, and I will give
orders concerning you." 9 And the
woman of Te·kō'ȧ said to the king,
"On me be the guilt, my lord the king,
and on my father's house; let the king
and his throne be guiltless." 10 The
king said, "If any one says anything
to you, bring him to me, and he shall
never touch you again." 11 Then she
said, "Pray let the king invoke the
LORD your God, that the avenger of
blood slay no more, and my son be
not destroyed." He said, "As the LORD
lives, not one hair of your son shall fall
to the ground."
12 Then the woman said, "Pray let
your handmaid speak a word to my
lord the king." He said, "Speak."
13 And the woman said, "Why then
have you planned such a thing against
the people of God? For in giving this
decision the king convicts himself, inasmuch as the king does not bring his
banished one home again. 14 We must
all die, we are like water spilt on the
ground, which cannot be gathered up
again; but God will not take away the
life of him who devises[i] means not to
keep his banished one an outcast.
15 Now I have come to say this to my
lord the king because the people have
made me afraid; and your handmaid
thought, 'I will speak to the king; it
may be that the king will perform the
request of his servant. 16 For the king
will hear, and deliver his servant from
the hand of the man who would destroy me and my son together from the
heritage of God.' 17 And your handmaid thought, 'The word of my lord
the king will set me at rest'; for my
lord the king is like the angel of God
to discern good and evil. The LORD
your God be with you!"
18 Then the king answered the
woman, "Do not hide from me anything I ask you." And the woman said,
"Let my lord the king speak." 19 The
king said, "Is the hand of Jō'ab with
you in all this?" The woman answered
and said, "As surely as you live, my
lord the king, one cannot turn to the
right hand or to the left from anything
that my lord the king has said. It was
your servant Joab who bade me; it was
he who put all these words in the
mouth of your handmaid. 20 In order
to change the course of affairs your
servant Jō'ab did this. But my lord
has wisdom like the wisdom of the
angel of God to know all things that
are on the earth."
21 Then the king said to Jō'ab,
"Behold now, I grant this; go, bring
back the young man Ab'sȧ·lòm."
22 And Jō'ab fell on his face to the
ground, and did obeisance, and blessed
the king; and Joab said, "Today your
servant knows that I have found favor
in your sight, my lord the king, in that
the king has granted the request of
his servant." 23 So Jō'ab arose and
went to Gē'shūr, and brought Ab'sȧ-
lòm to Jerusalem. 24 And the king said,
"Let him dwell apart in his own house;
he is not to come into my presence."
So Ab'sȧ·lòm dwelt apart in his own
house, and did not come into the
king's presence.
25 Now in all Israel there was no
one so much to be praised for his
beauty as Ab'sȧ·lòm; from the sole of
his foot to the crown of his head there
was no blemish in him. 26 And when
he cut the hair of his head (for at the
end of every year he used to cut it;
when it was heavy on him, he cut it),
he weighed the hair of his head, two
hundred shekels by the king's weight.
27 There were born to Ab'sȧ·lòm three
sons, and one daughter whose name
was Tā'mär; she was a beautiful
woman.
28 So Ab'sȧ·lòm dwelt two full
years in Jerusalem, without coming
into the king's presence. 29 Then
Ab'sȧ·lòm sent for Jō'ab, to send him

[i] Cn: Heb *and he devises*

to the king; but Joab would not come
to him. And he sent a second time, but
Joab would not come. 30 Then he said
to his servants, "See, Jō'ab's field is
next to mine, and he has barley there;
go and set it on fire." So Ab'sȧ·lȯm's
servants set the field on fire. 31 Then
Jō'ab arose and went to Ab'sȧ·lȯm at
his house, and said to him, "Why have
your servants set my field on fire?"
32 Ab'sȧ·lȯm answered Jō'ab, "Behold,
I sent word to you, 'Come here, that
I may send you to the king, to ask,
"Why have I come from Gē'shūr? It
would be better for me to be there
still." Now therefore let me go into the
presence of the king; and if there is
guilt in me, let him kill me.' " 33 Then
Jō'ab went to the king, and told him;
and he summoned Ab'sȧ·lȯm. So he
came to the king, and bowed himself
on his face to the ground before the
king; and the king kissed Absalom.

15 After this Ab'sȧ·lȯm got himself
a chariot and horses, and fifty
men to run before him. 2 And Ab'sȧ-
lȯm used to rise early and stand beside
the way of the gate; and when any man
had a suit to come before the king for
judgment, Absalom would call to him,
and say, "From what city are you?"
And when he said, "Your servant is of
such and such a tribe in Israel,"
3 Ab'sȧ·lȯm would say to him, "See,
your claims are good and right; but
there is no man deputed by the king
to hear you." 4 Ab'sȧ·lȯm said moreover, "Oh that I were judge in the
land! Then every man with a suit or
cause might come to me, and I would
give him justice." 5 And whenever a
man came near to do obeisance to him,
he would put out his hand, and take
hold of him, and kiss him. 6 Thus
Ab'sȧ·lȯm did to all of Israel who
came to the king for judgment; so
Absalom stole the hearts of the men of
Israel.

7 And at the end of four[j] years
Ab'sȧ·lȯm said to the king, "Pray let
me go and pay my vow, which I have
vowed to the LORD, in Hē'brȯn. 8 For
your servant vowed a vow while I
dwelt at Gē'shūr in Âr'ȧm, saying, 'If
the LORD will indeed bring me back
to Jerusalem, then I will offer worship
to the LORD.' " 9 The king said to him,
"Go in peace." So he arose, and went
to Hē'brȯn. 10 But Ab'sȧ·lȯm sent
secret messengers throughout all the
tribes of Israel, saying, "As soon as
you hear the sound of the trumpet,
then say, 'Absalom is king at Hē'-
brȯn!' " 11 With Ab'sȧ·lȯm went two
hundred men from Jerusalem who
were invited guests, and they went in
their simplicity, and knew nothing.
12 And while Ab'sȧ·lȯm was offering
the sacrifices, he sent for[k] Ȧ·hith'ȯ·phel
the Gī'lȯ·nīte, David's counselor, from
his city Gī'lōh. And the conspiracy
grew strong, and the people with
Absalom kept increasing.

13 And a messenger came to David,
saying, "The hearts of the men of
Israel have gone after Ab'sȧ·lȯm."
14 Then David said to all his servants
who were with him at Jerusalem,
"Arise, and let us flee; or else there
will be no escape for us from Ab'sȧ-
lȯm; go in haste, lest he overtake us
quickly, and bring down evil upon us,
and smite the city with the edge of the
sword." 15 And the king's servants said
to the king, "Behold, your servants are
ready to do whatever my lord the king
decides." 16 So the king went forth,
and all his household after him. And
the king left ten concubines to keep
the house. 17 And the king went forth,
and all the people after him; and they
halted at the last house. 18 And all his
servants passed by him; and all the
Cher'ė·thītes, and all the Pel'ė·thītes,
and all the six hundred Git'tītes who
had followed him from Gath, passed
on before the king.

19 Then the king said to It'tăi the
Git'tīte, "Why do you also go with us?
Go back, and stay with the king; for
you are a foreigner, and also an exile
from[l] your home. 20 You came only
yesterday, and shall I today make you
wander about with us, seeing I go I
know not where? Go back, and take
your brethren with you; and may the
LORD show[m] steadfast love and faithfulness to you." 21 But It'tăi answered
the king, "As the LORD lives, and as
my lord the king lives, wherever my
lord the king shall be, whether for
death or for life, there also will
your servant be." 22 And David said
to It'tăi, "Go then, pass on." So Ittai
the Git'tīte passed on, with all his men
and all the little ones who were with
him. 23 And all the country wept aloud
as all the people passed by, and the

[j] Gk Syr: Heb *forty* [k] Or *sent* [l] Gk Syr Vg: Heb *to*
[m] Gk: Heb lacks *may the* LORD *show*

king crossed the brook Kid′rȯn, and
all the people passed on toward the
wilderness.
24 And Ȧ·bī′ȧ·thär came up, and
lo, Zā′dok came also, with all the
Levites, bearing the ark of the covenant of God; and they set down the
ark of God, until the people had all
passed out of the city. 25 Then the
king said to Zā′dok, "Carry the ark of
God back into the city. If I find favor
in the eyes of the LORD, he will bring
me back and let me see both it and his
habitation; 26 but if he says, 'I have
no pleasure in you,' behold, here I am,
let him do to me what seems good to
him." 27 The king also said to Zā′dok
the priest, "Look,[n] go back to the city
in peace, you and Ȧ·bī′ȧ·thär,[o] with
your two sons, Ȧ·him′ȧ-az your son,
and Jonathan the son of Abiathar.
28 See, I wait at the fords of the wilderness, until word comes from you to
inform me." 29 So Zā′dok and Ȧ·bī′ȧ·
thär carried the ark of God back to
Jerusalem; and they remained there.
30 But David went up the ascent of
the Mount of Olives, weeping as he
went, barefoot and with his head
covered; and all the people who were
with him covered their heads, and
they went up, weeping as they went.
31 And it was told David, "Ȧ·hith′ȯ·phel
is among the conspirators with Ab′sȧ-
lȯm." And David said, "O LORD, I
pray thee, turn the counsel of Ahithophel into foolishness."
32 When David came to the summit, where God was worshiped, behold, Hū′shäi the Är′chīte came to
meet him with his coat rent and earth
upon his head. 33 David said to him,
"If you go on with me, you will be a
burden to me. 34 But if you return to
the city, and say to Ab′sȧ·lȯm, 'I will
be your servant, O king; as I have been
your father's servant in time past, so
now I will be your servant,' then you
will defeat for me the counsel of
Ȧ·hith′ȯ·phel. 35 Are not Zā′dok and
Ȧ·bī′ȧ·thär the priests with you there?
So whatever you hear from the king's
house, tell it to Zadok and Abiathar
the priests. 36 Behold, their two sons
are with them there, Ȧ·him′ȧ-az, Zā′-
dok's son, and Jonathan, Ȧ·bī′ȧ·thär's
son; and by them you shall send to me
everything you hear." 37 So Hū′shäi,
David's friend, came into the city, just
as Ab′sȧ·lȯm was entering Jerusalem.

16 When David had passed a little
beyond the summit, Zī′bȧ the
servant of Me·phib′ȯ·sheth met him,
with a couple of asses saddled, bearing
two hundred loaves of bread, a hundred bunches of raisins, a hundred of
summer fruits, and a skin of wine.
2 And the king said to Zī′bȧ, "Why
have you brought these?" Ziba answered, "The asses are for the king's
household to ride on, the bread and
summer fruit for the young men to
eat, and the wine for those who faint
in the wilderness to drink." 3 And the
king said, "And where is your master's
son?" Zī′bȧ said to the king, "Behold,
he remains in Jerusalem; for he said,
'Today the house of Israel will give me
back the kingdom of my father.' "
4 Then the king said to Zī′bȧ, "Behold,
all that belonged to Me·phib′ȯ·sheth is
now yours." And Ziba said, "I do
obeisance; let me ever find favor in
your sight, my lord the king."
5 When King David came to Bȧ-
hū′rim, there came out a man of the
family of the house of Saul, whose
name was Shim′ē-ī, the son of Gē′rȧ;
and as he came he cursed continually.
6 And he threw stones at David, and at
all the servants of King David; and all
the people and all the mighty men
were on his right hand and on his left.
7 And Shim′ē-ī said as he cursed, "Begone, begone, you man of blood, you
worthless fellow! 8 The LORD has
avenged upon you all the blood of the
house of Saul, in whose place you have
reigned; and the LORD has given the
kingdom into the hand of your son
Ab′sȧ·lȯm. See, your ruin is on you;
for you are a man of blood."
9 Then Ȧ·bi′shäi the son of Zė·rü′i-
ȧh said to the king, "Why should this
dead dog curse my lord the king? Let
me go over and take off his head."
10 But the king said, "What have I to
do with you, you sons of Zė·rü′i·ȧh? If
he is cursing because the LORD has
said to him, 'Curse David,' who then
shall say, 'Why have you done so?' "
11 And David said to Ȧ·bi′shäi and to
all his servants, "Behold, my own son
seeks my life; how much more now
may this Benjaminite! Let him alone,
and let him curse; for the LORD has
bidden him. 12 It may be that the
LORD will look upon my affliction,[p]
and that the LORD will repay me with
good for this cursing of me today."

[n] Gk: Heb *Are you a seer* or *Do you see?* [o] Cn: Heb lacks *and Abiathar* [p] Gk Vg: Heb *iniquity*

13 So David and his men went on the
road, while Shim'ē-ī went along on
the hillside opposite him and cursed
as he went, and threw stones at him
and flung dust. 14 And the king, and
all the people who were with him,
arrived weary at the Jordan;[q] and
there he refreshed himself.

15 Now Ab'sȧ·lȯm and all the people, the men of Israel, came to Jerusalem, and A·hith'ȯ·phel with him.
16 And when Hū'shäi the Är'chīte,
David's friend, came to Ab'sȧ·lȯm,
Hushai said to Absalom, "Long live
the king! Long live the king!" 17 And
Ab'sȧ·lȯm said to Hū'shäi, "Is this
your loyalty to your friend? Why did
you not go with your friend?" 18 And
Hū'shäi said to Ab'sȧ·lȯm, "No; for
whom the LORD and this people and
all the men of Israel have chosen, his
I will be, and with him I will remain.
19 And again, whom should I serve?
Should it not be his son? As I have
served your father, so I will serve you."

20 Then Ab'sȧ·lȯm said to A·hith'-
ȯ·phel, "Give your counsel; what shall
we do?" 21 A·hith'ȯ·phel said to Ab'sȧ-
lȯm, "Go in to your father's concubines, whom he has left to keep the
house; and all Israel will hear that you
have made yourself odious to your
father, and the hands of all who are
with you will be strengthened." 22 So
they pitched a tent for Ab'sȧ·lȯm upon
the roof; and Absalom went in to his
father's concubines in the sight of all
Israel. 23 Now in those days the
counsel which A·hith'ȯ·phel gave was
as if one consulted the oracle[r] of God;
so was all the counsel of Ahithophel
esteemed, both by David and by
Ab'sȧ·lȯm.

17 Moreover A·hith'ȯ·phel said to
Ab'sȧ·lȯm, "Let me choose twelve
thousand men, and I will set out and
pursue David tonight. 2 I will come
upon him while he is weary and discouraged, and throw him into a panic;
and all the people who are with him
will flee. I will strike down the king
only, 3 and I will bring all the people
back to you as a bride comes home to
her husband. You seek the life of only
one man,[s] and all the people will be
at peace." 4 And the advice pleased
Ab'sȧ·lȯm and all the elders of Israel.

5 Then Ab'sȧ·lȯm said, "Call Hū'-
shäi the Är'chīte also, and let us hear
what he has to say." 6 And when
Hū'shäi came to Ab'sȧ·lȯm, Absalom
said to him, "Thus has A·hith'ȯ·phel
spoken; shall we do as he advises? If
not, you speak." 7 Then Hū'shäi said
to Ab'sȧ·lȯm, "This time the counsel
which A·hith'ȯ·phel has given is not
good." 8 Hū'shäi said moreover, "You
know that your father and his men are
mighty men, and that they are enraged,
like a bear robbed of her cubs in the
field. Besides, your father is expert in
war; he will not spend the night with
the people. 9 Behold, even now he has
hidden himself in one of the pits, or
in some other place. And when some
of the people fall[t] at the first attack,
whoever hears it will say, 'There has
been a slaughter among the people
who follow Ab'sȧ·lȯm.' 10 Then even
the valiant man, whose heart is like the
heart of a lion, will utterly melt with
fear; for all Israel knows that your
father is a mighty man, and that those
who are with him are valiant men.
11 But my counsel is that all Israel be
gathered to you, from Dan to Beer-
sheba, as the sand by the sea for
multitude, and that you go to battle in
person. 12 So we shall come upon him
in some place where he is to be found,
and we shall light upon him as the dew
falls on the ground; and of him and all
the men with him not one will be left.
13 If he withdraws into a city, then all
Israel will bring ropes to that city, and
we shall drag it into the valley, until
not even a pebble is to be found
there." 14 And Ab'sȧ·lȯm and all the
men of Israel said, "The counsel of
Hū'shäi the Är'chīte is better than the
counsel of A·hith'ȯ·phel." For the
LORD had ordained to defeat the good
counsel of Ahithophel, so that the
LORD might bring evil upon Absalom.

15 Then Hū'shäi said to Zā'dok and
A·bī'ȧ·thär the priests, "Thus and so
did A·hith'ȯ·phel counsel Ab'sȧ·lȯm
and the elders of Israel; and thus and
so have I counseled. 16 Now therefore
send quickly and tell David, 'Do not
lodge tonight at the fords of the wilderness, but by all means pass over; lest
the king and all the people who are
with him be swallowed up.' " 17 Now
Jonathan and A·him'ȧ-az were waiting
at En-rō'gel; a maidservant used to go
and tell them, and they would go and

[q] Gk: Heb lacks *at the Jordan* [r] Heb *word*
[s] Gk: Heb *like the return of the whole (is) the man whom you seek* [t] Or *when he falls upon them*

tell King David; for they must not be
seen entering the city. 18 But a lad saw
them, and told Ab′sȧ·lȯm; so both of
them went away quickly, and came to
the house of a man at Bȧ·hū′rim, who
had a well in his courtyard; and they
went down into it. 19 And the woman
took and spread a covering over the
well's mouth, and scattered grain
upon it; and nothing was known of it.
20 When Ab′sȧ·lȯm's servants came to
the woman at the house, they said,
"Where are A·him′ȧ-az and Jonathan?" And the woman said to them,
"They have gone over the brook[u] of
water." And when they had sought and
could not find them, they returned to
Jerusalem.
21 After they had gone, the men
came up out of the well, and went and
told King David. They said to David,
"Arise, and go quickly over the water;
for thus and so has A·hith′ō·phel
counseled against you." 22 Then David
arose, and all the people who were
with him, and they crossed the Jordan;
by daybreak not one was left who had
not crossed the Jordan.
23 When A·hith′ō·phel saw that his
counsel was not followed, he saddled
his ass, and went off home to his own
city. And he set his house in order,
and hanged himself; and he died, and
was buried in the tomb of his father.
24 Then David came to Mā·hȧ·nā′-
im. And Ab′sȧ·lȯm crossed the Jordan
with all the men of Israel. 25 Now
Ab′sȧ·lȯm had set A·mā′sȧ over the
army instead of Jō′ab. Amasa was the
son of a man named Ith′rȧ the Ish′mȧ-
el·īte,[v] who had married Ab′i·gāl the
daughter of Nā′hash, sister of Zė·rü′i-
ȧh, Joab's mother. 26 And Israel and
Ab′sȧ·lȯm encamped in the land of
Gilead.
27 When David came to Mā·hȧ·nā′-
im, Shō′bī the son of Nā′hash from
Rab′bȧh of the Am′mȯ·nītes, and
Mā′chir the son of Am′mi-el from
Lō-dē′bär, and Bär·zil′lāi the Gileadite from Rō′gė·lim, 28 brought beds,
basins, and earthen vessels, wheat,
barley, meal, parched grain, beans and
lentils,[w] 29 honey and curds and sheep
and cheese from the herd, for David
and the people with him to eat; for
they said, "The people are hungry and
weary and thirsty in the wilderness."

18 Then David mustered the men
who were with him, and set over
them commanders of thousands and
commanders of hundreds. 2 And David
sent forth the army, one third under
the command of Jō′ab, one third under
the command of A·bi′shāi the son of
Zė·rü′i·ȧh, Joab's brother, and one
third under the command of It′tāi the
Git′tīte. And the king said to the men,
"I myself will also go out with you."
3 But the men said, "You shall not go
out. For if we flee, they will not care
about us. If half of us die, they will
not care about us. But you are worth
ten thousand of us;[x] therefore it is
better that you send us help from the
city." 4 The king said to them, "Whatever seems best to you I will do." So
the king stood at the side of the gate,
while all the army marched out by
hundreds and by thousands. 5 And the
king ordered Jō′ab and A·bi′shāi and
It′tāi, "Deal gently for my sake with
the young man Ab′sȧ·lȯm." And all
the people heard when the king gave
orders to all the commanders about
Absalom.
6 So the army went out into the
field against Israel; and the battle was
fought in the forest of E′phrȧ·im. 7 And
the men of Israel were defeated there
by the servants of David, and the
slaughter there was great on that day,
twenty thousand men. 8 The battle
spread over the face of all the country;
and the forest devoured more people
that day than the sword.
9 And Ab′sȧ·lȯm chanced to meet
the servants of David. Absalom was
riding upon his mule, and the mule
went under the thick branches of a
great oak, and his head caught fast in
the oak, and he was left hanging[y] between heaven and earth, while the
mule that was under him went on.
10 And a certain man saw it, and told
Jō′ab, "Behold, I saw Ab′sȧ·lȯm hanging in an oak." 11 Jō′ab said to the man
who told him, "What, you saw him!
Why then did you not strike him there
to the ground? I would have been glad
to give you ten pieces of silver and a
girdle." 12 But the man said to Jō′ab,
"Even if I felt in my hand the weight
of a thousand pieces of silver, I would
not put forth my hand against the
king's son; for in our hearing the king

[u] The meaning of the Hebrew word is uncertain [v] 1 Chron 2.17: Heb *Israelite*
[w] Heb *lentils and parched grain* [x] Gk Vg Symmachus: Heb *for now there are ten thousand such as we*
[y] Gk Syr Tg: Heb *was put*

commanded you and Ȧ·bi′shäi and
It′täi, 'For my sake protect the young
man Ab′sȧ·lȯm.' 13 On the other hand,
if I had dealt treacherously against his
life[z] (and there is nothing hidden from
the king), then you yourself would
have stood aloof." 14 Jō′ab said, "I
will not waste time like this with you."
And he took three darts in his hand,
and thrust them into the heart of
Ab′sȧ·lȯm, while he was still alive in
the oak. 15And ten young men, Jō′ab's
armor-bearers, surrounded Ab′sȧ·lȯm
and struck him, and killed him.

16 Then Jō′ab blew the trumpet,
and the troops came back from pursuing Israel; for Joab restrained them.
17And they took Ab′sȧ·lȯm, and threw
him into a great pit in the forest, and
raised over him a very great heap of
stones; and all Israel fled every one to
his own home. 18 Now Ab′sȧ·lȯm in
his lifetime had taken and set up for
himself the pillar which is in the King's
Valley, for he said, "I have no son to
keep my name in remembrance"; he
called the pillar after his own name,
and it is called Absalom's monument
to this day.

19 Then said Ȧ·him′ȧ-az the son of
Zā′dok, "Let me run, and carry tidings
to the king that the LORD has delivered
him from the power of his enemies."
20And Jō′ab said to him, "You are not
to carry tidings today; you may carry
tidings another day, but today you
shall carry no tidings, because the
king's son is dead." 21 Then Jō′ab said
to the Cushite, "Go, tell the king what
you have seen." The Cushite bowed
before Joab, and ran. 22 Then Ȧ·him′ȧ-
az the son of Zā′dok said again to
Jō′ab, "Come what may, let me also
run after the Cushite." And Joab said,
"Why will you run, my son, seeing
that you will have no reward for the
tidings?" 23 "Come what may," he
said, "I will run." So he said to him,
"Run." Then Ȧ·him′ȧ-az ran by the
way of the plain, and outran the
Cushite.

24 Now David was sitting between
the two gates; and the watchman went
up to the roof of the gate by the wall,
and when he lifted up his eyes and
looked, he saw a man running alone.
25And the watchman called out and
told the king. And the king said, "If
he is alone, there are tidings in his
mouth." And he came apace, and drew
near. 26And the watchman saw another
man running; and the watchman called
to the gate and said, "See, another man
running alone!" The king said, "He
also brings tidings." 27And the watchman said, "I think the running of the
foremost is like the running of Ȧ·him′-
ȧ-az the son of Zā′dok." And the king
said, "He is a good man, and comes
with good tidings."

28 Then Ȧ·him′ȧ-az cried out to
the king, "All is well." And he bowed
before the king with his face to the
earth, and said, "Blessed be the LORD
your God, who has delivered up the
men who raised their hand against my
lord the king." 29And the king said,
"Is it well with the young man
Ab′sȧ·lȯm?" Ȧ·him′ȧ-az answered,
"When Jō′ab sent your servant,[b] I saw
a great tumult, but I do not know what
it was." 30And the king said, "Turn
aside, and stand here." So he turned
aside, and stood still.

31 And behold, the Cushite came;
and the Cushite said, "Good tidings
for my lord the king! For the LORD has
delivered you this day from the power
of all who rose up against you." 32 The
king said to the Cushite, "Is it well
with the young man Ab′sȧ·lȯm?" And
the Cushite answered, "May the enemies of my lord the king, and all who
rise up against you for evil, be like
that young man." 33 [c]And the king was
deeply moved, and went up to the
chamber over the gate, and wept; and
as he went, he said, "O my son Ab′sȧ-
lȯm, my son, my son Absalom! Would
I had died instead of you, O Absalom,
my son, my son!"

19 It was told Jō′ab, "Behold, the
king is weeping and mourning for
Ab′sȧ·lȯm." 2 So the victory that day
was turned into mourning for all the
people; for the people heard that day,
"The king is grieving for his son."
3And the people stole into the city that
day as people steal in who are ashamed
when they flee in battle. 4 The king
covered his face, and the king cried
with a loud voice, "O my son Ab′sȧ-
lȯm, O Absalom, my son, my son!"
5 Then Jō′ab came into the house to
the king, and said, "You have today
covered with shame the faces of all
your servants, who have this day saved
your life, and the lives of your sons and
your daughters, and the lives of your
wives and your concubines, 6 because

[z] Another reading is *at the risk of my life* [b] Heb *the king's servant, your servant* [c] Ch 19.1 in Heb

you love those who hate you and hate
those who love you. For you have made
it clear today that commanders and
servants are nothing to you; for today
I perceive that if Ab'sȧ·lȯm were alive
and all of us were dead today, then
you would be pleased. 7 Now therefore
arise, go out and speak kindly to your
servants; for I swear by the LORD, if
you do not go, not a man will stay with
you this night; and this will be worse
for you than all the evil that has come
upon you from your youth until now."
8 Then the king arose, and took his
seat in the gate. And the people were
all told, "Behold, the king is sitting in
the gate"; and all the people came before the king.

Now Israel had fled every man to
his own home. 9 And all the people
were at strife throughout all the tribes
of Israel, saying, "The king delivered
us from the hand of our enemies, and
saved us from the hand of the Philistines; and now he has fled out of the
land from Ab'sȧ·lȯm. 10 But Ab'sȧ·lȯm,
whom we anointed over us, is dead in
battle. Now therefore why do you say
nothing about bringing the king back?"

11 And King David sent this message to Zā'dok and Ȧ·bī'ȧ·thär the
priests, "Say to the elders of Judah,
'Why should you be the last to bring
the king back to his house, when the
word of all Israel has come to the
king?[d] 12 You are my kinsmen, you are
my bone and my flesh; why then
should you be the last to bring back
the king?' 13 And say to Ȧ·mā'sȧ, 'Are
you not my bone and my flesh? God
do so to me, and more also, if you are
not commander of my army henceforth in place of Jō'ab.' " 14 And he
swayed the heart of all the men of
Judah as one man; so that they sent
word to the king, "Return, both you
and all your servants." 15 So the king
came back to the Jordan; and Judah
came to Gil'gȧl to meet the king and
to bring the king over the Jordan.

16 And Shim'ē-ī the son of Gē'rȧ,
the Benjaminite, from Bȧ·hū'rim,
made haste to come down with the men
of Judah to meet King David; 17 and
with him were a thousand men from
Benjamin. And Zī'bȧ the servant of
the house of Saul, with his fifteen sons
and his twenty servants, rushed down
to the Jordan before the king, 18 and
they crossed the ford[e] to bring over
the king's household, and to do his
pleasure. And Shim'ē-ī the son of
Gē'rȧ fell down before the king, as he
was about to cross the Jordan, 19 and
said to the king, "Let not my lord hold
me guilty or remember how your servant did wrong on the day my lord the
king left Jerusalem; let not the king
bear it in mind. 20 For your servant
knows that I have sinned; therefore,
behold, I have come this day, the first
of all the house of Joseph to come
down to meet my lord the king."
21 Ȧ·bi'shäi the son of Zė·rü'i·ȧh answered, "Shall not Shim'ē-ī be put to
death for this, because he cursed the
LORD's anointed?" 22 But David said,
"What have I to do with you, you sons
of Zė·rü'i·ȧh, that you should this day
be as an adversary to me? Shall any
one be put to death in Israel this day?
For do I not know that I am this day
king over Israel?" 23 And the king said
to Shim'ē-ī, "You shall not die." And
the king gave him his oath.

24 And Me·phib'ȯ·sheth the son of
Saul came down to meet the king; he
had neither dressed his feet, nor
trimmed his beard, nor washed his
clothes, from the day the king departed
until the day he came back in safety.
25 And when he came from[f] Jerusalem
to meet the king, the king said to him,
"Why did you not go with me, Me-
phib'ȯ·sheth?" 26 He answered, "My
lord, O king, my servant deceived me;
for your servant said to him, 'Saddle
an ass for me,[g] that I may ride upon
it and go with the king.' For your
servant is lame. 27 He has slandered
your servant to my lord the king. But
my lord the king is like the angel of
God; do therefore what seems good
to you. 28 For all my father's house
were but men doomed to death before
my lord the king; but you set your
servant among those who eat at your
table. What further right have I, then,
to cry to the king?" 29 And the king
said to him, "Why speak any more of
your affairs? I have decided: you and
Zī'bȧ shall divide the land." 30 And
Me·phib'ȯ·sheth said to the king, "Oh,
let him take it all, since my lord the
king has come safely home."

31 Now Bär·zil'läi the Gileadite had
come down from Rō'gė·lim; and he
went on with the king to the Jordan,

[d] Gk: Heb *to the king, to his house* [e] Cn: Heb *the ford crossed* [f] Heb *to*
[g] Gk Syr Vg: Heb *said, I will saddle an ass for myself*

to escort him over the Jordan. 32 Bär-
zil'läi was a very aged man, eighty
years old; and he had provided the
king with food while he stayed at
Mā·hȧ·nā'im; for he was a very wealthy
man. 33 And the king said to Bär·zil'läi,
"Come over with me, and I will provide for you with me in Jerusalem."
34 But Bär·zil'läi said to the king,
"How many years have I still to live,
that I should go up with the king to
Jerusalem? 35 I am this day eighty
years old; can I discern what is pleasant
and what is not? Can your servant
taste what he eats or what he drinks?
Can I still listen to the voice of singing
men and singing women? Why then
should your servant be an added burden to my lord the king? 36 Your
servant will go a little way over the
Jordan with the king. Why should the
king recompense me with such a reward? 37 Pray let your servant return,
that I may die in my own city, near
the grave of my father and my mother.
But here is your servant Chim'ham;
let him go over with my lord the king;
and do for him whatever seems good
to you." 38 And the king answered,
"Chim'ham shall go over with me, and
I will do for him whatever seems good
to you; and all that you desire of me
I will do for you." 39 Then all the
people went over the Jordan, and the
king went over; and the king kissed
Bär·zil'läi and blessed him, and he
returned to his own home. 40 The
king went on to Gil'gȧl, and Chim'ham
went on with him; all the people
of Judah, and also half the people
of Israel, brought the king on his
way.

41 Then all the men of Israel came
to the king, and said to the king, "Why
have our brethren the men of Judah
stolen you away, and brought the king
and his household over the Jordan,
and all David's men with him?" 42 All
the men of Judah answered the men
of Israel, "Because the king is near of
kin to us. Why then are you angry
over this matter? Have we eaten at all
at the king's expense? Or has he given
us any gift?" 43 And the men of Israel
answered the men of Judah, "We have
ten shares in the king, and in David
also we have more than you. Why
then did you despise us? Were we not
the first to speak of bringing back our
king?" But the words of the men of
Judah were fiercer than the words of
the men of Israel.

20 Now there happened to be there
a worthless fellow, whose name
was Sheba, the son of Bich'rī, a Benjaminite; and he blew the trumpet,
and said,

"We have no portion in David,
and we have no inheritance in the
son of Jesse;
every man to his tents, O Israel!"

2 So all the men of Israel withdrew
from David, and followed Sheba the
son of Bich'rī; but the men of Judah
followed their king steadfastly from
the Jordan to Jerusalem.

3 And David came to his house at
Jerusalem; and the king took the ten
concubines whom he had left to care
for the house, and put them in a house
under guard, and provided for them,
but did not go in to them. So they
were shut up until the day of their
death, living as if in widowhood.

4 Then the king said to Ȧ·mā'sȧ,
"Call the men of Judah together to me
within three days, and be here yourself." 5 So Ȧ·mā'sȧ went to summon
Judah; but he delayed beyond the set
time which had been appointed him.
6 And David said to Ȧ·bī'shäi, "Now
Sheba the son of Bich'rī will do us
more harm than Ab'sȧ·lȯm; take your
lord's servants and pursue him, lest
he get himself fortified cities, and
cause us trouble."[h] 7 And there went
out after Ȧ·bī'shäi, Jō'ab[l] and the
Cher'ē·thītes and the Pel'ē·thītes, and
all the mighty men; they went out
from Jerusalem to pursue Sheba the
son of Bich'rī. 8 When they were at
the great stone which is in Gib'ē·ȯn,
Ȧ·mā'sȧ came to meet them. Now
Jō'ab was wearing a soldier's garment,
and over it was a girdle with a sword
in its sheath fastened upon his loins,
and as he went forward it fell out.
9 And Jō'ab said to Ȧ·mā'sȧ, "Is it well
with you, my brother?" And Joab
took Amasa by the beard with his right
hand to kiss him. 10 But Ȧ·mā'sȧ did
not observe the sword which was in
Jō'ab's hand; so Joab struck him with
it in the body, and shed his bowels to
the ground, without striking a second
blow; and he died.

Then Joab and Ȧ·bī'shäi his brother
pursued Sheba the son of Bich'rī.
11 And one of Jō'ab's men took his
stand by Ȧ·mā'sȧ, and said, "Whoever

[h] Tg: Heb *snatch away our eyes* [l] Cn Compare Gk: Heb *after him Joab's men*

favors Joab, and whoever is for David,
let him follow Joab." 12 And A·mā'sȧ
lay wallowing in his blood in the highway. And any one who came by, seeing
him, stopped;[j] and when the man saw
that all the people stopped, he carried
Amasa out of the highway into the
field, and threw a garment over him.
13 When he was taken out of the highway, all the people went on after
Jō'ab to pursue Sheba the son of
Bich'rī.

14 And Sheba passed through all
the tribes of Israel to Abel of Beth-
mā'ȧ·cȧh;[k] and all the Bich'rītes[l] assembled, and followed him in. 15 And
all the men who were with Jō'ab came
and besieged him in Abel of Beth-
mā'ȧ·cȧh; they cast up a mound against
the city, and it stood against the rampart; and they were battering the wall,
to throw it down. 16 Then a wise
woman called from the city, "Hear!
Hear! Tell Jō'ab, 'Come here, that I
may speak to you.'" 17 And he came
near her; and the woman said, "Are
you Jō'ab?" He answered, "I am."
Then she said to him, "Listen to the
words of your maidservant." And he
answered, "I am listening." 18 Then
she said, "They were wont to say in
old time, 'Let them but ask counsel at
Abel'; and so they settled a matter.
19 I am one of those who are peaceable
and faithful in Israel; you seek to destroy a city which is a mother in Israel;
why will you swallow up the heritage
of the LORD?" 20 Jō'ab answered, "Far
be it from me, far be it, that I should
swallow up or destroy! 21 That is not
true. But a man of the hill country of
E'phrȧ·im, called Sheba the son of
Bich'rī, has lifted up his hand against
King David; give up him alone, and
I will withdraw from the city." And
the woman said to Jō'ab, "Behold, his
head shall be thrown to you over the
wall." 22 Then the woman went to all
the people in her wisdom. And they
cut off the head of Sheba the son of
Bich'rī, and threw it out to Jō'ab. So
he blew the trumpet, and they dispersed from the city, every man to his
home. And Joab returned to Jerusalem
to the king.

23 Now Jō'ab was in command of
all the army of Israel; and Be·nā'iȧh
the son of Je·hoi'ȧ·dȧ was in command
of the Cher'ė·thītes and the Pel'ė·thītes;
24 and A·dôr'ȧm was in charge of the
forced labor; and Je·hosh'ȧ·phat the
son of A·hi'lŭd was the recorder;
25 and Shē'vȧ was secretary; and Zā'-
dok and A·bī'ȧ·thär were priests;
26 and Ira the Jā'i·rīte was also David's
priest.

21 Now there was a famine in the
days of David for three years,
year after year; and David sought the
face of the LORD. And the LORD said,
"There is bloodguilt on Saul and on
his house, because he put the Gib'ē·ō-
nītes to death." 2 So the king called the
Gib'ē·ō·nītes.[m] Now the Gibeonites
were not of the people of Israel, but of
the remnant of the Am'ō·rītes; although the people of Israel had sworn
to spare them, Saul had sought to slay
them in his zeal for the people of Israel
and Judah. 3 And David said to the
Gib'ē·ō·nītes, "What shall I do for
you? And how shall I make expiation,
that you may bless the heritage of the
LORD?" 4 The Gib'ē·ō·nītes said to
him, "It is not a matter of silver or
gold between us and Saul or his house;
neither is it for us to put any man to
death in Israel." And he said, "What
do you say that I shall do for you?"
5 They said to the king, "The man
who consumed us and planned to
destroy us, so that we should have no
place in all the territory of Israel, 6 let
seven of his sons be given to us, so
that we may hang them up before the
LORD at Gib'ē·ŏn on the mountain of
the LORD."[n] And the king said, "I
will give them."

7 But the king spared Me·phib'ō-
sheth, the son of Saul's son Jonathan,
because of the oath of the LORD which
was between them, between David
and Jonathan the son of Saul. 8 The
king took the two sons of Riz'pȧh the
daughter of Ā'i'ȧh, whom she bore to
Saul, Är·mō'ni and Me·phib'ō·sheth;
and the five sons of Mē'rab[o] the daughter of Saul, whom she bore to Ā'dri-el
the son of Bär·zil'lāi the Mė·hō'lȧ·thīte;
9 and he gave them into the hands of
the Gib'ē·ō·nītes, and they hanged
them on the mountain before the

[j] This clause is transposed from the end of the verse [k] With 20.15: Heb *and Beth-maacah*
[l] Heb *Berites* [m] Heb *the Gibeonites and said to them*
[n] Cn Compare Gk and 21.9: Heb *at Gibeah of Saul, the chosen of the* LORD
[o] Two Hebrew Mss Gk: Heb *Michal*
20.23-26: 2 Sam 8.15-18; 1 Chron 18.14-17.

LORD, and the seven of them perished
together. They were put to death in
the first days of harvest, at the beginning of barley harvest.
10 Then Riz′pȧh the daughter of
Ā′i′ȧh took sackcloth, and spread it for
herself on the rock, from the beginning
of harvest until rain fell upon them
from the heavens; and she did not
allow the birds of the air to come upon
them by day, or the beasts of the field
by night. 11 When David was told
what Riz′pȧh the daughter of Ā′i′ȧh,
the concubine of Saul, had done,
12 David went and took the bones of
Saul and the bones of his son Jonathan
from the men of Jā′besh-gil′ē·ȧd, who
had stolen them from the public square
of Beth′-shan, where the Philistines
had hanged them, on the day the
Philistines killed Saul on Gil·bō′ȧ;
13 and he brought up from there the
bones of Saul and the bones of his son
Jonathan; and they gathered the bones
of those who were hanged. 14 And they
buried the bones of Saul and his son
Jonathan in the land of Benjamin in
Zē′lȧ, in the tomb of Kish his father;
and they did all that the king commanded. And after that God heeded
supplications for the land.
15 The Philistines had war again
with Israel, and David went down together with his servants, and they
fought against the Philistines; and
David grew weary. 16 And Ish′bī-
bē′nob, one of the descendants of the
giants, whose spear weighed three hundred shekels of bronze, and who was
girded with a new sword, thought to
kill David. 17 But A·bi′shāi the son of
Zė·rü′i·ȧh came to his aid, and attacked
the Philistine and killed him. Then
David's men adjured him, "You shall
no more go out with us to battle, lest
you quench the lamp of Israel."
18 After this there was again war
with the Philistines at Gob; then Sib′-
bė·chāi the Hū′shȧ·thīte slew Saph,
who was one of the descendants of the
giants. 19 And there was again war with
the Philistines at Gob; and El·hā′nȧn
the son of Jā′ȧ·rē-ôr′ė·gim, the Bethlehemite, slew Goliath the Git′tīte, the
shaft of whose spear was like a weaver's
beam. 20 And there was again war at
Gath, where there was a man of great
stature, who had six fingers on each
hand, and six toes on each foot, twenty-
four in number; and he also was
descended from the giants. 21 And
when he taunted Israel, Jonathan the
son of Shim′ē-ī, David's brother, slew
him. 22 These four were descended
from the giants in Gath; and they fell
by the hand of David and by the hand
of his servants.

22 And David spoke to the LORD
the words of this song on the
day when the LORD delivered him
from the hand of all his enemies, and
from the hand of Saul. 2 He said,

"The LORD is my rock, and my fortress, and my deliverer,
3 my[p] God, my rock, in whom I take refuge,
my shield and the horn of my salvation,
my stronghold and my refuge,
my savior; thou savest me from violence.
4 I call upon the LORD, who is worthy to be praised,
and I am saved from my enemies.

5 "For the waves of death encompassed me,
the torrents of perdition assailed me;
6 the cords of Shē′ōl entangled me,
the snares of death confronted me.

7 "In my distress I called upon the LORD;
to my God I called.
From his temple he heard my voice,
and my cry came to his ears.

8 "Then the earth reeled and rocked;
the foundations of the heavens trembled
and quaked, because he was angry.
9 Smoke went up from his nostrils,
and devouring fire from his mouth;
glowing coals flamed forth from him.
10 He bowed the heavens, and came down;
thick darkness was under his feet.
11 He rode on a cherub, and flew;
he was seen upon the wings of the wind.
12 He made darkness around him
his canopy, thick clouds, a gathering of water.

[p] Gk Ps 18.2: Heb lacks *my*
21.18-22: 1 Chron 20.4-8. **22.2-51:** Ps 18.2-50.

13 Out of the brightness before him
coals of fire flamed forth.
14 The LORD thundered from heaven,
and the Most High uttered his voice.
15 And he sent out arrows, and scattered them;
lightning, and routed them.
16 Then the channels of the sea were seen,
the foundations of the world were laid bare,
at the rebuke of the LORD,
at the blast of the breath of his nostrils.

17 "He reached from on high, he took me,
he drew me out of many waters,
18 He delivered me from my strong enemy,
from those who hated me;
for they were too mighty for me.
19 They came upon me in the day of my calamity;
but the LORD was my stay.
20 He brought me forth into a broad place;
he delivered me, because he delighted in me.

21 "The LORD rewarded me according to my righteousness;
according to the cleanness of my hands he recompensed me.
22 For I have kept the ways of the LORD,
and have not wickedly departed from my God.
23 For all his ordinances were before me,
and from his statutes I did not turn aside.
24 I was blameless before him,
and I kept myself from guilt.
25 Therefore the LORD has recompensed me according to my righteousness,
according to my cleanness in his sight.

26 "With the loyal thou dost show thyself loyal;
with the blameless man thou dost show thyself blameless;
27 with the pure thou dost show thyself pure,
and with the crooked thou dost show thyself perverse.
28 Thou dost deliver a humble people,
but thy eyes are upon the haughty to bring them down.
29 Yea, thou art my lamp, O LORD,
and my God lightens my darkness.
30 Yea, by thee I can crush a troop,
and by my God I can leap over a wall.
31 This God—his way is perfect;
the promise of the LORD proves true;
he is a shield for all those who take refuge in him.

32 "For who is God, but the LORD?
And who is a rock, except our God?
33 This God is my strong refuge,
and has made[r] my[s] way safe.
34 He made my[s] feet like hinds' feet,
and set me secure on the heights.
35 He trains my hands for war,
so that my arms can bend a bow of bronze.
36 Thou hast given me the shield of thy salvation,
and thy help[t] made me great.
37 Thou didst give a wide place for my steps under me,
and my feet[u] did not slip;
38 I pursued my enemies and destroyed them,
and did not turn back until they were consumed.
39 I consumed them; I thrust them through, so that they did not rise;
they fell under my feet.
40 For thou didst gird me with strength for the battle;
thou didst make my assailants sink under me.
41 Thou didst make my enemies turn their backs to me,
those who hated me, and I destroyed them.
42 They looked, but there was none to save;
they cried to the LORD, but he did not answer them.
43 I beat them fine as the dust of the earth,
I crushed them and stamped them down like the mire of the streets.

44 "Thou didst deliver me from strife with the peoples;[v]

[r] Ps 18.32: Heb *set free* [s] Another reading is *his* [t] Or *gentleness* [u] Heb *ankles*
[v] Gk: Heb *from strife with my people*

thou didst keep me as the head of
the nations;
people whom I had not known
served me.
45 Foreigners came cringing to me;
as soon as they heard of me, they
obeyed me.
46 Foreigners lost heart,
and came trembling[w] out of their
fastnesses.

47 "The LORD lives; and blessed be my
rock,
and exalted be my God, the rock
of my salvation,
48 the God who gave me vengeance
and brought down peoples under
me,
49 who brought me out from my
enemies;
thou didst exalt me above my
adversaries,
thou didst deliver me from men
of violence.

50 "For this I will extol thee, O LORD,
among the nations,
and sing praises to thy name.
51 Great triumphs he gives[x] to his king,
and shows steadfast love to his
anointed,
to David, and his descendants for
ever."

23 Now these are the last words
of David:
The oracle of David, the son of
Jesse,
the oracle of the man who was
raised on high,
the anointed of the God of Jacob,
the sweet psalmist of Israel:[y]

2 "The Spirit of the LORD speaks by
me,
his word is upon my tongue.
3 The God of Israel has spoken,
the Rock of Israel has said to
me:
When one rules justly over men,
ruling in the fear of God,
4 he dawns on them like the morning
light,
like the sun shining forth upon
a cloudless morning,
like rain[z] that makes grass to
sprout from the earth.
5 Yea, does not my house stand so
with God?
For he has made with me an everlasting covenant,
ordered in all things and secure.
For will he not cause to prosper
all my help and my desire?
6 But godless men[a] are all like thorns
that are thrown away;
for they cannot be taken with the
hand;
7 but the man who touches them
arms himself with iron and the
shaft of a spear,
and they are utterly consumed
with fire."[b]

8 These are the names of the mighty
men whom David had: Jō'sheb-bas-
shē'beth a Täh-chē'mȯ·nīte; he was
chief of the three;[c] he wielded his
spear[d] against eight hundred whom he
slew at one time.
9 And next to him among the three
mighty men was El·ē·ā'zär the son of
Dō'dō, son of Ȧ·hō'hī. He was with
David when they defied the Philistines
who were gathered there for battle,
and the men of Israel withdrew. 10 He
rose and struck down the Philistines
until his hand was weary, and his hand
cleaved to the sword; and the LORD
wrought a great victory that day; and
the men returned after him only to
strip the slain.
11 And next to him was Sham'mȧh,
the son of Ā'gee the Här'ȧ·rīte. The
Philistines gathered together at Lē'hī,
where there was a plot of ground full
of lentils; and the men fled from the
Philistines. 12 But he took his stand
in the midst of the plot, and defended
it, and slew the Philistines; and the
LORD wrought a great victory.
13 And three of the thirty chief men
went down, and came about harvest
time to David at the cave of Ȧ·dul'-
lȧm, when a band of Philistines was
encamped in the valley of Reph'ȧ·im.
14 David was then in the stronghold;
and the garrison of the Philistines was
then at Bethlehem. 15 And David said
longingly, "O that some one would
give me water to drink from the well
of Bethlehem which is by the gate!"
16 Then the three mighty men broke
through the camp of the Philistines,
and drew water out of the well of

[w] Ps 18.45: Heb *girded themselves* [x] Another reading is *He is a tower of salvation*
[y] Or *the favorite of the songs of Israel* [z] Heb *from rain* [a] Heb *worthlessness* [b] Heb *fire in the sitting*
[c] Or *captains* [d] 1 Chron 11.11: Heb obscure
22.50: Rom 15.9. **23.8-39**: 1 Chron 11 10-41.

Bethlehem which was by the gate, and
took and brought it to David. But he
would not drink of it; he poured it out
to the LORD, 17 and said, "Far be it
from me, O LORD, that I should do
this. Shall I drink the blood of the men
who went at the risk of their lives?"
Therefore he would not drink it. These
things did the three mighty men.

18 Now A·bi'shäi, the brother of
Jō'ab, the son of Zė·rü'i·ȧh, was chief
of the thirty.[e] And he wielded his
spear against three hundred men and
slew them, and won a name beside the
three. 19 He was the most renowned
of the thirty,[f] and became their commander; but he did not attain to the
three.

20 And Be·nā'iȧh the son of Je·hoi'-
ȧ·dȧ was a valiant man[g] of Kab'zē·ėl,
a doer of great deeds; he smote two
ariels[h] of Mō'ab. He also went down
and slew a lion in a pit on a day when
snow had fallen. 21 And he slew an
Egyptian, a handsome man. The
Egyptian had a spear in his hand; but
Be·nā'iȧh went down to him with a
staff, and snatched the spear out of
the Egyptian's hand, and slew him
with his own spear. 22 These things
did Be·nā'iȧh the son of Je·hoi'ȧ·dȧ,
and won a name beside the three
mighty men. 23 He was renowned
among the thirty, but he did not attain
to the three. And David set him over
his bodyguard.

24 As'ȧ·hel the brother of Jō'ab was
one of the thirty; El·hā'nȧn the son
of Dō'dō of Bethlehem, 25 Sham'mȧh
of Hâr'od, E·lī'kȧ of Harod, 26 Hē'lez
the Pal'tīte, Ira the son of Ik'kesh of
Te·kō'ȧ, 27 Ā·bi·ē'zėr, of An'ȧ·thoth,
Mė·bun'näi the Hū'shȧ·thīte, 28 Zal'-
mon the A·hō'hīte, Mā'hȧ·räi of Nė-
toph'ȧh, 29 Hē'leb the son of Bā'ȧ·nȧh
of Nė·toph'ȧh, It'täi the son of Rī'bäi
of Gib'ē-ȧh of the Benjaminites, 30 Be-
nā'iȧh of Pir'ȧ·thon, Hid'däi of the
brooks of Gā'ash, 31 Ā'bi-al'bȯn the
Är'bȧ·thīte, Az'mȧ·veth of Bȧ·hū'rim,
32 E·lī'ȧh·bȧ of Shā-al'bȯn, the sons of
Jā'shėn, Jonathan, 33 Sham'mȧh the
Hâr'ȧ·rīte, A·hī'ȧm the son of Shâr'ȧr
the Hararite, 34 E·liph'ė·let the son of
A·has'bäi of Mā'ȧ·cȧh, E·lī'ȧm the son
of A·hith'ō·phel of Gī'lō, 35 Hez'rō[i]
of Cär'mėl, Pā'ȧ·räi the Är'bīte, 36 I'gal
the son of Nathan of Zō'bȧh, Bā'nī
the Gad'īte, 37 Zē'lek the Am'mȯ·nīte,
Nā'hȧ·räi of Bė-ēr'ȯth, the armor-
bearer of Jō'ab the son of Zė·rü'i·ȧh,
38 Ira the Ith'rīte, Gâr'eb the Ithrite,
39 Ū·rī'ȧh the Hit'tīte: thirty-seven in
all.

24 Again the anger of the LORD
was kindled against Israel, and
he incited David against them, saying,
"Go, number Israel and Judah." 2 So
the king said to Jō'ab and the commanders of the army,[j] who were with
him, "Go through all the tribes of
Israel, from Dan to Beer-sheba, and
number the people, that I may know
the number of the people." 3 But
Jō'ab said to the king, "May the LORD
your God add to the people a hundred
times as many as they are, while the
eyes of my lord the king still see it;
but why does my lord the king delight
in this thing?" 4 But the king's word
prevailed against Jō'ab and the commanders of the army. So Joab and the
commanders of the army went out
from the presence of the king to number the people of Israel. 5 They crossed
the Jordan, and began from A·rō'ėr,[k]
and from the city that is in the middle
of the valley, toward Gad and on to
Jā'zėr. 6 Then they came to Gilead,
and to Kā'desh in the land of the
Hit'tītes;[l] and they came to Dan, and
from Dan[m] they went around to
Sī'don, 7 and came to the fortress of
Tȳre and to all the cities of the Hī'vītes
and Canaanites; and they went out to
the Negeb of Judah at Beer-sheba.
8 So when they had gone through all
the land, they came to Jerusalem at
the end of nine months and twenty
days. 9 And Jō'ab gave the sum of the
numbering of the people to the king:
in Israel there were eight hundred
thousand valiant men who drew the
sword, and the men of Judah were
five hundred thousand.

10 But David's heart smote him
after he had numbered the people.
And David said to the LORD, "I have
sinned greatly in what I have done.
But now, O LORD, I pray thee, take

[e] Two Hebrew Mss Syr: MT *three* [f] 1 Chron 11.25: Heb *Was he the most renowned of the three?*
[g] Another reading is *the son of Ish-hai* [h] The meaning of the word *ariel* is unknown
[i] Another reading is *Hezrai* [j] 1 Chron 21.2 Gk: Heb *to Joab the commander of the army*
[k] Gk: Heb *encamped in Aroer* [l] Gk: Heb *to the land of Tahtim-hodshi*
[m] Cn Compare Gk: Heb *they came to Dan-jaan and*
24.1-25: 1 Chron 21.1-27.

away the iniquity of thy servant; for
I have done very foolishly." 11And
when David arose in the morning, the
word of the LORD came to the prophet
Gad, David's seer, saying, 12 "Go and
say to David, 'Thus says the LORD,
Three things I offer[n] you; choose one
of them, that I may do it to you.' "
13 So Gad came to David and told
him, and said to him, "Shall three[o]
years of famine come to you in your
land? Or will you flee three months
before your foes while they pursue
you? Or shall there be three days'
pestilence in your land? Now consider,
and decide what answer I shall return
to him who sent me." 14 Then David
said to Gad, "I am in great distress;
let us fall into the hand of the LORD,
for his mercy is great; but let me not
fall into the hand of man."
15 So the LORD sent a pestilence
upon Israel from the morning until
the appointed time; and there died of
the people from Dan to Beer-sheba
seventy thousand men. 16And when
the angel stretched forth his hand
toward Jerusalem to destroy it, the
LORD repented of the evil, and said to
the angel who was working destruction
among the people, "It is enough; now
stay your hand." And the angel of the
LORD was by the threshing floor of
A·rau'nah the Jeb'ū·site. 17 Then David
spoke to the LORD when he saw the
angel who was smiting the people, and
said, "Lo, I have sinned, and I have
done wickedly; but these sheep, what
have they done? Let thy hand, I pray
thee, be against me and against my
father's house."
18 And Gad came that day to
David, and said to him, "Go up, rear
an altar to the LORD on the threshing
floor of A·rau'nah the Jeb'ū·site." 19 So
David went up at Gad's word, as the
LORD commanded. 20 And when A·rau'-
nah looked down, he saw the king and
his servants coming on toward him;
and Araunah went forth, and did
obeisance to the king with his face to
the ground. 21And A·rau'nah said,
"Why has my lord the king come to
his servant?" David said, "To buy the
threshing floor of you, in order to
build an altar to the LORD, that the
plague may be averted from the people." 22 Then A·rau'nah said to David,
"Let my lord the king take and offer
up what seems good to him; here are
the oxen for the burnt offering, and
the threshing sledges and the yokes of
the oxen for the wood. 23All this, O
king, A·rau'nah gives to the king."
And Araunah said to the king, "The
LORD your God accept you." 24 But
the king said to A·rau'nah, "No, but
I will buy it of you for a price; I will
not offer burnt offerings to the LORD
my God which cost me nothing." So
David bought the threshing floor and
the oxen for fifty shekels of silver.
25And David built there an altar to
the LORD, and offered burnt offerings
and peace offerings. So the LORD
heeded supplications for the land,
and the plague was averted from
Israel.

THE FIRST BOOK OF THE

KINGS

1 Now King David was old and
advanced in years; and although
they covered him with clothes, he
could not get warm. 2 Therefore his
servants said to him, "Let a young
maiden be sought for my lord the
king, and let her wait upon the king,
and be his nurse; let her lie in your
bosom, that my lord the king may be
warm." 3 So they sought for a beautiful maiden throughout all the territory
of Israel, and found Ab'i·shag the
Shū'nam·mīte, and brought her to the
king. 4 The maiden was very beautiful;
and she became the king's nurse and
ministered to him; but the king knew
her not.
5 Now Ad·o·nī'jah the son of Hag'-
gith exalted himself, saying, "I will be
king"; and he prepared for himself

[n] Or *hold over* [o] 1 Chron 21.12 Gk: Heb *seven*

chariots and horsemen, and fifty men
to run before him. 6 His father had
never at any time displeased him by
asking, "Why have you done thus and
so?" He was also a very handsome
man; and he was born next after
Ab'sȧ·lȯm. 7 He conferred with Jō'ab
the son of Zė·rü'i·ȧh and with Ȧ·bī'-
ȧ·thär the priest; and they followed
Ad·ȯ·nī'jȧh and helped him. 8 But
Zā'dok the priest, and Be·nā'iȧh the
son of Je·hoi'ȧ·dȧ, and Nathan the
prophet, and Shim'ē-ī, and Rē'ī, and
David's mighty men were not with
Ad·ȯ·nī'jȧh.

9 Ad·ȯ·nī'jȧh sacrificed sheep, oxen,
and fatlings by the Serpent's Stone,
which is beside En-rō'gėl, and he invited all his brothers, the king's sons,
and all the royal officials of Judah,
10 but he did not invite Nathan the
prophet or Be·nā'iȧh or the mighty
men or Solomon his brother.

11 Then Nathan said to Bath·shē'bȧ
the mother of Solomon, "Have you
not heard that Ad·ȯ·nī'jȧh the son of
Hag'gith has become king and David
our lord does not know it? 12 Now
therefore come, let me give you counsel,
that you may save your own life and
the life of your son Solomon. 13 Go in
at once to King David, and say to
him, 'Did you not, my lord the king,
swear to your maidservant, saying,
"Solomon your son shall reign after
me, and he shall sit upon my throne"?
Why then is Ad·ȯ·nī'jȧh king?' 14 Then
while you are still speaking with the
king, I also will come in after you and
confirm your words."

15 So Bath·shē'bȧ went to the king
into his chamber (now the king was
very old, and Ab'i·shag the Shü'nȧm-
mīte was ministering to the king).
16 Bath·shē'bȧ bowed and did obeisance to the king, and the king said,
"What do you desire?" 17 She said to
him, "My lord, you swore to your
maidservant by the LORD your God,
saying, 'Solomon your son shall reign
after me, and he shall sit upon my
throne.' 18 And now, behold, Ad·ȯ·nī'-
jȧh is king, although you, my lord the
king, do not know it. 19 He has sacrificed oxen, fatlings, and sheep in
abundance, and has invited all the
sons of the king, Ȧ·bī'ȧ·thär the priest,
and Jō'ab the commander of the army;
but Solomon your servant he has not
invited. 20 And now, my lord the king,
the eyes of all Israel are upon you, to
tell them who shall sit on the throne
of my lord the king after him. 21 Otherwise it will come to pass, when my
lord the king sleeps with his fathers,
that I and my son Solomon will be
counted offenders."

22 While she was still speaking with
the king, Nathan the prophet came in.
23 And they told the king, "Here is
Nathan the prophet." And when he
came in before the king, he bowed
before the king, with his face to the
ground. 24 And Nathan said, "My lord
the king, have you said, 'Ad·ȯ·nī'jȧh
shall reign after me, and he shall sit
upon my throne'? 25 For he has gone
down this day, and has sacrificed oxen,
fatlings, and sheep in abundance, and
has invited all the king's sons, Jō'ab
the commander[a] of the army, and
Ȧ·bī'ȧ·thär the priest; and behold, they
are eating and drinking before him,
and saying, 'Long live King Ad·ȯ·nī'-
jȧh!' 26 But me, your servant, and
Zā'dok the priest, and Be·nā'iȧh the
son of Je·hoi'ȧ·dȧ, and your servant
Solomon, he has not invited. 27 Has
this thing been brought about by my
lord the king and you have not told
your servants who should sit on the
throne of my lord the king after him?"

28 Then King David answered,
"Call Bath·shē'bȧ to me." So she came
into the king's presence, and stood
before the king. 29 And the king swore,
saying, "As the LORD lives, who has
redeemed my soul out of every adversity, 30 as I swore to you by the LORD,
the God of Israel, saying, 'Solomon
your son shall reign after me, and he
shall sit upon my throne in my stead';
even so will I do this day." 31 Then
Bath·shē'bȧ bowed with her face to
the ground, and did obeisance to the
king, and said, "May my lord King
David live for ever!"

32 King David said, "Call to me
Zā'dok the priest, Nathan the prophet,
and Be·nā'iȧh the son of Je·hoi'ȧ·dȧ."
So they came before the king. 33 And
the king said to them, "Take with you
the servants of your lord, and cause
Solomon my son to ride on my own
mule, and bring him down to Gī'hon;
34 and let Zā'dok the priest and Nathan
the prophet there anoint him king
over Israel; then blow the trumpet,
and say, 'Long live King Solomon!'
35 You shall then come up after him,

[a] Gk: Heb *commanders*

and he shall come and sit upon my
throne; for he shall be king in my
stead; and I have appointed him to be
ruler over Israel and over Judah."
36 And Be·nā′iȧh the son of Je·hoi′ȧ·dȧ
answered the king, "Amen! May the
LORD, the God of my lord the king,
say so. 37 As the LORD has been with
my lord the king, even so may he be
with Solomon, and make his throne
greater than the throne of my lord
King David."
38 So Zā′dok the priest, Nathan
the prophet, and Be·nā′iȧh the son of
Je·hoi′ȧ·dȧ, and the Cher′ė·thītes and
the Pel′ė·thītes, went down and caused
Solomon to ride on King David's
mule, and brought him to Gī′hon.
39 There Zā′dok the priest took the
horn of oil from the tent, and anointed
Solomon. Then they blew the trumpet;
and all the people said, "Long live
King Solomon!" 40 And all the people
went up after him, playing on pipes,
and rejoicing with great joy, so that
the earth was split by their noise.
41 Ad·ȯ·nī′jȧh and all the guests
who were with him heard it as they
finished feasting. And when Jō′ab
heard the sound of the trumpet, he
said, "What does this uproar in the
city mean?" 42 While he was still
speaking, behold, Jonathan the son of
A·bī′ȧ·thär the priest came; and Ad·ȯ-
nī′jȧh said, "Come in, for you are a
worthy man and bring good news."
43 Jonathan answered Ad·ȯ·nī′jȧh,
"No, for our lord King David has
made Solomon king; 44 and the king
has sent with him Zā′dok the priest,
Nathan the prophet, and Be·nā′iȧh
the son of Je·hoi′ȧ·dȧ, and the Cher′ė-
thītes and the Pel′ė·thītes; and they
have caused him to ride on the king's
mule; 45 and Zā′dok the priest and
Nathan the prophet have anointed him
king at Gī′hon; and they have gone
up from there rejoicing, so that the
city is in an uproar. This is the noise
that you have heard. 46 Solomon sits
upon the royal throne. 47 Moreover
the king's servants came to congratulate our lord King David, saying,
'Your God make the name of Solomon
more famous than yours, and make his
throne greater than your throne.' And
the king bowed himself upon the bed.
48 And the king also said, "Blessed be
the LORD, the God of Israel, who has
granted one of my offspring[b] to sit on
my throne this day, my own eyes
seeing it.' "
49 Then all the guests of Ad·ȯ·nī′-
jȧh trembled, and rose, and each went
his own way. 50 And Ad·ȯ·nī′jȧh feared
Solomon; and he arose, and went, and
caught hold of the horns of the altar.
51 And it was told Solomon, "Behold,
Ad·ȯ·nī′jȧh fears King Solomon; for,
lo, he has laid hold of the horns of the
altar, saying, 'Let King Solomon swear
to me first that he will not slay his
servant with the sword.' " 52 And Solomon said, "If he prove to be a worthy
man, not one of his hairs shall fall to
the earth; but if wickedness is found
in him, he shall die." 53 So King
Solomon sent, and they brought him
down from the altar. And he came
and did obeisance to King Solomon;
and Solomon said to him, "Go to your
house."

2 When David's time to die drew
near, he charged Solomon his son,
saying, 2 "I am about to go the way
of all the earth. Be strong, and show
yourself a man, 3 and keep the charge
of the LORD your God, walking in his
ways and keeping his statutes, his
commandments, his ordinances, and
his testimonies, as it is written in the
law of Moses, that you may prosper
in all that you do and wherever you
turn; 4 that the LORD may establish
his word which he spoke concerning
me, saying, 'If your sons take heed to
their way, to walk before me in faithfulness with all their heart and with
all their soul, there shall not fail you
a man on the throne of Israel.'
5 "Moreover you know also what
Jō′ab the son of Zė·rü′i·ȧh did to me,
how he dealt with the two commanders of the armies of Israel, Abner the
son of Nēr, and A·mā′sȧ the son of
Jē′thėr, whom he murdered, avenging[c]
in time of peace blood which had been
shed in war, and putting innocent
blood[d] upon the girdle about my[e] loins,
and upon the sandals on my[e] feet.
6 Act therefore according to your wisdom, but do not let his gray head go
down to Shē′ōl in peace. 7 But deal
loyally with the sons of Bär·zil′lāi the
Gileadite, and let them be among
those who eat at your table; for with
such loyalty they met me when I fled
from Ab′sȧ·lȯm your brother. 8 And
there is also with you Shim′ē-ī the
son of Gē′rȧ, the Benjaminite from

[b] Gk: Heb *one* [c] Gk: Heb *placing* [d] Gk: Heb *blood of war* [e] Gk: Heb *his*

Bȧ·hū′rim, who cursed me with a
grievous curse on the day when I went
to Mā·hȧ·nā′im; but when he came
down to meet me at the Jordan, I
swore to him by the LORD, saying,
'I will not put you to death with the
sword.' 9 Now therefore hold him not
guiltless, for you are a wise man; you
will know what you ought to do to
him, and you shall bring his gray head
down with blood to Shē′ōl."

10 Then David slept with his fathers, and was buried in the city of
David. 11 And the time that David
reigned over Israel was forty years; he
reigned seven years in Hē′brȯn, and
thirty-three years in Jerusalem. 12 So
Solomon sat upon the throne of David
his father; and his kingdom was firmly
established.

13 Then Ad·ȯ·nī′jȧh the son of
Hag′gith came to Bath·shē′bȧ the
mother of Solomon. And she said,
"Do you come peaceably?" He said,
"Peaceably." 14 Then he said, "I have
something to say to you." She said,
"Say on." 15 He said, "You know that
the kingdom was mine, and that all
Israel fully expected me to reign; however the kingdom has turned about
and become my brother's, for it was
his from the LORD. 16 And now I have
one request to make of you; do not
refuse me." She said to him, "Say
on." 17 And he said, "Pray ask King
Solomon—he will not refuse you—to
give me Ab′i·shag the Shü′nȧm·mīte
as my wife." 18 Bath·shē′bȧ said, "Very
well; I will speak for you to the king."

19 So Bath·shē′bȧ went to King
Solomon, to speak to him on behalf
of Ad·ȯ·nī′jȧh. And the king rose to
meet her, and bowed down to her;
then he sat on his throne, and had a
seat brought for the king's mother;
and she sat on his right. 20 Then she
said, "I have one small request to
make of you; do not refuse me." And
the king said to her, "Make your request, my mother; for I will not refuse
you." 21 She said, "Let Ab′i·shag the
Shü′nȧm·mīte be given to Ad·ȯ·nī′jȧh
your brother as his wife." 22 King
Solomon answered his mother, "And
why do you ask Ab′i·shag the Shü′-
nȧm·mīte for Ad·ȯ·nī′jȧh? Ask for him
the kingdom also; for he is my elder
brother, and on his side are Ȧ·bī′ȧ·thär[f]
the priest and Jō′ab the son of Zė·rü′-
i·ȧh." 23 Then King Solomon swore
by the LORD, saying, "God do so to
me and more also if this word does
not cost Ad·ȯ·nī′jȧh his life! 24 Now
therefore as the LORD lives, who has
established me, and placed me on the
throne of David my father, and who
has made me a house, as he promised,
Ad·ȯ·nī′jȧh shall be put to death this
day." 25 So King Solomon sent Be-
nā′iȧh the son of Je·hoi′ȧ·dȧ; and he
struck him down, and he died.

26 And to Ȧ·bī′ȧ·thär the priest the
king said, "Go to An′ȧ·thoth, to your
estate; for you deserve death. But I
will not at this time put you to death,
because you bore the ark of the Lord
GOD before David my father, and
because you shared in all the affliction
of my father." 27 So Solomon expelled
Ȧ·bī′ȧ·thär from being priest to the
LORD, thus fulfilling the word of the
LORD which he had spoken concerning
the house of Eli in Shī′lōh.

28 When the news came to Jō′ab—
for Joab had supported Ad·ȯ·nī′jȧh
although he had not supported Ab′sȧ-
lȯm—Joab fled to the tent of the LORD
and caught hold of the horns of the
altar. 29 And when it was told King
Solomon, "Jō′ab has fled to the tent
of the LORD, and behold, he is beside
the altar," Solomon sent Be·nā′iȧh the
son of Je·hoi′ȧ·dȧ, saying, "Go, strike
him down." 30 So Be·nā′iȧh came to
the tent of the LORD, and said to him,
"The king commands, 'Come forth.' "
But he said, "No, I will die here."
Then Benaiah brought the king word
again, saying, "Thus said Jō′ab, and
thus he answered me." 31 The king
replied to him, "Do as he has said,
strike him down and bury him; and
thus take away from me and from my
father's house the guilt for the blood
which Jō′ab shed without cause.
32 The LORD will bring back his
bloody deeds upon his own head, because, without the knowledge of my
father David, he attacked and slew
with the sword two men more righteous and better than himself, Abner
the son of Nēr, commander of the
army of Israel, and Ȧ·mā′sȧ the son
of Jē′thėr, commander of the army of
Judah. 33 So shall their blood come
back upon the head of Jō′ab and upon
the head of his descendants for ever;
but to David, and to his descendants,

[f] Gk Syr Vg: Heb *and for him and for Abiathar*
2.12: 1 Chron 29.23.

and to his house, and to his throne,
there shall be peace from the LORD
for evermore." 34 Then Be·nā'iȧh the
son of Je·hoi'ȧ·dȧ went up, and struck
him down and killed him; and he was
buried in his own house in the wilderness. 35 The king put Be·nā'iȧh the
son of Je·hoi'ȧ·dȧ over the army in
place of Jō'ab, and the king put Zā'-
dok the priest in the place of Ȧ·bī'ȧ-
thär.
36 Then the king sent and summoned Shim'ē-ī, and said to him,
"Build yourself a house in Jerusalem,
and dwell there, and do not go forth
from there to any place whatever.
37 For on the day you go forth, and
cross the brook Kid'rȯn, know for
certain that you shall die; your blood
shall be upon your own head." 38 And
Shim'ē-ī said to the king, "What you
say is good; as my lord the king has
said, so will your servant do." So
Shime-i dwelt in Jerusalem many
days.
39 But it happened at the end of
three years that two of Shim'ē-ī's
slaves ran away to Ā'chish, son of
Mā'ȧ·cȧh, king of Gath. And when it
was told Shime-i, "Behold, your slaves
are in Gath," 40 Shim'ē-ī arose and
saddled an ass, and went to Gath to
Ā'chish, to seek his slaves; Shime-i
went and brought his slaves from Gath.
41 And when Solomon was told that
Shim'ē-ī had gone from Jerusalem to
Gath and returned, 42 the king sent
and summoned Shim'ē-ī, and said to
him, "Did I not make you swear by
the LORD, and solemnly admonish
you, saying, 'Know for certain that
on the day you go forth and go to any
place whatever, you shall die'? And
you said to me, 'What you say is good;
I obey.' 43 Why then have you not
kept your oath to the LORD and the
commandment with which I charged
you?" 44 The king also said to Shim'ē-ī,
"You know in your own heart all the
evil that you did to David my father;
so the LORD will bring back your evil
upon your own head. 45 But King
Solomon shall be blessed, and the
throne of David shall be established
before the LORD for ever." 46 Then
the king commanded Be·nā'iȧh the son
of Je·hoi'ȧ·dȧ; and he went out and
struck him down, and he died.
So the kingdom was established in
the hand of Solomon.

3 Solomon made a marriage alliance
with Pharaoh king of Egypt; he
took Pharaoh's daughter, and brought
her into the city of David, until he
had finished building his own house
and the house of the LORD and the
wall around Jerusalem. 2 The people
were sacrificing at the high places,
however, because no house had yet
been built for the name of the LORD.
3 Solomon loved the LORD, walking
in the statutes of David his father;
only, he sacrificed and burnt incense
at the high places. 4 And the king went
to Gib'ē·ȯn to sacrifice there, for that
was the great high place; Solomon
used to offer a thousand burnt offerings upon that altar. 5 At Gib'ē·ȯn the
LORD appeared to Solomon in a dream
by night; and God said, "Ask what I
shall give you." 6 And Solomon said,
"Thou hast shown great and steadfast
love to thy servant David my father,
because he walked before thee in faithfulness, in righteousness, and in uprightness of heart toward thee; and
thou hast kept for him this great and
steadfast love, and hast given him a
son to sit on his throne this day. 7 And
now, O LORD my God, thou hast
made thy servant king in place of
David my father, although I am but a
little child; I do not know how to go
out or come in. 8 And thy servant is in
the midst of thy people whom thou
hast chosen, a great people, that cannot
be numbered or counted for multitude.
9 Give thy servant therefore an understanding mind to govern thy people,
that I may discern between good and
evil; for who is able to govern this thy
great people?"
10 It pleased the LORD that Solomon had asked this. 11 And God said
to him, "Because you have asked this,
and have not asked for yourself long
life or riches or the life of your enemies,
but have asked for yourself understanding to discern what is right,
12 behold, I now do according to your
word. Behold, I give you a wise and
discerning mind, so that none like you
has been before you and none like
you shall arise after you. 13 I give you
also what you have not asked, both
riches and honor, so that no other
king shall compare with you, all your
days. 14 And if you will walk in my
ways, keeping my statutes and my
commandments, as your father David

3.4-15: 2 Chron 1.3-13.

walked, then I will lengthen your
days."
15 And Solomon awoke, and behold, it was a dream. Then he came
to Jerusalem, and stood before the
ark of the covenant of the LORD, and
offered up burnt offerings and peace
offerings, and made a feast for all his
servants.
16 Then two harlots came to the
king, and stood before him. 17 The
one woman said, "Oh, my lord, this
woman and I dwell in the same house;
and I gave birth to a child while she
was in the house. 18 Then on the third
day after I was delivered, this woman
also gave birth; and we were alone;
there was no one else with us in the
house, only we two were in the house.
19 And this woman's son died in the
night, because she lay on it. 20 And
she arose at midnight, and took my
son from beside me, while your maidservant slept, and laid it in her bosom,
and laid her dead son in my bosom.
21 When I rose in the morning to
nurse my child, behold, it was dead;
but when I looked at it closely in the
morning, behold, it was not the child
that I had borne." 22 But the other
woman said, "No, the living child is
mine, and the dead child is yours."
The first said, "No, the dead child is
yours, and the living child is mine."
Thus they spoke before the king.
23 Then the king said, "The one
says, 'This is my son that is alive, and
your son is dead'; and the other says,
'No, but your son is dead, and my
son is the living one.'" 24 And the
king said, "Bring me a sword." So a
sword was brought before the king.
25 And the king said, "Divide the living
child in two, and give half to the one,
and half to the other." 26 Then the
woman whose son was alive said to
the king, because her heart yearned
for her son, "Oh, my lord, give her
the living child, and by no means slay
it." But the other said, "It shall be
neither mine nor yours; divide it."
27 Then the king answered and said,
"Give the living child to the first
woman, and by no means slay it; she
is its mother." 28 And all Israel heard
of the judgment which the king had
rendered; and they stood in awe of the
king, because they perceived that the
wisdom of God was in him, to render
justice.

4 King Solomon was king over all
Israel, 2 and these were his high
officials: Az·ȧ·rī'ȧh the son of Zā'dok
was the priest; 3 El·i·hôr'eph and Ȧ·hī'-
jȧh the sons of Shī'shȧ were secretaries;
Je·hosh'ȧ·phat the son of Ȧ·hī'lu̇d was
recorder; 4 Be·nā'iȧh the son of Je·hoi'-
ȧ·dȧ was in command of the army;
Zā'dok and Ȧ·bī'ȧ·thär were priests;
5 Az·ȧ·rī'ȧh the son of Nathan was over
the officers; Zā'bu̇d the son of Nathan
was priest and king's friend; 6 Ȧ·hī'shär
was in charge of the palace; and Ad·ō-
nī'rȧm the son of Ab'dȧ was in charge
of the forced labor.
7 Solomon had twelve officers over
all Israel, who provided food for the
king and his household; each man had
to make provision for one month in
the year. 8 These were their names:
Ben-hûr', in the hill country of
Ē'phrȧ·im; 9 Ben-dē'kėr, in Mā'kaz,
Shā-al'bim, Beth-shē'mesh, and Ē'lon-
beth-hā'nȧn; 10 Ben-hē'sed, in Ȧ·rŭb'-
both (to him belonged Sō'cōh and all
the land of Hē'phėr); 11 Ben-ȧ·bin'ȧ-
dab, in all Nā'phath-dôr (he had
Tā'phath the daughter of Solomon as
his wife); 12 Bā'ȧ·nȧ the son of Ȧ·hī'lu̇d,
in Tā'ȧ·nach, Mė·gid'dō, and all Beth-
shē'ȧn which is beside Zar'ė·than
below Jez'rē·ėl, and from Beth-shean
to Ā'bėl-mė·hō'lȧh, as far as the other
side of Jok'mē·ȧm; 13 Ben-gē'bėr, in
Rā'moth-gil'ē·ȧd (he had the villages
of Jā'ir the son of Mȧ·nas'sėh, which
are in Gilead, and he had the region
of Är'gȯb, which is in Bā'shȧn, sixty
great cities with walls and bronze bars);
14 Ȧ·hin'ȧ·dab the son of Id'dō, in Mā-
hȧ·nā'im; 15 Ȧ·him'ȧ·az, in Naph'tȧ·lī
(he had taken Bas'ė·math the daughter
of Solomon as his wife); 16 Bā'ȧ·nȧ the
son of Hū'shāi, in Ash'ėr and Be·ā'loth;
17 Je·hosh'ȧ·phat the son of Pȧ·rü'ȧh,
in Is'sȧ·chär; 18 Shim'ē-ī the son of
Ē'lȧ, in Benjamin; 19 Gē'bėr the son
of Ū'rī, in the land of Gilead, the
country of Sī'hon king of the Am'ō-
rītes and of Og king of Bā'shȧn. And
there was one officer in the land of
Judah.
20 Judah and Israel were as many
as the sand by the sea; they ate and
drank and were happy. 21[g] Solomon
ruled over all the kingdoms from the
Eū·phrā'tēs to the land of the Philistines and to the border of Egypt; they
brought tribute and served Solomon
all the days of his life.

[g] Ch 5.1 in Heb

22 Solomon's provision for one day
was thirty cors of fine flour, and sixty
cors of meal, 23 ten fat oxen, and
twenty pasture-fed cattle, a hundred
sheep, besides harts, gazelles, roe-
bucks, and fatted fowl. 24 For he had
dominion over all the region west of
the Eū·phrā'tēs from Tiph'sȧh to
Gā'zȧ, over all the kings west of the
Euphrates; and he had peace on all
sides round about him. 25 And Judah
and Israel dwelt in safety, from Dan
even to Beer-sheba, every man under
his vine and under his fig tree, all the
days of Solomon. 26 Solomon also had
forty thousand stalls of horses for his
chariots, and twelve thousand horsemen. 27 And those officers supplied
provisions for King Solomon, and for
all who came to King Solomon's table,
each one in his month; they let nothing
be lacking. 28 Barley also and straw
for the horses and swift steeds they
brought to the place where it was
required, each according to his charge.

29 And God gave Solomon wisdom
and understanding beyond measure,
and largeness of mind like the sand
on the seashore, 30 so that Solomon's
wisdom surpassed the wisdom of all
the people of the east, and all the
wisdom of Egypt. 31 For he was wiser
than all other men, wiser than Ethan
the Ez'rȧ·hīte, and Hē'mȧn, Cal'col,
and Där'dȧ, the sons of Mā'hol; and
his fame was in all the nations round
about. 32 He also uttered three thousand proverbs; and his songs were a
thousand and five. 33 He spoke of trees,
from the cedar that is in Lebanon to
the hyssop that grows out of the wall;
he spoke also of beasts, and of birds,
and of reptiles, and of fish. 34 And
men came from all peoples to hear the
wisdom of Solomon, and from all the
kings of the earth, who had heard of
his wisdom.

5[h] Now Hiram king of Tȳre sent
his servants to Solomon, when he
heard that they had anointed him king
in place of his father; for Hiram always
loved David. 2 And Solomon sent word
to Hiram, 3 "You know that David
my father could not build a house for
the name of the LORD his God because
of the warfare with which his enemies
surrounded him, until the LORD put
them under the soles of his feet. 4 But
now the LORD my God has given me
rest on every side; there is neither
adversary nor misfortune. 5 And so I
purpose to build a house for the name
of the LORD my God, as the LORD
said to David my father, 'Your son,
whom I will set upon your throne in
your place, shall build the house for
my name.' 6 Now therefore command
that cedars of Lebanon be cut for me;
and my servants will join your servants, and I will pay you for your
servants such wages as you set; for
you know that there is no one among
us who knows how to cut timber like
the Sī·dō'ni·ȧnṡ."

7 When Hiram heard the words of
Solomon, he rejoiced greatly, and said,
"Blessed be the LORD this day, who
has given to David a wise son to be
over this great people." 8 And Hiram
sent to Solomon, saying, "I have heard
the message which you have sent to
me; I am ready to do all you desire
in the matter of cedar and cypress
timber. 9 My servants shall bring it
down to the sea from Lebanon; and I
will make it into rafts to go by sea to
the place you direct, and I will have
them broken up there, and you shall
receive it; and you shall meet my
wishes by providing food for my
household." 10 So Hiram supplied
Solomon with all the timber of cedar
and cypress that he desired, 11 while
Solomon gave Hiram twenty thousand
cors of wheat as food for his household,
and twenty thousand[i] cors of beaten
oil. Solomon gave this to Hiram year
by year. 12 And the LORD gave Solomon
wisdom, as he promised him; and
there was peace between Hiram and
Solomon; and the two of them made a
treaty.

13 King Solomon raised a levy of
forced labor out of all Israel; and the
levy numbered thirty thousand men.
14 And he sent them to Lebanon, ten
thousand a month in relays; they
would be a month in Lebanon and
two months at home; Ad·ȯ·nī'rȧm was
in charge of the levy. 15 Solomon also
had seventy thousand burden-bearers
and eighty thousand hewers of stone
in the hill country, 16 besides Solomon's three thousand three hundred
chief officers who were over the work,
who had charge of the people who
carried on the work. 17 At the king's
command, they quarried out great,

[h] Ch 5.15 in Heb [i] Gk: Heb *twenty*
5.2-11: 2 Chron 2.3-16. **5.5:** 2 Chron 2.1. **5.15-16:** 2 Chron 2.2, 18.

costly stones in order to lay the foundation of the house with dressed stones.
18 So Solomon's builders and Hiram's
builders and the men of Gĕ'băl did the
hewing and prepared the timber and
the stone to build the house.

6 In the four hundred and eight-
ieth year after the people of Israel
came out of the land of Egypt, in the
fourth year of Solomon's reign over
Israel, in the month of Ziv, which is
the second month, he began to build
the house of the LORD. 2 The house
which King Solomon built for the
LORD was sixty cubits long, twenty
cubits wide, and thirty cubits high.
3 The vestibule in front of the nave of
the house was twenty cubits long,
equal to the width of the house, and
ten cubits deep in front of the house.
4 And he made for the house windows
with recessed frames. 5 He also built a
structure against the wall of the house,
running round the walls of the house,
both the nave and the inner sanctuary;
and he made side chambers all around.
6 The lowest story[j] was five cubits
broad, the middle one was six cubits
broad, and the third was seven cubits
broad; for around the outside of the
house he made offsets on the wall in
order that the supporting beams
should not be inserted into the walls
of the house.

7 When the house was built, it was
with stone prepared at the quarry; so
that neither hammer nor axe nor any
tool of iron was heard in the temple,
while it was being built.

8 The entrance for the lowest[k] story
was on the south side of the house;
and one went up by stairs to the
middle story, and from the middle
story to the third. 9 So he built the
house, and finished it; and he made
the ceiling of the house of beams and
planks of cedar. 10 He built the structure against the whole house, each
story[l] five cubits high, and it was joined
to the house with timbers of cedar.

11 Now the word of the LORD came
to Solomon, 12 "Concerning this house
which you are building, if you will
walk in my statutes and obey my
ordinances and keep all my commandments and walk in them, then I will
establish my word with you, which I
spoke to David your father. 13 And I
will dwell among the children of Israel,
and will not forsake my people Israel."

14 So Solomon built the house, and
finished it. 15 He lined the walls of the
house on the inside with boards of
cedar; from the floor of the house to
the rafters[m] of the ceiling, he covered
them on the inside with wood; and
he covered the floor of the house with
boards of cypress. 16 He built twenty
cubits of the rear of the house with
boards of cedar from the floor to the
rafters,[m] and he built this within as
an inner sanctuary, as the most holy
place. 17 The house, that is, the nave
in front of the inner sanctuary, was
forty cubits long. 18 The cedar within
the house was carved in the form of
gourds and open flowers; all was cedar,
no stone was seen. 19 The inner sanctuary he prepared in the innermost
part of the house, to set there the ark
of the covenant of the LORD. 20 The
inner sanctuary[n] was twenty cubits
long, twenty cubits wide, and twenty
cubits high; and he overlaid it with
pure gold. He also made[o] an altar of
cedar. 21 And Solomon overlaid the
inside of the house with pure gold,
and he drew chains of gold across, in
front of the inner sanctuary, and overlaid it with gold. 22 And he overlaid
the whole house with gold, until all
the house was finished. Also the whole
altar that belonged to the inner sanctuary he overlaid with gold.

23 In the inner sanctuary he made
two cherubim of olivewood, each ten
cubits high. 24 Five cubits was the
length of one wing of the cherub, and
five cubits the length of the other
wing of the cherub; it was ten cubits
from the tip of one wing to the tip of
the other. 25 The other cherub also
measured ten cubits; both cherubim
had the same measure and the same
form. 26 The height of one cherub was
ten cubits, and so was that of the other
cherub. 27 He put the cherubim in the
innermost part of the house; and the
wings of the cherubim were spread
out so that a wing of one touched the
one wall, and a wing of the other
cherub touched the other wall; their
other wings touched each other in the
middle of the house. 28 And he overlaid
the cherubim with gold.

29 He carved all the walls of the

[j] Gk: Heb *structure* [k] Gk Tg: Heb *middle* [l] Heb lacks *each story* [m] Gk: Heb *walls*
[n] Vg: Heb *and before the inner sanctuary* [o] Gk: Heb *covered*
6.1-28: 2 Chron 3.1-13; Acts 7.47.

house round about with carved figures
of cherubim and palm trees and open
flowers, in the inner and outer rooms.
30 The floor of the house he overlaid
with gold in the inner and outer rooms.
31 For the entrance to the inner
sanctuary he made doors of olivewood;
the lintel and the doorposts formed a
pentagon.[p] 32 He covered the two
doors of olivewood with carvings of
cherubim, palm trees, and open flowers; he overlaid them with gold, and
spread gold upon the cherubim and
upon the palm trees.
33 So also he made for the entrance
to the nave doorposts of olivewood, in
the form of a square, 34 and two doors
of cypress wood; the two leaves of the
one door were folding, and the two
leaves of the other door were folding.
35 On them he carved cherubim and
palm trees and open flowers; and he
overlaid them with gold evenly applied
upon the carved work. 36 He built the
inner court with three courses of hewn
stone and one course of cedar beams.
37 In the fourth year the foundation
of the house of the LORD was laid, in
the month of Ziv. 38 And in the eleventh year, in the month of Bul, which
is the eighth month, the house was
finished in all its parts, and according
to all its specifications. He was seven
years in building it.

7 Solomon was building his own
house thirteen years, and he finished his entire house.
2 He built the House of the Forest
of Lebanon; its length was a hundred
cubits, and its breadth fifty cubits,
and its height thirty cubits, and it was
built upon three[q] rows of cedar pillars,
with cedar beams upon the pillars.
3 And it was covered with cedar above
the chambers that were upon the forty-
five pillars, fifteen in each row. 4 There
were window frames in three rows,
and window opposite window in three
tiers. 5 All the doorways and windows[r]
had square frames, and window was
opposite window in three tiers.
6 And he made the Hall of Pillars;
its length was fifty cubits, and its
breadth thirty cubits; there was a porch
in front with pillars, and a canopy
before them.
7 And he made the Hall of the
Throne where he was to pronounce
judgment, even the Hall of Judgment;
it was finished with cedar from floor
to rafters.[s]
8 His own house where he was to
dwell, in the other court back of the
hall, was of like workmanship. Solomon also made a house like this hall
for Pharaoh's daughter whom he had
taken in marriage.
9 All these were made of costly
stones, hewn according to measure,
sawed with saws, back and front, even
from the foundation to the coping,
and from the court of the house of the
LORD[t] to the great court. 10 The foundation was of costly stones, huge
stones, stones of eight and ten cubits.
11 And above were costly stones, hewn
according to measurement, and cedar.
12 The great court had three courses
of hewn stone round about, and a
course of cedar beams; so had the
inner court of the house of the LORD,
and the vestibule of the house.
13 And King Solomon sent and
brought Hiram from Tyre. 14 He was
the son of a widow of the tribe of
Naph'ta-li, and his father was a man
of Tyre, a worker in bronze; and he
was full of wisdom, understanding,
and skill, for making any work in
bronze. He came to King Solomon,
and did all his work.
15 He cast two pillars of bronze.
Eighteen cubits was the height of one
pillar, and a line of twelve cubits
measured its circumference; it was
hollow, and its thickness was four
fingers; the second pillar was the
same.[u] 16 He also made two capitals
of molten bronze, to set upon the tops
of the pillars; the height of the one
capital was five cubits, and the height
of the other capital was five cubits.
17 Then he made two[v] nets of checker
work with wreaths of chain work for
the capitals upon the tops of the pillars; a net[w] for the one capital, and a
net[w] for the other capital. 18 Likewise
he made pomegranates;[x] in two rows
round about upon the one network, to
cover the capital that was upon the
top of the pillar; and he did the same
with the other capital. 19 Now the

[p] Heb obscure [q] Gk: Heb *four* [r] Gk: Heb *posts* [s] Syr Vg: Heb *floor*
[t] With 7.12: Heb *from the outside*
[u] Tg Syr Compare Gk and Jer 52.21: Heb *and a line of twelve cubits measured the circumference of the second pillar* [v] Gk: Heb lacks *he made two* [w] Gk: Heb *seven* [x] With 2 Mss Compare Gk: Heb *pillars*
7.15-21: 2 Chron 3.15-17.

capitals that were upon the tops of
the pillars in the vestibule were of
lily-work, four cubits. 20 The capitals
were upon the two pillars and also
above the rounded projection which
was beside the network; there were
two hundred pomegranates, in two
rows round about; and so with the
other capital. 21 He set up the pillars
at the vestibule of the temple; he set
up the pillar on the south and called
its name Jā'chin; and he set up the
pillar on the north and called its name
Bō'az. 22 And upon the tops of the
pillars was lily-work. Thus the work
of the pillars was finished.

23 Then he made the molten sea;
it was round, ten cubits from brim to
brim, and five cubits high, and a line
of thirty cubits measured its circumference. 24 Under its brim were gourds,
for thirty[y] cubits, compassing the sea
round about; the gourds were in two
rows, cast with it when it was cast.
25 It stood upon twelve oxen, three
facing north, three facing west, three
facing south, and three facing east; the
sea was set upon them, and all their
hinder parts were inward. 26 Its thickness was a handbreadth; and its brim
was made like the brim of a cup, like
the flower of a lily; it held two thousand baths.

27 He also made the ten stands of
bronze; each stand was four cubits
long, four cubits wide, and three cubits
high. 28 This was the construction of
the stands: they had panels, and the
panels were set in the frames 29 and
on the panels that were set in the
frames were lions, oxen, and cherubim.
Upon the frames, both above and
below the lions and oxen, there were
wreaths of beveled work. 30 Moreover
each stand had four bronze wheels and
axles of bronze; and at the four corners
were supports for a laver. The supports were cast, with wreaths at the
side of each. 31 Its opening was within
a crown which projected upward one
cubit; its opening was round, as a
pedestal is made, a cubit and a half
deep. At its opening there were carvings; and its panels were square, not
round. 32 And the four wheels were
underneath the panels; the axles of the
wheels were of one piece with the
stands; and the height of a wheel was
a cubit and a half. 33 The wheels were
made like a chariot wheel; their axles,
their rims, their spokes, and their
hubs, were all cast. 34 There were four
supports at the four corners of each
stand; the supports were of one piece
with the stands. 35 And on the top of
the stand there was a round band half
a cubit high; and on the top of the
stand its stays and its panels were of
one piece with it. 36 And on the sur-
faces of its stays and on its panels, he
carved cherubim, lions, and palm trees,
according to the space of each, with
wreaths round about. 37 After this
manner he made the ten stands; all
of them were cast alike, of the same
measure and the same form.

38 And he made ten lavers of
bronze; each laver held forty baths,
each laver measured four cubits, and
there was a laver for each of the ten
stands. 39 And he set the stands, five
on the south side of the house, and
five on the north side of the house;
and he set the sea on the southeast
corner of the house.

40 Hiram also made the pots, the
shovels, and the basins. So Hiram
finished all the work that he did for
King Solomon on the house of the
LORD: 41 the two pillars, the two bowls
of the capitals that were on the tops
of the pillars, and the two networks
to cover the two bowls of the capitals
that were on the tops of the pillars;
42 and the four hundred pomegranates
for the two networks, two rows of
pomegranates for each network, to
cover the two bowls of the capitals
that were upon the pillars; 43 the ten
stands, and the ten lavers upon the
stands; 44 and the one sea, and the
twelve oxen underneath the sea.

45 Now the pots, the shovels, and
the basins, all these vessels in the
house of the LORD, which Hiram made
for King Solomon, were of burnished
bronze. 46 In the plain of the Jordan
the king cast them, in the clay ground
between Suc'coth and Zar'ĕ·than.
47 And Solomon left all the vessels
unweighed, because there were so
many of them; the weight of the
bronze was not found out.

48 So Solomon made all the vessels
that were in the house of the LORD:
the golden altar, the golden table for
the bread of the Presence, 49 the lampstands of pure gold, five on the south

[y] Heb *ten*

7.23-26: 2 Chron 4.2-5. 7.38-51: 2 Chron 4.6, 5.1.

side and five on the north, before the
inner sanctuary; the flowers, the lamps,
and the tongs, of gold; 50 the cups,
snuffers, basins, dishes for incense,
and firepans, of pure gold; and the
sockets of gold, for the doors of the
innermost part of the house, the most
holy place, and for the doors of the
nave of the temple.

51 Thus all the work that King
Solomon did on the house of the LORD
was finished. And Solomon brought
in the things which David his father
had dedicated, the silver, the gold,
and the vessels, and stored them in the
treasuries of the house of the LORD.

8 Then Solomon assembled the
elders of Israel and all the heads
of the tribes, the leaders of the fathers'
houses of the people of Israel, before
King Solomon in Jerusalem, to bring
up the ark of the covenant of the LORD
out of the city of David, which is Zion.
2 And all the men of Israel assembled
to King Solomon at the feast in the
month Eth'a·nim, which is the seventh
month. 3 And all the elders of Israel
came, and the priests took up the ark.
4 And they brought up the ark of the
LORD, the tent of meeting, and all the
holy vessels that were in the tent; the
priests and the Levites brought them
up. 5 And King Solomon and all the
congregation of Israel, who had assembled before him, were with him before
the ark, sacrificing so many sheep and
oxen that they could not be counted or
numbered. 6 Then the priests brought
the ark of the covenant of the LORD to
its place, in the inner sanctuary of the
house, in the most holy place, underneath the wings of the cherubim. 7 For
the cherubim spread out their wings
over the place of the ark, so that the
cherubim made a covering above the
ark and its poles. 8 And the poles were
so long that the ends of the poles were
seen from the holy place before the
inner sanctuary; but they could not be
seen from outside; and they are there
to this day. 9 There was nothing in the
ark except the two tables of stone
which Moses put there at Hō'reb,
where the LORD made a covenant with
the people of Israel, when they came
out of the land of Egypt. 10 And when
the priests came out of the holy place,
a cloud filled the house of the LORD,
11 so that the priests could not stand
to minister because of the cloud; for
the glory of the LORD filled the house
of the LORD.

12 Then Solomon said,

"The LORD has set the sun in the
heavens,
but[z] has said that he would dwell
in thick darkness.
13 I have built thee an exalted house,
a place for thee to dwell in for
ever."

14 Then the king faced about, and
blessed all the assembly of Israel,
while all the assembly of Israel stood.
15 And he said, "Blessed be the LORD,
the God of Israel, who with his hand
has fulfilled what he promised with
his mouth to David my father, saying,
16 'Since the day that I brought my
people Israel out of Egypt, I chose no
city in all the tribes of Israel in which
to build a house, that my name might
be there; but I chose David to be over
my people Israel.' 17 Now it was in
the heart of David my father to build
a house for the name of the LORD,
the God of Israel. 18 But the LORD
said to David my father, 'Whereas it
was in your heart to build a house for
my name, you did well that it was in
your heart; 19 nevertheless you shall
not build the house, but your son who
shall be born to you shall build the
house for my name.' 20 Now the LORD
has fulfilled his promise which he
made; for I have risen in the place of
David my father, and sit on the throne
of Israel, as the LORD promised, and
I have built the house for the name of
the LORD, the God of Israel. 21 And
there I have provided a place for the
ark, in which is the covenant of the
LORD which he made with our fathers,
when he brought them out of the land
of Egypt."

22 Then Solomon stood before the
altar of the LORD in the presence of
all the assembly of Israel, and spread
forth his hands toward heaven; 23 and
said, "O LORD, God of Israel, there
is no God like thee, in heaven above
or on earth beneath, keeping covenant
and showing steadfast love to thy
servants who walk before thee with all
their heart; 24 who hast kept with thy
servant David my father what thou
didst declare to him; yea, thou didst
speak with thy mouth, and with thy
hand hast fulfilled it this day. 25 Now

[z] Gk: Heb lacks *has set the sun in the heavens, but*

8.1-6: Rev 11.19. 8.10-11: 2 Chron 5.13-14; Rev 15.8. 8.12-50: 2 Chron 6.1-39.

therefore, O LORD, God of Israel, keep
with thy servant David my father what
thou hast promised him, saying,
'There shall never fail you a man
before me to sit upon the throne of
Israel, if only your sons take heed to
their way, to walk before me as you
have walked before me.' 26 Now therefore, O God of Israel, let thy word be
confirmed, which thou hast spoken to
thy servant David my father.
27 "But will God indeed dwell on
the earth? Behold, heaven and the
highest heaven cannot contain thee;
how much less this house which I
have built! 28 Yet have regard to the
prayer of thy servant and to his supplication, O LORD my God, hearkening
to the cry and to the prayer which thy
servant prays before thee this day;
29 that thy eyes may be open night
and day toward this house, the place
of which thou hast said, 'My name
shall be there,' that thou mayest
hearken to the prayer which thy servant offers toward this place. 30 And
hearken thou to the supplication of
thy servant and of thy people Israel,
when they pray toward this place; yea,
hear thou in heaven thy dwelling
place; and when thou hearest, forgive.
31 "If a man sins against his neighbor and is made to take an oath, and
comes and swears his oath before
thine altar in this house, 32 then hear
thou in heaven, and act, and judge
thy servants, condemning the guilty
by bringing his conduct upon his own
head, and vindicating the righteous by
rewarding him according to his righteousness.
33 "When thy people Israel are defeated before the enemy because they
have sinned against thee, if they turn
again to thee, and acknowledge thy
name, and pray and make supplication
to thee in this house; 34 then hear
thou in heaven, and forgive the sin of
thy people Israel, and bring them
again to the land which thou gavest
to their fathers.
35 "When heaven is shut up and
there is no rain because they have
sinned against thee, if they pray toward this place, and acknowledge thy
name, and turn from their sin, when
thou dost afflict them, 36 then hear
thou in heaven, and forgive the sin of
thy servants, thy people Israel, when
thou dost teach them the good way in
which they should walk; and grant
rain upon thy land, which thou hast
given to thy people as an inheritance.
37 "If there is famine in the land,
if there is pestilence or blight or mildew or locust or caterpillar; if their
enemy besieges them in any[a] of their
cities; whatever plague, whatever sickness there is; 38 whatever prayer, whatever supplication is made by any man
or by all thy people Israel, each knowing the affliction of his own heart and
stretching out his hands toward this
house; 39 then hear thou in heaven thy
dwelling place, and forgive, and act,
and render to each whose heart thou
knowest, according to all his ways (for
thou, thou only, knowest the hearts of
all the children of men); 40 that they
may fear thee all the days that they
live in the land which thou gavest to
our fathers.
41 "Likewise when a foreigner, who
is not of thy people Israel, comes from
a far country for thy name's sake 42 (for
they shall hear of thy great name, and
thy mighty hand, and of thy outstretched arm), when he comes and
prays toward this house, 43 hear thou
in heaven thy dwelling place, and do
according to all for which the foreigner
calls to thee; in order that all the
peoples of the earth may know thy
name and fear thee, as do thy people
Israel, and that they may know that
this house which I have built is called
by thy name.
44 "If thy people go out to battle
against their enemy, by whatever way
thou shalt send them, and they pray
to the LORD toward the city which
thou hast chosen and the house which
I have built for thy name, 45 then hear
thou in heaven their prayer and their
supplication, and maintain their cause.
46 "If they sin against thee—for
there is no man who does not sin—
and thou art angry with them, and
dost give them to an enemy, so that
they are carried away captive to the
land of the enemy, far off or near;
47 yet if they lay it to heart in the land
to which they have been carried captive, and repent, and make supplication to thee in the land of their captors,
saying, 'We have sinned, and have
acted perversely and wickedly'; 48 if
they repent with all their mind and
with all their heart in the land of their
enemies, who carried them captive,

[a] Gk Syr: Heb *the land*

and pray to thee toward their land,
which thou gavest to their fathers, the
city which thou hast chosen, and the
house which I have built for thy name;
49 then hear thou in heaven thy dwelling place their prayer and their supplication, and maintain their cause
50 and forgive thy people who have
sinned against thee, and all their transgressions which they have committed
against thee; and grant them compassion in the sight of those who carried
them captive, that they may have compassion on them 51 (for they are thy
people, and thy heritage, which thou
didst bring out of Egypt, from the
midst of the iron furnace). 52 Let thy
eyes be open to the supplication of
thy servant, and to the supplication of
thy people Israel, giving ear to them
whenever they call to thee. 53 For thou
didst separate them from among all
the peoples of the earth, to be thy
heritage, as thou didst declare through
Moses, thy servant, when thou didst
bring our fathers out of Egypt, O Lord
GOD."

54 Now as Solomon finished offering all this prayer and supplication to
the LORD, he arose from before the
altar of the LORD, where he had knelt
with hands outstretched toward heav-
en; 55 and he stood, and blessed all
the assembly of Israel with a loud
voice, saying, 56 "Blessed be the LORD
who has given rest to his people Israel,
according to all that he promised; not
one word has failed of all his good
promise, which he uttered by Moses
his servant. 57 The LORD our God be
with us, as he was with our fathers;
may he not leave us or forsake us;
58 that he may incline our hearts to
him, to walk in all his ways, and to
keep his commandments, his statutes,
and his ordinances, which he commanded our fathers. 59 Let these words
of mine, wherewith I have made supplication before the LORD, be near to
the LORD our God day and night, and
may he maintain the cause of his
servant, and the cause of his people
Israel, as each day requires; 60 that all
the peoples of the earth may know
that the LORD is God; there is no
other. 61 Let your heart therefore be
wholly true to the LORD our God,
walking in his statutes and keeping
his commandments, as at this day."

62 Then the king, and all Israel
with him, offered sacrifice before the
LORD. 63 Solomon offered as peace
offerings to the LORD twenty-two thousand oxen and a hundred and twenty
thousand sheep. So the king and all
the people of Israel dedicated the
house of the LORD. 64 The same day
the king consecrated the middle of the
court that was before the house of the
LORD; for there he offered the burnt
offering and the cereal offering and
the fat pieces of the peace offerings,
because the bronze altar that was before the LORD was too small to receive
the burnt offering and the cereal
offering and the fat pieces of the peace
offerings.

65 So Solomon held the feast at that
time, and all Israel with him, a great
assembly, from the entrance of Hā′-
math to the Brook of Egypt, before
the LORD our God, seven days.[b] 66 On
the eighth day he sent the people
away; and they blessed the king, and
went to their homes joyful and glad
of heart for all the goodness that the
LORD had shown to David his servant
and to Israel his people.

9 When Solomon had finished
building the house of the LORD
and the king's house and all that Solomon desired to build, 2 the LORD appeared to Solomon a second time, as
he had appeared to him at Gib′ē·ŏn.
3 And the LORD said to him, "I have
heard your prayer and your supplication, which you have made before me;
I have consecrated this house which
you have built, and put my name there
for ever; my eyes and my heart will be
there for all time. 4 And as for you, if
you will walk before me, as David
your father walked, with integrity of
heart and uprightness, doing according
to all that I have commanded you, and
keeping my statutes and my ordinances, 5 then I will establish your
royal throne over Israel for ever, as I
promised David your father, saying,
'There shall not fail you a man upon
the throne of Israel.' 6 But if you turn
aside from following me, you or your
children, and do not keep my commandments and my statutes which I
have set before you, but go and serve
other gods and worship them, 7 then
I will cut off Israel from the land
which I have given them; and the

[b] Gk: Heb *seven days and seven days, fourteen days*
8.62-66: 2 Chron 7.4-10. **9.1-9:** 2 Chron 7.11-22.

house which I have consecrated for
my name I will cast out of my sight;
and Israel will become a proverb and
a byword among all peoples. 8 And
this house will become a heap of ruins;[c]
everyone passing by it will be astonished, and will hiss; and they will say,
'Why has the LORD done thus to this
land and to this house?' 9 Then they
will say, 'Because they forsook the
LORD their God who brought their
fathers out of the land of Egypt, and
laid hold on other gods, and worshiped them and served them; therefore the LORD has brought all this evil
upon them.'"

10 At the end of twenty years, in
which Solomon had built the two
houses, the house of the LORD and
the king's house, 11 and Hiram king of
Tȳre had supplied Solomon with cedar
and cypress timber and gold, as much
as he desired, King Solomon gave to
Hiram twenty cities in the land of
Galilee. 12 But when Hiram came from
Tȳre to see the cities which Solomon
had given him, they did not please
him. 13 Therefore he said, "What kind
of cities are these which you have
given me, my brother?" So they are
called the land of Cā'bụl to this day.
14 Hiram had sent to the king one
hundred and twenty talents of gold.

15 And this is the account of the
forced labor which King Solomon
levied to build the house of the LORD
and his own house and the Mil'lō and
the wall of Jerusalem and Hā'zôr and
Mẹ·gid'dō and Gē'zẹr 16 (Pharaoh
king of Egypt had gone up and captured Gē'zẹr and burnt it with fire,
and had slain the Canaanites who
dwelt in the city, and had given it as
dowry to his daughter, Solomon's wife;
17 so Solomon rebuilt Gē'zẹr) and
Lower Beth-hō'ron 18 and Bā'ȧ·lath
and Tā'mär in the wilderness, in the
land of Judah,[d] 19 and all the store-
cities that Solomon had, and the cities
for his chariots, and the cities for his
horsemen, and whatever Solomon desired to build in Jerusalem, in Lebanon,
and in all the land of his dominion.
20 All the people who were left of the
Am'ọ·rītes, the Hit'tītes, the Per'iz-
zītes, the Hī'vītes, and the Jeb'ū·sītes,
who were not of the people of Israel—
21 their descendants who were left
after them in the land, whom the
people of Israel were unable to destroy
utterly—these Solomon made a forced
levy of slaves, and so they are to this
day. 22 But of the people of Israel
Solomon made no slaves; they were
the soldiers, they were his officials, his
commanders, his captains, his chariot
commanders and his horsemen.

23 These were the chief officers
who were over Solomon's work: five
hundred and fifty, who had charge of
the people who carried on the work.

24 But Pharaoh's daughter went up
from the city of David to her own
house which Solomon had built for
her; then he built the Mil'lō.

25 Three times a year Solomon used
to offer up burnt offerings and peace
offerings upon the altar which he built
to the LORD, burning incense[e] before
the LORD. So he finished the house.

26 King Solomon built a fleet of
ships at Ē'zi·on-gē'bẹr, which is near
Ē'loth on the shore of the Red Sea,
in the land of Ē'dọm. 27 And Hiram
sent with the fleet his servants, seamen
who were familiar with the sea, together with the servants of Solomon;
28 and they went to Ō'phīr, and
brought from there gold, to the amount
of four hundred and twenty talents;
and they brought it to King Solomon.

10 Now when the queen of Sheba
heard of the fame of Solomon
concerning the name of the LORD, she
came to test him with hard questions.
2 She came to Jerusalem with a very
great retinue, with camels bearing
spices, and very much gold, and precious stones; and when she came to
Solomon, she told him all that was on
her mind. 3 And Solomon answered all
her questions; there was nothing hidden from the king which he could not
explain to her. 4 And when the queen
of Sheba had seen all the wisdom of
Solomon, the house that he had built,
5 the food of his table, the seating of
his officials, and the attendance of his
servants, their clothing, his cupbearers, and his burnt offerings which
he offered at the house of the LORD,
there was no more spirit in her.

6 And she said to the king, "The
report was true which I heard in my
own land of your affairs and of your
wisdom, 7 but I did not believe the
reports until I came and my own eyes
had seen it; and, behold, the half was

[c] Syr Old Latin: Heb *high* [d] Heb lacks *of Judah* [e] Gk: Heb *burning incense with it which*

9.10-28: 2 Chron 8.8-18. **10.1-29:** 2 Chron 9.1-28.

not told me; your wisdom and prosperity surpass the report which I heard.
8 Happy are your wives![f] Happy are
these your servants, who continually
stand before you and hear your wisdom! 9 Blessed be the LORD your God,
who has delighted in you and set you
on the throne of Israel! Because the
LORD loved Israel for ever, he has
made you king, that you may execute
justice and righteousness." 10 Then
she gave the king a hundred and
twenty talents of gold, and a very great
quantity of spices, and precious stones;
never again came such an abundance
of spices as these which the queen of
Sheba gave to King Solomon.

11 Moreover the fleet of Hiram,
which brought gold from Ō'phīr,
brought from Ophir a very great
amount of almug wood and precious
stones. 12 And the king made of the
almug wood supports for the house of
the LORD, and for the king's house,
lyres also and harps for the singers;
no such almug wood has come or been
seen, to this day.

13 And King Solomon gave to the
queen of Sheba all that she desired,
whatever she asked besides what was
given her by the bounty of King Solomon. So she turned and went back to
her own land, with her servants.

14 Now the weight of gold that
came to Solomon in one year was six
hundred and sixty-six talents of gold,
15 besides that which came from the
traders and from the traffic of the
merchants, and from all the kings of
Arabia and from the governors of the
land. 16 King Solomon made two hundred large shields of beaten gold; six
hundred shekels of gold went into each
shield. 17 And he made three hundred
shields of beaten gold; three minas of
gold went into each shield; and the
king put them in the House of the
Forest of Lebanon. 18 The king also
made a great ivory throne, and overlaid
it with the finest gold. 19 The throne
had six steps, and at the back of the
throne was a calf's head, and on each
side of the seat were arm rests and
two lions standing beside the arm rests,
20 while twelve lions stood there, one
on each end of a step on the six steps.
The like of it was never made in any
kingdom. 21 All King Solomon's drinking vessels were of gold, and all vessels
of the House of the Forest of Lebanon
were of pure gold; none were of silver,
it was not considered as anything in
the days of Solomon. 22 For the king
had a fleet of ships of Tär'shish at sea
with the fleet of Hiram. Once every
three years the fleet of ships of Tarshish used to come bringing gold,
silver, ivory, apes, and peacocks.[g]

23 Thus King Solomon excelled all
the kings of the earth in riches and in
wisdom. 24 And the whole earth sought
the presence of Solomon to hear his
wisdom, which God had put into his
mind. 25 Every one of them brought
his present, articles of silver and gold,
garments, myrrh, spices, horses, and
mules, so much year by year.

26 And Solomon gathered together
chariots and horsemen; he had fourteen hundred chariots and twelve
thousand horsemen, whom he stationed in the chariot cities and with
the king in Jerusalem. 27 And the king
made silver as common in Jerusalem
as stone, and he made cedar as plentiful as the sycamore of the She·phē'-
lȧh. 28 And Solomon's import of horses
was from Egypt and Kü'e, and the
king's traders received them from Kue
at a price. 29 A chariot could be imported from Egypt for six hundred
shekels of silver, and a horse for a
hundred and fifty; and so through the
king's traders they were exported to
all the kings of the Hit'tītes and the
kings of Syria.

11 Now King Solomon loved many
foreign women: the daughter of
Pharaoh, and Mō'ȧb·īte, Am'mȯ·nīte,
Ē'dȯm·īte, Sī·dō'ni·ȧn, and Hit'tīte
women, 2 from the nations concerning
which the LORD had said to the people
of Israel, "You shall not enter into
marriage with them, neither shall they
with you, for surely they will turn
away your heart after their gods";
Solomon clung to these in love. 3 He
had seven hundred wives, princesses,
and three hundred concubines; and
his wives turned away his heart. 4 For
when Solomon was old his wives
turned away his heart after other gods;
and his heart was not wholly true to
the LORD his God, as was the heart
of David his father. 5 For Solomon
went after Ash'tō·reth the goddess of
the Sī·dō'ni·ȧnṡ, and after Mil'com
the abomination of the Am'mȯ·nītes.
6 So Solomon did what was evil in the
sight of the LORD, and did not wholly

[f] Gk Syr: Heb *men* [g] Or *baboons*

follow the LORD, as David his father
had done. 7 Then Solomon built a
high place for Chē'mosh the abomination of Mō'ab, and for Mō'lech the
abomination of the Am'mȯ·nītes, on
the mountain east of Jerusalem. 8 And
so he did for all his foreign wives, who
burned incense and sacrificed to their
gods.

9 And the LORD was angry with
Solomon, because his heart had turned
away from the LORD, the God of Israel,
who had appeared to him twice, 10 and
had commanded him concerning this
thing, that he should not go after
other gods; but he did not keep what
the LORD commanded. 11 Therefore
the LORD said to Solomon, "Since this
has been your mind and you have not
kept my covenant and my statutes
which I have commanded you, I will
surely tear the kingdom from you and
will give it to your servant. 12 Yet for
the sake of David your father I will
not do it in your days, but I will tear
it out of the hand of your son. 13 However I will not tear away all the kingdom; but I will give one tribe to your
son, for the sake of David my servant
and for the sake of Jerusalem which I
have chosen."

14 And the LORD raised up an adversary against Solomon, Hā'dad the
Ē'dȯm·īte; he was of the royal house
in Ē'dȯm. 15 For when David was in
Ē'dȯm, and Jō'ab the commander of
the army went up to bury the slain,
he slew every male in Edom 16 (for
Jō'ab and all Israel remained there six
months, until he had cut off every
male in Ē'dȯm); 17 but Hā'dad fled to
Egypt, together with certain Ē'dȯm-
ītes of his father's servants, Hadad
being yet a little child. 18 They set
out from Mid'i·ȧn and came to Pâr'an,
and took men with them from Paran
and came to Egypt, to Pharaoh king
of Egypt, who gave him a house, and
assigned him an allowance of food,
and gave him land. 19 And Hā'dad
found great favor in the sight of Pharaoh, so that he gave him in marriage
the sister of his own wife, the sister
of Täh'pė·nēs the queen. 20 And the
sister of Täh'pė·nēs bore him Gė·nū'-
bȧth his son, whom Tahpenes weaned
in Pharaoh's house; and Genubath was
in Pharaoh's house among the sons of
Pharaoh. 21 But when Hā'dad heard
in Egypt that David slept with his
fathers and that Jō'ab the commander
of the army was dead, Hadad said to
Pharaoh, "Let me depart, that I may
go to my own country." 22 But Pharaoh said to him, "What have you lacked
with me that you are now seeking to
go to your own country?" And he said
to him, "Only let me go."

23 God also raised up as an adversary to him, Rē'zon the son of Ē·lī'ȧ·dȧ,
who had fled from his master Hā'dad-
ē'zėr king of Zō'bȧh. 24 And he gathered men about him and became leader
of a marauding band, after the slaughter by David; and they went to Damascus, and dwelt there, and made
him king in Damascus. 25 He was an
adversary of Israel all the days of
Solomon, doing mischief as Hā'dad
did; and he abhorred Israel, and
reigned over Syria.

26 Jer·ȯ·bō'ȧm the son of Nē'bat,
an Ē'phrȧ·im·īte of Zer'ė·dȧh, a servant
of Solomon, whose mother's name was
Zė·rü'ȧh, a widow, also lifted up his
hand against the king. 27 And this was
the reason why he lifted up his hand
against the king. Solomon built the
Mil'lō, and closed up the breach of the
city of David his father. 28 The man
Jer·ȯ·bō'ȧm was very able, and when
Solomon saw that the young man was
industrious he gave him charge over
all the forced labor of the house of
Joseph. 29 And at that time, when Jer-
ȯ·bō'ȧm went out of Jerusalem, the
prophet Ȧ·hī'jȧh the Shī'lȯ·nīte found
him on the road. Now Ahijah had clad
himself with a new garment; and the
two of them were alone in the open
country. 30 Then Ȧ·hī'jȧh laid hold of
the new garment that was on him, and
tore it into twelve pieces. 31 And he said
to Jer·ȯ·bō'ȧm, "Take for yourself ten
pieces; for thus says the LORD, the God
of Israel, 'Behold, I am about to tear
the kingdom from the hand of Solomon,
and will give you ten tribes 32 (but he
shall have one tribe, for the sake of
my servant David and for the sake of
Jerusalem, the city which I have
chosen out of all the tribes of Israel),
33 because he has[h] forsaken me, and
worshiped Ash'tō·reth the goddess of
the Sī·dō'ni·ȧns, Chē'mosh the god of
Mō'ab, and Mil'com the god of the
Am'mȯ·nītes, and has[h] not walked in
my ways, doing what is right in my
sight and keeping my statutes and my
ordinances, as David his father did.

[h] Gk Syr Vg: Heb *they have*

34 Nevertheless I will not take the
whole kingdom out of his hand; but I
will make him ruler all the days of his
life, for the sake of David my servant
whom I chose, who kept my commandments and my statutes; 35 but I
will take the kingdom out of his son's
hand, and will give it to you, ten
tribes. 36 Yet to his son I will give one
tribe, that David my servant may
always have a lamp before me in Jerusalem, the city where I have chosen
to put my name. 37 And I will take you,
and you shall reign over all that your
soul desires, and you shall be king
over Israel. 38 And if you will hearken
to all that I command you, and will
walk in my ways, and do what is right
in my eyes by keeping my statutes and
my commandments, as David my
servant did, I will be with you, and
will build you a sure house, as I built
for David, and I will give Israel to
you. 39 And I will for this afflict the
descendants of David, but not for
ever.' " 40 Solomon sought therefore
to kill Jer·o·bō'am; but Jeroboam
arose, and fled into Egypt, to Shī'shak
king of Egypt, and was in Egypt until
the death of Solomon.

41 Now the rest of the acts of Solomon, and all that he did, and his
wisdom, are they not written in the
book of the acts of Solomon? 42 And
the time that Solomon reigned in
Jerusalem over all Israel was forty
years. 43 And Solomon slept with his
fathers, and was buried in the city of
David his father; and Rē·ho·bō'am his
son reigned in his stead.

12 Rē·ho·bō'am went to Shē'chem,
for all Israel had come to Shechem to make him king. 2 And when
Jer·o·bō'am the son of Nē'bat heard
of it (for he was still in Egypt, whither
he had fled from King Solomon), then
Jeroboam returned from[i] Egypt. 3 And
they sent and called him; and Jer·o-
bō'am and all the assembly of Israel
came and said to Rē·ho·bō'am, 4 "Your
father made our yoke heavy. Now
therefore lighten the hard service of
your father and his heavy yoke upon
us, and we will serve you." 5 He said
to them, "Depart for three days, then
come again to me." So the people
went away.

6 Then King Rē·ho·bō'am took
counsel with the old men, who had
stood before Solomon his father while
he was yet alive, saying, "How do you
advise me to answer this people?"
7 And they said to him, "If you will
be a servant to this people today and
serve them, and speak good words to
them when you answer them, then
they will be your servants for ever."
8 But he forsook the counsel which
the old men gave him, and took counsel with the young men who had
grown up with him and stood before
him. 9 And he said to them, "What do
you advise that we answer this people
who have said to me, 'Lighten the
yoke that your father put upon us'?"
10 And the young men who had grown
up with him said to him, "Thus shall
you speak to this people who said to
you, 'Your father made our yoke
heavy, but do you lighten it for us';
thus shall you say to them, 'My little
finger is thicker than my father's loins.
11 And now, whereas my father laid
upon you a heavy yoke, I will add to
your yoke. My father chastised you
with whips, but I will chastise you
with scorpions.' "

12 So Jer·o·bō'am and all the people
came to Rē·ho·bō'am the third day, as
the king said, "Come to me again the
third day." 13 And the king answered
the people harshly, and forsaking the
counsel which the old men had given
him, 14 he spoke to them according to
the counsel of the young men, saying,
"My father made your yoke heavy,
but I will add to your yoke; my father
chastised you with whips, but I will
chastise you with scorpions." 15 So
the king did not hearken to the people;
for it was a turn of affairs brought
about by the LORD that he might fulfil
his word, which the LORD spoke by
A·hī'jah the Shī'lo·nīte to Jer·o·bō'am
the son of Nē'bat.

16 And when all Israel saw that the
king did not hearken to them, the
people answered the king,

"What portion have we in David?
We have no inheritance in the son
of Jesse.
To your tents, O Israel!
Look now to your own house,
David."

So Israel departed to their tents. 17 But
Rē·ho·bō'am reigned over the people
of Israel who dwelt in the cities of
Judah. 18 Then King Rē·ho·bō'am sent

[i] Gk Vg Compare 2 Chron 10.2: Heb *dwelt in*

11.42-43: 2 Chron 9.30-31. **12.1-19:** 2 Chron 10.1-19.

Ȧ·dō'ràm, who was taskmaster over
the forced labor, and all Israel stoned
him to death with stones. And King
Rehoboam made haste to mount his
chariot, to flee to Jerusalem. 19 So
Israel has been in rebellion against the
house of David to this day. 20 And
when all Israel heard that Jer·ȯ·bō'àm
had returned, they sent and called him
to the assembly and made him king
over all Israel. There was none that
followed the house of David, but the
tribe of Judah only.

21 When Rē·hȯ·bō'àm came to Jerusalem, he assembled all the house
of Judah, and the tribe of Benjamin,
a hundred and eighty thousand chosen
warriors, to fight against the house of
Israel, to restore the kingdom to Rehoboam the son of Solomon. 22 But the
word of God came to She·māi'àh the
man of God: 23 "Say to Rē·hȯ·bō'àm
the son of Solomon, king of Judah,
and to all the house of Judah and Benjamin, and to the rest of the people,
24 'Thus says the LORD, You shall not
go up or fight against your kinsmen
the people of Israel. Return every man
to his home, for this thing is from
me.'" So they hearkened to the word
of the LORD, and went home again,
according to the word of the LORD.

25 Then Jer·ȯ·bō'àm built Shē'-
chem in the hill country of Ē'phrȧ·im,
and dwelt there; and he went out from
there and built Pė·nū'el. 26 And Jer·ȯ-
bō'àm said in his heart, "Now the
kingdom will turn back to the house
of David; 27 if this people go up to
offer sacrifices in the house of the
LORD at Jerusalem, then the heart of
this people will turn again to their
lord, to Rē·hȯ·bō'àm king of Judah,
and they will kill me and return to
Rehoboam king of Judah." 28 So the
king took counsel, and made two calves
of gold. And he said to the people,
"You have gone up to Jerusalem long
enough. Behold your gods, O Israel,
who brought you up out of the land
of Egypt." 29 And he set one in Beth'ĕl,
and the other he put in Dan. 30 And
this thing became a sin, for the people
went to the one at Beth'ĕl and to the
other as far as Dan.[j] 31 He also made
houses on high places, and appointed
priests from among all the people, who
were not of the Levites. 32 And Jer·ȯ-
bō'àm appointed a feast on the fifteenth day of the eighth month like
the feast that was in Judah, and he
offered sacrifices upon the altar; so he
did in Beth'ĕl, sacrificing to the calves
that he had made. And he placed in
Bethel the priests of the high places
that he had made. 33 He went up to
the altar which he had made in Beth'ĕl
on the fifteenth day in the eighth
month, in the month which he had
devised of his own heart; and he ordained a feast for the people of Israel,
and went up to the altar to burn
incense.

13 And behold, a man of God came
out of Judah by the word of the
LORD to Beth'ĕl. Jer·ȯ·bō'àm was
standing by the altar to burn incense.
2 And the man cried against the altar
by the word of the LORD, and said,
"O altar, altar, thus says the LORD:
'Behold, a son shall be born to the
house of David, Jō·sī'àh by name; and
he shall sacrifice upon you the priests
of the high places who burn incense
upon you, and men's bones shall be
burned upon you.'" 3 And he gave a
sign the same day, saying, "This is the
sign that the LORD has spoken: 'Behold, the altar shall be torn down, and
the ashes that are upon it shall be
poured out.'" 4 And when the king
heard the saying of the man of God,
which he cried against the altar at
Beth'ĕl, Jer·ȯ·bō'àm stretched out his
hand from the altar, saying, "Lay hold
of him." And his hand, which he
stretched out against him, dried up,
so that he could not draw it back to
himself. 5 The altar also was torn
down, and the ashes poured out from
the altar, according to the sign which
the man of God had given by the word
of the LORD. 6 And the king said to
the man of God, "Entreat now the
favor of the LORD your God, and pray
for me, that my hand may be restored
to me." And the man of God entreated
the LORD; and the king's hand was
restored to him, and became as it was
before. 7 And the king said to the man
of God, "Come home with me, and
refresh yourself, and I will give you a
reward." 8 And the man of God said
to the king, "If you give me half your
house, I will not go in with you. And
I will not eat bread or drink water in
this place; 9 for so was it commanded
me by the word of the LORD, saying,

[j] Gk: Heb *went to the one as far as Dan*
12.22-24: 2 Chron 11.1-4.

'You shall neither eat bread, nor drink
water, nor return by the way that you
came.' " 10 So he went another way,
and did not return by the way that he
came to Beth'ĕl.
11 Now there dwelt an old prophet
in Beth'ĕl. And his sons[k] came and
told him all that the man of God had
done that day in Bethel; the words
also which he had spoken to the king,
they told to their father. 12And their
father said to them, "Which way did
he go?" And his sons showed him the
way which the man of God who came
from Judah had gone. 13And he said
to his sons, "Saddle the ass for me."
So they saddled the ass for him and
he mounted it. 14And he went after
the man of God, and found him sitting
under an oak; and he said to him,
"Are you the man of God who came
from Judah?" And he said, "I am."
15 Then he said to him, "Come home
with me and eat bread." 16And he said,
"I may not return with you, or go in
with you; neither will I eat bread nor
drink water with you in this place;
17 for it was said to me by the word
of the LORD, 'You shall neither eat
bread nor drink water there, nor return
by the way that you came.' " 18And
he said to him, "I also am a prophet
as you are, and an angel spoke to me
by the word of the LORD, saying,
'Bring him back with you into your
house that he may eat bread and drink
water.' " But he lied to him. 19 So he
went back with him, and ate bread in
his house, and drank water.
20 And as they sat at the table, the
word of the LORD came to the prophet
who had brought him back; 21 and he
cried to the man of God who came
from Judah, "Thus says the LORD,
'Because you have disobeyed the word
of the LORD, and have not kept the
commandment which the LORD your
God commanded you, 22 but have
come back, and have eaten bread and
drunk water in the place of which he
said to you, "Eat no bread, and drink
no water"; your body shall not come
to the tomb of your fathers.' " 23And
after he had eaten bread and drunk,
he saddled the ass for the prophet
whom he had brought back. 24And as
he went away a lion met him on the
road and killed him. And his body was
thrown in the road, and the ass stood
beside it; the lion also stood beside
the body. 25And behold, men passed
by, and saw the body thrown in the
road, and the lion standing by the
body. And they came and told it in
the city where the old prophet dwelt.
26 And when the prophet who had
brought him back from the way heard
of it, he said, "It is the man of God,
who disobeyed the word of the LORD;
therefore the LORD has given him to
the lion, which has torn him and slain
him, according to the word which the
LORD spoke to him." 27And he said
to his sons, "Saddle the ass for me."
And they saddled it. 28And he went
and found his body thrown in the
road, and the ass and the lion standing
beside the body. The lion had not
eaten the body or torn the ass. 29And
the prophet took up the body of the
man of God and laid it upon the ass,
and brought it back to the city,[l] to
mourn and to bury him. 30And he laid
the body in his own grave; and they
mourned over him, saying, "Alas, my
brother!" 31And after he had buried
him, he said to his sons, "When I die,
bury me in the grave in which the
man of God is buried; lay my bones
beside his bones. 32 For the saying
which he cried by the word of the
LORD against the altar in Beth'ĕl, and
against all the houses of the high
places which are in the cities of Sȧ-
mâr'i·ȧ, shall surely come to pass."
33 After this thing Jer·ȯ·bō'ăm did
not turn from his evil way, but made
priests for the high places again from
among all the people; any who would,
he consecrated to be priests of the
high places. 34And this thing became
sin to the house of Jer·ȯ·bō'ăm, so as
to cut it off and to destroy it from the
face of the earth.

14 At that time Ȧ·bī'jȧh the son of
Jer·ȯ·bō'ăm fell sick. 2And Jer·ȯ-
bō'ăm said to his wife, "Arise, and
disguise yourself, that it be not known
that you are the wife of Jeroboam,
and go to Shī'lōh; behold, Ȧ·hī'jȧh the
prophet is there, who said of me that
I should be king over this people.
3 Take with you ten loaves, some
cakes, and a jar of honey, and go to
him; he will tell you what shall happen
to the child."
4 Jer·ȯ·bō'ăm's wife did so; she
arose, and went to Shī'lōh, and came
to the house of Ȧ·hī'jȧh. Now Ahijah
could not see, for his eyes were dim

[k] Gk Syr Vg: Heb *son* [l] Gk: Heb *he came to the city of the old prophet*

because of his age. 5And the LORD
said to A·hī'jah, "Behold, the wife of
Jer·o·bō'am is coming to inquire of
you concerning her son; for he is
sick. Thus and thus shall you say to
her."

When she came, she pretended to
be another woman. 6 But when A·hī'jah
heard the sound of her feet, as she
came in at the door, he said, "Come
in, wife of Jer·o·bō'am; why do you
pretend to be another? For I am
charged with heavy tidings for you.
7 Go, tell Jer·o·bō'am, 'Thus says the
LORD, the God of Israel: "Because I
exalted you from among the people,
and made you leader over my people
Israel, 8 and tore the kingdom away
from the house of David and gave it
to you; and yet you have not been like
my servant David, who kept my commandments, and followed me with all
his heart, doing only that which was
right in my eyes, 9 but you have done
evil above all that were before you and
have gone and made for yourself other
gods, and molten images, provoking
me to anger, and have cast me behind
your back; 10 therefore behold, I will
bring evil upon the house of Jer·o-
bō'am, and will cut off from Jeroboam
every male, both bond and free in
Israel, and will utterly consume the
house of Jeroboam, as a man burns
up dung until it is all gone. 11Any one
belonging to Jer·o·bō'am who dies in
the city the dogs shall eat; and any one
who dies in the open country the birds
of the air shall eat; for the LORD has
spoken it." ' 12Arise therefore, go to
your house. When your feet enter the
city, the child shall die. 13And all Israel
shall mourn for him, and bury him;
for he only of Jer·o·bō'am shall come
to the grave, because in him there is
found something pleasing to the LORD,
the God of Israel, in the house of
Jeroboam. 14 Moreover the LORD will
raise up for himself a king over Israel,
who shall cut off the house of Jer·o-
bō'am today. And henceforth[m] 15 the
LORD will smite Israel, as a reed is
shaken in the water, and root up Israel
out of this good land which he gave
to their fathers, and scatter them beyond the Eū·phrā'tēs, because they
have made their A·shē'rim, provoking
the LORD to anger. 16And he will give
Israel up because of the sins of Jer·o-
bō'am, which he sinned and which he
made Israel to sin."

17 Then Jer·o·bō'am's wife arose,
and departed, and came to Tīr'zah.
And as she came to the threshold of
the house, the child died. 18And all
Israel buried him and mourned for
him, according to the word of the
LORD, which he spoke by his servant
A·hī'jah the prophet. 19 Now the rest
of the acts of Jer·o·bō'am, how he
warred and how he reigned, behold,
they are written in the Book of the
Chronicles of the Kings of Israel.
20And the time that Jer·o·bō'am
reigned was twenty-two years; and he
slept with his fathers, and Nā'dab his
son reigned in his stead.

21 Now Rē·ho·bō'am the son of
Solomon reigned in Judah. Rehoboam
was forty-one years old when he began
to reign, and he reigned seventeen
years in Jerusalem, the city which the
LORD had chosen out of all the tribes
of Israel, to put his name there. His
mother's name was Nā'a·mah the Am'-
mo·nīt·ess. 22And Judah did what was
evil in the sight of the LORD, and they
provoked him to jealousy with their
sins which they committed, more than
all that their fathers had done. 23 For
they also built for themselves high
places, and pillars, and A·shē'rim on
every high hill and under every green
tree; 24 and there were also male cult
prostitutes in the land. They did
according to all the abominations of
the nations which the LORD drove out
before the people of Israel.

25 In the fifth year of King Rē·ho-
bō'am, Shī'shak king of Egypt came
up against Jerusalem; 26 he took away
the treasures of the house of the LORD
and the treasures of the king's house;
he took away everything. He also took
away all the shields of gold which
Solomon had made; 27 and King Rē-
ho·bō'am made in their stead shields
of bronze, and committed them to the
hands of the officers of the guard, who
kept the door of the king's house.
28And as often as the king went into
the house of the LORD, the guard bore
them and brought them back to the
guardroom.

29 Now the rest of the acts of Rē-
ho·bō'am, and all that he did, are they
not written in the Book of the Chronicles of the Kings of Judah? 30And

[m] Heb obscure
14.25-31: 2 Chron 12.1-16.

there was war between Rē·hŏ·bō'ăm
and Jer·ŏ·bō'ăm continually. 31 And
Rē·hŏ·bō'ăm slept with his fathers and
was buried with his fathers in the
city of David. His mother's name
was Nā'ă·măh the Am'mŏ·nīt·ĕss.
And Ă·bī'jăm his son reigned in his
stead.

15 Now in the eighteenth year of
King Jer·ŏ·bō'ăm the son of
Nē'bat, Ă·bī'jăm began to reign over
Judah. 2 He reigned for three years in
Jerusalem. His mother's name was
Mā'ă·căh the daughter of Ă·bish'ă·lom.
3 And he walked in all the sins which
his father did before him; and his
heart was not wholly true to the LORD
his God, as the heart of David his
father. 4 Nevertheless for David's sake
the LORD his God gave him a lamp
in Jerusalem, setting up his son after
him, and establishing Jerusalem; 5 because David did what was right in the
eyes of the LORD, and did not turn
aside from anything that he commanded him all the days of his life,
except in the matter of Ū·rī'ăh the
Hit'tite. 6 Now there was war between
Rē·hŏ·bō'ăm and Jer·ŏ·bō'ăm all the
days of his life. 7 The rest of the acts
of Ă·bī'jăm, and all that he did, are
they not written in the Book of the
Chronicles of the Kings of Judah? And
there was war between Ă·bī'jăm and
Jer·ŏ·bō'ăm. 8 And Ă·bī'jăm slept with
his fathers; and they buried him in
the city of David. And Asa his son
reigned in his stead.

9 In the twentieth year of Jer·ŏ·
bō'ăm king of Israel Asa began to
reign over Judah, 10 and he reigned
forty-one years in Jerusalem. His
mother's name was Mā'ă·căh the
daughter of Ă·bish'ă·lom. 11 And Asa
did what was right in the eyes of the
LORD, as David his father had done.
12 He put away the male cult prostitutes out of the land, and removed all
the idols that his fathers had made.
13 He also removed Mā'ă·căh his
mother from being queen mother because she had an abominable image
made for Ă·shē'răh; and Asa cut down
her image and burned it at the brook
Kid'rŏn. 14 But the high places were
not taken away. Nevertheless the heart
of Asa was wholly true to the LORD all
his days. 15 And he brought into the
house of the LORD the votive gifts of
his father and his own votive gifts,
silver, and gold, and vessels.

16 And there was war between Asa
and Bā'ă·shă king of Israel all their
days. 17 Bā'ă·shă king of Israel went
up against Judah, and built Rā'măh,
that he might permit no one to go out
or come in to Asa king of Judah.
18 Then Asa took all the silver and the
gold that were left in the treasures of
the house of the LORD and the treasures
of the king's house, and gave them into
the hands of his servants; and King
Asa sent them to Ben-hā'dad the son
of Tab·rim'mon, the son of Hē'zi-on,
king of Syria, who dwelt in Damascus,
saying, 19 "Let there be a league between me and you, as between my
father and your father: behold, I am
sending to you a present of silver and
gold; go, break your league with Bā'ă-
shă king of Israel, that he may withdraw from me." 20 And Ben-hā'dad
hearkened to King Asa, and sent the
commanders of his armies against the
cities of Israel, and conquered Ī'jon,
Dan, Ā'bĕl-beth-mā'ă·căh, and all
Chin'nĕ·roth, with all the land of
Naph'tă·lī. 21 And when Bā'ă·shă
heard of it, he stopped building Rā'-
măh, and he dwelt in Tīr'zăh. 22 Then
King Asa made a proclamation to all
Judah, none was exempt, and they
carried away the stones of Rā'măh and
its timber, with which Bā'ă·shă had
been building; and with them King
Asa built Gē'bă of Benjamin and
Miz'păh. 23 Now the rest of all the
acts of Asa, all his might, and all that
he did, and the cities which he built,
are they not written in the Book of the
Chronicles of the Kings of Judah? But
in his old age he was diseased in his
feet. 24 And Asa slept with his fathers,
and was buried with his fathers in the
city of David his father; and Je·hosh'ă-
phat his son reigned in his stead.

25 Nā'dab the son of Jer·ŏ·bō'ăm
began to reign over Israel in the second
year of Asa king of Judah; and he
reigned over Israel two years. 26 He
did what was evil in the sight of the
LORD, and walked in the way of his
father, and in his sin which he made
Israel to sin.

27 Bā'ă·shă the son of Ă·hī'jăh, of
the house of Is'să·chăr, conspired
against him; and Bā'ă·shă struck him
down at Gib'bĕ·thon, which belonged

15.1-2, 7: 2 Chron 13.1-2. **15.8-12:** 2 Chron 14.1-5. **15.13-22:** 2 Chron 15.16-16.6.
15.23-24: 2 Chron 16.12-14. **15.24:** 2 Chron 17.1.

to the Philistines; for Nā'dab and all
Israel were laying siege to Gibbethon.
28 So Bā'ȧ·shȧ killed him in the third
year of Asa king of Judah, and reigned
in his stead. 29And as soon as he was
king, he killed all the house of Jer·ȯ-
bō'ȧm; he left to the house of Jeroboam
not one that breathed, until he had
destroyed it, according to the word of
the LORD which he spoke by his
servant Ȧ·hī'jȧh the Shī'lȯ·nīte; 30 it
was for the sins of Jer·ȯ·bō'ȧm which
he sinned and which he made Israel
to sin, and because of the anger to
which he provoked the LORD, the God
of Israel.

31 Now the rest of the acts of Nā'-
dab, and all that he did, are they not
written in the Book of the Chronicles
of the Kings of Israel? 32And there was
war between Asa and Bā'ȧ·shȧ king of
Israel all their days.

33 In the third year of Asa king of
Judah, Bā'ȧ·shȧ the son of Ȧ·hī'jȧh
began to reign over all Israel at Tīr'zȧh,
and reigned twenty-four years. 34 He
did what was evil in the sight of the
LORD, and walked in the way of
Jer·ȯ·bō'ȧm and in his sin which he
made Israel to sin.

16 And the word of the LORD came
to Jē'hū the son of Hȧ·nā'nī
against Bā'ȧ·shȧ, saying, 2 "Since I
exalted you out of the dust and made
you leader over my people Israel, and
you have walked in the way of Jer·ȯ-
bō'ȧm, and have made my people
Israel to sin, provoking me to anger
with their sins, 3 behold, I will utterly
sweep away Bā'ȧ·shȧ and his house,
and I will make your house like the
house of Jer·ȯ·bō'ȧm the son of Nē'bat.
4Any one belonging to Bā'ȧ·shȧ who
dies in the city the dogs shall eat; and
any one of his who dies in the field the
birds of the air shall eat."

5 Now the rest of the acts of Bā'ȧ-
shȧ, and what he did, and his might,
are they not written in the Book of
the Chronicles of the Kings of Israel?
6And Bā'ȧ·shȧ slept with his fathers,
and was buried at Tīr'zȧh; and Ē'lȧh
his son reigned in his stead. 7 Moreover the word of the LORD came by
the prophet Jē'hū the son of Hȧ·nā'nī
against Bā'ȧ·shȧ and his house, both
because of all the evil that he did in
the sight of the LORD, provoking him
to anger with the work of his hands,
in being like the house of Jer·ȯ·bō'ȧm,
and also because he destroyed it.

8 In the twenty-sixth year of Asa
king of Judah, Ē'lȧh the son of Bā'ȧ-
shȧ began to reign over Israel in Tīr'-
zȧh, and reigned two years. 9 But his
servant Zim'rī, commander of half his
chariots, conspired against him. When
he was at Tīr'zȧh, drinking himself
drunk in the house of Är'zȧ, who was
over the household in Tirzah, 10 Zim'rī
came in and struck him down and
killed him, in the twenty-seventh year
of Asa king of Judah, and reigned in
his stead.

11 When he began to reign, as soon
as he had seated himself on his throne,
he killed all the house of Bā'ȧ·shȧ; he
did not leave him a single male of his
kinsmen or his friends. 12 Thus Zim'rī
destroyed all the house of Bā'ȧ·shȧ,
according to the word of the LORD,
which he spoke against Baasha by
Jē'hū the prophet, 13 for all the sins of
Bā'ȧ·shȧ and the sins of Ē'lȧh his son
which they sinned, and which they
made Israel to sin, provoking the LORD
God of Israel to anger with their idols.
14 Now the rest of the acts of Ē'lȧh,
and all that he did, are they not written
in the Book of the Chronicles of the
Kings of Israel?

15 In the twenty-seventh year of
Asa king of Judah, Zim'rī reigned seven
days in Tīr'zȧh. Now the troops were
encamped against Gib'bė·thon, which
belonged to the Philistines, 16 and the
troops who were encamped heard it
said, "Zim'rī has conspired, and he
has killed the king"; therefore all Israel
made Om'rī, the commander of the
army, king over Israel that day in the
camp. 17 So Om'rī went up from
Gib'bė·thon, and all Israel with him,
and they besieged Tīr'zȧh. 18And when
Zim'rī saw that the city was taken, he
went into the citadel of the king's
house, and burned the king's house
over him with fire, and died, 19 because
of his sins which he committed, doing
evil in the sight of the LORD, walking
in the way of Jer·ȯ·bō'ȧm, and for his
sin which he committed, making Israel
to sin. 20 Now the rest of the acts of
Zim'rī, and the conspiracy which he
made, are they not written in the
Book of the Chronicles of the Kings
of Israel?

21 Then the people of Israel were
divided into two parts; half of the
people followed Tib'nī the son of
Gī'nath, to make him king, and half
followed Om'rī. 22 But the people who

followed Om′rī overcame the people
who followed Tib′nī the son of
Gī′nath; so Tibni died, and Omri became king. 23 In the thirty-first year of
Asa king of Judah, Om′rī began to reign
over Israel, and reigned for twelve
years; six years he reigned in Tīr′zȧh.
24 He bought the hill of Sȧ·mâr′i·ȧ
from Shē′mėr for two talents of silver;
and he fortified the hill, and called
the name of the city which he built,
Samaria, after the name of Shemer,
the owner of the hill.
25 Om′rī did what was evil in the
sight of the LORD, and did more evil
than all who were before him. 26 For
he walked in all the way of Jer·ȯ·bō′ȧm
the son of Nē′bat, and in the sins which
he made Israel to sin, provoking the
LORD, the God of Israel, to anger by
their idols. 27 Now the rest of the acts
of Om′rī which he did, and the might
that he showed, are they not written
in the Book of the Chronicles of the
Kings of Israel? 28 And Om′rī slept
with his fathers, and was buried in
Sȧ·mâr′i·ȧ; and Ā′hab his son reigned
in his stead.
29 In the thirty-eighth year of Asa
king of Judah, Ā′hab the son of Om′rī
began to reign over Israel, and Ahab
the son of Omri reigned over Israel in
Sȧ·mâr′i·ȧ twenty-two years. 30 And
Ā′hab the son of Om′rī did evil in the
sight of the LORD more than all that
were before him. 31 And as if it had
been a light thing for him to walk in
the sins of Jer·ȯ·bō′ȧm the son of
Nē′bat, he took for wife Jez′ė·bėl the
daughter of Eth·bā′ȧl king of the
Sī·dō′ni·ȧns, and went and served
Bā′ȧl, and worshiped him. 32 He
erected an altar for Bā′ȧl in the house
of Baal, which he built in Sȧ·mâr′i·ȧ.
33 And Ā′hab made an Ȧ·shē′rȧh. Ahab
did more to provoke the LORD, the
God of Israel, to anger than all the
kings of Israel who were before him.
34 In his days Hī′ėl of Beth′ėl built
Jericho; he laid its foundation at the
cost of Ȧ·bī′rȧm his first-born, and set
up its gates at the cost of his youngest
son Sē′gub, according to the word of
the LORD, which he spoke by Joshua
the son of Nun.

17 Now E·lī′jȧh the Tish′bīte, of
Tish′be[n] in Gilead, said to Ā′hab,
"As the LORD the God of Israel lives,
before whom I stand, there shall be
neither dew nor rain these years, except by my word." 2 And the word of
the LORD came to him. 3 "Depart from
here and turn eastward, and hide yourself by the brook Chē′rith, that is east
of the Jordan. 4 You shall drink from
the brook, and I have commanded the
ravens to feed you there." 5 So he
went and did according to the word of
the LORD; he went and dwelt by the
brook Chē′rith that is east of the
Jordan. 6 And the ravens brought him
bread and meat in the morning, and
bread and meat in the evening; and he
drank from the brook. 7 And after a
while the brook dried up, because there
was no rain in the land.
8 Then the word of the LORD came
to him. 9 "Arise, go to Zar′ė·phath,
which belongs to Sī′don, and dwell
there. Behold, I have commanded a
widow there to feed you." 10 So he
arose and went to Zar′ė·phath; and
when he came to the gate of the city,
behold, a widow was there gathering
sticks; and he called to her and said,
"Bring me a little water in a vessel,
that I may drink." 11 And as she was
going to bring it, he called to her and
said, "Bring me a morsel of bread in
your hand." 12 And she said, "As the
LORD your God lives, I have nothing
baked, only a handful of meal in a jar,
and a little oil in a cruse; and now, I
am gathering a couple of sticks, that I
may go in and prepare it for myself and
my son, that we may eat it, and die."
13 And E·lī′jȧh said to her, "Fear not;
go and do as you have said; but first
make me a little cake of it and bring it
to me, and afterward make for yourself
and your son. 14 For thus says the
LORD the God of Israel, 'The jar of
meal shall not be spent, and the cruse
of oil shall not fail, until the day that
the LORD sends rain upon the earth.'"
15 And she went and did as E·lī′jȧh
said; and she, and he, and her household ate for many days. 16 The jar of
meal was not spent, neither did the
cruse of oil fail, according to the word
of the LORD which he spoke by E·lī′jȧh.
17 After this the son of the woman,
the mistress of the house, became ill;
and his illness was so severe that there
was no breath left in him. 18 And she
said to E·lī′jȧh, "What have you
against me, O man of God? You have
come to me to bring my sin to remem-

[n] Gk: Heb *of the settlers*
16.34: Josh 6.26. **17.1:** Rev 11.6. **17.8-16:** Lk 4.25-26. **17.18:** Mt 8.29; Mk 1.24; Jn 2.4.

brance, and to cause the death of my
son!" 19 And he said to her, "Give me
your son." And he took him from her
bosom, and carried him up into the
upper chamber, where he lodged, and
laid him upon his own bed. 20 And he
cried to the LORD, "O LORD my God,
hast thou brought calamity even upon
the widow with whom I sojourn, by
slaying her son?" 21 Then he stretched
himself upon the child three times,
and cried to the LORD, "O LORD my
God, let this child's soul come into
him again." 22 And the LORD hearkened
to the voice of E·lī′jȧh; and the soul of
the child came into him again, and he
revived. 23 And E·lī′jȧh took the child,
and brought him down from the upper
chamber into the house, and delivered
him to his mother; and Elijah said,
"See, your son lives." 24 And the
woman said to E·lī′jȧh, "Now I know
that you are a man of God, and that
the word of the LORD in your mouth
is truth."

18 After many days the word of
the LORD came to E·lī′jȧh, in the
third year, saying, "Go, show yourself
to Ā′hab; and I will send rain upon
the earth." 2 So E·lī′jȧh went to show
himself to Ā′hab. Now the famine was
severe in Sȧ·mâr′i·ȧ. 3 And Ā′hab
called Ō·bȧ·dī′ȧh, who was over the
household. (Now Obadiah revered the
LORD greatly; 4 and when Jez′ė·bėl cut
off the prophets of the LORD, Ō·bȧ-
dī′ȧh took a hundred prophets and hid
them by fifties in a cave, and fed them
with bread and water.) 5 And Ā′hab
said to Ō·bȧ·dī′ȧh, "Go through the
land to all the springs of water and to
all the valleys; perhaps we may find
grass and save the horses and mules
alive, and not lose some of the animals." 6 So they divided the land
between them to pass through it;
Ā′hab went in one direction by himself, and Ō·bȧ·dī′ȧh went in another
direction by himself.

7 And as Ō·bȧ·dī′ȧh was on the way,
behold, E·lī′jȧh met him; and Obadiah
recognized him, and fell on his face,
and said, "Is it you, my lord Elijah?"
8 And he answered him, "It is I. Go,
tell your lord, 'Behold, E·lī′jȧh is
here.' " 9 And he said, "Wherein have
I sinned, that you would give your
servant into the hand of Ā′hab, to kill
me? 10 As the LORD your God lives,
there is no nation or kingdom whither
my lord has not sent to seek you; and
when they would say, 'He is not here,'
he would take an oath of the kingdom
or nation, that they had not found you.
11 And now you say, 'Go, tell your
lord, "Behold, E·lī′jȧh is here." '
12 And as soon as I have gone from
you, the Spirit of the LORD will carry
you whither I know not; and so, when
I come and tell Ā′hab and he cannot
find you, he will kill me, although I
your servant have revered the LORD
from my youth. 13 Has it not been
told my lord what I did when Jez′ė·bėl
killed the prophets of the LORD, how
I hid a hundred men of the LORD's
prophets by fifties in a cave, and fed
them with bread and water? 14 And
now you say, 'Go, tell your lord,
"Behold, E·lī′jȧh is here" '; and he
will kill me." 15 And E·lī′jȧh said, "As
the LORD of hosts lives, before whom
I stand, I will surely show myself to
him today." 16 So Ō·bȧ·dī′ȧh went to
meet Ā′hab, and told him; and Ahab
went to meet E·lī′jȧh.

17 When Ā′hab saw E·lī′jȧh, Ahab
said to him, "Is it you, you troubler
of Israel?" 18 And he answered, "I
have not troubled Israel; but you have,
and your father's house, because you
have forsaken the commandments of
the LORD and followed the Bā′ălṡ.
19 Now therefore send and gather all
Israel to me at Mount Cär′mėl, and
the four hundred and fifty prophets of
Bā′ăl and the four hundred prophets
of Ȧ·shē′rȧh, who eat at Jez′ė·bėl's
table."

20 So Ā′hab sent to all the people
of Israel, and gathered the prophets
together at Mount Cär′mėl. 21 And
E·lī′jȧh came near to all the people,
and said, "How long will you go
limping with two different opinions?
If the LORD is God, follow him; but if
Bā′ăl, then follow him." And the
people did not answer him a word.
22 Then E·lī′jȧh said to the people,
"I, even I only, am left a prophet of
the LORD; but Bā′ăl's prophets are
four hundred and fifty men. 23 Let
two bulls be given to us; and let them
choose one bull for themselves, and
cut it in pieces and lay it on the wood,
but put no fire to it; and I will prepare
the other bull and lay it on the wood,
and put no fire to it. 24 And you call on
the name of your god and I will call
on the name of the LORD; and the God
who answers by fire, he is God." And
all the people answered, "It is well

spoken." 25 Then E·lī'jȧh said to the
prophets of Bā'ȧl, "Choose for yourselves one bull and prepare it first, for
you are many; and call on the name of
your god, but put no fire to it." 26And
they took the bull which was given
them, and they prepared it, and called
on the name of Bā'ȧl from morning
until noon, saying, "O Baal, answer
us!" But there was no voice, and no
one answered. And they limped about
the altar which they had made. 27And
at noon E·lī'jȧh mocked them, saying,
"Cry aloud, for he is a god; either he
is musing, or he has gone aside, or he
is on a journey, or perhaps he is asleep
and must be awakened." 28And they
cried aloud, and cut themselves after
their custom with swords and lances,
until the blood gushed out upon them.
29And as midday passed, they raved
on until the time of the offering of the
oblation, but there was no voice; no
one answered, no one heeded.

30 Then E·lī'jȧh said to all the
people, "Come near to me"; and all
the people came near to him. And he
repaired the altar of the LORD that had
been thrown down; 31 E·lī'jȧh took
twelve stones, according to the number
of the tribes of the sons of Jacob, to
whom the word of the LORD came,
saying, "Israel shall be your name";
32 and with the stones he built an
altar in the name of the LORD. And he
made a trench about the altar, as great
as would contain two measures of
seed. 33And he put the wood in order,
and cut the bull in pieces and laid it
on the wood. And he said, "Fill four
jars with water, and pour it on the burnt
offering, and on the wood." 34And he
said, "Do it a second time"; and they
did it a second time. And he said, "Do
it a third time"; and they did it a third
time. 35And the water ran round about
the altar, and filled the trench also
with water.

36 And at the time of the offering
of the oblation, E·lī'jȧh the prophet
came near and said, "O LORD, God of
Abraham, Isaac, and Israel, let it be
known this day that thou art God in
Israel, and that I am thy servant, and
that I have done all these things at
thy word. 37Answer me, O LORD,
answer me, that this people may know
that thou, O LORD, art God, and that
thou hast turned their hearts back."
38 Then the fire of the LORD fell, and
consumed the burnt offering, and the
wood, and the stones, and the dust,
and licked up the water that was in
the trench. 39And when all the people
saw it, they fell on their faces; and
they said, "The LORD, he is God; the
LORD, he is God." 40And E·lī'jȧh said
to them, "Seize the prophets of Bā'ȧl;
let not one of them escape." And they
seized them; and Elijah brought them
down to the brook Kī'shon, and killed
them there.

41 And E·lī'jȧh said to Ā'hab, "Go
up, eat and drink; for there is a sound
of the rushing of rain." 42 So Ā'hab
went up to eat and to drink. And
E·lī'jȧh went up to the top of Cär'mĕl;
and he bowed himself down upon the
earth, and put his face between his
knees. 43And he said to his servant,
"Go up now, look toward the sea."
And he went up and looked, and said,
"There is nothing." And he said, "Go
again seven times." 44And at the
seventh time he said, "Behold, a little
cloud like a man's hand is rising out
of the sea." And he said, "Go up, say
to Ā'hab, 'Prepare your chariot and
go down, lest the rain stop you.' "
45And in a little while the heavens
grew black with clouds and wind, and
there was a great rain. And Ā'hab rode
and went to Jez'rē·ĕl. 46And the hand
of the LORD was on E·lī'jȧh; and he
girded up his loins and ran before
Ā'hab to the entrance of Jez'rē·ĕl.

19 Ā'hab told Jez'ė·bĕl all that
E·lī'jȧh had done, and how he had
slain all the prophets with the sword.
2 Then Jez'ė·bĕl sent a messenger to
E·lī'jȧh, saying, "So may the gods do
to me, and more also, if I do not make
your life as the life of one of them by
this time tomorrow." 3 Then he was
afraid, and he arose and went for his
life, and came to Beer-sheba, which
belongs to Judah, and left his servant
there.

4 But he himself went a day's
journey into the wilderness, and came
and sat down under a broom tree; and
he asked that he might die, saying, "It
is enough; now, O LORD, take away
my life; for I am no better than my
fathers." 5And he lay down and slept
under a broom tree; and behold, an
angel touched him, and said to him,
"Arise and eat." 6And he looked, and
behold, there was at his head a cake
baked on hot stones and a jar of water.
And he ate and drank, and lay down
again. 7And the angel of the LORD

came again a second time, and touched
him, and said, "Arise and eat, else the
journey will be too great for you."
8 And he arose, and ate and drank, and
went in the strength of that food forty
days and forty nights to Hō′reb the
mount of God.
9 And there he came to a cave, and
lodged there; and behold, the word of
the LORD came to him, and he said to
him, "What are you doing here,
E·lī′jȧh?" 10 He said, "I have been
very jealous for the LORD, the God of
hosts; for the people of Israel have
forsaken thy covenant, thrown down
thy altars, and slain thy prophets with
the sword; and I, even I only, am left;
and they seek my life, to take it away."
11 And he said, "Go forth, and stand
upon the mount before the LORD."
And behold, the LORD passed by, and
a great and strong wind rent the
mountains, and broke in pieces the
rocks before the LORD, but the LORD
was not in the wind; and after the wind
an earthquake, but the LORD was not
in the earthquake; 12 and after the
earthquake a fire, but the LORD was
not in the fire; and after the fire a still
small voice. 13 And when E·lī′jȧh heard
it, he wrapped his face in his mantle
and went out and stood at the entrance
of the cave. And behold, there came a
voice to him, and said, "What are
you doing here, Elijah?" 14 He said,
"I have been very jealous for the
LORD, the God of hosts; for the people
of Israel have forsaken thy covenant,
thrown down thy altars, and slain thy
prophets with the sword; and I, even
I only, am left; and they seek my life,
to take it away." 15 And the LORD said
to him, "Go, return on your way to
the wilderness of Damascus; and when
you arrive, you shall anoint Haz′ȧ·el
to be king over Syria; 16 and Jē′hū the
son of Nim′shī you shall anoint to be
king over Israel; and E·lī′shȧ the son
of Shā′phȧt of Ā′bėl-mė·hō′lȧh you
shall anoint to be prophet in your
place. 17 And him who escapes from
the sword of Haz′ȧ·el shall Jē′hū slay;
and him who escapes from the sword
of Jehu shall E·lī′shȧ slay. 18 Yet I will
leave seven thousand in Israel, all the
knees that have not bowed to Bā′ȧl,
and every mouth that has not kissed
him."
19 So he departed from there, and
found E·lī′shȧ the son of Shā′phȧt,
who was plowing, with twelve yoke of
oxen before him, and he was with the
twelfth. E·lī′jȧh passed by him and
cast his mantle upon him. 20 And he
left the oxen, and ran after E·lī′jȧh,
and said, "Let me kiss my father and
my mother, and then I will follow
you." And he said to him, "Go back
again; for what have I done to you?"
21 And he returned from following him,
and took the yoke of oxen, and slew
them, and boiled their flesh with the
yokes of the oxen, and gave it to the
people, and they ate. Then he arose
and went after E·lī′jȧh, and ministered
to him.

20 Ben-hā′dad the king of Syria
gathered all his army together;
thirty-two kings were with him, and
horses and chariots; and he went up
and besieged Sȧ·mâr′ĭ·ȧ, and fought
against it. 2 And he sent messengers
into the city of Ā′hab king of Israel,
and said to him, "Thus says Ben-
hā′dad: 3 'Your silver and your gold
are mine; your fairest wives and
children also are mine.' " 4 And the
king of Israel answered, "As you say,
my lord, O king, I am yours, and all
that I have." 5 The messengers came
again, and said, "Thus says Ben-hā′-
dad: 'I sent to you, saying, "Deliver
to me your silver and your gold, your
wives and your children"; 6 nevertheless I will send my servants to you tomorrow about this time, and they shall
search your house and the houses
of your servants, and lay hands on
whatever pleases them,[o] and take it
away.' "
7 Then the king of Israel called all
the elders of the land, and said,
"Mark, now, and see how this man is
seeking trouble; for he sent to me for
my wives and my children, and for
my silver and my gold, and I did not
refuse him." 8 And all the elders and
all the people said to him, "Do not
heed or consent." 9 So he said to the
messengers of Ben-hā′dad, "Tell my
lord the king, 'All that you first
demanded of your servant I will do;
but this thing I cannot do.' " And the
messengers departed and brought him
word again. 10 Ben-hā′dad sent to him
and said, "The gods do so to me, and
more also, if the dust of Sȧ·mâr′ĭ·ȧ
shall suffice for handfuls for all the

[o] Gk Syr Vg: Heb *you*
19.10: Rom 11.2-3. **19.18:** Rom 11.4.

people who follow me." 11And the
king of Israel answered, "Tell him,
'Let not him that girds on his armor
boast himself as he that puts it off.' "
12 When Ben-hā'dad heard this message as he was drinking with the kings
in the booths, he said to his men,
"Take your positions." And they
took their positions against the city.

13 And behold, a prophet came
near to Ā'hab king of Israel and said,
"Thus says the LORD, Have you seen
all this great multitude? Behold, I will
give it into your hand this day; and
you shall know that I am the LORD."
14And Ā'hab said, "By whom?" He
said, "Thus says the LORD, By the
servants of the governors of the
districts." Then he said, "Who shall
begin the battle?" He answered,
"You." 15 Then he mustered the
servants of the governors of the districts, and they were two hundred and
thirty-two; and after them he mustered
all the people of Israel, seven thousand.

16 And they went out at noon,
while Ben-hā'dad was drinking himself drunk in the booths, he and the
thiry-two kings who helped him.
17 The servants of the governors of the
districts went out first. And Ben-hā'-
dad sent out scouts, and they reported
to him, "Men are coming out from
Sȧ-mâr'i-ȧ." 18 He said, "If they have
come out for peace, take them alive;
or if they have come out for war, take
them alive."

19 So these went out of the city,
the servants of the governors of the
districts, and the army which followed
them. 20And each killed his man; the
Syrians fled and Israel pursued them,
but Ben-hā'dad king of Syria escaped
on a horse with horsemen. 21And the
king of Israel went out, and captured[p]
the horses and chariots, and killed the
Syrians with a great slaughter.

22 Then the prophet came near to
the king of Israel, and said to him,
"Come, strengthen yourself, and consider well what you have to do; for in
the spring the king of Syria will come
up against you."

23 And the servants of the king of
Syria said to him, "Their gods are
gods of the hills, and so they were
stronger than we; but let us fight
against them in the plain, and surely
we shall be stronger than they. 24And
do this: remove the kings, each from
his post, and put commanders in their
places; 25 and muster an army like the
army that you have lost, horse for
horse, and chariot for chariot; then we
will fight against them in the plain,
and surely we shall be stronger than
they." And he hearkened to their
voice, and did so.

26 In the spring Ben-hā'dad mustered the Syrians, and went up to
Ā'phek, to fight against Israel. 27And
the people of Israel were mustered and
were provisioned, and went against
them; the people of Israel encamped
before them like two little flocks of
goats, but the Syrians filled the
country. 28And a man of God came
near and said to the king of Israel,
"Thus says the LORD, 'Because the
Syrians have said, "The LORD is a god
of the hills but he is not a god of the
valleys," therefore I will give all this
great multitude into your hand, and
you shall know that I am the LORD.' "
29And they encamped opposite one
another seven days. Then on the
seventh day the battle was joined; and
the people of Israel smote of the
Syrians a hundred thousand foot
soldiers in one day. 30And the rest fled
into the city of Ā'phek; and the wall
fell upon twenty-seven thousand men
that were left.

Ben-hā'dad also fled, and entered
an inner chamber in the city. 31And
his servants said to him, "Behold
now, we have heard that the kings of
the house of Israel are merciful kings;
let us put sackcloth on our loins and
ropes upon our heads, and go out to
the king of Israel; perhaps he will
spare your life." 32 So they girded
sackcloth on their loins, and put ropes
on their heads, and went to the king of
Israel and said, "Your servant Ben-
hā'dad says, 'Pray, let me live.' " And
he said, "Does he still live? He is my
brother." 33 Now the men were
watching for an omen, and they
quickly took it up from him and said,
"Yes, your brother Ben-hā'dad." Then
he said, "Go and bring him." Then
Ben-hadad came forth to him; and he
caused him to come up into the
chariot. 34And Ben-hā'dad said to him,
"The cities which my father took from
your father I will restore; and you may
establish bazaars for yourself in
Damascus, as my father did in Sȧ-

[p] Gk: Heb *smote*

mâr′i·ȧ." And Ā′hab said, "I will let
you go on these terms." So he made
a covenant with him and let him
go.
35 And a certain man of the sons of
the prophets said to his fellow at the
command of the LORD, "Strike me, I
pray." But the man refused to strike
him. 36 Then he said to him, "Because
you have not obeyed the voice of the
LORD, behold, as soon as you have
gone from me, a lion shall kill you."
And as soon as he had departed from
him, a lion met him and killed him.
37 Then he found another man, and
said, "Strike me, I pray." And the
man struck him, smiting and wounding him. 38 So the prophet departed,
and waited for the king by the way,
disguising himself with a bandage over
his eyes. 39 And as the king passed,
he cried to the king and said, "Your
servant went out into the midst of the
battle; and behold, a soldier turned
and brought a man to me, and said,
'Keep this man; if by any means he
be missing, your life shall be for his
life, or else you shall pay a talent of
silver.' 40 And as your servant was busy
here and there, he was gone." The
king of Israel said to him, "So shall
your judgment be; you yourself have
decided it." 41 Then he made haste to
take the bandage away from his eyes;
and the king of Israel recognized him
as one of the prophets. 42 And he said
to him, "Thus says the LORD, 'Because
you have let go out of your hand the
man whom I had devoted to destruction, therefore your life shall go for his
life, and your people for his people.' "
43 And the king of Israel went to his
house resentful and sullen, and came
to Sȧ·mâr′i·ȧ.

21 Now Nā′both the Jez′rē·ė·līte
had a vineyard in Jez′rē·ėl, beside
the palace of Ā′hab king of Sȧ·mâr′i·ȧ.
2 And after this Ā′hab said to Nā′both,
"Give me your vineyard, that I may
have it for a vegetable garden, because
it is near my house; and I will give you
a better vineyard for it; or, if it seems
good to you, I will give you its value
in money." 3 But Nā′both said to
Ā′hab, "The LORD forbid that I should
give you the inheritance of my fathers."
4 And Ā′hab went into his house vexed
and sullen because of what Nā′both
the Jez′rē·ė·līte had said to him; for he
had said, "I will not give you the inheritance of my fathers." And he lay
down on his bed, and turned away his
face, and would eat no food.
5 But Jez′ė·bėl his wife came to
him, and said to him, "Why is your
spirit so vexed that you eat no food?"
6 And he said to her, "Because I spoke
to Nā′both the Jez′rē·ė·līte, and said
to him, 'Give me your vineyard for
money; or else, if it please you, I will
give you another vineyard for it'; and
he answered, 'I will not give you my
vineyard.' " 7 And Jez′ė·bėl his wife
said to him, "Do you now govern
Israel? Arise, and eat bread, and let
your heart be cheerful; I will give you
the vineyard of Nā′both the Jez′rē·ė-
līte."
8 So she wrote letters in Ā′hab's
name and sealed them with his seal,
and she sent the letters to the elders
and the nobles who dwelt with Nā′both
in his city. 9 And she wrote in the
letters, "Proclaim a fast, and set Nā′-
both on high among the people; 10 and
set two base fellows opposite him, and
let them bring a charge against him,
saying, 'You have cursed God and the
king.' Then take him out, and stone
him to death." 11 And the men of his
city, the elders and the nobles who
dwelt in his city, did as Jez′ė·bėl had
sent word to them. As it was written
in the letters which she had sent to
them, 12 they proclaimed a fast, and
set Nā′both on high among the people.
13 And the two base fellows came in
and sat opposite him; and the base
fellows brought a charge against Nā′-
both, in the presence of the people,
saying, "Naboth cursed God and the
king." So they took him outside the
city, and stoned him to death with
stones. 14 Then they sent to Jez′ė·bėl,
saying, "Nā′both has been stoned; he
is dead."
15 As soon as Jez′ė·bėl heard that
Nā′both had been stoned and was
dead, Jezebel said to Ā′hab, "Arise,
take possession of the vineyard of
Naboth the Jez′rē·ė·līte, which he refused to give you for money; for Naboth is not alive, but dead." 16 And as
soon as Ā′hab heard that Nā′both was
dead, Ahab arose to go down to the
vineyard of Naboth the Jez′rē·ė·līte,
to take possession of it.
17 Then the word of the LORD came
to E·lī′jȧh the Tish′bīte, saying,
18 "Arise, go down to meet Ā′hab king
of Israel, who is in Sȧ·mâr′i·ȧ; behold,
he is in the vineyard of Nā′both, where

he has gone to take possession. 19 And
you shall say to him, 'Thus says the
LORD, "Have you killed, and also
taken possession?" ' And you shall say
to him, 'Thus says the LORD: "In the
place where dogs licked up the blood
of Nā'both shall dogs lick your own
blood." ' "

20 Ā'hab said to E·lī'jȧh, "Have you
found me, O my enemy?" He answered, "I have found you, because
you have sold yourself to do what is
evil in the sight of the LORD. 21 Behold, I will bring evil upon you; I will
utterly sweep you away, and will cut
off from Ā'hab every male, bond or
free, in Israel; 22 and I will make your
house like the house of Jer·ȯ·bō'am the
son of Nē'bat, and like the house of
Bā'ȧ·shȧ the son of Ȧ·hī'jȧh, for the
anger to which you have provoked me,
and because you have made Israel to
sin. 23 And of Jez'ė·bėl the LORD also
said, 'The dogs shall eat Jezebel within
the bounds of Jez'rē·ėl.' 24 Any one belonging to Ā'hab who dies in the city
the dogs shall eat; and any one of his
who dies in the open country the birds
of the air shall eat."

25 (There was none who sold himself to do what was evil in the sight of
the LORD like Ā'hab, whom Jez'ė·bėl
his wife incited. 26 He did very abominably in going after idols, as the
Am'ȯ·rītes had done, whom the LORD
cast out before the people of Israel.)

27 And when Ā'hab heard those
words, he rent his clothes, and put
sackcloth upon his flesh, and fasted
and lay in sackcloth, and went about
dejectedly. 28 And the word of the
LORD came to E·lī'jȧh the Tish'bīte,
saying, 29 "Have you seen how Ā'hab
has humbled himself before me? Because he has humbled himself before
me, I will not bring the evil in his
days; but in his son's days I will bring
the evil upon his house."

22 For three years Syria and Israel continued without war.
2 But in the third year Je·hosh'ȧ·phat
the king of Judah came down to the
king of Israel. 3 And the king of Israel
said to his servants, "Do you know
that Rā'moth-gil'ē·ȧd belongs to us,
and we keep quiet and do not take it
out of the hand of the king of Syria?"
4 And he said to Je·hosh'ȧ·phat, "Will
you go with me to battle at Rā'moth-
gil'ē·ȧd?" And Jehoshaphat said to the
king of Israel, "I am as you are, my
people as your people, my horses as
your horses."

5 And Je·hosh'ȧ·phat said to the
king of Israel, "Inquire first for the
word of the LORD." 6 Then the king
of Israel gathered the prophets together, about four hundred men, and
said to them, "Shall I go to battle
against Rā'moth-gil'ē·ȧd, or shall I
forbear?" And they said, "Go up; for
the LORD will give it into the hand of
the king." 7 But Je·hosh'ȧ·phat said,
"Is there not here another prophet of
the LORD of whom we may inquire?"
8 And the king of Israel said to Je-
hosh'ȧ·phat, "There is yet one man by
whom we may inquire of the LORD,
Mī·cāi'ȧh the son of Im'lȧh; but I hate
him, for he never prophesies good concerning me, but evil." And Jehoshaphat said, "Let not the king say so."
9 Then the king of Israel summoned
an officer and said, "Bring quickly
Mī·cāi'ȧh the son of Im'lȧh." 10 Now
the king of Israel and Je·hosh'ȧ·phat
the king of Judah were sitting on their
thrones, arrayed in their robes, at the
threshing floor at the entrance of the
gate of Sȧ·mâr'i·ȧ; and all the prophets
were prophesying before them. 11 And
Zed·ė·kī'ȧh the son of Che·nā'ȧ·nȧh
made for himself horns of iron, and
said, "Thus says the LORD, 'With these
you shall push the Syrians until they
are destroyed.' " 12 And all the prophets
prophesied so, and said, "Go up to
Rā'moth-gil'ē·ȧd and triumph; the
LORD will give it into the hand of the
king."

13 And the messenger who went to
summon Mī·cāi'ȧh said to him, "Behold, the words of the prophets with
one accord are favorable to the king;
let your word be like the word of one
of them, and speak favorably." 14 But
Mī·cāi'ȧh said, "As the LORD lives,
what the LORD says to me, that I will
speak." 15 And when he had come to
the king, the king said to him, "Mī-
cāi'ȧh, shall we go to Rā'moth-gil'ē·ȧd
to battle, or shall we forbear?" And he
answered him, "Go up and triumph;
the LORD will give it into the hand of
the king." 16 But the king said to him,
"How many times shall I adjure you
that you speak to me nothing but the
truth in the name of the LORD?"
17 And he said, "I saw all Israel
scattered upon the mountains, as sheep

21.19: 2 Kings 9.26. **21.23:** 2 Kings 9.36. **22.1-35:** 2 Chron 18.1-34. **22.17:** Mt 9.36.

that have no shepherd; and the LORD
said, 'These have no master; let each
return to his home in peace.' " 18And
the king of Israel said to Je·hosh'ȧ-
phat, "Did I not tell you that he
would not prophesy good concerning
me, but evil?" 19And Mī·cāi'ȧh said,
"Therefore hear the word of the LORD:
I saw the LORD sitting on his throne,
and all the host of heaven standing beside him on his right hand and on his
left; 20 and the LORD said, 'Who will
entice Ā'hab, that he may go up and
fall at Rā'moth-gil'ē·ȧd?' And one said
one thing, and another said another.
21 Then a spirit came forward and
stood before the LORD, saying, 'I will
entice him.' 22And the LORD said to
him, 'By what means?' And he said,
'I will go forth, and will be a lying
spirit in the mouth of all his prophets.'
And he said, 'You are to entice him,
and you shall succeed; go forth and do
so.' 23 Now therefore behold, the LORD
has put a lying spirit in the mouth of
all these your prophets; the LORD has
spoken evil concerning you."

24 Then Zed·ė·kī'ȧh the son of
Che·nā'ȧ·nȧh came near and struck
Mī·cāi'ȧh on the cheek, and said,
"How did the Spirit of the LORD go
from me to speak to you?" 25And
Mī·cāi'ȧh said, "Behold, you shall see
on that day when you go into an inner
chamber to hide yourself." 26And the
king of Israel said, "Seize Mī·cāi'ȧh,
and take him back to Ā'mon the governor of the city and to Jō'ash the king's
son; 27 and say, 'Thus says the king,
"Put this fellow in prison, and feed him
with scant fare of bread and water,
until I come in peace." ' " 28And
Mī·cāi'ȧh said, "If you return in peace,
the LORD has not spoken by me." And
he said, "Hear, all you peoples!"

29 So the king of Israel and Je-
hosh'ȧ·phat the king of Judah went up
to Rā'moth-gil'ē·ȧd. 30And the king of
Israel said to Je·hosh'ȧ·phat, "I will
disguise myself and go into battle, but
you wear your robes." And the king
of Israel disguised himself and went
into battle. 31 Now the king of Syria
had commanded the thirty-two captains of his chariots, "Fight with
neither small nor great, but only with
the king of Israel." 32And when the
captains of the chariots saw Je·hosh'-
ȧ·phat, they said, "It is surely the
king of Israel." So they turned to
fight against him; and Jehoshaphat
cried out. 33And when the captains of
the chariots saw that it was not the
king of Israel, they turned back from
pursuing him. 34 But a certain man
drew his bow at a venture, and struck
the king of Israel between the scale
armor and the breastplate; therefore he
said to the driver of his chariot, "Turn
about, and carry me out of the battle,
for I am wounded." 35And the battle
grew hot that day, and the king was
propped up in his chariot facing the
Syrians, until at evening he died; and
the blood of the wound flowed into
the bottom of the chariot. 36And about
sunset a cry went through the army,
"Every man to his city, and every
man to his country!"

37 So the king died, and was
brought to Sȧ·mâr'i·ȧ; and they buried
the king in Samaria. 38And they
washed the chariot by the pool of
Sȧ·mâr'i·ȧ, and the dogs licked up his
blood, and the harlots washed themselves in it, according to the word of
the LORD which he had spoken.
39 Now the rest of the acts of Ā'hab,
and all that he did, and the ivory house
which he built, and all the cities that
he built, are they not written in the
Book of the Chronicles of the Kings
of Israel? 40 So Ā'hab slept with his
fathers; and Ā·hȧ·zī'ȧh his son reigned
in his stead.

41 Je·hosh'ȧ·phat the son of Asa
began to reign over Judah in the
fourth year of Ā'hab king of Israel.
42 Je·hosh'ȧ·phat was thirty-five years
old when he began to reign, and he
reigned twenty-five years in Jerusalem.
His mother's name was Ȧ·zü'bȧh the
daughter of Shil'hī. 43 He walked in
all the way of Asa his father; he did
not turn aside from it, doing what was
right in the sight of the LORD; yet the
high places were not taken away, and
the people still sacrificed and burned
incense on the high places. 44 Je·hosh'-
ȧ·phat also made peace with the king
of Israel.

45 Now the rest of the acts of Je-
hosh'ȧ·phat, and his might that he
showed, and how he warred, are they
not written in the Book of the Chronicles of the Kings of Judah? 46And the
remnant of the male cult prostitutes
who remained in the days of his father Asa, he exterminated from the
land.

22.41-43: 2 Chron 20.31-33.

47 There was no king in Ē'dȯm; a
deputy was king. 48 Je·hosh'ȧ·phat
made ships of Tär'shish to go to
Ō'phīr for gold; but they did not go,
for the ships were wrecked at Ē'zi·on-
gē'bėr. 49 Then Ā·hȧ·zī'ȧh the son of
Ā'hab said to Je·hosh'ȧ·phat, "Let my
servants go with your servants in the
ships," but Jehoshaphat was not willing. 50 And Je·hosh'ȧ·phat slept with
his fathers, and was buried with his
fathers in the city of David his father;
and Je·hō'rȧm his son reigned in his
stead.

51 Ā·hȧ·zī'ȧh the son of Ā'hab began to reign over Israel in Sȧ·mâr'i·ȧ
in the seventeenth year of Je·hosh'ȧ-
phat king of Judah, and he reigned
two years over Israel. 52 He did what
was evil in the sight of the LORD, and
walked in the way of his father, and
in the way of his mother, and in the
way of Jer·ȯ·bō'ȧm the son of Nē'bat,
who made Israel to sin. 53 He served
Bā'ăl and worshiped him, and provoked the LORD, the God of Israel, to
anger in every way that his father had
done.

THE SECOND BOOK OF THE

KINGS

1 After the death of Ā'hab, Mō'ab
rebelled against Israel.
2 Now Ā·hȧ·zī'ȧh fell through the
lattice in his upper chamber in Sȧ-
mâr'i·ȧ, and lay sick; so he sent messengers, telling them, "Go, inquire
of Bā'ăl-zē'bub, the god of Ek'rȯn,
whether I shall recover from this
sickness." 3 But the angel of the LORD
said to E·lī'jȧh the Tish'bīte, "Arise,
go up to meet the messengers of the
king of Sȧ·mâr'i·ȧ, and say to them,
'Is it because there is no God in Israel
that you are going to inquire of Bā'ăl-
zē'bub, the god of Ek'rȯn?' 4 Now
therefore thus says the LORD, 'You
shall not come down from the bed to
which you have gone, but you shall
surely die.' " So E·lī'jȧh went.
5 The messengers returned to the
king, and he said to them, "Why have
you returned?" 6 And they said to him,
"There came a man to meet us, and
said to us, 'Go back to the king who
sent you, and say to him, Thus says
the LORD, Is it because there is no God
in Israel that you are sending to inquire
of Bā'ăl-zē'bub, the god of Ek'rȯn?
Therefore you shall not come down
from the bed to which you have gone,
but shall surely die.' " 7 He said to
them, "What kind of man was he who
came to meet you and told you these
things?" 8 They answered him, "He
wore a garment of haircloth, with a
girdle of leather about his loins." And
he said, "It is E·lī'jȧh the Tish'bīte."
9 Then the king sent to him a
captain of fifty men with his fifty. He
went up to E·lī'jȧh, who was sitting on
the top of a hill, and said to him, "O
man of God, the king says, 'Come
down.' " 10 But E·lī'jȧh answered the
captain of fifty, "If I am a man of God,
let fire come down from heaven and
consume you and your fifty." Then
fire came down from heaven, and consumed him and his fifty.
11 Again the king sent to him another
captain of fifty men with his fifty.
And he went up[a] and said to him, "O
man of God, this is the king's order,
'Come down quickly!' " 12 But E·lī'jȧh
answered them, "If I am a man of
God, let fire come down from heaven
and consume you and your fifty." Then
the fire of God came down from heaven
and consumed him and his fifty.
13 Again the king sent the captain
of a third fifty with his fifty. And the
third captain of fifty went up, and
came and fell on his knees before
E·lī'jȧh, and entreated him, "O man
of God, I pray you, let my life, and
the life of these fifty servants of yours,
be precious in your sight. 14 Lo, fire
came down from heaven, and consumed the two former captains of fifty

[a] Gk Compare verses 9, 13: Heb *answered*

22.48-49: 2 Chron 20.35-37. **22.50:** 2 Chron 21.1. **1.10-12:** Lk 9.54; Rev 11.5; 20.9.

men with their fifties; but now let my
life be precious in your sight." 15 Then
the angel of the LORD said to E·lī′jȧh,
"Go down with him; do not be afraid
of him." So he arose and went down
with him to the king, 16 and said to
him, "Thus says the LORD, 'Because
you have sent messengers to inquire of
Bā′ȧl-zē′bub, the god of Ek′rŏn,—is it
because there is no God in Israel to
inquire of his word?—therefore you
shall not come down from the bed to
which you have gone, but you shall
surely die.' "

17 So he died according to the word
of the LORD which E·lī′jȧh had spoken.
Je·hō′rȧm, his brother,[b] became king
in his stead in the second year of
Jehoram the son of Je·hosh′ȧ·phat,
king of Judah, because Ā·hȧ·zī′ȧh had
no son. 18 Now the rest of the acts of
Ā·hȧ·zī′ȧh which he did, are they not
written in the Book of the Chronicles
of the Kings of Israel?

2 Now when the LORD was about
to take E·lī′jȧh up to heaven by a
whirlwind, Elijah and E·lī′shȧ were on
their way from Gil′gȧl. 2 And E·lī′jȧh
said to E·lī′shȧ, "Tarry here, I pray
you; for the LORD has sent me as far
as Beth′ĕl." But Elisha said, "As the
Lord lives, and as you yourself live, I
will not leave you." So they went down
to Bethel. 3 And the sons of the prophets who were in Beth′ĕl came out to
E·lī′shȧ, and said to him, "Do you
know that today the LORD will take
away your master from over you?"
And he said, "Yes, I know it; hold
your peace."

4 E·lī′jȧh said to him, "E·lī′shȧ,
tarry here, I pray you; for the LORD
has sent me to Jericho." But he said,
"As the LORD lives, and as you yourself live, I will not leave you." So they
came to Jericho. 5 The sons of the
prophets who were at Jericho drew
near to E·lī′shȧ, and said to him, "Do
you know that today the LORD will
take away your master from over you?"
And he answered, "Yes, I know it;
hold your peace."

6 Then E·lī′jȧh said to him, "Tarry
here, I pray you; for the LORD has sent
me to the Jordan." But he said, "As
the LORD lives, and as you yourself
live, I will not leave you." So the two
of them went on. 7 Fifty men of the
sons of the prophets also went, and
stood at some distance from them, as
they both were standing by the Jordan.
8 Then E·lī′jȧh took his mantle, and
rolled it up, and struck the water, and
the water was parted to the one side
and to the other, till the two of them
could go over on dry ground.

9 When they had crossed, E·lī′jȧh
said to E·lī′shȧ, "Ask what I shall do
for you, before I am taken from you."
And Elisha said, "I pray you, let me
inherit a double share of your spirit."
10 And he said, "You have asked a hard
thing; yet, if you see me as I am being
taken from you, it shall be so for you;
but if you do not see me, it shall not
be so." 11 And as they still went on
and talked, behold, a chariot of fire
and horses of fire separated the two of
them. And E·lī′jȧh went up by a whirlwind into heaven. 12 And E·lī′shȧ saw
it and cried, "My father, my father!
the chariots of Israel and its horsemen!" And he saw him no more.

Then he took hold of his own
clothes and rent them in two pieces.
13 And he took up the mantle of E·lī′jȧh
that had fallen from him, and went
back and stood on the bank of the
Jordan. 14 Then he took the mantle of
E·lī′jȧh that had fallen from him, and
struck the water, saying, "Where is
the LORD, the God of Elijah?" And
when he had struck the water, the
water was parted to the one side and
to the other; and E·lī′shȧ went over.

15 Now when the sons of the prophets who were at Jericho saw him over
against them, they said, "The spirit of
E·lī′jȧh rests on E·lī′shȧ." And they
came to meet him, and bowed to the
ground before him. 16 And they said to
him, "Behold now, there are with your
servants fifty strong men; pray, let
them go, and seek your master; it may
be that the Spirit of the LORD has
caught him up and cast him upon
some mountain or into some valley."
And he said, "You shall not send."
17 But when they urged him till he
was ashamed, he said, "Send." They
sent therefore fifty men; and for three
days they sought him but did not find
him. 18 And they came back to him,
while he tarried at Jericho, and he
said to them, "Did I not say to you,
Do not go?"

19 Now the men of the city said to
E·lī′shȧ, "Behold, the situation of this

[b] Gk Syr: Heb lacks *his brother*
2.11: Rev 11.12.

city is pleasant, as my lord sees; but
the water is bad, and the land is unfruitful." 20 He said, "Bring me a new
bowl, and put salt in it." So they
brought it to him. 21 Then he went to
the spring of water and threw salt in
it, and said, "Thus says the LORD, I
have made this water wholesome;
henceforth neither death nor miscarriage shall come from it." 22 So the
water has been wholesome to this day,
according to the word which E·lī′shȧ
spoke.

23 He went up from there to Beth′-
ėl; and while he was going up on the
way, some small boys came out of the
city and jeered at him, saying, "Go up,
you baldhead! Go up, you baldhead!"
24 And he turned around, and when he
saw them, he cursed them in the name
of the LORD. And two she-bears came
out of the woods and tore forty-two of
the boys. 25 From there he went on to
Mount Cär′mėl, and thence he returned to Sȧ·mâr′i·ȧ.

3 In the eighteenth year of Je-
hosh′ȧ·phat king of Judah, Je·hō′-
rȧm the son of Ā′hab became king over
Israel in Sȧ·mâr′i·ȧ, and he reigned
twelve years. 2 He did what was evil
in the sight of the LORD, though not
like his father and mother, for he put
away the pillar of Bā′ȧl which his
father had made. 3 Nevertheless he
clung to the sin of Jer·ȯ·bō′ȧm the son
of Nē′bat, which he made Israel to
sin; he did not depart from it.

4 Now Mē′shȧ king of Mō′ab was
a sheep breeder; and he had to deliver
annually[c] to the king of Israel a hundred thousand lambs, and the wool of
a hundred thousand rams. 5 But when
Ā′hab died, the king of Mō′ab rebelled
against the king of Israel. 6 So King
Je·hō′rȧm marched out of Sȧ·mâr′i·ȧ
at that time and mustered all Israel.
7 And he went and sent word to Je-
hosh′ȧ·phat king of Judah, "The king
of Mō′ab has rebelled against me; will
you go with me to battle against
Moab?" And he said, "I will go; I am
as you are, my people as your people,
my horses as your horses." 8 Then he
said, "By which way shall we march?"
Je·hō′rȧm answered, "By the way of
the wilderness of Ē′dȯm."

9 So the king of Israel went with
the king of Judah and the king of
Ē′dȯm. And when they had made a
circuitous march of seven days, there
was no water for the army or for the
beasts which followed them. 10 Then
the king of Israel said, "Alas! The
LORD has called these three kings to
give them into the hand of Mō′ab."
11 And Je·hosh′ȧ·phat said, "Is there no
prophet of the LORD here, through
whom we may inquire of the LORD?"
Then one of the king of Israel's servants answered, "E·lī′shȧ the son of
Shā′phȧt is here, who poured water on
the hands of E·lī′jȧh." 12 And Je·hosh′-
ȧ·phat said, "The word of the LORD is
with him." So the king of Israel and
Jehoshaphat and the king of Ē′dȯm
went down to him.

13 And E·lī′shȧ said to the king of
Israel, "What have I to do with you?
Go to the prophets of your father and
the prophets of your mother." But the
king of Israel said to him, "No; it is
the LORD who has called these three
kings to give them into the hand of
Mō′ab." 14 And E·lī′shȧ said, "As the
LORD of hosts lives, whom I serve,
were it not that I have regard for
Je·hosh′ȧ·phat the king of Judah, I
would neither look at you, nor see you.
15 But now bring me a minstrel." And
when the minstrel played, the power
of the LORD came upon him. 16 And he
said, "Thus says the LORD, 'I will
make this dry stream-bed full of pools.'
17 For thus says the LORD, 'You shall
not see wind or rain, but that stream-
bed shall be filled with water, so that
you shall drink, you, your cattle, and
your beasts.' 18 This is a light thing in
the sight of the LORD; he will also give
the Mō′ȧb·ītes into your hand, 19 and
you shall conquer every fortified city,
and every choice city, and shall fell
every good tree, and stop up all springs
of water, and ruin every good piece of
land with stones." 20 The next morning, about the time of offering the
sacrifice, behold, water came from the
direction of Ē′dȯm, till the country
was filled with water.

21 When all the Mō′ȧb·ītes heard
that the kings had come up to fight
against them, all who were able to put
on armor, from the youngest to the
oldest, were called out, and were drawn
up at the frontier. 22 And when they
rose early in the morning, and the sun
shone upon the water, the Mō′ȧb·ītes
saw the water opposite them as red as
blood. 23 And they said, "This is blood;
the kings have surely fought together,

[c] Tg: Heb lacks *annually*

and slain one another. Now then,
Mō'ab, to the spoil!" 24 But when they
came to the camp of Israel, the
Israelites rose and attacked the Mō'ab-
ites, till they fled before them; and they
went forward, slaughtering the Moabites as they went.[d] 25 And they overthrew the cities, and on every good
piece of land every man threw a stone,
until it was covered; they stopped
every spring of water, and felled all
the good trees; till only its stones were
left in Kīr-hâr'ė-seth, and the slingers
surrounded and conquered it. 26 When
the king of Mō'ab saw that the battle
was going against him, he took with
him seven hundred swordsmen to
break through, opposite the king of
E'dȯm; but they could not. 27 Then he
took his eldest son who was to reign
in his stead, and offered him for a
burnt offering upon the wall. And
there came great wrath upon Israel;
and they withdrew from him and
returned to their own land.

4 Now the wife of one of the sons
of the prophets cried to E·lī'shȧ,
"Your servant my husband is dead;
and you know that your servant feared
the LORD, but the creditor has come
to take my two children to be his
slaves." 2 And E·lī'shȧ said to her,
"What shall I do for you? Tell me;
what have you in the house?" And she
said, "Your maidservant has nothing
in the house, except a jar of oil."
3 Then he said, "Go outside, borrow
vessels of all your neighbors, empty
vessels and not too few. 4 Then go in,
and shut the door upon yourself and
your sons, and pour into all these
vessels; and when one is full, set it
aside." 5 So she went from him and
shut the door upon herself and her
sons; and as she poured they brought
the vessels to her. 6 When the vessels
were full, she said to her son, "Bring
me another vessel." And he said to
her, "There is not another." Then the
oil stopped flowing. 7 She came and
told the man of God, and he said,
"Go, sell the oil and pay your debts,
and you and your sons can live on the
rest."

8 One day E·lī'shȧ went on to Shü'-
nem, where a wealthy woman lived,
who urged him to eat some food. So
whenever he passed that way, he would
turn in there to eat food. 9 And she said
to her husband, "Behold now, I perceive that this is a holy man of God,
who is continually passing our way.
10 Let us make a small roof chamber
with walls, and put there for him a
bed, a table, a chair, and a lamp, so
that whenever he comes to us, he can
go in there."

11 One day he came there, and he
turned into the chamber and rested
there. 12 And he said to Ge·hā'zī his
servant, "Call this Shü'nȧm·mīte."
When he had called her, she stood
before him. 13 And he said to him,
"Say now to her, See, you have taken
all this trouble for us; what is to be
done for you? Would you have a word
spoken on your behalf to the king or
to the commander of the army?" She
answered, "I dwell among my own
people." 14 And he said, "What then
is to be done for her?" Ge·hā'zī answered, "Well, she has no son, and her
husband is old." 15 He said, "Call
her." And when he had called her, she
stood in the doorway. 16 And he said,
"At this season, when the time comes
round, you shall embrace a son." And
she said, "No, my lord, O man of God;
do not lie to your maidservant." 17 But
the woman conceived, and she bore a
son about that time the following
spring, as E·lī'shȧ had said to her.

18 When the child had grown, he
went out one day to his father among
the reapers. 19 And he said to his father,
"Oh, my head, my head!" The father
said to his servant, "Carry him to his
mother." 20 And when he had lifted
him, and brought him to his mother,
the child sat on her lap till noon, and
then he died. 21 And she went up and
laid him on the bed of the man of God,
and shut the door upon him, and went
out. 22 Then she called to her husband,
and said, "Send me one of the servants
and one of the asses, that I may quickly
go to the man of God, and come back
again." 23 And he said, "Why will you
go to him today? It is neither new
moon nor sabbath." She said, "It will
be well." 24 Then she saddled the ass,
and she said to her servant, "Urge the
beast on; do not slacken the pace for
me unless I tell you." 25 So she set out,
and came to the man of God at Mount
Cär'mėl.

When the man of God saw her
coming, he said to Ge·hā'zī his servant,
"Look, yonder is the Shü'nȧm·mīte;
26 run at once to meet her, and say to

[d] Gk: Heb uncertain

her, Is it well with you? Is it well with
your husband? Is it well with the
child?" And she answered, "It is well."
27 And when she came to the mountain
to the man of God, she caught hold of
his feet. And Ge·hā'zī came to thrust
her away. But the man of God said,
"Let her alone, for she is in bitter distress; and the LORD has hidden it from
me, and has not told me." 28 Then she
said, "Did I ask my lord for a son?
Did I not say, Do not deceive me?"
29 He said to Ge·hā'zī, "Gird up your
loins, and take my staff in your hand,
and go. If you meet any one, do not
salute him; and if any one salutes you,
do not reply; and lay my staff upon
the face of the child." 30 Then the
mother of the child said, "As the LORD
lives, and as you yourself live, I will
not leave you." So he arose and followed her. 31 Ge·hā'zī went on ahead
and laid the staff upon the face of the
child, but there was no sound or sign
of life. Therefore he returned to meet
him, and told him, "The child has not
awaked."

32 When E·lī'shȧ came into the
house, he saw the child lying dead on
his bed. 33 So he went in and shut the
door upon the two of them, and prayed
to the LORD. 34 Then he went up and
lay upon the child, putting his mouth
upon his mouth, his eyes upon his
eyes, and his hands upon his hands;
and as he stretched himself upon him,
the flesh of the child became warm.
35 Then he got up again, and walked
once to and fro in the house, and went
up, and stretched himself upon him;
the child sneezed seven times, and the
child opened his eyes. 36 Then he
summoned Ge·hā'zī and said, "Call
this Shü'nȧm·mīte." So he called her.
And when she came to him, he said,
"Take up your son." 37 She came and
fell at his feet, bowing to the ground;
then she took up her son and went out.

38 And E·lī'shȧ came again to Gil'-
gȧl when there was a famine in the
land. And as the sons of the prophets
were sitting before him, he said to his
servant, "Set on the great pot, and
boil pottage for the sons of the prophets." 39 One of them went out into the
field to gather herbs, and found a wild
vine and gathered from it his lap full
of wild gourds, and came and cut them
up into the pot of pottage, not knowing
what they were. 40 And they poured
out for the men to eat. But while they
were eating of the pottage, they cried
out, "O man of God, there is death in
the pot!" And they could not eat it.
41 He said, "Then bring meal." And
he threw it into the pot, and said,
"Pour out for the men, that they may
eat." And there was no harm in the
pot.

42 A man came from Bā'ȧl-shal'ĭ-
shȧh, bringing the man of God bread
of the first fruits, twenty loaves of
barley, and fresh ears of grain in his
sack. And E·lī'shȧ said, "Give to the
men, that they may eat." 43 But his
servant said, "How am I to set this
before a hundred men?" So he repeated, "Give them to the men, that
they may eat, for thus says the LORD,
'They shall eat and have some left.' "
44 So he set it before them. And they
ate, and had some left, according to
the word of the LORD.

5 Nā'ȧ·man, commander of the
army of the king of Syria, was a
great man with his master and in high
favor, because by him the LORD had
given victory to Syria. He was a
mighty man of valor, but he was a
leper. 2 Now the Syrians on one of
their raids had carried off a little maid
from the land of Israel, and she waited
on Nā'ȧ·man's wife. 3 She said to her
mistress, "Would that my lord were
with the prophet who is in Sȧ·mâr'ĭ·ȧ!
He would cure him of his leprosy." 4 So
Nā'ȧ·man went in and told his lord,
"Thus and so spoke the maiden from
the land of Israel." 5 And the king of
Syria said, "Go now, and I will send
a letter to the king of Israel."

So he went, taking with him ten
talents of silver, six thousand shekels
of gold, and ten festal garments. 6 And
he brought the letter to the king of
Israel, which read, "When this letter
reaches you, know that I have sent to
you Nā'ȧ·man my servant, that you
may cure him of his leprosy." 7 And
when the king of Israel read the letter,
he rent his clothes and said, "Am I
God, to kill and to make alive, that
this man sends word to me to cure a
man of his leprosy? Only consider, and
see how he is seeking a quarrel with
me."

8 But when E·lī'shȧ the man of God
heard that the king of Israel had rent
his clothes, he sent to the king, saying,
"Why have you rent your clothes? Let

4.33: Mt 6.6.

him come now to me, that he may
know that there is a prophet in Israel."
9 So Nā'ȧ·man came with his horses
and chariots, and halted at the door of
E·lī'shȧ's house. 10And E·lī'shȧ sent a
messenger to him, saying, "Go and
wash in the Jordan seven times, and
your flesh shall be restored, and you
shall be clean." 11 But Nā'ȧ·man was
angry, and went away, saying, "Behold, I thought that he would surely
come out to me, and stand, and call
on the name of the LORD his God, and
wave his hand over the place, and cure
the leper. 12Are not Ȧ·bā'nȧ[e] and
Phär'pär, the rivers of Damascus,
better than all the waters of Israel?
Could I not wash in them, and be
clean?" So he turned and went away
in a rage. 13 But his servants came
near and said to him, "My father, if
the prophet had commanded you to
do some great thing, would you not
have done it? How much rather, then,
when he says to you, 'Wash, and be
clean?'" 14 So he went down and
dipped himself seven times in the
Jordan, according to the word of the
man of God; and his flesh was restored
like the flesh of a little child, and he
was clean.

15 Then he returned to the man of
God, he and all his company, and he
came and stood before him; and he
said, "Behold, I know that there is no
God in all the earth but in Israel; so
accept now a present from your servant." 16 But he said, "As the LORD
lives, whom I serve, I will receive
none." And he urged him to take it,
but he refused. 17 Then Nā'ȧ·man
said, "If not, I pray you, let there be
given to your servant two mules'
burden of earth; for henceforth your
servant will not offer burnt offering or
sacrifice to any god but the LORD. 18 In
this matter may the LORD pardon your
servant: when my master goes into the
house of Rim'mon to worship there,
leaning on my arm, and I bow myself
in the house of Rimmon, when I bow
myself in the house of Rimmon, the
LORD pardon your servant in this
matter." 19 He said to him, "Go in
peace."

But when Nā'ȧ·man had gone from
him a short distance, 20 Ge·hā'zī, the
servant of E·lī'shȧ the man of God,
said, "See, my master has spared this
Nā'ȧ·man the Syrian, in not accepting
from his hand what he brought. As the
LORD lives, I will run after him, and
get something from him." 21 So
Ge·hā'zī followed Nā'ȧ·man. And
when Naaman saw some one running
after him, he alighted from the chariot
to meet him, and said, "Is all well?"
22And he said, "All is well. My master
has sent me to say, 'There have just
now come to me from the hill country
of E'phrȧ·im two young men of the
sons of the prophets; pray, give them
a talent of silver and two festal garments.'" 23And Nā'ȧ·man said, "Be
pleased to accept two talents." And he
urged him, and tied up two talents of
silver in two bags, with two festal
garments, and laid them upon two of
his servants; and they carried them
before Ge·hā'zī. 24And when he came
to the hill, he took them from their
hand, and put them in the house; and
he sent the men away, and they
departed. 25 He went in, and stood
before his master, and E·lī'shȧ said to
him, "Where have you been, Ge·hā'-
zī?" And he said, "Your servant went
nowhere." 26 But he said to him, "Did
I not go with you in spirit when the
man turned from his chariot to meet
you? Was it a time to accept money
and garments, olive orchards and vineyards, sheep and oxen, menservants
and maidservants? 27 Therefore the
leprosy of Nā'ȧ·man shall cleave to
you, and to your descendants for
ever." So he went out from his presence a leper, as white as snow.

6 Now the sons of the prophets
said to E·lī'shȧ, "See, the place
where we dwell under your charge is
too small for us. 2 Let us go to the
Jordan and each of us get there a log,
and let us make a place for us to dwell
there." And he answered, "Go."
3 Then one of them said, "Be pleased
to go with your servants." And he
answered, "I will go." 4 So he went
with them. And when they came to
the Jordan, they cut down trees. 5 But
as one was felling a log, his axe head
fell into the water; and he cried out,
"Alas, my master! It was borrowed."
6 Then the man of God said, "Where
did it fall?" When he showed him the
place, he cut off a stick, and threw it
in there, and made the iron float. 7And
he said, "Take it up." So he reached
out his hand and took it.

8 Once when the king of Syria was

[e] Another reading is *Amana*

warring against Israel, he took counsel
with his servants, saying, "At such
and such a place shall be my camp."
9 But the man of God sent word to the
king of Israel, "Beware that you do
not pass this place, for the Syrians are
going down there." 10 And the king of
Israel sent to the place of which the
man of God told him. Thus he used to
warn him, so that he saved himself
there more than once or twice.

11 And the mind of the king of
Syria was greatly troubled because of
this thing; and he called his servants
and said to them, "Will you not show
me who of us is for the king of Israel?"
12 And one of his servants said, "None,
my lord, O king; but E·lī'shȧ, the
prophet who is in Israel, tells the king
of Israel the words that you speak in
your bedchamber." 13 And he said,
"Go and see where he is, that I may
send and seize him." It was told him,
"Behold, he is in Dō'thȧn." 14 So he
sent there horses and chariots and a
great army; and they came by night,
and surrounded the city.

15 When the servant of the man of
God rose early in the morning and
went out, behold, an army with horses
and chariots was round about the city.
And the servant said, "Alas, my
master! What shall we do?" 16 He said,
"Fear not, for those who are with us are
more than those who are with them."
17 Then E·lī'shȧ prayed, and said, "O
LORD, I pray thee, open his eyes that
he may see." So the LORD opened the
eyes of the young man, and he saw;
and behold, the mountain was full of
horses and chariots of fire round about
Elisha. 18 And when the Syrians came
down against him, E·lī'shȧ prayed to
the LORD, and said, "Strike this people,
I pray thee, with blindness." So he
struck them with blindness in accordance with the prayer of Elisha. 19 And
E·lī'shȧ said to them, "This is not the
way, and this is not the city; follow
me, and I will bring you to the man
whom you seek." And he led them to
Sȧ·mâr'i·ȧ.

20 As soon as they entered Sȧ-
mâr'i·ȧ, E·lī'shȧ said, "O LORD, open
the eyes of these men, that they may
see." So the LORD opened their eyes,
and they saw; and lo, they were in the
midst of Samaria. 21 When the king of
Israel saw them he said to E·lī'shȧ,
"My father, shall I slay them? Shall I
slay them?" 22 He answered, "You
shall not slay them. Would you slay
those whom you have taken captive
with your sword and with your bow?
Set bread and water before them, that
they may eat and drink and go to their
master." 23 So he prepared for them
a great feast; and when they had eaten
and drunk, he sent them away, and
they went to their master. And the
Syrians came no more on raids into
the land of Israel.

24 Afterward Ben-hā'dad king of
Syria mustered his entire army, and
went up, and besieged Sȧ·mâr'i·ȧ.
25 And there was a great famine in
Sȧ·mâr'i·ȧ, as they besieged it, until
an ass's head was sold for eighty
shekels of silver, and the fourth part
of a kab of dove's dung for five shekels
of silver. 26 Now as the king of Israel
was passing by upon the wall, a
woman cried out to him, saying,
"Help, my lord, O king!" 27 And he
said, "If the LORD will not help you,
whence shall I help you? From the
threshing floor, or from the wine
press?" 28 And the king asked her,
"What is your trouble?" She answered,
"This woman said to me, 'Give your
son, that we may eat him today, and
we will eat my son tomorrow.' 29 So
we boiled my son, and ate him. And
on the next day I said to her, 'Give
your son, that we may eat him'; but
she has hidden her son." 30 When the
king heard the words of the woman he
rent his clothes—now he was passing
by upon the wall—and the people
looked, and behold, he had sackcloth
beneath upon his body—31 and he
said, "May God do so to me, and more
also, if the head of E·lī'shȧ the son of
Shā'phȧt remains on his shoulders
today."

32 E·lī'shȧ was sitting in his house,
and the elders were sitting with him.
Now the king had dispatched a man
from his presence; but before the
messenger arrived Elisha said to the
elders, "Do you see how this murderer
has sent to take off my head? Look,
when the messenger comes, shut the
door, and hold the door fast against
him. Is not the sound of his master's
feet behind him?" 33 And while he was
still speaking with them, the king[f]
came down to him and said, "This
trouble is from the LORD! Why should
I wait for the LORD any longer?"

[f] See 7.2: Heb *messenger*

7 1 But E·li'shȧ said, "Hear the
word of the LORD: thus says the
LORD, Tomorrow about this time a
measure of fine meal shall be sold for
a shekel, and two measures of barley
for a shekel, at the gate of Sȧ·mâr'i·ȧ."
2 Then the captain on whose hand the
king leaned said to the man of God,
"If the LORD himself should make
windows in heaven, could this thing
be?" But he said, "You shall see it
with your own eyes, but you shall not
eat of it."

3 Now there were four men who
were lepers at the entrance to the gate;
and they said to one another, "Why
do we sit here till we die? 4 If we say,
'Let us enter the city,' the famine is
in the city, and we shall die there; and
if we sit here, we die also. So now
come, let us go over to the camp of the
Syrians; if they spare our lives we
shall live, and if they kill us we shall
but die." 5 So they arose at twilight to
go to the camp of the Syrians; but
when they came to the edge of the
camp of the Syrians, behold, there was
no one there. 6 For the Lord had made
the army of the Syrians hear the
sound of chariots, and of horses, the
sound of a great army, so that they
said to one another, "Behold, the king
of Israel has hired against us the kings
of the Hit'tītes and the kings of Egypt
to come upon us." 7 So they fled
away in the twilight and forsook their
tents, their horses, and their asses,
leaving the camp as it was, and fled
for their lives. 8 And when these lepers
came to the edge of the camp, they
went into a tent, and ate and drank,
and they carried off silver and gold
and clothing, and went and hid them;
then they came back, and entered
another tent, and carried off things
from it, and went and hid them.

9 Then they said to one another,
"We are not doing right. This day is
a day of good news; if we are silent
and wait until the morning light,
punishment will overtake us; now
therefore come, let us go and tell the
king's household." 10 So they came
and called to the gatekeepers of the
city, and told them, "We came to the
camp of the Syrians, and behold, there
was no one to be seen or heard there,
nothing but the horses tied, and the
asses tied, and the tents as they were."
11 Then the gatekeepers called out,
and it was told within the king's
household. 12 And the king rose in the
night, and said to his servants, "I will
tell you what the Syrians have prepared against us. They know that we
are hungry; therefore they have gone
out of the camp to hide themselves in
the open country, thinking, 'When
they come out of the city, we shall
take them alive and get into the city.'"
13 And one of his servants said, "Let
some men take five of the remaining
horses, seeing that those who are left
here will fare like the whole multitude
of Israel that have already perished;
let us send and see." 14 So they took
two mounted men, and the king sent
them after the army of the Syrians,
saying, "Go and see." 15 So they went
after them as far as the Jordan; and,
lo, all the way was littered with garments and equipment which the
Syrians had thrown away in their
haste. And the messengers returned,
and told the king.

16 Then the people went out, and
plundered the camp of the Syrians. So
a measure of fine meal was sold for a
shekel, and two measures of barley for
a shekel, according to the word of the
LORD. 17 Now the king had appointed
the captain on whose hand he leaned
to have charge of the gate; and the
people trod upon him in the gate, so
that he died, as the man of God had
said when the king came down to him.
18 For when the man of God had said
to the king, "Two measures of barley
shall be sold for a shekel, and a measure of fine meal for a shekel, about this
time tomorrow in the gate of Sȧ·mâr'-
i·ȧ," 19 the captain had answered the
man of God, "If the LORD himself
should make windows in heaven,
could such a thing be?" And he had
said, "You shall see it with your own
eyes, but you shall not eat of it."
20 And so it happened to him, for the
people trod upon him in the gate and
he died.

8 Now E·li'shȧ had said to the
woman whose son he had restored
to life, "Arise, and depart with your
household, and sojourn wherever you
can; for the LORD has called for a
famine, and it will come upon the land
for seven years." 2 So the woman
arose, and did according to the word
of the man of God; she went with her
household and sojourned in the land
of the Philistines seven years. 3 And at
the end of the seven years, when the

woman returned from the land of the
Philistines, she went forth to appeal
to the king for her house and her land.
4 Now the king was talking with Ge-
hā'zī the servant of the man of God,
saying, "Tell me all the great things
that E·lī'shȧ has done." 5And while he
was telling the king how E·lī'shȧ had
restored the dead to life, behold, the
woman whose son he had restored to
life appealed to the king for her house
and her land. And Ge·hā'zī said, "My
lord, O king, here is the woman, and
here is her son whom Elisha restored
to life." 6And when the king asked the
woman, she told him. So the king
appointed an official for her, saying,
"Restore all that was hers, together
with all the produce of the fields from
the day that she left the land until
now."

7 Now E·lī'shȧ came to Damascus.
Ben-hā'dad the king of Syria was sick;
and when it was told him, "The man
of God has come here," 8 the king
said to Haz'ȧ·el, "Take a present with
you and go to meet the man of God,
and inquire of the LORD through him,
saying, 'Shall I recover from this sickness?' " 9 So Haz'ȧ·el went to meet
him, and took a present with him, all
kinds of goods of Damascus, forty
camel loads. When he came and stood
before him, he said, "Your son Ben-
hā'dad king of Syria has sent me to
you, saying, 'Shall I recover from this
sickness?' " 10And E·lī'shȧ said to him,
"Go, say to him, 'You shall certainly
recover'; but the LORD has shown me
that he shall certainly die." 11And he
fixed his gaze and stared at him, until
he was ashamed. And the man of God
wept. 12And Haz'ȧ·el said, "Why does
my lord weep?" He answered, "Because I know the evil that you will do
to the people of Israel; you will set on
fire their fortresses, and you will slay
their young men with the sword, and
dash in pieces their little ones, and rip
up their women with child." 13And
Haz'ȧ·el said, "What is your servant,
who is but a dog, that he should do
this great thing?" E·lī'shȧ answered,
"The LORD has shown me that you
are to be king over Syria." 14 Then he
departed from E·lī'shȧ, and came to
his master, who said to him, "What
did Elisha say to you?" And he answered, "He told me that you would
certainly recover." 15 But on the
morrow he took the coverlet and
dipped it in water and spread it over
his face, till he died. And Haz'ȧ·el
became king in his stead.

16 In the fifth year of Jō'rȧm the
son of Ā'hab, king of Israel,[g] Je·hō'-
rȧm the son of Je·hosh'ȧ·phat, king of
Judah, began to reign. 17 He was
thirty-two years old when he became
king, and he reigned eight years in
Jerusalem. 18And he walked in the
way of the kings of Israel, as the house
of Ā'hab had done, for the daughter of
Ahab was his wife. And he did what
was evil in the sight of the LORD.
19 Yet the LORD would not destroy
Judah, for the sake of David his
servant, since he promised to give a
lamp to him and to his sons for ever.

20 In his days Ē'dȯm revolted from
the rule of Judah, and set up a king of
their own. 21 Then Jō'rȧm passed over
to Zā'ir with all his chariots, and rose
by night, and he and his chariot commanders smote the Ē'dȯm·ītes who
had surrounded him; but his army fled
home. 22 So Ē'dȯm revolted from the
rule of Judah to this day. Then Lib'-
nȧh revolted at the same time. 23 Now
the rest of the acts of Jō'rȧm, and all
that he did, are they not written in the
Book of the Chronicles of the Kings
of Judah? 24 So Jō'rȧm slept with his
fathers, and was buried with his
fathers in the city of David; and Ā·hȧ-
zī'ȧh his son reigned in his stead.

25 In the twelfth year of Jō'rȧm
the son of Ā'hab, king of Israel, Ā·hȧ-
zī'ȧh the son of Je·hō'rȧm, king of
Judah, began to reign. 26 Ā·hȧ·zī'ȧh was
twenty-two years old when he began
to reign, and he reigned one year in
Jerusalem. His mother's name was
Ath·ȧ·lī'ȧh; she was a granddaughter
of Om'rī king of Israel. 27 He also
walked in the way of the house of
Ā'hab, and did what was evil in the
sight of the LORD, as the house of
Ahab had done, for he was son-in-law
to the house of Ahab.

28 He went with Jō'rȧm the son of
Ā'hab to make war against Haz'ȧ·el
king of Syria at Rā'moth-gil'ē·ȧd,
where the Syrians wounded Joram.
29And King Jō'rȧm returned to be
healed in Jez'rē·ėl of the wounds
which the Syrians had given him at
Rā'mȧh, when he fought against Haz'-

[g] Gk Syr: Heb *Israel, Jehoshaphat being king of Judah*
8.17-24: 2 Chron 21.5-10, 20. **8.24-29**: 2 Chron 22.1-6.

ȧ·el king of Syria. And A̅·hȧ·zī′ȧh the
son of Je·hō′rȧm king of Judah went
down to see Joram the son of A̅′hab
in Jezreel, because he was sick.

9 Then E·lī′shȧ the prophet called
one of the sons of the prophets and
said to him, "Gird up your loins, and
take this flask of oil in your hand,
and go to Rā′moth-gil′ē·ȧd. 2 And
when you arrive, look there for Jē′hū
the son of Je·hosh′ȧ·phat, son of
Nim′shī; and go in and bid him rise
from among his fellows, and lead him
to an inner chamber. 3 Then take the
flask of oil, and pour it on his head,
and say, 'Thus says the LORD, I anoint
you king over Israel.' Then open the
door and flee; do not tarry."

4 So the young man, the prophet,[h]
went to Rā′moth-gil′ē·ȧd. 5 And when
he came, behold, the commanders of
the army were in council; and he said,
"I have an errand to you, O commander." And Jē′hū said, "To which
of us all?" And he said, "To you, O
commander." 6 So he arose, and went
into the house; and the young man
poured oil on his head, saying to him,
"Thus says the LORD the God of
Israel, I anoint you king over the
people of the LORD, over Israel. 7 And
you shall strike down the house of
A̅′hab your master, that I may avenge
on Jez′ė·bėl the blood of my servants
the prophets, and the blood of all the
servants of the LORD. 8 For the whole
house of A̅′hab shall perish; and I will
cut off from Ahab every male, bond
or free, in Israel. 9 And I will make the
house of A̅′hab like the house of
Jer·ȯ·bō′ȧm the son of Nē′bat, and
like the house of Bā′ȧ·shȧ the son of
A·hī′jȧh. 10 And the dogs shall eat
Jez′ė·bėl in the territory of Jez′rē·ėl,
and none shall bury her." Then he
opened the door, and fled.

11 When Jē′hū came out to the
servants of his master, they said to
him, "Is all well? Why did this mad
fellow come to you?" And he said to
them, "You know the fellow and his
talk." 12 And they said, "That is not
true; tell us now." And he said, "Thus
and so he spoke to me, saying, 'Thus
says the LORD, I anoint you king over
Israel.' " 13 Then in haste every man
of them took his garment, and put it
under him on the bare[i] steps, and they
blew the trumpet, and proclaimed,
"Jē′hū is king."

14 Thus Jē′hū the son of Je·hosh′ȧ-
phat the son of Nim′shī conspired
against Jō′rȧm. (Now Joram with all
Israel had been on guard at Rā′moth-
gil′ē·ȧd against Haz′ȧ·el king of Syria;
15 but King Jō′rȧm had returned to
be healed in Jez′rē·ėl of the wounds
which the Syrians had given him,
when he fought with Haz′ȧ·el king of
Syria.) So Jē′hū said, "If this is your
mind, then let no one slip out of the
city to go and tell the news in Jezreel."
16 Then Jē′hū mounted his chariot,
and went to Jez′rē·ėl, for Jō′rȧm lay
there. And A̅·hȧ·zī′ȧh king of Judah
had come down to visit Joram.

17 Now the watchman was standing
on the tower in Jez′rē·ėl, and he spied
the company of Jē′hū as he came, and
said, "I see a company." And Jō′rȧm
said, "Take a horseman, and send to
meet them, and let him say, 'Is it
peace?' " 18 So a man on horseback
went to meet him, and said, "Thus
says the king, 'Is it peace?' " And
Jē′hū said, "What have you to do with
peace? Turn round and ride behind
me." And the watchman reported,
saying, "The messenger reached them,
but he is not coming back." 19 Then
he sent out a second horseman, who
came to them, and said, "Thus the
king has said, 'Is it peace?' " And
Jē′hū answered, "What have you to
do with peace? Turn round and ride
behind me." 20 Again the watchman
reported, "He reached them, but
he is not coming back. And the driving is like the driving of Jē′hū the
son of Nim′shī; for he drives furious-
ly."

21 Jō′rȧm said, "Make ready." And
they made ready his chariot. Then
Joram king of Israel and A̅·hȧ·zī′ȧh
king of Judah set out, each in his
chariot, and went to meet Jē′hū, and
met him at the property of Nā′both
the Jez′rē·ė·līte. 22 And when Jō′rȧm
saw Jē′hū, he said, "Is it peace,
Jehu?" He answered, "What peace
can there be, so long as the harlotries
and the sorceries of your mother Jez′-
ė·bėl are so many?" 23 Then Jō′rȧm
reined about and fled, saying to
A̅·hȧ·zī′ȧh, "Treachery, O Ahaziah!"
24 And Jē′hū drew his bow with his

[h] Gk Syr: Heb *the young man, the young man, the prophet*
[i] The meaning of the Hebrew word is uncertain
9.1-10: 2 Chron 22.7-9.

full strength, and shot Jō'rȧm between
the shoulders, so that the arrow pierced
his heart, and he sank in his chariot.
25 Jē'hū said to Bid'kär his aide, "Take
him up, and cast him on the plot of
ground belonging to Nā'both the Jez'-
rē·ė·līte; for remember, when you and
I rode side by side behind Ā'hab his
father, how the LORD uttered this
oracle against him: 26 'As surely as I
saw yesterday the blood of Nā'both
and the blood of his sons—says the
LORD—I will requite you on this plot
of ground.' Now therefore take him up
and cast him on the plot of ground, in
accordance with the word of the
LORD."
27 When Ā·hȧ·zī'ȧh the king of
Judah saw this, he fled in the direction
of Beth-hag'gȧn. And Jē'hū pursued
him, and said, "Shoot him also"; and
they shot him[j] in the chariot at the
ascent of Gūr, which is by Ib'lē·ȧm.
And he fled to Mė·gid'dō, and died
there. 28 His servants carried him in a
chariot to Jerusalem, and buried him
in his tomb with his fathers in the city
of David.
29 In the eleventh year of Jō'rȧm
the son of Ā'hab, Ā·hȧ·zī'ȧh began to
reign over Judah.
30 When Jē'hū came to Jez'rē·ėl,
Jez'ė·bėl heard of it; and she painted
her eyes, and adorned her head, and
looked out of the window. 31 And as
Jē'hū entered the gate, she said, "Is it
peace, you Zim'rī, murderer of your
master?" 32 And he lifted up his face
to the window, and said, "Who is on
my side? Who?" Two or three eunuchs
looked out at him. 33 He said, "Throw
her down." So they threw her down;
and some of her blood spattered on
the wall and on the horses, and they
trampled on her. 34 Then he went in
and ate and drank; and he said, "See
now to this cursed woman, and bury
her; for she is a king's daughter."
35 But when they went to bury her,
they found no more of her than the
skull and the feet and the palms of her
hands. 36 When they came back and
told him, he said, "This is the word
of the LORD, which he spoke by his
servant E·lī'jȧh the Tish'bīte, 'In the
territory of Jez'rē·ėl the dogs shall eat
the flesh of Jez'ė·bėl; 37 and the corpse
of Jez'ė·bėl shall be as dung upon the
face of the field in the territory of
Jez'rē·ėl, so that no one can say, This
is Jezebel.' "

10 Now Ā'hab had seventy sons in
Sȧ·mâr'i·ȧ. So Jē'hū wrote letters,
and sent them to Samaria, to the rulers
of the city,[k] to the elders, and to the
guardians of the sons of Ahab, saying,
2 "Now then, as soon as this letter
comes to you, seeing your master's
sons are with you, and there are with
you chariots and horses, fortified cities
also, and weapons, 3 select the best
and fittest of your master's sons and
set him on his father's throne, and
fight for your master's house." 4 But
they were exceedingly afraid, and said,
"Behold, the two kings could not stand
before him; how then can we stand?"
5 So he who was over the palace, and
he who was over the city, together
with the elders and the guardians, sent
to Jē'hū, saying, "We are your servants, and we will do all that you bid
us. We will not make any one king; do
whatever is good in your eyes." 6 Then
he wrote to them a second letter, saying, "If you are on my side, and if you
are ready to obey me, take the heads
of your master's sons, and come to me
at Jez'rē·ėl tomorrow at this time."
Now the king's sons, seventy persons,
were with the great men of the city,
who were bringing them up. 7 And
when the letter came to them, they
took the king's sons, and slew them,
seventy persons, and put their heads
in baskets, and sent them to him at
Jez'rē·ėl. 8 When the messenger came
and told him, "They have brought the
heads of the king's sons," he said,
"Lay them in two heaps at the entrance of the gate until the morning."
9 Then in the morning, when he went
out, he stood, and said to all the people, "You are innocent. It was I who
conspired against my master, and slew
him; but who struck down all these?
10 Know then that there shall fall to
the earth nothing of the word of the
LORD, which the LORD spoke concerning the house of Ā'hab; for the LORD
has done what he said by his servant
E·lī'jȧh." 11 So Jē'hū slew all that
remained of the house of Ā'hab in
Jez'rē·ėl, all his great men, and his
familiar friends, and his priests, until
he left him none remaining.
12 Then he set out and went to
Sȧ·mâr'i·ȧ. On the way, when he was

[j] Syr Vg Compare Gk: Heb lacks *and they shot him* [k] Gk Vg: Heb *Jezreel*
9.25: 1 Kings 21.19. **9.36:** 1 Kings 21.23; 2 Chron 22.7-9.

at Beth-ek'ed of the Shepherds, 13 Jē'-
hū met the kinsmen of Ā·hȧ·zī'ȧh king
of Judah, and he said, "Who are you?"
And they answered, "We are the kinsmen of Ahaziah, and we came down
to visit the royal princes and the sons
of the queen mother." 14 He said,
"Take them alive." And they took
them alive, and slew them at the pit
of Beth-ek'ed, forty-two persons, and
he spared none of them.
15 And when he departed from
there, he met Je·hon'ȧ·dab the son of
Rē'chab coming to meet him; and he
greeted him, and said to him, "Is your
heart true to my heart as mine is to
yours?"[l] And Je·hon'ȧ·dab answered,
"It is." Jē'hū said,[m] "If it is, give me
your hand." So he gave him his hand.
And Jehu took him up with him into
the chariot. 16 And he said, "Come
with me, and see my zeal for the
LORD." So he[n] had him ride in his
chariot. 17 And when he came to
Sȧ·mâr'i·ȧ, he slew all that remained
to Ā'hab in Samaria, till he had wiped
them out, according to the word of
the LORD which he spoke to E·lī'-
jȧh.
18 Then Jē'hū assembled all the
people, and said to them, "Ā'hab
served Bā'ȧl a little; but Jehu will serve
him much. 19 Now therefore call to
me all the prophets of Bā'ȧl, all his
worshipers and all his priests; let none
be missing, for I have a great sacrifice
to offer to Baal; whoever is missing
shall not live." But Jē'hū did it with
cunning in order to destroy the worshipers of Baal. 20 And Jē'hū ordered,
"Sanctify a solemn assembly for
Bā'ȧl." So they proclaimed it. 21 And
Jē'hū sent throughout all Israel; and
all the worshipers of Bā'ȧl came, so
that there was not a man left who did
not come. And they entered the house
of Baal, and the house of Baal was
filled from one end to the other. 22 He
said to him who was in charge of the
wardrobe, "Bring out the vestments
for all the worshipers of Bā'ȧl." So he
brought out the vestments for them.
23 Then Jē'hū went into the house of
Bā'ȧl with Je·hon'ȧ·dab the son of
Rē'chab; and he said to the worshipers
of Baal, "Search, and see that there is
no servant of the LORD here among
you, but only the worshipers of Baal."
24 Then he[o] went in to offer sacrifices
and burnt offerings.
Now Jē'hū had stationed eighty men
outside, and said, "The man who
allows any of those whom I give into
your hands to escape shall forfeit his
life." 25 So as soon as he had made an
end of offering the burnt offering,
Jē'hū said to the guard and to the
officers, "Go in and slay them; let not
a man escape." So when they put them
to the sword, the guard and the officers
cast them out and went into the inner
room[p] of the house of Bā'ȧl 26 and they
brought out the pillar that was in the
house of Bā'ȧl, and burned it. 27 And
they demolished the pillar of Bā'ȧl,
and demolished the house of Baal, and
made it a latrine to this day.
28 Thus Jē'hū wiped out Bā'ȧl from
Israel. 29 But Jē'hū did not turn aside
from the sins of Jer·ȯ·bō'ȧm the son
of Nē'bat, which he made Israel to sin,
the golden calves that were in Beth'ĕl,
and in Dan. 30 And the LORD said to
Jē'hū, "Because you have done well
in carrying out what is right in my
eyes, and have done to the house of
Ā'hab according to all that was in my
heart, your sons of the fourth generation shall sit on the throne of Israel."
31 But Jē'hū was not careful to walk
in the law of the LORD the God of
Israel with all his heart; he did not
turn from the sins of Jer·ȯ·bō'ȧm,
which he made Israel to sin.
32 In those days the LORD began to
cut off parts of Israel. Haz'ȧ·el defeated them throughout the territory
of Israel: 33 from the Jordan eastward,
all the land of Gilead, the Gadites, and
the Reubenites, and the Mȧ·nas'sītes,
from Ȧ·rō'ĕr, which is by the valley of
the Är'non, that is, Gilead and Bā'-
shȧn. 34 Now the rest of the acts of
Jē'hū, and all that he did, and all his
might, are they not written in the
Book of the Chronicles of the Kings
of Israel? 35 So Jē'hū slept with his
fathers, and they buried him in Sȧ-
mâr'i·ȧ. And Je·hō'ȧ·haz his son
reigned in his stead. 36 The time that
Jē'hū reigned over Israel in Sȧ·mâr'i·ȧ
was twenty-eight years.

11 Now when Ath·ȧ·lī'ȧh the
mother of Ā·hȧ·zī'ȧh saw that her
son was dead, she arose and destroyed
all the royal family. 2 But Je·hosh'ē·bȧ,

[l] Gk: Heb *Is it right with your heart, as my heart is with your heart?* [m] Gk: Heb lacks *Jehu said*
[n] Gk Syr Tg: Heb *they* [o] Gk Compare verse 25: Heb *they* [p] Cn: Heb *city*
11.1-20: 2 Chron 22.10-23.21.

the daughter of King Jō'răm, sister of A·hă·zī'ăh, took Jō'ash the son of Ahaziah, and stole him away from among the king's sons who were about to be slain, and she put[q] him and his nurse in a bedchamber. Thus she[r] hid him from Ath·ȧ·lī'ăh, so that he was not slain; 3 and he remained with her six years, hid in the house of the LORD, while Ath·ȧ·lī'ăh reigned over the land.

4 But in the seventh year Je·hoi'ȧ·dȧ sent and brought the captains of the Car'i·tēs and of the guards, and had them come to him in the house of the LORD; and he made a covenant with them and put them under oath in the house of the LORD, and he showed them the king's son. 5 And he commanded them, "This is the thing that you shall do: one third of you, those who come off duty on the sabbath and guard the king's house 6 (another third being at the gate Sūr and a third at the gate behind the guards), shall guard the palace; 7 and the two divisions of you, which come on duty in force on the sabbath and guard the house of the LORD,[s] 8 shall surround the king, each with his weapons in his hand; and whoever approaches the ranks is to be slain. Be with the king when he goes out and when he comes in."

9 The captains did according to all that Je·hoi'ȧ·dȧ the priest commanded, and each brought his men who were to go off duty on the sabbath, with those who were to come on duty on the sabbath, and came to Jehoiada the priest. 10 And the priest delivered to the captains the spears and shields that had been King David's, which were in the house of the LORD; 11 and the guards stood, every man with his weapons in his hand, from the south side of the house to the north side of the house, around the altar and the house.[t] 12 Then he brought out the king's son, and put the crown upon him, and gave him the testimony; and they proclaimed him king, and anointed him; and they clapped their hands, and said, "Long live the king!"

13 When Ath·ȧ·lī'ăh heard the noise of the guard and of the people, she went into the house of the LORD to the people; 14 and when she looked, there was the king standing by the pillar, according to the custom, and the captains and the trumpeters beside the king, and all the people of the land rejoicing and blowing trumpets. And Ath·ȧ·lī'ăh rent her clothes, and cried, "Treason! Treason!" 15 Then Je·hoi'ȧ·dȧ the priest commanded the captains who were set over the army, "Bring her out between the ranks; and slay with the sword any one who follows her." For the priest said, "Let her not be slain in the house of the LORD." 16 So they laid hands on her; and she went through the horses' entrance to the king's house, and there she was slain.

17 And Je·hoi'ȧ·dȧ made a covenant between the LORD and the king and people, that they should be the LORD's people; and also between the king and the people. 18 Then all the people of the land went to the house of Bā'ăl, and tore it down; his altars and his images they broke in pieces, and they slew Mat'tan the priest of Baal before the altars. And the priest posted watchmen over the house of the LORD. 19 And he took the captains, the Car'i·tēs, the guards, and all the people of the land; and they brought the king down from the house of the LORD, marching through the gate of the guards to the king's house. And he took his seat on the throne of the kings. 20 So all the people of the land rejoiced; and the city was quiet after Ath·ȧ·lī'ăh had been slain with the sword at the king's house.

21[u] Je·hō'ash was seven years old when he began to reign.

12 In the seventh year of Jē'hū Je·hō'ash began to reign, and he reigned forty years in Jerusalem. His mother's name was Zib'i·ăh of Beer-sheba. 2 And Je·hō'ash did what was right in the eyes of the LORD all his days, because Je·hoi'ȧ·dȧ the priest instructed him. 3 Nevertheless the high places were not taken away; the people continued to sacrifice and burn incense on the high places.

4 Je·hō'ash said to the priests, "All the money of the holy things which is brought into the house of the LORD, the money for which each man is assessed—the money from the assessment of persons—and the money which a man's heart prompts him to

[q] With 2 Chron 22.11: Heb lacks *and she put* [r] Gk Syr Vg Compare 2 Chron 22.11: Heb *they* [s] Heb *the* LORD *to the king* [t] Heb *the house to the king* [u] Ch 12.1 in Heb
11.21-12.14: 2 Chron 24.1-14.

bring into the house of the LORD, 5 let
the priests take, each from his ac-
quaintance; and let them repair the
house wherever any need of repairs is
discovered." 6 But by the twenty-third
year of King Je·hō′ash the priests had
made no repairs on the house. 7 Therefore King Je·hō′ash summoned Je-
hoi′ȧ·dȧ the priest and the other priests
and said to them, "Why are you not
repairing the house? Now therefore
take no more money from your acquaintances, but hand it over for the
repair of the house." 8 So the priests
agreed that they should take no more
money from the people, and that they
should not repair the house.
9 Then Je·hoi′ȧ·dȧ the priest took
a chest, and bored a hole in the lid of
it, and set it beside the altar on the
right side as one entered the house of
the LORD; and the priests who guarded
the threshold put in it all the money
that was brought into the house of
the LORD. 10 And whenever they saw
that there was much money in the
chest, the king's secretary and the
high priest came up and they counted
and tied up in bags the money that
was found in the house of the LORD.
11 Then they would give the money
that was weighed out into the hands
of the workmen who had the oversight
of the house of the LORD; and they paid
it out to the carpenters and the builders
who worked upon the house of the
LORD, 12 and to the masons and the
stonecutters, as well as to buy timber
and quarried stone for making repairs
on the house of the LORD, and for any
outlay upon the repairs of the house.
13 But there were not made for the
house of the LORD basins of silver,
snuffers, bowls, trumpets, or any
vessels of gold, or of silver, from the
money that was brought into the house
of the LORD, 14 for that was given to
the workmen who were repairing the
house of the LORD with it. 15 And they
did not ask an accounting from the
men into whose hand they delivered
the money to pay out to the workmen,
for they dealt honestly. 16 The money
from the guilt offerings and the money
from the sin offerings was not brought
into the house of the LORD; it belonged
to the priests.
17 At that time Haz′ȧ·el king of
Syria went up and fought against Gath,
and took it. But when Hazael set his
face to go up against Jerusalem, 18 Je-
hō′ash king of Judah took all the
votive gifts that Je·hosh′ȧ·phat and
Je·hō′ram and Ā·hȧ·zī′ah, his fathers,
the kings of Judah, had dedicated, and
his own votive gifts, and all the gold
that was found in the treasuries of the
house of the LORD and of the king's
house, and sent these to Haz′ȧ·el king
of Syria. Then Hazael went away from
Jerusalem.
19 Now the rest of the acts of
Jō′ash, and all that he did, are they not
written in the Book of the Chronicles
of the Kings of Judah? 20 His servants
arose and made a conspiracy, and slew
Jō′ash in the house of Mil′lō, on the
way that goes down to Sil′lȧ. 21 It was
Jō′zȧ·cär the son of Shim′ē·ath and
Je·hō′zȧ·bad the son of Shō′mėr, his
servants, who struck him down, so
that he died. And they buried him
with his fathers in the city of David,
and Am·ȧ·zī′ah his son reigned in his
stead.

13 In the twenty-third year of
Jō′ash the son of Ā·hȧ·zī′ah, king
of Judah, Je·hō′ȧ·haz the son of Jē′hū
began to reign over Israel in Sȧ·mâr′i·ȧ,
and he reigned seventeen years. 2 He
did what was evil in the sight of the
LORD, and followed the sins of Jer·ȯ-
bō′ȧm the son of Nē′bat, which he
made Israel to sin; he did not depart
from them. 3 And the anger of the
LORD was kindled against Israel, and
he gave them continually into the hand
of Haz′ȧ·el king of Syria and into the
hand of Ben-hā′dad the son of Hazael.
4 Then Je·hō′ȧ·haz besought the LORD,
and the LORD hearkened to him; for he
saw the oppression of Israel, how the
king of Syria oppressed them. 5 (Therefore the LORD gave Israel a savior, so
that they escaped from the hand of
the Syrians; and the people of Israel
dwelt in their homes as formerly.
6 Nevertheless they did not depart
from the sins of the house of Jer·ȯ-
bō′ȧm, which he made Israel to sin,
but walked[v] in them; and the Ȧ·shē′-
rȧh also remained in Sȧ·mâr′i·ȧ.) 7 For
there was not left to Je·hō′ȧ·haz an
army of more than fifty horsemen and
ten chariots and ten thousand footmen;
for the king of Syria had destroyed
them and made them like the dust at
threshing. 8 Now the rest of the acts of

[v] Gk Syr Tg Vg: Heb *he walked*
12.17-21: 2 Chron 24.23-26.

Je·hō'ȧ·haz and all that he did, and
his might, are they not written in the
Book of the Chronicles of the Kings
of Israel? 9 So Je·hō'ȧ·haz slept with
his fathers, and they buried him in
Sȧ·mâr'i·ȧ; and Jō'ash his son reigned
in his stead.

10 In the thirty-seventh year of
Jō'ash king of Judah Je·hō'ash the son
of Je·hō'ȧ·haz began to reign over
Israel in Sȧ·mâr'i·ȧ, and he reigned
sixteen years. 11 He also did what was
evil in the sight of the LORD; he did
not depart from all the sins of Jer·ȯ-
bō'ȧm the son of Nē'bat, which he
made Israel to sin, but he walked in
them. 12 Now the rest of the acts of
Jō'ash, and all that he did, and the
might with which he fought against
Am·ȧ·zī'ȧh king of Judah, are they not
written in the Book of the Chronicles
of the Kings of Israel? 13 So Jō'ash
slept with his fathers, and Jer·ȯ·bō'ȧm
sat upon his throne; and Joash was
buried in Sȧ·mâr'i·ȧ with the kings of
Israel.

14 Now when E·lī'shȧ had fallen sick
with the illness of which he was to die,
Jō'ash king of Israel went down to
him, and wept before him, crying,
"My father, my father! The chariots
of Israel and its horsemen!" 15 And
E·lī'shȧ said to him, "Take a bow and
arrows"; so he took a bow and arrows.
16 Then he said to the king of Israel,
"Draw the bow"; and he drew it. And
E·lī'shȧ laid his hands upon the king's
hands. 17 And he said, "Open the
window eastward"; and he opened it.
Then E·lī'shȧ said, "Shoot"; and he
shot. And he said, "The LORD's arrow
of victory, the arrow of victory over
Syria! For you shall fight the Syrians
in Ā'phek until you have made an end
of them." 18 And he said, "Take the
arrows"; and he took them. And he
said to the king of Israel, "Strike the
ground with them"; and he struck
three times, and stopped. 19 Then the
man of God was angry with him, and
said, "You should have struck five or
six times; then you would have struck
down Syria until you had made an end
of it, but now you will strike down
Syria only three times."

20 So E·lī'shȧ died, and they buried
him. Now bands of Mō'ȧb·ītes used to
invade the land in the spring of the
year. 21 And as a man was being buried,
lo, a marauding band was seen and
the man was cast into the grave of
E·lī'shȧ; and as soon as the man
touched the bones of Elisha, he revived, and stood on his feet.

22 Now Haz'ȧ·el king of Syria oppressed Israel all the days of Je·hō'ȧ-
haz. 23 But the LORD was gracious to
them and had compassion on them,
and he turned toward them, because
of his covenant with Abraham, Isaac,
and Jacob, and would not destroy
them; nor has he cast them from his
presence until now.

24 When Haz'ȧ·el king of Syria
died, Ben-hā'dad his son became king
in his stead. 25 Then Je·hō'ash the son
of Je·hō'ȧ·haz took again from Ben-
hā'dad the son of Haz'ȧ·el the cities
which he had taken from Jehoahaz his
father in war. Three times Jō'ash
defeated him and recovered the cities
of Israel.

14 In the second year of Jō'ash the
son of Jō'ȧ·haz, king of Israel,
Am·ȧ·zī'ȧh the son of Joash, king of
Judah, began to reign. 2 He was twenty-
five years old when he began to reign,
and he reigned twenty-nine years in
Jerusalem. His mother's name was
Jē'hō-ad'din of Jerusalem. 3 And he
did what was right in the eyes of the
LORD, yet not like David his father;
he did in all things as Jō'ash his father
had done. 4 But the high places were
not removed; the people still sacrificed
and burned incense on the high places.
5 And as soon as the royal power was
firmly in his hand he killed his servants
who had slain the king his father. 6 But
he did not put to death the children of
the murderers; according to what is
written in the book of the law of Moses,
where the LORD commanded, "The
fathers shall not be put to death for the
children, or the children be put to
death for the fathers; but every man
shall die for his own sin."

7 He killed ten thousand Ē'dȯm-
ītes in the Valley of Salt and took
Sē'lȧ by storm, and called it Jok'thē-el,
which is its name to this day.

8 Then Am·ȧ·zī'ȧh sent messengers
to Je·hō'ash the son of Je·hō'ȧ·haz, son
of Jē'hū, king of Israel, saying, "Come,
let us look one another in the face."
9 And Je·hō'ash king of Israel sent
word to Am·ȧ·zī'ȧh king of Judah, "A
thistle on Lebanon sent to a cedar on
Lebanon, saying, 'Give your daughter
to my son for a wife'; and a wild beast

14.2-6: 2 Chron 25.1-4. **14.7:** 2 Chron 25.11. **14.8-14:** 2 Chron 25.17-24.

of Lebanon passed by and trampled
down the thistle. 10 You have indeed
smitten Ē′dȯm, and your heart has
lifted you up. Be content with your
glory, and stay at home; for why should
you provoke trouble so that you fall,
you and Judah with you?"

11 But Am·ȧ·zī′ȧh would not listen.
So Je·hō′ash king of Israel went up,
and he and Amaziah king of Judah
faced one another in battle at Beth-
shē′mesh, which belongs to Judah.
12 And Judah was defeated by Israel,
and every man fled to his home. 13 And
Je·hō′ash king of Israel captured
Am·ȧ·zī′ȧh king of Judah, the son of
Jehoash, son of Ā·hȧ·zī′ȧh, at Beth-
shē′mesh, and came to Jerusalem, and
broke down the wall of Jerusalem for
four hundred cubits, from the Ē′phrȧ-
im Gate to the Corner Gate. 14 And he
seized all the gold and silver, and all
the vessels that were found in the
house of the LORD and in the treasuries
of the king's house, also hostages, and
he returned to Sȧ·mâr′i·ȧ.

15 Now the rest of the acts of
Je·hō′ash which he did, and his might,
and how he fought with Am·ȧ·zī′ȧh
king of Judah, are they not written in
the Book of the Chronicles of the Kings
of Israel? 16 And Je·hō′ash slept with
his fathers, and was buried in Sȧ·mâr′-
i·ȧ with the kings of Israel; and Jer·ȯ-
bō′ȧm his son reigned in his stead.

17 Am·ȧ·zī′ȧh the son of Jō′ash,
king of Judah, lived fifteen years after
the death of Je·hō′ash son of Je·hō′ȧ-
haz, king of Israel. 18 Now the rest of
the deeds of Am·ȧ·zī′ȧh, are they not
written in the Book of the Chronicles
of the Kings of Judah? 19 And they
made a conspiracy against him in
Jerusalem, and he fled to Lā′chish. But
they sent after him to Lachish, and
slew him there. 20 And they brought
him upon horses; and he was buried
in Jerusalem with his fathers in the
city of David. 21 And all the people of
Judah took Az·ȧ·rī′ȧh, who was sixteen
years old, and made him king instead
of his father Am·ȧ·zī′ȧh. 22 He built
Ē′lath and restored it to Judah, after
the king slept with his fathers.

23 In the fifteenth year of Am·ȧ-
zī′ȧh the son of Jō′ash, king of Judah,
Jer·ȯ·bō′ȧm the son of Joash, king of
Israel, began to reign in Sȧ·mâr′i·ȧ,
and he reigned forty-one years. 24 And
he did what was evil in the sight of the
LORD; he did not depart from all the
sins of Jer·ȯ·bō′ȧm the son of Nē′bat,
which he made Israel to sin. 25 He
restored the border of Israel from the
entrance of Hā′math as far as the Sea
of the Ar′ȧ·bȧh, according to the word
of the LORD, the God of Israel, which
he spoke by his servant Jonah the son
of Ā·mit′tāi, the prophet, who was
from Gath-hē′phėr. 26 For the LORD
saw that the affliction of Israel was
very bitter, for there was none left,
bond or free, and there was none to
help Israel. 27 But the LORD had not
said that he would blot out the name
of Israel from under heaven, so he
saved them by the hand of Jer·ȯ·bō′ȧm
the son of Jō′ash.

28 Now the rest of the acts of Jer·ȯ-
bō′ȧm, and all that he did, and his
might, how he fought, and how he
recovered for Israel Damascus and
Hā′math, which had belonged to
Judah, are they not written in the
Book of the Chronicles of the Kings
of Israel? 29 And Jer·ȯ·bō′ȧm slept with
his fathers, the kings of Israel, and
Zech·ȧ·rī′ȧh his son reigned in his
stead.

15 In the twenty-seventh year of
Jer·ȯ·bō′ȧm king of Israel Az·ȧ-
rī′ȧh the son of Am·ȧ·zī′ȧh, king of
Judah, began to reign. 2 He was sixteen years old when he began to reign,
and he reigned fifty-two years in Jerusalem. His mother's name was Jec·ȯ-
lī′ȧh of Jerusalem. 3 And he did what
was right in the eyes of the LORD,
according to all that his father Am·ȧ-
zī′ȧh had done. 4 Nevertheless the high
places were not taken away; the people
still sacrificed and burned incense on
the high places. 5 And the LORD smote
the king, so that he was a leper to the
day of his death, and he dwelt in a
separate house. And Jō′thȧm the
king's son was over the household,
governing the people of the land. 6 Now
the rest of the acts of Az·ȧ·rī′ȧh, and
all that he did, are they not written in
the Book of the Chronicles of the
Kings of Judah? 7 And Az·ȧ·rī′ȧh slept
with his fathers, and they buried him
with his fathers in the city of David,
and Jō′thȧm his son reigned in his
stead.

8 In the thirty-eighth year of Az·ȧ-
rī′ȧh king of Judah Zech·ȧ·rī′ȧh the

14.17-20: 2 Chron 25.25-28. **14.21-22:** 2 Chron 26.1-2. **15.2-3:** 2 Chron 26.3-4.
15.5-7: 2 Chron 26.20-23.

son of Jer·ȯ·bō'ȧm reigned over Israel
in Sȧ·mâr'i·ȧ six months. 9And he did
what was evil in the sight of the LORD,
as his fathers had done. He did not
depart from the sins of Jer·ȯ·bō'ȧm the
son of Nē'bat, which he made Israel
to sin. 10 Shal'lum the son of Jā'besh
conspired against him, and struck him
down at Ib'lē·ȧm,[w] and killed him, and
reigned in his stead. 11 Now the rest
of the deeds of Zech·ȧ·rī'ȧh, behold,
they are written in the Book of the
Chronicles of the Kings of Israel.
12 (This was the promise of the LORD
which he gave to Jē'hū, "Your sons
shall sit upon the throne of Israel to
the fourth generation." And so it came
to pass.)

13 Shal'lum the son of Jā'besh began to reign in the thirty-ninth year of
Uz·zī'ȧh king of Judah, and he reigned
one month in Sȧ·mâr'i·ȧ. 14 Then
Men'ȧ·hem the son of Gā'dī came up
from Tīr'zȧh and came to Sȧ·mâr'i·ȧ,
and he struck down Shal'lum the son
of Jā'besh in Samaria and slew him,
and reigned in his stead. 15 Now the
rest of the deeds of Shal'lum, and the
conspiracy which he made, behold,
they are written in the Book of the
Chronicles of the Kings of Israel. 16At
that time Men'ȧ·hem sacked Tap'-
pū-ȧh[x] and all who were in it and its
territory from Tīr'zȧh on; because
they did not open it to him, therefore
he sacked it, and he ripped up all the
women in it who were with child.

17 In the thirty-ninth year of Az·ȧ-
rī'ȧh king of Judah Men'ȧ·hem the son
of Gā'dī began to reign over Israel,
and he reigned ten years in Sȧ·mâr'i·ȧ.
18And he did what was evil in the
sight of the LORD; he did not depart
all his days from all the sins of Jer·ȯ-
bō'ȧm the son of Nē'bat, which he
made Israel to sin. 19 Pul the king of
Assyria came against the land; and
Men'ȧ·hem gave Pul a thousand talents
of silver, that he might help him to
confirm his hold of the royal power.
20 Men'ȧ·hem exacted the money from
Israel, that is, from all the wealthy
men, fifty shekels of silver from every
man, to give to the king of Assyria. So
the king of Assyria turned back, and
did not stay there in the land. 21 Now
the rest of the deeds of Men'ȧ·hem,
and all that he did, are they not written
in the Book of the Chronicles of the
Kings of Israel? 22And Men'ȧ·hem
slept with his fathers, and Pek·ȧ·hī'ȧh
his son reigned in his stead.

23 In the fiftieth year of Az·ȧ·rī'ȧh
king of Judah Pek·ȧ·hī'ȧh the son of
Men'ȧ·hem began to reign over Israel
in Sȧ·mâr'i·ȧ, and he reigned two
years. 24And he did what was evil in
the sight of the LORD; he did not turn
away from the sins of Jer·ȯ·bō'ȧm the
son of Nē'bat, which he made Israel
to sin. 25And Pē'kȧh the son of Rem-
ȧ·lī'ȧh, his captain, conspired against
him with fifty men of the Gileadites,
and slew him in Sȧ·mâr'i·ȧ, in the
citadel of the king's house;[y] he slew
him, and reigned in his stead. 26 Now
the rest of the deeds of Pek·ȧ·hī'ȧh,
and all that he did, behold, they are
written in the Book of the Chronicles
of the Kings of Israel.

27 In the fifty-second year of Az·ȧ-
rī'ȧh king of Judah Pē'kȧh the son of
Rem·ȧ·lī'ȧh began to reign over Israel
in Sȧ·mâr'i·ȧ, and reigned twenty
years. 28And he did what was evil in
the sight of the LORD; he did not depart from the sins of Jer·ȯ·bō'ȧm the
son of Nē'bat, which he made Israel
to sin.

29 In the days of Pē'kȧh king of
Israel Tig'lath-pī·lē'sėr king of Assyria
came and captured Ī'jon, Ā'bel-beth-
mā'ȧ·cȧh, Jȧ·nō'ȧh, Kē'desh, Hā'zôr,
Gilead, and Galilee, all the land of
Naph'tȧ·lī; and he carried the people
captive to Assyria. 30 Then Hō·shē'ȧ
the son of Ē'lȧh made a conspiracy
against Pē'kȧh the son of Rem·ȧ·lī'ȧh,
and struck him down, and slew him,
and reigned in his stead, in the
twentieth year of Jō'thȧm the son of
Uz·zī'ȧh. 31 Now the rest of the acts
of Pē'kȧh, and all that he did, behold,
they are written in the Book of the
Chronicles of the Kings of Israel.

32 In the second year of Pē'kȧh the
son of Rem·ȧ·lī'ȧh, king of Israel,
Jō'thȧm the son of Uz·zī'ȧh, king of
Judah, began to reign. 33 He was
twenty-five years old when he began
to reign, and he reigned sixteen years
in Jerusalem. His mother's name was
Je·rū'shȧ the daughter of Zā'dok.
34And he did what was right in the
eyes of the LORD, according to all that
his father Uz·zī'ȧh had done. 35 Never-

[w] Gk Compare 9.27: Heb *before the people* [x] Compare Gk: Heb *Tiphsah*
[y] Heb adds *Argob and Arieh*, which probably belong to the list of places in verse 29
15.33-35: 2 Chron 27.1-3.

theless the high places were not removed; the people still sacrificed and
burned incense on the high places. He
built the upper gate of the house of
the LORD. 36 Now the rest of the acts
of Jō'thȧm, and all that he did, are
they not written in the Book of the
Chronicles of the Kings of Judah? 37 In
those days the LORD began to send
Rē'zin the king of Syria and Pē'kȧh
the son of Rem·ȧ·lī'ȧh against Judah.
38 Jō'thȧm slept with his fathers, and
was buried with his fathers in the city
of David his father; and Ā'haz his son
reigned in his stead.

16 In the seventeenth year of Pē'-
kȧh the son of Rem·ȧ·lī'ȧh, Ā'haz
the son of Jō'thȧm, king of Judah,
began to reign. 2 Ā'haz was twenty
years old when he began to reign, and
he reigned sixteen years in Jerusalem.
And he did not do what was right in
the eyes of the LORD his God, as his
father David had done, 3 but he
walked in the way of the kings of Israel.
He even burned his son as an offering,[z]
according to the abominable practices
of the nations whom the LORD drove
out before the people of Israel. 4 And
he sacrificed and burned incense on
the high places, and on the hills, and
under every green tree.

5 Then Rē'zin king of Syria and
Pē'kȧh the son of Rem·ȧ·lī'ȧh, king of
Israel, came up to wage war on Jerusalem, and they besieged Ā'haz but
could not conquer him. 6 At that time[a]
the king of Ē'dȯm[b] recovered Ē'lath
for Edom,[b] and drove the men of
Judah from Elath; and the Ē'dȯm·ītes
came to Elath, where they dwell to
this day. 7 So Ā'haz sent messengers
to Tig'lath-pī·lē'ṡėr king of Assyria,
saying, "I am your servant and your
son. Come up, and rescue me from the
hand of the king of Syria and from
the hand of the king of Israel, who are
attacking me." 8 Ā'haz also took the
silver and gold that was found in the
house of the LORD and in the treasures
of the king's house, and sent a present
to the king of Assyria. 9 And the king
of Assyria hearkened to him; the king
of Assyria marched up against Damascus, and took it, carrying its people
captive to Kīr, and he killed Rē'zin.

10 When King Ā'haz went to Damascus to meet Tig'lath-pī·lē'ṡėr king
of Assyria, he saw the altar that was
at Damascus. And King Ahaz sent to
Ū·rī'ȧh the priest a model of the altar,
and its pattern, exact in all its details.
11 And Ū·rī'ȧh the priest built the
altar; in accordance with all that King
Ā'haz had sent from Damascus, so
Uriah the priest made it, before King
Ahaz arrived from Damascus. 12 And
when the king came from Damascus,
the king viewed the altar. Then the
king drew near to the altar, and went
up on it, 13 and burned his burnt offering and his cereal offering, and poured
his drink offering, and threw the blood
of his peace offerings upon the altar.
14 And the bronze altar which was before the LORD he removed from the
front of the house, from the place
between his altar and the house of the
LORD, and put it on the north side of
his altar. 15 And King Ā'haz commanded Ū·rī'ȧh the priest, saying,
"Upon the great altar burn the morning burnt offering, and the evening
cereal offering, and the king's burnt
offering, and his cereal offering, with
the burnt offering of all the people of
the land, and their cereal offering, and
their drink offering; and throw upon
it all the blood of the burnt offering,
and all the blood of the sacrifice; but
the bronze altar shall be for me to
inquire by." 16 Ū·rī'ȧh the priest did
all this, as King Ā'haz commanded.

17 And King Ā'haz cut off the
frames of the stands, and removed the
laver from them, and he took down
the sea from off the bronze oxen that
were under it, and put it upon a pedi-
ment of stone. 18 And the covered way
for the sabbath which had been built
inside the palace, and the outer entrance for the king he removed from[c]
the house of the LORD, because of the
king of Assyria. 19 Now the rest of the
acts of Ā'haz which he did, are they
not written in the Book of the Chronicles of the Kings of Judah? 20 And
Ā'haz slept with his fathers, and was
buried with his fathers in the city of
David; and Hez·ė·kī'ȧh his son reigned
in his stead.

17 In the twelfth year of Ā'haz
king of Judah Hō·shē'ȧ the son
of Ē'lȧh began to reign in Sȧ·mâr'ĭ·ȧ
over Israel, and he reigned nine years.
2 And he did what was evil in the sight

[z] Or *made his son to pass through the fire* [a] Heb *At that time Rezin* [b] Heb *Aram* (Syria)
[c] Cn: Heb *turned to*

15.38: 2 Chron 27.9. **16.2-4**: 2 Chron 28.1-4. **16.20**: 2 Chron 28.27.

of the LORD, yet not as the kings of Israel who were before him. 3 Against him came up Shal·măn·ē′ṡĕr king of Assyria; and Hō·shē′ȧ became his vassal, and paid him tribute. 4 But the king of Assyria found treachery in Hō·shē′ȧ; for he had sent messengers to Sō, king of Egypt, and offered no tribute to the king of Assyria, as he had done year by year; therefore the king of Assyria shut him up, and bound him in prison. 5 Then the king of Assyria invaded all the land and came to Sȧ·mâr′i·ȧ, and for three years he besieged it. 6 In the ninth year of Hō·shē′ȧ the king of Assyria captured Sȧ·mâr′i·ȧ, and he carried the Israelites away to Assyria, and placed them in Hā′lȧh, and on the Hā′bôr, the river of Gō′zan, and in the cities of the Medes.

7 And this was so, because the people of Israel had sinned against the LORD their God, who had brought them up out of the land of Egypt from under the hand of Pharaoh king of Egypt, and had feared other gods 8 and walked in the customs of the nations whom the LORD drove out before the people of Israel, and in the customs which the kings of Israel had introduced.[d] 9 And the people of Israel did secretly against the LORD their God things that were not right. They built for themselves high places at all their towns, from watchtower to fortified city; 10 they set up for themselves pillars and A·shē′rim on every high hill and under every green tree; 11 and there they burned incense on all the high places, as the nations did whom the LORD carried away before them. And they did wicked things, provoking the LORD to anger, 12 and they served idols, of which the LORD had said to them, "You shall not do this." 13 Yet the LORD warned Israel and Judah by every prophet and every seer, saying, "Turn from your evil ways and keep my commandments and my statutes, in accordance with all the law which I commanded your fathers, and which I sent to you by my servants the prophets." 14 But they would not listen, but were stubborn, as their fathers had been, who did not believe in the LORD their God. 15 They despised his statutes, and his covenant that he made with their fathers, and the warnings which he gave them. They went after false idols, and became false, and they followed the nations that were round about them, concerning whom the LORD had commanded them that they should not do like them. 16 And they forsook all the commandments of the LORD their God, and made for themselves molten images of two calves; and they made an A·shē′rȧh, and worshiped all the host of heaven, and served Bā′ăl. 17 And they burned their sons and their daughters as offerings,[e] and used divination and sorcery, and sold themselves to do evil in the sight of the LORD, provoking him to anger. 18 Therefore the LORD was very angry with Israel, and removed them out of his sight; none was left but the tribe of Judah only.

19 Judah also did not keep the commandments of the LORD their God, but walked in the customs which Israel had introduced. 20 And the LORD rejected all the descendants of Israel, and afflicted them, and gave them into the hand of spoilers, until he had cast them out of his sight.

21 When he had torn Israel from the house of David they made Jer·ȯ·bō′ăm the son of Nē′bat king. And Jeroboam drove Israel from following the LORD and made them commit great sin. 22 The people of Israel walked in all the sins which Jer·ȯ·bō′ăm did; they did not depart from them, 23 until the LORD removed Israel out of his sight, as he had spoken by all his servants the prophets. So Israel was exiled from their own land to Assyria until this day.

24 And the king of Assyria brought people from Babylon, Cū′thȧh, Av′vȧ, Hā′math, and Seph·är·vā′im, and placed them in the cities of Sȧ·mâr′i·ȧ instead of the people of Israel; and they took possession of Samaria, and dwelt in its cities. 25 And at the beginning of their dwelling there, they did not fear the LORD; therefore the LORD sent lions among them, which killed some of them. 26 So the king of Assyria was told, "The nations which you have carried away and placed in the cities of Sȧ·mâr′i·ȧ do not know the law of the god of the land; therefore he has sent lions among them, and behold, they are killing them, because they do not know the law of the god of the land." 27 Then the king of Assyria commanded, "Send there one of the

[d] Heb obscure [e] Or *made their sons and their daughters pass through the fire*

priests whom you carried away thence;
and let him[f] go and dwell there, and
teach them the law of the god of the
land." 28 So one of the priests whom
they had carried away from Sȧ·mâr'i·ȧ
came and dwelt in Beth'ėl, and taught
them how they should fear the
LORD.

29 But every nation still made gods
of its own, and put them in the shrines
of the high places which the Samaritans had made, every nation in the
cities in which they dwelt; 30 the men
of Babylon made Suc'coth-bē'noth,
the men of Cuth made Nēr'gal, the
men of Hā'math made Ȧ·shī'mȧ,
31 and the Av'vītes made Nib'haz and
Tär'tak; and the Sē·phär'vītes burned
their children in the fire to Ȧ·dram'mė-
lech and Ȧ·nam'mė·lech, the gods of
Seph·är·vā'im. 32 They also feared the
LORD, and appointed from among
themselves all sorts of people as priests
of the high places, who sacrificed for
them in the shrines of the high places.
33 So they feared the LORD but also
served their own gods, after the
manner of the nations from among
whom they had been carried away.
34 To this day they do according to the
former manner.

They do not fear the LORD, and
they do not follow the statutes or the
ordinances or the law or the commandment which the LORD commanded the
children of Jacob, whom he named
Israel. 35 The LORD made a covenant
with them, and commanded them,
"You shall not fear other gods or bow
yourselves to them or serve them or
sacrifice to them; 36 but you shall fear
the LORD, who brought you out of the
land of Egypt with great power and
with an outstretched arm; you shall
bow yourselves to him, and to him you
shall sacrifice. 37 And the statutes and
the ordinances and the law and the
commandment which he wrote for you,
you shall always be careful to do. You
shall not fear other gods, 38 and you
shall not forget the covenant that I
have made with you. You shall not
fear other gods, 39 but you shall fear
the LORD your God, and he will deliver
you out of the hand of all your enemies." 40 However they would not
listen, but they did according to their
former manner.

41 So these nations feared the
LORD, and also served their graven
images; their children likewise, and
their children's children—as their
fathers did, so they do to this day.

18 In the year of Hō·shē'ȧ son of
Ē'lȧh, king of Israel, Hez·ė·kī'ȧh
the son of Ā'haz, king of Judah, began
to reign. 2 He was twenty-five years
old when he began to reign, and he
reigned twenty-nine years in Jerusalem. His mother's name was Ā'bī
the daughter of Zech·ȧ·rī'ȧh. 3 And he
did what was right in the eyes of the
LORD, according to all that David his
father had done. 4 He removed the
high places, and broke the pillars, and
cut down the Ȧ·shē'rȧh. And he broke
in pieces the bronze serpent that Moses
had made, for until those days the
people of Israel had burned incense
to it; it was called Ne·hush'tȧn. 5 He
trusted in the LORD the God of Israel;
so that there was none like him among
all the kings of Judah after him, nor
among those who were before him.
6 For he held fast to the LORD; he did
not depart from following him, but
kept the commandments which the
LORD commanded Moses. 7 And the
LORD was with him; wherever he went
forth, he prospered. He rebelled
against the king of Assyria, and would
not serve him. 8 He smote the Philistines as far as Gā'zȧ and its territory, from watchtower to fortified
city.

9 In the fourth year of King Hez·ė-
kī'ȧh, which was the seventh year of
Hō·shē'ȧ son of Ē'lȧh, king of Israel,
Shal·mȧn·ē'ṡėr king of Assyria came
up against Sȧ·mâr'i·ȧ and besieged it
10 and at the end of three years he
took it. In the sixth year of Hez·ė·kī'ȧh,
which was the ninth year of Hō·shē'ȧ
king of Israel, Sȧ·mâr'i·ȧ was taken.
11 The king of Assyria carried the
Israelites away to Assyria, and put
them in Hā'lȧh, and on the Hā'bôr,
the river of Gō'zan, and in the cities
of the Medes, 12 because they did not
obey the voice of the LORD their God
but transgressed his covenant, even all
that Moses the servant of the LORD
commanded; they neither listened nor
obeyed.

13 In the fourteenth year of King
Hez·ė·kī'ȧh Sen·nach'ė·rib king of Assyria came up against all the fortified
cities of Judah and took them. 14 And

[f] Syr Vg: Heb *them*
18.1-3: 2 Chron 29.1-2. 18.13-19.37: 2 Chron 32.1-21; Is 36.1-37.38.

Hez·ė·kī'ȧh king of Judah sent to the
king of Assyria at Lā'chish, saying, "I
have done wrong; withdraw from me;
whatever you impose on me I will
bear." And the king of Assyria required of Hezekiah king of Judah
three hundred talents of silver and
thirty talents of gold. 15And Hez·ė-
kī'ȧh gave him all the silver that was
found in the house of the LORD, and
in the treasuries of the king's house.
16At that time Hez·ė·kī'ȧh stripped the
gold from the doors of the temple of
the LORD, and from the doorposts
which Hezekiah king of Judah had
overlaid and gave it to the king of
Assyria. 17And the king of Assyria sent
the Tär'tȧn, the Rab'sȧ·ris, and the
Rab'shȧ·kėh with a great army from
Lā'chish to King Hez·ė·kī'ȧh at Jerusalem. And they went up and came
to Jerusalem. When they arrived, they
came and stood by the conduit of the
upper pool, which is on the highway
to the Fuller's Field. 18And when they
called for the king, there came out to
them E·lī'ȧ·kim the son of Hil·kī'ȧh,
who was over the household, and
Sheb'nȧh the secretary, and Jō'ȧh the
son of Ā'saph, the recorder.
19 And the Rab'shȧ·kėh said to
them, "Say to Hez·ė·kī'ȧh, 'Thus says
the great king, the king of Assyria: On
what do you rest this confidence of
yours? 20 Do you think that mere
words are strategy and power for war?
On whom do you now rely, that you
have rebelled against me? 21 Behold,
you are relying now on Egypt, that
broken reed of a staff, which will pierce
the hand of any man who leans on it.
Such is Pharaoh king of Egypt to all
who rely on him. 22 But if you say to
me, "We rely on the LORD our God,"
is it not he whose high places and
altars Hez·ė·kī'ȧh has removed, saying
to Judah and to Jerusalem, "You shall
worship before this altar in Jerusalem"? 23 Come now, make a wager
with my master the king of Assyria:
I will give you two thousand horses, if
you are able on your part to set riders
upon them. 24 How then can you repulse a single captain among the least
of my master's servants, when you
rely on Egypt for chariots and for
horsemen? 25 Moreover, is it without
the LORD that I have come up against
this place to destroy it? The LORD said
to me, Go up against this land, and
destroy it.' "
26 Then E·lī'ȧ·kim the son of Hil-
kī'ȧh, and Sheb'nȧh, and Jō'ȧh, said
to the Rab'shȧ·kėh, "Pray, speak to
your servants in the Aramaic language,
for we understand it; do not speak to
us in the language of Judah within the
hearing of the people who are on the
wall." 27 But the Rab'shȧ·kėh said to
them, "Has my master sent me to
speak these words to your master and
to you, and not to the men sitting on
the wall, who are doomed with you to
eat their own dung and to drink their
own urine?"
28 Then the Rab'shȧ·kėh stood and
called out in a loud voice in the language of Judah: "Hear the word of the
great king, the king of Assyria! 29 Thus
says the king: 'Do not let Hez·ė·kī'ȧh
deceive you, for he will not be able to
deliver you out of my hand. 30 Do not
let Hez·ė·kī'ȧh make you to rely on the
LORD by saying, The LORD will surely
deliver us, and this city will not be
given into the hand of the king of
Assyria.' 31 Do not listen to Hez·ė-
kī'ȧh; for thus says the king of Assyria:
'Make your peace with me and come
out to me; then every one of you will
eat of his own vine, and every one of
his own fig tree, and every one of you
will drink the water of his own cistern;
32 until I come and take you away to
a land like your own land, a land of
grain and wine, a land of bread and
vineyards, a land of olive trees and
honey, that you may live, and not die.
And do not listen to Hez·ė·kī'ȧh when
he misleads you by saying, The LORD
will deliver us. 33 Has any of the gods
of the nations ever delivered his land
out of the hand of the king of Assyria?
34 Where are the gods of Hā'math and
Är'pad? Where are the gods of Seph-
är·vā'im, Hē'nȧ, and Ĭv'vȧh? Have
they delivered Sȧ·mâr'i·ȧ out of my
hand? 35 Who among all the gods of
the countries have delivered their
countries out of my hand, that the
LORD should deliver Jerusalem out of
my hand?' "
36 But the people were silent and
answered him not a word, for the
king's command was, "Do not answer
him." 37 Then E·lī'ȧ·kim the son of
Hil·kī'ȧh, who was over the household, and Sheb'nȧ the secretary, and
Jō'ȧh the son of Ā'saph, the recorder,
came to Hez·ė·kī'ȧh with their clothes
rent, and told him the words of the
Rab'shȧ·kėh.

19 When King Hez·ė·kī'ȧh heard
it, he rent his clothes, and covered
himself with sackcloth, and went into
the house of the LORD. 2 And he sent
E·lī'ȧ·kim, who was over the household, and Sheb'nȧ the secretary, and
the senior priests, covered with sackcloth, to the prophet Ī·ṡāi'ȧh the son
of Ā'moz. 3 They said to him, "Thus
says Hez·ė·kī'ȧh, This day is a day of
distress, of rebuke, and of disgrace;
children have come to the birth, and
there is no strength to bring them
forth. 4 It may be that the LORD your
God heard all the words of the Rab'-
shȧ·kėh, whom his master the king of
Assyria has sent to mock the living
God, and will rebuke the words which
the LORD your God has heard; therefore lift up your prayer for the remnant
that is left." 5 When the servants of
King Hez·ė·kī'ȧh came to Ī·ṡāi'ȧh,
6 Ī·ṡāi'ȧh said to them, "Say to your
master, 'Thus says the LORD: Do not
be afraid because of the words that
you have heard, with which the servants of the king of Assyria have reviled
me. 7 Behold, I will put a spirit in him,
so that he shall hear a rumor and return
to his own land; and I will cause
him to fall by the sword in his own
land.' "

8 The Rab'shȧ·kėh returned, and
found the king of Assyria fighting
against Lib'nȧh; for he heard that the
king had left Lā'chish. 9 And when the
king heard concerning Tīr·hā'kȧh king
of Ethiopia, "Behold, he has set out
to fight against you," he sent messengers again to Hez·ė·kī'ȧh, saying,
10 "Thus shall you speak to Hez·ė·kī'ȧh
king of Judah: 'Do not let your God
on whom you rely deceive you by
promising that Jerusalem will not be
given into the hand of the king of
Assyria. 11 Behold, you have heard
what the kings of Assyria have done
to all lands, destroying them utterly.
And shall you be delivered? 12 Have
the gods of the nations delivered them,
the nations which my fathers destroyed, Gō'zan, Hâr'ȧn, Rē'zeph, and
the people of Eden who were in Tel-
as'sȧr? 13 Where is the king of Hā'-
math, the king of Är'pad, the king of
the city of Seph·är·vā'im, the king of
Hē'nȧ, or the king of Iv'vȧh?' "

14 Hez·ė·kī'ȧh received the letter
from the hand of the messengers, and
read it; and Hezekiah went up to the
house of the LORD, and spread it before
the LORD. 15 And Hez·ė·kī'ȧh prayed
before the LORD, and said: "O LORD
the God of Israel, who art enthroned
above the cherubim, thou art the God,
thou alone, of all the kingdoms of the
earth; thou hast made heaven and
earth. 16 Incline thy ear, O LORD, and
hear; open thy eyes, O LORD, and see;
and hear the words of Sen·nach'ė·rib,
which he has sent to mock the living
God. 17 Of a truth, O LORD, the kings
of Assyria have laid waste the nations
and their lands, 18 and have cast their
gods into the fire; for they were no gods,
but the work of men's hands, wood
and stone; therefore they were destroyed. 19 So now, O LORD our God,
save us, I beseech thee, from his hand,
that all the kingdoms of the earth may
know that thou, O LORD, art God
alone."

20 Then Ī·ṡāi'ȧh the son of Ā'moz
sent to Hez·ė·kī'ȧh, saying, "Thus says
the LORD, the God of Israel: Your
prayer to me about Sen·nach'ė·rib
king of Assyria I have heard. 21 This
is the word that the LORD has spoken
concerning him:

"She despises you, she scorns you—
the virgin daughter of Zion;
she wags her head behind you—
the daughter of Jerusalem.

22 "Whom have you mocked and reviled?
Against whom have you raised your voice
and haughtily lifted your eyes?
Against the Holy One of Israel!
23 By your messengers you have mocked the Lord,
and you have said, 'With my many chariots
I have gone up the heights of the mountains,
to the far recesses of Lebanon;
I felled its tallest cedars,
its choicest cypresses;
I entered its farthest retreat,
its densest forest.
24 I dug wells
and drank foreign waters,
and I dried up with the sole of my foot
all the streams of Egypt.'

25 "Have you not heard
that I determined it long ago?
I planned from days of old
what now I bring to pass,

that you should turn fortified cities
into heaps of ruins,
26 while their inhabitants, shorn of
strength,
are dismayed and confounded,
and have become like plants of the
field,
and like tender grass,
like grass on the housetops;
blighted before it is grown?

27 "But I know your sitting down
and your going out and coming in,
and your raging against me.
28 Because you have raged against me
and your arrogance has come into
my ears,
I will put my hook in your nose
and my bit in your mouth,
and I will turn you back on the way
by which you came.

29 "And this shall be the sign for
you: this year you shall eat what grows
of itself, and in the second year what
springs of the same; then in the third
year sow, and reap, and plant vineyards, and eat their fruit. 30 And the
surviving remnant of the house of
Judah shall again take root downward,
and bear fruit upward; 31 for out of
Jerusalem shall go forth a remnant,
and out of Mount Zion a band of
survivors. The zeal of the LORD will
do this.
32 "Therefore thus says the LORD
concerning the king of Assyria, He
shall not come into this city or shoot
an arrow there, or come before it with
a shield or cast up a siege mound
against it. 33 By the way that he came,
by the same he shall return, and he
shall not come into this city, says the
LORD. 34 For I will defend this city to
save it, for my own sake and for the
sake of my servant David."
35 And that night the angel of the
LORD went forth, and slew a hundred
and eighty-five thousand in the camp
of the Assyrians; and when men arose
early in the morning, behold, these
were all dead bodies. 36 Then Sen-
nach′ė·rib king of Assyria departed,
and went home, and dwelt at Nin′ė-
vėh. 37 And as he was worshiping in
the house of Nis′roch his god,
A·dram′mė·lech and Shȧ·rē′zėr, his
sons, slew him with the sword, and
escaped into the land of Ar′ȧ·rat. And
E·sär·had′dȯn his son reigned in his
stead.

20 In those days Hez·ė·kī′ȧh became sick and was at the point
of death. And I·ṡāi′ȧh the prophet the
son of Ā′moz came to him, and said to
him, "Thus says the LORD, 'Set your
house in order; for you shall die, you
shall not recover.'" 2 Then Hez·ė-
kī′ȧh turned his face to the wall, and
prayed to the LORD, saying, 3 "Remember now, O LORD, I beseech thee,
how I have walked before thee in
faithfulness and with a whole heart,
and have done what is good in thy
sight." And Hez·ė·kī′ȧh wept bitterly.
4 And before I·ṡāi′ȧh had gone out of
the middle court, the word of the LORD
came to him: 5 "Turn back, and say
to Hez·ė·kī′ȧh the prince of my people,
Thus says the LORD, the God of David
your father: I have heard your prayer,
I have seen your tears; behold, I will
heal you; on the third day you shall
go up to the house of the LORD. 6 And
I will add fifteen years to your life. I
will deliver you and this city out of
the hand of the king of Assyria, and
I will defend this city for my own sake
and for my servant David's sake."
7 And I·ṡāi′ȧh said, "Bring a cake of
figs. And let them take and lay it on
the boil, that he may recover."
8 And Hez·ė·kī′ȧh said to I·ṡāi′ȧh,
"What shall be the sign that the LORD
will heal me, and that I shall go up to
the house of the LORD on the third
day?" 9 And I·ṡāi′ȧh said, "This is the
sign to you from the LORD, that the
LORD will do the thing that he has
promised: shall the shadow go forward
ten steps, or go back ten steps?" 10 And
Hez·ė·kī′ȧh answered, "It is an easy
thing for the shadow to lengthen ten
steps; rather let the shadow go back
ten steps." 11 And I·ṡāi′ȧh the prophet
cried to the LORD; and he brought the
shadow back ten steps, by which the
sun[g] had declined on the dial of Ā′haz.
12 At that time Mer′ȯ·dach-bal′ȧ-
dan the son of Bal′ȧ·dan, king of
Babylon, sent envoys with letters and
a present to Hez·ė·kī′ȧh; for he heard
that Hezekiah had been sick. 13 And
Hez·ė·kī′ȧh welcomed them, and he
showed them all his treasure house,
the silver, the gold, the spices, the
precious oil, his armory, all that was
found in his storehouses; there was

[g] Syr See Is 38.8 and Tg: Heb lacks *the sun*
20.1-21: 2 Chron 32.24-33; Is 38.1-39.8.

nothing in his house or in all his realm
that Hezekiah did not show them.
14 Then Ī·sāi'ah the prophet came to
King Hez·ė·kī'ah, and said to him,
"What did these men say? And whence
did they come to you?" And Hezekiah
said, "They have come from a far
country, from Babylon." 15 He said,
"What have they seen in your house?"
And Hez·ė·kī'ah answered, "They have
seen all that is in my house; there is
nothing in my storehouses that I did
not show them."

16 Then Ī·sāi'ah said to Hez·ė·kī'ah,
"Hear the word of the LORD: 17 Behold, the days are coming, when all
that is in your house, and that which
your fathers have stored up till this
day, shall be carried to Babylon;
nothing shall be left, says the LORD.
18 And some of your own sons, who
are born to you, shall be taken away;
and they shall be eunuchs in the
palace of the king of Babylon." 19 Then
said Hez·ė·kī'ah to Ī·sāi'ah, "The word
of the LORD which you have spoken is
good." For he thought, "Why not, if
there will be peace and security in my
days?"

20 The rest of the deeds of Hez·ė-
kī'ah, and all his might, and how he
made the pool and the conduit and
brought water into the city, are they
not written in the Book of the Chronicles of the Kings of Judah? 21 And
Hez·ė·kī'ah slept with his fathers;
and Ma·nas'seh his son reigned in his
stead.

21 Ma·nas'seh was twelve years old
when he began to reign, and he
reigned fifty-five years in Jerusalem.
His mother's name was Heph'zi·bah.
2 And he did what was evil in the sight
of the LORD, according to the abominable practices of the nations whom
the LORD drove out before the people
of Israel. 3 For he rebuilt the high
places which Hez·ė·kī'ah his father had
destroyed; and he erected altars for
Bā'al, and made an A·shē'rah, as Ā'hab
king of Israel had done, and worshiped
all the host of heaven, and served
them. 4 And he built altars in the house
of the LORD, of which the LORD had
said, "In Jerusalem will I put my
name." 5 And he built altars for all the
host of heaven in the two courts of the
house of the LORD. 6 And he burned
his son as an offering, and practiced
soothsaying and augury, and dealt
with mediums and with wizards. He
did much evil in the sight of the LORD,
provoking him to anger. 7 And the
graven image of A·shē'rah that he had
made he set in the house of which the
LORD said to David and to Solomon
his son, "In this house, and in Jerusalem, which I have chosen out of all
the tribes of Israel, I will put my name
for ever; 8 and I will not cause the feet
of Israel to wander any more out of
the land which I gave to their fathers,
if only they will be careful to do according to all that I have commanded
them, and according to all the law
that my servant Moses commanded
them." 9 But they did not listen, and
Ma·nas'seh seduced them to do more
evil than the nations had done whom
the LORD destroyed before the people
of Israel.

10 And the LORD said by his servants the prophets, 11 "Because Ma-
nas'seh king of Judah has committed
these abominations, and has done
things more wicked than all that the
Am'ō·rītes did, who were before him,
and has made Judah also to sin with
his idols; 12 therefore thus says the
LORD, the God of Israel, Behold, I
am bringing upon Jerusalem and
Judah such evil that the ears of every
one who hears of it will tingle. 13 And
I will stretch over Jerusalem the measuring line of Sa·mâr'i·a, and the
plummet of the house of Ā'hab; and I
will wipe Jerusalem as one wipes a
dish, wiping it and turning it upside
down. 14 And I will cast off the remnant
of my heritage, and give them into the
hand of their enemies, and they shall
become a prey and a spoil to all their
enemies, 15 because they have done
what is evil in my sight and have provoked me to anger, since the day their
fathers came out of Egypt, even to
this day."

16 Moreover Ma·nas'seh shed very
much innocent blood, till he had filled
Jerusalem from one end to another,
besides the sin which he made Judah
to sin so that they did what was evil
in the sight of the LORD.

17 Now the rest of the acts of Ma-
nas'seh, and all that he did, and the
sin that he committed, are they not
written in the Book of the Chronicles
of the Kings of Judah? 18 And Ma-
nas'seh slept with his fathers, and was
buried in the garden of his house, in

21.1-9: 2 Chron 33.1-9. **21.18:** 2 Chron 33.20.

the garden of Uz′zȧ; and Ā′mon his
son reigned in his stead.
19 Ā′mon was twenty-two years old
when he began to reign, and he
reigned two years in Jerusalem. His
mother's name was Me·shul′le·meth
the daughter of Hā′rūz of Jot′bȧh.
20 And he did what was evil in the sight
of the LORD, as Mȧ·nas′sėh his father
had done. 21 He walked in all the way
in which his father walked, and served
the idols that his father served, and
worshiped them; 22 he forsook the
LORD, the God of his fathers, and did
not walk in the way of the LORD. 23 And
the servants of Ā′mon conspired
against him, and killed the king in his
house. 24 But the people of the land
slew all those who had conspired
against King Ā′mon, and the people
of the land made Jō·sī′ȧh his son king
in his stead. 25 Now the rest of the acts
of Ā′mon which he did, are they not
written in the Book of the Chronicles
of the Kings of Judah? 26 And he was
buried in his tomb in the garden of
Uz′zȧ; and Jō·sī′ȧh his son reigned in
his stead.

22 Jō·sī′ȧh was eight years old
when he began to reign, and he
reigned thirty-one years in Jerusalem.
His mother's name was Je·dī′dȧh the
daughter of Ȧ·dāi′ȧh of Boz′kath. 2 And
he did what was right in the eyes of the
LORD, and walked in all the way of
David his father, and he did not turn
aside to the right hand or to the left.
3 In the eighteenth year of King
Jō·sī′ȧh, the king sent Shā′phȧn the
son of Az·ȧ·lī′ȧh, son of Me·shul′lȧm,
the secretary, to the house of the LORD,
saying, 4 "Go up to Hil·kī′ȧh the high
priest, that he may reckon the amount
of the money which has been brought
into the house of the LORD, which the
keepers of the threshold have collected
from the people; 5 and let it be given
into the hand of the workmen who
have the oversight of the house of the
LORD; and let them give it to the workmen who are at the house of the LORD,
repairing the house, 6 that is, to the
carpenters, and to the builders, and to
the masons, as well as for buying
timber and quarried stone to repair
the house. 7 But no accounting shall
be asked from them for the money
which is delivered into their hand, for
they deal honestly."
8 And Hil·kī′ȧh the high priest said
to Shā′phȧn the secretary, "I have
found the book of the law in the house
of the LORD." And Hilkiah gave the
book to Shaphan, and he read it. 9 And
Shā′phȧn the secretary came to the
king, and reported to the king, "Your
servants have emptied out the money
that was found in the house, and have
delivered it into the hand of the workmen who have the oversight of the
house of the LORD." 10 Then Shā′phȧn
the secretary told the king, "Hil·kī′ȧh
the priest has given me a book." And
Shaphan read it before the king.
11 And when the king heard the
words of the book of the law, he rent
his clothes. 12 And the king commanded
Hil·kī′ȧh the priest, and Ȧ·hī′kam the
son of Shā′phȧn, and Ach′bôr the son
of Mī·cāi′ȧh, and Shaphan the secretary, and Ȧ·sāi′ȧh the king's servant,
saying, 13 "Go, inquire of the LORD
for me, and for the people, and for all
Judah, concerning the words of this
book that has been found; for great is
the wrath of the LORD that is kindled
against us, because our fathers have
not obeyed the words of this book, to
do according to all that is written concerning us."
14 So Hil·kī′ȧh the priest, and
Ȧ·hī′kam, and Ach′bôr, and Shā′phȧn,
and Ȧ·sāi′ȧh went to Hul′dȧh the
prophetess, the wife of Shal′lŭm the
son of Tik′vȧh, son of Här′has, keeper
of the wardrobe (now she dwelt in
Jerusalem in the Second Quarter): and
they talked with her. 15 And she said
to them, "Thus says the LORD, the
God of Israel: 'Tell the man who sent
you to me, 16 Thus says the LORD,
Behold, I will bring evil upon this
place and upon its inhabitants, all the
words of the book which the king of
Judah has read. 17 Because they have
forsaken me and have burned incense
to other gods, that they might provoke
me to anger with all the work of their
hands, therefore my wrath will be
kindled against this place, and it will
not be quenched. 18 But as to the king
of Judah, who sent you to inquire of
the LORD, thus shall you say to him,
Thus says the LORD, the God of Israel:
Regarding the words which you have
heard, 19 because your heart was
penitent, and you humbled yourself
before the LORD, when you heard how
I spoke against this place, and against
its inhabitants, that they should be-

21.19-24: 2 Chron 33.21-25. **22.1-2:** 2 Chron 34.1-2. **22.3-7:** 2 Chron 34.8-12.

come a desolation and a curse, and you
have rent your clothes and wept before
me, I also have heard you, says the
LORD. 20 Therefore, behold, I will
gather you to your fathers, and you
shall be gathered to your grave in
peace, and your eyes shall not see all
the evil which I will bring upon this
place.' " And they brought back word
to the king.

23 Then the king sent, and all the
elders of Judah and Jerusalem
were gathered to him. 2And the king
went up to the house of the LORD, and
with him all the men of Judah
and all the inhabitants of Jerusalem,
and the priests and the prophets, all
the people, both small and great; and
he read in their hearing all the words
of the book of the covenant which had
been found in the house of the LORD.
3And the king stood by the pillar and
made a covenant before the LORD, to
walk after the LORD and to keep his
commandments and his testimonies
and his statutes, with all his heart and
all his soul, to perform the words of
this covenant that were written in this
book; and all the people joined in the
covenant.

4 And the king commanded Hil-
kī′ȧh the high priest, and the priests
of the second order, and the keepers
of the threshold, to bring out of the
temple of the LORD all the vessels
made for Bā′ȧl, for Ȧ·shē′rȧh, and for
all the host of heaven; he burned them
outside Jerusalem in the fields of the
Kid′rȯn, and carried their ashes to
Beth′ēl. 5And he deposed the idolatrous priests whom the kings of Judah
had ordained to burn incense in the
high places at the cities of Judah and
round about Jerusalem; those also
who burned incense to Bā′ȧl, to the sun,
and the moon, and the constellations,
and all the host of the heavens. 6And
he brought out the Ȧ·shē′rȧh from the
house of the LORD, outside Jerusalem,
to the brook Kid′rȯn, and burned it at
the brook Kidron, and beat it to dust
and cast the dust of it upon the graves
of the common people. 7And he broke
down the houses of the male cult prostitutes which were in the house of the
LORD, where the women wove hangings
for the Ȧ·shē′rȧh. 8And he brought all
the priests out of the cities of Judah,
and defiled the high places where the
priests had burned incense, from Gē′bȧ
to Beer-sheba; and he broke down the
high places of the gates that were at
the entrance of the gate of Joshua the
governor of the city, which were on
one's left at the gate of the city.
9 However, the priests of the high
places did not come up to the altar of
the LORD in Jerusalem, but they ate
unleavened bread among their brethren. 10And he defiled Tō′pheth, which
is in the valley of the sons of Hin′nȯm,
that no one might burn his son or his
daughter as an offering to Mō′lech.
11And he removed the horses that the
kings of Judah had dedicated to the
sun, at the entrance to the house of the
LORD, by the chamber of Nā′thȧn-
mē′lech the chamberlain, which was
in the precincts;[h] and he burned the
chariots of the sun with fire. 12And the
altars on the roof of the upper chamber
of Ā′haz, which the kings of Judah had
made, and the altars which Mȧ·nas′sėh
had made in the two courts of the
house of the LORD, he pulled down
and broke in pieces,[i] and cast the dust
of them into the brook Kid′rȯn. 13And
the king defiled the high places that
were east of Jerusalem, to the south
of the mount of corruption, which
Solomon the king of Israel had built
for Ash′tō·reth the abomination of the
Sī·dō′ni·ȧnṡ, and for Chē′mosh the
abomination of Mō′ab, and for Mil′-
com the abomination of the Am′mȯ-
nītes. 14And he broke in pieces the
pillars, and cut down the Ȧ·shē′rim,
and filled their places with the bones
of men.

15 Moreover the altar at Beth′ėl,
the high place erected by Jer·ȯ·bō′ȧm
the son of Nē′bat, who made Israel to
sin, that altar with the high place he
pulled down and he broke in pieces
its stones,[j] crushing them to dust; also
he burned the Ȧ·shē′rȧh. 16And as
Jō·sī′ȧh turned, he saw the tombs there
on the mount; and he sent and took
the bones out of the tombs, and burned
them upon the altar, and defiled it,
according to the word of the LORD
which the man of God proclaimed, who
had predicted these things. 17 Then he
said, "What is yonder monument that
I see?" And the men of the city told
him, "It is the tomb of the man of God

[h] The meaning of the Hebrew word is uncertain [i] Heb *pieces from there*
[j] Gk: Heb *he burned the high place*
23.4-20: 2 Chron 34.3-7.

who came from Judah and predicted
these things which you have done
against the altar at Beth′ėl." 18 And he
said, "Let him be; let no man move his
bones." So they let his bones alone,
with the bones of the prophet who
came out of Sȧ·mâr′ĭ·ȧ. 19 And all the
shrines also of the high places that
were in the cities of Sȧ·mâr′ĭ·ȧ, which
kings of Israel had made, provoking
the LORD to anger, Jō·sī′ȧh removed;
he did to them according to all that
he had done at Beth′ėl. 20 And he slew
all the priests of the high places who
were there, upon the altars, and burned
the bones of men upon them. Then he
returned to Jerusalem.

21 And the king commanded all the
people, "Keep the passover to the
LORD your God, as it is written in this
book of the covenant." 22 For no such
passover had been kept since the days
of the judges who judged Israel, or
during all the days of the kings of Israel
or of the kings of Judah; 23 but in the
eighteenth year of King Jō·sī′ȧh this
passover was kept to the LORD in
Jerusalem.

24 Moreover Jō·sī′ȧh put away the
mediums and the wizards and the teraphim and the idols and all the abominations that were seen in the land
of Judah and in Jerusalem, that he
might establish the words of the law
which were written in the book that
Hil·kī′ȧh the priest found in the house
of the LORD. 25 Before him there
was no king like him, who turned to
the LORD with all his heart and with
all his soul and with all his might,
according to all the law of Moses; nor
did any like him arise after him.

26 Still the LORD did not turn from
the fierceness of his great wrath, by
which his anger was kindled against
Judah, because of all the provocations
with which Mȧ·nas′sėh had provoked
him. 27 And the LORD said, "I will
remove Judah also out of my sight, as
I have removed Israel, and I will cast
off this city which I have chosen,
Jerusalem, and the house of which I
said, My name shall be there."

28 Now the rest of the acts of
Jō·sī′ȧh, and all that he did, are they
not written in the Book of the Chronicles of the Kings of Judah? 29 In his
days Pharaoh Nē′cō king of Egypt
went up to the king of Assyria to the
river Eū·phrā′tēṡ. King Jō·sī′ȧh went
to meet him; and Pharaoh Neco slew
him at Mė·gid′dō, when he saw him.
30 And his servants carried him dead
in a chariot from Mė·gid′dō, and
brought him to Jerusalem, and buried
him in his own tomb. And the people
of the land took Je·hō′ȧ·haz the son of
Jō·sī′ȧh, and anointed him, and made
him king in his father's stead.

31 Je·hō′ȧ·haz was twenty-three
years old when he began to reign, and
he reigned three months in Jerusalem.
His mother's name was Hȧ·mü′tal the
daughter of Jeremiah of Lib′nȧh.
32 And he did what was evil in the
sight of the LORD, according to all that
his fathers had done. 33 And Pharaoh
Nē′cō put him in bonds at Rib′lȧh in
the land of Hā′math, that he might not
reign in Jerusalem, and laid upon the
land a tribute of a hundred talents of
silver and a talent of gold. 34 And
Pharaoh Nē′cō made E·lī′ȧ·kim the
son of Jō·sī′ȧh king in the place of
Josiah his father, and changed his
name to Je·hoi′ȧ·kim. But he took
Je·hō′ȧ·haz away; and he came to
Egypt, and died there. 35 And Je·hoi′ȧ-
kim gave the silver and the gold to
Pharaoh, but he taxed the land to give
the money according to the command
of Pharaoh. He exacted the silver and
the gold of the people of the land, from
every one according to his assessment,
to give it to Pharaoh Nē′cō.

36 Je·hoi′ȧ·kim was twenty-five
years old when he began to reign, and
he reigned eleven years in Jerusalem.
His mother's name was Ze·bī′dȧh the
daughter of Pe·dāi′ȧh of Rü′mȧh.
37 And he did what was evil in the sight
of the LORD, according to all that his
fathers had done.

24 In his days Ne·bu·chȧd·nez′zȧr
king of Babylon came up, and
Je·hoi′ȧ·kim became his servant three
years; then he turned and rebelled
against him. 2 And the LORD sent
against him bands of the Chal·dē′ȧnṡ,
and bands of the Syrians, and bands
of the Mō′ȧb·ītes, and bands of the
Am′mo·nītes, and sent them against
Judah to destroy it, according to the
word of the LORD which he spoke by
his servants the prophets. 3 Surely this
came upon Judah at the command of
the LORD, to remove them out of his
sight, for the sins of Mȧ·nas′sėh,
according to all that he had done, 4 and
also for the innocent blood that he had

23.21-23: 2 Chron 35.1-19. 23.30-34: 2 Chron 36.1-4. 23.36-24.6: 2 Chron 36.5-8.

shed; for he filled Jerusalem with innocent blood, and the LORD would not
pardon. 5 Now the rest of the deeds of
Je·hoi′ȧ·kim, and all that he did, are
they not written in the Book of the
Chronicles of the Kings of Judah? 6 So
Je·hoi′ȧ·kim slept with his fathers, and
Je·hoi′ȧ·chin his son reigned in his
stead. 7 And the king of Egypt did not
come again out of his land, for the
king of Babylon had taken all that
belonged to the king of Egypt from
the Brook of Egypt to the river
Eū·phrā′tēṡ.

8 Je·hoi′ȧ·chin was eighteen years
old when he became king, and he
reigned three months in Jerusalem.
His mother's name was Ne·hush′tȧ the
daughter of El·nā′thȧn of Jerusalem.
9 And he did what was evil in the sight
of the LORD, according to all that his
father had done.

10 At that time the servants of
Ne·bu̇·chȧd·nez′zȧr king of Babylon
came up to Jerusalem, and the city was
besieged. 11 And Ne·bu̇·chȧd·nez′zȧr
king of Babylon came to the city,
while his servants were besieging it;
12 and Je·hoi′ȧ·chin the king of Judah
gave himself up to the king of Babylon,
himself, and his mother, and his servants, and his princes, and his palace
officials. The king of Babylon took him
prisoner in the eighth year of his reign,
13 and carried off all the treasures of
the house of the LORD, and the treasures of the king's house, and cut in
pieces all the vessels of gold in the
temple of the LORD, which Solomon
king of Israel had made, as the LORD
had foretold. 14 He carried away all
Jerusalem, and all the princes, and all
the mighty men of valor, ten thousand
captives, and all the craftsmen and the
smiths; none remained, except the
poorest people of the land. 15 And he
carried away Je·hoi′ȧ·chin to Babylon;
the king's mother, the king's wives, his
officials, and the chief men of the land,
he took into captivity from Jerusalem
to Babylon. 16 And the king of Babylon
brought captive to Babylon all the men
of valor, seven thousand, and the
craftsmen and the smiths, one thousand, all of them strong and fit for
war. 17 And the king of Babylon made
Mat·tȧ·nī′ȧh, Je·hoi′ȧ·chin's uncle,
king in his stead, and changed his
name to Zed·ė·kī′ȧh.

18 Zed·ė·kī′ȧh was twenty-one years
old when he became king, and he
reigned eleven years in Jerusalem. His
mother's name was Hȧ·mü′tal the
daughter of Jeremiah of Lib′nȧh.
19 And he did what was evil in the
sight of the LORD, according to all
that Je·hoi′ȧ·kim had done. 20 For because of the anger of the LORD it came
to the point in Jerusalem and Judah
that he cast them out from his presence.

And Zed·ė·kī′ȧh rebelled against
25 the king of Babylon. 1 And in
the ninth year of his reign, in
the tenth month, on the tenth day of
the month, Ne·bu̇·chȧd·nez′zȧr king
of Babylon came with all his army
against Jerusalem, and laid siege to it;
and they built siegeworks against it
round about. 2 So the city was besieged
till the eleventh year of King Zed·ė-
kī′ȧh. 3 On the ninth day of the fourth
month the famine was so severe in the
city that there was no food for the
people of the land. 4 Then a breach
was made in the city; the king with all
the men of war fled[k] by night by the
way of the gate between the two walls,
by the king's garden, though the Chal-
dē′ȧnṡ were around the city. And they
went in the direction of the Ar′ȧ·bȧh.
5 But the army of the Chal·dē′ȧnṡ
pursued the king, and overtook him
in the plains of Jericho; and all his
army was scattered from him. 6 Then
they captured the king, and brought
him up to the king of Babylon at
Rib′lȧh, who passed sentence upon
him. 7 They slew the sons of Zed·ė-
kī′ȧh before his eyes, and put out
the eyes of Zedekiah, and bound
him in fetters, and took him to Babylon.

8 In the fifth month, on the seventh
day of the month—which was the
nineteenth year of King Ne·bu̇·chȧd-
nez′zȧr, king of Babylon—Ne·bū′zȧ-
rad′ȧn, the captain of the bodyguard,
a servant of the king of Babylon, came
to Jerusalem. 9 And he burned the
house of the LORD, and the king's
house and all the houses of Jerusalem;
every great house he burned down.
10 And all the army of the Chal·dē′ȧnṡ,
who were with the captain of the guard,
broke down the walls around Jerusalem. 11 And the rest of the people
who were left in the city and the

[k] Gk Compare Jer 39.4; 52.7: Heb lacks *the king* and *fled*

24.8-17: 2 Chron 36.9-10. **24.18-25.21**: 2 Chron 36.11-21; Jer 52.1-27.

deserters who had deserted to the king
of Babylon, together with the rest of
the multitude, Ne·bū'zȧ·rad'ȧn the
captain of the guard carried into exile.
12 But the captain of the guard left
some of the poorest of the land to be
vinedressers and plowmen.
13 And the pillars of bronze that
were in the house of the LORD, and the
stands and the bronze sea that were in
the house of the LORD, the Chal·dē'ȧnṡ
broke in pieces, and carried the bronze
to Babylon. 14 And they took away the
pots, and the shovels, and the snuffers,
and the dishes for incense and all the
vessels of bronze used in the temple
service, 15 the firepans also, and the
bowls. What was of gold the captain
of the guard took away as gold, and
what was of silver, as silver. 16 As for
the two pillars, the one sea, and the
stands, which Solomon had made for
the house of the LORD, the bronze of
all these vessels was beyond weight.
17 The height of the one pillar was
eighteen cubits, and upon it was a
capital of bronze; the height of the
capital was three cubits; a network
and pomegranates, all of bronze, were
upon the capital round about. And the
second pillar had the like, with the
network.
18 And the captain of the guard
took Se·räi'ȧh the chief priest, and
Zeph·ȧ·nī'ȧh the second priest, and
the three keepers of the threshold;
19 and from the city he took an officer
who had been in command of the men
of war, and five men of the king's
council who were found in the city;
and the secretary of the commander
of the army who mustered the people
of the land; and sixty men of the people of the land who were found in the
city. 20 And Ne·bū'zȧ·rad'ȧn the captain of the guard took them, and
brought them to the king of Babylon
at Rib'lȧh. 21 And the king of Babylon
smote them, and put them to death at
Rib'lȧh in the land of Hā'math. So
Judah was taken into exile out of its
land.
22 And over the people who remained in the land of Judah, whom
Ne·bu̇·chȧd·nez'zȧr king of Babylon
had left, he appointed Ged·ȧ·lī'ȧh the
son of Ȧ·hī'kam, son of Shā'phȧn,
governor. 23 Now when all the captains of the forces in the open country[l]
and their men heard that the king of
Babylon had appointed Ged·ȧ·lī'ȧh
governor, they came with their men to
Gedaliah at Miz'pȧh, namely, Ish'-
mȧ·el the son of Neth·ȧ·nī'ȧh, and
Jō·hā'nȧn the son of Kȧ·rē'ȧh, and
Se·räi'ȧh the son of Tan'hu̇·meth the
Nė·toph'ȧ·thīte, and Jā-az·ȧ·nī'ȧh the
son of the Mā-ac'ȧ·thīte. 24 And Ged-
ȧ·lī'ȧh swore to them and their men,
saying, "Do not be afraid because of
the Chal·dē'ȧn officials; dwell in the
land, and serve the king of Babylon,
and it shall be well with you." 25 But
in the seventh month, Ish'mȧ·el the
son of Neth·ȧ·nī'ȧh, son of E·lish'ȧ-
mȧ, of the royal family, came with ten
men, and attacked and killed Ged·ȧ-
lī'ȧh and the Jews and the Chal·dē'-
ȧnṡ who were with him at Miz'pȧh.
26 Then all the people, both small and
great, and the captains of the forces
arose, and went to Egypt; for they
were afraid of the Chal·dē'ȧnṡ.
27 And in the thirty-seventh year
of the exile of Je·hoi'ȧ·chin king of
Judah, in the twelfth month, on the
twenty-seventh day of the month,
E'vil-mer'ȯ·dach king of Babylon, in
the year that he began to reign, graciously freed Jehoiachin king of Judah
from prison; 28 and he spoke kindly to
him, and gave him a seat above the
seats of the kings who were with him
in Babylon. 29 So Je·hoi'ȧ·chin put off
his prison garments. And every day of
his life he dined regularly at the king's
table; 30 and for his allowance, a
regular allowance was given him by the
king, every day a portion, as long as
he lived.

[l] With Jer 40.7: Heb lacks *in the open country*
25.22-26: Jer 40.7-43.7. **25.27-30:** Jer 52.31-34.

THE FIRST BOOK OF THE
CHRONICLES

1 Adam, Seth, Ē'nosh; 2 Kē'nȧn,
Mȧ-hal'ȧ·lel, Jâr'ed; 3 Ē'nȯch, Mė-
thü'ṡė·lȧh, Lā'mech; 4 Noah, Shem,
Ham, and Jā'pheth.
5 The sons of Jā'pheth: Gō'mėr,
Mā'gog, Mā'däi, Jā'vȧn, Tü'bȧl, Mē'-
shech, and Tī'rȧs. 6 The sons of Gō'-
mėr: Ash'kė·naz, Dī'phath, and Tō-
gär'mȧh. 7 The sons of Jā'vȧn:
Ē·lī'shȧh, Tär'shish, Kit'tim, and
Rō'dȧ·nim.
8 The sons of Ham: Cush, Egypt,
Püt, and Canaan. 9 The sons of Cush:
Sē'bȧ, Hav'i·lȧh, Sab'tȧ, Rā'ȧ·mȧ, and
Sab'te·cȧ. The sons of Rā'ȧ·mȧh: Sheba
and Dē'dan. 10 Cush was the father of
Nim'rod; he began to be a mighty one
in the earth.
11 Egypt was the father of Lü'dim,
An'ȧ·mim, Le·hā'bim, Naph'tü·him,
12 Path·rü'sim, Cas·lü'him (whence
came the Philistines), and Caph'tȯ·rim.
13 Canaan was the father of Sī'don
his first-born, and Heth, 14 and the
Jeb'ū·sītes, the Am'ȯ·rītes, the Gīr'gȧ-
shītes, 15 the Hī'vītes, the Är'kītes, the
Sī'nītes, 16 the Är'vȧ·dītes, the Zem'ȧ-
rītes, and the Hā'mȧ·thītes.
17 The sons of Shem: Ē'lȧm,
As'shür, Är·pach'shad, Lüd, Âr'ȧm,
Uz, Hul, Gē'thėr, and Mē'shech.
18 Är·pach'shad was the father of Shē'-
lȧh; and Shelah was the father of
Ē'bėr. 19 To Ē'bėr were born two sons:
the name of the one was Pē'leg (for in
his days the earth was divided), and
the name of his brother Jok'tan.
20 Jok'tan was the father of Al·mō'dad,
Shē'leph, Hā·zär·mā'veth, Jē'rȧh,
21 Hȧ·dôr'ȧm, Ū'zȧl, Dik'lȧh, 22 Ē'bȧl,
Ȧ·bim'ȧ-el, Sheba, 23 Ō'phīr, Hav'i-
lȧh, and Jō'bab; all these were the sons
of Jok'tan.
24 Shem, Är·pach'shad, Shē'lȧh;
25 Ē'bėr, Pē'leg, Rē'ü; 26 Sē'rüg, Nā'-
hôr, Tē'rȧh; 27 Abram, that is, Abraham.
28 The sons of Abraham: Isaac and
Ish'mȧ·el. 29 These are their genealogies: the first-born of Ish'mȧ·el, Ne-
bā'ioth; and Kē'där, Ad'bē·ėl, Mib'-
sȧm, 30 Mish'mȧ, Dü'mȧh, Mas'sȧ,
Hā'dad, Tē'mȧ, 31 Jē'tūr, Nā'phish,
and Ked'ė·mȧh. These are the sons of
Ish'mȧ·el. 32 The sons of Ke·tū'rȧh,
Abraham's concubine: she bore Zim'-
ran, Jok'shan, Mē'dan, Mid'i·ȧn,
Ish'bak, and Shü'ȧh. The sons of
Jokshan: Sheba and Dē'dan. 33 The
sons of Mid'i·ȧn: Ē'phȧh, Ē'phėr,
Hā'noch, Ȧ·bī'dȧ, and El·dā'ȧh. All
these were the descendants of Ke-
tū'rȧh.
34 Abraham was the father of Isaac.
The sons of Isaac: Esau and Israel.
35 The sons of Esau: E·lī'phaz, Reü'el,
Jē'ush, Jā'lȧm, and Kō'rȧh. 36 The
sons of E·lī'phaz: Tē'mȧn, Ō'mär,
Zē'phī, Gā'tȧm, Kē'naz, Tim'nȧ, and
Am'ȧ·lek. 37 The sons of Reü'el: Nā'-
hath, Zē'rȧh, Sham'mȧh, and Miz'-
zȧh.
38 The sons of Sē'ir: Lō'tan, Shō'-
bȧl, Zib'con, An'ȧh, Dī'shon, Ē'zėr,
and Dī'shan. 39 The sons of Lō'tan:
Hō'rī and Hō'mam; and Lotan's sister
was Tim'nȧ. 40 The sons of Shō'bȧl:
Al'i·an, Man'ȧ·hath, Ē'bȧl, Shē'phī,
and Ō'nȧm. The sons of Zib'ē·ȯn:
Ā'iȧh and An'ȧh. 41 The sons of
An'ȧh: Dī'shon. The sons of Dishon:
Ham'ran, Esh'ban, Ith'ran, and Chē'-
ran. 42 The sons of Ē'zėr: Bil'han,
Zā'ȧ·van, and Jā'ȧ·kan. The sons of
Dī'shan: Uz and Âr'ȧn.
43 These are the kings who reigned
in the land of Ē'dȯm before any king
reigned over the Israelites: Bē'lȧ the
son of Bē'ôr, the name of whose city
was Din'hȧ·bȧh. 44 When Bē'lȧ died,
Jō'bab the son of Zē'rȧh of Boz'rȧh
reigned in his stead. 45 When Jō'bab
died, Hū'sham of the land of the
Tē'mȧ·nītes reigned in his stead.
46 When Hū'sham died, Hā'dad the
son of Bē'dad, who defeated Mid'i·ȧn
in the country of Mō'ab, reigned in
his stead; and the name of his city was
Ā'vith. 47 When Hā'dad died, Sam'lȧh
of Mas·rē'kȧh reigned in his stead.
48 When Sam'lȧh died, Shā'ül of Re-
hō'both on the Eū·phrā'tēṡ reigned in
his stead. 49 When Shā'ül died, Bā'ȧl-
hā'nȧn, the son of Ach'bôr, reigned in

1.1-53: Gen 5; 10; 11; 25; 36.

his stead. 50 When Bā'ăl-hā'nȧn died,
Hā'dad reigned in his stead; and the
name of his city was Pā'ī, and his wife's
name Me·het'ȧ·bėl the daughter of
Mā'tred, the daughter of Mē'zȧ·hab.
51 And Hā'dad died.
The chiefs of Ē'dŏm were: chiefs
Tim'nȧ, Al'i·ȧh, Jē'theth, 52 Ō·hol·i-
bā'mȧh, Ē'lȧh, Pī'non, 53 Kē'naz,
Tē'mȧn, Mib'zär, 54 Mag'di-el, and
Ī'rȧm; these are the chiefs of Ē'dŏm.

2 These are the sons of Israel:
Reuben, Simeon, Levi, Judah,
Is'sȧ·chär, Zeb'ū·lŭn, 2 Dan, Joseph,
Benjamin, Naph'tȧ·lī, Gad, and Ash'-
ėr. 3 The sons of Judah: Ēr, Ō'nȧn,
and Shē'lȧh; these three Bath-shü'ȧ
the Canaanitess bore to him. Now Er,
Judah's first-born, was wicked in the
sight of the Lord, and he slew him.
4 His daughter-in-law Tā'mär also
bore him Per'ez and Zē'rȧh. Judah had
five sons in all.
5 The sons of Per'ez: Hez'rŏn and
Hā'mŭl. 6 The sons of Zē'rȧh: Zim'rī,
Ethan, Hē'mȧn, Cal'col, and Dâr'ȧ,
five in all. 7 The sons of Cär'mī:
Ā'chär, the troubler of Israel, who
transgressed in the matter of the devoted thing; 8 and Ethan's son was
Az·ȧ·rī'ȧh.
9 The sons of Hez'rŏn, that were
born to him: Jė·räh'mē·ėl, Räm, and
Chė·lü'bäi. 10 Räm was the father of
Am·min'ȧ·dab, and Amminadab was
the father of Näh'shŏn, prince of the
sons of Judah. 11 Näh'shŏn was the
father of Sal'mȧ, Salma of Bō'az,
12 Bō'az of Ō'bed, Obed of Jesse.
13 Jesse was the father of E·lī'ab his
first-born, Ȧ·bin'ȧ·dab the second,
Shim'ē-ȧ the third, 14 Nė·than'el the
fourth, Rad'däi the fifth, 15 Ō'zem the
sixth, David the seventh; 16 and their
sisters were Zė·rü'i·ȧh and Ab'i·gāil.
The sons of Zeruiah: Ȧ·bi'shäi, Jō'ab,
and As'ȧ·hel, three. 17 Ab'i·gāil bore
Ȧ·mā'sȧ, and the father of Amasa was
Jē'thėr the Ish'mȧ·el·īte.
18 Caleb the son of Hez'rŏn had
children by his wife Ȧ·zü'bȧh, and by
Jer'i·oth; and these were her sons:
Jē'shėr, Shō'bab, and Är'dŏn. 19 When
Ȧ·zü'bȧh died, Caleb married
Ē'phrath, who bore him Hūr. 20 Hūr
was the father of Ū'rī, and Uri was the
father of Bez'ȧ·lel.
21 Afterward Hez'rŏn went in to
the daughter of Mā'chir the father of
Gilead, whom he married when he
was sixty years old; and she bore him
Sē'gŭb; 22 and Sē'gŭb was the father
of Jā'ir, who had twenty-three cities
in the land of Gilead. 23 But Gē'shūr
and Âr'ȧm took from them Hav·voth-
jā'ir, Kē'nath and its villages, sixty
towns. All these were descendants of
Mā'chir, the father of Gilead. 24 After
the death of Hez'rŏn, Caleb went in
to Eph'rȧ·thȧh,[a] the wife of Hezron
his father, and she bore him Ash'hūr,
the father of Te·kō'ȧ.
25 The sons of Jė·räh'mē·ėl, the
first-born of Hez'rŏn: Räm, his first-
born, Bü'nȧh, Ō'ren, Ō'zem, and
Ȧ·hī'jȧh. 26 Jė·räh'mē·ėl also had
another wife, whose name was At'ȧ-
rȧh; she was the mother of Ō'nȧm.
27 The sons of Räm, the first-born of
Jė·räh'mē·ėl: Mā'az, Jā'min, and
Ē'kėr. 28 The sons of Ō'nȧm: Sham'mäi
and Jā'dȧ. The sons of Shammai: Nā'-
dab and Ȧ·bi'shūr. 29 The name of
Ȧ·bi'shūr's wife was Ab'i·hāil, and she
bore him Äh'ban and Mō'lid. 30 The
sons of Nā'dab: Sē'led and Ap'pȧ-im;
and Seled died childless. 31 The sons of
Ap'pȧ-im: Ish'ī. The sons of Ishi:
Shē'shan. The sons of Sheshan:
Äh'läi. 32 The sons of Jā'dȧ, Sham'-
mäi's brother: Jē'thėr and Jonathan;
and Jether died childless. 33 The sons
of Jonathan: Pē'leth and Zā'zȧ. These
were the descendants of Jė·räh'mē·ėl.
34 Now Shē'shan had no sons, only
daughters; but Sheshan had an Egyptian slave, whose name was Jär'hȧ.
35 So Shē'shan gave his daughter in
marriage to Jär'hȧ his slave; and she
bore him At'täi. 36 At'täi was the father
of Nathan and Nathan of Zā'bad.
37 Zā'bad was the father of Eph'lal,
and Ephlal of Ō'bed. 38 Ō'bed was the
father of Jē'hū, and Jehu of Az·ȧ·rī'ȧh.
39 Az·ȧ·rī'ȧh was the father of Hē'lez,
and Helez of El'e-ā'sȧh. 40 El'e-ā'sȧh
was the father of Sis'mäi, and Sismai
of Shal'lŭm. 41 Shal'lŭm was the father
of Jek·ȧ·mī'ȧh, and Jekamiah of
E·lish'ȧ·mȧ.
42 The sons of Caleb the brother
of Jė·räh'mē·ėl: Mȧ·rē'shȧh[b] his first-
born, who was the father of Ziph. The
sons of Mȧ·rē'shȧh: Hē'brŏn.[c] 43 The
sons of Hē'brŏn: Kō'rȧh, Tap'pū-ȧh,
Rē'kem, and Shē'mȧ. 44 Shē'mȧ was

[a] Gk Vg: Heb *in Caleb Ephrathah* [b] Gk: Heb *Mesha* [c] Heb *the father of Hebron*
2.1-2: Gen 35.23-26. **2.3-4:** Gen 38.3-7, 29-30; Num 26.19-20. **2.5:** Gen 46.12; Num 26.21.
2.6-8: Josh 7.1; 1 Kings 4.31.

the father of Rȧ'ham, the father of
Jôr'kē-ȧm; and Rē'kem was the father
of Sham'mäi. 45 The son of Sham'mäi:
Mā'on; and Maon was the father of
Beth'zûr. 46 Ē'phȧh also, Caleb's con-
cubine, bore Hâr'ȧn, Mō'zȧ, and
Gā'zez; and Haran was the father of
Gazez. 47 The sons of Jäh'däi: Rē'gem,
Jō'thȧm, Gē'shan, Pē'let, Ē'phȧh, and
Shā'aph. 48 Mā'ȧ·cȧh, Caleb's concu-
bine, bore Shē'bėr and Tīr'hȧ·nȧh.
49 She also bore Shā'aph the father of
Mad·man'nȧh, Shē'vȧ the father of
Mach·bē'nȧh and the father of Gib'ē-ȧ;
and the daughter of Caleb was Ach'-
sȧh. 50 These were the descendants of
Caleb.

The sons[d] of Hûr the first-born of
Eph'rȧ·thȧh: Shō'bȧl the father of
Kīr'i·ath-jē'ȧ·rim, 51 Sal'mȧ, the father
of Bethlehem, and Hâr'eph the father
of Beth-gā'dėr. 52 Shō'bȧl the father of
Kīr'i·ath-jē'ȧ·rim had other sons: Hȧ-
rō'ėh, half of the Me·nü'hoth. 53 And
the families of Kīr'i·ath-jē'ȧ·rim: the
Ith'rītes, the Pū'thītes, the Shü'mȧ-
thītes, and the Mish'rȧ·ītes; from these
came the Zō'rȧ·thītes and the Esh'tā-ȯ-
lītes. 54 The sons of Sal'mȧ: Bethlehem,
the Nė·toph'ȧ·thītes, At'roth-beth-
jō'ab, and half of the Man'ȧ·hā'thītes,
the Zō'rītes. 55 The families also of
the scribes that dwelt at Jā'bez: the
Tī'rȧ·thītes, the Shim'ē-ȧ·thītes, and
the Sü'chȧ·thītes. These are the Ken'-
ītes who came from Ham'math, the
father of the house of Rē'chab.

3 These are the sons of David that
were born to him in Hē'brȯn: the
first-born Am'non, by Ȧ·hin'ō-am the
Jez'rē·ė·līt·ėss; the second Daniel, by
Ab'i·gāil the Cär'mėl·īt·ėss, 2 the third
Ab'sȧ·lȯm, whose mother was Mā'ȧ-
cȧh, the daughter of Tal'mäi, king of
Gē'shûr; the fourth Ad·ȯ·nī'jȧh, whose
mother was Hag'gith; 3 the fifth Sheph-
ȧ·tī'ȧh, by Ȧ·bī'tal; the sixth Ith'rē-am,
by his wife Eg'lȧh; 4 six were born to
him in Hē'brȯn, where he reigned for
seven years and six months. And he
reigned thirty-three years in Jerusalem. 5 These were born to him in
Jerusalem: Shim'ē-ȧ, Shō'bab, Nathan,
and Solomon, four by Bath-shü'ȧ, the
daughter of Am'mi-el; 6 then Ib'här,
Ē·lish'ȧ·mȧ, Ē·liph'ė·let, 7 Nō'gȧh,
Nē'pheg, Jȧ·phī'ȧ, 8 Ē·lish'ȧ·mȧ, Ē·lī'-
ȧ·dȧ, and Ē·liph'ė·let, nine. 9 All these
were David's sons, besides the sons of
the concubines; and Tā'mär was their
sister.

10 The descendants of Solomon:
Rē·hȯ·bō'ȧm, Ȧ·bī'jȧh his son, Asa his
son, Je·hosh'ȧ·phat his son, 11 Jō'rȧm
his son, Ā·hȧ·zī'ȧh his son, Jō'ash his
son, 12 Am·ȧ·zī'ȧh his son, Az·ȧ·rī'ȧh
his son, Jō'thȧm his son, 13 Ā'haz his
son, Hez·ė·kī'ȧh his son, Mȧ·nas'sėh
his son, 14 Ā'mon his son, Jō·sī'ȧh his
son. 15 The sons of Jō·sī'ȧh: Jō·hā'nȧn
the first-born, the second Je·hoi'ȧ·kim,
the third Zed·ė·kī'ȧh, the fourth Shal'-
lŭm. 16 The descendants of Je·hoi'ȧ-
kim: Jec·ȯ·nī'ȧh his son, Zed·ė·kī'ȧh
his son; 17 and the sons of Jec·ȯ·nī'ȧh,
the captive: She-al'ti-el his son, 18 Mal-
chī'rȧm, Pe·dāi'ȧh, Shen·az'zär, Jek·ȧ-
mī'ȧh, Hosh'ȧ·mȧ, and Ned·ȧ·bī'ȧh;
19 and the sons of Pe·dāi'ȧh: Ze·rub'-
bȧ·bel and Shim'ē-ī; and the sons of
Ze·rub'bȧ·bel: Me·shul'lȧm and Han-
ȧ·nī'ȧh, and She·lō'mith was their
sister; 20 and Ha·shü'bȧh, Ō'hel, Ber-
ė·chī'ȧh, Has·ȧ·dī'ȧh, and Jü'shab-
hē'sed, five. 21 The sons of Han·ȧ·nī'-
ȧh: Pel·ȧ·tī'ȧh and Je·shā'iȧh, his son[e]
Reph·ā'iȧh, his son[e] Är'nȧn, his son[e]
Ō·bȧ·dī'ȧh, his son[e] Shec·ȧ·nī'ȧh.
22 The sons of Shec·ȧ·nī'ȧh: She-
māi'ȧh. And the sons of Shemaiah:
Hat'tŭsh, Ī'gal, Bȧ·rī'ȧh, Nē·ȧ·rī'ȧh,
and Shā'phȧt, six. 23 The sons of
Nē·ȧ·rī'ȧh: El'i-ō-ē'näi, Hiz·kī'ȧh, and
Az·rī'kam, three. 24 The sons of El'i-
ō-ē'näi: Hod'ȧ·vi'ȧh, Ē·lī'ȧ·shib, Pe-
lā'iȧh, Ak'kŭb, Jō·hā'nȧn, De·läi'ȧh,
and Ȧ·nā'nī, seven.

4 The sons of Judah: Per'ez, Hez'-
rȯn, Cär'mī, Hûr, and Shō'bȧl.
2 Rē-āi'ȧh the son of Shō'bȧl was the
father of Jā'hath, and Jahath was
the father of Ȧ·hü'mäi and Lā'had.
These were the families of the Zō'rȧ-
thītes. 3 These were the sons[f] of Ē'tam:
Jez'rē·ėl, Ish'mȧ, and Id'bash; and the
name of their sister was Haz·zė·lel-
pō'nī, 4 and Pė·nū'el was the father of
Gē'dôr, and Ē'zėr the father of Hū'-
shȧh. These were the sons of Hûr, the
first-born of Eph'rȧ·thah, the father
of Bethlehem. 5 Ash'hur, the father of
Te·kō'ȧ, had two wives, Hē'lȧh and
Nā'ȧ·rȧh; 6 Nā'ȧ·rȧh bore him Ȧ·huz'-
zȧm, Hē'phėr, Tē'mė·nī, and Hā-ȧ-
hash'tȧ·rī. These were the sons of
Naarah. 7 The sons of Hē'lȧh: Zē'reth,
Iz'här, and Eth'nan. 8 Koz was the
father of Ā'nub, Zō·bē'bȧh, and the

[d] Gk Vg: Heb *son* [e] Gk Compare Syr Vg: Heb *sons of* [f] Gk Compare Vg: Heb *father*
3.1-9: 2 Sam 3.2-5; 5.14-16; 1 Chron 14.3-6. 3.4: 2 Sam 5.4-5.

families of A·här'hel the son of Hâr'ŭm.
9 Jā'bez was more honorable than his
brothers; and his mother called his
name Jabez, saying, "Because I bore
him in pain." 10 Jā'bez called on the
God of Israel, saying, "Oh that thou
wouldst bless me and enlarge my
border, and that thy hand might be
with me, and that thou wouldst keep
me from harm so that it might not
hurt me!" And God granted what he
asked. 11 Chē'lub, the brother of
Shü'häh, was the father of Mē'hir,
who was the father of Esh'tȯn. 12 Esh'-
tȯn was the father of Beth·rā'phȧ,
Pȧ·sē'ȧh, and Te·hin'ȧh the father of
Ir·nā'hash. These are the men of
Rē'cȧh. 13 The sons of Kē'naz: Oth'ni-
el and Se·räi'ȧh; and the sons of
Othni-el: Hā'thath and Me·ō'nȯ·thäi.[g]
14 Me·ō'nȯ·thäi was the father of
Oph'rȧh; and Se·räi'ȧh was the father
of Jō'ab the father of Ge-hâr'ȧ·shim,[h]
so-called because they were craftsmen.
15 The sons of Caleb the son of Jė-
phün'nėh: Ī'rü, Ē'lȧh, and Nā'ȧm; and
the sons of Elah: Kē'naz. 16 The sons
of Je·hal'lel: Ziph, Zī'phȧh, Tir'i-ȧ,
and As'ȧ·rel. 17 The sons of Ez'rȧh:
Jē'thėr, Mē'red, Ē'phėr, and Jā'lȯn.
These are the sons of Bith'i-ȧh, the
daughter of Pharaoh, whom Mered
married;[i] and she conceived and bore[j]
Miriam, Sham'mäi, and Ish'bȧh, the
father of Esh·tė·mō'ȧ. 18 And his Jewish
wife bore Jē'red the father of Gē'dôr,
Hē'bėr the father of Sō'cōh, and Je-
kū'thi·el the father of Zȧ·nō'ȧh. 19 The
sons of the wife of Hō·dī'ȧh, the sister
of Nā'ham, were the fathers of Kē·ī'lȧh
the Gär'mīte and Esh·tė·mō'ȧ the Mā-
ac'ȧ·thīte. 20 The sons of Shī'mȯn:
Am'non, Rin'nȧh, Ben-hā'nȧn, and
Tī'lon. The sons of Ish'ī: Zō'heth and
Ben-zō'heth. 21 The sons of Shē'lȧh
the son of Judah: Ēr the father of
Lē'cȧh, Lā'ȧ·dȧh the father of Mȧ·rē'-
shȧh, and the families of the house of
linen workers at Beth-ash·bē'ȧ; 22 and
Jō'kim, and the men of Cō·zē'bȧ, and
Jō'ash, and Sâr'aph, who ruled in
Mō'ab and returned to Lē'hem[k] (now
the records[l] are ancient). 23 These
were the potters and inhabitants of
Ne·tā'im and Ge·dē'rȧh; they dwelt
there with the king for his work.
24 The sons of Simeon: Nem'ū-el,
Jā'min, Jâr'ib, Zē'rȧh, Shā'ŭl; 25 Shal'-
lŭm was his son, Mib'sȧm his son,
Mish'mȧ his son. 26 The sons of
Mish'mȧ: Ham'mū-el his son, Zac'cŭr
his son, Shim'ē-ī his son. 27 Shim'ē-ī
had sixteen sons and six daughters; but
his brothers had not many children,
nor did all their family multiply like
the men of Judah. 28 They dwelt in
Beer-sheba, Mō'lȧ·dȧh, Hā'zär-shü'ȧl,
29 Bil'hȧh, Ē'zem, Tō'lad, 30 Be·thū'el,
Hôr'mȧh, Zik'lag, 31 Beth-mär'cȧ·both,
Hā'zär-sü'sim, Beth-bir'ī, and Shā-
ȧ·rā'im. These were their cities until
David reigned. 32 And their villages
were Ē'tam, Ā'in, Rim'mon, Tō'chen,
and Ā'shȧn, five cities, 33 along with
all their villages which were round
about these cities as far as Bā'ȧl. These
were their settlements, and they kept
a genealogical record.

34 Me·shō'bab, Jam'lech, Jō'shȧh
the son of Am·ȧ·zī'ȧh, 35 Jō'ėl, Jē'hū
the son of Josh·i·bī'ȧh, son of Se·räi'-
ȧh, son of As'i-el, 36 El'i-ō-ē'näi,
Jā-ȧ·kō'bȧh, Jesh·ō·hāi'ȧh, A·sāi'ȧh,
Ad'i-el, Je·sim'i-el, Be·nā'iȧh, 37 Zī'zȧ
the son of Shī'phī, son of Al'lon, son
of Je·däi'ȧh, son of Shim'rī, son of
She·māi'ȧh—38 these mentioned by
name were princes in their families,
and their fathers' houses increased
greatly. 39 They journeyed to the
entrance of Gē'dôr, to the east side of
the valley, to seek pasture for their
flocks, 40 where they found rich, good
pasture, and the land was very broad,
quiet, and peaceful; for the former
inhabitants there belonged to Ham.
41 These, registered by name, came in
the days of Hez·ė·kī'ȧh, king of Judah,
and destroyed their tents and the
Me-ü'nim who were found there, and
exterminated them to this day, and
settled in their place, because there
was pasture there for their flocks.
42 And some of them, five hundred men
of the Simeonites, went to Mount
Sē'ir, having as their leaders Pel·ȧ·tī'-
ȧh, Nē-ȧ·rī'ȧh, Reph·ȧ'iȧh, and Uz'-
zi·el, the sons of Ish'ī; 43 and they
destroyed the remnant of the A·mal'ė-
kītes that had escaped, and they have
dwelt there to this day.

5 The sons of Reuben the first-
born of Israel (for he was the
first-born; but because he polluted his

[g] Gk Vg: Heb lacks *Meonothai* [h] That is *Valley of craftsmen*
[i] The clause: *These are . . . married* is transposed from verse 18 [j] Heb lacks *and bore*
[k] Vg Compare Gk: Heb *and Jashubi-lahem* [l] Or *matters*
4.24: Gen 46.10; Ex 6.15; Num 26.12-13. **4.28-33:** Josh 19.2-8. **5.1-26:** Gen 46.9; Num 26.5-6.

father's couch, his birthright was
given to the sons of Joseph the son of
Israel, so that he is not enrolled in the
genealogy according to the birthright;
2 though Judah became strong among
his brothers and a prince was from
him, yet the birthright belonged to
Joseph), 3 the sons of Reuben, the
first-born of Israel: Hā'noch, Pal'lū,
Hez'rȯn, and Cär'mī. 4 The sons of
Jō'ėl: She·māi'ȧh his son, Gog his son,
Shim'ē-ī his son, 5 Mī'cȧh his son,
Rē-äi'ȧh his son, Bā'ȧl his son, 6 Bė-
ēr'ȧh his son, whom Til'gath-pil·nē'-
sėr king of Assyria carried away into
exile; he was a chieftain of the Reubenites. 7 And his kinsmen by their
families, when the genealogy of their
generations was reckoned: the chief,
Je-ī'el, and Zech·ȧ·rī'ȧh, 8 and Bē'lȧ
the son of Ā'zaz, son of Shē'mȧ, son of
Jō'ėl, who dwelt in Ȧ·rō'ėr, as far as
Nē'bō and Bā'ȧl-mē'ȯn. 9 He also
dwelt to the east as far as the entrance
of the desert this side of the Eū·phrā'-
tēs, because their cattle had multiplied
in the land of Gilead. 10 And in the
days of Saul they made war on the
Hag'rītes, who fell by their hand; and
they dwelt in their tents throughout
all the region east of Gilead.

11 The sons of Gad dwelt over
against them in the land of Bā'shȧn as
far as Sal'ė·cȧh: 12 Jō'ėl the chief,
Shā'phȧm the second, Jā'näi, and Shā'-
phȧt in Bā'shȧn. 13 And their kinsmen
according to their fathers' houses:
Michael, Me·shul'lȧm, Sheba, Jō'räi,
Jā'cȧn, Zī'ȧ, and Ē'bėr, seven. 14 These
were the sons of Ab'i·hāil the son of
Hū'rī, son of Jȧ·rō'ȧh, son of Gilead,
son of Michael, son of Je·shish'äi, son
of Jäh'dō, son of Buz; 15 Ā'hī the son of
Ab'di-el, son of Gü'nī, was chief in
their fathers' houses; 16 and they dwelt
in Gilead, in Bā'shȧn and in its towns,
and in all the pasture lands of Sharon
to their limits. 17 All of these were
enrolled by genealogies in the days of
Jō'thȧm king of Judah, and in the
days of Jer·ȯ·bō'ȧm king of Israel.

18 The Reubenites, the Gadites,
and the half-tribe of Mȧ·nas'sėh had
valiant men, who carried shield and
sword, and drew the bow, expert in
war, forty-four thousand seven hundred and sixty, ready for service.
19 They made war upon the Hag'rītes,
Jē'tūr, Nā'phish, and Nō'dab; 20 and
when they received help against them,
the Hag'rītes and all who were with
them were given into their hands, for
they cried to God in the battle, and he
granted their entreaty because they
trusted in him. 21 They carried off
their livestock: fifty thousand of their
camels, two hundred and fifty thousand sheep, two thousand asses, and a
hundred thousand men alive. 22 For
many fell slain, because the war was
of God. And they dwelt in their place
until the exile.

23 The members of the half-tribe
of Mȧ·nas'sėh dwelt in the land; they
were very numerous from Bā'shȧn to
Bā'ȧl-hēr'mȯn, Sē'nir, and Mount
Hēr'mȯn. 24 These were the heads of
their fathers' houses: Ē'phėr,[m] Ish'ī,
E·lī'el, Az'ri-el, Jeremiah, Hod·ȧ·vī'ȧh,
and Jäh'di-el, mighty warriors, famous
men, heads of their fathers' houses.
25 But they transgressed against the
God of their fathers, and played the
harlot after the gods of the peoples of
the land, whom God had destroyed
before them. 26 So the God of Israel
stirred up the spirit of Pūl king of
Assyria, the spirit of Til'gath-pil·nē'-
sėr king of Assyria, and he carried
them away, namely, the Reubenites,
the Gadites, and the half-tribe of
Mȧ·nas'sėh, and brought them to
Hā'lȧh, Hā'bôr, Hâr'ȧ, and the river
Gō'zan, to this day.

6 [n] The sons of Levi: Gēr'shȯm,
Kō'hath, and Mė·râr'ī. 2 The sons
of Kō'hath: Am'ram, Iz'här, Hē'brȯn,
and Uz'zi·el. 3 The children of Am'-
ram: Aaron, Moses, and Miriam. The
sons of Aaron: Nā'dab, Ȧ·bī'hū, El·ē-
ā'zȧr, and Ith'ȧ·mär. 4 El·ē·ā'zȧr was
the father of Phin'ė·hȧs, Phinehas of
Ab·i·shü'ȧ, 5 Ab·i·shü'ȧ of Buk'kī,
Bukki of Uz'zī, 6 Uz'zī of Zer·ȧ·hī'ȧh,
Zerahiah of Me·rā'ioth, 7 Me·rā'ioth of
Am·ȧ·rī'ȧh, Amariah of Ȧ·hī'tūb, 8 Ȧ·hī'-
tūb of Zā'dok, Zadok of Ȧ·him'ȧ-az,
9 Ȧ·him'ȧ-az of Az·ȧ·rī'ȧh, Azariah of
Jō·hā'nȧn, 10 and Jō·hā'nȧn of Az·ȧ·rī'-
ȧh (it was he who served as priest in
the house that Solomon built in Jerusalem). 11 Az·ȧ·rī'ȧh was the father of
Am·ȧ·rī'ȧh, Amariah of Ȧ·hī'tūb,
12 Ȧ·hī'tūb of Zā'dok, Zadok of Shal'-
lūm, 13 Shal'lūm of Hil·kī'ȧh, Hilkiah
of Az·ȧ·rī'ȧh, 14 Az·ȧ·rī'ȧh of Se·räi'ȧh,
Seraiah of Je·hoz'ȧ·dak; 15 and Je·hoz'-
ȧ·dak went into exile when the LORD

[m] Gk Vg: Heb *and Epher* [n] Ch 5.27 in Heb
6.1-15: Gen 46.11; Ex 6.16-20; Num 3.2.

sent Judah and Jerusalem into exile
by the hand of Ne·bů·chad·nez′zȧr.

16[o] The sons of Levi: Gẽr′shȯm,
Kō′hath, and Mė·rȃr′ī. 17 And these
are the names of the sons of Gẽr′shȯm:
Lib′nī and Shim′ē-ī. 18 The sons of
Kō′hath: Am′ram, Iz′här, Hē′brȯn,
and Uz′zi·el. 19 The sons of Mė·rȃr′ī:
Mäh′lī and Mū′shī. These are the
families of the Levites according to
their fathers. 20 Of Gẽr′shȯm: Lib′nī
his son, Jā′hath his son, Zim′mȧh his
son, 21 Jō′ȧh his son, Id′dō his son,
Zē′rȧh his son, Jē-ath′ė·räi his son.
22 The sons of Kō′hath: Am·min′ȧ·dab
his son, Kō′rȧh his son, As′sir his son,
23 El·kā′nȧh his son, E·bī′ȧ·saph his
son, As′sir his son, 24 Tā′hath his son,
Ū·rī′ėl his son, Uz·zī′ȧh his son, and
Shā′ůl his son. 25 The sons of El·kā′-
nȧh: Ȧ·mā′säi and Ȧ·hī′moth, 26 El-
kā′nȧh his son, Zō′phäi his son, Nā′-
hath his son, 27 E·lī′ab his son, Je·rō′-
ham his son, El·kā′nȧh his son. 28 The
sons of Samuel: Jō′ėl[p] his first-born,
the second Ȧ·bī′jȧh.[q] 29 The sons of
Mė·rȃr′ī: Mäh′lī, Lib′nī his son,
Shim′ē-ī his son, Uz′zȧh his son,
30 Shim′ē-ȧ his son, Hag·gī′ȧh his son,
and Ȧ·sāi′ȧh his son.

31 These are the men whom David
put in charge of the service of song in
the house of the LORD, after the ark
rested there. 32 They ministered with
song before the tabernacle of the tent
of meeting, until Solomon had built
the house of the LORD in Jerusalem;
and they performed their service in
due order. 33 These are the men who
served and their sons. Of the sons of
the Kō′hȧ·thītes: Hē′mȧn the singer
the son of Jō′ėl, son of Samuel, 34 son
of El·kā′nȧh, son of Je·rō′ham, son of
E·lī′el, son of Tō′ȧh, 35 son of Zuph,
son of El·kā′nȧh, son of Mā′hath, son
of Ȧ·mā′säi, 36 son of El·kā′nȧh, son of
Jō′ėl, son of Az·ȧ·rī′ȧh, son of Zeph·ȧ-
nī′ȧh, 37 son of Tā′hath, son of As′sir,
son of E·bī′ȧ·saph, son of Kō′rȧh,
38 son of Iz′här, son of Kō′hath, son of
Levi, son of Israel; 39 and his brother
Ā′saph, who stood on his right hand,
namely, Asaph the son of Ber·ė·chī′ȧh,
son of Shim′ē-ȧ, 40 son of Michael, son
of Bā-ȧ·sē′iȧh, son of Mal·chī′jȧh,
41 son of Eth′nī, son of Zē′rȧh, son of
Ȧ·dāi′ȧh, 42 son of Ethan, son of Zim′-
mȧh, son of Shim′ē-ī, 43 son of Jā′hath,
son of Gẽr′shȯm, son of Levi. 44 On
the left hand were their brethren the
sons of Mė·rȃr′ī: Ethan the son of
Kish′ī, son of Ab′dī, son of Mal′lůch,
45 son of Hash·ȧ·bī′ȧh, son of Am·ȧ-
zī′ȧh, son of Hil·kī′ȧh, 46 son of Am′zī,
son of Bā′nī, son of Shē′mėr, 47 son of
Mäh′lī, son of Mū′shī, son of Mė·rȃr′ī,
son of Levi; 48 and their brethren the
Levites were appointed for all the
service of the tabernacle of the house
of God.

49 But Aaron and his sons made
offerings upon the altar of burnt offering and upon the altar of incense for
all the work of the most holy place,
and to make atonement for Israel,
according to all that Moses the servant
of God had commanded. 50 These are
the sons of Aaron: El·ē·ā′zȧr his son,
Phin′ė·hȧs his son, Ab·i·shü′ȧ his son,
51 Buk′kī his son, Uz′zī his son, Zer·ȧ-
hī′ȧh his son, 52 Me·rā′ioth his son,
Am·ȧ·rī′ȧh his son, Ȧ·hī′tůb his son,
53 Zā′dok his son, Ȧ·him′ȧ-az his son.

54 These are their dwelling places
according to their settlements within
their borders: to the sons of Aaron of
the families of Kō′hȧ·thītes, for theirs
was the lot, 55 to them they gave
Hē′brȯn in the land of Judah and its
surrounding pasture lands, 56 but the
fields of the city and its villages they
gave to Caleb the son of Jė·phün′nėh.
57 To the sons of Aaron they gave the
cities of refuge: Hē′brȯn, Lib′nȧh with
its pasture lands, Jat′tir, Esh·tė·mō′ȧ
with its pasture lands, 58 Hī′len with
its pasture lands, Dē′bir with its pasture lands, 59 Ā′shȧn with its pasture
lands, and Beth-shē′mesh with its
pasture lands; 60 and from the tribe of
Benjamin, Gē′bȧ with its pasture
lands, Al′ė·meth with its pasture lands,
and An′ȧ·thoth with its pasture lands.
All their cities throughout their families were thirteen.

61 To the rest of the Kō′hȧ·thītes
were given by lot out of the family of
the tribe, out of the half-tribe, the half
of Mȧ·nas′sėh, ten cities. 62 To the
Gẽr′shȯ·mītes according to their families were allotted thirteen cities out of
the tribes of Is′sȧ·chär, Ash′ẽr, Naph′-
tȧ·lī, and Mȧ·nas′sėh in Bā′shȧn. 63 To
the Mė·rȃr′ītes according to their
families were allotted twelve cities out
of the tribes of Reuben, Gad, and
Zeb′ū·lůn. 64 So the people of Israel
gave the Levites the cities with their

[o] Ch 6.1 in Heb [p] Gk Syr Compare verse 33 and 1 Sam 8.2: Heb lacks *Joel* [q] Heb *and Abijah*
6.16-53: Ex 6.16-24. **6.54-81:** Josh 21.1-42.

pasture lands. 65 They also gave them
by lot out of the tribes of Judah,
Simeon, and Benjamin these cities
which are mentioned by name.

66 And some of the families of the
sons of Kō'hath had cities of their
territory out of the tribe of Ē'phrȧ·im.
67 They were given the cities of refuge:
Shē'chem with its pasture lands in the
hill country of Ē'phrȧ·im, Gē'zėr with
its pasture lands, 68 Jok'mē·ȧm with
its pasture lands, Beth-hō'ron with its
pasture lands, 69 Ai'jȧ·lon with its pasture lands, Gath-rim'mon with its
pasture lands, 70 and out of the half-
tribe of Mȧ·nas'sėh, Ā'nėr with its
pasture lands, and Bil'ē-am with its
pasture lands, for the rest of the families of the Kō'hȧ·thītes.

71 To the Gēr'shȯ·mītes were given
out of the half-tribe of Mȧ·nas'sėh:
Gō'lȧn in Bā'shȧn with its pasture lands
and Ash'tȧ·roth with its pasture lands;
72 and out of the tribe of Is'sȧ·chär:
Kē'desh with its pasture lands, Dab'ė-
rath with its pasture lands, 73 Rā'moth
with its pasture lands, and Ā'nem with
its pasture lands; 74 out of the tribe of
Ash'ėr: Mā'shȧl with its pasture lands,
Ab'don with its pasture lands, 75 Hū'-
kok with its pasture lands, and Rē'hob
with its pasture lands; 76 and out of
the tribe of Naph'tȧ·lī: Kē'desh in
Galilee with its pasture lands, Ham'-
mȯn with its pasture lands, and Kīr·i-
ȧ·thā'im with its pasture lands. 77 To
the rest of the Mė·rär'ītes were allotted
out of the tribe of Zeb'ū·lŭn: Rim'-
mȯ·nō with its pasture lands, Tā'bôr
with its pasture lands, 78 and beyond
the Jordan at Jericho, on the east side
of the Jordan, out of the tribe of
Reuben: Bē'zėr in the steppe with its
pasture lands, Jäh'zȧh with its pasture
lands, 79 Ked'ė·moth with its pasture
lands, and Meph'ȧ-ath with its pasture
lands; 80 and out of the tribe of Gad:
Rā'moth in Gilead with its pasture
lands, Mā·hȧ·nā'im with its pasture
lands, 81 Hesh'bȯn with its pasture
lands, and Jā'zėr with its pasture lands.

7 The sons[r] of Is'sȧ·chär: Tō'lȧ,
Pū'ȧh, Jash'ŭb, and Shim'rȯn,
four. 2 The sons of Tō'lȧ: Uz'zī,
Reph·ā'iȧh, Jē'ri-el, Jäh'mäi, Ib'sȧm,
and She·mū'el, heads of their fathers'
houses, namely of Tola, mighty warriors of their generations, their number
in the days of David being twenty-two
thousand six hundred. 3 The sons of
Uz'zī: Iz·rȧ·hī'ȧh. And the sons of
Izrahiah: Michael, Ō·bȧ·dī'ȧh, Jō'ėl,
and Is·shī'ȧh, five, all of them chief
men; 4 and along with them, by their
generations, according to their fathers'
houses, were units of the army for war,
thirty-six thousand, for they had many
wives and sons. 5 Their kinsmen belonging to all the families of Is'sȧ·chär
were in all eighty-seven thousand
mighty warriors, enrolled by genealogy.

6 The sons of Benjamin: Bē'lȧ,
Bē'chėr, and Je·dī'ȧ-el, three. 7 The
sons of Bē'lȧ: Ez'bon, Uz'zī, Uz'zi·el,
Jer'i·moth, and Ī'rī, five, heads of
fathers' houses, mighty warriors; and
their enrollment by genealogies was
twenty-two thousand and thirty-four.
8 The sons of Bē'chėr: Ze·mī'rȧh,
Jō'ash, Ē·lī·ē'zėr, El·i·ō·ē'nāi, Om'rī,
Jer'ė·moth, Ȧ·bī'jȧh, An'ȧ·thoth, and
Al'ė·meth. All these were the sons of
Becher; 9 and their enrollment by
genealogies, according to their generations, as heads of their fathers' houses,
mighty warriors, was twenty thousand
two hundred. 10 The sons of Je·dī'ȧ-el:
Bil'han. And the sons of Bilhan: Jē'-
ush, Benjamin, Ē'hud, Che·nā'ȧ·nȧh,
Zē'thȧn, Tär'shish, and Ȧ·hish'ȧ·här.
11 All these were the sons of Je·dī'ȧ-el
according to the heads of their fathers'
houses, mighty warriors, seventeen
thousand and two hundred, ready for
service in war. 12 And Shup'pim and
Hup'pim were the sons of Īr, Hū'shim
the sons of Ā'hėr.

13 The sons of Naph'tȧ·lī: Jäh'-
zi-el, Gū'nī, Jē'zėr, and Shal'lŭm, the
offspring of Bil'hȧh.

14 The sons of Mȧ·nas'sėh: As'ri-el,
whom his Ar·ȧ·mē'ȧn concubine bore;
she bore Mā'chir the father of Gilead.
15 And Mā'chir took a wife for Hup'-
pim and for Shup'pim. The name of
his sister was Mā'ȧ·cȧh. And the name
of the second was Ze·loph'ė·had; and
Zelophehad had daughters. 16 And
Mā'ȧ·cȧh the wife of Mā'chir bore a
son, and she called his name Pē'resh;
and the name of his brother was
Shē'resh; and his sons were Ū'lȧm
and Rā'kėm. 17 The sons of Ū'lȧm:
Bē'dan. These were the sons of Gilead
the son of Mā'chir, son of Mȧ·nas'sėh.
18 And his sister Ham·mō'lė·cheth bore
Ish'hod, Ā·bi·ē'zėr, and Mäh'lȧh.
19 The sons of Shė·mī'dȧ were Ȧ·hī'ȧn,
Shē'chem, Lik'hī, and Ȧ·nī'ȧm.

[r] Syr Compare Vg: Heb *and to the sons*

20 The sons of E͞'phrȧ·im: Shü·the͞'-
lȧh, and Be͞'red his son, Ta͞'hath his
son, El·e͞-a͞'dȧh his son, Tahath his son,
21 Za͞'bad his son, Shü·the͞'lȧh his son,
and E͞'zėr and E͞'le͞-ad, whom the men
of Gath who were born in the land
slew, because they came down to raid
their cattle. 22 And E͞'phrȧ·im their
father mourned many days, and his
brothers came to comfort him. 23 And
E͞'phrȧ·im went in to his wife, and she
conceived and bore a son; and he called
his name Be͞·rī'ȧh, because evil had
befallen his house. 24 His daughter
was She͞'ė·rȧh, who built both Lower
and Upper Beth-ho͞'ron, and Uz'zėn-
she͞'ė·rȧh. 25 Re͞'phȧh was his son,
Re͞'sheph his son, Te͞'lȧh his son,
Ta͞'han his son, 26 La͞'dȧn his son,
Am·mī'hụ̈d his son, E·lish'ȧ·mȧ his
son, 27 Nun his son, Joshua his son.
28 Their possessions and settlements
were Beth'ėl and its towns, and eastward Na͞'ȧ·ran, and westward Ge͞'zėr
and its towns, She͞'chem and its towns,
and A͞y'yȧh and its towns; 29 also along
the borders of the Mȧ·nas'sītes, Beth-
she͞'ȧn and its towns, Ta͞'ȧ·nach and
its towns, Mė·gid'do͞ and its towns,
Dôr and its towns. In these dwelt
the sons of Joseph the son of Israel.

30 The sons of Ash'ėr: Im'nȧh,
Ish'vȧh, Ish'vī, Be͞·rī'ȧh, and their
sister Se͞'rȧh. 31 The sons of Be͞·rī'ȧh:
He͞'bėr and Mal'chi-el, who was the
father of Bir'za͞·ith. 32 He͞'bėr was the
father of Japh'let, Sho͞'mėr, Ho͞'thȧm,
and their sister Shü'ȧ. 33 The sons of
Japh'let: Pa͞'sach, Bim'hȧl, and Ash'-
vath. These are the sons of Japhlet.
34 The sons of She͞'mėr his brother:
Ro͞h'gȧh, Je·hub'bȧh, and Âr'ȧm.
35 The sons of He͞'lem his brother:
Zo͞'phȧh, Im'nȧ, She͞'lesh, and A͞'mȧl.
36 The sons of Zo͞'phȧh: Sü'ȧh, Här'-
ne·phėr, Shü'ȧl, Be͞'rī, Im'rȧh, 37 Be͞'-
zėr, Hod, Sham'mȧ, Shil'shȧh, Ith'ran,
and Be-e͞'rȧ. 38 The sons of Je͞'thėr:
Jė·phün'nėh, Pis'pȧ, and Âr'ȧ. 39 The
sons of Ul'lȧ: A͞'rȧh, Han'ni·el, and
Ri·zī'ȧ. 40 All of these were men of
Ash'ėr, heads of fathers' houses, approved, mighty warriors, chief of the
princes. Their number enrolled by
genealogies, for service in war, was
twenty-six thousand men.

8 Benjamin was the father of Be͞'lȧ
his first-born, Ash'bel the second,
A·hâr'ȧh the third, 2 No͞'hȧh the
fourth, and Ra͞'phȧ the fifth. 3 And
Be͞'lȧ had sons: Ad'där, Ge͞'rȧ, A·bī'-
hụ̈d, 4 Ab·i·shü'ȧ, Na͞'ȧ·man, A·ho͞'ȧh,
5 Ge͞'rȧ, She·phü'phȧn, and Hu͞'rȧm.
6 These are the sons of E͞'hud (they
were heads of fathers' houses of the
inhabitants of Ge͞'bȧ, and they were
carried into exile to Mȧ·na͞'hath):
7 Na͞'ȧ·man,[s] A·hī'jȧh, and Ge͞'rȧ, that
is, Heg'lȧm,[t] who was the father of
Uz'zȧ and A·hī'hụ̈d. 8 And Sha͞·hȧ·ra͞'im
sons in the country of Mo͞'ab after he
had sent away Hu͞'shim and Ba͞'ȧ·rȧ
his wives. 9 He had sons by Ho͞'desh
his wife: Jo͞'bab, Zib'i·ȧ, Me͞'shȧ, Mal'-
cȧm, 10 Je͞'ụ̈z, Sa·chī'ȧ, and Mīr'mȧh.
These were his sons, heads of fathers'
houses. 11 He also had sons by Hu͞'-
shim: A·bī'tụ̈b and El·pa͞'ȧl. 12 The
sons of El·pa͞'ȧl: E͞'bėr, Mī'shȧm, and
She͞'med, who built O͞'no͞ and Lod
with its towns, 13 and Be͞·rī'ȧh and
She͞'mȧ (they were heads of fathers'
houses of the inhabitants of Äi'jȧ·lon,
who put to flight the inhabitants of
Gath); 14 and A·hī'o͞, Sha͞'shak, and
Jer'ė·moth. 15 Zeb·ȧ·dī'ȧh, Âr'ȧd,
E͞'dėr, 16 Michael, Ish'pȧh, and Jo͞'hȧ
were sons of Be͞·rī'ȧh. 17 Zeb·ȧ·dī'ȧh,
Me·shul'lȧm, Hiz'kī, He͞'bėr, 18 Ish'mė-
räi, Iz·lī'ȧh, and Jo͞'bab were the sons
of El·pa͞'ȧl. 19 Ja͞'kim, Zich'rī, Zab'-
dī, 20 El'i-e͞'näi, Zil'lė·thäi, E·lī'el,
21 A·däi'ȧh, Be·ra͞'iȧh, and Shim'rath
were the sons of Shim'e͞-ī. 22 Ish'pan,
E͞'bėr, E·lī'el, 23 Ab'don, Zich'rī, Ha͞'-
nȧn, 24 Han·ȧ·nī'ȧh, E͞'lȧm, An·thȯ-
thī'jȧh, 25 Iph·dė'iȧh, and Pė·nu͞'el
were the sons of Sha͞'shak. 26 Sham'-
shė·räi, She͞·hȧ·rī'ȧh, Ath·ȧ·lī'ȧh, 27 Ja͞-
âr·ė·shī'ȧh, E·lī'jȧh, and Zich'ri were
the sons of Je·ro͞'ham. 28 These were
the heads of fathers' houses, according
to their generations, chief men. These
dwelt in Jerusalem.

29 Je-ī'el[u] the father of Gib'e͞·ȯn
dwelt in Gibeon, and the name of his
wife was Ma͞'ȧ·cȧh. 30 His first-born
son: Ab'don, then Zu͞r, Kish, Ba͞'ȧl,
Na͞'dab, 31 Ge͞'dôr, A·hī'o͞, Ze͞'chėr,
32 and Mik'loth (he was the father of
Shim'e͞-ȧh). Now these also dwelt opposite their kinsmen in Jerusalem,
with their kinsmen. 33 Ne͞r was the
father of Kish, Kish of Saul, Saul of
Jonathan, Mal'chī·shü'ȧ, A·bin'ȧ·dab,
and Esh·ba͞'ȧl; 34 and the son of Jonathan was Mer'ib-ba͞'ȧl; and Merib-baal
was the father of Mī'cȧh. 35 The sons
of Mī'cȧh: Pī'thon, Me͞'lech, Tȧ·re͞'ȧ,

[s] Heb *and Naaman* [t] Or *he carried them into exile* [u] Compare 9.35: Heb lacks *Jeiel*

and Ā'haz. 36Ā'haz was the father of
Je·hō'ad·dȧh; and Jehoaddah was the
father of Al'ė·meth, Az'mȧ·veth, and
Zim'rī; Zimri was the father of Mō'zȧ.
37 Mō'zȧ was the father of Bin'ē-ȧ;
Rā'phȧh was his son, El·e-ā'sȧh his
son, Ā'zel his son. 38Ā'zel had six sons,
and these are their names: Az·rī'kam,
Bō'che·rü, Ish'mȧ·el, Shē·ȧ·rī'ȧh, Ō·bȧ-
dī'ȧh, and Hā'nȧn. All these were the
sons of Azel. 39 The sons of Ē'shek his
brother: Ū'lȧm his first-born, Jē'ush
the second, and E·liph'ė·let the third.
40 The sons of Ū'lȧm were men who
were mighty warriors, bowmen, having
many sons and grandsons, one hundred and fifty. All these were Benjaminites.

9 So all Israel was enrolled by
genealogies; and these are written
in the Book of the Kings of Israel.
And Judah was taken into exile in
Babylon because of their unfaithfulness. 2 Now the first to dwell again in
their possessions in their cities were
Israel, the priests, the Levites, and the
temple servants. 3And some of the
people of Judah, Benjamin, Ē'phrȧ·im,
and Mȧ·nas'sėh dwelt in Jerusalem:
4 Ū'thäi the son of Am·mī'hụ̇d, son of
Om'rī, son of Im'rī, son of Bā'nī, from
the sons of Per'ez the son of Judah.
5And of the Shī'lȯ·nītes: Ȧ·sāi'ȧh the
first-born, and his sons. 6 Of the sons
of Zē'rȧh: Je·ü'el and their kinsmen,
six hundred and ninety. 7 Of the Benjaminites: Sal'lü the son of Me·shul'-
lȧm, son of Hod·ȧ·vī'ȧh, son of Has·sė-
nü'ȧh, 8 Ib·nē'iȧh the son of Je·rō'ham,
Ē'lȧh the son of Uz'zī, son of Mich'rī,
and Me·shul'lȧm the son of Sheph·ȧ-
tī'ȧh, son of Reü'el, son of Ib·nī'jȧh;
9 and their kinsmen according to their
generations, nine hundred and fifty-
six. All these were heads of fathers'
houses according to their fathers'
houses.

10 Of the priests: Je·däi'ȧh, Je·hoi'-
ȧ·rib, Jā'chin, 11 and Az·ȧ·rī'ȧh the son
of Hil·kī'ȧh, son of Me·shul'lȧm, son
of Zā'dok, son of Me·rā'ioth, son of
Ȧ·hī'tụ̇b, the chief officer of the house
of God; 12 and Ȧ·dāi'ȧh the son of
Je·rō'ham, son of Pash'hūr, son of
Mal·chī'jȧh, and Mā'ȧ·säi the son of
Ad'i-el, son of Jäh'zė·rȧh, son of Me-
shul'lȧm, son of Me·shil'lė·mith, son of
Im'mėr; 13 besides their kinsmen, heads
of their fathers' houses, one thousand
seven hundred and sixty, very able
men for the work of the service of the
house of God.

14 Of the Levites: She·māi'ȧh the
son of Has'shụ̇b, son of Az·rī'kam, son
of Hash·ȧ·bī'ȧh, of the sons of Mė·rȧr'ī;
15 and Bak·bak'kär, Hē'resh, Gā'lal,
and Mat·tȧ·nī'ȧh the son of Mī'cȧ, son
of Zich'rī, son of Ā'saph; 16 and
Ō·bȧ·dī'ȧh the son of She·māi'ȧh, son
of Gā'lal, son of Je·dü'thụ̇n, and Ber-
ė·chī'ȧh the son of Asa, son of El·kā'-
nȧh, who dwelt in the villages of the
Nė·toph'ȧ·thītes.

17 The gatekeepers were: Shal'lụ̇m,
Ak'kụ̇b, Tal'mȯn, Ȧ·hī'mȧn, and their
kinsmen (Shallum being the chief),
18 stationed hitherto in the king's gate
on the east side. These were the gatekeepers of the camp of the Levites.
19 Shal'lụ̇m the son of Kō're, son of
E·bī'ȧ·saph, son of Kō'rȧh, and his
kinsmen of his fathers' house, the
Kō'rȧ·hītes, were in charge of the
work of the service, keepers of the
thresholds of the tent, as their fathers
had been in charge of the camp of the
LORD, keepers of the entrance. 20And
Phin'ė·hȧs the son of El·ē·ā'zȧr was the
ruler over them in time past; the LORD
was with him. 21 Zech·ȧ·rī'ȧh the son
of Me·shel·ė·mī'ȧh was gatekeeper at
the entrance of the tent of meeting.
22All these, who were chosen as gatekeepers at the thresholds, were two
hundred and twelve. They were enrolled by genealogies in their villages.
David and Samuel the seer established
them in their office of trust. 23 So they
and their sons were in charge of the
gates of the house of the LORD, that
is, the house of the tent, as guards.
24 The gatekeepers were on the four
sides, east, west, north, and south;
25 and their kinsmen who were in their
villages were obliged to come in every
seven days, from time to time, to be
with these; 26 for the four chief gatekeepers, who were Levites, were in
charge of the chambers and the treasures of the house of God. 27And they
lodged round about the house of God;
for upon them lay the duty of watching,
and they had charge of opening it every
morning.

28 Some of them had charge of the
utensils of service, for they were required to count them when they were
brought in and taken out. 29 Others of
them were appointed over the furniture, and over all the holy utensils, also

9.1-2: Ezra 2.70; Neh 7.73; 11.3. **9.3-17:** Neh 11.4-19.

over the fine flour, the wine, the oil,
the incense, and the spices. 30 Others,
of the sons of the priests, prepared the
mixing of the spices, 31 and Mat·ti-
thī'ȧh, one of the Levites, the first-
born of Shal'lŭm the Kō'rȧ·hīte, was
in charge of making the flat cakes.
32 Also some of their kinsmen of the
Kō'hȧ·thītes had charge of the showbread, to prepare it every sabbath.

33 Now these are the singers, the
heads of fathers' houses of the Levites,
dwelling in the chambers of the temple
free from other service, for they were
on duty day and night. 34 These were
heads of fathers' houses of the Levites,
according to their generations, leaders,
who lived in Jerusalem.

35 In Gib'ē·ȯn dwelt the father of
Gibeon, Je-ī'el, and the name of his
wife was Mā'ȧ·cȧh, 36 and his first-
born son Ab'don, then Zŭr, Kish,
Bā'ȧl, Nēr, Nā'dab, 37 Gē'dôr, Ȧ·hī'ō,
Zech·ȧ·rī'ȧh, and Mik'loth; 38 and
Mikloth was the father of Shim'ē-am;
and these also dwelt opposite their
kinsmen in Jerusalem, with their kins-
men. 39 Nēr was the father of Kish,
Kish of Saul, Saul of Jonathan, Mal'-
chī·shü'ȧ, Ȧ·bin'ȧ·dab, and Esh·bā'ȧl;
40 and the son of Jonathan was Mer'ib-
bā'ȧl; and Merib-baal was the father of
Mī'cȧh. 41 The sons of Mī'cȧh: Pī'thon,
Mē'lech, Täh'rē-ȧ, and Ā'haz;[v] 42 and
Ā'haz was the father of Jâr'ȧh, and
Jarah of Al'ė·meth, Az'mȧ·veth, and
Zim'rī; and Zimri was the father of
Mō'zȧ. 43 Mō'zȧ was the father of
Bin'ē-ȧ; and Reph·ā'iȧh was his son,
El'e-ā'sȧh his son, Ā'zel his son.
44 Ā'zel had six sons and these are their
names: Az·rī'kam, Bō'che·rü, Ish'mȧ·el,
Shē·ȧ·rī'ȧh, Ō·bȧ·dī'ȧh, and Hā'nȧn;
these were the sons of Azel.

10 Now the Philistines fought
against Israel; and the men of
Israel fled before the Philistines, and
fell slain on Mount Gil·bō'ȧ. 2 And the
Philistines overtook Saul and his sons;
and the Philistines slew Jonathan and
Ȧ·bin'ȧ·dab and Mal'chī·shü'ȧ, the
sons of Saul. 3 The battle pressed hard
upon Saul, and the archers found him;
and he was wounded by the archers.
4 Then Saul said to his armor-bearer,
"Draw your sword, and thrust me
through with it, lest these uncircumcised come and make sport of me."
But his armor-bearer would not; for he
feared greatly. Therefore Saul took his
own sword, and fell upon it. 5 And
when his armor-bearer saw that Saul
was dead, he also fell upon his sword,
and died. 6 Thus Saul died; he and
his three sons and all his house died
together. 7 And when all the men of
Israel who were in the valley saw that
the army[w] had fled and that Saul and
his sons were dead, they forsook their
cities and fled; and the Philistines
came and dwelt in them.

8 On the morrow, when the Philistines came to strip the slain, they
found Saul and his sons fallen on
Mount Gil·bō'ȧ. 9 And they stripped
him and took his head and his armor,
and sent messengers throughout the
land of the Philistines, to carry the
good news to their idols and to the
people. 10 And they put his armor in
the temple of their gods, and fastened
his head in the temple of Dā'gon.
11 But when all Jā'besh-gil'ē·ȧd heard
all that the Philistines had done to
Saul, 12 all the valiant men arose, and
took away the body of Saul and the
bodies of his sons, and brought them
to Jā'besh. And they buried their bones
under the oak in Jabesh, and fasted
seven days.

13 So Saul died for his unfaithfulness; he was unfaithful to the LORD
in that he did not keep the command
of the LORD, and also consulted a
medium, seeking guidance, 14 and did
not seek guidance from the LORD.
Therefore the LORD slew him, and
turned the kingdom over to David
the son of Jesse.

11 Then all Israel gathered together to David at Hē'brȯn, and
said, "Behold, we are your bone and
flesh. 2 In times past, even when Saul
was king, it was you that led out and
brought in Israel; and the LORD your
God said to you, 'You shall be shepherd of my people Israel, and you
shall be prince over my people
Israel.' " 3 So all the elders of Israel
came to the king at Hē'brȯn; and David
made a covenant with them at Hebron
before the LORD, and they anointed
David king over Israel, according to
the word of the LORD by Samuel.

4 And David and all Israel went to
Jerusalem, that is Jē'bụs, where the
Jeb'ū·sītes were, the inhabitants of
the land. 5 The inhabitants of Jē'bụs

[v] Compare 8.35: Heb lacks *and Ahaz* [w] Heb *they*
10.1-12: 1 Sam 31.1-13. 11.1-3: 2 Sam 5.1-3. 11.4-9: 2 Sam 5.6-10.

said to David, "You will not come in
here." Nevertheless David took the
stronghold of Zion, that is, the city of
David. 6 David said, "Whoever shall
smite the Jeb'ū·sītes first shall be chief
and commander." And Jō'ab the son
of Zė·rü'i·ȧh went up first, so he became chief. 7And David dwelt in the
stronghold; therefore it was called the
city of David. 8And he built the city
round about from the Mil'lō in complete circuit; and Jō'ab repaired the
rest of the city. 9And David became
greater and greater, for the LORD of
hosts was with him.

10 Now these are the chiefs of
David's mighty men, who gave him
strong support in his kingdom, together with all Israel, to make him
king, according to the word of the
LORD concerning Israel. 11 This is an
account of David's mighty men: Jȧ-
shō'bē-ȧm, a Hach'mȯ·nīte, was chief
of the three;[x] he wielded his spear
against three hundred whom he slew
at one time.

12 And next to him among the
three mighty men was El·ē·ā'zȧr the
son of Dō'dō, the Ȧ·hō'hīte. 13 He was
with David at Pas-dam'mim when the
Philistines were gathered there for
battle. There was a plot of ground full
of barley, and the men fled from the
Philistines. 14 But he[y] took his[y] stand
in the midst of the plot, and defended
it, and slew the Philistines; and the
LORD saved them by a great victory.

15 Three of the thirty chief men
went down to the rock to David at the
cave of Ȧ·dul'lȧm, when the army of
Philistines was encamped in the valley
of Reph'ȧ·im. 16 David was then in
the stronghold; and the garrison of the
Philistines was then at Bethlehem.
17And David said longingly, "O that
some one would give me water to
drink from the well of Bethlehem
which is by the gate!" 18 Then the
three mighty men broke through the
camp of the Philistines, and drew
water out of the well of Bethlehem
which was by the gate, and took and
brought it to David. But David would
not drink of it; he poured it out to the
LORD, 19 and said, "Far be it from me
before my God that I should do this.
Shall I drink the lifeblood of these
men? For at the risk of their lives they
brought it." Therefore he would not
drink it. These things did the three
mighty men.

20 Now Ȧ·bi'shäi, the brother of
Jō'ab, was chief of the thirty.[z] And he
wielded his spear against three hundred men and slew them, and won a
name beside the three. 21 He was the
most renowned[a] of the thirty,[z] and became their commander; but he did not
attain to the three.

22 And Be·nā'iȧh the son of Je·hoi'-
ȧ·dȧ was a valiant man[b] of Kab'zē·ėl,
a doer of great deeds; he smote two
ariels[c] of Mō'ab. He also went down
and slew a lion in a pit on a day when
snow had fallen. 23And he slew an
Egyptian, a man of great stature, five
cubits tall. The Egyptian had in his
hand a spear like a weaver's beam; but
Be·nā'iȧh went down to him with a
staff, and snatched the spear out of
the Egyptian's hand, and slew him
with his own spear. 24 These things
did Be·nā'iȧh the son of Je·hoi'ȧ·dȧ,
and won a name beside the three
mighty men. 25 He was renowned
among the thirty, but he did not attain
to the three. And David set him over
his bodyguard.

26 The mighty men of the armies
were As'ȧ·hel the brother of Jō'ab,
El·hā'nȧn the son of Dō'dō of Bethlehem, 27 Sham'moth of Här'od,[d] Hē'lez
the Pel'ȯ·nīte, 28 Ira the son of Ik'kesh
of Te·kō'ȧ, Ā'bi·ē'zėr of An'ȧ·thoth,
29 Sib'bė·cāi the Hū'shȧ·thīte, Ī'lāi the
Ȧ·hō'hīte, 30 Mā'hȧ·räi of Nė·toph'ȧh,
Hē'led the son of Bā'ȧ·nȧh of Ne-
tophah, 31 Ith'äi the son of Rī'bäi of
Gib'ē-ȧh of the Benjaminites, Be·nā'-
iȧh of Pir'ȧ·thon, 32 Hū'räi of the
brooks of Gā'ash, Ȧ·bī'el the Är'bȧ-
thīte, 33Az'mȧ·veth of Bȧ·hā'rȯm,
Ē·lī'ȧh·bȧ of Shā-al'bȯn, 34 Hā'sheme[e]
the Gī'zȯ·nīte, Jonathan the son of
Shā'gee the Här'ȧ·rīte, 35Ȧ·hī'ȧm the
son of Sā'chär the Här'ȧ·rīte, Ē·lī'phal
the son of Ūr, 36 Hē'phėr the Me·chē'-
rȧ·thīte, Ȧ·hī'jȧh the Pel'ȯ·nīte, 37 Hez'-
rō of Cär'mėl, Nā'ȧ·räi the son of
Ez'bäi, 38 Jō'ėl the brother of Nathan,
Mib'här the son of Hag'räi, 39 Zē'lek
the Am'mȯ·nīte, Nā'hȧ·räi of Bė-ēr'-

[x] Compare 2 Sam 23.8: Heb *thirty* or *captains* [y] Compare 2 Sam 23.12: Heb *they . . . their*
[z] Syr: Heb *three* [a] Compare 2 Sam 23.19: Heb *more renowned among the two*
[b] Syr: Heb *the son of a valiant man* [c] The meaning of the word *ariel* is unknown
[d] Compare 2 Sam 23.25: Heb *the Harorite* [e] Compare Gk and 2 Sam 23.32: Heb *the sons of Hashem*
11.10-41: 2 Sam 23.8-39.

ȯth, the armor-bearer of Jō'ab the son
of Zė·rü'i·ȧh, 40 Ira the Ith'rīte, Gā'-
reb the Ithrite, 41 Ū·rī'ȧh the Hit'tīte,
Zā'bad the son of Ăh'läi, 42 Ad'i·nȧ
the son of Shī'zȧ the Reubenite, a
leader of the Reubenites, and thirty
with him, 43 Hā'nȧn the son of Mā'ȧ-
cȧh, and Josh'ȧ·phat the Mith'nīte,
44 Uz·zī'ȧ the Ash'te·rȧ·thīte, Shā'mȧ
and Je-ī'el the sons of Hō'thȧm the
Ȧ·rō'ė·rīte, 45 Je·dī'ȧ-el the son of
Shim'rī, and Jō'hȧ his brother, the
Tī'zīte, 46 E·lī'el the Mā'hȧ·vīte, and
Jer'i·bäi, and Josh·ȧ·vi'ȧh, the sons of
El'nā-ȧm, and Ith'mȧh the Mō'ȧb·īte,
47 E·lī'el, and Ō'bed, and Jā-ȧ·sī'el the
Me·zō'bȧ-īte.

12 Now these are the men who
came to David at Zik'lag, while
he could not move about freely because of Saul the son of Kish; and they
were among the mighty men who
helped him in war. 2 They were bowmen, and could shoot arrows and sling
stones with either the right or the left
hand; they were Benjaminites, Saul's
kinsmen. 3 The chief was Ă'hī-ē'zėr,
then Jō'ash, both sons of She·mā'ȧh of
Gib'ē-ȧh; also Jē'zi-el and Pē'let the
sons of Az'mȧ·veth; Ber'ȧ·cȧh, Jē'hū
of An'ȧ·thoth, 4 Ish·mā'iȧh of Gib'ē·ȯn,
a mighty man among the thirty and a
leader over the thirty; Jeremiah,[f] Jȧ-
hā'zi·el, Jō·hā'nȧn, Joz'ȧ·bad of Ge-
dē'rȧh, 5 E·lü'zäi,[g] Jer'i·moth, Be·ȧ-
lī'ȧh, Shem·ȧ·rī'ȧh, Sheph·ȧ·tī'ȧh the
Hâr'ū·phīte; 6 El·kā'nȧh, Is·shī'ȧh,
Az'ȧ·rel, Jō-ē'zėr, and Jȧ·shō'bē-ȧm,
the Kō'rȧ·hītes; 7 and Jō-ē'lȧh and
Zeb·ȧ·dī'ȧh, the sons of Je·rō'ham of
Gē'dôr.

8 From the Gadites there went over
to David at the stronghold in the
wilderness mighty and experienced
warriors, expert with shield and spear,
whose faces were like the faces of lions,
and who were swift as gazelles upon
the mountains: 9 Ē'zėr the chief, Ō·bȧ-
dī'ȧh second, E·lī'ab third, 10 Mish-
man'nȧh fourth, Jeremiah fifth, 11 At'-
täi sixth, E·lī'el seventh, 12 Jō·hā'nȧn
eighth, El·zā'bad ninth, 13 Jeremiah
tenth, Mach'bȧn·näi eleventh. 14 These
Gadites were officers of the army, the
lesser over a hundred and the greater
over a thousand. 15 These are the men
who crossed the Jordan in the first
month, when it was overflowing all its
banks, and put to flight all those in the
valleys, to the east and to the west.

16 And some of the men of Benjamin and Judah came to the stronghold to David. 17 David went out to
meet them and said to them, "If you
have come to me in friendship to help
me, my heart will be knit to you; but
if to betray me to my adversaries,
although there is no wrong in my
hands, then may the God of our fathers
see and rebuke you." 18 Then the
Spirit came upon Ȧ·mā'säi, chief of
the thirty, and he said,

"We are yours, O David;
and with you, O son of Jesse!
Peace, peace to you,
and peace to your helpers!
For your God helps you."

Then David received them, and made
them officers of his troops.

19 Some of the men of Mȧ·nas'sėh
deserted to David when he came with
the Philistines for the battle against
Saul. (Yet he did not help them, for
the rulers of the Philistines took
counsel and sent him away, saying,
"At peril to our heads he will desert
to his master Saul.") 20 As he went to
Zik'lag these men of Mȧ·nas'sėh
deserted to him: Ad'nȧh, Joz'ȧ·bad,
Je·dī'ȧ-el, Michael, Jozabad, E·lī'hū,
and Zil'lė·thäi, chiefs of thousands in
Manasseh. 21 They helped David
against the band of raiders;[h] for they
were all mighty men of valor, and were
commanders in the army. 22 For from
day to day men kept coming to David
to help him, until there was a great
army, like an army of God.

23 These are the numbers of the
divisions of the armed troops, who
came to David in Hē'brȯn, to turn the
kingdom of Saul over to him, according to the word of the LORD. 24 The
men of Judah bearing shield and spear
were six thousand eight hundred
armed troops. 25 Of the Simeonites,
mighty men of valor for war, seven
thousand one hundred. 26 Of the
Levites four thousand six hundred.
27 The prince Je·hoi'ȧ·dȧ, of the house
of Aaron, and with him three thousand
seven hundred. 28 Zā'dok, a young man
mighty in valor, and twenty-two commanders from his own father's house.
29 Of the Benjaminites, the kinsmen
of Saul, three thousand, of whom the
majority had hitherto kept their allegiance to the house of Saul. 30 Of the

[f] Heb verse 5 [g] Heb verse 6 [h] Or *as officers of his troops*

E'phrȧ·im·ītes twenty thousand eight hundred, mighty men of valor, famous men in their fathers' houses. 31 Of the half-tribe of Mȧ·nas'sėh eighteen thousand, who were expressly named to come and make David king. 32 Of Is'sȧ·chär men who had understanding of the times, to know what Israel ought to do, two hundred chiefs, and all their kinsmen under their command. 33 Of Zeb'ū·lủn fifty thousand seasoned troops, equipped for battle with all the weapons of war, to help David[i] with singleness of purpose. 34 Of Naph'tȧ·lī a thousand commanders with whom were thirty-seven thousand men armed with shield and spear. 35 Of the Danites twenty-eight thousand six hundred men equipped for battle. 36 Of Ash'ẻr forty thousand seasoned troops ready for battle. 37 Of the Reubenites and Gadites and the half-tribe of Mȧ·nas'sėh from beyond the Jordan, one hundred and twenty thousand men armed with all the weapons of war.

38 All these, men of war, arrayed in battle order, came to Hē'brȯn with full intent to make David king over all Israel; likewise all the rest of Israel were of a single mind to make David king. 39 And they were there with David for three days, eating and drinking, for their brethren had made preparation for them. 40 And also their neighbors, from as far as Is'sȧ·chär and Zeb'ū·lủn and Naph'tȧ·lī, came bringing food on asses and on camels and on mules and on oxen, abundant provisions of meal, cakes of figs, clusters of raisins, and wine and oil, oxen and sheep, for there was joy in Israel.

13 David consulted with the commanders of thousands and of hundreds, with every leader. 2 And David said to all the assembly of Israel, "If it seems good to you, and if it is the will of the LORD our God, let us send abroad to our brethren who remain in all the land of Israel, and with them to the priests and Levites in the cities that have pasture lands, that they may come together to us. 3 Then let us bring again the ark of our God to us; for we neglected it in the days of Saul." 4 All the assembly agreed to do so, for the thing was right in the eyes of all the people.

5 So David assembled all Israel from the Shī'hôr of Egypt to the entrance of Hā'math, to bring the ark of God from Kīr'i·ath-jē'ȧ·rim. 6 And David and all Israel went up to Bā'ȧ·lȧh, that is, to Kīr'i·ath-jē'ȧ·rim which belongs to Judah, to bring up from there the ark of God, which is called by the name of the LORD who sits enthroned above the cherubim. 7 And they carried the ark of God upon a new cart, from the house of Ȧ·bin'ȧ·dab, and Uz'zȧh and Ȧ·hī'ō[j] were driving the cart. 8 And David and all Israel were making merry before God with all their might, with song and lyres and harps and tambourines and cymbals and trumpets.

9 And when they came to the threshing floor of Chī'don, Uz'zȧh put out his hand to hold the ark, for the oxen stumbled. 10 And the anger of the LORD was kindled against Uz'zȧh; and he smote him because he put forth his hand to the ark; and he died there before God. 11 And David was angry because the LORD had broken forth upon Uz'zȧh; and that place is called Per'ez-uz'zȧ[k] to this day. 12 And David was afraid of God that day; and he said, "How can I bring the ark of God home to me?" 13 So David did not take the ark home into the city of David, but took it aside to the house of Ō'bed-ē'dȯm the Git'tīte. 14 And the ark of God remained with the household of Ō'bed-ē'dȯm in his house three months; and the LORD blessed the household of Obed-edom and all that he had.

14 And Hiram king of Tyre sent messengers to David, and cedar trees, also masons and carpenters to build a house for him. 2 And David perceived that the LORD had established him king over Israel, and that his kingdom was highly exalted for the sake of his people Israel.

3 And David took more wives in Jerusalem, and David begot more sons and daughters. 4 These are the names of the children whom he had in Jerusalem: Sham·mū'ȧ, Shō'bab, Nathan, Solomon, 5 Ib'här, E·lī'shü-ȧ, El'pelet, 6 Nō'gȧh, Nē'pheg, Jȧ·phī'ȧ, 7 E·lish'ȧ·mȧ, Bē·ė·lī'ȧ·dȧ, and E·liph'ė·let.

8 When the Philistines heard that David had been anointed king over all

[i] Gk: Heb lacks *David* [j] Or *and his brother* [k] That is *The breaking forth upon Uzzah*
13.1-14: 2 Sam 6.1-11. 14.1-2: 2 Sam 5.11-12. 14.3-7: 1 Chron 3.5-8; 2 Sam 5.14-16. 14.8-12: 2 Sam 5.17-21.

Israel, all the Philistines went up in
search of David; and David heard of it
and went out against them. 9 Now the
Philistines had come and made a raid
in the valley of Reph′ȧ·im. 10 And
David inquired of God, "Shall I go
up against the Philistines? Wilt thou
give them into my hand?" And the
LORD said to him, "Go up, and I will
give them into your hand." 11 And he
went up to Bā′ȧl-pe·rā′zim, and David
defeated them there; and David said,
"God has broken through[l] my enemies
by my hand, like a bursting flood."
Therefore the name of that place is
called Baal-perazim.[m] 12 And they left
their gods there, and David gave command, and they were burned.

13 And the Philistines yet again
made a raid in the valley. 14 And when
David again inquired of God, God
said to him, "You shall not go up after
them; go around and come upon them
opposite the balsam trees. 15 And when
you hear the sound of marching in the
tops of the balsam trees, then go out
to battle; for God has gone out before
you to smite the army of the Philistines." 16 And David did as God commanded him, and they smote the
Philistine army from Gib′ē·ȯn to Gē′-
zėr. 17 And the fame of David went
out into all lands, and the LORD
brought the fear of him upon all
nations.

15 David built houses for himself
in the city of David; and he prepared a place for the ark of God, and
pitched a tent for it. 2 Then David
said, "No one but the Levites may
carry the ark of God, for the LORD
chose them to carry the ark of the
LORD and to minister to him for ever."
3 And David assembled all Israel at
Jerusalem, to bring up the ark of the
LORD to its place, which he had prepared for it. 4 And David gathered together the sons of Aaron and the
Levites: 5 of the sons of Kō′hath,
Ū·rī′ėl the chief, with a hundred and
twenty of his brethren; 6 of the sons of
Mė·râr′ī, Ȧ·sāi′ȧh the chief, with two
hundred and twenty of his brethren;
7 of the sons of Gēr′shȯm, Jō′ėl the
chief, with a hundred and thirty of his
brethren; 8 of the sons of El·i·zā′phȧn,
She·māi′ȧh the chief, with two hundred of his brethren; 9 of the sons of
Hē′brȯn, E·lī′el the chief, with eighty
of his brethren; 10 of the sons of
Uz′zi·el, Am·min′ȧ·dab the chief, with
a hundred and twelve of his brethren.
11 Then David summoned the priests
Zā′dok and Ȧ·bī′ȧ·thär, and the Levites
Ū·rī′ėl, Ȧ·sāi′ȧh, Jō′ėl, Shė·māi′ȧh,
E·lī′el, and Am·min′ȧ·dab, 12 and said
to them, "You are the heads of the
fathers' houses of the Levites; sanctify
yourselves, you and your brethren, so
that you may bring up the ark of the
LORD, the God of Israel, to the place
that I have prepared for it. 13 Because
you did not carry it the first time,[n] the
LORD our God broke forth upon us,
because we did not care for it in the
way that is ordained." 14 So the priests
and the Levites sanctified themselves
to bring up the ark of the LORD, the
God of Israel. 15 And the Levites carried
the ark of God upon their shoulders
with the poles, as Moses had commanded according to the word of the
LORD.

16 David also commanded the
chiefs of the Levites to appoint their
brethren as the singers who should
play loudly on musical instruments,
on harps and lyres and cymbals, to
raise sounds of joy. 17 So the Levites
appointed Hē′mȧn the son of Jō′ėl;
and of his brethren Ā′saph the son of
Ber·ė·chī′ȧh; and of the sons of
Mė·râr′ī, their brethren, Ethan the son
of Kū·shā′iȧh; 18 and with them their
brethren of the second order, Zech·ȧ-
rī′ȧh, Jȧ·ā′zi·el, She·mir′ȧ·moth, Je-
hī′el, Un′nī, E·lī′ab, Be·nā′iȧh, Mā·ȧ-
sēi′ȧh, Mat·ti·thī′ȧh, E·liph′ė·le·hū,
and Mik·nē′iȧh, and the gatekeepers
Ō′bed-ē′dȯm and Je-i′el. 19 The singers, Hē′mȧn, Ā′saph, and Ethan,
were to sound bronze cymbals; 20 Zech-
ȧ·rī′ȧh, Ā′zi-el, She·mir′ȧ·moth, Je-
hī′el, Un′nī, E·lī′ab, Mā·ȧ·sēi′ȧh, and
Be·nā′iȧh were to play harps according
to Al′ȧ·moth; 21 but Mat·ti·thī′ȧh,
E·liph′ė·le·hū, Mik·nē′iȧh, Ō′bed-ē′-
dȯm, Je-ī′el, and Az·ȧ·zī′ȧh were to
lead with lyres according to the Sheminith. 22 Chen·ȧ·nī′ȧh, leader of the
Levites in music, should direct the
music, for he understood it. 23 Ber·ė-
chī′ȧh and El·kā′nȧh were to be gatekeepers for the ark. 24 Sheb·ȧ·nī′ȧh,
Josh′ȧ·phat, Nė·than′el, Ȧ·mā′sāi,
Zech·ȧ·rī′ȧh, Be·nā′iȧh, and E·li·ē′zėr,
the priests, should blow the trumpets
before the ark of God. Ō′bed-ē′dȯm

[l] Heb *paraz* [m] That is *Lord of breaking through* [n] The meaning of the Hebrew word is uncertain
14.13-16: 2 Sam 5.22-25. **15.1-16.3:** 2 Sam 6.12-19.

and Je·hī′ăh also were to be gatekeepers for the ark.
25 So David and the elders of
Israel, and the commanders of thousands, went to bring up the ark of the
covenant of the LORD from the house
of Ō′bed-ē′dŏm with rejoicing. 26 And
because God helped the Levites who
were carrying the ark of the covenant
of the LORD, they sacrificed seven
bulls and seven rams. 27 David was
clothed with a robe of fine linen, as
also were all the Levites who were
carrying the ark, and the singers, and
Chen·ă·nī′ăh the leader of the music
of the singers; and David wore a linen
ephod. 28 So all Israel brought up the
ark of the covenant of the LORD with
shouting, to the sound of the horn,
trumpets, and cymbals, and made loud
music on harps and lyres.
29 And as the ark of the covenant
of the LORD came to the city of David,
Mī′chăl the daughter of Saul looked
out of the window, and saw King
David dancing and making merry; and
she despised him in her heart.

16 And they brought in the ark of
God, and set it inside the tent
which David had pitched for it; and
they offered burnt offerings and peace
offerings before God. 2 And when
David had finished offering the burnt
offerings and the peace offerings, he
blessed the people in the name of the
LORD, 3 and distributed to all Israel,
both men and women, to each a loaf of
bread, a portion of meat,[o] and a cake
of raisins.
4 Moreover he appointed certain of
the Levites as ministers before the ark
of the Lord, to invoke, to thank, and
to praise the LORD, the God of Israel.
5 Ā′saph was the chief, and second to
him were Zech·ă·rī′ăh, Je-ī′el, She-
mir′ă·moth, Je·hī′el, Mat·ti·thī′ăh,
E·lī′ab, Be·nā′iăh, Ō′bed-ē′dŏm, and
Je-iel, who were to play harps and
lyres; Ā′saph was to sound the cymbals,
6 and Be·nā′iăh and Jă·hā′zi·el the
priests were to blow trumpets continually, before the ark of the covenant
of God.
7 Then on that day David first appointed that thanksgiving be sung to
the LORD by Ā′saph and his brethren.

8 O give thanks to the Lord, call on
his name,
make known his deeds among the
peoples!
9 Sing to him, sing praises to him,
tell of all his wonderful works!
10 Glory in his holy name;
let the hearts of those who seek
the LORD rejoice!
11 Seek the LORD and his strength,
seek his presence continually!
12 Remember the wonderful works
that he has done,
the wonders he wrought, the
judgments he uttered,
13 O offspring of Abraham his servant,
sons of Jacob, his chosen ones!

14 He is the LORD our God;
his judgments are in all the earth.
15 He is mindful of his covenant for
ever,
of the word that he commanded,
for a thousand generations,
16 the covenant which he made with
Abraham,
his sworn promise to Isaac,
17 which he confirmed as a statute to
Jacob,
as an everlasting covenant to
Israel,
18 saying, "To you I will give the land
of Canaan,
as your portion for an inheritance."

19 When they were few in number,
and of little account, and sojourners in it,
20 wandering from nation to nation,
from one kingdom to another
people,
21 he allowed no one to oppress them;
he rebuked kings on their account,
22 saying, "Touch not my anointed
ones,
do my prophets no harm!"

23 Sing to the LORD, all the earth!
Tell of his salvation from day to
day.
24 Declare his glory among the nations,
his marvelous works among all
the peoples!
25 For great is the LORD, and greatly
to be praised,
and he is to be held in awe above
all gods.
26 For all the gods of the peoples are
idols;
but the LORD made the heavens.

[o] Compare Gk Syr Vg: Heb uncertain
16.8-22: Ps 105.1-15. **16.23-33:** Ps 96.1-13.

27 Honor and majesty are before him;
strength and joy are in his place.

28 Ascribe to the LORD, O families of
the peoples,
ascribe to the LORD glory and
strength!
29 Ascribe to the LORD the glory due
his name;
bring an offering, and come before him!
Worship the LORD in holy array;
30 tremble before him, all the earth;
yea, the world stands firm, never
[illegible] be moved.
31 Let [illegible] heavens be glad, and let the
[illegible]th rejoice,
a[illegible] let them say among the na-
[illegible]ons, "The LORD reigns!"
32 Le[illegible]e sea roar, and all that fills it,
[illegible] the field exult, and everything
[illegible]n it!
33 T[illegible] shall the trees of the wood
sing for joy
[illegible]fore the LORD, for he comes to
judge the earth.
34 [illegible]ive thanks to the LORD, for he
is good;
[illegible]or his steadfast love endures for
ever!

[illegible]y also:
Deliver us, O God of our salvation,
and gather and save us from
among the nations,
[illegible]hat we may give thanks to thy holy
name,
and glory in thy praise.
Blessed be the LORD, the God of
Israel,
from everlasting to everlasting!"
[illegible]hen all the people said "Amen!" and
[illegible]raised the LORD.

37 So David left Ā'saph and his
brethren there before the ark of the
covenant of the LORD to minister continually before the ark as each day
required, 38 and also Ō'bed-ē'dŏm and
his[p] sixty-eight brethren; while Obed-
edom, the son of Je·dü'thŭn, and
Hō'sȧh were to be gatekeepers. 39 And
he left Zā'dok the priest and his
brethren the priests before the tabernacle of the LORD in the high place
that was at Gib'ē·ŏn, 40 to offer burnt
offerings to the LORD upon the altar
of burnt offering continually morning
and evening, according to all that is
written in the law of the LORD which
he commanded Israel. 41 With them
were Hē'mȧn and Je·dü'thŭn, and the
rest of those chosen and expressly
named to give thanks to the LORD, for
his steadfast love endures for ever.
42 Hē'mȧn and Je·dü'thŭn had trumpets and cymbals for the music and
instruments for sacred song. The sons
of Jeduthun were appointed to the
gate.

43 Then all the people departed
each to his house, and David went
home to bless his household.

17 Now when David dwelt in his
house, David said to Nathan the
prophet, "Behold, I dwell in a house
of cedar, but the ark of the covenant
of the LORD is under a tent." 2 And
Nathan said to David, "Do all that
is in your heart, for God is with
you."

3 But that same night the word of
the LORD came to Nathan, 4 "Go and
tell my servant David, 'Thus says the
LORD: You shall not build me a house
to dwell in. 5 For I have not dwelt in
a house since the day I led up Israel
to this day, but I have gone from tent
to tent and from dwelling to dwelling.
6 In all places where I have moved
with all Israel, did I speak a word with
any of the judges of Israel, whom I
commanded to shepherd my people,
saying, "Why have you not built me a
house of cedar?" ' 7 Now therefore
thus shall you say to my servant David,
'Thus says the LORD of hosts, I took
you from the pasture, from following
the sheep, that you should be prince
over my people Israel; 8 and I have
been with you wherever you went, and
have cut off all your enemies from
before you; and I will make for you a
name, like the name of the great ones
of the earth. 9 And I will appoint a
place for my people Israel, and will
plant them, that they may dwell in
their own place, and be disturbed no
more; and violent men shall waste
them no more, as formerly, 10 from
the time that I appointed judges over
my people Israel; and I will subdue
all your enemies. Moreover I declare
to you that the LORD will build you a
house. 11 When your days are fulfilled
to go to be with your fathers, I will
raise up your offspring after you, one
of your own sons, and I will establish
his kingdom. 12 He shall build a house

[p] Heb *their*
16.34: Ps 106.1. **16.35-36:** Ps 106.47-48. **17.1-27:** 2 Sam 7.1-29.

for me, and I will establish his throne
for ever. 13 I will be his father, and he
shall be my son; I will not take my
steadfast love from him, as I took it
from him who was before you, 14 but
I will confirm him in my house and
in my kingdom for ever and his throne
shall be established for ever.' " 15 In
accordance with all these words, and
in accordance with all this vision,
Nathan spoke to David.
16 Then King David went in and
sat before the LORD, and said, "Who
am I, O LORD God, and what is my
house, that thou hast brought me thus
far? 17 And this was a small thing in
thy eyes, O God; thou hast also spoken
of thy servant's house for a great while
to come, and hast shown me future
generations,[q] O LORD God! 18 And
what more can David say to thee for
honoring thy servant? For thou
knowest thy servant. 19 For thy servant's sake, O LORD, and according to
thy own heart, thou hast wrought all
this greatness, in making known all
these great things. 20 There is none
like thee, O LORD, and there is no God
besides thee, according to all that we
have heard with our ears. 21 What
other[r] nation on earth is like thy people Israel, whom God went to redeem
to be his people, making for thyself a
name for great and terrible things, in
driving out nations before thy people
whom thou didst redeem from Egypt?
22 And thou didst make thy people Israel
to be thy people for ever; and thou, O
LORD, didst become their God. 23 And
now, O LORD, let the word which thou
hast spoken concerning thy servant
and concerning his house be established
for ever, and do as thou hast spoken;
24 and thy name will be established
and magnified for ever, saying, 'The
LORD of hosts, the God of Israel, is
Israel's God,' and the house of thy
servant David will be established before thee. 25 For thou, my God, hast
revealed to thy servant that thou wilt
build a house for him; therefore thy
servant has found courage to pray before thee. 26 And now, O LORD, thou
art God, and thou hast promised this
good thing to thy servant; 27 now
therefore may it please thee to bless
the house of thy servant, that it may
continue for ever before thee; for what
thou, O LORD, hast blessed is blessed
for ever."

18 After this David defeated the
Philistines and subdued them,
and he took Gath and its villages out
of the hand of the Philistines.
2 And he defeated Mō'ab, and the
Mō'ȧb·ītes became servants to David
and brought tribute.
3 David also defeated Had·ȧ·dē'zėr
king of Zō'bȧh, toward Hā'math, as he
went to set up his monument[s] at the
river Eū·phrā'tēṡ. 4 And David took
from him a thousand chariots, seven
thousand horsemen, and twenty thousand foot soldiers; and David hamstrung all the chariot horses, but left
enough for a hundred chariots. 5 And
when the Syrians of Damascus came
to help Had·ȧ·dē'zėr king of Zō'bȧh,
David slew twenty-two thousand men
of the Syrians. 6 Then David put garrisons[t] in Syria of Damascus; and the
Syrians became servants to David,
and brought tribute. And the LORD
gave victory to David wherever he
went. 7 And David took the shields of
gold which were carried by the servants of Had·ȧ·dē'zėr, and brought
them to Jerusalem. 8 And from Tib'hath
and from Cün, cities of Had·ȧ·dē'zėr,
David took very much bronze; with
it Solomon made the bronze sea and
the pillars and the vessels of bronze.
9 When Tō'ū king of Hā'math
heard that David had defeated the
whole army of Had·ȧ·dē'zėr, king of
Zō'bȧh, 10 he sent his son Hȧ·dôr'ȧm
to King David, to greet him, and to
congratulate him because he had
fought against Had·ȧ·dē'zėr and defeated him; for Hadadezer had often
been at war with Tō'ū. And he sent
all sorts of articles of gold, of silver,
and of bronze; 11 these also King
David dedicated to the LORD, together
with the silver and gold which he had
carried off from all the nations, from
Ē'dȯm, Mō'ab, the Am'mȯ·nītes, the
Philistines, and Am'ȧ·lek.
12 And Ȧ·bi'shäi, the son of Zė·rü'-
i·ȧh, slew eighteen thousand Ē'dȯm-
ītes in the Valley of Salt. 13 And he put
garrisons in Ē'dȯm; and all the Ē'dȯm-
ītes became David's servants. And the
LORD gave victory to David wherever
he went.
14 So David reigned over all Israel;

[q] Cn: Heb uncertain [r] Gk Vg: Heb *one* [s] Heb *hand*
[t] Gk Vg 2 Sam 8.6 Compare Syr: Heb lacks *garrisons*
18.1-13: 2 Sam 8.1-14. 18.14-17: 2 Sam 8.15-18.

and he administered justice and equity
to all his people. 15And Jō'ab the son
of Zė·rü'i·ȧh was over the army; and
Je·hosh'ȧ·phat the son of Ȧ·hī'lu̇d was
recorder; 16 and Zā'dok the son of
Ȧ·hī'tu̇b and Ȧ·him'ė·lech the son of
Ȧ·bī'ȧ·thär were priests; and Shav'shȧ
was secretary; 17 and Be·nā'iȧh the son
of Je·hoi'ȧ·dȧ was over the Cher'ė-
thītes and the Pel'ė·thītes; and David's
sons were the chief officials in the
service of the king.

19 Now after this Nā'hash the king
of the Am'mȯ·nītes died, and his
son reigned in his stead. 2And David
said, "I will deal loyally with Hā'nu̇n
the son of Nā'hash, for his father dealt
loyally with me." So David sent messengers to console him concerning his
father. And David's servants came to
Hanun in the land of the Am'mȯ·nītes,
to console him. 3 But the princes of
the Am'mȯ·nītes said to Hā'nu̇n, "Do
you think, because David has sent
comforters to you, that he is honoring
your father? Have not his servants
come to you to search and to overthrow
and to spy out the land?" 4 So Hā'nu̇n
took David's servants, and shaved
them, and cut off their garments in the
middle, at their hips, and sent them
away; 5 and they departed. When
David was told concerning the men,
he sent to meet them, for the men were
greatly ashamed. And the king said,
"Remain at Jericho until your beards
have grown, and then return."

6 When the Am'mȯ·nītes saw that
they had made themselves odious to
David, Hā'nu̇n and the Ammonites
sent a thousand talents of silver to hire
chariots and horsemen from Mes·ȯ·pȯ-
tā'mi·ȧ, from Âr'ȧm-mā'ȧ·cȧh, and
from Zō'bȧh. 7 They hired thirty-two
thousand chariots and the king of
Mā'ȧ·cȧh with his army, who came
and encamped before Med'ė·bȧ. And
the Am'mȯ·nītes were mustered from
their cities and came to battle. 8 When
David heard of it, he sent Jō'ab and
all the army of the mighty men. 9And
the Am'mȯ·nītes came out and drew
up in battle array at the entrance of the
city, and the kings who had come were
by themselves in the open country.

10 When Jō'ab saw that the battle
was set against him both in front and
in the rear, he chose some of the picked
men of Israel, and arrayed them against
the Syrians; 11 the rest of his men he
put in the charge of Ȧ·bi'shäi his
brother, and they were arrayed against
the Am'mȯ·nītes. 12And he said, "If
the Syrians are too strong for me, then
you shall help me; but if the Am'mȯ-
nītes are too strong for you, then I will
help you. 13 Be of good courage, and
let us play the man for our people, and
for the cities of our God; and may
the LORD do what seems good to him."
14 So Jō'ab and the people who were
with him drew near before the Syrians
for battle; and they fled before him.
15And when the Am'mȯ·nītes saw that
the Syrians fled, they likewise fled
before Ȧ·bi'shäi, Jō'ab's brother, and
entered the city. Then Joab came to
Jerusalem.

16 But when the Syrians saw that
they had been defeated by Israel, they
sent messengers and brought out the
Syrians who were beyond the Eū-
phrā'tēs, with Shō'phach the commander of the army of Had·ȧ·dē'zėr at
their head. 17And when it was told
David, he gathered all Israel together,
and crossed the Jordan, and came to
them, and drew up his forces against
them. And when David set the battle
in array against the Syrians, they
fought with him. 18And the Syrians
fled before Israel; and David slew of
the Syrians the men of seven thousand
chariots, and forty thousand foot
soldiers, and killed also Shō'phach the
commander of their army. 19And when
the servants of Had·ȧ·dē'zėr saw that
they had been defeated by Israel, they
made peace with David, and became
subject to him. So the Syrians were
not willing to help the Am'mȯ·nītes
any more.

20 In the spring of the year, the
time when kings go forth to
battle, Jō'ab led out the army, and
ravaged the country of the Am'mȯ-
nītes, and came and besieged Rab'bȧh.
But David remained at Jerusalem. And
Jō'ab smote Rabbah, and overthrew it.
2And David took the crown of their
king[u] from his head; he found that it
weighed a talent of gold, and in it was
a precious stone; and it was placed on
David's head. And he brought forth
the spoil of the city, a very great
amount. 3And he brought forth the
people who were in it, and set them to
labor[v] with saws and iron picks and

[u] Or *Milcom* See 1 Kings 11.5 [v] Compare 2 Sam 12.31: Heb *he sawed*
19.1-19: 2 Sam 10.1-19. **20.1:** 2 Sam 11.1. **20.1-3:** 2 Sam 12.26-31.

axes;[w] and thus David did to all the
cities of the Am'mȯ·nītes. Then David
and all the people returned to Jerusalem.
4 And after this there arose war
with the Philistines at Gē'zėr; then
Sib'bė·cāi the Hū'shȧ·thīte slew Sip'-
päi, who was one of the descendants of
the giants; and the Philistines were
subdued. 5 And there was again war
with the Philistines; and El·hā'nȧn the
son of Jā'ir slew Läh'mī the brother
of Goliath the Git'tīte, the shaft of
whose spear was like a weaver's beam.
6 And there was again war at Gath,
where there was a man of great stature,
who had six fingers on each hand, and
six toes on each foot, twenty-four in
number; and he also was descended
from the giants. 7 And when he taunted
Israel, Jonathan the son of Shim'ē-ȧ,
David's brother, slew him. 8 These
were descended from the giants in
Gath; and they fell by the hand of
David and by the hand of his servants.
21 Satan stood up against Israel,
and incited David to number
Israel. 2 So David said to Jō'ab and
the commanders of the army, "Go,
number Israel, from Beer-sheba to
Dan, and bring me a report, that I may
know their number." 3 But Jō'ab said,
"May the LORD add to his people a
hundred times as many as they are!
Are they not, my lord the king, all of
them my lord's servants? Why then
should my lord require this? Why
should he bring guilt upon Israel?"
4 But the king's word prevailed against
Jō'ab. So Joab departed and went
throughout all Israel, and came back
to Jerusalem. 5 And Jō'ab gave the sum
of the numbering of the people to
David. In all Israel there were one
million one hundred thousand men
who drew the sword, and in Judah
four hundred and seventy thousand
who drew the sword. 6 But he did not
include Levi and Benjamin in the
numbering, for the king's command
was abhorrent to Jō'ab.
7 But God was displeased with this
thing, and he smote Israel. 8 And David
said to God, "I have sinned greatly in
that I have done this thing. But now,
I pray thee, take away the iniquity of
thy servant; for I have done very
foolishly." 9 And the LORD spoke to
Gad, David's seer, saying, 10 "Go and
say to David, 'Thus says the LORD,
Three things I offer you; choose one
of them, that I may do it to you.' "
11 So Gad came to David and said to
him, "Thus says the LORD, 'Take
which you will: 12 either three years of
famine; or three months of devastation
by your foes, while the sword of your
enemies overtakes you; or else three
days of the sword of the LORD, pestilence upon the land, and the angel of
the LORD destroying throughout all
the territory of Israel.' Now decide
what answer I shall return to him who
sent me." 13 Then David said to Gad,
"I am in great distress; let me fall into
the hand of the LORD, for his mercy is
very great; but let me not fall into the
hand of man."
14 So the LORD sent a pestilence
upon Israel; and there fell seventy
thousand men of Israel. 15 And God
sent the angel to Jerusalem to destroy
it; but when he was about to destroy
it, the LORD saw, and he repented of
the evil; and he said to the destroying
angel, "It is enough; now stay your
hand." And the angel of the LORD was
standing by the threshing floor of
Ôr'nȧn the Jeb'ū·sīte. 16 And David
lifted his eyes and saw the angel of the
LORD standing between earth and
heaven, and in his hand a drawn sword
stretched out over Jerusalem. Then
David and the elders, clothed in sackcloth, fell upon their faces. 17 And
David said to God, "Was it not I who
gave command to number the people?
It is I who have sinned and done very
wickedly. But these sheep, what have
they done? Let thy hand, I pray thee,
O LORD my God, be against me and
against my father's house; but let not
the plague be upon thy people."
18 Then the angel of the LORD
commanded Gad to say to David that
David should go up and rear an altar
to the LORD on the threshing floor of
Ôr'nȧn the Jeb'ū·sīte. 19 So David
went up at Gad's word, which he had
spoken in the name of the LORD.
20 Now Ôr'nȧn was threshing wheat;
he turned and saw the angel, and his
four sons who were with him hid
themselves. 21 As David came to Ôr'-
nȧn, Ornan looked and saw David and
went forth from the threshing floor,
and did obeisance to David with his
face to the ground. 22 And David said

[w] Compare 2 Sam 12.31: Heb *saws*
20.4-8: 2 Sam 21.18-22. **21.1-27:** 2 Sam 24.1-25.

to Ôr'nȧn, "Give me the site of the
threshing floor that I may build on it
an altar to the LORD—give it to me at
its full price—that the plague may be
averted from the people." 23 Then
Ôr'nȧn said to David, "Take it; and
let my lord the king do what seems
good to him; see, I give the oxen for
burnt offerings, and the threshing
sledges for the wood, and the wheat for
a cereal offering. I give it all." 24 But
King David said to Ôr'nȧn, "No, but
I will buy it for the full price; I will
not take for the LORD what is yours,
nor offer burnt offerings which cost
me nothing." 25 So David paid Ôr'nȧn
six hundred shekels of gold by weight
for the site. 26 And David built there
an altar to the LORD and presented
burnt offerings and peace offerings,
and called upon the LORD, and he
answered him with fire from heaven
upon the altar of burnt offering.
27 Then the LORD commanded the
angel; and he put his sword back into
its sheath.

28 At that time, when David saw
that the LORD had answered him at
the threshing floor of Ôr'nȧn the Jeb'ū-
sīte, he made his sacrifices there. 29 For
the tabernacle of the LORD, which
Moses had made in the wilderness, and
the altar of burnt offering were at that
time in the high place at Gib'ē·ȯn;
30 but David could not go before it to
inquire of God, for he was afraid of
the sword of the angel of the LORD.

22 Then David said, "Here shall
be the house of the LORD God
and here the altar of burnt offering for
Israel."

2 David commanded to gather together the aliens who were in the land
of Israel, and he set stonecutters to
prepare dressed stones for building the
house of God. 3 David also provided
great stores of iron for nails for the
doors of the gates and for clamps, as
well as bronze in quantities beyond
weighing, 4 and cedar timbers without
number; for the Sī·dō'ni·ȧnṡ and
Tȳ'ri·ȧnṡ brought great quantities of
cedar to David. 5 For David said,
"Solomon my son is young and inexperienced, and the house that is to
be built for the LORD must be exceedingly magnificent, of fame and glory
throughout all lands; I will therefore
make preparation for it." So David
provided materials in great quantity
before his death.

6 Then he called for Solomon his
son, and charged him to build a house
for the LORD, the God of Israel.
7 David said to Solomon, "My son, I
had it in my heart to build a house to
the name of the LORD my God. 8 But
the word of the LORD came to me,
saying, 'You have shed much blood and
have waged great wars; you shall not
build a house to my name, because
you have shed so much blood before me
upon the earth. 9 Behold, a son shall
be born to you; he shall be a man of
peace. I will give him peace from all
his enemies round about; for his name
shall be Solomon, and I will give peace
and quiet to Israel in his days. 10 He
shall build a house for my name. He
shall be my son, and I will be his
father, and I will establish his royal
throne in Israel for ever.' 11 Now, my
son, the LORD be with you, so that you
may succeed in building the house of
the LORD your God, as he has spoken
concerning you. 12 Only, may the LORD
grant you discretion and understanding, that when he gives you charge over
Israel you may keep the law of the
LORD your God. 13 Then you will prosper if you are careful to observe the
statutes and the ordinances which the
LORD commanded Moses for Israel. Be
strong, and of good courage. Fear not;
be not dismayed. 14 With great pains I
have provided for the house of the
LORD a hundred thousand talents of
gold, a million talents of silver, and
bronze and iron beyond weighing, for
there is so much of it; timber and stone
too I have provided. To these you must
add. 15 You have an abundance of
workmen: stonecutters, masons, carpenters, and all kinds of craftsmen
without number, skilled in working
16 gold, silver, bronze, and iron. Arise
and be doing! The LORD be with you!"

17 David also commanded all the
leaders of Israel to help Solomon his
son, saying, 18 "Is not the LORD your
God with you? And has he not given
you peace on every side? For he has
delivered the inhabitants of the land
into my hand; and the land is subdued
before the LORD and his people.
19 Now set your mind and heart to
seek the LORD your God. Arise and
build the sanctuary of the LORD God,
so that the ark of the covenant of the
LORD and the holy vessels of God may
be brought into a house built for the
name of the LORD."

23 When David was old and full of days, he made Solomon his son king over Israel.

2 David assembled all the leaders of Israel and the priests and the Levites. 3 The Levites, thirty years old and upward, were numbered, and the total was thirty-eight thousand men. 4 "Twenty-four thousand of these," David said, "shall have charge of the work in the house of the LORD, six thousand shall be officers and judges, 5 four thousand gatekeepers, and four thousand shall offer praises to the LORD with the instruments which I have made for praise." 6 And David organized them in divisions corresponding to the sons of Levi: Gẽr′shȯm, Kō′hath, and Mė·rãr′ī.

7 The sons of Gẽr′shȯm[x] were Lā′dȧn and Shim′ē-ī. 8 The sons of Lā′dȧn: Je·hī′el the chief, and Zē′thȧm, and Jō′ėl, three. 9 The sons of Shim′ē-ī: She·lō′moth, Hā′zi-el, and Hãr′ȧn, three. These were the heads of the fathers' houses of Lā′dȧn. 10 And the sons of Shim′ē-ī: Jā′hath, Zī′nȧ, and Jē′ush, and Bē·rī′ȧh. These four were the sons of Shime-i. 11 Jā′hath was the chief, and Zī′zȧh the second; but Jē′ush and Bē·rī′ȧh had not many sons, therefore they became a father's house in one reckoning.

12 The sons of Kō′hath: Am′ram, Iz′här, Hē′brȯn, and Uz′zi·el, four. 13 The sons of Am′ram: Aaron and Moses. Aaron was set apart to consecrate the most holy things, that he and his sons for ever should burn incense before the LORD, and minister to him and pronounce blessings in his name for ever. 14 But the sons of Moses the man of God were named among the tribe of Levi. 15 The sons of Moses: Gẽr′shȯm and Ē·lī·ē′zėr. 16 The sons of Gẽr′shȯm: She·bū′el the chief. 17 The sons of Ē·lī·ē′zėr: Rē·hȧ·bī′ȧh the chief; Eliezer had no other sons, but the sons of Rē·hȧ·bī′ȧh were very many. 18 The sons of Iz′här: She·lō′mith the chief. 19 The sons of Hē′brȯn: Je·rī′ȧh the chief, Am·ȧ·rī′ȧh the second, Jȧ·hā′zi·el the third, and Jek·ȧ·mē′ȧm the fourth. 20 The sons of Uz′zi·el: Mī′cȧh the chief and Is·shī′ȧh the second.

21 The sons of Mė·rãr′ī: Mäh′lī and Mū′shī. The sons of Mahli: El·ē·ā′zȧr and Kish. 22 El·ē·ā′zȧr died having no sons, but only daughters; their kinsmen, the sons of Kish, married them. 23 The sons of Mū′shī: Mäh′lī, Ē′dėr, and Jer′ė·moth, three.

24 These were the sons of Levi by their fathers' houses, the heads of fathers' houses as they were registered according to the number of the names of the individuals from twenty years old and upward who were to do the work for the service of the house of the LORD. 25 For David said, "The LORD, the God of Israel, has given peace to his people; and he dwells in Jerusalem for ever. 26 And so the Levites no longer need to carry the tabernacle or any of the things for its service"— 27 for by the last words of David these were the number of the Levites from twenty years old and upward— 28 "but their duty shall be to assist the sons of Aaron for the service of the house of the LORD, having the care of the courts and the chambers, the cleansing of all that is holy, and any work for the service of the house of God; 29 to assist also with the showbread, the flour for the cereal offering, the wafers of unleavened bread, the baked offering, the offering mixed with oil, and all measures of quantity or size. 30 And they shall stand every morning, thanking and praising the LORD, and likewise at evening, 31 and whenever burnt offerings are offered to the LORD on sabbaths, new moons, and feast days, according to the number required of them, continually before the LORD. 32 Thus they shall keep charge of the tent of meeting and the sanctuary, and shall attend the sons of Aaron, their brethren, for the service of the house of the LORD."

24 The divisions of the sons of Aaron were these. The sons of Aaron: Nā′dab, Ȧ·bī′hū, El·ē·ā′zȧr, and Ith′ȧ·mär. 2 But Nā′dab and Ȧ·bī′hū died before their father, and had no children, so El·ē·ā′zȧr and Ith′ȧ·mär became the priests. 3 With the help of Zā′dok of the sons of El·ē·ā′zȧr, and Ȧ·him′ė·lech of the sons of Ith′ȧ·mär, David organized them according to the appointed duties in their service. 4 Since more chief men were found among the sons of El·ē·ā′zȧr than among the sons of Ith′ȧ·mär, they organized them under sixteen heads of fathers' houses of the sons of Eleazar, and eight of the sons of Ithamar. 5 They organized them by lot, all

[x] Vg Compare Gk Syr: Heb *to the Gershonite*

alike, for there were officers of the sanctuary and officers of God among both
the sons of El·ē·ā'zȧr and the sons of
Ith'ȧ·mär. 6 And the scribe She·māi'ȧh
the son of Nė·than'el, a Levite, recorded them in the presence of the
king, and the princes, and Zā'dok the
priest, and Ȧ·him'ė·lech the son of
Ȧ·bī'ȧ·thär, and the heads of the
fathers' houses of the priests and of
the Levites; one father's house being
chosen for El·ē·ā'zȧr and one chosen
for Ith'ȧ·mär.

7 The first lot fell to Je·hoi'ȧ·rib,
the second to Je·dāi'ȧh, 8 the third to
Hā'rim, the fourth to Se-ō'rim, 9 the
fifth to Mal·ė·hī'jȧh, the sixth to Mij'-
ȧ·min, 10 the seventh to Hak'koz, the
eighth to Ȧ·bī'jȧh, 11 the ninth to
Jesh'ü·ȧ, the tenth to Shec·ȧ·nī'ȧh,
12 the eleventh to E·lī'ȧ·shib, the
twelfth to Jā'kim, 13 the thirteenth to
Hup'pȧh, the fourteenth to Je·sheb'e-
ȧb, 14 the fifteenth to Bil'gȧh, the
sixteenth to Im'mėr, 15 the seventeenth
to Hē'zir, the eighteenth to Hap'piz-
zez, 16 the nineteenth to Peth·ȧ·hī'ȧh,
the twentieth to Je·hez'kel, 17 the
twenty-first to Jā'chin, the twenty-
second to Gā'mụl, 18 the twenty-third
to De·lāi'ȧh, the twenty-fourth to
Mā-ȧ·zī'ȧh. 19 These had as their
appointed duty in their service to
come into the house of the LORD
according to the procedure established
for them by Aaron their father, as the
LORD God of Israel had commanded
him.

20 And of the rest of the sons of
Levi: of the sons of Am'ram, Shü'bȧ-el;
of the sons of Shuba-el, Jeh·dē'iȧh. 21 Of
Rē·hȧ·bī'ȧh: of the sons of Rehabiah,
Is·shī'ȧh the chief. 22 Of the Iz'hȧ-
rītes, She·lō'moth; of the sons of Shelo-
moth, Jā'hath. 23 The sons of Hē'brọn:[y]
Je·rī'ȧh the chief,[z] Am·ȧ·rī'ȧh the
second, Jȧ·hā'zi·el the third, Jek·ȧ-
mē'ȧm the fourth. 24 The sons of
Uz'zi·el, Mī'cȧh; of the sons of Micah,
Shā'mir. 25 The brother of Mī'cȧh,
Is·shī'ȧh; of the sons of Isshiah,
Zech·ȧ·rī'ȧh. 26 The sons of Mė·rȧr'ī:
Mäh'lī and Mū'shī. The sons of Jā-
ȧ·zī'ȧh: Bē'nō. 27 The sons of Mė·rȧr'ī:
of Jā-ȧ·zī'ȧh, Bē'nō, Shō'ham, Zac'cūr,
and Ib'rī. 28 Of Mäh'lī: El·ē·ā'zȧr, who
had no sons. 29 Of Kish, the sons of
Kish: Je·räh'mē·ėl. 30 The sons of
Mū'shī: Mäh'lī, Ē'dėr, and Jer'i·moth.
These were the sons of the Levites
according to their fathers' houses.
31 These also, the head of each father's
house and his younger brother alike,
cast lots, just as their brethren the sons
of Aaron, in the presence of King
David, Zā'dok, Ȧ·him'ė·lech, and the
heads of fathers' houses of the priests
and of the Levites.

25 David and the chiefs of the
service also set apart for the
service certain of the sons of Ā'saph,
and of Hē'mȧn, and of Je·dü'thụn,
who should prophesy with lyres, with
harps, and with cymbals. The list of
those who did the work and of their
duties was: 2 Of the sons of Ā'saph:
Zac'cūr, Joseph, Neth·ȧ·nī'ȧh, and
Ash·ȧ·rē'lȧh, sons of Asaph, under the
direction of Asaph, who prophesied
under the direction of the king. 3 Of
Je·dü'thụn, the sons of Jeduthun:
Ged·ȧ·lī'ȧh, Zē'rī, Je·shā'iȧh, Shim'ē-ī,[a]
Hash·ȧ·bī'ȧh, and Mat·ti·thī'ȧh, six,
under the direction of their father
Jeduthun, who prophesied with the
lyre in thanksgiving and praise to the
LORD. 4 Of Hē'mȧn, the sons of Heman: Buk·kī'ȧh, Mat·tȧ·nī'ȧh, Uz'zi·el,
She·bū'el, and Jer'i·moth, Han·ȧ·nī'-
ȧh, Hȧ·nā'nī, E·lī'ȧ·thȧh, Gid·dal'tī,
and Rō·mam'ti-ē'zėr, Josh·be·kash'ȧh,
Mal·lō'thī, Hō'thir, Mȧ·hā'zi-oth. 5 All
these were the sons of Hē'mȧn the
king's seer, according to the promise
of God to exalt him; for God had given
Heman fourteen sons and three
daughters. 6 They were all under the
direction of their father in the music
in the house of the LORD with cymbals,
harps, and lyres for the service of the
house of God. Ā'saph, Je·dü'thụn, and
Hē'mȧn were under the order of the
king. 7 The number of them along
with their brethren, who were trained
in singing to the LORD, all who were
skilful, was two hundred and eighty-
eight. 8 And they cast lots for their
duties, small and great, teacher and
pupil alike.

9 The first lot fell for Ā'saph to
Joseph; the second to Ged·ȧ·lī'ȧh, to
him and his brethren and his sons,
twelve; 10 the third to Zac'cūr, his sons
and his brethren, twelve; 11 the fourth
to Iz'rī, his sons and his brethren,
twelve; 12 the fifth to Neth·ȧ·nī'ȧh, his
sons and his brethren, twelve; 13 the
sixth to Buk·kī'ȧh, his sons and his
brethren, twelve; 14 the seventh to
Jesh·ȧ·rē'lȧh, his sons and his brethren,

[y] See 23.19: Heb lacks *Hebron* [z] See 23.19: Heb lacks *the chief* [a] One Ms: Gk: Heb lacks *Shimei*

twelve; 15 the eighth to Je·shā'iȧh, his
sons and his brethren, twelve; 16 the
ninth to Mat·tȧ·nī'ȧh, his sons and his
brethren, twelve; 17 the tenth to
Shim'ē-ī, his sons and his brethren,
twelve; 18 the eleventh to Az'ȧ·rel, his
sons and his brethren, twelve; 19 the
twelfth to Hash·ȧ·bī'ȧh, his sons and
his brethren, twelve; 20 to the thirteenth, Shü'bȧ-el, his sons and his
brethren, twelve; 21 to the fourteenth,
Mat·ti·thī'ȧh, his sons and his brethren, twelve; 22 to the fifteenth, to
Jer'ė·moth, his sons and his brethren,
twelve; 23 to the sixteenth, to Han·ȧ-
nī'ȧh, his sons and his brethren,
twelve; 24 to the seventeenth, to Josh-
be·kash'ȧh, his sons and his brethren,
twelve; 25 to the eighteenth, to Hȧ-
nā'nī, his sons and his brethren, twelve;
26 to the nineteenth, to Mal·lō'thī, his
sons and his brethren, twelve; 27 to the
twentieth, to E·lī'ȧ·thȧh, his sons and
his brethren, twelve; 28 to the twenty-
first, to Hō'thir, his sons and his
brethren, twelve; 29 to the twenty-
second, to Gid·dal'tī, his sons and his
brethren, twelve; 30 to the twenty-
third, to Mȧ·hā'zi-oth, his sons and
his brethren, twelve; 31 to the twenty-
fourth, to Rō·mam'ti-ē'zėr, his sons
and his brethren, twelve.

26 As for the divisions of the gatekeepers: of the Kō'rȧ·hītes, Me-
shel·ė·mī'ȧh the son of Kō're, of the
sons of Ā'saph. 2 And Me·shel·ė·mī'ȧh
had sons: Zech·ȧ·rī'ȧh the first-born,
Je·dī'ȧ-el the second, Zeb·ȧ·dī'ȧh the
third, Jath'ni-el the fourth, 3 Ē'lȧm the
fifth, Jē'hō-hā'nȧn the sixth, El'i·ē-hō-
ē'näi the seventh. 4 And Ō'bed-ē'dȯm
had sons: She·māi'ȧh the first-born,
Je·hō'zȧ·bad the second, Jō'ȧh the
third, Sā'chär the fourth, Nė·than'el
the fifth, 5 Am'mi-el the sixth, Is'sȧ-
chär the seventh, Pe-ul'lė·thäi the
eighth; for God blessed him. 6 Also to
his son She·māi'ȧh were sons born who
were rulers in their fathers' houses,
for they were men of great ability.
7 The sons of She·māi'ȧh: Oth'nī,
Reph'ȧ-el, Ō'bed, and El·zā'bad,
whose brethren were able men, E·lī'-
hū and Sem·ȧ·chī'ȧh. 8 All these were
of the sons of Ō'bed-ē'dȯm with their
sons and brethren, able men qualified
for the service; sixty-two of Obed-
edom. 9 And Me·shel·ė·mī'ȧh had sons
and brethren, able men, eighteen.
10 And Hō'sȧh, of the sons of Mė·rär'ī,
had sons: Shim'rī the chief (for though
he was not the first-born, his father
made him chief), 11 Hil·kī'ȧh the
second, Teb·ȧ·lī'ȧh the third, Zech·ȧ-
rī'ȧh the fourth: all the sons and brethren of Hō'sȧh were thirteen.

12 These divisions of the gatekeepers, corresponding to their chief
men, had duties, just as their brethren
did, ministering in the house of the
LORD; 13 and they cast lots by fathers'
houses, small and great alike, for their
gates. 14 The lot for the east fell to
Shel·ė·mī'ȧh. They cast lots also for
his son Zech·ȧ·rī'ȧh, a shrewd counselor, and his lot came out for the
north. 15 Ō'bed-ē'dȯm's came out for
the south, and to his sons was allotted
the storehouse. 16 For Shup'pim and
Hō'sȧh it came out for the west, at the
gate of Shal'lė·cheth on the road that
goes up. Watch corresponded to watch.
17 On the east there were six each day,[b]
on the north four each day, on the
south four each day, as well as two
and two at the storehouse; 18 and for
the parbar[c] on the west there were four
at the road and two at the parbar.
19 These were the divisions of the
gatekeepers among the Kō'rȧ·hītes and
the sons of Mė·rär'ī.

20 And of the Levites, Ȧ·hī'jȧh had
charge of the treasuries of the house of
God and the treasuries of the dedicated
gifts. 21 The sons of Lā'dȧn, the sons
of the Gēr'shȯ·nītes belonging to Ladan, the heads of the fathers' houses
belonging to Ladan the Gershonite:
Je·hī'ė·lī.[d]

22 The sons of Je·hī'ė·lī, Zē'thȧm
and Jō'ėl his brother, were in charge
of the treasuries of the house of the
LORD. 23 Of the Am'rȧ·mītes, the Iz'-
hȧ·rītes, the Hē'brȯ·nītes, and the
Uz'zi·ė·lītes—24 and She·bū'el the son
of Gēr'shȯm, son of Moses, was chief
officer in charge of the treasuries.
25 His brethren: from Ē·lī·ē'zėr were
his son Rē·hȧ·bī'ȧh, and his son Je·shā'-
iȧh, and his son Jō'rȧm, and his son
Zich'rī, and his son She·lō'moth.
26 This She·lō'moth and his brethren
were in charge of all the treasuries of
the dedicated gifts which David the
king, and the heads of the fathers'
houses, and the officers of the thousands and the hundreds, and the commanders of the army, had dedicated.

[b] Gk: Heb *Levites* [c] The meaning of the word *parbar* is unknown
[d] The Hebrew text of verse 21 is confused

27 From spoil won in battles they
dedicated gifts for the maintenance of
the house of the LORD. 28 Also all that
Samuel the seer, and Saul the son of
Kish, and Abner the son of Nēr, and
Jō'ab the son of Zė·rü'i·ȧh had dedicated—all dedicated gifts were in the
care of She·lō'moth[e] and his brethren.

29 Of the Iz'hȧ·rītes, Chen·ȧ·nī'ȧh
and his sons were appointed to outside
duties for Israel, as officers and judges.
30 Of the Hē'brȯ·nītes, Hash·ȧ·bī'ȧh
and his brethren, one thousand seven
hundred men of ability, had the oversight of Israel westward of the Jordan
for all the work of the LORD and for
the service of the king. 31 Of the
Hē'brȯ·nītes, Je·rī'jȧh was chief of the
Hebronites of whatever genealogy or
fathers' houses. (In the fortieth year
of David's reign search was made and
men of great ability among them were
found at Jā'zėr in Gilead.) 32 King
David appointed him and his brethren,
two thousand seven hundred men of
ability, heads of fathers' houses, to
have the oversight of the Reubenites,
the Gadites, and the half-tribe of the
Mȧ·nas'sītes for everything pertaining
to God and for the affairs of the king.

27 This is the list of the people
of Israel, the heads of fathers'
houses, the commanders of thousands
and hundreds, and their officers who
served the king in all matters concerning the divisions that came and went,
month after month throughout the
year, each division numbering twenty-
four thousand:

2 Jȧ·shō'bē·ȧm the son of Zab'di-el
was in charge of the first division in
the first month; in his division were
twenty-four thousand. 3 He was a
descendant of Per'ez, and was chief of
all the commanders of the army for
the first month. 4 Dō'däi the A·hō'hīte[f]
was in charge of the division of the
second month; in his division were
twenty-four thousand. 5 The third
commander, for the third month, was
Be·nā'iȧh, the son of Je·hoi'ȧ·dȧ the
priest, as chief; in his division were
twenty-four thousand. 6 This is the
Be·nā'iȧh who was a mighty man of
the thirty and in command of the
thirty; Am·miz'ȧ·bad his son was in
charge of his division.[g] 7 As'ȧ·hel the
brother of Jō'ab was fourth, for the
fourth month, and his son Zeb·ȧ·dī'ȧh
after him; in his division were twenty-
four thousand. 8 The fifth commander,
for the fifth month, was Sham'huth,
the Iz'rȧ·hīte; in his division were
twenty-four thousand. 9 Sixth, for the
sixth month, was Ira, the son of Ik'-
kesh the Te·kō'īte; in his division were
twenty-four thousand. 10 Seventh, for
the seventh month, was Hē'lez the
Pel'ȯ·nīte, of the sons of Ē'phrȧ·im; in
his division were twenty-four thousand. 11 Eighth, for the eighth month,
was Sib'bė·cäi the Hū'shȧ·thīte, of the
Zē'rȧ·hītes; in his division were twenty-
four thousand. 12 Ninth, for the ninth
month, was Ā'bi·ē'zėr of An'ȧ·thoth,
a Benjaminite; in his division were
twenty-four thousand. 13 Tenth, for
the tenth month, was Mā'hȧ·räi of
Nė·toph'ȧh, of the Zē'rȧ·hītes; in his
division were twenty-four thousand.
14 Eleventh, for the eleventh month,
was Be·nā'iȧh of Pir'ȧ·thon, of the sons
of Ē'phrȧ·im; in his division were
twenty-four thousand. 15 Twelfth, for
the twelfth month, was Hel'däi the
Nė·toph'ȧ·thīte, of Oth'ni-el; in his
division were twenty-four thousand.

16 Over the tribes of Israel, for the
Reubenites Ē·lī·ē'zėr the son of Zich'rī
was chief officer; for the Simeonites,
Sheph·ȧ·tī'ȧh the son of Mā'ȧ·cȧh;
17 for Levi, Hash·ȧ·bī'ȧh the son of
Ke·mū'el; for Aaron, Zā'dok; 18 for
Judah, E·lī'hū, one of David's
brothers; for Is'sȧ·chär, Om'rī the son
of Michael; 19 for Zeb'ū·lun, Ish·mā'-
iȧh the son of Ō·bȧ·dī'ȧh; for Naph'-
tȧ·lī, Jer'ė·moth the son of Az'ri-el;
20 for the Ē'phrȧ·im·ītes, Hō·shē'ȧ the
son of Az·ȧ·zī'ȧh; for the half-tribe of
Mȧ·nas'sėh, Jō'ėl the son of Pe·dāi'ȧh;
21 for the half-tribe of Mȧ·nas'sėh in
Gilead, Id'dō the son of Zech·ȧ·rī'ȧh;
for Benjamin, Jā·ȧ·sī'el, the son of Abner; 22 for Dan, Az'ȧ·rel the son of
Je·rō'ham. These were the leaders of
the tribes of Israel. 23 David did not
number those below twenty years of
age, for the LORD had promised to
make Israel as many as the stars of
heaven. 24 Jō'ab the son of Zė·rü'i·ȧh
began to number, but did not finish;
yet wrath came upon Israel for this,
and the number was not entered in
the chronicles of King David.

25 Over the king's treasuries was
Az'mȧ·veth the son of Ad'i-el; and
over the treasuries in the country, in

[e] Heb *Shelomith* [f] Gk: Heb *Ahohite and his division and Mikloth the chief officer*
[g] Gk Vg: Heb *was his division*

the cities, in the villages and in the
towers, was Jonathan the son of Uz-
zī'ăh; 26 and over those who did the
work of the field for tilling the soil was
Ez'rī the son of Chē'lŭb; 27 and over
the vineyards was Shim'ē-ī the Rā'mȧ-
thīte; and over the produce of the vineyards for the wine cellars was Zab'dī
the Shiph'mīte. 28 Over the olive and
sycamore trees in the She·phē'lȧh was
Bā'ȧl-hā'nȧn the Ge·dē'rīte; and over
the stores of oil was Jō'ash. 29 Over the
herds that pastured in Sharon was
Shit'răi the Shâr'ȯ·nīte; over the herds
in the valleys was Shā'phȧt the son of
Ad'lā·ī. 30 Over the camels was Ō'bil
the Ish'mȧ·el·īte; and over the she-
asses was Jeh·dē'iȧh the Me·ron'ȯ-
thīte. Over the flocks was Jā'ziz the
Hag'rīte. 31 All these were stewards of
King David's property.
32 Jonathan, David's uncle, was a
counselor, being a man of understanding and a scribe; he and Je·hī'el the son
of Hach'mȯ·nī attended the king's
sons. 33 Ȧ·hith'ȯ·phel was the king's
counselor, and Hū'shăi the Är'chīte
was the king's friend. 34 Ȧ·hith'ȯ·phel
was succeeded by Je·hoi'ȧ·dȧ the son
of Be·nā'iȧh, and Ȧ·bī'ȧ·thär. Jō'ab
was commander of the king's army.
28 David assembled at Jerusalem
all the officials of Israel, the
officials of the tribes, the officers of
the divisions that served the king, the
commanders of thousands, the commanders of hundreds, the stewards of
all the property and cattle of the king
and his sons, together with the palace
officials, the mighty men, and all the
seasoned warriors. 2 Then King David
rose to his feet and said: "Hear me,
my brethren and my people. I had it
in my heart to build a house of rest for
the ark of the covenant of the LORD,
and for the footstool of our God; and
I made preparations for building. 3 But
God said to me, 'You may not build a
house for my name, for you are a
warrior and have shed blood.' 4 Yet
the LORD God of Israel chose me from
all my father's house to be king over
Israel for ever; for he chose Judah as
leader, and in the house of Judah my
father's house, and among my father's
sons he took pleasure in me to make
me king over all Israel. 5 And of all my
sons (for the LORD has given me many
sons) he has chosen Solomon my son
to sit upon the throne of the kingdom
of the LORD over Israel. 6 He said to
me, 'It is Solomon your son who shall
build my house and my courts, for I
have chosen him to be my son, and I
will be his father. 7 I will establish his
kingdom for ever if he continues
resolute in keeping my commandments
and my ordinances, as he is today.'
8 Now therefore in the sight of all
Israel, the assembly of the LORD, and
in the hearing of our God, observe and
seek out all the commandments of the
LORD your God; that you may possess
this good land, and leave it for an
inheritance to your children after you
for ever.
9 "And you, Solomon my son,
know the God of your father, and
serve him with a whole heart and with
a willing mind; for the LORD searches
all hearts, and understands every plan
and thought. If you seek him, he will
be found by you; but if you forsake
him, he will cast you off for ever.
10 Take heed now, for the LORD has
chosen you to build a house for the
sanctuary; be strong, and do it."
11 Then David gave Solomon his
son the plan of the vestibule of the
temple, and of its houses, its treasuries, its upper rooms, and its inner
chambers, and of the room for the
mercy seat; 12 and the plan of all that
he had in mind for the courts of the
house of the LORD, all the surrounding
chambers, the treasuries of the house
of God, and the treasuries for dedicated gifts; 13 for the divisions of the
priests and of the Levites, and all the
work of the service in the house of the
LORD; for all the vessels for the service
in the house of the LORD, 14 the weight
of gold for all golden vessels for each
service, the weight of silver vessels for
each service, 15 the weight of the
golden lampstands and their lamps,
the weight of gold for each lampstand
and its lamp, the weight of silver for
a lampstand and its lamps, according
to the use of each lampstand in the
service, 16 the weight of gold for each
table for the showbread, the silver for
the silver tables, 17 and pure gold for
the forks, the basins, and the cups; for
the golden bowls and the weight of
each; for the silver bowls and the
weight of each; 18 for the altar of incense made of refined gold, and its
weight; also his plan for the golden
chariot of the cherubim that spread
their wings and covered the ark of the
covenant of the LORD. 19 All this he

made clear by the writing from the
hand of the LORD concerning it,[h] all
the work to be done according to the
plan.

20 Then David said to Solomon his
son, "Be strong and of good courage,
and do it. Fear not, be not dismayed;
for the LORD God, even my God, is
with you. He will not fail you or forsake you, until all the work for the
service of the house of the LORD is
finished. 21 And behold the divisions of
the priests and the Levites for all the
service of the house of God; and with
you in all the work will be every willing
man who has skill for any kind of
service; also the officers and all the
people will be wholly at your command."

29 And David the king said to all
the assembly, "Solomon my
son, whom alone God has chosen, is
young and inexperienced, and the
work is great; for the palace will not be
for man but for the LORD God. 2 So I
have provided for the house of my
God, so far as I was able, the gold for
the things of gold, the silver for the
things of silver, and the bronze for
the things of bronze, the iron for the
things of iron, and wood for the things
of wood, besides great quantities of
onyx and stones for setting, antimony,
colored stones, all sorts of precious
stones, and marble. 3 Moreover, in
addition to all that I have provided for
the holy house, I have a treasure of
my own of gold and silver, and because
of my devotion to the house of my God
I give it to the house of my God:
4 three thousand talents of gold, of the
gold of Ō'phĭr, and seven thousand
talents of refined silver, for overlaying
the walls of the house, 5 and for all the
work to be done by craftsmen, gold
for the things of gold and silver for
the things of silver. Who then will
offer willingly, consecrating himself
today to the LORD?"

6 Then the heads of fathers' houses
made their freewill offerings, as did
also the leaders of the tribes, the commanders of thousands and of hundreds,
and the officers over the king's work.
7 They gave for the service of the house
of God five thousand talents and ten
thousand darics of gold, ten thousand
talents of silver, eighteen thousand
talents of bronze, and a hundred thousand talents of iron. 8 And whoever had
precious stones gave them to the
treasury of the house of the LORD, in
the care of Je·hī'el the Gẽr'shŏ·nīte.
9 Then the people rejoiced because
these had given willingly, for with a
whole heart they had offered freely to
the LORD; David the king also rejoiced
greatly.

10 Therefore David blessed the
LORD in the presence of all the
assembly; and David said: "Blessed art
thou, O LORD, the God of Israel our
father, for ever and ever. 11 Thine, O
LORD, is the greatness, and the power,
and the glory, and the victory, and the
majesty; for all that is in the heavens
and in the earth is thine; thine is the
kingdom, O LORD, and thou art
exalted as head above all. 12 Both
riches and honor come from thee, and
thou rulest over all. In thy hand are
power and might; and in thy hand it
is to make great and to give strength
to all. 13 And now we thank thee, our
God, and praise thy glorious name.

14 "But who am I, and what is my
people, that we should be able thus to
offer willingly? For all things come
from thee, and of thy own have we
given thee. 15 For we are strangers before thee, and sojourners, as all our
fathers were; our days on the earth are
like a shadow, and there is no abiding.[i]
16 O LORD our God, all this abundance
that we have provided for building
thee a house for thy holy name comes
from thy hand and is all thy own. 17 I
know, my God, that thou triest the
heart, and hast pleasure in uprightness; in the uprightness of my heart I
have freely offered all these things,
and now I have seen thy people, who
are present here, offering freely and
joyously to thee. 18 O LORD, the God
of Abraham, Isaac, and Israel, our
fathers, keep for ever such purposes
and thoughts in the hearts of thy people, and direct their hearts toward
thee. 19 Grant to Solomon my son that
with a whole heart he may keep thy
commandments, thy testimonies, and
thy statutes, performing all, and that
he may build the palace for which I
have made provision."

20 Then David said to all the assembly, "Bless the LORD your God."
And all the assembly blessed the LORD,
the God of their fathers, and bowed

[h] Cn: Heb *upon me*
[i] Gk Vg: Heb *hope*

their heads, and worshiped the LORD,
and did obeisance to the king. 21 And
they performed sacrifices to the LORD,
and on the next day offered burnt
offerings to the LORD, a thousand bulls,
a thousand rams, and a thousand
lambs, with their drink offerings, and
sacrifices in abundance for all Israel;
22 and they ate and drank before the
LORD on that day with great gladness.
And they made Solomon the son of
David king the second time, and they
anointed him as prince for the LORD,
and Zā'dok as priest. 23 Then Solomon
sat on the throne of the LORD as king
instead of David his father; and he
prospered, and all Israel obeyed him.
24 All the leaders and the mighty men,
and also all the sons of King David,
pledged their allegiance to King Solomon. 25 And the LORD gave Solomon
great repute in the sight of all Israel,
and bestowed upon him such royal
majesty as had not been on any king
before him in Israel.

26 Thus David the son of Jesse
reigned over all Israel. 27 The time
that he reigned over Israel was forty
years; he reigned seven years in Hē'-
brŏn, and thirty-three years in Jerusalem. 28 Then he died in a good old
age, full of days, riches, and honor;
and Solomon his son reigned in his
stead. 29 Now the acts of King David,
from first to last, are written in the
Chronicles of Samuel the seer, and in
the Chronicles of Nathan the prophet,
and in the Chronicles of Gad the seer,
30 with accounts of all his rule and his
might and of the circumstances that
came upon him and upon Israel, and
upon all the kingdoms of the countries.

THE SECOND BOOK OF THE CHRONICLES

1 Solomon the son of David established himself in his kingdom, and
the LORD his God was with him and
made him exceedingly great.

2 Solomon spoke to all Israel, to the
commanders of thousands and of hundreds, to the judges, and to all the
leaders in all Israel, the heads of
fathers' houses. 3 And Solomon, and
all the assembly with him, went to the
high place that was at Gib'ē·ŏn; for the
tent of meeting of God, which Moses
the servant of the LORD had made in
the wilderness, was there. 4 (But David
had brought up the ark of God from
Kĭr'i·ath-jē'ā·rim to the place that
David had prepared for it, for he had
pitched a tent for it in Jerusalem.)
5 Moreover the bronze altar that Bez'-
ā·lel the son of Ū'rī, son of Hŭr, had
made, was there before the tabernacle
of the LORD. And Solomon and the
assembly sought the LORD. 6 And
Solomon went up there to the bronze
altar before the LORD, which was at
the tent of meeting, and offered a
thousand burnt offerings upon it.

7 In that night God appeared to
Solomon, and said to him, "Ask what
I shall give you." 8 And Solomon said
to God, "Thou hast shown great and
steadfast love to David my father, and
hast made me king in his stead. 9 O
LORD God, let thy promise to David
my father be now fulfilled, for thou
hast made me king over a people as
many as the dust of the earth. 10 Give
me now wisdom and knowledge to go
out and come in before this people,
for who can rule this thy people, that
is so great?" 11 God answered Solomon, "Because this was in your heart,
and you have not asked possessions,
wealth, honor, or the life of those who
hate you, and have not even asked long
life, but have asked wisdom and knowledge for yourself that you may rule my
people over whom I have made you
king, 12 wisdom and knowledge are
granted to you. I will also give you
riches, possessions, and honor, such as
none of the kings had who were before
you, and none after you shall have the
like." 13 So Solomon came from[a] the

[a] Gk Vg: Heb *to*

29.23: 1 Kings 2.12. **1.3-13:** 1 Kings 3.4-15.

high place at Gib'ē·ŏn, from before
the tent of meeting, to Jerusalem. And
he reigned over Israel.
14 Solomon gathered together chariots and horsemen; he had fourteen
hundred chariots and twelve thousand
horsemen, whom he stationed in the
chariot cities and with the king in
Jerusalem. 15 And the king made silver
and gold as common in Jerusalem as
stone, and he made cedar as plentiful
as the sycamore of the She·phē'lăh.
16 And Solomon's import of horses was
from Egypt and Kü'e, and the king's
traders received them from Kue for a
price. 17 They imported a chariot from
Egypt for six hundred shekels of silver,
and a horse for a hundred and fifty;
likewise through them these were exported to all the kings of the Hit'tītes
and the kings of Syria.
2[b] Now Solomon purposed to build
a temple for the name of the LORD,
and a royal palace for himself. 2[c] And
Solomon assigned seventy thousand
men to bear burdens and eighty thousand to quarry in the hill country, and
three thousand six hundred to oversee
them. 3 And Solomon sent word to
Hū'răm the king of Tȳre: "As you
dealt with David my father and sent
him cedar to build himself a house to
dwell in, so deal with me. 4 Behold, I
am about to build a house for the name
of the LORD my God and dedicate it
to him for the burning of incense of
sweet spices before him, and for the
continual offering of the showbread,
and for burnt offerings morning and
evening, on the sabbaths and the new
moons and the appointed feasts of the
LORD our God, as ordained for ever
for Israel. 5 The house which I am to
build will be great, for our God is
greater than all gods. 6 But who is able
to build him a house, since heaven,
even highest heaven, cannot contain
him? Who am I to build a house for
him, except as a place to burn incense
before him? 7 So now send me a man
skilled to work in gold, silver, bronze,
and iron, and in purple, crimson, and
blue fabrics, trained also in engraving,
to be with the skilled workers who are
with me in Judah and Jerusalem, whom
David my father provided. 8 Send me
also cedar, cypress, and algum timber
from Lebanon, for I know that your
servants know how to cut timber in
Lebanon. And my servants will be
with your servants, 9 to prepare timber
for me in abundance, for the house I
am to build will be great and wonderful. 10 I will give for your servants, the
hewers who cut timber, twenty thousand cors of crushed wheat, twenty
thousand cors of barley, twenty thousand baths of wine, and twenty thousand baths of oil."
11 Then Hū'răm the king of Tȳre
answered in a letter which he sent to
Solomon, "Because the LORD loves his
people he has made you king over
them." 12 Hū'răm also said, "Blessed
be the LORD God of Israel, who made
heaven and earth, who has given King
David a wise son, endued with discretion and understanding, who will build
a temple for the LORD, and a royal
palace for himself.
13 "Now I have sent a skilled man,
endued with understanding, Hū'răm-
ā'bĭ, 14 the son of a woman of the
daughters of Dan, and his father was
a man of Tȳre. He is trained to work
in gold, silver, bronze, iron, stone, and
wood, and in purple, blue, and crimson
fabrics and fine linen, and to do all
sorts of engraving and execute any
design that may be assigned him, with
your craftsmen, the craftsmen of my
lord, David your father. 15 Now therefore the wheat and barley, oil and wine,
of which my lord has spoken, let him
send to his servants; 16 and we will cut
whatever timber you need from
Lebanon, and bring it to you in rafts
by sea to Jop'pȧ, so that you may take
it up to Jerusalem."
17 Then Solomon took a census of
all the aliens who were in the land of
Israel, after the census of them which
David his father had taken; and there
were found a hundred and fifty-three
thousand six hundred. 18 Seventy
thousand of them he assigned to bear
burdens, eighty thousand to quarry in
the hill country, and three thousand
six hundred as overseers to make the
people work.
3 Then Solomon began to build the
house of the LORD in Jerusalem on
Mount Mō·rī'ăh, where the LORD had
appeared to David his father, at the
place that David had appointed, on
the threshing floor of Ôr'năn the Jeb'ū-

[b] Ch 1.18 in Heb [c] Ch 2.1 in Heb
1.14-17: 1 Kings 10.26-29. 2.1: 1 Kings 5.5. 2.2: 2 Chron 2.18; 1 Kings 5.15-16.
2.3-16: 1 Kings 5.2-11. 3.1-13: 1 Kings 6.1-28.

site. 2 He began to build in the second
month of the fourth year of his reign.
3 These are Solomon's measurements[d]
for building the house of God: the
length, in cubits of the old standard,
was sixty cubits, and the breadth
twenty cubits. 4 The vestibule in front
of the nave of the house was twenty
cubits long, equal to the width of the
house;[e] and its height was a hundred
and twenty cubits. He overlaid it on
the inside with pure gold. 5 The nave
he lined with cypress, and covered it
with fine gold, and made palms and
chains on it. 6 He adorned the house
with settings of precious stones. The
gold was gold of Pär·vā'im. 7 So he
lined the house with gold—its beams,
its thresholds, its walls, and its doors;
and he carved cherubim on the walls.
8 And he made the most holy place;
its length, corresponding to the breadth
of the house, was twenty cubits, and
its breadth was twenty cubits; he overlaid it with six hundred talents of fine
gold. 9 The weight of the nails was one
shekel[f] to fifty shekels of gold. And he
overlaid the upper chambers with
gold.
10 In the most holy place he made
two cherubim of wood[g] and overlaid[h]
them with gold. 11 The wings of the
cherubim together extended twenty
cubits: one wing of the one, of five
cubits, touched the wall of the house,
and its other wing, of five cubits,
touched the wing of the other cherub;
12 and of this cherub, one wing, of
five cubits, touched the wall of the
house, and the other wing, also of five
cubits, was joined to the wing of the
first cherub. 13 The wings of these
cherubim extended twenty cubits; the
cherubim[i] stood on their feet, facing
the nave. 14 And he made the veil of
blue and purple and crimson fabrics
and fine linen, and worked cherubim
on it.
15 In front of the house he made
two pillars thirty-five cubits high, with
a capital of five cubits on the top of
each. 16 He made chains like a necklace[j]
and put them on the tops of the pillars;
and he made a hundred pomegranates,
and put them on the chains. 17 He set
up the pillars in front of the temple,
one on the south, the other on the
north; that on the south he called
Jā'chin, and that on the north Bō'az.
4 He made an altar of bronze,
twenty cubits long, and twenty
cubits wide, and ten cubits high.
2 Then he made the molten sea; it was
round, ten cubits from brim to brim,
and five cubits high, and a line of
thirty cubits measured its circumference. 3 Under it were figures of
gourds,[k] for thirty[l] cubits, compassing
the sea round about; the gourds[k] were
in two rows, cast with it when it was
cast. 4 It stood upon twelve oxen, three
facing north, three facing west, three
facing south, and three facing east; the
sea was set upon them, and all their
hinder parts were inward. 5 Its thickness was a handbreadth; and its brim
was made like the brim of a cup, like
the flower of a lily; it held over three
thousand baths. 6 He also made ten
lavers in which to wash, and set five
on the south side, and five on the north
side. In these they were to rinse off
what was used for the burnt offering,
and the sea was for the priests to wash
in.
7 And he made ten golden lampstands as prescribed, and set them in
the temple, five on the south side and
five on the north. 8 He also made ten
tables, and placed them in the temple,
five on the south side and five on the
north. And he made a hundred basins
of gold. 9 He made the court of the
priests, and the great court, and doors
for the court, and overlaid their doors
with bronze; 10 and he set the sea at
the southeast corner of the house.
11 Hū'răm also made the pots, the
shovels, and the basins. So Huram
finished the work that he did for King
Solomon on the house of God: 12 the
two pillars, the bowls, and the two
capitals on the top of the pillars; and
the two networks to cover the two
bowls of the capitals that were on the
top of the pillars; 13 and the four hundred pomegranates for the two networks, two rows of pomegranates for
each network, to cover the two bowls
of the capitals that were upon the
pillars. 14 He made the stands also, and
the lavers upon the stands, 15 and the
one sea, and the twelve oxen underneath it. 16 The pots, the shovels, the

[d] Syr: Heb *foundations* [e] 1 Kings 6.3: Heb uncertain [f] Compare Gk: Heb lacks *one shekel*
[g] Gk: Heb uncertain [h] Heb *they overlaid* [i] Heb *they* [j] Cn: Heb *in the inner sanctuary*
[k] 1 Kings 7.24: Heb *oxen* [l] Compare verse 2: Heb *ten*
3.15-17: 1 Kings 7.15-21. **4.2-5:** 1 Kings 7.23-26. **4.6-5.1:** 1 Kings 7.38-51.

forks, and all the equipment for these
Hū'râm-ā'bī made of burnished bronze
for King Solomon for the house of the
LORD. 17 In the plain of the Jordan
the king cast them, in the clay ground
between Suc'coth and Zer'ĕ·dȧh.
18 Solomon made all these things in
great quantities, so that the weight of
the bronze was not ascertained.
19 So Solomon made all the things
that were in the house of God: the
golden altar, the tables for the bread
of the Presence, 20 the lampstands and
their lamps of pure gold to burn before the inner sanctuary, as prescribed;
21 the flowers, the lamps, and the
tongs, of purest gold; 22 the snuffers,
basins, dishes for incense, and firepans,
of pure gold; and the sockets[m] of the
temple, for the inner doors to the
most holy place and for the doors
of the nave of the temple were of
gold.

5 Thus all the work that Solomon
did for the house of the LORD was
finished. And Solomon brought in the
things which David his father had
dedicated, and stored the silver, the
gold, and all the vessels in the treasuries of the house of God.
2 Then Solomon assembled the
elders of Israel and all the heads of
the tribes, the leaders of the fathers'
houses of the people of Israel, in Jerusalem, to bring up the ark of the covenant of the LORD out of the city of
David, which is Zion. 3And all the men
of Israel assembled before the king at
the feast which is in the seventh
month. 4And all the elders of Israel
came, and the Levites took up the ark.
5And they brought up the ark, the tent
of meeting, and all the holy vessels
that were in the tent; the priests and
the Levites brought them up. 6And
King Solomon and all the congregation
of Israel, who had assembled before
him, were before the ark, sacrificing
so many sheep and oxen that they
could not be counted or numbered.
7 So the priests brought the ark of the
covenant of the LORD to its place, in
the inner sanctuary of the house, in
the most holy place, underneath the
wings of the cherubim. 8 For the
cherubim spread out their wings over
the place of the ark, so that the cherubim made a covering above the ark and
its poles. 9And the poles were so long
that the ends of the poles were seen
from the holy place before the inner
sanctuary; but they could not be seen
from outside; and they are there to
this day. 10 There was nothing in the
ark except the two tables which Moses
put there at Hō'reb, where the LORD
made a covenant with the people of
Israel, when they came out of Egypt.
11 Now when the priests came out of
the holy place (for all the priests who
were present had sanctified themselves,
without regard to their divisions; 12 and
all the Levitical singers, Ā'saph, Hē'-
mȧn, and Je·dü'thŭn, their sons and
kinsmen, arrayed in fine linen, with
cymbals, harps and lyres, stood east
of the altar with a hundred and twenty
priests who were trumpeters; 13 and
it was the duty of the trumpeters and
singers to make themselves heard in
unison in praise and thanksgiving to
the LORD), and when the song was
raised, with trumpets and cymbals and
other musical instruments, in praise
to the LORD,

"For he is good,
for his steadfast love endures for
ever,"

the house, the house of the LORD, was
filled with a cloud, 14 so that the priests
could not stand to minister because of
the cloud; for the glory of the LORD
filled the house of God.

6 Then Solomon said,
"The LORD has said that he would
dwell in thick darkness.
2 I have built thee an exalted house,
a place for thee to dwell in for
ever."

3 Then the king faced about, and
blessed all the assembly of Israel,
while all the assembly of Israel stood.
4And he said, "Blessed be the LORD,
the God of Israel, who with his hand
has fulfilled what he promised with
his mouth to David my father, saying,
5 'Since the day that I brought my
people out of the land of Egypt, I
chose no city in all the tribes of Israel
in which to build a house, that my
name might be there, and I chose no
man as prince over my people Israel;
6 but I have chosen Jerusalem that my
name may be there and I have chosen
David to be over my people Israel.'
7 Now it was in the heart of David my
father to build a house for the name
of the LORD, the God of Israel. 8 But

m 1 Kings 7.50: Heb *the door of the house*
5.13-14: 1 Kings 8.10-11. 6.1-39: 1 Kings 8.12-50.

the LORD said to David my father,
'Whereas it was in your heart to build
a house for my name, you did well
that it was in your heart; 9 nevertheless
you shall not build the house, but your
son who shall be born to you shall
build the house for my name.' 10 Now
the LORD has fulfilled his promise
which he made; for I have risen in the
place of David my father, and sit on
the throne of Israel, as the LORD
promised, and I have built the house
for the name of the LORD, the God of
Israel. 11 And there I have set the ark,
in which is the covenant of the LORD
which he made with the people of
Israel."

12 Then Solomon stood before the
altar of the LORD in the presence of all
the assembly of Israel, and spread
forth his hands. 13 Solomon had made
a bronze platform five cubits long, five
cubits wide, and three cubits high, and
had set it in the court; and he stood
upon it. Then he knelt upon his knees
in the presence of all the assembly of
Israel, and spread forth his hands toward heaven; 14 and said, "O LORD,
God of Israel, there is no God like
thee, in heaven or on earth, keeping
covenant and showing steadfast love
to thy servants who walk before thee
with all their heart; 15 who hast kept
with thy servant David my father what
thou didst declare to him; yea, thou
didst speak with thy mouth, and with
thy hand hast fulfilled it this day.
16 Now therefore, O LORD, God of
Israel, keep with thy servant David my
father what thou hast promised him,
saying, 'There shall never fail you a
man before me to sit upon the throne
of Israel, if only your sons take heed
to their way, to walk in my law as you
have walked before me.' 17 Now therefore, O LORD, God of Israel, let thy
word be confirmed, which thou hast
spoken to thy servant David.

18 "But will God dwell indeed with
man on the earth? Behold, heaven and
the highest heaven cannot contain
thee; how much less this house which
I have built! 19 Yet have regard to the
prayer of thy servant and to his supplication, O LORD my God, hearkening to the cry and to the prayer which
thy servant prays before thee; 20 that
thy eyes may be open day and night
toward this house, the place where
thou hast promised to set thy name,
that thou mayest hearken to the
prayer which thy servant offers toward
this place. 21 And hearken thou to the
supplications of thy servant and of thy
people Israel, when they pray toward
this place; yea, hear thou from heaven
thy dwelling place; and when thou
hearest, forgive.

22 "If a man sins against his neighbor and is made to take an oath, and
comes and swears his oath before thy
altar in this house, 23 then hear thou
from heaven, and act, and judge thy
servants, requiting the guilty by bringing his conduct upon his own head,
and vindicating the righteous by rewarding him according to his righteousness.

24 "If thy people Israel are defeated before the enemy because they
have sinned against thee, when they
turn again and acknowledge thy name,
and pray and make supplication to
thee in this house, 25 then hear thou
from heaven, and forgive the sin of thy
people Israel, and bring them again to
the land which thou gavest to them
and to their fathers.

26 "When heaven is shut up and
there is no rain because they have
sinned against thee, if they pray toward
this place, and acknowledge thy name,
and turn from their sin, when thou
dost afflict them, 27 then hear thou in
heaven, and forgive the sin of thy
servants, thy people Israel, when thou
dost teach them the good way[n] in which
they should walk; and grant rain upon
thy land, which thou hast given to thy
people as an inheritance.

28 "If there is famine in the land,
if there is pestilence or blight or mildew or locust or caterpillar; if their
enemies besiege them in any of their
cities; whatever plague, whatever sickness there is; 29 whatever prayer, whatever supplication is made by any man
or by all thy people Israel, each
knowing his own affliction, and his
own sorrow and stretching out his
hands toward this house; 30 then hear
thou from heaven thy dwelling place,
and forgive, and render to each whose
heart thou knowest, according to all
his ways (for thou, thou only, knowest
the hearts of the children of men);
31 that they may fear thee and walk in
thy ways all the days that they live in
the land which thou gavest to our
fathers.

[n] Gk Syr Vg: Heb *toward the good way*

32 "Likewise when a foreigner, who
is not of thy people Israel, comes from
a far country for the sake of thy great
name, and thy mighty hand, and thy
outstretched arm, when he comes and
prays toward this house, 33 hear thou
from heaven thy dwelling place, and
do according to all for which the foreigner calls to thee; in order that all
the peoples of the earth may know thy
name and fear thee, as do thy people
Israel, and that they may know that
this house which I have built is called
by thy name.

34 "If thy people go out to battle
against their enemies, by whatever
way thou shalt send them, and they
pray to thee toward this city which
thou hast chosen and the house which
I have built for thy name, 35 then hear
thou from heaven their prayer and
their supplication, and maintain their
cause.

36 "If they sin against thee—for
there is no man who does not sin—and
thou art angry with them, and dost
give them to an enemy, so that they
are carried away captive to a land far
or near; 37 yet if they lay it to heart in
the land to which they have been
carried captive, and repent, and make
supplication to thee in the land of
their captivity, saying, 'We have
sinned, and have acted perversely and
wickedly'; 38 if they repent with all
their mind and with all their heart in
the land of their captivity, to which
they were carried captive, and pray
toward their land, which thou gavest to
their fathers, the city which thou hast
chosen, and the house which I have
built for thy name, 39 then hear thou
from heaven thy dwelling place their
prayer and their supplications, and
maintain their cause and forgive thy
people who have sinned against thee.
40 Now, O my God, let thy eyes be
open and thy ears attentive to a prayer
of this place.

41 "And now arise, O LORD God, and
go to thy resting place,
thou and the ark of thy might.
Let thy priests, O LORD God, be
clothed with salvation,
and let thy saints rejoice in thy
goodness.
42 O LORD God, do not turn away the
face of thy anointed one!
Remember thy steadfast love for
David thy servant."

7 When Solomon had ended his
prayer, fire came down from
heaven and consumed the burnt offering and the sacrifices, and the glory of
the LORD filled the temple. 2 And the
priests could not enter the house of
the LORD, because the glory of the
LORD filled the LORD's house. 3 When
all the children of Israel saw the fire
come down and the glory of the LORD
upon the temple, they bowed down
with their faces to the earth on the
pavement, and worshiped and gave
thanks to the LORD, saying,
"For he is good,
for his steadfast love endures for
ever."

4 Then the king and all the people
offered sacrifice before the LORD.
5 King Solomon offered as a sacrifice
twenty-two thousand oxen and a hundred and twenty thousand sheep. So
the king and all the people dedicated
the house of God. 6 The priests stood
at their posts; the Levites also, with
the instruments for music to the LORD
which King David had made for giving
thanks to the LORD—for his steadfast
love endures for ever—whenever
David offered praises by their ministry; opposite them the priests sounded
trumpets; and all Israel stood.

7 And Solomon consecrated the
middle of the court that was before
the house of the LORD; for there he
offered the burnt offering and the fat
of the peace offerings, because the
bronze altar Solomon had made could
not hold the burnt offering and the
cereal offering and the fat.

8 At that time Solomon held the
feast for seven days, and all Israel with
him, a very great congregation, from
the entrance of Hā'math to the Brook
of Egypt. 9 And on the eighth day they
held a solemn assembly; for they had
kept the dedication of the altar seven
days and the feast seven days. 10 On
the twenty-third day of the seventh
month he sent the people away to their
homes, joyful and glad of heart for
the goodness that the LORD had shown
to David and to Solomon and to Israel
his people.

11 Thus Solomon finished the house
of the LORD and the king's house; all
that Solomon had planned to do in the
house of the LORD and in his own
house he successfully accomplished.
12 Then the LORD appeared to Solo-

6.41-42: Ps 132.8-10. **7.4-10:** 1 Kings 8.62-66. **7.11-22:** 1 Kings 9.1-9.

mon in the night and said to him: "I
have heard your prayer, and have
chosen this place for myself as a house
of sacrifice. 13 When I shut up the
heavens so that there is no rain, or
command the locust to devour the
land, or send pestilence among my
people, 14 if my people who are called
by my name humble themselves, and
pray and seek my face, and turn from
their wicked ways, then I will hear
from heaven, and will forgive their sin
and heal their land. 15 Now my eyes
will be open and my ears attentive to
the prayer that is made in this place.
16 For now I have chosen and consecrated this house that my name may
be there for ever; my eyes and my heart
will be there for all time. 17 And as for
you, if you walk before me, as David
your father walked, doing according
to all that I have commanded you and
keeping my statutes and my ordinances, 18 then I will establish your
royal throne, as I covenanted with
David your father, saying, 'There shall
not fail you a man to rule Israel.'

19 "But if you[o] turn aside and forsake my statutes and my commandments which I have set before you,
and go and serve other gods and
worship them, 20 then I will pluck
you[p] up from the land which I have
given you;[p] and this house, which I
have consecrated for my name, I will
cast out of my sight, and will make it
a proverb and a byword among all
peoples. 21 And at this house, which is
exalted, every one passing by will be
astonished, and say, 'Why has the
LORD done thus to this land and to
this house?' 22 Then they will say, 'Because they forsook the LORD the God
of their fathers who brought them out
of the land of Egypt, and laid hold on
other gods, and worshiped them and
served them; therefore he has brought
all this evil upon them.' "

8 At the end of twenty years, in
which Solomon had built the house
of the LORD and his own house,
2 Solomon rebuilt the cities which
Hū'ràm had given to him, and settled
the people of Israel in them.

3 And Solomon went to Hā'math-
zō'bàh, and took it. 4 He built Tad'-
môr in the wilderness and all the
store-cities which he built in Hā'math.
5 He also built Upper Beth-hō'ron and
Lower Beth-horon, fortified cities with
walls, gates, and bars, 6 and Bā'à·lath,
and all the store-cities that Solomon
had, and all the cities for his chariots,
and the cities for his horsemen, and
whatever Solomon desired to build in
Jerusalem, in Lebanon, and in all the
land of his dominion. 7 All the people
who were left of the Hit'tītes, the
Am'ò·rītes, the Per'iz·zītes, the Hī'-
vītes, and the Jeb'ū·sītes, who were
not of Israel, 8 from their descendants
who were left after them in the land,
whom the people of Israel had not
destroyed—these Solomon made a
forced levy and so they are to this day.
9 But of the people of Israel Solomon
made no slaves for his work; they were
soldiers, and his officers, the commanders of his chariots, and his horsemen. 10 And these were the chief
officers of King Solomon, two hundred
and fifty, who exercised authority over
the people.

11 Solomon brought Pharaoh's
daughter up from the city of David to
the house which he had built for her,
for he said, "My wife shall not live in
the house of David king of Israel, for
the places to which the ark of the
LORD has come are holy."

12 Then Solomon offered up burnt
offerings to the LORD upon the altar of
the LORD which he had built before
the vestibule, 13 as the duty of each
day required, offering according to
the commandment of Moses for the
sabbaths, the new moons, and the
three annual feasts—the feast of unleavened bread, the feast of weeks, and
the feast of tabernacles. 14 According
to the ordinance of David his father,
he appointed the divisions of the priests
for their service, and the Levites for
their offices of praise and ministry before the priests as the duty of each day
required, and the gatekeepers in their
divisions for the several gates; for so
David the man of God had commanded. 15 And they did not turn
aside from what the king had commanded the priests and Levites concerning any matter and concerning the
treasuries.

16 Thus was accomplished all the
work of Solomon from[q] the day the
foundation of the house of the LORD
was laid until it was finished. So the
house of the LORD was completed.

[o] The word *you* is plural here [p] Heb *them* [q] Gk Syr Vg: Heb *to*
8.1-18: 1 Kings 9.10-28.

17 Then Solomon went to E'zi·on-
gē'bėr and E'loth on the shore of the
sea, in the land of E'dŏm. 18 And
Hū'rȧm sent him by his servants ships
and servants familiar with the sea, and
they went to Ō'phīr together with the
servants of Solomon, and fetched from
there four hundred and fifty talents of
gold and brought it to King Solomon.
9 Now when the queen of Sheba
heard of the fame of Solomon she
came to Jerusalem to test him with
hard questions, having a very great
retinue and camels bearing spices and
very much gold and precious stones.
When she came to Solomon, she told
him all that was on her mind. 2 And
Solomon answered all her questions;
there was nothing hidden from Solomon which he could not explain to her.
3 And when the queen of Sheba had
seen the wisdom of Solomon, the
house that he had built, 4 the food of
his table, the seating of his officials,
and the attendance of his servants,
and their clothing, his cupbearers, and
their clothing, and his burnt offerings
which he offered at the house of the
LORD, there was no more spirit in
her.
5 And she said to the king, "The
report was true which I heard in my
own land of your affairs and of your
wisdom, 6 but I did not believe the[r]
reports until I came and my own eyes
had seen it; and behold, half the greatness of your wisdom was not told me;
you surpass the report which I heard.
7 Happy are your wives![s] Happy are
these your servants, who continually
stand before you and hear your wisdom! 8 Blessed be the LORD your God,
who has delighted in you and set you
on his throne as king for the LORD
your God! Because your God loved
Israel and would establish them for
ever, he has made you king over them,
that you may execute justice and righteousness." 9 Then she gave the king a
hundred and twenty talents of gold,
and a very great quantity of spices,
and precious stones: there were no
spices such as those which the queen
of Sheba gave to King Solomon.
10 Moreover the servants of Hū'-
rȧm and the servants of Solomon, who
brought gold from Ō'phīr, brought
algum wood and precious stones. 11 And
the king made of the algum wood
steps[t] for the house of the LORD and
for the king's house, lyres also and
harps for the singers; there never was
seen the like of them before in the land
of Judah.
12 And King Solomon gave to the
queen of Sheba all that she desired,
whatever she asked besides what she
had brought to the king. So she turned
and went back to her own land, with
her servants.
13 Now the weight of gold that
came to Solomon in one year was six
hundred and sixty-six talents of gold,
14 besides that which the traders and
merchants brought; and all the kings
of Arabia and the governors of the
land brought gold and silver to Solomon. 15 King Solomon made two hundred large shields of beaten gold; six
hundred shekels of beaten gold went
into each shield. 16 And he made three
hundred shields of beaten gold; three
hundred shekels of gold went into each
shield; and the king put them in the
House of the Forest of Lebanon. 17 The
king also made a great ivory throne,
and overlaid it with pure gold. 18 The
throne had six steps and a footstool of
gold, which were attached to the
throne, and on each side of the seat
were arm rests and two lions standing
beside the arm rests, 19 while twelve
lions stood there, one on each end of
a step on the six steps. The like of it
was never made in any kingdom. 20 All
King Solomon's drinking vessels were
of gold, and all the vessels of the
House of the Forest of Lebanon were
of pure gold; silver was not considered
as anything in the days of Solomon.
21 For the king's ships went to Tär'-
shish with the servants of Hū'rȧm;
once every three years the ships of
Tarshish used to come bringing gold,
silver, ivory, apes, and peacocks.[x]
22 Thus King Solomon excelled all
the kings of the earth in riches and in
wisdom. 23 And all the kings of the
earth sought the presence of Solomon
to hear his wisdom, which God had
put into his mind. 24 Every one of
them brought his present, articles of
silver and of gold, garments, myrrh,
spices, horses, and mules, so much
year by year. 25 And Solomon had four
thousand stalls for horses and chariots,

[r] Heb *their* [s] Gk Compare 1 Kings 10.8: Heb *men*
[t] Gk Vg: The meaning of the Hebrew word is uncertain [x] Or *baboons*
9.1-28: 1 Kings 10.1-29.

and twelve thousand horsemen, whom
he stationed in the chariot cities and
with the king in Jerusalem. 26 And he
ruled over all the kings from the
Eū·phrā′tēṡ to the land of the Philistines, and to the border of Egypt.
27 And the king made silver as common
in Jerusalem as stone, and cedar as
plentiful as the sycamore of the She-
phē′lȧh. 28 And horses were imported
for Solomon from Egypt and from all
lands.

29 Now the rest of the acts of Solomon, from first to last, are they not
written in the history of Nathan the
prophet, and in the prophecy of
Ȧ·hī′jȧh the Shī′lȯ·nīte, and in the
visions of Id′dō the seer concerning
Jer·ȯ·bō′ȧm the son of Nē′bat? 30 Solomon reigned in Jerusalem over all
Israel forty years. 31 And Solomon
slept with his fathers, and was buried
in the city of David his father; and
Rē·hȯ·bō′ȧm his son reigned in his
stead.

10 Rē·hȯ·bō′ȧm went to Shē′chem,
for all Israel had come to Shechem to make him king. 2 And when
Jer·ȯ·bō′ȧm the son of Nē′bat heard of
it (for he was in Egypt, whither he had
fled from King Solomon), then Jeroboam returned from Egypt. 3 And they
sent and called him; and Jer·ȯ·bō′ȧm
and all Israel came and said to Rē·hȯ-
bō′ȧm, 4 "Your father made our yoke
heavy. Now therefore lighten the hard
service of your father and his heavy
yoke upon us, and we will serve you."
5 He said to them, "Come to me again
in three days." So the people went
away.

6 Then King Rē·hȯ·bō′ȧm took
counsel with the old men, who had
stood before Solomon his father while
he was yet alive, saying, "How do you
advise me to answer this people?"
7 And they said to him, "If you will be
kind to this people and please them,
and speak good words to them, then
they will be your servants for ever."
8 But he forsook the counsel which the
old men gave him, and took counsel
with the young men who had grown
up with him and stood before him.
9 And he said to them, "What do you
advise that we answer this people who
have said to me, 'Lighten the yoke
that your father put upon us'?" 10 And
the young men who had grown up
with him said to him, "Thus shall you
speak to the people who said to you,
'Your father made our yoke heavy, but
do you lighten it for us'; thus shall you
say to them, 'My little finger is thicker
than my father's loins. 11 And now,
whereas my father laid upon you a
heavy yoke, I will add to your yoke.
My father chastised you with whips,
but I will chastise you with scorpions.' "

12 So Jer·ȯ·bō′ȧm and all the people came to Rē·hȯ·bō′ȧm the third day,
as the king said, "Come to me again
the third day." 13 And the king answered them harshly, and forsaking
the counsel of the old men, 14 King
Rē·hȯ·bō′ȧm spoke to them according
to the counsel of the young men, saying, "My father made your yoke
heavy, but I will add to it; my father
chastised you with whips, but I will
chastise you with scorpions." 15 So the
king did not hearken to the people; for
it was a turn of affairs brought about
by God that the LORD might fulfil his
word, which he spoke by Ȧ·hī′jȧh the
Shī′lȯ·nīte to Jer·ȯ·bō′ȧm the son of
Nē′bat.

16 And when all Israel saw that the
king did not hearken to them, the people answered the king,

"What portion have we in David?
We have no inheritance in the
son of Jesse.
Each of you to your tents, O Israel!
Look now to your own house,
David."

So all Israel departed to their tents.
17 But Rē·hȯ·bō′ȧm reigned over the
people of Israel who dwelt in the cities
of Judah. 18 Then King Rē·hȯ·bō′ȧm
sent Hȧ·dôr′ȧm, who was taskmaster
over the forced labor, and the people
of Israel stoned him to death with
stones. And King Rehoboam made
haste to mount his chariot, to flee to
Jerusalem. 19 So Israel has been in
rebellion against the house of David
to this day.

11 When Rē·hȯ·bō′ȧm came to
Jerusalem, he assembled the
house of Judah, and Benjamin, a hundred and eighty thousand chosen warriors, to fight against Israel, to restore
the kingdom to Rehoboam. 2 But the
word of the LORD came to She·māi′ȧh
the man of God: 3 "Say to Rē·hȯ·bō′ȧm
the son of Solomon king of Judah, and
to all Israel in Judah and Benjamin,
4 'Thus says the LORD, You shall not

9.30-31: 1 Kings 11.42-48. 10.1-19: 1 Kings 12.1-19. 11.1-4: 1 Kings 12.22-24.

go up or fight against your brethren.
Return every man to his home, for this
thing is from me.' " So they hearkened
to the word of the LORD, and returned
and did not go against Jer·o·bō'ăm.
5 Rē·hȯ·bō'ăm dwelt in Jerusalem,
and he built cities for defense in Judah.
6 He built Bethlehem, Ē'tam, Te·kō'ȧ,
7 Beth'-zūr, Sō'cōh, Ȧ·dul'lȧm, 8 Gath,
Mȧ·rē'shȧh, Ziph, 9Ad·ȯ·rā'im, Lā'-
chish, Ȧ·zē'kȧh, 10 Zō'rȧh, Äi'jȧ·lon,
and Hē'brȯn, fortified cities which are
in Judah and in Benjamin. 11 He made
the fortresses strong, and put commanders in them, and stores of food,
oil, and wine. 12And he put shields
and spears in all the cities, and made
them very strong. So he held Judah
and Benjamin.
13 And the priests and the Levites
that were in all Israel resorted to him
from all places where they lived. 14 For
the Levites left their common lands
and their holdings and came to Judah
and Jerusalem, because Jer·ȯ·bō'ăm
and his sons cast them out from serving as priests of the LORD, 15 and he
appointed his own priests for the high
places, and for the satyrs, and for the
calves which he had made. 16And
those who had set their hearts to seek
the LORD God of Israel came after
them from all the tribes of Israel to
Jerusalem to sacrifice to the LORD, the
God of their fathers. 17 They strengthened the kingdom of Judah, and for
three years they made Rē·hȯ·bō'ăm
the son of Solomon secure, for they
walked for three years in the way of
David and Solomon.
18 Rē·hȯ·bō'ăm took as wife Mā'-
hȧ·lath the daughter of Jer'i·moth the
son of David, and of Ab'i·hāil the
daughter of E·lī'ab the son of Jesse;
19 and she bore him sons, Jē'ush,
Shem·ȧ·rī'ȧh, and Zā'ham. 20After her
he took Mā'ȧ·cȧh the daughter of
Ab'sȧ·lȯm, who bore him Ȧ·bī'jȧh,
At'tāi, Zī'zȧ, and She·lō'mith. 21 Rē-
hȯ·bō'ăm loved Mā'ȧ·cȧh the daughter
of Ab'sȧ·lȯm above all his wives and
concubines (he took eighteen wives
and sixty concubines, and had twenty-
eight sons and sixty daughters); 22 and
Rē·hȯ·bō'ăm appointed Ȧ·bī'jȧh the
son of Mā'ȧ·cȧh as chief prince among
his brothers, for he intended to make
him king. 23And he dealt wisely, and
distributed some of his sons through
all the districts of Judah and Benjamin,
in all the fortified cities; and he gave
them abundant provisions, and pro-
cured wives for them.[u]

12 When the rule of Rē·hȯ·bō'ăm
was established and was strong,
he forsook the law of the LORD, and
all Israel with him. 2 In the fifth year
of King Rē·hȯ·bō'ăm, because they
had been unfaithful to the LORD,
Shī'shak king of Egypt came up
against Jerusalem 3 with twelve hundred chariots and sixty thousand
horsemen. And the people were without number who came with him from
Egypt—Libyans, Suk'ki·im, and Ethiopians. 4And he took the fortified cities
of Judah and came as far as Jerusalem.
5 Then She·māi'ȧh the prophet came
to Rē·hȯ·bō'ăm and to the princes of
Judah, who had gathered at Jerusalem
because of Shī'shak, and said to them,
"Thus says the LORD, 'You abandoned
me, so I have abandoned you to the
hand of Shishak.' " 6 Then the princes
of Israel and the king humbled themselves and said, "The LORD is righteous." 7 When the LORD saw that they
humbled themselves, the word of the
LORD came to She·māi'ȧh: "They have
humbled themselves; I will not destroy
them, but I will grant them some
deliverance, and my wrath shall not
be poured out upon Jerusalem by the
hand of Shī'shak. 8 Nevertheless they
shall be servants to him, that they may
know my service and the service of
the kingdoms of the countries."
9 So Shī'shak king of Egypt came
up against Jerusalem; he took away
the treasures of the house of the LORD
and the treasures of the king's house;
he took away everything. He also took
away the shields of gold which Solomon had made; 10 and King Rē·hȯ-
bō'ăm made in their stead shields of
bronze, and committed them to the
hands of the officers of the guard, who
kept the door of the king's house.
11And as often as the king went into
the house of the LORD, the guard came
and bore them, and brought them
back to the guardroom. 12And when
he humbled himself the wrath of the
LORD turned from him, so as not to
make a complete destruction; moreover, conditions were good in Judah.
13 So King Rē·hȯ·bō'ăm established
himself in Jerusalem and reigned.
Rehoboam was forty-one years old
when he began to reign, and he

[u] Cn: Heb *sought a multitude of wives* 12.1-16: 1 Kings 14.25-31.

reigned seventeen years in Jerusalem,
the city which the LORD had chosen
out of all the tribes of Israel to put his
name there. His mother's name was
Nā'ȧ·mȧh the Am'mȯ·nīt·ėss. 14 And
he did evil, for he did not set his heart
to seek the LORD.

15 Now the acts of Rē·hȯ·bō'ȧm,
from first to last, are they not written
in the chronicles of She·māi'ȧh the
prophet and of Id'dō the seer?[v] There
were continual wars between Rehoboam and Jer·ȯ·bō'ȧm. 16 And Rē·hȯ-
bō'ȧm slept with his fathers, and was
buried in the city of David; and
Ȧ·bī'jȧh his son reigned in his stead.

13 In the eighteenth year of King
Jer·ȯ·bō'ȧm Ȧ·bī'jȧh began to
reign over Judah. 2 He reigned for
three years in Jerusalem. His mother's
name was Mī·cāi'ȧh the daughter of
Ū'ri·el of Gib'ē-ȧh.

Now there was war between Ȧ·bī'jȧh
and Jer·ȯ·bō'ȧm. 3 Ȧ·bī'jȧh went out to
battle having an army of valiant men
of war, four hundred thousand picked
men; and Jer·ȯ·bō'ȧm drew up his line
of battle against him with eight hundred thousand picked mighty warriors.
4 Then Ȧ·bī'jȧh stood up on Mount
Zem·ȧ·rā'im which is in the hill
country of Ē'phrȧ·im, and said, "Hear
me, O Jer·ȯ·bō'ȧm and all Israel!
5 Ought you not to know that the
LORD God of Israel gave the kingship
over Israel for ever to David and his
sons by a covenant of salt? 6 Yet Jer·ȯ-
bō'ȧm the son of Nē'bat, a servant of
Solomon the son of David, rose up and
rebelled against his lord; 7 and certain
worthless scoundrels gathered about
him and defied Rē·hȯ·bō'ȧm the son
of Solomon, when Rehoboam was
young and irresolute and could not
withstand them.

8 "And now you think to withstand
the kingdom of the LORD in the hand
of the sons of David, because you are
a great multitude and have with you
the golden calves which Jer·ȯ·bō'ȧm
made you for gods. 9 Have you not
driven out the priests of the LORD, the
sons of Aaron, and the Levites, and
made priests for yourselves like the
peoples of other lands? Whoever comes
to consecrate himself with a young bull
or seven rams becomes a priest of what
are no gods. 10 But as for us, the LORD
is our God, and we have not forsaken
him. We have priests ministering to
the LORD who are sons of Aaron, and
Levites for their service. 11 They offer
to the LORD every morning and every
evening burnt offerings and incense of
sweet spices, set out the showbread on
the table of pure gold, and care for the
golden lampstand that its lamps may
burn every evening; for we keep the
charge of the LORD our God, but you
have forsaken him. 12 Behold, God is
with us at our head, and his priests
with their battle trumpets to sound
the call to battle against you. O sons
of Israel, do not fight against the
LORD, the God of your fathers; for
you cannot succeed."

13 Jer·ȯ·bō'ȧm had sent an ambush
around to come on them from behind;
thus his troops[w] were in front of
Judah, and the ambush was behind
them. 14 And when Judah looked, behold, the battle was before and behind
them; and they cried to the LORD, and
the priests blew the trumpets. 15 Then
the men of Judah raised the battle
shout. And when the men of Judah
shouted, God defeated Jer·ȯ·bō'ȧm
and all Israel before Ȧ·bī'jȧh and
Judah. 16 The men of Israel fled before
Judah, and God gave them into their
hand. 17 Ȧ·bī'jȧh and his people slew
them with a great slaughter; so there
fell slain of Israel five hundred thousand picked men. 18 Thus the men of
Israel were subdued at that time, and
the men of Judah prevailed, because
they relied upon the LORD, the God
of their fathers. 19 And Ȧ·bī'jȧh pursued Jer·ȯ·bō'ȧm, and took cities from
him, Beth'ėl with its villages and
Je·shā'nȧh with its villages and
Ē'phrȯn[x] with its villages. 20 Jer·ȯ-
bō'ȧm did not recover his power in the
days of Ȧ·bī'jȧh; and the LORD smote
him, and he died. 21 But Ȧ·bī'jȧh grew
mighty. And he took fourteen wives,
and had twenty-two sons and sixteen
daughters. 22 The rest of the acts of
Ȧ·bī'jȧh, his ways and his sayings, are
written in the story of the prophet
Id'dō.

14[y] So Ȧ·bī'jȧh slept with his
fathers, and they buried him in
the city of David; and Asa his son
reigned in his stead. In his days the land
had rest for ten years. 2[z] And Asa did

[v] Heb *seer, to enroll oneself* [w] Heb *they* [x] Another reading is *Ephrain* [y] Ch 13.23 in Heb
[z] Ch 14.1 in Heb
13.1-2: 1 Kings 15.1-2, 7. 14.1-5: 1 Kings 15.8-12.

what was good and right in the eyes of
the LORD his God. 3 He took away the
foreign altars and the high places, and
broke down the pillars and hewed
down the A·shē'rim, 4 and commanded
Judah to seek the LORD, the God of
their fathers, and to keep the law and
the commandment. 5 He also took out
of all the cities of Judah the high places
and the incense altars. And the kingdom had rest under him. 6 He built
fortified cities in Judah, for the land
had rest. He had no war in those years,
for the LORD gave him peace. 7 And he
said to Judah, "Let us build these
cities, and surround them with walls
and towers, gates and bars; the land is
still ours, because we have sought the
LORD our God; we have sought him,
and he has given us peace on every
side." So they built and prospered.
8 And Asa had an army of three hundred thousand from Judah, armed with
bucklers and spears, and two hundred
and eighty thousand men from Benjamin, that carried shields and drew
bows; all these were mighty men of
valor.

9 Zē'rȧh the Ethiopian came out
against them with an army of a million
men and three hundred chariots, and
came as far as Mȧ·rē'shȧh. 10 And Asa
went out to meet him, and they drew
up their lines of battle in the valley
of Zeph'ȧ·thȧh at Mȧ·rē'shȧh. 11 And
Asa cried to the LORD his God, "O
LORD, there is none like thee to help,
between the mighty and the weak.
Help us, O LORD our God, for we rely
on thee, and in thy name we have
come against this multitude. O LORD,
thou art our God; let not man prevail
against thee." 12 So the LORD defeated
the Ethiopians before Asa and before
Judah, and the Ethiopians fled. 13 Asa
and the people that were with him
pursued them as far as Gē'rär, and the
Ethiopians fell until none remained
alive; for they were broken before the
LORD and his army. The men of
Judah[a] carried away very much booty.
14 And they smote all the cities round
about Gē'rär, for the fear of the LORD
was upon them. They plundered all
the cities, for there was much plunder
in them. 15 And they smote the tents
of those who had cattle,[b] and carried
away sheep in abundance and camels.
Then they returned to Jerusalem.

15 The Spirit of God came upon
Az·ȧ·rī'ȧh the son of Ō'ded, 2 and
he went out to meet Asa, and said to
him, "Hear me, Asa, and all Judah
and Benjamin: The LORD is with you,
while you are with him. If you seek
him, he will be found by you, but if
you forsake him, he will forsake you.
3 For a long time Israel was without
the true God, and without a teaching
priest, and without law; 4 but when
in their distress they turned to the
LORD, the God of Israel, and sought
him, he was found by them. 5 In those
times there was no peace to him who
went out or to him who came in, for
great disturbances afflicted all the inhabitants of the lands. 6 They were
broken in pieces, nation against nation
and city against city, for God troubled
them with every sort of distress. 7 But
you, take courage! Do not let your
hands be weak, for your work shall be
rewarded."

8 When Asa heard these words,
the prophecy of Az·ȧ·rī'ȧh the son of
Ō'ded,[c] he took courage, and put away
the abominable idols from all the land
of Judah and Benjamin and from the
cities which he had taken in the hill
country of E'phrȧ·im, and he repaired
the altar of the LORD that was in front
of the vestibule of the house of the
LORD.[d] 9 And he gathered all Judah
and Benjamin, and those from E'phrȧ-
im, Mȧ·nas'sėh, and Simeon who were
sojourning with them, for great numbers had deserted to him from Israel
when they saw that the LORD his God
was with him. 10 They were gathered
at Jerusalem in the third month of the
fifteenth year of the reign of Asa.
11 They sacrificed to the LORD on that
day, from the spoil which they had
brought, seven hundred oxen and
seven thousand sheep. 12 And they
entered into a covenant to seek the
LORD, the God of their fathers, with
all their heart and with all their soul;
13 and that whoever would not seek
the LORD, the God of Israel, should be
put to death, whether young or old,
man or woman. 14 They took oath to
the LORD with a loud voice, and with
shouting, and with trumpets, and with
horns. 15 And all Judah rejoiced over
the oath; for they had sworn with all
their heart, and had sought him with
their whole desire, and he was found

[a] Heb *they* [b] Heb obscure [c] Compare Syr Vg: Heb *the prophecy, Oded the prophet*
[d] Heb *the vestibule of the* LORD

by them, and the LORD gave them rest
round about.
16 Even Mā'ȧ·cȧh, his mother, King
Asa removed from being queen mother
because she had made an abominable
image for Ȧ·shē'rȧh. Asa cut down her
image, crushed it, and burned it at the
brook Kid'rȯn. 17 But the high places
were not taken out of Israel. Nevertheless the heart of Asa was blameless
all his days. 18 And he brought into the
house of God the votive gifts of his
father and his own votive gifts, silver,
and gold, and vessels. 19 And there was
no more war until the thirty-fifth year
of the reign of Asa.
16 In the thirty-sixth year of the
reign of Asa, Bā'ȧ·shȧ king of
Israel went up against Judah, and
built Rā'mȧh, that he might permit no
one to go out or come in to Asa king
of Judah. 2 Then Asa took silver and
gold from the treasures of the house
of the LORD and the king's house, and
sent them to Ben-hā'dad king of Syria,
who dwelt in Damascus, saying, 3 "Let
there be a league between me and you,
as between my father and your father;
behold, I am sending to you silver and
gold; go, break your league with
Bā'ȧ·shȧ king of Israel, that he may
withdraw from me." 4 And Ben-hā'dad
hearkened to King Asa, and sent the
commanders of his armies against the
cities of Israel, and they conquered
I'jon, Dan, Ā'bėl-mā'im, and all the
store-cities of Naph'tȧ·lī. 5 And when
Bā'ȧ·shȧ heard of it, he stopped building Rā'mȧh, and let his work cease.
6 Then King Asa took all Judah, and
they carried away the stones of Rā'mȧh
and its timber, with which Bā'ȧ·shȧ
had been building, and with them he
built Gē'bȧ and Miz'pȧh.
7 At that time Hȧ·nā'nī the seer
came to Asa king of Judah, and said
to him, "Because you relied on the
king of Syria, and did not rely on the
LORD your God, the army of the king
of Syria has escaped you. 8 Were not
the Ethiopians and the Libyans a huge
army with exceedingly many chariots
and horsemen? Yet because you relied
on the LORD, he gave them into your
hand. 9 For the eyes of the LORD run
to and fro throughout the whole earth,
to show his might in behalf of those
whose heart is blameless toward him.
You have done foolishly in this; for
from now on you will have wars."
10 Then Asa was angry with the seer,
and put him in the stocks, in prison,
for he was in a rage with him because
of this. And Asa inflicted cruelties
upon some of the people at the same
time.
11 The acts of Asa, from first to
last, are written in the Book of the
Kings of Judah and Israel. 12 In the
thirty-ninth year of his reign Asa was
diseased in his feet, and his disease became severe; yet even in his disease he
did not seek the LORD, but sought
help from physicians. 13 And Asa slept
with his fathers, dying in the forty-
first year of his reign. 14 They buried
him in the tomb which he had hewn
out for himself in the city of David.
They laid him on a bier which had
been filled with various kinds of spices
prepared by the perfumer's art; and
they made a very great fire in his honor.
17 Je·hosh'ȧ·phat his son reigned
in his stead, and strengthened
himself against Israel. 2 He placed
forces in all the fortified cities of Judah,
and set garrisons in the land of Judah,
and in the cities of Ē'phrȧ·im which
Asa his father had taken. 3 The LORD was
with Je·hosh'ȧ·phat, because he walked
in the earlier ways of his father;[e] he
did not seek the Bā'ȧls, 4 but sought
the God of his father and walked in his
commandments, and not according to
the ways of Israel. 5 Therefore the
LORD established the kingdom in his
hand; and all Judah brought tribute to
Je·hosh'ȧ·phat; and he had great riches
and honor. 6 His heart was courageous
in the ways of the LORD; and furthermore he took the high places and the
Ȧ·shē'rim out of Judah.
7 In the third year of his reign he
sent his princes, Ben-hā'il, Ō·bȧ·dī'ȧh,
Zech·ȧ·rī'ȧh, Nė·than'el, and Mī·cāi'ȧh,
to teach in the cities of Judah; 8 and
with them the Levites, She·māi'ȧh,
Neth·ȧ·nī'ȧh, Zeb·ȧ·dī'ȧh, As'ȧ·hel,
She·mī'rȧ·moth, Je·hon'ȧ·thȧn, Ad·ȯ-
nī'jȧh, Tō·bī'jȧh, and Tob·ad·ȯ·nī'jȧh;
and with these Levites, the priests
Ė·lish'ȧ·mȧ and Je·hō'rȧm. 9 And they
taught in Judah, having the book of
the law of the LORD with them; they
went about through all the cities of
Judah and taught among the people.
10 And the fear of the LORD fell
upon all the kingdoms of the lands that

[e] Another reading is *his father David*
15.16-16.6: 1 Kings 15.13-22. **16.12-14:** 1 Kings 15.23-24. **17.1:** 1 Kings 15.24.

were round about Judah, and they
made no war against Je·hosh'ȧ·phat.
11 Some of the Philistines brought
Je·hosh'ȧ·phat presents, and silver for
tribute; and the Arabs also brought
him seven thousand seven hundred
rams and seven thousand seven hundred he-goats. 12 And Je·hosh'ȧ·phat
grew steadily greater. He built in
Judah fortresses and store-cities,
13 and he had great stores in the cities
of Judah. He had soldiers, mighty men
of valor, in Jerusalem. 14 This was the
muster of them by fathers' houses: Of
Judah, the commanders of thousands:
Ad'nȧh the commander, with three
hundred thousand mighty men of
valor, 15 and next to him Jē'hō-hā'nȧn
the commander, with two hundred and
eighty thousand, 16 and next to him
Am·ȧ·sī'ȧh the son of Zich'rī, a
volunteer for the service of the LORD,
with two hundred thousand mighty
men of valor. 17 Of Benjamin: E·lī'ȧ·dȧ,
a mighty man of valor, with two hundred thousand men armed with bow
and shield, 18 and next to him Je·hō'-
zȧ·bad with a hundred and eighty
thousand armed for war. 19 These
were in the service of the king, besides
those whom the king had placed in
the fortified cities throughout all
Judah.

18 Now Je·hosh'ȧ·phat had great
riches and honor; and he made a
marriage alliance with Ā'hab. 2 After
some years he went down to Ā'hab in
Sȧ·mâr'i·ȧ. And Ahab killed an abundance of sheep and oxen for him and
for the people who were with him, and
induced him to go up against Rā'moth-
gil'ē·ȧd. 3 Ā'hab king of Israel said to
Je·hosh'ȧ·phat king of Judah, "Will
you go with me to Rā'moth-gil'ē·ȧd?"
He answered him, "I am as you are,
my people as your people. We will be
with you in the war."

4 And Je·hosh'ȧ·phat said to the
king of Israel, "Inquire first for the
word of the LORD." 5 Then the king
of Israel gathered the prophets together, four hundred men, and said to
them, "Shall we go to battle against
Rā'moth-gil'ē·ȧd, or shall I forbear?"
And they said, "Go up; for God will
give it into the hand of the king."
6 But Je·hosh'ȧ·phat said, "Is there
not here another prophet of the LORD
of whom we may inquire?" 7 And the
king of Israel said to Je·hosh'ȧ·phat,
"There is yet one man by whom we
may inquire of the LORD, Mī·cāi'ȧh
the son of Im'lȧh; but I hate him, for
he never prophesies good concerning
me, but always evil." And Jehoshaphat
said, "Let not the king say so." 8 Then
the king of Israel summoned an officer
and said, "Bring quickly Mī·cāi'ȧh the
son of Im'lȧh." 9 Now the king of
Israel and Je·hosh'ȧ·phat the king of
Judah were sitting on their thrones,
arrayed in their robes; and they were
sitting at the threshing floor at the
entrance of the gate of Sȧ·mâr'i·ȧ; and
all the prophets were prophesying before them. 10 And Zed·ē·kī'ȧh the son
of Che·nā'ȧ·nȧh made for himself
horns of iron, and said, "Thus says
the LORD, 'With these you shall push
the Syrians until they are destroyed.'"
11 And all the prophets prophesied so,
and said, "Go up to Rā'moth-gil'ē·ȧd
and triumph; the LORD will give it into
the hand of the king."

12 And the messenger who went to
summon Mī·cāi'ȧh said to him, "Behold, the words of the prophets with
one accord are favorable to the king;
let your word be like the word of one
of them, and speak favorably." 13 But
Mī·cāi'ȧh said, "As the LORD lives,
what my God says, that I will speak."
14 And when he had come to the king,
the king said to him, "Mī·cāi'ȧh, shall
we go to Rā'moth-gil'ē·ȧd to battle, or
shall I forbear?" And he answered,
"Go up and triumph; they will be
given into your hand." 15 But the king
said to him, "How many times shall I
adjure you that you speak to me
nothing but the truth in the name of
the LORD?" 16 And he said, "I saw all
Israel scattered upon the mountains,
as sheep that have no shepherd; and
the LORD said, 'These have no master;
let each return to his home in peace.'"
17 And the king of Israel said to Je-
hosh'ȧ·phat, "Did I not tell you that
he would not prophesy good concerning me, but evil?" 18 And Mī·cāi'ȧh
said, "Therefore hear the word of the
LORD: I saw the LORD sitting on his
throne, and all the host of heaven
standing on his right hand and on his
left; 19 and the LORD said, 'Who will
entice Ā'hab the king of Israel, that he
may go up and fall at Rā'moth-
gil'ē·ȧd?' And one said one thing, and
another said another. 20 Then a spirit
came forward and stood before the

18.1-34: 1 Kings 22.1-35.

LORD, saying, 'I will entice him.' And
the LORD said to him, 'By what means?'
21 And he said, 'I will go forth, and
will be a lying spirit in the mouth of
all his prophets.' And he said, 'You are
to entice him, and you shall succeed;
go forth and do so.' 22 Now therefore
behold, the LORD has put a lying spirit
in the mouth of these your prophets;
the LORD has spoken evil concerning
you."

23 Then Zed·ė·kī'ȧh the son of
Che·nā'ȧ·nȧh came near and struck
Mī·cāi'ȧh on the cheek, and said,
"Which way did the Spirit of the LORD
go from me to speak to you?" 24 And
Mī·cāi'ȧh said, "Behold, you shall see
on that day when you go into an inner
chamber to hide yourself." 25 And the
king of Israel said, "Seize Mī·cāi'ȧh,
and take him back to Ā'mon the
governor of the city and to Jō'ash the
king's son; 26 and say, 'Thus says the
king, Put this fellow in prison, and
feed him with scant fare of bread and
water, until I return in peace.' " 27 And
Mī·cāi'ȧh said, "If you return in peace,
the LORD has not spoken by me." And
he said, "Hear, all you peoples!"

28 So the king of Israel and Je-
hosh'ȧ·phat the king of Judah went up
to Rā'moth-gil'ē·ȧd. 29 And the king of
Israel said to Je·hosh'ȧ·phat, "I will
disguise myself and go into battle, but
you wear your robes." And the king
of Israel disguised himself; and they
went into battle. 30 Now the king of
Syria had commanded the captains of
his chariots, "Fight with neither small
nor great, but only with the king of
Israel." 31 And when the captains of
the chariots saw Je·hosh'ȧ·phat, they
said, "It is the king of Israel." So they
turned to fight against him; and
Jehoshaphat cried out, and the LORD
helped him. God drew them away
from him, 32 for when the captains of
the chariots saw that it was not the
king of Israel, they turned back from
pursuing him. 33 But a certain man
drew his bow at a venture, and struck
the king of Israel between the scale
armor and the breastplate; therefore
he said to the driver of his chariot,
"Turn about, and carry me out of the
battle, for I am wounded." 34 And the
battle grew hot that day, and the king
of Israel propped himself up in his
chariot facing the Syrians until evening; then at sunset he died.

19 Je·hosh'ȧ·phat the king of
Judah returned in safety to his
house in Jerusalem. 2 But Jē'hū the son
of Hȧ·nā'nī the seer went out to meet
him, and said to King Je·hosh'ȧ·phat,
"Should you help the wicked and love
those who hate the LORD? Because of
this, wrath has gone out against you
from the LORD. 3 Nevertheless some
good is found in you, for you destroyed
the Ȧ·shē'rȧhṡ out of the land, and
have set your heart to seek God."

4 Je·hosh'ȧ·phat dwelt at Jerusalem; and he went out again among
the people, from Beer-sheba to the
hill country of Ē'phrȧ·im, and brought
them back to the LORD, the God of
their fathers. 5 He appointed judges in
the land in all the fortified cities of
Judah, city by city, 6 and said to the
judges, "Consider what you do, for
you judge not for man but for the
LORD; he is with you in giving judgment. 7 Now then, let the fear of the
LORD be upon you; take heed what
you do, for there is no perversion of
justice with the LORD our God, or
partiality, or taking bribes."

8 Moreover in Jerusalem Je·hosh'ȧ-
phat appointed certain Levites and
priests and heads of families of Israel,
to give judgment for the LORD and to
decide disputed cases. They had their
seat at Jerusalem. 9 And he charged
them: "Thus you shall do in the fear
of the LORD, in faithfulness, and with
your whole heart: 10 wherever a case
comes to you from your brethren who
live in their cities, concerning bloodshed, law or commandment, statutes
or ordinances, then you shall instruct
them, that they may not incur guilt
before the LORD and wrath may not
come upon you and your brethren.
Thus you shall do, and you will not
incur guilt. 11 And behold, Am·ȧ·rī'ȧh
the chief priest is over you in all
matters of the LORD; and Zeb·ȧ·dī'ȧh
the son of Ish'mȧ·el, the governor of
the house of Judah, in all the king's
matters; and the Levites will serve you
as officers. Deal courageously, and may
the LORD be with the upright!"

20 After this the Mō'ȧb·ītes and
Am'mȯ·nītes, and with them
some of the Me-ü'nītes,[f] came against
Je·hosh'ȧ·phat for battle. 2 Some men
came and told Je·hosh'ȧ·phat, "A great
multitude is coming against you from
Ē'dȯm,[g] from beyond the sea; and, be-

[f] Compare 26.7: Heb *Ammonites* [g] One Ms: Heb *Aram* (Syria)

hold, they are in Haz'ȧ·zon-tā'mär"
(that is, En-gē'dī). 3 Then Je·hosh'ȧ-
phat feared, and set himself to seek the
LORD, and proclaimed a fast throughout all Judah. 4 And Judah assembled
to seek help from the LORD; from all
the cities of Judah they came to seek
the LORD.
5 And Je·hosh'ȧ·phat stood in the
assembly of Judah and Jerusalem, in
the house of the LORD, before the new
court, 6 and said, "O LORD, God of
our fathers, art thou not God in
heaven? Dost thou not rule over all the
kingdoms of the nations? In thy hand
are power and might, so that none is
able to withstand thee. 7 Didst thou
not, O our God, drive out the inhabitants of this land before thy people
Israel, and give it for ever to the
descendants of Abraham thy friend?
8 And they have dwelt in it, and have
built thee in it a sanctuary for thy
name, saying, 9 'If evil comes upon us,
the sword, judgment,[h] or pestilence,
or famine, we will stand before this
house, and before thee, for thy name
is in this house, and cry to thee in our
affliction, and thou wilt hear and save.'
10 And now behold, the men of Am'-
mȯn and Mō'ab and Mount Sē'ir,
whom thou wouldest not let Israel invade when they came from the land of
Egypt, and whom they avoided and
did not destroy—11 behold, they reward us by coming to drive us out of
thy possession, which thou hast given
us to inherit. 12 O our God, wilt thou
not execute judgment upon them? For
we are powerless against this great
multitude that is coming against us.
We do not know what to do, but our
eyes are upon thee."
13 Meanwhile all the men of Judah
stood before the LORD, with their little
ones, their wives, and their children.
14 And the Spirit of the LORD came
upon Jȧ·hā'zi·el the son of Zech·ȧ-
rī'ah, son of Be·nā'iah, son of Je·ī'el,
son of Mat·tȧ·nī'ah, a Levite of the
sons of Ā'saph, in the midst of the
assembly. 15 And he said, "Hearken,
all Judah and inhabitants of Jerusalem,
and King Je·hosh'ȧ·phat: Thus says
the LORD to you, 'Fear not, and be not
dismayed at this great multitude; for
the battle is not yours but God's.
16 Tomorrow go down against them;
behold, they will come up by the
ascent of Ziz; you will find them at the
end of the valley, east of the wilderness
of Je·rü'el. 17 You will not need to
fight in this battle; take your position,
stand still, and see the victory of the
LORD on your behalf, O Judah and
Jerusalem.' Fear not, and be not dismayed; tomorrow go out against them,
and the LORD will be with you."
18 Then Je·hosh'ȧ·phat bowed his
head with his face to the ground, and
all Judah and the inhabitants of Jerusalem fell down before the LORD,
worshiping the LORD. 19 And the
Levites, of the Kō'hȧ·thītes and the
Kō'rȧ·hītes, stood up to praise the
LORD, the God of Israel, with a very
loud voice.
20 And they rose early in the morning and went out into the wilderness
of Te·kō'ȧ; and as they went out, Je-
hosh'ȧ phat stood and said, "Hear me,
Judah and inhabitants of Jerusalem!
Believe in the LORD your God, and
you will be established; believe his
prophets, and you will succeed." 21 And
when he had taken counsel with the
people, he appointed those who were
to sing to the LORD and praise him in
holy array, as they went before the
army, and say,

"Give thanks to the LORD,
for his steadfast love endures for
ever."

22 And when they began to sing and
praise, the LORD set an ambush against
the men of Am'mȯn, Mō'ab, and
Mount Sē'ir, who had come against
Judah, so that they were routed. 23 For
the men of Am'mȯn and Mō'ab rose
against the inhabitants of Mount Sē'ir,
destroying them utterly, and when
they had made an end of the inhabitants of Seir, they all helped to destroy
one another.
24 When Judah came to the watchtower of the wilderness, they looked
toward the multitude; and behold, they
were dead bodies lying on the ground;
none had escaped. 25 When Je·hosh'ȧ-
phat and his people came to take the
spoil from them, they found cattle[i] in
great numbers, goods, clothing, and
precious things, which they took for
themselves until they could carry no
more. They were three days in taking
the spoil, it was so much. 26 On the
fourth day they assembled in the
Valley of Be·rā'cah,[j] for there they

[h] Or *the sword of judgment* [i] Gk: Heb *among them* [j] That is *Blessing*
20.7: Jas 2.23.

blessed the LORD; therefore the name
of that place has been called the Valley
of Beracah to this day. 27 Then they
returned, every man of Judah and
Jerusalem, and Je·hosh'ȧ·phat at their
head, returning to Jerusalem with joy,
for the LORD had made them rejoice
over their enemies. 28 They came to
Jerusalem, with harps and lyres and
trumpets, to the house of the LORD.
29 And the fear of God came on all the
kingdoms of the countries when they
heard that the LORD had fought against
the enemies of Israel. 30 So the realm
of Je·hosh'ȧ·phat was quiet, for his
God gave him rest round about.

31 Thus Je·hosh'ȧ·phat reigned
over Judah. He was thirty-five years
old when he began to reign, and he
reigned twenty-five years in Jerusalem.
His mother's name was A·zü'bȧh the
daughter of Shil'hī. 32 He walked in
the way of Asa his father and did not
turn aside from it; he did what was
right in the sight of the LORD. 33 The
high places, however, were not taken
away; the people had not yet set their
hearts upon the God of their fathers.

34 Now the rest of the acts of Je-
hosh'ȧ·phat, from first to last, are
written in the chronicles of Jē'hū the
son of Hȧ·nā'nī, which are recorded in
the Book of the Kings of Israel.

35 After this Je·hosh'ȧ·phat king of
Judah joined with Ā·hȧ·zī'ȧh king of
Israel, who did wickedly. 36 He joined
him in building ships to go to Tär'-
shish, and they built the ships in
Ē'zi·on-gē'bėr. 37 Then Ē·lī·ē'zėr the
son of Dō·dav'ȧ·hū of Mȧ·rē'shȧh
prophesied against Je·hosh'ȧ·phat,
saying, "Because you have joined with
Ā·hȧ·zī'ȧh, the LORD will destroy what
you have made." And the ships were
wrecked and were not able to go to
Tär'shish.

21 Je·hosh'ȧ·phat slept with his
fathers, and was buried with his
fathers in the city of David; and Je-
hō'rȧm his son reigned in his stead.
2 He had brothers, the sons of Je-
hosh'ȧ·phat: Az·ȧ·rī'ȧh, Je·hī'el, Zech-
ȧ·rī'ȧh, Azariah, Michael, and Sheph-
ȧ·tī'ȧh; all these were the sons of
Jehoshaphat king of Judah. 3 Their
father gave them great gifts, of silver,
gold, and valuable possessions, together with fortified cities in Judah;
but he gave the kingdom to Je·hō'rȧm,
because he was the first-born. 4 When
Je·hō'rȧm had ascended the throne of
his father and was established, he slew
all his brothers with the sword and
also some of the princes of Israel.
5 Je·hō'rȧm was thirty-two years old
when he became king, and he reigned
eight years in Jerusalem. 6 And he
walked in the way of the kings of Israel,
as the house of Ā'hab had done; for
the daughter of Ahab was his wife.
And he did what was evil in the sight
of the LORD. 7 Yet the LORD would not
destroy the house of David, because
of the covenant which he had made
with David, and since he had promised to give a lamp to him and to his
sons for ever.

8 In his days Ē'dȯm revolted from
the rule of Judah, and set up a king of
their own. 9 Then Je·hō'rȧm passed
over with his commanders and all his
chariots, and he rose by night and
smote the Ē'dȯm·ītes who had surrounded him and his chariot commanders. 10 So Ē'dȯm revolted from
the rule of Judah to this day. At that
time Lib'nȧh also revolted from his
rule, because he had forsaken the
LORD, the God of his fathers.

11 Moreover he made high places
in the hill country of Judah, and led
the inhabitants of Jerusalem into unfaithfulness, and made Judah go
astray. 12 And a letter came to him
from E·lī'jȧh the prophet saying,
"Thus says the LORD, the God of David
your father, 'Because you have not
walked in the ways of Je·hosh'ȧ·phat
your father, or in the ways of Asa king
of Judah, 13 but have walked in the way
of the kings of Israel, and have led
Judah and the inhabitants of Jerusalem into unfaithfulness, as the house
of Ā'hab led Israel into unfaithfulness,
and also you have killed your brothers,
of your father's house, who were better
than yourself; 14 behold, the LORD will
bring a great plague on your people,
your children, your wives, and all your
possessions, 15 and you yourself will
have a severe sickness with a disease
of your bowels, until your bowels come
out because of the disease, day by
day.' "

16 And the LORD stirred up against
Je·hō'rȧm the anger of the Philistines
and of the Arabs who are near the
Ethiopians; 17 and they came up

20.31-33: 1 Kings 22.41-43. **20.35-37**: 1 Kings 22.48-49. **21.1**: 1 Kings 22.50.
21.5-10: 2 Kings 8.17-22.

against Judah, and invaded it, and
carried away all the possessions they
found that belonged to the king's
house, and also his sons and his wives,
so that no son was left to him except
Je·hō'ȧ·haz, his youngest son.
18 And after all this the LORD smote
him in his bowels with an incurable
disease. 19 In course of time, at the
end of two years, his bowels came out
because of the disease, and he died in
great agony. His people made no fire
in his honor, like the fires made for
his fathers. 20 He was thirty-two years
old when he began to reign, and he
reigned eight years in Jerusalem; and
he departed with no one's regret. They
buried him in the city of David, but
not in the tombs of the kings.

22 And the inhabitants of Jerusalem made Ā·hȧ·zī'ȧh his
youngest son king in his stead; for the
band of men that came with the Arabs
to the camp had slain all the older sons.
So Ahaziah the son of Je·hō'rȧm king
of Judah reigned. 2 Ā·hȧ·zī'ȧh was
forty-two years old when he began to
reign, and he reigned one year in Jerusalem. His mother's name was Ath·ȧ-
lī'ȧh, the granddaughter of Om'rī. 3 He
also walked in the ways of the house of
Ā'hab, for his mother was his counselor
in doing wickedly. 4 He did what was
evil in the sight of the LORD, as the
house of Ā'hab had done; for after the
death of his father they were his
counselors, to his undoing. 5 He even
followed their counsel, and went with
Je·hō'rȧm the son of Ā'hab king of
Israel to make war against Haz'ȧ·el
king of Syria at Rā'moth-gil'ē·ȧd. And
the Syrians wounded Jō'rȧm, 6 and he
returned to be healed in Jez'rē·ėl of
the wounds which he had received at
Rā'mȧh, when he fought against Haz'-
ȧ·el king of Syria. And Ā·hȧ·zī'ȧh the
son of Je·hō'rȧm king of Judah went
down to see Joram the son of Ā'hab in
Jez'rē·ėl, because he was sick.
7 But it was ordained by God that
the downfall of Ā·hȧ·zī'ȧh should come
about through his going to visit Jō'rȧm.
For when he came there he went out
with Je·hō'rȧm to meet Jē'hū the son
of Nim'shī, whom the LORD had
anointed to destroy the house of
Ā'hab. 8 And when Jē'hū was executing
judgment upon the house of Ā'hab, he
met the princes of Judah and the sons
of Ā·hȧ·zī'ȧh's brothers, who attended
Ahaziah, and he killed them. 9 He
searched for Ā·hȧ·zī'ȧh, and he was
captured while hiding in Sȧ·mâr'i·ȧ,
and he was brought to Jē'hū and put
to death. They buried him, for they
said, "He is the grandson of Je·hosh'ȧ-
phat, who sought the LORD with all
his heart." And the house of Ā·hȧ·zī'ȧh
had no one able to rule the kingdom.
10 Now when Ath·ȧ·lī'ȧh the mother
of Ā·hȧ·zī'ȧh saw that her son was
dead, she arose and destroyed all the
royal family of the house of Judah.
11 But Jē'hō-shab'ė-ath, the daughter
of the king, took Jō'ash the son of
Ā·hȧ·zī'ȧh, and stole him away from
among the king's sons who were about
to be slain, and she put him and his
nurse in a bedchamber. Thus Jeho-
shabe-ath, the daughter of King Je-
hō'rȧm and wife of Je·hoi'ȧ·dȧ the
priest, because she was a sister of
Ā·hȧ·zī'ȧh, hid him from Ath·ȧ·lī'ȧh,
so that she did not slay him; 12 and he
remained with them six years, hid in
the house of God, while Ath·ȧ·lī'ȧh
reigned over the land.

23 But in the seventh year Jehoi'ȧ·dȧ took courage, and entered into a compact with the commanders of hundreds, Az·ȧ·rī'ȧh the
son of Je·rō'ham, Ish'mȧ·el the son of
Jē'hō-hā'nȧn, Az·ȧ·rī'ȧh the son of
Ō'bed, Mā-ȧ·sēi'ȧh the son of Ȧ·dāi'ȧh,
and El·i·shā'phat the son of Zich'rī.
2 And they went about through Judah
and gathered the Levites from all the
cities of Judah, and the heads of
fathers' houses of Israel, and they
came to Jerusalem. 3 And all the assembly made a covenant with the king
in the house of God. And Je·hoi'ȧ·dȧ[l]
said to them, "Behold, the king's son!
Let him reign, as the LORD spoke concerning the sons of David. 4 This is the
thing that you shall do: of you priests
and Levites who come off duty on the
sabbath, one third shall be gatekeepers,
5 and one third shall be at the king's
house and one third at the Gate of the
Foundation; and all the people shall
be in the courts of the house of the
LORD. 6 Let no one enter the house of
the LORD except the priests and ministering Levites; they may enter, for
they are holy, but all the people shall

[l] Heb *he*

21.20: 2 Kings 8.17, 24. **22.1-6:** 2 Kings 8.24-29. **22.7-9:** 2 Kings 9.1-10.36.
22.10-23.21: 2 Kings 11.1-20.

keep the charge of the LORD. 7 The
Levites shall surround the king, each
with his weapons in his hand; and
whoever enters the house shall be
slain. Be with the king when he comes
in, and when he goes out."
8 The Levites and all Judah did
according to all that Je·hoi'ȧ·dȧ the
priest commanded. They each brought
his men, who were to go off duty on
the sabbath, with those who were to
come on duty on the sabbath; for
Jehoiada the priest did not dismiss the
divisions. 9 And Je·hoi'ȧ·dȧ the priest
delivered to the captains the spears
and the large and small shields that
had been King David's, which were
in the house of God; 10 and he set all
the people as a guard for the king,
every man with his weapon in his
hand, from the south side of the house
to the north side of the house, around
the altar and the house. 11 Then he
brought out the king's son, and put
the crown upon him, and gave him the
testimony; and they proclaimed him
king, and Je·hoi'ȧ·dȧ and his sons
anointed him, and they said, "Long
live the king."
12 When Ath·ȧ·lī'ȧh heard the noise
of the people running and praising the
king, she went into the house of the
LORD to the people; 13 and when she
looked, there was the king standing by
his pillar at the entrance, and the captains and the trumpeters beside the
king, and all the people of the land
rejoicing and blowing trumpets, and
the singers with their musical instruments leading in the celebration. And
Ath·ȧ·lī'ȧh rent her clothes, and cried,
"Treason! Treason!" 14 Then Jehoi'ȧ·dȧ the priest brought out the
captains who were set over the army,
saying to them, "Bring her out between the ranks; any one who follows
her is to be slain with the sword." For
the priest said, "Do not slay her in
the house of the LORD." 15 So they
laid hands on her; and she went into
the entrance of the horse gate of the
king's house, and they slew her there.
16 And Je·hoi'ȧ·dȧ made a covenant
between himself and all the people and
the king that they should be the LORD's
people. 17 Then all the people went to
the house of Bā'ȧl, and tore it down;
his altars and his images they broke in
pieces, and they slew Mat'tan the
priest of Bā'ȧl before the altars. 18 And
Je·hoi'ȧ·dȧ posted watchmen for the
house of the LORD under the direction
of the Levitical priests and the Levites
whom David had organized to be in
charge of the house of the LORD, to
offer burnt offerings to the LORD, as
it is written in the law of Moses, with
rejoicing and with singing, according
to the order of David. 19 He stationed
the gatekeepers at the gates of the
house of the LORD so that no one
should enter who was in any way unclean. 20 And he took the captains, the
nobles, the governors of the people,
and all the people of the land; and they
brought the king down from the house
of the LORD, marching through the
upper gate to the king's house. And
they set the king upon the royal
throne. 21 So all the people of the land
rejoiced; and the city was quiet, after
Ath·ȧ·lī'ȧh had been slain with the
sword.

24 Jō'ash was seven years old
when he began to reign, and he
reigned forty years in Jerusalem; his
mother's name was Zib'i·ȧh of Beer-
sheba. 2 And Jō'ash did what was right
in the eyes of the LORD all the days of
Je·hoi'ȧ·dȧ the priest. 3 Je·hoi'ȧ·dȧ got
for him two wives, and he had sons
and daughters.
4 After this Jō'ash decided to restore the house of the LORD. 5 And he
gathered the priests and the Levites,
and said to them, "Go out to the cities
of Judah, and gather from all Israel
money to repair the house of your God
from year to year; and see that you
hasten the matter." But the Levites
did not hasten it. 6 So the king summoned Je·hoi'ȧ·dȧ the chief, and said
to him, "Why have you not required
the Levites to bring in from Judah and
Jerusalem the tax levied by Moses, the
servant of the LORD, on[m] the congregation of Israel for the tent of testimony?" 7 For the sons of Ath·ȧ·lī'ȧh,
that wicked woman, had broken into
the house of God; and had also used
all the dedicated things of the house of
the LORD for the Bā'ȧls.
8 So the king commanded, and they
made a chest, and set it outside the
gate of the house of the LORD. 9 And
proclamation was made throughout
Judah and Jerusalem, to bring in for
the LORD the tax that Moses the

[m] Compare Vg: Heb *and*
24.1-14: 2 Kings 11.21-12.14.

servant of God laid upon Israel in the
wilderness. 10 And all the princes and
all the people rejoiced and brought
their tax and dropped it into the chest
until they had finished. 11 And whenever the chest was brought to the
king's officers by the Levites, when
they saw that there was much money
in it, the king's secretary and the
officer of the chief priest would come
and empty the chest and take it and
return it to its place. Thus they did
day after day, and collected money in
abundance. 12 And the king and Jehoi'ȧ·dȧ gave it to those who had
charge of the work of the house of the
LORD, and they hired masons and
carpenters to restore the house of the
LORD, and also workers in iron and
bronze to repair the house of the LORD.
13 So those who were engaged in the
work labored, and the repairing went
forward in their hands, and they restored the house of God to its proper
condition and strengthened it. 14 And
when they had finished, they brought
the rest of the money before the king
and Je·hoi'ȧ·dȧ, and with it were made
utensils for the house of the LORD,
both for the service and for the burnt
offerings, and dishes for incense, and
vessels of gold and silver. And they
offered burnt offerings in the house
of the LORD continually all the days of
Jehoiada.

15 But Je·hoi'ȧ·dȧ grew old and full
of days, and died; he was a hundred
and thirty years old at his death. 16 And
they buried him in the city of David
among the kings, because he had done
good in Israel, and toward God and
his house.

17 Now after the death of Je·hoi'ȧ-
dȧ the princes of Judah came and did
obeisance to the king; then the king
hearkened to them. 18 And they forsook the house of the LORD, the God
of their fathers, and served the A·shē'-
rim and the idols. And wrath came
upon Judah and Jerusalem for this
their guilt. 19 Yet he sent prophets
among them to bring them back to the
LORD; these testified against them, but
they would not give heed.

20 Then the Spirit of God took
possession of[n] Zech·ȧ·rī'ȧh the son of
Je·hoi'ȧ·dȧ the priest; and he stood
above the people, and said to them,
"Thus says God, 'Why do you transgress the commandments of the LORD,
so that you cannot prosper? Because
you have forsaken the LORD, he has
forsaken you.'" 21 But they conspired
against him, and by command of the
king they stoned him with stones in
the court of the house of the LORD.
22 Thus Jō'ash the king did not
remember the kindness which Jehoi'ȧ·dȧ, Zech·ȧ·rī'ȧh's father, had
shown him, but killed his son. And
when he was dying, he said, "May the
LORD see and avenge!"

23 At the end of the year the army
of the Syrians came up against Jō'ash.
They came to Judah and Jerusalem,
and destroyed all the princes of the
people from among the people, and
sent all their spoil to the king of
Damascus. 24 Though the army of the
Syrians had come with few men, the
LORD delivered into their hand a very
great army, because they had forsaken
the LORD, the God of their fathers.
Thus they executed judgment on
Jō'ash.

25 When they had departed from
him, leaving him severely wounded,
his servants conspired against him because of the blood of the son[o] of
Je·hoi'ȧ·dȧ the priest, and slew him on
his bed. So he died; and they buried
him in the city of David, but they did
not bury him in the tombs of the kings.
26 Those who conspired against him
were Zā'bad the son of Shim'ē-ath the
Am'mȯ·nīt·ėss, and Je·hō'zȧ·bad the
son of Shim'rith the Mō'ȧb·īt·ėss.
27 Accounts of his sons, and of the
many oracles against him, and of the
rebuilding[p] of the house of God are
written in the Commentary on the
Book of the Kings. And Am·ȧ·zī'ȧh his
son reigned in his stead.

25 Am·ȧ·zī'ȧh was twenty-five
years old when he began to
reign, and he reigned twenty-nine
years in Jerusalem. His mother's name
was Jē'hō-ad'dȧn of Jerusalem. 2 And
he did what was right in the eyes of
the LORD, yet not with a blameless
heart. 3 And as soon as the royal power
was firmly in his hand he killed his
servants who had slain the king his
father. 4 But he did not put their
children to death according to what is
written in the law, in the book of
Moses, where the LORD commanded,
"The fathers shall not be put to death

[n] Heb *clothed itself with* [o] Gk Vg: Heb *sons* [p] Heb *founding*
24.23-26: 2 Kings 12.17-18, 20-21. **25.1-4:** 2 Kings 14.2-6.

for the children, or the children be
put to death for the fathers; but every
man shall die for his own sin."
5 Then Am·ȧ·zī'ȧh assembled the
men of Judah, and set them by fathers'
houses under commanders of thousands and of hundreds for all Judah
and Benjamin. He mustered those
twenty years old and upward, and
found that they were three hundred
thousand picked men, fit for war, able
to handle spear and shield. 6 He hired
also a hundred thousand mighty men
of valor from Israel for a hundred talents of silver. 7 But a man of God came
to him and said, "O king, do not let
the army of Israel go with you, for the
LORD is not with Israel, with all these
Ē'phrȧ·im·ītes. 8 But if you suppose
that in this way you will be strong for
war,[q] God will cast you down before
the enemy; for God has power to help
or to cast down." 9 And Am·ȧ·zī'ȧh said
to the man of God, "But what shall we
do about the hundred talents which I
have given to the army of Israel?" The
man of God answered, "The LORD is
able to give you much more than this."
10 Then Am·ȧ·zī'ȧh discharged the
army that had come to him from
Ē'phrȧ·im, to go home again. And they
became very angry with Judah, and
returned home in fierce anger. 11 But
Am·ȧ·zī'ȧh took courage, and led out
his people, and went to the Valley of
Salt and smote ten thousand men of
Sē'ir. 12 The men of Judah captured
another ten thousand alive, and took
them to the top of a rock and threw
them down from the top of the rock;
and they were all dashed to pieces.
13 But the men of the army whom
Am·ȧ·zī'ȧh sent back, not letting them
go with him to battle, fell upon the
cities of Judah, from Sȧ·mâr'i·ȧ to
Beth-hō'ron, and killed three thousand
people in them, and took much spoil.
14 After Am·ȧ·zī'ȧh came from the
slaughter of the Ē'dȯm·ītes, he brought
the gods of the men of Sē'ir, and set
them up as his gods, and worshiped
them, making offerings to them.
15 Therefore the LORD was angry with
Am·ȧ·zī'ȧh and sent to him a prophet,
who said to him, "Why have you
resorted to the gods of a people, which
did not deliver their own people from
your hand?" 16 But as he was speaking
the king said to him, "Have we made
you a royal counselor? Stop! Why
should you be put to death?" So the
prophet stopped, but said, "I know
that God has determined to destroy
you, because you have done this and
have not listened to my counsel."
17 Then Am·ȧ·zī'ȧh king of Judah
took counsel and sent to Jō'ash the son
of Je·hō'ȧ·haz, son of Jē'hū, king of
Israel, saying, "Come, let us look one
another in the face." 18 And Jō'ash the
king of Israel sent word to Am·ȧ·zī'ȧh
king of Judah, "A thistle on Lebanon
sent to a cedar on Lebanon, saying,
'Give your daughter to my son for a
wife'; and a wild beast of Lebanon
passed by and trampled down the
thistle. 19 You say, 'See, I have smitten
Ē'dȯm,' and your heart has lifted you
up in boastfulness. But now stay at
home; why should you provoke trouble
so that you fall, you and Judah with
you?"
20 But Am·ȧ·zī'ȧh would not listen;
for it was of God, in order that he
might give them into the hand of their
enemies, because they had sought the
gods of Ē'dȯm. 21 So Jō'ash king of
Israel went up; and he and Am·ȧ·zī'ȧh
king of Judah faced one another in
battle at Beth-shē'mesh, which belongs
to Judah. 22 And Judah was defeated
by Israel, and every man fled to his
home. 23 And Jō'ash king of Israel
captured Am·ȧ·zī'ȧh king of Judah, the
son of Jō'ash, son of Ā·hȧ·zī'ȧh, at
Beth-shē'mesh, and brought him to
Jerusalem, and broke down the wall of
Jerusalem for four hundred cubits,
from the Ē'phrȧ·im Gate to the Corner
Gate. 24 And he seized all the gold and
silver, and all the vessels that were
found in the house of God, and Ō'bed-
ē'dȯm with them; he seized also the
treasuries of the king's house, and
hostages, and he returned to Sȧ·mâr'i·ȧ.
25 Am·ȧ·zī'ȧh the son of Jō'ash king
of Judah lived fifteen years after the
death of Joash the son of Je·hō'ȧ·haz,
king of Israel. 26 Now the rest of the
deeds of Am·ȧ·zī'ȧh, from first to last,
are they not written in the Book of
the Kings of Judah and Israel? 27 From
the time when he turned away from
the LORD they made a conspiracy
against him in Jerusalem, and he fled
to Lā'chish. But they sent after him
to Lachish, and slew him there. 28 And
they brought him upon horses; and he

[q] Gk: Heb *But if you go, act, be strong for the battle*
25.11: 2 Kings 14.7. 25.17-20, 21-24: 2 Kings 14.8-14. 25.25-28: 2 Kings 14.17-20.

was buried with his fathers in the city
of David.

26 And all the people of Judah
took Uz·zī'ah, who was sixteen
years old, and made him king instead
of his father Am·a·zī'ah. 2 He built
E'loth and restored it to Judah, after
the king slept with his fathers. 3 Uz-
zī'ah was sixteen years old when he
began to reign, and he reigned fifty-
two years in Jerusalem. His mother's
name was Jec·o·lī'ah of Jerusalem.
4And he did what was right in the eyes
of the LORD, according to all that his
father Am·a·zī'ah had done. 5 He set
himself to seek God in the days of
Zech·a·rī'ah, who instructed him in
the fear of God; and as long as he
sought the LORD, God made him
prosper.

6 He went out and made war
against the Philistines, and broke down
the wall of Gath and the wall of Jab'-
neh and the wall of Ash'dod; and he
built cities in the territory of Ashdod
and elsewhere among the Philistines.
7 God helped him against the Philistines, and against the Arabs that dwelt
in Gur·bā'al, and against the Me-
ü'nites. 8 The Am'mo·nites paid tribute to Uz·zī'ah, and his fame spread
even to the border of Egypt, for he
became very strong. 9 Moreover
Uz·zī'ah built towers in Jerusalem at
the Corner Gate and at the Valley
Gate and at the Angle, and fortified
them. 10And he built towers in the
wilderness, and hewed out many
cisterns, for he had large herds, both
in the She·phē'lah and in the plain,
and he had farmers and vinedressers
in the hills and in the fertile lands, for
he loved the soil. 11 Moreover Uz·zī'ah
had an army of soldiers, fit for war, in
divisions according to the numbers in
the muster made by Je-ī'el the secretary and Mā-a·sei'ah the officer, under
the direction of Han·a·nī'ah, one of
the king's commanders. 12 The whole
number of the heads of fathers' houses
of mighty men of valor was two thousand six hundred. 13 Under their command was an army of three hundred
and seven thousand five hundred, who
could make war with mighty power,
to help the king against the enemy.
14And Uz·zī'ah prepared for all the
army shields, spears, helmets, coats of
mail, bows, and stones for slinging.
15 In Jerusalem he made engines, in-
vented by skilful men, to be on the
towers and the corners, to shoot arrows
and great stones. And his fame spread
far, for he was marvelously helped, till
he was strong.

16 But when he was strong he grew
proud, to his destruction. For he was
false to the LORD his God, and entered
the temple of the LORD to burn incense
on the altar of incense. 17 But Az·a-
rī'ah the priest went in after him, with
eighty priests of the LORD who were
men of valor; 18 and they withstood
King Uz·zī'ah, and said to him, "It is
not for you, Uzziah, to burn incense
to the LORD, but for the priests the
sons of Aaron, who are consecrated to
burn incense. Go out of the sanctuary;
for you have done wrong, and it will
bring you no honor from the LORD
God." 19 Then Uz·zī'ah was angry.
Now he had a censer in his hand to
burn incense, and when he became
angry with the priests leprosy broke
out on his forehead, in the presence of
the priests in the house of the LORD,
by the altar of incense. 20And Az·a-
rī'ah the chief priest, and all the priests,
looked at him, and behold, he was
leprous in his forehead! And they
thrust him out quickly, and he himself
hastened to go out, because the LORD
had smitten him. 21And King Uz·zī'ah
was a leper to the day of his death, and
being a leper dwelt in a separate house,
for he was excluded from the house of
the LORD. And Jō'tham his son was
over the king's household, governing
the people of the land.

22 Now the rest of the acts of
Uz·zī'ah, from first to last, Ī·sāi'ah the
prophet the son of Ā'moz wrote. 23And
Uz·zī'ah slept with his fathers, and
they buried him with his fathers in the
burial field which belonged to the
kings, for they said, "He is a leper."
And Jō'tham his son reigned in his
stead.

27 Jō'tham was twenty-five years
old when he began to reign, and
he reigned sixteen years in Jerusalem.
His mother's name was Je·rü'shah the
daughter of Zā'dok. 2And he did what
was right in the eyes of the LORD according to all that his father Uz·zī'ah
had done—only he did not invade the
temple of the LORD. But the people
still followed corrupt practices. 3 He
built the upper gate of the house of
the LORD, and did much building on

26.1-4: 2 Kings 14.21-22; 15.2-3. **26.20-23:** 2 Kings 15.5-7. **27.1-3:** 2 Kings 15.33-35.

the wall of Ō'phel. 4 Moreover he built cities in the hill country of Judah, and forts and towers on the wooded hills. 5 He fought with the king of the Am'mȯ·nītes and prevailed against them. And the Ammonites gave him that year a hundred talents of silver, and ten thousand cors of wheat and ten thousand of barley. The Ammonites paid him the same amount in the second and the third years. 6 So Jō'thȧm became mighty, because he ordered his ways before the LORD his God. 7 Now the rest of the acts of Jō'thȧm, and all his wars, and his ways, behold, they are written in the Book of the Kings of Israel and Judah. 8 He was twenty-five years old when he began to reign, and he reigned sixteen years in Jerusalem. 9 And Jō'thȧm slept with his fathers, and they buried him in the city of David; and Ā'haz his son reigned in his stead.

28 Ā'haz was twenty years old when he began to reign, and he reigned sixteen years in Jerusalem. And he did not do what was right in the eyes of the LORD, like his father David, 2 but walked in the ways of the kings of Israel. He even made molten images for the Bā'ȧls; 3 and he burned incense in the valley of the son of Hin'nȯm, and burned his sons as an offering, according to the abominable practices of the nations whom the LORD drove out before the people of Israel. 4 And he sacrificed and burned incense on the high places, and on the hills, and under every green tree.

5 Therefore the LORD his God gave him into the hand of the king of Syria, who defeated him and took captive a great number of his people and brought them to Damascus. He was also given into the hand of the king of Israel, who defeated him with great slaughter. 6 For Pē'kȧh the son of Rem·ȧ·lī'ȧh slew a hundred and twenty thousand in Judah in one day, all of them men of valor, because they had forsaken the LORD, the God of their fathers. 7 And Zich'rī, a mighty man of Ē'phrȧ·im, slew Mā-ȧ·sē'i'ȧh the king's son and Az·rī'kam the commander of the palace and El·kā'nȧh the next in authority to the king.

8 The men of Israel took captive two hundred thousand of their kinsfolk, women, sons, and daughters; they also took much spoil from them and brought the spoil to Sȧ·mâr'i·ȧ. 9 But a prophet of the LORD was there, whose name was Ō'bed; and he went out to meet the army that came to Sȧ·mâr'i·ȧ, and said to them, "Behold, because the LORD, the God of your fathers, was angry with Judah, he gave them into your hand, but you have slain them in a rage which has reached up to heaven. 10 And now you intend to subjugate the people of Judah and Jerusalem, male and female, as your slaves. Have you not sins of your own against the LORD your God? 11 Now hear me, and send back the captives from your kinsfolk whom you have taken, for the fierce wrath of the LORD is upon you." 12 Certain chiefs also of the men of Ē'phrȧ·im, Az·ȧ·rī'ȧh the son of Jō·hā'nȧn, Ber·ė·chī'ȧh the son of Me·shil'lė·moth, Je·hiz·kī'ȧh the son of Shal'lŭm, and Ȧ·mā'sȧ the son of Had'läi, stood up against those who were coming from the war, 13 and said to them, "You shall not bring the captives in here, for you propose to bring upon us guilt against the LORD in addition to our present sins and guilt. For our guilt is already great, and there is fierce wrath against Israel." 14 So the armed men left the captives and the spoil before the princes and all the assembly. 15 And the men who have been mentioned by name rose and took the captives, and with the spoil they clothed all that were naked among them; they clothed them, gave them sandals, provided them with food and drink, and anointed them; and carrying all the feeble among them on asses, they brought them to their kinsfolk at Jericho, the city of palm trees. Then they returned to Sȧ·mâr'i·ȧ.

16 At that time King Ā'haz sent to the king[r] of Assyria for help. 17 For the Ē'dȯm·ītes had again invaded and defeated Judah, and carried away captives. 18 And the Philistines had made raids on the cities in the Shephē'lȧh and the Negeb of Judah, and had taken Beth-shē'mesh, Ȧi'jȧ·lon, Ge·dē'roth, Sō'cōh with its villages, Tim'nȧh with its villages, and Gim'zō with its villages; and they settled there. 19 For the LORD brought Judah low because of Ā'haz king of Israel, for he had dealt wantonly in Judah and had

[r] Gk Syr Vg Compare 2 Kings 16.7: Heb *kings*
27.9: 2 Kings 15.38. **28.1-4**: 2 Kings 16.2-4.

been faithless to the LORD. 20 So Til'-
gath-pil·nē'ṡėr king of Assyria came
against him, and afflicted him instead
of strengthening him. 21 For Ā'haz
took from the house of the LORD and
the house of the king and of the
princes, and gave tribute to the king
of Assyria; but it did not help him.

22 In the time of his distress he became yet more faithless to the LORD—
this same King Ā'haz. 23 For he sacrificed to the gods of Damascus which
had defeated him, and said, "Because
the gods of the kings of Syria helped
them, I will sacrifice to them that they
may help me." But they were the ruin
of him, and of all Israel. 24 And Ā'haz
gathered together the vessels of the
house of God and cut in pieces the
vessels of the house of God, and he
shut up the doors of the house of the
LORD; and he made himself altars in
every corner of Jerusalem. 25 In every
city of Judah he made high places to
burn incense to other gods, provoking
to anger the LORD, the God of his
fathers. 26 Now the rest of his acts and
all his ways, from first to last, behold,
they are written in the Book of the
Kings of Judah and Israel. 27 And
Ā'haz slept with his fathers, and they
buried him in the city, in Jerusalem,
for they did not bring him into the
tombs of the kings of Israel. And
Hez·ė·kī'ȧh his son reigned in his stead.

29 Hez·ė·kī'ȧh began to reign
when he was twenty-five years
old, and he reigned twenty-nine years
in Jerusalem. His mother's name was
A·bī'jȧh the daughter of Zech·ȧ·rī'ȧh.
2 And he did what was right in the
eyes of the LORD, according to all that
David his father had done.

3 In the first year of his reign, in
the first month, he opened the doors
of the house of the LORD, and repaired
them. 4 He brought in the priests and
the Levites, and assembled them in
the square on the east, 5 and said to
them, "Hear me, Levites! Now sanctify yourselves, and sanctify the house
of the LORD, the God of your fathers,
and carry out the filth from the holy
place. 6 For our fathers have been unfaithful and have done what was evil
in the sight of the LORD our God; they
have forsaken him, and have turned
away their faces from the habitation
of the LORD, and turned their backs.
7 They also shut the doors of the
vestibule and put out the lamps, and
have not burned incense or offered
burnt offerings in the holy place to the
God of Israel. 8 Therefore the wrath
of the LORD came on Judah and Jerusalem, and he has made them an object
of horror, of astonishment, and of
hissing, as you see with your own
eyes. 9 For lo, our fathers have fallen
by the sword and our sons and our
daughters and our wives are in captivity for this. 10 Now it is in my heart
to make a covenant with the LORD, the
God of Israel, that his fierce anger
may turn away from us. 11 My sons,
do not now be negligent, for the LORD
has chosen you to stand in his presence,
to minister to him, and to be his
ministers and burn incense to him."

12 Then the Levites arose, Mā'-
hath the son of A·mā'säi, and Jō'ėl the
son of Az·ȧ·rī'ȧh, of the sons of the
Kō'hȧ·thītes; and of the sons of Mė-
rär'ī, Kish the son of Ab'dī, and
Azariah the son of Je·hal'lė·lel; and of
the Gẽr'shȯ·nītes, Jō'ȧh the son of
Zim'mȧh, and Eden the son of Joah;
13 and of the sons of El·i·zā'phȧn,
Shim'rī and Je·ü'el; and of the sons
of Ā'saph, Zech·ȧ·rī'ȧh and Mat·tȧ-
nī'ȧh; 14 and of the sons of Hē'mȧn,
Je·hū'el and Shim'ē-ī; and of the sons
of Je·dü'thun, She·māi'ȧh and Uz'-
zi·el. 15 They gathered their brethren,
and sanctified themselves, and went
in as the king had commanded, by the
words of the LORD, to cleanse the
house of the LORD. 16 The priests went
into the inner part of the house of the
LORD to cleanse it, and they brought
out all the uncleanness that they found
in the temple of the LORD into the
court of the house of the LORD; and
the Levites took it and carried it out
to the brook Kid'rȯn. 17 They began
to sanctify on the first day of the first
month, and on the eighth day of the
month they came to the vestibule of
the LORD; then for eight days they
sanctified the house of the LORD, and
on the sixteenth day of the first month
they finished. 18 Then they went in to
Hez·ė·kī'ȧh the king and said, "We
have cleansed all the house of the
LORD, the altar of burnt offering and
all its utensils, and the table for the
showbread and all its utensils. 19 All
the utensils which King Ā'haz dis-
carded in his reign when he was faithless, we have made ready and sancti-

28.27: 2 Kings 16.20. **29.1-2**: 2 Kings 18.1-3.

fied; and behold, they are before the
altar of the LORD."
20 Then Hez·ė·kī'ăh the king rose
early and gathered the officials of the
city, and went up to the house of the
LORD. 21 And they brought seven bulls,
seven rams, seven lambs, and seven
he-goats for a sin offering for the kingdom and for the sanctuary and for
Judah. And he commanded the priests
the sons of Aaron to offer them on the
altar of the LORD. 22 So they killed the
bulls, and the priests received the
blood and threw it against the altar;
and they killed the rams and their
blood was thrown against the altar; and
they killed the lambs and their blood
was thrown against the altar. 23 Then
the he-goats for the sin offering were
brought to the king and the assembly,
and they laid their hands upon them,
24 and the priests killed them and made
a sin offering with their blood on the
altar, to make atonement for all Israel.
For the king commanded that the
burnt offering and the sin offering
should be made for all Israel.

25 And he stationed the Levites in
the house of the LORD with cymbals,
harps, and lyres, according to the
commandment of David and of Gad
the king's seer and of Nathan the
prophet; for the commandment was
from the LORD through his prophets.
26 The Levites stood with the instruments of David, and the priests with
the trumpets. 27 Then Hez·ė·kī'ăh
commanded that the burnt offering be
offered on the altar. And when the
burnt offering began, the song to the
LORD began also, and the trumpets,
accompanied by the instruments of
David king of Israel. 28 The whole
assembly worshiped, and the singers
sang, and the trumpeters sounded; all
this continued until the burnt offering
was finished. 29 When the offering was
finished, the king and all who were
present with him bowed themselves
and worshiped. 30 And Hez·ė·kī'ăh the
king and the princes commanded the
Levites to sing praises to the LORD
with the words of David and of Ā'saph
the seer. And they sang praises with
gladness, and they bowed down and
worshiped.

31 Then Hez·ė·kī'ăh said, "You
have now consecrated yourselves to
the LORD; come near, bring sacrifices
and thank offerings to the house of
the LORD." And the assembly brought
sacrifices and thank offerings; and all
who were of a willing heart brought
burnt offerings. 32 The number of the
burnt offerings which the assembly
brought was seventy bulls, a hundred
rams, and two hundred lambs; all these
were for a burnt offering to the LORD.
33 And the consecrated offerings were
six hundred bulls and three thousand
sheep. 34 But the priests were too few
and could not flay all the burnt offerings, so until other priests had sanctified themselves their brethren the Levites helped them, until the work was
finished—for the Levites were more
upright in heart than the priests in
sanctifying themselves. 35 Besides the
great number of burnt offerings there
was the fat of the peace offerings, and
there were the libations for the burnt
offerings. Thus the service of the house
of the LORD was restored. 36 And
Hez·ė·kī'ăh and all the people rejoiced
because of what God had done for the
people; for the thing came about
suddenly.

30 Hez·ė·kī'ăh sent to all Israel
and Judah, and wrote letters
also to Ē'phră·im and Mă·nas'sėh, that
they should come to the house of the
LORD at Jerusalem, to keep the passover to the LORD the God of Israel.
2 For the king and his princes and all
the assembly in Jerusalem had taken
counsel to keep the passover in the
second month—3 for they could not
keep it in its time because the priests
had not sanctified themselves in
sufficient number, nor had the people
assembled in Jerusalem—4 and the
plan seemed right to the king and all
the assembly. 5 So they decreed to
make a proclamation throughout all
Israel, from Beer-sheba to Dan, that
the people should come and keep the
passover to the LORD the God of Israel,
at Jerusalem; for they had not kept it
in great numbers as prescribed. 6 So
couriers went throughout all Israel
and Judah with letters from the king
and his princes, as the king had commanded, saying, "O people of Israel,
return to the LORD, the God of Abraham, Isaac, and Israel, that he may
turn again to the remnant of you who
have escaped from the hand of the
kings of Assyria. 7 Do not be like your
fathers and your brethren, who were
faithless to the LORD God of their
fathers, so that he made them a desolation, as you see. 8 Do not now be stiff-

necked as your fathers were, but yield yourselves to the LORD, and come to his sanctuary, which he has sanctified for ever, and serve the LORD your God, that his fierce anger may turn away from you. 9 For if you return to the LORD, your brethren and your children will find compassion with their captors, and return to this land. For the LORD your God is gracious and merciful, and will not turn away his face from you, if you return to him."

10 So the couriers went from city to city through the country of Ē'phrȧ·im and Mȧ·nas'sėh, and as far as Zeb'ū·lůn; but they laughed them to scorn, and mocked them. 11 Only a few men of Ash'ėr, of Mȧ·nas'sėh, and of Zeb'ū·lůn humbled themselves and came to Jerusalem. 12 The hand of God was also upon Judah to give them one heart to do what the king and the princes commanded by the word of the LORD.

13 And many people came together in Jerusalem to keep the feast of unleavened bread in the second month, a very great assembly. 14 They set to work and removed the altars that were in Jerusalem, and all the altars for burning incense they took away and threw into the Kid'rȯn valley. 15 And they killed the passover lamb on the fourteenth day of the second month. And the priests and the Levites were put to shame, so that they sanctified themselves, and brought burnt offerings into the house of the LORD. 16 They took their accustomed posts according to the law of Moses the man of God; the priests sprinkled the blood which they received from the hand of the Levites. 17 For there were many in the assembly who had not sanctified themselves; therefore the Levites had to kill the passover lamb for every one who was not clean, to make it holy to the LORD. 18 For a multitude of the people, many of them from Ē'phrȧ·im, Mȧ·nas'sėh, Is'sȧ·chär, and Zeb'ū·lůn, had not cleansed themselves, yet they ate the passover otherwise than as prescribed. For Hez·ė·kī'ȧh had prayed for them, saying, "The good LORD pardon every one 19 who sets his heart to seek God, the LORD the God of his fathers, even though not according to the sanctuary's rules of cleanness." 20 And the LORD heard Hez·ė·kī'ȧh, and healed the people. 21 And the people of Israel that were present at Jerusalem kept the feast of unleavened bread seven days with great gladness; and the Levites and the priests praised the LORD day by day, singing with all their might[s] to the LORD. 22 And Hez·ė·kī'ȧh spoke encouragingly to all the Levites who showed good skill in the service of the LORD. So the people ate the food of the festival for seven days, sacrificing peace offerings and giving thanks to the LORD the God of their fathers.

23 Then the whole assembly agreed together to keep the feast for another seven days; so they kept it for another seven days with gladness. 24 For Hez·ė·kī'ȧh king of Judah gave the assembly a thousand bulls and seven thousand sheep for offerings, and the princes gave the assembly a thousand bulls and ten thousand sheep. And the priests sanctified themselves in great numbers. 25 The whole assembly of Judah, and the priests and the Levites, and the whole assembly that came out of Israel, and the sojourners who came out of the land of Israel, and the sojourners who dwelt in Judah, rejoiced. 26 So there was great joy in Jerusalem, for since the time of Solomon the son of David king of Israel there had been nothing like this in Jerusalem. 27 Then the priests and the Levites arose and blessed the people, and their voice was heard, and their prayer came to his holy habitation in heaven.

31 Now when all this was finished, all Israel who were present went out to the cities of Judah and broke in pieces the pillars and hewed down the A·shē'rim and broke down the high places and the altars throughout all Judah and Benjamin, and in Ē'phrȧ·im and Mȧ·nas'sėh, until they had destroyed them all. Then all the people of Israel returned to their cities, every man to his possession.

2 And Hez·ė·kī'ȧh appointed the divisions of the priests and of the Levites, division by division, each according to his service, the priests and the Levites, for burnt offerings and peace offerings, to minister in the gates of the camp of the LORD and to give thanks and praise. 3 The contribution of the king from his own possessions was for the burnt offerings: the burnt offerings of morning and evening, and the burnt offerings for the sabbaths, the new moons, and the appointed

[s] Compare 1 Chron 13.8: Heb *with instruments of might*

feasts, as it is written in the law of the
LORD. 4And he commanded the people
who lived in Jerusalem to give the
portion due to the priests and the
Levites, that they might give themselves to the law of the LORD. 5As
soon as the command was spread
abroad, the people of Israel gave in
abundance the first fruits of grain,
wine, oil, honey, and of all the produce
of the field; and they brought in
abundantly the tithe of everything.
6And the people of Israel and Judah
who lived in the cities of Judah also
brought in the tithe of cattle and
sheep, and the dedicated things[t] which
had been consecrated to the LORD
their God, and laid them in heaps.
7 In the third month they began to
pile up the heaps, and finished them in
the seventh month. 8 When Hez·ė·kī'ȧh
and the princes came and saw the
heaps, they blessed the LORD and his
people Israel. 9And Hez·ė·kī'ȧh questioned the priests and the Levites
about the heaps. 10Az·ȧ·rī'ȧh the chief
priest, who was of the house of Zā'dok,
answered him, "Since they began to
bring the contributions into the house
of the LORD we have eaten and had
enough and have plenty left; for the
LORD has blessed his people, so that
we have this great store left."
11 Then Hez·ė·kī'ȧh commanded
them to prepare chambers in the house
of the LORD; and they prepared them.
12And they faithfully brought in the
contributions, the tithes and the dedicated things. The chief officer in charge
of them was Con·ȧ·nī'ȧh the Levite,
with Shim'ē-ī his brother as second;
13 while Je·hī'el, Az·ȧ·zī'ȧh, Nā'hath,
A·sā'ȧ·hel, Jer'i·moth, Jō'zȧ·bad, E·lī'-
el, Is·mȧ·chī'ȧh, Mā'hath, and Be·nā'-
iȧh were overseers assisting Con·ȧ·nī'ȧh
and Shim'ē-ī his brother, by the
appointment of Hez·ė·kī'ȧh the king
and Az·ȧ·rī'ȧh the chief officer of the
house of God. 14And Kō're the son of
Im'nȧh the Levite, keeper of the east
gate, was over the freewill offerings to
God, to apportion the contribution
reserved for the LORD and the most
holy offerings. 15 Eden, Mi·nī'ȧ·min,
Jesh'ü·ȧ, She·māi'ȧh, Am·ȧ·rī'ȧh, and
Shec·ȧ·nī'ȧh were faithfully assisting
him in the cities of the priests, to distribute the portions to their brethren,
old and young alike, by divisions,
16 except those enrolled by genealogy,
males from three years old and upwards, all who entered the house of
the LORD as the duty of each day
required, for their service according
to their offices, by their divisions.
17 The enrollment of the priests was
according to their fathers' houses; that
of the Levites from twenty years old
and upwards was according to their
offices, by their divisions. 18 The priests
were enrolled with all their little children, their wives, their sons, and their
daughters, the whole multitude; for
they were faithful in keeping themselves holy. 19And for the sons of
Aaron, the priests, who were in the
fields of common land belonging to
their cities, there were men in the
several cities who were designated by
name to distribute portions to every
male among the priests and to every one
among the Levites who was enrolled.
20 Thus Hez·ė·kī'ȧh did throughout
all Judah; and he did what was good
and right and faithful before the LORD
his God. 21And every work that he
undertook in the service of the house
of God and in accordance with the
law and the commandments, seeking
his God, he did with all his heart, and
prospered.

32 After these things and these
acts of faithfulness Sen·nach'ė-
rib king of Assyria came and invaded
Judah and encamped against the fortified cities, thinking to win them for
himself. 2And when Hez·ė·kī'ȧh saw
that Sen·nach'ė·rib had come and intended to fight against Jerusalem, 3 he
planned with his officers and his
mighty men to stop the water of the
springs that were outside the city; and
they helped him. 4A great many people
were gathered, and they stopped all the
springs and the brook that flowed
through the land, saying, "Why should
the kings of Assyria come and find
much water?" 5 He set to work
resolutely and built up all the wall that
was broken down, and raised towers
upon it,[u] and outside it he built
another wall; and he strengthened the
Mil'lō in the city of David. He also
made weapons and shields in abundance. 6And he set combat commanders over the people, and gathered
them together to him in the square at
the gate of the city and spoke encour-

[t] Heb *the tithe of the dedicated things* [u] Vg: Heb *and raised upon the towers*
32.1: 2 Kings 18.13.

agingly to them, saying, [7] "Be strong
and of good courage. Do not be afraid
or dismayed before the king of Assyria
and all the horde that is with him; for
there is one greater with us than with
him. [8] With him is an arm of flesh;
but with us is the LORD our God, to
help us and to fight our battles." And
the people took confidence from the
words of Hez·ė·kī'ȧh king of Judah.
9 After this Sen·nach'ė·rib king of
Assyria, who was besieging Lā'chish
with all his forces, sent his servants to
Jerusalem to Hez·ė·kī'ȧh king of Judah
and to all the people of Judah that
were in Jerusalem, saying, [10] "Thus
says Sen·nach'ė·rib king of Assyria,
'On what are you relying, that you
stand siege in Jerusalem? [11] Is not
Hez·ė·kī'ȧh misleading you, that he
may give you over to die by famine
and by thirst, when he tells you, "The
LORD our God will deliver us from the
hand of the king of Assyria"? [12] Has
not this same Hez·ė·kī'ȧh taken away
his high places and his altars and commanded Judah and Jerusalem, "Before one altar you shall worship, and
upon it you shall burn your sacrifices"?
[13] Do you not know what I and my
fathers have done to all the peoples of
other lands? Were the gods of the
nations of those lands at all able to
deliver their lands out of my hand?
[14] Who among all the gods of those
nations which my fathers utterly destroyed was able to deliver his people
from my hand, that your God should
be able to deliver you from my hand?
[15] Now therefore do not let Hez·ė·kī'ȧh
deceive you or mislead you in this
fashion, and do not believe him, for
no god of any nation or kingdom has
been able to deliver his people from
my hand or from the hand of my
fathers. How much less will your God
deliver you out of my hand!' "
16 And his servants said still more
against the Lord GOD and against his
servant Hez·ė·kī'ȧh. [17]And he wrote
letters to cast contempt on the LORD
the God of Israel and to speak against
him, saying, "Like the gods of the
nations of the lands who have not
delivered their people from my hands,
so the God of Hez·ė·kī'ȧh will not
deliver his people from my hand."
[18]And they shouted it with a loud
voice in the language of Judah to the
people of Jerusalem who were upon
the wall, to frighten and terrify them,
in order that they might take the city.
[19]And they spoke of the God of Jerusalem as they spoke of the gods of the
peoples of the earth, which are the
work of men's hands.
20 Then Hez·ė·kī'ȧh the king and
I·ṡāi'ȧh the prophet, the son of Ā'moz,
prayed because of this and cried to
heaven. [21]And the LORD sent an angel,
who cut off all the mighty warriors and
commanders and officers in the camp
of the king of Assyria. So he returned
with shame of face to his own land.
And when he came into the house of
his god, some of his own sons struck
him down there with the sword. [22] So
the LORD saved Hez·ė·kī'ȧh and the
inhabitants of Jerusalem from the hand
of Sen·nach'ė·rib king of Assyria and
from the hand of all his enemies; and
he gave them rest on every side. [23]And
many brought gifts to the LORD to
Jerusalem and precious things to Hez-
ė·kī'ȧh king of Judah, so that he was
exalted in the sight of all nations from
that time onward.
24 In those days Hez·ė·kī'ȧh became
sick and was at the point of death, and
he prayed to the LORD; and he answered him and gave him a sign.
[25] But Hez·ė·kī'ȧh did not make return
according to the benefit done to him,
for his heart was proud. Therefore
wrath came upon him and Judah and
Jerusalem. [26] But Hez·ė·kī'ȧh humbled
himself for the pride of his heart, both
he and the inhabitants of Jerusalem,
so that the wrath of the LORD did
not come upon them in the days of
Hezekiah.
27 And Hez·ė·kī'ȧh had very great
riches and honor; and he made for
himself treasuries for silver, for gold,
for precious stones, for spices, for
shields, and for all kinds of costly
vessels; [28] storehouses also for the
yield of grain, wine, and oil; and stalls
for all kinds of cattle, and sheepfolds.
[29] He likewise provided cities for himself, and flocks and herds in abundance; for God had given him very
great possessions. [30] This same Hez·ė-
kī'ȧh closed the upper outlet of the
waters of Gī'hon and directed them
down to the west side of the city of
David. And Hezekiah prospered in all
his works. [31]And so in the matter of
the envoys of the princes of Babylon,
who had been sent to him to inquire

32.9-21: 2 Kings 18.17-19.37. **32.24-33:** 2 Kings 20.1-21.

about the sign that had been done in
the land, God left him to himself, in
order to try him and to know all that
was in his heart.
32 Now the rest of the acts of Hez-
ė·kī'ȧh, and his good deeds, behold,
they are written in the vision of Ī·ṡāi'ȧh
the prophet the son of Ā'moz, in the
Book of the Kings of Judah and Israel.
33 And Hez·ė·kī'ȧh slept with his
fathers, and they buried him in the
ascent of the tombs of the sons of
David; and all Judah and the inhabitants of Jerusalem did him honor at
his death. And Mȧ·nas'sėh his son
reigned in his stead.

33 Mȧ·nas'sėh was twelve years old
when he began to reign, and he
reigned fifty-five years in Jerusalem.
2 He did what was evil in the sight of
the LORD, according to the abominable
practices of the nations whom the
LORD drove out before the people of
Israel. 3 For he rebuilt the high places
which his father Hez·ė·kī'ȧh had broken down, and erected altars to the
Bā'ălṡ, and made Ȧ·shē'rȧhṡ, and worshiped all the host of heaven, and
served them. 4 And he built altars in
the house of the LORD, of which the
LORD had said, "In Jerusalem shall
my name be for ever." 5 And he built
altars for all the host of heaven in the
two courts of the house of the LORD.
6 And he burned his sons as an offering
in the valley of the son of Hin'nŏm,
and practiced soothsaying and augury
and sorcery, and dealt with mediums
and with wizards. He did much evil
in the sight of the LORD, provoking
him to anger. 7 And the image of the
idol which he had made he set in the
house of God, of which God said to
David and to Solomon his son, "In
this house, and in Jerusalem, which
I have chosen out of all the tribes of
Israel, I will put my name for ever;
8 and I will no more remove the foot
of Israel from the land which I
appointed for your fathers, if only
they will be careful to do all that I
have commanded them, all the law,
the statutes, and the ordinances given
through Moses." 9 Mȧ·nas'sėh seduced
Judah and the inhabitants of Jerusalem, so that they did more evil than
the nations whom the LORD destroyed
before the people of Israel.
10 The LORD spoke to Mȧ·nas'sėh
and to his people, but they gave no
heed. 11 Therefore the LORD brought
upon them the commanders of the
army of the king of Assyria, who took
Mȧ·nas'sėh with hooks and bound him
with fetters of bronze and brought him
to Babylon. 12 And when he was in
distress he entreated the favor of the
LORD his God and humbled himself
greatly before the God of his fathers.
13 He prayed to him, and God received
his entreaty and heard his supplication
and brought him again to Jerusalem
into his kingdom. Then Mȧ·nas'sėh
knew that the LORD was God.
14 Afterwards he built an outer wall
for the city of David west of Gī'hon,
in the valley, and for the entrance into
the Fish Gate, and carried it round
Ō'phel, and raised it to a very great
height; he also put commanders of
the army in all the fortified cities in
Judah. 15 And he took away the foreign
gods and the idol from the house of
the LORD, and all the altars that he
had built on the mountain of the house
of the LORD and in Jerusalem, and he
threw them outside of the city. 16 He
also restored the altar of the LORD and
offered upon it sacrifices of peace
offerings and of thanksgiving; and he
commanded Judah to serve the LORD
the God of Israel. 17 Nevertheless the
people still sacrificed at the high places,
but only to the LORD their God.
18 Now the rest of the acts of Mȧ-
nas'sėh, and his prayer to his God, and
the words of the seers who spoke to
him in the name of the LORD the God
of Israel, behold, they are in the
Chronicles of the Kings of Israel.
19 And his prayer, and how God received his entreaty, and all his sin and
his faithlessness, and the sites on
which he built high places and set up
the Ȧ·shē'rim and the images, before
he humbled himself, behold, they are
written in the Chronicles of the Seers.[v]
20 So Mȧ·nas'sėh slept with his fathers,
and they buried him in his house; and
Ā'mon his son reigned in his stead.
21 Ā'mon was twenty-two years old
when he began to reign, and he
reigned two years in Jerusalem. 22 He
did what was evil in the sight of the
LORD, as Mȧ·nas'sėh his father had
done. Ā'mon sacrificed to all the images
that Manasseh his father had made,
and served them. 23 And he did not

[v] One Ms: Gk: Heb *of Hozai*
33.1-9: 2 Kings 21.1-9. 33.20: 2 Kings 21.18. 33.21-25: 2 Kings 21.19-24.

humble himself before the LORD, as
Må·nas'sėh his father had humbled
himself, but this Ā'mon incurred guilt
more and more. 24 And his servants
conspired against him and killed him
in his house. 25 But the people of the
land slew all those who conspired
against King Ā'mon; and the people
of the land made Jō·sī'ȧh his son king
in his stead.

34 Jō·sī'ȧh was eight years old
when he began to reign, and he
reigned thirty-one years in Jerusalem.
2 He did what was right in the eyes of
the LORD, and walked in the ways of
David his father; and he did not turn
aside to the right or to the left. 3 For
in the eighth year of his reign, while
he was yet a boy, he began to seek the
God of David his father; and in the
twelfth year he began to purge Judah
and Jerusalem of the high places, the
Ȧ·shē'rim, and the graven and the
molten images. 4 And they broke down
the altars of the Bā'ȧls in his presence;
and he hewed down the incense altars
which stood above them; and he broke
in pieces the Ȧ·shē'rim and the graven
and the molten images, and he made
dust of them and strewed it over the
graves of those who had sacrificed to
them. 5 He also burned the bones of
the priests on their altars, and purged
Judah and Jerusalem. 6 And in the cities
of Må·nas'sėh, Ē'phrȧ·im, and Simeon,
and as far as Naph'tȧ·lī, in their ruins[w]
round about, 7 he broke down the
altars, and beat the Ȧ·shē'rim and the
images into powder, and hewed down
all the incense altars throughout all
the land of Israel. Then he returned to
Jerusalem.

8 Now in the eighteenth year of his
reign, when he had purged the land
and the house, he sent Shā'phȧn the
son of Az·ȧ·lī'ȧh, and Mā·ȧ·sēi'ȧh the
governor of the city, and Jō'ȧh the son
of Jō'ȧ·haz, the recorder, to repair the
house of the LORD his God. 9 They
came to Hil·kī'ȧh the high priest and
delivered the money that had been
brought into the house of God, which
the Levites, the keepers of the threshold, had collected from Må·nas'sėh and
Ē'phrȧ·im and from all the remnant of
Israel and from all Judah and Benjamin
and from the inhabitants of Jerusalem.
10 They delivered it to the workmen
who had the oversight of the house of
the LORD; and the workmen who were
working in the house of the LORD gave
it for repairing and restoring the house.
11 They gave it to the carpenters and
the builders to buy quarried stone, and
timber for binders and beams for the
buildings which the kings of Judah
had let go to ruin. 12 And the men did
the work faithfully. Over them were
set Jā'hath and Ō·bȧ·dī'ȧh the Levites,
of the sons of Mė·rär'ī, and Zech·ȧ·rī'ȧh
and Me·shul'lȧm, of the sons of the
Kō'hȧ·thites, to have oversight. The
Levites, all who were skilful with
instruments of music, 13 were over the
burden bearers and directed all who
did work in every kind of service; and
some of the Levites were scribes, and
officials, and gatekeepers.

14 While they were bringing out
the money that had been brought into
the house of the LORD, Hil·kī'ȧh the
priest found the book of the law of the
LORD given through Moses. 15 Then
Hil·kī'ȧh said to Shā'phȧn the secretary, "I have found the book of the
law in the house of the LORD"; and
Hil·kī'ȧh gave the book to Shā'phȧn.
16 Shā'phȧn brought the book to the
king, and further reported to the king,
"All that was committed to your servants they are doing. 17 They have
emptied out the money that was found
in the house of the LORD and have
delivered it into the hand of the overseers and the workmen." 18 Then
Shā'phȧn the secretary told the king,
"Hil·kī'ȧh the priest has given me a
book." And Shaphan read it before
the king.

19 When the king heard the words
of the law he rent his clothes. 20 And
the king commanded Hil·kī'ȧh, Ȧ·hī'-
kam the son of Shā'phȧn, Ab'don the
son of Mī'cȧh, Shaphan the secretary,
and Ȧ·sāi'ȧh the king's servant, saying,
21 "Go, inquire of the LORD for me
and for those who are left in Israel and
in Judah, concerning the words of the
book that has been found; for great is
the wrath of the LORD that is poured
out on us, because our fathers have
not kept the word of the LORD, to do
according to all that is written in this
book."

22 So Hil·kī'ȧh and those whom the
king had sent[x] went to Hul'dȧh the
prophetess, the wife of Shal'lŭm the
son of Tok'hath, son of Has'rȧh,

[w] Heb uncertain [x] Syr Vg: Heb lacks *had sent*

34.1-2: 2 Kings 22.1-2. **34.3-7:** 2 Kings 23.4-20. **34.8-12:** 2 Kings 22.3-7.

keeper of the wardrobe (now she dwelt
in Jerusalem in the Second Quarter)
and spoke to her to that effect. 23And
she said to them, "Thus says the
LORD, the God of Israel: 'Tell the man
who sent you to me, 24 Thus says the
LORD, Behold, I will bring evil upon
this place and upon its inhabitants, all
the curses that are written in the book
which was read before the king of
Judah. 25 Because they have forsaken
me and have burned incense to other
gods, that they might provoke me to
anger with all the works of their hands,
therefore my wrath will be poured out
upon this place and will not be
quenched. 26 But to the king of Judah,
who sent you to inquire of the LORD,
thus shall you say to him, Thus says
the LORD, the God of Israel: Regarding the words which you have heard,
27 because your heart was penitent and
you humbled yourself before God
when you heard his words against this
place and its inhabitants, and you have
humbled yourself before me, and have
rent your clothes and wept before me,
I also have heard you, says the LORD.
28 Behold, I will gather you to your
fathers, and you shall be gathered to
your grave in peace, and your eyes
shall not see all the evil which I will
bring upon this place and its inhabitants.' " And they brought back word
to the king.

29 Then the king sent and gathered
together all the elders of Judah and
Jerusalem. 30And the king went up to
the house of the LORD, with all the men
of Judah and the inhabitants of Jerusalem and the priests and the Levites,
all the people both great and small;
and he read in their hearing all the
words of the book of the covenant
which had been found in the house of
the LORD. 31And the king stood in his
place and made a covenant before the
LORD, to walk after the LORD and to
keep his commandments and his
testimonies and his statutes, with all
his heart and all his soul, to perform
the words of the covenant that were
written in this book. 32 Then he made
all who were present in Jerusalem and
in Benjamin stand to it. And the inhabitants of Jerusalem did according
to the covenant of God, the God of
their fathers. 33And Jō·sī'ȧh took away
all the abominations from all the territory that belonged to the people of
Israel, and made all who were in Israel
serve the LORD their God. All his days
they did not turn away from following
the LORD the God of their fathers.

35 Jō·sī'ȧh kept a passover to the
LORD in Jerusalem; and they
killed the passover lamb on the fourteenth day of the first month. 2 He
appointed the priests to their offices
and encouraged them in the service of
the house of the LORD. 3And he said
to the Levites who taught all Israel
and who were holy to the LORD, "Put
the holy ark in the house which
Solomon the son of David, king of
Israel, built; you need no longer carry
it upon your shoulders. Now serve the
LORD your God and his people Israel.
4 Prepare yourselves according to your
fathers' houses by your divisions, following the directions of David king of
Israel and the directions of Solomon
his son. 5And stand in the holy place
according to the groupings of the
fathers' houses of your brethren the
lay people, and let there be for each a
part of a father's house of the Levites.[y]
6And kill the passover lamb, and
sanctify yourselves, and prepare for
your brethren, to do according to the
word of the LORD by Moses."

7 Then Jō·sī'ȧh contributed to the
lay people, as passover offerings for all
that were present, lambs and kids from
the flock to the number of thirty thousand, and three thousand bulls; these
were from the king's possessions. 8And
his princes contributed willingly to the
people, to the priests, and to the Levites. Hil·kī'ȧh, Zech·ȧ·rī'ȧh, and Je-
hī'el, the chief officers of the house of
God, gave to the priests for the passover offerings two thousand six hundred lambs and kids and three hundred
bulls. 9 Con·ȧ·nī'ȧh also, and She-
māi'ȧh and Nė·than'el his brothers,
and Hash·ȧ·bī'ȧh and Je-ī'el and Jō'zȧ-
bad, the chiefs of the Levites, gave to
the Levites for the passover offerings
five thousand lambs and kids and five
hundred bulls.

10 When the service had been prepared for, the priests stood in their
place, and the Levites in their divisions
according to the king's command.
11And they killed the passover lamb,
and the priests sprinkled the blood
which they received from them while

[y] Heb obscure
35.1-19: 2 Kings 23.21-23.

the Levites flayed the victims. 12 And
they set aside the burnt offerings that
they might distribute them according
to the groupings of the fathers' houses
of the lay people, to offer to the LORD,
as it is written in the book of Moses.
And so they did with the bulls. 13 And
they roasted the passover lamb with
fire according to the ordinance; and
they boiled the holy offerings in pots,
in caldrons, and in pans, and carried
them quickly to all the lay people.
14 And afterward they prepared for
themselves and for the priests, because
the priests the sons of Aaron were
busied in offering the burnt offerings
and the fat parts until night; so the
Levites prepared for themselves and
for the priests the sons of Aaron.
15 The singers, the sons of Ā'saph,
were in their place according to the
command of David, and Asaph, and
Hē'mȧn, and Je·dü'thŭn the king's
seer; and the gatekeepers were at each
gate; they did not need to depart from
their service, for their brethren the
Levites prepared for them.

16 So all the service of the LORD
was prepared that day, to keep the
passover and to offer burnt offerings
on the altar of the LORD, according to
the command of King Jō·sī'ȧh. 17 And
the people of Israel who were present
kept the passover at that time, and
the feast of unleavened bread seven
days. 18 No passover like it had been
kept in Israel since the days of Samuel
the prophet; none of the kings of Israel
had kept such a passover as was kept
by Jō·sī'ȧh, and the priests and the
Levites, and all Judah and Israel who
were present, and the inhabitants of
Jerusalem. 19 In the eighteenth year
of the reign of Jō·sī'ȧh this passover
was kept.

20 After all this, when Jō·sī'ȧh had
prepared the temple, Nē'cō king of
Egypt went up to fight at Cär'che·mish
on the Eū·phrā'tēs and Jō·sī'ȧh went
out against him. 21 But he sent envoys
to him, saying, "What have we to do
with each other, king of Judah? I am
not coming against you this day, but
against the house with which I am at
war; and God has commanded me to
make haste. Cease opposing God, who
is with me, lest he destroy you."
22 Nevertheless Jō·sī'ȧh would not
turn away from him, but disguised
himself in order to fight with him. He
did not listen to the words of Nē'cō
from the mouth of God, but joined
battle in the plain of Mė·gid'dō. 23 And
the archers shot King Jō·sī'ȧh; and the
king said to his servants, "Take me
away, for I am badly wounded." 24 So
his servants took him out of the chariot
and carried him in his second chariot
and brought him to Jerusalem. And
he died, and was buried in the tombs
of his fathers. All Judah and Jerusalem
mourned for Jō·sī'ȧh. 25 Jeremiah also
uttered a lament for Jō·sī'ȧh; and all
the singing men and singing women
have spoken of Josiah in their laments
to this day. They made these an ordinance in Israel; behold, they are
written in the Laments. 26 Now the
rest of the acts of Jō·sī'ȧh, and his good
deeds according to what is written in
the law of the LORD, 27 and his acts,
first and last, behold, they are written
in the Book of the Kings of Israel and
Judah.

36 The people of the land took
Je·hō'ȧ·haz the son of Jō·sī'ȧh
and made him king in his father's stead
in Jerusalem. 2 Je·hō'ȧ·haz was twenty-
three years old when he began to
reign; and he reigned three months in
Jerusalem. 3 Then the king of Egypt
deposed him in Jerusalem and laid
upon the land a tribute of a hundred
talents of silver and a talent of gold.
4 And the king of Egypt made E·lī'ȧ-
kim his brother king over Judah and
Jerusalem, and changed his name to
Je·hoi'ȧ·kim; but Nē'cō took Je·hō'ȧ-
haz his brother and carried him to
Egypt.

5 Je·hoi'ȧ·kim was twenty-five years
old when he began to reign, and he
reigned eleven years in Jerusalem. He
did what was evil in the sight of the
LORD his God. 6 Against him came up
Ne·bů·chȧd·nez'zȧr king of Babylon,
and bound him in fetters to take him
to Babylon. 7 Ne·bů·chȧd·nez'zȧr also
carried part of the vessels of the house
of the LORD to Babylon and put them
in his palace in Babylon. 8 Now the
rest of the acts of Je·hoi'ȧ·kim, and
the abominations which he did, and
what was found against him, behold,
they are written in the Book of the
Kings of Israel and Judah; and Jehoi'ȧ·chin his son reigned in his stead.

9 Je·hoi'ȧ·chin was eight years old
when he began to reign, and he reigned
three months and ten days in Jeru-

36.1-4: 2 Kings 23.30-34. **36.5-8:** 2 Kings 23.36-24.6. **36.9-10:** 2 Kings 24.8-17.

salem. He did what was evil in the
sight of the LORD. 10 In the spring of
the year King Ne·bu̇·chȧd·nez′zȧr sent
and brought him to Babylon, with the
precious vessels of the house of the
LORD, and made his brother Zed·ė-
kī′ȧh king over Judah and Jerusalem.
11 Zed·ė·kī′ȧh was twenty-one years
old when he began to reign, and he
reigned eleven years in Jerusalem.
12 He did what was evil in the sight of
the LORD his God. He did not humble
himself before Jeremiah the prophet,
who spoke from the mouth of the
LORD. 13 He also rebelled against King
Ne·bu̇·chȧd·nez′zȧr, who had made
him swear by God; he stiffened his
neck and hardened his heart against
turning to the LORD, the God of Israel.
14 All the leading priests and the people
likewise were exceedingly unfaithful,
following all the abominations of the
nations; and they polluted the house
of the LORD which he had hallowed in
Jerusalem.
15 The LORD, the God of their
fathers, sent persistently to them by
his messengers, because he had compassion on his people and on his dwelling place; 16 but they kept mocking
the messengers of God, despising his
words, and scoffing at his prophets, till
the wrath of the LORD rose against his
people, till there was no remedy.
17 Therefore he brought up against
them the king of the Chal·dē′ȧns, who
slew their young men with the sword
in the house of their sanctuary, and
had no compassion on young man or
virgin, old man or aged; he gave them
all into his hand. 18 And all the vessels
of the house of God, great and small,
and the treasures of the house of the
LORD, and the treasures of the king
and of his princes, all these he brought
to Babylon. 19 And they burned the
house of God, and broke down the wall
of Jerusalem, and burned all its palaces
with fire, and destroyed all its precious
vessels. 20 He took into exile in Babylon those who had escaped from the
sword, and they became servants to
him and to his sons until the establishment of the kingdom of Persia, 21 to
fulfil the word of the LORD by the
mouth of Jeremiah, until the land had
enjoyed its sabbaths. All the days that
it lay desolate it kept sabbath, to fulfil
seventy years.
22 Now in the first year of Cyrus
king of Persia, that the word of the
LORD by the mouth of Jeremiah might
be accomplished, the LORD stirred up
the spirit of Cyrus king of Persia so
that he made a proclamation throughout all his kingdom and also put it in
writing: 23 "Thus says Cyrus king of
Persia, 'The LORD, the God of heaven,
has given me all the kingdoms of the
earth, and he has charged me to build
him a house at Jerusalem, which is in
Judah. Whoever is among you of all
his people, may the LORD his God be
with him. Let him go up.' "

THE BOOK OF EZRA

1 In the first year of Cyrus king of
Persia, that the word of the LORD
by the mouth of Jeremiah might be
accomplished, the LORD stirred up the
spirit of Cyrus king of Persia so that
he made a proclamation throughout
all his kingdom and also put it in
writing:
2 "Thus says Cyrus king of Persia:
The LORD, the God of heaven, has
given me all the kingdoms of the earth,
and he has charged me to build him a
house at Jerusalem, which is in Judah.
3 Whoever is among you of all his people, may his God be with him, and let
him go up to Jerusalem, which is in
Judah, and rebuild the house of the
LORD, the God of Israel—he is the
God who is in Jerusalem; 4 and let
each survivor, in whatever place he
sojourns, be assisted by the men of his
place with silver and gold, with goods

36.11-21: 2 Kings 24.18-25.21. **36.22-23**: Ezra 1.1-3.
1.1-3: 2 Chron 36.22-23; Ezra 5.13; 6.3.

and with beasts, besides freewill offerings for the house of God which is in
Jerusalem."
5 Then rose up the heads of the
fathers' houses of Judah and Benjamin,
and the priests and the Levites, every
one whose spirit God had stirred to go
up to rebuild the house of the LORD
which is in Jerusalem; 6 and all who
were about them aided them with
vessels of silver, with gold, with goods,
with beasts, and with costly wares,
besides all that was freely offered.
7 Cyrus the king also brought out the
vessels of the house of the LORD which
Ne·bu̇·chȧd·nez'zȧr had carried away
from Jerusalem and placed in the
house of his gods. 8 Cyrus king of
Persia brought these out in charge of
Mith'rė·dath the treasurer, who
counted them out to Shesh-baz'zȧr
the prince of Judah. 9 And this was the
number of them: a thousand[a] basins
of gold, a thousand basins of silver,
twenty-nine censers, 10 thirty bowls of
gold, two thousand[b] four hundred and
ten bowls of silver, and a thousand
other vessels; 11 all the vessels of gold
and of silver were five thousand four
hundred and sixty-nine.[c] All these did
Shesh-baz'zȧr bring up, when the
exiles were brought up from Babylonia
to Jerusalem.

2 Now these were the people of the
province who came up out of the
captivity of those exiles whom Ne·bu̇·
chȧd·nez'zȧr the king of Babylon had
carried captive to Babylonia; they returned to Jerusalem and Judah, each
to his own town. 2 They came with
Ze·rub'bȧ·bel, Jesh'ü·ȧ, Nē·hė·mī'ȧh,
Se·räi'ȧh, Rē-el·āi'ȧh, Môr'de·cäi, Bil'-
shan, Mis'pȧr, Big'väi, Rē'hu̇m, and
Bā'ȧ·nȧh.
The number of the men of the people of Israel: 3 the sons of Pā'rosh, two
thousand one hundred and seventy-
two. 4 The sons of Sheph·ȧ·tī'ȧh, three
hundred and seventy-two. 5 The sons
of Ā'rȧh, seven hundred and seventy-
five. 6 The sons of Pā'hath-mō'ab,
namely the sons of Jesh'ü·ȧ and Jō'ab,
two thousand eight hundred and
twelve. 7 The sons of Ē'lȧm, one thousand two hundred and fifty-four. 8 The
sons of Zat'tü, nine hundred and
forty-five. 9 The sons of Zac'cäi, seven
hundred and sixty. 10 The sons of
Bā'nī, six hundred and forty-two.
11 The sons of Bē'bäi, six hundred and
twenty-three. 12 The sons of Az'gad,
one thousand two hundred and twenty-two. 13 The sons of Ad·ȯ·nī'kȧm, six
hundred and sixty-six. 14 The sons of
Big'väi, two thousand and fifty-six.
15 The sons of Ā'din, four hundred and
fifty-four. 16 The sons of Ā'tėr, namely
of Hez·ė·kī'ȧh, ninety-eight. 17 The
sons of Bē'zäi, three hundred and
twenty-three. 18 The sons of Jō'rȧh,
one hundred and twelve. 19 The sons
of Hā'shu̇m, two hundred and twenty-
three. 20 The sons of Gib'bär, ninety-
five. 21 The sons of Bethlehem, one
hundred and twenty-three. 22 The men
of Nė·toph'ȧh, fifty-six. 23 The men of
An'ȧ·thoth, one hundred and twenty-
eight. 24 The sons of Az'mȧ·veth,
forty-two. 25 The sons of Kīr'i·ath-
âr'im, Che·phī'rȧh, and Bė·ēr'ȯth,
seven hundred and forty-three. 26 The
sons of Rā'mȧh and Gē'bȧ, six hundred
and twenty-one. 27 The men of Mich'-
mȧs, one hundred and twenty-two.
28 The men of Beth'ėl and Ā̈i, two
hundred and twenty-three. 29 The
sons of Nē'bō, fifty-two. 30 The sons
of Mag'bish, one hundred and fifty-
six. 31 The sons of the other Ē'lȧm,
one thousand two hundred and fifty-
four. 32 The sons of Hā'rim, three hundred and twenty. 33 The sons of Lod,
Hā'did, and Ō'nō, seven hundred and
twenty-five. 34 The sons of Jericho,
three hundred and forty-five. 35 The
sons of Se·nā'ȧh, three thousand six
hundred and thirty.
36 The priests: the sons of Je·däi'ȧh,
of the house of Jesh'ü·ȧ, nine hundred
and seventy-three. 37 The sons of
Im'mėr, one thousand and fifty-two.
38 The sons of Pash'hûr, one thousand
two hundred and forty-seven. 39 The
sons of Hā'rim, one thousand and
seventeen.
40 The Levites: the sons of Jesh'ü·ȧ
and Kad'mi-el, of the sons of Hod·ȧ·
vī'ȧh, seventy-four. 41 The singers: the
sons of Ā'saph, one hundred and
twenty-eight. 42 The sons of the gatekeepers: the sons of Shal'lu̇m, the sons
of Ā'tėr, the sons of Tal'mȯn, the sons
of Ak'ku̇b, the sons of Hȧ·tī'tȧ, and
the sons of Shō'bäi, in all one hundred
and thirty-nine.
43 The temple servants:[d] the sons

[a] 1 Esdras 2.13: Heb *thirty* [b] 1 Esdras 2.13: Heb *of a second sort*
[c] 1 Esdras 2.14: Heb *five thousand four hundred* [d] Heb *nethinim*
2.1-70: Neh 7.6-73.

of Zī'hȧ, the sons of Hȧ·sü'phȧ, the
sons of Tab·bā'oth, 44 the sons of
Kē'ros, the sons of Sī'ȧ·hȧ, the sons of
Pā'don, 45 the sons of Le·bā'nȧh, the
sons of Hag'ȧ·bȧh, the sons of Ak'ku̇b,
46 the sons of Hā'gab, the sons of
Sham'lāi, the sons of Hā'nȧn, 47 the
sons of Gid'del, the sons of Gā'här,
the sons of Rē-äi'ȧh, 48 the sons of
Rē'zin, the sons of Ne·kō'dȧ, the sons
of Gaz'zȧm, 49 the sons of Uz'zȧ, the
sons of Pȧ·sē'ȧh, the sons of Bē'säi,
50 the sons of As'nȧh, the sons of Me-
ü'nim, the sons of Ne·phī'sim, 51 the
sons of Bak'bu̇k, the sons of Hȧ·kū'phȧ,
the sons of Här'hūr, 52 the sons of
Baz'lu̇th, the sons of Me·hī'dȧ, the
sons of Här'shȧ, 53 the sons of Bär'kos,
the sons of Sis'ėr·ȧ, the sons of Tē'mȧh,
54 the sons of Ne·zī'ȧh, and the sons
of Hȧ·tī'phȧ.

55 The sons of Solomon's servants:
the sons of Sō'täi, the sons of Has·sō'-
phė·reth, the sons of Pe·rü'dȧ, 56 the
sons of Jā'ȧ·lȧh, the sons of Där'kon,
the sons of Gid'del, 57 the sons of
Sheph·ȧ·tī'ȧh, the sons of Hat'til, the
sons of Pō'chė·reth-haz·zė·bā'im, and
the sons of Ā'mī.

58 All the temple servants[d] and the
sons of Solomon's servants were three
hundred and ninety-two.

59 The following were those who
came up from Tel-mē'lȧh, Tel-här'shȧ,
Chē'ru̇b, Ad'dȧn, and Im'mėr, though
they could not prove their fathers'
houses or their descent, whether they
belonged to Israel: 60 the sons of De-
läi'ȧh, the sons of Tō·bī'ȧh, and the
sons of Ne·kō'dȧ, six hundred and
fifty-two. 61 Also, of the sons of the
priests: the sons of Hȧ·bāi'ȧh, the sons
of Hak'koz, and the sons of Bär·zil'läi
(who had taken a wife from the
daughters of Barzillai the Gileadite,
and was called by their name). 62 These
sought their registration among those
enrolled in the genealogies, but they
were not found there, and so they were
excluded from the priesthood as unclean; 63 the governor told them that
they were not to partake of the most
holy food, until there should be a priest
to consult Ū'rim and Thum'mim.

64 The whole assembly together
was forty-two thousand three hundred
and sixty, 65 besides their menservants
and maidservants, of whom there were
seven thousand three hundred and
thirty-seven; and they had two hundred male and female singers. 66 Their
horses were seven hundred and thirty-
six, their mules were two hundred and
forty-five, 67 their camels were four
hundred and thirty-five, and their asses
were six thousand seven hundred and
twenty.

68 Some of the heads of families,
when they came to the house of the
LORD which is in Jerusalem, made
freewill offerings for the house of God,
to erect it on its site; 69 according to
their ability they gave to the treasury
of the work sixty-one thousand darics
of gold, five thousand minas of silver,
and one hundred priests' garments.

70 The priests, the Levites, and
some of the people lived in Jerusalem
and its vicinity;[e] and the singers, the
gatekeepers, and the temple servants
lived in their towns, and all Israel in
their towns.

3 When the seventh month came,
and the sons of Israel were in the
towns, the people gathered as one man
to Jerusalem. 2 Then arose Jesh'ü·ȧ
the son of Jō'zȧ·dak, with his fellow
priests, and Ze·rub'bȧ·bel the son of
She-al'ti-el with his kinsmen, and they
built the altar of the God of Israel, to
offer burnt offerings upon it, as it is
written in the law of Moses the man
of God. 3 They set the altar in its
place, for fear was upon them because
of the peoples of the lands, and they
offered burnt offerings upon it to the
LORD, burnt offerings morning and
evening. 4 And they kept the feast of
booths, as it is written, and offered the
daily burnt offerings by number according to the ordinance, as each day
required, 5 and after that the continual
burnt offerings, the offerings at the
new moon and at all the appointed
feasts of the LORD, and the offerings
of every one who made a freewill offering to the LORD. 6 From the first day
of the seventh month they began to
offer burnt offerings to the LORD. But
the foundation of the temple of the
LORD was not yet laid. 7 So they gave
money to the masons and the carpenters, and food, drink, and oil to the
Sī·dō'ni·ȧns and the Tyr'i·ȧns to bring
cedar trees from Lebanon to the sea,
to Jop'pȧ, according to the grant which
they had from Cyrus king of Persia.

8 Now in the second year of their
coming to the house of God at Jerusalem, in the second month, Ze·rub'-

[d] Heb *nethinim* [e] 1 Esdras 5.46: Heb lacks *lived in Jerusalem and its vicinity*

bȧ·bel the son of She-al′ti-el and
Jesh′ü·ȧ the son of Jō′zȧ·dak made a
beginning, together with the rest of
their brethren, the priests and the
Levites and all who had come to Jerusalem from the captivity. They appointed the Levites, from twenty years
old and upward, to have the oversight
of the work of the house of the LORD.
9 And Jesh′ü·ȧ with his sons and his
kinsmen, and Kad′mi-el and his sons,
the sons of Judah, together took the
oversight of the workmen in the house
of God, along with the sons of Hen′ȧ-
dad and the Levites, their sons and
kinsmen.

10 And when the builders laid the
foundation of the temple of the LORD,
the priests in their vestments came
forward with trumpets, and the Levites, the sons of Ā′saph, with cymbals,
to praise the LORD, according to the
directions of David king of Israel;
11 and they sang responsively, praising
and giving thanks to the LORD,

"For he is good,
for his steadfast love endures for
ever toward Israel."

And all the people shouted with a
great shout, when they praised the
LORD, because the foundation of the
house of the LORD was laid. 12 But
many of the priests and Levites and
heads of fathers' houses, old men who
had seen the first house, wept with a
loud voice when they saw the foundation of this house being laid, though
many shouted aloud for joy; 13 so that
the people could not distinguish the
sound of the joyful shout from the
sound of the people's weeping, for the
people shouted with a great shout, and
the sound was heard afar.

4 Now when the adversaries of
Judah and Benjamin heard that
the returned exiles were building a
temple to the LORD, the God of Israel,
2 they approached Ze·rub′bȧ·bel and
the heads of fathers' houses and said
to them, "Let us build with you; for
we worship your God as you do, and
we have been sacrificing to him ever
since the days of Ē′sär-had′dȯn king of
Assyria who brought us here." 3 But
Ze·rub′bȧ·bel, Jesh′ü·ȧ, and the rest
of the heads of fathers' houses in Israel
said to them, "You have nothing to do
with us in building a house to our God;
but we alone will build to the LORD,
the God of Israel, as King Cyrus the
king of Persia has commanded us."

4 Then the people of the land discouraged the people of Judah, and
made them afraid to build, 5 and hired
counselors against them to frustrate
their purpose, all the days of Cyrus
king of Persia, even until the reign of
Dȧ·rī′ůs king of Persia.

6 And in the reign of Ȧ·haṡ′ū-ē′růs,
in the beginning of his reign, they
wrote an accusation against the inhabitants of Judah and Jerusalem.

7 And in the days of Är-tȧ-x̆ērx′ēṡ,
Bish′lȧm and Mith′rė·dath and Tā′-
bē-ėl and the rest of their associates
wrote to Ar-ta-xerxes king of Persia;
the letter was written in Aramaic and
translated.[f] 8 Rē′hům the commander
and Shim′shäi the scribe wrote a letter
against Jerusalem to Är-tȧ-x̆ērx′ēṡ
the king as follows— 9 then wrote
Rē′hům the commander, Shim′shäi
the scribe, and the rest of their associates, the judges, the governors, the
officials, the Persians, the men of
Ē′rech, the Babylonians, the men of
Su′sȧ, that is, the Ē′lȧm·ītes, 10 and
the rest of the nations whom the great
and noble Os·nap′pȧr deported and
settled in the cities of Sȧ·mâr′i·ȧ and
in the rest of the province Beyond the
River, and now 11 this is a copy of the
letter that they sent—"To Är-tȧ-
x̆ērx′ēṡ the king: Your servants, the
men of the province Beyond the River,
send greeting. And now 12 be it known
to the king that the Jews who came up
from you to us have gone to Jerusalem.
They are rebuilding that rebellious
and wicked city; they are finishing the
walls and repairing the foundations.
13 Now be it known to the king that,
if this city is rebuilt and the walls
finished, they will not pay tribute,
custom, or toll, and the royal revenue
will be impaired. 14 Now because we
eat the salt of the palace and it is not
fitting for us to witness the king's dishonor, therefore we send and inform
the king, 15 in order that search may
be made in the book of the records of
your fathers. You will find in the book
of the records and learn that this city
is a rebellious city, hurtful to kings
and provinces, and that sedition was
stirred up in it from of old. That was
why this city was laid waste. 16 We
make known to the king that, if this

[f] Heb adds *in Aramaic*, indicating that 4.8-6.18 is in Aramaic. Another interpretation is *The letter was written in the Aramaic script and set forth in the Aramaic language.*

city is rebuilt and its walls finished,
you will then have no possession in the
province Beyond the River."
17 The king sent an answer: "To
Rē'hụm the commander and Shim'-
shäi the scribe and the rest of their
associates who live in Sȧ·mâr'i·ȧ and
in the rest of the province Beyond the
River, greeting. And now 18 the letter
which you sent to us has been plainly
read before me. 19 And I made a decree,
and search has been made, and it has
been found that this city from of old
has risen against kings, and that
rebellion and sedition have been made
in it. 20 And mighty kings have been
over Jerusalem, who ruled over the
whole province Beyond the River, to
whom tribute, custom, and toll were
paid. 21 Therefore make a decree that
these men be made to cease, and that
this city be not rebuilt, until a decree
is made by me. 22 And take care not
to be slack in this matter; why
should damage grow to the hurt of the
king?"
23 Then, when the copy of King
Ar-tȧ-xẽrx'ēṡ' letter was read before
Rē'hụm and Shim'shäi the scribe and
their associates, they went in haste to
the Jews at Jerusalem and by force
and power made them cease. 24 Then
the work on the house of God which
is in Jerusalem stopped: and it ceased
until the second year of the reign of
Dȧ·rī'ụs king of Persia.

5 Now the Prophets, Hag'gäi and
Zech·ȧ·rī'ȧh the son of Id'dō,
prophesied to the Jews who were in
Judah and Jerusalem, in the name of
the God of Israel who was over them.
2 Then Ze·rub'bȧ·bel the son of She-
al'ti-el and Jesh'ü·ȧ the son of Jō'zȧ-
dak arose and began to rebuild the
house of God which is in Jerusalem;
and with them were the prophets of
God, helping them.
3 At the same time Tat'tė·näi the
governor of the province Beyond the
River and Shē'thär-boz'ė·näi and their
associates came to them and spoke to
them thus, "Who gave you a decree
to build this house and to finish this
structure?" 4 They[g] also asked them
this, "What are the names of the men
who are building this building?" 5 But
the eye of their God was upon the
elders of the Jews, and they did not
stop them till a report should reach
Dȧ·rī'ụs and then answer be returned
by letter concerning it.
6 The copy of the letter which
Tat'tė·näi the governor of the province
Beyond the River and Shē'thär-boz'ė-
näi and his associates the governors
who were in the province Beyond the
River sent to Dȧ·rī'ụs the king; 7 they
sent him a report, in which was written
as follows: "To Dȧ·rī'ụs the king, all
peace. 8 Be it known to the king that
we went to the province of Judah, to
the house of the great God. It is being
built with huge stones, and timber is
laid in the walls; this work goes on
diligently and prospers in their hands.
9 Then we asked those elders and
spoke to them thus, 'Who gave you a
decree to build this house and to finish
this structure?' 10 We also asked them
their names, for your information, that
we might write down the names of the
men at their head. 11 And this was their
reply to us: 'We are the servants of the
God of heaven and earth, and we are
rebuilding the house that was built
many years ago, which a great king of
Israel built and finished. 12 But because our fathers had angered the God
of heaven, he gave them into the hand
of Ne·bụ·chȧd·nez'zȧr king of Babylon,
the Chal·dē'ȧn, who destroyed this
house and carried away the people to
Babylonia. 13 However in the first year
of Cyrus king of Babylon, Cyrus the
king made a decree that this house of
God should be rebuilt. 14 And the gold
and silver vessels of the house of God,
which Ne·bụ·chȧd·nez'zȧr had taken
out of the temple that was in Jerusalem
and brought into the temple of Babylon, these Cyrus the king took out of
the temple of Babylon, and they were
delivered to one whose name was
Shesh-baz'zȧr, whom he had made
governor; 15 and he said to him, "Take
these vessels, go and put them in the
temple which is in Jerusalem, and let
the house of God be rebuilt on its
site." 16 Then this Shesh-baz'zȧr came
and laid the foundations of the house
of God which is in Jerusalem; and
from that time until now it has been
in building, and it is not yet finished.'
17 Therefore, if it seem good to the
king, let search be made in the royal
archives there in Babylon, to see
whether a decree was issued by Cyrus
the king for the rebuilding of this

[g] Gk Syr: Aramaic *We*
5.1: Hag 1.1; Zech 1.1. 5.13: Ezra 1.1; 6.3.

house of God in Jerusalem. And let
the king send us his pleasure in this
matter."

6 Then Dȧ·rī'ŭs the king made a
decree, and search was made in
Babylonia, in the house of the archives
where the documents were stored.
2And in Ec·bat'ȧ·nȧ, the capital which
is in the province of Media, a scroll
was found on which this was written:
"A record. 3 In the first year of Cyrus
the king, Cyrus the king issued a
decree: Concerning the house of God
at Jerusalem, let the house be rebuilt,
the place where sacrifices are offered
and burnt offerings are brought; its
height shall be sixty cubits and its
breadth sixty cubits, 4 with three
courses of great stones and one course
of timber; let the cost be paid from the
royal treasury. 5And also let the gold
and silver vessels of the house of God,
which Ne·bŭ·chȧd·nez'zȧr took out of
the temple that is in Jerusalem and
brought to Babylon, be restored and
brought back to the temple which is
in Jerusalem, each to its place; you
shall put them in the house of God."
6 "Now therefore, Tat'tė·näi, governor of the province Beyond the
River, Shē'thär-boz'ė·näi, and your
associates the governors who are in the
province Beyond the River, keep away;
7 let the work on this house of God
alone; let the governor of the Jews
and the elders of the Jews rebuild this
house of God on its site. 8 Moreover
I make a decree regarding what you
shall do for these elders of the Jews for
the rebuilding of this house of God;
the cost is to be paid to these men in
full and without delay from the royal
revenue, the tribute of the province
from Beyond the River. 9And whatever is needed—young bulls, rams, or
sheep for burnt offerings to the God
of heaven, wheat, salt, wine, or oil, as
the priests at Jerusalem require—let
that be given to them day by day without fail, 10 that they may offer pleasing
sacrifices to the God of heaven, and
pray for the life of the king and his
sons. 11Also I make a decree that if any
one alters this edict, a beam shall be
pulled out of his house, and he shall
be impaled upon it, and his house shall
be made a dunghill. 12 May the God
who has caused his name to dwell there
overthrow any king or people that
shall put forth a hand to alter this, or
to destroy this house of God which is
in Jerusalem. I Dȧ·rī'ŭs make a decree;
let it be done with all diligence."
13 Then, according to the word sent
by Dȧ·rī'ŭs the king, Tat'tė·näi, the
governor of the province Beyond the
River, Shē'thär-boz'ė·näi, and their
associates did with all diligence what
Darius the king had ordered. 14And
the elders of the Jews built and prospered, through the prophesying of
Hag'gäi the prophet and Zech·ȧ·rī'ȧh
the son of Id'dō. They finished their
building by command of the God of
Israel and by decree of Cyrus and
Dȧ·rī'ŭs and Är-tȧ-x̌ẽrx'ēš king of
Persia; 15 and this house was finished
on the third day of the month of
Ȧ·där', in the sixth year of the reign
of Dȧ·rī'ŭs the king.
16 And the people of Israel, the
priests and the Levites, and the rest
of the returned exiles, celebrated the
dedication of this house of God with
joy. 17 They offered at the dedication
of this house of God one hundred bulls,
two hundred rams, four hundred
lambs, and as a sin offering for all
Israel twelve he-goats, according to
the number of the tribes of Israel.
18And they set the priests in their
divisions and the Levites in their
courses, for the service of God at
Jerusalem, as it is written in the book
of Moses.
19 On the fourteenth day of the
first month the returned exiles kept
the passover. 20 For the priests and
the Levites had purified themselves
together; all of them were clean. So
they killed the passover lamb for all
the returned exiles, for their fellow
priests, and for themselves; 21 it was
eaten by the people of Israel who had
returned from exile, and also by every
one who had joined them and separated
himself from the pollutions of the
peoples of the land to worship the
LORD, the God of Israel. 22And they
kept the feast of unleavened bread
seven days with joy; for the LORD had
made them joyful, and had turned the
heart of the king of Assyria to them,
so that he aided them in the work of
the house of God, the God of Israel.

7 Now after this, in the reign of
Är-tȧ-x̌ẽrx'ēš king of Persia, Ezra
the son of Se·räi'ȧh, son of Hil·kī'ȧh,
2 son of Shal'lŭm, son of Zā'dok, son
of Ȧ·hī'tŭb, 3 son of Am·ȧ·rī'ȧh, son of

6.3: Ezra 1.1; 5.13.

Az·ȧ·rī′ȧh, son of Me·rā′ioth, 4 son of
Zer·ȧ·hī′ȧh, son of Uz′zī, son of Buk′-
kī, 5 son of Ab·i·shü′ȧ, son of Phin′ė-
hȧs, son of El·ē·ā′zȧr, son of Aaron the
chief priest—6 this Ezra went up from
Babylonia. He was a scribe skilled in
the law of Moses which the LORD the
God of Israel had given; and the king
granted him all that he asked, for the
hand of the LORD his God was upon
him.
7 And there went up also to Jerusalem, in the seventh year of Är-tȧ-
xērx′ēṡ the king, some of the people
of Israel, and some of the priests and
Levites, the singers and gatekeepers,
and the temple servants. 8And he came
to Jerusalem in the fifth month, which
was in the seventh year of the king;
9 for on the first day of the first month
he began[h] to go up from Babylonia,
and on the first day of the fifth month
he came to Jerusalem, for the good
hand of his God was upon him. 10 For
Ezra had set his heart to study the law
of the LORD, and to do it, and to teach
his statutes and ordinances in Israel.
11 This is a copy of the letter which
King Är-tȧ-xērx′ēṡ gave to Ezra the
priest, the scribe, learned in matters of
the commandments of the LORD and
his statutes for Israel: 12 "Är-tȧ-xērx′-
ēṡ, king of kings, to Ezra the priest,
the scribe of the law of the God of
heaven.[x] And now 13 I make a decree
that any one of the people of Israel or
the priests or Levites in my kingdom,
who freely offers to go to Jerusalem,
may go with you. 14 For you are sent
by the king and his seven counselors
to make inquiries about Judah and
Jerusalem according to the law of your
God, which is in your hand, 15 and
also to convey the silver and gold
which the king and his counselors
have freely offered to the God of
Israel, whose dwelling is in Jerusalem,
16 with all the silver and gold which
you shall find in the whole province of
Babylonia, and with the freewill offerings of the people and the priests,
vowed willingly for the house of their
God which is in Jerusalem. 17 With
this money, then, you shall with all
diligence buy bulls, rams, and lambs,
with their cereal offerings and their
drink offerings, and you shall offer
them upon the altar of the house of
your God which is in Jerusalem.
18 Whatever seems good to you and
your brethren to do with the rest of
the silver and gold, you may do,
according to the will of your God.
19 The vessels that have been given
you for the service of the house of
your God, you shall deliver before the
God of Jerusalem. 20And whatever
else is required for the house of your
God, which you have occasion to provide, you may provide it out of the
king's treasury.
21 "And I, Är-tȧ-xērx′ēṡ the king,
make a decree to all the treasurers in
the province Beyond the River: Whatever Ezra the priest, the scribe of the
law of the God of heaven, requires of
you, be it done with all diligence, 22 up
to a hundred talents of silver, a hundred cors of wheat, a hundred baths
of wine, a hundred baths of oil, and
salt without prescribing how much.
23 Whatever is commanded by the God
of heaven, let it be done in full for the
house of the God of heaven, lest his
wrath be against the realm of the king
and his sons. 24 We also notify you
that it shall not be lawful to impose
tribute, custom, or toll upon any one
of the priests, the Levites, the singers,
the doorkeepers, the temple servants,
or other servants of this house of God.
25 "And you, Ezra, according to the
wisdom of your God which is in your
hand, appoint magistrates and judges
who may judge all the people in the
province Beyond the River, all such
as know the laws of your God; and
those who do not know them, you
shall teach. 26 Whoever will not obey
the law of your God and the law of the
king, let judgment be strictly executed
upon him, whether for death or for
banishment or for confiscation of his
goods or for imprisonment."
27 Blessed be the LORD, the God
of our fathers, who put such a thing as
this into the heart of the king, to
beautify the house of the LORD which
is in Jerusalem, 28 and who extended
to me his steadfast love before the
king and his counselors, and before all
the king's mighty officers. I took
courage, for the hand of the LORD my
God was upon me, and I gathered
leading men from Israel to go up with
me.
8 These are the heads of their
fathers' houses, and this is the
genealogy of those who went up with
me from Babylonia, in the reign of

[h] Vg See Syr: Heb *that was the foundation of the going up* [x] Aram adds a word of uncertain meaning

Ar-tȧ-xĕrx'ēs the king: 2 Of the sons
of Phin'ė·hȧs, Gĕr'shȯm. Of the sons
of Ith'ȧ·mär, Daniel. Of the sons of
David, Hat'tȯsh, 3 of the sons of Shec-
ȧ·nī'ȧh. Of the sons of Pā'rosh, Zech-
ȧ·rī'ȧh, with whom were registered one
hundred and fifty men. 4 Of the sons
of Pā'hath-mō'ab, El'i·ē-hō-ē'näi the
son of Zer·ȧ·hī'ȧh, and with him two
hundred men. 5 Of the sons of Zat'tü,[i]
Shec·ȧ·nī'ȧh the son of Jȧ·hā'zi·el, and
with him three hundred men. 6 Of the
sons of Ā'din, Ē'bed the son of Jonathan, and with him fifty men. 7 Of the
sons of Ē'lȧm, Je·shā'iȧh the son of
Ath·ȧ·lī'ȧh, and with him seventy men.
8 Of the sons of Sheph·ȧ·tī'ȧh, Zeb·ȧ-
dī'ȧh the son of Michael, and with him
eighty men. 9 Of the sons of Jō'ab,
Ō·bȧ·dī'ȧh the son of Je·hī'el, and with
him two hundred and eighteen men.
10 Of the sons of Bā'nī,[j] She·lō'mith
the son of Jos·i·phī'ȧh, and with him
a hundred and sixty men. 11 Of the
sons of Bē'bäi, Zech·ȧ·rī'ȧh, the son of
Bebai, and with him twenty-eight men.
12 Of the sons of Az'gad, Jō·hā'nȧn
the son of Hak'kȧ·tan, and with him a
hundred and ten men. 13 Of the sons
of Ad·ȯ·nī'kȧm, those who came later,
their names being E·liph'ė·let, Je·ü'el,
and She·māi'ȧh, and with them sixty
men. 14 Of the sons of Big'väi, Ū'thäi
and Zac'cûr, and with them seventy
men.

15 I gathered them to the river that
runs to Ȧ·hā'vȧ, and there we encamped three days. As I reviewed the
people and the priests, I found there
none of the sons of Levi. 16 Then I
sent for Ē·lī·ē'zėr, Âr'i·ėl, She·māi'ȧh,
El·nā'thȧn, Jâr'ib, Elnathan, Nathan,
Zech·ȧ·rī'ȧh, and Me·shul'lȧm, leading
men, and for Joi'ȧ·rib and Elnathan,
who were men of insight, 17 and sent
them to Id'dō, the leading man at the
place Cas·i·phī'ȧ, telling them what to
say to Iddo and his brethren the
temple servants[k] at the place Casiphia,
namely, to send us ministers for the
house of our God. 18 And by the good
hand of our God upon us, they brought
us a man of discretion, of the sons of
Mäh'lī the son of Levi, son of Israel,
namely Sher·ė·bī'ȧh with his sons and
kinsmen, eighteen; 19 also Hash·ȧ·bī'ȧh
and with him Je·shā'iȧh of the sons of
Mė·râr'ī, with his kinsmen and their
sons, twenty; 20 besides two hundred
and twenty of the temple servants,
whom David and his officials had set
apart to attend the Levites. These
were all mentioned by name.

21 Then I proclaimed a fast there,
at the river Ȧ·hā'vȧ, that we might
humble ourselves before our God, to
seek from him a straight way for ourselves, our children, and all our goods.
22 For I was ashamed to ask the king
for a band of soldiers and horsemen to
protect us against the enemy on our
way; since we had told the king, "The
hand of our God is for good upon all
that seek him, and the power of his
wrath is against all that forsake him."
23 So we fasted and besought our God
for this, and he listened to our entreaty.

24 Then I set apart twelve of the
leading priests: Sher·ė·bī'ȧh, Hash·ȧ-
bī'ȧh, and ten of their kinsmen with
them. 25 And I weighed out to them
the silver and the gold and the vessels,
the offering for the house of our God
which the king and his counselors and
his lords and all Israel there present
had offered; 26 I weighed out into their
hand six hundred and fifty talents of
silver, and silver vessels worth a hundred talents, and a hundred talents of
gold, 27 twenty bowls of gold worth a
thousand darics, and two vessels of
fine bright bronze as precious as gold.
28 And I said to them, "You are holy
to the LORD, and the vessels are holy;
and the silver and the gold are a freewill offering to the LORD, the God of
your fathers. 29 Guard them and keep
them until you weigh them before the
chief priests and the Levites and the
heads of fathers' houses in Israel at
Jerusalem, within the chambers of the
house of the LORD." 30 So the priests
and the Levites took over the weight
of the silver and the gold and the
vessels, to bring them to Jerusalem,
to the house of our God.

31 Then we departed from the river
Ȧ·hā'vȧ on the twelfth day of the first
month, to go to Jerusalem; the hand
of our God was upon us, and he
delivered us from the hand of the
enemy and from ambushes by the way.
32 We came to Jerusalem, and there
we remained three days. 33 On the
fourth day, within the house of our
God, the silver and the gold and the
vessels were weighed into the hands of
Mer'ė·moth the priest, son of Ū·rī'ȧh,
and with him was El·ē·ā'zȧr the son of
Phin'ė·hȧs, and with them were the

[i] Gk 1 Esdras 8.32: Heb lacks *of Zattu* [j] Gk 1 Esdras 8.36: Heb lacks *Bani* [k] Heb *nethinim*

Levites, Jō'zȧ·bad the son of Jesh'ü·ȧ
and Nō-ȧ·dī'āh the son of Bin'nü·ī.
34 The whole was counted and
weighed, and the weight of everything
was recorded.
35 At that time those who had come
from captivity, the returned exiles,
offered burnt offerings to the God of
Israel, twelve bulls for all Israel, ninety-
six rams, seventy-seven lambs, and as
a sin offering twelve he-goats; all this
was a burnt offering to the LORD.
36 They also delivered the king's com-
missions to the king's satraps and to
the governors of the province Beyond
the River; and they aided the people
and the house of God.

9 After these things had been done,
the officials approached me and
said, "The people of Israel and the
priests and the Levites have not
separated themselves from the peoples
of the lands with their abominations,
from the Canaanites, the Hit'tītes, the
Per'iz·zītes, the Jeb'ū·sītes, the Am'-
mȯ·nītes, the Mō'ȧb·ītes, the Egyptians, and the Am'ȯ·rītes. 2 For they
have taken some of their daughters to
be wives for themselves and for their
sons; so that the holy race has mixed
itself with the peoples of the lands.
And in this faithlessness the hand of
the officials and chief men has been
foremost." 3 When I heard this, I rent
my garments and my mantle, and
pulled hair from my head and beard,
and sat appalled. 4 Then all who
trembled at the words of the God of
Israel, because of the faithlessness of
the returned exiles, gathered round me
while I sat appalled until the evening
sacrifice. 5 And at the evening sacrifice
I rose from my fasting, with my garments and my mantle rent, and fell
upon my knees and spread out my
hands to the LORD my God, 6 saying:
"O my God, I am ashamed and
blush to lift my face to thee, my God,
for our iniquities have risen higher
than our heads, and our guilt has
mounted up to the heavens. 7 From
the days of our fathers to this day we
have been in great guilt; and for our
iniquities we, our kings, and our priests
have been given into the hand of the
kings of the lands, to the sword, to
captivity, to plundering, and to utter
shame, as at this day. 8 But now for a
brief moment favor has been shown by
the LORD our God, to leave us a remnant, and to give us a secure hold[l]
within his holy place, that our God
may brighten our eyes and grant us a
little reviving in our bondage. 9 For
we are bondmen; yet our God has not
forsaken us in our bondage, but has
extended to us his steadfast love before
the kings of Persia, to grant us some
reviving to set up the house of our
God, to repair its ruins, and to give
us protection[m] in Judea and Jerusalem.
10 "And now, O our God, what
shall we say after this? For we have
forsaken thy commandments, 11 which
thou didst command by thy servants
the prophets, saying, 'The land which
you are entering, to take possession of
it, is a land unclean with the pollutions
of the peoples of the lands, with their
abominations which have filled it from
end to end with their uncleanness.
12 Therefore give not your daughters
to their sons, neither take their daughters for your sons, and never seek their
peace or prosperity, that you may be
strong, and eat the good of the land,
and leave it for an inheritance to your
children for ever.' 13 And after all that
has come upon us for our evil deeds
and for our great guilt, seeing that thou,
our God, has punished us less than
our iniquities deserved and hast given
us such a remnant as this, 14 shall we
break thy commandments again and
intermarry with the peoples who
practice these abominations? Wouldst
thou not be angry with us till thou
wouldst consume us, so that there
should be no remnant, nor any to
escape? 15 O LORD the God of Israel,
thou art just, for we are left a remnant
that has escaped, as at this day. Behold, we are before thee in our guilt,
for none can stand before thee because
of this."

10 While Ezra prayed and made
confession, weeping and casting
himself down before the house of God,
a very great assembly of men, women,
and children, gathered to him out of
Israel; for the people wept bitterly.
2 And Shec·ȧ·nī'āh the son of Je·hī'el,
of the sons of E'lām, addressed Ezra:
"We have broken faith with our God
and have married foreign women from
the peoples of the land, but even now
there is hope for Israel in spite of this.
3 Therefore let us make a covenant
with our God to put away all these

[l] Heb *nail* or *tent-pin* [m] Heb *a wall*

wives and their children, according to
the counsel of my lord and of those
who tremble at the commandment of
our God; and let it be done according
to the law. 4 Arise, for it is your task,
and we are with you; be strong and do
it." 5 Then Ezra arose and made the
leading priests and Levites and all
Israel take oath that they would do
as had been said. So they took the
oath.

6 Then Ezra withdrew from before
the house of God, and went to the
chamber of Jē'hō-hā'nȧn the son of
E·lī'ȧ·shib, where he spent the night,[n]
neither eating bread nor drinking
water; for he was mourning over the
faithlessness of the exiles. 7 And a
proclamation was made throughout
Judah and Jerusalem to all the returned exiles that they should assemble
at Jerusalem, 8 and that if any one did
not come within three days, by order
of the officials and the elders all his
property should be forfeited, and he
himself banned from the congregation
of the exiles.

9 Then all the men of Judah and
Benjamin assembled at Jerusalem
within the three days; it was the ninth
month, on the twentieth day of the
month. And all the people sat in the
open square before the house of God,
trembling because of this matter and
because of the heavy rain. 10 And Ezra
the priest stood up and said to them,
"You have trespassed and married
foreign women, and so increased the
guilt of Israel. 11 Now then make confession to the LORD the God of your
fathers, and do his will; separate yourselves from the peoples of the land and
from the foreign wives." 12 Then all
the assembly answered with a loud
voice, "It is so; we must do as you
have said. 13 But the people are many,
and it is a time of heavy rain; we cannot stand in the open. Nor is this a
work for one day or for two; for we have
greatly transgressed in this matter.
14 Let our officials stand for the whole
assembly; let all in our cities who have
taken foreign wives come at appointed
times, and with them the elders and
judges of every city, till the fierce
wrath of our God over this matter be
averted from us." 15 Only Jonathan
the son of As'ȧ·hel and Jăh·zēi'ȧh the
son of Tik'vȧh opposed this, and Me-
shul'lȧm and Shab'bė·thāi the Levite
supported them.

16 Then the returned exiles did so.
Ezra the priest selected men,[o] heads
of fathers' houses, according to their
fathers' houses, each of them designated by name. On the first day of the
tenth month they sat down to examine
the matter; 17 and by the first day of
the first month they had come to the
end of all the men who had married
foreign women.

18 Of the sons of the priests who
had married foreign women were
found Mā-ȧ·sēi'ȧh, Ē·lī·ē'zėr, Jâr'ib,
and Ged·ȧ·lī'ȧh, of the sons of Jesh'ü·ȧ
the son of Jō'zȧ·dak and his brethren.
19 They pledged themselves to put
away their wives, and their guilt offering was a ram of the flock for their
guilt. 20 Of the sons of Im'mėr:
Hȧ·nā'nī and Zeb·ȧ·dī'ȧh. 21 Of the
sons of Hā'rim: Mā-ȧ·sēi'ȧh, E·lī'jȧh,
She·māi'ȧh, Je·hī'el, and Uz·zī'ȧh.
22 Of the sons of Pash'hūr: El'i-ō-ē'-
näi, Mā-ȧ·sēi'ȧh, Ish'mȧ·el, Nė·than'el,
Jō'zȧ·bad, and El·ā'sȧh.

23 Of the Levites: Jō'zȧ·bad, Shim'-
ē-ī, Ke·lāi'ȧh (that is, Ke·lī'tȧ), Peth'ȧ-
hī'ȧh, Judah, and Ē·lī·ē'zėr. 24 Of the
singers: E·lī'ȧ·shib. Of the gatekeepers:
Shal'lŭm, Tē'lem, and Ū'rī.

25 And of Israel: of the sons of
Pā'rosh: Rȧ·mī'ȧh, Iz·zī'ȧh, Mal·chī'-
jȧh, Mī'jȧ·min, El·ē·ā'zȧr, Hash·ȧ-
bī'ȧh,[p] and Be·nā'iȧh. 26 Of the sons
of Ē'lȧm: Mat·tȧ·nī'ȧh, Zech·ȧ·rī'ȧh,
Je·hī'el, Ab'dī, Jer'ė·moth, and E·lī'jȧh.
27 Of the sons of Zat'tü: El'i-ō-ē'näi,
E·lī'ȧ·shib, Mat·tȧ·nī'ȧh, Jer'ė·moth,
Zā'bad, and Ȧ·zī'zȧ. 28 Of the sons of
Bē'bäi were Jē'hō-hā'nȧn, Han·ȧ·nī'ȧh,
Zab'bäi, and Ath'läi. 29 Of the sons
of Bā'nī were Me·shul'lȧm, Mal'lŭch,
Ȧ·dāi'ȧh, Jash'ŭb, Shē'ȧl, and Jer'ė-
moth. 30 Of the sons of Pā'hath-mō'ab:
Ad'nȧ, Chē'lal, Be·nā'iȧh, Mā-ȧ·sēi'ȧh,
Mat·tȧ·nī'ȧh, Bez'ȧ·lel, Bin'nü·ī, and
Mȧ·nas'sėh. 31 Of the sons of Hā'rim:
Ē·lī·ē'zėr, Is·shī'jȧh, Mal·chī'jȧh, She-
māi'ȧh, Shim'ē-on, 32 Benjamin, Mal'-
lŭch, and Shem·ȧ·rī'ȧh. 33 Of the sons
of Hā'shŭm: Mat·tē'näi, Mat'tȧt·tȧh,
Zā'bad, E·liph'ė·let, Jer'ė·māi, Mȧ-
nas'sėh, and Shim'ē-ī. 34 Of the sons of
Bā'nī: Mā-ȧ·dā'ī, Am'ram, Ū'el, 35 Be-
nā'iȧh, Be·dēi'ȧh, Chel'ü·hī, 36 Vȧ·nī'-
ȧh, Mer'ė·moth, E·lī'ȧ·shib, 37 Mat·tȧ-
nī'ȧh, Mat·tē'näi, Jā'ȧ·sü. 38 Of the

[n] 1 Esdras 9.2: Heb *where he went* [o] 1 Esdras 9.16 Syr: Heb *and there were selected Ezra,* etc.
[p] 1 Esdras 9.26 Gk: Heb *Malchijah*

sons of Bin'nū·ī:[q] Shim'ē-ī, 39 Shel-
ė·mī'ȧh, Nathan, A·dāi'ȧh, 40 Mach-
nad'ė·bāi, Shā'shāi, Shā'rāi, 41 Az'ȧ·rel,
Shel·ė·mī'ȧh, Shem·ȧ·rī'ȧh, 42 Shal'-
lụm, Am·ȧ·rī'ȧh, and Joseph. 43 Of the
sons of Nē'bō: Je-ī'el, Mat·ti·thī'ȧh,
Zā'bad, Ze·bī'nȧ, Jad'dāi, Jō'ėl, and
Be·nā'iȧh. 44 All these had married
foreign women, and they put them
away with their children.[r]

THE BOOK OF NEHEMIAH

1 The words of Nē·hė·mī'ȧh the son
of Hac·ȧ·lī'ȧh.
Now it happened in the month of
Chis'lev, in the twentieth year, as I
was in Su'sȧ the capital, 2 that Hȧ·nā'nī,
one of my brethren, came with certain
men out of Judah; and I asked them
concerning the Jews that survived,
who had escaped exile, and concerning
Jerusalem. 3 And they said to me, "The
survivors there in the province who
escaped exile are in great trouble and
shame; the wall of Jerusalem is broken
down, and its gates are destroyed by
fire."
4 When I heard these words I sat
down and wept, and mourned for days;
and I continued fasting and praying
before the God of heaven. 5 And I said,
"O LORD God of heaven, the great and
terrible God who keeps covenant and
steadfast love with those who love him
and keep his commandments; 6 let thy
ear be attentive, and thy eyes open, to
hear the prayer of thy servant which
I now pray before thee day and night
for the people of Israel thy servants,
confessing the sins of the people of
Israel, which we have sinned against
thee. Yea, I and my father's house have
sinned. 7 We have acted very corruptly
against thee, and have not kept the
commandments, the statutes, and the
ordinances which thou didst command
thy servant Moses. 8 Remember the
word which thou didst command thy
servant Moses, saying, 'If you are unfaithful, I will scatter you among the
peoples; 9 but if you return to me and
keep my commandments and do them,
though your dispersed be under the
farthest skies, I will gather them thence
and bring them to the place which I
have chosen, to make my name dwell
there.' 10 They are thy servants and
thy people, whom thou hast redeemed
by thy great power and by thy strong
hand. 11 O Lord, let thy ear be attentive to the prayer of thy servant, and
to the prayer of thy servants who
delight to fear thy name; and give
success to thy servant today, and grant
him mercy in the sight of this man."
Now I was cupbearer to the king.
2 In the month of Nī'sȧn, in the
twentieth year of King Ȧr-tȧ-
x̆ĕrx'ēṡ, when wine was before him, I
took up the wine and gave it to the
king. Now I had not been sad in his
presence. 2 And the king said to me,
"Why is your face sad, seeing you are
not sick? This is nothing else but sadness of the heart." Then I was very
much afraid. 3 I said to the king, "Let
the king live for ever! Why should not
my face be sad, when the city, the
place of my fathers' sepulchres, lies
waste, and its gates have been destroyed by fire?" 4 Then the king said
to me, "For what do you make request?" So I prayed to the God of
heaven. 5 And I said to the king, "If it
pleases the king, and if your servant
has found favor in your sight, that you
send me to Judah, to the city of my
fathers' sepulchres, that I may rebuild
it." 6 And the king said to me (the
queen sitting beside him), "How long
will you be gone, and when will you
return?" So it pleased the king to send
me; and I set him a time. 7 And I said
to the king, "If it pleases the king, let
letters be given me to the governors of
the province Beyond the River, that
they may let me pass through until I
come to Judah; 8 and a letter to Ā'saph,
the keeper of the king's forest, that he
may give me timber to make beams for

[q] Gk: Heb *Bani, Binnui* [r] 1 Esdras 9.36: Heb obscure

the gates of the fortress of the temple,
and for the wall of the city, and for
the house which I shall occupy." And
the king granted me what I asked, for
the good hand of my God was upon
me.
9 Then I came to the governors of
the province Beyond the River, and
gave them the king's letters. Now the
king had sent with me officers of the
army and horsemen. 10 But when
San·bal'lȧt the Hôr'ȯ·nīte and Tō·bī'ȧh
the servant, the Am'mȯ·nīte, heard
this, it displeased them greatly that
some one had come to seek the welfare
of the children of Israel.
11 So I came to Jerusalem and was
there three days. 12 Then I arose in
the night, I and a few men with me;
and I told no one what my God had
put into my heart to do for Jerusalem.
There was no beast with me but the
beast on which I rode. 13 I went out
by night by the Valley Gate to the
Jackal's Well and to the Dung Gate,
and I inspected the walls of Jerusalem
which were broken down and its gates
which had been destroyed by fire.
14 Then I went on to the Fountain
Gate and to the King's Pool; but there
was no place for the beast that was
under me to pass. 15 Then I went up
in the night by the valley and inspected
the wall; and I turned back and entered by the Valley Gate, and so
returned. 16 And the officials did not
know where I had gone or what I was
doing; and I had not yet told the Jews,
the priests, the nobles, the officials,
and the rest that were to do the work.
17 Then I said to them, "You see
the trouble we are in, how Jerusalem
lies in ruins with its gates burned.
Come, let us build the wall of Jerusalem, that we may no longer suffer
disgrace." 18 And I told them of the
hand of my God which had been upon
me for good, and also of the words
which the king had spoken to me. And
they said, "Let us rise up and build."
So they strengthened their hands for
the good work. 19 But when San·bal'-
lȧt the Hôr'ȯ·nīte and Tō·bī'ȧh the
servant, the Am'mȯ·nīte, and Gē'shem
the Arab heard of it, they derided us
and despised us and said, "What is
this thing that you are doing? Are you
rebelling against the king?" 20 Then I
replied to them, "The God of heaven
will make us prosper, and we his servants will arise and build; but you have
no portion or right or memorial in
Jerusalem."

3 Then E·lī'ȧ·shib the high priest
rose up with his brethren the
priests and they built the Sheep Gate.
They consecrated it and set its doors;
they consecrated it as far as the Tower
of the Hundred, as far as the Tower
of Hȧ·nan'el. 2 And next to him the
men of Jericho built. And next to
them[a] Zac'cūr the son of Im'rī built.
3 And the sons of Has·sė·nā'ȧh built
the Fish Gate; they laid its beams and
set its doors, its bolts, and its bars.
4 And next to them Mer'ė·moth the son
of Ū·rī'ȧh, son of Hak'koz repaired.
And next to them Me·shul'lȧm the son
of Ber·ė·chī'ȧh, son of Me·shez'ȧ·bel
repaired. And next to them Zā'dok
the son of Bā'ȧ·nȧ repaired. 5 And next
to them the Te·kō'ītes repaired; but
their nobles did not put their necks to
the work of their Lord.[b]
6 And Joi'ȧ·dȧ the son of Pȧ·sē'ȧh
and Me·shul'lȧm the son of Bes·ȯ·dēi'-
ȧh repaired the Old Gate; they laid its
beams and set its doors, its bolts, and
its bars. 7 And next to them repaired
Mel·ȧ·tī'ȧh the Gib'ē·ȯ·nīte and Jā'don
the Me·rō'nȯ·thīte, the men of Gib'-
ē·ȯn and of Miz'pȧh, who were under
the jurisdiction of the governor of the
province Beyond the River. 8 Next to
them Uz'zi·el the son of Här·häi'ȧh,
goldsmiths, repaired. Next to him
Han·ȧ·nī'ȧh, one of the perfumers, repaired; and they restored[c] Jerusalem
as far as the Broad Wall. 9 Next to
them Reph·ā'iȧh the son of Hūr, ruler
of half the district of[d] Jerusalem, repaired. 10 Next to them Je·däi'ȧh the
son of Hȧ·rü'maph repaired opposite
his house; and next to him Hat'tȯsh
the son of Hash·ab·neī'ȧh repaired.
11 Mal·chī'jȧh the son of Hā'rim and
Has'shȯb the son of Pā'hath-mō'ab
repaired another section and the Tower
of the Ovens. 12 Next to him Shal'lȯm
the son of Hal·lō'hesh, ruler of half the
district of[d] Jerusalem, repaired, he
and his daughters.
13 Hā'nȯn and the inhabitants of
Zȧ·nō'ȧh repaired the Valley Gate;
they rebuilt it and set its doors, its
bolts, and its bars, and repaired a
thousand cubits of the wall, as far as
the Dung Gate.
14 Mal·chī'jȧh the son of Rē'chab,
ruler of the district of[d] Beth-hac·chē'-

[a] Heb *him* [b] Or *lords* [c] Or *abandoned* [d] Or *foreman of half the portion assigned to*

rem, repaired the Dung Gate; he rebuilt it and set its doors, its bolts, and
its bars.
15 And Shal'lŭm the son of Col-
hō'zėh, ruler of the district of[d] Miz'-
pȧh, repaired the Fountain Gate; he
rebuilt it and covered it and set its
doors, its bolts, and its bars; and he
built the wall of the Pool of Shē'lȧh of
the king's garden, as far as the stairs
that go down from the City of David.
16After him Nē·hė·mī'ȧh the son of
Az'bŭk, ruler of half the district of[d]
Beth'-zŭr, repaired to a point opposite
the sepulchres of David, to the artificial
pool, and to the house of the mighty
men. 17After him the Levites repaired:
Rē'hŭm the son of Bā'nī; next to him
Hash·ȧ·bī'ȧh, ruler of half the district
of[d] Kē·ī'lȧh, repaired for his district.
18After him their brethren repaired:
Bav'väi the son of Hen'ȧ·dad, ruler of
half the district of[d] Kē·ī'lȧh; 19 next to
him Ē'zėr the son of Jesh'ü·ȧ, ruler of
Miz'pȧh, repaired another section opposite the ascent to the armory at the
Angle. 20After him Bâr'ŭch the son of
Zab'bäi repaired another section from
the Angle to the door of the house of
E·lī'ȧ·shib the high priest. 21After him
Mer'ė·moth the son of Ū·rī'ȧh, son of
Hak'koz repaired another section from
the door of the house of E·lī'ȧ·shib to
the end of the house of Eliashib.
22After him the priests, the men of the
Plain, repaired. 23After them Benjamin
and Has'shŭb repaired opposite their
house. After them Az·ȧ·rī'ȧh the son
of Mā-ȧ·sēi'ȧh, son of An·ȧ·nī'ȧh repaired beside his own house. 24After
him Bin'nü·ī the son of Hen'ȧ·dad repaired another section, from the house
of Az·ȧ·rī'ȧh to the Angle 25 and to the
corner. Pā'lȧl the son of Ū'zäi repaired
opposite the Angle and the tower projecting from the upper house of the
king at the court of the guard. After
him Pe·dāi'ȧh the son of Pā'rosh 26 and
the temple servants living[e] on Ō'phel
repaired to a point opposite the Water
Gate on the east and the projecting
tower. 27After him the Te·kō'ītes repaired another section opposite the
great projecting tower as far as the
wall of Ō'phel.
28 Above the Horse Gate the priests
repaired, each one opposite his own
house. 29After them Zā'dok the son of
Im'mėr repaired opposite his own
house. After him She·māi'ȧh the son
of Shec·ȧ·nī'ȧh, the keeper of the East
Gate, repaired. 30After him Han·ȧ·nī'-
ȧh the son of Shel·ė·mī'ȧh and Hā'nŭn
the sixth son of Zā'laph repaired
another section. After him Me·shul'-
lȧm the son of Ber·ė·chī'ȧh repaired
opposite his chamber. 31After him
Mal·chī'jȧh, one of the goldsmiths, repaired as far as the house of the temple
servants and of the merchants, opposite the Muster Gate,[f] and to the
upper chamber of the corner. 32And
between the upper chamber of the
corner and the Sheep Gate the goldsmiths and the merchants repaired.

4[g] Now when San·bal'lȧt heard that
we were building the wall, he was
angry and greatly enraged, and he
ridiculed the Jews. 2And he said in
the presence of his brethren and of the
army of Sȧ·mâr'ĭ·ȧ, "What are these
feeble Jews doing? Will they restore
things? Will they sacrifice? Will they
finish up in a day? Will they revive
the stones out of the heaps of rubbish,
and burned ones at that?" 3 Tō·bī'ȧh
the Am'mȯ·nīte was by him, and he
said, "Yes, what they are building—if
a fox goes up on it he will break down
their stone wall!" 4 Hear, O our God,
for we are despised; turn back their
taunt upon their own heads, and give
them up to be plundered in a land
where they are captives. 5 Do not
cover their guilt, and let not their sin
be blotted out from thy sight; for they
have provoked thee to anger before
the builders.
6 So we built the wall; and all the
wall was joined together to half its
height. For the people had a mind to
work.
7[h] But when San·bal'lȧt and Tō-
bī'ȧh and the Arabs and the Am'mȯ-
nītes and the Ash'dȯ·dītes heard that
the repairing of the walls of Jerusalem
was going forward and that the
breaches were beginning to be closed,
they were very angry; 8 and they all
plotted together to come and fight
against Jerusalem and to cause confusion in it. 9And we prayed to our God,
and set a guard as a protection against
them day and night.
10 But Judah said, "The strength
of the burden-bearers is failing, and
there is much rubbish; we are not able
to work on the wall." 11And our

[d] Or *foreman of half the portion assigned to* [e] Cn: Heb *were living* [f] Or *Hammiphkad Gate*
[g] Ch 3.33 in Heb [h] Ch 4.1 in Heb

enemies said, "They will not know or
see till we come into the midst of them
and kill them and stop the work."
12 When the Jews who lived by them
came they said to us ten times, "From
all the places where they live[i] they
will come up against us."[j] 13 So in the
lowest parts of the space behind the
wall, in open places, I stationed the
people according to their families, with
their swords, their spears, and their
bows. 14 And I looked, and arose, and
said to the nobles and to the officials
and to the rest of the people, "Do not
be afraid of them. Remember the
Lord, who is great and terrible, and
fight for your brethren, your sons,
your daughters, your wives, and your
homes."

15 When our enemies heard that it
was known to us and that God had
frustrated their plan, we all returned
to the wall, each to his work. 16 From
that day on, half of my servants
worked on construction, and half held
the spears, shields, bows, and coats of
mail; and the leaders stood behind all
the house of Judah, 17 who were building on the wall. Those who carried
burdens were laden in such a way that
each with one hand labored on the
work and with the other held his
weapon. 18 And each of the builders
had his sword girded at his side while
he built. The man who sounded the
trumpet was beside me. 19 And I said
to the nobles and to the officials and
to the rest of the people, "The work
is great and widely spread, and we are
separated on the wall, far from one
another. 20 In the place where you
hear the sound of the trumpet, rally
to us there. Our God will fight for us."

21 So we labored at the work, and
half of them held the spears from the
break of dawn till the stars came out.
22 I also said to the people at that
time, "Let every man and his servant
pass the night within Jerusalem, that
they may be a guard for us by night
and may labor by day." 23 So neither
I nor my brethren nor my servants
nor the men of the guard who followed
me, none of us took off our clothes;
each kept his weapon in his hand.[k]

5 Now there arose a great outcry
of the people and of their wives
against their Jewish brethren. 2 For
there were those who said, "With our
sons and our daughters, we are many;
let us get grain, that we may eat and
keep alive." 3 There were also those
who said, "We are mortgaging our
fields, our vineyards, and our houses
to get grain because of the famine."
4 And there were those who said, "We
have borrowed money for the king's
tax upon our fields and our vineyards.
5 Now our flesh is as the flesh of our
brethren, our children are as their
children; yet we are forcing our sons
and our daughters to be slaves, and
some of our daughters have already
been enslaved; but it is not in our
power to help it, for other men have
our fields and our vineyards."

6 I was very angry when I heard
their outcry and these words. 7 I took
counsel with myself, and I brought
charges against the nobles and the
officials. I said to them, "You are
exacting interest, each from his
brother." And I held a great assembly
against them, 8 and said to them, "We,
as far as we are able, have bought back
our Jewish brethren who have been
sold to the nations; but you even sell
your brethren that they may be sold
to us!" They were silent, and could
not find a word to say. 9 So I said,
"The thing that you are doing is not
good. Ought you not to walk in the
fear of our God to prevent the taunts
of the nations our enemies? 10 Moreover I and my brethren and my servants are lending them money and
grain. Let us leave off this interest.
11 Return to them this very day their
fields, their vineyards, their olive
orchards, and their houses, and the
hundredth of money, grain, wine, and
oil which you have been exacting of
them." 12 Then they said, "We will
restore these and require nothing from
them. We will do as you say." And I
called the priests, and took an oath of
them to do as they had promised. 13 I
also shook out my lap and said, "So
may God shake out every man from
his house and from his labor who does
not perform this promise. So may he
be shaken out and emptied." And all
the assembly said "Amen" and praised
the LORD. And the people did as they
had promised.

14 Moreover from the time that I
was appointed to be their governor in
the land of Judah, from the twentieth
year to the thirty-second year of Ăr-
tă-xĕrx'ēs the king, twelve years,

[i] Cn: Heb *you return* [j] Compare Gk Syr: Heb uncertain [k] Cn: Heb *each his weapon the water*

neither I nor my brethren ate the food
allowance of the governor. 15 The
former governors who were before me
laid heavy burdens upon the people,
and took from them food and wine,
besides forty shekels of silver. Even
their servants lorded it over the people. But I did not do so, because of
the fear of God. 16 I also held to the
work on this wall, and acquired no
land; and all my servants were gathered there for the work. 17 Moreover
there were at my table a hundred and
fifty men, Jews and officials, besides
those who came to us from the nations
which were about us. 18 Now that
which was prepared for one day was
one ox and six choice sheep; fowls likewise were prepared for me, and every
ten days skins of wine in abundance;
yet with all this I did not demand the
food allowance of the governor, because the servitude was heavy upon
this people. 19 Remember for my good,
O my God, all that I have done for
this people.

6 Now when it was reported to
San·bal'lȧt and Tō·bī'ȧh and to
Gē'shem the Arab and to the rest of
our enemies that I had built the wall
and that there was no breach left in it
(although up to that time I had not
set up the doors in the gates), 2 Sanbal'lȧt and Gē'shem sent to me, saying, "Come and let us meet together
in one of the villages in the plain of
Ō'nō." But they intended to do me
harm. 3 And I sent messengers to them,
saying, "I am doing a great work and
I cannot come down. Why should the
work stop while I leave it and come
down to you?" 4 And they sent to me
four times in this way and I answered
them in the same manner. 5 In the
same way San·bal'lȧt for the fifth time
sent his servant to me with an open
letter in his hand. 6 In it was written,
"It is reported among the nations, and
Gē'shem[l] also says it, that you and the
Jews intend to rebel; that is why you
are building the wall; and you wish to
become their king, according to this
report. 7 And you have also set up
prophets to proclaim concerning you
in Jerusalem, 'There is a king in
Judah.' And now it will be reported
to the king according to these words.
So now come, and let us take counsel
together." 8 Then I sent to him, saying, "No such things as you say have
been done, for you are inventing them
out of your own mind." 9 For they all
wanted to frighten us, thinking, "Their
hands will drop from the work, and it
will not be done." But now, O God,
strengthen thou my hands.

10 Now when I went into the house
of She·māi'ȧh the son of De·lāi'ȧh, son
of Me·het'ȧ·bėl, who was shut up, he
said, "Let us meet together in the
house of God, within the temple, and
let us close the doors of the temple; for
they are coming to kill you, at night
they are coming to kill you." 11 But I
said, "Should such a man as I flee?
And what man such as I could go into
the temple and live?[m] I will not go in."
12 And I understood, and saw that God
had not sent him, but he had pronounced the prophecy against me because Tō·bī'ȧh and San·bal'lȧt had
hired him. 13 For this purpose he was
hired, that I should be afraid and act
in this way and sin, and so they could
give me an evil name, in order to taunt
me. 14 Remember Tō·bī'ȧh and Sanbal'lȧt, O my God, according to these
things that they did, and also the
prophetess Nō-ȧ·dī'ȧh and the rest of
the prophets who wanted to make me
afraid.

15 So the wall was finished on the
twenty-fifth day of the month Ē'lŭl,
in fifty-two days. 16 And when all our
enemies heard of it, all the nations
round about us were afraid[n] and fell
greatly in their own esteem; for they
perceived that this work had been
accomplished with the help of our
God. 17 Moreover in those days the
nobles of Judah sent many letters to
Tō·bī'ȧh, and Tobiah's letters came
to them. 18 For many in Judah were
bound by oath to him, because he was
the son-in-law of Shec·ȧ·nī'ȧh the son
of Ā'rȧh: and his son Jē'hō-hā'nȧn had
taken the daughter of Me·shul'lȧm the
son of Ber·ė·chī'ȧh as his wife. 19 Also
they spoke of his good deeds in my
presence, and reported my words to
him. And Tō·bī'ȧh sent letters to make
me afraid.

7 Now when the wall had been
built and I had set up the doors,
and the gatekeepers, the singers, and
the Levites had been appointed, 2 I
gave my brother Hȧ·nā'nī and Han·ȧ-
nī'ȧh the governor of the castle charge
over Jerusalem, for he was a more
faithful and God-fearing man than

[l] Heb *Gashmu* [m] Or *would go into the temple to save his life* [n] Another reading is *saw*

many. 3 And I said to them, "Let not
the gates of Jerusalem be opened until
the sun is hot; and while they are still
standing guard[o] let them shut and bar
the doors. Appoint guards from among
the inhabitants of Jerusalem, each to
his station and each opposite his own
house." 4 The city was wide and large,
but the people within it were few and
no houses had been built.

5 Then God put it into my mind to
assemble the nobles and the officials
and the people to be enrolled by
genealogy. And I found the book of
the genealogy of those who came up
at the first, and I found written in it:

6 These were the people of the
province who came up out of the
captivity of those exiles whom Ne·bu̇-
chȧd·nez'zȧr the king of Babylon had
carried into exile; they returned to
Jerusalem and Judah, each to his
town. 7 They came with Ze·rub'bȧ·bel,
Jesh'ü·ȧ, Nē·hė·mī'ȧh, Az·ȧ·rī'ȧh, Rā-
ȧ·mī'ȧh, Nā·ham'ȧ·nī, Môr'de·cäi, Bil'-
shan, Mis'pė·reth, Big'väi, Nē'hum,
Bā'ȧ·nȧh.

The number of the men of the people of Israel: 8 the sons of Pā'rosh, two
thousand a hundred and seventy-two.
9 The sons of Sheph·ȧ·tī'ȧh, three hundred and seventy-two. 10 The sons of
Ā'rȧh, six hundred and fifty-two.
11 The sons of Pā'hath-mō'ab, namely
the sons of Jesh'ü·ȧ and Jō'ab, two
thousand eight hundred and eighteen.
12 The sons of Ē'lȧm, a thousand two
hundred and fifty-four. 13 The sons of
Zat'tü, eight hundred and forty-five.
14 The sons of Zac'cäi, seven hundred
and sixty. 15 The sons of Bin'nü·ī, six
hundred and forty-eight. 16 The sons
of Bē'bäi, six hundred and twenty-
eight. 17 The sons of Az'gad, two thousand three hundred and twenty-two.
18 The sons of Ad·ȯ·nī'kȧm, six hundred and sixty-seven. 19 The sons of
Big'väi, two thousand and sixty-seven.
20 The sons of Ā'din, six hundred and
fifty-five. 21 The sons of Ā'tėr, namely
of Hez·ė·kī'ȧh, ninety-eight. 22 The
sons of Hā'shu̇m, three hundred and
twenty-eight. 23 The sons of Bē'zäi,
three hundred and twenty-four. 24 The
sons of Hā'riph, a hundred and twelve.
25 The sons of Gib'ē·ȯn, ninety-five.
26 The men of Bethlehem and Nė·toph'-
ȧh, a hundred and eighty-eight. 27 The
men of An'ȧ·thoth, a hundred and
twenty-eight. 28 The men of Beth-
az'mȧ·veth, forty-two. 29 The men of
Kĭr'i·ath-jē'ȧ·rim, Che·phī'rȧh, and
Bė-ēr'ȯth, seven hundred and forty-
three. 30 The men of Rā'mȧh and
Gē'bȧ, six hundred and twenty-one.
31 The men of Mich'mȧs, a hundred
and twenty-two. 32 The men of Beth'ėl
and Ā'i, a hundred and twenty-three.
33 The men of the other Nē'bō, fifty-
two. 34 The sons of the other Ē'lȧm, a
thousand two hundred and fifty-four.
35 The sons of Hā'rim, three hundred
and twenty. 36 The sons of Jericho,
three hundred and forty-five. 37 The
sons of Lod, Hā'did, and Ō'nō, seven
hundred and twenty-one. 38 The sons
of Se·nā'ȧh, three thousand nine hundred and thirty.

39 The priests: the sons of Je·däi'ȧh,
namely the house of Jesh'ü·ȧ, nine
hundred and seventy-three. 40 The
sons of Im'mėr, a thousand and fifty-
two. 41 The sons of Pash'hûr, a thousand two hundred and forty-seven.
42 The sons of Hā'rim, a thousand and
seventeen.

43 The Levites: the sons of Jesh'-
ü·ȧ, namely of Kad'mi-el of the sons
of Hō'dė·vȧh, seventy-four. 44 The
singers: the sons of Ā'saph, a hundred
and forty-eight. 45 The gatekeepers:
the sons of Shal'lu̇m, the sons of Ā'tėr,
the sons of Tal'mȯn, the sons of
Ak'ku̇b, the sons of Hȧ·tī'tȧ, the sons
of Shō'bäi, a hundred and thirty-eight.

46 The temple servants:[p] the sons
of Zī'hȧ, the sons of Hȧ·sü'phȧ, the
sons of Tab·bā'oth, 47 the sons of
Kē'ros, the sons of Sī'ȧ, the sons of
Pā'don, 48 the sons of Le·bā'nȧ, the
sons of Hag'ȧ·bȧ, the sons of Shal'mäi,
49 the sons of Hā'nȧn, the sons of
Gid'del, the sons of Gā'här, 50 the sons
of Rē-äi'ȧh, the sons of Rē'zin, the
sons of Ne·kō'dȧ, 51 the sons of Gaz'-
zȧm, the sons of Uz'zȧ, the sons of
Pȧ·sē'ȧh, 52 the sons of Bē'säi, the sons
of Me-ü'nim, the sons of Ne·phüsh'ė-
sim, 53 the sons of Bak'bu̇k, the sons of
Hȧ·kū'phȧ, the sons of Här'hûr, 54 the
sons of Baz'lith, the sons of Me·hī'dȧ,
the sons of Här'shȧ, 55 the sons of
Bär'kos, the sons of Sis'ėr·ȧ, the sons
of Tē'mȧh, 56 the sons of Ne·zī'ȧh, the
sons of Hȧ·tī'phȧ.

57 The sons of Solomon's servants:
the sons of Sō'täi, the sons of Sō'phė-
reth, the sons of Pe·rī'dȧ, 58 the sons

[o] Heb obscure [p] Heb *nethinim*

7.6-73: Ezra 2.1-70.

of Jā'ȧ·lȧ, the sons of Där'kon, the sons
of Gid'del, 59 the sons of Sheph·ȧ·tī'ȧh,
the sons of Hat'til, the sons of Pō'chė-
reth-haz·zė·bā'im, the sons of Ā'mon.
60 All the temple servants and the
sons of Solomon's servants were three
hundred and ninety-two.
61 The following were those who
came up from Tel-mē'lȧh, Tel-här'shȧ,
Chē'rŭb, Ad'don, and Im'mėr, but
they could not prove their fathers'
houses nor their descent, whether they
belonged to Israel: 62 the sons of De-
läi'ȧh, the sons of Tō·bī'ȧh, the sons of
Ne·kō'dȧ, six hundred and forty-two.
63 Also, of the priests: the sons of Hō-
bāi'ȧh, the sons of Hak'koz, the sons of
Bär·zil'läi (who had taken a wife of the
daughters of Barzillai the Gileadite
and was called by their name). 64 These
sought their registration among those
enrolled in the genealogies, but it was
not found there, so they were excluded
from the priesthood as unclean; 65 the
governor told them that they were not
to partake of the most holy food, until
a priest with Ū'rim and Thum'mim
should arise.
66 The whole assembly together
was forty-two thousand three hundred
and sixty, 67 besides their menservants
and maidservants, of whom there were
seven thousand three hundred and
thirty-seven; and they had two hundred and forty-five singers, male and
female. 68 Their horses were seven
hundred and thirty-six, their mules
two hundred and forty-five,[q] 69 their
camels four hundred and thirty-five,
and their asses six thousand seven
hundred and twenty.
70 Now some of the heads of
fathers' houses gave to the work. The
governor gave to the treasury a thousand darics of gold, fifty basins, five
hundred and thirty priests' garments.
71 And some of the heads of fathers'
houses gave into the treasury of the
work twenty thousand darics of gold
and two thousand two hundred minas
of silver. 72 And what the rest of the
people gave was twenty thousand
darics of gold, two thousand minas of
silver, and sixty-seven priests' garments.
73 So the priests, the Levites, the
gatekeepers, the singers, some of the
people, the temple servants, and all
Israel, lived in their towns.

And when the seventh month had
come, the children of Israel were in
8 their towns. 1 And all the people
gathered as one man into the
square before the Water Gate; and
they told Ezra the scribe to bring the
book of the law of Moses which the
LORD had given to Israel. 2 And Ezra
the priest brought the law before the
assembly, both men and women and
all who could hear with understanding,
on the first day of the seventh month.
3 And he read from it facing the square
before the Water Gate from early
morning until midday, in the presence
of the men and the women and those
who could understand; and the ears of
all the people were attentive to the
book of the law. 4 And Ezra the scribe
stood on a wooden pulpit which they
had made for the purpose; and beside
him stood Mat·ti·thī'ȧh, Shē'mȧ,
Ȧ·näi'ȧh, Ū·rī'ȧh, Hil·kī'ȧh, and Mā-
ȧ·sēi'ȧh on his right hand; and Pe-
dāi'ȧh, Mish'ȧ-el, Mal·chī'jȧh, Hā'-
shŭm, Hash-bad'dȧ·nȧh, Zech·ȧ·rī'ȧh,
and Me·shul'lȧm on his left hand.
5 And Ezra opened the book in the
sight of all the people, for he was
above all the people; and when he
opened it all the people stood. 6 And
Ezra blessed the LORD, the great God;
and all the people answered, "Amen,
Amen," lifting up their hands; and
they bowed their heads and worshiped
the LORD with their faces to the
ground. 7 Also Jesh'ü·ȧ, Bā'nī, Sher·ė-
bī'ȧh, Jā'min, Ak'kŭb, Shab'bė·thäi,
Hō·dī'ȧh, Mā-ȧ·sēi'ȧh, Ke·lī'tȧ, Az·ȧ-
rī'ȧh, Jō'zȧ·bad, Hā'nȧn, Pe·läi'ȧh, the
Levites,[r] helped the people to understand the law, while the people remained in their places. 8 And they read
from the book, from the law of God,
clearly;[s] and they gave the sense, so
that the people understood the reading.
9 And Nē·hė·mī'ȧh, who was the
governor, and Ezra the priest and
scribe, and the Levites who taught the
people said to all the people, "This
day is holy to the LORD your God; do
not mourn or weep." For all the people wept when they heard the words
of the law. 10 Then he said to them,
"Go your way, eat the fat and drink
sweet wine and send portions to him
for whom nothing is prepared; for this
day is holy to our Lord; and do not be
grieved, for the joy of the LORD is your

[q] Ezra 2.66 and the margins of some Hebrew Mss: Heb lacks *their horses . . . forty-five*
[r] 1 Esdras 9.48 Vg: Heb *and the Levites* [s] Or *with interpretation*

strength." 11 So the Levites stilled all
the people, saying, "Be quiet, for this
day is holy; do not be grieved." 12 And
all the people went their way to eat
and drink and to send portions and to
make great rejoicing, because they had
understood the words that were declared to them.

13 On the second day the heads of
fathers' houses of all the people, with
the priests and the Levites, came together to Ezra the scribe in order to
study the words of the law. 14 And
they found it written in the law that
the LORD had commanded by Moses
that the people of Israel should dwell
in booths during the feast of the
seventh month, 15 and that they should
publish and proclaim in all their towns
and in Jerusalem, "Go out to the hills
and bring branches of olive, wild olive,
myrtle, palm, and other leafy trees
to make booths, as it is written." 16 So
the people went out and brought them
and made booths for themselves, each
on his roof, and in their courts and in
the courts of the house of God, and
in the square at the Water Gate and
in the square at the Gate of E'phrȧ·im.
17 And all the assembly of those who
had returned from the captivity made
booths and dwelt in the booths; for
from the days of Jesh'ü·ȧ the son of
Nun to that day the people of Israel
had not done so. And there was very
great rejoicing. 18 And day by day, from
the first day to the last day, he read
from the book of the law of God. They
kept the feast seven days; and on the
eighth day there was a solemn assembly, according to the ordinance.

9 Now on the twenty-fourth day of
this month the people of Israel
were assembled with fasting and in
sackcloth, and with earth upon their
heads. 2 And the Israelites separated
themselves from all foreigners, and
stood and confessed their sins and the
iniquities of their fathers. 3 And they
stood up in their place and read from
the book of the law of the LORD their
God for a fourth of the day; for
another fourth of it they made confession and worshiped the LORD their
God. 4 Upon the stairs of the Levites
stood Jesh'ü·ȧ, Bā'nī, Kad'mi-el,
Sheb·ȧ·nī'ȧh, Bun'nī, Sher·ė·bī'ȧh,
Bani, and Che·nā'nī; and they cried
with a loud voice to the LORD their
God. 5 Then the Levites, Jesh'ü·ȧ,
Kad'mi-el, Bā'nī, Hash·ab·neī'ȧh,
Sher·ė·bī'ȧh, Hō·dī'ȧh, Sheb·ȧ·nī'ȧh,
and Peth·ȧ·hī'ȧh, said, "Stand up and
bless the LORD your God from everlasting to everlasting. Blessed be thy
glorious name which is exalted above
all blessing and praise."

6 And Ezra said:[t] "Thou art the
LORD, thou alone; thou hast made
heaven, the heaven of heavens, with
all their host, the earth and all that is
on it, the seas and all that is in them;
and thou preservest all of them; and
the host of heaven worships thee.
7 Thou art the LORD, the God who
didst choose Abram and bring him
forth out of Ūr of the Chal·dē'ȧns and
give him the name Abraham; 8 and thou
didst find his heart faithful before thee,
and didst make with him the covenant
to give to his descendants the land of
the Canaanite, the Hit'tīte, the Am'ō-
rīte, the Per'iz·zīte, the Jeb'ū·sīte, and
the Gīr'gȧ·shīte; and thou hast fulfilled thy promise, for thou art
righteous.

9 "And thou didst see the affliction
of our fathers in Egypt and hear their
cry at the Red Sea, 10 and didst perform
signs and wonders against Pharaoh
and all his servants and all the people
of his land, for thou knewest that they
acted insolently against our fathers;
and thou didst get thee a name, as it is
to this day. 11 And thou didst divide
the sea before them, so that they went
through the midst of the sea on dry
land; and thou didst cast their pursuers into the depths, as a stone into
mighty waters. 12 By a pillar of cloud
thou didst lead them in the day, and
by a pillar of fire in the night to light
for them the way in which they should
go. 13 Thou didst come down upon
Mount Sinai, and speak with them
from heaven and give them right
ordinances and true laws, good statutes
and commandments, 14 and thou didst
make known to them thy holy sabbath
and command them commandments
and statutes and a law by Moses thy
servant. 15 Thou didst give them
bread from heaven for their hunger
and bring forth water for them from
the rock for their thirst, and thou didst
tell them to go in to possess the land
which thou hadst sworn to give them.

16 "But they and our fathers acted
presumptuously and stiffened their
neck and did not obey thy command-

[t] Gk: Heb lacks *and Ezra said*

ments; 17 they refused to obey, and
were not mindful of the wonders
which thou didst perform among
them; but they stiffened their neck
and appointed a leader to return to
their bondage in Egypt. But thou art
a God ready to forgive, gracious and
merciful, slow to anger and abounding
in steadfast love, and didst not forsake
them. 18 Even when they had made
for themselves a molten calf and said,
'This is your God who brought you
up out of Egypt,' and had committed
great blasphemies, 19 thou in thy great
mercies didst not forsake them in the
wilderness; the pillar of cloud which
led them in the way did not depart
from them by day, nor the pillar of
fire by night which lighted for them
the way by which they should go.
20 Thou gavest thy good Spirit to
instruct them, and didst not withhold
thy manna from their mouth, and
gavest them water for their thirst.
21 Forty years didst thou sustain them
in the wilderness, and they lacked
nothing; their clothes did not wear out
and their feet did not swell. 22 And
thou didst give them kingdoms and
peoples, and didst allot to them every
corner; so they took possession of the
land of Sī'hon king of Hesh'bȯn and
the land of Og king of Bā'shȧn. 23 Thou
didst multiply their descendants as the
stars of heaven, and thou didst bring
them into the land which thou hadst
told their fathers to enter and possess.
24 So the descendants went in and
possessed the land, and thou didst subdue before them the inhabitants of the
land, the Canaanites, and didst give
them into their hands, with their kings
and the peoples of the land, that they
might do with them as they would.
25 And they captured fortified cities
and a rich land, and took possession
of houses full of all good things, cisterns hewn out, vineyards, olive
orchards and fruit trees in abundance;
so they ate, and were filled and became
fat, and delighted themselves in thy
great goodness.

26 "Nevertheless they were disobedient and rebelled against thee and
cast thy law behind their back and
killed thy prophets, who had warned
them in order to turn them back to
thee, and they committed great blasphemies. 27 Therefore thou didst give
them into the hand of their enemies,
who made them suffer; and in the time
of their suffering they cried to thee
and thou didst hear them from heaven;
and according to thy great mercies
thou didst give them saviors who saved
them from the hand of their enemies.
28 But after they had rest they did evil
again before thee, and thou didst
abandon them to the hand of their
enemies, so that they had dominion
over them; yet when they turned and
cried to thee thou didst hear from
heaven, and many times thou didst
deliver them according to thy mercies.
29 And thou didst warn them in order
to turn them back to thy law. Yet they
acted presumptuously and did not
obey thy commandments, but sinned
against thy ordinances, by the observance of which a man shall live, and
turned a stubborn shoulder and
stiffened their neck and would not
obey. 30 Many years thou didst bear
with them, and didst warn them by
thy Spirit through thy prophets; yet
they would not give ear. Therefore
thou didst give them into the hand of
the peoples of the lands. 31 Nevertheless in thy great mercies thou didst not
make an end of them or forsake them;
for thou art a gracious and merciful
God.

32 "Now therefore, our God, the
great and mighty and terrible God,
who keepest covenant and steadfast
love, let not all the hardship seem little
to thee that has come upon us, upon
our kings, our princes, our priests, our
prophets, our fathers, and all thy people, since the time of the kings of
Assyria until this day. 33 Yet thou
hast been just in all that has come upon
us, for thou hast dealt faithfully and
we have acted wickedly; 34 our kings,
our princes, our priests, and our
fathers have not kept thy law or heeded
thy commandments and thy warnings
which thou didst give them. 35 They
did not serve thee in their kingdom,
and in thy great goodness which thou
gavest them, and in the large and rich
land which thou didst set before them;
and they did not turn from their
wicked works. 36 Behold, we are slaves
this day; in the land that thou gavest
to our fathers to enjoy its fruit and its
good gifts, behold, we are slaves.
37 And its rich yield goes to the kings
whom thou hast set over us because of
our sins; they have power also over
our bodies and over our cattle at their
pleasure, and we are in great distress."

38[u] Because of all this we make a
firm covenant and write it, and our
princes, our Levites, and our priests
set their seal to it.

10[v] Those who set their seal are
Nē·hė·mī'ȧh the governor, the
son of Hac·ȧ·lī'ȧh, Zed·ė·kī'ȧh, 2 Se-
räi'ȧh, Az·ȧ·rī'ȧh, Jeremiah, 3 Pash'-
hŭr, Am·ȧ·rī'ȧh, Mal·chī'jȧh, 4 Hat'-
tŭsh, Sheb·ȧ·nī'ȧh, Mal'lŭch, 5 Hā'rim,
Mer'ė·moth, Ō·bȧ·dī'ȧh, 6 Daniel,
Gin'nė·thon, Bâr'ŭch, 7 Me·shul'lȧm,
Ȧ·bī'jȧh, Mī'jȧ·min, 8 Mā-ȧ·zī'ȧh, Bil'-
gäi, She·māi'ȧh; these are the priests.
9 And the Levites: Jesh'ü·ȧ the son of
Az·ȧ·nī'ȧh, Bin'nü·ī of the sons of
Hen'ȧ·dad, Kad'mi-el; 10 and their
brethren, Sheb·ȧ·nī'ȧh, Hō·dī'ȧh, Ke-
lī'tȧ, Pe·läi'ȧh, Hā'nȧn, 11 Mī'cȧ,
Rē'hob, Hash·ȧ·bī'ȧh, 12 Zac'cŭr, Sher-
ė·bī'ȧh, Sheb·ȧ·nī'ȧh, 13 Hō·dī'ȧh,
Bā'nī, Be·nī'nü. 14 The chiefs of the
people: Pā'rosh, Pā'hath-mō'ab, Ē'-
lȧm, Zat'tü, Bā'nī, 15 Bun'nī, Az'gad,
Bē'bäi, 16 Ad·ȯ·nī'jȧh, Big'väi, Ā'din,
17 Ā'tėr, Hez·ė·kī'ȧh, Az'zŭr, 18 Hō-
dī'ȧh, Hā'shŭm, Bē'zäi, 19 Hā'riph,
An'ȧ·thoth, Nē'bäi, 20 Mag'pi·ash,
Me·shul'lȧm, Hē'zir, 21 Me·shez'ȧ·bel,
Zā'dok, Jad'dü-ȧ, 22 Pel·ȧ·tī'ȧh, Hā'-
nȧn, Ȧ·näi'ȧh, 23 Hō·shē'ȧ, Han·ȧ-
nī'ȧh, Has'shŭb, 24 Hal·lō'hesh, Pil'hȧ,
Shō'bek, 25 Rē'hŭm, Hȧ·shab'nȧh, Mā-
ȧ·sēi'ȧh, 26 Ȧ·hī'ȧh, Hā'nȧn, Ā'nan,
27 Mal'lŭch, Hā'rim, Bā'ȧ·nȧh.

28 The rest of the people, the
priests, the Levites, the gatekeepers,
the singers, the temple servants, and
all who have separated themselves
from the peoples of the lands to the
law of God, their wives, their sons,
their daughters, all who have knowledge and understanding, 29 join with
their brethren, their nobles, and enter
into a curse and an oath to walk in
God's law which was given by Moses
the servant of God, and to observe and
do all the commandments of the LORD
our Lord and his ordinances and his
statutes. 30 We will not give our
daughters to the peoples of the land
or take their daughters for our sons;
31 and if the peoples of the land bring
in wares or any grain on the sabbath
day to sell, we will not buy from them
on the sabbath or on a holy day; and
we will forego the crops of the seventh
year and the exaction of every debt.

32 We also lay upon ourselves the
obligation to charge ourselves yearly
with the third part of a shekel for the
service of the house of our God: 33 for
the showbread, the continual cereal
offering, the continual burnt offering,
the sabbaths, the new moons, the
appointed feasts, the holy things, and
the sin offerings to make atonement
for Israel, and for all the work of the
house of our God. 34 We have likewise
cast lots, the priests, the Levites, and
the people, for the wood offering, to
bring it into the house of our God,
according to our fathers' houses, at
times appointed, year by year, to burn
upon the altar of the LORD our God,
as it is written in the law. 35 We
obligate ourselves to bring the first
fruits of our ground and the first fruits
of all fruit of every tree, year by year,
to the house of the LORD; 36 also to
bring to the house of our God, to the
priests who minister in the house of
our God, the first-born of our sons
and of our cattle, as it is written in the
law, and the firstlings of our herds and
of our flocks; 37 and to bring the first
of our coarse meal, and our contributions, the fruit of every tree, the wine
and the oil, to the priests, to the
chambers of the house of our God; and
to bring to the Levites the tithes from
our ground, for it is the Levites who
collect the tithes in all our rural towns.
38 And the priest, the son of Aaron,
shall be with the Levites when the
Levites receive the tithes; and the Levites shall bring up the tithe of the
tithes to the house of our God, to
the chambers, to the storehouse.
39 For the people of Israel and the sons
of Levi shall bring the contribution of
grain, wine, and oil to the chambers,
where are the vessels of the sanctuary,
and the priests that minister, and the
gatekeepers and the singers. We will
not neglect the house of our God.

11 Now the leaders of the people
lived in Jerusalem; and the rest
of the people cast lots to bring one
out of ten to live in Jerusalem the holy
city, while nine tenths remained in the
other towns. 2 And the people blessed
all the men who willingly offered to
live in Jerusalem.

3 These are the chiefs of the province who lived in Jerusalem; but in
the towns of Judah every one lived on
his property in their towns: Israel, the

[u] Ch 10.1 in Heb [v] Ch 10.2 in Heb
11.3-22: 1 Chron 9.2-34.

priests, the Levites, the temple servants, and the descendants of Solomon's servants. 4And in Jerusalem
lived certain of the sons of Judah and
of the sons of Benjamin. Of the sons of
Judah: Ȧ·thäi'ȧh the son of Uz·zī'ȧh,
son of Zech·ȧ·rī'ȧh, son of Am·ȧ·rī'ȧh,
son of Sheph·ȧ·tī'ȧh, son of Mȧ·hal'ȧ-
lel, of the sons of Per'ez; 5 and Mā-
ȧ·sēi'ȧh the son of Bâr'ŭch, son of
Col-hō'zėh, son of Hȧ·zāi'ȧh, son of
Ȧ·dāi'ȧh, son of Joi'ȧ·rib, son of Zech-
ȧ·rī'ȧh, son of the Shī'lō·nīte. 6All the
sons of Per'ez who lived in Jerusalem
were four hundred and sixty-eight
valiant men.

7 And these are the sons of Benjamin: Sal'lü the son of Me·shul'lȧm,
son of Jō'ed, son of Pe·dāi'ȧh, son of
Kō·läi'ȧh, son of Mā-ȧ·sēi'ȧh, son of
Ī'thi-el, son of Je·shā'iȧh. 8And after
him Gab·bā'ī, Sal'läi, nine hundred
and twenty-eight. 9 Jō'ėl the son of
Zich'rī was their overseer; and Judah
the son of Has·sė·nü'ȧh was second
over the city.

10 Of the priests: Je·däi'ȧh the son
of Joi'ȧ·rib, Jā'chin, 11 Se·räi'ȧh the
son of Hil·kī'ȧh, son of Me·shul'lȧm,
son of Zā'dok, son of Me·rā'ioth, son
of Ȧ·hī'tŭb, ruler of the house of God,
12 and their brethren who did the
work of the house, eight hundred and
twenty-two; and Ȧ·dāi'ȧh the son of
Je·rō'ham, son of Pel·ȧ·lī'ȧh, son of
Am'zī, son of Zech·ȧ·rī'ȧh, son of
Pash'hûr, son of Mal·chī'jȧh, 13 and
his brethren, heads of fathers' houses,
two hundred and forty-two; and
Ȧ·mash'säi, the son of Az'ȧ·rel, son of
Ăh'zäi, son of Me·shil'lė·moth, son of
Im'mėr, 14 and their brethren, mighty
men of valor, a hundred and twenty-
eight; their overseer was Zab'di·el the
son of Hag·gė·dō'lim.

15 And of the Levites: She·māi'ȧh
the son of Has'shŭb, son of Az·rī'kam,
son of Hash·ȧ·bī'ȧh, son of Bun'nī;
16 and Shab'bė·thāi and Jō'zȧ·bad, of
the chiefs of the Levites, who were
over the outside work of the house of
God; 17 and Mat·tȧ·nī'ȧh the son of
Mī'cȧ, son of Zab'dī, son of Ā'saph,
who was the leader to begin the thanksgiving in prayer, and Bak·bü·kī'ȧh, the
second among his brethren; and Ab'dȧ
the son of Sham'mū·ȧ, son of Gā'lal,
son of Je·dü'thŭn. 18All the Levites in
the holy city were two hundred and
eighty-four.

19 The gatekeepers, Ak'kŭb, Tal'-
mŏn and their brethren, who kept
watch at the gates, were a hundred
and seventy-two. 20And the rest of
Israel, and of the priests and the Levites, were in all the towns of Judah,
every one in his inheritance. 21 But
the temple servants lived on Ō'phel;
and Zī'hȧ and Gish'pȧ were over the
temple servants.

22 The overseer of the Levites in
Jerusalem was Uz'zī the son of Bā'nī,
son of Hash·ȧ·bī'ȧh, son of Mat·tȧ-
nī'ȧh, son of Mī'cȧ, of the sons of
Ā'saph, the singers, over the work of
the house of God. 23 For there was a
command from the king concerning
them, and a settled provision for the
singers, as every day required. 24And
Peth·ȧ·hī'ȧh the son of Me·shez'ȧ·bel,
of the sons of Zē'rȧh the son of Judah,
was at the king's hand in all matters
concerning the people.

25 And as for the villages, with
their fields, some of the people of
Judah lived in Kĭr'i·ath-är'bȧ and its
villages, and in Dī'bon and its villages,
and in Je·kab'zē·ėl and its villages,
26 and in Jesh'ü·ȧ and in Mō'lȧ·dȧh
and Beth-pel'et, 27 in Hā'zär-shü'ȧl,
in Beer-sheba and its villages, 28 in
Zik'lag, in Me·cō'nȧh and its villages,
29 in En-rim'mon, in Zō'rȧh, in Jär'-
muth, 30 Zȧ·nō'ȧh, Ȧ·dul'lȧm, and
their villages, Lā'chish and its fields,
and Ȧ·zē'kȧh and its villages. So they
encamped from Beer-sheba to the
valley of Hin'nȯm. 31 The people of
Benjamin also lived from Gē'bȧ onward, at Mich'mash, Ăi'jȧ, Beth'ėl and
its villages, 32An'ȧ·thoth, Nob, An·ȧ-
nī'ȧh, 33 Hā'zôr, Rā'mȧh, Git'tȧ·im,
34 Hā'did, Ze·bō'im, Ne·bal'lȧt, 35 Lod,
and Ō'nō, the valley of craftsmen.
36And certain divisions of the Levites
in Judah were joined to Benjamin.

12 These are the priests and the
Levites who came up with Ze-
rub'bȧ·bel the son of She-al'ti·el, and
Jesh'ü·ȧ: Se·räi'ȧh, Jeremiah, Ezra,
2Am·ȧ·rī'ȧh, Mal'lŭch, Hat'tŭsh,
3 Shec·ȧ·nī'ȧh, Rē'hŭm, Mer'ė·moth,
4 Id'dō, Gin'nė·thoi, Ȧ·bī'jȧh, 5 Mī'jȧ-
min, Mā-ȧ·dī'ȧh, Bil'gȧh, 6 She·māi'ȧh,
Joi'ȧ·rib, Je·däi'ȧh, 7 Sal'lü, Ā'mok,
Hil·kī'ȧh, Je·däi'ȧh. These were the
chiefs of the priests and of their
brethren in the days of Jesh'ü·ȧ.

8 And the Levites: Jesh'ü·ȧ, Bin'-
nü·ī, Kad'mi-el, Sher·ė·bī'ȧh, Judah,
and Mat·tȧ·nī'ȧh, who with his brethren was in charge of the songs of

thanksgiving. 9And Bak·bü·kī'ȧh and
Un'nō their brethren stood opposite
them in the service. 10And Jesh'ü·ȧ
was the father of Joi'ȧ·kim, Joiakim
the father of E·lī'ȧ·shib, Eliashib the
father of Joi'ȧ·dȧ, 11 Joi'ȧ·dȧ the father
of Jonathan, and Jonathan the father
of Jad'dü-ȧ.

12 And in the days of Joi'ȧ·kim
were priests, heads of fathers' houses:
of Se·räi'ȧh, Me·räi'ȧh; of Jeremiah,
Han·ȧ·nī'ȧh; 13 of Ezra, Me·shul'lȧm;
of Am·ȧ·rī'ȧh, Jē'hō-hā'nȧn; 14 of Mal'-
lū·chī, Jonathan; of Sheb·ȧ·nī'ȧh,
Joseph; 15 of Hā'rim, Ad'nȧ; of Me-
rā'ioth, Hel'käi; 16 of Id'dō, Zech·ȧ-
rī'ȧh; of Gin'nė·thon, Me·shul'lȧm;
17 of Ȧ·bī'jȧh, Zich'rī; of Mi·nī'ȧ·min,
of Mō·ȧ·dī'ȧh, Pil'täi; 18 of Bil'gȧh,
Sham'mū-ȧ; of She·māi'ȧh, Je·hon'ȧ-
thȧn; 19 of Joi'ȧ·rib, Mat·tē'näi; of
Je·däi'ȧh, Uz'zī; 20 of Sal'läi, Kal'läi;
of Ā'mok, Ē'bėr; 21 of Hil·kī'ȧh, Hash-
ȧ·bī'ȧh; of Je·däi'ȧh, Nė·than'el.

22 As for the Levites, in the days of
E·lī'ȧ·shib, Joi'ȧ·dȧ, Jō·hā'nȧn, and
Jad'dü-ȧ, there were recorded the
heads of fathers' houses; also the
priests until the reign of Dȧ·rī'ūs the
Persian. 23 The sons of Levi, heads
of fathers' houses, were written in the
Book of the Chronicles until the days of
Jō·hā'nȧn the son of E·lī'ȧ·shib. 24And
the chiefs of the Levites: Hash·ȧ·bī'ȧh,
Sher·ė·bī'ȧh, and Jesh'ü·ȧ the son of
Kad'mi-el, with their brethren over
against them, to praise and to give
thanks, according to the commandment of David the man of God, watch
corresponding to watch. 25 Mat·tȧ-
nī'ȧh, Bak·bü·kī'ȧh, Ō·bȧ·dī'ȧh, Me-
shul'lȧm, Tal'mȯn, and Ak'kūb were
gatekeepers standing guard at the
storehouses of the gates. 26 These
were in the days of Joi'ȧ·kim the son
of Jesh'ü·ȧ son of Jō'zȧ·dak, and in
the days of Nē·hė·mī'ȧh the governor
and of Ezra the priest the scribe.

27 And at the dedication of the wall
of Jerusalem they sought the Levites
in all their places, to bring them to
Jerusalem to celebrate the dedication
with gladness, with thanksgivings and
with singing, with cymbals, harps, and
lyres. 28And the sons of the singers
gathered together from the circuit
round Jerusalem and from the villages
of the Nė·toph'ȧ·thītes; 29 also from
Beth-gil'gȧl and from the region of
Gē'bȧ and Az'mȧ·veth; for the singers
had built for themselves villages
around Jerusalem. 30And the priests
and the Levites purified themselves;
and they purified the people and the
gates and the wall.

31 Then I brought up the princes
of Judah upon the wall, and appointed
two great companies which gave thanks
and went in procession. One went to
the right upon the wall to the Dung
Gate; 32 and after them went Hō·shäi'-
ȧh and half of the princes of Judah,
33 and Az·ȧ·rī'ȧh, Ezra, Me·shul'lȧm,
34 Judah, Benjamin, She·māi'ȧh, and
Jeremiah, 35 and certain of the priests'
sons with trumpets: Zech·ȧ·rī'ȧh the
son of Jonathan, son of She·māi'ȧh,
son of Mat·tȧ·nī'ȧh, son of Mī·cāi'ȧh,
son of Zac'cūr, son of Ā'saph; 36 and
his kinsmen, She·māi'ȧh, Az'ȧ·rel,
Mil'ȧ·läi, Gil'ȧ·läi, Mā'äi, Nė·than'el,
Judah, and Hȧ·nā'nī, with the musical
instruments of David the man of God;
and Ezra the scribe went before them.
37At the Fountain Gate they went up
straight before them by the stairs of
the city of David, at the ascent of the
wall, above the house of David, to the
Water Gate on the east.

38 The other company of those
who gave thanks went to the left, and
I followed them with half of the people, upon the wall, above the Tower of
the Ovens, to the Broad Wall, 39 and
above the Gate of Ē'phrȧ·im, and by
the Old Gate, and by the Fish Gate
and the Tower of Hȧ·nan'el and the
Tower of the Hundred, to the Sheep
Gate; and they came to a halt at the
Gate of the Guard. 40 So both companies of those who gave thanks stood
in the house of God, and I and half of
the officials with me; 41 and the priests
E·lī'ȧ·kim, Mā-ȧ·sēi'ȧh, Mi·nī'ȧ·min,
Mī·cāi'ȧh, El·i-ō-ē'näi, Zech·ȧ·rī'ȧh,
and Han·ȧ·nī'ȧh, with trumpets; 42 and
Mā-ȧ·sēi'ȧh, She·māi'ȧh, El·ē·ā'zȧr,
Uz'zī, Jē'hō-hā'nȧn, Mal·chī'jȧh,
Ē'lȧm, and Ē'zėr. And the singers sang
with Jez·rȧ·hī'ȧh as their leader. 43And
they offered great sacrifices that day
and rejoiced, for God had made them
rejoice with great joy; the women and
children also rejoiced. And the joy of
Jerusalem was heard afar off.

44 On that day men were appointed
over the chambers for the stores, the
contributions, the first fruits, and the
tithes, to gather into them the portions
required by the law for the priests and
for the Levites according to the fields
of the towns; for Judah rejoiced over

the priests and the Levites who ministered. 45 And they performed the
service of their God and the service of
purification, as did the singers and the
gatekeepers, according to the command of David and his son Solomon.
46 For in the days of David and Ā'saph
of old there was a chief of the singers,
and there were songs of praise and
thanksgiving to God. 47 And all Israel
in the days of Ze·rub'bȧ·bel and in
the days of Nē·hė·mī'ȧh gave the daily
portions for the singers and the gatekeepers; and they set apart that which
was for the Levites; and the Levites
set apart that which was for the sons
of Aaron.

13 On that day they read from the
book of Moses in the hearing of
the people; and in it was found written
that no Am'mȯ·nīte or Mō'ȧb·īte
should ever enter the assembly of God;
2 for they did not meet the children of
Israel with bread and water, but hired
Balaam against them to curse them—
yet our God turned the curse into a
blessing. 3 When the people heard the
law, they separated from Israel all
those of foreign descent.

4 Now before this, E·lī'ȧ·shib the
priest, who was appointed over the
chambers of the house of our God,
and who was connected with Tō·bī'ȧh,
5 prepared for Tō·bī'ȧh a large chamber
where they had previously put the
cereal offering, the frankincense, the
vessels, and the tithes of grain, wine,
and oil, which were given by commandment to the Levites, singers, and
gatekeepers, and the contributions for
the priests. 6 While this was taking
place I was not in Jerusalem, for in
the thirty-second year of Är-tȧ-xĕrx'ēs
king of Babylon I went to the king.
And after some time I asked leave of
the king 7 and came to Jerusalem, and
I then discovered the evil that E·lī'ȧ-
shib had done for Tō·bī'ȧh, preparing
for him a chamber in the courts of the
house of God. 8 And I was very angry,
and I threw all the household furniture
of Tō·bī'ȧh out of the chamber. 9 Then
I gave orders and they cleansed the
chambers; and I brought back thither
the vessels of the house of God, with
the cereal offering and the frankincense.

10 I also found out that the portions
of the Levites had not been given to
them; so that the Levites and the
singers, who did the work, had fled
each to his field. 11 So I remonstrated
with the officials and said, "Why is the
house of God forsaken?" And I
gathered them together and set them
in their stations. 12 Then all Judah
brought the tithe of the grain, wine,
and oil into the storehouses. 13 And I
appointed as treasurers over the storehouses Shel·ė·mī'ȧh the priest, Zā'dok
the scribe, and Pe·dāi'ah of the Levites, and as their assistant Hā'nȧn the
son of Zac'cŭr, son of Mat·tȧ·nī'ȧh,
for they were counted faithful; and
their duty was to distribute to their
brethren. 14 Remember me, O my
God, concerning this, and wipe not
out my good deeds that I have done
for the house of my God and for his
service.

15 In those days I saw in Judah
men treading wine presses on the
sabbath, and bringing in heaps of
grain and loading them on asses; and
also wine, grapes, figs, and all kinds
of burdens, which they brought into
Jerusalem on the sabbath day; and I
warned them on the day when they
sold food. 16 Men of Tȳre also, who
lived in the city, brought in fish and
all kinds of wares and sold them on
the sabbath to the people of Judah,
and in Jerusalem. 17 Then I remonstrated with the nobles of Judah and
said to them, "What is this evil thing
which you are doing, profaning the
sabbath day? 18 Did not your fathers
act in this way, and did not our God
bring all this evil on us and on this
city? Yet you bring more wrath upon
Israel by profaning the sabbath."

19 When it began to be dark at the
gates of Jerusalem before the sabbath,
I commanded that the doors should
be shut and gave orders that they
should not be opened until after the
sabbath. And I set some of my servants over the gates, that no burden
might be brought in on the sabbath
day. 20 Then the merchants and sellers
of all kinds of wares lodged outside
Jerusalem once or twice. 21 But I
warned them and said to them, "Why
do you lodge before the wall? If you
do so again I will lay hands on you."
From that time on they did not come
on the sabbath. 22 And I commanded
the Levites that they should purify
themselves and come and guard the
gates, to keep the sabbath day holy.

13.1: Deut 23.3-5.

Remember this also in my favor, O my God, and spare me according to the greatness of thy steadfast love.

23 In those days also I saw the Jews who had married women of Ash'dod, Am'mȯn, and Mō'ab; 24 and half of their children spoke the language of Ash'dod, and they could not speak the language of Judah, but the language of each people. 25 And I contended with them and cursed them and beat some of them and pulled out their hair; and I made them take oath in the name of God, saying, "You shall not give your daughters to their sons, or take their daughters for your sons or for yourselves. 26 Did not Solomon king of Israel sin on account of such women? Among the many nations there was no king like him, and he was beloved by his God, and God made him king over all Israel; nevertheless foreign women made even him to sin. 27 Shall we then listen to you and do all this great evil and act treacherously against our God by marrying foreign women?"

28 And one of the sons of Jehoi'ȧ·dȧ, the son of E·lī'ȧ·shib the high priest, was the son-in-law of Sanbal'lȧt the Hôr'ȯ·nīte; therefore I chased him from me. 29 Remember them, O my God, because they have defiled the priesthood and the covenant of the priesthood and the Levites.

30 Thus I cleansed them from everything foreign, and I established the duties of the priests and Levites, each in his work; 31 and I provided for the wood offering, at appointed times, and for the first fruits. Remember me, O my God, for good.

THE BOOK OF ESTHER

1 In the days of Ȧ·haṡ'ū-ē'rụs, the Ahasu-erus who reigned from India to Ethiopia over one hundred and twenty-seven provinces, 2 in those days when King Ȧ·haṡ'ū-ē'rụs sat on his royal throne in Su'sȧ the capital, 3 in the third year of his reign he gave a banquet for all his princes and servants, the army chiefs[a] of Persia and Media and the nobles and governors of the provinces being before him, 4 while he showed the riches of his royal glory and the splendor and pomp of his majesty for many days, a hundred and eighty days. 5 And when these days were completed, the king gave for all the people present in Su'sȧ the capital, both great and small, a banquet lasting for seven days, in the court of the garden of the king's palace. 6 There were white cotton curtains and blue hangings caught up with cords of fine linen and purple to silver rings[b] and marble pillars, and also couches of gold and silver on a mosaic pavement of porphyry, marble, mother-of-pearl and precious stones. 7 Drinks were served in golden goblets, goblets of different kinds, and the royal wine was lavished according to the bounty of the king. 8 And drinking was according to the law, no one was compelled; for the king had given orders to all the officials of his palace to do as every man desired. 9 Queen Vash'tī also gave a banquet for the women in the palace which belonged to King Ȧ·haṡ'ū-ē'rụs.

10 On the seventh day, when the heart of the king was merry with wine, he commanded Me·hü'mȧn, Biz'thȧ, Här·bō'nȧ, Big'thȧ and Ȧ·bag'thȧ, Zē'thär and Cär'kas, the seven eunuchs who served King Ȧ·haṡ'ū-ē'rụs as chamberlains, 11 to bring Queen Vash'tī before the king with her royal crown, in order to show the peoples and the princes her beauty; for she was fair to behold. 12 But Queen Vash'tī refused to come at the king's command conveyed by the eunuchs. At this the king was enraged, and his anger burned within him.

13 Then the king said to the wise men who knew the times—for this was the king's procedure toward all who were versed in law and judgment, 14 the

[a] Heb *the army* [b] Or *rods*

men next to him being Cär·shē′nȧ,
Shē′thär, Ad·mā′thȧ, Tär′shish, Mē′rēṡ,
Mär·sē′nȧ, and Me·mū′cȧn, the seven
princes of Persia and Media, who saw
the king's face, and sat first in the
kingdom—: 15 "According to the law,
what is to be done to Queen Vash′tī,
because she has not performed the
command of King Ȧ·haṡ′ū-ē′rŭs conveyed by the eunuchs?" 16 Then
Me·mū′cȧn said in presence of the
king and the princes, "Not only to the
king has Queen Vash′tī done wrong,
but also to all the princes and all the
peoples who are in all the provinces of
King Ȧ·haṡ′ū-ē′rŭs. 17 For this deed
of the queen will be made known to
all women, causing them to look with
contempt upon their husbands, since
they will say, 'King Ȧ·haṡ′ū-ē′rŭs
commanded Queen Vash′tī to be
brought before him, and she did not
come.' 18 This very day the ladies of
Persia and Media who have heard of
the queen's behavior will be telling it
to all the king's princes, and there will
be contempt and wrath in plenty. 19 If
it please the king, let a royal order go
forth from him, and let it be written
among the laws of the Persians and
the Medes so that it may not be
altered, that Vash′tī is to come no more
before King Ȧ·haṡ′ū-ē′rŭs; and let the
king give her royal position to another
who is better than she. 20 So when the
decree made by the king is proclaimed
throughout all his kingdom, vast as it
is, all women will give honor to their
husbands, high and low." 21 This advice pleased the king and the princes,
and the king did as Me·mū′cȧn pro-
posed; 22 he sent letters to all the royal
provinces, to every province in its own
script and to every people in its own
language, that every man be lord in
his own house and speak according to
the language of his people.

2 After these things, when the
anger of King Ȧ·haṡ′ū-ē′rŭs had
abated, he remembered Vash′tī and
what she had done and what had been
decreed against her. 2 Then the king's
servants who attended him said, "Let
beautiful young virgins be sought out
for the king. 3 And let the king appoint
officers in all the provinces of his kingdom to gather all the beautiful young
virgins to the harem in Su′sȧ the
capital, under custody of Heg′äi the
king's eunuch who is in charge of the
women; let their ointments be given
them. 4 And let the maiden who pleases
the king be queen instead of Vash′tī."
This pleased the king, and he did so.

5 Now there was a Jew in Su′sȧ the
capital whose name was Môr′de·cäi,
the son of Jā′ir, son of Shim′ē-ī, son of
Kish, a Benjaminite, 6 who had been
carried away from Jerusalem among
the captives carried away with Jec·ȯ-
nī′ȧh king of Judah, whom Ne·bŭ-
chȧd·nez′zȧr king of Babylon had carried away. 7 He had brought up Hȧ-
das′sȧh, that is Esther, the daughter
of his uncle, for she had neither father
nor mother; the maiden was beautiful
and lovely, and when her father and
her mother died, Môr′de·cäi adopted
her as his own daughter. 8 So when
the king's order and his edict were proclaimed, and when many maidens were
gathered in Su′sȧ the capital in custody
of Heg′äi, Esther also was taken into
the king's palace and put in custody
of Hegai who had charge of the
women. 9 And the maiden pleased him
and won his favor; and he quickly
provided her with her ointments and
her portion of food, and with seven
chosen maids from the king's palace,
and advanced her and her maids to the
best place in the harem. 10 Esther had
not made known her people or kindred,
for Môr′de·cäi had charged her not to
make it known. 11 And every day Môr′-
de·cäi walked in front of the court of
the harem, to learn how Esther was
and how she fared.

12 Now when the turn came for
each maiden to go in to King Ȧ·haṡ′ū-
ē′rŭs, after being twelve months under
the regulations for the women, since
this was the regular period of their
beautifying, six months with oil of
myrrh and six months with spices and
ointments for women—13 when the
maiden went in to the king in this way
she was given whatever she desired to
take with her from the harem to the
king's palace. 14 In the evening she
went, and in the morning she came
back to the second harem in custody
of Shȧ·ash′gaz the king's eunuch who
was in charge of the concubines; she
did not go in to the king again, unless
the king delighted in her and she was
summoned by name.

15 When the turn came for Esther
the daughter of Ab′i·hāil the uncle of
Môr′de·cäi, who had adopted her as
his own daughter, to go in to the king,
she asked for nothing except what

Heg'äi the king's eunuch, who had
charge of the women, advised. Now
Esther found favor in the eyes of all
who saw her. 16 And when Esther was
taken to King Ȧ·haṡ'ū-ē'rŭs into his
royal palace in the tenth month, which
is the month of Tē'beth, in the seventh
year of his reign, 17 the king loved
Esther more than all the women, and
she found grace and favor in his sight
more than all the virgins, so that he
set the royal crown on her head and
made her queen instead of Vash'tī.
18 Then the king gave a great banquet
to all his princes and servants; it was
Esther's banquet. He also granted a
remission of taxes[c] to the provinces,
and gave gifts with royal liberality.

19 When the virgins were gathered
together the second time, Môr'de·cäi
was sitting at the king's gate. 20 Now
Esther had not made known her kindred or her people, as Môr'de·cäi had
charged her; for Esther obeyed Mordecai just as when she was brought up
by him. 21 And in those days, as Môr'-
de·cäi was sitting at the king's gate,
Big'than and Tē'resh, two of the king's
eunuchs, who guarded the threshold,
became angry and sought to lay hands
on King Ȧ·haṡ'ū-ē'rŭs. 22 And this came
to the knowledge of Môr'de·cäi, and
he told it to Queen Esther, and Esther
told the king in the name of Mordecai.
23 When the affair was investigated
and found to be so, the men were both
hanged on the gallows. And it was
recorded in the Book of the Chronicles
in the presence of the king.

3 After these things King Ȧ·haṡ'ū-
ē'rŭs promoted Hā'măn the Ag'ȧ-
gīte, the son of Ham·mė·dā'thȧ, and
advanced him and set his seat above
all the princes who were with him.
2 And all the king's servants who were
at the king's gate bowed down and did
obeisance to Hā'măn; for the king had
so commanded concerning him. But
Môr'de·cäi did not bow down or do
obeisance. 3 Then the king's servants
who were at the king's gate said to
Môr'de·cäi, "Why do you transgress
the king's command?" 4 And when
they spoke to him day after day and
he would not listen to them, they told
Hā'măn, in order to see whether
Môr'de·cäi's words would avail; for he
had told them that he was a Jew. 5 And
when Hā'măn saw that Môr'de·cäi did
not bow down or do obeisance to him,
Haman was filled with fury. 6 But he
disdained to lay hands on Môr'de·cäi
alone. So, as they had made known to
him the people of Môr'de·cäi, Hā'măn
sought to destroy all the Jews, the
people of Mordecai, throughout the
whole kingdom of Ȧ·haṡ'ū-ē'rŭs.

7 In the first month, which is the
month of Nī'săn, in the twelfth year
of King Ȧ·haṡ'ū-ē'rŭs, they cast Pŭr,
that is the lot, before Hā'măn day after
day; and they cast it month after
month till the twelfth month, which is
the month of Ȧ·där'. 8 Then Hā'măn
said to King Ȧ·haṡ'ū-ē'rŭs, "There is
a certain people scattered abroad and
dispersed among the peoples in all the
provinces of your kingdom; their laws
are different from those of every other
people, and they do not keep the
king's laws, so that it is not for the
king's profit to tolerate them. 9 If it
please the king, let it be decreed that
they be destroyed, and I will pay ten
thousand talents of silver into the
hands of those who have charge of the
king's business, that they may put it
into the king's treasuries." 10 So the
king took his signet ring from his hand
and gave it to Hā'măn the Ag'ȧ·gīte,
the son of Ham·mė·dā'thȧ, the enemy
of the Jews. 11 And the king said to
Hā'măn, "The money is given to you,
the people also, to do with them as it
seems good to you."

12 Then the king's secretaries were
summoned on the thirteenth day of
the first month, and an edict, according to all that Hā'măn commanded,
was written to the king's satraps and
to the governors over all the provinces
and to the princes of all the peoples,
to every province in its own script and
every people in its own language; it
was written in the name of King
Ȧ·haṡ'ū-ē'rŭs and sealed with the
king's ring. 13 Letters were sent by
couriers to all the king's provinces, to
destroy, to slay, and to annihilate all
Jews, young and old, women and
children, in one day, the thirteenth
day of the twelfth month, which is the
month of Ȧ·där', and to plunder their
goods. 14 A copy of the document was
to be issued as a decree in every
province by proclamation to all the
peoples to be ready for that day. 15 The
couriers went in haste by order of the
king, and the decree was issued in
Su'sȧ the capital. And the king and

[c] Or *a holiday*

Hā'mȧn sat down to drink; but the city of Susa was perplexed.

4 When Môr'de·cäi learned all that had been done, Mordecai rent his clothes and put on sackcloth and ashes, and went out into the midst of the city, wailing with a loud and bitter cry; 2 he went up to the entrance of the king's gate, for no one might enter the king's gate clothed with sackcloth. 3 And in every province, wherever the king's command and his decree came, there was great mourning among the Jews, with fasting and weeping and lamenting, and most of them lay in sackcloth and ashes.

4 When Esther's maids and her eunuchs came and told her, the queen was deeply distressed; she sent garments to clothe Môr'de·cäi, so that he might take off his sackcloth, but he would not accept them. 5 Then Esther called for Hā'thach, one of the king's eunuchs, who had been appointed to attend her, and ordered him to go to Môr'de·cäi to learn what this was and why it was. 6 Hā'thach went out to Môr'de·cäi in the open square of the city in front of the king's gate, 7 and Môr'de·cäi told him all that had happened to him, and the exact sum of money that Hā'mȧn had promised to pay into the king's treasuries for the destruction of the Jews. 8 Môr'de·cäi also gave him a copy of the written decree issued in Su'sȧ for their destruction, that he might show it to Esther and explain it to her and charge her to go to the king to make supplication to him and entreat him for her people. 9 And Hā'thach went and told Esther what Môr'de·cäi had said. 10 Then Esther spoke to Hā'thach and gave him a message for Môr'de·cäi, saying, 11 "All the king's servants and the people of the king's provinces know that if any man or woman goes to the king inside the inner court without being called, there is but one law; all alike are to be put to death, except the one to whom the king holds out the golden scepter that he may live. And I have not been called to come in to the king these thirty days." 12 And they told Môr'de·cäi what Esther had said. 13 Then Môr'de·cäi told them to return answer to Esther, "Think not that in the king's palace you will escape any more than all the other Jews. 14 For if you keep silence at such a time as this, relief and deliverance will rise for the Jews from another quarter, but you and your father's house will perish. And who knows whether you have not come to the kingdom for such a time as this?" 15 Then Esther told them to reply to Môr'de·cäi, 16 "Go, gather all the Jews to be found in Su'sȧ, and hold a fast on my behalf, and neither eat nor drink for three days, night or day. I and my maids will also fast as you do. Then I will go to the king, though it is against the law; and if I perish, I perish." 17 Môr'de·cäi then went away and did everything as Esther had ordered him.

5 On the third day Esther put on her royal robes and stood in the inner court of the king's palace, opposite the king's hall. The king was sitting on his royal throne inside the palace opposite the entrance to the palace; 2 and when the king saw Queen Esther standing in the court, she found favor in his sight and he held out to Esther the golden scepter that was in his hand. Then Esther approached and touched the top of the scepter. 3 And the king said to her, "What is it, Queen Esther? What is your request? It shall be given you, even to the half of my kingdom." 4 And Esther said, "If it please the king, let the king and Hā'mȧn come this day to a dinner that I have prepared for the king." 5 Then said the king, "Bring Hā'mȧn quickly, that we may do as Esther desires." So the king and Haman came to the dinner that Esther had prepared. 6 And as they were drinking wine, the king said to Esther, "What is your petition? It shall be granted you. And what is your request? Even to the half of my kingdom, it shall be fulfilled." 7 But Esther said, "My petition and my request is: 8 If I have found favor in the sight of the king, and if it please the king to grant my petition and fulfil my request, let the king and Hā'mȧn come tomorrow[d] to the dinner which I will prepare for them, and tomorrow I will do as the king has said."

9 And Hā'mȧn went out that day joyful and glad of heart. But when Haman saw Môr'de·cäi in the king's gate, that he neither rose nor trembled

[d] Gk: Heb lacks *tomorrow*
5.3, 6: Mk 6.23.

before him, he was filled with wrath
against Mordecai. 10 Nevertheless
Hā'măn restrained himself, and went
home; and he sent and fetched his
friends and his wife Zē'resh. 11 And
Hā'măn recounted to them the splendor of his riches, the number of his
sons, all the promotions with which
the king had honored him, and how
he had advanced him above the princes
and the servants of the king. 12 And
Hā'măn added, "Even Queen Esther
let no one come with the king to the
banquet she prepared but myself. And
tomorrow also I am invited by her together with the king. 13 Yet all this
does me no good, so long as I see
Môr'de·cäi the Jew sitting at the king's
gate." 14 Then his wife Zē'resh and all
his friends said to him, "Let a gallows
fifty cubits high be made, and in the
morning tell the king to have Môr'de-
cäi hanged upon it; then go merrily
with the king to the dinner." This
counsel pleased Hā'măn, and he had
the gallows made.

6 On that night the king could not
sleep; and he gave orders to bring
the book of memorable deeds, the
chronicles, and they were read before
the king. 2 And it was found written
how Môr'de·cäi had told about Big-
thā'nȧ and Tē'resh, two of the king's
eunuchs, who guarded the threshold,
and who had sought to lay hands upon
King Ȧ·haś'ū-ē'rŭs. 3 And the king
said, "What honor or dignity has been
bestowed on Môr'de·cäi for this?" The
king's servants who attended him said,
"Nothing has been done for him."
4 And the king said, "Who is in the
court?" Now Hā'măn had just entered
the outer court of the king's palace to
speak to the king about having Môr'de-
cäi hanged on the gallows that he had
prepared for him. 5 So the king's
servants told him, "Hā'măn is there,
standing in the court." And the king
said, "Let him come in." 6 So Hā'măn
came in, and the king said to him,
"What shall be done to the man whom
the king delights to honor?" And
Haman said to himself, "Whom would
the king delight to honor more than
me?" 7 And Hā'măn said to the king,
"For the man whom the king delights
to honor, 8 let royal robes be brought,
which the king has worn, and the
horse which the king has ridden, and
on whose head a royal crown is set;
9 and let the robes and the horse be
handed over to one of the king's most
noble princes; let him[e] array the man
whom the king delights to honor, and
let him[e] conduct the man on horseback
through the open square of the city,
proclaiming before him: 'Thus shall it
be done to the man whom the king
delights to honor.' " 10 Then the king
said to Hā'măn, "Make haste, take
the robes and the horse, as you have
said, and do so to Môr'de·cäi the Jew
who sits at the king's gate. Leave out
nothing that you have mentioned."
11 So Hā'măn took the robes and the
horse, and he arrayed Môr'de·cäi and
made him ride through the open square
of the city, proclaiming, "Thus shall
it be done to the man whom the king
delights to honor."

12 Then Môr'de·cäi returned to the
king's gate. But Hā'măn hurried to his
house, mourning and with his head
covered. 13 And Hā'măn told his wife
Zē'resh and all his friends everything
that had befallen him. Then his wise
men and his wife Zeresh said to him,
"If Môr'de·cäi, before whom you have
begun to fall, is of the Jewish people,
you will not prevail against him but
will surely fall before him."

14 While they were yet talking with
him, the king's eunuchs arrived and
brought Hā'măn in haste to the banquet that Esther had prepared.

7 So the king and Hā'măn went in
to feast with Queen Esther. 2 And
on the second day, as they were drinking wine, the king again said to Esther,
"What is your petition, Queen Esther?
It shall be granted you. And what is
your request? Even to the half of my
kingdom, it shall be fulfilled." 3 Then
Queen Esther answered, "If I have
found favor in your sight, O king, and
if it please the king, let my life be
given me at my petition, and my people at my request. 4 For we are sold,
I and my people, to be destroyed, to
be slain, and to be annihilated. If we
had been sold merely as slaves, men
and women, I would have held my
peace; for our affliction is not to be
compared with the loss to the king."
5 Then King Ȧ·haś'ū-ē'rŭs said to
Queen Esther, "Who is he, and where
is he, that would presume to do this?"
6 And Esther said, "A foe and enemy!

[e] Heb *them*
7.2: Mk 6.23.

This wicked Hā′măn!" Then Haman
was in terror before the king and the
queen. 7And the king rose from the
feast in wrath and went into the palace
garden; but Hā′măn stayed to beg his
life from Queen Esther, for he saw that
evil was determined against him by
the king. 8And the king returned from
the palace garden to the place where
they were drinking wine, as Hā′măn
was falling on the couch where Esther
was; and the king said, "Will he even
assault the queen in my presence, in
my own house?" As the words left the
mouth of the king, they covered
Haman's face. 9 Then said Här·bō′nȧ,
one of the eunuchs in attendance on
the king, "Moreover, the gallows
which Hā′măn has prepared for Môr′-
de·cäi, whose word saved the king, is
standing in Haman's house, fifty cubits
high." 10And the king said, "Hang him
on that." So they hanged Hā′măn on
the gallows which he had prepared for
Môr′de·cäi. Then the anger of the
king abated.

8 On that day King Ȧ·haś′ū-ē′rŭs
gave to Queen Esther the house of
Hā′măn, the enemy of the Jews. And
Môr′de·cäi came before the king, for
Esther had told what he was to her;
2 and the king took off his signet ring,
which he had taken from Hā′măn,
and gave it to Môr′de·cäi. And Esther
set Mordecai over the house of Haman.

3 Then Esther spoke again to the
king; she fell at his feet and besought
him with tears to avert the evil design
of Hā′măn the Ag′ȧ·gīte and the plot
which he had devised against the Jews.
4And the king held out the golden
scepter to Esther, 5 and Esther rose
and stood before the king. And she
said, "If it please the king, and if I
have found favor in his sight, and if
the thing seem right before the king,
and I be pleasing in his eyes, let an
order be written to revoke the letters
devised by Hā′măn the Ag′ȧ·gīte, the
son of Ham·mė·dā′thȧ, which he wrote
to destroy the Jews who are in all the
provinces of the king. 6 For how can I
endure to see the calamity that is
coming to my people? Or how can I
endure to see the destruction of my
kindred?" 7 Then King Ȧ·haś′ū-ē′rŭs
said to Queen Esther and to Môr′de·cäi
the Jew, "Behold, I have given Esther
the house of Hā′măn, and they have
hanged him on the gallows, because
he would lay hands on the Jews. 8And
you may write as you please with
regard to the Jews, in the name of the
king, and seal it with the king's ring;
for an edict written in the name of the
king and sealed with the king's ring
cannot be revoked."

9 The king's secretaries were summoned at that time, in the third month,
which is the month of Sī′văn, on the
twenty-third day; and an edict was
written according to all that Môr′de-
cäi commanded concerning the Jews
to the satraps and the governors and
the princes of the provinces from India
to Ethiopia, a hundred and twenty-
seven provinces, to every province in
its own script and to every people in
its own language, and also to the Jews
in their script and their language.
10 The writing was in the name of
King Ȧ·haś′ū-ē′rŭs and sealed with
the king's ring, and letters were sent
by mounted couriers riding on swift
horses that were used in the king's
service, bred from the royal stud. 11 By
these the king allowed the Jews who
were in every city to gather and defend
their lives, to destroy, to slay, and to
annihilate any armed force of any people or province that might attack them,
with their children and women, and
to plunder their goods, 12 upon one
day throughout all the provinces of
King Ȧ·haś′ū-ē′rŭs, on the thirteenth
day of the twelfth month, which is the
month of Ȧ·där′. 13A copy of what was
written was to be issued as a decree in
every province, and by proclamation
to all peoples, and the Jews were to be
ready on that day to avenge themselves
upon their enemies. 14 So the couriers,
mounted on their swift horses that
were used in the king's service, rode
out in haste, urged by the king's command; and the decree was issued in
Su′sȧ the capital.

15 Then Môr′de·cäi went out from
the presence of the king in royal robes
of blue and white, with a great golden
crown and a mantle of fine linen and
purple, while the city of Su′sȧ shouted
and rejoiced. 16 The Jews had light and
gladness and joy and honor. 17And in
every province and in every city,
wherever the king's command and his
edict came, there was gladness and
joy among the Jews, a feast and a
holiday. And many from the peoples
of the country declared themselves
Jews, for the fear of the Jews had
fallen upon them.

9 Now in the twelfth month, which
is the month of Ȧ·där′, on the
thirteenth day of the same, when the
king's command and edict were about
to be executed, on the very day when
the enemies of the Jews hoped to get
the mastery over them, but which had
been changed to a day when the Jews
should get the mastery over their foes,
2 the Jews gathered in their cities
throughout all the provinces of King
Ȧ·has′ū-ē′rus to lay hands on such as
sought their hurt. And no one could
make a stand against them, for the fear
of them had fallen upon all peoples.
3 All the princes of the provinces and
the satraps and the governors and the
royal officials also helped the Jews, for
the fear of Môr′de·cäi had fallen upon
them. 4 For Môr′de·cäi was great in
the king's house, and his fame spread
throughout all the provinces; for the
man Mordecai grew more and more
powerful. 5 So the Jews smote all their
enemies with the sword, slaughtering,
and destroying them, and did as they
pleased to those who hated them. 6 In
Su′sȧ the capital itself the Jews slew
and destroyed five hundred men, 7 and
also slew Pär-shȧn-dā′thȧ and Dal′-
phon and As·pā′thȧ 8 and Pō·rā′thȧ
and Ȧ·dā′li·ȧ and Âr·i·dā′thȧ 9 and
Pȧr·mash′tȧ and Âr′i·säi and Âr′i·däi
and Väi·zā′thȧ, 10 the ten sons of
Hā′mȧn the son of Ham·mė·dā′thȧ,
the enemy of the Jews; but they laid
no hand on the plunder.

11 That very day the number of
those slain in Su′sȧ the capital was
reported to the king. 12 And the king
said to Queen Esther, "In Su′sȧ the
capital the Jews have slain five hundred
men and also the ten sons of Hā′mȧn.
What then have they done in the rest
of the king's provinces! Now what is
your petition? It shall be granted you.
And what further is your request? It
shall be fulfilled." 13 And Esther said,
"If it please the king, let the Jews who
are in Su′sȧ be allowed tomorrow also
to do according to this day's edict. And
let the ten sons of Hā′mȧn be hanged
on the gallows." 14 So the king commanded this to be done; a decree was
issued in Su′sȧ, and the ten sons of
Hā′mȧn were hanged. 15 The Jews
who were in Su′sȧ gathered also on
the fourteenth day of the month of
Ȧ·där′ and they slew three hundred
men in Susa; but they laid no hands
on the plunder.

16 Now the other Jews who were
in the king's provinces also gathered
to defend their lives, and got relief
from their enemies, and slew seventy-
five thousand of those who hated them;
but they laid no hands on the plunder.
17 This was on the thirteenth day of
the month of Ȧ·där′, and on the fourteenth day they rested and made that
a day of feasting and gladness. 18 But
the Jews who were in Su′sȧ gathered
on the thirteenth day and on the fourteenth, and rested on the fifteenth day,
making that a day of feasting and gladness. 19 Therefore the Jews of the
villages, who live in the open towns,
hold the fourteenth day of the month
of Ȧ·där′ as a day for gladness and
feasting and holiday-making, and a
day on which they send choice portions
to one another.

20 And Môr′de·cäi recorded these
things, and sent letters to all the Jews
who were in all the provinces of King
Ȧ·has′ū-ē′rus, both near and far,
21 enjoining them that they should
keep the fourteenth day of the month
Ȧ·där′ and also the fifteenth day of
the same, year by year, 22 as the days
on which the Jews got relief from their
enemies, and as the month that had
been turned for them from sorrow
into gladness and from mourning into
a holiday; that they should make them
days of feasting and gladness, days for
sending choice portions to one another
and gifts to the poor.

23 So the Jews undertook to do as
they had begun, and as Môr′de·cäi had
written to them. 24 For Hā′mȧn the
Ag′ȧ·gīte, the son of Ham·mė·dā′thȧ,
the enemy of all the Jews, had plotted
against the Jews to destroy them, and
had cast Pür, that is the lot, to crush
and destroy them; 25 but when Esther
came before the king, he gave orders
in writing that his wicked plot which
he had devised against the Jews should
come upon his own head, and that he
and his sons should be hanged on the
gallows. 26 Therefore they called these
days Pür′im, after the term Pür. And
therefore, because of all that was
written in this letter, and of what they
had faced in this matter, and of what
had befallen them, 27 the Jews ordained
and took it upon themselves and their
descendants and all who joined them,
that without fail they would keep these
two days according to what was written
and at the time appointed every year,

28 that these days should be remembered and kept throughout every generation, in every family, province, and
city, and that these days of Pür'im
should never fall into disuse among
the Jews, nor should the commemora-
tion of these days cease among their
descendants.
29 Then Queen Esther, the daughter of Ab'i·hāil, and Môr'de·cāi the
Jew gave full written authority, con-
firming this second letter about
Pür'im. 30 Letters were sent to all the
Jews, to the hundred and twenty-seven
provinces of the kingdom of A·haś'ū-
ē'rus, in words of peace and truth,
31 that these days of Pür'im should be
observed at their appointed seasons,
as Môr'de·cāi the Jew and Queen
Esther enjoined upon the Jews, and as
they had laid down for themselves and
for their descendants, with regard to
their fasts and their lamenting. 32 The
command of Queen Esther fixed these
practices of Pür'im, and it was recorded in writing.

10 King A·haś'ū-ē'rus laid tribute
on the land and on the coastlands
of the sea. 2 And all the acts of his
power and might, and the full account
of the high honor of Môr'de·cāi, to
which the king advanced him, are they
not written in the Book of the Chronicles of the kings of Media and Persia?
3 For Môr'de·cāi the Jew was next in
rank to King A·haś'ū-ē'rus, and he
was great among the Jews and popular
with the multitude of his brethren, for
he sought the welfare of his people
and spoke peace to all his people.

THE BOOK OF JOB

1 There was a man in the land of Uz,
whose name was Jōb; and that man
was blameless and upright, one who
feared God, and turned away from
evil. 2 There were born to him seven
sons and three daughters. 3 He had
seven thousand sheep, three thousand
camels, five hundred yoke of oxen, and
five hundred she-asses, and very many
servants; so that this man was the
greatest of all the people of the east.
4 His sons used to go and hold a feast
in the house of each on his day; and
they would send and invite their three
sisters to eat and drink with them.
5 And when the days of the feast had
run their course, Jōb would send and
sanctify them, and he would rise early
in the morning and offer burnt offerings according to the number of them
all; for Job said, "It may be that my
sons have sinned, and cursed God
in their hearts." Thus Job did continually.
6 Now there was a day when the
sons of God came to present themselves before the LORD, and Satan[a]
also came among them. 7 The LORD said
to Satan, "Whence have you come?"
Satan answered the LORD, "From going to and fro on the earth, and from
walking up and down on it." 8 And the
LORD said to Satan, "Have you considered my servant Jōb, that there is
none like him on the earth, a blameless
and upright man, who fears God and
turns away from evil?" 9 Then Satan
answered the LORD, "Does Jōb fear
God for nought? 10 Hast thou not put
a hedge about him and his house and
all that he has, on every side? Thou
hast blessed the work of his hands, and
his possessions have increased in the
land. 11 But put forth thy hand now,
and touch all that he has, and he will
curse thee to thy face." 12 And the
LORD said to Satan, "Behold, all that
he has is in your power; only upon
himself do not put forth your hand."
So Satan went forth from the presence
of the LORD.
13 Now there was a day when his
sons and daughters were eating and
drinking wine in their eldest brother's
house; 14 and there came a messenger
to Jōb, and said, "The oxen were
plowing and the asses feeding beside
them; 15 and the Sa·bē'ans fell upon

[a] Heb *the adversary*

them and took them, and slew the
servants with the edge of the sword;
and I alone have escaped to tell you."
16 While he was yet speaking, there
came another, and said, "The fire of
God fell from heaven and burned up
the sheep and the servants, and consumed them; and I alone have escaped
to tell you." 17 While he was yet speaking, there came another, and said,
"The Chal·dē'ăns formed three companies, and made a raid upon the
camels and took them, and slew the
servants with the edge of the sword;
and I alone have escaped to tell you."
18 While he was yet speaking, there
came another, and said, "Your sons
and daughters were eating and drinking wine in their eldest brother's
house; 19 and behold, a great wind
came across the wilderness, and struck
the four corners of the house, and it
fell upon the young people, and they
are dead; and I alone have escaped to
tell you."

20 Then Jōb arose, and rent his
robe, and shaved his head, and fell
upon the ground, and worshiped.
21 And he said, "Naked I came from
my mother's womb, and naked shall
I return; the LORD gave, and the LORD
has taken away; blessed be the name
of the LORD."

22 In all this Jōb did not sin or
charge God with wrong.

2 Again there was a day when the
sons of God came to present themselves before the LORD, and Satan also
came among them to present himself
before the LORD. 2 And the LORD said
to Satan, "Whence have you come?"
Satan answered the LORD, "From going to and fro on the earth, and from
walking up and down on it." 3 And the
LORD said to Satan, "Have you considered my servant Jōb, that there is
none like him on the earth, a blameless
and upright man, who fears God and
turns away from evil? He still holds
fast his integrity, although you moved
me against him, to destroy him without
cause." 4 Then Satan answered the
LORD, "Skin for skin! All that a man
has he will give for his life. 5 But put
forth thy hand now, and touch his
bone and his flesh, and he will curse
thee to thy face." 6 And the LORD said
to Satan, "Behold, he is in your power;
only spare his life."

7 So Satan went forth from the
presence of the LORD, and afflicted
Jōb with loathsome sores from the sole
of his foot to the crown of his head.
8 And he took a potsherd with which to
scrape himself, and sat among the ashes.

9 Then his wife said to him, "Do
you still hold fast your integrity? Curse
God, and die." 10 But he said to her,
"You speak as one of the foolish
women would speak. Shall we receive
good at the hand of God, and shall we
not receive evil?" In all this Jōb did
not sin with his lips.

11 Now when Jōb's three friends
heard of all this evil that had come
upon him, they came each from his
own place, E·lī'phaz the Tē'mȧ·nīte,
Bil'dad the Shü'hīte, and Zō'phär the
Nā'ȧ·mȧ·thīte. They made an appointment together to come to condole with
him and comfort him. 12 And when
they saw him from afar, they did not
recognize him; and they raised their
voices and wept; and they rent their
robes and sprinkled dust upon their
heads toward heaven. 13 And they sat
with him on the ground seven days
and seven nights, and no one spoke a
word to him, for they saw that his
suffering was very great.

3 After this Jōb opened his mouth
and cursed the day of his birth.
2 And Jōb said:

3 "Let the day perish wherein I was born,
and the night which said,
'A man-child is conceived.'
4 Let that day be darkness!
May God above not seek it,
nor light shine upon it.
5 Let gloom and deep darkness claim it.
Let clouds dwell upon it;
let the blackness of the day terrify it.
6 That night—let thick darkness seize it!
let it not rejoice among the days of the year,
let it not come into the number of the months.
7 Yea, let that night be barren;
let no joyful cry be heard[b] in it.
8 Let those curse it who curse the day,
who are skilled to rouse up Lė·vī'ȧ·thȧn.

[b] Heb *come*
3.3-19: Jer 20.14-18.

9 Let the stars of its dawn be dark;
let it hope for light, but have none,
nor see the eyelids of the morning;
10 because it did not shut the doors of my mother's womb,
nor hide trouble from my eyes.

11 "Why did I not die at birth,
come forth from the womb and expire?
12 Why did the knees receive me?
Or why the breasts, that I should suck?
13 For then I should have lain down and been quiet;
I should have slept; then I should have been at rest,
14 with kings and counselors of the earth
who rebuilt ruins for themselves,
15 or with princes who had gold,
who filled their houses with silver.
16 Or why was I not as a hidden untimely birth,
as infants that never see the light?
17 There the wicked cease from troubling,
and there the weary are at rest.
18 There the prisoners are at ease together;
they hear not the voice of the taskmaster.
19 The small and the great are there,
and the slave is free from his master.

20 "Why is light given to him that is in misery,
and life to the bitter in soul,
21 who long for death, but it comes not,
and dig for it more than for hid treasures;
22 who rejoice exceedingly,
and are glad, when they find the grave?
23 Why is light given to a man whose way is hid,
whom God has hedged in?
24 For my sighing comes as[c] my bread,
and my groanings are poured out like water.
25 For the thing that I fear comes upon me,
and what I dread befalls me.
26 I am not at ease, nor am I quiet;
I have no rest; but trouble comes."

4 Then E·lī'phaz the Tē'mȧ·nite answered:

2 "If one ventures a word with you, will you be offended?
Yet who can keep from speaking?
3 Behold, you have instructed many,
and you have strengthened the weak hands.
4 Your words have upheld him who was stumbling,
and you have made firm the feeble knees.
5 But now it has come to you, and you are impatient;
it touches you, and you are dismayed.
6 Is not your fear of God your confidence,
and the integrity of your ways your hope?

7 "Think now, who that was innocent ever perished?
Or where were the upright cut off?
8 As I have seen, those who plow iniquity
and sow trouble reap the same.
9 By the breath of God they perish,
and by the blast of his anger they are consumed.
10 The roar of the lion, the voice of the fierce lion,
the teeth of the young lions, are broken.
11 The strong lion perishes for lack of prey,
and the whelps of the lioness are scattered.

12 "Now a word was brought to me stealthily,
my ear received the whisper of it.
13 Amid thoughts from visions of the night,
when deep sleep falls on men,
14 dread came upon me, and trembling,
which made all my bones shake.
15 A spirit glided past my face;
the hair of my flesh stood up.
16 It stood still,
but I could not discern its appearance.
A form was before my eyes;
there was silence, then I heard a voice:
17 'Can mortal man be righteous before[d] God?
Can a man be pure before[d] his Maker?
18 Even in his servants he puts no trust,

[c] Heb *before* [d] Or *more than*

and his angels he charges with error;
19 how much more those who dwell in houses of clay,
whose foundation is in the dust,
who are crushed before the moth.
20 Between morning and evening they are destroyed;
they perish for ever without any regarding it.
21 If their tent-cord is plucked up within them,
do they not die, and that without wisdom?'

5 "Call now; is there any one who will answer you?
To which of the holy ones will you turn?
2 Surely vexation kills the fool,
and jealousy slays the simple.
3 I have seen the fool taking root,
but suddenly I cursed his dwelling.
4 His sons are far from safety,
they are crushed in the gate,
and there is no one to deliver them.
5 His harvest the hungry eat,
and he takes it even out of thorns;[e]
and the thirsty[f] pant after his[g] wealth.
6 For affliction does not come from the dust,
nor does trouble sprout from the ground;
7 but man is born to trouble
as the sparks fly upward.

8 "As for me, I would seek God,
and to God would I commit my cause;
9 who does great things and unsearchable,
marvelous things without number:
10 he gives rain upon the earth
and sends waters upon the fields;
11 he sets on high those who are lowly,
and those who mourn are lifted to safety.
12 He frustrates the devices of the crafty,
so that their hands achieve no success.
13 He takes the wise in their own craftiness;
and the schemes of the wily are brought to a quick end.
14 They meet with darkness in the daytime,
and grope at noonday as in the night.
15 But he saves the fatherless from their mouth,[h]
the needy from the hand of the mighty.
16 So the poor have hope,
and injustice shuts her mouth.

17 "Behold, happy is the man whom God reproves;
therefore despise not the chastening of the Almighty.
18 For he wounds, but he binds up;
he smites, but his hands heal.
19 He will deliver you from six troubles;
in seven there shall no evil touch you.
20 In famine he will redeem you from death,
and in war from the power of the sword.
21 You shall be hid from the scourge of the tongue,
and shall not fear destruction when it comes.
22 At destruction and famine you shall laugh,
and shall not fear the beasts of the earth.
23 For you shall be in league with the stones of the field,
and the beasts of the field shall be at peace with you.
24 You shall know that your tent is safe,
and you shall inspect your fold and miss nothing.
25 You shall know also that your descendants shall be many,
and your offspring as the grass of the earth.
26 You shall come to your grave in ripe old age,
as a shock of grain comes up to the threshing floor in its season.
27 Lo, this we have searched out; it is true.
Hear, and know it for your good."[i]

6 Then Jōb answered:
2 "O that my vexation were weighed,

[e] Heb obscure [f] Aquila Symmachus Syr Vg: Heb *snare* [g] Heb *their* [h] Cn: Heb uncertain
[i] Heb *for yourself*
5.12-13: 1 Cor 3.19.

and all my calamity laid in the balances!
3 For then it would be heavier than the sand of the sea;
therefore my words have been rash.
4 For the arrows of the Almighty are in me;
my spirit drinks their poison;
the terrors of God are arrayed against me.
5 Does the wild ass bray when he has grass,
or the ox low over his fodder?
6 Can that which is tasteless be eaten without salt,
or is there any taste in the slime of the purslane?[j]
7 My appetite refuses to touch them,
they are as food that is loathsome to me.[k]

8 "O that I might have my request,
and that God would grant my desire;
9 that it would please God to crush me,
that he would let loose his hand and cut me off!
10 This would be my consolation;
I would even exult[l] in pain unsparing;
for I have not denied the words of the Holy One.
11 What is my strength, that I should wait?
And what is my end, that I should be patient?
12 Is my strength the strength of stones,
or is my flesh bronze?
13 In truth I have no help in me,
and any resource is driven from me.

14 "He who withholds[m] kindness from a friend
forsakes the fear of the Almighty.
15 My brethren are treacherous as a torrent-bed,
as freshets that pass away,
16 which are dark with ice,
and where the snow hides itself.
17 In time of heat they disappear;
when it is hot, they vanish from their place.
18 The caravans turn aside from their course;
they go up into the waste, and perish.
19 The caravans of Tē'mȧ look,
the travelers of Sheba hope.
20 They are disappointed because they were confident;
they come thither and are confounded.
21 Such you have now become to me;[n]
you see my calamity, and are afraid.
22 Have I said, 'Make me a gift'?
Or, 'From your wealth offer a bribe for me'?
23 Or, 'Deliver me from the adversary's hand'?
Or, 'Ransom me from the hand of oppressors'?

24 "Teach me, and I will be silent;
make me understand how I have erred.
25 How forceful are honest words!
But what does reproof from you reprove?
26 Do you think that you can reprove words,
when the speech of a despairing man is wind?
27 You would even cast lots over the fatherless,
and bargain over your friend.

28 "But now, be pleased to look at me;
for I will not lie to your face.
29 Turn, I pray, let no wrong be done.
Turn now, my vindication is at stake.
30 Is there any wrong on my tongue?
Cannot my taste discern calamity?

7 "Has not man a hard service upon earth,
and are not his days like the days of a hireling?
2 Like a slave who longs for the shadow,
and like a hireling who looks for his wages,
3 so I am allotted months of emptiness,
and nights of misery are apportioned to me.
4 When I lie down I say, 'When shall I arise?'
But the night is long,
and I am full of tossing till the dawn.

[j] The meaning of the Hebrew word is uncertain [k] Heb obscure
[l] The meaning of the Hebrew word is uncertain [m] Syr Vg Compare Tg: Heb obscure
[n] Cn Compare Gk Syr: Heb obscure

5 My flesh is clothed with worms and dirt;
my skin hardens, then breaks out afresh.
6 My days are swifter than a weaver's shuttle,
and come to their end without hope.

7 "Remember that my life is a breath;
my eye will never again see good.
8 The eye of him who sees me will behold me no more;
while thy eyes are upon me, I shall be gone.
9 As the cloud fades and vanishes,
so he who goes down to Shē'ōl does not come up;
10 he returns no more to his house,
nor does his place know him any more.

11 "Therefore I will not restrain my mouth;
I will speak in the anguish of my spirit;
I will complain in the bitterness of my soul.
12 Am I the sea, or a sea monster,
that thou settest a guard over me?
13 When I say, 'My bed will comfort me,
my couch will ease my complaint,'
14 then thou dost scare me with dreams
and terrify me with visions,
15 so that I would choose strangling
and death rather than my bones.
16 I loathe my life; I would not live for ever.
Let me alone, for my days are a breath.
17 What is man, that thou dost make so much of him,
and that thou dost set thy mind upon him,
18 dost visit him every morning,
and test him every moment?
19 How long wilt thou not look away from me,
nor let me alone till I swallow my spittle?
20 If I sin, what do I do to thee, thou watcher of men?
Why hast thou made me thy mark?
Why have I become a burden to thee?
21 Why dost thou not pardon my transgression
and take away my iniquity?
For now I shall lie in the earth;
thou wilt seek me, but I shall not be."

8 Then Bil'dad the Shü'hīte answered:
2 "How long will you say these things,
and the words of your mouth be a great wind?
3 Does God pervert justice?
Or does the Almighty pervert the right?
4 If your children have sinned against him,
he has delivered them into the power of their transgression.
5 If you will seek God
and make supplication to the Almighty,
6 if you are pure and upright,
surely then he will rouse himself for you
and reward you with a rightful habitation.
7 And though your beginning was small,
your latter days will be very great.

8 "For inquire, I pray you, of bygone ages,
and consider what the fathers have found;
9 for we are but of yesterday, and know nothing,
for our days on earth are a shadow.
10 Will they not teach you, and tell you,
and utter words out of their understanding?

11 "Can papyrus grow where there is no marsh?
Can reeds flourish where there is no water?
12 While yet in flower and not cut down,
they wither before any other plant.
13 Such are the paths of all who forget God;
the hope of the godless man shall perish.
14 His confidence breaks in sunder,
and his trust is a spider's web.[o]
15 He leans against his house, but it does not stand;
he lays hold of it, but it does not endure.

[o] Heb *house*
7.17: Ps 8.4.

16 He thrives before the sun,
and his shoots spread over his garden.
17 His roots twine about the stoneheap;
he lives among the rocks.[p]
18 If he is destroyed from his place,
then it will deny him, saying, 'I have never seen you.'
19 Behold, this is the joy of his way;
and out of the earth others will spring.

20 "Behold, God will not reject a blameless man,
nor take the hand of evildoers.
21 He will yet fill your mouth with laughter,
and your lips with shouting.
22 Those who hate you will be clothed with shame,
and the tent of the wicked will be no more."

9 Then Jōb answered:
2 "Truly I know that it is so:
But how can a man be just before God?
3 If one wished to contend with him,
one could not answer him once in a thousand times.
4 He is wise in heart, and mighty in strength
—who has hardened himself against him, and succeeded?—
5 he who removes mountains, and they know it not,
when he overturns them in his anger;
6 who shakes the earth out of its place,
and its pillars tremble;
7 who commands the sun, and it does not rise;
who seals up the stars;
8 who alone stretched out the heavens,
and trampled the waves of the sea;[q]
9 who made the Bear and Ō rī'ŏn,
the Plēi'ȧ·dēṡ and the chambers of the south;
10 who does great things beyond understanding,
and marvelous things without number.
11 Lo, he passes by me, and I see him not;
he moves on, but I do not perceive him.
12 Behold, he snatches away; who can hinder him?
Who will say to him, 'What doest thou'?

13 "God will not turn back his anger;
beneath him bowed the helpers of Rā'hab.
14 How then can I answer him,
choosing my words with him?
15 Though I am innocent, I cannot answer him;
I must appeal for mercy to my accuser.[r]
16 If I summoned him and he answered me,
I would not believe that he was listening to my voice.
17 For he crushes me with a tempest,
and multiplies my wounds without cause;
18 he will not let me get my breath,
but fills me with bitterness.
19 If it is a contest of strength, behold him!
If it is a matter of justice, who can summon him?[s]
20 Though I am innocent, my own mouth would condemn me;
though I am blameless, he would prove me perverse.
21 I am blameless; I regard not myself;
I loathe my life.
22 It is all one; therefore I say,
he destroys both the blameless and the wicked.
23 When disaster brings sudden death,
he mocks at the calamity[t] of the innocent.
24 The earth is given into the hand of the wicked;
he covers the faces of its judges—
if it is not he, who then is it?

25 "My days are swifter than a runner;
they flee away, they see no good.
26 They go by like skiffs of reed,
like an eagle swooping on the prey.
27 If I say, 'I will forget my complaint,
I will put off my sad countenance,
and be of good cheer,'
28 I become afraid of all my suffering,
for I know thou wilt not hold me innocent.
29 I shall be condemned;
why then do I labour in vain?
30 If I wash myself with snow,

[p] Gk Vg: Heb uncertain [q] Or *trampled the back of the sea dragon* [r] Or *for my right*
[s] Compare Gk: Heb *me*. The text of the verse is uncertain
[t] The meaning of the Hebrew word is uncertain

and cleanse my hands with lye,
31 yet thou wilt plunge me into a pit,
and my own clothes will abhor me.
32 For he is not a man, as I am, that I might answer him,
that we should come to trial together.
33 There is no[u] umpire between us,
who might lay his hand upon us both.
34 Let him take his rod away from me,
and let not dread of him terrify me.
35 Then I would speak without fear of him,
for I am not so in myself.

10 "I loathe my life;
I will give free utterance to my complaint;
I will speak in the bitterness of my soul.
2 I will say to God, Do not condemn me;
let me know why thou dost contend against me.
3 Does it seem good to thee to oppress,
to despise the work of thy hands
and favor the designs of the wicked?
4 Hast thou eyes of flesh?
Dost thou see as man sees?
5 Are thy days as the days of man,
or thy years as man's years,
6 that thou dost seek out my iniquity
and search for my sin,
7 although thou knowest that I am not guilty,
and there is none to deliver out of thy hand?
8 Thy hands fashioned and made me;
and now thou dost turn about and destroy me.[v]
9 Remember that thou hast made me of clay;[w]
and wilt thou turn me to dust again?
10 Didst thou not pour me out like milk
and curdle me like cheese?
11 Thou didst clothe me with skin and flesh,
and knit me together with bones and sinews.
12 Thou hast granted me life and steadfast love;
and thy care has preserved my spirit.
13 Yet these things thou didst hide in thy heart;
I know that this was thy purpose.
14 If I sin, thou dost mark me,
and dost not acquit me of my iniquity.
15 If I am wicked, woe to me!
If I am righteous, I cannot lift up my head,
for I am filled with disgrace
and look upon my affliction.
16 And if I lift myself up,[x] thou dost hunt me like a lion,
and again work wonders against me;
17 thou dost renew thy witnesses against me,
and increase thy vexation toward me;
thou dost bring fresh hosts against me.[y]

18 "Why didst thou bring me forth from the womb?
Would that I had died before any eye had seen me,
19 and were as though I had not been,
carried from the womb to the grave.
20 Are not the days of my life few?[z]
Let me alone, that I may find a little comfort[a]
21 before I go whence I shall not return,
to the land of gloom and deep darkness,
22 the land of gloom[b] and chaos,
where light is as darkness."

11 Then Zō'phär the Nā'á·má·thīte answered:
2 "Should a multitude of words go unanswered,
and a man full of talk be vindicated?
3 Should your babble silence men,
and when you mock, shall no one shame you?
4 For you say, 'My doctrine is pure,
and I am clean in God's eyes.'
5 But oh, that God would speak,

[u] Another reading is *Would that there were*
[v] Cn Compare Gk Syr: Heb *made me together round about and thou dost destroy me*
[w] Gk: Heb *like clay* [x] Syr: Heb *he lifts himself up*
[y] Cn Compare Gk: Heb *changes and a host are with me*
[z] Cn Compare Gk Syr: Heb *Are not my days few? Let him cease* [a] Heb *brighten up*
[b] Heb *gloom as darkness, deep darkness*

and open his lips to you,
6 and that he would tell you the
secrets of wisdom!
For he is manifold in understanding.[c]
Know then that God exacts of you
less than your guilt deserves.

7 "Can you find out the deep things
of God?
Can you find out the limit of the
Almighty?
8 It is higher than heaven[d]—what can
you do?
Deeper than Shē'ōl—what can
you know?
9 Its measure is longer than the earth,
and broader than the sea.
10 If he passes through, and imprisons,
and calls to judgment, who can
hinder him?
11 For he knows worthless men;
when he sees iniquity, will he not
consider it?
12 But a stupid man will get understanding,
when a wild ass's colt is born a
man.

13 "If you set your heart aright,
you will stretch out your hands
toward him.
14 If iniquity is in your hand, put it
far away,
and let not wickedness dwell in
your tents.
15 Surely then you will lift up your
face without blemish;
you will be secure, and will not
fear.
16 You will forget your misery;
you will remember it as waters
that have passed away.
17 And your life will be brighter than
the noonday;
its darkness will be like the
morning.
18 And you will have confidence, because there is hope;
you will be protected[e] and take
your rest in safety.
19 You will lie down, and none will
make you afraid;
many will entreat your favor.
20 But the eyes of the wicked will fail;
all way of escape will be lost to
them,
and their hope is to breathe their
last."

12 Then Jōb answered:
2 "No doubt you are the people,
and wisdom will die with you.
3 But I have understanding as well as
you;
I am not inferior to you.
Who does not know such things
as these?
4 I am a laughingstock to my friends;
I, who called upon God and he
answered me,
a just and blameless man, am a
laughingstock.
5 In the thought of one who is at ease
there is contempt for misfortune;
it is ready for those whose feet
slip.
6 The tents of robbers are at peace,
and those who provoke God are
secure,
who bring their god in their hand.[f]

7 "But ask the beasts, and they will
teach you;
the birds of the air, and they will
tell you;
8 or the plants of the earth,[g] and they
will teach you;
and the fish of the sea will declare
to you.
9 Who among all these does not know
that the hand of the LORD has
done this?
10 In his hand is the life of every living
thing
and the breath of all mankind.
11 Does not the ear try words
as the palate tastes food?
12 Wisdom is with the aged,
and understanding in length of
days.

13 "With God[h] are wisdom and might;
he has counsel and understanding.
14 If he tears down, none can rebuild;
if he shuts a man in, none can
open.
15 If he withholds the waters, they dry
up;
if he sends them out, they overwhelm the land.
16 With him are strength and wisdom;
the deceived and the deceiver are
his.
17 He leads counselors away stripped,
and judges he makes fools.
18 He looses the bonds of kings,

[c] Heb obscure [d] Heb *The heights of heaven* [e] Or *you will look around* [f] Hebrew uncertain
[g] Or *speak to the earth* [h] Heb *him*

and binds a waistcloth on their
loins.
19 He leads priests away stripped,
and overthrows the mighty.
20 He deprives of speech those who
are trusted,
and takes away the discernment
of the elders.
21 He pours contempt on princes,
and looses the belt of the strong.
22 He uncovers the deeps out of darkness,
and brings deep darkness to light.
23 He makes nations great, and he
destroys them:
he enlarges nations, and leads
them away.
24 He takes away understanding from
the chiefs of the people of the
earth,
and makes them wander in a pathless waste.
25 They grope in the dark without
light;
and he makes them stagger like a
drunken man.

13 "Lo, my eye has seen all this,
my ear has heard and understood it.
2 What you know, I also know;
I am not inferior to you.
3 But I would speak to the Almighty,
and I desire to argue my case with
God.
4 As for you, you whitewash with lies;
worthless physicians are you all.
5 Oh that you would keep silent,
and it would be your wisdom!
6 Hear now my reasoning,
and listen to the pleadings of my
lips.
7 Will you speak falsely for God,
and speak deceitfully for him?
8 Will you show partiality toward him,
will you plead the case for God?
9 Will it be well with you when he
searches you out?
Or can you deceive him, as one
deceives a man?
10 He will surely rebuke you
if in secret you show partiality.
11 Will not his majesty terrify you,
and the dread of him fall upon
you?
12 Your maxims are proverbs of ashes,
your defenses are defenses of clay.

13 "Let me have silence, and I will
speak,
and let come on me what may.
14 I will take[i] my flesh in my teeth,
and put my life in my hand.
15 Behold, he will slay me; I have no
hope;
yet I will defend my ways to his
face.
16 This will be my salvation,
that a godless man shall not come
before him.
17 Listen carefully to my words,
and let my declaration be in your
ears.
18 Behold, I have prepared my case;
I know that I shall be vindicated.
19 Who is there that will contend with
me?
For then I would be silent and die.
20 Only grant two things to me,
then I will not hide myself from
thy face:
21 withdraw thy hand far from me,
and let not dread of thee terrify
me.
22 Then call, and I will answer;
or let me speak, and do thou reply
to me.
23 How many are my iniquities and
my sins?
Make me know my transgression
and my sin.
24 Why dost thou hide thy face,
and count me as thy enemy?
25 Wilt thou frighten a driven leaf
and pursue dry chaff?
26 For thou writest bitter things against
me,
and makest me inherit the iniquities of my youth.
27 Thou puttest my feet in the stocks,
and watchest all my paths;
thou settest a bound to the soles
of my feet.
28 Man[j] wastes away like a rotten thing,
like a garment that is moth-eaten.

14 "Man that is born of a woman is
of few days, and full of trouble.
2 He comes forth like a flower, and
withers;
he flees like a shadow, and continues not.
3 And dost thou open thy eyes upon
such a one
and bring him[k] into judgment
with thee?
4 Who can bring a clean thing out of
an unclean?
There is not one.
5 Since his days are determined,

[i] Gk: Heb *Why should I take?* [j] Heb *He* [k] Gk Syr Vg: Heb *me*

and the number of his months is with thee,
and thou hast appointed his bounds that he cannot pass,
6 look away from him, and desist,[l]
that he may enjoy, like a hireling, his day.

7 "For there is hope for a tree,
if it be cut down, that it will sprout again,
and that its shoots will not cease.
8 Though its root grow old in the earth,
and its stump die in the ground,
9 yet at the scent of water it will bud
and put forth branches like a young plant.
10 But man dies, and is laid low;
man breathes his last, and where is he?
11 As waters fail from a lake,
and a river wastes away and dries up,
12 so man lies down and rises not again;
till the heavens are no more he will not awake,
or be roused out of his sleep.
13 Oh that thou wouldest hide me in Shē'ōl,
that thou wouldest conceal me until thy wrath be past,
that thou wouldest appoint me a set time, and remember me!
14 If a man die, shall he live again?
All the days of my service I would wait,
till my release should come.
15 Thou wouldest call, and I would answer thee;
thou wouldest long for the work of thy hands.
16 For then thou wouldest number my steps,
thou wouldest not keep watch over my sin;
17 my transgression would be sealed up in a bag,
and thou wouldest cover over my iniquity.

18 "But the mountain falls and crumbles away,
and the rock is removed from its place;
19 the waters wear away the stones;
the torrents wash away the soil of the earth;
so thou destroyest the hope of man.
20 Thou prevailest for ever against him, and he passes;
thou changest his countenance, and sendest him away.
21 His sons come to honor, and he does not know it;
they are brought low, and he perceives it not.
22 He feels only the pain of his own body,
and he mourns only for himself."

15 Then E·lī'phaz the Tē'mȧ·nīte answered:
2 "Should a wise man answer with windy knowledge,
and fill himself with the east wind?
3 Should he argue in unprofitable talk,
or in words with which he can do no good?
4 But you are doing away with the fear of God,
and hindering meditation before God.
5 For your iniquity teaches your mouth,
and you choose the tongue of the crafty.
6 Your own mouth condemns you, and not I;
your own lips testify against you.

7 "Are you the first man that was born?
Or were you brought forth before the hills?
8 Have you listened in the council of God?
And do you limit wisdom to yourself?
9 What do you know that we do not know?
What do you understand that is not clear to us?
10 Both the gray-haired and the aged are among us,
older than your father.
11 Are the consolations of God too small for you,
or the word that deals gently with you?
12 Why does your heart carry you away,
and why do your eyes flash,
13 that you turn your spirit against God,
and let such words go out of your mouth?

[l] Cn: Heb *that he may desist*

14 What is man, that he can be clean?
Or he that is born of a woman,
that he can be righteous?
15 Behold, God puts no trust in his
holy ones,
and the heavens are not clean in
his sight;
16 how much less one who is abominable and corrupt,
a man who drinks iniquity like
water!

17 "I will show you, hear me;
and what I have seen I will declare
18 (what wise men have told,
and their fathers have not hidden,
19 to whom alone the land was given,
and no stranger passed among
them).
20 The wicked man writhes in pain all
his days,
through all the years that are laid
up for the ruthless.
21 Terrifying sounds are in his ears;
in prosperity the destroyer will
come upon him.
22 He does not believe that he will
return out of darkness,
and he is destined for the sword.
23 He wanders abroad for bread, saying, 'Where is it?'
He knows that a day of darkness
is ready at his hand;
24 distress and anguish terrify him;
they prevail against him, like a
king prepared for battle.
25 Because he has stretched forth his
hand against God,
and bids defiance to the Almighty,
26 running stubbornly against him
with a thick-bossed shield;
27 because he has covered his face with
his fat,
and gathered fat upon his loins,
28 and has lived in desolate cities,
in houses which no man should
inhabit,
which were destined to become
heaps of ruins;
29 he will not be rich, and his wealth
will not endure,
nor will he strike root in the
earth;[m]
30 he will not escape from darkness;
the flame will dry up his shoots,
and his blossom[n] will be swept
away[o] by the wind.
31 Let him not trust in emptiness,
deceiving himself;
for emptiness will be his recompense.
32 It will be paid in full before his
time,
and his branch will not be green.
33 He will shake off his unripe grape,
like the vine,
and cast off his blossom, like the
olive tree.
34 For the company of the godless is
barren,
and fire consumes the tents of
bribery.
35 They conceive mischief and bring
forth evil
and their heart prepares deceit."

16 Then Jōb answered:
2 "I have heard many such things;
miserable comforters are you all.
3 Shall windy words have an end?
Or what provokes you that you
answer?
4 I also could speak as you do,
if you were in my place;
I could join words together against
you,
and shake my head at you.
5 I could strengthen you with my
mouth,
and the solace of my lips would
assuage your pain.

6 "If I speak, my pain is not assuaged,
and if I forbear, how much of it
leaves me?
7 Surely now God has worn me out;
he has[p] made desolate all my
company.
8 And he has[p] shriveled me up,
which is a witness against me;
and my leanness has risen up against
me,
it testifies to my face.
9 He has torn me in his wrath, and
hated me;
he has gnashed his teeth at me;
my adversary sharpens his eyes
against me.
10 Men have gaped at me with their
mouth,
they have struck me insolently
upon the cheek,
they mass themselves together
against me.
11 God gives me up to the ungodly,
and casts me into the hands of
the wicked.
12 I was at ease, and he broke me
asunder;

[m] Vg: Heb obscure [n] Gk: Heb *mouth* [o] Cn: Heb *will depart* [p] Heb *thou hast*

he seized me by the neck and dashed me to pieces;
he set me up as his target,
13 his archers surround me.
He slashes open my kidneys, and does not spare;
he pours out my gall on the ground.
14 He breaks me with breach upon breach;
he runs upon me like a warrior.
15 I have sewed sackcloth upon my skin,
and have laid my strength in the dust.
16 My face is red with weeping,
and on my eyelids is deep darkness;
17 although there is no violence in my hands,
and my prayer is pure.

18 "O earth, cover not my blood,
and let my cry find no resting place.
19 Even now, behold, my witness is in heaven,
and he that vouches for me is on high.
20 My friends scorn me;
my eye pours out tears to God,
21 that he would maintain the right of a man with God,
like[q] that of a man with his neighbor.
22 For when a few years have come
I shall go the way whence I shall not return.

17 My spirit is broken, my days are extinct,
the grave is ready for me.
2 Surely there are mockers about me,
and my eye dwells on their provocation.

3 "Lay down a pledge for me with thyself;
who is there that will give surety for me?
4 Since thou hast closed their minds to understanding,
therefore thou wilt not let them triumph.
5 He who informs against his friends to get a share of their property,
the eyes of his children will fail.

6 "He has made me a byword of the peoples,
and I am one before whom men spit.
7 My eye has grown dim from grief,
and all my members are like a shadow.
8 Upright men are appalled at this,
and the innocent stirs himself up against the godless.
9 Yet the righteous holds to his way,
and he that has clean hands grows stronger and stronger.
10 But you, come on again, all of you,
and I shall not find a wise man among you.
11 My days are past, my plans are broken off,
the desires of my heart.
12 They make night into day;
'The light,' they say, 'is near to the darkness.'[r]
13 If I look for Shē'ōl as my house,
if I spread my couch in darkness,
14 if I say to the pit, 'You are my father,'
and to the worm, 'My mother,' or 'My sister,'
15 where then is my hope?
Who will see my hope?
16 Will it go down to the bars of Shē'ōl?
Shall we descend together into the dust?"

18 Then Bil'dad the Shü'hite answered:
2 "How long will you hunt for words?
Consider, and then we will speak.
3 Why are we counted as cattle?
Why are we stupid in your sight?
4 You who tear yourself in your anger,
shall the earth be forsaken for you,
or the rock be removed out of its place?

5 "Yea, the light of the wicked is put out,
and the flame of his fire does not shine.
6 The light is dark in his tent,
and his lamp above him is put out.
7 His strong steps are shortened
and his own schemes throw him down.
8 For he is cast into a net by his own feet,
and he walks on a pitfall.
9 A trap seizes him by the heel,
a snare lays hold of him.

[q] Syr Vg Tg: Heb *and* [r] Heb obscure

10 A rope is hid for him in the ground,
a trap for him in the path.
11 Terrors frighten him on every side,
and chase him at his heels.
12 His strength is hunger-bitten,
and calamity is ready for his stumbling.
13 By disease his skin is consumed,[s]
the first-born of death consumes his limbs.
14 He is torn from the tent in which he trusted,
and is brought to the king of terrors.
15 In his tent dwells that which is none of his;
brimstone is scattered upon his habitation.
16 His roots dry up beneath,
and his branches wither above.
17 His memory perishes from the earth,
and he has no name in the street.
18 He is thrust from light into darkness,
and driven out of the world.
19 He has no offspring or descendant among his people,
and no survivor where he used to live.
20 They of the west are appalled at his day,
and horror seizes them of the east.
21 Surely such are the dwellings of the ungodly,
such is the place of him who knows not God."

19 Then Jōb answered:
2 "How long will you torment me,
and break me in pieces with words?
3 These ten times you have cast reproach upon me;
are you not ashamed to wrong me?
4 And even if it be true that I have erred,
my error remains with myself.
5 If indeed you magnify yourselves against me,
and make my humiliation an argument against me,
6 know then that God has put me in the wrong,
and closed his net about me.
7 Behold, I cry out, 'Violence!' but I am not answered;
I call aloud, but there is no justice.
8 He has walled up my way, so that I cannot pass,
and he has set darkness upon my paths.
9 He has stripped from me my glory,
and taken the crown from my head.
10 He breaks me down on every side, and I am gone,
and my hope has he pulled up like a tree.
11 He has kindled his wrath against me,
and counts me as his adversary.
12 His troops come on together;
they have cast up siegeworks[t] against me,
and encamp round about my tent.

13 "He has put my brethren far from me,
and my acquaintances are wholly estranged from me.
14 My kinsfolk and my close friends have failed me;
15 the guests in my house have forgotten me;
my maidservants count me as a stranger;
I have become an alien in their eyes.
16 I call to my servant, but he gives me no answer;
I must beseech him with my mouth.
17 I am repulsive to my wife,
loathsome to the sons of my own mother.
18 Even young children despise me;
when I rise they talk against me.
19 All my intimate friends abhor me,
and those whom I loved have turned against me.
20 My bones cleave to my skin and to my flesh,
and I have escaped by the skin of my teeth.
21 Have pity on me, have pity on me,
O you my friends,
for the hand of God has touched me!
22 Why do you, like God, pursue me?
Why are you not satisfied with my flesh?

23 "Oh that my words were written!
Oh that they were inscribed in a book!
24 Oh that with an iron pen and lead

[s] Cn: Heb *it consumes the limbs of his skin* [t] Heb *their way*

they were graven in the rock for
ever!
25 For I know that my Redeemer[u] lives,
and at last he will stand upon the
earth;[v]
26 and after my skin has been thus
destroyed,
then from[w] my flesh I shall see
God,[x]
27 whom I shall see on my side,[y]
and my eyes shall behold, and
not another.
My heart faints within me!
28 If you say, 'How we will pursue
him!'
and, 'The root of the matter is
found in him';
29 be afraid of the sword,
for wrath brings the punishment
of the sword,
that you may know there is a
judgment."

20 Then Zō'phär the Nā'à-mà-
thīte answered:
2 "Therefore my thoughts answer
me,
because of my haste within me.
3 I hear censure which insults me,
and out of my understanding a
spirit answers me.
4 Do you not know this from of old,
since man was placed upon earth,
5 that the exulting of the wicked is
short,
and the joy of the godless but for
a moment?
6 Though his height mount up to the
heavens,
and his head reach to the clouds,
7 he will perish for ever like his own
dung;
those who have seen him will say,
'Where is he?'
8 He will fly away like a dream, and
not be found;
he will be chased away like a
vision of the night.
9 The eye which saw him will see
him no more,
nor will his place any more behold him.
10 His children will seek the favor of
the poor,
and his hands will give back his
wealth.
11 His bones are full of youthful vigor,
but it will lie down with him in
the dust.
12 "Though wickedness is sweet in his
mouth,
though he hides it under his
tongue,
13 though he is loath to let it go,
and holds it in his mouth,
14 yet his food is turned in his stomach;
it is the gall of asps within him.
15 He swallows down riches and vomits
them up again;
God casts them out of his belly.
16 He will suck the poison of asps;
the tongue of a viper will kill
him.
17 He will not look upon the rivers,
the streams flowing with honey
and curds.
18 He will give back the fruit of his
toil,
and will not swallow it down;
from the profit of his trading
he will get no enjoyment.
19 For he has crushed and abandoned
the poor,
he has seized a house which he
did not build.

20 "Because his greed knew no rest,
he will not save anything in which
he delights.
21 There was nothing left after he had
eaten;
therefore his prosperity will not
endure.
22 In the fulness of his sufficiency he
will be in straits;
all the force of misery will come
upon him.
23 To fill his belly to the full
God[z] will send his fierce anger
into him,
and rain it upon him as his food.[a]
24 He will flee from an iron weapon;
a bronze arrow will strike him
through.
25 It is drawn forth and comes out of
his body,
the glittering point comes out of
his gall;
terrors come upon him.
26 Utter darkness is laid up for his
treasures;
a fire not blown upon will devour
him;
what is left in his tent will be
consumed.
27 The heavens will reveal his iniquity,
and the earth will rise up against
him.

[u] Or *Vindicator* [v] Or *dust* [w] Or *without* [x] The meaning of this verse is uncertain [y] Or *for myself*
[z] Heb *he* [a] Cn: Heb *in his flesh*

[28] The possessions of his house will
be carried away,
dragged off in the day of God's[b]
wrath.
[29] This is the wicked man's portion
from God,
the heritage decreed for him by
God."

21 Then Jōb answered:
[2] "Listen carefully to my words,
and let this be your consolation.
[3] Bear with me, and I will speak,
and after I have spoken, mock on.
[4] As for me, is my complaint against
man?
Why should I not be impatient?
[5] Look at me, and be appalled,
and lay your hand upon your
mouth.
[6] When I think of it I am dismayed,
and shuddering seizes my flesh.
[7] Why do the wicked live,
reach old age, and grow mighty
in power?
[8] Their children are established in
their presence,
and their offspring before their
eyes.
[9] Their houses are safe from fear,
and no rod of God is upon them.
[10] Their bull breeds without fail;
their cow calves, and does not
cast her calf.
[11] They send forth their little ones like
a flock,
and their children dance.
[12] They sing to the tambourine and
the lyre,
and rejoice to the sound of the
pipe.
[13] They spend their days in prosperity,
and in peace they go down to
Shē'ōl.
[14] They say to God, 'Depart from us!
We do not desire the knowledge
of thy ways.
[15] What is the Almighty, that we
should serve him?
And what profit do we get if we
pray to him?'
[16] Behold, is not their prosperity in
their hand?
The counsel of the wicked is far
from me.

[17] "How often is it that the lamp of
the wicked is put out?
That their calamity comes upon
them?
That God[c] distributes pains in
his anger?
[18] That they are like straw before the
wind,
and like chaff that the storm
carries away?
[19] You say, 'God stores up their iniquity for their sons.'
Let him recompense it to themselves, that they may know it.
[20] Let their own eyes see their destruction,
and let them drink of the wrath
of the Almighty.
[21] For what do they care for their
houses after them,
when the number of their months
is cut off?
[22] Will any teach God knowledge,
seeing that he judges those that
are on high?
[23] One dies in full prosperity,
being wholly at ease and secure,
[24] his body[d] full of fat
and the marrow of his bones
moist.
[25] Another dies in bitterness of soul,
never having tasted of good.
[26] They lie down alike in the dust,
and the worms cover them.

[27] "Behold, I know your thoughts,
and your schemes to wrong
me.
[28] For you say, 'Where is the house
of the prince?
Where is the tent in which the
wicked dwelt?'
[29] Have you not asked those who travel
the roads,
and do you not accept their
testimony
[30] that the wicked man is spared in the
day of calamity,
that he is rescued in the day of
wrath?
[31] Who declares his way to his face,
and who requites him for what
he has done?
[32] When he is borne to the grave,
watch is kept over his tomb.
[33] The clods of the valley are sweet
to him;
all men follow after him,
and those who go before him are
innumerable.
[34] How then will you comfort me with
empty nothings?
There is nothing left of your
answers but falsehood."

[b] Heb *his* [c] Heb *he* [d] The meaning of the Hebrew word is uncertain

22 Then E·lī'phaz the Tē'mȧ·nīte answered:
2 "Can a man be profitable to God?
Surely he who is wise is profitable to himself.
3 Is it any pleasure to the Almighty if you are righteous,
or is it gain to him if you make your ways blameless?
4 Is it for your fear of him that he reproves you,
and enters into judgment with you?
5 Is not your wickedness great?
There is no end to your iniquities.
6 For you have exacted pledges of your brothers for nothing,
and stripped the naked of their clothing.
7 You have given no water to the weary to drink,
and you have withheld bread from the hungry.
8 The man with power possessed the land,
and the favored man dwelt in it.
9 You have sent widows away empty,
and the arms of the fatherless were crushed.
10 Therefore snares are round about you,
and sudden terror overwhelms you;
11 your light is darkened, so that[e] you cannot see,
and a flood of water covers you.

12 "Is not God high in the heavens?
See the highest stars, how lofty they are!
13 Therefore you say, 'What does God know?
Can he judge through the deep darkness?
14 Thick clouds enwrap him, so that he does not see,
and he walks on the vault of heaven.'
15 Will you keep to the old way
which wicked men have trod?
16 They were snatched away before their time;
their foundation was washed away.
17 They said to God, 'Depart from us,'
and 'What can the Almighty do to us?'[f]
18 Yet he filled their houses with good things—
but the counsel of the wicked is far from me.
19 The righteous see it and are glad;
the innocent laugh them to scorn,
20 saying, 'Surely our adversaries are cut off,
and what they left the fire has consumed.'

21 "Agree with God, and be at peace;
thereby good will come to you.
22 Receive instruction from his mouth,
and lay up his words in your heart.
23 If you return to the Almighty and humble yourself,[g]
if you remove unrighteousness far from your tents,
24 if you lay gold in the dust,
and gold of Ō'phīr among the stones of the torrent bed,
25 and if the Almighty is your gold,
and your precious silver;
26 then you will delight yourself in the Almighty,
and lift up your face to God.
27 You will make your prayer to him,
and he will hear you;
and you will pay your vows.
28 You will decide on a matter, and it will be established for you,
and light will shine on your ways.
29 For God abases the proud,[h]
but he saves the lowly.
30 He delivers the innocent man;[i]
you will be delivered through the cleanness of your hands."

23 Then Jōb answered:
2 "Today also my complaint is bitter,[j]
his[k] hand is heavy in spite of my groaning.
3 Oh, that I knew where I might find him,
that I might come even to his seat!
4 I would lay my case before him
and fill my mouth with arguments.
5 I would learn what he would answer me,
and understand what he would say to me.
6 Would he contend with me in the greatness of his power?
No; he would give heed to me.

[e] Cn Compare Gk: Heb *or darkness* [f] Gk Syr: Heb *them* [g] Gk: Heb *you will be built up*
[h] Cn: Heb *when they abased you said, Proud* [i] Gk Syr Vg: Heb *him that is not innocent*
[j] Syr Vg Tg: Heb *rebellious* [k] Gk Syr: Heb *my*
22.2-3: Job 35.6-8.

7 There an upright man could reason with him,
and I should be acquitted for ever by my judge.

8 "Behold, I go forward, but he is not there;
and backward, but I cannot perceive him;
9 on the left hand I seek him,[l] but I cannot behold him;
I[m] turn to the right hand, but I cannot see him.
10 But he knows the way that I take;
when he has tried me, I shall come forth as gold.
11 My foot has held fast to his steps;
I have kept his way and have not turned aside.
12 I have not departed from the commandment of his lips;
I have treasured in[n] my bosom the words of his mouth.
13 But he is unchangeable and who can turn him?
What he desires, that he does.
14 For he will complete what he appoints for me;
and many such things are in his mind.
15 Therefore I am terrified at his presence;
when I consider, I am in dread of him.
16 God has made my heart faint;
the Almighty has terrified me;
17 for I am[o] hemmed in by darkness,
and thick darkness covers my face.[p]

24 "Why are not times of judgment kept by the Almighty,
and why do those who know him never see his days?
2 Men remove landmarks;
they seize flocks and pasture them.
3 They drive away the ass of the fatherless;
they take the widow's ox for a pledge.
4 They thrust the poor off the road;
the poor of the earth all hide themselves.
5 Behold, like wild asses in the desert
they go forth to their toil,
seeking prey in the wilderness
as food[q] for their children.
6 They gather their[r] fodder in the field
and they glean the vineyard of the wicked man.
7 They lie all night naked, without clothing,
and have no covering in the cold.
8 They are wet with the rain of the mountains,
and cling to the rock for want of shelter.
9 (There are those who snatch the fatherless child from the breast,
and take in pledge the infant of the poor.)
10 They go about naked, without clothing;
hungry, they carry the sheaves;
11 among the olive rows of the wicked[s] they make oil;
they tread the wine presses, but suffer thirst.
12 From out of the city the dying groan,
and the soul of the wounded cries for help;
yet God pays no attention to their prayer.

13 "There are those who rebel against the light,
who are not acquainted with its ways,
and do not stay in its paths.
14 The murderer rises in the dark,[t]
that he may kill the poor and needy;
and in the night he is as a thief.
15 The eye of the adulterer also waits for the twilight,
saying, 'No eye will see me';
and he disguises his face.
16 In the dark they dig through houses;
by day they shut themselves up;
they do not know the light.
17 For deep darkness is morning to all of them;
for they are friends with the terrors of deep darkness.

18 "You say, 'They are swiftly carried away upon the face of the waters;
their portion is cursed in the land;
no treader turns toward their vineyards.
19 Drought and heat snatch away the snow waters;

[l] Compare Syr: Heb *on the left hand when he works* [m] Syr Vg: Heb *he* [n] Gk Vg: Heb *from*
[o] With one Ms: Heb *am not* [p] Vg: Heb *from my face* [q] Heb *food to him* [r] Heb *his*
[s] Heb *their olive rows* [t] Cn: Heb *at the light*

so does Shē'ōl those who have
sinned.
20 The squares of the town[u] forget
them;
their name[v] is no longer remembered;
so wickedness is broken like a
tree.'

21 "They feed on the barren childless
woman,
and do no good to the widow.
22 Yet God[w] prolongs the life of the
mighty by his power;
they rise up when they despair of
life.
23 He gives them security, and they
are supported;
and his eyes are upon their ways.
24 They are exalted a little while, and
then are gone;
they wither and fade like the
mallow;[x]
they are cut off like the heads of
grain.
25 If it is not so, who will prove me a
liar,
and show that there is nothing in
what I say?"

25 Then Bil'dad the Shü'hīte answered:
2 "Dominion and fear are with God;[y]
he makes peace in his high heaven.
3 Is there any number to his armies?
Upon whom does his light not
arise?
4 How then can man be righteous before God?
How can he who is born of woman
be clean?
5 Behold, even the moon is not bright
and the stars are not clean in his
sight;
6 how much less man, who is a
maggot,
and the son of man, who is a
worm!"

26 Then Jōb answered:
2 "How you have helped him
who has no power!
How you have saved the arm that
has no strength!
3 How you have counseled him who
has no wisdom,
and plentifully declared sound
knowledge!
4 With whose help have you uttered
words,
and whose spirit has come forth
from you?
5 The shades below tremble,
the waters and their inhabitants.
6 Shē'ōl is naked before God,
and Ȧ·bad'dôn has no covering.
7 He stretches out the north over the
void,
and hangs the earth upon nothing.
8 He binds up the waters in his thick
clouds,
and the cloud is not rent under
them.
9 He covers the face of the moon,[z]
and spreads over it his cloud.
10 He has described a circle upon the
face of the waters
at the boundary between light and
darkness.
11 The pillars of heaven tremble,
and are astounded at his rebuke.
12 By his power he stilled the sea;
by his understanding he smote
Rā'hab.
13 By his wind the heavens were made
fair;
his hand pierced the fleeing
serpent.
14 Lo, these are but the outskirts of
his ways;
and how small a whisper do we
hear of him!
But the thunder of his power who
can understand?"

27 And Jōb again took up his
discourse, and said:
2 "As God lives, who has taken away
my right,
and the Almighty, who has made
my soul bitter;
3 as long as my breath is in me,
and the spirit of God is in my
nostrils;
4 my lips will not speak falsehood,
and my tongue will not utter
deceit.
5 Far be it from me to say that you
are right;
till I die I will not put away my
integrity from me.
6 I hold fast my righteousness, and
will not let it go;
my heart does not reproach me
for any of my days.

7 "Let my enemy be as the wicked,
and let him that rises up against
me be as the unrighteous.

[u] Cn: Heb obscure [v] Cn: Heb *a worm* [w] Heb *he* [x] Gk: Heb *all* [y] Heb *him* [z] Or *his throne*

8 For what is the hope of the godless
when God cuts him off,
when God takes away his life?
9 Will God hear his cry,
when trouble comes upon him?
10 Will he take delight in the Almighty?
Will he call upon God at all times?
11 I will teach you concerning the
hand of God;
what is with the Almighty I will
not conceal.
12 Behold, all of you have seen it yourselves;
why then have you become altogether vain?

13 "This is the portion of a wicked man
with God,
and the heritage which oppressors
receive from the Almighty:
14 If his children are multiplied, it is
for the sword;
and his offspring have not enough
to eat.
15 Those who survive him the pestilence buries,
and their widows make no lamentation.
16 Though he heap up silver like dust,
and pile up clothing like clay;
17 he may pile it up, but the just will
wear it,
and the innocent will divide the
silver.
18 The house which he builds is like a
spider's web,[a]
like a booth which a watchman
makes.
19 He goes to bed rich, but will do so
no more;[b]
he opens his eyes, and his wealth
is gone.
20 Terrors overtake him like a flood;
in the night a whirlwind carries
him off.
21 The east wind lifts him up and he
is gone;
it sweeps him out of his place.
22 It[c] hurls at him without pity;
he flees from its[d] power in headlong flight.
23 It[c] claps its[d] hands at him,
and hisses at him from its[d] place.

28 "Surely there is a mine for
silver,
and a place for gold which they
refine.
2 Iron is taken out of the earth,
and copper is smelted from the
ore.
3 Men put an end to darkness,
and search out to the farthest
bound
the ore in gloom and deep darkness.
4 They open shafts in a valley away
from where men live;
they are forgotten by travelers,
they hang afar from men, they
swing to and fro.
5 As for the earth, out of it comes
bread;
but underneath it is turned up
as by fire.
6 Its stones are the place of sapphires,[e]
and it has dust of gold.

7 "That path no bird of prey knows,
and the falcon's eye has not seen
it.
8 The proud beasts have not trodden
it;
the lion has not passed over it.

9 "Man puts his hand to the flinty
rock,
and overturns mountains by the
roots.
10 He cuts out channels in the rocks,
and his eye sees every precious
thing.
11 He binds up the streams so that
they do not trickle,
and the thing that is hid he brings
forth to light.

12 "But where shall wisdom be found?
And where is the place of understanding?
13 Man does not know the way to
it,[f]
and it is not found in the land of
the living.
14 The deep says, 'It is not in me,'
and the sea says, 'It is not with
me.'
15 It cannot be gotten for gold,
and silver cannot be weighed as
its price.
16 It cannot be valued in the gold of
Ō'phīr,
in precious onyx or sapphire.[g]
17 Gold and glass cannot equal it,
nor can it be exchanged for jewels
of fine gold.

[a] Cn Compare Gk Syr: Heb *He builds his house like the moth*
[b] Gk Compare Syr: Heb *shall not be gathered* [c] Or *he* (that is God) [d] Or *his* [e] or *lapis lazuli*
[f] Gk: Heb *its price* [g] Or *lapis lazuli*

18 No mention shall be made of coral
or of crystal;
the price of wisdom is above
pearls.
19 The topaz of Ethiopia cannot compare with it,
nor can it be valued in pure gold.

20 "Whence then comes wisdom?
And where is the place of understanding?
21 It is hid from the eyes of all living,
and concealed from the birds of
the air.
22 A·bad'dȯn and Death say,
'We have heard a rumor of it with
our ears.'

23 "God understands the way to it,
and he knows its place.
24 For he looks to the ends of the earth,
and sees everything under the
heavens.
25 When he gave to the wind its
weight,
and meted out the waters by
measure;
26 when he made a decree for the rain,
and a way for the lightning of the
thunder;
27 then he saw it and declared it;
he established it, and searched it
out.
28 And he said to man,
'Behold, the fear of the Lord, that
is wisdom;
and to depart from evil is understanding.' "

29 And Jōb again took up his discourse, and said:
2 "Oh, that I were as in the months
of old,
as in the days when God watched
over me;
3 when his lamp shone upon my head,
and by his light I walked through
darkness;
4 as I was in my autumn days,
when the friendship of God was
upon my tent;
5 when the Almighty was yet with me,
when my children were about me;
6 when my steps were washed with
milk,
and the rock poured out for me
streams of oil!
7 When I went out to the gate of the
city,
when I prepared my seat in the
square,
8 the young men saw me and withdrew,
and the aged rose and stood;
9 the princes refrained from talking,
and laid their hand on their
mouth;
10 the voice of the nobles was hushed,
and their tongue cleaved to the
roof of their mouth.
11 When the ear heard, it called me
blessed,
and when the eye saw, it approved;
12 because I delivered the poor who
cried,
and the fatherless who had none
to help him.
13 The blessing of him who was about
to perish came upon me,
and I caused the widow's heart to
sing for joy.
14 I put on righteousness, and it
clothed me;
my justice was like a robe and a
turban.
15 I was eyes to the blind,
and feet to the lame.
16 I was a father to the poor,
and I searched out the cause of
him whom I did not know.
17 I broke the fangs of the unrighteous,
and made him drop his prey from
his teeth.
18 Then I thought, 'I shall die in my
nest,
and I shall multiply my days as
the sand,
19 my roots spread out to the waters,
with the dew all night on my
branches,
20 my glory fresh with me,
and my bow ever new in my
hand.'

21 "Men listened to me, and waited,
and kept silence for my counsel.
22 After I spoke they did not speak
again,
and my word dropped upon them.
23 They waited for me as for the
rain;
and they opened their mouths as
for the spring rain.
24 I smiled on them when they had no
confidence;
and the light of my countenance
they did not cast down.
25 I chose their way, and sat as chief,
and I dwelt like a king among his
troops,
like one who comforts mourners.

30 "But now they make sport of
me,
men who are younger than I,
whose fathers I would have disdained
to set with the dogs of my flock.
2 What could I gain from the strength
of their hands,
men whose vigor is gone?
3 Through want and hard hunger
they gnaw the dry and desolate
ground;[h]
4 they pick mallow and the leaves of
bushes,
and to warm themselves the roots
of the broom.
5 They are driven out from among
men;
they shout after them as after a
thief.
6 In the gullies of the torrents they
must dwell,
in holes of the earth and of the
rocks.
7 Among the bushes they bray;
under the nettles they huddle together.
8 A senseless, a disreputable brood,
they have been whipped out of
the land.

9 "And now I have become their song,
I am a byword to them.
10 They abhor me, they keep aloof
from me;
they do not hesitate to spit at the
sight of me.
11 Because God has loosed my cord
and humbled me,
they have cast off restraint in my
presence.
12 On my right hand the rabble rise,
they drive me[i] forth,
they cast up against me their ways
of destruction.
13 They break up my path,
they promote my calamity;
no one restrains[j] them.
14 As through[k] a wide breach they
come;
amid the crash they roll on.
15 Terrors are turned upon me;
my honor is pursued as by the
wind,
and my prosperity has passed
away like a cloud.

16 "And now my soul is poured out
within me;
days of affliction have taken hold
of me.
17 The night racks my bones,
and the pain that gnaws me takes
no rest.
18 With violence it seizes my garment;[l]
it binds me about like the collar
of my tunic.
19 God has cast me into the mire,
and I have become like dust and
ashes.
20 I cry to thee and thou dost not
answer me;
I stand, and thou dost not[m] heed
me.
21 Thou hast turned cruel to me;
with the might of thy hand thou
dost persecute me.
22 Thou liftest me up on the wind,
thou makest me ride on it,
and thou tossest me about in the
roar of the storm.
23 Yea, I know that thou wilt bring me
to death,
and to the house appointed for
all living.

24 "Yet does not one in a heap of ruins
stretch out his hand,
and in his disaster cry for help?[n]
25 Did not I weep for him whose day
was hard?
Was not my soul grieved for the
poor?
26 But when I looked for good, evil
came;
and when I waited for light, darkness came.
27 My heart is in turmoil, and is never
still;
days of affliction come to meet
me.
28 I go about blackened, but not by
the sun;
I stand up in the assembly, and
cry for help.
29 I am a brother of jackals,
and a companion of ostriches.
30 My skin turns black and falls from
me,
and my bones burn with heat.
31 My lyre is turned to mourning,
and my pipe to the voice of those
who weep.

31 "I have made a covenant with
my eyes;
how then could I look upon a
virgin?

[h] Heb *ground yesterday waste* [i] Heb *my feet* [j] Cn: Heb *helps* [k] Cn: Heb *like*
[l] Gk: Heb *my garment is disfigured* [m] One Heb Ms and Vg: Heb lacks *not* [n] Cn: Heb obscure

2 What would be my portion from God above,
and my heritage from the Almighty on high?
3 Does not calamity befall the unrighteous,
and disaster the workers of iniquity?
4 Does not he see my ways,
and number all my steps?

5 "If I have walked with falsehood,
and my foot has hastened to deceit;
6 (Let me be weighed in a just balance,
and let God know my integrity!)
7 if my step has turned aside from the way,
and my heart has gone after my eyes,
and if any spot has cleaved to my hands;
8 then let me sow, and another eat;
and let what grows for me be rooted out.

9 "If my heart has been enticed to a woman,
and I have lain in wait at my neighbor's door;
10 then let my wife grind for another,
and let others bow down upon her.
11 For that would be a heinous crime;
that would be an iniquity to be punished by the judges;
12 for that would be a fire which consumes unto A·bad'dòn,
and it would burn to the root all my increase.

13 "If I have rejected the cause of my manservant or my maidservant,
when they brought a complaint against me;
14 what then shall I do when God rises up?
When he makes inquiry, what shall I answer him?
15 Did not he who made me in the womb make him?
And did not one fashion us in the womb?

16 "If I have withheld anything that the poor desired,
or have caused the eyes of the widow to fail,
17 or have eaten my morsel alone,
and the fatherless has not eaten of it
18 (for from his youth I reared him as a father,
and from his mother's womb I guided him[o]);
19 if I have seen any one perish for lack of clothing,
or a poor man without covering;
20 if his loins have not blessed me,
and if he was not warmed with the fleece of my sheep;
21 if I have raised my hand against the fatherless,
because I saw help in the gate;
22 then let my shoulder blade fall from my shoulder,
and let my arm be broken from its socket.
23 For I was in terror of calamity from God,
and I could not have faced his majesty.

24 "If I have made gold my trust,
or called fine gold my confidence;
25 if I have rejoiced because my wealth was great,
or because my hand had gotten much;
26 if I have looked at the sun[p] when it shone,
or the moon moving in splendor,
27 and my heart has been secretly enticed,
and my mouth has kissed my hand;
28 this also would be an iniquity to be punished by the judges,
for I should have been false to God above.

29 "If I have rejoiced at the ruin of him that hated me,
or exulted when evil overtook him
30 (I have not let my mouth sin by asking for his life with a curse);
31 if the men of my tent have not said,
'Who is there that has not been filled with his meat?'
32 (the sojourner has not lodged in the street;
I have opened my doors to the wayfarer);
33 if I have concealed my transgressions from men,[q]

[o] Cn: Heb *for from my youth he grew up to me as a father, and from my mother's womb I guided her*
[p] Heb *the light* [q] Cn: Heb *like men* or *like Adam*

by hiding my iniquity in my
bosom,
34 because I stood in great fear of the
multitude,
and the contempt of families terrified me,
so that I kept silence, and did not
go out of doors—
35 Oh, that I had one to hear me!
(Here is my signature! let the
Almighty answer me!)
Oh, that I had the indictment
written by my adversary!
36 Surely I would carry it on my
shoulder;
I would bind it on me as a crown;
37 I would give him an account of all
my steps;
like a prince I would approach
him.

38 "If my land has cried out against
me,
and its furrows have wept together;
39 if I have eaten its yield without
payment,
and caused the death of its
owners;
40 let thorns grow instead of wheat,
and foul weeds instead of barley."

The words of Jōb are ended.

32 So these three men ceased to
answer Jōb, because he was
righteous in his own eyes. 2 Then
E·lī'hū the son of Bär'ạ·chel the Buzite,
of the family of Räm, became angry.
He was angry at Jōb because he justified himself rather than God; 3 he was
angry also at Jōb's three friends because they had found no answer,
although they had declared Job to be
in the wrong. 4 Now E·lī'hū had waited
to speak to Jōb because they were
older than he. 5 And when E·lī'hū saw
that there was no answer in the mouth
of these three men, he became angry.
6 And E·lī'hū the son of Bär'ȧ·chel
the Buzite answered:
"I am young in years,
and you are aged;
therefore I was timid and afraid
to declare my opinion to you.
7 I said, 'Let days speak,
and many years teach wisdom.'
8 But it is the spirit in a man,
the breath of the Almighty,
that makes him understand.
9 It is not the old[r] that are wise,
nor the aged that understand
what is right.
10 Therefore I say, 'Listen to me;
let me also declare my opinion.'
11 "Behold, I waited for your words,
I listened for your wise sayings,
while you searched out what to
say.
12 I gave you my attention,
and, behold, there was none that
confuted Jōb,
or that answered his words,
among you.
13 Beware lest you say, 'We have
found wisdom;
God may vanquish him, not
man.'
14 He has not directed his words
against me,
and I will not answer him with
your speeches.

15 "They are discomfited, they answer
no more;
they have not a word to say.
16 And shall I wait, because they do
not speak,
because they stand there, and
answer no more?
17 I also will give my answer;
I also will declare my opinion.
18 For I am full of words,
the spirit within me constrains
me.
19 Behold, my heart is like wine that
has no vent;
like new wineskins, it is ready to
burst.
20 I must speak, that I may find relief;
I must open my lips and answer.
21 I will not show partiality to any
person
or use flattery toward any man.
22 For I do not know how to flatter,
else would my Maker soon put
an end to me.

33 "But now, hear my speech,
O Jōb,
and listen to all my words.
2 Behold, I open my mouth;
the tongue in my mouth speaks.
3 My words declare the uprightness
of my heart,
and what my lips know they speak
sincerely.
4 The spirit of God has made me,

[r] Gk Syr Vg: Heb *many*

and the breath of the Almighty
gives me life.
5 Answer me, if you can;
set your words in order before
me; take your stand.
6 Behold, I am toward God as you are;
I too was formed from a piece of
clay.
7 Behold, no fear of me need terrify
you;
my pressure will not be heavy
upon you.

8 "Surely, you have spoken in my
hearing,
and I have heard the sound of
your words.
9 You say, 'I am clean, without
transgression;
I am pure, and there is no iniquity
in me.
10 Behold, he finds occasions against
me,
he counts me as his enemy;
11 he puts my feet in the stocks,
and watches all my paths.'

12 "Behold, in this you are not right.
I will answer you.
God is greater than man.
13 Why do you contend against him,
saying, 'He will answer none of
my[s] words'?
14 For God speaks in one way,
and in two, though man does not
perceive it.
15 In a dream, in a vision of the night,
when deep sleep falls upon men,
while they slumber on their beds,
16 then he opens the ears of men,
and terrifies them with warnings,
17 that he may turn man aside from
his deed,
and cut off[t] pride from man;
18 he keeps back his soul from the Pit,
his life from perishing by the
sword.

19 "Man is also chastened with pain
upon his bed,
and with continual strife in his
bones;
20 so that his life loathes bread,
and his appetite dainty food.
21 His flesh is so wasted away that it
cannot be seen;
and his bones which were not
seen stick out.
22 His soul draws near the Pit,
and his life to those who bring
death.
23 If there be for him an angel,
a mediator, one of the thousand,
to declare to man what is right
for him;
24 and he is gracious to him, and says,
'Deliver him from going down
into the Pit,
I have found a ransom;
25 let his flesh become fresh with
youth;
let him return to the days of his
youthful vigor';
26 then man prays to God, and he
accepts him,
he comes into his presence with
joy.
He recounts[u] to men his salvation,
27 and he sings before men, and
says:
'I sinned, and perverted what was
right,
and it was not requited to me.
28 He has redeemed my soul from
going down into the Pit,
and my life shall see the light.'

29 "Behold, God does all these things,
twice, three times, with a man,
30 to bring back his soul from the Pit,
that he may see the light of life.[v]
31 Give heed, O Jōb, listen to me;
be silent, and I will speak.
32 If you have anything to say, answer
me;
speak, for I desire to justify you.
33 If not, listen to me;
be silent, and I will teach you
wisdom."

34 Then E·lī'hū said:
2 "Hear my words, you wise
men,
and give ear to me, you who
know;
3 for the ear tests words
as the palate tastes food.
4 Let us choose what is right;
let us determine among ourselves
what is good.
5 For Jōb has said, 'I am innocent,
and God has taken away my right;
6 in spite of my right I am counted
a liar;
my wound is incurable, though
I am without transgression.'
7 What man is like Jōb,
who drinks up scoffing like water,

[s] Compare Gk: Heb *his* [t] Cn: Heb *hide* [u] Cn: Heb *returns*
[v] Syr: Heb *to be lighted with the light of life*

8 who goes in company with evildoers
and walks with wicked men?
9 For he has said, 'It profits a man
nothing
that he should take delight in
God.'

10 "Therefore, hear me, you men of
understanding,
far be it from God that he should
do wickedness,
and from the Almighty that he
should do wrong.
11 For according to the work of a man
he will requite him,
and according to his ways he will
make it befall him.
12 Of a truth, God will not do wickedly,
and the Almighty will not pervert
justice.
13 Who gave him charge over the earth
and who laid on him[w] the whole
world?
14 If he should take back his spirit[x] to
himself,
and gather to himself his breath,
15 all flesh would perish together,
and man would return to dust.

16 "If you have understanding, hear
this;
listen to what I say.
17 Shall one who hates justice govern?
Will you condemn him who is
righteous and mighty,
18 who says to a king, 'Worthless
one,'
and to nobles, 'Wicked man';
19 who shows no partiality to princes,
nor regards the rich more than
the poor,
for they are all the work of his
hands?
20 In a moment they die;
at midnight the people are shaken
and pass away,
and the mighty are taken away
by no human hand.

21 "For his eyes are upon the ways of
a man,
and he sees all his steps.
22 There is no gloom or deep darkness
where evildoers may hide themselves.
23 For he has not appointed a time[y] for
any man
to go before God in judgment.
24 He shatters the mighty without in-
vestigation,
and sets others in their place.
25 Thus, knowing their works,
he overturns them in the night,
and they are crushed.
26 He strikes them for their wickedness
in the sight of men,
27 because they turned aside from
following him,
and had no regard for any of his
ways,
28 so that they caused the cry of the
poor to come to him,
and he heard the cry of the
afflicted—
29 When he is quiet, who can condemn?
When he hides his face, who can
behold him,
whether it be a nation or a man?—
30 that a godless man should not reign,
that he should not ensnare the
people.

31 "For has any one said to God,
'I have borne chastisement; I will
not offend any more;
32 teach me what I do not see;
if I have done iniquity, I will do
it no more'?
33 Will he then make requital to suit
you,
because you reject it?
For you must choose, and not I;
therefore declare what you know.[z]
34 Men of understanding will say to
me,
and the wise man who hears me
will say:
35 'Jōb speaks without knowledge,
his words are without insight.'
36 Would that Jōb were tried to the
end,
because he answers like wicked
men.
37 For he adds rebellion to his sin;
he claps his hands among us,
and multiplies his words against
God."

35 And E·lī'hū said:
2 "Do you think this to be just?
Do you say, 'It is my right before
God,'
3 that you ask, 'What advantage have
I?
How am I better off than if I had
sinned?'
4 I will answer you

[w] Heb lacks *on him* [x] Heb *his heart his spirit* [y] Cn: Heb *yet*
[z] The Hebrew of verses 29-33 is obscure

and your friends with you.
5 Look at the heavens, and see;
and behold the clouds, which are
higher than you.
6 If you have sinned, what do you
accomplish against him?
And if your transgressions are
multiplied, what do you do to
him?
7 If you are righteous, what do you
give to him;
or what does he receive from
your hand?
8 Your wickedness concerns a man
like yourself,
and your righteousness a son of
man.

9 "Because of the multitude of oppressions people cry out;
they call for help because of the
arm of the mighty.
10 But none says, 'Where is God my
Maker,
who gives songs in the night,
11 who teaches us more than the beasts
of the earth,
and makes us wiser than the birds
of the air?'
12 There they cry out, but he does not
answer,
because of the pride of evil men.
13 Surely God does not hear an empty
cry,
nor does the Almighty regard it.
14 How much less when you say that
you do not see him,
that the case is before him, and
you are waiting for him!
15 And now, because his anger does
not punish,
and he does not greatly heed
transgression,[a]
16 Jōb opens his mouth in empty talk,
he multiplies words without
knowledge."

36 And E·lī'hū continued, and
said:
2 "Bear with me a little, and I will
show you,
for I have yet something to say
on God's behalf.
3 I will fetch my knowledge from
afar,
and ascribe righteousness to my
Maker.
4 For truly my words are not false;
one who is perfect in knowledge
is with you.

5 "Behold, God is mighty, and does
not despise any;
he is mighty in strength of understanding.
6 He does not keep the wicked alive,
but gives the afflicted their right.
7 He does not withdraw his eyes from
the righteous,
but with kings upon the throne
he sets them for ever, and they
are exalted.
8 And if they are bound in fetters
and caught in the cords of affliction,
9 then he declares to them their work
and their transgressions, that they
are behaving arrogantly.
10 He opens their ears to instruction,
and commands that they return
from iniquity.
11 If they hearken and serve him,
they complete their days in prosperity,
and their years in pleasantness.
12 But if they do not hearken, they
perish by the sword,
and die without knowledge.

13 "The godless in heart cherish anger;
they do not cry for help when he
binds them.
14 They die in youth,
and their life ends in shame.[b]
15 He delivers the afflicted by their
affliction,
and opens their ear by adversity.
16 He also allured you out of distress
into a broad place where there was
no cramping,
and what was set on your table
was full of fatness.

17 "But you are full of the judgment
on the wicked;
judgment and justice seize you.
18 Beware lest wrath entice you into
scoffing;
and let not the greatness of the
ransom turn you aside.
19 Will your cry avail to keep you from
distress,
or all the force of your strength?
20 Do not long for the night,
when peoples are cut off in their
place.

[a] Theodotion Symmachus Compare Vg: The meaning of the Hebrew word is uncertain
[b] Heb *among the cult prostitutes*
35.6-8: Job 22.2-3.

21 Take heed, do not turn to iniquity,
for this you have chosen rather
than affliction.
22 Behold, God is exalted in his power;
who is a teacher like him?
23 Who has prescribed for him his
way,
or who can say, 'Thou hast done
wrong?'

24 "Remember to extol his work,
of which men have sung.
25 All men have looked on it;
man beholds it from afar.
26 Behold, God is great, and we know
him not;
the number of his years is unsearchable.
27 For he draws up the drops of water,
he[c] distils his mist in rain
28 which the skies pour down,
and drop upon man abundantly.
29 Can any one understand the spreading of the clouds,
the thunderings of his pavilion?
30 Behold, he scatters his lightning
about him,
and covers the roots of the sea.
31 For by these he judges peoples;
he gives food in abundance.
32 He covers his hands with the
lightning,
and commands it to strike the
mark.
33 Its crashing declares concerning
him,
who is jealous with anger against
iniquity.

37 "At this also my heart
trembles,
and leaps out of its place.
2 Hearken to the thunder of his voice
and the rumbling that comes
from his mouth.
3 Under the whole heaven he lets it
go,
and his lightning to the corners
of the earth.
4 After it his voice roars;
he thunders with his majestic
voice
and he does not restrain the
lightnings[d] when his voice is
heard.
5 God thunders wondrously with his
voice;
he does great things which we
cannot comprehend.
6 For to the snow he says, 'Fall on
the earth';
and to the shower and the rain,[e]
'Be strong.'
7 He seals up the hand of every man,
that all men may know his work.[f]
8 Then the beasts go into their lairs,
and remain in their dens.
9 From its chamber comes the whirlwind,
and cold from the scattering
winds.
10 By the breath of God ice is given,
and the broad waters are frozen
fast.
11 He loads the thick cloud with
moisture;
the clouds scatter his lightning.
12 They turn round and round by his
guidance,
to accomplish all that he commands them
on the face of the habitable world.
13 Whether for correction, or for his
land,
or for love, he causes it to happen.

14 "Hear this, O Jōb;
stop and consider the wondrous
works of God.
15 Do you know how God lays his
command upon them,
and causes the lightning of his
cloud to shine?
16 Do you know the balancings of the
clouds,
the wondrous works of him who
is perfect in knowledge,
17 you whose garments are hot
when the earth is still because of
the south wind?
18 Can you, like him, spread out the
skies,
hard as a molten mirror?
19 Teach us what we shall say to him;
we cannot draw up our case because of darkness.
20 Shall it be told him that I would
speak?
Did a man ever wish that he
would be swallowed up?

21 "And now men cannot look on the
light
when it is bright in the skies,
when the wind has passed and
cleared them.
22 Out of the north comes golden
splendor;

[c] Cn: Heb *they distil* [d] Heb *them* [e] Cn Compare Syr: Heb *shower of rain and shower of rains*
[f] Vg Compare Syr Tg: Heb *that all men whom he has made may know it*

God is clothed with terrible
majesty.
23 The Almighty—we cannot find
him;
he is great in power and justice,
and abundant righteousness he
will not violate.
24 Therefore men fear him;
he does not regard any who are
wise in their own conceit."

38 Then the LORD answered Jōb
out of the whirlwind:
2 "Who is this that darkens counsel
by words without knowledge?
3 Gird up your loins like a man,
I will question you, and you shall
declare to me.

4 "Where were you when I laid the
foundation of the earth?
Tell me, if you have understanding.
5 Who determined its measurements
—surely you know!
Or who stretched the line upon it?
6 On what were its bases sunk,
or who laid its cornerstone,
7 when the morning stars sang together,
and all the sons of God shouted
for joy?

8 "Or who shut in the sea with doors,
when it burst forth from the
womb;
9 when I made clouds its garment,
and thick darkness its swaddling
band,
10 and prescribed bounds for it,
and set bars and doors,
11 and said, 'Thus far shall you come,
and no farther,
and here shall your proud waves
be stayed'?

12 'Have you commanded the morning
since your days began,
and caused the dawn to know its
place,
13 that it might take hold of the skirts
of the earth,
and the wicked be shaken out of it?
14 It is changed like clay under the
seal,
and it is dyed[g] like a garment.
15 From the wicked their light is withheld,
and their uplifted arm is broken.

16 "Have you entered into the springs
of the sea,
or walked in the recesses of the
deep?
17 Have the gates of death been revealed to you,
or have you seen the gates of deep
darkness?
18 Have you comprehended the ex-
panse of the earth?
Declare, if you know all this.

19 "Where is the way to the dwelling
of light,
and where is the place of darkness,
20 that you may take it to its territory
and that you may discern the
paths to its home?
21 You know, for you were born then,
and the number of your days is
great!

22 "Have you entered the storehouses
of the snow,
or have you seen the storehouses
of the hail,
23 which I have reserved for the time
of trouble,
for the day of battle and war?
24 What is the way to the place where
the light is distributed,
or where the east wind is scattered
upon the earth?

25 "Who has cleft a channel for the
torrents of rain,
and a way for the thunderbolt,
26 to bring rain on a land where no
man is,
on the desert in which there is
no man;
27 to satisfy the waste and desolate
land,
and to make the ground put forth
grass?

28 "Has the rain a father,
or who has begotten the drops of
dew?
29 From whose womb did the ice come
forth,
and who has given birth to the
hoarfrost of heaven?
30 The waters become hard like stone,
and the face of the deep is frozen.

31 "Can you bind the chains of the
Plēi'ā·dēs,

[g] Cn: Heb *they stand forth*
38.10: Jer 5.22.

or loose the cords of Ō·rī'ŏn?
32 Can you lead forth the Maz'zȧ·roth
in their season,
or can you guide the Bear with
its children?
33 Do you know the ordinances of the
heavens?
Can you establish their rule on
the earth?

34 "Can you lift up your voice to the
clouds,
that a flood of waters may cover
you?
35 Can you send forth lightnings, that
they may go
and say to you, 'Here we are'?
36 Who has put wisdom in the clouds,[h]
or given understanding to the
mists?[h]
37 Who can number the clouds by
wisdom?
Or who can tilt the waterskins of
the heavens,
38 when the dust runs into a mass
and the clods cleave fast together?

39 "Can you hunt the prey for the lion,
or satisfy the appetite of the young
lions,
40 when they crouch in their dens,
or lie in wait in their covert?
41 Who provides for the raven its
prey,
when its young ones cry to God,
and wander about for lack of food?

39 "Do you know when the
mountain goats bring forth?
Do you observe the calving of
the hinds?
2 Can you number the months that
they fulfil,
and do you know the time when
they bring forth,
3 when they crouch, bring forth their
offspring,
and are delivered of their young?
4 Their young ones become strong,
they grow up in the open;
they go forth, and do not return
to them.

5 "Who has let the wild ass go free?
Who has loosed the bonds of the
swift ass,
6 to whom I have given the steppe for
his home,
and the salt land for his dwelling
place?
7 He scorns the tumult of the city;
he hears not the shouts of the
driver.
8 He ranges the mountains as his
pasture,
and he searches after every green
thing.

9 "Is the wild ox willing to serve
you?
Will he spend the night at your
crib?
10 Can you bind him in the furrow
with ropes,
or will he harrow the valleys after
you?
11 Will you depend on him because
his strength is great,
and will you leave to him your
labor?
12 Do you have faith in him that he
will return,
and bring your grain to your
threshing floor?[i]

13 "The wings of the ostrich wave
proudly;
but are they the pinions and
plumage of love?[j]
14 For she leaves her eggs to the earth,
and lets them be warmed on the
ground,
15 forgetting that a foot may crush
them,
and that the wild beast may
trample them.
16 She deals cruelly with her young,
as if they were not hers;
though her labor be in vain, yet
she has no fear;
17 because God has made her forget
wisdom,
and given her no share in understanding.
18 When she rouses herself to flee,[k]
she laughs at the horse and his
rider.

19 "Do you give the horse his might?
Do you clothe his neck with
strength?[l]
20 Do you make him leap like the
locust?
His majestic snorting is terrible.
21 He paws[m] in the valley, and exults
in his strength;

[h] The meaning of the Hebrew word is uncertain [i] Heb *your grain and your threshing floor*
[j] Heb obscure [k] Heb obscure [l] Tg: The meaning of the Hebrew word is obscure
[m] Gk Syr Vg: Heb *they dig*

he goes out to meet the weapons.
22 He laughs at fear, and is not dismayed;
he does not turn back from the sword.
23 Upon him rattle the quiver,
the flashing spear and the javelin.
24 With fierceness and rage he swallows the ground;
he cannot stand still at the sound of the trumpet.
25 When the trumpet sounds, he says 'Aha!'
He smells the battle from afar,
the thunder of the captains, and the shouting.

26 "Is it by your wisdom that the hawk soars,
and spreads his wings toward the south?
27 Is it at your command that the eagle mounts up
and makes his nest on high?
28 On the rock he dwells and makes his home
in the fastness of the rocky crag.
29 Thence he spies out the prey;
his eyes behold it afar off.
30 His young ones suck up blood;
and where the slain are, there is he."

40 And the LORD said to Jōb:
2 "Shall a faultfinder contend with the Almighty?
He who argues with God, let him answer it."

3 Then Jōb answered the LORD:
4 "Behold, I am of small account;
what shall I answer thee?
I lay my hand on my mouth.
5 I have spoken once, and I will not answer;
twice, but I will proceed no further."

6 Then the LORD answered Jōb out of the whirlwind:
7 "Gird up your loins like a man;
I will question you, and you declare to me.
8 Will you even put me in the wrong?
Will you condemn me that you may be justified?
9 Have you an arm like God,
and can you thunder with a voice like his?
10 Deck yourself with majesty and dignity;
clothe yourself with glory and splendor.
11 Pour forth the overflowings of your anger,
and look on every one that is proud, and abase him.
12 Look on every one that is proud, and bring him low;
and tread down the wicked where they stand.
13 Hide them all in the dust together;
bind their faces in the world below.[n]
14 Then will I also acknowledge to you,
that your own right hand can give you victory.

15 "Behold, Bē'hė·mȯth,[o]
which I made as I made you;
he eats grass like an ox.
16 Behold, his strength in his loins,
and his power in the muscles of his belly.
17 He makes his tail stiff like a cedar;
the sinews of his thighs are knit together.
18 His bones are tubes of bronze,
his limbs like bars of iron.

19 "He is the first of the works[p] of God;
let him who made him bring near his sword!
20 For the mountains yield food for him
where all the wild beasts play.
21 Under the lotus plants he lies,
in the covert of the reeds and in the marsh.
22 For his shade the lotus trees cover him;
the willows of the brook surround him.
23 Behold, if the river is turbulent he is not frightened;
he is confident though Jordan rushes against his mouth.
24 Can one take him with hooks,[q]
or pierce his nose with a snare?

41[r] "Can you draw out Lė·vī'ȧ·thȧn[s] with a fishhook,
or press down his tongue with a cord?
2 Can you put a rope in his nose,
or pierce his jaw with a hook?

[n] Heb *hidden place* [o] Or *the hippopotamus* [p] Heb *ways* [q] Cn: Heb *in his eyes* [r] Ch 40.25 in Heb
[s] Or *the crocodile*

3 Will he make many supplications to you?
Will he speak to you soft words?
4 Will he make a covenant with you
to take him for your servant for ever?
5 Will you play with him as with a bird,
or will you put him on leash for your maidens?
6 Will traders bargain over him?
Will they divide him up among the merchants?
7 Can you fill his skin with harpoons,
or his head with fishing spears?
8 Lay hands on him;
think of the battle; you will not do it again!
9 [t] Behold, the hope of a man is disappointed;
he is laid low even at the sight of him.
10 No one is so fierce that he dares to stir him up.
Who then is he that can stand before me?
11 Who has given to me,[u] that I should repay him?
Whatever is under the whole heaven is mine.

12 "I will not keep silence concerning his limbs,
or his mighty strength, or his goodly frame.
13 Who can strip off his outer garment?
Who can penetrate his double coat of mail?[v]
14 Who can open the doors of his face?
Round about his teeth is terror.
15 His back[w] is made of rows of shields,
shut up closely as with a seal.
16 One is so near to another
that no air can come between them.
17 They are joined one to another;
they clasp each other and cannot be separated.
18 His sneezings flash forth light,
and his eyes are like the eyelids of the dawn.
19 Out of his mouth go flaming torches;
sparks of fire leap forth.
20 Out of his nostrils comes forth smoke,
as from a boiling pot and burning rushes.
21 His breath kindles coals,
and a flame comes forth from his mouth.
22 In his neck abides strength,
and terror dances before him.
23 The folds of his flesh cleave together,
firmly cast upon him and immovable.
24 His heart is hard as a stone,
hard as the nether millstone.
25 When he raises himself up the mighty[x] are afraid;
at the crashing they are beside themselves.
26 Though the sword reaches him, it does not avail;
nor the spear, the dart, or the javelin.
27 He counts iron as straw,
and bronze as rotten wood.
28 The arrow cannot make him flee;
for him slingstones are turned to stubble.
29 Clubs are counted as stubble;
he laughs at the rattle of javelins.
30 His underparts are like sharp potsherds;
he spreads himself like a threshing sledge on the mire.
31 He makes the deep boil like a pot;
he makes the sea like a pot of ointment.
32 Behind him he leaves a shining wake;
one would think the deep to be hoary.
33 Upon earth there is not his like,
a creature without fear.
34 He beholds everything that is high;
he is king over all the sons of pride."

42 Then Jōb answered the LORD:
2 "I know that thou canst do all things,
and that no purpose of thine can be thwarted.
3 'Who is this that hides counsel without knowledge?'
Therefore I have uttered what I did not understand,
things too wonderful for me,
which I did not know.
4 'Hear, and I will speak;
I will question you, and you declare to me.'
5 I had heard of thee by the hearing of the ear,

[t] Ch 41.1 in Heb [u] The meaning of the Hebrew is uncertain [v] Gk: Heb *bridle*
[w] Cn Compare Gk Vg: Heb *pride* [x] Or *gods*
41.11: Rom 11.35.

but now my eye sees thee;
6 therefore I despise myself,
and repent in dust and ashes."

7 After the LORD had spoken these
words to Jōb, the LORD said to E·lī'-
phaz the Tē'mȧ·nīte: "My wrath is
kindled against you and against your
two friends; for you have not spoken
of me what is right, as my servant Jōb
has. 8 Now therefore take seven bulls
and seven rams, and go to my servant
Jōb, and offer up for yourselves a
burnt offering; and my servant Job
shall pray for you, for I will accept his
prayer not to deal with you according
to your folly; for you have not spoken
of me what is right, as my servant Job
has." 9 So E·lī'phaz the Tē'mȧ·nīte
and Bil'dad the Shü'hīte and Zō'phär
the Nā'ȧ·mȧ·thīte went and did what
the LORD had told them; and the LORD
accepted Jōb's prayer.
10 And the LORD restored the fortunes of Jōb, when he had prayed for
his friends; and the LORD gave Job
twice as much as he had before.
11 Then came to him all his brothers
and sisters and all who had known him
before, and ate bread with him in his
house; and they showed him sympathy
and comforted him for all the evil that
the LORD had brought upon him; and
each of them gave him a piece of
money[y] and a ring of gold. 12 And the
LORD blessed the latter days of Jōb
more than his beginning; and he had
fourteen thousand sheep, six thousand
camels, a thousand yoke of oxen, and
a thousand she-asses. 13 He had also
seven sons and three daughters. 14 And
he called the name of the first Je·mī'-
mȧh; and the name of the second
Ke·zī'ȧh; and the name of the third
Ker'ĕn-hap'pŭch. 15 And in all the
land there were no women so fair as
Jōb's daughters; and their father gave
them inheritance among their brothers.
16 And after this Jōb lived a hundred
and forty years, and saw his sons, and
his sons' sons, four generations. 17 And
Jōb died, an old man, and full of days.

[y] Heb *qesitah*

THE PSALMS

BOOK I

1 Blessed is the man
who walks not in the counsel of the wicked,
nor stands in the way of sinners,
nor sits in the seat of scoffers;
2 but his delight is in the law of the LORD,
and on his law he meditates day and night.
3 He is like a tree
planted by streams of water,
that yields its fruit in its season,
and its leaf does not wither.
In all that he does, he prospers.

4 The wicked are not so,
but are like chaff which the wind drives away.
5 Therefore the wicked will not stand in the judgment,
nor sinners in the congregation of the righteous;
6 for the LORD knows the way of the righteous,
but the way of the wicked will perish.

2 Why do the nations conspire, and
the peoples plot in vain?
2 The kings of the earth set themselves,
and the rulers take counsel together,
against the LORD and his anointed, saying,
3 "Let us burst their bonds asunder,
and cast their cords from us."

4 He who sits in the heavens laughs;
the LORD has them in derision.
5 Then he will speak to them in his wrath,
and terrify them in his fury, saying,
6 "I have set my king
on Zion, my holy hill."

7 I will tell of the decree of the LORD:
He said to me, "You are my son,
today I have begotten you.
8 Ask of me, and I will make the nations your heritage,
and the ends of the earth your possession.
9 You shall break them with a rod of iron,
and dash them in pieces like a potter's vessel."

10 Now therefore, O kings, be wise;
be warned, O rulers of the earth.
11 Serve the LORD with fear,
with trembling 12 kiss his feet,[a]
lest he be angry, and you perish in the way;
for his wrath is quickly kindled.

Blessed are all who take refuge in him.

A Psalm of David, when he fled from Ab'sá·lóm his son.

3 O LORD, how many are my foes!
Many are rising against me;
2 many are saying of me,
there is no help for him in God. *Selah*

3 But thou, O LORD, art a shield about me,
my glory, and the lifter of my head.
4 I cry aloud to the LORD,
and he answers me from his holy hill. *Selah*

5 I lie down and sleep;
I wake again, for the LORD sustains me.
6 I am not afraid of ten thousands of people
who have set themselves against me round about.

7 Arise, O LORD!
Deliver me, O my God!
For thou dost smite all my enemies on the cheek,

[a] Cn: The Hebrew of 11b and 12a is uncertain
1.1-3: Jer 17.7-8. 2.1-2: Acts 4.25-26. 2.7: Mt 3.17; Acts 13.33; Heb 1.5; 5.5; 2 Pet 1.17.
2.8-9: Rev 2.26; 12.5; 19.15.

thou dost break the teeth of the wicked.

8 Deliverance belongs to the LORD;
thy blessing be upon thy people! *Selah*

To the choirmaster: with stringed instruments. A Psalm of David.

4 Answer me when I call, O God of my right!
Thou hast given me room when I was in distress.
Be gracious to me, and hear my prayer.

2 O men, how long shall my honor suffer shame?
How long will you love vain words, and seek after lies? *Selah*
3 But know that the LORD has set apart the godly for himself;
the LORD hears when I call to him.

4 Be angry, but sin not;
commune with your own hearts on your beds, and be silent. *Selah*
5 Offer right sacrifices,
and put your trust in the LORD.

6 There are many who say, "O that we might see some good!
Lift up the light of thy countenance upon us, O LORD!"
7 Thou hast put more joy in my heart
than they have when their grain and wine abound.

8 In peace I will both lie down and sleep;
for thou alone, O LORD, makest me dwell in safety.

To the choirmaster: for the flutes. A Psalm of David.

5 Give ear to my words, O LORD;
give heed to my groaning.
2 Hearken to the sound of my cry,
my King and my God,
for to thee do I pray.
3 O LORD, in the morning thou dost hear my voice;
in the morning I prepare a sacrifice for thee, and watch.

4 For thou art not a God who delights in wickedness;
evil may not sojourn with thee.
5 The boastful may not stand before thy eyes;
thou hatest all evildoers.
6 Thou destroyest those who speak lies;
the LORD abhors bloodthirsty and deceitful men.

7 But I through the abundance of thy steadfast love
will enter thy house,
I will worship toward thy holy temple
in the fear of thee.
8 Lead me, O LORD, in thy righteousness
because of my enemies;
make thy way straight before me.

9 For there is no truth in their mouth;
their heart is destruction,
their throat is an open sepulchre,
they flatter with their tongue.
10 Make them bear their guilt, O God;
let them fall by their own counsels;
because of their many transgressions cast them out,
for they have rebelled against thee.

11 But let all who take refuge in thee rejoice,
let them ever sing for joy;
and do thou defend them,
that those who love thy name may exult in thee.
12 For thou dost bless the righteous, O LORD;
thou dost cover him with favor as with a shield.

To the choirmaster: with stringed instruments; according to The Sheminith. A Psalm of David.

6 O LORD, rebuke me not in thy anger,
nor chasten me in thy wrath.
2 Be gracious to me, O LORD, for I am languishing;
O LORD, heal me, for my bones are troubled.

4.4: Eph 4.26.
5.9: Rom 3.13.

3 My soul also is sorely troubled.
But thou, O LORD—how long?

4 Turn, O LORD, save my life;
deliver me for the sake of thy steadfast love.
5 For in death there is no remembrance of thee;
in Shē'ōl who can give thee praise?

6 I am weary with my moaning;
every night I flood my bed with tears;
I drench my couch with my weeping.
7 My eye wastes away because of grief,
it grows weak because of all my foes.

8 Depart from me, all you workers of evil;
for the LORD has heard the sound of my weeping.
9 The LORD has heard my supplication;
the LORD accepts my prayer.
10 All my enemies shall be ashamed and sorely troubled;
they shall turn back, and be put to shame in a moment.

A Shiggaion of David, which he sang to the LORD concerning Cush a Benjaminite.

7 O LORD my God, in thee do I take refuge;
save me from all my pursuers, and deliver me,
2 lest like a lion they rend me,
dragging me away, with none to rescue.

3 O LORD my God, if I have done this,
if there is wrong in my hands,
4 if I have requited my friend with evil
or plundered my enemy without cause,
5 let the enemy pursue me and overtake me,
and let him trample my life to the ground,
and lay my soul in the dust. *Selah*

6 Arise, O LORD, in thy anger,
lift thyself up against the fury of my enemies;
awake, O my God;[b] thou hast appointed a judgment.
7 Let the assembly of the peoples be gathered about thee;
and over it take thy seat[c] on high.
8 The LORD judges the peoples;
judge me, O LORD, according to my righteousness
and according to the integrity that is in me.

9 O let the evil of the wicked come to an end,
but establish thou the righteous,
thou who triest the minds and hearts,
thou righteous God.
10 My shield is with God,
who saves the upright in heart.
11 God is a righteous judge,
and a God who has indignation every day.

12 If a man[d] does not repent, God[d] will whet his sword;
he has bent and strung his bow;
13 he has prepared his deadly weapons,
making his arrows fiery shafts.
14 Behold, the wicked man conceives evil,
and is pregnant with mischief,
and brings forth lies.
15 He makes a pit, digging it out,
and falls into the hole which he has made.
16 His mischief returns upon his own head,
and on his own pate his violence descends.

17 I will give to the LORD the thanks due to his righteousness,
and I will sing praise to the name of the LORD, the Most High.

To the choirmaster: according to The Gittith. A Psalm of David.

8 O LORD, our Lord,
how majestic is thy name in all the earth!

Thou whose glory above the heavens is chanted
2 by the mouth of babes and infants,

[b] Or *for me* [c] Cn: Heb *return* [d] Heb *he*
6.8: Mt 7.23; Lk 13.27. **7.9**: Rev 2.23. **8.2**: Mt 21.16.

thou hast founded a bulwark because of thy foes,
to still the enemy and the avenger.

3 When I look at thy heavens, the work of thy fingers,
the moon and the stars which thou hast established;
4 what is man that thou art mindful of him,
and the son of man that thou dost care for him?

5 Yet thou hast made him little less than God,
and dost crown him with glory and honor.
6 Thou hast given him dominion over the works of thy hands;
thou hast put all things under his feet,
7 all sheep and oxen,
and also the beasts of the field,
8 the birds of the air, and the fish of the sea,
whatever passes along the paths of the sea.

9 O LORD, our Lord,
how majestic is thy name in all the earth!

To the choirmaster: according to Muth-labben. A Psalm of David.

9 I will give thanks to the LORD with my whole heart;
I will tell of all thy wonderful deeds.
2 I will be glad and exult in thee,
I will sing praise to thy name, O Most High.

3 When my enemies turned back,
they stumbled and perished before thee.
4 For thou hast maintained my just cause;
thou hast sat on the throne giving righteous judgment.

5 Thou hast rebuked the nations, thou hast destroyed the wicked;
thou hast blotted out their name for ever and ever.
6 The enemy have vanished in everlasting ruins;
their cities thou hast rooted out;
the very memory of them has perished.

7 But the LORD sits enthroned for ever,
he has established his throne for judgment;
8 and he judges the world with righteousness,
he judges the peoples with equity.

9 The LORD is a stronghold for the oppressed,
a stronghold in times of trouble.
10 And those who know thy name put their trust in thee,
for thou, O LORD, hast not forsaken those who seek thee.

11 Sing praises to the LORD, who dwells in Zion!
Tell among the peoples his deeds!
12 For he who avenges blood is mindful of them;
he does not forget the cry of the afflicted.

13 Be gracious to me, O LORD!
Behold what I suffer from those who hate me,
O thou who liftest me up from the gates of death,
14 that I may recount all thy praises,
that in the gates of the daughter of Zion
I may rejoice in thy deliverance.

15 The nations have sunk in the pit which they made;
in the net which they hid has their own foot been caught.
16 The LORD has made himself known,
he has executed judgment;
the wicked are snared in the work of their own hands.
Higgaion. Selah

17 The wicked shall depart to Shē'ōl,
all the nations that forget God.

18 For the needy shall not always be forgotten,
and the hope of the poor shall not perish for ever.

19 Arise, O LORD! Let not man prevail;
let the nations be judged before thee!

8.4-6: Job 7.17-18; Ps 144.3; Heb 2.6-8.
8.6: 1 Cor 15.27; Eph 1.22. **9.8:** Acts 17.31.

20 Put them in fear, O LORD!
Let the nations know that they are but men! *Selah*

10 Why dost thou stand afar off, O LORD?
Why dost thou hide thyself in times of trouble?
2 In arrogance the wicked hotly pursue the poor;
let them be caught in the schemes which they have devised.

3 For the wicked boasts of the desires of his heart,
and the man greedy for gain curses and renounces the LORD.
4 In the pride of his countenance the wicked does not seek him;
all his thoughts are, "There is no God."

5 His ways prosper at all times;
thy judgments are on high, out of his sight;
as for all his foes, he puffs at them.
6 He thinks in his heart, "I shall not be moved;
throughout all generations I shall not meet adversity."

7 His mouth is filled with cursing and deceit and oppression;
under his tongue are mischief and iniquity.
8 He sits in ambush in the villages;
in hiding places he murders the innocent.

His eyes stealthily watch for the hapless,
9 he lurks in secret like a lion in his covert;
he lurks that he may seize the poor,
he seizes the poor when he draws him into his net.

10 The hapless is crushed, sinks down, and falls by his might.
11 He thinks in his heart, "God has forgotten,
he has hidden his face, he will never see it."

12 Arise, O LORD; O God, lift up thy hand;
forget not the afflicted.
13 Why does the wicked renounce God,
and say in his heart, "Thou wilt not call to account"?

14 Thou dost see; yea, thou dost note trouble and vexation,
that thou mayst take it into thy hands;
the hapless commits himself to thee;
thou hast been the helper of the fatherless.

15 Break thou the arm of the wicked and evildoer;
seek out his wickedness till thou find none.
16 The LORD is king for ever and ever;
the nations shall perish from his land.

17 O LORD, thou wilt hear the desire of the meek;
thou wilt strengthen their heart, thou wilt incline thy ear
18 to do justice to the fatherless and the oppressed,
so that man who is of the earth may strike terror no more.

To the choirmaster. Of David.

11 In the LORD I take refuge;
how can you say to me,
"Flee like a bird to the mountains;[e]
2 for lo, the wicked bend the bow,
they have fitted their arrow to the string,
to shoot in the dark at the upright in heart;
3 if the foundations are destroyed, what can the righteous do"?

4 The LORD is in his holy temple,
the LORD's throne is in heaven;
his eyes behold, his eyelids test, the children of men.
5 The LORD tests the righteous and the wicked,
and his soul hates him that loves violence.
6 On the wicked he will rain coals of fire and brimstone;
a scorching wind shall be the portion of their cup.
7 For the LORD is righteous, he loves righteous deeds;
the upright shall behold his face.

[e] Gk Syr Jerome Tg: Heb *flee to your mountain, O bird*
10.7: Rom 3.14.

To the choirmaster: according to The Sheminith. A Psalm of David.

12 Help, LORD; for there is no longer any that is godly;
for the faithful have vanished from among the sons of men.
2 Every one utters lies to his neighbor;
with flattering lips and a double heart they speak.

3 May the LORD cut off all flattering lips,
the tongue that makes great boasts,
4 those who say, "With our tongue we will prevail,
our lips are with us; who is our master?"

5 "Because the poor are despoiled,
because the needy groan,
I will now arise," says the LORD;
"I will place him in the safety for which he longs."
6 The promises of the LORD are promises that are pure,
silver refined in a furnace on the ground,
purified seven times.

7 Do thou, O LORD, protect us,
guard us ever from this generation.
8 On every side the wicked prowl,
as vileness is exalted among the sons of men.

To the choirmaster. A Psalm of David.

13 How long, O LORD? Wilt thou forget me for ever?
How long wilt thou hide thy face from me?
2 How long must I bear pain[f] in my soul,
and have sorrow in my heart all the day?
How long shall my enemy be exalted over me?

3 Consider and answer me, O LORD my God;
lighten my eyes, lest I sleep the sleep of death;
4 lest my enemy say, "I have prevailed over him";
lest my foes rejoice because I am shaken.

5 But I have trusted in thy steadfast love;
my heart shall rejoice in thy salvation.
6 I will sing to the LORD,
because he has dealt bountifully with me.

To the choirmaster. Of David.

14 The fool says in his heart, "There is no God."
They are corrupt, they do abominable deeds,
there is none that does good.

2 The LORD looks down from heaven upon the children of men,
to see if there are any that act wisely,
that seek after God.

3 They have all gone astray, they are all alike corrupt;
there is none that does good,
no, not one.

4 Have they no knowledge, all the evildoers
who eat up my people as they eat bread,
and do not call upon the LORD?

5 There they shall be in great terror,
for God is with the generation of the righteous.
6 You would confound the plans of the poor,
but the LORD is his refuge.

7 O that deliverance for Israel would come out of Zion!
When the LORD restores the fortunes of his people,
Jacob shall rejoice, Israel shall be glad.

A Psalm of David.

15 O LORD, who shall sojourn in thy tent?
Who shall dwell on thy holy hill?

2 He who walks blamelessly, and does what is right,
and speaks truth from his heart;

[f] Syr: Heb *hold counsels*
14.1-3: Rom 3.10-12. **14.1-7:** Ps 53.1-6.

3 who does not slander with his
tongue,
and does no evil to his friend,
nor takes up a reproach against
his neighbor;
4 in whose eyes a reprobate is despised,
but who honors those who fear
the LORD;
who swears to his own hurt and
does not change;
5 who does not put out his money at
interest,
and does not take a bribe against
the innocent.

He who does these things shall never
be moved.

A Miktam of David.

16 Preserve me, O God, for in thee
I take refuge.
2 I say to the LORD, "Thou art my
Lord;
I have no good apart from thee."[g]

3 As for the saints in the land, they
are the noble,
in whom is all my delight.

4 Those who choose another god
multiply their sorrows;[h]
their libations of blood I will not
pour out
or take their names upon my lips.

5 The LORD is my chosen portion and
my cup;
thou holdest my lot.
6 The lines have fallen for me in
pleasant places;
yea, I have a goodly heritage.

7 I bless the LORD who gives me
counsel;
in the night also my heart instructs me.
8 I keep the LORD always before me;
because he is at my right hand,
I shall not be moved.

9 Therefore my heart is glad, and my
soul rejoices;
my body also dwells secure.
10 For thou dost not give me up to
Shē'ōl,
or let thy godly one see the Pit.

11 Thou dost show me the path of life;
in thy presence there is fulness of
joy,
in thy right hand are pleasures
for evermore.

A Prayer of David.

17 Hear a just cause, O LORD;
attend to my cry!
Give ear to my prayer from lips
free of deceit!
2 From thee let my vindication come!
Let thy eyes see the right!

3 If thou triest my heart, if thou
visitest me by night,
if thou testest me, thou wilt find
no wickedness in me;
my mouth does not transgress.
4 With regard to the works of men,
by the word of thy lips
I have avoided the ways of the
violent.
5 My steps have held fast to thy paths,
my feet have not slipped.

6 I call upon thee, for thou wilt answer me, O God;
incline thy ear to me, hear my
words.
7 Wondrously show thy steadfast love,
O savior of those who seek refuge
from their adversaries at thy right
hand.

8 Keep me as the apple of the eye;
hide me in the shadow of thy
wings,
9 from the wicked who despoil me,
my deadly enemies who surround
me.

10 They close their hearts to pity;
with their mouths they speak
arrogantly.
11 They track me down; now they
surround me;
they set their eyes to cast me to
the ground.
12 They are like a lion eager to tear,
as a young lion lurking in ambush.

13 Arise, O LORD! confront them, overthrow them!
Deliver my life from the wicked
by thy sword,

[g] Jerome Tg: The meaning of the Hebrew is uncertain
[h] Cn: The meaning of the Hebrew is uncertain
16.8-11: Acts 2.25-28, 31. **16.10**: Acts 13.35.

14 from men by thy hand, O LORD,
from men whose portion in life is of the world.
May their belly be filled with what thou hast stored up for them;
may their children have more than enough;
may they leave something over to their babes.

15 As for me, I shall behold thy face in righteousness;
when I awake, I shall be satisfied with beholding thy form.

To the choirmaster. A Psalm of David the servant of the LORD, who addressed the words of this song to the LORD on the day when the LORD delivered him from the hand of all his enemies, and from the hand of Saul. He said:

18 I love thee, O LORD, my strength.
2 The LORD is my rock, and my fortress, and my deliverer,
my God, my rock, in whom I take refuge,
my shield, and the horn of my salvation, my stronghold.
3 I call upon the LORD, who is worthy to be praised,
and I am saved from my enemies.

4 The cords of death encompassed me,
the torrents of perdition assailed me;
5 the cords of Shē'ōl entangled me,
the snares of death confronted me.

6 In my distress I called upon the LORD;
to my God I cried for help.
From his temple he heard my voice,
and my cry to him reached his ears.

7 Then the earth reeled and rocked;
the foundations also of the mountains trembled
and quaked, because he was angry.
8 Smoke went up from his nostrils,
and devouring fire from his mouth;
glowing coals flamed forth from him.
9 He bowed the heavens, and came down;
thick darkness was under his feet.
10 He rode on a cherub, and flew;
he came swiftly upon the wings of the wind.
11 He made darkness his covering around him,
his canopy thick clouds dark with water.
12 Out of the brightness before him
there broke through his clouds
hailstones and coals of fire.
13 The LORD also thundered in the heavens,
and the Most High uttered his voice,
hailstones and coals of fire.
14 And he sent out his arrows, and scattered them;
he flashed forth lightnings, and routed them.
15 Then the channels of the sea were seen,
and the foundations of the world were laid bare,
at thy rebuke, O LORD,
at the blast of the breath of thy nostrils.

16 He reached from on high, he took me,
he drew me out of many waters.
17 He delivered me from my strong enemy,
and from those who hated me;
for they were too mighty for me.
18 They came upon me in the day of my calamity;
but the LORD was my stay.
19 He brought me forth into a broad place;
he delivered me, because he delighted in me.

20 The LORD rewarded me according to my righteousness;
according to the cleanness of my hands he recompensed me.
21 For I have kept the ways of the LORD,
and have not wickedly departed from my God.
22 For all his ordinances were before me,
and his statutes I did not put away from me.
23 I was blameless before him,
and I kept myself from guilt.
24 Therefore the LORD has recompensed me according to my righteousness,
according to the cleanness of my hands in his sight.

18:1-50: 2 Sam 22.2-51.

25 With the loyal thou dost show thyself loyal;
with the blameless man thou dost show thyself blameless;
26 with the pure thou dost show thyself pure;
and with the crooked thou dost show thyself perverse.
27 For thou dost deliver a humble people;
but the haughty eyes thou dost bring down.
28 Yea, thou dost light my lamp;
the LORD my God lightens my darkness.
29 Yea, by thee I can crush a troop;
and by my God I can leap over a wall.
30 This God—his way is perfect;
the promise of the LORD proves true;
he is a shield for all those who take refuge in him.

31 For who is God, but the LORD?
And who is a rock, except our God?—
32 the God who girded me with strength,
and made my way safe.
33 He made my feet like hinds' feet,
and set me secure on the heights.
34 He trains my hands for war,
so that my arms can bend a bow of bronze.
35 Thou hast given me the shield of thy salvation,
and thy right hand supported me,
and thy help[i] made me great.
36 Thou didst give a wide place for my steps under me,
and my feet did not slip.
37 I pursued my enemies and overtook them;
and did not turn back till they were consumed.
38 I thrust them through, so that they were not able to rise;
they fell under my feet.
39 For thou didst gird me with strength for the battle;
thou didst make my assailants sink under me.
40 Thou didst make my enemies turn their backs to me,
and those who hated me I destroyed.
41 They cried for help, but there was none to save,
they cried to the LORD, but he did not answer them.
42 I beat them fine as dust before the wind;
I cast them out like the mire of the streets.

43 Thou didst deliver me from strife with the peoples;[j]
thou didst make me the head of the nations;
people whom I had not known served me.
44 As soon as they heard of me they obeyed me;
foreigners came cringing to me.
45 Foreigners lost heart,
and came trembling out of their fastnesses.

46 The LORD lives; and blessed be my rock,
and exalted be the God of my salvation,
47 the God who gave me vengeance
and subdued peoples under me;
48 who delivered me from my enemies;
yea, thou didst exalt me above my adversaries;
thou didst deliver me from men of violence.

49 For this I will extol thee, O LORD, among the nations,
and sing praises to thy name.
50 Great triumphs he gives to his king,
and shows steadfast love to his anointed,
to David and his descendants for ever.

To the choirmaster. A Psalm of David.

19 The heavens are telling the glory of God;
and the firmament proclaims his handiwork.
2 Day to day pours forth speech,
and night to night declares knowledge.
3 There is no speech, nor are there words;
their voice is not heard;
4 yet their voice[k] goes out through all the earth,
and their words to the end of the world.

[i] Or *gentleness* [j] Gk Tg: Heb *people* [k] Gk Jerome Compare Syr: Heb *line*
18.49: Rom 15.9. **19.4**: Rom 10.18.

In them he has set a tent for the sun,
5 which comes forth like a bridegroom leaving his chamber,
and like a strong man runs its course with joy.
6 Its rising is from the end of the heavens,
and its circuit to the end of them;
and there is nothing hid from its heat.

7 The law of the LORD is perfect,
reviving the soul;
the testimony of the LORD is sure,
making wise the simple;
8 the precepts of the LORD are right,
rejoicing the heart;
the commandment of the LORD is pure,
enlightening the eyes;
9 the fear of the LORD is clean,
enduring for ever;
the ordinances of the LORD are true,
and righteous altogether.
10 More to be desired are they than gold,
even much fine gold;
sweeter also than honey
and drippings of the honeycomb.

11 Moreover by them is thy servant warned;
in keeping them there is great reward.
12 But who can discern his errors?
Clear thou me from hidden faults.
13 Keep back thy servant also from presumptuous sins;
let them not have dominion over me!
Then I shall be blameless,
and innocent of great transgression.

14 Let the words of my mouth and the meditation of my heart
be acceptable in thy sight,
O LORD, my rock and my redeemer.

To the choirmaster. A Psalm of David.

20 The LORD answer you in the day of trouble!
The name of the God of Jacob protect you!
2 May he send you help from the sanctuary,
and give you support from Zion!
3 May he remember all your offerings,
and regard with favor your burnt sacrifices! *Selah*

4 May he grant you your heart's desire,
and fulfil all your plans!
5 May we shout for joy over your victory,
and in the name of our God set up our banners!
May the LORD fulfil all your petitions!

6 Now I know that the LORD will help his anointed;
he will answer him from his holy heaven
with mighty victories by his right hand.
7 Some boast of chariots, and some of horses;
but we boast of the name of the LORD our God.
8 They will collapse and fall;
but we shall rise and stand upright.

9 Give victory to the king, O LORD;
answer us when we call.[l]

To the choirmaster. A Psalm of David.

21 In thy strength the king rejoices, O LORD;
and in thy help how greatly he exults!
2 Thou hast given him his heart's desire,
and hast not withheld the request of his lips. *Selah*
3 For thou dost meet him with goodly blessings;
thou dost set a crown of fine gold upon his head.
4 He asked life of thee; thou gavest it to him,
length of days for ever and ever.
5 His glory is great through thy help;
splendor and majesty thou dost bestow upon him.
6 Yea, thou dost make him most blessed for ever;
thou dost make him glad with the joy of thy presence.
7 For the king trusts in the LORD;
and through the steadfast love of the Most High he shall not be moved.

[l] Gk: Heb *give victory, O LORD, let the King answer us when we call*

8 Your hand will find out all your
enemies;
your right hand will find out
those who hate you.
9 You will make them as a blazing oven
when you appear.
The LORD will swallow them up in
his wrath;
and fire will consume them.
10 You will destroy their offspring
from the earth,
and their children from among
the sons of men.
11 If they plan evil against you,
if they devise mischief, they will
not succeed.
12 For you will put them to flight;
you will aim at their faces with
your bows.

13 Be exalted, O LORD, in thy strength!
We will sing and praise thy power.

To the choirmaster: according to The Hind of the Dawn. A Psalm of David.

22 My God, my God, why hast
thou forsaken me?
Why art thou so far from helping
me, from the words of my
groaning?
2 O my God, I cry by day, but thou
dost not answer;
and by night, but find no rest.

3 Yet thou art holy,
enthroned on the praises of Israel.
4 In thee our fathers trusted;
they trusted, and thou didst deliver them.
5 To thee they cried, and were saved;
in thee they trusted, and were
not disappointed.

6 But I am a worm, and no man;
scorned by men, and despised by
the people.
7 All who see me mock at me,
they make mouths at me, they
wag their heads;
8 "He committed his cause to the
LORD; let him deliver him,
let him rescue him, for he delights
in him!"

9 Yet thou art he who took me from
the womb;
thou didst keep me safe upon my
mother's breasts.
10 Upon thee was I cast from my birth,
and since my mother bore me
thou hast been my God.
11 Be not far from me,
for trouble is near
and there is none to help.

12 Many bulls encompass me,
strong bulls of Bā'shān surround
me;
13 they open wide their mouths at me,
like a ravening and roaring lion.

14 I am poured out like water,
and all my bones are out of joint;
my heart is like wax,
it is melted within my breast;
15 my strength is dried up like a potsherd,
and my tongue cleaves to my
jaws;
thou dost lay me in the dust of
death.

16 Yea, dogs are round about me;
a company of evildoers encircle
me;
they have pierced[m] my hands and
feet—
17 I can count all my bones—
they stare and gloat over me;
18 they divide my garments among
them,
and for my raiment they cast lots.

19 But thou, O LORD, be not far off!
O thou my help, hasten to my
aid!
20 Deliver my soul from the sword,
my life[n] from the power of the
dog!
21 Save me from the mouth of the
lion,
my afflicted soul[o] from the horns
of the wild oxen!

22 I will tell of thy name to my
brethren;
in the midst of the congregation
I will praise thee:
23 You who fear the LORD, praise him!
all you sons of Jacob, glorify him,
and stand in awe of him, all you
sons of Israel!
24 For he has not despised or abhorred
the affliction of the afflicted;

[m] Gk Syr Jerome: Heb *like a lion* [n] Heb *my only one* [o] Gk Syr: Heb *thou hast answered me*
22.1: Mt 27.46; Mk 15.34. **22.7-8:** Mt 27.39, 43; Mk 15.29; Lk 23.35.
22.18: Mt 27.35; Mk 15.24; Lk 23.34; Jn 19.24. **22.22:** Heb 2.12.

and he has not hid his face from him,
but has heard, when he cried to him.

25 From thee comes my praise in the great congregation;
my vows I will pay before those who fear him.
26 The afflicted[p] shall eat and be satisfied;
those who seek him shall praise the LORD!
May your hearts live for ever!

27 All the ends of the earth shall remember
and turn to the LORD;
and all the families of the nations shall worship before him.[q]
28 For dominion belongs to the LORD,
and he rules over the nations.

29 Yea, to him[r] shall all the proud of the earth bow down;
before him shall bow all who go down to the dust,
and he who cannot keep himself alive.
30 Posterity shall serve him;
men shall tell of the LORD to the coming generation,
31 and proclaim his deliverance to a people yet unborn,
that he has wrought it.

A Psalm of David.

23 The LORD is my shepherd, I shall not want;
2 he makes me lie down in green pastures.
He leads me beside still waters;[s]
3 he restores my soul.[t]
He leads me in paths of righteousness[u]
for his name's sake.

4 Even though I walk through the valley of the shadow of death,[v]
I fear no evil;
for thou art with me;
thy rod and thy staff,
they comfort me.

5 Thou preparest a table before me
in the presence of my enemies;
thou anointest my head with oil,
my cup overflows.
6 Surely[w] goodness and mercy[x] shall follow me
all the days of my life;
and I shall dwell in the house of the LORD
for ever.[y]

A Psalm of David.

24 The earth is the LORD's and the fulness thereof,
the world and those who dwell therein;
2 for he has founded it upon the seas,
and established it upon the rivers.

3 Who shall ascend the hill of the LORD?
And who shall stand in his holy place?
4 He who has clean hands and a pure heart,
who does not lift up his soul to what is false,
and does not swear deceitfully.
5 He will receive blessing from the LORD,
and vindication from the God of his salvation.
6 Such is the generation of those who seek him,
who seek the face of the God of Jacob.[z] *Selah*

7 Lift up your heads, O gates!
and be lifted up, O ancient doors!
that the King of glory may come in.
8 Who is the King of glory?
The LORD, strong and mighty,
the LORD, mighty in battle!
9 Lift up your heads, O gates!
and be lifted up,[a] O ancient doors!
that the King of glory may come in.
10 Who is this King of glory?
The LORD of hosts,
he is the King of glory! *Selah*

[p] Or *poor* [q] Gk Syr Jerome: Heb *thee*
[r] Cn: Heb *they have eaten and* [s] Heb *the waters of rest* [t] Or *life* [u] Or *right paths*
[v] Or *the valley of deep darkness* [w] Or *Only*
[x] Or *kindness* [y] Or *as long as I live* [z] Gk Syr: Heb *thy face, O Jacob*
[a] Gk Syr Jerome Tg Compare verse 7: Heb *lift up*
23.2: Rev 7.17. 24.1: 1 Cor 10.26. 24.4: Mt 5.8.

A Psalm of David.

25 To thee, O LORD, I lift up my soul.
2 O my God, in thee I trust,
let me not be put to shame;
let not my enemies exult over me.
3 Yea, let none that wait for thee be put to shame;
let them be ashamed who are wantonly treacherous.

4 Make me to know thy ways, O LORD;
teach me thy paths.
5 Lead me in thy truth, and teach me,
for thou art the God of my salvation;
for thee I wait all the day long

6 Be mindful of thy mercy, O LORD,
and of thy steadfast love,
for they have been from of old.
7 Remember not the sins of my youth,
or my transgressions;
according to thy steadfast love remember me,
for thy goodness' sake, O LORD!

8 Good and upright is the LORD;
therefore he instructs sinners in the way.
9 He leads the humble in what is right,
and teaches the humble his way.
10 All the paths of the LORD are steadfast love and faithfulness,
for those who keep his covenant and his testimonies.

11 For thy name's sake, O LORD,
pardon my guilt, for it is great.
12 Who is the man that fears the LORD?
Him will he instruct in the way that he should choose.
13 He himself shall abide in prosperity,
and his children shall possess the land.
14 The friendship of the LORD is for those who fear him,
and he makes known to them his covenant.
15 My eyes are ever toward the LORD,
for he will pluck my feet out of the net.

16 Turn thou to me, and be gracious to me;
for I am lonely and afflicted.
17 Relieve the troubles of my heart,
and bring me[b] out of my distresses.
18 Consider my affliction and my trouble,
and forgive all my sins.
19 Consider how many are my foes,
and with what violent hatred they hate me.
20 Oh guard my life, and deliver me;
let me not be put to shame, for I take refuge in thee.
21 May integrity and uprightness preserve me,
for I wait for thee.

22 Redeem Israel, O God,
out of all his troubles.

A Psalm of David.

26 Vindicate me, O LORD,
for I have walked in my integrity,
and I have trusted in the LORD without wavering.
2 Prove me, O LORD, and try me;
test my heart and my mind.
3 For thy steadfast love is before my eyes,
and I walk in faithfulness to thee.[c]

4 I do not sit with false men,
nor do I consort with dissemblers;
5 I hate the company of evildoers,
and I will not sit with the wicked.

6 I wash my hands in innocence,
and go about thy altar, O LORD,
7 singing aloud a song of thanksgiving,
and telling all thy wondrous deeds.

8 O LORD, I love the habitation of thy house,
and the place where thy glory dwells.
9 Sweep me not away with sinners,
nor my life with bloodthirsty men,
10 men in whose hands are evil devices,
and whose right hands are full of bribes.

11 But as for me, I walk in my integrity;
redeem me, and be gracious to me.
12 My foot stands on level ground;
in the great congregation I will bless the LORD.

[b] Or *The troubles of my heart are enlarged; bring me*
[c] Or *in thy faithfulness*

A Psalm of David.

27 The LORD is my light and my salvation;
whom shall I fear?
The LORD is the stronghold[d] of my life;
of whom shall I be afraid?

2 When evildoers assail me,
uttering slanders against me,[e]
my adversaries and foes,
they shall stumble and fall.

3 Though a host encamp against me,
my heart shall not fear;
though war arise against me,
yet I will be confident.

4 One thing have I asked of the LORD,
that will I seek after;
that I may dwell in the house of the LORD
all the days of my life,
to behold the beauty of the LORD,
and to inquire in his temple.

5 For he will hide me in his shelter
in the day of trouble;
he will conceal me under the cover of his tent,
he will set me high upon a rock.

6 And now my head shall be lifted up
above my enemies round about me;
and I will offer in his tent
sacrifices with shouts of joy;
I will sing and make melody to the LORD.

7 Hear, O LORD, when I cry aloud,
be gracious to me and answer me!
8 Thou hast said, "Seek ye my face."
My heart says to thee,
"Thy face, LORD, do I seek."
9 Hide not thy face from me.

Turn not thy servant away in anger,
thou who hast been my help.
Cast me not off, forsake me not,
O God of my salvation!
10 For my father and my mother have forsaken me,
but the LORD will take me up.

11 Teach me thy way, O LORD;
and lead me on a level path
because of my enemies.
12 Give me not up to the will of my adversaries;
for false witnesses have risen against me,
and they breathe out violence.

13 I believe that I shall see the goodness of the LORD
in the land of the living!
14 Wait for the LORD;
be strong, and let your heart take courage;
yea, wait for the LORD!

A Psalm of David.

28 To thee, O LORD, I call;
my rock, be not deaf to me,
lest, if thou be silent to me,
I become like those who go down to the Pit.
2 Hear the voice of my supplication,
as I cry to thee for help,
as I lift up my hands
toward thy most holy sanctuary.[f]

3 Take me not off with the wicked,
with those who are workers of evil,
who speak peace with their neighbors,
while mischief is in their hearts.
4 Requite them according to their work,
and according to the evil of their deeds;
requite them according to the work of their hands;
render them their due reward.
5 Because they do not regard the works of the LORD,
or the work of his hands,
he will break them down and build them up no more.

6 Blessed be the LORD!
for he has heard the voice of my supplications.
7 The LORD is my strength and my shield;
in him my heart trusts;
so I am helped, and my heart exults,
and with my song I give thanks to him.

8 The LORD is the strength of his people,
he is the saving refuge of his anointed.
9 O save thy people, and bless thy heritage;

[d] Or *refuge* [e] Heb *to eat up my flesh* [f] Heb *thy innermost sanctuary*

be thou their shepherd, and carry
them for ever.

A Psalm of David.

29 Ascribe to the LORD, O
heavenly beings,[g]
ascribe to the LORD glory and
strength.
2 Ascribe to the LORD the glory of his
name;
worship the LORD in holy array.

3 The voice of the LORD is upon the
waters;
the God of glory thunders,
the LORD, upon many waters.
4 The voice of the LORD is powerful,
the voice of the LORD is full of
majesty.

5 The voice of the LORD breaks the
cedars,
the LORD breaks the cedars of
Lebanon.
6 He makes Lebanon to skip like a
calf,
and Sir'i·on like a young wild ox.

7 The voice of the LORD flashes forth
flames of fire.
8 The voice of the LORD shakes the
wilderness,
the LORD shakes the wilderness
of Kā'desh.

9 The voice of the LORD makes the
oaks to whirl,[h]
and strips the forests bare;
and in his temple all cry, "Glory!"

10 The LORD sits enthroned over the
flood;
the LORD sits enthroned as king
for ever.
11 May the LORD give strength to his
people!
May the LORD bless his people
with peace!

A Psalm of David. A Song at the
dedication of the Temple.

30 I will extol thee, O LORD, for
thou hast drawn me up,
and hast not let my foes rejoice
over me.
2 O LORD my God, I cried to thee
for help,
and thou hast healed me.
3 O LORD, thou hast brought up my
soul from Shē'ōl,
restored me to life from among
those gone down to the Pit.[i]

4 Sing praises to the LORD, O you his
saints,
and give thanks to his holy name.
5 For his anger is but for a moment,
and his favor is for a lifetime.
Weeping may tarry for the night,
but joy comes with the morning.

6 As for me, I said in my prosperity,
"I shall never be moved."
7 By thy favor, O LORD,
thou hadst established me as a
strong mountain;
thou didst hide thy face,
I was dismayed.

8 To thee, O LORD, I cried;
and to the LORD I made supplication:
9 "What profit is there in my death,
if I go down to the Pit?
Will the dust praise thee?
Will it tell of thy faithfulness?
10 Hear, O LORD, and be gracious to
me!
O LORD, be thou my helper!"

11 Thou hast turned for me my mourning into dancing;
thou hast loosed my sackcloth
and girded me with gladness,
12 that my soul[j] may praise thee and
not be silent.
O LORD my God, I will give
thanks to thee for ever.

To the choirmaster. A Psalm of David.

31 In thee, O LORD, do I seek
refuge;
let me never be put to shame;
in thy righteousness deliver
me!
2 Incline thy ear to me,
rescue me speedily!
Be thou a rock of refuge for me,
a strong fortress to save me!

3 Yea, thou art my rock and my
fortress;

[g] Heb *sons of gods* [h] Or *makes the hinds to calve* [i] Or *that I should not go down to the Pit*
[j] Heb *that glory*

for thy name's sake lead me and
guide me,
4 take me out of the net which is
hidden for me,
for thou art my refuge.
5 Into thy hand I commit my spirit;
thou hast redeemed me, O LORD,
faithful God.

6 Thou hatest[k] those who pay regard
to vain idols;
but I trust in the LORD.
7 I will rejoice and be glad for thy
steadfast love,
because thou hast seen my affliction,
thou hast taken heed of my adversities,
8 and hast not delivered me into the
hand of the enemy;
thou hast set my feet in a broad
place.

9 Be gracious to me, O LORD, for I
am in distress;
my eye is wasted from grief,
my soul and my body also.
10 For my life is spent with sorrow,
and my years with sighing;
my strength fails because of my
misery,[l]
and my bones waste away.

11 I am the scorn of all my adversaries,
a horror[m] to my neighbors,
an object of dread to my acquaintances;
those who see me in the street
flee from me.
12 I have passed out of mind like one
who is dead;
I have become like a broken vessel.
13 Yea, I hear the whispering of
many—
terror on every side!—
as they scheme together against me,
as they plot to take my life.

14 But I trust in thee, O LORD,
I say, "Thou art my God."
15 My times are in thy hand;
deliver me from the hand of my
enemies and persecutors!
16 Let thy face shine on thy servant;
save me in thy steadfast love!
17 Let me not be put to shame, O LORD,
for I call on thee;
let the wicked be put to shame,
let them go dumbfounded to
Shē'ōl.
18 Let the lying lips be dumb,
which speak insolently against the
righteous
in pride and contempt.

19 O how abundant is thy goodness,
which thou hast laid up for those
who fear thee,
and wrought for those who take
refuge in thee,
in the sight of the sons of men!
20 In the covert of thy presence thou
hidest them
from the plots of men;
thou holdest them safe under thy
shelter
from the strife of tongues.

21 Blessed be the LORD,
for he has wondrously shown his
steadfast love to me
when I was beset as in a besieged
city.
22 I had said in my alarm,
"I am driven far[n] from thy sight."
But thou didst hear my supplications,
when I cried to thee for help.

23 Love the LORD, all you his saints!
The LORD preserves the faithful,
but abundantly requites him who
acts haughtily.
24 Be strong, and let your heart take
courage,
all you who wait for the LORD!

A Psalm of David. A Maskil.

32 Blessed is he whose transgression is forgiven,
whose sin is covered.
2 Blessed is the man to whom the
LORD imputes no iniquity,
and in whose spirit there is no
deceit.

3 When I declared not my sin, my
body wasted away
through my groaning all day
long.
4 For day and night thy hand was
heavy upon me;
my strength was dried up[o] as by
the heat of summer. *Selah*

[k] With one Heb Ms Gk Syr Jerome: Heb *I hate* [l] Gk Syr: Heb *iniquity* [m] Cn: Heb *exceedingly*
[n] Another reading is *cut off* [o] Heb obscure
31.5: Lk 23.46. **31.13:** Jer 6.25; 20.3, 10; 46.5; 49.29. **32.1-2:** Rom 4.7-8.

5 I acknowledged my sin to thee,
and I did not hide my iniquity;
I said, "I will confess my transgressions to the LORD";
then thou didst forgive the guilt of my sin. *Selah*

6 Therefore let every one who is godly offer prayer to thee;
at a time of distress,[p] in the rush of great waters,
they shall not reach him.
7 Thou art a hiding place for me,
thou preservest me from trouble;
thou dost encompass me with deliverance.[q] *Selah*

8 I will instruct you and teach you the way you should go;
I will counsel you with my eye upon you.
9 Be not like a horse or a mule, without understanding,
which must be curbed with bit and bridle,
else it will not keep with you.

10 Many are the pangs of the wicked;
but steadfast love surrounds him who trusts in the LORD.
11 Be glad in the LORD, and rejoice, O righteous,
and shout for joy, all you upright in heart!

33 Rejoice in the LORD, O you righteous!
Praise befits the upright.
2 Praise the LORD with the lyre,
make melody to him with the harp of ten strings!
3 Sing to him a new song,
play skilfully on the strings, with loud shouts.

4 For the word of the LORD is upright;
and all his work is done in faithfulness.
5 He loves righteousness and justice;
the earth is full of the steadfast love of the LORD.

6 By the word of the LORD the heavens were made,
and all their host by the breath of his mouth.
7 He gathered the waters of the sea as in a bottle;
he put the deeps in storehouses.
8 Let all the earth fear the LORD,
let all the inhabitants of the world stand in awe of him!
9 For he spoke, and it came to be;
he commanded, and it stood forth.

10 The LORD brings the counsel of the nations to nought;
he frustrates the plans of the peoples.
11 The counsel of the LORD stands for ever,
the thoughts of his heart to all generations.
12 Blessed is the nation whose God is the LORD,
the people whom he has chosen as his heritage!

13 The LORD looks down from heaven,
he sees all the sons of men;
14 from where he sits enthroned he looks forth
on all the inhabitants of the earth,
15 he who fashions the hearts of them all,
and observes all their deeds.
16 A king is not saved by his great army;
a warrior is not delivered by his great strength.
17 The war horse is a vain hope for victory,
and by its great might it cannot save.

18 Behold, the eye of the LORD is on those who fear him,
on those who hope in his steadfast love,
19 that he may deliver their soul from death,
and keep them alive in famine.

20 Our soul waits for the LORD;
he is our help and shield.
21 Yea, our heart is glad in him,
because we trust in his holy name.
22 Let thy steadfast love, O LORD, be upon us,
even as we hope in thee.

A Psalm of David, when he feigned madness before A·bim'ĕ·lech, so that he drove him out, and he went away.

34 I will bless the LORD at all times;
his praise shall continually be in my mouth.

[p] Cn: Heb *at a time of finding only* [q] Cn: Heb *shouts of deliverance*

2 My soul makes its boast in the LORD;
let the afflicted hear and be glad.
3 O magnify the LORD with me,
and let us exalt his name together!

4 I sought the LORD, and he answered me,
and delivered me from all my fears.
5 Look to him, and be radiant;
so your[r] faces shall never be ashamed.
6 This poor man cried, and the LORD heard him,
and saved him out of all his troubles.
7 The angel of the LORD encamps
around those who fear him, and delivers them.
8 O taste and see that the LORD is good!
Happy is the man who takes refuge in him!
9 O fear the LORD, you his saints,
for those who fear him have no want!
10 The young lions suffer want and hunger;
but those who seek the LORD lack no good thing.

11 Come, O sons, listen to me,
I will teach you the fear of the LORD.
12 What man is there who desires life,
and covets many days, that he may enjoy good?
13 Keep your tongue from evil,
and your lips from speaking deceit.
14 Depart from evil, and do good;
seek peace, and pursue it.

15 The eyes of the LORD are toward the righteous,
and his ears toward their cry.
16 The face of the LORD is against evildoers,
to cut off the remembrance of them from the earth.
17 When the righteous cry for help, the LORD hears,
and delivers them out of all their troubles.
18 The LORD is near to the brokenhearted,
and saves the crushed in spirit.
19 Many are the afflictions of the righteous;
but the LORD delivers him out of them all.
20 He keeps all his bones;
not one of them is broken.
21 Evil shall slay the wicked;
and those who hate the righteous will be condemned.
22 The LORD redeems the life of his servants;
none of those who take refuge in him will be condemned.

A Psalm of David.

35 Contend, O LORD, with those who contend with me;
fight against those who fight against me!
2 Take hold of shield and buckler,
and rise for my help!
3 Draw the spear and javelin
against my pursuers!
Say to my soul,
"I am your deliverance!"

4 Let them be put to shame and dishonor
who seek after my life!
Let them be turned back and confounded
who devise evil against me!
5 Let them be like chaff before the wind,
with the angel of the LORD driving them on!
6 Let their way be dark and slippery,
with the angel of the LORD pursuing them!

7 For without cause they hid their net for me;
without cause they dug a pit[s] for my life.
8 Let ruin come upon them unawares!
And let the net which they hid ensnare them;
let them fall therein to ruin!

9 Then my soul shall rejoice in the LORD,
exulting in his deliverance.
10 All my bones shall say,
"O LORD, who is like thee,
thou who deliverest the weak
from him who is too strong for him,

[r] Gk Syr Jerome: Heb *their* [s] The word *pit* is transposed from the preceding line
34.8: 1 Pet 2.3. 34.12-16: 1 Pet 3.10-12.

the weak and needy from him
who despoils him?"

11 Malicious witnesses rise up;
they ask me of things that I know
not.
12 They requite me evil for good;
my soul is forlorn.
13 But I, when they were sick—
I wore sackcloth,
I afflicted myself with fasting.
I prayed with head bowed[t] on my
bosom,
14 as though I grieved for my friend
or my brother;
I went about as one who laments
his mother,
bowed down and in mourning.

15 But at my stumbling they gathered
in glee,
they gathered together against
me;
cripples whom I knew not
slandered me without ceasing;
16 they impiously mocked more and
more,[u]
gnashing at me with their teeth.

17 How long, O LORD, wilt thou look
on?
Rescue me from their ravages,
my life from the lions!
18 Then I will thank thee in the great
congregation;
in the mighty throng I will praise
thee.

19 Let not those rejoice over me
who are wrongfully my foes,
and let not those wink the eye
who hate me without cause.
20 For they do not speak peace,
but against those who are quiet in
the land
they conceive words of deceit.
21 They open wide their mouths
against me;
they say, "Aha, Aha!
our eyes have seen it!"

22 Thou hast seen, O LORD; be not
silent!
O Lord, be not far from me!
23 Bestir thyself, and awake for my
right,
for my cause, my God and my
Lord!
24 Vindicate me, O LORD, my God,
according to thy righteousness;
and let them not rejoice over
me!
25 Let them not say to themselves,
"Aha, we have our heart's desire!"
Let them not say, "We have swallowed him up."

26 Let them be put to shame and confusion altogether
who rejoice at my calamity!
Let them be clothed with shame
and dishonor
who magnify themselves against
me!

27 Let those who desire my vindication
shout for joy and be glad,
and say evermore,
"Great is the LORD,
who delights in the welfare of his
servant!"
28 Then my tongue shall tell of thy
righteousness
and of thy praise all the day long.

To the choirmaster. A Psalm of David,
the servant of the LORD.

36 Transgression speaks to the
wicked
deep in his heart;
there is no fear of God
before his eyes.
2 For he flatters himself in his own
eyes
that his iniquity cannot be found
out and hated.
3 The words of his mouth are mischief
and deceit;
he has ceased to act wisely and do
good.
4 He plots mischief while on his bed;
he sets himself in a way that is
not good;
he spurns not evil.

5 Thy steadfast love, O LORD, extends
to the heavens,
thy faithfulness to the clouds.
6 Thy righteousness is like the mountains of God,
thy judgments are like the great
deep;
man and beast thou savest, O
LORD.

[t] Or *My prayer turned back*
[u] Cn Compare Gk: Heb *like the profanest of mockers of a cake*
35.19: Ps 69.4; Jn 15.25. **36.1:** Rom 3.18.

7 How precious is thy steadfast love, O God!
The children of men take refuge in the shadow of thy wings.
8 They feast on the abundance of thy house,
and thou givest them drink from the river of thy delights.
9 For with thee is the fountain of life;
in thy light do we see light.

10 O continue thy steadfast love to those who know thee,
and thy salvation to the upright of heart!
11 Let not the foot of arrogance come upon me,
nor the hand of the wicked drive me away.
12 There the evildoers lie prostrate,
they are thrust down, unable to rise.

A Psalm of David.

37 Fret not yourself because of the wicked,
be not envious of wrongdoers!
2 For they will soon fade like the grass,
and wither like the green herb.

3 Trust in the LORD, and do good;
so you will dwell in the land, and enjoy security.
4 Take delight in the LORD,
and he will give you the desires of your heart.

5 Commit your way to the LORD;
trust in him, and he will act.
6 He will bring forth your vindication as the light,
and your right as the noonday.

7 Be still before the LORD, and wait patiently for him;
fret not yourself over him who prospers in his way,
over the man who carries out evil devices!

8 Refrain from anger, and forsake wrath!
Fret not yourself; it tends only to evil.
9 For the wicked shall be cut off;
but those who wait for the LORD shall possess the land.

10 Yet a little while, and the wicked will be no more;
though you look well at his place, he will not be there.
11 But the meek shall possess the land,
and delight themselves in abundant prosperity.

12 The wicked plots against the righteous,
and gnashes his teeth at him;
13 but the LORD laughs at the wicked,
for he sees that his day is coming.

14 The wicked draw the sword and bend their bows,
to bring down the poor and needy,
to slay those who walk uprightly;
15 their sword shall enter their own heart,
and their bows shall be broken.

16 Better is a little that the righteous has
than the abundance of many wicked.
17 For the arms of the wicked shall be broken;
but the LORD upholds the righteous.

18 The LORD knows the days of the blameless,
and their heritage will abide for ever;
19 they are not put to shame in evil times,
in the days of famine they have abundance.

20 But the wicked perish;
the enemies of the LORD are like the glory of the pastures,
they vanish—like smoke they vanish away.

21 The wicked borrows, and cannot pay back,
but the righteous is generous and gives;
22 for those blessed by the LORD shall possess the land,
but those cursed by him shall be cut off.

23 The steps of a man are from the LORD,
and he establishes him in whose way he delights;

37.11: Mt 5.5.

24 though he fall, he shall not be cast
headlong,
for the LORD is the stay of his
hand.

25 I have been young, and now am old;
yet I have not seen the righteous
forsaken
or his children begging bread.
26 He is ever giving liberally and
lending,
and his children become a blessing.

27 Depart from evil, and do good;
so shall you abide for ever.
28 For the LORD loves justice;
he will not forsake his saints.

The righteous shall be preserved for
ever,
but the children of the wicked
shall be cut off.
29 The righteous shall possess the land,
and dwell upon it for ever.

30 The mouth of the righteous utters
wisdom,
and his tongue speaks justice.
31 The law of his God is in his heart;
his steps do not slip.

32 The wicked watches the righteous,
and seeks to slay him.
33 The LORD will not abandon him to
his power,
or let him be condemned when he
is brought to trial.

34 Wait for the LORD, and keep to his
way,
and he will exalt you to possess
the land;
you will look on the destruction
of the wicked.

35 I have seen a wicked man overbearing,
and towering like a cedar of
Lebanon.[v]
36 Again I[w] passed by, and, lo, he was
no more;
though I sought him, he could not
be found.

37 Mark the blameless man, and behold
the upright,
for there is posterity for the man
of peace.
38 But transgressors shall be altogether
destroyed;
the posterity of the wicked shall
be cut off.
39 The salvation of the righteous is
from the LORD;
he is their refuge in the time of
trouble.
40 The LORD helps them and delivers
them;
he delivers them from the wicked,
and saves them,
because they take refuge in him.

A Psalm of David, for the memorial
offering.

38 O LORD, rebuke me not in
thy anger,
nor chasten me in thy wrath!
2 For thy arrows have sunk into me,
and thy hand has come down on
me.

3 There is no soundness in my flesh
because of thy indignation;
there is no health in my bones
because of my sin.
4 For my iniquities have gone over
my head;
they weigh like a burden too
heavy for me.

5 My wounds grow foul and fester
because of my foolishness,
6 I am utterly bowed down and
prostrate;
all the day I go about mourning.
7 For my loins are filled with burning,
and there is no soundness in my
flesh.
8 I am utterly spent and crushed;
I groan because of the tumult of
my heart.

9 LORD, all my longing is known to
thee,
my sighing is not hidden from
thee.
10 My heart throbs, my strength fails
me;
and the light of my eyes—it also
has gone from me.
11 My friends and companions stand
aloof from my plague,
and my kinsmen stand afar off.

12 Those who seek my life lay their
snares,

[v] Gk: Heb obscure [w] Gk Syr Jerome: Heb *he*

those who seek my hurt speak of ruin,
and meditate treachery all the day long.

13 But I am like a deaf man, I do not hear,
like a dumb man who does not open his mouth.
14 Yea, I am like a man who does not hear,
and in whose mouth are no rebukes.

15 But for thee, O LORD, do I wait;
it is thou, O LORD my God, who wilt answer.
16 For I pray, "Only let them not rejoice over me,
who boast against me when my foot slips!"

17 For I am ready to fall,
and my pain is ever with me,
18 I confess my iniquity,
I am sorry for my sin.
19 Those who are my foes without cause[x] are mighty,
and many are those who hate me wrongfully.
20 Those who render me evil for good
are my adversaries because I follow after good.

21 Do not forsake me, O LORD!
O my God, be not far from me!
22 Make haste to help me,
O Lord, my salvation!

To the choirmaster: to Je·dü'thŭn. A Psalm of David.

39 I said, "I will guard my ways,
that I may not sin with tongue;
I will bridle[y] my mouth,
so long as the wicked are in my presence."
2 I was dumb and silent,
I held my peace to no avail;
my distress grew worse,
3 my heart became hot within me.
As I mused, the fire burned;
then I spoke with my tongue:

4 "LORD, let me know my end,
and what is the measure of my days;
let me know how fleeting my life is!
5 Behold, thou hast made my days a few handbreadths,
and my lifetime is as nothing in thy sight.
Surely every man stands as a mere breath! *Selah*
6 Surely man goes about as a shadow!
Surely for nought are they in turmoil;
man heaps up, and knows not who will gather!

7 "And now, Lord, for what do I wait?
My hope is in thee.
8 Deliver me from all my transgressions.
Make me not the scorn of the fool!
9 I am dumb, I do not open my mouth;
for it is thou who hast done it.
10 Remove thy stroke from me;
I am spent by the blows[z] of thy hand.
11 When thou dost chasten man
with rebukes for sin,
thou dost consume like a moth what is dear to him;
surely every man is a mere breath! *Selah*

12 "Hear my prayer, O LORD,
and give ear to my cry;
hold not thy peace at my tears!
for I am thy passing guest,
a sojourner, like all my fathers.
13 Look away from me, that I may know gladness,
before I depart and be no more!"

To the choirmaster. A Psalm of David.

40 I waited patiently for the LORD;
he inclined to me and heard my cry.
2 He drew me up from the desolate pit,[a]
out of the miry bog,
and set my feet upon a rock,
making my steps secure.
3 He put a new song in my mouth,
a song of praise to our God.
Many will see and fear,
and put their trust in the LORD.

4 Blessed is the man who makes
the LORD his trust,

[x] Cn: Heb *living* [y] Heb *muzzle* [z] Heb *hostility* [a] Cn: Heb *pit of tumult*

who does not turn to the proud,
to those who go astray after false gods!
5 Thou hast multiplied, O LORD my God,
thy wondrous deeds and thy thoughts toward us;
none can compare with thee!
Were I to proclaim and tell of them,
they would be more than can be numbered.

6 Sacrifice and offering thou dost not desire;
but thou hast given me an open ear.[b]
Burnt offering and sin offering
thou hast not required.
7 Then I said, "Lo, I come;
in the roll of the book it is written of me;
8 I delight to do thy will, O my God;
thy law is within my heart."

9 I have told the glad news of deliverance
in the great congregation;
lo, I have not restrained my lips,
as thou knowest, O LORD.
10 I have not hid thy saving help within my heart,
I have spoken of thy faithfulness and thy salvation;
I have not concealed thy steadfast love and thy faithfulness
from the great congregation.

11 Do not thou, O LORD, withhold
thy mercy from me,
let thy steadfast love and thy faithfulness
ever preserve me!
12 For evils have encompassed me
without number;
my iniquities have overtaken me,
till I cannot see;
they are more than the hairs of my head;
my heart fails me.

13 Be pleased, O LORD, to deliver me!
O LORD, make haste to help me!
14 Let them be put to shame and confusion altogether
who seek to snatch away my life;
let them be turned back and brought to dishonor
who desire my hurt!
15 Let them be appalled because of their shame
who say to me, "Aha, Aha!"

16 But may all who seek thee
rejoice and be glad in thee;
may those who love thy salvation
say continually, "Great is the LORD!"
17 As for me, I am poor and needy;
but the Lord takes thought for me.
Thou art my help and my deliverer;
do not tarry, O my God!

To the choirmaster. A Psalm of David.

41 Blessed is he who considers the poor![c]
The LORD delivers him in the day of trouble;
2 the LORD protects him and keeps him alive;
he is called blessed in the land;
thou dost not give him up to the will of his enemies.
3 The LORD sustains him on his sickbed;
in his illness thou healest all his infirmities.[d]

4 As for me, I said, "O LORD, be gracious to me;
heal me, for I have sinned against thee!"
5 My enemies say of me in malice;
"When will he die, and his name perish?"
6 And when one comes to see me, he utters empty words,
while his heart gathers mischief;
when he goes out, he tells it abroad.
7 All who hate me whisper together about me;
they imagine the worst for me.

8 They say, "A deadly thing has fastened upon him;
he will not rise again from where he lies."
9 Even my bosom friend in whom I trusted,
who ate of my bread, has lifted his heel against me.
10 But do thou, O LORD, be gracious to me,
and raise me up, that I may requite them!

[b] Heb *ears thou hast dug for me* [c] Or *weak* [d] Heb *thou changest all his bed*
40.6-8: Heb 10.5-9. 40.13-17: Ps 70.1-5. 41.9: Jn 13.18.

11 By this I know that thou art pleased
with me,
in that my enemy has not triumphed over me.
12 But thou hast upheld me because of
my integrity,
and set me in thy presence for ever.

13 Blessed be the LORD, the God of Israel,
from everlasting to everlasting!
Amen and Amen.

BOOK II

To the choirmaster. A Maskil of the Sons of Kō'răh.

42 As a hart longs
for flowing streams,
so longs my soul
for thee, O God.
2 My soul thirsts for God,
for the living God.
When shall I come and behold
the face of God?
3 My tears have been my food
day and night,
while men say to me continually,
"Where is your God?"

4 These things I remember,
as I pour out my soul:
how I went with the throng,
and led them in procession to the
house of God,
with glad shouts and songs of
thanksgiving,
a multitude keeping festival.
5 Why are you cast down, O my soul,
and why are you disquieted within me?
Hope in God; for I shall again praise
him,
my help 6 and my God.

My soul is cast down within me,
therefore I remember thee
from the land of Jordan and of
Hĕr'mŏn,
from Mount Mī'zär.
7 Deep calls to deep
at the thunder of thy cataracts;
all thy waves and thy billows
have gone over me.
8 By day the LORD commands his
steadfast love;
and at night his song is with me,
a prayer to the God of my life.

9 I say to God, my rock:
"Why hast thou forgotten me?
Why go I mourning
because of the oppression of the
enemy?"
10 As with a deadly wound in my body,
my adversaries taunt me,
while they say to me continually,
"Where is your God?"

11 Why are you cast down, O my soul,
and why are you disquieted within me?
Hope in God; for I shall again praise
him,
my help and my God.

43 Vindicate me, O God, and
defend my cause
against an ungodly people;
from deceitful and unjust men
deliver me!
2 For thou art the God in whom I
take refuge;
why hast thou cast me off?
Why go I mourning
because of the oppression of the
enemy?

3 Oh send out thy light and thy truth;
let them lead me,
let them bring me to thy holy hill
and to thy dwelling!
4 Then I will go to the altar of God,
to God my exceeding joy;
and I will praise thee with the lyre,
O God, my God.

5 Why are you cast down, O my soul,
and why are you disquieted within me?
Hope in God; for I shall again praise
him,
my help and my God.

To the choirmaster. A Maskil of the Sons of Kō'răh.

44 We have heard with our ears,
O God,
our fathers have told us,
what deeds thou didst perform in
their days,
in the days of old:
2 thou with thy own hand didst drive
out the nations,
but them thou didst plant;
thou didst afflict the peoples,
but them thou didst set free;
3 for not by their own sword did they
win the land,

nor did their own arm give them
victory;
but thy right hand, and thy arm,
and the light of thy countenance;
for thou didst delight in them.

4 Thou art my King and my God,
who ordainest[e] victories for Jacob.
5 Through thee we push down our
foes;
through thy name we tread down
our assailants.
6 For not in my bow do I trust,
nor can my sword save me.
7 But thou hast saved us from our foes,
and hast put to confusion those
who hate us.
8 In God we have boasted continually,
and we will give thanks to thy
name for ever. *Selah*

9 Yet thou hast cast us off and abased
us, and hast not gone out with
our armies.
10 Thou hast made us turn back from
the foe;
and our enemies have gotten spoil.
11 Thou hast made us like sheep for
slaughter,
and hast scattered us among the
nations.
12 Thou hast sold thy people for a
trifle,
demanding no high price for them.

13 Thou hast made us the taunt of our
neighbors;
the derision and scorn of those
about us.
14 Thou hast made us a byword among
the nations,
a laughingstock[f] among the
peoples.
15 All day long my disgrace is before
me,
and shame has covered my face,
16 at the words of the taunters and
revilers,
at the sight of the enemy and the
avenger.

17 All this has come upon us,
though we have not forgotten
thee,
or been false to thy covenant.
18 Our heart has not turned back,
nor have our steps departed from
thy way,
19 that thou shouldst have broken us
in the place of jackals,
and covered us with deep darkness.

20 If we had forgotten the name of our
God,
or spread forth our hands to a
strange god,
21 would not God discover this?
For he knows the secrets of the
heart.
22 Nay, for thy sake we are slain all
the day long,
and accounted as sheep for the
slaughter.

23 Rouse thyself! Why sleepest thou,
O Lord?
Awake! Do not cast us off for ever!
24 Why dost thou hide thy face?
Why dost thou forget our affliction and oppression?
25 For our soul is bowed down to the
dust;
our body cleaves to the ground.
26 Rise up, come to our help!
Deliver us for the sake of thy
steadfast love!

To the choirmaster: according to Lilies. A Maskil of the Sons of Kō′rah; a love song.

45 My heart overflows with a
goodly theme;
I address my verses to the king;
my tongue is like the pen of a
ready scribe.

2 You are the fairest of the sons of men;
grace is poured upon your lips;
therefore God has blessed you for
ever.
3 Gird your sword upon your thigh,
O mighty one,
in your glory and majesty!

4 In your majesty ride forth victori-
ously
for the cause of the truth and to
defend[g] the right;
let your right hand teach you
dread deeds!
5 Your arrows are sharp
in the heart of the king's enemies;
the peoples fall under you.

[e] Gk Syr: Heb *Thou are my King, O God; ordain* [f] Heb *a shaking of the head*
[g] Cn: Heb *and the meekness of*
44.22: Rom 8.36.

6 Your divine throne[h] endures for ever and ever.
Your royal scepter is a scepter of equity;
7 you love righteousness and hate wickedness.
Therefore God, your God, has anointed you
with the oil of gladness above your fellows;
8 your robes are all fragrant with myrrh and aloes and cassia.
From ivory palaces stringed instruments make you glad;
9 daughters of kings are among your ladies of honor;
at your right hand stands the queen in gold of Ō'phīr.

10 Hear, O daughter, consider, and incline your ear;
forget your people and your father's house;
11 and the king will desire your beauty.
Since he is your lord, bow to him;
12 the people[i] of Tȳre will sue your favor with gifts,
the richest of the people 13 with all kinds of wealth.

The princess is decked in her chamber with gold-woven robes;[j]
14 in many-colored robes she is led to the king,
with her virgin companions, her escort,[k] in her train.
15 With joy and gladness they are led along
as they enter the palace of the king.

16 Instead of your fathers shall be your sons;
you will make them princes in all the earth.
17 I will cause your name to be celebrated in all generations;
therefore the peoples will praise you for ever and ever.

To the choirmaster. A Psalm of the Sons of Kō'răh. According to Alamoth. A Song.

46 God is our refuge and strength,
a very present[l] help in trouble.
2 Therefore we will not fear though the earth should change,
though the mountains shake in the heart of the sea;
3 though its waters roar and foam,
though the mountains tremble with its tumult. *Selah*

4 There is a river whose streams make glad the city of God,
the holy habitation of the Most High.
5 God is in the midst of her, she shall not be moved;
God will help her right early.
6 The nations rage, the kingdoms totter;
he utters his voice, the earth melts.
7 The LORD of hosts is with us;
the God of Jacob is our refuge.[m] *Selah*

8 Come, behold the works of the LORD,
how he has wrought desolations in the earth.
9 He makes wars cease to the end of the earth;
he breaks the bow, and shatters the spear,
he burns the chariots with fire!
10 "Be still, and know that I am God.
I am exalted among the nations,
I am exalted in the earth!"
11 The LORD of hosts is with us;
the God of Jacob is our refuge.[m] *Selah*

To the choirmaster. A Psalm of the Sons of Kō'răh.

47 Clap your hands, all peoples!
Shout to God with loud songs of joy!
2 For the LORD, the Most High, is terrible,
a great king over all the earth.
3 He subdued peoples under us,
and nations under our feet.
4 He chose our heritage for us,
the pride of Jacob whom he loves. *Selah*

5 God has gone up with a shout,

[h] Or *Your throne is a throne of God*, or *Thy throne, O God* [i] Heb *daughter*
[j] Or *people. All glorious is the princess within, gold embroidery is her clothing* [k] Heb *those brought to you*
[l] Or *well proved* [m] Or *fortress*
45.6-7: Heb 1.8-9.

the LORD with the sound of a
trumpet.
6 Sing praises to God, sing praises!
Sing praises to our King, sing
praises!
7 For God is the king of all the earth;
sing praises with a psalm![n]

8 God reigns over the nations;
God sits on his holy throne.
9 The princes of the peoples gather
as the people of the God of
Abraham.
For the shields of the earth belong
to God;
he is highly exalted!

A Song. A Psalm of the Sons of
Kō'rȧh.

48 Great is the LORD and greatly
to be praised
in the city of our God!
His holy mountain, 2 beautiful in
elevation,
is the joy of all the earth,
Mount Zion, in the far north,
the city of the great King.
3 Within her citadels God
has shown himself a sure defense.

4 For lo, the kings assembled,
they came on together.
5 As soon as they saw it, they were
astounded,
they were in panic, they took to
flight;
6 trembling took hold of them there,
anguish as of a woman in travail.
7 By the east wind thou didst shatter
the ships of Tär'shish.
8 As we have heard, so have we seen
in the city of the LORD of hosts,
in the city of our God,
which God establishes for ever.
Selah

9 We have thought on thy steadfast
love, O God,
in the midst of thy temple.
10 As thy name, O God,
so thy praise reaches to the ends
of the earth.
Thy right hand is filled with victory;
11 let Mount Zion be glad!
Let the daughters of Judah rejoice
because of thy judgments!

12 Walk about Zion, go round about
her,
number her towers,
13 consider well her ramparts,
go through her citadels;
that you may tell the next generation
14 that this is God,
our God for ever and ever.
He will be our guide for ever.

To the choirmaster. A Psalm of the
Sons of Kō'rȧh.

49 Hear this, all peoples!
Give ear, all inhabitants of the
world,
2 both low and high,
rich and poor together!
3 My mouth shall speak wisdom;
the meditation of my heart shall
be understanding.
4 I will incline my ear to a proverb;
I will solve my riddle to the music
of the lyre.

5 Why should I fear in times of
trouble,
when the iniquity of my persecutors surrounds me,
6 men who trust in their wealth
and boast of the abundance of
their riches?
7 Truly no man can ransom himself,[o]
or give to God the price of his life,
8 for the ransom of his[p] life is costly,
and can never suffice,
9 that he should continue to live on
for ever,
and never see the Pit.

10 Yea, he shall see that even the wise
die,
the fool and the stupid alike must
perish
and leave their wealth to others.
11 Their graves[q] are their homes for
ever,
their dwelling places to all generations,
though they named lands their
own.
12 Man cannot abide in his pomp,
he is like the beasts that perish.

13 This is the fate of those who have
foolish confidence,

[n] Heb *Maskil* [o] Another reading is *no man can ransom his brother* [p] Gk: Heb *their*
[q] Gk Syr Compare Tg: Heb *their inward* (thought)
48.2: Mt 5.35.

the end of those[r] who are pleased
with their portion. *Selah*
14 Like sheep they are appointed for
Shē'ōl;
Death shall be their shepherd;
straight to the grave they descend,[s]
and their form shall waste away;
Sheol shall be their home.[t]
15 But God will ransom my soul from
the power of Shē'ōl,
for he will receive me. *Selah*

16 Be not afraid when one becomes rich,
when the glory[u] of his house
increases.
17 For when he dies he will carry
nothing away;
his glory[u] will not go down after
him.
18 Though, while he lives, he counts
himself happy,
and though a man gets praise
when he does well for himself,
19 he will go to the generation of his
fathers,
who will never more see the light.
20 Man cannot abide in his pomp,
he is like the beasts that perish.

A Psalm of Ā'saph.

50 The Mighty One, God the
LORD,
speaks and summons the earth
from the rising of the sun to its
setting.
2 Out of Zion, the perfection of
beauty,
God shines forth.

3 Our God comes, he does not keep
silence,
before him is a devouring fire,
round about him a mighty tempest.
4 He calls to the heavens above
and to the earth, that he may
judge his people:
5 "Gather to me my faithful ones,
who made a covenant with me by
sacrifice!"
6 The heavens declare his righteousness,
for God himself is judge! *Selah*

7 "Hear, O my people, and I will
speak,
O Israel, I will testify against you.
I am God, your God.
8 I do not reprove you for your
sacrifices;
your burnt offerings are continually before me.
9 I will accept no bull from your
house,
nor he-goat from your folds.
10 For every beast of the forest is mine,
the cattle on a thousand hills.
11 I know all the birds of the air,[v]
and all that moves in the field is
mine.

12 "If I were hungry, I would not tell
you;
for the world and all that is in it
is mine.
13 Do I eat the flesh of bulls,
or drink the blood of goats?
14 Offer to God a sacrifice of thanksgiving,[w]
and pay your vows to the Most
High;
15 and call upon me in the day of
trouble;
I will deliver you, and you shall
glorify me."

16 But to the wicked God says:
"What right have you to recite
my statutes,
or take my covenant on your lips?
17 For you hate discipline,
and you cast my words behind
you.
18 If you see a thief, you are a friend
of his;
and you keep company with
adulterers.

19 "You give your mouth free reign for
evil,
and your tongue frames deceit.
20 You sit and speak against your
brother;
you slander your own mother's
son.
21 These things you have done and
I have been silent;
you thought that I was one like
yourself.
But now I rebuke you, and lay the
charge before you.

22 "Mark this, then, you who forget
God,

[r] Tg: Heb *after them* [s] Cn: Heb *the upright shall have dominion over them in the morning*
[t] Heb uncertain [u] Or *wealth* [v] Gk Syr Tg: Heb *mountains*
[w] Or *make thanksgiving your sacrifice to God*

lest I rend, and there be none to
deliver!
23 He who brings thanksgiving as his
sacrifice honors me;
to him who orders his way aright
I will show the salvation of God!"

To the choirmaster. A Psalm of David, when Nathan the prophet came to him, after he had gone in to Bath-shē'bȧ.

51 Have mercy on me, O God,
according to thy steadfast love;
according to thy abundant mercy
blot out my transgressions.
2 Wash me thoroughly from my iniquity,
and cleanse me from my sin!

3 For I know my transgressions,
and my sin is ever before me.
4 Against thee, thee only, have I
sinned,
and done that which is evil in thy
sight,
so that thou art justified in thy
sentence
and blameless in thy judgment.
5 Behold, I was brought forth in iniquity,
and in sin did my mother conceive me.

6 Behold, thou desirest truth in the
inward being;
therefore teach me wisdom in my
secret heart.
7 Purge me with hyssop, and I shall
be clean;
wash me, and I shall be whiter
than snow.
8 Fill[x] me with joy and gladness;
let the bones which thou hast
broken rejoice.
9 Hide thy face from my sins,
and blot out all my iniquities.

10 Create in me a clean heart, O God,
and put a new and right[y] spirit
within me.
11 Cast me not away from thy presence,
and take not thy holy Spirit from
me.
12 Restore to me the joy of thy salvation,
and uphold me with a willing
spirit.
13 Then I will teach transgressors thy
ways,
and sinners will return to thee.
14 Deliver me from bloodguiltiness,[z]
O God,
thou God of my salvation,
and my tongue will sing aloud of
thy deliverance.

15 O Lord, open thou my lips,
and my mouth shall show forth
thy praise.
16 For thou hast no delight in sacrifice;
were I to give a burnt offering,
thou wouldst not be pleased.
17 The sacrifice acceptable to God[a] is
a broken spirit;
a broken and contrite heart, O
God, thou wilt not despise.

18 Do good to Zion in thy good
pleasure;
rebuild the walls of Jerusalem,
19 then wilt thou delight in right
sacrifices,
in burnt offerings and whole burnt
offerings;
then bulls will be offered on thy
altar.

To the choirmaster. A Maskil of David, when Dō'eg, the E'dȯm-ite, came and told Saul, "David has come to the house of Ȧ-him'ė-lech."

52 Why do you boast, O mighty
man,
of mischief done against the
godly?[b]
All the day 2 you are plotting
destruction.
Your tongue is like a sharp razor,
you worker of treachery.
3 You love evil more than good,
and lying more than speaking the
truth. *Selah*
4 You love all words that devour,
O deceitful tongue.

5 But God will break you down for
ever;
he will snatch and tear you from
your tent;
he will uproot you from the land
of the living. *Selah*
6 The righteous shall see, and fear,

[x] Syr: Heb *Make to hear* [y] Or *steadfast* [z] Or *death* [a] Or *My sacrifice, O God*
[b] Cn Compare Syr: Heb *the kindness of God*
51.4: Rom 3.4.

and shall laugh at him, saying,
7 "See the man who would not make God his refuge,
but trusted in the abundance of his riches,
and sought refuge in his wealth!"[c]

8 But I am like a green olive tree
in the house of God.
I trust in the steadfast love of God
for ever and ever.
9 I will thank thee for ever,
because thou hast done it.
I will proclaim[d] thy name, for it is good,
in the presence of the godly.

To the choirmaster: according to Mahalath. A Maskil of David.

53 The fool says in his heart,
"There is no God."
They are corrupt, doing abominable iniquity;
there is none that does good.

2 God looks down from heaven
upon the sons of men
to see if there are any that are wise,
that seek after God.

3 They have all fallen away;
they are all alike depraved;
there is none that does good,
no, not one.

4 Have those who work evil no understanding,
who eat up my people as they eat bread,
and do not call upon God?

5 There they are, in great terror,
in terror such as has not been!
For God will scatter the bones of the ungodly;[e]
they will be put to shame,[f] for God has rejected them.

6 O that deliverance for Israel would come from Zion!
When God restores the fortunes of his people,
Jacob will rejoice and Israel be glad.

To the choirmaster: with stringed instruments. A Maskil of David, when the Ziphites went and told Saul, "David is in hiding among us."

54 Save me, O God, by thy name,
and vindicate me by thy might.
2 Hear my prayer, O God;
give ear to the words of my mouth.

3 For insolent[g] men have risen against me,
ruthless men seek my life;
they do not set God before them.
Selah

4 Behold, God is my helper;
the Lord is the upholder[h] of my life.
5 He will requite my enemies with evil;
in thy faithfulness put an end to them.

6 With a freewill offering I will sacrifice to thee;
I will give thanks to thy name,
O LORD, for it is good.
7 For thou hast delivered me from every trouble,
and my eye has looked in triumph on my enemies.

To the choirmaster: with stringed instruments. A Maskil of David

55 Give ear to my prayer, O God;
and hide not thyself from my supplication!
2 Attend to me, and answer me;
I am overcome by my trouble.
I am distraught 3 by the noise of the enemy,
because of the oppression of the wicked.
For they bring[i] trouble upon me,
and in anger they cherish enmity against me.

4 My heart is in anguish within me,
the terrors of death have fallen upon me.
5 Fear and trembling come upon me,

[c] Syr Tg: Heb *his destruction* [d] Cn: Heb *wait for*
[e] Cn Compare Gk Syr: Heb *him who encamps against you* [f] Gk: Heb *you will put to shame*
[g] Another reading is *strangers* [h] Gk Syr Jerome: Heb *of* or *with those who uphold*
[i] Cn Compare Gk: Heb *they cause to totter*
53.1-3: Rom 3.10-12 53.1-6: Ps 14.1-7.

and horror overwhelms me.
6 And I say, "O that I had wings like a dove!
I would fly away and be at rest;
7 yea, I would wander afar,
I would lodge in the wilderness, *Selah*
8 I would haste to find me a shelter
from the raging wind and tempest."

9 Destroy their plans,[j] O Lord, confuse their tongues;
for I see violence and strife in the city.
10 Day and night they go around it on its walls;
and mischief and trouble are within it,
11 ruin is in its midst;
oppression and fraud
do not depart from its market place.

12 It is not an enemy who taunts me—
then I could bear it;
it is not an adversary who deals insolently with me—
then I could hide from him.
13 But it is you, my equal,
my companion, my familiar friend.
14 We used to hold sweet converse together;
within God's house we walked in fellowship.
15 Let death[k] come upon them;
let them go down to Shē′ōl alive;
let them go away in terror into their graves.[l]

16 But I call upon God;
and the LORD will save me.
17 Evening and morning and at noon
I utter my complaint and moan,
and he will hear my voice.
18 He will deliver my soul in safety
from the battle that I wage,
for many are arrayed against me.
19 God will give ear, and humble them,
he who is enthroned from of old;
because they keep no law,[m]
and do not fear God. *Selah*

20 My companion stretched out his hand against his friends,
he violated his covenant.
21 His speech was smoother than butter,
yet war was in his heart;
his words were softer than oil,
yet they were drawn swords.

22 Cast your burden[n] on the LORD,
and he will sustain you;
he will never permit
the righteous to be moved.

23 But thou, O God, wilt cast them down
into the lowest pit;
men of blood and treachery
shall not live out half their days.
But I will trust in thee.

To the choirmaster: according to The Dove on Far-off Terebinths. A Miktam of David, when the Philistines seized him in Gath.

56 Be gracious to me, O God,
for men trample upon me;
2 all day long foemen oppress me;
my enemies trample upon me all day long,
for many fight against me proudly.
3 When I am afraid,
I put my trust in thee.
4 In God, whose word I praise,
in God I trust without a fear.
What can flesh do to me?

5 All day long they seek to injure my cause;
all their thoughts are against me for evil.
6 They band themselves together, they lurk,
they watch my steps.
As they have waited for my life,
7 so recompense[o] them for their crime,
in wrath cast down the peoples, O God!

8 Thou hast kept count of my tossings;
put thou my tears in thy bottle!
Are they not in thy book?
9 Then my enemies will be turned back
in the day when I call.
This I know, that[p] God is for me.
10 In God, whose word I praise,
in the LORD, whose word I praise,

[j] Tg: Heb lacks *their plans* [k] Or *desolations* [l] Cn: Heb *evils are in their habitation, in their midst*
[m] Or *do not change* [n] Or *what he has given you* [o] Cn: Heb *deliver* [p] Or *because*
55.22: 1 Pet 5.7.

11 in God I trust without a fear.
What can man do to me?

12 My vows to thee I must perform, O God;
I will render thank offerings to thee.
13 For thou hast delivered my soul from death,
yea, my feet from falling,
that I may walk before God
in the light of life.

To the choirmaster: according to Do Not Destroy. A Miktam of David, when he fled from Saul, in the cave.

57 Be merciful to me, O God, be merciful to me,
for in thee my soul takes refuge;
in the shadow of thy wings I will take refuge,
till the storms of destruction pass by.
2 I cry to God Most High,
to God who fulfils his purpose for me.
3 He will send from heaven and save me,
he will put to shame those who trample upon me. *Selah*
God will send forth his steadfast love and his faithfulness!

4 I lie in the midst of lions
that greedily devour[q] the sons of men;
their teeth are spears and arrows,
their tongues sharp swords.

5 Be exalted, O God, above the heavens!
Let thy glory be over all the earth!

6 They set a net for my steps;
my soul was bowed down.
They dug a pit in my way,
but they have fallen into it themselves. *Selah*

7 My heart is steadfast, O God,
my heart is steadfast!
I will sing and make melody!
8 Awake, my soul!
Awake, O harp and lyre!
I will awake the dawn!
9 I will give thanks to thee, O Lord, among the peoples;
I will sing praises to thee among the nations.
10 For thy steadfast love is great to the heavens,
thy faithfulness to the clouds.

11 Be exalted, O God, above the heavens!
Let thy glory be over all the earth!

To the choirmaster: according to Do Not Destroy. A Miktam of David.

58 Do you indeed decree what is right, you gods?[s]
Do you judge the sons of men uprightly?
2 Nay, in your hearts you devise wrongs;
your hands deal out violence on earth.

3 The wicked go astray from the womb,
they err from their birth, speaking lies.
4 They have venom like the venom of a serpent,
like the deaf adder that stops its ear,
5 so that it does not hear the voice of charmers
or of the cunning enchanter.

6 O God, break the teeth in their mouths;
tear out the fangs of the young lions, O LORD!
7 Let them vanish like water that runs away;
like grass let them be trodden down and wither.[t]
8 Let them be like the snail which dissolves into slime,
like the untimely birth that never sees the sun.
9 Sooner than your pots can feel the heat of thorns,
whether green or ablaze, may he sweep them away!

10 The righteous will rejoice when he sees the vengeance;
he will bathe his feet in the blood of the wicked.
11 Men will say, "Surely there is a reward for the righteous;

[q] Cn: Heb *are aflame* [s] Or *mighty lords* [t] Cn: Heb uncertain
57.7-11: Ps 108.1-5.

surely there is a God who judges
on earth."

To the choirmaster: according to Do Not Destroy. A Miktam of David, when Saul sent men to watch his house in order to kill him.

59 Deliver me from my enemies,
O my God,
protect me from those who rise
up against me,
2 deliver me from those who work
evil,
and save me from bloodthirsty
men.

3 For, lo, they lie in wait for my life;
fierce men band themselves
against me.
For no transgression or sin of mine,
O LORD,
4 for no fault of mine, they run and
make ready.

Rouse thyself, come to my help,
and see!
5 Thou, LORD God of hosts, art
God of Israel.
Awake to punish all the nations;
spare none of those who treacherously plot evil. *Selah*

6 Each evening they come back,
howling like dogs
and prowling about the city.
7 There they are, bellowing with their
mouths,
and snarling with[u] their lips—
for "Who," they think, "will hear
us?"

8 But thou, O LORD, dost laugh at
them;
thou dost hold all the nations in
derision.
9 O my Strength, I will sing praises
to thee;[v]
for thou, O God, art my fortress.
10 My God in his steadfast love will
meet me;
my God will let me look in triumph on my enemies.

11 Slay them not, lest my people forget;
make them totter by thy power,
and bring them down,
O Lord, our shield!
12 For the sin of their mouths, the
words of their lips,
let them be trapped in their pride.
For the cursing and lies which they
utter,
13 consume them in wrath,
consume them till they are no
more,
that men may know that God rules
over Jacob
to the ends of the earth. *Selah*

14 Each evening they come back,
howling like dogs
and prowling about the city.
15 They roam about for food,
and growl if they do not get their
fill.

16 But I will sing of thy might;
I will sing aloud of thy steadfast
love in the morning.
For thou hast been to me a fortress
and a refuge in the day of my
distress.
17 O my Strength, I will sing praises
to thee,
for thou, O God, art my fortress,
the God who shows me steadfast
love.

To the choirmaster: according to Shushan Eduth. A Miktam of David; for instructions; when he strove with Âr′ȧm-nā·hȧ·rā′im and with Âr′ȧm-zō′bȧh, and when Jō′ab on his return killed twelve thousand of Ē′dȯm in the Valley of Salt.

60 O God, thou hast rejected us,
broken our defenses;
thou hast been angry; oh, restore
us.
2 Thou hast made the land to quake,
thou hast rent it open;
repair its breaches, for it totters.
3 Thou hast made thy people suffer
hard things;
thou hast given us wine to drink
that made us reel.

4 Thou hast set up a banner for those
who fear thee,
to rally to it from the bow.[w]
Selah
5 That thy beloved may be delivered,
give victory by thy right hand and
answer us!

[u] Cn: Heb *swords in* [v] Syr: Heb *I will watch for thee* [w] Gk Syr Jerome: Heb *truth*
60.5-12: Ps 108.6-13.

6 God has spoken in his sanctuary:[x]
"With exultation I will divide up Shē′chem
and portion out the Vale of Suc′coth.
7 Gilead is mine; Mȧ·nas′sėh is mine;
Ē′phrȧ·im is my helmet;
Judah is my scepter.
8 Mō′ab is my washbasin;
upon Ē′dȯm I cast my shoe;
over Phi·lis′ti·ȧ I shout in triumph."

9 Who will bring me to the fortified city?
Who will lead me to Ē′dȯm?
10 Hast thou not rejected us, O God?
Thou dost not go forth, O God, with our armies.
11 O grant us help against the foe,
for vain is the help of man!
12 With God we shall do valiantly;
it is he who will tread down our foes.

To the choirmaster: with stringed instruments. A Psalm of David.

61 Hear my cry, O God,
listen to my prayer;
2 from the end of the earth I call to thee,
when my heart is faint.

Lead thou me
to the rock that is higher than I;
3 for thou art my refuge,
a strong tower against the enemy.

4 Let me dwell in thy tent for ever!
Oh to be safe under the shelter of thy wings! *Selah*
5 For thou, O God, hast heard my vows,
thou hast given me the heritage of those who fear thy name.

6 Prolong the life of the king;
may his years endure to all generations!
7 May he be enthroned for ever before God;
bid steadfast love and faithfulness watch over him!

8 So will I ever sing praises to thy name,
as I pay my vows day after day.

To the choirmaster: according to Je·dū′thŭn. A Psalm of David.

62 For God alone my soul waits in silence;
from him comes my salvation.
2 He only is my rock and my salvation,
my fortress; I shall not be greatly moved.

3 How long will you set upon a man to shatter him, all of you,
like a leaning wall, a tottering fence?
4 They only plan to thrust him down from his eminence.
They take pleasure in falsehood.
They bless with their mouths,
but inwardly they curse. *Selah*

5 For God alone my soul waits in silence,
for my hope is from him.
6 He only is my rock and my salvation,
my fortress; I shall not be shaken.
7 On God rests my deliverance and my honor;
my mighty rock, my refuge is God.

8 Trust in him at all times, O people;
pour out your heart before him;
God is a refuge for us. *Selah*

9 Men of low estate are but a breath,
men of high estate are a delusion;
in the balances they go up;
they are together lighter than a breath.
10 Put no confidence in extortion,
set no vain hopes on robbery;
if riches increase, set not your heart on them.

11 Once God has spoken;
twice have I heard this:
that power belongs to God;
12 and that to thee, O Lord, belongs steadfast love.
For thou dost requite a man
according to his work.

A Psalm of David, when he was in the Wilderness of Judah.

63 O God, thou art my God, I seek thee,
my soul thirsts for thee;

[x] Or *by his holiness*
62.12: Jer 17.10; Rev 2.23; 22.12.

my flesh faints for thee,
as in a dry and weary land where no water is.
2 So I have looked upon thee in the sanctuary,
beholding thy power and glory.
3 Because thy steadfast love is better than life,
my lips will praise thee.
4 So I will bless thee as long as I live;
I will lift up my hands and call on thy name.

5 My soul is feasted as with marrow and fat,
and my mouth praises thee with joyful lips,
6 when I think of thee upon my bed,
and meditate on thee in the watches of the night;
7 for thou hast been my help,
and in the shadow of thy wings I sing for joy.
8 My soul clings to thee;
thy right hand upholds me.

9 But those who seek to destroy my life
shall go down into the depths of the earth;
10 they shall be given over to the power of the sword,
they shall be prey for jackals.
11 But the king shall rejoice in God;
all who swear by him shall glory;
for the mouths of liars will be stopped.

To the choirmaster. A Psalm of David.

64 Hear my voice, O God, in my complaint;
preserve my life from dread of the enemy,
2 hide me from the secret plots of the wicked,
from the scheming of evildoers,
3 who whet their tongues like swords,
who aim bitter words like arrows,
4 shooting from ambush at the blameless,
shooting at him suddenly and without fear.
5 They hold fast to their evil purpose;
they talk of laying snares secretly,
thinking, "Who can see us?[y]
6 Who can search out our crimes?[z]
We have thought out a cunningly conceived plot."
For the inward mind and heart of a man are deep!

7 But God will shoot his arrow at them;
they will be wounded suddenly.
8 Because of their tongue he will bring them to ruin;[a]
all who see them will wag their heads.
9 Then all men will fear;
they will tell what God has wrought,
and ponder what he has done.

10 Let the righteous rejoice in the LORD,
and take refuge in him!
Let all the upright in heart glory!

To the choirmaster. A Psalm of David. A Song.

65 Praise is due to thee,
O God, in Zion;
and to thee shall vows be performed,
2 O thou who hearest prayer!
To thee shall all flesh come
3 on account of sins.
When our transgressions prevail over us,[b]
thou dost forgive them.
4 Blessed is he whom thou dost choose and bring near,
to dwell in thy courts!
We shall be satisfied with the goodness of thy house,
thy holy temple!

5 By dread deeds thou dost answer us with deliverance,
O God of our salvation,
who art the hope of all the ends of the earth,
and of the farthest seas;
6 who by thy strength hast established the mountains,
being girded with might;
7 who dost still the roaring of the seas,
the roaring of their waves,
the tumult of the peoples;
8 so that those who dwell at earth's farthest bounds
are afraid at thy signs;

[y] Syr: Heb *them* [z] Cn: Heb *they search out crimes*
[a] Cn: Heb *They will bring him to ruin, their tongue being against them* [b] Gk: Heb *me*

thou makest the outgoings of the morning and the evening
to shout for joy.

9 Thou visitest the earth and waterest it,
thou greatly enrichest it;
the river of God is full of water;
thou providest their grain,
for so thou hast prepared it.
10 Thou waterest its furrows abundantly,
settling its ridges,
softening it with showers,
and blessing its growth.
11 Thou crownest the year with thy bounty;
the tracks of thy chariot drip with fatness.
12 The pastures of the wilderness drip,
the hills gird themselves with joy,
13 the meadows clothe themselves with flocks,
the valleys deck themselves with grain,
they shout and sing together for joy.

To the choirmaster. A Song. A Psalm.

66 Make a joyful noise to God, all the earth;
2 sing the glory of his name;
give to him glorious praise!
3 Say to God, "How terrible are thy deeds!
So great is thy power that thy enemies cringe before thee.
4 All the earth worships thee;
they sing praises to thee,
sing praises to thy name."
Selah
5 Come and see what God has done:
he is terrible in his deeds among men.
6 He turned the sea into dry land;
men passed through the river on foot.
There did we rejoice in him,
7 who rules by his might for ever,
whose eyes keep watch on the nations—
let not the rebellious exalt themselves. *Selah*

8 Bless our God, O peoples,
let the sound of his praise be heard,
9 who has kept us among the living,
and has not let our feet slip.
10 For thou, O God, hast tested us;
thou hast tried us as silver is tried.
11 Thou didst bring us into the net;
thou didst lay affliction on our loins;
12 thou didst let men ride over our heads;
we went through fire and through water;
yet thou hast brought us forth to a spacious place.[c]

13 I will come into thy house with burnt offerings;
I will pay thee my vows,
14 that which my lips uttered
and my mouth promised when I was in trouble.
15 I will offer to thee burnt offerings of fatlings,
with the smoke of the sacrifice of rams;
I will make an offering of bulls and goats. *Selah*

16 Come and hear, all you who fear God,
and I will tell what he has done for me.
17 I cried aloud to him,
and he was extolled with my tongue.
18 If I had cherished iniquity in my heart,
the Lord would not have listened.
19 But truly God has listened;
he has given heed to the voice of my prayer.

20 Blessed be God,
because he has not rejected my prayer
or removed his steadfast love from me!

To the choirmaster: with stringed instruments. A Psalm. A Song.

67 May God be gracious to us and bless us
and make his face to shine upon us, *Selah*
2 that thy way may be known upon earth,
thy saving power among all nations.

[c] Cn Compare Gk Syr Jerome Tg: Heb *saturation*

3 Let the peoples praise thee, O God;
let all the peoples praise thee!

4 Let the nations be glad and sing for joy,
for thou dost judge the peoples with equity
and guide the nations upon earth. *Selah*
5 Let the peoples praise thee, O God;
let all the peoples praise thee!

6 The earth has yielded its increase;
God, our God, has blessed us.
7 God has blessed us;
let all the ends of the earth fear him!

To the choirmaster. A Psalm of David. A Song.

68 Let God arise, let his enemies be scattered;
let those who hate him flee before him!
2 As smoke is driven away, so drive them away;
as wax melts before fire,
let the wicked perish before God!
3 But let the righteous be joyful;
let them exult before God;
let them be jubilant with joy!

4 Sing to God, sing praises to his name;
lift up a song to him who rides upon the clouds;[d]
his name is the LORD, exult before him!
5 Father of the fatherless and protector of widows
is God in his holy habitation.
6 God gives the desolate a home to dwell in;
he leads out the prisoners to prosperity;
but the rebellious dwell in a parched land.

7 O God, when thou didst go forth before thy people,
when thou didst march through the wilderness, *Selah*
8 the earth quaked, the heavens poured down rain,
at the presence of God;
yon Sinai quaked at the presence of God,
the God of Israel.
9 Rain in abundance, O God, thou didst shed abroad;
thou didst restore thy heritage as it languished;
10 thy flock found a dwelling in it;
in thy goodness, O God, thou didst provide for the needy.

11 The Lord gives the command;
great is the host of those who bore the tidings:
12 "The kings of the armies, they flee, they flee!"
The women at home divide the spoil,
13 though they stay among the sheepfolds—
the wings of a dove covered with silver,
its pinions with green gold.
14 When the Almighty scattered kings there,
snow fell on Zal'mon.

15 O mighty mountain, mountain of Bā'shȧn;
O many-peaked mountain, mountain of Bashan!
16 Why look you with envy, O many-peaked mountain,
at the mount which God desired for his abode,
yea, where the LORD will dwell for ever?

17 With mighty chariotry, twice ten thousand,
thousands upon thousands,
the Lord came from Sinai into the holy place.[e]
18 Thou didst ascend the high mount,
leading captives in thy train,
and receiving gifts among men,
even among the rebellious, that the LORD God may dwell there.

19 Blessed be the Lord,
who daily bears us up;
God is our salvation. *Selah*
20 Our God is a God of salvation;
and to GOD, the Lord, belongs escape from death.

21 But God will shatter the heads of his enemies,

[d] Or *cast up a highway for him who rides through the deserts*
[e] Cn: Heb *The Lord among them Sinai in the holy place*
68.18: Eph 4.8.

the hairy crown of him who walks
in his guilty ways.
22 The Lord said,
"I will bring them back from
Bā'shȧn,
I will bring them back from the
depths of the sea,
23 that you may bathe[f] your feet in
blood,
that the tongues of your dogs
may have their portion from
the foe."

24 Thy solemn processions are seen,[g]
O God,
the processions of my God, my
King, into the sanctuary—
25 the singers in front, the minstrels last,
between them maidens playing
timbrels:
26 "Bless God in the great congregation,
the LORD, O you who are of Israel's
fountain!"
27 There is Benjamin, the least of
them, in the lead,
the princes of Judah in their
throng,
the princes of Zeb'ū·lủn, the
princes of Naph'tȧ·lī.

28 Summon thy might, O God;
show thy strength, O God, thou
who hast wrought for us.
29 Because of thy temple at Jerusalem
kings bear gifts to thee.
30 Rebuke the beasts that dwell among
the reeds,
the herd of bulls with the calves
of the peoples.
Trample[h] under foot those who lust
after tribute;
scatter the peoples who delight in
war.[i]
31 Let bronze be brought from Egypt;
let Ethiopia hasten to stretch out
her hands to God.

32 Sing to God, O kingdoms of the
earth;
sing praises to the Lord, *Selah*
33 to him who rides in the heavens, the
ancient heavens;
lo, he sends forth his voice, his
mighty voice.
34 Ascribe power to God,
whose majesty is over Israel,
and his power is in the skies.
35 Terrible is God in his[j] sanctuary,
the God of Israel,
he gives power and strength to
his people.

Blessed be God!

To the choirmaster: according to
Lilies. A Psalm of David.

69 Save me, O God!
For the waters have come up
to my neck.
2 I sink in deep mire,
where there is no foothold;
I have come into deep waters,
and the flood sweeps over me.
3 I am weary with my crying;
my throat is parched.
My eyes grow dim
with waiting for my God.

4 More in number than the hairs of
my head
are those who hate me without
cause;
mighty are those who would destroy
me,
those who attack me with lies.
What I did not steal
must I now restore?
5 O God, thou knowest my folly;
the wrongs I have done are not
hidden from thee.

6 Let not those who hope in thee be
put to shame through me,
O Lord GOD of hosts;
let not those who seek thee be
brought to dishonor through
me,
O God of Israel.
7 For it is for thy sake that I have
borne reproach,
that shame has covered my face.
8 I have become a stranger to my
brethren,
an alien to my mother's sons.

9 For zeal for thy house has consumed
me,
and the insults of those who insult
thee have fallen on me.
10 When I humbled[k] my soul with
fasting,

[f] Gk Syr Tg: Heb *shatter* [g] Or *have been seen* [h] Cn: Heb *trampling*
[i] The Hebrew of verse 30 is obscure [j] Gk: Heb *from thy*
[k] Gk Syr: Heb *I wept with fasting my soul* or *I made my soul mourn with fasting*
69.4: Ps 35.19; Jn 15.25. **69.9:** Jn 2.17; Rom 15.3.

it became my reproach.
11 When I made sackcloth my clothing,
I became a byword to them.
12 I am the talk of those who sit in the gate,
and the drunkards make songs about me.

13 But as for me, my prayer is to thee, O LORD.
At an acceptable time, O God,
in the abundance of thy steadfast love answer me.
With thy faithful help 14 rescue me
from sinking in the mire;
let me be delivered from my enemies
and from the deep waters.
15 Let not the flood sweep over me,
or the deep swallow me up,
or the pit close its mouth over me.

16 Answer me, O LORD, for thy steadfast love is good;
according to thy abundant mercy, turn to me.
17 Hide not thy face from thy servant;
for I am in distress, make haste to answer me.
18 Draw near to me, redeem me,
set me free because of my enemies!

19 Thou knowest my reproach,
and my shame and my dishonor;
my foes are all known to thee.
20 Insults have broken my heart,
so that I am in despair.
I looked for pity, but there was none;
and for comforters, but I found none.
21 They gave me poison for food,
and for my thirst they gave me vinegar to drink.

22 Let their own table before them become a snare;
let their sacrificial feasts[l] be a trap.
23 Let their eyes be darkened, so that they cannot see;
and make their loins tremble continually.
24 Pour out thy indignation upon them,
and let thy burning anger overtake them.
25 May their camp be a desolation,
let no one dwell in their tents.
26 For they persecute him whom thou hast smitten,
and him[m] whom thou hast wounded, they afflict still more.[n]
27 Add to them punishment upon punishment;
may they have no acquittal from thee.
28 Let them be blotted out of the book of the living;
let them not be enrolled among the righteous.

29 But I am afflicted and in pain;
let thy salvation, O God, set me on high!

30 I will praise the name of God with a song;
I will magnify him with thanksgiving.
31 This will please the LORD more than an ox
or a bull with horns and hoofs.
32 Let the oppressed see it and be glad;
you who seek God, let your hearts revive.
33 For the LORD hears the needy,
and does not despise his own that are in bonds.

34 Let heaven and earth praise him,
the seas and everything that moves therein.
35 For God will save Zion
and rebuild the cities of Judah;
and his servants shall dwell[o] there and possess it;
36 the children of his servants shall inherit it,
and those who love his name shall dwell in it.

To the choirmaster. A Psalm of David, for the memorial offering.

70 Be pleased, O God, to deliver me!
O LORD, make haste to help me!
2 Let them be put to shame and confusion
who seek my life!
Let them be turned back and brought to dishonor

[l] Tg: Heb *for security* [m] One Ms Tg Compare Syr: Heb *those* [n] Gk Syr: Heb *recount the pain of* [o] Syr: Heb *and they shall dwell*

69.21: Mt 27.34, 48; Mk 15.36; Lk 23.36; Jn 19.29. **69.22-23**: Rom 11.9-10. **69.24**: Rev 16.1. **69.25**: Acts 1.20. **69.28**: Rev 3.5; 13.8; 17.8; 20.12, 15; 21.27. **70.1-5**: Ps 40.13-17.

who desire my hurt!
3 Let them be appalled because of their shame
who say, "Aha, Aha!"

4 May all who seek thee
rejoice and be glad in thee!
May those who love thy salvation
say evermore, "God is great!"
5 But I am poor and needy;
hasten to me, O God!
Thou art my help and my deliverer;
O LORD, do not tarry!

71 In thee, O LORD, do I take refuge;
let me never be put to shame!
2 In thy righteousness deliver me and rescue me;
incline thy ear to me, and save me!
3 Be thou to me a rock of refuge,
a strong fortress,[p] to save me,
for thou art my rock and my fortress.

4 Rescue me, O my God, from the hand of the wicked,
from the grasp of the unjust and cruel man.
5 For thou, O Lord, art my hope,
my trust, O LORD, from my youth.
6 Upon thee I have leaned from my birth;
thou art he who took me from my mother's womb.
My praise is continually of thee.

7 I have been as a portent to many;
but thou art my strong refuge.
8 My mouth is filled with thy praise,
and with thy glory all the day.
9 Do not cast me off in the time of old age;
forsake me not when my strength is spent.
10 For my enemies speak concerning me,
those who watch for my life consult together,
11 and say, "God has forsaken him;
pursue and seize him,
for there is none to deliver him."

12 O God, be not far from me;
O my God, make haste to help me!
13 May my accusers be put to shame and consumed;
with scorn and disgrace may they be covered
who seek my hurt.
14 But I will hope continually,
and will praise thee yet more and more.
15 My mouth will tell of thy righteous acts,
of thy deeds of salvation all the day,
for their number is past my knowledge.
16 With the mighty deeds of the Lord GOD I will come,
I will praise thy righteousness, thine alone.

17 O God, from my youth thou hast taught me,
and I still proclaim thy wondrous deeds.
18 So even to old age and gray hairs,
O God, do not forsake me,
till I proclaim thy might
to all the generations to come.[q]
Thy power 19 and thy righteousness,
O God,
reach the high heavens.

Thou who hast done great things,
O God, who is like thee?
20 Thou who hast made me see many sore troubles
wilt revive me again;
from the depths of the earth
thou wilt bring me up again.
21 Thou wilt increase my honor,
and comfort me again.

22 I will also praise thee with the harp
for thy faithfulness, O my God;
I will sing praises to thee with the lyre,
O Holy One of Israel.
23 My lips will shout for joy,
when I sing praises to thee;
my soul also, which thou hast rescued.
24 And my tongue will talk of thy righteous help
all the day long,
for they have been put to shame and disgraced
who sought to do me hurt.

A Psalm to Solomon.

72 Give the king thy justice, O God,
and thy righteousness to the royal son!

[p] Gk Compare 31.3: Heb *to come continually thou hast commanded*
[q] Gk Compare Syr: Heb *to a generation, to all that come*

2 May he judge thy people with righteousness,
and thy poor with justice!
3 Let the mountains bear prosperity for the people,
and the hills, in righteousness!
4 May he defend the cause of the poor of the people,
give deliverance to the needy,
and crush the oppressor!

5 May he live[r] while the sun endures,
and as long as the moon, throughout all generations!
6 May he be like rain that falls on the mown grass,
like showers that water the earth!
7 In his days may righteousness flourish,
and peace abound, till the moon be no more!

8 May he have dominion from sea to sea,
and from the River to the ends of the earth!
9 May his foes[s] bow down before him,
and his enemies lick the dust!
10 May the kings of Tär'shish and of the isles
render him tribute,
may the kings of Sheba and Sē'bȧ bring gifts!
11 May all kings fall down before him,
all nations serve him!

12 For he delivers the needy when he calls,
the poor and him who has no helper.
13 He has pity on the weak and the needy,
and saves the lives of the needy.
14 From oppression and violence he redeems their life;
and precious is their blood in his sight.

15 Long may he live,
may gold of Sheba be given to him!
May prayer be made for him continually,
and blessings invoked for him all the day!
16 May there be abundance of grain in the land;
on the tops of the mountains may it wave;
may its fruit be like Lebanon;
and may men blossom forth from the cities
like the grass of the field!
17 May his name endure for ever,
his fame continue as long as the sun!
May men bless themselves by him,
all nations call him blessed!

18 Blessed be the LORD, the God of Israel,
who alone does wondrous things.
19 Blessed be his glorious name for ever;
may his glory fill the whole earth!
Amen and Amen!

20 The prayers of David, the son of Jesse, are ended.

BOOK III

A Psalm of Ā'saph.

73 Truly God is good to the upright,
to those who are pure in heart.[t]
2 But as for me, my feet had almost stumbled,
my steps had well nigh slipped.
3 For I was envious of the arrogant,
when I saw the prosperity of the wicked.

4 For they have no pangs;
their bodies are sound and sleek.
5 They are not in trouble as other men are;
they are not stricken like other men.
6 Therefore pride is their necklace;
violence covers them as a garment.
7 Their eyes swell out with fatness,
their hearts overflow with follies.
8 They scoff and speak with malice;
loftily they threaten oppression.
9 They set their mouths against the heavens,
and their tongue struts through the earth.

10 Therefore the people turn and praise them;[u]

[r] Gk: Heb *may they fear thee* [s] Cn: Heb *those who dwell in the wilderness*
[t] Or *Truly God is good to Israel, to those who are pure in heart*
[u] Cn: Heb *his people return hither*

and find no fault in them.[v]
11 And they say, "How can God know?
Is there knowledge in the Most High?"
12 Behold, these are the wicked;
always at ease, they increase in riches.
13 All in vain have I kept my heart clean
and washed my hands in innocence.
14 For all the day long I have been stricken,
and chastened every morning.

15 If I had said, "I will speak thus,"
I would have been untrue to the generation of thy children.
16 But when I thought how to understand this,
it seemed to me a wearisome task,
17 until I went into the sanctuary of God;
then I perceived their end.
18 Truly thou dost set them in slippery places;
thou dost make them fall to ruin.
19 How they are destroyed in a moment,
swept away utterly by terrors!
20 They are[w] like a dream when one awakes,
on awaking you despise their phantoms.

21 When my soul was embittered,
when I was pricked in heart,
22 I was stupid and ignorant,
I was like a beast toward thee.
23 Nevertheless I am continually with thee;
thou dost hold my right hand.
24 Thou dost guide me with thy counsel,
and afterward thou wilt receive me to glory.[x]
25 Whom have I in heaven but thee?
And there is nothing upon earth that I desire besides thee.
26 My flesh and my heart may fail,
but God is the strength[y] of my heart and my portion for ever.

27 For lo, those who are far from thee shall perish;
thou dost put an end to those who are false to thee.
28 But for me it is good to be near God;
I have made the Lord GOD my refuge,
that I may tell of all thy works.

A Maskil of Ā'saph.

74 O God, why dost thou cast us off for ever?
Why does thy anger smoke against the sheep of thy pasture?
2 Remember thy congregation, which thou hast gotten of old,
which thou hast redeemed to be the tribe of thy heritage!
Remember Mount Zion, where thou hast dwelt.
3 Direct thy steps to the perpetual ruins;
the enemy has destroyed everything in the sanctuary!

4 Thy foes have roared in the midst of thy holy place;
they set up their own signs for signs.
5 At the upper entrance they hacked the wooden trellis with axes.[z]
6 And then all its carved wood
they broke down with hatchets and hammers.
7 They set thy sanctuary on fire;
to the ground they desecrated the dwelling place of thy name.
8 They said to themselves, "We will utterly subdue them";
they burned all the meeting places of God in the land.

9 We do not see our signs;
there is no longer any prophet,
and there is none among us who knows how long.
10 How long, O God, is the foe to scoff?
Is the enemy to revile thy name for ever?
11 Why dost thou hold back thy hand,
why dost thou keep thy right hand in[a] thy bosom?

12 Yet God my King is from of old,
working salvation in the midst of the earth.
13 Thou didst divide the sea by thy might;
thou didst break the heads of the dragons on the waters.

[v] Cn: Heb *abundant waters are drained by them*
[w] Cn: Heb *Lord* [x] Or *honor* [y] Heb *rock* [z] Cn Compare Gk Syr: Heb uncertain
[a] Cn: Heb *consume thy right hand from*

14 Thou didst crush the heads of Lė·vī'ȧ·thȧn,
thou didst give him as food[b] for the creatures of the wilderness.
15 Thou didst cleave open springs and brooks;
thou didst dry up ever-flowing streams.
16 Thine is the day, thine also the night;
thou hast established the luminaries and the sun.
17 Thou hast fixed all the bounds of the earth;
thou hast made summer and winter.

18 Remember this, O LORD, how the enemy scoffs,
and an impious people reviles thy name.
19 Do not deliver the soul of thy dove to the wild beasts;
do not forget the life of thy poor for ever.

20 Have regard for thy[c] covenant;
for the dark places of the land are full of the habitations of violence.
21 Let not the downtrodden be put to shame;
let the poor and needy praise thy name.

22 Arise, O God, plead thy cause;
remember how the impious scoff at thee all the day!
23 Do not forget the clamor of thy foes,
the uproar of thy adversaries which goes up continually!

To the choirmaster: according to Do Not Destroy. A Psalm of A̅'saph. A Song.

75 We give thanks to thee, O God; we give thanks;
we call on thy name and recount[d] thy wondrous deeds.

2 At the set time which I appoint
I will judge with equity.
3 When the earth totters, and all its inhabitants,
it is I who keep steady its pillars. *Selah*
4 I say to the boastful, "Do not boast,"
and to the wicked, "Do not lift up your horn;
5 do not lift up your horn on high,
or speak with insolent neck."

6 For not from the east or from the west
and not from the wilderness comes lifting up;
7 but it is God who executes judgment,
putting down one and lifting up another.
8 For in the hand of the LORD there is a cup,
with foaming wine, well mixed;
and he will pour a draught from it,
and all the wicked of the earth shall drain it down to the dregs.

9 But I will rejoice[e] for ever,
I will sing praises to the God of Jacob.
10 All the horns of the wicked he[f] will cut off,
but the horns of the righteous shall be exalted.

To the choirmaster: with stringed instruments. A Psalm of A̅'saph. A Song.

76 In Judah God is known,
his name is great in Israel.
2 His abode has been established in Salem,
his dwelling place in Zion.
3 There he broke the flashing arrows,
the shield, the sword, and the weapons of war. *Selah*

4 Glorious art thou, more majestic
than the everlasting mountains.[g]
5 The stouthearted were stripped of their spoil;
they sank into sleep;
all the men of war
were unable to use their hands.
6 At thy rebuke, O God of Jacob,
both rider and horse lay stunned.

7 But thou, terrible art thou!
Who can stand before thee
when once thy anger is roused?
8 From the heavens thou didst utter judgment;

[b] Heb *food for the people* [c] Gk Syr: Heb *the*
[d] Syr Compare Gk: Heb *and near is thy name. They recount* [e] Gk: Heb *declare* [f] Heb *I*
[g] Gk Heb *the mountains of prey*

the earth feared and was still,
9 when God arose to establish judgment
to save all the oppressed of the earth. *Selah*

10 Surely the wrath of men shall praise thee;
the residue of wrath thou wilt gird upon thee.
11 Make your vows to the LORD your God, and perform them;
let all around him bring gifts
to him who is to be feared,
12 who cuts off the spirit of princes,
who is terrible to the kings of the earth.

To the choirmaster: according to Je·dü'thün. A Psalm of Ā'saph.

77 I cry aloud to God,
aloud to God, that he may hear me.
2 In the day of my trouble I seek the Lord;
in the night my hand is stretched out without wearying;
my soul refuses to be comforted.

3 I think of God, and I moan;
I meditate, and my spirit faints. *Selah*
4 Thou dost hold my eyelids from closing;
I am so troubled that I cannot speak.
5 I consider the days of old,
I remember the years long ago.
6 I commune[h] with my heart in the night;
I meditate and search my spirit:[i]
7 "Will the Lord spurn for ever,
and never again be favorable?
8 Has his steadfast love for ever ceased?
Are his promises at an end for all time?
9 Has God forgotten to be gracious?
Has he in anger shut up his compassion?" *Selah*
10 And I say, "It is my grief
that the right hand of the Most High has changed."

11 I will call to mind the deeds of the LORD;
yea, I will remember thy wonders of old.
12 I will meditate on all thy work,
and muse on thy mighty deeds.
13 Thy way, O God, is holy.
What god is great like our God?
14 Thou are the God who workest wonders,
who has manifested thy might among the peoples.
15 Thou didst with thy arm redeem thy people,
the sons of Jacob and Joseph. *Selah*

16 When the waters saw thee, O God,
when the waters saw thee, they were afraid,
yea, the deep trembled.
17 The clouds poured out water;
the skies gave forth thunder;
thy arrows flashed on every side.
18 The crash of thy thunder was in the whirlwind;
thy lightnings lighted up the world;
the earth trembled and shook.
19 Thy way was through the sea,
thy path through the great waters;
yet thy footprints were unseen.
20 Thou didst lead thy people like a flock
by the hand of Moses and Aaron.

A Maskil of Ā'saph.

78 Give ear, O my people, to my teaching;
incline your ears to the words of my mouth!
2 I will open my mouth in a parable;
I will utter dark sayings from of old,
3 things that we have heard and known,
that our fathers have told us.
4 We will not hide them from their children,
but tell to the coming generation
the glorious deeds of the LORD, and his might,
and the wonders which he has wrought.

5 He established a testimony in Jacob,
and appointed a law in Israel,
which he commanded our fathers
to teach to their children;

[h] Gk Syr: Heb *my music* [i] Syr Jerome: Heb *my spirit searches*
78.2: Mt 13.35.

6 that the next generation might know
them,
the children yet unborn,
and arise and tell them to their
children,
7 so that they should set their hope
in God,
and not forget the works of God,
but keep his commandments;
8 and that they should not be like
their fathers,
a stubborn and rebellious generation,
a generation whose heart was not
steadfast,
whose spirit was not faithful to
God.

9 The E′phră·im·ītes, armed with[f]
the bow,
turned back on the day of battle.
10 They did not keep God's covenant,
but refused to walk according to
his law.
11 They forgot what he had done,
and the miracles that he had
shown them.
12 In the sight of their fathers he
wrought marvels
in the land of Egypt, in the fields
of Zō′ăn.
13 He divided the sea and let them
pass through it,
and made the waters stand like a
heap.
14 In the daytime he led them with a
cloud,
and all the night with a fiery light.
15 He cleft rocks in the wilderness,
and gave them drink abundantly
as from the deep.
16 He made streams come out of the
rock,
and caused waters to flow down
like rivers.

17 Yet they sinned still more against
him,
rebelling against the Most High
in the desert.
18 They tested God in their heart
by demanding the food they
craved.
19 They spoke against God, saying,
"Can God spread a table in the
wilderness?
20 He smote the rock so that water
gushed out
and streams overflowed.
Can he also give bread,
or provide meat for his people?"

21 Therefore, when the LORD heard,
he was full of wrath;
a fire was kindled against Jacob,
his anger mounted against Israel;
22 because they had no faith in God,
and did not trust his saving power.
23 Yet he commanded the skies above,
and opened the doors of heaven;
24 and he rained down upon them
manna to eat,
and gave them the grain of
heaven.
25 Man ate of the bread of the angels;
he sent them food in abundance.
26 He caused the east wind to blow in
the heavens,
and by his power he led out the
south wind;
27 he rained flesh upon them like dust,
winged birds like the sand of the
seas;
28 he let them fall in the midst of their
camp,
all around their habitations.
29 And they ate and were well filled,
for he gave them what they
craved.
30 But before they had sated their
craving,
while the food was still in their
mouths,
31 the anger of God rose against them
and he slew the strongest of them,
and laid low the picked men of
Israel.

32 In spite of all this they still sinned;
despite his wonders they did not
believe.
33 So he made their days vanish like a
breath,
and their years in terror.
34 When he slew them, they sought
for him;
they repented and sought God
earnestly.
35 They remembered that God was
their rock,
the Most High God their redeemer.
36 But they flattered him with their
mouths;
they lied to him with their
tongues.
37 Their heart was not steadfast toward him;

[f] Heb *armed with shooting*
78.24: Jn 6.31. **78.37:** Acts 8.21.

they were not true to his covenant.
38 Yet he, being compassionate,
forgave their iniquity,
and did not destroy them;
he restrained his anger often,
and did not stir up all his wrath.
39 He remembered that they were but flesh,
a wind that passes and comes not again.
40 How often they rebelled against him in the wilderness
and grieved him in the desert!
41 They tested him again and again,
and provoked the Holy One of Israel.
42 They did not keep in mind his power,
or the day when he redeemed them from the foe;
43 when he wrought his signs in Egypt,
and his miracles in the fields of Zō'ǎn.
44 He turned their rivers to blood,
so that they could not drink of their streams.
45 He sent among them swarms of flies,
which devoured them,
and frogs, which destroyed them.
46 He gave their crops to the caterpillar,
and the fruit of their labor to the locust.
47 He destroyed their vines with hail,
and their sycamores with frost.
48 He gave over their cattle to the hail,
and their flocks to thunderbolts.
49 He let loose on them his fierce anger,
wrath, indignation, and distress,
a company of destroying angels.
50 He made a path for his anger;
he did not spare them from death,
but gave their lives over to the plague.
51 He smote all the first-born in Egypt,
the first issue of their strength in the tents of Ham.
52 Then he led forth his people like sheep,
and guided them in the wilderness like a flock.
53 He led them in safety, so that they were not afraid;
but the sea overwhelmed their enemies.
54 And he brought them to his holy land,
to the mountain which his right hand had won.
55 He drove out nations before them;
he apportioned them for a possession
and settled the tribes of Israel in their tents.

56 Yet they tested and rebelled against the Most High God,
and did not observe his testimonies,
57 but turned away and acted treacherously like their fathers;
they twisted like a deceitful bow.
58 For they provoked him to anger with their high places;
they moved him to jealousy with their graven images.
59 When God heard, he was full of wrath,
and he utterly rejected Israel.
60 He forsook his dwelling at Shi'lōh,
the tent where he dwelt among men,
61 and delivered his power to captivity,
his glory to the hand of the foe.
62 He gave his people over to the sword,
and vented his wrath on his heritage.
63 Fire devoured their young men,
and their maidens had no marriage song.
64 Their priests fell by the sword,
and their widows made no lamentation.
65 Then the Lord awoke as from sleep,
like a strong man shouting because of wine.
66 And he put his adversaries to rout;
he put them to everlasting shame.

67 He rejected the tent of Joseph,
he did not choose the tribe of E'phrȧ·im;
68 but he chose the tribe of Judah,
Mount Zion, which he loves.
69 He built his sanctuary like the high heavens,
like the earth, which he has founded for ever.
70 He chose David his servant,
and took him from the sheepfolds;
71 from tending the ewes that had young he brought him
to be the shepherd of Jacob his people,
of Israel his inheritance.
72 With upright heart he tended them,
and guided them with skilful hand.

A Psalm of A'saph.

79 O God, the heathen have come into thy inheritance;
they have defiled thy holy temple;
they have laid Jerusalem in ruins.
2 They have given the bodies of thy servants
to the birds of the air for food,
the flesh of thy saints to the beasts of the earth.
3 They have poured out their blood like water
round about Jerusalem,
and there was none to bury them.
4 We have become a taunt to our neighbors,
mocked and derided by those round about us.

5 How long, O LORD? Wilt thou be angry for ever?
Will thy jealous wrath burn like fire?
6 Pour out thy anger on the nations
that do not know thee,
and on the kingdoms
that do not call on thy name!
7 For they have devoured Jacob,
and laid waste his habitation.

8 Do not remember against us the iniquities of our forefathers;
let thy compassion come speedily to meet us,
for we are brought very low.
9 Help us, O God of our salvation,
for the glory of thy name;
deliver us, and forgive our sins,
for thy name's sake!
10 Why should the nations say,
"Where is their God?"
Let the avenging of the outpoured blood of thy servants
be known among the nations before our eyes!

11 Let the groans of the prisoners come before thee;
according to thy great power preserve those doomed to die!
12 Return sevenfold into the bosom of our neighbors
the taunts with which they have taunted thee, O Lord!
13 Then we thy people, the flock of thy pasture,
will give thanks to thee for ever;
from generation to generation we will recount thy praise.

To the choirmaster: according to Lilies. A Testimony of A'saph. A Psalm.

80 Give ear, O Shepherd of Israel,
thou who leadest Joseph like a flock!
Thou who art enthroned upon the cherubim, shine forth
2 before E'phra·im and Benjamin and Ma·nas'seh!
Stir up thy might,
and come to save us!

3 Restore us, O God;
let thy face shine, that we may be saved!

4 O LORD God of hosts,
how long wilt thou be angry with thy people's prayers?
5 Thou hast fed them with the bread of tears,
and given them tears to drink in full measure.
6 Thou dost make us the scorn[k] of our neighbors;
and our enemies laugh among themselves.

7 Restore us, O God of hosts;
let thy face shine, that we may be saved!

8 Thou didst bring a vine out of Egypt;
thou didst drive out the nations and plant it.
9 Thou didst clear the ground for it;
it took deep root and filled the land.
10 The mountains were covered with its shade,
the mighty cedars with its branches;
11 it sent out its branches to the sea,
and its shoots to the River.
12 Why then hast thou broken down its walls,
so that all who pass along the way pluck its fruit?
13 The boar from the forest ravages it,
and all that move in the field feed on it.

14 Turn again, O God of hosts!
Look down from heaven, and see;
have regard for this vine,

[k] Syr: Heb *strife*

15 the stock which thy right hand
planted.[l]
16 They have burned it with fire, they
have cut it down;
may they perish at the rebuke of
thy countenance!
17 But let thy hand be upon the man
of thy right hand,
the son of man whom thou hast
made strong for thyself!
18 Then we will never turn back from
thee;
give us life, and we will call on
thy name!

19 Restore us, O LORD God of hosts!
let thy face shine, that we may be
saved!

To the choirmaster: according to The
Gittith. A Psalm of Ā'saph.

81 Sing aloud to God our
strength;
shout for joy to the God of Jacob!
2 Raise a song, sound the timbrel,
the sweet lyre with the harp.
3 Blow the trumpet at the new moon,
at the full moon, on our feast
day.
4 For it is a statute for Israel,
an ordinance of the God of Jacob.
5 He made it a decree in Joseph,
when he went out over[m] the land
of Egypt.

I hear a voice I had not known:
6 "I relieved your[n] shoulder of the
burden;
your[n] hands were freed from the
basket.
7 In distress you called, and I delivered you;
I answered you in the secret place
of thunder;
I tested you at the waters of
Mer'i·bah. *Selah*
8 Hear, O my people, while I admonish you!
O Israel, if you would but listen
to me!
9 There shall be no strange god
among you;
you shall not bow down to a
foreign god.
10 I am the LORD your God,
who brought you up out of the
land of Egypt.
Open your mouth wide, and I
will fill it.

11 "But my people did not listen to
my voice;
Israel would have none of me.
12 So I gave them over to their stubborn hearts,
to follow their own counsels.
13 O that my people would listen to
me,
that Israel would walk in my
ways!
14 I would soon subdue their enemies,
and turn my hand against their
foes.
15 Those who hate the LORD would
cringe toward him,
and their fate would last for ever.
16 I would feed you[o] with the finest
of the wheat,
and with honey from the rock I
would satisfy you."

A Psalm of Ā'saph.

82 God has taken his place in the
divine council;
in the midst of the gods he holds
judgment:
2 "How long will you judge unjustly
and show partiality to the wicked?
Selah
3 Give justice to the weak and the
fatherless;
maintain the right of the afflicted
and the destitute.
4 Rescue the weak and the needy;
deliver them from the hand of the
wicked."

5 They have neither knowledge nor
understanding,
they walk about in darkness;
all the foundations of the earth
are shaken.

6 I say, "You are gods,
sons of the Most High, all of you;
7 nevertheless, you shall die like men,
and fall like any prince."[p]

8 Arise, O God, judge the earth;
for to thee belong all the nations!

[l] Heb *planted and upon the son whom thou hast reared for thyself*
[m] Or *against* [n] Heb *his* [o] Cn Compare verse 16b: Heb *he would feed him*
[p] Or *fall as one man, O princes*
82.6: Jn 10.34.

A Song. A Psalm of Ā'saph.

83 O God, do not keep silence;
do not hold thy peace or be still, O God!
2 For lo, thy enemies are in tumult;
those who hate thee have raised their heads.
3 They lay crafty plans against thy people;
they consult together against thy protected ones.
4 They say, "Come, let us wipe them out as a nation;
let the name of Israel be remembered no more!"
5 Yea, they conspire with one accord;
against thee they make a covenant—
6 the tents of Ē'dȯm and the Ish'mȧ-el·ītes,
Mō'ab and the Hag'rītes,
7 Gē'bȧl and Am'mȯn and Am'ȧ·lek,
Phi·lis'ti·ȧ with the inhabitants of Tȳre;
8 Assyria also has joined them;
they are the strong arm of the children of Lot. *Selah*

9 Do to them as thou didst to Mid'i·ȧn,
as to Sis'ėr·ȧ and Jā'bın at the river Kī'shon,
10 who were destroyed at En'-dôr,
who became dung for the ground.
11 Make their nobles like Ôr'eb and Zē'eb,
all their princes like Zē'bȧh and Zal·mun'nȧ,
12 who said, "Let us take possession for ourselves
of the pastures of God."

13 O my God, make them like whirling dust,[q]
like chaff before the wind.
14 As fire consumes the forest,
as the flame sets the mountains ablaze,
15 so do thou pursue them with thy tempest
and terrify them with thy hurricane!
16 Fill their faces with shame,
that they may seek thy name, O LORD.
17 Let them be put to shame and dismayed for ever;
let them perish in disgrace.
18 Let them know that thou alone,
whose name is the LORD,
art the Most High over all the earth.

To the choirmaster: according to The Gittith. A Psalm of the Sons of Kō'rȧh.

84 How lovely is thy dwelling place,
O LORD of hosts!
2 My soul longs, yea, faints
for the courts of the LORD;
my heart and flesh sing for joy
to the living God.

3 Even the sparrow finds a home,
and the swallow a nest for herself,
where she may lay her young,
at thy altars, O LORD of hosts,
my King and my God.
4 Blessed are those who dwell in thy house,
ever singing thy praise! *Selah*

5 Blessed are the men whose strength is in thee,
in whose heart are the highways to Zion.[r]
6 As they go through the valley of Bā'cȧ
they make it a place of springs;
the early rain also covers it with pools.
7 They go from strength to strength;
the God of gods will be seen in Zion.

8 O LORD God of hosts, hear my prayer;
give ear, O God of Jacob! *Selah*
9 Behold our shield, O God;
look upon the face of thine anointed!

10 For a day in thy courts is better
than a thousand elsewhere.
I would rather be a doorkeeper in the house of my God
than dwell in the tents of wickedness.
11 For the LORD God is a sun and shield;
he bestows favor and honor.
No good thing does the LORD withhold
from those who walk uprightly.
12 O LORD of hosts,

[q] Or *a tumbleweed* [r] Heb lacks *to Zion*

blessed is the man who trusts in
thee!

To the choirmaster. A Psalm of the Sons of Kō'răh.

85 LORD, thou wast favorable to
thy land;
thou didst restore the fortunes of
Jacob.
2 Thou didst forgive the iniquity of
thy people;
thou didst pardon all their sin.
Selah
3 Thou didst withdraw all thy wrath;
thou didst turn from thy hot
anger.

4 Restore us again, O God of our
salvation,
and put away thy indignation toward
us!
5 Wilt thou be angry with us for ever?
Wilt thou prolong thy anger to
all generations?
6 Wilt thou not revive us again,
that thy people may rejoice in
thee?
7 Show us thy steadfast love, O LORD,
and grant us thy salvation.

8 Let me hear what God the LORD
will speak,
for he will speak peace to his
people,
to his saints, to those who turn
to him in their hearts.[s]
9 Surely his salvation is at hand for
those who fear him,
that glory may dwell in our land.

10 Steadfast love and faithfulness will
meet;
righteousness and peace will kiss
each other.
11 Faithfulness will spring up from the
ground,
and righteousness will look down
from the sky.
12 Yea, the LORD will give what is good,
and our land will yield its increase.
13 Righteousness will go before him,
and make his footsteps a way.

A Prayer of David.

86 Incline thy ear, O LORD, and
answer me,

[s] Gk: Heb *but let them not turn back to folly*

for I am poor and needy.
2 Preserve my life, for I am godly;
save thy servant who trusts in
thee.
Thou art my God; 3 be gracious to
me, O Lord,
for to thee do I cry all the day.
4 Gladden the soul of thy servant,
for to thee, O Lord, do I lift up
my soul.
5 For thou, O Lord, art good and
forgiving,
abounding in steadfast love to all
who call on thee.
6 Give ear, O LORD, to my prayer;
hearken to my cry of supplication.
7 In the day of my trouble I call on
thee,
for thou dost answer me.

8 There is none like thee among the
gods, O Lord,
nor are there any works like thine.
9 All the nations thou hast made shall
come
and bow down before thee, O
Lord,
and shall glorify thy name.
10 For thou art great and doest wondrous
things,
thou alone art God.
11 Teach me thy way, O LORD,
that I may walk in thy truth;
unite my heart to fear thy name.
12 I give thanks to thee, O Lord my
God, with my whole heart,
and I will glorify thy name for
ever.
13 For great is thy steadfast love toward
me;
thou hast delivered my soul from
the depths of Shē'ōl.

14 O God, insolent men have risen up
against me;
a band of ruthless men seek my
life,
and they do not set thee before
them.
15 But thou, O Lord, art a God merciful
and gracious,
slow to anger and abounding in
steadfast love and faithfulness.
16 Turn to me and take pity on me;
give thy strength to thy servant,
and save the son of thy handmaid.
17 Show me a sign of thy favor,
that those who hate me may see
and be put to shame

because thou, LORD, hast helped
me and comforted me.

A Psalm of the sons of Kō'rah.
A Song.

87 On the holy mount stands the
city he founded;
2 the LORD loves the gates of Zion
more than all the dwelling places
of Jacob.
3 Glorious things are spoken of you,
O city of God. *Selah*

4 Among those who know me I mention
Rā'hab and Babylon;
behold, Phi·lis'ti·à and Tȳre, with
Ethiopia—
"This one was born there," they
say.
5 And of Zion it shall be said,
"This one and that one were born
in her";
for the Most High himself will
establish her.
6 The LORD records as he registers the
peoples,
"This one was born there."
Selah

7 Singers and dancers alike say,
"All my springs are in you."

A Song. A Psalm of the Sons of Kō'rah.
To the choirmaster: according to
Mahalath Leannoth. A Maskil of
Hē'man the Ez'rà·hite.

88 O LORD, my God, I call for
help[t] by day;
I cry out in the night before thee.
2 Let my prayer come before thee,
incline thy ear to my cry!

3 For my soul is full of troubles,
and my life draws near to Shē'ōl.
4 I am reckoned among those who go
down to the Pit;
I am a man who has no strength,
5 like one forsaken among the dead,
like the slain that lie in the grave,
like those whom thou dost remember
no more,
for they are cut off from thy hand.
6 Thou hast put me in the depths of
the Pit,
in the regions dark and deep.
7 Thy wrath lies heavy upon me,
and thou dost overwhelm me with
all thy waves. *Selah*
8 Thou hast caused my companions
to shun me;
thou hast made me a thing of
horror to them.
I am shut in so that I cannot escape;
9 my eye grows dim through sorrow.
Every day I call upon thee, O
LORD;
I spread out my hands to thee.
10 Dost thou work wonders for the
dead?
Do the shades rise up to praise
thee? *Selah*
11 Is thy steadfast love declared in the
grave,
or thy faithfulness in A·bad'don?
12 Are thy wonders known in the
darkness,
or thy saving help in the land of
forgetfulness?

13 But I, O LORD, cry to thee;
in the morning my prayer comes
before thee.
14 O LORD, why dost thou cast me off?
Why dost thou hide thy face from
me?
15 Afflicted and close to death from
my youth up,
I suffer thy terrors; I am helpless.[u]
16 Thy wrath has swept over me;
thy dread assaults destroy me.
17 They surround me like a flood all
day long;
they close in upon me together.
18 Thou hast caused lover and friend
to shun me;
my companions are in darkness.

A Maskil of Ethan the Ez'rà·hite.

89 I will sing of thy steadfast
love, O LORD,[v] for ever;
with my mouth I will proclaim
thy faithfulness to all generations.
2 For thy steadfast love was established
for ever,
thy faithfulness is firm as the
heavens.
3 Thou hast said, "I have made a
covenant with my chosen one,
I have sworn to David my servant:

[t] Cn: Heb *O* LORD, *God of my salvation* [u] The meaning of the Hebrew word is uncertain
[v] Gk: Heb *the steadfast love of the* LORD
89.3-4: Ps 132.11; Acts 2.30.

4 'I will establish your descendants for ever,
and build your throne for all generations.' " *Selah*

5 Let the heavens praise thy wonders, O LORD,
thy faithfulness in the assembly of the holy ones!
6 For who in the skies can be compared to the LORD?
Who among the heavenly beings[w] is like the LORD,
7 a God feared in the council of the holy ones,
great and terrible[x] above all that are round about him?
8 O LORD God of hosts,
who is mighty as thou art, O LORD,
with thy faithfulness round about thee?
9 Thou dost rule the raging of the sea;
when its waves rise, thou stillest them.
10 Thou didst crush Rā'hab like a carcass,
thou didst scatter thy enemies with thy mighty arm.
11 The heavens are thine, the earth also is thine;
the world and all that is in it, thou hast founded them.
12 The north and the south, thou hast created them;
Tā'bôr and Hĕr'mòn joyously praise thy name.
13 Thou hast a mighty arm;
strong is thy hand, high thy right hand.
14 Righteousness and justice are the foundation of thy throne;
steadfast love and faithfulness go before thee.
15 Blessed are the people who know the festal shout,
who walk, O LORD, in the light of thy countenance,
16 who exult in thy name all the day,
and extol[y] thy righteousness.
17 For thou art the glory of their strength;
by thy favor our horn is exalted.
18 For our shield belongs to the LORD,
our king to the Holy One of Israel.

19 Of old thou didst speak in a vision to thy faithful one, and say:
"I have set the crown[z] upon one who is mighty,
I have exalted one chosen from the people.
20 I have found David, my servant;
with my holy oil I have anointed him;
21 so that my hand shall ever abide with him,
my arm also shall strengthen him.
22 The enemy shall not outwit him,
the wicked shall not humble him.
23 I will crush his foes before him
and strike down those who hate him.
24 My faithfulness and my steadfast love shall be with him,
and in my name shall his horn be exalted.
25 I will set his hand on the sea
and his right hand on the rivers.
26 He shall cry to me, 'Thou art my Father,
my God, and the Rock of my salvation.'
27 And I will make him the first-born,
the highest of the kings of the earth.
28 My steadfast love I will keep for him for ever,
and my covenant will stand firm for him.
29 I will establish his line for ever
and his throne as the days of the heavens.
30 If his children forsake my law
and do not walk according to my ordinances,
31 if they violate my statutes
and do not keep my commandments,
32 then I will punish their transgression with the rod
and their iniquity with scourges;
33 but I will not remove from him my steadfast love,
or be false to my faithfulness.
34 I will not violate my covenant,
or alter the word that went forth from my lips.
35 Once for all I have sworn by my holiness;
I will not lie to David.
36 His line shall endure for ever,
his throne as long as the sun before me.
37 Like the moon it shall be established for ever;

[w] Or *sons of gods* [x] Gk Syr: Heb *greatly terrible* [y] Cn: Heb *are exalted in*
[z] Cn: Heb *help*
89.20: Acts 13.22. **89.27:** Rev 1.5. **89.37:** Rev 1.5; 3.14.

it shall stand firm while the skies endure."[a] *Selah*

38 But now thou hast cast off and rejected,
thou art full of wrath against thy anointed.
39 Thou hast renounced the covenant with thy servant;
thou hast defiled his crown in the dust.
40 Thou hast breached all his walls;
thou hast laid his strongholds in ruins.
41 All that pass by despoil him;
he has become the scorn of his neighbors.
42 Thou hast exalted the right hand of his foes;
thou hast made all his enemies rejoice.
43 Yea, thou hast turned back the edge of his sword,
and thou hast not made him stand in battle.
44 Thou hast removed the scepter from his hand,[b]
and cast his throne to the ground.
45 Thou hast cut short the days of his youth;
thou hast covered him with shame. *Selah*

46 How long, O LORD? Wilt thou hide thyself for ever?
How long will thy wrath burn like fire?
47 Remember, O Lord,[c] what the measure of life is,
for what vanity thou hast created all the sons of men!
48 What man can live and never see death?
Who can deliver his soul from the power of Shē'ōl? *Selah*

49 Lord, where is thy steadfast love of old,
which by thy faithfulness thou didst swear to David?
50 Remember, O Lord, how thy servant is scorned;
how I bear in my bosom the insults[d] of the peoples,
51 with which thy enemies taunt, O LORD,
with which they mock the footsteps of thy anointed.

52 Blessed be the LORD for ever!
Amen and Amen.

BOOK IV

A Prayer of Moses, the man of God.

90

Lord, thou hast been our dwelling place[e]
in all generations.
2 Before the mountains were brought forth,
or ever thou hadst formed the earth and the world,
from everlasting to everlasting thou art God.

3 Thou turnest man back to the dust,
and sayest, "Turn back, O children of men!"
4 For a thousand years in thy sight are but as yesterday when it is past,
or as a watch in the night.

5 Thou dost sweep men away; they are like a dream,
like grass which is renewed in the morning:
6 in the morning it flourishes and is renewed;
in the evening it fades and withers.

7 For we are consumed by thy anger;
by thy wrath we are overwhelmed.
8 Thou hast set our iniquities before thee,
our secret sins in the light of thy countenance.

9 For all our days pass away under thy wrath,
our years come to an end[f] like a sigh.
10 The years of our life are threescore and ten,
or even by reason of strength fourscore;
yet their span[g] is but toil and trouble;
they are soon gone, and we fly away.

[a] Cn: Heb *the witness in the skies is sure* [b] Cn: Heb *removed his cleanness* [c] Cn: Heb *I*
[d] Cn: Heb *all of many* [e] Another reading is *refuge* [f] Syr: Heb *we bring our years to an end*
[g] Cn Compare Gk Syr Jerome Tg: Heb *pride*
90.4: 2 Pet 3.8.

11 Who considers the power of thy anger,
and thy wrath according to the fear of thee?
12 So teach us to number our days
that we may get a heart of wisdom.

13 Return, O LORD! How long?
Have pity on thy servants!
14 Satisfy us in the morning with thy steadfast love,
that we may rejoice and be glad all our days.
15 Make us glad as many days as thou hast afflicted us,
and as many years as we have seen evil.
16 Let thy work be manifest to thy servants,
and thy glorious power to their children.
17 Let the favor of the Lord our God be upon us,
and establish thou the work of our hands upon us,
yea, the work of our hands establish thou it.

91

He who dwells in the shelter of the Most High,
who abides in the shadow of the Almighty,
2 will say to the LORD, "My refuge and my fortress;
my God, in whom I trust."
3 For he will deliver you from the snare of the fowler
and from the deadly pestilence;
4 he will cover you with his pinions,
and under his wings you will find refuge;
his faithfulness is a shield and buckler.
5 You will not fear the terror of the night,
nor the arrow that flies by day,
6 nor the pestilence that stalks in darkness,
nor the destruction that wastes at noonday.

7 A thousand may fall at your side,
ten thousand at your right hand;
but it will not come near you.
8 You will only look with your eyes
and see the recompense of the wicked.

9 Because you have made the LORD your refuge,[h]
the Most High your habitation,
10 no evil shall befall you,
no scourge come near your tent.

11 For he will give his angels charge of you
to guard you in all your ways.
12 On their hands they will bear you up,
lest you dash your foot against a stone.
13 You will tread on the lion and the adder,
the young lion and the serpent you will trample under foot.

14 Because he cleaves to me in love,
I will deliver him;
I will protect him, because he knows my name.
15 When he calls to me, I will answer him;
I will be with him in trouble,
I will rescue him and honor him.
16 With long life I will satisfy him,
and show him my salvation.

A Psalm. A Song for the Sabbath.

92

It is good to give thanks to the LORD,
to sing praises to thy name, O Most High;
2 to declare thy steadfast love in the morning,
and thy faithfulness by night,
3 to the music of the lute and the harp,
to the melody of the lyre.
4 For thou, O LORD, hast made me glad by thy work;
at the works of thy hands I sing for joy.

5 How great are thy works, O LORD!
Thy thoughts are very deep!
6 The dull man cannot know,
the stupid cannot understand this:
7 that, though the wicked sprout like grass
and all evildoers flourish,
they are doomed to destruction for ever,
8 but thou, O LORD, art on high for ever.
9 For, lo, thy enemies, O LORD,

[h] Cn: Heb *Because thou,* LORD, *art my refuge; you have made*
91.11-12: Mt 4.6; Lk 4.10-11. 91.13: Lk 10.19.

for, lo, thy enemies shall perish;
all evildoers shall be scattered.

10 But thou hast exalted my horn like that of the wild ox;
thou hast poured over me[i] fresh oil.
11 My eyes have seen the downfall of my enemies,
my ears have heard the doom of my evil assailants.

12 The righteous flourish like the palm tree,
and grow like a cedar in Lebanon.
13 They are planted in the house of the LORD,
they flourish in the courts of our God.
14 They still bring forth fruit in old age,
they are ever full of sap and green,
15 to show that the LORD is upright;
he is my rock, and there is no unrighteousness in him.

93 The LORD reigns; he is robed in majesty;
the LORD is robed, he is girded with strength.
Yea, the world is established; it shall never be moved;
2 thy throne is established from of old;
thou art from everlasting.

3 The floods have lifted up, O LORD,
the floods have lifted up their voice,
the floods lift up their roaring.
4 Mightier than the thunders of many waters,
mightier than the waves[j] of the sea,
the LORD on high is mighty!

5 Thy decrees are very sure;
holiness befits thy house,
O LORD, for evermore.

94 O LORD, thou God of vengeance,
thou God of vengeance, shine forth!
2 Rise up, O judge of the earth;
render to the proud their deserts!
3 O LORD, how long shall the wicked,
how long shall the wicked exult?
4 They pour out their arrogant words,
they boast, all the evildoers.
5 They crush thy people, O LORD,
and afflict thy heritage.
6 They slay the widow and the sojourner,
and murder the fatherless;
7 and they say, "The LORD does not see;
the God of Jacob does not perceive."

8 Understand, O dullest of the people!
Fools, when will you be wise?
9 He who planted the ear, does he not hear?
He who formed the eye, does he not see?
10 He who chastens the nations, does he not chastise?
He who teaches men knowledge,
11 the LORD, knows the thoughts of man,
that they are but a breath.

12 Blessed is the man whom thou dost chasten, O LORD,
and whom thou dost teach out of thy law
13 to give him respite from days of trouble,
until a pit is dug for the wicked.
14 For the LORD will not forsake his people;
he will not abandon his heritage;
15 for justice will return to the righteous,
and all the upright in heart will follow it.

16 Who rises up for me against the wicked?
Who stands up for me against evildoers?
17 If the LORD had not been my help,
my soul would soon have dwelt in the land of silence.
18 When I thought, "My foot slips,"
thy steadfast love, O LORD, held me up.
19 When the cares of my heart are many,
thy consolations cheer my soul.
20 Can wicked rulers be allied with thee,
who frame mischief by statute?
21 They band together against the life of the righteous,

[i] Syr: Heb uncertain
[j] Cn: Heb *mighty the waves*
94.11: 1 Cor 3.20.

and condemn the innocent to death.
22 But the LORD has become my stronghold,
and my God the rock of my refuge.
23 He will bring back on them their iniquity
and wipe them out for their wickedness;
the LORD our God will wipe them out.

95 O come, let us sing to the LORD;
let us make a joyful noise to the rock of our salvation!
2 Let us come into his presence with thanksgiving;
let us make a joyful noise to him with songs of praise!
3 For the LORD is a great God,
and a great King above all gods.
4 In his hand are the depths of the earth;
the heights of the mountains are his also.
5 The sea is his, for he made it;
for his hands formed the dry land.

6 O come, let us worship and bow down,
let us kneel before the LORD, our Maker!
7 For he is our God,
and we are the people of his pasture,
and the sheep of his hand.

O that today you would hearken to his voice!
8 Harden not your hearts, as at Mer'i-bah,
as on the day at Mas'sah in the wilderness,
9 when your fathers tested me,
and put me to the proof, though they had seen my work.
10 For forty years I loathed that generation
and said, "They are a people who err in heart,
and they do not regard my ways."
11 Therefore I swore in my anger
that they should not enter my rest.

96 O sing to the LORD a new song;
sing to the LORD, all the earth!
2 Sing to the LORD, bless his name;
tell of his salvation from day to day.
3 Declare his glory among the nations,
his marvelous works among all the peoples!
4 For great is the LORD, and greatly to be praised;
he is to be feared above all gods.
5 For all the gods of the peoples are idols;
but the LORD made the heavens.
6 Honor and majesty are before him;
strength and beauty are in his sanctuary.

7 Ascribe to the LORD, O families of the peoples,
ascribe to the LORD glory and strength!
8 Ascribe to the LORD the glory due his name;
bring an offering, and come into his courts!
9 Worship the LORD in holy array;
tremble before him, all the earth!

10 Say among the nations, "The LORD reigns!
Yea, the world is established, it shall never be moved;
he will judge the peoples with equity."
11 Let the heavens be glad, and let the earth rejoice;
let the sea roar, and all that fills it;
12 let the field exult, and everything in it!
Then shall all the trees of the wood sing for joy
13 before the LORD, for he comes,
for he comes to judge the earth.
He will judge the world with righteousness,
and the peoples with his truth.

97 The LORD reigns; let the earth rejoice;
let the many coastlands be glad!
2 Clouds and thick darkness are round about him;
righteousness and justice are the foundation of his throne.
3 Fire goes before him,
and burns up his adversaries round about.
4 His lightnings lighten the world;
the earth sees and trembles.
5 The mountains melt like wax before the LORD,
before the Lord of all the earth.

95.7-11: Heb 3.7-11; 4.3-11. 96.1-13: 1 Chron 16.23-33.

6 The heavens proclaim his righteousness;
and all the peoples behold his glory.
7 All worshipers of images are put to shame,
who make their boast in worthless idols;
all gods bow down before him.
8 Zion hears and is glad,
and the daughters of Judah rejoice,
because of thy judgments, O God.
9 For thou, O LORD, art most high over all the earth;
thou art exalted far above all gods.

10 The LORD loves those who hate evil;[k]
he preserves the lives of his saints;
he delivers them from the hand of the wicked.
11 Light dawns[l] for the righteous,
and joy for the upright in heart.
12 Rejoice in the LORD, O you righteous,
and give thanks to his holy name!

A Psalm.

98 O sing to the LORD a new song,
for he has done marvelous things!
His right hand and his holy arm
have gotten him victory.
2 The LORD has made known his victory,
he has revealed his vindication in the sight of the nations.
3 He has remembered his steadfast love and faithfulness
to the house of Israel.
All the ends of the earth have seen
the victory of our God.

4 Make a joyful noise to the LORD, all the earth;
break forth into joyous song and sing praises!
5 Sing praises to the LORD with the lyre,
with the lyre and the sound of melody!
6 With trumpets and the sound of the horn
make a joyful noise before the King, the LORD!

7 Let the sea roar, and all that fills it;
the world and those who dwell in it!
8 Let the floods clap their hands;
let the hills sing for joy together
9 before the LORD, for he comes
to judge the earth.
He will judge the world with righteousness,
and the peoples with equity.

99 The LORD reigns; let the peoples tremble!
He sits enthroned upon the cherubim; let the earth quake!
2 The LORD is great in Zion;
he is exalted over all the peoples.
3 Let them praise thy great and terrible name!
Holy is he!
4 Mighty King,[m] lover of justice,
thou hast established equity;
thou hast executed justice
and righteousness in Jacob.
5 Extol the LORD our God;
worship at his footstool!
Holy is he!

6 Moses and Aaron were among his priests,
Samuel also was among those who called on his name.
They cried to the LORD, and he answered them.
7 He spoke to them in the pillar of cloud;
they kept his testimonies,
and the statutes that he gave them.

8 O LORD our God, thou didst answer them;
thou wast a forgiving God to them,
but an avenger of their wrongdoings.
9 Extol the LORD our God,
and worship at his holy mountain;
for the LORD our God is holy!

A Psalm for the thank offering.

100 Make a joyful noise to the LORD, all the lands![n]
2 Serve the LORD with gladness!
Come into his presence with singing!

[k] Cn: Heb *You who love the* LORD *hate evil* [l] Gk Syr Jerome: Heb *is sown* [m] Cn: Heb *and the king's strength*
[n] Heb *land* or *earth*
97.7: Heb 1.6.

3 Know that the LORD is God!
It is he that made us, and we are his;[o]
we are his people, and the sheep of his pasture.

4 Enter his gates with thanksgiving,
and his courts with praise!
Give thanks to him, bless his name!

5 For the LORD is good;
his steadfast love endures for ever,
and his faithfulness to all generations.

A Psalm of David.

101 I will sing of loyalty and of justice;
to thee, O LORD, I will sing.
2 I will give heed to the way that is blameless.
Oh when wilt thou come to me?

I will walk with integrity of heart within my house;
3 I will not set before my eyes
anything that is base.

I hate the work of those who fall away;
it shall not cleave to me.
4 Perverseness of heart shall be far from me;
I will know nothing of evil.

5 Him who slanders his neighbor secretly
I will destroy.
The man of haughty looks and arrogant heart
I will not endure.

6 I will look with favor on the faithful in the land,
that they may dwell with me;
he who walks in the way that is blameless
shall minister to me.

7 No man who practices deceit
shall dwell in my house;
no man who utters lies
shall continue in my presence.

8 Morning by morning I will destroy
all the wicked in the land,
cutting off all the evildoers
from the city of the LORD.

A prayer of one afflicted, when he is faint and pours out his complaint before the LORD.

102 Hear my prayer, O LORD;
let my cry come to thee!
2 Do not hide thy face from me
in the day of my distress!
Incline thy ear to me;
answer me speedily in the day when I call!

3 For my days pass away like smoke,
and my bones burn like a furnace.
4 My heart is smitten like grass, and withered;
I forgot to eat my bread.
5 Because of my loud groaning
my bones cleave to my flesh.
6 I am like a vulture[p] of the wilderness,
like an owl of the waste places;
7 I lie awake,
I am like a lonely bird on the housetop.
8 All the day my enemies taunt me,
those who deride me use my name for a curse.
9 For I eat ashes like bread,
and mingle tears with my drink,
10 because of thy indignation and anger;
for thou hast taken me up and thrown me away.
11 My days are like an evening shadow;
I wither away like grass.

12 But thou, O LORD, art enthroned for ever;
thy name endures to all generations.
13 Thou wilt arise and have pity on Zion;
it is the time to favor her;
the appointed time has come.
14 For thy servants hold her stones dear,
and have pity on her dust.
15 The nations will fear the name of the LORD,
and all the kings of the earth thy glory.
16 For the LORD will build up Zion,
he will appear in his glory;
17 he will regard the prayer of the destitute,

[o] Another reading is *and not we ourselves* [p] The meaning of the Hebrew word is uncertain

and will not despise their supplication.

18 Let this be recorded for a generation to come,
so that a people yet unborn may praise the LORD:
19 that he looked down from his holy height,
from heaven the LORD looked at the earth,
20 to hear the groans of the prisoners,
to set free those who were doomed to die;
21 that men may declare in Zion the name of the LORD,
and in Jerusalem his praise,
22 when peoples gather together,
and kingdoms, to worship the LORD.

23 He has broken my strength in mid-course;
he has shortened my days.
24 "O my God," I say, "take me not hence
in the midst of my days,
thou whose years endure
throughout all generations!"

25 Of old thou didst lay the foundation of the earth,
and the heavens are the work of thy hands.
26 They will perish, but thou dost endure;
they will all wear out like a garment.
Thou changest them like raiment, and they pass away;
27 but thou art the same, and thy years have no end.
28 The children of thy servants shall dwell secure;
their posterity shall be established before thee.

A Psalm of David.

103 Bless the LORD, O my soul; and all that is within me,
bless his holy name!
2 Bless the LORD, O my soul,
and forget not all his benefits,
3 who forgives all your iniquity,
who heals all your diseases,
4 who redeems your life from the Pit,
who crowns you with steadfast love and mercy,
5 who satisfies you with good as long as you live[q]
so that your youth is renewed like the eagle's.

6 The LORD works vindication
and justice for all who are oppressed.
7 He made known his ways to Moses,
his acts to the people of Israel.
8 The LORD is merciful and gracious,
slow to anger and abounding in steadfast love.
9 He will not always chide,
nor will he keep his anger for ever.
10 He does not deal with us according to our sins,
nor requite us according to our iniquities.
11 For as the heavens are high above the earth,
so great is his steadfast love toward those who fear him;
12 as far as the east is from the west,
so far does he remove our transgressions from us.
13 As a father pities his children,
so the LORD pities those who fear him.
14 For he knows our frame;
he remembers that we are dust.

15 As for man, his days are like grass;
he flourishes like a flower of the field;
16 for the wind passes over it, and it is gone,
and its place knows it no more.
17 But the steadfast love of the LORD is from everlasting to everlasting
upon those who fear him,
and his righteousness to children's children,
18 to those who keep his covenant
and remember to do his commandments.

19 The LORD has established his throne in the heavens,
and his kingdom rules over all.
20 Bless the LORD, O you his angels,
you mighty ones who do his word,
hearkening to the voice of his word!
21 Bless the LORD, all his hosts,
his ministers that do his will!

[q] Heb uncertain

102.25-27: Heb 1.10-12. 103.8: Jas 5.11. 103.17: Lk 1.50.

22 Bless the LORD, all his works,
in all places of his dominion.
Bless the LORD, O my soul!

104 Bless the LORD, O my soul!
O LORD my God, thou art very great!
Thou art clothed with honor and majesty,
2 who coverest thyself with light as with a garment,
who hast stretched out the heavens like a tent,
3 who hast laid the beams of thy chambers on the waters,
who makest the clouds thy chariot,
who ridest on the wings of the wind,
4 who makest the winds thy messengers,
fire and flame thy ministers.

5 Thou didst set the earth on its foundations,
so that it should never be shaken.
6 Thou didst cover it with the deep as with a garment;
the waters stood above the mountains.
7 At thy rebuke they fled;
at the sound of thy thunder they took to flight.
8 The mountains rose, the valleys sank down
to the place which thou didst appoint for them.
9 Thou didst set a bound which they should not pass,
so that they might not again cover the earth.

10 Thou makest springs gush forth in the valleys;
they flow between the hills,
11 they give drink to every beast of the field;
the wild asses quench their thirst.
12 By them the birds of the air have their habitation;
they sing among the branches.
13 From thy lofty abode thou waterest the mountains;
the earth is satisfied with the fruit of thy work.

14 Thou dost cause the grass to grow for the cattle,
and plants for man to cultivate,[r]
that he may bring forth food from the earth,
15 and wine to gladden the heart of man,
oil to make his face shine,
and bread to strengthen man's heart.
16 The trees of the LORD are watered abundantly,
the cedars of Lebanon which he planted.
17 In them the birds build their nests;
the stork has her home in the fir trees.
18 The high mountains are for the wild goats;
the rocks are a refuge for the badgers.
19 Thou hast made the moon to mark the seasons;
the sun knows its time for setting.
20 Thou makest darkness, and it is night,
when all the beasts of the forest creep forth.
21 The young lions roar for their prey,
seeking their food from God.
22 When the sun rises, they get them away
and lie down in their dens.
23 Man goes forth to his work
and to his labor until the evening.

24 O LORD, how manifold are thy works!
In wisdom hast thou made them all;
the earth is full of thy creatures.
25 Yonder is the sea, great and wide,
which teems with things innumerable,
living things both small and great.
26 There go the ships,
and Lė·vī'ă·thăn which thou didst form to sport in it.

27 These all look to thee,
to give them their food in due season.
28 When thou givest to them, they gather it up;
when thou openest thy hand,
they are filled with good things.
29 When thou hidest thy face, they are dismayed;
when thou takest away their breath, they die
and return to their dust.

[r] Or *fodder for the animals that serve man*
104.4: Heb 1.7.
104.12: Mt 13.32; Mk 4.32; Lk 13.19.

30 When thou sendest forth thy Spirit,[s]
they are created;
and thou renewest the face of the
ground.

31 May the glory of the LORD endure
for ever,
may the LORD rejoice in his
works,
32 who looks on the earth and it
trembles,
who touches the mountains and
they smoke!
33 I will sing to the LORD as long as
I live;
I will sing praise to my God
while I have being.
34 May my meditation be pleasing to
him,
for I rejoice in the LORD.
35 Let sinners be consumed from the
earth,
and let the wicked be no more!
Bless the LORD, O my soul!
Praise the LORD!

105 O give thanks to the LORD,
call on his name,
make known his deeds among the
peoples!
2 Sing to him, sing praises to him,
tell of all his wonderful works!
3 Glory in his holy name;
let the hearts of those who seek
the LORD rejoice!
4 Seek the LORD and his strength,
seek his presence continually!
5 Remember the wonderful works
that he has done,
his miracles, and the judgments
he uttered,
6 O offspring of Abraham his servant,
sons of Jacob, his chosen ones!

7 He is the LORD our God;
his judgments are in all the earth.
8 He is mindful of his covenant for
ever,
of the word that he commanded,
for a thousand generations,
9 the covenant which he made with
Abraham,
his sworn promise to Isaac,
10 which he confirmed to Jacob as a
statute,
to Israel as an everlasting covenant,
11 saying, "To you I will give the land
of Canaan
as your portion for an inheritance."

12 When they were few in number,
of little account, and sojourners
in it,
13 wandering from nation to nation,
from one kingdom to another
people,
14 he allowed no one to oppress them;
he rebuked kings on their account,
15 saying, "Touch not my anointed
ones,
do my prophets no harm!"

16 When he summoned a famine on
the land,
and broke every staff of bread,
17 he had sent a man ahead of them,
Joseph, who was sold as a slave.
18 His feet were hurt with fetters,
his neck was put in a collar of
iron;
19 until what he had said came to pass
the word of the LORD tested him.
20 The king sent and released him,
the ruler of the peoples set him
free;
21 he made him lord of his house,
and ruler of all his possessions,
22 to instruct[t] his princes at his pleasure,
and to teach his elders wisdom.

23 Then Israel came to Egypt;
Jacob sojourned in the land of
Ham.
24 And the LORD made his people very
fruitful,
and made them stronger than
their foes.
25 He turned their hearts to hate his
people,
to deal craftily with his servants.

26 He sent Moses his servant,
and Aaron whom he had chosen.
27 They wrought his signs among them,
and miracles in the land of Ham.
28 He sent darkness, and made the
land dark;
they rebelled[u] against his words.
29 He turned their waters into blood,
and caused their fish to die.
30 Their land swarmed with frogs,
even in the chambers of their
kings.
31 He spoke, and there came swarms
of flies,

[s] Or *breath* [t] Gk Syr Jerome: Heb *to bind* [u] Cn Compare Gk Syr: Heb *they did not rebel*
105.1-15: 1 Chron 16.8-22. 105.8-9: Lk 1.72-73.

and gnats throughout their country.
32 He gave them hail for rain,
and lightning that flashed through their land.
33 He smote their vines and fig trees,
and shattered the trees of their country.
34 He spoke, and the locusts came,
and young locusts without number;
35 which devoured all the vegetation in their land,
and ate up the fruit of their ground.
36 He smote all the first-born in their land,
the first issue of all their strength.

37 Then he led forth Israel with silver and gold,
and there was none among his tribes who stumbled.
38 Egypt was glad when they departed,
for dread of them had fallen upon it.
39 He spread a cloud for a covering,
and fire to give light by night.
40 They asked, and he brought quails
and gave them bread from heaven in abundance.
41 He opened the rock, and water gushed forth;
it flowed through the desert like a river.
42 For he remembered his holy promise,
and Abraham his servant.

43 So he led forth his people with joy,
his chosen ones with singing.
44 And he gave them the lands of the nations;
and they took possession of the fruit of the peoples' toil,
45 to the end that they should keep his statutes,
and observe his laws.
Praise the LORD!

106 Praise the LORD!
O give thanks to the LORD, for he is good;
for his steadfast love endures for ever!
2 Who can utter the mighty doings of the LORD,
or show forth all his praise?
3 Blessed are they who observe justice,
who do righteousness at all times!
4 Remember me, O LORD, when thou showest favor to thy people;
help me when thou deliverest them;
5 that I may see the prosperity of thy chosen ones,
that I may rejoice in the gladness of thy nation,
that I may glory with thy heritage.

6 Both we and our fathers have sinned;
we have committed iniquity, we have done wickedly.
7 Our fathers, when they were in Egypt,
did not consider thy wonderful works;
they did not remember the abundance of thy steadfast love,
but rebelled against the Most High[v] at the Red Sea.
8 Yet he saved them for his name's sake,
that he might make known his mighty power.
9 He rebuked the Red Sea, and it became dry;
and he led them through the deep as through a desert.
10 So he saved them from the hand of the foe,
and delivered them from the power of the enemy.
11 And the waters covered their adversaries;
not one of them was left.
12 Then they believed his words;
they sang his praise.

13 But they soon forgot his works;
they did not wait for his counsel.
14 But they had a wanton craving in the wilderness,
and put God to the test in the desert;
15 he gave them what they asked,
but sent a wasting disease among them.

16 When men in the camp were jealous of Moses
and Aaron, the holy one of the LORD,
17 the earth opened and swallowed up Dā'thăn,
and covered the company of Ȧ·bī'răm.

[v] Cn Compare 78.17, 56: Heb *at the sea*
106.1: 1 Chron 16.34.

18 Fire also broke out in their company;
the flame burned up the wicked.

19 They made a calf in Hō'reb
and worshiped a molten image.
20 They exchanged the glory of God
for the image of an ox that eats grass.
21 They forgot God, their Savior,
who had done great things in Egypt,
22 wondrous works in the land of Ham,
and terrible things by the Red Sea.
23 Therefore he said he would destroy them—
had not Moses, his chosen one,
stood in the breach before him,
to turn away his wrath from destroying them.

24 Then they despised the pleasant land,
having no faith in his promise.
25 They murmured in their tents,
and did not obey the voice of the LORD.
26 Therefore he raised his hand and swore to them
that he would make them fall in the wilderness,
27 and would disperse[w] their descendants among the nations,
scattering them over the lands.

28 Then they attached themselves to the Bā'ȧl of Pē'ôr,
and ate sacrifices offered to the dead;
29 they provoked the LORD to anger with their doings,
and a plague broke out among them.
30 Then Phin'ė·hȧs stood up and interposed,
and the plague was stayed.
31 And that has been reckoned to him as righteousness
from generation to generation for ever.

32 They angered him at the waters of Mer'i·bȧh,
and it went ill with Moses on their account;
33 for they made his spirit bitter,
and he spoke words that were rash.
34 They did not destroy the peoples,
as the LORD commanded them,
35 but they mingled with the nations
and learned to do as they did.
36 They served their idols,
which became a snare to them.
37 They sacrificed their sons
and their daughters to the demons;
38 they poured out innocent blood,
the blood of their sons and daughters,
whom they sacrificed to the idols of Canaan;
and the land was polluted with blood.
39 Thus they became unclean by their acts,
and played the harlot in their doings.

40 Then the anger of the LORD was kindled against his people,
and he abhorred his heritage;
41 he gave them into the hand of the nations,
so that those who hated them ruled over them.
42 Their enemies oppressed them,
and they were brought into subjection under their power.
43 Many times he delivered them,
but they were rebellious in their purposes,
and were brought low through their iniquity.
44 Nevertheless he regarded their distress,
when he heard their cry.
45 He remembered for their sake his covenant,
and relented according to the abundance of his steadfast love.
46 He caused them to be pitied
by all those who held them captive.

47 Save us, O LORD our God,
and gather us from among the nations,
that we may give thanks to thy holy name
and glory in thy praise.

48 Blessed be the LORD, the God of Israel,
from everlasting to everlasting!
And let all the people say, "Amen!"
Praise the LORD!

[w] Syr Compare Ezek 20.23: Heb *cause to fall*
106.47-48: 1 Chron 16.35-36.

BOOK V

107 O give thanks to the LORD,
for he is good;
for his steadfast love endures for ever!
2 Let the redeemed of the LORD say so,
whom he has redeemed from trouble
3 and gathered in from the lands,
from the east and from the west,
from the north and from the south.

4 Some wandered in desert wastes,
finding no way to a city to dwell in;
5 hungry and thirsty,
their soul fainted within them.
6 Then they cried to the LORD in their trouble,
and he delivered them from their distress;
7 he led them by a straight way,
till they reached a city to dwell in.
8 Let them thank the LORD for his steadfast love,
for his wonderful works to the sons of men!
9 For he satisfies him who is thirsty,
and the hungry he fills with good things.

10 Some sat in darkness and in gloom,
prisoners in affliction and in irons,
11 for they had rebelled against the words of God,
and spurned the counsel of the Most High.
12 Their hearts were bowed down with hard labor;
they fell down, with none to help.
13 Then they cried to the LORD in their trouble,
and he delivered them from their distress;
14 he brought them out of darkness and gloom,
and broke their bonds asunder.
15 Let them thank the LORD for his steadfast love,
for his wonderful works to the sons of men!
16 For he shatters the doors of bronze,
and cuts in two the bars of iron.

17 Some were sick[x] through their sinful ways,
and because of their iniquities suffered affliction;
18 they loathed any kind of food,
and they drew near to the gates of death.
19 Then they cried to the LORD in their trouble,
and he delivered them from their distress;
20 he sent forth his word, and healed them,
and delivered them from destruction.
21 Let them thank the LORD for his steadfast love,
for his wonderful works to the sons of men!
22 And let them offer sacrifices of thanksgiving,
and tell of his deeds in songs of joy!

23 Some went down to the sea in ships,
doing business on the great waters;
24 they saw the deeds of the LORD,
his wondrous works in the deep.
25 For he commanded, and raised the stormy wind,
which lifted up the waves of the sea.
26 They mounted up to heaven, they went down to the depths;
their courage melted away in their evil plight;
27 they reeled and staggered like drunken men,
and were at their wits' end.
28 Then they cried to the LORD in their trouble,
and he delivered them from their distress;
29 he made the storm be still,
and the waves of the sea were hushed.
30 Then they were glad because they had quiet,
and he brought them to their desired haven.
31 Let them thank the LORD for his steadfast love,
for his wonderful works to the sons of men!
32 Let them extol him in the congregation of the people,
and praise him in the assembly of the elders.

33 He turns rivers into a desert,

[x] Cn: Heb *fools*

springs of water into thirsty
ground,
34 a fruitful land into a salty waste,
because of the wickedness of its
inhabitants.
35 He turns a desert into pools of water,
a parched land into springs of
water.
36 And there he lets the hungry dwell,
and they establish a city to live
in;
37 they sow fields, and plant vineyards,
and get a fruitful yield.
38 By his blessing they multiply
greatly;
and he does not let their cattle
decrease.

39 When they are diminished and
brought low
through oppression, trouble, and
sorrow,
40 he pours contempt upon princes
and makes them wander in track-
less wastes;
41 but he raises up the needy out of
affliction,
and makes their families like
flocks.
42 The upright see it and are glad;
and all wickedness stops its
mouth.
43 Whoever is wise, let him give heed
to these things;
let men consider the steadfast love
of the LORD.

A Song. A Psalm of David.

108 My heart is steadfast, O God,
my heart is steadfast!
I will sing and make melody!
Awake, my soul!
2 Awake, O harp and lyre!
I will awake the dawn!
3 I will give thanks to thee, O LORD,
among the peoples,
I will sing praises to thee among
the nations.
4 For thy steadfast love is great above
the heavens,
thy faithfulness reaches to the
clouds.

5 Be exalted, O God, above the
heavens!
Let thy glory be over all the earth!
6 That thy beloved may be delivered,
give help by thy right hand, and
answer me!

7 God has promised in his sanctuary:[y]
"With exultation I will divide up
Shē'chem,
and portion out the Vale of
Suc'coth.
8 Gilead is mine; Mȧ·nas'sėh is mine;
Ē'phrȧ·im is my helmet;
Judah my scepter.
9 Mō'ab is my washbasin;
upon Ē'dȯm I cast my shoe;
over Phi·lis'ti·ȧ I shout in triumph."

10 Who will bring me to the fortified
city?
Who will lead me to Ē'dȯm?
11 Hast thou not rejected us, O God?
Thou dost not go forth, O God,
with our armies.
12 O grant us help against the foe,
for vain is the help of man!
13 With God we shall do valiantly;
it is he who will tread down our
foes.

To the choirmaster. A Psalm of David.

109 Be not silent, O God of my
praise!
2 For wicked and deceitful mouths
are opened against me,
speaking against me with lying
tongues.
3 They beset me with words of hate,
and attack me without cause.
4 In return for my love they accuse
me,
even as I make prayer for them.[z]
5 So they reward me evil for good,
and hatred for my love.

6 Appoint a wicked man against
him;
let an accuser bring him to trial.[a]
7 When he is tried, let him come forth
guilty;
let his prayer be counted as sin!
8 May his days be few;
may another seize his goods!
9 May his children be fatherless,
and his wife a widow!
10 May his children wander about and
beg;
may they be driven out of[b] the
ruins they inhabit!

[y] Or *by his holiness* [z] Syr: Heb *I prayer* [a] Heb *stand at his right hand* [b] Gk: Heb *and seek*
108.1-5: Ps 57.7-11. 108.6-13: Ps 60.5-12. 109.8: Acts 1.20.

11 May the creditor seize all that he has;
may strangers plunder the fruits of his toil!
12 Let there be none to extend kindness to him,
nor any to pity his fatherless children!
13 May his posterity be cut off;
may his name be blotted out in the second generation!
14 May the iniquity of his fathers be remembered before the LORD,
and let not the sin of his mother be blotted out!
15 Let them be before the LORD continually;
and may his[c] memory be cut off from the earth!
16 For he did not remember to show kindness,
but pursued the poor and needy and the brokenhearted to their death.
17 He loved to curse; let curses come on him!
He did not like blessing; may it be far from him!
18 He clothed himself with cursing as his coat,
may it soak into his body like water,
like oil into his bones!
19 May it be like a garment which he wraps round him,
like a belt with which he daily girds himself!

20 May this be the reward of my accusers from the LORD,
of those who speak evil against my life!
21 But thou, O GOD my Lord,
deal on my behalf for thy name's sake;
because thy steadfast love is good, deliver me!
22 For I am poor and needy,
and my heart is stricken within me.
23 I am gone, like a shadow at evening;
I am shaken off like a locust.
24 My knees are weak through fasting;
my body has become gaunt.
25 I am an object of scorn to my accusers;
when they see me, they wag their heads.

26 Help me, O LORD my God!
Save me according to thy steadfast love!
27 Let them know that this is thy hand;
thou, O LORD, hast done it!
28 Let them curse, but do thou bless!
Let my assailants be put to shame;[d] may thy servant be glad!
29 May my accusers be clothed with dishonor;
may they be wrapped in their own shame as in a mantle!

30 With my mouth I will give great thanks to the LORD;
I will praise him in the midst of the throng.
31 For he stands at the right hand of the needy,
to save him from those who condemn him to death.

A Psalm of David.

110 The LORD says to my lord:
"Sit at my right hand,
till I make your enemies
your footstool."

2 The LORD sends forth from Zion
your mighty scepter.
Rule in the midst of your foes!
3 Your people will offer themselves freely
on the day you lead your host
upon the holy mountains.[e]
From the womb of the morning
like dew your youth[f] will come to you.
4 The LORD has sworn
and will not change his mind,
"You are a priest for ever
after the order of Mel·chiz'ė·dek."

5 The Lord is at your right hand;
he will shatter kings on the day of his wrath.
6 He will execute judgment among the nations,
filling them with corpses;
he will shatter chiefs[g]

[c] Gk: Heb *their* [d] Gk: Heb *they have arisen and have been put to shame*
[e] Another reading is *in holy array* [f] Cn: Heb *the dew of your youth* [g] Or *the head*
109.25: Mt 27.39; Mk 15.29.
110.1: Mt 22.44; 26.64; Mk 12.36; 14.62; 16.19; Lk 20.42-43; 22.69; Acts 2.34; 1 Cor 15.25; Eph 1.20; Col 3.1; Heb 1.3, 13; 10.12-13; 12.2. **110.4:** Heb 5.6, 10; 6.20; 7.11, 15, 21.

over the wide earth.
7 He will drink from the brook by the way;
therefore he will lift up his head.

111

Praise the LORD.
I will give thanks to the LORD with my whole heart,
in the company of the upright, in the congregation.
2 Great are the works of the LORD,
studied by all who have pleasure in them.
3 Full of honor and majesty is his work,
and his righteousness endures for ever.
4 He has caused his wonderful works to be remembered;
the LORD is gracious and merciful.
5 He provides food for those who fear him;
he is ever mindful of his covenant.
6 He has shown his people the power of his works,
in giving them the heritage of the nations.
7 The works of his hands are faithful and just;
all his precepts are trustworthy,
8 they are established for ever and ever,
to be performed with faithfulness and uprightness.
9 He sent redemption to his people;
he has commanded his covenant for ever.
Holy and terrible is his name!
10 The fear of the LORD is the beginning of wisdom;
a good understanding have all those who practice it.
His praise endures for ever!

112

Praise the LORD.
Blessed is the man who fears the LORD,
who greatly delights in his commandments!
2 His descendants will be mighty in the land;
the generation of the upright will be blessed.
3 Wealth and riches are in his house;
and his righteousness endures for ever.
4 Light rises in the darkness for the upright;
the LORD[h] is gracious, merciful, and righteous.
5 It is well with the man who deals generously and lends,
who conducts his affairs with justice.
6 For the righteous will never be moved;
he will be remembered for ever.
7 He is not afraid of evil tidings;
his heart is firm, trusting in the LORD.
8 His heart is steady, he will not be afraid,
until he sees his desire on his adversaries.
9 He has distributed freely, he has given to the poor;
his righteousness endures for ever;
his horn is exalted in honor.
10 The wicked man sees it and is angry;
he gnashes his teeth and melts away;
the desire of the wicked man comes to nought.

113

Praise the LORD!
Praise, O servants of the LORD,
praise the name of the LORD!

2 Blessed be the name of the LORD
from this time forth and for evermore!
3 From the rising of the sun to its setting
the name of the LORD is to be praised!
4 The LORD is high above all nations,
and his glory above the heavens!

5 Who is like the LORD our God,
who is seated on high,
6 who looks far down
upon the heavens and the earth?
7 He raises the poor from the dust,
and lifts the needy from the ash heap,
8 to make them sit with princes,
with the princes of his people.
9 He gives the barren woman a home,
making her the joyous mother of children.
Praise the LORD!

114

When Israel went forth from Egypt,
the house of Jacob from a people of strange language,

[h] Gk: Heb lacks *the* LORD
112.9: 2 Cor 9.9.

2 Judah became his sanctuary,
Israel his dominion.

3 The sea looked and fled,
Jordan turned back.
4 The mountains skipped like rams,
the hills like lambs.

5 What ails you, O sea, that you flee?
O Jordan, that you turn back?
6 O mountains, that you skip like rams?
O hills, like lambs?

7 Tremble, O earth, at the presence of the LORD,
at the presence of the God of Jacob,
8 who turns the rock into a pool of water,
the flint into a spring of water.

115 Not to us, O LORD, not to us,
but to thy name give glory,
for the sake of thy steadfast love and thy faithfulness!
2 Why should the nations say,
"Where is their God?"

3 Our God is in the heavens;
he does whatever he pleases.
4 Their idols are silver and gold,
the work of men's hands.
5 They have mouths, but do not speak;
eyes, but do not see.
6 They have ears, but do not hear;
noses, but do not smell.
7 They have hands, but do not feel;
feet, but do not walk;
and they do not make a sound in their throat.
8 Those who make them are like them;
so are all who trust in them.

9 O Israel, trust in the LORD!
He is their help and their shield.
10 O house of Aaron, put your trust in the LORD!
He is their help and their shield.
11 You who fear the LORD, trust in the LORD!
He is their help and their shield.

12 The LORD has been mindful of us; he will bless us;
he will bless the house of Israel;
he will bless the house of Aaron;
13 he will bless those who fear the LORD,
both small and great.

14 May the LORD give you increase,
you and your children!
15 May you be blessed by the LORD,
who made heaven and earth!

16 The heavens are the LORD's heavens,
but the earth he has given to the sons of men.
17 The dead do not praise the LORD,
nor do any that go down into silence.
18 But we will bless the LORD
from this time forth and for evermore.
Praise the LORD!

116 I love the LORD, because he has heard
my voice and my supplications.
2 Because he inclined his ear to me,
therefore I will call on him as long as I live.
3 The snares of death encompassed me;
the pangs of Shē'ōl laid hold on me;
I suffered distress and anguish.
4 Then I called on the name of the LORD:
"O LORD, I beseech thee, save my life!"

5 Gracious is the LORD, and righteous;
our God is merciful.
6 The LORD preserves the simple;
when I was brought low, he saved me.
7 Return, O my soul, to your rest;
for the LORD has dealt bountifully with you.

8 For thou hast delivered my soul from death,
my eyes from tears,
my feet from stumbling;
9 I walk before the LORD
in the land of the living.
10 I kept my faith, even when I said,
"I am greatly afflicted";
11 I said in my consternation,
"Men are all a vain hope."

12 What shall I render to the LORD
for all his bounty to me?
13 I will lift up the cup of salvation
and call on the name of the LORD,

115.4-8: Ps 135.15-18. **115.13**: Rev 11.18; 19.5. **116.10**: 2 Cor 4.13.

14 I will pay my vows to the LORD
in the presence of all his people.
15 Precious in the sight of the LORD
is the death of his saints.
16 O LORD, I am thy servant;
I am thy servant, the son of thy handmaid.
Thou hast loosed my bonds.
17 I will offer to thee the sacrifice of thanksgiving
and call on the name of the LORD.
18 I will pay my vows to the LORD
in the presence of all his people,
19 in the courts of the house of the LORD,
in your midst, O Jerusalem.
Praise the LORD!

117 Praise the LORD, all nations!
Extol him, all peoples!
2 For great is his steadfast love toward us;
and the faithfulness of the LORD endures for ever.
Praise the LORD!

118 O give thanks to the LORD, for he is good;
his steadfast love endures for ever!

2 Let Israel say,
"His steadfast love endures for ever."
3 Let the house of Aaron say,
"His steadfast love endures for ever."
4 Let those who fear the LORD say,
"His steadfast love endures for ever."

5 Out of my distress I called on the LORD;
the LORD answered me and set me free.
6 With the LORD on my side I do not fear.
What can man do to me?
7 The LORD is on my side to help me;
I shall look in triumph on those who hate me.
8 It is better to take refuge in the LORD
than to put confidence in man.
9 It is better to take refuge in the LORD
than to put confidence in princes.
10 All nations surrounded me;
in the name of the LORD I cut them off!
11 They surrounded me, surrounded me on every side;
in the name of the LORD I cut them off!
12 They surrounded me like bees,
they blazed[i] like a fire of thorns;
in the name of the LORD I cut them off!
13 I was pushed hard,[j] so that I was falling,
but the LORD helped me.
14 The LORD is my strength and my song;
he has become my salvation.

15 Hark, glad songs of victory
in the tents of the righteous:
"The right hand of the LORD does valiantly,
16 the right hand of the LORD is exalted,
the right hand of the LORD does valiantly!"
17 I shall not die, but I shall live,
and recount the deeds of the LORD.
18 The LORD has chastened me sorely,
but he has not given me over to death.

19 Open to me the gates of righteousness,
that I may enter through them
and give thanks to the LORD.

20 This is the gate of the LORD;
the righteous shall enter through it.

21 I thank thee that thou hast answered me
and hast become my salvation.
22 The stone which the builders rejected
has become the head of the corner.
23 This is the LORD's doing;
it is marvelous in our eyes.
24 This is the day which the LORD has made;
let us rejoice and be glad in it.
25 Save us, we beseech thee, O LORD!
O LORD, we beseech thee, give us success!

[i] Gk: Heb *were extinguished* [j] Gk Syr Jerome: Heb *thou didst push me hard*
117.1: Rom 15.11. **118.6:** Heb 13.6.
118.22-23: Mt 21.42; Mk 12.10-11; Lk 20.17; Acts 4.11; 1 Pet 2.7.
118.25-26: Mt 21.9; 23.39; Mk 11.9-10; Lk 13.35; 19.38; Jn 12.13.

26 Blessed be he who enters in the name of the LORD!
We bless you from the house of the LORD.
27 The LORD is God,
and he has given us light.
Bind the festal procession with branches,
up to the horns of the altar!

28 Thou art my God, and I will give thanks to thee;
thou art my God, I will extol thee.

29 O give thanks to the LORD, for he is good;
for his steadfast love endures for ever!

119 Blessed are those whose way is blameless,
who walk in the law of the LORD!
2 Blessed are those who keep his testimonies,
who seek him with their whole heart,
3 who also do no wrong,
but walk in his ways!
4 Thou hast commanded thy precepts
to be kept diligently.
5 O that my ways may be steadfast
in keeping thy statutes!
6 Then I shall not be put to shame,
having my eyes fixed on all thy commandments.
7 I will praise thee with an upright heart,
when I learn thy righteous ordinances.
8 I will observe thy statutes;
O forsake me not utterly!

9 How can a young man keep his way pure?
By guarding it according to thy word.
10 With my whole heart I seek thee;
let me not wander from thy commandments!
11 I have laid up thy word in my heart,
that I might not sin against thee.
12 Blessed be thou, O LORD;
teach me thy statutes!
13 With my lips I declare
all the ordinances of thy mouth.
14 In the way of thy testimonies I delight
as much as in all riches.
15 I will meditate on thy precepts,
and fix my eyes on thy ways.
16 I will delight in thy statutes;
I will not forget thy word.

17 Deal bountifully with thy servant,
that I may live and observe thy word.
18 Open my eyes, that I may behold
wondrous things out of thy law.
19 I am a sojourner on earth;
hide not thy commandments from me!
20 My soul is consumed with longing
for thy ordinances at all times.
21 Thou dost rebuke the insolent, accursed ones,
who wander from thy commandments;
22 take away from me their scorn and contempt,
for I have kept thy testimonies.
23 Even though princes sit plotting against me,
thy servant will meditate on thy statutes.
24 Thy testimonies are my delight,
they are my counselors.

25 My soul cleaves to the dust;
revive me according to thy word!
26 When I told of my ways, thou didst answer me;
teach me thy statutes!
27 Make me understand the way of thy precepts,
and I will meditate on thy wondrous works.
28 My soul melts away for sorrow;
strengthen me according to thy word!
29 Put false ways far from me;
and graciously teach me thy law!
30 I have chosen the way of faithfulness,
I set thy ordinances before me.
31 I cleave to thy testimonies, O LORD;
let me not be put to shame!
32 I will run in the way of thy commandments
when thou enlargest my understanding!

33 Teach me, O LORD, the way of thy statutes;
and I will keep it to the end.
34 Give me understanding, that I may keep thy law
and observe it with my whole heart.
35 Lead me in the path of thy commandments,
for I delight in it.

36 Incline my heart to thy testimonies,
and not to gain!
37 Turn my eyes from looking at vanities;
and give me life in thy ways.
38 Confirm to thy servant thy promise,
which is for those who fear thee.
39 Turn away the reproach which I dread;
for thy ordinances are good.
40 Behold, I long for thy precepts;
in thy righteousness give me life!

41 Let thy steadfast love come to me, O LORD,
thy salvation according to thy promise;
42 then shall I have an answer for those who taunt me,
for I trust in thy word.
43 And take not the word of truth utterly out of my mouth,
for my hope is in thy ordinances.
44 I will keep thy law continually,
for ever and ever;
45 and I shall walk at liberty,
for I have sought thy precepts.
46 I will also speak of thy testimonies before kings,
and shall not be put to shame;
47 for I find my delight in thy commandments,
which I love.
48 I revere thy commandments, which I love,
and I will meditate on thy statutes.

49 Remember thy word to thy servant,
in which thou hast made me hope.
50 This is my comfort in my affliction
that thy promise gives me life.
51 Godless men utterly deride me,
but I do not turn away from thy law.
52 When I think of thy ordinances from of old,
I take comfort, O LORD.
53 Hot indignation seizes me because of the wicked,
who forsake thy law.
54 Thy statutes have been my songs
in the house of my pilgrimage.
55 I remember thy name in the night, O LORD,
and keep thy law.
56 This blessing has fallen to me,
that I have kept thy precepts.

57 The LORD is my portion;
I promise to keep thy words.
58 I entreat thy favor with all my heart;
be gracious to me according to thy promise.
59 When I think of thy ways,
I turn my feet to thy testimonies;
60 I hasten and do not delay
to keep thy commandments.
61 Though the cords of the wicked ensnare me,
I do not forget thy law.
62 At midnight I rise to praise thee,
because of thy righteous ordinances.
63 I am a companion of all who fear thee,
of those who keep thy precepts.
64 The earth, O LORD, is full of thy steadfast love;
teach me thy statutes!

65 Thou hast dealt well with thy servant,
O LORD, according to thy word.
66 Teach me good judgment and knowledge,
for I believe in thy commandments.
67 Before I was afflicted I went astray;
but now I keep thy word.
68 Thou art good and doest good;
teach me thy statutes.
69 The godless besmear me with lies,
but with my whole heart I keep thy precepts;
70 their heart is gross like fat,
but I delight in thy law.
71 It is good for me that I was afflicted,
that I might learn thy statutes.
72 The law of thy mouth is better to me
than thousands of gold and silver pieces.

73 Thy hands have made and fashioned me;
give me understanding that I may learn thy commandments.
74 Those who fear thee shall see me and rejoice,
because I have hoped in thy word.
75 I know, O LORD, that thy judgments are right,
and that in faithfulness thou hast afflicted me.
76 Let thy steadfast love be ready to comfort me
according to thy promise to thy servant.
77 Let thy mercy come to me, that I may live;
for thy law is my delight.

78 Let the godless be put to shame,
because they have subverted me with guile;
as for me, I will meditate on thy precepts.
79 Let those who fear thee turn to me,
that they may know thy testimonies.
80 May my heart be blameless in thy statutes,
that I may not be put to shame!

81 My soul languishes for thy salvation;
I hope in thy word.
82 My eyes fail with watching for thy promise;
I ask, "When wilt thou comfort me?"
83 For I have become like a wineskin in the smoke,
yet I have not forgotten thy statutes.
84 How long must thy servant endure?
When wilt thou judge those who persecute me?
85 Godless men have dug pitfalls for me,
men who do not conform to thy law.
86 All thy commandments are sure;
they persecute me with falsehood; help me!
87 They have almost made an end of me on earth;
but I have not forsaken thy precepts.
88 In thy steadfast love spare my life,
that I may keep the testimonies of thy mouth.

89 For ever, O LORD, thy word
is firmly fixed in the heavens.
90 Thy faithfulness endures to all generations;
thou hast established the earth, and it stands fast.
91 By thy appointment they stand this day;
for all things are thy servants.
92 If thy law had not been my delight,
I should have perished in my affliction.
93 I will never forget thy precepts;
for by them thou hast given me life.
94 I am thine, save me;
for I have sought thy precepts.
95 The wicked lie in wait to destroy me;
but I consider thy testimonies.
96 I have seen a limit to all perfection,
but thy commandment is exceedingly broad.

97 Oh, how I love thy law!
It is my meditation all the day.
98 Thy commandment makes me wiser than my enemies,
for it is ever with me.
99 I have more understanding than all my teachers,
for thy testimonies are my meditation.
100 I understand more than the aged,
for I keep thy precepts.
101 I hold back my feet from every evil way,
in order to keep thy word.
102 I do not turn aside from thy ordinances,
for thou hast taught me.
103 How sweet are thy words to my taste,
sweeter than honey to my mouth!
104 Through thy precepts I get understanding;
therefore I hate every false way.

105 Thy word is a lamp to my feet
and a light to my path.
106 I have sworn an oath and confirmed it,
to observe thy righteous ordinances.
107 I am sorely afflicted;
give me life, O LORD, according to thy word!
108 Accept my offerings of praise, O LORD,
and teach me thy ordinances.
109 I hold my life in my hand continually,
but I do not forget thy law.
110 The wicked have laid a snare for me,
but I do not stray from thy precepts.
111 Thy testimonies are my heritage for ever;
yea, they are the joy of my heart.
112 I incline my heart to perform thy statutes
for ever, to the end.

113 I hate double-minded men,
but I love thy law.
114 Thou art my hiding place and my shield;
I hope in thy word.
115 Depart from me, you evildoers,
that I may keep the commandments of my God.

116 Uphold me according to thy promise, that I may live,
and let me not be put to shame in my hope!
117 Hold me up, that I may be safe
and have regard for thy statutes continually!
118 Thou dost spurn all who go astray from thy statutes;
yea, their cunning is in vain.
119 All the wicked of the earth thou dost count as dross;
therefore I love thy testimonies.
120 My flesh trembles for fear of thee,
and I am afraid of thy judgments.

121 I have done what is just and right;
do not leave me to my oppressors.
122 Be surety for thy servant for good;
let not the godless oppress me.
123 My eyes fail with watching for thy salvation,
and for the fulfilment of thy righteous promise.
124 Deal with thy servant according to thy steadfast love,
and teach me thy statutes.
125 I am thy servant; give me understanding,
that I may know thy testimonies!
126 It is time for the LORD to act,
for thy law has been broken.
127 Therefore I love thy commandments
above gold, above fine gold.
128 Therefore I direct my steps by all thy precepts;[k]
I hate every false way.

129 Thy testimonies are wonderful;
therefore my soul keeps them.
130 The unfolding of thy words gives light;
it imparts understanding to the simple.
131 With open mouth I pant,
because I long for thy commandments.
132 Turn to me and be gracious to me,
as is thy wont toward those who love thy name.
133 Keep steady my steps according to thy promise,
and let no iniquity get dominion over me.
134 Redeem me from man's oppression,
that I may keep thy precepts.
135 Make thy face shine upon thy servant,
and teach me thy statutes.
136 My eyes shed streams of tears,
because men do not keep thy law.

137 Righteous art thou, O LORD,
and right are thy judgments.
138 Thou hast appointed thy testimonies in righteousness
and in all faithfulness.
139 My zeal consumes me,
because my foes forget thy words.
140 Thy promise is well tried,
and thy servant loves it.
141 I am small and despised,
yet I do not forget thy precepts.
142 Thy righteousness is righteous for ever,
and thy law is true.
143 Trouble and anguish have come upon me,
but thy commandments are my delight.
144 Thy testimonies are righteous for ever;
give me understanding that I may live.

145 With my whole heart I cry; answer me, O LORD!
I will keep thy statutes.
146 I cry to thee; save me,
that I may observe thy testimonies.
147 I rise before dawn and cry for help;
I hope in thy words.
148 My eyes are awake before the watches of the night,
that I may meditate upon thy promise.
149 Hear my voice in thy steadfast love;
O LORD, in thy justice preserve my life.
150 They draw near who persecute me with evil purpose;
they are far from thy law.
151 But thou art near, O LORD,
and all thy commandments are true.
152 Long have I known from thy testimonies
that thou hast founded them for ever.

153 Look on my affliction and deliver me,
for I do not forget thy law.
154 Plead my cause and redeem me;
give me life according to thy promise!
155 Salvation is far from the wicked,

[k] Gk Jerome: Heb uncertain

for they do not seek thy statutes.
156 Great is thy mercy, O LORD;
give me life according to thy justice.
157 Many are my persecutors and my adversaries,
but I do not swerve from thy testimonies.
158 I look at the faithless with disgust,
because they do not keep thy commands.
159 Consider how I love thy precepts!
Preserve my life according to thy steadfast love.
160 The sum of thy word is truth;
and every one of thy righteous ordinances endures for ever.

161 Princes persecute me without cause,
but my heart stands in awe of thy words.
162 I rejoice at thy word
like one who finds great spoil.
163 I hate and abhor falsehood,
but I love thy law.
164 Seven times a day I praise thee
for thy righteous ordinances.
165 Great peace have those who love thy law;
nothing can make them stumble.
166 I hope for thy salvation, O LORD,
and I do thy commandments.
167 My soul keeps thy testimonies;
I love them exceedingly.
168 I keep thy precepts and testimonies,
for all my ways are before thee.

169 Let my cry come before thee, O LORD;
give me understanding according to thy word!
170 Let my supplication come before thee;
deliver me according to thy word.
171 My lips will pour forth praise
that thou dost teach me thy statutes.
172 My tongue will sing of thy word,
for all thy commandments are right.
173 Let thy hand be ready to help me,
for I have chosen thy precepts.
174 I long for thy salvation, O LORD,
and thy law is my delight.
175 Let me live, that I may praise thee,
and let thy ordinances help me.
176 I have gone astray like a lost sheep;
seek thy servant,
for I do not forget thy commandments.

A Song of Ascents.

120 In my distress I cry to the LORD,
that he may answer me:
2 "Deliver me, O LORD,
from lying lips,
from a deceitful tongue."

3 What shall be given to you?
And what more shall be done to you,
you deceitful tongue?
4 A warrior's sharp arrows,
with glowing coals of the broom tree!

5 Woe is me, that I sojourn in Mē'shech,
that I dwell among the tents of Kē'där!
6 Too long have I had my dwelling
among those who hate peace.
7 I am for peace;
but when I speak,
they are for war!

A Song of Ascents.

121 I lift up my eyes to the hills.
From whence does my help come?
2 My help comes from the LORD,
who made heaven and earth.

3 He will not let your foot be moved,
he who keeps you will not slumber.
4 Behold, he who keeps Israel
will neither slumber nor sleep.

5 The LORD is your keeper;
the LORD is your shade
on your right hand.
6 The sun shall not smite you by day,
nor the moon by night.

7 The LORD will keep you from all evil;
he will keep your life.
8 The LORD will keep
your going out and your coming in
from this time forth and for evermore.

A Song of Ascents. Of David.

122 I was glad when they said to me,
"Let us go to the house of the LORD!"
2 Our feet have been standing
within your gates, O Jerusalem!

3 Jerusalem, built as a city
which is bound firmly together,
4 to which the tribes go up,
the tribes of the LORD,
as was decreed for Israel,
to give thanks to the name of the LORD.
5 There thrones for judgment were set,
the thrones of the house of David.

6 Pray for the peace of Jerusalem!
"May they prosper who love you!
7 Peace be within your walls,
and security within your towers!"
8 For my brethren and companions' sake
I will say, "Peace be within you!"
9 For the sake of the house of the LORD our God,
I will seek your good.

A Song of Ascents.

123 To thee I lift up my eyes,
O thou who art enthroned in the heavens!
2 Behold, as the eyes of servants
look to the hand of their master,
as the eyes of a maid
to the hand of her mistress,
so our eyes look to the LORD our God,
till he have mercy upon us.

3 Have mercy upon us, O LORD, have mercy upon us,
for we have had more than enough of contempt.
4 Too long our soul has been sated
with the scorn of those who are at ease,
the contempt of the proud.

A Song of Ascents. Of David.

124 If it had not been the LORD who was on our side,
let Israel now say—
2 if it had not been the LORD who was on our side,
when men rose up against us,
3 then they would have swallowed us up alive,
when their anger was kindled against us;
4 then the flood would have swept us away,
the torrent would have gone over us;
5 then over us would have gone the raging waters.

6 Blessed be the LORD,
who has not given us
as prey to their teeth!
7 We have escaped as a bird
from the snare of the fowlers;
the snare is broken,
and we have escaped!

8 Our help is in the name of the LORD,
who made heaven and earth.

A Song of Ascents.

125 Those who trust in the LORD are like Mount Zion,
which cannot be moved, but abides for ever.
2 As the mountains are round about Jerusalem,
so the LORD is round about his people,
from this time forth and for evermore.
3 For the scepter of wickedness shall not rest
upon the land allotted to the righteous,
lest the righteous put forth
their hands to do wrong.
4 Do good, O LORD, to those who are good,
and to those who are upright in their hearts!
5 But those who turn aside upon their crooked ways
the LORD will lead away with evildoers!
Peace be in Israel!

A Song of Ascents.

126 When the LORD restored the fortunes of Zion,[l]
we were like those who dream.

[l] Or *brought back those who returned to Zion*

2 Then our mouth was filled with laughter,
and our tongue with shouts of joy;
then they said among the nations,
"The LORD has done great things for them."
3 The LORD has done great things for us;
we are glad.

4 Restore our fortunes, O LORD,
like the watercourses in the Negeb!
5 May those who sow in tears
reap with shouts of joy!
6 He that goes forth weeping,
bearing the seed for sowing,
shall come home with shouts of joy,
bringing his sheaves with him.

A Song of Ascents. Of Solomon.

127 Unless the LORD builds the house,
those who build it labor in vain.
Unless the LORD watches over the city,
the watchman stays awake in vain.
2 It is in vain that you rise up early
and go late to rest,
eating the bread of anxious toil;
for[m] he gives to his beloved sleep.

3 Lo, sons are a heritage from the LORD,
the fruit of the womb a reward.
4 Like arrows in the hand of a warrior
are the sons of one's youth.
5 Happy is the man who has
his quiver full of them!
He shall not be put to shame
when he speaks with his enemies in the gate.

A Song of Ascents.

128 Blessed is every one who fears the LORD,
who walks in his ways!
2 You shall eat the fruit of the labor of your hands;
you shall be happy, and it shall be well with you.
3 Your wife will be like a fruitful vine
within your house;
your children will be like olive shoots
around your table.
4 Lo, thus shall the man be blessed
who fears the LORD.

5 The LORD bless you from Zion!
May you see the prosperity of Jerusalem
all the days of your life!
6 May you see your children's children!
Peace be upon Israel!

A Song of Ascents.

129 "Sorely have they afflicted me from my youth,"
let Israel now say—
2 "Sorely have they afflicted me from my youth,
yet they have not prevailed against me.
3 The plowers plowed upon my back;
they made long their furrows."
4 The LORD is righteous;
he has cut the cords of the wicked.
5 May all who hate Zion
be put to shame and turned backward!
6 Let them be like the grass on the housetops,
which withers before it grows up,
7 with which the reaper does not fill his hand
or the binder of sheaves his bosom,
8 while those who pass by do not say,
"The blessing of the LORD be upon you!
We bless you in the name of the LORD!"

A Song of Ascents.

130 Out of the depths I cry to thee, O LORD!
2 Lord, hear my voice!
Let thy ears be attentive
to the voice of my supplications!

3 If thou, O LORD, shouldst mark iniquities,
Lord, who could stand?

[m] Another reading is *so*
130.3: Ps 143.2; Rom 3.20; Gal 2.16.

4 But there is forgiveness with thee,
that thou mayest be feared.

5 I wait for the LORD, my soul waits,
and in his word I hope;
6 my soul waits for the LORD
more than watchmen for the morning,
more than watchmen for the morning.

7 O Israel, hope in the LORD!
For with the LORD there is steadfast love,
and with him is plenteous redemption.
8 And he will redeem Israel
from all his iniquities.

A Song of Ascents. Of David.

131 O LORD, my heart is not lifted up,
my eyes are not raised too high;
I do not occupy myself with things
too great and too marvelous for me.
2 But I have calmed and quieted my soul,
like a child quieted at its mother's breast;
like a child that is quieted is my soul.

3 O Israel, hope in the LORD
from this time forth and for evermore.

A Song of Ascents.

132 Remember, O LORD, in David's favor,
all the hardships he endured;
2 how he swore to the LORD
and vowed to the Mighty One of Jacob,
3 "I will not enter my house
or get into my bed;
4 I will not give sleep to my eyes
or slumber to my eyelids,
5 until I find a place for the LORD,
a dwelling place for the Mighty One of Jacob."

6 Lo, we heard of it in Eph'ra·thah,
we found it in the fields of Jā'är.
7 "Let us go to his dwelling place;
let us worship at his footstool!"

8 Arise, O LORD, and go to thy resting place,
thou and the ark of thy might.
9 Let thy priests be clothed with righteousness,
and let thy saints shout for joy.
10 For thy servant David's sake
do not turn away the face of thy anointed one.

11 The LORD swore to David a sure oath
from which he will not turn back:
"One of the sons of your body
I will set on your throne.
12 If your sons keep my covenant
and my testimonies which I shall teach them,
their sons also for ever
shall sit upon your throne."

13 For the LORD has chosen Zion;
he has desired it for his habitation:
14 "This is my resting place for ever;
here I will dwell, for I have desired it.
15 I will abundantly bless her provisions;
I will satisfy her poor with bread.
16 Her priests I will clothe with salvation,
and her saints will shout for joy.
17 There I will make a horn to sprout for David;
I have prepared a lamp for my anointed.
18 His enemies I will clothe with shame,
but upon himself his crown will shed its luster."

A Song of Ascents.

133 Behold, how good and pleasant it is
when brothers dwell in unity!
2 It is like the precious oil upon the head,
running down upon the beard,
upon the beard of Aaron,
running down on the collar of his robes!
3 It is like the dew of Hēr'mòn,
which falls on the mountains of Zion!
For there the LORD has commanded the blessing,
life for evermore.

132.11: Ps 89.3-4; Acts 2.30.

A Song of Ascents.

134 Come, bless the LORD,
all you servants of the LORD,
who stand by night in the house
of the LORD!
2 Lift up your hands to the holy place,
and bless the LORD!

3 May the LORD bless you from Zion,
he who made heaven and earth!

135 Praise the LORD.
Praise the name of the LORD,
give praise, O servants of the
LORD,
2 you that stand in the house of the
LORD,
in the courts of the house of our
God!
3 Praise the LORD, for the LORD is
good;
sing to his name, for he is gracious!
4 For the LORD has chosen Jacob for
himself,
Israel as his own possession.

5 For I know that the LORD is great,
and that our Lord is above all
gods.
6 Whatever the LORD pleases he does,
in heaven and on earth,
in the seas and all deeps.
7 He it is who makes the clouds rise
at the end of the earth,
who makes lightnings for the rain
and brings forth the wind from
his storehouses.

8 He it was who smote the first-born
of Egypt,
both of man and of beast;
9 who in thy midst, O Egypt,
sent signs and wonders
against Pharaoh and all his
servants;
10 who smote many nations
and slew mighty kings,
11 Sī'hon, king of the Am'ŏ·rītes,
and Og, king of Bā'shȧn,
and all the kingdoms of Canaan,
12 and gave their land as a heritage,
a heritage to his people Israel.

13 Thy name, O LORD, endures for
ever,
thy renown, O LORD, throughout
all ages.
14 For the LORD will vindicate his
people,
and have compassion on his
servants.

15 The idols of the nations are silver
and gold,
the work of men's hands.
16 They have mouths, but they speak
not,
they have eyes, but they see not,
17 they have ears, but they hear not,
nor is there any breath in their
mouths.
18 Like them be those who make
them!—
yea, every one who trusts in them!

19 O house of Israel, bless the LORD!
O house of Aaron, bless the LORD!
20 O house of Levi, bless the LORD!
You that fear the LORD, bless the
LORD!
21 Blessed be the LORD from Zion,
he who dwells in Jerusalem!
Praise the LORD!

136 O give thanks to the LORD,
for he is good,
for his steadfast love endures for
ever.
2 O give thanks to the God of gods,
for his steadfast love endures for
ever.
3 O give thanks to the Lord of lords,
for his steadfast love endures for
ever;

4 to him who alone does great wonders,
for his steadfast love endures for
ever;
5 to him who by understanding made
the heavens,
for his steadfast love endures for
ever;
6 to him who spread out the earth
upon the waters,
for his steadfast love endures for
ever;
7 to him who made the great lights,
for his steadfast love endures for
ever;
8 the sun to rule over the day,
for his steadfast love endures for
ever;
9 the moon and stars to rule over the
night,
for his steadfast love endures for
ever;

10 to him who smote the first-born of
Egypt,

135.14: Heb 10.30. **135.15-18:** Ps 115.4-8.

for his steadfast love endures for
ever;
11 and brought Israel out from among
them,
for his steadfast love endures for
ever;
12 with a strong hand and an outstretched arm,
for his steadfast love endures for
ever;
13 to him who divided the Red Sea in
sunder,
for his steadfast love endures for
ever;
14 and made Israel pass through the
midst of it,
for his steadfast love endures for
ever;
15 but overthrew Pharaoh and his host
in the Red Sea,
for his steadfast love endures for
ever;
16 to him who led his people through
the wilderness,
for his steadfast love endures for
ever;
17 to him who smote great kings,
for his steadfast love endures for
ever;
18 and slew famous kings,
for his steadfast love endures for
ever;
19 Sī'hon, king of the Am'ŏ-rītes,
for his steadfast love endures for
ever;
20 and Og, king of Bā'shăn,
for his steadfast love endures for
ever;
21 and gave their land as a heritage,
for his steadfast love endures for
ever;
22 a heritage to Israel his servant,
for his steadfast love endures for
ever.

23 It is he who remembered us in our
low estate,
for his steadfast love endures for
ever;
24 and rescued us from our foes,
for his steadfast love endures for
ever;
25 he who gives food to all flesh,
for his steadfast love endures for
ever.

26 O give thanks to the God of heaven,
for his steadfast love endures for
ever.

137 By the waters[o] of Babylon,
there we sat down and wept,
when we remembered Zion.
2 On the willows[p] there
we hung up our lyres.
3 For there our captors
required of us songs,
and our tormentors, mirth, saying,
"Sing us one of the songs of
Zion!"

4 How shall we sing the LORD's song
in a foreign land?
5 If I forget you, O Jerusalem,
let my right hand wither!
6 Let my tongue cleave to the roof of
my mouth,
if I do not remember you,
if I do not set Jerusalem
above my highest joy!

7 Remember, O LORD, against the
E'dŏm-ītes
the day of Jerusalem,
how they said, "Rase it, rase it!
Down to its foundations!"
8 O daughter of Babylon, you dev-
astator![q]
Happy shall he be who requites
you
with what you have done to us!
9 Happy shall he be who takes your
little ones
and dashes them against the rock!

A Psalm of David.

138 I give thee thanks, O LORD,
with my whole heart;
before the gods I sing thy praise;
2 I bow down toward thy holy temple
and give thanks to thy name for
thy steadfast love and thy
faithfulness;
for thou hast exalted above everything
thy name and thy word.[r]
3 On the day I called, thou didst
answer me,
my strength of soul thou didst
increase.[s]

4 All the kings of the earth shall praise
thee, O LORD,

[o] Heb *streams* [p] Or *poplars* [q] Or *you who are devastated*
[r] Cn: Heb *thou hast exalted thy word above all thy name*
[s] Syr Compare Gk Tg: Heb *thou didst make me arrogant in my soul* with *strength*

for they have heard the words of thy mouth;
5 and they shall sing of the ways of the LORD,
for great is the glory of the LORD.
6 For though the LORD is high, he regards the lowly;
but the haughty he knows from afar.

7 Though I walk in the midst of trouble,
thou dost preserve my life;
thou dost stretch out thy hand against the wrath of my enemies,
and thy right hand delivers me.
8 The LORD will fulfil his purpose for me;
thy steadfast love, O LORD, endures for ever.
Do not forsake the work of thy hands.

To the choirmaster. A Psalm of David.

139 O LORD, thou hast searched me and known me!
2 Thou knowest when I sit down and when I rise up;
thou discernest my thoughts from afar.
3 Thou searchest out my path and my lying down,
and art acquainted with all my ways.
4 Even before a word is on my tongue,
lo, O LORD, thou knowest it altogether.
5 Thou dost beset me behind and before,
and layest thy hand upon me.
6 Such knowledge is too wonderful for me;
it is high, I cannot attain it.

7 Whither shall I go from thy Spirit?
Or whither shall I flee from thy presence?
8 If I ascend to heaven, thou art there!
If I make my bed in Shē'ōl, thou art there!
9 If I take the wings of the morning
and dwell in the uttermost parts of the sea,
10 even there thy hand shall lead me,
and thy right hand shall hold me.
11 If I say, "Let only darkness cover me,
and the light about me be night,"
12 even the darkness is not dark to thee,
the night is bright as the day;
for darkness is as light with thee.

13 For thou didst form my inward parts,
thou didst knit me together in my mother's womb.
14 I praise thee, for thou art fearful and wonderful.[t]
Wonderful are thy works!
Thou knowest me right well;
15 my frame was not hidden from thee,
when I was being made in secret,
intricately wrought in the depths of the earth.
16 Thy eyes beheld my unformed substance;
in thy book were written, every one of them,
the days that were formed for me,
when as yet there was none of them.
17 How precious to me are thy thoughts, O God!
How vast is the sum of them!
18 If I would count them, they are more than the sand.
When I awake, I am still with thee.[u]

19 O that thou wouldst slay the wicked, O God,
and that men of blood would depart from me,
20 men who maliciously defy thee,
who lift themselves up against thee for evil![v]
21 Do I not hate them that hate thee, O LORD?
And do I not loathe them that rise up against thee?
22 I hate them with perfect hatred;
I count them my enemies.
23 Search me, O God, and know my heart!
Try me and know my thoughts!
24 And see if there be any wicked[w] way in me,
and lead me in the way everlasting![x]

[t] Cn Compare Gk Syr Jerome: Heb *fearful things I am wonderful*
[u] Or *were I to come to the end I would still be with thee* [v] Cn: Heb uncertain [w] Heb *hurtful*
[x] Or *the ancient way*. Compare Jer 6.16.

To the choirmaster. A Psalm of David.

140 Deliver me, O LORD, from evil men;
preserve me from violent men,
2 who plan evil things in their heart,
and stir up wars continually.
3 They make their tongue sharp as a serpent's,
and under their lips is the poison of vipers.
Selah

4 Guard me, O LORD, from the hands of the wicked;
preserve me from violent men,
who have planned to trip up my feet.
5 Arrogant men have hidden a trap for me,
and with cords they have spread a net,[y]
by the wayside they have set snares for me. *Selah*

6 I say to the LORD, Thou art my God;
give ear to the voice of my supplications, O LORD!
7 O LORD, my Lord, my strong deliverer,
thou hast covered my head in the day of battle.
8 Grant not, O LORD, the desires of the wicked;
do not further his evil plot!
Selah

9 Those who surround me lift up their head,[z]
let the mischief of their lips overwhelm them!
10 Let burning coals fall upon them!
Let them be cast into pits, no more to rise!
11 Let not the slanderer be established in the land;
let evil hunt down the violent man speedily!

12 I know that the LORD maintains the cause of the afflicted,
and executes justice for the needy.
13 Surely the righteous shall give thanks to thy name;
the upright shall dwell in thy presence.

A Psalm of David.

141 I call upon thee, O LORD; make haste to me!
Give ear to my voice, when I call to thee!
2 Let my prayer be counted as incense before thee,
and the lifting up of my hands as an evening sacrifice!

3 Set a guard over my mouth, O LORD,
keep watch over the door of my lips!
4 Incline not my heart to any evil,
to busy myself with wicked deeds
in company with men who work iniquity;
and let me not eat of their dainties!

5 Let a good man strike or rebuke me in kindness,
but let the oil of the wicked never anoint my head;[a]
for my prayer is continually[b] against their wicked deeds.
6 When they are given over to those who shall condemn them,
then they shall learn that the word of the LORD is true.
7 As a rock which one cleaves and shatters on the land,
so shall their bones be strewn at the mouth of Shē'ōl.[c]

8 But my eyes are toward thee, O LORD God;
in thee I seek refuge; leave me not defenseless!
9 Keep me from the trap which they have laid for me,
and from the snares of evildoers!
10 Let the wicked together fall into their own nets,
while I escape.

A Maskil of David, when he was in the cave. A Prayer.

142 I cry with my voice to the LORD,
with my voice I make supplication to the LORD,
2 I pour out my complaint before him,
I tell my trouble before him.

[y] Or *they have spread cords as a net*
[z] Cn Compare Gk: Heb *those who surround me are uplifted in head* [a] Gk: Heb obscure
[b] Cn: Heb *for continually and my prayer* [c] The Hebrew of verses 5-7 is obscure
140.3: Rom 3.13. 141.2: Rev 5.8; 8.3-4.

3 When my spirit is faint,
thou knowest my way!

In the path where I walk
they have hidden a trap for me.
4 I look to the right and watch,[d]
but there is none who takes notice
of me;
no refuge remains to me,
no man cares for me.

5 I cry to thee, O LORD;
I say, Thou art my refuge,
my portion in the land of the
living.
6 Give heed to my cry;
for I am brought very low!

Deliver me from my persecutors;
for they are too strong for me!
7 Bring me out of prison,
that I may give thanks to thy
name!
The righteous will surround me;
for thou wilt deal bountifully
with me.

A Psalm of David.

143 Hear my prayer, O LORD;
give ear to my supplications!
In thy faithfulness answer me, in
thy righteousness!
2 Enter not into judgment with thy
servant;
for no man living is righteous before thee.

3 For the enemy has pursued me;
he has crushed my life to the
ground;
he has made me sit in darkness
like those long dead.
4 Therefore my spirit faints within
me;
my heart within me is appalled.

5 I remember the days of old,
I meditate on all that thou hast
done;
I muse on what thy hands have
wrought.
6 I stretch out my hands to thee;
my soul thirsts for thee like a
parched land. *Selah*

7 Make haste to answer me, O LORD!
My spirit fails!
Hide not thy face from me,
lest I be like those who go down
to the Pit.
8 Let me hear in the morning of thy
steadfast love,
for in thee I put my trust.
Teach me the way I should go,
for to thee I lift up my soul.

9 Deliver me, O LORD, from my
enemies!
I have fled to thee for refuge![e]
10 Teach me to do thy will,
for thou art my God!
Let thy good spirit lead me
on a level path!

11 For thy name's sake, O LORD, preserve my life!
In thy righteousness bring me out
of trouble!
12 And in thy steadfast love cut off my
enemies,
and destroy all my adversaries,
for I am thy servant.

A Psalm of David.

144 Blessed be the LORD, my
rock,
who trains my hands for war,
and my fingers for battle;
2 my rock[f] and my fortress,
my stronghold and my deliverer,
my shield and he in whom I take
refuge,
who subdues the peoples under
him.[g]

3 O LORD, what is man that thou dost
regard him,
or the son of man that thou dost
think of him?
4 Man is like a breath,
his days are like a passing shadow.

5 Bow thy heavens, O LORD, and
come down!
Touch the mountains that they
smoke!
6 Flash forth the lightning and scatter
them,
send out thy arrows and rout
them!
7 Stretch forth thy hand from on
high,

[d] Or *Look to the right and watch* [e] One Heb Ms Gk: Heb *to thee I have hidden*
[f] With 18.2 2 Sam 22.2: Heb *my steadfast love* [g] Another reading is *my people under me*
143.2: Ps 130.3; Rom 3.20; Gal 2.16.

rescue me and deliver me from
the many waters,
from the hand of aliens,
8 whose mouths speak lies,
and whose right hand is a right
hand of falsehood.

9 I will sing a new song to thee, O
God;
upon a ten-stringed harp I will
play to thee,
10 who givest victory to kings,
who rescuest David thy[h] servant.
11 Rescue me from the cruel sword,
and deliver me from the hand of
aliens,
whose mouths speak lies,
and whose right hand is a right
hand of falsehood.

12 May our sons in their youth
be like plants full grown,
our daughters like corner pillars
cut for the structure of a palace;
13 may our garners be full,
providing all manner of store;
may our sheep bring forth thousands
and ten thousands in our fields;
14 may our cattle be heavy with young,
suffering no mischance or failure
in bearing;
may there be no cry of distress in
our streets!
15 Happy the people to whom such
blessings fall!
Happy the people whose God is
the LORD!

A Song of Praise. Of David.

145 I will extol thee, my God and
King,
and bless thy name for ever and
ever.
2 Every day I will bless thee,
and praise thy name for ever and
ever.
3 Great is the LORD, and greatly to
be praised,
and his greatness is unsearchable.

4 One generation shall laud thy works
to another,
and shall declare thy mighty acts.
5 On the glorious splendor of thy
majesty,
and on thy wondrous works, I
will meditate.
6 Men shall proclaim the might of thy
terrible acts,
and I will declare thy greatness.
7 They shall pour fourth the fame of
thy abundant goodness,
and shall sing aloud of thy righteousness.

8 The LORD is gracious and merciful,
slow to anger and abounding in
steadfast love.
9 The LORD is good to all,
and his compassion is over all
that he has made.

10 All thy works shall give thanks to
thee, O LORD,
and all thy saints shall bless thee!
11 They shall speak of the glory of thy
kingdom,
and tell of thy power,
12 to make known to the sons of men
thy[h] mighty deeds,
and the glorious splendor of thy[h]
kingdom.
13 Thy kingdom is an everlasting kingdom,
and thy dominion endures
throughout all generations.

The LORD is faithful in all his words,
and gracious in all his deeds.[i]
14 The LORD upholds all who are
falling,
and raises up all who are bowed
down.
15 The eyes of all look to thee,
and thou givest them their food
in due season.
16 Thou openest thy hand,
thou satisfiest the desire of every
living thing.
17 The LORD is just in all his ways,
and kind in all his doings.
18 The LORD is near to all who call
upon him,
to all who call upon him in truth.
19 He fulfils the desire of all who fear
him,
he also hears their cry, and saves
them.
20 The LORD preserves all who love
him;
but all the wicked he will destroy.

21 My mouth will speak the praise of
the LORD,
and let all flesh bless his holy
name for ever and ever.

[h] Heb *his* [i] These two lines are supplied by one Hebrew Ms, Gk and Syr

146 Praise the LORD!
Praise the LORD, O my soul!
2 I will praise the LORD as long as I live;
I will sing praises to my God while I have being.

3 Put not your trust in princes,
in a son of man, in whom there is no help.
4 When his breath departs he returns to his earth;
on that very day his plans perish.

5 Happy is he whose help is the God of Jacob,
whose hope is in the LORD his God,
6 who made heaven and earth,
the sea, and all that is in them;
who keeps faith for ever;
7 who executes justice for the oppressed;
who gives food to the hungry.

The LORD sets the prisoners free;
8 the LORD opens the eyes of the blind.
The LORD lifts up those who are bowed down;
the LORD loves the righteous.
9 The LORD watches over the sojourners,
he upholds the widow and the fatherless;
but the way of the wicked he brings to ruin.

10 The LORD will reign for ever,
thy God, O Zion, to all generations.
Praise the LORD!

147 Praise the LORD!
For it is good to sing praises to our God;
for he is gracious, and a song of praise is seemly.
2 The LORD builds up Jerusalem;
he gathers the outcasts of Israel.
3 He heals the brokenhearted,
and binds up their wounds.
4 He determines the number of the stars,
he gives to all of them their names.
5 Great is our LORD, and abundant in power;
his understanding is beyond measure.
6 The LORD lifts up the downtrodden,
he casts the wicked to the ground.

7 Sing to the LORD with thanksgiving;
make melody to our God upon the lyre!
8 He covers the heavens with clouds,
he prepares rain for the earth,
he makes grass grow upon the hills.
9 He gives to the beasts their food,
and to the young ravens which cry.
10 His delight is not in the strength of the horse,
nor his pleasure in the legs of a man;
11 but the LORD takes pleasure in those who fear him,
in those who hope in his steadfast love.

12 Praise the LORD, O Jerusalem!
Praise your God, O Zion!
13 For he strengthens the bars of your gates;
he blesses your sons within you.
14 He makes peace in your borders;
he fills you with the finest of the wheat.
15 He sends forth his command to the earth;
his word runs swiftly.
16 He gives snow like wool;
he scatters hoarfrost like ashes.
17 He casts forth his ice like morsels;
who can stand before his cold?
18 He sends forth his word, and melts them;
he makes his wind blow, and the waters flow.
19 He declares his word to Jacob,
his statutes and ordinances to Israel.
20 He has not dealt thus with any other nation;
they do not know his ordinances.
Praise the LORD!

148 Praise the LORD!
Praise the LORD from the heavens,
praise him in the heights!
2 Praise him, all his angels,
praise him, all his host!

3 Praise him, sun and moon,
praise him, all you shining stars!
4 Praise him, you highest heavens,
and you waters above the heavens!

5 Let them praise the name of the LORD!

For he commanded and they were
created.
6 And he established them for ever
and ever;
he fixed their bounds which cannot be passed.[l]

7 Praise the LORD from the earth,
you sea monsters and all deeps,
8 fire and hail, snow and frost,
stormy wind fulfilling his command!

9 Mountains and all hills,
fruit trees and all cedars!
10 Beasts and all cattle,
creeping things and flying birds!

11 Kings of the earth and all peoples,
princes and all rulers of the earth!
12 Young men and maidens together,
old men and children!

13 Let them praise the name of the
LORD,
for his name alone is exalted;
his glory is above earth and
heaven.
14 He has raised up a horn for his
people,
praise for all his saints,
for the people of Israel who are
near to him.
Praise the LORD!

149 Praise the LORD!
Sing to the LORD a new song,
his praise in the assembly of the
faithful!
2 Let Israel be glad in his Maker,
let the sons of Zion rejoice in
their King!
3 Let them praise his name with
dancing,

[l] Or *he set a law which cannot pass away*

making melody to him with
timbrel and lyre!
4 For the LORD takes pleasure in his
people;
he adorns the humble with victory.
5 Let the faithful exult in glory;
let them sing for joy on their
couches.
6 Let the high praises of God be in
their throats
and two-edged swords in their
hands,
7 to wreak vengeance on the nations
and chastisement on the peoples,
8 to bind their kings with chains
and their nobles with fetters of
iron,
9 to execute on them the judgment
written!
This is glory for all his faithful
ones.
Praise the LORD!

150 Praise the LORD!
Praise God in his sanctuary;
praise him in his mighty firmament!
2 Praise him for his mighty deeds;
praise him according to his exceeding greatness!

3 Praise him with trumpet sound;
praise him with lute and harp!
4 Praise him with timbrel and dance;
praise him with strings and
pipe!
5 Praise him with sounding cymbals;
praise him with loud clashing
cymbals!
6 Let everything that breathes praise
the LORD!
Praise the LORD!

THE PROVERBS

1 The proverbs of Solomon, son of David, king of Israel:

2 That men may know wisdom and instruction,
understanding words of insight,
3 receive instruction in wise dealing,
righteousness, justice, and equity;
4 that prudence may be given to the simple,
knowledge and discretion to the youth—
5 the wise man also may hear and increase in learning,
and the man of understanding acquire skill,
6 to understand a proverb and a figure,
the words of the wise and their riddles.

7 The fear of the LORD is the beginning of knowledge;
fools despise wisdom and instruction.

8 Hear, my son, your father's instruction,
and reject not your mother's teaching;
9 for they are a fair garland for your head,
and pendants for your neck.
10 My son, if sinners entice you,
do not consent.
11 If they say, "Come with us, let us lie in wait for blood,
let us wantonly ambush the innocent;
12 like Shē'ōl let us swallow them alive
and whole, like those who go down to the Pit;
13 we shall find all precious goods,
we shall fill our houses with spoil;
14 throw in your lot among us,
we will all have one purse"—
15 my son, do not walk in the way with them,
hold back your foot from their paths;
16 for their feet run to evil,
and they make haste to shed blood.
17 For in vain is a net spread
in the sight of any bird;
18 but these men lie in wait for their own blood,
they set an ambush for their own lives.
19 Such are the ways of all who get gain by violence;
it takes away the life of its possessors.

20 Wisdom cries aloud in the street;
in the markets she raises her voice;
21 on the top of the walls[a] she cries out;
at the entrance of the city gates she speaks:
22 "How long, O simple ones, will you love being simple?
How long will scoffers delight in their scoffing
and fools hate knowledge?
23 Give heed[b] to my reproof;
behold, I will pour out my thoughts[c] to you;
I will make my words known to you.
24 Because I have called and you refused to listen,
have stretched out my hand and no one has heeded,
25 and you have ignored all my counsel
and would have none of my reproof,
26 I also will laugh at your calamity;
I will mock when panic strikes you,
27 when panic strikes you like a storm,
and your calamity comes like a whirlwind,
when distress and anguish come upon you.
28 Then they will call upon me, but I will not answer;
they will seek me diligently but will not find me.
29 Because they hated knowledge
and did not choose the fear of the LORD,
30 would have none of my counsel,
and despised all my reproof,
31 therefore they shall eat the fruit of their way

[a] Heb uncertain [b] Heb *Turn* [c] Heb *spirit*
1.20-21: Prov 8.1-3.

and be sated with their own devices.
32 For the simple are killed by their
turning away,
and the complacence of fools destroys them;
33 but he who listens to me will dwell
secure
and will be at ease, without dread
of evil."

2 My son, if you receive my words
and treasure up my commandments with you,
2 making your ear attentive to wisdom
and inclining your heart to understanding;
3 yes, if you cry out for insight
and raise your voice for understanding,
4 if you seek it like silver
and search for it as for hidden
treasures;
5 then you will understand the fear
of the LORD
and find the knowledge of God.
6 For the LORD gives wisdom;
from his mouth come knowledge
and understanding;
7 he stores up sound wisdom for the
upright;
he is a shield to those who walk
in integrity,
8 guarding the paths of justice
and preserving the way of his
saints.
9 Then you will understand righteousness and justice
and equity, every good path;
10 for wisdom will come into your
heart,
and knowledge will be pleasant to
your soul;
11 discretion will watch over you;
understanding will guard you;
12 delivering you from the way of evil,
from men of perverted speech,
13 who forsake the paths of uprightness
to walk in the ways of darkness,
14 who rejoice in doing evil
and delight in the perverseness of
evil;
15 men whose paths are crooked,
and who are devious in their ways.

16 You will be saved from the loose[d]
woman,
from the adventuress[e] with her
smooth words,
17 who forsakes the companion of her
youth
and forgets the covenant of her
God;
18 for her house sinks down to death,
and her paths to the shades;
19 none who go to her come back
nor do they regain the paths of life.

20 So you will walk in the way of good
men
and keep to the paths of the
righteous.
21 For the upright will inhabit the land,
and men of integrity will remain
in it;
22 but the wicked will be cut off from
the land,
and the treacherous will be rooted
out of it.

3 My son, do not forget my teaching,
but let your heart keep my commandments;
2 for length of days and years of life
and abundant welfare will they
give you.

3 Let not loyalty and faithfulness forsake you;
bind them about your neck,
write them on the tablet of your
heart.
4 So you will find favor and good
repute[f]
in the sight of God and man.

5 Trust in the LORD with all your
heart,
and do not rely on your own
insight.
6 In all your ways acknowledge him,
and he will make straight your
paths.
7 Be not wise in your own eyes;
fear the LORD, and turn away
from evil.
8 It will be healing to your flesh[g]
and refreshment[h] to your bones.

9 Honor the LORD with your substance
and with the first fruits of all
your produce;
10 then your barns will be filled with
plenty,
and your vats will be bursting
with wine.

[d] Heb *strange* [e] Heb *foreign woman* [f] Cn: Heb *understanding* [g] Heb *navel* [h] Or *medicine*
3.4: Rom 12.17. **3.7:** Rom 12.16.

11 My son, do not despise the LORD's discipline
or be weary of his reproof,
12 for the LORD reproves him whom he loves,
as a father the son in whom he delights.

13 Happy is the man who finds wisdom,
and the man who gets understanding,
14 for the gain from it is better than gain from silver
and its profit better than gold.
15 She is more precious than jewels,
and nothing you desire can compare with her.
16 Long life is in her right hand;
in her left hand are riches and honor.
17 Her ways are ways of pleasantness,
and all her paths are peace.
18 She is a tree of life to those who lay hold of her;
those who hold her fast are called happy.

19 The LORD by wisdom founded the earth;
by understanding he established the heavens;
20 by his knowledge the deeps broke forth,
and the clouds drop down the dew.

21 My son, keep sound wisdom and discretion;
let them not escape from your sight,[i]
22 and they will be life for your soul
and adornment for your neck.
23 Then you will walk on your way securely
and your foot will not stumble.
24 If you sit down,[j] you will not be afraid;
when you lie down, your sleep will be sweet.
25 Do not be afraid of sudden panic,
or of the ruin[k] of the wicked, when it comes;
26 for the LORD will be your confidence
and will keep your foot from being caught.
27 Do not withhold good from those to whom it[l] is due,
when it is in your power to do it.
28 Do not say to your neighbor, "Go, and come again,
tomorrow I will give it"—when you have it with you.
29 Do not plan evil against your neighbor
who dwells trustingly beside you.
30 Do not contend with a man for no reason,
when he has done you no harm.
31 Do not envy a man of violence
and do not choose any of his ways;
32 for the perverse man is an abomination to the LORD,
but the upright are in his confidence.
33 The LORD's curse is on the house of the wicked,
but he blesses the abode of the righteous.
34 Toward the scorners he is scornful,
but to the humble he shows favor.
35 The wise will inherit honor,
but fools get[m] disgrace.

4 Hear, O sons, a father's instruction,
and be attentive, that you may gain[n] insight;
2 for I give you good precepts;
do not forsake my teaching.
3 When I was a son with my father,
tender, the only one in the sight of my mother,
4 he taught me, and said to me,
"Let your heart hold fast my words;
keep my commandments, and live;
5 do not forget, and do not turn away from the words of my mouth.
Get wisdom; get insight.[o]
6 Do not forsake her, and she will keep you;
love her, and she will guard you.
7 The beginning of wisdom is this: Get wisdom,
and whatever you get, get insight.
8 Prize her highly,[p] and she will exalt you;
she will honor you if you embrace her.
9 She will place on your head a fair garland;

[i] Reversing the order of the clauses [j] Gk: Heb *lie down* [k] Heb *storm*
[l] Heb *Do not withhold good from its owners* [m] Cn: Heb *exalt* [n] Heb *know*
[o] Reversing the order of the lines [p] The meaning of the Hebrew is uncertain
3.11-12: Heb 12.5-6. **3.34 (Gk):** Jas 4.6; 1 Pet 5.5.

she will bestow on you a beautiful
crown."

10 Hear, my son, and accept my words,
that the years of your life may be
many.
11 I have taught you the way of wisdom;
I have led you in the paths of
uprightness.
12 When you walk, your step will not
be hampered;
and if you run, you will not
stumble.
13 Keep hold of instruction, do not let
go;
guard her, for she is your life.
14 Do not enter the path of the wicked,
and do not walk in the way of
evil men.
15 Avoid it; do not go on it;
turn away from it and pass on.
16 For they cannot sleep unless they
have done wrong;
they are robbed of sleep unless
they have made some one
stumble.
17 For they eat the bread of wickedness
and drink the wine of violence.
18 But the path of the righteous is like
the light of dawn,
which shines brighter and brighter
until full day.
19 The way of the wicked is like deep
darkness;
they do not know over what they
stumble.

20 My son, be attentive to my words;
incline your ear to my sayings.
21 Let them not escape from your
sight;
keep them within your heart.
22 For they are life to him who finds
them,
and healing to all his flesh.
23 Keep your heart with all vigilance;
for from it flow the springs of
life.
24 Put away from you crooked speech,
and put devious talk far from you.
25 Let your eyes look directly forward,
and your gaze be straight before
you.
26 Take heed to[q] the path of your feet,
then all your ways will be sure.
27 Do not swerve to the right or to the
left;
turn your foot away from evil.

5 My son, be attentive to my wisdom,
incline your ear to my understanding;
2 that you may keep discretion,
and your lips may guard knowledge.
3 For the lips of a loose woman drip
honey,
and her speech[r] is smoother than
oil;
4 but in the end she is bitter as wormwood,
sharp as a two-edged sword.
5 Her feet go down to death;
her steps follow the path to[s] Shē'ōl;
6 she does not take heed to[t] the path
of life;
her ways wander, and she does
not know it.

7 And now, O sons, listen to me,
and do not depart from the words
of my mouth.
8 Keep your way far from her,
and do not go near the door of her
house;
9 lest you give your honor to others
and your years to the merciless;
10 lest strangers take their fill of your
strength,[u]
and your labors go to the house
of an alien;
11 and at the end of your life you groan,
when your flesh and body are
consumed,
12 and you say, "How I hated discipline,
and my heart despised reproof!
13 I did not listen to the voice of my
teachers
or incline my ear to my instruc-
tors.
14 I was at the point of utter ruin
in the assembled congregation."

15 Drink water from your own cistern,
flowing water from your own well.
16 Should your springs be scattered
abroad,
streams of water in the streets?
17 Let them be for yourself alone,
and not for strangers with you.
18 Let your fountain be blessed,
and rejoice in the wife of your
youth,
19 a lovely hind, a graceful doe.
Let her affection fill you at all times
with delight,

[q] The meaning of the Hebrew word is uncertain [r] Heb *palate* [s] Heb *lay hold of*
[t] The meaning of the Hebrew word is uncertain [u] Or *wealth*
4.26 (Gk): Heb 12.13.

be infatuated always with her
love.
20 Why should you be infatuated, my
son, with a loose woman
and embrace the bosom of an
adventuress?
21 For a man's ways are before the
eyes of the LORD,
and he watches[v] all his paths.
22 The iniquities of the wicked ensnare him,
and he is caught in the toils of his
sin.
23 He dies for lack of discipline,
and because of his great folly he
is lost.

6 My son, if you have become surety
for your neighbor,
have given your pledge for a
stranger;
2 if you are snared in the utterance
of your lips,[w]
caught in the words of your
mouth;
3 then do this, my son, and save
yourself,
for you have come into your
neighbor's power:
go, hasten,[x] and importune your
neighbor.
4 Give your eyes no sleep
and your eyelids no slumber;
5 save yourself like a gazelle from the
hunter,[y]
like a bird from the hand of the
fowler.

6 Go to the ant, O sluggard;
consider her ways, and be wise.
7 Without having any chief,
officer or ruler,
8 she prepares her food in summer,
and gathers her sustenance in
harvest.
9 How long will you lie there, O
sluggard?
When will you arise from your
sleep?
10 A little sleep, a little slumber,
a little folding of the hands to
rest,
11 and poverty will come upon you
like a vagabond,
and want like an armed man.

12 A worthless person, a wicked man,
goes about with crooked speech,
13 winks with his eyes, scrapes[z] with
his feet,
points with his finger,
14 with perverted heart devises evil,
continually sowing discord;
15 therefore calamity will come upon
him suddenly;
in a moment he will be broken
beyond healing.

16 There are six things which the
LORD hates,
seven which are an abomination
to him:
17 haughty eyes, a lying tongue,
and hands that shed innocent
blood,
18 a heart that devises wicked plans,
feet that make haste to run to
evil,
19 a false witness who breathes out lies,
and a man who sows discord
among brothers.

20 My son, keep your father's commandment,
and forsake not your mother's
teaching.
21 Bind them upon your heart always;
tie them about your neck.
22 When you walk, they[a] will lead
you;
when you lie down, they[a] will
watch over you;
and when you awake, they[a] will
talk with you.
23 For the commandment is a lamp
and the teaching a light,
and the reproofs of discipline are
the way of life,
24 to preserve you from the evil
woman,
from the smooth tongue of the
adventuress.
25 Do not desire her beauty in your
heart,
and do not let her capture you
with her eyelashes;
26 for a harlot may be hired for a loaf
of bread,[b]
but an adulteress[c] stalks a man's
very life.
27 Can a man carry fire in his bosom
and his clothes not be burned?
28 Or can one walk upon hot coals
and his feet not be scorched?
29 So is he who goes in to his neighbor's wife;

[v] The meaning of the Hebrew word is uncertain [w] Cn Compare Gk Syr: Heb *the words of your mouth*
[x] Or *humble yourself* [y] Cn: Heb *hand* [z] Or *taps* [a] Heb *it*
[b] Cn Compare Gk Syr Vg Tg: Heb *for because of a harlot to a piece of bread* [c] Heb *a man's wife*

none who touches her will go
unpunished.
30 Do not men despise[d] a thief if he
steals
to satisfy his appetite when he is
hungry?
31 And if he is caught, he will pay
sevenfold;
he will give all the goods of his
house.
32 He who commits adultery has no
sense;
he who does it destroys himself.
33 Wounds and dishonor will he get,
and his disgrace will not be wiped
away.
34 For jealousy makes a man furious,
and he will not spare when he
takes revenge.
35 He will accept no compensation,
nor be appeased though you
multiply gifts.

7 My son, keep my words
and treasure up my commandments with you;
2 keep my commandments and live,
keep my teachings as the apple
of your eye;
3 bind them on your fingers,
write them on the tablet of your
heart.
4 Say to wisdom, "You are my sister,"
and call insight your intimate
friend;
5 to preserve you from the loose
woman,
from the adventuress with her
smooth words.

6 For at the window of my house
I have looked out through my
lattice,
7 and I have seen among the simple,
I have perceived among the
youths,
a young man without sense,
8 passing along the street near her
corner,
taking the road to her house
9 in the twilight, in the evening,
at the time of night and darkness.

10 And lo, a woman meets him,
dressed as a harlot, wily of heart.[e]
11 She is loud and wayward,
her feet do not stay at home;
12 now in the street, now in the market,
and at every corner she lies in
wait.
13 She seizes him and kisses him,
and with impudent face she says
to him:
14 "I had to offer sacrifices,
and today I have paid my vows;
15 so now I have come out to meet you,
to seek you eagerly, and I have
found you.
16 I have decked my couch with
coverings,
colored spreads of Egyptian linen;
17 I have perfumed my bed with myrrh,
aloes, and cinnamon.
18 Come, let us take our fill of love till
morning;
let us delight ourselves with love.
19 For my husband is not at home;
he has gone on a long journey;
20 he took a bag of money with him;
at full moon he will come home."

21 With much seductive speech she
persuades him;
with her smooth talk she compels
him.
22 All at once he follows her,
as an ox goes to the slaughter,
or as a stag is caught fast[f]
23 till an arrow pierces its entrails;
as a bird rushes into a snare;
he does not know that it will cost
him his life.

24 And now, O sons, listen to me,
and be attentive to the words of
my mouth.
25 Let not your heart turn aside to her
ways,
do not stray into her paths;
26 for many a victim has she laid low;
yea, all her slain are a mighty
host.
27 Her house is the way to Shē'ōl,
going down to the chambers of
death.

8 Does not wisdom call,
does not understanding raise her
voice?
2 On the heights beside the way,
in the paths she takes her stand;
3 beside the gates in front of the town,
at the entrance of the portals she
cries aloud:
4 "To you, O men, I call,
and my cry is to the sons of men.

[d] Or *Men do not despise* [e] The meaning of the Hebrew is uncertain
[f] Cn Compare Gk: Heb uncertain
8.1-3: Prov 1.20-21.

5 O simple ones, learn prudence;
O foolish men, pay attention.
6 Hear, for I will speak noble things,
and from my lips will come what is right;
7 for my mouth will utter truth;
wickedness is an abomination to my lips.
8 All the words of my mouth are righteous;
there is nothing twisted or crooked in them.
9 They are all straight to him who understands
and right to those who find knowledge.
10 Take my instruction instead of silver,
and knowledge rather than choice gold;
11 for wisdom is better than jewels,
and all that you may desire cannot compare with her.
12 I, wisdom, dwell in prudence,[g]
and I find knowledge and discretion.
13 The fear of the LORD is hatred of evil.
Pride and arrogance and the way of evil
and perverted speech I hate.
14 I have counsel and sound wisdom,
I have insight, I have strength.
15 By me kings reign,
and rulers decree what is just;
16 by me princes rule,
and nobles govern[h] the earth.
17 I love those who love me,
and those who seek me diligently find me.
18 Riches and honor are with me,
enduring wealth and prosperity.
19 My fruit is better than gold, even fine gold,
and my yield than choice silver.
20 I walk in the way of righteousness,
in the paths of justice,
21 endowing with wealth those who love me,
and filling their treasuries.

22 The LORD created me at the beginning of his work,[i]
the first of his acts of old.
23 Ages ago I was set up,
at the first, before the beginning of the earth.
24 When there were no depths I was brought forth,
when there were no springs abounding with water.
25 Before the mountains had been shaped,
before the hills, I was brought forth;
26 before he had made the earth with its fields,[j]
or the first of the dust of the world.
27 When he established the heavens, I was there,
when he drew a circle on the face of the deep,
28 when he made firm the skies above,
when he established[j] the fountains of the deep,
29 when he assigned to the sea its limit,
so that the waters might not transgress his command,
when he marked out the foundations of the earth,
30 then I was beside him, like a master workman;[l]
and I was daily his[m] delight,
rejoicing before him always,
31 rejoicing in his inhabited world
and delighting in the sons of men.

32 And now, my sons, listen to me:
happy are those who keep my ways.
33 Hear instruction and be wise,
and do not neglect it.
34 Happy is the man who listens to me,
watching daily at my gates,
waiting beside my doors.
35 For he who finds me finds life
and obtains favor from the LORD;
36 but he who misses me injures himself;
all who hate me love death."

9 Wisdom has built her house,
she has set up[n] her seven pillars.
2 She has slaughtered her beasts,
she has mixed her wine,
she has also set her table.
3 She has sent out her maids to call
from the highest places in the town,
4 "Whoever is simple, let him turn in here!"
To him who is without sense she says,
5 "Come, eat of my bread
and drink of the wine I have mixed.

[g] Heb obscure [h] Gk: Heb *all the governors of* [i] Heb *way* [j] The meaning of the Hebrew is uncertain
[l] Another reading is *little child* [m] Gk: Heb lacks *his* [n] Gk Syr Tg: Heb *hewn*

6 Leave simpleness,[o] and live,
and walk in the way of insight."

7 He who corrects a scoffer gets himself abuse,
and he who reproves a wicked man incurs injury.
8 Do not reprove a scoffer, or he will hate you;
reprove a wise man, and he will love you.
9 Give instruction[p] to a wise man, and he will be still wiser;
teach a righteous man and he will increase in learning.
10 The fear of the LORD is the beginning of wisdom,
and the knowledge of the Holy One is insight.
11 For by me your days will be multiplied,
and years will be added to your life.
12 If you are wise, you are wise for yourself;
if you scoff, you alone will bear it.

13 A foolish woman is noisy;
she is wanton[q] and knows no shame.[r]
14 She sits at the door of her house,
she takes a seat on the high places of the town,
15 calling to those who pass by,
who are going straight on their way,
16 "Whoever is simple, let him turn in here!"
And to him who is without sense she says,
17 "Stolen water is sweet,
and bread eaten in secret is pleasant."
18 But he does not know that the dead[s] are there,
that her guests are in the depths of Shē'ōl.

10 The proverbs of Solomon.

A wise son makes a glad father,
but a foolish son is a sorrow to his mother.
2 Treasures gained by wickedness do not profit,
but righteousness delivers from death.
3 The LORD does not let the righteous go hungry,
but he thwarts the craving of the wicked.
4 A slack hand causes poverty,
but the hand of the diligent makes rich.
5 A son who gathers in summer is prudent,
but a son who sleeps in harvest brings shame.
6 Blessings are on the head of the righteous,
but the mouth of the wicked conceals violence.
7 The memory of the righteous is a blessing,
but the name of the wicked will rot.
8 The wise of heart will heed commandments,
but a prating fool will come to ruin.
9 He who walks in integrity walks securely,
but he who perverts his ways will be found out.
10 He who winks the eye causes trouble,
but he who boldly reproves makes peace.[t]
11 The mouth of the righteous is a fountain of life,
but the mouth of the wicked conceals violence.
12 Hatred stirs up strife,
but love covers all offenses.
13 On the lips of him who has understanding wisdom is found,
but a rod is for the back of him who lacks sense.
14 Wise men lay up knowledge,
but the babbling of a fool brings ruin near.
15 A rich man's wealth is his strong city;
the poverty of the poor is their ruin.
16 The wage of the righteous leads to life,
the gain of the wicked to sin.
17 He who heeds instruction is on the path to life,

[o] Gk Syr Vg Tg: Heb *simple ones*
[p] Heb lacks *instruction*
[q] Cn Compare Syr Vg: The meaning of the Hebrew is uncertain
[r] Gk Syr: The meaning of the Hebrew is uncertain [s] Heb *shades*
[t] Gk: Heb *but a prating fool will come to ruin*
10.12: Jas 5.20; 1 Pet 4.8.

but he who rejects reproof goes astray.
18 He who conceals hatred has lying lips,
and he who utters slander is a fool.
19 When words are many, transgression is not lacking,
but he who restrains his lips is prudent.
20 The tongue of the righteous is choice silver;
the mind of the wicked is of little worth.
21 The lips of the righteous feed many,
but fools die for lack of sense.
22 The blessing of the LORD makes rich,
and he adds no sorrow with it.[u]
23 It is like sport to a fool to do wrong,
but wise conduct is pleasure to a man of understanding.
24 What the wicked dreads will come upon him,
but the desire of the righteous will be granted.
25 When the tempest passes, the wicked is no more,
but the righteous is established for ever.
26 Like vinegar to the teeth, and smoke to the eyes,
so is the sluggard to those who send him.
27 The fear of the LORD prolongs life,
but the years of the wicked will be short.
28 The hope of the righteous ends in gladness,
but the expectation of the wicked comes to nought.
29 The LORD is a stronghold to him whose way is upright,
but destruction to evildoers.
30 The righteous will never be removed,
but the wicked will not dwell in the land.
31 The mouth of the righteous brings forth wisdom,
but the perverse tongue will be cut off.
32 The lips of the righteous know what is acceptable,
but the mouth of the wicked, what is perverse.

11 A false balance is an abomination to the LORD,
but a just weight is his delight.
2 When pride comes, then comes disgrace;
but with the humble is wisdom.
3 The integrity of the upright guides them,
but the crookedness of the treacherous destroys them.
4 Riches do not profit in the day of wrath,
but righteousness delivers from death.
5 The righteousness of the blameless keeps his way straight,
but the wicked falls by his own wickedness.
6 The righteousness of the upright delivers them,
but the treacherous are taken captive by their lust.
7 When the wicked dies, his hope perishes,
and the expectation of the godless comes to nought.
8 The righteous is delivered from trouble,
and the wicked gets into it instead.
9 With his mouth the godless man would destroy his neighbor,
but by knowledge the righteous are delivered.
10 When it goes well with the righteous, the city rejoices;
and when the wicked perish there are shouts of gladness.
11 By the blessing of the upright a city is exalted,
but it is overthrown by the mouth of the wicked.
12 He who belittles his neighbor lacks sense,
but a man of understanding remains silent.
13 He who goes about as a talebearer reveals secrets,
but he who is trustworthy in spirit keeps a thing hidden.
14 Where there is no guidance, a people falls;
but in an abundance of counselors there is safety.
15 He who gives surety for a stranger will smart for it,
but he who hates suretyship is secure.
16 A gracious woman gets honor,
and violent men get riches.
17 A man who is kind benefits himself,
but a cruel man hurts himself.
18 A wicked man earns deceptive wages,

[u] Or *and toil adds nothing to it*

but one who sows righteousness
gets a sure reward.
19 He who is steadfast in righteousness
will live,
but he who pursues evil will die.
20 Men of perverse mind are an abomination to the LORD,
but those of blameless ways are
his delight.
21 Be assured, an evil man will not go
unpunished,
but those who are righteous will
be delivered.
22 Like a gold ring in a swine's snout
is a beautiful woman without
discretion.
23 The desire of the righteous ends
only in good;
the expectation of the wicked in
wrath.
24 One man gives freely, yet grows all
the richer;
another withholds what he should
give, and only suffers want.
25 A liberal man will be enriched,
and one who waters will himself
be watered.
26 The people curse him who holds
back grain,
but a blessing is on the head of
him who sells it.
27 He who diligently seeks good seeks
favor,
but evil comes to him who
searches for it.
28 He who trusts in his riches will
wither,[v]
but the righteous will flourish like
a green leaf.
29 He who troubles his household will
inherit wind,
and the fool will be servant to the
wise.
30 The fruit of the righteous is a tree
of life,
but lawlessness[w] takes away lives.
31 If the righteous is requited on earth,
how much more the wicked and
the sinner!

12 Whoever loves discipline loves
knowledge,
but he who hates reproof is
stupid.
2 A good man obtains favor from the
LORD,
but a man of evil devices he
condemns.
3 A man is not established by wickedness,
but the root of the righteous will
never be moved.
4 A good wife is the crown of her
husband,
but she who brings shame is like
rottenness in his bones.
5 The thoughts of the righteous are
just;
the counsels of the wicked are
treacherous.
6 The words of the wicked lie in wait
for blood,
but the mouth of the upright
delivers men.
7 The wicked are overthrown and are
no more,
but the house of the righteous
will stand.
8 A man is commended according to
his good sense,
but one of perverse mind is
despised.
9 Better is a man of humble standing
who works for himself
than one who plays the great man
but lacks bread.
10 A righteous man has regard for the
life of his beast,
but the mercy of the wicked is
cruel.
11 He who tills his land will have plenty
of bread,
but he who follows worthless
pursuits has no sense.
12 The strong tower of the wicked
comes to ruin,
but the root of the righteous
stands firm.[x]
13 An evil man is ensnared by the
transgression of his lips,
but the righteous escapes from
trouble.
14 From the fruit of his words a man
is satisfied with good,
and the work of a man's hand
comes back to him.
15 The way of a fool is right in his own
eyes,
but a wise man listens to advice.
16 The vexation of a fool is known at
once,
but the prudent man ignores an
insult.
17 He who speaks the truth gives
honest evidence,
but a false witness utters deceit.
18 There is one whose rash words are
like sword thrusts,

[v] Cn: Heb *fall* [w] Cn Compare Gk Syr: Heb *a wise man* [x] Cn: The Hebrew of verse 12 is obscure
11.31 (Gk): 1 Pet 4.18.

but the tongue of the wise brings healing.
19 Truthful lips endure for ever,
but a lying tongue is but for a moment.
20 Deceit is in the heart of those who devise evil,
but those who plan good have joy.
21 No ill befalls the righteous,
but the wicked are filled with trouble.
22 Lying lips are an abomination to the LORD,
but those who act faithfully are his delight.
23 A prudent man conceals his knowledge,
but fools[y] proclaim their folly.
24 The hand of the diligent will rule,
while the slothful will be put to forced labor.
25 Anxiety in a man's heart weighs him down,
but a good word makes him glad.
26 A righteous man turns away from evil,[z]
but the way of the wicked leads them astray.
27 A slothful man will not catch his prey,[a]
but the diligent man will get precious wealth.[b]
28 In the path of righteousness is life,
but the way of error leads to death.[c]

13 A wise son hears his father's instruction,
but a scoffer does not listen to rebuke.
2 From the fruit of his mouth a good man eats good,
but the desire of the treacherous is for violence.
3 He who guards his mouth preserves his life;
he who opens wide his lips comes to ruin.
4 The soul of the sluggard craves, and gets nothing,
while the soul of the diligent is richly supplied.
5 A righteous man hates falsehood,
but a wicked man acts shamefully and disgracefully.
6 Righteousness guards him whose way is upright,
but sin overthrows the wicked.
7 One man pretends to be rich, yet has nothing;
another pretends to be poor, yet has great wealth.
8 The ransom of a man's life is his wealth,
but a poor man has no means of redemption.[d]
9 The light of the righteous rejoices,
but the lamp of the wicked will be put out.
10 By insolence the heedless make strife,
but with those who take advice is wisdom.
11 Wealth hastily gotten[e] will dwindle,
but he who gathers little by little will increase it.
12 Hope deferred makes the heart sick,
but a desire fulfilled is a tree of life.
13 He who despises the word brings destruction on himself,
but he who respects the commandment will be rewarded.
14 The teaching of the wise is a fountain of life,
that one may avoid the snares of death.
15 Good sense wins favor,
but the way of the faithless is their ruin.[f]
16 In everything a prudent man acts with knowledge,
but a fool flaunts his folly.
17 A bad messenger plunges men into trouble,
but a faithful envoy brings healing.
18 Poverty and disgrace come to him who ignores instruction,
but he who heeds reproof is honored.
19 A desire fulfilled is sweet to the soul;
but to turn away from evil is an abomination to fools.
20 He who walks with wise men becomes wise,
but the companion of fools will suffer harm.
21 Misfortune pursues sinners,
but prosperity rewards the righteous.

[y] Heb *the heart of fools* [z] Cn: The meaning of the Hebrew is uncertain
[a] Cn Compare Gk Syr: The meaning of the Hebrew is uncertain
[b] Cn: The meaning of the Hebrew is uncertain [c] Cn: The meaning of the Hebrew is uncertain
[d] Cn: Heb *does not hear rebuke* [e] Gk Vg: Heb *from vanity*
[f] Cn Compare Gk Syr Vg Tg: Heb *is enduring*

22 A good man leaves an inheritance to his children's children,
but the sinner's wealth is laid up for the righteous.
23 The fallow ground of the poor yields much food,
but it is swept away through injustice.
24 He who spares the rod hates his son,
but he who loves him is diligent to discipline him.
25 The righteous has enough to satisfy his appetite,
but the belly of the wicked suffers want.

14 Wisdom[g] builds her house,
but folly with her own hands tears it down.
2 He who walks in uprightness fears the LORD,
but he who is devious in his ways despises him.
3 The talk of a fool is a rod for his back,[h]
but the lips of the wise will preserve them.
4 Where there are no oxen, there is no[i] grain;
but abundant crops come by the strength of the ox.
5 A faithful witness does not lie,
but a false witness breathes out lies.
6 A scoffer seeks wisdom in vain,
but knowledge is easy for a man of understanding.
7 Leave the presence of a fool,
for there you do not meet words of knowledge.
8 The wisdom of a prudent man is to discern his way,
but the folly of fools is deceiving.
9 God scorns the wicked,[j]
but the upright enjoy his favor.
10 The heart knows its own bitterness,
and no stranger shares its joy.
11 The house of the wicked will be destroyed,
but the tent of the upright will flourish.
12 There is a way which seems right to a man,
but its end is the way to death.[k]
13 Even in laughter the heart is sad,
and the end of joy is grief.
14 A perverse man will be filled with the fruit of his ways,
and a good man with the fruit of his deeds.[l]
15 The simple believes everything,
but the prudent looks where he is going.
16 A wise man is cautious and turns away from evil,
but a fool throws off restraint and is careless.
17 A man of quick temper acts foolishly,
but a man of discretion is patient.[m]
18 The simple acquire folly,
but the prudent are crowned with knowledge.
19 The evil bow down before the good,
the wicked at the gates of the righteous.
20 The poor is disliked even by his neighbor,
but the rich has many friends.
21 He who despises his neighbor is a sinner,
but happy is he who is kind to the poor.
22 Do they not err that devise evil?
Those who devise good meet loyalty and faithfulness.
23 In all toil there is profit,
but mere talk tends only to want.
24 The crown of the wise is their wisdom,[n]
but folly is the garland[o] of fools.
25 A truthful witness saves lives,
but one who utters lies is a betrayer.
26 In the fear of the LORD one has strong confidence,
and his children will have a refuge.
27 The fear of the LORD is a fountain of life,
that one may avoid the snares of death.
28 In a multitude of people is the glory of a king,
but without people a prince is ruined.
29 He who is slow to anger has great understanding,
but he who has a hasty temper exalts folly.
30 A tranquil mind gives life to the flesh,
but passion makes the bones rot.
31 He who oppresses a poor man insults his Maker,

[g] Heb *Wisdom of women* [h] Cn: Heb *a rod of pride* [i] Cn: Heb *a manger of* [j] Cn: Heb obscure
[k] Heb *ways of death* [l] Cn: Heb *from upon him* [m] Gk: Heb *is hated* [n] Cn Compare Gk: Heb *riches*
[o] Cn: Heb *folly*

but he who is kind to the needy
honors him.
32 The wicked is overthrown through
his evil-doing,
but the righteous finds refuge
through his integrity.[p]
33 Wisdom abides in the mind of a
man of understanding,
but it is not[q] known in the heart
of fools.
34 Righteousness exalts a nation,
but sin is a reproach to any
people.
35 A servant who deals wisely has the
king's favor,
but his wrath falls on one who
acts shamefully.

15 A soft answer turns away
wrath,
but a harsh word stirs up anger.
2 The tongue of the wise dispenses
knowledge,[r]
but the mouths of fools pour out
folly.
3 The eyes of the LORD are in every
place,
keeping watch on the evil and the
good.
4 A gentle tongue is a tree of life,
but perverseness in it breaks the
spirit.
5 A fool despises his father's instruction,
but he who heeds admonition is
prudent.
6 In the house of the righteous there
is much treasure,
but trouble befalls the income of
the wicked.
7 The lips of the wise spread knowledge;
not so the minds of fools.
8 The sacrifice of the wicked is an
abomination to the LORD,
but the prayer of the upright is
his delight.
9 The way of the wicked is an
abomination to the LORD,
but he loves him who pursues
righteousness.
10 There is severe discipline for him
who forsakes the way;
he who hates reproof will die.
11 Shē'ōl and A·bad'dȯn lie open before the LORD,
how much more the hearts of
men!
12 A scoffer does not like to be reproved;
he will not go to the wise.
13 A glad heart makes a cheerful
countenance,
but by sorrow of heart the spirit
is broken.
14 The mind of him who has understanding seeks knowledge,
but the mouths of fools feed on
folly.
15 All the days of the afflicted are
evil,
but a cheerful heart has a continual feast.
16 Better is a little with the fear of the
LORD
than great treasure and trouble
with it.
17 Better is a dinner of herbs where
love is
than a fatted ox and hatred with
it.
18 A hot-tempered man stirs up strife,
but he who is slow to anger quiets
contention.
19 The way of a sluggard is overgrown
with thorns,
but the path of the upright is a
level highway.
20 A wise son makes a glad father,
but a foolish man despises his
mother.
21 Folly is a joy to him who has no
sense,
but a man of understanding walks
aright.
22 Without counsel plans go wrong,
but with many advisers they
succeed.
23 To make an apt answer is a joy to
a man,
and a word in season, how good
it is!
24 The wise man's path leads upward
to life,
that he may avoid Shē'ōl beneath.
25 The LORD tears down the house of
the proud,
but maintains the widow's
boundaries.
26 The thoughts of the wicked are an
abomination to the LORD,
the words of the pure are pleasing
to him.[s]
27 He who is greedy for unjust gain
makes trouble for his household,
but he who hates bribes will live.
28 The mind of the righteous ponders
how to answer,

[p] Gk Syr: Heb *in his death* [q] Gk Syr: Heb lacks *not* [r] Cn: Heb *makes knowledge good*
[s] Cn Compare Gk: Heb *pleasant words are pure*

but the mouth of the wicked pours out evil things.
29 The LORD is far from the wicked,
but he hears the prayer of the righteous.
30 The light of the eyes rejoices the heart,
and good news refreshes[t] the bones.
31 He whose ear heeds wholesome admonition
will abide among the wise.
32 He who ignores instruction despises himself,
but he who heeds admonition gains understanding.
33 The fear of the LORD is instruction in wisdom,
and humility goes before honor.

16 The plans of the mind belong to man,
but the answer of the tongue is from the LORD.
2 All the ways of a man are pure in his own eyes,
but the LORD weighs the spirit.
3 Commit your work to the LORD,
and your plans will be established.
4 The LORD has made everything for its purpose,
even the wicked for the day of trouble.
5 Every one who is arrogant is an abomination to the LORD;
be assured, he will not go unpunished.
6 By loyalty and faithfulness iniquity is atoned for,
and by the fear of the LORD a man avoids evil.
7 When a man's ways please the LORD,
he makes even his enemies to be at peace with him.
8 Better is a little with righteousness
than great revenues with injustice.
9 A man's mind plans his way,
but the LORD directs his steps.
10 Inspired decisions are on the lips of a king;
his mouth does not sin in judgment.
11 A just balance and scales are the LORD'S;
all the weights in the bag are his work.
12 It is an abomination to kings to do evil,
for the throne is established by righteousness.
13 Righteous lips are the delight of a king,
and he loves him who speaks what is right.
14 A king's wrath is a messenger of death,
and a wise man will appease it.
15 In the light of a king's face there is life,
and his favor is like the clouds that bring the spring rain.
16 To get wisdom is better[u] than gold;
to get understanding is to be chosen rather than silver.
17 The highway of the upright turns aside from evil;
he who guards his way preserves his life.
18 Pride goes before destruction,
and a haughty spirit before a fall.
19 It is better to be of a lowly spirit with the poor
than to divide the spoil with the proud.
20 He who gives heed to the word will prosper,
and happy is he who trusts in the LORD.
21 The wise of heart is called a man of discernment,
and pleasant speech increases persuasiveness.
22 Wisdom is a fountain of life to him who has it,
but folly is the chastisement of fools.
23 The mind of the wise makes his speech judicious,
and adds persuasiveness to his lips.
24 Pleasant words are like a honeycomb,
sweetness to the soul and health to the body.
25 There is a way which seems right to a man,
but its end is the way to death.[v]
26 A worker's appetite works for him;
his mouth urges him on.
27 A worthless man plots evil,
and his speech is like a scorching fire.
28 A perverse man spreads strife,
and a whisperer separates close friends.
29 A man of violence entices his neighbor
and leads him in a way that is not good.

[t] Heb *makes fat* [u] Gk Syr Vg Tg: Heb *how much better* [v] Heb *ways of death*

30 He who winks his eyes plans[w] perverse things,
he who compresses his lips brings evil to pass.
31 A hoary head is a crown of glory;
it is gained in a righteous life.
32 He who is slow to anger is better than the mighty,
and he who rules his spirit than he who takes a city.
33 The lot is cast into the lap,
but the decision is wholly from the LORD.

17 Better is a dry morsel with quiet
than a house full of feasting with strife.
2 A slave who deals wisely will rule over a son who acts shamefully,
and will share the inheritance as one of the brothers.
3 The crucible is for silver, and the furnace is for gold,
and the LORD tries hearts.
4 An evildoer listens to wicked lips;
and a liar gives heed to a mischievous tongue.
5 He who mocks the poor insults his Maker;
he who is glad at calamity will not go unpunished.
6 Grandchildren are the crown of the aged,
and the glory of sons is their fathers.
Fine speech is not becoming to a fool;
still less is false speech to a prince.
8 A bribe is like a magic stone in the eyes of him who gives it;
wherever he turns he prospers.
He who forgives an offense seeks love,
but he who repeats a matter alienates a friend.
10 A rebuke goes deeper into a man of understanding
than a hundred blows into a fool.
11 An evil man seeks only rebellion,
and a cruel messenger will be sent against him.
12 Let a man meet a she-bear robbed of her cubs,
rather than a fool in his folly.
13 If a man returns evil for good,
evil will not depart from his house.
14 The beginning of strife is like letting out water;
so quit before the quarrel breaks out.
15 He who justifies the wicked and he who condemns the righteous
are both alike in abomination to the LORD.
16 Why should a fool have a price in his hand to buy wisdom,
when he has no mind?
17 A friend loves at all times,
and a brother is born for adversity.
18 A man without sense gives a pledge,
and becomes surety in the presence of his neighbor.
19 He who loves transgression loves strife;
he who makes his door high seeks destruction.
20 A man of crooked mind does not prosper,
and one with a perverse tongue falls into calamity.
21 A stupid son is a grief to a father;
and the father of a fool has no joy.
22 A cheerful heart is a good medicine,
but a downcast spirit dries up the bones.
23 A wicked man accepts a bribe from the bosom
to pervert the ways of justice.
24 A man of understanding sets his face toward wisdom,
but the eyes of a fool are on the ends of the earth.
25 A foolish son is a grief to his father
and bitterness to her who bore him.
26 To impose a fine on a righteous man is not good;
to flog noble men is wrong.
27 He who restrains his words has knowledge,
and he who has a cool spirit is a man of understanding.
28 Even a fool who keeps silent is considered wise;
when he closes his lips, he is deemed intelligent.

18 He who is estranged[x] seeks pretexts[y]
to break out against all sound judgment.
2 A fool takes no pleasure in understanding,
but only in expressing his opinion.
3 When wickedness comes, contempt comes also;
and with dishonor comes disgrace.
4 The words of a man's mouth are deep waters;
the fountain of wisdom is a gushing stream.

[w] Gk Syr Vg Tg: Heb *to plan* [x] Heb *separated* [y] Gk Vg: Heb *desire*

5 It is not good to be partial to a wicked man,
or to deprive a righteous man of justice.
6 A fool's lips bring strife,
and his mouth invites a flogging.
7 A fool's mouth is his ruin,
and his lips are a snare to himself.
8 The words of a whisperer are like delicious morsels;
they go down into the inner parts of the body.
9 He who is slack in his work
is a brother to him who destroys.
10 The name of the LORD is a strong tower;
the righteous man runs into it and is safe.
11 A rich man's wealth is his strong city,
and like a high wall protecting him.[z]
12 Before destruction a man's heart is haughty,
but humility goes before honor.
13 If one gives answer before he hears,
it is his folly and shame.
14 A man's spirit will endure sickness;
but a broken spirit who can bear?
15 An intelligent mind acquires knowledge,
and the ear of the wise seeks knowledge.
16 A man's gift makes room for him
and brings him before great men.
17 He who states his case first seems right,
until the other comes and examines him.
18 The lot puts an end to disputes
and decides between powerful contenders.
19 A brother helped is like a strong city,[a]
but quarreling is like the bars of a castle.
20 From the fruit of his mouth a man is satisfied;
he is satisfied by the yield of his lips.
21 Death and life are in the power of the tongue,
and those who love it will eat its fruits.
22 He who finds a wife finds a good thing,
and obtains favor from the LORD.
23 The poor use entreaties,
but the rich answer roughly.
24 There are[b] friends who pretend to be friends,[c]
but there is a friend who sticks closer than a brother.

19 Better is a poor man who walks in his integrity
than a man who is perverse in speech, and is a fool.
2 It is not good for a man to be without knowledge,
and he who makes haste with his feet misses his way.
3 When a man's folly brings his way to ruin,
his heart rages against the LORD.
4 Wealth brings many new friends,
but a poor man is deserted by his friend.
5 A false witness will not go unpunished,
and he who utters lies will not escape.
6 Many seek the favor of a generous man,
and every one is a friend to a man who gives gifts.
7 All a poor man's brothers hate him;
how much more do his friends go far from him!
He pursues them with words, but does not have them.[d]
8 He who gets wisdom loves himself;
he who keeps understanding will prosper.
9 A false witness will not go unpunished,
and he who utters lies will perish.
10 It is not fitting for a fool to live in luxury,
much less for a slave to rule over princes.
11 Good sense makes a man slow to anger,
and it is his glory to overlook an offense.
12 A king's wrath is like the growling of a lion,
but his favor is like dew upon the grass.
13 A foolish son is ruin to his father,
and a wife's quarreling is a continual dripping of rain.
14 House and wealth are inherited from fathers,
but a prudent wife is from the LORD.
15 Slothfulness casts into a deep sleep,
and an idle person will suffer hunger.

z Or *in his imagination* a Gk Syr Vg Tg: The meaning of the Hebrew is uncertain
b Syr Tg: Heb *A man of* c Cn Compare Syr Vg Tg: Heb *to be broken* d Heb uncertain

16 He who keeps the commandment
keeps his life;
he who despises the word[e] will
die.
17 He who is kind to the poor lends
to the LORD,
and he will repay him for his
deed.
18 Discipline your son while there is
hope;
do not set your heart on his destruction.
19 A man of great wrath will pay the
penalty;
for if you deliver him, you will
only have to do it again.[f]
20 Listen to advice and accept instruction,
that you may gain wisdom for the
future.
21 Many are the plans in the mind of
a man,
but it is the purpose of the LORD
that will be established.
22 What is desired in a man is loyalty,
and a poor man is better than a
liar.
23 The fear of the LORD leads to life;
and he who has it rests satisfied;
he will not be visited by harm.
24 The sluggard buries his hand in the
dish,
and will not even bring it back
to his mouth.
25 Strike a scoffer, and the simple will
learn prudence;
reprove a man of understanding,
and he will gain knowledge.
26 He who does violence to his father
and chases away his mother
is a son who causes shame and
brings reproach.
27 Cease, my son, to hear instruction
only to stray from the words of
knowledge.
28 A worthless witness mocks at justice,
and the mouth of the wicked
devours iniquity.
29 Condemnation is ready for scoffers,
and flogging for the backs of
fools.

20 Wine is a mocker, strong drink
a brawler;
and whoever is led astray by it is
not wise.
2 The dread wrath of a king is like
the growling of a lion;
he who provokes him to anger
forfeits his life.
3 It is an honor for a man to keep
aloof from strife;
but every fool will be quarreling.
4 The sluggard does not plow in the
autumn;
he will seek at harvest and have
nothing.
5 The purpose in a man's mind is
like deep water,
but a man of understanding will
draw it out.
6 Many a man proclaims his own
loyalty,
but a faithful man who can find?
7 A righteous man who walks in his
integrity—
blessed are his sons after him!
8 A king who sits on the throne of
judgment
winnows all evil with his eyes.
9 Who can say, "I have made my
heart clean;
I am pure from my sin"?
10 Diverse weights and diverse measures
are both alike an abomination to
the LORD.
11 Even a child makes himself known
by his acts,
whether what he does is pure and
right.
12 The hearing ear and the seeing eye,
the LORD has made them both.
13 Love not sleep, lest you come to
poverty;
open your eyes, and you will have
plenty of bread.
14 "It is bad, it is bad," says the buyer;
but when he goes away, then he
boasts.
15 There is gold, and abundance of
costly stones;
but the lips of knowledge are a
precious jewel.
16 Take a man's garment when he has
given surety for a stranger,
and hold him in pledge when he
gives surety for foreigners.
17 Bread gained by deceit is sweet to
a man,
but afterward his mouth will be
full of gravel.
18 Plans are established by counsel;
by wise guidance wage war.
19 He who goes about gossiping reveals secrets;
therefore do not associate with
one who speaks foolishly.
20 If one curses his father or his
mother,

[e] Cn Compare 13.13: Heb *his ways* [f] Heb obscure

his lamp will be put out in utter darkness.
21 An inheritance gotten hastily in the beginning
will in the end not be blessed.
22 Do not say, "I will repay evil";
wait for the LORD, and he will help you.
23 Diverse weights are an abomination to the LORD,
and false scales are not good.
24 A man's steps are ordered by the LORD;
how then can man understand his way?
25 It is a snare for a man to say rashly, "It is holy,"
and to reflect only after making his vows.
26 A wise king winnows the wicked,
and drives the wheel over them.
27 The spirit of man is the lamp of the LORD,
searching all his innermost parts.
28 Loyalty and faithfulness preserve the king,
and his throne is upheld by righteousness.[g]
29 The glory of young men is their strength,
but the beauty of old men is their gray hair.
30 Blows that wound cleanse away evil;
strokes make clean the innermost parts.

21 The king's heart is a stream of water in the hand of the LORD;
he turns it wherever he will.
2 Every way of a man is right in his own eyes,
but the LORD weighs the heart.
3 To do righteousness and justice
is more acceptable to the LORD than sacrifice.
4 Haughty eyes and a proud heart,
the lamp of the wicked, are sin.
5 The plans of the diligent lead surely to abundance,
but every one who is hasty comes only to want.
6 The getting of treasures by a lying tongue
is a fleeting vapor and a snare of death.
7 The violence of the wicked will sweep them away,
because they refuse to do what is just.
8 The way of the guilty is crooked,
but the conduct of the pure is right.
9 It is better to live in a corner of the housetop
than in a house shared with a contentious woman.
10 The soul of the wicked desires evil;
his neighbor finds no mercy in his eyes.
11 When a scoffer is punished, the simple becomes wise;
when a wise man is instructed, he gains knowledge.
12 The righteous observes the house of the wicked;
the wicked are cast down to ruin.
13 He who closes his ear to the cry of the poor
will himself cry out and not be heard.
14 A gift in secret averts anger;
and a bribe in the bosom, strong wrath.
15 When justice is done, it is a joy to the righteous,
but dismay to evildoers.
16 A man who wanders from the way of understanding
will rest in the assembly of the dead.
17 He who loves pleasure will be a poor man;
he who loves wine and oil will not be rich.
18 The wicked is a ransom for the righteous,
and the faithless for the upright.
19 It is better to live in a desert land
than with a contentious and fretful woman.
20 Precious treasure remains[h] in a wise man's dwelling,
but a foolish man devours it.
21 He who pursues righteousness and kindness
will find life[i] and honor.
22 A wise man scales the city of the mighty
and brings down the stronghold in which they trust.
23 He who keeps his mouth and his tongue
keeps himself out of trouble.
24 "Scoffer" is the name of the proud, haughty man
who acts with arrogant pride.
25 The desire of the sluggard kills him
for his hands refuse to labor.

[g] Gk: Heb *loyalty*
[h] Gk: Heb *and oil* [i] Gk: Heb *life and righteousness*

26 All day long the wicked covets,[j]
but the righteous gives and does not hold back.
27 The sacrifice of the wicked is an abomination;
how much more when he brings it with evil intent.
28 A false witness will perish,
but the word of a man who hears will endure.
29 A wicked man puts on a bold face,
but an upright man considers[k] his ways.
30 No wisdom, no understanding, no counsel,
can avail against the LORD.
31 The horse is made ready for the day of battle,
but the victory belongs to the LORD.

22 A good name is to be chosen rather than great riches,
and favor is better than silver or gold.
2 The rich and the poor meet together;
the LORD is the maker of them all.
A prudent man sees danger and hides himself;
but the simple go on, and suffer for it.
4 The reward for humility and fear of the LORD
is riches and honor and life.
5 Thorns and snares are in the way of the perverse;
he who guards himself will keep far from them.
6 Train up a child in the way he should go,
and when he is old he will not depart from it.
7 The rich rules over the poor,
and the borrower is the slave of the lender.
8 He who sows injustice will reap calamity,
and the rod of his fury will fail.
9 He who has a bountiful eye will be blessed,
for he shares his bread with the poor.
10 Drive out a scoffer, and strife will go out,
and quarreling and abuse will cease.
11 He who loves purity of heart,
and whose speech is gracious, will have the king as his friend.
12 The eyes of the LORD keep watch over knowledge,
but he overthrows the words of the faithless.
13 The sluggard says, "There is a lion outside!
I shall be slain in the streets!"
14 The mouth of a loose woman is a deep pit;
he with whom the LORD is angry will fall into it.
15 Folly is bound up in the heart of a child,
but the rod of discipline drives it far from him.
16 He who oppresses the poor to increase his own wealth,
or gives to the rich, will only come to want.

17 Incline your ear, and hear the words of the wise,
and apply your mind to my knowledge;
18 for it will be pleasant if you keep them within you,
if all of them are ready on your lips.
19 That your trust may be in the LORD,
I have made them known to you today, even to you.

20 Have I not written for you thirty sayings
of admonition and knowledge,
21 to show you what is right and true,
that you may give a true answer to those who sent you?

22 Do not rob the poor, because he is poor,
or crush the afflicted at the gate;
23 for the LORD will plead their cause
and despoil of life those who despoil them.
24 Make no friendship with a man given to anger,
nor go with a wrathful man,
25 lest you learn his ways
and entangle yourself in a snare.
26 Be not one of those who give pledges,
who become surety for debts.
27 If you have nothing with which to pay,
why should your bed be taken from under you?
28 Remove not the ancient landmark
which your fathers have set.

[j] Gk: Heb *all day long he covets covetously* [k] Another reading is *establishes*
22.8 (Gk): 1 Cor 9.7.

29 Do you see a man skilful in his work?
he will stand before kings;
he will not stand before obscure men.

23 When you sit down to eat with a ruler,
observe carefully what[l] is before you;
2 and put a knife to your throat
if you are a man given to appetite.
3 Do not desire his delicacies,
for they are deceptive food.
4 Do not toil to acquire wealth;
be wise enough to desist.
5 When your eyes light upon it, it is gone;
for suddenly it takes to itself wings,
flying like an eagle toward heaven.
6 Do not eat the bread of a man who is stingy;
do not desire his delicacies;
7 for he is like one who is inwardly reckoning.[m]
"Eat and drink!" he says to you;
but his heart is not with you.
8 You will vomit up the morsels which you have eaten,
and waste your pleasant words.
9 Do not speak in the hearing of a fool,
for he will despise the wisdom of your words.

10 Do not remove an ancient landmark
or enter the fields of the fatherless;
11 for their Redeemer is strong;
he will plead their cause against you.
12 Apply your mind to instruction
and your ear to words of knowledge.
13 Do not withhold discipline from a child;
if you beat him with a rod, he will not die.
14 If you beat him with the rod
you will save his life from Shē'ōl.
15 My son, if your heart is wise,
my heart too will be glad.
16 My soul will rejoice
when your lips speak what is right.
17 Let not your heart envy sinners,
but continue in the fear of the LORD all the day.
18 Surely there is a future,
and your hope will not be cut off.

19 Hear, my son, and be wise,
and direct your mind in the way.
20 Be not among winebibbers,
or among gluttonous eaters of meat;
21 for the drunkard and the glutton will come to poverty,
and drowsiness will clothe a man with rags.

22 Hearken to your father who begot you,
and do not despise your mother when she is old.
23 Buy truth, and do not sell it;
buy wisdom, instruction, and understanding.
24 The father of the righteous will greatly rejoice;
he who begets a wise son will be glad in him.
25 Let your father and mother be glad,
let her who bore you rejoice.

26 My son, give me your heart,
and let your eyes observe[n] my ways.
27 For a harlot is a deep pit;
an adventuress is a narrow well.
28 She lies in wait like a robber
and increases the faithless among men.

29 Who has woe? Who has sorrow?
Who has strife? Who has complaining?
Who has wounds without cause?
Who has redness of eyes?
30 Those who tarry long over wine,
those who go to try mixed wine.
31 Do not look at wine when it is red,
when it sparkles in the cup
and goes down smoothly.
32 At the last it bites like a serpent,
and stings like an adder.
33 Your eyes will see strange things,
and your mind utter perverse things.
34 You will be like one who lies down in the midst of the sea,
like one who lies on the top of a mast.[o]
35 "They struck me," you will say,[p]
"but I was not hurt;
they beat me, but I did not feel it.
When shall I awake?
I will seek another drink."

24 Be not envious of evil men,
nor desire to be with them;
2 for their minds devise violence,
and their lips talk of mischief.

[l] Or *who* [m] Heb obscure [n] Another reading is *delight in* [o] Heb obscure
[p] Gk Syr Vg Tg: Heb lacks *you will say*

3 By wisdom a house is built,
and by understanding it is established;
4 by knowledge the rooms are filled
with all precious and pleasant riches.
5 A wise man is mightier than a strong man,[q]
and a man of knowledge than he who has strength;
6 for by wise guidance you can wage your war,
and in abundance of counselors there is victory.
7 Wisdom is too high for a fool;
in the gate he does not open his mouth.

8 He who plans to do evil
will be called a mischief-maker.
9 The devising of folly is sin,
and the scoffer is an abomination to men.

10 If you faint in the day of adversity,
your strength is small.
11 Rescue those who are being taken away to death;
hold back those who are stumbling to the slaughter.
12 If you say, "Behold, we did not know this,"
does not he who weighs the heart perceive it?
Does not he who keeps watch over your soul know it,
and will he not requite man according to his work?

13 My son, eat honey, for it is good,
and the drippings of the honeycomb are sweet to your taste.
14 Know that wisdom is such to your soul;
if you find it, there will be a future,
and your hope will not be cut off.

15 Lie not in wait as a wicked man against the dwelling of the righteous;
do not violence to his home;
16 for a righteous man falls seven times, and rises again;
but the wicked are overthrown by calamity.

17 Do not rejoice when your enemy falls,
and let not your heart be glad when he stumbles;
18 lest the LORD see it, and be displeased,
and turn away his anger from him.

19 Fret not yourself because of evildoers,
and be not envious of the wicked;
20 for the evil man has no future;
the lamp of the wicked will be put out.

21 My son, fear the LORD and the king,
and do not disobey either of them;[r]
22 for disaster from them will rise suddenly,
and who knows the ruin that will come from them both?

23 These also are sayings of the wise.

Partiality in judging is not good.
24 He who says to the wicked, "You are innocent,"
will be cursed by peoples, abhorred by nations;
25 but those who rebuke the wicked will have delight,
and a good blessing will be upon them.
26 He who gives a right answer
kisses the lips.

27 Prepare your work outside,
get everything ready for you in the field;
and after that build your house.

28 Be not a witness against your neighbor without cause,
and do not deceive with your lips.
29 Do not say, "I will do to him as he has done to me;
I will pay the man back for what he has done."

30 I passed by the field of a sluggard,
by the vineyard of a man without sense;
31 and lo, it was all overgrown with thorns;
the ground was covered with nettles,
and its stone wall was broken down.
32 Then I saw and considered it;
I looked and received instruction.
33 A little sleep, a little slumber,
a little folding of the hands to rest,

[q] Gk Compare Syr Tg: Heb *is in strength* [r] Gk: Heb *do not associate with those who change*

34 and poverty will come upon you
like a robber,
and want like an armed man.

25 These also are proverbs of Solomon which the men of Hez-ė-kī'ȧh king of Judah copied.

2 It is the glory of God to conceal
things,
but the glory of kings is to search
things out.
3 As the heavens for height, and the
earth for depth,
so the mind of kings is unsearchable.
4 Take away the dross from the silver,
and the smith has material for a
vessel;
5 take away the wicked from the
presence of the king,
and his throne will be established
in righteousness.
6 Do not put yourself forward in the
king's presence
or stand in the place of the great;
7 for it is better to be told, "Come up
here,"
than to be put lower in the
presence of the prince.

What your eyes have seen
8 do not hastily bring into court;
for[s] what will you do in the end,
when your neighbor puts you to
shame?
9 Argue your case with your neighbor
himself,
and do not disclose another's
secret;
10 lest he who hears you bring shame
upon you,
and your ill repute have no end.

11 A word fitly spoken
is like apples of gold in a setting
of silver.
12 Like a gold ring or an ornament of
gold
is a wise reprover to a listening
ear.
13 Like the cold of snow in the time of
harvest
is a faithful messenger to those
who send him,
he refreshes the spirit of his
masters.
14 Like clouds and wind without rain
is a man who boasts of a gift he
does not give.

15 With patience a ruler may be persuaded,
and a soft tongue will break a
bone.
16 If you have found honey, eat only
enough for you,
lest you be sated with it and
vomit it.
17 Let your foot be seldom in your
neighbor's house,
lest he become weary of you and
hate you.
18 A man who bears false witness
against his neighbor
is like a war club, or a sword, or
a sharp arrow.
19 Trust in a faithless man in time of
trouble
is like a bad tooth or a foot that
slips.
20 He who sings songs to a heavy heart
is like one who takes off a garment
on a cold day,
and like vinegar on a wound.[t]
21 If your enemy is hungry, give him
bread to eat;
and if he is thirsty, give him water
to drink;
22 for you will heap coals of fire on his
head,
and the LORD will reward you.
23 The north wind brings forth rain;
and a backbiting tongue, angry
looks.
24 It is better to live in a corner of the
housetop
than in a house shared with a
contentious woman.
25 Like cold water to a thirsty soul,
so is good news from a far country.
26 Like a muddied spring or a polluted
fountain
is a righteous man who gives way
before the wicked.
27 It is not good to eat much honey,
so be sparing of complimentary
words.[u]
28 A man without self-control
is like a city broken into and left
without walls.

26 Like snow in summer or rain
in harvest,
so honor is not fitting for a fool.
2 Like a sparrow in its flitting, like a
swallow in its flying,

[s] Cn: Heb *lest* [t] Gk: Heb *lye*
[u] Cn Compare Gk Syr Tg: Heb *searching out their glory is glory*
25.21-22: Rom 12.20.

a curse that is causeless does not alight.
3 A whip for the horse, a bridle for the ass,
and a rod for the back of fools.
4 Answer not a fool according to his folly,
lest you be like him yourself.
5 Answer a fool according to his folly,
lest he be wise in his own eyes.
6 He who sends a message by the hand of a fool
cuts off his own feet and drinks violence.
7 Like a lame man's legs, which hang useless,
is a proverb in the mouth of fools.
8 Like one who binds the stone in the sling
is he who gives honor to a fool.
9 Like a thorn that goes up into the hand of a drunkard
is a proverb in the mouth of fools.
10 Like an archer who wounds everybody
is he who hires a passing fool or drunkard.[v]
11 Like a dog that returns to his vomit
is a fool that repeats his folly.
12 Do you see a man who is wise in his own eyes?
There is more hope for a fool than for him.
13 The sluggard says, "There is a lion in the road!
There is a lion in the streets!"
14 As a door turns on its hinges,
so does a sluggard on his bed.
15 The sluggard buries his hand in the dish;
it wears him out to bring it back to his mouth.
16 The sluggard is wiser in his own eyes
than seven men who can answer discreetly.
17 He who meddles in a quarrel not his own
is like one who takes a passing dog by the ears.
18 Like a madman who throws firebrands,
arrows, and death,
19 is the man who deceives his neighbor
and says, "I am only joking!"
20 For lack of wood the fire goes out;
and where there is no whisperer, quarreling ceases.
21 As charcoal to hot embers and wood to fire,
so is a quarrelsome man for kindling strife.
22 The words of a whisperer are like delicious morsels;
they go down into the inner parts of the body.
23 Like the glaze[w] covering an earthen vessel
are smooth[x] lips with an evil heart.
24 He who hates, dissembles with his lips
and harbors deceit in his heart;
25 when he speaks graciously, believe him not,
for there are seven abominations in his heart;
26 though his hatred be covered with guile,
his wickedness will be exposed in the assembly.
27 He who digs a pit will fall into it,
and a stone will come back upon him who starts it rolling.
28 A lying tongue hates its victims,
and a flattering mouth works ruin.

27 Do not boast about tomorrow,
for you do not know what a day may bring forth.
2 Let another praise you, and not your own mouth;
a stranger, and not your own lips.
3 A stone is heavy, and sand is weighty,
but a fool's provocation is heavier than both.
4 Wrath is cruel, anger is overwhelming;
but who can stand before jealousy?
5 Better is open rebuke
than hidden love.
6 Faithful are the wounds of a friend;
profuse are the kisses of an enemy.
7 He who is sated loathes honey,
but to one who is hungry everything bitter is sweet.
8 Like a bird that strays from its nest,
is a man who strays from his home.
9 Oil and perfume make the heart glad,
but the soul is torn by trouble.[y]
10 Your friend, and your father's friend, do not forsake;
and do not go to your brother's house in the day of your calamity.

[v] The Hebrew text of this verse is uncertain [w] Cn: Heb *silver of dross* [x] Gk: Heb *burning*
[y] Gk: Heb *the sweetness of his friend from hearty counsel*
26.11: 2 Pet 2.22.

Better is a neighbor who is near
than a brother who is far away.
11 Be wise, my son, and make my heart glad,
that I may answer him who reproaches me.
12 A prudent man sees danger and hides himself;
but the simple go on, and suffer for it.
13 Take a man's garment when he has given surety for a stranger,
and hold him in pledge when he gives surety for foreigners.[z]
14 He who blesses his neighbor with a loud voice,
rising early in the morning,
will be counted as cursing.
15 A continual dripping on a rainy day
and a contentious woman are alike;
16 to restrain her is to restrain the wind[a]
or to grasp oil in his right hand.
17 Iron sharpens iron,
and one man sharpens another.
18 He who tends a fig tree will eat its fruit,
and he who guards his master will be honored.
19 As in water face answers to face,
so the mind of man reflects the man.
20 She'ōl and A·bad'dŏn are never satisfied,
and never satisfied are the eyes of man.
21 The crucible is for silver, and the furnace is for gold,
and a man is judged by his praise.
22 Crush a fool in a mortar with a pestle
along with crushed grain,
yet his folly will not depart from him.

23 Know well the condition of your flocks,
and give attention to your herds;
24 for riches do not last for ever;
and does a crown endure to all generations?
25 When the grass is gone, and the new growth appears,
and the herbage of the mountains is gathered,
26 the lambs will provide your clothing,
and the goats the price of a field;
27 there will be enough goats' milk for your food,
for the food of your household
and maintenance for your maidens.

28 The wicked flee when no one pursues,
but the righteous are bold as a lion.
2 When a land transgresses
it has many rulers;
but with men of understanding and knowledge
its stability will long continue.
3 A poor man who oppresses the poor
is a beating rain that leaves no food.
4 Those who forsake the law praise the wicked,
but those who keep the law strive against them.
5 Evil men do not understand justice,
but those who seek the LORD understand it completely.
6 Better is a poor man who walks in his integrity
than a rich man who is perverse in his ways.
7 He who keeps the law is a wise son,
but a companion of gluttons shames his father.
8 He who augments his wealth by interest and increase
gathers it for him who is kind to the poor.
9 If one turns away his ear from hearing the law,
even his prayer is an abomination.
10 He who misleads the upright into an evil way
will fall into his own pit;
but the blameless will have a goodly inheritance.
11 A rich man is wise in his own eyes,
but a poor man who has understanding will find him out.
12 When the righteous triumph, there is great glory;
but when the wicked rise, men hide themselves.
13 He who conceals his transgressions will not prosper,
but he who confesses and forsakes them will obtain mercy.
14 Blessed is the man who fears the LORD always;
but he who hardens his heart will fall into calamity.
15 Like a roaring lion or a charging bear

[z] Vg and 20.16: Heb *a foreign woman* [a] Heb obscure

is a wicked ruler over a poor
people.
16 A ruler who lacks understanding is
a cruel oppressor;
but he who hates unjust gain will
prolong his days.
17 If a man is burdened with the blood
of another,
let him be a fugitive until
death;
let no one help him.
18 He who walks in integrity will be
delivered,
but he who is perverse in his ways
will fall into a pit.[b]
19 He who tills his land will have
plenty of bread,
but he who follows worthless
pursuits will have plenty of
poverty.
20 A faithful man will abound with
blessings,
but he who hastens to be rich
will not go unpunished.
21 To show partiality is not good;
but for a piece of bread a man
will do wrong.
22 A miserly man hastens after wealth,
and does not know that want will
come upon him.
23 He who rebukes a man will afterward find more favor
than he who flatters with his
tongue.
24 He who robs his father or his mother
and says, "That is no transgression,"
is the companion of a man who
destroys.
25 A greedy man stirs up strife,
but he who trusts in the LORD
will be enriched.
26 He who trusts in his own mind is
a fool;
but he who walks in wisdom will
be delivered.
27 He who gives to the poor will not
want,
but he who hides his eyes will get
many a curse.
28 When the wicked rise, men hide
themselves,
but when they perish, the righteous increase.

29 He who is often reproved, yet
stiffens his neck
will suddenly be broken beyond
healing.
2 When the righteous are in authority,
the people rejoice;
but when the wicked rule, the
people groan.
3 He who loves wisdom makes his
father glad,
but one who keeps company with
harlots squanders his substance.
4 By justice a king gives stability to
the land,
but one who exacts gifts ruins
it.
5 A man who flatters his neighbor
spreads a net for his feet.
6 An evil man is ensnared in his
transgression,
but a righteous man sings and
rejoices.
7 A righteous man knows the rights
of the poor;
a wicked man does not understand
such knowledge.
8 Scoffers set a city aflame,
but wise men turn away wrath.
9 If a wise man has an argument with
a fool,
the fool only rages and laughs,
and there is no quiet.
10 Bloodthirsty men hate one who is
blameless,
and the wicked[c] seek his life.
11 A fool gives full vent to his anger,
but a wise man quietly holds it
back.
12 If a ruler listens to falsehood,
all his officials will be wicked.
13 The poor man and the oppressor
meet together;
the LORD gives light to the eyes
of both.
14 If a king judges the poor with equity
his throne will be established for
ever.
15 The rod and reproof give wisdom,
but a child left to himself brings
shame to his mother.
16 When the wicked are in authority,
transgression increases;
but the righteous will look upon
their downfall.
17 Discipline your son, and he will
give you rest;
he will give delight to your heart.
18 Where there is no prophecy the
people cast off restraint,
but blessed is he who keeps the
law.
19 By mere words a servant is not
disciplined,
for though he understands, he
will not give heed.

[b] Syr: Heb *in one* [c] Cn: Heb *upright*

20 Do you see a man who is hasty in his words?
There is more hope for a fool than for him.
21 He who pampers his servant from childhood,
will in the end find him his heir.[d]
22 A man of wrath stirs up strife,
and a man given to anger causes much transgression.
23 A man's pride will bring him low,
but he who is lowly in spirit will obtain honor.
24 The partner of a thief hates his own life;
he hears the curse, but discloses nothing.
25 The fear of man lays a snare,
but he who trusts in the LORD is safe.
26 Many seek the favor of a ruler,
but from the LORD a man gets justice.
27 An unjust man is an abomination to the righteous,
but he whose way is straight is an abomination to the wicked.

30 The words of A'gûr son of Jā'keh of Mas'så.[e]

The man says to Ith'i-el,
to Ithi-el and Ū'cal.[f]
2 Surely I am too stupid to be a man.
I have not the understanding of a man.
3 I have not learned wisdom,
nor have I knowledge of the Holy One.
4 Who has ascended to heaven and come down?
Who has gathered the wind in his fists?
Who has wrapped up the waters in a garment?
Who has established all the ends of the earth?
What is his name, and what is his son's name?
Surely you know!

5 Every word of God proves true;
he is a shield to those who take refuge in him.
6 Do not add to his words,
lest he rebuke you, and you be found a liar
7 Two things I ask of thee;
deny them not to me before I die:
8 Remove far from me falsehood and lying;
give me neither poverty nor riches;
feed me with the food that is needful for me,
9 lest I be full, and deny thee,
and say, "Who is the LORD?"
or lest I be poor, and steal,
and profane the name of my God.

10 Do not slander a servant to his master,
lest he curse you, and you be held guilty.

11 There are those who curse their fathers
and do not bless their mothers.
12 There are those who are pure in their own eyes
but are not cleansed of their filth.
13 There are those—how lofty are their eyes,
how high their eyelids lift!
14 There are those whose teeth are swords,
whose teeth are knives,
to devour the poor from off the earth,
the needy from among men.

15 The leech[g] has two daughters;
"Give, give," they cry.
Three things are never satisfied;
four never say, "Enough":
16 Shē'ōl, the barren womb,
the earth ever thirsty for water,
and the fire which never says, "Enough."[h]

17 The eye that mocks a father
and scorns to obey a mother
will be picked out by the ravens of the valley
and eaten by the vultures.

18 Three things are too wonderful for me;
four I do not understand:
19 the way of an eagle in the sky,
the way of a serpent on a rock,
the way of a ship on the high seas,
and the way of a man with a maiden.

[d] The meaning of the Hebrew word is uncertain [e] Or *the oracle*
[f] The Hebrew of this verse is obscure
[g] The meaning of the Hebrew word is uncertain
[h] Heb obscure

20 This is the way of an adulteress:
she eats, and wipes her mouth,
and says, "I have done no wrong."

21 Under three things the earth trembles;
under four it cannot bear up:
22 a slave when he becomes king,
and a fool when he is filled with food;
23 an unloved woman when she gets a husband,
and a maid when she succeeds her mistress.

24 Four things on earth are small,
but they are exceedingly wise:
25 the ants are a people not strong,
yet they provide their food in the summer;
26 the badgers are a people not mighty,
yet they make their homes in the rocks;
27 the locusts have no king,
yet all of them march in rank;
28 the lizard you can take in your hands,
yet it is in kings' palaces.

29 Three things are stately in their tread;
four are stately in their stride:
30 the lion, which is mightiest among beasts
and does not turn back before any;
31 the strutting cock,[i] the he-goat,
and a king striding before[j] his people.

32 If you have been foolish, exalting yourself,
or if you have been devising evil,
put your hand on your mouth.
33 For pressing milk produces curds,
pressing the nose produces blood,
and pressing anger produces strife.

31 The words of Lem'ū·ĕl, king of Mas'să,[k] which his mother taught him:

2 What, my son? What, son of my womb?
What, son of my vows?
3 Give not your strength to women,
your ways to those who destroy kings.
4 It is not for kings, O Lem'ū·ĕl,
it is not for kings to drink wine,
or for rulers to desire[l] strong drink;
5 lest they drink and forget what has been decreed,
and pervert the rights of all the afflicted.
6 Give strong drink to him who is perishing,
and wine to those in bitter distress;
7 let them drink and forget their poverty,
and remember their misery no more.
8 Open your mouth for the dumb,
for the rights of all who are left desolate.[m]
9 Open your mouth, judge righteously,
maintain the rights of the poor and needy.

10 A good wife who can find?
She is far more precious than jewels.
11 The heart of her husband trusts in her,
and he will have no lack of gain.
12 She does him good, and not harm,
all the days of her life.
13 She seeks wool and flax,
and works with willing hands.
14 She is like the ships of the merchant,
she brings her food from afar.
15 She rises while it is yet night
and provides food for her household
and tasks for her maidens.
16 She considers a field and buys it;
with the fruit of her hands she plants a vineyard.
17 She girds her loins with strength
and makes her arms strong.
18 She perceives that her merchandise is profitable.
Her lamp does not go out at night.
19 She puts her hands to the distaff,
and her hands hold the spindle.
20 She opens her hand to the poor,
and reaches out her hands to the needy.
21 She is not afraid of snow for her household,
for all her household are clothed in scarlet.
22 She makes herself coverings;
her clothing is fine linen and purple.

[i] Gk Syr Tg Compare Vg: Heb obscure [j] The meaning of the Hebrew is uncertain
[k] Or *King Lemuel, the oracle* [l] Cn: Heb *where* [m] Heb *are sons of passing away*

23 Her husband is known in the gates,
when he sits among the elders of the land.
24 She makes linen garments and sells them;
she delivers girdles to the merchant.
25 Strength and dignity are her clothing,
and she laughs at the time to come.
26 She opens her mouth with wisdom,
and the teaching of kindness is on her tongue.
27 She looks well to the ways of her household,
and does not eat the bread of idleness.
28 Her children rise up and call her blessed;
her husband also, and he praises her:
29 "Many women have done excellently,
but you surpass them all."
30 Charm is deceitful, and beauty is vain,
but a woman who fears the LORD is to be praised.
31 Give her of the fruit of her hands,
and let her works praise her in the gates.

ECCLESIASTES

OR THE PREACHER

1 The words of the Preacher,[a] the son of David, king in Jerusalem.
2 Vanity of vanities, says the Preacher,
vanity of vanities! All is vanity.
3 What does man gain by all the toil
at which he toils under the sun?
4 A generation goes, and a generation comes,
but the earth remains for ever.
5 The sun rises and the sun goes down,
and hastens to the place where it rises.
6 The wind blows to the south,
and goes round to the north;
round and round goes the wind,
and on its circuits the wind returns.
7 All streams run to the sea,
but the sea is not full;
to the place where the streams flow,
there they flow again.
8 All things are full of weariness;
a man cannot utter it;
the eye is not satisfied with seeing,
nor the ear filled with hearing.
9 What has been is what will be,
and what has been done is what will be done;
and there is nothing new under the sun.
10 Is there a thing of which it is said,
"See, this is new"?
It has been already,
in the ages before us.
11 There is no remembrance of former things,
nor will there be any remembrance
of later things yet to happen
among those who come after.

12 I the Preacher have been king
over Israel in Jerusalem. 13And I applied my mind to seek and to search
out by wisdom all that is done under
heaven; it is an unhappy business that
God has given to the sons of men to
be busy with. 14 I have seen everything that is done under the sun; and
behold, all is vanity and a striving after
wind.[b]

15 What is crooked cannot be made straight,
and what is lacking cannot be numbered.

16 I said to myself, "I have acquired great wisdom, surpassing all
who were over Jerusalem before me;
and my mind has had great experience
of wisdom and knowledge." 17And I
applied my mind to know wisdom and
to know madness and folly. I perceived
that this also is but a striving after
wind.

18 For in much wisdom is much vexation,

[a] Heb *Koheleth* [b] Or *a feeding on wind.* See Hos 12.1

and he who increases knowledge
increases sorrow.

2 I said to myself, "Come now, I
will make a test of pleasure; enjoy
yourself." But behold, this also was
vanity. 2 I said of laughter, "It is
mad," and of pleasure, "What use is
it?" 3 I searched with my mind how
to cheer my body with wine— my mind
still guiding me with wisdom—and
how to lay hold on folly, till I might
see what was good for the sons of men
to do under heaven during the few
days of their life. 4 I made great works;
I built houses and planted vineyards
for myself; 5 I made myself gardens
and parks, and planted in them all
kinds of fruit trees. 6 I made myself
pools from which to water the forest
of growing trees. 7 I bought male and
female slaves, and had slaves who
were born in my house; I had also
great possessions of herds and flocks,
more than any who had been before
me in Jerusalem. 8 I also gathered for
myself silver and gold and the treasure
of kings and provinces; I got singers,
both men and women, and many
concubines,[c] man's delight.

9 So I became great and surpassed
all who were before me in Jerusalem;
also my wisdom remained with me.
10 And whatever my eyes desired I did
not keep from them; I kept my heart
from no pleasure, for my heart found
pleasure in all my toil, and this was
my reward for all my toil. 11 Then I
considered all that my hands had done
and the toil I had spent in doing it,
and behold, all was vanity and a
striving after wind, and there was
nothing to be gained under the sun.

12 So I turned to consider wisdom
and madness and folly; for what can
the man do who comes after the king?
Only what he has already done. 13 Then
I saw that wisdom excels folly as light
excels darkness. 14 The wise man
has his eyes in his head, but the fool
walks in darkness; and yet I perceived
that one fate comes to all of them.
15 Then I said to myself, "What befalls
the fool will befall me also; why then
have I been so very wise?" And I said
to myself that this also is vanity. 16 For
of the wise man as of the fool there is
no enduring remembrance, seeing that
in the days to come all will have been
long forgotten. How the wise man dies
just like the fool! 17 So I hated life, because what is done under the sun was
grievous to me; for all is vanity and a
striving after wind.

18 I hated all my toil in which I had
toiled under the sun, seeing that I
must leave it to the man who will come
after me; 19 and who knows whether
he will be a wise man or a fool? Yet he
will be master of all for which I toiled
and used my wisdom under the sun.
This also is vanity. 20 So I turned
about and gave my heart up to despair
over all the toil of my labors under the
sun, 21 because sometimes a man who
has toiled with wisdom and knowledge
and skill must leave all to be enjoyed
by a man who did not toil for it. This
also is vanity and a great evil. 22 What
has a man from all the toil and strain
with which he toils beneath the sun?
23 For all his days are full of pain, and
his work is a vexation; even in the
night his mind does not rest. This also
is vanity.

24 There is nothing better for a
man than that he should eat and drink,
and find enjoyment in his toil. This
also, I saw, is from the hand of God;
25 for apart from him[d] who can eat or
who can have enjoyment? 26 For to
the man who pleases him God gives
wisdom and knowledge and joy; but
to the sinner he gives the work of
gathering and heaping, only to give to
one who pleases God. This also is
vanity and a striving after wind.

3 For everything there is a season
and a time for every matter under
heaven:

2 a time to be born, and a time to
die;
a time to plant, and a time to pluck
up what is planted:
3 a time to kill, and a time to heal;
a time to break down, and a time to
build up;
4 a time to weep, and a time to laugh;
a time to mourn, and a time to
dance;
5 a time to cast away stones, and a
time to gather stones together;
a time to embrace, and a time to refrain from embracing;
6 a time to seek, and a time to lose;
a time to keep, and a time to cast
away;
7 a time to rend, and a time to sew;
a time to keep silence, and a time to
speak;
8 a time to love, and a time to hate;

c The meaning of the Hebrew word is uncertain d Gk Syr: Heb *apart from me*

a time for war, and a time for peace.
9 What gain has the worker from his
toil?

10 I have seen the business that
God has given to the sons of men to
be busy with. 11 He has made everything beautiful in its time; also he has
put eternity into man's mind, yet so
that he cannot find out what God has
done from the beginning to the end.
12 I know that there is nothing better
for them than to be happy and enjoy
themselves as long as they live; 13 also
that it is God's gift to man that every
one should eat and drink and take
pleasure in all his toil. 14 I know that
whatever God does endures for ever;
nothing can be added to it, nor anything taken from it; God has made it
so, in order that men should fear before him. 15 That which is, already has
been; that which is to be, already has
been; and God seeks what has been
driven away.

16 Moreover I saw under the sun
that in the place of justice, even there
was wickedness, and in the place of
righteousness, even there was wickedness. 17 I said in my heart, God will
judge the righteous and the wicked,
for he has appointed a time for every
matter, and for every work. 18 I said
in my heart with regard to the sons of
men that God is testing them to show
them that they are but beasts. 19 For
the fate of the sons of men and the fate
of beasts is the same; as one dies, so
dies the other. They all have the same
breath, and man has no advantage over
the beasts; for all is vanity. 20 All go to
one place; all are from the dust, and
all turn to dust again. 21 Who knows
whether the spirit of man goes upward
and the spirit of the beast goes down
to the earth? 22 So I saw that there is
nothing better than that a man should
enjoy his work, for that is his lot; who
can bring him to see what will be after
him?

4 Again I saw all the oppressions
that are practiced under the sun.
And behold, the tears of the oppressed,
and they had no one to comfort them!
On the side of their oppressors there
was power, and there was no one to
comfort them. 2 And I thought the
dead who are already dead more
fortunate than the living who are still
alive; 3 but better than both is he who
has not yet been, and has not seen the
evil deeds that are done under the
sun.

4 Then I saw that all toil and all
skill in work come from a man's envy
of his neighbor. This also is vanity and
a striving after wind.

5 The fool folds his hands, and eats
his own flesh.

6 Better is a handful of quietness
than two hands full of toil and a
striving after wind.

7 Again, I saw vanity under the
sun: 8 a person who has no one, either
son or brother, yet there is no end to
all his toil, and his eyes are never
satisfied with riches, so that he never
asks, "For whom am I toiling and
depriving myself of pleasure?" This
also is vanity and an unhappy business.

9 Two are better than one, because
they have a good reward for their toil.
10 For if they fall, one will lift up his
fellow; but woe to him who is alone
when he falls and has not another to
lift him up. 11 Again, if two lie together,
they are warm; but how can one be
warm alone? 12 And though a man
might prevail against one who is alone,
two will withstand him. A threefold
cord is not quickly broken.

13 Better is a poor and wise youth
than an old and foolish king, who will
no longer take advice, 14 even though
he had gone from prison to the throne
or in his own kingdom had been born
poor. 15 I saw all the living who move
about under the sun, as well as that[f]
youth, who was to stand in his place;
16 there was no end of all the people;
he was over all of them. Yet those who
come later will not rejoice in him.
Surely this also is vanity and a striving
after wind.

5[g] Guard your steps when you go
to the house of God; to draw near
to listen is better than to offer the
sacrifice of fools; for they do not know
that they are doing evil. 2[h] Be not rash
with your mouth, nor let your heart be
hasty to utter a word before God, for
God is in heaven, and you upon earth;
therefore let your words be few.

3 For a dream comes with much
business, and a fool's voice with many
words.

4 When you vow a vow to God, do
not delay paying it; for he has no
pleasure in fools. Pay what you vow.
5 It is better that you should not vow

[f] Heb *the second* [g] Ch 4.17 in Heb [h] Ch 5.1 in Heb

than that you should vow and not pay.
6 Let not your mouth lead you into
sin, and do not say before the messenger[i] that it was a mistake; why
should God be angry at your voice,
and destroy the work of your hands?
7 For when dreams increase, empty
words grow many:[j] but do you fear
God.
8 If you see in a province the poor
oppressed and justice and right violently taken away, do not be amazed
at the matter; for the high official is
watched by a higher, and there are yet
higher ones over them. 9 But in all, a
king is an advantage to a land with
cultivated fields.[k]
10 He who loves money will not be
satisfied with money; nor he who loves
wealth, with gain: this also is vanity.
11 When goods increase, they increase who eat them; and what gain
has their owner but to see them with
his eyes?
12 Sweet is the sleep of a laborer,
whether he eats little or much; but the
surfeit of the rich will not let him
sleep.
13 There is a grievous evil which I
have seen under the sun: riches were
kept by their owner to his hurt, 14 and
those riches were lost in a bad venture;
and he is father of a son, but he has
nothing in his hand. 15 As he came
from his mother's womb he shall go
again, naked as he came, and shall
take nothing for his toil, which he may
carry away in his hand. 16 This also is
a grievous evil: just as he came, so
shall he go; and what gain has he that
he toiled for the wind, 17 and spent all
his days in darkness and grief,[l] in
much vexation and sickness and re-
sentment?
18 Behold, what I have seen to be
good and to be fitting is to eat and
drink and find enjoyment in all the
toil with which one toils under the sun
the few days of his life which God has
given him, for this is his lot. 19 Every
man also to whom God has given
wealth and possessions and power to
enjoy them, and to accept his lot and
find enjoyment in his toil—this is the
gift of God. 20 For he will not much
remember the days of his life because
God keeps him occupied with joy in
his heart.

6 There is an evil which I have seen
under the sun, and it lies heavy
upon men: 2 a man to whom God
gives wealth, possessions, and honor,
so that he lacks nothing of all that he
desires, yet God does not give him
power to enjoy them, but a stranger
enjoys them; this is vanity; it is a sore
affliction. 3 If a man begets a hundred
children, and lives many years, so that
the days of his years are many, but he
does not enjoy life's good things, and
also has no burial, I say that an untimely birth is better off than he. 4 For
it comes into vanity and goes into
darkness, and in darkness its name is
covered; 5 moreover it has not seen the
sun or known anything; yet it finds
rest rather than he. 6 Even though he
should live a thousand years twice
told, yet enjoy no good—do not all go
to the one place?
7 All the toil of man is for his
mouth, yet his appetite is not satisfied.
8 For what advantage has the wise man
over the fool? And what does the poor
man have who knows how to conduct
himself before the living? 9 Better is
the sight of the eyes than the wandering of desire; this also is vanity and a
striving after wind.
10 Whatever has come to be has
already been named, and it is known
what man is, and that he is not able
to dispute with one stronger than he.
11 The more words, the more vanity,
and what is man the better? 12 For who
knows what is good for man while he
lives the few days of his vain life,
which he passes like a shadow? For
who can tell man what will be after
him under the sun?

7 A good name is better than precious ointment;
and the day of death, than the
day of birth.
2 It is better to go to the house of
mourning
than to go to the house of feasting;
for this is the end of all men,
and the living will lay it to heart.
3 Sorrow is better than laughter,
for by sadness of countenance the
heart is made glad.
4 The heart of the wise is in the house
of mourning;
but the heart of fools is in the
house of mirth.

[i] Or *angel* [j] Or *For in a multitude of dreams there is futility, and ruin in a flood of words*
[k] Or *The profit of the land is among all of them; a cultivated field has a king*
[l] Gk: Heb *all his days also he eats in darkness*

5 It is better for a man to hear the
rebuke of the wise
than to hear the song of fools.
6 For as the crackling of thorns under
a pot,
so is the laughter of the fools;
this also is vanity.
7 Surely oppression makes the wise
man foolish,
and a bribe corrupts the mind.
8 Better is the end of a thing than its
beginning;
and the patient in spirit is better
than the proud in spirit.
9 Be not quick to anger,
for anger lodges in the bosom of
fools.
10 Say not, "Why were the former
days better than these?"
For it is not from wisdom that
you ask this.
11 Wisdom is good with an inheritance,
an advantage to those who see
the sun.
12 For the protection of wisdom is like
the protection of money;
and the advantage of knowledge
is that wisdom preserves the
life of him who has it.
13 Consider the work of God;
who can make straight what he
has made crooked?

14 In the day of prosperity be joyful, and in the day of adversity consider; God has made the one as well
as the other, so that man may not find
out anything that will be after him.

15 In my vain life I have seen
everything; there is a righteous man
who perishes in his righteousness, and
there is a wicked man who prolongs
his life in his evil-doing. 16 Be not
righteous overmuch, and do not make
yourself overwise; why should you destroy yourself? 17 Be not wicked overmuch, neither be a fool; why should
you die before your time? 18 It is good
that you should take hold of this, and
from that withhold not your hand; for
he who fears God shall come forth
from them all.

19 Wisdom gives strength to the
wise man more than ten rulers that
are in a city.

20 Surely there is not a righteous
man on earth who does good and never
sins.

21 Do not give heed to all the things
that men say, lest you hear your servant cursing you; 22 your heart knows
that many times you have yourself
cursed others.

23 All this I have tested by wisdom;
I said, "I will be wise"; but it was far
from me. 24 That which is, is far off,
and deep, very deep; who can find it
out? 25 I turned my mind to know and
to search out and to seek wisdom and
the sum of things, and to know the
wickedness of folly and the foolishness
which is madness. 26 And I found more
bitter than death the woman whose
heart is snares and nets, and whose
hands are fetters; he who pleases God
escapes her, but the sinner is taken by
her. 27 Behold, this is what I found,
says the Preacher, adding one thing to
another to find the sum, 28 which my
mind has sought repeatedly, but I have
not found. One man among a thousand
I found, but a woman among all these
I have not found. 29 Behold, this alone
I found, that God made man upright,
but they have sought out many devices.

8 Who is like the wise man?
And who knows the interpretation
of a thing?
A man's wisdom makes his face
shine,
and the hardness of his countenance is changed.

2 Keep[m] the king's command, and
because of your sacred oath be not
dismayed; 3 go from his presence, do
not delay when the matter is un-
pleasant, for he does whatever he
pleases. 4 For the word of the king is
supreme, and who may say to him,
"What are you doing?" 5 He who obeys
a command will meet no harm, and
the mind of a wise man will know the
time and way. 6 For every matter has
its time and way, although man's
trouble lies heavy upon him. 7 For he
does not know what is to be, for who
can tell him how it will be? 8 No man
has power to retain the spirit, or
authority over the day of death; there
is no discharge from war, nor will
wickedness deliver those who are given
to it. 9 All this I observed while apply-
ing my mind to all that is done under
the sun, while man lords it over man
to his hurt.

10 Then I saw the wicked buried;
they used to go in and out of the holy
place, and were praised in the city
where they had done such things. This
also is vanity. 11 Because sentence
against an evil deed is not executed

[m] Heb inserts an *I*

speedily, the heart of the sons of men
is fully set to do evil. 12 Though a
sinner does evil a hundred times and
prolongs his life, yet I know that it will
be well with those who fear God, because they fear before him; 13 but it
will not be well with the wicked,
neither will he prolong his days like a
shadow, because he does not fear before God.

14 There is a vanity which takes
place on earth, that there are righteous
men to whom it happens according to
the deeds of the wicked, and there are
wicked men to whom it happens according to the deeds of the righteous.
I said that this also is vanity. 15 And I
commend enjoyment, for man has no
good thing under the sun but to eat,
and drink, and enjoy himself, for this
will go with him in his toil through
the days of life which God gives him
under the sun.

16 When I applied my mind to
know wisdom, and to see the business
that is done on earth, how neither day
nor night one's eyes see sleep; 17 then
I saw all the work of God, that man
cannot find out the work that is done
under the sun. However much man
may toil in seeking, he will not find it
out; even though a wise man claims to
know, he cannot find it out.

9 But all this I laid to heart, examining it all, how the righteous
and the wise and their deeds are in the
hand of God; whether it is love or
hate man does not know. Everything
before them is vanity,[n] 2 since one fate
comes to all, to the righteous and the
wicked, to the good and the evil,[o] to
the clean and the unclean, to him who
sacrifices and him who does not sacrifice. As is the good man, so is the
sinner; and he who swears is as he who
shuns an oath. 3 This is an evil in all
that is done under the sun, that one
fate comes to all; also the hearts of
men are full of evil, and madness is in
their hearts while they live, and after
that they go to the dead. 4 But he who
is joined with all the living has hope,
for a living dog is better than a dead
lion. 5 For the living know that they
will die, but the dead know nothing,
and they have no more reward; but
the memory of them is lost. 6 Their
love and their hate and their envy have
already perished, and they have no
more for ever any share in all that is
done under the sun.

7 Go, eat your bread with enjoyment, and drink your wine with a
merry heart; for God has already
approved what you do.

8 Let your garments be always
white; let not oil be lacking on your
head.

9 Enjoy life with the wife whom
you love, all the days of your vain life
which he has given you under the sun,
because that is your portion in life and
in your toil at which you toil under the
sun. 10 Whatever your hand finds to
do, do it with your might; for there is
no work or thought or knowledge or
wisdom in Shē'ōl, to which you are
going.

11 Again I saw that under the sun
the race is not to the swift, nor the
battle to the strong, nor bread to the
wise, nor riches to the intelligent, nor
favor to the men of skill; but time and
chance happen to them all. 12 For man
does not know his time. Like fish
which are taken in an evil net, and like
birds which are caught in a snare, so
the sons of men are snared at an evil
time, when it suddenly falls upon them.

13 I have also seen this example of
wisdom under the sun, and it seemed
great to me. 14 There was a little city
with few men in it; and a great king
came against it and besieged it, building great siegeworks against it. 15 But
there was found in it a poor wise man,
and he by his wisdom delivered the
city. Yet no one remembered that
poor man. 16 But I say that wisdom is
better than might, though the poor
man's wisdom is despised, and his
words are not heeded.

17 The words of the wise heard in
quiet are better than the shouting of a
ruler among fools. 18 Wisdom is better
than weapons of war, but one sinner
destroys much good.

10 Dead flies make the perfumer's
ointment give off an evil odor;
so a little folly outweighs wisdom
and honor.
2 A wise man's heart inclines him toward the right,
but a fool's heart toward the left.
3 Even when the fool walks on the
road, he lacks sense,
and he says to every one that he
is a fool.

[n] Syr Compare Gk: Heb *Everything before them is everything*
[o] Gk Syr Vg: Heb lacks *and the evil*

4 If the anger of the ruler rises against
you, do not leave your place,
for deference will make amends
for great offenses.

5 There is an evil which I have seen
under the sun, as it were an error pro-
ceeding from the ruler: 6 folly is set
in many high places, and the rich sit
in a low place. 7 I have seen slaves on
horses, and princes walking on foot
like slaves.

8 He who digs a pit will fall into it;
and a serpent will bite him who
breaks through a wall.
9 He who quarries stones is hurt by
them;
and he who splits logs is en-
dangered by them.
10 If the iron is blunt, and one does
not whet the edge,
he must put forth more strength;
but wisdom helps one to succeed.
11 If the serpent bites before it is
charmed,
there is no advantage in a charmer.

12 The words of a wise man's mouth
win him favor,
but the lips of a fool consume him.
13 The beginning of the words of his
mouth is foolishness,
and the end of his talk is wicked
madness.
14 A fool multiplies words,
though no man knows what is to
be,
and who can tell him what will
be after him?
15 The toil of a fool wearies him,
so that he does not know the way
to the city.

16 Woe to you, O land, when your
king is a child,
and your princes feast in the
morning!
17 Happy are you, O land, when your
king is the son of free men,
and your princes feast at the
proper time,
for strength, and not for drunkenness!
18 Through sloth the roof sinks in,
and through indolence the house
leaks.
19 Bread is made for laughter,
and wine gladdens life,
and money answers everything.
20 Even in your thought, do not curse
the king,
nor in your bedchamber curse the
rich;
for a bird of the air will carry
your voice,
or some winged creature tell the
matter.

11 Cast your bread upon the waters,
for you will find it after many
days.
2 Give a portion to seven, or even to
eight,
for you know not what evil may
happen on earth.
3 If the clouds are full of rain,
they empty themselves on the
earth;
and if a tree falls to the south or to
the north,
in the place where the tree falls,
there it will lie.
4 He who observes the wind will not
sow;
and he who regards the clouds
will not reap.

5 As you do not know how the
spirit comes to the bones in the womb[p]
of a woman with child, so you do not
know the work of God who makes
everything.
6 In the morning sow your seed,
and at evening withhold not your
hand; for you do not know which will
prosper, this or that, or whether both
alike will be good.
7 Light is sweet, and it is pleasant
for the eyes to behold the sun.
8 For if a man lives many years, let
him rejoice in them all; but let him
remember that the days of darkness
will be many. All that comes is vanity.
9 Rejoice, O young man, in your
youth, and let your heart cheer you in
the days of your youth; walk in the
ways of your heart and the sight of
your eyes. But know that for all these
things God will bring you into
judgment.
10 Remove vexation from your
mind, and put away pain from your
body; for youth and the dawn of life
are vanity.

12 Remember also your Creator in
the days of your youth, before
the evil days come, and the years draw
nigh, when you will say, "I have no
pleasure in them"; 2 before the sun
and the light and the moon and the
stars are darkened and the clouds return after the rain; 3 in the day when

[p] Or *As you do not know the way of the wind, or how the bones grow in the womb*

the keepers of the house tremble, and
the strong men are bent, and the
grinders cease because they are few,
and those that look through the
windows are dimmed, 4 and the doors
on the street are shut; when the sound
of the grinding is low, and one rises
up at the voice of a bird, and all the
daughters of song are brought low;
5 they are afraid also of what is high,
and terrors are in the way; the almond
tree blossoms, the grasshopper drags
itself along[q] and desire fails; because
man goes to his eternal home, and the
mourners go about the streets; 6 before
the silver cord is snapped,[r] or the
golden bowl is broken, or the pitcher
is broken at the fountain, or the wheel
broken at the cistern, 7 and the dust
returns to the earth as it was, and the
spirit returns to God who gave it.
8 Vanity of vanities, says the Preacher;
all is vanity.

9 Besides being wise, the Preacher
also taught the people knowledge,
weighing and studying and arranging
proverbs with great care. 10 The
Preacher sought to find pleasing words,
and uprightly he wrote words of truth.

11 The sayings of the wise are like
goads, and like nails firmly fixed are
the collected sayings which are given
by one Shepherd. 12 My son, beware
of anything beyond these. Of making
many books there is no end, and much
study is a weariness of the flesh.

13 The end of the matter; all has
been heard. Fear God, and keep his
commandments; for this is the whole
duty of man.[s] 14 For God will bring
every deed into judgment, with[t] every
secret thing, whether good or evil.

THE SONG OF SOLOMON

1 The Song of Songs, which is Solomon's.

2 O that you[a] would kiss me with the
kisses of your[b] mouth!
For your love is better than wine,
3 your anointing oils are fragrant,
your name is oil poured out;
therefore the maidens love you.
4 Draw me after you, let us make
haste.
The king has brought me into his
chambers.
We will exult and rejoice in you;
we will extol your love more than
wine;
rightly do they love you.

5 I am very dark, but comely,
O daughters of Jerusalem,
like the tents of Kē'där,
like the curtains of Solomon.
6 Do not gaze at me because I am
swarthy,
because the sun has scorched me.
My mother's sons were angry with
me,
they made me keeper of the vineyards;
but, my own vineyard I have not
kept!
7 Tell me, you whom my soul loves,
where you pasture your flock,
where you make it lie down at
noon;
for why should I be like one who
wanders[c]
beside the flocks of your companions?

8 If you do not know,
O fairest among women,
follow in the tracks of the flock,
and pasture your kids
beside the shepherds' tents.

9 I compare you, my love,
to a mare of Pharaoh's chariots.
10 Your cheeks are comely with
ornaments,
your neck with strings of jewels.
11 We will make you ornaments of
gold,
studded with silver.

12 While the king was on his couch,
my nard gave forth its fragrance.
13 My beloved is to me a bag of myrrh,

[q] Or *is a burden* [r] Syr Vg Compare Gk: Heb *is removed* [s] Or *the duty of all men*
[t] Or *into the judgment on* [a] Heb *he* [b] Heb *his* [c] Gk Syr Vg: Heb *is veiled*

that lies between my breasts.
14 My beloved is to me a cluster of henna blossoms
in the vineyards of En gē′dī.

15 Behold, you are beautiful, my love;
behold, you are beautiful;
your eyes are doves.
16 Behold, you are beautiful, my beloved,
truly lovely.
Our couch is green;
17 the beams of our house are cedar,
our rafters[d] are pine.

2 I am a rose[e] of Sharon,
a lily of the valleys.

2 As a lily among brambles,
so is my love among maidens.

3 As an apple tree among the trees of the wood,
so is my beloved among young men.
With great delight I sat in his shadow,
and his fruit was sweet to my taste.
4 He brought me to the banqueting house,
and his banner over me was love.
5 Sustain me with raisins,
refresh me with apples;
for I am sick with love.
6 O that his left hand were under my head,
and that his right hand embraced me!
7 I adjure you, O daughters of Jerusalem,
by the gazelles or the hinds of the field,
that you stir not up nor awaken love
until it please.

8 The voice of my beloved!
Behold, he comes,
leaping upon the mountains,
bounding over the hills.
9 My beloved is like a gazelle,
or a young stag.
Behold, there he stands
behind our wall,
gazing in at the windows,
looking through the lattice.
10 My beloved speaks and says to me:
"Arise, my love, my fair one,
and come away;
11 for lo, the winter is past,
the rain is over and gone.
12 The flowers appear on the earth,
the time of singing has come,
and the voice of the turtledove
is heard in our land.
13 The fig tree puts forth its figs,
and the vines are in blossom;
they give forth fragrance.
Arise, my love, my fair one,
and come away.
14 O my dove, in the clefts of the rock,
in the covert of the cliff,
let me see your face,
let me hear your voice,
for your voice is sweet,
and your face is comely.
15 Catch us the foxes,
the little foxes,
that spoil the vineyards,
for our vineyards are in blossom."

16 My beloved is mine and I am his,
he pastures his flock among the lilies.
17 Until the day breathes
and the shadows flee,
turn, my beloved, be like a gazelle,
or a young stag upon rugged[f] mountains.

3 Upon my bed by night
I sought him whom my soul loves;
I sought him, but found him not;
I called him, but he gave no answer.[g]
2 "I will rise now and go about the city,
in the streets and in the squares;
I will seek him whom my soul loves."
I sought him, but found him not.
3 The watchmen found me,
as they went about in the city.
"Have you seen him whom my soul loves?"
4 Scarcely had I passed them,
when I found him whom my soul loves.
I held him, and would not let him go
until I had brought him into my mother's house,
and into the chamber of her that conceived me.
5 I adjure you, O daughters of Jerusalem,

[d] The meaning of the Hebrew word is uncertain [e] Heb *crocus*
[f] The meaning of the Hebrew word is unknown [g] Gk: Heb lacks this line

by the gazelles or the hinds of the field,
that you stir not up nor awaken love
until it please.

6 What is that coming up from the wilderness,
like a column of smoke,
perfumed with myrrh and frankincense,
with all the fragrant powders of the merchant?
7 Behold, it is the litter of Solomon!
About it are sixty mighty men
of the mighty men of Israel,
8 all girt with swords
and expert in war,
each with his sword at his thigh,
against alarms by night.
9 King Solomon made himself a palanquin
from the wood of Lebanon.
10 He made its posts of silver,
its back of gold, its seat of purple;
it was lovingly wrought within[h]
by the daughters of Jerusalem.
11 Go forth, O daughters of Zion,
and behold King Solomon,
with the crown with which his mother crowned him
on the day of his wedding,
on the day of the gladness of his heart.

4 Behold, you are beautiful, my love,
behold, you are beautiful!
Your eyes are doves
behind your veil.
Your hair is like a flock of goats,
moving down the slopes of Gilead.
2 Your teeth are like a flock of shorn ewes
that have come up from the washing,
all of which bear twins,
and not one among them is bereaved.
3 Your lips are like a scarlet thread,
and your mouth is lovely.
Your cheeks are like halves of a pomegranate
behind your veil.
4 Your neck is like the tower of David,
built for an arsenal,[i]
whereon hang a thousand bucklers,
all of them shields of warriors.
5 Your two breasts are like two fawns,
twins of a gazelle,
that feed among the lilies.
6 Until the day breathes
and the shadows flee,
I will hie me to the mountain of myrrh
and the hill of frankincense.
7 You are all fair, my love;
there is no flaw in you.
8 Come with me from Lebanon, my bride;
come with me from Lebanon.
Depart[j] from the peak of Ă·mä'nä,
from the peak of Sē'nir and Hĕr'mŏn,
from the dens of lions,
from the mountains of leopards.

9 You have ravished my heart, my sister, my bride,
you have ravished my heart with a glance of your eyes,
with one jewel of your necklace.
10 How sweet is your love, my sister, my bride!
how much better is your love than wine,
and the fragrance of your oils than any spice!
11 Your lips distil nectar, my bride;
honey and milk are under your tongue;
the scent of your garments is like the scent of Lebanon.
12 A garden locked is my sister, my bride,
a garden locked, a fountain sealed.
13 Your shoots are an orchard of pomegranates
with all choicest fruits,
henna with nard,
14 nard and saffron, calamus and cinnamon,
with all trees of frankincense,
myrrh and aloes,
with all chief spices—
15 a garden fountain, a well of living water,
and flowing streams from Lebanon.

16 Awake, O north wind,
and come, O south wind!
Blow upon my garden,
let its fragrance be wafted abroad.
Let my beloved come to his garden,
and eat its choicest fruits.

5 I come to my garden, my sister, my bride,
I gather my myrrh with my spice,

[h] The meaning of the Hebrew is uncertain [i] The meaning of the Hebrew word is uncertain [j] Or *look*

I eat my honeycomb with my honey,
I drink my wine with my milk.

Eat, O friends, and drink:
drink deeply, O lovers!

2 I slept, but my heart was awake.
Hark! my beloved is knocking.
"Open to me, my sister, my love,
my dove, my perfect one;
for my head is wet with dew,
my locks with the drops of the night."
3 I had put off my garment,
how could I put it on?
I had bathed my feet,
how could I soil them?
4 My beloved put his hand to the latch,
and my heart was thrilled within me.
5 I arose to open to my beloved,
and my hands dripped with myrrh,
my fingers with liquid myrrh,
upon the handles of the bolt.
6 I opened to my beloved,
but my beloved had turned and gone.
My soul failed me when he spoke.
I sought him, but found him not;
I called him, but he gave no answer.
7 The watchmen found me,
as they went about in the city;
they beat me, they wounded me,
they took away my mantle,
those watchmen of the walls.
8 I adjure you, O daughters of Jerusalem,
if you find my beloved,
that you tell him
I am sick with love.

9 What is your beloved more than another beloved,
O fairest among women?
What is your beloved more than another beloved,
that you thus adjure us?

10 My beloved is all radiant and ruddy,
distinguished among ten thousand.
11 His head is the finest gold;
his locks are wavy,
black as a raven.
12 His eyes are like doves
beside springs of water,
bathed in milk,
fitly set.[k]
13 His cheeks are like beds of spices,
yielding fragrance.
His lips are lilies,
distilling liquid myrrh.
14 His arms are rounded gold,
set with jewels.
His body is ivory work,[l]
encrusted with sapphires.[m]
15 His legs are alabaster columns,
set upon bases of gold.
His appearance is like Lebanon,
choice as the cedars.
16 His speech is most sweet,
and he is altogether desirable.
This is my beloved and this is my friend,
O daughters of Jerusalem.

6 Whither has your beloved gone,
O fairest among women?
Whither has your beloved turned,
that we may seek him with you?

2 My beloved has gone down to his garden,
to the beds of spices,
to pasture his flock in the gardens,
and to gather lilies.
3 I am my beloved's and my beloved is mine;
he pastures his flock among the lilies.

4 You are beautiful as Tĭr'zăh, my love,
comely as Jerusalem,
terrible as an army with banners.
5 Turn away your eyes from me,
for they disturb me—
Your hair is like a flock of goats,
moving down the slopes of Gilead.
6 Your teeth are like a flock of ewes,
that have come up from the washing,
all of them bear twins,
not one among them is bereaved.
7 Your cheeks are like halves of a pomegranate
behind your veil.
8 There are sixty queens and eighty concubines,
and maidens without number.
9 My dove, my perfect one, is only one,
the darling of her mother,

[k] The meaning of the Hebrew is uncertain [l] The meaning of the Hebrew word is uncertain
[m] Heb *lapis lazuli*

flawless to her that bore her.
The maidens saw her and called her happy;
the queens and concubines also, and they praised her.
10 "Who is this that looks forth like the dawn,
fair as the moon, bright as the sun,
terrible as an army with banners?"

11 I went down to the nut orchard,
to look at the blossoms of the valley,
to see whether the vines had budded,
whether the pomegranates were in bloom.
12 Before I was aware, my fancy set me
in a chariot beside my prince.[n]

13[o] Return, return, O Shü'lăm·mīte,
return, return, that we may look upon you.

Why should you look upon the Shulammite,
as upon a dance before two armies?[p]

7

How graceful are your feet in sandals,
O queenly maiden!
Your rounded thighs are like jewels,
the work of a master hand.
2 Your navel is a rounded bowl
that never lacks mixed wine.
Your belly is a heap of wheat,
encircled with lilies.
3 Your two breasts are like two fawns,
twins of a gazelle.
4 Your neck is like an ivory tower.
Your eyes are pools in Hesh'bŏn,
by the gate of Bath-rab'bim.
Your nose is like a tower of Lebanon,
overlooking Damascus.
5 Your head crowns you like Cär'mĕl,
and your flowing locks are like purple;
a king is held captive in the tresses.[q]

6 How fair and pleasant you are,
O loved one, delectable maiden![r]
7 You are stately[s] as a palm tree,
and your breasts are like its clusters.
8 I say I will climb the palm tree
and lay hold of its branches.
Oh, may your breasts be like clusters of the vine,
and the scent of your breath like apples,
9 and your kisses[t] like the best wine
that goes down[u] smoothly,
gliding over lips and teeth.[v]

10 I am my beloved's,
and his desire is for me.
11 Come, my beloved,
let us go forth into the fields,
and lodge in the villages;
12 let us go out early to the vineyards,
and see whether the vines have budded,
whether the grape blossoms have opened
and the pomegranates are in bloom.
There I will give you my love.
13 The mandrakes give forth fragrance,
and over our doors are all choice fruits,
new as well as old,
which I have laid up for you, O my beloved.

8

O that you were like a brother to me,
that nursed at my mother's breast!
If I met you outside, I would kiss you,
and none would despise me.
2 I would lead you and bring you
into the house of my mother,
and into the chamber of her that conceived me.[w]
I would give you spiced wine to drink,
the juice of my pomegranates.
3 O that his left hand were under my head,
and that his right hand embraced me!
4 I adjure you, O daughters of Jerusalem,
that you stir not up nor awaken love
until it please.

5 Who is that coming up from the wilderness,
leaning upon her beloved?

[n] Cn: The meaning of the Hebrew is uncertain [o] Ch 7.1 in Heb [p] Or *dance of Mahanaim*
[q] The meaning of the Hebrew word is uncertain [r] Syr: Heb *in delights* [s] Heb *This your stature is*
[t] Heb *palate* [u] Heb *down for my lover* [v] Gk Syr Vg: Heb *lips of sleepers*
[w] Gk Syr: Heb *mother; she* (or *you*) *will teach me*

Under the apple tree I awakened
you.
There your mother was in travail
with you,
there she who bore you was in
travail.

6 Set me as a seal upon your heart,
as a seal upon your arm;
for love is strong as death,
jealousy is cruel as the grave.
Its flashes are flashes of fire,
a most vehement flame.
7 Many waters cannot quench love,
neither can floods drown it.
If a man offered for love
all the wealth of his house,
it would be utterly scorned.

8 We have a little sister,
and she has no breasts.
What shall we do for our sister,
on the day when she is spoken
for?
9 If she is a wall,
we will build upon her a battlement of silver;
but if she is a door,
we will enclose her with boards
of cedar.
10 I was a wall,
and my breasts were like towers;
then I was in his eyes
as one who brings[x] peace.

11 Solomon had a vineyard at Bā'ăl-hā'mon;
he let out the vineyard to keepers;
each one was to bring for its fruit
a thousand pieces of silver.
12 My vineyard, my very own, is for
myself;
you, O Solomon, may have the
thousand,
and the keepers of the fruit two
hundred.

13 O you who dwell in the gardens,
my companions are listening for
your voice;
let me hear it.

14 Make haste, my beloved,
and be like a gazelle
or a young stag
upon the mountains of spices.

THE BOOK OF ISAIAH

1 The vision of I·sāi'ăh the son of
Ā'moz, which he saw concerning
Judah and Jerusalem in the days of
Ŭz·zī'ăh, Jō'thăm, Ā'haz, and Hez·ē-kī'ăh, kings of Judah.
2 Hear, O heavens, and give ear, O
earth;
for the LORD has spoken:
"Sons have I reared and brought
up,
but they have rebelled against me.
3 The ox knows its owner,
and the ass its master's crib;
but Israel does not know,
my people does not understand."

4 Ah, sinful nation,
a people laden with iniquity,
offspring of evildoers,
sons who deal corruptly!
They have forsaken the LORD,
they have despised the Holy One
of Israel,
they are utterly estranged.

5 Why will you still be smitten,
that you continue to rebel?
The whole head is sick,
and the whole heart faint.
6 From the sole of the foot even to
the head,
there is no soundness in it,
but bruises and sores
and bleeding wounds;
they are not pressed out, or bound
up,
or softened with oil.

7 Your country lies desolate,
your cities are burned with fire;
in your very presence
aliens devour your land;

x Or *finds*

it is desolate, as overthrown by aliens.
8 And the daughter of Zion is left
like a booth in a vineyard,
like a lodge in a cucumber field,
like a besieged city.

9 If the LORD of hosts
had not left us a few survivors,
we should have been like Sod'ŏm,
and become like Gŏ·môr'răh.

10 Hear the word of the LORD,
you rulers of Sod'ŏm!
Give ear to the teaching of our God,
you people of Gŏ·môr'răh!
11 "What to me is the multitude of your sacrifices?
says the LORD;
I have had enough of burnt offerings of rams
and the fat of fed beasts;
I do not delight in the blood of bulls,
or of lambs, or of he-goats.

12 "When you come to appear before me,
who requires of you
this trampling of my courts?
13 Bring no more vain offerings;
incense is an abomination to me.
New moon and sabbath and the calling of assemblies—
I cannot endure iniquity and solemn assembly.
14 Your new moons and your appointed feasts
my soul hates;
they have become a burden to me,
I am weary of bearing them.
15 When you spread forth your hands,
I will hide my eyes from you;
even though you make many prayers,
I will not listen;
your hands are full of blood.
16 Wash yourselves; make yourselves clean;
remove the evil of your doings
from before my eyes;
cease to do evil,
17 learn to do good;
seek justice,
correct oppression;
defend the fatherless,
plead for the widow.

18 "Come now, let us reason together,
says the LORD:
though your sins are like scarlet,
they shall be as white as snow;
though they are red like crimson,
they shall become like wool.
19 If you are willing and obedient,
you shall eat the good of the land;
20 But if you refuse and rebel,
you shall be devoured by the sword;
for the mouth of the LORD has spoken."

21 How the faithful city
has become a harlot,
she that was full of justice!
Righteousness lodged in her,
but now murderers.
22 Your silver has become dross,
your wine mixed with water.
23 Your princes are rebels
and companions of thieves.
Every one loves a bribe
and runs after gifts.
They do not defend the fatherless,
and the widow's cause does not come to them.

24 Therefore the Lord says,
the LORD of hosts,
the Mighty One of Israel:
"Ah, I will vent my wrath on my enemies,
and avenge myself on my foes.
25 I will turn my hand against you
and will smelt away your dross as with lye
and remove all your alloy.
26 And I will restore your judges as at the first,
and your counselors as at the beginning.
Afterward you shall be called the city of righteousness,
the faithful city."

27 Zion shall be redeemed by justice,
and those in her who repent, by righteousness.
28 But rebels and sinners shall be destroyed together,
and those who forsake the LORD shall be consumed.
29 For you shall be ashamed of the oaks
in which you delighted;
and you shall blush for the gardens
which you have chosen.
30 For you shall be like an oak
whose leaf withers,
and like a garden without water.
31 And the strong shall become tow,

1.9: Rom 9.29.

and his work a spark,
and both of them shall burn together,
with none to quench them.

2 The word which I·sai'ah the son of A'moz saw concerning Judah and Jerusalem.
2 It shall come to pass in the latter days
that the mountain of the house of the LORD
shall be established as the highest of the mountains,
and shall be raised above the hills;
and all the nations shall flow to it,
3 and many peoples shall come, and say:
"Come, let us go up to the mountain of the LORD,
to the house of the God of Jacob;
that he may teach us his ways
and that we may walk in his paths."
For out of Zion shall go forth the law,
and the word of the LORD from Jerusalem.
4 He shall judge between the nations,
and shall decide for many peoples;
and they shall beat their swords into plowshares,
and their spears into pruning hooks;
nation shall not lift up sword against nation,
neither shall they learn war any more.

5 O house of Jacob,
come, let us walk
in the light of the LORD.

6 For thou hast rejected thy people,
the house of Jacob,
because they are full of diviners[a]
from the east
and of soothsayers like the Philistines,
and they strike hands with foreigners.
7 Their land is filled with silver and gold,
and there is no end to their treasures;
their land is filled with horses,
and there is no end to their chariots.
8 Their land is filled with idols;
they bow down to the work of their hands,
to what their own fingers have made.
9 So man is humbled,
and men are brought low—
forgive them not!
10 Enter into the rock,
and hide in the dust
from before the terror of the LORD,
and from the glory of his majesty.
11 The haughty looks of man shall be brought low,
and the pride of men shall be humbled;
and the LORD alone will be exalted in that day.

12 For the LORD of hosts has a day
against all that is proud and lofty,
against all that is lifted up and high;[b]
13 against all the cedars of Lebanon,
lofty and lifted up;
and against all the oaks of Ba'shan;
14 against all the high mountains,
and against all the lofty hills;
15 against every high tower,
and against every fortified wall;
16 against all the ships of Tar'shish,
and against all the beautiful craft.
17 And the haughtiness of man shall be humbled,
and the pride of men shall be brought low;
and the LORD alone will be exalted in that day.
18 And the idols shall utterly pass away.
19 And men shall enter the caves of the rocks
and the holes of the ground,
from before the terror of the LORD,
and from the glory of his majesty,
when he rises to terrify the earth.

20 In that day men will cast forth
their idols of silver and their idols of gold,
which they made for themselves to worship,
to the moles and to the bats,
21 to enter the caverns of the rocks
and the clefts of the cliffs,
from before the terror of the LORD,
and from the glory of his majesty,
when he rises to terrify the earth.
22 Turn away from man

[a] Cn: Heb lacks *of diviners*
[b] Cn Compare Gk: Heb *low*
2.2-4: Mic 4.1-3

in whose nostrils is breath,
for of what account is he?

3 For, behold, the Lord, the LORD of hosts,
is taking away from Jerusalem and from Judah
stay and staff,
the whole stay of bread,
and the whole stay of water;
2 the mighty man and the soldier,
the judge and the prophet,
the diviner and the elder,
3 the captain of fifty
and the man of rank,
the counselor and the skilful magician
and the expert in charms.
4 And I will make boys their princes,
and babes shall rule over them.
5 And the people will oppress one another,
every man his fellow
and every man his neighbor;
the youth will be insolent to the elder,
and the base fellow to the honorable.

6 When a man takes hold of his brother
in the house of his father, saying:
"You have a mantle;
you shall be our leader,
and this heap of ruins
shall be under your rule";
7 in that day he will speak out, saying:
"I will not be a healer;
in my house there is neither bread nor mantle;
you shall not make me
leader of the people."
8 For Jerusalem has stumbled,
and Judah has fallen;
because their speech and their deeds
are against the LORD,
defying his glorious presence.

9 Their partiality witnesses against them;
they proclaim their sin like Sod'om,
they do not hide it.
Woe to them!
For they have brought evil upon themselves.
10 Tell the righteous that it shall be well with them,
for they shall eat the fruit of their deeds.
11 Woe to the wicked! It shall be ill with him,
for what his hands have done
shall be done to him.
12 My people—children are their oppressors,
and women rule over them.
O my people, your leaders mislead you,
and confuse the course of your paths.

13 The LORD has taken his place to contend,
he stands to judge his people.[d]
14 The LORD enters into judgment
with the elders and princes of his people:
"It is you who have devoured the vineyard,
the spoil of the poor is in your houses.
15 What do you mean by crushing my people,
by grinding the face of the poor?"
says the Lord GOD of hosts.

16 The LORD said:
Because the daughters of Zion are haughty
and walk with outstretched necks,
glancing wantonly with their eyes,
mincing along as they go,
tinkling with their feet;
17 the Lord will smite with a scab
the heads of the daughters of Zion,
and the LORD will lay bare their secret parts.

18 In that day the Lord will take
away the finery of the anklets, the
headbands, and the crescents; 19 the
pendants, the bracelets, and the scarfs;
20 the headdresses, the armlets, the
sashes, the perfume boxes, and the
amulets; 21 the signet rings and nose
rings; 22 the festal robes, the mantles,
the cloaks, and the handbags; 23 the
garments of gauze, the linen garments,
the turbans, and the veils.
24 Instead of perfume there will be rottenness;
and instead of a girdle, a rope;
and instead of well-set hair, baldness;
and instead of a rich robe, a girding of sackcloth;
instead of beauty, shame.[e]
25 Your men shall fall by the sword

[d] Gk Syr: Heb *judge peoples* [e] One ancient Ms: Heb lacks *shame*

and your mighty men in battle.
26 And her gates shall lament and mourn;
ravaged, she shall sit upon the ground.

4 And seven women shall take hold of one man in that day, saying, "We will eat our own bread and wear our own clothes, only let us be called by your name; take away our reproach."

2 In that day the branch of the
LORD shall be beautiful and glorious,
and the fruit of the land shall be the
pride and glory of the survivors of
Israel. 3 And he who is left in Zion and
remains in Jerusalem will be called
holy, every one who has been recorded
for life in Jerusalem, 4 when the Lord
shall have washed away the filth of the
daughters of Zion and cleansed the
bloodstains of Jerusalem from its midst
by a spirit of judgment and by a spirit
of burning. 5 Then the LORD will
create over the whole site of Mount
Zion and over her assemblies a cloud
by day, and smoke and the shining of
a flaming fire by night; for over all the
glory there will be a canopy and a
pavilion. 6 It will be for a shade by
day from the heat, and for a refuge
and a shelter from the storm and rain.

5 Let me sing for my beloved
a love song concerning his vineyard:
My beloved had a vineyard
on a very fertile hill.
2 He digged it and cleared it of stones,
and planted it with choice vines;
he built a watchtower in the midst of it,
and hewed out a wine vat in it;
and he looked for it to yield grapes,
but it yielded wild grapes.

3 And now, O inhabitants of Jerusalem
and men of Judah,
judge, I pray you, between me
and my vineyard.
4 What more was there to do for my vineyard,
that I have not done in it?
When I looked for it to yield grapes,
why did it yield wild grapes?

5 And now I will tell you
what I will do to my vineyard.
I will remove its hedge,
and it shall be devoured;
I will break down its wall,
and it shall be trampled down.
6 I will make it a waste;
it shall not be pruned or hoed,
and briers and thorns shall grow up,
I will also command the clouds
that they rain no rain upon it.

7 For the vineyard of the LORD of hosts
is the house of Israel,
and the men of Judah
are his pleasant planting;
and he looked for justice,
but behold, bloodshed;
for righteousness,
but behold, a cry!

8 Woe to those who join house to house,
who add field to field,
until there is no more room,
and you are made to dwell alone
in the midst of the land.
9 The LORD of hosts has sworn in my hearing:
"Surely many houses shall be desolate,
large and beautiful houses, without inhabitant.
10 For ten acres of vineyard shall yield
but one bath,
and a homer of seed shall yield but an ephah."

11 Woe to those who rise early in the morning,
that they may run after strong drink,
who tarry late into the evening
till wine inflames them!
12 They have lyre and harp,
timbrel and flute and wine at their feasts;
but they do not regard the deeds of the LORD,
or see the work of his hands.

13 Therefore my people go into exile
for want of knowledge;
their honored men are dying of hunger,
and their multitude is parched with thirst.
14 Therefore Shē'ōl has enlarged its appetite
and opened its mouth beyond measure,

4.2: Jer 23.5; 33.15; Zech 3.8; 6.12. **5.1-7:** Mt 21.33-46; Mk 12.1-12; Lk 20.9-19.

and the nobility of Jerusalem[f] and
her multitude go down,
her throng and he who exults in
her.
15 Man is bowed down, and men are
brought low,
and the eyes of the haughty are
humbled.
16 But the LORD of hosts is exalted in
justice,
and the Holy God shows himself
holy in righteousness.
17 Then shall the lambs graze as in
their pasture,
fatlings and kids[g] shall feed among
the ruins.

18 Woe to those who draw iniquity
with cords of falsehood,
who draw sin as with cart ropes,
19 who say: "Let him make haste,
let him speed his work
that we may see it;
let the purpose of the Holy One of
Israel draw near,
and let it come, that we may know
it!"
20 Woe to those who call evil good
and good evil,
who put darkness for light
and light for darkness,
who put bitter for sweet
and sweet for bitter!
21 Woe to those who are wise in their
own eyes,
and shrewd in their own sight!
22 Woe to those who are heroes at
drinking wine,
and valiant men in mixing strong
drink,
23 who acquit the guilty for a bribe,
and deprive the innocent of his
right!

24 Therefore, as the tongue of fire
devours the stubble,
and as dry grass sinks down in
the flame,
so their root will be as rottenness,
and their blossom go up like dust;
for they have rejected the law of
the LORD of hosts,
and have despised the word of
the Holy One of Israel.
25 Therefore the anger of the LORD
was kindled against his people,
and he stretched out his hand
against them and smote them,
and the mountains quaked;
and their corpses were as refuse
in the midst of the streets.
For all this his anger is not turned
away
and his hand is stretched out still.

26 He will raise a signal for a nation
afar off,
and whistle for it from the ends
of the earth;
and lo, swiftly, speedily it comes!
27 None is weary, none stumbles,
none slumbers or sleeps,
not a waistcloth is loose,
not a sandal-thong broken;
28 their arrows are sharp,
all their bows bent,
their horses' hoofs seem like flint,
and their wheels like the whirlwind.
29 Their roaring is like a lion,
like young lions they roar;
they growl and seize their prey,
they carry it off, and none can
rescue.
30 They will growl over it on that day,
like the roaring of the sea.
And if one look to the land,
behold, darkness and distress,
and the light is darkened by its
clouds.

6 In the year that King Uz-zī'ah
died I saw the Lord sitting upon
a throne, high and lifted up; and his
train filled the temple. 2Above him
stood the seraphim; each had six
wings: with two he covered his face,
and with two he covered his feet, and
with two he flew. 3And one called to
another and said:
"Holy, holy, holy is the LORD of
hosts;
the whole earth is full of his glory."
4And the foundations of the thresholds
shook at the voice of him who called,
and the house was filled with smoke.
5And I said: "Woe is me! For I am
lost; for I am a man of unclean lips,
and I dwell in the midst of a people of
unclean lips; for my eyes have seen
the King, the LORD of hosts!"
6 Then flew one of the seraphim to
me, having in his hand a burning coal
which he had taken with tongs from
the altar. 7And he touched my mouth,
and said: "Behold, this has touched
your lips; your guilt is taken away, and
your sin forgiven." 8And I heard the

[f] Heb *her nobility* [g] Cn Compare Gk: Heb *aliens*
6.3: Rev 4.8. 6.4: Rev 15.8

voice of the Lord saying, "Whom shall
I send, and who will go for us?" Then
I said, "Here am I! Send me." 9 And
he said, "Go and say to this people:
'Hear and hear, but do not understand;
see and see, but do not perceive.'
10 Make the heart of this people fat,
and their ears heavy,
and shut their eyes;
lest they see with their eyes,
and hear with their ears,
and understand with their hearts,
and turn and be healed."
11 Then I said, "How long, O Lord?"
And he said:
"Until cities lie waste
without inhabitant,
and houses without men,
and the land is utterly desolate,
12 and the LORD removes men far away,
and the forsaken places are many
in the midst of the land.
13 And though a tenth remain in it,
it will be burned again,
like a terebinth or an oak,
whose stump remains standing
when it is felled."
The holy seed is its stump.

7 In the days of Ā'haz the son of
Jō'thȧm, son of Uz·zi'ȧh, king of
Judah, Rē'zin the king of Syria and
Pē'kȧh the son of Rem·ȧ·lī'ȧh the king
of Israel came up to Jerusalem to wage
war against it, but they could not conquer
it. 2 When the house of David
was told, "Syria is in league with
Ē'phrȧ·im," his heart and the heart of
his people shook as the trees of the
forest shake before the wind.
3 And the LORD said to Ī·ṡāi'ȧh,
"Go forth to meet Ā'haz, you and
Shē'ȧr-jash'ụb[h] your son, at the end of
the conduit of the upper pool on the
highway to the Fuller's Field, 4 and
say to him, 'Take heed, be quiet, do
not fear, and do not let your heart be
faint because of these two smoldering
stumps of firebrands, at the fierce
anger of Rē'zin and Syria and the son
of Rem·ȧ·lī'ȧh. 5 Because Syria, with
Ē'phrȧ·im and the son of Rem·ȧ·lī'ȧh,
has devised evil against you, saying,
6 "Let us go up against Judah and
terrify it, and let us conquer it for ourselves,
and set up the son of Tā'bē-ėl
as king in the midst of it," 7 thus says
the Lord GOD:
It shall not stand,
and it shall not come to pass.
8 For the head of Syria is Damascus,
and the head of Damascus is Rē'zin.
(Within sixty-five years Ē'phrȧ·im
will be broken to pieces so that it will
no longer be a people.)
9 And the head of Ē'phrȧ·im is Sȧ·mâr'i·ȧ,
and the head of Samaria is the
son of Rem·ȧ·lī'ȧh.
If you will not believe,
surely you shall not be established.'"
10 Again the LORD spoke to Ā'haz,
11 "Ask a sign of the LORD your God;
let it be deep as Shē'ōl or high as
heaven." 12 But Ā'haz said, "I will not
ask, and I will not put the LORD to
the test." 13 And he said, "Hear then,
O house of David! Is it too little for
you to weary men, that you weary my
God also? 14 Therefore the Lord himself
will give you a sign. Behold, a
young woman[i] shall conceive and bear[j]
a son, and shall call his name Im·man'ū-ėl.[k] 15 He shall eat curds and honey
when he knows how to refuse the evil
and choose the good. 16 For before the
child knows how to refuse the evil and
choose the good, the land before whose
two kings you are in dread will be
deserted. 17 The LORD will bring upon
you and upon your people and upon
your father's house such days as have
not come since the day that Ē'phrȧ·im
departed from Judah—the king of
Assyria."
18 In that day the LORD will
whistle for the fly which is at the
sources of the streams of Egypt, and
for the bee which is in the land of
Assyria. 19 And they will all come and
settle in the steep ravines, and in the
clefts of the rocks, and on all the thornbushes,
and on all the pastures.
20 In that day the Lord will shave
with a razor which is hired beyond the
River—with the kings of Assyria—the
head and the hair of the feet, and it
will sweep away the beard also.
21 In that day a man will keep alive
a young cow and two sheep; 22 and because
of the abundance of milk which
they give, he will eat curds; for every

[h] That is *A remnant shall return* [i] Or *virgin* [j] Or *is with child and shall bear*
[k] That is *God is with us*
6.9-10: Mt 13.14-15; Mk 4.12; Lk 8.10; Jn 12.39-41; Acts 28.26-27. 7.14: Mt 1.23.

one that is left in the land will eat
curds and honey.
23 In that day every place where
there used to be a thousand vines,
worth a thousand shekels of silver, will
become briers and thorns. 24 With
bow and arrows men will come there,
for all the land will be briers and
thorns; 25 and as for all the hills which
used to be hoed with a hoe, you will
not come there for fear of briers and
thorns; but they will become a place
where cattle are let loose and where
sheep tread.

8 Then the LORD said to me, "Take
a large tablet and write upon it in
common characters, 'Belonging to
Mā'hėr-shal'al-hash'-baz.' "[l] 2And I
got reliable witnesses, Ū'rī·ȧh the priest
and Zech·ȧ·rī'ȧh the son of Je·ber·ė-
chī'ȧh, to attest for me. 3And I went
to the prophetess, and she conceived
and bore a son. Then the LORD said to
me, "Call his name Mā'hėr-shal'al-
hash'-baz; 4 for before the child knows
how to cry 'My father' or 'My mother,'
the wealth of Damascus and the spoil
of Sȧ·mâr'i·ȧ will be carried away before the king of Assyria."
5 The LORD spoke to me again:
6 "Because this people have refused
the waters of Shi·lō'ȧh that flow gently,
and melt in fear before[m] Rē'zin and
the son of Rem·ȧ·lī'ȧh; 7 therefore, behold, the Lord is bringing up against
them the waters of the River, mighty
and many, the king of Assyria and all
his glory; and it will rise over all its
channels and go over all its banks;
8 and it will sweep on into Judah, it
will overflow and pass on, reaching
even to the neck; and its outspread
wings will fill the breadth of your land,
O Im·man'ū-ėl."

9 Be broken, you peoples, and be dismayed;
give ear, all you far countries;
gird yourselves and be dismayed;
gird yourselves and be dismayed.
10 Take counsel together, but it will come to nought;
speak a word, but it will not stand,
for God is with us.[x]

11 For the LORD spoke thus to me
with his strong hand upon me, and
warned me not to walk in the way of
this people, saying: 12 "Do not call
conspiracy all that this people call
conspiracy, and do not fear what they
fear, nor be in dread. 13 But the LORD
of hosts, him you shall regard as holy;
let him be your fear, and let him be
your dread. 14And he will become a
sanctuary, and a stone of offense, and
a rock of stumbling to both houses of
Israel, a trap and a snare to the inhabitants of Jerusalem. 15And many
shall stumble thereon; they shall fall
and be broken; they shall be snared
and taken."

16 Bind up the testimony, seal the
teaching among my disciples. 17 I will
wait for the LORD, who is hiding his
face from the house of Jacob, and I
will hope in him. 18 Behold, I and the
children whom the LORD has given me
are signs and portents in Israel from
the LORD of hosts, who dwells on
Mount Zion. 19And when they say to
you, "Consult the mediums and the
wizards who chirp and mutter," should
not a people consult their God?
Should they consult the dead on behalf of the living? 20 To the teaching
and to the testimony! Surely for this
word which they speak there is no
dawn. 21 They will pass through the
land,[n] greatly distressed and hungry;
and when they are hungry, they will
be enraged and will curse[o] their king
and their God, and turn their faces upward; 22 and they will look to the
earth, but behold, distress and darkness, the gloom of anguish; and they
will be thrust into thick darkness.

9[p] But there will be no gloom for
her that was in anguish. In the
former time he brought into contempt
the land of Zeb'ū·lŭn and the land of
Naph'tȧ·lī, but in the latter time he
will make glorious the way of the sea,
the land beyond the Jordan, Galilee
of the nations.

2[q] The people who walked in darkness
have seen a great light;
those who dwelt in a land of deep darkness,
on them has light shined.
3 Thou hast multiplied the nation,
thou hast increased its joy;
they rejoice before thee

[l] That is *The spoil speeds, the prey hastes* [m] Cn: Heb *rejoices in* [x] Heb *immanu el* [n] Heb *it*
[o] Or *curse by* [p] Ch 8.23 in Heb [q] Ch 9.1 in Heb
8.12-13: 1 Pet 3.14-15. **8.14:** Rom 9.32-33; 1 Pet 2.8. **8.17-18:** Heb 2.13.
9.1-2: Mt 4.15-16; Lk 1.79.

as with joy at the harvest,
as men rejoice when they divide the spoil.
4 For the yoke of his burden,
and the staff for his shoulder,
the rod of his oppressor,
thou hast broken as on the day of Mid'i·ȧn.
5 For every boot of the tramping warrior in battle tumult
and every garment rolled in blood
will be burned as fuel for the fire.
6 For to us a child is born,
to us a son is given;
and the government will be upon his shoulder,
and his name will be called
"Wonderful Counselor, Mighty God,
Everlasting Father, Prince of Peace."
7 Of the increase of his government and of peace
there will be no end,
upon the throne of David, and over his kingdom,
to establish it, and to uphold it
with justice and with righteousness
from this time forth and for evermore.
The zeal of the LORD of hosts will do this.

8 The Lord has sent a word against Jacob,
and it will light upon Israel;
9 and all the people will know,
E'phrȧ·im and the inhabitants of Sȧ·mâr'i·ȧ,
who say in pride and in arrogance of heart:
10 "The bricks have fallen,
but we will build with dressed stones;
the sycamores have been cut down,
but we will put cedars in their place."
11 So the LORD raises adversaries[r] against them,
and stirs up their enemies.
12 The Syrians on the east and the Philistines on the west
devour Israel with open mouth.
For all this his anger is not turned away
and his hand is stretched out still.

13 The people did not turn to him who smote them,
nor seek the LORD of hosts.
14 So the LORD cut off from Israel head and tail,
palm branch and reed in one day—
15 the elder and honored man is the head,
and the prophet who teaches lies is the tail;
16 for those who lead this people lead them astray,
and those who are led by them are swallowed up.
17 Therefore the Lord does not rejoice over their young men,
and has no compassion on their fatherless and widows;
for every one is godless and an evildoer,
and every mouth speaks folly.
For all this his anger is not turned away
and his hand is stretched out still.

18 For wickedness burns like a fire,
it consumes briers and thorns;
it kindles the thickets of the forest,
and they roll upward in a column of smoke.
19 Through the wrath of the LORD of hosts
the land is burned,
and the people are like fuel for the fire;
no man spares his brother.
20 They snatch on the right, but are still hungry,
and they devour on the left, but are not satisfied;
each devours his neighbor's[s] flesh,
21 Mȧ·nas'sėh E'phrȧ·im, and Ephraim Manasseh,
and together they are against Judah.
For all this his anger is not turned away
and his hand is stretched out still.

10 Woe to those who decree iniquitous decrees,
and the writers who keep writing oppression,
2 to turn aside the needy from justice
and to rob the poor of my people of their right,
that widows may be their spoil,
and that they may make the fatherless their prey!
3 What will you do on the day of punishment,
in the storm which will come from afar?

[r] Cn: Heb *the adversaries of Rezin* [s] Tg Compare Gk: Heb *the flesh of his arm*

To whom will you flee for help,
and where will you leave your wealth?
4 Nothing remains but to crouch among the prisoners
or fall among the slain.
For all this his anger is not turned away
and his hand is stretched out still.

5 Ah, Assyria, the rod of my anger,
the staff of my fury![t]
6 Against a godless nation I send him,
and against the people of my wrath I command him,
to take spoil and seize plunder,
and to tread them down like the mire of the streets.
7 But he does not so intend,
and his mind does not so think;
but it is in his mind to destroy;
and to cut off nations not a few;
8 for he says:
"Are not my commanders all kings?
9 Is not Cal'nō like Cär'chė·mish?
Is not Hā'math like Ăr'pad?
Is not Så·mâr'i·å like Damascus?
10 As my hand has reached to the kingdoms of the idols
whose graven images were greater than those of Jerusalem and Så·mâr'i·å,
11 shall I not do to Jerusalem and her idols
as I have done to Så·mâr'i·å and her images?"

12 When the Lord has finished all
his work on Mount Zion and on Jerusalem he[u] will punish the arrogant
boasting of the king of Assyria and his
haughty pride. 13 For he says:
"By the strength of my hand I have done it,
and by my wisdom, for I have understanding;
I have removed the boundaries of peoples,
and have plundered their treasures;
like a bull I have brought down those who sat on thrones.
14 My hand has found like a nest
the wealth of the peoples;
and as men gather eggs that have been forsaken
so I have gathered all the earth;
and there was none that moved a wing,
or opened the mouth, or chirped."

15 Shall the axe vaunt itself over him who hews with it,
or the saw magnify itself against him who wields it?
As if a rod should wield him who lifts it,
or as if a staff should lift him who is not wood!
16 Therefore the Lord, the LORD of hosts,
will send wasting sickness among his stout warriors,
and under his glory a burning will be kindled,
like the burning of fire.
17 The light of Israel will become a fire,
and his Holy One a flame;
and it will burn and devour
his thorns and briers in one day.
18 The glory of his forest and of his fruitful land
the LORD will destroy, both soul and body,
and it will be as when a sick man wastes away.
19 The remnant of the trees of his forest will be so few
that a child can write them down.

20 In that day the remnant of Israel
and the survivors of the house of
Jacob will no more lean upon him that
smote them, but will lean upon the
LORD, the Holy One of Israel, in truth.
21 A remnant will return, the remnant
of Jacob, to the mighty God. 22 For
though your people Israel be as the
sand of the sea, only a remnant of them
will return. Destruction is decreed,
overflowing with righteousness. 23 For
the Lord, the LORD of hosts, will make
a full end, as decreed, in the midst of
all the earth.
24 Therefore thus says the Lord,
the LORD of hosts: "O my people, who
dwell in Zion, be not afraid of the
Assyrians when they smite with the
rod and lift up their staff against you
as the Egyptians did. 25 For in a very
little while my indignation will come
to an end, and my anger will be directed to their destruction. 26 And the
LORD of hosts will wield against them
a scourge, as when he smote Mid'i·ån
at the rock of Ō'reb; and his rod will

[t] Heb *a staff it is in their hand my fury* [u] Heb *I*
10.5-34: Nahum; Zeph 2.13-15. **10.22-23:** Rom 9.27-28.

be over the sea, and he will lift it as
he did in Egypt. 27And in that day his
burden will depart from your shoulder,
and his yoke will be destroyed from
your neck."

He has gone up from Rim'mon,[v]
28 he has come to Ä'i'ath;
he has passed through Mig'ron,
at Mich'mash he stores his baggage;
29 they have crossed over the pass,
at Gē'bȧ they lodge for the night;
Rā'mȧh trembles,
Gib'ē-ȧh of Saul has fled.
30 Cry aloud, O daughter of Gal'lim!
Hearken, O Lā'i·shȧh!
Answer her, O An'ȧ·thoth!
31 Mad·mē'nȧh is in flight,
the inhabitants of Gē'bim flee for safety.
32 This very day he will halt at Nob,
he will shake his fist
at the mount of the daughter of Zion,
the hill of Jerusalem.

33 Behold, the Lord, the LORD of hosts
will lop the boughs with terrifying power;
the great in height will be hewn down,
and the lofty will be brought low.
34 He will cut down the thickets of the forest with an axe,
and Lebanon with its majestic trees[w] will fall.

11 There shall come forth a shoot from the stump of Jesse,
and a branch shall grow out of his roots.
2 And the Spirit of the LORD shall rest upon him,
the spirit of wisdom and understanding,
the spirit of counsel and might,
the spirit of knowledge and the fear of the LORD.
3 And his delight shall be in the fear of the LORD.

He shall not judge by what his eyes see,
or decide by what his ears hear;
4 but with righteousness he shall judge the poor,
and decide with equity for the meek of the earth;
and he shall smite the earth with the rod of his mouth,
and with the breath of his lips he shall slay the wicked.
5 Righteousness shall be the girdle of his waist,
and faithfulness the girdle of his loins.

6 The wolf shall dwell with the lamb,
and the leopard shall lie down with the kid,
and the calf and the lion and the fatling together,
and a little child shall lead them.
7 The cow and the bear shall feed;
their young shall lie down together;
and the lion shall eat straw like the ox.
8 The sucking child shall play over the hole of the asp,
and the weaned child shall put his hand on the adder's den.
9 They shall not hurt or destroy
in all my holy mountain;
for the earth shall be full of the knowledge of the LORD
as the waters cover the sea.

10 In that day the root of Jesse
shall stand as an ensign to the peoples;
him shall the nations seek, and his
dwellings shall be glorious.
11 In that day the Lord will extend
his hand yet a second time to recover
the remnant which is left of his people, from Assyria, from Egypt, from
Path'ros, from Ethiopia, from Ē'lȧm,
from Shī'när, from Hā'math, and
from the coastlands of the sea.
12 He will raise an ensign for the nations,
and will assemble the outcasts of Israel,
and gather the dispersed of Judah
from the four corners of the earth.
13 The jealousy of Ē'phrȧ·im shall depart,
and those who harass Judah shall be cut off;
Ephraim shall not be jealous of Judah,
and Judah shall not harass Ephraim.

[v] Cn: Heb *and his yoke from your neck, and a yoke will be destroyed because of fatness*
[w] Cn Compare Gk Vg: Heb *with a majestic one*
11.1: Is 11.10; Rom 15.12. **11.2:** 1 Pet 4.14. **11.5:** Eph 6.14. **11.6-9:** Is 65.25; Hab 2.14.
11.10: Is 11.1; Rom 15.12.

14 But they shall swoop down upon
the shoulder of the Philistines
in the west,
and together they shall plunder
the people of the east.
They shall put forth their hand
against E'dom and Mō'ab,
and the Am'mo·nites shall obey
them.
15 And the LORD will utterly destroy
the tongue of the sea of Egypt;
and will wave his hand over the River
with his scorching wind,
and smite it into seven channels
that men may cross dryshod.
16 And there will be a highway from
Assyria
for the remnant which is left of
his people,
as there was for Israel
when they came up from the land
of Egypt.

12 You will say in that day:
"I will give thanks to thee, O
LORD,
for though thou wast angry with
me,
thy anger turned away,
and thou didst comfort me.

2 "Behold, God is my salvation;
I will trust, and will not be afraid;
for the LORD GOD is my strength
and my song,
and he has become my salvation."

3 With joy you will draw water
from the wells of salvation. 4And you
will say in that day:
"Give thanks to the LORD,
call upon his name;
make known his deeds among the
nations,
proclaim that his name is exalted.

5 "Sing praises to the LORD, for he
has done gloriously;
let this be known[x] in all the earth.
6 Shout, and sing for joy, O inhabitant of Zion,
for great in your midst is the Holy
One of Israel."

13 The oracle concerning Babylon
which I·sai'ah the son of Ā'moz
saw.
2 On a bare hill raise a signal,
cry aloud to them;
wave the hand for them to enter
the gates of the nobles.
3 I myself have commanded my consecrated ones,
have summoned my mighty men
to execute my anger,
my proudly exulting ones.

4 Hark, a tumult on the mountains
as of a great multitude!
Hark, an uproar of kingdoms,
of nations gathering together!
The LORD of hosts is mustering
a host for battle.
5 They come from a distant land,
from the end of the heavens,
the LORD and the weapons of his
indignation,
to destroy the whole earth.

6 Wail, for the day of the LORD is near;
as destruction from the Almighty
it will come!
7 Therefore all hands will be feeble,
and every man's heart will melt,
8 and they will be dismayed.
Pangs and agony will seize them;
they will be in anguish like a
woman in travail.
They will look aghast at one another;
their faces will be aflame.

9 Behold, the day of the LORD comes,
cruel, with wrath and fierce anger,
to make the earth a desolation
and to destroy its sinners from it.
10 For the stars of the heavens and
their constellations
will not give their light;
the sun will be dark at its rising
and the moon will not shed its
light.
11 I will punish the world for its evil,
and the wicked for their iniquity;
I will put an end to the pride of the
arrogant,
and lay low the haughtiness of
the ruthless.
12 I will make men more rare than fine
gold,
and mankind than the gold of
Ō'phir.
13 Therefore I will make the heavens
tremble,
and the earth will be shaken out
of its place,
at the wrath of the LORD of hosts
in the day of his fierce anger.
14 And like a hunted gazelle,

[x] Or *this is made known*
13.1-14.23: Is 47; Jer 50-51; Hab 1-2. 13.10: Mt 24.29; Mk 13.24; Rev 6.12; 8.12.

or like sheep with none to gather
them,
every man will turn to his own
people,
and every man will flee to his
own land.
15 Whoever is found will be thrust
through,
and whoever is caught will fall by
the sword.
16 Their infants will be dashed in pieces
before their eyes;
their houses will be plundered
and their wives ravished.

17 Behold, I am stirring up the Medes
against them,
who have no regard for silver
and do not delight in gold.
18 Their bows will slaughter the young
men;
they will have no mercy on the
fruit of the womb;
their eyes will not pity children.
19 And Babylon, the glory of kingdoms,
the splendor and pride of the
Chal·dē'ȧns,
will be like Sod'ȯm and Gȯ·môr'rȧh
when God overthrew them.
20 It will never be inhabited
or dwelt in for all generations;
no Arab will pitch his tent there,
no shepherds will make their
flocks lie down there.
21 But wild beasts will lie down there,
and its houses will be full of
howling creatures;
there ostriches will dwell,
and there satyrs will dance.
22 Hyenas will cry in its towers,
and jackals in the pleasant palaces;
its time is close at hand
and its days will not be prolonged.

14 The LORD will have compassion
on Jacob and will again choose
Israel, and will set them in their own
land, and aliens will join them and
will cleave to the house of Jacob. 2 And
the peoples will take them and bring
them to their place, and the house of
Israel will possess them in the LORD's
land as male and female slaves; they
will take captive those who were their
captors, and rule over those who
oppressed them.
3 When the LORD has given you
rest from your pain and turmoil and
the hard service with which you were
made to serve, 4 you will take up this
taunt against the king of Babylon:
"How the oppressor has ceased,
the insolent fury[y] ceased!
5 The LORD has broken the staff of
the wicked,
the scepter of rulers,
6 that smote the peoples in wrath
with unceasing blows,
that ruled the nations in anger
with unrelenting persecution.
7 The whole earth is at rest and quiet;
they break forth into singing.
8 The cypresses rejoice at you,
the cedars of Lebanon, saying,
'Since you were laid low,
no hewer comes up against us.'
9 Shē'ōl beneath is stirred up
to meet you when you come,
it rouses the shades to greet you,
all who were leaders of the earth;
it raises from their thrones
all who were kings of the nations.
10 All of them will speak
and say to you:
'You too have become as weak as
we!
You have become like us!'
11 Your pomp is brought down to
Shē'ōl,
the sound of your harps;
maggots are the bed beneath you,
and worms are your covering.

12 "How you are fallen from heaven,
O Day Star, son of Dawn!
How you are cut down to the
ground,
you who laid the nations low!
13 You said in your heart,
'I will ascend to heaven;
above the stars of God
I will set my throne on high;
I will sit on the mount of assembly
in the far north;
14 I will ascend above the heights of
the clouds,
I will make myself like the Most
High.'
15 But you are brought down to Shē'ōl,
to the depths of the Pit.
16 Those who see you will stare at you,
and ponder over you:
'Is this the man who made the earth
tremble,
who shook kingdoms,
17 who made the world like a desert
and overthrew its cities,

[y] One ancient Ms Compare Gk Syr Vg: The meaning of the Hebrew word is uncertain
13.21: Rev 18.2.

who did not let his prisoners go home?'
18 All the kings of the nations lie in glory,
each in his own tomb;
19 but you are cast out, away from your sepulchre,
like a loathed untimely birth,[z]
clothed with the slain, those pierced by the sword,
who go down to the stones of the Pit,
like a dead body trodden under foot.
20 You will not be joined with them in burial,
because you have destroyed your land,
you have slain your people.

"May the descendants of evildoers nevermore be named!
21 Prepare slaughter for his sons
because of the guilt of their fathers,
lest they rise and possess the earth,
and fill the face of the world with cities."

22 "I will rise up against them,"
says the LORD of hosts, "and will cut
off from Babylon name and remnant,
offspring and posterity, says the LORD.
23 And I will make it a possession of
the hedgehog, and pools of water, and
I will sweep it with the broom of
destruction, says the LORD of hosts."

24 The LORD of hosts has sworn:
"As I have planned,
so shall it be,
and as I have purposed,
so shall it stand,
25 that I will break the Assyrian in my land,
and upon my mountains trample him under foot;
and his yoke shall depart from them,
and his burden from their shoulder."
26 This is the purpose that is purposed concerning the whole earth;
and this is the hand that is stretched out
over all the nations.
27 For the LORD of hosts has purposed,
and who will annul it?
His hand is stretched out,
and who will turn it back?

28 In the year that King Ā'haz died
came this oracle:
29 "Rejoice not, O Phi·lis'ti·ȧ, all of you,
that the rod which smote you is broken,
for from the serpent's root will come forth an adder,
and its fruit will be a flying serpent.
30 And the first-born of the poor will feed,
and the needy lie down in safety;
but I will kill your root with famine,
and your remnant I[a] will slay.
31 Wail, O gate; cry, O city;
melt in fear, O Phi·lis'ti·ȧ, all of you!
For smoke comes out of the north,
and there is no straggler in his ranks."

32 What will one answer the messengers of the nation?
"The LORD has founded Zion,
and in her the afflicted of his people find refuge."

15 An oracle concerning Mō'ab.
Because Ăr is laid waste in a night
Moab is undone;
because Kīr is laid waste in a night
Moab is undone.
2 The daughter of Dī'bon[b] has gone up
to the high places to weep;
over Nē'bō and over Med'ė·bȧ
Mō'ab wails.
On every head is baldness,
every beard is shorn;
3 in the streets they gird on sackcloth;
on the housetops and in the squares
every one wails and melts in tears.
4 Hesh'bȯn and Ē·lė·ā'lėh cry out,
their voice is heard as far as Jā'haz;
therefore the armed men of Mō'ab cry aloud;
his soul trembles.
5 My heart cries out for Mō'ab;
his fugitives flee to Zō'ăr,
to Eg'lȧth-she·lish'i·yȧh.

[z] Cn Compare Tg Symmachus: Heb *a loathed branch* [a] One ancient Ms Vg; Heb *he*
[b] Cn: Heb *the house and Dibon*
14.29-31: Jer 47; Ezek 25.15-17; Joel 3.4-8; Amos 1.6-8; Zeph 2.4-7; Zech 9.5-7.
15-16: Is 25.10-12; Jer 48; Ezek 25.8-11; Amos 2.1-3; Zeph 2.8-11.

For at the ascent of Lū'hith
they go up weeping;
on the road to Hor·ō·nā'im
they raise a cry of destruction;
6 the waters of Nim'rim
are a desolation;
the grass is withered, the new growth fails,
the verdure is no more.
7 Therefore the abundance they have gained
and what they have laid up
they carry away
over the brook of the Willows.
8 For a cry has gone
round the land of Mō'ab;
the wailing reaches to Eg·lā'im,
the wailing reaches to Bē'ėr-ē'lim.
9 For the waters of Dī'bon[c] are full of blood;
yet I will bring upon Dibon[c] even more,
a lion for those of Mō'ab who escape,
for the remnant of the land.

16 They have sent lambs
to the ruler of the land,
from Sē'lȧ, by way of the desert,
to the mount of the daughter of Zion.
2 Like fluttering birds,
like scattered nestlings,
so are the daughters of Mō'ab
at the fords of the Ăr'non.
3 "Give counsel,
grant justice;
make your shade like night
at the height of noon;
hide the outcasts,
betray not the fugitive;
4 let the outcasts of Mō'ab
sojourn among you;
be a refuge to them
from the destroyer.
When the oppressor is no more,
and destruction has ceased,
and he who tramples under foot
has vanished from the land,
5 then a throne will be established in steadfast love
and on it will sit in faithfulness
in the tent of David
one who judges and seeks justice
and is swift to do righteousness."

6 We have heard of the pride of Mō'ab,
how proud he was;
of his arrogance, his pride, and his insolence—
his boasts are false.
7 Therefore let Mō'ab wail,
let every one wail for Moab.
Mourn, utterly stricken,
for the raisin-cakes of Kīr-hâr'ė·seth.

8 For the fields of Hesh'bȯn languish,
and the vine of Sib'mȧh;
the lords of the nations
have struck down its branches,
which reached to Jā'zėr
and strayed to the desert;
its shoots spread abroad
and passed over the sea.
9 Therefore I weep with the weeping of Jā'zėr
for the vine of Sib'mȧh;
I drench you with my tears,
O Hesh'bȯn and E·lė·ā'lėh;
for upon your fruit and your harvest
the battle shout has fallen.
10 And joy and gladness are taken away
from the fruitful field;
and in the vineyards no songs are sung,
no shouts are raised;
no treader treads out wine in the presses;
the vintage shout is hushed.[d]
11 Therefore my soul moans like a lyre for Mō'ab,
and my heart for Kīr-hē'res.

12 And when Mō'ab presents himself, when he wearies himself upon the
high place, when he comes to his
sanctuary to pray, he will not prevail.
13 This is the word which the LORD
spoke concerning Mō'ab in the past.
14 But now the LORD says, "In three
years, like the years of a hireling, the
glory of Mō'ab will be brought into
contempt, in spite of all his great
multitude, and those who survive will
be very few and feeble."

17 An oracle concerning Damascus.
Behold, Damascus will cease to be a city,
and will become a heap of ruins.
2 Her cities will be deserted for ever;[e]
they will be for flocks,
which will lie down, and none will make them afraid.

[c] One ancient Ms Vg Compare Syr: Heb *Dimon* [d] Gk: Heb *I have hushed*
[e] Cn Compare Gk: Heb *the cities of Aroer are deserted*
17.1-3: Jer 49.23-27; Amos 1.3-5; Zech 9.1.

3 The fortress will disappear from E'phră·im,
and the kingdom from Damascus;
and the remnant of Syria will be like the glory of the children of Israel,
says the LORD of hosts.

4 And in that day
the glory of Jacob will be brought low,
and the fat of his flesh will grow lean.
5 And it shall be as when the reaper gathers standing grain
and his arm harvests the ears,
and as when one gleans the ears of grain
in the Valley of Reph'ă·im.
6 Gleanings will be left in it,
as when an olive tree is beaten—
two or three berries
in the top of the highest bough,
four or five
on the branches of a fruit tree,
says the LORD God of Israel.

7 In that day men will regard their
Maker, and their eyes will look to the
Holy One of Israel; 8 they will not
have regard for the altars, the work of
their hands, and they will not look to
what their own fingers have made,
either the A·shē'rim or the altars of
incense.
9 In that day their strong cities will
be like the deserted places of the
Hi'vītes and the Am'ŏ·rites,[f] which
they deserted because of the children
of Israel, and there will be desolation.

10 For you have forgotten the God of your salvation,
and have not remembered the Rock of your refuge;
therefore, though you plant pleasant plants
and set out slips of an alien god,
11 though you make them grow on the day that you plant them,
and make them blossom in the morning that you sow;
yet the harvest will flee away
in a day of grief and incurable pain.

12 Ah, the thunder of many peoples,
they thunder like the thundering of the sea!
Ah, the roar of nations,
they roar like the roaring of mighty waters!
13 The nations roar like the roaring of many waters,
but he will rebuke them, and they will flee far away,
chased like chaff on the mountains before the wind
and whirling dust before the storm.
14 At evening time, behold, terror!
Before morning, they are no more!
This is the portion of those who despoil us,
and the lot of those who plunder us.

18 Ah, land of whirring wings which is beyond the rivers of Ethiopia;
2 which sends ambassadors by the Nile,
in vessels of papyrus upon the waters!
Go, you swift messengers,
to a nation, tall and smooth,
to a people feared near and far,
a nation mighty and conquering,
whose land the rivers divide.

3 All you inhabitants of the world,
you who dwell on the earth,
when a signal is raised on the mountains, look!
When a trumpet is blown, hear!
4 For thus the LORD said to me:
"I will quietly look from my dwelling
like clear heat in sunshine,
like a cloud of dew in the heat of harvest."
5 For before the harvest, when the blossom is over,
and the flower becomes a ripening grape,
he will cut off the shoots with pruning hooks,
and the spreading branches he will hew away.
6 They shall all of them be left
to the birds of prey of the mountains
and to the beasts of the earth.
And the birds of prey will summer upon them,
and all the beasts of the earth will winter upon them.

[f] Cn Compare Gk: Heb *the wood and the highest bough*
18: Zeph 2.12.

7 At that time gifts will be brought
to the LORD of hosts
from a people tall and smooth,
from a people feared near and far,
a nation mighty and conquering,
whose land the rivers divide,
to Mount Zion, the place of the name
of the LORD of hosts.

19 An oracle concerning Egypt.
Behold, the LORD is riding on a swift cloud
and comes to Egypt;
and the idols of Egypt will tremble at his presence,
and the heart of the Egyptians will melt within them.
2 And I will stir up Egyptians against Egyptians,
and they will fight, every man against his brother
and every man against his neighbor,
city against city, kingdom against kingdom;
3 and the spirit of the Egyptians within them will be emptied out,
and I will confound their plans;
and they will consult the idols and the sorcerers,
and the mediums and the wizards;
4 and I will give over the Egyptians into the hand of a hard master;
and a fierce king will rule over them,
says the Lord, the LORD of hosts.

5 And the waters of the Nile will be dried up,
and the river will be parched and dry;
6 and its canals will become foul,
and the branches of Egypt's Nile will diminish and dry up,
reeds and rushes will rot away.
7 There will be bare places by the Nile,
on the brink of the Nile,
and all that is sown by the Nile will dry up,
be driven away, and be no more.
8 The fishermen will mourn and lament,
all who cast hook in the Nile;
and they will languish
who spread nets upon the water.
9 The workers in combed flax will be in despair,
and the weavers of white cotton.
10 Those who are the pillars of the land will be crushed,
and all who work for hire will be grieved.

11 The princes of Zō'ǎn are utterly foolish;
the wise counselors of Pharaoh give stupid counsel.
How can you say to Pharaoh,
"I am a son of the wise,
a son of ancient kings"?
12 Where then are your wise men?
Let them tell you and make known
what the LORD of hosts has purposed against Egypt.
13 The princes of Zō'ǎn have become fools,
and the princes of Memphis are deluded;
those who are the cornerstones of her tribes
have led Egypt astray.
14 The LORD has mingled within her
a spirit of confusion;
and they have made Egypt stagger in all her doings
as a drunken man staggers in his vomit.
15 And there will be nothing for Egypt
which head or tail, palm branch
or reed, may do.

16 In that day the Egyptians will
be like women, and tremble with fear
before the hand which the LORD of
hosts shakes over them. 17 And the land
of Judah will become a terror to the
Egyptians; every one to whom it is
mentioned will fear because of the
purpose which the LORD of hosts has
purposed against them.
18 In that day there will be five
cities in the land of Egypt which speak
the language of Canaan and swear
allegiance to the LORD of hosts. One of
these will be called the City of the Sun.
19 In that day there will be an altar
to the LORD in the midst of the land of
Egypt, and a pillar to the LORD at its
border. 20 It will be a sign and a
witness to the LORD of hosts in the
land of Egypt; when they cry to the
LORD because of oppressors he will
send them a savior, and will defend
and deliver them. 21 And the LORD will
make himself known to the Egyptians;
and the Egyptians will know the LORD
in that day and worship with sacrifice
and burnt offering, and they will make
vows to the LORD and perform them.
22 And the LORD will smite Egypt,

19: Jer 46; Ezek 29-32; Zech 14.18-19.

smiting and healing, and they will return to the LORD, and he will heed
their supplications and heal them.
23 In that day there will be a highway from Egypt to Assyria, and the
Assyrian will come into Egypt, and the
Egyptian into Assyria, and the Egyptians will worship with the Assyrians.
24 In that day Israel will be the
third with Egypt and Assyria, a blessing in the midst of the earth, 25 whom
the LORD of hosts has blessed, saying,
"Blessed be Egypt my people, and
Assyria the work of my hands, and
Israel my heritage."

20 In the year that the commander in chief, who was sent
by Sär'gon the king of Assyria, came
to Ash'dod and fought against it and
took it,—2 at that time the LORD had
spoken by Ī·ṡāi'ȧh the son of Ā'moz,
saying, "Go, and loose the sackcloth
from your loins and take off your shoes
from your feet," and he had done so,
walking naked and barefoot—3 the
LORD said, "As my servant Ī·ṡāi'ȧh has
walked naked and barefoot for three
years as a sign and a portent against
Egypt and Ethiopia, 4 so shall the king
of Assyria lead away the Egyptians
captives and the Ethiopians exiles,
both the young and the old, naked and
barefoot, with buttocks uncovered, to
the shame of Egypt. 5 Then they shall
be dismayed and confounded because
of Ethiopia their hope and of Egypt
their boast. 6 And the inhabitants of
this coastland will say in that day,
'Behold, this is what has happened to
those in whom we hoped and to whom
we fled for help to be delivered from
the king of Assyria! And we, how shall
we escape?' "

21 The oracle concerning the wilderness of the sea.

As whirlwinds in the Negeb sweep on,
it comes from the desert,
from a terrible land.
2 A stern vision is told to me;
the plunderer plunders,
and the destroyer destroys.
Go up, O E'lȧm,
lay siege, O Media;
all the sighing she has caused
I bring to an end.
3 Therefore my loins are filled with anguish;
pangs have seized me,
like the pangs of a woman in travail;
I am bowed down so that I cannot hear,
I am dismayed so that I cannot see.
4 My mind reels, horror has appalled me;
the twilight I longed for
has been turned for me into trembling.
5 They prepare the table,
they spread the rugs,
they eat, they drink.
Arise, O princes,
oil the shield!
6 For thus the Lord said to me:
"Go, set a watchman,
let him announce what he sees.
7 When he sees riders, horsemen in pairs,
riders on asses, riders on camels,
let him listen diligently,
very diligently."
8 Then he who saw[g] cried:
"Upon a watchtower I stand, O Lord,
continually by day,
and at my post I am stationed
whole nights.
9 And, behold, here come riders,
horsemen in pairs!"
And he answered,
"Fallen, fallen is Babylon;
and all the images of her gods
he has shattered to the ground."
10 O my threshed and winnowed one,
what I have heard from the LORD of hosts,
the God of Israel, I announce to you.

11 The oracle concerning Dü'mȧh.
One is calling to me from Sē'ir,
"Watchman, what of the night?
Watchman, what of the night?"
12 The watchman says:
"Morning comes, and also the night.
If you will inquire, inquire;
come back again."

13 The oracle concerning Arabia.
In the thickets in Arabia you will lodge,
O caravans of Dē'dȧ·nītes.
14 To the thirsty bring water,
meet the fugitive with bread,
O inhabitants of the land of Tē'mȧ.
15 For they have fled from the swords,

[g] One ancient Ms: Heb *a lion*

from the drawn sword,
from the bent bow,
and from the press of battle.
16 For thus the Lord said to me,
"Within a year, according to the years
of a hireling, all the glory of Kē'dăr
will come to an end; 17 and the remainder of the archers of the mighty
men of the sons of Kē'dăr will be few;
for the LORD, the God of Israel, has
spoken."

22 The oracle concerning the
valley of vision.
What do you mean that you have
gone up,
all of you, to the housetops,
2 you who are full of shoutings,
tumultuous city, exultant town?
Your slain are not slain with the
sword
or dead in battle.
3 All your rulers have fled together,
without the bow they were captured.
All of you who were found were
captured,
though they had fled far away.[h]
4 Therefore I said:
"Look away from me,
let me weep bitter tears;
do not labor to comfort me
for the destruction of the daughter
of my people."

5 For the Lord GOD of hosts has a day
of tumult and trampling and
confusion
in the valley of vision,
a battering down of walls
and a shouting to the mountains.
6 And Ē'lȧm bore the quiver
with chariots and horsemen,[i]
and Kīr uncovered the shield.
7 Your choicest valleys were full of
chariots,
and the horsemen took their stand
at the gates.
8 He has taken away the covering of
Judah.

In that day you looked to the
weapons of the House of the Forest,
9 and you saw that the breaches of the
city of David were many, and you
collected the waters of the lower pool,
10 and you counted the houses of Jerusalem, and you broke down the houses
to fortify the wall. 11 You made a
reservoir between the two walls for
the water of the old pool. But you did
not look to him who did it, or have
regard for him who planned it long ago.

12 In that day the Lord GOD of hosts
called to weeping and mourning,
to baldness and girding with sackcloth;
13 and behold, joy and gladness,
slaying oxen and killing sheep,
eating flesh and drinking wine.
"Let us eat and drink,
for tomorrow we die."
14 The LORD of hosts has revealed himself in my ears;
"Surely this iniquity will not be forgiven you
till you die,"
says the Lord GOD of hosts.

15 Thus says the Lord GOD of
hosts, "Come, go to this steward, to
Sheb'nȧ, who is over the household,
and say to him: 16 What have you to
do here and whom have you here, that
you have hewn here a tomb for yourself, you who hew a tomb on the
height, and carve a habitation for
yourself in the rock? 17 Behold, the
LORD will hurl you away violently, O
you strong man. He will seize firm
hold on you, 18 and whirl you round
and round, and throw you like a ball
into a wide land; there you shall die,
and there shall be your splendid
chariots, you shame of your master's
house. 19 I will thrust you from your
office, and you will be cast down from
your station. 20 In that day I will call
my servant E·lī'ȧ·kim the son of Hil-
kī'ȧh, 21 and I will clothe him with
your robe, and will bind your girdle
on him, and will commit your authority to his hand; and he shall be a father
to the inhabitants of Jerusalem and to
the house of Judah. 22 And I will place
on his shoulder the key of the house
of David; he shall open, and none shall
shut; and he shall shut, and none shall
open. 23 And I will fasten him like a
peg in a sure place, and he will become
a throne of honor to his father's house.
24 And they will hang on him the whole
weight of his father's house, the offspring and issue, every small vessel,
from the cups to all the flagons. 25 In
that day, says the LORD of hosts, the
peg that was fastened in a sure place

[h] Gk Syr Vg: Heb *from far away* [i] The Hebrew of this line is obscure
22.22: Rev 3.7.

will give way; and it will be cut down
and fall, and the burden that was upon
it will be cut off, for the LORD has
spoken."

23 The oracle concerning Tȳre.
Wail, O ships of Tär'shish,
for Tyre is laid waste, without
house or haven!
From the land of Cyprus
it is revealed to them.
2 Be still, O inhabitants of the coast,
O merchants of Sī'don;
your messengers passed over the sea[j]
3 and were on many waters;
your revenue was the grain of
Shī'hôr,
the harvest of the Nile;
you were the merchant of the
nations.
4 Be ashamed, O Sī'don, for the sea
has spoken,
the stronghold of the sea, saying:
"I have neither travailed nor given
birth,
I have neither reared young men
nor brought up virgins."
5 When the report comes to Egypt,
they will be in anguish over the
report about Tȳre.
6 Pass over to Tär'shish,
wail, O inhabitants of the coast!
7 Is this your exultant city
whose origin is from days of old,
whose feet carried her
to settle afar?
8 Who has purposed this
against Tȳre, the bestower of
crowns,
whose merchants were princes,
whose traders were the honored
of the earth?
9 The LORD of hosts has purposed
it;
to defile the pride of all glory,
to dishonor all the honored of the
earth.
10 Overflow your land like the Nile,
O daughter of Tär'shish;
there is no restraint any more.
11 He has stretched out his hand over
the sea,
he has shaken the kingdoms;
the LORD has given command concerning Canaan
to destroy its strongholds.
12 And he said:
"You will no more exult,
O oppressed virgin daughter of
Sī'don;
arise, pass over to Cyprus,
even there you will have no rest."

13 Behold the land of the Chal·dē'-
ȧnṡ! This is the people; it was not
Assyria. They destined Tȳre for wild
beasts. They erected their siege
towers, they razed her palaces, they
made her a ruin.[k]
14 Wail, O ships of Tär'shish,
for your stronghold is laid waste.
15 In that day Tȳre will be forgotten
for seventy years, like the days of one
king. At the end of seventy years, it
will happen to Tyre as in the song of
the harlot:
16 "Take a harp,
go about the city,
O forgotten harlot!
Make sweet melody,
sing many songs,
that you may be remembered."
17 At the end of seventy years, the
LORD will visit Tȳre, and she will return to her hire, and will play the harlot with all the kingdoms of the world
upon the face of the earth. 18 Her
merchandise and her hire will be
dedicated to the LORD; it will not be
stored or hoarded, but her merchandise will supply abundant food and
fine clothing for those who dwell before the LORD.

24 Behold, the LORD will lay
waste the earth and make it
desolate,
and he will twist its surface and
scatter its inhabitants.
2 And it shall be, as with the people,
so with the priest;
as with the slave, so with his
master;
as with the maid, so with her
mistress;
as with the buyer, so with the seller;
as with the lender, so with the
borrower;
as with the creditor, so with the
debtor.
3 The earth shall be utterly laid waste,
and utterly despoiled;
for the LORD has spoken this
word.

4 The earth mourns and withers,

[j] One ancient Ms: Heb *who passed over the sea, they replenished you*
[k] The Hebrew of this verse is obscure
23: Ezek 26.1-28.19; Joel 3.4-8; Amos 1.9-10; Zech 9.3-4. 23.17: Rev 17.2.

the world languishes and withers;
the heavens languish together with the earth.
5 The earth lies polluted
under its inhabitants;
for they have transgressed the laws,
violated the statutes,
broken the everlasting covenant.
6 Therefore a curse devours the earth,
and its inhabitants suffer for their guilt;
therefore the inhabitants of the earth are scorched,
and few men are left.
7 The wine mourns,
the vine languishes,
all the merry-hearted sigh.
8 The mirth of the timbrels is stilled,
the noise of the jubilant has ceased,
the mirth of the lyre is stilled.
9 No more do they drink wine with singing;
strong drink is bitter to those who drink it.
10 The city of chaos is broken down,
every house is shut up so that none can enter.
11 There is an outcry in the streets for lack of wine;
all joy has reached its eventide;
the gladness of the earth is banished.
12 Desolation is left in the city,
the gates are battered into ruins.
13 For thus it shall be in the midst of the earth
among the nations,
as when an olive tree is beaten,
as at the gleaning when the vintage is done.

14 They lift up their voices, they sing for joy;
over the majesty of the LORD they shout from the west.
15 Therefore in the east give glory to the LORD;
in the coastlands of the sea, to the name of the LORD, the God of Israel.
16 From the ends of the earth we hear songs of praise,
of glory to the Righteous One.
But I say, "I pine away,
I pine away. Woe is me!
For the treacherous deal treacherously,
the treacherous deal very treacherously."

17 Terror, and the pit, and the snare
are upon you, O inhabitant of the earth!
18 He who flees at the sound of the terror
shall fall into the pit;
and he who climbs out of the pit
shall be caught in the snare.
For the windows of heaven are opened,
and the foundations of the earth tremble.
19 The earth is utterly broken,
the earth is rent asunder,
the earth is violently shaken.
20 The earth staggers like a drunken man,
it sways like a hut;
its transgression lies heavy upon it,
and it falls, and will not rise again.

21 On that day the LORD will punish
the host of heaven, in heaven,
and the kings of the earth, on the earth.
22 They will be gathered together
as prisoners in a pit;
they will be shut up in a prison,
and after many days they will be punished.
23 Then the moon will be confounded,
and the sun ashamed;
for the LORD of hosts will reign
on Mount Zion and in Jerusalem
and before his elders he will manifest his glory.

25 O LORD, thou art my God;
I will exalt thee, I will praise thy name;
for thou hast done wonderful things,
plans formed of old, faithful and sure.
2 For thou hast made the city a heap,
the fortified city a ruin;
the palace of aliens is a city no more,
it will never be rebuilt.
3 Therefore strong peoples will glorify thee;
cities of ruthless nations will fear thee.
4 For thou hast been a stronghold to the poor,
a stronghold to the needy in his distress,
a shelter from the storm and a shade from the heat;
for the blast of the ruthless is like a storm against a wall,
5 like heat in a dry place.

24.8: Rev 18.22.

Thou dost subdue the noise of the
aliens;
as heat by the shade of a cloud,
so the song of the ruthless is
stilled.

6 On this mountain the LORD of
hosts will make for all peoples a feast
of fat things, a feast of wine on
the lees, of fat things full of marrow,
of wine on the lees well refined.
7 And he will destroy on this mountain the covering that is cast over
all peoples, the veil that is spread
over all nations. 8 He will swallow
up death for ever, and the Lord GOD
will wipe away tears from all faces,
and the reproach of his people he will
take away from all the earth, for the
LORD has spoken.
9 It will be said on that day, "Lo,
this is our God; we have waited for
him, that he might save us. This is
the LORD; we have waited for him;
let us be glad and rejoice in his salvation."
10 For the hand of the LORD will
rest on this mountain, and Mō'ab shall
be trodden down in his place, as straw
is trodden down in a dungpit. 11 And
he will spread out his hands in the
midst of it as a swimmer spreads his
hands out to swim; but the LORD will
lay low his pride together with the
skill[l] of his hands. 12 And the high
fortifications of his walls he will bring
down, lay low, and cast to the ground,
even to the dust.

26

In that day this song will be sung in the land of Judah:
"We have a strong city;
he sets up salvation
as walls and bulwarks.
2 Open the gates,
that the righteous nation which
keeps faith
may enter in.
3 Thou dost keep him in perfect
peace,
whose mind is stayed on thee,
because he trusts in thee.
4 Trust in the LORD for ever,
for the LORD GOD
is an everlasting rock.
5 For he has brought low
the inhabitants of the height,
the lofty city.
He lays it low, lays it low to the
ground,
casts it to the dust.
6 The foot tramples it,
the feet of the poor,
the steps of the needy."

7 The way of the righteous is level;
thou[m] dost make smooth the path
of the righteous.
8 In the path of thy judgments,
O LORD, we wait for thee;
thy memorial name
is the desire of our soul.
9 My soul yearns for thee in the night,
my spirit within me earnestly
seeks thee.
For when thy judgments are in the
earth,
the inhabitants of the world learn
righteousness.
10 If favor is shown to the wicked,
he does not learn righteousness;
in the land of uprightness he deals
perversely
and does not see the majesty of
the LORD.
11 O LORD, thy hand is lifted up,
but they see it not.
Let them see thy zeal for thy people,
and be ashamed.
Let the fire for thy adversaries
consume them.
12 O LORD, thou wilt ordain peace for
us,
thou hast wrought for us all our
works.
13 O LORD our God,
other lords besides thee have
ruled over us,
but thy name alone we acknowledge.
14 They are dead, they will not live;
they are shades, they will not
arise;
to that end thou hast visited them
with destruction
and wiped out all remembrance
of them.
15 But thou hast increased the nation,
O LORD,
thou hast increased the nation;
thou art glorified;
thou hast enlarged all the borders
of the land.

l The meaning of the Hebrew word is uncertain
m Cn Compare Gk: Heb *thou* (*that art*) *upright*
25.8: 1 Cor 15.54; Rev 7.17; 21.4.
25.10-12: Is 15-16; Jer 48; Ezek 25.8-11; Amos 2.1-3; Zeph 2.8-11.

16 O LORD, in distress they sought thee,
they poured out a prayer[n]
when thy chastening was upon them.
17 Like a woman with child,
who writhes and cries out in her pangs,
when she is near her time,
so were we because of thee, O LORD;
18 we were with child, we writhed,
we have as it were brought forth wind.
We have wrought no deliverance in the earth,
and the inhabitants of the world have not fallen.
19 Thy dead shall live, their bodies[o] shall rise.
O dwellers in the dust, awake and sing for joy!
For thy dew is a dew of light,
and on the land of the shades thou wilt let it fall.

20 Come, my people, enter your chambers,
and shut your doors behind you;
hide yourselves for a little while
until the wrath is past.
21 For behold, the LORD is coming forth out of his place
to punish the inhabitants of the earth for their iniquity,
and the earth will disclose the blood shed upon her,
and will no more cover her slain.

27 In that day the LORD with his
hard and great and strong
sword will punish Lė·vī'ȧ·thȧn the
fleeing serpent, Leviathan the twisting
serpent, and he will slay the dragon
that is in the sea.

2 In that day:
"A pleasant vineyard, sing of it!
3 I, the LORD, am its keeper;
every moment I water it.
Lest any one harm it,
I guard it night and day;
4 I have no wrath.
Would that I had thorns and briers to battle!
I would set out against them,
I would burn them up together.
5 Or let them lay hold of my protection,
let them make peace with me,
let them make peace with me."

6 In days to come[q] Jacob shall take root,
Israel shall blossom and put forth shoots,
and fill the whole world with fruit.

7 Has he smitten them as he smote those who smote them?
Or have they been slain as their slayers were slain?
8 Measure by measure,[r] by exile thou didst contend with them;
he removed them with his fierce blast in the day of the east wind.
9 Therefore by this the guilt of Jacob will be expiated,
and this will be the full fruit of the removal of his sin:
when he makes all the stones of the altars
like chalkstones crushed to pieces,
no Ȧ·shē'rim or incense altars will remain standing.
10 For the fortified city is solitary,
a habitation deserted and forsaken, like the wilderness;
there the calf grazes,
there he lies down, and strips its branches.
11 When its boughs are dry, they are broken;
women come and make a fire of them.
For this is a people without discernment;
therefore he who made them will not have compassion on them,
he that formed them will show them no favor.

12 In that day from the river Eū-
phrā'tēs to the Brook of Egypt the
LORD will thresh out the grain, and
you will be gathered one by one, O
people of Israel. 13And in that day a
great trumpet will be blown, and those
who were lost in the land of Assyria and
those who were driven out to the land of
Egypt will come and worship the LORD
on the holy mountain at Jerusalem.

28 Woe to the proud crown of the drunkards of Ē'phrȧ·im,
and to the fading flower of its glorious beauty,

[n] Heb uncertain [o] Cn Compare Syr Tg: Heb *my body* [q] Heb *Those to come*
[r] Compare Syr Vg Tg: The meaning of the Hebrew word is unknown
27.13: Mt 24.31; 1 Cor 15.52; 1 Thess 4.16.

which is on the head of the rich
valley of those overcome with
wine!
2 Behold, the Lord has one who is
mighty and strong;
like a storm of hail, a destroying
tempest,
like a storm of mighty, overflowing
waters,
he will cast down to the earth
with violence.
3 The proud crown of the drunkards
of E'phră·im
will be trodden under foot;
4 and the fading flower of its glorious
beauty,
which is on the head of the rich
valley,
will be like a first-ripe fig before the
summer:
when a man sees it, he eats it up
as soon as it is in his hand.

5 In that day the LORD of hosts will
be a crown of glory,
and a diadem of beauty, to the
remnant of his people;
6 and a spirit of justice to him who
sits in judgment,
and strength to those who turn
back the battle at the gate.

7 These also reel with wine
and stagger with strong drink;
the priest and the prophet reel with
strong drink,
they are confused with wine,
they stagger with strong drink;
they err in vision,
they stumble in giving judgment.
8 For all tables are full of vomit,
no place is without filthiness.

9 "Whom will he teach knowledge,
and to whom will he explain the
message?
Those who are weaned from the
milk,
those taken from the breast?
10 For it is precept upon precept, precept upon precept,
line upon line, line upon line,
here a little, there a little."

11 Nay, but by men of strange lips
and with an alien tongue
the LORD will speak to this people,
12 to whom he has said,
"This is rest;
give rest to the weary;
and this is repose";
yet they would not hear.
13 Therefore the word of the LORD
will be to them
precept upon precept, precept
upon precept,
line upon line, line upon line,
here a little, there a little;
that they may go, and fall backward,
and be broken, and snared, and
taken.

14 Therefore hear the word of the
LORD, you scoffers,
who rule this people in Jerusalem!
15 Because you have said, "We have
made a covenant with death,
and with Shē'ōl we have an
agreement;
when the overwhelming scourge
passes through
it will not come to us;
for we have made lies our refuge,
and in falsehood we have taken
shelter";
16 therefore thus says the Lord GOD,
"Behold, I am laying in Zion for a
foundation
a stone, a tested stone,
a precious cornerstone, of a sure
foundation:
'He who believes will not be in
haste.'
17 And I will make justice the line,
and righteousness the plummet;
and hail will sweep away the refuge
of lies,
and waters will overwhelm the
shelter."
18 Then your covenant with death will
be annulled,
and your agreement with Shē'ōl
will not stand;
when the overwhelming scourge
passes through
you will be beaten down by it.
19 As often as it passes through it will
take you;
for morning by morning it will
pass through,
by day and by night;
and it will be sheer terror to understand the message.
20 For the bed is too short to stretch
oneself on it,
and the covering too narrow to
wrap oneself in it.
21 For the LORD will rise up as on
Mount Pe·rā'zim,

28.11-12: 1 Cor 14.21. **28.12:** Mt 11.29. **28.16:** Rom 9.33; 10.11; 1 Pet 2.4-6.

he will be wroth as in the valley of Gib'ē·ŏn;
to do his deed—strange is his deed!
and to work his work—alien is his work!
22 Now therefore do not scoff,
lest your bonds be made strong;
for I have heard a decree of destruction
from the Lord GOD of hosts upon the whole land.

23 Give ear, and hear my voice;
hearken, and hear my speech.
24 Does he who plows for sowing plow continually?
does he continually open and harrow his ground?
25 When he has leveled its surface,
does he not scatter dill, sow cummin,
and put in wheat in rows
and barley in its proper place,
and spelt as the border?
26 For he is instructed aright;
his God teaches him.

27 Dill is not threshed with a threshing sledge,
nor is a cart wheel rolled over cummin;
but dill is beaten out with a stick,
and cummin with a rod.
28 Does one crush bread grain?
No, he does not thresh it for ever;
when he drives his cart wheel over it
with his horses, he does not crush it.
29 This also comes from the LORD of hosts;
he is wonderful in counsel,
and excellent in wisdom.

29 Ho Âr'i·ĕl, Ariel,
the city where David encamped!
Add year to year;
let the feasts run their round.
2 Yet I will distress Âr'i·ĕl,
and there shall be moaning and lamentation,
and she shall be to me like an Ariel.
3 And I will encamp against you round about,
and will besiege you with towers
and I will raise siegeworks against you.
4 Then deep from the earth you shall speak,
from low in the dust your word shall come;
your voice shall come from the ground like the voice of a ghost,
and your speech shall whisper out of the dust.

5 But the multitude of your foes[s] shall be like small dust,
and the multitude of the ruthless like passing chaff.
And in an instant, suddenly,
6 you will be visited by the LORD of hosts
with thunder and with earthquake and great noise,
with whirlwind and tempest, and the flame of a devouring fire.
7 And the multitude of all the nations that fight against Âr'i·ĕl,
all that fight against her and her stronghold and distress her,
shall be like a dream, a vision of the night.
8 As when a hungry man dreams he is eating
and awakes with his hunger not satisfied,
or as when a thirsty man dreams he is drinking
and awakes faint, with his thirst not quenched,
so shall the multitude of all the nations be
that fight against Mount Zion.

9 Stupefy yourselves and be in a stupor,
blind yourselves and be blind!
Be drunk, but not with wine;
stagger, but not with strong drink!
10 For the LORD has poured out upon you
a spirit of deep sleep,
and has closed your eyes, the prophets,
and covered your heads, the seers.

11 And the vision of all this has become to you like the words of a book
that is sealed. When men give it to one
who can read, saying, "Read this," he
says, "I cannot, for it is sealed." 12 And
when they give the book to one who
cannot read, saying, "Read this," he
says, "I cannot read."

13 And the Lord said:

[s] Cn: Heb *strangers*
29.13: Mt 15.8-9; Mk 7.6-7.

"Because this people draw near with their mouth
and honor me with their lips,
while their hearts are far from me,
and their fear of me is a commandment of men learned by rote;
14 therefore, behold, I will again
do marvelous things with this people,
wonderful and marvelous;
and the wisdom of their wise men shall perish,
and the discernment of their discerning men shall be hid."

15 Woe to those who hide deep from the LORD their counsel,
whose deeds are in the dark,
and who say, "Who sees us? Who knows us?"
16 You turn things upside down!
Shall the potter be regarded as the clay;
that the thing made should say of its maker,
"He did not make me";
or the thing formed say of him who formed it,
"He has no understanding"?

17 Is it not yet a very little while
until Lebanon shall be turned into a fruitful field,
and the fruitful field shall be regarded as a forest?
18 In that day the deaf shall hear
the words of a book,
and out of their gloom and darkness
the eyes of the blind shall see.
19 The meek shall obtain fresh joy in the LORD,
and the poor among men shall exult in the Holy One of Israel.
20 For the ruthless shall come to nought and the scoffer cease,
and all who watch to do evil shall be cut off,
21 who by a word make a man out to be an offender,
and lay a snare for him who reproves in the gate,
and with an empty plea turn aside him who is in the right.

22 Therefore thus says the LORD,
who redeemed Abraham, concerning
the house of Jacob:
"Jacob shall no more be ashamed,
no more shall his face grow pale.
23 For when he sees his children,
the work of my hands, in his midst,
they will sanctify my name;
they will sanctify the Holy One of Jacob,
and will stand in awe of the God of Israel.
24 And those who err in spirit will come to understanding,
and those who murmur will accept instruction."

30 "Woe to the rebellious children," says the LORD,
"who carry out a plan, but not mine;
and who make a league, but not of my spirit,
that they may add sin to sin;
2 who set out to go down to Egypt,
without asking for my counsel,
to take refuge in the protection of Pharaoh,
and to seek shelter in the shadow of Egypt!
3 Therefore shall the protection of Pharaoh turn to your shame,
and the shelter in the shadow of Egypt to your humiliation.
4 For though his officials are at Zō'ăn
and his envoys reach Hā'nēṡ,
5 every one comes to shame
through a people that cannot profit them,
that brings neither help nor profit,
but shame and disgrace."

6 An oracle on the beasts of the Negeb.
Through a land of trouble and anguish,
from where come the lioness and the lion,
the viper and the flying serpent,
they carry their riches on the backs of asses,
and their treasures on the humps of camels,
to a people that cannot profit them.
7 For Egypt's help is worthless and empty,
therefore I have called her
"Rā'hab who sits still."

8 And now, go, write it before them on a tablet,
and inscribe it in a book,
that it may be for the time to come

29.14: 1 Cor 1.19. **29.16:** Is 45.9; Rom 9.20. **29.18-19:** Mt 11.5.

as a witness for ever.
9 For they are a rebellious people,
lying sons,
sons who will not hear
the instruction of the LORD;
10 who say to the seers, "See not";
and to the prophets, "Prophesy
not to us what is right;
speak to us smooth things,
prophesy illusions,
11 leave the way, turn aside from the
path,
let us hear no more of the Holy
One of Israel."
12 Therefore thus says the Holy One
of Israel,
"Because you despise this word,
and trust in oppression and perverseness,
and rely on them;
13 therefore this iniquity shall be to
you
like a break in a high wall, bulging
out, and about to collapse,
whose crash comes suddenly, in
an instant;
14 and its breaking is like that of a
potter's vessel
which is smashed so ruthlessly
that among its fragments not a sherd
is found
with which to take fire from the
hearth,
or to dip up water out of the
cistern."

15 For thus said the Lord GOD, the
Holy One of Israel,
"In returning and rest you shall
be saved;
in quietness and in trust shall be
your strength."
And you would not, 16 but you said,
"No! We will speed upon horses,"
therefore you shall speed away;
and, "We will ride upon swift
steeds,"
therefore your pursuers shall be
swift.
17 A thousand shall flee at the threat
of one,
at the threat of five you shall flee,
till you are left
like a flagstaff on the top of a
mountain,
like a signal on a hill.

18 Therefore the LORD waits to be
gracious to you;
therefore he exalts himself to
show mercy to you.
For the LORD is a God of justice;
blessed are all those who wait for
him.

19 Yea, O people in Zion who dwell
at Jerusalem; you shall weep no more.
He will surely be gracious to you at
the sound of your cry; when he hears
it, he will answer you. 20 And though
the Lord give you the bread of adversity and the water of affliction, yet your
Teacher will not hide himself any
more, but your eyes shall see your
Teacher. 21 And your ears shall hear a
word behind you, saying, "This is the
way, walk in it," when you turn to the
right or when you turn to the left.
22 Then you will defile your silver-covered graven images and your gold-plated molten images. You will scatter
them as unclean things; you will say
to them, "Begone!"

23 And he will give rain for the seed
with which you sow the ground, and
grain, the produce of the ground,
which will be rich and plenteous. In
that day your cattle will graze in large
pastures; 24 and the oxen and the asses
that till the ground will eat salted
provender, which has been winnowed
with shovel and fork. 25 And upon
every lofty mountain and every high
hill there will be brooks running with
water, in the day of the great slaughter,
when the towers fall. 26 Moreover the
light of the moon will be as the light
of the sun, and the light of the sun will
be sevenfold, as the light of seven days,
in the day when the LORD binds up
the hurt of his people, and heals the
wounds inflicted by his blow.

27 Behold, the name of the LORD comes
from far,
burning with his anger, and in
thick rising smoke;
his lips are full of indignation,
and his tongue is like a devouring
fire;
28 his breath is like an overflowing
stream
that reaches up to the neck;
to sift the nations with the sieve of
destruction,
and to place on the jaws of the
peoples a bridle that leads
astray.

29 You shall have a song as in the
night when a holy feast is kept; and
gladness of heart, as when one sets out
to the sound of the flute to go to the

mountain of the LORD, to the Rock of
Israel. 30And the LORD will cause his
majestic voice to be heard and the
descending blow of his arm to be seen,
in furious anger and a flame of devouring fire, with a cloudburst and tempest
and hailstones. 31 The Assyrians will
be terror-stricken at the voice of the
LORD, when he smites with his rod.
32And every stroke of the staff of
punishment which the LORD lays upon
them will be to the sound of timbrels
and lyres; battling with brandished
arm he will fight with them. 33 For a
burning place[t] has long been prepared;
yea, for the king[u] it is made ready, its
pyre made deep and wide, with fire
and wood in abundance; the breath of
the LORD, like a stream of brimstone,
kindles it.

31 Woe to those who go down to Egypt for help
and rely on horses,
who trust in chariots because they are many
and in horsemen because they are very strong,
but do not look to the Holy One of Israel
or consult the LORD!

2 And yet he is wise and brings disaster,
he does not call back his words,
but will arise against the house of the evildoers,
and against the helpers of those who work iniquity.

3 The Egyptians are men, and not God;
and their horses are flesh, and not spirit.
When the LORD stretches out his hand,
the helper will stumble, and he who is helped will fall,
and they will all perish together.

4 For thus the LORD said to me,
As a lion or a young lion growls over his prey,
and when a band of shepherds is called forth against him
is not terrified by their shouting
or daunted at their noise,
so the LORD of hosts will come down
to fight upon Mount Zion and upon its hill.

5 Like birds hovering, so the LORD of hosts
will protect Jerusalem;
he will protect and deliver it,
he will spare and rescue it.

6 Turn to him from whom you[v]
have deeply revolted, O people of
Israel. 7 For in that day every one shall
cast away his idols of silver and his
idols of gold, which your hands have
sinfully made for you.

8 "And the Assyrian shall fall by a sword, not of man;
and a sword, not of man, shall devour him;
and he shall flee from the sword,
and his young men shall be put to forced labor.

9 His rock shall pass away in terror,
and his officers desert the standard in panic,"
says the LORD, whose fire is in Zion,
and whose furnace is in Jerusalem.

32 Behold, a king will reign in righteousness,
and princes will rule in justice.

2 Each will be like a hiding place from the wind,
a covert from the tempest,
like streams of water in a dry place,
like the shade of a great rock in a weary land.

3 Then the eyes of those who see will not be closed,
and the ears of those who hear will hearken.

4 The mind of the rash will have good judgment,
and the tongue of the stammerers will speak readily and distinctly.

5 The fool will no more be called noble,
nor the knave said to be honorable.

6 For the fool speaks folly,
and his mind plots iniquity:
to practice ungodliness,
to utter error concerning the LORD,
to leave the craving of the hungry unsatisfied,
and to deprive the thirsty of drink.

7 The knaveries of the knave are evil;
he devises wicked devices
to ruin the poor with lying words,
even when the plea of the needy is right.

8 But he who is noble devises noble things,
and by noble things he stands.

[t] Or *Topheth* [u] Or *Moleck* [v] Heb *they*

9 Rise up, you women who are at ease, hear my voice;
you complacent daughters, give ear to my speech.
10 In little more than a year
you will shudder, you complacent women;
for the vintage will fail,
the fruit harvest will not come.
11 Tremble, you women who are at ease,
shudder, you complacent ones;
strip, and make yourselves bare,
and gird sackcloth upon your loins.
12 Beat upon your breasts for the pleasant fields,
for the fruitful vine,
13 for the soil of my people
growing up in thorns and briers;
yea, for all the joyous houses
in the joyful city.
14 For the palace will be forsaken,
the populous city deserted;
the hill and the watchtower
will become dens for ever,
a joy of wild asses,
a pasture of flocks;
15 until the Spirit is poured upon us from on high,
and the wilderness becomes a fruitful field,
and the fruitful field is deemed a forest.
16 Then justice will dwell in the wilderness,
and righteousness abide in the fruitful field.
17 And the effect of righteousness will be peace,
and the result of righteousness, quietness and trust for ever.
18 My people will abide in a peaceful habitation,
in secure dwellings, and in quiet resting places.
19 And the forest will utterly go down,[w]
and the city will be utterly laid low.
20 Happy are you who sow beside all waters,
who let the feet of the ox and the ass range free.

33 Woe to you, destroyer,
who yourself have not been destroyed;
you treacherous one,
with whom none has dealt treacherously!
When you have ceased to destroy,
you will be destroyed;
and when you have made an end of dealing treacherously,
you will be dealt with treacherously.

2 O LORD, be gracious to us; we wait for thee.
Be our arm every morning,
our salvation in the time of trouble.
3 At the thunderous noise peoples flee,
at the lifting up of thyself nations are scattered;
4 and spoil is gathered as the caterpillar gathers;
as locusts leap, men leap upon it.

5 The LORD is exalted, for he dwells on high;
he will fill Zion with justice and righteousness;
6 and he will be the stability of your times,
abundance of salvation, wisdom, and knowledge;
the fear of the LORD is his treasure.

7 Behold, the valiant ones[y] cry without;
the envoys of peace weep bitterly.
8 The highways lie waste,
the wayfaring man ceases.
Covenants are broken,
witnesses[z] are despised,
there is no regard for man.
9 The land mourns and languishes;
Lebanon is confounded and withers away;
Sharon is like a desert;
and Bā'shạn and Cär'mẹl shake off their leaves.

10 "Now I will arise," says the LORD,
"now I will lift myself up;
now I will be exalted.
11 You conceive chaff, you bring forth stubble;
your breath is a fire that will consume you.
12 And the peoples will be as if burned to lime,
like thorns cut down, that are burned in the fire."

13 Hear, you who are far off, what I have done;

[w] Cn: Heb *And it will hail when the forest comes down*
[y] The meaning of the Hebrew word is uncertain [z] One ancient Ms: Heb *cities*

and you who are near, acknowledge my might.
14 The sinners in Zion are afraid;
trembling has seized the godless:
"Who among us can dwell with the devouring fire?
Who among us can dwell with everlasting burnings?"
15 He who walks righteously and speaks uprightly,
who despises the gain of oppressions,
who shakes his hands, lest they hold a bribe,
who stops his ears from hearing of bloodshed
and shuts his eyes from looking upon evil,
16 he will dwell on the heights;
his place of defense will be the fortresses of rocks;
his bread will be given him, his water will be sure.

17 Your eyes will see the king in his beauty;
they will behold a land that stretches afar.
18 Your mind will muse on the terror:
"Where is he who counted,
where is he who weighed the tribute?
Where is he who counted the towers?"
19 You will see no more the insolent people,
the people of an obscure speech which you cannot comprehend,
stammering in a tongue which you cannot understand.
20 Look upon Zion, the city of our appointed feasts!
Your eyes will see Jerusalem,
a quiet habitation, an immovable tent,
whose stakes will never be plucked up,
nor will any of its cords be broken.
21 But there the LORD in majesty will be for us
a place of broad rivers and streams,
where no galley with oars can go,
nor stately ship can pass.
22 For the LORD is our judge, the LORD is our ruler,
the LORD is our king; he will save us.
23 Your tackle hangs loose;
it cannot hold the mast firm in its place,
or keep the sail spread out.

Then prey and spoil in abundance will be divided;
even the lame will take the prey.
24 And no inhabitant will say, "I am sick";
the people who dwell there will be forgiven their iniquity.

34 Draw near, O nations, to hear,
and hearken, O peoples!
Let the earth listen, and all that fills it;
the world, and all that comes from it.
2 For the LORD is enraged against all the nations,
and furious against all their host,
he has doomed them, has given them over for slaughter.
3 Their slain shall be cast out,
and the stench of their corpses shall rise;
the mountains shall flow with their blood.
4 All the host of heaven shall rot away,
and the skies roll up like a scroll.
All their host shall fall,
as leaves fall from the vine,
like leaves falling from the fig tree.

5 For my sword has drunk its fill in the heavens;
behold, it descends for judgment upon E'dŏm,
upon the people I have doomed.
6 The LORD has a sword; it is sated with blood,
it is gorged with fat,
with the blood of lambs and goats,
with the fat of the kidneys of rams.
For the LORD has a sacrifice in Boz'răh,
a great slaughter in the land of E'dŏm.
7 Wild oxen shall fall with them,
and young steers with the mighty bulls.
Their land shall be soaked with blood,
and their soil made rich with fat.

34: Is 63.1-6; Jer 49.7-22; Ezek 25.12-14; 35; Amos 1 11-12; Obad; Mal 1.2-5.
34.4: Rev 6.13-14.

8 For the LORD has a day of vengeance,
a year of recompense for the cause of Zion.
9 And the streams of E'dòm[a] shall be turned into pitch,
and her soil into brimstone;
her land shall become burning pitch.
10 Night and day it shall not be quenched;
its smoke shall go up for ever.
From generation to generation it shall lie waste;
none shall pass through it for ever and ever.
11 But the hawk and the porcupine shall possess it,
the owl and the raven shall dwell in it.
He shall stretch the line of confusion over it,
and the plummet of chaos over[b] its nobles.
12 They shall name it No Kingdom There,
and all its princes shall be nothing.

13 Thorns shall grow over its strongholds,
nettles and thistles in its fortresses.
It shall be the haunt of jackals,
an abode for ostriches.
14 And wild beasts shall meet with hyenas,
the satyr shall cry to his fellow;
yea, there shall the night hag alight,
and find for herself a resting place.

15 There shall the owl nest and lay
and hatch and gather her young in her shadow;
yea, there shall the kites be gathered,
each one with her mate.
16 Seek and read from the book of the LORD:
Not one of these shall be missing;
none shall be without her mate.
For the mouth of the LORD has commanded,
and his Spirit has gathered them.
17 He has cast the lot for them,
his hand has portioned it out to them with the line;
they shall possess it for ever,
from generation to generation they shall dwell in it.

35 The wilderness and the dry land shall be glad,
the desert shall rejoice and blossom;
like the crocus 2 it shall blossom abundantly,
and rejoice with joy and singing.
The glory of Lebanon shall be given to it,
the majesty of Cär'mĕl and Sharon.
They shall see the glory of the LORD,
the majesty of our God.

3 Strengthen the weak hands,
and make firm the feeble knees.
4 Say to those who are of a fearful heart,
"Be strong, fear not!
Behold, your God
will come with vengeance,
with the recompense of God.
He will come and save you."

5 Then the eyes of the blind shall be opened,
and the ears of the deaf unstopped;
6 then shall the lame man leap like a hart,
and the tongue of the dumb sing for joy.
For waters shall break forth in the wilderness,
and streams in the desert;
7 the burning sand shall become a pool,
and the thirsty ground springs of water;
the haunt of jackals shall become a swamp,[c]
the grass shall become reeds and rushes.

8 And a highway shall be there,
and it shall be called the Holy Way;
the unclean shall not pass over it,[d]
and fools shall not err therein.
9 No lion shall be there,
nor shall any ravenous beast come up on it;
they shall not be found there,
but the redeemed shall walk there.
10 And the ransomed of the LORD shall return,
and come to Zion with singing;

[a] Heb *her streams* [b] Heb lacks *over* [c] Cn: Heb *in the haunt of jackals is her resting place*
[d] Heb *it and he is for them a wayfarer*
34.9-10: Rev 19.3. 35.3: Heb 12.12. 35.5-6: Mt 11.5; Lk 7.22.

everlasting joy shall be upon their
heads;
they shall obtain joy and gladness,
and sorrow and sighing shall flee
away.

36 In the fourteenth year of King
Hez·ė·kī'ăh, Sen·nach'ė·rib king
of Assyria came up against all the
fortified cities of Judah and took them.
2 And the king of Assyria sent the
Rab'shȧ·kėh from Lā'chish to King
Hez·ė·kī'ăh at Jerusalem, with a great
army. And he stood by the conduit of
the upper pool on the highway to the
Fuller's Field. 3 And there came out to
him E·lī'ȧ·kim the son of Hil·kī'ăh,
who was over the household, and
Sheb'nȧ the secretary, and Jō'ăh the
son of Ā'saph, the recorder.
4 And the Rab'shȧ·kėh said to
them, "Say to Hez·ė·kī'ăh, 'Thus says
the great king, the king of Assyria: On
what do you rest this confidence of
yours? 5 Do you think that mere words
are strategy and power for war? On
whom do you now rely, that you have
rebelled against me? 6 Behold, you are
relying on Egypt, that broken reed of
a staff, which will pierce the hand of
any man who leans on it. Such is
Pharaoh king of Egypt to all who rely
on him. 7 But if you say to me, "We
rely on the LORD our God," is it not
he whose high places and altars Hez·ė-
kī'ăh has removed, saying to Judah
and to Jerusalem, "You shall worship
before this altar"? 8 Come now, make
a wager with my master the king of
Assyria: I will give you two thousand
horses, if you are able on your part to
set riders upon them. 9 How then can
you repulse a single captain among the
least of my master's servants, when
you rely on Egypt for chariots and for
horsemen? 10 Moreover, is it without
the LORD that I have come up against
this land to destroy it? The LORD said
to me, Go up against this land, and
destroy it.' "
11 Then E·lī'ȧ·kim, Sheb'nȧ, and
Jō'ăh said to the Rab'shȧ·kėh, "Pray,
speak to your servants in Aramaic,
for we understand it; do not speak to
us in the language of Judah within the
hearing of the people who are on the
wall." 12 But the Rab'shȧ·kėh said,
"Has my master sent me to speak these
words to your master and to you, and
not to the men sitting on the wall, who
are doomed with you to eat their own
dung and drink their own urine?"
13 Then the Rab'shȧ·kėh stood and
called out in a loud voice in the language of Judah: "Hear the words of
the great king, the king of Assyria!
14 Thus says the king: 'Do not let
Hez·ė·kī'ăh deceive you, for he will
not be able to deliver you. 15 Do not
let Hez·ė·kī'ăh make you rely on the
LORD by saying, "The LORD will surely
deliver us; this city will not be given
into the hand of the king of Assyria."
16 Do not listen to Hez·ė·kī'ăh; for
thus says the king of Assyria: Make
your peace with me and come out to
me; then every one of you will eat of
his own vine, and every one of his own
fig tree, and every one of you will
drink the water of his own cistern;
17 until I come and take you away to a
land like your own land, a land of grain
and wine, a land of bread and vineyards. 18 Beware lest Hez·ė·kī'ăh mislead you by saying, "The LORD will
deliver us." Has any of the gods of the
nations delivered his land out of the
hand of the king of Assyria? 19 Where
are the gods of Hā'math and Är'pad?
Where are the gods of Seph·är·vā'im?
Have they delivered Sȧ·mâr'i·ȧ out of
my hand? 20 Who among all the gods
of these countries have delivered their
countries out of my hand, that the
LORD should deliver Jerusalem out of
my hand?' "
21 But they were silent and answered him not a word, for the king's
command was, "Do not answer him."
22 Then E·lī'ȧ·kim the son of Hil·kī'ăh,
who was over the household, and
Sheb'nȧ the secretary, and Jō'ăh the
son of Ā'saph, the recorder, came to
Hez·ė·kī'ăh with their clothes rent,
and told him the words of the Rab'-
shȧ·kėh.

37 When King Hez·ė·kī'ăh heard
it, he rent his clothes, and
covered himself with sackcloth, and
went into the house of the LORD. 2 And
he sent E·lī'ȧ·kim, who was over the
household, and Sheb'nȧ the secretary,
and the senior priests, clothed with
sackcloth, to the prophet Ī·ṡāi'ăh the
son of Ā'moz. 3 They said to him,
"Thus says Hez·ė·kī'ăh, 'This day is
a day of distress, of rebuke, and of
disgrace; children have come to the
birth, and there is no strength to bring
them forth. 4 It may be that the LORD

36.1-38.8, 21-22: 2 Kings 18.13-20.11; 2 Chron 32.1-24.

your God heard the words of the
Rab'shȧ·kėh, whom his master the
king of Assyria has sent to mock the
living God, and will rebuke the words
which the LORD your God has heard;
therefore lift up your prayer for the
remnant that is left.' "
5 When the servants of King Hez-
ė·kī'ȧh came to I·ṡāi'ȧh, 6 I·ṡāi'ȧh said
to them, "Say to your master, 'Thus
says the LORD: Do not be afraid because of the words that you have
heard, with which the servants of the
king of Assyria have reviled me. 7 Behold, I will put a spirit in him, so that
he shall hear a rumor, and return to
his own land; and I will make him fall
by the sword in his own land.' "
8 The Rab'shȧ·kėh returned, and
found the king of Assyria fighting
against Lib'nȧh; for he had heard that
the king had left Lā'chish. 9 Now the
king heard concerning Tīr·hā'kȧh king
of Ethiopia, "He has set out to fight
against you." And when he heard it,
he sent messengers to Hez·ė·kī'ȧh,
saying, 10 "Thus shall you speak to
Hez·ė·kī'ȧh king of Judah: 'Do not let
your God on whom you rely deceive
you by promising that Jerusalem will
not be given into the hand of the king
of Assyria. 11 Behold, you have heard
what the kings of Assyria have done
to all lands, destroying them utterly.
And shall you be delivered? 12 Have
the gods of the nations delivered them,
the nations which my fathers destroyed, Gō'zȧn, Hâr'ȧn, Rē'zeph, and
the people of Eden who were in
Te·las'sȧr? 13 Where is the king of
Hā'math, the king of Är'pad, the king
of the city of Seph·är·vā'im, the king
of Hē'nȧ, or the king of Iv'vȧh?' "
14 Hez·ė·kī'ȧh received the letter
from the hand of the messengers, and
read it; and Hezekiah went up to the
house of the LORD, and spread it before the LORD. 15 And Hez·ė·kī'ȧh
prayed to the LORD: 16 "O LORD of
hosts, God of Israel, who art enthroned
above the cherubim, thou art the God,
thou alone, of all the kingdoms of the
earth; thou hast made heaven and
earth. 17 Incline thy ear, O LORD, and
hear; open thy eyes, O LORD, and see;
and hear all the words of Sen·nach'ė-
rib, which he has sent to mock the
living God. 18 Of a truth, O LORD, the
kings of Assyria have laid waste all the
nations and their lands, 19 and have
cast their gods into the fire; for they
were no gods, but the work of men's
hands, wood and stone; therefore they
were destroyed. 20 So now, O LORD
our God, save us from his hand, that
all the kingdoms of the earth may
know that thou alone art the LORD."
21 Then I·ṡāi'ȧh the son of Ā'moz
sent to Hez·ė·kī'ȧh, saying, "Thus
says the LORD, the God of Israel: Because you have prayed to me concerning Sen·nach'ė·rib king of Assyria,
22 this is the word that the LORD has
spoken concerning him:

'She despises you, she scorns you—
the virgin daughter of Zion;
she wags her head behind you—
the daughter of Jerusalem.

23 'Whom have you mocked and reviled?
Against whom have you raised
your voice
and haughtily lifted your eyes?
Against the Holy One of Israel!
24 By your servants you have mocked
the Lord,
and you have said, With my many
chariots
I have gone up the heights of the
mountains,
to the far recesses of Lebanon;
I felled its tallest cedars,
its choicest cypresses;
I came to its remotest height,
its densest forest.
25 I dug wells
and drank waters,
and I dried up with the sole of my
foot
all the streams of Egypt.

26 'Have you not heard
that I determined it long ago?
I planned from days of old
what now I bring to pass,
that you should make fortified cities
crash into heaps of ruins,
27 while their inhabitants, shorn of
strength,
are dismayed and confounded,
and have become like plants of the
field
and like tender grass,
like grass on the housetops,
blighted[e] before it is grown.

28 'I know your sitting down
and your going out and coming in,
and your raging against me.

[e] With 2 Kings 19.26: Heb *field*

29 Because you have raged against me
and your arrogance has come to my ears,
I will put my hook in your nose
and my bit in your mouth,
and I will turn you back on the way
by which you came.'

30 "And this shall be the sign for
you: this year eat what grows of itself,
and in the second year what springs of
the same; then in the third year sow
and reap, and plant vineyards, and eat
their fruit. 31 And the surviving remnant of the house of Judah shall again
take root downward, and bear fruit
upward; 32 for out of Jerusalem shall
go forth a remnant, and out of Mount
Zion a band of survivors. The zeal of
the LORD of hosts will accomplish this.
33 "Therefore thus says the LORD
concerning the king of Assyria: He
shall not come into this city, or shoot
an arrow there, or come before it with
a shield, or cast up a siege mound
against it. 34 By the way that he came,
by the same he shall return, and he
shall not come into this city, says the
LORD. 35 For I will defend this city to
save it, for my own sake and for the
sake of my servant David."

36 And the angel of the LORD went
forth, and slew a hundred and eighty-
five thousand in the camp of the
Assyrians; and when men arose early
in the morning, behold, these were all
dead bodies. 37 Then Sen·nach'ė·rib
king of Assyria departed, and went
home and dwelt at Nin'ė·vėh. 38 And
as he was worshiping in the house of
Nis'roch his god, A·dram'mė·lech and
Shȧ·rē'zėr, his sons, slew him with the
sword, and escaped into the land of
Ar'ȧ·rat. And E'sär-had'don his son
reigned in his stead.

38 In those days Hez·ė·kī'ăh became sick and was at the point
of death. And Ī·ṡāi'ăh the prophet the
son of Ā'moz came to him, and said
to him, "Thus says the LORD: Set
your house in order; for you shall die,
you shall not recover." 2 Then Hez·ė-
kī'ăh turned his face to the wall, and
prayed to the LORD, 3 and said, "Remember now, O LORD, I beseech thee,
how I have walked before thee in
faithfulness and with a whole heart,
and have done what is good in thy
sight." And Hez·ė·kī'ăh wept bitterly.
4 Then the word of the LORD came to
Ī·ṡāi'ăh: 5 "Go and say to Hez·ė·kī'ăh,
Thus says the LORD, the God of David
your father: I have heard your prayer,
I have seen your tears; behold, I will
add fifteen years to your life. 6 I will
deliver you and this city out of the
hand of the king of Assyria, and defend this city.
7 "This is the sign to you from the
LORD, that the LORD will do this thing
that he has promised: 8 Behold, I will
make the shadow cast by the declining
sun on the dial of Ā'haz turn back ten
steps." So the sun turned back on the
dial the ten steps by which it had
declined.[f]

9 A writing of Hez·ė·kī'ăh king of
Judah, after he had been sick and had
recovered from his sickness:

10 I said, In the noontide of my days
I must depart;
I am consigned to the gates of Shē'ōl
for the rest of my years.
11 I said, I shall not see the LORD
in the land of the living;
I shall look upon man no more
among the inhabitants of the world.
12 My dwelling is plucked up and removed from me
like a shepherd's tent;
like a weaver I have rolled up my life;
he cuts me off from the loom;
from day to night thou dost bring
me to an end;[g]
13 I cry for help[h] until morning;
like a lion he breaks all my bones;
from day to night thou dost bring
me to an end.[g]

14 Like a swallow or a crane[i] I clamor,
I moan like a dove.
My eyes are weary with looking upward.
O Lord, I am oppressed; be thou
my security!
15 But what can I say? For he has
spoken to me,
and he himself has done it.
All my sleep has fled[j]
because of the bitterness of my soul.

16 O Lord, by these things men live,

[f] The Hebrew of this verse is obscure [g] Heb uncertain [h] Cn: Heb obscure Heb uncertain
[j] Cn Compare Syr: Heb *I will walk slowly all my years*

and in all these is the life of my
spirit.[k]
Oh, restore me to health and
make me live!
17 Lo, it was for my welfare
that I had great bitterness;
but thou hast held back[l] my life
from the pit of destruction,
for thou hast cast all my sins
behind thy back.
18 For Shē′ōl cannot thank thee,
death cannot praise thee;
those who go down to the pit cannot
hope
for thy faithfulness.
19 The living, the living, he thanks
thee,
as I do this day;
the father makes known to the
children
thy faithfulness.

20 The LORD will save me,
and we will sing to stringed instruments[m]
all the days of our life,
at the house of the LORD.

21 Now Ī·ṡāi′ȧh had said, 'Let them
take a cake of figs, and apply it to the
boil, that he may recover." 22 Hez·ē-
kī′ȧh also had said, "What is the sign
that I shall go up to the house of the
LORD?"

39 At that time Mer′ȯ·dach-
bal′ȧ·dan the son of Bal′ȧ·dan,
king of Babylon, sent envoys with
letters and a present to Hez·ē·kī′ȧh,
for he heard that he had been sick and
had recovered. 2 And Hez·ē·kī′ȧh
welcomed them; and he showed them
his treasure house, the silver, the gold,
the spices, the precious oil, his whole
armory, all that was found in his storehouses. There was nothing in his
house or in all his realm that Hezekiah
did not show them. 3 Then Ī·ṡāi′ȧh the
prophet came to King Hez·ē·kī′ȧh, and
said to him, "What did these men say?
And whence did they come to you?"
Hezekiah said, "They have come to
me from a far country, from Babylon."
4 He said, "What have they seen in
your house?" Hez·ē·kī′ȧh answered,
"They have seen all that is in my
house; there is nothing in my storehouses that I did not show them."
5 Then Ī·ṡāi′ȧh said to Hez·ē·kī′ȧh,
"Hear the word of the LORD of hosts:
6 Behold, the days are coming, when
all that is in your house, and that which
your fathers have stored up till this
day, shall be carried to Babylon;
nothing shall be left, says the LORD.
7 And some of your own sons, who are
born to you, shall be taken away; and
they shall be eunuchs in the palace of
the king of Babylon." 8 Then said
Hez·ē·kī′ȧh to Ī·ṡāi′ȧh, "The word of
the LORD which you have spoken is
good." For he thought, "There will
be peace and security in my days."

40 Comfort, comfort my people,
says your God.
2 Speak tenderly to Jerusalem,
and cry to her
that her warfare[n] is ended,
that her iniquity is pardoned,
that she has received from the
LORD's hand
double for all her sins.

3 A voice cries:
"In the wilderness prepare the way
of the LORD,
make straight in the desert a
highway for our God.
4 Every valley shall be lifted up,
and every mountain and hill be
made low;
the uneven ground shall become
level,
and the rough places a plain.
5 And the glory of the LORD shall be
revealed,
and all flesh shall see it together,
for the mouth of the LORD has
spoken."

6 A voice says, "Cry!"
And I said, "What shall I cry?"
All flesh is grass,
and all its beauty is like the flower
of the field.
7 The grass withers, the flower fades,
when the breath of the LORD
blows upon it;
surely the people is grass.
8 The grass withers, the flower fades;
but the word of our God will
stand for ever.

9 Get you up to a high mountain,

[k] Heb uncertain [l] Cn Compare Gk Vg: Heb *loved* [m] Heb *my stringed instruments*
[n] Or *time of service*
39.1-8: 2 Kings 20.12-19; 2 Chron 32.31. 40.3: Mt 3.3; Mk 1.3; Lk 3.4; Jn 1.23. 40.4-5: Lk 3.5-6.
40.6-8: 1 Pet 1.24-25. 40.9: Is 52.7; Nahum 1.15; Acts 10.36; Rom 10.15.

O Zion, herald of good tidings;[o]
lift up your voice with strength,
O Jerusalem, herald of good tidings,[p]
lift it up, fear not;
say to the cities of Judah,
"Behold your God!"
10 Behold, the Lord GOD comes with might,
and his arm rules for him;
behold, his reward is with him,
and his recompense before him.
11 He will feed his flock like a shepherd,
he will gather the lambs in his arms,
he will carry them in his bosom,
and gently lead those that are with young.

12 Who has measured the waters in the hollow of his hand
and marked off the heavens with a span,
enclosed the dust of the earth in a measure
and weighed the mountains in scales
and the hills in a balance?
13 Who has directed the Spirit of the LORD,
or as his counselor has instructed him?
14 Whom did he consult for his enlightenment,
and who taught him the path of justice,
and taught him knowledge,
and showed him the way of understanding?
15 Behold, the nations are like a drop from a bucket,
and are accounted as the dust on the scales;
behold, he takes up the isles like fine dust.
16 Lebanon would not suffice for fuel,
nor are its beasts enough for a burnt offering.
17 All the nations are as nothing before him,
they are accounted by him as less than nothing and emptiness.

18 To whom then will you liken God,
or what likeness compare with him?
19 The idol! a workman casts it,
and a goldsmith overlays it with gold,
and casts for it silver chains.
20 He who is impoverished[q] chooses for an offering
wood that will not rot;
he seeks out a skilful craftsman
to set up an image that will not move.

21 Have you not known? Have you not heard?
Has it not been told you from the beginning?
Have you not understood from the foundations of the earth?
22 It is he who sits above the circle of the earth,
and its inhabitants are like grasshoppers;
who stretches out the heavens like a curtain,
and spreads them like a tent to dwell in;
23 who brings princes to nought,
and makes the rulers of the earth as nothing.

24 Scarcely are they planted, scarcely sown,
scarcely has their stem taken root in the earth,
when he blows upon them, and they wither,
and the tempest carries them off like stubble.

25 To whom then will you compare me,
that I should be like him?
says the Holy One.
26 Lift up your eyes on high and see:
who created these?
He who brings out their host by number,
calling them all by name;
by the greatness of his might,
and because he is strong in power
not one is missing.

27 Why do you say, O Jacob,
and speak, O Israel,
"My way is hid from the LORD,
and my right is disregarded by my God"?
28 Have you not known? Have you not heard?
The LORD is the everlasting God,
the Creator of the ends of the earth.
He does not faint or grow weary,

[o] Or *O herald of good tidings to Zion* [p] Or *O herald of good tidings to Jerusalem* [q] Heb uncertain
40.10: Rev 22.7, 12. **40.13:** Rom 11.34; 1 Cor 2.16.

his understanding is unsearchable.
29 He gives power to the faint,
and to him who has no might he increases strength.
30 Even youths shall faint and be weary,
and young men shall fall exhausted;
31 but they who wait for the LORD shall renew their strength,
they shall mount up with wings like eagles,
they shall run and not be weary,
they shall walk and not faint.

41 Listen to me in silence, O coastlands;
let the peoples renew their strength;
let them approach, then let them speak;
let us together draw near for judgment.

2 Who stirred up one from the east whom victory meets at every step?
He gives up nations before him,
so that he tramples kings under foot;
he makes them like dust with his sword,
like driven stubble with his bow.
3 He pursues them and passes on safely,
by paths his feet have not trod.
4 Who has performed and done this,
calling the generations from the beginning?
I, the LORD, the first,
and with the last; I am He.

5 The coastlands have seen and are afraid,
the ends of the earth tremble;
they have drawn near and come.
6 Every one helps his neighbor,
and says to his brother, "Take courage!"
7 The craftsman encourages the goldsmith,
and he who smooths with the hammer him who strikes the anvil,
saying of the soldering, "It is good";
and they fasten it with nails so that it cannot be moved.

8 But you, Israel, my servant,
Jacob, whom I have chosen,
the offspring of Abraham, my friend;
9 you whom I took from the ends of the earth,
and called from its farthest corners,
saying to you, "You are my servant,
I have chosen you and not cast you off";
10 fear not, for I am with you,
be not dismayed, for I am your God;
I will strengthen you, I will help you,
I will uphold you with my victorious right hand.

11 Behold, all who are incensed against you
shall be put to shame and confounded;
those who strive against you
shall be as nothing and shall perish.
12 You shall seek those who contend with you,
but you shall not find them;
those who war against you
shall be as nothing at all.
13 For I, the LORD your God,
hold your right hand;
it is I who say to you, "Fear not,
I will help you."

14 Fear not, you worm Jacob,
you men of Israel!
I will help you, says the LORD;
your Redeemer is the Holy One of Israel.
15 Behold, I will make of you a threshing sledge,
new, sharp, and having teeth;
you shall thresh the mountains and crush them,
and you shall make the hills like chaff;
16 you shall winnow them and the wind shall carry them away,
and the tempest shall scatter them.
And you shall rejoice in the LORD;
in the Holy One of Israel you shall glory.

17 When the poor and needy seek water,
and there is none,
and their tongue is parched with thirst,

41.8: Jas 2.23. **41.8-9:** Lk 1.54; Heb 2.16. **41.10:** Acts 18.10.

I the LORD will answer them,
I the God of Israel will not forsake them.
18 I will open rivers on the bare heights,
and fountains in the midst of the valleys;
I will make the wilderness a pool of water,
and the dry land springs of water.
19 I will put in the wilderness the cedar,
the acacia, the myrtle, and the olive;
I will set in the desert the cypress,
the plane and the pine together;
20 that men may see and know,
may consider and understand together,
that the hand of the LORD has done this,
the Holy One of Israel has created it.

21 Set forth your case, says the LORD;
bring your proofs, says the King of Jacob.
22 Let them bring them, and tell us what is to happen.
Tell us the former things, what they are,
that we may consider them,
that we may know their outcome;
or declare to us the things to come.
23 Tell us what is to come hereafter,
that we may know that you are gods;
do good, or do harm,
that we may be dismayed and terrified.
24 Behold, you are nothing,
and your work is nought;
an abomination is he who chooses you.

25 I stirred up one from the north, and he has come,
from the rising of the sun, and he shall call on my name;
he shall trample[r] on rulers as on mortar,
as the potter treads clay.
26 Who declared it from the beginning, that we might know,
and beforetime, that we might say, "He is right"?
There was none who declared it,
none who proclaimed,
none who heard your words.
27 I first have declared it to Zion,[s]
and I give to Jerusalem a herald of good tidings.
28 But when I look there is no one;
among these there is no counselor
who, when I ask, gives an answer.
29 Behold, they are all a delusion;
their works are nothing;
their molten images are empty wind.

42 Behold my servant, whom I uphold,
my chosen, in whom my soul delights;
I have put my Spirit upon him,
he will bring forth justice to the nations.
2 He will not cry or lift up his voice,
or make it heard in the street;
3 a bruised reed he will not break,
and a dimly burning wick he will not quench;
he will faithfully bring forth justice.
4 He will not fail[t] or be discouraged[u]
till he has established justice in the earth;
and the coastlands wait for his law.

5 Thus says God, the LORD,
who created the heavens and stretched them out,
who spread forth the earth and what comes from it,
who gives breath to the people upon it
and spirit to those who walk in it:
6 "I am the LORD, I have called you in righteousness,
I have taken you by the hand and kept you;
I have given you as a covenant to the people,
a light to the nations,
7 to open the eyes that are blind,
to bring out the prisoners from the dungeon,
from the prison those who sit in darkness.
8 I am the LORD, that is my name;
my glory I give to no other,
nor my praise to graven images.
9 Behold, the former things have come to pass,
and new things I now declare;

[r] Cn: Heb *come* [s] Cn: Heb *first to Zion, Behold, behold them* [t] Or *burn dimly* [u] Or *bruised*
42.1-4: Mt 12.18-21. **42.5**: Acts 17.24-25. **42.6**: Is 49.6; Lk 2.32; Acts 13.47; 26.23.
42.7: Acts 26.18.

before they spring forth
I tell you of them."

10 Sing to the LORD a new song,
his praise from the end of the earth!
Let the sea roar[v] and all that fills it,
the coastlands and their inhabitants.
11 Let the desert and its cities lift up their voice,
the villages that Kē'där inhabits;
let the inhabitants of Sē'lȧ sing for joy,
let them shout from the top of the mountains.
12 Let them give glory to the LORD,
and declare his praise in the coastlands.
13 The LORD goes forth like a mighty man,
like a man of war he stirs up his fury;
he cries out, he shouts aloud,
he shows himself mighty against his foes.

14 For a long time I have held my peace,
I have kept still and restrained myself;
now I will cry out like a woman in travail,
I will gasp and pant.
15 I will lay waste mountains and hills,
and dry up all their herbage;
I will turn the rivers into islands,
and dry up the pools.
16 And I will lead the blind
in a way that they know not,
in paths that they have not known
I will guide them.
I will turn the darkness before them into light,
the rough places into level ground.
These are the things I will do,
and I will not forsake them.
17 They shall be turned back and utterly put to shame,
who trust in graven images,
who say to molten images,
"You are our gods."

18 Hear, you deaf;
and look, you blind, that you may see!
19 Who is blind but my servant,
or deaf as my messenger whom I send?
Who is blind as my dedicated one,
or blind as the servant of the LORD?
20 He sees[w] many things, but does not observe them;
his ears are open, but he does not hear.
21 The LORD was pleased, for his righteousness' sake,
to magnify his law and make it glorious.
22 But this is a people robbed and plundered,
they are all of them trapped in holes
and hidden in prisons;
they have become a prey with none to rescue,
a spoil with none to say, "Restore!"
23 Who among you will give ear to this,
will attend and listen for the time to come?
24 Who gave up Jacob to the spoiler,
and Israel to the robbers?
Was it not the LORD, against whom we have sinned,
in whose ways they would not walk,
and whose law they would not obey?
25 So he poured upon him the heat of his anger
and the might of battle;
it set him on fire round about, but he did not understand;
it burned him, but he did not take it to heart.

43 But now thus says the LORD,
who created you, O Jacob,
he who formed you, O Israel:
"Fear not, for I have redeemed you;
I have called you by name, you are mine.
2 When you pass through the waters
I will be with you;
and through the rivers, they shall not overwhelm you;
when you walk through fire you shall not be burned,
and the flame shall not consume you.
3 For I am the LORD your God,
the Holy One of Israel, your Savior.
I give Egypt as your ransom,

[v] Cn Compare Ps 96.11; 98.7: Heb *Those who go down to the sea* [w] Heb *you see*
42.16: Acts 26.18.

Ethiopia and Sē'bȧ in exchange
for you.
4 Because you are precious in my
eyes,
and honored, and I love you,
I give men in return for you,
peoples in exchange for your life.
5 Fear not, for I am with you;
I will bring your offspring from
the east,
and from the west I will gather
you;
6 I will say to the north, Give up,
and to the south, Do not withhold;
bring my sons from afar
and my daughters from the end
of the earth,
7 every one who is called by my name,
whom I created for my glory,
whom I formed and made."

8 Bring forth the people who are
blind, yet have eyes,
who are deaf, yet have ears!
9 Let all the nations gather together,
and let the peoples assemble.
Who among them can declare this,
and show us the former things?
Let them bring their witnesses to
justify them,
and let them hear and say, It is
true.
10 "You are my witnesses," says the
LORD,
"and my servant whom I have
chosen,
that you may know and believe
me
and understand that I am He.
Before me no god was formed,
nor shall there be any after me.
11 I, I am the LORD,
and besides me there is no savior.
12 I declared and saved and proclaimed,
when there was no strange god
among you;
and you are my witnesses," says
the LORD.
13 "I am God, and also henceforth I
am He;
there is none who can deliver
from my hand;
I work and who can hinder it?"

14 Thus says the LORD,
your Redeemer, the Holy One of
Israel:
"For your sake I will send to
Babylon
and break down all the bars,
and the shouting of the Chal·dē'-
ȧnṡ will be turned to lamentations.[x]
15 I am the LORD, your Holy One,
the Creator of Israel, your King."
16 Thus says the LORD,
who makes a way in the sea,
a path in the mighty waters,
17 who brings forth chariot and horse,
army and warrior;
they lie down, they cannot rise,
they are extinguished,
quenched like a wick:
18 "Remember not the former things,
nor consider the things of old.
19 Behold, I am doing a new thing;
now it springs forth, do you not
perceive it?
I will make a way in the wilderness
and rivers in the desert.
20 The wild beasts will honor me,
the jackals and the ostriches;
for I give water in the wilderness,
rivers in the desert,
to give drink to my chosen people,
21 the people whom I formed for
myself
that they might declare my praise.

22 "Yet you did not call upon me, O
Jacob;
but you have been weary of me,
O Israel!
23 You have not brought me your
sheep for burnt offerings,
or honored me with your sacrifices.
I have not burdened you with offerings,
or wearied you with frankincense.
24 You have not bought me sweet
cane with money,
or satisfied me with the fat of
your sacrifices.
But you have burdened me with
your sins,
you have wearied me with your
iniquities.

25 "I, I am He
who blots out your transgressions
for my own sake,
and I will not remember your
sins.
26 Put me in remembrance, let us argue
together;
set forth your case, that you may
be proved right.
27 Your first father sinned,

[x] Heb obscure
43.5: Acts 18.10.

and your mediators transgressed
against me.
28 Therefore I profaned the princes of
the sanctuary,
I delivered Jacob to utter destruction
and Israel to reviling.

44 "But now hear, O Jacob my
servant,
Israel whom I have chosen!
2 Thus says the LORD who made you,
who formed you from the womb
and will help you:
Fear not, O Jacob my servant,
Jesh'u·run whom I have chosen.
3 For I will pour water on the thirsty
land,
and streams on the dry ground;
I will pour my Spirit upon your
descendants,
and my blessing on your offspring.
4 They shall spring up like grass amid
waters,[y]
like willows by flowing streams.
5 This one will say, 'I am the LORD's,'
another will call himself by the
name of Jacob,
and another will write on his hand,
'The LORD's,'
and surname himself by the name
of Israel."

6 Thus says the LORD, the King of
Israel
and his Redeemer, the LORD of
hosts:
"I am the first and I am the last;
besides me there is no god.
7 Who is like me? Let him proclaim
it,
let him declare and set it forth
before me.
Who has announced from of old the
things to come?[z]
Let them tell us[a] what is yet to
be.
8 Fear not, nor be afraid;
have I not told you from of old
and declared it?
And you are my witnesses!
Is there a God besides me?
There is no Rock; I know not
any."

9 All who make idols are nothing,
and the things they delight in do not
profit; their witnesses neither see nor
know, that they may be put to shame.
10 Who fashions a god or casts an
image, that is profitable for nothing?
11 Behold, all his fellows shall be put
to shame, and the craftsmen are but
men; let them all assemble, let them
stand forth, they shall be terrified,
they shall be put to shame together.
12 The ironsmith fashions it[b] and
works it over the coals; he shapes it
with hammers, and forges it with his
strong arm; he becomes hungry and
his strength fails, he drinks no water
and is faint. 13 The carpenter stretches
a line, he marks it out with a pencil;
he fashions it with planes, and marks
it with a compass; he shapes it into
the figure of a man, with the beauty
of a man, to dwell in a house. 14 He
cuts down cedars; or he chooses a
holm tree or an oak and lets it grow
strong among the trees of the forest;
he plants a cedar and the rain nourishes
it. 15 Then it becomes fuel for a man;
he takes a part of it and warms himself,
he kindles a fire and bakes bread; also
he makes a god and worships it, he
makes it a graven image and falls down
before it. 16 Half of it he burns in the
fire; over the half he eats flesh, he
roasts meat and is satisfied; also he
warms himself and says, "Aha, I am
warm, I have seen the fire!" 17 And the
rest of it he makes into a god, his idol;
and falls down to it and worships it;
he prays to it and says, "Deliver me,
for thou art my god!"
18 They know not, nor do they
discern; for he has shut their eyes, so
that they cannot see, and their minds,
so that they cannot understand. 19 No
one considers, nor is there knowledge
or discernment to say, "Half of it I
burned in the fire, I also baked bread
on its coals, I roasted flesh and have
eaten; and shall I make the residue of
it an abomination? Shall I fall down
before a block of wood?" 20 He feeds
on ashes; a deluded mind has led him
astray, and he cannot deliver himself
or say, "Is there not a lie in my right
hand?"

21 Remember these things, O Jacob,
and Israel, for you are my servant;
I formed you, you are my servant;
O Israel, you will not be forgotten
by me.

[y] Gk Compare Tg: Heb *They shall spring up in among grass*
[z] Cn: Heb *from my placing an eternal people and things to come* [a] Tg: Heb *them* [b] Cn: Heb *an axe*
44.6: Is 48.12; Rev 1.17; 2.8; 22.13.

22 I have swept away your transgressions like a cloud,
and your sins like mist;
return to me, for I have redeemed you.

23 Sing, O heavens, for the LORD has done it;
shout, O depths of the earth;
break forth into singing, O mountains,
O forest, and every tree in it!
For the LORD has redeemed Jacob,
and will be glorified in Israel.

24 Thus says the LORD, your Redeemer,
who formed you from the womb:
"I am the LORD, who made all things,
who stretched out the heavens alone,
who spread out the earth—Who was with me?[c]—
25 who frustrates the omens of liars,
and makes fools of diviners;
who turns wise men back,
and makes their knowledge foolish;
26 who confirms the word of his servant,
and performs the counsel of his messengers;
who says of Jerusalem, 'She shall be inhabited,'
and of the cities of Judah, 'They shall be built,
and I will raise up their ruins';
27 who says to the deep, 'Be dry,
I will dry up your rivers';
28 who says of Cyrus, 'He is my shepherd,
and he shall fulfil all my purpose';
saying of Jerusalem, 'She shall be built,'
and of the temple, 'Your foundation shall be laid.' "

45 Thus says the LORD to his anointed, to Cyrus,
whose right hand I have grasped,
to subdue nations before him
and ungird the loins of kings,
to open doors before him
that gates may not be closed:
2 "I will go before you
and level the mountains,[d]
I will break in pieces the doors of bronze
and cut asunder the bars of iron,
3 I will give you the treasures of darkness
and the hoards in secret places,
that you may know that it is I, the LORD,
the God of Israel, who call you by your name.
4 For the sake of my servant Jacob,
and Israel my chosen,
I call you by your name,
I surname you, though you do not know me.
5 I am the LORD, and there is no other,
besides me there is no God;
I gird you, though you do not know me,
6 that men may know, from the rising of the sun
and from the west, that there is none besides me;
I am the LORD, and there is no other.
7 I form light and create darkness,
I make weal and create woe,
I am the LORD, who do all these things.

8 "Shower, O heavens, from above,
and let the skies rain down righteousness;
let the earth open, that salvation may sprout forth,[e]
and let it cause righteousness to spring up also;
I the LORD have created it.

9 "Woe to him who strives with his Maker,
an earthen vessel with the potter![f]
Does the clay say to him who fashions it, 'What are you making'?
or 'Your work has no handles'?
10 Woe to him who says to a father,
'What are you begetting?'
or to a woman, 'With what are you in travail?' "
11 Thus says the LORD,
the Holy One of Israel, and his Maker:
"Will you question me[g] about my children,
or command me concerning the work of my hands?
12 I made the earth,

[c] Another reading is *who spread out the earth by myself* [d] One ancient Ms Gk: Heb *the swellings*
[e] One ancient Ms: Heb *that they may bring forth salvation* [f] Cn: Heb *potsherds* or *potters*
[g] Cn: Heb *Ask me of things to come*
44.23: Jer 51.48; Rev 12.12; 18.20. **44.25:** 1 Cor 1.20. **45.9:** Is 29.16; Rom 9.20.

and created man upon it;
it was my hands that stretched out the heavens,
and I commanded all their host.
13 I have aroused him in righteousness,
and I will make straight all his ways;
he shall build my city
and set my exiles free,
not for price or reward,"
says the LORD of hosts.

14 Thus says the LORD:
"The wealth of Egypt and the merchandise of Ethiopia,
and the Sȧ·bē′ȧns, men of stature,
shall come over to you and be yours,
they shall follow you;
they shall come over in chains
and bow down to you.
They will make supplication to you, saying:
'God is with you only, and there is no other,
no god besides him.' "
15 Truly, thou art a God who hidest thyself,
O God of Israel, the Savior.
16 All of them are put to shame and confounded,
the makers of idols go in confusion together.
17 But Israel is saved by the LORD
with everlasting salvation;
you shall not be put to shame or confounded
to all eternity.

18 For thus says the LORD,
who created the heavens
(he is God!),
who formed the earth and made it
(he established it;
he did not create it a chaos,
he formed it to be inhabited!):
"I am the LORD, and there is no other.
19 I did not speak in secret,
in a land of darkness;
I did not say to the offspring of Jacob,
'Seek me in chaos.'
I the LORD speak the truth,
I declare what is right.

20 "Assemble yourselves and come,
draw near together,
you survivors of the nations!
They have no knowledge
who carry about their wooden idols,
and keep on praying to a god
that cannot save.
21 Declare and present your case;
let them take counsel together!
Who told this long ago?
Who declared it of old?
Was it not I, the LORD?
And there is no other god besides me,
a righteous God and a Savior;
there is none besides me.

22 "Turn to me and be saved,
all the ends of the earth!
For I am God, and there is no other.
23 By myself I have sworn,
from my mouth has gone forth in righteousness
a word that shall not return:
'To me every knee shall bow,
every tongue shall swear.'

24 "Only in the LORD, it shall be said of me,
are righteousness and strength;
to him shall come and be ashamed,
all who were incensed against him.
25 In the LORD all the offspring of Israel
shall triumph in glory."

46 Bel bows down, Nē′bō stoops,
their idols are on beasts and cattle;
these things you carry are loaded
as burdens on weary beasts.
2 They stoop, they bow down together,
they cannot save the burden,
but themselves go into captivity.

3 "Hearken to me, O house of Jacob,
all the remnant of the house of Israel,
who have been borne by me from your birth,
carried from the womb;
4 even to your old age I am He,
and to gray hairs I will carry you.
I have made, and I will bear;
I will carry and will save.

5 "To whom will you liken me and make me equal,
and compare me, that we may be alike?

45.14: 1 Cor 14.25. **45.17:** Heb 5.9. **45.21:** Acts 15.18. **45.23:** Rom 14.11; Phil 2.10-11.

6 Those who lavish gold from the purse,
and weigh out silver in the scales,
hire a goldsmith, and he makes it into a god;
then they fall down and worship!
7 They lift it upon their shoulders, they carry it,
they set it in its place, and it stands there;
it cannot move from its place.
If one cries to it, it does not answer
or save him from his trouble.

8 "Remember this and consider,
recall it to mind, you transgressors,
9 remember the former things of old;
for I am God, and there is no other;
I am God, and there is none like me,
10 declaring the end from the beginning
and from ancient times things not yet done,
saying, 'My counsel shall stand,
and I will accomplish all my purpose,'
11 calling a bird of prey from the east,
the man of my counsel from a far country.
I have spoken, and I will bring it to pass;
I have purposed, and I will do it.

12 "Hearken to me, you stubborn of heart,
you who are far from deliverance:
13 I bring near my deliverance, it is not far off,
and my salvation will not tarry;
I will put salvation in Zion,
for Israel my glory."

47 Come down and sit in the dust,
O virgin daughter of Babylon;
sit on the ground without a throne,
O daughter of the Chal·dē′ăns!
For you shall no more be called
tender and delicate.
2 Take the millstones and grind meal,
put off your veil,
strip off your robe, uncover your legs,
pass through the rivers.
3 Your nakedness shall be uncovered,
and your shame shall be seen.
I will take vengeance,
and I will spare no man.
4 Our Redeemer—the LORD of hosts is his name—
is the Holy One of Israel.

5 Sit in silence, and go into darkness,
O daughter of the Chal·dē′ăns;
for you shall no more be called
the mistress of kingdoms.
6 I was angry with my people,
I profaned my heritage;
I gave them into your hand,
you showed them no mercy;
on the aged you made your yoke exceedingly heavy.
7 You said, "I shall be mistress for ever,"
so that you did not lay these things to heart
or remember their end.

8 Now therefore hear this, you lover of pleasures,
who sit securely,
who say in your heart,
"I am, and there is no one besides me;
I shall not sit as a widow
or know the loss of children":
9 These two things shall come to you
in a moment, in one day;
the loss of children and widowhood
shall come upon you in full measure,
in spite of your many sorceries
and the great power of your enchantments.

10 You felt secure in your wickedness,
you said, "No one sees me";
your wisdom and your knowledge
led you astray,
and you said in your heart,
"I am, and there is no one besides me."
11 But evil shall come upon you,
for which you cannot atone;
disaster shall fall upon you,
which you will not be able to expiate;
and ruin shall come on you suddenly,
of which you know nothing.

12 Stand fast in your enchantments
and your many sorceries,
with which you have labored from your youth;
perhaps you may be able to succeed,
perhaps you may inspire terror.

47: Is 13.1-14.23; Jer 50-51; Hab 1-2. **47.8:** Rev 18.7. **47.9:** Rev 18.8.

13 You are wearied with your many counsels;
let them stand forth and save you,
those who divide the heavens,
who gaze at the stars,
who at the new moons predict
what[h] shall befall you.

14 Behold, they are like stubble,
the fire consumes them;
they cannot deliver themselves
from the power of the flame.
No coal for warming oneself is this,
no fire to sit before!
15 Such to you are those with whom you have labored,
who have trafficked with you from your youth;
they wander about each in his own direction;
there is no one to save you.

48 Hear this, O house of Jacob,
who are called by the name of Israel,
and who came forth from the loins[i] of Judah;
who swear by the name of the LORD,
and confess the God of Israel,
but not in truth or right.
2 For they call themselves after the holy city,
and stay themselves on the God of Israel;
the LORD of hosts is his name.

3 "The former things I declared of old,
they went forth from my mouth and I made them known;
then suddenly I did them and they came to pass.
4 Because I know that you are obstinate,
and your neck is an iron sinew
and your forehead brass,
5 I declared them to you from of old,
before they came to pass I announced them to you,
lest you should say, 'My idol did them,
my graven image and my molten image commanded them.'

6 "You have heard; now see all this;
and will you not declare it?
From this time forth I make you hear new things,
hidden things which you have not known.
7 They are created now, not long ago;
before today you have never heard of them,
lest you should say, 'Behold, I knew them.'
8 You have never heard, you have never known,
from of old your ear has not been opened.
For I knew that you would deal very treacherously,
and that from birth you were called a rebel.

9 "For my name's sake I defer my anger,
for the sake of my praise I restrain it for you,
that I may not cut you off.
10 Behold, I have refined you, but not like[j] silver;
I have tried you in the furnace of affliction.
11 For my own sake, for my own sake, I do it,
for how should my name[k] be profaned?
My glory I will not give to another.

12 "Hearken to me, O Jacob,
and Israel, whom I called!
I am He, I am the first,
and I am the last.
13 My hand laid the foundation of the earth,
and my right hand spread out the heavens;
when I call to them,
they stand forth together.

14 Assemble, all of you, and hear!
Who among them has declared these things?
The LORD loves him;
he shall perform his purpose on Babylon,
and his arms shall be against the Chal·dē′ăns.
15 I, even I, have spoken and called him,
I have brought him, and he will prosper in his way.
16 Draw near to me, hear this:
from the beginning I have not spoken in secret,

[h] Gk Syr Compare Vg: Heb *from what* [i] Cn: Heb *waters* [j] Cn: Heb *with*
[k] Gk Old Latin: Heb lacks *my name*
48.12: Is 44.6; Rev 1.17; 2.8; 22.13.

from the time it came to be I
have been there."
And now the Lord GOD has sent me
and his Spirit.

17 Thus says the LORD,
your Redeemer, the Holy One of
Israel:
"I am the LORD your God,
who teaches you to profit,
who leads you in the way you
should go.
18 O that you had hearkened to my
commandments!
Then your peace would have been
like a river,
and your righteousness like the
waves of the sea;
19 your offspring would have been like
the sand,
and your descendants like its
grains;
their name would never be cut off
or destroyed from before me."

20 Go forth from Babylon, flee from
Chal·dē'ȧ,
declare this with a shout of joy,
proclaim it,
send it forth to the end of the earth;
say, "The LORD has redeemed
his servant Jacob!"
21 They thirsted not when he led them
through the deserts;
he made water flow for them from
the rock;
he cleft the rock and the water
gushed out.
22 "There is no peace," says the LORD,
"for the wicked."

49 Listen to me, O coastlands,
and hearken, you peoples from
afar.
The LORD called me from the
womb,
from the body of my mother he
named my name.
2 He made my mouth like a sharp
sword,
in the shadow of his hand he hid
me;
he made me a polished arrow,
in his quiver he hid me away.
3 And he said to me, "You are my
servant,
Israel, in whom I will be glorified."
4 But I said, "I have labored in vain,
I have spent my strength for
nothing and vanity;
yet surely my right is with the LORD,
and my recompense with my
God."

5 And now the LORD says,
who formed me from the womb
to be his servant,
to bring Jacob back to him,
and that Israel might be gathered
to him,
for I am honored in the eyes of the
LORD,
and my God has become my
strength—
6 he says:
"It is too light a thing that you
should be my servant
to raise up the tribes of Jacob
and to restore the preserved of
Israel;
I will give you as a light to the
nations,
that my salvation may reach to
the end of the earth."

7 Thus says the LORD,
the Redeemer of Israel and his
Holy One,
to one deeply despised, abhorred by
the nations,
the servant of rulers:
"Kings shall see and arise;
princes, and they shall prostrate
themselves;
because of the LORD, who is faithful,
the Holy One of Israel, who has
chosen you."

8 Thus says the LORD:
"In a time of favor I have answered
you,
in a day of salvation I have helped
you;
I have kept you and given you
as a covenant to the people,
to establish the land,
to apportion the desolate herit-
ages;
9 saying to the prisoners, 'Come
forth,'
to those who are in darkness,
'Appear.'
They shall feed along the ways,
on all bare heights shall be their
pasture;
10 they shall not hunger or thirst,

49.1: Jer 1.5; Gal 1.15. **49.4:** Phil 2.16. **49.6:** Is 42.6; Lk 2.32; Acts 13.47; 26.23.
49.8: 2 Cor 6.2. **49.10:** Rev 7.16.

neither scorching wind nor sun
shall smite them,
for he who has pity on them will
lead them,
and by springs of water will guide
them.
11 And I will make all my mountains
a way,
and my highways shall be raised
up.
12 Lo, these shall come from afar,
and lo, these from the north and
from the west,
and these from the land of
Sȳ·ē′nē."[l]
13 Sing for joy, O heavens, and exult,
O earth;
break forth, O mountains, into
singing!
For the LORD has comforted his
people,
and will have compassion on his
afflicted.

14 But Zion said, "The LORD has forsaken me,
my Lord has forgotten me."
15 "Can a woman forget her sucking
child,
that she should have no compassion on the son of her
womb?
Even these may forget,
yet I will not forget you.
16 Behold, I have graven you on the
palms of my hands;
your walls are continually before
me.
17 Your builders outstrip your destroyers,
and those who laid you waste go
forth from you.
18 Lift up your eyes round about and
see;
they all gather, they come to you.
As I live, says the LORD,
you shall put them all on as an
ornament,
you shall bind them on as a bride
does.

19 "Surely your waste and your desolate places
and your devastated land—
surely now you will be too narrow
for your inhabitants,
and those who swallowed you up
will be far away.
20 The children born in the time of
your bereavement
will yet say in your ears:
'The place is too narrow for me;
make room for me to dwell in.'
21 Then you will say in your heart:
'Who has borne me these?
I was bereaved and barren,
exiled and put away,
but who has brought up these?
Behold, I was left alone;
whence then have these come?'"

22 Thus says the Lord GOD:
"Behold, I will lift up my hand to
the nations,
and raise my signal to the peoples;
and they shall bring your sons in
their bosom,
and your daughters shall be carried on their shoulders.
23 Kings shall be your foster fathers,
and their queens your nursing
mothers.
With their faces to the ground they
shall bow down to you,
and lick the dust of your feet.
Then you will know that I am the
LORD;
those who wait for me shall not
be put to shame."

24 Can the prey be taken from the
mighty,
or the captives of a tyrant[m] be
rescued?
25 Surely, thus says the LORD:
"Even the captives of the mighty
shall be taken,
and the prey of the tyrant be
rescued,
for I will contend with those who
contend with you,
and I will save your children.
26 I will make your oppressors eat
their own flesh,
and they shall be drunk with their
own blood as with wine.
Then all flesh shall know
that I am the LORD your Savior,
and your Redeemer, the Mighty
One of Jacob."

50 Thus says the LORD:
"Where is your mother's bill of
divorce,
with which I put her away?
Or which of my creditors is it
to whom I have sold you?
Behold, for your iniquities you
were sold,

[l] Cn: Heb *Sinim* [m] One ancient Ms Syr Vg: Heb *righteous man*
49.13: Is 44.23; Jer 51.48; Rev 12.12; 18.20.

and for your transgressions your
mother was put away.
2 Why, when I came, was there no
man?
When I called, was there no one
to answer?
Is my hand shortened, that it cannot redeem?
Or have I no power to deliver?
Behold, by my rebuke I dry up the
sea,
I make the rivers a desert;
their fish stink for lack of water,
and die of thirst.
3 I clothe the heavens with blackness,
and make sackcloth their covering."

4 The Lord GOD has given me
the tongue of those who are
taught,
that I may know how to sustain with
a word
him that is weary.
Morning by morning he wakens,
he wakens my ear
to hear as those who are taught.
5 The Lord GOD has opened my ear,
and I was not rebellious,
I turned not backward.
6 I gave my back to the smiters,
and my cheeks to those who
pulled out the beard;
I hid not my face
from shame and spitting.

7 For the Lord GOD helps me;
therefore I have not been confounded;
therefore I have set my face like a
flint,
and I know that I shall not be
put to shame;
8 he who vindicates me is near.
Who will contend with me?
Let us stand up together.
Who is my adversary?
Let him come near to me.
9 Behold, the Lord GOD helps me;
who will declare me guilty?
Behold, all of them will wear out
like a garment;
the moth will eat them up.

10 Who among you fears the LORD
and obeys the voice of his servant,
who walks in darkness
and has no light,
yet trusts in the name of the LORD
and relies upon his God?
11 Behold, all you who kindle a fire,
who set brands alight![n]
Walk by the light of your fire,
and by the brands which you
have kindled!
This shall you have from my hand:
you shall lie down in torment.

51 "Hearken to me, you who pursue deliverance,
you who seek the LORD;
look to the rock from which you
were hewn,
and to the quarry from which
you were digged.
2 Look to Abraham your father
and to Sarah who bore you;
for when he was but one I called
him,
and I blessed him and made him
many.
3 For the LORD will comfort Zion;
he will comfort all her waste
places,
and will make her wilderness like
Eden,
her desert like the garden of the
LORD;
joy and gladness will be found in
her,
thanksgiving and the voice of
song.

4 "Listen to me, my people,
and give ear to me, my nation;
for a law will go forth from me,
and my justice for a light to the
peoples.
5 My deliverance draws near speedily,
my salvation has gone forth,
and my arms will rule the peoples;
the coastlands wait for me,
and for my arm they hope.
6 Lift up your eyes to the heavens,
and look at the earth beneath;
for the heavens will vanish like
smoke,
the earth will wear out like a
garment,
and they who dwell in it will die
like gnats;[o]
but my salvation will be for ever,
and my deliverance will never be
ended.

7 "Hearken to me, you who know
righteousness,

[n] Syr: Heb *gird yourselves with brands* [o] Or *in like manner*
50.8-9: Rom 8.33; Heb 1.11. 51.6: Heb 1.11.

the people in whose heart is my law;
fear not the reproach of men,
and be not dismayed at their revilings.
8 For the moth will eat them up like a garment,
and the worm will eat them like wool;
but my deliverance will be for ever,
and my salvation to all generations."

9 Awake, awake, put on strength,
O arm of the LORD;
awake, as in days of old,
the generations of long ago.
Was it not thou that didst cut Rā'hab in pieces,
that didst pierce the dragon?
10 Was it not thou that didst dry up the sea,
the waters of the great deep;
that didst make the depths of the sea a way
for the redeemed to pass over?
11 And the ransomed of the LORD shall return,
and come to Zion with singing;
everlasting joy shall be upon their heads;
they shall obtain joy and gladness,
and sorrow and sighing shall flee away.

12 "I, I am he that comforts you;
who are you that you are afraid of man who dies,
of the son of man who is made like grass,
13 and have forgotten the LORD, your Maker,
who stretched out the heavens
and laid the foundations of the earth,
and fear continually all the day
because of the fury of the oppressor,
when he sets himself to destroy?
And where is the fury of the oppressor?
14 He who is bowed down shall speedily be released;
he shall not die and go down to the Pit,
neither shall his bread fail.
15 For I am the LORD your God,
who stirs up the sea so that its waves roar—
the LORD of hosts is his name.
16 And I have put my words in your mouth,
and hid you in the shadow of my hand,
stretching out[p] the heavens
and laying the foundations of the earth,
and saying to Zion, 'You are my people.' "

17 Rouse yourself, rouse yourself,
stand up, O Jerusalem,
you who have drunk at the hand of the LORD
the cup of his wrath,
who have drunk to the dregs
the bowl of staggering.
18 There is none to guide her
among all the sons she has borne;
there is none to take her by the hand
among all the sons she has brought up.
19 These two things have befallen you—
who will condole with you?—
devastation and destruction, famine and sword;
who will comfort you?[q]
20 Your sons have fainted,
they lie at the head of every street
like an antelope in a net;
they are full of the wrath of the LORD,
the rebuke of your God.

21 Therefore hear this, you who are afflicted,
who are drunk, but not with wine:
22 Thus says your Lord, the LORD,
your God who pleads the cause of his people:
"Behold, I have taken from your hand
the cup of staggering;
the bowl of my wrath
you shall drink no more;
23 and I will put it into the hand of your tormentors,
who have said to you,
'Bow down, that we may pass over';
and you have made your back like the ground
and like the street for them to pass over."

[p] Syr: Heb *plant*
[q] One ancient Ms Gk Syr Vg: Heb *how may I comfort you*

52 Awake, awake,
put on your strength, O Zion;
put on your beautiful garments,
O Jerusalem, the holy city;
for there shall no more come into you
the uncircumcised and the unclean.
2 Shake yourself from the dust, arise,
O captive[r] Jerusalem;
loose the bonds from your neck,
O captive daughter of Zion.

3 For thus says the LORD: "You
were sold for nothing, and you shall
be redeemed without money. 4 For
thus says the Lord GOD: My people
went down at the first into Egypt to
sojourn there, and the Assyrian oppressed them for nothing. 5 Now
therefore what have I here, says the
LORD, seeing that my people are taken
away for nothing? Their rulers wail,
says the LORD, and continually all the
day my name is despised. 6 Therefore
my people shall know my name; therefore in that day they shall know that
it is I who speak; here am I."

7 How beautiful upon the mountains
are the feet of him who brings good tidings,
who publishes peace, who brings good tidings of good,
who publishes salvation,
who says to Zion, "Your God reigns."
8 Hark, your watchmen lift up their voice,
together they sing for joy;
for eye to eye they see
the return of the LORD to Zion.
9 Break forth together into singing,
you waste places of Jerusalem;
for the LORD has comforted his people,
he has redeemed Jerusalem.
10 The LORD has bared his holy arm
before the eyes of all the nations;
and all the ends of the earth shall see
the salvation of our God.

11 Depart, depart, go out thence,
touch no unclean thing;
go out from the midst of her, purify yourselves,
you who bear the vessels of the LORD.
12 For you shall not go out in haste,
and you shall not go in flight,
for the LORD will go before you,
and the God of Israel will be your rear guard.

13 Behold, my servant shall prosper,
he shall be exalted and lifted up,
and shall be very high.
14 As many were astonished at him[s]—
his appearance was so marred,
beyond human semblance,
and his form beyond that of the sons of men—
15 so shall he startle[t] many nations;
kings shall shut their mouths because of him;
for that which has not been told them they shall see,
and that which they have not heard they shall understand.

53 Who has believed what we have heard?
And to whom has the arm of the LORD been revealed?
2 For he grew up before him like a young plant,
and like a root out of dry ground;
he had no form or comeliness that we should look at him,
and no beauty that we should desire him.
3 He was despised and rejected[u] by men;
a man of sorrows,[v] and acquainted with grief;[w]
and as one from whom men hide their faces
he was despised, and we esteemed him not.

4 Surely he has borne our griefs[x]
and carried our sorrows;[y]
yet we esteemed him stricken,
smitten by God, and afflicted.
5 But he was wounded for our transgressions,
he was bruised for our iniquities;
upon him was the chastisement that made us whole,
and with his stripes we are healed.
6 All we like sheep have gone astray;

[r] Cn: Heb *sit* [s] Syr Tg: Heb *you* [t] The meaning of the Hebrew word is uncertain [u] Or *forsaken* [v] Or *pains* [w] Or *sickness* [x] Or *sicknesses* [y] Or *pains*

52.1: Rev 21.27. **52.5:** Rom 2.24. **52.7:** Acts 10.36; Rom 10.15; Eph 6.15. **52.10:** Lk 2.30; 3.6. **52.11:** 2 Cor 6.17. **52.15:** Rom 15.21. **53.1:** Jn 12.38; Rom 10.16. **53.4:** Mt 8.17. **53.5-6:** 1 Pet 2.24-25.

we have turned every one to his own way;
and the LORD has laid on him
the iniquity of us all.
7 He was oppressed, and he was afflicted,
yet he opened not his mouth;
like a lamb that is led to the slaughter,
and like a sheep that before its shearers is dumb,
so he opened not his mouth.
8 By oppression and judgment he was taken away;
and as for his generation, who considered
that he was cut off out of the land of the living,
stricken for the transgression of my people?
9 And they made his grave with the wicked
and with a rich man in his death,
although he had done no violence,
and there was no deceit in his mouth.

10 Yet it was the will of the LORD to bruise him;
he has put him to grief;[z]
when he makes himself[a] an offering for sin,
he shall see his offspring, he shall prolong his days;
the will of the LORD shall prosper in his hand;
11 he shall see the fruit of the travail of his soul and be satisfied;
by his knowledge shall the righteous one, my servant,
make many to be accounted righteous;
and he shall bear their iniquities.
12 Therefore I will divide him a portion with the great,
and he shall divide the spoil with the strong;
because he poured out his soul to death,
and was numbered with the transgressors;
yet he bore the sin of many,
and made intercession for the transgressors.

54 "Sing, O barren one, who did not bear;
break forth into singing and cry aloud,
you who have not been in travail!
For the children of the desolate one will be more
than the children of her that is married, says the LORD.
2 Enlarge the place of your tent,
and let the curtains of your habitations be stretched out;
hold not back, lengthen your cords
and strengthen your stakes.
3 For you will spread abroad to the right and to the left,
and your descendants will possess the nations
and will people the desolate cities.

4 "Fear not, for you will not be ashamed;
be not confounded, for you will not be put to shame;
for you will forget the shame of your youth,
and the reproach of your widowhood you will remember no more.
5 For your Maker is your husband,
the LORD of hosts is his name;
and the Holy One of Israel is your Redeemer,
the God of the whole earth he is called.
6 For the LORD has called you
like a wife forsaken and grieved in spirit,
like a wife of youth when she is cast off,
says your God.
7 For a brief moment I forsook you,
but with great compassion I will gather you.
8 In overflowing wrath for a moment
I hid my face from you,
but with everlasting love I will have compassion on you,
says the LORD, your Redeemer.

9 "For this is like the days of Noah to me:
as I swore that the waters of Noah
should no more go over the earth,
so I have sworn that I will not be angry with you
and will not rebuke you.
10 For the mountains may depart
and the hills be removed,
but my steadfast love shall not depart from you,

[z] **Heb** *made him sick* [a] **Vg**: **Heb** *thou makest his soul*
53.7-8: Acts 8.32-33. **53.9**: 1 Pet 2.22. **53.12**: Lk 22.37. **54.1**: Gal 4.27.

and my covenant of peace shall not be removed,
says the LORD, who has compassion on you.

11 "O afflicted one, storm-tossed, and not comforted,
behold, I will set your stones in antimony,
and lay your foundations with sapphires.[b]
12 I will make your pinnacles of agate,
your gates of carbuncles,
and all your wall of precious stones.
13 All your sons shall be taught by the LORD,
and great shall be the prosperity of your sons.
14 In righteousness you shall be established;
you shall be far from oppression, for you shall not fear;
and from terror, for it shall not come near you.
15 If any one stirs up strife,
it is not from me;
whoever stirs up strife with you
shall fall because of you.
16 Behold, I have created the smith
who blows the fire of coals,
and produces a weapon for its purpose.
I have also created the ravager to destroy;
17 no weapon that is fashioned against you shall prosper,
and you shall confute every tongue that rises against you in judgment.
This is the heritage of the servants of the LORD
and their vindication from me, says the LORD."

55 "Ho, every one who thirsts,
come to the waters;
and he who has no money,
come, buy and eat!
Come, buy wine and milk
without money and without price.
2 Why do you spend your money for that which is not bread,
and your labor for that which does not satisfy?
Hearken diligently to me, and eat what is good,
and delight yourselves in fatness.
3 Incline your ear, and come to me;
hear, that your soul may live;
and I will make with you an everlasting covenant,
my steadfast, sure love for David.
4 Behold, I made him a witness to the peoples,
a leader and commander for the peoples.
5 Behold, you shall call nations that you know not,
and nations that knew you not shall run to you,
because of the LORD your God, and of the Holy One of Israel,
for he has glorified you.

6 "Seek the LORD while he may be found,
call upon him while he is near;
7 let the wicked forsake his way,
and the unrighteous man his thoughts;
let him return to the LORD, that he may have mercy on him,
and to our God, for he will abundantly pardon.
8 For my thoughts are not your thoughts,
neither are your ways my ways, says the LORD.
9 For as the heavens are higher than the earth,
so are my ways higher than your ways
and my thoughts than your thoughts.

10 "For as the rain and the snow come down from heaven,
and return not thither but water the earth,
making it bring forth and sprout,
giving seed to the sower and bread to the eater,
11 so shall my word be that goes forth from my mouth;
it shall not return to me empty,
but it shall accomplish that which I purpose,
and prosper in the thing for which I sent it.

12 "For you shall go out in joy,
and be led forth in peace;
the mountains and the hills before you
shall break forth into singing,

[b] Or *lapis lazuli*

54.11-12: Rev 21.19. 54.13: Jn 6.45. 55.1: Rev 21.6; 22.17. 55.3: Acts 13.34; Heb 13.20. 55.10: 2 Cor 9.10.

and all the trees of the field shall
clap their hands.
13 Instead of the thorn shall come up
the cypress;
instead of the brier shall come up
the myrtle;
and it shall be to the LORD for a
memorial,
for an everlasting sign which shall
not be cut off."

56 Thus says the LORD:
"Keep justice, and do righteousness,
for soon my salvation will come,
and my deliverance be revealed.
2 Blessed is the man who does this,
and the son of man who holds it
fast,
who keeps the sabbath, not profaning it,
and keeps his hand from doing
any evil."

3 Let not the foreigner who has joined
himself to the LORD say,
"The LORD will surely separate
me from his people";
and let not the eunuch say,
"Behold, I am a dry tree."
4 For thus says the LORD:
"To the eunuchs who keep my
sabbaths,
who choose the things that please me
and hold fast my covenant,
5 I will give in my house and within
my walls
a monument and a name
better than sons and daughters;
I will give them an everlasting name
which shall not be cut off.

6 "And the foreigners who join themselves to the LORD,
to minister to him, to love the
name of the LORD,
and to be his servants,
every one who keeps the sabbath,
and does not profane it,
and holds fast my covenant—
7 these I will bring to my holy
mountain,
and make them joyful in my
house of prayer;
their burnt offerings and their
sacrifices
will be accepted on my altar;
for my house shall be called a house
of prayer
for all peoples.
8 Thus says the Lord GOD,
who gathers the outcasts of Israel,
I will gather yet others to him
besides those already gathered."[c]

9 All you beasts of the field, come to
devour—
all you beasts in the forest.
10 His watchmen are blind,
they are all without knowledge;
they are all dumb dogs,
they cannot bark;
dreaming, lying down,
loving to slumber.
11 The dogs have a mighty appetite;
they never have enough.
The shepherds also have no understanding;
they have all turned to their own
way,
each to his own gain, one and all.
12 "Come," they say, "let us[d] get wine,
let us fill ourselves with strong
drink;
and tomorrow will be like this day,
great beyond measure."

57 The righteous man perishes,
and no one lays it to heart;
devout men are taken away,
while no one understands.
For the righteous man is taken away
from calamity,
2 he enters into peace;
they rest in their beds
who walk in their uprightness.
3 But you, draw near hither,
sons of the sorceress,
offspring of the adulterer and the
harlot.
4 Of whom are you making sport?
Against whom do you open your
mouth wide
and put out your tongue?
Are you not children of transgression,
the offspring of deceit,
5 you who burn with lust among the
oaks,
under every green tree;
who slay your children in the valleys,
under the clefts of the rocks?
6 Among the smooth stones of the
valley is your portion;
they, they, are your lot;
to them you have poured out a
drink offering,
you have brought a cereal offering.

[c] Heb *his gathered ones* [d] One ancient Ms Syr Vg Tg: Heb *me*
56.7: Mt 21.13; Mk 11.17; Lk 19.46.

Shall I be appeased for these
things?
7 Upon a high and lofty mountain
you have set your bed,
and thither you went up to offer
sacrifice.
8 Behind the door and the doorpost
you have set up your symbol;
for, deserting me, you have uncovered your bed,
you have gone up to it,
you have made it wide;
and you have made a bargain for
yourself with them,
you have loved their bed,
you have looked on nakedness.[e]
9 You journeyed to Mē'loch[f] with oil
and multiplied your perfumes;
you sent your envoys far off,
and sent down even to Shē'ōl.
10 You were wearied with the length
of your way,
but you did not say, "It is hopeless";
you found new life for your strength,
and so you were not faint.

11 Whom did you dread and fear,
so that you lied,
and did not remember me,
did not give me a thought?
Have I not held my peace, even for
a long time,
and so you do not fear me?
12 I will tell of your righteousness and
your doings,
but they will not help you.
13 When you cry out, let your collection of idols deliver you!
The wind will carry them off,
a breath will take them away.
But he who takes refuge in me shall
possess the land,
and shall inherit my holy mountain.

14 And it shall be said,
"Build up, build up, prepare the
way,
remove every obstruction from
my people's way."
15 For thus says the high and lofty One
who inhabits eternity, whose
name is Holy:
"I dwell in the high and holy
place,
and also with him who is of a
contrite and humble spirit,
to revive the spirit of the humble,
and to revive the heart of the
contrite.
16 For I will not contend for ever,
nor will I always be angry;
for from me proceeds the spirit,
and I have made the breath of life.
17 Because of the iniquity of his covetousness I was angry,
I smote him, I hid my face and
was angry;
but he went on backsliding in the
way of his own heart.
18 I have seen his ways, but I will heal
him;
I will lead him and requite him
with comfort,
creating for his mourners the
fruit of the lips.
19 Peace, peace, to the far and to the
near, says the LORD;
and I will heal him.
20 But the wicked are like the tossing
sea;
for it cannot rest,
and its waters toss up mire and
dirt.
21 There is no peace, says my God,
for the wicked."

58 "Cry aloud, spare not,
lift up your voice like a trumpet;
declare to my people their transgression,
to the house of Jacob their sins.
2 Yet they seek me daily,
and delight to know my ways,
as if they were a nation that did
righteousness
and did not forsake the ordinance
of their God;
they ask of me righteous judgments,
they delight to draw near to God.
3 'Why have we fasted, and thou seest
it not?
Why have we humbled ourselves,
and thou takest no knowledge
of it?'
Behold, in the day of your fast you
seek your own pleasure,[g]
and oppress all your workers.
4 Behold, you fast only to quarrel and
to fight
and to hit with wicked fist.
Fasting like yours this day
will not make your voice to be
heard on high.
5 Is such the fast that I choose,
a day for a man to humble himself?

[e] The meaning of the Hebrew is uncertain [f] Or *the king* [g] Or *pursue your own business*
57.15: Mt 5.3. 57.19: Acts 2.39; Eph 2.13, 17.

Is it to bow down his head like a rush,
and to spread sackcloth and ashes under him?
Will you call this a fast,
and a day acceptable to the LORD?

6 "Is not this the fast that I choose:
to loose the bonds of wickedness,
to undo the thongs of the yoke,
to let the oppressed go free,
and to break every yoke?
7 Is it not to share your bread with the hungry,
and bring the homeless poor into your house;
when you see the naked, to cover him,
and not to hide yourself from your own flesh?
8 Then shall your light break forth like the dawn,
and your healing shall spring up speedily;
your righteousness shall go before you,
the glory of the LORD shall be your rear guard.
9 Then you shall call, and the LORD will answer;
you shall cry, and he will say, Here I am.

"If you take away from the midst of you the yoke,
the pointing of the finger, and speaking wickedness,
10 if you pour yourself out for the hungry
and satisfy the desire of the afflicted,
then shall your light rise in the darkness
and your gloom be as the noonday.
11 And the LORD will guide you continually,
and satisfy your desire with good things,[h]
and make your bones strong;
and you shall be like a watered garden,
like a spring of water,
whose waters fail not.
12 And your ancient ruins shall be rebuilt;
you shall raise up the foundations of many generations;
you shall be called the repairer of the breach,
the restorer of streets to dwell in.

13 "If you turn back your foot from the sabbath,
from doing your pleasure[i] on my holy day,
and call the sabbath a delight
and the holy day of the LORD honorable;
if you honor it, not going your own ways,
or seeking your own pleasure,[j] or talking idly;
14 then you shall take delight in the LORD,
and I will make you ride upon the heights of the earth;
I will feed you with the heritage of Jacob your father,
for the mouth of the LORD has spoken."

59 Behold, the LORD's hand is not shortened, that it cannot save,
or his ear dull, that it cannot hear;
2 but your iniquities have made a separation
between you and your God,
and your sins have hid his face from you
so that he does not hear.
3 For your hands are defiled with blood
and your fingers with iniquity;
your lips have spoken lies,
your tongue mutters wickedness.
4 No one enters suit justly,
no one goes to law honestly;
they rely on empty pleas, they speak lies,
they conceive mischief and bring forth iniquity.
5 They hatch adders' eggs,
they weave the spider's web;
he who eats their eggs dies,
and from one which is crushed a viper is hatched.
6 Their webs will not serve as clothing;
men will not cover themselves with what they make.
Their works are works of iniquity,
and deeds of violence are in their hands.
7 Their feet run to evil,
and they make haste to shed innocent blood;

[h] The meaning of the Hebrew word is uncertain [i] Or *business* [j] Or *pursuing your own business*
58.6: Acts 8.23. 59.7-8: Rom 3.15-17.

their thoughts are thoughts of iniquity,
desolation and destruction are in their highways.
8 The way of peace they know not,
and there is no justice in their paths;
they have made their roads crooked,
no one who goes in them knows peace.

9 Therefore justice is far from us,
and righteousness does not overtake us;
we look for light, and behold, darkness,
and for brightness, but we walk in gloom.
10 We grope for the wall like the blind,
we grope like those who have no eyes;
we stumble at noon as in the twilight,
among those in full vigor we are like dead men.
11 We all growl like bears,
we moan and moan like doves;
we look for justice, but there is none;
for salvation, but it is far from us.
12 For our transgressions are multiplied before thee,
and our sins testify against us;
for our transgressions are with us,
and we know our iniquities:
13 transgressing, and denying the LORD,
and turning away from following our God,
speaking oppression and revolt,
conceiving and uttering from the heart lying words.
14 Justice is turned back,
and righteousness stands afar off;
for truth has fallen in the public squares,
and uprightness cannot enter.
15 Truth is lacking,
and he who departs from evil makes himself a prey.

The LORD saw it, and it displeased him
that there was no justice.
16 He saw that there was no man,
and wondered that there was no one to intervene;
then his own arm brought him victory,
and his righteousness upheld him.
17 He put on righteousness as a breastplate,
and a helmet of salvation upon his head;
he put on garments of vengeance for clothing,
and wrapped himself in fury as a mantle.
18 According to their deeds, so will he repay,
wrath to his adversaries, requital to his enemies;
to the coastlands he will render requital.
19 So they shall fear the name of the LORD from the west,
and his glory from the rising of the sun;
for he will come like a rushing stream,
which the wind of the LORD drives.

20 "And he will come to Zion as Redeemer,
to those in Jacob who turn from transgression, says the LORD.
21 "And as for me, this is my covenant
with them, says the LORD: my spirit
which is upon you, and my words
which I have put in your mouth, shall
not depart out of your mouth, or out
of the mouth of your children, or out
of the mouth of your children's children, says the LORD, from this time
forth and for evermore."

60 Arise, shine; for your light has come,
and the glory of the LORD has risen upon you.
2 For behold, darkness shall cover the earth,
and thick darkness the peoples;
but the LORD will arise upon you,
and his glory will be seen upon you.
3 And nations shall come to your light,
and kings to the brightness of your rising.

4 Lift up your eyes round about, and see;
they all gather together, they come to you;
your sons shall come from far,
and your daughters shall be carried in the arms.
5 Then you shall see and be radiant,

59.17: Eph 6.14, 17; 1 Thess 5.8. **59.19**: Mt 8.11; Lk 13.29. **59.20-21**: Rom 11.26-27.

your heart shall thrill and rejoice;[k]
because the abundance of the sea
shall be turned to you,
the wealth of the nations shall
come to you.
6 A multitude of camels shall cover
you,
the young camels of Mid′i·ăn and
E′phăh;
all those from Sheba shall come.
They shall bring gold and frankincense,
and shall proclaim the praise of
the LORD.
7 All the flocks of Kē′där shall be
gathered to you,
the rams of Ne·bā′ioth shall
minister to you;
they shall come up with acceptance
on my altar,
and I will glorify my glorious
house.

8 Who are these that fly like a cloud,
and like doves to their windows?
9 For the coastlands shall wait for me,
the ships of Tär′shish first,
to bring your sons from far,
their silver and gold with them,
for the name of the LORD your God,
and for the Holy One of Israel,
because he has glorified you.

10 Foreigners shall build up your walls,
and their kings shall minister to
you;
for in my wrath I smote you,
but in my favor I have had mercy
on you.
11 Your gates shall be open continually;
day and night they shall not be
shut;
that men may bring to you the
wealth of the nations,
with their kings led in procession.
12 For the nation and kingdom
that will not serve you shall
perish;
those nations shall be utterly laid
waste.
13 The glory of Lebanon shall come to
you,
the cypress, the plane, and the
pine,
to beautify the place of my sanctuary;
and I will make the place of my
feet glorious.
14 The sons of those who oppressed
you
shall come bending low to you;
and all who despised you
shall bow down at your feet;
they shall call you the City of the
LORD,
the Zion of the Holy One of
Israel.

15 Whereas you have been forsaken
and hated,
with no one passing through,
I will make you majestic for ever,
a joy from age to age.
16 You shall suck the milk of nations,
you shall suck the breast of kings;
and you shall know that I, the LORD,
am your Savior
and your Redeemer, the Mighty
One of Jacob.

17 Instead of bronze I will bring gold,
and instead of iron I will bring
silver;
instead of wood, bronze,
instead of stones, iron.
I will make your overseers peace
and your taskmasters righteousness.
18 Violence shall no more be heard in
your land,
devastation or destruction within
your borders;
you shall call your walls Salvation,
and your gates Praise.

19 The sun shall be no more
your light by day,
nor for brightness shall the moon
give light to you by night;[l]
but the LORD will be your everlasting light,
and your God will be your glory.
20 Your sun shall no more go down,
nor your moon withdraw itself;
for the LORD will be your everlasting light,
and your days of mourning shall
be ended.
21 Your people shall all be righteous;
they shall possess the land for
ever,
the shoot of my planting, the work
of my hands,
that I might be glorified.
22 The least one shall become a clan,
and the smallest one a mighty
nation;

[k] Heb *be enlarged* [l] One ancient Ms Gk Old Latin Tg: Heb lacks *by night*
60.6: Mt 2.11. **60.11:** Rev 21.25-26. **60.14:** Rev 3.9. **60.19:** Rev 21.23; 22.5.

I am the LORD;
in its time I will hasten it.

61 The Spirit of the Lord GOD is upon me,
because the LORD has anointed me
to bring good tidings to the afflicted;[m]
he has sent me to bind up the brokenhearted,
to proclaim liberty to the captives,
and the opening of the prison[n] to those who are bound;
2 to proclaim the year of the LORD's favor,
and the day of vengeance of our God;
to comfort all who mourn;
3 to grant to those who mourn in Zion—
to give them a garland instead of ashes,
the oil of gladness instead of mourning,
the mantle of praise instead of a faint spirit;
that they may be called oaks of righteousness,
the planting of the LORD, that he may be glorified.
4 They shall build up the ancient ruins,
they shall raise up the former devastations;
they shall repair the ruined cities,
the devastations of many generations.

5 Aliens shall stand and feed your flocks,
foreigners shall be your plowmen and vinedressers;
6 but you shall be called the priests of the LORD,
men shall speak of you as the ministers of our God;
you shall eat the wealth of the nations,
and in their riches you shall glory.
7 Instead of your shame you shall have a double portion,
instead of dishonor you[o] shall rejoice in your[p] lot;
therefore in your[p] land you[o] shall possess a double portion;
yours[q] shall be everlasting joy.
8 For I the LORD love justice,
I hate robbery and wrong;[r]
I will faithfully give them their recompense,
and I will make an everlasting covenant with them.
9 Their descendants shall be known among the nations,
and their offspring in the midst of the peoples;
all who see them shall acknowledge them,
that they are a people whom the LORD has blessed.

10 I will greatly rejoice in the LORD,
my soul shall exult in my God;
for he has clothed me with the garments of salvation,
he has covered me with the robe of righteousness,
as a bridegroom decks himself with a garland,
and as a bride adorns herself with her jewels.
11 For as the earth brings forth its shoots,
and as a garden causes what is sown in it to spring up,
so the Lord GOD will cause righteousness and praise
to spring forth before all the nations.

62 For Zion's sake I will not keep silent,
and for Jerusalem's sake I will not rest,
until her vindication goes forth as brightness,
and her salvation as a burning torch.
2 The nations shall see your vindication,
and all the kings your glory;
and you shall be called by a new name
which the mouth of the LORD will give.
3 You shall be a crown of beauty in the hand of the LORD,
and a royal diadem in the hand of your God.
4 You shall no more be termed Forsaken,[s]
and your land shall no more be termed Desolate;[t]

[m] Or *poor* [n] Or *the opening of the eyes:* Heb *the opening* [o] Heb *they* [p] Heb *their* [q] Heb *theirs*
[r] Or *robbery with a burnt offering* [s] Heb *Azubah* [t] Heb *Shemamah*
61.1-2: Mt 11.5; Lk 4.18-19; 7.22. 61.6: Ex 19.6; 1 Pet 2.5; Rev 1.6; 5.10; 20.6. 62.2: Rev 2.17.

but you shall be called My delight
is in her,[u]
and your land Married;[v]
for the LORD delights in you,
and your land shall be married.
5 For as a young man marries a virgin,
so shall your sons marry you,
and as the bridegroom rejoices over
the bride,
so shall your God rejoice over you.

6 Upon your walls, O Jerusalem,
I have set watchmen;
all the day and all the night
they shall never be silent.
You who put the LORD in remembrance,
take no rest,
7 and give him no rest
until he establishes Jerusalem
and makes it a praise in the earth.
8 The LORD has sworn by his right
hand
and by his mighty arm:
"I will not again give your grain
to be food for your enemies,
and foreigners shall not drink your
wine
for which you have labored;
9 but those who garner it shall eat it
and praise the LORD,
and those who gather it shall drink
it
in the courts of my sanctuary."

10 Go through, go through the gates,
prepare the way for the people;
build up, build up the highway,
clear it of stones,
lift up an ensign over the peoples.
11 Behold, the LORD has proclaimed
to the end of the earth:
Say to the daughter of Zion,
"Behold, your salvation comes;
behold, his reward is with him,
and his recompense before him."
12 And they shall be called The holy
people,
The redeemed of the LORD;
and you shall be called Sought out,
a city not forsaken.

63 Who is this that comes from
E'dom,
in crimsoned garments from
Boz'rah,
he that is glorious in his apparel,
marching in the greatness of his
strength?
"It is I, announcing vindication,
mighty to save."

2 Why is thy apparel red,
and thy garments like his that
treads in the wine press?

3 "I have trodden the wine press
alone,
and from the peoples no one was
with me;
I trod them in my anger
and trampled them in my wrath;
their lifeblood is sprinkled upon my
garments,
and I have stained all my raiment.
4 For the day of vengeance was in my
heart,
and my year of redemption[w] has
come.
5 I looked, but there was no one to
help;
I was appalled, but there was no
one to uphold;
so my own arm brought me victory,
and my wrath upheld me.
6 I trod down the peoples in my anger,
I made them drunk in my wrath
and I poured out their lifeblood
on the earth."

7 I will recount the steadfast love of
the LORD,
the praises of the LORD,
according to all that the LORD has
granted us,
and the great goodness to the
house of Israel
which he has granted them according to his mercy,
according to the abundance of his
steadfast love.
8 For he said, Surely they are my
people,
sons who will not deal falsely;
and he became their Savior.
9 In all their affliction he was afflicted,[x]
and the angel of his presence
saved them;
in his love and in his pity he redeemed them;
he lifted them up and carried
them all the days of old.

10 But they rebelled
and grieved his holy Spirit;
therefore he turned to be their
enemy,
and himself fought against them.

[u] Heb *Hephzibah* [v] Heb *Beulah* [w] Or *the year of my redeemed* [x] Another reading is *he did not afflict*
63.1-6: Is 34; Jer 49.7-22; Ezek 25.12-14; 35; Amos 1.11-12; Obad; Mal 1.2-5. 63.3: Rev 19.15.

11 Then he remembered the days of old,
of Moses his servant.
Where is he who brought up out of the sea
the shepherds of his flock?
Where is he who put in the midst of them
his holy Spirit,
12 who caused his glorious arm
to go at the right hand of Moses,
who divided the waters before them
to make for himself an everlasting name,
13 who led them through the depths?
Like a horse in the desert,
they did not stumble.
14 Like cattle that go down into the valley,
the Spirit of the LORD gave them rest.
So thou didst lead thy people,
to make for thyself a glorious name.

15 Look down from heaven and see,
from thy holy and glorious habitation.
Where are thy zeal and thy might?
The yearning of thy heart and thy compassion
are withheld from me.
16 For thou art our Father,
though Abraham does not know us
and Israel does not acknowledge us;
thou, O LORD, art our Father,
our Redeemer from of old is thy name.
17 O LORD, why dost thou make us err from thy ways
and harden our heart, so that we fear thee not?
Return for the sake of thy servants,
the tribes of thy heritage.
18 Thy holy people possessed thy sanctuary a little while;
our adversaries have trodden it down.
19 We have become like those over whom thou hast never ruled,
like those who are not called by thy name.

64 O that thou wouldst rend the heavens and come down,
that the mountains might quake at thy presence—
2[y] as when fire kindles brushwood
and the fire causes water to boil—
to make thy name known to thy adversaries,
and that the nations might tremble at thy presence!
3 When thou didst terrible things which we looked not for,
thou camest down, the mountains quaked at thy presence.
4 From of old no one has heard
or perceived by the ear,
no eye has seen a God besides thee,
who works for those who wait for him.
5 Thou meetest him that joyfully works righteousness,
those that remember thee in thy ways.
Behold, thou wast angry, and we sinned;
in our sins we have been a long time, and shall we be saved?[z]
6 We have all become like one who is unclean,
and all our righteous deeds are like a polluted garment.
We all fade like a leaf,
and our iniquities, like the wind, take us away.
7 There is no one that calls upon thy name,
that bestirs himself to take hold of thee;
for thou hast hid thy face from us,
and hast delivered[a] us into the hand of our iniquities.

8 Yet, O LORD, thou art our Father;
we are the clay, and thou art our potter;
we are all the work of thy hand.
9 Be not exceedingly angry, O LORD,
and remember not iniquity for ever.
Behold, consider, we are all thy people.
10 Thy holy cities have become a wilderness,
Zion has become a wilderness,
Jerusalem a desolation.
11 Our holy and beautiful house,
where our fathers praised thee,
has been burned by fire,
and all our pleasant places have become ruins.
12 Wilt thou restrain thyself at these things, O LORD?

[y] Ch 64.1 in Heb [z] Hebrew obscure [a] Gk Syr Old Latin Tg: Heb *melted*
63.11: Heb 13.20. 64.4: 1 Cor 2.9.

Wilt thou keep silent, and afflict
us sorely?

65 I was ready to be sought by
those who did not ask for me;
I was ready to be found by those
who did not seek me.
I said, "Here am I, here am I,"
to a nation that did not call on
my name.
2 I spread out my hands all the day
to a rebellious people,
who walk in a way that is not good,
following their own devices;
3 a people who provoke me
to my face continually,
sacrificing in gardens
and burning incense upon bricks;
4 who sit in tombs,
and spend the night in secret
places;
who eat swine's flesh,
and broth of abominable things
is in their vessels;
5 who say, "Keep to yourself,
do not come near me, for I am
set apart from you."
These are a smoke in my nostrils,
a fire that burns all the day.
6 Behold, it is written before me:
"I will not keep silent, but I will
repay,
yea, I will repay into their bosom
7 their[b] iniquities and their[b] fathers'
iniquities together,
says the LORD;
because they burned incense upon
the mountains
and reviled me upon the hills,
I will measure into their bosom
payment for their former doings."

8 Thus says the LORD:
"As the wine is found in the cluster,
and they say, 'Do not destroy
it,
for there is a blessing in it,'
so I will do for my servants' sake,
and not destroy them all.
9 I will bring forth descendants from
Jacob,
and from Judah inheritors of my
mountains;
my chosen shall inherit it,
and my servants shall dwell there.
10 Sharon shall become a pasture for
flocks,
and the Valley of A'chôr a place
for herds to lie down,
for my people who have sought
me.
11 But you who forsake the LORD,
who forget my holy mountain,
who set a table for Fortune
and fill cups of mixed wine for
Destiny;
12 I will destine you to the sword,
and all of you shall bow down to
the slaughter;
because, when I called, you did not
answer,
when I spoke, you did not listen,
but you did what was evil in my
eyes,
and chose what I did not delight
in."

13 Therefore thus says the Lord GOD:
"Behold, my servants shall eat,
but you shall be hungry;
behold, my servants shall drink,
but you shall be thirsty;
behold, my servants shall rejoice,
but you shall be put to shame;
14 behold, my servants shall sing for
gladness of heart,
but you shall cry out for pain of
heart,
and shall wail for anguish of spirit.
15 You shall leave your name to my
chosen for a curse,
and the Lord GOD will slay you;
but his servants he will call by a
different name.
16 So that he who blesses himself in
the land
shall bless himself by the God of
truth,
and he who takes an oath in the land
shall swear by the God of truth;
because the former troubles are forgotten
and are hid from my eyes.

17 "For behold, I create new heavens
and a new earth;
and the former things shall not be
remembered
or come into mind.
18 But be glad and rejoice for ever
in that which I create;
for behold, I create Jerusalem a
rejoicing,
and her people a joy.
19 I will rejoice in Jerusalem,
and be glad in my people;
no more shall be heard in it the
sound of weeping

[b] Gk Syr: Heb *your*

65.1-2: Rom 10.20-21. 65.17: Is 66.22; 2 Pet 3.13; Rev 21.1.

and the cry of distress.
20 No more shall there be in it
an infant that lives but a few days,
or an old man who does not fill out his days,
for the child shall die a hundred years old,
and the sinner a hundred years old shall be accursed.
21 They shall build houses and inhabit them;
they shall plant vineyards and eat their fruit.
22 They shall not build and another inhabit;
they shall not plant and another eat;
for like the days of a tree shall the days of my people be,
and my chosen shall long enjoy the work of their hands.
23 They shall not labor in vain,
or bear children for calamity;[c]
for they shall be the offspring of the blessed of the LORD,
and their children with them.
24 Before they call I will answer,
while they are yet speaking I will hear.
25 The wolf and the lamb shall feed together,
the lion shall eat straw like the ox;
and dust shall be the serpent's food.
They shall not hurt or destroy
in all my holy mountain,
says the LORD."

66 Thus says the LORD:
"Heaven is my throne
and the earth is my footstool;
what is the house which you would build for me,
and what is the place of my rest?
2 All these things my hand has made,
and so all these things are mine,[d]
says the LORD.
But this is the man to whom I will look,
he that is humble and contrite in spirit,
and trembles at my word.

3 "He who slaughters an ox is like him who kills a man;
he who sacrifices a lamb, like him who breaks a dog's neck;
he who presents a cereal offering, like him who offers swine's blood;
he who makes a memorial offering of frankincense, like him who blesses an idol.
These have chosen their own ways,
and their soul delights in their abominations;
4 I also will choose affliction for them,
and bring their fears upon them;
because, when I called, no one answered,
when I spoke they did not listen;
but they did what was evil in my eyes,
and chose that in which I did not delight."

5 Hear the word of the LORD,
you who tremble at his word:
"Your brethren who hate you
and cast you out for my name's sake
have said, 'Let the LORD be glorified,
that we may see your joy';
but it is they who shall be put to shame.

6 "Hark, an uproar from the city!
A voice from the temple!
The voice of the LORD,
rendering recompense to his enemies!

7 "Before she was in labor
she gave birth;
before her pain came upon her
she was delivered of a son.
8 Who has heard such a thing?
Who has seen such things?
Shall a land be born in one day?
Shall a nation be brought forth in one moment?
For as soon as Zion was in labor
she brought forth her sons.
9 Shall I bring to the birth and not cause to bring forth?
says the LORD;
shall I, who cause to bring forth, shut the womb?
says your God.

10 "Rejoice with Jerusalem, and be glad for her,

[c] Or *sudden terror* [d] Gk Syr: Heb *came to be*
65.25: Is 11.6-9. **66.1-2:** Mt 5.34; Acts 7.49-50. **66.6:** Rev 16.1, 17.
66.7: Rev 12.5.

all you who love her;
rejoice with her in joy,
all you who mourn over her;
11 that you may suck and be satisfied
with her consoling breasts;
that you may drink deeply with
delight
from the abundance of her glory."

12 For thus says the LORD:
"Behold, I will extend prosperity to
her like a river,
and the wealth of the nations like
an overflowing stream;
and you shall suck, you shall be
carried upon her hip,
and dandled upon her knees.
13 As one whom his mother comforts,
so I will comfort you;
you shall be comforted in Jerusalem.
14 You shall see, and your heart shall
rejoice;
your bones shall flourish like the
grass;
and it shall be known that the hand
of the LORD is with his servants,
and his indignation is against his
enemies.

15 "For behold, the LORD will come in
fire,
and his chariots like the stormwind,
to render his anger in fury,
and his rebuke with flames of fire.
16 For by fire will the LORD execute
judgment,
and by his sword, upon all flesh;
and those slain by the LORD shall
be many.

17 "Those who sanctify and purify
themselves to go into the gardens,
following one in the midst, eating
swine's flesh and the abomination and
mice, shall come to an end together,
says the LORD.

18 "For I know[e] their works and
their thoughts, and I am[f] coming to
gather all nations and tongues; and
they shall come and shall see my glory,
19 and I will set a sign among them.
And from them I will send survivors
to the nations, to Tär'shish, Püt,[g] and
Lüd, who draw the bow, to Tü'bål and
Jā'vån, to the coastlands afar off, that
have not heard my fame or seen my
glory; and they shall declare my glory
among the nations. 20 And they shall
bring all your brethren from all the
nations as an offering to the LORD,
upon horses, and in chariots, and in
litters, and upon mules, and upon
dromedaries, to my holy mountain
Jerusalem, says the LORD, just as the
Israelites bring their cereal offering in
a clean vessel to the house of the LORD.
21 And some of them also I will take
for priests and for Levites, says the
LORD.

22 "For as the new heavens and the
new earth
which I will make
shall remain before me, says the
LORD;
so shall your descendants and
your name remain.
23 From new moon to new moon,
and from sabbath to sabbath,
all flesh shall come to worship before me,
says the LORD.

24 "And they shall go forth and
look on the dead bodies of the men
that have rebelled against me; for their
worm shall not die, their fire shall not
be quenched, and they shall be an
abhorrence to all flesh."

[e] Gk Syr: Heb lacks *know* [f] Gk Syr Vg Tg: Heb *it is* [g] Gk: Heb *Pul*
66.22: Is 65 17; 2 Pet 3 13; Rev 21.1. **66.24:** Mk 9 48.

THE BOOK OF

JEREMIAH

1 The words of Jeremiah, the son
of Hil·kī'ăh, of the priests who were
in An'ȧ·thoth in the land of Benjamin,
2 to whom the word of the LORD came
in the days of Jō sī'ăh the son of
Ā'mon, king of Judah, in the thirteenth
year of his reign. 3 It came also in the
days of Je·hoi'ȧ·kim the son of Jō-
sī'ăh, king of Judah, and until the end
of the eleventh year of Zed·ė·kī'ăh, the
son of Josiah, king of Judah, until the
captivity of Jerusalem in the fifth
month.

4 Now the word of the LORD came
to me saying,

5 "Before I formed you in the womb
I knew you,
and before you were born I consecrated you;
I appointed you a prophet to the nations."

6 Then I said, "Ah, Lord GOD! Behold,
I do not know how to speak, for I am
only a youth." 7 But the LORD said to
me,

"Do not say, 'I am only a youth';
for to all to whom I send you you
shall go,
and whatever I command you you
shall speak.
8 Be not afraid of them,
for I am with you to deliver you,
says the LORD."

9 Then the LORD put forth his hand
and touched my mouth; and the LORD
said to me,

"Behold, I have put my words in
your mouth.
10 See, I have set you this day over
nations and over kingdoms,
to pluck up and to break down,
to destroy and to overthrow,
to build and to plant."

11 And the word of the LORD came
to me, saying, "Jeremiah, what do you
see?" And I said, "I see a rod of
almond."[a] 12 Then the LORD said to
me, "You have seen well, for I am
watching[b] over my word to perform
it."

13 The word of the LORD came to
me a second time, saying, "What do
you see?" And I said, "I see a boiling
pot, facing away from the north."
14 Then the LORD said to me, "Out of
the north evil shall break forth upon
all the inhabitants of the land. 15 For,
lo, I am calling all the tribes of the
kingdoms of the north, says the LORD;
and they shall come and every one
shall set his throne at the entrance of
the gates of Jerusalem, against all its
walls round about, and against all the
cities of Judah. 16 And I will utter my
judgments against them, for all their
wickedness in forsaking me; they have
burned incense to other gods, and
worshiped the works of their own
hands. 17 But you, gird up your loins;
arise, and say to them everything that
I command you. Do not be dismayed
by them, lest I dismay you before
them. 18 And I, behold, I make you
this day a fortified city, an iron pillar,
and bronze walls, against the whole
land, against the kings of Judah, its
princes, its priests, and the people of
the land. 19 They will fight against
you; but they shall not prevail against
you, for I am with you, says the LORD,
to deliver you."

2 The word of the LORD came to
me, saying, 2 "Go and proclaim in
the hearing of Jerusalem, Thus says
the LORD,

I remember the devotion of your
youth,
your love as a bride,
how you followed me in the wilderness,
in a land not sown.
3 Israel was holy to the LORD,
the first fruits of his harvest.
All who ate of it became guilty;
evil came upon them,
says the LORD."

4 Hear the word of the LORD, O
house of Jacob, and all the families of
the house of Israel. 5 Thus says the
LORD:

[a] Heb *shaqed* [b] Heb *shoqed*

1.5: Is 49.1; Gal 1.15. **1.8:** Is 43.5; Acts 18.9-10. **1.10:** Rev 10.11.

"What wrong did your fathers find
in me
that they went far from me,
and went after worthlessness, and
became worthless?
6 They did not say, 'Where is the
LORD
who brought us up from the land
of Egypt,
who led us in the wilderness,
in a land of deserts and pits,
in a land of drought and deep
darkness,
in a land that none passes through,
where no man dwells?'
7 And I brought you into a plentiful
land
to enjoy its fruits and its good
things.
But when you came in you defiled
my land,
and made my heritage an abomination.
8 The priests did not say, 'Where is
the LORD?'
Those who handle the law did not
know me;
the rulers[c] transgressed against me;
the prophets prophesied by Bā'ăl,
and went after things that do not
profit.

9 "Therefore I still contend with you,
says the LORD,
and with your children's children
I will contend.
10 For cross to the coasts of Cyprus
and see,
or send to Kē'dăr and examine
with care;
see if there has been such a thing.
11 Has a nation changed its gods,
even though they are no gods?
But my people have changed their
glory
for that which does not profit.
12 Be appalled, O heavens, at this,
be shocked, be utterly desolate,
says the LORD,
13 for my people have committed two
evils:
they have forsaken me,
the fountain of living waters,
and hewed out cisterns for themselves,
broken cisterns,
that can hold no water.

14 "Is Israel a slave? Is he a homeborn servant?
Why then has he become a prey?
15 The lions have roared against him,
they have roared loudly.
They have made his land a waste;
his cities are in ruins, without
inhabitant.
16 Moreover, the men of Memphis and
Täh'păn·hēṡ
have broken the crown of your
head.
17 Have you not brought this upon
yourself
by forsaking the LORD your God,
when he led you in the way?
18 And now what do you gain by going
to Egypt,
to drink the waters of the Nile?
Or what do you gain by going to
Assyria,
to drink the waters of the Eū-
phrā'tēṡ?
19 Your wickedness will chasten you,
and your apostasy will reprove
you.
Know and see that it is evil and
bitter
for you to forsake the LORD your
God;
the fear of me is not in you,
says the Lord GOD of hosts.

20 "For long ago you broke your yoke
and burst your bonds;
and you said, 'I will not serve.'
Yea, upon every high hill
and under every green tree
you bowed down as a harlot.
21 Yet I planted you a choice vine,
wholly of pure seed.
How then have you turned de-
generate
and become a wild vine?
22 Though you wash yourself with lye
and use much soap,
the stain of your guilt is still before me,
says the Lord GOD.
23 How can you say, 'I am not defiled,
I have not gone after the Bā'ălṡ'?
Look at your way in the valley;
know what you have done—
a restive young camel interlacing
her tracks,
24 a wild ass used to the wilderness,
in her heat sniffing the wind!
Who can restrain her lust?
None who seek her need weary
themselves;
in her month they will find her.
25 Keep your feet from going unshod

[c] Heb *shepherds*

and your throat from thirst.
But you said, 'It is hopeless,
for I have loved strangers,
and after them I will go.'

26 "As a thief is shamed when caught,
so the house of Israel shall be shamed:
they, their kings, their princes,
their priests, and their prophets,
27 who say to a tree, 'You are my father,'
and to a stone, 'You gave me birth.'
For they have turned their back to me,
and not their face.
But in the time of their trouble they say,
'Arise and save us!'
28 But where are your gods
that you made for yourself?
Let them arise, if they can save you,
in your time of trouble;
for as many as your cities
are your gods, O Judah.

29 "Why do you complain against me?
You have all rebelled against me,
says the LORD.
30 In vain have I smitten your children,
they took no correction;
your own sword devoured your prophets
like a ravening lion.
31 And you, O generation, heed the word of the LORD.
Have I been a wilderness to Israel,
or a land of thick darkness?
Why then do my people say, 'We are free,
we will come no more to thee'?
32 Can a maiden forget her ornaments,
or a bride her attire?
Yet my people have forgotten me
days without number.

33 "How well you direct your course
to seek lovers!
So that even to wicked women
you have taught your ways.
34 Also on your skirts is found
the lifeblood of guiltless poor;
you did not find them breaking in.
Yet in spite of all these things
35 you say, 'I am innocent;
surely his anger has turned from me.'
Behold, I will bring you to judgment
for saying, 'I have not sinned.'
36 How lightly you gad about,
changing your way!
You shall be put to shame by Egypt
as you were put to shame by Assyria.
37 From it too you will come away
with your hands upon your head,
for the LORD has rejected those in whom you trust,
and you will not prosper by them.

3 "If[d] a man divorces his wife and she goes from him
and becomes another man's wife,
will he return to her?
Would not that land be greatly polluted?
You have played the harlot with many lovers;
and would you return to me?
says the LORD.
2 Lift up your eyes to the bare heights, and see!
Where have you not been lain with?
By the waysides you have sat awaiting lovers
like an Arab in the wilderness.
You have polluted the land
with your vile harlotry.
3 Therefore the showers have been withheld,
and the spring rain has not come;
yet you have a harlot's brow,
you refuse to be ashamed.
4 Have you not just now called to me,
'My father, thou art the friend of my youth—
5 will he be angry for ever,
will he be indignant to the end?'
Behold, you have spoken,
but you have done all the evil that you could."

6 The LORD said to me in the days
of King Jō·sī'ăh: "Have you seen what
she did, that faithless one, Israel, how
she went up on every high hill and
under every green tree, and there
played the harlot? 7And I thought,
'After she has done all this she will
return to me'; but she did not return,
and her false sister Judah saw it. 8 She
saw that for all the adulteries of that
faithless one, Israel, I had sent her
away with a decree of divorce; yet her
false sister Judah did not fear, but she
too went and played the harlot. 9 Because harlotry was so light to her, she

[d] Gk Syr: Heb *Saying, If*

polluted the land, committing adultery
with stone and tree. 10 Yet for all this
her false sister Judah did not return to
me with her whole heart, but in pretense, says the LORD."
11 And the LORD said to me,
"Faithless Israel has shown herself less
guilty than false Judah. 12 Go, and
proclaim these words toward the north,
and say,

'Return, faithless Israel,
says the LORD.
I will not look on you in anger,
for I am merciful,
says the LORD;
I will not be angry for ever.
13 Only acknowledge your guilt,
that you rebelled against the
LORD your God
and scattered your favors among
strangers under every green
tree,
and that you have not obeyed my
voice,
says the LORD.
14 Return, O faithless children,
says the LORD;
for I am your master;
I will take you, one from a city and
two from a family,
and I will bring you to Zion.

15 " 'And I will give you shepherds
after my own heart, who will feed you
with knowledge and understanding.
16 And when you have multiplied and
increased in the land, in those days,
says the LORD, they shall no more say,
"The ark of the covenant of the LORD."
It shall not come to mind, or be remembered, or missed; it shall not be
made again. 17 At that time Jerusalem
shall be called the throne of the LORD,
and all nations shall gather to it, to
the presence of the LORD in Jerusalem,
and they shall no more stubbornly
follow their own evil heart. 18 In those
days the house of Judah shall join the
house of Israel, and together they shall
come from the land of the north to the
land that I gave your fathers for a
heritage.

19 " 'I thought
how I would set you among my
sons,
and give you a pleasant land,
a heritage most beauteous of all
nations.
And I thought you would call me,
My Father,
and would not turn from following me.
20 Surely, as a faithless wife leaves her
husband,
so have you been faithless to me,
O house of Israel,
says the LORD.' "

21 A voice on the bare heights is heard,
the weeping and pleading of
Israel's sons,
because they have perverted their
way,
they have forgotten the LORD
their God.
22 "Return, O faithless sons,
I will heal your faithlessness."
"Behold, we come to thee;
for thou art the LORD our God.
23 Truly the hills are a delusion,
the orgies on the mountains.
Truly in the LORD our God
is the salvation of Israel.

24 "But from our youth the shameful thing has devoured all for which
our fathers labored, their flocks and
their herds, their sons and their
daughters. 25 Let us lie down in our
shame, and let our dishonor cover us;
for we have sinned against the LORD
our God, we and our fathers, from our
youth even to this day; and we have
not obeyed the voice of the LORD our
God."

4 "If you return, O Israel,
says the LORD,
to me you should return.
If you remove your abominations
from my presence,
and do not waver,
2 and if you swear, 'As the LORD
lives,'
in truth, in justice, and in uprightness,
then nations shall bless themselves
in him,
and in him shall they glory."

3 For thus says the LORD to the
men of Judah and to the inhabitants
of Jerusalem:

"Break up your fallow ground,
and sow not among thorns.
4 Circumcise yourselves to the
LORD,
remove the foreskin of your hearts,
O men of Judah and inhabitants
of Jerusalem;
lest my wrath go forth like fire,
and burn with none to quench
it,
because of the evil of your doings."

5 Declare in Judah, and proclaim
in Jerusalem, and say,
"Blow the trumpet through the land;
cry aloud and say,
'Assemble, and let us go
into the fortified cities!'
6 Raise a standard toward Zion,
flee for safety, stay not,
for I bring evil from the north,
and great destruction.
7 A lion has gone up from his thicket,
a destroyer of nations has set out;
he has gone forth from his place
to make your land a waste;
your cities will be ruins
without inhabitant.
8 For this gird you with sackcloth,
lament and wail;
for the fierce anger of the LORD
has not turned back from us."

9 "In that day, says the LORD, courage shall fail both king and princes;
the priests shall be appalled and the
prophets astounded." 10 Then I said,
"Ah, Lord GOD, surely thou hast
utterly deceived this people and Jerusalem, saying, 'It shall be well with
you'; whereas the sword has reached
their very life."

11 At that time it will be said to
this people and to Jerusalem, "A hot
wind from the bare heights in the
desert toward the daughter of my people, not to winnow or cleanse, 12 a
wind too full for this comes for me.
Now it is I who speak in judgment
upon them."

13 Behold, he comes up like clouds,
his chariots like the whirlwind;
his horses are swifter than eagles—
woe to us, for we are ruined!
14 O Jerusalem, wash your heart from wickedness,
that you may be saved.
How long shall your evil thoughts
lodge within you?
15 For a voice declares from Dan
and proclaims evil from Mount E'phra·im.
16 Warn the nations that he is coming;
announce to Jerusalem,
"Besiegers come from a distant land;
they shout against the cities of Judah.
17 Like keepers of a field are they
against her round about,
because she has rebelled against me,
says the LORD.
18 Your ways and your doings
have brought this upon you.
This is your doom, and it is bitter;
it has reached your very heart."

19 My anguish, my anguish! I writhe in pain!
Oh, the walls of my heart!
My heart is beating wildly;
I cannot keep silent;
for I hear the sound of the trumpet,
the alarm of war.
20 Disaster follows hard on disaster,
the whole land is laid waste.
Suddenly my tents are destroyed,
my curtains in a moment.
21 How long must I see the standard,
and hear the sound of the trumpet?
22 "For my people are foolish,
they know me not;
they are stupid children,
they have no understanding.
They are skilled in doing evil,
but how to do good they know not."

23 I looked on the earth, and lo, it was waste and void;
and to the heavens, and they had no light.
24 I looked on the mountains, and lo,
they were quaking,
and all the hills moved to and fro.
25 I looked, and lo, there was no man,
and all the birds of the air had fled.
26 I looked, and lo, the fruitful land
was a desert,
and all its cities were laid in ruins
before the LORD, before his fierce anger.

27 For thus says the LORD, "The
whole land shall be a desolation; yet I
will not make a full end.

28 For this the earth shall mourn,
and the heavens above be black;
for I have spoken, I have purposed;
I have not relented nor will I turn back."

29 At the noise of horseman and archer
every city takes to flight;
they enter thickets; they climb among rocks;
all the cities are forsaken,
and no man dwells in them.

30 And you, O desolate one,
what do you mean that you dress in scarlet,
that you deck yourself with ornaments of gold,
that you enlarge your eyes with paint?
In vain you beautify yourself.
Your lovers despise you;
they seek your life.
31 For I heard a cry as of a woman in travail,
anguish as of one bringing forth her first child,
the cry of the daughter of Zion gasping for breath,
stretching out her hands,
"Woe is me! I am fainting before murderers."

5 Run to and fro through the streets of Jerusalem,
look and take note!
Search her squares to see
if you can find a man,
one who does justice
and seeks truth;
that I may pardon her.
2 Though they say, "As the LORD lives,"
yet they swear falsely.
3 O LORD, do not thy eyes look for truth?
Thou hast smitten them,
but they felt no anguish;
thou hast consumed them,
but they refused to take correction.
They have made their faces harder than rock;
they have refused to repent.

4 Then I said, "These are only the poor,
they have no sense;
for they do not know the way of the LORD,
the law of their God.
5 I will go to the great,
and will speak to them;
for they know the way of the LORD,
the law of their God."
But they all alike had broken the yoke,
they had burst the bonds.

6 Therefore a lion from the forest shall slay them,
a wolf from the desert shall destroy them.
A leopard is watching against their cities,
every one who goes out of them shall be torn in pieces;
because their transgressions are many,
their apostasies are great.

7 "How can I pardon you?
Your children have forsaken me,
and have sworn by those who are no gods.
When I fed them to the full,
they committed adultery
and trooped to the houses of harlots.
8 They were well-fed lusty stallions,
each neighing for his neighbor's wife.
9 Shall I not punish them for these things?
says the LORD;
and shall I not avenge myself
on a nation such as this?

10 "Go up through her vine-rows and destroy,
but make not a full end;
strip away her branches,
for they are not the LORD's.
11 For the house of Israel and the house of Judah
have been utterly faithless to me,
says the LORD.
12 They have spoken falsely of the LORD,
and have said, 'He will do nothing;
no evil will come upon us,
nor shall we see sword or famine.
13 The prophets will become wind;
the word is not in them.
Thus shall it be done to them!' "

14 Therefore thus says the LORD, the God of hosts:
"Because they[e] have spoken this word,
behold, I am making my words in your mouth a fire,
and this people wood, and the fire shall devour them.
15 Behold, I am bringing upon you
a nation from afar, O house of Israel,
says the LORD.
It is an enduring nation,
it is an ancient nation,
a nation whose language you do not know,

[e] Heb *you*

nor can you understand what they say.
16 Their quiver is like an open tomb, they are all mighty men.
17 They shall eat up your harvest and your food;
they shall eat up your sons and your daughters;
they shall eat up your flocks and your herds;
they shall eat up your vines and your fig trees;
your fortified cities in which you trust
they shall destroy with the sword."

18 "But even in those days, says the
LORD, I will not make a full end of
you. 19And when your people say,
'Why has the LORD our God done all
these things to us?' you shall say to
them, 'As you have forsaken me and
served foreign gods in your land, so
you shall serve strangers in a land that
is not yours.' "

20 Declare this in the house of Jacob, proclaim it in Judah:
21 "Hear this, O foolish and senseless people,
who have eyes, but see not,
who have ears, but hear not.
22 Do you not fear me? says the LORD;
Do you not tremble before me?
I placed the sand as the bound for the sea,
a perpetual barrier which it cannot pass;
though the waves toss, they cannot prevail,
though they roar, they cannot pass over it.
23 But this people has a stubborn and rebellious heart;
they have turned aside and gone away.
24 They do not say in their hearts,
'Let us fear the LORD our God,
who gives the rain in its season,
the autumn rain and the spring rain,
and keeps for us
the weeks appointed for the harvest.'
25 Your iniquities have turned these away,
and your sins have kept good from you.
26 For wicked men are found among my people;
they lurk like fowlers lying in wait.[f]
They set a trap;
they catch men.
27 Like a basket full of birds,
their houses are full of treachery;
therefore they have become great and rich,
28 they have grown fat and sleek.
They know no bounds in deeds of wickedness;
they judge not with justice
the cause of the fatherless, to make it prosper,
and they do not defend the rights of the needy.
29 Shall I not punish them for these things?
says the LORD,
and shall I not avenge myself
on a nation such as this?"

30 An appalling and horrible thing
has happened in the land:
31 the prophets prophesy falsely,
and the priests rule at their direction;
my people love to have it so,
but what will you do when the end comes?

6 Flee for safety, O people of Benjamin,
from the midst of Jerusalem!
Blow the trumpet in Te·kō'ȧ,
and raise a signal on Beth-hac-chē'rem;
for evil looms out of the north,
and great destruction.
2 The comely and delicately bred I will destroy,
the daughter of Zion.
3 Shepherds with their flocks shall come against her;
they shall pitch their tents around her,
they shall pasture, each in his place.
4 "Prepare war against her;
up, and let us attack at noon!"
"Woe to us, for the day declines,
for the shadows of evening lengthen!"
5 "Up, and let us attack by night,
and destroy her palaces!"

6 For thus says the LORD of hosts:

[f] Heb uncertain
5.21: Is 6.9-10; Mt 13.10-15; Mk 8.17-18.

"Hew down her trees;
cast up a siege mound against Jerusalem.
This is the city which must be punished;
there is nothing but oppression within her.
7 As a well keeps its water fresh,
so she keeps fresh her wickedness;
violence and destruction are heard within her;
sickness and wounds are ever before me.
8 Be warned, O Jerusalem,
lest I be alienated from you;
lest I make you a desolation,
an uninhabited land."

9 Thus says the LORD of hosts:
"Glean[g] thoroughly as a vine
the remnant of Israel;
like a grape-gatherer pass your hand again
over its branches."
10 To whom shall I speak and give warning,
that they may hear?
Behold, their ears are closed,[h]
they cannot listen;
behold, the word of the LORD is to them an object of scorn,
they take no pleasure in it.
11 Therefore I am full of the wrath of the LORD;
I am weary of holding it in.
"Pour it out upon the children in the street,
and upon the gatherings of young men, also;
both husband and wife shall be taken,
the old folk and the very aged.
12 Their houses shall be turned over to others,
their fields and wives together;
for I will stretch out my hand
against the inhabitants of the land,"
says the LORD.
13 "For from the least to the greatest of them,
every one is greedy for unjust gain;
and from prophet to priest,
every one deals falsely.
14 They have healed the wound of my people lightly,
saying, 'Peace, peace,'
when there is no peace.
15 Were they ashamed when they committed abomination?
No, they were not at all ashamed;
they did not know how to blush.
Therefore they shall fall among those who fall;
at the time that I punish them,
they shall be overthrown,"
says the LORD.

16 Thus says the LORD:
"Stand by the roads, and look,
and ask for the ancient paths,
where the good way is; and walk in it,
and find rest for your souls.
But they said, 'We will not walk in it.'
17 I set watchmen over you, saying,
'Give heed to the sound of the trumpet!'
But they said, 'We will not give heed.'
18 Therefore hear, O nations,
and know, O congregation, what will happen to them.
19 Hear, O earth; behold, I am bringing evil upon this people,
the fruit of their devices,
because they have not given heed to my words;
and as for my law, they have rejected it.
20 To what purpose does frankincense come to me from Sheba,
or sweet cane from a distant land?
Your burnt offerings are not acceptable,
nor your sacrifices pleasing to me.
21 Therefore thus says the LORD:
'Behold, I will lay before this people
stumbling blocks against which they shall stumble;
fathers and sons together,
neighbor and friend shall perish.' "

22 Thus says the LORD:
"Behold, a people is coming from the north country,
a great nation is stirring from the farthest parts of the earth.
23 They lay hold on bow and spear,
they are cruel and have no mercy,
the sound of them is like the roaring sea;
they ride upon horses,
set in array as a man for battle,
against you, O daughter of Zion!"

[g] Cn: Heb *they shall glean* [h] Heb *uncircumcised*
6.16: Mt 11.29.

24 We have heard the report of it,
our hands fall helpless;
anguish has taken hold of us,
pain as of a woman in travail.
25 Go not forth into the field,
nor walk on the road;
for the enemy has a sword,
terror is on every side.
26 O daughter of my people, gird on
sackcloth,
and roll in ashes;
make mourning as for an only son,
most bitter lamentation;
for suddenly the destroyer
will come upon us.

27 "I have made you an assayer and
tester among my people,
that you may know and assay
their ways.
28 They are all stubbornly rebellious,
going about with slanders;
they are bronze and iron,
all of them act corruptly.
29 The bellows blow fiercely,
the lead is consumed by the fire;
in vain the refining goes on,
for the wicked are not removed.
30 Refuse silver they are called,
for the LORD has rejected them."

7 The word that came to Jeremiah
from the LORD: 2 Stand in the gate
of the LORD's house, and proclaim
there this word, and say, Hear the
word of the LORD, all you men of
Judah who enter these gates to worship the LORD. 3 Thus says the LORD
of hosts, the God of Israel, Amend
your ways and your doings, and I will
let you dwell in this place. 4 Do not
trust in these deceptive words: 'This
is the temple of the LORD, the temple
of the LORD, the temple of the LORD.'
5 "For if you truly amend your
ways and your doings, if you truly
execute justice one with another, 6 if
you do not oppress the alien, the
fatherless or the widow, or shed innocent blood in this place, and if you
do not go after other gods to your own
hurt, 7 then I will let you dwell in this
place, in the land that I gave of old to
your fathers for ever.
8 "Behold, you trust in deceptive
words to no avail. 9 Will you steal,
murder, commit adultery, swear
falsely, burn incense to Bā'ăl, and go
after other gods that you have not
known, 10 and then come and stand
before me in this house, which is
called by my name, and say, 'We are
delivered!'—only to go on doing all
these abominations? 11 Has this house,
which is called by my name, become a
den of robbers in your eyes? Behold,
I myself have seen it, says the LORD.
12 Go now to my place that was in
Shī'lōh, where I made my name dwell
at first, and see what I did to it for the
wickedness of my people Israel. 13 And
now, because you have done all these
things, says the LORD, and when I
spoke to you persistently you did not
listen, and when I called you, you did
not answer, 14 therefore I will do to
the house which is called by my name,
and in which you trust, and to the
place which I gave to you and to your
fathers, as I did to Shī'lōh. 15 And I
will cast you out of my sight, as I cast
out all your kinsmen, all the offspring
of Ē'phră·im.
16 "As for you, do not pray for this
people, or lift up cry or prayer for
them, and do not intercede with me,
for I do not hear you. 17 Do you not
see what they are doing in the cities of
Judah and in the streets of Jerusalem?
18 The children gather wood, the
fathers kindle fire, and the women
knead dough, to make cakes for the
queen of heaven; and they pour out
drink offerings to other gods, to provoke me to anger. 19 Is it I whom they
provoke? says the LORD. Is it not themselves, to their own confusion?
20 Therefore thus says the Lord GOD:
Behold, my anger and my wrath will
be poured out on this place, upon man
and beast, upon the trees of the field
and the fruit of the ground; it will burn
and not be quenched."
21 Thus says the LORD of hosts, the
God of Israel: "Add your burnt offerings to your sacrifices, and eat the
flesh. 22 For in the day that I brought
them out of the land of Egypt, I did
not speak to your fathers or command
them concerning burnt offerings and
sacrifices. 23 But this command I gave
them, 'Obey my voice, and I will be
your God, and you shall be my people;
and walk in all the way that I command
you, that it may be well with you.'
24 But they did not obey or incline
their ear, but walked in their own
counsels and the stubbornness of their
evil hearts, and went backward and
not forward. 25 From the day that

6.25: Jer 20.3, 10; 46.5; 49.29; Ps 31.13. **7.11:** Mt 21.13; Mk 11.17; Lk 19.46.

your fathers came out of the land of
Egypt to this day, I have persistently
sent all my servants the prophets to
them, day after day; 26 yet they did
not listen to me, or incline their ear,
but stiffened their neck. They did
worse than their fathers.
27 "So you shall speak all these
words to them, but they will not listen
to you. You shall call to them, but
they will not answer you. 28 And you
shall say to them, 'This is the nation
that did not obey the voice of the
LORD their God, and did not accept
discipline; truth has perished; it is cut
off from their lips.
29 Cut off your hair and cast it away;
raise a lamentation on the bare heights,
for the LORD has rejected and forsaken
the generation of his wrath.'
30 "For the sons of Judah have
done evil in my sight, says the LORD;
they have set their abominations in the
house which is called by my name, to
defile it. 31 And they have built the
high place[i] of Tō'pheth, which is in
the valley of the son of Hin'nom, to
burn their sons and their daughters in
the fire; which I did not command, nor
did it come into my mind. 32 Therefore, behold, the days are coming, says
the LORD, when it will no more be
called Tō'pheth, or the valley of the
son of Hin'nom, but the valley of
Slaughter: for they will bury in Topheth, because there is no room elsewhere. 33 And the dead bodies of this
people will be food for the birds of the
air, and for the beasts of the earth;
and none will frighten them away.
34 And I will make to cease from the
cities of Judah and from the streets of
Jerusalem the voice of mirth and the
voice of gladness, the voice of the
bridegroom and the voice of the bride;
for the land shall become a waste.

8 "At that time, says the LORD, the
bones of the kings of Judah, the
bones of its princes, the bones of the
priests, the bones of the prophets, and
the bones of the inhabitants of Jerusalem shall be brought out of their
tombs; 2 and they shall be spread before the sun and the moon and all the
host of heaven, which they have loved
and served, which they have gone
after, and which they have sought and
worshiped; and they shall not be
gathered or buried; they shall be as
dung on the surface of the ground.
3 Death shall be preferred to life by
all the remnant that remains of this
evil family in all the places where I
have driven them, says the LORD of
hosts.

4 "You shall say to them, Thus says the LORD:
When men fall, do they not rise again?
If one turns away, does he not return?
5 Why then has this people turned away
in perpetual backsliding?
They hold fast to deceit,
they refuse to return.
6 I have given heed and listened,
but they have not spoken aright;
no man repents of his wickedness,
saying, 'What have I done?'
Every one turns to his own course,
like a horse plunging headlong into battle.
7 Even the stork in the heavens
knows her times;
and the turtledove, swallow, and crane[j]
keep the time of their coming;
but my people know not
the ordinance of the LORD.

8 "How can you say, 'We are wise,
and the law of the LORD is with us'?
But, behold, the false pen of the scribes
has made it into a lie.
9 The wise men shall be put to shame,
they shall be dismayed and taken;
lo, they have rejected the word of the LORD,
and what wisdom is in them?
10 Therefore I will give their wives to others
and their fields to conquerors,
because from the least to the greatest
every one is greedy for unjust gain;
from prophet to priest
every one deals falsely.
11 They have healed the wound of my people lightly,
saying, 'Peace, peace,'
when there is no peace.

[i] Gk Tg: Heb *high places* [j] The meaning of the Hebrew word is uncertain
7.34: Rev 18.23.

12 Were they ashamed when they
committed abomination?
No, they were not at all ashamed;
they did not know how to blush.
Therefore they shall fall among the
fallen;
when I punish them, they shall
be overthrown,
says the LORD.
13 When I would gather them, says the
LORD,
there are no grapes on the vine,
nor figs on the fig tree;
even the leaves are withered,
and what I gave them has passed
away from them."[k]

14 Why do we sit still?
Gather together, let us go into the
fortified cities
and perish there;
for the LORD our God has doomed
us to perish,
and has given us poisoned water
to drink,
because we have sinned against
the LORD.
15 We looked for peace, but no good
came,
for a time of healing, but behold,
terror.

16 "The snorting of their horses is
heard from Dan;
at the sound of the neighing of
their stallions
the whole land quakes.
They come and devour the land and
all that fills it,
the city and those who dwell in it.
17 For behold, I am sending among
you serpents,
adders which cannot be charmed,
and they shall bite you,"
says the LORD.

18 My grief is beyond healing,[l]
my heart is sick within me.
19 Hark, the cry of the daughter of my
people
from the length and breadth of
the land:
"Is the LORD not in Zion?
Is her King not in her?"
"Why have they provoked me to
anger with their graven images,
and with their foreign idols?"
20 "The harvest is past, the summer is
ended,
and we are not saved."
21 For the wound of the daughter of
my people is my heart wounded,
I mourn, and dismay has taken
hold on me.

22 Is there no balm in Gilead?
Is there no physician there?
Why then has the health of the
daughter of my people
not been restored?

9[m] O that my head were waters,
and my eyes a fountain of tears,
that I might weep day and night
for the slain of the daughter of
my people!
2[n] O that I had in the desert
a wayfarers' lodging place,
that I might leave my people
and go away from them!
For they are all adulterers,
a company of treacherous men.
3 They bend their tongue like a
bow;
falsehood and not truth has grown
strong[o] in the land;
for they proceed from evil to evil,
and they do not know me, says
the LORD.

4 Let every one beware of his
neighbor,
and put no trust in any brother;
for every brother is a supplanter,
and every neighbor goes about as
a slanderer.
5 Every one deceives his neighbor,
and no one speaks the truth;
they have taught their tongue to
speak lies;
they commit iniquity and are too
weary to repent.[p]
6 Heaping oppression upon oppression, and deceit upon deceit,
they refuse to know me, says the
LORD.

7 Therefore thus says the LORD of
hosts:
"Behold, I will refine them and test
them,
for what else can I do, because of
my people?
8 Their tongue is a deadly arrow;
it speaks deceitfully;
with his mouth each speaks peaceably to his neighbor,
but in his heart he plans an
ambush for him.

[k] Heb uncertain [l] Cn Compare Gk: Heb uncertain [m] Ch 8.23 in Heb [n] Ch 9.1 in Heb
[o] Gk: Heb *and not for truth they have grown strong* [p] Cn Compare Gk: Heb *your dwelling*

9 Shall I not punish them for these
things? says the LORD;
and shall I not avenge myself
on a nation such as this?

10 "Take up[q] weeping and wailing for
the mountains,
and a lamentation for the pastures
of the wilderness,
because they are laid waste so that
no one passes through,
and the lowing of cattle is not
heard;
both the birds of the air and the
beasts
have fled and are gone.
11 I will make Jerusalem a heap of
ruins,
a lair of jackals;
and I will make the cities of Judah
a desolation,
without inhabitant."

12 Who is the man so wise that he
can understand this? To whom has
the mouth of the LORD spoken, that
he may declare it? Why is the land
ruined and laid waste like a wilderness,
so that no one passes through? 13 And
the LORD says: "Because they have
forsaken my law which I set before
them, and have not obeyed my voice,
or walked in accord with it, 14 but
have stubbornly followed their own
hearts and have gone after the Bā'als,
as their fathers taught them. 15 Therefore thus says the LORD of hosts, the
God of Israel: Behold, I will feed this
people with wormwood, and give
them poisonous water to drink. 16 I
will scatter them among the nations
whom neither they nor their fathers
have known; and I will send the sword
after them, until I have consumed
them."

17 Thus says the LORD of hosts:
"Consider, and call for the mourning women to come;
send for the skilful women to
come;
18 let them make haste and raise a
wailing over us,
that our eyes may run down with
tears,
and our eyelids gush with water.
19 For a sound of wailing is heard from
Zion:
'How we are ruined!
We are utterly shamed,
because we have left the land,
because they have cast down our
dwellings.' "

20 Hear, O women, the word of the
LORD,
and let your ear receive the word
of his mouth;
teach to your daughters a lament,
and each to her neighbor a dirge.
21 For death has come up into our
windows,
it has entered our palaces,
cutting off the children from the
streets
and the young men from the
squares.
22 Speak, "Thus says the LORD:
'The dead bodies of men shall fall
like dung upon the open field,
like sheaves after the reaper,
and none shall gather them.' "

23 Thus says the LORD: "Let not
the wise man glory in his wisdom, let
not the mighty man glory in his might,
let not the rich man glory in his riches;
24 but let him who glories glory in this,
that he understands and knows me,
that I am the LORD who practice steadfast love, justice, and righteousness in
the earth; for in these things I delight,
says the LORD."
25 "Behold, the days are coming,
says the LORD, when I will punish all
those who are circumcised but yet uncircumcised—26 Egypt, Judah, E'dom,
the sons of Am'mon, Mō'ab, and all
who dwell in the desert that cut the
corners of their hair; for all these
nations are uncircumcised, and all the
house of Israel is uncircumcised in
heart."

10 Hear the word which the LORD
speaks to you, O house of Israel.
2 Thus says the LORD:
"Learn not the way of the nations,
nor be dismayed at the signs of
the heavens
because the nations are dismayed
at them,
3 for the customs of the peoples are
false.
A tree from the forest is cut down,
and worked with an axe by the
hands of a craftsman.
4 Men deck it with silver and gold;

[q] Gk Syr: Heb *I will take up*
9.24: 1 Cor 1.31; 2 Cor 10.17. 9.26: Acts 7.51.

they fasten it with hammer and nails
so that it cannot move.
5 Their idols[r] are like scarecrows in a cucumber field,
and they cannot speak;
they have to be carried,
for they cannot walk.
Be not afraid of them,
for they cannot do evil,
neither is it in them to do good."

6 There is none like thee, O LORD;
thou art great, and thy name is great in might.
7 Who would not fear thee, O King of the nations?
For this is thy due;
for among all the wise ones of the nations
and in all their kingdoms
there is none like thee.
8 They are both stupid and foolish;
the instruction of idols is but wood!
9 Beaten silver is brought from Tär'shish,
and gold from Ū'phaz.
They are the work of the craftsman
and of the hands of the goldsmith;
their clothing is violet and purple;
they are all the work of skilled men.
10 But the LORD is the true God;
he is the living God and the everlasting King.
At his wrath the earth quakes,
and the nations cannot endure his indignation.

11 Thus shall you say to them:
"The gods who did not make the
heavens and the earth shall perish
from the earth and from under the
heavens."[s]

12 It is he who made the earth by his power,
who established the world by his wisdom,
and by his understanding stretched out the heavens.
13 When he utters his voice there is a tumult of waters in the heavens,
and he makes the mist rise from the ends of the earth.
He makes lightnings for the rain,
and he brings forth the wind from his storehouses.
14 Every man is stupid and without knowledge;
every goldsmith is put to shame by his idols;
for his images are false,
and there is no breath in them.
15 They are worthless, a work of delusion;
at the time of their punishment they shall perish.
16 Not like these is he who is the portion of Jacob,
for he is the one who formed all things,
and Israel is the tribe of his inheritance;
the LORD of hosts is his name.

17 Gather up your bundle from the ground,
O you who dwell under siege!
18 For thus says the LORD:
"Behold, I am slinging out the inhabitants of the land
at this time,
and I will bring distress on them,
that they may feel it."

19 Woe is me because of my hurt!
My wound is grievous.
But I said, "Truly this is an affliction,
and I must bear it."
20 My tent is destroyed,
and all my cords are broken;
my children have gone from me,
and they are not;
there is no one to spread my tent again,
and to set up my curtains.
21 For the shepherds are stupid,
and do not inquire of the LORD;
therefore they have not prospered,
and all their flock is scattered.

22 Hark, a rumor! Behold, it comes!—
a great commotion out of the north country
to make the cities of Judah a desolation,
a lair of jackals.

23 I know, O LORD, that the way of man is not in himself,
that it is not in man who walks to direct his steps.
24 Correct me, O LORD, but in just measure;
not in thy anger, lest thou bring me to nothing.

[r] Heb *They* [s] This verse is in Aramaic

25 Pour out thy wrath upon the nations
that know thee not,
and upon the peoples that call not
on thy name;
for they have devoured Jacob;
they have devoured him and consumed him,
and have laid waste his habitation.

11 The word that came to Jeremiah
from the LORD: 2 "Hear the words
of this covenant, and speak to the men
of Judah and the inhabitants of Jerusalem. 3 You shall say to them, Thus
says the LORD, the God of Israel:
Cursed be the man who does not heed
the words of this covenant 4 which I
commanded your fathers when I
brought them out of the land of Egypt,
from the iron furnace, saying, Listen
to my voice, and do all that I command
you. So shall you be my people, and I
will be your God, 5 that I may perform
the oath which I swore to your fathers,
to give them a land flowing with milk
and honey, as at this day." Then I
answered, "So be it, LORD."
6 And the LORD said to me, "Proclaim all these words in the cities of
Judah, and in the streets of Jerusalem:
Hear the words of this covenant and
do them. 7 For I solemnly warned
your fathers when I brought them up
out of the land of Egypt, warning them
persistently, even to this day, saying,
Obey my voice. 8 Yet they did not
obey or incline their ear, but every one
walked in the stubbornness of his evil
heart. Therefore I brought upon them
all the words of this covenant, which I
commanded them to do, but they did
not."
9 Again the LORD said to me, "There
is revolt among the men of Judah and
the inhabitants of Jerusalem. 10 They
have turned back to the iniquities of
their forefathers, who refused to hear
my words; they have gone after other
gods to serve them; the house of Israel
and the house of Judah have broken
my covenant which I made with their
fathers. 11 Therefore, thus says the
LORD, Behold, I am bringing evil upon
them which they cannot escape;
though they cry to me, I will not listen
to them. 12 Then the cities of Judah
and the inhabitants of Jerusalem will
go and cry to the gods to whom they
burn incense, but they cannot save
them in the time of their trouble.
13 For your gods have become as many
as your cities, O Judah; and as many
as the streets of Jerusalem are the
altars you have set up to shame, altars
to burn incense to Bā'ăl.
14 "Therefore do not pray for this
people, or lift up a cry or prayer on
their behalf, for I will not listen when
they call to me in the time of their
trouble. 15 What right has my beloved
in my house, when she has done vile
deeds? Can vows[t] and sacrificial flesh
avert your doom? Can you then exult?
16 The LORD once called you, 'A green
olive tree, fair with goodly fruit'; but
with the roar of a great tempest he will
set fire to it, and its branches will be
consumed. 17 The LORD of hosts, who
planted you, has pronounced evil
against you, because of the evil which
the house of Israel and the house of
Judah have done, provoking me to
anger by burning incense to Bā'ăl."

18 The LORD made it known to me and
I knew;
then thou didst show me their
evil deeds.
19 But I was like a gentle lamb
led to the slaughter.
I did not know it was against me
they devised schemes, saying,
"Let us destroy the tree with its
fruit,
let us cut him off from the land of
the living,
that his name be remembered no
more."
20 But, O LORD of hosts, who judgest
righteously,
who tries the heart and the mind,
let me see thy vengeance upon them,
for to thee have I committed my
cause.
21 Therefore thus says the LORD
concerning the men of An'ă·thoth,
who seek your life, and say, "Do not
prophesy in the name of the LORD, or
you will die by our hand"—22 therefore thus says the LORD of hosts:
"Behold, I will punish them; the
young men shall die by the sword;
their sons and their daughters shall die
by famine; 23 and none of them shall
be left. For I will bring evil upon the
men of An'ă·thoth, the year of their
punishment."

[t] Gk: Heb *many*
10.25: 1 Thess 4.5; Rev 16.1.

12 Righteous art thou, O LORD, when I complain to thee;
yet I would plead my case before thee.
Why does the way of the wicked prosper?
Why do all who are treacherous thrive?
2 Thou plantest them, and they take root;
they grow and bring forth fruit;
thou art near in their mouth
and far from their heart.
3 But thou, O LORD, knowest me;
thou seest me, and triest my mind toward thee.
Pull them out like sheep for the slaughter,
and set them apart for the day of slaughter.
4 How long will the land mourn,
and the grass of every field wither?
For the wickedness of those who dwell in it
the beasts and the birds are swept away,
because men said, "He will not see our latter end."

5 "If you have raced with men on foot,
and they have wearied you,
how will you compete with horses?
And if in a safe land you fall down,
how will you do in the jungle of the Jordan?
6 For even your brothers and the house of your father,
even they have dealt treacherously with you;
they are in full cry after you;
believe them not,
though they speak fair words to you."

7 "I have forsaken my house,
I have abandoned my heritage;
I have given the beloved of my soul
into the hands of her enemies.
8 My heritage has become to me
like a lion in the forest,
she has lifted up her voice against me;
therefore I hate her.
9 Is my heritage to me like a speckled bird of prey?
Are the birds of prey against her round about?
Go, assemble all the wild beasts;
bring them to devour.
10 Many shepherds have destroyed my vineyard,
they have trampled down my portion,
they have made my pleasant portion
a desolate wilderness.
11 They have made it a desolation;
desolate, it mourns to me.
The whole land is made desolate,
but no man lays it to heart.
12 Upon all the bare heights in the desert
destroyers have come;
for the sword of the LORD devours
from one end of the land to the other;
no flesh has peace.
13 They have sown wheat and have reaped thorns,
they have tired themselves out but profit nothing.
They shall be ashamed of their[u] harvests
because of the fierce anger of the LORD."

14 Thus says the LORD concerning
all my evil neighbors who touch the
heritage which I have given my people
Israel to inherit: "Behold, I will pluck
them up from their land, and I will
pluck up the house of Judah from
among them. 15 And after I have
plucked them up, I will again have
compassion on them, and I will bring
them again each to his heritage and
each to his land. 16 And it shall come
to pass, if they will diligently learn the
ways of my people, to swear by my
name, 'As the LORD lives,' even as they
taught my people to swear by Bā'ăl,
then they shall be built up in the midst
of my people. 17 But if any nation
will not listen, then I will utterly
pluck it up and destroy it, says the
LORD."

13 Thus said the LORD to me, "Go
and buy a linen waistcloth, and
put it on your loins, and do not dip it
in water." 2 So I bought a waistcloth
according to the word of the LORD,
and put it on my loins. 3 And the word
of the LORD came to me a second time,
4 "Take the waistcloth which you have
bought, which is upon your loins, and
arise, go to the Eū·phrā'tēs, and hide
it there in a cleft of the rock." 5 So I

[u] Heb *your*

went, and hid it by the Eū·phrā'tēs, as
the LORD commanded me. 6And after
many days the LORD said to me, "Arise,
go to the Eū·phrā'tēs, and take from
there the waistcloth which I commanded you to hide there." 7 Then I
went to the Eū·phrā'tēs, and dug, and
I took the waistcloth from the place
where I had hidden it. And behold,
the waistcloth was spoiled, it was good
for nothing.
8 Then the word of the LORD came
to me: 9 "Thus says the LORD: Even
so will I spoil the pride of Judah and
the great pride of Jerusalem. 10 This
evil people, who refuse to hear my
words, who stubbornly follow their
own heart and have gone after other
gods to serve them and worship them,
shall be like this waistcloth, which is
good for nothing. 11 For as the waistcloth clings to the loins of a man, so I
made the whole house of Israel and
the whole house of Judah cling to me,
says the LORD, that they might be
for me a people, a name, a praise,
and a glory, but they would not
listen.

12 "You shall speak to them this
word: 'Thus says the LORD, the God
of Israel, "Every jar shall be filled with
wine." ' And they will say to you, 'Do
we not indeed know that every jar will
be filled with wine?' 13 Then you shall
say to them, 'Thus says the LORD: Behold, I will fill with drunkenness all
the inhabitants of this land: the kings
who sit on David's throne, the priests,
the prophets, and all the inhabitants
of Jerusalem. 14And I will dash them
one against another, fathers and sons
together, says the LORD. I will not
pity or spare or have compassion, that
I should not destroy them.' "

15 Hear and give ear; be not proud,
for the LORD has spoken.
16 Give glory to the LORD your God
before he brings darkness,
before your feet stumble
on the twilight mountains,
and while you look for light
he turns it into gloom
and makes it deep darkness.
17 But if you will not listen,
my soul will weep in secret for
your pride;
my eyes will weep bitterly and run
down with tears,
because the LORD's flock has been
taken captive.

18 Say to the king and the queen
mother:
"Take a lowly seat,
for your beautiful crown
has come down from your head."[v]
19 The cities of the Negeb are shut up,
with none to open them;
all Judah is taken into exile,
wholly taken into exile.

20 "Lift up your eyes and see
those who come from the north.
Where is the flock that was given
you,
your beautiful flock?
21 What will you say when they set as
head over you
those whom you yourself have
taught
to be friends to you?
Will not pangs take hold of you,
like those of a woman in travail?
22 And if you say in your heart,
'Why have these things come
upon me?'
it is for the greatness of your iniquity
that your skirts are lifted up,
and you suffer violence.
23 Can the Ethiopian change his skin
or the leopard his spots?
Then also you can do good
who are accustomed to do evil.
24 I will scatter you[w] like chaff
driven by the wind from the
desert.
25 This is your lot,
the portion I have measured out
to you, says the LORD,
because you have forgotten me
and trusted in lies.
26 I myself will lift up your skirts over
your face,
and your shame will be seen.
27 I have seen your abominations,
your adulteries and neighings,
your lewd harlotries,
on the hills in the field.
Woe to you, O Jerusalem!
How long will it be
before you are made clean?"

14 The word of the LORD which
came to Jeremiah concerning
the drought:
2 "Judah mourns
and her gates languish;
her people lament on the ground,

[v] Gk Syr Vg: Heb obscure [w] Heb *them*

and the cry of Jerusalem goes up.
3 Her nobles send their servants for water;
they come to the cisterns,
they find no water,
they return with their vessels empty;
they are ashamed and confounded
and cover their heads.
4 Because of the ground which is dismayed,
since there is no rain on the land,
the farmers are ashamed,
they cover their heads.
5 Even the hind in the field forsakes her newborn calf
because there is no grass.
6 The wild asses stand on the bare heights,
they pant for air like jackals;
their eyes fail
because there is no herbage.

7 "Though our iniquities testify against us,
act, O LORD, for thy name's sake;
for our backslidings are many,
we have sinned against thee.
8 O thou hope of Israel,
its savior in time of trouble,
why shouldst thou be like a stranger in the land,
like a wayfarer who turns aside to tarry for a night?
9 Why shouldst thou be like a man confused?
like a mighty man who cannot save?
Yet thou, O LORD, art in the midst of us,
and we are called by thy name;
leave us not."

10 Thus says the LORD concerning this people:
"They have loved to wander thus,
they have not restrained their feet;
therefore the LORD does not accept them,
now he will remember their iniquity
and punish their sins."

11 The LORD said to me: "Do not
pray for the welfare of this people.
12 Though they fast, I will not hear
their cry, and though they offer burnt
offering and cereal offering I will not
accept them; but I will consume them
by the sword, by famine, and by
pestilence."

13 Then I said: "Ah, Lord GOD,
behold, the prophets say to them, 'You
shall not see the sword, nor shall you
have famine, but I will give you
assured peace in this place.' "
14 And
the LORD said to me: "The prophets
are prophesying lies in my name; I did
not send them, nor did I command
them or speak to them. They are
prophesying to you a lying vision,
worthless divination, and the deceit of
their own minds.
15 Therefore thus
says the LORD concerning the prophets
who prophesy in my name although I
did not send them, and who say, 'Sword
and famine shall not come on this
land': By sword and famine those
prophets shall be consumed.
16 And
the people to whom they prophesy
shall be cast out in the streets of Jerusalem,
victims of famine and sword,
with none to bury them—them, their
wives, their sons, and their daughters.
For I will pour out their wickedness
upon them.

17 "You shall say to them this word:
'Let my eyes run down with tears night and day,
and let them not cease,
for the virgin daughter of my people
is smitten with a great wound,
with a very grievous blow.
18 If I go out into the field,
behold, those slain by the sword!
And if I enter the city,
behold, the diseases of famine!
For both prophet and priest ply
their trade through the land,
and have no knowledge.' "

19 Hast thou utterly rejected Judah?
Does thy soul loathe Zion?
Why hast thou smitten us
so that there is no healing for us?
We looked for peace, but no good came;
for a time of healing, but behold, terror.
20 We acknowledge our wickedness, O LORD,
and the iniquity of our fathers,
for we have sinned against thee.
21 Do not spurn us, for thy name's sake;
do not dishonor thy glorious throne;

14.12: Rev 6.8.

remember and do not break thy
covenant with us.
22 Are there any among the false gods
of the nations that can bring
rain?
Or can the heavens give showers?
Art thou not he, O LORD our God?
We set our hope on thee,
for thou doest all these things.

15 Then the LORD said to me,
"Though Moses and Samuel
stood before me, yet my heart would
not turn toward this people. Send them
out of my sight, and let them go! 2 And
when they ask you, 'Where shall we
go?' you shall say to them, 'Thus says
the LORD:
"Those who are for pestilence, to
pestilence,
and those who are for the sword,
to the sword;
those who are for famine, to famine,
and those who are for captivity,
to captivity." '
3 "I will appoint over them four kinds
of destroyers, says the LORD: the
sword to slay, the dogs to tear, and the
birds of the air and the beasts of the
earth to devour and destroy. 4 And I
will make them a horror to all the
kingdoms of the earth because of what
Mȧ·nas′sėh the son of Hez·ė·kī′ȧh,
king of Judah, did in Jerusalem.

5 "Who will have pity on you, O
Jerusalem,
or who will bemoan you?
Who will turn aside
to ask about your welfare?
6 You have rejected me, says the
LORD,
you keep going backward;
so I have stretched out my hand
against you and destroyed
you;—
I am weary of relenting.
7 I have winnowed them with a
winnowing fork
in the gates of the land;
I have bereaved them, I have destroyed my people;
they did not turn from their ways.
8 I have made their widows more in
number
than the sand of the seas;
I have brought against the mothers
of young men
a destroyer at noonday;
I have made anguish and terror
fall upon them suddenly.
9 She who bore seven has languished;
she has swooned away;
her sun went down while it was yet
day;
she has been shamed and disgraced.
And the rest of them I will give to
the sword
before their enemies,
says the LORD."

10 Woe is me, my mother, that you
bore me, a man of strife and contention
to the whole land! I have not lent, nor
have I borrowed, yet all of them curse
me. 11 So let it be, O LORD,[x] if I have
not entreated[y] thee for their good, if I
have not pleaded with thee on behalf
of the enemy in the time of trouble
and in the time of distress! 12 Can one
break iron, iron from the north, and
bronze?
13 "Your wealth and your treasures
I will give as spoil, without price, for
all your sins, throughout all your
territory. 14 I will make you serve
your enemies in a land which you do
not know, for in my anger a fire is
kindled which shall burn for ever."

15 O LORD, thou knowest;
remember me and visit me,
and take vengeance for me on my
persecutors.
In thy forbearance take me not
away;
know that for thy sake I bear
reproach.
16 Thy words were found, and I ate
them,
and thy words became to me a
joy
and the delight of my heart;
for I am called by thy name,
O LORD, God of hosts.
17 I did not sit in the company of
merrymakers,
nor did I rejoice;
I sat alone, because thy hand was
upon me,
for thou hadst filled me with
indignation.
18 Why is my pain unceasing,
my wound incurable,
refusing to be healed?
Wilt thou be to me like a deceitful
brook,
like waters that fail?

[x] Gk Old Latin: Heb *the* LORD *said* [y] Cn: Heb obscure
15.2: Rev 13.10.

19 Therefore thus says the LORD:
"If you return, I will restore
you,
and you shall stand before me.
If you utter what is precious, and
not what is worthless,
you shall be as my mouth.
They shall turn to you,
but you shall not turn to them.
20 And I will make you to this people
a fortified wall of bronze;
they will fight against you,
but they shall not prevail over
you,
for I am with you
to save you and deliver you,
says the LORD.
21 I will deliver you out of the hand
of the wicked,
and redeem you from the grasp
of the ruthless."

16 The word of the LORD came to
me: 2 "You shall not take a wife,
nor shall you have sons or daughters
in this place. 3 For thus says the LORD
concerning the sons and daughters
who are born in this place, and concerning the mothers who bore them
and the fathers who begot them in this
land: 4 They shall die of deadly diseases. They shall not be lamented, nor
shall they be buried; they shall be as
dung on the surface of the ground.
They shall perish by the sword and by
famine, and their dead bodies shall be
food for the birds of the air and for the
beasts of the earth.
5 "For thus says the LORD: Do not
enter the house of mourning, or go to
lament, or bemoan them; for I have
taken away my peace from this people,
says the LORD, my steadfast love and
mercy. 6 Both great and small shall die
in this land; they shall not be buried,
and no one shall lament for them or
cut himself or make himself bald for
them. 7 No one shall break bread for
the mourner, to comfort him for the
dead; nor shall any one give him the
cup of consolation to drink for his
father or his mother. 8 You shall not
go into the house of feasting to sit with
them, to eat and drink. 9 For thus says
the LORD of hosts, the God of Israel:
Behold, I will make to cease from
this place, before your eyes and in
your days, the voice of mirth and
the voice of gladness, the voice of
the bridegroom and the voice of the
bride.
10 "And when you tell this people
all these words, and they say to you,
'Why has the LORD pronounced all
this great evil against us? What is our
iniquity? What is the sin that we have
committed against the LORD our God?'
11 then you shall say to them: 'Because
your fathers have forsaken me, says
the LORD, and have gone after other
gods and have served and worshiped
them, and have forsaken me and have
not kept my law, 12 and because you
have done worse than your fathers, for
behold, every one of you follows his
stubborn evil will, refusing to listen to
me; 13 therefore I will hurl you out of
this land into a land which neither you
nor your fathers have known, and
there you shall serve other gods day
and night, for I will show you no
favor.'
14 "Therefore, behold, the days are
coming, says the LORD, when it shall
no longer be said, 'As the LORD lives
who brought up the people of Israel
out of the land of Egypt,' 15 but 'As
the LORD lives who brought up the
people of Israel out of the north
country and out of all the countries where he had driven them.' For
I will bring them back to their
own land which I gave to their
fathers.
16 "Behold, I am sending for many
fishers, says the LORD, and they shall
catch them; and afterwards I will send
for many hunters, and they shall hunt
them from every mountain and every
hill, and out of the clefts of the rocks.
17 For my eyes are upon all their ways;
they are not hid from me, nor is their
iniquity concealed from my eyes.
18 And[z] I will doubly recompense their
iniquity and their sin, because they
have polluted my land with the carcasses of their detestable idols, and
have filled my inheritance with their
abominations."

19 O LORD, my strength and my
stronghold,
my refuge in the day of trouble,
to thee shall the nations come
from the ends of the earth and
say:
"Our fathers have inherited nought
but lies,

[z] Gk: Heb *And first*
16.9: Jer 7.34; 25.10; Rev 18.23.

worthless things in which there is
no profit.
20 Can man make for himself gods?
Such are no gods!"

21 "Therefore, behold, I will make
them know, this once I will make them
know my power and my might, and
they shall know that my name is the
LORD."

17 "The sin of Judah is written
with a pen of iron; with a point
of diamond it is engraved on the tablet
of their heart, and on the horns of their
altars, 2 while their children remember
their altars and their A·shē'rim, beside
every green tree, and on the high hills,
3 on the mountains in the open
country. Your wealth and all your
treasures I will give for spoil as the
price of your sin[a] throughout all your
territory. 4 You shall loosen your hand[b]
from your heritage which I gave to
you, and I will make you serve your
enemies in a land which you do not
know, for in my anger a fire is kindled
which shall burn for ever."

5 Thus says the LORD:
"Cursed is the man who trusts in
man
and makes flesh his arm,
whose heart turns away from the
LORD.
6 He is like a shrub in the desert,
and shall not see any good come.
He shall dwell in the parched places
of the wilderness,
in an uninhabited salt land.

7 "Blessed is the man who trusts in
the LORD,
whose trust is the LORD.
8 He is like a tree planted by water,
that sends out its roots by the
stream,
and does not fear when heat comes,
for its leaves remain green,
and is not anxious in the year of
drought,
for it does not cease to bear fruit."

9 The heart is deceitful above all
things,
and desperately corrupt;
who can understand it?
10 "I the LORD search the mind
and try the heart,
to give to every man according to
his ways,
according to the fruit of his
doings."

11 Like the partridge that gathers a
brood which she did not hatch,
so is he who gets riches but not
by right;
in the midst of his days they will
leave him,
and at his end he will be a fool.

12 A glorious throne set on high from
the beginning
is the place of our sanctuary.
13 O LORD, the hope of Israel,
all who forsake thee shall be put
to shame;
those who turn away from thee[c]
shall be written in the earth,
for they have forsaken the LORD,
the fountain of living water.

14 Heal me, O LORD, and I shall be
healed;
save me, and I shall be saved;
for thou art my praise.
15 Behold, they say to me,
"Where is the word of the LORD?
Let it come!"
16 I have not pressed thee to send evil,
nor have I desired the day of
disaster,
thou knowest;
that which came out of my lips
was before thy face.
17 Be not a terror to me;
thou art my refuge in the day of
evil.
18 Let those be put to shame who
persecute me,
but let me not be put to shame;
let them be dismayed,
but let me not be dismayed;
bring upon them the day of evil;
destroy them with double destruction!

19 Thus said the LORD to me: "Go
and stand in the Benjamin[d] Gate, by
which the kings of Judah enter and
by which they go out, and in all the
gates of Jerusalem, 20 and say: 'Hear
the word of the LORD, you kings of
Judah, and all Judah, and all the inhabitants of Jerusalem, who enter by
these gates. 21 Thus says the LORD:
Take heed for the sake of your lives,

[a] Cn: Heb *your high places for sin* [b] Cn: Heb *and in you* [c] Heb *me* [d] Cn: Heb *sons of people*
17.7-8: Ps 1.1-3. 17.10: Ps 62.12; Rev 2.23; 22.12.

and do not bear a burden on the sabbath day or bring it in by the gates of
Jerusalem. 22 And do not carry a
burden out of your houses on the
sabbath or do any work, but keep the
sabbath day holy, as I commanded
your fathers. 23 Yet they did not listen
or incline their ear, but stiffened their
neck, that they might not hear and
receive instruction.

24 " 'But if you listen to me, says
the LORD, and bring in no burden by
the gates of this city on the sabbath
day, but keep the sabbath day holy and
do no work on it, 25 then there shall
enter by the gates of this city kings[e]
who sit on the throne of David, riding
in chariots and on horses, they and
their princes, the men of Judah and
the inhabitants of Jerusalem; and this
city shall be inhabited for ever. 26 And
people shall come from the cities of
Judah and the places round about
Jerusalem, from the land of Benjamin,
from the She·phē'lȧh, from the hill
country, and from the Negeb, bringing burnt offerings and sacrifices,
cereal offerings and frankincense, and
bringing thank offerings to the house
of the LORD. 27 But if you do not listen
to me, to keep the sabbath day holy,
and not to bear a burden and enter by
the gates of Jerusalem on the sabbath
day, then I will kindle a fire in its gates,
and it shall devour the palaces of Jerusalem and shall not be quenched.' "

18 The word that came to Jeremiah
from the LORD: 2 "Arise, and go
down to the potter's house, and there
I will let you hear my words." 3 So I
went down to the potter's house, and
there he was working at his wheel.
4 And the vessel he was making of clay
was spoiled in the potter's hand, and
he reworked it into another vessel, as
it seemed good to the potter to do.

5 Then the word of the LORD came
to me: 6 "O house of Israel, can I not
do with you as this potter has done?
says the LORD. Behold, like the clay
in the potter's hand, so are you in my
hand, O house of Israel. 7 If at any
time I declare concerning a nation or
a kingdom, that I will pluck up and
break down and destroy it, 8 and if
that nation, concerning which I have
spoken, turns from its evil, I will repent of the evil that I intended to do
to it. 9 And if at any time I declare
concerning a nation or a kingdom that
I will build and plant it, 10 and if it
does evil in my sight, not listening to
my voice, then I will repent of the
good which I had intended to do to it.
11 Now, therefore, say to the men of
Judah and the inhabitants of Jerusalem: 'Thus says the LORD, Behold,
I am shaping evil against you and
devising a plan against you. Return,
every one from his evil way, and amend
your ways and your doings.'

12 "But they say, 'That is in vain!
We will follow our own plans, and will
every one act according to the stubbornness of his evil heart.'

13 "Therefore thus says the LORD:
Ask among the nations,
who has heard the like of this?
The virgin Israel
has done a very horrible thing.
14 Does the snow of Lebanon leave
the crags of Sir'i·ȯn?[f]
Do the mountain[g] waters run dry,[h]
the cold flowing streams?
15 But my people have forgotten me,
they burn incense to false gods;
they have stumbled[i] in their ways,
in the ancient roads,
and have gone into bypaths,
not the highway,
16 making their land a horror,
a thing to be hissed at for ever.
Every one who passes by it is horrified
and shakes his head.
17 Like the east wind I will scatter them
before the enemy.
I will show them my back, not my
face,
in the day of their calamity."

18 Then they said, "Come, let us
make plots against Jeremiah, for the
law shall not perish from the priest,
nor counsel from the wise, nor the
word from the prophet. Come, let us
smite him with the tongue, and let us
not heed any of his words."

19 Give heed to me, O LORD,
and hearken to my plea.[j]
20 Is evil a recompense for good?
Yet they have dug a pit for my
life.

[e] Cn: *kings and princes* [f] Cn: Heb *the field* [g] Cn: Heb *foreign* [h] Cn: Heb *Are . . . plucked up?*
[i] Gk Syr Vg: Heb *they made them stumble* [j] Gk Compare Syr Tg: Heb *my adversaries*
18.6: Rom 9.21.

Remember how I stood before thee
to speak good for them,
to turn away thy wrath from
them.
21 Therefore deliver up their children
to famine;
give them over to the power of
the sword,
let their wives become childless and
widowed.
May their men meet death by
pestilence,
their youths be slain by the
sword in battle.
22 May a cry be heard from their
houses,
when thou bringest the marauder
suddenly upon them!
For they have dug a pit to take me,
and laid snares for my feet.
23 Yet, thou, O LORD, knowest
all their plotting to slay me.
Forgive not their iniquity,
nor blot out their sin from thy
sight.
Let them be overthrown before thee;
deal with them in the time of
thine anger.

19 Thus said the LORD, "Go, buy
a potter's earthen flask, and take
some of the elders of the people and
some of the senior priests, 2 and go
out to the valley of the son of Hin'nom
at the entry of the Potsherd Gate, and
proclaim there the words that I tell
you. 3 You shall say, 'Hear the word
of the LORD, O kings of Judah and
inhabitants of Jerusalem. Thus says
the LORD of hosts, the God of Israel,
Behold, I am bringing such evil upon
this place that the ears of every one
who hears of it will tingle. 4 Because
the people have forsaken me, and have
profaned this place by burning incense
in it to other gods whom neither they
nor their fathers nor the kings of
Judah have known; and because they
have filled this place with the blood of
innocents, 5 and have built the high
places of Bā'ăl to burn their sons in
the fire as burnt offerings to Baal,
which I did not command or decree,
nor did it come into my mind; 6 therefore, behold, days are coming, says the
LORD, when this place shall no more
be called Tō'pheth, or the valley of
the son of Hin'nom, but the valley of
Slaughter. 7 And in this place I will
make void the plans of Judah and
Jerusalem, and will cause their people
to fall by the sword before their
enemies, and by the hand of those who
seek their life. I will give their dead
bodies for food to the birds of the air
and to the beasts of the earth. 8 And I
will make this city a horror, a thing to
be hissed at; every one who passes by
it will be horrified and will hiss because of all its disasters. 9 And I will
make them eat the flesh of their sons
and their daughters, and every one
shall eat the flesh of his neighbor in the
siege and in the distress, with which
their enemies and those who seek their
life afflict them.'

10 "Then you shall break the flask
in the sight of the men who go with
you, 11 and shall say to them, 'Thus
says the LORD of hosts: So will I break
this people and this city, as one breaks
a potter's vessel, so that it can never
be mended. Men shall bury in Tō'-
pheth because there will be no place
else to bury. 12 Thus will I do to this
place, says the LORD, and to its inhabitants, making this city like Tō'-
pheth. 13 The houses of Jerusalem and
the houses of the kings of Judah—all
the houses upon whose roofs incense
has been burned to all the host of
heaven, and drink offerings have been
poured out to other gods—shall be
defiled like the place of Tō'pheth.' "

14 Then Jeremiah came from Tō'-
pheth, where the LORD had sent him
to prophesy, and he stood in the court
of the LORD's house, and said to all
the people: 15 "Thus says the LORD
of hosts, the God of Israel, Behold, I
am bringing upon this city and upon
all its towns all the evil that I have
pronounced against it, because they
have stiffened their neck, refusing to
hear my words."

20 Now Pash'hūr the priest, the
son of Im'mėr, who was chief
officer in the house of the LORD, heard
Jeremiah prophesying these things.
2 Then Pash'hūr beat Jeremiah the
prophet, and put him in the stocks
that were in the upper Benjamin Gate
of the house of the LORD. 3 On the
morrow, when Pash'hūr released Jeremiah from the stocks, Jeremiah said
to him, "The LORD does not call your
name Pash'hūr, but Terror on every
side. 4 For thus says the LORD: Behold,
I will make you a terror to yourself
and to all your friends. They shall fall
by the sword of their enemies while

19.13: Acts 7.42. **20.3:** Jer 6.25; 46.5; 49.29; Ps 31.13.

you look on. And I will give all Judah
into the hand of the king of Babylon;
he shall carry them captive to Babylon,
and shall slay them with the sword.
5 Moreover, I will give all the wealth
of the city, all its gains, all its prized
belongings, and all the treasures of the
kings of Judah into the hand of their
enemies, who shall plunder them, and
seize them, and carry them to Babylon.
6 And you, Pash'hŭr, and all who dwell
in your house, shall go into captivity;
to Babylon you shall go; and there you
shall die, and there you shall be buried,
you and all your friends, to whom you
have prophesied falsely."

7 O LORD, thou hast deceived me,
and I was deceived;
thou art stronger than I,
and thou hast prevailed.
I have become a laughingstock all the day;
every one mocks me.
8 For whenever I speak, I cry out,
I shout, "Violence and destruction!"
For the word of the LORD has become for me
a reproach and derision all day long.
9 If I say, "I will not mention him,
or speak any more in his name,"
there is in my heart as it were a burning fire
shut up in my bones,
and I am weary with holding it in,
and I cannot.
10 For I hear many whispering.
Terror is on every side!
"Denounce him! Let us denounce him!"
say all my familiar friends,
watching for my fall.
"Perhaps he will be deceived,
then we can overcome him,
and take our revenge on him."
11 But the LORD is with me as a dread warrior;
therefore my persecutors will stumble,
they will not overcome me.
They will be greatly shamed,
for they will not succeed.
Their eternal dishonor
will never be forgotten.
12 O LORD of hosts, who triest the righteous,
who seest the heart and the mind,
let me see thy vengeance upon them,
for to thee have I committed my cause.

13 Sing to the LORD;
praise the LORD!
For he has delivered the life of the needy
from the hand of evildoers.

14 Cursed be the day
on which I was born!
The day when my mother bore me,
let it not be blessed!
15 Cursed be the man
who brought the news to my father,
"A son is born to you,"
making him very glad.
16 Let that man be like the cities
which the LORD overthrew without pity;
let him hear a cry in the morning
and an alarm at noon,
17 because he did not kill me in the womb;
so my mother would have been my grave,
and her womb for ever great.
18 Why did I come forth from the womb
to see toil and sorrow,
and spend my days in shame?

21 This is the word which came
to Jeremiah from the LORD, when
King Zed·ė·kī'ȧh sent to him Pash'hŭr
the son of Mal·chī'ȧh and Zeph·ȧ·nī'ȧh
the priest, the son of Mā·ȧ·sē'ȧh, saying, 2 "Inquire of the LORD for us, for
Ne·bu̇·chȧd·rez'zȧr king of Babylon is
making war against us; perhaps the
LORD will deal with us according to
all his wonderful deeds, and will make
him withdraw from us."
3 Then Jeremiah said to them:
4 "Thus you shall say to Zed·ė·kī'ȧh,
'Thus says the LORD, the God of Israel: Behold, I will turn back the
weapons of war which are in your
hands and with which you are fighting
against the king of Babylon and against
the Chal·dē'ȧns who are besieging you
outside the walls; and I will bring
them together into the midst of this
city. 5 I myself will fight against you
with outstretched hand and strong
arm, in anger, and in fury, and in great
wrath. 6 And I will smite the inhabit-

20.10: Jer 6.25; 46.5; 49.29; Ps 31.13. **20.14-18:** Job 3.3-13.

ants of this city, both man and beast;
they shall die of a great pestilence.
7 Afterward, says the LORD, I will give
Zed·ē·kī'ăh king of Judah, and his
servants, and the people in this city
who survive the pestilence, sword, and
famine, into the hand of Ne·bu·chăd-
rez'zăr king of Babylon and into the
hand of their enemies, into the hand
of those who seek their lives. He shall
smite them with the edge of the sword;
he shall not pity them, or spare them,
or have compassion.'

8 "And to this people you shall say:
'Thus says the LORD: Behold, I set
before you the way of life and the way
of death. 9 He who stays in this city
shall die by the sword, by famine, and
by pestilence; but he who goes out
and surrenders to the Chal·dē'ănṡ who
are besieging you shall live and shall
have his life as a prize of war. 10 For
I have set my face against this city for
evil and not for good, says the LORD:
it shall be given into the hand of the
king of Babylon, and he shall burn it
with fire.'

11 "And to the house of the king
of Judah say, 'Hear the word of the
LORD, 12 O house of David! Thus says
the LORD:

" 'Execute justice in the morning,
and deliver from the hand of the
oppressor
him who has been robbed,
lest my wrath go forth like fire,
and burn with none to quench it,
because of your evil doings.' "

13 "Behold, I am against you, O inhabitant of the valley,
O rock of the plain,
says the LORD;
you who say, 'Who shall come down
against us,
or who shall enter our habitations?'
14 I will punish you according to the
fruit of your doings,
says the LORD;
I will kindle a fire in her forest,
and it shall devour all that is
round about her."

22 Thus says the LORD: "Go
down to the house of the king
of Judah, and speak there this word,
2 and say, 'Hear the word of the LORD,
O King of Judah, who sit on the throne
of David, you, and your servants, and
your people who enter these gates.
3 Thus says the LORD: Do justice and
righteousness, and deliver from the
hand of the oppressor him who has
been robbed. And do no wrong or
violence to the alien, the fatherless,
and the widow, nor shed innocent
blood in this place. 4 For if you will
indeed obey this word, then there shall
enter the gates of this house kings who
sit on the throne of David, riding in
chariots and on horses, they, and their
servants, and their people. 5 But if you
will not heed these words, I swear by
myself, says the LORD, that this house
shall become a desolation. 6 For thus
says the LORD concerning the house
of the king of Judah:

" 'You are as Gilead to me,
as the summit of Lebanon,
yet surely I will make you a desert,
an uninhabited city.[k]
7 I will prepare destroyers against you,
each with his weapons;
and they shall cut down your
choicest cedars,
and cast them into the fire.

8 " 'And many nations will pass by
this city, and every man will say to his
neighbor, "Why has the LORD dealt
thus with this great city?" 9 And they
will answer, "Because they forsook the
covenant of the LORD their God, and
worshiped other gods and served
them." ' "

10 Weep not for him who is dead,
nor bemoan him;
but weep bitterly for him who goes
away,
for he shall return no more
to see his native land.

11 For thus says the LORD concerning Shal'lŭm the son of Jō·sī'ăh,
king of Judah, who reigned instead of
Josiah his father, and who went away
from this place: "He shall return here
no more, 12 but in the place where they
have carried him captive, there shall
he die, and he shall never see this land
again."

13 "Woe to him who builds his house
by unrighteousness,
and his upper rooms by injustice;
who makes his neighbor serve him
for nothing,
and does not give him his wages;

[k] Cn: Heb *cities*
22.5: Mt 23.38; Lk 13.35.

14 who says, 'I will build myself a great house
with spacious upper rooms,'
and cuts out windows for it,
paneling it with cedar,
and painting it with vermilion.
15 Do you think you are a king
because you compete in cedar?
Did not your father eat and drink
and do justice and righteousness?
Then it was well with him.
16 He judged the cause of the poor and needy;
then it was well.
Is not this to know me?
says the LORD.
17 But you have eyes and heart
only for your dishonest gain,
for shedding innocent blood,
and for practicing oppression and violence."

18 Therefore thus says the LORD
concerning Je·hoi'ă·kim the son of
Jō·sī'ăh, king of Judah:

"They shall not lament for him, saying,
'Ah my brother!' or 'Ah sister!'
they shall not lament for him, saying,
'Ah lord!' or 'Ah his majesty!'
19 With the burial of an ass he shall be buried,
dragged and cast forth beyond the gates of Jerusalem."

20 "Go up to Lebanon, and cry out,
and lift up your voice in Bā'shăn;
cry from Ab'ă·rim,
for all your lovers are destroyed:
21 I spoke to you in your prosperity,
but you said, 'I will not listen.'
This has been your way from your youth,
that you have not obeyed my voice.
22 The wind shall shepherd all your shepherds,
and your lovers shall go into captivity;
then you will be ashamed and confounded
because of all your wickedness.
23 O inhabitants of Lebanon,
nested among the cedars,
how you will groan[l] when pangs come upon you,
pain as of a woman in travail!"

24 "As I live, says the LORD,
though Cō·nī'ăh the son of Je·hoi'ă-
kim, king of Judah, were the signet
ring on my right hand, yet I would
tear you off 25 and give you into the
hand of those who seek your life, into
the hand of those of whom you are
afraid, even into the hand of Ne·bü-
chăd·rez'zăr king of Babylon and into
the hand of the Chal·dē'ăns. 26 I will
hurl you and the mother who bore
you into another country, where you
were not born, and there you shall die.
27 But to the land to which they will
long to return, there they shall not
return."

28 Is this man Cō·nī'ăh a despised, broken pot,
a vessel no one cares for?
Why are he and his children hurled and cast
into a land which they do not know?
29 O land, land, land,
hear the word of the LORD!
30 Thus says the LORD:
"Write this man down as childless,
a man who shall not succeed in his days;
for none of his offspring shall succeed
in sitting on the throne of David,
and ruling again in Judah."

23 "Woe to the shepherds who
destroy and scatter the sheep of
my pasture!" says the LORD. 2 Therefore thus says the LORD, the God of
Israel, concerning the shepherds who
care for my people: "You have
scattered my flock, and have driven
them away, and you have not attended
to them. Behold, I will attend to you
for your evil doings, says the LORD.
3 Then I will gather the remnant of
my flock out of all the countries where
I have driven them, and I will bring
them back to their fold, and they shall
be fruitful and multiply. 4 I will set
shepherds over them who will care for
them, and they shall fear no more, nor
be dismayed, neither shall any be
missing, says the LORD.

5 "Behold, the days are coming,
says the LORD, when I will raise up for
David a righteous Branch, and he
shall reign as king and deal wisely, and
shall execute justice and righteousness
in the land. 6 In his days Judah will

[l] Gk Vg Syr: Heb *be pitied*
23.5: Jer 33.15; Is 4.2; Zech 3.8; 6.12.

be saved, and Israel will dwell securely. And this is the name by which he will be called. 'The LORD is our righteousness.'

7 "Therefore, behold, the days are coming, says the LORD, when men shall no longer say, 'As the LORD lives who brought up the people of Israel out of the land of Egypt, [8] but 'As the LORD lives who brought up and led the descendants of the house of Israel out of the north country and out of all the countries where he[m] had driven them.' Then they shall dwell in their own land."

9 Concerning the prophets:
My heart is broken within me,
all my bones shake;
I am like a drunken man,
like a man overcome by wine,
because of the LORD
and because of his holy words.
10 For the land is full of adulterers;
because of the curse the land mourns,
and the pastures of the wilderness are dried up.
Their course is evil,
and their might is not right.
11 "Both prophet and priest are ungodly;
even in my house I have found their wickedness,
says the LORD.
12 Therefore their way shall be to them
like slippery paths in the darkness,
into which they shall be driven and fall;
for I will bring evil upon them
in the year of their punishment,
says the LORD.
13 In the prophets of Să·mâr'ĭ·ȧ
I saw an unsavory thing:
they prophesied by Bā'ȧl
and led my people Israel astray.
14 But in the prophets of Jerusalem
I have seen a horrible thing:
they commit adultery and walk in lies;
they strengthen the hands of evildoers,
so that no one turns from his wickedness;
all of them have become like Sod'ŏm to me,
and its inhabitants like Gŏ·môr'răh."

15 Therefore thus says the LORD of hosts concerning the prophets:
"Behold, I will feed them with wormwood,
and give them poisoned water to drink;
for from the prophets of Jerusalem
ungodliness has gone forth into all the land."

16 Thus says the LORD of hosts:
"Do not listen to the words of the
prophets who prophesy to you, filling
you with vain hopes; they speak visions
of their own minds, not from the
mouth of the LORD. [17] They say continually to those who despise the word
of the LORD, 'It shall be well with you';
and to every one who stubbornly
follows his own heart, they say, 'No
evil shall come upon you.' "

18 For who among them has stood in the council of the LORD
to perceive and to hear his word,
or who has given heed to his word and listened?
19 Behold, the storm of the LORD!
Wrath has gone forth,
a whirling tempest;
it will burst upon the head of the wicked.
20 The anger of the LORD will not turn back
until he has executed and accomplished
the intents of his mind.
In the latter days you will understand it clearly.

21 "I did not send the prophets,
yet they ran;
I did not speak to them,
yet they prophesied.
22 But if they had stood in my council,
then they would have proclaimed my words to my people,
and they would have turned them from their evil way,
and from the evil of their doings.

23 "Am I a God at hand, says the
LORD, and not a God afar off? [24] Can
a man hide himself in secret places so
that I cannot see him? says the LORD.
Do I not fill heaven and earth? says
the LORD. [25] I have heard what the
prophets have said who prophesy lies
in my name, saying, 'I have dreamed,
I have dreamed!' [26] How long shall

[m] Gk: Heb *I*

there be lies[n] in the heart of the
prophets who prophesy lies, and who
prophesy the deceit of their own heart,
27 who think to make my people forget
my name by their dreams which they
tell one another, even as their fathers
forgot my name for Bā'ȧl? 28 Let the
prophet who has a dream tell the
dream, but let him who has my word
speak my word faithfully. What has
straw in common with wheat? says the
LORD. 29 Is not my word like fire, says
the LORD, and like a hammer which
breaks the rock in pieces? 30 Therefore, behold, I am against the prophets,
says the LORD, who steal my words
from one another. 31 Behold, I am
against the prophets, says the LORD,
who use their tongues and say, 'Says
the LORD.' 32 Behold, I am against
those who prophesy lying dreams,
says the LORD, and who tell them and
lead my people astray by their lies and
their recklessness, when I did not
send them or charge them; so they do
not profit this people at all, says the
LORD.

33 "When one of this people, or a
prophet, or a priest asks you, 'What is
the burden of the LORD?' you shall say
to them, 'You are the burden,[o] and I
will cast you off, says the LORD.' 34 And
as for the prophet, priest, or one of the
people who says, 'The burden of the
LORD,' I will punish that man and his
household. 35 Thus shall you say, every
one to his neighbor and every one to
his brother, 'What has the LORD answered?' or 'What has the LORD
spoken?' 36 But 'the burden of the
LORD' you shall mention no more, for
the burden is every man's own word,
and you pervert the words of the
living God, the LORD of hosts, our
God. 37 Thus you shall say to the
prophet, 'What has the LORD answered you?' or 'What has the LORD
spoken?' 38 But if you say, 'The burden
of the LORD,' thus says the LORD, 'Because you have said these words, "The
burden of the LORD," when I sent to
you, saying, "You shall not say, 'The
burden of the LORD,'" 39 therefore,
behold, I will surely lift you up and
cast you away from my presence, you
and the city which I gave to you and
your fathers. 40 And I will bring upon
you everlasting reproach and perpetual shame, which shall not be forgotten.'"

24 After Ne·bu̇·chȧd·rez'zȧr king
of Babylon had taken into exile
from Jerusalem Jec·ȯ·nī'ȧh the son of
Je·hoi'ȧ·kim, king of Judah, together
with the princes of Judah, the craftsmen, and the smiths, and had brought
them to Babylon, the LORD showed me
this vision: Behold, two baskets of figs
placed before the temple of the LORD.
2 One basket had very good figs, like
first-ripe figs, but the other basket had
very bad figs, so bad that they could
not be eaten. 3 And the LORD said to
me, "What do you see, Jeremiah?" I
said, "Figs, the good figs very good,
and the bad figs very bad, so bad that
they cannot be eaten."

4 Then the word of the LORD came
to me: 5 "Thus says the LORD, the
God of Israel: Like these good figs, so
I will regard as good the exiles from
Judah, whom I have sent away from
this place to the land of the Chal·dē'-
ȧnṡ. 6 I will set my eyes upon them for
good, and I will bring them back to
this land. I will build them up, and
not tear them down; I will plant them,
and not uproot them. 7 I will give
them a heart to know that I am the
LORD; and they shall be my people
and I will be their God, for they shall
return to me with their whole heart.

8 "But thus says the LORD: Like
the bad figs which are so bad they cannot be eaten, so will I treat Zed·ė·kī'ȧh
the king of Judah, his princes, the
remnant of Jerusalem who remain in
this land, and those who dwell in the
land of Egypt. 9 I will make them a
horror[p] to all the kingdoms of the
earth, to be a reproach, a byword, a
taunt, and a curse in all the places
where I shall drive them. 10 And I will
send sword, famine, and pestilence
upon them, until they shall be utterly
destroyed from the land which I gave
to them and their fathers."

25 The word that came to Jeremiah concerning all the people
of Judah, in the fourth year of Je·hoi'ȧ-
kim the son of Jō·sī'ȧh, king of Judah
(that was the first year of Ne·bu̇·chȧd-
rez'zȧr king of Babylon), 2 which
Jeremiah the prophet spoke to all the
people of Judah and all the inhabitants
of Jerusalem: 3 "For twenty-three
years, from the thirteenth year of
Jō·sī'ȧh the son of Ā'mon, king of
Judah, to this day, the word of the

[n] Cn Compare Syr: Heb obscure [o] Gk Vg: Heb *What burden* [p] Compare Gk: Heb *horror for evil*

LORD has come to me, and I have
spoken persistently to you, but you
have not listened. 4 You have neither
listened nor inclined your ears to hear,
although the LORD persistently sent to
you all his servants the prophets, 5 saying, 'Turn now, every one of you, from
his evil way and wrong doings, and
dwell upon the land which the LORD
has given to you and your fathers from
of old and for ever; 6 do not go after
other gods to serve and worship them,
or provoke me to anger with the work
of your hands. Then I will do you no
harm.' 7 Yet you have not listened to
me, says the LORD, that you might
provoke me to anger with the work of
your hands to your own harm.

8 "Therefore thus says the LORD of
hosts: Because you have not obeyed
my words, 9 behold, I will send for all
the tribes of the north, says the LORD,
and for Ne·bů·chȧd·rez'zȧr the king of
Babylon, my servant, and I will bring
them against this land and its inhabitants, and against all these nations
round about; I will utterly destroy
them, and make them a horror, a
hissing, and an everlasting reproach.[q]
10 Moreover, I will banish from them
the voice of mirth and the voice of
gladness, the voice of the bridegroom
and the voice of the bride, the grinding
of the millstones and the light of the
lamp. 11 This whole land shall become
a ruin and a waste, and these nations
shall serve the king of Babylon seventy
years. 12 Then after seventy years are
completed, I will punish the king of
Babylon and that nation, the land of
the Chal·dē'ȧns, for their iniquity,
says the LORD, making the land an
everlasting waste. 13 I will bring upon
that land all the words which I have
uttered against it, everything written
in this book, which Jeremiah prophesied against all the nations. 14 For
many nations and great kings shall
make slaves even of them; and I will
recompense them according to their
deeds and the work of their hands."

15 Thus the LORD, the God of Israel, said to me: "Take from my hand
this cup of the wine of wrath, and
make all the nations to whom I send
you drink it. 16 They shall drink and
stagger and be crazed because of the
sword which I am sending among
them."

17 So I took the cup from the
LORD's hand, and made all the nations
to whom the LORD sent me drink it:
18 Jerusalem and the cities of Judah,
its kings and princes, to make them a
desolation and a waste, a hissing and
a curse, as at this day; 19 Pharaoh king
of Egypt, his servants, his princes, all
his people, 20 and all the foreign folk
among them; all the kings of the land
of Uz and all the kings of the land of
the Philistines (Ash'kė·lon, Gā'zȧ,
Ek'rȯn, and the remnant of Ash'dod);
21 Ē'dȯm, Mō'ab, and the sons of
Am'mȯn; 22 all the kings of Tȳre, all
the kings of Sī'don, and the kings of
the coastland across the sea; 23 Dē'dan,
Tē'mȧ, Buz, and all who cut the corners of their hair; 24 all the kings of
Arabia and all the kings of the mixed
tribes that dwell in the desert; 25 all
the kings of Zim'rī, all the kings of
Ē'lȧm, and all the kings of Media;
26 all the kings of the north, far and
near, one after another, and all the
kingdoms of the world which are on
the face of the earth. And after them
the king of Babylon[r] shall drink.

27 "Then you shall say to them,
'Thus says the LORD of hosts, the God
of Israel: Drink, be drunk and vomit,
fall and rise no more, because of the
sword which I am sending among
you.'

28 "And if they refuse to accept the
cup from your hand to drink, then you
shall say to them, 'Thus says the
LORD of hosts: You must drink! 29 For
behold, I begin to work evil at the
city which is called by my name, and
shall you go unpunished? You shall
not go unpunished, for I am summoning a sword against all the inhabitants
of the earth, says the LORD of hosts.'

30 "You, therefore, shall prophesy
against them all these words, and say
to them:

'The LORD will roar from on high,
and from his holy habitation utter
his voice;
he will roar mightily against his fold,
and shout, like those who tread
grapes,
against all the inhabitants of the
earth.
31 The clamor will resound to the ends
of the earth,
for the LORD has an indictment
against the nations;

[q] Gk Compare Syr: Heb *desolations* [r] Heb *Sheshach*, a cipher for Babylon
25.10: Jer 7.34; 16.9; Rev 18.23. **25.15:** Jer 51.7; Rev 14.8, 10; 16.19; 17.4; 18.3.

he is entering into judgment with
all flesh,
and the wicked he will put to the
sword,
says the LORD.'

32 "Thus says the LORD of hosts:
Behold, evil is going forth
from nation to nation,
and a great tempest is stirring
from the farthest parts of the
earth!

33 "And those slain by the LORD
on that day shall extend from one end
of the earth to the other. They shall
not be lamented, or gathered, or
buried; they shall be dung on the
surface of the ground.

34 "Wail, you shepherds, and cry,
and roll in ashes, you lords of the
flock,
for the days of your slaughter and
dispersion have come,
and you shall fall like choice
rams.[s]
35 No refuge will remain for the
shepherds,
nor escape for the lords of the
flock.
36 Hark, the cry of the shepherds,
and the wail of the lords of the
flock!
For the LORD is despoiling their
pasture,
37 and the peaceful folds are devastated,
because of the fierce anger of the
LORD.
38 Like a lion he has left his covert,
for their land has become a waste
because of the sword of the oppressor,
and because of his fierce anger."

26 In the beginning of the reign
of Je·hoi'ă·kim the son of
Jō·sī'ăh, king of Judah, this word came
from the LORD, 2 "Thus says the
LORD: Stand in the court of the LORD'S
house, and speak to all the cities of
Judah which come to worship in the
house of the LORD all the words that
I command you to speak to them; do
not hold back a word. 3 It may be they
will listen, and every one turn from
his evil way, that I may repent of the
evil which I intend to do to them because of their evil doings. 4 You shall
say to them, 'Thus says the LORD: If
you will not listen to me, to walk in
my law which I have set before you,
5 and to heed the words of my servants
the prophets whom I send to you
urgently, though you have not heeded,
6 then I will make this house like
Shī'lōh, and I will make this city a
curse for all the nations of the earth.' "

7 The priests and the prophets and
all the people heard Jeremiah speaking
these words in the house of the LORD.
8 And when Jeremiah had finished
speaking all that the LORD had commanded him to speak to all the people,
then the priests and the prophets and
all the people laid hold of him, saying,
"You shall die! 9 Why have you
prophesied in the name of the LORD,
saying, 'This house shall be like Shī'-
lōh, and this city shall be desolate,
without inhabitant'?" And all the
people gathered about Jeremiah in the
house of the LORD.

10 When the princes of Judah
heard these things, they came up from
the king's house to the house of the
LORD and took their seat in the entry
of the New Gate of the house of the
LORD. 11 Then the priests and the
prophets said to the princes and to all
the people, "This man deserves the
sentence of death, because he has
prophesied against this city, as you
have heard with your own ears."

12 Then Jeremiah spoke to all the
princes and all the people, saying,
"The LORD sent me to prophesy
against this house and this city all the
words you have heard. 13 Now therefore amend your ways and your doings, and obey the voice of the LORD
your God, and the LORD will repent
of the evil which he has pronounced
against you. 14 But as for me, behold,
I am in your hands. Do with me as
seems good and right to you. 15 Only
know for certain that if you put me to
death, you will bring innocent blood
upon yourselves and upon this city
and its inhabitants, for in truth the
LORD sent me to you to speak all these
words in your ears."

16 Then the princes and all the
people said to the priests and the
prophets, "This man does not deserve
the sentence of death, for he has
spoken to us in the name of the LORD
our God." 17 And certain of the elders
of the land arose and spoke to all the
assembled people, saying, 18 "Mī'căh
of Mō'rĕ·sheth prophesied in the days

[s] Gk: Heb *a choice vessel*

of Hez·ė·kī′ȧh king of Judah, and said
to all the people of Judah: 'Thus says
the LORD of hosts,

Zion shall be plowed as a field;
Jerusalem shall become a heap of ruins,
and the mountain of the house a wooded height.'

19 Did Hez·ė·kī′ȧh king of Judah and
all Judah put him to death? Did he not
fear the LORD and entreat the favor of
the LORD, and did not the LORD repent
of the evil which he had pronounced
against them? But we are about to
bring great evil upon ourselves."

20 There was another man who
prophesied in the name of the LORD,
Ū·rī′ȧh the son of She·māi′ȧh from
Kīr′i·ath-jē′ȧ·rim. He prophesied
against this city and against this land
in words like those of Jeremiah. 21 And
when King Je·hoi′ȧ·kim, with all his
warriors and all the princes, heard his
words, the king sought to put him to
death; but when Ū·rī′ȧh heard of it, he
was afraid and fled and escaped to
Egypt. 22 Then King Je·hoi′ȧ·kim
sent to Egypt certain men, El·nā′thȧn
the son of Ach′bôr and others with
him, 23 and they fetched Ū·rī′ȧh from
Egypt and brought him to King
Je·hoi′ȧ·kim, who slew him with the
sword and cast his dead body into the
burial place of the common people.

24 But the hand of Ȧ·hī′kȧm the son
of Shā′phȧn was with Jeremiah so that
he was not given over to the people to
be put to death.

27 In the beginning of the reign of
Zed·ė·kī′ȧh[u] the son of Jō·sī′ȧh,
king of Judah, this word came to
Jeremiah from the LORD. 2 Thus the
LORD said to me: "Make yourself
thongs and yoke-bars, and put them
on your neck. 3 Send word[v] to the
king of Ē′dȯm, the king of Mō′ab, the
king of the sons of Am′mȯn, the king
of Tȳre, and the king of Sī′don by the
hand of the envoys who have come to
Jerusalem to Zed·ė·kī′ȧh king of
Judah. 4 Give them this charge for
their masters: 'Thus says the LORD of
hosts, the God of Israel: This is what
you shall say to your masters: 5 "It is
I who by my great power and my outstretched arm have made the earth,
with the men and animals that are on
the earth, and I give it to whomever it
seems right to me. 6 Now I have given
all these lands into the hand of
Ne·bů·chȧd·nez′zȧr, the king of Babylon, my servant, and I have given him
also the beasts of the field to serve
him. 7 All the nations shall serve him
and his son and his grandson, until the
time of his own land comes; then
many nations and great kings shall
make him their slave.

8 " ' "But if any nation or kingdom
will not serve this Ne·bů·chȧd·nez′zȧr
king of Babylon, and put its neck under
the yoke of the king of Babylon, I will
punish that nation with the sword,
with famine, and with pestilence, says
the LORD, until I have consumed it by
his hand. 9 So do not listen to your
prophets, your diviners, your dreamers,[w] your soothsayers, or your
sorcerers, who are saying to you, 'You
shall not serve the king of Babylon.'
10 For it is a lie which they are prophesying to you, with the result that you
will be removed far from your land,
and I will drive you out, and you will
perish. 11 But any nation which will
bring its neck under the yoke of the
king of Babylon and serve him, I will
leave on its own land, to till it and
dwell there, says the LORD." ' "

12 To Zed·ė·kī′ȧh king of Judah I
spoke in like manner: "Bring your
necks under the yoke of the king of
Babylon, and serve him and his people, and live. 13 Why will you and
your people die by the sword, by
famine, and by pestilence, as the LORD
has spoken concerning any nation
which will not serve the king of Babylon? 14 Do not listen to the words of
the prophets who are saying to you,
'You shall not serve the king of Babylon,' for it is a lie which they are
prophesying to you. 15 I have not sent
them, says the LORD, but they are
prophesying falsely in my name, with
the result that I will drive you out
and you will perish, you and the
prophets who are prophesying to you."

16 Then I spoke to the priests and
to all this people, saying, "Thus says
the LORD: Do not listen to the words
of your prophets who are prophesying
to you, saying, 'Behold, the vessels of
the LORD's house will now shortly be
brought back from Babylon,' for it is
a lie which they are prophesying to
you. 17 Do not listen to them; serve
the king of Babylon and live. Why
should this city become a desolation?

[u] Another reading is *Jehoiakim* [v] Cn: Heb *send them* [w] Gk Syr Vg: Heb *dreams*

18 If they are prophets, and if the word
of the LORD is with them, then let
them intercede with the LORD of
hosts, that the vessels which are left in
the house of the LORD, in the house of
the king of Judah, and in Jerusalem
may not go to Babylon. 19 For thus
says the LORD of hosts concerning the
pillars, the sea, the stands, and the rest
of the vessels which are left in this
city, 20 which Ne·bu̇·chȧd·nez′zȧr king
of Babylon did not take away, when
he took into exile from Jerusalem to
Babylon Jec·ȯ·nī′ȧh the son of Je·hoi′ȧ-
kim, king of Judah, and all the nobles
of Judah and Jerusalem—21 thus says
the LORD of hosts, the God of Israel,
concerning the vessels which are left
in the house of the LORD, in the house
of the king of Judah, and in Jerusalem: 22 They shall be carried to
Babylon and remain there until the
day when I give attention to them,
says the LORD. Then I will bring
them back and restore them to this
place."

28 In that same year, at the beginning of the reign of Zed·ė-
kī′ȧh king of Judah, in the fifth month
of the fourth year, Han·ȧ·nī′ȧh the son
of Az′zŭr, the prophet from Gib′ē·ȯn,
spoke to me in the house of the LORD,
in the presence of the priests and all
the people, saying, 2 "Thus says the
LORD of hosts, the God of Israel: I
have broken the yoke of the king of
Babylon. 3 Within two years I will
bring back to this place all the vessels
of the LORD's house, which Ne·bu̇-
chȧd·nez′zȧr king of Babylon took
away from this place and carried to
Babylon. 4 I will also bring back to
this place Jec·ȯ·nī′ȧh the son of Je-
hoi′ȧ·kim, king of Judah, and all the
exiles from Judah who went to Babylon, says the LORD, for I will break
the yoke of the king of Babylon."

5 Then the prophet Jeremiah spoke
to Han·ȧ·nī′ȧh the prophet in the
presence of the priests and all the people who were standing in the house of
the LORD; 6 and the prophet Jeremiah
said, "Amen! May the LORD do so;
may the LORD make the words which
you have prophesied come true, and
bring back to this place from Babylon
the vessels of the house of the LORD,
and all the exiles. 7 Yet hear now this
word which I speak in your hearing
and in the hearing of all the people.
8 The prophets who preceded you and
me from ancient times prophesied war,
famine, and pestilence against many
countries and great kingdoms. 9 As for
the prophet who prophesies peace,
when the word of that prophet comes
to pass, then it will be known that the
LORD has truly sent the prophet."

10 Then the prophet Han·ȧ·nī′ȧh
took the yoke-bars from the neck of
Jeremiah the prophet, and broke
them. 11 And Han·ȧ·nī′ȧh spoke in the
presence of all the people, saying,
"Thus says the LORD: Even so will I
break the yoke of Ne·bu̇·chȧd·nez′zȧr
king of Babylon from the neck of all
the nations within two years." But
Jeremiah the prophet went his way.

12 Sometime after the prophet
Han·ȧ·nī′ȧh had broken the yoke-bars
from off the neck of Jeremiah the
prophet, the word of the LORD came
to Jeremiah: 13 "Go, tell Han·ȧ·nī′ȧh,
'Thus says the LORD: You have broken
wooden bars, but I[x] will make in their
place bars of iron. 14 For thus says the
LORD of hosts, the God of Israel: I
have put upon the neck of all these
nations an iron yoke of servitude to
Ne·bu̇·chȧd·nez′zȧr king of Babylon,
and they shall serve him, for I have
given to him even the beasts of the
field.' " 15 And Jeremiah the prophet
said to the prophet Han·ȧ·nī′ȧh,
"Listen, Hananiah, the LORD has not
sent you, and you have made this
people trust in a lie. 16 Therefore thus
says the LORD: 'Behold, I will remove
you from the face of the earth. This
very year you shall die, because you
have uttered rebellion against the
LORD.' "

17 In that same year, in the seventh
month, the prophet Han·ȧ·nī′ȧh died.

29 These are the words of the
letter which Jeremiah the
prophet sent from Jerusalem to the
elders[y] of the exiles, and to the priests,
the prophets, and all the people, whom
Ne·bu̇·chȧd·nez′zȧr had taken into
exile from Jerusalem to Babylon.
2 This was after King Jec·ȯ·nī′ȧh, and
the queen mother, the eunuchs, the
princes of Judah and Jerusalem, the
craftsmen, and the smiths had departed from Jerusalem. 3 The letter
was sent by the hand of El·ā′sȧh the
son of Shā′phȧn and Gem·ȧ·rī′ȧh the
son of Hil·kī′ȧh, whom Zed·ė·kī′ȧh
king of Judah sent to Babylon to

[x] Gk: Heb *you* [y] Gk: Heb *the rest of the elders*

Ne·bu̇·chȧd·nez'zȧr king of Babylon.
It said: 4 "Thus says the LORD of
hosts, the God of Israel, to all the
exiles whom I have sent into exile
from Jerusalem to Babylon: 5 Build
houses and live in them; plant gardens
and eat their produce. 6 Take wives
and have sons and daughters; take
wives for your sons, and give your
daughters in marriage, that they may
bear sons and daughters; multiply
there, and do not decrease. 7 But seek
the welfare of the city where I have
sent you into exile, and pray to the
LORD on its behalf, for in its welfare
you will find your welfare. 8 For thus
says the LORD of hosts, the God of
Israel: Do not let your prophets and
your diviners who are among you deceive you, and do not listen to the
dreams which they dream,[z] 9 for it is
a lie which they are prophesying to
you in my name; I did not send them,
says the LORD.

10 "For thus says the LORD: When
seventy years are completed for Babylon, I will visit you, and I will fulfil to
you my promise and bring you back
to this place. 11 For I know the plans
I have for you, says the LORD, plans
for welfare and not for evil, to give
you a future and a hope. 12 Then you
will call upon me and come and pray
to me, and I will hear you. 13 You
will seek me and find me; when you
seek me with all your heart, 14 I will
be found by you, says the LORD, and
I will restore your fortunes and gather
you from all the nations and all the
places where I have driven you, says
the LORD, and I will bring you back
to the place from which I sent you
into exile.

15 "Because you have said, 'The
LORD has raised up prophets for us in
Babylon,'—16 Thus says the LORD
concerning the king who sits on the
throne of David, and concerning all
the people who dwell in this city, your
kinsmen who did not go out with you
into exile: 17 'Thus says the LORD of
hosts, Behold, I am sending on them
sword, famine, and pestilence, and I
will make them like vile figs which are
so bad they cannot be eaten. 18 I will
pursue them with sword, famine, and
pestilence, and will make them a
horror to all the kingdoms of the
earth, to be a curse, a terror, a hissing,
and a reproach among all the nations
where I have driven them, 19 because
they did not heed my words, says the
LORD, which I persistently sent to
you by my servants the prophets, but
you would not listen, says the LORD.'—
20 Hear the word of the LORD, all you
exiles whom I sent away from Jerusalem to Babylon: 21 'Thus says the
LORD of hosts, the God of Israel, concerning Ā'hab the son of Kō·lāi'ȧh and
Zed·ė·kī'ȧh the son of Mā-ȧ·sēi'ȧh,
who are prophesying a lie to you in
my name: Behold, I will deliver them
into the hand of Ne·bu̇·chȧd·rez'zȧr
king of Babylon, and he shall slay them
before your eyes. 22 Because of them
this curse shall be used by all the exiles
from Judah in Babylon: "The LORD
make you like Zed·ė·kī'ȧh and Ā'hab,
whom the king of Babylon roasted in
the fire," 23 because they have committed folly in Israel, they have committed adultery with their neighbors'
wives, and they have spoken in my
name lying words which I did not
command them. I am the one who
knows, and I am witness, says the
LORD.' "

24 To She·māi'ȧh of Ne·hel'ȧm you
shall say: 25 "Thus says the LORD of
hosts, the God of Israel: You have
sent letters in your name to all the
people who are in Jerusalem, and to
Zeph·ȧ·nī'ȧh the son of Mā-ȧ·sēi'ȧh
the priest, and to all the priests, saying, 26 'The LORD has made you priest
instead of Je·hoi'ȧ·dȧ the priest, to
have charge in the house of the LORD
over every madman who prophesies,
to put him in the stocks and collar.
27 Now why have you not rebuked
Jeremiah of An'ȧ·thoth who is prophesying to you? 28 For he has sent to us
in Babylon, saying, "Your exile will be
long; build houses and live in them,
and plant gardens and eat their produce." ' "

29 Zeph·ȧ·nī'ȧh the priest read this
letter in the hearing of Jeremiah the
prophet. 30 Then the word of the LORD
came to Jeremiah: 31 "Send to all the
exiles, saying, 'Thus says the LORD
concerning She·māi'ȧh of Ne·hel'ȧm:
Because Shemaiah has prophesied to
you when I did not send him, and has
made you trust in a lie, 32 therefore
thus says the LORD: Behold, I will
punish She·māi'ȧh of Ne·hel'ȧm and
his descendants; he shall not have any
one living among this people to see[a]

[z] Cn: Heb *your dreams which you cause to dream* [a] Gk: Heb *and he shall not see*

the good that I will do to my people, says the LORD, for he has talked rebellion against the LORD.' "

30 The word that came to Jeremiah from the LORD:
2 "Thus says the LORD, the God of Israel: Write in a book all the words that I have spoken to you.
3 For behold, days are coming, says the LORD, when I will restore the fortunes of my people, Israel and Judah, says the LORD, and I will bring them back to the land which I gave to their fathers, and they shall take possession of it."

4 These are the words which the LORD spoke concerning Israel and Judah:

5 "Thus says the LORD:
We have heard a cry of panic,
of terror, and no peace.
6 Ask now, and see,
can a man bear a child?
Why then do I see every man
with his hands on his loins like a woman in labor?
Why has every face turned pale?
7 Alas! that day is so great
there is none like it;
it is a time of distress for Jacob;
yet he shall be saved out of it.

8 "And it shall come to pass in that day, says the LORD of hosts, that I will break the yoke from off their[b] neck, and I will burst their[b] bonds, and strangers shall no more make servants of them.[c]
9 But they shall serve the LORD their God and David their king, whom I will raise up for them.

10 "Then fear not, O Jacob my servant, says the LORD,
nor be dismayed, O Israel;
for lo, I will save you from afar,
and your offspring from the land of their captivity.
Jacob shall return and have quiet and ease,
and none shall make him afraid.
11 For I am with you to save you,
says the LORD;
I will make a full end of all the nations
among whom I scattered you,
but of you I will not make a full end.
I will chasten you in just measure,
and I will by no means leave you unpunished.

12 "For thus says the LORD:
Your hurt is incurable,
and your wound is grievous.
13 There is none to uphold your cause,
no medicine for your wound,
no healing for you.
14 All your lovers have forgotten you;
they care nothing for you;
for I have dealt you the blow of an enemy,
the punishment of a merciless foe,
because your guilt is great,
because your sins are flagrant.
15 Why do you cry out over your hurt?
Your pain is incurable.
Because your guilt is great,
because your sins are flagrant,
I have done these things to you.
16 Therefore all who devour you shall be devoured,
and all your foes, every one of them, shall go into captivity;
those who despoil you shall become a spoil,
and all who prey on you I will make a prey.
17 For I will restore health to you,
and your wounds I will heal,
says the LORD,
because they have called you an outcast:
'It is Zion, for whom no one cares!'

18 "Thus says the LORD:
Behold, I will restore the fortunes of the tents of Jacob,
and have compassion on his dwellings;
the city shall be rebuilt upon its mound,
and the palace shall stand where it used to be.
19 Out of them shall come songs of thanksgiving,
and the voices of those who make merry.
I will multiply them, and they shall not be few;
I will make them honored, and they shall not be small.
20 Their children shall be as they were of old,
and their congregation shall be established before me;
and I will punish all who oppress them.
21 Their prince shall be one of themselves,

[b] Gk Old Latin: Heb *your* [c] Heb *make a servant of him*

their ruler shall come forth from their midst;
I will make him draw near, and he shall approach me,
for who would dare of himself to approach me?
says the LORD.
22 And you shall be my people,
and I will be your God."

23 Behold the storm of the LORD!
Wrath has gone forth,
a whirling tempest;
it will burst upon the head of the wicked.
24 The fierce anger of the LORD will not turn back
until he has executed and accomplished
the intents of his mind.
In the latter days you will understand this.

31 "At that time, says the LORD, I will be the God of all the families of Israel, and they shall be my people."
2 Thus says the LORD:
"The people who survived the sword
found grace in the wilderness;
when Israel sought for rest,
3 the LORD appeared to him[d] from afar.
I have loved you with an everlasting love;
therefore I have continued my faithfulness to you.
4 Again I will build you, and you shall be built,
O virgin Israel!
Again you shall adorn yourself with timbrels,
and shall go forth in the dance of the merrymakers.
5 Again you shall plant vineyards
upon the mountains of Sȧ·mâr′i·ȧ;
the planters shall plant,
and shall enjoy the fruit.
6 For there shall be a day when watchmen will call
in the hill country of Ē′phrȧ·im:
'Arise, and let us go up to Zion,
to the LORD our God.' "

7 For thus says the LORD:
"Sing aloud with gladness for Jacob,
and raise shouts for the chief of the nations;
proclaim, give praise, and say,
'The LORD has saved his people,
the remnant of Israel.'
8 Behold, I will bring them from the north country,
and gather them from the farthest parts of the earth,
among them the blind and the lame,
the woman with child and her who is in travail, together;
a great company, they shall return here.
9 With weeping they shall come,
and with consolations[e] I will lead them back,
I will make them walk by brooks of water,
in a straight path in which they shall not stumble;
for I am a father to Israel,
and Ē′phrȧ·im is my first-born.

10 "Hear the word of the LORD, O nations,
and declare it in the coastlands afar off;
say, 'He who scattered Israel will gather him,
and will keep him as a shepherd keeps his flock.'
11 For the LORD has ransomed Jacob,
and has redeemed him from hands too strong for him.
12 They shall come and sing aloud on the height of Zion,
and they shall be radiant over the goodness of the LORD,
over the grain, the wine, and the oil,
and over the young of the flock and the herd;
their life shall be like a watered garden,
and they shall languish no more.
13 Then shall the maidens rejoice in the dance,
and the young men and the old shall be merry.
I will turn their mourning into joy,
I will comfort them, and give them gladness for sorrow.
14 I will feast the soul of the priests with abundance,
and my people shall be satisfied with my goodness,
says the LORD."

15 Thus says the LORD:
"A voice is heard in Rā′mȧh,

[d] Gk: Heb *me* [e] Gk Compare Vg Tg: Heb *supplications*
31.15: Mt 2.18.

lamentation and bitter weeping.
Rachel is weeping for her children;
she refuses to be comforted for her children,
because they are not."

16 Thus says the LORD:
"Keep your voice from weeping,
and your eyes from tears;
for your work shall be rewarded,
says the LORD,
and they shall come back from the land of the enemy.
17 There is hope for your future,
says the LORD,
and your children shall come back to their own country.
18 I have heard E'phră·im bemoaning,
'Thou hast chastened me, and I was chastened,
like an untrained calf;
bring me back that I may be restored,
for thou art the LORD my God.
19 For after I had turned away I repented;
and after I was instructed, I smote upon my thigh;
I was ashamed, and I was confounded,
because I bore the disgrace of my youth.'
20 Is E'phră·im my dear son?
Is he my darling child?
For as often as I speak against him,
I do remember him still.
Therefore my heart yearns for him;
I will surely have mercy on him,
says the LORD.

21 "Set up waymarks for yourself,
make yourself guideposts;
consider well the highway,
the road by which you went.
Return, O virgin Israel,
return to these your cities.
22 How long will you waver,
O faithless daughter?
For the LORD has created a new thing on the earth:
a woman protects a man."

23 Thus says the LORD of hosts,
the God of Israel: "Once more they
shall use these words in the land of
Judah and in its cities, when I restore
their fortunes:
'The LORD bless you, O habitation of righteousness,
O holy hill!'
24 And Judah and all its cities shall
dwell there together, and the farmers
and those who wander[f] with their
flocks. 25 For I will satisfy the weary
soul, and every languishing soul I will
replenish."
26 Thereupon I awoke and looked,
and my sleep was pleasant to me.
27 "Behold, the days are coming,
says the LORD, when I will sow the
house of Israel and the house of Judah
with the seed of man and the seed of
beast. 28 And it shall come to pass that
as I have watched over them to pluck
up and break down, to overthrow,
destroy, and bring evil, so I will watch
over them to build and to plant, says
the LORD. 29 In those days they shall
no longer say:
'The fathers have eaten sour grapes,
and the children's teeth are set on edge.'
30 But every one shall die for his own
sin; each man who eats sour grapes,
his teeth shall be set on edge.
31 "Behold, the days are coming,
says the LORD, when I will make a
new covenant with the house of Israel
and the house of Judah, 32 not like the
covenant which I made with their
fathers when I took them by the hand
to bring them out of the land of Egypt,
my covenant which they broke,
though I was their husband, says the
LORD. 33 But this is the covenant
which I will make with the house of
Israel after those days, says the LORD:
I will put my law within them, and I
will write it upon their hearts; and I
will be their God, and they shall be
my people. 34 And no longer shall each
man teach his neighbor and each his
brother, saying, 'Know the LORD,' for
they shall all know me, from the least
of them to the greatest, says the LORD;
for I will forgive their iniquity, and I
will remember their sin no more."

35 Thus says the LORD,
who gives the sun for light by day
and the fixed order of the moon
and the stars for light by night,
who stirs up the sea so that its waves roar—
the LORD of hosts is his name:
36 "If this fixed order departs

[f] Cn Compare Syr Vg Tg: Heb *and they shall wander*
31.31: Lk 22.20; 1 Cor 11.25. 31.31-34: Jer 32.38-40; Heb 8.8-12; 10.16-17.

from before me, says the LORD,
then shall the descendants of Israel
cease
from being a nation before me for
ever."

37 Thus says the LORD:
"If the heavens above can be
measured,
and the foundations of the earth
below can be explored,
then I will cast off all the descendants of Israel
for all that they have done,
says the LORD."

38 "Behold, the days are coming,
says the LORD, when the city shall be
rebuilt for the LORD from the tower
of Hȧ·nan'el to the Corner Gate.
39 And the measuring line shall go out
farther, straight to the hill Gā'reb,
and shall then turn to Gō'äh. 40 The
whole valley of the dead bodies and
the ashes, and all the fields as far as
the brook Kid'rŏn, to the corner of
the Horse Gate toward the east, shall
be sacred to the LORD. It shall not be
uprooted or overthrown any more for
ever."

32 The word that came to Jeremiah from the LORD in the
tenth year of Zed·ė·kī'äh king of Judah, which was the eighteenth year of
Ne·bu̇·chăd·rez'zăr. 2 At that time the
army of the king of Babylon was
besieging Jerusalem, and Jeremiah the
prophet was shut up in the court of
the guard which was in the palace of
the king of Judah. 3 For Zed·ė·kī'äh
king of Judah had imprisoned him,
saying, "Why do you prophesy and
say, 'Thus says the LORD: Behold, I am
giving this city into the hand of the
king of Babylon, and he shall take it;
4 Zed·ė·kī'äh king of Judah shall not
escape out of the hand of the Chal-
dē'ănṡ, but shall surely be given into
the hand of the king of Babylon, and
shall speak with him face to face and
see him eye to eye; 5 and he shall take
Zed·ė·kī'äh to Babylon, and there he
shall remain until I visit him, says the
LORD; though you fight against the
Chal·dē'ănṡ, you shall not succeed'?"
6 Jeremiah said, "The word of the
LORD came to me: 7 Behold, Han'ȧ·mel
the son of Shal'lu̇m your uncle will
come to you and say, 'Buy my field
which is at An'ȧ·thoth, for the right of
redemption by purchase is yours.'
8 Then Han'ȧ·mel my cousin came to
me in the court of the guard, in
accordance with the word of the LORD,
and said to me, 'Buy my field which
is at An'ȧ·thoth in the land of Benjamin, for the right of possession and
redemption is yours; buy it for yourself.' Then I knew that this was the
word of the LORD.
9 "And I bought the field at An'ȧ-
thoth from Han'ȧ·mel my cousin, and
weighed out the money to him, seventeen shekels of silver. 10 I signed the
deed, sealed it, got witnesses, and
weighed the money on scales. 11 Then
I took the sealed deed of purchase,
containing the terms and conditions,
and the open copy; 12 and I gave the
deed of purchase to Bâr'u̇ch the son
of Ne·rī'äh son of Mäh·sēi'äh, in the
presence of Han'ȧ·mel my cousin, in
the presence of the witnesses who
signed the deed of purchase, and in
the presence of all the Jews who were
sitting in the court of the guard. 13 I
charged Bâr'u̇ch in their presence,
saying, 14 'Thus says the LORD of
hosts, the God of Israel: Take these
deeds, both this sealed deed of purchase and this open deed, and put
them in an earthenware vessel, that
they may last for a long time. 15 For
thus says the LORD of hosts, the God
of Israel: Houses and fields and vineyards shall again be bought in this
land.'
16 "After I had given the deed of
purchase to Bâr'u̇ch the son of Ne-
rī'äh, I prayed to the LORD, saying:
17 'Ah Lord GOD! It is thou who hast
made the heavens and the earth by thy
great power and by thy outstretched
arm! Nothing is too hard for thee,
18 who showest steadfast love to thousands, but dost requite the guilt of
fathers to their children after them, O
great and mighty God whose name is
the LORD of hosts, 19 great in counsel
and mighty in deed; whose eyes are
open to all the ways of men, rewarding
every man according to his ways and
according to the fruit of his doings;
20 who hast shown signs and wonders
in the land of Egypt, and to this day
in Israel and among all mankind, and
hast made thee a name, as at this day.
21 Thou didst bring thy people Israel
out of the land of Egypt with signs
and wonders, with a strong hand and
outstretched arm, and with great

terror; 22 and thou gavest them this land, which thou didst swear to their fathers to give them, a land flowing with milk and honey; 23 and they entered and took possession of it. But they did not obey thy voice or walk in thy law; they did nothing of all thou didst command them to do. Therefore thou hast made all this evil come upon them. 24 Behold, the siege mounds have come up to the city to take it, and because of sword and famine and pestilence the city is given into the hands of the Chal·dē′ȧnṡ who are fighting against it. What thou didst speak has come to pass, and behold, thou seest it. 25 Yet thou, O Lord GOD, hast said to me, "Buy the field for money and get witnesses"—though the city is given into the hands of the Chal·dē′ȧnṡ.' "

26 The word of the LORD came to Jeremiah: 27 "Behold, I am the LORD, the God of all flesh; is anything too hard for me? 28 Therefore, thus says the LORD: Behold, I am giving this city into the hands of the Chal·dē′ȧnṡ and into the hands of Ne·bu̇·chȧd·rez′zȧr king of Babylon, and he shall take it. 29 The Chal·dē′ȧnṡ who are fighting against this city shall come and set this city on fire, and burn it, with the houses on whose roofs incense has been offered to Bā′ȧl and drink offerings have been poured out to other gods, to provoke me to anger. 30 For the sons of Israel and the sons of Judah have done nothing but evil in my sight from their youth; the sons of Israel have done nothing but provoke me to anger by the work of their hands, says the LORD. 31 This city has aroused my anger and wrath, from the day it was built to this day, so that I will remove it from my sight 32 because of all the evil of the sons of Israel and the sons of Judah which they did to provoke me to anger—their kings and their princes, their priests and their prophets, the men of Judah and the inhabitants of Jerusalem. 33 They have turned to me their back and not their face; and though I have taught them persistently they have not listened to receive instruction. 34 They set up their abominations in the house which is called by my name, to defile it. 35 They built the high places of Bā′ȧl in the valley of the son of Hin′nȯm, to offer up their sons and daughters to Mō′lech, though I did not command them, nor did it enter into my mind, that they should do this abomination, to cause Judah to sin.

36 "Now therefore thus says the LORD, the God of Israel, concerning this city of which you say, 'It is given into the hand of the king of Babylon by sword, by famine, and by pestilence': 37 Behold, I will gather them from all the countries to which I drove them in my anger and my wrath and in great indignation; I will bring them back to this place, and I will make them dwell in safety. 38 And they shall be my people, and I will be their God. 39 I will give them one heart and one way, that they may fear me for ever, for their own good and the good of their children after them. 40 I will make with them an everlasting covenant, that I will not turn away from doing good to them; and I will put the fear of me in their hearts, that they may not turn from me. 41 I will rejoice in doing them good, and I will plant them in this land in faithfulness, with all my heart and all my soul.

42 "For thus says the LORD: Just as I have brought all this great evil upon this people, so I will bring upon them all the good that I promise them. 43 Fields shall be bought in this land of which you are saying, It is a desolation, without man or beast; it is given into the hands of the Chal·dē′ȧnṡ. 44 Fields shall be bought for money, and deeds shall be signed and sealed and witnessed, in the land of Benjamin, in the places about Jerusalem, and in the cities of Judah, in the cities of the hill country, in the cities of the She·phē′lȧh, and in the cities of the Negeb; for I will restore their fortunes, says the LORD."

33 The word of the LORD came to Jeremiah a second time, while he was still shut up in the court of the guard: 2 "Thus says the LORD who made the earth,[g] the LORD who formed it to establish it—the LORD is his name: 3 Call to me and I will answer you, and will tell you great and hidden things which you have not known. 4 For thus says the LORD, the God of Israel, concerning the houses of this city and the houses of the kings of

[g] Gk: Heb *it*

32.38-40: Jer 31.31-34.

Judah which were torn down to make
a defense against the siege mounds
and before the sword:[h] 5 The Chal·dē′-
ȧnṡ are coming in to fight[i] and to fill
them with the dead bodies of men
whom I shall smite in my anger and
my wrath, for I have hidden my face
from this city because of all their
wickedness. 6 Behold, I will bring to
it health and healing, and I will heal
them and reveal to them abundance[j]
of prosperity and security. 7 I will restore the fortunes of Judah and the
fortunes of Israel, and rebuild them as
they were at first. 8 I will cleanse them
from all the guilt of their sin against
me, and I will forgive all the guilt of
their sin and rebellion against me.
9 And this city[k] shall be to me a name
of joy, a praise and a glory before all
the nations of the earth who shall hear
of all the good that I do for them; they
shall fear and tremble because of all
the good and all the prosperity I provide for it.

10 "Thus says the LORD: In this
place of which you say, 'It is a waste
without man or beast,' in the cities of
Judah and the streets of Jerusalem that
are desolate, without man or inhabitant or beast, there shall be heard again
11 the voice of mirth and the voice of
gladness, the voice of the bridegroom
and the voice of the bride, the voices
of those who sing, as they bring thank
offerings to the house of the LORD:

'Give thanks to the LORD of hosts,
for the LORD is good,
for his steadfast love endures for
ever!'

For I will restore the fortunes of the
land as at first, says the LORD.

12 "Thus says the LORD of hosts:
In this place which is waste, without
man or beast, and in all of its cities,
there shall again be habitations of
shepherds resting their flocks. 13 In
the cities of the hill country, in the
cities of the She·phē′lȧh, and in the
cities of the Negeb, in the land of
Benjamin, the places about Jerusalem,
and in the cities of Judah, flocks shall
again pass under the hands of the one
who counts them, says the LORD.

14 "Behold, the days are coming,
says the LORD, when I will fulfil the
promise I made to the house of Israel
and the house of Judah. 15 In those
days and at that time I will cause a
righteous Branch to spring forth for
David; and he shall execute justice and
righteousness in the land. 16 In those
days Judah will be saved and Jerusalem will dwell securely. And this is
the name by which it will be called:
'The LORD is our righteousness.'

17 "For thus says the LORD: David
shall never lack a man to sit on the
throne of the house of Israel, 18 and
the Levitical priests shall never lack a
man in my presence to offer burnt
offerings, to burn cereal offerings, and
to make sacrifices for ever."

19 The word of the LORD came to
Jeremiah: 20 "Thus says the LORD: If
you can break my covenant with the
day and my covenant with the night,
so that day and night will not come at
their appointed time, 21 then also my
covenant with David my servant may
be broken, so that he shall not have a
son to reign on his throne, and my
covenant with the Levitical priests my
ministers. 22 As the host of heaven cannot be numbered and the sands of the
sea cannot be measured, so I will
multiply the descendants of David my
servant, and the Levitical priests who
minister to me."

23 The word of the LORD came to
Jeremiah: 24 "Have you not observed
what these people are saying, 'The
LORD has rejected the two families
which he chose'? Thus they have
despised my people so that they are no
longer a nation in their sight. 25 Thus
says the LORD: If I have not established
my covenant with day and night and
the ordinances of heaven and earth,
26 then I will reject the descendants of
Jacob and David my servant and will
not choose one of his descendants to
rule over the seed of Abraham, Isaac,
and Jacob. For I will restore their
fortunes, and will have mercy upon
them."

34 The word which came to Jeremiah from the LORD, when
Ne·bū·chȧd·rez′zȧr king of Babylon
and all his army and all the kingdoms
of the earth under his dominion and
all the peoples were fighting against
Jerusalem and all of its cities: 2 "Thus
says the LORD, the God of Israel: Go
and speak to Zed·ė·kī′ȧh king of

[h] Heb obscure [i] Cn: Heb *They are coming in to fight against the Chaldeans* [j] Heb uncertain
[k] Heb *and it*

33.15: Jer 23.5; Is 4.2; Zech 3.8; 6.12.

Judah and say to him, 'Thus says the
LORD: Behold, I am giving this city
into the hand of the king of Babylon,
and he shall burn it with fire. 3 You
shall not escape from his hand, but
shall surely be captured and delivered
into his hand; you shall see the king
of Babylon eye to eye and speak with
him face to face; and you shall go to
Babylon.' 4 Yet hear the word of the
LORD, O Zed·ė·kī'ăh king of Judah!
Thus says the LORD concerning you:
'You shall not die by the sword. 5 You
shall die in peace. And as spices were
burned for your fathers, the former
kings who were before you, so men
shall burn spices for you and lament
for you, saying, "Alas, lord!" ' For I
have spoken the word, says the LORD."

6 Then Jeremiah the prophet spoke
all these words to Zed·ė·kī'ăh king of
Judah, in Jerusalem, 7 when the army
of the king of Babylon was fighting
against Jerusalem and against all the
cities of Judah that were left, Lā'chish
and A·zē'kăh; for these were the only
fortified cities of Judah that remained.

8 The word which came to Jeremiah from the LORD, after King
Zed·ė·kī'ăh had made a covenant with
all the people in Jerusalem to make a
proclamation of liberty to them, 9 that
every one should set free his Hebrew
slaves, male and female, so that no one
should enslave a Jew, his brother.
10 And they obeyed, all the princes and
all the people who had entered into the
covenant that every one would set free
his slave, male or female, so that they
would not be enslaved again; they
obeyed and set them free. 11 But afterward they turned around and took
back the male and female slaves they
had set free, and brought them into
subjection as slaves. 12 The word of the
LORD came to Jeremiah from the
LORD: 13 "Thus says the LORD, the
God of Israel: I made a covenant with
your fathers when I brought them out
of the land of Egypt, out of the house
of bondage, saying, 14 'At the end of
six[l] years each of you must set free
the fellow Hebrew who has been sold
to you and has served you six years;
you must set him free from your
service.' But your fathers did not
listen to me or incline their ears to me.
15 You recently repented and did what
was right in my eyes by proclaiming
liberty, each to his neighbor, and you
made a covenant before me in the
house which is called by my name;
16 but then you turned around and
profaned my name when each of you
took back his male and female slaves,
whom you had set free according to
their desire, and you brought them
into subjection to be your slaves.
17 Therefore, thus says the LORD: You
have not obeyed me by proclaiming
liberty, every one to his brother and
to his neighbor; behold, I proclaim to
you liberty to the sword, to pestilence,
and to famine, says the LORD. I will
make you a horror to all the kingdoms
of the earth. 18 And the men who transgressed my covenant and did not keep
the terms of the covenant which they
made before me, I will make like[m] the
calf which they cut in two and passed
between its parts—19 the princes of
Judah, the princes of Jerusalem, the
eunuchs, the priests, and all the people
of the land who passed between the
parts of the calf; 20 and I will give them
into the hand of their enemies and into the hand of those who seek their
lives. Their dead bodies shall be food
for the birds of the air and the beasts
of the earth. 21 And Zed·ė·kī'ăh king
of Judah, and his princes I will give
into the hand of their enemies and
into the hand of those who seek their
lives, into the hand of the army of the
king of Babylon which has withdrawn
from you. 22 Behold, I will command,
says the LORD, and will bring them
back to this city; and they will fight
against it, and take it, and burn it with
fire. I will make the cities of Judah a
desolation without inhabitant."

35 The word which came to Jeremiah from the LORD in the days
of Je·hoi'ȧ·kim the son of Jō·sī'ăh,
king of Judah: 2 "Go to the house of
the Rē'chȧ·bītes, and speak with them,
and bring them to the house of the
LORD, into one of the chambers; then
offer them wine to drink." 3 So I took
Jā-az·ȧ·nī'ăh the son of Jeremiah, son
of Hä·baz·zi·nī'ăh, and his brothers,
and all his sons, and the whole house
of the Rē'chȧ·bītes. 4 I brought them
to the house of the LORD into the
chamber of the sons of Hā'năn the son
of Ig·dȧ·lī'ăh, the man of God, which
was near the chamber of the princes,
above the chamber of Mā-ȧ·sē'ăh the
son of Shal'lŭm, keeper of the thresh-

[l] Gk: Heb *seven* [m] Cn: Heb lacks *like*

old. 5 Then I set before the Rē'chȧ-
bītes pitchers full of wine, and cups;
and I said to them, "Drink wine."
6 But they answered, "We will drink
no wine, for Jon'ȧ·dab the son of
Rē'chab, our father, commanded us,
'You shall not drink wine, neither you
nor your sons for ever; 7 you shall not
build a house; you shall not sow seed;
you shall not plant or have a vineyard;
but you shall live in tents all your days,
that you may live many days in the
land where you sojourn.' 8 We have
obeyed the voice of Jon'ȧ·dab the son
of Rē'chab, our father, in all that he
commanded us, to drink no wine all
our days, ourselves, our wives, our
sons, or our daughters, 9 and not to
build houses to dwell in. We have no
vineyard or field or seed; 10 but we
have lived in tents, and have obeyed
and done all that Jon'ȧ·dab our father
commanded us. 11 But when Ne·bŭ-
chȧd·rez'zȧr king of Babylon came up
against the land, we said, 'Come, and
let us go to Jerusalem for fear of the
army of the Chal·dē'ănṡ and the army
of the Syrians.' So we are living in
Jerusalem."

12 Then the word of the LORD
came to Jeremiah: 13 "Thus says the
LORD of hosts, the God of Israel: Go
and say to the men of Judah and the
inhabitants of Jerusalem, Will you not
receive instruction and listen to my
words? says the LORD. 14 The command which Jon'ȧ·dab the son of
Rē'chab gave to his sons, to drink no
wine, has been kept; and they drink
none to this day, for they have obeyed
their father's command. I have spoken
to you persistently, but you have not
listened to me. 15 I have sent to you
all my servants the prophets, sending
them persistently, saying, 'Turn now
every one of you from his evil way,
and amend your doings, and do not go
after other gods to serve them, and
then you shall dwell in the land which
I gave to you and your fathers.' But
you did not incline your ear or listen
to me. 16 The sons of Jon'ȧ·dab the
son of Rē'chab have kept the command
which their father gave them, but this
people has not obeyed me. 17 Therefore, thus says the LORD, the God of
hosts, the God of Israel: Behold, I am
bringing on Judah and all the inhabitants of Jerusalem all the evil that I
have pronounced against them; because I have spoken to them and they
have not listened, I have called to
them and they have not answered."

18 But to the house of the Rē'chȧ-
bītes Jeremiah said, "Thus says the
LORD of hosts, the God of Israel: Because you have obeyed the command
of Jon'ȧ·dab your father, and kept all
his precepts, and done all that he commanded you, 19 therefore thus says
the LORD of hosts, the God of Israel:
Jon'ȧ·dab the son of Rē'chab shall
never lack a man to stand before me."

36 In the fourth year of Je·hoi'ȧ-
kim the son of Jō·sī'ȧh, king of
Judah, this word came to Jeremiah
from the LORD: 2 "Take a scroll and
write on it all the words that I have
spoken to you against Israel and
Judah and all the nations, from the
day I spoke to you, from the days of
Jō·sī'ȧh until today. 3 It may be that
the house of Judah will hear all the
evil which I intend to do to them, so
that every one may turn from his evil
way, and that I may forgive their
iniquity and their sin."

4 Then Jeremiah called Bâr'ŭch the
son of Ne·rī'ȧh, and Baruch wrote
upon a scroll at the dictation of Jeremiah all the words of the LORD which
he had spoken to him. 5 And Jeremiah
ordered Bâr'ŭch, saying, "I am
debarred from going to the house of
the LORD; 6 so you are to go, and on
a fast day in the hearing of all the
people in the LORD's house you shall
read the words of the LORD from the
scroll which you have written at my
dictation. You shall read them also in
the hearing of all the men of Judah
who come out of their cities. 7 It may
be that their supplication will come
before the LORD, and that every one
will turn from his evil way, for great
is the anger and wrath that the LORD
has pronounced against this people."
8 And Bâr'ŭch the son of Ne·rī'ȧh did
all that Jeremiah the prophet ordered
him about reading from the scroll the
words of the LORD in the LORD's
house.

9 In the fifth year of Je·hoi'ȧ·kim
the son of Jō·sī'ȧh, king of Judah, in
the ninth month, all the people in
Jerusalem and all the people who came
from the cities of Judah to Jerusalem
proclaimed a fast before the LORD.
10 Then, in the hearing of all the people,
Bâr'ŭch read the words of Jeremiah
from the scroll, in the house of the

LORD, in the chamber of Gem·ȧ·rī'ȧh
the son of Shā'phȧn the secretary,
which was in the upper court, at the
entry of the New Gate of the LORD's
house.
11 When Mī·cāi'ȧh the son of
Gem·ȧ·rī'ȧh, son of Shā'phȧn, heard
all the words of the LORD from the
scroll, 12 he went down to the king's
house, into the secretary's chamber;
and all the princes were sitting there:
E·lish'ȧ·mȧ the secretary, De·lāi'ȧh the
son of She·māi'ȧh, El·nā'thȧn the son
of Ach'bôr, Gem·ȧ·rī'ȧh the son of
Shā'phȧn, Zed·ė·kī'ȧh the son of Han-
ȧ·nī'ȧh, and all the princes. 13 And
Mī·cāi'ȧh told them all the words that
he had heard, when Bâr'ŭch read the
scroll in the hearing of the people.
14 Then all the princes sent Je·hū'dī
the son of Neth·ȧ·nī'ȧh, son of Shel·ė-
mī'ȧh, son of Cū'shī, to say to Bâr'ŭch,
"Take in your hand the scroll that you
read in the hearing of the people, and
come." So Baruch the son of Ne·rī'ȧh
took the scroll in his hand and came
to them. 15 And they said to him, "Sit
down and read it." So Bâr'ŭch read it
to them. 16 When they heard all the
words, they turned one to another in
fear; and they said to Bâr'ŭch, "We
must report all these words to the
king." 17 Then they asked Bâr'ŭch,
"Tell us, how did you write all these
words? Was it at his dictation?"
18 Bâr'ŭch answered them, "He dic-
tated all these words to me, while I
wrote them with ink on the scroll."
19 Then the princes said to Bâr'ŭch,
"Go and hide, you and Jeremiah,
and let no one know where you
are."
20 So they went into the court to
the king, having put the scroll in the
chamber of E·lish'ȧ·mȧ the secretary;
and they reported all the words to the
king. 21 Then the king sent Je·hū'dī
to get the scroll, and he took it from
the chamber of E·lish'ȧ·mȧ the secretary; and Je·hū'dī read it to the king
and all the princes who stood beside
the king. 22 It was the ninth month,
and the king was sitting in the winter
house and there was a fire burning in
the brazier before him. 23 As Je·hū'dī
read three or four columns, the king
would cut them off with a penknife
and throw them into the fire in the
brazier, until the entire scroll was
consumed in the fire that was in the
brazier. 24 Yet neither the king, nor
any of his servants who heard all these
words, was afraid, nor did they rend
their garments. 25 Even when El·nā'-
thȧn and De·lāi'ȧh and Gem·ȧ·rī'ȧh
urged the king not to burn the scroll,
he would not listen to them. 26 And the
king commanded Jė·räh'mē·ėl the
king's son and Se·rāi'ȧh the son of
Az'ri-el and Shel·ė·mī'ȧh the son of
Ab'dē·ėl to seize Bâr'ŭch the secretary
and Jeremiah the prophet, but the
LORD hid them.
27 Now, after the king had burned
the scroll with the words which Bâr'-
ŭch wrote at Jeremiah's dictation, the
word of the LORD came to Jeremiah:
28 "Take another scroll and write on
it all the former words that were in
the first scroll, which Je·hoi'ȧ·kim the
king of Judah has burned. 29 And concerning Je·hoi'ȧ·kim king of Judah
you shall say, 'Thus says the LORD,
You have burned this scroll, saying,
"Why have you written in it that the
king of Babylon will certainly come
and destroy this land, and will cut off
from it man and beast?" 30 Therefore
thus says the LORD concerning Jehoi'ȧ·kim king of Judah, He shall have
none to sit upon the throne of David,
and his dead body shall be cast out to
the heat by day and the frost by night.
31 And I will punish him and his offspring and his servants for their iniquity; I will bring upon the inhabitants
of Jerusalem, and upon the men of
Judah, all the evil that I have pronounced against them, but they would
not hear.' "
32 Then Jeremiah took another
scroll and gave it to Bâr'ŭch the scribe,
the son of Ne·rī'ȧh, who wrote on it
at the dictation of Jeremiah all the
words of the scroll which Je·hoi'ȧ·kim
king of Judah had burned in the fire;
and many similar words were added
to them.

37 Zed·ė·kī'ȧh the son of Jō·sī'ȧh,
whom Ne·bū·chȧd·rez'zȧr king
of Babylon made king in the land of
Judah, reigned instead of Cō·nī'ȧh the
son of Je·hoi'ȧ·kim. 2 But neither he
nor his servants nor the people of the
land listened to the words of the LORD
which he spoke through Jeremiah the
prophet.
3 King Zed·ė·kī'ȧh sent Je·hū'cal
the son of Shel·ė·mī'ȧh, and Zeph·ȧ-
nī'ȧh the priest, the son of Mā·ȧ·sēi'ȧh,
to Jeremiah the prophet, saying, "Pray

for us to the LORD our God." 4 Now
Jeremiah was still going in and out
among the people, for he had not yet
been put in prison. 5 The army of
Pharaoh had come out of Egypt; and
when the Chal·dē'ȧnṡ who were besieging Jerusalem heard news of them,
they withdrew from Jerusalem.

6 Then the word of the LORD came
to Jeremiah the prophet: 7 "Thus says
the LORD, God of Israel: Thus shall
you say to the king of Judah who sent
you to me to inquire of me, 'Behold,
Pharaoh's army which came to help
you is about to return to Egypt, to its
own land. 8 And the Chal·dē'ȧnṡ shall
come back and fight against this city;
they shall take it and burn it with fire.
9 Thus says the LORD, Do not deceive
yourselves, saying, "The Chal·dē'ȧnṡ
will surely stay away from us," for
they will not stay away. 10 For even if
you should defeat the whole army of
Chal·dē'ȧnṡ who are fighting against
you, and there remained of them only
wounded men, every man in his tent,
they would rise up and burn this city
with fire.' "

11 Now when the Chal·dē'ȧn army
had withdrawn from Jerusalem at the
approach of Pharaoh's army, 12 Jeremiah set out from Jerusalem to go to
the land of Benjamin to receive his
portion[n] there among the people.
13 When he was at the Benjamin Gate,
a sentry there named I·rī'jȧh the son
of Shel·ė·mī'ȧh, son of Han·ȧ·nī'ȧh,
seized Jeremiah the prophet, saying,
"You are deserting to the Chal·dē'ȧnṡ."
14 And Jeremiah said, "It is false; I am
not deserting to the Chal·dē'ȧnṡ." But
I·rī'jȧh would not listen to him, and
seized Jeremiah and brought him to
the princes. 15 And the princes were
enraged at Jeremiah, and they beat
him and imprisoned him in the house
of Jonathan the secretary, for it had
been made a prison.

16 When Jeremiah had come to the
dungeon cells, and remained there
many days, 17 King Zed·ė·kī'ȧh sent
for him, and received him. The king
questioned him secretly in his house,
and said, "Is there any word from the
LORD?" Jeremiah said, "There is."
Then he said, "You shall be delivered
into the hand of the king of Babylon."
18 Jeremiah also said to King Zed·ė-
kī'ȧh, "What wrong have I done to
you or your servants or this people,
that you have put me in prison?
19 Where are your prophets who
prophesied to you, saying, 'The king
of Babylon will not come against you
and against this land'? 20 Now hear, I
pray you, O my lord the king: let my
humble plea come before you, and do
not send me back to the house of
Jonathan the secretary, lest I die
there." 21 So King Zed·ė·kī'ȧh gave
orders, and they committed Jeremiah
to the court of the guard; and a loaf
of bread was given him daily from the
bakers' street, until all the bread of
the city was gone. So Jeremiah remained in the court of the guard.

38 Now Sheph·ȧ·tī'ȧh the son of
Mat'tan, Ged·ȧ·lī'ȧh the son of
Pash'hŭr, Jū'cal the son of Shel·ė-
mī'ȧh, and Pash'hŭr the son of Mal-
chī'ȧh heard the words that Jeremiah
was saying to all the people, 2 "Thus
says the LORD, He who stays in this
city shall die by the sword, by famine,
and by pestilence; but he who goes
out to the Chal·dē'ȧnṡ shall live; he
shall have his life as a prize of war,
and live. 3 Thus says the LORD, This
city shall surely be given into the hand
of the army of the king of Babylon and
be taken." 4 Then the princes said to
the king, "Let this man be put to
death, for he is weakening the hands
of the soldiers who are left in this city,
and the hands of all the people, by
speaking such words to them. For this
man is not seeking the welfare of this
people, but their harm." 5 King Zed-
ė·kī'ȧh said, "Behold, he is in your
hands; for the king can do nothing
against you." 6 So they took Jeremiah
and cast him into the cistern of Mal-
chī'ȧh, the king's son, which was in
the court of the guard, letting Jeremiah
down by ropes. And there was no
water in the cistern, but only mire,
and Jeremiah sank in the mire.

7 When Ē'bed-mel'ech the Ethiopian, a eunuch, who was in the king's
house, heard that they had put Jeremiah into the cistern—the king was
sitting in the Benjamin Gate—8 Ē'bed-
mel'ech went from the king's house
and said to the king, 9 "My lord the
king, these men have done evil in all
that they did to Jeremiah the prophet
by casting him into the cistern, and
he will die there of hunger, for there
is no bread left in the city." 10 Then
the king commanded Ē'bed-mel'ech,

[n] Heb obscure

the Ethiopian, "Take three men with
you from here, and lift Jeremiah the
prophet out of the cistern before he
dies." 11 So Ē'bed-mel'ech took the
men with him and went to the house
of the king, to a wardrobe of[o] the
storehouse, and took from there old
rags and worn-out clothes, which he
let down to Jeremiah in the cistern by
ropes. 12 Then Ē'bed-mel'ech the
Ethiopian said to Jeremiah, "Put the
rags and clothes between your arm-
pits and the ropes." Jeremiah did so.
13 Then they drew Jeremiah up with
ropes and lifted him out of the cistern.
And Jeremiah remained in the court
of the guard.

14 King Zed·ė·kī'ȧh sent for Jeremiah the prophet and received him at
the third entrance of the temple of the
LORD. The king said to Jeremiah, "I
will ask you a question; hide nothing
from me." 15 Jeremiah said to Zed·ė-
kī'ȧh, "If I tell you, will you not be
sure to put me to death? And if I give
you counsel, you will not listen to me."
16 Then King Zed·ė·kī'ȧh swore
secretly to Jeremiah, "As the LORD
lives, who made our souls, I will not
put you to death or deliver you into
the hand of these men who seek your
life."

17 Then Jeremiah said to Zed·ė-
kī'ȧh, "Thus says the LORD, the God
of hosts, the God of Israel, If you will
surrender to the princes of the king
of Babylon, then your life shall be
spared, and this city shall not be
burned with fire, and you and your
house shall live. 18 But if you do not
surrender to the princes of the king
of Babylon, then this city shall be
given into the hand of the Chal·dē'ȧnṡ,
and they shall burn it with fire, and
you shall not escape from their hand."
19 King Zed·ė·kī'ȧh said to Jeremiah,
"I am afraid of the Jews who have
deserted to the Chal·dē'ȧnṡ, lest I be
handed over to them and they abuse
me." 20 Jeremiah said, "You shall not
be given to them. Obey now the voice
of the LORD in what I say to you, and
it shall be well with you, and your life
shall be spared. 21 But if you refuse to
surrender, this is the vision which the
LORD has shown to me: 22 Behold, all
the women left in the house of the
king of Judah were being led out to
the princes of the king of Babylon and
were saying,

'Your trusted friends have deceived
you
and prevailed against you;
now that your feet are sunk in the
mire,
they turn away from you.'

23 All your wives and your sons shall
be led out to the Chal·dē'ȧnṡ, and you
yourself shall not escape from their
hand, but shall be seized by the king
of Babylon; and this city shall be
burned with fire."

24 Then Zed·ė·kī'ȧh said to Jeremiah, "Let no one know of these
words and you shall not die. 25 If the
princes hear that I have spoken with
you and come to you and say to you,
'Tell us what you said to the king and
what the king said to you; hide nothing
from us and we will not put you to
death,' 26 then you shall say to them,
'I made a humble plea to the king that
he would not send me back to the
house of Jonathan to die there.' "
27 Then all the princes came to Jeremiah and asked him, and he answered
them as the king had instructed him.
So they left off speaking with him, for
the conversation had not been over-
heard. 28 And Jeremiah remained in
the court of the guard until the day
that Jerusalem was taken.

39 In the ninth year of Zed·ė-
kī'ȧh king of Judah, in the tenth
month, Ne·bů·chȧd·rez'zȧr king of
Babylon and all his army came against
Jerusalem and besieged it; 2 in the
eleventh year of Zed·ė·kī'ȧh, in the
fourth month, on the ninth day of the
month, a breach was made in the city.
3 When Jerusalem was taken,[p] all the
princes of the king of Babylon came
and sat in the middle gate: Nēr'gȧl-
shä·rē'zėr, Sam'gär-nē'bō, Sär'sė·chim
the Rab'sȧ·ris, Nergal-sharezer the
Rab'mag, with all the rest of the
officers of the king of Babylon. 4 When
Zed·ė·kī'ȧh king of Judah and all the
soldiers saw them, they fled, going out
of the city at night by way of the king's
garden through the gate between the
two walls; and they went toward the
Ar'ȧ·bȧh. 5 But the army of the Chal-
dē'ȧnṡ pursued them, and overtook
Zed·ė·kī'ȧh in the plains of Jericho;
and when they had taken him, they
brought him up to Ne·bů·chȧd·rez'zȧr
king of Babylon, at Rib'lȧh, in the
land of Hā'math; and he passed
sentence upon him. 6 The king of

[o] Cn: Heb *to under* [p] This clause has been transposed from the end of Chapter 38

Babylon slew the sons of Zed·ė·kī'ȧh
at Rib'lȧh before his eyes; and the
king of Babylon slew all the nobles of
Judah. 7 He put out the eyes of Zed·ė-
kī'ȧh, and bound him in fetters to
take him to Babylon. 8 The Chal·dē'-
ȧnṡ burned the king's house and the
house of the people, and broke down
the walls of Jerusalem. 9 Then Ne·bū'-
zȧ·rad'ȧn, the captain of the guard,
carried into exile to Babylon the rest
of the people who were left in the city,
those who had deserted to him, and
the people who remained. 10 Ne·bū'-
zȧ·rad'ȧn, the captain of the guard,
left in the land of Judah some of the
poor people who owned nothing, and
gave them vineyards and fields at the
same time.

11 Ne·bů·chȧd·rez'zȧr king of Babylon gave command concerning Jeremiah through Ne·bū'zȧ·rad'ȧn, the
captain of the guard, saying, 12 "Take
him, look after him well and do him
no harm, but deal with him as he tells
you." 13 So Ne·bū'zȧ·rad'ȧn the captain of the guard, Ne·bů·shaz'bȧn the
Rab'sȧ·ris, Nēr'gȧl-shä·rē'zėr the
Rab'mag, and all the chief officers of
the king of Babylon 14 sent and took
Jeremiah from the court of the guard.
They entrusted him to Ged·ȧ·lī'ȧh the
son of Ȧ·hī'kam, son of Shā'phȧn, that
he should take him home. So he dwelt
among the people.

15 The word of the LORD came to
Jeremiah while he was shut up in the
court of the guard: 16 "Go, and say
to Ē'bed-mel'ech the Ethiopian, 'Thus
says the LORD of hosts, the God of
Israel: Behold, I will fulfil my words
against this city for evil and not for
good, and they shall be accomplished
before you on that day. 17 But I will
deliver you on that day, says the
LORD, and you shall not be given into
the hand of the men of whom you are
afraid. 18 For I will surely save you,
and you shall not fall by the sword;
but you shall have your life as a prize
of war, because you have put your
trust in me, says the LORD.' "

40 The word that came to Jeremiah from the LORD after Ne-
bū'zȧ·rad'ȧn the captain of the guard
had let him go from Rā'mȧh, when he
took him bound in chains along with
all the captives of Jerusalem and
Judah who were being exiled to Babylon. 2 The captain of the guard took
Jeremiah and said to him, "The LORD
your God pronounced this evil against
this place; 3 the LORD has brought it
about, and has done as he said. Because
you sinned against the LORD, and did
not obey his voice, this thing has come
upon you. 4 Now, behold, I release
you today from the chains on your
hands. If it seems good to you to come
with me to Babylon, come, and I will
look after you well; but if it seems
wrong to you to come with me to
Babylon, do not come. See, the whole
land is before you; go wherever you
think it good and right to go. 5 If you
remain,[q] then return to Ged·ȧ·lī'ȧh the
son of Ȧ·hī'kam, son of Shā'phȧn,
whom the king of Babylon appointed
governor of the cities of Judah, and
dwell with him among the people; or
go wherever you think it right to go."
So the captain of the guard gave him
an allowance of food and a present, and
let him go. 6 Then Jeremiah went to
Ged·ȧ·lī'ȧh the son of Ȧ·hī'kam, at
Miz'pȧh, and dwelt with him among
the people who were left in the land.

7 When all the captains of the
forces in the open country and their
men heard that the king of Babylon
had appointed Ged·ȧ·lī'ȧh the son of
Ȧ·hī'kam governor in the land, and
had committed to him men, women,
and children, those of the poorest of
the land who had not been taken into
exile to Babylon, 8 they went to Ged·ȧ-
lī'ȧh at Miz'pȧh—Ish'mȧ·el the son of
Neth·ȧ·nī'ȧh, Jō·hā'nȧn the son of
Kȧ·rē'ȧh, Se·räi'ȧh the son of Tan'hū-
meth, the sons of Ē'phäi the Nė·toph'-
ȧ·thīte, Jez·ȧ·nī'ȧh the son of the Mā-
ac'ȧ·thīte, they and their men. 9 Ged-
ȧ·lī'ȧh the son of Ȧ·hī'kam, son of
Shā'phȧn, swore to them and their
men, saying, "Do not be afraid to
serve the Chal·dē'ȧnṡ. Dwell in the
land, and serve the king of Babylon,
and it shall be well with you. 10 As for
me, I will dwell at Miz'pȧh, to stand
for you before the Chal·dē'ȧnṡ who
will come to us; but as for you, gather
wine and summer fruits and oil, and
store them in your vessels, and dwell
in your cities that you have taken."
11 Likewise, when all the Jews who
were in Mō'ab and among the Am'-
mȯ·nītes and in Ē'dȯm and in other
lands heard that the king of Babylon
had left a remnant in Judah and had

[q] Syr: Heb obscure

appointed Ged·ȧ·lī'ȧh the son of Ȧ·hī'-
kam, son of Shā'phȧn, as governor over
them, 12 then all the Jews returned
from all the places to which they had
been driven and came to the land of
Judah, to Ged·ȧ·lī'ȧh at Miz'pȧh; and
they gathered wine and summer fruits
in great abundance.

13 Now Jō·hā'nȧn the son of
Kȧ·rē'ȧh and all the leaders of the
forces in the open country came to
Ged·ȧ·lī'ȧh at Miz'pȧh 14 and said to
him, "Do you know that Bā'ȧ·lis the
king of the Am'mȯ·nītes has sent Ish'-
mȧ·el the son of Neth·ȧ·nī'ȧh to take
your life?" But Ged·ȧ·lī'ȧh the son of
Ȧ·hī'kam would not believe them.
15 Then Jō·hā'nȧn the son of Kȧ·rē'ȧh
spoke secretly to Ged·ȧ·lī'ȧh at Miz'-
pȧh, "Let me go and slay Ish'mȧ·el
the son of Neth·ȧ·nī'ȧh, and no one
will know it. Why should he take your
life, so that all the Jews who are
gathered about you would be scattered,
and the remnant of Judah would
perish?" 16 But Ged·ȧ·lī'ȧh the son of
Ȧ·hī'kam said to Jō·hā'nȧn the son of
Kȧ·rē'ȧh, "You shall not do this thing,
for you are speaking falsely of Ish'-
mȧ·el."

41 In the seventh month, Ish'-
mȧ·el the son of Neth·ȧ·nī'ȧh, son
of E·lish'ȧ·mȧ, of the royal family, one
of the chief officers of the king, came
with ten men to Ged·ȧ·lī'ȧh the son
of Ȧ·hī'kam, at Miz'pȧh. As they ate
bread together there at Mizpah, 2 Ish'-
mȧ·el the son of Neth·ȧ·nī'ȧh and the
ten men with him rose up and struck
down Ged·ȧ·lī'ȧh the son of Ȧ·hī'kam,
son of Shā'phȧn, with the sword, and
killed him, whom the king of Babylon
had appointed governor in the land.
3 Ish'mȧ·el also slew all the Jews who
were with Ged·ȧ·lī'ȧh at Miz'pȧh, and
the Chal·dē'ȧn soldiers who happened
to be there.

4 On the day after the murder of
Ged·ȧ·lī'ȧh, before any one knew of it,
5 eighty men arrived from Shē'chem
and Shī'lōh and Sȧ·mâr'i·ȧ, with their
beards shaved and their clothes torn,
and their bodies gashed, bringing cereal
offerings and incense to present at the
temple of the LORD. 6 And Ish'mȧ·el
the son of Neth·ȧ·nī'ȧh came out from
Miz'pȧh to meet them, weeping as he
came. As he met them, he said to
them, "Come in to Ged·ȧ·lī'ȧh the son
of Ȧ·hī'kam." 7 When they came into
the city, Ish'mȧ·el the son of Neth·ȧ-
nī'ȧh and the men with him slew them,
and cast them into a cistern. 8 But
there were ten men among them who
said to Ish'mȧ·el, "Do not kill us, for
we have stores of wheat, barley, oil,
and honey hidden in the fields." So he
refrained and did not kill them with
their companions.

9 Now the cistern into which Ish'-
mȧ·el cast all the bodies of the men
whom he had slain was the large cistern[r] which King Asa had made for
defense against Bā'ȧ·shȧ king of Israel;
Ishmael the son of Neth·ȧ·nī'ȧh filled
it with the slain. 10 Then Ish'mȧ·el
took captive all the rest of the people
who were in Miz'pȧh, the king's
daughters and all the people who were
left at Mizpah, whom Ne·bū'zȧ·rad'ȧn,
the captain of the guard, had committed to Ged·ȧ·lī'ȧh the son of Ȧ·hī'-
kam. Ishmael the son of Neth·ȧ·nī'ȧh
took them captive and set out to cross
over to the Am'mȯ·nītes.

11 But when Jō·hā'nȧn the son of
Kȧ·rē'ȧh and all the leaders of the
forces with him heard of all the evil
which Ish'mȧ·el the son of Neth·ȧ-
nī'ȧh had done, 12 they took all their
men and went to fight against Ish'-
mȧ·el the son of Neth·ȧ·nī'ȧh. They
came upon him at the great pool which
is in Gib'ē·ȯn. 13 And when all the
people who were with Ish'mȧ·el saw
Jō·hā'nȧn the son of Kȧ·rē'ȧh and all
the leaders of the forces with him,
they rejoiced. 14 So all the people
whom Ish'mȧ·el had carried away
captive from Miz'pȧh turned about
and came back, and went to Jō·hā'nȧn
the son of Kȧ·rē'ȧh. 15 But Ish'mȧ·el
the son of Neth·ȧ·nī'ȧh escaped from
Jō·hā'nȧn with eight men, and went to
the Am'mȯ·nītes. 16 Then Jō·hā'nȧn
the son of Kȧ·rē'ȧh and all the leaders
of the forces with him took all the rest
of the people whom Ish'mȧ·el the son
of Neth·ȧ·nī'ȧh had carried away captives[s] from Miz'pȧh after he had slain
Ged·ȧ·lī'ȧh the son of Ȧ·hī'kam—
soldiers, women, children, and eunuchs, whom Jō·hā'nȧn brought back
from Gib'ē·ȯn. 17 And they went and
stayed at Gē'rüth Chim'hȧm near
Bethlehem, intending to go to Egypt
18 because of the Chal·dē'ȧns; for they
were afraid of them, because Ish'-
mȧ·el the son of Neth·ȧ·nī'ȧh had slain
Ged·ȧ·lī'ȧh the son of Ȧ·hī'kam, whom

[r] Gk: Heb *he had slain by the hand of Gedaliah* [s] Cn: Heb *whom he recovered from Ishmael*

the king of Babylon had made governor
over the land.

42 Then all the commanders of
the forces, and Jō·hā'nȧn the
son of Kȧ·rē'ȧh and Az·ȧ·rī'ȧh[t] the son
of Hō·shāi'ȧh, and all the people from
the least to the greatest, came near
2 and said to Jeremiah the prophet,
"Let our supplication come before
you, and pray to the LORD your God
for us, for all this remnant (for we are
left but a few of many, as your eyes
see us), 3 that the LORD your God may
show us the way we should go, and the
thing that we should do." 4 Jeremiah
the prophet said to them, "I have
heard you; behold, I will pray to the
LORD your God according to your
request, and whatever the LORD
answers you I will tell you; I will keep
nothing back from you." 5 Then they
said to Jeremiah, "May the LORD be a
true and faithful witness against us if
we do not act according to all the word
with which the LORD your God sends
you to us. 6 Whether it is good or evil,
we will obey the voice of the LORD our
God to whom we are sending you, that
it may be well with us when we obey
the voice of the LORD our God."

7 At the end of ten days the word
of the LORD came to Jeremiah. 8 Then
he summoned Jō·hā'nȧn the son of
Kȧ·rē'ȧh and all the commanders of
the forces who were with him, and all
the people from the least to the greatest, 9 and said to them, "Thus says
the LORD, the God of Israel, to whom
you sent me to present your supplication before him: 10 If you will remain
in this land, then I will build you up
and not pull you down; I will plant
you, and not pluck you up; for I
repent of the evil which I did to you.
11 Do not fear the king of Babylon, of
whom you are afraid; do not fear him,
says the LORD, for I am with you, to
save you and to deliver you from his
hand. 12 I will grant you mercy, that
he may have mercy on you and let you
remain in your own land. 13 But if you
say, 'We will not remain in this land,'
disobeying the voice of the LORD your
God 14 and saying, 'No, we will go to
the land of Egypt, where we shall not
see war, or hear the sound of the
trumpet, or be hungry for bread, and
we will dwell there,' 15 then hear the
word of the LORD, O remnant of
Judah. Thus says the LORD of hosts,
the God of Israel: If you set your faces
to enter Egypt and go to live there,
16 then the sword which you fear shall
overtake you there in the land of
Egypt; and the famine of which you
are afraid shall follow hard after you
to Egypt; and there you shall die. 17 All
the men who set their faces to go to
Egypt to live there shall die by the
sword, by famine, and by pestilence;
they shall have no remnant or survivor
from the evil which I will bring upon
them.

18 "For thus says the LORD of
hosts, the God of Israel: As my anger
and my wrath were poured out on the
inhabitants of Jerusalem, so my wrath
will be poured out on you when you
go to Egypt. You shall become an
execration, a horror, a curse, and a
taunt. You shall see this place no more.
19 The LORD has said to you, O remnant of Judah, 'Do not go to Egypt.'
Know for a certainty that I have
warned you this day 20 that you have
gone astray at the cost of your lives.
For you sent me to the LORD your
God, saying, 'Pray for us to the LORD
our God, and whatever the LORD our
God says declare to us and we will do
it.' 21 And I have this day declared it
to you, but you have not obeyed the
voice of the LORD your God in anything that he sent me to tell you.
22 Now therefore know for a certainty
that you shall die by the sword, by
famine, and by pestilence in the place
where you desire to go to live."

43 When Jeremiah finished speaking to all the people all these
words of the LORD their God, with
which the LORD their God had sent
him to them, 2 Az·ȧ·rī'ȧh the son of
Hō·shāi'ȧh and Jō·hā'nȧn the son of
Kȧ·rē'ȧh and all the insolent men said
to Jeremiah, "You are telling a lie. The
LORD our God did not send you to say,
'Do not go to Egypt to live there';
3 but Bâr'ŭch the son of Ne·rī'ȧh has
set you against us, to deliver us into
the hand of the Chal·dē'ȧnṡ, that they
may kill us or take us into exile in
Babylon." 4 So Jō·hā'nȧn the son of
Kȧ·rē'ȧh and all the commanders of
the forces and all the people did not
obey the voice of the LORD, to remain
in the land of Judah. 5 But Jō·hā'nȧn
the son of Kȧ·rē'ȧh and all the commanders of the forces took all the
remnant of Judah who had returned

[t] Gk: Heb *Jezaniah*

to live in the land of Judah from all the nations to which they had been driven—6 the men, the women, the children, the princesses, and every person whom Ne·bū'zȧ·rad'ȧn the captain of the guard had left with Ged·ȧ·li'ȧh the son of A·hi'kam, son of Shā'phȧn; also Jeremiah the prophet and Bâr'ŭch the son of Ne·ri'ȧh. 7 And they came into the land of Egypt, for they did not obey the voice of the LORD. And they arrived at Täh'pȧn·hēs.

8 Then the word of the LORD came to Jeremiah in Täh'pȧn·hēs: 9 "Take in your hands large stones, and hide them in the mortar in the pavement which is at the entrance to Pharaoh's palace in Täh'pȧn·hēs, in the sight of the men of Judah, 10 and say to them, 'Thus says the LORD of hosts, the God of Israel: Behold, I will send and take Ne·bu·chȧd·rez'zȧr the king of Babylon, my servant, and he[u] will set his throne above these stones which I have hid, and he will spread his royal canopy over them. 11 He shall come and smite the land of Egypt, giving to the pestilence those who are doomed to the pestilence, to captivity those who are doomed to captivity, and to the sword those who are doomed to the sword. 12 He[v] shall kindle a fire in the temples of the gods of Egypt; and he shall burn them and carry them away captive; and he shall clean the land of Egypt, as a shepherd cleans his cloak of vermin; and he shall go away from there in peace. 13 He shall break the obelisks of Hē·li·op'ō·lis which is in the land of Egypt; and the temples of the gods of Egypt he shall burn with fire.'"

44 The word that came to Jeremiah concerning all the Jews that dwelt in the land of Egypt, at Mig'dōl, at Täh'pȧn·hēs, at Memphis, and in the land of Path'ros, 2 "Thus says the LORD of hosts, the God of Israel: You have seen all the evil that I brought upon Jerusalem and upon all the cities of Judah. Behold, this day they are a desolation, and no one dwells in them, 3 because of the wickedness which they committed, provoking me to anger, in that they went to burn incense and serve other gods that they knew not, neither they, nor you, nor your fathers. 4 Yet I persistently sent to you all my servants the prophets, saying, 'Oh, do not do this abominable thing that I hate!' 5 But they did not listen or incline their ear, to turn from their wickedness and burn no incense to other gods. 6 Therefore my wrath and my anger were poured forth and kindled in the cities of Judah and in the streets of Jerusalem; and they became a waste and a desolation, as at this day. 7 And now thus says the LORD God of hosts, the God of Israel: Why do you commit this great evil against yourselves, to cut off from you man and woman, infant and child, from the midst of Judah, leaving you no remnant? 8 Why do you provoke me to anger with the works of your hands, burning incense to other gods in the land of Egypt where you have come to live, that you may be cut off and become a curse and a taunt among all the nations of the earth? 9 Have you forgotten the wickedness of your fathers, the wickedness of the kings of Judah, the wickedness of their[w] wives, your own wickedness, and the wickedness of your wives, which they committed in the land of Judah and in the streets of Jerusalem? 10 They have not humbled themselves even to this day, nor have they feared, nor walked in my law and my statutes which I set before you and before your fathers.

11 "Therefore thus says the LORD of hosts, the God of Israel: Behold, I will set my face against you for evil, to cut off all Judah. 12 I will take the remnant of Judah who have set their faces to come to the land of Egypt to live, and they shall all be consumed; in the land of Egypt they shall fall; by the sword and by famine they shall be consumed; from the least to the greatest, they shall die by the sword and by famine; and they shall become an execration, a horror, a curse, and a taunt. 13 I will punish those who dwell in the land of Egypt, as I have punished Jerusalem, with the sword, with famine, and with pestilence, 14 so that none of the remnant of Judah who have come to live in the land of Egypt shall escape or survive or return to the land of Judah, to which they desire to return to dwell there; for they shall not return, except some fugitives."

15 Then all the men who knew that their wives had offered incense to other gods, and all the women who stood by, a great assembly, all the people who

[u] Gk Syr: Heb *I* [v] Gk Syr Vg: Heb *I* [w] Heb *his*

dwelt in Path'ros in the land of Egypt,
answered Jeremiah: 16 "As for the
word which you have spoken to us in
the name of the LORD, we will not
listen to you. 17 But we will do everything that we have vowed, burn
incense to the queen of heaven and
pour out libations to her, as we did,
both we and our fathers, our kings and
our princes, in the cities of Judah and
in the streets of Jerusalem; for then we
had plenty of food, and prospered,
and saw no evil. 18 But since we left
off burning incense to the queen of
heaven and pouring out libations to
her, we have lacked everything and
have been consumed by the sword and
by famine." 19 And the women said,[x]
"When we burned incense to the
queen of heaven and poured out libations to her, was it without our husbands' approval that we made cakes
for her bearing her image and poured
out libations to her?"

20 Then Jeremiah said to all the
people, men and women, all the people
who had given him this answer: 21 "As
for the incense that you burned in the
cities of Judah and in the streets of
Jerusalem, you and your fathers, your
kings and your princes, and the people
of the land, did not the LORD remember it?[y] Did it not come into his mind?
22 The LORD could no longer bear
your evil doings and the abominations
which you committed; therefore your
land has become a desolation and a
waste and a curse, without inhabitant,
as it is this day. 23 It is because you
burned incense, and because you
sinned against the LORD and did not
obey the voice of the LORD or walk in
his law and in his statutes and in his
testimonies, that this evil has befallen
you, as at this day."

24 Jeremiah said to all the people
and all the women, "Hear the word of
the LORD, all you of Judah who are in
the land of Egypt, 25 Thus says the
LORD of hosts, the God of Israel: You
and your wives have declared with
your mouths, and have fulfilled it with
your hands, saying, 'We will surely
perform our vows that we have made,
to burn incense to the queen of heaven
and to pour out libations to her.' Then
confirm your vows and perform your
vows! 26 Therefore hear the word of
the LORD, all you of Judah who dwell
in the land of Egypt: Behold, I have
sworn by my great name, says the
LORD, that my name shall no more be
invoked by the mouth of any man of
Judah in all the land of Egypt, saying,
'As the Lord GOD lives.' 27 Behold, I
am watching over them for evil and
not for good; all the men of Judah who
are in the land of Egypt shall be consumed by the sword and by famine,
until there is an end of them. 28 And
those who escape the sword shall return from the land of Egypt to the
land of Judah, few in number; and all
the remnant of Judah, who came to
the land of Egypt to live, shall know
whose word will stand, mine or theirs.
29 This shall be the sign to you, says
the LORD, that I will punish you in
this place, in order that you may know
that my words will surely stand against
you for evil: 30 Thus says the LORD,
Behold, I will give Pharaoh Hoph'rȧ
king of Egypt into the hand of his
enemies and into the hand of those
who seek his life, as I gave Zed·ė·kī'ȧh
king of Judah into the hands of Ne·bů-
chȧd·rez'zȧr king of Babylon, who
was his enemy and sought his life."

45 The word that Jeremiah the
prophet spoke to Bâr'ůch the
son of Ne·rī'ȧh, when he wrote these
words in a book at the dictation of
Jeremiah, in the fourth year of Je·hoi'-
ȧ·kim the son of Jō·sī'ȧh, king of
Judah: 2 "Thus says the LORD, the
God of Israel, to you, O Bâr'ůch: 3 You
said, 'Woe is me! for the LORD has
added sorrow to my pain; I am weary
with my groaning, and I find no rest.'
4 Thus shall you say to him, Thus
says the LORD: Behold, what I have
built I am breaking down, and what I
have planted I am plucking up—that
is, the whole land. 5 And do you seek
great things for yourself? Seek them
not; for, behold, I am bringing evil
upon all flesh, says the LORD; but
I will give you your life as a prize of
war in all places to which you may
go."

46 The word of the LORD which
came to Jeremiah the prophet
concerning the nations.

2 About Egypt. Concerning the
army of Pharaoh Nē'cō, king of Egypt,
which was by the river Eū·phrā'tēṡ at

[x] Compare Syr: Heb lacks *And the women said* [y] Syr: Heb *them*
46: Is 19; Ezek 29-32; Zech 14.18-19.

Cär'chẹ̇·mish and which Ne·bụ̇·chȧd-
rez'zȧr king of Babylon defeated in the
fourth year of Je·hoi'ȧ·kim the son of
Jō·sī'ȧh, king of Judah:
3 "Prepare buckler and shield,
and advance for battle!
4 Harness the horses;
mount, O horsemen!
Take your stations with your helmets,
polish your spears,
put on your coats of mail!
5 Why have I seen it?
They are dismayed
and have turned backward.
Their warriors are beaten down,
and have fled in haste;
they look not back—
terror on every side!
says the LORD.
6 The swift cannot flee away,
nor the warrior escape;
in the north by the river Eū·phrā'tēṡ
they have stumbled and fallen.

7 "Who is this, rising like the Nile,
like rivers whose waters surge?
8 Egypt rises like the Nile,
like rivers whose waters surge.
He said, I will rise, I will cover the earth,
I will destroy cities and their inhabitants.
9 Advance, O horses,
and rage, O chariots!
Let the warriors go forth:
men of Ethiopia and Püt who handle the shield,
men of Lüd, skilled in handling the bow.
10 That day is the day of the Lord GOD of hosts,
a day of vengeance,
to avenge himself on his foes.
The sword shall devour and be sated,
and drink its fill of their blood.
For the LORD GOD of hosts holds a sacrifice
in the north country by the river Eū·phrā'tēṡ.
11 Go up to Gilead, and take balm,
O virgin daughter of Egypt!
In vain you have used many medicines;
there is no healing for you.
12 The nations have heard of your shame,
and the earth is full of your cry;
for warrior has stumbled against warrior;
they have both fallen together."

13 The word which the LORD spoke
to Jeremiah the prophet about the
coming of Ne·bụ̇·chȧd·rez'zȧr king of
Babylon to smite the land of Egypt:
14 "Declare in Egypt, and proclaim in Mig'dōl;
proclaim in Memphis and Täh'pȧn·hēṡ;
Say, 'Stand ready and be prepared,
for the sword shall devour round about you.'
15 Why has Ā'pis fled?[z]
Why did not your bull stand?
Because the LORD thrust him down.
16 Your multitude stumbled[a] and fell,
and they said one to another,
'Arise, and let us go back to our own people
and to the land of our birth,
because of the sword of the oppressor.'
17 Call the name of Pharaoh, king of Egypt,
'Noisy one who lets the hour go by.'

18 "As I live, says the King,
whose name is the LORD of hosts,
like Tā'bôr among the mountains,
and like Cär'mẹ̇l by the sea, shall one come.
19 Prepare yourselves baggage for exile,
O inhabitants of Egypt!
For Memphis shall become a waste,
a ruin, without inhabitant.

20 "A beautiful heifer is Egypt,
but a gadfly from the north has come upon her.
21 Even her hired soldiers in her midst
are like fatted calves;
yea, they have turned and fled together,
they did not stand;
for the day of their calamity has come upon them,
the time of their punishment.

22 "She makes a sound like a serpent gliding away;
for her enemies march in force,
and come against her with axes,
like those who fell trees.

[z] Gk: Heb *Why was it swept away* [a] Gk: Heb *He made many stumble*
46.5: Ps 31.13; Jer 6.25; 20.3, 10; 49.29.

23 They shall cut down her forest,
says the LORD,
though it is impenetrable,
because they are more numerous
than locusts;
they are without number.
24 The daughter of Egypt shall be put
to shame,
she shall be delivered into the hand
of a people from the north."

25 The LORD of hosts, the God of
Israel, said: "Behold, I am bringing
punishment upon Ā'mon of Thebes,
and Pharaoh, and Egypt and her gods
and her kings, upon Pharaoh and those
who trust in him. 26 I will deliver them
into the hand of those who seek their
life, into the hand of Ne·bu̇·chȧd·rez'-
zȧr king of Babylon and his officers.
Afterward Egypt shall be inhabited as
in the days of old, says the LORD.

27 "But fear not, O Jacob my servant,
nor be dismayed, O Israel;
for lo, I will save you from afar,
and your offspring from the land
of their captivity.
Jacob shall return and have quiet
and ease,
and none shall make him afraid.
28 Fear not, O Jacob my servant,
says the LORD,
for I am with you.
I will make a full end of all the
nations
to which I have driven you,
but of you I will not make a full end.
I will chasten you in just measure,
and I will by no means leave you
unpunished."

47 The word of the LORD that
came to Jeremiah the prophet
concerning the Philistines, before
Pharaoh smote Gā'zȧ.
2 "Thus says the LORD:
Behold, waters are rising out of the
north,
and shall become an overflowing
torrent;
they shall overflow the land and all
that fills it,
the city and those who dwell in it.
Men shall cry out,
and every inhabitant of the land
shall wail.
3 At the noise of the stamping of the
hoofs of his stallions,
at the rushing of his chariots, at
the rumbling of their wheels,
the fathers look not back to their
children,
so feeble are their hands,
4 because of the day that is coming
to destroy
all the Philistines,
to cut off from Tȳre and Sī'don
every helper that remains.
For the LORD is destroying the
Philistines,
the remnant of the coastland of
Caph'tor.
5 Baldness has come upon Gā'zȧ,
Ash'kė·lon has perished.
O remnant of the An'ȧ·kim,[b]
how long will you gash yourselves?
6 Ah, sword of the LORD!
How long till you are quiet?
Put yourself into your scabbard,
rest and be still!
7 How can it[c] be quiet,
when the LORD has given it a
charge?
Against Ash'kė·lon and against the
seashore
he has appointed it."

48 Concerning Mō'ab.
Thus says the LORD of hosts, the
God of Israel:
"Woe to Nē'bō, for it is laid waste!
Kīr·i·ȧ·thā'im is put to shame, it
is taken;
the fortress is put to shame and
broken down;
2 the renown of Mō'ab is no more.
In Hesh'bȯn they planned evil
against her:
'Come, let us cut her off from
being a nation!'
You also, O Madmen, shall be
brought to silence;
the sword shall pursue you.

3 "Hark! a cry from Hor·ō·nā'im,
'Desolation and great destruction!'
4 Mō'ab is destroyed;
a cry is heard as far as Zō'är.[d]
5 For at the ascent of Lū'hith
they go up weeping;[e]
for at the descent of Hor·ō·nā'im

[b] Gk: Heb *their valley* [c] Gk Vg: Heb *you* [d] Gk: Heb *her little ones*
[e] Cn: Heb *weeping goes up with weeping*
47: Is 14.29-31; Ezek 25.15-17; Amos 1.6-8; Zeph 2.4-7; Zech 9.5-7.
48: Is 15-16; 25.10-12; Ezek 25.8-11; Amos 2.1-3; Zeph 2.8-11.

they have heard the cry[f] of destruction.
6 Flee! Save yourselves!
Be like a wild ass[g] in the desert!
7 For, because you trusted in your
strongholds[h] and your treasures,
you also shall be taken;
and Chē'mosh shall go forth into
exile,
with his priests and his princes.
8 The destroyer shall come upon every
city,
and no city shall escape;
the valley shall perish,
and the plain shall be destroyed,
as the LORD has spoken.

9 "Give wings to Mō'ab,
for she would fly away;
her cities shall become a desolation,
with no inhabitant in them.

10 "Cursed is he who does the work of the LORD with slackness; and cursed is he who keeps back his sword from bloodshed.

11 "Mō'ab has been at ease from his
youth
and has settled on his lees;
he has not been emptied from vessel
to vessel,
nor has he gone into exile;
so his taste remains in him,
and his scent is not changed.

12 "Therefore, behold, the days are
coming, says the LORD, when I shall
send to him tilters who will tilt him,
and empty his vessels, and break his[i]
jars in pieces. 13 Then Mō'ab shall be
ashamed of Chē'mosh, as the house of
Israel was ashamed of Beth'ĕl, their
confidence.

14 "How do you say, 'We are heroes
and mighty men of war'?
15 The destroyer of Mō'ab and his
cities has come up,
and the choicest of his young men
have gone down to slaughter,
says the King, whose name is the
LORD of hosts.
16 The calamity of Mō'ab is near at
hand
and his affliction hastens apace.
17 Bemoan him, all you who are round
about him,
and all who know his name;
say, 'How the mighty scepter is
broken,
the glorious staff.'

18 "Come down from your glory,
and sit on the parched ground,
O inhabitant of Dī'bon!
For the destroyer of Mō'ab has come
up against you;
he has destroyed your strongholds.
19 Stand by the way and watch,
O inhabitant of A·rō'ĕr!
Ask him who flees and her who
escapes;
say, 'What has happened?'
20 Mō'ab is put to shame, for it is
broken;
wail and cry!
Tell it by the Är'non,
that Moab is laid waste.

21 "Judgment has come upon the
tableland, upon Hō'lon, and Jäh'zȧh,
and Meph'ȧ-ath, 22 and Dī'bon, and
Nē'bō, and Beth-dib·lȧ·thā'im, 23 and
Kīr·i·ȧ·thā'im, and Beth-gā'mul, and
Beth-mē'on, 24 and Ker'i·oth, and
Boz'rȧh, and all the cities of the land
of Mō'ab, far and near. 25 The horn of
Mō'ab is cut off, and his arm is broken,
says the LORD.

26 "Make him drunk, because he
magnified himself against the LORD;
so that Mō'ab shall wallow in his
vomit, and he too shall be held in
derision. 27 Was not Israel a derision
to you? Was he found among thieves,
that whenever you spoke of him you
wagged your head?

28 "Leave the cities, and dwell in the
rock,
O inhabitants of Mō'ab!
Be like the dove that nests
in the sides of the mouth of a
gorge.
29 We have heard of the pride of
Mō'ab—
he is very proud—
of his loftiness, his pride, and his
arrogance,
and the haughtiness of his heart.
30 I know his insolence, says the LORD;
his boasts are false,
his deeds are false.
31 Therefore I wail for Mō'ab;
I cry out for all Moab;
for the men of Kīr-hē'res I mourn.

[f] Gk Compare Is 15.5: Heb *the distress of the cry* [g] Gk Aquila: Heb *like Aroer* [h] Gk: Heb *works*
[i] Gk Aquila: Heb *their*

32 More than for Jā'zėr I weep for
you,
O vine of Sib'māh!
Your branches passed over the sea,
reached as far as Jazer;[j]
upon your summer fruits and your
vintage
the destroyer has fallen.
33 Gladness and joy have been taken
away
from the fruitful land of Mō'ab;
I have made the wine cease from
the wine presses;
no one treads them with shouts
of joy;
the shouting is not the shout of
joy.

34 "Hesh'bȯn and E·lė·ā'lėh cry
out;[k] as far as Jā'haz they utter their
voice, from Zō'ăr to Hor·ō·nā'im and
Eg'lăth-she·lish'i·yȧh. For the waters
of Nim'rim also have become desolate.
35 And I will bring to an end in Mō'ab,
says the LORD, him who offers sacrifice
in the high place and burns incense to
his god. 36 Therefore my heart moans
for Mō'ab like a flute, and my heart
moans like a flute for the men of Kīr-
hē'res; therefore the riches they gained
have perished.
37 "For every head is shaved and
every beard cut off; upon all the hands
are gashes, and on the loins is sackcloth. 38 On all the housetops of Mō'ab
and in the squares there is nothing but
lamentations; for I have broken Moab
like a vessel for which no one cares,
says the LORD. 39 How it is broken!
How they wail! How Mō'ab has turned
his back in shame! So Moab has become a derision and a horror to all that
are round about him."
40 For thus says the LORD:
"Behold, one shall fly swiftly like
an eagle,
and spread his wings against
Mō'ab;
41 the cities shall be taken
and the strongholds seized.
The heart of the warriors of Mō'ab
shall be in that day
like the heart of a woman in her
pangs;
42 Mō'ab shall be destroyed and be
no longer a people,
because he magnified himself
against the LORD.
43 Terror, pit, and snare
are before you, O inhabitant of
Mō'ab!
says the LORD.
44 He who flees from the terror
shall fall into the pit,
and he who climbs out of the pit
shall be caught in the snare.
For I will bring these things[l] upon
Mō'ab
in the year of their punishment,
says the LORD.

45 "In the shadow of Hesh'bȯn
fugitives stop without strength;
for a fire has gone forth from
Heshbon,
a flame from the house of Sī'hon;
it has destroyed the forehead of
Mō'ab,
the crown of the sons of tumult.
46 Woe to you, O Mō'ab!
The people of Chē'mosh is undone;
for your sons have been taken
captive,
and your daughters into captivity.
47 Yet I will restore the fortunes of
Mō'ab
in the latter days, says the LORD."
Thus far is the judgment on Mō'ab.

49 Concerning the Am'mȯ·nītes.
Thus says the LORD:
"Has Israel no sons?
Has he no heir?
Why then has Mil'com dispossessed
Gad,
and his people settled in its cities?
2 Therefore, behold, the days are
coming,
says the LORD,
when I will cause the battle cry to
be heard
against Rab'bȧh of the Am'mȯ-
nītes;
it shall become a desolate mound,
and its villages shall be burned
with fire;
then Israel shall dispossess those
who dispossessed him,
says the LORD.

3 "Wail, O Hesh'bȯn, for Ăi is laid
waste!
Cry, O daughters of Rab'bȧh!
Gird yourselves with sackcloth,
lament, and run to and fro among
the hedges!
For Mil'com shall go into exile,

[j] Cn: Heb *the sea of Jazer* [k] Cn: Heb *From the cry of Heshbon to Elealeh* [l] Gk Syr: Heb *to her*
49.1-6: Ezek 21.28-32; 25.1-7; Amos 1.13-15; Zeph 2.8-11.

with his priests and his princes.
4 Why do you boast of your valleys,[m]
O faithless daughter,
who trusted in her treasures, saying,
'Who will come against me?'
5 Behold, I will bring terror upon you,
says the Lord GOD of hosts,
from all who are round about you,
and you shall be driven out, every man straight before him,
with none to gather the fugitives.
6 But afterward I will restore the
fortunes of the Am'mo·nites, says the
LORD."

7 Concerning E'dom.
Thus says the LORD of hosts:
"Is wisdom no more in Te'man?
Has counsel perished from the prudent?
Has their wisdom vanished?
8 Flee, turn back, dwell in the depths,
O inhabitants of De'dan!
For I will bring the calamity of Esau upon him,
the time when I punish him.
9 If grape-gatherers came to you,
would they not leave gleanings?
If thieves came by night,
would they not destroy only enough for themselves?
10 But I have stripped Esau bare,
I have uncovered his hiding places,
and he is not able to conceal himself.
His children are destroyed, and his brothers,
and his neighbors; and he is no more.
11 Leave your fatherless children, I will keep them alive;
and let your widows trust in me."
12 For thus says the LORD: "If
those who did not deserve to drink the
cup must drink it, will you go unpunished? You shall not go unpunished, but you must drink. 13 For I
have sworn by myself, says the LORD,
that Boz'rah shall become a horror, a
taunt, a waste, and a curse; and all her
cities shall be perpetual wastes."
14 I have heard tidings from the LORD,
and a messenger has been sent among the nations:
"Gather yourselves together and come against her,
and rise up for battle!"
15 For behold, I will make you small among the nations,
despised among men.
16 The horror you inspire has deceived you,
and the pride of your heart,
you who live in the clefts of the rock,[n]
who hold the height of the hill.
Though you make your nest as high as the eagle's,
I will bring you down from there,
says the LORD.
17 "E'dom shall become a horror;
every one who passes by it will be
horrified and will hiss because of all
its disasters. 18 As when Sod'om and
Go·mor'rah and their neighbor cities
were overthrown, says the LORD, no
man shall dwell there, no man shall
sojourn in her. 19 Behold, like a lion
coming up from the jungle of the
Jordan against a strong sheepfold, I
will suddenly make them[o] run away
from her; and I will appoint over her
whomever I choose. For who is like
me? Who will summon me? What
shepherd can stand before me?
20 Therefore hear the plan which the
LORD has made against E'dom and the
purposes which he has formed against
the inhabitants of Te'man: Even the
little ones of the flock shall be dragged
away; surely their fold shall be
appalled at their fate. 21 At the sound
of their fall the earth shall tremble; the
sound of their cry shall be heard at the
Red Sea. 22 Behold, one shall mount
up and fly swiftly like an eagle, and
spread his wings against Boz'rah, and
the heart of the warriors of E'dom shall
be in that day like the heart of a
woman in her pangs."

23 Concerning Damascus.
"Ha'math and Ar'pad are confounded,
for they have heard evil tidings;
they melt in fear, they are troubled like the sea[p]
which cannot be quiet.
24 Damascus has become feeble, she turned to flee,
and panic seized her;
anguish and sorrows have taken hold of her,
as of a woman in travail.

[m] Heb *valleys, your valley flows* [n] Or *Sela* [o] Gk Syr: Heb *him* [p] Cn: Heb *there is trouble in the sea*
49.7-22: Is 34; 63.1-6; Ezek 25.12-14; 35; Amos 1.11-12; Obad; Mal 1.2-5.
49.23-27: Is 17.1-3; Amos 1.3-5; Zech 9.1.

25 How the famous city is forsaken,[q]
the joyful city![r]
26 Therefore her young men shall fall
in her squares,
and all her soldiers shall be destroyed in that day,
says the LORD of hosts.
27 And I will kindle a fire in the wall
of Damascus,
and it shall devour the strongholds of Ben-hā'dad."

28 Concerning Kē'där and the kingdoms of Hā'zôr which Ne·bu·chad'rez'zar king of Babylon smote.
Thus says the LORD:
"Rise up, advance against Kedar!
Destroy the people of the east!
29 Their tents and their flocks shall be
taken,
their curtains and all their goods;
their camels shall be borne away
from them,
and men shall cry to them:
'Terror on every side!'
30 Flee, wander far away, dwell in the
depths,
O inhabitants of Hā'zôr!
says the LORD.
For Ne·bu·chad·rez'zar king of
Babylon
has made a plan against you,
and formed a purpose against
you.

31 "Rise up, advance against a nation
at ease,
that dwells securely,
says the LORD,
that has no gates or bars,
that dwells alone.
32 Their camels shall become booty,
their herds of cattle a spoil.
I will scatter to every wind
those who cut the corners of their
hair,
an I will bring their calamity
from every side of them,
says the LORD.
33 Hā'zôr shall become a haunt of
jackals,
an everlasting waste;
no man shall dwell there,
no man shall sojourn in her."

34 The word of the LORD that came to Jeremiah the prophet concerning Ē'lam, in the beginning of the reign of Zed·e·kī'ah king of Judah.

35 Thus says the LORD of hosts:
"Behold, I will break the bow of
Ē'lam, the mainstay of their might;
36 and I will bring upon Ē'lam the
four winds from the four quarters of
heaven; and I will scatter them to all
those winds, and there shall be no
nation to which those driven out of
Elam shall not come. 37 I will terrify
Ē'lam before their enemies, and before
those who seek their life; I will bring
evil upon them, my fierce anger, says
the LORD. I will send the sword after
them, until I have consumed them;
38 and I will set my throne in Ē'lam,
and destroy their king and princes,
says the LORD.
39 "But in the latter days I will
restore the fortunes of Ē'lam, says the
LORD."

50

The word which the LORD spoke concerning Babylon, concerning the land of the Chal·dē'ans, by Jeremiah the prophet:
2 "Declare among the nations and
proclaim,
set up a banner and proclaim,
conceal it not, and say:
'Babylon is taken,
Bel is put to shame,
Mer'o·dach is dismayed.
Her images are put to shame,
her idols are dismayed.'
3 "For out of the north a nation has
come up against her, which shall make
her land a desolation, and none shall
dwell in it; both man and beast shall
flee away.

4 "In those days and in that time,
says the LORD, the people of Israel and
the people of Judah shall come together, weeping as they come; and
they shall seek the LORD their God.
5 They shall ask the way to Zion, with
faces turned toward it, saying, 'Come,
let us join ourselves to the LORD in an
everlasting covenant which will never
be forgotten.'

6 "My people have been lost sheep;
their shepherds have led them astray,
turning them away on the mountains;
from mountain to hill they have gone,
they have forgotten their fold. 7 All
who found them have devoured them,
and their enemies have said, 'We are
not guilty, for they have sinned against

[q] Vg: Heb *not forsaken* [r] Syr Vg Tg: Heb *city of my joy*
49.29: Ps 31.13; Jer 6.25; 20.3, 10; 46.5. **50-51:** Is 13.1-14.23; 47; Hab 1-2.

the LORD, their true habitation, the
LORD, the hope of their fathers.'

8 "Flee from the midst of Babylon,
and go out of the land of the Chal·dē′-
ȧnṡ, and be as he-goats before the
flock. 9 For behold, I am stirring up
and bringing against Babylon a company of great nations, from the north
country; and they shall array themselves against her; from there she shall
be taken. Their arrows are like a skilled
warrior who does not return empty-
handed. 10 Chal·dē′ȧ shall be plundered; all who plunder her shall be
sated, says the LORD.

11 "Though you rejoice, though you
exult,
O plunderers of my heritage,
though you are wanton as a heifer
at grass,
and neigh like stallions,
12 your mother shall be utterly shamed,
and she who bore you shall be
disgraced.
Lo, she shall be the last of the
nations,
a wilderness dry and desert.
13 Because of the wrath of the LORD
she shall not be inhabited,
but shall be an utter desolation;
every one who passes by Babylon
shall be appalled,
and hiss because of all her
wounds.
14 Set yourselves in array against
Babylon round about,
all you that bend the bow;
shoot at her, spare no arrows,
for she has sinned against the
LORD.
15 Raise a shout against her round
about,
she has surrendered;
her bulwarks have fallen,
her walls are thrown down.
For this is the vengeance of the
LORD:
take vengeance on her,
do to her as she has done.
16 Cut off from Babylon the sower,
and the one who handles the
sickle in time of harvest;
because of the sword of the oppressor,
every one shall turn to his own
people,
and every one shall flee to his own
land.

17 "Israel is a hunted sheep driven
away by lions. First the king of
Assyria devoured him, and now at last
Ne·bu̇·chȧd·rez′zȧr king of Babylon
has gnawed his bones. 18 Therefore,
thus says the LORD of hosts, the God
of Israel: Behold, I am bringing punishment on the king of Babylon and
his land, as I punished the king of
Assyria. 19 I will restore Israel to his
pasture, and he shall feed on Cär′mėl
and in Bā′shȧn, and his desire shall be
satisfied on the hills of Ē′phrȧ·im and
in Gilead. 20 In those days and in that
time, says the LORD, iniquity shall be
sought in Israel, and there shall be
none; and sin in Judah, and none shall
be found; for I will pardon those whom
I leave as a remnant.

21 "Go up against the land of Mer·ȧ-
thā′im,[s]
and against the inhabitants of
Pē′kod.[t]
Slay, and utterly destroy after
them,
says the LORD,
and do all that I have commanded
you.
22 The noise of battle is in the land,
and great destruction!
23 How the hammer of the whole
earth
is cut down and broken!
How Babylon has become
a horror among the nations!
24 I set a snare for you and you were
taken, O Babylon,
and you did not know it;
you were found and caught,
because you strove against the
LORD.
25 The LORD has opened his armory,
and brought out the weapons of
his wrath,
for the Lord GOD of hosts has a
work to do
in the land of the Chal·dē′ȧnṡ.
26 Come against her from every
quarter;
open her granaries;
pile her up like heaps of grain, and
destroy her utterly;
let nothing be left of her.
27 Slay all her bulls,
let them go down to the slaughter.

[s] Or *Double Rebellion* [t] Or *Punishment*
50.8: Jer 51.6, 9, 45; 2 Cor 6.17; Rev 18.4.

Woe to them, for their day has come,
the time of their punishment.

28 "Hark! they flee and escape from
the land of Babylon, to declare in Zion
the vengeance of the LORD our God,
vengeance for his temple.

29 "Summon archers against Babylon, all those who bend the bow. Encamp round about her; let no one
escape. Requite her according to her
deeds, do to her according to all that
she has done; for she has proudly
defied the LORD, the Holy One of
Israel. 30 Therefore her young men
shall fall in her squares, and all her
soldiers shall be destroyed on that day,
says the LORD.

31 "Behold, I am against you, O proud one,
says the Lord GOD of hosts;
for your day has come,
the time when I will punish you.
32 The proud one shall stumble and fall,
with none to raise him up,
and I will kindle a fire in his cities,
and it will devour all that is round about him.

33 "Thus says the LORD of hosts:
The people of Israel are oppressed,
and the people of Judah with them;
all who took them captive have held
them fast, they refuse to let them go.
34 Their Redeemer is strong; the LORD
of hosts is his name. He will surely
plead their cause, that he may give rest
to the earth, but unrest to the inhabitants of Babylon.

35 "A sword upon the Chal·dē′ȧnṡ,
says the LORD,
and upon the inhabitants of Babylon,
and upon her princes and her wise men!
36 A sword upon the diviners,
that they may become fools!
A sword upon her warriors,
that they may be destroyed!
37 A sword upon her horses and upon her chariots,
and upon all the foreign troops in her midst,
that they may become women!
A sword upon all her treasures,
that they may be plundered!
38 A drought upon her waters,
that they may be dried up!
For it is a land of images,
and they are mad over idols.

39 "Therefore wild beasts shall
dwell with hyenas in Babylon, and
ostriches shall dwell in her; she shall
be peopled no more for ever, nor inhabited for all generations. 40As when
God overthrew Sod′ŏm and Gȯ·môr′-
rȧh and their neighbor cities, says the
LORD, so no man shall dwell there, and
no son of man shall sojourn in her.

41 "Behold, a people comes from the north;
a mighty nation and many kings
are stirring from the farthest parts of the earth.
42 They lay hold of bow and spear;
they are cruel, and have no mercy.
The sound of them is like the roaring of the sea;
they ride upon horses,
arrayed as a man for battle
against you, O daughter of Babylon!

43 "The king of Babylon heard the report of them,
and his hands fell helpless;
anguish seized him,
pain as of a woman in travail.

44 "Behold, like a lion coming up
from the jungle of the Jordan against
a strong sheepfold, I will suddenly
make them run away from her; and I
will appoint over her whomever I
choose. For who is like me? Who will
summon me? What shepherd can
stand before me? 45 Therefore hear the
plan which the LORD has made against
Babylon, and the purposes which he
has formed against the land of the
Chal·dē′ȧnṡ: Surely the little ones of
their flock shall be dragged away;
surely their fold shall be appalled at
their fate. 46At the sound of the capture
of Babylon the earth shall tremble,
and her cry shall be heard among the
nations."

51 Thus says the LORD:
"Behold, I will stir up the spirit of a destroyer
against Babylon,
against the inhabitants of Chal-dē′ȧ;[u]

[u] Heb *Leb-qamai*, a cipher for Chaldea

2 and I will send to Babylon winnowers,
and they shall winnow her,
and they shall empty her land,
when they come against her from every side
on the day of trouble.
3 Let not the archer bend his bow,
and let him not stand up in his coat of mail.
Spare not her young men;
utterly destroy all her host.
4 They shall fall down slain in the land of the Chal·dē'ăns,
and wounded in her streets.
5 For Israel and Judah have not been forsaken
by their God, the LORD of hosts;
but the land of the Chal·dē'ăns[v] is full of guilt
against the Holy One of Israel.

6 "Flee from the midst of Babylon,
let every man save his life!
Be not cut off in her punishment,
for this is the time of the LORD's vengeance,
the requital he is rendering her.
7 Babylon was a golden cup in the LORD's hand,
making all the earth drunken;
the nations drank of her wine,
therefore the nations went mad.
8 Suddenly Babylon has fallen and been broken;
wail for her!
Take balm for her pain;
perhaps she may be healed.
9 We would have healed Babylon,
but she was not healed.
Forsake her, and let us go
each to his own country;
for her judgment has reached up to heaven
and has been lifted up even to the skies.
10 The LORD has brought forth our vindication;
come, let us declare in Zion
the work of the LORD our God.

11 "Sharpen the arrows!
Take up the shields!
The LORD has stirred up the spirit of
the kings of the Medes, because his
purpose concerning Babylon is to destroy it, for that is the vengeance of
the LORD, the vengeance for his temple.

12 Set up a standard against the walls of Babylon;
make the watch strong;
set up watchmen;
prepare the ambushes;
for the LORD has both planned and done
what he spoke concerning the inhabitants of Babylon.
13 O you who dwell by many waters,
rich in treasures,
your end has come,
the thread of your life is cut.
14 The LORD of hosts has sworn by himself;
Surely I will fill you with men, as many as locusts,
and they shall raise the shout of victory over you.

15 "It is he who made the earth by his power,
who established the world by his wisdom,
and by his understanding
stretched out the heavens.
16 When he utters his voice there is a tumult of waters in the heavens,
and he makes the mist rise from the ends of the earth.
He makes lightnings for the rain,
and he brings forth the wind from his storehouses.
17 Every man is stupid and without knowledge;
every goldsmith is put to shame by his idols;
for his images are false,
and there is no breath in them.
18 They are worthless, a work of delusion;
at the time of their punishment they shall perish.
19 Not like these is he who is the portion of Jacob,
for he is the one who formed all things,
and Israel is the tribe of his inheritance;
the LORD of hosts is his name.

20 "You are my hammer and weapon of war:
with you I break nations in pieces;
with you I destroy kingdoms;
21 with you I break in pieces the horse and his rider;

[v] Heb *their land*

51.6, 9, 45: Jer 50.8; 2 Cor 6.17; Rev 18.4. 51.7-8: Jer 25.15; Rev 14.8, 10; 16.19; 17.4; 18.3.
51.13: Rev 17.1.

with you I break in pieces the chariot and the charioteer;
22 with you I break in pieces man and woman;
with you I break in pieces the old man and the youth;
with you I break in pieces the young man and the maiden;
23 with you I break in pieces the shepherd and his flock;
with you I break in pieces the farmer and his team;
with you I break in pieces governors and commanders.

24 "I will requite Babylon and all the inhabitants of Chal·dē′à before your very eyes for all the evil that they have done in Zion, says the LORD.

25 "Behold, I am against you, O destroying mountain,
says the LORD,
which destroys the whole earth;
I will stretch out my hand against you,
and roll you down from the crags,
and make you a burnt mountain.
26 No stone shall be taken from you for a corner
and no stone for a foundation,
but you shall be a perpetual waste,
says the LORD.

27 "Set up a standard on the earth,
blow the trumpet among the nations;
prepare the nations for war against her,
summon against her the kingdoms,
Ar′à·rat, Min′nī, and Ash′kė·naz;
appoint a marshal against her,
bring up horses like bristling locusts.
28 Prepare the nations for war against her,
the kings of the Medes, with their governors and deputies,
and every land under their dominion.
29 The land trembles and writhes in pain,
for the LORD's purposes against Babylon stand,
to make the land of Babylon a desolation,
without inhabitant.
30 The warriors of Babylon have ceased fighting,
they remain in their strongholds;
their strength has failed,
they have become women;
her dwellings are on fire,
her bars are broken.
31 One runner runs to meet another,
and one messenger to meet another,
to tell the king of Babylon
that his city is taken on every side;
32 the fords have been seized,
the bulwarks are burned with fire,
and the soldiers are in panic.
33 For thus says the LORD of hosts, the God of Israel:
The daughter of Babylon is like a threshing floor
at the time when it is trodden;
yet a little while
and the time of her harvest will come."

34 "Ne·bu̇·chad·rez′zȧr the king of Babylon has devoured me,
he has crushed me;
he has made me an empty vessel,
he has swallowed me like a monster;
he has filled his belly with my delicacies,
he has rinsed me out.
35 The violence done to me and to my kinsmen be upon Babylon,"
let the inhabitant of Zion say.
"My blood be upon the inhabitants of Chal·dē′ȧ,"
let Jerusalem say.
36 Therefore thus says the LORD:
"Behold, I will plead your cause
and take vengeance for you.
I will dry up her sea
and make her fountain dry;
37 and Babylon shall become a heap of ruins,
the haunt of jackals,
a horror and a hissing,
without inhabitant.

38 "They shall roar together like lions;
they shall growl like lions' whelps.
39 While they are inflamed I will prepare them a feast
and make them drunk, till they swoon away[w]
and sleep a perpetual sleep
and not wake, says the LORD.
40 I will bring them down like lambs to the slaughter,
like rams and he-goats.

[w] Gk Vg: Heb *rejoice*

41 "How Babylon[x] is taken,
the praise of the whole earth seized!
How Babylon has become
a horror among the nations!
42 The sea has come up on Babylon;
she is covered with its tumultuous waves.
43 Her cities have become a horror,
a land of drought and a desert,
a land in which no one dwells,
and through which no son of man passes.
44 And I will punish Bel in Babylon,
and take out of his mouth what he has swallowed.
The nations shall no longer flow to him;
the wall of Babylon has fallen.

45 "Go out of the midst of her, my people!
Let every man save his life
from the fierce anger of the LORD!
46 Let not your heart faint, and be not fearful
at the report heard in the land,
when a report comes in one year
and afterward a report in another year,
and violence is in the land,
and ruler is against ruler.

47 "Therefore, behold, the days are coming
when I will punish the images of Babylon;
her whole land shall be put to shame,
and all her slain shall fall in the midst of her.
48 Then the heavens and the earth,
and all that is in them,
shall sing for joy over Babylon;
for the destroyers shall come
against them out of the north,
says the LORD.
49 Babylon must fall for the slain of Israel,
as for Babylon have fallen the slain of all the earth.

50 "You that have escaped from the sword,
go, stand not still!
Remember the LORD from afar,
and let Jerusalem come into your mind:
51 'We are put to shame, for we have heard reproach;
dishonor has covered our face,
for aliens have come
into the holy places of the LORD's house.'

52 "Therefore, behold, the days are coming, says the LORD,
when I will execute judgment upon her images,
and through all her land
the wounded shall groan.
53 Though Babylon should mount up to heaven,
and though she should fortify her strong height,
yet destroyers would come from me upon her,
says the LORD.

54 "Hark! a cry from Babylon!
The noise of great destruction
from the land of the Chal·dē'ȧns!
55 For the LORD is laying Babylon waste,
and stilling her mighty voice.
Their waves roar like many waters,
the noise of their voice is raised;
56 for a destroyer has come upon her,
upon Babylon;
her warriors are taken,
their bows are broken in pieces;
for the LORD is a God of recompense,
he will surely requite.
57 I will make drunk her princes and her wise men,
her governors, her commanders,
and her warriors;
they shall sleep a perpetual sleep
and not wake,
says the King, whose name is the LORD of hosts.

58 "Thus says the LORD of hosts:
The broad wall of Babylon
shall be leveled to the ground
and her high gates
shall be burned with fire.
The peoples labor for nought,
and the nations weary themselves
only for fire."

59 The word which Jeremiah the
prophet commanded Se·räi'ȧh the son
of Ne·rī'ȧh, son of Mäh·sēi'ȧh, when
he went with Zed·ė·kī'ȧh king of Judah
to Babylon, in the fourth year of his
reign. Seraiah was the quartermaster.

x Heb *Sheshach*, a cipher for Babylon
51.48: Is 44.23; Rev 12.12; 18.20.

60 Jeremiah wrote in a book all the
evil that should come upon Babylon,
all these words that are written concerning Babylon. 61 And Jeremiah said
to Se·rāi'ȧh: "When you come to
Babylon, see that you read all these
words, 62 and say, 'O LORD, thou hast
said concerning this place that thou
wilt cut it off, so that nothing shall
dwell in it, neither man nor beast, and
it shall be desolate for ever.' 63 When
you finish reading this book, bind a
stone to it, and cast it into the midst
of the Eū·phrā'tēs, 64 and say, 'Thus
shall Babylon sink, to rise no more,
because of the evil that I am bringing
upon her.' "[y]

Thus far are the words of Jeremiah.

52 Zed·ė·kī'ȧh was twenty-one
years old when he became king;
and he reigned eleven years in Jerusalem. His mother's name was Hȧ·mü'-
tal the daughter of Jeremiah of
Lib'nȧh. 2 And he did what was evil in
the sight of the LORD, according to all
that Je·hoi'ȧ·kim had done. 3 Surely
because of the anger of the LORD
things came to such a pass in Jerusalem
and Judah that he cast them out from
his presence.

And Zed·ė·kī'ȧh rebelled against the
king of Babylon. 4 And in the ninth
year of his reign, in the tenth month,
on the tenth day of the month,
Ne·bu̇·chȧd·rez'zȧr king of Babylon
came with all his army against Jerusalem, and they laid siege to it and
built siegeworks against it round about.
5 So the city was besieged till the
eleventh year of King Zed·ė·kī'ȧh.
6 On the ninth day of the fourth
month the famine was so severe in the
city, that there was no food for the
people of the land. 7 Then a breach
was made in the city; and all the men
of war fled and went out from the city
by night by the way of a gate between
the two walls, by the king's garden,
while the Chal·dē'ȧnṡ were round
about the city. And they went in the
direction of the Ar'ȧ·bȧh. 8 But the
army of the Chal·dē'ȧnṡ pursued the
king, and overtook Zed·ė·kī'ȧh in the
plains of Jericho; and all his army was
scattered from him. 9 Then they captured the king, and brought him up
to the king of Babylon at Rib'lȧh in
the land of Hā'math, and he passed
sentence upon him. 10 The king of
Babylon slew the sons of Zed·ė·kī'ȧh
before his eyes, and also slew all the
princes of Judah at Rib'lȧh. 11 He put
out the eyes of Zed·ė·kī'ȧh, and bound
him in fetters, and the king of Babylon
took him to Babylon, and put him in
prison till the day of his death.

12 In the fifth month, on the tenth
day of the month—which was the
nineteenth year of King Ne·bu̇·chȧd-
rez'zȧr, king of Babylon—Ne·bū'zȧ-
rad'ȧn the captain of the bodyguard
who served the king of Babylon,
entered Jerusalem. 13 And he burned
the house of the LORD, and the king's
house and all the houses of Jerusalem;
every great house he burned down.
14 And all the army of the Chal·dē'ȧnṡ,
who were with the captain of the
guard, broke down all the walls round
about Jerusalem. 15 And Ne·bū'zȧ-
rad'ȧn the captain of the guard carried
away captive some of the poorest of
the people and the rest of the people
who were left in the city and the
deserters who had deserted to the king
of Babylon, together with the rest of
the artisans. 16 But Ne·bū'zȧ·rad'ȧn
the captain of the guard left some of
the poorest of the land to be vinedressers and plowmen.

17 And the pillars of bronze that
were in the house of the LORD, and the
stands and the bronze sea that were in
the house of the LORD, the Chal·dē'ȧnṡ
broke in pieces, and carried all the
bronze to Babylon. 18 And they took
away the pots, and the shovels, and
the snuffers, and the basins, and the
dishes for incense, and all the vessels
of bronze used in the temple service;
19 also the small bowls, and the firepans, and the basins, and the pots, and
the lampstands, and the dishes for
incense, and the bowls for libation.
What was of gold the captain of the
guard took away as gold, and what was
of silver, as silver. 20 As for the two
pillars, the one sea, the twelve bronze
bulls which were under the sea,[z] and
the stands, which Solomon the king
had made for the house of the LORD,
the bronze of all these things was beyond weight. 21 As for the pillars, the
height of the one pillar was eighteen
cubits, its circumference was twelve
cubits, and its thickness was four

[y] Gk: Heb *upon her. And they shall weary themselves* [z] Heb lacks *the sea*

51.63-64: Rev 18.21. **52:** 2 Kings 24.18-25.30; 2 Chron 36.11-13.

fingers, and it was hollow. 22 Upon it
was a capital of bronze; the height of
the one capital was five cubits; a network and pomegranates, all of bronze,
were upon the capital round about.
And the second pillar had the like,
with pomegranates. 23 There were
ninety-six pomegranates on the sides;
all the pomegranates were a hundred
upon the network round about.
24 And the captain of the guard
took Se·räi′ȧh the chief priest, and
Zeph·ȧ·nī′ȧh the second priest, and
the three keepers of the threshold;
25 and from the city he took an officer
who had been in command of the men
of war, and seven men of the king's
council, who were found in the city;
and the secretary of the commander
of the army who mustered the people
of the land; and sixty men of the people of the land, who were found in the
midst of the city. 26 And Ne·bū′zȧ-
rad′ȧn the captain of the guard took
them, and brought them to the king of
Babylon at Rib′lȧh. 27 And the king of
Babylon smote them, and put them to
death at Rib′lȧh in the land of Hā′-
math. So Judah was carried captive
out of its land.
28 This is the number of the people
whom Ne·bů·chȧd·rez′zȧr carried away
captive: in the seventh year, three
thousand and twenty-three Jews; 29 in
the eighteenth year of Ne·bů·chȧd-
rez′zȧr he carried away captive from
Jerusalem eight hundred and thirty-
two persons; 30 in the twenty-third
year of Ne·bů·chȧd·rez′zȧr, Ne·bū′zȧ-
rad′ȧn the captain of the guard carried
away captive of the Jews seven hundred and forty-five persons; all the
persons were four thousand and six
hundred.
31 And in the thirty-seventh year of
the captivity of Je·hoi′ȧ·chin king of
Judah, in the twelfth month, on the
twenty-fifth day of the month, E′vil-
mer′ō·dach king of Babylon, in the
year that he became king, lifted up the
head of Je·hoi′ȧ·chin king of Judah
and brought him out of prison; 32 and
he spoke kindly to him, and gave him
a seat above the seats of the kings who
were with him in Babylon. 33 So
Je·hoi′ȧ·chin put off his prison garments. And every day of his life he
dined regularly at the king's table;
34 as for his allowance, a regular
allowance was given him by the king
according to his daily need, until the
day of his death as long as he lived.

THE LAMENTATIONS

OF JEREMIAH

1 How lonely sits the city
that was full of people!
How like a widow has she become,
she that was great among the nations!
She that was a princess among the cities
has become a vassal.

2 She weeps bitterly in the night,
tears on her cheeks;
among all her lovers
she has none to comfort her;
all her friends have dealt treacherously with her,
they have become her enemies.

3 Judah has gone into exile because of affliction
and hard servitude;
she dwells now among the nations,
but finds no resting place;
her pursuers have all overtaken her
in the midst of her distress.

4 The roads to Zion mourn,
for none come to the appointed feasts;
all her gates are desolate,
her priests groan;
her maidens have been dragged away,[a]
and she herself suffers bitterly.

5 Her foes have become the head,

[a] Gk Old Latin: Heb *afflicted*

her enemies prosper,
because the LORD has made her suffer
for the multitude of her transgressions;
her children have gone away,
captives before the foe.

6 From the daughter of Zion has departed
all her majesty.
Her princes have become like harts
that find no pasture;
they fled without strength
before the pursuer.

7 Jerusalem remembers
in the days of her affliction and bitterness[b]
all the precious things
that were hers from days of old.
When her people fell into the hand of the foe,
and there was none to help her,
the foe gloated over her,
mocking at her downfall.

8 Jerusalem sinned grievously,
therefore she became filthy;
all who honored her despise her,
for they have seen her nakedness;
yea, she herself groans,
and turns her face away.

9 Her uncleanness was in her skirts;
she took no thought of her doom;
therefore her fall is terrible,
she has no comforter.
"O LORD, behold my affliction,
for the enemy has triumphed!"

10 The enemy has stretched out his hands
over all her precious things;
yea, she has seen the nations
invade her sanctuary,
those whom thou didst forbid
to enter thy congregation.

11 All her people groan
as they search for bread;
they trade their treasures for food
to revive their strength.
"Look, O LORD, and behold,
for I am despised."

12 "Is it nothing to you,[c] all you who pass by?
Look and see
if there is any sorrow like my sorrow
which was brought upon me,
which the LORD inflicted
on the day of his fierce anger.

13 "From on high he sent fire;
into my bones[d] he made it descend;
he spread a net for my feet;
he turned me back;
he has left me stunned,
faint all the day long.

14 "My transgressions were bound[e] into a yoke;
by his hand they were fastened together;
they were set upon my neck;
he caused my strength to fail;
the Lord gave me into the hands
of those whom I cannot withstand.

15 "The LORD flouted all my mighty men
in the midst of me;
he summoned an assembly against me
to crush my young men;
the Lord has trodden as in a wine press
the virgin daughter of Judah.

16 "For these things I weep;
my eyes flow with tears;
for a comforter is far from me,
one to revive my courage;
my children are desolate,
for the enemy has prevailed."

17 Zion stretches out her hands,
but there is none to comfort her;
the LORD has commanded against Jacob
that his neighbors should be his foes;
Jerusalem has become
a filthy thing among them.

18 "The LORD is in the right,
for I have rebelled against his word;
but hear, all you peoples,
and behold my suffering;
my maidens and my young men
have gone into captivity.

19 "I called to my lovers
but they deceived me;
my priests and elders
perished in the city,

[b] Cn: Heb *wandering* [c] Heb uncertain [d] Gk: Heb *bones and* [e] Cn: Heb uncertain

while they sought food
to revive their strength.

20 "Behold, O LORD, for I am in distress,
my soul is in tumult,
my heart is wrung within me,
because I have been very rebellious.
In the street the sword bereaves;
in the house it is like death.

21 "Hear[f] how I groan;
there is none to comfort me.
All my enemies have heard of my trouble;
they are glad that thou hast done it.
Bring thou[g] the day thou hast announced,
and let them be as I am.

22 "Let all their evil doing come before thee;
and deal with them
as thou hast dealt with me
because of all my transgressions;
for my groans are many
and my heart is faint."

2 How the Lord in his anger
has set the daughter of Zion under a cloud!
He has cast down from heaven to earth
the splendor of Israel;
he has not remembered his footstool
in the day of his anger.

2 The Lord has destroyed without mercy
all the habitations of Jacob;
in his wrath he has broken down
the strongholds of the daughter of Judah;
he has brought down to the ground in dishonor
the kingdom and its rulers.

3 He has cut down in fierce anger
all the might of Israel;
he has withdrawn from them his right hand
in the face of the enemy;
he has burned like a flaming fire in Jacob,
consuming all around.

4 He has bent his bow like an enemy,
with his right hand set like a foe;
and he has slain all the pride of our eyes
in the tent of the daughter of Zion;
he has poured out his fury like fire.

5 The Lord has become like an enemy,
he has destroyed Israel;
he has destroyed all its palaces,
laid in ruins its strongholds;
and he has multiplied in the daughter of Judah
mourning and lamentation.

6 He has broken down his booth like that of a garden,
laid in ruins the place of his appointed feasts;
the LORD has brought to an end in Zion
appointed feast and sabbath,
and in his fierce indignation has spurned
king and priest.

7 The Lord has scorned his altar,
disowned his sanctuary;
he has delivered into the hand of the enemy
the walls of her palaces;
a clamor was raised in the house of the LORD
as on the day of an appointed feast.

8 The LORD determined to lay in ruins
the wall of the daughter of Zion;
he marked it off by the line;
he restrained not his hand from destroying;
he caused rampart and wall to lament,
they languish together.

9 Her gates have sunk into the ground;
he has ruined and broken her bars;
her king and princes are among the nations;
the law is no more,
and her prophets obtain
no vision from the LORD.

10 The elders of the daughter of Zion
sit on the ground in silence;
they have cast dust on their heads
and put on sackcloth;
the maidens of Jerusalem

[f] Gk Syr: Heb *they heard* [g] Syr: Heb *thou hast brought*

have bowed their heads to the
ground.

11 My eyes are spent with weeping;
my soul is in tumult;
my heart is poured out in grief[h]
because of the destruction of the
daughter of my people,
because infants and babes faint
in the streets of the city.

12 They cry to their mothers,
"Where is bread and wine?"
as they faint like wounded men
in the streets of the city,
as their life is poured out
on their mothers' bosom.

13 What can I say for you, to what
compare you,
O daughter of Jerusalem?
What can I liken to you, that I may
comfort you,
O virgin daughter of Zion?
For vast as the sea is your ruin;
who can restore you?

14 Your prophets have seen for you
false and deceptive visions;
they have not exposed your iniquity
to restore your fortunes,
but have seen for you oracles
false and misleading.

15 All who pass along the way
clap their hands at you;
they hiss and wag their heads
at the daughter of Jerusalem;
"Is this the city which was called
the perfection of beauty,
the joy of all the earth?"

16 All your enemies
rail against you;
they hiss, they gnash their teeth,
they cry: "We have destroyed her!
Ah, this is the day we longed for;
now we have it; we see it!"

17 The LORD has done what he purposed,
has carried out his threat;
as he ordained long ago,
he has demolished without pity;
he has made the enemy rejoice over
you,
and exalted the might of your
foes.

18 Cry aloud[i] to the Lord!
O[j] daughter of Zion!
Let tears stream down like a torrent
day and night!
Give yourself no rest,
your eyes no respite!

19 Arise, cry out in the night,
at the beginning of the watches!
Pour out your heart like water
before the presence of the Lord!
Lift your hands to him
for the lives of your children,
who faint for hunger
at the head of every street.

20 Look, O LORD, and see!
With whom hast thou dealt thus?
Should women eat their offspring,
the children of their tender care?
Should priest and prophet be slain
in the sanctuary of the Lord?

21 In the dust of the streets
lie the young and the old;
my maidens and my young men
have fallen by the sword;
in the day of thy anger thou hast
slain them,
slaughtering without mercy.

22 Thou didst invite as to the day of
an appointed feast
my terrors on every side;
and on the day of the anger of the
LORD
none escaped or survived;
those whom I dandled and reared
my enemy destroyed.

3 I am the man who has seen
affliction
under the rod of his wrath;
2 he has driven and brought me
into darkness without any light;
3 surely against me he turns his hand
again and again the whole day
long.

4 He has made my flesh and my skin
waste away,
and broken my bones;
5 he has besieged and enveloped me
with bitterness and tribulation;
6 he has made me dwell in darkness
like the dead of long ago.

7 He has walled me about so that I
cannot escape;
he has put heavy chains on me;
8 though I call and cry for help,

[h] Heb *to the ground* [i] Cn: Heb *Their heart cried* [j] Cn: Heb *O wall of*

he shuts out my prayer,
9 he has blocked my ways with hewn stones,
he has made my paths crooked.

10 He is to me like a bear lying in wait,
like a lion in hiding;
11 he led me off my way and tore me to pieces;
he has made me desolate;
12 he bent his bow and set me
as a mark for his arrow.

13 He drove into my heart
the arrows of his quiver;
14 I have become the laughingstock of all peoples,
the burden of their songs all day long.
15 He has filled me with bitterness,
he has sated me with wormwood.

16 He has made my teeth grind on gravel,
and made me cower in ashes;
17 my soul is bereft of peace,
I have forgotten what happiness is;
18 so I say, "Gone is my glory,
and my expectation from the LORD."

19 Remember my affliction and my bitterness,[k]
the wormwood and the gall!
20 My soul continually thinks of it
and is bowed down within me.
21 But this I call to mind,
and therefore I have hope:

22 The steadfast love of the LORD never ceases,[l]
his mercies never come to an end;
23 they are new every morning;
great is thy faithfulness.
24 "The LORD is my portion," says my soul,
"therefore I will hope in him."

25 The LORD is good to those who wait for him,
to the soul that seeks him.
26 It is good that one should wait quietly
for the salvation of the LORD.
27 It is good for a man that he bear
the yoke in his youth.

28 Let him sit alone in silence
when he has laid it on him;
29 let him put his mouth in the dust—
there may yet be hope;
30 let him give his cheek to the smiter,
and be filled with insults.

31 For the Lord will not
cast off for ever,
32 but, though he cause grief, he will have compassion
according to the abundance of his steadfast love;
33 for he does not willingly afflict
or grieve the sons of men.

34 To crush under foot
all the prisoners of the earth,
35 to turn aside the right of a man
in the presence of the Most High,
36 to subvert a man in his cause,
the Lord does not approve.

37 Who has commanded and it came to pass,
unless the Lord has ordained it?
38 Is it not from the mouth of the Most High
that good and evil come?
39 Why should a living man complain,
a man, about the punishment of his sins?

40 Let us test and examine our ways,
and return to the LORD!
41 Let us lift up our hearts and hands
to God in heaven:
42 "We have transgressed and rebelled,
and thou hast not forgiven.

43 "Thou hast wrapped thyself with anger and pursued us,
slaying without pity;
44 thou hast wrapped thyself with a cloud
so that no prayer can pass through.
45 Thou hast made us offscouring and refuse
among the peoples.

46 "All our enemies
rail against us;
47 panic and pitfall have come upon us,
devastation and destruction;
48 my eyes flow with rivers of tears
because of the destruction of the daughter of my people.

49 "My eyes will flow without ceasing,
without respite,
50 until the LORD from heaven
looks down and sees;

[k] Cn: Heb *wandering* [l] Syr Tg: Heb *we are not cut off*

51 my eyes cause me grief
at the fate of all the maidens of my city.

52 "I have been hunted like a bird
by those who were my enemies without cause;
53 they flung me alive into the pit
and cast stones on me;
54 water closed over my head;
I said, 'I am lost.'

55 "I called on thy name, O LORD,
from the depths of the pit;
56 thou didst hear my plea, 'Do not close
thine ear to my cry for help!'[m]
57 Thou didst come near when I called on thee;
thou didst say, 'Do not fear!'

58 "Thou hast taken up my cause, O Lord,
thou hast redeemed my life.
59 Thou hast seen the wrong done to me, O LORD;
judge thou my cause.
60 Thou hast seen all their vengeance,
all their devices against me.

61 "Thou hast heard their taunts, O LORD,
all their devices against me.
62 The lips and thoughts of my assailants
are against me all the day long.
63 Behold their sitting and their rising;
I am the burden of their songs.

64 "Thou wilt requite them, O LORD,
according to the work of their hands.
65 Thou wilt give them dullness of heart;
thy curse will be on them
66 Thou wilt pursue them in anger and destroy them
from under thy heavens, O LORD."[n]

4 How the gold has grown dim,
how the pure gold is changed!
The holy stones lie scattered
at the head of every street.

2 The precious sons of Zion,
worth their weight in fine gold,
how they are reckoned as earthen pots,
the work of a potter's hands!

3 Even the jackals give the breast
and suckle their young,
but the daughter of my people has become cruel,
like the ostriches in the wilderness.

4 The tongue of the nursling cleaves
to the roof of its mouth for thirst;
the children beg for food,
but no one gives to them.

5 Those who feasted on dainties
perish in the streets;
those who were brought up in purple
lie on ash heaps.

6 For the chastisement[o] of the daughter of my people has been greater
than the punishment[p] of Sod'om,
which was overthrown in a moment,
no hand being laid on it.[q]

7 Her princes were purer than snow,
whiter than milk;
their bodies were more ruddy than coral,
the beauty of their form[r] was like sapphire.[s]

8 Now their visage is blacker than soot,
they are not recognized in the streets;
their skin has shriveled upon their bones,
it has become as dry wood.

9 Happier were the victims of the sword
than the victims of hunger,
who pined away, stricken
by want of the fruits of the field.

10 The hands of compassionate women
have boiled their own children;
they became their food
in the destruction of the daughter of my people.

11 The LORD gave full vent to his wrath,
he poured out his hot anger;

[m] Heb uncertain [n] Syr Compare Gk Vg: Heb *the heavens of the* LORD [o] Or *iniquity* [p] Or *sin*
[q] Heb uncertain [r] Heb uncertain [s] Heb *lapis lazuli*

and he kindled a fire in Zion,
which consumed its foundations.

12 The kings of the earth did not believe,
or any of the inhabitants of the world,
that foe or enemy could enter
the gates of Jerusalem.

13 This was for the sins of her prophets
and the iniquities of her priests,
who shed in the midst of her
the blood of the righteous.

14 They wandered, blind, through the streets,
so defiled with blood
that none could touch
their garments.

15 "Away! Unclean!" men cried at them;
"Away! Away! Touch not!"
So they became fugitives and wanderers;
men said among the nations,
"They shall stay with us no longer."

16 The LORD himself has scattered them,
he will regard them no more;
no honor was shown to the priests,
no favor to the elders.

17 Our eyes failed, ever watching
vainly for help;
in our watching[t] we watched
for a nation which could not save.

18 Men dogged our steps
so that we could not walk in our streets;
our end drew near; our days were numbered;
for our end had come.

19 Our pursuers were swifter
than the vultures in the heavens;
they chased us on the mountains,
they lay in wait for us in the wilderness.

20 The breath of our nostrils, the LORD's anointed,
was taken in their pits,
he of whom we said, "Under his shadow
we shall live among the nations."

21 Rejoice and be glad, O daughter of E'dom,
dweller in the land of Uz;
but to you also the cup shall pass;
you shall become drunk and strip yourself bare.

22 The punishment of your iniquity, O daughter of Zion, is accomplished,
he will keep you in exile no longer;
but your iniquity, O daughter of E'dom, he will punish,
he will uncover your sins.

5 Remember, O LORD, what has befallen us;
behold, and see our disgrace!
2 Our inheritance has been turned over to strangers,
our homes to aliens.
3 We have become orphans, fatherless;
our mothers are like widows.
4 We must pay for the water we drink,
the wood we get must be bought.
5 With a yoke[u] on our necks we are hard driven;
we are weary, we are given no rest.
6 We have given the hand to Egypt,
and to Assyria, to get bread enough.
7 Our fathers sinned, and are no more;
and we bear their iniquities.
8 Slaves rule over us;
there is none to deliver us from their hand.
9 We get our bread at the peril of our lives,
because of the sword in the wilderness.
10 Our skin is hot as an oven
with the burning heat of famine.
11 Women are ravished in Zion,
virgins in the towns of Judah.
12 Princes are hung up by their hands;
no respect is shown to the elders.
13 Young men are compelled to grind at the mill;
and boys stagger under loads of wood.
14 The old men have quit the city gate,
the young men their music.
15 The joy of our hearts has ceased;
our dancing has been turned to mourning.
16 The crown has fallen from our head;
woe to us, for we have sinned!
17 For this our heart has become sick,

[t] Heb uncertain [u] Symmachus: Heb lacks *with a yoke*

for these things our eyes have
grown dim,
18 for Mount Zion which lies desolate;
jackals prowl over it.

19 But thou, O LORD, dost reign for
ever;
thy throne endures to all generations.
20 Why dost thou forget us for ever,
why dost thou so long forsake
us?
21 Restore us to thyself, O LORD, that
we may be restored!
Renew our days as of old!
22 Or hast thou utterly rejected us?
Art thou exceedingly angry with
us?

THE BOOK OF
EZEKIEL

1 In the thirtieth year, in the fourth
month, on the fifth day of the
month, as I was among the exiles by
the river Chē'bär, the heavens were
opened, and I saw visions of God.
2 On the fifth day of the month (it was
the fifth year of the exile of King
Je·hoi'ȧ·chin), 3 the word of the LORD
came to E·zēk'i·ėl the priest, the son
of Bū'zī, in the land of the Chal·dē'-
ȧnṡ by the river Chē'bär; and the hand
of the LORD was upon him there.
4 As I looked, behold, a stormy
wind came out of the north, and a great
cloud, with brightness round about it,
and fire flashing forth continually, and
in the midst of the fire, as it were
gleaming bronze. 5And from the midst
of it came the likeness of four living
creatures. And this was their appearance: they had the form of men, 6 but
each had four faces, and each of them
had four wings. 7 Their legs were
straight, and the soles of their feet
were like the sole of a calf's foot; and
they sparkled like burnished bronze.
8 Under their wings on their four sides
they had human hands. And the four
had their faces and their wings thus:
9 their wings touched one another;
they went every one straight forward,
without turning as they went. 10As for
the likeness of their faces, each had
the face of a man in front;[a] the four had
the face of a lion on the right side, the
four had the face of an ox on the left
side, and the four had the face of an
eagle at the back.[b] 11 Such were their
faces. And their wings were spread out
above; each creature had two wings,
each of which touched the wing of
another, while two covered their
bodies. 12And each went straight forward; wherever the spirit would go,
they went, without turning as they
went. 13 In the midst of[c] the living
creatures there was something that
looked like burning coals of fire, like
torches moving to and fro among the
living creatures; and the fire was bright,
and out of the fire went forth lightning.
14And the living creatures darted to
and fro, like a flash of lightning.
15 Now as I looked at the living
creatures, I saw a wheel upon the
earth beside the living creatures, one
for each of the four of them.[d] 16As for
the appearance of the wheels and their
construction: their appearance was like
the gleaming of a chrysolite; and the
four had the same likeness, their construction being as it were a wheel
within a wheel. 17 When they went,
they went in any of their four directions[e] without turning as they went.
18 The four wheels had rims and they
had spokes;[f] and their rims were full
of eyes round about. 19And when the
living creatures went, the wheels went
beside them; and when the living
creatures rose from the earth, the
wheels rose. 20 Wherever the spirit
would go, they went, and the wheels
rose along with them; for the spirit of
the living creatures was in the wheels.
21 When those went, these went; and

[a] Cn: Heb lacks *in front* [b] Cn: Heb lacks *at the back* [c] Gk Old Latin: Heb *And the likeness of*
[d] Heb *of their faces* [e] Heb *on their four sides* [f] Cn: Heb uncertain

1.1: Rev 19.11. **1.5, 18:** Rev 4.6. **1.10:** Rev 4.7. **1.13:** Rev 4.5. **1.18:** Ezek 10.12; Rev 4.8.

when those stood, these stood; and
when those rose from the earth, the
wheels rose along with them; for the
spirit of the living creatures was in the
wheels.

22 Over the heads of the living
creatures there was the likeness of a
firmament, shining like crystal,[g] spread
out above their heads. 23 And under
the firmament their wings were
stretched out straight, one toward
another; and each creature had two
wings covering its body. 24 And when
they went, I heard the sound of their
wings like the sound of many waters,
like the thunder of the Almighty, a
sound of tumult like the sound of a
host; when they stood still, they let
down their wings. 25 And there came
a voice from above the firmament over
their heads; when they stood still, they
let down their wings.

26 And above the firmament over
their heads there was the likeness of a
throne, in appearance like sapphire;[h]
and seated above the likeness of a
throne was a likeness as it were of
a human form. 27 And upward from
what had the appearance of his loins
I saw as it were gleaming bronze, like
the appearance of fire enclosed round
about; and downward from what had
the appearance of his loins I saw as it
were the appearance of fire, and there
was brightness round about him.[i]
28 Like the appearance of the bow that
is in the cloud on the day of rain, so
was the appearance of the brightness
round about.

Such was the appearance of the likeness of the glory of the LORD. And
when I saw it, I fell upon my face, and
I heard the voice of one speaking.

2 And he said to me, "Son of man,
stand upon your feet, and I will
speak with you." 2 And when he spoke
to me, the Spirit entered into me and
set me upon my feet; and I heard him
speaking to me. 3 And he said to me,
"Son of man, I send you to the people
of Israel, to a nation[j] of rebels, who
have rebelled against me; they and
their fathers have transgressed against
me to this very day. 4 The people also
are impudent and stubborn: I send you
to them; and you shall say to them,
'Thus says the Lord GOD.' 5 And
whether they hear or refuse to hear
(for they are a rebellious house) they
will know that there has been a prophet
among them. 6 And you, son of man,
be not afraid of them, nor be afraid of
their words, though briers and thorns
are with you and you sit upon scorpions; be not afraid of their words, nor
be dismayed at their looks, for they
are a rebellious house. 7 And you shall
speak my words to them, whether they
hear or refuse to hear; for they are a
rebellious house.

8 "But you, son of man, hear what
I say to you; be not rebellious like that
rebellious house; open your mouth,
and eat what I give you." 9 And when
I looked, behold, a hand was stretched
out to me, and, lo, a written scroll was
in it; 10 and he spread it before me;
and it had writing on the front and on
the back, and there were written on it
words of lamentation and mourning
3 and woe. 1 And he said to me, "Son
of man, eat what is offered to you;
eat this scroll, and go, speak to the
house of Israel." 2 So I opened my
mouth, and he gave me the scroll to
eat. 3 And he said to me, "Son of man,
eat this scroll that I give you and fill
your stomach with it." Then I ate it;
and it was in my mouth as sweet as
honey.

4 And he said to me, "Son of man,
go, get you to the house of Israel, and
speak with my words to them. 5 For
you are not sent to a people of foreign
speech and a hard language, but to the
house of Israel— 6 not to many peoples of foreign speech and a hard
language, whose words you cannot
understand. Surely, if I sent you to
such, they would listen to you. 7 But
the house of Israel will not listen to
you; for they are not willing to listen
to me; because all the house of Israel
are of a hard forehead and of a stubborn heart. 8 Behold, I have made
your face hard against their faces, and
your forehead hard against their foreheads. 9 Like adamant harder than
flint have I made your forehead; fear
them not, nor be dismayed at their
looks, for they are a rebellious house."
10 Moreover he said to me, "Son of
man, all my words that I shall speak
to you receive in your heart, and hear
with your ears. 11 And go, get you to
the exiles, to your people, and say to
them, 'Thus says the Lord GOD';
whether they hear or refuse to hear."

[g] Gk: Heb *awesome crystal* [h] Heb *lapis lazuli* [i] Or *it* [j] Syr: Heb *nations*

1.24: Ezek 43.2; Rev 1.15: 14.2; 19.6. **1.26:** Rev 1.13; 4.2. **2.8-3.3:** Rev 5.1; 10.8-10.

12 Then the Spirit lifted me up,
and as the glory of the LORD arose[k]
from its place, I heard behind me the
sound of a great earthquake; 13 it was
the sound of the wings of the living
creatures as they touched one another,
and the sound of the wheels beside
them, that sounded like a great earthquake. 14 The Spirit lifted me up and
took me away, and I went in bitterness
in the heat of my spirit, the hand of
the LORD being strong upon me; 15 and
I came to the exiles at Tel-ā'bib, who
dwelt by the river Chē'bär.[l] And I sat
there overwhelmed among them seven
days.

16 And at the end of seven days,
the word of the LORD came to me:
17 "Son of man, I have made you a
watchman for the house of Israel;
whenever you hear a word from my
mouth, you shall give them warning
from me. 18 If I say to the wicked,
'You shall surely die,' and you give
him no warning, nor speak to warn
the wicked from his wicked way, in
order to save his life, that wicked man
shall die in his iniquity; but his blood
I will require at your hand. 19 But if
you warn the wicked, and he does not
turn from his wickedness, or from his
wicked way, he shall die in his iniquity;
but you will have saved your life.
20 Again, if a righteous man turns from
his righteousness and commits iniquity, and I lay a stumbling block
before him, he shall die; because you
have not warned him, he shall die for
his sin, and his righteous deeds which
he has done shall not be remembered;
but his blood I will require at your
hand. 21 Nevertheless if you warn the
righteous man not to sin, and he does
not sin, he shall surely live, because he
took warning; and you will have saved
your life."

22 And the hand of the LORD was
there upon me; and he said to me,
"Arise, go forth into the plain,[m] and
there I will speak with you." 23 So I
arose and went forth into the plain;[m]
and, lo, the glory of the LORD stood
there, like the glory which I had seen
by the river Chē'bär; and I fell on my
face. 24 But the Spirit entered into me,
and set me upon my feet; and he spoke
with me and said to me, "Go, shut
yourself within your house. 25 And
you, O son of man, behold, cords will
be placed upon you, and you shall be
bound with them, so that you cannot
go out among the people; 26 and I will
make your tongue cleave to the roof
of your mouth, so that you shall be
dumb and unable to reprove them; for
they are a rebellious house. 27 But
when I speak with you, I will open
your mouth, and you shall say to them,
'Thus says the Lord GOD'; he that
will hear, let him hear; and he that
will refuse to hear, let him refuse; for
they are a rebellious house.

4 "And you, O son of man, take a
brick and lay it before you, and
portray upon it a city, even Jerusalem;
2 and put siegeworks against it, and
build a siege wall against it, and cast
up a mound against it; set camps also
against it, and plant battering rams
against it round about. 3 And take an
iron plate, and place it as an iron wall
between you and the city; and set your
face toward it, and let it be a state of
siege, and press the siege against it.
This is a sign for the house of Israel.

4 "Then lie upon your left side, and
I will lay the punishment of the house
of Israel upon you;[n] for the number of
the days that you lie upon it, you shall
bear their punishment. 5 For I assign
to you a number of days, three hundred and ninety days, equal to the
number of the years of their punishment; so long shall you bear the punishment of the house of Israel. 6 And
when you have completed these, you
shall lie down a second time, but on
your right side, and bear the punishment of the house of Judah; forty days
I assign you, a day for each year. 7 And
you shall set your face toward the
siege of Jerusalem, with your arm
bared; and you shall prophesy against
the city. 8 And, behold, I will put cords
upon you, so that you cannot turn
from one side to the other, till you have
completed the days of your siege.

9 "And you, take wheat and barley,
beans and lentils, millet and spelt, and
put them into a single vessel, and make
bread of them. During the number of
days that you lie upon your side, three
hundred and ninety days, you shall eat
it. 10 And the food which you eat shall

[k] Cn: Heb *blessed be the glory of the* LORD
[l] Heb *Chebar, and to where they dwelt*. Another reading is *Chebar, and I sat where they sat* [m] Or *valley*
[n] Cn: Heb *you shall lay . . . upon it*
3.16-21: Ezek 33.1-9.

be by weight, twenty shekels a day;
once a day you shall eat it. 11 And
water you shall drink by measure, the
sixth part of a hin; once a day you shall
drink. 12 And you shall eat it as a barley
cake, baking it in their sight on human
dung." 13 And the LORD said, "Thus
shall the people of Israel eat their
bread unclean, among the nations
whither I will drive them." 14 Then I
said, "Ah Lord GOD! behold, I have
never defiled myself; from my youth
up till now I have never eaten what
died of itself or was torn by beasts,
nor has foul flesh come into my
mouth." 15 Then he said to me, "See,
I will let you have cow's dung instead
of human dung, on which you may
prepare your bread." 16 Moreover he
said to me, "Son of man, behold, I
will break the staff of bread in Jerusalem; they shall eat bread by weight
and with fearfulness; and they shall
drink water by measure and in dismay.
17 I will do this that they may lack
bread and water, and look at one
another in dismay, and waste away
under their punishment.

5 "And you, O son of man, take a
sharp sword; use it as a barber's
razor and pass it over your head and
your beard; then take balances for
weighing, and divide the hair. 2 A third
part you shall burn in the fire in the
midst of the city, when the days of the
siege are completed; and a third part
you shall take and strike with the
sword round about the city; and a
third part you shall scatter to the wind,
and I will unsheathe the sword after
them. 3 And you shall take from these
a small number, and bind them in the
skirts of your robe. 4 And of these again
you shall take some, and cast them
into the fire, and burn them in the fire;
from there a fire will come forth into
all the house of Israel. 5 Thus says the
Lord GOD: This is Jerusalem; I have
set her in the center of the nations,
with countries round about her. 6 And
she has wickedly rebelled against my
ordinances[o] more than the nations, and
against my statutes more than the
countries round about her, by rejecting
my ordinances and not walking in my
statutes. 7 Therefore thus says the
Lord GOD: Because you are more
turbulent than the nations that are
round about you, and have not walked
in my statutes or kept my ordinances,
but have acted[p] according to the
ordinances of the nations that are
round about you; 8 therefore thus says
the Lord GOD: Behold, I, even I, am
against you; and I will execute judgments in the midst of you in the sight
of the nations. 9 And because of all
your abominations I will do with you
what I have never yet done, and the
like of which I will never do again.
10 Therefore fathers shall eat their sons
in the midst of you, and sons shall eat
their fathers; and I will execute judgments on you, and any of you who
survive I will scatter to all the winds.
11 Wherefore, as I live, says the Lord
GOD, surely, because you have defiled
my sanctuary with all your detestable
things and with all your abominations,
therefore I will cut you down;[q] my eye
will not spare, and I will have no pity.
12 A third part of you shall die of pestilence and be consumed with famine in
the midst of you; a third part shall fall
by the sword round about you; and a
third part I will scatter to all the winds
and will unsheathe the sword after
them.

13 "Thus shall my anger spend itself, and I will vent my fury upon them
and satisfy myself; and they shall know
that I, the LORD, have spoken in my
jealousy, when I spend my fury upon
them. 14 Moreover I will make you a
desolation and an object of reproach
among the nations round about you
and in the sight of all that pass by.
15 You shall be[r] a reproach and a taunt,
a warning and a horror, to the nations
round about you, when I execute
judgments on you in anger and fury,
and with furious chastisements—I, the
LORD, have spoken—16 when I loose
against you[s] my deadly arrows of
famine, arrows for destruction, which
I will loose to destroy you, and when
I bring more and more famine upon
you, and break your staff of bread. 17 I
will send famine and wild beasts
against you, and they will rob you of
your children; pestilence and blood
shall pass through you; and I will
bring the sword upon you. I, the LORD,
have spoken."

6 The word of the LORD came to
me: 2 "Son of man, set your face
toward the mountains of Israel, and
prophesy against them, 3 and say, You

[o] Or *changed my ordinances into wickedness* [p] Another reading is *and have not acted*
[q] Another reading is *I will withdraw* [r] Gk Syr Vg Tg: Heb *And it shall be* [s] Heb *them*

mountains of Israel, hear the word of
the Lord GOD! Thus says the Lord
GOD to the mountains and the hills,
to the ravines and the valleys: Behold,
I, even I, will bring a sword upon you,
and I will destroy your high places.
4 Your altars shall become desolate,
and your incense altars shall be broken;
and I will cast down your slain before
your idols. 5And I will lay the dead
bodies of the people of Israel before
their idols; and I will scatter your
bones round about your altars.
6 Wherever you dwell your cities shall
be waste and your high places ruined,
so that your altars will be waste and
ruined,[t] your idols broken and destroyed, your incense altars cut down,
and your works wiped out. 7And the
slain shall fall in the midst of you, and
you shall know that I am the LORD.
8 "Yet I will leave some of you
alive. When you have among the
nations some who escape the sword,
and when you are scattered through
the countries, 9 then those of you who
escape will remember me among the
nations where they are carried captive,
when I have broken[u] their wanton
heart which has departed from me,
and blinded their eyes which turn
wantonly after their idols; and they
will be loathsome in their own sight
for the evils which they have committed, for all their abominations.
10And they shall know that I am the
LORD; I have not said in vain that I
would do this evil to them."
11 Thus says the Lord GOD: "Clap
your hands, and stamp your foot, and
say, Alas! because of all the evil
abominations of the house of Israel;
for they shall fall by the sword, by
famine, and by pestilence. 12 He that
is far off shall die of pestilence; and he
that is near shall fall by the sword; and
he that is left and is preserved shall die
of famine. Thus I will spend my fury
upon them. 13And you shall know that
I am the LORD, when their slain lie
among their idols round about their
altars, upon every high hill, on all the
mountain tops, under every green tree,
and under every leafy oak, wherever
they offered pleasing odor to all their
idols. 14And I will stretch out my hand
against them, and make the land
desolate and waste, throughout all
their habitations, from the wilderness
to Rib'lah.[v] Then they will know that
I am the LORD."

7 The word of the LORD came to
me: 2 "And you, O son of man,
thus says the Lord GOD to the land
of Israel: An end! The end has come
upon the four corners of the land.
3 Now the end is upon you, and I will
let loose my anger upon you, and will
judge you according to your ways; and
I will punish you for all your abominations. 4And my eye will not spare you,
nor will I have pity; but I will punish
you for your ways, while your abominations are in your midst. Then you
will know that I am the LORD.
5 "Thus says the Lord GOD: Disaster after disaster! Behold, it comes.
6An end has come, the end has come;
it has awakened against you. Behold,
it comes. 7 Your doom[w] has come to
you, O inhabitant of the land; the time
has come, the day is near, a day of
tumult, and not of joyful shouting
upon the mountains. 8 Now I will
soon pour out my wrath upon you,
and spend my anger against you, and
judge you according to your ways; and
I will punish you for all your abominations. 9And my eye will not spare,
nor will I have pity; I will punish you
according to your ways, while your
abominations are in your midst. Then
you will know that I am the LORD,
who smite.
10 "Behold, the day! Behold, it
comes! Your doom[w] has come, injustice[x] has blossomed, pride has
budded. 11 Violence has grown up into
a rod of wickedness; none of them shall
remain, nor their abundance, nor their
wealth; neither shall there be pre-
eminence among them.[y] 12 The time
has come, the day draws near. Let not
the buyer rejoice, nor the seller mourn,
for wrath is upon all their multitude.
13 For the seller shall not return to
what he has sold, while they live. For
wrath[z] is upon all their multitude; it
shall not turn back; and because of his
iniquity, none can maintain his life.[a]
14 "They have blown the trumpet
and made all ready; but none goes to
battle, for my wrath is upon all their
multitude. 15 The sword is without,

[t] Syr Vg Tg: Heb *and be made guilty* [u] Syr Vg Tg: Heb *I have been broken*
[v] Another reading is *Diblah* [w] The meaning of the Hebrew word is uncertain [x] Or *the rod*
[y] The Hebrew of verse 11 is uncertain [z] Cn: Heb *vision* [a] Heb obscure
6.9: Ezek 20.43; 36.31. **7.2**: Rev 7.1; 20.8.

pestilence and famine are within; he
that is in the field dies by the sword;
and him that is in the city famine
and pestilence devour. 16 And if any
survivors escape, they will be on the
mountains, like doves of the valleys,
all of them moaning, every one over
his iniquity. 17 All hands are feeble,
and all knees weak as water. 18 They
gird themselves with sackcloth, and
horror covers them; shame is upon all
faces, and baldness on all their heads.
19 They cast their silver into the
streets, and their gold is like an unclean
thing; their silver and gold are not able
to deliver them in the day of the wrath
of the LORD; they cannot satisfy their
hunger or fill their stomachs with it.
For it was the stumbling block of their
iniquity. 20 Their[b] beautiful ornament
they used for vainglory, and they made
their abominable images and their detestable things of it; therefore I will
make it an unclean thing to them.
21 And I will give it into the hands of
foreigners for a prey, and to the wicked
of the earth for a spoil; and they shall
profane it. 22 I will turn my face from
them, that they may profane my
precious[c] place; robbers shall enter
and profane it, 23 and make a desolation.[d]

"Because the land is full of bloody
crimes and the city is full of violence,
24 I will bring the worst of the nations
to take possession of their houses; I
will put an end to their proud might,
and their holy places shall be profaned.
25 When anguish comes, they will seek
peace, but there shall be none. 26 Disaster comes upon disaster, rumor
follows rumor; they seek a vision from
the prophet, but the law perishes from
the priest, and counsel from the elders.
27 The king mourns, the prince is
wrapped in despair, and the hands of
the people of the land are palsied by
terror. According to their way I will
do to them, and according to their own
judgments I will judge them; and they
shall know that I am the LORD."

8 In the sixth year, in the sixth
month, on the fifth day of the
month, as I sat in my house, with the
elders of Judah sitting before me, the
hand of the Lord GOD fell there upon
me. 2 Then I beheld, and, lo, a form
that had the appearance of a man;[e]
below what appeared to be his loins
it was fire, and above his loins it was
like the appearance of brightness, like
gleaming bronze. 3 He put forth the
form of a hand, and took me by a lock
of my head; and the Spirit lifted me
up between earth and heaven, and
brought me in visions of God to Jerusalem, to the entrance of the gateway
of the inner court that faces north,
where was the seat of the image of
jealousy, which provokes to jealousy.
4 And behold, the glory of the God of
Israel was there, like the vision that I
saw in the plain.

5 Then he said to me, "Son of man,
lift up your eyes now in the direction
of the north." So I lifted up my eyes
toward the north, and behold, north
of the altar gate, in the entrance, was
this image of jealousy. 6 And he said to
me, "Son of man, do you see what
they are doing, the great abominations
that the house of Israel are committing
here, to drive me far from my sanctuary? But you will see still greater
abominations."

7 And he brought me to the door of
the court; and when I looked, behold,
there was a hole in the wall. 8 Then
said he to me, "Son of man, dig in the
wall"; and when I dug in the wall, lo,
there was a door. 9 And he said to me,
"Go in, and see the vile abominations
that they are committing here." 10 So
I went in and saw; and there, portrayed
upon the wall round about, were all
kinds of creeping things, and loathsome beasts, and all the idols of the
house of Israel. 11 And before them
stood seventy men of the elders of the
house of Israel, with Jā-az·ȧ·nī'ȧh the
son of Shā'phȧn standing among them.
Each had his censer in his hand, and
the smoke of the cloud of incense went
up. 12 Then he said to me, "Son of
man, have you seen what the elders of
the house of Israel are doing in the
dark, every man in his room[f] of pic-
tures? For they say, 'The LORD does
not see us, the LORD has forsaken the
land.' " 13 He said also to me, "You
will see still greater abominations
which they commit."

14 Then he brought me to the entrance of the north gate of the house
of the LORD; and behold, there sat
women weeping for Täm'müz. 15 Then
he said to me, "Have you seen this, O

[b] Syr Symmachus: Heb *Its* [c] Or *secret* [d] Cn: Heb *make the chain* [e] Gk: Heb *fire*
[f] Gk Syr Vg Tg: Heb *rooms*

son of man? You will see still greater
abominations than these."
16 And he brought me into the
inner court of the house of the LORD;
and behold, at the door of the temple
of the LORD, between the porch and
the altar, were about twenty-five men,
with their backs to the temple of the
LORD, and their faces toward the east,
worshiping the sun toward the east.
17 Then he said to me, "Have you
seen this, O son of man? Is it too slight
a thing for the house of Judah to commit the abominations which they commit here, that they should fill the land
with violence, and provoke me further
to anger? Lo, they put the branch to
their nose. 18 Therefore I will deal in
wrath; my eye will not spare, nor will
I have pity; and though they cry in my
ears with a loud voice, I will not hear
them."

9 Then he cried in my ears with a
loud voice, saying, "Draw near,
you executioners of the city, each with
his destroying weapon in his hand."
2 And lo, six men came from the direction of the upper gate, which faces
north, every man with his weapon for
slaughter in his hand, and with them
was a man clothed in linen, with a
writing case at his side. And they went
in and stood beside the bronze altar.
3 Now the glory of the God of
Israel had gone up from the cherubim
on which it rested to the threshold of
the house; and he called to the man
clothed in linen, who had the writing
case at his side. 4 And the LORD said
to him, "Go through the city, through
Jerusalem, and put a mark upon the
foreheads of the men who sigh and
groan over all the abominations that
are committed in it." 5 And to the
others he said in my hearing, "Pass
through the city after him, and smite;
your eye shall not spare, and you shall
show no pity; 6 slay old men outright,
young men and maidens, little children
and women, but touch no one upon
whom is the mark. And begin at my
sanctuary." So they began with the
elders who were before the house.
7 Then he said to them, "Defile the
house, and fill the courts with the
slain. Go forth." So they went forth,
and smote in the city. 8 And while they
were smiting, and I was left alone, I
fell upon my face, and cried, "Ah
Lord GOD! wilt thou destroy all that
remains of Israel in the outpouring of
thy wrath upon Jerusalem?"
9 Then he said to me, "The guilt
of the house of Israel and Judah is
exceedingly great; the land is full of
blood, and the city full of injustice; for
they say, 'The LORD has forsaken the
land, and the LORD does not see.' 10 As
for me, my eye will not spare, nor will
I have pity, but I will requite their
deeds upon their heads."
11 And lo, the man clothed in linen,
with the writing case at his side,
brought back word, saying, "I have
done as thou didst command me."

10 Then I looked, and behold, on
the firmament that was over the
heads of the cherubim there appeared
above them something like a sapphire,
in form resembling a throne. 2 And he
said to the man clothed in linen, "Go
in among the whirling wheels underneath the cherubim; fill your hands
with burning coals from between the
cherubim, and scatter them over the
city."
And he went in before my eyes.
3 Now the cherubim were standing on
the south side of the house, when the
man went in; and a cloud filled the
inner court. 4 And the glory of the
LORD went up from the cherubim to
the threshold of the house; and the
house was filled with the cloud, and
the court was full of the brightness of
the glory of the LORD. 5 And the sound
of the wings of the cherubim was
heard as far as the outer court, like
the voice of God Almighty when he
speaks.
6 And when he commanded the
man clothed in linen, "Take fire from
between the whirling wheels, from between the cherubim," he went in and
stood beside a wheel. 7 And a cherub
stretched forth his hand from between
the cherubim to the fire that was
between the cherubim and took some
of it, and put it into the hands of the
man clothed in linen, who took it and
went out. 8 The cherubim appeared to
have the form of a human hand under
their wings.
9 And I looked, and behold, there
were four wheels beside the cherubim,
one beside each cherub; and the
appearance of the wheels was like
sparkling chrysolite. 10 And as for their
appearance, the four had the same
likeness, as if a wheel were within a

9.4, 6: 1 Pet 4.17; Rev 7.3; 9.4; 14.1. **10.1:** Rev 4.2. **10.2:** Rev 8.5.

wheel. 11 When they went, they went
in any of their four directions[g] without
turning as they went, but in whatever
direction the front wheel faced the
others followed without turning as
they went. 12And[h] their rims, and their
spokes,[i] and the wheels were full of
eyes round about—the wheels that the
four of them had. 13As for the wheels,
they were called in my hearing the
whirling wheels. 14And every one had
four faces: the first face was the face
of the cherub, and the second face was
the face of a man, and the third the
face of a lion, and the fourth the face
of an eagle.
15 And the cherubim mounted up.
These were the living creatures that I
saw by the river Chē'bär. 16And when
the cherubim went, the wheels went
beside them; and when the cherubim
lifted up their wings to mount up from
the earth, the wheels did not turn from
beside them. 17 When they stood still,
these stood still, and when they
mounted up, these mounted up with
them; for the spirit of the living
creatures[j] was in them.
18 Then the glory of the LORD
went forth from the threshold of the
house, and stood over the cherubim.
19And the cherubim lifted up their
wings and mounted up from the earth
in my sight as they went forth, with
the wheels beside them; and they stood
at the door of the east gate of the house
of the LORD; and the glory of the God
of Israel was over them.
20 These were the living creatures
that I saw underneath the God of
Israel by the river Chē'bär; and I
knew that they were cherubim. 21 Each
had four faces, and each four wings,
and underneath their wings the
semblance of human hands. 22And as
for the likeness of their faces, they
were the very faces whose appearance
I had seen by the river Chē'bär. They
went every one straight forward.

11 The Spirit lifted me up, and
brought me to the east gate of the
house of the LORD, which faces east.
And behold, at the door of the gateway
there were twenty-five men; and I saw
among them Jā-az·à·nī'ǎh the son of
Az'zũr, and Pel·à·tī'ǎh the son of Be-
nā'iǎh, princes of the people. 2And he
said to me, "Son of man, these are the
men who devise iniquity and who give
wicked counsel in this city; 3 who say,
'The time is not near[k] to build houses;
this city is the caldron, and we are the
flesh.' 4 Therefore prophesy against
them, prophesy, O son of man."
5 And the Spirit of the LORD fell
upon me, and he said to me, "Say,
Thus says the LORD: So you think, O
house of Israel; for I know the things
that come into your mind. 6 You have
multiplied your slain in this city, and
have filled its streets with the slain.
7 Therefore thus says the Lord GOD:
Your slain whom you have laid in the
midst of it, they are the flesh, and this
city is the caldron; but you shall be
brought forth out of the midst of it.
8 You have feared the sword; and I
will bring the sword upon you, says
the Lord GOD. 9And I will bring you
forth out of the midst of it, and give
you into the hands of foreigners, and
execute judgments upon you. 10 You
shall fall by the sword; I will judge you
at the border of Israel; and you shall
know that I am the LORD. 11 This city
shall not be your caldron, nor shall
you be the flesh in the midst of it; I
will judge you at the border of Israel;
12 and you shall know that I am the
LORD; for you have not walked in my
statutes, nor executed my ordinances,
but have acted according to the ordinances of the nations that are round
about you."
13 And it came to pass, while I was
prophesying, that Pel·à·tī'ǎh the son
of Be·nā'iǎh died. Then I fell down
upon my face, and cried with a loud
voice, and said, "Ah Lord GOD! wilt
thou make a full end of the remnant
of Israel?"
14 And the word of the LORD came
to me: 15 "Son of man, your brethren,
even your brethren, your fellow exiles,[l]
the whole house of Israel, all of them,
are those of whom the inhabitants of
Jerusalem have said, 'They have gone
far from the LORD; to us this land is
given for a possession.' 16 Therefore
say, 'Thus says the Lord GOD: Though
I removed them far off among the
nations, and though I scattered them
among the countries, yet I have been
a sanctuary to them for a while[m] in
the countries where they have gone.'
17 Therefore say, 'Thus says the Lord

[g] Heb *on their four sides* [h] Gk: Heb *And their whole body and* [i] Heb *spokes and their wings*
[j] Or *of life* [k] Or *Is not the time near . . .?* [l] Gk Syr: Heb *men of your kindred* [m] Or *in small measure*
10.12: Ezek 1.18; Rev 4.8. **10.14:** Ezek 1.10; Rev 4.7.

GOD: I will gather you from the peoples, and assemble you out of the
countries where you have been
scattered, and I will give you the land
of Israel.' 18And when they come there,
they will remove from it all its detestable things and all its abominations.
19And I will give them one[n] heart, and
put a new spirit within them; I will
take the stony heart out of their flesh
and give them a heart of flesh, 20 that
they may walk in my statutes and keep
my ordinances and obey them; and
they shall be my people, and I will be
their God. 21 But as for those[o] whose
heart goes after their detestable things
and their abominations, I will requite
their deeds upon their own heads, says
the Lord GOD."

22 Then the cherubim lifted up
their wings, with the wheels beside
them; and the glory of the God of
Israel was over them. 23And the glory
of the LORD went up from the midst
of the city, and stood upon the mountain which is on the east side of the
city. 24And the Spirit lifted me up and
brought me in the vision by the Spirit
of God into Chal·dē'ȧ, to the exiles.
Then the vision that I had seen went
up from me. 25And I told the exiles all
the things that the LORD had showed
me.

12 The word of the LORD came to
me: 2 "Son of man, you dwell in
the midst of a rebellious house, who
have eyes to see, but see not, who have
ears to hear, but hear not; 3 for they
are a rebellious house. Therefore, son
of man, prepare for yourself an exile's
baggage, and go into exile by day in
their sight; you shall go like an exile
from your place to another place in
their sight. Perhaps they will understand, though[p] they are a rebellious
house. 4 You shall bring out your
baggage by day in their sight, as
baggage for exile; and you shall go
forth yourself at evening in their sight,
as men do who must go into exile.
5 Dig through the wall in their sight,
and go[q] out through it. 6 In their sight
you shall lift the baggage upon your
shoulder, and carry it out in the dark;
you shall cover your face, that you
may not see the land; for I have made
you a sign for the house of Israel."

7 And I did as I was commanded.
I brought out my baggage by day, as
baggage for exile, and in the evening
I dug through the wall with my own
hands; I went forth in the dark, carrying my outfit upon my shoulder in
their sight.

8 In the morning the word of the
LORD came to me: 9 "Son of man, has
not the house of Israel, the rebellious
house, said to you, 'What are you doing?' 10 Say to them, 'Thus says the
Lord GOD: This oracle concerns the
prince in Jerusalem and all the house
of Israel who are in it.'[r] 11 Say, 'I am
a sign for you: as I have done, so shall
it be done to them; they shall go into
exile, into captivity.' 12And the prince
who is among them shall lift his
baggage upon his shoulder in the dark,
and shall go forth; he[s] shall dig through
the wall and go[t] out through it; he
shall cover his face, that he may not
see the land with his eyes. 13And I
will spread my net over him, and he
shall be taken in my snare; and I will
bring him to Babylon in the land of
the Chal·dē'ȧnṡ, yet he shall not see
it; and he shall die there. 14And I will
scatter toward every wind all who are
round about him, his helpers[u] and all
his troops; and I will unsheathe the
sword after them. 15And they shall
know that I am the LORD, when I
disperse them among the nations and
scatter them through the countries.
16 But I will let a few of them escape
from the sword, from famine and
pestilence, that they may confess all
their abominations among the nations
where they go, and may know that I
am the LORD."

17 Moreover the word of the LORD
came to me: 18 "Son of man, eat your
bread with quaking, and drink water
with trembling and with fearfulness;
19 and say of the people of the land,
Thus says the Lord GOD concerning
the inhabitants of Jerusalem in the
land of Israel: They shall eat their
bread with fearfulness, and drink water
in dismay, because their land will be
stripped of all it contains, on account
of the violence of all those who dwell

[n] Another reading is *a new*
[o] Cn: Heb *To the heart of their detestable things and their abominations their heart goes*
[p] Or *will see that* [q] Gk Syr Vg Tg: Heb *bring* [r] Heb *in the midst of them* [s] Gk Syr: Heb *they*
[t] Gk Syr Tg: Heb *bring* [u] Gk Syr Tg: Heb *his help*
11.19: Ezek 18.31; 36.26; 2 Cor 3.3. **12.2**: Mk 8.18.

in it. 20 And the inhabited cities shall
be laid waste, and the land shall become a desolation; and you shall know
that I am the LORD."
21 And the word of the LORD came
to me: 22 "Son of man, what is this
proverb that you have about the land
of Israel, saying, 'The days grow long,
and every vision comes to nought'?
23 Tell them therefore, 'Thus says the
Lord GOD: I will put an end to this
proverb, and they shall no more use it
as a proverb in Israel.' But say to
them, The days are at hand, and the
fulfilment[v] of every vision. 24 For
there shall be no more any false vision
of flattering divination within the
house of Israel. 25 But I the LORD will
speak the word which I will speak, and
it will be performed. It will no longer
be delayed, but in your days, O rebellious house, I will speak the word and
perform it, says the Lord GOD."
26 Again the word of the LORD
came to me: 27 "Son of man, behold,
they of the house of Israel say, 'The
vision that he sees is for many days
hence, and he prophesies of times far
off.' 28 Therefore say to them, Thus
says the Lord GOD: None of my words
will be delayed any longer, but the
word which I speak will be performed,
says the Lord GOD."

13 The word of the LORD came to
me: 2 "Son of man, prophesy
against the prophets of Israel, prophesy[w] and say to those who prophesy
out of their own minds: 'Hear the
word of the LORD!' 3 Thus says the
Lord GOD, Woe to the foolish prophets
who follow their own spirit, and have
seen nothing! 4 Your prophets have
been like foxes among ruins, O Israel.
5 You have not gone up into the
breaches, or built up a wall for the
house of Israel, that it might stand in
battle in the day of the LORD. 6 They
have spoken falsehood and divined a
lie; they say, 'Says the LORD,' when
the LORD has not sent them, and yet
they expect him to fulfil their word.
7 Have you not seen a delusive vision,
and uttered a lying divination, whenever you have said, 'Says the LORD,'
although I have not spoken?"
8 Therefore thus says the Lord
GOD: "Because you have uttered de-
lusions and seen lies, therefore behold, I am against you, says the Lord
GOD. 9 My hand will be against the
prophets who see delusive visions and
who give lying divinations; they shall
not be in the council of my people, nor
be enrolled in the register of the house
of Israel, nor shall they enter the land
of Israel; and you shall know that I
am the Lord GOD. 10 Because, yea, because they have misled my people,
saying, 'Peace,' when there is no peace;
and because, when the people build a
wall, these prophets daub it with
whitewash; 11 say to those who daub
it with whitewash that it shall fall!
There will be a deluge of rain,[x] great
hailstones will fall, and a stormy wind
break out; 12 and when the wall falls,
will it not be said to you, 'Where is
the daubing with which you daubed
it?' 13 Therefore thus says the Lord
GOD: I will make a stormy wind break
out in my wrath; and there shall be a
deluge of rain in my anger, and great
hailstones in wrath to destroy it.
14 And I will break down the wall that
you have daubed with whitewash, and
bring it down to the ground, so that
its foundation will be laid bare; when
it falls, you shall perish in the midst
of it; and you shall know that I am the
LORD. 15 Thus will I spend my wrath
upon the wall, and upon those who
have daubed it with whitewash; and I
will say to you, The wall is no more,
nor those who daubed it, 16 the prophets of Israel who prophesied concerning Jerusalem and saw visions of peace
for her, when there was no peace, says
the Lord GOD.
17 "And you, son of man, set your
face against the daughters of your people, who prophesy out of their own
minds; prophesy against them 18 and
say, Thus says the Lord GOD: Woe to
the women who sew magic bands upon
all wrists, and make veils for the heads
of persons of every stature, in the hunt
for souls! Will you hunt down souls
belonging to my people, and keep
other souls alive for your profit? 19 You
have profaned me among my people
for handfuls of barley and for pieces
of bread, putting to death persons who
should not die and keeping alive persons who should not live, by your
lies to my people, who listen to lies.
20 "Wherefore thus says the Lord
GOD: Behold, I am against your magic
bands with which you hunt the souls,[y]

[v] Heb *word* [w] Gk: Heb *who prophesy* [x] Heb *rain and you*
[y] Gk Syr: Heb *souls for birds*

and I will tear them from your arms; and I will let the souls that you hunt go free[z] like birds. 21 Your veils also I will tear off, and deliver my people out of your hand, and they shall be no more in your hand as prey; and you shall know that I am the LORD. 22 Because you have disheartened the righteous falsely, although I have not disheartened him, and you have encouraged the wicked, that he should not turn from his wicked way to save his life; 23 therefore you shall no more see delusive visions nor practice divination; I will deliver my people out of your hand. Then you will know that I am the LORD."

14 Then came certain of the elders of Israel to me, and sat before me. 2 And the word of the LORD came to me: 3 "Son of man, these men have taken their idols into their hearts, and set the stumbling block of their iniquity before their faces; should I let myself be inquired of at all by them? 4 Therefore speak to them, and say to them, Thus says the Lord GOD: Any man of the house of Israel who takes his idols into his heart and sets the stumbling block of his iniquity before his face, and yet comes to the prophet, I the LORD will answer him myself[a] because of the multitude of his idols, 5 that I may lay hold of the hearts of the house of Israel, who are all estranged from me through their idols.

6 "Therefore say to the house of Israel, Thus says the Lord GOD: Repent and turn away from your idols; and turn away your faces from all your abominations. 7 For any one of the house of Israel, or of the strangers that sojourn in Israel, who separates himself from me, taking his idols into his heart and putting the stumbling block of his iniquity before his face, and yet comes to a prophet to inquire for himself of me, I the LORD will answer him myself; 8 and I will set my face against that man, I will make him a sign and a byword and cut him off from the midst of my people; and you shall know that I am the LORD. 9 And if the prophet be deceived and speak a word, I, the LORD, have deceived that prophet, and I will stretch out my hand against him, and will destroy him from the midst of my people Israel. 10 And they shall bear their punishment—the punishment of the prophet and the punishment of the inquirer shall be alike—11 that the house of Israel may go no more astray from me, nor defile themselves any more with all their transgressions, but that they may be my people and I may be their God, says the Lord GOD."

12 And the word of the LORD came to me: 13 "Son of man, when a land sins against me by acting faithlessly, and I stretch out my hand against it, and break its staff of bread and send famine upon it, and cut off from it man and beast, 14 even if these three men, Noah, Daniel, and Jōb, were in it, they would deliver but their own lives by their righteousness, says the Lord GOD. 15 If I cause wild beasts to pass through the land, and they ravage it, and it be made desolate, so that no man may pass through because of the beasts; 16 even if these three men were in it, as I live, says the Lord GOD, they would deliver neither sons nor daughters; they alone would be delivered, but the land would be desolate. 17 Or if I bring a sword upon that land, and say, Let a sword go through the land; and I cut off from it man and beast; 18 though these three men were in it, as I live, says the Lord GOD, they would deliver neither sons nor daughters, but they alone would be delivered. 19 Or if I send a pestilence into that land, and pour out my wrath upon it with blood, to cut off from it man and beast; 20 even if Noah, Daniel, and Jōb were in it, as I live, says the Lord GOD, they would deliver neither son nor daughter; they would deliver but their own lives by their righteousness.

21 "For thus says the Lord GOD: How much more when I send upon Jerusalem my four sore acts of judgment, sword, famine, evil beasts, and pestilence, to cut off from it man and beast! 22 Yet, if there should be left in it any survivors to lead out sons and daughters, when they come forth to you, and you see their ways and their doings, you will be consoled for the evil that I have brought upon Jerusalem, for all that I have brought upon it. 23 They will console you, when you see their ways and their doings; and you shall know that I have not done without cause all that I have done in it, says the Lord GOD."

[z] Cn: Heb *the souls* [a] Cn Compare Tg: Heb uncertain
14.21: Rev 6.8.

15 And the word of the LORD came to me: 2 "Son of man, how does the wood of the vine surpass any wood, the vine branch which is among the trees of the forest? 3 Is wood taken from it to make anything? Do men take a peg from it to hang any vessel on? 4 Lo, it is given to the fire for fuel; when the fire has consumed both ends of it, and the middle of it is charred, is it useful for anything? 5 Behold, when it was whole, it was used for nothing; how much less, when the fire has consumed it and it is charred, can it ever be used for anything! 6 Therefore thus says the Lord GOD: Like the wood of the vine among the trees of the forest, which I have given to the fire for fuel, so will I give up the inhabitants of Jerusalem. 7 And I will set my face against them; though they escape from the fire, the fire shall yet consume them; and you will know that I am the LORD, when I set my face against them. 8 And I will make the land desolate, because they have acted faithlessly, says the Lord GOD."

16 Again the word of the LORD came to me: 2 "Son of man, make known to Jerusalem her abominations, 3 and say, Thus says the Lord GOD to Jerusalem: Your origin and your birth are of the land of the Canaanites; your father was an Am'ŏ·rīte, and your mother a Hit'tīte. 4 And as for your birth, on the day you were born your navel string was not cut, nor were you washed with water to cleanse you, nor rubbed with salt, nor swathed with bands. 5 No eye pitied you, to do any of these things to you out of compassion for you; but you were cast out on the open field, for you were abhorred, on the day that you were born.

6 "And when I passed by you, and saw you weltering in your blood, I said to you in your blood, 'Live, 7 and grow up[b] like a plant of the field.' And you grew up and became tall and arrived at full maidenhood;[c] your breasts were formed, and your hair had grown; yet you were naked and bare.

8 "When I passed by you again and looked upon you, behold, you were at the age for love; and I spread my skirt over you, and covered your nakedness: yea, I plighted my troth to you and entered into a covenant with you, says the Lord GOD, and you became mine. 9 Then I bathed you with water and washed off your blood from you, and anointed you with oil. 10 I clothed you also with embroidered cloth and shod you with leather, I swathed you in fine linen and covered you with silk. 11 And I decked you with ornaments, and put bracelets on your arms, and a chain on your neck. 12 And I put a ring on your nose, and earrings in your ears, and a beautiful crown upon your head. 13 Thus you were decked with gold and silver; and your raiment was of fine linen, and silk, and embroidered cloth; you ate fine flour and honey and oil. You grew exceedingly beautiful, and came to regal estate. 14 And your renown went forth among the nations because of your beauty, for it was perfect through the splendor which I had bestowed upon you, says the Lord GOD.

15 "But you trusted in your beauty, and played the harlot because of your renown, and lavished your harlotries on any passer-by. 16 You took some of your garments, and made for yourself gaily decked shrines, and on them played the harlot; the like has never been, nor ever shall be. 17 You also took your fair jewels of my gold and of my silver, which I had given you, and made for yourself images of men, and with them played the harlot; 18 and you took your embroidered garments to cover them, and set my oil and my incense before them. 19 Also my bread which I gave you—I fed you with fine flour and oil and honey—you set before them for a pleasing odor, says the Lord GOD.[d] 20 And you took your sons and your daughters, whom you had borne to me, and these you sacrificed to them to be devoured. Were your harlotries so small a matter 21 that you slaughtered my children and delivered them up as an offering by fire to them? 22 And in all your abominations and your harlotries you did not remember the days of your youth, when you were naked and bare, weltering in your blood.

23 "And after all your wickedness (woe, woe to you! says the Lord GOD), 24 you built yourself a vaulted chamber, and made yourself a lofty place in

[b] Gk Syr: Heb *I made you a myriad* [c] Cn: Heb *ornament of ornaments*
[d] Syr: Heb *and it was, says the Lord* GOD
16.3: Ezek 16.45.

every square; 25 at the head of every
street you built your lofty place and
prostituted your beauty, offering yourself to any passer-by, and multiplying
your harlotry. 26 You also played the
harlot with the Egyptians, your lustful
neighbors, multiplying your harlotry,
to provoke me to anger. 27 Behold,
therefore, I stretched out my hand
against you, and diminished your
allotted portion, and delivered you to
the greed of your enemies, the daughters of the Philistines, who were
ashamed of your lewd behavior. 28 You
played the harlot also with the Assyrians, because you were insatiable; yea,
you played the harlot with them, and
still you were not satisfied. 29 You
multiplied your harlotry also with the
trading land of Chal·dē′à; and even
with this you were not satisfied.

30 "How lovesick is your heart,
says the Lord GOD, seeing you did all
these things, the deeds of a brazen
harlot; 31 building your vaulted chamber at the head of every street, and
making your lofty place in every
square. Yet you were not like a harlot,
because you scorned hire. 32 Adulterous
wife, who receives strangers instead of
her husband! 33 Men give gifts to all
harlots; but you gave your gifts to all
your lovers, bribing them to come to
you from every side for your harlotries.
34 So you were different from other
women in your harlotries: none so-
licited you to play the harlot; and you
gave hire, while no hire was given to
you; therefore you were different.

35 "Wherefore, O harlot, hear the
word of the LORD: 36 Thus says the
Lord GOD, Because your shame was
laid bare and your nakedness uncovered in your harlotries with your
lovers, and because of all your idols,
and because of the blood of your children that you gave to them, 37 therefore, behold, I will gather all your
lovers, with whom you took pleasure,
all those you loved and all those you
loathed; I will gather them against you
from every side, and will uncover your
nakedness to them, that they may see
all your nakedness. 38 And I will judge
you as women who break wedlock and
shed blood are judged, and bring upon
you the blood of wrath and jealousy.
39 And I will give you into the hand of
your lovers, and they shall throw down
your vaulted chamber and break down
your lofty places; they shall strip you
of your clothes and take your fair
jewels, and leave you naked and bare.
40 They shall bring up a host against
you, and they shall stone you and cut
you to pieces with their swords. 41 And
they shall burn your houses and
execute judgments upon you in the
sight of many women; I will make you
stop playing the harlot, and you shall
also give hire no more. 42 So will I
satisfy my fury on you, and my jealousy shall depart from you; I will be
calm, and will no more be angry.
43 Because you have not remembered
the days of your youth, but have
enraged me with all these things; therefore, behold, I will requite your deeds
upon your head, says the Lord GOD.

"Have you not committed lewdness
in addition to all your abominations?
44 Behold, every one who uses proverbs
will use this proverb about you, 'Like
mother, like daughter.' 45 You are the
daughter of your mother, who loathed
her husband and her children; and you
are the sister of your sisters, who
loathed their husbands and their children. Your mother was a Hit′tīte and
your father an Am′ò·rīte. 46 And your
elder sister is Sà·mâr′i·à, who lived
with her daughters to the north of you;
and your younger sister, who lived to
the south of you, is Sod′òm with her
daughters. 47 Yet you were not content
to walk in their ways, or do according
to their abominations; within a very
little time you were more corrupt than
they in all your ways. 48 As I live, says
the Lord GOD, your sister Sod′òm and
her daughters have not done as you
and your daughters have done. 49 Behold, this was the guilt of your sister
Sod′òm: she and her daughters had
pride, surfeit of food, and prosperous
ease, but did not aid the poor and
needy. 50 They were haughty, and did
abominable things before me; therefore I removed them, when I saw it.
51 Sà·mâr′i·à has not committed half
your sins; you have committed more
abominations than they, and have
made your sisters appear righteous by
all the abominations which you have
committed. 52 Bear your disgrace, you
also, for you have made judgment
favorable to your sisters; because of
your sins in which you acted more
abominably than they, they are more
in the right than you. So be ashamed,

16.45: Ezek 16.3.

you also, and bear your disgrace, for
you have made your sisters appear
righteous.
53 "I will restore their fortunes,
both the fortunes of Sod'ŏm and her
daughters, and the fortunes of Să-
mâr'i·ȧ and her daughters, and I will
restore your own fortunes in the midst
of them, 54 that you may bear your
disgrace and be ashamed of all that
you have done, becoming a consolation to them. 55 As for your sisters,
Sod'ŏm and her daughters shall return
to their former estate, and Să·mâr'i·ȧ
and her daughters shall return to their
former estate; and you and your
daughters shall return to your former
estate. 56 Was not your sister Sod'ŏm
a byword in your mouth in the day of
your pride, 57 before your wickedness
was uncovered? Now you have become
like her[e] an object of reproach for the
daughters of E'dŏm[f] and all her
neighbors, and for the daughters of
the Philistines, those round about who
despise you. 58 You bear the penalty
of your lewdness and your abominations, says the LORD.
59 "Yea, thus says the Lord GOD:
I will deal with you as you have done,
who have despised the oath in breaking
the covenant, 60 yet I will remember
my covenant with you in the days of
your youth, and I will establish with
you an everlasting covenant. 61 Then
you will remember your ways, and be
ashamed when I[g] take your sisters,
both your elder and your younger, and
give them to you as daughters, but not
on account of the covenant with you.
62 I will establish my covenant with
you, and you shall know that I am the
LORD, 63 that you may remember and
be confounded, and never open your
mouth again because of your shame,
when I forgive you all that you have
done, says the Lord GOD."
17 The word of the LORD came to
me: 2 "Son of man, propound a
riddle, and speak an allegory to the
house of Israel; 3 say, Thus says the
Lord GOD: A great eagle with great
wings and long pinions, rich in
plumage of many colors, came to
Lebanon and took the top of the cedar;
4 he broke off the topmost of its young
twigs and carried it to a land of trade,
and set it in a city of merchants. 5 Then
he took of the seed of the land and
planted it in fertile soil; he placed it
beside abundant waters. He set it like
a willow twig, 6 and it sprouted and
became a low spreading vine, and its
branches turned toward him, and its
roots remained where it stood. So it
became a vine, and brought forth
branches and put forth foliage.
7 "But there was another great
eagle with great wings and much
plumage; and behold, this vine bent
its roots toward him, and shot forth
its branches toward him that he might
water it. From the bed where it was
planted 8 he transplanted it[h] to good
soil by abundant waters, that it might
bring forth branches, and bear fruit,
and become a noble vine. 9 Say, Thus
says the Lord GOD: Will it thrive?
Will he not pull up its roots and cut
off its branches,[i] so that all its fresh
sprouting leaves wither? It will not
take a strong arm or many people to
pull it from its roots. 10 Behold, when
it is transplanted, will it thrive? Will it
not utterly wither when the east wind
strikes it—wither away on the bed
where it grew?"
11 Then the word of the LORD came
to me: 12 "Say now to the rebellious
house, Do you not know what these
things mean? Tell them, Behold, the
king of Babylon came to Jerusalem,
and took her king and her princes and
brought them to him to Babylon.
13 And he took one of the seed royal
and made a covenant with him, putting
him under oath. (The chief men of the
land he had taken away, 14 that the
kingdom might be humble and not
lift itself up, and that by keeping his
covenant it might stand.) 15 But he
rebelled against him by sending ambassadors to Egypt, that they might
give him horses and a large army. Will
he succeed? Can a man escape who
does such things? Can he break the
covenant and yet escape? 16 As I live,
says the Lord GOD, surely in the
place where the king dwells who made
him king, whose oath he despised, and
whose covenant with him he broke, in
Babylon he shall die. 17 Pharaoh with
his mighty army and great company
will not help him in war, when mounds
are cast up and siege walls built to cut
off many lives. 18 Because he despised
the oath and broke the covenant, because he gave his hand and yet did all

[e] Cn: Heb uncertain [f] Another reading is *Aram* [g] Syr: Heb *you* [h] Cn: Heb *it was transplanted*
[i] Cn: Heb *fruit*

these things, he shall not escape.
19 Therefore thus says the Lord God:
As I live, surely my oath which he
despised, and my covenant which he
broke, I will requite upon his head.
20 I will spread my net over him, and
he shall be taken in my snare, and I
will bring him to Babylon and enter
into judgment with him there for the
treason he has committed against me.
21 And all the pick[j] of his troops shall
fall by the sword, and the survivors
shall be scattered to every wind; and
you shall know that I, the Lord, have
spoken."

22 Thus says the Lord God: "I myself will take a sprig from the lofty
top of the cedar, and will set it out; I
will break off from the topmost of its
young twigs a tender one, and I myself
will plant it upon a high and lofty
mountain; 23 on the mountain height
of Israel will I plant it, that it may
bring forth boughs and bear fruit, and
become a noble cedar; and under it will
dwell all kinds of beasts;[k] in the shade
of its branches birds of every sort will
nest. 24 And all the trees of the field
shall know that I the Lord bring low
the high tree, and make high the low
tree, dry up the green tree, and make
the dry tree flourish. I the Lord have
spoken, and I will do it."

18 The word of the Lord came to
me again: 2 "What do you mean
by repeating this proverb concerning
the land of Israel, 'The fathers have
eaten sour grapes, and the children's
teeth are set on edge'? 3 As I live, says
the Lord God, this proverb shall no
more be used by you in Israel. 4 Behold, all souls are mine; the soul of the
father as well as the soul of the son is
mine: the soul that sins shall die.

5 "If a man is righteous and does
what is lawful and right—6 if he does
not eat upon the mountains or lift up
his eyes to the idols of the house of
Israel, does not defile his neighbor's
wife or approach a woman in her time
of impurity, 7 does not oppress any
one, but restores to the debtor his
pledge, commits no robbery, gives his
bread to the hungry and covers the
naked with a garment, 8 does not lend
at interest or take any increase, withholds his hand from iniquity, executes
true justice between man and man,
9 walks in my statutes, and is careful
to observe my ordinances[l]—he is
righteous, he shall surely live, says the
Lord God.

10 "If he begets a son who is a
robber, a shedder of blood,[m] 11 who
does none of these duties, but eats
upon the mountains, defiles his
neighbor's wife, 12 oppresses the poor
and needy, commits robbery, does not
restore the pledge, lifts up his eyes to
the idols, commits abomination,
13 lends at interest, and takes increase;
shall he then live? He shall not live.
He has done all these abominable
things; he shall surely die; his blood
shall be upon himself.

14 "But if this man begets a son
who sees all the sins which his father
has done, and fears, and does not do
likewise, 15 who does not eat upon the
mountains or lift up his eyes to the
idols of the house of Israel, does not
defile his neighbor's wife, 16 does not
wrong any one, exacts no pledge, commits no robbery, but gives his bread to
the hungry and covers the naked with
a garment, 17 withholds his hand from
iniquity,[n] takes no interest or increase,
observes my ordinances, and walks in
my statutes; he shall not die for his
father's iniquity; he shall surely live.
18 As for his father, because he practiced extortion, robbed his brother,
and did what is not good among his
people, behold, he shall die for his
iniquity.

19 "Yet you say, 'Why should not
the son suffer for the iniquity of the
father?' When the son has done what
is lawful and right, and has been careful to observe all my statutes, he shall
surely live. 20 The soul that sins shall
die. The son shall not suffer for the
iniquity of the father, nor the father
suffer for the iniquity of the son;
the righteousness of the righteous
shall be upon himself, and the wickedness of the wicked shall be upon
himself.

21 "But if a wicked man turns
away from all his sins which he has
committed and keeps all my statutes
and does what is lawful and right, he

[j] Another reading is *fugitives* [k] Gk: Heb lacks *all kinds of beasts*
[l] Gk: Heb *has kept my ordinances, to deal truly* [m] Heb *blood, and he does any one of these things*
[n] Gk: Heb *the poor*
17.23: Ezek 31.6; Mt 13.32; Mk 4.32; Lk 13.19. **18.2**: Jer 31.29. **18.4**: Ezek 18.20.
18.20: Ezek 18.4.

shall surely live; he shall not die.
22 None of the transgressions which
he has committed shall be remembered
against him; for the righteousness
which he has done he shall live.
23 Have I any pleasure in the death of
the wicked, says the Lord GOD, and
not rather that he should turn from
his way and live? 24 But when a
righteous man turns away from his
righteousness and commits iniquity
and does the same abominable things
that the wicked man does, shall he
live? None of the righteous deeds
which he has done shall be remembered; for the treachery of which he
is guilty and the sin he has committed,
he shall die.
25 "Yet you say, 'The way of the
Lord is not just.' Hear now, O house
of Israel: Is my way not just? Is it not
your ways that are not just? 26 When a
righteous man turns away from his
righteousness and commits iniquity,
he shall die for it; for the iniquity
which he has committed he shall die.
27 Again, when a wicked man turns
away from the wickedness he has
committed and does what is lawful and
right, he shall save his life. 28 Because
he considered and turned away from
all the transgressions which he had
committed, he shall surely live, he shall
not die. 29 Yet the house of Israel says,
'The way of the Lord is not just.' O
house of Israel, are my ways not just?
Is it not your ways that are not just?
30 "Therefore I will judge you, O
house of Israel, every one according
to his ways, says the Lord GOD. Repent
and turn from all your transgressions,
lest iniquity be your ruin.[o] 31 Cast
away from you all the transgressions
which you have committed against me,
and get yourselves a new heart and a
new spirit! Why will you die, O house
of Israel? 32 For I have no pleasure in
the death of any one, says the Lord
GOD; so turn, and live."

19 And you, take up a lamentation
for the princes of Israel, 2 and
say:

What a lioness was your mother
among lions!
She couched in the midst of young
lions,
rearing her whelps.
3 And she brought up one of her
whelps;
he became a young lion,
and he learned to catch prey;
he devoured men.
4 The nations sounded an alarm
against him;
he was taken in their pit;
and they brought him with hooks
to the land of Egypt.
5 When she saw that she was baffled,[p]
that her hope was lost,
she took another of her whelps
and made him a young lion.
6 He prowled among the lions;
he became a young lion,
and he learned to catch prey;
he devoured men.
7 And he ravaged their strongholds,[q]
and laid waste their cities;
and the land was appalled and all
who were in it
at the sound of his roaring.
8 Then the nations set against him
snares[r] on every side;
they spread their net over him;
he was taken in their pit.
9 With hooks they put him in a cage,
and brought him to the king of
Babylon;
they brought him into custody,
that his voice should no more be
heard
upon the mountains of Israel.

10 Your mother was like a vine in a
vineyard[s]
transplanted by the water,
fruitful and full of branches
by reason of abundant water.
11 Its strongest stem became
a ruler's scepter;
it towered aloft
among the thick boughs;
it was seen in its height
with the mass of its branches.
12 But the vine was plucked up in fury,
cast down to the ground;
the east wind dried it up;
its fruit was stripped off,
its strong stem was withered;
the fire consumed it.
13 Now it is transplanted in the
wilderness,
in a dry and thirsty land.
14 And fire has gone out from its stem,

[o] Or *so that they shall not be a stumbling block of iniquity to you* [p] Heb *had waited*
[q] Tg Compare Theodotion: Heb *knew his widows* [r] Cn: Heb *from the provinces*
[s] Cn: Heb *in your blood*
18.23: Ezek 18.32; 33.11. **18.31:** Ezek 11.19; 36.26. **18.32:** Ezek 18.23; 33.11.

has consumed its branches and
fruit,
so that there remains in it no strong
stem,
no scepter for a ruler.

This is a lamentation, and has become a lamentation.

20 In the seventh year, in the
fifth month, on the tenth day
of the month, certain of the elders of
Israel came to inquire of the LORD,
and sat before me. 2And the word of
the LORD came to me: 3 "Son of man,
speak to the elders of Israel, and say
to them, Thus says the Lord GOD, Is
it to inquire of me that you come? As
I live, says the Lord GOD, I will not
be inquired of by you. 4 Will you
judge them, son of man, will you judge
them? Then let them know the abominations of their fathers, 5 and say to
them, Thus says the Lord GOD: On
the day when I chose Israel, I swore
to the seed of the house of Jacob, making myself known to them in the land
of Egypt, I swore to them, saying, I
am the LORD your God. 6 On that day
I swore to them that I would bring
them out of the land of Egypt into a
land that I had searched out for them,
a land flowing with milk and honey,
the most glorious of all lands. 7And I
said to them, Cast away the detestable
things your eyes feast on, every one of
you, and do not defile yourselves with
the idols of Egypt; I am the LORD your
God. 8 But they rebelled against me
and would not listen to me; they did
not every man cast away the detestable
things their eyes feasted on, nor did
they forsake the idols of Egypt.

"Then I thought I would pour out
my wrath upon them and spend my
anger against them in the midst of
the land of Egypt. 9 But I acted for
the sake of my name, that it should
not be profaned in the sight of the
nations among whom they dwelt, in
whose sight I made myself known to
them in bringing them out of the land
of Egypt. 10 So I led them out of the
land of Egypt and brought them into
the wilderness. 11 I gave them my
statutes and showed them my ordinances, by whose observance man
shall live. 12 Moreover I gave them my
sabbaths, as a sign between me and
them, that they might know that I the
LORD sanctify them. 13 But the house
of Israel rebelled against me in the
wilderness; they did not walk in my
statutes but rejected my ordinances,
by whose observance man shall live;
and my sabbaths they greatly profaned.

"Then I thought I would pour out
my wrath upon them in the wilderness,
to make a full end of them. 14 But I
acted for the sake of my name, that it
should not be profaned in the sight of
the nations, in whose sight I had
brought them out. 15 Moreover I
swore to them in the wilderness that
I would not bring them into the land
which I had given them, a land flowing
with milk and honey, the most glorious
of all lands, 16 because they rejected
my ordinances and did not walk in my
statutes, and profaned my sabbaths;
for their heart went after their idols.
17 Nevertheless my eye spared them,
and I did not destroy them or make a
full end of them in the wilderness.

18 "And I said to their children in
the wilderness, Do not walk in the
statutes of your fathers, nor observe
their ordinances, nor defile yourselves
with their idols. 19 I the LORD am
your God; walk in my statutes, and be
careful to observe my ordinances,
20 and hallow my sabbaths that they
may be a sign between me and you,
that you may know that I the LORD
am your God. 21 But the children
rebelled against me; they did not walk
in my statutes, and were not careful
to observe my ordinances, by whose
observance man shall live; they profaned my sabbaths.

"Then I thought I would pour out
my wrath upon them and spend my
anger against them in the wilderness.
22 But I withheld my hand, and acted
for the sake of my name, that it should
not be profaned in the sight of the
nations, in whose sight I had brought
them out. 23 Moreover I swore to
them in the wilderness that I would
scatter them among the nations and
disperse them through the countries,
24 because they had not executed my
ordinances, but had rejected my
statutes and profaned my sabbaths,
and their eyes were set on their
fathers' idols. 25 Moreover I gave them
statutes that were not good and ordinances by which they could not have
life; 26 and I defiled them through
their very gifts in making them offer
by fire all their first-born, that I might

horrify them; I did it that they might
know that I am the LORD.
27 "Therefore, son of man, speak
to the house of Israel and say to them,
Thus says the Lord GOD: In this
again your fathers blasphemed me, by
dealing treacherously with me. 28 For
when I had brought them into the
land which I swore to give them, then
wherever they saw any high hill or
any leafy tree, there they offered their
sacrifices and presented the provocation of their offering; there they sent
up their soothing odors, and there they
poured out their drink offerings. 29 (I
said to them, What is the high place
to which you go? So its name is called
Bā'măh[t] to this day.) 30 Wherefore say
to the house of Israel, Thus says the
Lord GOD: Will you defile yourselves
after the manner of your fathers and
go astray after their detestable things?
31 When you offer your gifts and
sacrifice your sons by fire, you defile
yourselves with all your idols to this
day. And shall I be inquired of by you,
O house of Israel? As I live, says the
Lord GOD, I will not be inquired of
by you.
32 "What is in your mind shall
never happen—the thought, 'Let us
be like the nations, like the tribes of
the countries, and worship wood and
stone.'
33 "As I live, says the Lord GOD,
surely with a mighty hand and an outstretched arm, and with wrath poured
out, I will be king over you. 34 I will
bring you out from the peoples and
gather you out of the countries where
you are scattered, with a mighty hand
and an outstretched arm, and with
wrath poured out; 35 and I will bring
you into the wilderness of the peoples,
and there I will enter into judgment
with you face to face. 36 As I entered
into judgment with your fathers in
the wilderness of the land of Egypt,
so I will enter into judgment with you,
says the Lord GOD. 37 I will make you
pass under the rod, and I will let you
go in by number.[u] 38 I will purge out
the rebels from among you, and those
who transgress against me; I will bring
them out of the land where they sojourn, but they shall not enter the land
of Israel. Then you will know that I
am the LORD.
39 "As for you, O house of Israel,
thus says the Lord GOD: Go serve
every one of you his idols, now and
hereafter, if you will not listen to me;
but my holy name you shall no more
profane with your gifts and your idols.
40 "For on my holy mountain, the
mountain height of Israel, says the
Lord GOD, there all the house of Israel, all of them, shall serve me in the
land; there I will accept them, and
there I will require your contributions
and the choicest of your gifts, with all
your sacred offerings. 41 As a pleasing
odor I will accept you, when I bring
you out from the peoples, and gather
you out of the countries where you
have been scattered; and I will manifest my holiness among you in the
sight of the nations. 42 And you shall
know that I am the LORD, when I
bring you into the land of Israel, the
country which I swore to give to your
fathers. 43 And there you shall remember your ways and all the doings
with which you have polluted yourselves; and you shall loathe yourselves
for all the evils that you have committed. 44 And you shall know that I
am the LORD, when I deal with you for
my name's sake, not according to your
evil ways, nor according to your
corrupt doings, O house of Israel, says
the Lord GOD."
45[v] And the word of the LORD came
to me: 46 "Son of man, set your face
toward the south, preach against the
south, and prophesy against the forest
land in the Negeb; 47 say to the forest
of the Negeb, Hear the word of the
LORD: Thus says the Lord GOD, Behold, I will kindle a fire in you, and it
shall devour every green tree in you
and every dry tree; the blazing flame
shall not be quenched, and all faces
from south to north shall be scorched
by it. 48 All flesh shall see that I the
LORD have kindled it; it shall not be
quenched." 49 Then I said, "Ah Lord
GOD! they are saying of me, 'Is he not
a maker of allegories?' "

21 [w] The word of the LORD came to
me: 2 "Son of man, set your face
toward Jerusalem and preach against
the sanctuaries; prophesy against the
land of Israel 3 and say to the land of
Israel, Thus says the LORD: Behold,
I am against you, and will draw forth

[t] That is *High Place* [u] Gk: Heb *bring you into the bond of the covenant* [v] Ch 21.1 in Heb
[w] Ch 21.6 in Heb
20.41: Eph 5.2; Phil 4.18. **20.43**: Ezek 6.9; 36.31.

my sword out of its sheath, and will
cut off from you both righteous and
wicked. 4 Because I will cut off from
you both righteous and wicked, therefore my sword shall go out of its
sheath against all flesh from south to
north; 5 and all flesh shall know that
I the LORD have drawn my sword out
of its sheath; it shall not be sheathed
again. 6 Sigh therefore, son of man;
sigh with breaking heart and bitter
grief before their eyes. 7 And when they
say to you, 'Why do you sigh?' you
shall say, 'Because of the tidings. When
it comes, every heart will melt and all
hands will be feeble, every spirit will
faint and all knees will be weak as
water. Behold, it comes and it will be
fulfilled,' " says the Lord GOD.
8 And the word of the LORD came
to me: 9 "Son of man, prophesy and
say, Thus says the Lord, Say:
A sword, a sword is sharpened
and also polished,
10 sharpened for slaughter,
polished to flash like lightning!
Or do we make mirth? You have
despised the rod, my son, with everything of wood. 11 So the sword is given
to be polished, that it may be handled;
it is sharpened and polished to be
given into the hand of the slayer.
12 Cry and wail, son of man, for it is
against my people; it is against all the
princes of Israel; they are delivered
over to the sword with my people.
Smite therefore upon your thigh.
13 For it will not be a testing—what
could it do if you despise the rod?"
says the Lord GOD.
14 "Prophesy therefore, son of
man; clap your hands and let the sword
come down twice, yea thrice, the
sword for those to be slain; it is the
sword for the great slaughter, which
encompasses them, 15 that their hearts
may melt, and many fall at all their
gates. I have given the glittering sword;
ah! it is made like lightning, it is
polished[x] for slaughter. 16 Cut sharply
to right[y] and left where your edge is
directed. 17 I also will clap my hands,
and I will satisfy my fury; I the LORD
have spoken."
18 The word of the LORD came to
me again: 19 "Son of man, mark two
ways for the sword of the king of
Babylon to come; both of them shall
come forth from the same land. And
make a signpost, make it at the head
of the way to a city; 20 mark a way for
the sword to come to Rab'bah of the
Am'mo·nites and to Judah and to[z]
Jerusalem the fortified. 21 For the king
of Babylon stands at the parting of the
way, at the head of the two ways, to
use divination; he shakes the arrows,
he consults the teraphim, he looks at
the liver. 22 Into his right hand comes
the lot for Jerusalem,[a] to open the
mouth with a cry,[b] to lift up the voice
with shouting, to set battering rams
against the gates, to cast up mounds,
to build siege towers. 23 But to them
it will seem like a false divination; they
have sworn solemn oaths; but he brings
their guilt to remembrance, that they
may be captured.
24 "Therefore thus says the Lord
GOD: Because you have made your
guilt to be remembered, in that your
transgressions are uncovered, so that
in all your doings your sins appear—
because you have come to remembrance, you shall be taken in them.[c]
25 And you, O unhallowed wicked one,
prince of Israel, whose day has come,
the time of your final punishment,
26 thus says the Lord GOD: Remove
the turban, and take off the crown;
things shall not remain as they are;
exalt that which is low, and abase that
which is high. 27 A ruin, ruin, ruin I
will make it; there shall not be even a
trace[d] of it until he comes whose right
it is; and to him I will give it.
28 "And you, son of man, prophesy,
and say, Thus says the Lord GOD concerning the Am'mo·nites, and concerning their reproach; say, A sword, a
sword is drawn for the slaughter, it is
polished to glitter[e] and to flash like
lightning—29 while they see for you
false visions, while they divine lies for
you—to be laid on the necks of the
unhallowed wicked, whose day has
come, the time of their final punishment. 30 Return it to its sheath. In the
place where you were created, in the
land of your origin, I will judge you.
31 And I will pour out my indignation
upon you; I will blow upon you with
the fire of my wrath; and I will deliver
you into the hands of brutal men, skil-

[x] Tg: Heb *wrapped up* [y] Gk Syr Vg: Heb *right, set* [z] Gk Syr: Heb *in*
[a] Heb *Jerusalem, to set battering rams* [b] Gk: Heb *with slaughter* [c] Gk: Heb *with the hand*
[d] Cn: Heb *not even this* [e] Cn: Heb *to contain*
21.28-32: Ezek 25.1-7; Jer 49.1-6; Amos 1.13-15; Zeph 2.8-11.

ful to destroy. 32 You shall be fuel for
the fire; your blood shall be in the
midst of the land; you shall be no more
remembered; for I the LORD have
spoken."

22 Moreover the word of the
LORD came to me, saying,
2 "And you, son of man, will you
judge, will you judge the bloody city?
Then declare to her all her abominable
deeds. 3 You shall say, Thus says the
Lord GOD: A city that sheds blood in
the midst of her, that her time may
come, and that makes idols to defile
herself! 4 You have become guilty by
the blood which you have shed, and
defiled by the idols which you have
made; and you have brought your day
near, the appointed time[f] of your years
has come. Therefore I have made you
a reproach to the nations, and a mocking to all the countries. 5 Those who
are near and those who are far from
you will mock you, you infamous one,
full of tumult.

6 "Behold, the princes of Israel in
you, every one according to his power,
have been bent on shedding blood.
7 Father and mother are treated with
contempt in you; the sojourner suffers
extortion in your midst; the fatherless
and the widow are wronged in you.
8 You have despised my holy things,
and profaned my sabbaths. 9 There
are men in you who slander to shed
blood, and men in you who eat upon
the mountains; men commit lewdness
in your midst. 10 In you men uncover
their fathers' nakedness; in you they
humble women who are unclean in
their impurity. 11 One commits abomination with his neighbor's wife;
another lewdly defiles his daughter-in-
law; another in you defiles his sister,
his father's daughter. 12 In you men
take bribes to shed blood; you take
interest and increase and make gain
of your neighbors by extortion; and
you have forgotten me, says the Lord
GOD.

13 "Behold, therefore, I strike my
hands together at the dishonest gain
which you have made, and at the
blood which has been in the midst of
you. 14 Can your courage endure, or
can your hands be strong, in the days
that I shall deal with you? I the LORD
have spoken, and I will do it. 15 I will
scatter you among the nations and
disperse you through the countries,
and I will consume your filthiness out
of you. 16 And I[g] shall be profaned
through you in the sight of the nations;
and you shall know that I am the
LORD."

17 And the word of the LORD came
to me: 18 "Son of man, the house of
Israel has become dross to me; all of
them, silver[h] and bronze and tin and
iron and lead in the furnace, have
become dross. 19 Therefore thus says
the Lord GOD: Because you have all
become dross, therefore, behold, I will
gather you into the midst of Jerusalem.
20 As men gather silver and bronze and
iron and lead and tin into a furnace,
to blow the fire upon it in order to
melt it; so I will gather you in my
anger and in my wrath, and I will put
you in and melt you. 21 I will gather
you and blow upon you with the fire
of my wrath, and you shall be melted
in the midst of it. 22 As silver is melted
in a furnace, so you shall be melted in
the midst of it; and you shall know
that I the LORD have poured out my
wrath upon you."

23 And the word of the LORD came
to me: 24 "Son of man, say to her, You
are a land that is not cleansed, or rained
upon in the day of indignation. 25 Her
princes[i] in the midst of her are like a
roaring lion tearing the prey; they have
devoured human lives; they have taken
treasure and precious things; they have
made many widows in the midst of
her. 26 Her priests have done violence
to my law and have profaned my holy
things; they have made no distinction
between the holy and the common,
neither have they taught the difference
between the unclean and the clean, and
they have disregarded my sabbaths, so
that I am profaned among them. 27 Her
princes in the midst of her are like
wolves tearing the prey, shedding
blood, destroying lives to get dishonest
gain. 28 And her prophets have daubed
for them with whitewash, seeing false
visions and divining lies for them, saying, 'Thus says the Lord GOD,' when
the LORD has not spoken. 29 The people of the land have practiced extortion
and committed robbery; they have
oppressed the poor and needy, and
have extorted from the sojourner without redress. 30 And I sought for a man
among them who should build up the

[f] Two Mss Gk Syr Vg Tg: Heb *until* [g] Gk Syr Vg: Heb *you*
[h] Transposed from the end of the verse. Compare verse 20 [i] Gk: Heb *a conspiracy of her prophets*

wall and stand in the breach before me
for the land, that I should not destroy
it; but I found none. 31 Therefore I
have poured out my indignation upon
them; I have consumed them with the
fire of my wrath; their way have I
requited upon their heads, says the
Lord GOD."

23 The word of the LORD came
to me: 2 "Son of man, there
were two women, the daughters of one
mother; 3 they played the harlot in
Egypt; they played the harlot in their
youth; there their breasts were pressed
and their virgin bosoms handled.
4 Ō·hō′lȧh was the name of the elder
and Ō·hol′i·bȧh the name of her sister.
They became mine, and they bore
sons and daughters. As for their
names, Ō·hō′lȧh is Sȧ·mâr′i·ȧ, and
Ō·hol′i·bȧh is Jerusalem.

5 "Ō·hō′lȧh played the harlot
while she was mine; and she doted on
her lovers the Assyrians, 6 warriors
clothed in purple, governors and
commanders, all of them desirable
young men, horsemen riding on
horses. 7 She bestowed her harlotries
upon them, the choicest men of
Assyria all of them; and she defiled
herself with all the idols of every one
on whom she doted. 8 She did not
give up her harlotry which she had
practiced since her days in Egypt; for
in her youth men had lain with her
and handled her virgin bosom and
poured out their lust upon her.
9 Therefore I delivered her into the
hands of her lovers, into the hands of
the Assyrians, upon whom she doted.
10 These uncovered her nakedness;
they seized her sons and her daughters;
and her they slew with the sword; and
she became a byword among women,
when judgment had been executed
upon her.

11 "Her sister Ō·hol′i·bȧh saw this,
yet she was more corrupt than she in
her doting and in her harlotry, which
was worse than that of her sister.
12 She doted upon the Assyrians,
governors and commanders, warriors
clothed in full armor, horsemen riding
on horses, all of them desirable young
men. 13 And I saw that she was defiled;
they both took the same way. 14 But
she carried her harlotry further; she
saw men portrayed upon the wall, the
images of the Chal·dē′ȧnṡ portrayed in
vermilion, 15 girded with belts on their
loins, with flowing turbans on their
heads, all of them looking like officers,
a picture of Babylonians whose native
land was Chal·dē′ȧ. 16 When she saw
them she doted upon them, and sent
messengers to them in Chal·dē′ȧ.
17 And the Babylonians came to her
into the bed of love, and they defiled
her with their lust; and after she was
polluted by them, she turned from
them in disgust. 18 When she carried
on her harlotry so openly and flaunted
her nakedness, I turned in disgust
from her, as I had turned from her
sister. 19 Yet she increased her harlotry, remembering the days of her
youth, when she played the harlot in
the land of Egypt 20 and doted upon
her paramours there, whose members
were like those of asses, and whose
issue was like that of horses. 21 Thus
you longed for the lewdness of your
youth, when the Egyptians[j] handled
your bosom and pressed[k] your young
breasts."

22 Therefore, O Ō·hol′i·bȧh, thus
says the Lord GOD: "Behold, I will
rouse against you your lovers from
whom you turned in disgust, and I
will bring them against you from
every side: 23 the Babylonians and all
the Chal·dē′ȧnṡ, Pē′kod and Shō′ȧ and
Kō′ȧ, and all the Assyrians with them,
desirable young men, governors and
commanders all of them, officers and
warriors,[l] all of them riding on horses.
24 And they shall come against you
from the north[m] with chariots and
wagons and a host of peoples; they
shall set themselves against you on
every side with buckler, shield, and
helmet, and I will commit the judgment to them, and they shall judge you
according to their judgments. 25 And I
will direct my indignation against you,
that they may deal with you in fury.
They shall cut off your nose and your
ears, and your survivors shall fall by
the sword. They shall seize your sons
and your daughters, and your survivors
shall be devoured by fire. 26 They shall
also strip you of your clothes and take
away your fine jewels. 27 Thus I will
put an end to your lewdness and your
harlotry brought from the land of
Egypt; so that you shall not lift up
your eyes to the Egyptians or remember them any more. 28 For thus says

[j] Two Mss: Heb *from Egypt* [k] Cn: Heb *for the sake of* [l] Compare verses 6 and 12: Heb *called*
[m] Gk: The meaning of the Hebrew word is unknown

the Lord GOD: Behold, I will deliver
you into the hands of those whom you
hate, into the hands of those from
whom you turned in disgust; 29 and
they shall deal with you in hatred, and
take away all the fruit of your labor,
and leave you naked and bare, and the
nakedness of your harlotry shall be
uncovered. Your lewdness and your
harlotry 30 have brought this upon you,
because you played the harlot with the
nations, and polluted yourself with
their idols. 31 You have gone the way
of your sister; therefore I will give her
cup into your hand. 32 Thus says the
Lord GOD:

"You shall drink your sister's cup
 which is deep and large;
you shall be laughed at and held in
 derision,
 for it contains much;
33 you will be filled with drunkenness
 and sorrow.
A cup of horror and desolation,
 is the cup of your sister Sȧ·mâr'i·ȧ;
34 you shall drink it and drain it out,
 and pluck out your hair,[n]
 and tear your breasts;
for I have spoken, says the Lord GOD.

35 Therefore thus says the Lord GOD:
Because you have forgotten me and
cast me behind your back, therefore
bear the consequences of your lewdness and harlotry."

36 The LORD said to me: "Son of
man, will you judge Ō·hō'lȧh and
Ō·hol'i·bȧh? Then declare to them
their abominable deeds. 37 For they
have committed adultery, and blood is
upon their hands; with their idols they
have committed adultery; and they
have even offered up to them for food
the sons whom they had borne to me.
38 Moreover this they have done to
me: they have defiled my sanctuary on
the same day and profaned my sabbaths. 39 For when they had slaughtered their children in sacrifice to their
idols, on the same day they came into
my sanctuary to profane it. And lo,
this is what they did in my house.
40 They even sent for men to come
from far, to whom a messenger was
sent, and lo, they came. For them you
bathed yourself, painted your eyes,
and decked yourself with ornaments;
41 you sat upon a stately couch, with
a table spread before it on which you
had placed my incense and my oil.
42 The sound of a carefree multitude
was with her; and with men of the
common sort drunkards[o] were brought
from the wilderness; and they put
bracelets upon the hands of the
women, and beautiful crowns upon
their heads.

43 "Then I said, Do not men now
commit adultery[p] when they practice
harlotry with her? 44 For they have
gone in to her, as men go in to a
harlot. Thus they went in to Ō·hō'lȧh
and to Ō·hol'i·bȧh to commit lewdness.[q] 45 But righteous men shall pass
judgment on them with the sentence
of adulteresses, and with the sentence
of women that shed blood; because
they are adulteresses, and blood is
upon their hands."

46 For thus says the Lord GOD:
"Bring up a host against them, and
make them an object of terror and a
spoil. 47 And the host shall stone them
and dispatch them with their swords;
they shall slay their sons and their
daughters, and burn up their houses.
48 Thus will I put an end to lewdness
in the land, that all women may take
warning and not commit lewdness as
you have done. 49 And your lewdness
shall be requited upon you, and you
shall bear the penalty for your sinful
idolatry; and you shall know that I
am the Lord GOD."

24 In the ninth year, in the tenth
month, on the tenth day of the
month, the word of the LORD came to
me: 2 "Son of man, write down the
name of this day, this very day. The
king of Babylon has laid siege to Jerusalem this very day. 3 And utter an
allegory to the rebellious house and
say to them, Thus says the Lord GOD:

Set on the pot, set it on,
 pour in water also;
4 put in it the pieces of flesh,
 all the good pieces, the thigh and
 the shoulder;
 fill it with choice bones.
5 Take the choicest one of the flock,
 pile the logs[r] under it;
boil its pieces,[s]
 seethe[t] also its bones in it.

6 "Therefore thus says the Lord
GOD: Woe to the bloody city, to the
pot whose rust is in it, and whose rust
has not gone out of it! Take out of it

[n] Compare Syr: Heb *gnaw its sherds* [o] Heb uncertain [p] Compare Gk: Heb obscure
[q] Gk: Heb *a woman of lewdness* [r] Compare verse 10: Heb *the bones* [s] Two Mss: Heb *its boilings*
[t] Cn: Heb *its bones seethe*

piece after piece, without making any
choice.[u] 7 For the blood she has shed
is still in the midst of her; she put it
on the bare rock, she did not pour it
upon the ground to cover it with dust.
8 To rouse my wrath, to take vengeance, I have set on the bare rock the
blood she has shed, that it may not be
covered. 9 Therefore thus says the
Lord GOD: Woe to the bloody city! I
also will make the pile great. 10 Heap
on the logs, kindle the fire, boil well
the flesh, and empty out the broth,[v]
and let the bones be burned up.
11 Then set it empty upon the coals,
that it may become hot, and its copper
may burn, that its filthiness may be
melted in it, its rust consumed. 12 In
vain I have wearied myself;[w] its thick
rust does not go out of it by fire. 13 Its
rust is your filthy lewdness. Because
I would have cleansed you and you
were not cleansed from your filthiness,
you shall not be cleansed any more till
I have satisfied my fury upon you. 14 I
the LORD have spoken; it shall come
to pass, I will do it; I will not go back,
I will not spare, I will not repent;
according to your ways and your doings I will judge you, says the Lord
GOD."

15 Also the word of the LORD came
to me: 16 "Son of man, behold, I am
about to take the delight of your eyes
away from you at a stroke; yet you
shall not mourn or weep nor shall your
tears run down. 17 Sigh, but not aloud;
make no mourning for the dead. Bind
on your turban, and put your shoes on
your feet; do not cover your lips, nor
eat the bread of mourners."[x] 18 So I
spoke to the people in the morning,
and at evening my wife died. And on
the next morning I did as I was commanded.

19 And the people said to me,
"Will you not tell us what these things
mean for us, that you are acting thus?"
20 Then I said to them, "The word of
the LORD came to me: 21 'Say to the
house of Israel, Thus says the Lord
GOD: Behold, I will profane my
sanctuary, the pride of your power,
the delight of your eyes, and the desire
of your soul; and your sons and your
daughters whom you left behind shall
fall by the sword. 22 And you shall do
as I have done; you shall not cover
your lips, nor eat the bread of mourners.[x] 23 Your turbans shall be on your
heads and your shoes on your feet; you
shall not mourn or weep, but you shall
pine away in your iniquities and groan
to one another. 24 Thus shall E·zēk'i·ėl
be to you a sign; according to all that
he has done you shall do. When this
comes, then you will know that I am
the Lord GOD.'

25 "And you, son of man, on the
day when I take from them their
stronghold, their joy and glory, the
delight of their eyes and their heart's
desire, and also their sons and daughters, 26 on that day a fugitive will come
to you to report to you the news. 27 On
that day your mouth will be opened to
the fugitive, and you shall speak and
be no longer dumb. So you will be a
sign to them; and they will know that
I am the LORD."

25

The word of the LORD came
to me: 2 "Son of man, set your
face toward the Am'mȯ·nītes, and
prophesy against them. 3 Say to the
Am'mȯ·nītes, Hear the word of the
Lord GOD: Thus says the Lord GOD,
Because you said, 'Aha!' over my
sanctuary when it was profaned, and
over the land of Israel when it was
made desolate, and over the house of
Judah when it went into exile; 4 therefore I am handing you over to the
people of the East for a possession,
and they shall set their encampments
among you and make their dwellings
in your midst; they shall eat your fruit,
and they shall drink your milk. 5 I will
make Rab'bȧh a pasture for camels and
the cities of the Am'mȯ·nītes[y] a fold
for flocks. Then you will know that I
am the LORD. 6 For thus says the Lord
GOD: Because you have clapped your
hands and stamped your feet and
rejoiced with all the malice within you
against the land of Israel, 7 therefore,
behold, I have stretched out my hand
against you, and will hand you over
as spoil to the nations; and I will cut
you off from the peoples and will make
you perish out of the countries; I will
destroy you. Then you will know that
I am the LORD.

8 "Thus says the Lord GOD: Be-

[u] Heb *no lot has fallen upon it* [v] Compare Gk: Heb *mix the spices* [w] Cn: Heb uncertain
[x] Vg Tg: Heb *men* [y] Cn: Heb lacks *the cities of*

25.1-7: Ezek 21.28-32; Jer 49.1-6; Amos 1.13-15; Zeph 2.8-11.
25.8-11: Is 15-16; 25.10-12; Jer 48; Amos 2.1-3; Zeph 2.8-11.

cause Mō'ab[z] said, Behold, the house
of Judah is like all the other nations,
9 therefore I will lay open the flank of
Mō'ab from the cities[a] on its frontier,
the glory of the country, Beth-jesh'i-
moth, Bā'ăl-mē'ŏn, and Kĭr·ĭ·ă·thā'im.
10 I will give it along with the Am'mŏ-
nītes to the people of the East as a
possession, that it[b] may be remembered no more among the nations,
11 and I will execute judgments upon
Mō'ab. Then they will know that I am
the LORD.

12 "Thus says the Lord GOD:
Because Ē'dŏm acted revengefully
against the house of Judah and has
grievously offended in taking vengeance upon them, 13 therefore thus says
the Lord GOD, I will stretch out my
hand against Ē'dŏm, and cut off from
it man and beast; and I will make it
desolate; from Tē'măn even to Dē'dan
they shall fall by the sword. 14 And I
will lay my vengeance upon Ē'dŏm by
the hand of my people Israel; and they
shall do in Edom according to my
anger and according to my wrath; and
they shall know my vengeance, says
the Lord GOD.

15 "Thus says the Lord GOD: Because the Philistines acted revengefully and took vengeance with malice
of heart to destroy in never-ending
enmity; 16 therefore thus says the
Lord GOD, Behold, I will stretch out
my hand against the Philistines, and I
will cut off the Cher'ĕ·thites, and
destroy the rest of the seacoast. 17 I
will execute great vengeance upon
them with wrathful chastisements.
Then they will know that I am the
LORD, when I lay my vengeance upon
them."

26 In the eleventh year, on the
first day of the month, the word
of the LORD came to me: 2 "Son of
man, because Tȳre said concerning
Jerusalem, 'Aha, the gate of the peoples is broken, it has swung open to
me; I shall be replenished, now that
she is laid waste,' 3 therefore thus says
the Lord GOD: Behold, I am against
you, O Tȳre, and will bring up many
nations against you, as the sea brings
up its waves. 4 They shall destroy the
walls of Tȳre, and break down her
towers; and I will scrape her soil from
her, and make her a bare rock. 5 She
shall be in the midst of the sea a place
for the spreading of nets; for I have
spoken, says the Lord GOD; and she
shall become a spoil to the nations;
6 and her daughters on the mainland
shall be slain by the sword. Then they
will know that I am the LORD.

7 "For thus says the Lord GOD:
Behold, I will bring upon Tȳre from
the north Ne·bŭ·chăd·rez'zăr king of
Babylon, king of kings, with horses
and chariots, and with horsemen and
a host of many soldiers. 8 He will slay
with the sword your daughters on the
mainland; he will set up a siege wall
against you, and throw up a mound
against you, and raise a roof of shields
against you. 9 He will direct the shock
of his battering rams against your
walls, and with his axes he will break
down your towers. 10 His horses will
be so many that their dust will cover
you; your walls will shake at the noise
of the horsemen and wagons and
chariots, when he enters your gates as
one enters a city which has been
breached. 11 With the hoofs of his
horses he will trample all your streets;
he will slay your people with the
sword; and your mighty pillars will
fall to the ground. 12 They will make
a spoil of your riches and a prey of
your merchandise; they will break
down your walls and destroy your
pleasant houses; your stones and timber and soil they will cast into the midst
of the waters. 13 And I will stop the
music of your songs, and the sound of
your lyres shall be heard no more. 14 I
will make you a bare rock; you shall
be a place for the spreading of nets;
you shall never be rebuilt; for I
the LORD have spoken, says the Lord
GOD.

15 "Thus says the Lord GOD to
Tȳre: Will not the coastlands shake at
the sound of your fall, when the
wounded groan, when slaughter is
made in the midst of you? 16 Then all
the princes of the sea will step down
from their thrones, and remove their
robes, and strip off their embroidered
garments; they will clothe themselves
with trembling; they will sit upon the
ground and tremble every moment,
and be appalled at you. 17 And they

[z] Gk Old Latin: Heb *Moab and Seir* [a] Heb *cities from its cities* [b] Cn: Heb *the Ammonites*
25.12-14: Ezek 35; Is 34; 63.1-6; Jer 49.7-22; Amos 1.11-12; Obad; Mal 1.2-5.
25.15-17: Is 14.29-31; Jer 47; Amos 1.6-8; Zeph 2.4-7; Zech 9.5-7.
26.1-28.19: Is 23; Joel 3.4-8; Amos 1.9-10; Zech 9.3-4. **26.13:** Rev 18.22. **26.16-17:** Rev 18.9-10.

will raise a lamentation over you, and
say to you,
'How you have vanished[c] from the
seas,
O city renowned,
that was mighty on the sea,
you and your inhabitants,
who imposed your terror
on all the mainland![d]
18 Now the isles tremble
on the day of your fall;
yea, the isles that are in the sea
are dismayed at your passing.'
19 "For thus says the Lord GOD:
When I make you a city laid waste,
like the cities that are not inhabited,
when I bring up the deep over you,
and the great waters cover you, 20 then
I will thrust you down with those who
descend into the Pit, to the people of
old, and I will make you to dwell in
the nether world, among primeval
ruins, with those who go down to the
Pit, so that you will not be inhabited
or have a place[e] in the land of the
living. 21 I will bring you to a dreadful
end, and you shall be no more; though
you be sought for, you will never
be found again, says the Lord
GOD."

27 The word of the LORD came to
me: 2 "Now you, son of man,
raise a lamentation over Tȳre, 3 and
say to Tȳre, who dwells at the
entrance to the sea, merchant of the
peoples on many coastlands, thus says
the Lord GOD:
"O Tyre, you have said,
'I am perfect in beauty.'
4 Your borders are in the heart of the
seas;
your builders made perfect your
beauty.
5 They made all your planks
of fir trees from Sē'nir;
they took a cedar from Lebanon
to make a mast for you.
6 Of oaks of Bā'shȧn
they made your oars;
they made your deck of pines
from the coasts of Cyprus,
inlaid with ivory.
7 Of fine embroidered linen from
Egypt
was your sail,
serving as your ensign;
blue and purple from the coasts of
E·lī'shȧh
was your awning.
8 The inhabitants of Sī'don and
Är'vad
were your rowers;
skilled men of Zē'mėr[f] were in you,
they were your pilots.
9 The elders of Gē'bȧl and her skilled
men were in you,
caulking your seams;
all the ships of the sea with their
mariners were in you,
to barter for your wares.
10 "Persia and Lüd and Püt were
in your army as your men of war; they
hung the shield and helmet in you;
they gave you splendor. 11 The men of
Är'vad and Hē'lech[g] were upon your
walls round about, and men of Gā'mad
were in your towers; they hung their
shields upon your walls round about;
they made perfect your beauty.
12 "Tär'shish trafficked with you
because of your great wealth of every
kind; silver, iron, tin, and lead they
exchanged for your wares. 13 Jā'vȧn,
Tü'bȧl, and Mē'shech traded with you;
they exchanged the persons of men and
vessels of bronze for your merchandise. 14 Beth-tō·gär'mȧh exchanged
for your wares horses, war horses, and
mules. 15 The men of Rhodes[h] traded
with you; many coastlands were your
own special markets, they brought you
in payment ivory tusks and ebony.
16 Ē'dŏm[i] trafficked with you because of
your abundant goods; they exchanged
for your wares emeralds, purple,
embroidered work, fine linen, coral,
and agate. 17 Judah and the land of
Israel traded with you; they exchanged
for your merchandise wheat, olives
and early figs,[j] honey, oil, and balm.
18 Damascus trafficked with you for
your abundant goods, because of your
great wealth of every kind; wine of
Hel'bon, and white wool, 19 and wine[k]
from Ū'zȧl they exchanged for your
wares; wrought iron, cassia, and
calamus were bartered for your merchandise. 20 Dē'dan traded with you
in saddlecloths for riding. 21 Arabia
and all the princes of Kē'där were
your favored dealers in lambs, rams,
and goats; in these they trafficked with

[c] Gk Old Latin Aquila: Heb *vanished, O inhabited one,* [d] Cn: Heb *her inhabitants*
[e] Gk: Heb *I will give beauty* [f] Compare Gen 10.18: Heb *your skilled men, O Tyre*
[g] Or *and your army* [h] Gk: Heb *Dedan* [i] Another reading is *Aram*
[j] Cn: Heb *wheat of minnith and pannag* [k] Gk: Heb *Vedan and Javan*
27.13: Rev 18.13.

you. 22 The traders of Sheba and
Rā'ȧ·mȧh traded with you; they exchanged for your wares the best of all
kinds of spices, and all precious stones,
and gold. 23 Hâr'ȧn, Can'nėh, Eden,[l]
As'shŭr, and Chil'mad traded with
you. 24 These traded with you in
choice garments, in clothes of blue and
embroidered work, and in carpets of
colored stuff, bound with cords and
made secure; in these they traded with
you.[m] 25 The ships of Tär'shish traveled for you with your merchandise.[n]

"So you were filled and heavily laden
in the heart of the seas.
26 Your rowers have brought you out into the high seas.
The east wind has wrecked you
in the heart of the seas.
27 Your riches, your wares, your merchandise,
your mariners and your pilots,
your caulkers, your dealers in merchandise,
and all your men of war who are in you,
with all your company
that is in your midst,
sink into the heart of the seas
on the day of your ruin.
28 At the sound of the cry of your pilots
the countryside shakes,
29 and down from their ships
come all that handle the oar.
The mariners and all the pilots of the sea
stand on the shore
30 and wail aloud over you,
and cry bitterly.
They cast dust on their heads
and wallow in ashes;
31 they make themselves bald for you,
and gird themselves with sackcloth,
and they weep over you in bitterness of soul,
with bitter mourning.
32 In their wailing they raise a lamentation for you,
and lament over you:
'Who was ever destroyed[o] like Tȳre
in the midst of the sea?
33 When your wares came from the seas,
you satisfied many peoples;
with your abundant wealth and merchandise
you enriched the kings of the earth.
34 Now you are wrecked by the seas,
in the depths of the waters;
your merchandise and all your crew
have sunk with you.
35 All the inhabitants of the coastlands
are appalled at you;
and their kings are horribly afraid,
their faces are convulsed.
36 The merchants among the peoples
hiss at you;
you have come to a dreadful end
and shall be no more for ever.' "

28 The word of the LORD came
to me: 2 "Son of man, say to
the prince of Tȳre, Thus says the
Lord GOD:

"Because your heart is proud,
and you have said, 'I am a god,
I sit in the seat of the gods,
in the heart of the seas,'
yet you are but a man, and no god,
though you consider yourself as wise as a god—
3 you are indeed wiser than Daniel;
no secret is hidden from you;
4 by your wisdom and your understanding
you have gotten wealth for yourself,
and have gathered gold and silver
into your treasuries;
5 by your great wisdom in trade
you have increased your wealth,
and your heart has become proud
in your wealth—
6 therefore thus says the Lord GOD:
"Because you consider yourself
as wise as a god,
7 therefore, behold, I will bring
strangers upon you,
the most terrible of the nations;
and they shall draw their swords
against the beauty of your wisdom
and defile your splendor.
8 They shall thrust you down into the Pit,
and you shall die the death of the slain
in the heart of the seas.
9 Will you still say, 'I am a god,'
in the presence of those who slay you,

[l] Cn: Heb *Eden the traders of Sheba*
[m] Cn: Heb *in your market* [n] Cn: Heb *your travelers your merchandise*
[o] Tg Vg: Heb *like silence*
27.27-36: Rev 18.9-19. **28.2:** Dan 11.36; 2 Thess 2.4; Rev 13.5.

though you are but a man, and no god,
in the hands of those who wound you?
10 You shall die the death of the uncircumcised
by the hand of foreigners;
for I have spoken, says the Lord GOD."

11 Moreover the word of the LORD
came to me: 12 "Son of man, raise a
lamentation over the king of Tyre,
and say to him, Thus says the Lord
GOD:

"You were the signet of perfection,[p]
full of wisdom
and perfect in beauty.
13 You were in Eden, the garden of God;
every precious stone was your covering,
carnelian, topaz, and jasper,
chrysolite, beryl, and onyx;
sapphire,[q] carbuncle, and emerald;
and wrought in gold were your settings
and your engravings.[r]
On the day that you were created
they were prepared.
14 With an anointed guardian cherub
I placed you;[s]
you were on the holy mountain of God;
in the midst of the stones of fire
you walked.
15 You were blameless in your ways
from the day you were created,
till iniquity was found in you.
16 In the abundance of your trade
you were filled with violence, and you sinned;
so I cast you as a profane thing from the mountain of God,
and the guardian cherub drove you out
from the midst of the stones of fire.
17 Your heart was proud because of your beauty;
you corrupted your wisdom for the sake of your splendor.
I cast you to the ground;
I exposed you before kings,
to feast their eyes on you.
18 By the multitude of your iniquities,
in the unrighteousness of your trade
you profaned your sanctuaries;
so I brought forth fire from the midst of you;
it consumed you,
and I turned you to ashes upon the earth
in the sight of all who saw you.
19 All who know you among the peoples
are appalled at you;
you have come to a dreadful end
and shall be no more for ever."

20 The word of the LORD came to
me: 21 "Son of man, set your face toward Sī'don, and prophesy against her
22 and say, Thus says the Lord GOD:

"Behold, I am against you, O Sī'don,
and I will manifest my glory in the midst of you.
And they shall know that I am the LORD
when I execute judgments in her,
and manifest my holiness in her;
23 for I will send pestilence into her,
and blood into her streets;
and the slain shall fall in the midst of her,
by the sword that is against her on every side.
Then they will know that I am the LORD.

24 "And for the house of Israel
there shall be no more a brier to prick
or a thorn to hurt them among all
their neighbors who have treated them
with contempt. Then they will know
that I am the Lord GOD.

25 "Thus says the Lord GOD:
When I gather the house of Israel
from the peoples among whom they
are scattered, and manifest my holiness
in them in the sight of the nations,
then they shall dwell in their own land
which I gave to my servant Jacob.
26 And they shall dwell securely in it,
and they shall build houses and plant
vineyards. They shall dwell securely,
when I execute judgments upon all
their neighbors who have treated them
with contempt. Then they will know
that I am the LORD their God."

29 In the tenth year, in the tenth
month, on the twelfth day of
the month, the word of the LORD came
to me: 2 "Son of man, set your face
against Pharaoh king of Egypt, and
prophesy against him and against all
Egypt; 3 speak, and say, Thus says the
Lord GOD:

[p] Heb obscure [q] Or *lapis lazuli* [r] Heb uncertain [s] Heb uncertain
28.20-26: Joel 3.4-8; Zech 9.2. 29-32: Is 19; Jer 46; Zech 14.18-19.

"Behold, I am against you,
Pharaoh king of Egypt,
the great dragon that lies
in the midst of his streams,
that says, 'My Nile is my own;
I made it.'[t]
4 I will put hooks in your jaws,
and make the fish of your streams
stick to your scales;
and I will draw you up out of the
midst of your streams,
with all the fish of your streams
which stick to your scales.
5 And I will cast you forth into the
wilderness,
you and all the fish of your
streams;
you shall fall upon the open field,
and not be gathered and buried.
To the beasts of the earth and to
the birds of the air
I have given you as food.

6 "Then all the inhabitants of Egypt
shall know that I am the LORD. Because you[u] have been a staff of reed to
the house of Israel; 7 when they
grasped you with the hand, you broke,
and tore all their shoulders; and when
they leaned upon you, you broke, and
made all their loins to shake;[v] 8 therefore thus says the Lord GOD: Behold,
I will bring a sword upon you, and
will cut off from you man and beast;
9 and the land of Egypt shall be a
desolation and a waste. Then they will
know that I am the LORD.

"Because you[w] said, 'The Nile is
mine, and I made it,' 10 therefore,
behold, I am against you, and against
your streams, and I will make the land
of Egypt an utter waste and desolation,
from Mig'dōl to Sy̆·ē'nē, as far as the
border of Ethiopia. 11 No foot of man
shall pass through it, and no foot of
beast shall pass through it; it shall be
uninhabited forty years. 12 And I will
make the land of Egypt a desolation
in the midst of desolated countries;
and her cities shall be a desolation forty
years among cities that are laid waste.
I will scatter the Egyptians among the
nations, and disperse them among the
countries.

13 "For thus says the Lord GOD: At
the end of forty years I will gather the
Egyptians from the peoples among
whom they were scattered; 14 and I
will restore the fortunes of Egypt, and
bring them back to the land of Path'-
ros, the land of their origin; and there
they shall be a lowly kingdom. 15 It
shall be the most lowly of the kingdoms, and never again exalt itself
above the nations; and I will make
them so small that they will never again
rule over the nations. 16 And it shall
never again be the reliance of the
house of Israel, recalling their iniquity,
when they turn to them for aid. Then
they will know that I am the Lord
GOD."

17 In the twenty-seventh year, in
the first month, on the first day of the
month, the word of the LORD came to
me: 18 "Son of man, Ne·bu̇·chȧd·rez'-
zȧr king of Babylon made his army
labor hard against Ty̆re; every head
was made bald and every shoulder was
rubbed bare; yet neither he nor his
army got anything from Tyre to pay
for the labor that he had performed
against it. 19 Therefore thus says the
Lord GOD: Behold, I will give the land
of Egypt to Ne·bu̇·chȧd·rez'zȧr king
of Babylon; and he shall carry off its
wealth[x] and despoil it and plunder it;
and it shall be the wages for his army.
20 I have given him the land of Egypt
as his recompense for which he
labored, because they worked for me,
says the Lord GOD.

21 "On that day I will cause a horn
to spring forth to the house of Israel,
and I will open your lips among them.
Then they will know that I am the
LORD."

30 The word of the LORD came to
me: 2 "Son of man, prophesy,
and say, Thus says the Lord GOD:
"Wail, 'Alas for the day!'
3 For the day is near,
the day of the LORD is near;
it will be a day of clouds,
a time of doom for the nations.
4 A sword shall come upon Egypt,
and anguish shall be in Ethiopia,
when the slain fall in Egypt,
and her wealth is carried away,
and her foundations are torn
down.
5 Ethiopia, and Pu̇t, and Lu̇d, and all
Arabia, and Libya,[y] and the people of
the land that is in league, shall fall
with them by the sword.

6 "Thus says the LORD:
Those who support Egypt shall fall,

[t] Syr Compare Gk: Heb *I have made myself* [u] Gk Syr Vg: Heb *they* [v] Syr: Heb *stand*
[w] Gk Syr Vg: Heb *he* [x] Or *multitude* [y] Gk Compare Syr Vg: Heb *Cub*

and her proud might shall come
down;
from Mig'dōl to Sȳ·ē'nē
they shall fall within her by the
sword,
says the Lord GOD.
7 And she[z] shall be desolated in the
midst of desolated countries
and her cities shall be in the midst
of cities that are laid waste.
8 Then they will know that I am the
LORD,
when I have set fire to Egypt,
and all her helpers are broken.
9 "On that day swift[a] messengers
shall go forth from me to terrify the
unsuspecting Ethiopians; and anguish
shall come upon them on the day of
Egypt's doom; for, lo, it comes!

10 "Thus says the Lord GOD:
I will put an end to the wealth[b] of
Egypt,
by the hand of Ne·bu·chad·rez'-
zar king of Babylon.
11 He and his people with him, the
most terrible of the nations,
shall be brought in to destroy the
land;
and they shall draw their swords
against Egypt,
and fill the land with the slain.
12 And I will dry up the Nile,
and will sell the land into the
hand of evil men;
I will bring desolation upon the land
and everything in it,
by the hand of foreigners;
I, the LORD, have spoken.

13 "Thus says the Lord GOD:
I will destroy the idols,
and put an end to the images, in
Memphis;
there shall no longer be a prince in
the land of Egypt;
so I will put fear in the land of
Egypt.
14 I will make Path'ros a desolation,
and will set fire to Zō'an,
and will execute acts of judgment
upon Thebes.
15 And I will pour my wrath upon
Pe·lü'si·um,
the stronghold of Egypt,
and cut off the multitude of
Thebes.
16 And I will set fire to Egypt;
Pe·lü'si·um shall be in great
agony;
Thebes shall be breached,
and its walls broken down.[c]
17 The young men of On and of Pī-
bē'seth shall fall by the sword;
and the women shall go into captivity.
18 At Te·haph'ne·hēs the day shall be
dark,
when I break there the dominion
of Egypt,
and her proud might shall come to
an end;
she shall be covered by a cloud,
and her daughters shall go into
captivity.
19 Thus I will execute acts of judgment
upon Egypt.
Then they will know that I am
the LORD."

20 In the eleventh year, in the first
month, on the seventh day of the
month, the word of the LORD came to
me: 21 "Son of man, I have broken the
arm of Pharaoh king of Egypt; and lo,
it has not been bound up, to heal it
by binding it with a bandage, so that
it may become strong to wield the
sword. 22 Therefore thus says the Lord
GOD: Behold, I am against Pharaoh
king of Egypt, and will break his
arms, both the strong arm and the one
that was broken; and I will make the
sword fall from his hand. 23 I will
scatter the Egyptians among the
nations, and disperse them throughout
the lands. 24 And I will strengthen the
arms of the king of Babylon, and put
my sword in his hand; but I will break
the arms of Pharaoh, and he will groan
before him like a man mortally
wounded. 25 I will strengthen the arms
of the king of Babylon, but the arms
of Pharaoh shall fall; and they shall
know that I am the LORD. When I put
my sword into the hand of the king
of Babylon, he shall stretch it out
against the land of Egypt; 26 and I will
scatter the Egyptians among the nations and disperse them throughout
the countries. Then they will know
that I am the LORD."

31 In the eleventh year, in the
third month, on the first day of
the month, the word of the LORD came
to me: 2 "Son of man, say to Pharaoh
king of Egypt and to his multitude:

[z] Gk: Heb *they*
[a] Gk Syr: Heb *in ships* [b] Or *multitude*
[c] Cn: Heb *and Memphis, distresses by day*

"Whom are you like in your greatness?
3 Behold, I will liken you to[d] a cedar in Lebanon,
with fair branches and forest shade,
and of great height,
its top among the clouds.[e]
4 The waters nourished it,
the deep made it grow tall,
making its river flow[f]
round the place of its planting,
sending forth its streams
to all the trees of the forest.
5 So it towered high
above all the trees of the forest;
its boughs grew large
and its branches long,
from abundant water in its shoots.
6 All the birds of the air
made their nests in its boughs;
under its branches all the beasts of the field
brought forth their young;
and under its shadow
dwelt all great nations.
7 It was beautiful in its greatness,
in the length of its branches;
for its roots went down
to abundant waters.
8 The cedars in the garden of God
could not rival it,
nor the fir trees equal its boughs;
the plane trees were as nothing
compared with its branches;
no tree in the garden of God
was like it in beauty.
9 I made it beautiful
in the mass of its branches,
and all the trees of Eden envied it,
that were in the garden of God.

10 "Therefore thus says the Lord
GOD: Because it[g] towered high and set
its top among the clouds,[h] and its heart
was proud of its height, 11 I will give
it into the hand of a mighty one of the
nations; he shall surely deal with it as
its wickedness deserves. I have cast it
out. 12 Foreigners, the most terrible of
the nations, will cut it down and leave
it. On the mountains and in all the
valleys its branches will fall, and its
boughs will lie broken in all the watercourses of the land; and all the peoples
of the earth will go from its shadow
and leave it. 13 Upon its ruin will
dwell all the birds of the air, and upon
its branches will be all the beasts of
the field. 14 All this is in order that no
trees by the waters may grow to lofty
height or set their tops among the
clouds,[h] and that no trees that drink
water may reach up to them in height;
for they are all given over to death, to
the nether world among mortal men,
with those who go down to the Pit.

15 "Thus says the Lord GOD: When
it goes down to Shē'ōl I will make the
deep mourn for[i] it, and restrain its
rivers, and many waters shall be
stopped; I will clothe Lebanon in
gloom for it, and all the trees of the
field shall faint because of it. 16 I will
make the nations quake at the sound
of its fall, when I cast it down to
Shē'ōl with those who go down to the
Pit; and all the trees of Eden, the
choice and best of Lebanon, all that
drink water, will be comforted in the
nether world. 17 They also shall go
down to Shē'ōl with it, to those who
are slain by the sword; yea, those who
dwelt under its shadow among the
nations shall perish.[j] 18 Whom are you
thus like in glory and in greatness
among the trees of Eden? You shall
be brought down with the trees of
Eden to the nether world; you shall
lie among the uncircumcised, with
those who are slain by the sword.

"This is Pharaoh and all his multitude, says the Lord GOD."

32 In the twelfth year, in the
twelfth month, on the first day
of the month, the word of the LORD
came to me: 2 "Son of man, raise a
lamentation over Pharaoh king of
Egypt, and say to him:

"You consider yourself a lion among the nations,
but you are like a dragon in the seas;
you burst forth in your rivers,
trouble the waters with your feet,
and foul their rivers.
3 Thus says the Lord GOD:
I will throw my net over you
with a host of many peoples;
and I[k] will haul you up in my dragnet.
4 And I will cast you on the ground,
on the open field I will fling you,
and will cause all the birds of the air to settle on you,

[d] Cn: Heb *Behold, Assyria* [e] Gk: Heb *thick boughs* [f] Gk: Heb *going* [g] Syr Vg: Heb *you*
[h] Gk: Heb *thick boughs* [i] Gk: Heb *mourn for, I have covered* [j] Compare Gk: Heb obscure
[k] Gk Vg: Heb *they*
31.6: Ezek 17.23; Dan 4.12-21; Mt 13.32; Mk 4.32; Lk 13.19. **31.8** (Gk): Rev 2.7.

and I will gorge the beasts of the
whole earth with you.
5 I will strew your flesh upon the
mountains,
and fill the valleys with your
carcass.[l]
6 I will drench the land even to the
mountains
with your flowing blood;
and the watercourses will be full
of you.
7 When I blot you out, I will cover
the heavens,
and make their stars dark;
I will cover the sun with a cloud,
and the moon shall not give its
light.
8 All the bright lights of heaven
will I make dark over you,
and put darkness upon your land,
says the Lord GOD.

9 "I will trouble the hearts of many
peoples, when I carry you captive[m]
among the nations, into the countries
which you have not known. 10 I will
make many peoples appalled at you,
and their kings shall shudder because
of you, when I brandish my sword
before them; they shall tremble every
moment, every one for his own life, on
the day of your downfall. 11 For thus
says the Lord GOD: The sword of the
king of Babylon shall come upon you.
12 I will cause your multitude to fall
by the swords of mighty ones, all of
them most terrible among the nations.

"They shall bring to nought the
pride of Egypt,
and all its multitudes shall perish.
13 I will destroy all its beasts
from beside many waters;
and no foot of man shall trouble
them any more,
nor shall the hoofs of beasts
trouble them.
14 Then I will make their waters clear,
and cause their rivers to run like
oil, says the Lord GOD.
15 When I make the land of Egypt
desolate
and when the land is stripped of
all that fills it,
when I smite all who dwell in it,
then they will know that I am the
LORD.
16 This is a lamentation which shall be
chanted; the daughters of the nations
shall chant it; over Egypt, and over all
her multitude, shall they chant it, says
the Lord GOD."

17 In the twelfth year, in the first
month,[n] on the fifteenth day of the
month, the word of the LORD came to
me: 18 "Son of man, wail over the
multitude of Egypt, and send them
down, her and the daughters of majestic nations, to the nether world, to
those who have gone down to the Pit:
19 'Whom do you surpass in beauty?
Go down, and be laid with the
uncircumcised.'
20 They shall fall amid those who are
slain by the sword,[o] and with her shall
lie all her multitudes.[p] 21 The mighty
chiefs shall speak of them, with their
helpers, out of the midst of Shē'ōl:
'They have come down, they lie still,
the uncircumcised, slain by the sword.'

22 "Assyria is there, and all her
company, their graves round about
her, all of them slain, fallen by the
sword; 23 whose graves are set in the
uttermost parts of the Pit, and her
company is round about her grave; all
of them slain, fallen by the sword, who
spread terror in the land of the living.

24 "Ē'lȧm is there, and all her
multitude about her grave; all of them
slain, fallen by the sword, who went
down uncircumcised into the nether
world, who spread terror in the land
of the living, and they bear their shame
with those who go down to the Pit.
25 They have made her a bed among
the slain with all her multitude, their
graves round about her, all of them
uncircumcised, slain by the sword; for
terror of them was spread in the land
of the living, and they bear their shame
with those who go down to the Pit;
they are placed among the slain.

26 "Mē'shech and Tü'bȧl are there,
and all their multitude, their graves
round about them, all of them uncircumcised, slain by the sword; for
they spread terror in the land of the
living. 27 And they do not lie with the
fallen mighty men of old[q] who went
down to Shē'ōl with their weapons of
war, whose swords were laid under
their heads, and whose shields[r] are
upon their bones; for the terror of the
mighty men was in the land of the
living. 28 So you shall be broken and

[l] Symmachus Syr Vg: Heb *your height* [m] Gk: Heb *bring your destruction*
[n] Gk: Heb lacks *in the first month* [o] Gk Syr: Heb *sword, the sword is delivered*
[p] Gk: Heb *they have drawn her away and all her multitudes* [q] Gk Old Latin: Heb *of the uncircumcised*
[r] Cn: Heb *iniquities*

lie among the uncircumcised, with
those who are slain by the sword.
29 "E'dom is there, her kings and
all her princes, who for all their might
are laid with those who are slain by
the sword; they lie with the uncircumcised, with those who go down to
the Pit.
30 "The princes of the north are
there, all of them, and all the Si·dō'ni-
ans, who have gone down in shame
with the slain, for all the terror which
they caused by their might; they lie
uncircumcised with those who are
slain by the sword, and bear their
shame with those who go down to the
Pit.
31 "When Pharaoh sees them, he
will comfort himself for all his multitude, Pharaoh and all his army, slain
by the sword, says the Lord GOD.
32 For he[s] spread terror in the land of
the living; therefore he shall be laid
among the uncircumcised, with those
who are slain by the sword, Pharaoh
and all his multitude, says the Lord
GOD."
33 The word of the LORD came
to me: 2 "Son of man, speak to
your people and say to them, If I bring
the sword upon a land, and the people
of the land take a man from among
them, and make him their watchman;
3 and if he sees the sword coming upon
the land and blows the trumpet and
warns the people; 4 then if any one
who hears the sound of the trumpet
does not take warning, and the sword
comes and takes him away, his blood
shall be upon his own head. 5 He heard
the sound of the trumpet, and did not
take warning; his blood shall be upon
himself. But if he had taken warning,
he would have saved his life. 6 But if
the watchman sees the sword coming
and does not blow the trumpet, so that
the people are not warned, and the
sword comes, and takes any one of
them; that man is taken away in his
iniquity, but his blood I will require at
the watchman's hand.
7 "So you, son of man, I have made
a watchman for the house of Israel;
whenever you hear a word from my
mouth, you shall give them warning
from me. 8 If I say to the wicked, O
wicked man, you shall surely die, and
you do not speak to warn the wicked
to turn from his way, that wicked man
shall die in his iniquity, but his blood
I will require at your hand. 9 But if
you warn the wicked to turn from his
way, and he does not turn from his
way; he shall die in his iniquity, but
you will have saved your life.
10 "And you, son of man, say to
the house of Israel, Thus have you
said: 'Our transgressions and our sins
are upon us, and we waste away because of them; how then can we live?'
11 Say to them, As I live, says the
Lord GOD, I have no pleasure in the
death of the wicked, but that the
wicked turn from his way and live;
turn back, turn back from your evil
ways; for why will you die, O house
of Israel? 12 And you, son of man, say
to your people, The righteousness of
the righteous shall not deliver him
when he transgresses; and as for the
wickedness of the wicked, he shall not
fall by it when he turns from his
wickedness; and the righteous shall not
be able to live by his righteousness[t]
when he sins. 13 Though I say to the
righteous that he shall surely live, yet
if he trusts in his righteousness and
commits iniquity, none of his righteous
deeds shall be remembered; but in the
iniquity that he has committed he shall
die. 14 Again, though I say to the
wicked, 'You shall surely die,' yet if
he turns from his sin and does what
is lawful and right, 15 if the wicked
restores the pledge, gives back what he
has taken by robbery, and walks in the
statutes of life, committing no iniquity;
he shall surely live, he shall not die.
16 None of the sins that he has committed shall be remembered against
him; he has done what is lawful and
right, he shall surely live.
17 "Yet your people say, 'The way
of the Lord is not just'; when it is their
own way that is not just. 18 When the
righteous turns from his righteousness,
and commits iniquity, he shall die for
it. 19 And when the wicked turns from
his wickedness, and does what is lawful and right, he shall live by it. 20 Yet
you say, 'The way of the Lord is not
just.' O house of Israel, I will judge
each of you according to his ways."
21 In the twelfth year of our exile,
in the tenth month, on the fifth day of
the month, a man who had escaped
from Jerusalem came to me and said,
"The city has fallen." 22 Now the

[s] Cn: Heb *I* [t] Heb *by it*
33.1-9: Ezek 3.16-21. 33.11: Ezek 18.23, 32.

hand of the LORD had been upon me
the evening before the fugitive came;
and he had opened my mouth by the
time the man came to me in the
morning; so my mouth was opened,
and I was no longer dumb.
23 The word of the LORD came to
me: 24 "Son of man, the inhabitants
of these waste places in the land of
Israel keep saying, 'Abraham was only
one man, yet he got possession of the
land; but we are many; the land is
surely given us to possess.' 25 Therefore say to them, Thus says the Lord
GOD: You eat flesh with the blood, and
lift up your eyes to your idols, and
shed blood; shall you then possess the
land? 26 You resort to the sword, you
commit abominations and each of you
defiles his neighbor's wife; shall you
then possess the land? 27 Say this to
them, Thus says the Lord GOD: As I
live, surely those who are in the waste
places shall fall by the sword; and him
that is in the open field I will give to
the beasts to be devoured; and those
who are in strongholds and in caves
shall die by pestilence. 28 And I will
make the land a desolation and a
waste; and her proud might shall come
to an end; and the mountains of Israel
shall be so desolate that none will pass
through. 29 Then they will know that
I am the LORD, when I have made the
land a desolation and a waste because
of all their abominations which they
have committed.
30 "As for you, son of man, your
people who talk together about you by
the walls and at the doors of the houses,
say to one another, each to his brother,
'Come, and hear what the word is that
comes forth from the LORD.' 31 And
they come to you as people come, and
they sit before you as my people, and
they hear what you say but they will
not do it; for with their lips they show
much love, but their heart is set on
their gain. 32 And, lo, you are to them
like one who sings love songs[u] with a
beautiful voice and plays well on an
instrument, for they hear what you
say, but they will not do it. 33 When
this comes—and come it will!—then
they will know that a prophet has been
among them."
34 The word of the LORD came
to me: 2 "Son of man, prophesy
against the shepherds of Israel, prophesy, and say to them, even to the
shepherds, Thus says the Lord GOD:
Ho, shepherds of Israel who have been
feeding yourselves! Should not shepherds feed the sheep? 3 You eat the
fat, you clothe yourselves with the
wool, you slaughter the fatlings; but
you do not feed the sheep. 4 The weak
you have not strengthened, the sick
you have not healed, the crippled you
have not bound up, the strayed you
have not brought back, the lost you
have not sought, and with force and
harshness you have ruled them. 5 So
they were scattered, because there was
no shepherd; and they became food
for all the wild beasts. 6 My sheep
were scattered, they wandered over
all the mountains and on every high
hill; my sheep were scattered over all
the face of the earth, with none to
search or seek for them.
7 "Therefore, you shepherds, hear
the word of the LORD: 8 As I live, says
the Lord GOD, because my sheep have
become a prey, and my sheep have
become food for all the wild beasts,
since there was no shepherd; and because my shepherds have not searched
for my sheep, but the shepherds have
fed themselves, and have not fed my
sheep; 9 therefore, you shepherds, hear
the word of the LORD: 10 Thus says
the Lord GOD, Behold, I am against
the shepherds; and I will require my
sheep at their hand, and put a stop to
their feeding the sheep; no longer shall
the shepherds feed themselves. I will
rescue my sheep from their mouths,
that they may not be food for them.
11 "For thus says the Lord GOD:
Behold, I, I myself will search for my
sheep, and will seek them out. 12 As a
shepherd seeks out his flock when
some of his sheep[v] have been scattered
abroad, so will I seek out my sheep;
and I will rescue them from all places
where they have been scattered on a
day of clouds and thick darkness.
13 And I will bring them out from the
peoples, and gather them from the
countries, and will bring them into
their own land; and I will feed them
on the mountains of Israel, by the
fountains, and in all the inhabited
places of the country. 14 I will feed
them with good pasture, and upon
the mountain heights of Israel shall be
their pasture; there they shall lie down

[u] Cn: Heb *like a love song* [v] Cn: Heb *when he is among his sheep*
34.5: Mt 9.36; Mk 6.34.

in good grazing land, and on fat pasture they shall feed on the mountains
of Israel. 15 I myself will be the shepherd of my sheep, and I will make
them lie down, says the Lord GOD.
16 I will seek the lost, and I will bring
back the strayed, and I will bind up
the crippled, and I will strengthen the
weak, and the fat and the strong I will
watch over;[w] I will feed them in
justice.

17 "As for you, my flock, thus says
the Lord GOD: Behold, I judge between sheep and sheep, rams and he-
goats. 18 Is it not enough for you to
feed on the good pasture, that you
must tread down with your feet the
rest of your pasture; and to drink of
clear water, that you must foul the
rest with your feet? 19And must my
sheep eat what you have trodden with
your feet, and drink what you have
fouled with your feet?

20 "Therefore, thus says the Lord
GOD to them: Behold, I, I myself will
judge between the fat sheep and the
lean sheep. 21 Because you push with
side and shoulder, and thrust at all the
weak with your horns, till you have
scattered them abroad, 22 I will save
my flock, they shall no longer be a
prey; and I will judge between sheep
and sheep. 23And I will set up over
them one shepherd, my servant David,
and he shall feed them: he shall feed
them and be their shepherd. 24And I,
the LORD, will be their God, and my
servant David shall be prince among
them; I, the LORD, have spoken.

25 "I will make with them a covenant of peace and banish wild beasts
from the land, so that they may dwell
securely in the wilderness and sleep
in the woods. 26And I will make them
and the places round about my hill a
blessing; and I will send down the
showers in their season; they shall be
showers of blessing. 27And the trees
of the field shall yield their fruit, and
the earth shall yield its increase, and
they shall be secure in their land; and
they shall know that I am the LORD,
when I break the bars of their yoke,
and deliver them from the hand of
those who enslaved them. 28 They
shall no more be a prey to the nations,
nor shall the beasts of the land devour
them; they shall dwell securely, and
none shall make them afraid. 29And I
will provide for them prosperous[x]
plantations so that they shall no more
be consumed with hunger in the land,
and no longer suffer the reproach of
the nations. 30And they shall know
that I, the LORD their God, am with
them, and that they, the house of Israel,
are my people, says the Lord GOD.
31And you are my sheep, the sheep of
my pasture,[y] and I am your God, says
the Lord GOD."

35 The word of the LORD came to
me: 2 "Son of man, set your face
against Mount Sē'ir, and prophesy
against it, 3 and say to it, Thus says
the Lord GOD: Behold, I am against
you, Mount Sē'ir, and I will stretch
out my hand against you, and I will
make you a desolation and a waste. 4 I
will lay your cities waste, and you
shall become a desolation; and you
shall know that I am the LORD. 5 Because you cherished perpetual enmity,
and gave over the people of Israel to
the power of the sword at the time of
their calamity, at the time of their
final punishment; 6 therefore, as I live,
says the Lord GOD, I will prepare you
for blood, and blood shall pursue you;
because you are guilty of blood,[z] therefore blood shall pursue you. 7 I will
make Mount Sē'ir a waste and a desolation; and I will cut off from it all who
come and go. 8And I will fill your
mountains with the slain; on your hills
and in your valleys and in all your
ravines those slain with the sword
shall fall. 9 I will make you a perpetual
desolation, and your cities shall not be
inhabited. Then you will know that I
am the LORD.

10 "Because you said, 'These two
nations and these two countries shall
be mine, and we will take possession
of them'—although the LORD was
there—11 therefore, as I live, says the
Lord GOD, I will deal with you
according to the anger and envy which
you showed because of your hatred
against them; and I will make myself
known among you,[a] when I judge you.
12And you shall know that I, the LORD,
have heard all the revilings which you
uttered against the mountains of Israel, saying, 'They are laid desolate,
they are given us to devour.' 13And
you magnified yourselves against me

[w] Gk Syr Vg: Heb *destroy* [x] Gk Syr Old Latin: Heb *for renown*
[y] Gk Old Latin: Heb *pasture you are men* [z] Gk: Heb *you have hated blood* [a] Gk: Heb *them*
34.16: Lk 19.10. **34.23:** Ezek 37.24.

with your mouth, and multiplied your
words against me; I heard it. 14 Thus
says the Lord GOD: For the rejoicing
of the whole earth I will make you
desolate. 15 As you rejoiced over the
inheritance of the house of Israel, because it was desolate, so I will deal
with you; you shall be desolate, Mount
Sē'ir, and all E'dŏm, all of it. Then
they will know that I am the LORD.

36 "And you, son of man, prophesy
to the mountains of Israel, and
say, O mountains of Israel, hear the
word of the LORD. 2 Thus says the
Lord GOD: Because the enemy said of
you, 'Aha!' and, 'The ancient heights
have become our possession,' 3 therefore prophesy, and say, Thus says the
Lord GOD: Because, yea, because they
made you desolate, and crushed you
from all sides, so that you became the
possession of the rest of the nations,
and you became the talk and evil
gossip of the people; 4 therefore, O
mountains of Israel, hear the word of
the Lord GOD: Thus says the Lord
GOD to the mountains and the hills,
the ravines and the valleys, the desolate wastes and the deserted cities,
which have become a prey and derision
to the rest of the nations round about;
5 therefore thus says the Lord GOD: I
speak in my hot jealousy against the
rest of the nations, and against all
E'dŏm, who gave my land to themselves as a possession with whole-
hearted joy and utter contempt, that
they might possess[b] it and plunder it.
6 Therefore prophesy concerning the
land of Israel, and say to the mountains and hills, to the ravines and
valleys, Thus says the Lord GOD:
Behold, I speak in my jealous wrath,
because you have suffered the reproach of the nations; 7 therefore thus
says the Lord GOD: I swear that the
nations that are round about you shall
themselves suffer reproach.

8 "But you, O mountains of Israel,
shall shoot forth your branches, and
yield your fruit to my people Israel;
for they will soon come home. 9 For,
behold, I am for you, and I will turn
to you, and you shall be tilled and
sown; 10 and I will multiply men upon
you, the whole house of Israel, all of
it; the cities shall be inhabited and the
waste places rebuilt; 11 and I will
multiply upon you man and beast; and
they shall increase and be fruitful; and
I will cause you to be inhabited as in
your former times, and will do more
good to you than ever before. Then
you will know that I am the LORD.
12 Yea, I will let men walk upon you,
even my people Israel; and they shall
possess you, and you shall be their
inheritance, and you shall no longer
bereave them of children. 13 Thus
says the Lord GOD: Because men say
to you, 'You devour men and you
bereave your nation of children,'
14 therefore you shall no longer devour
men and no longer bereave your nation
of children, says the Lord GOD; 15 and
I will not let you hear any more the
reproach of the nations, and you shall
no longer bear the disgrace of the
peoples and no longer cause your
nation to stumble, says the Lord GOD."

16 The word of the LORD came to
me: 17 "Son of man, when the house
of Israel dwelt in their own land, they
defiled it by their ways and their doings; their conduct before me was like
the uncleanness of a woman in her
impurity. 18 So I poured out my wrath
upon them for the blood which they
had shed in the land, for the idols with
which they had defiled it. 19 I scattered
them among the nations, and they
were dispersed through the countries;
in accordance with their conduct and
their deeds I judged them. 20 But
when they came to the nations, wherever they came, they profaned my holy
name, in that men said of them, 'These
are the people of the LORD, and yet
they had to go out of his land.' 21 But
I had concern for my holy name,
which the house of Israel caused to be
profaned among the nations to which
they came.

22 "Therefore say to the house of
Israel, Thus says the Lord GOD: It is
not for your sake, O house of Israel,
that I am about to act, but for the
sake of my holy name, which you have
profaned among the nations to which
you came. 23 And I will vindicate the
holiness of my great name, which has
been profaned among the nations, and
which you have profaned among
them; and the nations will know that
I am the LORD, says the Lord GOD,
when through you I vindicate my
holiness before their eyes. 24 For I
will take you from the nations, and
gather you from all the countries, and
bring you into your own land. 25 I

[b] One Ms: Heb *drive out*

will sprinkle clean water upon you,
and you shall be clean from all your
uncleannesses, and from all your idols
I will cleanse you. 26A new heart I will
give you, and a new spirit I will put
within you; and I will take out of your
flesh the heart of stone and give you a
heart of flesh. 27And I will put my
spirit within you, and cause you to
walk in my statutes and be careful to
observe my ordinances. 28 You shall
dwell in the land which I gave to your
fathers; and you shall be my people,
and I will be your God. 29And I will
deliver you from all your uncleannesses; and I will summon the grain
and make it abundant and lay no
famine upon you. 30 I will make the
fruit of the tree and the increase of
the field abundant, that you may never
again suffer the disgrace of famine
among the nations. 31 Then you will
remember your evil ways, and your
deeds that were not good; and you will
loathe yourselves for your iniquities
and your abominable deeds. 32 It is not
for your sake that I will act, says the
Lord GOD; let that be known to you.
Be ashamed and confounded for your
ways, O house of Israel.

33 "Thus says the Lord GOD: On
the day that I cleanse you from all
your iniquities, I will cause the cities
to be inhabited, and the waste places
shall be rebuilt. 34And the land that
was desolate shall be tilled, instead of
being the desolation that it was in the
sight of all who passed by. 35And they
will say, 'This land that was desolate
has become like the garden of Eden;
and the waste and desolate and ruined
cities are now inhabited and fortified.'
36 Then the nations that are left round
about you shall know that I, the LORD,
have rebuilt the ruined places, and
replanted that which was desolate; I,
the LORD, have spoken, and I will do
it.

37 "Thus says the Lord GOD: This
also I will let the house of Israel ask
me to do for them: to increase their
men like a flock. 38 Like the flock for
sacrifices,[c] like the flock at Jerusalem
during her appointed feasts, so shall
the waste cities be filled with flocks of
men. Then they will know that I am
the LORD."

37 The hand of the LORD was
upon me, and he brought me
out by the Spirit of the LORD, and set
me down in the midst of the valley;[d]
it was full of bones. 2And he led me
round among them; and behold, there
were very many upon the valley;[d] and
lo, they were very dry. 3And he said
to me, "Son of man, can these bones
live?" And I answered, "O Lord GOD,
thou knowest." 4Again he said to me,
"Prophesy to these bones, and say to
them, O dry bones, hear the word of
the LORD. 5 Thus says the Lord GOD
to these bones: Behold, I will cause
breath[e] to enter you, and you shall
live. 6And I will lay sinews upon you,
and will cause flesh to come upon you,
and cover you with skin, and put
breath[e] in you, and you shall live; and
you shall know that I am the LORD."

7 So I prophesied as I was commanded; and as I prophesied, there
was a noise, and behold, a rattling; and
the bones came together, bone to its
bone. 8And as I looked, there were
sinews on them, and flesh had come
upon them, and skin had covered
them; but there was no breath in
them. 9 Then he said to me, "Prophesy
to the breath, prophesy, son of man,
and say to the breath,[f] Thus says the
Lord GOD: Come from the four winds,
O breath,[f] and breathe upon these
slain, that they may live." 10 So I
prophesied as he commanded me, and
the breath came into them, and they
lived, and stood upon their feet, an
exceedingly great host.

11 Then he said to me, "Son of
man, these bones are the whole house
of Israel. Behold, they say, 'Our bones
are dried up, and our hope is lost; we
are clean cut off.' 12 Therefore prophesy, and say to them, Thus says the
Lord GOD: Behold, I will open your
graves, and raise you from your graves,
O my people; and I will bring you
home into the land of Israel. 13And
you shall know that I am the LORD,
when I open your graves, and raise
you from your graves, O my people.
14And I will put my Spirit within you,
and you shall live, and I will place
you in your own land; then you shall
know that I, the LORD, have spoken,
and I have done it, says the LORD."

[c] Heb *flock of holy things* [d] Or *plain* [e] Or *spirit*
[f] Or *wind* or *spirit*

36.26: Ezek 11.19; 18.31; 2 Cor 3.3. **36.27:** Ezek 37.14; 1 Thess 4.8. **36.31:** Ezek 6.9; 20.43.
37.5, 10: Rev 11.11. **37.14:** Ezek 36.27; 1 Thess 4.8.

15 The word of the LORD came to
me: 16 "Son of man, take a stick and
write on it, 'For Judah, and the children of Israel associated with him';
then take another stick and write upon
it, 'For Joseph (the stick of E'phră·im)
and all the house of Israel associated
with him'; 17 and join them together
into one stick, that they may become
one in your hand. 18 And when your
people say to you, 'Will you not show
us what you mean by these?' 19 say to
them, Thus says the Lord GOD: Behold, I am about to take the stick of
Joseph (which is in the hand of E'phră-
im) and the tribes of Israel associated
with him; and I will join[g] with it the
stick of Judah, and make them one
stick, that they may be one in my hand.
20 When the sticks on which you write
are in your hand before their eyes,
21 then say to them, Thus says the
Lord GOD: Behold, I will take the
people of Israel from the nations
among which they have gone, and
will gather them from all sides, and
bring them to their own land; 22 and
I will make them one nation in the
land, upon the mountains of Israel;
and one king shall be king over them
all; and they shall be no longer two
nations, and no longer divided into
two kingdoms. 23 They shall not defile
themselves any more with their idols
and their detestable things, or with
any of their transgressions; but I will
save them from all the backslidings in
which they have sinned, and will
cleanse them; and they shall be my
people, and I will be their God.
24 "My servant David shall be king
over them; and they shall all have one
shepherd. They shall follow my ordinances and be careful to observe my
statutes. 25 They shall dwell in the
land where your fathers dwelt that I
gave to my servant Jacob; they and
their children and their children's
children shall dwell there for ever; and
David my servant shall be their prince
for ever. 26 I will make a covenant of
peace with them; it shall be an everlasting covenant with them; and I will
bless[h] them and multiply them, and
will set my sanctuary in the midst of
them for evermore. 27 My dwelling
place shall be with them; and I will
be their God, and they shall be my
people. 28 Then the nations will know
that I the LORD sanctify Israel, when
my sanctuary is in the midst of them
for evermore."

38 The word of the LORD came
to me: 2 "Son of man, set your
face toward Gog, of the land of Mā'-
gog, the chief prince of Mē'shech and
Tü'băl, and prophesy against him
3 and say, Thus says the Lord GOD:
Behold, I am against you, O Gog, chief
prince of Mē'shech and Tü'băl; 4 and
I will turn you about, and put hooks
into your jaws, and I will bring you
forth, and all your army, horses and
horsemen, all of them clothed in full
armor, a great company, all of them
with buckler and shield, wielding
swords; 5 Persia, Cush, and Püt are
with them, all of them with shield and
helmet; 6 Gō'mėr and all his hordes;
Beth-tō·gär'măh from the uttermost
parts of the north with all his hordes—
many peoples are with you.
7 "Be ready and keep ready, you
and all the hosts that are assembled
about you, and be a guard for them.
8 After many days you will be mustered; in the latter years you will go
against the land that is restored from
war, the land where people were
gathered from many nations upon the
mountains of Israel, which had been
a continual waste; its people were
brought out from the nations and
now dwell securely, all of them. 9 You
will advance, coming on like a storm,
you will be like a cloud covering the
land, you and all your hordes, and
many peoples with you.
10 "Thus says the Lord GOD: On
that day thoughts will come into your
mind, and you will devise an evil
scheme 11 and say, 'I will go up against
the land of unwalled villages; I will
fall upon the quiet people who dwell
securely, all of them dwelling without
walls, and having no bars or gates';
12 to seize spoil and carry off plunder;
to assail the waste places which are
now inhabited, and the people who
were gathered from the nations, who
have gotten cattle and goods, who
dwell at the center of the earth.
13 Sheba and Dē'dan and the merchants of Tär'shish and all its villages
will say to you, 'Have you come to
seize spoil? Have you assembled your

[g] Heb *join them* [h] Tg: Heb *give*
37.26: Heb 13.20. 37.27: Ex 25.8; 29.45; Lev 26.12; Jer 31.1; 2 Cor 6.16; Rev 21.3.
38.2, 9, 15: Rev 20.8.

hosts to carry off plunder, to carry
away silver and gold, to take away
cattle and goods, to seize great spoil?'
14 "Therefore, son of man, prophesy, and say to Gog, Thus says the Lord
GOD: On that day when my people
Israel are dwelling securely, you will
bestir yourself[i] 15 and come from your
place out of the uttermost parts of the
north, you and many peoples with you,
all of them riding on horses, a great
host, a mighty army; 16 you will come
up against my people Israel, like a
cloud covering the land. In the latter
days I will bring you against my land,
that the nations may know me, when
through you, O Gog, I vindicate my
holiness before their eyes.
17 "Thus says the Lord GOD: Are
you he of whom I spoke in former
days by my servants the prophets of
Israel, who in those days prophesied
for years that I would bring you against
them? 18 But on that day, when Gog
shall come against the land of Israel,
says the Lord GOD, my wrath will be
roused. 19 For in my jealousy and in
my blazing wrath I declare, On that
day there shall be a great shaking in
the land of Israel; 20 the fish of the
sea, and the birds of the air, and the
beasts of the field, and all creeping
things that creep on the ground, and
all the men that are upon the face of
the earth, shall quake at my presence,
and the mountains shall be thrown
down, and the cliffs shall fall, and
every wall shall tumble to the ground.
21 I will summon every kind of terror[j]
against Gog,[k] says the Lord GOD;
every man's sword will be against his
brother. 22 With pestilence and bloodshed I will enter into judgment with
him; and I will rain upon him and his
hordes and the many peoples that are
with him, torrential rains and hailstones, fire and brimstone. 23 So I
will show my greatness and my holiness and make myself known in the
eyes of many nations. Then they will
know that I am the LORD.

39 "And you, son of man, prophesy against Gog, and say, Thus
says the Lord GOD: Behold, I am
against you, O Gog, chief prince of
Mē'shech and Tū'bal; 2 and I will
turn you about and drive you forward,
and bring you up from the uttermost
parts of the north, and lead you against
the mountains of Israel; 3 then I will
strike your bow from your left hand,
and will make your arrows drop out of
your right hand. 4 You shall fall upon
the mountains of Israel, you and all
your hordes and the peoples that are
with you; I will give you to birds of prey
of every sort and to the wild beasts to
be devoured. 5 You shall fall in the
open field; for I have spoken, says the
Lord GOD. 6 I will send fire on Mā'gog
and on those who dwell securely in the
coastlands; and they shall know that
I am the LORD.
7 "And my holy name I will make
known in the midst of my people Israel; and I will not let my holy name
be profaned any more; and the nations
shall know that I am the LORD, the
Holy One in Israel. 8 Behold, it is
coming and it will be brought about,
says the Lord GOD. That is the day of
which I have spoken.
9 "Then those who dwell in the
cities of Israel will go forth and make
fires of the weapons and burn them,
shields and bucklers, bows and arrows,
handpikes and spears, and they will
make fires of them for seven years;
10 so that they will not need to take
wood out of the field or cut down any
out of the forests, for they will make
their fires of the weapons; they will
despoil those who despoiled them, and
plunder those who plundered them,
says the Lord GOD.
11 "On that day I will give to Gog
a place for burial in Israel, the Valley
of the Travelers[l] east of the sea; it will
block the travelers, for there Gog and
all his multitude will be buried; it will
be called the Valley of Hā'mon-gog.[m]
12 For seven months the house of Israel will be burying them, in order to
cleanse the land. 13 All the people of
the land will bury them; and it will
redound to their honor on the day that
I show my glory, says the Lord GOD.
14 They will set apart men to pass
through the land continually and bury[n]
those remaining upon the face of the
land, so as to cleanse it; at the end of
seven months they will make their
search. 15 And when these pass through
the land and any one sees a man's
bone, then he shall set up a sign by it,
till the buriers have buried it in the

[i] Gk: Heb *will you not know?* [j] Gk: Heb *a sword to all my mountains* [k] Heb *him* [l] Or *Abarim*
[m] That is *the multitude of Gog* [n] Gk Syr: Heb *bury the travelers*
38.22: Rev 8.7; 14.10. **39.4, 17-20:** Rev 19.17, 18, 21.

Valley of Hā'mon-gog. 16 (A city
Hȧ·mō'nȧh[o] is there also.) Thus shall
they cleanse the land.
17 "As for you, son of man, thus
says the Lord GOD: Speak to the birds
of every sort and to all beasts of the
field, 'Assemble and come, gather
from all sides to the sacrificial feast
which I am preparing for you, a great
sacrificial feast upon the mountains of
Israel, and you shall eat flesh and
drink blood. 18 You shall eat the flesh
of the mighty, and drink the blood of
the princes of the earth—of rams, of
lambs, and of goats, of bulls, all of
them fatlings of Bā'shȧn. 19 And you
shall eat fat till you are filled, and
drink blood till you are drunk, at the
sacrificial feast which I am preparing
for you. 20 And you shall be filled at
my table with horses and riders, with
mighty men and all kinds of warriors,'
says the Lord GOD.
21 "And I will set my glory among
the nations; and all the nations shall
see my judgment which I have executed, and my hand which I have laid
on them. 22 The house of Israel shall
know that I am the LORD their God,
from that day forward. 23 And the
nations shall know that the house of
Israel went into captivity for their
iniquity, because they dealt so treacherously with me that I hid my face
from them and gave them into the
hand of their adversaries, and they all
fell by the sword. 24 I dealt with them
according to their uncleanness and
their transgressions, and hid my face
from them.
25 "Therefore thus says the Lord
GOD: Now I will restore the fortunes
of Jacob, and have mercy upon the
whole house of Israel; and I will be
jealous for my holy name. 26 They
shall forget their shame, and all the
treachery they have practiced against
me, when they dwell securely in their
land with none to make them afraid,
27 when I have brought them back
from the peoples and gathered them
from their enemies' lands, and through
them have vindicated my holiness in
the sight of many nations. 28 Then
they shall know that I am the LORD
their God because I sent them into
exile among the nations, and then
gathered them into their own land. I
will leave none of them remaining
among the nations any more; 29 and I
will not hide my face any more from
them, when I pour out my Spirit upon
the house of Israel, says the Lord
GOD."

40 In the twenty-fifth year of our
exile, at the beginning of the
year, on the tenth day of the month,
in the fourteenth year after the city
was conquered, on that very day, the
hand of the LORD was upon me, 2 and
brought me in the visions of God into
the land of Israel, and set me down
upon a very high mountain, on which
was a structure like a city opposite
me.[p] 3 When he brought me there,
behold, there was a man, whose appearance was like bronze, with a line
of flax and a measuring reed in his
hand; and he was standing in the gateway. 4 And the man said to me, "Son
of man, look with your eyes, and hear
with your ears, and set your mind upon
all that I shall show you, for you were
brought here in order that I might
show it to you; declare all that you
see to the house of Israel."
5 And behold, there was a wall all
around the outside of the temple area,
and the length of the measuring reed
in the man's hand was six long cubits,
each being a cubit and a handbreadth
in length; so he measured the thickness
of the wall, one reed; and the height,
one reed. 6 Then he went into the
gateway facing east, going up its steps,
and measured the threshold of the
gate, one reed deep;[q] 7 and the side
rooms, one reed long, and one reed
broad; and the space between the side
rooms, five cubits; and the threshold
of the gate by the vestibule of the gate
at the inner end, one reed. 8 Then he
measured the vestibule of the gateway,
eight cubits; 9 and its jambs, two
cubits; and the vestibule of the gate
was at the inner end. 10 And there were
three side rooms on either side of the
east gate; the three were of the same
size; and the jambs on either side
were of the same size. 11 Then he
measured the breadth of the opening
of the gateway, ten cubits; and the
breadth of the gateway, thirteen cubits. 12 There was a barrier before the
side rooms, one cubit on either side;
and the side rooms were six cubits on
either side. 13 Then he measured the

[o] That is *Multitude* [p] Gk: Heb *on the south* [q] Heb *deep, and one threshold, one reed deep*
40.1-43.17: 1 Kings 6-7; 2 Chron 3-4. 40.2: Rev 21.10. 40.3, 5: Rev 21.15.

gate from the back[r] of the one side
room to the back[r] of the other, a
breadth of five and twenty cubits,
from door to door. 14 He measured also
the vestibule, twenty cubits; and round
about the vestibule of the gateway
was the court.[s] 15 From the front of
the gate at the entrance to the end of
the inner vestibule of the gate was
fifty cubits. 16 And the gateway had
windows round about, narrowing in-
wards into their jambs in the side
rooms, and likewise the vestibule had
windows round about inside, and on
the jambs were palm trees.

17 Then he brought me into the
outer court; and behold, there were
chambers and a pavement, round
about the court; thirty chambers
fronted on the pavement. 18 And the
pavement ran along the side of the
gates, corresponding to the length of
the gates; this was the lower pavement.
19 Then he measured the distance
from the inner front of[t] the lower gate
to the outer front of the inner court,
a hundred cubits.

Then he went before me to the
north, 20 and behold, there was a
gate[u] which faced toward the north,
belonging to the outer court. He measured its length and its breadth. 21 Its
side rooms, three on either side, and
its jambs and its vestibule were of the
same size as those of the first gate; its
length was fifty cubits, and its breadth
twenty-five cubits. 22 And its windows,
its vestibule, and its palm trees were
of the same size as those of the gate
which faced toward the east; and
seven steps led up to it; and its vestibule was on the inside. 23 And opposite
the gate on the north, as on the east,
was a gate to the inner court; and he
measured from gate to gate, a hundred
cubits.

24 And he led me toward the south,
and behold, there was a gate on the
south; and he measured its jambs and
its vestibule; they had the same size as
the others. 25 And there were windows
round about in it and in its vestibule,
like the windows of the others; its
length was fifty cubits, and its breadth
twenty-five cubits. 26 And there were
seven steps leading up to it, and its
vestibule was on the inside; and it had
palm trees on its jambs, one on either
side. 27 And there was a gate on the
south of the inner court; and he measured from gate to gate toward the
south, a hundred cubits.

28 Then he brought me to the
inner court by the south gate, and he
measured the south gate; it was of the
same size as the others. 29 Its side
rooms, its jambs, and its vestibule were
of the same size as the others; and
there were windows round about in it
and in its vestibule; its length was
fifty cubits, and its breadth twenty-five
cubits. 30 And there were vestibules
round about, twenty-five cubits long
and five cubits broad. 31 Its vestibule
faced the outer court, and palm trees
were on its jambs, and its stairway had
eight steps.

32 Then he brought me to the inner
court on the east side, and he measured the gate; it was of the same size
as the others. 33 Its side rooms, its
jambs, and its vestibule were of the
same size as the others; and there were
windows round about in it and in its
vestibule; its length was fifty cubits,
and its breadth twenty-five cubits.
34 Its vestibule faced the outer court,
and it had palm trees on its jambs, one
on either side; and its stairway had
eight steps.

35 Then he brought me to the
north gate, and he measured it; it had
the same size as the others. 36 Its side
rooms, its jambs, and its vestibule
were of the same size as the others;[v]
and it had windows round about; its
length was fifty cubits, and its breadth
twenty-five cubits. 37 Its vestibule[w]
faced the outer court, and it had palm
trees on its jambs, one on either side;
and its stairway had eight steps.

38 There was a chamber with its
door in the vestibule of the gate,[x]
where the burnt offering was to be
washed. 39 And in the vestibule of the
gate were two tables on either side, on
which the burnt offering and the sin
offering and the guilt offering were to
be slaughtered. 40 And on the outside
of the vestibule[y] at the entrance of the

[r] Compare Gk: Heb *roof*
[s] Compare Gk: Heb *and he made the jambs sixty cubits, and to the jamb of the court was the gateway round about* [t] Compare Gk: Heb *from before*
[u] Gk: Heb *a hundred cubits on the east and on the north.*[20]*And the gate*
[v] One Ms Compare verses 29 and 33: Heb lacks *were of the same size as the others*
[w] Gk Vg Compare verses 26, 31, 34: Heb *jambs* [x] Cn: Heb *at the jambs of the gates*
[y] Cn: Heb *to him who goes up*

north gate were two tables; and on the other side of the vestibule of the gate were two tables. 41 Four tables were on the inside, and four tables on the outside of the side of the gate, eight tables, on which the sacrifices were to be slaughtered. 42 And there were also four tables of hewn stone for the burnt offering, a cubit and a half long, and a cubit and a half broad, and one cubit high, on which the instruments were to be laid with which the burnt offerings and the sacrifices were slaughtered. 43 And hooks, a handbreadth long, were fastened round about within. And on the tables the flesh of the offering was to be laid.

44 Then he brought me from without into the inner court, and behold, there were two chambers[z] in the inner court, one[a] at the side of the north gate facing south, the other at the side of the south[b] gate facing north. 45 And he said to me, This chamber which faces south is for the priests who have charge of the temple, 46 and the chamber which faces north is for the priests who have charge of the altar; these are the sons of Zā'dok, who alone among the sons of Levi may come near to the LORD to minister to him. 47 And he measured the court, a hundred cubits long, and a hundred cubits broad, foursquare; and the altar was in front of the temple.

48 Then he brought me to the vestibule of the temple and measured the jambs of the vestibule, five cubits on either side; and the breadth of the gate was fourteen cubits; and the sidewalls of the gate were three cubits[c] on either side. 49 The length of the vestibule was twenty cubits, and the breadth twelve[d] cubits; and ten steps led up[e] to it; and there were pillars beside the jambs on either side.

41 Then he brought me to the nave, and measured the jambs; on each side six cubits was the breadth of the jambs.[f] 2 And the breadth of the entrance was ten cubits; and the sidewalls of the entrance were five cubits on either side; and he measured the length of the nave forty cubits, and its breadth, twenty cubits. 3 Then he went into the inner room and measured the jambs of the entrance, two cubits; and the breadth of the entrance, six cubits; and the sidewalls[g] of the entrance, seven cubits. 4 And he measured the length of the room, twenty cubits, and its breadth, twenty cubits, beyond the nave. And he said to me, This is the most holy place.

5 Then he measured the wall of the temple, six cubits thick; and the breadth of the side chambers, four cubits, round about the temple. 6 And the side chambers were in three stories, one over another, thirty in each story. There were offsets[h] all around the wall of the temple to serve as supports for the side chambers, so that they should not be supported by the wall of the temple. 7 And the side chambers became broader as they rose[i] from story to story, corresponding to the enlargement of the offset[j] from story to story round about the temple; on the side of the temple a stairway led upward, and thus one went up from the lowest story to the top story through the middle story. 8 I saw also that the temple had a raised platform round about; the foundations of the side chambers measured a full reed of six long cubits. 9 The thickness of the outer wall of the side chambers was five cubits; and the part of the platform which was left free was five cubits.[k] Between the platform[l] of the temple and the 10 chambers of the court was a breadth of twenty cubits round about the temple on every side. 11 And the doors of the side chambers opened on the part of the platform that was left free, one door toward the north, and another door toward the south; and the breadth of the part that was left free was five cubits round about.

12 The building that was facing the temple yard on the west side was seventy cubits broad; and the wall of the building was five cubits thick round about, and its length ninety cubits.

13 Then he measured the temple, a hundred cubits long; and the yard and the building with its walls, a hundred cubits long; 14 also the breadth

[z] Gk: Heb *and from without to the inner gate were chambers for singers* [a] Gk: Heb *which*
[b] Gk: Heb *east* [c] Gk: Heb *and the breadth of the gates was three cubits* [d] Gk: Heb *eleven*
[e] Gk: Heb *and by steps which went up* [f] Compare Gk: Heb *tent* [g] Gk: Heb *breadth*
[h] Gk Compare 1 Kings 6.6: Heb *they entered* [i] Cn: Heb *it was surrounded*
[j] Gk: Heb *for the encompassing of the temple* [k] Syr: Heb lacks *five cubits*
[l] Cn: Heb *house of the side chambers*

of the east front of the temple and the
yard, a hundred cubits.

15 Then he measured the length of
the building facing the yard which was
at the west and its walls[m] on either
side, a hundred cubits.

The nave of the temple and the
inner room and the outer[n] vestibule
16 were paneled[o] and round about all
three had windows with recessed[p]
frames. Over against the threshold the
temple was paneled with wood round
about, from the floor up to the
windows (now the windows were
covered), 17 to the space above the
door, even to the inner room, and on
the outside. And on all the walls round
about in the inner room and the nave
were carved likenesses[q] 18 of cherubim
and palm trees, a palm tree between
cherub and cherub. Every cherub had
two faces: 19 the face of a man toward
the palm tree on the one side, and the
face of a young lion toward the palm
tree on the other side. They were
carved on the whole temple round
about; 20 from the floor to above the
door cherubim and palm trees were
carved on the wall.[r]

21 The doorposts of the nave were
squared; and in front of the holy place
was something resembling 22 an altar
of wood, three cubits high, two cubits
long, and two cubits broad;[s] its corners, its base,[t] and its walls were of
wood. He said to me, "This is the
table which is before the LORD."
23 The nave and the holy place had
each a double door. 24 The doors had
two leaves apiece, two swinging leaves
for each door. 25 And on the doors of
the nave were carved cherubim and
palm trees, such as were carved on
the walls; and there was a canopy of
wood in front of the vestibule outside.
26 And there were recessed windows
and palm trees on either side, on the
sidewalls of the vestibule.[u]

42 Then he led me out into the
inner[v] court, toward the north,
and he brought me to the chambers
which were opposite the temple yard
and opposite the building on the
north. 2 The length of the building
which was on the north side[w] was[x] a
hundred cubits, and the breadth fifty
cubits. 3 Adjoining the twenty cubits
which belonged to the inner court,
and facing the pavement which belonged to the outer court, was gallery[y]
against gallery[y] in three stories. 4 And
before the chambers was a passage inward, ten cubits wide and a hundred
cubits long,[z] and their doors were on
the north. 5 Now the upper chambers
were narrower, for the galleries[y] took
more away from them than from the
lower and middle chambers in the
building. 6 For they were in three
stories, and they had no pillars like
the pillars of the outer[a] court; hence
the upper chambers were set back
from the ground more than the lower
and the middle ones. 7 And there was
a wall outside parallel to the chambers,
toward the outer court, opposite the
chambers, fifty cubits long. 8 For the
chambers on the outer court were fifty
cubits long, while those opposite the
temple were a hundred cubits long.
9 Below these chambers was an entrance on the east side, as one enters
them from the outer court, 10 where
the outside wall begins.[b]

On the south[c] also, opposite the
yard and opposite the building, there
were chambers 11 with a passage in
front of them; they were similar to the
chambers on the north, of the same
length and breadth, with the same
exits[d] and arrangements and doors.
12 And below the south chambers was
an entrance on the east side, where one
enters the passage, and opposite them
was a dividing wall.[e]

13 Then he said to me, "The north
chambers and the south chambers
opposite the yard are the holy chambers, where the priests who approach
the LORD shall eat the most holy
offerings; there they shall put the most
holy offerings—the cereal offering, the

[m] Cn: The meaning of the Hebrew term is unknown [n] Gk: Heb *of the court* [o] Gk: Heb *the thresholds*
[p] Cn Compare Gk 1 Kings 6.4: The meaning of the Hebrew term is unknown
[q] Cn: Heb *measures and carved* [r] Cn Compare verse 25: Heb *and the wall*
[s] Gk: Heb lacks *two cubits broad* [t] Gk: Heb *length*
[u] Cn: Heb *vestibule. And the side chambers of the temple and the canopies* [v] Gk: Heb *outer*
[w] Gk: Heb *door* [x] Gk: Heb *before the length*
[y] The meaning of the Hebrew word is unknown
[z] Gk Syr: Heb *a way of one cubit* [a] Gk: Heb lacks *outer*
[b] Cn Compare Gk: Heb *in the breadth of the wall of the court* [c] Gk: Heb *east*
[d] Heb *and all their exits*
[e] Cn: Heb *And according to the entrances of the chambers that were toward the south was an entrance at the head of the way, the way before the dividing wall toward the east as one enters them*

sin offering, and the guilt offering, for
the place is holy. 14 When the priests
enter the holy place, they shall not go
out of it into the outer court without
laying there the garments in which
they minister, for these are holy; they
shall put on other garments before
they go near to that which is for the
people."

15 Now when he had finished measuring the interior of the temple area,
he led me out by the gate which faced
east, and measured the temple area
round about. 16 He measured the east
side with the measuring reed, five
hundred cubits by the measuring reed.
17 Then he turned and measured[f] the
north side, five hundred cubits by the
measuring reed. 18 Then he turned
and measured[f] the south side, five
hundred cubits by the measuring reed.
19 Then he turned to the west side and
measured, five hundred cubits by the
measuring reed. 20 He measured it on
the four sides. It had a wall around it,
five hundred cubits long and five hundred cubits broad, to make a separation between the holy and the common.

43 Afterward he brought me to
the gate, the gate facing east.
2 And behold, the glory of the God of
Israel came from the east; and the
sound of his coming was like the
sound of many waters; and the earth
shone with his glory. 3 And[g] the vision
I saw was like the vision which I had
seen when he came to destroy the city,
and[h] like the vision which I had seen
by the river Chē′bär; and I fell upon
my face. 4 As the glory of the LORD
entered the temple by the gate facing
east, 5 the Spirit lifted me up, and
brought me into the inner court; and
behold, the glory of the LORD filled
the temple.

6 While the man was standing beside me, I heard one speaking to me
out of the temple; 7 and he said to me,
"Son of man, this is the place of my
throne and the place of the soles of my
feet, where I will dwell in the midst
of the people of Israel for ever. And
the house of Israel shall no more defile
my holy name, neither they, nor their
kings, by their harlotry, and by the
dead bodies[i] of their kings, 8 by setting
their threshold by my threshold and
their doorposts beside my doorposts,
with only a wall between me and them.
They have defiled my holy name by
their abominations which they have
committed, so I have consumed them
in my anger. 9 Now let them put away
their idolatry and the dead bodies[i] of
their kings far from me, and I will
dwell in their midst for ever.

10 "And you, son of man, describe
to the house of Israel the temple and
its appearance and plan,[j] that they
may be ashamed of their iniquities.
11 And if they are ashamed of all that
they have done, portray[k] the temple,
its arrangement, its exits and its entrances, and its whole form; and make
known to them all its ordinances and
all its laws; and write it down in their
sight, so that they may observe and
perform all its laws[l] and all its ordinances. 12 This is the law of the
temple: the whole territory round
about upon the top of the mountain
shall be most holy. Behold, this is the
law of the temple.

13 "These are the dimensions of the
altar by cubits (the cubit being a cubit
and a handbreadth): its base shall be
one cubit high,[m] and one cubit broad,
with a rim of one span around its edge.
And this shall be the height[x] of the
altar: 14 from the base on the ground
to the lower ledge, two cubits, with a
breadth of one cubit; and from the
smaller ledge to the larger ledge, four
cubits, with a breadth of one cubit;
15 and the altar hearth, four cubits;
and from the altar hearth projecting
upward, four horns, one cubit high.[n]
16 The altar hearth shall be square,
twelve cubits long by twelve broad.
17 The ledge also shall be square, fourteen cubits long by fourteen broad,
with a rim around it half a cubit broad,
and its base one cubit round about.
The steps of the altar shall face east."

18 And he said to me, "Son of man,
thus says the Lord GOD: These are
the ordinances for the altar: On the
day when it is erected for offering
burnt offerings upon it and for throwing blood against it, 19 you shall give

[f] Gk: Heb *measuring reed round about. He measured* [g] Gk: Heb *And like the vision*
[h] Syr: Heb *and the visions* [i] Or *the monuments*
[j] Gk: Heb *the temple that they may measure the pattern* [k] Gk: Heb *the form of*
[l] Compare Gk: Heb *its whole form* [m] Gk: Heb lacks *high* [x] Gk: Heb *back*
[n] Gk: Heb lacks *one cubit high*
43.2: Ezek 1.24; Rev 1.15; 14.2; 19.6.

to the Levitical priests of the family
of Zā'dok, who draw near to me to
minister to me, says the Lord GOD, a
bull for a sin offering. 20 And you shall
take some of its blood, and put it on
the four horns of the altar, and on the
four corners of the ledge, and upon
the rim round about; thus you shall
cleanse the altar and make atonement
for it. 21 You shall also take the bull of
the sin offering, and it shall be burnt
in the appointed place belonging to
the temple, outside the sacred area.
22 And on the second day you shall
offer a he-goat without blemish for a
sin offering; and the altar shall be
cleansed, as it was cleansed with the
bull. 23 When you have finished
cleansing it, you shall offer a bull without blemish and a ram from the flock
without blemish. 24 You shall present
them before the LORD, and the priests
shall sprinkle salt upon them and offer
them up as a burnt offering to the
LORD. 25 For seven days you shall
provide daily a goat for a sin offering;
also a bull and a ram from the flock,
without blemish, shall be provided.
26 Seven days shall they make atonement for the altar and purify it, and
so consecrate it. 27 And when they
have completed these days, then from
the eighth day onward the priests shall
offer upon the altar your burnt offerings and your peace offerings; and I
will accept you, says the Lord GOD."

44 Then he brought me back to
the outer gate of the sanctuary,
which faces east; and it was shut.
2 And he[o] said to me, "This gate shall
remain shut; it shall not be opened,
and no one shall enter by it; for the
LORD, the God of Israel, has entered
by it; therefore it shall remain shut.
3 Only the prince may sit in it to eat
bread before the LORD; he shall enter
by way of the vestibule of the gate,
and shall go out by the same way."

4 Then he brought me by way of
the north gate to the front of the
temple; and I looked, and behold, the
glory of the LORD filled the temple of
the LORD; and I fell upon my face.
5 And the LORD said to me, "Son of
man, mark well, see with your eyes,
and hear with your ears all that I shall
tell you concerning all the ordinances
of the temple of the LORD and all its
laws; and mark well those who may
be admitted to[p] the temple and all
those who are to be excluded from the
sanctuary. 6 And say to the rebellious
house,[q] to the house of Israel, Thus
says the Lord GOD: O house of Israel,
let there be an end to all your abominations, 7 in admitting foreigners, uncircumcised in heart and flesh, to be
in my sanctuary, profaning it,[r] when
you offer to me my food, the fat and
the blood. You[s] have broken my covenant, in addition to all your abominations. 8 And you have not kept charge
of my holy things; but you have set
foreigners to keep my charge in my
sanctuary.

9 "Therefore[t] thus says the Lord
GOD: No foreigners, uncircumcised in
heart and flesh, of all the foreigners
who are among the people of Israel,
shall enter my sanctuary. 10 But the
Levites who went far from me, going
astray from me after their idols when
Israel went astray, shall bear their
punishment. 11 They shall be ministers
in my sanctuary, having oversight at
the gates of the temple, and serving in
the temple; they shall slay the burnt
offering and the sacrifice for the people, and they shall attend on the
people, to serve them. 12 Because they
ministered to them before their idols
and became a stumbling block of
iniquity to the house of Israel, therefore I have sworn concerning them,
says the Lord GOD, that they shall
bear their punishment. 13 They shall
not come near to me, to serve me as
priest, nor come near any of my
sacred things and the things that are
most sacred; but they shall bear their
shame, because of the abominations
which they have committed. 14 Yet I
will appoint them to keep charge of
the temple, to do all its service and all
that is to be done in it.

15 "But the Levitical priests, the
sons of Zā'dok, who kept the charge of
my sanctuary when the people of
Israel went astray from me, shall come
near to me to minister to me; and they
shall attend on me to offer me the fat
and the blood, says the Lord GOD;
16 they shall enter my sanctuary, and
they shall approach my table, to
minister to me, and they shall keep my
charge. 17 When they enter the gates

[o] Cn: Heb *the* LORD [p] Cn: Heb *the entrance of* [q] Gk: Heb lacks *house* [r] Gk: Heb *it my temple*
[s] Gk Syr Vg: Heb *they* [t] Gk: Heb *for you*
44.4: Rev 15.8.

of the inner court, they shall wear
linen garments; they shall have nothing
of wool on them, while they minister
at the gates of the inner court, and
within. 18 They shall have linen turbans upon their heads, and linen
breeches upon their loins; they shall
not gird themselves with anything that
causes sweat. 19 And when they go out
into the outer court to the people, they
shall put off the garments in which
they have been ministering, and lay
them in the holy chambers; and they
shall put on other garments, lest they
communicate holiness to the people
with their garments. 20 They shall not
shave their heads or let their locks
grow long; they shall only trim the hair
of their heads. 21 No priest shall drink
wine, when he enters the inner court.
22 They shall not marry a widow, or a
divorced woman, but only a virgin of
the stock of the house of Israel, or a
widow who is the widow of a priest.
23 They shall teach my people the
difference between the holy and the
common, and show them how to distinguish between the unclean and the
clean. 24 In a controversy they shall
act as judges, and they shall judge it
according to my judgments. They
shall keep my laws and my statutes in
all my appointed feasts, and they shall
keep my sabbaths holy. 25 They shall
not defile themselves by going near to
a dead person; however, for father or
mother, for son or daughter, for
brother or unmarried sister they may
defile themselves. 26 After he is defiled,[u] he shall count for himself seven
days, and then he shall be clean.[v]
27 And on the day that he goes into the
holy place, into the inner court, to
minister in the holy place, he shall
offer his sin offering, says the Lord
GOD.

28 "They shall have no[w] inheritance; I am their inheritance: and you
shall give them no possession in Israel;
I am their possession. 29 They shall eat
the cereal offering, the sin offering,
and the guilt offering; and every devoted thing in Israel shall be theirs.
30 And the first of all the first fruits of
all kinds, and every offering of all
kinds from all your offerings, shall
belong to the priests; you shall also
give to the priests the first of your
coarse meal, that a blessing may rest
on your house. 31 The priests shall not
eat of anything, whether bird or beast,
that has died of itself or is torn.

45 "When you allot the land as a
possession, you shall set apart
for the LORD a portion of the land as
a holy district, twenty-five thousand
cubits long and twenty[x] thousand
cubits broad; it shall be holy throughout its whole extent. 2 Of this a square
plot of five hundred by five hundred
cubits shall be for the sanctuary, with
fifty cubits for an open space around
it. 3 And in the holy district you shall
measure off a section twenty-five
thousand cubits long and ten thousand
broad, in which shall be the sanctuary,
the most holy place. 4 It shall be the
holy portion of the land; it shall be for
the priests, who minister in the sanctuary and approach the LORD to minister to him; and it shall be a place for
their houses and a holy place for the
sanctuary. 5 Another section, twenty-
five thousand cubits long and ten
thousand cubits broad, shall be for the
Levites who minister at the temple,
as their possession for cities to live in.[y]

6 "Alongside the portion set apart
as the holy district you shall assign for
the possession of the city an area five
thousand cubits broad, and twenty-
five thousand cubits long; it shall belong to the whole house of Israel.

7 "And to the prince shall belong
the land on both sides of the holy
district and the property of the city,
alongside the holy district and the
property of the city, on the west and
on the east, corresponding in length
to one of the tribal portions, and extending from the western to the eastern
boundary of the land. 8 It is to be his
property in Israel. And my princes
shall no more oppress my people; but
they shall let the house of Israel have
the land according to their tribes.

9 "Thus says the Lord GOD:
Enough, O princes of Israel! Put away
violence and oppression, and execute
justice and righteousness; cease your
evictions of my people, says the Lord
GOD.

10 "You shall have just balances, a
just ephah, and a just bath. 11 The
ephah and the bath shall be of the same
measure, the bath containing one
tenth of a homer, and the ephah one
tenth of a homer; the homer shall be

[u] Syr: Heb *cleansed* [v] Syr: Heb lacks *and then he shall be clean* [w] Vg: Heb *as an* [x] Gk: Heb *ten*
[y] Gk: Heb *twenty chambers*

the standard measure. 12 The shekel shall be twenty gerahs; five shekels
shall be five shekels, and ten shekels shall be ten shekels, and your mina
shall be fifty shekels.[z]
13 "This is the offering which you
shall make: one sixth of an ephah from
each homer of wheat, and one sixth of
an ephah from each homer of barley,
14 and as the fixed portion of oil,[a] one
tenth of a bath from each cor (the cor,[b]
like the homer, contains ten baths);
15 and one sheep from every flock of
two hundred, from the families[c] of
Israel. This is the offering for cereal
offerings, burnt offerings, and peace
offerings, to make atonement for them,
says the Lord GOD. 16 All the people
of the land shall give[d] this offering to
the prince in Israel. 17 It shall be the
prince's duty to furnish the burnt
offerings, cereal offerings, and drink
offerings, at the feasts, the new moons,
and the sabbaths, all the appointed
feasts of the house of Israel: he shall
provide the sin offerings, cereal offerings, burnt offerings, and peace offerings, to make atonement for the house
of Israel.
18 "Thus says the Lord GOD: In
the first month, on the first day of the
month, you shall take a young bull
without blemish, and cleanse the
sanctuary. 19 The priest shall take
some of the blood of the sin offering
and put it on the doorposts of the
temple, the four corners of the ledge
of the altar, and the posts of the gate
of the inner court. 20 You shall do the
same on the seventh day of the month
for any one who has sinned through
error or ignorance; so you shall make
atonement for the temple.
21 "In the first month, on the
fourteenth day of the month, you shall
celebrate the feast of the passover, and
for seven days unleavened bread shall
be eaten. 22 On that day the prince
shall provide for himself and all the
people of the land a young bull for a
sin offering. 23 And on the seven days
of the festival he shall provide as a
burnt offering to the LORD seven young
bulls and seven rams without blemish,
on each of the seven days; and a he-
goat daily for a sin offering. 24 And
he shall provide as a cereal offering an
ephah for each bull, an ephah for each
ram, and a hin of oil to each ephah.
25 In the seventh month, on the
fifteenth day of the month and for the
seven days of the feast, he shall make
the same provision for sin offerings,
burnt offerings, and cereal offerings,
and for the oil.

46 "Thus says the Lord GOD:
The gate of the inner court that
faces east shall be shut on the six working days; but on the sabbath day it
shall be opened and on the day of the
new moon it shall be opened. 2 The
prince shall enter by the vestibule of
the gate from without, and shall take
his stand by the post of the gate. The
priests shall offer his burnt offering
and his peace offerings, and he shall
worship at the threshold of the gate.
Then he shall go out, but the gate
shall not be shut until evening. 3 The
people of the land shall worship at the
entrance of that gate before the LORD
on the sabbaths and on the new moons.
4 The burnt offering that the prince
offers to the LORD on the sabbath day
shall be six lambs without blemish and
a ram without blemish; 5 and the cereal
offering with the ram shall be an
ephah, and the cereal offering with the
lambs shall be as much as he is able,
together with a hin of oil to each
ephah. 6 On the day of the new moon
he shall offer a young bull without
blemish, and six lambs and a ram,
which shall be without blemish; 7 as a
cereal offering he shall provide an
ephah with the bull and an ephah
with the ram, and with the lambs as
much as he is able, together with a hin
of oil to each ephah. 8 When the prince
enters, he shall go in by the vestibule
of the gate, and he shall go out by the
same way.
9 "When the people of the land
come before the LORD at the appointed
feasts, he who enters by the north gate
to worship shall go out by the south
gate; and he who enters by the south
gate shall go out by the north gate: no
one shall return by way of the gate by
which he entered, but each shall go
out straight ahead. 10 When they go
in, the prince shall go in with them;
and when they go out, he shall go out.
11 "At the feasts and the appointed
seasons the cereal offering with a
young bull shall be an ephah, and with

[z] Gk: Heb *twenty shekels, twenty-five shekels, fifteen shekels shall be your mina*
[a] Cn: Heb *oil, the bath the oil* [b] Vg: Heb *homer* [c] Gk: Heb *watering places*
[d] Gk Compare Syr: Heb *shall be to*

a ram an ephah, and with the lambs
as much as one is able to give, together
with a hin of oil to an ephah. 12 When
the prince provides a freewill offering,
either a burnt offering or peace offerings as a freewill offering to the LORD,
the gate facing east shall be opened
for him; and he shall offer his burnt
offering or his peace offerings as he
does on the sabbath day. Then he
shall go out, and after he has gone out
the gate shall be shut.

13 "He shall provide a lamb a year
old without blemish for a burnt offering to the LORD daily; morning by
morning he shall provide it. 14 And he
shall provide a cereal offering with it
morning by morning, one sixth of an
ephah, and one third of a hin of oil to
moisten the flour, as a cereal offering
to the LORD; this is the ordinance for
the continual burnt offering.[e] 15 Thus
the lamb and the meal offering and the
oil shall be provided, morning by
morning, for a continual burnt offering.

16 "Thus says the Lord GOD: If
the prince makes a gift to any of his
sons out of[f] his inheritance, it shall
belong to his sons, it is their property
by inheritance. 17 But if he makes a gift
out of his inheritance to one of his
servants, it shall be his to the year of
liberty; then it shall revert to the
prince; only his sons may keep a gift
from his inheritance. 18 The prince
shall not take any of the inheritance of
the people, thrusting them out of their
property; he shall give his sons their
inheritance out of his own property,
so that none of my people shall be dispossessed of his property."

19 Then he brought me through the
entrance, which was at the side of the
gate, to the north row of the holy
chambers for the priests; and there I
saw a place at the extreme western end
of them. 20 And he said to me, "This
is the place where the priests shall boil
the guilt offering and the sin offering,
and where they shall bake the cereal
offering, in order not to bring them
out into the outer court and so communicate holiness to the people."

21 Then he brought me forth to the
outer court, and led me to the four
corners of the court; and in each
corner of the court there was a court—
22 in the four corners of the court were
small[g] courts, forty cubits long and
thirty broad; the four were of the same
size. 23 On the inside, around each of
the four courts was a row of masonry,
with hearths made at the bottom of
the rows round about. 24 Then he said
to me, "These are the kitchens where
those who minister at the temple shall
boil the sacrifices of the people."

47 Then he brought me back to
the door of the temple; and behold, water was issuing from below
the threshold of the temple toward the
east (for the temple faced east); and
the water was flowing down from
below the south end of the threshold
of the temple, south of the altar.
2 Then he brought me out by way of
the north gate, and led me round on
the outside to the outer gate, that faces
toward the east;[h] and the water was
coming out on the south side.

3 Going on eastward with a line in
his hand, the man measured a thousand cubits, and then led me through
the water; and it was ankle-deep.
4 Again he measured a thousand, and
led me through the water; and it was
knee-deep. Again he measured a thousand, and led me through the water;
and it was up to the loins. 5 Again he
measured a thousand, and it was a
river that I could not pass through, for
the water had risen; it was deep
enough to swim in, a river that could
not be passed through. 6 And he said
to me, "Son of man, have you seen
this?"

Then he led me back along the bank
of the river. 7 As I went back, I saw
upon the bank of the river very many
trees on the one side and on the other.
8 And he said to me, "This water flows
toward the eastern region and goes
down into the Ar'ā·bāh; and when it
enters the stagnant waters of the sea,[i]
the water will become fresh. 9 And
wherever the river[j] goes every living
creature which swarms will live, and
there will be very many fish; for this
water goes there, that the waters of the
sea[k] may become fresh; so everything
will live where the river goes. 10 Fishermen will stand beside the sea; from

[e] Cn: Heb *perpetual ordinances continually* [f] Gk: Heb *it is his inheritance*
[g] Gk Syr Vg: The meaning of the Hebrew word is uncertain [h] Heb obscure
[i] Compare Syr: Heb *into the sea to the sea those that were made to issue forth*
[j] Gk Syr Vg Tg: Heb *two rivers* [k] Compare Syr: Heb lacks *the waters of the sea*
47.1-2: Zech 14.8; Rev 22.1-2.

En-gē′dī to En-eg′lā·im it will be a
place for the spreading of nets; its
fish will be of very many kinds, like
the fish of the Great Sea. 11 But its
swamps and marshes will not become
fresh; they are to be left for salt.
12 And on the banks, on both sides of
the river, there will grow all kinds of
trees for food. Their leaves will not
wither nor their fruit fail, but they
will bear fresh fruit every month, because the water for them flows from
the sanctuary. Their fruit will be for
food, and their leaves for healing."

13 Thus says the Lord GOD: "These
are the boundaries by which you shall
divide the land for inheritance among
the twelve tribes of Israel. Joseph
shall have two portions. 14 And you
shall divide it equally; I swore to give
it to your fathers, and this land shall
fall to you as your inheritance.

15 "This shall be the boundary of
the land: On the north side, from the
Great Sea by way of Heth′lon to the
entrance of Hā′math, and on to Zē′-
dad,[l] 16 Be·rō′thȧh, Sib′rȧ·im (which
lies on the border between Damascus
and Hā′math), as far as Hā·zėr-
hat′ti·con, which is on the border of
Hau′rän. 17 So the boundary shall run
from the sea to Hā′zär-ē′non, which
is on the northern border of Damascus,
with the border of Hā′math to the
north.[m] This shall be the north side.

18 "On the east side, the boundary
shall run from Hā′zär-ē′non[n] between
Hau′rän and Damascus;[m] along the
Jordan between Gilead and the land
of Israel; to the eastern sea and as far
as Tā′mär.[o] This shall be the east side.

19 "On the south side, it shall run
from Tā′mär as far as the waters of
Mer′i·bath-kā′desh, thence along the
Brook of Egypt to the Great Sea. This
shall be the south side.

20 "On the west side, the Great Sea
shall be the boundary to a point opposite the entrance of Hā′math. This
shall be the west side.

21 "So you shall divide this land
among you according to the tribes of
Israel. 22 You shall allot it as an inheritance for yourselves and for the
aliens who reside among you and have
begotten children among you. They
shall be to you as native-born sons of
Israel; with you they shall be allotted
an inheritance among the tribes of
Israel. 23 In whatever tribe the alien
resides, there you shall assign him his
inheritance, says the Lord GOD.

48 "These are the names of the
tribes: Beginning at the northern border, from the sea by way[p] of
Heth′lon to the entrance of Hā′math,
as far as Hā′zär-ē′non (which is on the
northern border of Damascus over
against Hamath), and[q] extending from
the east side to the west,[r] Dan, one
portion. 2 Adjoining the territory of
Dan, from the east side to the west,
Ash′ėr, one portion. 3 Adjoining the
territory of Ash′ėr, from the east side
to the west, Naph′tȧ·lī, one portion.
4 Adjoining the territory of Naph′tȧ·lī,
from the east side to the west, Mȧ-
nas′sėh, one portion. 5 Adjoining the
territory of Mȧ·nas′sėh, from the east
side to the west, Ē′phrȧ·im, one portion. 6 Adjoining the territory of
Ē′phrȧ·im, from the east side to the
west, Reuben, one portion. 7 Adjoining
the territory of Reuben, from the east
side to the west, Judah, one portion.

8 "Adjoining the territory of Judah,
from the east side to the west, shall be
the portion which you shall set apart,
twenty-five thousand cubits in
breadth, and in length equal to one of
the tribal portions, from the east side
to the west, with the sanctuary in the
midst of it. 9 The portion which you
shall set apart for the LORD shall be
twenty-five thousand cubits in length,
and twenty[s] thousand in breadth.
10 These shall be the allotments of the
holy portion: the priests shall have an
allotment measuring twenty-five thousand cubits on the northern side, ten
thousand cubits in breadth on the
western side, ten thousand in breadth
on the eastern side, and twenty-five
thousand in length on the southern
side, with the sanctuary of the LORD
in the midst of it. 11 This shall be for
the consecrated priests, the sons[t] of
Zā′dok, who kept my charge, who did
not go astray when the people of Israel
went astray, as the Levites did. 12 And
it shall belong to them as a special
portion from the holy portion of the
land, a most holy place, adjoining the
territory of the Levites. 13 And along-

[l] Gk: Heb *the entrance of Zedad, Hamath* [m] Heb obscure [n] Cn: Heb lacks *Hazar-enon*
[o] Compare Syr: Heb *you shall measure* [p] Compare 47.15: Heb *by the side of the way*
[q] Cn: Heb *and they shall be his* [r] Gk Compare verses 2-8: Heb *the east side the west*
[s] Compare 45.1: Heb *ten* [t] One Ms Gk: Heb *of the sons*

side the territory of the priests, the
Levites shall have an allotment
twenty-five thousand cubits in length
and ten thousand in breadth. The
whole length shall be twenty-five thousand cubits and the breadth twenty[u]
thousand. 14 They shall not sell or
exchange any of it; they shall not
alienate this choice portion of the land,
for it is holy to the LORD.

15 "The remainder, five thousand
cubits in breadth and twenty-five
thousand in length, shall be for ordinary use for the city, for dwellings
and for open country. In the midst of
it shall be the city; 16 and these shall
be its dimensions: the north side four
thousand five hundred cubits, the
south side four thousand five hundred,
the east side four thousand five hundred, and the west side four thousand
and five hundred. 17 And the city shall
have open land: on the north two hundred and fifty cubits, on the south two
hundred and fifty, on the east two
hundred and fifty, and on the west
two hundred and fifty. 18 The remainder of the length alongside the
holy portion shall be ten thousand
cubits to the east, and ten thousand to
the west, and it shall be alongside the
holy portion. Its produce shall be food
for the workers of the city. 19 And the
workers of the city, from all the tribes
of Israel, shall till it. 20 The whole portion which you shall set apart shall be
twenty-five thousand cubits square,
that is, the holy portion together with
the property of the city.

21 "What remains on both sides of
the holy portion and of the property
of the city shall belong to the prince.
Extending from the twenty-five thousand cubits of the holy portion to the
east border, and westward from the
twenty-five thousand cubits to the
west border, parallel to the tribal portions, it shall belong to the prince. The
holy portion with the sanctuary of the
temple in its midst, 22 and the property
of the Levites and the property of the
city,[v] shall be in the midst of that
which belongs to the prince. The portion of the prince shall lie between the
territory of Judah and the territory of
Benjamin.

23 "As for the rest of the tribes:
from the east side to the west, Benjamin, one portion. 24 Adjoining the
territory of Benjamin, from the east
side to the west, Simeon, one portion.
25 Adjoining the territory of Simeon,
from the east side to the west, Is'sȧ-
chär, one portion. 26 Adjoining the
territory of Is'sȧ·chär, from the east
side to the west, Zeb'ū·lůn, one portion. 27 Adjoining the territory of Zeb'-
ū·lůn, from the east side to the west,
Gad, one portion. 28 And adjoining the
territory of Gad to the south, the
boundary shall run from Tā'mär to the
waters of Mer'i·bath-kā'desh, thence
along the Brook of Egypt to the Great
Sea. 29 This is the land which you
shall allot as an inheritance among
the tribes of Israel, and these are
their several portions, says the Lord
GOD.

30 "These shall be the exits of the
city: On the north side, which is to be
four thousand five hundred cubits by
measure, 31 three gates, the gate of
Reuben, the gate of Judah, and the
gate of Levi, the gates of the city being
named after the tribes of Israel. 32 On
the east side, which is to be four thousand five hundred cubits, three gates,
the gate of Joseph, the gate of Benjamin, and the gate of Dan. 33 On the
south side, which is to be four thousand five hundred cubits by measure,
three gates, the gate of Simeon, the
gate of Is'sȧ·chär, and the gate of
Zeb'ū·lůn. 34 On the west side, which
is to be four thousand five hundred
cubits, three gates,[w] the gate of Gad,
the gate of Ash'ėr, and the gate of
Naph'tȧ·lī. 35 The circumference of
the city shall be eighteen thousand
cubits. And the name of the city
henceforth shall be, The LORD is
there."

[u] Gk: Heb *ten* [v] Cn: Heb *and from the property of the Levites and from the property of the city*
[w] One Ms Gk Syr: Heb *their gates three*
48.16: Rev 21.16. **48.31-35:** Rev 21.12-13.

THE BOOK OF
DANIEL

1 In the third year of the reign of Je·hoi'ȧ·kim king of Judah, Ne·bu̇-chȧd·nez'zȧr king of Babylon came to Jerusalem and besieged it. 2 And the Lord gave Je·hoi'ȧ·kim king of Judah into his hand, with some of the vessels of the house of God; and he brought them to the land of Shī'när, to the house of his god, and placed the vessels in the treasury of his god. 3 Then the king commanded Ash'pė·naz, his chief eunuch, to bring some of the people of Israel, both of the royal family and of the nobility, 4 youths without blemish, handsome and skilful in all wisdom, endowed with knowledge, understanding learning, and competent to serve in the king's palace, and to teach them the letters and language of the Chal·dē'ȧnṡ. 5 The king assigned them a daily portion of the rich food which the king ate, and of the wine which he drank. They were to be educated for three years, and at the end of that time they were to stand before the king. 6 Among these were Daniel, Han·ȧ·nī'ȧh, Mish'ȧ-el, and Az·ȧ·rī'ȧh of the tribe of Judah. 7 And the chief of the eunuchs gave them names: Daniel he called Bel·tė·shaz'zȧr, Han·ȧ·nī'ȧh he called Shad'rach, Mish'ȧ-el he called Mē'shach, and Az·ȧ·rī'ȧh he called Ȧ·bed'ne·gō.

8 But Daniel resolved that he would not defile himself with the king's rich food, or with the wine which he drank; therefore he asked the chief of the eunuchs to allow him not to defile himself. 9 And God gave Daniel favor and compassion in the sight of the chief of the eunuchs; 10 and the chief of the eunuchs said to Daniel, "I fear lest my lord the king, who appointed your food and your drink, should see that you were in poorer condition than the youths who are of your own age. So you would endanger my head with the king." 11 Then Daniel said to the steward whom the chief of the eunuchs had appointed over Daniel, Han·ȧ·nī'ȧh, Mish'ȧ-el, and Az·ȧ·rī'ȧh; 12 "Test your servants for ten days; let us be given vegetables to eat and water to drink. 13 Then let our appearance and the appearance of the youths who eat the king's rich food be observed by you, and according to what you see deal with your servants." 14 So he hearkened to them in this matter, and tested them for ten days. 15 At the end of ten days it was seen that they were better in appearance and fatter in flesh than all the youths who ate the king's rich food. 16 So the steward took away their rich food and the wine they were to drink, and gave them vegetables.

17 As for these four youths, God gave them learning and skill in all letters and wisdom; and Daniel had understanding in all visions and dreams. 18 At the end of the time, when the king had commanded that they should be brought in, the chief of the eunuchs brought them in before Ne·bu̇·chȧd·nez'zȧr. 19 And the king spoke with them, and among them all none was found like Daniel, Han·ȧ·nī'ȧh, Mish'ȧ-el, and Az·ȧ·rī'ȧh; therefore they stood before the king. 20 And in every matter of wisdom and understanding concerning which the king inquired of them, he found them ten times better than all the magicians and enchanters that were in all his kingdom. 21 And Daniel continued until the first year of King Cyrus.

2 In the second year of the reign of Ne·bu̇·chȧd·nez'zȧr, Nebuchadnezzar had dreams; and his spirit was troubled, and his sleep left him. 2 Then the king commanded that the magicians, the enchanters, the sorcerers, and the Chal·dē'ȧnṡ be summoned, to tell the king his dreams. So they came in and stood before the king. 3 And the king said to them, "I had a dream, and my spirit is troubled to know the dream." 4 Then the Chal·dē'ȧnṡ said to the king,[a] "O king, live for ever! Tell your servants the dream, and we will show the interpretation." 5 The king answered the Chal·dē'ȧnṡ, "The word from me is sure: if you do not make known to me the dream and its

[a] Heb adds *in Aramaic*, indicating that the text from this point to the end of chapter 7 is in Aramaic

interpretation, you shall be torn limb
from limb, and your houses shall be
laid in ruins. 6 But if you show the
dream and its interpretation, you shall
receive from me gifts and rewards and
great honor. Therefore show me the
dream and its interpretation." 7 They
answered a second time, "Let the
king tell his servants the dream, and
we will show its interpretation." 8 The
king answered, "I know with certainty
that you are trying to gain time, because you see that the word from me
is sure 9 that if you do not make the
dream known to me, there is but one
sentence for you. You have agreed to
speak lying and corrupt words before
me till the times change. Therefore
tell me the dream, and I shall know
that you can show me its interpretation." 10 The Chal·dē′ȧnṡ answered
the king, "There is not a man on earth
who can meet the king's demand; for
no great and powerful king has asked
such a thing of any magician or enchanter or Chaldean. 11 The thing
that the king asks is difficult, and none
can show it to the king except the
gods, whose dwelling is not with flesh."

12 Because of this the king was
angry and very furious, and commanded that all the wise men of
Babylon be destroyed. 13 So the decree
went forth that the wise men were to
be slain, and they sought Daniel and
his companions, to slay them. 14 Then
Daniel replied with prudence and discretion to Âr′i·och, the captain of the
king's guard, who had gone out to slay
the wise men of Babylon; 15 he said to
Âr′i·och, the king's captain, "Why is
the decree of the king so severe?" Then
Arioch made the matter known to
Daniel. 16 And Daniel went in and
besought the king to appoint him a
time, that he might show to the king
the interpretation.

17 Then Daniel went to his house
and made the matter known to Han·ȧ-
nī′ȧh, Mish′ȧ-el, and Az·ȧ·rī′ȧh, his
companions, 18 and told them to seek
mercy of the God of heaven concerning
this mystery, so that Daniel and his
companions might not perish with the
rest of the wise men of Babylon.
19 Then the mystery was revealed to
Daniel in a vision of the night. Then
Daniel blessed the God of heaven.
20 Daniel said:

"Blessed be the name of God for
ever and ever,
to whom belong wisdom and
might.
21 He changes times and seasons;
he removes kings and sets up
kings;
he gives wisdom to the wise
and knowledge to those who have
understanding;
22 he reveals deep and mysterious
things;
he knows what is in the darkness,
and the light dwells with him.
23 To thee, O God of my fathers,
I give thanks and praise,
for thou hast given me wisdom
and strength,
and hast now made known to me
what we asked of thee,
for thou hast made known to us
the king's matter."

24 Therefore Daniel went in to
Âr′i·och, whom the king had appointed
to destroy the wise men of Babylon;
he went and said thus to him, "Do
not destroy the wise men of Babylon;
bring me in before the king, and I will
show the king the interpretation."

25 Then Âr′i·och brought in Daniel
before the king in haste, and said thus
to him: "I have found among the
exiles from Judah a man who can
make known to the king the interpretation." 26 The king said to Daniel,
whose name was Bel·tė·shaz′zȧr, "Are
you able to make known to me the
dream that I have seen and its interpretation?" 27 Daniel answered the
king, "No wise men, enchanters,
magicians, or astrologers can show to
the king the mystery which the king
has asked, 28 but there is a God in
heaven who reveals mysteries, and he
has made known to King Ne·bu̇·chȧd-
nez′zȧr what will be in the latter days.
Your dream and the visions of your
head as you lay in bed are these: 29 To
you, O king, as you lay in bed came
thoughts of what would be hereafter,
and he who reveals mysteries made
known to you what is to be. 30 But as
for me, not because of any wisdom
that I have more than all the living has
this mystery been revealed to me, but
in order that the interpretation may
be made known to the king, and that
you may know the thoughts of your
mind.

31 "You saw, O king, and behold,
a great image. This image, mighty and
of exceeding brightness, stood before

you, and its appearance was frightening. 32 The head of this image was of
fine gold, its breast and arms of silver,
its belly and thighs of bronze, 33 its
legs of iron, its feet partly of iron and
partly of clay. 34 As you looked, a stone
was cut out by no human hand, and it
smote the image on its feet of iron and
clay, and broke them in pieces; 35 then
the iron, the clay, the bronze, the
silver, and the gold, all together were
broken in pieces, and became like the
chaff of the summer threshing floors;
and the wind carried them away, so
that not a trace of them could be
found. But the stone that struck the
image became a great mountain and
filled the whole earth.

36 "This was the dream; now we
will tell the king its interpretation.
37 You, O king, the king of kings, to
whom the God of heaven has given the
kingdom, the power, and the might,
and the glory, 38 and into whose hand
he has given, wherever they dwell, the
sons of men, the beasts of the field,
and the birds of the air, making you
rule over them all—you are the head
of gold. 39 After you shall arise another
kingdom inferior to you, and yet a
third kingdom of bronze, which shall
rule over all the earth. 40 And there
shall be a fourth kingdom, strong as
iron, because iron breaks to pieces and
shatters all things; and like iron which
crushes, it shall break and crush all
these. 41 And as you saw the feet and
toes partly of potter's clay and partly
of iron, it shall be a divided kingdom;
but some of the firmness of iron shall
be in it, just as you saw iron mixed
with the miry clay. 42 And as the toes
of the feet were partly iron and partly
clay, so the kingdom shall be partly
strong and partly brittle. 43 As you
saw the iron mixed with miry clay, so
they will mix with one another in
marriage,[b] but they will not hold together, just as iron does not mix with
clay. 44 And in the days of those kings
the God of heaven will set up a kingdom which shall never be destroyed,
nor shall its sovereignty be left to
another people. It shall break in pieces
all these kingdoms and bring them to
an end, and it shall stand for ever;
45 just as you saw that a stone was cut
from a mountain by no human hand,
and that it broke in pieces the iron, the
bronze, the clay, the silver, and the
gold. A great God has made known
to the king what shall be hereafter.
The dream is certain, and its interpretation sure."

46 Then King Ne·bu̇·chȧd·nez'zȧr
fell upon his face, and did homage to
Daniel, and commanded that an offering and incense be offered up to him.
47 The king said to Daniel, "Truly,
your God is God of gods and Lord
of kings, and a revealer of mysteries,
for you have been able to reveal this
mystery." 48 Then the king gave
Daniel high honors and many great
gifts, and made him ruler over the
whole province of Babylon, and chief
prefect over all the wise men of Babylon. 49 Daniel made request of the
king, and he appointed Shad'rach,
Mē'shach, and Ȧ·bed'ne·gō over the
affairs of the province of Babylon; but
Daniel remained at the king's court.

3 King Ne·bu̇·chȧd·nez'zȧr made
an image of gold, whose height
was sixty cubits and its breadth six
cubits. He set it up on the plain of
Dü'rȧ, in the province of Babylon.
2 Then King Ne·bu̇·chȧd·nez'zȧr sent
to assemble the satraps, the prefects,
and the governors, the counselors, the
treasurers, the justices, the magistrates, and all the officials of the
provinces to come to the dedication of
the image which King Nebuchadnezzar
had set up. 3 Then the satraps, the
prefects, and the governors, the counselors, the treasurers, the justices, the
magistrates, and all the officials of the
provinces, were assembled for the
dedication of the image that King Ne-
bu̇·chȧd·nez'zȧr had set up; and they
stood before the image that Nebuchadnezzar had set up. 4 And the herald proclaimed aloud, "You are commanded,
O peoples, nations, and languages,
5 that when you hear the sound of the
horn, pipe, lyre, trigon, harp, bagpipe,
and every kind of music, you are to fall
down and worship the golden image
that King Ne·bu̇·chȧd·nez'zȧr has set
up; 6 and whoever does not fall down
and worship shall immediately be cast
into a burning fiery furnace." 7 Therefore, as soon as all the peoples heard
the sound of the horn, pipe, lyre,
trigon, harp, bagpipe, and every kind
of music, all the peoples, nations, and
languages fell down and worshiped the

[b] Aram *by the seed of men*
2.44: Rev 11.15. 3.5-6: Rev 13.15.

golden image which King Ne·bu̇·chȧd-
nez'zȧr had set up.
8 Therefore at that time certain
Chal·dē'ȧnṡ came forward and maliciously accused the Jews. 9 They said
to King Ne·bu̇·chȧd·nez'zȧr, "O king,
live for ever! 10 You, O king, have
made a decree, that every man who
hears the sound of the horn, pipe, lyre,
trigon, harp, bagpipe, and every kind
of music, shall fall down and worship
the golden image; 11 and whoever does
not fall down and worship shall be
cast into a burning fiery furnace.
12 There are certain Jews whom you
have appointed over the affairs of the
province of Babylon: Shad'rach, Mē'-
shach, and Ȧ·bed'ne·gō. These men,
O king, pay no heed to you; they do
not serve your gods or worship the
golden image which you have set up."
13 Then Ne·bu̇·chȧd·nez'zȧr in
furious rage commanded that Shad'-
rach, Mē'shach, and Ȧ·bed'ne·gō be
brought. Then they brought these men
before the king. 14 Ne·bu̇·chȧd·nez'zȧr
said to them, "Is it true, O Shad'rach,
Mē'shach, and Ȧ·bed'ne·gō, that you
do not serve my gods or worship the
golden image which I have set up?
15 Now if you are ready when you
hear the sound of the horn, pipe, lyre,
trigon, harp, bagpipe, and every kind
of music, to fall down and worship the
image which I have made, well and
good; but if you do not worship, you
shall immediately be cast into a burning fiery furnace; and who is the god
that will deliver you out of my hands?"
16 Shad'rach, Mē'shach, and Ȧ·bed'-
ne·gō answered the king, "O Ne·bu̇-
chȧd·nez'zȧr, we have no need to
answer you in this matter. 17 If it be
so, our God whom we serve is able to
deliver us from the burning fiery
furnace; and he will deliver us out of
your hand, O king.[c] 18 But if not, be
it known to you, O king, that we will
not serve your gods or worship the
golden image which you have set up."
19 Then Ne·bu̇·chȧd·nez'zȧr was full
of fury, and the expression of his face
was changed against Shad'rach, Mē'-
shach, and Ȧ·bed'ne·gō. He ordered
the furnace heated seven times more
than it was wont to be heated. 20 And
he ordered certain mighty men of his
army to bind Shad'rach, Mē'shach,
and Ȧ·bed'ne·gō, and to cast them into
the burning fiery furnace. 21 Then these
men were bound in their mantles,[d]
their tunics,[d] their hats, and their
other garments, and they were cast
into the burning fiery furnace. 22 Because the king's order was strict and
the furnace very hot, the flame of the
fire slew those men who took up Shad'-
rach, Mē'shach, and Ȧ·bed'ne·gō.
23 And these three men, Shad'rach,
Mē'shach, and Ȧ·bed'ne·gō, fell bound
into the burning fiery furnace.
24 Then King Ne·bu̇·chȧd·nez'zȧr
was astonished and rose up in haste.
He said to his counselors, "Did we not
cast three men bound into the fire?"
They answered the king, "True, O
king." 25 He answered, "But I see four
men loose, walking in the midst of the
fire, and they are not hurt; and the
appearance of the fourth is like a son
of the gods."
26 Then Ne·bu̇·chȧd·nez'zȧr came
near to the door of the burning fiery
furnace and said, "Shad'rach, Mē'-
shach, and Ȧ·bed'ne·gō, servants of
the Most High God, come forth, and
come here!" Then Shadrach, Meshach,
and Abednego came out from the fire.
27 And the satraps, the prefects, the
governors, and the king's counselors
gathered together and saw that the
fire had not had any power over the
bodies of those men; the hair of their
heads was not singed, their mantles[d]
were not harmed, and no smell of fire
had come upon them. 28 Ne·bu̇·chȧd-
nez'zȧr said, "Blessed be the God of
Shad'rach, Mē'shach, and Ȧ·bed'ne·gō,
who has sent his angel and delivered
his servants, who trusted in him, and
set at nought the king's command, and
yielded up their bodies rather than
serve and worship any god except their
own God. 29 Therefore I make a decree:
Any people, nation, or language that
speaks anything against the God of
Shad'rach, Mē'shach, and Ȧ·bed'ne·gō
shall be torn limb from limb, and their
houses laid in ruins; for there is no
other god who is able to deliver in this
way." 30 Then the king promoted
Shad'rach, Mē'shach, and Ȧ·bed'ne·gō
in the province of Babylon.
4[e] King Ne·bu̇·chȧd·nez'zȧr to all
peoples, nations, and languages,
that dwell in all the earth: Peace be

[c] Or *Behold, our God . . . king.* Or *If our God is able to deliver us, he will deliver us from the burning fiery furnace and out of your hand, O king*
[d] The meaning of the Aramaic word is uncertain [e] Ch 3.31 in Aram

multiplied to you! 2 It has seemed
good to me to show the signs and
wonders that the Most High God has
wrought toward me.

3 How great are his signs,
how mighty his wonders!
His kingdom is an everlasting
kingdom,
and his dominion is from generation to generation.

4[f] I, Ne·bu̇·chȧd·nez′zȧr, was at
ease in my house and prospering in
my palace. 5 I had a dream which
made me afraid; as I lay in bed the
fancies and the visions of my head
alarmed me. 6 Therefore I made a
decree that all the wise men of Babylon should be brought before me, that
they might make known to me the
interpretation of the dream. 7 Then
the magicians, the enchanters, the
Chal·dē′ȧnṡ, and the astrologers came
in; and I told them the dream, but
they could not make known to me its
interpretation. 8 At last Daniel came in
before me—he who was named Bel·tė-
shaz′zȧr after the name of my god, and
in whom is the spirit of the holy gods[g]
—and I told him the dream, saying,
9 "O Bel·tė·shaz′zȧr, chief of the
magicians, because I know that the
spirit of the holy gods[g] is in you and
that no mystery is difficult for you,
here is[h] the dream which I saw; tell me
its interpretation. 10 The visions of my
head as I lay in bed were these: I saw,
and behold, a tree in the midst of the
earth; and its height was great. 11 The
tree grew and became strong, and its
top reached to heaven, and it was
visible to the end of the whole earth.
12 Its leaves were fair and its fruit
abundant, and in it was food for all.
The beasts of the field found shade
under it, and the birds of the air dwelt
in its branches, and all flesh was fed
from it.

13 "I saw in the visions of my head
as I lay in bed, and behold, a watcher,
a holy one, came down from heaven.
14 He cried aloud and said thus, 'Hew
down the tree and cut off its branches,
strip off its leaves and scatter its fruit;
let the beasts flee from under it and the
birds from its branches. 15 But leave
the stump of its roots in the earth,
bound with a band of iron and bronze,
amid the tender grass of the field. Let
him be wet with the dew of heaven;
let his lot be with the beasts in the
grass of the earth; 16 let his mind be
changed from a man's, and let a
beast's mind be given to him; and let
seven times pass over him. 17 The
sentence is by the decree of the
watchers, the decision by the word of
the holy ones, to the end that the
living may know that the Most High
rules the kingdom of men, and gives it
to whom he will, and sets over it the
lowliest of men.' 18 This dream I, King
Ne·bu̇·chȧd·nez′zȧr, saw. And you, O
Bel·tė·shaz′zȧr, declare the interpretation, because all the wise men of my
kingdom are not able to make known
to me the interpretation, but you are
able, for the spirit of the holy gods[i] is
in you."

19 Then Daniel, whose name was
Bel·tė·shaz′zȧr, was dismayed for a
moment, and his thoughts alarmed
him. The king said, "Belteshazzar, let
not the dream or the interpretation
alarm you." Belteshazzar answered,
"My lord, may the dream be for those
who hate you and its interpretation
for your enemies! 20 The tree you saw,
which grew and became strong, so that
its top reached to heaven, and it was
visible to the end of the whole earth;
21 whose leaves were fair and its fruit
abundant, and in which was food for
all; under which beasts of the field
found shade, and in whose branches
the birds of the air dwelt—22 it is you,
O king, who have grown and become
strong. Your greatness has grown and
reaches to heaven, and your dominion
to the ends of the earth. 23 And whereas
the king saw a watcher, a holy one,
coming down from heaven and saying,
'Hew down the tree and destroy it, but
leave the stump of its roots in the
earth, bound with a band of iron and
bronze, in the tender grass of the field;
and let him be wet with the dew of
heaven; and let his lot be with the
beasts of the field, till seven times pass
over him'; 24 this is the interpretation,
O king: It is a decree of the Most High,
which has come upon my lord the
king, 25 that you shall be driven from
among men, and your dwelling shall
be with the beasts of the field; you
shall be made to eat grass like an ox,
and you shall be wet with the dew of
heaven, and seven times shall pass
over you, till you know that the Most

[f] Ch 4.1 in Aram [g] Or *Spirit of the holy God* [h] Cn: Aram *visions of* [i] Or *Spirit of the holy God*
4.12, 21: Ezek 17.23; 31.6; Mt 13.32; Mk 4.32; Lk 13.19.

High rules the kingdom of men, and
gives it to whom he will. 26 And as it
was commanded to leave the stump
of the roots of the tree, your kingdom
shall be sure for you from the time
that you know that Heaven rules.
27 Therefore, O king, let my counsel
be acceptable to you; break off your
sins by practicing righteousness, and
your iniquities by showing mercy to
the oppressed, that there may perhaps
be a lengthening of your tranquility."
28 All this came upon King Ne·bu̇-
chȧd·nez'zȧr. 29 At the end of twelve
months he was walking on the roof of
the royal palace of Babylon, 30 and the
king said, "Is not this great Babylon,
which I have built by my mighty
power as a royal residence and for the
glory of my majesty?" 31 While the
words were still in the king's mouth,
there fell a voice from heaven, "O
King Ne·bu̇·chȧd·nez'zȧr, to you it is
spoken: The kingdom has departed
from you, 32 and you shall be driven
from among men, and your dwelling
shall be with the beasts of the field;
and you shall be made to eat grass like
an ox; and seven times shall pass over
you, until you have learned that the
Most High rules the kingdom of men
and gives it to whom he will." 33 Immediately the word was fulfilled upon
Ne·bu̇·chȧd·nez'zȧr. He was driven
from among men, and ate grass like an
ox, and his body was wet with the dew
of heaven till his hair grew as long as
eagles' feathers, and his nails were like
birds' claws.
34 At the end of the days I, Ne·bu̇-
chȧd·nez'zȧr, lifted my eyes to heaven,
and my reason returned to me, and I
blessed the Most High, and praised
and honored him who lives for ever;

for his dominion is an everlasting
dominion,
and his kingdom endures from
generation to generation;
35 all the inhabitants of the earth are
accounted as nothing;
and he does according to his will
in the host of heaven
and among the inhabitants of the
earth;
and none can stay his hand
or say to him, "What doest thou?"

36 At the same time my reason returned
to me; and for the glory of my kingdom, my majesty and splendor returned to me. My counselors and my
lords sought me, and I was established
in my kingdom, and still more greatness was added to me. 37 Now I,
Ne·bu̇·chȧd·nez'zȧr, praise and extol
and honor the King of heaven; for all
his works are right and his ways are
just; and those who walk in pride he
is able to abase.

5 King Bel·shaz'zȧr made a great
feast for a thousand of his lords,
and drank wine in front of the
thousand.
2 Bel·shaz'zȧr, when he tasted the
wine, commanded that the vessels of
gold and of silver which Ne·bu̇·chȧd-
nez'zȧr his father had taken out of the
temple in Jerusalem be brought, that
the king and his lords, his wives, and
his concubines might drink from them.
3 Then they brought in the golden and
silver vessels[j] which had been taken
out of the temple, the house of God
in Jerusalem; and the king and his
lords, his wives, and his concubines
drank from them. 4 They drank wine,
and praised the gods of gold and silver,
bronze, iron, wood, and stone.
5 Immediately the fingers of a
man's hand appeared and wrote on the
plaster of the wall of the king's palace,
opposite the lampstand; and the king
saw the hand as it wrote. 6 Then the
king's color changed, and his thoughts
alarmed him; his limbs gave way, and
his knees knocked together. 7 The king
cried aloud to bring in the enchanters,
the Chal·dē'ȧnṡ, and the astrologers.
The king said to the wise men of
Babylon, "Whoever reads this writing,
and shows me its interpretation, shall
be clothed with purple, and have a
chain of gold about his neck, and shall
be the third ruler in the kingdom."
8 Then all the king's wise men came
in, but they could not read the writing
or make known to the king the interpretation. 9 Then King Bel·shaz'zȧr
was greatly alarmed, and his color
changed; and his lords were perplexed.
10 The queen, because of the words
of the king and his lords, came into the
banqueting hall; and the queen said,
"O king, live for ever! Let not your
thoughts alarm you or your color
change. 11 There is in your kingdom
a man in whom is the spirit of the holy
gods.[k] In the days of your father light
and understanding and wisdom, like
the wisdom of the gods, were found in
him, and King Ne·bu̇·chȧd·nez'zȧr,

[j] Theodotion Vg: Aram *golden vessles* [k] Or *Spirit of the holy God*

your father, made him chief of the
magicians, enchanters, Chal·dē′ȧnṡ,
and astrologers,[l] 12 because an excellent spirit, knowledge, and understanding to interpret dreams, explain
riddles, and solve problems were found
in this Daniel, whom the king named
Bel·tė·shaz′zȧr. Now let Daniel be
called, and he will show the interpretation."
13 Then Daniel was brought in before the king. The king said to Daniel,
"You are that Daniel, one of the exiles
of Judah, whom the king my father
brought from Judah. 14 I have heard
of you that the spirit of the holy gods[k]
is in you, and that light and understanding and excellent wisdom are
found in you. 15 Now the wise men,
the enchanters, have been brought in
before me to read this writing and
make known to me its interpretation;
but they could not show the interpretation of the matter. 16 But I have
heard that you can give interpretations
and solve problems. Now if you can
read the writing and make known to
me its interpretation, you shall be
clothed with purple, and have a chain
of gold about your neck, and shall be
the third ruler in the kingdom."
17 Then Daniel answered before
the king, "Let your gifts be for yourself, and give your rewards to another;
nevertheless I will read the writing to
the king and make known to him the
interpretation. 18 O king, the Most
High God gave Ne·bu̇·chȧd·nez′zȧr
your father kingship and greatness and
glory and majesty; 19 and because of
the greatness that he gave him, all
peoples, nations, and languages trembled and feared before him; whom he
would he slew, and whom he would
he kept alive; whom he would he
raised up, and whom he would he put
down. 20 But when his heart was lifted
up and his spirit was hardened so that
he dealt proudly, he was deposed from
his kingly throne, and his glory was
taken from him; 21 he was driven from
among men, and his mind was made
like that of a beast, and his dwelling
was with the wild asses; he was fed
grass like an ox, and his body was wet
with the dew of heaven, until he knew
that the Most High God rules the
kingdom of men, and sets over it whom
he will. 22 And you his son, Bel·shaz′-
zȧr, have not humbled your heart,
though you knew all this, 23 but you
have lifted up yourself against the
Lord of heaven; and the vessels of his
house have been brought in before
you, and you and your lords, your
wives, and your concubines have drunk
wine from them; and you have praised
the gods of silver and gold, of bronze,
iron, wood, and stone, which do not
see or hear or know, but the God in
whose hand is your breath, and whose
are all your ways, you have not
honored.
24 "Then from his presence the
hand was sent, and this writing was
inscribed. 25 And this is the writing
that was inscribed: MĒ′NĒ, MĒ′NĒ,
TEK′ĖL, and PÄR′SIN. 26 This is the interpretation of the matter: MĒ′NĒ, God
has numbered the days of your kingdom and brought it to an end; 27 TEK′-
ĖL, you have been weighed in the
balances and found wanting; 28 PĒ′RES,
your kingdom is divided and given to
the Medes and Persians."
29 Then Bel·shaz′zȧr commanded,
and Daniel was clothed with purple,
a chain of gold was put about his neck,
and proclamation was made concerning him, that he should be the third
ruler in the kingdom.
30 That very night Bel·shaz′zȧr the
Chal·dē′ȧn king was slain. 31 And
Dȧ·rī′u̇s the Mede received the kingdom, being about sixty-two years old.
6 It pleased Dȧ·rī′u̇s to set over the
kingdom a hundred and twenty
satraps, to be throughout the whole
kingdom; 2 and over them three presidents, of whom Daniel was one, to
whom these satraps should give
account, so that the king might suffer
no loss. 3 Then this Daniel became
distinguished above all the other
presidents and satraps, because an excellent spirit was in him; and the king
planned to set him over the whole
kingdom. 4 Then the presidents and
the satraps sought to find a ground for
complaint against Daniel with regard
to the kingdom; but they could find
no ground for complaint or any fault,
because he was faithful, and no error
or fault was found in him. 5 Then
these men said, "We shall not find any
ground for complaint against this
Daniel unless we find it in connection
with the law of his God."
6 Then these presidents and satraps
came by agreement[m] to the king and

[l] Aram repeats *the king your father* [m] Or *thronging*

said to him, "O King Dȧ·rī'ŭs, live for
ever! 7 All the presidents of the kingdom, the prefects and the satraps, the
counselors and the governors are
agreed that the king should establish
an ordinance and enforce an interdict,
that whoever makes petition to any
god or man for thirty days, except to
you, O king, shall be cast into the den
of lions. 8 Now, O king, establish the
interdict and sign the document, so
that it cannot be changed, according
to the law of the Medes and the
Persians, which cannot be revoked."
9 Therefore King Dȧ·rī'ŭs signed the
document and interdict.

10 When Daniel knew that the
document had been signed, he went to
his house where he had windows in
his upper chamber open toward Jerusalem; and he got down upon his
knees three times a day and prayed
and gave thanks before his God, as he
had done previously. 11 Then these
men came by agreement[m] and found
Daniel making petition and supplication before his God. 12 Then they
came near and said before the king,
concerning the interdict, "O king! Did
you not sign an interdict, that any man
who makes petition to any god or man
within thirty days except to you, O
king, shall be cast into the den of
lions?" The king answered, "The
thing stands fast, according to the law
of the Medes and Persians, which cannot be revoked." 13 Then they answered before the king, "That Daniel,
who is one of the exiles from Judah,
pays no heed to you, O king, or the
interdict you have signed, but makes
his petition three times a day."

14 Then the king, when he heard
these words, was much distressed, and
set his mind to deliver Daniel; and he
labored till the sun went down to
rescue him. 15 Then these men came
by agreement[m] to the king, and said
to the king, "Know, O king, that it is
a law of the Medes and Persians that
no interdict or ordinance which the
king establishes can be changed."

16 Then the king commanded, and
Daniel was brought and cast into the
den of lions. The king said to Daniel,
"May your God, whom you serve continually, deliver you!" 17 And a stone
was brought and laid upon the mouth
of the den, and the king sealed it with
his own signet and with the signet of
his lords, that nothing might be
changed concerning Daniel. 18 Then
the king went to his palace, and spent
the night fasting; no diversions were
brought to him, and sleep fled from
him.

19 Then, at break of day, the king
arose and went in haste to the den of
lions. 20 When he came near to the den
where Daniel was, he cried out in a
tone of anguish and said to Daniel, "O
Daniel, servant of the living God, has
your God, whom you serve continually, been able to deliver you from the
lions?" 21 Then Daniel said to the
king, "O king, live for ever! 22 My
God sent his angel and shut the lions'
mouths, and they have not hurt me,
because I was found blameless before
him; and also before you, O king, I
have done no wrong." 23 Then the
king was exceedingly glad, and commanded that Daniel be taken up out
of the den. So Daniel was taken up out
of the den, and no kind of hurt was
found upon him, because he had
trusted in his God. 24 And the king
commanded, and those men who had
accused Daniel were brought and cast
into the den of lions—they, their
children, and their wives; and before
they reached the bottom of the den
the lions overpowered them and broke
all their bones in pieces.

25 Then King Dȧ·rī'ŭs wrote to all
the peoples, nations, and languages
that dwell in all the earth: "Peace be
multiplied to you. 26 I make a decree,
that in all my royal dominion men
tremble and fear before the god of
Daniel,

for he is the living God,
  enduring for ever;
his kingdom shall never be de-
    stroyed,
  and his dominion shall be to the
    end.
27 He delivers and rescues,
  he works signs and wonders
  in heaven and on earth,
he who has saved Daniel
  from the power of the lions."

28 So this Daniel prospered during
the reign of Dȧ·rī'ŭs and the reign of
Cyrus the Persian.

7 In the first year of Bel·shaz'zȧr
king of Babylon, Daniel had a
dream and visions of his head as he lay
in his bed. Then he wrote down the

[m] Or *thronging* 6.22: 2 Tim 4.17.

dream, and told the sum of the matter.
2 Daniel said, "I saw in my vision by
night, and behold, the four winds of
heaven were stirring up the great sea.
3 And four great beasts came up out
of the sea, different from one another.
4 The first was like a lion and had
eagles' wings. Then as I looked its
wings were plucked off, and it was
lifted up from the ground and made to
stand upon two feet like a man; and
the mind of a man was given to it.
5 And behold, another beast, a second
one, like a bear. It was raised up on
one side; it had three ribs in its mouth
between its teeth; and it was told,
'Arise, devour much flesh.' 6 After this
I looked, and lo, another, like a leopard,
with four wings of a bird on its back;
and the beast had four heads; and
dominion was given to it. 7 After this
I saw in the night visions, and behold,
a fourth beast, terrible and dreadful
and exceedingly strong; and it had
great iron teeth; it devoured and broke
in pieces, and stamped the residue
with its feet. It was different from all
the beasts that were before it; and it
had ten horns. 8 I considered the
horns, and behold, there came up
among them another horn, a little one,
before which three of the first horns
were plucked up by the roots; and behold, in this horn were eyes like the
eyes of a man, and a mouth speaking
great things. 9 As I looked,

thrones were placed
  and one that was ancient of days
    took his seat;
his raiment was white as snow,
  and the hair of his head like pure
    wool;
his throne was fiery flames,
  its wheels were burning fire.
10 A stream of fire issued
  and came forth from before him;
a thousand thousands served him,
  and ten thousand times ten thou-
    sand stood before him;
the court sat in judgment,
  and the books were opened.

11 I looked then because of the sound
of the great words which the horn was
speaking. And as I looked, the beast
was slain, and its body destroyed and
given over to be burned with fire.
12 As for the rest of the beasts, their
dominion was taken away, but their
lives were prolonged for a season and
a time. 13 I saw in the night visions,

and behold, with the clouds of
    heaven
  there came one like a son of man,
and he came to the Ancient of Days
  and was presented before him.
14 And to him was given dominion
  and glory and kingdom,
that all peoples, nations, and languages
  should serve him;
his dominion is an everlasting dominion,
  which shall not pass away,
and his kingdom one
  that shall not be destroyed.

15 "As for me, Daniel, my spirit
within me was anxious and the visions
of my head alarmed me. 16 I approached one of those who stood there
and asked him the truth concerning
all this. So he told me, and made
known to me the interpretation of the
things. 17 'These four great beasts are
four kings who shall arise out of the
earth. 18 But the saints of the Most
High shall receive the kingdom, and
possess the kingdom for ever, for ever
and ever.'

19 "Then I desired to know the
truth concerning the fourth beast,
which was different from all the rest,
exceedingly terrible, with its teeth of
iron and claws of bronze; and which
devoured and broke in pieces, and
stamped the residue with its feet;
20 and concerning the ten horns that
were on its head, and the other horn
which came up and before which three
of them fell, the horn which had eyes
and a mouth that spoke great things,
and which seemed greater than its
fellows. 21 As I looked, this horn made
war with the saints, and prevailed over
them, 22 until the Ancient of Days
came, and judgment was given for the
saints of the Most High, and the time
came when the saints received the
kingdom.

23 "Thus he said: 'As for the fourth
    beast,
  there shall be a fourth kingdom on
    earth,
  which shall be different from all
    the kingdoms,

7.3: Rev 13.1. **7.3, 7, 21:** Rev 11.7. **7.4-6:** Rev 13.2. **7.7:** Rev 12.3; 13.1; 17.3. **7.8, 11:** Rev 13.5.
7.9: Rev 1.14; 20.4, 11. **7.10:** Rev 5.11; 20.12.
7.13-14: Mt 24.30; 26.64; Mk 13.26; 14.62; Lk 21.27; 22.69; Rev 1.7, 13; 14.14.
7.14, 18, 22, 27: Rev 11.15. **7.20, 24:** Rev 17.12. **7.21:** Rev 13.7.

and it shall devour the whole earth,
and trample it down, and break
it to pieces.
24 As for the ten horns,
out of this kingdom
ten kings shall arise,
and another shall arise after
them;
he shall be different from the
former ones,
and shall put down three kings.
25 He shall speak words against the
Most High,
and shall wear out the saints
of the Most High,
and shall think to change the
times and the law;
and they shall be given into his
hand
for a time, two times, and half
a time.
26 But the court shall sit in judgment,
and his dominion shall be taken
away,
to be consumed and destroyed
to the end.
27 And the kingdom and the dominion
and the greatness of the kingdoms under the whole heaven
shall be given to the people of
the saints of the Most High;
their kingdom shall be an everlasting kingdom,
and all dominions shall serve
and obey them.'

28 "Here is the end of the matter.
As for me, Daniel, my thoughts
greatly alarmed me, and my color
changed; but I kept the matter in my
mind."

8 In the third year of the reign of
King Bel·shaz'zar a vision appeared to me, Daniel, after that which
appeared to me at the first. 2 And I
saw in the vision; and when I saw, I
was in Su'sȧ the capital, which is in
the province of E'lăm; and I saw in
the vision, and I was at the river
Ū'lăi. 3 I raised my eyes and saw, and
behold, a ram standing on the bank of
the river. It had two horns; and both
horns were high, but one was higher
than the other, and the higher one
came up last. 4 I saw the ram charging
westward and northward and southward; no beast could stand before him,
and there was no one who could rescue
from his power; he did as he pleased
and magnified himself.

5 As I was considering, behold, a
he-goat came from the west across the
face of the whole earth, without
touching the ground; and the goat had
a conspicuous horn between his eyes.
6 He came to the ram with the two
horns, which I had seen standing on
the bank of the river, and he ran at
him in his mighty wrath. 7 I saw him
come close to the ram, and he was
enraged against him and struck the
ram and broke his two horns; and the
ram had no power to stand before him,
but he cast him down to the ground
and trampled upon him; and there was
no one who could rescue the ram from
his power. 8 Then the he-goat magnified himself exceedingly; but when he
was strong, the great horn was broken,
and instead of it there came up four
conspicuous horns toward the four
winds of heaven.

9 Out of one of them came forth a
little horn, which grew exceedingly
great toward the south, toward the
east, and toward the glorious land.
10 It grew great, even to the host of
heaven; and some of the host of the
stars it cast down to the ground, and
trampled upon them. 11 It magnified
itself, even up to the Prince of the
host; and the continual burnt offering
was taken away from him, and the
place of his sanctuary was overthrown.
12 And the host was given over to it together with the continual burnt offering through transgression;[n] and truth
was cast down to the ground, and the
horn acted and prospered. 13 Then I
heard a holy one speaking; and another
holy one said to the one that spoke,
"For how long is the vision concerning
the continual burnt offering, the transgression that makes desolate, and the
giving over of the sanctuary and host
to be trampled underfoot?"[o] 14 And he
said to him,[p] "For two thousand and
three hundred evenings and mornings;
then the sanctuary shall be restored to
its rightful state."

15 When I, Daniel, had seen the
vision, I sought to understand it; and
behold, there stood before me one
having the appearance of a man. 16 And
I heard a man's voice between the
banks of the Ū'lăi, and it called,
"Gabriel, make this man understand
the vision." 17 So he came near where
I stood; and when he came, I was

[n] Heb obscure [o] Heb obscure [p] Theodotion Gk Syr Vg: Heb *me*
7.25: Rev 12.14. **8.10**: Rev 12.4. **8.13**: Lk 21.24.

frightened and fell upon my face. But
he said to me, "Understand, O son of
man, that the vision is for the time of
the end."

18 As he was speaking to me, I fell
into a deep sleep with my face to the
ground; but he touched me and set me
on my feet. 19 He said, "Behold, I will
make known to you what shall be at
the latter end of the indignation; for it
pertains to the appointed time of the
end. 20 As for the ram which you saw
with the two horns, these are the kings
of Media and Persia. 21 And the he-
goat[q] is the king of Greece; and the
great horn between his eyes is the first
king. 22 As for the horn that was broken,
in place of which four others arose,
four kingdoms shall arise from his[r]
nation, but not with his power. 23 And
at the latter end of their rule, when the
transgressors have reached their full
measure, a king of bold countenance,
one who understands riddles, shall
arise. 24 His power shall be great,[s] and
he shall cause fearful destruction, and
shall succeed in what he does, and
destroy mighty men and the people of
the saints. 25 By his cunning he shall
make deceit prosper under his hand,
and in his own mind he shall magnify
himself. Without warning he shall
destroy many; and he shall even rise
up against the Prince of princes; but,
by no human hand, he shall be broken.
26 The vision of the evenings and the
mornings which has been told is true;
but seal up the vision, for it pertains
to many days hence."

27 And I, Daniel, was overcome
and lay sick for some days; then I rose
and went about the king's business;
but I was appalled by the vision and
did not understand it.

9 In the first year of Dȧ·rī′ůs the
son of Ȧ·has̆′ū-ē′růs, by birth a
Mede, who became king over the realm
of the Chal·dē′ȧns—2 in the first year
of his reign, I, Daniel, perceived in
the books the number of years which,
according to the word of the LORD to
Jeremiah the prophet, must pass before the end of the desolations of Jerusalem, namely, seventy years.

3 Then I turned my face to the
Lord God, seeking him by prayer and
supplications with fasting and sackcloth and ashes. 4 I prayed to the
LORD my God and made confession,
saying, "O Lord, the great and terrible
God, who keepest covenant and steadfast love with those who love him and
keep his commandments, 5 we have
sinned and done wrong and acted
wickedly and rebelled, turning aside
from thy commandments and ordinances; 6 we have not listened to thy
servants the prophets, who spoke in
thy name to our kings, our princes,
and our fathers, and to all the people
of the land. 7 To thee, O Lord, belongs
righteousness, but to us confusion of
face, as at this day, to the men of
Judah, to the inhabitants of Jerusalem,
and to all Israel, those that are near
and those that are far away, in all the
lands to which thou hast driven them,
because of the treachery which they
have committed against thee. 8 To us,
O Lord, belongs confusion of face, to
our kings, to our princes, and to our
fathers, because we have sinned
against thee. 9 To the Lord our God
belong mercy and forgiveness; because
we have rebelled against him, 10 and
have not obeyed the voice of the LORD
our God by following his laws, which
he set before us by his servants the
prophets. 11 All Israel has transgressed
thy law and turned aside, refusing to
obey thy voice. And the curse and
oath which are written in the law of
Moses the servant of God have been
poured out upon us, because we have
sinned against him. 12 He has confirmed his words, which he spoke
against us and against our rulers who
ruled us, by bringing upon us a great
calamity; for under the whole heaven
there has not been done the like of
what has been done against Jerusalem.
13 As it is written in the law of Moses,
all this calamity has come upon us, yet
we have not entreated the favor of the
LORD our God, turning from our iniquities and giving heed to thy truth.
14 Therefore the LORD has kept ready
the calamity and has brought it upon
us; for the LORD our God is righteous
in all the works which he has done,
and we have not obeyed his voice.
15 And now, O Lord our God, who
didst bring thy people out of the land
of Egypt with a mighty hand, and hast
made thee a name, as at this day, we
have sinned, we have done wickedly.
16 O Lord, according to all thy
righteous acts, let thy anger and thy

[q] Or *shaggy he-goat* [r] Theodotion Gk Vg: Heb *the*
[s] Theodotion and Beatty papyrus of Gk: Heb repeats *but not with his power* from verse 22

wrath turn away from thy city Jerusalem, thy holy hill; because for our sins, and for the iniquities of our fathers, Jerusalem and thy people have become a byword among all who are round about us. 17 Now therefore, O our God, hearken to the prayer of thy servant and to his supplications, and for thy own sake, O Lord,[t] cause thy face to shine upon thy sanctuary, which is desolate. 18 O my God, incline thy ear and hear; open thy eyes and behold our desolations, and the city which is called by thy name; for we do not present our supplications before thee on the ground of our righteousness, but on the ground of thy great mercy. 19 O LORD, hear; O LORD, forgive; O LORD, give heed and act; delay not, for thy own sake, O my God, because thy city and thy people are called by thy name."

20 While I was speaking and praying, confessing my sin and the sin of my people Israel, and presenting my supplication before the LORD my God for the holy hill of my God; 21 while I was speaking in prayer, the man Gabriel, whom I had seen in the vision at the first, came to me in swift flight at the time of the evening sacrifice. 22 He came[u] and he said to me, "O Daniel, I have now come out to give you wisdom and understanding. 23 At the beginning of your supplications a word went forth, and I have come to tell it to you, for you are greatly beloved; therefore consider the word and understand the vision.

24 "Seventy weeks of years are decreed concerning your people and your holy city, to finish the transgression, to put an end to sin, and to atone for iniquity, to bring in everlasting righteousness, to seal both vision and prophet, and to anoint a most holy place.[v] 25 Know therefore and understand that from the going forth of the word to restore and build Jerusalem to the coming of an anointed one, a prince, there shall be seven weeks. Then for sixty-two weeks it shall be built again with squares and moat, but in a troubled time. 26 And after the sixty-two weeks, an anointed one shall be cut off, and shall have nothing; and the people of the prince who is to come shall destroy the city and the sanctuary. Its[w] end shall come with a flood, and to the end there shall be war; desolations are decreed. 27 And he shall make a strong covenant with many for one week; and for half of the week he shall cause sacrifice and offering to cease; and upon the wing of abominations shall come one who makes desolate, until the decreed end is poured out on the desolator."

10 In the third year of Cyrus king of Persia a word was revealed to Daniel, who was named Bel·tĕ·shaz′zär. And the word was true, and it was a great conflict. And he understood the word and had understanding of the vision.

2 In those days I, Daniel, was mourning for three weeks. 3 I ate no delicacies, no meat or wine entered my mouth, nor did I anoint myself at all, for the full three weeks. 4 On the twenty-fourth day of the first month, as I was standing on the bank of the great river, that is, the Tī′gris, 5 I lifted up my eyes and looked, and behold, a man clothed in linen, whose loins were girded with gold of Ū′phaz. 6 His body was like beryl, his face like the appearance of lightning, his eyes like flaming torches, his arms and legs like the gleam of burnished bronze, and the sound of his words like the noise of a multitude. 7 And I, Daniel, alone saw the vision, for the men who were with me did not see the vision, but a great trembling fell upon them, and they fled to hide themselves. 8 So I was left alone and saw this great vision, and no strength was left in me; my radiant appearance was fearfully changed, and I retained no strength. 9 Then I heard the sound of his words; and when I heard the sound of his words, I fell on my face in a deep sleep with my face to the ground.

10 And behold, a hand touched me and set me trembling on my hands and knees. 11 And he said to me, "O Daniel, man greatly beloved, give heed to the words that I speak to you, and stand upright, for now I have been sent to you." While he was speaking this word to me, I stood up trembling. 12 Then he said to me, "Fear not, Daniel, for from the first day that you set your mind to understand and humbled yourself before your God,

[t] Theodotion Vg Compare Syr: Heb *for the Lord's sake* [u] Gk Syr: Heb *made to understand*
[v] Or *thing* or *one* [w] Or *his*
9.27: Dan 11.31; 12.11; Mt 24.15; Mk 13.14. **10.5-6:** Rev 1.13-14; 2.18.

your words have been heard, and I
have come because of your words.
13 The prince of the kingdom of Persia
withstood me twenty-one days; but
Michael, one of the chief princes, came
to help me, so I left him there with the
prince of the kingdom of Persia[x] 14 and
came to make you understand what is
to befall your people in the latter
days. For the vision is for days yet to
come."

15 When he had spoken to me
according to these words, I turned my
face toward the ground and was dumb.
16 And behold, one in the likeness of
the sons of men touched my lips; then
I opened my mouth and spoke. I said
to him who stood before me, "O my
lord, by reason of the vision pains
have come upon me, and I retain no
strength. 17 How can my lord's servant
talk with my lord? For now no strength
remains in me, and no breath is left
in me."

18 Again one having the appearance
of a man touched me and strengthened
me. 19 And he said, "O man greatly
beloved, fear not, peace be with you;
be strong and of good courage." And
when he spoke to me, I was strengthened and said, "Let my lord speak, for
you have strengthened me." 20 Then
he said, "Do you know why I have
come to you? But now I will return to
fight against the prince of Persia; and
when I am through with him, lo, the
prince of Greece will come. 21 But I
will tell you what is inscribed in the
book of truth: there is none who contends by my side against these except
Michael, your prince. 1 And as for me,
11 in the first year of Da·rī'us the
Mede, I stood up to confirm and
strengthen him.

2 "And now I will show you the
truth. Behold, three more kings shall
arise in Persia; and a fourth shall be
far richer than all of them; and when
he has become strong through his
riches, he shall stir up all against the
kingdom of Greece. 3 Then a mighty
king shall arise, who shall rule with
great dominion and do according to
his will. 4 And when he has arisen, his
kingdom shall be broken and divided
toward the four winds of heaven, but
not to his posterity, nor according to
the dominion with which he ruled; for
his kingdom shall be plucked up and
go to others besides these.

5 "Then the king of the south shall
be strong, but one of his princes shall
be stronger than he and his dominion
shall be a great dominion. 6 After some
years they shall make an alliance, and
the daughter of the king of the south
shall come to the king of the north to
make peace; but she shall not retain
the strength of her arm, and he and his
offspring shall not endure; but she
shall be given up, and her attendants,
her child, and he who got possession
of[y] her.

7 "In those times a branch[z] from
her roots shall arise in his place; he
shall come against the army and enter
the fortress of the king of the north,
and he shall deal with them and shall
prevail. 8 He shall also carry off to
Egypt their gods with their molten
images and with their precious vessels
of silver and of gold; and for some
years he shall refrain from attacking
the king of the north. 9 Then the latter
shall come into the realm of the king
of the south but shall return into his
own land.

10 "His sons shall wage war and
assemble a multitude of great forces,
which shall come on and overflow and
pass through, and again shall carry the
war as far as his fortress. 11 Then the
king of the south, moved with anger,
shall come out and fight with the king
of the north; and he shall raise a great
multitude, but it shall be given into
his hand. 12 And when the multitude is
taken, his heart shall be exalted, and he
shall cast down tens of thousands, but
he shall not prevail. 13 For the king of
the north shall again raise a multitude,
greater than the former; and after
some years[a] he shall come on with a
great army and abundant supplies.

14 "In those times many shall rise
against the king of the south; and the
men of violence among your own people shall lift themselves up in order to
fulfil the vision; but they shall fail.
15 Then the king of the north shall
come and throw up siegeworks, and
take a well-fortified city. And the
forces of the south shall not stand, or
even his picked troops, for there shall
be no strength to stand. 16 But he who
comes against him shall do according

[x] Theodotion Compare Gk: Heb *I was left there with the kings of Persia* [y] Or *supported*
[z] Gk: Heb *from a branch* [a] Heb *at the end of the times years*
10.13, 21: Rev 12.7.

to his own will, and none shall stand
before him; and he shall stand in the
glorious land, and all of it shall be in
his power. 17 He shall set his face to
come with the strength of his whole
kingdom, and he shall bring terms of
peace[b] and perform them. He shall
give him the daughter of women to
destroy the kingdom;[c] but it shall not
stand or be to his advantage. 18 Afterward he shall turn his face to the
coastlands, and shall take many of
them; but a commander shall put an
end to his insolence; indeed[d] he shall
turn his insolence back upon him.
19 Then he shall turn his face back
toward the fortresses of his own land;
but he shall stumble and fall, and shall
not be found.

20 "Then shall arise in his place one
who shall send an exactor of tribute
through the glory of the kingdom; but
within a few days he shall be broken,
neither in anger nor in battle. 21 In his
place shall arise a contemptible person
to whom royal majesty has not been
given; he shall come in without warning and obtain the kingdom by flat-
teries. 22 Armies shall be utterly swept
away before him and broken, and the
prince of the covenant also. 23 And
from the time that an alliance is made
with him he shall act deceitfully; and
he shall become strong with a small
people. 24 Without warning he shall
come into the richest parts[e] of the
province; and he shall do what neither
his fathers nor his fathers' fathers have
done, scattering among them plunder,
spoil, and goods. He shall devise plans
against strongholds, but only for a
time. 25 And he shall stir up his power
and his courage against the king of the
south with a great army; and the king
of the south shall wage war with an
exceedingly great and mighty army;
but he shall not stand, for plots shall
be devised against him. 26 Even those
who eat his rich food shall be his undoing; his army shall be swept away,
and many shall fall down slain. 27 And
as for the two kings, their minds shall
be bent on mischief; they shall speak
lies at the same table, but to no avail;
for the end is yet to be at the time
appointed. 28 And he shall return to his
land with great substance, but his
heart shall be set against the holy
covenant. And he shall work his will,
and return to his own land.

29 "At the time appointed he shall
return and come into the south; but it
shall not be this time as it was before.
30 For ships of Kit'tim shall come
against him, and he shall be afraid and
withdraw, and shall turn back and be
enraged and take action against the
holy covenant. He shall turn back and
give heed to those who forsake the
holy covenant. 31 Forces from him
shall appear and profane the temple
and fortress, and shall take away the
continual burnt offering. And they
shall set up the abomination that
makes desolate. 32 He shall seduce with
flattery those who violate the covenant; but the people who know their
God shall stand firm and take action.
33 And those among the people who
are wise shall make many understand,
though they shall fall by sword and
flame, by captivity and plunder, for
some days. 34 When they fall, they
shall receive a little help. And many
shall join themselves to them with
flattery; 35 and some of those who are
wise shall fall, to refine and to cleanse
them[f] and to make them white, until
the time of the end, for it is yet for the
time appointed.

36 "And the king shall do according
to his will; he shall exalt himself and
magnify himself above every god, and
shall speak astonishing things against
the God of gods. He shall prosper till
the indignation is accomplished; for
what is determined shall be done.
37 He shall give no heed to the gods of
his fathers, or to the one beloved by
women; he shall not give heed to any
other god, for he shall magnify himself
above all. 38 He shall honor the god of
fortresses instead of these; a god whom
his fathers did not know he shall honor
with gold and silver, with precious
stones and costly gifts. 39 He shall deal
with the strongest fortresses by the
help of a foreign god; those who acknowledge him he shall magnify with
honor. He shall make them rulers over
many and shall divide the land for a
price.

40 "At the time of the end the king
of the south shall attack[g] him; but the
king of the north shall rush upon him
like a whirlwind, with chariots and

[b] Gk: Heb *upright ones* [c] Heb *her* or *it* [d] Heb obscure [e] Or *among the richest men*
[f] Gk: Heb *among them* [g] Heb *thrust at*

11.31: Dan 9.27; 12.11; Mt 24.15; Mk 13.14. **11.36:** Ezek 28.2; 2 Thess 2.4; Rev 13.5.

horsemen, and with many ships; and
he shall come into countries and shall
overflow and pass through. 41 He shall
come into the glorious land. And tens
of thousands shall fall, but these shall
be delivered out of his hand: Ē'dȯm
and Mō'ab and the main part of the
Am'mȯ·nītes. 42 He shall stretch out
his hand against the countries, and the
land of Egypt shall not escape. 43 He
shall become ruler of the treasures of
gold and of silver, and all the precious
things of Egypt; and the Libyans and
the Ethiopians shall follow in his train.
44 But tidings from the east and the
north shall alarm him, and he shall go
forth with great fury to exterminate
and utterly destroy many. 45 And he
shall pitch his palatial tents between
the sea and the glorious holy mountain;
yet he shall come to his end, with none
to help him.

12 "At that time shall arise Michael, the great prince who has
charge of your people. And there shall
be a time of trouble, such as never has
been since there was a nation till that
time; but at that time your people
shall be delivered, every one whose
name shall be found written in the
book. 2 And many of those who sleep in
the dust of the earth shall awake, some
to everlasting life, and some to shame
and everlasting contempt. 3 And those
who are wise shall shine like the brightness of the firmament; and those who
turn many to righteousness, like the
stars for ever and ever. 4 But you,
Daniel, shut up the words, and seal
the book, until the time of the end.
Many shall run to and fro, and knowledge shall increase."
5 Then I Daniel looked, and behold, two others stood, one on this
bank of the stream and one on that
bank of the stream. 6 And I[h] said to the
man clothed in linen, who was above
the waters of the stream, "How long
shall it be till the end of these wonders?" 7 The man clothed in linen,
who was above the waters of the
stream, raised his right hand and his
left hand toward heaven; and I heard
him swear by him who lives for ever
that it would be for a time, two times,
and half a time; and that when the
shattering of the power of the holy
people comes to an end all these things
would be accomplished. 8 I heard, but
I did not understand. Then I said, "O
my lord, what shall be the issue of
these things?" 9 He said, "Go your
way, Daniel, for the words are shut up
and sealed until the time of the end.
10 Many shall purify themselves, and
make themselves white, and be refined; but the wicked shall do wickedly;
and none of the wicked shall understand; but those who are wise shall
understand. 11 And from the time that
the continual burnt offering is taken
away, and the abomination that makes
desolate is set up, there shall be a thousand two hundred and ninety days.
12 Blessed is he who waits and comes
to the thousand three hundred and
thirty-five days. 13 But go your way till
the end; and you shall rest, and shall
stand in your allotted place at the end
of the days."

THE BOOK OF

HOSEA

1 The word of the LORD that came
to Hō·ṡē'ȧ the son of Be-ē'rī, in the
days of Uz·zī'ȧh, Jō'thȧm, Ā'haz, and
Hez·ė·kī'ȧh, kings of Judah, and in the
days of Jer·ȯ·bō'ȧm the son of Jō'ash,
king of Israel.
2 When the LORD first spoke
through Hō·ṡē'ȧ, the LORD said to
Hosea, "Go, take to yourself a wife of
harlotry and have children of harlotry,
for the land commits great harlotry
by forsaking the LORD." 3 So he went

h Gk Vg: Heb *he*
12.1: Mt 24.21; Mk 13.19; Rev 12.7; 16.18.
12.2: Mt 25.46. **12.3**: Mt 13.43. **12.4**: Rev 22.10.
12.7: Rev 4.9; 10.5; 12.14. **12.11**: Dan 9.27; 11.31; Mt 24.15; Mk 13.14.

and took Gō'mĕr the daughter of Dib-
lā'im, and she conceived and bore him
a son.
4 And the LORD said to him, "Call
his name Jez'rē·ĕl; for yet a little while,
and I will punish the house of Jē'hū
for the blood of Jezreel, and I will put
an end to the kingdom of the house of
Israel. 5 And on that day, I will break
the bow of Israel in the valley of
Jez'rē·ĕl."
6 She conceived again and bore a
daughter. And the LORD said to him,
"Call her name Not pitied, for I will
no more have pity on the house of
Israel, to forgive them at all. 7 But I
will have pity on the house of Judah,
and I will deliver them by the LORD
their God; I will not deliver them by
bow, nor by sword, nor by war, nor
by horses, nor by horsemen."
8 When she had weaned Not pitied,
she conceived and bore a son. 9 And
the LORD said, "Call his name Not my
people, for you are not my people and
I am not your God."[a]
10[b] Yet the number of the people of
Israel shall be like the sand of the sea,
which can be neither measured nor
numbered; and in the place where it
was said to them, "You are not my
people," it shall be said to them, "Sons
of the living God." 11 And the people
of Judah and the people of Israel shall
be gathered together, and they shall
appoint for themselves one head; and
they shall go up from the land, for
great shall be the day of Jez'rē·ĕl.

2[c] Say to your brother,[d] "My people," and to your sister,[e] "She has
obtained pity."

2 "Plead with your mother, plead—
for she is not my wife,
and I am not her husband—
that she put away her harlotry from
her face,
and her adultery from between
her breasts;
3 lest I strip her naked
and make her as in the day she
was born,
and make her like a wilderness,
and set her like a parched land,
and slay her with thirst.
4 Upon her children also I will have
no pity,
because they are children of
harlotry.
5 For their mother has played the
harlot;
she that conceived them has acted
shamefully.
For she said, 'I will go after my
lovers,
who give me my bread and my
water,
my wool and my flax, my oil and
my drink.'
6 Therefore I will hedge up her[f] way
with thorns;
and I will build a wall against
her,
so that she cannot find her paths.
7 She shall pursue her lovers,
but not overtake them;
and she shall seek them,
but shall not find them.
Then she shall say, 'I will go
and return to my first husband,
for it was better with me then
than now.'
8 And she did not know
that it was I who gave her
the grain, the wine, and the oil,
and who lavished upon her silver
and gold which they used for
Bā'ăl.
9 Therefore I will take back
my grain in its time,
and my wine in its season;
and I will take away my wool and
my flax,
which were to cover her nakedness.
10 Now I will uncover her lewdness
in the sight of her lovers,
and no one shall rescue her out of
my hand.
11 And I will put an end to all her
mirth,
her feasts, her new moons, her
sabbaths,
and all her appointed feasts.
12 And I will lay waste her vines and
her fig trees,
of which she said,
'These are my hire,
which my lovers have given me.'
I will make them a forest,
and the beasts of the field shall
devour them.
13 And I will punish her for the feast
days of the Bā'ălṡ
when she burned incense to them
and decked herself with her ring
and jewelry,

[a] Heb *I am not yours* [b] Ch 2.1 in Heb [c] Ch 2.3 in Heb [d] Gk: Heb *brothers* [e] Gk Vg: Heb *sisters*
[f] Gk Syr: Heb *your*

1.6, 9: Hos 2.23; 1 Pet 2.10. **1.10:** Rom 9.26. **2.1, 23:** Rom 9.25; 1 Pet 2.10.

and went after her lovers,
and forgot me, says the LORD.

14 "Therefore, behold, I will allure her,
and bring her into the wilderness,
and speak tenderly to her.
15 And there I will give her her vineyards,
and make the Valley of Ā'chôr a door of hope.
And there she shall answer as in the days of her youth,
as at the time when she came out of the land of Egypt.

16 "And in that day, says the LORD,
you will call me, 'My husband,' and no
longer will you call me, 'My Bā'ăl.'
17 For I will remove the names of the
Bā'ăls from her mouth, and they shall
be mentioned by name no more. 18 And
I will make for you[g] a covenant on that
day with the beasts of the field, the
birds of the air, and the creeping things
of the ground; and I will abolish[h] the
bow, the sword, and war from the
land; and I will make you lie down in
safety. 19 And I will betroth you to me
for ever; I will betroth you to me in
righteousness and in justice, in steadfast love, and in mercy. 20 I will betroth you to me in faithfulness; and
you shall know the LORD.

21 "And in that day, says the LORD,
I will answer the heavens
and they shall answer the earth;
22 and the earth shall answer the grain, the wine, and the oil,
and they shall answer Jez'rē-ĕl;[i]
23 and I will sow him[j] for myself in the land.
And I will have pity on Not pitied,
and I will say to Not my people,
'You are my people';
and he shall say, 'Thou art my God.' "

3 And the LORD said to me, "Go
again, love a woman who is beloved
of a paramour and is an adulteress;
even as the LORD loves the people of
Israel, though they turn to other gods
and love cakes of raisins." 2 So I bought
her for fifteen shekels of silver and a
homer and a lethech of barley. 3 And I
said to her, "You must dwell as mine
for many days; you shall not play the
harlot, or belong to another man; so
will I also be to you." 4 For the children of Israel shall dwell many days
without king or prince, without sacrifice or pillar, without ephod or teraphim. 5 Afterward the children of Israel
shall return and seek the LORD their
God, and David their king; and they
shall come in fear to the LORD and to
his goodness in the latter days.

4 Hear the word of the LORD, O people of Israel;
for the LORD has a controversy with the inhabitants of the land.
There is no faithfulness or kindness,
and no knowledge of God in the land;
2 there is swearing, lying, killing, stealing, and committing adultery;
they break all bounds and murder follows murder.
3 Therefore the land mourns,
and all who dwell in it languish,
and also the beasts of the field,
and the birds of the air;
and even the fish of the sea are taken away.

4 Yet let no one contend,
and let none accuse,
for with you is my contention, O priest.[k]
5 You shall stumble by day,
the prophet also shall stumble with you by night;
and I will destroy your mother.
6 My people are destroyed for lack of knowledge;
because you have rejected knowledge,
I reject you from being a priest to me.
And since you have forgotten the law of your God,
I also will forget your children.

7 The more they increased,
the more they sinned against me;
I will change their glory into shame.
8 They feed on the sin of my people;
they are greedy for their iniquity.
9 And it shall be like people, like priest;
I will punish them for their ways,
and requite them for their deeds.
10 They shall eat, but not be satisfied;
they shall play the harlot, but not multiply;
because they have forsaken the LORD to cherish harlotry.

11 Wine and new wine

[g] Heb *them* [h] Heb *break* [i] That is *God sows* [j] Cn: Heb *her* [k] Cn: Heb uncertain

take away the understanding.
12 My people inquire of a thing of wood,
and their staff gives them oracles.
For a spirit of harlotry has led them astray,
and they have left their God to play the harlot.
13 They sacrifice on the tops of the mountains,
and make offerings upon the hills,
under oak, poplar, and terebinth,
because their shade is good.

Therefore your daughters play the harlot,
and your brides commit adultery.
14 I will not punish your daughters when they play the harlot,
nor your brides when they commit adultery;
for the men themselves go aside with harlots,
and sacrifice with cult prostitutes,
and a people without understanding shall come to ruin.

15 Though you play the harlot, O Israel,
let not Judah become guilty.
Enter not into Gil'găl,
nor go up to Beth-ā'vėn,
and swear not, "As the LORD lives."
16 Like a stubborn heifer,
Israel is stubborn;
can the LORD now feed them
like a lamb in a broad pasture?

17 E'phrȧ·im is joined to idols,
let him alone.
18 A band[l] of drunkards, they give themselves to harlotry;
they love shame more than their glory.[m]
19 A wind has wrapped them[n] in its wings,
and they shall be ashamed because of their altars.[o]

5 Hear this, O priests!
Give heed, O house of Israel!
Hearken, O house of the king!
For the judgment pertains to you;
for you have been a snare at Miz'pȧh,
and a net spread upon Tā'bôr.
2 And they have made deep the pit of Shit'tim[p];
but I will chastise all of them.

3 I know E'phrȧ·im,
and Israel is not hid from me;
for now, O Ephraim, you have played the harlot,
Israel is defiled.
4 Their deeds do not permit them
to return to their God.
For the spirit of harlotry is within them,
and they know not the LORD.

5 The pride of Israel testifies to his face;
E'phrȧ·im[q] shall stumble in his guilt;
Judah also shall stumble with them.
6 With their flocks and herds they shall go
to seek the LORD,
but they will not find him;
he has withdrawn from them.
7 They have dealt faithlessly with the LORD;
for they have borne alien children.
Now the new moon shall devour them with their fields.

8 Blow the horn in Gib'ē-ȧh,
the trumpet in Rā'mȧh.
Sound the alarm at Beth-ā'vėn;
tremble,[r] O Benjamin!
9 E'phrȧ·im shall become a desolation
in the day of punishment;
among the tribes of Israel
I declare what is sure.
10 The princes of Judah have become
like those who remove the landmark;
upon them I will pour out
my wrath like water.
11 E'phrȧ·im is oppressed, crushed in judgment,
because he was determined to go after vanity.[s]
12 Therefore I am like a moth to E'phrȧ·im,
and like dry rot to the house of Judah.

13 When E'phrȧ·im saw his sickness,
and Judah his wound,
then Ephraim went to Assyria,
and sent to the great king.[t]
But he is not able to cure you
or heal your wound.
14 For I will be like a lion to E'phrȧ·im,

[l] Cn: Heb uncertain [m] Cn Compare Gk: Heb of this line uncertain [n] Heb *her*
[o] Gk Syr: Heb *sacrifices* [p] Cn: Heb uncertain [q] Heb *Israel and Ephraim*
[r] Cn Compare Gk: Heb *after you* [s] Gk: Heb *a command* [t] Cn: Heb *a king that will contend*

and like a young lion to the house
of Judah.
I, even I, will rend and go away,
I will carry off, and none shall
rescue.

15 I will return again to my place,
until they acknowledge their guilt
and seek my face,
and in their distress they seek me,
saying,

6 "Come, let us return to the LORD;
for he has torn, that he may heal
us;
he has stricken, and he will bind
us up.
2 After two days he will revive us;
on the third day he will raise us
up,
that we may live before him.
3 Let us know, let us press on to know
the LORD;
his going forth is sure as the
dawn;
he will come to us as the showers,
as the spring rains that water the
earth."

4 What shall I do with you, O
E'phră·im?
What shall I do with you, O
Judah?
Your love is like a morning cloud,
like the dew that goes early away.
5 Therefore I have hewn them by the
prophets,
I have slain them by the words
of my mouth,
and my judgment goes forth as
the light.[u]
6 For I desire steadfast love and not
sacrifice,
the knowledge of God, rather than
burnt offerings.

7 But at[v] Adam they transgressed the
covenant;
there they dealt faithlessly with
me.
8 Gilead is a city of evildoers,
tracked with blood.
9 As robbers lie in wait[w] for a man,
so the priests are banded together;[x]
they murder on the way to Shē'chem,
yea, they commit villainy.
10 In the house of Israel I have seen a
horrible thing;
E'phră·im's harlotry is there, Israel is defiled.

11 For you also, O Judah, a harvest is
appointed.

When I would restore the fortunes
of my people,

7 1 when I would heal Israel,
the corruption of E'phră·im is revealed,
and the wicked deeds of Să-
mâr'i·ă;
for they deal falsely,
the thief breaks in,
and the bandits raid without.
2 But they do not consider
that I remember all their evil
works.
Now their deeds encompass them,
they are before my face.
3 By their wickedness they make the
king glad,
and the princes by their treachery.
4 They are all adulterers;
they are like a heated oven,
whose baker ceases to stir the fire,
from the kneading of the dough
until it is leavened.
5 On the day of our king the princes
became sick with the heat of wine;
he stretched out his hand with
mockers.
6 For like an oven their hearts burn[y]
with intrigue;
all night their anger smolders;
in the morning it blazes like a
flaming fire.
7 All of them are hot as an oven,
and they devour their rulers.
All their kings have fallen;
and none of them calls upon me.

8 E'phră·im mixes himself with the
peoples;
Ephraim is a cake not turned.
9 Aliens devour his strength,
and he knows it not;
gray hairs are sprinkled upon him,
and he knows it not.
10 The pride of Israel witnesses against
him;
yet they do not return to the LORD
their God,
nor seek him, for all this.

11 E'phră·im is like a dove,
silly and without sense,

[u] Gk Syr: Heb *thy judgment goes forth* [v] Cn: Heb *like* [w] Cn: Heb uncertain [x] Syr: Heb *a company*
[y] Gk Syr: Heb *brought near*
6.6: Mt 9.13; 12.7.

calling to Egypt, going to Assyria.
12 As they go, I will spread over them
my net;
I will bring them down like birds
of the air;
I will chastise them for their
wicked deeds.[z]
13 Woe to them, for they have strayed
from me!
Destruction to them, for they
have rebelled against me!
I would redeem them,
but they speak lies against me.

14 They do not cry to me from the
heart,
but they wail upon their beds;
for grain and wine they gash themselves,
they rebel against me.
15 Although I trained and strengthened
their arms,
yet they devise evil against me.
16 They turn to Bā'ăl;[a]
they are like a treacherous bow,
their princes shall fall by the sword
because of the insolence of their
tongue.
This shall be their derision in the
land of Egypt.

8 Set the trumpet to your lips,
for[b] a vulture is over the house
of the LORD,
because they have broken my covenant,
and transgressed my law.
2 To me they cry,
My God, we Israel know thee.
3 Israel has spurned the good;
the enemy shall pursue him.

4 They made kings, but not through
me.
They set up princes, but without
my knowledge.
With their silver and gold they made
idols
for their own destruction.
5 I have[c] spurned your calf, O Să-
mâr'i·ȧ.
My anger burns against them.
How long will it be
till they are pure 6 in Israel?[d]

A workman made it;
it is not God.
The calf of Să·mâr'i·ȧ
shall be broken to pieces.[e]

7 For they sow the wind,
and they shall reap the whirlwind.
The standing grain has no heads,
it shall yield no meal;
if it were to yield,
aliens would devour it.
8 Israel is swallowed up;
already they are among the
nations
as a useless vessel.
9 For they have gone up to Assyria,
a wild ass wandering alone;
Ē'phrȧ·im has hired lovers.
10 Though they hire allies among the
nations,
I will soon gather them up.
And they shall cease[f] for a little
while
from anointing[g] king and princes.

11 Because Ē'phrȧ·im has multiplied
altars for sinning,
they have become to him altars
for sinning.
12 Were I to write for him my laws by
ten thousands,
they would be regarded as a
strange thing.
13 They love sacrifice;[h]
they sacrifice flesh and eat it;
but the LORD has no delight in
them.
Now he will remember their iniquity,
and punish their sins;
they shall return to Egypt.
14 For Israel has forgotten his Maker,
and built palaces;
and Judah has multiplied fortified
cities;
but I will send a fire upon his
cities,
and it shall devour his strongholds.

9 Rejoice not, O Israel!
Exult not[i] like the peoples;
for you have played the harlot, forsaking your God.
You have loved a harlot's hire
upon all threshing floors.
2 Threshing floor and winevat shall
not feed them,

[z] Cn: Heb *according to the report to their congregation* [a] Cn: Heb uncertain [b] Cn: Heb *as*
[c] Heb *He has* [d] Gk: Heb *for from Israel* [e] Or *shall go up in flames* [f] Gk: Heb *begin*
[g] Gk: Heb *burden* [h] Cn: Heb uncertain [i] Gk: Heb *to exultation*
8.14: Amos 1.4, 7, 10, 12, 14; 2.2, 5.

and the new wine shall fail them.
3 They shall not remain in the land of the LORD;
but E'phrȧ·im shall return to Egypt,
and they shall eat unclean food in Assyria.

4 They shall not pour libations of wine to the LORD;
and they shall not please him with their sacrifices.
Their bread[j] shall be like mourners' bread;
all who eat of it shall be defiled;
for their bread shall be for their hunger only;
it shall not come to the house of the LORD.

5 What will you do on the day of appointed festival,
and on the day of the feast of the LORD?
6 For behold, they are going to Assyria;[k]
Egypt shall gather them,
Memphis shall bury them.
Nettles shall possess their precious things of silver;
thorns shall be in their tents.

7 The days of punishment have come,
the days of recompense have come;
Israel shall know it.
The prophet is a fool,
the man of the spirit is mad,
because of your great iniquity
and great hatred.
8 The prophet is the watchman of E'phrȧ·im,
the people of my God,
yet a fowler's snare is on all his ways,
and hatred in the house of his God.
9 They have deeply corrupted themselves
as in the days of Gib'ē-ȧh:
he will remember their iniquity,
he will punish their sins.

10 Like grapes in the wilderness,
I found Israel.
Like the first fruit on the fig tree,
in its first season,
I saw your fathers.
But they came to Bā'ȧl-pē'ôr,
and consecrated themselves to Bā'ȧl,[l]
and became detestable like the thing they loved.
11 E'phrȧ·im's glory shall fly away like a bird—
no birth, no pregnancy, no conception!
12 Even if they bring up children,
I will bereave them till none is left.
Woe to them
when I depart from them!
13 E'phrȧ·im's sons, as I have seen,
are destined for a prey;[m]
Ephraim must lead forth his sons to slaughter.
14 Give them, O LORD—
what wilt thou give?
Give them a miscarrying womb
and dry breasts.

15 Every evil of theirs is in Gil'gȧl;
there I began to hate them.
Because of the wickedness of their deeds
I will drive them out of my house.
I will love them no more;
all their princes are rebels.

16 E'phrȧ·im is stricken,
their root is dried up,
they shall bear no fruit.
Even though they bring forth,
I will slay their beloved children.
17 My God will cast them off,
because they have not hearkened to him;
they shall be wanderers among the nations.

10 Israel is a luxuriant vine
that yields its fruit.
The more his fruit increased
the more altars he built;
as his country improved
he improved his pillars.
2 Their heart is false;
now they must bear their guilt.
The LORD[n] will break down their altars,
and destroy their pillars.

3 For now they will say:
"We have no king,
for we fear not the LORD,

[j] Cn: Heb *to them* [k] Cn: Heb *from destruction* [l] Heb *shame* [m] Cn Compare Gk: Heb uncertain
[n] Heb *he*
9.7: Lk 21.22.

and a king, what could he do for
us?"
4 They utter mere words;
with empty oaths they make
covenants;
so judgment springs up like poisonous weeds
in the furrows of the field.
5 The inhabitants of Să·mâr'ĭ·ȧ tremble
for the calf[o] of Beth-ā'vėn.
Its people shall mourn for it,
and its idolatrous priests shall
wail[p] over it,
over its glory which has departed
from it.
6 Yea, the thing itself shall be carried
to Assyria,
as tribute to the great king.[q]
E'phrȧ·im shall be put to shame,
and Israel shall be ashamed of his
idol.[r]

7 Să·mâr'ĭ·ȧ's king shall perish,
like a chip on the face of the
waters.
8 The high places of Ā'vėn, the sin of
Israel,
shall be destroyed.
Thorn and thistle shall grow up
on their altars;
and they shall say to the mountains,
Cover us,
and to the hills, Fall upon us.

9 From the days of Gib'ē-ȧh, you
have sinned, O Israel;
there they have continued.
Shall not war overtake them in
Gibe-ah?
10 I will come[s] against the wayward
people to chastise them;
and nations shall be gathered
against them
when they are chastised[t] for their
double iniquity.

11 E'phrȧ·im was a trained heifer
that loved to thresh,
and I spared her fair neck;
but I will put Ephraim to the yoke,
Judah must plow,
Jacob must harrow for himself.
12 Sow for yourselves righteousness,
reap the fruit[u] of steadfast love;
break up your fallow ground,
for it is the time to seek the LORD,
that he may come and rain salvation upon you.

13 You have plowed iniquity,
you have reaped injustice,
you have eaten the fruit of lies.
Because you have trusted in your
chariots[v]
and in the multitude of your
warriors,
14 therefore the tumult of war shall
arise among your people,
and all your fortresses shall be
destroyed,
as Shal'mȧn destroyed Beth-är'bėl
on the day of battle;
mothers were dashed in pieces
with their children.
15 Thus it shall be done to you, O
house of Israel,[w]
because of your great wickedness.
In the storm[x] the king of Israel
shall be utterly cut off.

11 When Israel was a child, I loved
him,
and out of Egypt I called my son.
2 The more I[y] called them,
the more they went from me;[z]
they kept sacrificing to the Bā'ȧls,
and burning incense to idols.

3 Yet it was I who taught E'phrȧ·im
to walk,
I took them up in my[a] arms;
but they did not know that I
healed them.
4 I led them with cords of compassion,[b]
with the bands of love,
and I became to them as one
who eases the yoke on their jaws,
and I bent down to them and fed
them.

5 They shall return to the land of
Egypt,
and Assyria shall be their king,
because they have refused to
return to me.
6 The sword shall rage against their
cities,
consume the bars of their gates,
and devour them in their fortresses.[c]

[o] Gk Syr: Heb *calves* [p] Cn: Heb *exult* [q] Cn: Heb *a king that will contend* [r] Cn: Heb *counsel*
[s] Cn Compare Gk: Heb *in my desire* [t] Gk: Heb *bound* [u] Gk: Heb *according to* [v] Gk: Heb *way*
[w] Gk: Heb *O Bethel* [x] Cn: Heb *dawn* [y] Gk: Heb *they* [z] Gk: Heb *them* [a] Gk Syr Vg: Heb *his*
[b] Heb *man* [c] Cn: Heb *counsels*
10.8: Lk 23.30; Rev 6.16. 10.12: 2 Cor 9.10. 11.1: Mt 2.15.

7 My people are bent on turning away
from me;[d]
so they are appointed to the yoke,
and none shall remove it.

8 How can I give you up, O E'phrȧ·im!
How can I hand you over, O
Israel!
How can I make you like Ad'mȧh!
How can I treat you like Ze·boi'-
im!
My heart recoils within me,
my compassion grows warm and
tender.
9 I will not execute my fierce anger,
I will not again destroy E'phrȧ·im;
for I am God and not man,
the Holy One in your midst,
and I will not come to destroy.[e]

10 They shall go after the LORD,
he will roar like a lion;
yea, he will roar,
and his sons shall come trembling
from the west;
11 they shall come trembling like birds
from Egypt,
and like doves from the land of
Assyria;
and I will return them to their
homes, says the LORD.
12[f] E'phrȧ·im has encompassed me
with lies,
and the house of Israel with deceit;
but Judah is still known by[g] God,
and is faithful to the Holy One.

12 E'phrȧ·im herds the wind,
and pursues the east wind all
day long;
they multiply falsehood and violence;
they make a bargain with Assyria,
and oil is carried to Egypt.

2 The LORD has an indictment against
Judah,
and will punish Jacob according
to his ways,
and requite him according to his
deeds.
3 In the womb he took his brother by
the heel,
and in his manhood he strove
with God.
4 He strove with the angel and prevailed,
he wept and sought his favor.
He met God at Beth'ĕl,
and there God spoke with him[h]—
5 the LORD the God of hosts,
the LORD is his name:
6 "So you, by the help of your God,
return,
hold fast to love and justice,
and wait continually for your
God."

7 A trader, in whose hands are false
balances,
he loves to oppress.
8 E'phrȧ·im has said, "Ah, but I am
rich,
I have gained wealth for myself";
but all his riches can never offset[i]
the guilt he has incurred.
9 I am the LORD your God
from the land of Egypt;
I will again make you dwell in tents,
as in the days of the appointed
feast.

10 I spoke to the prophets;
it was I who multiplied visions,
and through the prophets gave
parables.
11 If there is iniquity in Gilead
they shall surely come to nought;
if in Gil'găl they sacrifice bulls,
their altars also shall be like stone
heaps
on the furrows of the field.
12 (Jacob fled to the land of Âr'ăm,
there Israel did service for a wife,
and for a wife he herded sheep.)
13 By a prophet the LORD brought
Israel up from Egypt,
and by a prophet he was preserved.
14 E'phrȧ·im has given bitter provocation;
so his LORD will leave his bloodguilt upon him,
and will turn back upon him his
reproaches.

13 When E'phrȧ·im spoke, men
trembled;
he was exalted in Israel;
but he incurred guilt through
Bā'ăl and died.
2 And now they sin more and more,
and make for themselves molten
images,
idols skilfully made of their silver,

[d] The meaning of the Hebrew is uncertain [e] Cn: Heb *into the city* [f] Ch 12.1 in Heb
[g] Cn Compare Gk: Heb *roams with* [h] Gk Syr: Heb *us* [i] Cn Compare Gk: Heb obscure
12.8: Rev 3.17.

all of them the work of craftsmen.
Sacrifice to these, they say.[j]
Men kiss calves!
3 Therefore they shall be like the morning mist
or like the dew that goes early away,
like the chaff that swirls from the threshing floor
or like smoke from a window.

4 I am the LORD your God
from the land of Egypt;
you know no God but me,
and besides me there is no savior.
5 It was I who knew you in the wilderness,
in the land of drought;
6 but when they had fed[k] to the full,
they were filled, and their heart was lifted up;
therefore they forgot me.
7 So I will be to them like a lion,
like a leopard I will lurk beside the way.
8 I will fall upon them like a bear robbed of her cubs,
I will tear open their breast,
and there I will devour them like a lion,
as a wild beast would rend them.

9 I will destroy you, O Israel;
who[l] can help you?
10 Where[m] now is your king, to save you;
where are all[n] your princes,[o] to defend you[p]—
those of whom you said,
"Give me a king and princes"?
11 I have given you kings in my anger,
and I have taken them away in my wrath.

12 The iniquity of E'phrȧ·im is bound up,
his sin is kept in store.
13 The pangs of childbirth come for him,
but he is an unwise son;
for now he does not present himself
at the mouth of the womb.

14 Shall I ransom them from the power of Shē'ōl?
Shall I redeem them from Death?
O Death, where[q] are your plagues?
O Sheol, where[q] is your destruction?
Compassion is hid from my eyes.

15 Though he may flourish as the reed plant,[r]
the east wind, the wind of the LORD, shall come,
rising from the wilderness;
and his fountain shall dry up,
his spring shall be parched;
it shall strip his treasury
of every precious thing.
16[s] Sȧ·mâr'i·ȧ shall bear her guilt,
because she has rebelled against her God;
they shall fall by the sword,
their little ones shall be dashed in pieces,
and their pregnant women ripped open.

14 Return, O Israel, to the LORD your God,
for you have stumbled because of your iniquity.
2 Take with you words
and return to the LORD;
say to him,
"Take away all iniquity;
accept that which is good
and we will render
the fruit[t] of our lips.
3 Assyria shall not save us,
we will not ride upon horses;
and we will say no more, 'Our God',
to the work of our hands.
In thee the orphan finds mercy."

4 I will heal their faithlessness;
I will love them freely,
for my anger has turned from them.
5 I will be as the dew to Israel;
he shall blossom as the lily,
he shall strike root as the poplar;[u]
6 his shoots shall spread out;
his beauty shall be like the olive,
and his fragrance like Lebanon.
7 They shall return and dwell beneath my[v] shadow,
they shall flourish as a garden;[w]
they shall blossom as the vine,

[j] Gk: Heb *to these they say sacrifices of* [k] Cn: Heb *according to their pasture* [l] Gk Syr: Heb *for in me*
[m] Gk Syr Vg: Heb *I will be* [n] Cn: Heb *in all* [o] Cn: Heb *cities*
[p] Cn Compare Gk: Heb *and your judges* [q] Gk Syr: Heb *I will be* [r] Cn: Heb *among brothers*
[s] Ch 14.1 in Heb [t] Gk Syr: Heb *bulls* [u] Cn: Heb *Lebanon* [v] Heb *his*
[w] Cn: Heb *they shall grow grain*
13.14: 1 Cor 15.55. **14.2:** Heb 13.15.

their fragrance shall be like the
wine of Lebanon.

8 O E'phră·im, what have I to do with
idols?
it is I who answer and look after
you.[x]
I am like an evergreen cypress,
from me comes your fruit.

9 Whoever is wise, let him understand these things;
whoever is discerning, let him
know them;
for the ways of the LORD are
right,
and the upright walk in them,
but transgressors stumble in
them.

THE BOOK OF JOEL

1 The word of the LORD that came
to Jō'ĕl, the son of Pe·thū'el:

2 Hear this, you aged men,
give ear, all inhabitants of the
land!
Has such a thing happened in your
days,
or in the days of your fathers?
3 Tell your children of it,
and let your children tell their
children,
and their children another generation.

4 What the cutting locust left,
the swarming locust has eaten.
What the swarming locust left,
the hopping locust has eaten,
and what the hopping locust left,
the destroying locust has eaten.

5 Awake, you drunkards, and weep;
and wail, all you drinkers of wine,
because of the sweet wine,
for it is cut off from your mouth.
6 For a nation has come up against
my land,
powerful and without number;
its teeth are lions' teeth,
and it has the fangs of a lioness.
7 It has laid waste my vines,
and splintered my fig trees;
it has stripped off their bark and
thrown it down;
their branches are made white.

8 Lament like a virgin girded with
sackcloth
for the bridegroom of her youth.
9 The cereal offering and the drink
offering are cut off
from the house of the LORD.
The priests mourn,
the ministers of the LORD.
10 The fields are laid waste,
the ground mourns;
because the grain is destroyed,
the wine fails,
the oil languishes.

11 Be confounded, O tillers of the soil,
wail, O vinedressers,
for the wheat and the barley;
because the harvest of the field
has perished.
12 The vine withers,
the fig tree languishes.
Pomegranate, palm, and apple,
all the trees of the field are
withered;
and gladness fails
from the sons of men.

13 Gird on sackcloth and lament, O
priests,
wail, O ministers of the altar.
Go in, pass the night in sackcloth,
O ministers of my God!
Because cereal offering and drink
offering
are withheld from the house of
your God.

14 Sanctify a fast,
call a solemn assembly.
Gather the elders
and all the inhabitants of the land

x Heb *him*
14.9: Acts 13.10. **1.6:** Rev 9.8.

to the house of the LORD your God;
and cry to the LORD.

15 Alas for the day!
For the day of the LORD is near,
and as destruction from the Almighty it comes.
16 Is not the food cut off
before our eyes,
joy and gladness
from the house of our God?

17 The seed shrivels under the clods,[a]
the storehouses are desolate;
the granaries are ruined
because the grain has failed.
18 How the beasts groan!
The herds of cattle are perplexed
because there is no pasture for them;
even the flocks of sheep are dismayed.

19 Unto thee, O LORD, I cry.
For fire has devoured
the pastures of the wilderness,
and flame has burned
all the trees of the field.
20 Even the wild beasts cry to thee
because the water brooks are dried up,
and fire has devoured
the pastures of the wilderness.

2 Blow the trumpet in Zion;
sound the alarm on my holy mountain!
Let all the inhabitants of the land tremble,
for the day of the LORD is coming, it is near,
2 a day of darkness and gloom,
a day of clouds and thick darkness!
Like blackness there is spread upon the mountains
a great and powerful people;
their like has never been from of old,
nor will be again after them
through the years of all generations.

3 Fire devours before them,
and behind them a flame burns.
The land is like the garden of Eden before them,
but after them a desolate wilderness,
and nothing escapes them.

4 Their appearance is like the appearance of horses,
and like war horses they run.
5 As with the rumbling of chariots,
they leap on the tops of the mountains,
like the crackling of a flame of fire
devouring the stubble,
like a powerful army
drawn up for battle.

6 Before them peoples are in anguish,
all faces grow pale.
7 Like warriors they charge,
like soldiers they scale the wall.
They march each on his way,
they do not swerve[b] from their paths.
8 They do not jostle one another,
each marches in his path;
they burst through the weapons
and are not halted.
9 They leap upon the city,
they run upon the walls;
they climb up into the houses,
they enter through the windows
like a thief.

10 The earth quakes before them,
the heavens tremble.
The sun and the moon are darkened,
and the stars withdraw their shining.
11 The LORD utters his voice
before his army,
for his host is exceedingly great;
he that executes his word is powerful.
For the day of the LORD is great and very terrible;
who can endure it?

12 "Yet even now," says the LORD,
"return to me with all your heart,
with fasting, with weeping, and with mourning;
13 and rend your hearts and not your garments."
Return to the LORD, your God,
for he is gracious and merciful,
slow to anger, and abounding in steadfast love,
and repents of evil.
14 Who knows whether he will not turn and repent,
and leave a blessing behind him,
a cereal offering and a drink offering
for the LORD, your God?

[a] Heb uncertain [b] Gk Syr Vg: Heb *take a pledge*
2.4-5: Rev 9.7,9. **2.10:** Rev 9.2.
2.11: Rev 6.17.

15 Blow the trumpet in Zion;
sanctify a fast;
call a solemn assembly;
16 gather the people.
Sanctify the congregation;
assemble the elders;
gather the children,
even nursing infants.
Let the bridegroom leave his room,
and the bride her chamber.

17 Between the vestibule and the altar
let the priests, the ministers of the LORD, weep
and say, "Spare thy people, O LORD,
and make not thy heritage a reproach,
a byword among the nations.
Why should they say among the peoples,
'Where is their God?' "

18 Then the LORD became jealous for his land,
and had pity on his people.
19 The LORD answered and said to his people,
"Behold, I am sending to you
grain, wine, and oil,
and you will be satisfied;
and I will no more make you
a reproach among the nations.

20 "I will remove the northerner far from you,
and drive him into a parched and desolate land,
his front into the eastern sea,
and his rear into the western sea;
the stench and foul smell of him will rise,
for he has done great things.

21 "Fear not, O land;
be glad and rejoice,
for the LORD has done great things!
22 Fear not, you beasts of the field,
for the pastures of the wilderness are green;
the tree bears its fruit,
the fig tree and vine give their full yield.

23 "Be glad, O sons of Zion,
and rejoice in the LORD, your God;
for he has given the early rain for your vindication,
he has poured down for you abundant rain,
the early and the latter rain, as before.

24 "The threshing floors shall be full of grain,
the vats shall overflow with wine and oil.
25 I will restore to you the years
which the swarming locust has eaten,
the hopper, the destroyer, and the cutter,
my great army, which I sent among you.

26 "You shall eat in plenty and be satisfied,
and praise the name of the LORD your God,
who has dealt wondrously with you.
And my people shall never again be put to shame.
27 You shall know that I am in the midst of Israel,
and that I, the LORD, am your God and there is none else.
And my people shall never again be put to shame.

28[c] "And it shall come to pass afterward,
that I will pour out my spirit on all flesh;
your sons and your daughters shall prophesy,
your old men shall dream dreams,
and your young men shall see visions.
29 Even upon the menservants and maidservants
in those days, I will pour out my spirit.

30 "And I will give portents in the
heavens and on the earth, blood and
fire and columns of smoke. 31 The sun
shall be turned to darkness, and the
moon to blood, before the great and
terrible day of the LORD comes. 32 And
it shall come to pass that all who call
upon the name of the LORD shall be
delivered; for in Mount Zion and in
Jerusalem there shall be those who
escape, as the LORD has said, and
among the survivors shall be those
whom the LORD calls.

[c] Ch 3.1 in Heb

2.28-32: Acts 2.17-21. **2.31:** Rev 6.12. **2.32:** Rom 10.13.

3[d] "For behold, in those days and
at that time, when I restore the
fortunes of Judah and Jerusalem, 2 I
will gather all the nations and bring
them down to the valley of Je·hosh'ȧ-
phat, and I will enter into judgment
with them there, on account of my
people and my heritage Israel, because
they have scattered them among the
nations, and have divided up my land,
3 and have cast lots for my people, and
have given a boy for a harlot, and have
sold a girl for wine, and have drunk it.
4 "What are you to me, O Tȳre and
Sī'don, and all the regions of Phi·lis'-
ti·ȧ? Are you paying me back for something? If you are paying me back, I
will requite your deed upon your own
head swiftly and speedily. 5 For you
have taken my silver and my gold, and
have carried my rich treasures into
your temples.[e] 6 You have sold the
people of Judah and Jerusalem to the
Greeks, removing them far from their
own border. 7 But now I will stir them
up from the place to which you have
sold them, and I will requite your deed
upon your own head. 8 I will sell your
sons and your daughters into the hand
of the sons of Judah, and they will sell
them to the Sȧ·bē'ȧns, to a nation far
off; for the LORD has spoken."

9 Proclaim this among the nations:
Prepare war,
stir up the mighty men.
Let all the men of war draw near,
let them come up.
10 Beat your plowshares into swords,
and your pruning hooks into spears;
let the weak say, "I am a warrior."

11 Hasten and come,
all you nations round about,
gather yourselves there.
Bring down thy warriors, O LORD.
12 Let the nations bestir themselves,
and come up to the valley of Je·hosh'ȧ·phat;
for there I will sit to judge
all the nations round about.

13 Put in the sickle,
for the harvest is ripe.
Go in, tread,
for the wine press is full.
The vats overflow,
for their wickedness is great.

14 Multitudes, multitudes,
in the valley of decision!
For the day of the LORD is near
in the valley of decision.
15 The sun and the moon are darkened,
and the stars withdraw their shining.

16 And the LORD roars from Zion,
and utters his voice from Jerusalem,
and the heavens and the earth shake.
But the LORD is a refuge to his people,
a stronghold to the people of Israel.

17 "So you shall know that I am the LORD your God,
who dwell in Zion, my holy mountain.
And Jerusalem shall be holy
and strangers shall never again pass through it.

18 "And in that day
the mountains shall drip sweet wine,
and the hills shall flow with milk,
and all the stream beds of Judah
shall flow with water;
and a fountain shall come forth from the house of the LORD
and water the valley of Shit'tim.

19 "Egypt shall become a desolation
and Ē'dŏm a desolate wilderness,
for the violence done to the people of Judah,
because they have shed innocent blood in their land.
20 But Judah shall be inhabited for ever,
and Jerusalem to all generations.
21 I will avenge their blood, and I will not clear the guilty,[g]
for the LORD dwells in Zion."

[d] Ch 4.1 in Heb [e] Or *palaces*
[g] Gk Syr: Heb *I will hold innocent their blood which I have not held innocent*
3.4-8: Is 23; Ezek 26.1-28.19; Amos 1.9-10; Zech 9.3-4; Ezek 28.20-26; Zech 9.2; Is 14.29-31; Jer 47; Ezek 25.15-17; Amos 1.6-8; Zeph 2.4-7; Zech 9.5-7.
3.10: Is 2.4; Mic 4.3. **3.13:** Mk 4.29; Rev 14.15, 18-19. **3.16:** Amos 1.2.
3.18: Ezek 47.1-12; Amos 9.13; Zech 14.8; Rev 22.1.

THE BOOK OF

AMOS

1 The words of Amos, who was
among the shepherds of Te·kō′ȧ,
which he saw concerning Israel in the
days of Uz·zī′ȧh king of Judah and in
the days of Jer·ȯ·bō′ȧm the son of
Jō′ash, king of Israel, two years[a]
before the earthquake. 2 And he
said:
"The LORD roars from Zion,
and utters his voice from Jerusalem;
the pastures of the shepherds mourn,
and the top of Cär′mėl withers."

3 Thus says the LORD:
"For three transgressions of Damascus,
and for four, I will not revoke the punishment;[b]
because they have threshed Gilead
with threshing sledges of iron.
4 So I will send a fire upon the house of Haz′ȧ·el,
and it shall devour the strongholds of Ben-hā′dad.
5 I will break the bar of Damascus,
and cut off the inhabitants from the Valley of Ā′vėn,[c]
and him that holds the scepter from Beth-ē′dėn;
and the people of Syria shall go into exile to Kīr,"
says the LORD.

6 Thus says the LORD:
"For three transgressions of Gā′zȧ,
and for four, I will not revoke the punishment;[b]
because they carried into exile a whole people
to deliver them up to Ē′dȯm.
7 So I will send a fire upon the wall of Gā′zȧ,
and it shall devour her strongholds.
8 I will cut off the inhabitants from Ash′dod,
and him that holds the scepter from Ash′kė·lon;
I will turn my hand against Ek′rȯn;
and the remnant of the Philistines shall perish,"
says the Lord GOD.

9 Thus says the LORD:
"For three transgressions of Tȳre,
and for four, I will not revoke the punishment;[b]
because they delivered up a whole people to Ē′dȯm,
and did not remember the covenant of brotherhood.
10 So I will send a fire upon the wall of Tȳre,
and it shall devour her strongholds."

11 Thus says the LORD:
"For three transgressions of Ē′dȯm,
and for four, I will not revoke the punishment;[b]
because he pursued his brother with the sword,
and cast off all pity,
and his anger tore perpetually,
and he kept his wrath[d] for ever.
12 So I will send a fire upon Tē′mȧn,
and it shall devour the strongholds of Boz′rȧh."

13 Thus says the LORD:
"For three transgressions of the Am′mȯ·nītes,
and for four, I will not revoke the punishment;[b]
because they have ripped up women with child in Gilead,
that they might enlarge their border.
14 So I will kindle a fire in the wall of Rab′bȧh,
and it shall devour her strongholds,

[a] Or *during two years* [b] Heb *cause it to return* [c] Or *On* [d] Gk Syr Vg: Heb *his wrath kept*

1.2: Joel 3.16. 1.3-5: Is 17.1-3; Jer 49.23-27; Zech 9.1.
1.6-8: Is 14.29-31; Jer 47; Ezek 25.15-17; Joel 3.4-8; Zeph 2.4-7; Zech 9.5-7.
1.9-10: Is 23; Ezek 26.1-28.19; Joel 3.4-8; Zech 9.3-4.
1.11-12: Is 34; 63.1-6; Jer 49.7-22; Ezek 25.12-14; 35; Obad; Mal. 1.2-5.
1.13-15: Jer 49.1-6; Ezek 21.28-32; 25.1-7; Zeph 2.8-11.

with shouting in the day of battle,
with a tempest in the day of the whirlwind;
15 and their king shall go into exile,
he and his princes together,"
says the LORD.

2 Thus says the LORD:
"For three transgressions of Mō'ab,
and for four, I will not revoke the punishment;[e]
because he burned to lime
the bones of the king of E'dom.
2 So I will send a fire upon Mō'ab,
and it shall devour the strongholds of Ker'i·oth,
and Moab shall die amid uproar,
amid shouting and the sound of the trumpet;
3 I will cut off the ruler from its midst,
and will slay all its princes with him,"
says the LORD.

4 Thus says the LORD:
"For three transgressions of Judah,
and for four, I will not revoke the punishment;[e]
because they have rejected the law of the LORD,
and have not kept his statutes,
but their lies have led them astray,
after which their fathers walked.
5 So I will send a fire upon Judah,
and it shall devour the strongholds of Jerusalem."

6 Thus says the LORD:
"For three transgressions of Israel,
and for four, I will not revoke the punishment;[e]
because they sell the righteous for silver,
and the needy for a pair of shoes—
7 they that trample the head of the poor into the dust of the earth,
and turn aside the way of the afflicted;
a man and his father go in to the same maiden,
so that my holy name is profaned;
8 they lay themselves down beside every altar
upon garments taken in pledge;
and in the house of their God they drink
the wine of those who have been fined.
9 "Yet I destroyed the Am'ò·rite before them,
whose height was like the height of the cedars,
and who was as strong as the oaks;
I destroyed his fruit above,
and his roots beneath.
10 Also I brought you up out of the land of Egypt,
and led you forty years in the wilderness,
to possess the land of the Am'ò·rite.
11 And I raised up some of your sons for prophets,
and some of your young men for Naz'i·rites.
Is it not indeed so, O people of Israel?"
says the LORD.

12 "But you made the Naz'i·rites drink wine,
and commanded the prophets,
saying, 'You shall not prophesy.'

13 "Behold, I will press you down in your place,
as a cart full of sheaves presses down.
14 Flight shall perish from the swift,
and the strong shall not retain his strength,
nor shall the mighty save his life;
15 he who handles the bow shall not stand,
and he who is swift of foot shall not save himself,
nor shall he who rides the horse save his life;
16 and he who is stout of heart among the mighty
shall flee away naked in that day,"
says the LORD.

3 Hear this word that the LORD has
spoken against you, O people of
Israel, against the whole family which
I brought up out of the land of Egypt:
2 "You only have I known
of all the families of the earth;
therefore I will punish you
for all your iniquities.

3 "Do two walk together,
unless they have made an appointment?
4 Does a lion roar in the forest,
when he has no prey?

[e] Heb *cause it to return*
2.1-3: Is 15-16; 25.10-12; Jer 48; Ezek 25.8-11; Zeph 2.8-11.

Does a young lion cry out from his den,
if he has taken nothing?
5 Does a bird fall in a snare on the earth,
when there is no trap for it?
Does a snare spring up from the ground,
when it has taken nothing?
6 Is a trumpet blown in a city,
and the people are not afraid?
Does evil befall a city,
unless the LORD has done it?
7 Surely the Lord GOD does nothing,
without revealing his secret
to his servants the prophets.
8 The lion has roared;
who will not fear?
The Lord GOD has spoken;
who can but prophesy?"

9 Proclaim to the strongholds in Assyria,[f]
and to the strongholds in the land of Egypt,
and say, "Assemble yourselves upon the mountains of Sȧ·mâr′i·ȧ,
and see the great tumults within her,
and the oppressions in her midst."
10 "They do not know how to do right," says the LORD,
"those who store up violence and robbery in their strongholds."
11 Therefore thus says the Lord GOD:
"An adversary shall surround the land,
and bring down your defenses from you,
and your strongholds shall be plundered."

12 Thus says the LORD: "As the
shepherd rescues from the mouth of
the lion two legs, or a piece of an ear,
so shall the people of Israel who dwell
in Sȧ·mâr′i·ȧ be rescued, with the
corner of a couch and part[g] of a bed."

13 "Hear, and testify against the house of Jacob,"
says the Lord GOD, the God of hosts,
14 "that on the day I punish Israel for his transgressions,
I will punish the altars of Beth′ĕl,
and the horns of the altar shall be cut off
and fall to the ground.
15 I will smite the winter house with the summer house;
and the houses of ivory shall perish,
and the great houses[h] shall come to an end,"
says the LORD.

4 "Hear this word, you cows of Bā′shȧn,
who are in the mountain of Sȧ·mâr′i·ȧ,
who oppress the poor, who crush the needy,
who say to their husbands,
'Bring, that we may drink!'
2 The Lord GOD has sworn by his holiness
that, behold, the days are coming upon you,
when they shall take you away with hooks,
even the last of you with fishhooks.
3 And you shall go out through the breaches,
every one straight before her;
and you shall be cast forth into Här′mȯn,"
says the LORD.

4 "Come to Beth′ĕl, and transgress;
to Gil′găl, and multiply transgression;
bring your sacrifices every morning,
your tithes every three days;
5 offer a sacrifice of thanksgiving of that which is leavened,
and proclaim freewill offerings,
publish them;
for so you love to do, O people of Israel!"
says the Lord GOD.

6 "I gave you cleanness of teeth in all your cities,
and lack of bread in all your places,
yet you did not return to me,"
says the LORD.

7 "And I also withheld the rain from you
when there were yet three months to the harvest;
I would send rain upon one city,
and send no rain upon another city;
one field would be rained upon,

[f] Gk: Heb *Ashdod*
[g] The meaning of the Hebrew word is uncertain [h] Or *many houses*
3.7: Rev 10.7.

and the field on which it did not
rain withered;
8 so two or three cities wandered to
one city
to drink water, and were not
satisfied;
yet you did not return to me,"
says the LORD.

9 "I smote you with blight and mildew;
I laid waste[i] your gardens and
your vineyards;
your fig trees and your olive trees
the locust devoured;
yet you did not return to me,"
says the LORD.

10 "I sent among you a pestilence after
the manner of Egypt;
I slew your young men with the
sword;
I carried away your horses;[j]
and I made the stench of your
camp go up into your nostrils;
yet you did not return to me,"
says the LORD.

11 "I overthrew some of you,
as when God overthrew Sod'ŏm
and Gȯ·môr'răh,
and you were as a brand plucked
out of the burning;
yet you did not return to me,"
says the LORD.

12 "Therefore thus I will do to you, O
Israel;
because I will do this to you,
prepare to meet your God, O
Israel!"

13 For lo, he who forms the mountains,
and creates the wind,
and declares to man what is his
thought;
who makes the morning darkness,
and treads on the heights of the
earth—
the LORD, the God of hosts, is his
name!

5 Hear this word which I take up
over you in lamentation, O house
of Israel:
2 "Fallen, no more to rise,
is the virgin Israel;
forsaken on her land,
with none to raise her up."

3 For thus says the Lord GOD:
"The city that went forth a thousand
shall have a hundred left,
and that which went forth a hundred
shall have ten left
to the house of Israel."

4 For thus says the LORD to the house
of Israel:
"Seek me and live;
5 but do not seek Beth'ĕl,
and do not enter into Gil'găl
or cross over to Beer-sheba;
for Gilgal shall surely go
into exile;
and Bethel shall come to nought."

6 Seek the LORD and live,
lest he break out like fire in the
house of Joseph,
and it devour, with none to
quench it for Beth'ĕl,
7 O you who turn justice to wormwood,
and cast down righteousness to
the earth!

8 He who made the Plē'ĭ·dēṡ and
Ō·rī'ŏn,
and turns deep darkness into the
morning,
and darkens the day into night,
who calls for the waters of the sea,
and pours them out upon the
surface of the earth,
the LORD is his name,
9 who makes destruction flash forth
against the strong,
so that destruction comes upon
the fortress.

10 They hate him who reproves in the
gate,
and they abhor him who speaks
the truth.
11 Therefore because you trample
upon the poor
and take from him exactions of
wheat,
you have built houses of hewn stone,
but you shall not dwell in them;
you have planted pleasant vineyards,
but you shall not drink their wine.
12 For I know how many are your
transgressions,
and how great are your sins—
you who afflict the righteous, who
take a bribe,

[i] Cn: Heb *the multitude of* [j] Heb *with the captivity of your horses*

and turn aside the needy in the gate.
13 Therefore he who is prudent will keep silent in such a time;
for it is an evil time.

14 Seek good, and not evil,
that you may live;
and so the LORD, the God of hosts,
will be with you,
as you have said.
15 Hate evil, and love good,
and establish justice in the gate;
it may be that the LORD, the God of hosts,
will be gracious to the remnant of Joseph.

16 Therefore thus says the LORD, the God of hosts, the Lord:
"In all the squares there shall be wailing;
and in all the streets they shall say, 'Alas! alas!'
They shall call the farmers to mourning
and to wailing those who are skilled in lamentation,
17 and in all vineyards there shall be wailing,
for I will pass through the midst of you,"
says the LORD.

18 Woe to you who desire the day of the LORD!
Why would you have the day of the LORD?
It is darkness, and not light;
19 as if a man fled from a lion,
and a bear met him;
or went into the house and leaned with his hand against the wall,
and a serpent bit him.
20 Is not the day of the LORD darkness,
and not light,
and gloom with no brightness in it?

21 "I hate, I despise your feasts,
and I take no delight in your solemn assemblies.
22 Even though you offer me your burnt offerings and cereal offerings,
I will not accept them,
and the peace offerings of your fatted beasts
I will not look upon.
23 Take away from me the noise of your songs;
to the melody of your harps I will not listen.
24 But let justice roll down like waters,
and righteousness like an ever-flowing stream.

25 "Did you bring to me sacrifices
and offerings the forty years in the
wilderness, O house of Israel? 26 You
shall take up Sak'kůth your king, and
Käi'wän your star-god, your images,[k]
which you made for yourselves;
27 therefore I will take you into exile
beyond Damascus," says the LORD,
whose name is the God of hosts.

6 "Woe to those who are at ease in Zion,
and to those who feel secure on the mountain of Sȧ·mâr'i·ȧ,
the notable men of the first of the nations,
to whom the house of Israel come!
2 Pass over to Cal'nėh, and see;
and thence go to Hā'math the great;
then go down to Gath of the Philistines.
Are they better than these kingdoms?
Or is their territory greater than your territory,
3 O you who put far away the evil day,
and bring near the seat of violence?

4 Woe to those who lie upon beds of ivory,
and stretch themselves upon their couches,
and eat lambs from the flock,
and calves from the midst of the stall;
5 who sing idle songs to the sound of the harp,
and like David invent for themselves instruments of music;
6 who drink wine in bowls, and anoint themselves with the finest oils,
but are not grieved over the ruin of Joseph!
7 Therefore they shall now be the first of those to go into exile,
and the revelry of those who stretch themselves shall pass away."

[k] Heb *your images, your star-god*
5.25-27: Acts 7.42-43.

8 The Lord God has sworn by himself
(says the Lord, the God of hosts):
"I abhor the pride of Jacob,
and hate his strongholds;
and I will deliver up the city and all that is in it."

9 And if ten men remain in one
house, they shall die. 10And when a
man's kinsman, he who burns him,[l]
shall take him up to bring the bones
out of the house, and shall say to him
who is in the innermost parts of the
house, "Is there still any one with
you?" he shall say, "No"; and he shall
say, "Hush! We must not mention the
name of the Lord."

11 For behold, the Lord commands,
and the great house shall be smitten into fragments,
and the little house into bits.
12 Do horses run upon rocks?
Does one plow the sea with oxen?
But you have turned justice into poison
and the fruit of righteousness into wormwood—
13 you who rejoice in Lō-dē'bär,[n]
who say, "Have we not by our own strength
taken Kär·nā'im[o] for ourselves?"
14 "For behold, I will raise up against you a nation,
O house of Israel," says the Lord, the God of hosts;
"and they shall oppress you from the entrance of Hā'math
to the brook of the Ar·ȧ·bȧh."

7 Thus the Lord God showed me:
behold, he was forming locusts in
the beginning of the shooting up of the
latter growth; and lo, it was the latter
growth after the king's mowings.
2 When they had finished eating the
grass of the land, I said,
"O Lord God, forgive, I beseech thee!
How can Jacob stand?
He is so small!"
3 The Lord repented concerning this;
"It shall not be," said the Lord.

4 Thus the Lord God showed me:
behold, the Lord God was calling for
a judgment by fire, and it devoured
the great deep and was eating up the
land.
5 Then I said,
"O Lord God, cease, I beseech thee!
How can Jacob stand?
He is so small!"
6 The Lord repented concerning this;
"This also shall not be," said the Lord God.

7 He showed me: behold, the Lord
was standing beside a wall built with
a plumb line, with a plumb line in his
hand. 8And the Lord said to me,
"Amos, what do you see?" And I said,
"A plumb line." Then the Lord said,
"Behold, I am setting a plumb line
in the midst of my people Israel;
I will never again pass by them;
9 the high places of Isaac shall be made desolate,
and the sanctuaries of Israel shall be laid waste,
and I will rise against the house of Jer·ȯ·bō'ȧm with the sword."

10 Then Am·ȧ·zī'ȧh the priest of
Beth'ĕl sent to Jer·ȯ·bō'ȧm king of Israel, saying, "Amos has conspired
against you in the midst of the house
of Israel; the land is not able to bear
all his words. 11 For thus Amos has
said,
'Jer·ȯ·bō'ȧm shall die by the sword,
and Israel must go into exile
away from his land.' "
12And Am·ȧ·zī'ȧh said to Amos, "O
seer, go, flee away to the land of Judah,
and eat bread there, and prophesy
there; 13 but never again prophesy at
Beth'ĕl, for it is the king's sanctuary,
and it is a temple of the kingdom."
14 Then Amos answered Am·ȧ-
zī'ȧh, "I am no prophet, nor a prophet's son;[p] but I am a herdsman, and a
dresser of sycamore trees, 15 and the
Lord took me from following the
flock, and the Lord said to me, 'Go,
prophesy to my people Israel.'
16 "Now therefore hear the word of the Lord.
You say, 'Do not prophesy against Israel,
and do not preach against the house of Isaac.'
17 Therefore thus says the Lord:
'Your wife shall be a harlot in the city,

[l] Or *who makes a burning for him*
[n] Or *a thing of nought* [o] Or *horns*
[p] Or *one of the sons of the prophets*

and your sons and your daughters
shall fall by the sword,
and your land shall be parceled
out by line;
you yourself shall die in an unclean
land,
and Israel shall surely go into
exile away from its land.' "

8 Thus the Lord GOD showed me:
behold, a basket of summer fruit.[q]
2 And he said, "Amos, what do you
see?" And I said, "A basket of summer
fruit."[q] Then the LORD said to me,
"The end[r] has come upon my people Israel;
I will never again pass by them.
3 The songs of the temple[s] shall become wailings in that day,"
says the Lord GOD;
"the dead bodies shall be many;
in every place they shall be cast
out in silence."[t]

4 Hear this, you who trample upon
the needy,
and bring the poor of the land to
an end,
5 saying, "When will the new moon
be over,
that we may sell grain?
And the sabbath,
that we may offer wheat for sale,
that we may make the ephah small
and the shekel great,
and deal deceitfully with false
balances,
6 that we may buy the poor for silver
and the needy for a pair of
sandals,
and sell the refuse of the wheat?"
7 The LORD has sworn by the pride
of Jacob:
"Surely I will never forget any of
their deeds.
8 Shall not the land tremble on this
account,
and every one mourn who dwells
in it,
and all of it rise like the Nile,
and be tossed about and sink
again, like the Nile of Egypt?"

9 "And on that day," says the Lord
GOD,
"I will make the sun go down at
noon,
and darken the earth in broad
daylight.
10 I will turn your feasts into mourning,
and all your songs into lamentation;
I will bring sackcloth upon all loins,
and baldness on every head;
I will make it like the mourning for
an only son,
and the end of it like a bitter day.

11 "Behold, the days are coming," says
the Lord GOD,
"when I will send a famine on
the land;
not a famine of bread, nor a thirst
for water,
but of hearing the words of the
LORD.
12 They shall wander from sea to sea,
and from north to east;
they shall run to and fro, to seek the
word of the LORD,
but they shall not find it.

13 "In that day the fair virgins and the
young men
shall faint for thirst.
14 Those who swear by Ash'i·mȧh of
Sȧ·mâr'i·ȧ,
and say, 'As thy god lives, O Dan,'
and, 'As the way of Beer-sheba lives,'
they shall fall, and never rise
again."

9 I saw the LORD standing beside[u]
the altar, and he said:
"Smite the capitals until the thresholds shake,
and shatter them on the heads of
all the people;[v]
and what are left of them I will slay
with the sword;
not one of them shall flee away,
not one of them shall escape.

2 "Though they dig into Shē'ōl,
from there shall my hand take
them;
though they climb up to heaven,
from there I will bring them down.
3 Though they hide themselves on the
top of Cär'mėl,
from there I will search out and
take them;
and though they hide from my sight
at the bottom of the sea,
there I will command the serpent,
and it shall bite them.
4 And though they go into captivity
before their enemies,

[q] Heb *qayits* [r] Heb *qets* [s] Or *palace* [t] Or *be silent!* [u] Or *upon* [v] Heb *all of them*

there I will command the sword,
and it shall slay them;
and I will set my eyes upon them
for evil and not for good."

5 The Lord, GOD of hosts,
he who touches the earth and it
melts,
and all who dwell in it mourn,
and all of it rises like the Nile,
and sinks again, like the Nile of
Egypt;
6 who builds his upper chambers in
the heavens,
and founds his vault upon the
earth;
who calls for the waters of the sea,
and pours them out upon the
surface of the earth—
the LORD is his name.

7 "Are you not like the Ethiopians to
me,
O people of Israel?" says the LORD.
"Did I not bring up Israel from the
land of Egypt,
and the Philistines from Caph'tor
and the Syrians from Kīr?
8 Behold, the eyes of the Lord GOD
are upon the sinful kingdom,
and I will destroy it from the
surface of the ground;
except that I will not utterly destroy the house of Jacob,"
says the LORD.

9 "For lo, I will command,
and shake the house of Israel
among all the nations
as one shakes with a sieve,
but no pebble shall fall upon the
earth.
10 All the sinners of my people shall
die by the sword,
who say, 'Evil shall not overtake
or meet us.'

11 "In that day I will raise up
the booth of David that is fallen
and repair its breaches,
and raise up its ruins,
and rebuild it as in the days of old;
12 that they may possess the remnant
of E'dŏm
and all the nations who are called
by my name,"
says the LORD who does this.

13 "Behold, the days are coming," says
the LORD,
"when the plowman shall overtake the reaper
and the treader of grapes him who
sows the seed;
the mountains shall drip sweet wine,
and all the hills shall flow with it.
14 I will restore the fortunes of my
people Israel,
and they shall rebuild the ruined
cities and inhabit them;
they shall plant vineyards and drink
their wine,
and they shall make gardens and
eat their fruit.
15 I will plant them upon their land,
and they shall never again be
plucked up
out of the land which I have given
them,"
says the LORD your God.

THE BOOK OF

OBADIAH

1 The vision of Ō·bȧ·dī'ȧh.

Thus says the Lord GOD concerning
E'dŏm:
We have heard tidings from the
LORD,
and a messenger has been sent
among the nations:
"Rise up! let us rise against her for
battle!"
2 Behold, I will make you small among
the nations,
you shall be utterly
despised.
3 The pride of your heart has deceived
you,

9.11-12: Acts 15.16-17. **9.13:** Joel 3.18.
1-21: Is 34; 63.1-6; Jer 49.7-22; Ezek 25.12-14; 35; Amos 1.11-12; Mal 1.2-5.

you who live in the clefts of the rock,[a]
whose dwelling is high,
who say in your heart,
"Who will bring me down to the ground?"
4 Though you soar aloft like the eagle,
though your nest is set among the stars,
thence I will bring you down,
says the LORD.

5 If thieves came to you,
if plunderers by night—
how you have been destroyed!—
would they not steal only enough for themselves?
If grape gatherers came to you,
would they not leave gleanings?
6 How Esau has been pillaged,
his treasures sought out!
7 All your allies have deceived you,
they have driven you to the border;
your confederates have prevailed against you;
your trusted friends have set a trap under you—
there is no understanding of it.
8 Will I not on that day, says the LORD,
destroy the wise men out of E'dŏm,
and understanding out of Mount Esau?
9 And your mighty men shall be dismayed, O Tē'măn,
so that every man from Mount Esau will be cut off by slaughter.
10 For the violence done to your brother Jacob,.
shame shall cover you,
and you shall be cut off for ever.
11 On the day that you stood aloof,
on the day that strangers carried off his wealth,
and foreigners entered his gates
and cast lots for Jerusalem,
you were like one of them.
12 But you should not have gloated over the day of your brother
in the day of his misfortune;
you should not have rejoiced over the people of Judah
in the day of their ruin;
you should not have boasted
in the day of distress.
13 You should not have entered the gate of my people
in the day of his calamity;
you should not have gloated over his disaster
in the day of his calamity;
you should not have looted his goods
in the day of his calamity.
14 You should not have stood at the parting of the ways
to cut off his fugitives;
you should not have delivered up his survivors
in the day of distress.

15 For the day of the LORD is near
upon all the nations.
As you have done, it shall be done to you,
your deeds shall return on your own head.
16 For as you have drunk upon my holy mountain,
all the nations round about shall drink;
they shall drink, and stagger,[b]
and shall be as though they had not been.
17 But in Mount Zion there shall be those that escape,
and it shall be holy;
and the house of Jacob shall possess their own possessions.
18 The house of Jacob shall be a fire,
and the house of Joseph a flame,
and the house of Esau stubble;
they shall burn them and consume them,
and there shall be no survivor to the house of Esau;
for the LORD has spoken.
19 Those of the Negeb shall possess Mount Esau,
and those of the She·phē'lăh the land of the Philistines;
they shall possess the land of E'phrȧ·im and the land of Sȧ·mâr'i·ȧ
and Benjamin shall possess Gilead.
20 The exiles in Hā'lăh[c] who are of the people of Israel
shall possess[d] Phoenicia as far as Zar'ė·phath;
and the exiles of Jerusalem who are in Se·phär'ad
shall possess the cities of the Negeb.
21 Saviors shall go up to Mount Zion
to rule Mount Esau;
and the kingdom shall be the LORD's.

[a] Or *Sela* [b] Cn: Heb *swallow* [c] Cn: Heb *this army* [d] Cn: Heb *which*

THE BOOK OF

JONAH

1 Now the word of the LORD came
to Jō'nȧh the son of Ȧ·mit'tāi, saying, 2 "Arise, go to Nin'ė·vėh, that
great city, and cry against it; for their
wickedness has come up before me."
3 But Jō'nȧh rose to flee to Tär'shish
from the presence of the LORD. He
went down to Jop'pȧ and found a ship
going to Tarṣhish; so he paid the fare,
and went on board, to go with them
to Tarshish, away from the presence
of the LORD.

4 But the LORD hurled a great wind
upon the sea, and there was a mighty
tempest on the sea, so that the ship
threatened to break up. 5 Then the
mariners were afraid, and each cried
to his god; and they threw the wares
that were in the ship into the sea, to
lighten it for them. But Jō'nȧh had
gone down into the inner part of the
ship and had lain down, and was fast
asleep. 6 So the captain came and said
to him, "What do you mean, you
sleeper? Arise, call upon your god!
Perhaps the god will give a thought to
us, that we do not perish."

7 And they said to one another,
"Come, let us cast lots, that we may
know on whose account this evil has
come upon us." So they cast lots, and
the lot fell upon Jō'nȧh. 8 Then they
said to him, "Tell us, on whose
account this evil has come upon us?
What is your occupation? And whence
do you come? What is your country?
And of what people are you?" 9 And he
said to them, "I am a Hebrew; and I
fear the LORD, the God of heaven,
who made the sea and the dry land."
10 Then the men were exceedingly
afraid, and said to him, "What is this
that you have done!" For the men
knew that he was fleeing from the
presence of the LORD, because he had
told them.

11 Then they said to him, "What
shall we do to you, that the sea may
quiet down for us?" For the sea grew
more and more tempestuous. 12 He
said to them, "Take me up and throw
me into the sea; then the sea will quiet
down for you; for I know it is because
of me that this great tempest has come
upon you." 13 Nevertheless the men
rowed hard to bring the ship back to
land, but they could not, for the sea
grew more and more tempestuous
against them. 14 Therefore they cried
to the LORD, "We beseech thee, O
LORD, let us not perish for this man's
life, and lay not on us innocent blood;
for thou, O LORD, hast done as it
pleased thee." 15 So they took up
Jō'nȧh and threw him into the sea; and
the sea ceased from its raging. 16 Then
the men feared the LORD exceedingly,
and they offered a sacrifice to the LORD
and made vows.

17[a] And the LORD appointed a great
fish to swallow up Jō'nȧh; and Jonah
was in the belly of the fish three days
and three nights.

2 Then Jō'nȧh prayed to the LORD
his God from the belly of the fish,
2 saying,

"I called to the LORD, out of my
distress,
and he answered me;
out of the belly of Shē'ōl I cried,
and thou didst hear my voice.
3 For thou didst cast me into the deep,
into the heart of the seas,
and the flood was round about
me;
all thy waves and thy billows
passed over me.
4 Then I said, 'I am cast out
from thy presence;
how shall I again look
upon thy holy temple?'
5 The waters closed in over me,
the deep was round about me;
weeds were wrapped about my head
6 at the roots of the mountains.
I went down to the land
whose bars closed upon me for
ever;
yet thou didst bring up my life from
the Pit,
O LORD my God.
7 When my soul fainted within me,

[a] Ch 2.1 in Heb
1.17: Mt 12.40.

I remembered the LORD;
and my prayer came to thee,
into thy holy temple.
8 Those who pay regard to vain idols
forsake their true loyalty.
9 But I with the voice of thanksgiving
will sacrifice to thee;
what I have vowed I will pay.
Deliverance belongs to the LORD!"
10 And the LORD spoke to the fish, and
it vomited out Jō'nȧh upon the dry
land.

3 Then the word of the LORD came
to Jō'nȧh the second time, saying,
2 "Arise, go to Nin'ė·vėh, that great
city, and proclaim to it the message
that I tell you." 3 So Jō'nȧh arose and
went to Nin'ė·vėh, according to the
word of the LORD. Now Nineveh was
an exceedingly great city, three days'
journey in breadth. 4 Jō'nȧh began to
go into the city, going a day's journey.
And he cried, "Yet forty days, and
Nin'ė·vėh shall be overthrown!" 5 And
the people of Nin'ė·vėh believed God;
they proclaimed a fast, and put on
sackcloth, from the greatest of them
to the least of them.
6 Then tidings reached the king of
Nin'ė·vėh, and he arose from his
throne, removed his robe, and covered
himself with sackcloth, and sat in
ashes. 7 And he made proclamation and
published through Nin'ė·vėh, "By the
decree of the king and his nobles: Let
neither man nor beast, herd nor flock,
taste anything; let them not feed, or
drink water, 8 but let man and beast
be covered with sackcloth, and let
them cry mightily to God; yea, let
every one turn from his evil way and
from the violence which is in his hands.
9 Who knows, God may yet repent and
turn from his fierce anger, so that we
perish not?"
10 When God saw what they did,
how they turned from their evil way,
God repented of the evil which he had
said he would do to them; and he did
not do it.

4 But it displeased Jō'nȧh exceedingly, and he was angry. 2 And he
prayed to the LORD and said, "I pray
thee, LORD, is not this what I said
when I was yet in my country? That
is why I made haste to flee to Tär'-
shish; for I knew that thou art a
gracious God and merciful, slow to
anger, and abounding in steadfast love,
and repentest of evil. 3 Therefore now,
O LORD, take my life from me, I
beseech thee, for it is better for me to
die than to live." 4 And the LORD said,
"Do you do well to be angry?" 5 Then
Jō'nȧh went out of the city and sat to
the east of the city, and made a booth
for himself there. He sat under it in the
shade, till he should see what would
become of the city.
6 And the LORD God appointed a
plant,[b] and made it come up over
Jō'nȧh, that it might be a shade over
his head, to save him from his discom-
fort. So Jonah was exceedingly glad
because of the plant.[b] 7 But when
dawn came up the next day, God
appointed a worm which attacked the
plant,[b] so that it withered. 8 When the
sun rose, God appointed a sultry east
wind, and the sun beat upon the head
of Jō'nȧh so that he was faint; and he
asked that he might die, and said, "It
is better for me to die than to live."
9 But God said to Jō'nȧh, "Do you do
well to be angry for the plant?"[b] And
he said, "I do well to be angry, angry
enough to die." 10 And the LORD said,
"You pity the plant,[b] for which you
did not labor, nor did you make it
grow, which came into being in a
night, and perished in a night. 11 And
should not I pity Nin'ė·vėh, that great
city, in which there are more than a
hundred and twenty thousand persons
who do not know their right hand
from their left, and also much cattle?"

[b] Heb *qiqayon*, probably *the castor oil plant*
3.9: Joel 2.14. 4.2: Ex 34.6.

THE BOOK OF

MICAH

1 The word of the LORD that came
to Mī'căh of Mō'rė·sheth in the
days of Jō'thăm, Ā'haz, and Hez·ė-
kī'ăh, kings of Judah, which he saw
concerning Să·mâr'i·ă and Jerusalem.

2 Hear, you peoples, all of you;
hearken, O earth, and all that is in it;
and let the Lord GOD be a witness against you,
the Lord from his holy temple.
3 For behold, the LORD is coming forth out of his place,
and will come down and tread upon the high places of the earth.
4 And the mountains will melt under him
and the valleys will be cleft,
like wax before the fire,
like waters poured down a steep place.
5 All this is for the transgression of Jacob
and for the sins of the house of Israel.
What is the transgression of Jacob?
Is it not Să·mâr'i·ă?
And what is the sin of the house[a] of Judah?
Is it not Jerusalem?
6 Therefore I will make Să·mâr'i·ă a heap in the open country,
a place for planting vineyards;
and I will pour down her stones into the valley,
and uncover her foundations.
7 All her images shall be beaten to pieces,
all her hires shall be burned with fire,
and all her idols I will lay waste;
for from the hire of a harlot she gathered them,
and to the hire of a harlot they shall return.

8 For this I will lament and wail;
I will go stripped and naked;
I will make lamentation like the jackals,
and mourning like the ostriches.
9 For her wound[b] is incurable;
and it has come to Judah,
it has reached to the gate of my people,
to Jerusalem.

10 Tell it not in Gath,
weep not at all;
in Beth-le-aph'răh
roll yourselves in the dust.
11 Pass on your way,
inhabitants of Shā'phir,
in nakedness and shame;
the inhabitants of Zā'ă·nan
do not come forth;
the wailing of Beth-ē'zel
shall take away from you its standing place.
12 For the inhabitants of Mā'roth
wait anxiously for good,
because evil has come down from the LORD
to the gate of Jerusalem.
13 Harness the steeds to the chariots,
inhabitants of Lā'chish;
you were[c] the beginning of sin
to the daughter of Zion,
for in you were found
the transgressions of Israel.
14 Therefore you shall give parting gifts
to Mō'rė·sheth-gath;
the houses of Ach'zib shall be a deceitful thing
to the kings of Israel.
15 I will again bring a conqueror upon you,
inhabitants of Mă·rē'shăh;
the glory of Israel
shall come to Ă·dul'lăm.
16 Make yourselves bald and cut off your hair,
for the children of your delight;
make yourselves as bald as the eagle,
for they shall go from you into exile.

[a] Gk Tg Compare Syr: Heb *what are the high places* [b] Gk Syr Vg: Heb *wounds*
[c] Cn: Heb *it was*
1.2: 1 Kings 22.28.

2 Woe to those who devise wickedness
and work evil upon their beds!
When the morning dawns, they perform it,
because it is in the power of their hand.
2 They covet fields, and seize them;
and houses, and take them away;
they oppress a man and his house,
a man and his inheritance.
3 Therefore thus says the LORD:
Behold, against this family I am devising evil,
from which you cannot remove your necks;
and you shall not walk haughtily,
for it will be an evil time.
4 In that day they shall take up a taunt song against you,
and wail with bitter lamentation,
and say, "We are utterly ruined;
he changes the portion of my people;
how he removes it from me!
Among our captors[d] he divides our fields."
5 Therefore you will have none to cast the line by lot
in the assembly of the LORD.

6 "Do not preach"—thus they preach—
"one should not preach of such things;
disgrace will not overtake us."
7 Should this be said, O house of Jacob?
Is the Spirit of the LORD impatient?
Are these his doings?
Do not my words do good
to him who walks uprightly?
8 But you rise against my people[e] as an enemy;
you strip the robe from the peaceful,[f]
from those who pass by trustingly
with no thought of war.
9 The women of my people you drive out
from their pleasant houses;
from their young children you take away
my glory for ever.
10 Arise and go,
for this is no place to rest;
because of uncleanness that destroys
with a grievous destruction.
11 If a man should go about and utter wind and lies,
saying, "I will preach to you of wine and strong drink,"
he would be the preacher for this people!

12 I will surely gather all of you, O Jacob,
I will gather the remnant of Israel;
I will set them together
like sheep in a fold,
like a flock in its pasture,
a noisy multitude of men.
13 He who opens the breach will go up before them;
they will break through and pass the gate,
going out by it.
Their king will pass on before them,
the LORD at their head.

3 And I said:
Hear, you heads of Jacob
and rulers of the house of Israel!
Is it not for you to know justice?—
2 you who hate the good and love the evil,
who tear the skin from off my people,
and their flesh from off their bones;
3 who eat the flesh of my people,
and flay their skin from off them,
and break their bones in pieces,
and chop them up like meat[g] in a kettle,
like flesh in a caldron.

4 Then they will cry to the LORD,
but he will not answer them;
he will hide his face from them at that time,
because they have made their deeds evil.

5 Thus says the LORD concerning the prophets
who lead my people astray,
who cry "Peace"
when they have something to eat,
but declare war against him
who puts nothing into their mouths.
6 Therefore it shall be night to you, without vision,
and darkness to you, without divination.

[d] Cn: Heb *the rebellious* [e] Cn: Heb *yesterday my people rose* [f] Cn: Heb *from before a garment*
[g] Gk: Heb *as*

The sun shall go down upon the prophets,
and the day shall be black over them;
7 the seers shall be disgraced,
and the diviners put to shame;
they shall all cover their lips,
for there is no answer from God.
8 But as for me, I am filled with power,
with the Spirit of the LORD,
and with justice and might,
to declare to Jacob his transgression
and to Israel his sin.

9 Hear this, you heads of the house of Jacob
and rulers of the house of Israel,
who abhor justice
and pervert all equity,
10 who build Zion with blood
and Jerusalem with wrong.
11 Its heads give judgment for a bribe,
its priests teach for hire,
its prophets divine for money;
yet they lean upon the LORD and say,
"Is not the LORD in the midst of us?
No evil shall come upon us."
12 Therefore because of you
Zion shall be plowed as a field;
Jerusalem shall become a heap of ruins,
and the mountain of the house a wooden height.

4 It shall come to pass in the latter days
that the mountain of the house of the LORD
shall be established as the highest of the mountains,
and shall be raised up above the hills;
and peoples shall flow to it,
2 and many nations shall come, and say:
"Come, let us go up to the mountain of the LORD,
to the house of the God of Jacob;
that he may teach us his ways
and we may walk in his paths."
For out of Zion shall go forth the law,
and the word of the LORD from Jerusalem.
3 He shall judge between many peoples,
and shall decide for strong nations afar off;
and they shall beat their swords into plowshares,
and their spears into pruning hooks;
nation shall not lift up sword against nation,
neither shall they learn war any more;
4 but they shall sit every man under his vine and under his fig tree,
and none shall make them afraid;
for the mouth of the LORD of hosts has spoken.

5 For all the peoples walk
each in the name of its god,
but we will walk in the name of the LORD our God
for ever and ever.

6 In that day, says the LORD,
I will assemble the lame
and gather those who have been driven away,
and those whom I have afflicted;
7 and the lame I will make the remnant;
and those who were cast off, a strong nation;
and the LORD will reign over them in Mount Zion
from this time forth and for evermore.

8 And you, O tower of the flock,
hill of the daughter of Zion,
to you shall it come,
the former dominion shall come,
the kingdom of the daughter of Jerusalem.

9 Now why do you cry aloud?
Is there no king in you?
Has your counselor perished,
that pangs have seized you like a woman in travail?
10 Writhe and groan,[h] O daughter of Zion,
like a woman in travail;
for now you shall go forth from the city
and dwell in the open country;
you shall go to Babylon.
There you shall be rescued,
there the LORD will redeem you
from the hand of your enemies.

[h] Heb uncertain
4.1-3: Is 2.2-4. **4.4:** Zech 3.10.

11 Now many nations
are assembled against you,
saying, "Let her be profaned,
and let our eyes gaze upon
Zion."
12 But they do not know
the thoughts of the LORD,
they do not understand his plan,
that he has gathered them as
sheaves to the threshing floor.
13 Arise and thresh,
O daughter of Zion,
for I will make your horn iron
and your hoofs bronze;
you shall beat in pieces many peoples,
and shall[i] devote their gain to the
LORD,
their wealth to the Lord of the
whole earth.

5[j] Now you are walled about with
a wall;[k]
siege is laid against us;
with a rod they strike upon the
cheek
the ruler of Israel.

2[l] But you, O Bethlehem Eph'rȧ·thȧh,
who are little to be among the
clans of Judah,
from you shall come forth for me
one who is to be ruler in Israel,
whose origin is from of old,
from ancient days.
3 Therefore he shall give them up
until the time
when she who is in travail has
brought forth;
then the rest of his brethren shall
return
to the people of Israel.
4 And he shall stand and feed his
flock in the strength of the
LORD,
in the majesty of the name of the
LORD his God.
And they shall dwell secure, for
now he shall be great
to the ends of the earth.

5 And this shall be peace,
when the Assyrian comes into our
land
and treads upon our soil,[m]
that we will raise against him seven
shepherds
and eight princes of men;
6 they shall rule the land of Assyria
with the sword,
and the land of Nim'rod with the
drawn sword;[n]
and they[o] shall deliver us from the
Assyrian
when he comes into our land
and treads within our border.

7 Then the remnant of Jacob shall be
in the midst of many peoples
like dew from the LORD,
like showers upon the grass,
which tarry not for men
nor wait for the sons of men.
8 And the remnant of Jacob shall be
among the nations,
in the midst of many peoples,
like a lion among the beasts of the
forest,
like a young lion among the flocks
of sheep,
which, when it goes through, treads
down
and tears in pieces, and there is
none to deliver.
9 Your hand shall be lifted up over
your adversaries,
and all your enemies shall be cut
off.

10 And in that day, says the LORD,
I will cut off your horses from
among you
and will destroy your chariots;
11 and I will cut off the cities of your
land
and throw down all your strongholds;
12 and I will cut off sorceries from your
hand,
and you shall have no more soothsayers;
13 and I will cut off your images
and your pillars from among you,
and you shall bow down no more
to the work of your hands;
14 and I will root out your A·shē'rim
from among you
and destroy your cities.
15 And in anger and wrath I will execute vengeance
upon the nations that did not
obey.

6 Hear what the LORD says:
Arise, plead your case before the
mountains,

[i] Gk Syr Tg: Heb *I will* [j] Ch 4.14 in Heb [k] Cn Compare Gk: Heb obscure [l] Ch 5.1 in Heb
[m] Gk: Heb *in our palaces* [n] Cn: Heb *in its entrances* [o] Heb *he*
5.2: Mt 2.6; Jn 7.42.

and let the hills hear your voice.
2 Hear, you mountains, the controversy of the LORD,
and you enduring foundations of the earth;
for the LORD has a controversy with his people,
and he will contend with Israel.

3 "O my people, what have I done to you?
In what have I wearied you?
Answer me!
4 For I brought you up from the land of Egypt,
and redeemed you from the house of bondage;
and I sent before you Moses,
Aaron, and Miriam.
5 O my people, remember what Bā'lak king of Mō'ab devised,
and what Balaam the son of Bē'ôr answered him,
and what happened from Shit'tim to Gil'găl,
that you may know the saving acts of the LORD."

6 "With what shall I come before the LORD,
and bow myself before God on high?
Shall I come before him with burnt offerings,
with calves a year old?
7 Will the LORD be pleased with thousands of rams,
with ten thousands of rivers of oil?
Shall I give my first-born for my transgression,
the fruit of my body for the sin of my soul?"
8 He has showed you, O man, what is good;
and what does the LORD require of you
but to do justice, and to love kindness,[p]
and to walk humbly with your God?

9 The voice of the LORD cries to the city—
and it is sound wisdom to fear thy name:
"Hear, O tribe and assembly of the city![q]
10 Can I forget[r] the treasures of wickedness in the house of the wicked,
and the scant measure that is accursed?
11 Shall I acquit the man with wicked scales
and with a bag of deceitful weights?
12 Your[s] rich men are full of violence;
your[s] inhabitants speak lies,
and their tongue is deceitful in their mouth.
13 Therefore I have begun[t] to smite you,
making you desolate because of your sins.
14 You shall eat, but not be satisfied,
and there shall be hunger in your inward parts;
you shall put away, but not save,
and what you save I will give to the sword.
15 You shall sow, but not reap;
you shall tread olives, but not anoint yourselves with oil;
you shall tread grapes, but not drink wine.
16 For you have kept the statutes of Om'rī,[u]
and all the works of the house of Ā'hab;
and you have walked in their counsels;
that I may make you a desolation,
and your[v] inhabitants a hissing;
so you shall bear the scorn of the peoples."[w]

7 Woe is me! For I have become
as when the summer fruit has been gathered,
as when the vintage has been gleaned:
there is no cluster to eat,
no first-ripe fig which my soul desires.
2 The godly man has perished from the earth,
and there is none upright among men;
they all lie in wait for blood,
and each hunts his brother with a net.
3 Their hands are upon what is evil,
to do it diligently;
the prince and the judge ask for a bribe,

[p] Or *steadfast love* [q] Cn Compare Gk: Heb *and who has appointed it yet* [r] Cn: Heb uncertain
[s] Heb *whose* [t] Gk Syr Vg: Heb *have made sick* [u] Gk Syr Vg Tg: Heb *the statutes of Omri are kept*
[v] Heb *its* [w] Gk: Heb *my people*

and the great man utters the evil
desire of his soul;
thus they weave it together.
4 The best of them is like a brier,
the most upright of them a thorn
hedge.
The day of their[x] watchmen, of
their[x] punishment, has come;
now their confusion is at hand.
5 Put no trust in a neighbor,
have no confidence in a friend;
guard the doors of your mouth
from her who lies in your bosom;
6 for the son treats the father with
contempt,
the daughter rises up against her
mother,
the daughter-in-law against her
mother-in-law;
a man's enemies are the men of
his own house.
7 But as for me, I will look to the
LORD,
I will wait for the God of my
salvation;
my God will hear me.

8 Rejoice not over me, O my enemy;
when I fall, I shall rise;
when I sit in darkness,
the LORD will be a light to me.
9 I will bear the indignation of the
LORD
because I have sinned against
him,
until he pleads my cause
and executes judgment for me.
He will bring me forth to the light;
I shall behold his deliverance.
10 Then my enemy will see,
and shame will cover her who said
to me,
"Where is the LORD your God?"
My eyes will gloat over her;
now she will be trodden down
like the mire of the streets.

11 A day for the building of your walls!
In that day the boundary shall be
far extended.
12 In that day they will come to you,
from Assyria to[y] Egypt,
and from Egypt to the River,
from sea to sea and from mountain
to mountain.
13 But the earth will be desolate
because of its inhabitants,
for the fruit of their doings.

14 Shepherd thy people with thy staff,
the flock of thy inheritance,
who dwell alone in a forest
in the midst of a garden land;
let them feed in Bā'shȧn and Gilead
as in the days of old.

15 As in the days when you came out
of the land of Egypt
I will show them[z] marvelous
things.

16 The nations shall see and be
ashamed
of all their might;
they shall lay their hands on their
mouths;
their ears shall be deaf;
17 they shall lick the dust like a serpent,
like the crawling things of the
earth;
they shall come trembling out of
their strongholds,
they shall turn in dread to the
LORD our God,
and they shall fear because of
thee.

18 Who is a God like thee, pardoning
iniquity
and passing over transgression
for the remnant of his inheritance?
He does not retain his anger for ever
because he delights in steadfast
love.
19 He will again have compassion upon
us,
he will tread our iniquities under
foot.
Thou wilt cast all our[a] sins
into the depths of the sea.
20 Thou wilt show faithfulness to
Jacob
and steadfast love to Abraham,
as thou hast sworn to our fathers
from the days of old.

[x] Heb *your* [y] Cn: Heb *and cities of* [z] Heb *him* [a] Gk Syr Vg Tg: Heb *their*
7.6: Mt 10.21, 35-36; Mk 13.12; Lk 12.53. **7.20:** Lk 1.55.

THE BOOK OF
NAHUM

1 An oracle concerning Nin′ĕ·vĕh. The book of the vision of Nā′hŭm of El′kosh.

2 The LORD is a jealous God and avenging,
the LORD is avenging and wrathful;
the LORD takes vengeance on his adversaries
and keeps wrath for his enemies.
3 The LORD is slow to anger and of great might,
and the LORD will by no means clear the guilty.

His way is in whirlwind and storm,
and the clouds are the dust of his feet.
4 He rebukes the sea and makes it dry,
he dries up all the rivers;
Bā′shăn and Cär′mĕl wither,
the bloom of Lebanon fades.
5 The mountains quake before him,
the hills melt;
the earth is laid waste before him,
the world and all that dwell therein.

6 Who can stand before his indignation?
Who can endure the heat of his anger?
His wrath is poured out like fire,
and the rocks are broken asunder by him.
7 The LORD is good,
a stronghold in the day of trouble;
he knows those who take refuge in him.
8 But with an overflowing flood
he will make a full end of his adversaries,[a]
and will pursue his enemies into darkness.
9 What do you plot against the LORD?
He will make a full end;
he will not take vengeance[b] twice on his foes.[c]
10 Like entangled thorns they are consumed,[d]
like dry stubble.
11 Did one not[e] come out from you,
who plotted evil against the LORD,
and counseled villainy?

12 Thus says the LORD,
"Though they be strong and many,[f]
they will be cut off and pass away.
Though I have afflicted you,
I will afflict you no more.
13 And now I will break his yoke from off you
and will burst your bonds asunder."

14 The LORD has given commandment about you:
"No more shall your name be perpetuated;
from the house of your gods I will cut off
the graven image and the molten image.
I will make your grave, for you are vile."

15[g] Behold, on the mountains the feet of him
who brings good tidings,
who proclaims peace!
Keep your feasts, O Judah,
fulfil your vows,
for never again shall the wicked come against you,
he is utterly cut off.

2 The shatterer has come up against you.
Man the ramparts;
watch the road;
gird your loins;
collect all your strength.

2 (For the LORD is restoring the majesty of Jacob
as the majesty of Israel,
for plunderers have stripped them
and ruined their branches.)

[a] Gk: Heb *her place* [b] Gk: Heb *rise up* [c] Cn: Heb *distress*
[d] Heb *are consumed, drunken as with their drink* [e] Cn: Heb *fully* [f] Heb uncertain [g] Ch 2.1 in Heb
1.3: Is 10.5-34; Zeph 2.12-15. 1.15: Is 40.9; 52.7; Acts 10.36; Rom 10.15.

3 The shield of his mighty men is red,
his soldiers are clothed in scarlet.
The chariots flash like flame[h]
when mustered in array;
the chargers[i] prance.
4 The chariots rage in the streets,
they rush to and fro through the squares;
they gleam like torches,
they dart like lightning.
5 The officers are summoned,
they stumble as they go,
they hasten to the wall,
the mantelet is set up.
6 The river gates are opened,
the palace is in dismay;
7 its mistress[j] is stripped, she is carried off,
her maidens lamenting,
moaning like doves,
and beating their breasts.
8 Nin'ė·vėh is like a pool
whose waters[k] run away.
"Halt! Halt!" they cry;
but none turns back.
9 Plunder the silver,
plunder the gold!
There is no end of treasure,
or wealth of every precious thing.

10 Desolate! Desolation and ruin!
Hearts faint and knees tremble,
anguish is on all loins,
all faces grow pale!
11 Where is the lions' den,
the cave[l] of the young lions,
where the lion brought his prey,
where his cubs were, with none to disturb?
12 The lion tore enough for his whelps
and strangled prey for his lionesses;
he filled his caves with prey
and his dens with torn flesh.

13 Behold, I am against you, says
the LORD of hosts, and I will burn
your[m] chariots in smoke, and the sword
shall devour your young lions; I will
cut off your prey from the earth, and
the voice of your messengers shall no
more be heard.

3 Woe to the bloody city,
all full of lies and booty—
no end to the plunder!
2 The crack of whip, and rumble of wheel,
galloping horse and bounding chariot!
3 Horsemen charging,
flashing sword and glittering spear,
hosts of slain,
heaps of corpses,
dead bodies without end—
they stumble over the bodies!
4 And all for the countless harlotries of the harlot,
graceful and of deadly charms,
who betrays nations with her harlotries,
and peoples with her charms.

5 Behold, I am against you,
says the LORD of hosts,
and will lift up your skirts over your face;
and I will let nations look on your nakedness
and kingdoms on your shame.
6 I will throw filth at you
and treat you with contempt,
and make you a gazingstock.
7 And all who look on you will shrink from you and say,
Wasted is Nin'ė·vėh; who will bemoan her?
whence shall I seek comforters for her?[n]

8 Are you better than Thebes[o]
that sat by the Nile,
with water around her,
her rampart a sea,
and water her wall?
9 Ethiopia was her strength,
Egypt too, and that without limit;
Püt and the Libyans were her[p] helpers.

10 Yet she was carried away,
she went into captivity;
her little ones were dashed in pieces
at the head of every street;
for her honored men lots were cast,
and all her great men were bound in chains.
11 You also will be drunken,
you will be dazed;
you will seek
a refuge from the enemy.
12 All your fortresses are like fig trees
with first-ripe figs—

[h] Cn: The meaning of the Hebrew word is uncertain [i] Cn Compare Gk Syr: Heb *cypresses*
[j] The meaning of the Hebrew is uncertain
[k] Cn Compare Gk: Heb *from the days that she has become, and they* [l] Cn: Heb *pasture* [m] Heb *her*
[n] Gk: Heb *you* [o] Heb *No-amon* [p] Gk: Heb *your*

if shaken they fall
into the mouth of the eater.
13 Behold, your troops
are women in your midst.
The gates of your land
are wide open to your foes;
fire has devoured your bars.

14 Draw water for the siege,
strengthen your forts;
go into the clay,
tread the mortar,
take hold of the brick mold!
15 There will the fire devour you,
the sword will cut you off.
It will devour you like the locust.

Multiply yourselves like the locust,
multiply like the grasshopper!
16 You increased your merchants
more than the stars of the heavens.
The locust spreads its wings and flies away.
17 Your princes are like grasshoppers,
your scribes[q] like clouds of locusts
settling on the fences
in a day of cold—
when the sun rises, they fly away;
no one knows where they are.

18 Your shepherds are asleep,
O king of Assyria;
your nobles slumber.
Your people are scattered on the mountains
with none to gather them.
19 There is no assuaging your hurt,
your wound is grievous.
All who hear the news of you
clap their hands over you.
For upon whom has not come
your unceasing evil?

THE BOOK OF

HABAKKUK

1 The oracle of God which Hȧ·bak′-kŭk the prophet saw.
2 O LORD, how long shall I cry for help,
and thou wilt not hear?
Or cry to thee "Violence!"
and thou wilt not save?
3 Why dost thou make me see wrongs
and look upon trouble?
Destruction and violence are before me;
strife and contention arise.
4 So the law is slacked
and justice never goes forth.
For the wicked surround the righteous,
so justice goes forth perverted.

5 Look among the nations, and see;
wonder and be astounded.
For I am doing a work in your days
that you would not believe if told.
6 For lo, I am rousing the Chal·dē′ȧnṡ,
that bitter and hasty nation,
who march through the breadth of the earth,
to seize habitations not their own.
7 Dread and terrible are they;
their justice and dignity proceed from themselves.
8 Their horses are swifter than leopards,
more fierce than the evening wolves;
their horsemen press proudly on.
Yea, their horsemen come from afar;
they fly like an eagle swift to devour.
9 They all come for violence;
terror[a] of them goes before them.
They gather captives like sand.
10 At kings they scoff,
and of rulers they make sport.
They laugh at every fortress,
for they heap up earth and take it.
11 Then they sweep by like the wind
and go on,
guilty men, whose own might is their god!

12 Art thou not from everlasting,
O LORD my God, my Holy One?

[q] Or *marshals* [a] Cn: Heb uncertain
1-2: Is 13.1-14.23; 47; Jer 50-51. **1.5:** Acts 13.41. **1.6:** Rev 20.9.

We shall not die.
O LORD, thou hast ordained them as a judgment;
and thou, O Rock, hast established them for chastisement.
13 Thou who art of purer eyes than to behold evil
and canst not look on wrong,
why dost thou look on faithless men,
and art silent when the wicked swallows up
the man more righteous than he?
14 For thou makest men like the fish of the sea,
like crawling things that have no ruler.
15 He brings all of them up with a hook,
he drags them out with his net,
he gathers them in his seine;
so he rejoices and exults.
16 Therefore he sacrifices to his net
and burns incense to his seine;
for by them he lives in luxury,[b]
and his food is rich.
17 Is he then to keep on emptying his net,
and mercilessly slaying nations for ever?

2 I will take my stand to watch,
and station myself on the tower,
and look forth to see what he will say to me,
and what I will answer concerning my complaint.
2 And the LORD answered me:
"Write the vision;
make it plain upon tablets,
so he may run who reads it.
3 For still the vision awaits its time;
it hastens to the end—it will not lie.
If it seem slow, wait for it;
it will surely come, it will not delay.
4 Behold, he whose soul is not upright in him shall fail,[c]
but the righteous shall live by his faith.[d]
5 Moreover, wine is treacherous;
the arrogant man shall not abide.[e]
His greed is as wide as Shē'ōl;
like death he has never enough.
He gathers for himself all nations,
and collects as his own all peoples."

6 Shall not all these take up their taunt against him, in scoffing derision of him, and say,
"Woe to him who heaps up what is not his own—
for how long?—
and loads himself with pledges!"
7 Will not your debtors suddenly arise,
and those awake who will make you tremble?
Then you will be booty for them.
8 Because you have plundered many nations,
all the remnant of the peoples shall plunder you,
for the blood of men and violence to the earth,
to cities and all who dwell therein.

9 Woe to him who gets evil gain for his house,
to set his nest on high,
to be safe from the reach of harm!
10 You have devised shame to your house
by cutting off many peoples;
you have forfeited your life.
11 For the stone will cry out from the wall,
and the beam from the woodwork respond.

12 Woe to him who builds a town with blood,
and founds a city on iniquity!
13 Behold, is it not from the LORD of hosts
that peoples labor only for fire,
and nations weary themselves for nought?
14 For the earth will be filled
with the knowledge of the glory of the LORD,
as the waters cover the sea.

15 Woe to him who makes his neighbors drink
of the cup of his wrath,[f] and makes them drunk,
to gaze on their shame!
16 You will be sated with contempt instead of glory.
Drink, yourself, and stagger![g]
The cup in the LORD's right hand
will come around to you,

[b] Heb *his portion is fat* [c] Cn: Heb *is puffed up* [d] Or *faithfulness*
[e] The Hebrew of these two lines is obscure [f] Cn: Heb *joining to your wrath*
[g] Cn Compare Gk Syr: Heb *be uncircumcised*
2.1: Is 21.8. **2.3:** Heb 10.37. **2.4:** Rom 1.17; Gal 3.11; Heb 10.38-39. **2.14:** Is 11.9.

and shame will come upon your
glory!
17 The violence done to Lebanon will
overwhelm you;
the destruction of the beasts will
terrify you,[h]
for the blood of men and violence
to the earth,
to cities and all who dwell therein.

18 What profit is an idol
when its maker has shaped it,
a metal image, a teacher of lies?
For the workman trusts in his own
creation
when he makes dumb idols!
19 Woe to him who says to a wooden
thing, Awake;
to a dumb stone, Arise!
Can this give revelation?
Behold, it is overlaid with gold and
silver,
and there is no breath at all in it.

20 But the LORD is in his holy temple;
let all the earth keep silence before him.

3 A prayer of Hȧ·bak′kủk the
prophet, according to Shig·i·ōn′-
oth.
2 O LORD, I have heard the report of
thee,
and thy work, O LORD, do I fear.
In the midst of the years renew it;
in the midst of the years make it
known;
in wrath remember mercy.
3 God came from Tē′mȧn,
and the Holy One from Mount
Pâr′an.
His glory covered the heavens,
and the earth was full of his
praise. *Selah*
4 His brightness was like the light,
rays flashed from his hand;
and there he veiled his power.
5 Before him went pestilence,
and plague followed close behind.
6 He stood and measured the earth;
he looked and shook the nations;
then the eternal mountains were
scattered,
the everlasting hills sank low.
His ways were as of old.
7 I saw the tents of Cü′shan in affliction;
the curtains of the land of Mid′i-
ȧn did tremble.
8 Was thy wrath against the rivers,
O LORD?
Was thy anger against the rivers,
or thy indignation against the sea,
when thou didst ride upon thy
horses,
upon thy chariot of victory?
9 Thou didst strip the sheath from thy
bow,
and put the arrows to the string.[i]
Selah
Thou didst cleave the earth with
rivers.
10 The mountains saw thee, and
writhed;
the raging waters swept on;
the deep gave forth its voice,
it lifted its hands on high.
11 The sun and moon stood still in
their habitation[j]
at the light of thine arrows as they
sped,
at the flash of thy glittering spear.
12 Thou didst bestride the earth in
fury,
thou didst trample the nations in
anger.
13 Thou wentest forth for the salvation
of thy people,
for the salvation of thy anointed.
Thou didst crush the head of the
wicked,[k]
laying him bare from thigh to
neck.[l] *Selah*
14 Thou didst pierce with thy[m] shafts
the head of his warriors,[n]
who came like a whirlwind to
scatter me,
rejoicing as if to devour the poor
in secret.
15 Thou didst trample the sea with thy
horses,
the surging of mighty waters.

16 I hear, and my body trembles,
my lips quiver at the sound;
rottenness enters into my bones,
my steps totter[o] beneath me.
I will quietly wait for the day of
trouble
to come upon people who invade
us.

17 Though the fig tree do not blossom,
nor fruit be on the vines,

[h] Gk Syr: Heb *them* [i] Cn: Heb obscure [j] Heb uncertain [k] Cn: Heb *head from the house of the wicked*
[l] Heb obscure [m] Heb *his* [n] Vg Compare Gk Syr: Heb uncertain
[o] Cn Compare Gk: Heb *I tremble because*
2.20: Zeph 1.7; Zech 2.13.

the produce of the olive fail
and the fields yield no food,
the flock be cut off from the fold
and there be no herd in the stalls,
18 yet I will rejoice in the LORD,
I will joy in the God of my salvation.
19 GOD, the Lord, is my strength;
he makes my feet like hinds' feet,
he makes me tread upon my high places.

To the choirmaster: with stringed[p] instruments.

THE BOOK OF

ZEPHANIAH

1 The word of the LORD which came
to Zeph·ȧ·nī′ȧh the son of Cū′shī,
son of Ged·ȧ·lī′ȧh, son of Am·ȧ·rī′ȧh,
son of Hez·ė·kī′ȧh, in the days of
Jō·sī′ȧh the son of Ā′mon, king of
Judah.

2 "I will utterly sweep away everything
from the face of the earth," says the LORD.
3 "I will sweep away man and beast;
I will sweep away the birds of the air
and the fish of the sea.
I will overthrow[a] the wicked;
I will cut off mankind
from the face of the earth," says the LORD.
4 "I will stretch out my hand against Judah,
and against all the inhabitants of Jerusalem;
and I will cut off from this place
the remnant of Bā′ȧl
and the name of the idolatrous priests;[b]
5 those who bow down on the roofs
to the host of the heavens;
those who bow down and swear to the LORD
and yet swear by Mil′com;
6 those who have turned back from following the LORD,
who do not seek the LORD or inquire of him."

7 Be silent before the Lord GOD!
For the day of the LORD is at hand;
the LORD has prepared a sacrifice
and consecrated his guests.
8 And on the day of the LORD's sacrifice—
"I will punish the officials and the king's sons
and all who array themselves in foreign attire.
9 On that day I will punish
every one who leaps over the threshold,
and those who fill their master's house
with violence and fraud."

10 "On that day," says the LORD,
"a cry will be heard from the Fish Gate,
a wail from the Second Quarter,
a loud crash from the hills.
11 Wail, O inhabitants of the Mortar!
For all the traders are no more;
all who weigh out silver are cut off.
12 At that time I will search Jerusalem with lamps,
and I will punish the men
who are thickening upon their lees,
those who say in their hearts,
'The LORD will not do good,
nor will he do ill.'
13 Their goods shall be plundered,
and their houses laid waste.
Though they build houses,
they shall not inhabit them;
though they plant vineyards,
they shall not drink wine from them."

14 The great day of the LORD is near,
near and hastening fast;
the sound of the day of the LORD is bitter,

[p] Heb *my stringed* [a] Cn: Heb *the stumbling blocks*
[b] Compare Gk: Heb *idolatrous priests with the priests*
1.7: Hab 2.20; Zech 2.13.

the mighty man cries aloud there.
15 A day of wrath is that day,
a day of distress and anguish,
a day of ruin and devastation,
a day of darkness and gloom,
a day of clouds and thick darkness,
16 a day of trumpet blast and battle cry
against the fortified cities
and against the lofty battlements.

17 I will bring distress on men,
so that they shall walk like the blind,
because they have sinned against the LORD;
their blood shall be poured out like dust,
and their flesh like dung.
18 Neither their silver nor their gold
shall be able to deliver them
on the day of the wrath of the LORD.
In the fire of his jealous wrath,
all the earth shall be consumed;
for a full, yea, sudden end
he will make of all the inhabitants of the earth.

2 Come together and hold assembly,
O shameless nation,
2 before you are driven away
like the drifting chaff,[c]
before there comes upon you
the fierce anger of the LORD,
before there comes upon you
the day of the wrath of the LORD.
3 Seek the LORD, all you humble of the land,
who do his commands;
seek righteousness, seek humility;
perhaps you may be hidden
on the day of the wrath of the LORD.
4 For Gā'zȧ shall be deserted,
and Ash'kė·lon shall become a desolation;
Ash'dod's people shall be driven out at noon,
and Ek'ron shall be uprooted.

5 Woe to you inhabitants of the seacoast,
you nation of the Cher'ė·thītes!
The word of the LORD is against you,
O Canaan, land of the Philistines;
and I will destroy you till no inhabitant is left.
6 And you, O seacoast, shall be pastures,
meadows for shepherds
and folds for flocks.
7 The seacoast shall become the possession
of the remnant of the house of Judah,
on which they shall pasture,
and in the houses of Ash'kė·lon
they shall lie down at evening.
For the LORD their God will be mindful of them
and restore their fortunes.

8 "I have heard the taunts of Mō'ab
and the revilings of the Am'mȯ-nītes,
how they have taunted my people
and made boasts against their territory.
9 Therefore, as I live," says the LORD of hosts,
the God of Israel,
"Mō'ab shall become like Sod'ȯm,
and the Am'mȯ·nītes like Gȯ-môr'rȧh,
a land possessed by nettles and salt pits,
and a waste for ever.
The remnant of my people shall plunder them,
and the survivors of my nation
shall possess them."
10 This shall be their lot in return for their pride,
because they scoffed and boasted
against the people of the LORD of hosts.
11 The LORD will be terrible against them;
yea, he will famish all the gods of the earth,
and to him shall bow down,
each in its place,
all the lands of the nations.

12 You also, O Ethiopians,
shall be slain by my sword.

13 And he will stretch out his hand
against the north,
and destroy Assyria;
and he will make Nin'ė·vėh a desolation,

[c] Cn Compare Gk Syr: Heb *before a decree is born; like chaff a day has passed away*
2.4-7: Is 14.29-31; Jer 47; Ezek 25.15-17; Joel 3.4-8; Amos 1.6-8; Zech 9.5-7.
2.8-11: Is 15-16; 25.10-12; Jer 48; Ezek 25.8-11; Amos 2.1-3. **2.12:** Is 18.
2.13-15: Is 10.5-34; Nahum.

a dry waste like the desert.
14 Herds shall lie down in the midst
of her,
all the beasts of the field;[d]
the vulture[e] and the hedgehog
shall lodge in her capitals;
the owl[f] shall hoot in the window,
the raven[g] croak on the threshold;
for her cedar work will be laid
bare.
15 This is the exultant city
that dwelt secure,
that said to herself,
"I am and there is none else."
What a desolation she has become,
a lair for wild beasts!
Every one who passes by her
hisses and shakes his fist.

3 Woe to her that is rebellious and
defiled,
the oppressing city!
2 She listens to no voice,
she accepts no correction.
She does not trust in the LORD,
she does not draw near to her
God.

3 Her officials within her
are roaring lions;
her judges are evening wolves
that leave nothing till the morning.
4 Her prophets are wanton, faithless
men;
her priests profane what is sacred,
they do violence to the law.
5 The LORD within her is righteous,
he does no wrong;
every morning he shows forth his
justice,
each dawn he does not fail;
but the unjust knows no shame.

6 "I have cut off nations;
their battlements are in ruins;
I have laid waste their streets
so that none walks in them;
their cities have been made desolate,
without a man, without an inhabitant.
7 I said, 'Surely she will fear me,
she will accept correction;
she will not lose sight[h]
of all that I have enjoined upon
her.'
But all the more they were eager
to make all their deeds corrupt."

8 "Therefore wait for me," says the
LORD,
"for the day when I arise as a
witness.
For my decision is to gather nations,
to assemble kingdoms,
to pour out upon them my indignation,
all the heat of my anger;
for in the fire of my jealous wrath
all the earth shall be consumed.

9 "Yea, at that time I will change the
speech of the peoples
to a pure speech,
that all of them may call on the
name of the LORD
and serve him with one accord.
10 From beyond the rivers of Ethiopia
my suppliants, the daughter of
my dispersed ones,
shall bring my offering.

11 "On that day you shall not be put
to shame
because of the deeds by which
you have rebelled against me;
for then I will remove from your
midst
your proudly exultant ones,
and you shall no longer be haughty
in my holy mountain.
12 For I will leave in the midst of you
a people humble and lowly.
They shall seek refuge in the name
of the LORD,
13 those who are left in Israel;
they shall do no wrong
and utter no lies,
nor shall there be found in their
mouth
a deceitful tongue.
For they shall pasture and lie down,
and none shall make them afraid."

14 Sing aloud, O daughter of Zion;
shout, O Israel!
Rejoice and exult with all your
heart,
O daughter of Jerusalem!
15 The LORD has taken away the judgments against you,
he has cast out your enemies.
The King of Israel, the LORD, is in
your midst;
you shall fear evil no more.
16 On that day it shall be said to
Jerusalem:

[d] Tg Compare Gk: Heb *nation* [e] The meaning of the Hebrew word is uncertain [f] Cn: Heb *a voice*
[g] Gk Vg: Heb *desolation* [h] Gk Syr: Heb *and her dwelling will not be cut off*
3.13: Rev 14.5.

"Do not fear, O Zion;
let not your hands grow weak.
17 The LORD, your God, is in your midst,
a warrior who gives victory;
he will rejoice over you with gladness,
he will renew you[i] in his love;
he will exult over you with loud singing
18 as on a day of festival.[j]
"I will remove disaster[k] from you,
so that you will not bear reproach for it.
19 Behold, at that time I will deal
with all your oppressors.
And I will save the lame
and gather the outcast,
and I will change their shame into praise
and renown in all the earth.
20 At that time I will bring you home,
at the time when I gather you together;
yea, I will make you renowned and praised
among all the peoples of the earth,
when I restore your fortunes
before your eyes," says the LORD.

THE BOOK OF

HAGGAI

1 In the second year of Dȧ·rī'ŭs the
king, in the sixth month, on the first
day of the month, the word of the
LORD came by Hag'gäi the prophet to
Ze·rub'bȧ·bel the son of She-al'ti-el,
governor of Judah, and to Joshua the
son of Je·hoz'ȧ·dak, the high priest,
2 "Thus says the LORD of hosts: This
people say the time has not yet come
to rebuild the house of the LORD."
3 Then the word of the LORD came by
Hag'gäi the prophet, 4 "Is it a time for
you yourselves to dwell in your paneled
houses, while this house lies in ruins?
5 Now therefore thus says the LORD of
hosts: Consider how you have fared.
6 You have sown much, and harvested
little; you eat, but you never have
enough; you drink, but you never have
your fill; you clothe yourselves, but no
one is warm; and he who earns wages
earns wages to put them into a bag
with holes.

7 "Thus says the LORD of hosts:
Consider how you have fared. 8 Go up
to the hills and bring wood and build
the house, that I may take pleasure in
it and that I may appear in my glory,
says the LORD. 9 You have looked for
much, and, lo, it came to little; and
when you brought it home, I blew it
away. Why? says the LORD of hosts.
Because of my house that lies in ruins,
while you busy yourselves each with
his own house. 10 Therefore the
heavens above you have withheld the
dew, and the earth has withheld its
produce. 11 And I have called for a
drought upon the land and the hills,
upon the grain, the new wine, the oil,
upon what the ground brings forth,
upon men and cattle, and upon all
their labors."

12 Then Ze·rub'bȧ·bel the son of
She-al'ti-el, and Joshua the son of
Je·hoz'ȧ·dak, the high priest, with all
the remnant of the people, obeyed the
voice of the LORD their God, and
the words of Hag'gäi the prophet, as
the LORD their God had sent him; and
the people feared before the LORD.
13 Then Hag'gäi, the messenger of the
LORD, spoke to the people with the
LORD's message, "I am with you, says
the LORD." 14 And the LORD stirred up
the spirit of Ze·rub'bȧ·bel the son of
She-al'ti-el, governor of Judah, and
the spirit of Joshua the son of Je·hoz'ȧ·dak, the high priest, and the spirit
of all the remnant of the people; and
they came and worked on the house of
the LORD of hosts, their God, 15 on the
twenty-fourth day of the month, in
the sixth month.

2 In the second year of Dȧ·rī'ŭs the
king, 1 in the seventh month, on
the twenty-first day of the month, the
word of the LORD came by Hag'gäi

[i] Gk Syr: Heb *he will be silent* [j] Gk Syr: Heb obscure [k] Cn: Heb *they were*

the prophet, 2 "Speak now to Ze·rub'bȧ·bel the son of She-al'ti-el, governor of Judah, and to Joshua the son of Je·hoz'ȧ·dak, the high priest, and to all the remnant of the people, and say, 3 'Who is left among you that saw this house in its former glory? How do you see it now? Is it not in your sight as nothing? 4 Yet now take courage, O Ze·rub'bȧ·bel, says the LORD; take courage, O Joshua, son of Je·hoz'ȧ·dak, the high priest; take courage, all you people of the land, says the LORD; work, for I am with you, says the LORD of hosts, 5 according to the promise that I made you when you came out of Egypt. My Spirit abides among you; fear not. 6 For thus says the LORD of hosts: Once again, in a little while, I will shake the heavens and the earth and the sea and the dry land; 7 and I will shake all nations, so that the treasures of all nations shall come in, and I will fill this house with splendor, says the LORD of hosts. 8 The silver is mine, and the gold is mine, says the LORD of hosts. 9 The latter splendor of this house shall be greater then the former, says the LORD of hosts; and in this place I will give prosperity, says the LORD of hosts.' "

10 On the twenty-fourth day of the ninth month, in the second year of Dȧ·rī'ŭs, the word of the LORD came by Hag'gäi the prophet, 11 "Thus says the LORD of hosts: Ask the priests to decide this question, 12 'If one carries holy flesh in the skirt of his garment, and touches with his skirt bread, or pottage, or wine, or oil, or any kind of food, does it become holy?' " The priests answered, "No." 13 Then said Hag'gäi, "If one who is unclean by contact with a dead body touches any of these, does it become unclean?" The priests answered, "It does become unclean." 14 Then Hag'gäi said, "So is it with this people, and with this nation before me, says the LORD; and so with every work of their hands; and what they offer there is unclean. 15 Pray now, consider what will come to pass from this day onward. Before a stone was placed upon a stone in the temple of the LORD, 16 how did you fare?[a] When one came to a heap of twenty measures, there were but ten; when one came to the winevat to draw fifty measures, there were but twenty. 17 I smote you and all the products of your toil with blight and mildew and hail; yet you did not return to me, says the LORD. 18 Consider from this day onward, from the twenty-fourth day of the ninth month. Since the day that the foundation of the LORD's temple was laid, consider: 19 Is the seed yet in the barn? Do the vine, the fig tree, the pomegranate, and the olive tree still yield nothing? From this day on I will bless you."

20 The word of the LORD came a second time to Hag'gäi on the twenty-fourth day of the month, 21 "Speak to Ze·rub'bȧ·bel, governor of Judah, saying, I am about to shake the heavens and the earth, 22 and to overthrow the throne of kingdoms; I am about to destroy the strength of the kingdoms of the nations, and overthrow the chariots and their riders; and the horses and their riders shall go down, every one by the sword of his fellow. 23 On that day, says the LORD of hosts, I will take you, O Ze·rub'bȧ·bel my servant, the son of She-al'ti-el, says the LORD, and make you like a signet ring; for I have chosen you, says the LORD of hosts."

[a] Gk: Heb *since they were*
2.6: Heb 12.26.

THE BOOK OF

ZECHARIAH

1 In the eighth month, in the second
year of Dȧ·rī′ŭs, the word of the
LORD came to Zech·ȧ·rī′ȧh the son of
Ber·ė·chī′ȧh, son of Id′dō, the prophet,
saying, 2 "The LORD was very angry
with your fathers. 3 Therefore say to
them, Thus says the LORD of hosts:
Return to me, says the LORD of hosts,
and I will return to you, says the LORD
of hosts. 4 Be not like your fathers, to
whom the former prophets cried out,
'Thus says the LORD of hosts, Return
from your evil ways and from your evil
deeds.' But they did not hear or heed
me, says the LORD. 5 Your fathers,
where are they? And the prophets, do
they live for ever? 6 But my words and
my statutes, which I commanded my
servants the prophets, did they not
overtake your fathers? So they repented and said, As the LORD of hosts
purposed to deal with us for our ways
and deeds, so has he dealt with us."

7 On the twenty-fourth day of the
eleventh month which is the month
of Shė·bät′, in the second year of
Dȧ·rī′ŭs, the word of the LORD came
to Zech·ȧ·rī′ȧh the son of Ber·ė·chī′ȧh,
son of Id′dō, the prophet; and Zechariah said, 8 "I saw in the night, and
behold, a man riding upon a red horse!
He was standing among the myrtle
trees in the glen; and behind him were
red, sorrel, and white horses. 9 Then I
said, 'What are these, my lord?' The
angel who talked with me said to me,
'I will show you what they are.' 10 So
the man who was standing among the
myrtle trees answered, 'These are they
whom the LORD has sent to patrol the
earth.' 11 And they answered the angel
of the LORD who was standing among
the myrtle trees, 'We have patrolled
the earth, and behold, all the earth
remains at rest.' 12 Then the angel of
the LORD said, 'O LORD of hosts, how
long wilt thou have no mercy on Jerusalem and the cities of Judah, against
which thou hast had indignation these
seventy years?' 13 And the LORD answered gracious and comforting words
to the angel who talked with me. 14 So
the angel who talked with me said to
me, 'Cry out, Thus says the LORD of
hosts: I am exceedingly jealous for
Jerusalem and for Zion. 15 And I am
very angry with the nations that are at
ease; for while I was angry but a little
they furthered the disaster. 16 Therefore, thus says the LORD, I have
returned to Jerusalem with compassion; my house shall be built in it, says
the LORD of hosts, and the measuring
line shall be stretched out over Jerusalem. 17 Cry again, Thus says the
LORD of hosts: My cities shall again
overflow with prosperity, and the
LORD will again comfort Zion and
again choose Jerusalem.' "

18[a] And I lifted my eyes and saw,
and behold, four horns! 19 And I said
to the angel who talked with me,
"What are these?" And he answered
me, "These are the horns which have
scattered Judah, Israel, and Jerusalem." 20 Then the LORD showed me
four smiths. 21 And I said, "What are
these coming to do?" He answered,
"These are the horns which scattered
Judah, so that no man raised his head;
and these have come to terrify them,
to cast down the horns of the nations
who lifted up their horns against the
land of Judah to scatter it."

2[b] And I lifted my eyes and saw,
and behold, a man with a measuring line in his hand! 2 Then I said,
"Where are you going?" And he said
to me, "To measure Jerusalem, to see
what is its breadth and what is its
length." 3 And behold, the angel who
talked with me came forward, and
another angel came forward to meet
him, 4 and said to him, "Run, say to
that young man, 'Jerusalem shall be
inhabited as villages without walls, because of the multitude of men and
cattle in it. 5 For I will be to her a wall
of fire round about, says the LORD, and
I will be the glory within her.' "

6 Ho! ho! Flee from the land of the
north, says the LORD; for I have spread
you abroad as the four winds of the
heavens, says the LORD. 7 Ho! Escape

[a] Ch 2.1 in Heb [b] Ch 2.5 in Heb

to Zion, you who dwell with the
daughter of Babylon. 8 For thus said
the LORD of hosts, after his glory sent
me to the nations who plundered you,
for he who touches you touches the
apple of his eye: 9 "Behold, I will shake
my hand over them, and they shall
become plunder for those who served
them. Then you will know that the
LORD of hosts has sent me. 10 Sing and
rejoice, O daughter of Zion; for lo, I
come and I will dwell in the midst of
you, says the LORD. 11 And many nations shall join themselves to the LORD
in that day, and shall be my people;
and I will dwell in the midst of you,
and you shall know that the LORD of
hosts has sent me to you. 12 And the
LORD will inherit Judah as his portion
in the holy land, and will again choose
Jerusalem."

13 Be silent, all flesh, before the
LORD; for he has roused himself from
his holy dwelling.

3 Then he showed me Joshua the
high priest standing before the
angel of the LORD, and Satan standing
at his right hand to accuse him. 2 And
the LORD said to Satan, "The LORD
rebuke you, O Satan! The LORD who
has chosen Jerusalem rebuke you! Is
not this a brand plucked from the
fire?" 3 Now Joshua was standing
before the angel, clothed with filthy
garments. 4 And the angel said to those
who were standing before him, "Remove the filthy garments from him."
And to him he said, "Behold, I have
taken your iniquity away from you,
and I will clothe you with rich apparel."
5 And I said, "Let them put a clean
turban on his head." So they put a
clean turban on his head and clothed
him with garments; and the angel of
the LORD was standing by.

6 And the angel of the LORD enjoined Joshua, 7 "Thus says the LORD
of hosts: If you will walk in my ways
and keep my charge, then you shall
rule my house and have charge of my
courts, and I will give you the right of
access among those who are standing
here. 8 Hear now, O Joshua the high
priest, you and your friends who sit before you, for they are men of good
omen: behold, I will bring my servant
the Branch. 9 For behold, upon the
stone which I have set before Joshua,
upon a single stone with seven facets,
I will engrave its inscription, says the
LORD of hosts, and I will remove the
guilt of this land in a single day. 10 In
that day, says the LORD of hosts, every
one of you will invite his neighbor
under his vine and under his fig tree."

4 And the angel who talked with
me came again, and waked me,
like a man that is wakened out of his
sleep. 2 And he said to me, "What do
you see?" I said, "I see, and behold, a
lampstand all of gold, with a bowl on
the top of it, and seven lamps on it,
with seven lips on each of the lamps
which are on the top of it. 3 And there
are two olive trees by it, one on the
right of the bowl and the other on its
left." 4 And I said to the angel who
talked with me, "What are these, my
lord?" 5 Then the angel who talked
with me answered me, "Do you not
know what these are?" I said, "No,
my lord." 6 Then he said to me, "This
is the word of the LORD to Ze·rub'ba-
bel: Not by might, nor by power, but
by my Spirit, says the LORD of hosts.
7 What are you, O great mountain?
Before Ze·rub'ba·bel you shall become
a plain; and he shall bring forward the
top stone amid shouts of 'Grace, grace
to it!' " 8 Moreover the word of the
LORD came to me, saying, 9 "The
hands of Ze·rub'ba·bel have laid the
foundation of this house; his hands
shall also complete it. Then you will
know that the LORD of hosts has sent
me to you. 10 For whoever has despised
the day of small things shall rejoice,
and shall see the plummet in the hand
of Ze·rub'ba·bel.

"These seven are the eyes of the
LORD, which range through the whole
earth." 11 Then I said to him, "What
are these two olive trees on the right
and the left of the lampstand?" 12 And
a second time I said to him, "What are
these two branches of the olive trees,
which are beside the two golden pipes
from which the oil[c] is poured out?"
13 He said to me, "Do you not know
what these are?" I said, "No, my
lord." 14 Then he said, "These are
the two anointed who stand by the
Lord of the whole earth."

5 Again I lifted my eyes and saw,
and behold, a flying scroll! 2 And
he said to me, "What do you see?" I

[c] Cn: Heb *gold*

2.13: Hab 2.20; Zeph 1.7. **3.2:** Jude 9. **3.8:** Is 4.2; Jer 23.5; 33.15; Zech 6.12. **3.10:** Mic 4.4. **4.3, 11-14:** Rev 11.4. **4.10:** Rev 5.6.

answered, "I see a flying scroll; its
length is twenty cubits, and its breadth
ten cubits." 3 Then he said to me,
"This is the curse that goes out over
the face of the whole land; for every
one who steals shall be cut off henceforth according to it, and every one
who swears falsely shall be cut off
henceforth according to it. 4 I will
send it forth, says the LORD of hosts,
and it shall enter the house of the thief,
and the house of him who swears
falsely by my name; and it shall abide
in his house and consume it, both
timber and stones."
5 Then the angel who talked with
me came forward and said to me,
"Lift your eyes, and see what this is
that goes forth." 6 And I said, "What
is it?" He said, "This is the ephah that
goes forth." And he said, "This is
their iniquity[d] in all the land." 7 And
behold, the leaden cover was lifted,
and there was a woman sitting in the
ephah! 8 And he said, "This is Wickedness." And he thrust her back into the
ephah, and thrust down the leaden
weight upon its mouth. 9 Then I lifted
my eyes and saw, and behold, two
women coming forward! The wind was
in their wings; they had wings like the
wings of a stork, and they lifted up
the ephah between earth and heaven.
10 Then I said to the angel who talked
with me, "Where are they taking the
ephah?" 11 He said to me, "To the
land of Shī'när, to build a house for it;
and when this is prepared, they will
set the ephah down there on its base."
6 And again I lifted my eyes and
saw, and behold, four chariots
came out from between two mountains;
and the mountains were mountains of
bronze. 2 The first chariot had red
horses, the second black horses, 3 the
third white horses, and the fourth
chariot dappled gray[e] horses. 4 Then I
said to the angel who talked with me,
"What are these, my lord?" 5 And the
angel answered me, "These are going
forth to the four winds of heaven, after
presenting themselves before the LORD
of all the earth. 6 The chariot with the
black horses goes toward the north
country, the white ones go toward the
west country,[f] and the dappled ones go
toward the south country." 7 When
the steeds came out, they were impatient to get off and patrol the earth.
And he said, "Go, patrol the earth."
So they patrolled the earth. 8 Then he
cried to me, "Behold, those who go
toward the north country have set my
Spirit at rest in the north country."
9 And the word of the LORD came
to me: 10 "Take from the exiles Hel'-
däi, Tō·bī'jȧh, and Je·däi'ȧh, who have
arrived from Babylon; and go the same
day to the house of Jō·sī'ȧh, the son of
Zeph·ȧ·nī'ȧh. 11 Take from them silver
and gold, and make a crown,[g] and set
it upon the head of Joshua, the son of
Je·hoz'ȧ·dak, the high priest; 12 and
say to him, 'Thus says the LORD of
hosts, "Behold, the man whose name
is the Branch: for he shall grow up in
his place, and he shall build the temple
of the LORD. 13 It is he who shall build
the temple of the LORD, and shall bear
royal honor, and shall sit and rule upon
his throne. And there shall be a priest
by his throne, and peaceful understanding shall be between them
both." ' 14 And the crown[h] shall be in
the temple of the LORD as a reminder
to Hel'däi,[i] Tō·bī'jȧh, Je·däi'ȧh, and
Jō·sī'ȧh[j] the son of Zeph·ȧ·nī'ȧh.
15 "And those who are far off shall
come and help to build the temple of
the LORD; and you shall know that the
LORD of hosts has sent me to you. And
this shall come to pass, if you will
diligently obey the voice of the LORD
your God."
7 In the fourth year of King Dȧ·rī'-
ŭs, the word of the LORD came to
Zech·ȧ·rī'ȧh in the fourth day of the
ninth month, which is Chis'lev. 2 Now
the people of Beth'ĕl had sent Shȧ·rē'-
zėr and Reg'em-mel'ech and their
men, to entreat the favor of the LORD,
3 and to ask the priests of the house of
the LORD of hosts and the prophets,
"Should I mourn and fast in the fifth
month, as I have done for so many
years?" 4 Then the word of the LORD
of hosts came to me; 5 "Say to all the
people of the land and the priests,
When you fasted and mourned in the
fifth month and in the seventh, for
these seventy years, was it for me that
you fasted? 6 And when you eat and
when you drink, do you not eat for
yourselves and drink for yourselves?

[d] Gk Compare Syr: Heb *eye* [e] Compare Gk: The meaning of the Hebrew word is uncertain
[f] Cn: Heb *after them* [g] Gk Mss: Heb *crowns* [h] Gk: Heb *crowns* [i] With verse 10: Heb *Helem*
[j] With verse 10: Heb *Hen*

6.1-3: Rev 6.2-8. **6.5:** Rev 7.1. **6.12:** Zech 3.8; Is 4.2; Jer 23.5; 33.15.

7 When Jerusalem was inhabited and
in prosperity, with her cities round
about her, and the South and the lowland were inhabited, were not these
the words which the LORD proclaimed
by the former prophets?"
8 And the word of the LORD came
to Zech·a·ri'ah, saying, 9 "Thus says
the LORD of hosts, Render true judgments, show kindness and mercy each
to his brother, 10 do not oppress the
widow, the fatherless, the sojourner,
or the poor; and let none of you devise
evil against his brother in your heart."
11 But they refused to hearken, and
turned a stubborn shoulder, and
stopped their ears that they might not
hear. 12 They made their hearts like
adamant lest they should hear the law
and the words which the LORD of
hosts had sent by his Spirit through
the former prophets. Therefore great
wrath came from the LORD of hosts.
13 "As I called, and they would not
hear, so they called, and I would not
hear," says the LORD of hosts, 14 "and
I scattered them with a whirlwind
among all the nations which they had
not known. Thus the land they left was
desolate, so that no one went to and
fro, and the pleasant land was made
desolate."

8 And the word of the LORD of
hosts came to me, saying, 2 "Thus
says the LORD of hosts: I am jealous
for Zion with great jealousy, and I am
jealous for her with great wrath. 3 Thus
says the LORD: I will return to Zion,
and will dwell in the midst of Jerusalem, and Jerusalem shall be called
the faithful city, and the mountain of
the LORD of hosts, the holy mountain.
4 Thus says the LORD of hosts: Old
men and old women shall again sit in
the streets of Jerusalem, each with
staff in hand for very age. 5 And the
streets of the city shall be full of boys
and girls playing in its streets. 6 Thus
says the LORD of hosts: If it is marvelous in the sight of the remnant of this
people in these days, should it also be
marvelous in my sight, says the LORD
of hosts? 7 Thus says the LORD of
hosts: Behold, I will save my people
from the east country and from the
west country; 8 and I will bring them
to dwell in the midst of Jerusalem; and
they shall be my people and I will be
their God, in faithfulness and in righteousness."
9 Thus says the LORD of hosts:
"Let your hands be strong, you who
in these days have been hearing these
words from the mouth of the prophets,
since the day that the foundation of
the house of the LORD of hosts was
laid, that the temple might be built.
10 For before those days there was no
wage for man or any wage for beast,
neither was there any safety from the
foe for him who went out or came in;
for I set every man against his fellow.
11 But now I will not deal with the
remnant of this people as in the former
days, says the LORD of hosts. 12 For
there shall be a sowing of peace; the vine
shall yield its fruit, and the ground
shall give its increase, and the heavens
shall give their dew; and I will cause
the remnant of this people to possess
all these things. 13 And as you have
been a byword of cursing among the
nations, O house of Judah and house
of Israel, so will I save you and you
shall be a blessing. Fear not, but let
your hands be strong."
14 For thus says the LORD of hosts:
"As I purposed to do evil to you, when
your fathers provoked me to wrath,
and I did not relent, says the LORD of
hosts, 15 so again have I purposed in
these days to do good to Jerusalem and
to the house of Judah; fear not. 16 These
are the things that you shall do: Speak
the truth to one another, render in
your gates judgments that are true and
make for peace, 17 do not devise evil
in your hearts against one another, and
love no false oath, for all these things
I hate, says the LORD."
18 And the word of the LORD of
hosts came to me, saying, 19 "Thus
says the LORD of hosts: The fast of the
fourth month, and the fast of the fifth,
and the fast of the seventh, and the
fast of the tenth, shall be to the house
of Judah seasons of joy and gladness,
and cheerful feasts; therefore love
truth and peace.
20 "Thus says the LORD of hosts:
Peoples shall yet come, even the inhabitants of many cities; 21 the inhabitants of one city shall go to another,
saying, 'Let us go at once to entreat
the favor of the LORD, and to seek the
LORD of hosts; I am going.' 22 Many
peoples and strong nations shall come
to seek the LORD of hosts in Jerusalem,
and to entreat the favor of the LORD.
23 Thus says the LORD of hosts: In

8.16: Eph 4.25.

those days ten men from the nations of every tongue shall take hold of the robe of a Jew, saying, 'Let us go with you, for we have heard that God is with you.' "

9 An Oracle

The word of the LORD is against
the land of Had'rach
and will rest upon Damascus.
For to the LORD belong the cities of
Âr'âm,[k]
even as all the tribes of Israel;
2 Hā'math also, which borders thereon,
Tȳre and Sī'don, though they are
very wise.
3 Tȳre has built herself a rampart,
and heaped up silver like dust,
and gold like the dirt of the
streets.
4 But lo, the Lord will strip her of her
possessions
and hurl her wealth into the sea,
and she shall be devoured by fire.

5 Ash'kė·lon shall see it, and be afraid;
Gā'zȧ too, and shall writhe in
anguish;
Ek'rȯn also, because its hopes are
confounded.
The king shall perish from Gaza;
Ashkelon shall be uninhabited;
6 a mongrel people shall dwell in
Ash'dod;
and I will make an end of the
pride of Phi·lis'ti·ȧ.
7 I will take away its blood from its
mouth,
and its abominations from between its teeth;
it too shall be a remnant for our
God;
it shall be like a clan in Judah,
and Ek'rȯn shall be like the
Jeb'ū·sītes.
8 Then I will encamp at my house as
a guard,
so that none shall march to and
fro;
no oppressor shall again overrun
them,
for now I see with my own eyes.

9 Rejoice greatly, O daughter of Zion!
Shout aloud, O daughter of Jerusalem!
Lo, your king comes to you;
triumphant and victorious is he,
humble and riding on an ass,
on a colt the foal of an ass.
10 I will cut off the chariot from
Ē'phrȧ·im
and the war horse from Jerusalem;
and the battle bow shall be cut off,
and he shall command peace to
the nations;
his dominion shall be from sea to
sea,
and from the River to the ends of
the earth.

11 As for you also, because of the blood
of my covenant with you,
I will set your captives free from
the waterless pit.
12 Return to your stronghold, O
prisoners of hope;
today I declare that I will restore
to you double.
13 For I have bent Judah as my bow;
I have made Ē'phrȧ·im its arrow.
I will brandish your sons, O Zion,
over your sons, O Greece,
and wield you like a warrior's
sword.

14 Then the LORD will appear over
them,
and his arrow go forth like
lightning;
the Lord GOD will sound the
trumpet,
and march forth in the whirlwinds
of the south.
15 The LORD of hosts will protect them,
and they shall devour and tread
down the slingers;[l]
and they shall drink their blood[m]
like wine,
and be full like a bowl,
drenched like the corners of the
altar.

16 On that day the LORD their God
will save them
for they are the flock of his people;
for like the jewels of a crown
they shall shine on his land.
17 Yea, how good and how fair it shall
be!
Grain shall make the young men
flourish,
and new wine the maidens.

[k] Cn: Heb *the eye of Adam* (or *man*) [l] Cn: Heb *the slingstones* [m] Gk: Heb *be turbulent*
9.9: Mt 21.5; Jn 12.15.

10 Ask rain from the LORD
in the season of the spring
rain,
from the LORD who makes the storm
clouds,
who gives men showers of rain,
to every one the vegetation in the
field.
2 For the teraphim utter nonsense,
and the diviners see lies;
the dreamers tell false dreams,
and give empty consolation.
Therefore the people wander like
sheep;
they are afflicted for want of a
shepherd.

3 "My anger is hot against the shepherds,
and I will punish the leaders;[n]
for the LORD of hosts cares for his
flock, the house of Judah,
and will make them like his proud
steed in battle.
4 Out of them shall come the cornerstone,
out of them the tent peg,
out of them the battle bow,
out of them every ruler.
5 Together they shall be like mighty
men in battle,
trampling the foe in the mud of
the streets;
they shall fight because the LORD is
with them,
and they shall confound the riders
on horses.

6 "I will strengthen the house of
Judah,
and I will save the house of
Joseph.
I will bring them back because I
have compassion on them,
and they shall be as though I had
not rejected them;
for I am the LORD their God and
I will answer them.
7 Then E'phrȧ·im shall become like a
mighty warrior,
and their hearts shall be glad as
with wine.
Their children shall see it and rejoice,
their hearts shall exult in the
LORD.

8 "I will signal for them and gather
them in,
for I have redeemed them,
and they shall be as many as of
old.
9 Though I scattered them among the
nations,
yet in far countries they shall
remember me,
and with their children they shall
live and return.
10 I will bring them home from the
land of Egypt,
and gather them from Assyria;
and I will bring them to the land of
Gilead and to Lebanon,
till there is no room for them.
11 They shall pass through the sea of
Egypt,[o]
and the waves of the sea shall be
smitten,
and all the depths of the Nile
dried up.
The pride of Assyria shall be laid
low,
and the scepter of Egypt shall
depart.
12 I will make them strong in the LORD
and they shall glory[p] in his name,"
says the LORD.

11 Open your doors, O Lebanon,
that the fire may devour your
cedars!
2 Wail, O cypress, for the cedar has
fallen,
for the glorious trees are ruined!
Wail, oaks of Bā'shȧn,
for the thick forest has been
felled!
3 Hark, the wail of the shepherds,
for their glory is despoiled!
Hark, the roar of the lions,
for the jungle of the Jordan is
laid waste!

4 Thus said the LORD my God:
"Become shepherd of the flock doomed
to slaughter. 5 Those who buy them
slay them and go unpunished; and
those who sell them say, 'Blessed be
the LORD, I have become rich'; and
their own shepherds have no pity on
them. 6 For I will no longer have pity
on the inhabitants of this land, says the
LORD. Lo, I will cause men to fall each
into the hand of his shepherd, and
each into the hand of his king; and
they shall crush the earth, and I will
deliver none from their hand."
7 So I became the shepherd of the
flock doomed to be slain for those who
trafficked in the sheep. And I took two

[n] Or *he-goats* [o] Cn: Heb *distress* [p] Gk: Heb *walk*

staffs; one I named Grace, the other I
named Union. And I tended the sheep.
8 In one month I destroyed the three
shepherds. But I became impatient
with them, and they also detested me.
9 So I said, "I will not be your shepherd. What is to die, let it die; what is
to be destroyed, let it be destroyed;
and let those that are left devour the
flesh of one another." 10 And I took my
staff Grace, and I broke it, annulling
the covenant which I had made with
all the peoples. 11 So it was annulled
on that day, and the traffickers in the
sheep, who were watching me, knew
that it was the word of the LORD.
12 Then I said to them, "If it seems
right to you, give me my wages; but if
not, keep them." And they weighed
out as my wages thirty shekels of silver.
13 Then the LORD said to me, "Cast it
into the treasury"[q]—the lordly price
at which I was paid off by them. So
I took the thirty shekels of silver and
cast them into the treasury[q] in the
house of the LORD. 14 Then I broke
my second staff Union, annulling the
brotherhood between Judah and Israel.

15 Then the LORD said to me,
"Take once more the implements of a
worthless shepherd. 16 For lo, I am
raising up in the land a shepherd who
does not care for the perishing, or seek
the wandering,[r] or heal the maimed,
or nourish the sound, but devours the
flesh of the fat ones, tearing off even
their hoofs.

17 Woe to my worthless shepherd,
    who deserts the flock!
May the sword smite his arm
    and his right eye!
Let his arm be wholly withered,
    his right eye utterly blinded!"

12 An Oracle

The word of the LORD concerning
Israel: Thus says the LORD, who
stretched out the heavens and founded
the earth and formed the spirit of man
within him: 2 "Lo, I am about to make
Jerusalem a cup of reeling to all the
peoples round about; it will be against
Judah also in the siege against Jerusalem. 3 On that day I will make
Jerusalem a heavy stone for all the
peoples; all who lift it shall grievously
hurt themselves. And all the nations
of the earth will come together against
it. 4 On that day, says the LORD, I will
strike every horse with panic, and its
rider with madness. But upon the
house of Judah I will open my eyes,
when I strike every horse of the peoples with blindness. 5 Then the clans
of Judah shall say to themselves, 'The
inhabitants of Jerusalem have strength
through the LORD of hosts, their
God.'

6 "On that day I will make the
clans of Judah like a blazing pot in the
midst of wood, like a flaming torch
among sheaves; and they shall devour
to the right and to the left all the peoples round about, while Jerusalem shall
still be inhabited in its place, in
Jerusalem.

7 "And the LORD will give victory
to the tents of Judah first, that the
glory of the house of David and the
glory of the inhabitants of Jerusalem
may not be exalted over that of Judah.
8 On that day the LORD will put a
shield about the inhabitants of Jerusalem so that the feeblest among them
on that day shall be like David, and
the house of David shall be like God,
like the angel of the LORD, at their
head. 9 And on that day I will seek to
destroy all the nations that come
against Jerusalem.

10 "And I will pour out on the
house of David and the inhabitants of
Jerusalem a spirit of compassion and
supplication, so that, when they look
on him whom they have pierced, they
shall mourn for him, as one mourns
for an only child, and weep bitterly
over him, as one weeps over a first-
born. 11 On that day the mourning in
Jerusalem will be as great as the
mourning for Hā'dad-rim'mon in the
plain of Mė·gid'dō. 12 The land shall
mourn, each family by itself; the family of the house of David by itself, and
their wives by themselves; the family
of the house of Nathan by itself, and
their wives by themselves; 13 the family
of the house of Levi by itself, and their
wives by themselves; the family of the
Shim'ē-ites by itself, and their wives
by themselves; 14 and all the families
that are left, each by itself, and their
wives by themselves.

13

"On that day there shall be a
fountain opened for the house of
David and the inhabitants of Jeru-

[q] Syr: Heb *to the potter* [r] Syr Compare Gk Vg: Heb *the youth*
11.12-13: Mt 26.15; 27.9. **12.10:** Jn 19.37.

salem to cleanse them from sin and
uncleanness.
2 "And on that day, says the LORD
of hosts, I will cut off the names of the
idols from the land, so that they shall
be remembered no more; and also I
will remove from the land the prophets
and the unclean spirit. 3 And if any one
again appears as a prophet, his father
and mother who bore him will say to
him, 'You shall not live, for you speak
lies in the name of the LORD'; and his
father and mother who bore him shall
pierce him through when he prophesies. 4 On that day every prophet will
be ashamed of his vision when he
prophesies; he will not put on a hairy
mantle in order to deceive, 5 but he
will say, 'I am no prophet, I am a tiller
of the soil; for the land has been my
possession[t] since my youth.' 6 And if
one asks him, 'What are these wounds
on your back?' he will say, 'The
wounds I received in the house of my
friends.' "

7 "Awake, O sword, against my shepherd,
against the man who stands next
to me,"
says the LORD of hosts.
"Strike the shepherd, that the sheep
may be scattered;
I will turn my hand against the
little ones.
8 In the whole land, says the LORD,
two thirds shall be cut off and
perish,
and one third shall be left alive.
9 And I will put this third into the
fire,
and refine them as one refines
silver,
and test them as gold is tested.
They will call on my name,
and I will answer them.
I will say, 'They are my people';
and they will say, 'The LORD is
my God.' "

14 Behold, a day of the LORD is
coming, when the spoil taken
from you will be divided in the midst
of you. 2 For I will gather all the nations against Jerusalem to battle, and
the city shall be taken and the houses
plundered and the women ravished;
half of the city shall go into exile, but
the rest of the people shall not be cut
off from the city. 3 Then the LORD will
go forth and fight against those nations
as when he fights on a day of battle.
4 On that day his feet shall stand on
the Mount of Olives which lies before
Jerusalem on the east; and the Mount
of Olives shall be split in two from east
to west by a very wide valley; so that
one half of the Mount shall withdraw
northward, and the other half southward. 5 And the valley of my mountains
shall be stopped up, for the valley of
the mountains shall touch the side of
it; and you shall flee as you fled from
the earthquake in the days of Uz·zī'ăh
king of Judah. Then the LORD your[u]
God will come, and all the holy ones
with him.[v]
6 On that day there shall be neither
cold nor frost.[w] 7 And there shall
be continuous day (it is known to
the LORD), not day and not night,
for at evening time there shall be
light.
8 On that day living waters shall
flow out from Jerusalem, half of them
to the eastern sea and half of them to
the western sea; it shall continue in
summer as in winter.
9 And the LORD will become king
over all the earth; on that day the LORD
will be one and his name one.
10 The whole land shall be turned
into a plain from Gē'bȧ to Rim'mon
south of Jerusalem. But Jerusalem
shall remain aloft upon its site from
the Gate of Benjamin to the place of
the former gate, to the Corner Gate,
and from the Tower of Hȧ·nan'el to
the king's wine presses. 11 And it shall
be inhabited, for there shall be no
more curse;[x] Jerusalem shall dwell in
security.
12 And this shall be the plague with
which the LORD will smite all the peoples that wage war against Jerusalem:
their flesh shall rot while they are still
on their feet, their eyes shall rot in
their sockets, and their tongues shall
rot in their mouths. 13 And on that day
a great panic from the LORD shall fall
on them, so that each will lay hold on
the hand of his fellow, and the hand
of the one will be raised against the
hand of the other; 14 even Judah will
fight against Jerusalem. And the
wealth of all the nations round about

[t] Cn: Heb *for man has caused me to possess* [u] Heb *my* [v] Gk Syr Vg Tg: Heb *you*
[w] Compare Gk Syr Vg Tg: Heb uncertain [x] Or *ban of utter destruction*
13.7: Mt 26.31; Mk 14.27. **14.8:** Ezek 47.1-12; Rev 22.1-2. **14.11:** Rev 22.3.

shall be collected, gold, silver, and garments in great abundance. 15 And a
plague like this plague shall fall on the
horses, the mules, the camels, the
asses, and whatever beasts may be in
those camps.
16 Then every one that survives of
all the nations that have come against
Jerusalem shall go up year after year
to worship the King, the LORD of
hosts, and to keep the feast of booths.
17 And if any of the families of the
earth do not go up to Jerusalem to
worship the King, the LORD of hosts,
there will be no rain upon them. 18 And
if the family of Egypt do not go up and
present themselves, then upon them
shall[y] come the plague with which the
LORD afflicts the nations that do not go
up to keep the feast of booths. 19 This
shall be the punishment to Egypt and
the punishment to all the nations that
do not go up to keep the feast of
booths.
20 And on that day there shall be
inscribed on the bells of the horses,
"Holy to the LORD." And the pots in
the house of the LORD shall be as the
bowls before the altar; 21 and every pot
in Jerusalem and Judah shall be sacred
to the LORD of hosts, so that all who
sacrifice may come and take of them
and boil the flesh of the sacrifice in
them. And there shall no longer be a
trader in the house of the LORD of
hosts on that day.

THE BOOK OF

MALACHI

1 The oracle of the word of the
LORD to Israel by Mal'a·chi.[a]
2 "I have loved you," says the
LORD. But you say, "How hast thou
loved us?" "Is not Esau Jacob's
brother?" says the LORD. "Yet I have
loved Jacob 3 but I have hated Esau;
I have laid waste his hill country and
left his heritage to jackals of the
desert." 4 If E'dom says, "We are shattered but we will rebuild the ruins,"
the LORD of hosts says, "They may
build, but I will tear down, till they
are called the wicked country, the
people with whom the LORD is angry
for ever." 5 Your own eyes shall see
this, and you shall say, "Great is the
LORD, beyond the border of Israel!"
6 "A son honors his father, and a
servant his master. If then I am a
father, where is my honor? And if I am
a master, where is my fear? says the
LORD of hosts to you, O priests, who
despise my name. You say, 'How have
we despised thy name?' 7 By offering
polluted food upon my altar. And you
say, 'How have we polluted it?'[b] By
thinking that the LORD's table may be
despised. 8 When you offer blind
animals in sacrifice, is that no evil?
And when you offer those that are
lame or sick, is that no evil? Present
that to your governor; will he be
pleased with you or show you favor?
says the LORD of hosts. 9 And now
entreat the favor of God, that he may
be gracious to us. With such a gift from
your hand, will he show favor to any
of you? says the LORD of hosts. 10 Oh,
that there were one among you who
would shut the doors, that you might
not kindle fire upon my altar in vain!
I have no pleasure in you, says the
LORD of hosts, and I will not accept an
offering from your hand. 11 For from
the rising of the sun to its setting my
name is great among the nations, and
in every place incense is offered to my
name, and a pure offering; for my
name is great among the nations, says
the LORD of hosts. 12 But you profane
it when you say that the LORD's table
is polluted, and the food for it[c] may be
despised. 13 'What a weariness this is,'
you say, and you sniff at me,[d] says the
LORD of hosts. You bring what has

[y] Gk Syr: Heb *shall not* [a] Or *my messenger* [b] Gk: Heb *thee* [c] Heb *its fruit, its food*
[d] Another reading is *it*
14.18-19: Is 19; Jer 46; Ezek 29-32. **1.2-3:** Rom 9.13.
1.2-5: Is 34; 63.1-6; Jer 49.7-22; Ezek 25.12-14; 35; Amos 1.11-12; Obad.

been taken by violence or is lame or
sick, and this you bring as your offering! Shall I accept that from your
hand? says the LORD. 14 Cursed be the
cheat who has a male in his flock, and
vows it, and yet sacrifices to the Lord
what is blemished; for I am a great
King, says the LORD of hosts, and my
name is feared among the nations.

2 "And now, O priests, this command is for you. 2 If you will not
listen, if you will not lay it to heart to
give glory to my name, says the LORD
of hosts, then I will send the curse
upon you and I will curse your blessings; indeed I have already cursed
them, because you do not lay it to
heart. 3 Behold, I will rebuke your offspring, and spread dung upon your
faces, the dung of your offerings, and
I will put you out of my presence.[e]
4 So shall you know that I have sent
this command to you, that my covenant with Levi may hold, says the
LORD of hosts. 5 My covenant with
him was a covenant of life and peace,
and I gave them to him, that he might
fear; and he feared me, he stood in awe
of my name. 6 True instruction[f] was
in his mouth, and no wrong was found
on his lips. He walked with me in peace
and uprightness, and he turned many
from iniquity. 7 For the lips of a priest
should guard knowledge, and men
should seek instruction[f] from his
mouth, for he is the messenger of the
LORD of hosts. 8 But you have turned
aside from the way; you have caused
many to stumble by your instruction;[f]
you have corrupted the covenant of
Levi, says the LORD of hosts, 9 and so
I make you despised and abased before
all the people, inasmuch as you have
not kept my ways but have shown
partiality in your instruction."[f]

10 Have we not all one father? Has
not one God created us? Why then are
we faithless to one another, profaning
the covenant of our fathers? 11 Judah
has been faithless, and abomination
has been committed in Israel and in
Jerusalem; for Judah has profaned the
sanctuary of the LORD, which he loves,
and has married the daughter of a
foreign god. 12 May the LORD cut off
from the tents of Jacob, for the man
who does this, any to witness[g] or
answer, or to bring an offering to the
LORD of hosts!

13 And this again you do. You cover
the LORD's altar with tears, with weeping and groaning because he no longer
regards the offering or accepts it with
favor at your hand. 14 You ask, "Why
does he not?" Because the LORD was
witness to the covenant between you
and the wife of your youth, to whom
you have been faithless, though she is
your companion and your wife by
covenant. 15 Has not the one God
made[h] and sustained for us the spirit
of life?[i] And what does he desire?
Godly offspring. So take heed to yourselves, and let none be faithless to the
wife of his youth. 16 "For I hate[j]
divorce, says the LORD the God of
Israel, and covering one's garment with
violence, says the LORD of hosts. So
take heed to yourselves and do not be
faithless."

17 You have wearied the LORD with
your words. Yet you say, "How have
we wearied him?" By saying, "Every
one who does evil is good in the sight
of the LORD, and he delights in them."
Or by asking, "Where is the God of
justice?"

3 "Behold, I send my messenger to
prepare the way before me, and
the Lord whom you seek will suddenly
come to his temple; the messenger of
the covenant in whom you delight, behold, he is coming, says the LORD of
hosts. 2 But who can endure the day
of his coming, and who can stand when
he appears?

"For he is like a refiner's fire and
like fullers' soap; 3 he will sit as a refiner and purifier of silver, and he will
purify the sons of Levi and refine them
like gold and silver, till they present
right offerings to the LORD. 4 Then
the offering of Judah and Jerusalem
will be pleasing to the LORD as in the
days of old and as in former years.

5 "Then I will draw near to you
for judgment; I will be a swift witness
against the sorcerers, against the adulterers, against those who swear falsely,
against those who oppress the hireling
in his wages, the widow and the
orphan, against those who thrust aside
the sojourner, and do not fear me, says
the LORD of hosts.

[e] Cn Compare Gk Syr: Heb *and he shall bear you to it* [f] Or *law* [g] Cn Compare Gk: Heb *arouse*
[h] Or *has he not made one?* [i] Cn: Heb *and a remnant of spirit was his* [j] Cn: Heb *he hates*
3.1: Mt 11.10; Mk 1.2; Lk 1.17, 76; 7.27. **3.2:** Rev 6.17.

6 "For I the LORD do not change;
therefore you, O sons of Jacob, are not
consumed. 7 From the days of your
fathers you have turned aside from my
statutes and have not kept them. Return to me, and I will return to you,
says the LORD of hosts. But you say,
'How shall we return?' 8 Will man rob
God? Yet you are robbing me. But
you say, 'How are we robbing thee?'
In your tithes and offerings. 9 You are
cursed with a curse, for you are
robbing me; the whole nation of you.
10 Bring the full tithes into the storehouse, that there may be food in my
house; and thereby put me to the test,
says the LORD of hosts, if I will not
open the windows of heaven for you
and pour down for you an overflowing
blessing. 11 I will rebuke the devourer[k]
for you, so that it will not destroy the
fruits of your soil; and your vine in the
field shall not fail to bear, says the
LORD of hosts. 12 Then all nations will
call you blessed, for you will be a land
of delight, says the LORD of hosts.

13 "Your words have been stout
against me, says the LORD. Yet you
say, 'How have we spoken against
thee?' 14 You have said, 'It is vain to
serve God. What is the good of our
keeping his charge or of walking as in
mourning before the LORD of hosts?
15 Henceforth we deem the arrogant
blessed; evildoers not only prosper but
when they put God to the test they
escape.'"

16 Then those who feared the LORD
spoke with one another; the LORD
heeded and heard them, and a book
of remembrance was written before
him of those who feared the LORD and
thought on his name. 17 "They shall
be mine, says the LORD of hosts, my
special possession on the day when I
act, and I will spare them as a man
spares his son who serves him. 18 Then
once more you shall distinguish between the righteous and the wicked,
between one who serves God and one
who does not serve him.

4[l] "For behold, the day comes,
burning like an oven, when all the
arrogant and all evildoers will be
stubble; the day that comes shall burn
them up, says the LORD of hosts, so
that it will leave them neither root nor
branch. 2 But for you who fear my
name the sun of righteousness shall
rise, with healing in its wings. You
shall go forth leaping like calves from
the stall. 3 And you shall tread down
the wicked, for they will be ashes under
the soles of your feet, on the day when
I act, says the LORD of hosts.

4 "Remember the law of my servant
Moses, the statutes and ordinances
that I commanded him at Hō'reb for
all Israel.

5 "Behold, I will send you E·lī'jah
the prophet before the great and terrible day of the LORD comes. 6 And he
will turn the hearts of fathers to their
children and the hearts of children to
their fathers, lest I come and smite the
land with a curse."[m]

[k] Or *devouring locust* [l] Ch 4.1-6 are Ch 3.19-24 in the Hebrew [m] Or *ban of utter destruction*
4.5: Mt 17.11; Mk 9.12. **4.6:** Lk 1.17.

THE
New Testament

OF OUR LORD AND SAVIOR

Jesus Christ

REVISED STANDARD VERSION

THE GOSPEL ACCORDING TO

MATTHEW

1 The book of the genealogy of Jesus
Christ, the son of David, the son of
Abraham.
2 Abraham was the father of Isaac,
and Isaac the father of Jacob, and
Jacob the father of Judah and his
brothers, 3 and Judah the father of
Per'ez and Zē'rȧh by Tā'mär, and
Perez the father of Hez'rȯn, and Hezron the father of Räm,[a] 4 and Räm[a]
the father of Am·min'ȧ·dab, and Am-
minadab the father of Näh'shȯn, and
Nahshon the father of Sal'mȯn, 5 and
Sal'mȯn the father of Bō'az by Rā'hab,
and Boaz the father of Ō'bed by Ruth,
and Obed the father of Jesse, 6 and
Jesse the father of David the king.
And David was the father of Sol-
omon by the wife of Ū·rī'ȧh, 7 and
Solomon the father of Rē·hȯ·bō'ȧm,
and Rehoboam the father of Ȧ·bī'jȧh,
and Abijah the father of Asa,[b] 8 and
Asa[b] the father of Je·hosh'ȧ·phat, and
Jehoshaphat the father of Jō'rȧm, and
Joram the father of Uz·zī'ȧh, 9 and Uz-
zī'ȧh the father of Jō'thȧm, and Jotham
the father of Ā'haz, and Ahaz the
father of Hez·ė·kī'ȧh, 10 and Hez·ė·kī'-
ȧh the father of Mȧ·nas'sėh, and
Manasseh the father of Amos,[c] and
Amos[c] the father of Jō·sī'ȧh, 11 and
Jō·sī'ȧh the father of Jech·ȯ·nī'ȧh and
his brothers, at the time of the deportation to Babylon.
12 And after the deportation to
Babylon: Jech·ȯ·nī'ȧh was the father
of She-al'ti-el,[d] and She-alti-el[d] the
father of Ze·rub'bȧ·bel, 13 and Ze·rub'-
bȧ·bel the father of Ȧ·bī'ŭd, and Abiud
the father of E·lī'ȧ·kim, and Eliakim
the father of Ā'zôr, 14 and Ā'zôr the
father of Zā'dok, and Zadok the father
of Ā'chim, and Achim the father of
E·lī'ŭd, 15 and E·lī'ŭd the father of
El·ē·ā'zȧr, and Eleazar the father of
Mat'thȧn, and Matthan the father of
Jacob, 16 and Jacob the father of
Joseph the husband of Mary, of
whom Jesus was born, who is called
Christ.
17 So all the generations from
Abraham to David were fourteen
generations, and from David to the
deportation to Babylon fourteen generations, and from the deportation to
Babylon to the Christ fourteen gen-
erations.

18 Now the birth of Jesus Christ[f]
took place in this way. When his
mother Mary had been betrothed to
Joseph, before they came together she
was found to be with child of the Holy
Spirit; 19 and her husband Joseph, being a just man and unwilling to put
her to shame, resolved to divorce her
quietly. 20 But as he considered this,
behold, an angel of the Lord appeared
to him in a dream, saying, "Joseph,
son of David, do not fear to take Mary
your wife, for that which is conceived
in her is of the Holy Spirit; 21 she will
bear a son, and you shall call his name
Jesus, for he will save his people from
their sins." 22 All this took place to fulfil what the Lord had spoken by the
prophet:
23 "Behold, a virgin shall conceive and
bear a son,
and his name shall be called
Em·man'ū-ėl"
(which means, God with us). 24 When
Joseph woke from sleep, he did as
the angel of the Lord commanded
him; he took his wife, 25 but knew her
not until she had borne a son; and he
called his name Jesus.

2 Now when Jesus was born in
Bethlehem of Judea in the days of
Her'ȯd the king, behold, wise men
from the East came to Jerusalem, saying, 2 "Where is he who has been born
king of the Jews? For we have seen his
star in the East, and have come to
worship him." 3 When Her'ȯd the
king heard this, he was troubled, and

[a] Greek *Aram* [b] Greek *Asaph* [c] Other authorities read *Amon* [d] Greek *Salathiel*
[f] Other ancient authorities read *of the Christ*

1.1-17: Lk 3.23-38. **1.3-6:** Ruth 4.18-22; 1 Chron 2.1-15. **1.11:** 2 Kings 24.14; Jer 27.20.
1.18: Lk 1.26-38. **1.21:** Lk 2.21; Jn 1.29; Acts 13.23. **1.23:** Is 7.14. **2.1:** Lk 2.4-7; 1.5.
2.2: Jer 23.5; Zech 9.9; Mk 15.2; Jn 1.49; Num 24.17.

all Jerusalem with him; 4 and assembling all the chief priests and scribes
of the people, he inquired of them
where the Christ was to be born.
5 They told him, "In Bethlehem of
Judea; for so it is written by the
prophet:

6 'And you, O Bethlehem, in the land
of Judah,
are by no means least among the
rulers of Judah;
for from you shall come a ruler
who will govern my people Israel.' "

7 Then Her′ȯd summoned the wise
men secretly and ascertained from
them what time the star appeared;
8 and he sent them to Bethlehem, saying, "Go and search diligently for the
child, and when you have found him
bring me word, that I too may come
and worship him." 9 When they had
heard the king they went their way;
and lo, the star which they had seen
in the East went before them, till it
came to rest over the place where the
child was. 10 When they saw the star,
they rejoiced exceedingly with great
joy; 11 and going into the house they
saw the child with Mary his mother,
and they fell down and worshiped him.
Then, opening their treasures, they
offered him gifts, gold and frankincense and myrrh. 12 And being warned
in a dream not to return to Her′ȯd,
they departed to their own country by
another way.

13 Now when they had departed,
behold, an angel of the Lord appeared
to Joseph in a dream and said, "Rise,
take the child and his mother, and
flee to Egypt, and remain there till I
tell you; for Her′ȯd is about to search
for the child, to destroy him." 14 And
he rose and took the child and his
mother by night, and departed to
Egypt, 15 and remained there until the
death of Her′ȯd. This was to fulfil
what the Lord had spoken by the
prophet, "Out of Egypt have I called
my son."

16 Then Her′ȯd, when he saw that
he had been tricked by the wise men,
was in a furious rage, and he sent and
killed all the male children in Bethlehem and in all that region who were
two years old or under, according to
the time which he had ascertained
from the wise men. 17 Then was fulfilled what was spoken by the prophet
Jeremiah:

18 "A voice was heard in Rā′mȧh,
wailing and loud lamentation,
Rachel weeping for her children;
she refused to be consoled,
because they were no more."

19 But when Her′ȯd died, behold,
an angel of the Lord appeared in a
dream to Joseph in Egypt, saying,
20 "Rise, take the child and his mother,
and go to the land of Israel, for those
who sought the child's life are dead."
21 And he rose and took the child and
his mother, and went to the land of
Israel. 22 But when he heard that
Är·chė·lā′ŭs reigned over Judea in
place of his father Her′ȯd, he was
afraid to go there, and being warned
in a dream he withdrew to the district
of Galilee. 23 And he went and dwelt in
a city called Nazareth, that what was
spoken by the prophets might be fulfilled, "He shall be called a Nazarene."

3 In those days came John the
Baptist, preaching in the wilderness of Judea, 2 "Repent, for the kingdom of heaven is at hand." 3 For this
is he who was spoken of by the prophet
Ī·ṡāi′ȧh when he said,

"The voice of one crying in the
wilderness:
Prepare the way of the Lord,
make his paths straight."

4 Now John wore a garment of camel's
hair, and a leather girdle around his
waist; and his food was locusts and
wild honey. 5 Then went out to him
Jerusalem and all Judea and all the
region about the Jordan, 6 and they
were baptized by him in the river
Jordan, confessing their sins.

7 But when he saw many of the
Pharisees and Sad′dū·ċeeṡ coming for
baptism, he said to them, "You brood
of vipers! Who warned you to flee
from the wrath to come? 8 Bear fruit
that befits repentance, 9 and do not
presume to say to yourselves, 'We
have Abraham as our father'; for I tell
you, God is able from these stones to
raise up children to Abraham. 10 Even

2.5: Jn 7.42. **2.6:** Mic 5.2; Jn 21.16. **2.11:** Mt 1.18; 12.46. **2.12:** Mt 2.22; Acts 10.22; Heb 11.7.
2.15: Hos 11.1; Ex 4.22. **2.18:** Jer 31.15. **2.19:** Mt 1.20; 2.13. **2.23:** Lk 1.26; Is 11.1; Mk 1.24.
3.1-12: Mk 1.3-8; Lk 3.2-17; Jn 1.6-8, 19-28. **3.2:** Mt 4.17; Dan 2.44; 4.17; Mt 10.7. **3.3:** Is 40.3.
3.4: 2 Kings 1.8; Zech 13.4; Lev 11.22. **3.7:** Mt 12.34; 23.33; 1 Thess 1.10.
3.9: Jn 8.33; Rom 4.16. **3.10:** Mt 7.19.

now the axe is laid to the root of the
trees; every tree therefore that does
not bear good fruit is cut down and
thrown into the fire.

11 "I baptize you with water for
repentance, but he who is coming
after me is mightier than I, whose
sandals I am not worthy to carry; he
will baptize you with the Holy Spirit
and with fire. 12 His winnowing fork
is in his hand, and he will clear his
threshing floor and gather his wheat
into the granary, but the chaff he will
burn with unquenchable fire."

13 Then Jesus came from Galilee
to the Jordan to John, to be baptized
by him. 14 John would have prevented
him, saying, "I need to be baptized by
you, and do you come to me?" 15 But
Jesus answered him, "Let it be so now;
for thus it is fitting for us to fulfil all
righteousness." Then he consented.
16 And when Jesus was baptized, he
went up immediately from the water,
and behold, the heavens were opened[g]
and he saw the Spirit of God descending like a dove, and alighting on him;
17 and lo, a voice from heaven, saying,
"This is my beloved Son,[h] with whom
I am well pleased."

4 Then Jesus was led up by the
Spirit into the wilderness to be
tempted by the devil. 2 And he fasted
forty days and forty nights, and afterward he was hungry. 3 And the tempter
came and said to him, "If you are the
Son of God, command these stones to
become loaves of bread." 4 But he
answered, "It is written,

'Man shall not live by bread alone,
but by every word that proceeds
from the mouth of God.' "

5 Then the devil took him to the holy
city, and set him on the pinnacle of the
temple, 6 and said to him, "If you are
the Son of God, throw yourself down;
for it is written,

'He will give his angels charge of
you,'

and

'On their hands they will bear you
up,
lest you strike your foot against a
stone.' "

7 Jesus said to him, "Again it is written, 'You shall not tempt the Lord
your God.' " 8 Again, the devil took
him to a very high mountain, and
showed him all the kingdoms of the
world and the glory of them; 9 and he
said to him, "All these I will give you,
if you will fall down and worship me."
10 Then Jesus said to him, "Begone,
Satan! for it is written,

'You shall worship the Lord your
God
and him only shall you serve.' "

11 Then the devil left him, and behold, angels came and ministered to
him.

12 Now when he heard that John
had been arrested, he withdrew into
Galilee; 13 and leaving Nazareth he
went and dwelt in Cȧ·pĕr'nȧ-ŭm by
the sea, in the territory of Zeb'ū·lŭn
and Naph'tȧ·lī, 14 that what was
spoken by the prophet Ī·ṡāi'ȧh might
be fulfilled:

15 "The land of Zeb'ū·lŭn and the land
of Naph'tȧ·lī,
toward the sea, across the Jordan,
Galilee of the Gentiles—
16 the people who sat in darkness
have seen a great light,
and for those who sat in the region
and shadow of death
light has dawned."

17 From that time Jesus began to
preach, saying, "Repent, for the kingdom of heaven is at hand."

18 As he walked by the Sea of
Galilee, he saw two brothers, Simon
who is called Peter and Andrew his
brother, casting a net into the sea; for
they were fishermen. 19 And he said to
them, "Follow me, and I will make
you fishers of men." 20 Immediately
they left their nets and followed him.
21 And going on from there he saw two
other brothers, James the son of Zeb'-
ė·dee and John his brother, in the boat
with Zebedee their father, mending
their nets, and he called them. 22 Immediately they left the boat and their
father, and followed him.

23 And he went about all Galilee,
teaching in their synagogues and

[g] Other ancient authorities add *to him* [h] Or *my Son, my* (or *the*) *Beloved*

3.12: Mt 13.30. **3.13-17:** Mk 1.9-11; Lk 3.21-22; Jn 1.31-34.
3.17: Mt 12.18; 17.5; Mk 9.7; Lk 9.35; Ps 2.7; Is 42.1. **4.1-11:** Mk 1.12-13; Lk 4.1-13; Heb 2.18; 4.15.
4.2: Ex 34.28; 1 Kings 19.8. **4.4:** Deut 8.3. **4.5:** Mt 27.53; Neh 11.1; Dan 9.24; Rev 21.10.
4.6: Ps 91.11-12. **4.7:** Deut 6.16. **4.10:** Deut 6.13; Mk 8.33. **4.11:** Mt 26.53; Lk 22.43.
4.12: Mk 1.14; Lk 4.14; Mt 14.3; Jn 1.43. **4.13:** Jn 2.12; Mk 1.21; Lk 4.23. **4.15:** Is 9.1-2.
4.17: Mk 1.15; Mt 3.2; 10.7. **4.18-22:** Mk 1.16-20; Lk 5.1-11; Jn 1.35-42.
4.23-25: Mk 1.39; Lk 4.15, 44; Mt 9.35; Mk 3.7-8; Lk 6.17.

preaching the gospel of the kingdom
and healing every disease and every
infirmity among the people. 24 So his
fame spread throughout all Syria, and
they brought him all the sick, those
afflicted with various diseases and
pains, demoniacs, epileptics, and para-
lytics, and he healed them. 25 And
great crowds followed him from Galilee
and the De-cap'o-lis and Jerusalem and
Judea and from beyond the Jordan.

5 Seeing the crowds, he went up
on the mountain, and when he sat
down his disciples came to him. 2 And
he opened his mouth and taught them,
saying:

3 "Blessed are the poor in spirit,
for theirs is the kingdom of heaven.
4 "Blessed are those who mourn,
for they shall be comforted.
5 "Blessed are the meek, for they
shall inherit the earth.
6 "Blessed are those who hunger
and thirst for righteousness, for they
shall be satisfied.
7 "Blessed are the merciful, for
they shall obtain mercy.
8 "Blessed are the pure in heart,
for they shall see God.
9 "Blessed are the peacemakers, for
they shall be called sons of God.
10 "Blessed are those who are persecuted for righteousness' sake, for
theirs is the kingdom of heaven.
11 "Blessed are you when men revile you and persecute you and utter
all kinds of evil against you falsely on
my account. 12 Rejoice and be glad,
for your reward is great in heaven, for
so men persecuted the prophets who
were before you.

13 "You are the salt of the earth;
but if salt has lost its taste, how shall
its saltness be restored? It is no longer
good for anything except to be thrown
out and trodden under foot by men.

14 "You are the light of the world.
A city set on a hill cannot be hid.
15 Nor do men light a lamp and put it
under a bushel, but on a stand, and it
gives light to all in the house. 16 Let
your light so shine before men, that
they may see your good works and
give glory to your Father who is in
heaven.

17 "Think not that I have come to
abolish the law and the prophets; I
have come not to abolish them but to
fulfil them. 18 For truly, I say to you,
till heaven and earth pass away, not
an iota, not a dot, will pass from the
law until all is accomplished. 19 Whoever then relaxes one of the least of
these commandments and teaches men
so, shall be called least in the kingdom
of heaven; but he who does them and
teaches them shall be called great in
the kingdom of heaven. 20 For I tell
you, unless your righteousness exceeds
that of the scribes and Pharisees, you
will never enter the kingdom of
heaven.

21 "You have heard that it was said
to the men of old, 'You shall not kill;
and whoever kills shall be liable to
judgment.' 22 But I say to you that
every one who is angry with his
brother[i] shall be liable to judgment;
whoever insults[j] his brother shall be
liable to the council, and whoever says,
'You fool!' shall be liable to the hell[k]
of fire. 23 So if you are offering your
gift at the altar, and there remember
that your brother has something
against you, 24 leave your gift there
before the altar and go; first be reconciled to your brother, and then come
and offer your gift. 25 Make friends
quickly with your accuser, while you
are going with him to court, lest your
accuser hand you over to the judge,
and the judge to the guard, and you
be put in prison; 26 truly, I say to you,
you will never get out till you have
paid the last penny.

27 "You have heard that it was said,
'You shall not commit adultery.' 28 But
I say to you that every one who looks
at a woman lustfully has already committed adultery with her in his heart.
29 If your right eye causes you to sin,
pluck it out and throw it away; it is
better that you lose one of your members than that your whole body be
thrown into hell.[k] 30 And if your right
hand causes you to sin, cut it off and

[i] Other ancient authorities insert *without cause* [j] Greek *says Raca to* (an obscure term of abuse)
[k] Greek *Gehenna*

5.1-12: Lk 6.17, 20-23; Mk 3.13; Jn 6.3. **5.3:** Mk 10.14; Lk 22.29. **5.4:** Is 61.2; Jn 16.20; Rev 7.17.
5.5: Ps 37.11. **5.6:** Is 55.1-2; Jn 4.14; 6.48-51. **5.8:** Ps 24.4; Heb 12.14; 1 Jn 3.2; Rev 22.4.
5.10: 1 Pet 3.14; 4.14. **5.12:** 2 Chron 36.16; Mt 23.37; Acts 7.52; 1 Thess 2.15; Jas 5.10.
5.13: Mk 9.49-50; Lk 14.34-35. **5.14:** Eph 5.8; Phil 2.15; Jn 8.12.
5.15-16: Lk 11.33; Mk 4.21; 1 Pet 2.12. **5.18:** Lk 16.17; Mk 13.31. **5.19:** Jas 2.10.
5.21: Ex 20.13; Deut 5.17; 16.18. **5.25-26:** Lk 12.57-59. **5.27:** Ex 20.14; Deut 5.18.
5.29-30: Mk 9.43-48; Mt 18.8-9.

throw it away; it is better that you lose
one of your members than that your
whole body go into hell.[k]
31 "It was also said, 'Whoever divorces his wife, let him give her a
certificate of divorce.' 32 But I say to
you that every one who divorces his
wife, except on the ground of unchastity, makes her an adulteress; and
whoever marries a divorced woman
commits adultery.
33 "Again you have heard that it
was said to the men of old, 'You shall
not swear falsely, but shall perform to
the Lord what you have sworn.' 34 But
I say to you, Do not swear at all, either
by heaven, for it is the throne of God,
35 or by the earth, for it is his footstool,
or by Jerusalem, for it is the city of
the great King. 36 And do not swear by
your head, for you cannot make one
hair white or black. 37 Let what you
say be simply 'Yes' or 'No'; anything
more than this comes from evil.[l]
38 "You have heard that it was said,
'An eye for an eye and a tooth for a
tooth.' 39 But I say to you, Do not
resist one who is evil. But if any one
strikes you on the right cheek, turn to
him the other also; 40 and if any one
would sue you and take your coat, let
him have your cloak as well; 41 and if
any one forces you to go one mile, go
with him two miles. 42 Give to him
who begs from you, and do not refuse
him who would borrow from you.
43 "You have heard that it was said,
'You shall love your neighbor and hate
your enemy.' 44 But I say to you, Love
your enemies and pray for those who
persecute you, 45 so that you may be
sons of your Father who is in heaven;
for he makes his sun rise on the evil
and on the good, and sends rain on the
just and on the unjust. 46 For if you
love those who love you, what reward
have you? Do not even the tax collectors do the same? 47 And if you salute
only your brethren, what more are you
doing than others? Do not even the
Gentiles do the same? 48 You, therefore, must be perfect, as your heavenly
Father is perfect.

6 "Beware of practicing your piety
before men in order to be seen by
them; for then you will have no reward
from your Father who is in heaven.
2 "Thus, when you give alms,
sound no trumpet before you, as the
hypocrites do in the synagogues and
in the streets, that they may be praised
by men. Truly, I say to you, they have
their reward. 3 But when you give
alms, do not let your left hand know
what your right hand is doing, 4 so
that your alms may be in secret; and
your Father who sees in secret will
reward you.
5 "And when you pray, you must
not be like the hypocrites; for they love
to stand and pray in the synagogues
and at the street corners, that they may
be seen by men. Truly, I say to you,
they have their reward. 6 But when
you pray, go into your room and shut
the door and pray to your Father who
is in secret; and your Father who sees
in secret will reward you.
7 "And in praying do not heap up
empty phrases as the Gentiles do; for
they think that they will be heard for
their many words. 8 Do not be like
them, for your Father knows what you
need before you ask him. 9 Pray then
like this:
Our Father who art in heaven,
Hallowed be thy name.
10 Thy kingdom come,
Thy will be done,
On earth as it is in heaven.
11 Give us this day our daily bread;[m]
12 And forgive us our debts,
As we also have forgiven our
debtors;
13 And lead us not into temptation,
But deliver us from evil.[n]
14 For if you forgive men their trespasses, your heavenly Father also will
forgive you; 15 but if you do not forgive
men their trespasses, neither will your
Father forgive your trespasses.
16 "And when you fast, do not look

[k] Greek *Gehenna* [l] Or *the evil one* [m] Or *our bread for the morrow*
[n] Or *the evil one*. Other authorities, some ancient, add, in some form, *For thine is the kingdom and the power and the glory, for ever. Amen.*

5.31-32: Lk 16.18; Mk 10.11-12; Mt 19.9; 1 Cor 7.10-11; Deut 24.1-4.
5.33-37: Mt 23.16-22; Jas 5.12; Lev 19.12; Num 30.2; Deut 23.21. **5.35:** Is 66.1; Acts 7.49; Ps 48.2.
5.38: Ex 21.24; Lev 24.20; Deut 19.21.
5.39-42: Lk 6.29-30; 1 Cor 6.7; Rom 12.17; 1 Pet 2.19; 3.9; Prov 24.29.
5.43-48: Lk 6.27-28, 32-36; Lev 19.18; Prov 25.21-22. **5.48:** Lev 19.2. **6.1:** Mt 23.5.
6.4: Col 3.23-24. **6.5:** Mk 11.25; Lk 18.10-14. **6.7:** 1 Kings 18.25-29. **6.8:** Mt 6.32; Lk 12.30.
6.9-13: Lk 11.2-4. **6.13:** 2 Thess 3.3; Jn 17.15; Jas 1.13.
6.14-15: Mt 18.35; Mk 11.25; Eph 4.32; Col 3.13. **6.16:** Is 58.5.

dismal, like the hypocrites, for they
disfigure their faces that their fasting
may be seen by men. Truly, I say to
you, they have their reward. 17 But
when you fast, anoint your head and
wash your face, 18 that your fasting
may not be seen by men but by your
Father who is in secret; and your Father who sees in secret will reward you.
19 "Do not lay up for yourselves
treasures on earth, where moth and
rust[o] consume and where thieves
break in and steal, 20 but lay up for
yourselves treasures in heaven, where
neither moth nor rust[o] consumes and
where thieves do not break in and
steal. 21 For where your treasure is,
there will your heart be also.
22 "The eye is the lamp of the body.
So, if your eye is sound, your whole
body will be full of light; 23 but if your
eye is not sound, your whole body will
be full of darkness. If then the light in
you is darkness, how great is the darkness!
24 "No one can serve two masters;
for either he will hate the one and love
the other, or he will be devoted to the
one and despise the other. You cannot
serve God and mammon.
25 "Therefore I tell you, do not be
anxious about your life, what you shall
eat or what you shall drink, nor about
your body, what you shall put on. Is
not life more than food, and the body
more than clothing? 26 Look at the
birds of the air: they neither sow nor
reap nor gather into barns, and yet
your heavenly Father feeds them. Are
you not of more value than they? 27 And
which of you by being anxious can add
one cubit to his span of life?[p] 28 And
why are you anxious about clothing?
Consider the lilies of the field, how
they grow; they neither toil nor spin;
29 yet I tell you, even Solomon in all
his glory was not arrayed like one of
these. 30 But if God so clothes the
grass of the field, which today is alive
and tomorrow is thrown into the oven,
will he not much more clothe you, O
men of little faith? 31 Therefore do not
be anxious, saying, 'What shall we eat?'
or 'What shall we drink?' or 'What
shall we wear?' 32 For the Gentiles
seek all these things; and your heavenly
Father knows that you need them all.
33 But seek first his kingdom and his
righteousness, and all these things
shall be yours as well.
34 "Therefore do not be anxious
about tomorrow, for tomorrow will be
anxious for itself. Let the day's own
trouble be sufficient for the day.

7 "Judge not, that you be not
judged. 2 For with the judgment
you pronounce you will be judged,
and the measure you give will be the
measure you get. 3 Why do you see the
speck that is in your brother's eye, but
do not notice the log that is in your
own eye? 4 Or how can you say to your
brother, 'Let me take the speck out of
your eye,' when there is the log in your
own eye? 5 You hypocrite, first take
the log out of your own eye, and then
you will see clearly to take the speck
out of your brother's eye.
6 "Do not give dogs what is holy;
and do not throw your pearls before
swine, lest they trample them under
foot and turn to attack you.
7 "Ask, and it will be given you;
seek, and you will find; knock, and it
will be opened to you. 8 For every one
who asks receives, and he who seeks
finds, and to him who knocks it will
be opened. 9 Or what man of you, if
his son asks him for bread, will give
him a stone? 10 Or if he asks for a fish,
will give him a serpent? 11 If you then,
who are evil, know how to give good
gifts to your children, how much more
will your Father who is in heaven give
good things to those who ask him!
12 So whatever you wish that men
would do to you, do so to them; for
this is the law and the prophets.
13 "Enter by the narrow gate; for
the gate is wide and the way is easy,[q]
that leads to destruction, and those
who enter by it are many. 14 For the
gate is narrow and the way is hard,
that leads to life, and those who find
it are few.
15 "Beware of false prophets, who

[o] Or *worm* [p] Or *to his stature* [q] Other ancient authorities read *for the way is wide and easy*

6.18: Mt 6.4, 6. **6.19-21:** Lk 12.33-34; Mk 10.21; 1 Tim 6.17-19; Jas 5.1-3.
6.22-23: Lk 11.34-36; Mt 20.15; Mk 7.22. **6.24:** Lk 16.13.
6.25-33: Lk 12.22-31; 10.41; 12.11; Phil 4.6; 1 Pet 5.7. **6.26:** Mt 10.29. **6.27:** Ps 39.5.
6.29: 1 Kings 10.4-7. **6.30:** Mt 8.26; 14.31; 16.8. **6.33:** Mt 19.28; Mk 10.29-30; Lk 18.29-30.
7.1-2: Lk 6.37-38; Mk 4.24; Rom 2.1; 14.10. **7.3-5:** Lk 6.41-42.
7.7-11: Lk 11.9-13; Mk 11.24; Jn 15.7; 16.23-24; Jas 4.3; 1 Jn 3.22; 5.14. **7.12:** Lk 6.31.
7.13-14: Lk 13.23-24; Jer 21.8; Deut 30.19; Jn 14.6; 10.7.
7.15: Mt 24.11, 24; Ezek 22.27; 1 Jn 4.1; Jn 10.12.

come to you in sheep's clothing but
inwardly are ravenous wolves. 16 You
will know them by their fruits. Are
grapes gathered from thorns, or figs
from thistles? 17 So, every sound tree
bears good fruit, but the bad tree bears
evil fruit. 18 A sound tree cannot bear
evil fruit, nor can a bad tree bear good
fruit. 19 Every tree that does not bear
good fruit is cut down and thrown into
the fire. 20 Thus you will know them
by their fruits.

21 "Not every one who says to me,
'Lord, Lord,' shall enter the kingdom
of heaven, but he who does the will of
my Father who is in heaven. 22 On
that day many will say to me, 'Lord,
Lord, did we not prophesy in your
name, and cast out demons in your
name, and do many mighty works in
your name?' 23 And then will I declare
to them, 'I never knew you; depart
from me, you evildoers.'

24 "Every one then who hears these
words of mine and does them will be
like a wise man who built his house
upon the rock; 25 and the rain fell, and
the floods came, and the winds blew
and beat upon that house, but it did
not fall, because it had been founded
on the rock. 26 And every one who
hears these words of mine and does
not do them will be like a foolish man
who built his house upon the sand;
27 and the rain fell, and the floods
came, and the winds blew and beat
against that house, and it fell; and great
was the fall of it."

28 And when Jesus finished these
sayings, the crowds were astonished at
his teaching, 29 for he taught them as
one who had authority, and not as their
scribes.

8 When he came down from the
mountain, great crowds followed
him; 2 and behold, a leper came to him
and knelt before him, saying, "Lord,
if you will, you can make me clean."
3 And he stretched out his hand and
touched him, saying, "I will; be clean."
And immediately his leprosy was
cleansed. 4 And Jesus said to him, "See
that you say nothing to any one; but
go, show yourself to the priest, and
offer the gift that Moses commanded,
for a proof to the people."[r]

5 As he entered Că·pĕr'nȧ-ŭm, a
centurion came forward to him, beseeching him 6 and saying, "Lord, my
servant is lying paralyzed at home, in
terrible distress." 7 And he said to him,
"I will come and heal him." 8 But the
centurion answered him, "Lord, I am
not worthy to have you come under
my roof; but only say the word, and
my servant will be healed. 9 For I am
a man under authority, with soldiers
under me; and I say to one, 'Go,' and
he goes, and to another, 'Come,' and
he comes, and to my slave, 'Do this,'
and he does it." 10 When Jesus heard
him, he marveled, and said to those who
followed him, "Truly, I say to you, not
even[s] in Israel have I found such faith.
11 I tell you, many will come from east
and west and sit at table with Abraham,
Isaac, and Jacob in the kingdom of
heaven, 12 while the sons of the kingdom will be thrown into the outer
darkness; there men will weep and
gnash their teeth." 13 And to the centurion Jesus said, "Go; be it done for
you as you have believed." And the
servant was healed at that very moment.

14 And when Jesus entered Peter's
house, he saw his mother-in-law lying
sick with a fever; 15 he touched her
hand, and the fever left her, and she
rose and served him. 16 That evening
they brought to him many who were
possessed with demons; and he cast
out the spirits with a word, and healed
all who were sick. 17 This was to fulfil
what was spoken by the prophet
Ī·ṡăi'ȧh, "He took our infirmities and
bore our diseases."

18 Now when Jesus saw great
crowds around him, he gave orders to
go over to the other side. 19 And a scribe
came up and said to him, "Teacher, I
will follow you wherever you go."
20 And Jesus said to him, "Foxes have
holes, and birds of the air have nests;
but the Son of man has nowhere to lay
his head." 21 Another of the disciples
said to him, "Lord, let me first go and

[r] Greek *to them* [s] Other ancient authorities read *with no one*

7.16-20: Lk 6.43-44; Mt 12.33-35; Mt 3.10; Jas 3.12; Lk 13.7. **7.21:** Lk 6.46.
7.22-23: Lk 13.26-27; Mt 25.12; Ps 6.8. **7.24-27:** Lk 6.47-49; Jas 1.22-25.
7.28-29: Mk 1.22; Lk 4.32; Mt 11.1; 13.53; 19.1; 26.1. **8.2-4:** Mk 1.40-44; Lk 5.12-14.
8.2: Mt 9.18; 15.25; 18.26; 20.20; Jn 9.38. **8.4:** Mk 3.12; 5.43; 7.36; 8.30; 9.9; Lev 14.2.
8.5-13: Lk 7.1-10; Jn 4.46-53. **8.11-12:** Lk 13.28-29; Is 49.12; 59.19; Mal 1.11; Ps 107.3.
8.12: Mt 13.42, 50; 22.13; 24.51; 25.30; Lk 13.28. **8.14-16:** Mk 1.29-34; Lk 4.38-41; Mt 4.23-24.
8.17: Is 53.4. **8.18-22:** Lk 9.57-60; Mk 4.35; Lk 8.22.

bury my father." 22 But Jesus said to
him, "Follow me, and leave the dead
to bury their own dead."

23 And when he got into the boat,
his disciples followed him. 24 And behold, there arose a great storm on the
sea, so that the boat was being
swamped by the waves; but he was
asleep. 25 And they went and woke him,
saying, "Save, Lord; we are perishing."
26 And he said to them, "Why are you
afraid, O men of little faith?" Then he
rose and rebuked the winds and the
sea; and there was a great calm. 27 And
the men marveled, saying, "What sort
of man is this, that even winds and sea
obey him?"

28 And when he came to the other
side, to the country of the Gad'a-
rēnes,[t] two demoniacs met him, coming
out of the tombs, so fierce that no one
could pass that way. 29 And behold,
they cried out, "What have you to do
with us, O Son of God? Have you come
here to torment us before the time?"
30 Now a herd of many swine was feeding at some distance from them. 31 And
the demons begged him, "If you cast
us out, send us away into the herd of
swine." 32 And he said to them, "Go."
So they came out and went into the
swine; and behold, the whole herd
rushed down the steep bank into the
sea, and perished in the waters. 33 The
herdsmen fled, and going into the city
they told everything, and what had
happened to the demoniacs. 34 And behold, all the city came out to meet
Jesus; and when they saw him, they
begged him to leave their neighborhood.

9 And getting into a boat he
crossed over and came to his own
city. 2 And behold, they brought to him
a paralytic, lying on his bed; and when
Jesus saw their faith he said to the
paralytic, "Take heart, my son; your
sins are forgiven." 3 And behold, some
of the scribes said to themselves, "This
man is blaspheming." 4 But Jesus,
knowing[u] their thoughts, said, "Why
do you think evil in your hearts? 5 For
which is easier, to say, 'Your sins are
forgiven,' or to say, 'Rise and walk'?
6 But that you may know that the Son
of man has authority on earth to forgive sins"—he then said to the paralytic—"Rise, take up your bed and go
home." 7 And he rose and went home.
8 When the crowds saw it, they were
afraid, and they glorified God, who
had given such authority to men.

9 As Jesus passed on from there, he
saw a man called Matthew sitting at
the tax office; and he said to him,
"Follow me." And he rose and followed him.

10 And as he sat at table[v] in the
house, behold, many tax collectors and
sinners came and sat down with Jesus
and his disciples. 11 And when the
Pharisees saw this, they said to his
disciples, "Why does your teacher eat
with tax collectors and sinners?" 12 But
when he heard it, he said, "Those who
are well have no need of a physician,
but those who are sick. 13 Go and learn
what this means, 'I desire mercy, and
not sacrifice.' For I came not to call
the righteous, but sinners."

14 Then the disciples of John came
to him, saying, "Why do we and the
Pharisees fast,[w] but your disciples do
not fast?" 15 And Jesus said to them,
"Can the wedding guests mourn as
long as the bridegroom is with them?
The days will come, when the bridegroom is taken away from them, and
then they will fast. 16 And no one puts
a piece of unshrunk cloth on an old
garment, for the patch tears away
from the garment, and a worse tear is
made. 17 Neither is new wine put into
old wineskins; if it is, the skins burst,
and the wine is spilled, and the skins
are destroyed; but new wine is put
into fresh wineskins, and so both are
preserved."

18 While he was thus speaking to
them, behold, a ruler came in and
knelt before him, saying, "My daughter has just died; but come and lay your
hand on her, and she will live." 19 And
Jesus rose and followed him, with his
disciples. 20 And behold, a woman who
had suffered from a hemorrhage for
twelve years came up behind him and
touched the fringe of his garment; 21 for

[t] Other ancient authorities read *Gergesenes;* some, *Gerasenes* [u] Other ancient authorities read *seeing*
[v] Greek *reclined* [w] Other ancient authorities add *much* or *often*

8.22: Mt 9.9; Jn 1.43; 21.19. **8.23-27:** Mk 4.36-41; Lk 8.22-25. **8.26:** Mt 6.30; 14.31; 16.8.
8.28-34: Mk 5.1-17; Lk 8.26-37. **8.29:** Judg 11.12; 2 Sam 16.10; Mk 1.24; Jn 2.4.
9.1-8: Mk 2.1-12; Lk 5.17-26. **9.2:** Mt 9.22; Mk 6.50; 10.49; Jn 16.33; Acts 23.11; Lk 7.48.
9.9-13: Mk 2.13-17; Lk 5.27-32; 15.1-2; 7.34. **9.13:** Hos 6.6; Mt 12.7; 1 Tim 1.15.
9.14-17: Mk 2.18-22; Lk 5.33-39; 18.12. **9.18-26:** Mk 5.21-43; Lk 8.40-56.
9.18: Mt 8.2; 15.25; 18.26; 20.20; Jn 9.38. **9.20:** Num 15.38; Deut 22.12; Mt 14.36; Mk 3.10.

she said to herself, "If I only touch
his garment, I shall be made well."
22 Jesus turned, and seeing her he said,
"Take heart, daughter; your faith has
made you well." And instantly the
woman was made well. 23 And when
Jesus came to the ruler's house, and
saw the flute players, and the crowd
making a tumult, 24 he said, "Depart;
for the girl is not dead but sleeping."
And they laughed at him. 25 But when
the crowd had been put outside, he
went in and took her by the hand, and
the girl arose. 26 And the report of this
went through all that district.

27 And as Jesus passed on from
there, two blind men followed him,
crying aloud, "Have mercy on us, Son
of David." 28 When he entered the
house, the blind men came to him;
and Jesus said to them, "Do you
believe that I am able to do this?"
They said to him, "Yes, Lord."
29 Then he touched their eyes, saying,
"According to your faith be it done to
you." 30 And their eyes were opened.
And Jesus sternly charged them, "See
that no one knows it." 31 But they went
away and spread his fame through all
that district.

32 As they were going away, behold, a dumb demoniac was brought
to him. 33 And when the demon had
been cast out, the dumb man spoke;
and the crowds marveled, saying,
"Never was anything like this seen in
Israel." 34 But the Pharisees said, "He
casts out demons by the prince of
demons."

35 And Jesus went about all the
cities and villages, teaching in their
synagogues and preaching the gospel
of the kingdom, and healing every
disease and every infirmity. 36 When
he saw the crowds, he had compassion
for them, because they were harassed
and helpless, like sheep without a
shepherd. 37 Then he said to his
disciples, "The harvest is plentiful,
but the laborers are few; 38 pray therefore the Lord of the harvest to send
out laborers into his harvest."

10 And he called to him his twelve
disciples and gave them authority
over unclean spirits, to cast them out,
and to heal every disease and every
infirmity. 2 The names of the twelve
apostles are these: first, Simon, who is
called Peter, and Andrew his brother;
James the son of Zeb'ė·dee, and John
his brother; 3 Philip and Bartholomew;
Thomas and Matthew the tax collector;
James the son of Al·phaē'ŭs, and
Thăd·daē'ŭs;[x] 4 Simon the Că·nă·naē'-
ăn, and Judas Is·car'ĭ·ŏt, who betrayed
him.

5 These twelve Jesus sent out,
charging them, "Go nowhere among
the Gentiles, and enter no town of the
Samaritans, 6 but go rather to the lost
sheep of the house of Israel. 7 And
preach as you go, saying, 'The kingdom of heaven is at hand.' 8 Heal the
sick, raise the dead, cleanse lepers, cast
out demons. You received without
pay, give without pay. 9 Take no gold,
nor silver, nor copper in your belts,
10 no bag for your journey, nor two
tunics, nor sandals, nor a staff; for the
laborer deserves his food. 11 And whatever town or village you enter, find out
who is worthy in it, and stay with him
until you depart. 12 As you enter the
house, salute it. 13 And if the house is
worthy, let your peace come upon it;
but if it is not worthy, let your peace
return to you. 14 And if any one will
not receive you or listen to your words,
shake off the dust from your feet as
you leave that house or town. 15 Truly,
I say to you, it shall be more tolerable
on the day of judgment for the land of
Sod'ŏm and Gŏ·môr'răh than for that
town.

16 "Behold, I send you out as sheep
in the midst of wolves; so be wise as
serpents and innocent as doves. 17 Beware of men; for they will deliver you
up to councils, and flog you in their
synagogues, 18 and you will be dragged
before governors and kings for my
sake, to bear testimony before them
and the Gentiles. 19 When they deliver
you up, do not be anxious how you are
to speak or what you are to say; for

[x] Other ancient authorities read *Lebbaeus* or *Lebbaeus called Thaddaeus*

9.22: Mk 10.52; Lk 7.50; 17.19; Mt 15.28; 9.29. **9.27-31:** Mt 20.29-34.
9.32-34: Lk 11.14-15; Mt 12.22-24; Mk 3.22; Jn 7.20. **9.35:** Mt 4.23; Mk 6.6.
9.36: Mk 6.34; Mt 14.14; 15.32; Num 27.17; Zech 10.2. **9.37-38:** Lk 10.2; Jn 4.35.
10.1-4: Mk 6.7; 3.16-19; Lk 9.1; 6.14-16; Acts 1.13. **10.5:** Lk 9.52; Jn 4.9; Acts 8.5, 25.
10.6: Mt 15.24; 10.23. **10.7-8:** Lk 9.2; 10.9-11; Mt 4.17.
10.9-14: Mk 6.8-11; Lk 9.3-5; 10.4-12; 22.35-36. **10.10:** 1 Cor 9.14; 1 Tim 5.18. **10.14:** Acts 13.51.
10.15: Mt 11.24; Lk 10.12; Jude 7; 2 Pet 2.6. **10.16:** Lk 10.3; Gen 3.1; Rom 16.19.
10.17-22: Mk 13.9-13; Lk 12.11-12; 21 12-19; Jn 16.2. **10.18:** Acts 25.24-26.

what you are to say will be given to
you in that hour; 20 for it is not you who
speak, but the Spirit of your Father
speaking through you. 21 Brother will
deliver up brother to death, and the
father his child, and children will rise
against parents and have them put to
death; 22 and you will be hated by all for
my name's sake. But he who endures
to the end will be saved. 23 When they
persecute you in one town, flee to the
next; for truly, I say to you, you will
not have gone through all the towns of
Israel, before the Son of man comes.
24 "A disciple is not above his
teacher, nor a servant[y] above his
master; 25 it is enough for the disciple
to be like his teacher, and the servant[y]
like his master. If they have called the
master of the house Bē-el'zė·bul, how
much more will they malign those of
his household.

26 "So have no fear of them; for
nothing is covered that will not be
revealed, or hidden that will not be
known. 27 What I tell you in the dark,
utter in the light; and what you hear
whispered, proclaim upon the housetops. 28 And do not fear those who kill
the body but cannot kill the soul; rather
fear him who can destroy both soul and
body in hell.[z] 29 Are not two sparrows
sold for a penny? And not one of them
will fall to the ground without your
Father's will. 30 But even the hairs of
your head are all numbered. 31 Fear
not, therefore; you are of more value
than many sparrows. 32 So every one
who acknowledges me before men, I
also will acknowledge before my
Father who is in heaven; 33 but whoever denies me before men, I also will
deny before my Father who is in
heaven.
34 "Do not think that I have come
to bring peace on earth; I have not
come to bring peace, but a sword.
35 For I have come to set a man against
his father, and a daughter against her
mother, and a daughter-in-law against
her mother-in-law; 36 and a man's foes
will be those of his own household.
37 He who loves father or mother more
than me is not worthy of me; and he
who loves son or daughter more than
me is not worthy of me; 38 and he who
does not take his cross and follow me
is not worthy of me. 39 He who finds
his life will lose it, and he who loses
his life for my sake will find it.
40 "He who receives you receives
me, and he who receives me receives
him who sent me. 41 He who receives
a prophet because he is a prophet shall
receive a prophet's reward, and he who
receives a righteous man because he
is a righteous man shall receive a
righteous man's reward. 42 And whoever gives to one of these little ones
even a cup of cold water because he is
a disciple, truly, I say to you, he shall
not lose his reward."

11 And when Jesus had finished
instructing his twelve disciples,
he went on from there to teach and
preach in their cities.
2 Now when John heard in prison
about the deeds of the Christ, he sent
word by his disciples 3 and said to
him, "Are you he who is to come, or
shall we look for another?" 4 And Jesus
answered them, "Go and tell John
what you hear and see: 5 the blind
receive their sight and the lame walk,
lepers are cleansed and the deaf hear,
and the dead are raised up, and the
poor have good news preached to them.
6 And blessed is he who takes no offense
at me."
7 As they went away, Jesus began
to speak to the crowds concerning
John: "What did you go out into the
wilderness to behold? A reed shaken
by the wind? 8 Why then did you go
out? To see a man[a] clothed in soft
raiment? Behold, those who wear soft
raiment are in kings' houses. 9 Why
then did you go out? To see a prophet?[b]
Yes, I tell you, and more than a
prophet. 10 This is he of whom it is
written,

[y] Or *slave* [z] Greek *Gehenna* [a] Or *What then did you go out to see? A man . . .*
[b] Other ancient authorities read *What then did you go out to see? A prophet?*

10.20: Jn 16.7-11. **10.21:** Mt 10.35-36; Lk 12.52-53. **10.22:** Jn 15.18; Mt 24.9.
10.23: Mt 16.27; 1 Thess 4.17. **10.24:** Lk 6.40; Jn 13.16; 15.20.
10.25: Mt 9.34; 12.24; Mk 3.22; Lk 11.15; 2 Kings 1.2. **10.26-33:** Lk 12.2-9.
10.26: Mk 4.22; Lk 8.17; Eph 5.13. **10.28:** Heb 10.31. **10.31:** Mt 12.12.
10.32: Mk 8.38; Lk 9.26; Rev 3.5; 2 Tim 2.12. **10.34-36:** Lk 12.51-53; Mt 10.21; Mk 13.12; Mic 7.6.
10.37-39: Lk 14.25-27; 17.33; 9.23-24; Mt 16.24-25; Mk 8.34-35; Jn 12.25.
10.40: Lk 10.16; Jn 13.20; Gal 4.14; Mk 9.37; Mt 18.5; Lk 9.48. **10.42:** Mk 9.41; Mt 25.40.
11.1: Mt 7.28; 13.53; 19.1; 26.1. **11.2-19:** Lk 7.18-35. **11.3:** Mk 1.7-8; Hab 2.3; Jn 11.27.
11.5: Is 35.5-6; 61.1; Lk 4.18-19. **11.9:** Mt 14.5; 21.26; Lk 1.76. **11.10:** Mal 3.1; Mk 1.2.

'Behold, I send my messenger before thy face,
who shall prepare thy way before
thee.'
11 Truly, I say to you, among those
born of women there has risen no one
greater than John the Baptist; yet he
who is least in the kingdom of heaven
is greater than he. 12 From the days of
John the Baptist until now the kingdom of heaven has suffered violence,[c]
and men of violence take it by force.
13 For all the prophets and the law
prophesied until John; 14 and if you
are willing to accept it, he is E·lī'jah
who is to come. 15 He who has ears to
hear,[d] let him hear.
16 "But to what shall I compare
this generation? It is like children
sitting in the market places and calling
to their playmates,
17 'We piped to you, and you did not
dance;
we wailed, and you did not mourn.'
18 For John came neither eating nor
drinking, and they say, 'He has a
demon'; 19 the Son of man came eating
and drinking, and they say, 'Behold, a
glutton and a drunkard, a friend of tax
collectors and sinners!' Yet wisdom is
justified by her deeds."[e]
20 Then he began to upbraid the
cities where most of his mighty works
had been done, because they did not
repent. 21 "Woe to you, Chō·rā'zin!
woe to you, Beth-sā'i·då! for if the
mighty works done in you had been
done in Tȳre and Sī'don, they would
have repented long ago in sackcloth
and ashes. 22 But I tell you, it shall be
more tolerable on the day of judgment
for Tȳre and Sī'don than for you.
23 And you, Cȧ·pĕr'nȧ-ŭm, will you
be exalted to heaven? You shall be
brought down to Hades. For if the
mighty works done in you had been
done in Sod'ŏm, it would have remained until this day. 24 But I tell you
that it shall be more tolerable on the
day of judgment for the land of Sod'-
ŏm than for you."
25 At that time Jesus declared, "I
thank thee, Father, Lord of heaven
and earth, that thou hast hidden these
things from the wise and understanding and revealed them to babes; 26 yea,
Father, for such was thy gracious will.[f]
27 All things have been delivered to me
by my Father; and no one knows the
Son except the Father, and no one
knows the Father except the Son and
any one to whom the Son chooses to
reveal him. 28 Come to me, all who
labor and are heavy laden, and I will
give you rest. 29 Take my yoke upon
you, and learn from me; for I am
gentle and lowly in heart, and you will
find rest for your souls. 30 For my yoke
is easy, and my burden is light."

12 At that time Jesus went through
the grainfields on the sabbath;
his disciples were hungry, and they
began to pluck ears of grain and to eat.
2 But when the Pharisees saw it, they
said to him, "Look, your disciples are
doing what is not lawful to do on the
sabbath." 3 He said to them, "Have
you not read what David did, when he
was hungry, and those who were with
him: 4 how he entered the house of
God and ate the bread of the Presence,
which it was not lawful for him to eat
nor for those who were with him, but
only for the priests? 5 Or have you not
read in the law how on the sabbath the
priests in the temple profane the sabbath, and are guiltless? 6 I tell you,
something greater than the temple is
here. 7 And if you had known what this
means, 'I desire mercy, and not sacrifice,' you would not have condemned
the guiltless. 8 For the Son of man is
lord of the sabbath."
9 And he went on from there, and
entered their synagogue. 10 And behold, there was a man with a withered
hand. And they asked him, "Is it lawful to heal on the sabbath?" so that
they might accuse him. 11 He said to
them, "What man of you, if he has one
sheep and it falls into a pit on the
sabbath, will not lay hold of it and lift
it out? 12 Of how much more value is a
man than a sheep! So it is lawful to do

[c] Or *has been coming violently* [d] Other ancient authorities omit *to hear*
[e] Other ancient authorities read *children* (Luke 7.35) [f] Or *so it was well-pleasing before thee*

11.12-13: Lk 16.16. **11.14:** Mal 4.5; Mt 17.10-13; Jn 1.21; Lk 1.17.
11.15: Mt 13.9, 43; Mk 4.23; Rev 13.9; 2.7. **11.16-19:** Lk 7.31-35. **11.20-24:** Lk 10.13-15.
11.24: Mt 10.15; Lk 10.12. **11.25-27:** Lk 10.21-22. **11.25:** 1 Cor 1.26-29.
11.27: Jn 3.35; 5.20; 13.3; 7.29; 10.15; 17.25; Mt 28.18.
11.29: Jn 13.15; Phil 2.5; 1 Pet 2.21; Jer 6.16. **12.1-8:** Mk 2.23-28; Lk 6.1-5. **12.1:** Deut 23.25.
12.3: 1 Sam 21.1-6; Lev 24.9. **12.5:** Num 28.9-10. **12.6:** Mt 12.41-42; Lk 11.31-32.
12.7: Hos 6.6; Mt 9.13. **12.8:** Jn 5.1-18; 7.19-24; 9.1-41. **12.9-14:** Mk 3.1-6; Lk 6.6-11.
12.11: Lk 14.5. **12.12:** Mt 10.31.

good on the sabbath." 13 Then he said
to the man, "Stretch out your hand."
And the man stretched it out, and it
was restored, whole like the other.
14 But the Pharisees went out and took
counsel against him, how to destroy
him.

15 Jesus, aware of this, withdrew
from there. And many followed him,
and he healed them all, 16 and ordered
them not to make him known. 17 This
was to fulfil what was spoken by the
prophet Ī·ṣāi′ȧh:

18 "Behold, my servant whom I have
chosen,
my beloved with whom my soul
is well pleased.
I will put my Spirit upon him,
and he shall proclaim justice to
the Gentiles.
19 He will not wrangle or cry aloud,
nor will any one hear his voice in
the streets;
20 he will not break a bruised reed
or quench a smoldering wick,
till he brings justice to victory;
21 and in his name will the Gentiles
hope."

22 Then a blind and dumb demoniac was brought to him, and he
healed him, so that the dumb man
spoke and saw. 23 And all the people
were amazed, and said, "Can this be
the Son of David?" 24 But when the
Pharisees heard it they said, "It is only
by Bē-el′zė·bul, the prince of demons,
that this man casts out demons."
25 Knowing their thoughts, he said to
them, "Every kingdom divided against
itself is laid waste, and no city or house
divided against itself will stand; 26 and
if Satan casts out Satan, he is divided
against himself; how then will his
kingdom stand? 27 And if I cast out
demons by Bē-el′zė·bul, by whom do
your sons cast them out? Therefore
they shall be your judges. 28 But if it
is by the Spirit of God that I cast out
demons, then the kingdom of God has
come upon you. 29 Or how can one
enter a strong man's house and plunder
his goods, unless he first binds the
strong man? Then indeed he may
plunder his house. 30 He who is not
with me is against me, and he who does
not gather with me scatters. 31 Therefore I tell you, every sin and blasphemy
will be forgiven men, but the blasphemy against the Spirit will not be
forgiven. 32 And whoever says a word
against the Son of man will be forgiven; but whoever speaks against the
Holy Spirit will not be forgiven, either
in this age or in the age to come.

33 "Either make the tree good, and
its fruit good; or make the tree bad,
and its fruit bad; for the tree is known
by its fruit. 34 You brood of vipers!
how can you speak good, when you
are evil? For out of the abundance of
the heart the mouth speaks. 35 The
good man out of his good treasure
brings forth good, and the evil man out
of his evil treasure brings forth evil.
36 I tell you, on the day of judgment
men will render account for every
careless word they utter; 37 for by your
words you will be justified, and by
your words you will be condemned."

38 Then some of the scribes and
Pharisees said to him, "Teacher, we
wish to see a sign from you." 39 But he
answered them, "An evil and adulterous generation seeks for a sign; but no
sign shall be given to it except the sign
of the prophet Jō′nȧh. 40 For as Jō′nȧh
was three days and three nights in the
belly of the whale, so will the Son of
man be three days and three nights in
the heart of the earth. 41 The men of
Nin′ė·vėh will arise at the judgment
with this generation and condemn it;
for they repented at the preaching of
Jō′nȧh, and behold, something greater
than Jonah is here. 42 The queen of
the South will arise at the judgment
with this generation and condemn it;
for she came from the ends of the
earth to hear the wisdom of Solomon,
and behold, something greater than
Solomon is here.

43 "When the unclean spirit has
gone out of a man, he passes through
waterless places seeking rest, but he
finds none. 44 Then he says, 'I will
return to my house from which I
came.' And when he comes he finds
it empty, swept, and put in order.
45 Then he goes and brings with him
seven other spirits more evil than him-

12.14: Mk 14.1; Jn 7.30; 8.59; 10.39; 11.53. **12.15-16:** Mk 3.7-12; Lk 6.17-19. **12.18-21:** Is 42.1-4.
12.22-29: Mk 3.22-27; Lk 11.14-22. **12.22:** Mt 9.32-33. **12.24:** Mt 9.34; 10.25; Jn 7.20; 8.52; 10.20.
12.30: Lk 11.23; Mk 9.40. **12.31-32:** Mk 3.28-30; Lk 12.10.
12.33-35: Lk 6.43-45; Mt 7.16-20; Jas 3.11-12; Mt 15.18.
12.38-42: Lk 11.16, 29-32; Mk 8.11-12; Mt 16.1-4; Jn 2.18; 6.30; 1 Cor 1.22. **12.40:** Jon 1.17.
12.41: Jon 3.5. **12.42:** 1 Kings 10.1-10; 2 Chron 9.1-12. **12.43-45:** Lk 11.24-26; 2 Pet 2.20.

self, and they enter and dwell there;
and the last state of that man becomes
worse than the first. So shall it be also
with this evil generation."

46 While he was still speaking to
the people, behold, his mother and his
brothers stood outside, asking to speak
to him.[g] 48 But he replied to the man
who told him, "Who is my mother,
and who are my brothers?" 49 And
stretching out his hand toward his
disciples, he said, "Here are my mother
and my brothers! 50 For whoever does
the will of my Father in heaven is my
brother, and sister, and mother."

13 That same day Jesus went out
of the house and sat beside the
sea. 2 And great crowds gathered about
him, so that he got into a boat and sat
there; and the whole crowd stood on
the beach. 3 And he told them many
things in parables, saying: "A sower
went out to sow. 4 And as he sowed,
some seeds fell along the path, and the
birds came and devoured them. 5 Other
seeds fell on rocky ground, where they
had not much soil, and immediately
they sprang up, since they had no
depth of soil, 6 but when the sun rose
they were scorched; and since they had
no root they withered away. 7 Other
seeds fell upon thorns, and the thorns
grew up and choked them. 8 Other
seeds fell on good soil and brought
forth grain, some a hundredfold, some
sixty, some thirty. 9 He who has ears,[h]
let him hear."

10 Then the disciples came and said
to him, "Why do you speak to them in
parables?" 11 And he answered them,
"To you it has been given to know the
secrets of the kingdom of heaven, but
to them it has not been given. 12 For
to him who has will more be given,
and he will have abundance; but from
him who has not, even what he has
will be taken away. 13 This is why I
speak to them in parables, because
seeing they do not see, and hearing
they do not hear, nor do they understand. 14 With them indeed is fulfilled
the prophecy of I·sāi′ăh which says:

'You shall indeed hear but never
understand,
and you shall indeed see but
never perceive.
15 For this people's heart has grown
dull,
and their ears are heavy of hearing,
and their eyes they have closed,
lest they should perceive with their
eyes,
and hear with their ears,
and understand with their heart,
and turn for me to heal them.'

16 But blessed are your eyes, for they
see, and your ears, for they hear.
17 Truly, I say to you, many prophets
and righteous men longed to see what
you see, and did not see it, and to hear
what you hear, and did not hear it.

18 "Hear then the parable of the
sower. 19 When any one hears the
word of the kingdom and does not
understand it, the evil one comes and
snatches away what is sown in his
heart; this is what was sown along the
path. 20 As for what was sown on rocky
ground, this is he who hears the word
and immediately receives it with joy;
21 yet he has no root in himself, but
endures for a while, and when tribulation or persecution arises on account
of the word, immediately he falls away.[i]
22 As for what was sown among thorns,
this is he who hears the word, but the
cares of the world and the delight in
riches choke the word, and it proves
unfruitful. 23 As for what was sown on
good soil, this is he who hears the word
and understands it; he indeed bears
fruit, and yields, in one case a hundredfold, in another sixty, and in
another thirty."

24 Another parable he put before
them, saying, "The kingdom of
heaven may be compared to a man
who sowed good seed in his field; 25 but
while men were sleeping, his enemy
came and sowed weeds among the
wheat, and went away. 26 So when the
plants came up and bore grain, then
the weeds appeared also. 27 And the
servants[j] of the householder came and
said to him, 'Sir, did you not sow

[g] Other ancient authorities insert verse 47, *Some one told him, "Your mother and your brothers are standing outside, asking to speak to you"*
[h] Other ancient authorities add here and in verse 43 *to hear* [i] Or *stumbles* [j] Or *slaves*

12.46-50: Mk 3.31-35; Lk 8.19-21. **12.46:** Jn 2.1-12; 19.25-27; 7.1-10; Mk 6.3; 1 Cor 9.5.
12.50: Jn 15.14. **13.1-9:** Mk 4.1-9; Lk 8.4-8; 5.1-3. **13.10-13:** Mk 4.10-12; Lk 8.9-10.
13.12: Mk 4.25; Lk 8.18; Mt 25.29; Lk 19.26.
13.14-15: Is 6.9-10; Mk 8.18; Jn 12.39-41; Acts 28.26-27.
13.16-17: Lk 10.23-24; Jn 8.56; Heb 11.13; 1 Pet 1.10-12. **13.18-23:** Mk 4.13-20; Lk 8.11-15.
13.22: Mt 19.23; 1 Tim 6.9-10, 17. **13.24-30:** Mk 4.26-29.

good seed in your field? How then has
it weeds?' 28 He said to them, 'An
enemy has done this.' The servants[l]
said to him, 'Then do you want us to
go and gather them?' 29 But he said,
'No; lest in gathering the weeds you
root up the wheat along with them.
30 Let both grow together until the
harvest; and at harvest time I will tell
the reapers, Gather the weeds first and
bind them in bundles to be burned,
but gather the wheat into my barn.' "

31 Another parable he put before
them, saying, "The kingdom of heaven
is like a grain of mustard seed which a
man took and sowed in his field; 32 it
is the smallest of all seeds, but when it
has grown it is the greatest of shrubs
and becomes a tree, so that the birds
of the air come and make nests in its
branches."

33 He told them another parable.
"The kingdom of heaven is like leaven
which a woman took and hid in three
measures of meal, till it was all
leavened."

34 All this Jesus said to the crowds
in parables; indeed he said nothing to
them without a parable. 35 This was
to fulfil what was spoken by the
prophet:[k]

"I will open my mouth in parables,
I will utter what has been hidden
since the foundation of the
world."

36 Then he left the crowds and
went into the house. And his disciples
came to him, saying, "Explain to us
the parable of the weeds of the field."
37 He answered, "He who sows the
good seed is the Son of man; 38 the
field is the world, and the good seed
means the sons of the kingdom; the
weeds are the sons of the evil one,
39 and the enemy who sowed them is
the devil; the harvest is the close of the
age, and the reapers are angels. 40 Just
as the weeds are gathered and burned
with fire, so will it be at the close of
the age. 41 The Son of man will send
his angels, and they will gather out of
his kingdom all causes of sin and all
evildoers, 42 and throw them into the
furnace of fire; there men will weep
and gnash their teeth. 43 Then the
righteous will shine like the sun in the
kingdom of their Father. He who has
ears, let him hear.

44 "The kingdom of heaven is like
treasure hidden in a field, which a man
found and covered up; then in his joy
he goes and sells all that he has and
buys that field.

45 "Again, the kingdom of heaven
is like a merchant in search of fine
pearls, 46 who, on finding one pearl of
great value, went and sold all that he
had and bought it.

47 "Again, the kingdom of heaven
is like a net which was thrown into
the sea and gathered fish of every kind;
48 when it was full, men drew it ashore
and sat down and sorted the good into
vessels but threw away the bad. 49 So
it will be at the close of the age. The
angels will come out and separate the
evil from the righteous, 50 and throw
them into the furnace of fire; there
men will weep and gnash their teeth.

51 "Have you understood all this?"
They said to him, "Yes." 52 And he
said to them, "Therefore every scribe
who has been trained for the kingdom
of heaven is like a householder who
brings out of his treasure what is new
and what is old."

53 And when Jesus had finished
these parables, he went away from
there, 54 and coming to his own
country he taught them in their
synagogue, so that they were astonished, and said, "Where did this man
get this wisdom and these mighty
works? 55 Is not this the carpenter's
son? Is not his mother called Mary?
And are not his brothers James and
Joseph and Simon and Judas? 56 And
are not all his sisters with us? Where
then did this man get all this?" 57 And
they took offense at him. But Jesus
said to them, "A prophet is not without
honor except in his own country and
in his own house." 58 And he did not do
many mighty works there, because of
their unbelief.

14 At that time Her'od the tetrarch
heard about the fame of Jesus;
2 and he said to his servants, "This is
John the Baptist, he has been raised

[l] Or *slaves* [k] Other ancient authorities read *the prophet Isaiah*

13.31-32: Mk 4.30-32; Lk 13.18-19; Mt 17.20. **13.33:** Lk 13.20-21; Gal 5.9; Gen 18.6.
13.34: Mk 4.33-34; Jn 10.6; 16.25. **13.35:** Ps 78.2. **13.38:** Jn 8.44; 1 Jn 3.10. **13.41:** Mt 24.31.
13.42: Mt 13.50; 8.12; 22.13; 24.51; 25.30; Lk 13.28. **13.47-50:** Mt 13.40-42.
13.53: Mt 7.28; 11.1; 19.1; 26.1. **13.54-58:** Mk 6.1-6; Lk 4.16-30.
14.1-2: Mk 6.14-16; Lk 9.7-9; Mk 8.28.

from the dead; that is why these powers
are at work in him." 3 For Her'od had
seized John and bound him and put
him in prison, for the sake of He-rō'-
di-as, his brother Philip's wife;[l] 4 because John said to him, "It is not lawful for you to have her." 5And though
he wanted to put him to death, he
feared the people, because they held
him to be a prophet. 6 But when
Her'od's birthday came, the daughter
of He-rō'di-as danced before the company, and pleased Herod, 7 so that he
promised with an oath to give her
whatever she might ask. 8 Prompted
by her mother, she said, "Give me the
head of John the Baptist here on a
platter." 9And the king was sorry; but
because of his oaths and his guests he
commanded it to be given; 10 he sent
and had John beheaded in the prison,
11 and his head was brought on a
platter and given to the girl, and she
brought it to her mother. 12And his
disciples came and took the body and
buried it; and they went and told
Jesus.

13 Now when Jesus heard this, he
withdrew from there in a boat to a
lonely place apart. But when the
crowds heard it, they followed him on
foot from the towns. 14As he went
ashore he saw a great throng; and he
had compassion on them, and healed
their sick. 15 When it was evening, the
disciples came to him and said, "This
is a lonely place, and the day is now
over; send the crowds away to go into
the villages and buy food for themselves." 16 Jesus said, "They need not
go away; you give them something to
eat." 17 They said to him, "We have
only five loaves here and two fish."
18And he said, "Bring them here to
me." 19 Then he ordered the crowds
to sit down on the grass; and taking
the five loaves and the two fish he
looked up to heaven, and blessed, and
broke and gave the loaves to the
disciples, and the disciples gave them
to the crowds. 20And they all ate and
were satisfied. And they took up
twelve baskets full of the broken pieces
left over. 21And those who ate were
about five thousand men, besides
women and children.

22 Then he made the disciples get
into the boat and go before him to the
other side, while he dismissed the
crowds. 23And after he had dismissed
the crowds, he went up into the hills
by himself to pray. When evening
came, he was there alone, 24 but the
boat by this time was many furlongs
distant from the land,[m] beaten by the
waves; for the wind was against them.
25And in the fourth watch of the night
he came to them, walking on the sea.
26 But when the disciples saw him
walking on the sea, they were terrified,
saying, "It is a ghost!" And they cried
out for fear. 27 But immediately he
spoke to them, saying, "Take heart,
it is I; have no fear."

28 And Peter answered him, "Lord,
if it is you, bid me come to you on the
water." 29 He said, "Come." So Peter
got out of the boat and walked on the
water and came to Jesus; 30 but when
he saw the wind,[n] he was afraid, and
beginning to sink he cried out, "Lord,
save me." 31 Jesus immediately reached
out his hand and caught him, saying
to him, "O man of little faith, why did
you doubt?" 32And when they got into
the boat, the wind ceased. 33And those
in the boat worshiped him, saying,
"Truly you are the Son of God."

34 And when they had crossed
over, they came to land at Gen-nes'a-
ret. 35And when the men of that place
recognized him, they sent round to all
that region and brought to him all that
were sick, 36 and besought him that
they might only touch the fringe of his
garment; and as many as touched it
were made well.

15 Then Pharisees and scribes
came to Jesus from Jerusalem
and said, 2 "Why do your disciples
transgress the tradition of the elders?
For they do not wash their hands when
they eat." 3 He answered them, "And
why do you transgress the commandment of God for the sake of your
tradition? 4 For God commanded,
'Honor your father and your mother,'
and, 'He who speaks evil of father or

[l] Other ancient authorities read *his brother's wife* [m] Other ancient authorities read *was out on the sea*
[n] Other ancient authorities read *strong wind*

14.3-4: Mk 6.17-18; Lk 3.19-20; Lev 18.16; 20.21. **14.5-12:** Mk 6.19-29.
14.13-21: Mk 6.32-44; Lk 9.10-17; Jn 6.1-13; Mt 15.32-38. **14.19:** Mk 14.22; Lk 24.30.
14.22-23: Mk 6.45-46; Jn 6.15-17. **14.24-33:** Mk 6.47-52; Jn 6.16-21. **14.26:** Lk 24.37.
14.29: Jn 21.7. **14.31:** Mt 6.30; 8.26; 16.8. **14.33:** Mt 28.9, 17. **14.34-36:** Mk 6.53-56; Jn 6.22-26.
14.36: Mk 3.10; Num 15.38; Mt 9.20. **15.1-20:** Mk 7.1-23.
15.4: Ex 20.12; Deut 5.16; Ex 21.17; Lev 20.9.

mother, let him surely die.' 5 But you
say, 'If any one tells his father or his
mother, What you would have gained
from me is given to God,[o] he need not
honor his father.' 6 So for the sake of
your tradition, you have made void
the word[p] of God. 7 You hypocrites!
Well did Ī·ṡāi'ȧh prophesy of you,
when he said:

8 'This people honors me with their
lips,
but their heart is far from me;
9 in vain do they worship me,
teaching as doctrines the precepts
of men.' "

10 And he called the people to him
and said to them, "Hear and understand: 11 not what goes into the mouth
defiles a man, but what comes out of
the mouth, this defiles a man." 12 Then
the disciples came and said to him,
"Do you know that the Pharisees were
offended when they heard this saying?" 13 He answered, "Every plant
which my heavenly Father has not
planted will be rooted up. 14 Let them
alone; they are blind guides. And if a
blind man leads a blind man, both will
fall into a pit." 15 But Peter said to
him, "Explain the parable to us."
16 And he said, "Are you also still without understanding? 17 Do you not see
that whatever goes into the mouth
passes into the stomach, and so passes
on?[q] 18 But what comes out of the
mouth proceeds from the heart, and
this defiles a man. 19 For out of the
heart come evil thoughts, murder,
adultery, fornication, theft, false witness, slander. 20 These are what defile
a man; but to eat with unwashed hands
does not defile a man."

21 And Jesus went away from there
and withdrew to the district of Tȳre
and Sī'don. 22 And behold, a Canaanite
woman from that region came out and
cried, "Have mercy on me, O Lord,
Son of David; my daughter is severely
possessed by a demon." 23 But he did
not answer her a word. And his
disciples came and begged him, saying,
"Send her away, for she is crying after
us." 24 He answered, "I was sent only
to the lost sheep of the house of Israel."
25 But she came and knelt before him,
saying, "Lord, help me." 26 And he
answered, "It is not fair to take the
children's bread and throw it to the
dogs." 27 She said, "Yes, Lord, yet
even the dogs eat the crumbs that fall
from their master's table." 28 Then
Jesus answered her, "O woman, great
is your faith! Be it done for you as you
desire." And her daughter was healed
instantly.

29 And Jesus went on from there
and passed along the Sea of Galilee.
And he went up into the hills, and sat
down there. 30 And great crowds came
to him, bringing with them the lame,
the maimed, the blind, the dumb, and
many others, and they put them at his
feet, and he healed them, 31 so that the
throng wondered, when they saw the
dumb speaking, the maimed whole,
the lame walking, and the blind seeing;
and they glorified the God of Israel.

32 Then Jesus called his disciples
to him and said, "I have compassion
on the crowd, because they have been
with me now three days, and have
nothing to eat; and I am unwilling to
send them away hungry, lest they faint
on the way." 33 And the disciples said
to him, "Where are we to get bread
enough in the desert to feed so great a
crowd?" 34 And Jesus said to them,
"How many loaves have you?" They
said, "Seven, and a few small fish."
35 And commanding the crowd to sit
down on the ground, 36 he took the
seven loaves and the fish, and having
given thanks he broke them and gave
them to the disciples, and the disciples
gave them to the crowds. 37 And they
all ate and were satisfied; and they
took up seven baskets full of the
broken pieces left over. 38 Those who
ate were four thousand men, besides
women and children. 39 And sending
away the crowds, he got into the boat
and went to the region of Mag'ȧ·dan.

16 And the Pharisees and Sad'dū-
ċeeṡ came, and to test him they
asked him to show them a sign from
heaven. 2 He answered them,[r] "When
it is evening, you say, 'It will be fair
weather; for the sky is red.' 3 And in

[o] Or *an offering* [p] Other ancient authorities read *law* [q] Or *is evacuated*
[r] Other ancient authorities omit the following words to the end of verse 3

15.8-9: Is 29.13. **15.11:** Acts 10.14-15; 1 Tim 4.3. **15.13:** Is 60.21; Jn 15.2.
15.14: Lk 6.39; Mt 23.16, 24; Rom 2.19. **15.19:** Gal 5.19-21; 1 Cor 6.9-10; Rom 14.14.
15.21-28: Mk 7.24-30. **15.24:** Mt 10.6, 23. **15.25:** Mt 8.2; 18.26; 20.20; Jn 9.38.
15.28: Mt 9.22, 28; Mk 10.52; Lk 7.50; 17.19. **15.29-31:** Mk 7.31-37.
15.32-39: Mk 8.1-10; Mt 14.13-21. **15.32:** Mt 9.36.
16.1-4: Mk 8.11-12; Lk 11.16, 29; 12.54-56; Mt 12.38-39; Jn 2.18; 6.30.

the morning, 'It will be stormy today,
for the sky is red and threatening.'
You know how to interpret the appearance of the sky, but you cannot
interpret the signs of the times. 4 An
evil and adulterous generation seeks
for a sign, but no sign shall be given to
it except the sign of Jō'nah." So he
left them and departed.

5 When the disciples reached the
other side, they had forgotten to bring
any bread. 6 Jesus said to them, "Take
heed and beware of the leaven of the
Pharisees and Sad'dū·cees." 7 And they
discussed it among themselves, saying,
"We brought no bread." 8 But Jesus,
aware of this, said, "O men of little
faith, why do you discuss among yourselves the fact that you have no bread?
9 Do you not yet perceive? Do you not
remember the five loaves of the five
thousand, and how many baskets you
gathered? 10 Or the seven loaves of the
four thousand, and how many baskets
you gathered? 11 How is it that you
fail to perceive that I did not speak
about bread? Beware of the leaven of
the Pharisees and Sad'dū·cees."
12 Then they understood that he did
not tell them to beware of the leaven
of bread, but of the teaching of the
Pharisees and Sad'dū·cees.

13 Now when Jesus came into the
district of Caes·ȧ·rē'ȧ Phi·lip'pī, he
asked his disciples, "Who do men say
that the Son of man is?" 14 And they
said, "Some say John the Baptist,
others say E·lī'jah, and others Jeremiah
or one of the prophets." 15 He said to
them, "But who do you say that I am?"
16 Simon Peter replied, "You are the
Christ, the Son of the living God."
17 And Jesus answered him, "Blessed
are you, Simon Bär-Jō'nȧ! For flesh
and blood has not revealed this to you,
but my Father who is in heaven. 18 And
I tell you, you are Peter,[s] and on this
rock[t] I will build my church, and the
powers of death[u] shall not prevail
against it. 19 I will give you the keys of
the kingdom of heaven, and whatever
you bind on earth shall be bound in
heaven, and whatever you loose on
earth shall be loosed in heaven."
20 Then he strictly charged the disciples to tell no one that he was the
Christ.

21 From that time Jesus began to
show his disciples that he must go to
Jerusalem and suffer many things from
the elders and chief priests and scribes,
and be killed, and on the third day be
raised. 22 And Peter took him and began to rebuke him, saying, "God
forbid, Lord! This shall never happen
to you." 23 But he turned and said to
Peter, "Get behind me, Satan! You
are a hindrance[v] to me; for you are not
on the side of God, but of men."

24 Then Jesus told his disciples,
"If any man would come after me, let
him deny himself and take up his
cross and follow me. 25 For whoever
would save his life will lose it, and
whoever loses his life for my sake will
find it. 26 For what will it profit a man,
if he gains the whole world and forfeits
his life? Or what shall a man give in
return for his life? 27 For the Son of
man is to come with his angels in the
glory of his Father, and then he will
repay every man for what he has done.
28 Truly, I say to you, there are some
standing here who will not taste death
before they see the Son of man coming
in his kingdom."

17 And after six days Jesus took
with him Peter and James and
John his brother, and led them up a
high mountain apart. 2 And he was
transfigured before them, and his face
shone like the sun, and his garments
became white as light. 3 And behold,
there appeared to them Moses and
E·lī'jah, talking with him. 4 And Peter
said to Jesus, "Lord, it is well that we
are here; if you wish, I will make three
booths here, one for you and one for
Moses and one for E·lī'jah." 5 He was
still speaking, when lo, a bright cloud
overshadowed them, and a voice from
the cloud said, "This is my beloved

[s] Greek *Petros* [t] Greek *petra* [u] Greek *the gates of Hades* [v] Greek *stumbling block*

16.4: Jon 3.4-5. **16.5-12:** Mk 8.13-21. **16.6:** Lk 12.1. **16.8:** Mt 6.30; 8.26; 14.31. **16.9:** Mt 14.17-21.
16.10: Mt 15.34-38. **16.13-16:** Mk 8.27-30; Lk 9.18-21. **16.14:** Mt 14.2; Mk 6.15; Lk 9.7-8; Jn 1.21.
16.16: Mt 1.16; Jn 11.27; 1.49. **16.17:** 1 Cor 15.50; Gal 1.16; Eph 6.12; Heb 2.14.
16.18: Jn 1.40-42; 21.15-17; 1 Cor 15.5. **16.19:** Is 22.22; Rev 1.18; Mt 18.18; Jn 20.23.
16.20: Mt 8.4; Mk 3.12; 5.43; 7.36; 9.9. **16.21-28:** Mk 8.31-9.1; Lk 9.22-27.
16.21: Mt 17.22-23; 20.17-19; Lk 17.25; Mt 17.12; 26.2. **16.23:** Mt 4.10.
16.24-26: Mt 10.38-39; Lk 14.27; 17.33; Jn 12.25.
16.27: Mt 10.33; Lk 12.9; 1 Jn 2.28; Rom 2.6; Rev 22.12.
16.28: Mt 10.23; 1 Cor 16.22; 1 Thess 4.15-18; Rev 1.7; Jas 5.7.
17.1-9: Mk 9.2-10; Lk 9.28-36; 2 Pet 1.17-18. **17.1:** Mt 26.37; Mk 5.37; 13.3.
17.5: Mt 3.17; Is 42.1; Ps 2.7; Jn 12.28.

Son,[w] with whom I am well pleased;
listen to him." 6 When the disciples
heard this, they fell on their faces, and
were filled with awe. 7 But Jesus came
and touched them, saying, "Rise, and
have no fear." 8 And when they lifted
up their eyes, they saw no one but
Jesus only.

9 And as they were coming down
the mountain, Jesus commanded them,
"Tell no one the vision, until the Son
of man is raised from the dead." 10 And
the disciples asked him, "Then why do
the scribes say that first E·lī'jȧh must
come?" 11 He replied, "E·lī'jȧh does
come, and he is to restore all things;
12 but I tell you that E·lī'jȧh has
already come, and they did not know
him, but did to him whatever they
pleased. So also the Son of man will
suffer at their hands." 13 Then the
disciples understood that he was
speaking to them of John the Baptist.

14 And when they came to the
crowd, a man came up to him and
kneeling before him said, 15 "Lord,
have mercy on my son, for he is an
epileptic and he suffers terribly; for
often he falls into the fire, and often
into the water. 16 And I brought him
to your disciples, and they could not
heal him." 17 And Jesus answered, "O
faithless and perverse generation, how
long am I to be with you? How long
am I to bear with you? Bring him here
to me." 18 And Jesus rebuked him, and
the demon came out of him, and the
boy was cured instantly. 19 Then the
disciples came to Jesus privately and
said, "Why could we not cast it out?"
20 He said to them, "Because of your
little faith. For truly, I say to you, if
you have faith as a grain of mustard
seed, you will say to this mountain,
'Move hence to yonder place,' and it
will move; and nothing will be impossible to you."[x]

22 As they were gathering[y] in
Galilee, Jesus said to them, "The Son
of man is to be delivered into the
hands of men, 23 and they will kill him,
and he will be raised on the third day."
And they were greatly distressed.

24 When they came to Cȧ·pĕr'nȧ·ŭm, the collectors of the half-shekel
tax went up to Peter and said, "Does
not your teacher pay the tax?" 25 He
said, "Yes." And when he came home,
Jesus spoke to him first, saying, "What
do you think, Simon? From whom do
kings of the earth take toll or tribute?
From their sons or from others?"
26 And when he said, "From others,"
Jesus said to him, "Then the sons are
free. 27 However, not to give offense
to them, go to the sea and cast a hook,
and take the first fish that comes up,
and when you open its mouth you will
find a shekel; take that and give it to
them for me and for yourself."

18 At that time the disciples came
to Jesus, saying, "Who is the
greatest in the kingdom of heaven?"
2 And calling to him a child, he put
him in the midst of them, 3 and said,
"Truly, I say to you, unless you turn
and become like children, you will
never enter the kingdom of heaven.
4 Whoever humbles himself like this
child, he is the greatest in the kingdom
of heaven.

5 "Whoever receives one such child
in my name receives me; 6 but whoever causes one of these little ones who
believe in me to sin,[z] it would be better
for him to have a great millstone
fastened round his neck and to be
drowned in the depth of the sea.

7 "Woe to the world for temptations
to sin![a] For it is necessary that temptations come, but woe to the man by
whom the temptation comes! 8 And if
your hand or your foot causes you to
sin,[z] cut it off and throw it from you;
it is better for you to enter life maimed
or lame than with two hands or two
feet to be thrown into the eternal fire.
9 And if your eye causes you to sin,[z]
pluck it out and throw it from you; it
is better for you to enter life with one

[w] Or *my Son, my* (or *the*) *Beloved*
[x] Other ancient authorities insert verse 21, "*But this kind never comes out except by prayer and fasting*"
[y] Other ancient authorities read *abode* [z] Greek *causes . . . to stumble* [a] Greek *stumbling blocks*

17.9: Mt 8.4; 16.20; Mk 3.12; 5.43; 7.36. **17.10-13:** Mk 9.11-13; Mt 11.14; Mal 4.5.
17.12: Mt 16.21; 17.22; 20.17; 26.2; Lk 17.25. **17.14-18:** Mk 9.14-27; Lk 9.37-43.
17.19-21: Mk 9.28-29. **17.20:** Lk 17.6; Mt 21.21; Mk 11.22-23; 1 Cor 13.2; Mk 9.23.
17.22-23: Mk 9.30-32; Lk 9.43-45; Mt 16.21; 20.17-19; 26.2. **17.24:** Ex 30.13; 38.26.
17.25: Rom 13.7; Mt 22.17-21.
17.27: Mt 5.29; 18.6-9; Jn 6.61; 1 Cor 8.13.
18.1-5: Mk 9.33-37; Lk 9.46-48. **18.3:** Mk 10.15; Lk 18.17; 1 Pet 2.2.
18.5: Mt 10.40; Lk 10.16; Jn 13.20. **18.6-9:** Mk 9.42-48; Lk 17.1-2. **18.8-9:** Mt 5.29-30; 17.27.

eye than with two eyes to be thrown
into the hell[b] of fire.
10 "See that you do not despise one
of these little ones; for I tell you that
in heaven their angels always behold
the face of my Father who is in heaven.[c]
12 What do you think? If a man has a
hundred sheep, and one of them has
gone astray, does he not leave the
ninety-nine on the hills and go in
search of the one that went astray?
13 And if he finds it, truly, I say to you,
he rejoices over it more than over the
ninety-nine that never went astray.
14 So it is not the will of my[d] Father
who is in heaven that one of these little
ones should perish.
15 "If your brother sins against
you, go and tell him his fault, between
you and him alone. If he listens to
you, you have gained your brother.
16 But if he does not listen, take one or
two others along with you, that every
word may be confirmed by the evidence of two or three witnesses. 17 If
he refuses to listen to them, tell it to
the church; and if he refuses to listen
even to the church, let him be to you
as a Gentile and a tax collector.
18 Truly, I say to you, whatever you
bind on earth shall be bound in heav-
en, and whatever you loose on earth
shall be loosed in heaven. 19 Again I
say to you, if two of you agree on
earth about anything they ask, it will
be done for them by my Father in
heaven. 20 For where two or three are
gathered in my name, there am I in
the midst of them."
21 Then Peter came up and said to
him, "Lord, how often shall my
brother sin against me, and I forgive
him? As many as seven times?" 22 Jesus
said to him, "I do not say to you seven
times, but seventy times seven.[e]
23 "Therefore the kingdom of
heaven may be compared to a king
who wished to settle accounts with his
servants. 24 When he began the reckoning, one was brought to him who
owed him ten thousand talents;[f] 25 and
as he could not pay, his lord ordered
him to be sold, with his wife and
children and all that he had, and payment to be made. 26 So the servant fell
on his knees, imploring him, 'Lord,
have patience with me, and I will pay
you everything.' 27 And out of pity for
him the lord of that servant released
him and forgave him the debt. 28 But
that same servant, as he went out,
came upon one of his fellow servants
who owed him a hundred denarii;[g] and
seizing him by the throat he said, 'Pay
what you owe.' 29 So his fellow servant
fell down and besought him, 'Have
patience with me, and I will pay you.'
30 He refused and went and put him
in prison till he should pay the debt.
31 When his fellow servants saw what
had taken place, they were greatly distressed, and they went and reported
to their lord all that had taken place.
32 Then his lord summoned him and
said to him, 'You wicked servant! I
forgave you all that debt because you
besought me; 33 and should not you
have had mercy on your fellow servant, as I had mercy on you?' 34 And in
anger his lord delivered him to the
jailers,[h] till he should pay all his debt.
35 So also my heavenly Father will do
to every one of you, if you do not forgive your brother from your heart."

19 Now when Jesus had finished
these sayings, he went away from
Galilee and entered the region of
Judea beyond the Jordan; 2 and large
crowds followed him, and he healed
them there.
3 And Pharisees came up to him
and tested him by asking, "Is it lawful
to divorce one's wife for any cause?"
4 He answered, "Have you not read
that he who made them from the
beginning made them male and female, 5 and said, 'For this reason a
man shall leave his father and mother
and be joined to his wife, and the two
shall become one'?[i] 6 So they are no
longer two but one.[i] What therefore
God has joined together, let no man
put asunder." 7 They said to him,

[b] Greek *Gehenna* [c] Other ancient authorities add verse 11, *For the Son of man came to save the lost*
[d] Other ancient authorities read *your* [e] Or *seventy-seven times*
[f] This talent was probably worth about a thousand dollars
[g] The denarius was worth about twenty cents [h] Greek *torturers* [i] Greek *one flesh*
18.10: Acts 12.11. **18.11:** Lk 19.10. **18.12-14:** Lk 15.3-7.
18.15-17: Lk 17.3; 1 Cor 6.1-6; Gal 6.1; Jas 5.19-20; Lev 19.17; Deut 19.15.
18.18: Mt 16.19; Jn 20.23. **18.19-20:** Mt 7.7; 21.22; Jas 1.5-7; 1 Jn 5.14; Jn 14.13.
18.21-22: Lk 17.4; Gen 4.24. **18.23:** Mt 25.19. **18.25:** Lk 7.42. **18.26:** Mt 8.2. **18.35:** Mt 6.14.
19.1: Mt 7.28; 11.1; 13.53; 26.1. **19.1-9:** Mk 10.1-12. **19.5:** Gen 1.27; 2.24; Eph 5.31; 1 Cor 6.16.
19.7: Deut 24.1-4.

"Why then did Moses command one
to give a certificate of divorce, and to
put her away?" 8 He said to them,
"For your hardness of heart Moses
allowed you to divorce your wives, but
from the beginning it was not so. 9 And
I say to you: whoever divorces his
wife, except for unchastity,[j] and
marries another, commits adultery."[k]

10 The disciples said to him, "If
such is the case of a man with his wife,
it is not expedient to marry." 11 But
he said to them, "Not all men can
receive this precept, but only those
to whom it is given. 12 For there are
eunuchs who have been so from birth,
and there are eunuchs who have been
made eunuchs by men, and there are
eunuchs who have made themselves
eunuchs for the sake of the kingdom
of heaven. He who is able to receive
this, let him receive it."

13 Then children were brought to
him that he might lay his hands on
them and pray. The disciples rebuked
the people; 14 but Jesus said, "Let the
children come to me, and do not hinder
them; for to such belongs the kingdom
of heaven." 15 And he laid his hands
on them and went away.

16 And behold, one came up to him,
saying, "Teacher, what good deed
must I do, to have eternal life?" 17 And
he said to him, "Why do you ask me
about what is good? One there is who
is good. If you would enter life, keep
the commandments." 18 He said to
him, "Which?" And Jesus said, "You
shall not kill, You shall not commit
adultery, You shall not steal, You
shall not bear false witness, 19 Honor
your father and mother, and, You
shall love your neighbor as yourself."
20 The young man said to him, "All
these I have observed; what do I still
lack?" 21 Jesus said to him, "If you
would be perfect, go, sell what you
possess and give to the poor, and you
will have treasure in heaven; and
come, follow me." 22 When the young
man heard this he went away sorrowful; for he had great possessions.

23 And Jesus said to his disciples,
"Truly, I say to you, it will be hard
for a rich man to enter the kingdom of
heaven. 24 Again I tell you, it is easier
for a camel to go through the eye of a
needle than for a rich man to enter the
kingdom of God." 25 When the disciples heard this they were greatly
astonished, saying, "Who then can be
saved?" 26 But Jesus looked at them
and said to them, "With men this is
impossible, but with God all things are
possible." 27 Then Peter said in reply,
"Lo, we have left everything and followed you. What then shall we have?"
28 Jesus said to them, "Truly, I say
to you, in the new world, when the
Son of man shall sit on his glorious
throne, you who have followed me will
also sit on twelve thrones, judging the
twelve tribes of Israel. 29 And every
one who has left houses or brothers or
sisters or father or mother or children
or lands, for my name's sake, will
receive a hundredfold,[l] and inherit
eternal life. 30 But many that are first
will be last, and the last first.

20 "For the kingdom of heaven is
like a householder who went out
early in the morning to hire laborers
for his vineyard. 2 After agreeing with
the laborers for a denarius[m] a day, he
sent them into his vineyard. 3 And going out about the third hour he saw
others standing idle in the market
place; 4 and to them he said, 'You go
into the vineyard too, and whatever
is right I will give you.' So they went.
5 Going out again about the sixth
hour and the ninth hour, he did the
same. 6 And about the eleventh hour
he went out and found others standing; and he said to them, 'Why do you
stand here idle all day?' 7 They said to
him, 'Because no one has hired us.'
He said to them, 'You go into the
vineyard too.' 8 And when evening
came, the owner of the vineyard said
to his steward, 'Call the laborers and
pay them their wages, beginning with
the last, up to the first.' 9 And when
those hired about the eleventh hour

[j] Other ancient authorities, after *unchastity*, read *makes her commit adultery*
[k] Other ancient authorities insert *and he who marries a divorced woman commits adultery*
[l] Other ancient authorities read *manifold* [m] The denarius was worth about twenty cents

19.9: Mt 5.32; Lk 16.18; 1 Cor 7.10-13. **19.11:** 1 Cor 7.7-9.
19.13-15: Mk 10.13-16; Lk 18.15-17; Mt 18.2-3; 1 Cor 14.20. **19.16-22:** Mk 10.17-22; Lk 18.18-23.
19.16: Lk 10.25; Lev 18.5. **19.18:** Ex 20.12-16; Deut 5.16-20; Rom 13.9; Jas 2.11.
19.19: Lev 19.18; Mt 22.39. **19.21:** Lk 12.33; Acts 2.45; 4.34; Mt 6.20.
19.23-26: Mk 10.23-27; Lk 18.24-27. **19.26:** Gen 18 14; Job 42.2.
19.27-30: Mk 10.28-31; Lk 18.28-30; Mt 4 18-22. **19.28:** Lk 22.30; Mt 20.21; Rev 3.21.
19.30: Mt 20.16; Lk 13.30. **20.1:** Mt 21.28, 33. **20.8:** Lev 19.13; Deut 24.15.

came, each of them received a denarius. 10 Now when the first came, they
thought they would receive more; but
each of them also received a denarius.
11 And on receiving it they grumbled
at the householder, 12 saying, 'These
last worked only one hour, and you
have made them equal to us who have
borne the burden of the day and the
scorching heat.' 13 But he replied to
one of them, 'Friend, I am doing you
no wrong; did you not agree with me
for a denarius? 14 Take what belongs
to you, and go; I choose to give to this
last as I give to you. 15 Am I not
allowed to do what I choose with what
belongs to me? Or do you begrudge
my generosity?[n] 16 So the last will be
first, and the first last."

17 And as Jesus was going up to
Jerusalem, he took the twelve disciples
aside, and on the way he said to them,
18 "Behold, we are going up to Jerusalem; and the Son of man will be
delivered to the chief priests and
scribes, and they will condemn him to
death, 19 and deliver him to the Gentiles to be mocked and scourged and
crucified, and he will be raised on the
third day."

20 Then the mother of the sons of
Zeb'ė·dee came up to him with her
sons, and kneeling before him she
asked him for something. 21 And he
said to her, "What do you want?" She
said to him, "Command that these
two sons of mine may sit, one at your
right hand and one at your left, in your
kingdom." 22 But Jesus answered,
"You do not know what you are asking. Are you able to drink the cup that
I am to drink?" They said to him,
"We are able." 23 He said to them,
"You will drink my cup, but to sit at
my right hand and at my left is not
mine to grant, but it is for those for
whom it has been prepared by my
Father." 24 And when the ten heard it,
they were indignant at the two brothers. 25 But Jesus called them to him
and said, "You know that the rulers of
the Gentiles lord it over them, and
their great men exercise authority over
them. 26 It shall not be so among you;
but whoever would be great among
you must be your servant, 27 and whoever would be first among you must be
your slave; 28 even as the Son of man
came not to be served but to serve,
and to give his life as a ransom for
many."

29 And as they went out of Jericho,
a great crowd followed him. 30 And
behold, two blind men sitting by the
roadside, when they heard that Jesus
was passing by, cried out,[o] "Have
mercy on us, Son of David!" 31 The
crowd rebuked them, telling them to
be silent; but they cried out the more,
"Lord, have mercy on us, Son of
David!" 32 And Jesus stopped and
called them, saying, "What do you
want me to do for you?" 33 They said
to him, "Lord, let our eyes be
opened." 34 And Jesus in pity touched
their eyes, and immediately they received their sight and followed him.

21 And when they drew near to
Jerusalem and came to Beth'-
phȧ·ḡē, to the Mount of Olives, then
Jesus sent two disciples, 2 saying to
them, "Go into the village opposite
you, and immediately you will find an
ass tied, and a colt with her; untie
them and bring them to me. 3 If any
one says anything to you, you shall
say, 'The Lord has need of them,' and
he will send them immediately."
4 This took place to fulfil what was
spoken by the prophet, saying,
5 "Tell the daughter of Zion,
Behold, your king is coming to you,
humble, and mounted on an ass,
and on a colt, the foal of an ass."
6 The disciples went and did as Jesus
had directed them; 7 they brought the
ass and the colt, and put their garments on them, and he sat thereon.
8 Most of the crowd spread their garments on the road, and others cut
branches from the trees and spread
them on the road. 9 And the crowds
that went before him and that followed
him shouted, "Hosanna to the Son of
David! Blessed is he who comes in the
name of the Lord! Hosanna in the
highest!" 10 And when he entered
Jerusalem, all the city was stirred,

[n] Or *is your eye evil because I am good?* [o] Other ancient authorities insert *Lord*

20.13: Mt 22.12; 26.50. **20.15:** Mt 6.23; Mk 7.22; Deut 15.9. **20.16:** Lk 13.30; Mt 19.30; Mk 10.31.
20.17-19: Mk 10.32-34; Lk 18.31-34; Mt 16.21; 17.12, 22-23; 26.2. **20.20-24:** Mk 10.35-41.
20.20: Mt 8.2; 9.18; 15.25; 18.26; Jn 9.38. **20.21:** Mt 19.28. **20.22:** Mt 26.39; Jn 18.11.
20.23: Acts 12.2; Rev 1.9; Mt 13.11. **20.25-28:** Mk 10.42-45; Lk 22.25-27.
20.26: Mt 23.11; Mk 9.35; Lk 9.48. **20.28:** Mt 26.28; 1 Tim 2.5-6; Jn 13.15-16; Tit 2.14; 1 Pet 1.18.
20.29-34: Mk 10.46-52; Lk 18.35-43; Mt 9.27-31. **21.1-9:** Mk 11.1-10; Lk 19.29-38; Jn 12.12-18.
21.5: Is 62.11; Zech 9.9. **21.8:** 2 Kings 9.13. **21.9:** Ps 118.26; Lk 2.14: Mt 21.15; 23.39.

saying, "Who is this?" 11 And the
crowds said, "This is the prophet
Jesus from Nazareth of Galilee."
12 And Jesus entered the temple of
God[p] and drove out all who sold and
bought in the temple, and he overturned the tables of the money-
changers and the seats of those who
sold pigeons. 13 He said to them, "It
is written, 'My house shall be called a
house of prayer'; but you make it a
den of robbers."
14 And the blind and the lame came
to him in the temple, and he healed
them. 15 But when the chief priests
and the scribes saw the wonderful
things that he did, and the children
crying out in the temple, "Hosanna to
the Son of David!" they were indignant; 16 and they said to him, "Do you
hear what these are saying?" And
Jesus said to them, "Yes; have you
never read,

'Out of the mouth of babes and
sucklings
thou hast brought perfect praise'?"

17 And leaving them, he went out of
the city to Beth'a·ny and lodged there.
18 In the morning, as he was returning to the city, he was hungry.
19 And seeing a fig tree by the wayside
he went to it, and found nothing on it
but leaves only. And he said to it,
"May no fruit ever come from you
again!" And the fig tree withered at
once. 20 When the disciples saw it they
marveled, saying, "How did the fig
tree wither at once?" 21 And Jesus
answered them, "Truly, I say to you,
if you have faith and never doubt, you
will not only do what has been done
to the fig tree, but even if you say to
this mountain, 'Be taken up and cast
into the sea,' it will be done. 22 And
whatever you ask in prayer, you will
receive, if you have faith."
23 And when he entered the temple,
the chief priests and the elders of the
people came up to him as he was
teaching, and said, "By what authority are you doing these things, and
who gave you this authority?" 24 Jesus
answered them, "I also will ask you a
question; and if you tell me the answer, then I also will tell you by what
authority I do these things. 25 The
baptism of John, whence was it? From
heaven or from men?" And they
argued with one another, "If we say,
'From heaven,' he will say to us, 'Why
then did you not believe him?' 26 But
if we say, 'From men,' we are afraid of
the multitude; for all hold that John
was a prophet." 27 So they answered
Jesus, "We do not know." And he
said to them, "Neither will I tell you
by what authority I do these things.
28 "What do you think? A man had
two sons; and he went to the first and
said, 'Son, go and work in the vineyard today.' 29 And he answered, 'I will
not'; but afterward he repented and
went. 30 And he went to the second and
said the same; and he answered, 'I go,
sir,' but did not go. 31 Which of the
two did the will of his father?" They
said, "The first." Jesus said to them,
"Truly, I say to you, the tax collectors
and the harlots go into the kingdom of
God before you. 32 For John came to
you in the way of righteousness, and
you did not believe him, but the tax
collectors and the harlots believed
him; and even when you saw it, you
did not afterward repent and believe
him.

33 "Hear another parable. There
was a householder who planted a vineyard, and set a hedge around it, and
dug a wine press in it, and built a
tower, and let it out to tenants, and
went into another country. 34 When
the season of fruit drew near, he sent
his servants to the tenants, to get his
fruit; 35 and the tenants took his servants and beat one, killed another,
and stoned another. 36 Again he sent
other servants, more than the first;
and they did the same to them. 37 Afterward he sent his son to them, saying,
'They will respect my son.' 38 But
when the tenants saw the son, they
said to themselves, 'This is the heir;
come, let us kill him and have his inheritance.' 39 And they took him and
cast him out of the vineyard, and killed
him. 40 When therefore the owner of
the vineyard comes, what will he do

[p] Other ancient authorities omit *of God*

21.11: Jn 6.14; 7.40; Acts 3.22; Mk 6.15; Lk 13.33.
21.12-13: Mk 11.15-17; Lk 19.45-46; Jn 2.13-17; Ex 30.13; Lev 1.14. **21.13:** Is 56.7; Jer 7.11.
21.15: Lk 19.39; Mt 21.9. **21.16:** Ps 8.2. **21.17-19:** Mk 11.11-14; Lk 13.6-9.
21.20-22: Mk 11.20-24. **21.21:** Mt 17.20; Lk 17.6; 1 Cor 13.2; Jas 1.6. **21.22:** Jn 14.13-14; 16.23.
21.23-27: Mk 11.27-33; Lk 20.1-8; Jn 2.18-22. **21.26:** Mt 11.9; 14.5; Lk 1.76.
21.28: Mt 20.1; 21.33. **21.32:** Lk 7.29-30. **21.33-46:** Mk 12.1-12; Lk 20.9-19; Is 5.1-7.
21.34: Mt 22.3.

to those tenants?" 41 They said to him,
"He will put those wretches to a
miserable death, and let out the vineyard to other tenants who will give
him the fruits in their seasons."
42 Jesus said to them, "Have you
never read in the scriptures:

'The very stone which the builders
rejected
has become the head of the corner;
this was the Lord's doing,
and it is marvelous in our eyes'?

43 Therefore I tell you, the kingdom
of God will be taken away from you
and given to a nation producing the
fruits of it."[q]

45 When the chief priests and the
Pharisees heard his parables, they
perceived that he was speaking about
them. 46 But when they tried to arrest
him, they feared the multitudes, because they held him to be a prophet.

22 And again Jesus spoke to them
in parables, saying, 2 "The kingdom of heaven may be compared to a
king who gave a marriage feast for his
son, 3 and sent his servants to call
those who were invited to the marriage
feast; but they would not come.
4 Again he sent other servants, saying,
'Tell those who are invited, Behold, I
have made ready my dinner, my oxen
and my fat calves are killed, and everything is ready; come to the marriage
feast.' 5 But they made light of it and
went off, one to his farm, another to
his business, 6 while the rest seized his
servants, treated them shamefully,
and killed them. 7 The king was angry,
and he sent his troops and destroyed
those murderers and burned their city.
8 Then he said to his servants, 'The
wedding is ready, but those invited
were not worthy. 9 Go therefore to the
thoroughfares, and invite to the marriage feast as many as you find.' 10 And
those servants went out into the
streets and gathered all whom they
found, both bad and good; so the
wedding hall was filled with guests.

11 "But when the king came in to
look at the guests, he saw there a man
who had no wedding garment; 12 and
he said to him, 'Friend, how did you
get in here without a wedding garment?' And he was speechless. 13 Then
the king said to the attendants, 'Bind
him hand and foot, and cast him into
the outer darkness; there men will
weep and gnash their teeth.' 14 For
many are called, but few are chosen."

15 Then the Pharisees went and
took counsel how to entangle him in
his talk. 16 And they sent their disciples
to him, along with the He·rō'di-ȧnṡ,
saying, "Teacher, we know that you
are true, and teach the way of God
truthfully, and care for no man; for
you do not regard the position of men.
17 Tell us, then, what you think. Is it
lawful to pay taxes to Caesar, or not?"
18 But Jesus, aware of their malice,
said, "Why put me to the test, you
hypocrites? 19 Show me the money for
the tax." And they brought him a
coin.[r] 20 And Jesus said to them,
"Whose likeness and inscription is
this?" 21 They said, "Caesar's." Then
he said to them, "Render therefore to
Caesar the things that are Caesar's,
and to God the things that are God's."
22 When they heard it, they marveled;
and they left him and went away.

23 The same day Sad'dū·ċeeṡ came
to him, who say that there is no resurrection; and they asked him a question, 24 saying, "Teacher, Moses said,
'If a man dies, having no children, his
brother must marry the widow, and
raise up children for his brother.'
25 Now there were seven brothers
among us; the first married, and died,
and having no children left his wife to
his brother. 26 So too the second and
third, down to the seventh. 27 After
them all, the woman died. 28 In the
resurrection, therefore, to which of the
seven will she be wife? For they all
had her."

29 But Jesus answered them, "You
are wrong, because you know neither
the scriptures nor the power of God.
30 For in the resurrection they neither
marry nor are given in marriage, but
are like angels[s] in heaven. 31 And as for
the resurrection of the dead, have you
not read what was said to you by God,
32 'I am the God of Abraham, and the
God of Isaac, and the God of Jacob'?
He is not God of the dead, but of the

[q] Other ancient authorities add verse 44, "*And he who falls on this stone will be broken to pieces; but when it falls on any one, it will crush him*" [r] Greek *a denarius* [s] Other ancient authorities add *of God*

21.41: Mt 8.11; Acts 13.46; 18.6; 28.28. **21.42:** Ps 118.22-23; Acts 4.11; 1 Pet 2.7.
22.1-10: Lk 14.16-24. **22.3:** Mt 21.34. **22.10:** Mt 13.47. **22.12:** Mt 20.13; 26.50.
22.13: Mt 8.12; 13.42, 50; 24.51; 25.30; Lk 13.28. **22.15-22:** Mk 12.13-17; Lk 20.20-26.
22.15: Mk 3.6; 8.15. **22.21:** Rom 13.7. **22.23-33:** Mk 12.18-27; Lk 20.27-38.
22.23: Acts 4.1-2; 23.6-10. **22.24:** Deut 25.5. **22.32:** Ex 3.6.

living." 33And when the crowd heard
it, they were astonished at his teaching.
34 But when the Pharisees heard
that he had silenced the Sad'dū·cees,
they came together. 35And one of
them, a lawyer, asked him a question,
to test him. 36 "Teacher, which is the
great commandment in the law?"
37And he said to him, "You shall love
the Lord your God with all your heart,
and with all your soul, and with all
your mind. 38 This is the great and
first commandment. 39And a second is
like it, You shall love your neighbor as
yourself. 40 On these two commandments depend all the law and the
prophets."
41 Now while the Pharisees were
gathered together, Jesus asked them
a question, 42 saying, "What do you
think of the Christ? Whose son is he?"
They said to him, "The son of David."
43 He said to them, "How is it then
that David, inspired by the Spirit,[t]
calls him Lord, saying,
44 'The Lord said to my Lord,
Sit at my right hand,
till I put thy enemies under thy
feet'?
45 If David thus calls him Lord, how
is he his son?" 46And no one was able
to answer him a word, nor from that
day did any one dare to ask him any
more questions.

23 Then said Jesus to the crowds
and to his disciples, 2 "The
scribes and the Pharisees sit on Moses'
seat; 3 so practice and observe whatever they tell you, but not what they
do; for they preach, but do not practice. 4 They bind heavy burdens, hard
to bear,[u] and lay them on men's
shoulders; but they themselves will
not move them with their finger.
5 They do all their deeds to be seen by
men; for they make their phylacteries
broad and their fringes long, 6 and
they love the place of honor at feasts
and the best seats in the synagogues,
7 and salutations in the market places,
and being called rabbi by men. 8 But
you are not to be called rabbi, for you
have one teacher, and you are all
brethren. 9And call no man your father
on earth, for you have one Father,
who is in heaven. 10 Neither be called
masters, for you have one master, the
Christ. 11 He who is greatest among
you shall be your servant; 12 whoever
exalts himself will be humbled, and
whoever humbles himself will be
exalted.
13 "But woe to you, scribes and
Pharisees, hypocrites! because you
shut the kingdom of heaven against
men; for you neither enter yourselves,
nor allow those who would enter to
go in.[v] 15 Woe to you, scribes and
Pharisees, hypocrites! for you traverse
sea and land to make a single proselyte, and when he becomes a proselyte,
you make him twice as much a child
of hell[w] as yourselves.
16 "Woe to you, blind guides, who
say, 'If any one swears by the temple,
it is nothing; but if any one swears by
the gold of the temple, he is bound by
his oath.' 17 You blind fools! For
which is greater, the gold or the temple
that has made the gold sacred? 18And
you say, 'If any one swears by the
altar, it is nothing; but if any one
swears by the gift that is on the altar,
he is bound by his oath.' 19 You blind
men! For which is greater, the gift or
the altar that makes the gift sacred?
20 So he who swears by the altar,
swears by it and by everything on it;
21 and he who swears by the temple,
swears by it and by him who dwells in
it; 22 and he who swears by heaven,
swears by the throne of God and by
him who sits upon it.
23 "Woe to you, scribes and Pharisees, hypocrites! for you tithe mint
and dill and cummin, and have neglected the weightier matters of the law,
justice and mercy and faith; these you
ought to have done, without neglecting the others. 24 You blind guides,

[t] Or *David in the Spirit* [u] Other ancient authorities omit *hard to bear*
[v] Other authorities add here (or after verse 12) verse 14, *Woe to you, scribes and Pharisees, hypocrites! for you devour widows' houses and for a pretense you make long prayers; therefore you will receive the greater condemnation* [w] Greek *Gehenna*

22.33: Mt 7.28. **22.34-40:** Mk 12.28-34; Lk 20.39-40; 10.25-28. **22.35:** Lk 7.30; 11.45; 14.3.
22.37: Deut 6.5. **22.39:** Lev 19.18; Mt 19.19; Gal 5.14; Rom 13.9; Jas 2.8.
22.41-46: Mk 12.35-37; Lk 20.41-44. **22.44:** Ps 110.1; Acts 2.34-35; Heb 1.13; 10.13.
22.46: Mk 12.34; Lk 20.40. **23.4:** Lk 11.46; Acts 15.10.
23.5: Mt 6.1, 5, 16; Ex 13.9; Deut 6.8; Mt 9.20. **23.6-7:** Mk 12.38-39; Lk 20.46; 14.7-11; 11.43.
23.8: Jas 3.1. **23.11:** Mt 20.26; Mk 9.35; 10.43; Lk 9.48; 22.26.
23.12: Lk 14.11; 18.14; Mt 18.4; 1 Pet 5.6. **23.13:** Lk 11.52. **23.15:** Acts 2.10; 6.5; 13.43.
23.16-22: Mt 5.33-37; 15.14. **23.17:** Ex 30.29. **23.21:** 1 Kings 8.13; Ps 26.8.
23.23-24: Lk 11.42; Lev 27.30; Mic 6.8.

straining out a gnat and swallowing
a camel!
25 "Woe to you, scribes and Pharisees, hypocrites! for you cleanse the
outside of the cup and of the plate, but
inside they are full of extortion and
rapacity. 26 You blind Pharisee! first
cleanse the inside of the cup and of the
plate, that the outside also may be
clean.
27 "Woe to you, scribes and Pharisees, hypocrites! for you are like
whitewashed tombs, which outwardly
appear beautiful, but within they are
full of dead men's bones and all uncleanness. 28 So you also outwardly
appear righteous to men, but within
you are full of hypocrisy and iniquity.
29 "Woe to you, scribes and Pharisees, hypocrites! for you build the
tombs of the prophets and adorn the
monuments of the righteous, 30 saying,
'If we had lived in the days of our
fathers, we would not have taken part
with them in shedding the blood of the
prophets.' 31 Thus you witness against
yourselves, that you are sons of those
who murdered the prophets. 32 Fill up,
then, the measure of your fathers.
33 You serpents, you brood of vipers,
how are you to escape being sentenced
to hell?[w] 34 Therefore I send you
prophets and wise men and scribes,
some of whom you will kill and crucify,
and some you will scourge in your
synagogues and persecute from town
to town, 35 that upon you may come all
the righteous blood shed on earth,
from the blood of innocent Abel to the
blood of Zech·ȧ·rī'ȧh the son of Bar·ȧ-
chi'ȧh, whom you murdered between
the sanctuary and the altar. 36 Truly,
I say to you, all this will come upon
this generation.
37 "O Jerusalem, Jerusalem, killing
the prophets and stoning those who
are sent to you! How often would I
have gathered your children together
as a hen gathers her brood under her
wings, and you would not! 38 Behold,
your house is forsaken and desolate.[x]
39 For I tell you, you will not see me
again, until you say, 'Blessed is he who
comes in the name of the Lord.' "

24 Jesus left the temple and was
going away, when his disciples
came to point out to him the buildings
of the temple. 2 But he answered them,
"You see all these, do you not? Truly,
I say to you, there will not be left here
one stone upon another, that will not
be thrown down."
3 As he sat on the Mount of Olives,
the disciples came to him privately,
saying, "Tell us, when will this be, and
what will be the sign of your coming
and of the close of the age?" 4 And
Jesus answered them, "Take heed that
no one leads you astray. 5 For many
will come in my name, saying, 'I am
the Christ,' and they will lead many
astray. 6 And you will hear of wars and
rumors of wars; see that you are not
alarmed; for this must take place, but
the end is not yet. 7 For nation will
rise against nation, and kingdom
against kingdom, and there will be
famines and earthquakes in various
places: 8 all this is but the beginning
of the sufferings.
9 "Then they will deliver you up to
tribulation, and put you to death; and
you will be hated by all nations for my
name's sake. 10 And then many will
fall away,[y] and betray one another,
and hate one another. 11 And many
false prophets will arise and lead many
astray. 12 And because wickedness is
multiplied, most men's love will grow
cold. 13 But he who endures to the end
will be saved. 14 And this gospel of the
kingdom will be preached throughout
the whole world, as a testimony to all
nations; and then the end will come.
15 "So when you see the desolating
sacrilege spoken of by the prophet
Daniel, standing in the holy place (let
the reader understand), 16 then let
those who are in Judea flee to the
mountains; 17 let him who is on the
housetop not go down to take what is
in his house; 18 and let him who is in
the field not turn back to take his

[w] Greek *Gehenna* [x] Other ancient authorities omit *and desolate* [y] Or *stumble*

23.25-26: Lk 11.39-41; Mk 7.4. **23.27-28:** Lk 11.44; Acts 23.3; Ps 5.9.
23.29-32: Lk 11.47-48; Acts 7.51-53. **23.33:** Mt 3.7; Lk 3.7.
23.34-36: Lk 11.49-51; 2 Chron 36.15-16. **23.34:** Mt 10.17, 23.
23.35: Gen 4.8; Heb 11.4; Zech 1.1; 2 Chron 24.21. **23.36:** Mt 10.23; 16.28; 24.34.
23.37-39: Lk 13.34-35. **23.38:** 1 Kings 9.7; Jer 22.5. **23.39:** Mt 21.9; Ps 118.26.
24.1-35: Mk 13.1-31; Lk 21.1-33. **24.2:** Mt 26.61; 27.39-40; Lk 19.44; Jn 2.19.
24.3: Lk 17.20; Mt 13.39, 40, 49; 28.20; 16.27. **24.5:** Mt 24.11, 23-24; 1 Jn 2.18.
24.6-7: Rev 6.3-8, 12-17; Is 19.2. **24.9:** Mt 10.17-18, 22; Jn 15.18; 16.2. **24.13:** Mt 10.22; Rev 2.7.
24.14: Mt 28.19; Rom 10.18. **24.15:** Dan 9.27; 11.31; 12.11. **24.17-18:** Lk 17.31.

mantle. 19 And alas for those who are
with child and for those who give suck
in those days! 20 Pray that your flight
may not be in winter or on a sabbath.
21 For then there will be great tribulation, such as has not been from the
beginning of the world until now, no,
and never will be. 22 And if those days
had not been shortened, no human being would be saved; but for the sake
of the elect those days will be shortened. 23 Then if any one says to you,
'Lo, here is the Christ!' or 'There he
is!' do not believe it. 24 For false
Christs and false prophets will arise
and show great signs and wonders, so
as to lead astray, if possible, even the
elect. 25 Lo, I have told you beforehand. 26 So, if they say to you, 'Lo, he
is in the wilderness,' do not go out; if
they say, 'Lo, he is in the inner rooms,'
do not believe it. 27 For as the lightning comes from the east and shines
as far as the west, so will be the coming
of the Son of man. 28 Wherever the body
is, there the eagles[z] will be gathered
together.

29 "Immediately after the tribulation of those days the sun will be
darkened, and the moon will not give
its light, and the stars will fall from
heaven, and the powers of the heavens
will be shaken; 30 then will appear the
sign of the Son of man in heaven, and
then all the tribes of the earth will
mourn, and they will see the Son of
man coming on the clouds of heaven
with power and great glory; 31 and he
will send out his angels with a loud
trumpet call, and they will gather his
elect from the four winds, from one
end of heaven to the other.

32 "From the fig tree learn its lesson:
as soon as its branch becomes tender
and puts forth its leaves, you know
that summer is near. 33 So also, when
you see all these things, you know that
he is near, at the very gates. 34 Truly,
I say to you, this generation will not
pass away till all these things take
place. 35 Heaven and earth will pass
away, but my words will not pass away.

36 "But of that day and hour no
one knows, not even the angels of
heaven, nor the Son,[a] but the Father
only. 37 As were the days of Noah, so
will be the coming of the Son of man.
38 For as in those days before the flood
they were eating and drinking, marrying and giving in marriage, until the
day when Noah entered the ark, 39 and
they did not know until the flood came
and swept them all away, so will be
the coming of the Son of man. 40 Then
two men will be in the field; one is
taken and one is left. 41 Two women
will be grinding at the mill; one is
taken and one is left. 42 Watch therefore, for you do not know on what day
your Lord is coming. 43 But know this,
that if the householder had known in
what part of the night the thief was
coming, he would have watched and
would not have let his house be broken
into. 44 Therefore you also must be
ready; for the Son of man is coming
at an hour you do not expect.

45 "Who then is the faithful and
wise servant, whom his master has set
over his household, to give them their
food at the proper time? 46 Blessed is
that servant whom his master when
he comes will find so doing. 47 Truly,
I say to you, he will set him over all
his possessions. 48 But if that wicked
servant says to himself, 'My master
is delayed,' 49 and begins to beat his
fellow servants, and eats and drinks
with the drunken, 50 the master of that
servant will come on a day when he
does not expect him and at an hour he
does not know, 51 and will punish[b] him,
and put him with the hypocrites; there
men will weep and gnash their teeth.

25 "Then the kingdom of heaven
shall be compared to ten
maidens who took their lamps and
went to meet the bridegroom.[c] 2 Five
of them were foolish, and five were
wise. 3 For when the foolish took their
lamps, they took no oil with them;
4 but the wise took flasks of oil with
their lamps. 5 As the bridegroom was
delayed, they all slumbered and slept.

[z] Or *vultures* [a] Other ancient authorities omit *nor the Son* [b] Or *cut him in pieces*
[c] Other ancient authorities add *and the bride*

24.19: Lk 23.29. **24.21:** Dan 12.1; Joel 2.2. **24.26-27:** Lk 17.22-24; Rev 1.7.
24.28: Lk 17.37; Job 39.30. **24.29:** Rev 8.12; Is 13.10; Ezek 32.7; Joel 2.10-11; Zeph 1.15.
24.30: Mt 16.27; Dan 7.13; Rev 1.7. **24.31:** 1 Cor 15.52; 1 Thess 4.16; Is 27.13; Zech 9.14.
24.34: Mt 16.28. **24.35:** Mt 5.18; Lk 16.17. **24.36:** Acts 1.6-7.
24.37-39: Lk 17.26-27; Gen 6.5-8; 7.6-24. **24.40-41:** Lk 17.34-35.
24.42: Mk 13.35; Lk 12.40; Mt 25.13. **24.43-51:** Lk 12.39-46.
24.43: 1 Thess 5.2; Rev 3.3; 16.15; 2 Pet 3.10. **24.45:** Mt 25.21, 23. **24.49:** Lk 21.34.
24.51: Mt 8.12; 13.42, 50; 22.13; 25.30; Lk 13.28. **25.1:** Lk 12.35-38; Mk 13.34. **25.2:** Mt 7.24-27.

6 But at midnight there was a cry,
'Behold, the bridegroom! Come out to
meet him.' 7 Then all those maidens
rose and trimmed their lamps. 8 And
the foolish said to the wise, 'Give us
some of your oil, for our lamps are
going out.' 9 But the wise replied,
'Perhaps there will not be enough for
us and for you; go rather to the dealers
and buy for yourselves.' 10 And while
they went to buy, the bridegroom
came, and those who were ready went
in with him to the marriage feast; and
the door was shut. 11 Afterward the
other maidens came also, saying,
'Lord, lord, open to us.' 12 But he
replied, 'Truly, I say to you, I do not
know you.' 13 Watch therefore, for you
know neither the day nor the hour.

14 "For it will be as when a man
going on a journey called his servants
and entrusted to them his property;
15 to one he gave five talents,[d] to
another two, to another one, to each
according to his ability. Then he went
away. 16 He who had received the five
talents went at once and traded with
them; and he made five talents more.
17 So also, he who had the two talents
made two talents more. 18 But he who
had received the one talent went and
dug in the ground and hid his master's
money. 19 Now after a long time the
master of those servants came and
settled accounts with them. 20 And he
who had received the five talents came
forward, bringing five talents more,
saying, 'Master, you delivered to me
five talents; here I have made five
talents more.' 21 His master said to
him, 'Well done, good and faithful
servant; you have been faithful over a
little, I will set you over much; enter
into the joy of your master.' 22 And he
also who had the two talents came
forward, saying, 'Master, you delivered
to me two talents; here I have made
two talents more.' 23 His master said
to him, 'Well done, good and faithful
servant; you have been faithful over a
little, I will set you over much; enter
into the joy of your master.' 24 He also
who had received the one talent came
forward, saying, 'Master, I knew you
to be a hard man, reaping where you
did not sow, and gathering where you
did not winnow; 25 so I was afraid, and
I went and hid your talent in the
ground. Here you have what is yours.'
26 But his master answered him, 'You
wicked and slothful servant! You knew
that I reap where I have not sowed,
and gather where I have not winnowed? 27 Then you ought to have
invested my money with the bankers,
and at my coming I should have
received what was my own with
interest. 28 So take the talent from him,
and give it to him who has the ten
talents. 29 For to every one who has
will more be given, and he will have
abundance; but from him who has not,
even what he has will be taken away.
30 And cast the worthless servant into
the outer darkness; there men will
weep and gnash their teeth.'

31 "When the Son of man comes in
his glory, and all the angels with him,
then he will sit on his glorious throne.
32 Before him will be gathered all the
nations, and he will separate them one
from another as a shepherd separates
the sheep from the goats, 33 and he will
place the sheep at his right hand, but
the goats at the left. 34 Then the King
will say to those at his right hand,
'Come, O blessed of my Father, inherit
the kingdom prepared for you from
the foundation of the world; 35 for I
was hungry and you gave me food, I
was thirsty and you gave me drink,
I was a stranger and you welcomed
me, 36 I was naked and you clothed
me, I was sick and you visited me, I
was in prison and you came to me.'
37 Then the righteous will answer him,
"Lord, when did we see thee hungry
and feed thee, or thirsty and give thee
drink? 38 And when did we see thee a
stranger and welcome thee, or naked
and clothe thee? 39 And when did we
see thee sick or in prison and visit
thee?' 40 And the King will answer
them, 'Truly, I say to you, as you did
it to one of the least of these my
brethren, you did it to me.' 41 Then
he will say to those at his left hand,
'Depart from me, you cursed, into the
eternal fire prepared for the devil and
his angels; 42 for I was hungry and you

[d] This talent was probably worth about a thousand dollars

25.10: Rev 19.9. **25.11-12:** Lk 13.25; Mt 7.21-23. **25.13:** Mt 24.42; Mk 13.35; Lk 12.40.
25.14-30: Lk 19.12-28. **25.19:** Mt 18.23. **25.21:** Lk 16.10; Mt 24.45.
25.29: Mt 13.12; Mk 4.25; Lk 8.18. **25.30:** Mt 8.12; 13.42, 50; 22.13; Lk 13.28.
25.31: Mt 16.27; 19.28. **25.32:** Ezek 34.17. **25.34:** Lk 12.32; Mt 5.3; Rev 13.8; 17.8.
25.35-36: Is 58.7; Jas 1.27; 2.15-16; Heb 13.2; 2 Tim 1.16.
25.40: Mt 10.42; Mk 9.41; Heb 6.10; Prov 19.17. **25.41:** Mk 9.48; Lk 16.23; Rev 20.10.

gave me no food, I was thirsty and
you gave me no drink, 43 I was a
stranger and you did not welcome me,
naked and you did not clothe me, sick
and in prison and you did not visit me.'
44 Then they also will answer, 'Lord,
when did we see thee hungry or thirsty
or a stranger or naked or sick or in
prison, and did not minister to thee?'
45 Then he will answer them, 'Truly,
I say to you, as you did it not to one
of the least of these, you did it not to
me.' 46 And they will go away into
eternal punishment, but the righteous
into eternal life."

26 When Jesus had finished all
these sayings, he said to his
disciples, 2 "You know that after two
days the Passover is coming, and the
Son of man will be delivered up to be
crucified."

3 Then the chief priests and the
elders of the people gathered in the
palace of the high priest, who was
called Că'iȧ·phȧs, 4 and took counsel
together in order to arrest Jesus by
stealth and kill him. 5 But they said,
"Not during the feast, lest there be a
tumult among the people."

6 Now when Jesus was at Beth'ȧ·ny
in the house of Simon the leper, 7 a
woman came up to him with an alabaster jar of very expensive ointment,
and she poured it on his head, as he
sat at table. 8 But when the disciples
saw it, they were indignant, saying,
"Why this waste? 9 For this ointment
might have been sold for a large sum,
and given to the poor." 10 But Jesus,
aware of this, said to them, "Why do
you trouble the woman? For she has
done a beautiful thing to me. 11 For
you always have the poor with you,
but you will not always have me. 12 In
pouring this ointment on my body she
has done it to prepare me for burial.
13 Truly, I say to you, wherever this
gospel is preached in the whole world,
what she has done will be told in
memory of her."

14 Then one of the twelve, who was
called Judas Is·car'i·ŏt, went to the
chief priests 15 and said, "What will
you give me if I deliver him to you?"
And they paid him thirty pieces of
silver. 16 And from that moment
he sought an opportunity to betray
him.

17 Now on the first day of Unleavened Bread the disciples came to
Jesus, saying, "Where will you have
us prepare for you to eat the passover?"
18 He said, "Go into the city to such
a one, and say to him, 'The Teacher
says, My time is at hand; I will keep
the passover at your house with my
disciples.' " 19 And the disciples did as
Jesus had directed them, and they
prepared the passover.

20 When it was evening, he sat at
table with the twelve disciples;[e] 21 and
as they were eating, he said, "Truly, I
say to you, one of you will betray me."
22 And they were very sorrowful, and
began to say to him one after another,
"Is it I, Lord?" 23 He answered, "He
who has dipped his hand in the dish
with me, will betray me. 24 The Son
of man goes as it is written of him, but
woe to that man by whom the Son of
man is betrayed! It would have been
better for that man if he had not been
born." 25 Judas, who betrayed him,
said, "Is it I, Master?"[f] He said to
him, "You have said so."

26 Now as they were eating, Jesus
took bread, and blessed, and broke it,
and gave it to the disciples and said,
"Take, eat; this is my body." 27 And
he took a cup, and when he had given
thanks he gave it to them, saying,
"Drink of it, all of you; 28 for this is
my blood of the[g] covenant, which is
poured out for many for the forgiveness of sins. 29 I tell you I shall not
drink again of this fruit of the vine
until that day when I drink it new with
you in my Father's kingdom."

30 And when they had sung a
hymn, they went out to the Mount of
Olives. 31 Then Jesus said to them,

[e] Other authorities omit *disciples* [f] Or *Rabbi* [g] Other ancient authorities insert *new*

25.46: Dan 12.2; Jn 5.29. **26.1:** Mt 7.28; 11.1; 13.53; 19.1.
26.2-5: Mk 14.1-2; Lk 22.1-2; Jn 11.47-53. **26.6-13:** Mk 14.3-9; Jn 12.1-8; Lk 7.36-38.
26.11: Deut 15.11. **26.12:** Jn 19.40. **26.14-16:** Mk 14.10-11; Lk 22.3-6.
26.15: Ex 21.32; Zech 11.12. **26.17-19:** Mk 14.12-16; Lk 22.7-13.
26.18: Mt 26.45; Jn 7.6; 12.23; 13.1; 17.1. **26.19:** Mt 21.6; Deut 16.5-8.
26.20-24: Mk 14.17-21; Lk 22.14, 21-23; Jn 13.21-30.
26.24: Ps 41.9; Lk 24.25; 1 Cor 15.3; Acts 17.2-3; Mt 18.7.
26.26-29: Mk 14.22-25; Lk 22.17-19; 1 Cor 10.16; 11.23-26; Mt 14.19; 15.36.
26.28: Heb 9.20; Mt 20.28; Mk 1.4; Ex 24.6-8.
26.30-35: Mk 14.26-31; Lk 22.33-34, 39; Jn 14.31; 18.1; 13.36-38.
26.31: Zech 13.7; Jn 16.32.

"You will all fall away because of me
this night; for it is written, 'I will
strike the shepherd, and the sheep of
the flock will be scattered.' 32 But after
I am raised up, I will go before you
to Galilee." 33 Peter declared to him,
"Though they all fall away because of
you, I will never fall away." 34 Jesus
said to him, "Truly, I say to you, this
very night, before the cock crows, you
will deny me three times." 35 Peter
said to him, "Even if I must die with
you, I will not deny you." And so said
all the disciples.

36 Then Jesus went with them to
a place called Geth·sem'ȧ·nē, and he
said to his disciples, "Sit here, while
I go yonder and pray." 37And taking
with him Peter and the two sons of
Zeb'ė·dee, he began to be sorrowful
and troubled. 38 Then he said to them,
"My soul is very sorrowful, even to
death; remain here, and watch[h] with
me." 39And going a little farther he
fell on his face and prayed, "My
Father, if it be possible, let this cup
pass from me; nevertheless, not as I
will, but as thou wilt." 40And he came
to the disciples and found them sleeping; and he said to Peter, "So, could
you not watch[h] with me one hour?
41 Watch[h] and pray that you may not
enter into temptation; the spirit indeed
is willing, but the flesh is weak."
42Again, for the second time, he went
away and prayed, "My Father, if this
cannot pass unless I drink it, thy will
be done." 43And again he came and
found them sleeping, for their eyes
were heavy. 44 So, leaving them again,
he went away and prayed for the third
time, saying the same words. 45 Then
he came to the disciples and said to
them, "Are you still sleeping and
taking your rest? Behold, the hour is
at hand, and the Son of man is betrayed into the hands of sinners. 46 Rise,
let us be going; see, my betrayer is at
hand."

47 While he was still speaking,
Judas came, one of the twelve, and
with him a great crowd with swords
and clubs, from the chief priests and
the elders of the people. 48 Now the
betrayer had given them a sign, saying,
"The one I shall kiss is the man; seize
him." 49And he came up to Jesus at
once and said, "Hail, Master!"[i] And
he kissed him. 50 Jesus said to him,
"Friend, why are you here?"[j] Then
they came up and laid hands on Jesus
and seized him. 51And behold, one of
those who were with Jesus stretched
out his hand and drew his sword, and
struck the slave of the high priest, and
cut off his ear. 52 Then Jesus said to
him, "Put your sword back into its
place; for all who take the sword will
perish by the sword. 53 Do you think
that I cannot appeal to my Father, and
he will at once send me more than
twelve legions of angels? 54 But how
then should the scriptures be fulfilled,
that it must be so?" 55At that hour
Jesus said to the crowds, "Have you
come out as against a robber, with
swords and clubs to capture me? Day
after day I sat in the temple teaching,
and you did not seize me. 56 But all
this has taken place, that the scriptures
of the prophets might be fulfilled."
Then all the disciples forsook him and
fled.

57 Then those who had seized
Jesus led him to Cā'iȧ·phȧs the high
priest, where the scribes and the elders
had gathered. 58 But Peter followed
him at a distance, as far as the courtyard of the high priest, and going
inside he sat with the guards to see
the end. 59 Now the chief priests and
the whole council sought false testimony against Jesus that they might
put him to death, 60 but they found
none, though many false witnesses
came forward. At last two came forward 61 and said, "This fellow said, 'I
am able to destroy the temple of God,
and to build it in three days.' " 62And
the high priest stood up and said,
"Have you no answer to make? What
is it that these men testify against
you?" 63 But Jesus was silent. And the
high priest said to him, "I adjure you
by the living God, tell us if you are the
Christ, the Son of God." 64 Jesus said
to him, "You have said so. But I tell
you, hereafter you will see the Son of
man seated at the right hand of Power,
and coming on the clouds of heaven."

[h] Or *keep awake* [i] Or *Rabbi* [j] Or *do that for which you have come*

26.32: Mt 28.7, 10, 16. **26.36-46:** Mk 14.32-42; Lk 22.40-46. **26.38:** Jn 12.27; Heb 5 7-8.
26.39: Jn 18.11; Mt 20.22. **26.41:** Mt 6.13; Lk 11.4. **26.42:** Jn 4.34; 5.30; 6.38.
26.45: Mt 26.18; Jn 12.23; 13.1; 17.1. **26.47-56:** Mk 14.43-50; Lk 22.47-53; Jn 18.2-11.
26.50: Mt 20.13; 22.12. **26.52:** Gen 9.6; Rev 13.10. **26.55:** Lk 19.47; Jn 18.19-21.
26.57-75: Mk 14.53-72; Lk 22.54-71; Jn 18.12-27. **26.61:** Mt 24.2; 27.40; Acts 6.14; Jn 2.19.
26.63: Mt 27.11; Jn 18.33. **26.64:** Mt 16.28; Dan 7.13; Ps 110.1.

65 Then the high priest tore his robes,
and said, "He has uttered blasphemy.
Why do we still need witnesses? You
have now heard his blasphemy. 66 What
is your judgment?" They answered,
"He deserves death." 67 Then they
spat in his face, and struck him; and
some slapped him, 68 saying, "Prophesy
to us, you Christ! Who is it that struck
you?"

69 Now Peter was sitting outside in
the courtyard. And a maid came up to
him, and said, "You also were with
Jesus the Galilean." 70 But he denied
it before them all, saying, "I do not
know what you mean." 71 And when
he went out to the porch, another
maid saw him, and she said to the bystanders, "This man was with Jesus
of Nazareth." 72 And again he denied
it with an oath, "I do not know the
man." 73 After a little while the bystanders came up and said to Peter,
"Certainly you are also one of them,
for your accent betrays you." 74 Then
he began to invoke a curse on himself
and to swear, "I do not know the
man." And immediately the cock
crowed. 75 And Peter remembered the
saying of Jesus, "Before the cock
crows, you will deny me three times."
And he went out and wept bitterly.

27 When morning came, all the
chief priests and the elders of
the people took counsel against Jesus
to put him to death; 2 and they bound
him and led him away and delivered
him to Pilate the governor.

3 When Judas, his betrayer, saw
that he was condemned, he repented
and brought back the thirty pieces of
silver to the chief priests and the
elders, 4 saying, "I have sinned in
betraying innocent blood." They said,
"What is that to us? See to it yourself."
5 And throwing down the pieces of
silver in the temple, he departed; and
he went and hanged himself. 6 But the
chief priests, taking the pieces of silver,
said, "It is not lawful to put them into
the treasury, since they are blood
money." 7 So they took counsel, and
bought with them the potter's field,
to bury strangers in. 8 Therefore that
field has been called the Field of Blood
to this day. 9 Then was fulfilled what
had been spoken by the prophet Jeremiah, saying, "And they took the
thirty pieces of silver, the price of him
on whom a price had been set by some
of the sons of Israel, 10 and they gave
them for the potter's field, as the Lord
directed me."

11 Now Jesus stood before the
governor; and the governor asked him,
"Are you the King of the Jews?"
Jesus said to him, "You have said so."
12 But when he was accused by the
chief priests and elders, he made no
answer. 13 Then Pilate said to him,
"Do you not hear how many things
they testify against you?" 14 But he
gave him no answer, not even to a
single charge; so that the governor
wondered greatly.

15 Now at the feast the governor
was accustomed to release for the
crowd any one prisoner whom they
wanted. 16 And they had then a no-
torious prisoner, called Bȧ·rab′bȧs.[k]
17 So when they had gathered, Pilate
said to them, "Whom do you want me
to release for you, Bȧ·rab′bȧs[k] or Jesus
who is called Christ?" 18 For he knew
that it was out of envy that they had
delivered him up. 19 Besides, while he
was sitting on the judgment seat, his
wife sent word to him, "Have nothing
to do with that righteous man, for I
have suffered much over him today in
a dream." 20 Now the chief priests and
the elders persuaded the people to ask
for Bȧ·rab′bȧs and destroy Jesus.
21 The governor again said to them,
"Which of the two do you want me to
release for you?" And they said,
"Bȧ·rab′bȧs." 22 Pilate said to them,
"Then what shall I do with Jesus who
is called Christ?" They all said, "Let
him be crucified." 23 And he said,
"Why, what evil has he done?" But
they shouted all the more, "Let him
be crucified."

24 So when Pilate saw that he was
gaining nothing, but rather that a riot
was beginning, he took water and
washed his hands before the crowd,
saying, "I am innocent of this man's
blood;[l] see to it yourselves." 25 And all
the people answered, "His blood be

[k] Other ancient authorities read *Jesus Barabbas*

[l] Other authorities read *this righteous blood* or *this righteous man's blood*

26.65: Num 14.6; Acts 14.14; Lev 24.16. **26.75:** Mt 26.34. **27.1-2:** Mk 15.1; Lk 23.1; Jn 18.28. **27.3-10:** Acts 1.16-20. **27.3:** Mt 26.15; Ex 21.32. **27.6:** Deut 23.18. **27.9:** Zech 11.12-13; Jer 32.6-15; 18.2-3. **27.11-26:** Mk 15.2-15; Lk 23.3, 18-25; Jn 18.29-19.16. **27.14:** Lk 23.9; Mt 26.62; Mk 14.60; 1 Tim 6.13. **27.19:** Lk 23.4. **27.21:** Acts 3.13-14. **27.24:** Deut 21.6-9; Ps 26.6. **27.25:** Acts 5.28; Josh 2.19.

on us and on our children!" 26 Then
he released for them Bȧ·rab'bȧs, and
having scourged Jesus, delivered him
to be crucified.

27 Then the soldiers of the governor
took Jesus into the praetorium, and
they gathered the whole battalion before him. 28And they stripped him and
put a scarlet robe upon him, 29 and
plaiting a crown of thorns they put it
on his head, and put a reed in his right
hand. And kneeling before him they
mocked him, saying, "Hail, King of
the Jews!" 30And they spat upon him,
and took the reed and struck him on
the head. 31And when they had
mocked him, they stripped him of
the robe, and put his own clothes on
him, and led him away to crucify
him.

32 As they were marching out, they
came upon a man of Cȳ·rē'nē, Simon
by name; this man they compelled to
carry his cross. 33And when they came
to a place called Gol'gȯ·thȧ (which
means the place of a skull), 34 they
offered him wine to drink, mingled
with gall; but when he tasted it, he
would not drink it. 35And when they
had crucified him, they divided his
garments among them by casting lots;
36 then they sat down and kept watch
over him there. 37And over his head
they put the charge against him, which
read, "This is Jesus the King of the
Jews." 38 Then two robbers were
crucified with him, one on the right
and one on the left. 39And those who
passed by derided him, wagging their
heads 40 and saying, "You who would
destroy the temple and build it in
three days, save yourself! If you are
the Son of God, come down from the
cross." 41 So also the chief priests,
with the scribes and elders, mocked
him, saying, 42 "He saved others; he
cannot save himself. He is the King of
Israel; let him come down now from
the cross, and we will believe in him.
43 He trusts in God; let God deliver
him now, if he desires him; for he said,
'I am the Son of God.' " 44And the
robbers who were crucified with him
also reviled him in the same way.

45 Now from the sixth hour there
was darkness over all the land[m] until
the ninth hour. 46And about the ninth
hour Jesus cried with a loud voice,
"Ē'lī, Ē'lī, lä'mȧ sȧ·bach'-thā'nī?"
that is, "My God, my God, why hast
thou forsaken me?" 47And some of the
bystanders hearing it said, "This man
is calling E·lī'jȧh." 48And one of them
at once ran and took a sponge, filled it
with vinegar, and put it on a reed, and
gave it to him to drink. 49 But the
others said, "Wait, let us see whether
E·lī'jȧh will come to save him."[n] 50And
Jesus cried again with a loud voice
and yielded up his spirit.

51 And behold, the curtain of the
temple was torn in two, from top to
bottom; and the earth shook, and the
rocks were split; 52 the tombs also
were opened, and many bodies of the
saints who had fallen asleep were
raised, 53 and coming out of the tombs
after his resurrection they went into
the holy city and appeared to many.
54 When the centurion and those who
were with him, keeping watch over
Jesus, saw the earthquake and what
took place, they were filled with awe,
and said, "Truly this was the Son[x] of
God!"

55 There were also many women
there, looking on from afar, who had
followed Jesus from Galilee, ministering to him; 56 among whom were Mary
Mag'dȧ·lēne, and Mary the mother of
James and Joseph, and the mother of
the sons of Zeb'ė·dee.

57 When it was evening, there came
a rich man from Ar·i·mȧ·thē'ȧ, named
Joseph, who also was a disciple of
Jesus. 58 He went to Pilate and asked
for the body of Jesus. Then Pilate
ordered it to be given to him. 59And
Joseph took the body, and wrapped it
in a clean linen shroud, 60 and laid it
in his own new tomb, which he had
hewn in the rock; and he rolled a great
stone to the door of the tomb, and
departed. 61 Mary Mag'dȧ·lēne and the
other Mary were there, sitting opposite
the sepulchre.

62 Next day, that is, after the day
of Preparation, the chief priests and

[m] Or *earth*
[n] Other ancient authorities insert *And another took a spear and pierced his side, and out came water and blood* [x] Or *a son*

27.27-31: Mk 15.16-20; Lk 23.11; Jn 19.2-3. **27.32:** Mk 15.21; Lk 23.26; Jn 19.17; Heb 13.12.
27.33-44: Mk 15.22-32; Lk 23.33-39; Jn 19.17-24. **27.35:** Ps 22.18. **27.39:** Ps 22.7-8; 109.25.
27.40: Mt 26.61; Acts 6.14; Jn 2.19. **27.45-56:** Mk 15.33-41; Lk 23.44-54; Jn 19.28-30.
27.46: Ps 22.1. **27.48:** Ps 69.21. **27.51:** Heb 9.8; 10.19; Ex 26.31-35; Mt 28.2. **27.54:** Mt 3.17; 17.5.
27.56: Lk 24.10. **27.57-61:** Mk 15.42-47; Lk 23.50-56; Jn 19.38-42; Acts 13.29.

the Pharisees gathered before Pilate
63 and said, "Sir, we remember how
that impostor said, while he was still
alive, 'After three days I will rise
again.' 64 Therefore order the sepulchre to be made secure until the third
day, lest his disciples go and steal him
away, and tell the people, 'He has
risen from the dead,' and the last fraud
will be worse than the first." 65 Pilate
said to them, "You have a guard[o] of
soldiers; go, make it as secure as you
can."[p] 66 So they went and made the
sepulchre secure by sealing the stone
and setting a guard.

28 Now after the sabbath, toward
the dawn of the first day of the
week, Mary Mag'dȧ·lēne and the other
Mary went to see the sepulchre. 2And
behold, there was a great earthquake;
for an angel of the Lord descended
from heaven and came and rolled back
the stone, and sat upon it. 3 His
appearance was like lightning, and his
raiment white as snow. 4And for fear
of him the guards trembled and became like dead men. 5 But the angel
said to the women, "Do not be afraid;
for I know that you seek Jesus who
was crucified. 6 He is not here; for he
has risen, as he said. Come, see the
place where he[q] lay. 7 Then go quickly
and tell his disciples that he has risen
from the dead, and behold, he is going
before you to Galilee; there you will
see him. Lo, I have told you." 8 So
they departed quickly from the tomb
with fear and great joy, and ran to tell
his disciples. 9And behold, Jesus met
them and said, "Hail!" And they came
up and took hold of his feet and
worshiped him. 10 Then Jesus said to
them, "Do not be afraid; go and tell
my brethren to go to Galilee, and there
they will see me."

11 While they were going, behold,
some of the guard went into the city
and told the chief priests all that had
taken place. 12And when they had
assembled with the elders and taken
counsel, they gave a sum of money to
the soldiers 13 and said, "Tell people,
'His disciples came by night and stole
him away while we were asleep.' 14And
if this comes to the governor's ears, we
will satisfy him and keep you out of
trouble." 15 So they took the money
and did as they were directed; and this
story has been spread among the Jews
to this day.

16 Now the eleven disciples went
to Galilee, to the mountain to which
Jesus had directed them. 17And when
they saw him they worshiped him; but
some doubted. 18And Jesus came and
said to them, "All authority in heaven
and on earth has been given to me.
19 Go therefore and make disciples of
all nations, baptizing them in the
name of the Father and of the Son and
of the Holy Spirit, 20 teaching them to
observe all that I have commanded
you; and lo, I am with you always, to
the close of the age."

THE GOSPEL ACCORDING TO

MARK

1 The beginning of the gospel of
Jesus Christ, the son of God.[a]
2 As it is written in I·sāi'ah the
prophet,[b]
"Behold, I send my messenger before thy face,
who shall prepare thy way;
3 the voice of one crying in the
wilderness:
Prepare the way of the Lord,
make his paths straight—"
4 John the baptizer appeared[c] in the

[o] Or *Take a guard* [p] Greek *know* [q] Other ancient authorities read *the Lord*
[a] Other ancient authorities omit *the Son of God* [b] Other ancient authorities read *in the prophets*
[c] Other ancient authorities read *John was baptizing*

27.63: Mt 16.21; 17.23; 20.19. **27.66:** Mt 27.60; 28.11-15. **28.1-8:** Mk 16.1-8; Lk 24.1-9; Jn 20.1-2.
28.1: Lk 8.2; Mt 27.56. **28.2:** Mt 27.51, 60. **28.4:** Mt 27.62-66. **28.7:** Mt 26.32; 28.16; Jn 21.1-23.
28.9: Jn 20.14-18. **28.11:** Mt 27.62-66. **28.16-17:** 1 Cor 15.5; Jn 21.1-23.
28.18: Mt 11.27; Lk 10.22; Phil 2.9; Eph 1.20-22. **28.19:** Lk 24.47; Acts 1.8.
28.20: Mt 13.39, 49; 24.3; 18.20; Acts 18.10. **1.2-8:** Mt 3.1-12; Lk 3.2-16; Jn 1.6, 15, 19-28.
1.2: Mal 3.1; Mt 11.10; Lk 7.27. **1.3:** Is 40.3. **1.4:** Acts 13.24.

wilderness, preaching a baptism of
repentance for the forgiveness of sins.
5 And there went out to him all the
country of Judea, and all the people
of Jerusalem; and they were baptized
by him in the river Jordan, confessing
their sins. 6 Now John was clothed
with camel's hair, and had a leather
girdle around his waist, and ate locusts
and wild honey. 7 And he preached,
saying, "After me comes he who is
mightier than I, the thong of whose
sandals I am not worthy to stoop down
and untie. 8 I have baptized you with
water; but he will baptize you with the
Holy Spirit."

9 In those days Jesus came from
Nazareth of Galilee and was baptized
by John in the Jordan. 10 And when
he came up out of the water, immediately he saw the heavens opened and
the Spirit descending upon him like a
dove; 11 and a voice came from heaven,
"Thou art my beloved Son;[d] with thee
I am well pleased."

12 The Spirit immediately drove
him out into the wilderness. 13 And he
was in the wilderness forty days,
tempted by Satan; and he was with
the wild beasts; and the angels ministered to him.

14 Now after John was arrested,
Jesus came into Galilee, preaching the
gospel of God, 15 and saying, "The
time is fulfilled, and the kingdom of
God is at hand; repent, and believe in
the gospel."

16 And passing along by the Sea
of Galilee, he saw Simon and Andrew
the brother of Simon casting a net in
the sea; for they were fishermen. 17 And
Jesus said to them, "Follow me and I
will make you become fishers of men."
18 And immediately they left their nets
and followed him. 19 And going on a
little farther, he saw James the son of
Zeb'ė·dee and John his brother, who
were in their boat mending the nets.
20 And immediately he called them;
and they left their father Zeb'ė·dee in
the boat with the hired servants, and
followed him.

21 And they went into Cȧ·pēr'nȧ·
ŭm; and immediately on the sabbath
he entered the synagogue and taught.
22 And they were astonished at his
teaching, for he taught them as one
who had authority, and not as the
scribes. 23 And immediately there was
in their synagogue a man with an unclean spirit; 24 and he cried out, "What
have you to do with us, Jesus of
Nazareth? Have you come to destroy
us? I know who you are, the Holy One
of God." 25 But Jesus rebuked him,
saying, "Be silent, and come out of
him!" 26 And the unclean spirit, convulsing him and crying with a loud
voice, came out of him. 27 And they
were all amazed, so that they questioned among themselves, saying,
"What is this? A new teaching! With
authority he commands even the unclean spirits, and they obey him."
28 And at once his fame spread everywhere throughout all the surrounding
region of Galilee.

29 And immediately he[e] left the
synagogue, and entered the house of
Simon and Andrew, with James and
John. 30 Now Simon's mother-in-law
lay sick with a fever, and immediately
they told him of her. 31 And he came
and took her by the hand and lifted
her up, and the fever left her; and she
served them.

32 That evening, at sundown, they
brought to him all who were sick or
possessed with demons. 33 And the
whole city was gathered together about
the door. 34 And he healed many
who were sick with various diseases,
and cast out many demons; and
he would not permit the demons
to speak, because they knew
him.

35 And in the morning, a great
while before day, he rose and went out
to a lonely place, and there he prayed.
36 And Simon and those who were with
him followed him, 37 and they found
him and said to him, "Every one is
searching for you." 38 And he said to
them, "Let us go on to the next towns,
that I may preach there also; for that
is why I came out." 39 And he went
throughout all Galilee, preaching in
their synagogues and casting out
demons.

40 And a leper came to him be-

[d] Or *my Son, my* (or *the*) *Beloved* [e] Other ancient authorities read *they*

1.9-11: Mt 3.13-17; Lk 3.21-22; Jn 1.29-34. **1.11:** Ps 2.7; Is 42.1. **1.12-13:** Mt 4.1-11; Lk 4.1-13.
1.14-15: Mt 4.12-17; Lk 4.14-15. **1.16-20:** Mt 4.18-22; Lk 5.1-11; Jn 1.40-42.
1.21-22: Mt 7.28-29; Lk 4.31-32. **1.23-28:** Lk 4.33-37. **1.24:** Jn 6.69.
1.29-31: Mt 8.14-15; Lk 4.38-39. **1.32-34:** Mt 8.16-17; Lk 4.40-41. **1.35-38:** Lk 4.42-43.
1.39: Mt 4.23-25; Lk 4.44.

seeching him, and kneeling said to
him, "If you will, you can make me
clean." 41 Moved with pity, he
stretched out his hand and touched
him, and said to him, "I will; be
clean." 42 And immediately the leprosy
left him, and he was made clean.
43 And he sternly charged him, and
sent him away at once, 44 and said to
him, "See that you say nothing to any
one; but go, show yourself to the priest,
and offer for your cleansing what Moses
commanded, for a proof to the people."[f] 45 But he went out and began
to talk freely about it, and to spread
the news, so that Jesus[g] could no longer
openly enter a town, but was out in
the country; and people came to him
from every quarter.

2 And when he returned to Cȧ-
pēr'nȧ-ŭm after some days, it was
reported that he was at home. 2 And
many were gathered together, so that
there was no longer room for them,
not even about the door; and he was
preaching the word to them. 3 And
they came, bringing to him a paralytic
carried by four men. 4 And when they
could not get near him because of the
crowd, they removed the roof above
him; and when they had made an
opening, they let down the pallet on
which the paralytic lay. 5 And when
Jesus saw their faith, he said to the
paralytic, "My son, your sins are forgiven." 6 Now some of the scribes
were sitting there, questioning in their
hearts, 7 "Why does this man speak
thus? It is blasphemy! Who can forgive sins but God alone?" 8 And immediately Jesus, perceiving in his
spirit that they thus questioned within
themselves, said to them, "Why do
you question thus in your hearts?
9 Which is easier, to say to the paralytic, 'Your sins are forgiven,' or to
say, 'Rise, take up your pallet and
walk'? 10 But that you may know that
the Son of man has authority on earth
to forgive sins"—he said to the paralytic—11 "I say to you, rise, take up
your pallet and go home." 12 And he
rose, and immediately took up the
pallet and went out before them all; so
that they were all amazed and glorified
God, saying, "We never saw anything
like this!"

13 He went out again beside the
sea; and all the crowd gathered about
him, and he taught them. 14 And as he
passed on, he saw Levi the son of
Al·phaē'ŭs sitting at the tax office, and
he said to him, "Follow me." And he
rose and followed him.

15 And as he sat at table in his
house, many tax collectors and sinners
were sitting with Jesus and his disciples; for there were many who
followed him. 16 And the scribes of[h]
the Pharisees, when they saw that he
was eating with sinners and tax collectors, said to his disciples, "Why
does he eat[i] with tax collectors and
sinners?" 17 And when Jesus heard it,
he said to them, "Those who are well
have no need of a physician, but those
who are sick; I came not to call the
righteous, but sinners."

18 Now John's disciples and the
Pharisees were fasting; and people
came and said to him, "Why do
John's disciples and the disciples of
the Pharisees fast, but your disciples
do not fast?" 19 And Jesus said to
them, "Can the wedding guests fast
while the bridegroom is with them?
As long as they have the bridegroom
with them, they cannot fast. 20 The
days will come, when the bridegroom
is taken away from them, and then
they will fast in that day. 21 No one
sews a piece of unshrunk cloth on an
old garment; if he does, the patch
tears away from it, the new from the
old, and a worse tear is made. 22 And
no one puts new wine into old wineskins; if he does, the wine will burst
the skins, and the wine is lost, and so
are the skins; but new wine is for fresh
skins."[j]

23 One sabbath he was going
through the grainfields; and as they
made their way his disciples began to
pluck ears of grain. 24 And the Pharisees said to him, "Look, why are they
doing what is not lawful on the sabbath?" 25 And he said to them, "Have
you never read what David did, when
he was in need and was hungry, he and
those who were with him: 26 how he

[f] Greek *to them* [g] Greek *he* [h] Other ancient authorities read *and*
[i] Other ancient authorities add *and drink*
[j] Other ancient authorities omit *but new wine is for fresh skins*
1.44: Lev 13.49; 14.2-32. **1.40-45:** Mt 8.2-4; Lk 5.12-16. **2.3-12:** Mt 9.2-8; Lk 5.18-26.
2.12: Mt 9.33. **2.14-17:** Mt 9.9-13; Lk 5.27-32. **2.16:** Acts 23.9. **2.18-22:** Mt 9.14-17; Lk 5.33-38.
2.20: Lk 17.22. **2.23-28:** Mt 12.1-8; Lk 6.1-5. **2.23:** Deut 23.25. **2.26:** 1 Sam 21.1-6; 2 Sam 8.17.

entered the house of God, when
A·bī'ȧ·thär was high priest, and ate the
bread of the Presence, which is not
lawful for any but the priests to eat,
and also gave it to those who were
with him?" 27 And he said to them,
"The sabbath was made for man, not
man for the sabbath; 28 so the Son of
man is lord even of the sabbath."

3 Again he entered the synagogue,
and a man was there who had a
withered hand. 2 And they watched
him, to see whether he would heal him
on the sabbath, so that they might
accuse him. 3 And he said to the man
who had the withered hand, "Come
here." 4 And he said to them, "Is it
lawful on the sabbath to do good or
to do harm, to save life or to kill?"
But they were silent. 5 And he looked
around at them with anger, grieved at
their hardness of heart, and said to the
man, "Stretch out your hand." He
stretched it out, and his hand was
restored. 6 The Pharisees went out,
and immediately held counsel with
the He·rō'di-ȧns against him, how to
destroy him.

7 Jesus withdrew with his disciples
to the sea, and a great multitude from
Galilee followed; also from Judea
8 and Jerusalem and Id·ū·mē'ȧ and
from beyond the Jordan and from
about Tȳre and Sī'don a great multitude, hearing all that he did, came to
him. 9 And he told his disciples to have
a boat ready for him because of the
crowd, lest they should crush him;
10 for he had healed many, so that all
who had diseases pressed upon him to
touch him. 11 And whenever the unclean spirits beheld him, they fell
down before him and cried out, "You
are the Son of God." 12 And he
strictly ordered them not to make him
known.

13 And he went up into the hills,
and called to him those whom he
desired; and they came to him. 14 And
he appointed twelve,[k] to be with him,
and to be sent out to preach 15 and
have authority to cast out demons:
16 Simon whom he surnamed Peter;
17 James the son of Zeb'ė·dee and
John the brother of James, whom he
surnamed Bō-ȧ·nēr'gēs, that is, sons
of thunder; 18 Andrew, and Philip, and
Bartholomew, and Matthew, and
Thomas, and James the son of Al-
phaē'ůs, and Thȧd·daē'ůs, and Simon
the Cā·nȧ·naē'ȧn, 19 and Judas Is·car'-
i·ȯt, who betrayed him.

Then he went home; 20 and the
crowd came together again, so that
they could not even eat. 21 And when
his friends heard it, they went out to
seize him, for they said, "He is beside
himself." 22 And the scribes who came
down from Jerusalem said, "He is
possessed by Bē-el'zė·bul, and by the
prince of demons he casts out the
demons." 23 And he called them to
him, and said to them in parables,
"How can Satan cast out Satan? 24 If
a kingdom is divided against itself,
that kingdom cannot stand. 25 And if a
house is divided against itself, that
house will not be able to stand. 26 And
if Satan has risen up against himself
and is divided, he cannot stand, but is
coming to an end. 27 But no one can
enter a strong man's house and
plunder his goods, unless he first binds
the strong man; then indeed he may
plunder his house.

28 "Truly, I say to you, all sins will
be forgiven the sons of men, and whatever blasphemies they utter; 29 but
whoever blasphemes against the Holy
Spirit never has forgiveness, but is
guilty of an eternal sin"—30 for they
had said, "He has an unclean spirit."

31 And his mother and his brothers
came; and standing outside they sent
to him and called him. 32 And a crowd
was sitting about him; and they said
to him, "Your mother and your
brothers[l] are outside, asking for you."
33 And he replied, "Who are my mother
and my brothers?" 34 And looking
around on those who sat about him,
he said, "Here are my mother and my
brother! 35 Whoever does the will of
God is my brother, and sister, and
mother."

[k] Other ancient authorities add *whom also he named apostles*
[l] Other early authorities add *and your sisters*

2.27: Ex 23.12; Deut 5.14. **3.1-6:** Mt 12.9-14; Lk 6.6-11. **3.2:** Lk 11.54. **3.6:** Mk 12.13.
3.7-12: Mt 4.24-25; 12.15-16; Lk 6.17-19.
3.8: Mt 11.21. **3.10:** Mk 5.29, 34; 6.56. **3.12:** Mk 1.45.
3.13: Mt 5.1; Lk 6.12. **3.14-15:** Mt 10.1. **3.16-19:** Mt 10.2-4; Lk 6.14-16; Acts 1.13.
3.19: Mk 2.1; 7.17. **3.20:** Mk 6.31. **3.21:** Mk 3.31-35; Jn 10.20.
3.22-27: Mt 12.24-29; Lk 11.15-22. **3.22:** Mt 9.34; 10.25. **3.27:** Is 49.24-25.
3.28-30: Mt 12.31-32; Lk 12.10. **3.31-35:** Mt 12.46-50; Lk 8.19-21.

4 Again he began to teach beside the sea. And a very large crowd gathered about him, so that he got into a boat and sat in it on the sea; and the whole crowd was beside the sea on the land. 2 And he taught them many things in parables, and in his teaching he said to them: 3 "Listen! A sower went out to sow. 4 And as he sowed, some seed fell along the path, and the birds came and devoured it. 5 Other seed fell on rocky ground, where it had not much soil, and immediately it sprang up, since it had no depth of soil; 6 and when the sun rose it was scorched, and since it had no root it withered away. 7 Other seed fell among thorns and the thorns grew up and choked it, and it yielded no grain. 8 And other seeds fell into good soil and brought forth grain, growing up and increasing and yielding thirtyfold and sixtyfold and a hundredfold." 9 And he said, "He who has ears to hear, let him hear."

10 And when he was alone, those who were about him with the twelve asked him concerning the parables. 11 And he said to them, "To you has been given the secret of the kingdom of God, but for those outside everything is in parables; 12 so that they may indeed see but not perceive, and may indeed hear but not understand; lest they should turn again, and be forgiven." 13 And he said to them, "Do you not understand this parable? How then will you understand all the parables? 14 The sower sows the word. 15 And these are the ones along the path, where the word is sown; when they hear, Satan immediately comes and takes away the word which is sown in them. 16 And these in like manner are the ones sown upon rocky ground, who, when they hear the word, immediately receive it with joy; 17 and they have no root in themselves, but endure for a while; then, when tribulation or persecution arises on account of the word, immediately they fall away.[m] 18 And others are the ones sown among thorns; they are those who hear the word, 19 but the cares of the world, and the delight in riches, and the desire for other things, enter in and choke the word, and it proves unfruitful. 20 But those that were sown upon the good soil are the ones who hear the word and accept it and bear fruit, thirtyfold and sixtyfold and a hundredfold."

21 And he said to them, "Is a lamp brought in to be put under a bushel, or under a bed, and not on a stand? 22 For there is nothing hid, except to be made manifest; nor is anything secret, except to come to light. 23 If any man has ears to hear, let him hear." 24 And he said to them, "Take heed what you hear; the measure you give will be the measure you get, and still more will be given you. 25 For to him who has will more be given; and from him who has not, even what he has will be taken away."

26 And he said, "The kingdom of God is as if a man should scatter seed upon the ground, 27 and should sleep and rise night and day, and the seed should sprout and grow, he knows not how. 28 The earth produces of itself, first the blade, then the ear, then the full grain in the ear. 29 But when the grain is ripe, at once he puts in the sickle, because the harvest has come."

30 And he said, "With what can we compare the kingdom of God, or what parable shall we use for it? 31 It is like a grain of mustard seed, which, when sown upon the ground, is the smallest of all the seeds on earth; 32 yet when it is sown it grows up and becomes the greatest of all shrubs, and puts forth large branches, so that the birds of the air can make nests in its shade."

33 With many such parables he spoke the word to them, as they were able to hear it; 34 he did not speak to them without a parable, but privately to his own disciples he explained everything.

35 On that day, when evening had come, he said to them, "Let us go across to the other side." 36 And leaving the crowd, they took him with them, just as he was, in the boat. And other boats were with him. 37 And a great storm of wind arose, and the

m Or *stumble*

4.1-9: Mt 13.1-9; Lk 8.4-8. **4.10-12:** Mt 13.10-15; Lk 8.9-10.
4.11: 1 Cor 5.12-13; Col 4.5; 1 Thess 4.12; 1 Tim 3.7. **4.12:** Is 6.9-10.
4.13-20: Mt 13.18-23; Lk 8.11-15. **4.21:** Mt 5.15; Lk 8.16; 11.33. **4.22:** Mt 10.26; Lk 8.17; 12.2.
4.23: Mt 11.15; Mk 4.9. **4.24:** Mt 7.2; Lk 6.38. **4.25:** Mt 13.12; 25.29; Lk 8.18; 19.26.
4.26-29: Mt 13.24-30. **4.30-32:** Mt 13.31-32; Lk 13.18-19. **4.34:** Mt 13.34; Jn 16.25.
4.35-41: Mt 8.18, 23-27; Lk 8.22-25.

waves beat into the boat, so that the
boat was already filling. 38 But he was
in the stern, asleep on the cushion;
and they woke him and said to him,
"Teacher, do you not care if we
perish?" 39And he awoke and rebuked
the wind, and said to the sea, "Peace!
Be still!" And the wind ceased, and
there was a great calm. 40 He said to
them, "Why are you afraid? Have you
no faith?" 41And they were filled with
awe, and said to one another, "Who
then is this, that even wind and sea
obey him?"

5 They came to the other side of
the sea, to the country of the
Ger'á·senes.[n] 2And when he had come
out of the boat, there met him out of
the tombs a man with an unclean
spirit, 3 who lived among the tombs;
and no one could bind him any more,
even with a chain; 4 for he had often
been bound with fetters and chains,
but the chains he wrenched apart, and
the fetters he broke in pieces; and no
one had the strength to subdue him.
5 Night and day among the tombs and
on the mountains he was always crying
out, and bruising himself with stones.
6And when he saw Jesus from afar, he
ran and worshiped him; 7 and crying
out with a loud voice, he said, "What
have you to do with me, Jesus, Son of
the Most High God? I adjure you by
God, do not torment me." 8 For he
had said to him, "Come out of the
man, you unclean spirit!" 9And Jesus[o]
asked him, "What is your name?" He
replied, "My name is Legion; for we
are many." 10And he begged him
eagerly not to send them out of the
country. 11 Now a great herd of swine
was feeding there on the hillside; 12 and
they begged him, "Send us to the
swine, let us enter them." 13 So he
gave them leave. And the unclean
spirits came out, and entered the
swine; and the herd, numbering about
two thousand, rushed down the steep
bank into the sea, and were drowned
in the sea.

14 The herdsmen fled, and told it
in the city and in the country. And
people came to see what it was that
had happened. 15And they came to
Jesus, and saw the demoniac sitting
there, clothed and in his right mind,
the man who had had the legion; and
they were afraid. 16And those who had
seen it told what had happened to the
demoniac and to the swine. 17And they
began to beg Jesus[p] to depart from
their neighborhood. 18And as he was
getting into the boat, the man who had
been possessed with demons begged
him that he might be with him. 19 But
he refused, and said to him, "Go home
to your friends, and tell them how
much the Lord has done for you, and
how he has had mercy on you." 20And
he went away and began to proclaim
in the De·cap'ō·lis how much Jesus
had done for him; and all men
marveled.

21 And when Jesus had crossed
again in the boat to the other side, a
great crowd gathered about him; and
he was beside the sea. 22 Then came
one of the rulers of the synagogue,
Jā'ī·rŭs by name; and seeing him, he
fell at his feet, 23 and besought him,
saying, "My little daughter is at the
point of death. Come and lay your
hands on her, so that she may be made
well, and live." 24And he went with
him.

And a great crowd followed him and
thronged about him. 25And there was
a woman who had had a flow of blood
for twelve years, 26 and who had
suffered much under many physicians,
and had spent all that she had, and
was no better but rather grew worse.
27 She had heard the reports about
Jesus, and came up behind him in the
crowd and touched his garment. 28 For
she said, "If I touch even his garments, I shall be made well." 29And
immediately the hemorrhage ceased;
and she felt in her body that she was
healed of her disease. 30And Jesus,
perceiving in himself that power had
gone forth from him, immediately
turned about in the crowd, and said,
"Who touched my garments?" 31And
his disciples said to him, "You see the
crowd pressing around you, and yet
you say, 'Who touched me?' " 32And
he looked around to see who had done
it. 33 But the woman, knowing what
had been done to her, came in fear
and trembling and fell down before
him, and told him the whole truth.
34And he said to her, "Daughter,

[n] Other ancient authorities read *Gergesenes*, some *Gadarenes* [o] Greek *he* [p] Greek *him*

5.1-20: Mt 8.28-34; Lk 8.26-39. **5.7:** Acts 16.17; Heb 7.1; Mk 1.24. **5.20:** Mk 7.31.
5.21-43: Mt 9.18-26; Lk 8.40-56. **5.22:** Lk 13.14; Acts 13.15; 18.8, 17.
5.23: Mk 6.5; 7.32; 8.23; Acts 9.17; 28.8. **5.30:** Lk 5.17. **5.34:** Lk 7.50; Mk 10.52.

your faith has made you well; go
in peace, and be healed of your
disease."
35 While he was still speaking, there
came from the ruler's house some who
said, "Your daughter is dead. Why
trouble the Teacher any further?"
36 But ignoring[q] what they said, Jesus
said to the ruler of the synagogue, "Do
not fear, only believe." 37 And he
allowed no one to follow him except
Peter and James and John the brother
of James. 38 When they came to the
house of the ruler of the synagogue, he
saw a tumult, and people weeping and
wailing loudly. 39 And when he had
entered, he said to them, "Why do you
make a tumult and weep? The child
is not dead but sleeping." 40 And they
laughed at him. But he put them all
outside, and took the child's father
and mother and those who were with
him, and went in where the child was.
41 Taking her by the hand he said to
her, "Tal'i·thȧ cü'mī"; which means,
"Little girl, I say to you, arise." 42 And
immediately the girl got up and
walked; for she was twelve years old.
And immediately they were overcome
with amazement. 43 And he strictly
charged them that no one should
know this, and told them to give her
something to eat.

6 He went away from there and
came to his own country; and his
disciples followed him. 2 And on the
sabbath he began to teach in the
synagogue; and many who heard him
were astonished, saying, "Where did
this man get all this? What is the
wisdom given to him? What mighty
works are wrought by his hands! 3 Is
not this the carpenter, the son of Mary
and brother of James and Jō'sēṡ and
Judas and Simon, and are not his
sisters here with us?" And they took
offense[r] at him. 4 And Jesus said to
them, "A prophet is not without
honor, except in his own country, and
among his own kin, and in his own
house." 5 And he could do no mighty
work there, except that he laid his
hands upon a few sick people and
healed them. 6 And he marveled because of their unbelief.
And he went about among the villages teaching.
7 And he called to him the twelve,
and began to send them out two by
two, and gave them authority over
the unclean spirits. 8 He charged them
to take nothing for their journey except a staff; no bread, no bag, no
money in their belts; 9 but to wear
sandals and not put on two tunics.
10 And he said to them, "Where you
enter a house, stay there until you
leave the place. 11 And if any place will
not receive you and they refuse to
hear you, when you leave, shake off
the dust that is on your feet for a
testimony against them." 12 So they
went out and preached that men
should repent. 13 And they cast out
many demons, and anointed with oil
many that were sick and healed them.
14 King Her'ȯd heard of it; for
Jesus's[s] name had become known.
Some[t] said, "John the baptizer has
been raised from the dead; that is why
these powers are at work in him."
15 But others said, "It is E·lī'jȧh."
And others said, "It is a prophet, like
one of the prophets of old." 16 But
when Her'ȯd heard of it he said,
"John, whom I beheaded, has been
raised." 17 For Her'ȯd had sent and
seized John, and bound him in prison
for the sake of He·rō'di-ȧs, his brother
Philip's wife; because he had married
her. 18 For John said to Her'ȯd, "It is
not lawful for you to have your
brother's wife." 19 And He·rō'di-ȧs had
a grudge against him, and wanted to
kill him. But she could not, 20 for
Her'ȯd feared John, knowing that he
was a righteous and holy man, and
kept him safe. When he heard him, he
was much perplexed; and yet he heard
him gladly. 21 But an opportunity came
when Her'ȯd on his birthday gave a
banquet for his courtiers and officers
and the leading men of Galilee. 22 For
when He·rō'di-ȧs' daughter came in
and danced, she pleased Her'ȯd and
his guests; and the king said to the girl,
"Ask me for whatever you wish, and I
will grant it." 23 And he vowed to her,
"Whatever you ask me, I will give
you, even half of my kingdom." 24 And

[q] Or *overhearing*. Other ancient authorities read *hearing* [r] Or *stumbled* [s] Greek *his*
[t] Other ancient authorities read *he*

5.37: Mk 9.2; 13.3. **5.41:** Lk 7.14; Acts 9.40. **5.43:** Mk 1.43-44; 7.36.
6.1-6: Mt 13.53-58; Lk 4.16-30. **6.2:** Mk 1.21; Mt 7.28. **6.3:** Mt 11.6. **6.5:** Mk 5.23; 7.32; 8.23.
6.6: Mt 9.35. **6.7-11:** Mt 10.1, 5, 7-11; Lk 9.1-5. **6.7:** Lk 10.1. **6.11:** Mt 10.14.
6.12-13: Mt 11.1; Lk 9.6. **6.13:** Jas 5.14. **6.14-16:** Mt 14.1-2; Lk 9.7-9; 9.19; Mt 21.11.
6.17-18: Mt 14.3-4; Lk 3.19-20. **6.19-29:** Mt 14.5-12. **6.20:** Mt 21.26. **6.23:** Esther 5.3, 6.

she went out, and said to her mother,
"What shall I ask?" And she said,
"The head of John the baptizer."
25 And she came in immediately with
haste to the king, and asked, saying,
"I want you to give me at once the
head of John the Baptist on a platter."
26 And the king was exceedingly sorry;
but because of his oaths and his guests
he did not want to break his word to
her. 27 And immediately the king sent
a soldier of the guard and gave orders
to bring his head. He went and beheaded him in the prison, 28 and
brought his head on a platter, and
gave it to the girl; and the girl gave it
to her mother. 29 When his disciples
heard of it, they came and took his
body, and laid it in a tomb.

30 The apostles returned to Jesus,
and told him all that they had done
and taught. 31 And he said to them,
"Come away by yourselves to a lonely
place, and rest a while." For many
were coming and going, and they had
no leisure even to eat. 32 And they went
away in the boat to a lonely place by
themselves. 33 Now many saw them
going, and knew them, and they ran
there on foot from all the towns, and
got there ahead of them. 34 As he
landed he saw a great throng, and he
had compassion on them, because they
were like sheep without a shepherd;
and he began to teach them many
things. 35 And when it grew late, his
disciples came to him and said, "This
is a lonely place, and the hour is now
late; 36 send them away, to go into the
country and villages round about and
buy themselves something to eat."
37 But he answered them, "You give
them something to eat." And they said
to him, "Shall we go and buy two
hundred denarii[u] worth of bread, and
give it to them to eat? 38 And he said
to them, "How many loaves have you?
Go and see." And when they had
found out, they said, "Five, and two
fish." 39 Then he commanded them
all to sit down by companies upon the
green grass. 40 So they sat down in
groups, by hundreds and by fifties.
41 And taking the five loaves and the
two fish he looked up to heaven, and
blessed, and broke the loaves, and
gave them to the disciples to set before the people; and he divided the two
fish among them all. 42 And they all ate
and were satisfied. 43 And they took
up twelve baskets full of broken pieces
and of the fish. 44 And those who
ate the loaves were five thousand
men.

45 Immediately he made his disciples get into the boat and go before
him to the other side, to Beth-sā'i·dȧ,
while he dismissed the crowd. 46 And
after he had taken leave of them, he
went into the hills to pray. 47 And when
evening came, the boat was out on the
sea, and he was alone on the land.
48 And he saw that they were distressed
in rowing, for the wind was against
them. And about the fourth watch of
the night he came to them, walking on
the sea. He meant to pass by them,
49 but when they saw him walking on
the sea they thought it was a ghost,
and cried out; 50 for they all saw him,
and were terrified. But immediately
he spoke to them and said, "Take
heart, it is I; have no fear." 51 And he
got into the boat with them and the
wind ceased. And they were utterly
astounded, 52 for they did not understand about the loaves, but their
hearts were hardened.

53 And when they had crossed over,
they came to land at Gen·nes'ȧ·ret,
and moored to the shore. 54 And when
they got out of the boat, immediately
the people recognized him, 55 and ran
about the whole neighborhood and
began to bring sick people on their
pallets to any place where they heard
he was. 56 And wherever he came, in
villages, cities, or country, they laid
the sick in the market places, and besought him that they might touch
even the fringe of his garment; and as
many as touched it were made well.

7 Now when the Pharisees gathered
together to him, with some of the
scribes, who had come from Jerusalem, 2 they saw that some of his disciples ate with hands defiled, that is,
unwashed. 3 (For the Pharisees, and
all the Jews, do not eat unless they
wash their hands,[v] observing the tra-

[u] The denarius was worth about twenty cents
[v] One Greek word is of uncertain meaning and is not translated

6.30-31: Lk 9.10; Mk 3.20. **6.32-44:** Mt 14.13-21; Lk 9.11-17; Jn 6.5-13; Mk 8.1-10; Mt 15.32-39. **6.34:** Mt 9.36. **6.37:** 2 Kings 4.42-44. **6.41:** Mk 14.22; Lk 24.30-31. **6.45-52:** Mt 14.22-33; Jn 6.15-21. **6.48:** Mk 13.35. **6.50:** Mt 9.2. **6.52:** Mk 8.17. **6.53-56:** Mt 14.34-36. **6.56:** Mk 3.10; Mt 9.20. **7.1-15:** Mt 15.1-11; Lk 11.38.

dition of the elders; 4 and when they
come from the market place, they do
not eat unless they purify[w] themselves;
and there are many other traditions
which they observe, the washing of
cups and pots and vessels of bronze.[x])
5 And the Pharisees and the scribes
asked him, "Why do your disciples
not live[y] according to the tradition of
the elders, but eat with hands defiled?" 6 And he said to them, "Well
did Ī·ṡāi′ȧh prophesy of you hypocrites, as it is written,

'This people honors me with their
lips,
but their heart is far from me;
7 in vain do they worship me,
teaching as doctrines the precepts
of men.'

8 You leave the commandment of
God, and hold fast the tradition of
men."

9 And he said to them, "You have
a fine way of rejecting the commandment of God, in order to keep your
tradition! 10 For Moses said, 'Honor
your father and your mother'; and,
'He who speaks evil of father or
mother, let him surely die'; 11 but you
say, 'If a man tell his father or his
mother, What you would have gained
from me is Côr′bȧn' (that is, given to
God)[z]—12 then you no longer permit
him to do anything for his father or
mother, 13 thus making void the word
of God through your tradition which
you hand on. And many such things
you do."

14 And he called the people to him
again, and said to them, "Hear me, all
of you, and understand: 15 there is
nothing outside a man which by going
into him can defile him; but the things
which come out of a man are what
defile him."[a] 17 And when he had
entered the house, and left the people,
his disciples asked him about the
parable. 18 And he said to them, "Then
are you also without understanding?
Do you not see that whatever goes
into a man from outside cannot defile
him, 19 since it enters, not his heart
but his stomach, and so passes on?"[b]
(Thus he declared all foods clean.)
20 And he said, "What comes out of a
man is what defiles a man. 21 For from
within, out of the heart of man, come
evil thoughts, fornication, theft, murder, adultery, 22 coveting, wickedness,
deceit, licentiousness, envy, slander,
pride, foolishness. 23 All these evil
things come from within, and they
defile a man."

24 And from there he arose and
went away to the region of Tȳre and
Sī′don.[c] And he entered a house, and
would not have any one know it; yet
he could not be hid. 25 But immediately a woman, whose little daughter
was possessed by an unclean spirit,
heard of him, and came and fell down
at his feet. 26 Now the woman was a
Greek, a Sȳ·rō·phȯe·ni′ċiȧn by birth.
And she begged him to cast the demon
out of her daughter. 27 And he said to
her, "Let the children first be fed, for
it is not right to take the children's
bread and throw it to the dogs." 28 But
she answered him, "Yes, Lord; yet
even the dogs under the table eat the
children's crumbs." 29 And he said to
her, "For this saying you may go your
way; the demon has left your daughter." 30 And she went home, and found
the child lying in bed, and the demon
gone.

31 Then he returned from the region of Tȳre, and went through Sī′don
to the Sea of Galilee, through the
region of the De·cap′ȯ·lis. 32 And they
brought to him a man who was deaf
and had an impediment in his speech;
and they besought him to lay his hand
upon him. 33 And taking him aside
from the multitude privately, he put
his fingers into his ears, and he spat
and touched his tongue; 34 and looking
up to heaven, he sighed, and said to
him, "Eph′phȧ·thȧ," that is, "Be
opened." 35 And his ears were opened,
his tongue was released, and he spoke
plainly. 36 And he charged them to tell
no one; but the more he charged them,
the more zealously they proclaimed it.
37 And they were astonished beyond
measure, saying, "He has done all
things well; he even makes the deaf
hear and the dumb speak."

[w] Other ancient authorities read *baptize* [x] Other ancient authorities add *and beds* [y] Greek *walk*
[z] Or *an offering* [a] Other ancient authorities add verse 16, "*If any man has ears to hear, let him hear*"
[b] Or *is evacuated* [c] Other ancient authorities omit *and Sidon*

7.4: Mt 23.25; Lk 11.39. **7.5:** Gal 1.14. **7.6-7:** Is 29.13.
7.10: Ex 20.12; Deut 5.16; Ex 21.17; Lev 20.9. **7.17-23:** Mt 15.15-20; Mk 4.10.
7.18-19: 1 Cor 10.25-27; Rom 14.14; Tit 1.15; Acts 10.15. **7.20-23:** Rom 1.28-31; Gal 5.19-21.
7.22: Mt 6.23; 20.15. **7.24-30:** Mt 15.21-28. **7.31-37:** Mt 15.29-31. **7.32:** Mk 5.23.
7.33: Mk 8.23. **7.36:** Mk 1.44; 5.43.

8 In those days, when again a great
crowd had gathered, and they had
nothing to eat, he called his disciples
to him, and said to them, 2 "I have
compassion on the crowd, because
they have been with me now three
days, and have nothing to eat; 3 and if
I send them away hungry to their
homes, they will faint on the way; and
some of them have come a long way."
4And his disciples answered him,
"How can one feed these men with
bread here in the desert?" 5And he
asked them, "How many loaves have
you?" They said, "Seven." 6And he
commanded the crowd to sit down on
the ground; and he took the seven
loaves, and having given thanks he
broke them and gave them to his disciples to set before the people; and
they set them before the crowd. 7And
they had a few small fish; and having
blessed them, he commanded that
these also should be set before them.
8And they ate, and were satisfied; and
they took up the broken pieces left
over, seven baskets full. 9And there
were about four thousand people.
10And he sent them away and immediately he got into the boat with
his disciples, and went to the district
of Dal·ma·nü'tha.[d]

11 The Pharisees came and began
to argue with him, seeking from him
a sign from heaven, to test him. 12And
he sighed deeply in his spirit, and
said, "Why does this generation seek
a sign? Truly, I say to you, no sign
shall be given to this generation."
13And he left them, and getting into
the boat again he departed to the
other side.

14 Now they had forgotten to bring
bread; and they had only one loaf with
them in the boat. 15And he cautioned
them, saying, "Take heed, beware of
the leaven of the Pharisees and the
leaven of Her'od."[e] 16And they discussed it with one another, saying,
"We have no bread." 17And being
aware of it, Jesus said to them, "Why
do you discuss the fact that you have
no bread? Do you not yet perceive or
understand? Are your hearts hardened? 18 Having eyes do you not see,
and having ears do you not hear? And
do you not remember? 19 When I
broke the five loaves for the five thousand, how many baskets full of broken
pieces did you take up?" They said to
him, "Twelve." 20 "And the seven for
the four thousand, how many baskets
full of broken pieces did you take up?"
And they said to him, "Seven." 21And
he said to them, "Do you not yet
understand?"

22 And they came to Beth-sā'i·da.
And some people brought to him a
blind man, and begged him to touch
him. 23And he took the blind man by
the hand, and led him out of the
village; and when he had spit on his
eyes and laid his hands upon him, he
asked him, "Do you see anything?"
24And he looked up and said, "I see
men; but they look like trees, walking." 25 Then again he laid his hands
upon his eyes; and he looked intently
and was restored, and saw everything
clearly. 26And he sent him away to his
home, saying, "Do not even enter the
village."

27 And Jesus went on with his disciples, to the villages of Caes·a·rē'a
Phi·lip'pī; and on the way he asked
his disciples, "Who do men say that
I am?" 28And they told him, "John
the Baptist; and others say, E·lī'jah;
and others one of the prophets." 29And
he asked them, "But who do you say
that I am?" Peter answered him, "You
are the Christ." 30And he charged
them to tell no one about him.

31 And he began to teach them that
the Son of man must suffer many
things, and be rejected by the elders
and the chief priests and the scribes,
and be killed, and after three days rise
again. 32And he said this plainly. And
Peter took him, and began to rebuke
him. 33 But turning and seeing his
disciples, he rebuked Peter, and said,
"Get behind me, Satan! For you are
not on the side of God, but of men."

34 And he called to him the multitude with his disciples, and said to
them, "If any man would come after
me, let him deny himself and take up

[d] Other ancient authorities read *Magadan* or *Magdala*
[e] Other ancient authorities read *the Herodians*

8.1-10: Mt 15.32-39; Mk 6.32-44; Mt 14.13-21; Lk 9.11-17; Jn 6.5-13.
8.11-12: Mt 16.1-4; 12.38-39; Lk 11.29. **8.13-21:** Mt 16.4-12. **8.15:** Lk 12.1; Mk 6.14; 12.13.
8.17: Mk 6.52; Jer 5.21; Is 6.9-10; Mt 13.10-15. **8.19:** Mk 6.41-44. **8.20:** Mk 8.1-10.
8.22-26: Mk 10.46-52; Jn 9.1-7. **8.22:** Mk 6.45; Lk 9.10. **8.23:** Mk 7.33; 5.23.
8.27-30: Mt 16.13-20; Lk 9.18-21; Jn 6.66-69. **8.28:** Mk 6.14. **8.30:** Mk 9.9; 1.34.
8.31-9.1: Mt 16.21-28; Lk 9.22-27. **8.33:** Mt 4.10. **8.34:** Mt 10.38; Lk 14.27.

his cross and follow me. 35 For whoever would save his life will lose it;
and whoever loses his life for my sake
and the gospel's will save it. 36 For
what does it profit a man, to gain the
whole world and forfeit his life? 37 For
what can a man give in return for his
life? 38 For whoever is ashamed of me
and of my words in this adulterous
and sinful generation, of him will the
Son of man also be ashamed, when he
comes in the glory of his Father with
9 the holy angels." 1And he said to
them, "Truly, I say to you, there
are some standing here who will not
taste death before they see the kingdom of God come with power."

2 And after six days Jesus took with
him Peter and James and John, and
led them up a high mountain apart by
themselves; and he was transfigured
before them, 3 and his garments became glistening, intensely white, as no
fuller on earth could bleach them.
4And there appeared to them E·lī'jȧh
with Moses; and they were talking to
Jesus. 5And Peter said to Jesus,
"Master,[f] it is well that we are here;
let us make three booths, one for you
and one for Moses and one for E·lī'-
jȧh." 6 For he did not know what to
say, for they were exceedingly afraid.
7And a cloud overshadowed them, and
a voice came out of the cloud, "This
is my beloved Son;[g] listen to him."
8And suddenly looking around they
no longer saw any one with them but
Jesus only.

9 And as they were coming down
the mountain, he charged them to tell
no one what they had seen, until the
Son of man should have risen from
the dead. 10 So they kept the matter
to themselves, questioning what the
rising from the dead meant. 11And
they asked him, "Why do the scribes
say that first E·lī'jȧh must come?"
12And he said to them, "E·lī'jȧh does
come first to restore all things; and
how is it written of the Son of man,
that he should suffer many things and
be treated with contempt? 13 But I tell
you that E·lī'jȧh has come, and they
did to him whatever they pleased, as
it is written of him."

14 And when they came to the disciples, they saw a great crowd about
them, and scribes arguing with them.
15And immediately all the crowd,
when they saw him, were greatly
amazed, and ran up to him and
greeted him. 16And he asked them,
"What are you discussing with them?"
17And one of the crowd answered him,
"Teacher, I brought my son to you,
for he has a dumb spirit; 18 and wherever it seizes him, it dashes him down;
and he foams and grinds his teeth and
becomes rigid; and I asked your disciples to cast it out, and they were not
able." 19And he answered them, "O
faithless generation, how long am I to
be with you? How long am I to bear
with you? Bring him to me." 20And
they brought the boy to him; and when
the spirit saw him, immediately it
convulsed the boy, and he fell on the
ground and rolled about, foaming at
the mouth. 21And Jesus[h] asked his
father, "How long has he had this?"
And he said, "From childhood. 22And
it has often cast him into the fire and
into the water, to destroy him; but if
you can do anything, have pity on us
and help us." 23And Jesus said to him,
"If you can! All things are possible to
him who believes." 24 Immediately the
father of the child cried out[i] and said,
"I believe; help my unbelief!" 25And
when Jesus saw that a crowd came
running together, he rebuked the unclean spirit, saying to it, "You dumb
and deaf spirit, I command you, come
out of him, and never enter him
again." 26And after crying out and
convulsing him terribly, it came out,
and the boy was like a corpse; so that
most of them said, "He is dead."
27 But Jesus took him by the hand and
lifted him up, and he arose. 28And
when he had entered the house, his
disciples asked him privately, "Why
could we not cast it out?" 29And he
said to them, "This kind cannot be
driven out by anything but prayer."[j]

30 They went on from there and
passed through Galilee. And he would
not have any one know it; 31 for he was
teaching his disciples, saying to them,
"The Son of man will be delivered

[f] Or *Rabbi* [g] Or *my Son, my* (or *the*) *Beloved* [h] Greek *he* [i] Other ancient authorities add *with tears*
[j] Other ancient authorities add *and fasting*

8.35: Mt 10.39; Lk 17.33; Jn 12.25. **8.38:** Mt 10.33; Lk 12.9. **9.1:** Mk 13.30; Mt 10.23; Lk 22.18.
9.2-8: Mt 17.1-8; Lk 9.28-36. **9.2:** Mk 5.37; 13.3. **9.3:** Mt 28.3.
9.7: 2 Pet 1.17-18; Mt 3.17; Jn 12.28-29. **9.9-13:** Mt 17.9-13; Lk 9.36. **9.9:** Mk 8.30; 5.43; 7.36.
9.11: Mt 11.14. **9.12:** Mk 8.31; 9.31; 10.33. **9.14-27:** Mt 17.14-18; Lk 9.37-43.
9.23: Mt 17.20; Lk 17.6; Mk 11.22-24. **9.30-32:** Mt 17.22-23; Lk 9.43-45. **9.31:** Mk 8.31; 10.33.

into the hands of men, and they will
kill him; and when he is killed, after
three days he will rise." 32 But they
did not understand the saying, and
they were afraid to ask him.

33 And they came to Cȧ·pẽr′nȧ·ŭm;
and when he was in the house he
asked them, "What were you discussing on the way?" 34 But they were
silent; for on the way they had discussed with one another who was the
greatest. 35And he sat down and called
the twelve; and he said to them, "If
any one would be first, he must be
last of all and servant of all." 36And
he took a child, and put him in the
midst of them; and taking him in his
arms, he said to them, 37 "Whoever
receives one such child in my name
receives me; and whoever receives me,
receives not me but him who sent me."

38 John said to him, "Teacher, we
saw a man casting out demons in your
name,[k] and we forbade him, because
he was not following us." 39 But Jesus
said, "Do not forbid him; for no one
who does a mighty work in my name
will be able soon after to speak evil of
me. 40 For he that is not against us is
for us. 41 For truly, I say to you, whoever gives you a cup of water to drink
because you bear the name of Christ,
will by no means lose his reward.

42 "Whoever causes one of these
little ones who believe in me to sin,[l] it
would be better for him if a great millstone were hung round his neck and
he were thrown into the sea. 43And if
your hand causes you to sin,[l] cut it
off; it is better for you to enter life
maimed than with two hands to go to
hell,[m] to the unquenchable fire.[n] 45And
if your foot causes you to sin,[l] cut it
off; it is better for you to enter life
lame than with two feet to be thrown
into hell.[m,n] 47And if your eye causes
you to sin,[l] pluck it out; it is better for
you to enter the kingdom of God with
one eye than with two eyes to be
thrown into hell,[m] 48 where their worm
does not die, and the fire is not
quenched. 49 For every one will be
salted with fire.[o] 50 Salt is good; but
if the salt has lost its saltness, how will
you season it? Have salt in yourselves,
and be at peace with one another."

10 And he left there and went to
the region of Judea and beyond
the Jordan, and crowds gathered to
him again; and again, as his custom
was, he taught them.

2 And Pharisees came up and in
order to test him asked, "Is it lawful
for a man to divorce his wife?" 3 He
answered them, "What did Moses
command you?" 4 They said, "Moses
allowed a man to write a certificate of
divorce, and to put her away." 5 But
Jesus said to them, "For your hardness
of heart he wrote you this commandment. 6 But from the beginning of
creation, 'God made them male and
female.' 7 'For this reason a man shall
leave his father and mother and be
joined to his wife,[p] 8 and the two shall
become one.'[q] So they are no longer
two but one.[q] 9 What therefore God
has joined together, let not man put
asunder."

10 And in the house the disciples
asked him again about this matter.
11And he said to them, "Whoever
divorces his wife and marries another,
commits adultery against her; 12 and if
she divorces her husband and marries
another, she commits adultery."

13 And they were bringing children
to him, that he might touch them; and
the disciples rebuked them. 14 But
when Jesus saw it he was indignant,
and said to them, "Let the children
come to me, do not hinder them; for
to such belongs the kingdom of God.
15 Truly, I say to you, whoever does
not receive the kingdom of God like a
child shall not enter it." 16And he took
them in his arms and blessed them,
laying his hands upon them.

17 And as he was setting out on his
journey, a man ran up and knelt before
him, and asked him, "Good Teacher,

[k] Other ancient authorities add *who does not follow us* [l] Greek *stumble* [m] Greek *Gehenna*
[n] Verses 44 and 46 (which are identical with verse 48) are omitted by the best ancient authorities
[o] Other ancient authorities add *and every sacrifice will be salted with salt*
[p] Other ancient authorities omit *and be joined to his wife* [q] Greek *one flesh*

9.32: Jn 12.16. **9.33-37:** Mt 18.1-5; Lk 9.46-48. **9.34:** Lk 22.24.
9.35: Mk 10.43-44; Mt 20.26-27; 23.11; Lk 22.26. **9.36:** Mk 10.16.
9.37: Mt 10.40; Lk 10.16; Jn 12.44; 13.20. **9.38-40:** Lk 9.49-50; 11.23; Mt 12.30; Num 11.27-29.
9.41: Mt 10.42. **9.42-48:** Mt 18.6-9; 5.29-30; Lk 17.1-2. **9.48:** Is 66.24.
9.49-50: Mt 5.13; Lk 14.34-35. **9.50:** Col 4.6; 1 Thess 5.13. **10.1-12:** Mt 19.1-9.
10.1: Lk 9.51; Jn 10.40; 11.7. **10.4:** Deut 24.1-4. **10.6:** Gen 1.27; 5.2. **10.7-8:** Gen 2.24.
10.11: Mt 5.32; Lk 16.18; 1 Cor 7.10-11; Rom 7.2-3. **10.13-16:** Mt 19.13-15; 18.3; Lk 18.15-17.
10.16: Mk 9.36. **10.17-31:** Mt 19.16-30; Lk 18.18-30. **10.17:** Lk 10.25; Mk 1.40.

what must I do to inherit eternal
life?" 18 And Jesus said to him, "Why
do you call me good? No one is good
but God alone. 19 You know the commandments: 'Do not kill, Do not
commit adultery, Do not steal, Do not
bear false witness, Do not defraud,
Honor your father and mother.' "
20 And he said to him, "Teacher, all
these I have observed from my
youth." 21 And Jesus looking upon him
loved him, and said to him, "You lack
one thing; go, sell what you have, and
give to the poor, and you will have
treasure in heaven; and come, follow
me." 22 At that saying his countenance
fell, and he went away sorrowful; for
he had great possessions.

23 And Jesus looked around and
said to his disciples, "How hard it will
be for those who have riches to enter
the kingdom of God!" 24 And the disciples were amazed at his words. But
Jesus said to them again, "Children,
how hard it is[r] to enter the kingdom of
God! 25 It is easier for a camel to go
through the eye of a needle than for a
rich man to enter the kingdom of God."
26 And they were exceedingly astonished, and said to him,[s] "Then who
can be saved?" 27 Jesus looked at them
and said, "With men it is impossible,
but not with God; for all things are
possible with God." 28 Peter began to
say to him, "Lo, we have left everything and followed you." 29 Jesus said,
"Truly, I say to you, there is no one
who has left house or brothers or
sisters or mother or father or children
or lands, for my sake and for the
gospel, 30 who will not receive a hundredfold now in this time, houses and
brothers and sisters and mothers and
children and lands, with persecutions,
and in the age to come eternal life.
31 But many that are first will be last,
and the last first."

32 And they were on the road,
going up to Jerusalem, and Jesus was
walking ahead of them; and they were
amazed, and those who followed were
afraid. And taking the twelve again,
he began to tell them what was to
happen to him, 33 saying, "Behold, we
are going up to Jerusalem; and the Son
of man will be delivered to the chief
priests and the scribes, and they will
condemn him to death, and deliver
him to the Gentiles; 34 and they will
mock him, and spit upon him, and
scourge him, and kill him; and after
three days he will arise."

35 And James and John, the sons
of Zeb'ĕ·dee, came forward to him,
and said to him, "Teacher, we want
you to do for us whatever we ask of
you." 36 And he said to them, "What
do you want me to do for you?" 37 And
they said to him, "Grant us to sit, one
at your right hand and one at your
left, in your glory." 38 But Jesus said
to them, "You do not know what you
are asking. Are you able to drink the
cup that I drink, or to be baptized
with the baptism with which I am
baptized?" 39 And they said to him,
"We are able." And Jesus said to
them, "The cup that I drink you will
drink; and with the baptism with
which I am baptized, you will be
baptized; 40 but to sit at my right hand
or at my left is not mine to grant, but
it is for those for whom it has been
prepared." 41 And when the ten heard
it, they began to be indignant at James
and John. 42 And Jesus called them to
him and said to them, "You know that
those who are supposed to rule over
the Gentiles lord it over them, and
their great men exercise authority over
them. 43 But it shall not be so among
you; but whoever would be great
among you must be your servant, 44 and
whoever would be first among you
must be slave of all. 45 For the Son of
man also came not to be served but to
serve, and to give his life as a ransom
for many."

46 And they came to Jericho; and
as he was leaving Jericho with his
disciples and a great multitude, Bär-
ti·maē'ŭs, a blind beggar, the son of
Tī·maē'ŭs, was sitting by the roadside. 47 And when he heard that it was
Jesus of Nazareth, he began to cry out
and say, "Jesus, Son of David, have
mercy on me!" 48 And many rebuked
him, telling him to be silent; but he

[r] Other ancient authorities add *for those who trust in riches*
[s] Other ancient authorities read *to one another*

10.19: Ex 20.12-16; Deut 5.16-20. **10.21:** Mt 6.20; Lk 12.33; Acts 2.45; 4.34-35. **10.28:** Mk 1.16-20.
10.30: Mt 6.33. **10.31:** Mt 20.16; Lk 13.30. **10.32-34:** Mt 20.17-19; Lk 18.31-34.
10.33: Mk 8.31; 9.12, 33. **10.34:** Mk 14.65; 15.19, 26-32. **10.35-45:** Mt 20.20-28.
10.37: Mt 19.28; Lk 22.30. **10.38:** Lk 12.50; Jn 18.11. **10.39:** Acts 12.2; Rev 1.9.
10.42-45: Lk 22.25-27. **10.43:** Mk 9.35. **10.45:** 1 Tim 2.5-6.
10.46-52: Mt 20.29-34; Lk 18.35-43; Mk 8.22-26. **10.47:** Mt 9.27.

cried out all the more, "Son of David,
have mercy on me!" 49And Jesus
stopped and said, "Call him." And
they called the blind man, saying to
him, "Take heart; rise, he is calling
you." 50And throwing off his mantle
he sprang up and came to Jesus.
51And Jesus said to him, "What do
you want me to do for you?" And the
blind man said to him, "Master,[t] let
me receive my sight." 52And Jesus
said to him, "Go your way; your faith
has made you well." And immediately
he received his sight and followed him
on the way.

11 And when they drew near to
Jerusalem, to Beth'phȧ·ġē and
Beth'ȧ·ny, at the Mount of Olives, he
sent two of his disciples, 2 and said to
them, "Go into the village opposite
you, and immediately as you enter it
you will find a colt tied, on which no
one has ever sat; untie it and bring it.
3 If any one says to you, 'Why are you
doing this?' say, 'The Lord has need
of it and will send it back here immediately.' " 4And they went away,
and found a colt tied at the door out
in the open street; and they untied it.
5And those who stood there said to
them, "What are you doing, untying
the colt?" 6And they told them what
Jesus had said; and they let them go.
7And they brought the colt to Jesus,
and threw their garments on it; and
he sat upon it. 8And many spread their
garments on the road, and others
spread leafy branches which they had
cut from the fields. 9And those who
went before and those who followed
cried out, "Hosanna! Blessed is he
who comes in the name of the Lord!
10 Blessed is the kingdom of our father
David that is coming! Hosanna in the
highest!"

11 And he entered Jerusalem, and
went into the temple; and when he had
looked round at everything, as it was
already late, he went out to Beth'ȧ·ny
with the twelve.

12 On the following day, when they
came from Beth'ȧ·ny, he was hungry.
13And seeing in the distance a fig tree
in leaf, he went to see if he could find
anything on it. When he came to it,
he found nothing but leaves, for it was
not the season for figs. 14And he said
to it, "May no one ever eat fruit from
you again." And his disciples heard it.

15 And they came to Jerusalem.
And he entered the temple and began
to drive out those who sold and those
who bought in the temple, and he
overturned the tables of the money-
changers and the seats of those who
sold pigeons; 16 and he would not
allow any one to carry anything
through the temple. 17And he taught,
and said to them, "Is it not written,
'My house shall be called a house of
prayer for all the nations'? But you
have made it a den of robbers." 18And
the chief priests and the scribes heard
it and sought a way to destroy him; for
they feared him, because all the multitude was astonished at his teaching.
19And when evening came they[u] went
out of the city.

20 As they passed by in the morning, they saw the fig tree withered
away to its roots. 21And Peter remembered and said to him, "Master,[v] look!
The fig tree which you cursed has
withered." 22And Jesus answered
them, "Have faith in God. 23 Truly,
I say to you, whoever says to this
mountain, 'Be taken up and cast into
the sea,' and does not doubt in his
heart, but believes that what he says
will come to pass, it will be done for
him. 24 Therefore I tell you, whatever
you ask in prayer, believe that you
receive it, and you will. 25And whenever you stand praying, forgive, if you
have anything against any one; so that
your Father also who is in heaven may
forgive you your trespasses."[w]

27 And they came again to Jerusalem. And as he was walking in the
temple, the chief priests and the scribes
and the elders came to him, 28 and
they said to him, "By what authority
are you doing these things, or who
gave you this authority to do them?"
29 Jesus said to them, "I will ask you
a question; answer me, and I will tell

[t] Or *Rabbi* [u] Other ancient authorities read *he* [v] Or *Rabbi*
[w] Other ancient authorities add verse 26, "*But if you do not forgive, neither will your Father who is in heaven forgive your trespasses*"

10.52: Mt 9.22; Mk 5.34; Lk 7.50; 8.48; 17.19. **11.1-10:** Mt 21.1-9; Lk 19.29-38. **11.4:** Mk 14.16.
11.7-10: Jn 12.12-15. **11.9:** Ps 118.26; Mt 21.15; 23.39. **11.11:** Mt 21.10-11, 17.
11.12-14: Mt 21.18-19; Lk 13.6-9. **11.15-18:** Mt 21.12-16; Lk 19.45-48; Jn 2.13-16.
11.17: Is 56.7; Jer 7.11. **11.19:** Lk 21.37. **11.20-25:** Mt 21.20-22; Mt 17.20; Lk 17.6.
11.24: Jn 14.13-14; 16.23; Mt 7.7-11. **11.25:** Mt 6.14-15; 18.35.
11.27-33: Mt 21.23-27; Lk 20.1-8; Jn 2.18.

you by what authority I do these
things. 30 Was the baptism of John
from heaven or from men? Answer
me." 31 And they argued with one
another, "If we say, 'From heaven,'
he will say, 'Why then did you not
believe him?' 32 But shall we say,
'From men'?"—they were afraid of
the people, for all held that John was
a real prophet. 33 So they answered
Jesus, "We do not know." And Jesus
said to them, "Neither will I tell you
by what authority I do these things."

12 And he began to speak to them
in parables. "A man planted a
vineyard, and set a hedge around it,
and dug a pit for the wine press, and
built a tower, and let it out to tenants,
and went into another country. 2 When
the time came, he sent a servant to the
tenants, to get from them some of the
fruit of the vineyard. 3 And they took
him and beat him, and sent him away
empty-handed. 4 Again he sent to them
another servant, and they wounded
him in the head, and treated him
shamefully. 5 And he sent another, and
him they killed; and so with many
others, some they beat and some they
killed. 6 He had still one other, a beloved son; finally he sent him to them,
saying, 'They will respect my son.'
7 But those tenants said to one another,
'This is the heir; come, let us kill him,
and the inheritance will be ours.' 8 And
they took him and killed him, and cast
him out of the vineyard. 9 What will
the owner of the vineyard do? He will
come and destroy the tenants, and
give the vineyard to others. 10 Have
you not read this scripture:

'The very stone which the builders
rejected
has become the head of the corner;
11 this was the Lord's doing,
and it is marvelous in our eyes'?"

12 And they tried to arrest him, but
feared the multitude, for they perceived that he had told the parable
against them; so they left him and
went away.

13 And they sent to him some of
the Pharisees and some of the He·rō′-
di-ȧnṡ, to entrap him in his talk. 14 And
they came and said to him, "Teacher,
we know that you are true, and care
for no man; for you do not regard the
position of men, but truly teach the
way of God. Is it lawful to pay taxes
to Caesar, or not? 15 Should we pay
them, or should we not?" But knowing
their hypocrisy, he said to them,
"Why put me to the test? Bring me a
coin,[x] and let me look at it." 16 And
they brought one. And he said to them,
"Whose likeness and inscription is
this?" They said to him, "Caesar's."
17 Jesus said to them, "Render to
Caesar the things that are Caesar's,
and to God the things that are God's."
And they were amazed at him.

18 And Sad′dū·ċeeṡ came to him,
who say that there is no resurrection;
and they asked him a question, saying,
19 "Teacher, Moses wrote for us that
if a man's brother dies and leaves a
wife, but leaves no child, the man[y]
must take the wife, and raise up
children for his brother. 20 There
were seven brothers; the first took a
wife, and when he died left no children; 21 and the second took her, and
died, leaving no children; and the
third likewise; 22 and the seven left no
children. Last of all the woman also
died. 23 In the resurrection whose
wife will she be? For the seven had
her as wife."

24 Jesus said to them, "Is not this
why you are wrong, that you know
neither the scriptures nor the power
of God? 25 For when they rise from
the dead, they neither marry nor are
given in marriage, but are like angels
in heaven. 26 And as for the dead being
raised, have you not read in the book
of Moses, in the passage about the
bush, how God said to him, 'I am the
God of Abraham, and the God of
Isaac, and the God of Jacob'? 27 He is
not God of the dead, but of the living;
you are quite wrong."

28 And one of the scribes came up
and heard them disputing with one
another, and seeing that he answered
them well, asked him, "Which commandment is the first of all?" 29 Jesus
answered, "The first is, 'Hear, O
Israel: The Lord our God, the Lord
is one; 30 and you shall love the Lord
your God with all your heart, and with
all your soul, and with all your mind,

[x] Greek *a denarius* [y] Greek *his brother*

12.1-12: Mt 21.33-46; Lk 20.9-19; Is 5.1-7. **12.10-11:** Ps 118.22-23; Acts 4.11; 1 Pet 2.7.
12.12: Mk 11.18. **12.13-17:** Mt 22.15-22; Lk 20.20-26. **12.13:** Mk 3.6; Lk 11.54. **12.17:** Rom 13.7.
12.18-27: Mt 22.23-33; Lk 20.27-38. **12.19:** Deut 25.5. **12.26:** Ex 3.6.
12.28-34: Mt 22.34-40; Lk 20.39-40; 10.25-28. **12.29:** Deut 6.4.

and with all your strength.' 31 The
second is this, 'You shall love your
neighbor as yourself.' There is no
other commandment greater than
these." 32 And the scribe said to him,
"You are right, Teacher; you have
truly said that he is one, and there is
no other but he; 33 and to love him
with all the heart, and with all the
understanding, and with all the
strength, and to love one's neighbor
as oneself, is much more than all
whole burnt offerings and sacrifices."
34 And when Jesus saw that he answered wisely, he said to him, "You
are not far from the kingdom of God."
And after that no one dared to ask him
any question.

35 And as Jesus taught in the temple, he said, "How can the scribes say
that the Christ is the son of David?
36 David himself, inspired by[z] the
Holy Spirit, declared,

'The Lord said to my Lord,
Sit at my right hand,
till I put thy enemies under thy feet.'

37 David himself calls him Lord; so
how is he his son?" And the great
throng heard him gladly.

38 And in his teaching he said,
"Beware of the scribes, who like to go
about in long robes, and to have salutations in the market places 39 and the
best seats in the synagogues and the
places of honor at feasts, 40 who devour
widows' houses and for a pretense
make long prayers. They will receive
the greater condemnation."

41 And he sat down opposite the
treasury, and watched the multitude
putting money into the treasury.
Many rich people put in large sums.
42 And a poor widow came, and put
in two copper coins, which make a
penny. 43 And he called his disciples
to him, and said to them, "Truly, I
say to you, this poor widow has put in
more than all those who are contrib-
uting to the treasury. 44 For they all
contributed out of their abundance;
but she out of her poverty has put in
everything she had, her whole living."

13 And as he came out of the temple, one of his disciples said to
him, "Look, Teacher, what wonderful
stones and what wonderful buildings!"
2 And Jesus said to him, "Do you see
these great buildings? There will not
be left here one stone upon another,
that will not be thrown down."

3 And as he sat on the Mount of
Olives opposite the temple, Peter and
James and John and Andrew asked him
privately, 4 "Tell us, when will this
be, and what will be the sign when
these things are all to be accomplished?" 5 And Jesus began to say to
them, "Take heed that no one leads
you astray. 6 Many will come in my
name, saying, 'I am he!' and they will
lead many astray. 7 And when you hear
of wars and rumors of wars, do not be
alarmed; this must take place, but the
end is not yet. 8 For nation will rise
against nation, and kingdom against
kingdom; there will be earthquakes in
various places, there will be famines;
this is but the beginning of the sufferings.

9 "But take heed to yourselves; for
they will deliver you up to councils;
and you will be beaten in synagogues;
and you will stand before governors
and kings for my sake, to bear testimony before them. 10 And the gospel
must first be preached to all nations.
11 And when they bring you to trial
and deliver you up, do not be anxious
beforehand what you are to say; but
say whatever is given you in that hour,
for it is not you who speak, but the
Holy Spirit. 12 And brother will deliver
up brother to death, and the father his
child, and children will rise against
parents and have them put to death;
13 and you will be hated by all for my
name's sake. But he who endures to
the end will be saved.

14 "But when you see the desolating sacrilege set up where it ought
not to be (let the reader understand),
then let those who are in Judea flee to
the mountains; 15 let him who is on
the housetop not go down, nor enter his
house, to take anything away; 16 and
let him who is in the field not turn
back to take his mantle. 17 And alas for
those who are with child and for those
who give suck in those days! 18 Pray

[z] Or *himself, in*

12.31: Lev 19.18; Rom 13.9; Gal 5.14; Jas 2.8. **12.33:** 1 Sam 15.22; Hos 6.6; Mic 6.6-8; Mt 9.13.
12.35-37: Mt 22.41-46; Lk 20.41-44. **12.36:** Ps 110.1; Acts 2.34-35; Heb 1.13.
12.38-40: Mt 23.5-7; Lk 20.46-47; 11.43. **12.41-44:** Lk 21.1-4; Jn 8.20. **13.1-37:** Mt 24; Lk 21.5-36.
13.2: Lk 19.43-44; Mk 14.58; 15.29; Jn 2.19; Acts 6.14. **13.3:** Mk 5.37; 9.2. **13.4:** Lk 17.20.
13.6: Jn 8.24; 1 Jn 2.18. **13.9-13:** Mt 10.17-22. **13.11:** Jn 14.26; 16.7-11; Lk 12.11-12.
13.13: Jn 15.21. **13.14:** Dan 9.27; 11.31; 12.11. **13.17:** Lk 23.29.

that it may not happen in winter.
19 For in those days there will be such
tribulation as has not been from the
beginning of the creation which God
created until now, and never will be.
20 And if the Lord had not shortened
the days, no human being would be
saved; but for the sake of the elect,
whom he chose, he shortened the
days. 21 And then if any one says to
you, 'Look, here is the Christ!' or
'Look, there he is!' do not believe it.
22 False Christs and false prophets
will arise and show signs and wonders,
to lead astray, if possible, the elect.
23 But take heed; I have told you all
things beforehand.
24 "But in those days, after that
tribulation, the sun will be darkened,
and the moon will not give its light,
25 and the stars will be falling from
heaven, and the powers in the heavens
will be shaken. 26 And then they will
see the Son of man coming in clouds
with great power and glory. 27 And then
he will send out the angels, and gather
his elect from the four winds, from the
ends of the earth to the ends of
heaven.
28 "From the fig tree learn its lesson: as soon as its branch becomes
tender and puts forth its leaves, you
know that summer is near. 29 So also,
when you see these things taking place,
you know that he is near, at the very
gates. 30 Truly, I say to you, this
generation will not pass away before
all these things take place. 31 Heaven
and earth will pass away, but my
words will not pass away.
32 "But of that day or that hour no
one knows, not even the angels in
heaven, nor the Son, but only the
Father. 33 Take heed, watch;[a] for you
do not know when the time will come.
34 It is like a man going on a journey,
when he leaves home and puts his
servants in charge, each with his work,
and commands the doorkeeper to be
on the watch. 35 Watch therefore—for
you do not know when the master of
the house will come, in the evening, or at midnight, or at cockcrow,
or in the morning—36 lest he come
suddenly and find you asleep. 37 And
what I say to you I say to all:
Watch."

14 It was now two days before the
Passover and the feast of Unleavened Bread. And the chief priests
and the scribes were seeking how to
arrest him by stealth, and kill him;
2 for they said, "Not during the feast,
lest there be a tumult of the people."
3 And while he was at Beth'à·ny in
the house of Simon the leper, as he
sat at table, a woman came with an
alabaster jar of ointment of pure nard,
very costly, and she broke the jar and
poured it over his head. 4 But there
were some who said to themselves
indignantly, "Why was the ointment
thus wasted? 5 For this ointment might
have been sold for more than three
hundred denarii,[b] and given to the
poor." And they reproached her. 6 But
Jesus said, "Let her alone; why do you
trouble her? She has done a beautiful
thing to me. 7 For you always have the
poor with you, and whenever you will,
you can do good to them; but you will
not always have me. 8 She has done
what she could; she has anointed my
body beforehand for burying. 9 And
truly, I say to you, wherever the gospel is preached in the whole world,
what she has done will be told in
memory of her."
10 Then Judas Is·car'i·ȯt, who was
one of the twelve, went to the chief
priests in order to betray him to them.
11 And when they heard it they were
glad, and promised to give him money.
And he sought an opportunity to
betray him.
12 And on the first day of Unleavened Bread, when they sacrificed the
passover lamb, his disciples said to
him, "Where will you have us go and
prepare for you to eat the passover?"
13 And he sent two of his disciples, and
said to them, "Go into the city, and a
man carrying a jar of water will meet
you; follow him, 14 and wherever he
enters, say to the householder, 'The
Teacher says, Where is my guest
room, where I am to eat the passover
with my disciples? 15 And he will show
you a large upper room furnished and

[a] Other ancient authorities add *and pray* [b] The denarius was worth about twenty cents
13.22: Mt 7.15; Jn 4.48. **13.26:** Mk 8.38; Mt 10.23; Dan 7.13. **13.30:** Mk 9.1.
13.31: Mt 5.18; Lk 16.17. **13.32:** Acts 1.7. **13.33:** Eph 6.18; Col 4.2. **13.34:** Mt 25.14.
13.35: Lk 12.35-40. **14.1-2:** Mt 26.1-5; Lk 22.1-2; Jn 11.47-53.
14.3-9: Mt 26.6-13; Lk 7.36-38; Jn 12.1-8. **14.7:** Deut 15.11. **14.8:** Jn 19.40.
14.10-11: Mt 26.14-16; Lk 22.3-6. **14.12-16:** Mt 26.17-19; Lk 22.7-13.

ready; there prepare for us." 16 And
the disciples set out and went to the
city, and found it as he had told them;
and they prepared the passover.

17 And when it was evening he
came with the twelve. 18 And as they
were at table eating, Jesus said, "Truly,
I say to you, one of you will betray me,
one who is eating with me." 19 They
began to be sorrowful, and to say to
him one after another, "Is it I?" 20 He
said to them, "It is one of the twelve,
one who is dipping bread in the same
dish with me. 21 For the Son of man
goes as it is written of him, but woe
to that man by whom the Son of man
is betrayed! It would have been better for that man if he had not been
born."

22 And as they were eating, he
took bread, and blessed, and broke it,
and gave it to them, and said, "Take;
this is my body." 23 And he took a cup,
and when he had given thanks he gave
it to them, and they all drank of it.
24 And he said to them, "This is my
blood of the[c] covenant, which is
poured out for many. 25 Truly, I say
to you, I shall not drink again of the
fruit of the vine until that day when
I drink it new in the kingdom of
God."

26 And when they had sung a
hymn, they went out to the Mount of
Olives. 27 And Jesus said to them,
"You will all fall away; for it is written,
'I will strike the shepherd, and the
sheep will be scattered.' 28 But after I
am raised up, I will go before you to
Galilee." 29 Peter said to him, "Even
though they all fall away, I will not."
30 And Jesus said to him, "Truly, I say
to you, this very night, before the
cock crows twice, you will deny me
three times." 31 But he said vehemently, "If I must die with you, I will
not deny you." And they all said the
same.

32 And they went to a place which
was called Geth·sem'a·ne; and he said
to his disciples, "Sit here, while I
pray." 33 And he took with him Peter
and James and John, and began to be
greatly distressed and troubled. 34 And
he said to them, "My soul is very
sorrowful, even to death; remain here,
and watch."[d] 35 And going a little
farther, he fell on the ground and
prayed that, if it were possible, the
hour might pass from him. 36 And he
said, "Ab'ba, Father, all things are
possible to thee; remove this cup from
me; yet not what I will, but what thou
wilt." 37 And he came and found them
sleeping, and he said to Peter, "Simon,
are you asleep? Could you not watch[d]
one hour? 38 Watch[d] and pray that you
may not enter into temptation; the
spirit indeed is willing, but the flesh
is weak." 39 And again he went away
and prayed, saying the same words.
40 And again he came and found them
sleeping, for their eyes were very
heavy; and they did not know what to
answer him. 41 And he came the third
time, and said to them, "Are you still
sleeping and taking your rest? It is
enough; the hour has come; the Son
of man is betrayed into the hands of
sinners. 42 Rise, let us be going; see,
my betrayer is at hand."

43 And immediately, while he was
still speaking, Judas came, one of the
twelve, and with him a crowd with
swords and clubs, from the chief
priests and the scribes and the elders.
44 Now the betrayer had given them
a sign, saying, "The one I shall kiss is
the man; seize him and lead him away
safely." 45 And when he came, he went
up to him at once, and said, "Master!"[e]
And he kissed him. 46 And they laid
hands on him and seized him. 47 But
one of those who stood by drew his
sword, and struck the slave of the
high priest and cut off his ear. 48 And
Jesus said to them, "Have you come
out as against a robber, with swords
and clubs to capture me? 49 Day after
day I was with you in the temple
teaching, and you did not seize me.
But let the scriptures be fulfilled."
50 And they all forsook him and fled.

51 And a young man followed him,
with nothing but a linen cloth about
his body; and they seized him, 52 but
he left the linen cloth and ran away
naked.

[c] Other ancient authorities insert *new* [d] Or *keep awake* [e] Or *Rabbi*

14.17-21: Mt 26.20-25; Lk 22.14, 21-23; Jn 13.21-30; Ps 41.9.
14.22-25: Mt 26.26-29; Lk 22.17-19; 1 Cor 11.23-26. **14.22:** Mk 6.41; 8.6; Lk 24.30.
14.23: 1 Cor 10.16. **14.24:** Ex 24.8; Heb 9.20. **14.26-31:** Mt 26.30-35; Lk 22.39, 33-34.
14.27: Zech 13.7; Jn 16.32. **14.28:** Mk 16.7. **14.30:** Mk 14.66-72; Jn 13.36-38; 18.17-18, 25-27.
14.32-42: Mt 26.36-46; Lk 22.40-46; Heb 5.7-8. **14.34:** Jn 12.27.
14.36: Rom 8.15; Gal 4.6; Mk 10.38; Jn 18.11. **14.38:** Mt 6.13; Lk 11.4.
14.43-50: Mt 26.47-56; Lk 22.47-53; Jn 18.2-11. **14.49:** Lk 19.47; Jn 18.19-21.

53 And they led Jesus to the high
priest; and all the chief priests and the
elders and the scribes were assembled.
54And Peter had followed him at a
distance, right into the courtyard of
the high priest; and he was sitting
with the guards, and warming himself
at the fire. 55 Now the chief priests
and the whole council sought testimony
against Jesus to put him to death; but
they found none. 56 For many bore
false witness against him, and their
witness did not agree. 57And some
stood up and bore false witness against
him, saying, 58 "We heard him say,
'I will destroy this temple that is made
with hands, and in three days I will
build another, not made with hands.'"
59 Yet not even so did their testimony
agree. 60And the high priest stood up
in the midst, and asked Jesus, "Have
you no answer to make? What is it that
these men testify against you?" 61 But
he was silent and made no answer.
Again the high priest asked him, "Are
you the Christ, the Son of the Blessed?"
62And Jesus said, "I am; and you will
see the Son of man sitting at the right
hand of Power, and coming with the
clouds of heaven." 63And the high
priest tore his mantle, and said, "Why
do we still need witnesses? 64 You have
heard his blasphemy. What is your
decision?" And they all condemned
him as deserving death. 65And some
began to spit on him, and to cover his
face, and to strike him, saying to him,
"Prophesy!" And the guards received
him with blows.

66 And as Peter was below in the
courtyard, one of the maids of the
high priest came; 67 and seeing Peter
warming himself, she looked at him,
and said, "You also were with the
Nazarene, Jesus." 68 But he denied it,
saying, "I neither know nor understand what you mean." And he went
out into the gateway.[f] 69And the maid
saw him, and began again to say to
the bystanders, "This man is one of
them." 70 But again he denied it. And
after a little while again the bystanders
said to Peter, "Certainly you are one
of them; for you are a Galilean."
71 But he began to invoke a curse on
himself and to swear, "I do not know
this man of whom you speak." 72And
immediately the cock crowed a second
time. And Peter remembered how
Jesus had said to him, "Before the
cock crows twice, you will deny me
three times." And he broke down and
wept.

15 And as soon as it was morning
the chief priests, with the elders
and scribes, and the whole council held
a consultation; and they bound Jesus
and led him away and delivered him
to Pilate. 2And Pilate asked him, "Are
you the King of the Jews?" And he
answered him, "You have said so."
3And the chief priests accused him of
many things. 4And Pilate again asked
him, "Have you no answer to make?
See how many charges they bring
against you." 5 But Jesus made no
further answer, so that Pilate wondered.

6 Now at the feast he used to
release for them one prisoner whom
they asked. 7And among the rebels in
prison, who had committed murder in
the insurrection, there was a man
called Ba·rab'bas. 8And the crowd
came up and began to ask Pilate to do
as he was wont to do for them. 9And
he answered them, "Do you want me
to release for you the King of the
Jews?" 10 For he perceived that it was
out of envy that the chief priests had
delivered him up. 11 But the chief
priests stirred up the crowd to have
him release for them Ba·rab'bas instead. 12And Pilate again said to them,
"Then what shall I do with the man
whom you call the King of the Jews?"
13And they cried out again, "Crucify
him." 14And Pilate said to them,
"Why, what evil has he done?" But
they shouted all the more, "Crucify
him." 15 So Pilate, wishing to satisfy
the crowd, released for them Ba·rab'-
bas; and having scourged Jesus, he
delivered him to be crucified.

16 And the soldiers led him away
inside the palace (that is, the praetorium); and they called together the
whole battalion. 17And they clothed
him in a purple cloak, and plaiting a
crown of thorns they put it on him.

[f] Or *fore-court.* Other ancient authorities add *and the cock crowed*

14.53-65: Mt 26.57-68; Lk 22.54-55, 63-71; Jn 18.12-24. **14.58:** Mk 13.2; 15.29; Acts 6.14; Jn 2.19.
14.62: Dan 7.13; Mk 9.1; 13.26. **14.63:** Acts 14.14; Num 14.6. **14.64:** Lev 24.16.
14.66-72: Mt 26.69-75; Lk 22.56-62; Jn 18.16-18, 25-27; Mk 14.30.
15.1: Mt 27.1-2; Lk 23.1; Jn 18.28. **15.2-15:** Mt 27.11-26; Lk 23.2-3, 18-25; Jn 18.29-19.16.
15.11: Acts 3.14. **15.16-20:** Mt 27.27-31; Lk 23.11; Jn 19.2-3.

18And they began to salute him, "Hail,
King of the Jews!" 19And they struck
his head with a reed, and spat upon
him, and they knelt down in homage
to him. 20And when they had mocked
him, they stripped him of the purple
cloak, and put his own clothes on him.
And they led him out to crucify him.

21 And they compelled a passerby,
Simon of Cȳ·rē′nē, who was coming
in from the country, the father of
Alexander and Rufus, to carry his
cross. 22And they brought him to the
place called Gol′gȯ·thȧ (which means
the place of a skull). 23And they offered
him wine mingled with myrrh; but he
did not take it. 24And they crucified
him, and divided his garments among
them, casting lots for them, to decide
what each should take. 25And it was
the third hour, when they crucified
him. 26And the inscription of the
charge against him read, "The King
of the Jews." 27And with him they
crucified two robbers, one on his right
and one on his left.[g] 29And those who
passed by derided him, wagging their
heads, and saying, "Aha! You who
would destroy the temple and build it
in three days, 30 save yourself, and
come down from the cross!" 31 So also
the chief priests mocked him to one
another with the scribes, saying, "He
saved others; he cannot save himself.
32 Let the Christ, the King of Israel,
come down now from the cross, that
we may see and believe." Those who
were crucified with him also reviled
him.

33 And when the sixth hour had
come, there was darkness over the
whole land[h] until the ninth hour.
34And at the ninth hour Jesus cried
with a loud voice, "E′lō-ī, E′lō-ī,
lä′mȧ sȧ·bach′-thā′nī?" which means,
"My God, my God, why hast thou
forsaken me?" 35And some of the bystanders hearing it said, "Behold, he
is calling E·lī′jȧh." 36And one ran and,
filling a sponge full of vinegar, put it
on a reed and gave it to him to drink,
saying, "Wait, let us see whether
E·lī′jȧh will come to take him down."
37And Jesus uttered a loud cry, and
breathed his last. 38And the curtain of
the temple was torn in two, from top
to bottom. 39And when the centurion,
who stood facing him, saw that he
thus[i] breathed his last, he said, "Truly
this man was the Son[x] of God!"

40 There were also women looking
on from afar, among whom were Mary
Mag′dȧ·lēne, and Mary the mother of
James the younger and of Jō′sēṡ, and
Sȧ·lō′mē, 41 who, when he was in
Galilee, followed him, and ministered
to him; and also many other women
who came up with him to Jerusalem.

42 And when evening had come,
since it was the day of Preparation,
that is, the day before the sabbath,
43 Joseph of Ar·i·mȧ·thē′ȧ, a respected
member of the council, who was also
himself looking for the kingdom of
God, took courage and went to Pilate,
and asked for the body of Jesus. 44And
Pilate wondered if he were already
dead; and summoning the centurion,
he asked him whether he was already
dead.[j] 45And when he learned from the
centurion that he was dead, he granted
the body to Joseph. 46And he bought
a linen shroud, and taking him down,
wrapped him in the linen shroud, and
laid him in a tomb which had been
hewn out of the rock; and he rolled a
stone against the door of the tomb.
47 Mary Mag′dȧ·lēne and Mary the
mother of Jō′sēṡ saw where he was laid.

16 And when the sabbath was past,
Mary Mag′dȧ·lēne, and Mary the
mother of James, and Sȧ·lō′mē,
bought spices, so that they might go
and anoint him. 2And very early on
the first day of the week they went to
the tomb when the sun had risen.
3And they were saying to one another,
"Who will roll away the stone for us
from the door of the tomb?" 4And
looking up, they saw that the stone was
rolled back; for it was very large. 5And
entering the tomb, they saw a young
man sitting on the right side, dressed
in a white robe; and they were amazed.
6And he said to them, "Do not be
amazed; you seek Jesus of Nazareth,

[g] Other ancient authorities insert verse 28, *And the scripture was fulfilled which says, "He was reckoned with the transgressors"* [h] Or *earth* [i] Other ancient authorities insert *cried out and* [x] Or *a son* [j] Other ancient authorities read *whether he had been some time dead*

15.21: Mt 27.32; Lk 23.26; Rom 16.13. **15.22-32:** Mt 27.33-44; Lk 23.33-39; Jn 19.17-24.
15.24: Ps 22.18. **15.29:** Mk 13.2; 14.58; Jn 2.19. **15.31:** Ps 22.7-8.
15.33-41: Mt 27.45-56; Lk 23.44-49; Jn 19.28-30. **15.34:** Ps 22.1. **15.36:** Ps 69.21.
15.38: Heb 10.19-20. **15.39:** Mk 1.11; 9.7. **15.40:** Jn 19.25. **15.41:** Lk 8.1-3.
15.42-47: Mt 27.57-61; Lk 23.50-56; Jn 19.38-42; Acts 13.29. **15.42:** Deut 21.22-23.
16.1-8: Mt 28.1-8; Lk 24.1-10; Jn 20.1-2. **16.1:** Lk 23.56; Jn 19.39.

who was crucified. He has risen, he is
not here; see the place where they laid
him. 7 But go, tell his disciples and
Peter that he is going before you to
Galilee; there you will see him, as he
told you." 8 And they went out and
fled from the tomb; for trembling and
astonishment had come upon them;
and they said nothing to any one, for
they were afraid.[k]

THE GOSPEL ACCORDING TO

LUKE

1 Inasmuch as many have undertaken to compile a narrative of the
things which have been accomplished
among us, 2 just as they were delivered
to us by those who from the beginning
were eyewitnesses and ministers of
the word, 3 it seemed good to me
also, having followed all things closely[a] for some time past, to write
an orderly account for you, most excellent Thē·oph'i lus, 4 that you
may know the truth concerning the
things of which you have been informed.

5 In the days of Her'ȯd, king of
Judea, there was a priest named Zech-
ȧ·rī'ȧh,[b] of the division of Ȧ·bī'jȧh;
and he had a wife of the daughters of
Aaron, and her name was Elizabeth.
6 And they were both righteous before
God, walking in all the commandments
and ordinances of the Lord blameless.
7 But they had no child, because
Elizabeth was barren, and both were
advanced in years.

8 Now while he was serving as
priest before God when his division
was on duty, 9 according to the custom
of the priesthood, it fell to him by lot
to enter the temple of the Lord and
burn incense. 10 And the whole multitude of the people were praying outside at the hour of incense. 11 And
there appeared to him an angel of the
Lord standing on the right side of the
altar of incense. 12 And Zech·ȧ·rī'ȧh
was troubled when he saw him, and
fear fell upon him. 13 But the angel
said to him, "Do not be afraid, Zech-
ȧ·rī'ȧh, for your prayer is heard, and
your wife Elizabeth will bear you a
son, and you shall call his name John.
14 And you will have joy and gladness,
and many will rejoice at his birth;
15 for he will be great before the Lord,

[k] Other texts and versions add as 16.9-20 the following passage:

9 *Now when he rose early on the first day of the week, he appeared first to Mary Magdalene, from whom he had cast out seven demons.* 10 *She went and told those who had been with him, as they mourned and wept.* 11 *But when they heard that he was alive and had been seen by her, they would not believe it.*

12 *After this he appeared in another form to two of them, as they were walking into the country.* 13 *And they went back and told the rest, but they did not believe them.*

14 *Afterward he appeared to the eleven themselves as they sat at table; and he upbraided them for their unbelief and hardness of heart, because they had not believed those who saw him after he had risen.* 15 *And he said to them, "Go into all the world and preach the gospel to the whole creation.* 16 *He who believes and is baptized will be saved; but he who does not believe will be condemned.* 17 *And these signs will accompany those who believe: in my name they will cast out demons; they will speak in new tongues;* 18 *they will pick up serpents, and if they drink any deadly thing, it will not hurt them; they will lay their hands on the sick, and they will recover."*

19 *So then the Lord Jesus, after he had spoken to them, was taken up into heaven, and sat down at the right hand of God.* 20 *And they went forth and preached everywhere, while the Lord worked with them and confirmed the message by the signs that attended it. Amen.*

Other ancient authorities add after verse 8 the following: *But they reported briefly to Peter and those with him all that they had been told. And after this, Jesus himself sent out by means of them, from east to west, the sacred and imperishable proclamation of eternal salvation.*

[a] Or *accurately* [b] Greek *Zacharias*

16.7: Mk 14.28; Jn 21.1-23; Mt 28.7. **1.2:** 1 Jn 1.1; Acts 1.21; Heb 2.3. **1.3:** Acts 1.1.
1.4: Jn 20.31. **1.5:** Mt 2.1; 1 Chron 24.10; 2 Chron 31.2.
1.9: Ex 30.7. **1.11:** Lk 2.9; Acts 5.19.
1.13: Lk 1.30, 60. **1.15:** Num 6.3; Lk 7.33.

and he shall drink no wine nor
strong drink,
and he will be filled with the Holy
Spirit,
even from his mother's womb.
16 And he will turn many of the sons
of Israel to the Lord their God,
17 And he will go before him in the
spirit and power of E·lī'jah,
to turn the hearts of the fathers to
the children,
and the disobedient to the wisdom
of the just,
to make ready for the Lord a people
prepared."
18 And Zech·a·rī'ah said to the angel,
"How shall I know this? For I am an
old man, and my wife is advanced in
years." 19 And the angel answered him,
"I am Gabriel, who stand in the
presence of God; and I was sent to
speak to you, and to bring you this
good news. 20 And behold, you will be
silent and unable to speak until the
day that these things come to pass,
because you did not believe my words,
which will be fulfilled in their time."
21 And the people were waiting for
Zech·a·rī'ah, and they wondered at his
delay in the temple. 22 And when he
came out, he could not speak to them,
and they perceived that he had seen a
vision in the temple; and he made
signs to them and remained dumb.
23 And when his time of service was
ended, he went to his home.

24 After these days his wife Elizabeth conceived, and for five months
she hid herself, saying, 25 "Thus the
Lord has done to me in the days when
he looked on me, to take away my
reproach among men."

26 In the sixth month the angel
Gabriel was sent from God to a city
of Galilee named Nazareth, 27 to a
virgin betrothed to a man whose name
was Joseph, of the house of David; and
the virgin's name was Mary. 28 And he
came to her and said, "Hail, O favored
one, the Lord is with you!"[c] 29 But she
was greatly troubled at the saying, and
considered in her mind what sort of
greeting this might be. 30 And the
angel said to her, "Do not be afraid,
Mary, for you have found favor with
God. 31 And behold, you will conceive
in your womb and bear a son, and you
shall call his name Jesus.
32 He will be great, and will be called
the Son of the Most High;
and the Lord God will give to him
the throne of his father David,
33 and he will reign over the house of
Jacob for ever;
and of his kingdom there will be no
end."
34 And Mary said to the angel, "How
can this be, since I have no husband?"
35 And the angel said to her,
"The Holy Spirit will come upon
you,
and the power of the Most High
will overshadow you;
therefore the child to be born[d] will
be called holy,
the Son of God.
36 And behold, your kinswoman Elizabeth in her old age has also conceived
a son; and this is the sixth month with
her who was called barren. 37 For with
God nothing will be impossible."
38 And Mary said, "Behold, I am the
handmaid of the Lord; let it be to me
according to your word." And the
angel departed from her.

39 In those days Mary arose and
went with haste into the hill country,
to a city of Judah, 40 and she entered
the house of Zech·a·rī'ah and greeted
Elizabeth. 41 And when Elizabeth
heard the greeting of Mary, the babe
leaped in her womb; and Elizabeth was
filled with the Holy Spirit 42 and she
exclaimed with a loud cry, "Blessed
are you among women, and blessed is
the fruit of your womb! 43 And why is
this granted me, that the mother of my
Lord should come to me? 44 For behold, when the voice of your greeting
came to my ears, the babe in my
womb leaped for joy. 45 And blessed is
she who believed that there would be[e]
fulfilment of what was spoken to her
from the Lord."
46 And Mary said,
"My soul magnifies the Lord,
47 and my spirit rejoices in God my
Savior,
48 for he has regarded the low estate of
his handmaiden.

[c] Other ancient authorities add "*Blessed are you among women!*"
[d] Other ancient authorities add *of you* [e] Or *believed, for there will be*
1.17: Mt 11.14; 17.13; Mal 4.5. **1.18:** Lk 1.34. **1.19:** Dan 8.16; 9.21; Mt 18.10.
1.25: Gen 30.23; Is 4.1. **1.30:** Lk 1.13. **1.31:** Lk 2.21; Mt 1.21. **1.33:** Mt 28.18; Dan 2.44.
1.34: Lk 1.18. **1.35:** Mt 1.20. **1.37:** Gen 18.14. **1.42:** Lk 11.27-28. **1.46-55:** 1 Sam 2.1-10.
1.47: 1 Tim 2.3; Tit 2.10; Jude 25.

For behold, henceforth all generations will call me blessed;
49 for he who is mighty has done great things for me,
and holy is his name.
50 And his mercy is on those who fear him
from generation to generation.
51 He has shown strength with his arm,
he has scattered the proud in the imagination of their hearts,
52 he has put down the mighty from their thrones,
and exalted those of low degree;
53 he has filled the hungry with good things,
and the rich he has sent empty away.
54 He has helped his servant Israel,
in remembrance of his mercy,
55 as he spoke to our fathers,
to Abraham and to his posterity for ever."

56And Mary remained with her about
three months, and returned to her
home.

57 Now the time came for Elizabeth
to be delivered, and she gave birth to
a son. 58And her neighbors and kinsfolk heard that the Lord had shown
great mercy to her, and they rejoiced
with her. 59And on the eighth day they
came to circumcise the child; and they
would have named him Zech·ȧ·rī'ȧh
after his father, 60 but his mother said,
"Not so; he shall be called John."
61And they said to her, "None of your
kindred is called by this name." 62And
they made signs to his father, inquir-
ing what he would have him called.
63And he asked for a writing tablet,
and wrote, "His name is John." And
they all marveled. 64And immediately
his mouth was opened and his tongue
loosed, and he spoke, blessing God.
65And fear came on all their neighbors.
And all these things were talked about
through all the hill country of Judea;
66 and all who heard them laid them
up in their hearts, saying, "What then
will this child be?" For the hand of
the Lord was with him.

67 And his father Zech·ȧ·rī'ȧh was
filled with the Holy Spirit, and prophesied, saying,

68 "Blessed be the Lord God of Israel,
for he has visited and redeemed his people,
69 and has raised up a horn of salvation for us
in the house of his servant David,
70 as he spoke by the mouth of his holy prophets from of old,
71 that we should be saved from our enemies,
and from the hand of all who hate us;
72 to perform the mercy promised to our fathers,
and to remember his holy covenant,
73 the oath which he swore to our
father Abraham, 74 to grant us
that we, being delivered from the hand of our enemies,
might serve him without fear,
75 in holiness and righteousness before him all the days of our life.
76 And you, child, will be called the prophet of the Most High;
for you will go before the Lord to prepare his ways,
77 to give knowledge of salvation to his people
in the forgiveness of their sins,
78 through the tender mercy of our God,
when the day shall dawn upon[f] us from on high
79 to give light to those who sit in darkness and in the shadow of death,
to guide our feet into the way of peace."

80And the child grew and became
strong in spirit, and he was in the
wilderness till the day of his manifestation to Israel.

2 In those days a decree went out
from Caesar Augustus that all the
world should be enrolled. 2 This was
the first enrollment, when Quī·rin'i-us
was governor of Syria. 3And all went
to be enrolled, each to his own city.
4And Joseph also went up from
Galilee, from the city of Nazareth, to
Judea, to the city of David, which is
called Bethlehem, because he was of
the house and lineage of David, 5 to be
enrolled with Mary his betrothed, who
was with child. 6And while they were
there, the time came for her to be
delivered. 7And she gave birth to her
first-born son and wrapped him in
swaddling cloths, and laid him in a
manger, because there was no place
for them in the inn.

[f] Or *whereby the dayspring will visit*. Other ancient authorities read *since the dayspring has visited*
1.55: Mic 7.20; Gen 17.7; 18.18; 22.17. **1.59:** Lev 12.3; Gen 17.12. **1.63:** Lk 1.13.
1.76: Lk 7.26; Mal 4.5. **1.77:** Mk 1.4. **1.78:** Mal 4.2; Eph 5.14. **1.79:** Is 9.2; Mt 4.16.
1.80: Lk 2.40; 2.52. **2.1:** Lk 3.1. **2.4:** Lk 1.27.

8 And in that region there were
shepherds out in the field, keeping
watch over their flock by night. 9 And
an angel of the Lord appeared to them,
and the glory of the Lord shone
around them, and they were filled
with fear. 10 And the angel said to
them, "Be not afraid; for behold, I
bring you good news of a great joy
which will come to all the people;
11 for to you is born this day in the city
of David a Savior, who is Christ the
Lord. 12 And this will be a sign for you:
you will find a babe wrapped in
swaddling cloths and lying in a manger." 13 And suddenly there was with
the angel a multitude of the heavenly
host praising God and saying,

14 "Glory to God in the highest,
and on earth peace among men
with whom he is pleased!"[g]

15 When the angels went away
from them into heaven, the shepherds
said to one another, "Let us go over
to Bethlehem and see this thing that
has happened, which the Lord has
made known to us." 16 And they went
with haste, and found Mary and
Joseph, and the babe lying in a manger. 17 And when they saw it they made
known the saying which had been told
them concerning this child; 18 and all
who heard it wondered at what the
shepherds told them. 19 But Mary
kept all these things, pondering them
in her heart. 20 And the shepherds returned, glorifying and praising God
for all they had heard and seen, as it
had been told them.

21 And at the end of eight days,
when he was circumcised, he was
called Jesus, the name given by the
angel before he was conceived in the
womb.

22 And when the time came for
their purification according to the law
of Moses, they brought him up to
Jerusalem to present him to the Lord
23 (as it is written in the law of the
Lord, "Every male that opens the
womb shall be called holy to the
Lord") 24 and to offer a sacrifice according to what is said in the law of
the Lord, "a pair of turtledoves, or
two young pigeons." 25 Now there was
a man in Jerusalem, whose name was
Simeon, and this man was righteous
and devout, looking for the consolation of Israel, and the Holy Spirit was
upon him. 26 And it had been revealed
to him by the Holy Spirit that he
should not see death before he had
seen the Lord's Christ. 27 And inspired
by the Spirit[h] he came into the temple;
and when the parents brought in the
child Jesus, to do for him according to
the custom of the law, 28 he took him
up in his arms and blessed God and
said,

29 "Lord, now lettest thou thy servant
depart in peace,
according to thy word;
30 for mine eyes have seen thy salvation
31 which thou hast prepared in the
presence of all peoples,
32 a light for revelation to the Gentiles,
and for glory to thy people Israel."

33 And his father and his mother
marveled at what was said about him;
34 and Simeon blessed them and said
to Mary his mother,

"Behold, this child is set for the fall
and rising of many in Israel,
and for a sign that is spoken against
35 (and a sword will pierce through
your own soul also),
that thoughts out of many hearts
may be revealed."

36 And there was a prophetess,
Anna, the daughter of Phan′ū-el, of
the tribe of Ash′ėr; she was of a great
age, having lived with her husband
seven years from her virginity, 37 and
as a widow till she was eighty-four.
She did not depart from the temple,
worshiping with fasting and prayer
night and day. 38 And coming up at
that very hour she gave thanks to God,
and spoke of him to all who were looking for the redemption of Jerusalem.

39 And when they had performed
everything according to the law of the
Lord, they returned into Galilee, to
their own city, Nazareth. 40 And the
child grew and became strong, filled
with wisdom; and the favor of God
was upon him.

41 Now his parents went to Jerusalem every year at the feast of the

[g] Other ancient authorities read *peace, good will among men* [h] Or *in the Spirit*

2.9: Lk 1.11; Acts 5.19. **2.11:** Jn 4.42; Acts 5.31; Mt 16.16; Acts 2.36.
2.12: 1 Sam 2.34; 2 Kings 19.29; Is 7.14. **2.14:** Lk 19.38; 3.22. **2.19:** Lk 2.51.
2.21: Lk 1.59, 31; Mt 1.25. **2.22-24:** Lev 12.2-8. **2.23:** Ex 13.2, 12. **2.25:** Lk 2.38; 23.51.
2.30: Is 52.10; Lk 3.6. **2.32:** Is 42.6; 49.6; Acts 13.47; 26.23. **2.36:** Acts 21.9; Josh 19.24; 1 Tim 5.9.
2.40: Judg 13.24; 1 Sam 2.26. **2.41:** Deut 16.1-8; Ex 23.15.

Passover. 42 And when he was twelve
years old, they went up according to
custom; 43 and when the feast was
ended, as they were returning, the boy
Jesus stayed behind in Jerusalem.
His parents did not know it, 44 but
supposing him to be in the company
they went a day's journey, and they
sought him among their kinsfolk and
acquaintances; 45 and when they did
not find him, they returned to Jerusalem, seeking him. 46 After three days
they found him in the temple, sitting
among the teachers, listening to them
and asking them questions; 47 and all
who heard him were amazed at his
understanding and his answers. 48 And
when they saw him they were astonished; and his mother said to him,
"Son, why have you treated us so?
Behold, your father and I have been
looking for you anxiously." 49 And he
said to them, "How is it that you
sought me? Did you not know that I
must be in my Father's house?" 50 And
they did not understand the saying
which he spoke to them. 51 And he
went down with them and came to
Nazareth, and was obedient to them;
and his mother kept all these things
in her heart.

52 And Jesus increased in wisdom
and in stature,[l] and in favor with God
and man.

3 In the fifteenth year of the reign of
Tī·bē′ri-ŭs Caesar, Pontius Pilate
being governor of Judea, and Her′ŏd
being tetrarch of Galilee, and his
brother Philip tetarch of the region of
Ī·tu·raē′ȧ and Trach·ȯ·nī′tis, and Lȳ-
sā′ni-ȧs tetrarch of Ab·ĭ·lē′nē, 2 in the
high-priesthood of An′nas and Cā′iȧ-
phȧs, the word of God came to John
the son of Zech·ȧ·rī′ȧh in the wilderness; 3 and he went into all the region
about the Jordan, preaching a baptism
of repentance for the forgiveness of
sins. 4 As it is written in the book of
the words of Ī·ṡāi′ȧh the prophet,

"The voice of one crying in the
wilderness:
Prepare the way of the Lord,
make his paths straight.
5 Every valley shall be filled,
and every mountain and hill shall
be brought low,
and the crooked shall be made
straight,
and the rough ways shall be made
smooth;
6 and all flesh shall see the salvation
of God."

7 He said therefore to the multitudes that came out to be baptized by
him, "You brood of vipers! Who
warned you to flee from the wrath to
come? 8 Bear fruits that befit repentance, and do not begin to say to yourselves, 'We have Abraham as our
father'; for I tell you, God is able from
these stones to raise up children to
Abraham. 9 Even now the axe is laid
to the root of the trees; every tree
therefore that does not bear good fruit
is cut down and thrown into the fire."

10 And the multitudes asked him,
"What then shall we do?" 11 And he
answered them, "He who has two
coats, let him share with him who has
none; and he who has food, let him do
likewise." 12 Tax collectors also came
to be baptized, and said to him,
"Teacher, what shall we do?" 13 And
he said to them, "Collect no more than
is appointed you." 14 Soldiers also
asked him, "And we, what shall we
do?" And he said to them, "Rob no
one by violence or by false accusation,
and be content with your wages."

15 As the people were in expectation, and all men questioned in their
hearts concerning John, whether perhaps he were the Christ, 16 John answered them all, "I baptize you with
water; but he who is mightier than I
is coming, the thong of whose sandals
I am not worthy to untie; he will
baptize you with the Holy Spirit and
with fire. 17 His winnowing fork is in
his hand, to clear his threshing floor,
and to gather the wheat into his
granary, but the chaff he will burn
with unquenchable fire."

18 So, with many other exhortations, he preached good news to the
people. 19 But Her′ŏd the tetrarch,
who had been reproved by him for
He·rō′di-ȧs, his brother's wife, and for
all the evil things that Herod had

[l] Or *years*

2.48: Mk 3.31-35. **2.51:** Lk 2.19. **2.52:** Lk 1.80; 2.40. **3.1:** Lk 23.1; 9.7; 13.31; 23.7. **3.2:** Jn 18.13; Acts 4.6; Mt 26.3; Jn 11.49. **3.3-9:** Mt 3.1-10; Mk 1.1-5; Jn 1.6, 23. **3.4-6:** Is 40 3-5. **3.6:** Lk 2.30. **3.7:** Mt 12.34; 23.33. **3.8:** Jn 8.33, 39. **3.9:** Mt 7.19; Heb 6.7-8. **3.11:** Lk 6.29. **3.15:** Acts 13.25, Jn 1.19-22. **3.16-18:** Mt 3.11-12; Mk 1.7-8; Jn 1.26-27, 33; Acts 1.5; 11.16; 19 4. **3.19-20:** Mt 14.3-4; Mk 6.17-18.

done, 20 added this to them all, that
he shut up John in prison.
21 Now when all the people were
baptized, and when Jesus also had
been baptized and was praying, the
heaven was opened, 22 and the Holy
Spirit descended upon him in bodily
form, as a dove, and a voice came from
heaven, "Thou art my beloved Son;[j]
with thee I am well pleased."[k]

23 Jesus, when he began his ministry, was about thirty years of age,
being the son (as was supposed) of
Joseph, the son of Hē'lī, 24 the son of
Mat'thȧt, the son of Levi, the son of
Mel'chī, the son of Jan'nȧ-ī, the son
of Joseph, 25 the son of Mat·tȧ·thī'ȧs,
the son of Amos, the son of Nā'hụm,
the son of Es'lī, the son of Nag'gȧ-ī,
26 the son of Mā'ath, the son of Mat-
tȧ·thī'ȧs, the son of Sem'ē-in, the son
of Jō'sech, the son of Jō'dȧ, 27 the son
of Jō-an'ȧn, the son of Rhē'sȧ, the
son of Ze·rub'bȧ·bel, the son of She-
al'ti-el,[l] the son of Nē'rī, 28 the son of
Mel'chī, the son of Ad'dī, the son of
Cō'sȧm, the son of El·mā'dȧm, the son
of Ēr, 29 the son of Joshua, the son of
Ē·li·ē'zėr, the son of Jō'rim, the son
of Mat'thȧt, the son of Levi, 30 the
son of Simeon, the son of Judah, the
son of Joseph, the son of Jō'nȧm,
the son of Ē·lī'ȧ·kim, 31 the son of
Mē'le-ä, the son of Men'nȧ, the son
of Mat'tȧ·thȧ, the son of Nathan, the
son of David, 32 the son of Jesse, the
son of Ō'bed, the son of Bō'az, the son
of Sā'lȧ, the son of Näh'shȯn, 33 the
son of Am·min'ȧ·dab, the son of
Ad'min, the son of Är'nī, the son of
Hez'rȯn, the son of Per'ez, the son
of Judah, 34 the son of Jacob, the son
of Isaac, the son of Abraham, the
son of Tē'rȧh, the son of Nā'hôr,
35 the son of Sē'rụg, the son of Rē'ü,
the son of Pē'leg, the son of Ē'bėr, the
son of Shē'lȧh, 36 the son of Cā-ī'nȧn,
the son of Är·phā'ẋad, the son of
Shem, the son of Noah, the son of
Lā'mech, 37 the son of Mė·thü'sė·lȧh,
the son of Ē'nȯch, the son of Jâr'ėd,
the son of Mȧ·hā'lȧ·lē-el, the son of
Cā-ī'nȧn, 38 the son of Ē'nȯs, the son
of Seth, the son of Adam, the son of
God.

4 And Jesus, full of the Holy Spirit,
returned from the Jordan, and was
led by the Spirit 2 for forty days in the
wilderness, tempted by the devil. And
he ate nothing in those days; and
when they were ended, he was hungry.
3 The devil said to him, "If you are
the Son of God, command this stone
to become bread." 4And Jesus answered him, "It is written, 'Man shall
not live by bread alone.' " 5And the
devil took him up, and showed him
all the kingdoms of the world in a
moment of time, 6 and said to him,
"To you I will give all this authority
and their glory; for it has been delivered to me, and I give it to whom I
will. 7 If you, then, will worship me,
it shall all be yours." 8And Jesus answered him, "It is written,

'You shall worship the Lord your
God,
and him only shall you serve.' "

9And he took him to Jerusalem, and
set him on the pinnacle of the temple,
and said to him, "If you are the Son of
God, throw yourself down from here;
10 for it is written,

'He will give his angels charge of
you, to guard you,'

11 and

'On their hands they will bear you
up,
lest you strike your foot against a
stone.' "

12And Jesus answered him, "It is said,
'You shall not tempt the Lord your
God.' " 13And when the devil had
ended every temptation, he departed
from him until an opportune time.

14 And Jesus returned in the power
of the Spirit into Galilee, and a report
concerning him went out through all
the surrounding country. 15And he
taught in their synagogues, being
glorified by all.

16 And he came to Nazareth, where
he had been brought up; and he went
to the synagogue, as his custom was,

[j] Or *my Son, my* (or *the*) *Beloved* [k] Other ancient authorities read *today I have begotten thee*
[l] Greek *Salathiel*

3.21-22: Mt 3 13-17; Mk 1.9-11; Jn 1.29-34. **3.21.** Lk 5 16; 6.12; 9.18; 9.28; 11.1; Mk 1.35.
3.22. Ps 2.7; Is 42 1; Lk 9.35; Acts 10.38; 2 Pet 1 17.
3.23-38: Mt 1 1-17; Gen 5.3-32; 11.10-26; Ruth 4.18-22; 1 Chron 1.1-4, 24-28; 2.1-15.
3.23. Jn 8 57; Lk 1.27. **4.1-13:** Mt 4 1-11; Mk 1.12-13. **4.2:** Deut 9 9; 1 Kings 19.8.
4.4. Deut 8 3. **4.6:** 1 Jn 5.19. **4.8:** Deut 6 13. **4.10-11:** Ps 91.11-12. **4.12:** Deut 6.16.
4.13: Lk 22 28. **4.14.** Mt 4 12; Mk 1 14; Mt 9.26; Lk 4 37. **4.15:** Mt 4.23; 9.35; 11.1.
4.16-30: Mt 13 53-58; Mk 6 1-6; Acts 13.14-16

on the sabbath day. And he stood up
to read; 17 and there was given to him
the book of the prophet Ī·ṡāi′ȧh. He
opened the book and found the place
where it was written,
18 "The Spirit of the Lord is upon me,
because he has anointed me to
preach good news to the poor.
He has sent me to proclaim release
to the captives
and recovering of sight to the blind,
to set at liberty those who are oppressed,
19 to proclaim the acceptable year of
the Lord."
20 And he closed the book, and gave it
back to the attendant, and sat down;
and the eyes of all in the synagogue
were fixed on him. 21 And he began to
say to them, "Today this scripture has
been fulfilled in your hearing." 22 And
all spoke well of him, and wondered at
the gracious words which proceeded
out of his mouth; and they said, "Is
not this Joseph's son?" 23 And he said
to them, "Doubtless you will quote to
me this proverb, 'Physician, heal yourself; what we have heard you did at
Cȧ·pēr′nȧ·ŭm, do here also in your
own country.' " 24 And he said, "Truly,
I say to you, no prophet is acceptable
in his own country. 25 But in truth, I
tell you, there were many widows in
Israel in the days of E·lī′jȧh, when the
heaven was shut up three years and
six months, when there came a great
famine over all the land; 26 and E·lī′jȧh
was sent to none of them but only to
Zar′ė·phath, in the land of Sī′don, to
a woman who was a widow. 27 And
there were many lepers in Israel in the
time of the prophet E·lī′shȧ; and none
of them was cleansed, but only Nā′ȧ-
man the Syrian." 28 When they heard
this, all in the synagogue were filled
with wrath. 29 And they rose up and
put him out of the city, and led him to
the brow of the hill on which their city
was built, that they might throw him
down headlong. 30 But passing through
the midst of them he went away.

31 And he went down to Cȧ·pēr′nȧ-
ŭm, a city of Galilee. And he was
teaching them on the sabbath; 32 and
they were astonished at his teaching,
for his word was with authority. 33 And
in the synagogue there was a man who
had the spirit of an unclean demon;
and he cried out with a loud voice,
34 "Ah![m] What have you to do with
us, Jesus of Nazareth? Have you come
to destroy us? I know who you are,
the Holy One of God." 35 But Jesus
rebuked him, saying, "Be silent, and
come out of him!" And when the
demon had thrown him down in the
midst, he came out of him, having
done him no harm. 36 And they were
all amazed and said to one another,
"What is this word? For with authority
and power he commands the unclean
spirits, and they come out." 37 And
reports of him went out into every
place in the surrounding region.

38 And he arose and left the synagogue, and entered Simon's house.
Now Simon's mother-in-law was ill
with a high fever, and they besought
him for her. 39 And he stood over her
and rebuked the fever, and it left her;
and immediately she rose and served
them.

40 Now when the sun was setting,
all those who had any that were sick
with various diseases brought them to
him; and he laid his hands on every
one of them and healed them. 41 And
demons also came out of many, crying,
"You are the Son of God!" But he
rebuked them, and would not allow
them to speak, because they knew
that he was the Christ.

42 And when it was day he departed
and went into a lonely place. And the
people sought him and came to him,
and would have kept him from leaving
them; 43 but he said to them, "I must
preach the good news of the kingdom
of God to the other cities also; for I was
sent for this purpose." 44 And he was
preaching in the synagogues of Judea.[n]

5 While the people pressed upon
him to hear the word of God, he
was standing by the lake of Gen·nes′ȧ-
ret. 2 And he saw two boats by the
lake; but the fishermen had gone out
of them and were washing their nets.
3 Getting into one of the boats, which
was Simon's, he asked him to put out
a little from the land. And he sat down

[m] Or *Let us alone* [n] Other ancient authorities read *Galilee*

4.18-19: Is 61.1-2. **4.22:** Jn 6.42; 7.15. **4.23:** Mk 1.21, 2.1; Jn 4.46. **4.24:** Jn 4.44
4.25: 1 Kings 17.1, 8-16; 18.1; Jas 5.17-18. **4.27:** 2 Kings 5.1-14. **4.29:** Acts 7.58; Num 15.35.
4.30: Jn 8.59; 10.39. **4.31-37:** Mk 1.21-28. **4.32:** Mt 7.28; 13.54; 22.33; Mk 11.18; Jn 7 46.
4.37: Lk 4.14; 5.15; Mt 9.26. **4.38-41:** Mt 8.14-17; Mk 1.29-34. **4.42-43:** Mk 1.35-38.
4.44: Mt 4.23; Mk 1.39; Mt 9.35. **5.1-11:** Mt 4.18-22; Mk 1.16-20; Jn 1.40-42; 21 1-19.
5.3: Mt 13.1-2; Mk 4.1.

and taught the people from the boat.
4And when he had ceased speaking,
he said to Simon, "Put out into the
deep and let down your nets for a
catch." 5And Simon answered, "Master, we toiled all night and took
nothing! But at your word I will let
down the nets." 6And when they had
done this, they enclosed a great shoal
of fish; and as their nets were breaking,
7 they beckoned to their partners in
the other boat to come and help them.
And they came and filled both the
boats, so that they began to sink. 8 But
when Simon Peter saw it, he fell down
at Jesus' knees, saying, "Depart from
me, for I am a sinful man, O Lord."
9 For he was astonished, and all that
were with him, at the catch of fish
which they had taken; 10 and so also
were James and John, sons of Zeb′ĕ-
dee, who were partners with Simon.
And Jesus said to Simon, "Do not be
afraid; henceforth you will be catching
men." 11And when they had brought
their boats to land, they left everything and followed him.

12 While he was in one of the cities,
there came a man full of leprosy; and
when he saw Jesus, he fell on his face
and besought him, "Lord, if you will,
you can make me clean." 13And he
stretched out his hand, and touched
him, saying, "I will; be clean." And
immediately the leprosy left him.
14And he charged him to tell no one;
but "go and show yourself to the
priest, and make an offering for your
cleansing, as Moses commanded, for a
proof to the people."[o] 15 But so much
the more the report went abroad concerning him; and great multitudes
gathered to hear and to be healed of
their infirmities. 16 But he withdrew
to the wilderness and prayed.

17 On one of those days, as he was
teaching, there were Pharisees and
teachers of the law sitting by, who had
come from every village of Galilee and
Judea and from Jerusalem; and the
power of the Lord was with him to
heal.[p] 18And behold, men were bringing on a bed a man who was paralyzed,
and they sought to bring him in and
lay him before Jesus;[q] 19 but finding
no way to bring him in, because of the
crowd, they went up on the roof and
let him down with his bed through the
tiles into the midst before Jesus. 20And
when he saw their faith he said, "Man,
your sins are forgiven you." 21And the
scribes and the Pharisees began to
question, saying, "Who is this that
speaks blasphemies? Who can forgive
sins but God only?" 22 When Jesus
perceived their questionings, he answered them, "Why do you question
in your hearts? 23 Which is easier, to
say, 'Your sins are forgiven you,' or to
say, 'Rise and walk'? 24 But that you
may know that the Son of man has
authority on earth to forgive sins"—
he said to the man who was paralyzed—"I say to you, rise, take up
your bed and go home." 25And immediately he rose before them, and
took up that on which he lay, and went
home, glorifying God. 26And amazement seized them all, and they glorified
God and were filled with awe, saying,
"We have seen strange things today."

27 After this he went out, and saw
a tax collector, named Levi, sitting at
the tax office; and he said to him,
"Follow me." 28And he left everything, and rose and followed him.

29 And Levi made him a great
feast in his house; and there was a
large company of tax collectors and
others sitting at table[r] with them.
30And the Pharisees and their scribes
murmured against his disciples, saying,
"Why do you eat and drink with tax
collectors and sinners?" 31And Jesus
answered them, "Those who are well
have no need of a physician, but those
who are sick; 32 I have not come to
call the righteous, but sinners to
repentance.

33 And they said to him, "The disciples of John fast often and offer
prayers, and so do the disciples of the
Pharisees, but yours eat and drink."
34And Jesus said to them, "Can you
make wedding guests fast while the
bridegroom is with them? 35 The days
will come, when the bridegroom is
taken away from them, and then they
will fast in those days." 36 He told
them a parable also: "No one tears a

[o] Greek *to them* [p] Other ancient authorities read *was present to heal them* [q] Greek *him*
[r] Greek *reclining*

5.5: Lk 8.24, 45; 9.33, 49; 17.13. **5.12-16:** Mt 8.1-4; Mk 1.40-45; Lk 17.11-19.
5.14: Lev 13.49; 14.2-32. **5.15:** Lk 4.14, 37; Mt 9.26. **5.16:** Lk 3.21; 6.12, 9.18, 28, 11.1
5.17-26: Mt 9.1-8; Mk 2.1-12; Jn 5.1-9. **5.17:** Mt 15.1; Mk 5.30; Lk 6.19 **5.20:** Lk 7.48-49.
5.27-32: Mt 9.9-13; Mk 2.13-17. **5.30:** Lk 15.1-2. **5.32:** 1 Tim 1.15.
5.33-38: Mt 9.14-17; Mk 2.18-22. **5.33:** Lk 7.18; 11.1; Jn 3.25-26 **5.35:** Lk 9.22; 17.22.

piece from a new garment and puts it
upon an old garment; if he does, he
will tear the new, and the piece from
the new will not match the old. 37 And
no one puts new wine into old wineskins; if he does, the new wine will
burst the skins and it will be spilled,
and the skins will be destroyed. 38 But
new wine must be put into fresh wineskins. 39 And no one after drinking old
wine desires new; for he says, 'The old
is good.' "[s]

6 On a sabbath,[t] while he was going
through the grainfields, his disciples plucked and ate some ears of grain,
rubbing them in their hands. 2 But
some of the Pharisees said, "Why are
you doing what is not lawful to do on
the sabbath?" 3 And Jesus answered,
"Have you not read what David did
when he was hungry, he and those
who were with him: 4 how he entered
the house of God, and took and ate the
bread of the Presence, which it is not
lawful for any but the priests to eat,
and also gave it to those with him?"
5 And he said to them, "The Son of
man is lord of the sabbath."

6 On another sabbath, when he
entered the synagogue and taught, a
man was there whose right hand was
withered. 7 And the scribes and the
Pharisees watched him, to see whether
he would heal on the sabbath, so that
they might find an accusation against
him. 8 But he knew their thoughts, and
he said to the man who had the
withered hand, "Come and stand
here." And he rose and stood there.
9 And Jesus said to them, "I ask you,
is it lawful on the sabbath to do good
or to do harm, to save life or to destroy
it?" 10 And he looked around on them
all, and said to him, "Stretch out your
hand." And he did so, and his hand
was restored. 11 But they were filled
with fury and discussed with one
another what they might do to Jesus.

12 In these days he went out into
the hills to pray; and all night he continued in prayer to God. 13 And when
it was day, he called his disciples, and
chose from them twelve, whom he
named apostles; 14 Simon, whom he
named Peter, and Andrew his brother,
and James and John, and Philip, and
Bartholomew, 15 and Matthew, and
Thomas, and James the son of Al-
phaē'ŭs, and Simon who was called
the Zealot, 16 and Judas the son of
James, and Judas Is·car'i·ŏt, who became a traitor.

17 And he came down with them
and stood on a level place, with a great
crowd of his disciples and a great multitude of people from all Judea and
Jerusalem and the seacoast of Tȳre
and Sī'don, who came to hear him
and to be healed of their diseases;
18 and those who were troubled with
unclean spirits were cured. 19 And all
the crowd sought to touch him, for
power came forth from him and healed
them all.

20 And he lifted up his eyes on his
disciples, and said:
"Blessed are you poor, for yours is
the kingdom of God.
21 "Blessed are you that hunger
now, for you shall be satisfied.
"Blessed are you that weep now, for
you shall laugh.
22 "Blessed are you when men hate
you, and when they exclude you and
revile you, and cast out your name as
evil, on account of the Son of man!
23 Rejoice in that day, and leap for joy,
for behold, your reward is great in
heaven; for so their fathers did to the
prophets.
24 "But woe to you that are rich,
for you have received your consolation.
25 "Woe to you that are full now,
for you shall hunger.
"Woe to you that laugh now, for
you shall mourn and weep.
26 "Woe to you, when all men
speak well of you, for so their fathers
did to the false prophets.
27 "But I say to you that hear,
Love your enemies, do good to those
who hate you, 28 bless those who curse
you, pray for those who abuse you.
29 To him who strikes you on the
cheek, offer the other also; and from
him who takes away your cloak do not
withhold your coat as well. 30 Give to

[s] Other ancient authorities read *better*
[t] Other ancient authorities read *On the second first sabbath* (on the second sabbath after the first)

6.1-5: Mt 12.1-8; Mk 2.23-28. **6.1:** Deut 23.25. **6.2:** Ex 20.10; 23.12, Deut 5.14. **6.3:** 1 Sam 21.1-6.
6.4: Lev 24.9. **6.6-11:** Mt 12.9-14; Mk 3.1-6. **6.12-16:** Mk 3.13-19; Mt 10.2-4; Acts 1.13.
6.12: Lk 3.21; 5.16; 9.18, 28; 11.1. **6.17-19:** Mt 5.1-2; 4.24-25; Mk 3.7-12.
6.19: Mk 3.10; Mt 9.21; 14.36; Lk 5.17. **6.20-23:** Mt 5.3-12. **6.22:** 1 Pet 4.14; Jn 9.22; 16.2.
6.24-26: Lk 10.13-15; 11.38-52; 17.1; 21.23, 22.22. **6.24:** Lk 16.25, Jas 5.1-5; Mt 6.2.
6.27-30: Mt 5.39-44; Rom 12.17; 1 Cor 6.7.

every one who begs from you; and of
him who takes away your goods do not
ask them again. 31 And as you wish
that men would do to you, do so to
them.

32 "If you love those who love you,
what credit is that to you? For even
sinners love those who love them.
33 And if you do good to those who do
good to you, what credit is that to
you? For even sinners do the same.
34 And if you lend to those from whom
you hope to receive, what credit is that
to you? Even sinners lend to sinners,
to receive as much again. 35 But love
your enemies, and do good, and lend,
expecting nothing in return;[v] and
your reward will be great, and you will
be sons of the Most High; for he is
kind to the ungrateful and the selfish.
36 Be merciful, even as your Father is
merciful.

37 "Judge not, and you will not be
judged; condemn not, and you will not
be condemned; forgive, and you will
be forgiven; 38 give, and it will be
given to you; good measure, pressed
down, shaken together, running over,
will be put into your lap. For the
measure you give will be the measure
you get back."

39 He also told them a parable:
"Can a blind man lead a blind man?
Will they not both fall into a pit? 40 A
disciple is not above his teacher, but
every one when he is fully taught will
be like his teacher. 41 Why do you see
the speck that is in your brother's eye,
but do not notice the log that is in
your own eye? 42 Or how can you say
to your brother, 'Brother, let me take
out the speck that is in your eye,' when
you yourself do not see the log that is
in your own eye? You hypocrite, first
take the log out of your own eye, and
then you will see clearly to take out
the speck that is in your brother's eye.

43 "For no good tree bears bad
fruit, nor again does a bad tree bear
good fruit; 44 for each tree is known
by its own fruit. For figs are not
gathered from thorns, nor are grapes
picked from a bramble bush. 45 The
good man out of the good treasure of
his heart produces good, and the evil
man out of his evil treasure produces
evil; for out of the abundance of the
heart his mouth speaks.

46 "Why do you call me 'Lord,
Lord,' and not do what I tell you?
47 Every one who comes to me and
hears my words and does them, I will
show you what he is like: 48 he is like
a man building a house, who dug deep,
and laid the foundation upon rock;
and when a flood arose, the stream
broke against that house and could not
shake it, because it had been well
built.[w] 49 But he who hears and does
not do them is like a man who built a
house on the ground without a foundation; against which the stream broke,
and immediately it fell, and the ruin
of that house was great."

7 After he had ended all his sayings
in the hearing of the people he
entered Cȧ·pẽr′nȧ-ŭm. 2 Now a centurion had a slave who was dear[x] to
him, who was sick and at the point of
death. 3 When he heard of Jesus, he
sent to him elders of the Jews, asking
him to come and heal his slave. 4 And
when they came to Jesus, they besought him earnestly, saying, "He is
worthy to have you do this for him,
5 for he loves our nation, and he built
us our synagogue." 6 And Jesus went
with them. When he was not far from
the house, the centurion sent friends
to him, saying to him, "Lord, do not
trouble yourself, for I am not worthy
to have you come under my roof;
7 therefore I did not presume to come
to you. But say the word, and let my
servant be healed. 8 For I am a man
set under authority, with soldiers
under me: and I say to one, 'Go,' and
he goes; and to another, 'Come,' and
he comes; and to my slave, 'Do this,'
and he does it." 9 When Jesus heard
this he marveled at him, and turned
and said to the multitude that followed
him, "I tell you, not even in Israel
have I found such faith." 10 And when
those who had been sent returned to
the house, they found the slave well.

11 Soon afterward[y] he went to a

[v] Other ancient authorities read *despairing of no man*
[w] Other ancient authorities read *founded upon the rock* [x] Or *valuable*
[y] Other ancient authorities read *Next day*

6.31: Mt 7.12. **6.32-36:** Mt 5.44-48. **6.35:** Mt 5.9. **6.37-38:** Mt 7.1-2; Rom 2.1.
6.38: Mk 4.24; Acts 20.35. **6.39:** Mt 15.14. **6.40:** Mt 10.24-25; Jn 13.16; 15.20. **6.41-42:** Mt 7.3-5.
6.43-45: Mt 7.18-19; 12.33-35; Jas 3.11-12. **6.45:** Mk 7.20. **6.46:** Mt 7.21.
6.47-49: Mt 7.24-27; Jas 1.22-25. **7.1-10:** Mt 8.5-10, 13; Jn 4.46-53. **7.5:** Acts 10.2.
7.11-17: Mk 5.21-24, 35-43; Jn 11.1-44; 1 Kings 17.17-24; 2 Kings 4.32-37.

city called Nā'in, and his disciples
and a great crowd went with him. 12 As
he drew near to the gate of the city,
behold, a man who had died was being
carried out, the only son of his mother,
and she was a widow; and a large
crowd from the city was with her.
13 And when the Lord saw her, he had
compassion on her and said to her,
"Do not weep." 14 And he came and
touched the bier, and the bearers stood
still. And he said, "Young man, I say
to you, arise." 15 And the dead man
sat up, and began to speak. And he
gave him to his mother. 16 Fear seized
them all; and they glorified God, saying, "A great prophet has arisen
among us!" and "God has visited his
people!" 17 And this report concerning him spread through the whole of
Judea and all the surrounding country.

18 The disciples of John told him
of all these things. 19 And John, calling
to him two of his disciples, sent them
to the Lord, saying, "Are you he who
is to come, or shall we look for
another?" 20 And when the men had
come to him, they said, "John the
Baptist has sent us to you, saying,
'Are you he who is to come, or shall
we look for another?' " 21 In that hour
he cured many of diseases and plagues
and evil spirits, and on many that were
blind he bestowed sight. 22 And he
answered them, "Go and tell John
what you have seen and heard: the
blind receive their sight, the lame
walk, lepers are cleansed, and the deaf
hear, the dead are raised up, the poor
have good news preached to them.
23 And blessed is he who takes no
offense at me."

24 When the messengers of John
had gone, he began to speak to the
crowds concerning John: "What did
you go out into the wilderness to behold? A reed shaken by the wind?
25 What then did you go out to see?
A man clothed in soft raiment? Behold, those who are gorgeously ap-
pareled and live in luxury are in kings'
courts. 26 What then did you go out
to see? A prophet? Yes, I tell you, and
more than a prophet. 27 This is he of
whom it is written,

'Behold, I send my messenger before thy face,
who shall prepare thy way before
thee.'

28 I tell you, among those born of
women none is greater than John; yet
he who is least in the kingdom of God
is greater than he." 29 (When they
heard this all the people and the tax
collectors justified God, having been
baptized with the baptism of John;
30 but the Pharisees and the lawyers
rejected the purpose of God for themselves, not having been baptized by
him.)

31 "To what then shall I compare
the men of this generation, and what
are they like? 32 They are like children
sitting in the market place and calling
to one another,

'We piped to you, and you did not
dance;
we wailed, and you did not weep.'

33 For John the Baptist has come eating no bread and drinking no wine;
and you say, 'He has a demon.' 34 The
Son of man has come eating and
drinking; and you say, 'Behold, a
glutton and a drunkard, a friend of
tax collectors and sinners!' 35 Yet
wisdom is justified by all her children."

36 One of the Pharisees asked him
to eat with him, and he went into the
Pharisee's house, and sat at table.
37 And behold, a woman of the city,
who was a sinner, when she learned
that he was sitting at table in the
Pharisee's house, brought an alabaster
flask of ointment, 38 and standing behind him at his feet, weeping, she began to wet his feet with her tears, and
wiped them with the hair of her head,
and kissed his feet, and anointed them
with the ointment. 39 Now when the
Pharisee who had invited him saw it,
he said to himself, "If this man were
a prophet, he would have known who
and what sort of woman this is who
is touching him, for she is a sinner."
40 And Jesus answering said to him,
"Simon, I have something to say to
you." And he answered, "What is it,
Teacher?" 41 "A certain creditor had
two debtors; one owed five hundred
denarii, and the other fifty. 42 When
they could not pay, he forgave them

7.13: Lk 7.19; 10.1; 11.39; 12.42; 13.15; 17.5-6; 18.6; 19.8; 22.61; 24.3.
7.16: Lk 7.39; 24.19; Mt 21.11; Jn 6.14. **7.18-35:** Mt 11.2-19. **7.21:** Mt 4.23; Mk 3.10.
7.22: Is 29.18-19; 35.5-6; 61.1; Lk 4.18-19. **7.27:** Mal 3.1; Mk 1.2. **7.29-30:** Mt 21.32; Lk 3.12.
7.33: Lk 1.15. **7.34:** Lk 5.29; 15.1-2; 7.36-50. **7.36-50:** Mt 26.6-13; Mk 14.3-9; Jn 12.1-8.
7.36: Lk 11.37; 14.1. **7.39:** Lk 7.16; 24.19; Mt 21.11; Jn 6.14. **7.42:** Mt 18.25.

both. Now which of them will love
him more?" 43 Simon answered, "The
one, I suppose, to whom he forgave
more." And he said to him, "You
have judged rightly." 44 Then turning
toward the woman he said to Simon,
"Do you see this woman? I entered
your house, you gave me no water for
my feet, but she has wet my feet with
her tears and wiped them with her
hair. 45 You gave me no kiss, but from
the time I came in she has not ceased
to kiss my feet. 46 You did not anoint
my head with oil, but she has anointed
my feet with ointment. 47 Therefore
I tell you, her sins, which are many,
are forgiven, for she loved much; but
he who is forgiven little, loves little."
48 And he said to her, "Your sins are
forgiven." 49 Then those who were at
table with him began to say among
themselves, "Who is this, who even
forgives sins?" 50 And he said to the
woman, "Your faith has saved you;
go in peace."

8 Soon afterward he went on
through cities and villages, preaching and bringing the good news of the
kingdom of God. And the twelve were
with him, 2 and also some women who
had been healed of evil spirits and
infirmities: Mary, called Mag'dȧ·lēne,
from whom seven demons had gone
out, 3 and Jō-an'nȧ, the wife of
Chü'zȧ, Her'ȯd's steward, and Su-
sanna, and many others, who provided
for them[z] out of their means.

4 And when a great crowd came
together and people from town after
town came to him, he said in a parable:
5 "A sower went out to sow his seed;
and as he sowed, some fell along the
path, and was trodden under foot, and
the birds of the air devoured it. 6 And
some fell on the rock; and as it grew
up, it withered away, because it had
no moisture. 7 And some fell among
thorns; and the thorns grew with it
and choked it. 8 And some fell into
good soil and grew, and yielded a
hundredfold." As he said this, he
called out, "He who has ears to hear,
let him hear."

9 And when his disciples asked him
what this parable meant, 10 he said,
"To you it has been given to know the
secrets of the kingdom of God; but for
others they are in parables, so that
seeing they may not see, and hearing
they may not understand. 11 Now the
parable is this: The seed is the word
of God. 12 The ones along the path are
those who have heard; then the devil
comes and takes away the word from
their hearts, that they may not believe
and be saved. 13 And the ones on the
rock are those who, when they hear
the word, receive it with joy; but these
have no root, they believe for a while
and in time of temptation fall away.
14 And as for what fell among the
thorns, they are those who hear, but
as they go on their way they are
choked by the cares and riches and
pleasures of life, and their fruit does
not mature. 15 And as for that in the
good soil, they are those who, hearing
the word, hold it fast in an honest and
good heart, and bring forth fruit with
patience.

16 "No one after lighting a lamp
covers it with a vessel, or puts it under
a bed, but puts it on a stand, that those
who enter may see the light. 17 For
nothing is hid that shall not be made
manifest, nor anything secret that
shall not be known and come to light.
18 Take heed then how you hear; for
to him who has will more be given,
and from him who has not, even what
he thinks that he has will be taken
away."

19 Then his mother and his brothers
came to him, but they could not
reach him for the crowd. 20 And he was
told, "Your mother and your brothers
are standing outside, desiring to see
you." 21 But he said to them, "My
mother and my brothers are those
who hear the word of God and do it."

22 One day he got into a boat with
his disciples, and he said to them,
"Let us go across to the other side of
the lake." So they set out, 23 and as
they sailed he fell asleep. And a storm
of wind came down on the lake, and
they were filling with water, and were
in danger. 24 And they went and woke

z Other ancient authorities read *him*

7.43: Lk 10.28. **7.48:** Mt 9.2; Mk 2.5; Lk 5.20. **7.50:** Mt 9.22; Mk 5.34; Lk 8.48.
8.1-3: Lk 4.15; Mk 15.40-41; Mt 27.55-56; Lk 23.49. **8.4-8:** Mt 13.1-9; Mk 4.1-9. **8.8:** Mt 11.15.
8.9-10: Mt 13.10-13; Mk 4.10-12; Is 6.9-10; Jer 5.21; Ezek 12.2. **8.11-15:** Mt 13.18-23; Mk 4.13-20.
8.11: 1 Thess 2.13; 1 Pet 1.23. **8.16:** Mk 4.21; Mt 5.15; Lk 11.33.
8.17: Mk 4.22-23; Mt 10.26-27; Lk 12.2-3; Eph 5.13. **8.18:** Mk 4.24-25; Mt 13.12; 25.29; Lk 19.26.
8.19-21: Mt 12.46-50; Mk 3.31-35. **8.21:** Lk 11.28; Jn 15.14.
8.22-25: Mt 8.23-27; Mk 4.35-41; 6.47-52; Jn 6.16-21. **8.24:** Lk 5.5; 8.45; 9.33, 49; 17.13.

him saying, "Master, Master, we are
perishing!" And he awoke and rebuked
the wind and the raging waves; and
they ceased, and there was a calm.
25 He said to them, "Where is your
faith?" And they were afraid, and they
marveled, saying to one another, "Who
then is this, that he commands even
wind and water, and they obey him?"

26 Then they arrived at the country
of the Ger'ȧ·senes,[a] which is opposite
Galilee. 27 And as he stepped out on
land there met him a man from the
city who had demons; for a long time
he had worn no clothes, and he lived
not in a house but among the tombs.
28 When he saw Jesus, he cried out
and fell down before him, and said
with a loud voice, "What have you to
do with me, Jesus, Son of the Most
High God? I beseech you, do not
torment me." 29 For he had commanded the unclean spirit to come out
of the man. (For many a time it had
seized him; he was kept under guard,
and bound with chains and fetters, but
he broke the bonds and was driven by
the demon into the desert.) 30 Jesus
then asked him, "What is your name?"
And he said, "Legion"; for many
demons had entered him. 31 And they
begged him not to command them to
depart into the abyss. 32 Now a large
herd of swine was feeding there on the
hillside; and they begged him to let
them enter these. So he gave them
leave. 33 Then the demons came out of
the man and entered the swine, and
the herd rushed down the steep bank
into the lake and were drowned.

34 When the herdsmen saw what
had happened, they fled, and told it
in the city and in the country. 35 Then
people went out to see what had
happened, and they came to Jesus, and
found the man from whom the demons
had gone, sitting at the feet of Jesus,
clothed and in his right mind; and
they were afraid. 36 And those who had
seen it told them how he who had
been possessed with demons was
healed. 37 Then all the people of the
surrounding country of the Ger'ȧ-
senes[a] asked him to depart from them;
for they were seized with great fear;
so he got into the boat and returned.
38 The man from whom the demons
had gone begged that he might be with
him; but he sent him away, saying,
39 "Return to your home, and declare
how much God has done for you."
And he went away, proclaiming
throughout the whole city how much
Jesus had done for him.

40 Now when Jesus returned, the
crowd welcomed him, for they were
all waiting for him. 41 And there came
a man named Jā'ī·rŭs, who was a ruler
of the synagogue; and falling at Jesus'
feet he besought him to come to his
house, 42 for he had an only daughter,
about twelve years of age, and she was
dying.

As he went, the people pressed
round him. 43 And a woman who had
had a flow of blood for twelve years[b]
and could not be healed by any one,
44 came up behind him, and touched
the fringe of his garment; and immediately her flow of blood ceased.
45 And Jesus said, "Who was it that
touched me?" When all denied it,
Peter[c] said, "Master, the multitudes
surround you and press upon you!"
46 But Jesus said, "Some one touched
me; for I perceive that power has gone
forth from me." 47 And when the
woman saw that she was not hidden,
she came trembling, and falling down
before him declared in the presence of
all the people why she had touched
him, and how she had been immediately healed. 48 And he said to her,
"Daughter, your faith has made you
well; go in peace."

49 While he was still speaking, a
man from the ruler's house came and
said, "Your daughter is dead; do not
trouble the Teacher any more." 50 But
Jesus on hearing this answered him,
"Do not fear; only believe, and she
shall be well." 51 And when he came
to the house, he permitted no one to
enter with him, except Peter and John
and James, and the father and mother
of the child. 52 And all were weeping
and bewailing her; but he said, "Do
not weep; for she is not dead but
sleeping." 53 And they laughed at him,
knowing that she was dead. 54 But
taking her by the hand he called, saying, "Child, arise." 55 And her spirit

[a] Other ancient authorities read *Gadarenes*, others *Gergesenes*
[b] Other ancient authorities add *and had spent all her living upon physicians*
[c] Other ancient authorities add *and those who were with him*

8.26-39: Mt 8.28-34; Mk 5.1-20. **8.28:** Mk 1.24; Jn 2.4. **8.40-56:** Mt 9.18-26; Mk 5.21-43.
8.45: Lk 8.24. **8.46:** Lk 5.17; 6.19. **8.48:** Mt 9.22; Lk 7.50; 17.19; 18.42.

returned, and she got up at once; and
he directed that something should be
given her to eat. 56And her parents
were amazed; but he charged them to
tell no one what had happened.

9 And he called the twelve together
and gave them power and authority
over all demons and to cure diseases,
2 and he sent them out to preach the
kingdom of God and to heal. 3And he
said to them, "Take nothing for your
journey, no staff, nor bag, nor bread,
nor money; and do not have two
tunics. 4And whatever house you enter,
stay there, and from there depart.
5And wherever they do not receive
you, when you leave that town shake
off the dust from your feet as a
testimony against them." 6And they
departed and went through the villages, preaching the gospel and healing
everywhere.

7 Now Her'od the tetrarch heard
of all that was done, and he was
perplexed, because it was said by some
that John had been raised from the
dead, 8 by some that E·lī'jah had
appeared, and by others that one of
the old prophets had risen. 9 Her'od
said, "John I beheaded; but who is
this about whom I hear such things?"
And he sought to see him.

10 On their return the apostles told
him what they had done. And he took
them and withdrew apart to a city
called Beth-sā'i·da. 11 When the
crowds learned it, they followed him;
and he welcomed them and spoke to
them of the kingdom of God, and
cured those who had need of healing.
12 Now the day began to wear away;
and the twelve came and said to him,
"Send the crowd away, to go into the
villages and country round about, to
lodge and get provisions; for we are
here in a lonely place." 13 But he said
to them, "You give them something
to eat." They said, "We have no more
than five loaves and two fish—unless
we are to go and buy food for all these
people." 14 For there were about five
thousand men. And he said to his disciples, "Make them sit down in companies, about fifty each." 15And they
did so, and made them all sit down.
16And taking the five loaves and the
two fish he looked up to heaven, and
blessed and broke them, and gave
them to the disciples to set before the
crowd. 17And all ate and were satisfied.
And they took up what was left over,
twelve baskets of broken pieces.

18 Now it happened that as he was
praying alone the disciples were with
him; and he asked them, "Who do
the people say that I am?" 19And they
answered, "John the Baptist; but
others say, E·lī'jah; and others, that
one of the old prophets has risen."
20And he said to them, "But who do
you say that I am?" And Peter answered, "The Christ of God." 21 But
he charged and commanded them to
tell this to no one, 22 saying, "The Son
of man must suffer many things, and
be rejected by the elders and chief
priests and scribes, and be killed, and
on the third day be raised."

23 And he said to all, "If any man
would come after me, let him deny
himself and take up his cross daily and
follow me. 24 For whoever would save
his life will lose it; and whoever loses
his life for my sake, he will save it.
25 For what does it profit a man if he
gains the whole world and loses or
forfeits himself? 26 For whoever is
ashamed of me and of my words, of
him will the Son of man be ashamed
when he comes in his glory and the
glory of the Father and of the holy
angels. 27 But I tell you truly, there
are some standing here who will not
taste death before they see the kingdom of God."

28 Now about eight days after these
sayings he took with him Peter and
John and James, and went up on the
mountain to pray. 29And as he was
praying, the appearance of his countenance was altered, and his raiment
became dazzling white. 30And behold,
two men talked with him, Moses and
E·lī'jah, 31 who appeared in glory and

8.56: Mt 8.4; Mk 3.12; 7.36; Lk 9.21. **9.1-6:** Mt 10.1, 5, 7-11, 14; Mk 6.7-12; Lk 10.4-11.
9.5: Acts 13.51. **9.7-9:** Mt 14.1-2; Mk 6.14-16; Lk 9.19. **9.9:** Lk 23.8.
9.10: Mk 6.30-31; Lk 10.17; Jn 1.44. **9.11-17:** Mt 14.13-21; Mk 6.32-44; Jn 6.1-14; Mk 8.4-10.
9.13: 2 Kings 4.42-44. **9.16:** Lk 22.19; 24.30-31; Acts 2.42; 20.11; 27.35.
9.18-21: Mt 16.13-20; Mk 8.27-30; Jn 1.49; 11.27; 6.66-69. **9.18:** Lk 3.21; 5.16; 6.12; 9.28; 11.1.
9.19: Lk 9.9; Mk 9.11-13. **9.22:** Mt 16.21; Mk 8.31; Lk 9.43-45; 18.31-34; 17.25.
9.23-27: Mt 16.24-28; Mk 8.34-9.1. **9.24-25:** Mt 10.38-39; Lk 14.27; 17.33; Jn 12.25.
9.26: Mt 10.33; Lk 12.9; 1 Jn 2.28. **9.27:** Lk 22.18; Mt 10.23; 1 Thess 4.15-18; Jn 21.22.
9.28-36: Mt 17.1-8; Mk 9.2-8; 2 Pet 1.17-18. **9.28:** Lk 8.51; 3.21; 5.16; 6.12; 9.18; 11.1.
9.30: Acts 1.9-11.

spoke of his departure, which he was
to accomplish at Jerusalem. 32 Now
Peter and those who were with him
were heavy with sleep but kept awake,
and they saw his glory and the two
men who stood with him. 33 And as
the men were parting from him, Peter
said to Jesus, "Master, it is well that
we are here; let us make three booths,
one for you and one for Moses and one
for E·lī'jah"—not knowing what he
said. 34 As he said this, a cloud came
and overshadowed them; and they
were afraid as they entered the cloud.
35 And a voice came out of the cloud,
saying, "This is my Son, my Chosen;[d]
listen to him!" 36 And when the voice
had spoken, Jesus was found alone.
And they kept silence and told no one
in those days anything of what they
had seen.

37 On the next day, when they had
come down from the mountain, a
great crowd met him. 38 And behold,
a man from the crowd cried, "Teacher,
I beg you to look upon my son, for he
is my only child; 39 and behold, a spirit
seizes him, and he suddenly cries out;
it convulses him till he foams, and
shatters him, and will hardly leave
him. 40 And I begged your disciples to
cast it out, but they could not."
41 Jesus answered, "O faithless and
perverse generation, how long am I to
be with you and bear with you? Bring
your son here." 42 While he was
coming, the demon tore him and convulsed him. But Jesus rebuked the
unclean spirit, and healed the boy, and
gave him back to his father. 43 And all
were astonished at the majesty of God.

But while they were all marveling
at everything he did, he said to his
disciples, 44 "Let these words sink into
your ears; for the Son of man is to be
delivered into the hands of men."
45 But they did not understand this
saying, and it was concealed from
them, that they should not perceive
it; and they were afraid to ask him
about this saying.

46 And an argument arose among
them as to which of them was the
greatest. 47 But when Jesus perceived
the thought of their hearts, he took a
child and put him by his side, 48 and
said to them, "Whoever receives this
child in my name receives me, and
whoever receives me receives him who
sent me; for he who is least among you
all is the one who is great."

49 John answered, "Master, we saw
a man casting out demons in your
name, and we forbade him, because he
does not follow with us." 50 But Jesus
said to him, "Do not forbid him; for
he that is not against you is for you."

51 When the days drew near for
him to be received up, he set his face
to go to Jerusalem. 52 And he sent messengers ahead of him, who went and
entered a village of the Samaritans, to
make ready for him; 53 but the people
would not receive him, because his
face was set toward Jerusalem. 54 And
when his disciples James and John
saw it, they said, "Lord, do you want
us to bid fire come down from heaven
and consume them?"[e] 55 But he turned
and rebuked them.[f] 56 And they went
on to another village.

57 As they were going along the
road, a man said to him, "I will follow
you wherever you go." 58 And Jesus
said to him, "Foxes have holes, and
birds of the air have nests; but the
Son of man has nowhere to lay his
head." 59 To another he said, "Follow
me." But he said, "Lord, let me first
go and bury my father." 60 But he
said to him, "Leave the dead to bury
their own dead; but as for you, go and
proclaim the kingdom of God."
61 Another said, "I will follow you,
Lord; but let me first say farewell to
those at my home." 62 Jesus said to
him, "No one who puts his hand to
the plow and looks back is fit for the
kingdom of God."

10 After this the Lord appointed
seventy[g] others, and sent them on
ahead of him, two by two, into every
town and place where he himself was

[d] Other ancient authorities read *my Beloved* [e] Other ancient authorities add *as Elijah did*
[f] Other ancient authorities add *and he said, "You do not know what manner of spirit you are of; for the Son of man came not to destroy men's lives but to save them"*
[g] Other ancient authorities read *seventy-two*

9.32: Jn 1.14. **9.33:** Lk 5.5; 8.24, 45; 9.49; 17.13. **9.35:** Lk 3.22; Jn 12.28-30.
9.36: Mt 17.9; Mk 9.9-10. **9.37-43:** Mt 17.14-18; Mk 9.14-27.
9.43-45: Mt 17.22-23; Mk 9.30-32; Lk 9.22; 18.31-34; 17.25. **9.46-48:** Mt 18.1-5; Mk 9.33-37.
9.48: Lk 10.16; Mt 10.40. **9.49-50:** Mk 9.38-40; Lk 11.23. **9.49:** Lk 5.5; 8.24, 45; 9.33; 17.13.
9.51-56: Mk 10.1; Lk 17.11; Jn 4.40-42. **9.52:** Mt 10.5; Jn 4.4. **9.54:** Mk 3.17; 2 Kings 1.9-16.
9.57-60: Mt 8.19-22. **9.61:** 1 Kings 19.20; Phil 3.13. **10.1:** Lk 9.1-2, 51-52; 7.13.

about to come. 2 And he said to them,
"The harvest is plentiful, but the
laborers are few; pray therefore the
Lord of the harvest to send out
laborers into his harvest. 3 Go your
way; behold, I send you out as lambs
in the midst of wolves. 4 Carry no
purse, no bag, no sandals; and salute
no one on the road. 5 Whatever house
you enter, first say, 'Peace be to this
house!' 6 And if a son of peace is there,
your peace shall rest upon him; but if
not, it shall return to you. 7 And remain
in the same house, eating and drinking
what they provide, for the laborer
deserves his wages; do not go from
house to house. 8 Whenever you enter
a town and they receive you, eat what
is set before you; 9 heal the sick in it
and say to them, 'The kingdom of
God has come near to you.' 10 But
whenever you enter a town and they
do not receive you, go into its streets
and say, 11 'Even the dust of your
town that clings to our feet, we wipe
off against you; nevertheless know
this, that the kingdom of God has
come near.' 12 I tell you, it shall be
more tolerable on that day for Sod'ŏm
than for that town.

13 "Woe to you, Chō·rā'zin! woe to
you, Beth-sā'i·dȧ! for if the mighty
works done in you had been done in
Tȳre and Sī'don, they would have
repented long ago, sitting in sackcloth
and ashes. 14 But it shall be more
tolerable in the judgment for Tȳre and
Sī'don than for you. 15 And you,
Cȧ·pẽr'nȧ·ŭm, will you be exalted to
heaven? You shall be brought down
to Hades.

16 "He who hears you hears me,
and he who rejects you rejects me, and
he who rejects me rejects him who
sent me."

17 The seventy[g] returned with joy,
saying, "Lord, even the demons are
subject to us in your name!" 18 And he
said to them, "I saw Satan fall like
lightning from heaven. 19 Behold, I
have given you authority to tread upon
serpents and scorpions, and over all
the power of the enemy; and nothing
shall hurt you. 20 Nevertheless do not
rejoice in this, that the spirits are subject to you; but rejoice that your names
are written in heaven."

21 In that same hour he rejoiced in
the Holy Spirit and said, "I thank thee,
Father, Lord of heaven and earth, that
thou hast hidden these things from the
wise and understanding and revealed
them to babes; yea, Father, for such
was thy gracious will.[h] 22 All things
have been delivered to me by my
Father; and no one knows who the Son
is except the Father, or who the Father
is except the Son and any one to whom
the Son chooses to reveal him."

23 Then turning to the disciples he
said privately, "Blessed are the eyes
which see what you see! 24 For I tell
you that many prophets and kings
desired to see what you see, and did
not see it, and to hear what you hear,
and did not hear it."

25 And behold, a lawyer stood up to
put him to the test, saying, "Teacher,
what shall I do to inherit eternal life?"
26 He said to him, "What is written in
the law? How do you read?" 27 And he
answered, "You shall love the Lord
your God with all your heart, and
with all your soul, and with all your
strength, and with all your mind; and
your neighbor as yourself." 28 And he
said to him, "You have answered
right; do this, and you will live."

29 But he, desiring to justify himself, said to Jesus, "And who is my
neighbor?" 30 Jesus replied, "A man
was going down from Jerusalem to
Jericho, and he fell among robbers,
who stripped him and beat him, and
departed, leaving him half dead.
31 Now by chance a priest was going
down that road; and when he saw him
he passed by on the other side. 32 So
likewise a Levite, when he came to the
place and saw him, passed by on the
other side. 33 But a Samaritan, as he
journeyed, came to where he was; and
when he saw him, he had compassion,
34 and went to him and bound up his

[g] Other ancient authorities read *seventy-two* [h] Or *so it was well-pleasing before thee*

10.2: Mt 9.37-38; Jn 4.35. **10.3-12:** Mt 10.7-16; Mk 6.8-11; Lk 9.2-5; 22.35-36. **10.5:** 1 Sam 25.6.
10.7: 1 Cor 10.27; 9.14; 1 Tim 5.18; Deut 24.15. **10.11:** Acts 13.51.
10.12: Mt 11.24; Gen 19.24-28; Jude 7. **10.13-15:** Mt 11.21-23; Lk 6.24-26.
10.16: Mt 10.40; 18.5; Mk 9.37; Lk 9.48; Jn 13.20; 12.48. **10.18:** Rev 12.9; Jn 12.31.
10.20: Ex 32.32; Ps 69.28; Dan 12.1; Phil 4.3; Heb 12.23; Rev 3.5; 13.8; 21.27.
10.21-22: Mt. 11.25-27. **10.21:** 1 Cor 1.26-29. **10.22:** Mt 28.18; Jn 3.35; 13.3; 10.15; 17.25.
10.23-24: Mt 13.16-17; Jn 8.56; Heb 11.13; 1 Pet 1.10-12. **10.25-28:** Mt 22.34-39; Mk 12.28-31.
10.25: Mk 10.17; Mt 19.16; Lk 18.18. **10.27:** Deut 6.5; Lev 19.18; Rom 13.9; Gal 5.14; Jas 2.8.
10.28: Lk 20.39; Lev 18.5. **10.33:** Lk 9.51-56; 17.11-19; Jn 4.4-42.

wounds, pouring on oil and wine; then
he set him on his own beast and
brought him to an inn, and took care
of him. 35And the next day he took out
two denarii[i] and gave them to the inn-
keeper, saying, 'Take care of him; and
whatever more you spend, I will repay
you when I come back.' 36 Which of
these three, do you think, proved
neighbor to the man who fell among
the robbers?" 37 He said, "The one
who showed mercy on him." And Jesus
said to him, "Go and do likewise."

38 Now as they went on their way,
he entered a village; and a woman
named Martha received him into her
house. 39And she had a sister called
Mary, who sat at the Lord's feet and
listened to his teaching. 40 But Martha
was distracted with much serving; and
she went to him and said, "Lord, do
you not care that my sister has left me
to serve alone? Tell her then to help
me." 41 But the Lord answered her,
"Martha, Martha, you are anxious and
troubled about many things; 42 one
thing is needful.[j] Mary has chosen the
good portion, which shall not be taken
away from her."

11 He was praying in a certain
place, and when he ceased, one
of his disciples said to him, "Lord,
teach us to pray, as John taught his
disciples." 2And he said to them,
"When you pray, say:

"Father, hallowed be thy name. Thy
kingdom come. 3 Give us each day our
daily bread;[k] 4 and forgive us our sins,
for we ourselves forgive every one who
is indebted to us; and lead us not into
temptation."

5 And he said to them, "Which of
you who has a friend will go to him at
midnight and say to him, 'Friend, lend
me three loaves; 6 for a friend of mine
has arrived on a journey, and I have
nothing to set before him'; 7 and he
will answer from within, 'Do not
bother me; the door is now shut, and
my children are with me in bed; I cannot get up and give you anything'? 8 I
tell you, though he will not get up and
give him anything because he is his
friend, yet because of his importunity
he will rise and give him whatever he
needs. 9And I tell you, Ask, and it will
be given you; seek, and you will find;
knock, and it will be opened to you.
10 For every one who asks receives,
and he who seeks finds, and to him
who knocks it will be opened. 11 What
father among you, if his son asks for[l]
a fish, will instead of a fish give him a
serpent; 12 or if he asks for an egg, will
give him a scorpion? 13 If you then,
who are evil, know how to give good
gifts to your children, how much more
will the heavenly Father give the Holy
Spirit to those who ask him!"

14 Now he was casting out a demon
that was dumb; when the demon had
gone out, the dumb man spoke, and
the people marveled. 15 But some of
them said, "He casts out demons by
Bē-el'zė·bul, the prince of demons";
16 while others, to test him, sought
from him a sign from heaven. 17 But
he, knowing their thoughts, said to
them, "Every kingdom divided against
itself is laid waste, and house falls
upon house. 18And if Satan also is
divided against himself, how will his
kingdom stand? For you say that I
cast out demons by Bē-el'zė·bul.
19And if I cast out demons by Bē-el'zė-
bul, by whom do your sons cast them
out? Therefore they shall be your
judges. 20 But if it is by the finger of
God that I cast out demons, then the
kingdom of God has come upon you.
21 When a strong man, fully armed,
guards his own palace, his goods are
in peace; 22 but when one stronger
than he assails him and overcomes
him, he takes away his armor in which
he trusted, and divides his spoil. 23 He
who is not with me is against me, and
he who does not gather with me
scatters.

24 "When the unclean spirit has
gone out of a man, he passes through
waterless places seeking rest; and finding none he says, 'I will return to my
house from which I came.' 25And
when he comes he finds it swept and
put in order. 26 Then he goes and

[i] The denarius was worth about twenty cents [j] Other ancient authorities read *few things are needful, or only one* [k] Or *our bread for the morrow*
[l] Other ancient authorities insert *bread, will give him a stone; or if he asks for*

10.38-42: Jn 12.1-3; 11.1-45. **10.41:** Lk 7.13.
11.1: Mk 1.35; Lk 3.21; 5.16; 6.12; 9.18, 28; 5.33; 7.18. **11.2-4:** Mt 6.9-13.
11.4: Mk 11.25; Mt 18.35. **11.5-8:** Lk 18.1-8. **11.9-13:** Mt 7.7-11.
11.9: Mt 18.19; 21.22; Mk 11.24; Jas 1.5-8; 1 Jn 5.14-15; Jn 15.7; 16.23-24.
11.14-23: Mt 12.22-30; 10.25; Mk 3.23-27. **11.14-15:** Mt 9.32-34.
11.16: Mt 12.38; 16.1; Mk 8.11; Jn 2.18; 6.30. **11.23:** Lk 9.50. **11.24-26:** Mt 12.43-45.

brings seven other spirits more evil
than himself, and they enter and dwell
there; and the last state of that man
becomes worse than the first."
27 As he said this, a woman in the
crowd raised her voice and said to him,
"Blessed is the womb that bore you,
and the breasts that you sucked!"
28 But he said, "Blessed rather are
those who hear the word of God and
keep it!"
29 When the crowds were increasing, he began to say, "This generation
is an evil generation; it seeks a sign,
but no sign shall be given to it except
the sign of Jō'nȧh. 30 For as Jō'nȧh
became a sign to the men of Nin'ė·vėh,
so will the Son of man be to this generation. 31 The queen of the South
will arise at the judgment with the men
of this generation and condemn them;
for she came from the ends of the
earth to hear the wisdom of Solomon,
and behold, something greater than
Solomon is here. 32 The men of Nin'-
ė·vėh will arise at the judgment with
this generation and condemn it; for
they repented at the preaching of
Jō'nȧh, and behold, something greater
than Jonah is here.
33 "No one after lighting a lamp
puts it in a cellar or under a bushel,
but on a stand, that those who enter
may see the light. 34 Your eye is the
lamp of your body; when your eye is
sound, your whole body is full of
light; but when it is not sound, your
body is full of darkness. 35 Therefore
be careful lest the light in you be darkness. 36 If then your whole body is full
of light, having no part dark, it will be
wholly bright, as when a lamp with its
rays gives you light."
37 While he was speaking, a Pharisee asked him to dine with him; so he
went in and sat at table. 38 The Pharisee was astonished to see that he did
not first wash before dinner. 39 And the
Lord said to him, "Now you Pharisees
cleanse the outside of the cup and of
the dish, but inside you are full of
extortion and wickedness. 40 You fools!
Did not he who made the outside make
the inside also? 41 But give for alms
those things which are within; and behold, everything is clean for you.
42 "But woe to you Pharisees! for
you tithe mint and rue and every herb,
and neglect justice and the love of
God; these you ought to have done,
without neglecting the others. 43 Woe
to you Pharisees! for you love the best
seat in the synagogues and salutations
in the market places. 44 Woe to you;
for you are like graves which are not
seen, and men walk over them without
knowing it."
45 One of the lawyers answered
him, "Teacher, in saying this you
reproach us also." 46 And he said,
"Woe to you lawyers also! for you load
men with burdens hard to bear, and
you yourselves do not touch the
burdens with one of your fingers.
47 Woe to you! for you build the tombs
of the prophets whom your fathers
killed. 48 So you are witnesses and
consent to the deeds of your fathers;
for they killed them, and you build
their tombs. 49 Therefore also the
Wisdom of God said, 'I will send them
prophets and apostles, some of whom
they will kill and persecute,' 50 that
the blood of all the prophets, shed
from the foundation of the world, may
be required of this generation, 51 from
the blood of Ā'bėl to the blood of
Zech·ȧ·rī'ȧh, who perished between
the altar and the sanctuary. Yes, I tell
you, it shall be required of this generation. 52 Woe to you lawyers! for you
have taken away the key of knowledge;
you did not enter yourselves, and you
hindered those who were entering."
53 As he went away from there, the
scribes and the Pharisees began to
press him hard, and to provoke him to
speak of many things, 54 lying in wait
for him, to catch at something he
might say.

12 In the meantime, when so many
thousands of the multitude had
gathered together that they trod upon
one another, he began to say to his
disciples first, "Beware of the leaven
of the Pharisees, which is hypocrisy.
2 Nothing is covered up that will not
be revealed, or hidden that will not be

11.27: Lk 1.42; 23.29. **11.28:** Lk 8.21; Jn 15.14. **11.29-32:** Mt 12.39-42.
11.29: Mt 16.4; Mk 8.12; Lk 11.16; Jon 3.4-5. **11.31:** 1 Kings 10.1-10; 2 Chron 9.1-12.
11.32: Mt 12.6. **11.33:** Mt 5.15; Mk 4.21; Lk 8.16. **11.34-35:** Mt 6.22-23. **11.37:** Lk 7.36; 14.1.
11.38: Mk 7.1-5. **11.39-41:** Mt 23.25-26. **11.39:** Lk 7.13. **11.41:** Tit 1.15; Mk 7.19.
11.42: Mt 23.23-24; Lev 27.30; Mic 6.8. **11.43:** Mt 23.6-7; Mk 12.38-39; Lk 20.46. **11.44:** Mt 23.27.
11.46: Mt 23.4. **11.47-48:** Mt 23.29-32; Acts 7.51-53. **11.49-51:** Mt 23.34-36.
11.49: 1 Cor 1.24; Col 2.3. **11.51:** Gen 4.8; 2 Chron 24.20-21; Zech 1.1. **11.52:** Mt 23.13.
11.53-54: Mk 12.13. **12.1:** Mt 16.6; Mk 8.15. **12.2-3:** Mt 10.26-27; Mk 4.22; Lk 8.17; Eph 5.13.

known. 3 Whatever you have said in
the dark shall be heard in the light,
and what you have whispered in
private rooms shall be proclaimed
upon the housetops.

4 "I tell you, my friends, do not
fear those who kill the body, and after
that have no more that they can do.
5 But I will warn you whom to fear:
fear him who, after he has killed, has
power to cast into hell;[m] yes, I tell
you, fear him! 6 Are not five sparrows
sold for two pennies? And not one of
them is forgotten before God. 7 Why,
even the hairs of your head are all
numbered. Fear not; you are of more
value than many sparrows.

8 "And I tell you, every one who
acknowledges me before men, the Son
of man also will acknowledge before
the angels of God; 9 but he who denies
me before men will be denied before
the angels of God. 10 And every one
who speaks a word against the Son of
man will be forgiven; but he who
blasphemes against the Holy Spirit
will not be forgiven. 11 And when they
bring you before the synagogues and
the rulers and the authorities, do not
be anxious how or what you are to
answer or what you are to say; 12 for
the Holy Spirit will teach you in that
very hour what you ought to say."

13 One of the multitude said to
him, "Teacher, bid my brother divide
the inheritance with me." 14 But he
said to him, "Man, who made me a
judge or divider over you?" 15 And he
said to them, "Take heed, and beware
of all covetousness; for a man's life
does not consist in the abundance of
his possessions." 16 And he told them a
parable, saying, "The land of a rich
man brought forth plentifully; 17 and
he thought to himself, 'What shall I
do, for I have nowhere to store my
crops?' 18 And he said, 'I will do this;
I will pull down my barns, and build
larger ones; and there I will store all
my grain and my goods. 19 And I will
say to my soul, Soul, you have ample
goods laid up for many years; take
your ease, eat, drink, be merry.' 20 But
God said to him, 'Fool! This night
your soul is required of you; and the
things you have prepared, whose will
they be?' 21 So is he who lays up
treasure for himself, and is not rich
toward God."

22 And he said to his disciples,
"Therefore I tell you, do not be anxious about your life, what you shall
eat, nor about your body, what you
shall put on. 23 For life is more than
food, and the body more than clothing.
24 Consider the ravens: they neither
sow nor reap, they have neither storehouse nor barn, and yet God feeds
them. Of how much more value are
you than the birds! 25 And which of
you by being anxious can add a cubit
to his span of life?[n] 26 If then you are
not able to do as small a thing as that,
why are you anxious about the rest?
27 Consider the lilies, how they grow;
they neither toil nor spin;[o] yet I tell
you, even Solomon in all his glory was
not arrayed like one of these. 28 But if
God so clothes the grass which is alive
in the field today and tomorrow is
thrown into the oven, how much more
will he clothe you, O men of little
faith! 29 And do not seek what you are
to eat and what you are to drink, nor
be of anxious mind. 30 For all the nations of the world seek these things;
and your Father knows that you need
them. 31 Instead, seek his[p] kingdom,
and these things shall be yours as well.

32 "Fear not, little flock, for it is
your Father's good pleasure to give
you the kingdom. 33 Sell your possessions, and give alms; provide yourselves with purses that do not grow
old, with a treasure in the heavens
that does not fail, where no thief
approaches and no moth destroys.
34 For where your treasure is, there
will your heart be also.

35 "Let your loins be girded and
your lamps burning, 36 and be like
men who are waiting for their master
to come home from the marriage feast,
so that they may open to him at once
when he comes and knocks. 37 Blessed
are those servants whom the master

[m] Greek *Gehenna* [n] Or *to his stature*
[o] Other ancient authorities read *Consider the lilies; they neither spin nor weave*
[p] Other ancient authorities read *God's*

12.4: Jn 15.14-15. **12.4-9:** Mt 10.28-33. **12.5:** Heb 10.31. **12.7:** Lk 21.18; Acts 27.34; Mt 12.12.
12.9: Mk 8.38; Lk 9.26; 2 Tim 2.12. **12.10:** Mt 12.31-32; Mk 3.28-29.
12.11-12: Mt 10.19-20; Mk 13.11; Lk 21.14-15. **12.15:** 1 Tim 6.6-10.
12.20: Jer 17.11; Job 27.8; Ps 39.6; Lk 12.33-34. **12.22-31:** Mt 6.25-33. **12.24:** Lk 12.6-7.
12.27: 1 Kings 10.1-10. **12.30:** Mt 6.8. **12.32:** Jn 21.15-17. **12.33-34:** Mt 6.19-21; Lk 18.22.
12.35: Eph 6.14; Mt 25.1-13; Mk 13.33-37. **12.37:** Jn 13.3-5; Mt 24.42; Lk 21.36.

finds awake when he comes; truly, I
say to you, he will gird himself and
have them sit at table, and he will
come and serve them. 38 If he comes
in the second watch, or in the third,
and finds them so, blessed are those
servants! 39 But know this, that if the
householder had known at what hour
the thief was coming, he would have
been awake and[q] would not have left
his house to be broken into. 40 You
also must be ready; for the Son of man
is coming at an hour you do not
expect."

41 Peter said, "Lord, are you telling
this parable for us or for all?" 42 And
the Lord said, "Who then is the faithful and wise steward, whom his master
will set over his household, to give
them their portion of food at the
proper time? 43 Blessed is that servant
whom his master when he comes will
find so doing. 44 Truly I tell you, he
will set him over all his possessions.
45 But if that servant says to himself,
'My master is delayed in coming,' and
begins to beat the menservants and the
maidservants, and to eat and drink and
get drunk, 46 the master of that servant
will come on a day when he does not
expect him and at an hour he does not
know, and will punish[r] him, and put
him with the unfaithful. 47 And that
servant who knew his master's will, but
did not make ready or act according
to his will, shall receive a severe beating. 48 But he who did not know, and
did what deserved a beating, shall
receive a light beating. Every one to
whom much is given, of him will much
be required; and of him to whom men
commit much they will demand the
more.

49 "I came to cast fire upon the
earth; and would that it were already
kindled! 50 I have a baptism to be
baptized with; and how I am con-
strained until it is accomplished! 51 Do
you think that I have come to give
peace on earth? No, I tell you, but
rather division; 52 for henceforth in
one house there will be five divided,
three against two and two against
three; 53 they will be divided, father
against son and son against father,
mother against daughter and daughter
against her mother, mother-in-law
against her daughter-in-law and
daughter-in-law against her mother-
in-law."

54 He also said to the multitudes,
"When you see a cloud rising in the
west, you say at once, 'A shower is
coming'; and so it happens. 55 And
when you see the south wind blowing,
you say, 'There will be scorching heat';
and it happens. 56 You hypocrites! You
know how to interpret the appearance
of earth and sky; but why do you not
know how to interpret the present
time?

57 "And why do you not judge for
yourselves what is right? 58 As you go
with your accuser before the magis-
trate, make an effort to settle with him
on the way, lest he drag you to the
judge, and the judge hand you over to
the officer, and the officer put you in
prison. 59 I tell you, you will never get
out till you have paid the very last
copper."

13 There were some present at that
very time who told him of the
Galileans whose blood Pilate had
mingled with their sacrifices. 2 And he
answered them, "Do you think that
these Galileans were worse sinners
than all the other Galileans, because
they suffered thus? 3 I tell you, No;
but unless you repent you will all
likewise perish. 4 Or those eighteen
upon whom the tower in Sī·lō'ăm fell
and killed them, do you think that they
were worse offenders than all the
others who dwelt in Jerusalem? 5 I tell
you, No; but unless you repent you
will all likewise perish."

6 And he told this parable: "A man
had a fig tree planted in his vineyard;
and he came seeking fruit on it and
found none. 7 And he said to the vinedresser, 'Lo, these three years I have
come seeking fruit on this fig tree, and
I find none. Cut it down; why should
it use up the ground?' 8 And he answered him, 'Let it alone, sir, this
year also, till I dig about it and put on
manure. 9 And if it bears fruit next
year, well and good; but if not, you
can cut it down.' "

[q] Other ancient authorities omit *would have been awake and*
[r] Or *cut him in pieces*

12.39-40: Mt 24.43-44; 1 Thess 5.2; Rev 3.3; 16.15; 2 Pet 3.10. **12.42-46:** Mt 24.45-51.
12.42: Lk 7.13. **12.47-48:** Deut 25.2-3; Num 15.29-30; Lk 8.18; 19.26. **12.49:** Lk 22.15.
12.50: Mk 10.38-39; Jn 12.27. **12.51-53:** Mt 10.34-36; Lk 21.16; Mic 7.6. **12.54-56:** Mt 16.2-3.
12.57-59: Mt 5.25-26. **13.2:** Jn 9.1-3. **13.6-9:** Mt 21.18-20; Mk 11.12-14, 20-21.
13.7: Mt 3.10; 7.19; Lk 3.9.

10 Now he was teaching in one of
the synagogues on the sabbath. 11 And
there was a woman who had had a
spirit of infirmity for eighteen years;
she was bent over and could not fully
straighten herself. 12 And when Jesus
saw her, he called her and said to her,
"Woman, you are freed from your
infirmity." 13 And he laid his hands
upon her, and immediately she was
made straight, and she praised God.
14 But the ruler of the synagogue,
indignant because Jesus had healed on
the sabbath, said to the people, "There
are six days on which work ought to
be done; come on those days and be
healed, and not on the sabbath day."
15 Then the Lord answered him, "You
hypocrites! Does not each of you on
the sabbath untie his ox or his ass from
the manger, and lead it away to water
it? 16 And ought not this woman, a
daughter of Abraham whom Satan
bound for eighteen years, be loosed
from this bond on the sabbath day?"
17 As he said this, all his adversaries
were put to shame; and all the people
rejoiced at all the glorious things that
were done by him.

18 He said therefore, "What is the
kingdom of God like? And to what
shall I compare it? 19 It is like a grain
of mustard seed which a man took and
sowed in his garden; and it grew and
became a tree, and the birds of the air
made nests in its branches."

20 And again he said, "To what
shall I compare the kingdom of God?
21 It is like leaven which a woman
took and hid in three measures of
meal, till it was all leavened."

22 He went on his way through
towns and villages, teaching, and
journeying toward Jerusalem. 23 And
some one said to him, "Lord, will
those who are saved be few?" And he
said to them, 24 "Strive to enter by the
narrow door; for many, I tell you, will
seek to enter and will not be able.
25 When once the householder has
risen up and shut the door, you will
begin to stand outside and to knock
at the door, saying, 'Lord, open to us.'
He will answer you, 'I do not know
where you come from.' 26 Then you
will begin to say, 'We ate and drank in
your presence, and you taught in our
streets.' 27 But he will say, 'I tell you,
I do not know where you come from;
depart from me, all you workers of
iniquity!' 28 There you will weep and
gnash your teeth, when you see Abraham and Isaac and Jacob and all the
prophets in the kingdom of God and
you yourselves thrust out. 29 And men
will come from east and west, and
from north and south, and sit at table
in the kingdom of God. 30 And behold, some are last who will be first,
and some are first who will be last."

31 At that very hour some Pharisees
came, and said to him, "Get away from
here, for Her'od wants to kill you."
32 And he said to them, "Go and tell
that fox, 'Behold, I cast out demons
and perform cures today and tomorrow, and the third day I finish my
course. 33 Nevertheless I must go on
my way today and tomorrow and the
day following; for it cannot be that a
prophet should perish away from
Jerusalem.' 34 O Jerusalem, Jerusalem,
killing the prophets and stoning those
who are sent to you! How often would
I have gathered your children together
as a hen gathers her brood under her
wings, and you would not! 35 Behold,
your house is forsaken. And I tell you,
you will not see me until you say,
'Blessed is he who comes in the name
of the Lord!' "

14 One sabbath when he went to
dine at the house of a ruler who
belonged to the Pharisees, they were
watching him. 2 And behold, there was
a man before him who had dropsy.
3 And Jesus spoke to the lawyers and
Pharisees, saying, "Is it lawful to heal
on the sabbath, or not?" 4 But they
were silent. Then he took him and
healed him, and let him go. 5 And he
said to them, "Which of you, having
an ass[s] or an ox that has fallen into a
well, will not immediately pull him
out on a sabbath day?" 6 And they
could not reply to this.

7 Now he told a parable to those
who were invited, when he marked
how they chose the places of honor,
saying to them, 8 "When you are in-

[s] Other ancient authorities read *a son*

13.14: Ex 20.9-10; Lk 6.6-11; 14.1-6; Jn 5.1-18. **13.15:** Lk 7.13; 14.5; Mt 12.11. **13.16:** Lk 19.9.
13.18-19: Mt 13.31-32; Mk 4.30-32. **13.20-21:** Mt 13.33. **13.22:** Lk 9.51; 17.11; 18.31; 19.11.
13.23-24: Mt 7.13-14; Jn 10.7. **13.25:** Mt 25.10-12. **13.26-27:** Mt 7.21-23; 25.41; Lk 6.46.
13.28-29: Mt 8.11-12. **13.30:** Mt 19.30; Mk 10.31. **13.32:** Heb 2.10; 7.28.
13.34-35: Mt 23.37-39; Lk 19.41. **13.35:** Jer 22.5; Ps 118.26; Lk 19.38. **14.1:** Lk 7.36; 11.37; Mk 3.2.
14.3: Mt 12.10; Mk 3.4; Lk 6.9. **14.5:** Mt 12.11; Lk 13.15. **14.8:** Prov 25.6-7; Lk 11.43; 20.46.

vited by any one to a marriage feast,
do not sit down in a place of honor,
lest a more eminent man than you be
invited by him; 9 and he who invited
you both will come and say to you,
'Give place to this man,' and then you
will begin with shame to take the
lowest place. 10 But when you are
invited, go and sit in the lowest place,
so that when your host comes he may
say to you, 'Friend, go up higher';
then you will be honored in the
presence of all who sit at table with
you. 11 For every one who exalts himself will be humbled, and he who
humbles himself will be exalted."

12 He said also to the man who had
invited him, "When you give a dinner
or a banquet, do not invite your
friends or your brothers or your kinsmen or rich neighbors, lest they also
invite you in return, and you be repaid.
13 But when you give a feast, invite the
poor, the maimed, the lame, the blind,
14 and you will be blessed, because
they cannot repay you. You will be repaid at the resurrection of the just."

15 When one of those who sat at
table with him heard this, he said to
him, "Blessed is he who shall eat bread
in the kingdom of God!" 16 But he
said to him, "A man once gave a great
banquet, and invited many; 17 and at
the time for the banquet he sent his
servant to say to those who had been
invited, 'Come; for all is now ready.'
18 But they all alike began to make
excuses. The first said to him, 'I have
bought a field, and I must go out and
see it; I pray you, have me excused.'
19 And another said, 'I have bought five
yoke of oxen, and I go to examine
them; I pray you, have me excused.'
20 And another said, 'I have married a
wife, and therefore I cannot come.'
21 So the servant came and reported
this to his master. Then the householder in anger said to his servant, 'Go
out quickly to the streets and lanes of
the city, and bring in the poor and
maimed and blind and lame.' 22 And
the servant said, 'Sir, what you commanded has been done, and still there
is room.' 23 And the master said to the
servant, 'Go out to the highways and
hedges, and compel people to come in,
that my house may be filled. 24 For I
tell you, none of those men who were
invited shall taste my banquet.' "

25 Now great multitudes accompanied him; and he turned and said
to them, 26 "If any one comes to me
and does not hate his own father and
mother and wife and children and
brothers and sisters, yes, and even his
own life, he cannot be my disciple.
27 Whoever does not bear his own
cross and come after me, cannot be
my disciple. 28 For which of you,
desiring to build a tower, does not
first sit down and count the cost,
whether he has enough to complete
it? 29 Otherwise, when he has laid a
foundation, and is not able to finish,
all who see it begin to mock him,
30 saying, 'This man began to build,
and was not able to finish.' 31 Or what
king, going to encounter another king
in war, will not sit down first and take
counsel whether he is able with ten
thousand to meet him who comes
against him with twenty thousand?
32 And if not, while the other is yet a
great way off, he sends an embassy and
asks terms of peace. 33 So therefore,
whoever of you does not renounce all
that he has cannot be my disciple.

34 "Salt is good; but if salt has lost
its taste, how shall its saltness be
restored? 35 It is fit neither for the land
nor for the dunghill; men throw it
away. He who has ears to hear, let him
hear."

15 Now the tax collectors and
sinners were all drawing near to
hear him. 2 And the Pharisees and the
scribes murmured, saying, "This man
receives sinners and eats with them."

3 So he told them this parable:
4 "What man of you, having a hundred
sheep, if he has lost one of them, does
not leave the ninety-nine in the wilderness, and go after the one which is lost,
until he finds it? 5 And when he has
found it, he lays it on his shoulders,
rejoicing. 6 And when he comes home,
he calls together his friends and his
neighbors, saying to them, 'Rejoice
with me, for I have found my sheep
which was lost.' 7 Just so, I tell you,
there will be more joy in heaven over
one sinner who repents than over

14.11: Mt 23.12; Lk 18.14; Mt 18.4; 1 Pet 5.6. **14.12:** Jas 2.2-4. **14.13:** Lk 14.21. **14.15:** Rev 19.9.
14.16-24: Mt 22.1-10. **14.20:** Deut 24.5; 1 Cor 7.33. **14.21:** Lk 14.13. **14.26-27:** Mt 10.37-38.
14.27: Mt 16.24; Mk 8.34; Lk 9.23. **14.33:** Lk 18.29-30; Phil 3.7.
14.34-35: Mt 5.13; Mk 9.49-50; Mt 11.15. **15.1-2:** Lk 5.29-30; 19.7. **15.4-7:** Mt 18.10-14.
15.7: Jas 5.20; Lk 19.10; 15.10.

ninety-nine righteous persons who
need no repentance.
8 "Or what woman, having ten
silver coins,[t] if she loses one coin, does
not light a lamp and sweep the house
and seek diligently until she finds it?
9 And when she has found it, she calls
together her friends and neighbors,
saying, 'Rejoice with me, for I have
found the coin which I had lost.'
10 Just so, I tell you, there is joy before the angels of God over one sinner
who repents."
11 And he said, "There was a man
who had two sons; 12 and the younger
of them said to his father, 'Father,
give me the share of property that falls
to me.' And he divided his living
between them. 13 Not many days
later, the younger son gathered all he
had and took his journey into a far
country, and there he squandered his
property in loose living. 14 And when
he had spent everything, a great
famine arose in that country, and he
began to be in want. 15 So he went
and joined himself to one of the
citizens of that country, who sent him
into his fields to feed swine. 16 And he
would gladly have fed on[u] the pods
that the swine ate; and no one gave
him anything. 17 But when he came to
himself he said, 'How many of my
father's hired servants have bread
enough and to spare, but I perish here
with hunger! 18 I will arise and go to
my father, and I will say to him,
"Father, I have sinned against heaven
and before you; 19 I am no longer
worthy to be called your son; treat me
as one of your hired servants." '
20 And he arose and came to his father.
But while he was yet at a distance, his
father saw him and had compassion,
and ran and embraced him and kissed
him. 21 And the son said to him,
'Father, I have sinned against heaven
and before you; I am no longer worthy
to be called your son.'[v] 22 But the
father said to his servants, 'Bring
quickly the best robe, and put it on
him; and put a ring on his hand, and
shoes on his feet; 23 and bring the fatted
calf and kill it, and let us eat and make
merry; 24 for this my son was dead,
and is alive again; he was lost, and is
found.' And they began to make merry.
25 "Now his elder son was in the
field; and as he came and drew near to
the house, he heard music and dancing.
26 And he called one of the servants
and asked what this meant. 27 And he
said to him, 'Your brother has come,
and your father has killed the fatted
calf, because he has received him safe
and sound.' 28 But he was angry and
refused to go in. His father came out
and entreated him, 29 but he answered
his father, 'Lo, these many years I
have served you, and I never disobeyed your command; yet you never
gave me a kid, that I might make
merry with my friends. 30 But when
this son of yours came, who has
devoured your living with harlots, you
killed for him the fatted calf! 31 And
he said to him, 'Son, you are always
with me, and all that is mine is yours.
32 It was fitting to make merry and be
glad, for this your brother was dead,
and is alive; he was lost and is found.' "

16 He also said to the disciples,
"There was a rich man who had
a steward, and charges were brought
to him that this man was wasting his
goods. 2 And he called him and said to
him, 'What is this that I hear about
you? Turn in the account of your
stewardship, for you can no longer be
steward.' 3 And the steward said to
himself, 'What shall I do, since my
master is taking the stewardship away
from me? I am not strong enough to
dig, and I am ashamed to beg. 4 I have
decided what to do, so that people may
receive me into their houses when I
am put out of the stewardship.' 5 So,
summoning his master's debtors one
by one, he said to the first, 'How much
do you owe my master?' 6 He said, 'A
hundred measures of oil.' And he said
to him, 'Take your bill, and sit down
quickly and write fifty.' 7 Then he
said to another, 'And how much do
you owe?' He said, 'A hundred measures of wheat.' He said to him, 'Take
your bill, and write eighty.' 8 The
master commended the dishonest
steward for his prudence; for the sons
of this world[w] are wiser in their own

[t] The drachma, rendered here by *silver coin*, was about sixteen cents
[u] Other ancient authorities read *filled his belly with*
[v] Other ancient authorities add *treat me as one of your hired servants*
[w] Greek *age*
15.11: Mt 21.28. **15.12:** Deut 21.15-17. **15.22:** Gen 41.42; Zech 3.4.
15.24: 1 Tim 5.6; Eph 2.1; Lk 9.60. **16.8:** 1 Thess 5.5; Eph 5.8; Lk 20.34; Jn 12.36.

generation than the sons of light. 9 And
I tell you, make friends for yourselves
by means of unrighteous mammon, so
that when it fails they may receive you
into the eternal habitations.

10 "He who is faithful in a very
little is faithful also in much; and he
who is dishonest in a very little is dishonest also in much. 11 If then you
have not been faithful in the unrighteous mammon, who will entrust to
you the true riches? 12 And if you have
not been faithful in that which is
another's, who will give you that which
is your own? 13 No servant can serve
two masters; for either he will hate the
one and love the other, or he will be
devoted to the one and despise the
other. You cannot serve God and
mammon."

14 The Pharisees, who were lovers
of money, heard all this, and they
scoffed at him. 15 But he said to them,
"You are those who justify yourselves
before men, but God knows your
hearts; for what is exalted among men
is an abomination in the sight of God.

16 "The law and the prophets were
until John; since then the good news
of the kingdom of God is preached,
and every one enters it violently. 17 But
it is easier for heaven and earth to
pass away, than for one dot of the law
to become void.

18 "Every one who divorces his
wife and marries another commits
adultery, and he who marries a woman
divorced from her husband commits
adultery.

19 "There was a rich man, who was
clothed in purple and fine linen and
who feasted sumptuously every day.
20 And at his gate lay a poor man
named Laz'ȧ·rŭs, full of sores, 21 who
desired to be fed with what fell from
the rich man's table; moreover the
dogs came and licked his sores. 22 The
poor man died and was carried by the
angels to Abraham's bosom. The rich
man also died and was buried; 23 and
in Hades, being in torment, he lifted
up his eyes, and saw Abraham far off
and Laz'ȧ·rŭs in his bosom. 24 And he
called out, 'Father Abraham, have
mercy upon me, and send Laz'ȧ·rŭs to
dip the end of his finger in water and
cool my tongue; for I am in anguish in
this flame.' 25 But Abraham said, 'Son,
remember that you in your lifetime
received your good things, and Laz'ȧ-
rŭs in like manner evil things; but now
he is comforted here, and you are in
anguish. 26 And besides all this, between us and you a great chasm has
been fixed, in order that those who
would pass from here to you may not
be able, and none may cross from
there to us.' 27 And he said, 'Then I
beg you, father, to send him to my
father's house, 28 for I have five
brothers, so that he may warn them,
lest they also come into this place of
torment.' 29 But Abraham said, 'They
have Moses and the prophets; let them
hear them.' 30 And he said, 'No, father
Abraham; but if some one goes to
them from the dead, they will repent.'
31 He said to him, 'If they do not hear
Moses and the prophets, neither will
they be convinced if some one should
rise from the dead.' "

17 And he said to his disciples,
"Temptations to sin[x] are sure to
come; but woe to him by whom they
come! 2 It would be better for him if
a millstone were hung round his neck
and he were cast into the sea, than
that he should cause one of these little
ones to sin.[y] 3 Take heed to yourselves;
if your brother sins, rebuke him, and
if he repents, forgive him; 4 and if he
sins against you seven times in the
day, and turns to you seven times, and
says, 'I repent,' you must forgive him."

5 The apostles said to the Lord,
"Increase our faith!" 6 And the Lord
said, "If you had faith as a grain of
mustard seed, you could say to this
sycamine tree, 'Be rooted up, and be
planted in the sea,' and it would obey
you.

7 "Will any one of you, who has a
servant plowing or keeping sheep, say
to him when he has come in from the
field, 'Come at once and sit down at
table'? 8 Will he not rather say to him,
'Prepare supper for me, and gird yourself and serve me, till I eat and drink;
and afterward you shall eat and drink'?
9 Does he thank the servant because

[x] Greek *stumbling blocks* [y] Greek *stumble*

16.9: Lk 12.33; 18.22. **16.10:** Mt 25.21; Lk 19.17. **16.13:** Mt 6.24.
16.15: 1 Sam 16.7; Prov 21.2; Acts 1.24; Lk 10.29. **16.16:** Mt 11.12-13. **16.17:** Mt 5.17-18; Lk 21.33.
16.18: Mt 5.31-32; 19.9; Mk 10.11-12; 1 Cor 7.10-11. **16.20:** Jn 11.1-44; 12.1, 9. **16.22:** Jn 13.23.
16.25: Lk 6.24. **16.29:** Jn 5.45-47; Acts 15.21; Lk 4.17. **16.30:** Lk 3.8; 19.9.
17.1-2: Mt 18.6-7; Mk 9.42; 1 Cor 8.12. **17.3-4:** Mt 18.15, 21-22.
17.5-6: Mt 17.20; 21.21; Mk 11.22-23. **17.5:** Lk 7.13. **17.8:** Lk 12.37; Jn 13.3-5.

he did what was commanded? 10 So
you also, when you have done all that
is commanded you, say, 'We are unworthy servants; we have only done
what was our duty.' "

11 On the way to Jerusalem he was
passing along between Sȧ·mâr'i·ȧ and
Galilee. 12 And as he entered a village,
he was met by ten lepers, who stood at
a distance 13 and lifted up their voices
and said, "Jesus, Master, have mercy
on us." 14 When he saw them he said
to them, "Go and show yourselves to
the priests." And as they went they
were cleansed. 15 Then one of them,
when he saw that he was healed, turned
back, praising God with a loud voice;
16 and he fell on his face at Jesus' feet,
giving him thanks. Now he was a
Samaritan. 17 Then said Jesus, "Were
not ten cleansed? Where are the nine?
18 Was no one found to return and
give praise to God except this foreigner?" 19 And he said to him, "Rise
and go your way; your faith has made
you well."

20 Being asked by the Pharisees
when the kingdom of God was coming, he answered them, "The kingdom
of God is not coming with signs to be
observed; 21 nor will they say, 'Lo, here
it is!' or 'There!' for behold, the kingdom of God is in the midst of you."[z]

22 And he said to the disciples,
"The days are coming when you will
desire to see one of the days of the Son
of man, and you will not see it. 23 And
they will say to you, 'Lo, there!' or
'Lo, here!' Do not go, do not follow
them. 24 For as the lightning flashes
and lights up the sky from one side to
the other, so will the Son of man be in
his day.[a] 25 But first he must suffer
many things and be rejected by this
generation. 26 As it was in the days of
Noah, so will it be in the days of the
Son of man. 27 They ate, they drank,
they married, they were given in
marriage, until the day when Noah
entered the ark, and the flood came
and destroyed them all. 28 Likewise as
it was in the days of Lot—they ate,
they drank, they bought, they sold,
they planted, they built, 29 but on the
day when Lot went out from Sod'ȯm
fire and brimstone rained from heaven
and destroyed them all—30 so will it
be on the day when the Son of man is
revealed. 31 On that day, let him who
is on the housetop, with his goods in
the house, not come down to take
them away; and likewise let him who
is in the field not turn back. 32 Remember Lot's wife. 33 Whoever seeks
to gain his life will lose it, but whoever
loses his life will preserve it. 34 I tell
you, in that night there will be two
men in one bed; one will be taken and
the other left. 35 There will be two
women grinding together; one will be
taken and the other left."[b] 37 And they
said to him, "Where, Lord?" He said
to them, "Where the body is, there the
eagles[c] will be gathered together."

18 And he told them a parable, to
the effect that they ought always
to pray and not lose heart. 2 He said,
"In a certain city there was a judge
who neither feared God nor regarded
man; 3 and there was a widow in that
city who kept coming to him and saying, 'Vindicate me against my adversary.' 4 For a while he refused; but
afterward he said to himself, 'Though
I neither fear God nor regard man,
5 yet because this widow bothers me,
I will vindicate her, or she will wear
me out by her continual coming.' "
6 And the Lord said, "Hear what the
unrighteous judge says. 7 And will not
God vindicate his elect, who cry to
him day and night? Will he delay long
over them? 8 I tell you, he will vindicate them speedily. Nevertheless,
when the Son of man comes, will he
find faith on earth?"

9 He also told this parable to some
who trusted in themselves that they
were righteous and despised others:
10 "Two men went up into the temple
to pray, one a Pharisee and the other
a tax collector. 11 The Pharisee stood

[z] Or *within you* [a] Other ancient authorities omit *in his day*
[b] Other ancient authorities add verse 36, "*Two men will be in the field; one will be taken and the other left*"
[c] Or *vultures*

17.11: Lk 9.51; 13.22; 19.11. **17.12:** Lev 13.45-46. **17.13:** Lk 5.5; 8.24, 45; 9.33, 49.
17.14: Lk 5.14; Mt 8.4; Mk 1.44; Lev 14.2-32. **17.19:** Mt 9.22; Mk 5.34; Lk 8.48; 18.42.
17.20: Lk 19.11; 21.7; Acts 1.6. **17.22:** Mt 9.15; Mk 2.20; Lk 5.35. **17.23:** Mt 24.23; Mk 13.21.
17.24: Mt 24.27; Rev 1.7. **17.25:** Lk 9.22. **17.26-27:** Mt 24.37-39; Gen 6.5-8; 7.6-24.
17.28-30: Gen 18.20-33; 19.24-25. **17.31:** Mt 24.17-18; Mk 13.15-16; Lk 21.21. **17.32:** Gen 19.26.
17.33: Mt 10.39; 16.25; Mk 8.35; Lk 9.24; Jn 12.25. **17.34-35:** Mt 24.40-41. **17.37:** Mt 24.28.
18.1-8: Lk 11.5-8. **18.6:** Lk 7.13. **18.7:** Rev 6.10; Mt 24.22; Rom 8.33; Col 3.12; 2 Tim 2.10.
18.11: Mt 6.5; Mk 11.25.

and prayed thus with himself, 'God,
I thank thee that I am not like other
men, extortioners, unjust, adulterers,
or even like this tax collector. 12 I fast
twice a week, I give tithes of all that I
get.' 13 But the tax collector, standing
far off, would not even lift up his eyes
to heaven, but beat his breast, saying,
'God, be merciful to me a sinner!' 14 I
tell you, this man went down to his
house justified rather than the other;
for every one who exalts himself will
be humbled, but he who humbles himself will be exalted."

15 Now they were bringing even
infants to him that he might touch
them; and when the disciples saw it,
they rebuked them. 16 But Jesus called
them to him, saying, "Let the children
come to me, and do not hinder them;
for to such belongs the kingdom of
God. 17 Truly, I say to you, whoever
does not receive the kingdom of God
like a child shall not enter it."

18 And a ruler asked him, "Good
Teacher, what shall I do to inherit
eternal life?" 19 And Jesus said to him,
"Why do you call me good? No one is
good but God alone. 20 You know the
commandments: 'Do not commit
adultery, Do not kill, Do not steal, Do
not bear false witness, Honor your
father and mother.' " 21 And he said,
"All these I have observed from my
youth." 22 And when Jesus heard it,
he said to him, "One thing you still
lack. Sell all that you have and distribute to the poor, and you will have
treasure in heaven; and come, follow
me." 23 But when he heard this he
became sad, for he was very rich.
24 Jesus looking at him said, "How
hard it is for those who have riches to
enter the kingdom of God! 25 For it is
easier for a camel to go through the
eye of a needle than for a rich man to
enter the kingdom of God." 26 Those
who heard it said, "Then who can be
saved?" 27 But he said, "What is impossible with men is possible with
God." 28 And Peter said, "Lo, we have
left our homes and followed you."
29 And he said to them, "Truly, I say
to you, there is no man who has left
house or wife or brothers or parents or
children, for the sake of the kingdom
of God, 30 who will not receive manifold more in this time, and in the age
to come eternal life."

31 And taking the twelve, he said
to them, "Behold, we are going up to
Jerusalem, and everything that is
written of the Son of man by the
prophets will be accomplished. 32 For
he will be delivered to the Gentiles,
and will be mocked and shamefully
treated and spit upon, 33 they will
scourge him and kill him, and on the
third day he will rise." 34 But they
understood none of these things; this
saying was hid from them, and they
did not grasp what was said.

35 As he drew near to Jericho, a
blind man was sitting by the roadside
begging; 36 and hearing a multitude
going by, he inquired what this meant.
37 They told him, "Jesus of Nazareth
is passing by." 38 And he cried, "Jesus,
Son of David, have mercy on me!"
39 And those who were in front rebuked
him, telling him to be silent; but he
cried out all the more, "Son of David,
have mercy on me!" 40 And Jesus
stopped, and commanded him to be
brought to him; and when he came
near, he asked him, 41 "What do you
want me to do for you?" He said,
"Lord, let me receive my sight."
42 And Jesus said to him, "Receive
your sight; your faith has made you
well." 43 And immediately he received
his sight and followed him, glorifying
God; and all the people, when they
saw it, gave praise to God.

19 He entered Jericho and was
passing through. 2 And there was
a man named Zac·chae'us; he was a
chief tax collector, and rich. 3 And he
sought to see who Jesus was, but
could not, on account of the crowd,
because he was small of stature. 4 So
he ran on ahead and climbed up into
a sycamore tree to see him, for he was
to pass that way. 5 And when Jesus
came to the place, he looked up and
said to him, "Zac·chae'us, make haste
and come down; for I must stay at
your house today." 6 So he made haste

18.12: Lk 5.33; 11.42. **18.14:** Mt 18.4; 23.12; Lk 14.11; 1 Pet 5.6.
18.15-17: Mt 19.13-15; 18.3; Mk 10.13-16. **18.18-23:** Mt 19.16-22; Mk 10.17-22. **18.18:** Lk 10.25.
18.20: Ex 20.12-16; Deut 5.16-20; Rom 13.9; Jas 2.11. **18.22:** Lk 12.33; Acts 2.45; 4.32.
18.24-27: Mt 19.23-26; Mk 10.23-27. **18.27:** Gen 18.14; Job 42.2; Jer 32.17; Lk 1.37.
18.28-30: Mt 19.27-30; Mk 10.28-31; Lk 5.1-11.
18.31-34: Mt 20.17-19; Mk 10.32-34; Lk 9.22, 44-45; 17.25.
18.35-43: Mt 20.29-34; Mk 10.46-52; Mt 9.27-31; Mk 8.22; Jn 9.1-7.
18.42: Mt 9.22; Mk 5.34; 10.52; Lk 7.50; 8.48; 17.19. **19.1:** Mk 10.46.

and came down, and received him
joyfully. 7And when they saw it they
all murmured, "He has gone in to be
the guest of a man who is a sinner."
8And Zac·chae̅'ŭs stood and said to
the Lord, "Behold, Lord, the half of
my goods I give to the poor; and if I
have defrauded any one of anything,
I restore it fourfold." 9And Jesus said
to him, "Today salvation has come to
this house, since he also is a son of
Abraham. 10 For the Son of man came
to seek and to save the lost."

11 As they heard these things, he
proceeded to tell a parable, because he
was near to Jerusalem, and because
they supposed that the kingdom of
God was to appear immediately. 12 He
said therefore, "A nobleman went into
a far country to receive kingly power[d]
and then return. 13 Calling ten of his
servants, he gave them ten pounds,[e]
and said to them, 'Trade with these
till I come.' 14 But his citizens hated
him and sent an embassy after him,
saying, 'We do not want this man to
reign over us.' 15 When he returned,
having received the kingly power,[d] he
commanded these servants, to whom
he had given the money, to be called to
him, that he might know what they
had gained by trading. 16 The first
came before him, saying, 'Lord, your
pound has made ten pounds more.'
17And he said to him, 'Well done, good
servant! Because you have been faithful in a very little, you shall have
authority over ten cities.' 18And the
second came, saying, 'Lord, your
pound has made five pounds.' 19And
he said to him, 'And you are to be
over five cities.' 20 Then another came,
saying, 'Lord, here is your pound,
which I kept laid away in a napkin;
21 for I was afraid of you, because you
are a severe man; you take up what
you did not lay down, and reap what
you did not sow.' 22 He said to him, 'I
will condemn you out of your own
mouth, you wicked servant! You knew
that I was a severe man, taking up what
I did not lay down and reaping what
I did not sow? 23 Why then did you
not put my money into the bank, and
at my coming I should have collected it
with interest?' 24And he said to those
who stood by, 'Take the pound from
him, and give it to him who has the
ten pounds.' 25 (And they said to him,
'Lord, he has ten pounds!') 26 'I tell
you, that to every one who has will
more be given; but from him who has
not, even what he has will be taken
away. 27 But as for these enemies of
mine, who did not want me to reign
over them, bring them here and slay
them before me.' "

28 And when he had said this, he
went on ahead, going up to Jerusalem.
29 When he drew near to Beth'phȧ·ge̅
and Beth'ȧ·ny, at the mount that is
called Ol'i·vet, he sent two of the disciples, 30 saying, "Go into the village
opposite, where on entering you will
find a colt tied, on which no one has
ever yet sat; untie it and bring it here.
31 If any one asks you, 'Why are you
untying it?' you shall say this, 'The
Lord has need of it.' " 32 So those who
were sent went away and found it as
he had told them. 33And as they were
untying the colt, its owners said to
them, "Why are you untying the colt?"
34And they said, "The Lord has need
of it." 35And they brought it to Jesus,
and throwing their garments on the
colt they set Jesus upon it. 36And as he
rode along, they spread their garments
on the road. 37As he was now drawing
near, at the descent of the Mount of
Olives, the whole multitude of the disciples began to rejoice and praise God
with a loud voice for all the mighty
works that they had seen, 38 saying,
"Blessed is the King who comes in the
name of the Lord! Peace in heaven and
glory in the highest!" 39And some of the
Pharisees in the multitude said to him,
"Teacher, rebuke your disciples."
40 He answered, "I tell you, if these
were silent, the very stones would cry
out."

41 And when he drew near and saw
the city he wept over it, 42 saying,
"Would that even today you knew the
things that make for peace! But now
they are hid from your eyes. 43 For the
days shall come upon you, when your
enemies will cast up a bank about you
and surround you, and hem you in on

[d] Greek *a kingdom* [e] The mina, rendered here by *pound*, was equal to about twenty dollars

19.7: Lk 5.29-30; 15.1-2. **19.8:** Lk 7.13; 3.14; Ex 22.1; Lev 6.5; Num 5.6-7.
19.9: Lk 3.8; 13.16; Rom 4.16. **19.11:** Lk 9.51; 13.22; 17.11; 18.31; 9.27. **19.12-28:** Mt 25.14-30.
19.12: Mk 13.34. **19.17:** Lk 16.10. **19.26:** Mt 13.12; Mk 4.25; Lk 8.18. **19.28:** Mk 10.32.
19.29-38: Mt 21.1-9; Mk 11.1-10; Jn 12.12-18. **19.32:** Lk 22.13. **19.34:** Lk 7.13.
19.36: 2 Kings 9.13. **19.38:** Ps 118.26; Lk 13.35; 2.14. **19.39-40:** Mt 21.15-16; Hab 2.11.
19.41: Lk 13.33-34. **19.43:** Lk 21.21-24; 21.6; Is 29.3; Jer 6.6; Ezek 4.2.

every side, 44 and dash you to the
ground, you and your children within
you, and they will not leave one stone
upon another in you; because you did
not know the time of your visitation."
45 And he entered the temple and
began to drive out those who sold,
46 saying to them, "It is written,
'My house shall be a house of prayer';
but you have made it a den of robbers."
47 And he was teaching daily in the
temple. The chief priests and the
scribes and the principal men of the
people sought to destroy him; 48 but
they did not find anything they could
do, for all the people hung upon his
words.

20 One day, as he was teaching
the people in the temple and
preaching the gospel, the chief priests
and the scribes with the elders came
up 2 and said to him, "Tell us by what
authority you do these things, or who
it is that gave you this authority."
3 He answered them, "I also will ask
you a question; now tell me, 4 Was the
baptism of John from heaven or from
men?" 5And they discussed it with
one another, saying, "If we say, 'From
heaven,' he will say, 'Why did you not
believe him?' 6 But if we say, 'From
men,' all the people will stone us; for
they are convinced that John was a
prophet." 7 So they answered that they
did not know whence it was. 8And
Jesus said to them, "Neither will I
tell you by what authority I do these
things."
9 And he began to tell the people
this parable: "A man planted a vineyard, and let it out to tenants, and
went into another country for a long
while. 10 When the time came, he sent
a servant to the tenants, that they
should give him some of the fruit of
the vineyard; but the tenants beat him,
and sent him away empty-handed.
11And he sent another servant; him
also they beat and treated shamefully,
and sent him away empty-handed.
12And he sent yet a third; this one they
wounded and cast out. 13 Then the
owner of the vineyard said, 'What shall
I do? I will send my beloved son; it
may be they will respect him.' 14 But
when the tenants saw him, they said
to themselves, 'This is the heir; let us
kill him, that the inheritance may be
ours.' 15And they cast him out of the
vineyard and killed him. What then
will the owner of the vineyard do to
them? 16 He will come and destroy
those tenants, and give the vineyard
to others." When they heard this, they
said, "God forbid!" 17 But he looked
at them and said, "What then is this
that is written:

'The very stone which the builders
rejected
has become the head of the corner'?

18 Every one who falls on that stone
will be broken to pieces; but when it
falls on any one it will crush him."
19 The scribes and the chief priests
tried to lay hands on him at that very
hour, but they feared the people; for
they perceived that he had told this
parable against them. 20 So they
watched him, and sent spies, who
pretended to be sincere, that they
might take hold of what he said, so as
to deliver him up to the authority and
jurisdiction of the governor. 21 They
asked him, "Teacher, we know that
you speak and teach rightly, and show
no partiality, but truly teach the way
of God. 22 Is it lawful for us to give
tribute to Caesar, or not?" 23 But he
perceived their craftiness, and said to
them, 24 "Show me a coin.[f] Whose
likeness and inscription has it?" They
said, "Caesar's." 25 He said to them,
"Then render to Caesar the things that
are Caesar's, and to God the things
that are God's." 26And they were not
able in the presence of the people to
catch him by what he said; but marveling at his answer they were silent.
27 There came to him some Sad'-
dū·cees, those who say that there is no
resurrection, 28 and they asked him a
question, saying, "Teacher, Moses
wrote for us that if a man's brother
dies, having a wife but no children,
the man[g] must take the wife and raise
up children for his brother. 29 Now
there were seven brothers; the first
took a wife, and died without children;
30 and the second 31 and the third took
her, and likewise all seven left no chil-

[f] Greek *denarius* [g] Greek *his brother*

19.44: 1 Pet 2.12. **19.45-46:** Mt 21.12-13; Mk 11.15-17; Jn 2.13-17.
19.47-48: Mk 11.18; Lk 21.37; 22.53. **20.1-8:** Mt 21.23-27; Mk 11.27-33. **20.2:** Jn 2.18.
20.6: Mt 14.5; Lk 7.29. **20.9-19:** Mt 21.33-46; Mk 12.1-12. **20.9:** Is 5.1-7; Mt 25.14.
20.16: Acts 13.46; 18.6; 28.28. **20.17:** Ps 118.22-23; Acts 4.11; 1 Pet 2.6-7. **20.18:** Is 8.14-15.
20.19: Lk 19.47. **20.20-26:** Mt 22.15-22; Mk 12.13-17. **20.21:** Jn 3.2. **20.25:** Rom 13.7; Lk 23.2.
20.27-38: Mt 22.23-33; Mk 12.18-27. **20.27:** Acts 4.1-2; 23.6-10. **20.28:** Deut 25.5.

dren and died. 32 Afterward the woman
also died. 33 In the resurrection, therefore, whose wife will the woman be?
For the seven had her as wife."

34 And Jesus said to them, "The
sons of this age marry and are given
in marriage; 35 but those who are
accounted worthy to attain to that age
and to the resurrection from the dead
neither marry nor are given in marriage, 36 for they cannot die any more,
because they are equal to angels and
are sons of God, being sons of the
resurrection. 37 But that the dead are
raised, even Moses showed, in the
passage about the bush, where he calls
the Lord the God of Abraham and the
God of Isaac and the God of Jacob.
38 Now he is not God of the dead, but
of the living; for all live to him."
39 And some of the scribes answered,
"Teacher, you have spoken well."
40 For they no longer dared to ask him
any question.

41 But he said to them, "How can
they say that the Christ is David's
son? 42 For David himself says in the
Book of Psalms,

'The Lord said to my Lord,
Sit at my right hand,
43 till I make thy enemies a stool for
thy feet.'

44 David thus calls him Lord; so how
is he his son?"

45 And in the hearing of all the
people he said to his disciples, 46 "Beware of the scribes, who like to go
about in long robes, and love salutations in the market places and the best
seats in the synagogues and the places
of honor at feasts, 47 who devour
widows' houses and for a pretense
make long prayers. They will receive
the greater condemnation."

21 He looked up and saw the rich
putting their gifts into the treasury; 2 and he saw a poor widow put in
two copper coins. 3 And he said, "Truly
I tell you, this poor widow has put in
more than all of them; 4 for they all
contributed out of their abundance,
but she out of her poverty put in all
the living that she had."

5 And as some spoke of the temple,
how it was adorned with noble stones
and offerings, he said, 6 "As for these
things which you see, the days will
come when there shall not be left here
one stone upon another that will not
be thrown down." 7 And they asked
him, "Teacher, when will this be, and
what will be the sign when this is
about to take place?" 8 And he said,
"Take heed that you are not led astray;
for many will come in my name, saying, 'I am he!' and, 'The time is at
hand!' Do not go after them. 9 And
when you hear of wars and tumults, do
not be terrified; for this must first take
place, but the end will not be at once."

10 Then he said to them, "Nation
will rise against nation, and kingdom
against kingdom; 11 there will be great
earthquakes, and in various places
famines and pestilences; and there will
be terrors and great signs from
heaven. 12 But before all this they will
lay their hands on you and persecute
you, delivering you up to the synagogues and prisons, and you will be
brought before kings and governors
for my name's sake. 13 This will be a
time for you to bear testimony.
14 Settle it therefore in your minds,
not to meditate beforehand how to
answer; 15 for I will give you a mouth
and wisdom, which none of your
adversaries will be able to withstand
or contradict. 16 You will be delivered
up even by parents and brothers and
kinsmen and friends, and some of you
they will put to death; 17 you will be
hated by all for my name's sake. 18 But
not a hair of your head will perish.
19 By your endurance you will gain
your lives.

20 "But when you see Jerusalem
surrounded by armies, then know that
its desolation has come near. 21 Then
let those who are in Judea flee to the
mountains, and let those who are inside the city depart, and let not those
who are out in the country enter it;
22 for these are days of vengeance, to
fulfil all that is written. 23 Alas for
those who are with child and for those

20.37: Ex 3.6. **20.39:** Mk 12.28. **20.40:** Mk 12.34; Mt 22.46.
20.41-44: Mt 22.41-45; Mk 12.35-37; Ps 110.1.
20.45-47: Mk 12.38-40; Mt 23.6-7; Lk 11.43; 14.7-11. **21.1-4:** Mk 12.41-44.
21.5-23: Mt 24.1-19; Mk 13.1-17. **21.6:** Lk 19.43-44; Mk 14.58; 15.29; Acts 6.14.
21.7: Lk 17.20; Acts 1.6. **21.8:** Lk 17.23; Mk 13.21; 1 Jn 2.18. **21.10:** 2 Chron 15.6; Is 19.2.
21.12-17: Mt 10.17-21. **21.12:** Acts 25.24; Jn 16.2. **21.13:** Phil 1.12. **21.14-15:** Lk 12.11-12.
21.16: Lk 12.52-53. **21.17:** Mt 10.22; Jn 15.18-25.
21.18: Lk 12.7; Mt 10.30; Acts 27.34; 1 Sam 14.45. **21.19:** Mt 10.22; Rev 2.7.
21.20-22: Lk 19.41-44; 23.28-31; 17.31. **21.23:** Lk 23.29.

who give suck in those days! For great
distress shall be upon the earth and
wrath upon this people; 24 they will
fall by the edge of the sword, and be
led captive among all nations; and
Jerusalem will be trodden down by the
Gentiles, until the times of the Gentiles are fulfilled.

25 "And there will be signs in sun
and moon and stars, and upon the
earth distress of nations in perplexity
at the roaring of the sea and the waves,
26 men fainting with fear and with
foreboding of what is coming on the
world; for the powers of the heavens
will be shaken. 27 And then they will
see the Son of man coming in a cloud
with power and great glory. 28 Now
when these things begin to take place,
look up and raise your heads, because
your redemption is drawing near."

29 And he told them a parable:
"Look at the fig tree, and all the trees;
30 as soon as they come out in leaf, you
see for yourselves and know that the
summer is already near. 31 So also,
when you see these things taking
place, you know that the kingdom of
God is near. 32 Truly, I say to you,
this generation will not pass away till
all has taken place. 33 Heaven and
earth will pass away, but my words
will not pass away.

34 "But take heed to yourselves
lest your hearts be weighed down with
dissipation and drunkenness and cares
of this life, and that day come upon
you suddenly like a snare; 35 for it will
come upon all who dwell upon the face
of the whole earth. 36 But watch at all
times, praying that you may have
strength to escape all these things that
will take place, and to stand before the
Son of man."

37 And every day he was teaching
in the temple, but at night he went out
and lodged on the mount called Ol'i-
vet. 38 And early in the morning all the
people came to him in the temple to
hear him.

22 Now the feast of Unleavened
Bread drew near, which is called
the Passover. 2 And the chief priests
and the scribes were seeking how to
put him to death; for they feared the
people.

3 Then Satan entered into Judas
called Is-car'i-ot, who was of the number of the twelve; 4 he went away and
conferred with the chief priests and
captains how he might betray him to
them. 5 And they were glad, and
engaged to give him money. 6 So he
agreed, and sought an opportunity to
betray him to them in the absence of
the multitude.

7 Then came the day of Unleavened
Bread, on which the passover lamb had
to be sacrificed. 8 So Jesus[h] sent Peter
and John, saying, "Go and prepare the
passover for us, that we may eat it."
9 They said to him, "Where will you
have us prepare it?" 10 He said to
them, "Behold, when you have
entered the city, a man carrying a jar
of water will meet you; follow him into
the house which he enters, 11 and tell
the householder, 'The Teacher says to
you, Where is the guest room, where
I am to eat the passover with my disciples?' 12 And he will show you a large
upper room furnished; there make
ready." 13 And they went, and found it
as he had told them; and they prepared
the passover.

14 And when the hour came, he sat
at table, and the apostles with him.
15 And he said to them, "I have
earnestly desired to eat this passover
with you before I suffer; 16 for I tell
you I shall not eat it[i] until it is fulfilled
in the kingdom of God." 17 And he
took a cup, and when he had given
thanks he said, "Take this, and divide
it among yourselves; 18 for I tell you
that from now on I shall not drink of
the fruit of the vine until the kingdom
of God comes." 19 And he took bread,
and when he had given thanks he
broke it and gave it to them, saying,

[h] Greek *he* [i] Other ancient authorities read *never eat it again*

21.24: Rom 11.25; Is 63.18; Dan 8.13; Rev 11.2. **21.25-27**: Mt 24.29-30; Mk 13.24-26.
21.25: Rev 6.12-13; Is 13.10; Joel 2.10; Zeph 1.15.
21.27: Lk 9.27; Dan 7.13-14. **21.28**: Lk 18.7-8.
21.29-33: Mt 24.32-35; Mk 13.28-31. **21.32**: Lk 9.27. **21.33**: Lk 16.17.
21.34: Lk 12.45; Mk 4.19; 1 Thess 5.6-7.
21.36: Mk 13.33. **21.37**: Lk 19.47; Mk 11.19.
22.1-2: Mt 26.2-5; Mk 14.1-2; Jn 11.47-53. **22.3-6**: Mt 26.14-16; Mk 14.10-11; Jn 13.2.
22.7-13: Mt 26.17-19; Mk 14.12-16. **22.7**: Ex 12.18-20; Deut 16.5-8. **22.8**: Acts 3.1; Lk 19.29.
22.14: Mt 26.20; Mk 14.17; Jn 13.17. **22.15**: Lk 12.49-50. **22.16**: Lk 14.15.
22.17: Mt 26.27; Mk 14.23; 1 Cor 10.16. **22.18**: Mt 26.29; Mk 14.25.
22.19: Mt 26.26; Mk 14.22; 1 Cor 10.16; 11.23-26; Lk 9.16.

"This is my body.[j] 21 But behold the
hand of him who betrays me is with
me on the table. 22 For the Son of man
goes as it has been determined; but
woe to that man by whom he is betrayed!" 23And they began to question
one another, which of them it was that
would do this.

24 A dispute also arose among them,
which of them was to be regarded as
the greatest. 25And he said to them,
"The kings of the Gentiles exercise lord-
ship over them; and those in authority
over them are called benefactors. 26 But
not so with you; rather let the greatest
among you become as the youngest,
and the leader as one who serves.
27 For which is the greater, one who
sits at table, or one who serves? Is it
not the one who sits at table? But I
am among you as one who serves.

28 "You are those who have continued with me in my trials; 29 as my
Father appointed a kingdom for me,
so do I appoint for you 30 that you
may eat and drink at my table in my
kingdom, and sit on thrones judging
the twelve tribes of Israel.

31 "Simon, Simon, behold, Satan
demanded to have you,[k] that he might
sift you[k] like wheat, 32 but I have
prayed for you that your faith may not
fail; and when you have turned again,
strengthen your brethren." 33And he
said to him, "Lord, I am ready to go
with you to prison and to death." 34 He
said, "I tell you, Peter, the cock will
not crow this day, until you three
times deny that you know me."

35 And he said to them, "When I
sent you out with no purse or bag or
sandals, did you lack anything?" They
said, "Nothing." 36 He said to them,
"But now, let him who has a purse
take it, and likewise a bag. And let him
who has no sword sell his mantle and
buy one. 37 For I tell you that this
scripture must be fulfilled in me, 'And
he was reckoned with transgressors';
for what is written about me has its
fulfilment." 38And they said, "Look,
Lord, here are two swords." And he
said to them, "It is enough."

39 And he came out, and went, as
was his custom, to the Mount of
Olives; and the disciples followed him.
40And when he came to the place he
said to them, "Pray that you may not
enter into temptation." 41And he withdrew from them about a stone's throw,
and knelt down and prayed, 42 "Father,
if thou art willing, remove this cup
from me; nevertheless not my will, but
thine, be done." 43And there appeared
to him an angel from heaven, strengthening him. 44And being in an agony
he prayed more earnestly; and his
sweat became like great drops of blood
falling down upon the ground.[l] 45And
when he rose from prayer, he came to
the disciples and found them sleeping
for sorrow, 46 and he said to them,
"Why do you sleep? Rise and pray that
you may not enter into temptation."

47 While he was still speaking,
there came a crowd, and the man
called Judas, one of the twelve, was
leading them. He drew near to Jesus
to kiss him; 48 but Jesus said to him,
"Judas, would you betray the Son of
man with a kiss?" 49And when those
who were about him saw what would
follow, they said, "Lord, shall we
strike with the sword?" 50And one of
them struck the slave of the high priest
and cut off his right ear. 51 But Jesus
said, "No more of this!" And he
touched his ear and healed him.
52 Then Jesus said to the chief priests
and captains of the temple and elders,
who had come out against him, "Have
you come out as against a robber, with
swords and clubs? 53 When I was with
you day after day in the temple, you
did not lay hands on me. But this is
your hour, and the power of darkness."

54 Then they seized him and led
him away, bringing him into the high
priest's house. Peter followed at a
distance; 55 and when they had kindled

[j] Other ancient authorities add *which is given for you. Do this in remembrance of me."* 20 *And likewise the cup after supper, saying, "This cup which is poured out for you is the new covenant in my blood."*
[k] The Greek word for *you* here is plural; in verse 32 it is singular
[l] Other ancient authorities omit verses 43 and 44

22.21-23: Mt 26.21-24; Mk 14.18-21; Ps 41.9; Jn 13.21-30. **22.24:** Lk 9.46; Mk 9.34.
22.25-27: Mt 20.25-28; Mk 10.42-45; Jn 13.3-16. **22.26:** Lk 9.48. **22.28-30:** Mt 19.28.
22.28: Lk 4.13; Heb 2.18; 4.15. **22.29:** Mk 14.24; Heb 9.20. **22.30:** Mk 10.37; Rev 3.21; 20.4.
22.31: Job 1.6-12; Amos 9.9. **22.32:** Jn 17.15; 21.15-17.
22.33-34: Mt 26.33-35; Mk 14.29-31; Jn 13.37-38. **22.35:** Lk 10.4; Mt 10.9. **22.36:** Lk 22.49-50.
22.37: Is 53.12. **22.39:** Mt 26.30; Mk 14.26; Jn 18.1.
22.40-46: Mt 26.36-46; Mk 14.32-42; Heb 5.7-8. **22.40:** Lk 11.4. **22.42:** Mk 10.38; Jn 18.11; 5.30.
22.47-53: Mt. 26.47-56; Mk 14.43-49; Jn 18.3-11. **22.49:** Lk 22.38. **22.53:** Lk 19.47.
22.54-55: Mt 26.57-58; Mk 14.53-54; Jn 18.12-16.

a fire in the middle of the courtyard
and sat down together, Peter sat
among them. 56 Then a maid, seeing
him as he sat in the light and gazing
at him, said, "This man also was with
him." 57 But he denied it, saying,
"Woman, I do not know him." 58 And
a little later some one else saw him
and said, "You also are one of them."
But Peter said, "Man, I am not."
59 And after an interval of about an
hour still another insisted, saying,
"Certainly this man also was with him;
for he is a Galilean." 60 But Peter said,
"Man, I do not know what you are
saying." And immediately, while he
was still speaking, the cock crowed.
61 And the Lord turned and looked at
Peter. And Peter remembered the
word of the Lord, how he had said to
him, "Before the cock crows today,
you will deny me three times." 62 And
he went out and wept bitterly.

63 Now the men who were holding
Jesus mocked him and beat him;
64 they also blindfolded him and asked
him, "Prophesy! Who is it that struck
you?" 65 And they spoke many other
words against him, reviling him.

66 When day came, the assembly of
the elders of the people gathered together, both chief priests and scribes;
and they led him away to their council,
and they said, 67 "If you are the Christ,
tell us." But he said to them, "If I tell
you, you will not believe; 68 and if I
ask you, you will not answer. 69 But
from now on the Son of man shall be
seated at the right hand of the power
of God." 70 And they all said, "Are you
the Son of God, then?" And he said to
them, "You say that I am." 71 And
they said, "What further testimony do
we need? We have heard it ourselves
from his own lips."

23 Then the whole company of
them arose, and brought him
before Pilate. 2 And they began to
accuse him, saying, "We found this
man perverting our nation, and for-
bidding us to give tribute to Caesar,
and saying that he himself is Christ a
king." 3 And Pilate asked him, "Are
you the King of the Jews?" And he
answered him, "You have said so."
4 And Pilate said to the chief priests
and the multitudes, "I find no crime
in this man." 5 But they were urgent,
saying, "He stirs up the people, teaching throughout all Judea, from Galilee
even to this place."

6 When Pilate heard this, he asked
whether the man was a Galilean. 7 And
when he learned that he belonged to
Her'ȯd's jurisdiction, he sent him over
to Herod, who was himself in Jerusalem at that time. 8 When Her'ȯd saw
Jesus, he was very glad, for he had long
desired to see him, because he had
heard about him, and he was hoping
to see some sign done by him. 9 So he
questioned him at some length; but he
made no answer. 10 The chief priests
and the scribes stood by, vehemently
accusing him. 11 And Her'ȯd with his
soldiers treated him with contempt
and mocked him; then, arraying him
in gorgeous apparel, he sent him back
to Pilate. 12 And Her'ȯd and Pilate became friends with each other that very
day, for before this they had been at
enmity with each other.

13 Pilate then called together the
chief priests and the rulers and the
people, 14 and said to them, "You
brought me this man as one who was
perverting the people; and after examining him before you, behold, I did
not find this man guilty of any of your
charges against him; 15 neither did
Her'ȯd, for he sent him back to us.
Behold, nothing deserving death has
been done by him; 16 I will therefore
chastise him and release him."[m]

18 But they all cried out together,
"Away with this man, and release to
us Bȧ·rab'bȧs"—19 a man who had
been thrown into prison for an insurrection started in the city, and for
murder. 20 Pilate addressed them once
more, desiring to release Jesus; 21 but
they shouted out, "Crucify, crucify
him!" 22 A third time he said to them,
"Why, what evil has he done? I have

[m] Here, or after verse 19, other ancient authorities add verse 17, *Now he was obliged to release one man to them at the festival*

22.56-62: Mt 26.69-75; Mk 14.66-72; Jn 18.16-18, 25-27.
22.61: Lk 7.13; 22.34.
22.63-65: Mt 26.67-68; Mk 14.65; Jn 18.22-24. **22.66:** Mt 26.57; Mk 14.53; Lk 22.54.
22.67-71: Mt 26.63-66; Mk 14.61-64; Jn 18.19-21. **22.70:** Lk 23.3; Mt 27.11.
23.1: Mt 27.1-2; Mk 15.1; Jn 18.28. **23.2:** Lk 20.25.
23.3: Mt 27.11-12; Mk 15.2-3; Jn 18.29-38; Lk 22.70.
23.4: Lk 23.14, 22, 41; Mt 27.24; Jn 19.4, 6; Acts 13.28. **23.8:** Lk 9.9; Acts 4.27-28.
23.9: Mk 15.5. **23.11:** Mk 15.17-19; Jn 19.2-3. **23.14:** Lk 23.4, 22, 41. **23.16:** Lk 23.22; Jn 19.12-14.
23.18-23: Mt 27.20-23; Mk 15.11-14; Acts 3.13-14; Jn 18.38-40; 19.14-15.

found in him no crime deserving
death; I will therefore chastise him and
release him." 23 But they were urgent,
demanding with loud cries that he
should be crucified. And their voices
prevailed. 24 So Pilate gave sentence
that their demand should be granted.
25 He released the man who had been
thrown into prison for insurrection
and murder, whom they asked for;
but Jesus he delivered up to their
will.

26 And as they led him away, they
seized one Simon of Cȳ·rē′nē, who was
coming in from the country, and laid
on him the cross, to carry it behind
Jesus. 27 And there followed him a
great multitude of the people, and of
women who bewailed and lamented
him. 28 But Jesus turning to them said,
"Daughters of Jerusalem, do not weep
for me, but weep for yourselves and
for your children. 29 For behold, the
days are coming when they will say,
'Blessed are the barren, and the wombs
that never bore, and the breasts that
never gave suck!' 30 Then they will
begin to say to the mountains, 'Fall on
us'; and to the hills, 'Cover us.' 31 For
if they do this when the wood is green,
what will happen when it is dry?"

32 Two others also, who were
criminals, were led away to be put to
death with him. 33 And when they
came to the place which is called The
Skull, there they crucified him, and
the criminals, one on the right and one
on the left. 34 And Jesus said, "Father,
forgive them; for they know not what
they do."[n] And they cast lots to divide
his garments. 35 And the people stood
by, watching; but the rulers scoffed at
him, saying, "He saved others; let him
save himself, if he is the Christ of God,
his Chosen One!" 36 The soldiers also
mocked him, coming up and offering
him vinegar, 37 and saying, "If you
are the King of the Jews, save yourself!" 38 There was also an inscription
over him,[o] "This is the King of the
Jews."

39 One of the criminals who were
hanged railed at him, saying, "Are you
not the Christ? Save yourself and us!"
40 But the other rebuked him, saying,
"Do you not fear God, since you are
under the same sentence of condemnation? 41 And we indeed justly; for we
are receiving the due reward of our
deeds; but this man has done nothing
wrong." 42 And he said, "Jesus, remember me when you come in your
kingly power."[p] 43 And he said to him,
"Truly, I say to you, today you will
be with me in Paradise."

44 It was now about the sixth hour,
and there was darkness over the whole
land[q] until the ninth hour, 45 while the
sun's light failed;[r] and the curtain of
the temple was torn in two. 46 Then
Jesus, crying with a loud voice, said,
"Father, into thy hands I commit my
spirit!" And having said this he
breathed his last. 47 Now when the
centurion saw what had taken place,
he praised God, and said, "Certainly
this man was innocent!" 48 And all the
multitudes who assembled to see the
sight, when they saw what had taken
place, returned home beating their
breasts. 49 And all his acquaintances
and the women who had followed him
from Galilee stood at a distance and
saw these things.

50 Now there was a man named
Joseph from the Jewish town of Ar·i-
mȧ·thē′ȧ. He was a member of the
council, a good and righteous man,
51 who had not consented to their
purpose and deed, and he was looking
for the kingdom of God. 52 This man
went to Pilate and asked for the body
of Jesus. 53 Then he took it down and
wrapped it in a linen shroud, and laid
him in a rock-hewn tomb, where no
one had ever yet been laid. 54 It was
the day of Preparation, and the sabbath was beginning.[s] 55 The women
who had come with him from Galilee
followed, and saw the tomb, and how
his body was laid; 56 then they returned,
and prepared spices and ointments.

On the sabbath they rested according to the commandment.

[n] Other ancient authorities omit the sentence *And Jesus . . . what they do*
[o] Other ancient authorities add *in letters of Greek and Latin and Hebrew*
[p] Greek *kingdom* [q] Or *earth*
[r] Or *the sun was eclipsed.* Other ancient authorities read *the sun was darkened* [s] Greek *was dawning*

23.23-25: Mt 27.26; Mk 15.15. **23.26:** Mt 27.32; Mk 15.21; Jn 19.17.
23.28-31: Lk 21.23-24; 19.41-44. **23.33-39:** Mt 27.33-44; Mk 15.22-32; Jn 19.17-24.
23 34: Acts 7.60; Ps 22.18. **23.35:** Lk 4.23. **23.36:** Mk 15.23; Ps 69.21. **23.41:** Lk 23.4, 14, 22.
23.43: 2 Cor 12.3; Rev 2.7. **23.44-49:** Mt 27.45-56; Mk 15.33-41; Jn 19.25-30.
23.45: Ex 26.31-35; Heb 9.8; 10.19. **23.46:** Ps 31.5. **23.49:** Lk 8.1-3; 23.55-56; 24.10.
23.50-56: Mt 27.57-61; Mk 15.42-47; Jn 19.38-42; Acts 13.29. **23.56:** Mk 16.1; Ex 12.16; 20.10.

24 But on the first day of the
week, at early dawn, they went
to the tomb, taking the spices which
they had prepared. 2 And they found
the stone rolled away from the tomb,
3 but when they went in they did not
find the body.[t] 4 While they were
perplexed about this, behold, two men
stood by them in dazzling apparel;
5 and as they were frightened and
bowed their faces to the ground, the
men said to them, "Why do you seek
the living among the dead?[u] 6 Remember how he told you, while he was still
in Galilee, 7 that the Son of man must
be delivered into the hands of sinful
men, and be crucified, and on the third
day rise." 8 And they remembered his
words, 9 and returning from the tomb
they told all this to the eleven and to
all the rest. 10 Now it was Mary Mag′-
dȧ·lēne and Jō-an′nȧ and Mary the
mother of James and the other women
with them who told this to the apostles;
11 but these words seemed to them an
idle tale, and they did not believe
them.[v]

13 That very day two of them were
going to a village named Em·mā′ŭs,
about seven miles[w] from Jerusalem,
14 and talking with each other about
all these things that had happened.
15 While they were talking and discussing together, Jesus himself drew
near and went with them. 16 But their
eyes were kept from recognizing him.
17 And he said to them, "What is this
conversation which you are holding
with each other as you walk?" And
they stood still, looking sad. 18 Then
one of them, named Clē′ȯ·pȧs, answered him, "Are you the only visitor
to Jerusalem who does not know the
things that have happened there in
these days?" 19 And he said to them,
"What things?" And they said to him,
"Concerning Jesus of Nazareth, who
was a prophet mighty in deed and
word before God and all the people,
20 and how our chief priests and rulers
delivered him up to be condemned to
death, and crucified him. 21 But we
had hoped that he was the one to
redeem Israel. Yes, and besides all
this, it is now the third day since this
happened. 22 Moreover, some women
of our company amazed us. They were
at the tomb early in the morning 23 and
did not find his body; and they came
back saying that they had even seen a
vision of angels, who said that he was
alive. 24 Some of those who were with
us went to the tomb, and found it just
as the women had said; but him they
did not see." 25 And he said to them,
"O foolish men, and slow of heart to
believe all that the prophets have
spoken! 26 Was it not necessary that
the Christ should suffer these things
and enter into his glory?" 27 And beginning with Moses and all the
prophets, he interpreted to them in all
the scriptures the things concerning
himself.

28 So they drew near to the village
to which they were going. He appeared
to be going further, 29 but they con-
strained him, saying, "Stay with us,
for it is toward evening and the day is
now far spent." So he went in to stay
with them. 30 When he was at table
with them, he took the bread and
blessed, and broke it, and gave it to
them. 31 And their eyes were opened
and they recognized him; and he
vanished out of their sight. 32 They
said to each other, "Did not our hearts
burn within us while he talked to us
on the road, while he opened to us the
scriptures?" 33 And they rose that same
hour and returned to Jerusalem; and
they found the eleven gathered together and those who were with them,
34 who said, "The Lord has risen
indeed, and has appeared to Simon!"
35 Then they told what had happened
on the road, and how he was known to
them in the breaking of the bread.

36 As they were saying this, Jesus
himself stood among them.[x] 37 But
they were startled and frightened, and
supposed that they saw a spirit. 38 And

[t] Other ancient authorities add *of the Lord Jesus*
[u] Other ancient authorities add *He is not here, but has risen*
[v] Other ancient authorities add verse 12, *But Peter rose and ran to the tomb; stooping and looking in, he saw the linen cloths by themselves; and he went home wondering at what had happened*
[w] Greek *sixty stadia;* some ancient authorities read *a hundred and sixty stadia*
[x] Other ancient authorities add *and said to them, "Peace to you!"*

24.1-9: Mt 28.1-8; Mk 16.1-7; Jn 20.1, 11-13. **24.6:** Lk 9.22; 13 32-33.
24.10: Mk 16.1; Lk 8.1-3; Jn 20.2. **24.16:** Jn 20.14; 21.4.
24.19: Mt 21.11; Lk 7.16; 13.33; Acts 3.22. **24.24:** Jn 20.3-10.
24.27: Lk 24.44-45; Acts 28.23; 1 Pet 1.11. **24.28:** Mk 6.48. **24.30:** Lk 9.16; 22.19.
24.34: 1 Cor 15 5. **24.36-43:** Jn 20.19-20, 27; Jn 21.5, 9-13; 1 Cor 15.5; Acts 10.40-41.

he said to them, "Why are you
troubled, and why do questionings
rise in your hearts? 39 See my hands
and my feet, that it is I myself; handle
me, and see; for a spirit has not flesh
and bones as you see that I have."[y]
41 And while they still disbelieved for
joy, and wondered, he said to them,
"Have you anything here to eat?"
42 They gave him a piece of broiled
fish, 43 and he took it and ate before
them.

44 Then he said to them, "These
are my words which I spoke to you,
while I was still with you, that everything written about me in the law of
Moses and the prophets and the psalms
must be fulfilled." 45 Then he opened
their minds to understand the scriptures, 46 and said to them, "Thus it
is written, that the Christ should suffer
and on the third day rise from the
dead, 47 and that repentance and forgiveness of sins should be preached in
his name to all nations,[z] beginning
from Jerusalem. 48 You are witnesses
of these things. 49 And behold, I send
the promise of my Father upon you;
but stay in the city, until you
are clothed with power from on
high."

50 Then he led them out as far as
Beth'a·ny, and lifting up his hands he
blessed them. 51 While he blessed
them, he parted from them.[a] 52 And
they[b] returned to Jerusalem with great
joy, 53 and were continually in the
temple blessing God.

THE GOSPEL ACCORDING TO
JOHN

1 In the beginning was the Word,
and the Word was with God, and
the Word was God. 2 He was in the
beginning with God; 3 all things were
made through him, and without him
was not anything made that was made.
4 In him was life,[a] and the life was the
light of men. 5 The light shines in the
darkness, and the darkness has not
overcome it.

6 There was a man sent from God,
whose name was John. 7 He came for
testimony, to bear witness to the light,
that all might believe through him.
8 He was not the light, but came to
bear witness to the light.

9 The true light that enlightens
every man was coming into the world.
10 He was in the world, and the world
was made through him, yet the world
knew him not. 11 He came to his own
home, and his own people received
him not. 12 But to all who received
him, who believed in his name, he
gave power to become children of
God; 13 who were born, not of blood
nor of the will of the flesh nor of the
will of man, but of God.

14 And the Word became flesh and
dwelt among us, full of grace and
truth; we have beheld his glory, glory
as of the only Son from the Father.
15 (John bore witness to him, and
cried, "This was he of whom I said,
'He who comes after me ranks before
me, for he was before me.' ") 16 And
from his fulness have we all received,
grace upon grace. 17 For the law was
given through Moses; grace and truth
came through Jesus Christ. 18 No one

[y] Other ancient authorities add verse 40, *And when he had said this, he showed them his hands and his feet*
[z] Or *nations. Beginning from Jerusalem you are witnesses*
[a] Other ancient authorities add *and was carried up into heaven*
[b] Other ancient authorities add *worshiped him, and*
[a] Or *was not anything made. That which has been made was life in him*

24.39: 1 Jn 1.1. **24.44:** Lk 24.26-27; Acts 28.23. **24.46:** Hos 6.2; 1 Cor 15.3-4.
24.47: Acts 1.4-8; Mt 28.19. **24.49:** Acts 2.1-4; Jn 14.26; 20.21-23. **24.51:** Acts 1.9-11.
24.52-53: Acts 1.12-14. **1.1:** Gen 1.1; 1 Jn 1.1; Rev 19.13; Jn 17.5.
1.3: Col 1.16; 1 Cor 8.6; Heb 1.2. **1.4:** Jn 5.26; 11.25; 14.6. **1.5:** Jn 9.5; 12.46.
1.6: Mk 1.4; Mt 3.1; Lk 3.3; Jn 1.19-23. **1.9:** 1 Jn 2.8. **1.12:** Gal 3.26; Jn 3.18; 1 Jn 5.13.
1.13: Jn 3.5; 1 Pet 1.23; Jas 1.18; 1 Jn 3.9.
1.14: Rom 1.3; Gal 4.4; Phil 2.7; 1 Tim 3.16; Heb 2.14; 1 Jn 4.2. **1.15:** Jn 1.30.
1.16: Col 1.19; 2.9; Eph 1.23; Rom 5.21. **1.17:** Jn 7.19. **1.18:** Ex 33.20; Jn 6.26; 1 Jn 4.12; Jn 3.11.

has ever seen God; the only Son,[b] who
is in the bosom of the Father, he has
made him known.

19 And this is the testimony of
John, when the Jews sent priests and
Levites from Jerusalem to ask him,
"Who are you?" 20 He confessed, he
did not deny, but confessed, "I am
not the Christ." 21 And they asked him,
"What then? Are you E·lī'jȧh?" He
said, "I am not." "Are you the prophet?" And he answered, "No." 22 They
said to him then, "Who are you? Let
us have an answer for those who sent
us. What do you say about yourself?"
23 He said, "I am the voice of one
crying in the wilderness, 'Make
straight the way of the Lord,' as the
prophet Ī·ṡāi'ȧh said."

24 Now they had been sent from
the Pharisees. 25 They asked him,
"Then why are you baptizing, if you
are neither the Christ, nor E·lī'jȧh, nor
the prophet?" 26 John answered them,
"I baptize with water; but among you
stands one whom you do not know,
27 even he who comes after me, the
thong of whose sandal I am not worthy
to untie." 28 This took place in Beth'-
ȧ·ny beyond the Jordan, where John
was baptizing.

29 The next day he saw Jesus
coming toward him, and said, "Behold, the Lamb of God, who takes
away the sin of the world! 30 This is
he of whom I said, 'After me comes a
man who ranks before me, for he was
before me.' 31 I myself did not know
him; but for this I came baptizing with
water, that he might be revealed to
Israel." 32 And John bore witness, "I
saw the Spirit descend as a dove from
heaven, and it remained on him. 33 I
myself did not know him; but he who
sent me to baptize with water said to
me, 'He on whom you see the Spirit
descend and remain, this is he who
baptizes with the Holy Spirit.' 34 And
I have seen and have borne witness
that this is the Son of God."

35 The next day again John was
standing with two of his disciples;
36 and he looked at Jesus as he walked,
and said, "Behold, the Lamb of God!"
37 The two disciples heard him say
this, and they followed Jesus. 38 Jesus
turned, and saw them following, and
said to them, "What do you seek?"
And they said to him, "Rabbi" (which
means Teacher), "where are you staying?" 39 He said to them, "Come and
see." They came and saw where he
was staying; and they stayed with him
that day, for it was about the tenth
hour. 40 One of the two who heard
John speak, and followed him, was
Andrew, Simon Peter's brother. 41 He
first found his brother Simon, and said
to him, "We have found the Messiah"
(which means Christ). 42 He brought
him to Jesus. Jesus looked at him, and
said, "So you are Simon the son of
John? You shall be called Cē'phȧs"
(which means Peter[c]).

43 The next day Jesus decided to
go to Galilee. And he found Philip and
said to him, "Follow me." 44 Now
Philip was from Beth-sā'i·dȧ, the city
of Andrew and Peter. 45 Philip found
Nȧ·than'ȧ-el, and said to him, "We
have found him of whom Moses in the
law and also the prophets wrote, Jesus
of Nazareth, the son of Joseph."
46 Nȧ·than'ȧ-el said to him, "Can anything good come out of Nazareth?"
Philip said to him, "Come and see."
47 Jesus saw Nȧ·than'ȧ-el coming to
him, and said of him, "Behold, an
Israelite indeed, in whom is no guile!"
48 Nȧ·than'ȧ-el said to him, "How do
you know me?" Jesus answered him,
"Before Philip called you, when you
were under the fig tree, I saw you."
49 Nȧ·than'ȧ-el answered him, "Rabbi, you are the Son of God! You are
the King of Israel!" 50 Jesus answered
him, "Because I said to you, I saw you
under the fig tree, do you believe? You
shall see greater things than these."
51 And he said to him, "Truly, truly,
I say to you, you will see heaven
opened, and the angels of God ascending and descending upon the Son of
man."

2 On the third day there was a
marriage at Cā'nȧ in Galilee, and
the mother of Jesus was there; 2 Jesus

[b] Other ancient authorities read *God* [c] From the word for *rock* in Aramaic and Greek respectively

1.19: Jn 1.6. **1.20:** Jn 3.28. **1.21:** Mt 11.14; 16.14; Mk 9.13; Mt 17.13; Deut 18.15, 18.
1.23: Is 40.3; Mk 1.3; Mt 3.3; Lk 3.4. **1.26-27:** Mk 1.7-8; Mt 3.11; Lk 3.16. **1.28:** Jn 3.26; 10.40.
1.29: Jn 1.36; Is 53.7; Acts 8.32; 1 Pet 1.19; Rev 5.6; 1 Jn 3.5. **1.30:** Jn 1.15.
1.32: Mk 1.10; Mt 3.16; Lk 3.22. **1.35:** Lk 7.18. **1.40-42:** Mt 4.18-22; Mk 1.16-20; Lk 5.2-11.
1.41: Dan 9.25; Jn 4.25. **1.42:** Jn 21.15-17; 1 Cor 15.5; Mt 16.18. **1.43:** Mt 10.3; Jn 6.5; 12.21; 14.8.
1.45: Lk 24.27. **1.46:** Jn 7.41; Mk 6.2. **1.49:** Ps 2.7; Mk 15.32; Jn 12.13. **1.51:** Lk 3.21; Gen 28.12.
2.1: Jn 4.46; 21.2.

also was invited to the marriage, with his disciples. 3 When the wine failed, the mother of Jesus said to him, "They have no wine." 4 And Jesus said to her, "O woman, what have you to do with me? My hour has not yet come." 5 His mother said to the servants, "Do whatever he tells you." 6 Now six stone jars were standing there, for the Jewish rites of purification, each holding twenty or thirty gallons. 7 Jesus said to them, "Fill the jars with water." And they filled them up to the brim. 8 He said to them, "Now draw some out, and take it to the steward of the feast." So they took it. 9 When the steward of the feast tasted the water now become wine, and did not know where it came from (though the servants who had drawn the water knew), the steward of the feast called the bridegroom 10 and said to him, "Every man serves the good wine first; and when men have drunk freely, then the poor wine; but you have kept the good wine until now." 11 This, the first of his signs, Jesus did at Cā′nȧ in Galilee, and manifested his glory; and his disciples believed in him.

12 After this he went down to Cȧ-pẽr′nȧ-ŭm, with his mother and his brothers and his disciples; and there they stayed for a few days.

13 The Passover of the Jews was at hand, and Jesus went up to Jerusalem. 14 In the temple he found those who were selling oxen and sheep and pigeons, and the money-changers at their business. 15 And making a whip of cords, he drove them all, with the sheep and oxen, out of the temple; and he poured out the coins of the money-changers and overturned their tables. 16 And he told those who sold the pigeons, "Take these things away; you shall not make my Father's house a house of trade." 17 His disciples remembered that it was written, "Zeal for thy house will consume me." 18 The Jews then said to him, "What sign have you to show us for doing this?" 19 Jesus answered them, "Destroy this temple, and in three days I will raise it up." 20 The Jews then said, "It has taken forty-six years to build this temple, and will you raise it up in three days?" 21 But he spoke of the temple of his body. 22 When therefore he was raised from the dead, his disciples remembered that he had said this; and they believed the scripture and the word which Jesus had spoken.

23 Now when he was in Jerusalem at the Passover feast, many believed in his name when they saw the signs which he did; 24 but Jesus did not trust himself to them, 25 because he knew all men and needed no one to bear witness of man; for he himself knew what was in man.

3 Now there was a man of the Pharisees, named Nic·ȯ·dē′mŭs, a ruler of the Jews. 2 This man came to Jesus[d] by night and said to him, "Rabbi, we know that you are a teacher come from God; for no one can do these signs that you do, unless God is with him." 3 Jesus answered him, "Truly, truly, I say to you, unless one is born anew,[e] he cannot see the kingdom of God." 4 Nic·ȯ·dē′mŭs said to him, "How can a man be born when he is old? Can he enter a second time into his mother's womb and be born?" 5 Jesus answered, "Truly, truly, I say to you, unless one is born of water and the Spirit, he cannot enter the kingdom of God. 6 That which is born of the flesh is flesh, and that which is born of the Spirit is spirit.[f] 7 Do not marvel that I said to you, 'You must be born anew.'[e] 8 The wind[f] blows where it wills, and you hear the sound of it, but you do not know whence it comes or whither it goes; so it is with every one who is born of the Spirit." 9 Nic·ȯ·dē′mŭs said to him, "How can this be?" 10 Jesus answered him, "Are you a teacher of Israel, and yet you do not understand this? 11 Truly, truly, I say to you, we speak of what we know, and bear witness to what we have seen; but you do not receive our testimony. 12 If I have told you earthly things and you do not believe, how can you

[d] Greek *him* [e] Or *from above* [f] The same Greek word means both *wind* and *spirit*

2.3: Jn 19.26; Mk 3.31. **2.4:** Mk 1.24; 5.7; Jn 7.6, 30; 8.20. **2.6:** Mk 7.3; Jn 3.25.
2.11: Jn 2.23; 3.2; 4.54; 6.2. **2.12:** Mt 4.13; Jn 7.3; Mk 3.31.
2.13: Jn 6.4; 11.55; Deut 16.1-6; Lk 2.41. **2.14-16:** Mt 21.12-13; Mk 11.15-17; Lk 19.45-46.
2.16: Lk 2.49. **2.17:** Ps 69.9. **2.18:** Mk 11.28; Mt 21.23; Lk 20.2. **2.19:** Mk 14.58; Acts 6.14.
2.21: 1 Cor 6.19; Jn 8.57. **2.22:** Jn 12.16; 14.26. **2.25:** Jn 1.47; 6.61; 13.11; Mk 2.8.
3.1: Jn 7.50; 19.39; Lk 23.13; Jn 7.26. **3.2:** Jn 2.11; 7.31; 9.16; Acts 10.38.
3.3: Jn 1.13; 1 Pet 1.23; Jas 1.18; 1 Jn 3.9. **3.5:** Ezek 36.25-27; Eph 5.26; Tit 3.5. **3.6:** 1 Cor 15.50.
3.8: Ezek 37.9. **3.11:** Jn 8.26; 1.18; 3.32.

believe if I tell you heavenly things?
13 No one has ascended into heaven
but he who descended from heaven,
the Son of man.[g] 14 And as Moses
lifted up the serpent in the wilderness,
so must the Son of man be lifted up,
15 that whoever believes in him may
have eternal life."[h]

16 For God so loved the world that
he gave his only Son, that whoever
believes in him should not perish but
have eternal life. 17 For God sent the
Son into the world, not to condemn
the world, but that the world might
be saved through him. 18 He who
believes in him is not condemned; he
who does not believe is condemned
already, because he has not believed
in the name of the only Son of God.
19 And this is the judgment, that the
light has come into the world, and
men loved darkness rather than light,
because their deeds were evil. 20 For
every one who does evil hates the light,
and does not come to the light, lest his
deeds should be exposed. 21 But he
who does what is true comes to the
light, that it may be clearly seen that
his deeds have been wrought in God.

22 After this Jesus and his disciples
went into the land of Judea; there he
remained with them and baptized.
23 John also was baptizing at Aē′non
near Sā′lim, because there was much
water there; and people came and
were baptized. 24 For John had not
yet been put in prison.

25 Now a discussion arose between
John's disciples and a Jew over purifying. 26 And they came to John, and
said to him, "Rabbi, he who was with
you beyond the Jordan, to whom you
bore witness, here he is, baptizing, and
all are going to him." 27 John answered, "No one can receive anything
except what is given him from heaven.
28 You yourselves bear me witness,
that I said, I am not the Christ, but I
have been sent before him. 29 He who
has the bride is the bridegroom; the
friend of the bridegroom, who stands
and hears him, rejoices greatly at the
bridegroom's voice; therefore this joy
of mine is now full. 30 He must increase, but I must decrease."[i]

31 He who comes from above is
above all; he who is of the earth belongs to the earth, and of the earth he
speaks; he who comes from heaven is
above all. 32 He bears witness to what
he has seen and heard, yet no one
receives his testimony; 33 he who
receives his testimony sets his seal to
this, that God is true. 34 For he whom
God has sent utters the words of God,
for it is not by measure that he gives
the Spirit; 35 the Father loves the Son,
and has given all things into his hand.
36 He who believes in the Son has
eternal life; he who does not obey the
Son shall not see life, but the wrath of
God rests upon him.

4 Now when the Lord knew that
the Pharisees had heard that Jesus
was making and baptizing more disciples than John 2 (although Jesus
himself did not baptize, but only his
disciples), 3 he left Judea and departed
again to Galilee. 4 He had to pass
through Sȧ·mâr′i·ȧ. 5 So he came to a
city of Sȧ·mâr′i·ȧ, called Sȳ′chär, near
the field that Jacob gave to his son
Joseph. 6 Jacob's well was there, and
so Jesus, wearied as he was with his
journey, sat down beside the well. It
was about the sixth hour.

7 There came a woman of Sȧ·mâr′i·ȧ
to draw water. Jesus said to her, "Give
me a drink." 8 For his disciples had
gone away into the city to buy food.
9 The Samaritan woman said to him,
"How is it that you, a Jew, ask a drink
of me, a woman of Sȧ·mâr′i·ȧ?" For
Jews have no dealings with Samaritans. 10 Jesus answered her, "If you
knew the gift of God, and who it is that
is saying to you, 'Give me a drink,' you
would have asked him and he would
have given you living water." 11 The
woman said to him, "Sir, you have
nothing to draw with, and the well is
deep; where do you get that living
water? 12 Are you greater than our
father Jacob, who gave us the well,
and drank from it himself, and his

[g] Other ancient authorities add *who is in heaven*
[h] Some interpreters hold that the quotation continues through verse 21
[i] Some interpreters hold that the quotation continues through verse 36

3.13: Rom 10.6; Eph 4.9. **3.14:** Num 21.9; Jn 8.28; 12.34. **3.16:** Rom 5.8; 8.32; Eph 2.4; 1 Jn 4.9-10. **3.17:** Jn 8.15; 12.47; Lk 19.10; 1 Jn 4.14. **3.19:** Jn 1.4; 8.12; Eph 5.11, 13. **3.21:** 1 Jn 1.6. **3.22:** Jn 4.2. **3.24:** Mk 1.14; 6.17-18. **3.26:** Jn 1.7, 28. **3.27:** 1 Cor 4.7. **3.28:** Jn 1.20, 23. **3.29:** Mk 2.19-20; Mt 25.1; Jn 15.11. **3.31:** Jn 3.13; 8.23; 1 Jn 4.5. **3.32:** Jn 3.11. **3.36:** Jn 3.16; 5.24. **4.1:** Jn 3.22. **4.4:** Lk 9.52; 17.11. **4.5:** Gen 33.19; 48.22; Josh 24.32. **4.9:** Mt 10.5; Jn 8.48; Ezra 4.3-6. **4.10:** Jn 7.37; Rev 21.6; 22.17.

sons, and his cattle?" 13 Jesus said to
her, "Every one who drinks of this
water will thirst again, 14 but whoever
drinks of the water that I shall give
him will never thirst; the water that I
shall give him will become in him a
spring of water welling up to eternal
life." 15 The woman said to him, "Sir,
give me this water, that I may not
thirst, nor come here to draw."

16 Jesus said to her, "Go, call your
husband, and come here." 17 The
woman answered him, "I have no
husband." Jesus said to her, "You are
right in saying, 'I have no husband';
18 for you have had five husbands, and
he whom you now have is not your
husband; this you said truly." 19 The
woman said to him, "Sir, I perceive
that you are a prophet. 20 Our fathers
worshiped on this mountain; and you
say that in Jerusalem is the place
where men ought to worship." 21 Jesus
said to her, "Woman, believe me, the
hour is coming when neither on this
mountain nor in Jerusalem will you
worship the Father. 22 You worship
what you do not know; we worship
what we know, for salvation is from
the Jews. 23 But the hour is coming,
and now is, when the true worshipers
will worship the Father in spirit and
truth, for such the Father seeks to
worship him. 24 God is spirit, and
those who worship him must worship
in spirit and truth." 25 The woman
said to him, "I know that Messiah is
coming (he who is called Christ); when
he comes, he will show us all things."
26 Jesus said to her, "I who speak to
you am he."

27 Just then his disciples came.
They marveled that he was talking
with a woman, but none said, "What
do you wish?" or, "Why are you talking with her?" 28 So the woman left
her water jar, and went away into the
city, and said to the people, 29 "Come,
see a man who told me all that I ever
did. Can this be the Christ?" 30 They
went out of the city and were coming
to him.

31 Meanwhile the disciples besought him, saying, "Rabbi, eat."
32 But he said to them, "I have food
to eat of which you do not know."
33 So the disciples said to one another,
"Has any one brought him food?"
34 Jesus said to them, "My food is to
do the will of him who sent me, and
to accomplish his work. 35 Do you not
say, 'There are yet four months, then
comes the harvest'? I tell you, lift up
your eyes, and see how the fields are
already white for harvest. 36 He who
reaps receives wages, and gathers fruit
for eternal life, so that sower and
reaper may rejoice together. 37 For
here the saying holds true, 'One sows
and another reaps.' 38 I sent you to
reap that for which you did not labor;
others have labored, and you have
entered into their labor."

39 Many Samaritans from that city
believed in him because of the
woman's testimony, "He told me all
that I ever did." 40 So when the Samaritans came to him, they asked him
to stay with them; and he stayed there
two days. 41 And many more believed
because of his word. 42 They said to
the woman, "It is no longer because
of your words that we believe, for we
have heard for ourselves, and we know
that this is indeed the Savior of the
world."

43 After the two days he departed
to Galilee. 44 For Jesus himself testified that a prophet has no honor in
his own country. 45 So when he came
to Galilee, the Galileans welcomed
him, having seen all that he had done
in Jerusalem at the feast, for they too
had gone to the feast.

46 So he came again to Cā'nȧ in
Galilee, where he had made the water
wine. And at Cȧ·pĕr'nȧ-ŭm there was
an official whose son was ill. 47 When
he heard that Jesus had come from
Judea to Galilee, he went and begged
him to come down and heal his son,
for he was at the point of death.
48 Jesus therefore said to him, "Unless
you see signs and wonders you will not
believe." 49 The official said to him,
"Sir, come down before my child
dies." 50 Jesus said to him, "Go; your
son will live." The man believed the
word that Jesus spoke to him and went
his way. 51 As he was going down, his

4.14: Jn 6.35; 7.38. **4.15:** Jn 6.34. **4.18:** 2 Kings 17.24; Hos 2.7.
4.20: Deut 11.29; Josh 8.33; Lk 9.53. **4.21:** Jn 5.25; 16.2, 32; Mal 1.11.
4.22: 2 Kings 17.28-41; Is 2.3; Rom 9.4. **4.24:** Phil 3.3. **4.26:** Jn 8.24. **4.29:** Jn 7.26; Mt 12.23.
4.32: Mt 4.4. **4.34:** Jn 5.30; 6.38; 17.4. **4.35:** Lk 10.2; Mt 9.37. **4.37:** Job 31.8; Mic 6.15.
4.42: 1 Jn 4.14; 2 Tim 1.10. **4.44:** Mk 6.4; Mt 13.57. **4.46:** Jn 2.1-11; Mt 8.5-10; Lk 7.2-10.
4.48: Dan 4.2; Mk 13.22; Acts 2.19; 4.30; Rom 15.19; Heb 2.4.

servants met him and told him that
his son was living. 52 So he asked them
the hour when he began to mend, and
they said to him, "Yesterday at the
seventh hour the fever left him."
53 The father knew that was the hour
when Jesus had said to him, "Your
son will live"; and he himself believed,
and all his household. 54 This was now
the second sign that Jesus did when
he had come from Judea to Galilee.

5 After this there was a feast of the
Jews, and Jesus went up to Jerusalem.

2 Now there is in Jerusalem by the
Sheep Gate a pool, in Hebrew called
Beth-zā'thȧ,[j] which has five porticoes.
3 In these lay a multitude of invalids,
blind, lame, paralyzed.[k] 5 One man
was there, who had been ill for thirty-
eight years. 6 When Jesus saw him and
knew that he had been lying there a
long time, he said to him, "Do you
want to be healed?" 7 The sick man
answered him, "Sir, I have no man to
put me into the pool when the water
is troubled, and while I am going
another steps down before me."
8 Jesus said to him, "Rise, take up
your pallet, and walk." 9 And at once
the man was healed, and he took up
his pallet and walked.

Now that day was the sabbath. 10 So
the Jews said to the man who was
cured, "It is the sabbath, it is not lawful for you to carry your pallet." 11 But
he answered them, "The man who
healed me said to me, 'Take up your
pallet, and walk.' " 12 They asked him,
"Who is the man who said to you,
'Take up your pallet, and walk'?"
13 Now the man who had been healed
did not know who it was, for Jesus had
withdrawn, as there was a crowd in
the place. 14 Afterward, Jesus found
him in the temple, and said to him,
"See, you are well! Sin no more, that
nothing worse befall you." 15 The man
went away and told the Jews that it
was Jesus who had healed him. 16 And
this was why the Jews persecuted
Jesus, because he did this on the sabbath. 17 But Jesus answered them,
"My Father is working still, and I am
working." 18 This was why the Jews
sought all the more to kill him, because
he not only broke the sabbath but also
called God his Father, making himself
equal with God.

19 Jesus said to them, "Truly,
truly, I say to you, the Son can do
nothing of his own accord, but only
what he sees the Father doing; for
whatever he does, that the Son does
likewise. 20 For the Father loves the
Son, and shows him all that he himself
is doing; and greater works than these
will he show him, that you may marvel.
21 For as the Father raises the dead
and gives them life, so also the Son
gives life to whom he will. 22 The
Father judges no one, but has given
all judgment to the Son, 23 that all
may honor the Son, even as they honor
the Father. He who does not honor the
Son does not honor the Father who
sent him. 24 Truly, truly, I say to you,
he who hears my word and believes
him who sent me, has eternal life; he
does not come into judgment, but has
passed from death to life.

25 "Truly, truly, I say to you, the
hour is coming, and now is, when the
dead will hear the voice of the Son of
God, and those who hear will live.
26 For as the Father has life in himself,
so he has granted the Son also to have
life in himself, 27 and has given him
authority to execute judgment, because he is the Son of man. 28 Do not
marvel at this; for the hour is coming
when all who are in the tombs will hear
his voice 29 and come forth, those who
have done good, to the resurrection of
life, and those who have done evil, to
the resurrection of judgment.

30 "I can do nothing on my own
authority; as I hear, I judge; and my
judgment is just, because I seek not
my own will but the will of him who
sent me. 31 If I bear witness to myself,
my testimony is not true; 32 there is
another who bears witness to me, and

[j] Other ancient authorities read *Bethesda*, others *Bethsaida*

[k] Other ancient authorities insert, wholly or in part, *waiting for the moving of the water; 4 for an angel of the Lord went down at certain seasons into the pool, and troubled the water: whoever stepped in first after the troubling of the water was healed of whatever disease he had*

4.53: Acts 11.14. **4.54:** Jn 2.11. **5.2:** Neh 3.1; 12.39. **5.8:** Mk 2.11; Mt 9.6; Lk 5.24.
5.10: Neh 13.19; Jer 17.21; Jn 7.23; 9.16; Mk 2.24. **5.14:** Mk 2.5. **5.17:** Gen 2.3.
5.18: Jn 7.1; 10.33. **5.19:** Jn 5.30; 8.28; 14.10. **5.20:** Jn 14.12. **5.21:** Rom 4.17; 8.11; Jn 11.25.
5.23: Lk 10.16; 1 Jn 2.23. **5.24:** Jn 3.18. **5.25:** Jn 4.21; 16,.2 32.
5.29: Dan 12.2; Acts 24.15; Jn 11.24; Mt 25.46; 1 Cor 15.52. **5.30:** Jn 5.19; 8.16; 6.38.
5.31-37: Jn 8.14-18.

I know that the testimony which he
bears to me is true. 33 You sent to
John, and he has borne witness to the
truth. 34 Not that the testimony which
I receive is from man; but I say this
that you may be saved. 35 He was a
burning and shining lamp, and you
were willing to rejoice for a while in
his light. 36 But the testimony which I
have is greater than that of John; for
the works which the Father has
granted me to accomplish, these very
works which I am doing, bear me
witness that the Father has sent me.
37 And the Father who sent me has
himself borne witness to me. His voice
you have never heard, his form you
have never seen; 38 and you do not
have his word abiding in you, for you
do not believe him whom he has sent.
39 You search the scriptures, because
you think that in them you have
eternal life; and it is they that bear
witness to me; 40 yet you refuse to
come to me that you may have life.
41 I do not receive glory from men.
42 But I know that you have not the
love of God within you. 43 I have come
in my Father's name, and you do not
receive me; if another comes in his own
name, him you will receive. 44 How can
you believe, who receive glory from
one another and do not seek the glory
that comes from the only God? 45 Do
not think that I shall accuse you to
the Father; it is Moses who accuses you,
on whom you set your hope. 46 If you
believed Moses, you would believe me,
for he wrote of me. 47 But if you do
not believe his writings, how will you
believe my words?"

6 After this Jesus went to the other
side of the Sea of Galilee, which is
the Sea of Tī·bē'ri-ȧs. 2 And a multitude followed him, because they saw
the signs which he did on those who
were diseased. 3 Jesus went up into the
hills, and there sat down with his disciples. 4 Now the Passover, the feast
of the Jews, was at hand. 5 Lifting up
his eyes, then, and seeing that a multitude was coming to him, Jesus said
to Philip, "How are we to buy bread,
so that these people may eat?" 6 This
he said to test him, for he himself knew
what he would do. 7 Philip answered
him, "Two hundred denarii[l] would
not buy enough bread for each of them
to get a little." 8 One of his disciples,
Andrew, Simon Peter's brother, said
to him, 9 "There is a lad here who has
five barley loaves and two fish; but
what are they among so many?"
10 Jesus said, "Make the people sit
down." Now there was much grass in
the place; so the men sat down, in
number about five thousand. 11 Jesus
then took the loaves, and when he had
given thanks, he distributed them to
those who were seated; so also the fish,
as much as they wanted. 12 And when
they had eaten their fill, he told his
disciples, "Gather up the fragments
left over, that nothing may be lost."
13 So they gathered them up and filled
twelve baskets with fragments from
the five barley loaves, left by those who
had eaten. 14 When the people saw the
sign which he had done, they said,
"This is indeed the prophet who is to
come into the world!"

15 Perceiving then that they were
about to come and take him by force
to make him king, Jesus withdrew
again to the hills by himself.

16 When evening came, his disciples went down to the sea, 17 got into
a boat, and started across the sea to
Cȧ·pēr'nȧ-ŭm. It was now dark, and
Jesus had not yet come to them. 18 The
sea rose because a strong wind was
blowing. 19 When they had rowed
about three or four miles,[m] they saw
Jesus walking on the sea and drawing
near to the boat. They were frightened,
20 but he said to them, "It is I; do not
be afraid." 21 Then they were glad to
take him into the boat, and immediately the boat was at the land to which
they were going.

22 On the next day the people who
remained on the other side of the sea
saw that there had been only one boat
there, and that Jesus had not entered
the boat with his disciples, but that
his disciples had gone away alone.
23 However, boats from Tī·bē'ri-ȧs
came near the place where they ate the
bread after the Lord had given thanks.
24 So when the people saw that Jesus
was not there, nor his disciples, they

[l] The denarius was worth about twenty cents [m] Greek *twenty-five or thirty stadia*

5.33: Jn 1.7, 19. **5.34:** 1 Jn 5.9. **5.36:** Jn 10.25; 14.11; 15.24; Mt 11.4. **5.39:** Lk 24.27; Acts 13.27.
5.43: Mt 24.5. **5.45:** Jn 9.28; Rom 2.17. **5.47:** Lk 16.29, 31.
6.1-13: Mt 14.13-21; Mk 6.32-44; Lk 9.10-17. **6.5:** Jn 1.43; 12.21. **6.8:** Jn 1.40; 12.22.
6.9: Jn 21.9-13. **6.14:** Mt 21.11. **6.15:** Jn 6.3; 18.36. **6.16-21:** Mt 14.22-27; Mk 6.45-51.

themselves got into the boats and went
to Cȧ·pẽr′nȧ-ŭm, seeking Jesus.
25 When they found him on the
other side of the sea, they said to him,
"Rabbi, when did you come here?"
26 Jesus answered them, "Truly, truly,
I say to you, you seek me, not because
you saw signs, but because you ate
your fill of the loaves. 27 Do not labor
for the food which perishes, but for
the food which endures to eternal life,
which the Son of man will give to you;
for on him has God the Father set his
seal." 28 Then they said to him, "What
must we do, to be doing the works of
God?" 29 Jesus answered them, "This
is the work of God, that you believe
in him whom he has sent." 30 So they
said to him, "Then what sign do you
do, that we may see, and believe you?
What work do you perform? 31 Our
fathers ate the manna in the wilderness; as it is written, 'He gave them
bread from heaven to eat.' " 32 Jesus
then said to them, "Truly, truly, I say
to you, it was not Moses who gave you
the bread from heaven; my Father
gives you the true bread from heaven.
33 For the bread of God is that which
comes down from heaven, and gives
life to the world." 34 They said to him,
"Lord, give us this bread always."
35 Jesus said to them, "I am the
bread of life; he who comes to me
shall not hunger, and he who believes
in me shall never thirst. 36 But I said
to you that you have seen me and yet
do not believe. 37 All that the Father
gives me will come to me; and him
who comes to me I will not cast out.
38 For I have come down from heaven,
not to do my own will, but the will of
him who sent me; 39 and this is the
will of him who sent me, that I should
lose nothing of all that he has given
me, but raise it up at the last day.
40 For this is the will of my Father,
that every one who sees the Son and
believes in him should have eternal
life; and I will raise him up at the last
day."
41 The Jews then murmured at
him, because he said, "I am the bread
which came down from heaven."
42 They said, "Is not this Jesus, the
son of Joseph, whose father and
mother we know? How does he now
say, 'I have come down from heaven'?"
43 Jesus answered them, "Do not
murmur among yourselves. 44 No one
can come to me unless the Father who
sent me draws him; and I will raise
him up at the last day. 45 It is written
in the prophets, 'And they shall all be
taught by God.' Every one who has
heard and learned from the Father
comes to me. 46 Not that any one has
seen the Father except him who is from
God; he has seen the Father. 47 Truly,
truly, I say to you, he who believes has
eternal life. 48 I am the bread of life.
49 Your fathers ate the manna in the
wilderness, and they died. 50 This is
the bread which comes down from
heaven, that a man may eat of it and
not die. 51 I am the living bread which
came down from heaven; if any one
eats of this bread, he will live for ever;
and the bread which I shall give
for the life of the world is my flesh."
52 The Jews then disputed among
themselves, saying, "How can this man
give us his flesh to eat?" 53 So Jesus
said to them, "Truly, truly, I say to
you, unless you eat the flesh of the
Son of man and drink his blood, you
have no life in you; 54 he who eats my
flesh and drinks my blood has eternal
life, and I will raise him up at the last
day. 55 For my flesh is food indeed,
and my blood is drink indeed. 56 He
who eats my flesh and drinks my blood
abides in me, and I in him. 57 As the
living Father sent me, and I live because of the Father, so he who eats me
will live because of me. 58 This is the
bread which came down from heaven,
not such as the fathers ate and died;
he who eats this bread will live for
ever." 59 This he said in the synagogue,
as he taught at Cȧ·pẽr′nȧ-ŭm.
60 Many of his disciples, when they
heard it, said, "This is a hard saying;
who can listen to it?" 61 But Jesus,
knowing in himself that his disciples
murmured at it, said to them, "Do you
take offense at this? 62 Then what if
you were to see the Son of man ascending where he was before? 63 It is the
spirit that gives life, the flesh is of no

6.27: Is 55.2. **6.29:** 1 Thess 1.3; 1 Jn 3.23. **6.30:** Mt 12.38; Mk 8.11.
6.31: Ex 16.4, 15; Num 11.8; Neh 9.15; Ps 78.24; 105.40. **6.34:** Jn 4.15; Mt 6.11.
6.35: Jn 6.48-50; 4.14. **6.37:** Jn 17.2. **6.38:** Jn 4.34; 5.30. **6.39:** Jn 17.12; 18.9.
6.40: Jn 5.29; 11.24; 6.54. **6.42:** Lk 4.22; Jn 7.27. **6.44:** Jer 31.3; Hos 11.4; Jn 12.32; 6.65.
6.45: 1 Thess 4.9; 1 Jn 2.27; Is 54.13. **6.46:** Jn 1.18. **6.52:** Jn 3.4; 4.9.
6.56: Jn 15.4; 1 Jn 3.24; 4.15. **6.58:** Jn 6.41, 51. **6.59:** Jn 6.25. **6.61:** Mt 11.6. **6.62:** Jn 3.13; 17.5.
6.63: 2 Cor 3.6; Jn 6.68.

avail; the words that I have spoken to
you are spirit and life. 64 But there are
some of you that do not believe." For
Jesus knew from the first who those
were that did not believe, and who it
was that should betray him. 65 And he
said, "This is why I told you that no
one can come to me unless it is granted
him by the Father."

66 After this many of his disciples
drew back and no longer went about
with him. 67 Jesus said to the twelve,
"Will you also go away?" 68 Simon
Peter answered him, "Lord, to whom
shall we go? You have the words of
eternal life; 69 and we have believed,
and have come to know, that you are
the Holy One of God." 70 Jesus answered them, "Did I not choose you,
the twelve, and one of you is a devil?"
71 He spoke of Judas the son of Simon
Is·car'i·ot, for he, one of the twelve,
was to betray him.

7 After this Jesus went about in
Galilee; he would not go about in
Judea, because the Jews[n] sought to kill
him. 2 Now the Jews' feast of Tabernacles was at hand. 3 So his brothers
said to him, "Leave here and go to
Judea, that your disciples may see the
works you are doing. 4 For no man
works in secret if he seeks to be
known openly. If you do these things,
show yourself to the world." 5 For
even his brothers did not believe in
him. 6 Jesus said to them, "My time
has not yet come, but your time is
always here. 7 The world cannot hate
you, but it hates me because I testify
of it that its works are evil. 8 Go to the
feast yourselves; I am not[o] going up to
this feast, for my time has not yet fully
come." 9 So saying, he remained in
Galilee.

10 But after his brothers had gone
up to the feast, then he also went up,
not publicly, but in private. 11 The
Jews were looking for him at the feast,
and saying, "Where is he?" 12 And
there was much muttering about him
among the people. While some said,
"He is a good man," others said,
"No, he is leading the people astray."
13 Yet for fear of the Jews no one spoke
openly of him.

14 About the middle of the feast
Jesus went up into the temple and
taught. 15 The Jews marveled at it,
saying, "How is it that this man has
learning,[p] when he has never studied?"
16 So Jesus answered them, "My
teaching is not mine, but his who sent
me; 17 if any man's will is to do his
will, he shall know whether the teaching is from God or whether I am
speaking on my own authority. 18 He
who speaks on his own authority seeks
his own glory; but he who seeks the
glory of him who sent him is true, and
in him there is no falsehood. 19 Did
not Moses give you the law? Yet none
of you keeps the law. Why do you seek
to kill me?" 20 The people answered,
"You have a demon! Who is seeking
to kill you?" 21 Jesus answered them,
"I did one deed, and you all marvel at
it. 22 Moses gave you circumcision
(not that it is from Moses, but from
the fathers), and you circumcise a man
upon the sabbath. 23 If on the sabbath
a man receives circumcision, so that
the law of Moses may not be broken,
are you angry with me because on the
sabbath I made a man's whole body
well? 24 Do not judge by appearances,
but judge with right judgment."

25 Some of the people of Jerusalem
therefore said, "Is not this the man
whom they seek to kill? 26 And here he
is, speaking openly, and they say
nothing to him! Can it be that the
authorities really know that this is the
Christ? 27 Yet we know where this man
comes from; and when the Christ
appears, no one will know where he
comes from." 28 So Jesus proclaimed,
as he taught in the temple, "You know
me, and you know where I come from?
But I have not come of my own accord;
he who sent me is true, and him you
do not know. 29 I know him, for I come
from him, and he sent me." 30 So they
sought to arrest him; but no one laid
hands on him, because his hour had
not yet come. 31 Yet many of the peo-

[n] Or *Judeans* [o] Other ancient authorities add *yet* [p] Or *this man knows his letters*

6.64: Jn 2.25. **6.65:** Jn 6.44; 3.27. **6.68-69:** Mk 8.27-30. **6.70:** Jn 15.16, 19.
6.71: Jn 13.2, 27; 17.12. **7.2:** Lev 23.34; Deut 16.16. **7.3:** Mk 3.21, 31; Mt 12.46.
7.6: Mt 26.18; Jn 2.4; 7.30. **7.7:** Jn 15.18-21. **7.12:** Jn 7.40-43. **7.13:** Jn 19.38; 20.19.
7.19: Jn 1.17. **7.20:** Jn 8.48; 10.20; Mt 11.18; Mk 3.22.
7.21: Jn 5.2-9. **7.22:** Lev 12.3; Gen 17.10; 21.4.
7.23: Mk 3.5; Lk 13.12; 14.4. **7.24:** Jn 8.15; Is 11.3; Zech 7.9. **7.27:** Jn 6.42; 7.41; 9.29.
7.28: Jn 8.42. **7.29:** Jn 8.55; 17.25; Mt 11.27. **7.30:** Jn 7.44; 10.39; Mk 12.12; Jn 8.20.
7.31: Jn 8.30; 10.42; 11.45.

ple believed him; they said, "When the
Christ appears, will he do more signs
than this man has done?"
32 The Pharisees heard the crowd
thus muttering about him, and the
chief priests and Pharisees sent officers
to arrest him. 33 Jesus then said, "I
shall be with you a little longer, and
then I go to him who sent me; 34 you
will seek me and you will not find me;
where I am you cannot come." 35 The
Jews said to one another, "Where does
this man intend to go that we shall not
find him? Does he intend to go to the
Dispersion among the Greeks and
teach the Greeks? 36 What does he
mean by saying, 'You will seek me and
you will not find me,' and, 'Where I
am you cannot come'?"
37 On the last day of the feast, the
great day, Jesus stood up and proclaimed, "If any one thirst, let him
come to me and drink. 38 He who
believes in me, as[q] the scripture has
said, 'Out of his heart shall flow rivers
of living water.'" 39 Now this he said
about the Spirit, which those who
believed in him were to receive; for as
yet the Spirit had not been given,
because Jesus was not yet glorified.
40 When they heard these words,
some of the people said, "This is
really the prophet." 41 Others said,
"This is the Christ." But some said,
"Is the Christ to come from Galilee?
42 Has not the scripture said that the
Christ is descended from David, and
comes from Bethlehem, the village
where David was?" 43 So there was a
division among the people over him.
44 Some of them wanted to arrest him,
but no one laid hands on him.
45 The officers then went back to
the chief priests and Pharisees, who
said to them, "Why did you not bring
him?" 46 The officers answered, "No
man ever spoke like this man!" 47 The
Pharisees answered them, "Are you
led astray, you also? 48 Have any of the
authorities or of the Pharisees believed
in him? 49 But this crowd, who do not
know the law, are accursed." 50 Nic·ō-
dē'mus, who had gone to him before,
and who was one of them, said to them,
51 "Does our law judge a man without
first giving him a hearing and learning
what he does?" 52 They replied, "Are
you from Galilee too? Search and you
will see that no prophet is to rise from
Galilee."[r]

8 12 Again Jesus spoke to them,
saying, "I am the light of the
world; he who follows me will not walk
in darkness, but will have the light of
life." 13 The Pharisees then said to
him, "You are bearing witness to yourself; your testimony is not true."
14 Jesus answered, "Even if I do bear
witness to myself, my testimony is
true, for I know whence I have come
and whither I am going, but you do not
know whence I come or whither I am
going. 15 You judge according to the
flesh, I judge no one. 16 Yet even if I
do judge, my judgment is true, for it
is not I alone that judge, but I and he[s]
who sent me. 17 In your law it is
written that the testimony of two men
is true; 18 I bear witness to myself, and
the Father who sent me bears witness
to me." 19 They said to him therefore,
"Where is your Father?" Jesus answered, "You know neither me nor
my Father; if you knew me, you would

[q] Or *let him come to me, and let him who believes in me drink. As*
[r] Other ancient authorities add 7.53-8.11 either here or at the end of this gospel or after Luke 21.38, with variations of the text:

8 53 *They went each to his own house,* 1 *but Jesus went to the Mount of Olives.* 2 *Early in the morning he
came again to the temple; all the people came to him, and he sat down and taught them.* 3 *The scribes
and the Pharisees brought a woman who had been caught in adultery, and placing her in the midst* 4 *they
said to him, "Teacher, this woman has been caught in the act of adultery.* 5 *Now in the law Moses commanded us to stone such. What do you say about her?"* 6 *This they said to test him, that they might have
some charge to bring against him. Jesus bent down and wrote with his finger on the ground.* 7 *And as they
continued to ask him, he stood up and said to them, "Let him who is without sin among you be the first
to throw a stone at her."* 8 *And once more he bent down and wrote with his finger on the ground.* 9 *But when
they heard it, they went away, one by one, beginning with the eldest, and Jesus was left alone with the
woman standing before him.* 10 *Jesus looked up and said to her, "Woman, where are they? Has no one condemned you?"* 11 *She said, "No one, Lord." And Jesus said, "Neither do I condemn you; go, and do not
sin again."*

[s] Other ancient authorities read *the Father*

7.33: Jn 8.21; 12.35; 13.33; 14.19; 16.16-19. **7.35:** Jas 1.1; 1 Pet 1.1; Jn 12.20; Acts 11.20.
7.37: Lev 23.36; Jn 4.10, 14. **7.38:** Is 44.3; 55.1; 58.11. **7.39:** Jn 20.22; 12.23.
7.40: Jn 1.21; Mt 21.11. **7.42:** Mic 5.2; Mt 1.1; Lk 2.4. **7.44:** Jn 7.30; 10.39. **7.46:** Mt 7.28.
7.50: Jn 3.1; 19.39. **7.51:** Deut 17.6; Ex 23.1. **7.52:** 2 Kings 14.25. **8.12:** Jn 9.5; 12.35; 1.4.
8.13-18: Jn 5.31-39. **8.15:** Jn 7.24; 3.17. **8.16:** Jn 5.30. **8.17:** Deut 19.15; Mt 18.16. **8.19:** Jn 14.7.

know my Father also." 20 These words
he spoke in the treasury, as he taught
in the temple; but no one arrested him,
because his hour had not yet come.

21 Again he said to them, "I go
away, and you will seek me and die in
your sin; where I am going, you cannot
come." 22 Then said the Jews, "Will
he kill himself, since he says, 'Where
I am going, you cannot come'?" 23 He
said to them, "You are from below, I
am from above; you are of this world,
I am not of this world. 24 I told you
that you would die in your sins, for
you will die in your sins unless you believe that I am he." 25 They said to
him, "Who are you?" Jesus said to
them, "Even what I have told you
from the beginning.[t] 26 I have much
to say about you and much to judge;
but he who sent me is true, and I
declare to the world what I have heard
from him." 27 They did not understand that he spoke to them of the
Father. 28 So Jesus said, "When you
have lifted up the Son of man, then
you will know that I am he, and that
I do nothing on my own authority but
speak thus as the Father taught me.
29 And he who sent me is with me; he
has not left me alone, for I always do
what is pleasing to him." 30 As he
spoke thus, many believed in him.

31 Jesus then said to the Jews who
had believed in him, "If you continue
in my word, you are truly my disciples,
32 and you will know the truth, and
the truth will make you free." 33 They
answered him, "We are descendants
of Abraham, and have never been in
bondage to any one. How is it that you
say, 'You will be made free'?"

34 Jesus answered them, "Truly,
truly, I say to you, every one who
commits sin is a slave to sin. 35 The
slave does not continue in the house
for ever; the son continues for ever.
36 So if the Son makes you free, you
will be free indeed. 37 I know that you
are descendants of Abraham; yet you
seek to kill me, because my word finds
no place in you. 38 I speak of what I
have seen with my Father, and you do
what you have heard from your
father."

39 They answered him, "Abraham
is our father." Jesus said to them, "If
you were Abraham's children, you
would do what Abraham did, 40 but
now you seek to kill me, a man who
has told you the truth which I heard
from God; this is not what Abraham
did. 41 You do what your father did."
They said to him, "We were not born
of fornication; we have one Father,
even God." 42 Jesus said to them, "If
God were your Father, you would love
me, for I proceeded and came forth
from God; I came not of my own
accord, but he sent me. 43 Why do you
not understand what I say? It is because you cannot bear to hear my
word. 44 You are of your father the
devil, and your will is to do your
father's desires. He was a murderer
from the beginning, and has nothing
to do with the truth, because there is
no truth in him. When he lies, he
speaks according to his own nature,
for he is a liar and the father of lies.
45 But, because I tell the truth, you do
not believe me. 46 Which of you convicts me of sin? If I tell the truth, why
do you not believe me? 47 He who is
of God hears the words of God; the
reason why you do not hear them is
that you are not of God."

48 The Jews answered him, "Are
we not right in saying that you are a
Samaritan and have a demon?" 49 Jesus
answered, "I have not a demon; but
I honor my Father, and you dishonor
me. 50 Yet I do not seek my own
glory; there is One who seeks it and he
will be the judge. 51 Truly, truly, I
say to you, if any one keeps my word,
he will never see death." 52 The Jews
said to him, "Now we know that you
have a demon. Abraham died, as did
the prophets; and you say, 'If any one
keeps my word, he will never taste
death.' 53 Are you greater than our
father Abraham, who died? And the
prophets died! Who do you claim to
be?" 54 Jesus answered, "If I glorify
myself, my glory is nothing; it is my
Father who glorifies me, of whom you
say that he is your God. 55 But you
have not known him; I know him. If
I said, I do not know him, I should be

[t] Or *Why do I talk to you at all?*

8.20: Mk 12.41; Jn 7.30. **8.21-22:** Jn 7.33-36. **8.23:** Jn 3.31; 17.14; 1 Jn 4.5.
8.24: Jn 8.28; 4.26; 13.19; Mk 13.6. **8.28:** Jn 3.14; 12.32. **8.30:** Jn 7.31; 10.42; 11.45.
8.31: Jn 15.7; 2 Jn 9. **8.32:** 2 Cor 3.17; Gal 5.1. **8.33:** Mt 3.9; Gal 3.7. **8.34:** Rom 6.16; 2 Pet 2.19.
8.35: Gen 21.10; Gal 4.30. **8.41:** Deut 32.6; Is 63.16; 64.8. **8.42:** Jn 13.3; 16.28.
8.44: 1 Jn 3.8, 15; Gen 3.4; 1 Jn 2.4; Mt 12.34. **8.46:** 1 Jn 3.5; Jn 18.37. **8.48:** Jn 7.20; 10.20; 4.9.
8.53: Jn 4.12.

a liar like you; but I do know him and
I keep his word. 56 Your father Abraham rejoiced that he was to see my
day; he saw it and was glad." 57 The
Jews then said to him, "You are not
yet fifty years old, and have you seen
Abraham?"[u] 58 Jesus said to them,
"Truly, truly, I say to you, before
Abraham was, I am." 59 So they took
up stones to throw at him; but Jesus
hid himself, and went out of the
temple.

9 As he passed by, he saw a man
blind from his birth. 2 And his
disciples asked him, "Rabbi, who
sinned, this man or his parents, that
he was born blind?" 3 Jesus answered,
"It was not that this man sinned, or
his parents, but that the works of God
might be made manifest in him. 4 We
must work the works of him who sent
me, while it is day; night comes, when
no one can work. 5 As long as I am in
the world, I am the light of the world."
6 As he said this, he spat on the ground
and made clay of the spittle and
anointed the man's eyes with the clay,
7 saying to him, "Go, wash in the pool
of Sī·lō'ȧm" (which means Sent). So
he went and washed and came back
seeing. 8 The neighbors and those who
had seen him before as a beggar, said,
"Is not this the man who used to sit
and beg?" 9 Some said, "It is he";
others said, "No, but he is like him."
He said, "I am the man." 10 They said
to him, "Then how were your eyes
opened?" 11 He answered, "The man
called Jesus made clay and anointed
my eyes and said to me, 'Go to Sī·lō'-
ȧm and wash'; so I went and washed
and received my sight." 12 They said
to him, "Where is he?" He said, "I do
not know."

13 They brought to the Pharisees
the man who had formerly been blind.
14 Now it was a sabbath day when
Jesus made the clay and opened his
eyes. 15 The Pharisees again asked him
how he had received his sight. And he
said to them, "He put clay on my eyes,
and I washed, and I see." 16 Some of
the Pharisees said, "This man is not
from God, for he does not keep the
sabbath." But others said, "How can
a man who is a sinner do such signs?"
There was a division among them.
17 So they again said to the blind man,
"What do you say about him, since he
has opened your eyes?" He said, "He
is a prophet."

18 The Jews did not believe that he
had been blind and had received his
sight, until they called the parents of
the man who had received his sight,
19 and asked them, "Is this your son,
who you say was born blind? How
then does he now see?" 20 His parents
answered, "We know that this is our
son, and that he was born blind; 21 but
how he now sees we do not know, nor
do we know who opened his eyes. Ask
him; he is of age, he will speak for himself." 22 His parents said this because
they feared the Jews, for the Jews had
already agreed that if any one should
confess him to be Christ, he was to be
put out of the synagogue. 23 Therefore
his parents said, "He is of age, ask
him."

24 So for the second time they
called the man who had been blind,
and said to him, "Give God the praise;
we know that this man is a sinner."
25 He answered, "Whether he is a
sinner, I do not know; one thing I
know, that though I was blind, now I
see." 26 They said to him, "What did
he do to you? How did he open your
eyes?" 27 He answered them, "I have
told you already, and you would not
listen. Why do you want to hear it
again? Do you too want to become his
disciples?" 28 And they reviled him,
saying, "You are his disciple, but we
are disciples of Moses. 29 We know
that God has spoken to Moses, but as
for this man, we do not know where
he comes from." 30 The man answered, "Why, this is a marvel! You
do not know where he comes from,
and yet he opened my eyes. 31 We
know that God does not listen to
sinners, but if any one is a worshiper
of God and does his will, God listens
to him. 32 Never since the world began
has it been heard that any one opened
the eyes of a man born blind. 33 If this
man were not from God, he could do
nothing." 34 They answered him, "You
were born in utter sin, and would you
teach us?" And they cast him out.

[u] Other ancient authorities read *has Abraham seen you?*

8.56: Mt 13.17; Heb 11.13. **8.57:** Jn 2.20. **8.58:** Jn 1.1; 17.5, 24. **8.59:** Jn 10.31; 11.8.
9.2: Lk 13.2; Acts 28.4; Ezek 18.20; Ex 20.5. **9.3:** Jn 11.4. **9.4:** Jn 11.9; 12.35.
9.5: Jn 1.4; 8.12; 12.46. **9.6:** Mk 7.33; 8.23. **9.7:** Lk 13.4. **9.16:** Mt 12.2; Jn 5.9; 7.43; 10.19.
9.22: Jn 7.13; 12.42; Lk 6.22. **9.28:** Jn 5.45.

35 Jesus heard that they had cast
him out, and having found him he
said, "Do you believe in the Son of
man?"[v] 36 He answered, "And who is
he, sir, that I may believe in him?"
37 Jesus said to him, "You have seen
him, and it is he who speaks to you."
38 He said, "Lord, I believe"; and he
worshiped him. 39 Jesus said, "For
judgment I came into this world, that
those who do not see may see, and
that those who see may become blind."
40 Some of the Pharisees near him
heard this, and they said to him, "Are
we also blind?" 41 Jesus said to them,
"If you were blind, you would have no
guilt; but now that you say, 'We see,'
your guilt remains.

10 "Truly, truly, I say to you, he
who does not enter the sheepfold
by the door but climbs in by another
way, that man is a thief and a robber;
2 but he who enters by the door is the
shepherd of the sheep. 3 To him the
gatekeeper opens; the sheep hear his
voice, and he calls his own sheep by
name and leads them out. 4 When he
has brought out all his own, he goes
before them, and the sheep follow him,
for they know his voice. 5 A stranger
they will not follow, but they will flee
from him, for they do not know the
voice of strangers." 6 This figure Jesus
used with them, but they did not understand what he was saying to them.

7 So Jesus again said to them,
"Truly, truly, I say to you, I am the
door of the sheep. 8 All who came before me are thieves and robbers; but
the sheep did not heed them. 9 I am
the door; if any one enters by me, he
will be saved, and will go in and out
and find pasture. 10 The thief comes
only to steal and kill and destroy; I
came that they may have life, and have
it abundantly. 11 I am the good shepherd. The good shepherd lays down
his life for the sheep. 12 He who is a
hireling and not a shepherd, whose
own the sheep are not, sees the wolf
coming and leaves the sheep and flees;
and the wolf snatches them and scatters
them. 13 He flees because he is a
hireling and cares nothing for the
sheep. 14 I am the good shepherd; I
know my own and my own know me,
15 as the Father knows me and I know
the Father; and I lay down my life for
the sheep. 16 And I have other sheep,
that are not of this fold; I must bring
them also, and they will heed my
voice. So there shall be one flock, one
shepherd. 17 For this reason the Father
loves me, because I lay down my life,
that I may take it again. 18 No one
takes it from me, but I lay it down of
my own accord. I have power to lay
it down, and I have power to take it
again; this charge I have received from
my Father."

19 There was again a division among
the Jews because of these words.
20 Many of them said, "He has a
demon, and he is mad; why listen to
him?" 21 Others said, "These are not
the sayings of one who has a demon.
Can a demon open the eyes of the
blind?"

22 It was the feast of the Dedication
at Jerusalem; 23 it was winter, and
Jesus was walking in the temple, in
the portico of Solomon. 24 So the Jews
gathered round him and said to him,
"How long will you keep us in suspense? If you are the Christ, tell us
plainly." 25 Jesus answered them, "I
told you, and you do not believe. The
works that I do in my Father's name,
they bear witness to me; 26 but you do
not believe, because you do not belong
to my sheep. 27 My sheep hear my
voice, and I know them, and they
follow me; 28 and I give them eternal
life, and they shall never perish, and
no one shall snatch them out of my
hand. 29 My Father, who has given
them to me,[w] is greater than all, and
no one is able to snatch them out of
the Father's hand. 30 I and the Father
are one."

31 The Jews took up stones again
to stone him. 32 Jesus answered them,
"I have shown you many good works
from the Father; for which of these do
you stone me?" 33 The Jews answered
him, "We stone you for no good work

[v] Other ancient authorities read *the Son of God*
[w] Other ancient authorities read *What my Father has given to me*

9.38: Mt 28.9. **9.39:** Jn 5.27; 3.19; Mt 15.14. **9.41:** Jn 15.22. **10.2:** Mk 6.34. **10.6:** Jn 16.25. **10.8:** Jer 23.1; Ezek 34.2. **10.11:** Is 40.11; Ezek 34.11-16; Heb 13.20; 1 Pet 5.4; Rev 7.17; 1 Jn 3.16; Jn 15.13. **10.15:** Mt 11.27. **10.16:** Is 56.8; Jn 11.52; 17.20; Eph 2.13-18; 1 Pet 2.25. **10.18:** Jn 14.31; 15.10; Phil 2.8; Heb 5.8. **10.19:** Jn 7.43; 9.16. **10.20:** Jn 7.20; 8.48; Mt 11.18. **10.21:** Jn 9.32; Ex 4.11. **10.23:** Acts 3.11; 5.12. **10.25:** Jn 5.36; 10.38. **10.26:** Jn 8.47. **10.28:** Jn 17.2; 1 Jn 2.25. **10.30:** Jn 17.21. **10.31:** Jn 8.59; 11.8. **10.33:** Lev 24.16; Mk 14.64.

but for blasphemy; because you, being
a man, make yourself God." 34 Jesus
answered them, "Is it not written in
your law, 'I said, you are gods'? 35 If
he called them gods to whom the word
of God came (and scripture cannot be
broken), 36 do you say of him whom
the Father consecrated and sent into
the world, 'You are blaspheming,' because I said, I am the Son of God'?
37 If I am not doing the works of my
Father, then do not believe me; 38 but
if I do them, even though you do not
believe me, believe the works, that you
may know and understand that the
Father is in me and I am in the
Father." 39 Again they tried to arrest
him, but he escaped from their hands.

40 He went away again across the
Jordan to the place where John at first
baptized, and there he remained.
41 And many came to him; and they
said, "John did no sign, but everything that John said about this man
was true." 42 And many believed in
him there.

11 Now a certain man was ill,
Laz'à·rùs of Beth'à·ny, the village of Mary and her sister Martha. 2 It
was Mary who anointed the Lord with
ointment and wiped his feet with her
hair, whose brother Laz'à·rùs was ill.
3 So the sisters sent to him, saying,
"Lord, he whom you love is ill." 4 But
when Jesus heard it he said, "This illness is not unto death; it is for the
glory of God, so that the Son of God
may be glorified by means of it."

5 Now Jesus loved Martha and her
sister and Laz'à·rùs. 6 So when he
heard that he was ill, he stayed two
days longer in the place where he was.
7 Then after this he said to the disciples, "Let us go into Judea again."
8 The disciples said to him, "Rabbi,
the Jews were but now seeking to
stone you, and are you going there
again?" 9 Jesus answered, "Are there
not twelve hours in the day? If any one
walks in the day, he does not stumble,
because he sees the light of this world.
10 But if any one walks in the night,
he stumbles, because the light is not
in him." 11 Thus he spoke, and then
he said to them, "Our friend Laz'à·rùs
has fallen asleep, but I go to awake him
out of sleep." 12 The disciples said to
him, "Lord, if he has fallen asleep, he
will recover." 13 Now Jesus had spoken
of his death, but they thought that he
meant taking rest in sleep. 14 Then
Jesus told them plainly, "Laz'à·rùs is
dead; 15 and for your sake I am glad
that I was not there, so that you may
believe. But let us go to him."
16 Thomas, called the Twin, said to
his fellow disciples, "Let us also go,
that we may die with him."

17 Now when Jesus came, he found
that Laz'à·rùs[x] had already been in the
tomb four days. 18 Beth'à·ny was near
Jerusalem, about two miles[y] off, 19 and
many of the Jews had come to Martha
and Mary to console them concerning
their brother. 20 When Martha heard
that Jesus was coming, she went and
met him, while Mary sat in the house.
21 Martha said to Jesus, "Lord, if you
had been here, my brother would not
have died. 22 And even now I know
that whatever you ask from God, God
will give you." 23 Jesus said to her,
"Your brother will rise again."
24 Martha said to him, "I know that he
will rise again in the resurrection at
the last day." 25 Jesus said to her, "I
am the resurrection and the life;[z] he
who believes in me, though he die, yet
shall he live, 26 and whoever lives and
believes in me shall never die. Do you
believe this?" 27 She said to him, "Yes,
Lord; I believe that you are the Christ,
the Son of God, he who is coming into
the world."

28 When she had said this, she went
and called her sister Mary, saying
quietly, "The Teacher is here and is
calling for you." 29 And when she heard
it, she rose quickly and went to him.
30 Now Jesus had not yet come to the
village, but was still in the place where
Martha had met him. 31 When the
Jews who were with her in the house,
consoling her, saw Mary rise quickly
and go out, they followed her, supposing that she was going to the tomb to
weep there. 32 Then Mary, when she
came where Jesus was and saw him,
fell at his feet, saying to him, "Lord,
if you had been here, my brother

[x] Greek *he* [y] Greek *fifteen stadia* [z] Other ancient authorities omit *and the life*

10.34: Jn 8.17; Ps 82.6. **10.39:** Jn 7.30; 8.59; Lk 4.30. **10.40:** Jn 1.28. **10.42:** Jn 7.31; 11.45.
11.1: Mk 11.1; Lk 10.38. **11.2:** Jn 12.3; Lk 7.38; Mk 14.3. **11.4:** Jn 9.3. **11.8:** Jn 8.59; 10.31
11.9: Jn 9.4; 12.35; Lk 13.33. **11.11:** Mk 5.39; Acts 7.60. **11.16:** Mt 10.3; Jn 20.24-28.
11.19: Job 2.11. **11.24:** Dan 12.2; Jn 5.28; Acts 24.15. **11.25:** Jn 1.4; 5.26; Rev 1.18.
11.26: Jn 6.47; 8.51. **11.27:** Mt 16.16. **11.32:** Jn 11.22.

would not have died." 33 When Jesus
saw her weeping, and the Jews who
came with her also weeping, he was
deeply moved in spirit and troubled;
34 and he said, "Where have you laid
him?" They said to him, "Lord, come
and see." 35 Jesus wept. 36 So the
Jews said, "See how he loved him!"
37 But some of them said, "Could not
he who opened the eyes of the blind
man have kept this man from dying?"

38 Then Jesus, deeply moved again,
came to the tomb; it was a cave, and a
stone lay upon it. 39 Jesus said, "Take
away the stone." Martha, the sister of
the dead man, said to him, "Lord, by
this time there will be an odor, for he
has been dead four days." 40 Jesus said
to her, "Did I not tell you that if you
would believe you would see the glory
of God?" 41 So they took away the
stone. And Jesus lifted up his eyes and
said, "Father, I thank thee that thou
hast heard me. 42 I knew that thou
hearest me always, but I have said this
on account of the people standing by,
that they may believe that thou didst
send me." 43 When he had said this,
he cried with a loud voice, "Laz'ȧ·rŭs,
come out." 44 The dead man came
out, his hands and feet bound with
bandages, and his face wrapped with
a cloth. Jesus said to them, "Unbind
him, and let him go."

45 Many of the Jews therefore, who
had come with Mary and had seen
what he did, believed in him; 46 but
some of them went to the Pharisees
and told them what Jesus had done.
47 So the chief priests and the Pharisees gathered the council, and said,
"What are we to do? For this man
performs many signs. 48 If we let him
go on thus, every one will believe in
him, and the Romans will come and
destroy both our holy place[a] and our
nation." 49 But one of them, Cā'iȧ-
phȧs, who was high priest that year,
said to them, "You know nothing at
all; 50 you do not understand that it is
expedient for you that one man should
die for the people, and that the whole
nation should not perish." 51 He did
not say this of his own accord, but
being high priest that year he prophesied that Jesus should die for the
nation, 52 and not for the nation only,
but to gather into one the children of
God who are scattered abroad. 53 So
from that day on they took counsel
how to put him to death.

54 Jesus therefore no longer went
about openly among the Jews, but
went from there to the country near
the wilderness, to a town called
Ē'phrȧ·im; and there he stayed with
the disciples.

55 Now the Passover of the Jews
was at hand, and many went up from
the country to Jerusalem before the
Passover, to purify themselves. 56 They
were looking for Jesus and saying to
one another as they stood in the
temple, "What do you think? That he
will not come to the feast?" 57 Now
the chief priests and the Pharisees had
given orders that if any one knew
where he was, he should let them
know, so that they might arrest
him.

12 Six days before the Passover,
Jesus came to Beth'ȧ·ny, where
Laz'ȧ·rŭs was, whom Jesus had raised
from the dead. 2 There they made him
a supper; Martha served, and Laz'ȧ-
rŭs was one of those at table with him.
3 Mary took a pound of costly ointment of pure nard and anointed the
feet of Jesus and wiped his feet with
her hair; and the house was filled with
the fragrance of the ointment. 4 But
Judas Is·car'i·ŏt, one of his disciples
(he who was to betray him), said,
5 "Why was this ointment not sold for
three hundred denarii[b] and given to
the poor?" 6 This he said, not that he
cared for the poor but because he was
a thief, and as he had the money box
he used to take what was put into it.
7 Jesus said, "Let her alone, let her
keep it for the day of my burial. 8 The
poor you always have with you, but
you do not always have me."

9 When the great crowd of the Jews
learned that he was there, they came,
not only on account of Jesus but also
to see Laz'ȧ·rŭs, whom he had raised
from the dead. 10 So the chief priests
planned to put Laz'ȧ·rŭs also to death,
11 because on account of him many of

[a] Greek *our place* [b] The denarius was worth about twenty cents

11.35: Lk 19.41. **11.37:** Jn 9.7. **11.38:** Mt 27.60; Mk 15.46; Lk 24.2; Jn 20.1.
11.41: Jn 17.1; Mt 11.25. **11.42:** Jn 12.30. **11.44:** Jn 19.40; 20.7. **11.49:** Mt 26.3.
11.52: Jn 10.16; 17.21. **11.55:** Mt 26.1; Mk 14.1; Lk 22.1; Jn 13.1. **11.56:** Jn 7.11.
12.1-8: Mt 26.6-13; Mk 14.3-9; Lk 7.37-38. **12.4:** Jn 6.71; 13.26. **12.6:** Lk 8.3. **12.7:** Jn 19.40.
12.10: Mk 14.1.

the Jews were going away and believing
in Jesus.
12 The next day a great crowd who
had come to the feast heard that Jesus
was coming to Jerusalem. 13 So they
took branches of palm trees and went
out to meet him, crying, "Hosanna!
Blessed is he who comes in the name
of the Lord, even the King of Israel!"
14 And Jesus found a young ass and
sat upon it; as it is written,
15 "Fear not, daughter of Zion;
behold, your king is coming,
sitting on an ass's colt!"
16 His disciples did not understand
this at first; but when Jesus was
glorified, then they remembered that
this had been written of him and had
been done to him. 17 The crowd that
had been with him when he called
Laz'å·rus out of the tomb and raised
him from the dead bore witness. 18 The
reason why the crowd went to meet him
was that they heard he had done this
sign. 19 The Pharisees then said to one
another, "You see that you can do
nothing; look, the world has gone after
him."

20 Now among those who went up
to worship at the feast were some
Greeks. 21 So these came to Philip,
who was from Beth-sā'i·dȧ in Galilee,
and said to him, "Sir, we wish to see
Jesus." 22 Philip went and told Andrew; Andrew went with Philip and
they told Jesus. 23 And Jesus answered
them, "The hour has come for the Son
of man to be glorified. 24 Truly, truly,
I say to you, unless a grain of wheat
falls into the earth and dies, it remains
alone; but if it dies, it bears much
fruit. 25 He who loves his life loses it,
and he who hates his life in this world
will keep it for eternal life. 26 If any
one serves me, he must follow me; and
where I am, there shall my servant be
also; if any one serves me, the Father
will honor him.

27 "Now is my soul troubled. And
what shall I say? 'Father, save me from
this hour'? No, for this purpose I have
come to this hour. 28 Father, glorify
thy name." Then a voice came from
heaven, "I have glorified it, and I will
glorify it again." 29 The crowd standing by heard it and said that it had
thundered. Others said, "An angel has
spoken to him." 30 Jesus answered,
"This voice has come for your sake,
not for mine. 31 Now is the judgment
of this world, now shall the ruler of
this world be cast out; 32 and I, when
I am lifted up from the earth, will
draw all men to myself." 33 He said
this to show by what death he was to
die. 34 The crowd answered him, "We
have heard from the law that the
Christ remains for ever. How can you
say that the Son of man must be lifted
up? Who is this Son of man?" 35 Jesus
said to them, "The light is with you
for a little longer. Walk while you have
the light, lest the darkness overtake
you; he who walks in the darkness does
not know where he goes. 36 While you
have the light, believe in the light, that
you may become sons of light."

When Jesus had said this, he departed and hid himself from them.
37 Though he had done so many signs
before them, yet they did not believe
in him; 38 it was that the word spoken
by the prophet Ī·ṡāi'ȧh might be fulfilled:
"Lord, who has believed our report,
and to whom has the arm of the
Lord been revealed?"
39 Therefore they could not believe.
For Ī·ṡāi'ȧh again said,
40 "He has blinded their eyes and
hardened their heart,
lest they should see with their eyes
and perceive with their heart,
and turn for me to heal them."
41 Ī·ṡāi'ȧh said this because he saw his
glory and spoke of him. 42 Nevertheless many even of the authorities
believed in him, but for fear of the
Pharisees they did not confess it, lest
they should be put out of the synagogue: 43 for they loved the praise of
men more than the praise of God.

44 And Jesus cried out and said,
"He who believes in me, believes not
in me but in him who sent me. 45 And
he who sees me sees him who sent me.
46 I have come as light into the world,
that whoever believes in me may not

12.12-15: Mt 21.4-9; Mk 11.7-10; Lk 19.35-38. **12.13:** Ps 118.25; Jn 1.49. **12.15:** Zech 9.9.
12.16: Mk 9.32; Jn 2.22. **12.20:** Jn 7.35; Acts 11.20. **12.21:** Jn 1.44; 6.5.
12.23: Jn 13.1; 17.1; Mk 14.35, 41. **12.24:** 1 Cor 15.36. **12.25:** Mt 10.39; Mk 8.35; Lk 9.24; 14.26.
12.27: Jn 11.33; Mt 26.38; Mk 14.34. **12.28:** Mk 1.11; 9.7. **12.31:** Jn 16.11; 2 Cor 4.4; Eph 2.2.
12.32: Jn 3.14; 8.28. **12.34:** Ps 110.4; Is 9.7; Ezek 37.25; Dan 7.14.
12.35: Jn 7.33; 9.4; Eph 5.8; 1 Jn 2.11. **12.36:** Lk 16.8; Jn 8.59. **12.38:** Is 53.1; Rom 10.16.
12.40: Is 6.10; Mt 13.14. **12.41:** Is 6.1; Lk 24.27. **12.42:** Jn 9.22; Lk 6.22. **12.44:** Mt 10.40; Jn 5.24.
12.45: Jn 14.9. **12.46:** Jn 1.4; 8.12; 9.5.

remain in darkness. 47 If any one hears
my sayings and does not keep them, I
do not judge him; for I did not come
to judge the world but to save the
world. 48 He who rejects me and does
not receive my sayings has a judge; the
word that I have spoken will be his
judge on the last day. 49 For I have not
spoken on my own authority; the
Father who sent me has himself
given me commandment what to say
and what to speak. 50 And I know that
his commandment is eternal life. What
I say, therefore, I say as the Father has
bidden me."

13 Now before the feast of the
Passover, when Jesus knew that
his hour had come to depart out of this
world to the Father, having loved his
own who were in the world, he loved
them to the end. 2 And during supper,
when the devil had already put it into
the heart of Judas Is·car'i·ot, Simon's
son, to betray him, 3 Jesus, knowing
that the Father had given all things
into his hands, and that he had come
from God and was going to God,
4 rose from supper, laid aside his garments, and girded himself with a towel.
5 Then he poured water into a basin,
and began to wash the disciples' feet,
and to wipe them with the towel with
which he was girded. 6 He came to
Simon Peter; and Peter said to him,
"Lord, do you wash my feet?" 7 Jesus
answered him, "What I am doing you
do not know now, but afterward you
will understand." 8 Peter said to him,
"You shall never wash my feet."
Jesus answered him, "If I do not wash
you, you have no part in me." 9 Simon
Peter said to him, "Lord, not my feet
only but also my hands and my head!"
10 Jesus said to him, "He who has
bathed does not need to wash, except
for his feet,[c] but he is clean all over;
and you are clean, but not all of you."
11 For he knew who was to betray
him; that was why he said, "You are
not all clean."

12 When he had washed their feet,
and taken his garments, and resumed
his place, he said to them, "Do you
know what I have done to you? 13 You
call me Teacher and Lord; and you
are right, for so I am. 14 If I then, your
Lord and Teacher, have washed your
feet, you also ought to wash one
another's feet. 15 For I have given you
an example, that you also should do
as I have done to you. 16 Truly, truly,
I say to you, a servant[d] is not greater
than his master; nor is he who is sent
greater than he who sent him. 17 If
you know these things, blessed are you
if you do them. 18 I am not speaking
of you all; I know whom I have chosen;
it is that the scripture may be fulfilled,
'He who ate my bread has lifted his
heel against me.' 19 I tell you this now,
before it takes place, that when it does
take place you may believe that I am
he. 20 Truly, truly, I say to you, he
who receives any one whom I send
receives me; and he who receives me
receives him who sent me."

21 When Jesus had thus spoken, he
was troubled in spirit, and testified,
"Truly, truly, I say to you, one of you
will betray me." 22 The disciples
looked at one another, uncertain of
whom he spoke. 23 One of his disciples,
whom Jesus loved, was lying close to
the breast of Jesus; 24 so Simon Peter
beckoned to him and said, "Tell us
who it is of whom he speaks." 25 So
lying thus, close to the breast of Jesus,
he said to him, "Lord, who is it?"
26 Jesus answered, "It is he to whom
I shall give this morsel when I have
dipped it." So when he had dipped the
morsel, he gave it to Judas, the son of
Simon Is·car'i·ot. 27 Then after the
morsel, Satan entered into him. Jesus
said to him, "What you are going to
do, do quickly." 28 Now no one at the
table knew why he said this to him.
29 Some thought that, because Judas
had the money box, Jesus was telling
him, "Buy what we need for the
feast"; or, that he should give something to the poor. 30 So, after receiving
the morsel, he immediately went out;
and it was night.

31 When he had gone out, Jesus
said, "Now is the Son of man glorified,
and in him God is glorified; 32 if God
is glorified in him, God will also
glorify him in himself, and glorify him

[c] Other ancient authorities omit *except for his feet* [d] Or *slave*

12.47: Jn 3.17. **12.48:** Mt 10.14-15. **13.1:** Jn 11.55; 12.23; 16.28. **13.2:** Jn 6.71; Mk 14.10. **13.5:** Lk 7.44; 22.27. **13.8:** Deut 12.12; Jn 3.5; 9.7. **13.11:** Jn 13.2. **13.15:** 1 Pet 2.21. **13.16:** Mt 10.24; Lk 6.40. **13.17:** Lk 11.28; Jas 1.25. **13.18:** Ps 41.9. **13.19:** Jn 14.29; 8.28. **13.20:** Mt 10.40; Lk 10.16. **13.21-26:** Mt 26.21-25; Mk 14.18-21; Lk 22.21-23. **13.23:** Jn 19.26; 20.2; 21.7, 20. **13.26:** Jn 6.71. **13.29:** Jn 12.6. **13.30:** Lk 22.53. **13.31-32:** Jn 17.1.

at once. 33 Little children, yet a little
while I am with you. You will seek
me; and as I said to the Jews so now I
say to you, 'Where I am going you
cannot come.' 34 A new commandment
I give to you, that you love one another;
even as I have loved you, that you also
love one another. 35 By this all men
will know that you are my disciples,
if you have love for one another."

36 Simon Peter said to him, "Lord,
where are you going?" Jesus answered, "Where I am going you cannot
follow me now; but you shall follow
afterward." 37 Peter said to him, "Lord,
why cannot I follow you now? I will
lay down my life for you." 38 Jesus
answered, "Will you lay down your
life for me? Truly, truly, I say to you,
the cock will not crow, till you have
denied me three times.

14 "Let not your hearts be
troubled; believe[e] in God, believe
also in me. 2 In my Father's house are
many rooms; if it were not so, would
I have told you that I go to prepare a
place for you? 3 And when I go and
prepare a place for you, I will come
again and will take you to myself, that
where I am you may be also. 4 And you
know the way where I am going."[f]
5 Thomas said to him, "Lord, we do
not know where you are going; how
can we know the way?" 6 Jesus said to
him, "I am the way, and the truth, and
the life; no one comes to the Father,
but by me. 7 If you had known me,
you would have known my Father
also; henceforth you know him and
have seen him."

8 Philip said to him, "Lord, show
us the Father, and we shall be satisfied." 9 Jesus said to him, "Have I
been with you so long, and yet you do
not know me, Philip? He who has seen
me has seen the Father; how can you
say, 'Show us the Father'? 10 Do you
not believe that I am in the Father and
the Father in me? The words that I
say to you I do not speak on my own
authority; but the Father who dwells
in me does his works. 11 Believe me
that I am in the Father and the Father
in me; or else believe me for the sake
of the works themselves.

12 "Truly, truly, I say to you, he
who believes in me will also do the
works that I do; and greater works
than these will he do, because I go to
the Father. 13 Whatever you ask in
my name, I will do it, that the Father
may be glorified in the Son; 14 if you
ask[g] anything in my name, I will do it.

15 "If you love me, you will keep
my commandments. 16 And I will pray
the Father, and he will give you
another Counselor, to be with you for
ever, 17 even the Spirit of truth, whom
the world cannot receive, because it
neither sees him nor knows him; you
know him, for he dwells with you, and
will be in you.

18 "I will not leave you desolate; I
will come to you. 19 Yet a little while,
and the world will see me no more, but
you will see me; because I live, you
will live also. 20 In that day you will
know that I am in my Father, and you
in me, and I in you. 21 He who has my
commandments and keeps them, he it
is who loves me; and he who loves me
will be loved by my Father, and I will
love him and manifest myself to him."
22 Judas (not Is·car'i·ot) said to him,
"Lord, how is it that you will manifest
yourself to us, and not to the world?"
23 Jesus answered him, "If a man loves
me, he will keep my word, and my
Father will love him, and we will come
to him and make our home with him.
24 He who does not love me does not
keep my words; and the word which
you hear is not mine but the Father's
who sent me.

25 "These things I have spoken to
you, while I am still with you. 26 But
the Counselor, the Holy Spirit, whom
the Father will send in my name, he
will teach you all things, and bring to
your remembrance all that I have said
to you. 27 Peace I leave with you; my
peace I give to you; not as the world
gives do I give to you. Let not your
hearts be troubled, neither let them be
afraid. 28 You heard me say to you, 'I
go away, and I will come to you.' If

[e] Or *you believe* [f] Other ancient authorities read *where I am going you know, and the way you know*
[g] Other ancient authorities add *me*

13.33: 1 Jn 2.1; Jn 7.33.
13.34: Jn 15.12, 17; 1 Jn 3.23; 2 Jn 5; Lev 19.18; 1 Thess 4.9; 1 Pet 1.22; Heb 13.1; Eph 5.2; 1 Jn 4.10.
13.36: Jn 21.18; 2 Pet 1.14. **13.37-38:** Mt 26.33-35; Mk 14.29-31; Lk 22.33-34.
14.2: Jn 13.33. **14.5:** Jn 11.16. **14.6:** Jn 10.9; 1.4, 14. **14.9:** Jn 12.45. **14.11:** Jn 10.38.
14.13: Mt 7.7; Jn 15.7, 16; 16.23; Jas 1.5. **14.15:** Jn 15.10; 1 Jn 5.3; 2 Jn 6.
14.16: Jn 14.26; 15.26; 16.7; 1 Jn 2.1. **14.19:** Jn 7.33. **14.22:** Acts 1.13; 10.40-41.
14.23: 1 Jn 2.24; Rev 21.3. **14.27:** Jn 16.33; Phil 4.7; Col 3.15; Jn 20.19.

you loved me, you would have rejoiced, because I go to the Father; for the Father is greater than I. 29 And now I have told you before it takes place, so that when it does take place, you may believe. 30 I will no longer talk much with you, for the ruler of this world is coming. He has no power over me; 31 but I do as the Father has commanded me, so that the world may know that I love the Father. Rise, let us go hence.

15 "I am the true vine, and my Father is the vinedresser. 2 Every branch of mine that bears no fruit, he takes away, and every branch that does bear fruit he prunes, that it may bear more fruit. 3 You are already made clean by the word which I have spoken to you. 4 Abide in me, and I in you. As the branch cannot bear fruit by itself, unless it abides in the vine, neither can you, unless you abide in me. 5 I am the vine, you are the branches. He who abides in me, and I in him, he it is that bears much fruit, for apart from me you can do nothing. 6 If a man does not abide in me, he is cast forth as a branch and withers; and the branches are gathered, thrown into the fire and burned. 7 If you abide in me, and my words abide in you, ask whatever you will, and it shall be done for you. 8 By this my Father is glorified, that you bear much fruit, and so prove to be my disciples. 9 As the Father has loved me, so have I loved you; abide in my love. 10 If you keep my commandments, you will abide in my love, just as I have kept my Father's commandments and abide in his love. 11 These things I have spoken to you, that my joy may be in you, and that your joy may be full.

12 "This is my commandment, that you love one another as I have loved you. 13 Greater love has no man than this, that a man lay down his life for his friends. 14 You are my friends if you do what I command you. 15 No longer do I call you servants,[h] for the servant[i] does not know what his master is doing; but I have called you friends, for all that I have heard from my Father I have made known to you. 16 You did not choose me, but I chose you and appointed you that you should go and bear fruit and that your fruit should abide; so that whatever you ask the Father in my name, he may give it to you. 17 This I command you, to love one another.

18 "If the world hates you, know that it has hated me before it hated you. 19 If you were of the world, the world would love its own; but because you are not of the world, but I chose you out of the world, therefore the world hates you. 20 Remember the word that I said to you, 'A servant[i] is not greater than his master.' If they persecuted me, they will persecute you; if they kept my word, they will keep yours also. 21 But all this they will do to you on my account, because they do not know him who sent me. 22 If I had not come and spoken to them, they would not have sin; but now they have no excuse for their sin. 23 He who hates me hates my Father also. 24 If I had not done among them the works which no one else did, they would not have sin; but now they have seen and hated both me and my Father. 25 It is to fulfil the word that is written in their law, 'They hated me without a cause.' 26 But when the Counselor comes, whom I shall send to you from the Father, even the Spirit of truth, who proceeds from the Father, he will bear witness to me; 27 and you also are witnesses, because you have been with me from the beginning.

16 "I have said all this to you to keep you from falling away. 2 They will put you out of the synagogues; indeed, the hour is coming when whoever kills you will think he is offering service to God. 3 And they will do this because they have not known the Father, nor me. 4 But I have said these things to you, that when their hour comes you may remember that I told you of them.

"I did not say these things to you from the beginning, because I was

[h] Or *slaves* [i] Or *slave*

14.29: Jn 13.19. **14.30:** Jn 12.31. **14.31:** Mk 14.42; Jn 18.1.
15.1: Is 5.1-7; Ezek 19.10; Mk 12.1-9; Mt 15.13; Rom 11.17. **15.3:** Jn 13.10.
15.4: Jn 6.56; 1 Jn 2.6. **15.7:** Jn 14.13; 16.23; Mt 7.7; Jas 1.5. **15.8:** Mt 5.16.
15.10: Jn 14.15; 1 Jn 5.3. **15.12:** Jn 13.34. **15.13:** Rom 5.7; Jn 10.11. **15.14:** Lk 12.4.
15.16: Jn 6.70; 13.18; 14.13; 16.23. **15.18:** Jn 7.7; 1 Jn 3.13; Mt 10.22; 24.9.
15.20: Jn 13.16; Mt 10.24; 1 Cor 4.12; Acts 4.17; 1 Pet 4.14; Rev 2.3. **15.22:** Jn 9.41.
15.25: Ps 35.19; 69.4. **15.26:** Jn 14.16, 26; 16.7; 1 Jn 2.1; 5.7. **15.27:** Jn 19.35; 21.24; 1 Jn 4.14.
16.2: Jn 9.22; Acts 26.9-11; Is 66.5.

with you. 5 But now I am going to him who sent me; yet none of you asks me, 'Where are you going?' 6 But because I have said these things to you, sorrow has filled your hearts. 7 Nevertheless I tell you the truth: it is to your advantage that I go away, for if I do not go away, the Counselor will not come to you; but if I go, I will send him to you. 8 And when he comes, he will convince the world of sin and of righteousness and of judgment: 9 of sin, because they do not believe in me; 10 of righteousness, because I go to the Father, and you will see me no more; 11 of judgment, because the ruler of this world is judged.

12 "I have yet many things to say to you, but you cannot bear them now. 13 When the Spirit of truth comes, he will guide you into all the truth; for he will not speak on his own authority, but whatever he hears he will speak, and he will declare to you the things that are to come. 14 He will glorify me, for he will take what is mine and declare it to you. 15 All that the Father has is mine; therefore I said that he will take what is mine and declare it to you.

16 "A little while, and you will see me no more; again a little while, and you will see me." 17 Some of his disciples said to one another, "What is this that he says to us, 'A little while, and you will not see me, and again a little while, and you will see me'; and, 'because I go to the Father'? 18 They said, "What does he mean by 'a little while'? We do not know what he means." 19 Jesus knew that they wanted to ask him; so he said to them, "Is this what you are asking yourselves, what I meant by saying, 'A little while, and you will not see me, and again a little while, and you will see me'? 20 Truly, truly, I say to you, you will weep and lament, but the world will rejoice; you will be sorrowful, but your sorrow will turn into joy. 21 When a woman is in travail she has sorrow, because her hour has come; but when she is delivered of the child, she no longer remembers the anguish, for joy that a child[j] is born into the world. 22 So you have sorrow now, but I will see you again and your hearts will rejoice, and no one will take your joy from you. 23 In that day you will ask nothing of me. Truly, truly, I say to you, if you ask anything of the Father, he will give it to you in my name. 24 Hitherto you have asked nothing in my name; ask, and you will receive, that your joy may be full.

25 "I have said this to you in figures; the hour is coming when I shall no longer speak to you in figures but tell you plainly of the Father. 26 In that day you will ask in my name; and I do not say to you that I shall pray the Father for you; 27 for the Father himself loves you, because you have loved me and have believed that I came from the Father. 28 I came from the Father and have come into the world; again, I am leaving the world and going to the Father."

29 His disciples said, "Ah, now you are speaking plainly, not in any figure! 30 Now we know that you know all things, and need none to question you; by this we believe that you came from God." 31 Jesus answered them, "Do you now believe? 32 The hour is coming, indeed it has come, when you will be scattered, every man to his home, and will leave me alone; yet I am not alone, for the Father is with me. 33 I have said this to you, that in me you may have peace. In the world you have tribulation; but be of good cheer, I have overcome the world."

17 When Jesus had spoken these words, he lifted up his eyes to heaven and said, "Father, the hour has come; glorify thy Son that the Son may glorify thee, 2 since thou hast given him power over all flesh, to give eternal life to all whom thou hast given him. 3 And this is eternal life, that they know thee the only true God, and Jesus Christ whom thou hast sent. 4 I glorified thee on earth, having accomplished the work which thou gavest me to do; 5 and now, Father, glorify thou me in thy own presence with the glory which I had with thee before the world was made.

[j] Greek *a human being*

16.5: Jn 7.33; 14.5. **16.7:** Jn 14.16, 26; 15.26. **16.9:** Jn 15.22. **16.10:** Acts 3.14; 7.52; 1 Pet 3.18. **16.11:** Jn 12.31. **16.14:** Jn 7.39. **16.16-24:** Jn 14.18-24. **16.20:** Jn 20.20. **16.21:** Is 13.8; Hos 13.13; Mic 4.9; 1 Thess 5.3. **16.24:** Jn 14.14; 15.11. **16.25:** Jn 10.6; Mt 13.34. **16.32:** Jn 4.23; Mk 14.27; Zech 13.7. **16.33:** Jn 14.27; 15.18; Rom 8.37; 2 Cor 2.14; Rev 3.21. **17.1:** Jn 11.41; 13.31. **17.5:** Jn 1.1; 8.58; Phil 2.6.

6 "I have manifested thy name to the men whom thou gavest me out of the world; thine they were, and thou gavest them to me, and they have kept thy word. 7 Now they know that everything that thou hast given me is from thee; 8 for I have given them the words which thou gavest me, and they have received them and know in truth that I came from thee; and they have believed that thou didst send me. 9 I am praying for them; I am not praying for the world but for those whom thou hast given me, for they are thine; 10 all mine are thine, and thine are mine, and I am glorified in them. 11 And now I am no more in the world, but they are in the world, and I am coming to thee. Holy Father, keep them in thy name, which thou hast given me, that they may be one, even as we are one. 12 While I was with them, I kept them in thy name, which thou hast given me; I have guarded them, and none of them is lost but the son of perdition, that the scripture might be fulfilled. 13 But now I am coming to thee; and these things I speak in the world, that they may have my joy fulfilled in themselves. 14 I have given them thy word; and the world has hated them because they are not of the world, even as I am not of the world. 15 I do not pray that thou shouldst take them out of the world, but that thou shouldst keep them from the evil one.[k] 16 They are not of the world, even as I am not of the world. 17 Sanctify them in the truth; thy word is truth. 18 As thou didst send me into the world, so I have sent them into the world. 19 And for their sake I consecrate myself, that they also may be consecrated in truth.

20 "I do not pray for these only, but also for those who believe in me through their word, 21 that they may all be one; even as thou, Father, art in me, and I in thee, that they also may be in us, so that the world may believe that thou hast sent me. 22 The glory which thou hast given me I have given to them, that they may be one even as we are one, 23 I in them and thou in me, that they may become perfectly one, so that the world may know that thou hast sent me and hast loved them even as thou hast loved me. 24 Father, I desire that they also, whom thou hast given me, may be with me where I am, to behold my glory which thou hast given me in thy love for me before the foundation of the world. 25 O righteous Father, the world has not known thee, but I have known thee; and these know that thou hast sent me. 26 I made known to them thy name, and I will make it known, that the love with which thou hast loved me may be in them, and I in them."

18 When Jesus had spoken these words, he went forth with his disciples across the Kid'rŏn valley, where there was a garden, which he and his disciples entered. 2 Now Judas, who betrayed him, also knew the place; for Jesus often met there with his disciples. 3 So Judas, procuring a band of soldiers and some officers from the chief priests and the Pharisees, went there with lanterns and torches and weapons. 4 Then Jesus, knowing all that was to befall him, came forward and said to them, "Whom do you seek?" 5 They answered him, "Jesus of Nazareth." Jesus said to them, "I am he." Judas, who betrayed him, was standing with them. 6 When he said to them, "I am he," they drew back and fell to the ground. 7 Again he asked them, "Whom do you seek?" And they said, "Jesus of Nazareth." 8 Jesus answered, "I told you that I am he; so, if you seek me, let these men go." 9 This was to fulfil the word which he had spoken, "Of those whom thou gavest me I lost not one." 10 Then Simon Peter, having a sword, drew it and struck the high priest's slave and cut off his right ear. The slave's name was Mal'chŭs. 11 Jesus said to Peter, "Put your sword into its sheath; shall I not drink the cup which the Father has given me?"

12 So the band of soldiers and their captain and the officers of the Jews seized Jesus and bound him. 13 First they led him to An'nas; for he was the father-in-law of Cā'iȧ·phȧs, who was high priest that year. 14 It was Cā'iȧ-

[k] Or *from evil*

17.9: Lk 22.32; Jn 14.16. **17.11:** Phil 2.9; Rev 19.12; Rom 12.5; Gal 3.28; Jn 17.21. **17.12:** Ps 41.9; Jn 6.70; 18.9. **17.14:** Jn 15.19; 8.23. **17.21:** Jn 10.38; 17.11. **17.24:** Jn 1.14; 17.5; Mt 25.34. **18.1:** Mt 26.30, 36; Mk 14.26, 32; Lk 22.39; 2 Sam 15.23. **18.3-11:** Mt 26.47-56; Mk 14.43-50; Lk 22.47-53. **18.4:** Jn 6.64; 13.1. **18.9:** Jn 17.12; 6.39. **18.11:** Mk 10.38; 14.36. **18.12-13:** Mt 26.57; Mk 14.53; Lk 22.54; 3.2. **18.14:** Jn 11.49-51.

phas who had given counsel to the
Jews that it was expedient that one
man should die for the people.
15 Simon Peter followed Jesus, and
so did another disciple. As this disciple
was known to the high priest, he
entered the court of the high priest
along with Jesus, 16 while Peter stood
outside at the door. So the other disciple, who was known to the high priest,
went out and spoke to the maid who
kept the door, and brought Peter in.
17 The maid who kept the door said
to Peter, "Are not you also one of this
man's disciples?" He said, "I am
not." 18 Now the servants[l] and officers
had made a charcoal fire, because it
was cold, and they were standing and
warming themselves; Peter also was
with them, standing and warming
himself.
19 The high priest then questioned
Jesus about his disciples and his teaching. 20 Jesus answered him, "I have
spoken openly to the world; I have
always taught in synagogues and in the
temple, where all Jews come together;
I have said nothing secretly. 21 Why
do you ask me? Ask those who have
heard me, what I said to them; they
know what I said." 22 When he had
said this, one of the officers standing
by struck Jesus with his hand, saying,
"Is that how you answer the high
priest?" 23 Jesus answered him, "If I
have spoken wrongly, bear witness to
the wrong; but if I have spoken rightly,
why do you strike me?" 24 An'nas then
sent him bound to Cā'iȧ·phȧs the high
priest.
25 Now Simon Peter was standing
and warming himself. They said to
him, "Are not you also one of his disciples?" He denied it and said, "I am
not." 26 One of the servants[l] of the
high priest, a kinsman of the man
whose ear Peter had cut off, asked,
"Did I not see you in the garden with
him?" 27 Peter again denied it; and at
once the cock crowed.
28 Then they led Jesus from the
house of Cā'iȧ·phȧs to the praetorium.
It was early. They themselves did not
enter the praetorium, so that they
might not be defiled, but might eat the
passover. 29 So Pilate went out to them
and said, "What accusation do you
bring against this man?" 30 They answered him, "If this man were not an
evildoer, we would not have handed
him over." 31 Pilate said to them,
"Take him yourselves and judge him
by your own law." The Jews said to
him, "It is not lawful for us to put any
man to death." 32 This was to fulfil the
word which Jesus had spoken to show
by what death he was to die.
33 Pilate entered the praetorium
again and called Jesus, and said to him,
"Are you the King of the Jews?"
34 Jesus answered, "Do you say this
of your own accord, or did others say
it to you about me?" 35 Pilate answered,
"Am I a Jew? Your own nation and
the chief priests have handed you over
to me; what have you done?" 36 Jesus
answered, "My kingship is not of this
world; if my kingship were of this
world, my servants would fight, that
I might not be handed over to the
Jews; but my kingship is not from the
world." 37 Pilate said to him, "So you
are a king?" Jesus answered, "You say
that I am a king. For this I was born,
and for this I have come into the
world, to bear witness to the truth.
Every one who is of the truth hears
my voice." 38 Pilate said to him, "What
is truth?"
After he had said this, he went out
to the Jews again, and told them, "I
find no crime in him. 39 But you have
a custom that I should release one man
for you at the Passover; will you have
me release for you the King of the
Jews?" 40 They cried out again, "Not
this man, but Bȧ·rab'bȧs!" Now
Barabbas was a robber.

19 Then Pilate took Jesus and
scourged him. 2 And the soldiers
plaited a crown of thorns, and put it
on his head, and arrayed him in a
purple robe; 3 they came up to him,
saying, "Hail, King of the Jews!" and
struck him with their hands. 4 Pilate
went out again, and said to them,
"Behold, I am bringing him out to
you, that you may know that I find no

[l] Or *slaves*

18.15-16: Mt 26.58; Mk 14.54; Lk 22.54. **18.17-18:** Mt 26.69-72; Mk 14.66-69; Lk 22.56-58.
18.19-23: Mt 26.59-66; Mk 14.55-64; Lk 22.67-71. **18.23:** Mt 5.39; Acts 23.2-5.
18.24: Jn 18.13; Lk 3.2. **18.25-27:** Mt 26.73-75; Mk 14.70-72; Lk 22.59-62.
18.28: Jn 11.55; Mt 27.1-2; Mk 15.1; Lk 23.1. **18.29-38:** Mt 27.11-14; Mk 15.2-5; Lk 23.2-3.
18.32: Jn 3.14; 12.32. **18.36:** Jn 6.15; Mt 26.53. **18.37:** Jn 3.32; 8.14, 47; 1 Jn 4.6.
18.38-40: Mt 27.15-26; Mk 15.6-15; Lk 23.18-19; Acts 3.14.
19.2-3: Mt 27.27-31; Mk 15.16-20; Lk 22.63-65; 23.11. **19.4:** Jn 18.38; 19.6; Lk 23.4.

crime in him." 5 So Jesus came out,
wearing the crown of thorns and the
purple robe. Pilate said to them, "Here
is the man!" 6 When the chief priests
and the officers saw him, they cried
out, "Crucify him, crucify him!"
Pilate said to them, "Take him yourselves and crucify him, for I find no
crime in him." 7 The Jews answered
him, "We have a law, and by that law
he ought to die, because he has made
himself the Son of God." 8 When
Pilate heard these words, he was the
more afraid; 9 he entered the praetorium again and said to Jesus, "Where
are you from?" But Jesus gave no
answer. 10 Pilate therefore said to him,
"You will not speak to me? Do you
not know that I have power to release
you, and power to crucify you?"
11 Jesus answered him, "You would
have no power over me unless it had
been given you from above; therefore
he who delivered me to you has the
greater sin."

12 Upon this Pilate sought to release him, but the Jews cried out, "If
you release this man, you are not
Caesar's friend; every one who makes
himself a king sets himself against
Caesar." 13 When Pilate heard these
words, he brought Jesus out and sat
down on the judgment seat at a place
called The Pavement, and in Hebrew,
Gab'ba·tha. 14 Now it was the day of
Preparation of the Passover; it was
about the sixth hour. He said to the
Jews, "Here is your King!" 15 They
cried out, "Away with him, away with
him, crucify him!" Pilate said to them,
"Shall I crucify your King?" The chief
priests answered, "We have no king
but Caesar." 16 Then he handed him
over to them to be crucified.

17 So they took Jesus, and he went
out, bearing his own cross, to the
place called the place of a skull, which
is called in Hebrew Gol'go·tha.
18 There they crucified him, and with
him two others, one on either side, and
Jesus between them. 19 Pilate also
wrote a title and put it on the cross; it
read, "Jesus of Nazareth, the King of
the Jews." 20 Many of the Jews read
this title, for the place where Jesus was
crucified was near the city; and it was
written in Hebrew, in Latin, and in
Greek. 21 The chief priests of the Jews
then said to Pilate, "Do not write, 'The
King of the Jews,' but, 'This man
said, I am King of the Jews.'"
22 Pilate answered, "What I have
written I have written."

23 When the soldiers had crucified
Jesus they took his garments and made
four parts, one for each soldier; also
his tunic. But the tunic was without
seam, woven from top to bottom; 24 so
they said to one another, "Let us not
tear it, but cast lots for it to see whose
it shall be." This was to fulfil the
scripture,

"They parted my garments among
them,
and for my clothing they cast lots."

25 So the soldiers did this. But
standing by the cross of Jesus were his
mother, and his mother's sister, Mary
the wife of Clō'pas, and Mary Mag'da-
lēne. 26 When Jesus saw his mother,
and the disciple whom he loved standing near, he said to his mother,
"Woman, behold, your son!" 27 Then
he said to the disciple, "Behold, your
mother!" And from that hour the disciple took her to his own home.

28 After this Jesus, knowing that
all was now finished, said (to fulfil the
scripture), "I thirst." 29 A bowl full of
vinegar stood there; so they put a
sponge full of the vinegar on hyssop
and held it to his mouth. 30 When
Jesus had received the vinegar, he said,
"It is finished"; and he bowed his
head and gave up his spirit.

31 Since it was the day of Preparation, in order to prevent the bodies
from remaining on the cross on the
sabbath (for that sabbath was a high
day), the Jews asked Pilate that their
legs might be broken, and that they
might be taken away. 32 So the soldiers
came and broke the legs of the first,
and of the other who had been crucified with him; 33 but when they came
to Jesus and saw that he was already
dead, they did not break his legs.
34 But one of the soldiers pierced his
side with a spear, and at once there
came out blood and water. 35 He who

19.7: Lev 24.16; Mk 14.61-64; Jn 5.18; 10.33. **19.11:** Rom 13.1; Jn 18.28. **19.12:** Lk 23.2.
19.14: Mk 15.42; Jn 19.31, 42; Mk 15.25, 33. **19.17-24:** Mt 27.33-44; Mk 15.22-32; Lk 23.33-43.
19.24: Ex 28.32; Ps 22.18.
19.25: Mt 27.55-56; Mk 15.40-41; Lk 23.49; Jn 2.3; Mk 3.31; Lk 24.18; Jn 20.1, 18.
19.26: Jn 13.23; 20.2; 21.20. **19.28-30:** Ps 69.21; Mt 27.45-50; Mk 15.33-37; Lk 23.44-46; Jn 17.4.
19.31: Deut 21.23; Ex 12.16. **19.34:** 1 Jn 5.6-8. **19.35:** Jn 15.27; 21.24.

saw it has borne witness—his testimony is true, and he knows that he
tells the truth—that you also may
believe. 36 For these things took place
that the scripture might be fulfilled,
"Not a bone of him shall be broken."
37 And again another scripture says,
"They shall look on him whom they
have pierced."

38 After this Joseph of Ar·i·mȧ-
thē'ȧ, who was a disciple of Jesus, but
secretly, for fear of the Jews, asked
Pilate that he might take away the
body of Jesus, and Pilate gave him
leave. So he came and took away his
body. 39 Nic·ȯ·dē'mus also, who had
at first come to him by night, came
bringing a mixture of myrrh and aloes,
about a hundred pounds' weight.
40 They took the body of Jesus, and
bound it in linen cloths with the
spices, as is the burial custom of the
Jews. 41 Now in the place where he
was crucified there was a garden, and
in the garden a new tomb where no
one had ever been laid. 42 So because
of the Jewish day of Preparation, as
the tomb was close at hand, they laid
Jesus there.

20 Now on the first day of the
week Mary Mag'dȧ·lēne came to
the tomb early, while it was still dark,
and saw that the stone had been taken
away from the tomb. 2 So she ran, and
went to Simon Peter and the other
disciple, the one whom Jesus loved,
and said to them, "They have taken
the Lord out of the tomb, and we do
not know where they have laid him."
3 Peter then came out with the other
disciple, and they went toward the
tomb. 4 They both ran, but the other
disciple outran Peter and reached the
tomb first; 5 and stooping to look in,
he saw the linen cloths lying there, but
he did not go in. 6 Then Simon Peter
came, following him, and went into
the tomb; he saw the linen cloths lying,
7 and the napkin, which had been on
his head, not lying with the linen
cloths but rolled up in a place by itself.
8 Then the other disciple, who reached
the tomb first, also went in, and he
saw and believed; 9 for as yet they did
not know the scripture, that he must
rise from the dead. 10 Then the disciples
went back to their homes.

11 But Mary stood weeping outside
the tomb, and as she wept she stooped
to look into the tomb; 12 and she saw
two angels in white, sitting where the
body of Jesus had lain, one at the head
and one at the feet. 13 They said to
her, "Woman, why are you weeping?"
She said to them, "Because they have
taken away my Lord, and I do not
know where they have laid him."
14 Saying this, she turned round and
saw Jesus standing, but she did not
know that it was Jesus. 15 Jesus said
to her, "Woman, why are you weeping? Whom do you seek?" Supposing
him to be the gardener, she said to
him, "Sir, if you have carried him
away, tell me where you have laid him,
and I will take him away." 16 Jesus
said to her, "Mary." She turned and
said to him in Hebrew, "Rȧb-bō'nī!"
(which means Teacher). 17 Jesus said
to her, "Do not hold me, for I have
not yet ascended to the Father; but go
to my brethren and say to them, I am
ascending to my Father and your
Father, to my God and your God."
18 Mary Mag'dȧ·lēne went and said to
the disciples, "I have seen the Lord";
and she told them that he had said
these things to her.

19 On the evening of that day, the
first day of the week, the doors being
shut where the disciples were, for fear
of the Jews, Jesus came and stood
among them and said to them, "Peace
be with you." 20 When he had said
this, he showed them his hands and
his side. Then the disciples were glad
when they saw the Lord. 21 Jesus said
to them again, "Peace be with you. As
the Father has sent me, even so I send
you." 22 And when he had said this, he
breathed on them, and said to them,
"Receive the Holy Spirit. 23 If you
forgive the sins of any, they are forgiven; if you retain the sins of any,
they are retained."

24 Now Thomas, one of the twelve,
called the Twin, was not with them
when Jesus came. 25 So the other disciples told him, "We have seen the
Lord." But he said to them, "Unless

19.36: Ex 12.46; Num 9.12; Ps 34.20. **19.37:** Zech 12.10.
19.38-42: Mt 27.57-61; Mk 15.42-47; Lk 23.50-56. **19.39:** Jn 3.1; 7.50. **19.40:** Mk 16.1; 14.8.
20.1-10: Mt 28.1-8; Mk 16.1-8; Lk 24.1-10. **20.3-10:** Lk 24.11-12. **20.9:** Lk 24.26, 46.
20.12: Lk 24.4; Mt 28.5; Mk 16.5. **20.13:** Jn 20.2. **20.14:** Mt 28.9; Jn 21.4.
20.17: Jn 20.27; Mt 28.10; Jn 7.33. **20.18:** Lk 24.10, 23. **20.19-20:** Lk 24.36-39.
20.21: Jn 17.18; Mt 28.19. **20.22:** Acts 2.4, 33. **20.23:** Mt 16.19; 18.18. **20.24:** Jn 11.16.

I see in his hands the print of the nails,
and place my finger in the mark of the
nails, and place my hand in his side, I
will not believe."
26 Eight days later, his disciples
were again in the house, and Thomas
was with them. The doors were shut,
but Jesus came and stood among
them, and said, "Peace be with you."
27 Then he said to Thomas, "Put your
finger here, and see my hands; and put
out your hand, and place it in my side;
do not be faithless, but believing."
28 Thomas answered him, "My Lord
and my God!" 29 Jesus said to him,
"Have you believed because you have
seen me? Blessed are those who have
not seen and yet believe."
30 Now Jesus did many other signs
in the presence of the disciples, which
are not written in this book; 31 but
these are written that you may believe
that Jesus is the Christ, the Son of
God, and that believing you may have
life in his name.

21 After this Jesus revealed himself
again to the disciples by the Sea
of Tī·bē'ri·ȧs; and he revealed himself
in this way. 2 Simon Peter, Thomas
called the Twin, Nȧ·than'ȧ-el of Cā'nȧ
in Galilee, the sons of Zeb'ė·dee, and
two others of his disciples were together. 3 Simon Peter said to them, "I
am going fishing." They said to him,
"We will go with you." They went
out and got into the boat; but that
night they caught nothing.
4 Just as day was breaking, Jesus
stood on the beach; yet the disciples
did not know that it was Jesus. 5 Jesus
said to them, "Children, have you any
fish?" They answered him, "No."
6 He said to them, "Cast the net on
the right side of the boat, and you will
find some." So they cast it, and now
they were not able to haul it in, for the
quantity of fish. 7 That disciple whom
Jesus loved said to Peter, "It is the
Lord!" When Simon Peter heard that
it was the Lord, he put on his clothes,
for he was stripped for work, and
sprang into the sea. 8 But the other
disciples came in the boat, dragging
the net full of fish, for they were not
far from the land, but about a hundred
yards[m] off.
9 When they got out on land, they
saw a charcoal fire there, with fish
lying on it, and bread. 10 Jesus said to
them, "Bring some of the fish that
you have just caught." 11 So Simon
Peter went aboard and hauled the net
ashore, full of large fish, a hundred and
fifty-three of them; and although there
were so many, the net was not torn.
12 Jesus said to them, "Come and have
breakfast." Now none of the disciples
dared ask him, "Who are you?" They
knew it was the Lord. 13 Jesus came
and took the bread and gave it to them,
and so with the fish. 14 This was now
the third time that Jesus was revealed
to the disciples after he was raised from
the dead.
15 When they had finished breakfast, Jesus said to Simon Peter, "Simon, son of John, do you love me more
than these?" He said to him, "Yes,
Lord; you know that I love you." He
said to him, "Feed my lambs." 16 A
second time he said to him, "Simon,
son of John, do you love me?" He said
to him, "Yes, Lord; you know that I
love you." He said to him, "Tend my
sheep." 17 He said to him the third
time, "Simon, son of John, do you
love me?" Peter was grieved because
he said to him the third time, "Do you
love me?" And he said to him, "Lord,
you know everything; you know that
I love you." Jesus said to him, "Feed
my sheep. 18 Truly, truly, I say to you,
when you were young, you girded
yourself and walked where you would;
but when you are old, you will stretch
out your hands, and another will gird
you and carry you where you do not
wish to go." 19 (This he said to show
by what death he was to glorify God.)
And after this he said to him, "Follow
me."
20 Peter turned and saw following
them the disciple whom Jesus loved,
who had lain close to his breast at the
supper and had said, "Lord, who is it
that is going to betray you?" 21 When
Peter saw him, he said to Jesus, "Lord,
what about this man?" 22 Jesus said to
him, "If it is my will that he remain

[m] Greek *two hundred cubits*

20.27: Lk 24.40. **20.29:** 1 Pet 1.8. **20.30:** Jn 21.25. **20.31:** Jn 3.15. **21.2:** Jn 11.16; 1.45; Lk 5.10.
21.3-6: Lk 5.3-7. **21.4:** Jn 20.14; Lk 24.16. **21.5:** Lk 24.41. **21.7:** Jn 13.23; 19.26; 20.2; 21.20.
21.14: Jn 20.19, 26. **21.15:** Jn 1.42; 13.37; Mk 14.29-31; Lk 12.32.
21.16: Mt 2.6; Acts 20.28; 1 Pet 5.2; Rev 7.17. **21.19:** 2 Pet 1.14; Mk 1.17. **21.20:** Jn 13.25.
21.22: 1 Cor 4.5; Jas 5.7; Rev 2.25; Mt 16.28.

until I come, what is that to you?
Follow me!" 23 The saying spread
abroad among the brethren that this
disciple was not to die; yet Jesus did
not say to him that he was not to die,
but, "If it is my will that he remain
until I come, what is that to you?"
24 This is the disciple who is bearing witness to these things, and who
has written these things; and we know
that his testimony is true.
25 But there are also many other
things which Jesus did; were every one
of them to be written, I suppose that
the world itself could not contain the
books that would be written.

THE ACTS OF THE APOSTLES

1 In the first book, O Thē-oph'i·lŭs,
I have dealt with all that Jesus
began to do and teach, 2 until the day
when he was taken up, after he had
given commandment through the Holy
Spirit to the apostles whom he had
chosen. 3 To them he presented himself alive after his passion by many
proofs, appearing to them during forty
days, and speaking of the kingdom of
God. 4 And while staying[a] with them
he charged them not to depart from
Jerusalem, but to wait for the promise
of the Father, which, he said, "you
heard from me, 5 for John baptized
with water, but before many days
you shall be baptized with the Holy
Spirit."
6 So when they had come together,
they asked him, "Lord, will you at
this time restore the kingdom to
Israel?" 7 He said to them, "It is not
for you to know times or seasons which
the Father has fixed by his own
authority. 8 But you shall receive
power when the Holy Spirit has come
upon you; and you shall be my witnesses in Jerusalem and in all Judea
and Sȧ·mâr'i·ȧ and to the end of the
earth." 9 And when he had said this, as
they were looking on, he was lifted up,
and a cloud took him out of their sight.
10 And while they were gazing into
heaven as he went, behold, two men
stood by them in white robes, 11 and
said, "Men of Galilee, why do you
stand looking into heaven? This Jesus,
who was taken up from you into
heaven, will come in the same way as
you saw him go into heaven."
12 Then they returned to Jerusalem
from the mount called Ol'i·vet, which
is near Jerusalem, a sabbath day's
journey away; 13 and when they had
entered, they went up to the upper
room, where they were staying, Peter
and John and James and Andrew,
Philip and Thomas, Bartholomew and
Matthew, James the son of Al·phaē'ŭs
and Simon the Zealot and Judas the
son of James. 14 All these with one
accord devoted themselves to prayer,
together with the women and Mary the
mother of Jesus, and with his brothers.
15 In those days Peter stood up
among the brethren (the company of
persons was in all about a hundred and
twenty), and said, 16 "Brethren, the
scripture had to be fulfilled, which the
Holy Spirit spoke beforehand by the
mouth of David, concerning Judas who
was guide to those who arrested Jesus.
17 For he was numbered among us,
and was allotted his share in this
ministry. 18 (Now this man bought a
field with the reward of his wickedness; and falling headlong[b] he burst
open in the middle and all his bowels
gushed out. 19 And it became known
to all the inhabitants of Jerusalem, so
that the field was called in their
language A·kel'dȧ·mȧ, that is, Field of
Blood.) 20 For it is written in the book
of Psalms,

'Let his habitation become desolate,
and let there be no one to live in it';

[a] Or *eating* [b] Or *swelling up*

21.24: Jn 15 27; 19.35. **21.25:** Jn 20.30. **1.1:** Lk 1.1-4. **1.4:** Lk 24.49. **1.8:** Lk 24.48-49. **1.9-12:** Lk 24.50-53. **1.13:** Mt 10.2-4; Mk 3.16-19; Lk 6.14-16. **1.16-19:** Mt 27.3-10. **1.20:** Ps 69.25; 109.8.

and
'His office let another take.'
21 So one of the men who have accompanied us during all the time that
the Lord Jesus went in and out among
us, 22 beginning from the baptism of
John until the day when he was taken
up from us—one of these men must
become with us a witness to his resurrection." 23And they put forward two,
Joseph called Bär'sab·bȧs, who was
surnamed Justus, and Mat·thī'ȧs.
24And they prayed and said, "Lord,
who knowest the hearts of all men,
show which one of these two thou hast
chosen 25 to take the place in this
ministry and apostleship from which
Judas turned aside, to go to his own
place." 26And they cast lots for them,
and the lot fell on Mat·thī'ȧs; and he
was enrolled with the eleven apostles.

2 When the day of Pentecost had
come, they were all together in one
place. 2And suddenly a sound came
from heaven like the rush of a mighty
wind, and it filled all the house where
they were sitting. 3And there appeared
to them tongues as of fire, distributed
and resting on each one of them. 4And
they were all filled with the Holy Spirit
and began to speak in other tongues,
as the Spirit gave them utterance.

5 Now there were dwelling in Jerusalem Jews, devout men from every
nation under heaven. 6And at this
sound the multitude came together,
and they were bewildered, because each
one heard them speaking in his own
language. 7And they were amazed and
wondered, saying, "Are not all these
who are speaking Galileans? 8And how
is it that we hear, each of us in his own
native language? 9 Pär'thi·ȧns and
Medes and Ē'lȧ·mītes and residents of
Mes·ȯ·pȯ·tā'mi·ȧ, Judea and Cap·pȧ-
dō'ci·ȧ, Pon'tŭs and Asia, 10 Phryg'i·ȧ
and Pam·phyl'i·ȧ, Egypt and the parts
of Libya belonging to Cȳ·rē'nē, and
visitors from Rome, both Jews and
proselytes, 11 Cretans and Arabians,
we hear them telling in our own
tongues the mighty works of God."
12And all were amazed and perplexed,
saying to one another, "What does
this mean?" 13 But others mocking
said, "They are filled with new wine."

14 But Peter, standing with the
eleven, lifted up his voice and addressed them, "Men of Judea and all
who dwell in Jerusalem, let this be
known to you, and give ear to my
words. 15 For these men are not drunk,
as you suppose, since it is only the
third hour of the day; 16 but this is
what was spoken by the prophet Jō'ĕl:
17 'And in the last days it shall be, God declares,
that I will pour out my Spirit upon all flesh,
and your sons and your daughters shall prophesy,
and your young men shall see visions,
and your old men shall dream dreams;
18 yea, and on my menservants and my maidservants in those days
I will pour out my Spirit; and they shall prophesy.
19 And I will show wonders in the heaven above
and signs on the earth beneath,
blood, and fire, and vapor of smoke;
20 the sun shall be turned into darkness
and the moon into blood,
before the day of the Lord comes,
the great and manifest day.
21 And it shall be that whoever calls on the name of the Lord shall be saved.'

22 "Men of Israel, hear these words:
Jesus of Nazareth, a man attested to
you by God with mighty works and
wonders and signs which God did
through him in your midst, as you
yourselves know—23 this Jesus, delivered up according to the definite
plan and foreknowledge of God, you
crucified and killed by the hands of
lawless men. 24 But God raised him
up, having loosed the pangs of death,
because it was not possible for him to
be held by it. 25 For David says concerning him,
'I saw the Lord always before me,
for he is at my right hand that I may not be shaken;
26 therefore my heart was glad, and my tongue rejoiced;
moreover my flesh will dwell in hope.
27 For thou wilt not abandon my soul to Hades,
nor let thy Holy One see corruption.
28 Thou hast made known to me the ways of life;
thou wilt make me full of gladness with thy presence.'

29 "Brethren, I may say to you
confidently of the patriarch David that

2.17-21: Joel 2.28-32. **2.25-28:** Ps 16.8-11.

he both died and was buried, and his
tomb is with us to this day. 30 Being
therefore a prophet, and knowing that
God had sworn with an oath to him
that he would set one of his descendants upon his throne, 31 he foresaw
and spoke of the resurrection of the
Christ, that he was not abandoned to
Hades, nor did his flesh see corruption.
32 This Jesus God raised up, and of
that we all are witnesses. 33 Being
therefore exalted at the right hand of
God, and having received from the
Father the promise of the Holy Spirit,
he has poured out this which you see
and hear. 34 For David did not ascend
into the heavens; but he himself says,

'The Lord said to my Lord, Sit at
my right hand,
35 till I make thy enemies a stool for
thy feet.'

36 Let all the house of Israel therefore
know assuredly that God has made
him both Lord and Christ, this Jesus
whom you crucified."

37 Now when they heard this they
were cut to the heart, and said to Peter
and the rest of the apostles, "Brethren,
what shall we do?" 38And Peter said
to them, "Repent, and be baptized
every one of you in the name of Jesus
Christ for the forgiveness of your sins;
and you shall receive the gift of the
Holy Spirit. 39 For the promise is to
you and to your children and to all
that are far off, every one whom the
Lord our God calls to him." 40And he
testified with many other words and
exhorted them, saying, "Save yourselves from this crooked generation."
41 So those who received his word
were baptized, and there were added
that day about three thousand souls.
42And they devoted themselves to the
apostles' teaching and fellowship, to
the breaking of bread and the prayers.

43 And fear came upon every soul;
and many wonders and signs were
done through the apostles. 44And all
who believed were together and had
all things in common; 45 and they sold
their possessions and goods and distributed them to all, as any had need.
46And day by day, attending the temple together and breaking bread in
their homes, they partook of food with
glad and generous hearts, 47 praising
God and having favor with all the
people. And the Lord added to their
number day by day those who were
being saved.

3 Now Peter and John were going
up to the temple at the hour of
prayer, the ninth hour. 2And a man
lame from birth was being carried,
whom they laid daily at that gate of
the temple which is called Beautiful
to ask alms of those who entered the
temple. 3 Seeing Peter and John about
to go into the temple, he asked for
alms. 4And Peter directed his gaze at
him, with John, and said, "Look at
us." 5And he fixed his attention upon
them, expecting to receive something
from them. 6 But Peter said, "I have
no silver and gold, but I give you what
I have; in the name of Jesus Christ of
Nazareth, walk." 7And he took him by
the right hand and raised him up; and
immediately his feet and ankles were
made strong. 8And leaping up he
stood and walked and entered the
temple with them, walking and leaping
and praising God. 9And all the people
saw him walking and praising God,
10 and recognized him as the one who
sat for alms at the Beautiful Gate of
the temple; and they were filled with
wonder and amazement at what had
happened to him.

11 While he clung to Peter and
John, all the people ran together to
them in the portico called Solomon's,
astounded. 12And when Peter saw it
he addressed the people, "Men of
Israel, why do you wonder at this, or
why do you stare at us, as though by
our own power or piety we had made
him walk? 13 The God of Abraham
and of Isaac and of Jacob, the God of
our fathers, glorified his servant[c]
Jesus, whom you delivered up and
denied in the presence of Pilate, when
he had decided to release him. 14 But
you denied the Holy and Righteous
One, and asked for a murderer to be
granted to you, 15 and killed the
Author of life, whom God raised from
the dead. To this we are witnesses.
16And his name, by faith in his name,
has made this man strong whom you
see and know; and the faith which is
through Jesus[d] has given the man this
perfect health in the presence of you
all.

17 "And now, brethren, I know that

[c] Or *child* [d] Greek *him*

2.30: Ps 132.11. **2.31:** Ps 16.10. **2.34-35:** Ps 110.1. **2.39:** Is 57.19; Joel 2.32.
2.44-45: Acts 4.32-35. **3.13:** Ex 3.6; Is 52.13.

you acted in ignorance, as did also
your rulers. 18 But what God foretold
by the mouth of all the prophets, that
his Christ should suffer, he thus fulfilled. 19 Repent therefore, and turn
again, that your sins may be blotted
out, that times of refreshing may
come from the presence of the Lord,
20 and that he may send the Christ
appointed for you, Jesus, 21 whom
heaven must receive until the time for
establishing all that God spoke by the
mouth of his holy prophets from of old.
22 Moses said, 'The Lord God will
raise up for you a prophet from your
brethren as he raised me up. You shall
listen to him in whatever he tells you.
23 And it shall be that every soul that
does not listen to that prophet shall be
destroyed from the people.' 24 And all
the prophets who have spoken, from
Samuel and those who came afterwards, also proclaimed these days.
25 You are the sons of the prophets
and of the covenant which God gave
to your fathers, saying to Abraham,
'And in your posterity shall all the
families of the earth be blessed.'
26 God, having raised up his servant,[c]
sent him to you first, to bless you in
turning every one of you from your
wickedness."

4 And as they were speaking to the
people, the priests and the captain
of the temple and the Sad'dū·ceeṡ
came upon them, 2 annoyed because
they were teaching the people and
proclaiming in Jesus the resurrection
from the dead. 3 And they arrested
them and put them in custody until
the morrow, for it was already evening.
4 But many of those who heard the
word believed; and the number of the
men came to about five thousand.

5 On the morrow their rulers and
elders and scribes were gathered together in Jerusalem, 6 with An'nas the
high priest and Cā'iȧ·phȧs and John
and Alexander, and all who were of
the high-priestly family. 7 And when
they had set them in the midst, they
inquired, "By what power or by what
name did you do this?" 8 Then Peter,
filled with the Holy Spirit, said to
them, "Rulers of the people and elders,
9 if we are being examined today concerning a good deed done to a cripple,
by what means this man has been
healed, 10 be it known to you all, and
to all the people of Israel, that by the
name of Jesus Christ of Nazareth,
whom you crucified, whom God raised
from the dead, by him this man is
standing before you well. 11 This is
the stone which was rejected by you
builders, but which has become the
head of the corner. 12 And there is
salvation in no one else, for there is no
other name under heaven given among
men by which we must be saved."

13 Now when they saw the boldness
of Peter and John, and perceived that
they were uneducated, common men,
they wondered; and they recognized
that they had been with Jesus. 14 But
seeing the man that had been healed
standing beside them, they had
nothing to say in opposition. 15 But
when they had commanded them to
go aside out of the council, they conferred with one another, 16 saying,
"What shall we do with these men?
For that a notable sign has been
performed through them is manifest
to all the inhabitants of Jerusalem, and
we cannot deny it. 17 But in order that
it may spread no further among the
people, let us warn them to speak no
more to any one in this name." 18 So
they called them and charged them
not to speak or teach at all in the name
of Jesus. 19 But Peter and John answered them, "Whether it is right in
the sight of God to listen to you rather
than to God, you must judge; 20 for
we cannot but speak of what we have
seen and heard." 21 And when they had
further threatened them, they let them
go, finding no way to punish them,
because of the people; for all men
praised God for what had happened.
22 For the man on whom this sign of
healing was performed was more than
forty years old.

23 When they were released they
went to their friends and reported
what the chief priests and the elders
had said to them. 24 And when they
heard it, they lifted their voices together to God and said, "Sovereign
Lord, who didst make the heaven and
the earth and the sea and everything
in them, 25 who by the mouth of our
father David, thy servant,[c] didst say
by the Holy Spirit,

'Why did the Gentiles rage,

[c] Or *child*

3.22: Deut 18.15-16. **3.23:** Deut 18.19; Lev 23.29. **3.25:** Gen 22.18. **4.11:** Ps 118.22.
4.24: Ex 20.11; Ps 146.6. **4.25-26:** Ps 2.1-2.

and the peoples imagine vain things?
26 The kings of the earth set themselves in array,
and the rulers were gathered together,
against the Lord and against his
Anointed'—[e]
27 for truly in this city there were
gathered together against thy holy servant[c] Jesus, whom thou didst anoint,
both Her′ȯd and Pontius Pilate, with
the Gentiles and the peoples of Israel,
28 to do whatever thy hand and thy
plan had predestined to take place.
29 And now, Lord, look upon their
threats, and grant to thy servants[f] to
speak thy word with all boldness,
30 while thou stretchest out thy hand
to heal, and signs and wonders are
performed through the name of thy
holy servant[c] Jesus." 31 And when they
had prayed, the place in which they
were gathered together was shaken;
and they were all filled with the Holy
Spirit and spoke the word of God with
boldness.

32 Now the company of those who
believed were of one heart and soul,
and no one said that any of the things
which he possessed was his own, but
they had everything in common.
33 And with great power the apostles
gave their testimony to the resurrection of the Lord Jesus, and great grace
was upon them all. 34 There was not
a needy person among them, for as
many as were possessors of lands or
houses sold them, and brought the
proceeds of what was sold 35 and laid
it at the apostles' feet; and distribution
was made to each as any had need.
36 Thus Joseph who was surnamed by
the apostles Bär′nȧ·bȧs (which means,
Son of encouragement), a Levite, a
native of Cyprus, 37 sold a field which
belonged to him, and brought the
money and laid it at the apostles' feet.

5 But a man named An·ȧ·nī′ȧs with
his wife Sap·phī′rȧ sold a piece of
property, 2 and with his wife's knowledge he kept back some of the proceeds, and brought only a part and
laid it at the apostles' feet. 3 But Peter
said, "An·ȧ·nī′ȧs, why has Satan filled
your heart to lie to the Holy Spirit and
to keep back part of the proceeds of
the land? 4 While it remained unsold,
did it not remain your own? And after
it was sold, was it not at your disposal?
How is it that you have contrived this
deed in your heart? You have not lied
to men but to God." 5 When An·ȧ·nī′ȧs
heard these words, he fell down and
died. And great fear came upon all
who heard of it. 6 The young men
rose and wrapped him up and carried
him out and buried him.

7 After an interval of about three
hours his wife came in, not knowing
what had happened. 8 And Peter said
to her, "Tell me whether you sold the
land for so much." And she said, "Yes,
for so much." 9 But Peter said to her,
"How is it that you have agreed together to tempt the Spirit of the Lord?
Hark, the feet of those that have buried
your husband are at the door, and they
will carry you out." 10 Immediately
she fell down at his feet and died.
When the young men came in they
found her dead, and they carried her
out and buried her beside her husband. 11 And great fear came upon the
whole church, and upon all who
heard of these things.

12 Now many signs and wonders
were done among the people by the
hands of the apostles. And they were
all together in Solomon's Portico.
13 None of the rest dared join them,
but the people held them in high
honor. 14 And more than ever believers were added to the Lord, multitudes both of men and women, 15 so
that they even carried out the sick into
the streets, and laid them on beds and
pallets, that as Peter came by at least
his shadow might fall on some of them.
16 The people also gathered from the
towns around Jerusalem, bringing the
sick and those afflicted with unclean
spirits, and they were all healed.

17 But the high priest rose up and
all who were with him, that is, the
party of the Sad′dū·cees, and filled
with jealousy 18 they arrested the
apostles and put them in the common
prison. 19 But at night an angel of the
Lord opened the prison doors and
brought them out and said, 20 "Go
and stand in the temple and speak to
the people all the words of this Life."
21 And when they heard this, they
entered the temple at daybreak and
taught.

Now the high priest came and those
who were with him and called together
the council and all the senate of Israel,

[e] Or *Christ* [c] Or *child* [f] Or *slaves*
4.27: Ps 2.2; 2.1. **4.32-35:** Acts 2.44-45.

and sent to the prison to have them
brought. 22 But when the officers came,
they did not find them in the prison,
and they returned and reported,
23 "We found the prison securely
locked and the sentries standing at the
doors, but when we opened it we
found no one inside." 24 Now when
the captain of the temple and the chief
priests heard these words, they were
much perplexed about them, wondering what this would come to. 25And
some one came and told them, "The
men whom you put in prison are
standing in the temple and teaching
the people." 26 Then the captain with
the officers went and brought them,
but without violence, for they were
afraid of being stoned by the people.

27 And when they had brought
them, they set them before the council.
And the high priest questioned them,
28 saying, "We strictly charged you
not to teach in this name, yet here you
have filled Jerusalem with your teaching and you intend to bring this man's
blood upon us." 29 But Peter and the
apostles answered, "We must obey
God rather than men. 30 The God of
our fathers raised Jesus whom you
killed by hanging him on a tree. 31 God
exalted him at his right hand as Leader
and Savior, to give repentance to
Israel and forgiveness of sins. 32And
we are witnesses to these things, and
so is the Holy Spirit whom God has
given to those who obey him."

33 When they heard this they were
enraged and wanted to kill them. 34 But
a Pharisee in the council named Gȧ-
mā'li·ėl, a teacher of the law, held in
honor by all the people, stood up and
ordered the men to be put outside for
a while. 35And he said to them, "Men
of Israel, take care what you do with
these men. 36 For before these days
Theū'dȧs arose, giving himself out to
be somebody, and a number of men,
about four hundred, joined him; but
he was slain and all who followed him
were dispersed and came to nothing.
37After him Judas the Galilean arose
in the days of the census and drew
away some of the people after him; he
also perished, and all who followed
him were scattered. 38 So in the
present case I tell you, keep away from
these men and let them alone; for if
this plan or this undertaking is of men,
it will fail; 39 but if it is of God, you
will not be able to overthrow them.
You might even be found opposing
God!"

40 So they took his advice, and
when they had called in the apostles,
they beat them and charged them not
to speak in the name of Jesus, and let
them go. 41 Then they left the presence of the council, rejoicing that they
were counted worthy to suffer dishonor
for the name. 42And every day in the
temple and at home they did not
cease teaching and preaching Jesus as
the Christ.

6 Now in these days when the disciples were increasing in number,
the Hellenists murmured against the
Hebrews because their widows were
neglected in the daily distribution.
2And the twelve summoned the body
of the disciples and said, "It is not
right that we should give up preaching
the word of God to serve tables.
3 Therefore, brethren, pick out from
among you seven men of good repute,
full of the Spirit and of wisdom, whom
we may appoint to this duty. 4 But we
will devote ourselves to prayer and to
the ministry of the word." 5And what
they said pleased the whole multitude,
and they chose Stephen, a man full of
faith and of the Holy Spirit, and Philip,
and Proch'ȯ·rŭs, and Nī·cā'nŏr, and
Tī'mŏn, and Pär'mė·nas, and Nic·ȯ-
lā'ŭs, a proselyte of An'ti·och. 6 These
they set before the apostles, and they
prayed and laid their hands upon
them.

7 And the word of God increased;
and the number of the disciples multiplied greatly in Jerusalem, and a
great many of the priests were obedient
to the faith.

8 And Stephen, full of grace and
power, did great wonders and signs
among the people. 9 Then some of
those who belonged to the synagogue
of the Freedmen (as it was called), and
of the Cȳ·rē'ni·ȧnṡ, and of the Alexan-
drians, and of those from Ci·li'ci·ȧ and
Asia, arose and disputed with Stephen.
10 But they could not withstand the
wisdom and the Spirit with which he
spoke. 11 Then they secretly instigated
men, who said, "We have heard him
speak blasphemous words against
Moses and God." 12And they stirred
up the people and the elders and the
scribes, and they came upon him and

5.30: Deut 21.22-23.

seized him and brought him before the
council, 13 and set up false witnesses
who said, "This man never ceases to
speak words against this holy place and
the law; 14 for we have heard him say
that this Jesus of Nazareth will destroy
this place, and will change the customs
which Moses delivered to us." 15And
gazing at him, all who sat in the
council saw that his face was like the
face of an angel.

7 And the high priest said, "Is this
so?" 2And Stephen said:
"Brethren and fathers, hear me. The
God of glory appeared to our father
Abraham, when he was in Mes·ȯ·pȯ-
tā'mi·ȧ, before he lived in Hâr'ȧn,
3 and said to him, 'Depart from your
land and from your kindred and go
into the land which I will show you.'
4 Then he departed from the land of
the Chal·dē'ȧnṡ, and lived in Hâr'ȧn.
And after his father died, God removed him from there into this land
in which you are now living; 5 yet he
gave him no inheritance in it, not even
a foot's length, but promised to give
it to him in possession and to his
posterity after him, though he had no
child. 6And God spoke to this effect,
that his posterity would be aliens in a
land belonging to others, who would
enslave them and ill-treat them four
hundred years. 7 'But I will judge the
nation which they serve,' said God,
'and after that they shall come out and
worship me in this place.' 8And he
gave him the covenant of circumcision. And so Abraham became the
father of Isaac, and circumcised him
on the eighth day; and Isaac became
the father of Jacob, and Jacob of the
twelve patriarchs.

9 "And the patriarchs, jealous of
Joseph, sold him into Egypt; but God
was with him, 10 and rescued him out
of all his afflictions, and gave him
favor and wisdom before Pharaoh,
king of Egypt, who made him governor
over Egypt and over all his household.
11 Now there came a famine throughout all Egypt and Canaan, and great
affliction, and our fathers could find
no food. 12 But when Jacob heard that
there was grain in Egypt, he sent forth
our fathers the first time. 13And at the
second visit Joseph made himself
known to his brothers, and Joseph's
family became known to Pharaoh.
14And Joseph sent and called to him
Jacob his father and all his kindred,
seventy-five souls; 15 and Jacob went
down into Egypt. And he died, himself and our fathers, 16 and they were
carried back to Shē'chem and laid in
the tomb that Abraham had bought
for a sum of silver from the sons of
Hā'mor in Shechem.

17 "But as the time of the promise
drew near, which God had granted to
Abraham, the people grew and multiplied in Egypt 18 till there arose over
Egypt another king who had not
known Joseph. 19 He dealt craftily
with our race and forced our fathers to
expose their infants, that they might
not be kept alive. 20At this time Moses
was born, and was beautiful before
God. And he was brought up for three
months in his father's house; 21 and
when he was exposed, Pharaoh's
daughter adopted him and brought
him up as her own son. 22And Moses
was instructed in all the wisdom of the
Egyptians, and he was mighty in his
words and deeds.

23 "When he was forty years old,
it came into his heart to visit his
brethren, the sons of Israel. 24And seeing one of them being wronged, he
defended the oppressed man and
avenged him by striking the Egyptian.
25 He supposed that his brethren
understood that God was giving them
deliverance by his hand, but they did
not understand. 26And on the following day he appeared to them as they
were quarreling and would have reconciled them, saying, 'Men, you are
brethren, why do you wrong each
other?' 27 But the man who was
wronging his neighbor thrust him
aside, saying, 'Who made you a ruler
and a judge over us? 28 Do you want
to kill me as you killed the Egyptian
yesterday?' 29At this retort Moses fled,
and became an exile in the land of
Mid'i·ȧn, where he became the father
of two sons.

30 "Now when forty years had

7.2: Ps 29.3; Gen 11.31; 15.7. **7.3:** Gen 12.1. **7.4:** Gen 11.31; 15.7; 12.5.
7.5: Deut 2.5; Gen 12.7; 17.8. **7.6-7:** Gen 15.13-14. **7.7:** Ex 3.12.
7.8: Gen 17.10-14; 21.2-4; 25.26; 29.31-35; 30.1-24; 35.16-18, 23-26. **7.9:** Gen 37.11, 28; 45.4.
7.9-10: Gen 39.2-3, 21. **7.10:** Gen 41.40-46; Ps 105.21. **7.11:** Gen 41.54-55; 42.5. **7.12:** Gen 42.2.
7.13: Gen 45.1-4. **7.14:** Gen 45.9-10. **7.14-15:** Deut 10.22. **7.16:** Josh 24.32; Gen 50.13.
7.17-18: Ex 1.7-8. **7.19:** Ex 1.10-11, 15-22. **7.20:** Ex 2.2. **7.21:** Ex 2.5-6, 10. **7.23-29:** Ex 2.11-15.
7.29: Ex 2.22; 18.3-4. **7.30-34:** Ex 3.1-10.

passed, an angel appeared to him in
the wilderness of Mount Sinai, in a
flame of fire in a bush. 31 When Moses
saw it he wondered at the sight; and as
he drew near to look, the voice of the
Lord came, 32 'I am the God of your
fathers, the God of Abraham and of
Isaac and of Jacob.' And Moses
trembled and did not dare to look.
33 And the Lord said to him, 'Take off
the shoes from your feet, for the place
where you are standing is holy ground.
34 I have surely seen the ill-treatment
of my people that are in Egypt and
heard their groaning, and I have come
down to deliver them. And now come,
I will send you to Egypt.'

35 "This Moses whom they refused, saying, 'Who made you a ruler
and a judge?' God sent as both ruler
and deliverer by the hand of the angel
that appeared to him in the bush.
36 He led them out, having performed
wonders and signs in Egypt and at the
Red Sea, and in the wilderness for
forty years. 37 This is the Moses who
said to the Israelites, 'God will raise
up for you a prophet from your
brethren as he raised me up.' 38 This
is he who was in the congregation in
the wilderness with the angel who
spoke to him at Mount Sinai, and with
our fathers; and he received living
oracles to give to us. 39 Our fathers
refused to obey him, but thrust him
aside, and in their hearts they turned
to Egypt, 40 saying to Aaron, 'Make
for us gods to go before us; as for this
Moses who led us out from the land
of Egypt, we do not know what has
become of him.' 41 And they made a
calf in those days, and offered a
sacrifice to the idol and rejoiced in the
works of their hands. 42 But God
turned and gave them over to worship
the host of heaven, as it is written in
the book of the prophets:

'Did you offer to me slain beasts
and sacrifices,
forty years in the wilderness, O
house of Israel?
43 And you took up the tent of Mō'loch,
and the star of the god Rē'phăn,
the figures which you made to
worship;
and I will remove you beyond
Babylon.'

44 "Our fathers had the tent of
witness in the wilderness, even as he
who spoke to Moses directed him to
make it, according to the pattern that
he had seen. 45 Our fathers in turn
brought it in with Joshua when they
dispossessed the nations which God
thrust out before our fathers. So it was
until the days of David, 46 who found
favor in the sight of God and asked
leave to find a habitation for the God
of Jacob. 47 But it was Solomon who
built a house for him. 48 Yet the Most
High does not dwell in houses made
with hands; as the prophet says,
49 'Heaven is my throne,
and earth my footstool.
What house will you build for me,
says the Lord,
or what is the place of my rest?
50 Did not my hand make all these
things?'

51 "You stiff-necked people, uncircumcised in heart and ears, you
always resist the Holy Spirit. As your
fathers did, so do you. 52 Which of the
prophets did not your fathers persecute? And they killed those who
announced beforehand the coming of
the Righteous One, whom you have
now betrayed and murdered, 53 you
who received the law as delivered by
angels and did not keep it."

54 Now when they heard these
things they were enraged, and they
ground their teeth against him. 55 But
he, full of the Holy Spirit, gazed into
heaven and saw the glory of God, and
Jesus standing at the right hand of
God; 56 and he said, "Behold, I see
the heavens opened, and the Son of
man standing at the right hand of
God." 57 But they cried out with a
loud voice and stopped their ears and
rushed together upon him. 58 Then
they cast him out of the city and
stoned him; and the witnesses laid
down their garments at the feet of a
young man named Saul. 59 And as they
were stoning Stephen, he prayed,
"Lord Jesus, receive my spirit."
60 And he knelt down and cried with a
loud voice, "Lord, do not hold this
sin against them." And when he had
said this, he fell asleep. 1 And Saul
8 was consenting to his death.
And on that day a great persecution

7.35: Ex 2.14. 7.36: Ex 7.3; 14.21; Num 14.33. 7.37: Deut 18.15, 18. 7.38: Ex 19.
7.39: Num 14.3-4. 7.40: Ex 32.1, 23. 7.41: Ex 32.4, 6. 7.42: Jer 19.13. 7.42-43: Amos 5.25-27.
7.44: Ex 25.9, 40. 7.45: Josh 3.14-17; Deut 32.49. 7.46: 2 Sam 7.8-16; Ps 132.1-5. 7.47: 1 Kings 6.
7.49-50: Is 66.1-2. 7.51: Ex 33.3, 5; Jer 9.26; 6.10; Num 27.14; Is 63.10. 8.1: Acts 11.19.

arose against the church in Jerusalem;
and they were all scattered throughout
the region of Judea and Sȧ·mâr'i·ȧ,
except the apostles. 2 Devout men
buried Stephen, and made great lamentation over him. 3 But Saul laid
waste the church, and entering house
after house, he dragged off men
and women and committed them to
prison.

4 Now those who were scattered
went about preaching the word.
5 Philip went down to a city of Sȧ-
mâr'i·ȧ, and proclaimed to them the
Christ. 6 And the multitudes with one
accord gave heed to what was said by
Philip, when they heard him and saw
the signs which he did. 7 For unclean
spirits came out of many who were
possessed, crying with a loud voice;
and many who were paralyzed or lame
were healed. 8 So there was much joy
in that city.

9 But there was a man named
Simon who had previously practiced
magic in the city and amazed the
nation of Sȧ·mâr'i·ȧ, saying that he
himself was somebody great. 10 They
all gave heed to him, from the least to
the greatest, saying, "This man is that
power of God which is called Great."
11 And they gave heed to him, because
for a long time he had amazed them
with his magic. 12 But when they believed Philip as he preached good news
about the kingdom of God and the
name of Jesus Christ, they were baptized, both men and women. 13 Even
Simon himself believed, and after being baptized he continued with Philip.
And seeing signs and great miracles
performed, he was amazed.

14 Now when the apostles at Jerusalem heard that Sȧ·mâr'i·ȧ had received the word of God, they sent to
them Peter and John, 15 who came
down and prayed for them that they
might receive the Holy Spirit; 16 for
it had not yet fallen on any of them,
but they had only been baptized in the
name of the Lord Jesus. 17 Then they
laid their hands on them and they
received the Holy Spirit. 18 Now when
Simon saw that the Spirit was given
through the laying on of the apostles'
hands, he offered them money, 19 saying, "Give me also this power, that
any one on whom I lay my hands may
receive the Holy Spirit." 20 But Peter
said to him, "Your silver perish with
you, because you thought you could
obtain the gift of God with money!
21 You have neither part nor lot in this
matter, for your heart is not right before God. 22 Repent therefore of this
wickedness of yours, and pray to the
Lord that, if possible, the intent of
your heart may be forgiven you. 23 For
I see that you are in the gall of bitterness and in the bond of iniquity."
24 And Simon answered, "Pray for me
to the Lord, that nothing of what you
have said may come upon me."

25 Now when they had testified and
spoken the word of the Lord, they
returned to Jerusalem, preaching the
gospel to many villages of the Samaritans.

26 But an angel of the Lord said to
Philip, "Rise and go toward the south[g]
to the road that goes down from Jerusalem to Gā'zȧ." This is a desert road.
27 And he rose and went. And behold,
an Ethiopian, a eunuch, a minister of
Can·dā'ċē the queen of the Ethiopians,
in charge of all her treasure, had come
to Jerusalem to worship 28 and was returning; seated in his chariot, he was
reading the prophet Ī·ṡāi'ȧh. 29 And the
Spirit said to Philip, "Go up and join
this chariot." 30 So Philip ran to him,
and heard him reading Ī·ṡāi'ȧh the
prophet, and asked, "Do you understand what you are reading?" 31 And he
said, "How can I, unless some one
guides me?" And he invited Philip to
come up and sit with him. 32 Now the
passage of the scripture which he was
reading was this:

"As a sheep led to the slaughter
or a lamb before its shearer is dumb,
so he opens not his mouth.
33 In his humiliation justice was denied
him.
Who can describe his generation?
For his life is taken up from the
earth."

34 And the eunuch said to Philip,
"About whom, pray, does the prophet
say this, about himself or about some
one else?" 35 Then Philip opened his
mouth, and beginning with this scripture he told him the good news of
Jesus. 36 And as they went along the
road they came to some water, and the
eunuch said, "See, here is water! What

[g] Or *at noon*

8.21: Ps 78.37. **8.23:** Is 58.6.
8.32-33: Is 53.7-8.

is to prevent my being baptized?"[h] 38 And he commanded the chariot to stop, and they both went down into the water, Philip and the eunuch, and he baptized him. 39 And when they came up out of the water, the Spirit of the Lord caught up Philip; and the eunuch saw him no more, and went on his way rejoicing. 40 But Philip was found at Ȧ·zō'tŭs, and passing on he preached the gospel to all the towns till he came to Caes·ȧ·rē'ȧ.

9 But Saul, still breathing threats and murder against the disciples of the Lord, went to the high priest 2 and asked him for letters to the synagogues at Damascus, so that if he found any belonging to the Way, men or women, he might bring them bound to Jerusalem. 3 Now as he journeyed he approached Damascus, and suddenly a light from heaven flashed about him. 4 And he fell to the ground and heard a voice saying to him, "Saul, Saul, why do you persecute me?" 5 And he said, "Who are you, Lord?" And he said, "I am Jesus, whom you are persecuting; 6 but rise and enter the city, and you will be told what you are to do." 7 The men who were traveling with him stood speechless, hearing the voice but seeing no one. 8 Saul arose from the ground; and when his eyes were opened, he could see nothing; so they led him by the hand and brought him into Damascus. 9 And for three days he was without sight, and neither ate nor drank.

10 Now there was a disciple at Damascus named An·ȧ·nī'ȧs. The Lord said to him in a vision, "Ananias." And he said, "Here I am, Lord." 11 And the Lord said to him, "Rise and go to the street called Straight, and inquire in the house of Judas for a man of Tär'sŭs named Saul; for behold, he is praying, 12 and he has seen a man named An·ȧ·nī'ȧs come in and lay his hands on him so that he might regain his sight." 13 But An·ȧ·nī'ȧs answered, "Lord, I have heard from many about this man, how much evil he has done to thy saints at Jerusalem; 14 and here he has authority from the chief priests to bind all who call upon thy name." 15 But the Lord said to him, "Go, for he is a chosen instrument of mine to carry my name before the Gentiles and kings and the sons of Israel; 16 for I will show him how much he must suffer for the sake of my name." 17 So An·ȧ·nī'ȧs departed and entered the house. And laying his hands on him he said, "Brother Saul, the Lord Jesus who appeared to you on the road by which you came, has sent me that you may regain your sight and be filled with the Holy Spirit." 18 And immediately something like scales fell from his eyes and he regained his sight. Then he rose and was baptized, 19 and took food and was strengthened.

For several days he was with the disciples at Damascus. 20 And in the synagogues immediately he proclaimed Jesus, saying, "He is the Son of God." 21 And all who heard him were amazed, and said, "Is not this the man who made havoc in Jerusalem of those who called on this name? And he has come here for this purpose, to bring them bound before the chief priests." 22 But Saul increased all the more in strength, and confounded the Jews who lived in Damascus by proving that Jesus was the Christ.

23 When many days had passed, the Jews plotted to kill him, 24 but their plot became known to Saul. They were watching the gates day and night, to kill him; 25 but his disciples took him by night and let him down over the wall, lowering him in a basket.

26 And when he had come to Jerusalem he attempted to join the disciples; and they were all afraid of him, for they did not believe that he was a disciple. 27 But Bär'nȧ·bȧs took him, and brought him to the apostles, and declared to them how on the road he had seen the Lord, who spoke to him, and how at Damascus he had preached boldly in the name of Jesus. 28 So he went in and out among them at Jerusalem, 29 preaching boldly in the name of the Lord. And he spoke and disputed against the Hellenists; but they were seeking to kill him. 30 And when the brethren knew it, they brought him down to Caes·ȧ·rē'ȧ, and sent him off to Tär'sŭs.

31 So the church throughout all Judea and Galilee and Sȧ·mâr'i·ȧ had peace and was built up; and walking in the fear of the Lord and in the com-

[h] Other ancient authorities add all or most of verse 37, *And Philip said, "If you believe with all your heart, you may." And he replied, "I believe that Jesus Christ is the Son of God."*

9.1-19: Acts 22.4-16; 26.9-18. **9.24-25:** 2 Cor 11.32-33.

fort of the Holy Spirit it was multiplied.

32 Now as Peter went here and
there among them all, he came down
also to the saints that lived at Lyd'dȧ.
33 There he found a man named Aē-
nē'ȧs, who had been bedridden for
eight years and was paralyzed. 34 And
Peter said to him, "Aē·nē'ȧs, Jesus
Christ heals you; rise and make your
bed." And immediately he rose. 35 And
all the residents of Lyd'dȧ and Sharon
saw him, and they turned to the Lord.
36 Now there was at Jop'pȧ a disciple named Tab'i·thȧ, which means
Dôr'cȧs or Gȧ·zelle'. She was full of
good works and acts of charity. 37 In
those days she fell sick and died; and
when they had washed her, they laid
her in an upper room. 38 Since Lyd'dȧ
was near Jop'pȧ, the disciples, hearing
that Peter was there, sent two men to
him entreating him, "Please come to
us without delay." 39 So Peter rose
and went with them. And when he had
come, they took him to the upper
room. All the widows stood beside him
weeping, and showing coats and garments which Dôr'cȧs made while she
was with them. 40 But Peter put them
all outside and knelt down and prayed;
then turning to the body he said,
"Tab'i·thȧ, rise." And she opened her
eyes, and when she saw Peter she sat
up. 41 And he gave her his hand and
lifted her up. Then calling the saints
and widows he presented her alive.
42 And it became known throughout all
Jop'pȧ, and many believed in the Lord.
43 And he stayed in Jop'pȧ for many
days with one Simon, a tanner.

10 At Caes·ȧ·rē'ȧ there was a man
named Cornelius, a centurion of
what was known as the Italian Cohort,
2 a devout man who feared God with
all his household, gave alms liberally
to the people, and prayed constantly
to God. 3 About the ninth hour of the
day he saw clearly in a vision an angel
of God coming in and saying to him,
"Cornelius." 4 And he stared at him in
terror, and said, "What is it, Lord?"
And he said to him, "Your prayers and
your alms have ascended as a memorial
before God. 5 And now send men to
Jop'pȧ, and bring one Simon who is
called Peter; 6 he is lodging with
Simon, a tanner, whose house is by
the seaside." 7 When the angel who
spoke to him had departed, he called
two of his servants and a devout
soldier from among those that waited
on him, 8 and having related everything to them, he sent them to Jop'pȧ.
9 The next day, as they were on
their journey and coming near the city,
Peter went up on the housetop to pray,
about the sixth hour. 10 And he became
hungry and desired something to eat;
but while they were preparing it, he
fell into a trance 11 and saw the heaven
opened, and something descending,
like a great sheet, let down by four
corners upon the earth. 12 In it were
all kinds of animals and reptiles and
birds of the air. 13 And there came a
voice to him, "Rise, Peter; kill and
eat." 14 But Peter said, "No, Lord; for
I have never eaten anything that is
common or unclean." 15 And the voice
came to him again a second time,
"What God has cleansed, you must not
call common." 16 This happened three
times, and the thing was taken up at
once to heaven.
17 Now while Peter was inwardly
perplexed as to what the vision which
he had seen might mean, behold, the
men that were sent by Cornelius,
having made inquiry for Simon's
house, stood before the gate 18 and
called out to ask whether Simon who
was called Peter was lodging there.
19 And while Peter was pondering the
vision, the Spirit said to him, "Behold,
three men are looking for you. 20 Rise
and go down, and accompany them
without hesitation; for I have sent
them." 21 And Peter went down to the
men and said, "I am the one you are
looking for; what is the reason for
your coming?" 22 And they said,
"Cornelius, a centurion, an upright
and God-fearing man, who is well
spoken of by the whole Jewish nation,
was directed by a holy angel to send
for you to come to his house, and to
hear what you have to say." 23 So he
called them in to be his guests.
The next day he rose and went off
with them, and some of the brethren
from Jop'pȧ accompanied him. 24 And
on the following day they entered
Caes·ȧ·rē'ȧ. Cornelius was expecting
them and had called together his kinsmen and close friends. 25 When Peter
entered, Cornelius met him and fell
down at his feet and worshiped him.
26 But Peter lifted him up, saying,

10.1-48: Acts 11.4-17.

"Stand up; I too am a man." 27 And as
he talked with him, he went in and
found many persons gathered; 28 and
he said to them, "You yourselves
know how unlawful it is for a Jew to
associate with or to visit any one of
another nation, but God has shown me
that I should not call any man common or unclean. 29 So when I was sent
for, I came without objection. I ask
then why you sent for me."

30 And Cornelius said, "Four days
ago, about this hour, I was keeping the
ninth hour of prayer in my house; and
behold, a man stood before me in
bright apparel, 31 saying, 'Cornelius,
your prayer has been heard and your
alms have been remembered before
God. 32 Send therefore to Jop'pȧ and
ask for Simon who is called Peter; he
is lodging in the house of Simon, a
tanner, by the seaside.' 33 So I sent to
you at once, and you have been kind
enough to come. Now therefore we are
all here present in the sight of God,
to hear all that you have been commanded by the Lord."

34 And Peter opened his mouth and
said: "Truly I perceive that God shows
no partiality, 35 but in every nation
any one who fears him and does what
is right is acceptable to him. 36 You
know the word which he sent to
Israel, preaching good news of peace
by Jesus Christ (he is Lord of all),
37 the word which was proclaimed
throughout all Judea, beginning from
Galilee after the baptism which John
preached: 38 how God anointed Jesus
of Nazareth with the Holy Spirit and
with power; how he went about doing
good and healing all that were oppressed by the devil, for God was with
him. 39 And we are witnesses to all that
he did both in the country of the Jews
and in Jerusalem. They put him to
death by hanging him on a tree; 40 but
God raised him on the third day and
made him manifest; 41 not to all the
people but to us who were chosen by
God as witnesses, who ate and drank
with him after he rose from the dead.
42 And he commanded us to preach to
the people, and to testify that he is the
one ordained by God to be judge of
the living and the dead. 43 To him all
the prophets bear witness that every
one who believes in him receives forgiveness of sins through his name."

44 While Peter was still saying this,
the Holy Spirit fell on all who heard
the word. 45 And the believers from
among the circumcised who came with
Peter were amazed, because the gift of
the Holy Spirit had been poured out
even on the Gentiles. 46 For they heard
them speaking in tongues and extolling
God. Then Peter declared, 47 "Can
any one forbid water for baptizing
these people who have received the
Holy Spirit just as we have?" 48 And
he commanded them to be baptized in
the name of Jesus Christ. Then
they asked him to remain for some
days.

11 Now the apostles and the
brethren who were in Judea heard
that the Gentiles also had received the
word of God. 2 So when Peter went up
to Jerusalem, the circumcision party
criticized him, 3 saying, "Why did you
go to uncircumcised men and eat with
them?" 4 But Peter began and explained to them in order: 5 "I was in
the city of Jop'pȧ praying; and in a
trance I saw a vision, something
descending, like a great sheet, let down
from heaven by four corners; and it
came down to me. 6 Looking at it
closely I observed animals and beasts
of prey and reptiles and birds of the
air. 7 And I heard a voice saying to me,
'Rise, Peter; kill and eat.' 8 But I said,
'No, Lord; for nothing common or unclean has ever entered my mouth.'
9 But the voice answered a second time
from heaven, 'What God has cleansed
you must not call common.' 10 This
happened three times, and all was
drawn up again into heaven. 11 At that
very moment three men arrived at the
house in which we were, sent to me
from Caes·ȧ·rē'ȧ. 12 And the Spirit told
me to go with them, making no distinction. These six brethren also accompanied me, and we entered the man's
house. 13 And he told us how he had
seen the angel standing in his house
and saying, 'Send to Jop'pȧ and bring
Simon called Peter; 14 he will declare
to you a message by which you will be
saved, you and all your household.'
15 As I began to speak, the Holy Spirit
fell on them just as on us at the beginning. 16 And I remembered the word
of the Lord, how he said, 'John baptized with water, but you shall be
baptized with the Holy Spirit.' 17 If
then God gave the same gift to them
as he gave to us when we believed in

11.4-17: Acts 10.1-48. **11.16:** Acts 1.5.

the Lord Jesus Christ, who was I that
I could withstand God?" 18 When they
heard this they were silenced. And
they glorified God, saying, "Then to
the Gentiles also God has granted
repentance unto life."
19 Now those who were scattered
because of the persecution that arose
over Stephen traveled as far as Phoė-
ni'ċi·ȧ and Cyprus and An'ti·och,
speaking the word to none except
Jews. 20 But there were some of them,
men of Cyprus and Ċȳ·rē'nē, who on
coming to An'ti·och spoke to the
Greeks[i] also, preaching the Lord
Jesus. 21 And the hand of the Lord was
with them, and a great number that
believed turned to the Lord. 22 News
of this came to the ears of the church
in Jerusalem, and they sent Bär'nȧ·bȧs
to An'ti·och. 23 When he came and
saw the grace of God, he was glad; and
he exhorted them all to remain faithful
to the Lord with steadfast purpose;
24 for he was a good man, full of the
Holy Spirit and of faith. And a large
company was added to the Lord. 25 So
Bär'nȧ·bȧs went to Tär'su̇s to look for
Saul; 26 and when he had found him,
he brought him to An'ti·och. For a
whole year they met with[j] the church,
and taught a large company of people;
and in Antioch the disciples were for
the first time called Christians.
27 Now in these days prophets
came down from Jerusalem to An'ti-
och. 28 And one of them named Ag'ȧ-
bu̇s stood up and foretold by the Spirit
that there would be a great famine over
all the world; and this took place in the
days of Claudius. 29 And the disciples
determined, every one according to his
ability, to send relief to the brethren
who lived in Judea; 30 and they did so,
sending it to the elders by the hand of
Bär'nȧ·bȧs and Saul.

12 About that time Her'ȯd the king
laid violent hands upon some who
belonged to the church. 2 He killed
James the brother of John with the
sword; 3 and when he saw that it
pleased the Jews, he proceeded to
arrest Peter also. This was during the
days of Unleavened Bread. 4 And when
he had seized him, he put him in
prison, and delivered him to four
squads of soldiers to guard him,
intending after the Passover to bring
him out to the people. 5 So Peter was
kept in prison; but earnest prayer for
him was made to God by the church.
6 The very night when Her'ȯd was
about to bring him out, Peter was
sleeping between two soldiers, bound
with two chains, and sentries before
the door were guarding the prison;
7 and behold, an angel of the Lord
appeared, and a light shone in the
cell; and he struck Peter on the side
and woke him, saying, "Get up
quickly." And the chains fell off his
hands. 8 And the angel said to him,
"Dress yourself and put on your
sandals." And he did so. And he said
to him, "Wrap your mantle around
you and follow me." 9 And he went out
and followed him; he did not know
that what was done by the angel was
real, but thought he was seeing a
vision. 10 When they had passed the
first and the second guard, they came
to the iron gate leading into the city.
It opened to them of its own accord,
and they went out and passed on
through one street; and immediately
the angel left him. 11 And Peter came
to himself, and said, "Now I am sure
that the Lord has sent his angel and
rescued me from the hand of Her'ȯd
and from all that the Jewish people
were expecting."
12 When he realized this, he went
to the house of Mary, the mother of
John whose other name was Mark,
where many were gathered together
and were praying. 13 And when he
knocked at the door of the gateway, a
maid named Rhō'dȧ came to answer.
14 Recognizing Peter's voice, in her
joy she did not open the gate but ran
in and told that Peter was standing at
the gate. 15 They said to her, "You are
mad." But she insisted that it was so.
They said, "It is his angel!" 16 But
Peter continued knocking; and when
they opened, they saw him and were
amazed. 17 But motioning to them
with his hand to be silent, he described
to them how the Lord had brought
him out of the prison. And he said,
"Tell this to James and to the brethren." Then he departed and went to
another place.
18 Now when day came, there was
no small stir among the soldiers over
what had become of Peter. 19 And
when Her'ȯd had sought for him and
could not find him, he examined the

[i] Other ancient authorities read *Hellenists* [j] Or *were guests of*
11.19: Acts 8.4.

sentries and ordered that they should
be put to death. Then he went down
from Judea to Caes·ȧ·rē'ȧ, and remained there.
20 Now Her'ȯd was angry with the
people of Tȳre and Sī'don; and they
came to him in a body, and having
persuaded Blas'tu̇s, the king's chamberlain, they asked for peace, because
their country depended on the king's
country for food. 21 On an appointed
day Her'ȯd put on his royal robes,
took his seat upon the throne, and
made an oration to them. 22 And the
people shouted, "The voice of a god,
and not of man!" 23 Immediately an
angel of the Lord smote him, because
he did not give God the glory; and he
was eaten by worms and died.
24 But the word of God grew and
multiplied.
25 And Bär'nȧ·bȧs and Saul returned from[k] Jerusalem when they
had fulfilled their mission, bringing
with them John whose other name was
Mark.

13 Now in the church at An'ti·och
there were prophets and teachers,
Bär'nȧ·bȧs, Sym'ē·ọn who was called
Nī'ġėr, Lucius of Cȳ·rē'nē, Man'ȧ-en
a member of the court of Her'ȯd the
tetrarch, and Saul. 2 While they were
worshiping the Lord and fasting, the
Holy Spirit said, "Set apart for me
Bär'nȧ·bȧs and Saul for the work to
which I have called them." 3 Then
after fasting and praying they laid their
hands on them and sent them off.
4 So, being sent out by the Holy
Spirit, they went down to Sė·leü'ċi·ȧ;
and from there they sailed to Cyprus.
5 When they arrived at Sal'ȧ·mis, they
proclaimed the word of God in the
synagogues of the Jews. And they had
John to assist them. 6 When they had
gone through the whole island as far
as Pā'phos, they came upon a certain
magician, a Jewish false prophet,
named Bär-Jē'șu̇s. 7 He was with the
proconsul, Sẽr'ġi·u̇s Päul'u̇s, a man of
intelligence, who summoned Bär'nȧ-
bȧs and Saul and sought to hear the
word of God. 8 But El'y·mȧs the
magician (for that is the meaning of
his name) withstood them, seeking to
turn away the proconsul from the
faith. 9 But Saul, who is also called
Paul, filled with the Holy Spirit,
looked intently at him 10 and said,
"You son of the devil, you enemy of
all righteousness, full of all deceit and
villainy, will you not stop making
crooked the straight paths of the Lord?
11 And now, behold, the hand of the
Lord is upon you, and you shall be
blind and unable to see the sun for a
time." Immediately mist and darkness
fell upon him and he went about seeking people to lead him by the hand.
12 Then the proconsul believed, when
he saw what had occurred, for he was
astonished at the teaching of the Lord.
13 Now Paul and his company set
sail from Pā'phos, and came to Pẽr'gȧ
in Pam·phyl'i·ȧ. And John left them
and returned to Jerusalem; 14 but they
passed on from Pẽr'gȧ and came to
An'ti·och of Pi·sid'i·ȧ. And on the
sabbath day they went into the synagogue and sat down. 15 After the reading of the law and the prophets, the
rulers of the synagogue sent to them,
saying, "Brethren, if you have any
word of exhortation for the people,
say it." 16 So Paul stood up, and
motioning with his hand said:
"Men of Israel, and you that fear
God, listen. 17 The God of this people
Israel chose our fathers and made the
people great during their stay in the
land of Egypt, and with uplifted arm
he led them out of it. 18 And for about
forty years he bore with[m] them in the
wilderness. 19 And when he had destroyed seven nations in the land of
Canaan, he gave them their land as an
inheritance, for about four hundred
and fifty years. 20 And after that he
gave them judges until Samuel the
prophet. 21 Then they asked for a
king; and God gave them Saul the son
of Kish, a man of the tribe of Benjamin, for forty years. 22 And when he
had removed him, he raised up David
to be their king; of whom he testified
and said, 'I have found in David the
son of Jesse a man after my heart, who
will do all my will.' 23 Of this man's
posterity God has brought to Israel a
Savior, Jesus, as he promised. 24 Before his coming John had preached a
baptism of repentance to all the people
of Israel. 25 And as John was finishing
his course, he said, 'What do you
suppose that I am? I am not he. No,

[k] Other ancient authorities read *to* [m] Other ancient authorities read *cared for* (Deut 1.31)
13.10: Hos 14.9. **13.17:** Ex 6.1, 6. **13.18:** Deut 1.31. **13.19:** Deut 7.1; Josh 14.1.
13.22: Ps 89.20; 1 Sam 13.14; Is 44.28. **13.24:** Mk 1.1-4. **13.25:** Jn 1.20; Mt 3.11; Mk 1.7; Lk 3.16.

but after me one is coming, the sandals
of whose feet I am not worthy to untie.'
26 "Brethren, sons of the family of
Abraham, and those among you that
fear God, to us has been sent the message of this salvation. 27 For those who
live in Jerusalem and their rulers, because they did not recognize him nor
understand the utterances of the
prophets which are read every sabbath,
fulfilled these by condemning him.
28 Though they could charge him with
nothing deserving death, yet they
asked Pilate to have him killed. 29 And
when they had fulfilled all that was
written of him, they took him down
from the tree, and laid him in a tomb.
30 But God raised him from the dead;
31 and for many days he appeared to
those who came up with him from
Galilee to Jerusalem, who are now his
witnesses to the people. 32 And we
bring you the good news that what
God promised to the fathers, 33 this
he has fulfilled to us their children by
raising Jesus; as also it is written in
the second psalm,

'Thou art my Son,
today I have begotten thee.'

34 And as for the fact that he raised him
from the dead, no more to return to
corruption, he spoke in this way,

'I will give you the holy and sure
blessings of David.'

35 Therefore he says also in another
psalm,

'Thou wilt not let thy Holy One see
corruption.'

36 For David, after he had served the
counsel of God in his own generation,
fell asleep, and was laid with his
fathers, and saw corruption; 37 but he
whom God raised up saw no corruption. 38 Let it be known to you therefore, brethren, that through this man
forgiveness of sins is proclaimed to
you, 39 and by him every one that
believes is freed from everything from
which you could not be freed by the
law of Moses. 40 Beware, therefore,
lest there come upon you what is said
in the prophets:

41 'Behold, you scoffers, and wonder,
and perish;
for I do a deed in your days,
a deed you will never believe, if one
declares it to you.'"

42 As they went out, the people
begged that these things might be told
them the next sabbath. 43 And when
the meeting of the synagogue broke
up, many Jews and devout converts
to Judaism followed Paul and Bär'nȧ-
bȧs, who spoke to them and urged
them to continue in the grace of God.

44 The next sabbath almost the
whole city gathered together to hear
the word of God. 45 But when the
Jews saw the multitudes, they were
filled with jealousy, and contradicted
what was spoken by Paul, and reviled
him. 46 And Paul and Bär'nȧ·bȧs spoke
out boldly, saying, "It was necessary
that the word of God should be spoken
first to you. Since you thrust it from
you, and judge yourselves unworthy
of eternal life, behold, we turn to the
Gentiles. 47 For so the Lord has commanded us, saying,

'I have set you to be a light for the
Gentiles,
that you may bring salvation to the
uttermost parts of the earth.'"

48 And when the Gentiles heard
this, they were glad and glorified the
word of God; and as many as were
ordained to eternal life believed.
49 And the word of the Lord spread
throughout all the region. 50 But the
Jews incited the devout women of
high standing and the leading men of
the city, and stirred up persecution
against Paul and Bär'nȧ·bȧs, and drove
them out of their district. 51 But they
shook off the dust from their feet
against them, and went to Ī·cō'ni·ŭm.
52 And the disciples were filled with joy
and with the Holy Spirit.

14 Now at Ī·cō'ni·ŭm they entered
together into the Jewish synagogue, and so spoke that a great company believed, both of Jews and of
Greeks. 2 But the unbelieving Jews
stirred up the Gentiles and poisoned
their minds against the brethren. 3 So
they remained for a long time, speaking
boldly for the Lord, who bore witness
to the word of his grace, granting signs
and wonders to be done by their hands.
4 But the people of the city were divided; some sided with the Jews, and
some with the apostles. 5 When an
attempt was made by both Gentiles
and Jews, with their rulers, to molest
them and to stone them, 6 they learned
of it and fled to Lys'trȧ and Dẽr'bē,
cities of Lyc·ā·ō'ni·ȧ, and to the surrounding country; 7 and there they
preached the gospel.

8 Now at Lys'trȧ there was a man

13.26: Ps 107.20. **13.33:** Ps 2.7. **13.34:** Is 55.3. **13.35:** Ps 16.10. **13.41:** Hab 1.5. **13.47:** Is 49.6.

sitting, who could not use his feet; he
was a cripple from birth, who had
never walked. 9 He listened to Paul
speaking; and Paul, looking intently
at him and seeing that he had faith to
be made well, 10 said in a loud voice,
"Stand upright on your feet." And he
sprang up and walked. 11And when
the crowds saw what Paul had done,
they lifted up their voices, saying in
Lyc·ā·ō'ni·ȧn, "The gods have come
down to us in the likeness of men!"
12 Bär'nȧ·bȧs they called Zeus, and
Paul, because he was the chief speaker,
they called Hẽr'mēṡ. 13And the priest
of Zeus, whose temple was in front of
the city, brought oxen and garlands to
the gates and wanted to offer sacrifice
with the people. 14 But when the
apostles Bär'nȧ·bȧs and Paul heard of
it, they tore their garments and rushed
out among the multitude, crying,
15 "Men, why are you doing this? We
also are men, of like nature with you,
and bring you good news, that you
should turn from these vain things to
a living God who made the heaven
and the earth and the sea and all that
is in them. 16 In past generations he
allowed all the nations to walk in their
own ways; 17 yet he did not leave himself without witness, for he did good
and gave you from heaven rains and
fruitful seasons, satisfying your hearts
with food and gladness." 18 With these
words they scarcely restrained the
people from offering sacrifice to them.
19 But Jews came there from An'ti-
och and Ī·cō'ni·ŭm; and having persuaded the people, they stoned Paul
and dragged him out of the city, supposing that he was dead. 20 But when
the disciples gathered about him, he
rose up and entered the city; and on
the next day he went on with Bär'nȧ-
bȧs to Dẽr'bē. 21 When they had
preached the gospel to that city and
had made many disciples, they returned to Lys'trȧ and to Ī·cō'ni·ŭm
and to An'ti·och, 22 strengthening the
souls of the disciples, exhorting them
to continue in the faith, and saying
that through many tribulations we
must enter the kingdom of God. 23And
when they had appointed elders for
them in every church, with prayer and
fasting, they committed them to the
Lord in whom they believed.
24 Then they passed through Pi-
sid'i·ȧ, and came to Pam·phyl'i·ȧ.
25And when they had spoken the word
in Pẽr'gȧ, they went down to At·tȧ·lī'ȧ;
26 and from there they sailed to An'ti-
och, where they had been commended
to the grace of God for the work which
they had fulfilled. 27And when they
arrived, they gathered the church together and declared all that God had
done with them, and how he had
opened a door of faith to the Gentiles.
28And they remained no little time
with the disciples.

15 But some men came down from
Judea and were teaching the
brethren, "Unless you are circumcised
according to the custom of Moses, you
cannot be saved." 2And when Paul
and Bär'nȧ·bȧs had no small dissension
and debate with them, Paul and Barnabas and some of the others were
appointed to go up to Jerusalem to the
apostles and the elders about this
question. 3 So, being sent on their way
by the church, they passed through
both Phoė·ni'ċi·ȧ and Sȧ·mâr'i·ȧ, re-
porting the conversion of the Gentiles,
and they gave great joy to all the brethren. 4 When they came to Jerusalem,
they were welcomed by the church and
the apostles and the elders, and they
declared all that God had done with
them. 5 But some believers who belonged to the party of the Pharisees
rose up, and said, "It is necessary to
circumcise them, and to charge them
to keep the law of Moses."
6 The apostles and the elders were
gathered together to consider this
matter. 7And after there had been
much debate, Peter rose and said to
them, "Brethren, you know that in the
early days God made choice among
you, that by my mouth the Gentiles
should hear the word of the gospel and
believe. 8And God who knows the
heart bore witness to them, giving
them the Holy Spirit just as he did to
us; 9 and he made no distinction between us and them, but cleansed their
hearts by faith. 10 Now therefore why
do you make trial of God by putting a
yoke upon the neck of the disciples
which neither our fathers nor we have
been able to bear? 11 But we believe
that we shall be saved through the grace
of the Lord Jesus, just as they will."
12 And all the assembly kept silence; and they listened to Bär'nȧ·bȧs
and Paul as they related what signs
and wonders God had done through

14.15: Ex 20.11; Ps 146.6. **14.19:** 2 Cor 11.25. **15.1-30:** Gal 2.1-10.

them among the Gentiles. 13After they
finished speaking, James replied,
"Brethren, listen to me. 14 Sym'ē·ȯn
has related how God first visited the
Gentiles, to take out of them a people
for his name. 15And with this the
words of the prophets agree, as it is
written,

16 'After this I will return,
and I will rebuild the dwelling of
David, which has fallen;
I will rebuild its ruins,
and I will set it up,
17 that the rest of men may seek the
Lord,
and all the Gentiles who are called
by my name,
18 says the Lord, who has made these
things known from of old.'

19 Therefore my judgment is that we
should not trouble those of the Gentiles who turn to God, 20 but should
write to them to abstain from the
pollutions of idols and from unchastity
and from what is strangled[n] and from
blood. 21 For from early generations
Moses has had in every city those who
preach him, for he is read every sabbath in the synagogues."

22 Then it seemed good to the
apostles and the elders, with the whole
church, to choose men from among
them and send them to An'ti·och with
Paul and Bär'nȧ·bȧs. They sent Judas
called Bär'sab·bȧs, and Silas, leading
men among the brethren, 23 with the
following letter: "The brethren, both
the apostles and the elders, to the
brethren who are of the Gentiles in
An'ti·och and Syria and Ċi·li'ċi·ȧ,
greeting. 24 Since we have heard that
some persons from us have troubled
you with words, unsettling your minds,
although we gave them no instructions, 25 it has seemed good to us in
assembly to choose men and send them
to you with our beloved Bär'nȧ·bȧs
and Paul, 26 men who have risked
their lives for the sake of our Lord
Jesus Christ. 27 We have therefore
sent Judas and Silas, who themselves
will tell you the same things by word
of mouth. 28 For it has seemed good
to the Holy Spirit and to us to lay
upon you no greater burden than these
necessary things: 29 that you abstain
from what has been sacrificed to idols
and from blood and from what is
strangled[n] and from unchastity. If you
keep yourselves from these, you will
do well. Farewell."

30 So when they were sent off, they
went down to An'ti·och; and having
gathered the congregation together,
they delivered the letter. 31And when
they read it, they rejoiced at the exhortation. 32And Judas and Silas, who
were themselves prophets, exhorted
the brethren with many words and
strengthened them. 33And after they
had spent some time, they were sent
off in peace by the brethren to those
who had sent them.[o] 35 But Paul and
Bär'nȧ·bȧs remained in An'ti·och,
teaching and preaching the word of
the Lord, with many others also.

36 And after some days Paul said
to Bär'nȧ·bȧs, "Come, let us return
and visit the brethren in every city
where we proclaimed the word of the
Lord, and see how they are." 37And
Bär'nȧ·bȧs wanted to take with them
John called Mark. 38 But Paul thought
best not to take with them one who
had withdrawn from them in Pam-
phyl'i·ȧ, and had not gone with them
to the work. 39And there arose a sharp
contention, so that they separated
from each other; Bär'nȧ·bȧs took Mark
with him and sailed away to Cyprus,
40 but Paul chose Silas and departed,
being commended by the brethren to
the grace of the Lord. 41And he went
through Syria and Ċi·li'ċi·ȧ, strengthening the churches.

16 And he came also to Dẽr'bē and
to Lys'trȧ. A disciple was there,
named Timothy, the son of a Jewish
woman who was a believer; but his
father was a Greek. 2 He was well
spoken of by the brethren at Lys'trȧ
and Ī·cō'ni·ŭm. 3 Paul wanted Timothy
to accompany him; and he took him
and circumcised him because of the
Jews that were in those places, for they
all knew that his father was a Greek.
4As they went on their way through
the cities, they delivered to them for
observance the decisions which had
been reached by the apostles and
elders who were at Jerusalem. 5 So the
churches were strengthened in the
faith, and they increased in numbers
daily.

6 And they went through the region

[n] Other early authorities omit *and from what is strangled*
[o] Other ancient authorities insert verse 34, *But it seemed good to Silas to remain there*
15.16-18: Amos 9.11-12; Jer 12.15; Is 45.21.

of Phryġ'i·ȧ and Galatia, having been
forbidden by the Holy Spirit to speak
the word in Asia. 7And when they had
come opposite My'si·ȧ, they attempted
to go into Bi·thyn'i·ȧ, but the Spirit of
Jesus did not allow them; 8 so, passing
by My'si·ȧ, they went down to Trō'as.
9And a vision appeared to Paul in the
night: a man of Maċ·ė·dō'ni·ȧ was
standing beseeching him and saying,
"Come over to Macedonia and help
us." 10And when he had seen the
vision, immediately we sought to go
on into Maċ·ė·dō'ni·ȧ, concluding that
God had called us to preach the gospel
to them.

11 Setting sail therefore from Trō'-
as, we made a direct voyage to Sam'ȯ-
thrāċe, and the following day to Nē-
ap'ȯ·lis, 12 and from there to Phi·lip'pī,
which is the leading city of the district[x]
of Maċ·ė·dō'ni·ȧ, and a Roman colony.
We remained in this city some days;
13 and on the sabbath day we went
outside the gate to the riverside, where
we supposed there was a place of
prayer; and we sat down and spoke to
the women who had come together.
14 One who heard us was a woman
named Lyd'i·ȧ, from the city of Thȳ·ȧ-
tī'rȧ, a seller of purple goods, who was
a worshiper of God. The Lord opened
her heart to give heed to what was said
by Paul. 15And when she was baptized,
with her household, she besought us,
saying, "If you have judged me to be
faithful to the Lord, come to my
house and stay." And she prevailed
upon us.

16 As we were going to the place of
prayer, we were met by a slave girl
who had a spirit of divination and
brought her owners much gain by
soothsaying. 17 She followed Paul and
us, crying, "These men are servants
of the Most High God, who proclaim
to you the way of salvation." 18And
this she did for many days. But Paul
was annoyed, and turned and said to
the spirit, "I charge you in the name
of Jesus Christ to come out of her."
And it came out that very hour.

19 But when her owners saw that
their hope of gain was gone, they
seized Paul and Silas and dragged
them into the market place before the
rulers; 20 and when they had brought
them to the magistrates they said,
"These men are Jews and they are
disturbing our city. 21 They advocate
customs which it is not lawful for us
Romans to accept or practice." 22 The
crowd joined in attacking them; and
the magistrates tore the garments off
them and gave orders to beat them
with rods. 23And when they had inflicted many blows upon them, they
threw them into prison, charging the
jailer to keep them safely. 24 Having
received this charge, he put them into
the inner prison and fastened their feet
in the stocks.

25 But about midnight Paul and
Silas were praying and singing hymns
to God, and the prisoners were listening to them, 26 and suddenly there was
a great earthquake, so that the foundations of the prison were shaken; and
immediately all the doors were opened
and every one's fetters were unfas-
tened. 27 When the jailer woke and saw
that the prison doors were open, he
drew his sword and was about to kill
himself, supposing that the prisoners
had escaped. 28 But Paul cried with a
loud voice, "Do not harm yourself, for
we are all here." 29And he called for
lights and rushed in, and trembling
with fear he fell down before Paul and
Silas, 30 and brought them out and
said, "Men, what must I do to be
saved?" 31And they said, "Believe in
the Lord Jesus, and you will be saved,
you and your household." 32And they
spoke the word of the Lord to him and
to all that were in his house. 33And he
took them the same hour of the night,
and washed their wounds, and he was
baptized at once, with all his family.
34 Then he brought them up into his
house, and set food before them; and
he rejoiced with all his household that
he had believed in God.

35 But when it was day, the magistrates sent the police, saying, "Let
those men go." 36And the jailer reported the words to Paul, saying, "The
magistrates have sent to let you go;
now therefore come out and go in
peace." 37 But Paul said to them,
"They have beaten us publicly, uncondemned, men who are Roman
citizens, and have thrown us into
prison; and do they now cast us out
secretly? No! let them come themselves and take us out." 38 The police
reported these words to the magistrates, and they were afraid when they

[x] The Greek text is uncertain
16.22-23: 2 Cor 11.25.

heard that they were Roman citizens;
39 so they came and apologized to
them. And they took them out and
asked them to leave the city. 40 So
they went out of the prison, and visited
Lyd'i·ȧ; and when they had seen the
brethren they exhorted them and
departed.

17 Now when they had passed
through Am·phip'ȯ·lis and Ap-
ȯl·lō'ni·ȧ, they came to Thes·sȧ·lȯ-
nī'cȧ, where there was a synagogue of
the Jews. 2 And Paul went in, as was
his custom, and for three weeks[p] he
argued with them from the scriptures,
3 explaining and proving that it was
necessary for the Christ to suffer and
to rise from the dead, and saying,
"This Jesus, whom I proclaim to you,
is the Christ." 4 And some of them
were persuaded, and joined Paul and
Silas; as did a great many of the devout
Greeks and not a few of the leading
women. 5 But the Jews were jealous,
and taking some wicked fellows of the
rabble, they gathered a crowd, set the
city in an uproar, and attacked the
house of Jason, seeking to bring them
out to the people. 6 And when they
could not find them, they dragged
Jason and some of the brethren before
the city authorities, crying, "These
men who have turned the world upside
down have come here also, 7 and Jason
has received them; and they are all
acting against the decrees of Caesar,
saying that there is another king,
Jesus." 8 And the people and the city
authorities were disturbed when they
heard this. 9 And when they had taken
security from Jason and the rest, they
let them go.

10 The brethren immediately sent
Paul and Silas away by night to Be-
roē'ȧ; and when they arrived they went
into the Jewish synagogue. 11 Now
these Jews were more noble than those
in Thes·sȧ·lȯ·nī'cȧ, for they received
the word with all eagerness, examining
the scriptures daily to see if these
things were so. 12 Many of them therefore believed, with not a few Greek
women of high standing as well as men.
13 But when the Jews of Thes·sȧ·lȯ-
nī'cȧ learned that the word of God was
proclaimed by Paul at Be·roē'ȧ also,
they came there too, stirring up and
inciting the crowds. 14 Then the brethren immediately sent Paul off on his
way to the sea, but Silas and Timothy
remained there. 15 Those who conducted Paul brought him as far as
Athens; and receiving a command for
Silas and Timothy to come to him as
soon as possible, they departed.

16 Now while Paul was waiting for
them at Athens, his spirit was provoked within him as he saw that the
city was full of idols. 17 So he argued
in the synagogue with the Jews and
the devout persons, and in the market
place every day with those who
chanced to be there. 18 Some also of
the Epicurean and Stoic philosophers
met him. And some said, "What
would this babbler say?" Others said,
"He seems to be a preacher of foreign
divinities"—because he preached Jesus
and the resurrection. 19 And they took
hold of him and brought him to the
Ar'ē-op'ȧ·gus, saying, "May we know
what this new teaching is which you
present? 20 For you bring some strange
things to our ears; we wish to know
therefore what these things mean."
21 Now all the Athenians and the
foreigners who lived there spent their
time in nothing except telling or hearing something new.

22 So Paul, standing in the middle
of the Ar'ē-op'ȧ·gus, said: "Men of
Athens, I perceive that in every way
you are very religious. 23 For as I
passed along, and observed the objects
of your worship, I found also an altar
with this inscription, 'To an unknown
god.' What therefore you worship as
unknown, this I proclaim to you.
24 The God who made the world and
everything in it, being Lord of heaven
and earth, does not live in shrines made
by man, 25 nor is he served by human
hands, as though he needed anything,
since he himself gives to all men life
and breath and everything. 26 And he
made from one every nation of men to
live on all the face of the earth, having
determined allotted periods and the
boundaries of their habitation, 27 that
they should seek God, in the hope
that they might feel after him and find
him. Yet he is not far from each one
of us, 28 for

'In him we live and move and have
our being';

as even some of your poets have said,

'For we are indeed his offspring.'

29 Being then God's offspring, we

[p] Or *sabbaths*

17.24-25: Is 42.5. **17.28:** Epimenides; Aratus, *Phaenomena*, 5.

ought not to think that the Deity is
like gold, or silver, or stone, a representation by the art and imagination
of man. 30 The times of ignorance God
overlooked, but now he commands all
men everywhere to repent, 31 because
he has fixed a day on which he will
judge the world in righteousness by a
man whom he has appointed, and of
this he has given assurance to all men
by raising him from the dead."
32 Now when they heard of the
resurrection of the dead, some mocked;
but others said, "We will hear you
again about this." 33 So Paul went out
from among them. 34 But some men
joined him and believed, among them
Dī·ȯ·nys'ĭ·ůs the Ar'ē-op'ȧ·ġite and a
woman named Dam'ȧ·ris and others
with them.
18 After this he left Athens and
went to Corinth. 2And he found
a Jew named Aq'ui·lȧ, a native of
Pon'tůs, lately come from Italy with
his wife Priscilla, because Claudius had
commanded all the Jews to leave
Rome. And he went to see them; 3 and
because he was of the same trade he
stayed with them, and they worked, for
by trade they were tentmakers. 4And
he argued in the synagogue every
sabbath, and persuaded Jews and
Greeks.
5 When Silas and Timothy arrived
from Maċ·ė·dō'ni·ȧ, Paul was occupied
with preaching, testifying to the Jews
that the Christ was Jesus. 6And when
they opposed and reviled him, he
shook out his garments and said to
them, "Your blood be upon your
heads! I am innocent. From now on I
will go to the Gentiles." 7And he left
there and went to the house of a man
named Tit'ĭ·ůs[q] Justus, a worshiper of
God; his house was next door to the
synagogue. 8 Cris'půs, the ruler of the
synagogue, believed in the Lord, together with all his household; and
many of the Corinthians hearing Paul
believed and were baptized. 9And the
Lord said to Paul one night in a vision,
"Do not be afraid, but speak and do
not be silent; 10 for I am with you, and
no man shall attack you to harm you;
for I have many people in this city."
11And he stayed a year and six months,
teaching the word of God among them.
12 But when Gal'lĭ·ō was proconsul
of Ȧ·chā'ĭȧ, the Jews made a united
attack upon Paul and brought him before the tribunal, 13 saying, "This man
is persuading men to worship God
contrary to the law." 14 But when Paul
was about to open his mouth, Gal'lĭ·ō
said to the Jews, "If it were a matter
of wrongdoing or vicious crime, I
should have reason to bear with you,
O Jews; 15 but since it is a matter of
questions about words and names and
your own law, see to it yourselves; I
refuse to be a judge of these things."
16And he drove them from the tribunal.
17And they all seized Sos'thė·nēs, the
ruler of the synagogue, and beat him
in front of the tribunal. But Gal'lĭ·ō
paid no attention to this.
18 After this Paul stayed many days
longer, and then took leave of the
brethren and sailed for Syria, and with
him Priscilla and Aq'ui·lȧ. At Ċen'-
chrē-ȧe he cut his hair, for he had a
vow. 19And they came to Eph'ė·sůs,
and he left them there; but he himself
went into the synagogue and argued
with the Jews. 20 When they asked him
to stay for a longer period, he declined;
21 but on taking leave of them he said,
"I will return to you if God wills," and
he set sail from Eph'ė·sůs.
22 When he had landed at Ċaes·ȧ-
rē'ȧ, he went up and greeted the
church, and then went down to An'tĭ-
och. 23After spending some time there
he departed and went from place to
place through the region of Galatia
and Phryġ'ĭ·ȧ, strengthening all the
disciples.
24 Now a Jew named Ȧ·pol'los, a
native of Alexandria, came to Eph'ė-
sůs. He was an eloquent man, well
versed in the scriptures. 25 He had
been instructed in the way of the Lord;
and being fervent in spirit, he spoke
and taught accurately the things concerning Jesus, though he knew only
the baptism of John. 26 He began to
speak boldly in the synagogue; but
when Priscilla and Aq'ui·lȧ heard him,
they took him and expounded to him
the way of God more accurately.
27And when he wished to cross to
Ȧ·chā'ĭȧ, the brethren encouraged him,
and wrote to the disciples to receive
him. When he arrived, he greatly
helped those who through grace had
believed, 28 for he powerfully confuted
the Jews in public, showing by the
scriptures that the Christ was Jesus.

[q] Other early authorities read *Titus*
17.31: Ps 9.8; 96.13; 98.9. 18.9-10: Is 43.5; Jer 1.8.

19 While Ȧ·pol′los was at Corinth,
Paul passed through the upper
country and came to Eph′ė·sŭs. There
he found some disciples. 2 And he said
to them, "Did you receive the Holy
Spirit when you believed?" And they
said, "No, we have never even heard
that there is a Holy Spirit." 3 And he
said, "Into what then were you baptized?" They said, "Into John's baptism." 4 And Paul said, "John baptized
with the baptism of repentance, telling
the people to believe in the one who
was to come after him, that is, Jesus."
5 On hearing this, they were baptized
in the name of the Lord Jesus. 6 And
when Paul had laid his hands upon
them, the Holy Spirit came on them;
and they spoke with tongues and
prophesied. 7 There were about twelve
of them in all.

8 And he entered the synagogue
and for three months spoke boldly,
arguing and pleading about the kingdom of God; 9 but when some were
stubborn and disbelieved, speaking
evil of the Way before the congregation, he withdrew from them, taking
the disciples with him, and argued
daily in the hall of Tȳ·ran′nŭs.[r] 10 This
continued for two years, so that all the
residents of Asia heard the word of
the Lord, both Jews and Greeks.

11 And God did extraordinary miracles by the hands of Paul, 12 so that
handkerchiefs or aprons were carried
away from his body to the sick, and
diseases left them and the evil spirits
came out of them. 13 Then some of the
itinerant Jewish exorcists undertook
to pronounce the name of the Lord
Jesus over those who had evil spirits,
saying, "I adjure you by the Jesus
whom Paul preaches." 14 Seven sons
of a Jewish high priest named Sċē′vȧ
were doing this. 15 But the evil spirit
answered them, "Jesus I know, and
Paul I know; but who are you?" 16 And
the man in whom the evil spirit was
leaped on them, mastered all of them,
and overpowered them, so that they
fled out of that house naked and
wounded. 17 And this became known
to all residents of Eph′ė·sŭs, both Jews
and Greeks; and fear fell upon them
all; and the name of the Lord Jesus
was extolled. 18 Many also of those
who were now believers came, confessing and divulging their practices.
19 And a number of those who practiced
magic arts brought their books together and burned them in the sight
of all; and they counted the value of
them and found it came to fifty thousand pieces of silver. 20 So the word of
the Lord grew and prevailed mightily.

21 Now after these events Paul
resolved in the Spirit to pass through
Maċ·ė·dō′ni·ȧ and Ȧ·chā′iȧ and go to
Jerusalem, saying, "After I have been
there, I must also see Rome." 22 And
having sent into Maċ·ė·dō′ni·ȧ two of
his helpers, Timothy and E·ras′tŭs, he
himself stayed in Asia for a while.

23 About that time there arose no
little stir concerning the Way. 24 For
a man named De·mē′tri·ŭs, a silversmith, who made silver shrines of
Är′tė·mis, brought no little business
to the craftsmen. 25 These he gathered
together, with the workmen of like
occupation, and said, "Men, you know
that from this business we have our
wealth. 26 And you see and hear that
not only at Eph′ė·sŭs but almost
throughout all Asia this Paul has
persuaded and turned away a considerable company of people, saying that
gods made with hands are not gods.
27 And there is danger not only that
this trade of ours may come into disrepute but also that the temple of the
great goddess Är′tė·mis may count for
nothing, and that she may even be
deposed from her magnificence, she
whom all Asia and the world worship."

28 When they heard this they were
enraged, and cried out, "Great is
Är′tė·mis of the E·phē′ṡiȧnṡ!" 29 So
the city was filled with the confusion;
and they rushed together into the
theater, dragging with them Gā′iŭs
and Ar·is·tär′chŭs, Maċ·ė·dō′ni·ȧnṡ
who were Paul's companions in travel.
30 Paul wished to go in among the
crowd, but the disciples would not let
him; 31 some of the Ā′si·ärchs also,
who were friends of his, sent to him
and begged him not to venture into
the theater. 32 Now some cried one
thing, some another; for the assembly
was in confusion, and most of them
did not know why they had come together. 33 Some of the crowd prompted
Alexander, whom the Jews had put
forward. And Alexander motioned
with his hand, wishing to make a
defense to the people. 34 But when
they recognized that he was a Jew, for

[r] Other ancient authorities add *from the fifth hour to the tenth*

about two hours they all with one
voice cried out, "Great is Är′tė·mis of
the E·phē′ṡiȧnṡ!" 35And when the
town clerk had quieted the crowd, he
said, "Men of Eph′ė·sus, what man is
there who does not know that the city
of the Ephesians is temple keeper of
the great Är′tė·mis, and of the sacred
stone that fell from the sky?[s] 36 Seeing
then that these things cannot be contradicted, you ought to be quiet and
do nothing rash. 37 For you have
brought these men here who are
neither sacrilegious nor blasphemers
of our goddess. 38 If therefore De·mē′-
tri·ůs and the craftsmen with him have
a complaint against any one, the courts
are open, and there are proconsuls; let
them bring charges against one
another. 39 But if you seek anything
further,[t] it shall be settled in the regular assembly. 40 For we are in danger
of being charged with rioting today,
there being no cause that we can give
to justify this commotion." 41And
when he had said this, he dismissed
the assembly.

20 After the uproar ceased, Paul
sent for the disciples and having
exhorted them took leave of them and
departed for Maċ·ė·dō′ni·ȧ. 2 When he
had gone through these parts and had
given them much encouragement, he
came to Greece. 3 There he spent
three months, and when a plot was
made against him by the Jews as he
was about to set sail for Syria, he
determined to return through Maċ·ė-
dō′ni·ȧ. 4 Sop′ȧ·tėr of Be·roē′ȧ, the
son of Pyr′rhůs, accompanied him;
and of the Thes·sȧ·lō′ni·ȧnṡ, Ar·is·tär′-
chůs and Se·cun′důs; and Gā′iůs of
Dẽr′bē, and Timothy; and the Asians,
Tych′i·cůs and Troph′i·můs. 5 These
went on and were waiting for us at
Trō′as, 6 but we sailed away from
Phi·lip′pī after the days of Unleavened
Bread, and in five days we came to
them at Trō′as, where we stayed for
seven days.

7 On the first day of the week, when
we were gathered together to break
bread, Paul talked with them, intending to depart on the morrow; and he
prolonged his speech until midnight.
8 There were many lights in the upper
chamber where we were gathered.
9And a young man named Eū′ty·chůs
was sitting in the window. He sank
into a deep sleep as Paul talked still
longer; and being overcome by sleep,
he fell down from the third story and
was taken up dead. 10 But Paul went
down and bent over him, and embracing him said, "Do not be alarmed, for
his life is in him." 11And when Paul
had gone up and had broken bread and
eaten, he conversed with them a long
while, until daybreak, and so departed.
12And they took the lad away alive,
and were not a little comforted.

13 But going ahead to the ship, we
set sail for As′sos, intending to take
Paul aboard there; for so he had
arranged, intending himself to go by
land. 14And when he met us at As′sos,
we took him on board and came to
Mit·y·lē′nē. 15And sailing from there
we came the following day opposite
Chī′os; the next day we touched at
Sā′mos; and[u] the day after that we
came to Mī·lē′tůs. 16 For Paul had
decided to sail past Eph′ė·sůs, so that
he might not have to spend time in
Asia; for he was hastening to be at
Jerusalem, if possible, on the day of
Pentecost.

17 And from Mī·lē′tůs he sent to
Eph′ė·sůs and called to him the elders
of the church. 18And when they came
to him, he said to them:

"You yourselves know how I lived
among you all the time from the first
day that I set foot in Asia, 19 serving
the Lord with all humility and with
tears and with trials which befell me
through the plots of the Jews; 20 how
I did not shrink from declaring to you
anything that was profitable, and
teaching you in public and from house
to house, 21 testifying both to Jews and
to Greeks of repentance to God and
of faith in our Lord Jesus Christ.
22And now, behold, I am going to
Jerusalem, bound in the Spirit, not
knowing what shall befall me there;
23 except that the Holy Spirit testifies
to me in every city that imprisonment
and afflictions await me. 24 But I do
not account my life of any value nor as
precious to myself, if only I may
accomplish my course and the ministry
which I received from the Lord Jesus,
to testify to the gospel of the grace of
God. 25And now, behold, I know that
all you among whom I have gone about
preaching the kingdom will see my
face no more. 26 Therefore I testify to

[s] The meaning of the Greek is uncertain [t] Other ancient authorities read *about other matters*
[u] Other ancient authorities add *after remaining at Trogyllium*

you this day that I am innocent of the
blood of all of you, 27 for I did not
shrink from declaring to you the whole
counsel of God. 28 Take heed to yourselves and to all the flock, in which the
Holy Spirit has made you guardians,
to feed the church of the Lord[v] which
he obtained with his own blood.[w] 29 I
know that after my departure fierce
wolves will come in among you, not
sparing the flock; 30 and from among
your own selves will arise men speaking perverse things, to draw away the
disciples after them. 31 Therefore be
alert, remembering that for three years
I did not cease night or day to admonish every one with tears. 32 And
now I commend you to God and to the
word of his grace, which is able to
build you up and to give you the
inheritance among all those who are
sanctified. 33 I coveted no one's silver
or gold or apparel. 34 You yourselves
know that these hands ministered to
my necessities, and to those who were
with me. 35 In all things I have shown
you that by so toiling one must help
the weak, remembering the words of
the Lord Jesus, how he said, 'It is
more blessed to give than to receive.' "

36 And when he had spoken thus, he
knelt down and prayed with them all.
37 And they all wept and embraced Paul
and kissed him, 38 sorrowing most
of all because of the word he had spok-
en, that they should see his face no
more. And they brought him to the
ship.

21 And when we had parted from
them and set sail, we came by a
straight course to Cos, and the next
day to Rhodes, and from there to
Pat'ȧ·rȧ.[x] 2 And having found a ship
crossing to Phoė·ni'ċi·ȧ, we went
aboard, and set sail. 3 When we had
come in sight of Cyprus, leaving it on
the left we sailed to Syria, and landed
at Tȳre; for there the ship was to un-
load its cargo. 4 And having sought out
the disciples, we stayed there for seven
days. Through the Spirit they told
Paul not to go on to Jerusalem. 5 And
when our days there were ended, we
departed and went on our journey; and
they all, with wives and children,
brought us on our way till we were
outside the city; and kneeling down on
the beach we prayed and bade one
another farewell. 6 Then we went on
board the ship, and they returned
home.

7 When we had finished the voyage
from Tȳre, we arrived at Ptol·ė·mā'is;
and we greeted the brethren and
stayed with them for one day. 8 On the
morrow we departed and came to
Ċaes·ȧ·rē'ȧ; and we entered the house
of Philip the evangelist, who was one
of the seven, and stayed with him.
9 And he had four unmarried daughters,
who prophesied. 10 While we were
staying for some days, a prophet
named Ag'ȧ·bŭs came down from
Judea. 11 And coming to us he took
Paul's girdle and bound his own feet
and hands, and said, "Thus says the
Holy Spirit, 'So shall the Jews at Jerusalem bind the man who owns this
girdle and deliver him into the hands
of the Gentiles.' " 12 When we heard
this, we and the people there begged
him not to go up to Jerusalem. 13 Then
Paul answered, "What are you doing,
weeping and breaking my heart? For I
am ready not only to be imprisoned but
even to die at Jerusalem for the name
of the Lord Jesus." 14 And when
he would not be persuaded, we ceased
and said, "The will of the Lord be
done."

15 After these days we made ready
and went up to Jerusalem. 16 And some
of the disciples from Ċaes·ȧ·rē'ȧ went
with us, bringing us to the house of
Mnā'sŏn of Cyprus, an early disciple,
with whom we should lodge.

17 When we had come to Jerusalem,
the brethren received us gladly. 18 On
the following day Paul went in with us
to James; and all the elders were
present. 19 After greeting them, he
related one by one the things that God
had done among the Gentiles through
his ministry. 20 And when they heard
it, they glorified God. And they said to
him, "You see, brother, how many
thousands there are among the Jews
of those who have believed; they are
all zealous for the law, 21 and they have
been told about you that you teach all
the Jews who are among the Gentiles
to forsake Moses, telling them not to
circumcise their children or observe
the customs. 22 What then is to be
done? They will certainly hear that you
have come. 23 Do therefore what we

[v] Other ancient authorities read *of God* [w] Or *with the blood of his Own*
[x] Other ancient authorities add *and Myra*

tell you. We have four men who are
under a vow; 24 take these men and
purify yourself along with them and
pay their expenses, so that they may
shave their heads. Thus all will know
that there is nothing in what they have
been told about you but that you yourself live in observance of the law.
25 But as for the Gentiles who have
believed, we have sent a letter with our
judgment that they should abstain
from what has been sacrificed to idols
and from blood and from what is
strangled[y] and from unchastity."
26 Then Paul took the men, and the
next day he purified himself with them
and went into the temple, to give
notice when the days of purification
would be fulfilled and the offering
presented for every one of them.

27 When the seven days were almost
completed, the Jews from Asia, who
had seen him in the temple, stirred up
all the crowd, and laid hands on him,
28 crying out, "Men of Israel, help!
This is the man who is teaching men
everywhere against the people and the
law and this place; moreover he also
brought Greeks into the temple, and
he has defiled this holy place." 29 For
they had previously seen Troph'i·mus
the E·phe'sian with him in the city,
and they supposed that Paul had
brought him into the temple. 30 Then
all the city was aroused, and the people ran together; they seized Paul and
dragged him out of the temple, and at
once the gates were shut. 31 And as
they were trying to kill him, word came
to the tribune of the cohort that all
Jerusalem was in confusion. 32 He at
once took soldiers and centurions, and
ran down to them; and when they saw
the tribune and the soldiers, they
stopped beating Paul. 33 Then the
tribune came up and arrested him, and
ordered him to be bound with two
chains. He inquired who he was and
what he had done. 34 Some in the
crowd shouted one thing, some
another; and as he could not learn the
facts because of the uproar, he ordered
him to be brought into the barracks.
35 And when he came to the steps, he
was actually carried by the soldiers,
because of the violence of the crowd;
36 for the mob of the people followed,
crying, "Away with him!"

37 As Paul was about to be brought
into the barracks, he said to the
tribune, "May I say something to you?"
And he said, "Do you know Greek?
38 Are you not the Egyptian, then, who
recently stirred up a revolt and led the
four thousand men of the Assassins
out into the wilderness?" 39 Paul
replied, "I am a Jew, from Tär'sus in
Ci·li'ci·a, a citizen of no mean city; I
beg you, let me speak to the people."
40 And when he had given him leave,
Paul, standing on the steps, motioned
with his hand to the people; and when
there was a great hush, he spoke to
them in the Hebrew language, saying:

22 "Brethren and fathers, hear
the defense which I now make
before you."

2 And when they heard that he
addressed them in the Hebrew language, they were the more quiet. And
he said:

3 "I am a Jew, born at Tär'sus in
Ci·li'ci·a, but brought up in this city
at the feet of Ga·mā'li·el, educated
according to the strict manner of the
law of our fathers, being zealous for
God as you all are this day. 4 I persecuted this Way to the death, binding
and delivering to prison both men and
women, 5 as the high priest and the
whole council of elders bear me witness. From them I received letters to
the brethren, and I journeyed to
Damascus to take those also who were
there and bring them in bonds to
Jerusalem to be punished.

6 "As I made my journey and drew
near to Damascus, about noon a great
light from heaven suddenly shone
about me. 7 And I fell to the ground
and heard a voice saying to me, 'Saul,
Saul, why do you persecute me?' 8 And
I answered, 'Who are you, Lord?' And
he said to me, 'I am Jesus of Nazareth
whom you are persecuting.' 9 Now
those who were with me saw the light
but did not hear the voice of the one
who was speaking to me. 10 And I said,
'What shall I do, Lord?' And the Lord
said to me, 'Rise, and go into Damascus, and there you will be told all that
is appointed for you to do.' 11 And
when I could not see because of the
brightness of that light, I was led by
the hand by those who were with me,
and came into Damascus.

12 "And one An·a·nī'as, a devout
man according to the law, well spoken

[y] Other early authorities omit *and from what is strangled*
22.4-16: Acts 9.1-19; 26.9-18; Gal 1.14.

of by all the Jews who lived there,
13 came to me, and standing by me
said to me, 'Brother Saul, receive your
sight.' And in that very hour I received
my sight and saw him. 14And he said,
'The God of our fathers appointed you
to know his will, to see the Just One
and to hear a voice from his mouth;
15 for you will be a witness for him to
all men of what you have seen and
heard. 16And now why do you wait?
Rise and be baptized, and wash away
your sins, calling on his name.'

17 "When I had returned to Jerusalem and was praying in the temple,
I fell into a trance 18 and saw him saying to me, 'Make haste and get quickly
out of Jerusalem, because they will not
accept your testimony about me.'
19And I said, 'Lord, they themselves
know that in every synagogue I imprisoned and beat those who believed
in thee. 20And when the blood of
Stephen thy witness was shed, I also
was standing by and approving, and
keeping the garments of those who
killed him.' 21And he said to me, 'Depart; for I will send you far away to
the Gentiles.' "

22 Up to this word they listened to
him; then they lifted up their voices
and said, "Away with such a fellow
from the earth! For he ought not to
live." 23And as they cried out and
waved their garments and threw dust
into the air, 24 the tribune commanded him to be brought into the
barracks, and ordered him to be examined by scourging, to find out why
they shouted thus against him. 25 But
when they had tied him up with the
thongs, Paul said to the centurion who
was standing by, "Is it lawful for you
to scourge a man who is a Roman
citizen, and uncondemned?" 26 When
the centurion heard that, he went to
the tribune and said to him, "What
are you about to do? For this man is a
Roman citizen." 27 So the tribune
came and said to him, "Tell me, are
you a Roman citizen?" And he said,
"Yes." 28 The tribune answered, "I
bought this citizenship for a large
sum." Paul said, "But I was born a
citizen." 29 So those who were about
to examine him withdrew from him
instantly; and the tribune also was
afraid, for he realized that Paul was a
Roman citizen and that he had bound
him.

30 But on the morrow, desiring to
know the real reason why the Jews
accused him, he unbound him, and
commanded the chief priests and all
the council to meet, and he brought
Paul down and set him before them.

23 And Paul, looking intently at
the council, said, "Brethren, I
have lived before God in all good
conscience up to this day." 2And the
high priest An·ȧ·nī′ȧs commanded
those who stood by him to strike him
on the mouth. 3 Then Paul said to
him, "God shall strike you, you whitewashed wall! Are you sitting to judge
me according to the law, and yet contrary to the law you order me to be
struck?" 4 Those who stood by said,
"Would you revile God's high priest?"
5And Paul said, "I did not know,
brethren, that he was the high priest;
for it is written, 'You shall not speak
evil of a ruler of your people.' "

6 But when Paul perceived that one
part were Sad′dū·ċeeṡ and the other
Pharisees, he cried out in the council,
"Brethren, I am a Pharisee, a son of
Pharisees; with respect to the hope and
the resurrection of the dead I am on
trial." 7And when he had said this, a
dissension arose between the Pharisees
and the Sad′dū·ċeeṡ; and the assembly
was divided. 8 For the Sad′dū·ċeeṡ say
that there is no resurrection, nor angel,
nor spirit; but the Pharisees acknowledge them all. 9 Then a great clamor
arose; and some of the scribes of the
Pharisees' party stood up and contended, "We find nothing wrong in
this man. What if a spirit or an angel
spoke to him?" 10And when the dissension became violent, the tribune,
afraid that Paul would be torn in pieces
by them, commanded the soldiers to
go down and take him by force from
among them and bring him into the
barracks.

11 The following night the Lord
stood by him and said, "Take courage,
for as you have testified about me at
Jerusalem, so you must bear witness
also at Rome."

12 When it was day, the Jews made
a plot and bound themselves by an
oath neither to eat nor drink till they
had killed Paul. 13 There were more
than forty who made this conspiracy.
14And they went to the chief priests
and elders, and said, "We have strictly
bound ourselves by an oath to taste

23.5: Ex 22.28.

no food till we have killed Paul. 15 You
therefore, along with the council, give
notice now to the tribune to bring him
down to you, as though you were going
to determine his case more exactly.
And we are ready to kill him before he
comes near."

16 Now the son of Paul's sister
heard of their ambush; so he went and
entered the barracks and told Paul.
17 And Paul called one of the centurions
and said, "Bring this young man to the
tribune; for he has something to tell
him." 18 So he took him and brought
him to the tribune and said, "Paul the
prisoner called me and asked me to
bring this young man to you, as he has
something to say to you." 19 The
tribune took him by the hand, and
going aside asked him privately, "What
is it that you have to tell me?" 20 And
he said, "The Jews have agreed to ask
you to bring Paul down to the council
tomorrow, as though they were going
to inquire somewhat more closely
about him. 21 But do not yield to them;
for more than forty of their men lie in
ambush for him, having bound themselves by an oath neither to eat nor
drink till they have killed him; and
now they are ready, waiting for the
promise from you." 22 So the tribune
dismissed the young man, charging
him, "Tell no one that you have informed me of this."

23 Then he called two of the centurions and said, "At the third hour of
the night get ready two hundred
soldiers with seventy horsemen and
two hundred spearmen to go as far as
Caes·a·rē'a. 24 Also provide mounts for
Paul to ride, and bring him safely to
Felix the governor." 25 And he wrote a
letter to this effect:

26 "Claudius Lys'i·as to his Excel-
lency the governor Felix, greeting.
27 This man was seized by the Jews,
and was about to be killed by them,
when I came upon them with the
soldiers and rescued him, having
learned that he was a Roman citizen.
28 And desiring to know the charge on
which they accused him, I brought
him down to their council. 29 I found
that he was accused about questions
of their law, but charged with nothing
deserving death or imprisonment.
30 And when it was disclosed to me
that there would be a plot against the
man, I sent him to you at once, order-
ing his accusers also to state before you
what they have against him."

31 So the soldiers, according to
their instructions, took Paul and
brought him by night to An·tip'a·tris.
32 And on the morrow they returned to
the barracks, leaving the horsemen to
go on with him. 33 When they came
to Caes·a·rē'a and delivered the letter
to the governor, they presented Paul
also before him. 34 On reading the
letter, he asked to what province he
belonged. When he learned that he
was from Ci·li'ci·a 35 he said, "I will
hear you when your accusers arrive."
And he commanded him to be guarded
in Her'od's praetorium.

24 And after five days the high
priest An·a·nī'as came down
with some elders and a spokesman, one
Ter·tul'lus. They laid before the
governor their case against Paul; 2 and
when he was called, Ter·tul'lus began
to accuse him, saying:

"Since through you we enjoy much
peace, and since by your provision,
most excellent Felix, reforms are introduced on behalf of this nation, 3 in
every way and everywhere we accept
this with all gratitude. 4 But, to detain
you no further, I beg you in your kindness to hear us briefly. 5 For we have
found this man a pestilent fellow, an
agitator among all the Jews throughout
the world, and a ringleader of the sect
of the Nazarenes. 6 He even tried to
profane the temple, but we seized
him.[z] 8 By examining him yourself you
will be able to learn from him about
everything of which we accuse him."

9 The Jews also joined in the
charge, affirming that all this was so.

10 And when the governor had
motioned to him to speak, Paul replied:
"Realizing that for many years you
have been judge over this nation, I
cheerfully make my defense. 11 As you
may ascertain, it is not more than
twelve days since I went up to worship
at Jerusalem; 12 and they did not find
me disputing with any one or stirring
up a crowd, either in the temple or
in the synagogues, or in the city.
13 Neither can they prove to you what
they now bring up against me. 14 But
this I admit to you, that according to

z Other ancient authorities add *and we would have judged him according to our law. 7 But the chief captain Lysias came and with great violence took him out of our hands, 8 commanding his accusers to come before you.*

the Way, which they call a sect, I worship the God of our fathers, believing
everything laid down by the law or
written in the prophets, 15 having a
hope in God which these themselves
accept, that there will be a resurrection
of both the just and the unjust. 16 So
I always take pains to have a clear
conscience toward God and toward
men. 17 Now after some years I came
to bring to my nation alms and offerings. 18 As I was doing this, they found
me purified in the temple, without any
crowd or tumult. But some Jews from
Asia—19 they ought to be here before
you and to make an accusation, if they
have anything against me. 20 Or else
let these men themselves say what
wrongdoing they found when I stood
before the council, 21 except this one
thing which I cried out while standing
among them, 'With respect to the
resurrection of the dead I am on trial
before you this day.' "

22 But Felix, having a rather accurate knowledge of the Way, put them
off, saying, "When Lys′i·ȧs the tribune
comes down, I will decide your case."
23 Then he gave orders to the centurion that he should be kept in
custody but should have some liberty,
and that none of his friends should be
prevented from attending to his needs.

24 After some days Felix came with
his wife Drü·sil′lȧ, who was a Jewess;
and he sent for Paul and heard him
speak upon faith in Christ Jesus. 25 And
as he argued about justice and self-
control and future judgment, Felix was
alarmed and said, "Go away for the
present; when I have an opportunity I
will summon you." 26 At the same time
he hoped that money would be given
him by Paul. So he sent for him often
and conversed with him. 27 But when
two years had elapsed, Felix was succeeded by Pôr′ci·ŭs Fes′tŭs; and desiring to do the Jews a favor, Felix left
Paul in prison.

25 Now when Fes′tŭs had come
into his province, after three
days he went up to Jerusalem from
Caes·ȧ·rē′ȧ. 2 And the chief priests and
the principal men of the Jews informed
him against Paul; and they urged him,
3 asking as a favor to have the man sent
to Jerusalem, planning an ambush to
kill him on the way. 4 Fes′tŭs replied
that Paul was being kept at Caes·ȧ·rē′ȧ,
and that he himself intended to go
there shortly. 5 "So," said he, "let the
men of authority among you go down
with me, and if there is anything wrong
about the man, let them accuse him."

6 When he had stayed among them
not more than eight or ten days, he
went down to Caes·ȧ·rē′ȧ; and the next
day he took his seat on the tribunal
and ordered Paul to be brought. 7 And
when he had come, the Jews who had
gone down from Jerusalem stood about
him, bringing against him many serious charges which they could not
prove. 8 Paul said in his defense,
"Neither against the law of the Jews,
nor against the temple, nor against
Caesar have I offended at all." 9 But
Fes′tŭs, wishing to do the Jews a favor,
said to Paul, "Do you wish to go up to
Jerusalem, and there be tried on these
charges before me?" 10 But Paul said,
"I am standing before Caesar's tribunal, where I ought to be tried; to
the Jews I have done no wrong, as you
know very well. 11 If then I am a
wrongdoer, and have committed anything for which I deserve to die, I do
not seek to escape death; but if there
is nothing in their charges against me,
no one can give me up to them. I appeal to Caesar." 12 Then Fes′tŭs, when
he had conferred with his council,
answered, "You have appealed to
Caesar; to Caesar you shall go."

13 Now when some days had passed,
Ȧ·grip′pȧ the king and Bėr·nī′cē
arrived at Caes·ȧ·rē′ȧ to welcome
Fes′tŭs. 14 And as they stayed there
many days, Fes′tŭs laid Paul's case before the king, saying, "There is a man
left prisoner by Felix; 15 and when I
was at Jerusalem, the chief priests and
the elders of the Jews gave information
about him, asking for sentence against
him. 16 I answered them that it was
not the custom of the Romans to give
up any one before the accused met the
accusers face to face, and had opportunity to make his defense concerning
the charge laid against him. 17 When
therefore they came together here, I
made no delay, but on the next day
took my seat on the tribunal and
ordered the man to be brought in.
18 When the accusers stood up, they
brought no charge in his case of such
evils as I supposed; 19 but they had
certain points of dispute with him
about their own superstition and about
one Jesus, who was dead, but whom
Paul asserted to be alive. 20 Being at a
loss how to investigate these questions,

I asked whether he wished to go to
Jerusalem and be tried there regarding
them. 21 But when Paul had appealed
to be kept in custody for the decision
of the emperor, I commanded him to
be held until I could send him to
Caesar." 22 And Ȧ·grip′pȧ said to
Fes′tu̇s, "I should like to hear the
man myself." "Tomorrow," said he,
"you shall hear him."

23 So on the morrow Ȧ·grip′pȧ and
Bėr·nī′ċē came with great pomp, and
they entered the audience hall with the
military tribunes and the prominent
men of the city. Then by command of
Fes′tu̇s Paul was brought in. 24 And
Fes′tu̇s said, "King Ȧ·grip′pȧ and all
who are present with us, you see this
man about whom the whole Jewish
people petitioned me, both at Jerusalem and here, shouting that he
ought not to live any longer. 25 But I
found that he had done nothing
deserving death; and as he himself
appealed to the emperor, I decided to
send him. 26 But I have nothing definite to write to my lord about him.
Therefore I have brought him before
you, and, especially before you, King
Ȧ·grip′pȧ, that, after we have examined him, I may have something to
write. 27 For it seems to me unreason-
able, in sending a prisoner, not to
indicate the charges against him."

26 Ȧ·grip′pȧ said to Paul, "You
have permission to speak for
yourself." Then Paul stretched out his
hand and made his defense:

2 "I think myself fortunate that it
is before you, King Ȧ·grip′pȧ, I am to
make my defense today against all the
accusations of the Jews, 3 because you
are especially familiar with all customs and controversies of the Jews;
therefore I beg you to listen to me
patiently.

4 "My manner of life from my
youth, spent from the beginning
among my own nation and at Jerusalem, is known by all the Jews. 5 They
have known for a long time, if they
are willing to testify, that according to
the strictest party of our religion I have
lived as a Pharisee. 6 And now I stand
here on trial for hope in the promise
made by God to our fathers, 7 to
which our twelve tribes hope to attain,
as they earnestly worship night and
day. And for this hope I am accused
by Jews, O king! 8 Why is it thought
incredible by any of you that God
raises the dead?

9 "I myself was convinced that I
ought to do many things in opposing
the name of Jesus of Nazareth. 10 And
I did so in Jerusalem; I not only shut
up many of the saints in prison, by
authority from the chief priests, but
when they were put to death I cast my
vote against them. 11 And I punished
them often in all the synagogues and
tried to make them blaspheme; and in
raging fury against them, I persecuted
them even to foreign cities.

12 "Thus I journeyed to Damascus
with the authority and commission of
the chief priests. 13 At midday, O king,
I saw on the way a light from heaven,
brighter than the sun, shining round
me and those who journeyed with me.
14 And when we had all fallen to the
ground, I heard a voice saying to me
in the Hebrew language, 'Saul, Saul,
why do you persecute me? It hurts you
to kick against the goads.' 15 And I
said, 'Who are you, Lord?' And the
Lord said, 'I am Jesus whom you are
persecuting. 16 But rise and stand upon
your feet; for I have appeared to you
for this purpose, to appoint you to
serve and bear witness to the things in
which you have seen me and to those
in which I will appear to you, 17 delivering you from the people and from
the Gentiles—to whom I send you
18 to open their eyes, that they may
turn from darkness to light and from
the power of Satan to God, that they
may receive forgiveness of sins and a
place among those who are sanctified
by faith in me.'

19 "Wherefore, O King Ȧ·grip′pȧ,
I was not disobedient to the heavenly
vision, 20 but declared first to those at
Damascus, then at Jerusalem and
throughout all the country of Judea,
and also to the Gentiles, that they
should repent and turn to God and
perform deeds worthy of their repentance. 21 For this reason the Jews seized
me in the temple and tried to kill me.
22 To this day I have had the help that
comes from God, and so I stand here
testifying both to small and great, saying nothing but what the prophets and
Moses said would come to pass: 23 that
the Christ must suffer, and that, by
being the first to rise from the dead,
he would proclaim light both to the
people and to the Gentiles."

26.9-18: Acts 9.1-8; 22.4-16. **26.16-17:** Ezek 2.1, 3. **26.18:** Is 42.7, 16.

24 And as he thus made his defense,
Fes'tu̇s said with a loud voice, "Paul,
you are mad; your great learning is
turning you mad." 25 But Paul said,
"I am not mad, most excellent Fes'tu̇s,
but I am speaking the sober truth.
26 For the king knows about these
things, and to him I speak freely; for I
am persuaded that none of these things
has escaped his notice, for this was not
done in a corner. 27 King Ȧ·grip'pȧ,
do you believe the prophets? I know
that you believe." 28 And Ȧ·grip'pȧ
said to Paul, "In a short time you
think to make me a Christian!" 29 And
Paul said, "Whether short or long, I
would to God that not only you but
also all who hear me this day might
become such as I am—except for these
chains."

30 Then the king rose, and the
governor and Bėr·nī'ċē and those who
were sitting with them; 31 and when
they had withdrawn, they said to one
another, "This man is doing nothing
to deserve death or imprisonment."
32 And Ȧ·grip'pȧ said to Fes'tu̇s, "This
man could have been set free if he had
not appealed to Caesar."

27 And when it was decided that
we should sail for Italy, they
delivered Paul and some other prisoners to a centurion of the Augustan
Cohort, named Julius. 2 And embark-
ing in a ship of Ad·rȧ·myt'ti·u̇m,
which was about to sail to the ports
along the coast of Asia, we put to sea,
accompanied by Ar·is·tär'chu̇s, a
Maċ·ė·dō'ni·ȧn from Thes·sȧ·lȯ·nī'cȧ.
3 The next day we put in at Sī'don;
and Julius treated Paul kindly, and
gave him leave to go to his friends and
be cared for. 4 And putting to sea from
there we sailed under the lee of Cyprus,
because the winds were against us.
5 And when we had sailed across the
sea which is off Ċi·li'ċi·ȧ and Pam-
phyl'i·ȧ, we came to Myra in Ly'ċi·ȧ.
6 There the centurion found a ship of
Alexandria sailing for Italy, and put us
on board. 7 We sailed slowly for a
number of days, and arrived with
difficulty off Cnī'du̇s, and as the wind
did not allow us to go on, we sailed
under the lee of Crete off Sal·mō'nē.
8 Coasting along it with difficulty, we
came to a place called Fair Havens,
near which was the city of Lȧ·sē'ȧ.

9 As much time had been lost, and
the voyage was already dangerous because the fast had already gone by,
Paul advised them, 10 saying, "Sirs, I
perceive that the voyage will be with
injury and much loss, not only of the
cargo and the ship, but also of our
lives." 11 But the centurion paid more
attention to the captain and to the
owner of the ship than to what Paul
said. 12 And because the harbor was
not suitable to winter in, the majority
advised to put to sea from there, on
the chance that somehow they could
reach Phoenix, a harbor of Crete,
looking northeast and southeast,[a] and
winter there.

13 And when the south wind blew
gently, supposing that they had obtained their purpose, they weighed
anchor and sailed along Crete, close
inshore. 14 But soon a tempestuous
wind, called the northeaster, struck
down from the land; 15 and when the
ship was caught and could not face
the wind, we gave way to it and were
driven. 16 And running under the lee
of a small island called Cäu'dȧ,[b] we
managed with difficulty to secure the
boat; 17 after hoisting it up, they took
measures[c] to undergird the ship; then,
fearing that they should run on the
Syr'tis, they lowered the gear, and so
were driven. 18 As we were violently
storm-tossed, they began next day to
throw the cargo overboard; 19 and the
third day they cast out with their own
hands the tackle of the ship. 20 And
when neither sun nor stars appeared for
many a day, and no small tempest lay
on us, all hope of our being saved was
at last abandoned.

21 As they had been long without
food, Paul then came forward among
them and said, "Men, you should have
listened to me, and should not have
set sail from Crete and incurred this
injury and loss. 22 I now bid you take
heart; for there will be no loss of life
among you, but only of the ship. 23 For
this very night there stood by me an
angel of the God to whom I belong
and whom I worship, 24 and he said,
'Do not be afraid, Paul; you must stand
before Caesar; and lo, God has granted
you all those who sail with you.' 25 So
take heart, men, for I have faith in
God that it will be exactly as I have
been told. 26 But we shall have to run
on some island."

27 When the fourteenth night had
come, as we were drifting across the

[a] Or *southwest and northwest* [b] Other ancient authorities read *Clauda* [c] Greek *helps*

sea of Ā'dri·ȧ, about midnight the
sailors suspected that they were near-
ing land. 28 So they sounded and
found twenty fathoms; a little farther
on they sounded again and found
fifteen fathoms. 29 And fearing that we
might run on the rocks, they let out
four anchors from the stern, and
prayed for day to come. 30 And as the
sailors were seeking to escape from
the ship, and had lowered the boat
into the sea, under pretense of laying
out anchors from the bow, 31 Paul said
to the centurion and the soldiers,
"Unless these men stay in the ship,
you cannot be saved." 32 Then the
soldiers cut away the ropes of the boat,
and let it go.

33 As day was about to dawn, Paul
urged them all to take some food, saying, "Today is the fourteenth day that
you have continued in suspense and
without food, having taken nothing.
34 Therefore I urge you to take some
food; it will give you strength, since
not a hair is to perish from the head of
any of you." 35 And when he had said
this, he took bread, and giving thanks
to God in the presence of all he broke
it and began to eat. 36 Then they all
were encouraged and ate some food
themselves. 37 (We were in all two
hundred and seventy-six[d] persons in
the ship.) 38 And when they had eaten
enough, they lightened the ship,
throwing out the wheat into the sea.

39 Now when it was day, they did
not recognize the land, but they
noticed a bay with a beach, on which
they planned if possible to bring the
ship ashore. 40 So they cast off the
anchors and left them in the sea, at
the same time loosening the ropes that
tied the rudders; then hoisting the
foresail to the wind they made for the
beach. 41 But striking a shoal[e] they ran
the vessel aground; the bow stuck and
remained immovable, and the stern
was broken up by the surf. 42 The
soldiers' plan was to kill the prisoners,
lest any should swim away and escape;
43 but the centurion, wishing to save
Paul, kept them from carrying out
their purpose. He ordered those who
could swim to throw themselves overboard first and make for the land,
44 and the rest on planks or on pieces
of the ship. And so it was that all
escaped to land.

28 After we had escaped, we then
learned that the island was
called Malta. 2 And the natives showed
us unusual kindness, for they kindled
a fire and welcomed us all, because it
had begun to rain and was cold. 3 Paul
had gathered a bundle of sticks and
put them on the fire, when a viper
came out because of the heat and
fastened on his hand. 4 When the
natives saw the creature hanging from
his hand, they said to one another,
"No doubt this man is a murderer.
Though he has escaped from the sea,
justice has not allowed him to live."
5 He, however, shook off the creature
into the fire and suffered no harm.
6 They waited, expecting him to swell
up or suddenly fall down dead; but
when they had waited a long time and
saw no misfortune come to him, they
changed their minds and said that he
was a god.

7 Now in the neighborhood of that
place were lands belonging to the chief
man of the island, named Pub'li·ŭs,
who received us and entertained us
hospitably for three days. 8 It happened that the father of Pub'li·ŭs lay
sick with fever and dysentery; and
Paul visited him and prayed, and
putting his hands on him healed him.
9 And when this had taken place, the
rest of the people on the island who
had diseases also came and were cured.
10 They presented many gifts to us;[f]
and when we sailed, they put on board
whatever we needed.

11 After three months we set sail
in a ship which had wintered in the
island, a ship of Alexandria, with the
Twin Brothers as figurehead. 12 Putting in at Syracuse, we stayed there for
three days. 13 And from there we made
a circuit and arrived at Rhē'ġi·ŭm;
and after one day a south wind sprang
up, and on the second day we came to
Pū·tē'ō·lī. 14 There we found brethren,
and were invited to stay with them for
seven days. And so we came to Rome.
15 And the brethren there, when they
heard of us, came as far as the Forum
of Ap'pi·ŭs and Three Taverns to
meet us. On seeing them Paul thanked
God and took courage. 16 And when
we came into Rome, Paul was allowed
to stay by himself, with the soldier
that guarded him.

17 After three days he called to-

[d] Other ancient authorities read *seventy-six* or *about seventy-six* [e] Greek *place of two seas*
[f] Or *honored us with many honors*

gether the local leaders of the Jews;
and when they had gathered, he said
to them, "Brethren, though I had done
nothing against the people or the
customs of our fathers, yet I was
delivered prisoner from Jerusalem into the hands of the Romans. 18 When
they had examined me, they wished
to set me at liberty, because there was
no reason for the death penalty in my
case. 19 But when the Jews objected,
I was compelled to appeal to Caesar—
though I had no charge to bring against
my nation. 20 For this reason therefore
I have asked to see you and speak with
you, since it is because of the hope of
Israel that I am bound with this chain."
21 And they said to him, "We have
received no letters from Judea about
you, and none of the brethren coming
here has reported or spoken any evil
about you. 22 But we desire to hear
from you what your views are; for with
regard to this sect we know that everywhere it is spoken against."

23 When they had appointed a day
for him, they came to him at his
lodging in great numbers. And he
expounded the matter to them from
morning till evening, testifying to the
kingdom of God and trying to convince them about Jesus both from the
law of Moses and from the prophets.
24 And some were convinced by what
he said, while others disbelieved. 25 So,
as they disagreed among themselves,
they departed, after Paul had made
one statement: "The Holy Spirit was
right in saying to your fathers through
Ī·sāi'ȧh the prophet:

26 'Go to this people, and say,
You shall indeed hear but never
understand,
and you shall indeed see but never
perceive.
27 For this people's heart has grown
dull,
and their ears are heavy of hearing,
and their eyes they have closed;
lest they should perceive with their
eyes,
and hear with their ears,
and understand with their heart,
and turn for me to heal them.'
28 Let it be known to you then that
this salvation of God has been sent to
the Gentiles; they will listen."[g]

30 And he lived there two whole
years at his own expense,[h] and welcomed all who came to him, 31 preaching the kingdom of God and teaching
about the Lord Jesus Christ quite
openly and unhindered.

THE LETTER OF PAUL TO THE

ROMANS

1 Paul, a servant[a] of Jesus Christ,
called to be an apostle, set apart for
the gospel of God 2 which he promised
beforehand through his prophets in
the holy scriptures, 3 the gospel concerning his Son, who was descended
from David according to the flesh
4 and designated Son of God in power
according to the Spirit of holiness by
his resurrection from the dead, Jesus
Christ our Lord, 5 through whom we
have received grace and apostleship to
bring about the obedience of faith for
the sake of his name among all the
nations, 6 including yourselves who are
called to belong to Jesus Christ;

7 To all God's beloved in Rome,
who are called to be saints:

Grace to you and peace from
God our Father and the Lord Jesus
Christ.

8 First, I thank my God through
Jesus Christ for all of you, because

[g] Other ancient authorities add verse 29, *And when he had said these words, the Jews departed, holding much dispute among themselves*
[h] Or *in his own hired dwelling* [a] Or *slave*

28.26-27: Is 6.9-10. **28.28:** Ps 67.2. **1.1:** Acts 9.15; 13.2; 1 Cor 1.1; 2 Cor 1.1; Gal 1.15.
1.5: Acts 26.16-18; Rom 15.18; Gal 2.7, 9.
1.7: 1 Cor 1.3; 2 Cor 1.2; Gal 1.3; Eph 1.2; Phil 1.2; Col 1.2; 1 Thess 1.2; 2 Thess 1.2; 1 Tim 1.2; 2 Tim 1.2; Tit 1.4; Philem 3; 2 Jn 3. **1.8:** Rom 16.19.

your faith is proclaimed in all the world. 9 For God is my witness, whom I serve with my spirit in the gospel of his Son, that without ceasing I mention you always in my prayers, 10 asking that somehow by God's will I may now at last succeed in coming to you. 11 For I long to see you, that I may impart to you some spiritual gift to strengthen you, 12 that is, that we may be mutually encouraged by each other's faith, both yours and mine. 13 I want you to know, brethren, that I have often intended to come to you (but thus far have been prevented), in order that I may reap some harvest among you as well as among the rest of the Gentiles. 14 I am under obligation both to Greeks and to barbarians, both to the wise and to the foolish: 15 so I am eager to preach the gospel to you also who are in Rome.

16 For I am not ashamed of the gospel: it is the power of God for salvation to every one who has faith, to the Jew first and also to the Greek. 17 For in it the righteousness of God is revealed through faith for faith; as it is written, "He who through faith is righteous shall live."[b]

18 For the wrath of God is revealed from heaven against all ungodliness and wickedness of men who by their wickedness suppress the truth. 19 For what can be known about God is plain to them, because God has shown it to them. 20 Ever since the creation of the world his invisible nature, namely, his eternal power and deity, has been clearly perceived in the things that have been made. So they are without excuse; 21 for although they knew God they did not honor him as God or give thanks to him, but they became futile in their thinking and their senseless minds were darkened. 22 Claiming to be wise, they became fools, 23 and exchanged the glory of the immortal God for images resembling mortal man or birds or animals or reptiles.

24 Therefore God gave them up in the lusts of their hearts to impurity, to the dishonoring of their bodies among themselves, 25 because they exchanged the truth about God for a lie and worshiped and served the creature rather than the Creator, who is blessed for ever! Amen.

26 For this reason God gave them up to dishonorable passions. Their women exchanged natural relations for unnatural, 27 and the men likewise gave up natural relations with women and were consumed with passion for one another, men committing shameless acts with men and receiving in their own persons the due penalty for their error.

28 And since they did not see fit to acknowledge God, God gave them up to a base mind and to improper conduct. 29 They were filled with all manner of wickedness, evil, covetousness, malice. Full of envy, murder, strife, deceit, malignity, they are gossips, 30 slanderers, haters of God, insolent, haughty, boastful, inventors of evil, disobedient to parents, 31 foolish, faithless, heartless, ruthless. 32 Though they know God's decree that those who do such things deserve to die, they not only do them but approve those who practice them.

2 Therefore you have no excuse, O man, whoever you are, when you judge another; for in passing judgment upon him you condemn yourself, because you, the judge, are doing the very same things. 2 We know that the judgment of God rightly falls upon those who do such things. 3 Do you suppose, O man, that when you judge those who do such things and yet do them yourself, you will escape the judgment of God? 4 Or do you presume upon the riches of his kindness and forbearance and patience? Do you not know that God's kindness is meant to lead you to repentance? 5 But by your hard and impenitent heart you are storing up wrath for yourself on the day of wrath when God's righteous judgment will be revealed. 6 For he will render to every man according to his works: 7 to those who by patience in well-doing seek for glory and honor and immortality, he will give eternal life; 8 but for those who are factious and do not obey the truth, but obey wickedness, there will be wrath and fury. 9 There will be tribulation and distress for

b Or *The righteous shall live by faith*

1.10: Rom 15.23, 32; Acts 19.21. **1.13:** Rom 15.22. **1.14:** 1 Cor 9.16. **1.16:** 1 Cor 1.18, 24. **1.17:** Rom 3.21; Gal 3.11; Phil 3.9; Heb 10.38; Hab 2.4. **1.18:** Eph 5.6; Col 3.6. **1.20:** Ps 19.1-4. **1.21:** Eph 4.17-18. **1.23:** Acts 17.29. **2.1:** Rom 14.22. **2.4:** Eph 1.7; 2.7; Phil 4.19; Col 1.27. **2.6:** Mt 16.27; 1 Cor 3.8; 2 Cor 5.10; Rev 22.12.

every human being who does evil, the
Jew first and also the Greek, 10 but
glory and honor and peace for every one
who does good, the Jew first and also
the Greek. 11 For God shows no
partiality.
12 All who have sinned without the
law will also perish without the law,
and all who have sinned under the
law will be judged by the law. 13 For
it is not the hearers of the law who are
righteous before God, but the doers
of the law who will be justified. 14 When
Gentiles who have not the law do by
nature what the law requires, they are
a law to themselves, even though they
do not have the law. 15 They show
that what the law requires is written
on their hearts, while their conscience
also bears witness and their conflicting
thoughts accuse or perhaps excuse
them 16 on that day when, according
to my gospel, God judges the secrets
of men by Christ Jesus.
17 But if you call yourself a Jew
and rely upon the law and boast of
your relation to God 18 and know his
will and approve what is excellent, because you are instructed in the law,
19 and if you are sure that you are a
guide to the blind, a light to those who
are in darkness, 20 a corrector of the
foolish, a teacher of children, having
in the law the embodiment of knowledge and truth—21 you then who teach
others, will you not teach yourself?
While you preach against stealing, do
you steal? 22 You who say that one
must not commit adultery, do you
commit adultery? You who abhor
idols, do you rob temples? 23 You who
boast in the law, do you dishonor God
by breaking the law? 24 For, as it is
written, "The name of God is blasphemed among the Gentiles because
of you."
25 Circumcision indeed is of value
if you obey the law; but if you break
the law, your circumcision becomes
uncircumcision. 26 So, if a man who is
uncircumcised keeps the precepts of
the law, will not his uncircumcision be
regarded as circumcision? 27 Then
those who are physically uncircumcised but keep the law will condemn
you who have the written code and
circumcision but break the law. 28 For
he is not a real Jew who is one outwardly, nor is true circumcision something external and physical. 29 He is a
Jew who is one inwardly, and real
circumcision is a matter of the heart,
spiritual and not literal. His praise is
not from men but from God.

3 Then what advantage has the
Jew? Or what is the value of circumcision? 2 Much in every way. To
begin with, the Jews are entrusted
with the oracles of God. 3 What if some
were unfaithful? Does their faithlessness nullify the faithfulness of God?
4 By no means! Let God be true
though every man be false, as it is
written,
"That thou mayest be justified in
thy words,
and prevail when thou art judged."
5 But if our wickedness serves to show
the justice of God, what shall we say?
That God is unjust to inflict wrath on
us? (I speak in a human way.) 6 By no
means! For then how could God judge
the world? 7 But if through my falsehood God's truthfulness abounds to
his glory, why am I still being condemned as a sinner? 8 And why not do
evil that good may come?—as some
people slanderously charge us with
saying. Their condemnation is just.
9 What then? Are we Jews any
better off?[c] No, not at all; for I[d] have
already charged that all men, both
Jews and Greeks, are under the power
of sin, 10 as it is written:
"None is righteous, no, not one;
11 no one understands, no one seeks
for God.
12 All have turned aside, together they
have gone wrong;
no one does good, not even one."
13 "Their throat is an open grave,
they use their tongues to deceive."
"The venom of asps is under their
lips."
14 "Their mouth is full of curses and
bitterness."
15 "Their feet are swift to shed blood,
16 in their paths are ruin and misery,

[c] Or *at any disadvantage?* [d] Greek *we*

2.11: Deut 10.17; 2 Chron 19.7; Gal 2.6; Eph 6.9; Col 3.25; 1 Pet 1.17. **2.12:** Rom 3.19; 1 Cor 9.21.
2.13: Jas 1.22-23, 25. **2.16:** Eccles 12.14; Rom 16.25; 1 Cor 4.5. **2.18:** Phil 1.10.
2.20: Rom 6.17; 2 Tim 1.13. **2.21:** Mt 23.3-4. **2.24:** Is 52.5. **2.25:** Jer 9.25.
2.26: 1 Cor 7.19; Acts 10.35. **2.27:** Mt 12.41. **2.28:** Mt 3.9; Jn 8.39; Rom 9.6-7; Gal 6.15.
2.29: 2 Cor 3.6; Phil 3.3; Col 2.11; 1 Pet 3.4. **3.2:** Ps 147.19; Rom 9.4. **3.4:** Ps 51.4.
3.5: Rom 5.9; 6.19; 1 Cor 9.8; Gal 3.15. **3.8:** Rom 6.1, 15. **3.9:** Rom 1.18-32; 2.1-29; 11.32; 3.23.
3.10-12: Ps 14.1-2; 53.1-2. **3.13:** Ps 5.9; 140.3. **3.14:** Ps 10.7. **3.15-17:** Is 59.7-8.

17 and the way of peace they do not
know."
18 "There is no fear of God before
their eyes."
19 Now we know that whatever the
law says it speaks to those who are
under the law, so that every mouth
may be stopped, and the whole world
may be held accountable to God.
20 For no human being will be justified in his sight by works of the law,
since through the law comes knowledge of sin.
21 But now the righteousness of
God has been manifested apart from
law, although the law and the prophets
bear witness to it, 22 the righteousness
of God through faith in Jesus Christ
for all who believe. For there is no
distinction; 23 since all have sinned and
fall short of the glory of God, 24 they
are justified by his grace as a gift,
through the redemption which is in
Christ Jesus, 25 whom God put forward as an expiation by his blood, to
be received by faith. This was to show
God's righteousness, because in his
divine forbearance he had passed over
former sins; 26 it was to prove at the
present time that he himself is righteous and that he justifies him who has
faith in Jesus.
27 Then what becomes of our
boasting? It is excluded. On what
principle? On the principle of works?
No, but on the principle of faith.
28 For we hold that a man is justified
by faith apart from works of law. 29 Or
is God the God of Jews only? Is he not
the God of Gentiles also? Yes, of Gentiles also, 30 since God is one; and he
will justify the circumcised on the
ground of their faith and the uncircumcised through their faith. 31 Do we
then overthrow the law by this faith?
By no means! On the contrary, we uphold the law.
4 What then shall we say about[e]
Abraham, our forefather according to the flesh? 2 For if Abraham was
justified by works, he has something
to boast about, but not before God.
3 For what does the scripture say?
"Abraham believed God, and it was
reckoned to him as righteousness."
4 Now to one who works, his wages
are not reckoned as a gift but as his
due. 5 And to one who does not work
but trusts him who justifies the ungodly, his faith is reckoned as righteousness. 6 So also David pronounces
a blessing upon the man to whom God
reckons righteousness apart from
works:
7 "Blessed are those whose iniquities
are forgiven, and whose sins are
covered;
8 blessed is the man against whom the
Lord will not reckon his sin."
9 Is this blessing pronounced only
upon the circumcised, or also upon the
uncircumcised? We say that faith was
reckoned to Abraham as righteousness.
10 How then was it reckoned to him?
Was it before or after he had been
circumcised? It was not after, but before he was circumcised. 11 He received circumcision as a sign or seal of
the righteousness which he had by
faith while he was still uncircumcised.
The purpose was to make him the
father of all who believe without being
circumcised and who thus have righteousness reckoned to them, 12 and
likewise the father of the circumcised
who are not merely circumcised but
also follow the example of the faith
which our father Abraham had before
he was circumcised.
13 The promise to Abraham and
his descendants, that they should inherit the world, did not come through
the law but through the righteousness
of faith. 14 If it is the adherents of the
law who are to be the heirs, faith is
null and the promise is void. 15 For the
law brings wrath, but where there is
no law there is no transgression.
16 That is why it depends on faith,
in order that the promise may rest on
grace and be guaranteed to all his
descendants—not only to the adherents of the law but also to those
who share the faith of Abraham, for he
is the father of us all, 17 as it is written,
"I have made you the father of many
nations"—in the presence of the God
in whom he believed, who gives life to

[e] Other ancient authorities read *was gained by*

3.18: Ps 36.1. **3.19:** Rom 2.12. **3.20:** Ps 143.2; Acts 13.39; Gal 2.16; 3.11; Rom 7.7.
3.21: Rom 1.17; Phil 3.9; 2 Pet 1.1. **3.22:** Rom 4.5; 9.30; 10.12; Gal 2.16. **3.23:** Rom 3.9.
3.24: Rom 4.16; 5.9; Eph 2.8; Tit 3.7; Eph 1.7; Col 1.14; Heb 9.15. **3.26:** 1 Jn 2.2; Col 1.20.
3.28: Acts 13.39; Rom 5.1; Eph 2.9. **3.29:** Rom 9.24; Acts 10.34-35. **3.30:** Rom 4.11-12, 16.
3.31: Rom 8.4; Mt 5.17. **4.2:** 1 Cor 1.31. **4.3:** Gen 15.6; Rom 4.9, 22; Gal 3.6; Jas 2.23.
4.4: Rom 11.6. **4.5:** Rom 3.22. **4.7:** Ps 32.1-2. **4.11:** Gen 17.10; Rom 3.22, 30.
4.13: Gen 17.4-6; 22.17-18; Gal 3.29. **4.14:** Gal 3.18. **4.15:** Gal 3.10. **4.17:** Gen 17.5; Jn 5.21.

the dead and calls into existence the
things that do not exist. 18 In hope he
believed against hope, that he should
become the father of many nations; as
he had been told, "So shall your
descendants be." 19 He did not weaken
in faith when he considered his own
body, which was as good as dead because he was about a hundred years old,
or when he considered the barrenness
of Sarah's womb. 20 No distrust made
him waver concerning the promise of
God, but he grew strong in his faith as
he gave glory to God, 21 fully convinced that God was able to do what
he had promised. 22 That is why his
faith was "reckoned to him as righteousness." 23 But the words, "it was
reckoned to him," were written not for
his sake alone, 24 but for ours also. It
will be reckoned to us who believe in
him that raised from the dead Jesus
our Lord, 25 who was put to death for
our trespasses and raised for our
justification.

5 Therefore, since we are justified
by faith, we[f] have peace with God
through our Lord Jesus Christ.
2 Through him we have obtained
access[g] to this grace in which we stand,
and we[h] rejoice in our hope of sharing
the glory of God. 3 More than that,
we[h] rejoice in our sufferings, knowing
that suffering produces endurance,
4 and endurance produces character,
and character produces hope, 5 and
hope does not disappoint us, because
God's love has been poured into our
hearts through the Holy Spirit which
has been given to us.
6 While we were yet helpless, at the
right time Christ died for the ungodly.
7 Why, one will hardly die for a righteous man—though perhaps for a good
man one will dare even to die. 8 But
God shows his love for us in that while
we were yet sinners Christ died for us.
9 Since, therefore, we are now justified
by his blood, much more shall we be
saved by him from the wrath of God.
10 For if while we were enemies we
were reconciled to God by the death
of his Son, much more, now that we
are reconciled, shall we be saved by
his life. 11 Not only so, but we also
rejoice in God through our Lord Jesus
Christ, through whom we have now
received our reconciliation.
12 Therefore as sin came into the
world through one man and death
through sin, and so death spread to all
men because all men sinned—13 sin
indeed was in the world before the
law was given, but sin is not counted
where there is no law. 14 Yet death
reigned from Adam to Moses, even
over those whose sins were not like the
transgression of Adam, who was a type
of the one who was to come.
15 But the free gift is not like the
trespass. For if many died through one
man's trespass, much more have the
grace of God and the free gift in the
grace of that one man Jesus Christ
abounded for many. 16 And the free
gift is not like the effect of that one
man's sin. For the judgment following
one trespass brought condemnation,
but the free gift following many trespasses brings justification. 17 If, because of one man's trespass, death
reigned through that one man, much
more will those who receive the
abundance of grace and the free gift of
righteousness reign in life through the
one man Jesus Christ.
18 Then as one man's trespass led
to condemnation for all men, so one
man's act of righteousness leads to
acquittal and life for all men. 19 For
as by one man's disobedience many
were made sinners, so by one man's
obedience many will be made righteous. 20 Law came in, to increase the
trespass; but where sin increased,
grace abounded all the more, 21 so
that, as sin reigned in death, grace also
might reign through righteousness to
eternal life through Jesus Christ our
Lord.

6 What shall we say then? Are we
to continue in sin that grace may
abound? 2 By no means! How can we
who died to sin still live in it? 3 Do
you not know that all of us who have

[f] Other ancient authorities read *let us* [g] Other ancient authorities add *by faith* [h] Or *let us*

4.18: Gen 15.5. **4.19**: Heb 11.12; Gen 17.17; 18.11. **4.22**: Rom 4.3.
4.23-24: Rom 15.4; 1 Cor 9.10; 10.11. **4.25**: Rom 8.32. **5.1**: Rom 3.28.
5.2: Eph 2.18; 3.12; Heb 10.19-20. **5.3**: Rom 5.11; 2 Cor 12.10; Jas 1.3.
5.5: Ps 119.116; Acts 2.33; Phil 1.20. **5.8**: Jn 15.13; Rom 8.32; 1 Pet 3.18; 1 Jn 3.16; 4.10.
5.9: Rom 3.5, 24-25; Eph 1.7; 1 Thess 1.10. **5.10**: Col 1.21. **5.11**: Rom 5.3.
5.12: 1 Cor 15.21-22; Rom 6.23; Jas 1.15. **5.14**: 1 Cor 15.22, 45. **5.15**: Acts 15.11. **5.16**: Rom 8.1.
5.19: Phil 2.8. **5.20**: Rom 7.7-8; Gal 3.19; 1 Tim 1.14. **5.21**: Rom 6.23. **6.1**: Rom 3.8; 6.15.
6.2: Rom 7.4, 6; Gal 2.19; 1 Pet 2.24. **6.3**: Acts 2.38; 8.16; 19.5.

been baptized into Christ Jesus were
baptized into his death? 4 We were
buried therefore with him by baptism
into death, so that as Christ was raised
from the dead by the glory of the
Father, we too might walk in newness
of life.

5 For if we have been united with
him in a death like his, we shall certainly be united with him in a resurrection like his. 6 We know that our
old self was crucified with him so that
the sinful body might be destroyed,
and we might no longer be enslaved
to sin. 7 For he who has died is freed
from sin. 8 But if we have died with
Christ, we believe that we shall also
live with him. 9 For we know that
Christ being raised from the dead will
never die again; death no longer has
dominion over him. 10 The death he
died he died to sin, once for all, but
the life he lives he lives to God. 11 So
you also must consider yourselves
dead to sin and alive to God in Christ
Jesus.

12 Let not sin therefore reign in
your mortal bodies, to make you obey
their passions. 13 Do not yield your
members to sin as instruments of
wickedness, but yield yourselves to
God as men who have been brought
from death to life, and your members
to God as instruments of righteousness. 14 For sin will have no dominion
over you, since you are not under law
but under grace.

15 What then? Are we to sin because we are not under law but under
grace? By no means! 16 Do you not
know that if you yield yourselves to
any one as obedient slaves, you are
slaves of the one whom you obey,
either of sin, which leads to death, or
of obedience, which leads to righteousness? 17 But thanks be to God,
that you who were once slaves of sin
have become obedient from the heart
to the standard of teaching to which
you were committed, 18 and, having
been set free from sin, have become
slaves of righteousness. 19 I am speaking in human terms, because of your
natural limitations. For just as you
once yielded your members to impurity and to greater and greater
iniquity, so now yield your members
to righteousness for sanctification.

20 When you were slaves of sin, you
were free in regard to righteousness.
21 But then what return did you get
from the things of which you are now
ashamed? The end of those things is
death. 22 But now that you have been
set free from sin and have become
slaves of God, the return you get is
sanctification and its end, eternal life.
23 For the wages of sin is death, but
the free gift of God is eternal life in
Christ Jesus our Lord.

7 Do you not know, brethren—for
I am speaking to those who know
the law—that the law is binding on a
person only during his life? 2 Thus a
married woman is bound by law to her
husband as long as he lives; but if her
husband dies she is discharged from
the law concerning the husband.
3 Accordingly, she will be called an
adulteress if she lives with another man
while her husband is alive. But if her
husband dies she is free from that law,
and if she marries another man she is
not an adulteress.

4 Likewise, my brethren, you have
died to the law through the body of
Christ, so that you may belong to
another, to him who has been raised
from the dead in order that we may
bear fruit for God. 5 While we were
living in the flesh, our sinful passions,
aroused by the law, were at work in
our members to bear fruit for death.
6 But now we are discharged from the
law, dead to that which held us captive,
so that we serve not under the old
written code but in the new life of the
Spirit.

7 What then shall we say? That the
law is sin? By no means! Yet, if it had
not been for the law, I should not have
known sin. I should not have known
what it is to covet if the law had not
said, "You shall not covet." 8 But sin,
finding opportunity in the commandment, wrought in me all kinds of
covetousness. Apart from the law sin
lies dead. 9 I was once alive apart from
the law, but when the commandment
came, sin revived and I died; 10 the

6.4: Col 2.12. **6.5**: 2 Cor 4.10; Col 2.12. **6.6**: Rom 7.24; Col 2.13. **6.7**: 1 Pet 4.1.
6.8: 2 Tim 2.11. **6.9**: Acts 2.24; Rev 1.18. **6.11**: Rom 7.4, 6; Gal 2.19; 1 Pet 2.24.
6.13: Rom 6.19; 7.5; 12.1. **6.14**: Rom 8.2. **6.15**: Rom 3.8; 6.1. **6.16**: Mt 6.24; Jn 8.34; Rom 12.1.
6.18: Rom 8.2. **6.19**: Rom 3.5; 6.13; 12.1. **6.20**: Mt 6.24; Jn 8.34. **6.21**: Rom 7.5; 8.6, 13, 21.
6.23: Rom 5.12, 21; Gal 6.7-8. **7.2**: 1 Cor 7.39. **7.4**: Rom 6.2, 11; Gal 2.19; Col 1.22.
7.5: Rom 6.13, 21; 8.8; Jas 1.15. **7.7**: Rom 3.20; 5.20; Ex 20.17; Deut 5.21. **7.8**: 1 Cor 15.56.
7.10: Lev 18.5; Rom 10.5.

very commandment which promised
life proved to be death to me. 11 For sin,
finding opportunity in the commandment, deceived me and by it killed me.
12 So the law is holy, and the commandment is holy and just and good.

13 Did that which is good, then,
bring death to me? By no means! It
was sin, working death in me through
what is good, in order that sin might
be shown to be sin, and through the
commandment might become sinful
beyond measure. 14 We know that the
law is spiritual; but I am carnal, sold
under sin. 15 I do not understand my
own actions. For I do not do what I
want, but I do the very thing I hate.
16 Now if I do what I do not want, I
agree that the law is good. 17 So then
it is no longer I that do it, but sin
which dwells within me. 18 For I know
that nothing good dwells within me,
that is, in my flesh. I can will what is
right, but I cannot do it. 19 For I do
not do the good I want, but the evil I
do not want is what I do. 20 Now if I
do what I do not want, it is no longer
I that do it, but sin which dwells within me.

21 So I find it to be a law that when
I want to do right, evil lies close at
hand. 22 For I delight in the law of
God, in my inmost self, 23 but I see in
my members another law at war with
the law of my mind and making me
captive to the law of sin which dwells
in my members. 24 Wretched man that
I am! Who will deliver me from this
body of death? 25 Thanks be to God
through Jesus Christ our Lord! So
then, I of myself serve the law of God
with my mind, but with my flesh I
serve the law of sin.

8 There is therefore now no condemnation for those who are in
Christ Jesus. 2 For the law of the Spirit
of life in Christ Jesus has set me free
from the law of sin and death. 3 For
God has done what the law, weakened
by the flesh, could not do: sending his
own Son in the likeness of sinful flesh
and for sin,[i] he condemned sin in the
flesh, 4 in order that the just requirement of the law might be fulfilled in
us, who walk not according to the
flesh but according to the Spirit. 5 For
those who live according to the flesh
set their minds on the things of the
flesh, but those who live according to
the Spirit set their minds on the things
of the Spirit. 6 To set the mind on the
flesh is death, but to set the mind on
the Spirit is life and peace. 7 For the
mind that is set on the flesh is hostile
to God; it does not submit to God's
law, indeed it cannot; 8 and those
who are in the flesh cannot please
God.

9 But you are not in the flesh, you
are in the Spirit, if the Spirit of God
really dwells in you. Any one who does
not have the Spirit of Christ does not
belong to him. 10 But if Christ is in
you, although your bodies are dead
because of sin, your spirits are alive
because of righteousness. 11 If the
Spirit of him who raised Jesus from
the dead dwells in you, he who raised
Christ Jesus from the dead will give
life to your mortal bodies also through
his Spirit which dwells in you.

12 So then, brethren, we are debtors, not to the flesh, to live according
to the flesh—13 for if you live according to the flesh you will die, but if by
the Spirit you put to death the deeds
of the body you will live. 14 For all
who are led by the Spirit of God are
sons of God. 15 For you did not receive
the spirit of slavery to fall back into
fear, but you have received the spirit
of sonship. When we cry, "Ab'bȧ!
Father!" 16 it is the Spirit himself
bearing witness with our spirit that we
are children of God, 17 and if children,
then heirs, heirs of God and fellow
heirs with Christ, provided we suffer
with him in order that we may also
be glorified with him.

18 I consider that the sufferings of
this present time are not worth comparing with the glory that is to be
revealed to us. 19 For the creation
waits with eager longing for the revealing of the sons of God; 20 for the creation was subjected to futility, not of

[i] Or *and as a sin offering*

7.12: 1 Tim 1.8. **7.14:** 1 Cor 3.1. **7.15:** Gal 5.17. **7.22:** Ps 1.2. **7.23:** Gal 5.17.
7.24: Rom 6.6; Col 2.11. **8.1:** Rom 5.16. **8.2:** 1 Cor 15.45; Rom 6.14, 18.
8.3: Acts 13.39; Heb 7.18; 10.1-2; Phil 2.7; Heb 2.14. **8.4:** Rom 3.31; Gal 5.16, 25.
8.5: Gal 5.19-25. **8.6:** Rom 6.21; 8.13, 27; Gal 6.8. **8.8:** Rom 7.5.
8.9: 1 Cor 3.16; 6.19; 2 Cor 6.16; 2 Tim 1.14. **8.10:** Gal 2.20; Eph 3.17. **8.11:** Jn 5.21.
8.13: Rom 8.6; Col 3.5. **8.14:** Gal 5.18. **8.15:** Rom 9.4; Gal 4.5-7; Mk 14.36. **8.16:** Acts 5.32.
8.17: Gal 3.29; 4.7; 2 Cor 1.5, 7; 2 Tim 2.12; 1 Pet 4.13. **8.18:** 2 Cor 4.17; Col 3.4; 1 Pet 5.1.
8.19: 1 Pet 1.7, 13; 1 Jn 3.2. **8.20:** Eccles 1.2.

its own will but by the will of him who
subjected it in hope; 21 because the
creation itself will be set free from its
bondage to decay and obtain the
glorious liberty of the children of God.
22 We know that the whole creation
has been groaning in travail together
until now; 23 and not only the creation,
but we ourselves, who have the first
fruits of the Spirit, groan inwardly as
we wait for adoption as sons, the redemption of our bodies. 24 For in this
hope we were saved. Now hope that is
seen is not hope. For who hopes for
what he sees? 25 But if we hope for
what we do not see, we wait for it with
patience.

26 Likewise the Spirit helps us in
our weakness; for we do not know how
to pray as we ought, but the Spirit
himself intercedes for us with sighs
too deep for words. 27 And he who
searches the hearts of men knows what
is the mind of the Spirit, because[j] the
Spirit intercedes for the saints according to the will of God.

28 We know that in everything God
works for good[k] with those who love
him,[l] who are called according to his
purpose. 29 For those whom he foreknew he also predestined to be conformed to the image of his Son, in
order that he might be the first-born
among many brethren. 30 And those
whom he predestined he also called;
and those whom he called he also
justified; and those whom he justified
he also glorified.

31 What then shall we say to this?
If God is for us, who is against us?
32 He who did not spare his own Son
but gave him up for us all, will he not
also give us all things with him? 33 Who
shall bring any charge against God's
elect? It is God who justifies; 34 who is
to condemn? Is it Christ Jesus, who
died, yes, who was raised from the
dead, who is at the right hand of God,
who indeed intercedes for us?[m]
35 Who shall separate us from the love
of Christ? Shall tribulation, or distress,
or persecution, or famine, or nakedness, or peril, or sword? 36 As it is
written,

"For thy sake we are being killed all
the day long;
we are regarded as sheep to be
slaughtered."

37 No, in all these things we are more
than conquerors through him who
loved us. 38 For I am sure that neither
death, nor life, nor angels, nor principalities, nor things present, nor things
to come, nor powers, 39 nor height,
nor depth, nor any thing else in all
creation, will be able to separate us
from the love of God in Christ Jesus
our Lord.

9 I am speaking the truth in Christ,
I am not lying; my conscience
bears me witness in the Holy Spirit,
2 that I have great sorrow and unceasing anguish in my heart. 3 For I could
wish that I myself were accursed and
cut off from Christ for the sake of my
brethren, my kinsmen by race. 4 They
are Israelites, and to them belong the
sonship, the glory, the covenants, the
giving of the law, the worship, and the
promises; 5 to them belong the patriarchs, and of their race, according to
the flesh, is the Christ. God who is
over all be blessed for ever.[n] Amen.

6 But it is not as though the word
of God had failed. For not all who are
descended from Israel belong to Israel,
7 and not all are children of Abraham
because they are his descendants; but
"Through Isaac shall your descendants
be named." 8 This means that it is not
the children of the flesh who are the
children of God, but the children of
the promise are reckoned as descendants. 9 For this is what the promise
said, "About this time I will return and
Sarah shall have a son." 10 And not
only so, but also when Rebecca had
conceived children by one man, our
forefather Isaac, 11 though they were
not yet born and had done nothing
either good or bad, in order that God's
purpose of election might continue,
not because of works but because of
his call, 12 she was told, "The elder
will serve the younger." 13 As it is
written, "Jacob I loved, but Esau I
hated."

[j] Or *that* [k] Other ancient authorities read *in everything he works for good*, or *everything works for good* [l] Greek *God* [m] Or *It is Christ Jesus . . . for us* [n] Or *Christ, who is God over all, blessed for ever*

8.21: Acts 3.21; Rom 6.21; 2 Pet 3.13; Rev 21.1. **8.22:** Jer 12.4, 11. **8.23:** 2 Cor 1.22; 5.2, 4; Gal 5.5. **8.24:** 2 Cor 5.7; Heb 11.1. **8.27:** Ps 139.1-2; Lk 16.15; Rev 2.23; Rom 8.6, 34. **8.29:** Rom 9.23; 11.2; 1 Pet 1.2, 20; Eph 1.5, 11. **8.31:** Ps 118.6. **8.32:** Jn 3.16; Rom 4.25; 5.8. **8.33:** Lk 18.7; Is 50.8-9. **8.34:** Rom 8.27. **8.36:** Ps 44.22. **8.37:** 1 Cor 15.57. **9.3:** Ex 32.32. **9.4:** Rom 3.2; 8.15. **9.6:** Rom 2.28-29. **9.7:** Gen 21.12; Heb 11.18. **9.8:** Gal 3.29; 4.28. **9.9:** Gen 18.10. **9.10:** Gen 25.21. **9.12:** Gen 25.23. **9.13:** Mal 1.2-3.

14 What shall we say then? Is there
injustice on God's part? By no means!
15 For he says to Moses, "I will have
mercy on whom I have mercy, and I
will have compassion on whom I have
compassion." 16 So it depends not
upon man's will or exertion, but upon
God's mercy. 17 For the scripture says
to Pharaoh, "I have raised you up for
the very purpose of showing my power
in you, so that my name may be proclaimed in all the earth." 18 So then he
has mercy upon whomever he wills,
and he hardens the heart of whomever
he wills.

19 You will say to me then, "Why
does he still find fault? For who can
resist his will?" 20 But who are you, a
man, to answer back to God? Will what
is molded say to its molder, "Why have
you made me thus?" 21 Has the potter
no right over the clay, to make out of
the same lump one vessel for beauty
and another for menial use? 22 What if
God, desiring to show his wrath and
to make known his power, has endured
with much patience the vessels of
wrath made for destruction, 23 in order
to make known the riches of his glory
for the vessels of mercy, which he has
prepared beforehand for glory, 24 even
us whom he has called, not from the
Jews only but also from the Gentiles?
25 As indeed he says in Hō·ṡē'ȧ,

"Those who were not my people
I will call 'my people,'
and her who was not beloved
I will call 'my beloved.' "
26 "And in the very place where it was
said to them, 'You are not my
people,'
they will be called 'sons of the living
God.' "

27 And Ī·ṡāi'ȧh cries out concerning
Israel: "Though the number of the
sons of Israel be as the sand of the sea,
only a remnant of them will be saved;
28 for the Lord will execute his sentence upon the earth with rigor and
dispatch." 29 And as Ī·ṡāi'ȧh predicted,

"If the Lord of hosts had not left us
children,
we would have fared like Sod'ȯm
and been made like Gȯ·môr'-
rȧh."

30 What shall we say, then? That
Gentiles who did not pursue righteousness have attained it, that is, righteousness through faith; 31 but that
Israel who pursued the righteousness
which is based on law did not succeed
in fulfilling that law. 32 Why? Because
they did not pursue it through faith,
but as if it were based on works. They
have stumbled over the stumbling
stone, 33 as it is written,

"Behold, I am laying in Zion a stone
that will make men stumble,
a rock that will make them fall;
and he who believes in him will not
be put to shame."

10 Brethren, my heart's desire and
prayer to God for them is that
they may be saved. 2 I bear them witness that they have a zeal for God, but
it is not enlightened. 3 For, being
ignorant of the righteousness that
comes from God, and seeking to establish their own, they did not submit to
God's righteousness. 4 For Christ is
the end of the law, that every one who
has faith may be justified.

5 Moses writes that the man who
practices the righteousness which is
based on the law shall live by it. 6 But
the righteousness based on faith says,
Do not say in your heart, "Who will
ascend into heaven?" (that is, to bring
Christ down) 7 or "Who will descend
into the abyss?" (that is, to bring
Christ up from the dead). 8 But what
does it say? The word is near you, on
your lips and in your heart (that is, the
word of faith which we preach); 9 because, if you confess with your lips
that Jesus is Lord and believe in your
heart that God raised him from the
dead, you will be saved. 10 For man
believes with his heart and so is justified, and he confesses with his lips and
so is saved. 11 The scripture says, "No
one who believes in him will be put to
shame." 12 For there is no distinction
between Jew and Greek; the same
Lord is Lord of all and bestows his
riches upon all who call upon him.

9.14: 2 Chron 19.7. **9.15:** Ex 33.19. **9.17:** Ex 9.16. **9.18:** Rom 11.7. **9.20:** Is 29.16; 45.9.
9.21: 2 Tim 2.20. **9.22:** Prov 16.4. **9.23:** Rom 8.29. **9.24:** Rom 3.29. **9.25:** Hos 2.23; 1 Pet 2.10.
9.26: Hos 1.10. **9.27:** Is 10.22-23; Gen 22.17; Hos 1.10; Rom 11.5; 2 Kings 19.4; Is 11.11.
9.29: Is 1.9. **9.30:** Rom 3.22; 10.6, 20; Gal 2.16; 3.24; Phil 3.9; Heb 11.7.
9.31: Is 51.1; Rom 10.2-3; 11.7. **9.32:** 1 Pet 2.8. **9.33:** Is 28.16; Rom 10.11. **10.2-4:** Rom 9.31.
10.3: Rom 1.17. **10.4:** Gal 3.24; Rom 3.22; 7.1-4.
10.5: Lev 18.5; Neh 9.29; Ezek 20.11, 13, 21; Rom 7.10. **10.6:** Deut 30.12-13; Rom 9.30.
10.8: Deut 30.14. **10.9:** Mt 10.32; Lk 12.8; Acts 16.31. **10.11:** Is 28.16; Rom 9.33.
10.12: Rom 3.22, 29; Gal 3.28; Col 3.11; Acts 10.36.

13 For, "every one who calls upon the
name of the Lord will be saved."
14 But how are men to call upon
him in whom they have not believed?
And how are they to believe in him of
whom they have never heard? And
how are they to hear without a
preacher? 15 And how can men preach
unless they are sent? As it is written,
"How beautiful are the feet of those
who preach good news!" 16 But they
have not all heeded the gospel; for
Ī·ṡāi'ăh says, "Lord, who has believed
what he has heard from us?" 17 So
faith comes from what is heard, and
what is heard comes by the preaching
of Christ.
18 But I ask, have they not heard?
Indeed they have; for
"Their voice has gone out to all the
earth,
and their words to the ends of the
world."
19 Again I ask, did Israel not understand? First Moses says,
"I will make you jealous of those
who are not a nation;
with a foolish nation I will make you
angry."
20 Then Ī·ṡāi'ăh is so bold as to say;
"I have been found by those who
did not seek me;
I have shown myself to those who
did not ask for me."
21 But of Israel he says, "All day long
I have held out my hands to a disobedient and contrary people."

11 I ask, then, has God rejected his
people? By no means! I myself am
an Israelite, a descendant of Abraham,
a member of the tribe of Benjamin.
2 God has not rejected his people
whom he foreknew. Do you not know
what the scripture says of E·lī'jăh,
how he pleads with God against Israel?
3 "Lord, they have killed thy prophets,
they have demolished thy altars, and I
alone am left, and they seek my life."
4 But what is God's reply to him? "I
have kept for myself seven thousand
men who have not bowed the knee to
Bā'ăl." 5 So too at the present time
there is a remnant, chosen by grace.
6 But if it is by grace, it is no longer on
the basis of works; otherwise grace
would no longer be grace.
7 What then? Israel failed to obtain
what it sought. The elect obtained it,
but the rest were hardened, 8 as it is
written,
"God gave them a spirit of stupor,
eyes that should not see and ears
that should not hear,
down to this very day."
9 And David says,
"Let their feast become a snare and
a trap,
a pitfall and a retribution for them;
10 let their eyes be darkened so that
they cannot see,
and bend their backs for ever."
11 So I ask, have they stumbled so
as to fall? By no means! But through
their trespass salvation has come to
the Gentiles, so as to make Israel
jealous. 12 Now if their trespass means
riches for the world, and if their failure
means riches for the Gentiles, how
much more will their full inclusion
mean!
13 Now I am speaking to you Gentiles. Inasmuch then as I am an apostle
to the Gentiles, I magnify my ministry
14 in order to make my fellow Jews
jealous, and thus save some of them.
15 For if their rejection means the
reconciliation of the world, what will
their acceptance mean but life from
the dead? 16 If the dough offered as
first fruits is holy, so is the whole
lump; and if the root is holy, so are the
branches.
17 But if some of the branches were
broken off, and you, a wild olive shoot,
were grafted in their place to share the
richness[o] of the olive tree, 18 do not
boast over the branches. If you do
boast, remember it is not you that
support the root, but the root that supports you. 19 You will say, "Branches
were broken off so that I might be
grafted in." 20 That is true. They were
broken off because of their unbelief,
but you stand fast only through faith.
So do not become proud, but stand in
awe. 21 For if God did not spare the
natural branches, neither will he spare

[o] Other ancient authorities read *rich root*

10.13: Joel 2.32; Acts 2.21. **10.15:** Is 52.7. **10.16:** Is 53.1; Jn 12.38. **10.18:** Ps 19.4; Col 1.6, 23.
10.19: Deut 32.21; Rom 11.11, 14. **10.20:** Is 65.1; Rom 9.30. **10.21:** Is 65.2.
11.1: 1 Sam 12.22; Jer 31.37; 33.24-26; 2 Cor 11.22; Phil 3.5. **11.2:** Ps 94.14; 1 Kings 19.10.
11.4: 1 Kings 19.18. **11.5:** 2 Kings 19.4; Is 11.11; Rom 9.27. **11.6:** Rom 4.4.
11.7: Rom 9.18, 31; 11.25. **11.8:** Is 29.10; Deut 29.4; Mt 13.13-14. **11.9:** Ps 69.22-23.
11.11: Rom 10.19; 11.14. **11.13:** Acts 9.15. **11.14:** Rom 10.19; 11.11; 1 Cor 9.22.
11.15: Lk 15.24, 32. **11.20:** 2 Cor 1.24.

you. 22 Note then the kindness and
the severity of God: severity toward
those who have fallen, but God's
kindness to you, provided you continue
in his kindness; otherwise you too will
be cut off. 23 And even the others, if
they do not persist in their unbelief,
will be grafted in, for God has the
power to graft them in again. 24 For
if you have been cut from what is by
nature a wild olive tree, and grafted,
contrary to nature, into a cultivated
olive tree, how much more will these
natural branches be grafted back into
their own olive tree.

25 Lest you be wise in your own
conceits, I want you to understand
this mystery, brethren: a hardening has
come upon part of Israel, until the full
number of the Gentiles come in, 26 and
so all Israel will be saved; as it is
written,

"The Deliverer will come from
Zion,
he will banish ungodliness from
Jacob";
27 "and this will be my covenant with
them
when I take away their sins."

28 As regards the gospel they are enemies of God, for your sake; but as
regards election they are beloved for
the sake of their forefathers. 29 For
the gifts and the call of God are ir-
revocable. 30 Just as you were once
disobedient to God but now have received mercy because of their disobedience, 31 so they have now been
disobedient in order that by the mercy
shown to you they also may[p] receive
mercy. 32 For God has consigned all
men to disobedience, that he may
have mercy upon all.

33 O the depth of the riches and
wisdom and knowledge of God! How
unsearchable are his judgments and
how inscrutable his ways!
34 "For who has known the mind of
the Lord,
or who has been his counselor?"
35 "Or who has given a gift to him
that he might be repaid?"
36 For from him and through him and
to him are all things. To him be glory
for ever. Amen.

12 I appeal to you therefore, brethren, by the mercies of God, to
present your bodies as a living sacrifice, holy and acceptable to God,
which is your spiritual worship. 2 Do
not be conformed to this world[q] but
be transformed by the renewal of your
mind, that you may prove what is the
will of God, what is good and acceptable and perfect.[r]

3 For by the grace given to me I
bid every one among you not to think
of himself more highly than he ought
to think, but to think with sober judgment, each according to the measure
of faith which God has assigned him.
4 For as in one body we have many
members, and all the members do not
have the same function, 5 so we,
though many, are one body in Christ,
and individually members one of
another. 6 Having gifts that differ according to the grace given to us, let us
use them: if prophecy, in proportion to
our faith; 7 if service, in our serving; he
who teaches, in his teaching; 8 he
who exhorts, in his exhortation;
he who contributes, in liberality;
he who gives aid, with zeal; he who
does acts of mercy, with cheer-
fulness.

9 Let love be genuine; hate what is
evil, hold fast to what is good; 10 love
one another with brotherly affection;
outdo one another in showing honor.
11 Never flag in zeal, be aglow with the
Spirit, serve the Lord. 12 Rejoice in
your hope, be patient in tribulation,
be constant in prayer. 13 Contribute to
the needs of the saints, practice
hospitality.

14 Bless those who persecute you;
bless and do not curse them. 15 Rejoice
with those who rejoice, weep with
those who weep. 16 Live in harmony
with one another; do not be haughty,
but associate with the lowly;[s] never be
conceited. 17 Repay no one evil for

[p] Other ancient authorities add *now* [q] Greek *age*
[r] Or *what is the good and acceptable and perfect will of God* [s] Or *give yourselves to humble tasks*

11.25: 1 Cor 2.7-10; Eph 3.3-5, 9; Rom 9.18; 11.7; Lk 21.24. **11.26:** Is 59. 20-21.
11.27: Jer 31.33; Is 27.9. **11.32:** Rom 3.9; Gal 3.22-29. **11.33:** Col 2.3.
11.34: Is 40.13-14; 1 Cor 2.16. **11.35:** Job 35.7; 41.11. **11.36:** 1 Cor 8.6; 11.12; Col 1.16; Heb 2.10.
12.1: Rom 6.13, 16, 19; 1 Pet 2.5. **12.2:** 1 Jn 2.15; Eph 4.23; 5.10. **12.4:** 1 Cor 12.12-14; Eph 4.4, 16.
12.5: 1 Cor 10.17; 12.20, 27; Eph 4.25. **12.6-8:** 1 Cor 7.7; 12.4-11; 1 Pet 4.10-11.
12.12: Acts 1.14; Rom 5.2; 1 Thess 5.17. **12.14:** Mt 5.44; Lk 6.28.
12.16: Rom 11.25; 15.5; 1 Cor 1.10; 2 Cor 13.11; Phil 2.2; 4.2; Prov 3.7; 26.12.
12.17: Prov 20.22; 2 Cor 8.21; 1 Thess 5.15.

evil, but take thought for what is noble
in the sight of all. 18 If possible, so far
as it depends upon you, live peaceably
with all. 19 Beloved, never avenge
yourselves, but leave it[t] to the wrath
of God; for it is written, "Vengeance
is mine, I will repay, says the Lord."
20 No, "if your enemy is hungry, feed
him; if he is thirsty, give him drink;
for by so doing you will heap burning
coals upon his head." 21 Do not be
overcome by evil, but overcome evil
with good.

13 Let every person be subject to
the governing authorities. For
there is no authority except from God,
and those that exist have been insti-
tuted by God. 2 Therefore he who
resists the authorities resists what God
has appointed, and those who resist
will incur judgment. 3 For rulers are
not a terror to good conduct, but to
bad. Would you have no fear of him
who is in authority? Then do what is
good, and you will receive his approval,
4 for he is God's servant for your good.
But if you do wrong, be afraid, for he
does not bear the sword in vain; he is
the servant of God to execute his
wrath on the wrongdoer. 5 Therefore
one must be subject, not only to avoid
God's wrath but also for the sake of
conscience. 6 For the same reason you
also pay taxes, for the authorities are
ministers of God, attending to this
very thing. 7 Pay all of them their dues,
taxes to whom taxes are due, revenue
to whom revenue is due, respect to
whom respect is due, honor to whom
honor is due.

8 Owe no one anything, except to
love one another; for he who loves his
neighbor has fulfilled the law. 9 The
commandments, "You shall not commit adultery, You shall not kill, You
shall not steal, You shall not covet,"
and any other commandment, are
summed up in this sentence, "You
shall love your neighbor as yourself."
10 Love does no wrong to a neighbor;
therefore love is the fulfilling of the
law.

11 Besides this you know what hour
it is, how it is full time now for you to
wake from sleep. For salvation is
nearer to us now than when we first
believed; 12 the night is far gone, the
day is at hand. Let us then cast off the
works of darkness and put on the
armor of light; 13 let us conduct ourselves becomingly as in the day, not in
reveling and drunkenness, not in
debauchery and licentiousness, not in
quarreling and jealousy. 14 But put on
the Lord Jesus Christ, and make no
provision for the flesh, to gratify its
desires.

14 As for the man who is weak in
faith, welcome him, but not for
disputes over opinions. 2 One believes
he may eat anything, while the weak
man eats only vegetables. 3 Let not him
who eats despise him who abstains,
and let not him who abstains pass
judgment on him who eats; for God
has welcomed him. 4 Who are you to
pass judgment on the servant of
another? It is before his own master
that he stands or falls. And he will be
upheld, for the Master is able to make
him stand.

5 One man esteems one day as
better than another, while another man
esteems all days alike. Let every one
be fully convinced in his own mind.
6 He who observes the day, observes
it in honor of the Lord. He also who
eats, eats in honor of the Lord, since
he gives thanks to God; while he who
abstains, abstains in honor of the Lord
and gives thanks to God. 7 None of us
lives to himself, and none of us dies to
himself. 8 If we live, we live to the
Lord, and if we die, we die to the Lord;
so then, whether we live or whether
we die, we are the Lord's. 9 For to this
end Christ died and lived again, that
he might be Lord both of the dead and
of the living.

10 Why do you pass judgment on
your brother? Or you, why do you
despise your brother? For we shall all
stand before the judgment seat of God;
11 for it is written,

[t] Greek *give place*
12.18: Mk 9.50; Rom 14.19. **12.19:** Lev 19.18; Deut 32.35; Heb 10.30.
12.20: Prov 25.21-22; Mt 5.44; Lk 6.27. **13.1:** Tit 3.1; 1 Pet 2.13-14; Prov 8.15; Jn 19.11.
13.3: 1 Pet 2.14. **13.4:** 1 Thess 4.6. **13.7:** Mt 22.21; Mk 12.17; Lk 20.25.
13.8: Mt 22.39-40; Rom 13.10; Gal 5.14; Col 3.14; Jas 2.8.
13.9: Ex 20.13-14; Deut 5.17-18; Lev 19.18; Mt 19.19.
13.10: Mt 22.39-40; Rom 13.8; Gal 5.14; Jas 2.8. **13.11:** Eph 5.14; 1 Thess 5.6.
13.12: 1 Jn 2.8; Eph 5.11; 1 Thess 5.8. **13.13:** 1 Thess 4.12; Gal 5.19-21. **13.14:** Gal 3.27; 5.16.
14.3: Col 2.16. **14.5:** Gal 4.10. **14.7:** Gal 2.20; 2 Cor 5.15. **14.8:** Phil 1.20. **14.10:** 2 Cor 5.10.
14.11: Is 45.23; Phil 2.10-11.

"As I live, says the Lord, every knee
shall bow to me,
and every tongue shall give praise[u]
to God."
12 So each of us shall give account of
himself to God.
13 Then let us no more pass judgment on one another, but rather decide
never to put a stumbling block or
hindrance in the way of a brother. 14 I
know and am persuaded in the Lord
Jesus that nothing is unclean in itself;
but it is unclean for any one who thinks
it unclean. 15 If your brother is being
injured by what you eat, you are no
longer walking in love. Do not let what
you eat cause the ruin of one for whom
Christ died. 16 So do not let what is
good to you be spoken of as evil. 17 For
the kingdom of God does not mean
food and drink but righteousness and
peace and joy in the Holy Spirit; 18 he
who thus serves Christ is acceptable to
God and approved by men. 19 Let us
then pursue what makes for peace and
for mutual upbuilding. 20 Do not, for
the sake of food, destroy the work of
God. Everything is indeed clean, but
it is wrong for any one to make others
fall by what he eats; 21 it is right not
to eat meat or drink wine or do anything that makes your brother stumble.[v] 22 The faith that you have, keep
between yourself and God; happy is
he who has no reason to judge himself
for what he approves. 23 But he who has
doubts is condemned, if he eats, because he does not act from faith; for
whatever does not proceed from faith
is sin.[w]

15 We who are strong ought to bear
with the failings of the weak, and
not to please ourselves; 2 let each of us
please his neighbor for his good, to
edify him. 3 For Christ did not please
himself; but, as it is written, "The
reproaches of those who reproached
thee fell on me." 4 For whatever was
written in former days was written for
our instruction, that by steadfastness
and by the encouragement of the scriptures we might have hope. 5 May the
God of steadfastness and encouragement grant you to live in such harmony
with one another, in accord with Christ
Jesus, 6 that together you may with
one voice glorify the God and Father
of our Lord Jesus Christ.
7 Welcome one another, therefore,
as Christ has welcomed you, for the
glory of God. 8 For I tell you that
Christ became a servant to the circumcised to show God's truthfulness,
in order to confirm the promises given
to the patriarchs, 9 and in order that
the Gentiles might glorify God for his
mercy. As it is written,
"Therefore I will praise thee among
the Gentiles,
and sing to thy name";
10 and again it is said,
"Rejoice, O Gentiles, with his
people";
11 and again,
"Praise the Lord, all Gentiles,
and let all the peoples praise him";
12 and further Ī·ṡāi′ăh says,
"The root of Jesse shall come,
he who rises to rule the Gentiles;
in him shall the Gentiles hope."
13 May the God of hope fill you with
all joy and peace in believing, so that
by the power of the Holy Spirit you
may abound in hope.
14 I myself am satisfied about you,
my brethren, that you yourselves are
full of goodness, filled with all knowledge, and able to instruct one another.
15 But on some points I have written
to you very boldly by way of reminder,
because of the grace given me by God
16 to be a minister of Christ Jesus to
the Gentiles in the priestly service of
the gospel of God, so that the offering
of the Gentiles may be acceptable,
sanctified by the Holy Spirit. 17 In
Christ Jesus, then, I have reason to be
proud of my work for God. 18 For I
will not venture to speak of anything
except what Christ has wrought
through me to win obedience from the
Gentiles, by word and deed, 19 by the
power of signs and wonders, by the
power of the Holy Spirit, so that from
Jerusalem and as far round as Il·lyr′i-
cŭm I have fully preached the gospel
of Christ, 20 thus making it my ambition to preach the gospel, not where

[u] Or *confess* [v] Other ancient authorities add *or be upset or be weakened*
[w] Other authorities, some ancient, insert here Ch. 16.25-27

14.13: Mt 7.1; 1 Cor 8.13. **14.15:** Rom 14.20; 1 Cor 8.11. **14.16:** 1 Cor 10.30.
14.19: Mk 9.50; Rom 12.18; 1 Thess 5.11. **14.20:** Rom 14.15; 1 Cor 8.9-12. **14.21:** 1 Cor 8.13.
14.22: Rom 2.1. **15.3:** Ps 69.9. **15.4:** Rom 4.23-24; 1 Cor 9.10; 2 Tim 3.16.
15.5: Rom 12.16; 1 Cor 1.10; 2 Cor 13.11; Phil 2.2; 4.2. **15.9:** Ps 18.49; 2 Sam 22.50.
15.10: Deut 32.43. **15.11:** Ps 117.1. **15.12:** Is 11.10; Mt 12.21. **15.16:** Acts 9.15.
15.18: Rom 1.5; Acts 15.12; 21.19. **15.19:** Acts 19.11; 2 Cor 12.12. **15.20:** 2 Cor 10.15-16.

Christ has already been named, lest I
build on another man's foundation,
21 but as it is written,

"They shall see who have never
been told of him,
and they shall understand who have
never heard of him."

22 This is the reason why I have so
often been hindered from coming to
you. 23 But now, since I no longer
have any room for work in these
regions, and since I have longed for
many years to come to you, 24 I hope
to see you in passing as I go to Spain,
and to be sped on my journey there by
you, once I have enjoyed your company for a little. 25 At present, however,
I am going to Jerusalem with aid for
the saints. 26 For Maċ·ė·dō'ni·ȧ and
A·chā'iȧ have been pleased to make
some contribution for the poor among
the saints at Jerusalem; 27 they were
pleased to do it, and indeed they are
in debt to them, for if the Gentiles
have come to share in their spiritual
blessings, they ought also to be of
service to them in material blessings.
28 When therefore I have completed
this, and have delivered to them what
has been raised,[x] I shall go on by way
of you to Spain; 29 and I know that
when I come to you I shall come in the
fulness of the blessing[y] of Christ.

30 I appeal to you, brethren, by our
Lord Jesus Christ and by the love of
the Spirit, to strive together with me
in your prayers to God on my behalf,
31 that I may be delivered from the
unbelievers in Judea, and that my
service for Jerusalem may be acceptable to the saints, 32 so that by God's
will I may come to you with joy and
be refreshed in your company. 33 The
God of peace be with you all. Amen.

16 I commend to you our sister
Phoebe, a deaconess of the church
at Ċen'chrē-ȧe, 2 that you may receive
her in the Lord as befits the saints,
and help her in whatever she may
require from you, for she has been
a helper of many and of myself as well.

3 Greet Pris'cȧ and Aq'ui·lȧ, my
fellow workers in Christ Jesus, 4 who
risked their necks for my life, to whom
not only I but also all the churches of
the Gentiles give thanks; 5 greet also
the church in their house. Greet my
beloved E·paē'nė·tus, who was the
first convert in Asia for Christ. 6 Greet
Mary, who has worked hard among
you. 7 Greet An·dron'i·cus and Jü'-
ni·ȧs, my kinsmen and my fellow
prisoners; they are men of note among
the apostles, and they were in Christ
before me. 8 Greet Am·pli·ā'tus, my
beloved in the Lord. 9 Greet Ŭr·bā'-
nus, our fellow worker in Christ, and
my beloved Stā'chys. 10 Greet A·pel'-
lēs, who is approved in Christ. Greet
those who belong to the family of
Ar·is·tob'ū·lus. 11 Greet my kinsman
He·rō'di·on. Greet those in the Lord
who belong to the family of När·ċis'-
sus. 12 Greet those workers in the
Lord, Trȳ·phaē'nȧ and Trȳ·phō'sȧ.
Greet the beloved Per'sis, who has
worked hard in the Lord. 13 Greet
Rufus, eminent in the Lord, also his
mother and mine. 14 Greet A·syn'cri-
tus, Phlē'gon, Hēr'mēs, Pat'rō·bȧs,
Hēr'mȧs, and the brethren who are
with them. 15 Greet Phi·lol'ȯ·gus,
Julia, Nē'rė·us and his sister, and
Ō·lym'pȧs, and all the saints who are
with them. 16 Greet one another with
a holy kiss. All the churches of Christ
greet you.

17 I appeal to you, brethren, to
take note of those who create dissensions and difficulties, in opposition to
the doctrine which you have been
taught; avoid them. 18 For such persons do not serve our Lord Christ, but
their own appetites,[z] and by fair and
flattering words they deceive the
hearts of the simple-minded. 19 For
while your obedience is known to all,
so that I rejoice over you, I would have
you wise as to what is good and guile-
less as to what is evil; 20 then the God
of peace will soon crush Satan under
your feet. The grace of our Lord Jesus
Christ be with you.[a]

[x] Greek *sealed to them this fruit*
[y] Other ancient authorities insert *of the gospel* [z] Greek *their own belly* (Phil 3.19)
[a] Other ancient authorities omit this sentence

15.21: Is 52.15. **15.22:** Rom 1.13. **15.23:** Acts 19.21; Rom 1.10-11; 15.32. **15.24:** Rom 15.28.
15.25: Acts 19.21; 24.17; 15.31. **15.26:** 2 Cor 8.1-5; 9.2; 1 Thess 1. 7-8. **15.27:** 1 Cor 9.11.
15.28: Rom 15.24. **15.29:** Acts 19.21. **15.31:** 2 Thess 3.2; Rom 15.25-26; 2 Cor 8.4; 9.1.
15.32: Rom 1.10; Acts 19.21. **15.33:** 2 Cor 13.11; Phil 4.9. **16.3:** Acts 18.2. **16.5:** 1 Cor 16.19.
16.16: 2 Cor 13.12; 1 Thess 5.26; 1 Pet 5.14. **16.17:** Gal 1.8-9; 2 Thess 3.6, 14; 2 Jn 10.
16.19: Rom 1.8; 1 Cor 14.20.
16.20: 1 Cor 16.23; 2 Cor 13.14; Gal 6.18, Phil 4.23; 1 Thess 5.28; 2 Thess 3.18; Rev 22.21.

21 Timothy, my fellow worker,
greets you; so do Lucius and Jason
and Sō·sip′ȧ·tėr, my kinsmen.
22 I Tertius, the writer of this letter, greet you in the Lord.
23 Gā′iŭs, who is host to me and to
the whole church, greets you. E·ras′-
tŭs, the city treasurer, and our brother
Quär′tŭs, greet you.[b]

25 Now to him who is able to
strengthen you according to my gospel
and the preaching of Jesus Christ, according to the revelation of the mystery
which was kept secret for long ages
26 but is now disclosed and through
the prophetic writings is made known
to all nations, according to the command of the eternal God, to bring
about the obedience of faith—27 to the
only wise God be glory for evermore
through Jesus Christ! Amen.

THE FIRST LETTER OF PAUL TO THE

CORINTHIANS

1 Paul, called by the will of God to
be an apostle of Christ Jesus, and
our brother Sos′thė·nēṡ,
2 To the church of God which is at
Corinth, to those sanctified in Christ
Jesus, called to be saints together with
all those who in every place call on the
name of our Lord Jesus Christ, both
their Lord and ours:
3 Grace to you and peace from
God our Father and the Lord Jesus
Christ.

4 I give thanks to God[a] always for
you because of the grace of God which
was given you in Christ Jesus, 5 that
in every way you were enriched in him
with all speech and all knowledge—
6 even as the testimony to Christ was
confirmed among you—7 so that you
are not lacking in any spiritual gift, as
you wait for the revealing of our Lord
Jesus Christ; 8 who will sustain you
to the end, guiltless in the day of our
Lord Jesus Christ. 9 God is faithful,
by whom you were called into the
fellowship of his Son, Jesus Christ our
Lord.
10 I appeal to you, brethren, by the
name of our Lord Jesus Christ, that all
of you agree and that there be no dissensions among you, but that you be
united in the same mind and the same
judgment. 11 For it has been reported
to me by Chlō′ē's people that there is
quarreling among you, my brethren.
12 What I mean is that each one of
you says, "I belong to Paul," or "I
belong to A·pol′los," or "I belong to
Cē′phȧs," or "I belong to Christ."
13 Is Christ divided? Was Paul crucified for you? Or were you baptized in
the name of Paul? 14 I am thankful[b]
that I baptized none of you except
Cris′pŭs and Gā′iŭs; 15 lest any one
should say that you were baptized in
my name. 16 (I did baptize also the
household of Steph′ȧ·nȧs. Beyond that,
I do not know whether I baptized any
one else.) 17 For Christ did not send
me to baptize but to preach the gospel,
and not with eloquent wisdom, lest
the cross of Christ be emptied of its
power.
18 For the word of the cross is folly
to those who are perishing, but to us
who are being saved it is the power of
God. 19 For it is written,
"I will destroy the wisdom of the
wise,
and the cleverness of the clever I
will thwart."
20 Where is the wise man? Where is
the scribe? Where is the debater of
this age? Has not God made foolish
the wisdom of the world? 21 For since,

[b] Other ancient authorities insert verse 24, *The grace of our Lord Jesus Christ be with you all. Amen.*
[a] Other ancient authorities read *my God* [b] Other ancient authorities read *I thank God*
16.21: Acts 16.1. **16.23:** 1 Cor 1.14. **1.1:** Rom 1.1; Acts 18.17. **1.2:** Acts 18.1. **1.3:** Rom 1.7.
1.4: Rom 1.8. **1.8:** 1 Cor 5.5; 2 Cor 1.14. **1.9:** Rom 8.28; 1 Jn 1.3.
1.12: 1 Cor 3.4; Acts 18.24; 1 Cor 3.22; Jn 1.42; 1 Cor 9.5; 15.5. **1.13:** Mt 28.19; Acts 2.38.
1.14: Acts 18.8; Rom 16.23. **1.16:** 1 Cor 16.15. **1.17:** Jn 4.2; Acts 10.48; 1 Cor 2.1, 4, 13.
1.19: Is 29.14.

in the wisdom of God, the world did
not know God through wisdom, it
pleased God through the folly of what
we preach to save those who believe.
22 For Jews demand signs and Greeks
seek wisdom, 23 but we preach Christ
crucified, a stumbling block to Jews
and folly to Gentiles, 24 but to those
who are called, both Jews and Greeks,
Christ the power of God and the wisdom of God. 25 For the foolishness of
God is wiser than men, and the weakness of God is stronger than men.

26 For consider your call, brethren;
not many of you were wise according
to worldly standards, not many were
powerful, not many were of noble
birth; 27 but God chose what is foolish
in the world to shame the wise, God
chose what is weak in the world to
shame the strong, 28 God chose what
is low and despised in the world, even
things that are not, to bring to nothing
things that are, 29 so that no human
being might boast in the presence of
God. 30 He is the source of your life
in Christ Jesus, whom God made our
wisdom, our righteousness and sanctification and redemption; 31 therefore,
as it is written, "Let him who boasts,
boast of the Lord."

2 When I came to you, brethren,
I did not come proclaiming to you
the testimony[c] of God in lofty words
or wisdom. 2 For I decided to know
nothing among you except Jesus Christ
and him crucified. 3 And I was with
you in weakness and in much fear and
trembling; 4 and my speech and my
message were not in plausible words of
wisdom, but in demonstration of the
Spirit and power, 5 that your faith
might not rest in the wisdom of men
but in the power of God.

6 Yet among the mature we do impart wisdom, although it is not a
wisdom of this age or of the rulers of
this age, who are doomed to pass away.
7 But we impart a secret and hidden
wisdom of God, which God decreed
before the ages for our glorification.
8 None of the rulers of this age understood this; for if they had, they would
not have crucified the Lord of glory.
9 But, as it is written,

"What no eye has seen, nor ear
heard,
nor the heart of man conceived,
what God has prepared for those
who love him,"

10 God has revealed to us through the
Spirit. For the Spirit searches everything, even the depths of God. 11 For
what person knows a man's thoughts
except the spirit of the man which is
in him? So also no one comprehends
the thoughts of God except the Spirit
of God. 12 Now we have received not
the spirit of the world, but the Spirit
which is from God, that we might
understand the gifts bestowed on us
by God. 13 And we impart this in words
not taught by human wisdom but
taught by the Spirit, interpreting
spiritual truths to those who possess
the Spirit.[d]

14 The unspiritual[e] man does not
receive the gifts of the Spirit of God,
for they are folly to him, and he is not
able to understand them because they
are spiritually discerned. 15 The spiritual man judges all things, but is himself to be judged by no one. 16 "For
who has known the mind of the Lord
so as to instruct him?" But we have
the mind of Christ.

3 But I, brethren, could not address
you as spiritual men, but as men
of the flesh, as babes in Christ. 2 I fed
you with milk, not solid food; for you
were not ready for it; and even yet you
are not ready, 3 for you are still of the
flesh. For while there is jealousy and
strife among you, are you not of the
flesh, and behaving like ordinary men?
4 For when one says, "I belong to
Paul," and another, "I belong to
A·pol'los," are you not merely men?

5 What then is A·pol'los? What is
Paul? Servants through whom you
believed, as the Lord assigned to each.
6 I planted, A·pol'los watered, but God

[c] Other ancient authorities read *mystery* (or *secret*)
[d] Or *interpreting spiritual truths in spiritual language;* or *comparing spiritual things with spiritual*
[e] Or *natural*

1.22: Mt 12.38. **1.23:** 1 Cor 2.2; Gal 3.1; 5.11. **1.27:** Jas 2.5. **1.28:** Rom 4.17. **1.29:** Eph 2.9.
1.30: 1 Cor 4.15; Rom 8.1; 2 Cor 5.21; 1 Cor 6.11; 1 Thess 5.23; Eph 1.7, 14; Col 1.14; Rom 3.24.
1.31: Jer 9.24; 2 Cor 10.17. **2.1:** 1 Cor 1.17. **2.2:** Gal 6.14; 1 Cor 1.23.
2.3: Acts 18.1, 6, 12; 1 Cor 4.10; 2 Cor 11.30. **2.4:** Rom 15.19; 1 Cor 4.20.
2.5: 2 Cor 4.7; 6.7; 1 Cor 12.9. **2.6:** Eph 4.13. **2.7:** Rom 8.29-30. **2.8:** Acts 7.2; Jas 2.1.
2.9: Is 64.4; 65.17. **2.10:** Mt 11.25; 13.11; 16.17; Eph 3.3, 5. **2.12:** Rom 8.15. **2.13:** 1 Cor 1.17.
2.14: 1 Cor 1.18; Jas 3.15. **2.15:** 1 Cor 3.1; 14.37; Gal 6.1. **2.16:** Is 40.13; Rom 11.34.
3.1: Rom 7.14; Heb 5.13. **3.2:** Heb 5.12-13; 1 Pet 2.2. **3.4:** 1 Cor 1.12.
3.5: 2 Cor 6.4; Eph 3.7; Col 1.25. **3.6:** Acts 18.4-11, 24-27; 1 Cor 1.12.

gave the growth. 7 So neither he who plants nor he who waters is anything, but only God who gives the growth. 8 He who plants and he who waters are equal, and each shall receive his wages according to his labor. 9 For we are fellow workers for God;[f] you are God's field, God's building.

10 According to the commission of God given to me, like a skilled master builder I laid a foundation, and another man is building upon it. Let each man take care how he builds upon it. 11 For no other foundation can any one lay than that which is laid, which is Jesus Christ. 12 Now if any one builds on the foundation with gold, silver, precious stones, wood, hay, stubble—13 each man's work will become manifest; for the Day will disclose it, because it will be revealed with fire, and the fire will test what sort of work each one has done. 14 If the work which any man has built on the foundation survives, he will receive a reward. 15 If any man's work is burned up, he will suffer loss, though he himself will be saved, but only as through fire.

16 Do you not know that you are God's temple and that God's Spirit dwells in you? 17 If any one destroys God's temple, God will destroy him. For God's temple is holy, and that temple you are.

18 Let no one deceive himself. If any one among you thinks that he is wise in this age, let him become a fool that he may become wise. 19 For the wisdom of this world is folly with God. For it is written, "He catches the wise in their craftiness," 20 and again, "The Lord knows that the thoughts of the wise are futile." 21 So let no one boast of men. For all things are yours, 22 whether Paul or A·pol'los or Cē'phȧs or the world or life or death or the present or the future, all are yours; 23 and you are Christ's; and Christ is God's.

4 This is how one should regard us, as servants of Christ and stewards of the mysteries of God. 2 Moreover it is required of stewards that they be found trustworthy. 3 But with me it is a very small thing that I should be judged by you or by any human court. I do not even judge myself. 4 I am not aware of anything against myself, but I am not thereby acquitted. It is the Lord who judges me. 5 Therefore do not pronounce judgment before the time, before the Lord comes, who will bring to light the things now hidden in darkness and will disclose the purposes of the heart. Then every man will receive his commendation from God.

6 I have applied all this to myself and A·pol'los for your benefit, brethren, that you may learn by us to live according to scripture, that none of you may be puffed up in favor of one against another. 7 For who sees anything different in you? What have you that you did not receive? If then you received it, why do you boast as if it were not a gift?

8 Already you are filled! Already you have become rich! Without us you have become kings! And would that you did reign, so that we might share the rule with you! 9 For I think that God has exhibited us apostles as last of all, like men sentenced to death; because we have become a spectacle to the world, to angels and to men. 10 We are fools for Christ's sake, but you are wise in Christ. We are weak, but you are strong. You are held in honor, but we are in disrepute. 11 To the present hour we hunger and thirst, we are ill-clad and buffeted and homeless, 12 and we labor, working with our own hands. When reviled, we bless; when persecuted, we endure; 13 when slandered, we try to conciliate; we have become, and are now, as the refuse of the world, the offscouring of all things.

14 I do not write this to make you ashamed, but to admonish you as my beloved children. 15 For though you have countless guides in Christ, you do not have many fathers. For I became your father in Christ Jesus through the

[f] Greek *God's fellow workers*

3.9: Is 61.3; Eph 2.20-22; 1 Pet 2.5. **3.10:** Rom 12.3; 1 Cor 15.10. **3.11:** Eph 2.20.
3.13: 2 Thess 1.7-10. **3.15:** Job 23.10. **3.16:** 1 Cor 6.19; 2 Cor 6.16.
3.18: Is 5.21; 1 Cor 8.2; Gal 6.3. **3.19:** Job 5.13; 1 Cor 1.20. **3.20:** Ps 94.11.
3.21: 1 Cor 4.6; Rom 8.32. **3.22:** 1 Cor 1.12; Rom 8.38. **4.1:** 1 Cor 9.17; Rom 11.25; 16.25.
4.4: 2 Cor 1.12. **4.5:** Rom 2.16; 1 Cor 3.13; 2 Cor 10.18; Rom 2.29.
4.6: 1 Cor 1.19, 31; 3.19-20; 1.12; 3.4. **4.9:** 1 Cor 15.31; 2 Cor 11.23; Rom 8.36; Heb 10.33.
4.10: 1 Cor 1.18; 2 Cor 11.19; 1 Cor 3.18; 2 Cor 13.9; 1 Cor 2.3. **4.11:** Rom 8.35; 2 Cor 11.23-27.
4.12: Acts 18.3; 1 Pet 3.9. **4.15:** 1 Cor 1.30; Philem 10.

gospel. 16 I urge you, then, be imitators of me. 17 Therefore I sent[g] to you Timothy, my beloved and faithful child in the Lord, to remind you of my ways in Christ, as I teach them everywhere in every church. 18 Some are arrogant, as though I were not coming to you. 19 But I will come to you soon, if the Lord wills, and I will find out not the talk of these arrogant people but their power. 20 For the kingdom of God does not consist in talk but in power. 21 What do you wish? Shall I come to you with a rod, or with love in a spirit of gentleness?

5 It is actually reported that there is immorality among you, and of a kind that is not found even among pagans; for a man is living with his father's wife. 2 And you are arrogant! Ought you not rather to mourn? Let him who has done this be removed from among you.

3 For though absent in body I am present in spirit, and as if present, I have already pronounced judgment 4 in the name of the Lord Jesus on the man who has done such a thing. When you are assembled, and my spirit is present, with the power of our Lord Jesus, 5 you are to deliver this man to Satan for the destruction of the flesh, that his spirit may be saved in the day of the Lord Jesus.[h]

6 Your boasting is not good. Do you not know that a little leaven leavens the whole lump? 7 Cleanse out the old leaven that you may be a new lump, as you really are unleavened. For Christ, our paschal lamb, has been sacrificed. 8 Let us, therefore, celebrate the festival, not with the old leaven, the leaven of malice and evil, but with the unleavened bread of sincerity and truth.

9 I wrote to you in my letter not to associate with immoral men; 10 not at all meaning the immoral of this world, or the greedy and robbers, or idolators, since then you would need to go out of the world. 11 But rather I wrote[i] to you not to associate with any one who bears the name of brother if he is guilty of immorality or greed, or is an idolator, reviler, drunkard, or robber—not even to eat with such a one. 12 For what have I to do with judging outsiders? Is it not those inside the church whom you are to judge? 13 God judges those outside. "Drive out the wicked person from among you."

6 When one of you has a grievance against a brother, does he dare go to law before the unrighteous instead of the saints? 2 Do you not know that the saints will judge the world? And if the world is to be judged by you, are you incompetent to try trivial cases? 3 Do you not know that we are to judge angels? How much more, matters pertaining to this life! 4 If then you have such cases, why do you lay them before those who are least esteemed by the church? 5 I say this to your shame. Can it be that there is no man among you wise enough to decide between members of the brotherhood, 6 but brother goes to law against brother, and that before unbelievers?

7 To have lawsuits at all with one another is defeat for you. Why not rather suffer wrong? Why not rather be defrauded? 8 But you yourselves wrong and defraud, and that even your own brethren.

9 Do you not know that the unrighteous will not inherit the kingdom of God? Do not be deceived; neither the immoral, nor idolators, nor adulterers, nor homosexuals,[j] 10 nor thieves, nor the greedy, nor drunkards, nor revilers, nor robbers will inherit the kingdom of God. 11 And such were some of you. But you were washed, you were sanctified, you were justified in the name of the Lord Jesus Christ and in the Spirit of our God.

12 "All things are lawful for me," but not all things are helpful. "All things are lawful for me," but I will not be enslaved by anything. 13 "Food is meant for the stomach and the stomach for food"—and God will destroy both one and the other. The body is not meant for immorality, but

[g] Or *am sending* [h] Other ancient authorities omit *Jesus* [i] Or *now I write*
[j] Two Greek words are rendered by this expression

4.17: 1 Cor 16.10; Acts 16.1; 1 Cor 7.17. **4.21:** 2 Cor 1.23. **5.1:** Deut 22.30; 27.20. **5.3:** Col 2.5. **5.4:** 2 Thess 3.6. **5.5:** Mt 4.10; 1 Cor 1.8. **5.6:** Gal 5.9. **5.8:** Ex 12.19; 13.7; Deut 16.3. **5.9:** 2 Cor 6.14. **5.10:** 1 Cor 10.27. **5.11:** 2 Thess 3.6; 1 Cor 10.7, 14, 20-21. **5.12:** Mk 4.11. **5.13:** Deut 17.7; 1 Cor 5.2. **6.1:** Mt 18.17. **6.7:** Mt 5.39-40. **6.9:** 1 Cor 15.50. **6.11:** Acts 22.16; Rom 8.30. **6.12:** 1 Cor 10.23.

for the Lord, and the Lord for the
body. 14 And God raised the Lord and
will also raise us up by his power.
15 Do you not know that your bodies
are members of Christ? Shall I therefore take the members of Christ and
make them members of a prostitute?
Never! 16 Do you not know that he
who joins himself to a prostitute becomes one body with her? For, as it is
written, "The two shall become one."[k]
17 But he who is united to the Lord
becomes one spirit with him. 18 Shun
immorality. Every other sin which a
man commits is outside the body; but
the immoral man sins against his own
body. 19 Do you not know that your
body is a temple of the Holy Spirit
within you, which you have from God?
You are not your own; 20 you were
bought with a price. So glorify God in
your body.

7 Now concerning the matters
about which you wrote. It is well
for a man not to touch a woman. 2 But
because of the temptation to immorality, each man should have his own wife
and each woman her own husband.
3 The husband should give to his wife
her conjugal rights, and likewise the
wife to her husband. 4 For the wife
does not rule over her own body, but
the husband does; likewise the husband does not rule over his own body,
but the wife does. 5 Do not refuse one
another except perhaps by agreement
for a season, that you may devote
yourselves to prayer; but then come
together again, lest Satan tempt you
through lack of self-control. 6 I say
this by way of concession, not of command. 7 I wish that all were as I myself
am. But each has his own special gift
from God, one of one kind and one of
another.

8 To the unmarried and the widows
I say that it is well for them to remain
single as I do. 9 But if they cannot
exercise self-control, they should
marry. For it is better to marry than
to be aflame with passion.

10 To the married I give charge, not
I but the Lord, that the wife should
not separate from her husband 11 (but
if she does, let her remain single or
else be reconciled to her husband)—
and that the husband should not divorce his wife.

12 To the rest I say, not the Lord,
that if any brother has a wife who is an
unbeliever, and she consents to live
with him, he should not divorce her.
13 If any woman has a husband who is
an unbeliever, and he consents to live
with her, she should not divorce him.
14 For the unbelieving husband is
consecrated through his wife, and the
unbelieving wife is consecrated through
her husband. Otherwise, your children
would be unclean, but as it is they are
holy. 15 But if the unbelieving partner
desires to separate, let it be so; in such
a case the brother or sister is not
bound. For God has called us[l] to
peace. 16 Wife, how do you know
whether you will save your husband?
Husband, how do you know whether
you will save your wife?

17 Only, let every one lead the life
which the Lord has assigned to him,
and in which God has called him. This
is my rule in all the churches. 18 Was
any one at the time of his call already
circumcised? Let him not seek to remove the marks of circumcision. Was
any one at the time of his call uncircumcised? Let him not seek circumcision. 19 For neither circumcision
counts for anything nor uncircumcision, but keeping the commandments
of God. 20 Every one should remain
in the state in which he was called.
21 Were you a slave when called? Never
mind. But if you can gain your freedom, avail yourself of the opportunity.[x]
22 For he who was called in the Lord
as a slave is a freedman of the Lord.
Likewise he who was free when called
is a slave of Christ. 23 You were bought
with a price; do not become slaves of
men. 24 So, brethren, in whatever
state each was called, there let him remain with God.

25 Now concerning the unmarried,
I have no command of the Lord, but
I give my opinion as one who by the
Lord's mercy is trustworthy. 26 I think
that in view of the impending[m] distress
it is well for a person to remain as he

[k] Greek *one flesh* [l] Other ancient authorities read *you*
[x] Or *make use of your present condition instead* [m] Or *present*

6.15: Rom 12.5; 1 Cor 12.27. **6.16:** Gen 2.24; Mt 19.5; Mk 10.8; Eph 5.31.
6.17: Jn 17.21-23; Rom 8.9; Gal 2.20. **6.19:** 1 Cor 3.16; Jn 2.21.
6.20: 1 Cor 7.23; Acts 20.28; Rom 12.1. **7.5:** Ex 19.15. **7.7:** 1 Cor 7.8; 9.5. **7.9:** 1 Tim 5.14.
7.12: 2 Cor 11.17. **7.16:** 1 Pet 3.1. **7.17:** Rom 12.3; 1 Cor 14.33; 2 Cor 8.18; 11.28.
7.18: 1 Maccabees 1.15; Acts 15.1-2. **7.19:** Gal 5.6; 6.15; Rom 2.25. **7.22:** Jn 8.32, 36. **7.23:** 1 Cor 6.20.

is. 27 Are you bound to a wife? Do not
seek to be free. Are you free from a
wife? Do not seek marriage. 28 But if
you marry, you do not sin, and if a girl
marries she does not sin. Yet those who
marry will have worldly troubles, and
I would spare you that. 29 I mean,
brethren, the appointed time has
grown very short; from now on, let
those who have wives live as though
they had none, 30 and those who mourn
as though they were not mourning,
and those who rejoice as though they
were not rejoicing, and those who buy
as though they had no goods, 31 and
those who deal with the world as
though they had no dealings with it.
For the form of this world is passing
away.

32 I want you to be free from
anxieties. The unmarried man is anxious about the affairs of the Lord, how
to please the Lord; 33 but the married
man is anxious about worldly affairs,
how to please his wife, 34 and his
interests are divided. And the unmarried woman or girl is anxious about
the affairs of the Lord, how to be holy
in body and spirit; but the married
woman is anxious about worldly affairs, how to please her husband. 35 I
say this for your own benefit, not to
lay any restraint upon you, but to
promote good order and to secure
your undivided devotion to the Lord.

36 If any one thinks that he is not
behaving properly toward his betrothed, if his passions are strong, and
it has to be, let him do as he wishes; let
them marry—it is no sin. 37 But whoever is firmly established in his heart,
being under no necessity but having
his desire under control, and has determined this in his heart, to keep her
as his betrothed, he will do well. 38 So
that he who marries his betrothed does
well; and he who refrains from marriage will do better.

39 A wife is bound to her husband
as long as he lives. If the husband dies,
she is free to be married to whom she
wishes, only in the Lord. 40 But in my
judgment she is happier if she remains
as she is. And I think that I have the
Spirit of God.

8 Now concerning food offered to
idols: we know that "all of us
possess knowledge." "Knowledge"
puffs up, but love builds up. 2 If any
one imagines that he knows something,
he does not yet know as he ought to
know. 3 But if one loves God, one is
known by him.

4 Hence, as to the eating of food
offered to idols, we know that "an idol
has no real existence," and that "there
is no God but one." 5 For although
there may be so-called gods in heaven
or on earth—as indeed there are many
"gods" and many "lords"— 6 yet for
us there is one God, the Father, from
whom are all things and for whom we
exist, and one Lord, Jesus Christ,
through whom are all things and
through whom we exist.

7 However, not all possess this
knowledge. But some, through being
hitherto accustomed to idols, eat food
as really offered to an idol; and their
conscience, being weak, is defiled.
8 Food will not commend us to God.
We are no worse off if we do not eat,
and no better off if we do. 9 Only take
care lest this liberty of yours somehow
become a stumbling block to the weak.
10 For if any one sees you, a man of
knowledge, at table in an idol's temple,
might he not be encouraged, if his
conscience is weak, to eat food offered
to idols? 11 And so by your knowledge
this weak man is destroyed, the brother
for whom Christ died. 12 Thus, sinning
against your brethren and wounding
their conscience when it is weak, you
sin against Christ. 13 Therefore, if
food is a cause of my brother's falling,
I will never eat meat, lest I cause my
brother to fall.

9 Am I not free? Am I not an
apostle? Have I not seen Jesus our
Lord? Are not you my workmanship
in the Lord? 2 If to others I am not an
apostle, at least I am to you; for you
are the seal of my apostleship in the
Lord.

3 This is my defense to those who
would examine me. 4 Do we not have
the right to our food and drink? 5 Do
we not have the right to be accom-

7.29: Rom 13.11-12; 1 Cor 7.31. **7.32**: 1 Tim 5.5. **7.39**: Rom 7.2. **7.40**: 1 Cor 7.25.
8.1: Rom 15.14. **8.2**: 1 Cor 3.18; 13.8, 9, 12. **8.3**: Gal 4.9; Rom 8.29. **8.4**: 1 Cor 10.19; Deut 6.4.
8.6: Mal 2.10; Eph 4.6; Rom 11.36; 1 Cor 1.2; Eph 4.5; Jn 1.3; Col 1.16. **8.7**: 1 Cor 8.4-5.
8.8: Rom 14.17. **8.9**: 1 Cor 8.10-11; Rom 14.1. **8.11**: Rom 14.15, 20. **8.12**: Mt 18.6; Rom 14.20.
18.13: Rom 14.21. **9.1**: 1 Cor 9.19; 2 Cor 12.12; 1 Thess 2.6; Acts 9.3, 17; 1 Cor 15.8.
9.4: 1 Cor 9.14. **9.5**: 1 Cor 7.7-8; Mt 12.46; 8.14; Jn 1.42.

panied by a wife,[n] as the other apostles and the brothers of the Lord and Cē′phȧs? 6 Or is it only Bär′nȧ·bȧs and I who have no right to refrain from working for a living? 7 Who serves as a soldier at his own expense? Who plants a vineyard without eating any of its fruit? Who tends a flock without getting some of the milk?

8 Do I say this on human authority? Does not the law say the same? 9 For it is written in the law of Moses, "You shall not muzzle an ox when it is treading out the grain." Is it for oxen that God is concerned? 10 Does he not speak entirely for our sake? It was written for our sake, because the plowman should plow in hope and the thresher thresh in hope of a share in the crop. 11 If we have sown spiritual good among you, is it too much if we reap your material benefits? 12 If others share this rightful claim upon you, do not we still more?

Nevertheless, we have not made use of this right, but we endure anything rather than put an obstacle in the way of the gospel of Christ. 13 Do you not know that those who are employed in the temple service get their food from the temple, and those who serve at the altar share in the sacrificial offerings? 14 In the same way, the Lord commanded that those who proclaim the gospel should get their living by the gospel.

15 But I have made no use of any of these rights, nor am I writing this to secure any such provision. For I would rather die than have any one deprive me of my ground for boasting. 16 For if I preach the gospel, that gives me no ground for boasting. For necessity is laid upon me. Woe to me if I do not preach the gospel! 17 For if I do this of my own will, I have a reward; but if not of my own will, I am entrusted with a commission. 18 What then is my reward? Just this: that in my preaching I may make the gospel free of charge, not making full use of my right in the gospel.

19 For though I am free from all men, I have made myself a slave to all, that I might win the more. 20 To the Jews I became as a Jew, in order to win Jews; to those under the law I became as one under the law—though not being myself under the law—that I might win those under the law. 21 To those outside the law I became as one outside the law—not being without law toward God but under the law of Christ—that I might win those outside the law. 22 To the weak I became weak, that I might win the weak. I have become all things to all men, that I might by all means save some. 23 I do it all for the sake of the gospel, that I may share in its blessings.

24 Do you not know that in a race all the runners compete, but only one receives the prize? So run that you may obtain it. 25 Every athlete exercises self-control in all things. They do it to receive a perishable wreath, but we an imperishable. 26 Well, I do not run aimlessly, I do not box as one beating the air; 27 but I pommel my body and subdue it, lest after preaching to others I myself should be disqualified.

10 I want you to know, brethren, that our fathers were all under the cloud, and all passed through the sea, 2 and all were baptized into Moses in the cloud and in the sea, 3 and all ate the same supernatural[o] food 4 and all drank the same supernatural[o] drink. For they drank from the supernatural[o] Rock which followed them, and the Rock was Christ. 5 Nevertheless with most of them God was not pleased; for they were overthrown in the wilderness.

6 Now these things are warnings for us, not to desire evil as they did. 7 Do not be idolaters as some of them were; as it is written, "The people sat down to eat and drink and rose up to dance." 8 We must not indulge in immorality as some of them did, and twenty-three thousand fell in a single day. 9 We must not put the Lord[p] to the test, as some of them did and were destroyed by serpents; 10 nor grumble, as some

[n] Greek *a sister as wife* [o] Greek *spiritual* [p] Other ancient authorities read *Christ*

9.6: Acts 4.36. **9.9:** Deut 25.4; 1 Tim 5.18.
9.10: 2 Tim 2.6. **9.11:** Rom 15.27. **9.12:** 2 Cor 6.3. **9.13:** Deut 18.1. **9.14:** Mt 10.10; Lk 10.7-8.
9.15: 2 Cor 11.10. **9.17:** 1 Cor 4.1; Gal 2.7. **9.18:** 2 Cor 11.7. **9.20:** Rom 11.14.
9.21: Rom 2.12, 14. **9.22:** 2 Cor 11.29; Rom 15.1; 1 Cor 10.33; Rom 11.14. **9.24:** Heb 12.1.
9.25: 2 Tim 2.5; 4.8; Jas 1.12; 1 Pet 5.4. **10.1:** Rom 1.13; Ex 13.21; 14.22, 29.
10.2: Rom 6.3; Gal 3.27. **10.3:** Ex 16.4, 35. **10.4:** Ex 17.6; Num 20.11. **10.5:** Num 14.29-30.
10.6: Num 11.4, 34. **10.7:** Ex 32.4, 6. **10.8:** Num 25.1-18. **10.9:** Num 21.5-6.
10.10: Num 16.41, 49.

of them did and were destroyed by the
Destroyer. 11 Now these things happened to them as a warning, but they
were written down for our instruction,
upon whom the end of the ages has
come. 12 Therefore let any one who
thinks that he stands take heed lest he
fall. 13 No temptation has overtaken
you that is not common to man. God
is faithful, and he will not let you be
tempted beyond your strength, but
with the temptation will also provide
the way of escape, that you may be
able to endure it.

14 Therefore, my beloved, shun the
worship of idols. 15 I speak as to
sensible men; judge for yourselves
what I say. 16 The cup of blessing
which we bless, is it not a participation[q]
in the blood of Christ? The bread
which we break, is it not a participation[q] in the body of Christ? 17 Because
there is one bread, we who are many
are one body, for we all partake of the
one bread. 18 Consider the practice of
Israel; are not those who eat the sacrifices partners in the altar? 19 What do I
imply then? That food offered to idols
is anything, or that an idol is anything?
20 No, I imply that what pagans sacrifice they offer to demons and not to
God. I do not want you to be partners
with demons. 21 You cannot drink the
cup of the Lord and the cup of demons.
You cannot partake of the table of the
Lord and the table of demons. 22 Shall
we provoke the Lord to jealousy? Are
we stronger than he?

23 "All things are lawful," but not
all things are helpful. "All things are
lawful," but not all things build up.
24 Let no one seek his own good, but
the good of his neighbor. 25 Eat whatever is sold in the meat market without
raising any question on the ground of
conscience. 26 For "the earth is the
Lord's, and everything in it." 27 If one
of the unbelievers invites you to dinner
and you are disposed to go, eat whatever is set before you without raising
any question on the ground of conscience. 28 (But if some one says to
you, "This has been offered in sacrifice," then out of consideration for the
man who informed you, and for conscience' sake—29 I mean his conscience, not yours—do not eat it.) For
why should my liberty be determined
by another man's scruples? 30 If I partake with thankfulness, why am I
denounced because of that for which
I give thanks?

31 So, whether you eat or drink, or
whatever you do, do all to the glory of
God. 32 Give no offense to Jews or to
Greeks or to the church of God, 33 just
as I try to please all men in everything
I do, not seeking my own advantage,
but that of many, that they may be
11 saved. 1 Be imitators of me, as I
am of Christ.

2 I commend you because you remember me in everything and maintain the traditions even as I have delivered them to you. 3 But I want you
to understand that the head of every
man is Christ, the head of a woman is
her husband, and the head of Christ
is God. 4 Any man who prays or prophesies with his head covered dishonors
his head, 5 but any woman who prays
or prophesies with her head unveiled
dishonors her head—it is the same as
if her head were shaven. 6 For if a
woman will not veil herself, then she
should cut off her hair; but if it is dis-
graceful for a woman to be shorn or
shaven, let her wear a veil. 7 For a man
ought not to cover his head, since he
is the image and glory of God; but
woman is the glory of man. 8 (For man
was not made from woman, but woman
from man. 9 Neither was man created
for woman, but woman for man.)
10 That is why a woman ought to have
a veil[r] on her head, because of the
angels. 11 (Nevertheless, in the Lord
woman is not independent of man nor
man of woman; 12 for as woman was
made from man, so man is now born
of woman. And all things are from
God.) 13 Judge for yourselves; is it
proper for a woman to pray to God
with her head uncovered? 14 Does not
nature itself teach you that for a man
to wear long hair is degrading to him,
15 but if a woman has long hair, it is
her pride? For her hair is given to her
for a covering. 16 If any one is disposed

[q] Or *communion* [r] Greek *authority* (the veil being a symbol of this)

10.13: 1 Cor 1.9. **10.14:** 1 Jn 5.21. **10.16:** Mt 26.27-28; Acts 2.42. **10.17:** Rom 12.5.
10.18: Lev 7.6. **10.20:** Deut 32.17. **10.21:** 2 Cor 6.16. **10.22:** Deut 32.21; Eccles 6.10; Is 45.9.
10.23: 1 Cor 6.12; Phil 2.21. **10.26:** Ps 24.1; 50.12. **10.28:** 1 Cor 8.7, 10-12. **10.32:** 1 Cor 8.13.
10.33: 1 Cor 9.22; Rom 15.2; 1 Cor 13.5. **11.1:** 1 Cor 4.16. **11.2:** 2 Thess 2.15.
11.3: Eph 1.22; 4.15; 5.23; Col 1.8; 2.19. **11.5:** Lk 2.36; Acts 21.9; 1 Cor 14.34. **11.7:** Gen 1.26.
11.8: Gen 2.21-23. **11.9:** Gen 2.18. **11.12:** 2 Cor 5.18; Rom 11.36. **11.16:** 1 Cor 7.17.

to be contentious, we recognize no
other practice, nor do the churches of
God.

17 But in the following instructions
I do not commend you, because when
you come together it is not for the
better but for the worse. 18 For, in the
first place, when you assemble as a
church, I hear that there are divisions
among you; and I partly believe it,
19 for there must be factions among
you in order that those who are genuine
among you may be recognized. 20 When
you meet together, it is not the Lord's
supper that you eat. 21 For in eating,
each one goes ahead with his own
meal, and one is hungry and another
is drunk. 22 What! Do you not have
houses to eat and drink in? Or do you
despise the church of God and humili-
ate those who have nothing? What
shall I say to you? Shall I commend
you in this? No, I will not.

23 For I received from the Lord
what I also delivered to you, that the
Lord Jesus on the night when he was
betrayed took bread, 24 and when he
had given thanks, he broke it, and said,
"This is my body which is for[s] you.
Do this in remembrance of me." 25 In
the same way also the cup, after supper,
saying, "This cup is the new covenant
in my blood. Do this, as often as you
drink it, in remembrance of me."
26 For as often as you eat this bread
and drink the cup, you proclaim the
Lord's death until he comes.

27 Whoever, therefore, eats the
bread or drinks the cup of the Lord in
an unworthy manner will be guilty of
profaning the body and blood of the
Lord. 28 Let a man examine himself,
and so eat of the bread and drink of
the cup. 29 For any one who eats and
drinks without discerning the body
eats and drinks judgment upon himself. 30 That is why many of you are
weak and ill, and some have died.[t]
31 But if we judged ourselves truly, we
should not be judged. 32 But when we
are judged by the Lord, we are chastened[u] so that we may not be condemned along with the world.

33 So then, my brethren, when you
come together to eat, wait for one
another—34 if any one is hungry, let
him eat at home—lest you come together to be condemned. About the
other things I will give directions when
I come.

12 Now concerning spiritual gifts,
brethren, I do not want you to
be uninformed. 2 You know that when
you were heathen, you were led astray
to dumb idols, however you may have
been moved. 3 Therefore I want you
to understand that no one speaking by
the Spirit of God ever says "Jesus be
cursed!" and no one can say "Jesus is
Lord!" except by the Holy Spirit.

4 Now there are varieties of gifts,
but the same Spirit; 5 and there are
varieties of service, but the same Lord;
6 and there are varieties of working,
but it is the same God who inspires
them all in every one. 7 To each is
given the manifestation of the Spirit
for the common good. 8 To one is
given through the Spirit the utterance
of wisdom, and to another the utterance of knowledge according to the
same Spirit, 9 to another faith by the
same Spirit, to another gifts of healing
by the one Spirit, 10 to another the
working of miracles, to another prophecy, to another the ability to distinguish between spirits, to another
various kinds of tongues, to another
the interpretation of tongues. 11 All
these are inspired by one and the same
Spirit who apportions to each one
individually as he wills.

12 For just as the body is one and
has many members, and all the members of the body, though many, are one
body, so it is with Christ. 13 For by
one Spirit we were all baptized into
one body—Jews or Greeks, slaves or
free—and all were made to drink of
one Spirit.

14 For the body does not consist of
one member but of many. 15 If the
foot should say, "Because I am not a
hand, I do not belong to the body,"
that would not make it any less a part
of the body. 16 And if the ear should
say, "Because I am not an eye, I do
not belong to the body," that would
not make it any less a part of the body.

[s] Other ancient authorities read *broken for* [t] Greek *have fallen asleep* (as in 15.6, 20)
[u] Or *when we are judged we are being chastened by the Lord*

11.18: 1 Cor 1.10. **11.23:** 1 Cor 15.3.
11.23-25: Mt 26.26-28; Mk 14.22-24; Lk 22.17-19; 1 Cor 10.16. **11.25:** 2 Cor 3.6; Lk 22.20.
11.26: 1 Cor 4.5. **11.32:** 1 Cor 1.20. **11.34:** 1 Cor 4.19. **12.2:** Eph 2.11-12. **12.3:** Rom 10.9.
12.10: 1 Cor 14.26. **12.12:** Rom 12.4. **12.13:** Gal 3.28; Col 3.11; Eph 2.13-18; Jn 7.37-39.

17 If the whole body were an eye,
where would be the hearing? If the
whole body were an ear, where would
be the sense of smell? 18 But as it is,
God arranged the organs in the body,
each one of them, as he chose. 19 If all
were a single organ, where would the
body be? 20 As it is, there are many
parts, yet one body. 21 The eye cannot
say to the hand, "I have no need of
you," nor again the head to the feet,
"I have no need of you." 22 On the
contrary, the parts of the body which
seem to be weaker are indispensable,
23 and those parts of the body which
we think less honorable we invest with
the greater honor, and our unpresent-
able parts are treated with greater
modesty, 24 which our more present-
able parts do not require. But God has
so adjusted the body, giving the greater
honor to the inferior part, 25 that there
may be no discord in the body, but
that the members may have the same
care for one another. 26 If one member
suffers, all suffer together; if one member is honored, all rejoice together.

27 Now you are the body of Christ
and individually members of it. 28 And
God has appointed in the church first
apostles, second prophets, third teachers, then workers of miracles, then
healers, helpers, administrators,
speakers in various kinds of tongues.
29 Are all apostles? Are all prophets?
Are all teachers? Do all work miracles?
30 Do all possess gifts of healing? Do
all speak with tongues? Do all interpret? 31 But earnestly desire the higher
gifts.

And I will show you a still more
excellent way.

13 If I speak in the tongues of men
and of angels, but have not love,
I am a noisy gong or a clanging cymbal.
2 And if I have prophetic powers, and
understand all mysteries and all knowledge, and if I have all faith, so as to
remove mountains, but have not love,
I am nothing. 3 If I give away all I
have, and if I deliver my body to be
burned,[v] but have not love, I gain
nothing.

4 Love is patient and kind; love is
not jealous or boastful; 5 it is not arrogant or rude. Love does not insist on
its own way; it is not irritable or resentful; 6 it does not rejoice at wrong,
but rejoices in the right. 7 Love bears
all things, believes all things, hopes all
things, endures all things.

8 Love never ends; as for prophecies,
they will pass away; as for tongues,
they will cease; as for knowledge, it
will pass away. 9 For our knowledge is
imperfect and our prophecy is imperfect; 10 but when the perfect comes,
the imperfect will pass away. 11 When
I was a child, I spoke like a child, I
thought like a child, I reasoned like a
child; when I became a man, I gave up
childish ways. 12 For now we see in a
mirror dimly, but then face to face.
Now I know in part; then I shall understand fully, even as I have been fully
understood. 13 So faith, hope, love
abide, these three; but the greatest of
these is love.

14 Make love your aim, and earnestly desire the spiritual gifts,
especially that you may prophesy.
2 For one who speaks in a tongue
speaks not to men but to God; for no
one understands him, but he utters
mysteries in the Spirit. 3 On the other
hand, he who prophesies speaks to men
for their upbuilding and encouragement and consolation. 4 He who speaks
in a tongue edifies himself, but he who
prophesies edifies the church. 5 Now I
want you all to speak in tongues, but
even more to prophesy. He who
prophesies is greater than he who
speaks in tongues, unless someone
interprets, so that the church may be
edified.

6 Now, brethren, if I come to you
speaking in tongues, how shall I
benefit you unless I bring you some
revelation or knowledge or prophecy
or teaching? 7 If even lifeless instruments, such as the flute or the harp, do
not give distinct notes, how will any
one know what is played? 8 And if the
bugle gives an indistinct sound, who
will get ready for battle? 9 So with
yourselves; if you in a tongue utter
speech that is not intelligible, how will
any one know what is said? For you
will be speaking into the air. 10 There
are doubtless many different languages
in the world, and none is without
meaning; 11 but if I do not know the
meaning of the language, I shall be a
foreigner to the speaker and the
speaker a foreigner to me. 12 So with

[v] Other ancient authorities read *body that I may glory*

12.27: Eph 1.23; 4.12; Col 1.18, 24; Eph 5.30; Rom 12.5. **12.28:** Eph 4.11; 2.20; 3.5. **13.1:** Ps 150.5. **13.2:** 1 Cor 14.2; Mt 17.20; 21.21. **13.5:** 1 Cor 10.24. **13.7:** 1 Cor 9.12.

yourselves; since you are eager for
manifestations of the Spirit, strive to
excel in building up the church.
13 Therefore, he who speaks in a
tongue should pray for the power to
interpret. 14 For if I pray in a tongue,
my spirit prays but my mind is unfruitful. 15 What am I to do? I will
pray with the spirit and I will pray
with the mind also; I will sing with the
spirit and I will sing with the mind also.
16 Otherwise, if you bless[w] with the
spirit, how can any one in the position
of an outsider[x] say the "Amen" to your
thanksgiving when he does not know
what you are saying? 17 For you may
give thanks well enough, but the other
man is not edified. 18 I thank God that
I speak in tongues more than you all;
19 nevertheless, in church I would
rather speak five words with my mind,
in order to instruct others, than ten
thousand words in a tongue.
20 Brethren, do not be children in
your thinking; be babes in evil, but in
thinking be mature. 21 In the law it is
written, "By men of strange tongues
and by the lips of foreigners will I
speak to this people, and even then
they will not listen to me, says the
Lord." 22 Thus, tongues are a sign not
for believers but for unbelievers, while
prophecy is not for unbelievers but for
believers. 23 If, therefore, the whole
church assembles and all speak in
tongues, and outsiders or unbelievers
enter, will they not say that you are
mad? 24 But if all prophesy, and an
unbeliever or outsider enters, he is
convicted by all, he is called to account
by all, 25 the secrets of his heart are
disclosed; and so, falling on his face,
he will worship God and declare that
God is really among you.
26 What then, brethren? When you
come together, each one has a hymn,
a lesson, a revelation, a tongue, or an
interpretation. Let all things be done
for edification. 27 If any speak in a
tongue, let there be only two or at
most three, and each in turn; and let
one interpret. 28 But if there is no one
to interpret, let each of them keep
silence in church and speak to himself
and to God. 29 Let two or three
prophets speak, and let the others
weigh what is said. 30 If a revelation is
made to another sitting by, let the first
be silent. 31 For you can all prophesy
one by one, so that all may learn and
all be encouraged; 32 and the spirits of
prophets are subject to prophets.
33 For God is not a God of confusion
but of peace.
As in all the churches of the saints,
34 the women should keep silence in
the churches. For they are not permitted to speak, but should be sub-
ordinate, as even the law says. 35 If
there is anything they desire to know,
let them ask their husbands at home.
For it is shameful for a woman to
speak in church. 36 What! Did the
word of God originate with you, or
are you the only ones it has reached?
37 If any one thinks that he is a
prophet, or spiritual, he should acknowledge that what I am writing to
you is a command of the Lord. 38 If
any one does not recognize this, he is
not recognized. 39 So, my brethren,
earnestly desire to prophesy, and do
not forbid speaking in tongues; 40 but
all things should be done decently and
in order.

15 Now I would remind you, brethren, in what terms I preached to
you the gospel, which you received, in
which you stand, 2 by which you are
saved, if you hold it fast—unless you
believed in vain.
3 For I delivered to you as of first
importance what I also received, that
Christ died for our sins in accordance
with the scriptures, 4 that he was
buried, that he was raised on the third
day in accordance with the scriptures,
5 and that he appeared to Cē′phȧs,
then to the twelve. 6 Then he appeared
to more than five hundred brethren at
one time, most of whom are still alive,
though some have fallen asleep. 7 Then
he appeared to James, then to all the
apostles. 8 Last of all, as to one untimely born, he appeared also to me.
9 For I am the least of the apostles,
unfit to be called an apostle, because I
persecuted the church of God. 10 But
by the grace of God I am what I am,
and his grace toward me was not in
vain. On the contrary, I worked harder

[w] That is, *give thanks to God* [x] Or *him that is without gifts*
14.15: Eph 5.19; Col 3.16. **14.16:** 1 Chron 16.36; Ps 106.48; Mt 15.36. **14.20:** Eph 4.14.
14.21: Is 28.11-12. **14.26:** Eph 5.19. **14.34:** 1 Tim 2.11-12; 1 Pet 3.1.
15.3: 1 Cor 11.23; 1 Pet 2.24; Is 53.5-12. **15.4:** Mt 16.21; Ps 16.8-9. **15.5:** Lk 24.34; Mt 28.17.
15.8: 1 Cor 9.1; Gal 1.16; Acts 9.3-6. **15.9:** Acts 8.3.

than any of them, though it was not
I, but the grace of God which is with
me. 11 Whether then it was I or they,
so we preach and so you believed.

12 Now if Christ is preached as
raised from the dead, how can some
of you say that there is no resurrection
of the dead? 13 But if there is no resurrection of the dead, then Christ has
not been raised; 14 if Christ has not
been raised, then our preaching is in
vain and your faith is in vain. 15 We
are even found to be misrepresenting
God, because we testified of God that
he raised Christ, whom he did not
raise if it is true that the dead are not
raised. 16 For if the dead are not raised,
then Christ has not been raised. 17 If
Christ has not been raised, your faith
is futile and you are still in your sins.
18 Then those also who have fallen
asleep in Christ have perished. 19 If
for this life only we have hoped in
Christ, we are of all men most to be
pitied.

20 But in fact Christ has been
raised from the dead, the first fruits of
those who have fallen asleep. 21 For as
by a man came death, by a man has
come also the resurrection of the dead.
22 For as in Adam all die, so also in
Christ shall all be made alive. 23 But
each in his own order: Christ the first
fruits, then at his coming those who
belong to Christ. 24 Then comes the
end, when he delivers the kingdom to
God the Father after destroying every
rule and every authority and power.
25 For he must reign until he has put
all his enemies under his feet. 26 The
last enemy to be destroyed is death.
27 "For God[z] has put all things in
subjection under his feet." But when
it says, "All things are put in subjection under him," it is plain that he is
excepted who put all things under
him. 28 When all things are subjected
to him, then the Son himself will also
be subjected to him who put all things
under him, that God may be everything to every one.

29 Otherwise, what do people mean
by being baptized on behalf of the
dead? If the dead are not raised at all,
why are people baptized on their behalf? 30 Why am I in peril every hour?
31 I protest, brethren, by my pride in
you which I have in Christ Jesus our
Lord, I die every day! 32 What do I
gain if, humanly speaking, I fought
with beasts at Eph'ĕ·sŭs? If the dead
are not raised, "Let us eat and drink,
for tomorrow we die." 33 Do not be
deceived: "Bad company ruins good
morals." 34 Come to your right mind,
and sin no more. For some have no
knowledge of God. I say this to your
shame.

35 But some one will ask, "How are
the dead raised? With what kind of
body do they come?" 36 You foolish
man! What you sow does not come to
life unless it dies. 37 And what you sow
is not the body which is to be, but a
bare kernel, perhaps of wheat or of
some other grain. 38 But God gives it
a body as he has chosen, and to each
kind of seed its own body. 39 For not
all flesh is alike, but there is one kind
for men, another for animals, another
for birds, and another for fish. 40 There
are celestial bodies and there are terrestrial bodies; but the glory of the
celestial is one, and the glory of the
terrestrial is another. 41 There is one
glory of the sun, and another glory
of the moon, and another glory of
the stars; for star differs from star in
glory.

42 So is it with the resurrection of
the dead. What is sown is perishable,
what is raised is imperishable. 43 It is
sown in dishonor, it is raised in glory.
It is sown in weakness, it is raised in
power. 44 It is sown a physical body,
it is raised a spiritual body. If there is
a physical body, there is also a spiritual
body. 45 Thus it is written, "The first
man Adam became a living being";
the last Adam became a life-giving
spirit. 46 But it is not the spiritual
which is first but the physical, and
then the spiritual. 47 The first man was
from the earth, a man of dust; the
second man is from heaven. 48 As was
the man of dust, so are those who are
of the dust; and as is the man of
heaven, so are those who are of heaven.
49 Just as we have borne the image of
the man of dust, we shall[a] also bear
the image of the man of heaven. 50 I
tell you this, brethren: flesh and blood

[z] Greek *he* [a] Other ancient authorities read *let us*

15.14: 1 Thess 4.14. **15.18:** 1 Thess 4.16. **15.21:** Rom 5.12. **15.22:** Rom 5.14-18.
15.23: 1 Thess 2.19. **15.25:** Ps 110.1. **15.27:** Ps 8.6; Eph 1.22. **15.28:** Phil 3.21. **15.30:** 2 Esdras 7.89.
15.31: Rom 8.36. **15.32:** 2 Cor 1.8, 9; Is 22.13. **15.33:** Menander, *Thais*. **15.34:** Rom 13.11.
15.36: Jn 12.24. **15.38:** Gen 1.11. **15.42:** Dan 12.3. **15.45:** Gen 2.7.

cannot inherit the kingdom of God,
nor does the perishable inherit the
imperishable.
51 Lo! I tell you a mystery. We
shall not all sleep, but we shall all be
changed, 52 in a moment, in the twin-
kling of an eye, at the last trumpet.
For the trumpet will sound, and the
dead will be raised imperishable, and
we shall be changed. 53 For this perishable nature must put on the imperishable, and this mortal nature must
put on immortality. 54 When the
perishable puts on the imperishable,
and the mortal puts on immortality,
then shall come to pass the saying that
is written:
"Death is swallowed up in victory."
55 "O death, where is thy victory?
O death, where is thy sting?"
56 The sting of death is sin, and the
power of sin is the law. 57 But thanks
be to God, who gives us the victory
through our Lord Jesus Christ.
58 Therefore, my beloved brethren,
be steadfast, immovable, always
abounding in the work of the Lord,
knowing that in the Lord your labor is
not in vain.

16 Now concerning the contribution for the saints: as I directed
the churches of Galatia, so you also are
to do. 2 On the first day of every week,
each of you is to put something aside
and store it up, as he may prosper, so
that contributions need not be made
when I come. 3 And when I arrive, I
will send those whom you accredit by
letter to carry your gift to Jerusalem.
4 If it seems advisable that I should go
also, they will accompany me.
5 I will visit you after passing
through Mac·e·dō'ni·a, for I intend to
pass through Macedonia, 6 and perhaps I will stay with you or even spend
the winter, so that you may speed me
on my journey, wherever I go. 7 For I
do not want to see you now just in
passing; I hope to spend some time
with you, if the Lord permits. 8 But I
will stay in Eph'e·sus until Pentecost,
9 for a wide door for effective work has
opened to me, and there are many
adversaries.
10 When Timothy comes, see that
you put him at ease among you, for he
is doing the work of the Lord, as I am.
11 So let no one despise him. Speed
him on his way in peace, that he may
return to me; for I am expecting him
with the brethren.
12 As for our brother A·pol'los, I
strongly urged him to visit you with
the other brethren, but it was not at
all his will[b] to come now. He will come
when he has opportunity.
13 Be watchful, stand firm in your
faith, be courageous, be strong. 14 Let
all that you do be done in love.
15 Now, brethren, you know that
the household of Steph'a·nas were the
first converts in A·chā'ia, and they have
devoted themselves to the service of
the saints; 16 I urge you to be subject
to such men and to every fellow worker
and laborer. 17 I rejoice at the coming
of Steph'a·nas and Fôr·tū·nā'tus and
A·chā'i·cus, because they have made
up for your absence; 18 for they refreshed my spirit as well as yours.
Give recognition to such men.
19 The churches of Asia send greetings. Aq'ui·la and Pris'ca, together
with the church in their house, send
you hearty greetings in the Lord.
20 All the brethren send greetings.
Greet one another with a holy kiss.

21 I, Paul, write this greeting with
my own hand. 22 If any one has no
love for the Lord, let him be accursed.
Our Lord, come![c] 23 The grace of
the Lord Jesus be with you. 24 My
love be with you all in Christ Jesus.
Amen.

[b] Or *God's will for him* [c] Greek *Maranatha*

15.51-52: 1 Thess 4.15-17. **15.54:** Is 25.8. **15.55:** Hos 13.14. **16.1:** Acts 24.17.
16.2: Acts 20.7; 2 Cor 9.4-5. **16.3:** 2 Cor 8.18-19. **16.5:** Rom 15.26; Acts 19.21. **16.7:** Acts 18.21.
16.8: Acts 18.19. **16.9:** Acts 19.9. **16.10:** Acts 16.1. **16.12:** Acts 18.24. **16.13:** Ps 31.24; Eph 6.10.
16.19: Acts 18.2; Rom 16.5. **16.20:** Rom 16.16. **16.21:** Col 4.18; Gal 6.11; 2 Thess 3.17.
16.22: Rom 9.3. **16.23:** Rom 16.20.

THE SECOND LETTER OF PAUL TO THE

CORINTHIANS

1 Paul, an apostle of Christ Jesus
by the will of God, and Timothy
our brother.
To the church of God which is at
Corinth, with all the saints who are in
the whole of A·chā'ia:
2 Grace to you and peace from God
our Father and the Lord Jesus Christ.

3 Blessed be the God and Father of
our Lord Jesus Christ, the Father of
mercies and God of all comfort, 4 who
comforts us in all our affliction, so that
we may be able to comfort those who
are in any affliction, with the comfort
with which we ourselves are comforted by God. 5 For as we share
abundantly in Christ's sufferings, so
through Christ we share abundantly
in comfort too.[a] 6 If we are afflicted, it
is for your comfort and salvation; and
if we are comforted, it is for your comfort, which you experience when you
patiently endure the same sufferings
that we suffer. 7 Our hope for you is
unshaken; for we know that as you
share in our sufferings, you will also
share in our comfort.
8 For we do not want you to be
ignorant, brethren, of the affliction we
experienced in Asia; for we were so
utterly, unbearably crushed that we
despaired of life itself. 9 Why, we felt
that we had received the sentence of
death; but that was to make us rely
not on ourselves but on God who
raises the dead; 10 he delivered us from
so deadly a peril, and he will deliver
us; on him we have set our hope that
he will deliver us again. 11 You also
must help us by prayer, so that many
will give thanks on our behalf for the
blessing granted us in answer to many
prayers.
12 For our boast is this, the testimony of our conscience that we have
behaved in the world, and still more
toward you, with holiness and godly
sincerity, not by earthly wisdom but
by the grace of God. 13 For we write
you nothing but what you can read
and understand; I hope you will understand fully, 14 as you have understood in part, that you can be proud
of us as we can be of you, on the day
of the Lord Jesus.
15 Because I was sure of this, I
wanted to come to you first, so that
you might have a double pleasure;[b]
16 I wanted to visit you on my way to
Mac·e·dō'ni·a, and to come back to
you from Macedonia and have you
send me on my way to Judea. 17 Was I
vacillating when I wanted to do this?
Do I make my plans like a worldly
man, ready to say Yes and No at
once? 18 As surely as God is faithful,
our word to you has not been Yes and
No. 19 For the Son of God, Jesus
Christ, whom we preached among you,
Sil·vā'nus and Timothy and I, was not
Yes and No; but in him it is always
Yes. 20 For all the promises of God
find their Yes in him. That is why we
utter the Amen through him, to the
glory of God. 21 But it is God who
establishes us with you in Christ, and
has commissioned us; 22 he has put his
seal upon us and given us his Spirit in
our hearts as a guarantee.
23 But I call God to witness against
me—it was to spare you that I refrained from coming to Corinth. 24 Not
that we lord it over your faith; we
work with you for your joy, for you
2 stand firm in your faith. 1 For I
made up my mind not to make you
another painful visit. 2 For if I cause
you pain, who is there to make me
glad but the one whom I have pained?
3 And I wrote as I did, so that when I
came I might not be pained by those
who should have made me rejoice, for
I felt sure of all of you, that my joy
would be the joy of you all. 4 For I
wrote you out of much affliction and
anguish of heart and with many tears,
not to cause you pain but to let you

[a] Or, *For as the sufferings of Christ abound for us, so also our comfort abounds though Christ*
[b] Other ancient authorities read *favor*

1.1: Eph 1.1; Col 1.1; 2 Cor 1.19; Acts 16.1; 18.1. **1.2:** Rom 1.7. **1.3:** Eph 1.3; 1 Pet 1.3; Rom 15.5. **1.4:** 2 Cor 7.6-7, 13. **1.16:** Acts 19.21. **1.19:** 1 Thess 1.1; Acts 15.22. **1.20:** 1 Cor 14.16; Rev 3.14.

know the abundant love that I have
for you.
5 But if any one has caused pain, he
has caused it not to me, but in some
measure—not to put it too severely—
to you all. 6 For such a one this punishment by the majority is enough;
7 so you should rather turn to forgive
and comfort him, or he may be overwhelmed by excessive sorrow. 8 So I
beg you to reaffim your love for him.
9 For this is why I wrote, that I might
test you and know whether you are
obedient in everything. 10 Any one
whom you forgive, I also forgive.
What I have forgiven, if I have forgiven anything, has been for your
sake in the presence of Christ, 11 to
keep Satan from gaining the advantage over us; for we are not ignorant
of his designs.
12 When I came to Trō'as to preach
the gospel of Christ, a door was opened
for me in the Lord; 13 but my mind
could not rest because I did not find
my brother Titus there. So I took
leave of them and went on to Mac·ė-
dō'ni·ȧ.
14 But thanks be to God, who in
Christ always leads us in triumph, and
through us spreads the fragrance of
the knowledge of him everywhere.
15 For we are the aroma of Christ to
God among those who are being saved
and among those who are perishing,
16 to one a fragrance from death to
death, to the other a fragrance from
life to life. Who is sufficient for these
things? 17 For we are not, like so many,
peddlers of God's word; but as men
of sincerity, as commissioned by God,
in the sight of God we speak in Christ.

3 Are we beginning to commend
ourselves again? Or do we need, as
some do, letters of recommendation to
you, or from you? 2 You yourselves are
our letter of recommendation, written
on your[c] hearts, to be known and read
by all men; 3 and you show that you
are a letter from Christ delivered by
us, written not with ink but with the
Spirit of the living God, not on tablets
of stone but on tablets of human
hearts.
4 Such is the confidence that we
have through Christ toward God.
5 Not that we are sufficient of ourselves to claim anything as coming
from us; our sufficiency is from God,
6 who has qualified us to be ministers
of a new covenant, not in a written
code but in the Spirit; for the written
code kills, but the Spirit gives life.
7 Now if the dispensation of death,
carved in letters on stone, came with
such splendor that the Israelites could
not look at Moses' face because of its
brightness, fading as this was, 8 will
not the dispensation of the Spirit be
attended with greater splendor? 9 For
if there was splendor in the dispensation of condemnation, the dispensation of righteousness must far exceed
it in splendor. 10 Indeed, in this case,
what once had splendor has come to
have no splendor at all, because of the
splendor that surpasses it. 11 For if
what faded away came with splendor,
what is permanent must have much
more splendor.
12 Since we have such a hope, we
are very bold, 13 not like Moses, who
put a veil over his face so that the Israelites might not see the end of the
fading splendor. 14 But their minds
were hardened; for to this day, when
they read the old covenant, that same
veil remains unlifted, because only
through Christ is it taken away. 15 Yes,
to this day whenever Moses is read a
veil lies over their minds; 16 but when
a man turns to the Lord the veil is
removed. 17 Now the Lord is the
Spirit, and where the Spirit of the
Lord is, there is freedom. 18 And we
all, with unveiled face, beholding[d] the
glory of the Lord, are being changed
into his likeness from one degree of
glory to another; for this comes from
the Lord who is the Spirit.

4 Therefore, having this ministry
by the mercy of God,[e] we do not
lose heart. 2 We have renounced dis-
graceful, underhanded ways; we refuse
to practice cunning or to tamper with
God's word, but by the open statement of the truth we would commend
ourselves to every man's conscience in
the sight of God. 3 And even if our gospel is veiled, it is veiled only to those
who are perishing. 4 In their case the
god of this world has blinded the
minds of the unbelievers, to keep them
from seeing the light of the gospel of
the glory of Christ, who is the likeness
of God. 5 For what we preach is not

[c] Other ancient authorities read *our* [d] Or *reflecting* [e] Greek *as we have received mercy*

2.12: Acts 16.8. **3.1:** Acts 18.27; Rom 16.1; 1 Cor 16.3. **3.3:** Ex 24.12; 31.18; 32.15-16; Jer 31.33.
3.6: Jer 31.31. **3.7:** Ex 34.29-35. **3.17:** Is 61.1-2. **4.4:** Jn 12.31; Col 1.15.

ourselves, but Jesus Christ as Lord,
with ourselves as your servants[f] for
Jesus' sake. 6 For it is the God who
said, "Let light shine out of darkness,"
who has shone in our hearts to give
the light of the knowledge of the glory
of God in the face of Christ.

7 But we have this treasure in
earthen vessels, to show that the tran-
scendent power belongs to God and
not to us. 8 We are afflicted in every
way, but not crushed; perplexed, but
not driven to despair; 9 persecuted,
but not forsaken; struck down, but
not destroyed; 10 always carrying in
the body the death of Jesus, so that
the life of Jesus may also be manifested in our bodies. 11 For while we
live we are always being given up to
death for Jesus' sake, so that the life
of Jesus may be manifested in our
mortal flesh. 12 So death is at work in
us, but life in you.

13 Since we have the same spirit of
faith as he had who wrote, "I believed, and so I spoke," we too believe,
and so we speak, 14 knowing that he
who raised the Lord Jesus will raise
us also with Jesus and bring us with
you into his presence. 15 For it is all
for your sake, so that as grace extends
to more and more people it may increase thanksgiving, to the glory of
God.

16 So we do not lose heart. Though
our outer nature is wasting away, our
inner nature is being renewed every
day. 17 For this slight momentary
affliction is preparing for us an eternal
weight of glory beyond all comparison, 18 because we look not to the
things that are seen but to the things
that are unseen; for the things that
are seen are transient, but the things
that are unseen are eternal.

5 For we know that if the earthly
tent we live in is destroyed, we
have a building from God, a house not
made with hands, eternal in the heavens. 2 Here indeed we groan, and long
to put on our heavenly dwelling, 3 so
that by putting it on we may not be
found naked. 4 For while we are still
in this tent, we sigh with anxiety; not
that we would be unclothed, but that
we would be further clothed, so that
what is mortal may be swallowed up
by life. 5 He who has prepared us for
this very thing is God, who has given
us the Spirit as a guarantee.

6 So we are always of good courage;
we know that while we are at home in
the body we are away from the Lord,
7 for we walk by faith, not by sight.
8 We are of good courage, and we
would rather be away from the body
and at home with the Lord. 9 So
whether we are at home or away, we
make it our aim to please him. 10 For
we must all appear before the judgment seat of Christ, so that each one
may receive good or evil, according to
what he has done in the body.

11 Therefore, knowing the fear of
the Lord, we persuade men; but what
we are is known to God, and I hope it
is known also to your conscience.
12 We are not commending ourselves
to you again but giving you cause to
be proud of us, so that you may be
able to answer those who pride themselves on a man's position and not on
his heart. 13 For if we are beside ourselves, it is for God; if we are in our
right mind, it is for you. 14 For the
love of Christ controls us, because we
are convinced that one has died for all;
therefore all have died. 15 And he died
for all, that those who live might live
no longer for themselves but for
him who for their sake died and was
raised.

16 From now on, therefore, we regard no one from a human point of
view; even though we once regarded
Christ from a human point of view, we
regard him thus no longer. 17 Therefore, if any one is in Christ, he is a new
creation;[g] the old has passed away, behold, the new has come. 18 All this is
from God, who through Christ reconciled us to himself and gave us the
ministry of reconciliation; 19 that is,
God was in Christ reconciling[h] the
world to himself, not counting their
trespasses against them, and entrust-
ing to us the message of reconciliation. 20 So we are ambassadors for
Christ, God making his appeal through
us. We beseech you on behalf of
Christ, be reconciled to God. 21 For
our sake he made him to be sin who
knew no sin, so that in him we might
become the righteousness of God.

[f] Or *slaves* [g] Or *creature* [h] Or *in Christ God was reconciling*
4.6: Gen 1.3. **4.13:** Ps 116.10. **4.14:** 1 Thess 4.14. **5.10:** Mt 16.27. **5.12:** 2 Cor 3.1.
5.14: Rom 5.15; 6.6-7. **5.17:** Rom 16.7; Gal 6.15. **5.18:** 1 Cor 11.12; Col 1.20; Rom 5.10.
5.20: Eph 6.20. **5.21:** Heb 4.15; 7.25; 1 Pet 2.22; 1 Jn 3.5; Acts 3.14.

6 Working together with him, then,
we entreat you not to accept the
grace of God in vain. 2 For he says,
"At the acceptable time I have listened to you,
and helped you on the day of
salvation."
Behold, now is the acceptable time; behold, now is the day of salvation. 3 We
put no obstacle in any one's way, so
that no fault may be found with our
ministry, 4 but as servants of God we
commend ourselves in every way:
through great endurance, in afflictions, hardships, calamities, 5 beatings, imprisonments, tumults, labors,
watching, hunger; 6 by purity, knowledge, forbearance, kindness, the Holy
Spirit, genuine love, 7 truthful speech,
and the power of God; with the weapons of righteousness for the right hand
and for the left; 8 in honor and dishonor, in ill repute and good repute.
We are treated as impostors, and yet
are true; 9 as unknown, and yet well
known; as dying, and behold we live;
as punished, and yet not killed; 10 as
sorrowful, yet always rejoicing; as
poor, yet making many rich; as having
nothing, and yet possessing everything.
11 Our mouth is open to you, Corinthians; our heart is wide. 12 You are
not restricted by us, but you are restricted in your own affections. 13 In
return—I speak as to children—widen
your hearts also.

14 Do not be mismated with unbelievers. For what partnership have
righteousness and iniquity? Or what
fellowship has light with darkness?
15 What accord has Christ with Bē'li-
ȧl?[i] Or what has a believer in common
with an unbeliever? 16 What agreement has the temple of God with
idols? For we are the temple of the
living God; as God said,
"I will live in them and move among
them,
and I will be their God,
and they shall be my people.
17 Therefore come out from them,
and be separate from them, says the
Lord,
and touch nothing unclean;
then I will welcome you,
18 and I will be a father to you,
and you shall be my sons and
daughters,
says the Lord Almighty."

7 Since we have these promises,
beloved, let us cleanse ourselves
from every defilement of body and
spirit, and make holiness perfect in
the fear of God.

2 Open your hearts to us; we have
wronged no one, we have corrupted no
one, we have taken advantage of no
one. 3 I do not say this to condemn
you, for I said before that you are in
our hearts, to die together and to live
together. 4 I have great confidence in
you; I have great pride in you; I am
filled with comfort. With all our affliction, I am overjoyed.
5 For even when we came into
Maċ·ė·dō'ni·ȧ, our bodies had no rest
but we were afflicted at every turn—
fighting without and fear within. 6 But
God, who comforts the downcast,
comforted us by the coming of Titus,
7 and not only by his coming but also
by the comfort with which he was
comforted in you, as he told us of your
longing, your mourning, your zeal for
me, so that I rejoiced still more. 8 For
even if I made you sorry with my letter, I do not regret it (though I did
regret it), for I see that that letter
grieved you, though only for a while.
9 As it is, I rejoice, not because you
were grieved, but because you were
grieved into repenting; for you felt a
godly grief, so that you suffered no
loss through us. 10 For godly grief
produces a repentance that leads to
salvation and brings no regret, but
worldly grief produces death. 11 For
see what earnestness this godly grief
has produced in you, what eagerness
to clear yourselves, what indignation,
what alarm, what longing, what zeal,
what punishment! At every point you
have proved yourselves guiltless in the
matter. 12 So although I wrote to you,
it was not on account of the one who
did the wrong, nor on account of the
one who suffered the wrong, but in

[i] Greek *Beliar*

6.2: Is 49.8. **6.4:** 2 Cor 4.8-11; 11.23-27. **6.5:** Acts 16.23.
6.7: 2 Cor 10.4; Rom 13.12; Eph 6.11-12. **6.9:** Rom 8.36. **6.10:** Rom 8.32; 1 Cor 3.21.
6.11: Ezek 33.22; Is 60.5. **6.16:** 1 Cor 10.21; 3.16; Ex 25.8; 29.45; Lev 26.12; Ezek 37.27; Jer 31.1.
6.17: Is 52.11. **6.18:** Hos 1.10; Is 43.6. **7.2:** 2 Cor 6.12-13. **7.3:** 2 Cor 6.11-12.
7.5: 2 Cor 2.13; 4.8. **7.6:** 2 Cor 2.13; 7.13-14. **7.8:** 2 Cor 2.2. **7.12:** 2 Cor 7.8; 2.3, 9.

order that your zeal for us might be
revealed to you in the sight of God.
13 Therefore we are comforted.
And besides our own comfort we
rejoiced still more at the joy of Titus,
because his mind has been set at rest
by you all. 14 For if I have expressed
to him some pride in you, I was not
put to shame; but just as everything
we said to you was true, so our boasting before Titus has proved true.
15 And his heart goes out all the more
to you, as he remembers the obedience
of you all, and the fear and trembling
with which you received him. 16 I
rejoice, because I have perfect confidence in you.

8 We want you to know, brethren,
about the grace of God which has
been shown in the churches of Mac·e-
dō'ni·a, 2 for in a severe test of affliction, their abundance of joy and their
extreme poverty have overflowed in a
wealth of liberality on their part. 3 For
they gave according to their means, as
I can testify, and beyond their means,
of their own free will, 4 begging us
earnestly for the favor of taking part
in the relief of the saints—5 and this,
not as we expected, but first they gave
themselves to the Lord and to us by
the will of God. 6 Accordingly we have
urged Titus that as he had already
made a beginning, he should also complete among you this gracious work.
7 Now as you excel in everything—in
faith, in utterance, in knowledge, in
all earnestness, and in your love for
us—see that you excel in this gracious
work also.
8 I say this not as a command, but
to prove by the earnestness of others
that your love also is genuine. 9 For
you know the grace of our Lord Jesus
Christ, that though he was rich, yet
for your sake he became poor, so that
by his poverty you might become rich.
10 And in this matter I give my advice:
it is best for you now to complete what
a year ago you began not only to do
but to desire, 11 so that your readiness
in desiring it may be matched by your
completing it out of what you have.
12 For if the readiness is there, it is
acceptable according to what a man
has, not according to what he has not.
13 I do not mean that others should be
eased and you burdened, 14 but that
as a matter of equality your abundance at the present time should supply their want, so that their abundance may supply your want, that
there may be equality. 15 As it is
written, "He who gathered much had
nothing over, and he who gathered
little had no lack."
16 But thanks be to God who puts
the same earnest care for you into the
heart of Titus. 17 For he not only
accepted our appeal, but being himself very earnest he is going to you of
his own accord. 18 With him we are
sending the brother who is famous
among all the churches for his preaching of the gospel; 19 and not only that,
but he has been appointed by the
churches to travel with us in this
gracious work which we are carrying
on, for the glory of the Lord and to
show our good will. 20 We intend that
no one should blame us about this
liberal gift which we are administer-
ing, 21 for we aim at what is honorable
not only in the Lord's sight but also in
the sight of men. 22 And with them we
are sending our brother whom we have
often tested and found earnest in
many matters, but who is now more
earnest than ever because of his great
confidence in you. 23 As for Titus, he is
my partner and fellow worker in your
service; and as for our brethren, they
are messengers[j] of the churches, the
glory of Christ. 24 So give proof, before the churches, of your love and
of our boasting about you to these
men.

9 Now it is superfluous for me to
write to you about the offering for
the saints, 2 for I know your readiness,
of which I boast about you to the people of Mac·e·dō'ni·a, saying that
A·chā'ia has been ready since last
year; and your zeal has stirred up most
of them. 3 But I am sending the brethren so that our boasting about you
may not prove vain in this case, so
that you may be ready, as I said you
would be; 4 lest if some Mac·e·dō'ni-
ans come with me and find that you
are not ready, we be humiliated—to
say nothing of you—for being so
confident. 5 So I thought it necessary

[j] Greek *apostles*

8.3: 1 Cor 16.2. **8.4:** Acts 24.17; Rom 15.31. **8.6:** 2 Cor 8.16, 23; 2.13. **8.9:** 2 Cor 6.10.
8.10: 2 Cor 9.2; 1 Cor 16.2-3. **8.15:** Ex 16.18. **8.18:** 2 Cor 12.18. **8.19:** 1 Cor 16.3-4.
9.1: 2 Cor 8.4. **9.2:** Rom 15.26; 2 Cor 8.10. **9.3:** 1 Cor 16.2.

to urge the brethren to go on to you
before me, and arrange in advance for
this gift you have promised, so that it
may be ready not as an exaction but
as a willing gift.

6 The point is this: he who sows
sparingly will also reap sparingly, and
he who sows bountifully will also reap
bountifully. 7 Each one must do as he
has made up his mind, not reluctantly
or under compulsion, for God loves a
cheerful giver. 8 And God is able to
provide you with every blessing in
abundance, so that you may always
have enough of everything and may
provide in abundance for every good
work. 9 As it is written,

"He scatters abroad, he gives to the
poor;
his righteousness[k] endures for ever."

10 He who supplies seed to the sower
and bread for food will supply and
multiply your resources[l] and increase
the harvest of your righteousness.[k]
11 You will be enriched in every way
for great generosity, which through us
will produce thanksgiving to God;
12 for the rendering of this service not
only supplies the wants of the saints
but also overflows in many thanksgivings to God. 13 Under the test of this
service, you[m] will glorify God by your
obedience in acknowledging the gospel
of Christ, and by the generosity of
your contribution for them and for all
others; 14 while they long for you and
pray for you, because of the surpassing grace of God in you. 15 Thanks be
to God for his inexpressible gift!

10 I, Paul, myself entreat you, by
the meekness and gentleness of
Christ—I who am humble when face
to face with you, but bold to you when
I am away!— 2 I beg of you that when
I am present I may not have to show
boldness with such confidence as I
count on showing against some who
suspect us of acting in worldly fashion.
3 For though we live in the world we
are not carrying on a worldly war, 4 for
the weapons of our warfare are not
worldly but have divine power to destroy strongholds. 5 We destroy arguments and every proud obstacle to the
knowledge of God, and take every
thought captive to obey Christ, 6 being ready to punish every disobedience, when your obedience is complete.

7 Look at what is before your eyes.
If any one is confident that he is
Christ's, let him remind himself that
as he is Christ's, so are we. 8 For even
if I boast a little too much of our
authority, which the Lord gave for
building you up and not for destroying you, I shall not be put to shame.
9 I would not seem to be frightening
you with letters. 10 For they say,
"His letters are weighty and strong,
but his bodily presence is weak, and
his speech of no account." 11 Let such
people understand that what we say
by letter when absent, we do when
present. 12 Not that we venture to
class or compare outselves with some
of those who commend themselves.
But when they measure themselves
by one another, and compare themselves with one another, they are
without understanding.

13 But we will not boast beyond
limit, but will keep to the limits God
has apportioned us, to reach even to
you. 14 For we are not overextending
ourselves, as though we did not reach
you; we were the first to come all the
way to you with the gospel of Christ.
15 We do not boast beyond limit, in
other men's labors; but our hope is
that as your faith increases, our field
among you may be greatly enlarged,
16 so that we may preach the gospel in
lands beyond you, without boasting of
work already done in another's field.
17 "Let him who boasts, boast of the
Lord." 18 For it is not the man who
commends himself that is accepted,
but the man whom the Lord commends.

11 I wish you would bear with me
in a little foolishness. Do bear
with me! 2 I feel a divine jealousy for
you, for I betrothed you to Christ to
present you as a pure bride to her one
husband. 3 But I am afraid that as the
serpent deceived Eve by his cunning,
your thoughts will be led astray from
a sincere and pure devotion to Christ.
4 For if some one comes and preaches

[k] Or *benevolence* [l] Greek *sowing* [m] Or *they*

9.7: Prov 22.8 (Gk.). **9.8:** Eph 3.20. **9.9:** Ps 112.9. **9.10:** Is 55.10; Hos 10.12.
9.13: 2 Cor 8.4; Rom 15.31. **9.15:** Rom 5.15-16. **10.1:** 2 Cor 10.10.
10.2: 2 Cor 13.2, 10; 1 Cor 4.21. **10.6:** 2 Cor 2.9. **10.7:** 1 Cor 1.12. **10.10:** 1 Cor 2.3.
10.15: Rom 15.20. **10.17:** Jer 9.24. **11.1:** 2 Cor 11.21. **11.2:** Hos 2.19-20; Eph 5.26-27.
11.3: Gen 3.4. **11.4:** Gal 1.6.

another Jesus than the one we
preached, or if you receive a different
spirit from the one you received, or if
you accept a different gospel from the
one you accepted, you submit to it
readily enough. 5 I think that I am
not in the least inferior to these superlative apostles. 6 Even if I am unskilled in speaking, I am not in
knowledge; in every way we have
made this plain to you in all things.

7 Did I commit a sin in abasing myself so that you might be exalted, because I preached God's gospel without
cost to you? 8 I robbed other churches
by accepting support from them in
order to serve you. 9 And when I was
with you and was in want, I did not
burden any one, for my needs were
supplied by the brethren who came
from Mac·e·dō'ni·a. So I refrained and
will refrain from burdening you in any
way. 10 As the truth of Christ is in me,
this boast of mine shall not be silenced
in the regions of A·chā'ia. 11 And why?
Because I do not love you? God knows
I do!

12 And what I do I will continue to
do, in order to undermine the claim
of those who would like to claim that
in their boasted mission they work on
the same terms as we do. 13 For such
men are false apostles, deceitful workmen, disguising themselves as apostles
of Christ. 14 And no wonder, for even
Satan disguises himself as an angel of
light. 15 So it is not strange if his servants also disguise themselves as
servants of righteousness. Their end
will correspond to their deeds.

16 I repeat, let no one think me
foolish; but even if you do, accept me
as a fool, so that I too may boast a
little. 17 (What I am saying I say not
with the Lord's authority but as a fool,
in this boastful confidence; 18 since
many boast of worldly things, I too
will boast.) 19 For you gladly bear
with fools, being wise yourselves!
20 For you bear it if a man makes
slaves of you, or preys upon you, or
takes advantage of you, or puts on
airs, or strikes you in the face. 21 To
my shame, I must say, we were too
weak for that!

But whatever any one dares to
boast of—I am speaking as a fool—I
also dare to boast of that. 22 Are they
Hebrews? So am I. Are they Israelites? So am I. Are they descendants of
Abraham? So am I. 23 Are they servants of Christ? I am a better one—I
am talking like a madman—with far
greater labors, far more imprisonments, with countless beatings, and
often near death. 24 Five times I have
received at the hands of the Jews the
forty lashes less one. 25 Three times I
have been beaten with rods; once I
was stoned. Three times I have been
shipwrecked; a night and a day I have
been adrift at sea; 26 on frequent
journeys, in danger from rivers,
danger from robbers, danger from
my own people, danger from Gentiles,
danger in the city, danger in the
wilderness, danger at sea, danger from
false brethren; 27 in toil and hardship,
through many a sleepless night, in
hunger and thirst, often without food,
in cold and exposure. 28 And, apart
from other things, there is the daily
pressure upon me of my anxiety for
all the churches. 29 Who is weak, and
I am not weak? Who is made to fall,
and I am not indignant?

30 If I must boast, I will boast of
the things that show my weakness.
31 The God and Father of the Lord
Jesus, he who is blessed for ever,
knows that I do not lie. 32 At Damascus, the governor under King Ar'e·tas
guarded the city of Damascus in order
to seize me, 33 but I was let down in a
basket through a window in the wall,
and escaped his hands.

12 I must boast; there is nothing to
be gained by it, but I will go on
to visions and revelations of the Lord.
2 I know a man in Christ who fourteen
years ago was caught up to the third
heaven—whether in the body or out
of the body I do not know, God knows.
3 And I know that this man was caught
up into Paradise—whether in the body
or out of the body I do not know, God
knows— 4 and he heard things that
cannot be told, which man may not
utter. 5 On behalf of this man I will
boast, but on my own behalf I will not
boast, except of my weaknesses.
6 Though if I wish to boast, I shall not
be a fool, for I shall be speaking the
truth. But I refrain from it, so that no

11.5: 2 Cor 12.11; Gal 2.6. **11.6:** 1 Cor 1.17. **11.7:** 2 Cor 12.13; 1 Cor 9.18. **11.8:** Phil 4.15, 18. **11.10:** 1 Cor 9.15. **11.11:** 2 Cor 12.15. **11.12:** 1 Cor 9.12. **11.17:** 1 Cor 7.12, 25. **11.19:** 1 Cor 4.10. **11.23:** Acts 16.23; 2 Cor 6.5. **11.24:** Deut 25.3. **11.25:** Acts 16.22; 14.19. **11.26:** Acts 9.23; 14.5. **11.27:** 1 Cor 4.11. **11.29:** 1 Cor 9.22. **11.32-33:** Acts 9.24-25. **12.4:** Lk 23.43.

one may think more of me than he
sees in me or hears from me. 7 And to
keep me from being too elated by the
abundance of revelations, a thorn was
given me in the flesh, a messenger of
Satan, to harass me, to keep me from
being too elated. 8 Three times I besought the Lord about this, that it
should leave me; 9 but he said to me,
"My grace is sufficient for you, for my
power is made perfect in weakness."
I will all the more gladly boast of my
weaknesses, that the power of Christ
may rest upon me. 10 For the sake of
Christ, then, I am content with weaknesses, insults, hardships, persecutions, and calamities; for when I am
weak, then I am strong.

11 I have been a fool! You forced
me to it, for I ought to have been commended by you. For I am not at all
inferior to these superlative apostles,
even though I am nothing. 12 The
signs of a true apostle were performed
among you in all patience, with signs
and wonders and mighty works. 13 For
in what were you less favored than the
rest of the churches, except that I myself did not burden you? Forgive me
this wrong!

14 Here for the third time I am
ready to come to you. And I will not
be a burden, for I seek not what is
yours but you; for children ought not
to lay up for their parents, but parents
for their children. 15 I will most gladly
spend and be spent for your souls. If
I love you the more, am I to be loved
the less? 16 But granting that I myself
did not burden you, I was crafty, you
say, and got the better of you by
guile. 17 Did I take advantage of you
through any of those whom I sent to
you? 18 I urged Titus to go, and sent
the brother with him. Did Titus take
advantage of you? Did we not act in
the same spirit? Did we not take the
same steps?

19 Have you been thinking all along
that we have been defending ourselves
before you? It is in the sight of God
that we have been speaking in Christ,
and all for your upbuilding, beloved.
20 For I fear that perhaps I may come
and find you not what I wish, and that
you may find me not what you wish;
that perhaps there may be quarreling,
jealousy, anger, selfishness, slander,
gossip, conceit, and disorder. 21 I fear
that when I come again my God may
humble me before you, and I may
have to mourn over many of those
who sinned before and have not
repented of the impurity, immorality,
and licentiousness which they have
practiced.

13 This is the third time I am
coming to you. Any charge must
be sustained by the evidence of two or
three witnesses. 2 I warned those who
sinned before and all the others, and I
warn them now while absent, as I did
when present on my second visit, that
if I come again I will not spare them—
3 since you desire proof that Christ is
speaking in me. He is not weak in dealing with you, but is powerful in you.
4 For he was crucified in weakness, but
lives by the power of God. For we are
weak in him, but in dealing with you
we shall live with him by the power of
God.

5 Examine yourselves, to see
whether you are holding to your faith.
Test yourselves. Do you not realize
that Jesus Christ is in you?—unless
indeed you fail to meet the test! 6 I
hope you will find out that we have
not failed. 7 But we pray God that you
may not do wrong—not that we may
appear to have met the test, but that
you may do what is right, though we
may seem to have failed. 8 For we cannot do anything against the truth, but
only for the truth. 9 For we are glad
when we are weak and you are strong.
What we pray for is your improve-
ment. 10 I write this while I am away
from you, in order that when I come
I may not have to be severe in my use
of the authority which the Lord has
given me for building up and not for
tearing down.

11 Finally, brethren, farewell. Mend
your ways, heed my appeal, agree
with one another, live in peace, and
the God of love and peace will be
with you. 12 Greet one another with
a holy kiss. 13 All the saints greet
you.

14 The grace of the Lord Jesus
Christ and the love of God and the
fellowship of[n] the Holy Spirit be with
you all.

[n] Or *and participation in*

12.7: Job 2.6. **12.10:** Rom 5.3; 2 Cor 6.4-5. **12.11:** 2 Cor 11.5. **12.13:** 2 Cor 11.7. **12.16:** 2 Cor 11.9.
12.18: 2 Cor 2.13; 8.18. **12.20:** 2 Cor 2.1-4; 1 Cor 1.11; 3.3. **13.1:** 2 Cor 12.14; Deut 19.15.
13.4: Phil 2.7-8; Rom 6.8. **13.10:** 2 Cor 2.3. **13.12:** Rom 16.16. **13.13:** Phil 4.22. **13.14:** Rom 16.20.

THE LETTER OF PAUL TO THE

GALATIANS

1 Paul an apostle—not from men
nor through man, but through
Jesus Christ and God the Father, who
raised him from the dead— 2 and all
the brethren who are with me,
To the churches of Galatia:
3 Grace to you and peace from God
the Father and our Lord Jesus Christ,
4 who gave himself for our sins to
deliver us from the present evil age,
according to the will of our God and
Father; 5 to whom be the glory for
ever and ever. Amen.

6 I am astonished that you are so
quickly deserting him who called you
in the grace of Christ and turning to a
different gospel— 7 not that there is
another gospel, but there are some
who trouble you and want to pervert
the gospel of Christ. 8 But even if we,
or an angel from heaven, should
preach to you a gospel contrary to
that which we preached to you, let
him be accursed. 9 As we have said
before, so now I say again, If any one
is preaching to you a gospel contrary
to that which you received, let him be
accursed.
10 Am I now seeking the favor of
men, or of God? Or am I trying to
please men? If I were still pleasing
men, I should not be a servant[a] of
Christ.
11 For I would have you know,
brethren, that the gospel which was
preached by me is not man's[b] gospel.
12 For I did not receive it from man,
nor was I taught it, but it came
through a revelation of Jesus Christ.
13 For you have heard of my former
life in Judaism, how I persecuted the
church of God violently and tried to
destroy it; 14 and I advanced in Judaism beyond many of my own age
among my people, so extremely zealous was I for the traditions of my
fathers. 15 But when he who had set
me apart before I was born, and had
called me through his grace, 16 was
pleased to reveal his Son to[c] me, in
order that I might preach him among
the Gentiles, I did not confer with
flesh and blood, 17 nor did I go up to
Jerusalem to those who were apostles
before me, but I went away into
Arabia; and again I returned to
Damascus.
18 Then after three years I went up
to Jerusalem to visit Cē′phȧs, and remained with him fifteen days. 19 But
I saw none of the other apostles except
James the Lord's brother. 20 (In what
I am writing to you, before God, I do
not lie!) 21 Then I went into the regions of Syria and Ċi·li′ċi·ȧ. 22 And I
was still not known by sight to the
churches of Christ in Judea; 23 they
only heard it said, "He who once
persecuted us is now preaching
the faith he once tried to destroy."
24 And they glorified God because of
me.

2 Then after fourteen years I went
up again to Jerusalem with Bär′-
nȧ·bȧs, taking Titus along with me.
2 I went up by revelation; and I laid
before them (but privately before
those who were of repute) the gospel
which I preach among the Gentiles,
lest somehow I should be running or
had run in vain. 3 But even Titus, who
was with me, was not compelled to be
circumcised, though he was a Greek.
4 But because of false brethren secretly
brought in, who slipped in to spy out
our freedom which we have in Christ
Jesus, that they might bring us into
bondage— 5 to them we did not yield
submission even for a moment, that
the truth of the gospel might be preserved for you. 6 And from those who
were reputed to be something (what
they were makes no difference to me;
God shows no partiality)—those, I
say, who were of repute added nothing to me; 7 but on the contrary, when
they saw that I had been entrusted

[a] Or *slave* [b] Greek *according to man* [c] Greek *in*
1.3: Rom 1.7. **1.4:** Gal 2.20; 1 Tim 2.6. **1.5:** Rom 16.27. **1.8:** 2 Cor 11.4. **1.10:** 1 Thess 2.4.
1.11: Rom 1.16-17. **1.13:** Acts 8.3. **1.14:** Acts 22.3. **1.15:** Acts 9.1-19; Is 49.1; Jer 1.5.
1.18: Acts 9.26-30; 11.30. **2.1:** Acts 15.2. **2.5:** Acts 15.23-29. **2.6:** Deut 10.17.

with the gospel to the uncircumcised,
just as Peter had been entrusted with
the gospel to the circumcised 8 (for he
who worked through Peter for the
mission to the circumcised worked
through me also for the Gentiles), 9and
when they perceived the grace that
was given to me, James and Cē'phȧs
and John, who were reputed to be
pillars, gave to me and Bär'nȧ·bȧs the
right hand of fellowship, that we
should go to the Gentiles and they to
the circumcised; 10 only they would
have us remember the poor, which
very thing I was eager to do.
11 But when Cē'phȧs came to An'-
ti·och I opposed him to his face, because he stood condemned. 12 For before certain men came from James, he
ate with the Gentiles; but when they
came he drew back and separated
himself, fearing the circumcision
party. 13And with him the rest of the
Jews acted insincerely, so that even
Bär'nȧ·bȧs was carried away by their
insincerity. 14 But when I saw that
they were not straightforward about
the truth of the gospel, I said to Cē'-
phȧs before them all, "If you, though
a Jew, live like a Gentile and not like a
Jew, how can you compel the Gentiles
to live like Jews?" 15 We ourselves,
who are Jews by birth and not Gentile
sinners, 16 yet who know that a man is
not justified[d] by works of the law but
through faith in Jesus Christ, even we
have believed in Christ Jesus, in order
to be justified by faith in Christ, and
not by works of the law, because by
works of the law shall no one be
justified. 17 But if, in our endeavor to
be justified in Christ, we ourselves
were found to be sinners, is Christ
then an agent of sin? Certainly not!
18 But if I build up again those things
which I tore down, then I prove myself a transgressor. 19 For I through
the law died to the law, that I might
live to God. 20 I have been crucified
with Christ; it is no longer I who live,
but Christ who lives in me; and the
life I now live in the flesh I live by
faith in the Son of God, who loved me
and gave himself for me. 21 I do not
nullify the grace of God; for if justification[e] were through the law, then
Christ died to no purpose.

3 O foolish Galatians! Who has be-
witched you, before whose eyes
Jesus Christ was publicly portrayed as
crucified? 2 Let me ask you only this:
Did you receive the Spirit by works of
the law, or by hearing with faith? 3Are
you so foolish? Having begun with the
Spirit, are you now ending with the
flesh? 4 Did you experience so many
things in vain?—if it really is in vain.
5 Does he who supplies the Spirit to
you and works miracles among you do
so by works of the law, or by hearing
with faith?
6 Thus Abraham "believed God,
and it was reckoned to him as righteousness." 7 So you see that it is men
of faith who are the sons of Abraham.
8And the scripture, foreseeing that
God would justify the Gentiles by
faith, preached the gospel beforehand
to Abraham, saying, "In you shall all
the nations be blessed." 9 So then,
those who are men of faith are
blessed with Abraham who had faith.
10 For all who rely on works of the
law are under a curse; for it is written,
"Cursed be every one who does not
abide by all things written in the book
of the law, and do them." 11 Now it is
evident that no man is justified before
God by the law; for "He who through
faith is righteous shall live";[f] 12 but
the law does not rest on faith, for "He
who does them shall live by them."
13 Christ redeemed us from the curse
of the law, having become a curse for
us—for it is written, "Cursed be every
one who hangs on a tree"— 14 that in
Christ Jesus the blessing of Abraham
might come upon the Gentiles, that
we might receive the promise of the
Spirit through faith.
15 To give a human example,
brethren: no one annuls even a man's
will,[g] or adds to it, once it has been
ratified. 16 Now the promises were
made to Abraham and to his offspring.
It does not say, "And to offsprings,"
referring to many; but, referring to
one, "And to your offspring," which
is Christ. 17 This is what I mean: the

[d] Or *reckoned righteous;* and so elsewhere [e] Or *righteousness* [f] Or *the righteous shall live by faith*
[g] Or *covenant* (as in verse 17)
2.11: Acts 11.19-26. **2.16:** Ps 143.2; Rom 3.20. **2.20:** Gal 1.4. **3.6:** Gen 15.6; Rom 4.3.
3.8: Gen 12.3; 18.18; Acts 3.25. **3.9:** Rom 4.16. **3.10:** Deut 27.26.
3.11: Hab 2.4; Rom 1.17; Heb 10.38. **3.12:** Lev 18.5; Rom 10.5. **3.13:** Deut 21.23.
3.16: Gen 12.7. **3.17:** Ex 12.40.

law, which came four hundred and
thirty years afterward, does not annul
a covenant previously ratified by God,
so as to make the promise void. 18 For
if the inheritance is by the law, it is no
longer by promise; but God gave it to
Abraham by a promise.
19 Why then the law? It was added
because of transgressions, till the offspring should come to whom the
promise had been made; and it was
ordained by angels through an intermediary. 20 Now an intermediary
implies more than one; but God is
one.
21 Is the law then against the promises of God? Certainly not; for if a law
had been given which could make
alive, then righteousness would indeed
be by the law. 22 But the scripture
consigned all things to sin, that what
was promised to faith in Jesus Christ
might be given to those who believe.
23 Now before faith came, we were
confined under the law, kept under
restraint until faith should be revealed. 24 So that the law was our
custodian until Christ came, that we
might be justified by faith. 25 But now
that faith has come, we are no longer
under a custodian; 26 for in Christ
Jesus you are all sons of God, through
faith. 27 For as many of you as were
baptized into Christ have put on
Christ. 28 There is neither Jew nor
Greek, there is neither slave nor free,
there is neither male nor female; for
you are all one in Christ Jesus. 29 And
if you are Christ's, then you are Abraham's offspring, heirs according to
promise.

4 I mean that the heir, as long as
he is a child, is no better than a
slave, though he is the owner of all the
estate; 2 but he is under guardians and
trustees until the date set by the
father. 3 So with us; when we were
children, we were slaves to the elemental spirits of the universe. 4 But
when the time had fully come, God
sent forth his Son, born of woman,
born under the law, 5 to redeem those
who were under the law, so that we
might receive adoption as sons. 6 And
because you are sons, God has sent the
Spirit of his Son into our hearts, crying, "Ab'bà! Father!" 7 So through
God you are no longer a slave but a
son, and if a son then an heir.
8 Formerly, when you did not know
God, you were in bondage to beings
that by nature are no gods; 9 but now
that you have come to know God, or
rather to be known by God, how can
you turn back again to the weak and
beggarly elemental spirits, whose
slaves you want to be once more?
10 You observe days, and months, and
seasons, and years! 11 I am afraid I
have labored over you in vain.
12 Brethren, I beseech you, become
as I am, for I also have become as you
are. You did me no wrong; 13 you
know it was because of a bodily ail-
ment that I preached the gospel to you
at first; 14 and though my condition
was a trial to you, you did not scorn or
despise me, but received me as an
angel of God, as Christ Jesus. 15 What
has become of the satisfaction you
felt? For I bear you witness that, if
possible, you would have plucked out
your eyes and given them to me.
16 Have I then become your enemy by
telling you the truth?[h] 17 They make
much of you, but for no good purpose;
they want to shut you out, that you
may make much of them. 18 For a
good purpose it is always good to be
made much of, and not only when I
am present with you. 19 My little children, with whom I am again in travail
until Christ be formed in you! 20 I
could wish to be present with you now
and to change my tone, for I am perplexed about you.
21 Tell me, you who desire to be
under law, do you not hear the law?
22 For it is written that Abraham had
two sons, one by a slave and one by a
free woman. 23 But the son of the
slave was born according to the flesh,
the son of the free woman through
promise. 24 Now this is an allegory:
these women are two covenants. One
is from Mount Sinai, bearing children
for slavery; she is Hā'gàr. 25 Now Hā'-
gàr is Mount Sinai in Arabia;[i] she
corresponds to the present Jerusalem,
for she is in slavery with her children.
26 But the Jerusalem above is free, and
she is our mother. 27 For it is written,
"Rejoice, O barren one that dost
not bear;

[h] Or *by dealing truly with you*
[i] Other ancient authorities read *For Sinai is a mountain in Arabia*
3.18: Rom 11.6. **3.19**: Rom 5.20. **3.21**: Rom 8.2-4. **3.22**: Rom 3.9-19; 11.32. **3.28**: Rom 10.12. **4.3**: Col 2.20. **4.6**: Rom 8.15. **4.13**: Acts 16.6. **4.19**: 1 Cor 4.15. **4.22**: Gen 16.15; 21.2, 9. **4.23**: Rom 9.7-9. **4.27**: Is 54.1.

break forth and shout, thou who art
not in travail;
for the desolate hath more children
than she who hath a husband."
28 Now we,[j] brethren, like Isaac, are
children of promise. 29 But as at that
time he who was born according to the
flesh persecuted him who was born
according to the Spirit, so it is now.
30 But what does the scripture say?
"Cast out the slave and her son; for
the son of the slave shall not inherit
with the son of the free woman."
31 So, brethren, we are not children of
the slave but of the free woman.

5 For freedom Christ has set us
free; stand fast therefore, and do
not submit again to a yoke of slavery.
2 Now I, Paul, say to you that if
you receive circumcision, Christ will
be of no advantage to you. 3 I testify
again to every man who receives circumcision that he is bound to keep the
whole law. 4 You are severed from
Christ, you who would be justified by
the law; you have fallen away from
grace. 5 For through the Spirit, by
faith, we wait for the hope of righteousness. 6 For in Christ Jesus neither
circumcision nor uncircumcision is of
any avail, but faith working through
love. 7 You were running well; who
hindered you from obeying the truth?
8 This persuasion is not from him who
called you. 9 A little leaven leavens the
whole lump. 10 I have confidence in
the Lord that you will take no other
view than mine; and he who is troubling you will bear his judgment, whoever he is. 11 But if I, brethren, still
preach circumcision, why am I still
persecuted? In that case the stumbling
block of the cross has been removed.
12 I wish those who unsettle you would
mutilate themselves!
13 For you were called to freedom,
brethren; only do not use your freedom as an opportunity for the flesh,
but through love be servants of one
another. 14 For the whole law is fulfilled in one word, "You shall love
your neighbor as yourself." 15 But if
you bite and devour one another take
heed that you are not consumed by
one another.
16 But I say, walk by the Spirit,
and do not gratify the desires of the
flesh. 17 For the desires of the flesh are
against the Spirit, and the desires of
the Spirit are against the flesh; for
these are opposed to each other, to
prevent you from doing what you
would. 18 But if you are led by the
Spirit you are not under the law.
19 Now the works of the flesh are plain:
immorality, impurity, licentiousness,
20 idolatry, sorcery, enmity, strife,
jealousy, anger, selfishness, dissension, party spirit, 21 envy,[k] drunkenness, carousing, and the like. I warn
you, as I warned you before, that
those who do such things shall not inherit the kingdom of God. 22 But the
fruit of the Spirit is love, joy, peace,
patience, kindness, goodness, faithfulness, 23 gentleness, self-control; against
such there is no law. 24 And those who
belong to Christ Jesus have crucified
the flesh with its passions and desires.
25 If we live by the Spirit, let us
also walk by the Spirit. 26 Let us have
no self-conceit, no provoking of one
another, no envy of one another.

6 Brethren, if a man is overtaken in
any trespass, you who are spiritual
should restore him in a spirit of gentleness. Look to yourself, lest you too be
tempted. 2 Bear one another's burdens, and so fulfill the law of Christ.
3 For if any one thinks he is something,
when he is nothing, he deceives himself. 4 But let each one test his own
work, and then his reason to boast
will be in himself alone and not in his
neighbor. 5 For each man will have to
bear his own load.
6 Let him who is taught the word
share all good things with him who
teaches.
7 Do not be deceived; God is not
mocked, for whatever a man sows,
that he will also reap. 8 For he who
sows to his own flesh will from the
flesh reap corruption; but he who sows
to the Spirit will from the Spirit reap
eternal life. 9 And let us not grow
weary in well-doing, for in due season
we shall reap, if we do not lose heart.
10 So then, as we have opportunity,
let us do good to all men, and especially to those who are of the household of faith.

11 See with what large letters I am
writing to you with my own hand. 12 It

[j] Other ancient authorities read *you* [k] Other ancient authorities add *murder*

4.29: Gen 21.9. **4.30:** Gen 21.10-12. **5.6:** 1 Cor 7.19; Gal 6.15. **5.9:** 1 Cor 5.6.
5.14: Lev 19.18; Rom 13.8-10. **5.17:** Rom 7.15-23. **5.19:** Rom 1.28. **6.11:** 1 Cor 16.21.

is those who want to make a good
showing in the flesh that would compel you to be circumcised, and only in
order that they may not be persecuted
for the cross of Christ. 13 For even
those who receive circumcision do not
themselves keep the law, but they
desire to have you circumcised that
they may glory in your flesh. 14 But
far be it from me to glory except in the
cross of our Lord Jesus Christ, by
which[l] the world has been crucified to
me, and I to the world. 15 For neither
circumcision counts for anything, nor
uncircumcision, but a new creation.
16 Peace and mercy be upon all who
walk by this rule, upon the Israel of
God.

17 Henceforth let no man trouble
me; for I bear on my body the marks
of Jesus.

18 The grace of our Lord Jesus
Christ be with your spirit, brethren.
Amen.

THE LETTER OF PAUL TO THE

EPHESIANS

1 Paul, an apostle of Christ Jesus
by the will of God,

To the saints who are also faithful[a]
in Christ Jesus:

2 Grace to you and peace from God
our Father and the Lord Jesus Christ.

3 Blessed be the God and Father of
our Lord Jesus Christ, who has blessed
us in Christ with every spiritual blessing in the heavenly places, 4 even as
he chose us in him before the foundation of the world, that we should be
holy and blameless before him. 5 He
destined us in love[b] to be his sons
through Jesus Christ, according to the
purpose of his will, 6 to the praise of
his glorious grace which he freely bestowed on us in the Beloved. 7 In him
we have redemption through his
blood, the forgiveness of our trespasses, according to the riches of his
grace 8 which he lavished upon us.
9 For he has made known to us in all
wisdom and insight the mystery of his
will, according to his purpose which
he set forth in Christ 10 as a plan for
the fulness of time, to unite all things
in him, things in heaven and things
on earth.

11 In him, according to the purpose
of him who accomplishes all things
according to the counsel of his will,
12 we who first hoped in Christ have
been destined and appointed to live
for the praise of his glory. 13 In him
you also, who have heard the word of
truth, the gospel of your salvation,
and have believed in him, were sealed
with the promised Holy Spirit,
14 which is the guarantee of our inheritance until we acquire possession
of it, to the praise of his glory.

15 For this reason, because I have
heard of your faith in the Lord Jesus
and your love[c] toward all the saints,
16 I do not cease to give thanks for
you, remembering you in my prayers,
17 that the God of our Lord Jesus
Christ, the Father of glory, may give
you a spirit of wisdom and of revelation in the knowledge of him, 18 having the eyes of your hearts enlightened, that you may know what is the
hope to which he has called you, what
are the riches of his glorious inheritance in the saints, 19 and what is the
immeasurable greatness of his power
in us who believe, according to the
working of his great might 20 which
he accomplished in Christ when he
raised him from the dead and made
him sit at his right hand in the heavenly places, 21 far above all rule and
authority and power and dominion,
and above every name that is named,

[l] Or *through whom* [a] Other ancient authorities read *who are at Ephesus and faithful*
[b] Or *before him in love, having destined us*
[c] Other ancient authorities omit *your love*

6.16: Ps 125.5. **1.3:** 2 Cor 1.3. **1.6:** Col 1.13. **1.7:** Col 1.14. **1.10:** Gal 4.4.
1.14: 2 Cor 1.22.
1.15: Col 1.9. **1.16:** Col 1.3. **1.18:** Deut 33.3. **1.20:** Ps 110.1.
1.21: Col 1.6; 2.10, 15.

not only in this age but also in that
which is to come; 22 and he has put all
things under his feet and has made
him the head over all things for the
church, 23 which is his body, the fullness of him who fills all in all.

2 And you he made alive, when you
were dead through the trespasses
and sins 2 in which you once walked,
following the course of this world,
following the prince of the power of
the air, the spirit that is now at work
in the sons of disobedience. 3 Among
these we all once lived in the passions
of our flesh, following the desires of
body and mind, and so we were by
nature children of wrath, like the rest
of mankind. 4 But God, who is rich in
mercy, out of the great love with
which he loved us, 5 even when we
were dead through our trespasses,
made us alive together with Christ
(by grace you have been saved), 6 and
raised us up with him, and made us
sit with him in the heavenly places in
Christ Jesus, 7 that in the coming ages
he might show the immeasurable
riches of his grace in kindness toward
us in Christ Jesus. 8 For by grace you
have been saved through faith; and
this is not your own doing, it is the
gift of God— 9 not because of works,
lest any man should boast. 10 For we
are his workmanship, created in Christ
Jesus for good works, which God
prepared beforehand, that we should
walk in them.

11 Therefore remember that at one
time you Gentiles in the flesh, called
the uncircumcision by what is called
the circumcision, which is made in the
flesh by hands— 12 remember that you
were at that time separated from
Christ, alienated from the commonwealth of Israel, and strangers to the
covenants of promise, having no hope
and without God in the world. 13 But
now in Christ Jesus you who once
were far off have been brought near in
the blood of Christ. 14 For he is our
peace, who has made us both one, and
has broken down the dividing wall of
hostility, 15 by abolishing in his flesh
the law of commandments and ordinances, that he might create in himself one new man in place of the two,
so making peace, 16 and might reconcile us both to God in one body
through the cross, thereby bringing
the hostility to an end. 17 And he came
and preached peace to you who were
far off and peace to those who were
near; 18 for through him we both have
access in one Spirit to the Father.
19 So then you are no longer strangers
and sojourners, but you are fellow
citizens with the saints and members
of the household of God, 20 built upon
the foundation of the apostles and
prophets, Christ Jesus himself being
the cornerstone, 21 in whom the whole
structure is joined together and grows
into a holy temple in the Lord; 22 in
whom you also are built into it for a
dwelling place of God in the Spirit.

3 For this reason I, Paul, a prisoner
for Christ Jesus on behalf of you
Gentiles— 2 assuming that you have
heard of the stewardship of God's
grace that was given to me for you,
3 how the mystery was made known to
me by revelation, as I have written
briefly. 4 When you read this you can
perceive my insight into the mystery
of Christ, 5 which was not made known
to the sons of men in other generations as it has now been revealed to
his holy apostles and prophets by the
Spirit; 6 that is, how the Gentiles are
fellow heirs, members of the same
body, and partakers of the promise in
Christ Jesus through the gospel.

7 Of this gospel I was made a minister according to the gift of God's
grace which was given me by the
working of his power. 8 To me, though
I am the very least of all the saints,
this grace was given, to preach to the
Gentiles the unsearchable riches of
Christ, 9 and to make all men see what
is the plan of the mystery hidden for
ages in[d] God who created all things;
10 that through the church the manifold wisdom of God might now be
made known to the principalities and
powers in the heavenly places. 11 This
was according to the eternal purpose
which he has realized in Christ Jesus
our Lord, 12 in whom we have boldness and confidence of access through
our faith in him. 13 So I ask you not
to[e] lose heart over what I am suffering
for you, which is your glory.

14 For this reason I bow my knees
before the Father, 15 from whom every
family in heaven and on earth is

[d] Or *by* [e] Or *I ask that I may not*

1.22: Ps 8.6; Col 1.19. **1.23:** Rom 12.5; Col 2.17. **2.2:** Col 1.13. **2.8:** Gal 2.16. **2.12:** Is 57.19.
2.17: Is 57.19. **3.2:** Col 1.25. **3.6:** Col 1.27. **3.9:** Col 1.26.

named, 16 that according to the riches
of his glory he may grant you to be
strengthened with might through his
Spirit in the inner man, 17 and that
Christ may dwell in your hearts
through faith; that you, being rooted
and grounded in love, 18 may have
power to comprehend with all the
saints what is the breadth and length
and height and depth, 19 and to know
the love of Christ which surpasses
knowledge, that you may be filled
with all the fulness of God.

20 Now to him who by the power
at work within us is able to do far
more abundantly than all that we ask
or think, 21 to him be glory in the
church and in Christ Jesus to all
generations, for ever and ever. Amen.

4 I therefore, a prisoner for the
Lord, beg you to lead a life worthy
of the calling to which you have been
called, 2 with all lowliness and meekness, with patience, forbearing one another in love, 3 eager to maintain the
unity of the Spirit in the bond of
peace. 4 There is one body and one
Spirit, just as you were called to the
one hope that belongs to your call,
5 one Lord, one faith, one baptism,
6 one God and Father of us all, who is
above all and through all and in all.
7 But grace was given to each of us
according to the measure of Christ's
gift. 8 Therefore it is said,

"When he ascended on high he led
a host of captives,
and he gave gifts to men."

9 (In saying, "He ascended," what
does it mean but that he had also
descended into the lower parts of the
earth? 10 He who descended is he who
also ascended far above all the heavens, that he might fill all things.)
11 And his gifts were that some should
be apostles, some prophets, some
evangelists, some pastors and teachers, 12 for the equipment of the saints,
for the work of ministry, for building
up the body of Christ, 13 until we all
attain to the unity of the faith and of
the knowledge of the Son of God, to
mature manhood, to the measure of
the stature of the fullness of Christ;
14 so that we may no longer be children, tossed to and fro and carried
about with every wind of doctrine,
by the cunning of men, by their craftiness in deceitful wiles. 15 Rather,
speaking the truth in love, we are to
grow up in every way into him who
is the head, into Christ, 16 from whom
the whole body, joined and knit together by every joint with which it is
supplied, when each part is working
properly, makes bodily growth and
upbuilds itself in love.

17 Now this I affirm and testify in
the Lord, that you must no longer live
as the Gentiles do, in the futility of
their minds; 18 they are darkened in
their understanding, alienated from
the life of God because of the ignorance that is in them, due to their
hardness of heart; 19 they have become callous and have given themselves up to licentiousness, greedy to
practice every kind of uncleanness.
20 You did not so learn Christ!—
21 assuming that you have heard
about him and were taught in him, as
the truth is in Jesus. 22 Put off your
old nature which belongs to your
former manner of life and is corrupt
through deceitful lusts, 23 and be renewed in the spirit of your minds,
24 and put on the new nature, created
after the likeness of God in true righteousness and holiness.

25 Therefore, putting away falsehood, let every one speak the truth
with his neighbor, for we are members
one of another. 26 Be angry but do not
sin; do not let the sun go down on your
anger, 27 and give no opportunity to
the devil. 28 Let the thief no longer
steal, but rather let him labor, doing
honest work with his hands, so that he
may be able to give to those in need.
29 Let no evil talk come out of your
mouths, but only such as is good for
edifying, as fits the occasion, that it
may impart grace to those who hear.
30 And do not grieve the Holy Spirit of
God, in whom you were sealed for the
day of redemption. 31 Let all bitterness and wrath and anger and clamor
and slander be put away from you,
with all malice, 32 and be kind to one
another, tenderhearted, forgiving one
another, as God in Christ forgave you.

5 Therefore be imitators of God,
as beloved children. 2 And walk in
love, as Christ loved us and gave himself up for us, a fragrant offering and
sacrifice to God.

3 But immorality and all impurity

4.2: Col 3.12-13. **4.8:** Ps 68.18. **4.15:** Col 1.18. **4.16:** Col 2.19. **4.25:** Zech 8.16; Rom 12.5.
5.2: Ex 29.18; Ezek 20.41.

or covetousness must not even be
named among you, as is fitting among
saints. 4 Let there be no filthiness, nor
silly talk, nor levity, which are not
fitting; but instead let there be thanksgiving. 5 Be sure of this, that no immoral or impure man, or one who is
covetous (that is an idolater), has any
inheritance in the kingdom of Christ
and of God. 6 Let no one deceive you
with empty words, for it is because of
these things that the wrath of God
comes upon the sons of disobedience.
7 Therefore do not associate with
them, 8 for once you were darkness,
but now you are light in the Lord;
walk as children of light 9 (for the
fruit of light is found in all that is
good and right and true), 10 and try to
learn what is pleasing to the Lord.
11 Take no part in the unfruitful works
of darkness, but instead expose them.
12 For it is a shame even to speak of
the things that they do in secret; 13 but
when anything is exposed by the light
it becomes visible, for anything that
becomes visible is light. 14 Therefore
it is said,

"Awake, O sleeper, and arise from
the dead,
and Christ shall give you light."

15 Look carefully then how you
walk, not as unwise men but as wise,
16 making the most of the time, because the days are evil. 17 Therefore
do not be foolish, but understand
what the will of the Lord is. 18 And do
not get drunk with wine, for that is
debauchery; but be filled with the
Spirit, 19 addressing one another in
psalms and hymns and spiritual songs,
singing and making melody to the
Lord with all your heart, 20 always
and for everything giving thanks in
the name of our Lord Jesus Christ to
God the Father.

21 Be subject to one another out of
reverence for Christ. 22 Wives, be subject to your husbands, as to the Lord.
23 For the husband is the head of the
wife as Christ is the head of the
church, his body, and is himself its
Savior. 24 As the church is subject to
Christ, so let wives also be subject in
everything to their husbands. 25 Husbands, love your wives, as Christ
loved the church and gave himself up
for her, 26 that he might sanctify her,
having cleansed her by the washing
of water with the word, 27 that he
might present the church to himself in
splendor, without spot or wrinkle or
any such thing, that she might be
holy and without blemish. 28 Even so
husbands should love their wives as
their own bodies. He who loves his
wife loves himself. 29 For no man ever
hates his own flesh, but nourishes and
cherishes it, as Christ does the church,
30 because we are members of his
body. 31 "For this reason a man shall
leave his father and mother and be
joined to his wife, and the two shall
become one." 32 This is a great mystery, and I take it to mean Christ
and the church; 33 however, let each
one of you love his wife as himself,
and let the wife see that she respects
her husband.

6 Children, obey your parents in
the Lord, for this is right. 2 "Honor
your father and mother" (this is the
first commandment with a promise),
3 "that it may be well with you and
that you may live long on the earth."
4 Fathers, do not provoke your children to anger, but bring them up in
the discipline and instruction of the
Lord.

5 Slaves, be obedient to those who
are your earthly masters, with fear
and trembling, in singleness of heart,
as to Christ; 6 not in the way of eyeservice, as men-pleasers, but as servants[f] of Christ, doing the will of God
from the heart, 7 rendering service
with a good will as to the Lord and
not to men, 8 knowing that whatever
good any one does, he will receive the
same again from the Lord, whether he
is a slave or free. 9 Masters, do the
same to them, and forbear threatening, knowing that he who is both their
Master and yours is in heaven, and
that there is no partiality with him.

10 Finally, be strong in the Lord
and in the strength of his might. 11 Put
on the whole armor of God, that you
may be able to stand against the wiles
of the devil. 12 For we are not contending against flesh and blood, but
against the principalities, against the
powers, against the world rulers of
this present darkness, against the
spiritual hosts of wickedness in the
heavenly places. 13 Therefore take the

[f] Or *slaves*

5.16: Col 4.5. **5.19:** Col 3.16-17. **5.22-6.9:** Col 3.18-4 1. **5.31:** Gen 2.24. **6.2:** Ex 20.12.
6.3: Deut 5.16.

whole armor of God, that you may be
able to withstand in the evil day, and
having done all, to stand. 14 Stand
therefore, having girded your loins
with truth, and having put on the
breastplate of righteousness, 15 and
having shod your feet with the equipment of the gospel of peace; 16 above
all taking the shield of faith, with
which you can quench all the flaming
darts of the evil one. 17 And take the
helmet of salvation, and the sword
of the Spirit, which is the word of
God. 18 Pray at all times in the Spirit,
with all prayer and supplication. To
that end keep alert with all perseverance, making supplication for all
the saints, 19 and also for me, that
utterance may be given me in opening
my mouth boldly to proclaim the
mystery of the gospel, 20 for which I
am an ambassador in chains; that I
may declare it boldly, as I ought to
speak.

21 Now that you also may know
how I am and what I am doing, Tych'-
i·cus the beloved brother and faithful
minister in the Lord will tell you
everything. 22 I have sent him to you
for this very purpose, that you may
know how we are, and that he may
encourage your hearts.
23 Peace be to the brethren, and
love with faith, from God the Father
and the Lord Jesus Christ. 24 Grace
be with all who love our Lord Jesus
Christ with love undying.

THE LETTER OF PAUL TO THE

PHILIPPIANS

1 Paul and Timothy, servants[a] of
Christ Jesus,
To all the saints in Christ Jesus who
are at Phi·lip'pī, with the bishops[b] and
deacons:
2 Grace to you and peace from God
our Father and the Lord Jesus Christ.

3 I thank my God in all my remembrance of you, 4 always in every
prayer of mine for you all making my
prayer with joy, 5 thankful for your
partnership in the gospel from the
first day until now. 6 And I am sure
that he who began a good work in you
will bring it to completion at the day
of Jesus Christ. 7 It is right for me to
feel thus about you all, because I hold
you in my heart, for you are all partakers with me of grace, both in my
imprisonment and in the defense and
confirmation of the gospel. 8 For God
is my witness, how I yearn for you all
with the affection of Christ Jesus.
9 And it is my prayer that your love
may abound more and more, with
knowledge and all discernment, 10 so
that you may approve what is excellent, and may be pure and blameless
for the day of Christ, 11 filled with the
fruits of righteousness which come
through Jesus Christ, to the glory and
praise of God.
12 I want you to know, brethren,
that what has happened to me has
really served to advance the gospel,
13 so that it has become known
through out the whole praetorian
guard[c] and to all the rest that my
imprisonment is for Christ; 14 and
most of the brethren have been made
confident in the Lord because of my
imprisonment, and are much more
bold to speak the word of God without
fear.
15 Some indeed preach Christ from
envy and rivalry, but others from
good will. 16 The latter do it out of
love, knowing that I am put here for
the defense of the gospel; 17 the
former proclaim Christ out of parti-
sanship, not sincerely but thinking to

[a] Or *slaves* [b] Or *overseers* [c] Greek *in the whole praetorium*
6.14: Is 11.5; 59.17; 1 Thess 5.8. **6.15:** Is 52.7. **6.21-22:** Col 4.7-8.
1.1: Acts 16.1, 12-40; Rom 1.1; 2 Cor 1.1; Gal 1.10; Col 1.1; 1 Thess 1.1; 2 Thess 1.1; Philem 1.
1.2: Rom 1.7. **1.6, 10:** 1 Cor 1.8. **1.7:** Acts 21.33; 2 Cor 7.3; Eph 6.20. **1.12:** Lk 21.13.
1.13: Acts 28.30; 2 Tim 2.9.

afflict me in my imprisonment. 18 What then? Only that in every way, whether in pretense or in truth, Christ is proclaimed; and in that I rejoice.

19 Yes, and I shall rejoice. For I know that through your prayers and the help of the Spirit of Jesus Christ this will turn out for my deliverance, 20 as it is my eager expectation and hope that I shall not be at all ashamed, but that with full courage now as always Christ will be honored in my body, whether by life or by death. 21 For to me to live is Christ, and to die is gain. 22 If it is to be life in the flesh, that means fruitful labor for me. Yet which I shall choose I cannot tell. 23 I am hard pressed between the two. My desire is to depart and be with Christ, for that is far better. 24 But to remain in the flesh is more necessary on your account. 25 Convinced of this, I know that I shall remain and continue with you all, for your progress and joy in the faith, 26 so that in me you may have ample cause to glory in Christ Jesus, because of my coming to you again.

27 Only let your manner of life be worthy of the gospel of Christ, so that whether I come and see you or am absent, I may hear of you that you stand firm in one spirit, with one mind striving side by side for the faith of the gospel, 28 and not frightened in anything by your opponents. This is a clear omen to them of their destruction, but of your salvation, and that from God. 29 For it has been granted to you that for the sake of Christ you should not only believe in him but also suffer for his sake, 30 engaged in the same conflict which you saw and now hear to be mine.

2 So if there is any encouragement in Christ, any incentive of love, any participation in the Spirit, any affection and sympathy, 2 complete my joy by being of the same mind, having the same love, being in full accord and of one mind. 3 Do nothing from selfishness or conceit, but in humility count others better than yourselves. 4 Let each of you look not only to his own interests, but also to the interests of others. 5 Have this mind among yourselves, which you have in Christ Jesus, 6 who, though he was in the form of God, did not count equality with God a thing to be grasped, 7 but emptied himself, taking the form of a servant,[d] being born in the likeness of men. 8 And being found in human form he humbled himself and became obedient unto death, even death on a cross. 9 Therefore God has highly exalted him and bestowed on him the name which is above every name, 10 that at the name of Jesus every knee should bow, in heaven and on earth and under the earth, 11 and every tongue confess that Jesus Christ is Lord, to the glory of God the Father.

12 Therefore, my beloved, as you have always obeyed, so now, not only as in my presence but much more in my absence, work out your own salvation with fear and trembling; 13 for God is at work in you, both to will and to work for his good pleasure.

14 Do all things without grumbling or questioning, 15 that you may be blameless and innocent, children of God without blemish in the midst of a crooked and perverse generation, among whom you shine as lights in the world, 16 holding fast the word of life, so that in the day of Christ I may be proud that I did not run in vain or labor in vain. 17 Even if I am to be poured as a libation upon the sacrificial offering of your faith, I am glad and rejoice with you all. 18 Likewise you also should be glad and rejoice with me.

19 I hope in the Lord Jesus to send Timothy to you soon, so that I may be cheered by news of you. 20 I have no one like him, who will be genuinely anxious for your welfare. 21 They all look after their own interests, not those of Jesus Christ. 22 But Timothy's worth you know, how as a son with a father he has served with me in the gospel. 23 I hope therefore to send him just as soon as I see how it will go with me; 24 and I trust in the Lord that shortly I myself shall come also.

25 I have thought it necessary to send to you Ep·aph·rō·dī'tus my brother and fellow worker and fellow

[d] Or *slave*

1.19: Acts 16.7; 2 Cor 1.11. **1.20:** Rom 14.8. **1.21:** Gal 2.20. **1.28:** 2 Thess 1.5.
1.30: Acts 16.19-40; 1 Thess 2.2. **2.1:** 2 Cor 13.14. **2.3-4:** Rom 12.10; 15.1-2.
2.5-8: Mt 11.29; 20.28; Jn 1.1; 2 Cor 8.9; Heb 5.8. **2.9-11:** Rom 10.9; 14.9; Eph 1.20-21.
2.13: 1 Cor 15.10. **2.15:** Mt 5.45, 48.

soldier, and your messenger and minister to my need, 26 for he has been
longing for you all, and has been distressed because you heard that he was
ill. 27 Indeed he was ill, near to death.
But God had mercy on him, and not
only on him but on me also, lest I
should have sorrow upon sorrow. 28 I
am the more eager to send him, therefore, that you may rejoice at seeing
him again, and that I may be less
anxious. 29 So receive him in the Lord
with all joy; and honor such men,
30 for he nearly died for the work of
Christ, risking his life to complete
your service to me.

3 Finally, my brethren, rejoice in
the Lord. To write the same things
to you is not irksome to me, and is
safe for you.

2 Look out for the dogs, look out
for the evil-workers, look out for those
who mutilate the flesh. 3 For we are
the true circumcision, who worship
God in spirit,[e] and glory in Christ
Jesus, and put no confidence in the
flesh. 4 Though I myself have reason
for confidence in the flesh also. If any
other man thinks he has reason for
confidence in the flesh, I have more:
5 circumcised on the eighth day, of the
people of Israel, of the tribe of Benjamin, a Hebrew born of Hebrews; as to
the law a Pharisee, 6 as to zeal a perse-
cutor of the church, as to righteousness under the law blameless. 7 But
whatever gain I had, I counted as loss
for the sake of Christ. 8 Indeed I count
everything as loss because of the surpassing worth of knowing Christ Jesus
my Lord. For his sake I have suffered
the loss of all things, and count them
as refuse, in order that I may gain
Christ 9 and be found in him, not
having a righteousness of my own,
based on law, but that which is
through faith in Christ, the righteousness from God that depends on faith;
10 that I may know him and the power
of his resurrection, and may share his
sufferings, becoming like him in his
death, 11 that if possible I may attain
the resurrection from the dead.

12 Not that I have already obtained this or am already perfect; but
I press on to make it my own, because
Christ Jesus has made me his own.
13 Brethren, I do not consider that I
have made it my own; but one thing I
do, forgetting what lies behind and
straining forward to what lies ahead,
14 I press on toward the goal for the
prize of the upward call of God in
Christ Jesus. 15 Let those of us who
are mature be thus minded; and if in
anything you are otherwise minded,
God will reveal that also to you.
16 Only let us hold true to what we
have attained.

17 Brethren, join in imitating me,
and mark those who so live as you
have an example in us. 18 For many, of
whom I have often told you and now
tell you even with tears, live as enemies of the cross of Christ. 19 Their
end is destruction, their god is the
belly, and they glory in their shame,
with minds set on earthly things.
20 But our commonwealth is in
heaven, and from it we await a Savior,
the Lord Jesus Christ, 21 who will
change our lowly body to be like his
glorious body, by the power which
enables him even to subject all things
to himself.

4 Therefore, my brethren, whom
I love and long for, my joy and
crown, stand firm thus in the Lord,
my beloved.

2 I entreat Eū-ō'di·ȧ and I entreat
Syn'ty·chē to agree in the Lord. 3 And
I ask you also, true yokefellow, help
these women, for they have labored
side by side with me in the gospel together with Clement and the rest of
my fellow workers, whose names are
in the book of life.

4 Rejoice in the Lord always; again
I will say, Rejoice. 5 Let all men know
your forbearance. The Lord is at
hand. 6 Have no anxiety about anything, but in everything by prayer and
supplication with thanksgiving let
your requests be made known to God.
7 And the peace of God, which passes
all understanding, will keep your
hearts and your minds in Christ
Jesus.

8 Finally, brethren, whatever is
true, whatever is honorable, whatever
is just, whatever is pure, whatever is
lovely, whatever is gracious, if there
is any excellence, if there is anything
worthy of praise, think about these

[e] Other ancient authorities read *worship by the Spirit of God*

3.3: Rom 2.28-29; Gal 6.14-15. 3.4-7: Acts 8.3; 22.3-21; 23.6; 26.4-23; Rom 11.1; 2 Cor 11.18-31. 3.17: 1 Cor 4.15-17. 3.21: 1 Cor 15.35-58; Col 3.4. 4.3: Lk 10.20. 4.6: Mt 6.25-34.

things. 9 What you have learned and
received and heard and seen in me,
do; and the God of peace will be with
you.
10 I rejoice in the Lord greatly that
now at length you have revived your
concern for me; you were indeed concerned for me, but you had no opportunity. 11 Not that I complain of
want; for I have learned, in whatever
state I am, to be content. 12 I know
how to be abased, and I know how to
abound; in any and all circumstances
I have learned the secret of facing
plenty and hunger, abundance and
want. 13 I can do all things in him
who strengthens me.
14 Yet it was kind of you to share
my trouble. 15And you Phi·lip′pi·ȧnṡ
yourselves know that in the beginning
of the gospel, when I left Mač·ė·dō′-
ni·ȧ, no church entered into partnership with me in giving and receiving
except you only; 16 for even in Thes-
sȧ·lȯ·nī′cȧ you sent me help[f] once and
again. 17 Not that I seek the gift; but
I seek the fruit which increases to
your credit. 18 I have received full
payment, and more; I am filled, having received from Ep·aph·rō·dī′tůs
the gifts you sent, a fragrant offering,
a sacrifice acceptable and pleasing to
God. 19And my God will supply every
need of yours according to his riches in
glory in Christ Jesus. 20 To our God
and Father be glory for ever and ever.
Amen.

21 Greet every saint in Christ Jesus.
The brethren who are with me greet
you. 22All the saints greet you, especially those of Caesar's household.
23 The grace of the Lord Jesus
Christ be with your spirit.

THE LETTER OF PAUL TO THE

COLOSSIANS

1 Paul, an apostle of Christ Jesus
by the will of God, and Timothy
our brother,
2 To the saints and faithful brethren in Christ at Cȯ·los′saē:
Grace to you and peace from God
our Father.

3 We always thank God, the Father
of our Lord Jesus Christ, when we
pray for you, 4 because we have heard
of your faith in Christ Jesus and of the
love which you have for all the saints,
5 because of the hope laid up for you
in heaven. Of this you have heard before in the word of the truth, the
gospel 6 which has come to you, as
indeed in the whole world it is bearing
fruit and growing—so among yourselves, from the day you heard and
understood the grace of God in truth,
7 as you learned it from Ep′ȧ·phras
our beloved fellow servant. He is a
faithful minister of Christ on our[a] behalf 8 and has made known to us your
love in the Spirit.
9 And so, from the day we heard of
it, we have not ceased to pray for you,
asking that you may be filled with the
knowledge of his will in all spiritual
wisdom and understanding, 10 to lead
a life worthy of the Lord, fully pleasing to him, bearing fruit in every good
work and increasing in the knowledge
of God. 11 May you be strengthened
with all power, according to his glorious might, for all endurance and patience with joy, 12 giving thanks to the
Father, who has qualified us[b] to share
in the inheritance of the saints in light.
13 He has delivered us from the dominion of darkness and transferred us
to the kingdom of his beloved Son,
14 in whom we have redemption, the
forgiveness of sins.
15 He is the image of the invisible

[f] Other ancient authorities read *money for my needs* [a] Other ancient authorities read *your*
[b] Other ancient authorities read *you*
4.9: Rom 15.33. **4.10:** 2 Cor 11.9. **4.13:** 2 Cor 12.9. **4.16:** Acts 17.1-9; 1 Thess 2.9.
4.23: Gal 6.18; Philem 25. **1.2:** Rom 1.7. **1.3:** Eph 1.16. **1.7:** Col 4.12; Philem 23.
1.9: Eph 1.15-17. **1.13:** Eph 1.21; 2.2. **1.15:** 2 Cor 4.4.

God, the first-born of all creation;
16 for in him all things were created,
in heaven and on earth, visible and
invisible, whether thrones or dominions or principalities or authorities—
all things were created through him
and for him. 17 He is before all things,
and in him all things hold together.
18 He is the head of the body, the
church; he is the beginning, the first-
born from the dead, that in everything he might be pre-eminent.
19 For in him all the fulness of God
was pleased to dwell, 20 and through
him to reconcile to himself all things,
whether on earth or in heaven, making peace by the blood of his cross.

21 And you, who once were estranged and hostile in mind, doing
evil deeds, 22 he has now reconciled in
his body of flesh by his death, in order
to present you holy and blameless and
irreproachable before him, 23 provided that you continue in the faith,
stable and steadfast, not shifting from
the hope of the gospel which you
heard, which has been preached to
every creature under heaven, and of
which I, Paul, became a minister.

24 Now I rejoice in my sufferings
for your sake, and in my flesh I complete what is lacking in Christ's afflictions for the sake of his body, that is,
the church, 25 of which I became a
minister according to the divine office
which was given to me for you, to
make the word of God fully known,
26 the mystery hidden for ages and
generations[c] but now made manifest
to his saints. 27 To them God chose to
make known how great among the
Gentiles are the riches of the glory of
this mystery, which is Christ in you,
the hope of glory. 28 Him we proclaim,
warning every man and teaching
every man in all wisdom, that we may
present every man mature in Christ.
29 For this I toil, striving with all the
energy which he mightily inspires
within me.

2 For I want you to know how
greatly I strive for you, and for
those at Lā-ŏ·di·ċē′ȧ, and for all who
have not seen my face, 2 that their
hearts may be encouraged as they are
knit together in love, to have all the
riches of assured understanding and
the knowledge of God's mystery, of
Christ, 3 in whom are hid all the
treasures of wisdom and knowledge.
4 I say this in order that no one may
delude you with beguiling speech.
5 For though I am absent in body, yet
I am with you in spirit, rejoicing to see
your good order and the firmness of
your faith in Christ.

6 As therefore you received Christ
Jesus the Lord, so live in him, 7 rooted
and built up in him and established in
the faith, just as you were taught,
abounding in thanksgiving.

8 See to it that no one makes a prey
of you by philosophy and empty deceit,
according to human tradition, according to the elemental spirits of the
universe, and not according to Christ.
9 For in him the whole fulness of deity
dwells bodily, 10 and you have come
to fulness of life in him, who is the
head of all rule and authority. 11 In
him also you were circumcised with a
circumcision made without hands, by
putting off the body of flesh in the
circumcision of Christ; 12 and you
were buried with him in baptism, in
which you were also raised with him
through faith in the working of God,
who raised him from the dead. 13 And
you, who were dead in trespasses and
the uncircumcision of your flesh, God
made alive together with him, having
forgiven us all our trespasses, 14 having canceled the bond which stood
against us with its legal demands;
this he set aside, nailing it to the cross.
15 He disarmed the principalities and
powers and made a public example of
them, triumphing over them in him.[d]

16 Therefore let no one pass judgment on you in questions of food and
drink or with regard to a festival or a
new moon or a sabbath. 17 These are
only a shadow of what is to come; but
the substance belongs to Christ. 18 Let
no one disqualify you, insisting on
self-abasement and worship of angels,
taking his stand on visions, puffed up
without reason by his sensuous mind,
19 and not holding fast to the Head,
from whom the whole body, nourished
and knit together through its joints and
ligaments, grows with a growth that is
from God.

20 If with Christ you died to the
elemental spirits of the universe, why

[c] Or *from angels and men* [d] Or *in it* (that is, the cross)

1.17: Prov 8.22-31. **1.18:** Eph 4.15. **1.25:** Eph 3.2. **1.26:** Eph 3.9. **2.3:** Is 45.3. **2.10:** Eph 1.21-22. **2.15:** Eph 1.21. **2.16:** Rom 14.1-12. **2.17:** Eph 1.23. **2.19:** Eph 1.22; 4.16. **2.20:** Gal 4.3.

do you live as if you still belonged to
the world? Why do you submit to
regulations, 21 "Do not handle, Do
not taste, Do not touch" 22 (referring
to things which all perish as they are
used), according to human precepts
and doctrines? 23 These have indeed
an appearance of wisdom in promot-
ing rigor of devotion and self-abasement and severity to the body, but
they are of no value in checking the
indulgence of the flesh.[e]

3 If then you have been raised with
Christ, seek the things that are
above, where Christ is, seated at the
right hand of God. 2 Set your minds
on things that are above, not on
things that are on earth. 3 For you
have died, and your life is hid with
Christ in God. 4 When Christ who is
our life appears, then you also will
appear with him in glory.

5 Put to death therefore what is
earthly in you: immorality, impurity,
passion, evil desire, and covetousness,
which is idolatry. 6 On account of
these the wrath of God is coming.[f]
7 In these you once walked, when you
lived in them. 8 But now put them all
away: anger, wrath, malice, slander,
and foul talk from your mouth. 9 Do
not lie to one another, seeing that you
have put off the old nature with its
practices 10 and have put on the new
nature, which is being renewed in
knowledge after the image of its
creator. 11 Here there cannot be Greek
and Jew, circumcised and uncircumcised, barbarian, Scyth'i·ȧn, slave,
free man, but Christ is all, and in all.

12 Put on then, as God's chosen
ones, holy and beloved, compassion,
kindness, lowliness, meekness, and
patience, 13 forbearing one another
and, if one has a complaint against
another, forgiving each other; as the
Lord has forgiven you, so you also
must forgive. 14 And above all these
put on love, which binds everything
together in perfect harmony. 15 And
let the peace of Christ rule in your
hearts, to which indeed you were
called in the one body. And be thankful. 16 Let the word of Christ dwell in
you richly, as you teach and admonish
one another in all wisdom, and as you
sing psalms and hymns and spiritual
songs with thankfulness in your hearts
to God. 17 And whatever you do, in
word or deed, do everything in the
name of the Lord Jesus, giving thanks
to God the Father through him.

18 Wives, be subject to your husbands, as is fitting in the Lord. 19 Husbands, love your wives, and do not be
harsh with them. 20 Children, obey
your parents in everything, for this
pleases the Lord. 21 Fathers, do not
provoke your children, lest they become discouraged. 22 Slaves, obey in
everything those who are your earthly
masters, not with eyeservice, as men-
pleasers, but in singleness of heart,
fearing the Lord. 23 Whatever your
task, work heartily, as serving the
Lord and not men, 24 knowing that
from the Lord you will receive the inheritance as your reward; you are
serving the Lord Christ. 25 For the
wrongdoer will be paid back for the
wrong he has done, and there is no
partiality.

4 Masters, treat your slaves justly
and fairly, knowing that you also
have a Master in heaven.

2 Continue steadfastly in prayer,
being watchful in it with thanksgiving; 3 and pray for us also, that God
may open to us a door for the word, to
declare the mystery of Christ, on
account of which I am in prison, 4 that
I may make it clear, as I ought to
speak.

5 Conduct yourselves wisely toward
outsiders, making the most of the
time. 6 Let your speech always be
gracious, seasoned with salt, so that
you may know how you ought to
answer every one.

7 Tych'i·cus will tell you all about
my affairs; he is a beloved brother and
faithful minister and fellow servant in
the Lord. 8 I have sent him to you for
this very purpose, that you may know
how we are and that he may encourage
your hearts, 9 and with him Ō·nes'i-
mus, the faithful and beloved brother,
who is one of yourselves. They will
tell you of everything that has taken
place here.

10 Ar·is·tär'chus my fellow prisoner

[e] Or *are of no value, serving only to indulge the flesh*
[f] Other ancient authorities add *upon the sons of disobedience*

2.22: Is 29.13; Mk 7.7. **3.1:** Ps 110.1. **3.10:** Gen 1.26. **3.12-13:** Eph 4.2. **3.16-17:** Eph 5.19. **3.18-4.1:** Eph 5.22-6.9. **3.23:** Rom 12.11. **4.1:** Lev 25.43, 53. **4.2:** Rom 12.12. **4.5:** Eph 5.16. **4.7-8:** Eph 6.21-22. **4.9:** Philem 10. **4.10-11:** Acts 19.29; 27.2; Philem 24.

greets you, and Mark the cousin of Bär'nȧ·bȧs (concerning whom you have received instructions—if he comes to you, receive him), 11 and Jesus who is called Justus. These are the only men of the circumcision among my fellow workers for the kingdom of God, and they have been a comfort to me. 12 Ep'ȧ·phras, who is one of yourselves, a servant[g] of Christ Jesus, greets you, always remembering you earnestly in his prayers, that you may stand mature and fully assured in all the will of God. 13 For I bear him witness that he has worked hard for you and for those in Lā-ȯ·di·ċē'ȧ and in Hī-ĕr·ap'ȯ·lis. 14 Luke the beloved physician and Dē'mȧs greet you. 15 Give my greetings to the brethren at Lā-ȯ·di·ċē'ȧ, and to Nym'phȧ and the church in her house. 16 And when this letter has been read among you, have it read also in the church of the Lā-ȯ·di·ċē'ȧns; and see that you read also the letter from Lā-ȯ·di·ċē'ȧ. 17 And say to Är·chip'pŭs, "See that you fulfil the ministry which you have received in the Lord."

18 I, Paul, write this greeting with my own hand. Remember my fetters. Grace be with you.

THE FIRST LETTER OF PAUL TO THE

THESSALONIANS

1 Paul, Sil·vā'nŭs, and Timothy, To the church of the Thes·sȧ·lō'ni·ȧns in God the Father and the Lord Jesus Christ:

Grace to you and peace.

2 We give thanks to God always for you all, constantly mentioning you in our prayers, 3 remembering before our God and Father your work of faith and labor of love and steadfastness of hope in our Lord Jesus Christ. 4 For we know, brethren beloved by God, that he has chosen you; 5 for our gospel came to you not only in word, but also in power and in the Holy Spirit and with full conviction. You know what kind of men we proved to be among you for your sake. 6 And you became imitators of us and of the Lord, for you received the word in much affliction, with joy inspired by the Holy Spirit; 7 so that you became an example to all the believers in Maċ·ė·dō'ni·ȧ and in Ā·chā'iȧ. 8 For not only has the word of the Lord sounded forth from you in Maċ·ė·dō'ni·ȧ and Ā·chā'iȧ, but your faith in God has gone forth everywhere, so that we need not say anything. 9 For they themselves report concerning us what a welcome we had among you, and how you turned to God from idols, to serve a living and true God, 10 and to wait for his Son from heaven, whom he raised from the dead, Jesus who delivers us from the wrath to come.

2 For you yourselves know, brethren, that our visit to you was not in vain; 2 but though we had already suffered and been shamefully treated at Phi·lip'pī, as you know, we had courage in our God to declare to you the gospel of God in the face of great opposition. 3 For our appeal does not spring from error or uncleanness, nor is it made with guile; 4 but just as we have been approved by God to be entrusted with the gospel, so we speak, not to please men, but to please God who tests our hearts. 5 For we never used either words of flattery, as you know, or a cloak for greed, as God is witness; 6 nor did we seek glory from men, whether from you or from

[g] Or *slave*

4.12: Col 1.7; Philem 23. **4.14:** 2 Tim 4.10-11; Philem 24. **4.18:** 1 Cor 16.21.
1.1: 2 Thess 1.1; 2 Cor 1.19; Acts 16.1; Acts 17.1; Rom 1.7. **1.2:** 2 Thess 1.3; 2.13; Rom 1.9.
1.3: 2 Thess 1.11; 1.3; Rom 8.25; 15.4; Gal 1.4. **1.4:** 2 Thess 2.13; Rom 1.7; 2 Pet 1.10.
1.5: 2 Thess 2.14; Rom 15.19. **1.6:** Col 2.2; 1 Thess 2.10; 1 Cor 4.16; 11.1; Acts 17.5.-10; 13.52.
1.7: Rom 15.26; Acts 18.12. **1.8:** 2 Thess 3.1; Rom 1.8. **1.10:** Mt 3.7.
2.2: Acts 16.19-24; 17.1-9; Rom 1.1. **2.5:** Acts 20.33. **2.6:** 1 Cor 9.1.

others, though we might have made
demands as apostles of Christ. 7 But
we were gentle[a] among you, like a
nurse taking care of her children. 8 So,
being affectionately desirous of you,
we were ready to share with you not
only the gospel of God but also our
own selves, because you had become
very dear to us.

9 For you remember our labor and
toil, brethren; we worked night and
day, that we might not burden any of
you, while we preached to you the
gospel of God. 10 You are witnesses,
and God also, how holy and righteous
and blameless was our behavior to you
believers; 11 for you know how, like a
father with his children, we exhorted
each one of you and encouraged you
and charged you 12 to lead a life
worthy of God, who calls you into his
own kingdom and glory.

13 And we also thank God constantly for this, that when you received the word of God which you
heard from us, you accepted it not as
the word of men but as what it really
is, the word of God, which is at work
in you believers. 14 For you, brethren,
became imitators of the churches of
God in Christ Jesus which are in
Judea; for you suffered the same
things from your own countrymen as
they did from the Jews, 15 who killed
both the Lord Jesus and the prophets, and drove us out, and displease
God and oppose all men 16 by hindering us from speaking to the Gentiles
that they may be saved—so as always to fill up the measure of their
sins. But God's wrath has come upon
them at last![b]

17 But since we were bereft of you,
brethren, for a short time, in person
not in heart, we endeavored the more
eagerly and with great desire to see
you face to face; 18 because we wanted
to come to you—I, Paul, again and
again—but Satan hindered us. 19 For
what is our hope or joy or crown of
boasting before our Lord Jesus at his
coming? Is it not you? 20 For you are
our glory and joy.

3 Therefore when we could bear it
no longer, we were willing to be
left behind at Athens alone, 2 and we
sent Timothy, our brother and God's
servant in the gospel of Christ, to
establish you in your faith and to exhort you, 3 that no one be moved by
these afflictions. You yourselves know
that this is to be our lot. 4 For when
we were with you, we told you beforehand that we were to suffer affliction;
just as it has come to pass, and as you
know. 5 For this reason, when I could
bear it no longer, I sent that I might
know your faith, for fear that somehow the tempter had tempted you and
that our labor would be in vain.

6 But now that Timothy has come
to us from you, and has brought us the
good news of your faith and love and
reported that you always remember us
kindly and long to see us, as we long
to see you— 7 for this reason, brethren, in all our distress and affliction
we have been comforted about you
through your faith; 8 for now we live,
if you stand fast in the Lord. 9 For
what thanksgiving can we render to
God for you, for all the joy which we
feel for your sake before our God,
10 praying earnestly night and day
that we may see you face to face
and supply what is lacking in your
faith?

11 Now may our God and Father
himself, and our Lord Jesus, direct
our way to you; 12 and may the Lord
make you increase and abound in love
to one another and to all men, as we
do to you, 13 so that he may establish
your hearts unblamable in holiness
before our God and Father, at the
coming of our Lord Jesus with all his
saints.

4 Finally, brethren, we beseech and
exhort you in the Lord Jesus, that
as you learned from us how you ought
to live and to please God, just as you
are doing, you do so more and more.
2 For you know what instructions we
gave you through the Lord Jesus.
3 For this is the will of God, your sanc-

[a] Other ancient authorities read *babes* [b] Or *completely*, or *for ever*

2.7: 1 Thess 2.11; Gal 4.19. **2.8:** 2 Cor 12.15; 1 Jn 3.16. **2.11:** 1 Cor 4.14. **2.12:** 1 Pet 5.10.
2.13: 1 Thess 1.2. **2.14:** 1 Thess 1.6; 1 Cor 7.17; Gal 1.22; Acts 17.5; 2 Thess 1.4.
2.15: Lk 24.20; Acts 2.23; 7.52.
2.16: Acts 9.23; 13.45, 50; 14.2, 5, 19; 17.5, 13; 18.12; 21.21, 27; 25.2, 7; 1 Cor 10.33; Gen 15.16; 1 Thess 1.10.
2.17: 1 Cor 5.3. **2.19:** Phil 4.1; 1 Thess 3.13; 4.15; 5.23; Mt 16.27; Mk 8.38. **2.20:** 2 Cor 1.14.
3.1: Phil 2.19; Acts 17.15. **3.2:** 2 Cor 1.1; Col 1.1. **3.3:** Acts 14.22. **3.4:** 1 Thess 2.14.
3.5: Mt 4.3; Phil 2.16. **3.6:** Acts 18.5. **3.13:** 1 Cor 1.8; 1 Thess 2.19; 4.17. **4.3:** 1 Cor 6.18.

tification: that you abstain from immorality; 4 that each one of you know
how to take a wife for himself in holiness and honor, 5 not in the passion of
lust like heathen who do not know
God; 6 that no man transgress, and
wrong his brother in this matter,[c]
because the Lord is an avenger
in all these things, as we solemnly
forewarned you. 7 For God has not
called us for uncleanness, but in
holiness. 8 Therefore whoever disregards this, disregards not man
but God, who gives his Holy Spirit to
you.

9 But concerning love of the brethren you have no need to have any one
write to you, for you yourselves have
been taught by God to love one another; 10 and indeed you do love all
the brethren throughout Mac·e·dō′-
ni·a. But we exhort you, brethren, to
do so more and more, 11 to aspire to
live quietly, to mind your own affairs,
and to work with your hands, as we
charged you; 12 so that you may command the respect of outsiders, and be
dependent on nobody.

13 But we would not have you
ignorant, brethren, concerning those
who are asleep, that you may not
grieve as others do who have no hope.
14 For since we believe that Jesus died
and rose again, even so, through Jesus,
God will bring with him those who
have fallen asleep. 15 For this we declare to you by the word of the Lord,
that we who are alive, who are left
until the coming of the Lord, shall not
precede those who have fallen asleep.
16 For the Lord himself will descend
from heaven with a cry of command,
with the archangel's call, and with the
sound of the trumpet of God. And the
dead in Christ will rise first; 17 then we
who are alive, who are left, shall be
caught up together with them in the
clouds to meet the Lord in the air; and
so we shall always be with the Lord.
18 Therefore comfort one another with
these words.

5 But as to the times and the seasons, brethren, you have no need
to have anything written to you. 2 For
you yourselves know well that the day
of the Lord will come like a thief in
the night. 3 When people say, "There
is peace and security," then sudden
destruction will come upon them as
travail comes upon a woman with
child, and there will be no escape.
4 But you are not in darkness, brethren, for that day to surprise you like a
thief. 5 For you are all sons of light
and sons of the day; we are not of the
night or of darkness. 6 So then let us
not sleep, as others do, but let us keep
awake and be sober. 7 For those who
sleep sleep at night, and those who get
drunk are drunk at night. 8 But, since
we belong to the day, let us be sober,
and put on the breastplate of faith and
love, and for a helmet the hope of
salvation. 9 For God has not destined
us for wrath, but to obtain salvation
through our Lord Jesus Christ, 10 who
died for us so that whether we wake
or sleep we might live with him.
11 Therefore encourage one another
and build one another up, just as you
are doing.

12 But we beseech you, brethren,
to respect those who labor among you
and are over you in the Lord and
admonish you, 13 and to esteem them
very highly in love because of their
work. Be at peace among yourselves.
14 And we exhort you, brethren, admonish the idle, encourage the fainthearted, help the weak, be patient
with them all. 15 See that none of you
repays evil for evil, but always seek to
do good to one another and to all.
16 Rejoice always, 17 pray constantly,
18 give thanks in all circumstances;
for this is the will of God in Christ
Jesus for you. 19 Do not quench the
Spirit, 20 do not despise prophesying,
21 but test everything; hold fast what
is good, 22 abstain from every form of
evil.

23 May the God of peace himself

[c] Or *defraud his brother in business*

4.4: 1 Cor 7.2; 1 Pet 3.7. **4.11:** 2 Thess 3.12; Eph 4.28; 2 Thess 3.10-12. **4.13:** Eph 2.12.
4.14: 2 Cor 4.14. **4.16:** Mt 24.31; 1 Cor 15.23; 2 Thess 2.1. **5.1:** Acts 1.7. **5.2:** 1 Cor 1.8.
5.3: 2 Thess 1.9. **5.4:** 1 Jn 2.8; Acts 26.18. **5.5:** Lk 16.8. **5.6:** Rom 13.11; 1 Pet 1.13.
5.7: Acts 2.15; 2 Pet 2.13. **5.8:** Eph 6.14, 23, 17; Rom 8.24.
5.9: 1 Thess 1.10; 2 Thess 2.13; Rom 14.9.
5.12: 1 Cor 16.18; 1 Tim 5.17; 1 Cor 16.16; Rom 16.6, 12; 1 Cor 15.10; Heb 13.17.
5.13: Mk 9.50. **5.14:** Is 35.4; Rom 14.1; 1 Cor 8.7; 2 Thess 3.6, 7, 11.
5.15: Rom 12.17; 1 Pet 3.9. **5.16:** Phil 4.4. **5.17:** Eph 6.18.
5.18: Eph 5.20. **5.19:** Eph 4.30. **5.20:** 1 Cor 14.31. **5.21:** 1 Cor 14.29; 1 Jn 4.1.
5.23: Rom 15.33.

sanctify you wholly; and may your
spirit and soul and body be kept sound
and blameless at the coming of our
Lord Jesus Christ. 24 He who calls you
is faithful, and he will do it.
25 Brethren, pray for us.
26 Greet all the brethren with a
holy kiss.
27 I adjure you by the Lord that
this letter be read to all the brethren.
28 The grace of our Lord Jesus
Christ be with you.

THE SECOND LETTER OF PAUL TO THE

THESSALONIANS

1 Paul, Sil·vā'nŭs, and Timothy,
To the church of the Thes·sȧ·lō'-
ni·ȧnṡ in God our Father and the Lord
Jesus Christ:
2 Grace to you and peace from
God the Father and the Lord Jesus
Christ.

3 We are bound to give thanks to
God always for you, brethren, as is
fitting, because your faith is growing
abundantly, and the love of every one
of you for one another is increasing.
4 Therefore we ourselves boast of you
in the churches of God for your steadfastness and faith in all your persecutions and in the afflictions which you
are enduring.
5 This is evidence of the righteous
judgment of God, that you may be
made worthy of the kingdom of God,
for which you are suffering— 6 since
indeed God deems it just to repay with
affliction those who afflict you, 7 and
to grant rest with us to you who are
afflicted, when the Lord Jesus is revealed from heaven with his mighty
angels in flaming fire, 8 inflicting
vengeance upon those who do not
know God and upon those who do not
obey the gospel of our Lord Jesus.
9 They shall suffer the punishment of
eternal destruction and exclusion from
the presence of the Lord and from the
glory of his might, 10 when he comes
on that day to be glorified in his
saints, and to be marveled at in all
who have believed, because our testimony to you was believed. 11 To this
end we always pray for you, that our
God may make you worthy of his call,
and may fulfil every good resolve and
work of faith by his power, 12 so that
the name of our Lord Jesus may be
glorified in you, and you in him, according to the grace of our God and
the Lord Jesus Christ.

2 Now concerning the coming of
our Lord Jesus Christ and our
assembling to meet him, we beg you,
brethren, 2 not to be quickly shaken in
mind or excited, either by spirit or by
word, or by letter purporting to be
from us, to the effect that the day of
the Lord has come. 3 Let no one
deceive you in any way; for that day
will not come, unless the rebellion
comes first, and the man of lawlessness[a] is revealed, the son of perdition,
4 who opposes and exalts himself
against every so-called god or object
of worship, so that he takes his seat in
the temple of God, proclaiming himself to be God. 5 Do you not remember
that when I was still with you I told
you this? 6 And you know what is re-
straining him now so that he may be
revealed in his time. 7 For the mystery
of lawlessness is already at work; only
he who now restrains it will do so until
he is out of the way. 8 And then the
lawless one will be revealed, and the
Lord Jesus will slay him with the
breath of his mouth and destroy him
by his appearing and his coming. 9 The

[a] Other ancient authorities read *sin*

5.26: Rom 16.16. **5.27:** Col 4.16. **5.28:** Rom 16.20; 2 Thess 3.18.
1.1: 1 Thess 1.1; 2 Cor 1.19; Acts 16.1. **1.2:** Rom 1.7. **1.3:** 1 Thess 1.2. **1.8:** Gal 4.8.
1.11: 1 Thess 1.3. **2.1:** 1 Thess 4.15-17. **2.2:** 2 Thess 3.17.
2.3: Eph 5.6-8; Dan 7.25; 8.25; 11.36; Rev 13.5; Jn 17.12. **2.4:** Ezek 28.2. **2.5:** 1 Thess 3.4.
2.8: Is 11.4. **2.9:** Mt 24.24; Jn 4.48.

coming of the lawless one by the
activity of Satan will be with all power
and with pretended signs and wonders, 10 and with all wicked deception
for those who are to perish, because
they refused to love the truth and so
be saved. 11 Therefore God sends upon
them a strong delusion, to make them
believe what is false, 12 so that all may
be condemned who did not believe the
truth but had pleasure in unrighteousness.

13 But we are bound to give thanks
to God always for you, brethren beloved by the Lord, because God chose
you from the beginning[b] to be saved
through sanctification by the Spirit[c]
and belief in the truth. 14 To this he
called you through our gospel, so that
you may obtain the glory of our Lord
Jesus Christ. 15 So then, brethren,
stand firm and hold to the traditions
which you were taught by us, either
by word of mouth or by letter.

16 Now may our Lord Jesus Christ
himself, and God our Father, who
loved us and gave us eternal comfort
and good hope through grace, 17 comfort your hearts and establish them in
every good work and word.

3 Finally, brethren, pray for us,
that the word of the Lord may
speed on and triumph, as it did among
you, 2 and that we may be delivered
from wicked and evil men; for not all
have faith. 3 But the Lord is faithful;
he will strengthen you and guard you
from evil.[d] 4 And we have confidence in
the Lord about you, that you are doing and will do the things which we
command. 5 May the Lord direct your
hearts to the love of God and to the
steadfastness of Christ.

6 Now we command you, brethren,
in the name of our Lord Jesus Christ,
that you keep away from any brother
who is living in idleness and not in
accord with the tradition that you
received from us. 7 For you yourselves
know how you ought to imitate us; we
were not idle when we were with you,
8 we did not eat any one's bread without paying, but with toil and labor we
worked night and day, that we might
not burden any of you. 9 It was not
because we have not that right, but to
give you in our conduct an example to
imitate. 10 For even when we were
with you, we gave you this command:
If any one will not work, let him not
eat. 11 For we hear that some of you
are living in idleness, mere busybodies,
not doing any work. 12 Now such persons we command and exhort in the
Lord Jesus Christ to do their work in
quietness and to earn their own living.
13 Brethren, do not be weary in well-
doing.

14 If any one refuses to obey what
we say in this letter, note that man,
and have nothing to do with him, that
he may be ashamed. 15 Do not look on
him as an enemy, but warn him as a
brother.

16 Now may the Lord of peace himself give you peace at all times in all
ways. The Lord be with you all.

17 I, Paul, write this greeting with
my own hand. This is the mark in
every letter of mine; it is the way I
write. 18 The grace of our Lord Jesus
Christ be with you all.

[b] Other ancient authorities read *as the first converts* [c] Or *of spirit* [d] Or *the evil one*

2.11: Rom 1.28. **2.13:** 2 Thess 1.3; Eph 1.4; 1 Pet 1.2. **2.15:** 1 Cor 16.13; 11.2.
2.16: 1 Thess 3.11; 1 Pet 1.3. **3.1:** 1 Thess 5.25; 1.8. **3.2:** Rom 15.31. **3.3:** 1 Cor 1.9; 1 Thess 5.24.
3.6: 1 Cor 5.4, 5, 11; 1 Thess 5.14. **3.7:** 1 Thess 1.6, 9. **3.8:** 1 Thess 2.9; Acts 18.3; Eph 4.28.
3.9: 2 Thess 3.7. **3.10:** 1 Thess 4.11. **3.11:** 2 Thess 3.6. **3.12:** 1 Thess 4.1, 11. **3.13:** Gal 6.9.
3.16: Ruth 2.4. **3.17:** 1 Cor 16.21. **3.18:** Rom 16.20; 1 Thess 5.28.

THE FIRST LETTER OF PAUL TO

TIMOTHY

1 Paul, an apostle of Christ Jesus
by command of God our Savior
and of Christ Jesus our hope,
2 To Timothy, my true child in the
faith:
Grace, mercy, and peace from God
the Father and Christ Jesus our
Lord.
3 As I urged you when I was going
to Mac·e·do'ni·a, remain at Eph'e·sus
that you may charge certain persons
not to teach any different doctrine,
4 nor to occupy themselves with myths
and endless genealogies which promote speculations rather than the
divine training[a] that is in faith;
5 whereas the aim of our charge is love
that issues from a pure heart and a
good conscience and sincere faith.
6 Certain persons by swerving from
these have wandered away into vain
discussion, 7 desiring to be teachers of
the law, without understanding either
what they are saying or the things
about which they make assertions.
8 Now we know that the law is
good, if any one uses it lawfully, 9 understanding this, that the law is not
laid down for the just but for the lawless and disobedient, for the ungodly
and sinners, for the unholy and profane, for murderers of fathers and
murderers of mothers, for manslayers,
10 immoral persons, sodomites, kid-
napers, liars, perjurers, and whatever
else is contrary to sound doctrine,
11 in accordance with the glorious gospel of the blessed God with which I
have been entrusted.
12 I thank him who has given me
strength for this, Christ Jesus our
Lord, because he judged me faithful
by appointing me to his service,
13 though I formerly blasphemed and
persecuted and insulted him; but I
received mercy because I had acted
ignorantly in unbelief, 14 and the grace
of our Lord overflowed for me with
the faith and love that are in Christ
Jesus. 15 The saying is sure and worthy
of full acceptance, that Christ Jesus
came into the world to save sinners.
And I am the foremost of sinners;
16 but I received mercy for this reason,
that in me, as the foremost, Jesus
Christ might display his perfect patience for an example to those who
were to believe in him for eternal life.
17 To the King of ages, immortal, invisible, the only God, be honor and
glory for ever and ever.[b] Amen.
18 This charge I commit to you,
Timothy, my son, in accordance with
the prophetic utterances which pointed
to you, that inspired by them you may
wage the good warfare, 19 holding
faith and a good conscience. By rejecting conscience, certain persons have
made shipwreck of their faith,
20 among them Hy·me·nae'us and
Alexander, whom I have delivered to
Satan that they may learn not to
blaspheme.

2 First of all, then, I urge that supplications, prayers, intercessions,
and thanksgivings be made for all
men, 2 for kings and all who are in
high positions, that we may lead a
quiet and peaceable life, godly and
respectful in every way. 3 This is
good, and it is acceptable in the sight
of God our Savior, 4 who desires all
men to be saved and to come to the
knowledge of the truth. 5 For there is
one God, and there is one mediator
between God and men, the man
Christ Jesus, 6 who gave himself as a
ransom for all, the testimony to which
was borne at the proper time. 7 For
this I was appointed a preacher and
apostle (I am telling the truth, I am
not lying), a teacher of the Gentiles in
faith and truth.
8 I desire then that in every place
the men should pray, lifting holy
hands without anger or quarreling;
9 also that women should adorn themselves modestly and sensibly in seemly
apparel, not with braided hair or gold
or pearls or costly attire 10 but by good
deeds, as befits women who profess
religion. 11 Let a woman learn in
silence with all submissiveness. 12 I
permit no woman to teach or to have

[a] Or *stewardship*, or *order* [b] Greek *to the ages of ages*

authority over men; she is to keep
silent. 13 For Adam was formed first,
then Eve; 14 and Adam was not deceived, but the woman was deceived
and became a transgressor. 15 Yet
woman will be saved through bearing
children,[c] if she continues[d] in faith
and love and holiness, with modesty.

3 The saying is sure: If any one
aspires to the office of bishop, he
desires a noble task. 2 Now a bishop
must be above reproach, the husband
of one wife, temperate, sensible, digni-
fied, hospitable, an apt teacher, 3 no
drunkard, not violent but gentle, not
quarrelsome, and no lover of money.
4 He must manage his own household
well, keeping his children submissive
and respectful in every way; 5 for if a
man does not know how to manage his
own household, how can he care for
God's church? 6 He must not be a
recent convert, or he may be puffed
up with conceit and fall into the condemnation of the devil;[f] 7 moreover
he must be well thought of by outsiders, or he may fall into reproach
and the snare of the devil.[f]

8 Deacons likewise must be serious,
not double-tongued, not addicted to
much wine, not greedy for gain; 9 they
must hold the mystery of the faith
with a clear conscience. 10 And let them
also be tested first; then if they prove
themselves blameless let them serve
as deacons. 11 The women likewise
must be serious, no slanderers, but
temperate, faithful in all things.
12 Let deacons be the husband of one
wife, and let them manage their children and their households well; 13 for
those who serve well as deacons gain a
good standing for themselves and also
great confidence in the faith which is
in Christ Jesus.

14 I hope to come to you soon, but
I am writing these instructions to you
so that, 15 if I am delayed, you may
know how one ought to behave in the
household of God, which is the church
of the living God, the pillar and bulwark of the truth. 16 Great indeed, we
confess, is the mystery of our religion:

He[h] was manifested in the flesh,
vindicated[i] in the Spirit,
seen by angels,
preached among the nations,
believed on in the world,
taken up in glory.

4 Now the Spirit expressly says
that in later times some will depart from the faith by giving heed to
deceitful spirits and doctrines of demons, 2 through the pretensions of
liars whose consciences are seared,
3 who forbid marriage and enjoin
abstinence from foods which God
created to be received with thanksgiving by those who believe and know
the truth. 4 For everything created by
God is good, and nothing is to be
rejected if it is received with thanksgiving; 5 for then it is consecrated by
the word of God and prayer.

6 If you put these instructions before the brethren, you will be a good
minister of Christ Jesus, nourished on
the words of the faith and of the good
doctrine which you have followed.
7 Have nothing to do with godless and
silly myths. Train yourself in godliness; 8 for while bodily training is of
some value, godliness is of value in
every way, as it holds promise for the
present life and also for the life to
come. 9 The saying is sure and worthy
of full acceptance. 10 For to this end
we toil and strive,[j] because we have
our hope set on the living God, who
is the Savior of all men, especially of
those who believe.

11 Command and teach these
things. 12 Let no one despise your
youth, but set the believers an example in speech and conduct, in love, in
faith, in purity. 13 Till I come, attend
to the public reading of scripture, to
preaching, to teaching. 14 Do not neglect the gift you have, which was given
you by prophetic utterance when the
elders laid their hands upon you.
15 Practice these duties, devote yourself to them, so that all may see your
progress. 16 Take heed to yourself and
to your teaching: hold to that, for by
so doing you will save both yourself
and your hearers.

5 Do not rebuke an older man but
exhort him as you would a father;
treat younger men like brothers,
2 older women like mothers, younger
women like sisters, in all purity.

3 Honor widows who are real widows. 4 If a widow has children or

[c] Or *by the birth of the child* [d] Greek *they continue* [f] Or *slanderer*
[h] Greek *Who;* other ancient authorities read *God;* others, *Which* [i] Or *justified*
[j] Other ancient authorities read *suffer reproach*
2.13: Gen 2.7, 21-22. **2.14:** Gen 3.1-6.

grandchildren, let them first learn
their religious duty to their own family and make some return to their
parents; for this is acceptable in the
sight of God. 5 She who is a real
widow, and is left all alone, has set
her hope on God and continues in
supplications and prayers night and
day; 6 whereas she who is self-indul-
gent is dead even while she lives.
7 Command this, so that they may be
without reproach. 8 If any one does
not provide for his relatives, and
especially for his own family, he has
disowned the faith and is worse than
an unbeliever.

9 Let a widow be enrolled if she is
not less than sixty years of age, having been the wife of one husband;
10 and she must be well attested for
her good deeds, as one who has
brought up children, shown hospitality, washed the feet of the saints, relieved the afflicted, and devoted
herself to doing good in every way.
11 But refuse to enroll younger widows;
for when they grow wanton against
Christ they desire to marry, 12 and so
they incur condemnation for having
violated their first pledge. 13 Besides
that, they learn to be idlers, gadding
about from house to house, and not
only idlers but gossips and busybodies, saying what they should not.
14 So I would have younger widows
marry, bear children, rule their households, and give the enemy no occasion
to revile us. 15 For some have already
strayed after Satan. 16 If any believing woman[l] has relatives who are
widows, let her assist them; let the
church not be burdened, so that it
may assist those who are real widows.

17 Let the elders who rule well be
considered worthy of double honor,
especially those who labor in preaching and teaching; 18 for the scripture
says, "You shall not muzzle an ox
when it is treading out the grain,"
and, "The laborer deserves his wages."
19 Never admit any charge against an
elder except on the evidence of two or
three witnesses. 20 As for those who
persist in sin, rebuke them in the
presence of all, so that the rest may
stand in fear. 21 In the presence of
God and of Christ Jesus and of the
elect angels I charge you to keep these
rules without favor, doing nothing
from partiality. 22 Do not be hasty in
the laying on of hands, nor partici-
pate in another man's sins; keep yourself pure.

23 No longer drink only water, but
use a little wine for the sake of your
stomach and your frequent ailments.

24 The sins of some men are conspicuous, pointing to judgment, but
the sins of others appear later. 25 So
also good deeds are conspicuous; and
even when they are not, they cannot
remain hidden.

6 Let all who are under the yoke of
slavery regard their masters as
worthy of all honor, so that the name
of God and the teaching may not be
defamed. 2 Those who have believing
masters must not be disrespectful on
the ground that they are brethren;
rather they must serve all the better
since those who benefit by their service are believers and beloved.

Teach and urge these duties. 3 If
any one teaches otherwise and does
not agree with the sound words of our
Lord Jesus Christ and the teaching
which accords with godliness, 4 he is
puffed up with conceit, he knows
nothing; he has a morbid craving for
controversy and for disputes about
words, which produce envy, dissension, slander, base suspicions, 5 and
wrangling among men who are depraved in mind and bereft of the
truth, imagining that godliness is a
means of gain. 6 There is great gain in
godliness with contentment; 7 for we
brought nothing into the world, and[m]
we cannot take anything out of the
world; 8 but if we have food and
clothing, with these we shall be content. 9 But those who desire to be
rich fall into temptation, into a snare,
into many senseless and hurtful desires that plunge men into ruin and
destruction. 10 For the love of money
is the root of all evils; it is through
this craving that some have wandered
away from the faith and pierced their
hearts with many pangs.

11 But as for you, man of God,
shun all this; aim at righteousness,
godliness, faith, love, steadfastness,
gentleness. 12 Fight the good fight of
the faith; take hold of the eternal life
to which you were called when you

l Other ancient authorities read *man or woman;* others, simply *man*
m Other ancient authorities insert *it is certain that*
5.18: Deut 25.4; 1 Cor 9.9; Mt 10.10; Lk 10.7; 1 Cor 9.14. **5.19:** Deut 19.15.

made the good confession in the
presence of many witnesses. 13 In the
presence of God who gives life to all
things, and of Christ Jesus who in his
testimony before Pontius Pilate made
the good confession, 14 I charge you
to keep the commandment unstained
and free from reproach until the
appearing of our Lord Jesus Christ;
15 and this will be made manifest at
the proper time by the blessed and
only Sovereign, the King of kings and
Lord of lords, 16 who alone has immortality and dwells in unapproach-
able light, whom no man has ever
seen or can see. To him be honor and
eternal dominion. Amen.

17 As for the rich in this world,
charge them not to be haughty, nor to
set their hopes on uncertain riches but
on God who richly furnishes us with
everything to enjoy. 18 They are to do
good, to be rich in good deeds, liberal
and generous, 19 thus laying up for
themselves a good foundation for the
future, so that they may take hold of
the life which is life indeed.

20 O Timothy, guard what has been
entrusted to you. Avoid the godless
chatter and contradictions of what is
falsely called knowledge, 21 for by pro-
fessing it some have missed the mark
as regards the faith.

Grace be with you.

THE SECOND LETTER OF PAUL TO

TIMOTHY

1 Paul, an apostle of Christ Jesus
by the will of God according to the
promise of the life which is in Christ
Jesus,

2 To Timothy, my beloved child:

Grace, mercy, and peace from
God the Father and Christ Jesus our
Lord.

3 I thank God whom I serve with a
clear conscience, as did my fathers,
when I remember you constantly in
my prayers. 4 As I remember your
tears, I long night and day to see you,
that I may be filled with joy. 5 I am
reminded of your sincere faith, a faith
that dwelt first in your grandmother
Lō'is and your mother Eunice and
now, I am sure, dwells in you. 6 Hence
I remind you to rekindle the gift of
God that is within you through the
laying on of my hands; 7 for God did
not give us a spirit of timidity but a
spirit of power and love and self-
control.

8 Do not be ashamed then of testifying to our Lord, nor of me his
prisoner, but take your share of suffering for the gospel in the power of God,
9 who saved us and called us with a
holy calling, not in virtue of our works
but in virtue of his own purpose and
the grace which he gave us in Christ
Jesus ages ago, 10 and now has manifested through the appearing of our
Savior Christ Jesus, who abolished
death and brought life and immortality to light through the gospel. 11 For
this gospel I was appointed a preacher
and apostle and teacher, 12 and therefore I suffer as I do. But I am not
ashamed, for I know whom I have
believed, and I am sure that he is
able to guard until that Day what
has been entrusted to me.[a] 13 Follow
the pattern of the sound words which
you have heard from me, in the faith
and love which are in Christ Jesus;
14 guard the truth that has been entrusted to you by the Holy Spirit who
dwells within us.

15 You are aware that all who are
in Asia turned away from me, and
among them Phy̆'gĕ·lus and Hẽr·mog'-
ĕ·nēs. 16 May the Lord grant mercy to
the household of On·ĕ·siph'ō·rŭs, for
he often refreshed me; he was not
ashamed of my chains, 17 but when he
arrived in Rome he searched for me
eagerly and found me— 18 may the
Lord grant him to find mercy from the
Lord on that Day—and you well

[a] Or *what I have entrusted to him*

6.13: Jn 18.37. **1.5:** Acts 16.1.

know all the service he rendered at
Eph'ĕ·sŭs.

2 You then, my son, be strong in
the grace that is in Christ Jesus,
2 and what you have heard from me
before many witnesses entrust to
faithful men who will be able to teach
others also. 3 Take your share of suffering as a good soldier of Christ
Jesus. 4 No soldier on service gets
entangled in civilian pursuits, since
his aim is to satisfy the one who en-
listed him. 5 An athlete is not crowned
unless he competes according to the
rules. 6 It is the hard-working farmer
who ought to have the first share of
the crops. 7 Think over what I say,
for the Lord will grant you understanding in everything.

8 Remember Jesus Christ, risen
from the dead, descended from David,
as preached in my gospel, 9 the gospel
for which I am suffering and wearing
fetters like a criminal. But the word of
God is not fettered. 10 Therefore I endure everything for the sake of the
elect, that they also may obtain the
salvation which in Christ Jesus goes
with eternal glory. 11 The saying is
sure:

If we have died with him, we shall
also live with him;
12 if we endure, we shall also reign
with him;
if we deny him, he also will deny us;
13 if we are faithless, he remains
faithful—
for he cannot deny himself.

14 Remind them of this, and charge
them before the Lord[b] to avoid disputing about words, which does no
good, but only ruins the hearers. 15 Do
your best to present yourself to God
as one approved, a workman who has
no need to be ashamed, rightly handling the word of truth. 16 Avoid such
godless chatter, for it will lead people
into more and more ungodliness, 17 and
their talk will eat its way like gan-
grene. Among them are Hy̆·mĕ·naē'ŭs
and Phi·lē'tŭs, 18 who have swerved
from the truth by holding that the
resurrection is past already. They are
upsetting the faith of some. 19 But
God's firm foundation stands, bearing
this seal: "The Lord knows those who
are his," and, "Let every one who
names the name of the Lord depart
from iniquity."

20 In a great house there are not
only vessels of gold and silver but also
of wood and earthenware, and some
for noble use, some for ignoble. 21 If
any one purifies himself from what is
ignoble, then he will be a vessel for
noble use, consecrated and useful to
the master of the house, ready for any
good work. 22 So shun youthful passions and aim at righteousness, faith,
love, and peace, along with those who
call upon the Lord from a pure heart.
23 Have nothing to do with stupid,
senseless controversies; you know that
they breed quarrels. 24 And the Lord's
servant must not be quarrelsome but
kindly to every one, an apt teacher,
forbearing, 25 correcting his opponents
with gentleness. God may perhaps
grant that they will repent and come
to know the truth, 26 and they may
escape from the snare of the devil,
after being captured by him to do his
will.[c]

3 But understand this, that in the
last days there will come times of
stress. 2 For men will be lovers of self,
lovers of money, proud, arrogant,
abusive, disobedient to their parents,
ungrateful, unholy, 3 inhuman, impla-
cable, slanderers, profligates, fierce,
haters of good, 4 treacherous, reckless,
swollen with conceit, lovers of pleasure rather than lovers of God, 5 holding the form of religion but denying
the power of it. Avoid such people.
6 For among them are those who make
their way into households and capture
weak women, burdened with sins and
swayed by various impulses, 7 who
will listen to anybody and can never
arrive at a knowledge of the truth.
8 As Jan'nēs and Jam'brēs opposed
Moses, so these men also oppose the
truth, men of corrupt mind and coun-
terfeit faith; 9 but they will not get
very far, for their folly will be plain
to all, as was that of those two men.

10 Now you have observed my
teaching, my conduct, my aim in life,
my faith, my patience, my love, my
steadfastness, 11 my persecutions, my
sufferings, what befell me at An'ti·och,
at Ī·cō'ni·ŭm, and at Lys'tră, what
persecutions I endured; yet from them
all the Lord rescued me. 12 Indeed all
who desire to live a godly life in Christ
Jesus will be persecuted, 13 while evil
men and impostors will go on from

[b] other ancient authorities read *God*

[c] Or *by him, to do his* (that is, God's) *will*

2.19: Num 16.5; Is 26.13. **3.8:** Ex 7.11. **3.11:** Acts 13 14-52; 14 1-20; 16.1-5.

bad to worse, deceivers and deceived.
14 But as for you, continue in what
you have learned and have firmly believed, knowing from whom you
learned it 15 and how from childhood
you have been acquainted with the
sacred writings which are able to
instruct you for salvation through
faith in Christ Jesus. 16All scripture is
inspired by God and[d] profitable for
teaching, for reproof, for correction,
and for training in righteousness,
17 that the man of God may be complete, equipped for every good work.

4 I charge you in the presence of
God and of Christ Jesus who is to
judge the living and the dead, and by
his appearing and his kingdom:
2 preach the word, be urgent in season
and out of season, convince, rebuke,
and exhort, be unfailing in patience
and in teaching. 3 For the time is
coming when people will not endure
sound teaching, but having itching
ears they will accumulate for themselves teachers to suit their own lik-
ings, 4 and will turn away from listening to the truth and wander into
myths. 5As for you, always be steady,
endure suffering, do the work of an
evangelist, fulfill your ministry.

6 For I am already on the point of
being sacrificed; the time of my departure has come. 7 I have fought the
good fight, I have finished the race, I
have kept the faith. 8 Henceforth
there is laid up for me the crown of
righteousness, which the Lord, the
righteous judge, will award to me on
that Day, and not only to me but
also to all who have loved his appearing.

9 Do your best to come to me soon.
10 For Dē'màs, in love with this present world, has deserted me and gone
to Thes·sȧ·lȯ·nī'cȧ; Cres'ċenṡ has gone
to Galatia,[e] Titus to Dalmatia. 11 Luke
alone is with me. Get Mark and bring
him with you; for he is very useful in
serving me. 12 Tych'ĭ·cŭs I have sent
to Eph'ė·sŭs. 13 When you come, bring
the cloak that I left with Cär'pŭs at
Trō'as, also the books, and above all
the parchments. 14Alexander the cop-
persmith did me great harm; the Lord
will requite him for his deeds. 15 Beware of him yourself, for he strongly
opposed our message. 16At my first
defense no one took my part; all
deserted me. May it not be charged
against them! 17 But the Lord stood
by me and gave me strength to proclaim the word fully, that all the Gentiles might hear it. So I was rescued
from the lion's mouth. 18 The Lord
will rescue me from every evil and
save me for his heavenly kingdom. To
him be the glory for ever and ever.
Amen.

19 Greet Pris'cȧ and Aq'ui·lȧ, and
the household of On·ė·siph'ō·rŭs.
20 E·ras'tŭs remained at Corinth;
Troph'ĭ·mŭs I left ill at Mī·lē'tŭs.
21 Do your best to come before winter.
Eu·bū'lŭs sends greetings to you, as
do Pū'denṡ and Lī'nŭs and Claudia
and all the brethren.

22 The Lord be with your spirit.
Grace be with you.

THE LETTER OF PAUL TO

TITUS

1 Paul, a servant[a] of God and an
apostle of Jesus Christ, to further
the faith of God's elect and their
knowledge of the truth which accords
with godliness, 2 in hope of eternal
life which God, who never lies, promised ages ago 3 and at the proper time
manifested in his word through the
preaching with which I have been
entrusted by command of God our
Savior;

4 To Titus, my true child in a common faith:

Grace and peace from God the
Father and Christ Jesus our Savior.

5 This is why I left you in Crete,
that you might amend what was de-

[d] Or *Every scripture inspired by God is also* [e] Other ancient authorities read *Gaul* [a] Or *slave*

fective, and appoint elders in every
town as I directed you, 6 if any man is
blameless, the husband of one wife,
and his children are believers and not
open to the charge of being profligate
or insubordinate. 7 For a bishop, as
God's steward, must be blameless; he
must not be arrogant or quick-tem-
pered or a drunkard or violent or
greedy for gain, 8 but hospitable, a
lover of goodness, master of himself,
upright, holy, and self-controlled; 9 he
must hold firm to the sure word as
taught, so that he may be able to give
instruction in sound doctrine and also
to confute those who contradict it.
10 For there are many insubordinate
men, empty talkers and deceivers,
especially the circumcision party;
11 they must be silenced, since they are
upsetting whole families by teaching
for base gain what they have no right
to teach. 12 One of themselves, a
prophet of their own, said, "Cretans
are always liars, evil beasts, lazy gluttons." 13 This testimony is true.
Therefore rebuke them sharply, that
they may be sound in the faith, 14 instead of giving heed to Jewish myths
or to commands of men who reject the
truth. 15 To the pure all things are
pure, but to the corrupt and unbelieving nothing is pure; their very
minds and consciences are corrupted.
16 They profess to know God, but they
deny him by their deeds; they are
detestable, disobedient, unfit for any
good deed.

2 But as for you, teach what befits
sound doctrine. 2 Bid the older
men be temperate, serious, sensible,
sound in faith, in love, and in steadfastness. 3 Bid the older women likewise to be reverent in behavior, not to
be slanderers or slaves to drink; they
are to teach what is good, 4 and so
train the young women to love their
husbands and children, 5 to be sensible, chaste, domestic, kind, and submissive to their husbands, that the
word of God may not be discredited.
6 Likewise urge the younger men to
control themselves. 7 Show yourself in
all respects a model of good deeds, and
in your teaching show integrity, grav-
ity, 8 and sound speech that cannot be
censured, so that an opponent may be
put to shame, having nothing evil to
say of us. 9 Bid slaves to be submissive
to their masters and to give satisfaction in every respect; they are not to
be refractory, 10 nor to pilfer, but to
show entire and true fidelity, so that in
everything they may adorn the doctrine of God our Savior.

11 For the grace of God has appeared for the salvation of all men,
12 training us to renounce irreligion
and worldly passions, and to live
sober, upright, and godly lives in this
world, 13 awaiting our blessed hope,
the appearing of the glory of our great
God and Savior[c] Jesus Christ, 14 who
gave himself for us to redeem us from
all iniquity and to purify for himself a
people of his own who are zealous for
good deeds.

15 Declare these things; exhort and
reprove with all authority. Let no one
disregard you.

3 Remind them to be submissive to
rulers and authorities, to be obedient, to be ready for any honest work,
2 to speak evil of no one, to avoid
quarreling, to be gentle, and to show
perfect courtesy toward all men. 3 For
we ourselves were once foolish, disobedient, led astray, slaves to various
passions and pleasures, passing our
days in malice and envy, hated by
men and hating one another; 4 but
when the goodness and loving kindness of God our Savior appeared,
5 he saved us, not because of deeds
done by us in righteousness, but in
virtue of his own mercy, by the washing of regeneration and renewal in the
Holy Spirit, 6 which he poured out
upon us richly through Jesus Christ
our Savior, 7 so that we might be
justified by his grace and become
heirs in hope of eternal life. 8 The
saying is sure.

I desire you to insist on these things,
so that those who have believed in
God may be careful to apply themselves to good deeds;[d] these are excellent and profitable to men. 9 But
avoid stupid controversies, genealogies, dissensions, and quarrels over
the law, for they are unprofitable and
futile. 10 As for a man who is factious,
after admonishing him once or twice,
have nothing more to do with him,
11 knowing that such a person is perverted and sinful; he is self-con-
demned.

[c] Or *of the great God and our Savior* [d] Or *enter honorable occupations*
1.12: Epimenides 2.14: Ps 130.8; Ezek 37.23: Deut 14.2.

12 When I send Ar'tė·mȧs or Tych'-
i·cŭs to you, do your best to come to
me at Ni·cop'ō·lis, for I have decided
to spend the winter there. 13 Do your
best to speed Zē'nȧs the lawyer and
Ȧ·pol'los on their way; see that they
lack nothing. 14 And let our people
learn to apply themselves to good
deeds,[d] so as to help cases of urgent
need, and not to be unfruitful.
15 All who are with me send greetings to you. Greet those who love us
in the faith.
Grace be with you all.

THE LETTER OF PAUL TO

PHILEMON

1 Paul, a prisoner for Christ Jesus,
and Timothy our brother,
To Phi·lē'mŏn our beloved fellow
worker 2 and Ap'phi·ȧ our sister and
Ar·chip'pŭs our fellow soldier, and the
church in your house:
3 Grace to you and peace from God
our Father and the Lord Jesus Christ.

4 I thank my God always when I
remember you in my prayers, 5 because I hear of your love and of the
faith which you have toward the Lord
Jesus and all the saints, 6 and I pray
that the sharing of your faith may promote the knowledge of all the good
that is ours in Christ. 7 For I have
derived much joy and comfort from
your love, my brother, because the
hearts of the saints have been refreshed through you.
8 Accordingly, though I am bold
enough in Christ to command you to
do what is required, 9 yet for love's
sake I prefer to appeal to you—I,
Paul, an ambassador[a] and now a
prisoner also for Christ Jesus— 10 I
appeal to you for my child, Ō·nes'-
i·mŭs, whose father I have become in
my imprisonment. 11 (Formerly he
was useless to you, but now he is
indeed useful[b] to you and to me.)
12 I am sending him back to you,
sending my very heart. 13 I would
have been glad to keep him with me,
in order that he might serve me on
your behalf during my imprisonment
for the gospel; 14 but I preferred to do
nothing without your consent in order
that your goodness might not be by
compulsion but of your own free will.
15 Perhaps this is why he was
parted from you for a while, that you
might have him back for ever, 16 no
longer as a slave but more than a
slave, as a beloved brother, especially
to me but how much more to you, both
in the flesh and in the Lord. 17 So if
you consider me your partner, receive
him as you would receive me. 18 If he
has wronged you at all, or owes you
anything, charge that to my account.
19 I, Paul, write this with my own
hand, I will repay it—to say nothing
of your owing me even your own self.
20 Yes, brother, I want some benefit
from you in the Lord. Refresh my
heart in Christ.
21 Confident of your obedience, I
write to you, knowing that you will do
even more than I say. 22 At the same
time, prepare a guest room for me, for
I am hoping through your prayers to
be granted to you.
23 Ep'ȧ·phras, my fellow prisoner
in Christ Jesus, sends greetings to you,
24 and so do Mark, Ar·is·tär'chŭs,
Dē'mȧs, and Luke, my fellow workers.
25 The grace of the Lord Jesus
Christ be with your spirit.

[d] Or *enter honorable occupations* [a] Or *an old man*
[b] The name Onesimus means *useful* or (compare verse 20) *beneficial*
3: Rom 1.7. **4:** Rom 1.8. **10:** Col 4.9. **23:** Col 1.7; 4.12. **24:** Col 4.10, 14.

THE LETTER TO THE

HEBREWS

1 In many and various ways God
spoke of old to our fathers by the
prophets; 2 but in these last days he
has spoken to us by a Son, whom he
appointed the heir of all things,
through whom also he created the
world. 3 He reflects the glory of God
and bears the very stamp of his nature, upholding the universe by his
word of power. When he had made
purification for sins, he sat down at
the right hand of the Majesty on high,
4 having become as much superior to
angels as the name he has obtained is
more excellent than theirs.

5 For to what angel did God ever
say,

"Thou art my Son,
today I have begotten thee"?

Or again,

"I will be to him a father,
and he shall be to me a son"?

6 And again, when he brings the first-
born into the world, he says,

"Let all God's angels worship him."

7 Of the angels he says,

"Who makes his angels winds,
and his servants flames of fire."

8 But of the Son he says,

"Thy throne, O God,[a] is for ever
and ever,
the righteous scepter is the scepter
of thy[b] kingdom.
9 Thou hast loved righteousness and
hated lawlessness;
therefore God, thy God, has
anointed thee
with the oil of gladness beyond thy
comrades."

10 And,

"Thou, Lord, didst found the earth
in the beginning,
and the heavens are the work of
thy hands;
11 they will perish, but thou remain-
est;
they will all grow old like a garment,
12 like a mantle thou wilt roll them up,
and they will be changed.[c]
But thou art the same,
and thy years will never end."

13 But to what angel has he ever said,

"Sit at my right hand,
till I make thy enemies
a stool for thy feet"?

14 Are they not all ministering spirits
sent forth to serve, for the sake of
those who are to obtain salvation?

2 Therefore we must pay the closer
attention to what we have heard,
lest we drift away from it. 2 For if the
message declared by angels was valid
and every transgression or disobedience received a just retribution, 3 how
shall we escape if we neglect such a
great salvation? It was declared at
first by the Lord, and it was attested
to us by those who heard him, 4 while
God also bore witness by signs and
wonders and various miracles and by
gifts of the Holy Spirit distributed
according to his own will.

5 For it was not to angels that God
subjected the world to come, of which
we are speaking. 6 It has been testified
somewhere,

"What is man that thou art mindful
of him,
or the son of man, that thou carest
for him?
7 Thou didst make him for a little
while lower than the angels,
thou hast crowned him with glory
and honor,[d]
8 putting everything in subjection
under his feet."

Now in putting everything in subjection to him, he left nothing outside his
control. As it is, we do not yet see
everything in subjection to him. 9 But
we see Jesus, who for a little while was
made lower than the angels, crowned
with glory and honor because of the
suffering of death, so that by the grace
of God he might taste death for every
one.

[a] Or *God is thy throne* [b] Other ancient authorities read *his*
[c] Other ancient authorities add *like a garment*
[d] Other ancient authorities insert *and didst set him over the works of thy hands*
1.5: Ps 2.7; 2 Sam 7.14. **1.6:** Deut 32.43 (Gk.); Ps 97.7. **1.7:** Ps 104.4. **1.8-9:** Ps 45.6-7.
1.10-12: Ps 102.25-27. **1.13:** Ps 110.1. **2.6-9:** Ps 8.4-6.

10 For it was fitting that he, for
whom and by whom all things exist,
in bringing many sons to glory, should
make the pioneer of their salvation
perfect through suffering. 11 For he
who sanctifies and those who are
sanctified have all one origin. That is
why he is not ashamed to call them
brethren, 12 saying,

"I will proclaim thy name to my
brethren,
in the midst of the congregation I
will praise thee."

13 And again,

"I will put my trust in him."

And again,

"Here am I, and the children God
has given me."

14 Since therefore the children
share in flesh and blood, he himself
likewise partook of the same nature,
that through death he might destroy
him who has the power of death, that
is, the devil, 15 and deliver all those
who through fear of death were subject to lifelong bondage. 16 For surely
it is not with angels that he is concerned but with the descendants of
Abraham. 17 Therefore he had to be
made like his brethren in every respect, so that he might become a
merciful and faithful high priest in the
service of God, to make expiation for
the sins of the people. 18 For because
he himself has suffered and been
tempted, he is able to help those who
are tempted.

3 Therefore, holy brethren, who
share in a heavenly call, consider
Jesus, the apostle and high priest of
our confession. 2 He was faithful to
him who appointed him, just as Moses
also was faithful in[e] God's house. 3 Yet
Jesus has been counted worthy of as
much more glory than Moses as the
builder of a house has more honor
than the house. 4 (For every house is
built by some one, but the builder of
all things is God.) 5 Now Moses was
faithful in all God's house as a servant,
to testify to the things that were to be
spoken later, 6 but Christ was faithful
over God's[f] house as a son. And we
are his house if we hold fast our confidence and pride in our hope.[g]

7 Therefore, as the Holy Spirit says,

"Today, when you hear his voice,
8 do not harden your hearts as in the
rebellion,
on the day of testing in the wilderness,
9 where your fathers put me to the
test
and saw my works for forty years.
10 Therefore I was provoked with that
generation,
and said, 'They always go astray in
their hearts;
they have not known my ways.'
11 As I swore in my wrath,
'They shall never enter my rest.' "

12 Take care, brethren, lest there be in
any of you an evil, unbelieving heart,
leading you to fall away from the living God. 13 But exhort one another
every day, as long as it is called
"today," that none of you may be
hardened by the deceitfulness of sin.
14 For we share in Christ, if only we
hold our first confidence firm to the
end, 15 while it is said,

"Today, when you hear his voice,
do not harden your hearts
as in the rebellion."

16 Who were they that heard and yet
were rebellious? Was it not all those
who left Egypt under the leadership
of Moses? 17 And with whom was he
provoked forty years? Was it not with
those who sinned, whose bodies fell
in the wilderness? 18 And to whom did
he swear that they should never enter
his rest, but to those who were disobedient? 19 So we see that they were
unable to enter because of unbelief.

4 Therefore, while the promise of
entering his rest remains, let us
fear lest any of you be judged to have
failed to reach it. 2 For good news
came to us just as to them; but the
message which they heard did not
benefit them, because it did not meet
with faith in the hearers.[h] 3 For we
who have believed enter that rest, as
he has said,

"As I swore in my wrath,
'They shall never enter my rest,' "

although his works were finished from
the foundation of the world. 4 For he
has somewhere spoken of the seventh
day in this way, "And God rested on

[e] Other ancient authorities insert *all* [f] Greek *his* [g] Other ancient authorities insert *firm to the end*
[h] Other manuscripts read *they were not united in faith with the hearers*

2.12: Ps 22.22. **2.13:** Is 8.17-18. **2.16:** Is 41.8-9. **3.2:** Num 12.7. **3.5:** Num 12.7.
3.7-11: Ps 95.7-11. **3.15:** Ps 95.7-8. **3.16-19:** Num 14.1-35. **3.17:** Num 14.29. **4.3:** Ps 95.11.
4.4: Gen 2.2.

the seventh day from all his works."
5 And again in this place he said,
"They shall never enter my rest."
6 Since therefore it remains for some
to enter it, and those who formerly
received the good news failed to enter
because of disobedience, 7 again he
sets a certain day, "Today," saying
through David so long afterward, in
the words already quoted,
"Today, when you hear his voice,
do not harden your hearts."
8 For if Joshua had given them rest,
God[i] would not speak later of another
day. 9 So then, there remains a sabbath rest for the people of God; 10 for
whoever enters God's rest also ceases
from his labors as God did from
his.
11 Let us therefore strive to enter
that rest, that no one fall by the same
sort of disobedience. 12 For the word
of God is living and active, sharper
than any two-edged sword, piercing
to the division of soul and spirit, of
joints and marrow, and discerning the
thoughts and intentions of the heart.
13 And before him no creature is hidden, but all are open and laid bare to
the eyes of him with whom we have
to do.

14 Since then we have a great high
priest who has passed through the
heavens, Jesus, the Son of God, let us
hold fast our confession. 15 For we
have not a high priest who is unable to
sympathize with our weaknesses, but
one who in every respect has been
tempted as we are, yet without sinning. 16 Let us then with confidence
draw near to the throne of grace, that
we may receive mercy and find grace
to help in time of need.

5 For every high priest chosen from
among men is appointed to act on
behalf of men in relation to God, to
offer gifts and sacrifices for sins. 2 He
can deal gently with the ignorant and
wayward, since he himself is beset
with weakness. 3 Because of this he is
bound to offer sacrifice for his own
sins as well as for those of the people.
4 And one does not take the honor upon
himself, but he is called by God, just
as Aaron was.
5 So also Christ did not exalt himself to be made a high priest, but was
appointed by him who said to him,
"Thou art my Son,
today I have begotten thee";
6 as he says also in another place,
"Thou art a priest for ever,
after the order of Mel·chiz'ĕ·dek."
7 In the days of his flesh, Jesus[j]
offered up prayers and supplications,
with loud cries and tears, to him who
was able to save him from death, and
he was heard for his godly fear.
8 Although he was a Son, he learned
obedience through what he suffered;
9 and being made perfect he became
the source of eternal salvation to all
who obey him, 10 being designated by
God a high priest after the order of
Mel·chiz'ĕ·dek.
11 About this we have much to say
which is hard to explain, since you
have become dull of hearing. 12 For
though by this time you ought to be
teachers, you need some one to teach
you again the first principles of God's
word. You need milk, not solid food;
13 for every one who lives on milk is
unskilled in the word of righteousness,
for he is a child. 14 But solid food is for
the mature, for those who have their
faculties trained by practice to distinguish good from evil.

6 Therefore let us leave the ele-
mentary doctrines of Christ and
go on to maturity, not laying again a
foundation of repentance from dead
works and of faith toward God, 2 with
instruction[k] about ablutions, the laying on of hands, the resurrection of the
dead, and eternal judgment. 3 And
this we will do if God permits.[l] 4 For
it is impossible to restore again to
repentance those who have once been
enlightened, who have tasted the
heavenly gift, and have become partakers of the Holy Spirit, 5 and have
tasted the goodness of the word of
God and the powers of the age to
come, 6 if they then commit apostasy,
since they crucify the Son of God on
their own account and hold him up to
contempt. 7 For land which has drunk
the rain that often falls upon it, and
brings forth vegetation useful to those
for whose sake it is cultivated, receives a blessing from God. 8 But if it

[i] Greek *he* [j] Greek *he* [k] Other ancient manuscripts read *of instruction*
[l] Other ancient manuscripts read *let us do this if God permits*
4.5: Ps 95.11. **4.7:** Ps 95.7-8. **4.10:** Gen 2.2. **5.5:** Ps 2.7. **5.6:** Ps 110.4.
5.7: Mt 26.36-46; Mk 14.32-42; Lk 22.40-46. **5.9:** Is 45.17. **5.10:** Ps 110.4. **6.8:** Gen 3.17-18.

bears thorns and thistles, it is worthless and near to being cursed; its end
is to be burned.

9 Though we speak thus, yet in
your case, beloved, we feel sure of
better things that belong to salvation.
10 For God is not so unjust as to overlook your work and the love which
you showed for his sake in serving the
saints, as you still do. 11 And we desire
each one of you to show the same
earnestness in realizing the full assurance of hope until the end, 12 so that
you may not be sluggish, but imitators
of those who through faith and patience inherit the promises.

13 For when God made a promise
to Abraham, since he had no one
greater by whom to swear, he swore
by himself, 14 saying, "Surely I will
bless you and multiply you." 15 And
thus Abraham,[m] having patiently endured, obtained the promise. 16 Men
indeed swear by a greater than themselves, and in all their disputes an
oath is final for confirmation. 17 So
when God desired to show more con-
vincingly to the heirs of the promise
the unchangeable character of his
purpose, he interposed with an oath,
18 so that through two unchangeable
things, in which it is impossible that
God should prove false, we who have
fled for refuge might have strong encouragement to seize the hope set
before us. 19 We have this as a sure
and steadfast anchor of the soul, a
hope that enters into the inner shrine
behind the curtain, 20 where Jesus
has gone as a forerunner on our
behalf, having become a high priest
for ever after the order of Mel·chiz'-
ė·dek.

7 For this Mel·chiz'ė·dek, king of
Salem, priest of the Most High
God, met Abraham returning from
the slaughter of the kings and blessed
him; 2 and to him Abraham apportioned a tenth part of everything. He
is first, by translation of his name,
king of righteousness, and then he is
also king of Salem, that is, king of
peace. 3 He is without father or mother
or genealogy, and has neither beginning of days nor end of life, but resembling the Son of God he continues
a priest for ever.

4 See how great he is! Abraham the
patriarch gave him a tithe of the
spoils. 5 And those descendants of Levi
who receive the priestly office have a
commandment in the law to take
tithes from the people, that is, from
their brethren, though these also are
descended from Abraham. 6 But this
man who has not their genealogy received tithes from Abraham and
blessed him who had the promises.
7 It is beyond dispute that the inferior is blessed by the superior.
8 Here tithes are received by mortal
men; there, by one of whom it is
testified that he lives. 9 One might
even say that Levi himself, who receives tithes, paid tithes through
Abraham, 10 for he was still in the
loins of his ancestor when Mel·chiz'-
ė·dek met him.

11 Now if perfection had been at-
tainable through the Lė·vit'i·cal
priesthood (for under it the people
received the law), what further need
would there have been for another
priest to arise after the order of
Mel·chiz'ė·dek, rather than one named
after the order of Aaron? 12 For when
there is a change in the priesthood,
there is necessarily a change in the
law as well. 13 For the one of whom
these things are spoken belonged to
another tribe, from which no one has
ever served at the altar. 14 For it is
evident that our Lord was descended
from Judah, and in connection with
that tribe Moses said nothing about
priests.

15 This becomes even more evident
when another priest arises in the likeness of Mel·chiz'ė·dek, 16 who has become a priest, not according to a legal
requirement concerning bodily descent but by the power of an inde-
structible life. 17 For it is witnessed of
him,

"Thou art a priest for ever,
after the order of Mel·chiz'ė·dek."

18 On the one hand, a former commandment is set aside because of its
weakness and uselessness 19 (for the
law made nothing perfect); on the
other hand, a better hope is introduced, through which we draw near
to God.

20 And it was not without an oath.

[m] Greek *he*

6.13-14: Gen 22.16-17. **6.19:** Lev 16.2.
6.20: Ps 110.4. **7.1-10:** Gen 14.17-20.
7.11, 15, 17: Ps 110.4.

21 Those who formerly became priests
took their office without an oath, but
this one was addressed with an oath,

"The Lord has sworn
and will not change his mind,
'Thou art a priest for ever.' "

22 This makes Jesus the surety of a
better covenant.

23 The former priests were many
in number, because they were prevented by death from continuing in
office; 24 but he holds his priesthood
permanently, because he continues for
ever. 25 Consequently he is able for all
time to save those who draw near to
God through him, since he always lives
to make intercession for them.

26 For it was fitting that we should
have such a high priest, holy, blameless, unstained, separated from sinners, exalted above the heavens. 27 He
has no need, like those high priests, to
offer sacrifices daily, first for his own
sins and then for those of the people;
he did this once for all when he offered
up himself. 28 Indeed, the law appoints
men in their weakness as high priests,
but the word of the oath, which came
later than the law, appoints a Son who
has been made perfect for ever.

8 Now the point in what we are
saying is this: we have such a high
priest, one who is seated at the right
hand of the throne of the Majesty in
heaven, 2 a minister in the sanctuary
and the true tent[n] which is set up not
by man but by the Lord. 3 For every
high priest is appointed to offer gifts
and sacrifices; hence it is necessary for
this priest also to have something to
offer. 4 Now if he were on earth, he
would not be a priest at all, since there
are priests who offer gifts according to
the law. 5 They serve a copy and
shadow of the heavenly sanctuary; for
when Moses was about to erect the
tent,[n] he was instructed by God, saying, "See that you make everything
according to the pattern which was
shown you on the mountain." 6 But as
it is, Christ[o] has obtained a ministry
which is as much more excellent than
the old as the convenant he mediates
is better, since it is enacted on better
promises. 7 For if that first covenant
had been faultless, there would have
been no occasion for a second.

8 For he finds fault with them when
he says:

"The days will come, says the Lord,
when I will establish a new covenant with the house of Israel
and with the house of Judah;
9 not like the covenant that I made with their fathers
on the day when I took them by the hand
to lead them out of the land of Egypt;
for they did not continue in my covenant,
and so I paid no heed to them, says the Lord.
10 This is the covenant that I will make with the house of Israel
after those days, says the Lord:
I will put my laws into their minds,
and write them on their hearts,
and I will be their God,
and they shall be my people.
11 And they shall not teach every one his fellow
or every one his brother, saying, 'Know the Lord,'
for all shall know me,
from the least of them to the greatest.
12 For I will be merciful toward their iniquities,
and I will remember their sins no more."

13 In speaking of a new covenant he
treats the first as obsolete. And what
is becoming obsolete and growing old
is ready to vanish away.

9 Now even the first covenant had
regulations for worship and an
earthly sanctuary. 2 For a tent[p] was
prepared, the outer one, in which were
the lampstand and the table and the
bread of the Presence;[q] it is called the
Holy Place. 3 Behind the second curtain stood a tent[p] called the Holy of
Holies, 4 having the golden altar of
incense and the ark of the covenant
covered on all sides with gold, which
contained a golden urn holding the
manna, and Aaron's rod that budded,
and the tables of the covenant; 5 above
it were the cherubim of glory overshadowing the mercy seat. Of these
things we cannot now speak in detail.

6 These preparations having thus
been made, the priests go continually

[n] Or *tabernacle* [o] Greek *he* [p] Or *tabernacle* [q] Greek *the presentation of the loaves*

7.21, 28: Ps 110.4. **8.1:** Ps 110.1. **8.5:** Ex 25.40. **8.8-12:** Jer 31.31-34. **9.1-10:** Ex 25.10-40.
9.2: Lev 24.5. **9.3:** Ex 26.31-33. **9.4:** Ex 30.1-5; 16.32-33; Num 17.8-10.

into the outer tent,[p] performing their
ritual duties; 7 but into the second
only the high priest goes, and he but
once a year, and not without taking
blood which he offers for himself and
for the errors of the people. 8 By this
the Holy Spirit indicates that the way
into the sanctuary is not yet opened
as long as the outer tent[p] is still
standing 9 (which is symbolic for the
present age). According to this arrangement, gifts and sacrifices are
offered which cannot perfect the conscience of the worshiper, 10 but deal
only with food and drink and various
ablutions, regulations for the body
imposed until the time of reforma-
tion.

11 But when Christ appeared as a
high priest of the good things that
have come,[r] then through the greater
and more perfect tent[p] (not made with
hands, that is, not of this creation)
12 he entered once for all into the Holy
Place, taking[s] not the blood of goats
and calves but his own blood, thus
securing an eternal redemption. 13 For
if the sprinkling of defiled persons with
the blood of goats and bulls and with
the ashes of a heifer sanctifies for the
purification of the flesh, 14 how much
more shall the blood of Christ, who
through the eternal Spirit offered
himself without blemish to God,
purify your[t] conscience from dead
works to serve the living God.

15 Therefore he is the mediator of
a new covenant, so that those who are
called may receive the promised
eternal inheritance, since a death has
occurred which redeems them from
the transgressions under the first covenant.[u] 16 For where a will[u] is involved,
the death of the one who made it must
be established. 17 For a will[u] takes
effect only at death, since it is not in
force as long as the one who made it
is alive. 18 Hence even the first covenant was not ratified without blood.
19 For when every commandment of
the law had been declared by Moses
to all the people, he took the blood of
calves and goats, with water and
scarlet wool and hyssop, and sprinkled
both the book itself and all the people,
20 saying, "This is the blood of the
covenant which God commanded
you." 21 And in the same way he
sprinkled with the blood both the
tent[p] and all the vessels used in worship. 22 Indeed, under the law almost
everything is purified with blood, and
without the shedding of blood there is
no forgiveness of sins.

23 Thus it was necessary for the
copies of the heavenly things to be
purified with these rites, but the
heavenly things themselves with better sacrifices than these. 24 For Christ
has entered, not into a sanctuary
made with hands, a copy of the true
one, but into heaven itself, now to
appear in the presence of God on our
behalf. 25 Nor was it to offer himself
repeatedly, as the high priest enters
the Holy Place yearly with blood not
his own; 26 for then he would have
had to suffer repeatedly since the
foundation of the world. But as it is,
he has appeared once for all at the
end of the age to put away sin by the
sacrifice of himself. 27 And just as it is
appointed for men to die once, and
after that comes judgment, 28 so
Christ, having been offered once to
bear the sins of many, will appear a
second time, not to deal with sin but
to save those who are eagerly waiting
for him.

10 For since the law has but a
shadow of the good things to
come instead of the true form of these
realities, it can never, by the same
sacrifices which are continually offered
year after year, make perfect those
who draw near. 2 Otherwise, would
they not have ceased to be offered?
If the worshipers had once been
cleansed, they would no longer have
any consciousness of sin. 3 But in
these sacrifices there is a reminder of
sin year after year. 4 For it is impossible that the blood of bulls and goats
should take away sins.

5 Consequently, when Christ[v] came
into the world, he said,

"Sacrifices and offerings thou hast
not desired,
but a body hast thou prepared for
me;
6 in burnt offerings and sin offerings
thou hast taken no pleasure.
7 Then I said, 'Lo, I have come to do
thy will, O God,'

[p] Or *tabernacle* [r] Other manuscripts read *good things to come* [s] Greek *through*
[t] Other manuscripts read *our* [u] The Greek word here used means both *covenant* and *will*
[v] Greek *he*

9.7: Lev 16. **9.13**: Lev 16.6, 16; Num 19.9, 17-18. **9.19-20**: Ex 24.6-8. **10.5-9**: Ps 40.6-8.

as it is written of me in the roll of
the book."
8 When he said above, "Thou hast
neither desired nor taken pleasure in
sacrifices and offerings and burnt
offerings and sin offerings" (these are
offered according to the law), 9 then
he added, "Lo, I have come to do thy
will." He abolishes the first in order
to establish the second. 10 And by that
will we have been sanctified through
the offering of the body of Jesus Christ
once for all.

11 And every priest stands daily at
his service, offering repeatedly the
same sacrifices, which can never take
away sins. 12 But when Christ[w] had
offered for all time a single sacrifice
for sins, he sat down at the right hand
of God, 13 then to wait until his enemies should be made a stool for his
feet. 14 For by a single offering he has
perfected for all time those who are
sanctified. 15 And the Holy Spirit also
bears witness to us; for after saying,
16 "This is the covenant that I will
make with them
after those days, says the Lord:
I will put my laws on their hearts,
and write them on their minds,"
17 then he adds,
"I will remember their sins and
their misdeeds no more."
18 Where there is forgiveness of these,
there is no longer any offering for sin.

19 Therefore, brethren, since we
have confidence to enter the sanctuary
by the blood of Jesus, 20 by the new
and living way which he opened for us
through the curtain, that is, through
his flesh, 21 and since we have a great
priest over the house of God, 22 let us
draw near with a true heart in full
assurance of faith, with our hearts
sprinkled clean from an evil conscience
and our bodies washed with pure
water. 23 Let us hold fast the confession of our hope without wavering, for
he who promised is faithful; 24 and let
us consider how to stir up one another
to love and good works, 25 not neglecting to meet together, as is the habit of
some, but encouraging one another,
and all the more as you see the Day
drawing near.

26 For if we sin deliberately after
receiving the knowledge of the truth,
there no longer remains a sacrifice for
sins, 27 but a fearful prospect of judgment, and a fury of fire which will
consume the adversaries. 28 A man
who has violated the law of Moses dies
without mercy at the testimony of
two or three witnesses. 29 How much
worse punishment do you think will
be deserved by the man who has
spurned the Son of God, and profaned
the blood of the covenant by which he
was sanctified, and outraged the
Spirit of grace? 30 For we know him
who said, "Vengeance is mine, I will
repay." And again, "The Lord will
judge his people." 31 It is a fearful
thing to fall into the hands of the
living God.

32 But recall the former days when,
after you were enlightened, you endured a hard struggle with sufferings,
33 sometimes being publicly exposed
to abuse and affliction, and sometimes
being partners with those so treated.
34 For you had compassion on the
prisoners, and you joyfully accepted
the plundering of your property, since
you knew that you yourselves had a
better possession and an abiding one.
35 Therefore do not throw away your
confidence, which has a great reward.
36 For you have need of endurance, so
that you may do the will of God and
receive what is promised.
37 "For yet a little while,
and the coming one shall come and
shall not tarry;
38 but my righteous one shall live by
faith,
and if he shrinks back,
my soul has no pleasure in him."
39 But we are not of those who shrink
back and are destroyed, but of those
who have faith and keep their souls.

11 Now faith is the assurance of
things hoped for, the conviction
of things not seen. 2 For by it the men
of old received divine approval. 3 By
faith we understand that the world
was created by the word of God, so
that what is seen was made out of
things which do not appear.

4 By faith Abel offered to God a
more acceptable sacrifice than Cain,
through which he received approval as
righteous, God bearing witness by
accepting his gifts; he died, but
through his faith he is still speaking.

[w] Greek *this one*

10.12-13: Ps 110.1. **10.16-17:** Jer 31.33-34. **10.27:** Is 26 11. **10.28:** Deut 17.2-6. **10.29:** Ex 24.8. **10.30:** Deut 32.35-36. **10.37:** Is 26.20 (Gk.). **10.37-38:** Hab 2.3-4. **11.4:** Gen 4.3-10.

5 By faith E'nóch was taken up so that
he should not see death; and he was
not found, because God had taken
him. Now before he was taken he was
attested as having pleased God. 6 And
without faith it is impossible to please
him. For whoever would draw near to
God must believe that he exists and
that he rewards those who seek him.
7 By faith Noah, being warned by God
concerning events as yet unseen, took
heed and constructed an ark for the
saving of his household; by this he
condemned the world and became an
heir of the righteousness which comes
by faith.

8 By faith Abraham obeyed when
he was called to go out to a place
which he was to receive as an inheritance; and he went out, not knowing
where he was to go. 9 By faith he
sojourned in the land of promise, as
in a foreign land, living in tents with
Isaac and Jacob, heirs with him of
the same promise. 10 For he looked
forward to the city which has foundations, whose builder and maker is
God. 11 By faith Sarah herself received
power to conceive, even when she was
past the age, since she considered him
faithful who had promised. 12 Therefore from one man, and him as good
as dead, were born descendants as
many as the stars of heaven and as
the innumerable grains of sand by the
seashore.

13 These all died in faith, not having received what was promised, but
having seen it and greeted it from afar,
and having acknowledged that they
were strangers and exiles on the earth.
14 For people who speak thus make it
clear that they are seeking a homeland. 15 If they had been thinking of
that land from which they had gone
out, they would have had opportunity
to return. 16 But as it is, they desire a
better country, that is, a heavenly
one. Therefore God is not ashamed to
be called their God, for he has prepared for them a city.

17 By faith Abraham, when he was
tested, offered up Isaac, and he who
had received the promises was ready
to offer up his only son, 18 of whom it
was said, "Through Isaac shall your
descendants be named." 19 He considered that God was able to raise men
even from the dead; hence, figur-
atively speaking, he did receive him
back. 20 By faith Isaac invoked future
blessings on Jacob and Esau. 21 By
faith Jacob, when dying, blessed each
of the sons of Joseph, bowing in
worship over the head of his staff.
22 By faith Joseph, at the end of his
life, made mention of the exodus of
the Israelites and gave directions
concerning his burial.[x]

23 By faith Moses, when he was
born, was hid for three months by his
parents, because they saw that the
child was beautiful; and they were not
afraid of the king's edict. 24 By faith
Moses, when he was grown up, refused to be called the son of Pharaoh's
daughter, 25 choosing rather to share
ill-treatment with the people of God
than to enjoy the fleeting pleasures of
sin. 26 He considered abuse suffered
for the Christ greater wealth than the
treasures of Egypt, for he looked to
the reward. 27 By faith he left Egypt,
not being afraid of the anger of the
king; for he endured as seeing him
who is invisible. 28 By faith he kept
the Passover and sprinkled the blood,
so that the Destroyer of the first-born
might not touch them.

29 By faith the people crossed the
Red Sea as if on dry land; but the
Egyptians, when they attempted to
do the same, were drowned. 30 By
faith the walls of Jericho fell down
after they had been encircled for
seven days. 31 By faith Rā'hab the
harlot did not perish with those who
were disobedient, because she had
given friendly welcome to the spies.

32 And what more shall I say? For
time would fail me to tell of Gideon,
Bâr'ȧk, Samson, Jeph'thȧh, of David
and Samuel and the prophets— 33 who
through faith conquered kingdoms,
enforced justice, received promises,
stopped the mouths of lions,
34 quenched raging fire, escaped the
edge of the sword, won strength out of

[x] Greek *bones*

11.5: Gen 5.21-24. **11.7:** Gen 6.13-22. **11.8-9:** Gen 12.1-8. **11.11:** Gen 17.19; 18.11-14; 21.2.
11.12: Gen 15.5-6; 22.17; 32.12. **11.13:** Ps 39.12; Gen 23.4. **11:16:** Ex 3.6, 15; 4.5.
11.17: Gen 22.1-10. **11.18:** Gen 21.12. **11.20:** Gen 27.27-29, 39-40. **11.21:** Gen 48; 47.31 (Gk.).
11.22: Gen 50.24-25; Ex 13.19. **11.23:** Ex 2.2; 1.22. **11.24:** Ex 2.10, 11-15. **11.27:** Ex 2.15.
11.28: Ex 12.21-28, 29-30. **11.29:** Ex 14.21-31. **11.30:** Josh 6.12-21. **11.31:** Josh 2.1-21; 6.22-25.
11.32: Judg 6-8; 4-5; 13-16; 11-12; 1 Sam 16-30; 2 Sam 1-24; 1 Kings 1-2.11; 1 Sam 1-12; 15;
16.1-13. **11.33:** Dan 6. **11.34:** Dan 3.

weakness, became mighty in war, put foreign armies to flight. 35 Women received their dead by resurrection. Some were tortured, refusing to accept release, that they might rise again to a better life. 36 Others suffered mocking and scourging, and even chains and imprisonment. 37 They were stoned, they were sawn in two,[y] they were killed with the sword; they went about in skins of sheep and goats, destitute, afflicted, ill-treated— 38 of whom the world was not worthy—wandering over deserts and mountains, and in dens and caves of the earth.

39 And all these, though well attested by their faith, did not receive what was promised, 40 since God had foreseen something better for us, that apart from us they should not be made perfect.

12 Therefore, since we are surrounded by so great a cloud of witnesses, let us also lay aside every weight, and sin which clings so closely, and let us run with perseverance the race that is set before us, 2 looking to Jesus the pioneer and perfecter of our faith, who for the joy that was set before him endured the cross, despising the shame, and is seated at the right hand of the throne of God.

3 Consider him who endured from sinners such hostility against himself, so that you may not grow weary or fainthearted. 4 In your struggle against sin you have not yet resisted to the point of shedding your blood. 5 And have you forgotten the exhortation which addresses you as sons?—

"My son, do not regard lightly the
discipline of the Lord,
nor lose courage when you are
punished by him.
6 For the Lord disciplines him whom
he loves,
and chastises every son whom he
receives."

7 It is for discipline that you have to endure. God is treating you as sons; for what son is there whom his father does not discipline? 8 If you are left without discipline, in which all have participated, then you are illegitimate children and not sons. 9 Besides this, we have had earthly fathers to discipline us and we respected them. Shall we not much more be subject to the Father of spirits and live? 10 For they disciplined us for a short time at their pleasure, but he disciplines us for our good, that we may share his holiness. 11 For the moment all discipline seems painful rather than pleasant; later it yields the peaceful fruit of righteousness to those who have been trained by it.

12 Therefore lift your drooping hands and strengthen your weak knees, 13 and make straight paths for your feet, so that what is lame may not be put out of joint but rather be healed. 14 Strive for peace with all men, and for the holiness without which no one will see the Lord. 15 See to it that no one fail to obtain the grace of God; that no "root of bitterness" spring up and cause trouble, and by it the many become defiled; 16 that no one be immoral or irreligious like Esau, who sold his birthright for a single meal. 17 For you know that afterward, when he desired to inherit the blessing, he was rejected, for he found no chance to repent, though he sought it with tears.

18 For you have not come to what may be touched, a blazing fire, and darkness, and gloom, and a tempest, 19 and the sound of a trumpet, and a voice whose words made the hearers entreat that no further messages be spoken to them. 20 For they could not endure the order that was given, "If even a beast touches the mountain, it shall be stoned." 21 Indeed, so terrifying was the sight that Moses said, "I tremble with fear." 22 But you have come to Mount Zion and to the city of the living God, the heavenly Jerusalem, and to innumerable angels in festal gathering, 23 and to the assembly[z] of the first-born who are enrolled in heaven, and to a judge who is God of all, and to the spirits of just men made perfect, 24 and to Jesus, the mediator of a new covenant, and to the sprinkled blood that speaks more graciously than the blood of Abel.

25 See that you do not refuse him

[y] Other manuscripts add *they were tempted* [z] Or *angels, and to the festal gathering and assembly*

11.35: 1 Kings 17.17-24; 2 Kings 4.25-37. **12.2:** Ps 110.1. **12.5-8:** Prov 3.11-12. **12.12:** Is 35.3. **12.13:** Prov 4.26 (Gk.). **12.15:** Deut 29.18 (Gk.). **12.16:** Gen 25.29-34. **12.17:** Gen 27.30-40. **12.18-19:** Ex 19.12-22; 20.18-21; Deut 4.11-12; 5.22-27. **12.20:** Ex 19.12-13. **12.21:** Deut 9.19. **12.24:** Gen 4.10. **12.25:** Ex 20.19.

who is speaking. For if they did not
escape when they refused him who
warned them on earth, much less shall
we escape if we reject him who warns
from heaven. 26 His voice then shook
the earth; but now he has promised,
"Yet once more I will shake not only
the earth but also the heaven." 27 This
phrase, "Yet once more," indicates
the removal of what is shaken, as of
what has been made, in order that
what cannot be shaken may remain.
28 Therefore let us be grateful for
receiving a kingdom that cannot be
shaken, and thus let us offer to God
acceptable worship, with reverence
and awe; 29 for our God is a consuming
fire.

13 Let brotherly love continue.
2 Do not neglect to show hospitality to strangers, for thereby some
have entertained angels unawares.
3 Remember those who are in prison,
as though in prison with them; and
those who are ill-treated, since you
also are in the body. 4 Let marriage be
held in honor among all, and let the
marriage bed be undefiled; for God
will judge the immoral and adulterous. 5 Keep your life free from love of
money, and be content with what you
have; for he has said, "I will never fail
you nor forsake you." 6 Hence we can
confidently say,

"The Lord is my helper,
I will not be afraid;
what can man do to me?"

7 Remember your leaders, those
who spoke to you the word of God;
consider the outcome of their life, and
imitate their faith. 8 Jesus Christ is
the same yesterday and today and for
ever. 9 Do not be led away by diverse
and strange teachings; for it is well
that the heart be strengthened by
grace, not by foods, which have not
benefited their adherents. 10 We have
an altar from which those who serve
the tent[a] have no right to eat. 11 For
the bodies of those animals whose
blood is brought into the sanctuary
by the high priest as a sacrifice for sin
are burned outside the camp. 12 So
Jesus also suffered outside the gate
in order to sanctify the people through
his own blood. 13 Therefore let us go
forth to him outside the camp, bearing abuse for him. 14 For here we have
no lasting city, but we seek the city
which is to come. 15 Through him
then let us continually offer up a
sacrifice of praise to God, that is, the
fruit of lips that acknowledge his
name. 16 Do not neglect to do good
and to share what you have, for such
sacrifices are pleasing to God.

17 Obey your leaders and submit to
them; for they are keeping watch over
your souls, as men who will have to
give account. Let them do this joyfully, and not sadly, for that would be
of no advantage to you.

18 Pray for us, for we are sure that
we have a clear conscience, desiring to
act honorably in all things. 19 I urge
you the more earnestly to do this in
order that I may be restored to you
the sooner.

20 Now may the God of peace who
brought again from the dead our Lord
Jesus, the great shepherd of the sheep,
by the blood of the eternal covenant,
21 equip you with everything good
that you may do his will, working
in you[b] that which is pleasing in
his sight, through Jesus Christ; to
whom be glory for ever and ever.
Amen.

22 I appeal to you, brethren, bear
with my word of exhortation, for I
have written to you briefly. 23 You
should understand that our brother
Timothy has been released, with
whom I shall see you if he comes soon.
24 Greet all your leaders and all the
saints. Those who come from Italy
send you greetings. 25 Grace be with
all of you. Amen.

[a] Or *tabernacle* [b] Other ancient authorities read *us*

12.26: Hag 2.6. **12.29:** Deut 4.24. **13.2:** Gen 18.1-8; 19.1-3. **13.5:** Deut 31.6, 8; Josh 1.5.
13.6: Ps 118.6. **13.11, 13:** Lev 16.27. **13.15:** Lev 7.12; Is 57.19; Hos 14.2.
13.20: Is 63.11; Zech 9.11; Is 55.3; Ezek 37.26.

THE LETTER OF

JAMES

1 James, a servant of God and of
the Lord Jesus Christ,
To the twelve tribes in the Dispersion:
Greeting.

2 Count it all joy, my brethren,
when you meet various trials, 3 for you
know that the testing of your faith
produces steadfastness. 4 And let
steadfastness have its full effect, that
you may be perfect and complete,
lacking in nothing.
5 If any of you lacks wisdom, let
him ask God who gives to all men
generously and without reproaching,
and it will be given him. 6 But let him
ask in faith, with no doubting, for he
who doubts is like a wave of the sea
that is driven and tossed by the wind.
7, 8 For that person must not suppose
that a double-minded man, unstable
in all his ways, will receive anything
from the Lord.
9 Let the lowly brother boast in his
exaltation, 10 and the rich in his humiliation, because like the flower of
the grass he will pass away. 11 For the
sun rises with its scorching heat and
withers the grass; its flower falls, and
its beauty perishes. So will the rich
man fade away in the midst of his
pursuits.
12 Blessed is the man who endures
trial, for when he has stood the test he
will receive the crown of life which
God has promised to those who love
him. 13 Let no one say when he is
tempted, "I am tempted by God"; for
God cannot be tempted with evil and
he himself tempts no one; 14 but each
person is tempted when he is lured
and enticed by his own desire. 15 Then
desire when it has conceived gives
birth to sin; and sin when it is full-
grown brings forth death.
16 Do not be deceived, my beloved
brethren. 17 Every good endowment
and every perfect gift is from above,
coming down from the Father of lights
with whom there is no variation or
shadow due to change.[a] 18 Of his own
will he brought us forth by the word
of truth that we should be a kind of
first fruits of his creatures.
19 Know this, my beloved brethren. Let every man be quick to hear,
slow to speak, slow to anger, 20 for the
anger of man does not work the righteousness of God. 21 Therefore put
away all filthiness and rank growth of
wickedness and receive with meekness
the implanted word, which is able to
save your souls.
22 But be doers of the word, and
not hearers only, deceiving yourselves.
23 For if any one is a hearer of the
word and not a doer, he is like a man
who observes his natural face in a
mirror; 24 for he observes himself and
goes away and at once forgets what he
was like. 25 But he who looks into the
perfect law, the law of liberty, and
perseveres, being no hearer that forgets but a doer that acts, he shall be
blessed in his doing.
26 If any one thinks he is religious,
and does not bridle his tongue but
deceives his heart, this man's religion
is vain. 27 Religion that is pure and
undefiled before God and the Father
is this: to visit orphans and widows in
their affliction, and to keep onself unstained from the world.

2 My brethren, show no partiality
as you hold the faith of our Lord
Jesus Christ, the Lord of glory. 2 For
if a man with gold rings and in fine
clothing comes into your assembly,
and a poor man in shabby clothing
also comes in, 3 and you pay attention
to the one who wears the fine clothing
and say, "Have a seat here, please,"
while you say to the poor man, "Stand
there," or, "Sit at my feet," 4 have
you not made distinctions among
yourselves, and become judges with
evil thoughts? 5 Listen, my beloved
brethren. Has not God chosen those
who are poor in the world to be rich in
faith and heirs of the kingdom which

[a] Other ancient authorities read *variation due to a shadow of turning*
1.10-11: Is 40.6-7.

he has promised to those who love
him? 6 But you have dishonored the
poor man. Is it not the rich who
oppress you, is it not they who drag
you into court? 7 Is it not they who
blaspheme that honorable name by
which you are called?

8 If you really fulfil the royal law,
according to the scripture, "You shall
love your neighbor as yourself," you
do well. 9 But if you show partiality,
you commit sin, and are convicted by
the law as transgressors. 10 For whoever keeps the whole law but fails in
one point has become guilty of all of
it. 11 For he who said, "Do not commit adultery," said also, "Do not
kill." If you do not commit adultery
but do kill, you have become a transgressor of the law. 12 So speak and so
act as those who are to be judged
under the law of liberty. 13 For judgment is without mercy to one who
has shown no mercy; yet mercy
triumphs over judgment.

14 What does it profit, my brethren, if a man says he has faith but has
not works? Can his faith save him?
15 If a brother or sister is ill-clad and
in lack of daily food, 16 and one of you
says to them, "Go in peace, be warmed
and filled," without giving them the
things needed for the body, what does
it profit? 17 So faith by itself, if it has
no works, is dead.

18 But some one will say, "You
have faith and I have works." Show
me your faith apart from your works,
and I by my works will show you my
faith. 19 You believe that God is one;
you do well. Even the demons believe
—and shudder. 20 Do you want to be
shown, you foolish fellow, that faith
apart from works is barren? 21 Was
not Abraham our father justified by
works, when he offered his son Isaac
upon the altar? 22 You see that faith
was active along with his works, and
faith was completed by works, 23 and
the scripture was fulfilled which says,
"Abraham believed God, and it was
reckoned to him as righteousness";
and he was called the friend of God.
24 You see that a man is justified by
works and not by faith alone. 25 And in
the same way was not also Rā'hab the
harlot justified by works when she
received the messengers and sent them
out another way? 26 For as the body
apart from the spirit is dead, so faith
apart from works is dead.

3 Let not many of you become
teachers, my brethren, for you
know that we who teach shall be
judged with greater strictness. 2 For
we all make many mistakes, and if
any one makes no mistakes in what he
says he is a perfect man, able to bridle
the whole body also. 3 If we put bits
into the mouths of horses that they
may obey us, we guide their whole
bodies. 4 Look at the ships also;
though they are so great and are driven
by strong winds, they are guided by a
very small rudder wherever the will of
the pilot directs. 5 So the tongue is a
little member and boasts of great
things. How great a forest is set
ablaze by a small fire!

6 And the tongue is a fire. The
tongue is an unrighteous world among
our members, staining the whole body,
setting on fire the cycle of nature,[b] and
set on fire by hell.[c] 7 For every kind of
beast and bird, of reptile and sea
creature, can be tamed and has been
tamed by humankind, 8 but no human
being can tame the tongue—a restless
evil, full of deadly poison. 9 With it we
bless the Lord and Father, and with it
we curse men, who are made in the
likeness of God. 10 From the same
mouth come blessing and cursing. My
brethren, this ought not to be so.
11 Does a spring pour forth from the
same opening fresh water and brack-
ish? 12 Can a fig tree, my brethren,
yield olives, or a grapevine figs? No
more can salt water yield fresh.

13 Who is wise and understanding
among you? By his good life let him
show his works in the meekness of
wisdom. 14 But if you have bitter
jealousy and selfish ambition in your
hearts, do not boast and be false to
the truth. 15 This wisdom is not such
as comes down from above, but is
earthly, unspiritual, devilish. 16 For
where jealousy and selfish ambition
exist, there will be disorder and every
vile practice. 17 But the wisdom from
above is first pure, then peaceable,
gentle, open to reason, full of mercy
and good fruits, without uncertainty
or insincerity. 18 And the harvest of

b Or *wheel of birth* *c* Greek *Gehenna*

2.8: Lev 19.18. **2.11:** Ex 20.13-14; Deut 5.17-18. **2.21:** Gen 22.1-14.
2.23: Gen 15.6; Is 41.8; 2 Chron 20.7. **2.25:** Josh 2.1-21.

righteousness is sown in peace by
those who make peace.

4 What causes wars, and what
causes fightings among you? Is it
not your passions that are at war in
your members? 2 You desire and do
not have; so you kill. And you covet[d]
and cannot obtain; so you fight and
wage war. You do not have, because
you do not ask. 3 You ask and do not
receive, because you ask wrongly, to
spend it on your passions. 4 Unfaithful
creatures! Do you not know that
friendship with the world is enmity
with God? Therefore whoever wishes
to be a friend of the world makes himself an enemy of God. 5 Or do you
suppose it is in vain that the scripture
says, "He yearns jealously over the
spirit which he has made to dwell in
us"? 6 But he gives more grace; therefore it says, "God opposes the proud,
but gives grace to the humble." 7 Submit yourselves therefore to God. Resist the devil and he will flee from you.
8 Draw near to God and he will draw
near to you. Cleanse your hands, you
sinners, and purify your hearts, you
men of double mind. 9 Be wretched
and mourn and weep. Let your laughter be turned to mourning and your
joy to dejection. 10 Humble yourselves
before the Lord and he will exalt you.

11 Do not speak evil against one
another, brethren. He that speaks evil
against a brother or judges his brother,
speaks evil against the law and judges
the law. But if you judge the law, you
are not a doer of the law but a judge.
12 There is one lawgiver and judge, he
who is able to save and to destroy.
But who are you that you judge your
neighbor?

13 Come now, you who say, "Today or tomorrow we will go into such
and such a town and spend a year
there and trade and get gain";
14 whereas you do not know about
tomorrow. What is your life? For you
are a mist that appears for a little
time and then vanishes. 15 Instead
you ought to say, "If the Lord wills,
we shall live and we shall do this or
that." 16 As it is, you boast in your
arrogance. All such boasting is evil.
17 Whoever knows what is right to do
and fails to do it, for him it is sin.

5 Come now, you rich, weep and
howl for the miseries that are
coming upon you. 2 Your riches have
rotted and your garments are moth-
eaten. 3 Your gold and silver have
rusted, and their rust will be evidence
against you and will eat your flesh
like fire. You have laid up treasure[e]
for the last days. 4 Behold, the wages
of the laborers who mowed your fields,
which you kept back by fraud, cry
out; and the cries of the harvesters
have reached the ears of the Lord of
hosts. 5 You have lived on the earth
in luxury and in pleasure; you have
fattened your hearts in a day of
slaughter. 6 You have condemned,
you have killed the righteous man;
he does not resist you.

7 Be patient, therefore, brethren,
until the coming of the Lord. Behold,
the farmer waits for the precious fruit
of the earth, being patient over it until
it receives the early and the late rain.
8 You also be patient. Establish your
hearts, for the coming of the Lord is
at hand. 9 Do not grumble, brethren,
against one another, that you may not
be judged; behold, the Judge is standing at the doors. 10 As an example of
suffering and patience, brethren, take
the prophets who spoke in the name
of the Lord. 11 Behold, we call those
happy who were steadfast. You have
heard of the steadfastness of Job, and
you have seen the purpose of the
Lord, how the Lord is compassionate
and merciful.

12 But above all, my brethren, do
not swear, either by heaven or by earth
or with any other oath, but let your
yes be yes and your no be no, that you
may not fall under condemnation.

13 Is any one among you suffering?
Let him pray. Is any cheerful? Let
him sing praise. 14 Is any among you
sick? Let him call for the elders of the
church, and let them pray over him,
anointing him with oil in the name of
the Lord; 15 and the prayer of faith
will save the sick man, and the Lord
will raise him up; and if he has committed sins, he will be forgiven.
16 Therefore confess your sins to one
another, and pray for one another,
that you may be healed. The prayer
of a righteous man has great power
in its effects. 17 E·lī'jah was a man of

[d] Or *you kill and you covet* [e] Or *will eat your flesh, since you have stored up fire*

4.6: Prov 3.34. **5.11:** Job 1.21-22; 2.10; Ps 103.8; 111.4. **5.12:** Mt 5.37.
5.17: 1 Kings 17 1; 18.1; Lk 4.25.

like nature with ourselves and he
prayed fervently that it might not
rain, and for three years and six
months it did not rain on the earth.
18 Then he prayed again and the
heaven gave rain, and the earth
brought forth its fruit.
19 My brethren, if any one among
you wanders from the truth and some
one brings him back, 20 let him know
that whoever brings back a sinner
from the error of his way will save his
soul from death and will cover a
multitude of sins.

THE FIRST LETTER OF

PETER

1 Peter, an apostle of Jesus Christ,
To the exiles of the Dispersion in
Pon'tŭs, Galatia, Cap·pȧ·dō'ci·ȧ, Asia,
and Bi·thyn'i·ȧ, 2 chosen and destined
by God the Father and sanctified
by the Spirit for obedience to Jesus
Christ and for sprinkling with his
blood:
May grace and peace be multiplied
to you.

3 Blessed be the God and Father of
our Lord Jesus Christ! By his great
mercy we have been born anew to a
living hope through the resurrection
of Jesus Christ from the dead, 4 and to
an inheritance which is imperishable,
undefiled, and unfading, kept in
heaven for you, 5 who by God's power
are guarded through faith for a salvation ready to be revealed in the last
time. 6 In this you rejoice,[a] though
now for a little while you may have to
suffer various trials, 7 so that the
genuineness of your faith, more precious than gold which though perishable is tested by fire, may redound to
praise and glory and honor at the
revelation of Jesus Christ. 8 Without
having seen[b] him you[c] love him;
though you do not now see him you[c]
believe in him and rejoice with unut-
terable and exalted joy. 9 As the
outcome of your faith you obtain the
salvation of your souls.
10 The prophets who prophesied of
the grace that was to be yours
searched and inquired about this salvation; 11 they inquired what person
or time was indicated by the Spirit of
Christ within them when predicting
the sufferings of Christ and the subsequent glory. 12 It was revealed to
them that they were serving not
themselves but you, in the things
which have now been announced to
you by those who preached the good
news to you through the Holy Spirit
sent from heaven, things into which
angels long to look.
13 Therefore gird up your minds,
be sober, set your hope fully upon the
grace that is coming to you at the
revelation of Jesus Christ. 14 As obedient children, do not be conformed to
the passions of your former ignorance,
15 but as he who called you is holy, be
holy yourselves in all your conduct;
16 since it is written, "You shall be
holy, for I am holy." 17 And if you invoke as Father him who judges each
one impartially according to his deeds,
conduct yourselves with fear throughout the time of your exile. 18 You
know that you were ransomed from
the futile ways inherited from your
fathers, not with perishable things
such as silver or gold, 19 but with the
precious blood of Christ, like that of a
lamb without blemish or spot. 20 He
was destined before the foundation of
the world but was made manifest at
the end of the times for your sake.
21 Through him you have confidence
in God, who raised him from the dead
and gave him glory, so that your faith
and hope are in God.[d]
22 Having purified your souls by
your obedience to the truth for a sincere love of the brethren, love one

[a] Or *Rejoice in this* [b] Other ancient authorities read *known* [c] Or omit *you*
[d] Or *so that your faith is hope in God*
5.18: 1 Kings 18.42. **1.16:** Lev 11.44-45.

another earnestly from the heart.
23 You have been born anew, not of
perishable seed but of imperishable,
through the living and abiding word
of God; 24 for

"All flesh is like grass
and all its glory like the flower of grass.
The grass withers, and the flower falls,
25 but the word of the Lord abides for ever."

That word is the good news which was
preached to you.

2 So put away all malice and all
guile and insincerity and envy and
all slander. 2 Like newborn babes, long
for the pure spiritual milk, that by it
you may grow up to salvation; 3 for
you have tasted the kindness of the
Lord.

4 Come to him, to that living stone,
rejected by men but in God's sight
chosen and precious; 5 and like living
stones be yourselves built into a
spiritual house, to be a holy priesthood, to offer spiritual sacrifices
acceptable to God through Jesus
Christ. 6 For it stands in scripture:

"Behold, I am laying in Zion a stone,
a cornerstone chosen and precious,
and he who believes in him will not be put to shame."

7 To you therefore who believe, he is
precious, but for those who do not
believe,

"The very stone which the builders rejected
has become the head of the corner,"

8 and

"A stone that will make men stumble,
a rock that will make them fall";

for they stumble because they disobey
the word, as they were destined to do.

9 But you are a chosen race, a royal
priesthood, a holy nation, God's own
people,[e] that you may declare the
wonderful deeds of him who called
you out of darkness into his marvelous light. 10 Once you were no people
but now you are God's people; once
you had not received mercy but now
you have received mercy.

11 Beloved, I beseech you as aliens
and exiles to abstain from the passions
of the flesh that wage war against
your soul. 12 Maintain good conduct
among the Gentiles, so that in case
they speak against you as wrongdoers,
they may see your good deeds and
glorify God on the day of visitation.

13 Be subject for the Lord's sake
to every human institution,[f] whether
it be to the emperor as supreme, 14 or
to governors as sent by him to punish
those who do wrong and to praise
those who do right. 15 For it is God's
will that by doing right you should
put to silence the ignorance of foolish
men. 16 Live as free men, yet without
using your freedom as a pretext for
evil; but live as servants of God.
17 Honor all men. Love the brotherhood. Fear God. Honor the emperor.

18 Servants, be submissive to your
masters with all respect, not only to
the kind and gentle but also to the
overbearing. 19 For one is approved if,
mindful of God, he endures pain while
suffering unjustly. 20 For what credit
is it, if when you do wrong and are
beaten for it you take it patiently?
But if when you do right and suffer
for it you take it patiently, you have
God's approval. 21 For to this you
have been called, because Christ also
suffered for you, leaving you an example, that you should follow in his
steps. 22 He committed no sin; no
guile was found on his lips. 23 When
he was reviled, he did not revile in
return; when he suffered, he did not
threaten; but he trusted to him who
judges justly. 24 He himself bore our
sins in his body on the tree,[g] that we
might die to sin and live to righteousness. By his wounds you have been
healed. 25 For you were straying like
sheep, but have now returned to the
Shepherd and Guardian of your souls.

3 Likewise you wives, be submissive to your husbands, so that
some, though they do not obey the
word, may be won without a word by
the behavior of their wives, 2 when
they see your reverent and chaste behavior. 3 Let not yours be the outward
adorning with braiding of hair, deco-
ration of gold, and wearing of robes,
4 but let it be the hidden person of the
heart with the imperishable jewel of a

[e] Greek *a people for his possession* [f] Or *every institution ordained for men* [g] Or *carried up . . . to the tree*
1.24-25: Is 40.6-9. **2.3:** Ps 34.8. **2.4:** Ps 118.22; Is 28.16. **2.6:** Is 28.16. **2.7:** Ps 118 22.
2.8: Is 8.14-15. **2.9:** Ex 19.5-6. **2.10:** Hos 2.23. **2.22:** Is 53 9. **2.24:** Is 53.12 (Gk.).
2.24-25: Is 53.5-6.

gentle and quiet spirit, which in God's
sight is very precious. 5 So once the
holy women who hoped in God used
to adorn themselves and were submissive to their husbands, 6 as Sarah
obeyed Abraham, calling him lord.
And you are now her children if you
do right and let nothing terrify you.
7 Likewise you husbands, live con-
siderately with your wives, bestowing
honor on the woman as the weaker
sex, since you are joint heirs of the
grace of life, in order that your
prayers may not be hindered.
8 Finally, all of you, have unity of
spirit, sympathy, love of the brethren,
a tender heart and a humble mind.
9 Do not return evil for evil or reviling for reviling; but on the contrary
bless, for to this you have been called,
that you may obtain a blessing. 10 For

"He that would love life
and see good days,
let him keep his tongue from evil
and his lips from speaking guile;
11 let him turn away from evil and do
right;
let him seek peace and pursue it.
12 For the eyes of the Lord are upon
the righteous,
and his ears are open to their prayer.
But the face of the Lord is against
those that do evil."

13 Now who is there to harm you if
you are zealous for what is right?
14 But even if you do suffer for righteousness' sake, you will be blessed.
Have no fear of them, nor be troubled,
15 but in your hearts reverence Christ
as Lord. Always be prepared to make
a defense to any one who calls you to
account for the hope that is in you,
yet do it with gentleness and reverence; 16 and keep your conscience
clear, so that, when you are abused,
those who revile your good behavior
in Christ may be put to shame. 17 For
it is better to suffer for doing right, if
that should be God's will, than for
doing wrong. 18 For Christ also died[h]
for sins once for all, the righteous for
the unrighteous, that he might bring
us to God, being put to death in the
flesh but made alive in the spirit;
19 in which he went and preached to
the spirits in prison, 20 who formerly
did not obey, when God's patience
waited in the days of Noah, during
the building of the ark, in which a
few, that is, eight persons, were saved
through water. 21 Baptism, which
corresponds to this, now saves you,
not as a removal of dirt from the body
but as an appeal to God for a clear
conscience, through the resurrection
of Jesus Christ, 22 who has gone into
heaven and is at the right hand of God,
with angels, authorities, and powers
subject to him.

4 Since therefore Christ suffered
in the flesh,[i] arm yourselves with
the same thought, for whoever has
suffered in the flesh has ceased from
sin, 2 so as to live for the rest of the
time in the flesh no longer by human
passions but by the will of God. 3 Let
the time that is past suffice for doing
what the Gentiles like to do, living in
licentiousness, passions, drunkenness,
revels, carousing, and lawless idolatry.
4 They are surprised that you do not
now join them in the same wild
profligacy, and they abuse you; 5 but
they will give account to him who is
ready to judge the living and the dead.
6 For this is why the gospel was
preached even to the dead, that
though judged in the flesh like men,
they might live in the spirit like God.
7 The end of all things is at hand;
therefore keep sane and sober for your
prayers. 8 Above all hold unfailing
your love for one another, since love
covers a multitude of sins. 9 Practice
hospitality ungrudgingly to one another. 10 As each has received a gift,
employ it for one another, as good
stewards of God's varied grace:
11 whoever speaks, as one who utters
oracles of God; whoever renders service, as one who renders it by the
strength which God supplies; in order
that in everything God may be glorified through Jesus Christ. To him
belong glory and dominion for ever
and ever. Amen.
12 Beloved, do not be surprised at
the fiery ordeal which comes upon you
to prove you, as though something
strange were happening to you. 13 But
rejoice in so far as you share Christ's
sufferings, that you may also rejoice
and be glad when his glory is revealed.
14 If you are reproached for the name
of Christ, you are blessed, because the
spirit of glory[j] and of God rests upon

[h] Other ancient authorities read *suffered* [i] Other ancient authorities add *for us; some for you*
[j] Other ancient authorities insert *and of power*

3.6: Gen 18.12. **3.10-12:** Ps 34.12-16. **3.14-15:** Is 8.12-13. **3.20:** Gen 6-8. **4.14:** Is 11.2.

you. 15 But let none of you suffer as a
murderer, or a thief, or a wrongdoer,
or a mischief-maker; 16 yet if one
suffers as a Christian, let him not be
ashamed, but under that name let him
glorify God. 17 For the time has come
for judgment to begin with the household of God; and if it begins with us,
what will be the end of those who do
not obey the gospel of God? 18 And

"If the righteous man is scarcely saved,
where will the impious and sinner appear?"

19 Therefore let those who suffer according to God's will do right and entrust their souls to a faithful Creator.

5 So I exhort the elders among you,
as a fellow elder and a witness of
the sufferings of Christ as well as a
partaker in the glory that is to be
revealed. 2 Tend the flock of God that
is your charge,[k] not by constraint but
willingly,[l] not for shameful gain but
eagerly, 3 not as domineering over
those in your charge but being examples to the flock. 4 And when the
chief Shepherd is manifested you will
obtain the unfading crown of glory.
5 Likewise you that are younger be
subject to the elders. Clothe yourselves, all of you, with humility toward one another, for "God opposes
the proud, but gives grace to the
humble."

6 Humble yourselves therefore under the mighty hand of God, that in
due time he may exalt you. 7 Cast all
your anxieties on him, for he cares
about you. 8 Be sober, be watchful.
Your adversary the devil prowls
around like a roaring lion, seeking
some one to devour. 9 Resist him,
firm in your faith, knowing that the
same experience of suffering is required of your brotherhood throughout the world. 10 And after you have
suffered a little while, the God of all
grace, who has called you to his
eternal glory in Christ, will himself
restore, establish, and strengthen[m]
you. 11 To him be the dominion for
ever and ever. Amen.

12 By Sil·vā'nŭs, a faithful brother
as I regard him, I have written
briefly to you, exhorting and declaring that this is the true grace of God;
stand fast in it. 13 She who is at
Babylon, who is likewise chosen,
sends you greetings; and so does my
son Mark. 14 Greet one another with
the kiss of love.

Peace to all of you that are in
Christ.

THE SECOND LETTER OF

PETER

1 Simon Peter, a servant and
apostle of Jesus Christ,

To those who have obtained a faith
of equal standing with ours in the
righteousness of our God and Savior
Jesus Christ:[a]

2 May grace and peace be multiplied to you in the knowledge of God
and of Jesus our Lord.

3 His divine power has granted to
us all things that pertain to life and
godliness, through the knowledge of
him who called us to[b] his own glory
and excellence, 4 by which he has
granted to us his precious and very
great promises, that through these
you may escape from the corruption
that is in the world because of passion,
and become partakers of the divine
nature. 5 For this very reason make
every effort to supplement your faith
with virtue, and virtue with knowledge, 6 and knowledge with self-

[k] Other ancient authorities add *exercising the oversight*
[l] Other ancient authorities add *as God would have you*
[m] Other ancient authorities read *restore, establish, strengthen and settle*
[a] Or *of our God and the Savior Jesus Christ* [b] Or *by*
4.18: Prov 11.31 (Gk.). **5.5:** Prov 3.34. **5.7:** Ps 55.22.

control, and self-control with steadfastness, and steadfastness with godliness, 7 and godliness with brotherly
affection, and brotherly affection with
love. 8 For if these things are yours
and abound, they keep you from
being ineffective or unfruitful in the
knowledge of our Lord Jesus Christ.
9 For whoever lacks these things is
blind and shortsighted and has forgotten that he was cleansed from his
old sins. 10 Therefore, brethren, be the
more zealous to confirm your call and
election, for if you do this you will
never fall; 11 so there will be richly
provided for you an entrance into
the eternal kingdom of our Lord and
Savior Jesus Christ.

12 Therefore I intend always to
remind you of these things, though
you know them and are established in
the truth that you have. 13 I think it
right, as long as I am in this body,[c] to
arouse you by way of reminder,
14 since I know that the putting off of
my body[c] will be soon, as our Lord
Jesus Christ showed me. 15 And I will
see to it that after my departure you
may be able at any time to recall
these things.

16 For we did not follow cleverly
devised myths when we made known
to you the power and coming of our
Lord Jesus Christ, but we were eyewitnesses of his majesty. 17 For when
he received honor and glory from God
the Father and the voice was borne to
him by the Majestic Glory, "This is
my beloved Son,[d] with whom I am
well pleased," 18 we heard this voice
borne from heaven, for we were with
him on the holy mountain. 19 And we
have the prophetic word made more
sure. You will do well to pay attention
to this as to a lamp shining in a dark
place, until the day dawns and the
morning star rises in your hearts.
20 First of all you must understand
this, that no prophecy of scripture is
a matter of one's own interpretation,
21 because no prophecy ever came by
the impulse of man, but men moved
by the Holy Spirit spoke from God.[e]

2 But false prophets also arose
among the people, just as there
will be false teachers among you, who
will secretly bring in destructive here-
sies, even denying the Master who
bought them, bringing upon themselves swift destruction. 2 And many
will follow their licentiousness, and because of them the way of truth will be
reviled. 3 And in their greed they will
exploit you with false words; from of
old their condemnation has not been
idle, and their destruction has not
been asleep.

4 For if God did not spare the
angels when they sinned, but cast
them into hell[f] and committed them
to pits of nether gloom to be kept
until the judgment; 5 if he did not
spare the ancient world, but preserved Noah, a herald of righteousness, with seven other persons, when
he brought a flood upon the world of
the ungodly; 6 if by turning the cities
of Sod'ŏm and Gŏ·môr'răh to ashes he
condemned them to extinction and
made them an example to those who
were to be ungodly; 7 and if he rescued
righteous Lot, greatly distressed by
the licentiousness of the wicked 8 (for
by what that righteous man saw and
heard as he lived among them, he was
vexed in his righteous soul day after
day with their lawless deeds), 9 then
the Lord knows how to rescue the
godly from trial, and to keep the
unrighteous under punishment until
the day of judgment, 10 and especially
those who indulge in the lust of
defiling passion and despise authority.

Bold and wilful, they are not afraid
to revile the glorious ones, 11 whereas
angels, though greater in might and
power, do not pronounce a reviling
judgment upon them before the Lord.
12 But these, like irrational animals,
creatures of instinct, born to be caught
and killed, reviling in matters of which
they are ignorant, will be destroyed in
the same destruction with them, 13 suffering wrong for their wrongdoing.
They count it pleasure to revel in the
daytime. They are blots and blemishes, reveling in their dissipation,[g]
carousing with you. 14 They have eyes
full of adultery, insatiable for sin.
They entice unsteady souls. They
have hearts trained in greed. Accursed
children! 15 Forsaking the right way

[c] Greek *tent*
[d] Or *my Son, my* (or *the*) *Beloved*
[e] Other authorities read *moved by the Holy Spirit holy men of God spoke* [f] Greek *Tartarus*
[g] Other ancient authorities read *love feasts*
1.17-18: Mt 17.1-8; Mk 9.2-8; Lk 9.28-36. **2.1-18:** Jude 4-16. **2.5:** Gen 8.18; 6.6-8. **2.6:** Gen 19.24.
2.7: Gen 19.16, 29. **2.15:** Num 22.5, 7.

they have gone astray; they have
followed the way of Balaam, the son
of Bē'ôr, who loved gain from wrongdoing, 16 but was rebuked for his own
transgression; a dumb ass spoke with
human voice and restrained the
prophet's madness.

17 These are waterless springs and
mists driven by a storm; for them the
nether gloom of darkness has been
reserved. 18 For, uttering loud boasts
of folly, they entice with licentious
passions of the flesh men who have
barely escaped from those who live in
error. 19 They promise them freedom,
but they themselves are slaves of corruption; for whatever overcomes a
man, to that he is enslaved. 20 For if,
after they have escaped the defile-
ments of the world through the knowledge of our Lord and Savior Jesus
Christ, they are again entangled in
them and overpowered, the last state
has become worse for them than the
first. 21 For it would have been better
for them never to have known the
way of righteousness than after knowing it to turn back from the holy commandment delivered to them. 22 It
has happened to them according to
the true proverb, The dog turns back
to his own vomit, and the sow is
washed only to wallow in the mire.

3 This is now the second letter that
I have written to you, beloved,
and in both of them I have aroused
your sincere mind by way of reminder;
2 that you should remember the predictions of the holy prophets and the
commandment of the Lord and Savior
through your apostles. 3 First of all
you must understand this, that scoffers will come in the last days with
scoffing, following their own passions
4 and saying, "Where is the promise
of his coming? For ever since the
fathers fell asleep, all things have
continued as they were from the
beginning of creation." 5 They deliberately ignore this fact, that by the
word of God heavens existed long
ago, and an earth formed out of water
and by means of water, 6 through
which the world that then existed
was deluged with water and perished.
7 But by the same word the heavens
and earth that now exist have been
stored up for fire, being kept until
the day of judgment and destruction
of ungodly men.

8 But do not ignore this one fact,
beloved, that with the Lord one day
is as a thousand years, and a thousand
years as one day. 9 The Lord is not
slow about his promise as some count
slowness, but is forbearing toward
you,[h] not wishing that any should
perish, but that all should reach
repentance. 10 But the day of the
Lord will come like a thief, and then
the heavens will pass away with a
loud noise, and the elements will be
dissolved with fire, and the earth and
the works that are upon it will be
burned up.

11 Since all these things are thus to
be dissolved, what sort of persons
ought you to be in lives of holiness and
godliness, 12 waiting for and hastening[i] the coming of the day of God,
because of which the heavens will be
kindled and dissolved, and the elements will melt with fire! 13 But
according to his promise we wait for
new heavens and a new earth in which
righteousness dwells.

14 Therefore, beloved, since you
wait for these, be zealous to be found
by him without spot or blemish, and
at peace. 15 And count the forbearance
of our Lord as salvation. So also our
beloved brother Paul wrote to you according to the wisdom given him,
16 speaking of this as he does in all his
letters. There are some things in them
hard to understand, which the ignorant and unstable twist to their own
destruction, as they do the other
scriptures. 17 You therefore, beloved,
knowing this beforehand, beware lest
you be carried away with the error of
lawless men and lose your own stability. 18 But grow in the grace and
knowledge of our Lord and Savior
Jesus Christ. To him be the glory
both now and to the day of eternity.
Amen.

[h] Other ancient authorities read *on your account* [i] Or *earnestly desiring*

2.16: Num 22.21, 23, 28, 30-31. **2.22:** Prov 26.11. **3.5-6:** Gen 1.6-8; 7.11. **3.8:** Ps 90.4.
3.12: Is 34.4. **3.13:** Is 65.17; 66.22.

THE FIRST LETTER OF

JOHN

1 That which was from the beginning, which we have heard, which
we have seen with our eyes, which we
have looked upon and touched with
our hands, concerning the word of
life— 2 the life was made manifest,
and we saw it, and testify to it, and
proclaim to you the eternal life which
was with the Father and was made
manifest to us— 3 that which we have
seen and heard we proclaim also to
you, so that you may have fellowship
with us; and our fellowship is with
the Father and with his Son Jesus
Christ. 4 And we are writing this that
our[a] joy may be complete.

5 This is the message we have
heard from him and proclaim to you,
that God is light and in him is no
darkness at all. 6 If we say we have
fellowship with him while we walk in
darkness, we lie and do not live according to the truth; 7 but if we walk
in the light, as he is in the light, we
have fellowship with one another, and
the blood of Jesus his Son cleanses us
from all sin. 8 If we say we have no
sin, we deceive ourselves, and the
truth is not in us. 9 If we confess our
sins, he is faithful and just, and will
forgive our sins and cleanse us from
all unrighteousness. 10 If we say we
have not sinned, we make him a liar,
and his word is not in us.

2 My little children, I am writing
this to you so that you may not
sin; but if any one does sin, we have
an advocate with the Father, Jesus
Christ the righteous; 2 and he is the
expiation for our sins, and not for
ours only but also for the sins of the
whole world. 3 And by this we may be
sure that we know him, if we keep his
commandments. 4 He who says "I
know him" but disobeys his commandments is a liar, and the truth is
not in him; 5 but whoever keeps his
word, in him truly love for God is
perfected. By this we may be sure
that we are in him: 6 he who says he
abides in him ought to walk in the
same way in which he walked.

7 Beloved, I am writing you no new
commandment, but an old commandment which you had from the beginning; the old commandment is the
word which you have heard. 8 Yet I
am writing you a new commandment,
which is true in him and in you, because[b] the darkness is passing away
and the true light is already shining.
9 He who says he is in the light and
hates his brother is in the darkness
still. 10 He who loves his brother
abides in the light, and in it[c] there is
no cause for stumbling. 11 But he who
hates his brother is in the darkness
and walks in the darkness, and
does not know where he is going,
because the darkness has blinded his
eyes.

12 I am writing to you, little children, because your sins are forgiven
for his sake. 13 I am writing to you,
fathers, because you know him who is
from the beginning. I am writing to
you, young men, because you have
overcome the evil one. I write to you,
children, because you know the Father. 14 I write to you, fathers, because
you know him who is from the beginning. I write to you, young men,
because you are strong, and the word
of God abides in you, and you have
overcome the evil one.

15 Do not love the world or the
things in the world. If any one loves
the world, love for the Father is not in
him. 16 For all that is in the world, the
lust of the flesh and the lust of the
eyes and the pride of life, is not of
the Father but is of the world. 17 And
the world passes away, and the lust of

[a] Other ancient authorities read *your* [b] Or *that* [c] Or *him*

1.1-2: Lk 24.39; Jn 1.1; 4.14; 15.27; 20.20, 25; Acts 4.20; 1 Jn 2.13. **1.4:** Jn 15.11; 2 Jn 12.
1.5: 1 Jn 3.11. **1.6-8:** Jn 3.21; 1 Jn 2.4, 11. **1.7:** Rev 1.5. **1.10:** 1 Jn 5.10. **2.1:** Jn 14.16.
2.2: Jn 1.29; 3.14-16; 11.51-52; 1 Jn 4.10. **2.3:** Jn 15.10. **2.4:** 1 Jn 1.6-8; 4.20.
2.5: Jn 14.21, 23; 1 Jn 5.3. **2.6:** Jn 13.15. **2.7:** Jn 13.34. **2.8:** Jn 8.12.
2.10-11: Jn 11.9-10; 1 Jn 1.6. **2.13:** Jn 1.1; 1 Jn 1.1.

it; but he who does the will of God
abides for ever.

18 Children, it is the last hour; and
as you have heard that antichrist is
coming, so now many antichrists have
come; therefore we know that it is the
last hour. 19 They went out from us,
but they were not of us; for if they
had been of us, they would have continued with us; but they went out,
that it might be plain that they all
are not of us. 20 But you have been
anointed by the Holy One, and you
all know.[d] 21 I write to you, not because you do not know the truth, but
because you know it, and know that
no lie is of the truth. 22 Who is the
liar but he who denies that Jesus is
the Christ? This is the antichrist, he
who denies the Father and the Son.
23 No one who denies the Son has the
Father. He who confesses the Son has
the Father also. 24 Let what you heard
from the beginning abide in you. If
what you heard from the beginning
abides in you, then you will abide in
the Son and in the Father. 25And this
is what he has promised us,[e] eternal
life.

26 I write this to you about those
who would deceive you; 27 but the
anointing which you received from
him abides in you, and you have no
need that any one should teach you;
as his anointing teaches you about
everything, and is true, and is no lie,
just as it has taught you, abide in him.

28 And now, little children, abide
in him, so that when he appears we
may have confidence and not shrink
from him in shame at his coming.
29 If you know that he is righteous,
you may be sure that every one who
does right is born of him.

3 See what love the Father has
given us, that we should be called
children of God; and so we are. The
reason why the world does not know
us is that it did not know him. 2 Beloved, we are God's children now; it
does not yet appear what we shall be,
but we know that when he appears
we shall be like him, for we shall see
him as he is. 3And every one who thus
hopes in him purifies himself as he is
pure.

4 Every one who commits sin is
guilty of lawlessness; sin is lawlessness. 5 You know that he appeared to
take away sins, and in him there is no
sin. 6 No one who abides in him sins;
no one who sins has either seen him or
known him. 7 Little children, let no
one deceive you. He who does right is
righteous, as he is righteous. 8 He who
commits sin is of the devil; for the
devil has sinned from the beginning.
The reason the Son of God appeared
was to destroy the works of the devil.
9 No one born of God commits sin; for
God's[f] nature abides in him, and he
cannot sin because he is[g] born of God.
10 By this it may be seen who are the
children of God, and who are the children of the devil: whoever does not do
right is not of God, nor he who does
not love his brother.

11 For this is the message which
you have heard from the beginning,
that we should love one another,
12 and not be like Cain who was of the
evil one and murdered his brother.
And why did he murder him? Because
his own deeds were evil and his
brother's righteous. 13 Do not wonder,
brethren, that the world hates you.
14 We know that we have passed out
of death into life, because we love the
brethren. He who does not love remains in death. 15Any one who hates
his brother is a murderer, and you
know that no murderer has eternal
life abiding in him. 16 By this we
know love, that he laid down his life
for us; and we ought to lay down our
lives for the brethren. 17 But if any
one has the world's goods and sees his
brother in need, yet closes his heart
against him, how does God's love
abide in him? 18 Little children, let us
not love in word or speech but in
deed and in truth.

19 By this we shall know that we
are of the truth, and reassure our
hearts before him 20 whenever our
hearts condemn us, for God is greater
than our hearts, and he knows everything. 21 Beloved, if our hearts do not

[d] Other ancient authorities read *you know everything* [e] Other ancient authorities read *you*
[f] Greek *his* [g] Or *for the offspring of God abide in him, and they cannot sin because they are*
2.18: 1 Jn 4.3. **2.22:** 2 Jn 7. **2.23:** 1 Jn 4.15; 2 Jn 9. **2.27:** Jn 14.26. **2.28:** 1 Jn 4.17.
2.29: 1 Jn 3.7-10; 4.7. **3.1:** Jn 1.12; 16.3. **3.5:** Jn 1.29. **3.8:** Jn 8.34, 44. **3.9:** 1 Jn 5.18.
3.11: 1 Jn 1.5. **3.13:** Jn 15.18-19. **3.14:** Jn 5.24. **3.15:** Jn 8.44. **3.16:** Jn 13.1; 15.13.
3.18: Jas 1.22. **3.21:** 1 Jn 5.14.

condemn us, we have confidence before God; 22 and we receive from him
whatever we ask, because we keep his
commandments and do what pleases
him. 23And this is his commandment,
that we should believe in the name of
his Son Jesus Christ and love one another, just as he has commanded us.
24All who keep his commandments
abide in him, and he in them. And by
this we know that he abides in us, bv
the Spirit which he has given us.

4 Beloved, do not believe every
spirit, but test the spirits to see
whether they are of God; for many
false prophets have gone out into the
world. 2 By this you know the Spirit
of God: every spirit which confesses
that Jesus Christ has come in the flesh
is of God, 3 and every spirit which
does not confess Jesus is not of God.
This is the spirit of antichrist, of which
you heard that it was coming, and
now it is in the world already. 4 Little
children, you are of God, and have
overcome them; for he who is in you
is greater than he who is in the world.
5 They are of the world, therefore
what they say is of the world, and the
world listens to them. 6 We are of God.
Whoever knows God listens to us, and
he who is not of God does not listen
to us. By this we know the spirit of
truth and the spirit of error.

7 Beloved, let us love one another;
for love is of God, and he who loves
is born of God and knows God. 8 He
who does not love does not know God;
for God is love. 9 In this the love of
God was made manifest among us,
that God sent his only Son into the
world, so that we might live through
him. 10 In this is love, not that we
loved God but that he loved us and
sent his Son to be the expiation for
our sins. 11 Beloved, if God so loved
us, we also ought to love one another.
12 No man has ever seen God; if we
love one another, God abides in us
and his love is perfected in us.

13 By this we know that we abide
in him and he in us, because he has
given us of his own Spirit. 14And we
have seen and testify that the Father
has sent his Son as the Savior of the
world. 15 Whoever confesses that Jesus is the Son of God, God abides in
him, and he in God. 16 So we know and
believe the love God has for us. God
is love, and he who abides in love
abides in God, and God abides in him.
17 In this is love perfected with us,
that we may have confidence for the
day of judgment, because as he is so
are we in this world. 18 There is no
fear in love, but perfect love casts out
fear. For fear has to do with punishment, and he who fears is not perfected in love. 19 We love, because he
first loved us. 20 If any one says, "I
love God," and hates his brother, he is
a liar; for he who does not love his
brother whom he has seen, cannot[h]
love God whom he has not seen.
21And this commandment we have
from him, that he who loves God
should love his brother also.

5 Every one who believes that
Jesus is the Christ is a child of
God, and every one who loves the
parent loves the child. 2 By this we
know that we love the children of God,
when we love God and obey his commandments. 3 For this is the love of
God, that we keep his commandments. And his commandments are
not burdensome. 4 For whatever is
born of God overcomes the world; and
this is the victory that overcomes the
world, our faith. 5 Who is it that overcomes the world but he who believes
that Jesus is the Son of God?

6 This is he who came by water and
blood, Jesus Christ, not with the
water only but with the water and the
blood. 7And the Spirit is the witness,
because the Spirit is the truth. 8 There
are three witnesses, the Spirit, the
water, and the blood; and these three
agree. 9 If we receive the testimony of
men, the testimony of God is greater;
for this is the testimony of God that
he has borne witness to his Son. 10 He
who believes in the Son of God has the
testimony in himself. He who does
not believe God has made him a liar,
because he has not believed in the
testimony that God has borne to his
Son. 11And this is the testimony, that

h Other ancient authorities read *how can he*

3.23: Jn 6.29; 13.34; 15.17. **3.24:** 1 Jn 4.13. **4.3:** 1 Jn 2.18. **4.5:** Jn 15.19. **4.6:** Jn 8.47. **4.7:** 1 Jn 2.29. **4.9:** Jn 3.16. **4.10:** Jn 15.12; 1 Jn 4.19; 2.2. **4.12:** Jn 1.18. **4.13:** 1 Jn 3.24. **4.14:** Jn 4.42; 3.17. **4.17:** 1 Jn 2.28. **4.19:** 1 Jn 4.10. **4.20:** 1 Jn 2.4. **5.1:** Jn 8.42. **5.3:** Jn 14.15; 1 Jn 2.5; 2 Jn 6. **5.4:** Jn 16.33. **5.6-8:** Jn 19.34; 4.23; 15.26. **5.9:** Jn 5.32, 36; 8.18. **5.10:** 1 Jn 1.10.

God gave us eternal life, and this life
is in his Son. 12 He who has the Son
has life; he who has not the Son of
God has not life.

13 I write this to you who believe
in the name of the Son of God, that
you may know that you have eternal
life. 14 And this is the confidence which
we have in him, that if we ask anything according to his will he hears us.
15 And if we know that he hears us in
whatever we ask, we know that we
have obtained the requests made of
him. 16 If any one sees his brother
committing what is not a mortal sin,
he will ask, and God[i] will give him
life for those whose sin is not mortal.
There is sin which is mortal; I do not
say that one is to pray for that. 17 All
wrongdoing is sin, but there is sin
which is not mortal.

18 We know that any one born of
God does not sin, but He who was
born of God keeps him, and the evil
one does not touch him.

19 We know that we are of God,
and the whole world is in the power of
the evil one.

20 And we know that the Son of
God has come and has given us understanding, to know him who is true;
and we are in him who is true, in his
Son Jesus Christ. This is the true God
and eternal life. 21 Little children, keep
yourselves from idols.

THE SECOND LETTER OF JOHN

1 The elder to the elect lady and
her children, whom I love in the truth,
and not only I but also all who know
the truth, 2 because of the truth which
abides in us and will be with us for
ever:

3 Grace, mercy, and peace will be
with us, from God the Father and
from Jesus Christ the Father's Son,
in truth and love.

4 I rejoiced greatly to find some of
your children following the truth, just
as we have been commanded by the
Father. 5 And now I beg you, lady, not
as though I were writing you a new
commandment, but the one we have
had from the beginning, that we love
one another. 6 And this is love, that we
follow his commandments; this is the
commandment, as you have heard
from the beginning, that you follow
love. 7 For many deceivers have gone
out into the world, men who will not
acknowledge the coming of Jesus
Christ in the flesh; such a one is the
deceiver and the antichrist. 8 Look to
yourselves, that you may not lose
what you[a] have worked for, but may
win a full reward. 9 Any one who goes
ahead and does not abide in the doctrine of Christ does not have God; he
who abides in the doctrine has both
the Father and the Son. 10 If any one
comes to you and does not bring this
doctrine, do not receive him into the
house or give him any greeting; 11 for he
who greets him shares his wicked work.

12 Though I have much to write to
you, I would rather not use paper and
ink, but I hope to come to see you and
talk with you face to face, so that our
joy may be complete.

13 The children of your elect sister
greet you.

[i] Greek *he* [a] Other ancient authorities read *we*

5.12: Jn 3.36. **5.13:** Jn 20.31. **5.14:** Mt 7.7; 1 Jn 3.21. **5.18:** Jn 17.15; 1 Jn 3.9.
5.20-21: Jn 17.3; Rev 3.7. **1:** 3 Jn 1. **5:** Jn 13.34. **6:** 1 Jn 5.3. **7:** 1 Jn 2.22. **12:** 1 Jn 1.4; 3 Jn 13.

THE THIRD LETTER OF

JOHN

1 The elder to the beloved Gā'ius,
whom I love in the truth.
2 Beloved, I pray that all may go
well with you and that you may be in
health; I know that it is well with your
soul. 3 For I greatly rejoiced when
some of the brethren arrived and testified to the truth of your life, as indeed
you do follow the truth. 4 No greater
joy can I have than this, to hear that
my children follow the truth.
5 Beloved, it is a loyal thing you do
when you render any service to the
brethren, especially to strangers, 6 who
have testified to your love before the
church. You will do well to send them
on their journey as befits God's service. 7 For they have set out for his
sake and have accepted nothing from
the heathen. 8 So we ought to support
such men, that we may be fellow
workers in the truth.
9 I have written something to the
church; but Dī·ot'rė·phēs, who likes
to put himself first, does not acknowledge my authority. 10 So if I come, I
will bring up what he is doing, prating
against me with evil words. And not
content with that, he refuses himself to welcome the brethren, and
also stops those who want to welcome them and puts them out of the
church.
11 Beloved, do not imitate evil but
imitate good. He who does good is of
God; he who does evil has not seen
God. 12 Dė·mē'tri·us has testimony
from every one, and from the truth
itself; I testify to him too, and you
know my testimony is true.

13 I had much to write to you, but
I would rather not write with pen and
ink; 14 I hope to see you soon, and we
will talk together face to face.
15 Peace be to you. The friends
greet you. Greet the friends, every one
of them.

THE LETTER OF

JUDE

1 Jude, a servant of Jesus Christ
and brother of James,
To those who are called, beloved in
God the Father and kept for Jesus
Christ:
2 May mercy, peace, and love be
multiplied to you.

3 Beloved, being very eager to write
to you of our common salvation, I
found it necessary to write appealing
to you to contend for the faith which
was once for all delivered to the
saints. 4 For admission has been
secretly gained by some who long ago
were designated for this condemnation, ungodly persons who pervert
the grace of our God into licentiousness and deny our only Master and
Lord, Jesus Christ.[a]
5 Now I desire to remind you,
though you were once for all fully informed, that he[b] who saved a people
out of the land of Egypt, afterward
destroyed those who did not believe.
6 And the angels that did not keep
their own position but left their proper
dwelling have been kept by him in
eternal chains in the nether gloom
until the judgment of the great day;
7 just as Sŏd'ŏm and Gŏ·mŏr'rah and
the surrounding cities, which likewise

[a] Or *the only Master and our Lord Jesus Christ* [b] Ancient authorities read *Jesus* or *the Lord* or *God*

1: Acts 19.29; 2 Jn 1. **12**: Jn 21.24. **13**: 2 Jn 12. **4-16** (Jude): 2 Pet 2.1-18. **7** (Jude): Gen 19.

acted immorally and indulged in unnatural lust, serve as an example by
undergoing a punishment of eternal
fire.
8 Yet in like manner these men in
their dreamings defile the flesh, reject
authority, and revile the glorious
ones.[c] 9 But when the archangel
Michael, contending with the devil,
disputed about the body of Moses, he
did not presume to pronounce a reviling judgment upon him, but said,
"The Lord rebuke you." 10 But these
men revile whatever they do not understand, and by those things that
they know by instinct as irrational
animals do, they are destroyed. 11 Woe
to them! For they walk in the way of
Cain, and abandon themselves for the
sake of gain to Balaam's error, and
perish in Kō'răh's rebellion. 12 These
are blemishes[d] on your love feasts, as
they boldly carouse together, looking
after themselves; waterless clouds,
carried along by winds; fruitless trees
in late autumn, twice dead, uprooted;
13 wild waves of the sea, casting up
the foam of their own shame; wandering stars for whom the nether gloom
of darkness has been reserved for ever.
14 It was of these also that Ē'nŏch
in the seventh generation from Adam
prophesied, saying, "Behold, the Lord
came with his holy myriads, 15 to execute judgment on all, and to convict
all the ungodly of all their deeds of
ungodliness which they have committed in such an ungodly way, and
of all the harsh things which ungodly
sinners have spoken against him."
16 These are grumblers, malcontents,
following their own passions, loud-
mouthed boasters, flattering people
to gain advantage.
17 But you must remember, beloved, the predictions of the apostles
of our Lord Jesus Christ; 18 they said
to you, "In the last time there will be
scoffers, following their own ungodly
passions." 19 It is these who set up
divisions, worldly people, devoid of
the Spirit. 20 But you, beloved, build
yourselves up on your most holy faith;
pray in the Holy Spirit; 21 keep yourselves in the love of God; wait for the
mercy of our Lord Jesus Christ unto
eternal life. 22 And convince some, who
doubt; 23 save some, by snatching
them out of the fire; on some have
mercy with fear, hating even the garment spotted by the flesh.[e]

24 Now to him who is able to keep
you from falling and to present you
without blemish before the presence
of his glory with rejoicing, 25 to the
only God, our Savior through Jesus
Christ our Lord, be glory, majesty,
dominion, and authority, before all
time and now and for ever. Amen.

THE

REVELATION TO JOHN

1 The revelation of Jesus Christ,
which God gave him to show to his
servants what must soon take place;
and he made it known by sending his
angel to his servant John, 2 who bore
witness to the word of God and to the
testimony of Jesus Christ, even to all
that he saw. 3 Blessed is he who reads
aloud the words of the prophecy, and
blessed are those who hear, and who
keep what is written therein; for the
time is near.
4 John to the seven churches that
are in Asia:
Grace to you and peace from him
who is and who was and who is to
come, and from the seven spirits who
are before his throne, 5 and from Jesus
Christ the faithful witness, the first-
born of the dead, and the ruler of kings
on earth.
To him who loves us and has freed
us from our sins by his blood 6 and
made us a kingdom, priests to his God

[c] Greek *glories* [d] Or *reefs* [e] The Greek text in this sentence is uncertain at several points
9: Zech 3.2. **11:** Gen 4.3-8; Num 22-24; 16. **14-15:** Enoch 1.9. **23:** Zech 3.3-4.
1.4: Ex 3.14. **1.5:** Ps 89.27. **1.6:** Ex 19.6; Is 61.6.

and Father, to him be glory and
dominion for ever and ever. Amen.
7 Behold, he is coming with the clouds,
and every eye will see him, every one
who pierced him; and all tribes of the
earth will wail on account of him.
Even so. Amen.
8 "I am the Alpha and the Omega,"
says the Lord God, who is and
who was and who is to come, the
Almighty.
9 I John, your brother, who share
with you in Jesus the tribulation and
the kingdom and the patient endurance, was on the island called Pat'mȯs
on account of the word of God and the
testimony of Jesus. 10 I was in the
Spirit on the Lord's day, and I heard
behind me a loud voice like a trumpet
11 saying, "Write what you see in a
book and send it to the seven churches,
to Eph'ė·sůs and to Smyr'nȧ and to
Pẽr'gȧ·mům and to Thȳ·ȧ·tī'rȧ and
to Sär'dis and to Philadelphia and to
Lā-ȯ·di·ċē'ȧ."
12 Then I turned to see the voice
that was speaking to me, and on turning I saw seven golden lampstands,
13 and in the midst of the lampstands
one like a son of man, clothed with a
long robe and with a golden girdle
round his breast; 14 his head and his
hair were white as white wool, white
as snow; his eyes were like a flame of
fire, 15 his feet were like burnished
bronze, refined as in a furnace, and his
voice was like the sound of many
waters; 16 in his right hand he held
seven stars, from his mouth issued a
sharp two-edged sword, and his face
was like the sun shining in full
strength.
17 When I saw him, I fell at his feet
as though dead. But he laid his right
hand upon me, saying, "Fear not, I
am the first and the last, 18 and the
living one; I died, and behold I am
alive for evermore, and I have the
keys of Death and Hades. 19 Now
write what you see, what is and what
is to take place hereafter. 20 As for the
mystery of the seven stars which you
saw in my right hand, and the seven
golden lampstands, the seven stars
are the angels of the seven churches
and the seven lampstands are the
seven churches.

2 "To the angel of the church in
Eph'ė·sůs write: 'The words of
him who holds the seven stars in his
right hand, who walks among the
seven golden lampstands.
2 " 'I know your works, your toil
and your patient endurance, and how
you cannot bear evil men but have
tested those who call themselves apostles but are not, and found them to be
false; 3 I know you are enduring patiently and bearing up for my name's
sake, and you have not grown weary.
4 But I have this against you, that you
have abandoned the love you had at
first. 5 Remember then from what you
have fallen, repent and do the works
you did at first. If not, I will come to
you and remove your lampstand from
its place, unless you repent. 6 Yet this
you have, you hate the works of the
Nic·ō·lā'i·tȧnṡ, which I also hate.
7 He who has an ear, let him hear
what the Spirit says to the churches.
To him who conquers I will grant to
eat of the tree of life, which is in the
paradise of God.'
8 "And to the angel of the church
in Smyr'nȧ write: 'The words of the
first and the last, who died and came
to life.
9 " 'I know your tribulation and
your poverty (but you are rich) and
the slander of those who say that they
are Jews and are not, but are a synagogue of Satan. 10 Do not fear what
you are about to suffer. Behold, the
devil is about to throw some of you
into prison, that you may be tested,
and for ten days you will have tribulation. Be faithful unto death, and I
will give you the crown of life. 11 He
who has an ear, let him hear what the
Spirit says to the churches. He who
conquers shall not be hurt by the
second death.'
12 "And to the angel of the church
in Pẽr'gȧ·mům write: 'The words of
him who has the sharp two-edged
sword.
13 " 'I know where you dwell,
where Satan's throne is; you hold fast
my name and you did not deny my
faith even in the days of An'ti·pas my
witness, my faithful one, who was
killed among you, where Satan dwells.
14 But I have a few things against you:

1.7: Dan 7.13; Mt 24.30; Mk 14.62; Zech 12.10. **1.8:** Ex 3.14. **1.13:** Dan 7.13; 10.5.
1.15: Ezek 1.24. **1.16:** Ex 34.29. **1.17:** Is 44.2, 6.
2.7: Gen 2.9. **2.8:** Is 44.6. **2.10:** Dan 1.12.
2.14: Num 31.16; 25.1-2.

you have some there who hold the
teaching of Balaam, who taught Bā'-
lak to put a stumbling block before
the sons of Israel, that they might eat
food sacrificed to idols and practice
immorality. 15 So you also have some
who hold the teaching of the Nic·ō-
lā'i·tăns. 16 Repent then. If not, I will
come to you soon and war against
them with the sword of my mouth.
17 He who has an ear, let him hear
what the Spirit says to the churches.
To him who conquers I will give some
of the hidden manna, and I will give
him a white stone, with a new name
written on the stone which no one
knows except him who receives it.'

18 "And to the angel of the church
in Thy̆·ȧ·tī'rȧ write: 'The words of the
Son of God, who has eyes like a flame
of fire, and whose feet are like burnished bronze.

19 " 'I know your works, your love
and faith and service and patient endurance, and that your latter works
exceed the first. 20 But I have this
against you, that you tolerate the
woman Jez'ė·bĕl, who calls herself a
prophetess and is teaching and beguiling my servants to practice immorality and to eat food sacrificed to idols.
21 I gave her time to repent, but she
refuses to repent of her immorality.
22 Behold, I will throw her on a sickbed, and those who commit adultery
with her I will throw into great
tribulation, unless they repent of her
doings; 23 and I will strike her children dead. And all the churches shall
know that I am he who searches mind
and heart, and I will give to each of
you as your works deserve. 24 But
to the rest of you in Thy̆·ȧ·tī'rȧ, who
do not hold this teaching, who have
not learned what some call the deep
things of Satan, to you I say, I do not
lay upon you any other burden;
25 only hold fast what you have, until
I come. 26 He who conquers and who
keeps my works until the end, I will
give him power over the nations,
27 and he shall rule them with a rod of
iron, as when earthen pots are broken
in pieces, even as I myself have received power from my Father; 28 and
I will give him the morning star.
29 He who has an ear, let him hear
what the Spirit says to the churches.'

3 "And to the angel of the church
in Sär'dis write: 'The words of
him who has the seven spirits of God
and the seven stars.

" 'I know your works; you have the
name of being alive, and you are dead.
2 Awake, and strengthen what remains
and is on the point of death, for I have
not found your works perfect in the
sight of my God. 3 Remember then
what you received and heard; keep
that, and repent. If you will not
awake, I will come like a thief, and
you will not know at what hour I will
come upon you. 4 Yet you have still a
few names in Sär'dis, people who have
not soiled their garments; and they
shall walk with me in white, for they
are worthy. 5 He who conquers shall
be clad thus in white garments, and
I will not blot his name out of the
book of life; I will confess his name
before my Father and before his
angels. 6 He who has an ear, let
him hear what the Spirit says to the
churches.'

7 "And to the angel of the church
in Philadelphia write: 'The words of
the holy one, the true one, who has
the key of David, who opens and no
one shall shut, who shuts and no one
opens.

8 " 'I know your works. Behold, I
have set before you an open door,
which no one is able to shut; I know
that you have but little power, and
yet you have kept my word and have
not denied my name. 9 Behold, I will
make those of the synagogue of Satan
who say that they are Jews and are
not, but lie—behold, I will make them
come and bow down before your feet,
and learn that I have loved you.
10 Because you have kept my word of
patient endurance, I will keep you
from the hour of trial which is coming
on the whole world, to try those who
dwell upon the earth. 11 I am coming
soon; hold fast what you have, so that
no one may seize your crown. 12 He
who conquers, I will make him a pillar
in the temple of my God; never shall
he go out of it, and I will write on
him the name of my God, and the
name of the city of my God, the new
Jerusalem which comes down from
my God out of heaven, and my own
new name. 13 He who has an ear, let

2.17: Ps 78.24; Is 62.2. **2.18:** Dan 10.6. **2.20:** 1 Kings 16.31; 2 Kings 9.22, 30; Num 25.1.
2.23: Jer 17.10; Ps 62.12. **2.26:** Ps 2.8-9. **3.5:** Ex 32.32; Ps 69.28; Dan 12.1; Mt 10.32.
3.7: Is 22.22. **3.9:** Is 60.14; 49.23; 43.4. **3.12:** Is 62.2; Ezek 48.35; Rev 21.2.

him hear what the Spirit says to the
churches.'
14 "And to the angel of the church
in Lā-ŏ·di·ċē'ȧ write: 'The words of
the Amen, the faithful and true witness, the beginning of God's creation.
15 " 'I know your works: you are
neither cold nor hot. Would that you
were cold or hot! 16 So, because you
are lukewarm, and neither cold nor
hot, I will spew you out of my mouth.
17 For you say, I am rich, I have prospered, and I need nothing; not knowing that you are wretched, pitiable,
poor, blind, and naked. 18 Therefore I
counsel you to buy from me gold refined by fire, that you may be rich,
and white garments to clothe you and
to keep the shame of your nakedness
from being seen, and salve to anoint
your eyes, that you may see. 19 Those
whom I love, I reprove and chasten;
so be zealous and repent. 20 Behold, I
stand at the door and knock; if any
one hears my voice and opens the
door, I will come in to him and eat
with him, and he with me. 21 He who
conquers, I will grant him to sit with
me on my throne, as I myself conquered and sat down with my Father
on his throne. 22 He who has an ear,
let him hear what the Spirit says to
the churches.' "

4 After this I looked, and lo, in
heaven an open door! And the
first voice, which I had heard speaking
to me like a trumpet, said, "Come up
hither, and I will show you what must
take place after this." 2At once I was
in the Spirit, and lo, a throne stood in
heaven, with one seated on the throne!
3And he who sat there appeared like
jasper and carnelian, and round the
throne was a rainbow that looked like
an emerald. 4 Round the throne were
twenty-four thrones, and seated on
the thrones were twenty-four elders,
clad in white garments, with golden
crowns upon their heads. 5 From the
throne issue flashes of lightning, and
voices and peals of thunder, and before
the throne burn seven torches of fire,
which are the seven spirits of God;
6 and before the throne there is as it
were a sea of glass, like crystal.
And round the throne, on each side
of the throne, are four living creatures, full of eyes in front and behind:
7 the first living creature like a lion,
the second living creature like an ox,
the third living creature with the face
of a man, and the fourth living creature like a flying eagle. 8And the four
living creatures, each of them with six
wings, are full of eyes all round and
within, and day and night they never
cease to sing,

"Holy, holy, holy, is the Lord God
Almighty,
who was and is and is to come!"

9And whenever the living creatures
give glory and honor and thanks to
him who is seated on the throne, who
lives for ever and ever, 10 the twenty-
four elders fall down before him who
is seated on the throne and worship
him who lives for ever and ever; they
cast their crowns before the throne,
singing,

11 "Worthy art thou, our Lord and
God,
to receive glory and honor and
power,
for thou didst create all things,
and by thy will they existed and
were created."

5 And I saw in the right hand of
him who was seated on the throne
a scroll written within and on the
back, sealed with seven seals; 2 and I
saw a strong angel proclaiming with a
loud voice, "Who is worthy to open
the scroll and break its seals?" 3And
no one in heaven or on earth or under
the earth was able to open the scroll
or to look into it, 4 and I wept much
that no one was found worthy to open
the scroll or to look into it. 5 Then one
of the elders said to me, "Weep not;
lo, the Lion of the tribe of Judah, the
Root of David, has conquered, so that
he can open the scroll and its seven
seals."
6 And between the throne and the
four living creatures and among the
elders, I saw a Lamb standing, as
though it had been slain, with seven
horns and with seven eyes, which are
the seven spirits of God sent out into
all the earth; 7 and he went and took
the scroll from the right hand of him
who was seated on the throne. 8And
when he had taken the scroll, the four
living creatures and the twenty-four
elders fell down before the Lamb, each

3.14: Ps 89.28; Prov 8.22; Jn 1.1-3. **3.17:** Hos 12.8. **3.19:** Prov 3.12. **4.1:** Ex 19.16, 24.
4.2: Ezek 1.26-28. **4.5:** Ex 19.16; Zech 4.2. **4.6:** Ezek 1.5, 18. **4.7:** Ezek 1.10. **4.8:** Is 6.2-3.
4.9: Ps 47.8. **5.1:** Ezek 2.9; Is 29.11. **5.5:** Gen 49.9. **5.6:** Is 53.7; Zech 4.10. **5.8:** Ps 141.2.

holding a harp, and with golden bowls
full of incense, which are the prayers
of the saints; 9 and they sang a new
song, saying,

"Worthy art thou to take the scroll
and to open its seals,
for thou wast slain and by thy blood
didst ransom men for God
from every tribe and tongue and
people and nation,
10 and hast made them a kingdom and
priests to our God,
and they shall reign on earth."

11 Then I looked, and I heard around
the throne and the living creatures
and the elders the voice of many
angels, numbering myriads of myriads
and thousands of thousands, 12 saying
with a loud voice, "Worthy is the
Lamb who was slain, to receive power
and wealth and wisdom and might
and honor and glory and blessing!"
13And I heard every creature in
heaven and on earth and under the
earth and in the sea, and all therein,
saying, "To him who sits upon the
throne and to the Lamb be blessing
and honor and glory and might for
ever and ever!" 14And the four living
creatures said, "Amen!" and the
elders fell down and worshiped.

6 Now I saw when the Lamb
opened one of the seven seals, and
I heard one of the four living creatures say, as with a voice of thunder,
"Come!" 2And I saw, and behold, a
white horse, and its rider had a bow;
and a crown was given to him, and he
went out conquering and to conquer.

3 When he opened the second seal,
I heard the second living creature say,
"Come!" 4And out came another
horse, bright red; its rider was permitted to take peace from the earth,
so that men should slay one another;
and he was given a great sword.

5 When he opened the third seal,
I heard the third living creature say,
"Come!" And I saw, and behold, a
black horse, and its rider had a balance in his hand; 6 and I heard what
seemed to be a voice in the midst of
the four living creatures saying, "A
quart of wheat for a denarius,[a] and
three quarts of barley for a denarius;[a]
but do not harm oil and wine!"

7 When he opened the fourth seal,
I heard the voice of the fourth living
creature say, "Come!" 8And I saw,
and behold, a pale horse, and its
rider's name was Death, and Hades
followed him; and they were given
power over a fourth of the earth, to
kill with sword and with famine and
with pestilence and by wild beasts of
the earth.

9 When he opened the fifth seal, I
saw under the altar the souls of those
who had been slain for the word of
God and for the witness they had
borne; 10 they cried out with a loud
voice, "O Sovereign Lord, holy and
true, how long before thou wilt judge
and avenge our blood on those who
dwell upon the earth?" 11 Then they
were each given a white robe and told
to rest a little longer, until the number
of their fellow servants and their
brethren should be complete, who
were to be killed as they themselves
had been.

12 When he opened the sixth seal,
I looked, and behold, there was a
great earthquake; and the sun became
black as sackcloth, the full moon became like blood, 13 and the stars of
the sky fell to the earth as the fig tree
sheds its winter fruit when shaken by
a gale; 14 the sky vanished like a scroll
that is rolled up, and every mountain
and island was removed from its
place. 15 Then the kings of the earth
and the great men and the generals
and the rich and the strong, and every
one, slave and free, hid in the caves
and among the rocks of the mountains,
16 calling to the mountains and rocks,
"Fall on us and hide us from the face
of him who is seated on the throne,
and from the wrath of the Lamb;
17 for the great day of their wrath has
come, and who can stand before it?"

7 After this I saw four angels standing at the four corners of the earth,
holding back the four winds of the
earth, that no wind might blow on
earth or sea or against any tree. 2 Then
I saw another angel ascend from the
rising of the sun, with the seal of the
living God, and he called with a loud
voice to the four angels who had been
given power to harm earth and sea,
3 saying, "Do not harm the earth or

[a] The denarius was worth about twenty cents

5.9: Ps 33.3. **5.10:** Ex 19.6; Is 61.6. **5.11:** Dan 7.10. **6.2:** Zech 1.8; 6.1-3. **6.6:** 2 Kings 6.25. **6.8:** Hos 13.14; Ezek 5.12. **6.10:** Zech 1.12; Ps 79.5; Gen 4.10. **6.12:** Joel 2.31; Acts 2.20. **6.13:** Is 34.4. **6.15:** Is 2.10. **6.16:** Hos 10.8. **6.17:** Joel 2.11; Mal 3.2. **7.1:** Zech 6.5. **7.3:** Ezek 9.4.

the sea or the trees, till we have sealed
the servants of our God upon their
foreheads." 4And I heard the number
of the sealed, a hundred and forty-
four thousand sealed, out of every
tribe of the sons of Israel, 5 twelve
thousand sealed out of the tribe of
Judah, twelve thousand of the tribe
of Reuben, twelve thousand of the
tribe of Gad, 6 twelve thousand of the
tribe of Ash'ėr, twelve thousand of
the tribe of Naph'tȧ·lī, twelve thousand of the tribe of Mȧ·nas'sėh,
7twelve thousand of the tribe of
Simeon, twelve thousand of the tribe
of Levi, twelve thousand of the tribe
of Is'sȧ·chär, 8 twelve thousand of the
tribe of Zeb'ū·lun, twelve thousand of
the tribe of Joseph, twelve thousand
sealed out of the tribe of Benjamin.
9 After this I looked, and behold,
a great multitude which no man could
number, from every nation, from all
tribes and peoples and tongues, standing before the throne and before the
Lamb, clothed in white robes, with
palm branches in their hands, 10 and
crying out with a loud voice, "Salvation belongs to our God who sits upon
the throne, and to the Lamb!" 11And
all the angels stood round the throne
and round the elders and the four
living creatures, and they fell on their
faces before the throne and worshiped
God, 12 saying, "Amen! Blessing and
glory and wisdom and thanksgiving
and honor and power and might be to
our God for ever and ever! Amen."
13 Then one of the elders addressed
me, saying, "Who are these, clothed
in white robes, and whence have they
come?" 14 I said to him, "Sir, you
know." And he said to me, "These are
they who have come out of the great
tribulation; they have washed their
robes and made them white in the
blood of the Lamb.

15 Therefore are they before the throne
of God,
and serve him day and night
within his temple;
and he who sits upon the throne
will shelter them with his
presence.
16 They shall hunger no more, neither
thirst any more;
the sun shall not strike them, nor
any scorching heat.
17 For the Lamb in the midst of the
throne will be their shepherd,
and he will guide them to springs
of living water;
and God will wipe away every tear
from their eyes."

8 When the Lamb opened the
seventh seal, there was silence in
heaven for about half an hour. 2 Then
I saw the seven angels who stand before God, and seven trumpets were
given to them. 3And another angel
came and stood at the altar with a
golden censer; and he was given much
incense to mingle with the prayers of
all the saints upon the golden altar
before the throne; 4 and the smoke of
the incense rose with the prayers of
the saints from the hand of the angel
before God. 5 Then the angel took the
censer and filled it with fire from the
altar and threw it on the earth; and
there were peals of thunder, loud
noises, flashes of lightning, and an
earthquake.
6 Now the seven angels who had
the seven trumpets made ready to
blow them.
7 The first angel blew his trumpet,
and there followed hail and fire, mixed
with blood, which fell on the earth;
and a third of the earth was burnt up,
and a third of the trees were burnt up,
and all green grass was burnt up.
8 The second angel blew his trumpet, and something like a great mountain, burning with fire, was thrown
into the sea; 9 and a third of the sea
became blood, a third of the living
creatures in the sea died, and a third
of the ships were destroyed.
10 The third angel blew his trumpet, and a great star fell from heaven,
blazing like a torch, and it fell on a
third of the rivers and on the fountains of water. 11 The name of the
star is Wormwood. A third of the
waters became wormwood, and many
men died of the water, because it was
made bitter.
12 The fourth angel blew his trumpet, and a third of the sun was struck,
and a third of the moon and a third of
the stars, so that a third of their light
was darkened; a third of the day was
kept from shining, and likewise a third
of the night.
13 Then I looked, and I heard an

7.14: Dan 12.1; Gen 49.11. **7.16**: Is 49.10; Ps 121.6. **7.17**: Ezek 34.23; Ps 23.2; Is 25.8.
8.3: Amos 9.1; Ps 141.2. **8.5**: Lev 16.12; Ezek 10.2. **8.7**: Ex 9.23-25. **8.8**: Jer 51.25.
8.10: Is 14.12.

eagle crying with a loud voice, as it
flew in midheaven, "Woe, woe, woe
to those who dwell on the earth, at the
blasts of the other trumpets which the
three angels are about to blow!"

9 And the fifth angel blew his
trumpet, and I saw a star fallen
from heaven to earth, and he was
given the key of the shaft of the bottomless pit; 2 he opened the shaft of
the bottomless pit, and from the shaft
rose smoke like the smoke of a great
furnace, and the sun and the air were
darkened with the smoke from the
shaft. 3 Then from the smoke came
locusts on the earth, and they were
given power like the power of scorpions of the earth; 4 they were told
not to harm the grass of the earth or
any green growth or any tree, but
only those of mankind who have not
the seal of God upon their foreheads;
5 they were allowed to torture them
for five months, but not to kill them,
and their torture was like the torture
of a scorpion, when it stings a man.
6 And in those days men will seek
death and will not find it; they will
long to die, and death will fly from
them.

7 In appearance the locusts were
like horses arrayed for battle; on their
heads were what looked like crowns of
gold; their faces were like human
faces, 8 their hair like women's hair,
and their teeth like lions' teeth; 9 they
had scales like iron breastplates, and
the noise of their wings was like the
noise of many chariots with horses
rushing into battle. 10 They have tails
like scorpions, and stings, and their
power of hurting men for five months
lies in their tails. 11 They have as king
over them the angel of the bottomless
pit; his name in Hebrew is Ȧ·bad'dȯn,
and in Greek he is called Ȧ·pol'lyȯn.[b]

12 The first woe has passed; behold, two woes are still to come.

13 Then the sixth angel blew his
trumpet, and I heard a voice from the
four horns of the golden altar before
God, 14 saying to the sixth angel who
had the trumpet, "Release the four
angels who are bound at the great
river Eū·phrā'tēṡ." 15 So the four angels were released, who had been held
ready for the hour, the day, the
month, and the year, to kill a third of
mankind. 16 The number of the troops
of cavalry was twice ten thousand
times ten thousand; I heard their
number. 17 And this was how I saw
the horses in my vision: the riders
wore breastplates the color of fire and
of sapphire[c] and of sulphur, and the
heads of the horses were like lions'
heads, and fire and smoke and sulphur
issued from their mouths. 18 By these
three plagues a third of mankind was
killed, by the fire and smoke and
sulphur issuing from their mouths.
19 For the power of the horses is in
their mouths and in their tails; their
tails are like serpents, with heads, and
by means of them they wound.

20 The rest of mankind, who were
not killed by these plagues, did not
repent of the works of their hands nor
give up worshiping demons and idols
of gold and silver and bronze and
stone and wood, which cannot either
see or hear or walk; 21 nor did they
repent of their murders or their sorceries or their immorality or their
thefts.

10 Then I saw another mighty angel coming down from heaven,
wrapped in a cloud, with a rainbow
over his head, and his face was like the
sun, and his legs like pillars of fire.
2 He had a little scroll open in his
hand. And he set his right foot on the
sea, and his left foot on the land, 3 and
called out with a loud voice, like a lion
roaring; when he called out, the seven
thunders sounded. 4 And when the
seven thunders had sounded, I was
about to write, but I heard a voice
from heaven saying, "Seal up what
the seven thunders have said, and do
not write it down." 5 And the angel
whom I saw standing on sea and land
lifted up his right hand to heaven
6 and swore by him who lives for ever
and ever, who created heaven and
what is in it, the earth and what is in
it, and the sea and what is in it, that
there should be no more delay, 7 but
that in the days of the trumpet call to
be sounded by the seventh angel, the
mystery of God, as he announced to
his servants the prophets, should be
fulfilled.

8 Then the voice which I had heard

[b] Or *Destroyer* [c] Greek *hyacinth*

9.2: Gen 19.28; Ex 19.18; Joel 2.10. **9.3:** Ex 10.12-15. **9.4:** Ezek 9.4. **9.6:** Job 3.21. **9.7:** Joel 2.4. **9.8:** Joel 1.6. **9.9:** Joel 2.5. **9.13:** Ex 30.1-3. **9.20:** Is 17.8; Ps 115.4-7; 135.15-17. **10.5:** Deut 32.40; Dan 12.7.

from heaven spoke to me again, saying, "Go, take the scroll which is open
in the hand of the angel who is standing on the sea and on the land."
9 So I went to the angel and told him
to give me the little scroll; and he said
to me, "Take it and eat; it will be
bitter to your stomach, but sweet as
honey in your mouth." 10 And I took
the little scroll from the hand of the
angel and ate it; it was sweet as
honey in my mouth, but when I had
eaten it my stomach was made bitter.
11 And I was told, "You must again
prophesy about many peoples and
nations and tongues and kings."

11 Then I was given a measuring
rod like a staff, and I was told:
"Rise and measure the temple of God
and the altar and those who worship
there, 2 but do not measure the court
outside the temple; leave that out, for
it is given over to the nations, and
they will trample over the holy city
for forty-two months. 3 And I will
grant my two witnesses power to
prophesy for one thousand two hundred and sixty days, clothed in sackcloth."

4 These are the two olive trees and
the two lampstands which stand before the Lord of the earth. 5 And if any
one would harm them, fire pours from
their mouth and consumes their foes;
if any one would harm them, thus he
is doomed to be killed. 6 They have
power to shut the sky, that no rain
may fall during the days of their
prophesying, and they have power
over the waters to turn them into
blood, and to smite the earth with
every plague, as often as they desire.
7 And when they have finished their
testimony, the beast that ascends
from the bottomless pit will make war
upon them and conquer them and kill
them, 8 and their dead bodies will
lie in the street of the great city which
is allegorically[d] called Sod'om and
Egypt, where their Lord was crucified.
9 For three days and a half men from
the peoples and tribes and tongues
and nations gaze at their dead bodies
and refuse to let them be placed in a
tomb, 10 and those who dwell on the
earth will rejoice over them and make
merry and exchange presents, because
these two prophets had been a torment to those who dwell on the earth.
11 But after the three and a half days
a breath of life from God entered
them, and they stood up on their
feet, and great fear fell on those who
saw them. 12 Then they heard a loud
voice from heaven saying to them,
"Come up hither!" And in the sight
of their foes they went up to heaven
in a cloud. 13 And at that hour there
was a great earthquake, and a tenth
of the city fell; seven thousand people
were killed in the earthquake, and the
rest were terrified and gave glory to
the God of heaven.

14 The second woe has passed; behold, the third woe is soon to come.

15 Then the seventh angel blew his
trumpet, and there were loud voices
in heaven, saying, "The kingdom of
the world has become the kingdom of
our Lord and of his Christ, and he
shall reign for ever and ever." 16 And
the twenty-four elders who sit on their
thrones before God fell on their faces
and worshiped God, 17 saying,

"We give thanks to thee, Lord God
Almighty, who art and who
wast,
that thou hast taken thy great
power and begun to reign.
18 The nations raged, but thy wrath
came,
and the time for the dead to be
judged,
for rewarding thy servants, the
prophets and saints,
and those who fear thy name,
both small and great,
and for destroying the destroyers of
the earth."

19 Then God's temple in heaven
was opened, and the ark of his covenant was seen within his temple; and
there were flashes of lightning, loud
noises, peals of thunder, an earthquake, and heavy hail.

12 And a great portent appeared
in heaven, a woman clothed
with the sun, with the moon under
her feet, and on her head a crown of
twelve stars; 2 she was with child and

[d] Greek *spiritually*

10.9: Ezek 2.8; 3.1-3. **10.11:** Jer 1.10. **11.1:** Ezek 40.3. **11.2:** Zech 12.3; Is 63.18; Lk 21.24.
11.4: Zech 4.3, 11-14. **11.5:** 2 Kings 1.10; Jer 5.14. **11.6:** 1 Kings 17.1; Ex 7.17, 19.
11.7: Dan 7.3, 7, 21. **11.8:** Is 1.9. **11.11:** Ezek 37.5, 10. **11.12:** 2 Kings 2.11. **11.15:** Ps 22.28; Dan 7.14, 27. **11.18:** Ps 2.1. **11.19:** 1 Kings 8.1-6; 2 Maccabees 2.4-8. **12.2:** Mic 4.10.

she cried out in her pangs of birth, in
anguish for delivery. 3 And another
portent appeared in heaven; behold, a
great red dragon, with seven heads
and ten horns, and seven diadems
upon his heads. 4 His tail swept down
a third of the stars of heaven, and
cast them to the earth. And the
dragon stood before the woman who
was about to bear a child, that he
might devour her child when she
brought it forth; 5 she brought forth a
male child, one who is to rule all the
nations with a rod of iron, but her
child was caught up to God and to his
throne, 6 and the woman fled into the
wilderness, where she has a place prepared by God, in which to be nourished for one thousand two hundred
and sixty days.

7 Now war arose in heaven, Michael
and his angels fighting against the
dragon; and the dragon and his angels
fought, 8 but they were defeated and
there was no longer any place for them
in heaven. 9 And the great dragon was
thrown down, that ancient serpent,
who is called the Devil and Satan, the
deceiver of the whole world—he was
thrown down to the earth, and his
angels were thrown down with him.
10 And I heard a loud voice in heaven,
saying, "Now the salvation and the
power and the kingdom of our God
and the authority of his Christ have
come, for the accuser of our brethren
has been thrown down, who accuses
them day and night before our God.
11 And they have conquered him by
the blood of the Lamb and by the
word of their testimony, for they
loved not their lives even unto death.
12 Rejoice then, O heaven and you
that dwell therein! But woe to you,
O earth and sea, for the devil has
come down to you in great wrath,
because he knows that his time is
short!"

13 And when the dragon saw that
he had been thrown down to the earth,
he pursued the woman who had borne
the male child. 14 But the woman was
given the two wings of the great eagle
that she might fly from the serpent
into the wilderness, to the place where
she is to be nourished for a time, and
times, and half a time. 15 The serpent
poured water like a river out of his
mouth after the woman, to sweep her
away with the flood. 16 But the earth
came to the help of the woman, and
the earth opened its mouth and swallowed the river which the dragon had
poured from his mouth. 17 Then the
dragon was angry with the woman,
and went off to make war on the rest
of her offspring, on those who keep
the commandments of God and bear
testimony to Jesus. And he stood[e]
on the sand of the sea.

13 And I saw a beast rising out of
the sea, with ten horns and
seven heads, with ten diadems upon
its horns and a blasphemous name
upon its heads. 2 And the beast that
I saw was like a leopard, its feet were
like a bear's, and its mouth was like a
lion's mouth. And to it the dragon
gave his power and his throne and
great authority. 3 One of its heads
seemed to have a mortal wound, but
its mortal wound was healed, and the
whole earth followed the beast with
wonder. 4 Men worshiped the dragon,
for he had given his authority to the
beast, and they worshiped the beast,
saying, "Who is like the beast, and
who can fight against it?"

5 And the beast was given a mouth
uttering haughty and blasphemous
words, and it was allowed to exercise
authority for forty-two months; 6 it
opened its mouth to utter blasphemies
against God, blaspheming his name
and his dwelling, that is, those who
dwell in heaven. 7 Also it was allowed
to make war on the saints and to conquer them.[f] And authority was given
it over every tribe and people and
tongue and nation, 8 and all who dwell
on earth will worship it, every one
whose name has not been written before the foundation of the world in the
book of life of the Lamb that was slain.
9 If any one has an ear, let him hear:
10 If any one is to be taken captive,
to captivity he goes;
if any one slays with the sword,
with the sword must he be slain.
Here is a call for the endurance and
faith of the saints.

11 Then I saw another beast which

[e] Other ancient authorities read *And I stood*, connecting the sentence with 13.1
[f] Other ancient authorities omit this sentence

12.3: Dan 7.7. **12.4:** Dan 8.10. **12.5:** Is 66.7; Ps 2.9. **12.7:** Dan 10.13.
12.9: Gen 3.1, 14-15; Zech 3.1. **12.10:** Job 1.9-11. **12.12:** Is 44.23; 49.13. **12.14:** Dan 7.25; 12.7.
13.1: Dan 7.1-6. **13.5:** Dan 7.8. **13.7:** Dan 7.21. **13.9:** Mk 4.23. **13.10:** Jer 15.2.

rose out of the earth; it had two horns
like a lamb and it spoke like a dragon.
12 It exercises all the authority of the
first beast in its presence, and makes
the earth and its inhabitants worship
the first beast, whose mortal wound
was healed. 13 It works great signs,
even making fire come down from
heaven to earth in the sight of men;
14 and by the signs which it is allowed
to work in the presence of the beast, it
deceives those who dwell on earth,
bidding them make an image for the
beast which was wounded by the
sword and yet lived; 15 and it was
allowed to give breath to the image of
the beast so that the image of the
beast should even speak, and to cause
those who would not worship the
image of the beast to be slain. 16 Also
it causes all, both small and great,
both rich and poor, both free and
slave, to be marked on the right hand
or the forehead, 17 so that no one can
buy or sell unless he has the mark,
that is, the name of the beast or the
number of its name. 18 This calls for
wisdom: let him who has understanding reckon the number of the beast,
for it is a human number, its number
is six hundred and sixty-six.[g]

14 Then I looked, and lo, on
Mount Zion stood the Lamb,
and with him a hundred and forty-
four thousand who had his name and
his Father's name written on their
foreheads. 2 And I heard a voice from
heaven like the sound of many waters
and like the sound of loud thunder;
the voice I heard was like the sound
of harpers playing on their harps, 3 and
they sing a new song before the
throne and before the four living
creatures and before the elders. No
one could learn that song except the
hundred and forty-four thousand who
had been redeemed from the earth.
4 It is these who have not defiled
themselves with women, for they
are chaste;[h] it is these who follow the
Lamb wherever he goes; these have
been redeemed from mankind as first
fruits for God and the Lamb, 5 and in
their mouth no lie was found, for they
are spotless.

6 Then I saw another angel flying
in midheaven, with an eternal gospel
to proclaim to those who dwell on
earth, to every nation and tribe and
tongue and people; 7 and he said with
a loud voice, "Fear God and give him
glory, for the hour of his judgment has
come; and worship him who made
heaven and earth, the sea and the
fountains of water."

8 Another angel, a second, followed, saying, "Fallen, fallen is Babylon the great, she who made all
nations drink the wine of her impure
passion."

9 And another angel, a third, followed them, saying with a loud voice,
"If any one worships the beast and its
image, and receives a mark on his
forehead or on his hand, 10 he also
shall drink the wine of God's wrath,
poured unmixed into the cup of his
anger, and he shall be tormented with
fire and brimstone in the presence of
the holy angels and in the presence of
the Lamb. 11 And the smoke of their
torment goes up for ever and ever; and
they have no rest, day or night, these
worshipers of the beast and its image,
and whoever receives the mark of its
name."

12 Here is a call for the endurance
of the saints, those who keep the commandments of God and the faith of
Jesus.

13 And I heard a voice from heaven
saying, "Write this: Blessed are the
dead who die in the Lord henceforth."
"Blessed indeed," says the Spirit,
"that they may rest from their labors,
for their deeds follow them!"

14 Then I looked, and lo, a white
cloud, and seated on the cloud one
like a son of man, with a golden crown
on his head, and a sharp sickle in his
hand. 15 And another angel came out
of the temple, calling with a loud voice
to him who sat upon the cloud, "Put
in your sickle, and reap, for the hour
to reap has come, for the harvest of
the earth is fully ripe." 16 So he who
sat upon the cloud swung his sickle on
the earth, and the earth was reaped.

17 And another angel came out of
the temple in heaven, and he too had
a sharp sickle. 18 Then another angel
came out from the altar, the angel
who has power over fire, and he called
with a loud voice to him who had the
sharp sickle, "Put in your sickle, and
gather the clusters of the vine of the

[g] Other ancient authorities read *six hundred and sixteen* [h] Greek *virgins*
13.14: Deut 13.1-5. **13.15:** Dan 3.5. **14.1:** Ezek 9.4. **14.8:** Is 21.9. **14.10:** Jer 51 7; Gen 19.24.
14.11: Is 34.10. **14.14:** Dan 7.13. **14.15:** Joel 3 13; Mt 13.30.

earth, for its grapes are ripe." 19 So
the angel swung his sickle on the earth
and gathered the vintage of the earth,
and threw it into the great wine press
of the wrath of God; 20 and the wine
press was trodden outside the city,
and blood flowed from the wine press,
as high as a horse's bridle, for one
thousand six hundred stadia.[i]

15 Then I saw another portent in
heaven, great and wonderful,
seven angels with seven plagues,
which are the last, for with them the
wrath of God is ended.

2 And I saw what appeared to be a
sea of glass mingled with fire, and
those who had conquered the beast
and its image and the number of its
name, standing beside the sea of glass
with harps of God in their hands.
3 And they sing the song of Moses, the
servant of God, and the song of the
Lamb, saying,

"Great and wonderful are thy
deeds,
O Lord God the Almighty!
Just and true are thy ways,
O King of the ages![j]
4 Who shall not fear and glorify thy
name, O Lord?
For thou alone art holy.
All nations shall come and worship
thee,
for thy judgments have been revealed."

5 After this I looked, and the temple of the tent of witness in heaven
was opened, 6 and out of the temple
came the seven angels with the seven
plagues, robed in pure bright linen,
and their breasts girded with golden
girdles. 7 And one of the four living
creatures gave the seven angels seven
golden bowls full of the wrath of God
who lives for ever and ever; 8 and the
temple was filled with smoke from the
glory of God and from his power, and
no one could enter the temple until
the seven plagues of the seven angels
were ended.

16 Then I heard a loud voice from
the temple telling the seven
angels, "Go and pour out on the earth
the seven bowls of the wrath of God."

2 So the first angel went and poured
his bowl on the earth, and foul and
evil sores came upon the men who
bore the mark of the beast and worshiped its image.

3 The second angel poured his bowl
into the sea, and it became like the
blood of a dead man, and every living
thing died that was in the sea.

4 The third angel poured his bowl
into the rivers and the fountains of
water, and they became blood. 5 And
I heard the angel of water say,

"Just art thou in these thy judgments,
thou who art and wast, O Holy One.
6 For men have shed the blood of
saints and prophets,
and thou hast given them blood to
drink.
It is their due!"

7 And I heard the altar cry,

"Yea, Lord God the Almighty,
true and just are thy judgments!"

8 The fourth angel poured his bowl
on the sun, and it was allowed to
scorch men with fire; 9 men were
scorched by the fierce heat, and they
cursed the name of God who had
power over these plagues, and they
did not repent and give him glory.

10 The fifth angel poured his bowl
on the throne of the beast, and its
kingdom was in darkness; men gnawed
their tongues in anguish 11 and cursed
the God of heaven for their pain and
sores, and did not repent of their
deeds.

12 The sixth angel poured his bowl
on the great river Eū·phrā'tēs, and its
water was dried up, to prepare the
way for the kings from the east. 13 And
I saw, issuing from the mouth of the
dragon and from the mouth of the
beast and from the mouth of the false
prophet, three foul spirits like frogs;
14 for they are demonic spirits, performing signs, who go abroad to the
kings of the whole world, to assemble
them for battle on the great day of
God the Almighty. 15 ("Lo, I am coming like a thief! Blessed is he who is
awake, keeping his garments that he
may not go naked and be seen exposed!") 16 And they assembled them

[i] About two hundred miles [j] Other ancient authorities read *the nations*

14.20: Joel 3.13. **15.1**: Lev 26.21. **15.3**: Ex 15.1; Ps 145.17. **15.4**: Jer 10.7; Ps 86.9-10.
15.5: Ex 40.34. **15.8**: 1 Kings 8.10; Is 6.4; Ezek 44.4. **16.1**: Is 66.6; Ps 69.24.
16.2: Ex 9.10-11; Deut 28.35. **16.3-4**: Ex 7.17-21. **16.6**: Ps 79.3. **16.7**: Ps 119.137.
16.10: Ex 10.21. **16.12**: Is 11.15-16. **16.13**: 1 Kings 22.21-23; Ex 8.3. **16.15**: 1 Thess 5.2.
16.16: 2 Kings 9.27.

at the place which is called in Hebrew
Är·mȧ·ged′dȯn.
17 The seventh angel poured his
bowl into the air, and a great voice
came out of the temple, from the
throne, saying, "It is done!" 18And
there were flashes of lightning, loud
noises, peals of thunder, and a great
earthquake such as had never been
since men were on the earth, so great
was that earthquake. 19 The great
city was split into three parts, and the
cities of the nations fell, and God remembered great Babylon, to make
her drain the cup of the fury of his
wrath. 20And every island fled away,
and no mountains were to be found;
21 and great hailstones, heavy as a
hundredweight, dropped on men from
heaven, till men cursed God for the
plague of the hail, so fearful was that
plague.

17 Then one of the seven angels
who had the seven bowls came
and said to me, "Come, I will show
you the judgment of the great harlot
who is seated upon many waters,
2 with whom the kings of the earth
have committed fornication, and with
the wine of whose fornication the
dwellers on earth have become drunk."
3And he carried me away in the Spirit
into a wilderness, and I saw a woman
sitting on a scarlet beast which was
full of blasphemous names, and it had
seven heads and ten horns. 4 The
woman was arrayed in purple and
scarlet, and bedecked with gold and
jewels and pearls, holding in her hand
a golden cup full of abominations and
the impurities of her fornication; 5 and
on her forehead was written a name
of mystery: "Babylon the great,
mother of harlots and of earth's
abominations." 6And I saw the
woman, drunk with the blood of the
saints and the blood of the martyrs of
Jesus.
When I saw her I marveled greatly.
7 But the angel said to me, "Why
marvel? I will tell you the mystery of
the woman, and of the beast with
seven heads and ten horns that carries
her. 8 The beast that you saw was, and
is not, and is to ascend from the bottomless pit and go to perdition; and
the dwellers on earth whose names
have not been written in the book of
life from the foundation of the world,
will marvel to behold the beast, because it was and is not and is to come.
9 This calls for a mind with wisdom:
the seven heads are seven hills on
which the woman is seated; 10 they are
also seven kings five of whom have
fallen, one is, the other has not yet
come, and when he comes he must remain only a little while. 11As for the
beast that was and is not, it is an
eighth but it belongs to the seven, and
it goes to perdition. 12And the ten
horns that you saw are ten kings who
have not yet received royal power,
but they are to receive authority as
kings for one hour, together with the
beast. 13 These are of one mind and
give over their power and authority
to the beast; 14 they will make war on
the Lamb, and the Lamb will conquer
them, for he is Lord of lords and King
of kings, and those with him are
called and chosen and faithful."
15 And he said to me, "The waters
that you saw, where the harlot is
seated, are peoples and multitudes
and nations and tongues. 16And the
ten horns that you saw, they and the
beast will hate the harlot; they will
make her desolate and naked, and
devour her flesh and burn her up with
fire, 17 for God has put it into their
hearts to carry out his purpose by
being of one mind and giving over
their royal power to the beast, until
the words of God shall be fulfilled.
18And the woman that you saw is the
great city which has dominion over
the kings of the earth."
18 After this I saw another angel
coming down from heaven, having great authority; and the earth was
made bright with his splendor. 2And
he called out with a mighty voice,
"Fallen, fallen is Babylon the
great!
It has become a dwelling place of
demons,
a haunt of every foul spirit,
a haunt of every foul and hateful
bird;
3 for all nations have drunk[k] the wine
of her impure passion,
and the kings of the earth have

[k] Other ancient authorities read *fallen by*
16.17: Is 66.6. **16.18**: Ex 19.16; Dan 12.1. **16.21**: Ex 9.23. **17.1**: Jer 51.13.
17.2: Is 23.17; Jer 25.15-16. **17.4**: Jer 51.7. **17.8**: Dan 7.3; Rev 3.5. **17.12**: Dan 7.20-24.
17.14: Dan 2.47. **18.2**: Is 21.9; Jer 50.39. **18.3**: Jer 25.15, 27.

committed fornication with her,
and the merchants of the earth have grown rich with the wealth of her wantonness."
4 Then I heard another voice from
heaven saying,
"Come out of her, my people,
lest you take part in her sins,
lest you share in her plagues;
5 for her sins are heaped high as heaven,
and God has remembered her iniquities.
6 Render to her as she herself has rendered,
and repay her double for her deeds;
mix a double draught for her in the cup she mixed.
7 As she glorified herself and played the wanton,
so give her a like measure of torment and mourning.
Since in her heart she says, 'A queen I sit,
I am no widow, mourning I shall never see,'
8 so shall her plagues come in a single day,
pestilence and mourning and famine,
and she shall be burned with fire;
for mighty is the Lord God who judges her."
9 And the kings of the earth, who
committed fornication and were wanton with her, will weep and wail over
her when they see the smoke of her
burning; 10 they will stand far off, in
fear of her torment, and say,
"Alas! alas! thou great city,
thou mighty city, Babylon!
In one hour has thy judgment come."
11 And the merchants of the earth
weep and mourn for her, since no one
buys their cargo any more, 12 cargo of
gold, silver, jewels and pearls, fine
linen, purple, silk and scarlet, all kinds
of scented wood, all articles of ivory,
all articles of costly wood, bronze, iron
and marble, 13 cinnamon, spice, incense, myrrh, frankincense, wine, oil,
fine flour and wheat, cattle and sheep,
horses and chariots, and slaves, that
is, human souls.
14 "The fruit for which thy soul longed has gone from thee,
and all thy dainties and thy splendor are lost to thee, never to be found again!"
15 The merchants of these wares, who
gained wealth from her, will stand far
off, in fear of her torment, weeping
and mourning aloud,
16 "Alas, alas, for the great city
that was clothed in fine linen, in purple and scarlet,
bedecked with gold, with jewels, and with pearls!
17 In one hour all this wealth has been laid waste."
And all shipmasters and seafaring
men, sailors and all whose trade is on
the sea, stood far off 18 and cried out
as they saw the smoke of her burning,
"What city was like the great city?"
19 And they threw dust on their heads,
as they wept and mourned, crying out,
"Alas, alas, for the great city
where all who had ships at sea grew rich by her wealth!
In one hour she has been laid waste.
20 Rejoice over her, O heaven,
O saints and apostles and prophets,
for God has given judgment for you against her!"
21 Then a mighty angel took up a
stone like a great millstone and threw
it into the sea, saying,
"So shall Babylon the great city be thrown down with violence,
and shall be found no more;
22 and the sound of harpers and minstrels, of flute players and trumpeters,
shall be heard in thee no more;
and a craftsman of any craft
shall be found in thee no more;
and the sound of the millstone
shall be heard in thee no more;
23 and the light of a lamp
shall shine in thee no more;
and the voice of bridegroom and bride
shall be heard in thee no more;
for thy merchants were the great men of the earth,
and all nations were deceived by thy sorcery.
24 And in her was found the blood of prophets and of saints,

18.4: Is 48.20; Jer 50.8. **18.5:** Jer 51.9. **18.6:** Ps 137.8. **18.7:** Is 47.8-9. **18.9:** Ezek 26.16-17.
18.11: Ezek 27.36. **18.12:** Ezek 27.12-13, 22. **18.15:** Ezek 27.36, 31.
18.17: Is 23.14; Ezek 27.26-30. **18.19:** Ezek 27.30-34. **18.20:** Is 44.23; Jer 51.48.
18.21: Jer 51.63; Ezek 26.21. **18.22:** Is 24.8; Ezek 26.13. **18.23:** Jer 25.10.
18.24: Jer 51.49.

and of all who have been slain on
earth."

19 After this I heard what seemed
to be the mighty voice of a great
multitude in heaven, crying,
"Hallelujah! Salvation and glory
and power belong to our God,
2 for his judgments are true and
just;
he has judged the great harlot who
corrupted the earth with her
fornication,
and he has avenged on her the blood
of his servants."
3 Once more they cried,
"Hallelujah! The smoke from her
goes up for ever and ever."
4 And the twenty-four elders and the
four living creatures fell down and
worshiped God who is seated on the
throne, saying, "Amen. Hallelujah!"
5 And from the throne came a voice
crying,
"Praise our God, all you his servants,
you who fear him, small and great."
6 Then I heard what seemed to be the
voice of a great multitude, like the
sound of many waters and like the
sound of mighty thunderpeals, crying,
"Hallelujah! For the Lord our God
the Almighty reigns.
7 Let us rejoice and exult and give
him the glory,
for the marriage of the Lamb has
come,
and his Bride has made herself
ready;
8 it was granted her to be clothed with
fine linen, bright and pure"—
for the fine linen is the righteous deeds
of the saints.
9 And the angel said[l] to me, "Write
this: Blessed are those who are invited
to the marriage supper of the Lamb."
And he said to me, "These are true
words of God." 10 Then I fell down at
his feet to worship him, but he said to
me, "You must not do that! I am a
fellow servant with you and your
brethren who hold the testimony of
Jesus. Worship God." For the testimony of Jesus is the spirit of prophecy.
11 Then I saw heaven opened, and
behold, a white horse! He who sat
upon it is called Faithful and True,
and in righteousness he judges and
makes war. 12 His eyes are like a flame
of fire, and on his head are many diadems; and he has a name inscribed
which no one knows but himself.
13 He is clad in a robe dipped in[m]
blood, and the name by which he is
called is The Word of God. 14 And the
armies of heaven, arrayed in fine linen,
white and pure, followed him on white
horses. 15 From his mouth issues a
sharp sword with which to smite the
nations, and he will rule them with a
rod of iron; he will tread the wine press
of the fury of the wrath of God the
Almighty. 16 On his robe and on his
thigh he has a name inscribed, King of
kings and Lord of lords.
17 Then I saw an angel standing in
the sun, and with a loud voice he
called to all the birds that fly in midheaven, "Come, gather for the great
supper of God, 18 to eat the flesh of
kings, the flesh of captains, the flesh
of mighty men, the flesh of horses and
their riders, and the flesh of all men,
both free and slave, both small and
great." 19 And I saw the beast and the
kings of the earth with their armies
gathered to make war against him who
sits upon the horse and against his
army. 20 And the beast was captured,
and with it the false prophet who in
its presence had worked the signs by
which he deceived those who had
received the mark of the beast and
those who worshiped its image. These
two were thrown alive into the lake of
fire that burns with brimstone. 21 And
the rest were slain by the sword of him
who sits upon the horse, the sword
that issues from his mouth; and all the
birds were gorged with their flesh.

20 Then I saw an angel coming
down from heaven, holding in
his hand the key of the bottomless pit
and a great chain. 2 And he seized the
dragon, that ancient serpent, who is
the Devil and Satan, and bound him
for a thousand years, 3 and threw him
into the pit, and shut it and sealed it
over him, that he should deceive the
nations no more, till the thousand
years were ended. After that he must
be loosed for a little while.
4 Then I saw thrones, and seated
on them were those to whom judg-

[l] Greek *he said* [m] Other ancient authorities read *sprinkled with*
19.2: Deut 32.43. **19.3:** Is 34.10. **19.5:** Ps 115.13. **19.7:** Ps 118.24. **19.11:** Ezek 1.1.
19.12: Dan 10.6. **19.15:** Ps 2.9. **19.16:** Deut 10.17; Dan 2.47. **19.17:** Ezek 39.4, 17-20.
20.4: Dan 7.9, 22, 27.

ment was committed. Also I saw the
souls of those who had been beheaded
for their testimony to Jesus and for
the word of God, and who had not
worshiped the beast or its image and
had not received its mark on their
foreheads or their hands. They came
to life, and reigned with Christ a thousand years. 5 The rest of the dead did
not come to life until the thousand
years were ended. This is the first
resurrection. 6 Blessed and holy is he
who shares in the first resurrection!
Over such the second death has no
power, but they shall be priests of
God and of Christ, and they shall
reign with him a thousand years.
7 And when the thousand years are
ended, Satan will be loosed from his
prison 8 and will come out to deceive
the nations which are at the four
corners of the earth, that is, Gog and
Mā'gog, to gather them for battle;
their number is like the sand of the
sea. 9 And they marched up over the
broad earth and surrounded the
camp of the saints and the beloved
city; but fire came down from heaven[n]
and consumed them, 10 and the devil
who had deceived them was thrown
into the lake of fire and brimstone
where the beast and the false prophet
were, and they will be tormented day
and night for ever and ever.
11 Then I saw a great white throne
and him who sat upon it; from his
presence earth and sky fled away, and
no place was found for them. 12 And I
saw the dead, great and small, standing before the throne, and books were
opened. Also another book was
opened, which is the book of life. And
the dead were judged by what was
written in the books, by what they
had done. 13 And the sea gave up the
dead in it, Death and Hades gave up
the dead in them, and all were judged
by what they had done. 14 Then
Death and Hades were thrown into
the lake of fire. This is the second
death, the lake of fire; 15 and if any
one's name was not found written in
the book of life, he was thrown into
the lake of fire.

21 Then I saw a new heaven and a
new earth; for the first heaven
and the first earth had passed away,
and the sea was no more. 2 And I saw
the holy city, new Jerusalem, coming
down out of heaven from God, prepared as a bride adorned for her husband; 3 and I heard a great voice from
the throne saying, "Behold, the dwelling of God is with men. He will dwell
with them, and they shall be his people,[o] and God himself will be with
them;[p] 4 he will wipe away every tear
from their eyes, and death shall be no
more, neither shall there be mourning
nor crying nor pain any more, for the
former things have passed away."
5 And he who sat upon the throne
said, "Behold, I make all things new."
Also he said, "Write this, for these
words are trustworthy and true."
6 And he said to me, "It is done! I am
the Alpha and the Omega, the beginning and the end. To the thirsty I will
give water without price from the
fountain of the water of life. 7 He who
conquers shall have this heritage, and
I will be his God and he shall be my
son. 8 But as for the cowardly, the
faithless, the polluted, as for murderers, fornicators, sorcerers, idolaters,
and all liars, their lot shall be in the
lake that burns with fire and brimstone, which is the second death."
9 Then came one of the seven angels
who had the seven bowls full of the
seven last plagues, and spoke to me,
saying, "Come, I will show you the
Bride, the wife of the Lamb." 10 And
in the Spirit he carried me away to a
great, high mountain, and showed me
the holy city Jerusalem coming down
out of heaven from God, 11 having the
glory of God, its radiance like a most
rare jewel, like a jasper, clear as
crystal. 12 It had a great, high wall,
with twelve gates, and at the gates
twelve angels, and on the gates the
names of the twelve tribes of the sons
of Israel were inscribed; 13 on the east
three gates, on the north three gates,
on the south three gates, and on the
west three gates. 14 And the wall of the
city had twelve foundations, and on

[n] Other ancient authorities read *from God, out of heaven,* or *out of heaven from God*
[o] Other ancient authorities read *peoples* [p] Other ancient authorities add *and be their God*

20.8: Ezek 38.2, 9, 15. **20.9:** 2 Kings 1.10-12. **20.11-12:** Dan 7.9-10.
20.15: Rev 3.5. **21.1:** Is 66.22. **21.2:** Rev 3.12. **21.3:** Ezek 37.27.
21.4: Is 25.8; 35.10. **21.5:** Is 43.19. **21.6:** Is 55.1. **21.7:** Ps 89.27-28.
21.8: Is 30.33. **21.10:** Ezek 40.2.
21.12: Ezek 48.30-35; Ex 28.21.

them the twelve names of the twelve
apostles of the Lamb.

15 And he who talked to me had a
measuring rod of gold to measure the
city and its gates and walls. 16 The
city lies foursquare, its length the
same as its breadth; and he measured the city with his rod, twelve
thousand stadia;[q] its length and
breadth and height are equal. 17 He
also measured its wall, a hundred and
forty-four cubits by a man's measure,
that is, an angel's. 18 The wall was
built of jasper, while the city was
pure gold, clear as glass. 19 The foundations of the wall of the city were
adorned with every jewel; the first
was jasper, the second sapphire, the
third agate, the fourth emerald,
20 the fifth onyx, the sixth carnelian,
the seventh chrysolite, the eighth
beryl, the ninth topaz, the tenth
chrysoprase, the eleventh jacinth, the
twelfth amethyst. 21 And the twelve
gates were twelve pearls, each of the
gates made of a single pearl, and the
street of the city was pure gold, trans-
parent as glass.

22 And I saw no temple in the city,
for its temple is the Lord God the
Almighty and the Lamb. 23 And the
city has no need of sun or moon to
shine upon it, for the glory of God is
its light, and its lamp is the Lamb.
24 By its light shall the nations walk;
and the kings of the earth shall bring
their glory into it, 25 and its gates shall
never be shut by day—and there shall
be no night there; 26 they shall bring
into it the glory and the honor of the
nations. 27 But nothing unclean shall
enter it, nor any one who practices
abomination or falsehood, but only
those who are written in the Lamb's
book of life.

22 Then he showed me the river
of the water of life, bright as
crystal, flowing from the throne of
God and of the Lamb 2 through the
middle of the street of the city; also,
on either side of the river, the tree of
life[r] with its twelve kinds of fruit,
yielding its fruit each month; and the
leaves of the tree were for the healing
of the nations. 3 There shall no more
be anything accursed, but the throne
of God and of the Lamb shall be in it,
and his servants shall worship him;
4 they shall see his face, and his name
shall be on their foreheads. 5 And
night shall be no more; they need no
light of lamp or sun, for the Lord God
will be their light, and they shall
reign for ever and ever.

6 And he said to me, "These words
are trustworthy and true. And the
Lord, the God of the spirits of the
prophets, has sent his angel to show
his servants what must soon take
place. 7 And behold, I am coming
soon."

Blessed is he who keeps the words
of the prophecy of this book.

8 I John am he who heard and saw
these things. And when I heard and
saw them, I fell down to worship at
the feet of the angel who showed them
to me; 9 but he said to me, "You must
not do that! I am a fellow servant
with you and your brethren the
prophets, and with those who keep
the words of this book. Worship God."

10 And he said to me, "Do not seal
up the words of the prophecy of this
book, for the time is near. 11 Let the
evildoer still do evil, and the filthy
still be filthy, and the righteous still
do right, and the holy still be holy."

12 "Behold, I am coming soon,
bringing my recompense, to repay
every one for what he has done. 13 I
am the Alpha and the Omega, the
first and the last, the beginning and
the end."

14 Blessed are those who wash their
robes,[s] that they may have the right
to the tree of life and that they may
enter the city by the gates. 15 Outside
are the dogs and sorcerers and fornicators and murderers and idolaters, and
every one who loves and practices
falsehood.

16 "I Jesus have sent my angel to
you with this testimony for the
churches. I am the root and the offspring of David, the bright morning
star."

17 The Spirit and the Bride say,
"Come." And let him who hears say,

[q] About fifteen hundred miles

[r] Or *the Lamb. In the midst of the street of the city, and on either side of the river, was the tree of life,* etc.

[s] Other ancient authorities read *do his commandments*

21.15: Ezek 40.5. **21.19:** Is 54.11-12. **21.23:** Is 24.23; 60.1, 19. **21.25:** Is 60.11.
21.27: Is 52.1; Rev 3.5. **22.2:** Gen 2.9. **22.3:** Zech 14.11. **22.4:** Ps 17.15. **22.11:** Dan 12.10.
22.12: Is 40.1; Jer 17.10. **22.13:** Is 44.6; 48.12. **22.14:** Gen 2.9; 3.22. **22.16:** Is 11.1, 10.
22.17: Is 55.1.

"Come." And let him who is thirsty
come, let him who desires take the
water of life without price.
18 I warn every one who hears the
words of the prophecy of this book: if
any one adds to them, God will add
to him the plagues described in this
book, 19 and if any one takes away
from the words of the book of this
prophecy, God will take away his
share in the tree of life and in the
holy city, which are described in this
book.
20 He who testifies to these things
says, "Surely I am coming soon."
Amen. Come, Lord Jesus!
21 The grace of the Lord Jesus be
with all the saints.[t] Amen.

[t] Other ancient authorities omit *all;* others omit *the saints*
22.21: 2 Thess 3.18.

A Summary
Of The Books Of The Bible

BRIEF CHRONOLOGICAL OUTLINE OF NEW TESTAMENT HISTORY

A SUMMARY OF THE BOOKS OF THE BIBLE

THE OLD TESTAMENT

GENESIS—Genesis, a Greek word meaning "a beginning or origin," is the title given to the first book of the Bible, which tells of the creation of the earth and of mankind. This Book relates the early history of Israel from the creation until the death of Joseph, including accounts of the Flood and the dispersion of Noah and his descendants throughout the world. *Genesis* also contains the history of the great patriarchs, Abraham, Isaac, and Jacob, and the story of Joseph in Egypt.

EXODUS—The second book of the Bible deals with the departure, or *exodus*, of the Israelites from Egypt under the leadership of Moses. Included here are descriptions of the Israelites' oppression at the hands of the Egyptian kings, Moses' dealings with the Pharaoh, the overthrow of the Egyptians, and an account of the Israelites' long journey to Sinai. During their sojourn there they received the Ten Commandments from Moses, who had been given them by God. The Book concludes with the erection of the Tabernacle.

LEVITICUS—This is the book of the Levites, the members of the tribe of Levi who were chosen to assist the Jewish priests. *Leviticus* is concerned mostly with the laws and rules of worship the Levites were expected to follow. It also contains rules governing the personal and social life of the people.

NUMBERS—The title *Numbers* is a translation of the name of the Greek version, so called because it contains accounts of two censuses, or *numberings*, of the Hebrews, taken after their departure from Egypt. The history of the peoples' wanderings from Egypt to the Promised Land, begun in *Exodus*, is continued here. This Book also tells of the appointment of Joshua as Moses' successor.

DEUTERONOMY—*Deuteronomy* means "the second law"; in this Book the law of Moses is set down for the second time. In *Leviticus* it was written for the priests; here, in *Deuteronomy*, it is intended for the instruction of the ordinary people. *Deuteronomy* continues the history told in the closing chapters of *Numbers;* however, it is made up mostly of addresses given by Moses to his people.

These first five books of the Old Testament are called the Pentateuch, a Greek word meaning "a book of five volumes." According to Jewish tradition these books are ascribed to Moses.

JOSHUA—Here we have the history of the Israelites' conquest of Canaan, the Promised Land. This Book tells how Joshua, Moses' successor, led the people across the river Jordan, captured the city of Jericho, drove out the Canaanites, and divided their land among the twelve tribes of Israel.

JUDGES—After the death of Joshua, Israel was under the control of a series of leaders who, because they settled disputes, were called judges. This Book tells of many of these leaders, some of whom were great men of supreme courage and wisdom, who, in times of crisis, came forward to deliver the people from evil and suffering.

The *Book of Judges* covers the history of Israel from the time of Joshua's death until the death of Samson.

RUTH—This Book is the story of Ruth of Moab, a widow who left her own people to accompany Naomi, her mother-in-law, back to her homeland in Israel. There Ruth worked in the fields of Boaz, whom she later married. Most authorities agree that the historical significance of this Book lies in its establishment of the ancestry of David, who is shown to be the son of Jesse, who was, in turn, the grandson of Ruth and Boaz.

SAMUEL, 1 and 2—The two books of *Samuel* continue the history of Israel from the times written of in *Judges* until the death of David. The Books were originally one book and are named after Samuel because he is the most prominent figure in the opening chapters.

The first Book deals with the history of Samuel during his judgeship and the history of Saul from his accession as king until his death.

The second Book of Samuel is concerned mostly with the reign of David.

KINGS, 1 and 2—The history discussed in the first and second books of *Samuel* is carried on in the books of *Kings*. The first Book deals principally with the reign of Solomon, David's son, and the building of the first Temple. The latter part of the first Book and the first part of the second relate the history of Israel and, especially, Judah during the reigns of many kings who succeeded Solomon; particular emphasis is placed on the work of the prophets Elijah and Elisha. *Kings* concludes with an account of the destruction of Israel by invading Babylonian armies and the beginning of the Israelites' long, bitter exile in Babylonia.

CHRONICLES, 1 and 2—These two Books supplement and continue the history of the period dealt with in the two books of *Samuel* and the two books of *Kings*. The first Book contains genealogical lists outlining the ancestry of David; it also provides an account of the period of David's reign. The second Book deals with the reign of Solomon and the history of Judah until the time of the Babylonian captivity.

EZRA—The Books of *Ezra* and *Nehemiah* tell of the Jews' return to Jerusalem after the Babylonian exile. The *Book of Ezra* deals mainly with the rebuilding of the Temple, a task carried on in the face of many dangers and difficulties. Ezra, a priest and scribe, encouraged the people during those difficult times and began teaching them how they were to worship God and follow His law after the Temple was rebuilt.

NEHEMIAH—Nehemiah, one of the Jewish exiles, returned to Jerusalem in order to rally the people to rebuild the city's walls. This Book relates how Nehemiah achieved this goal despite great hostility and how, later, he cleansed the people of everything foreign. *Nehemiah* also describes the efforts of Ezra to restore religion to the people.

ESTHER—This narrative recounts how Esther, a Jewish maiden, became queen of Ahasuerus, a Persian king, and was instrumental in rescuing the Jews in Persia from the destruction prepared for them by Haman, the king's minister.

JOB—In the form of a long poem, the *Book of Job* is the account of a wealthy man who loses his wealth and his children, and is afflicted with disease. The bulk of the Book is a discussion between him and his friends about why he has suffered. Job is rebuked by God for questioning His ways, which are beyond the power of man to understand. Job then repents and his wealth is restored twofold.

PSALMS—*Psalms* consists of 150 poems with a varied subject matter. Some were set to music and meant to be sung as part of religious ceremonies. Other psalms are prayers, lamentations, expressions of faith or joy, pleas for help, or songs of praise or gratitude. Some contain historical or national material; others are of a didactic nature, dealing with matters of religion or morality.

PROVERBS—The authorship of this Book is attributed to Solomon by some authorities. Others say, however, that Solomon only collected the proverbs. In any case, this is a collection of wise sayings concerning life and behavior expressed in maxims and intended for the moral instruction and guidance of the people of Israel.

ECCLESIASTES—The words of the author, thought by some to have been Solomon, are generally of a discouraging nature. He laments over the impossibility of achieving real happiness through material means. He points out that the end for the wise and the foolish is the same and that riches bring no satisfaction. He concludes that life in general has no meaning and that man should enjoy such pleasures as God provides for him during his short stay on earth. The author demonstrates again and again the vanity of all things, particularly all actions of men.

SONG OF SOLOMON—This Book is a series of poems about two lovers. Opinions differ widely as to how this Book should be interpreted. Some consider the lover to represent God and the maiden to represent the people of Israel. Others see the lover as symbolic of Christ and the maiden as the Church. Still others regard this Book simply as a love story in which true and genuine affection triumphs over the advantages of wealth and position. The *Song* is traditionally supposed to have been composed by Solomon.

ISAIAH—Isaiah is called the greatest of the Hebrew prophets. In this Book, the first of the prophetical Books, are his many prophecies, including those foretelling the Babylonian captivity and how Israel would benefit from it, the failure of Assyrian armies to capture Jerusalem, and the downfall of Babylon. Furthermore, he saw beyond these events to the redemption of the Israelites and their return to Israel from exile. One other prophecy was later interpreted by Matthew as having foretold the virgin birth of Jesus.

JEREMIAH—The Lord came to Jeremiah and called upon him to become a prophet. This Book is a collection of God's messages and warnings carried by Jeremiah to the people of Israel, predicting the conquest and ruin of their country at the hands of the Babylonians. It gives considerable attention to the personal feelings of Jeremiah, particularly the sadness and discouragement he felt when his warnings went unheeded. He felt forsaken even by the Lord because of the long delay in the fulfillment of his prophecies. Although his predictions are chiefly predictions of impending doom, he does express hope for the renewal of God's covenant with the Jews and for their restoration as God's chosen people.

LAMENTATIONS—The five poems that constitute this Book, called *The Lamentations of Jeremiah*, are concerned with the destruction of Jerusalem and the great suffering of the people following that event. The Book includes the confession of the people, based on the realization that disaster had befallen them because of their sins.

Jeremiah is believed by many authorities to have been the author of this Book.

EZEKIEL—The prophet Ezekiel was one of those carried in captivity to Babylonia. His prophecies, made both before and after the destruction of Jerusalem, deal with the impending downfall of Jerusalem, the foreign nations that rejoiced at its fall, and the restoration of Israel. His messages are delivered as threats, arguments, prophecies, and, most strikingly, as descriptions of visions which had come to him.

DANIEL—Daniel, a prophet, lived during the time of the Babylonian conquest. The first part of this Book is mainly historical, beginning with the capture of Daniel by Nebuchadnezzar. Episodes include those of Daniel's being thrown into the den of lions, Nebuchadnezzar's dream and its interpretation by Daniel, Daniel's three friends who were thrown into the fiery furnace, and Belshazzer's feast and his seeing the handwriting on the wall.

The last part of the Book contains descriptions of Daniel's visions—visions of promise and encouragement for the Jewish people.

HOSEA—The *Book of Hosea* is the first of twelve bearing the name of those who are often called the minor prophets. Hosea was a native of Israel, toward which most of his prophecies are directed. He warns the Israelites of their infidelity to God; he rebukes them for their unfaithfulness and for their sins;

he threatens them with punishment if they will not renounce their evil ways. But Hosea does speak of God's never-failing love for the people of Israel and His willingness to forgive those who seek forgiveness.

JOEL—Probably a Judaean prophet, Joel set forth his lamentations over the devastation of his land by a plague of locusts and then a drought. Joel tells his people they are being punished for their sins; he exhorts them to repent, promising that God will pour forth His goodness upon them if they do so.

AMOS—Although he claimed to be no prophet, Amos carried the word of God to the people of Israel. He prophesies that God's judgment will fall on Damascus, Tyre, Edom, Ammon, and Judah, but will fall most heavily on Israel, which, in spite of all God's gifts, had still done evil. The Book concludes with a promise that the kingdom of God shall again be restored.

OBADIAH—The "vision" of Obadiah constitutes the shortest of the Old Testament prophecies. It is concerned with the Edomites, long the enemies and tormentors of Israel. When Edom is destroyed, Obadiah looks upon its downfall as no accident but, rather, the judgment of God upon a proud and cruel people.

JONAH—Jonah, a Hebrew prophet, was commanded by God to preach to the heathen and hostile city of Nineveh. Jonah disobeyed this command and fled in a ship, but, as punishment, he was overtaken by a storm, thrown into the sea, and swallowed by a great fish. The prophet prayed and was vomited out upon dry land. He then obeyed God's command and preached at Nineveh, and the people of Nineveh repented.

MICAH—The sermons, prophecies, and exhortations of Micah form the substance of this Book. He urges the people to repent and to relinquish their wicked ways, threatening them with punishment if they do not. He concludes by warning them that, because of their unfaithfulness, they do not deserve to be saved. In one of his prophecies some Biblical authorities see a foretelling of the coming of Jesus.

NAHUM—Nahum's vision deals exclusively with the impending and, as it seems to him, inevitable doom of Nineveh. He points out that no nation as evil as Nineveh can withstand the judgment of God.

HABAKKUK—The Chaldean invasion of Judah is the basic theme of Habakkuk's prophecy. The Book is constructed in the form of a dialogue between Habakkuk and God. It contains the prophet's complaints that, although his people deserve to be punished, the punishment should not be administered by the wicked Chaldeans. God replies that His judgment will fall on all the wicked and that only the righteous will survive.

ZEPHANIAH—Zephaniah, born into an age of corruption following the reigns of several wicked kings, is certain that a great day of wrath will fall upon the nations of the earth, and especially on Judah and Jerusalem.

He describes this impending destruction graphically, and he calls upon the people to repent, turn sincerely to the Lord, and thus escape the doom that threatens them.

HAGGAI—This Book consists of four addresses delivered by the prophet Haggai and a description of their effect on the people. In these addresses Haggai rebukes the Jews for their failure to rebuild the Temple. He describes the glory of the future Temple and promises them God's blessings if they will continue their work.

ZECHARIAH—Zechariah, along with Haggai, encouraged the Jews to rebuild the Temple. However, Haggai had used reproofs, whereas Zechariah inspires the people with messages that have come to him in the form of visions. He promises them the destruction of their enemies and the enjoyment of peace and prosperity if they will rebuild God's Temple. Another of

Zechariah's prophecies, according to many authorities, foretells the coming of Jesus.

MALACHI—The last Book of the Old Testament was written after the Babylonian captivity and the reconstruction of the Temple. The prophet Malachi attacks the wickedness of the people, which he finds especially reprehensible in view of the fact that they are once again able to worship God as their people had before the Exile. He urges them to serve God with greater sincerity and obey the laws of Moses more strictly. The Book ends with the prediction that God will send a messenger to prepare His way.

THE NEW TESTAMENT

MATTHEW—The *Gospel of Matthew*, although perhaps not written first, is placed first probably because it contains the closest ties with the Old Testament. Through frequent quotations from the Old Testament, Matthew attempts to show that the coming of Jesus was the fulfillment of Old Testament prophecy and that He was, therefore, the long-awaited Savior of the Jews.

The four Gospels all deal with the life of Jesus, His teachings, and His crucifixion and resurrection. They differ, however, in approach and aspect and even in the episodes and teachings they record. The *Gospel of Matthew* is particularly noted for the Sermon on the Mount, which appears only here, and for the most widely known account of Jesus' last days in Jerusalem and His crucifixion.

MARK—According to tradition, much of the material used by Mark was gleaned from the preachings of Peter, one of Jesus' original disciples. It is thought that Matthew and Luke, whose Gospels seem to have been written later, used the writings of Mark as a basis from which they prepared their own versions of the story of Jesus.

The *Gospel of Mark* is concerned mostly with the actions and influences of Jesus and the ways in which He used His divine power, especially in vanquishing the powers of evil by healing demoniacs. In thus laying his emphasis on the representation of Jesus as a spiritual conqueror, Mark reports nothing of His birth or youth.

LUKE—Luke apparently worked from the *Gospel of Mark*, but went on to compile a much fuller account of Jesus' life than is found in any of the other Gospels, especially as far as detail and content are concerned. For instance, only in *Luke* is there an account of the birth of John the Baptist, a record of Mary's song of thankfulness (*The Magnificat*), the tale of the shepherds and the song of the angels at the birth of Jesus, the incident of Jesus at the Temple questioning the learned men, and the description of the visit to the house of the hated tax collector. Furthermore, *Luke* treats Jesus' birth and early boyhood with much greater detail than the other Gospels.

Throughout this Book, Luke seems to see Jesus as the Savior of all men and not just as the fulfillment of Old Testament prophecy.

JOHN—The *Gospel of John*, unlike the other Gospels, is not primarily given over to the recording of historical data but rather is concerned with emphasizing the divine nature of Jesus and interpreting the purpose of His appearance on earth. The other Gospels focus attention on the birth, infancy, baptism, temptation, transfiguration, and actual deeds of Jesus; the fourth Gospel concentrates on telling who Jesus was, what He stood for, and what He would do for those who loved Him and believed in Him.

It is thought that no other Book has done more than the *Gospel of John* to establish the teachings of Jesus as a universal religion, namely Christianity.

ACTS—*The Acts of the Apostles*, the full name of this Book, traces the travels and records the early teachings of the disciples after the death and resurrection of Jesus. *Acts* is particularly devoted to the journeys and teachings of Paul, who, more than any other person, is responsible for the spread of Christianity. The beginnings and the early triumphant progress of the Christian Church are set down in this Book, the author of which is almost certainly Luke, who also wrote the third Gospel.

ROMANS—While Paul was in Corinth, he wrote this Letter to the Christians in Rome in anticipation of his intended visit. The letter is rather like a treatise in which Paul expounds his faith in God and points out that Christianity is a divine plan intended to produce righteousness in man.

Paul explains to the Christians that Jesus died for them while they were still sinners, and he outlines how they should behave in the new life that He has brought them.

CORINTHIANS, 1 and 2—Paul wrote the first of the two Letters to the Christians in Corinth when he heard of the monstrous wickedness in which they were indulging. He rebukes them for their evil ways, points out how they have sinned, and exhorts them to relinquish their wicked habits and conform to the standards of unselfishness and purity taught by Christ. He also answers the many questions they have asked.

In his second Letter Paul thanks the Christians for listening to his entreaties and for trying to live the life Jesus expected of His followers. Answering an earlier complaint about the difficulties of leading a Christian life, Paul cites himself as an example of one who had suffered a great deal in preaching the gospel of Christ. But he explains how one can enrich his soul by following and teaching others to follow Jesus.

GALATIANS—Prior to the writing of this Letter Paul had been in Galatia and had apparently been detained there because of illness. During his long stay Paul converted the Galatians to Christianity. But after Paul's departure, false teachers arrived and denounced Paul as a mere convert. These teachers warned the Galatians that if they wished to be loyal Christians they must live by the Mosaic law. In answer to these arguments Paul wrote this Letter. In it he makes it clear that the Mosaic law, although handed down by God, is not to be strictly binding on Christians because it has been superseded by faith in Jesus. Paul appeals to the Galatians to trust in the love and forgiveness of God as Jesus had taught.

EPHESIANS—Paul founded a church at Ephesus, and later he wrote this Letter to the Christians of that church, expounding his conception of the ideal church and outlining what he thinks should be its accomplishments. He explains that it is the duty of all Christians to see that this dream of the ideal church is realized. He points out that this can be achieved only through Christian unity, that is, unity among Christians of the community and the world, but, most importantly, unity among members of a Christian household. By means of this unity and the strength of a unified church, Christians will be able to withstand the wickedness that will confront them everywhere.

PHILIPPIANS—While he was in prison, Paul wrote this Letter, as well as the letter to the Ephesians. Paul had visited Philippi in the course of his travels (as described in *Acts*), and this letter is one of gratitude to the Philippians who had shown him so much kindness during his stay. Paul does caution the Philippians against those who are enemies of the gospel, and he concludes by expressing hope that they will continue their Christian practices.

COLOSSIANS—Although there is no record of his ever having been in Colossae, Paul wrote this Letter to the Christians there asserting his intense interest in them. He warns them against the faulty doctrines and philosophies preached by those who were trying to shake their faith in Jesus. He tells the Colossians of the danger of believing that salvation can be gained by laws or rituals or by any means other than faith in God. Paul insists that Christ is the one mediator between God and man and that only through Him can man be saved.

Paul goes on to state that they will become a new people when they abandon their sinful ways and turn to a life of Christian unity and fellowship.

THESSALONIANS, I and 2—The first of these two Letters to the Christians at Thessalonica was written by Paul not long after he had preached there. In this Letter he expresses his thanks for the many kindnesses shown him. He reminds the Thessalonians of the richness of their new life now that they have become Christians, and he advises them what to do in order to make this life endure.

Paul learned that the Christians of Thessalonica were being disturbed by rumors of the early return of Christ to earth. He hastened to write a second letter to them warning them that the coming of Jesus is not imminent and will not take place until after a period of testing in which the true believers will be separated from the unrighteous. He admonishes some of them for stopping their work and living in idleness and advises all of them that the way to be ready for the Lord is to work quietly and hard with patience and faith.

TIMOTHY, I and 2—Timothy was a friend of Paul's who traveled with him on several missionary journeys. These two Letters to Timothy are personal letters as contrasted with Paul's previous Letters, which have been directed to the congregations of various Christian churches.

In his first Letter Paul discusses the false beliefs that were being taught in the churches. In order to halt this trend, he suggests that the ministers and other church officers be chosen with particular care and then he outlines just what they ought to teach.

Paul looks to Timothy as his successor, so his second Letter contains instructions to Timothy detailing how he, as a minister, should carry on the work of bringing the word of God to the people. He advises Timothy that his task will not be an easy one and that he will have to remain strong if he is to achieve success in leading the people to salvation.

TITUS—Titus, like Timothy, was a close and trusted friend of Paul. Paul's object in writing him this Letter seems to have been to instruct him in the ways of carrying on the work Paul felt he had left incomplete.

The work immediately at hand was the organization of a church at Crete. Paul explains how this should be done and how the needs of the church are to be fulfilled in spite of certain opposition. The letter also offers personal advice to Titus stressing the sobriety of conduct and religion that he should expect and seek to instill in all men.

PHILEMON—This Letter from Paul to Philemon concerns Philemon's slave Onesimus, who had fled because of a crime he had committed against his master. Onesimus had met Paul, who converted him and became deeply attached to him. Paul sent Onesimus back with this letter beseeching Philemon to receive him no longer as a slave but as a beloved brother.

HEBREWS—Because the Hebrews' religion has its foundation in the Old Testament, it is thought that they, in particular, should derive encouragement from this Letter. The unknown author shows his audience that, while God had, in earlier times, spoken through the prophets and had handed down his law through Moses, He was now speaking to them in a new and more wonderful way, through Jesus, His Son. And because Jesus is superior to the prophets, to Moses, and even to the angels it is possible for everyone to become closer to God by believing in Jesus and following His teachings.

The author goes on to show the Christians that they can face life with a new courage and gladness that should rise from the confidence that God will forgive their sins. In return for this confidence they must approach God with a greater faith.

Finally, the author sets down a list of duties which all Christians are to perform in offering acceptable worship to God.

JAMES—According to tradition, James, the brother of Jesus, wrote this Letter. He seems to have written it for Christians in general rather than to a particular church or people as Paul did.

James is concerned with giving advice on Christian behavior. He counsels against faultfinding, swearing, impatience, jealousy, selfish ambition, and arrogance. He advises them on worship, sickness, and prayer, and he encourages them to show their faith in God by means of action rather than words.

PETER, 1 and 2—One of the twelve apostles of Jesus, Peter wrote the first of his two Letters to a group of exiles who were being cruelly mistreated. He tells them that they must endure this persecution, and he reminds them that Jesus too had suffered. As Christ withstood his tormentors through patience and holiness, they too can stand up before danger and trouble in order to receive, as Jesus did, glory from God. They must love and help one another, work and pray together, and the strength of God through Jesus will be with them.

The second Letter has to do with conditions in the church when false teachers were causing keen disappointment among the people by encouraging them to believe that it was futile to hope for better things since Jesus had not returned as they had been told He would. Peter tells the Christians to ignore these teachers and be patient and brave, for God will fulfil His promise of a new heaven and a new earth, but, in the meantime, to be careful to lead the virtuous and peaceful life of true Christians.

JOHN, 1, 2, and 3—Most authorities agree that these three short Letters were written by the apostle John, the author of the fourth Gospel. The basic theme of the three Letters seems to be that people ought to love one another as God loves them. In the first Letter John talks about fellowship and brotherly love and what benefits Christians can expect to gain from them. Whether the second Letter is addressed to a real lady or to a church disguised under the metaphor *the elect lady* makes no difference to the message, which is a warning against taking in unbelievers. The third Letter is written to a man called Gaius, whom John commends for his hospitality to his fellow Christians.

JUDE—The last of the Letters is thought by some authorities to have been written by Jude, a brother of Jesus. In this Letter addressed to all Christians, Jude urges them to work against the wicked behavior and wrong ideas that are creeping into the church. He encourages them to a steadfast defense of the truth and he asks them to be compassionate in helping those who have strayed into wickedness.

REVELATION—The only prophecies appearing in the New Testament are contained in this Book, sometimes called *Apocalypse*, which means "revelation" or "a sudden disclosure that contains a prophecy." Many authorities believe that this Book, called *The Revelation to John*, like the three letters of John, was written by the author of the fourth Gospel.

The Book seems to be a collection of earlier prophecies which had to do with the advent of a Savior and the founding of the kingdom of God on earth, and a transformation of these prophecies into a foretelling of the second coming of Jesus and the formation of a new heaven and a new earth.

Between the opening and closing passage of the Book, seven visions are described—visions which are full of symbols and allegories, many of which have defied positive interpretation.

The principal message of the author seems to be that Jesus who had died and risen will always be alive and will always surpass in strength all the power of evil in the world. The Book ends as it began, with the assurance that Jesus will come again and be victorious over His enemies.

BRIEF CHRONOLOGICAL OUTLINE OF NEW TESTAMENT HISTORY

Note on the Birth of Jesus—From Josephus, a Jewish historian of the 1st century A.D., we learn that Herod died in the thirty-seventh year of his reign. Now Herod was made king of Judea in the consulship of Domitius Calvinus and Asinius Pollio, *i.e.*, 40 B.C. (714 A.U.C.*). Most writers have supposed that the year is reckoned by Josephus from the month Nisan, seventh month of the Jewish year; moreover, we may conclude from Josephus that Herod died at the beginning of the thirty-seventh year, or immediately before Passover. Consequently we must add thirty-six years to 714 A.U.C. Hence we get 750 A.U.C. = 4 B.C. as the date of Herod's death, and since this took place subsequent to the birth of Jesus, 4 B.C. is the *latest possible date that can be assigned* to His birth.

Thus, the Christian era is really calculated from a wrong starting-point. This was derived from the defective chronology of *Dionysius Exiguus* (6th cent.), who made the year of Jesus' birth, or A.D. 1, to correspond to 754 A.U.C.

B.C.

4. Probable date of Jesus' birth. Herod's death. Archelaus becomes ethnarch (or governor) of Judea, Samaria, and Idumea.

A.D.

8. Jesus visits Jerusalem at the age of twelve and talks with the rabbis in the Temple.

26. Ministry of John the Baptist.

27. Baptism of Jesus Christ at the age of thirty. His temptation, and inauguration of his ministry (Mt 3.1-6, 13-17; Mk 1.1-11; Lk 3.15-18, 21-22). First miracle at Cana in Galilee (Jn 2.1-11). First Passover (April 9). Discourse with Nicodemus (Jn 3.1-21). John the Baptist is imprisoned by Herod, the Tetrarch of Galilee (Lk 3.18-20). Christ leaves Judea for Galilee and on the way visits Sychar. He talks with the Samaritan woman, visits Cana, and heals the nobleman's son (Mt 4.12; Mk 1.14; Jn 4.46-54). Revisits Nazareth, gives address at the Synagogue, and escapes with his life (Lk 4.14-30). Gathers four disciples—Andrew, Simon, James, and John (Mt 4.18-22; Mk 1.16-20). First Galilean Circuit with the disciples (Mt 4.23-25; Mk 1.35-39; Lk 4.42-44).

27-28. Sermon on the Mount (probably not one, but separate sermons and sayings collected). Subsequent miracles. Call of Levi or Matthew to be a disciple (Mt 5.1-9.9; Mk 1.40; 2.14; Lk 5.1-28).

28. March 29. Christ's Second Passover (June 5). Discussions with the Pharisees. Heals the man with a withered hand (Mt 12.1-13; Mk 2.23-3.6; Lk 6.1-11). Returns to Galilee and chooses the Apostles (Mt 10.2-4; Mk 3.13-19; Lk 6.12-16). Further miracles. Message from John the Baptist (Mt 8.5-13; 11.2-30; Lk 7.1-35).

Second Galilean Circuit (Lk 8.1-3). Christ's teaching with parables (Mt 13.1-53; Mk 4.1-34; Lk 8.4-18). (These parables were delivered on separate occasions at intervals which cannot be determined.) Quelling of the Storm. Heals the Gadarene demoniac and performs other miracles (Mt 8.18-34; 9.18-34; Mk 5.1-43; Lk 8.22-56).

29. Third Galilean Circuit (Mt 10.1 foll.; 11.1; Mk 6.7-13; Lk 10.1-6). Feeding of the five thousand (Mt 14.13-23; Mk 6.30-46; Lk 9.10-17; Jn 6.1-14). Jesus walks on the sea and quells the storm, afterwards returns to Capernaum and performs many acts of healing (Mt

* A.U.C. is the abbreviation for the Latin *anno urbis conditae*, which means "year from the building of Rome."

A.D. 14.22-36; Mk 6.47-56; Jn 6.16-24). Sermon in the Synagogue of
29. Capernaum on the bread of life (Jn 6.25-71).

Third Passover (April 16). Jesus stays in Galilee (Jn 7.1). Controversy with scribes and Pharisees sent from Jerusalem. Jesus heals a dumb man and the demoniac daughter of the Syrophoenician woman (Mt 15.1-28; Mk 7.1-37). Feeding of the four thousand and voyage to Magadan (Mt 15.32-39; Mk 8.1-9). Jesus prophesies his coming death and resurrection, and subsequent persecution of his disciples. The transfiguration. Healing of a dumb demoniac (Mt 16.21-23; 17.23; Mk 8.31; 9.31; Lk 9.18-45). Seventy evangelists sent forth (Lk 10.1-20).

At this point in the life of Jesus it becomes especially difficult to arrange the events with any approximation to their actual sequence. We seem to be dependent on two Gospels for the next series of events, viz., in the order:—(1) Jn 7.2-8.59; (2) Lk 10.25-11.13; (3) Jn 9.1-11.54. According to some authorities there are the following parallels:—(*a*) Lk 9.51-13.21 runs parallel with Jn 7.10-10.42, the departure of Jesus in Lk 9.51, being the same as that referred to in Jn 7.10. (*b*) Lk 13.22-17.10 is parallel with Jn 11.1-54, both having certain common features. (*c*) Lk 17.11-19.28 is parallel with Jn 11.55-12.11.

In this series of narratives the following dates have been assigned by some scholars:—(1) Jesus leaves Galilee about the time of the Feast of the Tabernacles, 15th Tishri-October 12, A.D. 29. He reaches Jerusalem and teaches in the Temple in the middle of the feast after having passed through Samaria and sent forth the seventy. On the sabbath of the Feast occur the events described in Jn 7.14-53, *i.e.*, 22nd Tishri (October 19). On this sabbath also occurred the events of Jn 8.1-2,12-10.21; 11.1-54 (cf. Lk 8.22-17.10) which treats of Jesus' *last journey except one to Judea.*

Feast of Tabernacles (October) (Jn 7.2 foll.). Jesus goes to the feast privately.

Feast of Dedication (Dec.), Jn 10.22. Christ again visits Jerusalem.

30. Raising of Lazarus (Jn 11.6-54). Arrival in Bethany six days before the Passover (Jn 12.1-9).

Christ anointed by Mary (Mt 26.6-13; Mk 14.3-9; Lk 7.36-50).

Plot against Jesus and Lazarus (Jn 12.10-11).

Christ enters Jerusalem and cleanses the Temple (Mt 21.1-16; Mk 11.1-19; Lk 19.29-48).

Parables and Sermons (Mt 21-25; Mk 11-13; Lk 20-21).

Last Passover (April 5): (Mt 26.1-5; Mk 14.1-2; Lk 22.1-2).

Conspiracy of the Jews. Paschal Supper (Mt 26.1-35; Mk 14.1-31; Lk 22.1-38; Jn 13.1-38).

Sermons in John 14-17.

Gethsemane, Betrayal, Trial, Crucifixion, Resurrection, and Ascension (Mt 26.36-28.20; Mk 14.32-16.8; Lk 22.39-24.53; Jn 18-21).

Ascension of Jesus Christ. Matthias appointed by lot to fill Judas' place (Acts 1).

Day of Pentecost and Descent of the Holy Spirit (Acts 2).

Imprisonment of Peter and John by order of Sanhedrin (Acts 4).

31. Growth of the Christian community. Death of Ananias and Sapphira. Increasing activity and influence of the Christians awaken the hostility of the Sanhedrin. Imprisonment of the Apostles. They are miraculously liberated, and, on the advice of Gamaliel, the Sanhedrin ultimately allows them to depart.

36. Trial and martyrdom of Stephen (Acts 6.9-7.60).

Rapid growth in numbers of the Christians. They are persecuted by their Jewish brethren, in which persecution Saul takes an active part. Philip the deacon preached in Samaria, to which place Peter and John follow. Philip converts the Ethiopian eunuch (Acts 8).

A.D.

37. Conversion of Saul. He spends three years in Arabia.

40. Paul (formerly Saul) returns to Jerusalem. The Jews plot to take away his life. He departs for Tarsus (Acts 9).
Cessation of persecution and increase of Christian believers.
Peter visits and baptizes Cornelius, a Roman centurion. Christianity extended to the Gentiles (Acts 10.1-11.18).

41. Growth in numbers of the Gentile Christians in Antioch. They are visited by Barnabas. They are now first called Christians.

43. Paul brought by Barnabas from Tarsus, and they labor together at Antioch. Severe famine prophesied by Agabus (Acts 11.21-30).

44. Herod Agrippa puts James, brother of John, to death, and imprisons Peter. Herod dies at Caesarea (Acts 12).

45. Paul and Barnabas set apart to preach to the Gentiles. Their *first missionary journey* (Acts 13-14).

48. Dissensions awakened at Antioch. Paul and Barnabas sent as representatives to Jerusalem. *Decree in favor of Gentile liberty.*

40-50. Paul's *second missionary journey* with Silas (Acts 15-17).

51. After preaching in Phrygia, Galatia, Mysia, and Troas, he is joined by Luke and crosses over into Macedonia and visits Philippi, Thessalonica, and Berea, from where Jewish opposition drives him to Athens.

52. Paul at Corinth with Aquila and Priscilla. *Letter to Thessalonians.*

53. Proconsulship of Gallio in Achaia. Paul leaves Corinth for Ephesus (Acts 18.1-21).

54-55. Paul at Jerusalem. *Third missionary journey.*

56-57. Sets out from Antioch for Galatia and Phrygia. Paul at Ephesus for two years. Perhaps writes *First Letter to Corinthians*, and perhaps also *Letter to Galatians.*
After a tumult at Ephesus he leaves for Macedonia (Acts 19.21-41).

57. Writes *Second Letter to Corinthians.* Paul reaches Corinth probably at the end of the year.

58. Stays three months at Corinth. *Letter to the Romans.* He leaves Corinth in the early part of the year, returns to Macedonia, revisits Philippi in company with Luke, and departs after Passover (Acts 20.1-6). Leaves Troas; bids farewell to Ephesian elders at Miletus (Acts 20.7-38).

59. Visits Tyre, then Caesarea, and arrives at Jerusalem before Pentecost. Violent outburst of feeling against Paul. He is rescued by Claudius Lysias at the head of his troops. Defends himself before the Jews; is sent to Caesarea. Defends himself before Felix. (Acts 21-24)

60. Paul still prisoner at Caesarea. Defends himself before Festus and Agrippa (Acts 25-26). He is delivered with other prisoners to the centurion Julius. Voyage to Rome. Shipwreck at Malta, where he winters.

61. Sails for Rome. Visits Syracuse, Rhegium, Puteoli. At length he reaches Rome and is placed under custody of a Pretorian prefect. Lives two years in his hired house. (Acts 27-28)

A.D.
62-63. Writes Letters to the *Ephesians* and *Colossians*, to *Philemon*, and to *Philippians*.

64. Persecution by Nero.
The martyrdom of Paul is placed by most authorities somewhere between A.D. 64 and 66.

Note.—The chronological scheme set forth above can only be regarded as the best approximation that can be obtained from a careful examination of the facts of the narrative both of Jesus' life, described in the Gospels, and of the followers of Jesus related in *The Acts of the Apostles*, supplemented by occasional references in the Letters. Particular importance belongs to all allusions to the occurrence of Jewish festivals as a means of marking the progress of time. The occasional mention of the name of the reigning Roman Emperor at any rate furnishes certain time limits. A few of the more important indications of date arising out of the Scripture narrative may here be specified.

(1) The reference to Herod's death (Mt 2.1-19) has been already discussed in the note at the beginning of this section. Jesus may have been born as early as 6 B.C. This seems to be supported by the fact that the census of Palestine conducted under the *legatus* (governor) Sentius Saturninus, cannot be placed later than A.D. 6.

(2) Lk 3.1, "fifteenth year of the reign of Tiberius" would, if taken according to Roman usage, mean A.D. 28-29. According to Jewish usage, it might perhaps signify the year beginning 1st Tishri, A.D. 27.

(3) Jn 2.20, "It has taken forty-six years to build this temple" hardly gives us a very definite clue, since the statements of Josephus differ between the 15th and 18th year of Herod as the date of the start of the building. We may therefore make the 46th year as approximately A.D. 21-27.

(4) Acts 12.3, Death of Herod Agrippa. This took place in A.D. 44 according to some historians.